D0586201

American and British Theatrical Biography:

A Directory

by

J. P. WEARING

The Scarecrow Press, Inc.

Metuchen, N.J. & London

1979

INSTITUTE OF
UNITED STATES
STUDIES

Library of Congress Cataloging in Publication Data

Wearing, J   P
  American and British theatrical biography.

  1. Theater--United States--Biography--Dictories.
2. Theater--Great Britain--Biography--Directories.
I. Title.
PN2285.W42   792'.0295   78-31162
ISBN 0-8108-1201-0

INTRODUCTION

This directory is intended as a reference tool to locate
biographical information about figures connected with the American and British theatre. For each person the following information is provided: name (with cross-references to stage
names, pseudonyms, etc.), dates of birth and death, national-
ity, theatrical occupation(s), and a code to the source(s) containing fuller biographical information.

It should be noted that a person might not appear under
the same name in each source. Sometimes a person changed
names in the course of his or her career; this is particularly
true of women in earlier centuries, who would perform under
their maiden names until they married, and who would then perform under their married names. In some cases, some female performers were known by several names, since they
married two or three times. In these instances I have listed
such people under the name by which they were best known,
with cross-references to their other names. Thus, in locating
such people in various sources, users should be aware that the
person may appear under the various names I have given (as
additional information in square brackets), and not necessarily
under the <u>main</u> name-entry in the directory. Also, some
sources have the practice of dealing with <u>all</u> members of the
same theatrical family under a single entry; hence, such en-
tries may have to be scanned to locate the information indi-
cated by this directory. Users should also check any appen-
dices or addenda which may contain the relevant information.
And while the directory is alphabetized strictly on a letter-by-
letter basis, such may not be the case with all the sources
surveyed; thus, for example, I make no alphabetical distinction
between "Mac" and "Mc", while a specific source may list
these prefixes separately. (I have attempted to resolve all
variant spellings of names, but I am conscious that some in-

advertant duplications may still remain. Users should, there-fore, check similar spellings of names: for example, Abbott, Abbot, Abott, or, Smith, Smythe, etc.)

The question of birth (and occasionally death) dates is vexed, to say the least. I have attempted to give the best con-sensus of such dates; when there is no such consensus I pro-vide all dates given in the various sources. Where the age at death is known (but the birth year is not), I provide the age at death in square brackets after the year of death: for example, (d. 1977 [49]).

While the focus of the directory is on American and British figures, I have also included "foreign" personalities when the sources surveyed make some mention of their contri-bution to the American or British theatre. In addition, the di-rectory embraces the spheres of ballet, opera, music, circus, music-hall and the like to the extent that some figures from those spheres are included in the sources surveyed, and might be considered to have contributed to "the theatre" in the wid-est sense of that word.

I have also thought it useful to include basic informa-tion derived from necrologies which sometimes form part of some of the volumes surveyed: such information is designated by the appropriate code and an asterisk (*). In every instance, users will find it worthwhile to consult such necrologies, since all kinds of information are buried therein.

I would be grateful if users would bring to my attention any errors or omissions, as well as suggestions for additional sources which might be surveyed for future editions of this di-rectory.

I am grateful to the staffs of the British Library, Lon-don, and of the several libraries which have furnished books via the interlibrary loan program. I owe a special debt of thanks to the staff of the Central Reference Department of the University of Arizona Library who helped make my task easier than it would otherwise have been. My research assistant, Miss Paula Pranka, provided help with parts of the bibliogra-phy of sources and with some of the proofreading, for which I am grateful. As ever, I remain indebted to my friends who have materially helped me during the preparation of this book--

in particular Mr. Peter Turnbull and Miss Lesley Whitbourn of London, England.

J. P. Wearing
University of Arizona
April 1978

SOURCES INDEXED

AAS   Robin May. A Companion to the Theatre: The Anglo-American Stage from 1920. Guildford & London: Lutterworth, 1973.

BD   Philip H. Highfill, Jr., et al. A Biographical Dictionary of Actors, Actresses, Musicians, Dancers, Managers, & Other Stage Personnel in London, 1660-1800. 4 vols. to date. Carbondale: Southern Illinois University Press, 1973- .

BE   Walter Rigdon, ed. The Biographical Encyclopedia and Who's Who of the American Theatre. New York: Heinemann, 1966.

BP/1   John Chapman and Garrison P. Sherwood, eds. The Best Plays of 1894-1899. New York: Dodd, Mead, 1955.

BP/2   Burns Mantle and Garrison P. Sherwood, eds. The Best Plays of 1899-1909 and the Year Book of the Drama in America. New York: Dodd, Mead, 1944.

BP/3   _____ and _____. The Best Plays of 1909-1919 and the Year Book of the Drama in America. New York: Dodd, Mead, 1933.

BP/4   Burns Mantle, ed. The Best Plays of 1919-20 and the Year Book of the Drama in America. Boston: Small, Maynard, 1920.

BP/5   _____. The Best Plays of 1920-21 and the Year Book of the Drama in America. Boston: Small, Maynard, 1921.

BP/6   _____. The Best Plays of 1921-22 and the Year Book of the Drama in America. Boston: Small, Maynard, 1922.

BP/7   _____. The Best Plays of 1922-23 and the Year Book of the Drama in America. Boston: Small, Maynard, 1923.

BP/8   _____. The Best Plays of 1923-24 and the Year Book of the Drama in America. Boston: Small, Maynard, 1924.

BP/9   _____. The Best Plays of 1924-25 and the Year Book of the Drama in America. Boston: Small, Maynard, 1925.

BP/10   _____. The Best Plays of 1925-26 and the Year Book of the Drama in America. New York: Dodd, Mead, 1926.

BP/11   _____. The Best Plays of 1926-27 and the Year Book of the Drama in America. New York: Dodd, Mead, 1928.

BP/12   _____. The Best Plays of 1927-28 and the Year Book of the Drama in America. New York: Dodd, Mead, 1928.

BP/13   _____ . The Best Plays of 1928-29 and the Year Book of the Drama in America. New York: Dodd, Mead, 1929.

BP/14   _____ . The Best Plays of 1929-30 and the Year Book of the Drama in America. New York: Dodd, Mead, 1931.

BP/15   _____ . The Best Plays of 1930-31 and the Year Book of the Drama in America. New York: Dodd, Mead, 1931.

BP/16   _____ . The Best Plays of 1931-32 and the Year Book of the Drama in America. New York: Dodd, Mead, 1932.

BP/17   _____ . The Best Plays of 1932-33 and the Year Book of the Drama in America. New York: Dodd, Mead, 1933.

BP/18   _____ . The Best Plays of 1933-34 and the Year Book of the Drama in America. New York: Dodd, Mead, 1934.

BP/19   _____ . The Best Plays of 1934-35 and the Year Book of the Drama in America. New York: Dodd, Mead, 1935.

BP/20   _____ . The Best Plays of 1935-36 and the Year Book of the Drama in America. New York: Dodd, Mead, 1937.

BP/21   _____ . The Best Plays of 1936-37 and the Year Book of the Drama in America. New York: Dodd, Mead, 1937.

BP/22   _____ . The Best Plays of 1937-38 and the Year Book of the Drama in America. New York: Dodd, Mead, 1938.

BP/23   _____ . The Best Plays of 1938-39 and the Year Book of the Drama in America. New York: Dodd, Mead, 1939.

BP/24   _____ . The Best Plays of 1939-40 and the Year Book of the Drama in America. New York: Dodd, Mead, 1940.

BP/25   _____ . The Best Plays of 1940-41 and the Year Book of the Drama in America. New York: Dodd, Mead, 1941.

BP/26   _____ . The Best Plays of 1941-42 and the Year Book of the Drama in America. New York: Dodd, Mead, 1942.

BP/27   _____ . The Best Plays of 1942-43 and the Year Book of the Drama in America. New York: Dodd, Mead, 1943.

BP/28   _____ . The Best Plays of 1943-44 and the Year Book of the Drama in America. New York: Dodd, Mead, 1944.

BP/29   _____ . The Best Plays of 1944-45 and the Year Book of the Drama in America. New York: Dodd, Mead, 1945.

BP/30   _____ . The Best Plays of 1945-46 and the Year Book of the Drama in America. New York: Dodd, Mead, 1946.

BP/31   _____ . The Best Plays of 1946-47 and the Year Book of the Drama in America. New York: Dodd, Mead, 1947.

BP/32   John Chapman, ed. The Burns Mantle Best Plays of 1947-48 and the Year Book of the Drama in America. New York: Dodd, Mead, 1948.

BP/33   . The Burns Mantle Best Plays of 1948-49 and the Year Book of Drama in America. New York: Dodd, Mead, 1949.

BP/34   . The Burns Mantle Best Plays of 1949-50 and the Year Book of Drama in America. New York: Dodd, Mead, 1950.

BP/35   . The Burns Mantle Best Plays of 1950-51 and the Year Book of the Drama in America. New York: Dodd, Mead, 1951.

BP/36   . The Burns Mantle Best Plays of 1951-52 and the Year Book of the Drama in America. New York: Dodd, Mead, 1952.

BP/37 Louis Kronenberger, ed. The Burns Mantle Yearbook. The Best Plays of 1952-1953. New York & Toronto: Dodd, Mead, 1953.

BP/38   . The Burns Mantle Yearbook: The Best Plays of 1953-1954. New York & Toronto: Dodd, Mead, 1954.

BP/39   . The Burns Mantle Yearbook: The Best Plays of 1954-1955. New York & Toronto: Dodd, Mead, 1955.

BP/40   . The Burns Mantle Yearbook: The Best Plays of 1955-1956. New York & Toronto: Dodd, Mead, 1956.

BP/41   . The Burns Mantle Yearbook: The Best Plays of 1956-1957. New York & Toronto: Dodd, Mead, 1957.

BP/42   . The Burns Mantle Yearbook: The Best Plays of 1957-1958. New York & Toronto: Dodd, Mead, 1958.

BP/43   . The Burns Mantle Yearbook: The Best Plays of 1958-1959. New York & Toronto: Dodd, Mead, 1959.

BP/44   . The Burns Mantle Yearbook: The Best Plays of 1959-1960. New York & Toronto: Dodd, Mead, 1960.

BP/45   . The Burns Mantle Yearbook: The Best Plays of 1960-1961. New York & Toronto: Dodd, Mead, 1961.

BP/46 Henry Hewes, ed. The Burns Mantle Yearbook: The Best Plays of 1961-1962. New York & Toronto: Dodd, Mead, 1962.

BP/47   . The Burns Mantle Yearbook: The Best Plays of 1962-1963. New York & Toronto: Dodd, Mead, 1963.

BP/48   . The Burns Mantle Yearbook: The Best Plays of 1963-1964. New York & Toronto: Dodd, Mead, 1964.

BP/49 Guernsey, Otis L., Jr. The Burns Mantle Yearbook: The Best Plays of 1964-1965. New York & Toronto: Dodd, Mead, 1965.

BP/50   . The Burns Mantle Yearbook: The Best Plays of 1965-1966. New York & Toronto: Dodd, Mead, 1966.

BP/51   _____ . The Burns Mantle Yearbook: The Best Plays of 1966-1967. New York & Toronto: Dodd, Mead, 1967.

BP/52   _____ . The Burns Mantle Yearbook: The Best Plays of 1967-1968. New York & Toronto: Dodd, Mead, 1968.

BP/53   _____ . The Burns Mantle Yearbook: The Best Plays of 1968-1969. New York & Toronto: Dodd, Mead, 1969.

BP/54   _____ . The Burns Mantle Yearbook: The Best Plays of 1969-1970. New York & Toronto: Dodd, Mead, 1970.

BP/55   _____ . The Burns Mantle Yearbook: The Best Plays of 1970-1971. New York & Toronto: Dodd, Mead, 1971.

BP/56   _____ . The Burns Mantle Yearbook: The Best Plays of 1971-1972. New York & Toronto: Dodd, Mead, 1972.

BP/57   _____ . The Burns Mantle Yearbook: The Best Plays of 1972-1973. New York & Toronto: Dodd, Mead, 1973.

BP/58   _____ . The Burns Mantle Yearbook: The Best Plays of 1973-1974. New York & Toronto: Dodd, Mead, 1974.

BP/59   _____ . The Burns Mantle Yearbook: The Best Plays of 1974-1975. New York & Toronto: Dodd, Mead, 1975.

BP/60   _____ . The Burns Mantle Yearbook: The Best Plays of 1975-1976. New York & Toronto: Dodd, Mead, 1976.

BS   The Biography of the British Stage: Being Correct Narratives of the Lives of all the Principal Actors & Actresses at Drury-Lane, Covent-Garden, the Haymarket, the Lyceum, the Surrey, the Coburg, and the Adelphi Theatres. London: Sherwood, Jones, 1824.

BTR/74   Eric Johns, ed. British Theatre Review 1974. Eastbourne: Vance-Offord, 1975.

CB   Current Biography. New York: Wilson, 1940-1976. [Annual.]

CD   James Vinson, ed. Contemporary Dramatists. 2nd ed. London: St. James Press; New York: St. Martin's Press, 1977.

CDP   Lillian Arvilla Hall. Catalogue of Dramatic Portraits in the Theatre Collection of the Harvard College Library. 4 vols. Cambridge, Mass.: Harvard University Press, 1930-1934.

CH   Michael Anderson, et al. Crowell's Handbook of Contemporary Drama. New York: Crowell, 1971.

COC   Phyllis Hartnoll, ed. The Concise Oxford Companion to the Theatre. London: Oxford University Press, 1972.

CP/1   David E. Baker. The Companion to the Play-House; or, An Historical Account of all the Dramatic Writers (and their works) that have appeared in Great Britain and Ireland, from the Commencement of our Theatrical Exhibitions, down to the Present Year, 1764. 2 vols. London: Becker & Dehondt, 1764.

CP/2   Isaac Reed. Biographica Dramatica; or, A Companion to the
          Playhouse. 2 vols. London: Rivington, 1782. [A revision
          of CP/1.]

CP/3   Stephen Jones. Biographica Dramatica; or, A Companion to the
          Playhouse. 3 vols. London: Longman, Hurst, et al., 1812.
          [A revision of CP/1, CP/2.]

DA   Edwin Nungezer. A Dictionary of Actors and of Other Persons
          Associated with the Public Representation of Plays in England
          before 1642. New Haven, Conn.: Yale University Press,
          1929.

DAB   Dictionary of American Biography. 20 vols. & 4 suppls. New
          York: Scribner's, 1928-74.

DD   W. Davenport Adams. A Dictionary of the Drama: A Guide to
          the Plays, Playwrights, Players, and Playhouses of the United
          Kingdom and America from the Earliest Times to the Present.
          London: Chatto & Windus, 1904. [Only vol. 1., A-G, pub-
          lished.]

DNB   Dictionary of National Biography. 22 vols., & 7 suppls. London,
          1885-1971.

DP   Erskine Reid & Herbert Compton. The Dramatic Peerage, 1891:
          Personal Notes and Professional Sketches of the Actors and
          Actresses of the London Stage. London: General Publishing
          Co. [1891].

EA/68-   The Era Almanack and Annual. Published annually 1868-1919 by
EA/19   The Era office, London. [EA/68-EA/99 indicates the alman-
          acks for the years 1868-1899; EA/00-EA/19 indicates the al-
          manacks for 1900-1919.]

EAP   Oscar Wegelin. Early American Plays 1714-1830. New York:
          Dunlap Society, 1900.

ES   Enciclopedia dello spettacolo. 10 vols., & suppl. Rome: Casa
          Editrice le Maschere, 1954-1966.

FGF   Frederick Gard Fleay. A Biographical Chronicle of the English
          Drama 1559-1642. 2 vols. London: Reeves & Turner, 1891.

GC   William L. Keese. A Group of Comedians. New York: Dunlap
          Society, 1901.

GRB/1   Bampton Hunt, ed. The Green Room Book, or, Who's Who on
          the Stage: An Annual Biographical Record of the Dramatic,
          Musical and Variety World, 1906. London: T. Sealey Clark,
          1906.

GRB/2   John Parker, ed. The Green Room Book or Who's Who on the
          Stage, 1907. London: T. Sealey Clark, 1907.

GRB/3   _____. The Green Room Book or Who's Who on the Stage,
          1908. London: T. Sealey Clark, 1908.

GRB/4   _____ . The Green Room Book or Who's Who on the Stage,
                 1909. London: T. Sealey Clark, 1909.

GT   Thomas Gilliland. The Dramatic Mirror: Including a Biograph-
                 ical and Critical Account of all the Dramatic Writers and Per-
                 formers and a History of the Country Theatres in England,
                 Ireland and Scotland. 2 vols. London: Chapple, 1808.

HAS   T. Allston Brown. History of the American Stage: Containing
                 Biographical Sketches of Nearly Every Member of the Pro-
                 fession that has appeared on the American Stage, from 1773
                 to 1870. New York: Dick & Fitzgerald, 1870.

HJD   James D. Hart. The Oxford Companion to American Literature.
                 4th ed. New York: Oxford University Press, 1965.

HP   Sir Paul Harvey, ed. The Oxford Companion to English Litera-
                 ture. 4th ed. Rev. Dorothy Eagle. Oxford: Clarendon
                 Press, 1967.

MD   Siegfried Melchinger. The Concise Encyclopedia of Modern
                 Drama. New York: Horizon, 1964.

MH   McGraw-Hill Encyclopedia of World Drama. 4 vols. New York:
                 McGraw-Hill, 1972.

MWD   Myron Matlaw. Modern World Drama: An Encyclopedia. New
                 York: Dutton, 1972.

NTH   Bernard Sobel, ed. The New Theatre Handbook and Digest of
                 Plays. New York: Crown, 1959.

NYM   Harrison Grey Fiske, ed. The New York Mirror Annual and Di-
                 rectory of the Theatrical Profession for 1888. New York:
                 New York Mirror, 1888.

OAA/1   Charles Eyre Pascoe, ed. The Dramatic List: A Record of the
                 Principal Performances of Living Actors and Actresses of the
                 British Stage; With Criticisms from Contemporary Journals.
                 1st ed. London: Hardwicke & Bogue, 1879.

OAA/2   _____ . Our Actors and Actresses: The Dramatic List: A
                 Record of the Performances of Living Actors and Actresses of
                 the British Stage. 2nd ed. London: David Bogue, 1880.

OC/1   Phyllis Hartnoll, ed. The Oxford Companion to the Theatre. 1st
                 ed. London: Oxford University Press, 1951.

OC/2   _____ . The Oxford Companion to the Theatre. 2nd ed. Lon-
                 don: Oxford University Press, 1957.

OC/3   _____ . The Oxford Companion to the Theatre. 3rd ed. Lon-
                 don: Oxford University Press, 1967.

OX   William Oxberry. Oxberry's Dramatic Biography and Histrionic
                 Anecdotes. London: George Virtue, 1825-27. [Title and im-
                 print varies.]

PDT   John Russell Taylor. The Penguin Dictionary of the Theatre.
         Rev. ed. Harmondsworth: Penguin, 1970.

PP/1   John Bouve Clapp and Edwin Francis Edgett. Players of the
         Present. Pt. 1. New York: Dunlap Society, 1899.

PP/2   _____. Players of the Present. Pt. 2. New York: Dunlap
         Society, 1900.

PP/3   _____. Players of the Present. Pt. 3. New York: Dunlap
         Society, 1901.

RE   John Gassner and Edward Quinn, eds. The Reader's Encyclo-
         pedia of World Drama. New York: Crowell, 1969.

RJ   James Rees. The Dramatic Authors of America. Philadelphia:
         G. B. Zieber, 1845.

SR   Robert L. Sherman. Actors and Authors with Composers who
         helped make them famous: A Chronological Record and Brief
         Biography of Theatrical Celebrities from 1750 to 1950. Chi-
         cago: The Author, 1951.

TD/1   The Thespian Dictionary; or, Dramatic Biography of the Eight-
         eenth Century: Containing Sketches of the Lives, Productions,
         &c. of All the Principal Managers, Dramatists, Composers,
         Commentators, Actors, and Actresses, of the United Kingdom:
         Interspersed with Several Original Anecdotes; and Forming a
         Concise History of the English Stage. London: T. Hurst,
         1802.

TD/2   The Thespian Dictionary ... of the English Stage. 2nd ed. Lon-
         don: James Cundee, 1805.

TW/1   Daniel Blum, ed. Theatre World (1944-45 Season). Vol. 1.
         New York: Blum, 1945.

TW/2   _____. Theatre World (1945-46 Season). Vol. 2. New York:
         Blum, 1946.

TW/3   _____. Theatre World (1946-47 Season). Vol. 3. New York:
         Blum, 1947.

TW/4   _____. Theatre World (1947-48 Season). Vol. 4. New York:
         Blum, 1948.

TW/5   _____. Theatre World (1948-49 Season). Vol. 5. New York:
         Greenberg, 1950.

TW/6   _____. Theatre World (1949-50 Season). Vol. 6. New York:
         Greenberg, 1950.

TW/7   _____. Theatre World (1950-51 Season). Vol. 7. New York:
         Greenberg, 1951.

TW/8   _____. Theatre World (1951-52 Season). Vol. 8. New York:
         Greenberg, 1952.

TW/9   _____. Theatre World (1952-53 Season). Vol. 9. New York: Greenberg, 1953.

TW/10   _____. Theatre World (1953-54 Season). Vol. 10. New York: Greenberg, 1954.

TW/11   _____. Theatre World (1954-55 Season). Vol. 11. New York: Greenberg, 1955.

TW/12   _____. Theatre World (1955-56 Season). Vol. 12. New York: Greenberg, 1956.

TW/13   _____. Theatre World (1956-57 Season). Vol. 13. New York: Greenberg, 1957.

TW/14   _____. Theatre World (1957-58 Season). Vol. 14. Philadelphia: Chilton, 1958.

TW/15   _____. Theatre World (1958-59 Season). Vol. 15. Philadelphia: Chilton, 1959.

TW/16   _____. Theatre World (1959-60 Season). Vol. 16. Philadelphia: Chilton, 1960.

TW/17   _____. Theatre World (1960-61 Season). Vol. 17. Philadelphia: Chilton, 1961.

TW/18   _____. Theatre World (1961-62 Season). Vol. 18. Philadelphia: Chilton, 1962.

TW/19   _____. Theatre World (1962-63 Season). Vol. 19. Philadelphia: Chilton, 1963.

TW/20   _____. Theatre World (1963-64 Season). Vol. 20. Philadelphia: Chilton, 1964.

TW/21   John Willis, ed. Theatre World (1964-65 Season). Vol. 21. New York: Crown, 1965.

TW/22   _____. Theatre World (1965-66 Season). Vol. 22. New York: Crown, 1966.

TW/23   _____. Theatre World (1966-67 Season). Vol. 23. New York: Crown, 1967.

TW/24   _____. Theatre World (1967-68 Season). Vol. 24. New York: Crown, 1968.

TW/25   _____. Theatre World (1968-69 Season). Vol. 25. New York: Crown, 1969.

TW/26   _____. Theatre World (1969-70 Season). Vol. 26. New York: Crown, 1970.

TW/27   _____. Theatre World (1970-71 Season). Vol. 27. New York: Crown, 1971.

TW/28   _____. Theatre World (1971-72 Season). Vol. 28. New York: Crown, 1973.

TW/29   _____ . Theatre World (1972-73 Season). Vol. 29. New
           York: Crown, 1974.

TW/30   _____ . Theatre World (1973-74 Season). Vol. 30. New
           York: Crown, 1975.

WWA/H   Who Was Who in America: Historical Volume 1607-1896. Chi-
           cago: Marquis, 1963.

WWA/1   Who Was Who in America: Vol. 1: 1897-1942. Chicago: Mar-
           quis, 1966.

WWA/2   Who Was Who in America: Vol. 2: 1943-1950. Chicago: Mar-
           quis, 1966.

WWA/3   Who Was Who in America: Vol. 3: 1951-1960. Chicago: Mar-
           quis, 1966.

WWA/4   Who Was Who in America: Vol. 4: 1961-1968. Chicago: Mar-
           quis, 1968.

WWA/5   Who Was Who in America: Vol. 5: 1969-1973. Chicago: Mar-
           quis, 1973.

WWM   Dixie Hines and Harry Prescott Hanaford, eds. Who's Who in
           Music and Drama. New York: H. P. Hanaford, 1914.

WWS   Walter Browne and E. de Roy Koch. Who's Who on the Stage
           1908: The Dramatic Reference Book and Biographical Diction-
           ary of the Theatre: Containing Careers of Actors, Actresses,
           Managers and Playwrights of the American Stage. New York:
           Dodge, 1908.

WWT/1   John Parker, ed. The New Dramatic List: Who's Who in the
           Theatre: A Biographical Record of the Contemporary Stage.
           1st ed. London: Pitman, 1912.

WWT/2   _____ . The New Dramatic List: Who's Who in the Theatre:
           A Biographical Record of the Contemporary Stage: With a
           Foreword by Sir Herbert Beerbohm Tree. 2nd ed. London:
           Pitman, 1914.

WWT/3   _____ . The New Dramatic List: Who's Who in the Theatre:
           A Biographical Record of the Contemporary Stage. 3rd ed.,
           rev. London: Pitman, 1916.

WWT/4   _____ . The New Dramatic List: Who's Who in the Theatre:
           A Biographical Record of the Contemporary Stage. 4th ed.,
           rev. London: Pitman, 1922.

WWT/5   _____ . The Dramatic List: Who's Who in the Theatre: A
           Biographical Record of the Contemporary Stage. 5th ed., rev.
           London: Pitman, 1925.

WWT/6   _____ . The Dramatic List: Who's Who in the Theatre: A
           Biographical Record of the Contemporary Stage. 6th ed., rev.
           London: Pitman, 1930.

WWT/7   _____ . The Dramatic List: Who's Who in the Theatre: A Biographical Record of the Contemporary Stage. 7th ed., rev. London: Pitman, 1933.

WWT/8   _____ . The Dramatic List: Who's Who in the Theatre: A Biographical Record of the Contemporary Stage. 8th ed., rev. London: Pitman, 1936.

WWT/9   _____ . The Dramatic List: Who's Who in the Theatre: A Biographical Record of the Contemporary Stage. 9th ed., rev. London: Pitman, 1939.

WWT/10   _____ . The Dramatic List: Who's Who in the Theatre: A Biographical Record of the Contemporary Stage. 10th ed., rev. London: Pitman, 1947.

WWT/11   _____ . The Dramatic List: Who's Who in the Theatre: A Biographical Record of the Contemporary Stage. 11th ed., rev. London: Pitman, 1952.

WWT/12   _____ . Who's Who in the Theatre: A Biographical Record of the Contemporary Stage. 12th ed. London: Pitman, 1957.

WWT/13   Freda Gaye, ed. Who's Who in the Theatre: A Biographical Record of the Contemporary Stage. 13th ed. London: Pitman, 1961.

WWT/14   _____ . Who's Who in the Theatre: A Biographical Record of the Contemporary Stage. 14th ed. London: Pitman, 1967.

WWT/15   Who's Who in the Theatre: A Biographical Record of the Contemporary Stage. 15th ed. London: Pitman, 1972.

WWT/16   Ian Herbert, ed. Who's Who in the Theatre: A Biographical Record of the Contemporary Stage. 16th ed. London: Pitman; Detroit: Gale Research, 1977.

WWW/1   Who Was Who: Vol. 1: 1897-1915. 5th ed. London: Black, 1967.

WWW/2   Who Was Who: Vol. 2: 1916-1928. 4th ed. London: Black, 1967.

WWW/3   Who Was Who: Vol. 3: 1929-1940. 2nd ed. London: Black, 1967.

WWW/4   Who Was Who: Vol. 4: 1941-1950. 3rd ed. London: Black, 1964.

WWW/5   Who Was Who: Vol. 5: 1951-1960. 2nd ed. London: Black, 1964.

WWW/6   Who Was Who: Vol. 6: 1961-1970. London: Black, 1972.

A., R. (fl early 17th cent) drama-
tist CP/2-3
AARON, David (b 1947) American
actor TW/29-30
AARON, Jack (b 1933) American
actor TW/26-30
AARONOFF, Alma S. (d 1969
[53]) public relations BP/54*
AARONS, Alexander A. (d 1943
[52]) producing manager SR,
WWT/6-8
AARONS, Alfred E. (d 1936
[71]) American producing
manager, composer SR,
WWS, WWT/6-8
AARONSON, Irving (d 1963 [68])
composer, bandleader BE*
AARONSON, Rudolph (d 1919)
manager WWT/14*
AASEN, John (d 1938 [51]) per-
former BE*
ABA, Marika (d 1972) publicist
BP/57*
ABALDO, Joseph American actor
TW/30
ABARBANELL, Jacob Ralph
(1852-1922) American drama-
tist WWA/1
ABARBANELL, Lina (1880-1963)
German actress, singer ES,
TW/19, WWM, WWS, WWT/
1-2, 6-9
ABBA, Marta (b 1900/07) Italian
actress ES, WWT/9
ABBAS, Hector (1884-1942) Dutch
actor WWT/6-8
ABBE, Charles Smith (d 1932
[73]) American actor PP/1
ABBE, Josephine A. CDP
ABBEY, Henry Eugène (1846-96)
American manager CDP,
COC, DAB, OC/1-3, SR,
WWA/H
ABBEY, Mrs. Henry Eugène see

Girard, Florence
ABBEY, May Evers [Mrs. George
Lessey] (d 1952 [80]) American
performer BE*
ABBOT, Elizabeth Bradshaw see
Abbott, Mrs. William
ABBOT, John (d 1744) singer BD
ABBOT, Marie singer CDP
ABBOT, William see Abbott,
William
ABBOT, Mrs. William see Ab-
bott, Mrs. William
ABBOTT, Mr. (fl 1718-19) numberer
BD
ABBOTT, Mr. (fl 1799) instrumen-
talist BD
ABBOTT, Al (d 1962 [78]) perform-
er BE*
ABBOTT, Alf (d 1887 [40]) variety
artist EA/88*
ABBOTT, Amy (d 1904) music-hall
performer EA/05*
ABBOTT, Annie ["The Georgia Mag-
net"; Priscilla Rawlinson]
(1868-1943) American perform-
er SR
ABBOTT, Anthony Duke (fl 1795-
99) English musician BD
ABBOTT, Bessie Pickens (1878-
1919) American singer GRB/1-
2, SR, WWA/1, WWM, WWS
ABBOTT, Betty (b 1924) American
actress TW/4
ABBOTT, Bud [William] (1900-74)
American comedian CB, ES,
SR, TW/30
ABBOTT, C. (d 1817 [89]) performer BE*
ABBOTT, Charles (fl second half
19th cent) actor SR
ABBOTT, Charles (d 1874 [32])
pantomimist EA/75*
ABBOTT, Clara Barnes (d 1956
[82]) musical director BE*

---

*An asterisk indicates that information appears in a necrology portion of the
book cited.

ABBOTT, Dolly (d 1955 [68])
American performer BE*
ABBOTT, Dorothy L. (d 1937
[51]) American performer
BE*
ABBOTT, Edward B. (d 1932
[50]) performer BE*
ABBOTT, Edward S. [né Sanders]
(d 1936 [22]) American per-
former BE*
ABBOTT, Emma (1850-91) Amer-
ican singer CDP, DAB, ES,
SR, WWA/H
ABBOTT, Frank (d 1899 [25])
descriptive vocalist EA/00*
ABBOTT, George (fl 1740) mu-
sician BD
ABBOTT, George Francis (b 1887)
American actor, dramatist,
producer, director AAS, BE,
CB, CD, COC, ES, HJD,
MD, MH, MWD, NTH, OC/
1-3, PDT, SR, TW/2-8,
WWT/6-16
ABBOTT, Harriet (d 1874) dancer
EA/75*
ABBOTT, Harry (1861-1942)
press representative, actor
SR
ABBOTT, Henry (fl 1762-84)
stage doorkeeper BD
ABBOTT, John (b 1905) English
actor BE, ES, TW/2, 6,
13, WWT/9-11
ABBOTT, Judith American cast-
ing director, director, actress
BE
ABBOTT, Marion (1866-1937)
American performer SR
ABBOTT, Michael Ann (d 1972
[44]) performer BP/57*
ABBOTT, Nancy Ann (d 1964
[63]) American actress BE*
ABBOTT, Paul (d 1872) panto-
mimist EA/73*
ABBOTT, Percy (d 1960 [74])
Australian magician BE*
ABBOTT, Philip (b 1924) Amer-
ican actor BE, TW/16
ABBOTT, Richard (b 1899) Bel-
gian/American actor BE
ABBOTT, T. (fl 1788?-1821?)
actor, singer BD
ABBOTT, William (1789-1843)
English actor, dramatist BS,
CDP, COC, DD, DNB, ES,
HAS, OC/1-3, SR, WWA/H
ABBOTT, Mrs. William [née Bu-

loid; Mrs. William Bradshaw]
(c. 1820-58) American actress
CDP, DD, HAS, SR
ABBOTT, Yarnell (d 1938 [67])
American writer BE*
ABDULLAH, Achmed (1881-1945)
Syrian dramatist CB, SR
ABDUSHELLI, Zurab (1913-57) Rus-
sian announcer BE*
A'BECKET, Thomas (1808-90) Eng-
lish actor, singer, composer,
musician HAS, SR
A BECKETT, Arthur William (1844-
1909) English dramatist DD,
DNB, WWW/1
A BECKETT, Gilbert Abbott (1811-
56) English dramatist DD, DNB,
ES, HP
A BECKETT, Gilbert Arthur (1837-
91) English dramatist DD, DNB,
HP, SR
ABEGG, Mrs. (fl 1758-63) actress,
singer BD
ABEGGLEN, Homer N. (b 1901)
American educator, director
BE
ABEL, Alfred (d 1937 [72]) actor
BE*
ABEL, George (d 1916 [46]) Irish?
lessee EA/18*
ABEL, Grover Cleveland (d 1972
[79]) dance teacher BP/57*
ABEL, Harry Nelson (d 1882) ad-
vance agent EA/83*
ABEL, Karl Friedrich (1723-87)
German instrumentalist, com-
poser BD, CDP, DNB
ABEL, Lionel (b 1910) American
dramatist, critic ES, MD,
MWD
ABEL, Mala (d 1905) EA/07*
ABEL, Neal (d 1952 [70]) perform-
er BE*
ABEL, Walter (b 1898) American
actor BE, ES, SR, TW/2-8,
14-15, 17, 19, 24, WWT/7-16
ABEL, William Henry (d 1887 [53])
EA/88*
ABELES, Edward S. (1869-1919)
American actor GRB/2-4, SR,
WWM, WWS, WWT/1-3
ABELES, Joseph (b 1911) American
theatrical photographer BE
ABELES, Julian T. (d 1973 [80])
lawyer BP/57*
ABELL, Edith (d 1926 [78]) singer
CDP
ABELL, John (1650?-1724?) Scottish

singer, instrumentalist BD, DNB

ABELL, Kjeld (1901-61) Danish dramatist, designer COC, ES, MWD, OC/1-3

ABELL BROTHERS (fl 1726-27) house servants? BD

ABELMAN, Lester (d 1972 [58]) critic BP/56*

ABELS, Gregory (b 1941) American actor TW/28, 30

ABELS, Marcella Ruth see Cisney, Marcella

ABELSON, Hope (b 1919) American producer BE

ABEND, Sheldon (b 1929) American literary representative BE

ABERCROMBIE, Lascelles (1881-1938) English critic, dramatist DNB, ES, OC/1, WWT/2-8, WWW/3

ABERDEIN, Mr. (fl 1782-96) Scottish actor, singer BD

ABERDEIN, Mr. (fl 1783-1819) dresser, scene man? BD

ABERT, Johann Joseph (1832-1915) Bohemian composer, conductor ES

ABINGDON, Marie [Mrs. Charles Glenny] (d 1898 [39]) actress EA/99*, WWT/14*

ABINGDON, William (1888-1959) English director WWT/6-12

ABINGDON, W[illiam] L. (1859-1918) English actor DD, DP, EA/95, GRB/1-4, WWM, WWS, WWT/1-3

ABINGDON, Mrs. W[illiam] L. see Fernandez, Bijou

ABINGTON, Frances see Abington, Mrs. James

ABINGTON, James (d 1806) trumpeter, singer BD

ABINGTON, Mrs. James [Frances Barton] (1737-1815) English actress BD, CDP, COC, DD, DNB, ES, GT, NTH, OC/2-3, TD/1-2

ABINGTON, Joseph (d 1744) violinist BD

ABINGTON, Leonard (d 1767) violinist, trumpeter, composer, singer? BD

ABINGTON, Leonard Joseph (fl 1794) singer BD

ABINGTON, William (fl 1774-94) composer, instrumentalist BD

ABLAMOWICZ, Anna singer CDP

ABLE, Frank [J. H. R. Penrose] (d 1893) EA/94*

ABLE, Will B. (b 1923) American actor, singer, dancer, comedian, mimist, choreographer BE, TW/25-26

ABLEMAN, Paul (b 1927) English dramatist CD

ABORN, Louis H. (b 1912) American executive BE

ABORN, Milton (1864-1933) American manager DAB, SR, WWA/1, WWM, WWT/7

ABORN, Sargent (1866-1956) American impresario SR, WWM

ABOS, Gerolamo (1700-60) Italian composer ES

ABOTT, Bessie Pickens see Abbott, Bessie Pickens

ABOUCHAR, Joan (b 1937) Chinese/American children's theatre manager BE

ABRAHALL, Mr. (fl 1700) musician BD

ABRAHAM, Mr. (fl 1793) presenter BD

ABRAHAM, F. Murray (b 1939) American actor TW/24-30

ABRAHAM, John (fl 1688) instrumentalist BD

ABRAHAM, Louis (d 1975 [51]) producer/director/choreographer BP/60*

ABRAHAM, Paul (1892-1960) composer ES, WWT/8-10

ABRAHAMS, A. E. (1873-1966) English proprietor WWT/6-10

ABRAHAMS, Barney (d 1969 [62]) manager BP/54*

ABRAHAMS, David Bramah (1775-1837) English violist, violinist, singer BD

ABRAHAMS, Doris Cole (b 1925) American producing manager WWT/15-16

ABRAHAMS, Elizabeth (d 1906) EA/07*

ABRAHAMS, Frederick (d 1912 [90]) music-hall proprietor EA/13*

ABRAHAMS, John (fl 1775-79) house servant? BD

ABRAHAMS, Joseph B. (d 1969 [84]) designer BP/54*

ABRAHAMS, Louis William (d 1890 [33]) EA/91*

ABRAHAMS, Mrs. M. (d 1870 [29]) EA/71*

ABRAHAMS, Morris (d 1915 [84])
manager WWT/14*
ABRAHAMS, Mrs. Morris (d 1885)
EA/87*
ABRAHAMSOHN, Otto see
Brahm, Otto
ABRAM, Lancelot Arthur (d 1899)
musical director EA/00*
ABRAM, Launcelot Sharpe see
Sharpe, L.
ABRAMS, Bill (b 1943) American
actor TW/27
ABRAMS, Charles (fl 1794) Vio-
loncellist BD
ABRAMS, Eliza (b 1763?) singer
BD
ABRAMS, Flora (fl 1778) singer
BD
ABRAMS, Miss G. (fl 1778-80)
singer, actress BD
ABRAMS, Harriet (1760-1825?)
singer, composer BD,
CDP
ABRAMS, Jane (fl 1799) singer?
BD
ABRAMS, Theodosia [Mrs.
Thomas Fisher; Mrs. Joseph
Garrow] (c 1761-1849)
singer BD
ABRAMS, William (fl 1794) vio-
linist, violist BD
ABRAMSON, Charles H. (b 1902)
American producer BE
ABRAVANEL, Maurice (b 1903)
Greek/American musical
director, conductor, educa-
tor BE, ES
ABRUZZO, Raffaella Julia Thérésa
see Allen, Rae
ABSE, Dannie (b 1923) Welsh
dramatist CD
ABT, Frank (d 1885 [65]) com-
poser EA/86*
ABUD, Charles J. (d 1926 [71])
manager WWT/14*
ABUZA, Sophie see Tucker,
Sophie
ABYNGDON, Henry (fl 1455-78)
master of the Chapel Royal
DA
ACE, Jane (d 1974 [74]) actress
BP/59*, WWT/16*
ACHARD, Marcel (1900-74) French
dramatist, director BE,
BTR/74, MWD
ACHENBACH, Maximilian see
Alvary, Max
ACHILLE, Mons. (fl 1827)

French dancer HAS
ACHILLE, Mme. (b 1797) French
dancer CDP, HAS
ACHMAN, Mr. actor TD/2
ACHMET, Mrs. [Mrs. William
Cairns; Catherine Ann Egan]
(b 1766) actress BD, DD,
TD/1-2
ACHMET, Miss (fl 1794) actress
BD
ACHURCH, Janet [née Janet Achurch
Sharp; Mrs. Charles Charring-
ton] (1864-1916) English actress,
COC, DD, DP, EA/95, ES,
GRB/1-4, OC/1-3, WWT/1-3,
WWW/2
ACHURCH, Thomas (d 1771) actor
BD
ACHURCH, Mrs. [Thomas?] (fl
1734) actress BD
ACKER, Iris American actress
TW/30
ACKER, Mabel actress TW/1, 3
ACKERILL, Mr. (fl 1793-95) slack-
wire dancer, equestrian, tum-
bler BD
ACKERILL, Master (fl 1793-95)
slack-wire dancer, violinist
BD
ACKERMAN, Al (d 1971 [90])
performer BP/56*
ACKERMAN, Floyd F. (b 1927)
American producer, personal
manager, theatre representative
BE
ACKERMAN, Irene (d 1916 [45])
American actress CDP, WWS
ACKERMAN, Irving (d 1970 [85])
theatre owner BP/55*
ACKERMAN, Loni Zoe (b 1949)
American actress TW/26-30
ACKERMAN, P. Dodd, Sr. (d
1963 [87]) American designer
BE*
ACKERMANN, Charlotte (1757-74)
actress BE*
ACKERMANN, Dorothea (1752-1821)
actress BE*
ACKERMANN, Konrad Ernst (1710-
71) actor, manager BE*,
WWT/14*
ACKERY, Mr. (fl 1787) actor BD
ACKERY, Cecil (d 1963 [70]) magi-
cian BE*
ACKLAND, Henry (d 1900 [52])
singer EA/01*
ACKLAND, Joss (b 1928) English
actor AAS, WWT/15-16

ACKLAND, Rodney (b 1908) English actor, dramatist AAS, BE, CD, ES, PDT, WWT/7-15

ACKMAN, Mrs. (fl 1779) house servant? BD

ACKMAN, Ellis (d 1774) actor BD

ACKROYD, David (b 1940) American actor TW/28, 30

ACKTE, Aino (1876-1944) Finnish singer ES, WWM

ACOSTA, Rodolfo (d 1974 [54]) performer BP/59*

ACTE, Aino see Ackté, Aino

ACTMAN, Irving (d 1967 [60]) composer/lyricist BP/52*

ACTON-BOND, Acton see Bond, Acton

ACTON-PHILLIPS, Sophia Matilda (d 1900) EA/01*

ADAIR, Alice (d 1895) EA/97*

ADAIR, Jean (d 1953 [80]) Canadian actress TW/1, 6-7, 9, WWT/8-11

ADAIR, Robert (d 1954 [54]) actor WWT/14*

ADAIR, Yvonne (b 1925) American singer, dancer, actress BE

ADAM, Adolph (d 1856 [53]) composer EA/72*

ADAM, Noelle (b 1933) French dancer, actress BE, TW/19

ADAM, Ronald (b 1896) English actor, manager, dramatist AAS, WWT/8-16

ADAM, V. equestrian performer CDP

ADAM, William (d 1879 [18]) violinist EA/80*

ADAMBERGER, Valentin (1743-1804) German singer BD

ADAMOV, Arthur (1908-70) Russian/French dramatist CH, COC, MH, OC/3

ADAMS (d 1887 [82]) aeronaut EA/88*

ADAMS, Mr. equestrian performer CDP

ADAMS, Mr. (fl 1669-73) actor BD

ADAMS, Mr. (fl 1728) actor BD

ADAMS, Mr. (fl 1736-48) dancer, actor BD

ADAMS, Mr. (fl 1763-70?) singer BD

ADAMS, Mr. (fl 1782-1800) bird imitator, tumbler, equestrian BD

ADAMS, Mr. (fl 1788) actor BD

ADAMS, Mrs. (fl 1731) actress BD

ADAMS, Mrs. (fl 1748) dancer/actress BD

ADAMS, Mrs. (fl 1750) actress, singer BD

ADAMS, Mrs. (fl 1798-1800) box-office keeper BD

ADAMS, Master (fl 1763-66) singer BD

ADAMS, Master (fl 1795) bird imitator BD

ADAMS, Miss see Barrymore, Mrs. William

ADAMS, Abigail (d 1955 [37]) actress BE*

ADAMS, Mrs. A. A. see Duff, Mary

ADAMS, Albert F. (d 1965 [82]) performer BP/50*

ADAMS, Alice (d 1877) EA/78*

ADAMS, Alice Baldwin [Mrs. Burton Adams] (d 1936 [83]) actress BE*

ADAMS, Anna Matilda (fl 1800?-08?) dancer, actress? BD

ADAMS, Annie [Mrs. H. Wall] (d 1905 [61]) variety artist CDP, ES, GRB/1, SR

ADAMS, Annie (d 1916 [69]) actress WWT/14*

ADAMS, Arthur Henry (1872-1936) New Zealand dramatist WWW/3

ADAMS, Augustus A. see Addams, Augustus A.

ADAMS, Bert (d 1904) manager EA/05*

ADAMS, Blake (d 1913) Scottish actor GRB/2-3

ADAMS, Bob (d 1948 [74]) comedian WWT/14*

ADAMS, Bret (b 1930) American producer, talent representative BE

ADAMS, Mrs. Burton see Adams, Alice Baldwin

ADAMS, Caroline (d 1889) actress EA/90*

ADAMS, Casey see Showalter, Max

ADAMS, C. F. (d 1854) American actor HAS

ADAMS, Mrs. C. F. (fl 1850) American actress HAS

ADAMS, Charles (fl c.1745-51) actor BD

ADAMS, Charles (d 1880 [52])
circus manager EA/82*
ADAMS, Charles R. (1834-1900)
American singer CDP, DAB,
ES, WWA/H
ADAMS, Claire (fl 1920s) actress
ES
ADAMS, Constance see De Mille,
Mrs. Cecil
ADAMS, Diana (b 1926) American
dancer CB, ES
ADAMS, Dick (b 1889) Irish mana-
ger WWT/2
ADAMS, Miss E. (fl 1800-08)
dancer, singer BD
ADAMS, Earl P. actor SR
ADAMS, Edie American actress,
entertainer BE, WWT/16
ADAMS, Edith [Edith Enke] (b
1927) American singer,
actress CB, TW/9-19
ADAMS, Edwin (1834-77) Ameri-
can actor CDP, COC, DAB,
DD, ES, HAS, OC/1-3, SR,
WWA/H
ADAMS, Mrs. Edwin (fl c1820s)
American actress, dancer
HAS
ADAMS, Frances Sale (d 1969
[77]) performer BP/54*
ADAMS, Mrs. Francis (d 1972
[86]) performer BP/57*
ADAMS, Frank Ramsay (1883-
1963) American dramatist
WWA/4
ADAMS, Frank Steward (d 1964
[79]) organist BE*
ADAMS, Franklin Pierce (1881-
1960) American performer,
writer BE*
ADAMS, Franklin R. dramatist
SR
ADAMS, George (fl 1729) drama-
tist CP/1-3, DD, GT
ADAMS, George (1777-1810)
English instrumental musi-
cian BD
ADAMS, George (d 1870 [47])
actor EA/71*
ADAMS, George Frederick (d
1917 [40]) EA/18*
ADAMS, George H. (1853-1935)
English clown CDP
ADAMS, G. G., the Elder (d
1853) American actor HAS,
SR
ADAMS, Miss H. (fl 1800-08)
dancer, singer BD

ADAMS, Ida (d 1960 [72]) actress
WWT/4-5
ADAMS, Isabel [Mrs. Ernest Clif-
ton] (d 1893 [62]) actress
EA/94*, WWT/14*
ADAMS, Jack (fl 1667?) clown BD
ADAMS, James (b c.1771) violinist,
organist BD
ADAMS, James Blake (b c.1749)
organist, violoncellist, violinist
BD
ADAMS, Jill (d 1964 [41]) dancer
BE*
ADAMS, Joey (b 1911) American
comedian, producer, toastmaster
BE
ADAMS, John (fl 1576-91) actor
DA
ADAMS, John (fl 1739) musician
BD
ADAMS, John (fl 1739) musician
BD [sic]
ADAMS, John (fl 1794) horn player,
organist BD
ADAMS, John (d 1873) minstrel
EA/74*
ADAMS, John B. (1830-63) American
actor HAS, SR
ADAMS, John Cranford (b 1903)
American writer, educator BE
ADAMS, John F. American actor
HAS
ADAMS, John Jay (fl 1822) American
actor DD
ADAMS, Joseph Quincy (1881-1946)
American scholar CB, DAB,
OC/1-2, WWA/2
ADAMS, J. P. (d 1853) American
comedian HAS, SR
ADAMS, Julian (d 1887 [62]) con-
ductor EA/88*
ADAMS, Justin actor, dramatist
SR
ADAMS, Kathryn (d 1959 [65])
American actress BE*
ADAMS, Lee (b 1924) American
lyricist BE
ADAMS, Leslie (1887-1936) Ameri-
can actor SR
ADAMS, Lionel (d 1952 [86]) actor
TW/9
ADAMS, Margaret (d 1873 [63])
EA/74*
ADAMS, Margie [Mrs. H. Wilmot
Young] (1881-1937) Canadian
actress BE*
ADAMS, Mason (b 1919) American
actor TW/16, 26-28, 30

ADAMS, Maude [Maude Kiskadden] (1872-1953) American actress ES, GRB/2-4, HJD, NTH, OC/1-3, PP/1, SR, TW/10, WWA/3, WWM, WWS, WWT/1-11

ADAMS, Milward (b 1857) American manager WWM

ADAMS, Miriam (b 1907) English actress WWT/7-9

ADAMS, Nicholas [Nathan Anspach] (d 1935 [64]) American actor BE*

ADAMS, Nick (d 1968 [36]) performer BP/52*

ADAMS, Rebecca (d 1865) American actress HAS

ADAMS, Robert British Guianan actor WWT/10-11

ADAMS, Robert K. (b 1909) American producer, director, actor BE, ES

ADAMS, Roger (b 1917) English composer BE

ADAMS, Ronald (b 1896) English manager ES, WWT/7

ADAMS, Miss S. (fl 1800-08) dancer, singer BD

ADAMS, Mrs. Sam see Nott, Cicely

ADAMS, Samuel (d 1893 [55]) lessee EA/94*

ADAMS, Samuel Hopkins (1871-1958) American writer BE*

ADAMS, Sarah Ann see Nott, Cicely

ADAMS, Selby (1872-1943) American actor, showboat manager SR

ADAMS, Sheila K. (b 1950) American actress TW/30

ADAMS, Stanley (b 1907) American lyricist, executive BE

ADAMS, Stephen see Maybrick, Michael

ADAMS, Suzanne (1872/73-1953) American singer SR, WWS, WWA/5

ADAMS, Thomas (b 1783) oboist, organist BD

ADAMS, Trude (b 1931) American actress TW/22

ADAMS, Virginia (d 1975 [62]) performer BP/59*

ADAMS, William (d 1897) business manager EA/98*

ADAMS, Mrs. William (d 1877) EA/78*

ADAMS, William Davenport (1851-1904) English critic, scholar DNB, WWW/1

ADAMS, William Henry Davenport (1828-91) English scholar DNB

ADAMS, William P. (d 1972 [85]) actor TW/29

ADAMS, W. J. singer CDP

ADAMSON, Mr. (fl 1816) English actor SR

ADAMSON, John (fl 1808) translator CP/3, DD

ADAMSON, Owen (d 1672) singer BD

ADAMSON, Patrick (fl 1572) dramatist FGF

ADAMSON, Richard (fl 1661) singer BD

ADCOCK, Mr. (d 1753) English actor DD, SR

ADCOCK, Mr. (fl 1794?-1803?) actor, singer?, manager? BD

ADCOCK, Miss (fl 1782-83) singer BD

ADCOCK, Miss see Wilson, Mrs.

ADCOCK, Abraham (d 1773) trumpeter, organist, violinist, organ builder BD

ADCOCK, William (fl 1752-72) English actor BD, HAS

ADCOCK, Mrs. William [Mary Palmer] (d 1773) BD

ADDAMS, Augustus A. (d 1851) American actor CDP, DD, HAS, SR

ADDAMS, Dawn (b 1930) English actress ES, WWT/15-16

ADDAMS, John dramatist RJ

ADDAMS, Mrs. J. P. see Provost, Mary

ADDERLEY, James (d 1917) EA/18*

ADDERSLEY, T. G. (d 1879 [28]) agent EA/80*

ADDIE, Harriet Frances [Fanny Hamilton] (1816-75) actress DD

ADDINGTON, Sir William (d 1811 [83]) dramatist CP/3

ADDINSELL, Richard Stewart [or Stuart] (1904-77) English composer BE, ES, WWT/7-16

ADDIS, George actor TW/24-25

ADDIS, John B. (b 1804) English actor, stage manager HAS, SR

ADDISON, Mrs. (fl 1747-52)

dancer BD
ADDISON, Mrs. (fl 1796) singer
TD/1-2
ADDISON, Anne see Howard,
Anne
ADDISON, Carlotta [Mrs. Charles
La Trobe] (1849/50-1914)
English actress DD, DP,
EA/95, GRB/1-4, OAA/1-2,
WWT/1-2
ADDISON, Edward Phillips (1808-
74) actor DD
ADDISON, Fanny (b 1847) English
actress DD, OAA/1-2
ADDISON, Col. Henry Robert
(1805-76) dramatist DD,
EA/68
ADDISON, John (d 1799) musician
BD
ADDISON, John (c.1766-1844)
English double bass player,
violoncellist, composer BD,
DD, DNB, ES
ADDISON, John English composer
BE
ADDISON, Mrs. John [Elizabeth
Willems] (fl 1785?-1840)
BD, DD
ADDISON, Joseph (1672-1719)
English dramatist CDP,
COC, CP/1-3, DD, DNB,
ES, GT, HP, MH, NTH,
OC/1-3, SR, TD/1-2
ADDISON, Laura (1822-52) Eng-
lish actress CDP, DD,
DNB, ES, HAS
ADDISON, R. (d 1868 [71]) music
publisher EA/69*
ADDISON, Thomas dramatist SR
ADDISON, Victoria (d 1971 [92])
performer BP/55*
ADDY, Wesley (b 1912/13) Amer-
ican actor BE, TW/2-4, 6-
7, 10-18, 26, 29, WWT/11-16
ADE, George (1866-1944) American
dramatist CB, COC, DAB,
ES, GRB/2-4, HJD, MH,
MWD, NTH, OC/1-3, SR,
WWA/2, WWM, WWS,
WWT/1-9
ADEANE, Mr. (fl 1786) dancer?
BD
ADELAIDE, Mlle. (fl 1788-89)
dancer BD
ADELAIDE, Mary see Whytal,
Mrs. Russ
ADELINE, Mlle. (fl 1840-50)
dancer HAS

A'DELL, E. (b 1875) English actor
GRB/1
ADESON, Beatrice (d 1917) EA/18*
ADESON, Martin (d 1936) actor
WWT/14*
ADESON, Stephen (d 1945) actor
WWT/14*
ADINY-MILLET, Ada [Addie Chap-
man] (1855-1924) French singer
ES
ADIX, Vern (b 1912) American edu-
cator, director, designer BE
ADKIN, Elizabeth A. (d 1892 [53])
actress EA/93*
ADKINS, Gilbert (d 1967) comedian,
singer TW/24
ADKINS, Morton (b 1877) American
singer WWM
ADKINSON, Will (fl 1625) actor
DA
ADLER, Adolph J. (d 1961 [77])
theatre owner-manager BE*
ADLER, Allen A. (d 1964 [47])
American producer, writer
BE*
ADLER, Benjamin (d 1974 [84])
theatrical backer TW/30
ADLER, Celia (b 1898) American
actress TW/11
ADLER, Eleanor (d 1974 [34]) per-
former BP/59*
ADLER, Felix (1897-1960) American
clown BE*
ADLER, Frances (1891-1964) Amer-
ican actress, teacher BE,
TW/21
ADLER, Harriet (d 1974 [55]) per-
former BP/58*
ADLER, Harry (d 1973 [66]) per-
sonal manager, agent BP/57*
ADLER, Hyman (d 1945 [62]) actor,
producer WWT/14*
ADLER, Jacob (d 1974 [101])
dramatist BP/59*
ADLER, Jacob P. (1855-1926)
Russian actor ES, GRB/3-4,
NTH, SR, WWT/1-5
ADLER, Larry (b 1914) American
musician, composer, performer
BE, CB, SR
ADLER, Luther (b 1903) American
actor, director AAS, BE, ES,
SR, TW/1-9, 12-13, 16, 20-
26, WWT/8-16
ADLER, Richard (b 1921) American
composer, lyricist, director,
producer AAS, BE, ES, WWT/
15-16

ADLER, Sarah (d 1953 [45])
American actress NTH
ADLER, Stella (b 1902) American
actress, director, teacher
BE, ES, TW/2-7, WWT/
8-16
ADMIRE, Jere American actor
TW/26-27
ADOLPHUS, John (d 1845 [79])
barrister EA/72*
ADOREE, Renée [Renée de la
Fointe] (1902-33) French
actress BE*
ADRIAN, G[ilbert] (1903-58)
American costume designer
WWA/3
ADRIAN, James American actor
TW/28
ADRIAN, Max (1903-73) English
actor, director AAS, BE,
ES, TW/13, 15-17, 24, 29,
WWT/10-15
ADRIANA, Cora (fl 1871) Amer-
ican dancer CDP
ADRIANI, Mr. (fl 1765-67)
dancer BD
ADRIENNE, Jean (b 1905) Indian/
English actress, singer,
dancer WWT/7-11
ADSON, F. (fl 1634) actor DA
ADYE, Algernon (d 1897 [36])
actor EA/97*
ADYE, Harriette see Howard,
Inez
ADYE, Oscar (d 1914 [55]) Eng-
lish actor GRB/3-4, WWT/
1-2
A. E. [George William Russell]
(1867-1935) Irish dramatist
COC, MH, MWD, OC/2-3
AENEA [Mrs. Letitia Dando]
English dancer GRB/1
AESCHYLUS (525-456 B.C.)
Greek dramatist ES
AFFELDER, Paul B. (d 1975
[59]) critic BP/59*
AFINOGENOV, Alexander Niko-
laevich (1904-41) Russian
dramatist COC, MWD,
OC/1-3
AFRICAN, The (fl 1793-95)
equestrian, tumbler BD
AFRIQUE [Alexander Watkin]
(d 1961 [54]) South African
performer BE*
AFTON, Effie American actress
TW/8, 10
AGAOGLU, Adalet (b 1929)

Turkish dramatist RE
AGAR, Mr. actor CDP
AGAR, Dan (b 1881) English actor
WWT/4-7
AGAR, Grace Hale (d 1963 [74])
actress BE*
AGATE, James Evershed (1877-
1947) English critic AAS,
COC, DNB, ES, NTH, OC/1-3,
PDT, WWT/5-10, WWW/4
AGATE, May (1892-1960) English
actress COC, ES, OC/2-3,
WWT/6-10
AGGAS, Robert (c.1619-79) English
scene painter BD, COC, DD,
DNB, ES, OC/1-3
AGGAS, Robert (fl 1662-79) drum-
mer BD
AGLGAZE, Julia Cohn (d 1975 [73])
lawyer BP/59*
AGNESI, Luigi (1838-75) Belgian
composer, singer ES
AGNETTA, Signora (fl 1747-51)
singer BD
AGNEW, Beatrice actress GRB/
3-4, WWT/1
AGOSTINELLI-QUIROLI, Adelina
(b 1882) Italian singer ES
AGOUST [William Bridge] (d 1894)
circus clown EA/95*
AGRATI, Signora (d 1887) actress
EA/88*
AGRESS, Ted (b 1945) American
actor TW/25, 28
AGUE, James W. (d 1975 [75])
performer BP/60*
AGUGLIA-FERRAU, Mimi (1884-
1970) Italian actress ES,
WWT/3
AGUIARI, Lucrezia [Mme. Giuseppe
Colla] (1743-83) Italian singer
BD
AGUS, Joseph (fl 1763?) violinist,
composer? BD
AGUS, Joseph (1749-1803?) violin-
ist, composer? BD
AHEARNE, Tom (1904-69) American
actor TW/22-23, 25
AHERNE, Brian (b 1902) English
actor AAS, BE, CB, ES, SR,
TW/1-8, 10-18, WWT/6-15
AHERNE, Patrick (d 1970 [69])
performer BP/55*
AHLERS, Anny (1906-33) German
actress, singer NTH, WWT/7
AHLERT, Fred E. (1892-1953)
American composer BE*
AHMED, Raju (d 1972 [35])

performer BP/57*

AHRENDT, Carl Frederick William (1842-1909) German actor
BE*

AICARD, Jean (1848-1921) French dramatist GRB/2-4

AICKIN, Elinor (d 1914 [80])
actress DD, EA/95

AICKIN, Francis (d 1805) Irish
actor BD, CDP, DD, DNB,
ES, TD/1-2

AICKIN, Graves (d 1799) actor
BD

AICKIN, Mrs. Graves (1770-1814)
actress BD

AICKIN, James (c. 1735-1803)
Irish actor BD, CDP, DD,
DNB, TD/1-2

AIDE, Hamilton (1826-1906)
French/English dramatist
DD, DNB, GRB/1, WWW/1

AIDMAN, Charles (b 1925) American actor, director BE

AIDOO, Ama Ata (b 1942) Ghanian
dramatist CD

AIKEN, Albert W. (1846-94)
American actor, singer,
dramatist CDP, HAS

AIKEN, Conrad (1889-1973)
American poet, dramatist
MD, MWD

AIKEN, Frank Eugene (1840-1910)
American actor, manager
CDP, HAS, PP/1, SR,
WWA/1, WWS

AIKEN, George L. (1830-76)
American actor, dramatist
COC, DAB, DD, ES, HAS,
HJD, MH, NTH, OC/1-3,
RE, SR, WWA/H

AIKEN, Peter (d 1876) comic
singer EA/77*

AIKEN, Mrs. Peter (d 1869 [32])
EA/70*

AILEY, Alvin (b 1931) American
actor, dancer, choreographer,
director, dance coach
BE, CB, ES, TW/14, 19

AIME, Mlle. (fl 1791) dancer
BD

AIMEE, Kirsten (b 1969) American
actor TW/29

AIMEE, Marie [Marie Trochon]
(1852-87) French actress,
singer CDP, DD, NYM, SR

AINLEY, Beatrice (d 1939)
actress WWT/14*

AINLEY, Henry Hinchliffe (1879-

1945) English actor AAS, COC,
DNB, ES, GRB/1-4, OC/1-3,
SR, TW/2, WWT/1-9, WWW/4

AINLEY, Mrs. Henry Hinchliffe
see Sheldon, Suzanne

AINLEY, Richard (1910-56) English
actor ES, WWT/7-14

AINLEY, Mrs. Thomas (d 1884)
EA/85*

AINSLEE, Adra (d 1963 [87])
actress BE*

AINSLEY, Mary (d 1906) EA/07*

AINSLEY, Paul (b 1945) American
actor TW/28-29

AINSWORTH, Mr. (fl 1788-90)
house servant BD

AINSWORTH, Frank K. (d 1879)
American business manager,
advance agent EA/80*

AINSWORTH, George dramatist
FGF

AINSWORTH, Helen Shumate (d
1961 [59]) American performer,
talent representative BE*

AINSWORTH, Sydney (d 1922 [50])
English actor WWM

AIRE, James (fl 1794) singer BD

AISTON, Arthur C. (1868-1924)
American producer SR

AITCHISON, Ivy see St. Helier,
Ivy

AITKEN, Alice (d 1868 [25]) singer
EA/69*

AITKEN, Grover Robert see Dale,
Grover

AITKEN, James (d 1891 [38]) advance agent EA/92*

AITKEN, Kate (d 1971 [81]) performer BP/56*

AITKEN, Margaret Edith [Margaret
Edith Bunten] (d 1909) elocutionist EA/10*

AITKEN, Maria (b 1945) Irish
actress WWT/16

AITKEN, William (d 1882 [55])
dramatist, actor EA/83*

AITKIN, John (fl 1764-1774) singer
BD

AITKINS, Anna (fl 1851) actress
HAS

AITKINS, Edward (d 1883 [64])
comedian EA/84*

AKAR, John (d 1975 [48]) performer
BP/60*

AKBAR (d 1911) gymnast EA/12*

AKED, Muriel (1887-1955) English
actress WWT/7-11

AKEMAN, David (d 1973 [57])

performer BP/58*
AKEROYDE, Samuel (b c.1650)
English composer, instru-
mentalist BD
AKERS, Andra (b 1946) American
actress TW/28, 30
AKERSTROM, Ullie (fl 1890s)
actress, dramatist SR
AKERY, Mr. (fl 1767-88) house
servant? BD
AKHURST, Herbert George (d
1888 [38]) actor EA/89*
AKHURST, Walter James (d 1880
[24]) actor EA/81*
AKHURST, William (d 1878 [55])
English/Australian dramatist
EA/79*
AKID, Everard (d 1879 [65])
musician EA/80*
AKIMOV, Nikolai (d 1968 [67])
producer/director/choreog-
rapher BP/53*
AKINS, Zoe (1886-1958) American
dramatist COC, ES, HJD,
MD, MH, MWD, NTH,
OC/3, SR, TW/14, WWA/3,
WWT/5-12
AKSENFELD, Israel (1787-1866)
Russian dramatist ES
AKST, Harry (1894-1963) song-
writer BE*, BP/47*
ALABASTER, William (1567-
1640) English dramatist
CP/2-3, DD, FGF
ALAINO, Caroline (b 1832)
Italian actress, singer
HAS, SR
ALARCON Y MENDOZA, Juan
Ruiz de (c.1581-1639)
Mexican dramatist COC
ALBA, Alney (b 1910) American
actor TW/9
ALBAN, Jean-Pierre (d 1973
[38]) performer BP/57*
ALBANESE, Francesco (b 1912)
Italian singer ES
ALBANESE, Licia (b 1913/14)
Italian singer CB, ES
ALBANESI, Meggie (1899-1923)
English actress AAS, WWT/4
ALBANI, Mme. [Marie Louise
Emma Cecile Albani-Gye]
(1852-1930) Canadian singer
CDP, DNB, ES, GRB/1-4,
WWA/3-4, WWS, WWW/3
ALBANI-GYE, Marie Louise
Emma Cecile see Albani,
Mme.

ALBAUGH, John W. (1837-1909)
American actor, manager CDP,
DD, HAS, PP/1, SR, WWA/1,
WWS
ALBAUGH, John W., Jr. (1867-
1910) American actor, manager
WWS
ALBAUGH, Mrs. John W., Jr. see
May, Olive
ALBEE, Edward [Franklin] (b 1928)
American dramatist, producer
AAS, BE, CB, CD, CH, COC,
ES, HJD, MD, MH, MWD,
OC/3, PDT, RE, WWT/14-16
ALBEE, Edward Franklin (1857-
1930) American manager DAB,
ES, OC/1-3, SR, WWA/1,
WWS
ALBEE, Portia (b 1860) American
actress PP/1
ALBENIZ, Isaac (1860-1909) Spanish
composer, pianist ES
ALBER, David O. (d 1969 [59])
public relations BP/53*
ALBERG, Mildred Freed (b 1920)
Canadian producer BE
ALBERGHETTI, Anna Maria (b
1936) Italian singer BE, CB,
TW/14, 18
ALBERGHETTI, Carla (b 1939)
Italian singer BE
ALBERGOTTI, Vittoria (fl 1713)
Italian singer BD
ALBERNI, Luis (d 1962 [75]) Spanish
actor BE*
ALBERS, Henry (1866-1926) Dutch/
French singer ES
ALBERT (1789-1865) French dancer,
choreographer ES
ALBERT, Arthur comedian, singer
CDP
ALBERT, Ben English comedian
CDP
ALBERT, Mrs. C. S. see Traux,
Sarah
ALBERT, Eddie (b 1908) American
actor BE, CB, ES, TW/29,
WWT/16
ALBERT, Eugène d' (1864-1932)
Scottish pianist, composer ES
ALBERT, Frank [J. J. Hughes] (d
1902 [68]) EA/03*
ALBERT, Fred English singer,
composer CDP
ALBERT, Margot (b 1943) American
actress TW/26
ALBERT, Mark [Mark Albert Bing-
ham] (d 1890) vocal comedian

EA/91*

ALBERT, Rose [Mrs. Fred Evans] (d 1903 [32]) music-hall performer EA/04*

ALBERT, Wil (b 1930) American actor TW/30

ALBERT, William (1863-1941) West Indian business manager WWT/4-7

ALBERTA, Laura actress CDP

ALBERTARELLI, Francesco (fl 1788-92) Italian singer BD

ALBERTAZZI, Emma [Emma Howson] (1813/14-47) singer CDP, DD, DNB, ES

ALBERTAZZI, Giorgio (b 1923) Italian actor ES

ALBERTIERI, Luigi (1860-1930) Italian dancer, choreographer ES

ALBERTINE, Hannah [Hannah Manchester] (1831-89) actress, dancer CDP, HAS

ALBERTINI, Mme. (fl 1859) singer CDP

ALBERTO, Thomas (d 1871 [31]) music-hall performer ? EA/72*

ALBERTSON, Frank (1909-64) American actor TW/8-11, 20

ALBERTSON, Jack (b 1910?) American actor CB, TW/6, 8, 20, 29-30, WWT/16

ALBERTSON, Lillian (d 1962 [81]) American actress, producer TW/19

ALBERY, Sir Bronson James (1881-1971) English manager ES, OC/1-3, WWA/5, WWT/5-14

ALBERY, Donald Arthur Rolleston (b 1914) English producer BE, OC/3, WWT/10-16

ALBERY, James (1838-89) English dramatist DD, DNB, ES, OC/1-3, SR

ALBIN, J. (d 1886) bicycle performer EA/87*

ALBINI, Lieut. [Frederick Baxter Ewing] (b 1849) English illusionist, humorist GRB/1

ALBONE, James (fl 1740) singer BD

ALBONI, Mme. Marietta [Mme. Zeiger, Countess Pepoli] (1824-94) Italian singer CDP, ES, HAS, SR

ALBRECHT, Caterina K. (d 1896) pianist EA/97*

ALBRECHT, Johanna (b 1940) American actress TW/27

ALBRICI, Bartolomeo (b c.1630) Italian instrumentalist, singer, composer BD

ALBRICI, Leonora (fl 1662-71) Italian singer BD

ALBRICI, Vincenzo (1631-96) Italian instrumentalist, singer, composer BD

ALBRIGHT, Bob (d 1971 [87]) performer BP/55*

ALBRIGHT, Hardie (1903-75) American actor WWT/7-11

ALBRIGHT, H. Darkes (b 1907) American educator, writer, editor BE

ALBU, Annie (fl 1881-90) English singer, actress CDP, DD, DP

ALBUZIO, Mr. (fl 1753-54) singer BD

ALCALDE, Mario (b 1926) American actor TW/10-12, 21

ALCHORNE, Mrs. (1683-87) strong woman BD

ALCIDOR [Philippe Toubel] (fl 1662-68) actor BD

ALCOCK, Mr. (fl 1714) actor BD

ALCOCK, Mrs. (fl 1714) actress BD

ALCOCK, Merle (d 1975 [85]) performer BP/59*

ALCORN, M. (d 1912) sketch performer EA/13*

ALCOTT, Mrs. Margaret see Leighton, Margaret

ALDA, Alan (b 1936) American actor BE, TW/20-24, WWT/15-16

ALDA, Frances [Frances Davis] (1883-1952) New Zealand singer ES

ALDA, Robert (b 1914) American actor AAS, BE, ES, TW/7-8, 13, 21-22, 25-26, WWT/15-16

ALDAY, Paul (1764-1835?) French violinist, composer BD

ALDEN, Hortense (b 1903) American actress BE, WWT/9-10

ALDEN, John (d 1962 [55]) Australian actor, director WWT/14*

ALDEN, Mary Maguire (d 1946 [63]) American actress BE*

ALDERMAN, John (b 1937) American actor TW/16, 21

ALDERSON, Clifton (1864-1930) English actor EA/97, WWT/3-6

ALDERSON, Mrs. Clifton see
Thorne, May
ALDERSON, William (fl 1509-13)
member of the Chapel Royal
DA
ALDERSON, William (b 1935)
American actor TW/25
ALDERTON, John (b 1940) Eng-
lish actor WWT/15-16
ALDIN, Arthur (b 1872) English
manager WWT/3
ALDINI, Mme. (fl 1857) singer
HAS
ALDOUS, Lucette (b 1938) New
Zealand dancer ES
ALDREDGE, Theoni V. Greek
costume designer BE,
WWT/15-16
ALDREDGE, Thomas (b 1928)
American actor, producer,
director BE, TW/22-30,
WWT/16
ALDRICH, Louis [Louis Lyon]
(1843-1901) American actor
CDP, COC, DAB, ES,
OC/1-3, PP/1, SR, WWA/H
ALDRICH, Mariska (b 1881)
American singer ES, WWM
ALDRICH, Perley Dunn (b 1863)
American vocal teacher
WWM
ALDRICH, Richard (1863-1937)
American critic BE*,
BP/21*
ALDRICH, Richard Stoddard
(b 1902) American manager,
producer BE, CB, ES,
TW/2-8, WWT/9-15
ALDRICH, Thomas Baily (1836-
1907) American writer ES,
HJD, WWW/1
ALDRIDGE, Mr. (d 1768) per-
former? BD
ALDRIDGE, Mr. (fl 1790) per-
former? BD
ALDRIDGE, Arthur (b 1879)
English singer WWM
ALDRIDGE, Carrie [Carrie
Southall] (d 1907) EA/08*,
GRB/3*
ALDRIDGE, Ira (d 1886 [24])
pianist EA/87*
ALDRIDGE, Ira Frederick (1804-
67) American actor CDP,
COC, DAB, DD, ES, HAS,
OC/1-3, PDT, WWA/H
ALDRIDGE, John Franklin (d
1899 [54]) actor EA/00*

ALDRIDGE, John Stratten (d 1973
[59]) critic BP/58*
ALDRIDGE, Michael (b 1920) Eng-
lish actor AAS, WWT/11-16
ALDRIDGE, Robert (d 1793) dancer,
ballet master BD
ALDWIN, Mr. (fl 1741) singer BD
ALEDORE (fl 1711) singer? BD
ALEICHEM, Sholom (1859-1916)
Russian/American dramatist
COC, OC/1-3, PDT
ALETTER, Frank (b 1926) American
actor TW/12-13, 16
ALEWORTH, Jeoffrey (d 1687) in-
strumentalist, singer BD
ALEWORTH, William (fl 1662-69)
violinist BD
ALEXANDER, Mr. (fl 1666-67)
actor BD
ALEXANDER, Mr. (fl 1849) actor
HAS
ALEXANDER, Master (fl 1759)
actor BD
ALEXANDER, Miss (fl 1864-69)
American actress HAS
ALEXANDER, Ada music-hall singer
CDP
ALEXANDER, Mrs. Adam see
Blake, Joanna
ALEXANDER, Annie Emma [Mrs.
A. Bradley] (d 1908) EA/09*
ALEXANDER, Arthur (d 1899 [45])
comedian EA/01*
ALEXANDER, Augustine (d 1907
[46]) EA/08*
ALEXANDER, Ben (d 1969 [58])
performer BP/54*
ALEXANDER, Benjamin (fl 1794-95)
violinist BD
ALEXANDER, Brandy (b 1943)
American actress TW/25
ALEXANDER, Charles K. (b 1919/
20/23) Egyptian actor BE,
TW/3, 27-28
ALEXANDER, Cris (b 1920) Amer-
ican actor, photographer BE,
TW/1-3, 9-11, 13, 16, 22
ALEXANDER, David (d 1973 [65])
critic BP/57*
ALEXANDER, Franz (d 1910) EA/
11*
ALEXANDER, George (d 1813)
"Spotted Boy" CDP
ALEXANDER, Sir George [George
Alexander Gibb Samson] (1858-
1918) English actor, manager
COC, EA/96, DD, DNB, DP,
ES, GRB/1-4, NTH, OC/1-3,

SR, WWS, WWT/1-3, WWW/2
ALEXANDER, Hugh (b 1939) Canadian actor TW/26
ALEXANDER, James (d 1962 [46]) musical comedian TW/18
ALEXANDER, James (b 1941) American actor TW/25, 30
ALEXANDER, Jane (b 1939) American actress TW/25, 29-30, WWT/16
ALEXANDER, Janet (d 1961) English actress GRB/1-4, WWT/2-6
ALEXANDER, J. F. (d 1876 [58]) EA/88*
ALEXANDER, John (1796-1851) Scottish manager, actor DD
ALEXANDER, John (b 1897) American actor BE, ES, TW/4-7, 10-20, WWT/9-16
ALEXANDER, Katherine (b 1901) American actress BE, ES, TW/2-7, WWT/7-13
ALEXANDER, Lois (d 1968 [77]) performer BP/52*
ALEXANDER, Mara (d 1965) performer BP/49*
ALEXANDER, Muriel [Muriel Marsh] (1898-1975) Irish actress WWT/5-8
ALEXANDER, Rod (b 1919/22) American educator, actor, director BE, TW/4, 6
ALEXANDER, Rod (b 1920) American dancer, choreographer, director BE
ALEXANDER, Ronald (b 1917) American dramatist, actor BE
ALEXANDER, Ross [Ross Alexander Smith] (1907-37) American actor BE*, BP/21*
ALEXANDER, Sidney (1845-1911) actor SR
ALEXANDER, S. King [W. B. Codrington Ball] Irish manager GRB/1-2
ALEXANDER, Terence (b 1923) English actor WWT/15-16
ALEXANDER, Terry (b 1947) American actor TW/28, 30
ALEXANDER, William, Earl of Stirling (1567/68-1640) dramatist CP/1-3, DD, ES, FGF
ALEXANDRA, Ada (d 1907)

Dutch/English comedienne EA/08*, GRB/3*
ALEXANDRE [Alexander Vattenmare] (1796-1864) French ventriloquist, impersonator CDP, DAB, HAS, WWA/H
ALEXANDRE, Mme. (fl 1859) tight-rope dancer HAS
ALEXANDRE, Rene (d 1946) French actor SR
ALEXANDRE, W. B. (d 1878) ventriloquist EA/79*
ALEXANDRINA dancer CDP
ALEXIS, Mr. (fl 1794) violinist BD
ALFASA, Joe (b 1914) American actor TW/23-26
ALFIERI, Vittorio Amedeo (1749-1803) Italian dramatist ES, OC/1-3
ALFORD, Fred (d 1878) comic singer EA/79*
ALFORD, Walter (b 1912) Canadian press representative BE
ALFORD-MASON, T. (b 1877) English actor, singer, mimic, hypnotist, mesmerist GRB/1
ALFRED, Edward (d 1793) actor, house servant, singer BD
ALFRED, William (b 1922) American scholar, dramatist CD, CH, MH
ALFRIEND, Edward Morrisson (b 1843) American dramatist WWA/4
ALGERANOFF, Harcourt [Harcourt Essex] English dancer ES
ALGERANOVA, Claudie Italian dancer ES
ALI, George (d 1947 [81]) animal impersonator WWT/14*
ALIAS, Charles (d 1921) costumier WWT/14*
ALIAS, Sarah Anne (d 1897) costumier EA/98*
ALICE, Mary (b 1941) American actress TW/24, 26, 28-30
ALINDER, Dallas (b 1941) American actor TW/30
ALISON, George (1866-1936) English actor SR, WWM
ALIVE AND TRUCKING THEATRE CO., The theatre collective CD
ALIX, Mina [Florence Exton] (d 1904) cyclist EA/05*
ALIZA, Ben (b 1938) American actor TW/21

ALKER, Theo (d 1906) comedian EA/07*

ALKOK, John (fl 1554) actor DA

ALLABY, William (fl 1641-62) musician BD

ALLAN, Mrs. (d 1909) dancing teacher EA/10*

ALLAN, Alexander (b 1806) dramatist CDP

ALLAN, Alf (d 1902 [49]) comedian WWT/14*

ALLAN, Alfred Thomas see Perry, Alf

ALLAN, Andrew (d 1974 [66]) performer BP/58*

ALLAN, Charles G. (1852-1911) English actor DD, EA/97, GRB/1-4

ALLAN, Christopher (d 1973 [46]) agent BP/58*

ALLAN, Dot (d 1964) dramatist BP/49*

ALLAN, Elizabeth (b 1910) English actress ES, WWT/7-14

ALLAN, Emily (d 1889) EA/90*

ALLAN, Ernest (d 1903 [33]) pianist, composer EA/04*

ALLAN, Jed (b 1938) American actor TW/23

ALLAN, John, Jr. (d 1878 [24]) musical director EA/79*

ALLAN, Louise Rosalie [née Despréaux] (1810-56) actress BE*

ALLAN, Maud (1879-1956) Canadian dancer ES, GRB/4, WWT/1-11, WWW/5

ALLAN, Oswald (d 1893 [45]) dramatist EA/94*

ALLAN, Ted (b 1916) Canadian dramatist CD

ALLAN, Watty (d 1903 [35]) comedian WWT/14*

ALLAN CARADORI, Mme. (d 1865 [65]) singer HAS, SR

ALLANDALE, Fred [Frederick Arnold] (1872-1921) English actor, singer GRB/1-3

ALLANO clown CDP

ALLANSON, Charles (fl 1691-96) singer BD

ALLARD, Sieur (fl 1702) French dancer BD

ALLARDICE, James (d 1966 [46]) dramatist BP/50*

ALLARDICE, Robert Barclay (1779-1854) pedestrian CDP

ALLDEN, Mr. S. (fl 1794) violinist BD

ALLEGRANTI, Teresa Maddalena [Mrs. Harrison] (c.1750-c.1802) Italian singer BD

ALLEGRET, Marc (d 1973 [73]) producer/director/choreographer BP/58*

ALLEGRO, Anita (d 1964) actress BE*

ALLEN, Mr. (fl 1732-33) actor BD

ALLEN, Mr. (fl 1733-34) treasurer BD

ALLEN, Mr. (fl 1737-40) house servant BD

ALLEN, Mr. (fl 1746-57) actor BD

ALLEN, Mr. (fl 1761-74?) house servant? BD

ALLEN, Mr. (fl 1764-65) dresser BD

ALLEN, Mr. (fl 1764-98) dramatist CP/3

ALLEN, Mr. (fl 1793) dancer BD

ALLEN, Mr. (fl 1828) American actor HAS

ALLEN, Mrs. (fl 1746-67) house servant? BD

ALLEN, Mrs. (fl 1789-92) BD

ALLEN, Adrianne (b 1907) English actress BE, ES, TW/3, 5-6, 13, WWT/7-14

ALLEN, A. Hylton (b 1879) English actor ES, WWT/4-12

ALLEN, Alfred (1866-1947) American dramatist WWA/2, WWM

ALLEN, Andrew Jackson (1776-1853) American actor, costumier CDP, DD, HAS, SR, WWA/H

ALLEN, Ann (fl 1742-69) actress, house servant? BD

ALLEN, Mrs. Annie (d 1893) EA/94*

ALLEN, Mme. Caradori see Allan Caradori, Mme.

ALLEN, Charles Leslie (1830-1917) American actor GRB/3-4, PP/1, WWM, WWS, WWT/1-3

ALLEN, Chesney [William E. Allen] (b 1896) English music-hall comedian COC, WWT/10-11

ALLEN, Mrs. Clarissa [Mrs. Lacombe or La Coomb] (d 1851) American actress DD, HAS, SR

ALLEN, C. Leslie (b 1830) American actor HAS

ALLEN, Mrs. C. Leslie [Sarah Lyon] (fl c.1850s) English actress HAS

ALLEN, David (d 1903 [72]) theatrical printer EA/04*

ALLEN, Deborah (b 1950) American actress TW/30

ALLEN, Dennis R. (b 1940) American actor TW/25

ALLEN, Dion (b 1922) American actor TW/7-8

ALLEN, Dorothy (d 1970 [74]) performer BP/55*

ALLEN, Mrs. Edwin (d 1905 [51]) EA/06*

ALLEN, Elizabeth [Elizabeth Ellen Gillease] (b 1934) American actress, singer BE, TW/16-17, 21-23, WWT/15-16

ALLEN, Emily Louisa (d 1905 [45]) EA/06*

ALLEN, Mrs. F. (d 1874) EA/75*

ALLEN, Frank (b 1851) English manager, proprietor GRB/1-4, WWT/1-2

ALLEN, Fred [John Florence Sullivan] (1894-1956) American actor ES, NTH, SR, TW/12

ALLEN, Frederick (d 1879) circus proprietor EA/80*

ALLEN, G. (d 1870) circus proprietor? EA/71*

ALLEN, George (d 1877) singer EA/78*

ALLEN, Gracie (1905-64) American comedienne CB, ES, SR, TW/21, WWA/4

ALLEN, Harry actor CDP

ALLEN, Harry (d 1876) equestrian EA/77*

ALLEN, Harry (d 1906 [24]) music-hall comedian EA/07*

ALLEN, Henry (d 1867 [48]) comedian EA/68*

ALLEN, Henry Robinson (1809-76) Irish singer ES

ALLEN, H. Marsh English actor GRB/3-4, WWT/1-6

ALLEN, Horace (d 1896 [40]) actor EA/97*

ALLEN, Inglis (1879-1943) English dramatist WWW/4

ALLEN, Jack (b 1907) English actor WWT/9-16

ALLEN, James (fl 1732) singer

BD

ALLEN, Mrs. James see Grahame, Cissy

ALLEN, James Lane (1849-1915) American dramatist WWM, WWW/2

ALLEN, Jay (b 1922) American dramatist MH

ALLEN, Jeremy (fl 1640) actor DA

ALLEN, Jerrard Grant (b 1878) English manager GRB/2-4, WWT/1

ALLEN, J. H. American actor DD

ALLEN, Mrs. J. H. see Allen, Louise

ALLEN, Mrs. J. H. see Vaidis, Lizzie

ALLEN, John (1570?-93?) actor DA

ALLEN, John (d 1722) violinist BD

ALLEN, John (fl 1761) musician? BD

ALLEN, Johnny [George Erb] (1844-85) minstrel CDP

ALLEN, John Piers (b 1912) English principal of the Central School of Speech and Drama WWT/16

ALLEN, Jonelle (b 1944) American actress TW/28-30

ALLEN, Jonny (b 1962) American actor TW/26

ALLEN, Joseph (1840-1917) English actor SR

ALLEN, Joseph (d 1952 [80]) American actor TW/9

ALLEN, Joseph, Jr. (d 1963 [44]) American actor BE*

ALLEN, Joyce (b 1926) American actress TW/3

ALLEN, Judith (fl 1933-50) American actress ES

ALLEN, Judy (b 1945) American actress TW/24, 28

ALLEN, Kelcey (1875-1951) American critic NTH, TW/8, WWT/7-11

ALLEN, Kenneth (d 1976 [72]) performer BP/60*

ALLEN, Leslie (fl 1759-61) English actor SR

ALLEN, Mrs. Leslie (fl 1759-61) English actress SR

ALLEN, Lester (d 1949 [58]) comedian TW/6

ALLEN, Lewis (b 1905) English actor ES

ALLEN, Lewis (b 1922) American

producer BE
ALLEN, Louise [Mrs. J. H.
Allen] (fl 1856) American?
actress CDP
ALLEN, Louise [Mrs. William
Collier] (d 1909 [36]) Amer-
ican actress GRB/2-4, WWS
ALLEN, Marc, III (b 1943) Amer-
ican actor TW/26-27
ALLEN, Marie [Mrs. Wilkinson]
(d 1880 [27]) actress EA/81*
ALLEN, Marsh see Allen,
H. Marsh
ALLEN, Michael K. (b 1940)
American actor TW/24
ALLEN, Neal (d 1974 [22]) com-
poser/lyricist BP/58*
ALLEN, Norman (b 1939) English
actor TW/21-23, 25-26,
28-29
ALLEN, Patrick (b 1927) actor
WWT/16
ALLEN, Paul Hastings (b 1883)
American composer ES
ALLEN, Percy (d 1959 [86])
critic WWT/14*
ALLEN, Rae [Raffaella Julia
Thérésa Abruzzo] (b 1926)
American actress BE, TW/
16, 21-23, 25-27, 29,
WWT/14-16
ALLEN, Ralph Donkin (d 1906
[69]) EA/07*
ALLEN, Reginald (b 1905) Amer-
ican administrator, writer
BE
ALLEN, Richard (fl 1609-13)
actor DA
ALLEN, Rita (d 1968 [56])
producer BE, TW/25
ALLEN, Robert (b 1906) Amer-
ican actor TW/1-3, 13, 16
ALLEN, Robert H. (d 1912)
EA/13*
ALLEN, Mrs. Robert W. (1865-
91) actress SR
ALLEN, Seth (b 1941) American
actor TW/25-26, 28-30
ALLEN, Sheila (b 1932) English
actress WWT/14-16
ALLEN, Steve (b 1921) American
comedian, composer, writer
BE
ALLEN, Susan Westford (d 1944
[79]) performer TW/1
ALLEN, Theodore singer CDP
ALLEN, Thomas (1696?-1738)
house servant, pugilist BD

ALLEN, Thomas (b c.1757) dwarf
BD, CDP
ALLEN, Thomas (fl 1794) musician
BD
ALLEN, Tomasso (d 1898 [37])
equestrian EA/99*
ALLEN, Vera (b 1897) American
actress BE, TW/2-3, 10-11,
WWT/10-14
ALLEN, Viola [Mrs. Peter Duryea]
(1869-1948) American actress
COC, DAB, ES, GRB/2-4,
NTH, OC/1-3, PP/1, SR,
TW/4, WWA/2, WWM, WWS,
WWT/1-10
ALLEN, Mrs. Vivian Beaumont (d
1962 [70]) philanthropist BE*,
BP/47*
ALLEN, Vivienne (d 1963 [42])
performer BP/48*
ALLEN, W. (fl 1794) musician BD
ALLEN, Walter (b 1940) actor
TW/25
ALLEN, Walter C. (d 1903) music-
hall comedian EA/04*
ALLEN, W. H. (d 1884) pedestal
clog dancer EA/85*
ALLEN, William (d 1647) English
actor COC, DA, DD, ES,
OC/1-3
ALLEN, William E. see Allen,
Chesney
ALLEN, Woody (b 1935) American
comedian, writer CB, TW/25-
26, WWT/16
ALLENBY, Frank (1898-1953) Tas-
manian actor ES, TW/4,
WWT/7-12
ALLENBY, Peggy [Eleanor Byrne
Fox] (1905-67) American
actress WWT/7-8
ALLENSON, Mr. (fl 1669-70) actor?
BD
ALLENTUCK, Max (b 1911) Ameri-
can business manager, manager
BE
ALLERS, Mr. (fl 1793) actor BD
ALLERS, Franz (b 1905) Czech
conductor BE
ALLESTREE, Mary [Geraldine Ed-
dowes] (d 1912) English actress
GRB/1
ALLEYN, Annie [Mrs. Charles
Bernard] (1860-96) English
actress DD
ALLEYN, Edward (1566-1626) Eng-
lish actor CDP, COC, DA, DD,
DNB, ES, GT, HP, NTH,

OC/1-3, PDT
ALLEYN, Hilda (d 1897 [18])
singer EA/98*
ALLEYN, John (1556/57-96)
actor DA
ALLEYN, Richard (d 1601) actor
DA
ALLEYN, W. (d 1895) comedian
EA/96*
ALLEYNE, Miss [?=Muriel
Alleyne] actress DD
ALLEYNE, J. M. (d 1874 [40])
music-hall chairman EA/75*
ALLEYNE, Muriel [Flora Mid-
dleton Stanley] English
actress GRB/1
ALLEYNE-BARRETT, Elise Bar-
bara see Craven, Elise
ALLEYN'S BOY (fl 1600-01)
actor DA
ALLFORD, Mrs. Emma (d 1871)
EA/72*
ALLFORD, Mary (d 1875) EA/
76*
ALLGOOD, Sara (1883-1950)
Irish actress COC, ES,
OC/1-3, TW/2-7, WWT/
2-10
ALLIN, Norman (b 1885) English
singer, chorus master ES
ALLINGHAM, Mr. (fl 1798)
house servant BD
ALLINGHAM, John (fl 1636)
actor DA
ALLINGHAM, John Till (fl 1799-
1810) English dramatist
CDP, CP/3, DD, DNB,
ES, GT, TD/1-2
ALLINGHAM, Maria Caroline
[Mrs. Samuel Ricketts] (d
1811) English actress BD
ALLINGHAM, William (1828-89)
dramatist DD
ALLINSON, Mrs. (fl 1699) singer
BD
ALLINSON, Michael English
actor BE, TW/22-23, 26-
27, WWT/16
ALLIO, René (b 1921) French
scene designer, costume
designer ES
ALLISON, Mr. (fl 1735) actor
BD
ALLISON, Mr. (fl 1788-92)
dancer BD
ALLISON, Mrs. (fl 1703-05)
actress BD
ALLISON, Miss (b 1819) see

Seymour, Mrs.
ALLISON, Betty (fl 1693-97) actress
BD
ALLISON, George (d 1936 [70])
actor WWT/14*
ALLISON, James (d 1890) Australian
manager EA/91*
ALLISON, Laura (d 1879 [59])
actress, manager CDP
ALLISON, Maria (fl 1698-99)
actress, singer BD
ALLISON, Ralph (fl 1690s) singer
BD
ALLISTER, Claud (1891-1967/70)
English actor ES, TW/4,
WWT/7-13
ALLITEN, Mary Frances (d 1912
[63]) composer EA/13*
ALLMON, Clinton (b 1941) Ameri-
can actor TW/25-26
ALLNUTT, Alfred (d 1867 [17])
singer? EA/68*
ALLNUTT, Eugénie (d 1901) ballet
mistress, actress EA/02*
ALLNUTT, Sarah (d 1887 [80])
EA/88*
ALLSBROOKE, Bill (b 1945) Amer-
ican actor TW/26-28
ALLWOOD, Frederick William (d
1903) composer, conductor
EA/04*
ALLWOOD, Thomas (d 1886) actor,
composer EA/88*
ALLYN, Adam (d 1768) actor BD,
HAS
ALLYN, Mrs. Adam (fl 1759-61) HAS
ALLYN, Alyce (d 1975) performer
BP/60*
ALLYN, William (b 1927) American
actor TW/3
ALLYSON, June (b 1923/26) Amer-
ican actress CB, ES, TW/26
ALMAR, C. Norman (d 1900 [33])
advance agent EA/01*
ALMAR, George (b 1802) actor,
dramatist, manager CDP, DD
ALMAR, Joe (d 1897) gymnast
EA/98*
ALMA-TADEMA, Sir Lawrence
(1836-1912) Dutch/English de-
signer, painter COC, DNB,
OC/1-3, WWW/1
ALMERS, Walter (d 1916) EA/17*
ALMOND, Emma [Miss E. Romer]
(1814-68) English singer
CDP, DD
ALMOND, John (d 1885) comedian,
scenic artist EA/86*

ALMOND, R. P. (d 1878 [54])
theatrical and musical caterer
EA/79*

ALMONTE, Charlie [Charles
Frederick Burgess] (d 1892
[48]) founder of the Almonte
Troupe EA/93*

ALMONTE, Marie A. (d 1973)
performer BP/58*

ALMONTE, William [William Bur-
gess] (d 1900 [43]) pantomimist EA/01*

ALMONTI, Ada Burgess (d 1899)
EA/00*

ALMORAVIDS, Tchaka (b 1939)
American actor TW/26

ALONSO, Alicia (b 1921) Cuban
dancer CB, ES

ALONSO, Fernando (b 1914)
Cuban dancer ES

ALONSO, Master [of the Tremaine Family] CDP

ALPAR, Gita (b 1900) Hungarian
actress, singer WWT/8-10

ALPERN, Morris Mark (b 1940)
American actor TW/23

ALPERN, Susan (b 1955) American actress TW/24

ALPERSON, Edward L. (d 1969
[73]) producer/director/
choreographer BP/54*

ALPORT, Sidney (d 1906 [59])
manager EA/07*

ALSEDGER, Mr. (fl 1794) musician BD

ALSKA, Daisy (d 1892) EA/93*

ALSKA, Walter [Walter Pollard]
(d 1896) variety performer
EA/97*

ALSOP, Mrs. Frances (d 1821)
English actress CDP, DD,
HAS, SR

ALSWANG, Ralph (b 1916) American designer, director,
producer BE, TW/2-8,
WWT/12-16

ALT, Natalie American singer,
actress WWT/4-5

ALTEMUS, J. K. (d 1854) actor
HAS

ALTEMUS, Mrs. J. K. (fl 1842)
actress HAS

ALTER, Lottie (fl 1890-1900)
American actress WWM,
WWS

ALTER, Martha (b 1904) American composer ES

ALTGLASS, Max Mayer (1895-

1952) Polish singer WWA/3

ALTHOFF, Charles R. (d 1962 [72])
actor BE*

ALTHOUSE, Earl F. (d 1971 [78])
performer BP/55*

ALTHOUSE, Paul Shearer (1889-
1954) American singer ES,
WWA/3

ALTIER, William B. (d 1971)
founder of the first dinner
theatre BP/56*

ALTIERE, Guiditta singer CDP

ALTMAN, Charles American stage
lighting executive BE

ALTMAN, Frieda (b 1904) American
actress BE, ES, TW/2-6

ALTMAN, Richard (b 1932) American director, actor BE, ES

ALTMAN, Ruth American actress,
singer BE, WWT/8-10

ALTON, George (d 1875 [48]) singer
EA/76*

ALTON, Robert (d 1957 [54]) American director, choreographer
TW/13

ALVA, Mme. [Mrs. Hettie St. John
Brenon] (d 1904) lyric artist
EA/05*

ALVAREZ [Albert Raymond Gour-
ron] (1861-1933) French singer
ES, GRB/1-4, WWS

ALVAREZ, Anita (b 1920) American
actress TW/3-4, 6

ALVAREZ, Carmen American
dancer, singer, actress BE,
TW/24-26, 29-30

ALVAREZ, Julio (d 1969 [63])
performer BP/54*

ALVAREZ, Luis (b 1872) Spanish
singer GRB/3

ALVAREZ, Marguerite d' (b c.1886)
English singer ES

ALVAREZ QUINTERO, Joaquin
(1873-1944) Spanish dramatist
CB, COC, MWD, OC/2-3,
PDT

ALVAREZ QUINTERO, Serafin
(1871-1938) Spanish dramatist
COC, MWD, OC/2-3, PDT

ALVARY, Lorenzo (b 1909) American singer ES

ALVARY, Max [Maximilian Achen-
bach] (1856-98) German singer
ES

ALVO, Henry [Henry Thorpe] (d
1901 [43]) circus proprietor
EA/02*

ALVORD, Ned (d 1970 [87])

publicist BP/55*

ALZAR, Mme. [Mrs. T. Stevens] (d 1907 [43]) costumier EA/08*, GRB/3*

AMADEI, Alexander (fl 1684) mountebank BD

AMADEI, Filippo (b c.1683) Italian instrumentalist, composer BD

AMADI, Mme. [Annie Tremaine] actress, singer DD

AMALIA, Miss (fl. 1869-88) actress DD, OAA/2

AMAN, John American actor TW/25, 28

AMANTINI, Sig. (fl 1778) singer BD

AMATO, Pasquale (1879-1942) Italian singer CB, ES, WWA/2

AMAYA, Carmen (1913-63) Spanish dancer, choreographer ES, TW/20

AMBER, Mabel (1866-1945) American actress SR

AMBER, Maude (d 1938 [66]) American actress BE*

AMBER, Norton (fl 1744-54) patentee, banker, pit-door-keeper BD

AMBERG, George H. (1901-71) critic, curator ES

AMBERG, Gustave (1844-1921) manager BP/5*, WWT/14*

AMBIENT, Mark (1860-1937) English dramatist, actor DD, GRB/1-3, WWT/2-7

AMBLER, Mr. (fl 1661) singer BD

AMBLER, Johnson (d 1873) manager EA/74*

AMBRE, Emilie (d 1898) singer CDP

AMBROISE, Antonio (fl 1752-78) puppet-showman BD

AMBROSE, Mr. (fl 1735-36) house servant BD

AMBROSE, Mrs. [Mrs. Jona] (fl c.1739-1813) actress BD

AMBROSE, Mrs. (fl 1735-36) house servant? BD

AMBROSE, Mrs. [née Mahon] (fl 1770-89) singer BD

AMBROSE, Miss (fl 1731-32) dancer BD

AMBROSE, Miss [Mrs. Kelf; Mrs. Egerton] (fl 1739-1813) Gibraltan actress

BD, DD

AMBROSE, Miss E. (fl 1756-87) actress BD

AMBROSE, John (b 1763) English instrumentalist, composer BD

AMBROSE, Kay English critic ES

AMBROSINI, Antonia (fl 1754) singer BD

AMBURGH, Van see Van Amburgh, Isaac A.

AMCOTTS, Vincent (d 1881) dramatist, manager DD

AMECHE, Don [Dominic Felix Amici] (b 1908) American actor CB, SR, TW/24, WWT/15-16

AMENDOLIA, Don (b 1945) American actor TW/28

AMERICAN WOMAN, The (fl 1781) dwarf? BD

AMERIS, Giovanna (d 1891) singer EA/92*

AMES, Adrienne (d 1947 [39]) American actress TW/2-3

AMES, Amy (d 1916) actress SR

AMES, Cindy American actress TW/26, 28

AMES, Ed (b 1929) American actor TW/20

AMES, Emma see Girdlestone, Amy

AMES, Florenz (b 1884) American actor, singer TW/1, 8, WWT/10-12

AMES, Gerald (1881-1933) English actor ES, WWT/4-7

AMES, Harry (d 1969 [76]) performer BP/54*

AMES, Leon (b 1903) American actor BE, TW/24, WWT/10-11

AMES, Michael see Andrews, Tod

AMES, Percy (d 1936 [62]) English actor SR

AMES, Robert (1893-1931) American actor ES, WWT/5-6

AMES, Rosemary (b 1906) American actress WWT/8-9

AMES, Winthrop (1871-1937) American manager COC, DAB, ES, NTH, OC/1-3, SR, WWA/1, WWT/3-8

AMHERST, G. A. see Amherst, J. H.

AMHERST, J. H. [or G. A.] (1776-1851) English actor, dramatist DD, HAS, SR

AMIC, Henry (d 1929 [75]) dramatist BE*

AMICA, V. (fl 1848) chorus

master HAS
AMIC-ANGELO, Andrew (b 1943)
American actor TW/24, 27
AMICI, Dominic Felix see
Ameche, Don
AMICONI, Jacopo (c. 1675-1752)
Italian scene painter BD
AMIEL, Josette (b 1933) French
dancer ES
AMMIDON, Hoyt (b 1909) Ameri-
can executive BE
AMNER, Ralph (c. 1584-1664)
English singer BD
AMODIO, Alessandro (fl 1855)
singer CDP
AMORE, James (d 1974 [27])
performer BP/58*
AMORETTI, Giustina (fl 1748-49)
Italian singer BD
AMOREVOLI, Angelo (1716-98)
Italian singer BD, ES
AMOS, Ruth American actress
TW/4
"AMOS AND ANDY" see Gosden,
Charles Freeman
AMPHLETT, Mr. (fl 1802)
dramatist CP/3
AMRAM, David Werner (b 1930)
American composer, con-
ductor, musician BE, CB
AMSDEN, Minneola (d 1962 [75])
performer BE*
AMSTEL, Jane (d 1949 [48])
actress WWT/14*
ANALEAU, Mr. (fl 1687-88)
singer? BD
ANANIA, John (b 1923) Italian
actor TW/26-28
ANATO, Marie (d 1889) EA/90*
ANATO, Nina see Melbourne,
Mrs. Walter
ANATO, Palmyra equestrienne
CDP
ANCEY, Georges (1860-1926)
dramatist BE*
ANCHUTZ, Miss see Zimmer-
man, Mlle.
ANCLIFFE, Charles (d 1953
[72]) composer WWT/14*
ANCONA, Mario (1860-1931) Italian
singer ES
ANCOT, Jean (1779-1848) violinist,
pianist, composer CDP
ANDERMAN, Maureen (b 1946)
American actress TW/27-29
ANDERS, Glenn (b 1890) American
actor BE, ES, TW/1-18,
WWT/6-14

ANDERS, Katie (b 1942) American
actress TW/25, 28
ANDERSEN, Gerald (b 1910) English
actor TW/3
ANDERSEN, Hans Christian (1805-
75) Danish dramatist BE*
ANDERSEN, Lale (d 1972 [59]) per-
former BP/57*
ANDERSON, Mr. (d 1767) actor
BD
ANDERSON, Mr. (fl 1794) musician
BD
ANDERSON, Mr. (fl 1850s) English
prompter HAS
ANDERSON, Mrs. (fl 1743?-50)
actress BD
ANDERSON, Mrs. see Hill, Mrs.
ANDERSON, Miss (fl 1733-37)
dancer BD
ANDERSON, Miss (fl 1782) actress
BD
ANDERSON, Addie (1844/58-84)
American actress HAS
ANDERSON, A. G. (d 1904) pro-
prietor EA/05*
ANDERSON, Alfred (d 1876 [28])
pianist EA/77*
ANDERSON, Anne Renée (b 1920)
American actress TW/5
ANDERSON, Beverly (b 1932) Amer-
ican talent representative BE
ANDERSON, Bronco Billy (d 1971
[88]) performer BP/55*
ANDERSON, Mrs. Caroline Amelia
Sophia (d 1868) EA/69*
ANDERSON, Cecil (d 1968 [62])
composer/lyricist BP/53*
ANDERSON, Christian Oscar (d
1876 [59]) EA/77*
ANDERSON, Clair Mathes (d 1964
[68]) American actress BE*
ANDERSON, Dallas (d 1934 [60])
Scottish performer BE*, BP/
19*, WWT/14*
ANDERSON, Daphne (b 1922) English
actress, singer WWT/11-16
ANDERSON, David (fl 1874-82)
critic DD
ANDERSON, David C. (1813-84)
American actor CDP, DD,
HAS, SR
ANDERSON, Mrs. David C. (d
1840) actress DD, HAS, SR
ANDERSON, David-Rhys (b 1945)
Welsh actor TW/23
ANDERSON, Douglas (b 1948)
American actor TW/30
ANDERSON, E. Abbot see

Aynesworth, E. Allan

ANDERSON, Edith (b 1816) American actress SR

ANDERSON, Elizabeth (d 1887) EA/89*

ANDERSON, Elizabeth see Thomas, Mrs. Jacob Wonderly, I

ANDERSON, Flora (d 1870 [17]) EA/71*

ANDERSON, Florence (d 1962 [80]) English wardrobe mistress, performer BE*, BP/47*

ANDERSON, Fred see Sutherland, Fred

ANDERSON, Garland (d 1939 [53]) American dramatist BE*, WWT/14*

ANDERSON, George composer CDP

ANDERSON, George Frederick (d 1876 [83]) violinist EA/78*

ANDERSON, G. H. (d 1867 [36]) comedian, singer EA/68*

ANDERSON, G. H. (b 1861) actor SR

ANDERSON, Gwen actress TW/1

ANDERSON, Harry English comedian, singer CDP

ANDERSON, Harry (d 1918) EA/19*

ANDERSON, Mrs. Henry see Macfarren, Alice

ANDERSON, Hugh (d 1965 [75]) dramatist BP/50*

ANDERSON, James (fl 1820s) American? actor, prompter CDP, DD, HAS

ANDERSON, James (d 1893) Irish actor EA/94*

ANDERSON, James (d 1969) performer BP/54*

ANDERSON, James P. (1837-1911) American circus performer and manager SR

ANDERSON, James Robertson (1811-95) Scottish actor CDP, DD, DNB, ES, HAS, OAA/1-2, SR, WWA/H

ANDERSON, Mrs. James Robertson (fl 1831) English actress HAS

ANDERSON, Jane see Germon, Mrs. C. G.

ANDERSON, J. F. R. (d 1905) journalist EA/06*

ANDERSON, J. Grant (b 1897) Scottish actor, producer WWT/11-16

ANDERSON, Mrs. J. H. see Levey, Nellie

ANDERSON, John (b 1922) American actor TW/13

ANDERSON, John Hargis (1896-1943) American critic, dramatist CB, NTH, SR, WWA/2, WWT/9

ANDERSON, John Henry [Wizard of the North] (1815-74) Scottish magician, actor CDP, DNB, SR

ANDERSON, John Henry (d 1878 [34]) EA/79*

ANDERSON, John Murray (1886-1954) Canadian producer, lyricist, dancer, ES, TW/2-8, 10, WWA/3, WWT/5-11

ANDERSON, Josephine [née Bartolozzi] (1807-48) English actress CDP, DD, HAS

ANDERSON, Joshua R. (fl 1831) actor, singer CDP, DD, SR

ANDERSON, Dame Judith (b 1898) Australian/American actress AAS, BE, CB, COC, ES, NTH, OC/1-3, PDT, SR, TW/2-21, 23, 27, WWT/6-16

ANDERSON, Julia (d 1950 [86]) Danish/American dramatist, actress BE*, BP/36*

ANDERSON, Katherine American actress TW/8

ANDERSON, Lawrence (1893-1939) English actor WWT/5-8

ANDERSON, Lee (d 1889 [41]) manager EA/91*

ANDERSON, Leroy (1908-75) American composer, conductor BE, CB

ANDERSON, L. G. Abbot see Goodrich, Louis

ANDERSON, Linda (d 1975 [36]) producer/director/choreographer BP/60*

ANDERSON, Lindsay Gordon (b 1923) English director AAS, CB, COC, PDT, WWT/14-16

ANDERSON, Lizzie (d 1878 [16]) EA/79*

ANDERSON, Louise (d 1877) American actress EA/78*

ANDERSON, Lucy (1790-1878) pianist CDP

ANDERSON, Maggie (d 1876 [36]) EA/78*

ANDERSON, Marian (b 1908)
American singer CB, SR
ANDERSON, Marie (d 1900)
actress EA/97
ANDERSON, Mary [Mme. de
Navarro] (1859-1940) Amer-
ican actress CB, CDP,
COC, DAB, DD, ES, GRB/1,
3, NTH, OC/1-3, PP/1,
SR, WWA/4, WWM, WWS,
WWT/4-9
ANDERSON, Mary American
actress TW/11
ANDERSON, Max (d 1943) mana-
ger SR
ANDERSON, Maxwell (1888-1959)
American dramatist AAS,
CB, CH, COC, ES, HJD,
MD, MH, MWD, NTH,
OC/1-3, PDT, RE, SR,
TW/14, WWA/3, WWT/6-
12, WWW/5
ANDERSON, Millar (b 1880)
Irish actor GRB/1-2
ANDERSON, Ophelia [née Pelby]
(1813-52) American actress
DD, HAS, SR
ANDERSON, P. August (1839-
1919) actor SR
ANDERSON, Paul American
actor TW/5-6
ANDERSON, Percy (d 1928 [77])
designer WWT/14*
ANDERSON, Phyllis Stohl (d
1956 [49]) American literary
representative BE*, BP/41*
ANDERSON, Reddick (d 1907)
English actor CDP
ANDERSON, Richard (b 1926)
American actor BE
ANDERSON, Robert W. (d 1971
[31]) performer BP/55*
ANDERSON, Robert W[oodruff]
(b 1917) American dramatist
AAS, BE, CB, CD, CH, ES,
HJD, MD, MWD, PDT,
WWT/13-16
ANDERSON, Robina (d 1900 [54])
actress EA/01*
ANDERSON, Rona (b 1928) Scot-
tish actress WWT/12-16
ANDERSON, Ruth (d 1975 [64])
performer BP/60*
ANDERSON, Sara (b 1920)
American actress TW/4
ANDERSON, Sherwood (1876-1941)
American dramatist DAB,
NTH, WWW/4

ANDERSON, Stuart [Stuart Newman]
(d 1911 [25]) box-office keeper
EA/12*
ANDERSON, Thomas (d 1891 [70])
musician EA/92*
ANDERSON, Thomas (b 1906) Amer-
ican actor TW/25-29
ANDERSON, T. J. (d 1897) stage
manager EA/98*
ANDERSON, Victoria (d 1875) wire-
walker EA/76*
ANDERSON, Weldon see Ather-
stone, Weldon
ANDERSON, Will (d 1869 [34])
music-hall performer? EA/70*
ANDERSON, William (d 1869) Amer-
ican actor DD
ANDERSON, Mrs. William (d 1831)
American actress DD, HAS,
SR
ANDERTON, Mr. actor CDP
ANDERTON, Sarah [née Coxer]
(d 1869) English actress DD,
HAS
ANDES, Keith (b 1920) American
actor, singer BE, TW/3-9
ANDETON, Mr. actor CDP
ANDO, Flavio Italian actor, mana-
ger WWT/2-3
ANDOGA, Victor (d 1969 [91])
producer/director/choreographer
BP/54*
ANDRA, Fern (d 1974 [80]) perform-
er BP/58*
ANDRE, Frank (b 1942) American
actor TW/24-26
ANDRE, Gaby (d 1972) performer
BP/57*
ANDRE, Gwili (d 1959 [51]) Danish
actress BE*
ANDRE, Joan (b 1929) American
actress TW/3
ANDRE, Mjr. John (1751-80) Eng-
lish designer NTH, SR
ANDRE, Theodore see Van Griet-
huysen, Ted
ANDREA, Sieur (fl 1781) whistler
BD
ANDREAE, Otto Stuart see
Stuart, Otto
ANDREAS, Miss (fl 1779-80) dancer
BD
ANDREE, Emilie see D'Alençon,
Emilienne
ANDREEV, Leonid Nikolaevich see
Andreyev, Leonid Nikolaivich
ANDREINI, Isabella (1562-1604)
actress, singer CDP

ANDREONI, Mr. (fl 1739-42)
Italian singer BD
ANDRES, Barbara (b 1939) American actress TW/26
ANDRESEN, Hans (b 1869) German actor, manager GRB/4, WWT/1-2
ANDREWE, Henry (fl 1509-11) member of the Chapel Royal DA
ANDREWES, Richard (fl 1584) actor DA
ANDREWS, Mr. (fl 1752) actor BD
ANDREWS, Mr. (fl 1792-99?) dresser, house servant BD
ANDREWS, Mr. (fl 1794) music porter BD
ANDREWS, Mr. (fl 1794) singer BD
ANDREWS, Mrs. (fl 1696-97) actress BD
ANDREWS, Mrs. (d 1907) "coon" singer EA/08*
ANDREWS, Miss (fl 1796-98) singer, actress BD, DD, TD/1-2
ANDREWS, Miss actress HAS
ANDREWS, A. [né Isaacs] (b 1807) Jamaican actor DD, HAS
ANDREWS, Adora (d 1956 [84]) American actress BE*
ANDREWS, Albert Garcia (d 1950 [93]) American actor OAA/1-2, TW/7
ANDREWS, Ann (b 1895) American actress BE, TW/3-8, WWT/7-11
ANDREWS, Bobbie (b 1894) English actor WWT/1-4
ANDREWS, Charles Bond (d 1899 [42]) composer, conductor EA/00*
ANDREWS, Dana (b 1912) American actor BE, CB, ES, WWT/14-16
ANDREWS, Mr. E. (fl 1760-70?) singer BD
ANDREWS, E. A. (d 1893 [28]) EA/94*
ANDREWS, Edward (b 1914) American actor TW/5, 8, 17
ANDREWS, Elizabeth (1821-1910) English actress BE*, WWT/14*
ANDREWS, George H. (1798-

1866) English actor CDP, DD, HAS, SR
ANDREWS, George Lee (b 1942) American actor TW/28-30
ANDREWS, Harry (b 1911) English actor AAS, ES, TW/2, 8, WWT/11-16
ANDREWS, Henry (d 1890) actor EA/91*
ANDREWS, James Glen (d 1880 [40]) actor EA/81*
ANDREWS, James Petit (d 1797) English dramatist CP/3, DD
ANDREWS, Jane (d 1883 [50]) EA/84*
ANDREWS, Jane see Germon, Mrs. Greene C.
ANDREWS, Jane A. singer CDP
ANDREWS, Julie [Julia Elizabeth Wells] (b 1935) English actress, singer AAS, BE, CB, ES, TW/11-20, WWT/11-15
ANDREWS, Lois (d 1968 [44]) actress TW/24
ANDREWS, Louise [Mrs. Arthur Baer] (d 1950) performer BE*
ANDREWS, Lyle D. (d 1950 [79]) American proprietor, manager BE*, BP/34*, WWT/14*
ANDREWS, Maidie English actress WWT/6-14
ANDREWS, Marie American actress TW/27
ANDREWS, Maxene American actress TW/30
ANDREWS, Miles Peter (c. 1750-1814) English dramatist CDP, CP/2-3, DD, DNB, ES, GT, TD/1-2
ANDREWS, Nancy (b 1924) American actress, singer BE, TW/6-9, 11-21, 26-27, WWT/14-16
ANDREWS, Richard Hoffman (d 1891 [88]) composer EA/92*
ANDREWS, Robert (1895-1976?) English actor ES, WWT/5-13
ANDREWS, Robert C. (fl 1789-1819) scene painter, proprietor BD
ANDREWS, Stanley (d 1969 [77]) performer BP/54*
ANDREWS, Tod [Michael Ames] (1914/20-72) American actor BE, TW/1-3, 5-13, 16, 29, WWT/12-15
ANDREWS, Walter English comedian CDP
ANDREWS, W. C. (fl 1878)

American actor SR
ANDREWS, William (d 1878 [42])
Australian comedian EA/79*
ANDREWS, W. S. (fl 1860s)
actor HAS
ANDREYEV, Leonid Nikolaivich
(1871-1919) Russian dramatist
COC, MWD, OC/1-3, PDT
ANDRIESSEN, Pelagie (b 1863)
Austrian singer ES
ANDROWES, George (fl 1608)
theatre share-holder DA
ANDRUSS, Mrs. Albert <u>see</u>
Herndon, Agnes
ANELLO, Jerome (b 1939) Amer-
ican actor TW/28
ANEREAU, John (fl 1794-97)
singer BD
ANFOSSI, Pasquale (1727-97)
Italian composer, musical
director BD
ANGEL, Mr. (fl 1720-32) Harper
BD
ANGEL, Edward (fl 1660-73)
English actor BD, COC,
DD, ES, OC/1-3
ANGEL, Heather (b 1909) English
actress ES, WWT/7-10
ANGEL, Lou (b 1940) American
actor TW/23-24
ANGEL, Morris (d 1941) cos-
tumier WWT/14*
ANGELA, June (b 1959) American
actress TW/27
ANGELELLI, Augusta [Mrs. Vit-
torio Correr; Augusta Wynne]
(fl 1798) singer BD
ANGELES, Aimee [Mrs. George
Considine] (b 1880) actress,
dancer WWS
ANGELES, Victoria de los [Vic-
toria Gamez Cima] (b 1923)
Spanish singer CB
ANGELI, Francesco (fl 1678-79)
Italian actor BD
ANGELI, Pier (d 1971 [39]) per-
former BP/56*
ANGELICA, Mrs. (fl 1785) singer
BD
ANGELINA (fl 1827) actress
CDP
ANGELINA, La Petite American?
dancer CDP
ANGELINA, Giuseppi (d 1916)
conductor SR
ANGELIQUE, Mlle. (fl 1828)
dancer HAS
ANGELL, Edythe (d 1966 [68])

performer BP/51*
ANGELL, George (fl 1736-39) musi-
cian BD
ANGELL, Victor (d 1874) gymnast
EA/75*
ANGELL, W. H. (d 1872 [74])
comedian, manager EA/72*
ANGELO, Mme. [Margaret Ann
Ashworth] (d 1911 [40]) per-
former EA/12*
ANGELO, Sig. (d c.1663) musician
BD
ANGELO, Sig. (fl 1723-24) scene
painter? BD
ANGELO, Signora (fl 1714-15)
singer? BD
ANGELO, Henry (1760-1839?)
fencing-master CDP, DNB
ANGELOU, Maya [Marguerite John-
son] (b 1928) American writer,
entertainer CB
ANGELUS, Muriel (b 1909/12) Eng-
lish actress WWT/7-10
ANGER, Al (d 1966 [65]) performer
BP/50*
ANGERS, Avril (b 1922) English
actress, singer WWT/11-16
ANGIER, Mr. (fl 1784-85) singer
BD
ANGLER, Mr. (fl 1786) performer
BD
ANGLIN, Margaret (1876-1958)
Canadian/American actress
COC, ES, GRB/2-4, NTH,
OC/1-3, SR, TW/2-3, 5-7,
15, WWA/5, WWM, WWS,
WWT/1-11
ANGOLD, Edith (d 1971 [76]) per-
former BP/56*
ANGRASINI, Sig. (fl 1831) singer
HAS
ANGRASINI, Signorina (fl 1825)
singer HAS
ANGUS, J. Keith (b 1848) Scottish
dramatist DD
ANKRUM, Morris (d 1964 [68])
performer BP/49*
ANNA, Signora (fl 1703) singer BD
ANNABELLA [Suzanne Georgette
Charpentier] (b 1912/13)
French actress TW/3, WWT/10
ANNALS, Michael (b 1938) English
designer AAS, WWT/15-16
ANNATO, Palmyre equestrienne
CDP
ANNEGAN, J. B. (b 1944) American
actor TW/26
ANNESLEY, Mr. (fl 1800)

manager? BD
ANNESLEY, Mrs. (fl 1744-49)
dancer BD
ANNESLEY, Lady Constance see
O'Niel, Colette
ANNIBALI, Domenico (1705-79?)
Italian singer BD
ANOUILH, Jean (b 1910) French
dramatist BE, CB, COC,
ES, HP, MH, MWD, NTH,
OC/1-3, PDT
ANSALDO, Pericle (b 1889) Italian
stage manager ES
ANSANI, Giovanni (1744-1826)
Italian singer, composer BD
ANSCHUTZ, Carl Friedrich Niko-
laus (1813/15/18-70) German
conductor CDP, ES, WWA/H
ANSEIMI, Rosina (d 1965 [85])
performer BP/49*
ANSELL, Mr. (fl 1785) dancer
BD
ANSELL, Mr. (fl 1827) English
actor HAS
ANSELL, Mrs. (fl 1788-91) house
servant? BD
ANSELL, Mrs. (fl 1800) actress
DD
ANSELL, Miss (fl 1787-88) house
servant? BD
ANSELL, Albert E. (d 1912)
advance manager EA/13*
ANSELL, Eva (d 1894 [22])
serio-comic EA/95*
ANSELL, John (fl 1761-88) box-
keeper BD
ANSELL, John (1874-1948) Eng-
lish composer, conductor
GRB/4, WWT/1-10, WWW/4
ANSELL, Mary (d 1950 [83])
actress DD
ANSELL, Thomas (d 1788) house
servant BD
ANSELL, William (fl 1762-90)
house servant, bill-sticker
BD
ANSELMO, Mr. (fl 1786-1803)
house servant BD
ANSELMO, Mrs. (fl 1794-1804)
dresser BD
ANSERMET, Ernest Alexandre
(1883-1969) Swiss conductor
CB
ANSKY [Solomon Rappoport]
(1863-1920) dramatist COC,
OC/1-3
ANSLEY, Abraham (d 1662)
trumpeter BD

ANSLEY, Edmond [Buster Brown]
(d 1972 [84]) midget BP/57*
ANSON, A. E. (1879-1936) English
actor SR, WWT/1-8
ANSON, Barbara American actress
TW/25
ANSON, Carlotta [Mrs. Wilson
Howard] English actress GRB/1
ANSON, Cecile E. [Mrs. John H.
R. Penrose] English actress
GRB/1
ANSON, C. W. (d 1944) actor
WWT/14*
ANSON, E. (fl 1833) actress HAS
ANSON, Frank (d 1897 [39]) actor
EA/98*
ANSON, George William (1847-1920)
Scottish actor DD, EA/95,
GRB/3-4, OAA/2, WWT/1-3
ANSON, John William (1817-81)
English actor DD, OAA/1-2
ANSON, Reginald F. (d 1919) actor
WWT/14*
ANSPACH, Elizabeth, Margravine
of (1750-1828) English dramatist
CDP, CP/3, DD, DNB, GT,
TD/1-2
ANSPACH, Nathan see Adams,
Nicholas
ANSPACHER, Florence S. (d 1971
[84]) patron BP/56*
ANSPACHER, Louis Kaufman (1878-
1947) American dramatist ES,
SR, WWA/2, WWM, WWS,
WWT/4-7
ANSPACHER, Mrs. Louis Kaufman
see Kidder, Kathryn
"ANSTEY, F."[Thomas Anstey
Gutherie] (1856-1934) English
dramatist DD, ES, GRB/2-4,
HP, WWM, WWT/1-7, WWW/3
ANSTEY, Percy [Percy Page-Phil-
lips] (1876-1920) French actor
GRB/1-3, WWW/2
ANSTISS, Jessie (d 1881) actress
EA/82*
ANSTRUTHER, Harold [Harold Ed-
ward Archer] English actor
WWT/4-6
ANTHEIL, George (1900-59) Amer-
ican composer CB, ES,
WWA/3
ANTHES, Georg (1863-1922) German
singer ES
ANTHONY, Mr. (fl 1733) French
horn player BD
ANTHONY, Carl (d 1930 [52]) actor
BE*, BP/15*, WWT/14*

ANTHONY, C. F. (d 1871) English musician EA/72*

ANTHONY, C. L. see Smith, Dodie

ANTHONY, Edward (d 1971 [76]) author BP/56*

ANTHONY, Jack [John Anthony Herbertson] (d 1962 [61]) Scottish performer BE*

ANTHONY, John J. (d 1970) performer BP/55*

ANTHONY, Joseph [né Deuster] (b 1912) American director, actor, dramatist BE, ES, TW/8-9, 23, WWT/14-16

ANTHONY, Michael (b 1943) Australian actor TW/26

ANTHONY, Peter (fl 1672-73) trumpeter BD

ANTHONY, Robert (b 1941) American actor TW/25, 27-29

ANTINORI, Luigi (fl 1726) singer BD

ANTLEY, George (d 1910) actor EA/11*

ANTOGNINI, Cirillo (fl 1843) Italian singer CDP

ANTOINE, André (1858-1943) French actor, producer, manager COC, GRB/1-4, NTH, OC/1-3, WWT/1

ANTOINE, Josephine Louise (1908-71) American singer CB

ANTOINE, Robert (b 1932) American actor TW/5

ANTOINE, Theophil (d 1891 [70]) EA/91*

ANTON, Pauline see Marvel, Pauline

ANTONELLI, Sig. (d 1895) conductor EA/96*

ANTONET [Umberto Guillaume] (1872-1935) Italian clown ES

ANTONIADOU, Koula (b 1945) Cypriot actor TW/28

ANTONIE, Mons. (d 1732) actor, acrobat BD

ANTONINO, Teresa dancer CDP

ANTONIO [Antonio Ruiz Soler] (b 1921/23) Spanish dancer, choreographer CB, ES, WWT/12

ANTONIO, Carl horse trainer CDP

ANTONIO, Lou (b 1934) American actor, director BE,

TW/14-15, 17-21

ANTONOVA, Helene A. (d 1973 [75]) performer BP/58*

ANTONY, Hilda (b 1886) Chilean actress GRB/4, WWT/1-10

ANTOON, A. J. (b 1944) American director WWT/16

ANTRIM, Harry (d 1967 [72]) actor TW/23

ANTROBUS, John (b 1933) English actor, dramatist AAS, CD, WWT/15-16

ANUNCIATI, Signora (fl 1766-67) singer BD

AP ARTHUR, Jeffrey (fl 1759) dancer BD

APFEL, Oscar (d 1938) American producer, director ES

APILEUTTER, Christopher (fl 1615) actor DA

APLIN, Emma H. (d 1965 [48]) executive BP/50*

APLON, Boris American actor TW/26-29

APOTHEOLA Indian chief CDP

APPEL, Anna (d 1963 [75]) Rumanian actress TW/20

APPELBAUM, Gertrude (b 1918) American business manager BE

APPELL, Don American librettist, producer, director, actor BE, CD

APPERLEY, John (fl 1613-20) musician DA

APPLEBY, Mr. (fl 1696-99) acrobat BD

APPLEBY, Mr. (fl 1792) puppet-show man BD

APPLEBY, Master (fl 1798-1819) dancer BD

APPLEBY, Dorothy (b 1908) American actress WWT/8-19

APPLEBY, Mrs. Emma (d 1885 [59]) EA/86*

APPLEBY, Louie (d 1902 [40]) actress EA/03*

APPLEBY, Thomas Bilton (d 1892 [47]) English actor, lessee DD, OAA/2

APPLEBY, William (fl 1787-1818) messenger, porter BD

APPLETON, Master (fl 1790-93?) musician BD

APPLETON, George J. (d 1926 [82]) manager BE*, BP/11*, WWT/14*

APPLEWHITE, Eric Leon (d 1973

[76]) performer BP/58*
APPLEYARD, Beatrice (b 1918)
English dancer, choreographer
ES
APPLIN, Arthur (d 1949 [76])
English actor GRB/1-4
APPLIN, Mrs. Arthur see
Olive, Edyth
APPLIN, George (d 1949 [76])
dramatist BE*
APPY, Henry (b 1828) violinist
CDP
APSTEIN, Theodore (b 1918)
Russian/American dramatist
BE
APTHORP, William Foster (b
1848) American critic WWA/
4, WWM
APTOMMAS, John S. (d 1917
[20]) EA/18*
APTOMMAS, Priscilla (d 1907)
harpist EA/08*
AQUILANTI, Chiaretta (fl 1742-
63) dancer BD
ARBAN, Mr. (d 1889 [63]) con-
ductor EA/90*
ARBEIT, Herman (b 1925) Amer-
ican actor TW/29
ARBENINA, Stella (1887-1976)
Russian actress WWT/5-10
ARBOS, Enrique Fernández
(1863-1939) Spanish musical
director, composer, violinist
ES
ARBUCKLE, Maclyn (1866-1931)
American actor ES, GRB/
3-4, SR, WWA/1, WWM,
WWS, WWT/1-6
ARBUCKLE, Matthew (1828-83)
musician, bandmaster CDP
ARBUCKLE, Minta Durfee (d
1975 [85]) performer BP/60*
ARBUCKLE, Roscoe [Fatty]
(1887-1933) American actor,
director BE*, BP/18*, ES
ARBURY, Guy (d 1972 [65])
actor TW/29
ARBUTHNOT, Dr. John (d 1735)
Scottish dramatist CP/3
ARBUZOV, Aleksei Nikolayevich
(b 1908) Russian dramatist
COC, PDT
ARCARO, Flavia (1876/82-1937)
American actress WWM
ARCE, Juan F. Acosts (d 1968
[78]) composer/lyricist
BP/53*
ARCEDECKNE, Mrs. see

Elsworthy, Miss
ARCHELL, Mr. (fl 1794) trumpeter
BD
ARCHER, Mr. (fl 1735-42) actor
BD
ARCHER, Mr. (fl 1786-1803) Scot-
tish actor DD, TD/1-2
ARCHER, Mrs. (fl 1848) actress
HAS
ARCHER, Alexander (1757?-1817)
actor BD
ARCHER, Belle (1860-1900) Ameri-
can actress WWA/1
ARCHER, Charles (1861-1941)
Scottish writer WWW/4
ARCHER, Charles George (d 1901
[41]) EA/02*
ARCHER, C. J. (d 1905) manager
EA/06*
ARCHER, Elisha (1760-1800) Eng-
lish violinist BD
ARCHER, Eugene (d 1973 [42])
critic BP/57*
ARCHER, Frank [Frank Bishop
Arnold] (d 1917 [72]) English
actor DD, OAA/1-2
ARCHER, Mrs. Frederick see
Pritchard, Marie
ARCHER, Harold Edward see
Anstruther, Harold
ARCHER, Harry (1888-1960) Amer-
ican composer BE*, BP/44*
ARCHER, Joe English comedian
CDP
ARCHER, John (1835-1921) English
actor DD, OAA/1-2
ARCHER, John B. (b 1915) Ameri-
can actor BE, TW/1-8, WWT/
11-13
ARCHER, Osceola American actress
TW/24, 28
ARCHER, Richard (fl 1603) actor
DA
ARCHER, Thomas (1789-1848)
English comedian, dramatist,
BS, CDP, DD, DNB, ES, HAS
ARCHER, Thomas (d 1851) English
singer HAS, SR
ARCHER, Mrs. Thomas American
actress DD
ARCHER, William (1856-1924)
Scottish critic, dramatist
COC, DD, DNB, ES, GRB/1-4,
HP, MD, MWD, NTH, OC/1-3,
PDT, WWT/1-4, WWW/2
ARCHEVEQUE, Mr. (fl 1773-74)
box-office keeper BD
ARCHEY, Mr. (fl 1708) house

servant BD
ARCHIBALD, Mrs. (fl 1856)
    actress HAS
ARCHIBALD, Douglas (b 1919)
    Trinidadian dramatist CD
ARCHIBALD, William (1915/24-70)
    West Indian dramatist, direc-
    tor, singer, dancer BE, ES,
    MH, TW/1-3, 6-7, 27
ARCHIPOVA, Irina Konstantinovna
    (b 1925) Russian singer ES
ARDEN, Edwin Hunter Pendleton
    (1864-1918) American drama-
    tist, actor, manager DAB,
    ES, GRB/3-4, SR, WWA/1,
    WWM, WWS, WWT/2-3
ARDEN, Eliza (fl 1850s) actress
    DD
ARDEN, Eve [Eunice Quedens]
    (b 1912) American actress
    BE, CB, ES, TW/23, WWT/
    10-16
ARDEN, H. T. see Arnold,
    Henry Thomas
ARDEN, Jane Welsh dramatist,
    actress CD
ARDEN, John (b 1930) English
    dramatist, director AAS,
    CD, CH, COC, ES, MD,
    MWD, OC/3, PDT, RE,
    WWT/14-16
ARDEN, Milly see Chaplin,
    Amelia
ARDEN, Victor (d 1962 [69])
    composer BP/47*
ARDEN, Wallace (d 1903) actor
    EA/04*
ARDITI, Luigi (1822-1903) Italian
    composer, conductor, musi-
    cian CDP, DNB, ES, WWW/1
ARDITI, Virginia (d 1909) EA/10*
ARDREY, Robert (b 1908) Ameri-
    can dramatist BE, CB, CD,
    ES, MD, MWD, WWT/9-14
ARDRON, Samuel singer, com-
    poser CDP
ARENA, Giuseppe (fl 1738-46)
    Italian composer ES
ARENT, Arthur (1904/05/06-72)
    American dramatist BE,
    ES, MD, MH, MWD
ARGENTINA [Antonia Mercé]
    (1890-1936) Argentinian dancer,
    choreographer ES, WWT/8
ARGENTINITA [Encarnación López
    Julves] (1905-45) Argentinian
    dancer CB, ES, TW/2
ARGO, Allison (b 1953) American

actress TW/30
ARGYLE, Fanny Austin (d 1917)
    American actress SR
ARGYLE, Gertrude [Gertrude F.
    DeVingut] (fl 1861) actress
    HAS
ARGYLE, Pearl [Pearl Wellman]
    (1910-47) South African dancer
    ES, SR, WWT/8-10
ARIMONDI, Vittorio (1861-1928)
    Italian singer ES
ARIOSTI, Attilio Malachia (d 1666)
    Italian composer, violist BD
ARIS, Ben (b 1937) English actor
    TW/25
ARISHIMA, Takeo (1878-1923)
    Japanese dramatist ES
ARISTIPPE [Félix Bernier de Mal-
    igny] (d 1865) French actor
    ES
ARKELL, Elizabeth English actress
    WWT/5-9
ARKELL, Monique see Berendt,
    Rachel
ARKELL, Reginald (1882-1959)
    English dramatist, lyricist
    WWT/4-12, WWW/5
ARKELL, Rosy (d 1897 [28]) EA/
    98*
ARKIN, Alan (b 1934) American
    actor, writer, composer BE,
    CB, ES, TW/19-22, WWT/15-16
ARKINSTALL, Beatrice K. [Beatrice
    K. Court] (d 1917) EA/18*
ARKINSTALL, John (fl 1603) actor
    DA
ARLEN, Bill (b 1951) American
    actor TW/30
ARLEN, Harold [Hyman Arluck] (b
    1905) American composer BE,
    CB, ES, PDT, WWT/15-16
ARLEN, Jerry American musical
    director BE
ARLEN, Michael (1895-1956) Bul-
    garian/English dramatist
    DNB, WWT/6-10, WWW/5
ARLEN, Richard (1899-1976) Amer-
    ican actor TW/1
ARLEN, Stephen Walter [né Badham]
    (1913-72) English manager,
    director WWT/15
ARLING, Joyce (b 1911) American
    actress BE, WWT/9-11
ARLINGTON, Billy (1835-91) min-
    strel SR
ARLINGTON, Billy (b 1873) Ameri-
    can actor WWT/6
ARLINGTON, Mrs. Eddie [née

Nettie Bowne] (1877-1947)
actress SR

ARLINGTON, Eleanor (d 1973)
performer BP/58*

ARLINGTON, Maggie [Margaret
Ryerson] (1853-77) American
actress NYM

ARLINGTON, May (b 1847) American actress HAS

ARLINGTON, William [né Burnell]
American comedian HAS

ARLISS, Dimitra American actress
TW/27

ARLISS, Florence Montgomery
(d 1950 [77]) English actress
TW/6

ARLISS, George (1868-1946)
English actor CB, DAB,
DNB, ES, GRB/3-4, NTH,
OC/1-3, SR, TW/2, WWA/
2, WWM, WWS, WWT/1-9,
WWW/4

ARLISS, Mrs. George see
Montgomery, Florence

ARLUCK, Hyman see Arlen,
Harold

ARMALENA, Mr. (fl 1777) musician? BD

ARMAND, Joseph (b 1833) American actor HAS

ARMAND'ARY, Mlle. French
singer CDP

ARMBRUSTER, Carl (1846-1917)
German musical director
ES

ARMBRUSTER, Violet actress
EA/95

ARMEN, Johnny (b 1938) American actor TW/27-29

ARMENDARIZ, Pedro (d 1963)
Mexican actor BE*

ARMETTA, Henry (1888-1945)
Italian actor TW/2

ARMIGER, Edward (d 1635) actor
DA

ARMIN, Robert (c.1568-c.1611)
English clown, actor, drama-
tist CDP, COC, CP/1-3,
DA, DD, DNB, ES, FGF,
GT, NTH, OC/1-3

ARMISTEAD, Horace (b 1898)
English scene designer ES

ARMITAGE, Bessie (d 1918)
EA/19*

ARMITAGE, Buford (b 1898)
American manager, stage
manager, actor BE

ARMITAGE, Merle (b 1893)

American impresario ES

ARMITAGE, R. A. see Gay, Noel

ARMITAGE, Sarah (d 1913) EA/14*

ARMITAGE, Walter W. (d 1953
[46]) South African actor, producer BE*, BP/37*

ARMONDOS, George (d 1965 [64])
performer BP/50*

ARMOUR, A. C. (d 1893 [38])
comedian EA/95*

ARMOUR, William Alexander (d
1916 [44]) EA/17*

ARMSTEAD, Mrs. [Elizabeth Brid-
get Blane; Mrs. Charles James
Fox] (1750-1842) English actress
BD

ARMSTRONG, Mr. (fl 1717-19)
singer BD

ARMSTRONG, Mr. (fl 1722) dancer
BD

ARMSTRONG, Mr. (fl 1726)
trumpeter BD

ARMSTRONG, Anna (1863-1948)
actress, trapezist SR

ARMSTRONG, Anthony (1897-1976)
Canadian/English dramatist
AAS, ES, WWT/7-14

ARMSTRONG, Mrs. Charles see
Melba, Nellie

ARMSTRONG, Charlotte (d 1969
[64]) dramatist BP/54*

ARMSTRONG, Charlotte Eva (d
1901) EA/02*

ARMSTRONG, Clara [Mrs. Felix
Pitt] (d 1894 [39]) actress
EA/95*

ARMSTRONG, Mjr. Edwin H. (1890-
1954) American inventor, engineer BE*

ARMSTRONG, Elizabeth [Kitty Ann
Worlock; Mrs. John Moody, II]
(1763-1846) English dancer BD

ARMSTRONG, Eunice B. (d 1971
[84]) dramatist BP/56*

ARMSTRONG, Gordon E. (d 1965
[64]) critic BP/50*

ARMSTRONG, Harry (1879-1951)
American songwriter BE*,
BP/35*

ARMSTRONG, Sir Harry Gloster
(d 1938 [77]) English actor
BE*, WWT/14*

ARMSTRONG, Helen (fl 1858)
actress HAS

ARMSTRONG, Henry (d 1877 [62])
actor EA/78*

ARMSTRONG, John (fl 1769) proprietor BD

ARMSTRONG, Dr. John (c.1709-79) English dramatist CP/2-3, DD, GT

ARMSTRONG, John (1893-1973) English scene designer ES

ARMSTRONG, John A. (d 1974 [60]) theatre operator BP/59*

ARMSTRONG, Louis (1900-71) American musician CB, ES

ARMSTRONG, Ned (d 1961 [55]) press representative BE*, BP/46*

ARMSTRONG, Paul (1869-1915) American dramatist DAB, ES, GRB/3-4, OC/1-3, SR, WWA/1, WWM, WWS, WWT/1-2

ARMSTRONG, Robert (1896-1973) American actor ES, TW/1, 29, WWT/6-10

ARMSTRONG, Sydney [Mrs. W. G. Smyth] American actress WWM, WWS

ARMSTRONG, Mr. W. (fl 1708-13) violist BD

ARMSTRONG, Will H. (d 1943 [74]) performer BE*

ARMSTRONG, William [William D'Alvini; "Jap of Japs"] (d. 1889 [42]) EA/90*

ARMSTRONG, William (d 1895) clown EA/96*

ARMSTRONG, William [William M. Devine] (d 19--?) American performer BE*

ARMSTRONG, Sir William (1882-1952) Scottish actor, producer, director AAS, COC, DNB, ES, OC/1-3, WWT/4-11, WWW/5

ARMSTRONG, William Dawson (1868-1936) American composer ES, WWM

ARMSTRONG, Will Steven (1930-69) American designer BE, ES, TW/26, WWT/14

ARMUS, Sidney (b 1924) American actor TW/11, 17, 21-24

ARMYTAGE, Grace [Mrs. Campbell Bradley] (d 1907) actress EA/08*, GRB/3*

ARMYTAGE, Seul (d 1897 [21]) music-hall performer EA/98*

ARNATT, John (b 1917) English actor WWT/12-16

ARNAUD, Yvonne Germaine (1892-1958) French actress,

singer AAS, COC, ES, OC/3, TW/14, WWT/2-12, WWW/5

ARNAULD, Mons. (fl 1764-70) dancer BD

ARNAUT, John (d 1965 [65]) performer BP/50*

ARNAZ, Desi (b 1917) Cuban musician CB

ARNDT, Felix (1889-1918) American composer BE*

ARNE, Miss (fl 1795) singer DD, TD/1-2

ARNE, Cecilia see Arne, Mrs. Thomas Augustine

ARNE, Michael (c.1740-86) composer, singer, musician BD, DD, DNB, ES

ARNE, Mrs. Michael, II [Elizabeth Wright] (1751?-69) singer BD

ARNE, Mrs. Michael, III [Ann Venables] (fl 1772-1820) singer BD

ARNE, Richard (b 1719) English singer, actor BD

ARNE, Susanna Maria see Cibber, Mrs. Theophilus, II

ARNE, Thomas (1682-1736) English box-numberer, manager? BD

ARNE, Dr. Thomas Augustine (1710-78) English composer BD, CDP, CP/1-3, DD, DNB, ES, TD/1-2

ARNE, Mrs. Thomas Augustine [Cecilia Young] (1711-89) English singer BD, DNB

ARNEEL, Eugen (d 1972 [52]) critic BP/57*

ARNELL, Nydia (d 1970 [74]) musical comedian TW/26

ARNELL, Patricia (b 1950) American actress TW/29

ARNELL, Richard (b 1917) English composer ES

ARNESS, James (b 1923) American actor CB

ARNO, Sig. (1895-1975) German actor, singer, director BE, TW/1-2, 16-17

ARNO, Owen G. (d 1969 [35]) dramatist BP/54*

ARNOLD, Mr. (fl 1696-1702) actor BD

ARNOLD, Mr. (fl 1771-85?) proprietor BD

ARNOLD, Mrs. singer DD, HAS

ARNOLD, Mrs. see Belfille, Mrs.

ARNOLD, Miss (fl 1794-96) actress

BD

ARNOLD, Charles (1854-1905) Swiss/English actor, singer DD, GRB/1

ARNOLD, Charles (d 1917 [77]) actor EA/18*

ARNOLD, Cornelius (fl 1757) dramatist CP/2-3, DD, GT

ARNOLD, Doris (d 1969 [61]) producer/director/choreographer BP/54*

ARNOLD, Eddie (d 1962 [34]) performer BE*

ARNOLD, Eddy (b 1918) American singer CB

ARNOLD, Edward [Gunther Schneider] (1890-1956) American actor ES, TW/12, WWA/3, WWT/8-10

ARNOLD, Elizabeth (fl 1797-1809) actress, singer, dancer SR

ARNOLD, Elizabeth see Clendining, Mrs. William

ARNOLD, Emily C. (d 1900 [40]) descriptive singer EA/01*

ARNOLD, Frank Bishop see Archer, Frank

ARNOLD, Franz (1878-1960) German dramatist WWT/11-12

ARNOLD, Frederick see Allandale, Fred

ARNOLD, G. J. (fl 1846) actor HAS

ARNOLD, Mrs. Henry [Elizabeth Smith; Mrs. Charles Tubbs] (fl 1784-c.1799) actress, singer BD

ARNOLD, Henry C. English comedian CDP

ARNOLD, Henry Thomas [H. T. Arden] (1840-76) dramatist DD

ARNOLD, H. Somerfield (d 1900) actor EA/01*

ARNOLD, J. (d 1878) Negro artist EA/79*

ARNOLD, Jack [Arnold Jack Gluck] (d 1962 [59]) performer BE*

ARNOLD, James A. (d 1905) singer, actor, manager GRB/1

ARNOLD, Jeanne American actress TW/26-28, 30

ARNOLD, Jonas (d 1975 [72])

publicist BP/60*

ARNOLD, Laura (d 1963 [c.73]) American actress, talent representative BE*

ARNOLD, Lilian (d 1974 [69]) producer/director/choreographer BP/59*

ARNOLD, Lilian American talent representative BE

ARNOLD, Madison (b 1935) American actor TW/25, 27

ARNOLD, Mary Sophia see Bailey, Mrs. William

ARNOLD, Mat [Charles Kerr] (d 1894) pantomimist, comedian EA/95*

ARNOLD, Matthew (1822-88) English critic, dramatist COC, DD, ES, HP, NTH, OC/1-3

ARNOLD, Maurice (b 1865) American composer WWA/4, WWM

ARNOLD, Phil (d 1968 [55]) performer BP/52*

ARNOLD, Phyl (d 1941 [38]) actress WWT/7-8

ARNOLD, Priscilla (d 1898) EA/99*

ARNOLD, Reggie (d 1963 [43]) performer BE*

ARNOLD, Dr. Samuel (1740-1802) English composer, conductor, manager, organist, musical editor BD, CDP, DD, DNB, ES, TD/1-2

ARNOLD, Samuel James (1774-1852) English manager, dramatist CP/3, DD, DNB, ES, GT, TD/1-2

ARNOLD, Seth (d 1955 [70]) English/American actor TW/1, 6-7

ARNOLD, T. (fl 1799) proprietor BD

ARNOLD, Tom (d 1969 [72]) manager WWT/9-14, WWW/6

ARNOLD, Victor (b 1936) American actor TW/22-26, 28, 30

ARNOLD, Wade (d 1975) producer/director/choreographer BP/59*

ARNOLD, W. H. dramatist DD

ARNOLDI, Sig. (fl 1848) singer HAS

ARNOLDSON, Sigrid (1861-1943) Swedish singer ES, WWA/5

ARNOT, Edwin (d 1885) actor EA/86*

ARNOT, Louise [Mrs. Mary Louise Gunn] (d 1919 [76]) actress BE*

ARNOTT, Emma (d 1891 [47])

EA /93*

ARNOTT, Peter Douglas (b 1931)
English educator, puppeteer
BE

ARNOULD, Mr. (fl 1687-88)
singer BD

ARNOULD, Sophie (1740-1802)
French actress, singer BE*,
WWT /14*

ARNOULD-PLESSY, Mme. (d 1897
[78]) actress WWT /14*

ARNSTEIN, Alexander (d 1895)
musician EA /96*

ARNULL, Mr. (fl 1784-1817)
musician BD

ARON, Robert (fl 1702) mountebank BD

ARONS, Morris (d 1877 [29])
advance agent EA /78*

ARONSON, Boris Solomon (b
1900/04) American designer
AAS, BE, COC, ES, OC/3,
WWT /11-16

ARONSON, Edward (d 1888 [29])
American actor EA /89*

ARONSON, Rudolph (1856-1919)
American composer, mana-
ger CDP, SR, WWA /1,
WWS

ARONSTEIN, Martin (b 1936)
American lighting designer
WWT /16

AROVA, Sonia (b 1927) Bulgarian/
English dancer ES

ARPER, Mrs. Clarence F.
see Atwood, Lorena E.

ARPINO, Gerald (b 1929) American dancer, choreographer
ES

ARQUETTE, Cliff[ord] (1905-74)
American comedian CB

ARRABAL, Fernando [Fernando
Arrabal Téran] (b 1932)
Spanish dramatist CB, CH,
COC, RE, WWT /15-16

ARRANDALE, Gilbert (d 1908
[39]) EA /09*

ARRIGHI, Mel (b 1933) American
actor TW /18

ARRIGONI, Carlo (b 1697) Italian
composer, band leader,
musician BD

ARRINGTON, Lillie see Burroughs, Marie

ARROWSMITH, Mr. (fl 1673)
dramatist CP /1-3

ARROWSMITH, Daniel (fl 1783-
94) singer, composer BD

ARROWSMITH, William (fl 1673)
dramatist DD

ARROWSMITH, William (b 1924)
American translator, editor,
educator BE

ARROYO, Martina (b 1936?) American singer CB

ARTAUD, Antonin (1896-1948)
French actor, theorist CH,
COC, PDT

ARTAUD, Stephen (d 1886 [71])
actor EA /87*

ARTELL, R. F. [Robert Frederick
Corson] (d 1885) gymnast
EA /86*

ARTHUR, Beatrice (b 1926?) American actress BE, CB, TW /15,
21-24, WWT /16

ARTHUR, Carol (b 1935) American
actress, singer, comedienne
BE, TW /22

ARTHUR, Daniel V. (d 1939 [72])
manager WWT /14*

ARTHUR, Daphne (b 1925) English
actress WWT /11-13

ARTHUR, George K. [George Brest]
(b 1899) Scottish actor ES

ARTHUR, Hartney J. (b 1917) Australian producer, director,
actor BE

ARTHUR, Helen (d 1939 [60]) American press representative BE*

ARTHUR, Hope American actress
TW /24

ARTHUR, Jean [Gladys Green] (b
1905/08) American actress
BE, CB, ES, TW /6-7, WWT /
8-12

ARTHUR, John (1708?-72) English
actor, machinist, manager,
dramatist BD, CDP, CP /2-3
DD, GT, TD /1-2

ARTHUR, John (d 1916 [44]) actor,
stage manager WWT /14*

ARTHUR, Mrs. John, II [Grace
Read; Mrs. Daniel Williams]
(fl 1760-74) actress, singer
BD

ARTHUR, Johnny American actor
ES, TW /5

ARTHUR, Joseph (1848-1906) American dramatist BE*, WWT /14*

ARTHUR, Julia [Mrs. B. P. Cheney, Jr.] (1869-1950) Canadian
actress ES, GRB /2-4, PP /1,
SR, TW /6, WWA /5, WWS,
WWT /1-9

ARTHUR, Lee American agent,

dramatist SR

ARTHUR, Paul (1856/59-1928)
American actor GRB/2-4,
WWS, WWT/1-5

ARTHUR, Phil (b 1923) American
actor TW/3, 6-18

ARTHUR, Robert (d 1929 [73])
manager GRB/4, WWT/1-5

ARTHUR, Roger (fl 1669) musician BD

ARTHUR, Sam [Sam Geary] (d
1908 [39]) EA/09*

ARTHUR, Thomas dramatist
FGF

ARTHUR, Thomas (fl 1528-29)
actor DA

ARTHUR, Wallis English comedian CDP

ARTHUR-JONES, Winifred [Mrs.
Leslie Faber] (b 1880)
English actress GRB/3-4,
WWT/1-6

ARTHURS, George (1875-1944)
English lyricist, librettist
WWT/4-9

ARTHURSON, Mr. (fl 1847)
Singer CDP, HAS

ARTIMA, Baldassare (fl 1669-71)
scenekeeper BD

ARTINGSTALL, William (d 1868
[36]) musician EA/68*

ARTOIS, Jack (d 1910 [34])
acrobat EA/12*

ARUNDALE, Grace [Grace Kelly]
actress GRB/2-4, WWT/1-5

ARUNDALE, Sybil [Sybil Kelly]
(1879/82-1965) English
actress ES, GRB/1-4,
WWT/1-11

ARUNDEL, Honor (d 1973) dramatist BP/58*

ARUNDELL, Dennis (b 1898)
English actor, producer,
musician, composer, director
AAS, ES, WWT/9-15

ARVOLD, Alfred G. (1882-1957)
American educator, little
theatre initiator BE*

ARZSCHAR, Robert (fl 1608-1616)
English actor DA

ASBRIDGE, John (1725-1800)
musician BD

ASBURY, Mr. pantaloon CDP

ASCH, Sholom (1880-1957)
Polish/American dramatist
MH, MWD, NTH, OC/1-3,
RE, WWW/5

ASCHE, Oscar [John Stanger

Heiss] (1871-1936) Australian/
English actor COC, DNB,
ES, GRB/1-4, NTH, OC/1-3,
WWT/1-8, WWW/3

ASCHE, Mrs. Oscar see Brayton,
Lily

ASCHER, Anton (d 1884) composer
EA/85*

ASCHER, Joseph (d 1869 [39])
pianist EA/70*

ASCHER, Leo (1880-1942) Austrian
composer CB

ASCOUGH, Charles Edward (d
1779) dramatist CP/2, GT,
TD/1-2

ASH, Arty (d 1954 [61]) comedian
WWT/14*

ASH, Gordon (d 1929 [52]) actor
WWT/4-5

ASH, Ingram (d 1974 [55]) executive
BP/59*

ASH, Joe (fl 1680s?) boxkeeper
BD

ASH, Maie (1888-1923) English
actress, dancer GRB/1-4,
WWT/1-2

ASH, Paul R. (d 1958 [57]) bandleader BE*

ASHBEE, Ashton (d 1898 [29])
actor EA/99*

ASHBORNE, Edward (fl 1624) actor
DA

ASHBUNY, Mr. (fl 1689) house servant? BD

ASHBURTON, Lady [Frances Bel-
mont] (b 1884) American
actress GRB/1

ASHBURY, Mr. (fl 1767-69) house
servant? BD

ASHBURY, John (fl 1690-1700) fifer
BD

ASHBURY, Joseph (1638-1720)
English actor, manager DD,
DNB, ES

ASHCROFT, Dame Peggy (b 1907)
English actress AAS, BE,
CB, COC, ES, OC/2-3, PDT,
TW/5-7, WWT/7-16

ASHCROFT, William E. (d 1906)
EA/07*

ASHCROFT, W. J. (d 1918 [73])
EA/19*

ASHE, Andrew (c.1759-1838) Irish
musician BD

ASHE, Martin (b 1909) American
actor TW/13

ASHE, Warren (d 1947 [44]) American actor TW/1

ASHER, Mrs. (d 1899) EA/00*
ASHER, Angelo Andrew musical
    director GRB/1
ASHER, Jane (b 1946) English
    actress TW/23, 27, WWT/
    15-16
ASHER, Max (d 1957 [77]) actor
    BE*
ASHER, Morris (d 1895) EA/96*
ASHERMANN, Otto (b 1903) Aus-
    trian educator, director BE
ASHERSON, Renée (b 1915) Eng-
    lish actress AAS, ES, WWT/
    10-16
ASHFORD, Charles (1850-1903)
    English actor DD, OAA/2
ASHFORD, Daisy (d 1972 [90])
    dramatist BP/56*
ASHFORD, Harry (d 1903 [40])
    variety comedian EA/05*
ASHFORD, Harry (1858-1926)
    English actor SR
ASHFORD, Tom (d 1887) music-
    hall artist EA/88*
ASHLEY, Annie (d 1947 [82])
    American actress BE*,
    WWT/14*
ASHLEY, Barbara American
    singer, actress BE, TW/7-
    19
ASHLEY, Celeste American theatre
    librarian BE
ASHLEY, Charles (d 1888) acting
    manager EA/89*
ASHLEY, Charles Jane (c.1773-
    1843) musician BD, DNB
ASHLEY, Charles Milton (d
    1910) proprietor EA/11*
ASHLEY, Gen. Christopher (1767-
    1818) English violinist BD
ASHLEY, Elizabeth [née Cole]
    (b 1939) American actress
    BE, TW/18, 20, 28, WWT/
    15-16
ASHLEY, Esther Potter [née
    McCormac] (d 1887) Ameri-
    can actress NYM
ASHLEY, Helen [Mrs. Clarence
    S. Spencer; née Hurt] (d
    1954 [75]) actress, writer
    BE*
ASHLEY, Henry Jeffries (d 1890
    [59]) English actor, singer
    CDP, DD, DP, OAA/1-2
ASHLEY, Iris (b 1909) Irish
    actress, singer WWT/8-9
ASHLEY, Jane (1740-1809) bas-
    soonist BD

ASHLEY, Jane Jeffries (d 1909)
    EA/11*
ASHLEY, J. B. [Henry Thomas Buz-
    zard] (d 1892 [36]) actor EA/
    93*
ASHLEY, Mrs. J. B. see Uns-
    worth, Evelyn
ASHLEY, Joel American actor
    TW/1
ASHLEY, John (1734-1805) bassoon-
    ist, oratorio manager BD,
    DNB
ASHLEY, John James (1771-1815)
    English musician, composer
    BD, DNB
ASHLEY, Minne [Mrs. William Astor
    Chanler] (1875-1945) American
    actress, singer, dancer WWM,
    WWS
ASHLEY, Richard Godfrey (1774-
    1836) English musician BD,
    DNB
ASHLEY, Stephen W. (fl 1863)
    actor CDP
ASHLEY, Ted American talent rep-
    resentative BE
ASHLEY, William (fl 1672) musi-
    cian BD
ASHMER, James G. [né Gollicker]
    (1826-63) English actor HAS
ASHMORE, Basil (b 1915) English
    producer WWT/11-16
ASHMORE, Dorothy (d 1892) EA/
    93*
ASHMORE, Joseph (fl 1794) singer
    BD
ASHMORE, Peter (b 1916) English
    director, actor BE, WWT/11-
    14
ASHTON, Mr. (fl 1624-25?) actor
    DA
ASHTON, Mr. (fl 1698) actor BD
ASHTON, Amelia (d 1868) EA/69*
ASHTON, Florence (d 1973 [69])
    performer BP/58*
ASHTON, Frederick (b 1906) English
    dancer, choreographer CB,
    ES, OC/1-2, WWT/8-12
ASHTON, George (d 1935 [82])
    agent GRB/2-4
ASHTON, Gordon (d 1874) actor
    EA/75*
ASHTON, Henrietta [Mrs. Walter
    Ashton] (d 1912) EA/13*
ASHTON, Robert (fl 1675-79) vio-
    linist BD
ASHTON, Robert (fl 1727) Irish
    dramatist CP/2, DD, TD/1

ASHTON, Sylvia (d 1940 [60])
American actress BE*
ASHTON, Thomas (fl 1673)
musician BD
ASHTON, Thomas (fl 1737-58)
musician BD
ASHTON, Mrs. Walter see
Ashton, Henrietta
ASHTON, Winifred see Dane,
Clemence
ASHWELL, Charles (d 1916 [34])
EA/17*
ASHWELL, Lena [Mrs. Arthur
Playfair] (1872-1957) English
actress COC, DNB, EA/96,
ES, GRB/1-4, OC/1-3,
WWM, WWS, WWT/1-12,
WWW/5
ASHWIN, Mr. (fl 1795-1813?)
tailor, actor, dancer? BD
ASHWORTH, John Henry (d 1916
[50]) advance manager EA/
17*
ASHWORTH, Margaret Ann see
Angelo, Mme.
ASHWYNNE, Muriel [Muriel
Walker] English actress
GRB/3-4
ASKAM, Perry (d 1961 [60])
American singer, actor TW/
18
ASKEN, Aaron (fl 1627-40)
dancer DA
ASKER, Mrs. (fl 1782-84) actress,
equestrienne? BD
ASKER, Mrs. Catherine (d 1867)
actress EA/68*
ASKEW, John (d 1895) violin
maker EA/96*
ASKEW, Mary Jane (d 1909)
EA/10*
ASKEY, Mr. (fl 1794) singer
BD
ASKEY, Arthur Bowden (b 1900)
English comedian ES,
WWT/10-16
ASKIN, Harry (d 1934 [67])
American manager, producer
BE*, BP/19*
ASKINS, Mr. (fl 1796) ventrilo-
quist BD
ASKWIN, Mr. (fl 1793) scene
painter BD
ASPEY, Mr. (fl 1742-44) singer,
actor BD
ASPINALL, T. H. (d 1897) pro-
prietor EA/98*
ASPINALL, Mrs. W. E. see

Mason, Kitty
ASPINWALL, Stanhope (d 1771)
dramatist CP/2-3
ASPLAND, George V. (d 1911)
showman EA/10*
ASPULL, George (1813-32) pianist
CDP, DNB
ASQUITH, Anthony (1902-68) English
actor, producer ES, WWT/10,
WWW/6
ASQUITH, Lady Cynthia Mary Evelyn
(1887-1960) English dramatist
DNB
ASQUITH, Mary (d 1942 [69])
actress BE*, WWT/14*
ASSELIN, Mr. (fl 1772-75) dancer
BD
ASSELIN, Mlle. (fl 1759-66) dancer
BD
ASSONI, Sig. (d 1860) singer HAS
ASTAIRE, Adele (b 1898) American
actress, dancer BE, SR,
WWT/5-11
ASTAIRE, Ann Geilus (d 1975 [96])
BP/60*
ASTAIRE, Fred (b 1899/1900)
American actor, dancer AAS,
BE, CB, ES, SR, WWT/5-11
ASTAR, Ben Palestinian actor
TW/10-11
ASTHER, Nils (b 1901) Swedish
actor ES
ASTLEY, Miss (fl 1773) equestri-
enne, actress? BD
ASTLEY, Edward (fl 1782-93) door-
keeper, bill-sticker, hostler
BD
ASTLEY, Hannah Waldo (fl 1820s)
equestrienne CDP
ASTLEY, Hugh F. L. (d 1910 [78])
chairman EA/11*
ASTLEY, Jessie Marion (d 1880)
EA/82*
ASTLEY, John English actor WWT/
4-6
ASTLEY, John Philip Conway (1767-
1821) equestrian, actor, mana-
ger, dramatist BD, CDP
ASTLEY, Philip (1742-1814) English
equestrian, manager BD, CDP,
DD, DNB, ES, HP, OC/3
ASTLEY, Mrs. Philip [Patty Jones]
(d 1794) equestrienne BD
ASTON, Anthony (c. 1682-c.1753)
English actor, singer, dancer,
manager, composer, dramatist
BD, CDP, COC, CP/1-3, DD,
DNB, ES, GT, HJD, NTH,

OC/1-3, SR, TD/1-2,
WWA/H
ASTON, Mrs. Anthony (fl 1704-
35?) actress BD
ASTON, Frank (b 1897) American
critic NTH
ASTON, Joseph (1762-1844) Eng-
lish dramatist DD
ASTON, Kate CDP
ASTON, Mrs. Knight see Brent,
Mabel
ASTON, Robert Irish dramatist
TD/2
ASTON, Walter (fl 1733) drama-
tist CP/2-3, DD, GT
ASTON, Walter (c.1706-c.39)
actor BD
ASTOR, Adelaide [Mrs. George
Grossmith] (d 1951) English
actress BE*, WWT/14*
ASTOR, George (d 1970 [77])
performer BP/55*
ASTOR, June (d 1967 [49]) per-
former BP/52*
ASTOR, Mary (b 1906) American
actress, writer BE, CB,
TW/1
ASTOR, Richard (b 1927) Ameri-
can talent representative
BE
ASTREDO, Humbert Allen Amer-
ican actor TW/24, 27-28
ASTROP, Maggie (d 1882) singer
EA/83*
ASTRUC, Gabriel (1864-1938)
French impresario ES
ATCHESON, Mr. (fl 1722) actor
BD
ATCHINSON-ELY, Edgar English
comedian CDP
ATCHISON, Prof. D. L. (d 1878)
American aeronaut EA/79*
ATCHLEY, Hooper (d 1943 [57])
actor BE*
ATES, Roscoe (d 1962 [67])
American actor BE*,
BP/46*
ATHAS, Nick (b 1937) American
actor TW/23-24
ATHAY, W. (d 1874) musician
EA/75*
ATHERLEY, Frank actor GRB/
1-3
ATHERSTONE, Weldon [Weldon
Anderson] (d 1910) actor
EA/11*
ATHERTON, Miss (fl 1732-44)
dancer, singer, actress BD

ATHERTON, Miss (fl 1790-91)
actress BD
ATHERTON, Alice [Mrs. Willie
Edouin] (1854-99) actress,
singer CDP, DD
ATHERTON, Daisy (d 1961 [80])
English actress BE*
ATHERTON, Gertrude American
dramatist WWM
ATHERTON, James (d 1898 [54])
animal trainer EA/99*
ATHERTON, Joshua (fl 1745-94?)
musician BD
ATHERTON, Mary (d 1877) EA/79*
ATHERTON, William (b 1947)
American actor TW/28-29
ATHEY, Bertha (d 1897) singer
EA/98*
ATHOL, Katherine Phoebe Mary
see Seymour, Katie
"ATHOL FORBES" see Phillips,
Rev. Forbes Alexander
ATHYA, Cpt. F. see Solomon,
Solomon
ATIENZA, Edward (b 1924) English
actor AAS, BE, TW/16, 19,
22-23, WWT/15-16
ATKIN, Charles (b 1910) English
stage manager, director, actor
BE
ATKIN, David (d 1917) EA/18*
ATKIN, John A. (d 1907 [49])
actor, manager GRB/3
ATKIN, Mrs. John A. see Nelson,
Florence
ATKIN, Nancy (b 1904) English
actress WWT/5-6
ATKINS, Mr. (d 1725?) pit door-
keeper BD
ATKINS, Mr. (fl 1783-92) house
servant BD
ATKINS, Mr. (fl late 18th cent)
actor, manager DD, TD/2
ATKINS, Mrs. (fl 1722?-39) box-
keeper BD
ATKINS, Mrs. (fl 1797) actress,
singer DD
ATKINS, Mrs. (d 1886) actress
EA/87*
ATKINS, Alfred (d 1941 [41]) actor
WWT/14*
ATKINS, Charles (d 1775) dancer,
singer, actor BD
ATKINS, Edward (1819-83) actor
CDP, DD
ATKINS, Eileen (b 1934) English
actress AAS, TW/23-24, 28
WWT/14-16

ATKINS, Eliza (fl 1797-1806)
actress CDP
ATKINS, James (fl 1794) singer
BD
ATKINS, John (d 1671) composer,
violinist BD
ATKINS, Michael (fl 1755-75)
singer, actor BD
ATKINS, Michael (c.1747-1812)
actor, manager, scene
painter, dancer, composer,
singer BD
ATKINS, Norton (d 1903 [39])
songwriter EA/04*
ATKINS, Robert (1886-1972)
English actor, director
AAS, COC, ES, OC/1-3,
WWT/4-14
ATKINS, Mrs. Selenear (d 1892)
EA/93*
ATKINS, Thomas C. (d 1968
[80]) dramatist BP/53*
ATKINS, Tom American actor
TW/24-26, 28-30
ATKINS, Will (d 1912 [58])
vocal comedian EA/13*
ATKINS, William (1763-1831)
singer, actor BD
ATKINS, Mrs. William [Eliza
Warrell; Mrs. Hill] (fl
1787-1808?) singer, actress
BD, TD/1-2
ATKINSON, Mr. (fl 1747-51)
doorkeeper BD
ATKINSON, Mr. (fl 1750) actor
BD
ATKINSON, Mr. (fl 1781) actor
BD
ATKINSON, Mrs. (d 1887) EA/88*
ATKINSON, Master (fl 1783)
dancer BD
ATKINSON, Miss (fl 1771-82)
actress BD
ATKINSON, Miss [The pig-faced
lady] CDP
ATKINSON, Miss (fl 1853-64)
actress DD
ATKINSON, Alex (d 1962 [45])
dramatist WWT/14*
ATKINSON, Brooks see Atkinson,
Justin Brooks
ATKINSON, Charles H. (d 1909
[72]) minstrel BE*
ATKINSON, Clinton (b 1927)
actor TW/25
ATKINSON, David (b 1921) Cana-
dian actor, singer BE,
TW/12-13, 15-17, 23-30

ATKINSON, Elizabeth (d 1880 [70])
EA/81*
ATKINSON, E. Philip (d 1902 [46])
manager EA/03*
ATKINSON, Frank (d 1963 [72])
performer BE*
ATKINSON, Frederick (d 1879 [36])
proprietor EA/80*
ATKINSON, George Aytoun see
Aytoun, George
ATKINSON, Mrs. George Aytoun
(d 1888) EA/89*
ATKINSON, George H. (d 1955 [75])
press representative BE*
ATKINSON, Harry [Harry Atkinson
Fitts] (b 1866) Australian vari-
ety artist GRB/1
ATKINSON, Howard T. (d 1975
[75]) performer BP/60*
ATKINSON, Isabella (d 1898)
actress EA/99*
ATKINSON, James Henry (d 1916)
actor EA/17*
ATKINSON, John B. (d 1868 [35])
musician EA/69*
ATKINSON, Joseph (1743-1818)
Irish dramatist CP/3, DD,
DNB, GT, TD/1-2
ATKINSON, Justin Brooks (b 1894)
American critic AAS, BE,
CB, COC, ES, HJD, NTH,
OC/1-3, PDT, WWT/6-16
ATKINSON, L. (fl 1848) actor
HAS
ATKINSON, Matthew (b 1963) Amer-
ican actor TW/27
ATKINSON, Peggy [Peggy Longo]
(b 1943) American actress
TW/30
ATKINSON, Rosalind (b 1900) New
Zealand/English actress AAS,
BE, ES, WWT/9-16
ATKINSON, Thomas (1600-39) Eng-
lish dramatist DD, FGF
ATLAS (fl 1787) strong man BD
ATLAS, Leopold (1907-54) Ameri-
can dramatist BE*
ATLEE, Howard (b 1926) American
press representative BE
ATOM, Willie [William Henry War-
ren] (b 1875) English actor
GRB/1
ATTAWAY, Ruth American actress
BE
ATTENBOROUGH, Sir Richard (b
1923) English actor ES, WWT/
10-16
ATTERBURY, Luffman (d 1796)

musician BD, DNB
ATTERIDGE, Harold Richard
(1886-1938) American drama-
tist ES, SR, WWA/1-2,
WWT/5-8
ATTERINO, Sig. (fl 1754) dancer
BD
ATTERSOLL, Mrs. (d 1893 [66])
EA/94*
ATTEWELL, George (fl 1590-95)
actor DA, DD
ATTIE, Paulette (b 1936) Ameri-
can actress TW/27
ATTLE, John C. American actor
TW/24-30
ATTLES, Joseph (b 1903) Amer-
ican actor TW/25-26, 28-29
ATTWELL, Hugh (d 1621) English
actor DA, DD, DNB, ES,
OC/1-3
ATTWELLS, Frank (d 1892 [49])
lessee EA/93*
ATTWOOD, Mr. (fl 1784) vio-
linist BD
ATTWOOD, Miss (fl 1794) musi-
cian BD
ATTWOOD, Francis (b 1775)
musician BD
ATTWOOD, Herbert (d 1911)
EA/12*
ATTWOOD, Thomas (b 1737)
musician BD
ATTWOOD, Thomas (1765-1838)
English singer, composer,
violoncellist BD, DD,
DNB, ES, TD/1-2
ATWATER, Edith (b 1911) Amer-
ican actress BE, TW/3-8,
WWT/10-15
ATWELL, Ben H. (d 1951 [74])
American manager, press
agent WWM
ATWELL, Grace [Mrs. Edwin
Mordant] American actress
WWM
ATWELL, Hugh see Attwell,
Hugh
ATWELL, Roy (1880-1962) Amer-
ican comedian TW/18, WWM
ATWILL, Lionel (1885-1946)
English actor CB, ES, SR,
TW/2, WWA/2, WWT/3-9
ATWOOD, Mr. (fl 1734-35)
house servant? BD
ATWOOD, Alban [Alban Gwynne
Atwood] English actor GRB/
1-4
ATWOOD, Alban Gwynne see

Atwood, Alban
ATWOOD, Donna (b 1926) American
dancer, ice skater CB
ATWOOD, G. C. (fl 1858) American
actor HAS
ATWOOD, Mrs. G. C. (fl 1854)
actress HAS
ATWOOD, John (fl 1735) musician?
BD
ATWOOD, Lorena E. [Mrs. Clar-
ence F. Arper] (d 1947) Amer-
ican actress WWS
ATWOOD, Neill (fl 1850s) comedian
HAS
ATWOOD, Roland (d 1903) actor
EA/04*
AUBE, Mrs. C. L. (d 1894 [23])
EA/95*
AUBER, Daniel François Esprit
(1782-1871) French composer
DD, DNB, ES
AUBERJONOIS, René (b 1940)
American actor TW/25-30,
WWT/15-16
AUBERT, Mrs. (fl 1719) dramatist
CP/3, DD
AUBERT, Mons. (fl 1 715-1725)
dancer BD
AUBERT, Isabella (fl 1715-20)
singer, author BD
AUBERT, Jeanne (b 1906) French
actress, singer WWT/8-9
AUBERT, John (fl 1695-1716) oboist
BD
AUBIN, Mrs. (fl 1730) dramatist
CP/3, DD
AUBIN, Mrs. (fl 1724-29) orator
BD
AUBREY, Bob (d 1903) music-hall
performer? EA/04*
AUBREY, Georges (d 1975 [47])
performer BP/60*
AUBREY, Mrs. James see Hen-
derson, Marie
AUBREY, Kate (fl 1874) English
actress DD, OAA/1-2
AUBREY, Lizzie [Mrs. Charles
Dodsworth] (d 1900) EA/01*
AUBREY, Madge [Marjorie Alex-
andra Witham] (1902-70) Eng-
lish actress WWT/8-9
AUBREY, Mrs. W. [Mrs. W.
Aubrey Chandler] (b 1838) Eng-
lish actress GRB/1
AUBUCHON, Jacques (b 1924) Amer-
ican actor TW/9-10
AUCKLAND, Marie [Mrs. Charles
Herrick Jennings] English

actress GRB/1

AUDE, Joseph (1755-1841)
dramatist BE*

AUDEN, W[ystan] H[ugh] (1907-
73) English/American drama-
tist AAS, BE, CB, COC,
ES, HJD, HP, MD, MH,
MWD, NTH, OC/1-3, PDT,
WWT/9-15

AUDLEY, Joseph (d 1896 [65])
EA/97*

AUDLEY, Maxine (b 1923) English
actress AAS, WWT/12-16

AUDLEY, Sarah (d 1898) EA/00*

AUDRAN, Alfred (d 1884 [35])
singer EA/85*

AUDRAN, Edmond (1917-51)
French dancer ES

AUDRE, Olga [Mrs. Mabel Win-
penny] (d 1917 [49]) actress
EA/18*

AUDREY, May (d 1909) actress
EA/10*

AUER, Florence (d 1962 [82])
actress TW/18

AUER, Mischa (1905-67) Russian
actor TW/3, 23

AUERBACH, Artie (d 1957 [54])
American performer BE*

AUERBACH, George (d 1973
[68]) dramatist BP/58*

AUERBACH, Leonard stage
manager BE

AUERBACH-LEVY, William (d
1961 [75]) caricaturist,
artist BE*

AUG, Edna (1878-1938) American
performer BE*, BP/23*

AUGARDE, Adrienne (d 1913)
actress, singer GRB/1-4,
WWS, WWT/1

AUGARDE, Amy (1868-1959)
English actress DD,
GRB/2-4, WWT/1-9

AUGARDE, Gertrude [Mrs.
George Henry Trader] (d
1959) actress BE*

AUGER, Mr. (fl 1783) dancer
BD

AUGER, Genevieve see Genevieve

AUGUST, Edwin (d 1964 [81])
actor, director BE*

AUGUST, Harold (d 1909) clown
EA/11*

AUGUSTA, Mlle. (1806-1901)
French dancer CDP, HAS,
SR

AUGUSTA, Mlle. [Augusta Rabineau]
(1848-63) American HAS

AUGUSTE, Mlle. M. (fl 1741-53)
dancer BD

AUGUSTEN, William (fl 1595-97)
actor DA

AULICK, W. W. (b 1873) American
press representative WWM

AULISI, Joseph G. costume designer
WWT/16

AULT, Marie (1870-1951) English
actress ES, WWT/5-11

AUMONT, Jean-Pierre (b 1909/13)
French actor TW/5-6, 12, 15,
19, 26, 28, WWT/15-16

AURELIUS, Mary American actress
TW/6-7

AURETTI, Anne (1742-54) dancer
BD, CDP

AURETTI, Janneton (fl 1742-63)
dancer BD

AURIOL, Mme. (d 1862 [33]) EA/
72*

AURIOL, Francesca dancer CDP

AURIOL, Jean Baptiste (d 1881
[76]) clown, acrobat CDP

AURTHUR, Robert Alan (b 1922)
American dramatist, producer
BE

AUSTA, Amber [Mrs. William
Haines] (d 1910 [27]) variety
comedienne EA/11*

AUSTEN, Mr. (fl 1744) actor BD

AUSTEN-LEE, Cyril (b 1870) English actor GRB/1-4

AUSTIN, Mr. (fl late 18th cent)
actor, manager DD

AUSTIN, Mr. (fl 1757-67) scene
painter, candle snuffer BD

AUSTIN, Mr. (fl 1794) singer BD

AUSTIN, Mr. (fl 1794) violinist
BD

AUSTIN, Mr. (fl 1830s) English
actor, musician HAS

AUSTIN, Miss (fl 1766-67) actress
BD

AUSTIN, Miss (fl 1794) pianist BD

AUSTIN, Miss (fl 1846) singer HAS

AUSTIN, Albert English actor ES

AUSTIN, Alfred (1835-1913) English
dramatist DNB, ES, WWW/1

AUSTIN, Anslow J. (d 1939) honor-
ary secretary of Actors'
Orphanage WWT/14*

AUSTIN, Billy (d 1967 [59]) performer BP/51*

AUSTIN, Charles (1878-1944) English music-hall performer

COC, OC/1-3

AUSTIN, Charles (fl 1967) actor
TW/24

AUSTIN, Charlotte Stuart (d
1900) EA/01*

AUSTIN, Edgar [William Edgar
Piercey] (d 1893) "The
Lightning Cartoonist" EA/
94*

AUSTIN, Elizabeth (fl 1827) English actress, singer CDP,
DD, HAS

AUSTIN, Emma (d 1900 [62])
EA/01*

AUSTIN, Ernest Collier (d 1916
[23]) composer EA/17*

AUSTIN, F. (d 1904 [36])
comedian EA/05*

AUSTIN, Frederic (1872-1952)
English singer, composer
WWW/5

AUSTIN, Frederick Britten (1885-
1941) English dramatist CB,
WWW/4

AUSTIN, Gene (d 1972 [71])
singer, composer BP/52*,
WWWT/16*

AUSTIN, George (d 1905 [80])
EA/06*

AUSTIN, George [Ross Johnstone
Smith] (b 1879) Indian/
English actor GRB/1

AUSTIN, G. H. (d 1907 [28])
comedian EA/08*

AUSTIN, Henry [né Oates] (d
1912) EA/14*

AUSTIN, Jennie [Mrs. Joseph
Hurtig] (d 1938) performer
BE*

AUSTIN, José (d 1881) circus
performer EA/82*

AUSTIN, Joseph (1735-1821)
actor, manager BD

AUSTIN, J. W. (d 1905) musical
director EA/06*

AUSTIN, Kenneth S. (d 1898)
EA/00*

AUSTIN, Lizzie (d 1892) EA/93*

AUSTIN, Louis Frederick (d
1905) critic, dramatist
WWT/14*

AUSTIN, Lyn (b 1922) American
producer BE

AUSTIN, Mary (d 1880 [75])
EA/81*

AUSTIN, Mary [née Hunter]
(1868-1934) American dramatist ES, WWA/1

AUSTIN, Mary Elizabeth (d 1898)
EA/99*

AUSTIN, Mrs. Noel [Louisa Crad-
dock] (d 1869 [21]) burlesque
actress EA/70*

AUSTIN, Rumbo [Thomas William
Rumbo] (d 1917 [59]) EA/18*

AUSTIN, Samuel (d 1886 [77])
EA/87*

AUSTIN, S. H. (d 1918 [62]) EA/
19*

AUSTIN, Sumner Francis (b 1888)
English singer, impresario
ES

AUSTIN-LEIGH, Mrs. see
O'Reilly, Emmie

AUSTIN-LEIGH, Anthony (b 1860)
English actor-manager GRB/1

AUSTIN-MORTIMER (d 1911 [29])
EA/12*

AUSTRAL, Florence (1894-1968)
Australian singer WWW/6

AUSTRALIAN CHILDREN CDP

AVALOS, Luis (b 1946) Cuban actor
TW/26-30

AVEDON, Doe (b 1925) American
TW/5-7

AVELING, Mrs. H. see Willett,
Miss W.

AVELLONI, Casimiro (fl 1721)
musician BD

AVELLONI, Signora Casimiro see
Durastanti, Margherita

AVENEL, Mlle. (d 1857) actress
HAS

AVERAY, Robert (fl 1756) dramatist
CP/2-3, DD, GT

AVERELL, Robert see Averill,
Robert

AVERILL, Robert (d 1913) actor
WWT/14*

AVERY, Brian (b 1940) American
actor TW/23

AVERY, Madge (d 1909) actress
EA/11*

AVERY, Phyllis (b 1924) American
actress BE, TW/2

AVERY, Thomas (fl 1768) master
carpenter BD

AVERY, Val (b 1924) American
actress TW/26

AVES, Dreda (d 1942) American
singer WWA/2

AVES, Rosetta (d 1883 [70]) EA/
84*

AVISON, Charles (1709-70) English
musician, composer BD, DNB

AVOGLIO, Christina Maria (fl

1740-44) Italian singer BD
AVOLA, Little (d 1886 [11])
    EA/87*
"AVOLINA" see Chadwick,
    Sophia
AVONDALE, Mrs. Walter (d
    1886 [35]) EA/87*
AVONE, Thomas L. (d 1912
    [60]) music-hall artist EA/
    13*
AVORY, Mr. (fl 1738) house
    servant? BD
AVRIL, Suzanne [Suzanne Dela-
    roche] French actress
    WWT/2-3
AWAD, Jacqueline (b 1941)
    actress TW/25-26
AXELROD, George (b 1922)
    American dramatist, pro-
    ducer, director AAS, BE,
    CD, MD, MH
AXELROD, Jack (b 1930) Amer-
    ican actor TW/27
AXEN, Robert (fl 1631-35) actor
    DA
AXER, Erwin (b 1917) Polish
    actor ES
AXT, John Mitchell (fl 1748)
    kettle drummer BD
AXT, William L. (d 1959 [71])
    composer, conductor BE*
AXWORTHY, Geoffrey (b 1923)
    English director of drama
    WWT/15-16
AYCKBOURN, Alan (b 1939)
    English dramatist, director,
    actor AAS, CD, WWT/15-
    16
AYED, Aly Ben (d 1972 [40])
    performer BP/56*
AYER, Harriet Hubbard adapter
    DD
AYER, Nat D. (d 1952 [65])
    American composer WWT/
    4-6
AYERS, Agnes (1896-1940)
    American actress BE*
AYERS, Christine American
    actress TW/1
AYERS, David H. (b 1924)
    American executive, direc-
    tor, educator BE
AYERS, Lemuel (1915-55)
    American scene designer,
    costumier, producer ES,
    TW/2-8, 12, WWA/3
AYERS, Shirley Osborn (d 1967
    [50]) actress, producer,

costume designer TW/24
AYERTON, Randle (1869-1940)
    English performer BE*
AYLETT, Mr. (fl 1726-29) gallery
    doorkeeper BD
AYLETT, Mrs. (fl 1716-26) gallery
    doorkeeper BD
AYLEWORTH, Mr. (fl 1721) dancer
    BD
AYLEWORTH, Jonathan (fl 1739)
    musician BD
AYLEWORTH [Joseph?] (fl 1708-10)
    violinist BD
AYLIFF, Mrs. (fl 1690-97) singer,
    actress BD, DD
AYLIFF, Henry Kiell (1872-1949)
    South African actor, producer,
    director AAS, WWT/5-10,
    WWW/4
AYLIFFE, John (1803-47) comedian
    DD
AYLING, W. L. (1816-57) American
    actor HAS
AYLING, Mrs. W. L. (b 1819)
    American actress HAS
AYLMER, Christopher (fl 1662)
    musician BD
AYLMER, David (d 1964 [31]) actor
    BE*, BP/49*
AYLMER, Sir Felix (b 1889) English
    actor AAS, BE, ES, WWT/5-
    15
AYLMER, George (fl 1787-1801)
    singer, actor BD
AYLWARD, Emily (d 1895) EA/96*
AYLWARD, Theodore (1730-1801)
    English singer, organist, com-
    poser BD, DNB
AYLWYN, Jean (1885-1964) Scottish
    actress GRB/4, WWT/1-6
AYMAR, William T. (d 1883) clown
    CDP
AYME [Mr. ?] (fl 1726-27) house
    servant BD
AYME, Marcel (1902-67) French
    dramatist BE, MWD
AYNESWORTH, E. Allan [E. Abbot
    Anderson] (1865-1959) English
    actor DD, DP, EA/96, ES,
    GRB/1-4, WWT/1-11
AYNSCOMB, Mr. (fl 1761-62)
    singer BD
AYNSTEY, Howard (b 1864) English
    musical director GRB/1
AYNSWORTH, John (d 1581) actor
    DA
AYRE, William (fl 1737-40) trans-
    lator CP/1-3, DD, GT

AYRES, Miss (fl 1840s) English
  actress HAS
AYRES, Ames (d 1872 [23])
  trapezist EA/72*
AYRES [James?] (fl 1729-44)
  actor, dramatist? BD,
  CP/1-3, DD, GT
AYRES, Matthew (fl 1702) actor
  BD
AYRES, Philip Bernard Chinery
  (d 1899) EA/00*
AYRES, Robert (d 1968 [54])
  performer BP/53*
AYRTON, Edmund (1734-1808)
  English organist, composer,
  concert organizer, singer
  BD, DNB
AYRTON, Edward Edmund (fl
  1784-94) singer, organist
  BD
AYRTON, Michael (1921-75)
  English scene designer ES
AYRTON, Norman (b 1924) Eng-
  lish principal of the London
  Academy of Music and
  Dramatic Art WWT/15-16
AYRTON, Randle (1869-1940)
  English actor AAS, WWT/
  4-9
AYRTON, Robert (d 1924) actor
  BE*, WWT/14*
AYRTON, William (1777-1858)
  English singer, music critic,
  manager BD, DD, DNB,
  ES
AYRTON, William Francis Mor-
  rall (1778-1850) English
  singer, organist BD, DD
AYRTOUN, Margaret (fl 1884)
  actress CDP, DD
AYSCOUGH, Cpt. George Edward
  (d 1779) dramatist CDP,
  CP/3, DD, DNB
AYSCOUGH, Samuel (1745-1804)
  scholar DD, DNB
AYTON, Fanny (b 1806?) English
  singer CDP, ES
AYTON, Richard (1786-1823)
  English dramatist DD, DNB
AYTOUN, George [George Aytoun
  Atkinson] Scottish dramatic
  and variety agent GRB/1
AYTOUN, Mrs. George see
  Sipple, Rosina
AYTOUN, William Edmonstoune
  (1813-65) dramatist DD,
  DNB
AZA, Bert (d 1953 [70]) agent

WWT/14*
AZITO, (b 1948) American actor
  TW/30
AZNAVOUR, Charles (b 1924)
  French singer, composer, actor
  CB
AZTEC CHILDREN [Bartola (b 1840);
  Maximo (b 1832)] CDP, HAS
AZUMA IV, Tokuho Japanese dancer
  CB
AZZARA, Candy (b 1945) American
  actress TW/25-26

- B -

B., G. (fl 1704) dramatist CP/3
B., H. H. (fl 1659) dramatist
  CP/3
B., J. dramatist CP/1
B., J. (fl 1809) dramatist CP/3
B., P. see Belon, Peter
B., R. [?=Richard Bower, q.v.]
  English dramatist FGF
B., W. (fl 1717-18) dramatist
  CP/1-3
BABB, Mrs. (fl 1706-07) actress
  BD
BABBINI, Matteo (1754-1816) Italian
  singer BD
BABCOCK, Barbara actress TW/26
BABCOCK, Edward Chester see
  Van Heusen, James
BABEL, Charles (fl 1697-1716)
  instrumentalist BD
BABEL, Isaak (1894-1941) Russian
  dramatist MWD
BABEL, William (c.1690-1723)
  English composer, instrumental-
  ist BD
BABER, Jane (d 1873) actress
  EA/74*
BABHAM, Christopher (fl 1632)
  English actor DA
BABILEE, Jean [né Guttman] (b
  1923) French dancer, choreog-
  rapher ES
BABIN, Victor (d 1972 [63]) com-
  poser/lyricist BP/56*
BABNIGG, Emma (d 1904 [80])
  singer EA/05*
"BABY BENSON" see Fish, Mar-
  guerite
BACALL, Lauren [Betty Joan
  Perske] (b 1924) American
  actress AAS, BE, CB, ES,
  TW/22-25, 27-28, WWT/15-16
BACCALA, Dona (b 1945) American

actress TW/22-23

BACCALONI, Salvatore (1900-69)
Italian singer CB, TW/26,
WWA/5

BACCELLI, Giovanna (b 1801)
Italian dancer BD, CDP

BACCELY, Mrs. (b. c. 1730)
English actress SR

BACCHELLI, Signorina see
Corri, Signora Domenico

BACCHUS, Mrs. Reginald see
Bowman, Isa

BACH, Fernand (d 1953 [72])
comedian WWT/14*

BACH, Johann Christian (1735-82)
German composer, instru-
mentalist, entrepreneur
BD, ES

BACH, Johann Christoph (b 1764)
German musician, teacher
BD

BACH, Leonhard Emil (1849-
1902) German musician,
composer ES

BACH, Dr. Otto (d 1893 [60])
conductor EA/94*

BACH, Reginald (1886-1941)
English actor, producer
CB, WWT/4-9

BACHARACH, Burt (b 1929)
American composer CB

BACHE, Walter (d 1888 [45])
pianist EA/89*

BACKER, George (d 1974 [70s])
dramatist BP/58*

BACKINGTON, Miss (fl 1734)
actress BD

BACKSTEAD, Will see Bark-
sted, William

BACKSTER, Richard see
Baxter, Richard

BACKUS, Charles (1831-83)
American minstrel CDP,
HAS, SR

BACKUS, E. Y. (d 1914 [62])
American actor, stage manager BE*

BACKUS, George (1857-1939)
American actor, dramatist
WWM

BACKUS, Richard (b 1945)
American actor TW/27-30,
WWT/16

BACLANOVA, Olga (1899-1974)
Russian actress ES, TW/
2-3, 6-7, WWT/8-10

BACON, Mr. (fl 1784) singer
BD

BACON, Catherine (b 1947) American actress TW/26, 28

BACON, Charles (d 1886) sculptor
EA/87*

BACON, David Gaspar, Jr. (1914-
42) American actor BE*

BACON, Delia Salter (1811-59)
American dramatist, writer
DD, HJD, WWA/H

BACON, Elizabeth see Poole,
Elizabeth

BACON, Ernst (b 1898) American
composer, pianist, conductor
ES

BACON, Faith (d 1956 [c. 45])
performer BE*

BACON, Sir Francis (1561-1626)
English dramatist FGF, NTH

BACON, Frank (1864-1922) Ameri-
can actor, dramatist, manager
COC, DAB, ES, MWD, NTH,
OC/1-3, SR, WWA/1, WWT/4

BACON, James (fl 1795) dramatist
CP/3, DD

BACON, James (1821-58) American
actor HAS, SR

BACON, Jane (d 1956 [89]) actress
BE*

BACON, Jane (b 1894/95) English
actress ES, WWT/6-9

BACON, Job [or John] (fl 1624-25)
actor DA

BACON, John see Bacon, Job

BACON, Lloyd (b 1890) American
actor ES

BACON, Mai (b 1897) English
actress WWT/5-14

BACON, Max (d 1969 [65]) performer BP/54*

BACON, Dr. Phanuel (1700-83)
English dramatist CP/2-3,
DD, DNB, GT

BACON, Walter Scott (d 1973 [82])
producer/director/choreographer
BP/58*

BADA, Angelo (1875-1941) Italian
singer CB

BADCOCK, [Mr. ?] (fl 1796-99)
house servant BD

BADDELEY, Jr. (fl 1781) actor
BD

BADDELEY, Angela (1904-76) English actress AAS, COC, ES,
WWT/6-16

BADDELEY, Clinton (d 1918 [46])
EA/19*

BADDELEY, Hermione (b 1906)
English actress AAS, BE,

COC, TW/18-19, 24-25,
WWT/5-16
BADDELEY, Richard (fl 1661-62)
sub-treasurer BD
BADDELEY, Robert (1732-94)
English actor BD, CDP,
COC, DD, DNB, ES, GT,
OC/1-3, TD/1-2
BADDELEY, Mrs. Robert see
Baddeley, Sophia
BADDELEY, Sophia [Mrs. Robert
Baddeley; née Snow] (1745-
86) English actress BD,
CDP, DD, DNB, OC/1-3,
TD/1-2
BADDELEY, W. St. Clair (fl
1878-79) dramatist DD
BADDOW (d 1911) ventriloquist
EA/13*
BADEL, Alan Fernand (b 1923)
English actor, director,
producer AAS, BE, COC,
ES, TW/20, WWT/11-16
BADEL, Sarah (b 1943) English
actress WWT/15-16
BADER, Merwin O. (d 1975
[80]) theatre builder BP/
60*
BADERNA, Maria (b 1830)
Italian dancer ES
BADHAM, Stephen see Arlen,
Stephen
BADIA, Leopold (b 1905) Spanish
actor TW/3
BADIA, Luigi (1819-99) Italian
composer, singing master
ES
BADIALI, Cesare (1810-65)
Italian singer CDP, ES,
HAS
BADILAI, Signora Frederic
(b c.1817) actress, singer
SR
BADINI, Signora (fl 1792) singer
BD
BADINI, Carlo Francesco (fl
1770-93) Italian librettist,
manager BD
BADLEY, Robert A. (1865-
1918) producer SR
BADLOWE, Richard (fl 1594)
actor DA
BADY, Berthe (d 1921 [49])
actress WWT/14*
BAER, Mr. (fl 1774) clarinetist
BD
BAER, Mrs. Arthur see
Andrews, Louise

BAER, Marian (b 1926) American
actress TW/29
BAER, Max (1909-59) American
boxer, performer TW/16
BAER, Richard see Barr, Richard
BAERWITZ, Sam (d 1974 [82])
producer/director/choreographer
BP/59*
BAETTY, Mr. (fl 1795-97) house
servant? BD
BAFF, Reggie (b 1949) American
actress TW/26
BAFF, Regina American actress
TW/30
BAGDASARIAN, Ross S. (d 1972
[52]) composer/lyricist BP/56*
BAGG, Mr. (fl 1767-69) doorkeeper
BD
BAGGOT, King (1880-1948) Ameri-
can actor ES, TW/5
BAGGS, Zachary (fl 1685-1710)
treasurer BD
BAGLEY, Ben (b 1933) American
producer, director BE
BAGLEY, Caroline [Mrs. Edgar
Bagley] (d 1908) EA/09*
BAGLEY, Mrs. Edgar see Bagley,
Caroline
BAGLEY, Eleanore (b 1924) Amer-
ican actress TW/4
BAGLEY, Sam (d 1968 [65]) per-
former BP/53*
BAGNAGE, Mr. (fl 1716-17) pit-
keeper BD
BAGNAL, Mrs. (fl 1764-65) candle-
woman BD
BAGNALL, Mr. (fl 1734) harpsi-
chordist BD
BAGNALL, Joshua L. (d 1894 [69])
EA/95*
BAGNALL, Sam (d 1885) singer,
composer CDP
BAGNALL, Walter Wilcock (d 1885
[33]) EA/86*
BAGNOLD, Enid [Lady Roderick
Jones] (b 1889) English drama-
tist AAS, BE, CB, CD, COC,
MD, MWD, PDT, WWT/14-16
BAGNOLESI, Anna [Giovanni Battista
Pinacci] (fl 1731-32) singer
BD
BAGOT, A. G. (fl 1885-90) drama-
tist DD
BAGSTARE, Richard (fl 1636) actor
DA
BAGWELL, Marsha (b 1946) Amer-
ican actress TW/30
BAHN, Chester B. (d 1962 [68])

English journalist, editor
BE*
BAHR-MILDENBURG, Anna (1872-
1947) Austrian singer ES
BAILDON, Joseph (1727-74) Eng-
lish composer, organist,
singer BD
BAILDON, Thomas (d 1760)
English singer, composer
BD
BAILDON, Thomas (d 1762) Eng-
lish singer, composer BD
BAILEY, Mr. (fl 1800) actor
HAS
BAILEY, Mrs. [née Watson]
(b 1815) English actress
HAS
BAILEY, Abraham (fl 1667) drama-
tist CP/1-3, DD
BAILEY, Alison (d 1965 [51])
performer BP/49*
BAILEY, Bill (d 1966 [80])
performer BP/50*
BAILEY, Bryan (1922-60) Eng-
lish actor, manager COC,
OC/3
BAILEY, Charles (d 1903 [36])
EA/04*
BAILEY, Consuela (fl 1905-11)
actress WWM
BAILEY, Francis (d 1902 [65])
EA/03*
BAILEY, Frankie (1859-1953)
American showgirl TW/10
BAILEY, Frank J. (d 1971 [32])
producer/director/choreog-
rapher BP/56*
BAILEY, Gordon (b 1875) English
actor GRB/1-2, WWT/2-6
BAILEY, Hackaliah (1770-1845)
circus performer SR
BAILEY, H. C. (1878-1961)
English critic WWT/2-3
BAILEY, Henry (d 1893 [75])
marionette proprietor EA/94*
BAILEY, Prof. James (d 1890
[58]) EA/92*
BAILEY, James Anthony (1847-
1906) American circus owner
and manager, showman
CDP, DAB, ES, SR, WWA/1
BAILEY, Dr. John (d 1746) Eng-
lish dramatist CP/1
BAILEY, John Cann (1864-1931)
critic DNB
BAILEY, Joseph (d 1972 [61])
lawyer BP/57*
BAILEY, Lilian [Mrs. Georg

Henschel] (1860-1901) singer
CDP
BAILEY, Margery (1891-1963)
American scholar BE*
BAILEY, Mary [née Nellie de Vere]
(d 1878 [25]) EA/79*
BAILEY, Mary (d 1902) EA/04*
BAILEY, Mildred (d 1951 [48])
American singer BE*
BAILEY, Pearl (b 1918) American
actress, singer BE, CB,
TW/2, 6-8, 11-12, 24-26,
WWT/15-16
BAILEY, Robin (b 1919) English
actor AAS, BE, TW/20, WWT/
11-16
BAILEY, Ruth American producer,
actress BE
BAILEY, Samuel (fl 1694-1707)
actor BD
BAILEY, Mrs. Thomas [Charlotte
Watson] (b 1815) actress
CDP, SR
BAILEY, William [William O'Reilly]
(d 1791) English actor, manager
BD
BAILEY, William (d 1927 [82])
manager WWT/14*
BAILEY, Mrs. William [Mrs. Wil-
liam O'Reilly; née Mary Sophia
Arnold] (fl 1778-82) actress,
singer BD
BAILEY, William H. (b 1826)
American actor HAS
BAILEY, William N. (d 1962 [76])
American director, actor BE*
BAILHE, Edilou see Claire, Ludi
BAILLIE, Joanna (1762-1851) Scot-
tish dramatist CDP, CP/3,
DD, DNB, ES, HP
BAILLIE, John (fl 1736) Scottish
lawyer, dramatist CP/3, DD
BAILLIE, Dr. John (d 1743) drama-
tist CP/2-3, DD, GT
BAILY, Mrs. (fl 1742-46) actress
BD
BAILY, Georgina F. [Mrs. Har-
rington Baily] (d 1909 [54])
manager EA/11*
BAILY, Harrington (d 1908) mana-
ger, agent EA/10*, GRB/3*
BAILY, Mrs. Harrington see
Baily, Georgina F.
BAIN, Conrad (b 1923) Canadian
actor BE, TW/14, 21-30,
WWT/15-16
BAIN, Donald (b 1922) English actor
TW/3

BAIN, W. J. (d 1895) elocution-
ist EA/96*
BAINBRIDGE, A. E. (fl 1900)
manager, agent SR
BAINBRIDGE, Cecil J. W. (d
1944) manager WWT/14*
BAINBRIDGE, Clement actor,
manager SR
BAINBRIDGE, Julian (d 1969
[91]) performer BP/53*
BAINBRIDGE, Mrs. Richard see
Fayne, Kate
BAINBRIDGE, Richard Bousfield
(d 1904) lessee EA/05*,
WWT/14*
BAINES, Florence (1877-1918)
English actress GRB/2-4,
WWT/1
BAINES, Mary Lavinia (d 1910
[59]) actress EA/11*
BAINES, Richard Thomas jour-
nalist GRB/2-3
BAINI, Cecilia (fl 1763-64) singer
BD
BAINTER, Fay (1892-1968) Amer-
ican actress BE, ES, TW/
2-16, 24, WWA/5, WWT/4-14
BAINTON, Edgar Leslie (b 1880)
English composer ES
BAIRD, Bill (b 1904) American
puppeteer, writer, designer
BE, CB, ES
BAIRD, Claribel (b 1904) Amer-
ican educator, director,
actress BE, TW/22-23
BAIRD, Cora (1912-67) American
puppeteer, actress BE, CB,
TW/24, WWA/5
BAIRD, Dorothea [Mrs. H. B.
Irving] (1875-1933) English
actress CDP, COC, GRB/
1-4, OC/1-3, WWS, WWT/
1-6, WWW/3
BAIRD, Ethel English actress
WWT/3-7
BAIRD, Leah (d 1971 [60]) per-
former BP/56*
BAIRD, Stewart (d 1947 [66])
American singer, actress
TW/4
BAIRD, Tom (d 1976) composer/
lyricist BP/60*
BAIRNSFATHER, Bruce (1887-
1959) English dramatist
BE*
BAJOR, Gisi (d 1951 [55])
actress WWT/14*
BAKER, Mr. (fl 1683) actor BD

BAKER, Mr. (fl 1729-30) singer
BD
BAKER, Mr. (fl 1732) dancer, actor
BD
BAKER, Mr. (fl 1740) actor BD
BAKER, Mr. (fl 1742-45) pit door-
keeper BD
BAKER, Mr. (fl 1744-45) singer
BD
BAKER, Mr. (fl 1749-50) singer
BD
BAKER, Mr. (fl 1752-57) house
servant BD
BAKER, Mr. (fl 1760-61) box-office
keeper BD
BAKER, Mr. (fl 1760-69?) dancer,
actor BD
BAKER, Mr. (fl 1770) singer BD
BAKER, Mr. (fl 1775) actor BD
BAKER, Mr. (fl 1776-77) actor
BD
BAKER, Mr. (fl 1794) actor CDP
BAKER, Mr. (fl 1820) actor DD
BAKER, Mr. (fl 1821) actor CDP
BAKER, Mr. (d 1897 [41]) entre-
preneur EA/98*
BAKER, Mrs. (d 1760?) singer,
actress, dancer BD
BAKER, Mrs. (fl 1770) puppeteer
BD
BAKER, Mrs. (fl 1780) actress
BD
BAKER, Mrs. (b 1800) English
actress BS
BAKER, Mrs. manager, dancer
DD
BAKER, Mrs. (d 1899 [87]) custo-
dian of Anne Hathaway's cottage
EA/00*
BAKER, Miss (fl 1746-47) dancer
BD
BAKER, [Miss?] (fl 1766-67)
singer BD
BAKER, Miss (fl 1828) see
Nichols, Mrs. Horace F.
BAKER, Alexina [Mrs. John Lewis]
(1821-87) American actress
CDP, DD, HAS, NYM, SR
BAKER, Mrs. Alfred see Wright,
Nelly
BAKER, Ann (1761-1817) actress
BD
BAKER, Arthur (d 1911 [31]) per-
former EA/12*
BAKER, Bartholomew (fl 1615?-
1679) actor BD
BAKER, Basil (d 1859 [54]) come-
dian EA/72*, WWT/14*

BAKER, Belle (d 1957 [67])
American vaudevillian
TW/13
BAKER, Benjamin (fl 1730-36)
kettle-drummer BD
BAKER, Benjamin A. (1818-90)
American actor, manager,
dramatist CDP, COC,
DAB, DD, ES, HAS, HJD,
OC/1-3, SR
BAKER, Benny (b 1907) Ameri-
can actor TW/28-30,
WWT/10-11
BAKER, Berkley (fl 1775-1805)
actor, manager BD, TD/1-2
BAKER, Bertha Kunz (d 1943)
American dramatic reader
WWA/2
BAKER, Blanche CDP
BAKER, Carroll (b 1931) Amer-
ican actress BE, ES,
TW/10, 12-13, 19
BAKER, Charles (fl 1758-70)
gallery office keeper BD
BAKER, Charles (d 1844)
comedian EA/72*
BAKER, Clara L. [Mrs. George
L. Baker] (d 1858) singer?
HAS
BAKER, Mrs. C. W. see
Baker, Matilda
BAKER, Daniel E. (d 1939 [78])
American performer BE*
BAKER, David (b 1926) Ameri-
can composer, pianist BE
BAKER, David Lionel Erskine
(1730-67?) English actor,
dramatist, historian BD,
CDP, CP/2-3, DD, DNB,
ES, GT, TD/1-2
BAKER, Mrs. David Lionel
Erskine [née Elizabeth Clen-
don] (d 1778) English actress
BD
BAKER, Dorothy (1907-68) Amer-
ican dramatist BE, CB,
HJD, WWA/5
BAKER, Elizabeth (1879-1962)
English dramatist ES,
NTH, WWT/2-11
BAKER, Ellis (b 1898) American
actor TW/2-3, 6-7
BAKER, Elsie (d 1971 [78]) per-
former BP/56*
BAKER, Emma Mabella singer
CDP
BAKER, Fay American actress
TW/3

BAKER, Fletcher (d 1879) singer,
composer EA/80*
BAKER, Frances (fl 1677) actress
BD
BAKER, Francis (fl 1670-90) actor
BD
BAKER, Frank (d 1909 [23]) proper-
ty master EA/10*
BAKER, Frederick (d 1888) singer,
actor EA/89*
BAKER, George (1773?-1847) Eng-
lish musician, composer BD,
DNB
BAKER, George (1885-1976) English
actor, singer, script-writer
WWT/9-15
BAKER, George (b 1931) Bulgarian/
English actor, director, pro-
ducer TW/15, WWT/14-16
BAKER, George E. singer CDP
BAKER, Mrs. George L. see
Baker, Clara L.
BAKER, George Pierce (1866-1935)
American dramatist, scholar
COC, DAB, ES, HJD, MH,
NTH, OC/1-3, WWT/6-7
BAKER, G. T. Howard, Jr. (d
1886) performer EA/88*
BAKER, Harry (fl 1592) actor DA
BAKER, Henrietta see Chanfrau,
Henrietta
BAKER, Henry Barton (d 1906 [60])
historian, actor DD
BAKER, Henry Chichester see
Chichester, Henry
BAKER, Howard (d 1907 [53]) EA/
08*
BAKER, Howard (b 1905) American
dramatist, educator BE
BAKER, Iris (b 1901) Indian/English
actress ES, WWT/7-13
BAKER, Jane King (d 1971 [75])
performer BP/56*
BAKER, Janet (b 1933) English
singer CB
BAKER, Job (fl 1709-44) kettle-
drummer BD
BAKER, John (d 1679) trumpeter
BD
BAKER, John E. (d 1966) director
BP/51*
BAKER, [John] Lewis (d 1873 [50])
American actor CDP, HAS,
SR, WWA/H
BAKER, Josephine (1906-75) Amer-
ican performer BE, CB, ES,
SR, WWT/15-16
BAKER, Josephine Turck (d 1942)

American dramatist WWA/2

BAKER, J. S. (fl 1787-1800) actor, manager BD

BAKER, J. S. (b 1830) American actor HAS, SR

BAKER, Mrs. J. S. (fl 1785-1800) actress, singer, dancer BD

BAKER, Mrs. J. S. [née Porter] (fl 1838) American actress HAS, SR

BAKER, Katherine (d 1729) actress BD

BAKER, Kenny (b 1912) American singer, actor BE

BAKER, Lee (1880-1948) American actor ES, SR, TW/4, WWT/4-10

BAKER, Lenny (b 1945) American actor TW/25-27, 30

BAKER, Lewis see Baker, John Lewis

BAKER, Lewis J. (d 1962 [79]) Russian/American performer BE*

BAKER, Mark (b 1946) American actor TW/28-30

BAKER, Matilda [Mrs. C. W. Baker] (b 1801) actress CDP, OX

BAKER, Norah see Baring, Norah

BAKER, Paul (b 1911) American producer, director, educator BE

BAKER, Peter F. (fl 1886) actor CDP, SR

BAKER, Phil (1898-1963) American comedian SR, TW/20, WWA/4

BAKER, R. (fl 1737) see Baker, Robert

BAKER, Ray (d 1976 [35]) producer/director/choreographer BP/60*

BAKER, Richard (fl 1778-79) singer, actor BD

BAKER, Mrs. Richard see D'Elmar, Camille

BAKER, Robert (fl 1574) actor DA

BAKER, Robert (fl 1737) dramatist CP/2-3, DD, GT

BAKER, Sarah [née Wakelin] (1736-1816) English proprietor, manager, dancer, actress BD, COC, OC/2-3

BAKER, Sir Stanley (1928-76)

Welsh actor ES, TW/8

BAKER, Tarkington (d 1924 [45]) press representative, critic BE*, BP/8*

BAKER, Thomas (fl 1700-09) English dramatist CP/1-3, DD, DNB, GT, TD/1-2

BAKER, Thomas (c. 1686-1745) singer BD

BAKER, Thomas (fl 1745-85?) actor, singer, dancer BD

BAKER, Thomas (c. 1765-1801) actor, singer BD, TD/1-2

BAKER, Thomas (fl 1832-50) English musician, conductor, composer CDP, HAS, SR

BAKER, Mrs. Thomas [née Elizabeth Miller] (fl 1761-92) actress, singer, dancer BD

BAKER, Walter see Bray, Walter

BAKER, W. F. (d 1899 [60]) singer EA/00*

BAKER, William (fl 1784-96) singer BD

BAKER, William (d 1879 [42]) singer EA/80*

BAKER, William K. (d 1976 [50]) critic BP/60*

BAKER, W. J. see Fleming, William J.

BAKER, Word (b 1923) American producer, director BE

BAKEWELL, [Mary] (fl 1771-87) actress BD

BAKLANOFF, Georges (1882-1938) Russian singer WWA/1

BAKST, Léon (1866-1924) Russian costume designer COC

BALABAN, A. J. (d 1962 [73]) American executive BE*

BALABAN, Emanuel (1895-1973) American conductor WWA/5

BALABAN, Robert (b 1945) American actor TW/24-26, 28-29

BALANCHINE, George (b 1904) Russian/American choreographer BE, CB, ES, TW/2-8, WWT/10-16

BALATRI, Filippo (1676-1756) Italian singer BD

BALBI, Rosina (fl 1748-60) Italian dancer BD

BALBIRNIE, Robert T. G. de Vaux see Gore, Ivan Pat

BALCH, Marston (b 1901) American educator, director BE

BALDASSARI, Benedetto (fl 1712-25) singer BD

BALDAUFF, Patrick (b 1938)
American actor TW/24, 26
BALDERSTON, John Lloyd (1889-
1954) American dramatist
ES, MD, MH, MWD, NTH,
SR, WWT/7-11, WWW/5
BALDI, Antonio (fl 1726-28)
Italian singer BD, ES
BALDIE, Dacre (d 1907 [70])
actor EA/08*, GRB/3*
BALDUCCI, Sig. (fl 1739) ma-
chinist BD
BALDWIN, Mr. (fl 1774-75)
actor BD
BALDWIN, Annie actress EA/97
BALDWIN, Caroline (d 1896)
EA/98*
BALDWIN, Earl (d 1970 [69])
dramatist BP/55*
BALDWIN, J. (fl 1783-94)
music-porter, musician?
BD
BALDWIN, James Arthur (b
1924) American dramatist
CD, CH, ES, HJD, MH,
MWD
BALDWIN, Joseph (1787-1820)
English actor DD, HAS, SR
BALDWIN, Joseph B. (b 1918)
American educator, drama-
tist BE
BALDWIN, Mary (fl 1703-06)
singer BD
BALDWIN, Robert (d 1866)
actor HAS
BALDWIN, Silas (1825-67)
American contortionist,
musician, juggler HAS, SR
BALDWIN, Thomas Scott (b
1857) American acrobat
SR
BALE, Edwin (d 1912) EA/13*
BALE, Emma (d 1897 [43])
EA/99*
BALE, Frank (d 1899) music-
hall performer EA/01*
BALE, John (1495-1563) Irish
dramatist CP/1-3, DD,
ES, FGF, HP, MH, OC/1-3
BALE, W. (d 1916) EA/17*
BALELLI, Antonio (fl 1786-89)
Italian singer BD
BALENTYNE, James [or James
Valentine] (d 1889) wire-
walker, juggler EA/90*
BALES, William (b 1915) Ameri-
can dancer, choreographer,
dance master ES

BALETTI, Sig. (fl 1755-56) dancer
BD
BALFE, Lizzie (d 1890) EA/91*
BALFE, Louise (b 1864) actress,
singer SR
BALFE, Michael William (1808-70)
Irish composer, singer CDP,
DD, DNB, ES, SR
BALFE, Victoria [Duchesse de
Frias] (d 1871 [34]) singer
CDP
BALFOUR, Betty (b 1903) English
actress ES
BALFOUR, Ethel [Ethel Alice Win-
ton] (b 1885) English actress
GRB/1
BALFOUR, Thomas (b 1849) English
actor OAA/2
BALFOUR, William (d 1964 [89])
actor BE*
BALHATCHET, Bob (b 1944) Amer-
ican actor TW/30
BALICOURT, Simon (fl 1735-48)
flutist BD
BALIEFF, Nikita (1877-1936)
Russian compere, cabaret de-
viser COC, OC/1-3
BALIN, Ina (b 1937) American
actress BE, TW/14-17
BALIN, Mireille (d 1968 [59]) per-
former BP/53*
BALL, Mr. (fl 1799-1804) house
servant BD
BALL, Mrs. (fl 1789) singer BD
BALL, Miss (fl 1781) actress BD
BALL, Miss see Bass, Mrs.
Charles
BALL, Donald I. (d 1974 [69])
producer/director/choreographer
BP/58*
BALL, Edmund (fl 1778) dramatist
CP/3, DD
BALL, Edward see Fitzball, Ed-
ward
BALL, Eleanor [Mrs. Meredith
Ball] (d 1903) EA/05*
BALL, Ernest R. (1878-1927)
American composer SR, WWM
BALL, Frank see Thornton,
Frank
BALL, Harry [William Henry
Powles] (d 1888) singer EA/89*
BALL, James (d 1889) proprietor
EA/90*
BALL, J. H. (d 1885) EA/86*
BALL, J. Meredith (d 1915 [77])
conductor, composer BE*
BALL, Joseph (d 1906)

proprietor EA/07*

BALL, Lewis (1820-1905) Welsh actor DD, GRB/1

BALL, Mrs. Lewis see Ball, Margaret

BALL, Lucille (b 1911) American actress, producer BE, CB

BALL, Margaret [Mrs. Lewis Ball] (d 1880 [56]) EA/81*

BALL, Matilda Powles (d 1901 [58]) EA/02*

BALL, Mrs. Meredith see Ball, Eleanor

BALL, Robert Hamilton (b 1902) American educator, historian BE

BALL, Sarah (d 1904) EA/05*

BALL, Suzan (1933-55) American actress BE*

BALL, Mr. W. (d. 1869 [84]) composer EA/70*

BALL, W. B. Codrington see Alexander, S. King

BALL, Wilfred (d 1897 [49]) musical director EA/98*

BALL, William (b 1931) American actor, director, producer AAS, BE, CB, ES, WWT/15-16

BALLANGER, G. N. (d 1916 [48]) American manager EA/17*

BALLANTINE, Edward (d 1971 [84]) composer/lyricist BP/56*

BALLANTINE, E. J. (d 1968 [80]) actor, director TW/25

BALLANTYNE, Paul (b 1909) American actor BE, TW/9-20, 25, 27, WWT/15-16

BALLARD, Sig. (fl 1752-53) Italian animal trainer BD

BALLARD, Florence (d 1976 [32]) performer BP/60*

BALLARD, Frederick (1884-1957) American dramatist ES

BALLARD, J. G. dramatist SR

BALLARD, Jonathan (fl 1755-62) treasurer BD

BALLARD, Kaye (b 1926) American actress, singer BE, CB, TW/9, 11-12, 17-23, 30, WWT/16

BALLARD, Lucinda (b 1908) American designer BE, ES, TW/2-8

BALLARD, Sarah see Terry,

Sarah Ballard

BALLARD, Thomas (d 1908) scene artist EA/09*

BALLARINI, Mr. (fl 1778) puppet-show man BD

BALLERINO, Virginia (d 1974) performer BP/58*

"BALLETINO, Sig." (fl 1753-54) dancer? BD

"BALLETINO, Signora" (fl 1753-54) dancer? BD

BALLEW, Leighton M. (b 1916) American educator BE

BALLIN, Hugo (d 1956 [76]) American producer, director, painter BE*, BP/41*

BALLIN, Mrs. Hugo Ballin see Ballin, Mabel

BALLIN, Mabel [Mrs. Hugo Ballin] (d 1958 [73]) American actress BE*

BALLOCH, George S. (d 1971 [46]) producer/director/choreographer BP/56*

BALLS (fl 1631) actor DA

BALLS, Mrs. CDP

BALLS, John S. (1799-1844) English actor CDP, DD, HAS, SR

BALMAIN, Andrew (d 1893 [75]) EA/94*

BALMAIN, Rollo (186?-1920) Scottish actor, manager GRB/1-4

BALMAIN, Mrs. Rollo see Mignon, Sara

BALMAT, Mr. (fl 1785-87) acrobat BD

BALMER, Edwin (1883-1959) American writer WWA/3

BALMFORTH, [John?] (fl 1784) singer BD

BALON, Jean (fl 1698-99) dancer BD

BALPH, Mme. (fl 1784) equestrienne BD

BALSAM, Martin (b 1919) American actor AAS, BE, TW/12-14, 22-24, WWT/15-16

BALSHAW, Jarvis (fl 1794) singer BD

BALSHAW, Peter (fl 1794) singer BD

BALTHAZAR, Mr. (fl 1760-63) dancer BD

BALTIMORE, Jake (d 1898) singer EA/99*

BALTZAR, Thomas (c.1630-63) Swedish violinist BD, DNB

BAMATTRE, Martha (d 1970 [78])

performer BP/55*

BAMBER, Willis (d 1878) master
carpenter EA/79*

BAMBERGER, Theron (d 1953
[59]) American producer,
press agent TW/10

BAMBOSCHEK, Giuseppe (1890/
91-1969) Italian conductor
ES, WWA/5

BAMBRIDGE, Mr. (fl 1731-43)
actor BD

BAMBRIDGE, Mrs. (fl 1731-38)
actress BD

BAMBRIDGE, Mrs. (fl 1749)
house servant? BD

BAMBRIDGE, Mrs. (fl 1757-67)
dancer BD

BAMBRIDGE, Thomas (d 1867
[82]) musician EA/68*

BAMBRIDGE, William Herbert
(d 1917 [28]) singer, actor
EA/18*

BAMFIELD, Mr. (fl 1671) actor,
dancer BD

BAMFIELD, Edward (1732-68)
giant BD

BAMFORD, Mr. (fl 1847) actor
HAS

BAMPTON, Rose (b 1908) American singer ES

BANASTER, Gilbert (fl 1478-84?)
master of the Chapel Royal
DA

"BANBAREGINES, Sig." (fl 1752-
54) dancer BD

BANBERRY, Mr. (fl 1746) actor,
singer, dancer BD

BANBURY, Frith (b 1912) English director, actor, manager
AAS, COC, ES, WWT/10-16

BANCKER, James W. (1790-1866)
American? equestrian mana-
ger, actor, circus performer
HAS, SR

BANCROFT, Anne [née Italiano]
(b 1931) American actress
AAS, BE, CB, ES, TW/14-
22, 24-25, WWT/13-16

BANCROFT, Charles (d 1969
[58]) performer BP/54*

BANCROFT, George (1882-1956)
American actor ES, TW/13

BANCROFT, George P. see
Pleydell, George

BANCROFT, John (d 1969) English dramatist CP/1-3, DD,
GT

BANCROFT, Lady Marie [Marie

Effie Wilton] (1839-1921) Eng-
lish actress, manager CDP,
COC, DD, DNB, ES, GRB/1-4,
NTH, OAA/1-2, OC/1-3, SR,
WWT/1-3, WWW/2

BANCROFT, Sir Squire Bancroft
(1841-1926) English actor,
manager CDP, COC, DD,
DNB, DP, ES, GRB/1-4,
OAA/1-2, OC/1-3, WWT/1-5,
WWW/2

BAND, Thomas see Bond, Thomas

BANDEL, Emma Frederick (d 1969
[3]) performer BP/54*

BANDIERA, Anna (fl 1756) singer
BD

BANDMANN, Daniel Edward (1840-
1905) German actor CDP, DD,
HAS, OAA/1-2, SR, WWA/1

BANDMANN, Maurice E. (d 1922
[49]) manager WWT/14*

BANDMANN-PALMER, Mrs. [née
Millicent Palmer] (d 1926 [81])
English actress CDP, DD,
EA/96, GRB/1-4, OAA/1-2

BANDURRIA, George [né Haydock]
(d 1907 [69]) musician EA/09*

BANE, Paula American actress
TW/2-3

BANFORD, Mr. (fl 1728) box keeper
BD

BANG, Herman Joachim (1857-1912)
dramatist BE*

BANGS, Frank C. (1833-1908)
American actor CDP, DAB,
DD, ES, GRB/3-4, HAS,
OC/1-3, PP/1

BANGS, John Kendrick (1862-1922)
American dramatist DAB,
GRB/2-4, WWA/1, WWS,
WWT/1-4, WWW/2

BANIM, John (1798-1842) Irish
dramatist CDP, DD, DNB,
ES, HP

BANISTER, Mr. (fl c.1676) dancer
BD

BANISTER, Ella (fl 1886-90) American actress DP

BANISTER, James (fl 1676-86)
violinist BD

BANISTER, Rev. James (fl 1780)
translator CP/3

BANISTER, Jeoffrey (1641-84)
violinist BD

BANISTER, John (1630?-79) English
instrumentalist, composer,
impresario BD, DD, DNB,
ES

BANISTER, John (1662-1736)
English violinist BD
BANISTER, John (b 1686) Eng-
lish flutist BD
BANISTER, Thomas (fl 1673)
musician BD
BANKES, William (fl 1635) actor
DA
BANKHEAD, Tallulah Brockman
(1903-68) American actress
AAS, BE, CB, COC, ES,
NTH, PDT, SR, TW/1-21,
25, WWA/5, WWT/5-14
BANKS, Mr. (fl 1588-1637)
Scottish equestrian CDP,
DNB
BANKS, Mr. (fl 1723) actor
BD
BANKS, Mr. (fl 1746-49?)
actor BD
BANKS, Mr. (d 1752) doorkeep-
er, office keeper BD
BANKS, Mr. (fl 1780) carver?
actor BD
BANKS, Mr. (fl 1789) actor
BD
BANKS, Mr. (fl 1800-27) dancer,
actor BD
BANKS, Mrs. (fl 1789) actress
BD
BANKS, Aaron (d 1883) minstrel
EA/84*
BANKS, Bertram (d 1916 [39])
child impersonator EA/17*
BANKS, "Billy" (d 1886) minstrel
EA/87*
BANKS, Charles Eugene (1852-
1932) American dramatist
WWA/1
BANKS, Clara (d 1891 [34])
EA/92*
BANKS, Emily [Mrs. James
Banks] (d 1882 [29]) EA/83*
BANKS, Ern (d 1893) actor
EA/95*
BANKS, George Linnaeus (1821-
81) dramatist DD
BANKS, Henry (1744-1829)
tailor, wardrobe keeper
BD
BANKS, Mrs. James see
Banks, Emily
BANKS, Joe singer CDP
BANKS, John (c.1650-1706)
English dramatist COC,
CP/1-3, DD, DNB, ES,
GT, OC/1-3
BANKS, Leslie James (1890-1952)

English actor AAS, COC,
DNB, ES, OC/3, TW/6-8,
WWT/4-11, WWW/5
BANKS, Louisa see Brower, Mrs.
Frank
BANKS, Monty (1897-1950) French
actor, director BE*
BANKS, Nathaniel P. (fl 1839)
American actor HAS, SR
BANKS, Thomas (1756-1810) English
scene painter, dancer, actor
BD
BANKS, W. (fl 1796-1812?) actor,
singer, dancer BD
BANKS, Walter (d 1903 [42]) humor-
ist EA/05*
BANKS, William (d 1776) dancer,
actor, designer BD
BANNEN, Ian (b 1928) Scottish actor
AAS, WWT/13-16
BANNER, Mr. (d 1800?) doorkeeper
BD
BANNER, Mr. (fl 1801) doorkeeper
BD
BANNER, Mr. (fl 1801) sweeper
BD
BANNER, Jack (d 1974 [67]) jour-
nalist, publicist BP/58*
BANNER, John (1910-73) Polish/
American actor TW/29, WWA/
5
BANNERMAN, Celia (b 1946) Eng-
lish actress WWT/15-16
BANNERMAN, Mrs. G. L. see
Evelyne, Alma
BANNERMAN, Kay (b 1919) English
dramatist, actress ES, WWT/
10-16
BANNERMAN, Margaret (1896-1976)
Canadian actress BE, TW/1,
3, WWT/4-15
BANNISTER, Mr. (fl 1790-97)
puppet-showman BD
BANNISTER, Mrs. (fl 1793-94?)
actress BD
BANNISTER, Charles (1741-1804)
English actor, singer BD,
CDP, DD, DNB, ES, OC/1-3,
TD/1-2
BANNISTER, Harry (1893-1961)
American actor TW/5-11, 13,
17, WWT/11-13
BANNISTER, Master J. (fl 1773)
actor BD
BANNISTER, J. (fl 1879-80) actor
DD
BANNISTER, James (fl 1771-83)
actor BD

BANNISTER, John see
Banister, John
BANNISTER, John (d 1725) violinist CDP
BANNISTER, John (1760-1836)
English actor BD, CDP,
COC, DD, DNB, ES, GT,
OC/1-3, OX, TD/1-2
BANNISTER, Mrs. John [née
Elizabeth Harper] (1757-
1849) English actress BD,
CDP, COC, TD/1-2
BANNISTER, Matilda (d 1879
[62]) EA/80*
BANNISTER, Nathaniel Harring-
ton (1813-47) American
actor, dramatist DAB, DD,
ES, HAS, HJD, OC/1-3,
RJ, SR, WWA/H
BANNISTER, Mrs. Nathaniel
Harrington [née Amelia
Green] (fl 1817-53) American
actress DD, HAS
BANNISTER, T. B. (fl 1871-93)
dramatist DD
BANSON, Richard (fl 1777-94)
scene painter BD
BANTI, Signora (fl 1756-58)
dancer BD, CDP
BANTI, Signora (fl 1860) Spanish
singer HAS
BANTI, Felicita (fl 1777-88?)
dancer BD
BANTI, Zaccaria (fl 1758?-1802)
dancer BD
BANTI, Signora Zaccaria [née
Brigitta Giorgi] (c. 1756-
1806) Italian singer BD,
CDP, ES
BANTI-GIORGI, Brigida see
Banti, Signora Zaccaria
BANTOCK, Sir Granville Ran-
some (1868-1946) English
composer DNB, ES, WWW/4
BANTOCK, Leedham (d 1928
[58]) dramatist, actor BE*,
WWT/14*
BANVARD, Fifi (d 1962) Aus-
tralian actress WWT/14*
BANVARD, John (1820-91) ex-
hibitor CDP
BANWELL, Louisa (d 1891
[43]) EA/92*
BANYAI, George (b 1905) Hun-
garian/American general
manager, house manager
BE
BANYARD, Mr. (fl 1785) actor

BD
BAPTIST, Mr. (fl 1691) oboist BD
BAPTIST, Mr. (fl 1784-85) dancer
BD
BAPTISTE, Mr. (fl 1724) flutist
BD
BAPTISTE, Mr. (fl 1782) clown,
equestrian, tumbler BD
BARA, Theda (1890-1955) Ameri-
can actress TW/11
BARAGREY, John (1918-75) Ameri-
can actor BE, TW/6-8, 22-
23, 28
BARAGWANATH, John G. (d 1965
[76]) dramatist BP/50*
BARAKA, Imamu Amiri [Leroi
Jones] (b 1934) American
dramatist, educator, adminis-
trator CB, CD, CH, HJD,
MH, MWD, WWT/16
BARAL, Robert (b 1910) American
writer BE
BARAS, Charles (1826-73) American
actor, dramatist SR
BARASCH, Norman (b 1922) Ameri-
can dramatist BE
BARATOW BEN-ZWI [Paul Brenner]
(1878-1952) Russian actor ES
BARATTI, Francesco (fl 1754-55)
Italian singer BD
BARBALONGA, Signor (d 1911)
singer EA/13*
BARBANDT, Charles (fl 1754-61)
musician, composer, teacher
BD
BARBARINA see Campanini,
Barbarina
BARBAT, Percy D. (d 1965 [82])
performer BP/50*
BARBEAU, Adrienne (b 1945) Amer-
ican actress TW/27-29
BARBEE, Richard (b 1887) Ameri-
can actor WWT/5-8
BARBER, Miss see Mason, Mrs.
BARBER, [Mr. ?] (fl 1708) house
servant BD
BARBER, Mr. (fl 1725-28) house
servant? BD
BARBER, Mr. (fl 1780) actor BD
BARBER, Mr. (fl 1784?-94) violist
BD
BARBER, Mrs. Charles J. see
Newton, Elizabeth Blanche
BARBER, Samuel (b 1910) American
composer, conductor CB, ES,
HJD
BARBER, William Charles (d 1912
[58]) journalist EA/13*

"BARBERINI, La" see Campanini, Barbarina

BARBERRE, Mons. (fl 1827-31) French dancer HAS

BARBERRE, Mme. (fl 1825) French singer HAS

BARBETTE, Yander (d 1973 [68]) performer BP/58*

BARBIER, George W. (1866-1945) American actor CB, ES, SR

BARBIER, Jane (d 1757) singer BD

BARBIERE, M. G. (fl 1827) French dancer CDP

BARBIERI, Fedora (b 1919/20) Italian singer CB, ES

BARBILI, Signorina (fl 1848) Italian singer SR

BARBIROLLI, Sir John (1899-1970) English conductor ES

BARBOR, H. R. (1893-1933) English journalist WWT/6-7

BARBOTT, Mr. (fl 1794) violinist, dancing master? BD

BARBOUR, Edwin (b 1841) actor, dramatist SR

BARBOUR, Joyce (b 1901) English actress ES, WWT/5-15

BARBOUR, Oliver (d 1968 [63]) actor, director, producer TW/24

BARBOUR, Robert MacDermot see MacDermot, Robert

BARBOUR, Thomas (b 1921) American actor TW/22, 24-27, 29-30

BARBOUR, William (d 1910 [47]) electrician EA/11*

BARCAVELLE [Mrs. ?] (fl 1786) dancer? house servant? BD

BARCELLA, Ernest L. (d 1974 [63]) publicist BP/58*

BARCLAY, Mr. (fl 1741-44) actor BD

BARCLAY, Arthur J. English manager GRB/1-3

BARCLAY, Caroline [Mrs. Caroline Whalley] (fl 1792-94) actress BD, CDP, TD/1-2

BARCLAY, Delancey (d 1917) American actor SR

BARCLAY, Don Van Tassel (d 1975 [83]) performer BP/60*

BARCLAY, James M. (fl 1836) dramatist DD

BARCLAY, Jered American

actor TW/23, 26

BARCLAY, Sir William see Berkley, Sir William

BARCOCK, Mr. (fl 1730-33) actor BD

BARCROFT, Judith American actress TW/23

BARD, Wilkie [Billie Smith] (1870-1944) English music-hall artist CDP, COC, OC/1-3, SR

BARDIN, Peter (d 1773) actor BD

BARDOLEAU, Mr. (1794-1801?) singer BD

BARDOLY, Dr. Louis S. (d 1969 [75]) dramatist BP/54*

BARDON, Henry (b 1923) Czech actor WWT/15-16

BARDSLEY, John (d 1916 [33]) singer WWT/14*

BARE, Carl (d 1975 [15]) performer BP/60*

BARE, Thomas (d 1908) EA/09*

BARER, Marshall (b 1923) American lyricist, director, dramatist BE

BARETTA, Mlle. (fl 1869-79) dancer CDP

BARETTI, Giuseppe Marc Antonio (1719-89) Italian writer CDP, ES

BARFIELD, Mr. (fl 1784) actor BD

BARFIELD, Roger (fl 1606) actor DA

BARFOOT, Mrs. see Bates, Miss

BARFOOT, Harry (d 1870) comedian EA/71*

BARFORD, Mr. (fl 1794) musician, music seller, actor? BD

BARFORD, Richard (fl 1729) dramatist CP/1-3, DD, GT

BARGE, Fred (d 1900) actor EA/01*

BARGE, Gillian (b 1940) English actress WWT/16

BARGY, Roy (d 1974 [79]) composer/lyricist BP/58*

BARI, Lenny (b 1955) American actor TW/28

BARILI, Clotida (fl 1847-48) singer CDP, HAS

BARING, Hon. Maurice (1874-1945) dramatist WWT/2-7

BARING, Norah [Norah Baker] English actress ES

BARK, John Daly (c. 1775-1808) Irish dramatist WWA/H

BARKANY, Marie (b 1862) German

actress WWT/2

BARKENTIN, Marjorie (d 1974
[83]) dramatist TW/30

BARKER (fl 1603) actor DA

BARKER, Mr. (fl 1690) English
dramatist CP/1-3

BARKER, Mr. (fl 1752) actor
BD

BARKER, Mrs. see Grattan,
Mrs. Henry P.

BARKER, Annie A. (d 1908)
actress EA/09*

BARKER, Bernard (d 1917) EA/
18*

BARKER, Carrie [Carrie Ender-
son] (d 1887) EA/88*

BARKER, Clive (b 1931) English
actor, director, dramatist
WWT/15-16

BARKER, Felix English critic
AAS

BARKER, George (d 1876 [64])
singer, composer EA/77*

BARKER, George see Murray,
G. W.

BARKER, Harley Granville see
Granville-Barker, Harley

BARKER, Henry Aston (fl 1787?-
1823) panorama exhibitor
BD

BARKER, Howard (b 1946) English dramatist CD, WWT/
16

BARKER, Jack (d 1950 [55])
musical comedy actor TW/7

BARKER, James Nelson (1784-
1858) American dramatist
COC, DAB, DD, EAP, ES,
HJD, MH, OC/1-3, RE,
RJ, SR, WWA/H

BARKER, John (d 1897) roundabout proprietor EA/98*

BARKER, Joseph (b 1862)
Scottish actor GRB/1

BARKER, Lex (d 1973 [53])
performer BP/57*

BARKER, Margaret (b 1908)
American actress TW/5-12

BARKER, Mike (d 1976 [60])
executive BP/60*

BARKER, Mrs. R. see
Cruise, Marie

BARKER, Reginald (1886-1937)
Scottish actor ES

BARKER, Reginald (1895-1945)
American? actor, manager
SR

BARKER, Richard (d 1903 [69])

actor, stage manager BE*,
EA/04*, WWT/14*

BARKER, Robert (c.1739-1806)
panorama exhibitor BD, CDP

BARKER, Ronnie (b 1929) English
actor WWT/15-16

BARKER, Thomas (fl 1620) dramatist CP/1-3

BARKER, William H. (d 1863)
American minstrel HAS

BARKHURST, Mr. (fl 1691-92)
musician BD

BARKOW, Arthur A. (d 1972 [58])
stage manager BP/56*

BARKSHIRE, Percy E. (b 1882)
English singer GRB/1

BARKSTED, William (fl 1606-11)
English dramatist, actor CP/
1-3, DA, DD, DNB, FGF

BARKSTEED see Barksted, William

BARKWELL, Mr. (fl 1686) musician
BD

BARKWORTH, Peter (b 1929) English actor WWT/14-16

BARLETTE, Sophie [Mrs. W.
Bryant] (d 1905) music-hall
performer EA/06*

BARLEY-CLARKE, Lily (b 1886)
English actress GRB/1

BARLEY-CLARKE, Marion [Mrs.
Albert H. Clarke] (d 1917 [56])
EA/18*

BARLING, Violet see Brandon,
Violet

BARLOG, Boleslaw (b 1906) German
director WWT/14

BARLOW ["The Great Australian
Vocalist"] singer CDP

BARLOW, Mr. (fl 1745-46) actor,
singer BD

BARLOW, Billie (1862/65-1937)
English actress, singer CDP,
WWT/4-6

BARLOW, Edward (fl 1785-1800)
treasurer BD

BARLOW, Harriet (d 1878 [22])
actress EA/79*

BARLOW, H. J. (1892-1970) English manager WWT/11-14

BARLOW, Howard (1892-1972)
American conductor CB

BARLOW, Milt G. (1843-1904)
minstrel performer and manager
CDP, SR

BARLOW, Nevett (d 1973 [39])
composer/lyricist BP/58*

BARLOW, Reginald (1867?-1943)

American actor CB, SR

BARLOW, Samuel L. M. (b
1892) American composer,
conductor ES

BARLOW, Seaghan (d 1972 [80s])
member of the National
Dramatic Society BP/57*

BARMAN, Mr. (fl 1735-36) actor?
house servant? BD

BARMORE, S. Wesley see
Harris, Samuel

BARNABE, Bruno (b 1905) English actor ES, WWT/10-16

BARNABEE, Henry Clay (1833-
1917) American actor,
singer CDP, DAB, ES,
NTH, SR, WWA/1, WWM,
WWS

BARNARD, Mr. (fl 1744-48) actor
BD

BARNARD, Mr. (fl 1750-54)
house servant BD

BARNARD, Mrs. (fl 1744) actress
BD

BARNARD, Mrs. (fl 1779-85)
actress BD

BARNARD, Miss (fl 1783) actress
BD

BARNARD, Amelia (d 1891)
EA/93*

BARNARD, Annie (d 1941)
actress BE*

BARNARD, Barney (d 1924 [46])
American comedian BP/8*

BARNARD, Bert (d 1917 [31])
variety agent EA/18*

BARNARD, Mrs. C. (d 1869)
composer EA/70*

BARNARD, Cecil (d 1896 [31])
performer EA/97*

BARNARD, Charles (1838-1920)
American dramatist ES,
WWA/1

BARNARD, Mrs. Charles (d
1911) EA/12*

BARNARD, Daniel (d 1879)
proprietor EA/80*

BARNARD, Edward (fl 1741-57)
dramatist CP/2-3, GT

BARNARD, Henry (b 1921)
American actor TW/2-6, 9

BARNARD, Henry see Guinard,
John

BARNARD, Ivor (1887-1953)
English actor ES, WWT/6-11

BARNARD, Sir John (fl 1722-37)
parliamentarian TD/1-2

BARNARD, John (d 1773?)

musician BD

BARNARD, John (1812-95) musical
director, composer DD

BARNARD, Mollie (b 1830) English
actress HAS

BARNARD, Sophye (b 1888) American singer WWM

BARNAY, Ludwig (b 1842) German
manager GRB/4, WWT/1-2

BARNBY, Sir Joseph (1838-96)
principal of Guildhall School of
Music EA/97*

BARNE, Will (fl 1602) actor DA

BARNES, Mr. (fl 1721) actor BD

BARNES, Mr. (fl 1743?-59) doorkeeper BD

BARNES, Mr. (fl 1757-60) constable
BD

BARNES, Mr. (fl 1777-82) actor
BD

BARNES, Mr. (fl 1795-98) dancer
BD

BARNES, Mrs. (fl 1782-1808?)
actress BD, CDP

BARNES, Mrs. (d 1916) EA/17*

BARNES, Miss (fl 1781-92) actress,
singer, dancer BD

BARNES, Barnaby (1569-c.1609)
English dramatist CP/1-3,
ES, FGF, RE

BARNES, Barry K. (1906-65) English actor ES, WWT/9-12,
WWW/6

BARNES, Billy (b 1927) American
lyricist, composer, singer BE

BARNES, Binnie [Gertrude Maude
Barnes] (b 1905/08) English
actress ES, TW/8, WWT/7-9

BARNES, Charles (d 1711) singer
BD

BARNES, Charlotte Mary Sanford
(1818-63) American actress,
dramatist COC, DAB, ES,
HJD, OC/1-3, RJ, SR, WWA/H

BARNES, Clive (b 1927) English
critic AAS, CB, WWT/16

BARNES, Djuna (b 1892) American
dramatist, actress CD, HJD,
MD

BARNES, Edward (d c.1703) ropedancer, booth operator BD

BARNES, Mrs. Edward (fl 1704-11)
fair booth operator BD

BARNES, Elliott (b 1843) dramatist
SR

BARNES, Emily Jane (d 1911)
equestrienne EA/12*

BARNES, E. S. (d 1905)

music-hall manager EA/06*

BARNES, F. E. (d 1880) actor,
musician EA/81*

BARNES, Fred singer CDP

BARNES, Fred (d 1917) EA/18*

BARNES, George (d 1878) proprietor EA/79*

BARNES, Howard (1904-68) English critic TW/24, WWA/5,
WWT/10-13

BARNES, James (d 1838 [51])
actor CDP, DD

BARNES, James (d 1888) clown
EA/89*

BARNES, J. H. see Barnes,
John H.

BARNES, Joe (d 1964 [59]) performer BE*

BARNES, John (1761-1841)
English actor CDP, COC,
DD, HAS, SR

BARNES, Mrs. John (d 1841)
English actress SR,
WWA/H

BARNES, John H. (1850/52-
1925) English actor DD,
EA/96, GRB/1-4, OAA/2,
SR, WWS, WWT/1-5

BARNES, Joshua (1654-1712)
English translator, dramatist
CP/3

BARNES, Kempster (b 1923)
South African actor TW/3

BARNES, Sir Kenneth Ralph
(1878-1957) English prin-
cipal of the Royal Academy
of Dramatic Art, dramatist
COC, DNB, ES, OC/1-3,
WWT/4-12, WWW/5

BARNES, Mabel Thomas (d
1962) performer BE*

BARNES, Mae (b 1907) American singer, dancer, actress
BE, TW/10-12

BARNES, Margaret Ayer (1886-
1967) American dramatist
HJD, TW/24

BARNES, Mary (1780-1864)
English actress DD, HAS

BARNES, Mary (d 1869 [51])
actress? EA/70*

BARNES, Peter (b 1931) English dramatist, director
AAS, CD, WWT/15-16

BARNES, Price [John Price
Burnham] (d 1877 [31])
singer EA/78*

BARNES, Richard (fl 1675-91)

actor, singer BD

BARNES, Sidney (d 1889) actor,
singer CDP

BARNES, Thomas (fl 1629) actor
DA

BARNES, Thomas (1785-1841) English critic COC, OC/1-3

BARNES, T. Roy (d 1937 [56])
English actor BE*, BP/21*

BARNES, Verona actress TW/25-
26, 28, 30

BARNES, William A. (fl 1870)
dramatist SR

BARNES, William Augustus (1826-
68) actor CDP, HAS, SR

BARNES, Winifred (1892/94-1935)
actress, singer WWT/3-7

BARNET, Mr. (fl 1778-1845?)
actor BD

BARNET, Mrs. (fl 1795) singer
BD

BARNET, Mrs. (fl 1848) actress
HAS

BARNET, Master (fl 1750) actor
BD

BARNET, Jarvis (fl 1748-50) actor
BD

BARNET, Robert Ayers (1850/53-
1933) American dramatist,
librettist WWM

BARNETT, Mrs. (fl 1729) actress
BD

BARNETT, Mrs. (d 1905) EA/06*

BARNETT, Alice [Mrs. Dickins]
(d 1901) actress, singer DD

BARNETT, Benjamin (fl c.1855)
actor DD

BARNETT, Catherine (fl 1786-1800)
actress, singer BD

BARNETT, Chester A. (d 1947
[62]) actor TW/4

BARNETT, C. Z. (d 1890 [88])
dramatist, librettist, performer
DD

BARNETT, Domenico J. (d 1911
[70]) professor of music EA/
13*

BARNETT, Mrs. E. F. Kemble (d
1895) EA/96*

BARNETT, Emma (d 1877) actress
EA/78*

BARNETT, Mrs. Frances (d 1870
[71]) actress EA/71*

BARNETT, Henry (d 1868 [76])
manager EA/68*

BARNETT, Humphrey (d 1874 [62])
acting manager EA/75*

BARNETT, John (fl 1794) bass

viol-player BD

BARNETT, John (1802-90) English composer, singer, musical director CDP, DD, DNB, ES

BARNETT, John Francis (1838-1916) composer, pianist DD

BARNETT, Millie see Soutten, Mme.

BARNETT, Morris (1800-56) French?/English actor, dramatist CDP, DD, DNB

BARNETT, Orlando (b 1867) English actor GRB/1

BARNETT, R. A. (b c.1860) dramatist SR

BARNETT, Richard (d 1892 [21]) actor, singer EA/94*

BARNETT, Mrs. Richard (d 1873) actress, singer EA/75*

BARNETT, Thomas (fl 1794) musician BD

BARNEY, Jay (b 1918) American actor, stage manager BE, TW/12-15, 22, 24-25, 28

BARNEY, Ludwig (b 1845) actor SR

BARNEY, Phil (d 1975 [81]) critic BP/60*

BARNHARD, Lawrence C. (d 1975 [71]) producer/director/choreographer BP/59*

BARNHART, Franklin (d 1976 [49]) union executive BP/60*

BARNHILL, James (b 1922) American educator, actor, director BE

BARNS, Mr. (fl 1794-95) house servant BD

BARNS, Mrs. (fl 1725) actress? BD

BARNSHAW, John (fl 1768-83) actor, singer BD

BARNUM, Bush (d 1971 [60]) publicist BP/56*

BARNUM, George William (1853-1937) American actor WWM

BARNUM, John (fl 1876) actor, singer CDP

BARNUM, Phineas Taylor (1810-91) American circus showman CDP, COC, DAB, DD, ES, HAS, HJD, HP, NTH, OC/1-3, PDT, SR, WWA/H

BARNWELL, Mr. (fl 1794-95)

dresser BD

BARON, Mr. (fl 1800) singer BD

BARON, Louis [or Lewis] (d 1920 [62]) actor BE*, WWT/14*

BARON, Milton (d 1972 [76]) producer/director/choreographer BP/57*

BARON, Robert (b 1630) English dramatist CP/1-3, DD, DNB, FGF

BARON, Robert Alex (b 1920) American company manager, general manager, director, press representative BE

BARON, Sandy (b 1938) American actor TW/22-24, 28-29

BARON, Sheldon (b 1935) American actor TW/23

"BARONESS, The" [Joanna Maria Lindelheim] (fl 1703-17) Italian singer BD

BARONOVA, Irina (b 1919) Russian dancer ES, TW/1, WWT/9-12

BAROWBY, Miss (fl 1766) actress, dancer BD

BARR, Mr. (fl 1749-50) stage door-keeper BD

BARR, Mr. (fl 1788-95) actor BD

BARR, Benjamin (fl 1794) bass viol player? BD

BARR, Byron Ellsworth see Young, Gig

BARR, Geoffrey (b 1924) American personal manager, actor BE, TW/7

BARR, Ida (d 1967 [85]) performer BP/52*

BARR, Jeanne (d 1967 [35]) actress TW/24

BARR, Margaret English dancer, choreographer ES

BARR, Olive (d 1912 [88]) EA/13*

BARR, Patrick (b 1908) Indian/English actor WWT/10-16

BARR, Richard [né Baer] (b 1917) American producer, director BE, WWT/14-16

BARR, Richard M. (d 1972 [64]) publicist BP/57*

BARRACLOUGH, Sydney (1869/71-1930) English actor, singer GRB/1-4

BARRAND, William (fl 1793) bass viol player? BD

BARRAS, Charles M. (1826-73) American actor, dramatist BE*

BARRAS, Joseph (fl 1756)

proprietor BD

BARRASFORD, Elizabeth (d 1894 [32]) EA/95*

BARRASFORD, Thomas (1860-1910) English manager GRB/1

BARRASFORD, Mrs. [Thomas; Maude D'Almaine] English singer GRB/1

BARRAT, Mr. (d 1795) actor TD/1

BARRAT, Robert (1891-1970) American actor ES, TW/26

BARRATT, Mr. (fl 1784?-94) bass viol player BD

BARRATT, Augustus English composer, lyricist WWT/4-6

BARRATT, Walter Augustus (d 1947 [73]) Scottish composer, producer, conductor BE*

BARRATT, Watson (1884-1962) American scene designer ES, TW/2-8, WWT/7-13

BARRAUD, George (b 1893) English actor ES

BARRAUD, Mark H. (d 1887 [39]) scene artist EA/89*

BARRAULT, Jean-Louis (b 1910) French director, actor BE, CB, COC, ES, NTH, OC/3, WWT/11-14

BARRE, Mons. (fl 1796-98) choreographer, dance director BD

BARRE, Mlle. (fl 1795-96) dancer BD

BARRE, Albert (d 1910 [54]) dramatist BE*, WWT/14*

BARRE, George (d 1892) EA/93*

BARRE, Mrs. [Joseph?; née Groce] (fl 1768-97?) actress, singer BD

BARREM, Mr. (fl 1795) house servant? BD

BARRERA, José (b 1929) Spanish dancer TW/26

BARRERE, Jean (b 1918) American stage manager, director BE

BARRESFORD, Mrs. see Bulkeley, Mrs. George

BARRET, Mr. (fl 1730-32) actor BD

BARRET, Mr. (fl 1789) actor, manager TD/2

BARRET, John (fl 1635) actor DA

BARRET, R. (fl 1784-85) actor BD

BARRETT, Mr. (fl 1722) actor BD

BARRETT, Mr. (fl 1736-37) musician? BD

BARRETT, Mr. (fl 1776-1805?) box-keeper, constable BD

BARRETT, Mr. (d 1777?) actor BD

BARRETT, Mr. (fl 1784-94) double-bass player BD

BARRETT, Mr. (fl 1797-1800) violinist BD

BARRETT, Mrs. (fl 1776) actress BD

BARRETT, Mrs. (fl 1790-1816) actress, dancer, singer BD

BARRETT, Mrs. (fl 1797) BD

BARRETT, Miss (fl 1776) actress/singer BD

BARRETT, Miss (fl 1784) actress BD

BARRETT, Ann Jane (1801-53) actress CDP, HAS

BARRETT, Edith (1906-77) American actress ES, WWT/7-10

BARRETT, Eliza [Mrs. Oscar Barrett] (d 1908) EA/10*

BARRETT, Ellen Anna (d 1892) EA/93*

BARRETT, George (1869-1935) English actor DP, GRB/3-4, WWT/1-7

BARRETT, Mrs. George [Mrs. Henry] (1801-53) American actress DD

BARRETT, Mrs. George see Vincent, Nellie

BARRETT, George Edward (1849-94) English actor DD, OC/1-3

BARRETT, George Horton (1794-1860) American/English actor CDP, COC, DAB, DD, ES, HAS, OC/1-3, SR, WWA/H

BARRETT, Mrs. George Horton [née Stockwell; Mrs. Drummond; Mrs. Henry] (d 1857 [55]) actress HAS, SR

BARRETT, Georgianna (b 1829) American actress HAS

BARRETT, Giles Linnett (1744-1809) actor, manager BD, CDP, DD, HAS

BARRETT, Mrs. Giles Linnett [née Ranoe; Mrs. Rivers; Mrs. Belfield] (d 1832) actress BD, DD, HAS

BARRETT, Henry J. (d 1908) EA/09*

BARRETT, Henry Michael (d
1872 [68]) English actor
BE*, EA/73*
BARRETT, Ivy Rice (d 1962
[64]) performer BE*
BARRETT, Jane (d 1969) per-
former BP/54*
BARRETT, J. H. (b 1831) Amer-
ican actor HAS
BARRETT, Mrs. J. H. [Emily
Viola Crocker] (d 1869)
American actress HAS
BARRETT, Jimmie (d 1964
[80]) performer BE*
BARRETT, John (c.1674-c.1720)
organist, composer BD
BARRETT, John (d 1795) actor
BD, TD/2
BARRETT, [John?] (fl 1799)
actor BD
BARRETT, John L. (d 1874
[50]) comedian EA/75*
BARRETT, John Peter (b 1937)
American actor TW/30
BARRETT, J. Pritchard (d
1900) scene artist EA/01*
BARRETT, Laurinda (b 1931)
American actress TW/13,
24, 30
BARRETT, Lawrence (1838-91)
American actor, producer
CDP, COC, DAB, DD, ES,
HAS, NTH, OC/1-3, SR,
WWA/H
BARRETT, Leslie (b 1919)
American actor TW/23-
24, 30
BARRETT, Lester (fl 1894)
singer CDP
BARRETT, Lester (d 1970 [68])
performer BP/55*
BARRETT, Lillian Foster (1884-
1963) American dramatist
WWA/4
BARRETT, Louis F. (1843-96)
American actor SR
BARRETT, Mary Anne (d 1893)
EA/94*
BARRETT, Minnette (d 1964
[80]) actress TW/21
BARRETT, Nora Cunneen (d
1965 [65]) performer BP/50*
BARRETT, Oscar, Sr. (d 1941
[95]) composer, conductor,
producer BE*
BARRETT, Oscar, Jr. (1875-
1943) English manager DD,
WWT/3-9

BARRETT, Mrs. Oscar see Bar-
rett, Eliza
BARRETT, Raina (b 1941) American
actress TW/26-29
BARRETT, Ray (d 1973 [65]) per-
former BP/57*
BARRETT, Reginald (1861-1940)
English composer WWA/1,
WWM
BARRETT, Robert Reville see
Reville, Robert
BARRETT, Roger (d 1968 [47])
performer BP/53*
BARRETT, Sidney Harrison (d 1901
[36]) comedian EA/02*
BARRETT, T. A. see Stuart,
Leslie
BARRETT, T. W. singer, com-
poser CDP
BARRETT, Viola Crocker see
Barrett, Mrs. J. H.
BARRETT, W. A. (fl 1882) librett-
tist DD
BARRETT, Walter (fl 1623) actor
DA
BARRETT, Wilson (1846-1904) Eng-
lish actor, manager CDP,
COC, DD, DNB, DP, EA/96,
ES, GRB/1, OAA/2, OC/1-3,
SR, WWA/1, WWW/1
BARRETT, Wilson (b 1900) English
actor, manager WWT/9-13
BARRETT, Mrs. Wilson see
Heath, Caroline
BARREY, Lodowick see Barry,
Lodowick
BARRIE, Amanda [née Broadhurst]
(b 1939) English actress WWT/
14-16
BARRIE, Barbara (b 1931) American
actress TW/25-30, WWT/16
BARRIE, Frank (b 1940) English
actor TW/23
BARRIE, Sir James Matthew (1860-
1937) Scottish dramatist AAS,
COC, DD, DNB, ES, GRB/1-4,
HP, MD, MH, MWD, NTH,
OC/1-3, PDT, RE, SR, WWS,
WWT/1-8, WWW/3
BARRIE, Mona (b 1909) English
actress ES
BARRIE, Wendy (b 1912) English
actress ES
BARRIERE, Hippolite (fl 1823-24)
theatre owner WWA/H
BARRINGER, Ned (d 1976 [87])
performer BP/60*
BARRINGTON, Mr. (fl 1783) actor,

singer BD
BARRINGTON, Mrs. (fl 1732-33)
actress? BD
BARRINGTON, Henry Harding
(d 1908) actor EA/09*,
GRB/4*
BARRINGTON, John (1715-73)
Irish actor BD
BARRINGTON, Mrs. John [née
Ann Hallam (fl 1733-73)
actress BD
BARRINGTON, Josephine (d 1973)
performer BP/57*
BARRINGTON, Pattie [Mary Kay]
(d 1906 [22]) EA/07*
BARRINGTON, Roland (d 1893
[40]) actor EA/94*
BARRINGTON, Rutland [George
Rutland Fleet] (1853-1922)
English actor CDP, DD,
DNB, DP, EA/95, ES,
GRB/1-4, OAA/2, WWT/1-4
BARRIS, Harry (d 1962 [57])
American composer, per-
former BE*
BARRISCALE, Bessie (d 1965
[81]) performer BP/50*
BARRISFORD, Mrs. Ebenezer
see Bulkley, Mrs. George
BARRISON, Mabel (1882-1912)
actress CDP
BARROIS, Mons. (fl 1754-55)
dancer BD
BARRON, [Mrs. ?] (fl 1760-61)
charwoman BD
BARRON, Mlle. (d 1852) dancer
HAS
BARRON, Carter Tate (1905-50)
American executive WWA/3
BARRON, Charles (1840-1918)
American actor CDP, HAS,
SR, PP/1
BARRON, Elwyn Alfred (1855-
1929) American dramatist
GRB/2-3, SR, WWA/1,
WWM, WWW/3
BARRON, John (fl 1784-94)
singer, pianist, violinist?
BD
BARRON, Madge Douglas [Mrs.
Charles Harley] (d 1900
[35]) EA/01*
BARRON, Marcus (1925-44)
actor WWT/8-9
BARRON, Mark (1905-60) Amer-
ican critic NTH, WWA/4
BARRON, Muriel (b 1906) Scot-
tish actress, singer

WWT/10-12
BARRON, William (d 1890) EA/91*
BARRON, William Augustus (fl
1760?-94) violoncellist BD
BARROW, Bernard (b 1927) Ameri-
can educator, director, actor
BE
BARROW, D. (fl 1850) actor HAS
BARROW, James O. see Barrows,
James O.
BARROW, Janet (d 1965?) English
actress TW/7
BARROW, John (d 1904) stage
manager EA/05*
BARROW, Julia Bennet (b 1824)
English actress, manager
CDP, HAS
BARROW, Thomas (1722?-89)
Welsh singer, harpsichord
teacher BD
BARROW, William (d 1902 [36])
music-hall manager EA/04*
BARROWS, James O. (1857-1925)
American actor PP/1, SR,
WWS
BARRS, Georgina (d 1902) EA/03*
BARRS, Norman (b 1917) English
actor TW/4, 6, 13, 20, 22-
24, 26-28, 30
BARR-SMITH, A. (b 1905) Australian
actor ES
BARRY, Mr. (fl 1699) actor? BD
BARRY, Mr. (fl 1799) actor BD
BARRY, Ann see Barry, Mrs.
Spranger
BARRY, Bob [Oscar Mills] (d 1918)
EA/19*
BARRY, Bobby (1887-1964) Ameri-
can actor TW/3
BARRY, Charles Whittle (d 1889)
actor EA/90*
BARRY, Christine [Grace Under-
wood] (b 1911) Welsh actress
WWT/9-10
BARRY, David Loring (d 1610)
lessee DA
BARRY, Donna American actress
TW/26
BARRY, Edwin (fl 1879) singer
CDP
BARRY, Elaine (d 1948) dancer
TW/4
BARRY, Elizabeth (1658-1713) Eng-
lish actress BD, CDP, COC,
DD, DNB, ES, HP, NTH,
OC/1-3
BARRY, Elizabeth (d 1873 [68])
EA/74*

BARRY, Fred (d 1964) English
dancer TW/1
BARRY, Frederick (b 1876)
American composer WWM
BARRY, Gene (b 1919) American
actor TW/2-3, 6-8
BARRY, H. C. [F. W. Russell]
(d 1909) singer, composer
CDP
BARRY, Helen [Mrs. Alexander
Rolls] (d 1904 [51]) English
actress CDP, DD, OAA/
1-2, SR
BARRY, Joan (b 1901/02/03)
actress WWT/4-8
BARRY, John (b 1915) American
singer TW/1-3
BARRY, John D. (b 1866) Amer-
ican dramatist WWM
BARRY, Leonard (fl 1890s) singer
CDP
BARRY, Leonard (d 1972 [50])
performer BP/57*
BARRY, Lodowick [Lodowick
Barrey] (fl c.1620) English
dramatist CP/1-3, DD,
DNB, FGF
BARRY, Lydia [Mrs. George
Felix] (d 1932 [56]) American
vaudevillian CDP, SR,
WWM
BARRY, Mary (fl 1698) actress
BD
BARRY, Mary Ann (d 1891 [85])
EA/92*
BARRY, Matthew (b 1962) Amer-
ican actor TW/29
BARRY, Pat (d 1879 [29]) Irish
comedian EA/80*
BARRY, Philip (1896-1949)
American dramatist AAS,
COC, DAB, ES, HJD, MD,
MH, MWD, NTH, OC/1-3,
PDT, RE, SR, TW/6,
WWA/1, WWT/6-10
BARRY, Shiel (1842/43-97) Irish
actor DD, DP, OAA/1-2
BARRY, Shiel (1882-1916) Eng-
lish actor GRB/4, WWT/
1-3
BARRY, Mrs. Shiel see Minto,
Dorothy
BARRY, Spranger (1719-77) Irish
actor, manager BD, CDP,
COC, DD, DNB, ES, GT,
NTH, OC/1-3, TD/1-2
BARRY, Mrs. Spranger [née
Ann Street; Mrs. William

Dancer; Mrs. Thomas Craw-
ford] (1734-1801) English act-
ress BD, CDP, DD, DNB,
ES, GT, TD/1-2
BARRY, Thomas (c.1743-68) Irish
actor BD
BARRY, Thomas (d 1857 [47])
clown, actor CDP, DD, HAS,
SR
BARRY, Thomas (1798-1876) Eng-
lish actor, manager CDP
BARRY, Mrs. Thomas (fl 1766-74)
actress BD
BARRY, Mrs. Thomas (d 1854)
actress DD, HAS
BARRY, Mrs. Thomas see
Biddles, Clara S.
BARRY, Mrs. Thomas see
Redmund, Clara S.
BARRY, Tom (d 1857 [47]) clown
BE*, WWT/14*
BARRY, Tom (d 1931 [47]) Ameri-
can dramatist BE*
BARRY, Viola (d 1964 [70]) actress
BE*
BARRY, W. H. (d 1893) mana-
ger EA/94*
BARRY, William (d 1780) actor,
treasurer BD
BARRY, Mrs. William [née Jane
Osborne] (1739-71) English
actress BD
BARRY, William J. (d 1898 [38])
EA/99*
BARRY AND FAY actors, variety
performers SR
BARRYMORE, Miss (fl 1785) actress
BD
BARRYMORE, Earl of (1769-93)
English actor, patron CDP,
COC, DD, OC/1-3
BARRYMORE, Ann (d 1862 [62])
actress CDP
BARRYMORE, Diana (1921-60)
American actress ES, TW/1,
3-16, WWT/10-12
BARRYMORE, Ethel (1879-1959)
American actress AAS, CB,
COC, ES, GRB/2-4, NTH,
OC/1-3, PTD, SR, TW/1-15,
WWA/3, WWM, WWS, WWT/
1-12, WWW/5
BARRYMORE, Georgiana Emma
Drew (1856-93) American actress
DAB, ES, NTH, OC/1-3,
WWA/H
BARRYMORE, John (1882-1942)
American actor AAS, CB,

COC, DAB, ES, GRB/3-4,
NTH, OC/1-3, PDT, SR,
WWA/2, WWT/1-9, WWW/4
BARRYMORE, Lionel (1878-1954)
English actor AAS, CB,
COC, ES, NTH, OC/1-3,
PDT, SR, TW/11, WWA/3,
WWT/1-11, WWW/5
BARRYMORE, Mrs. Lionel see
Rankin, Doris
BARRYMORE, Maurice [Herman
Blythe] (1847-1905) American
actor, dramatist COC, DAB,
DD, ES, GRB/1, NTH,
OC/1-3, PP/1, SR, WWA/1
BARRYMORE, William (1759-
1830) English actor, drama-
tist, manager BD, COC,
GT, OC/1-3, TD/1
BARRYMORE, Mrs. William
[Miss Adams] (d 1862)
actress DD, HAS, SR
BARRYMORE, William Henry
(d 1845) actor, dramatist
CDP, DD, HAS, SR,
OC/1-3
BARSACQ, André (1909-73)
French scene designer ES
BARSANTI, Francesco (b
c.1690) Italian instrumen-
talist, composer BD
BARSANTI, Jane [Mrs. John
Richard Kirwan Lyster;
Mrs. Richard Daly; Mrs.
Lisley] (d 1795) actress,
singer BD, CDP, DD
BARSBY, Mrs. E. A. [Mrs.
Frank Barsby] (d 1906)
EA/07*
BARSBY, Frank (d 1892) actor
EA/93*
BARSBY, Mrs. Frank see
Barsby, Mrs. E. A.
BARSTOW, Edith (d 1960)
American choreographer
WWA/3
BARSTOW, James S., Jr. (d
1968 [49]) critic BP/53*
BART, Jan (d 1971 [52]) com-
poser/lyricist BP/56*
BART, Lionel (b 1930) English
composer, lyricist, drama-
tist, director AAS, BE,
CD, PDT, WWT/14-16
BARTEESKE, John (fl 1660)
drummer BD
BARTELL, Bob (d 1903) music-
hall artist EA/04*

BARTELL, Jerry (b 1942) American
actor TW/30
BARTELL, Richard (d 1967 [69])
performer BP/52*
BARTELLE, Jennie Dickerson
[née Maude Dickerson] (1856-
1943) singer SR
BARTELMAN, Mrs. (fl 1767) singer
BD
BARTELS, Louis John (1896-1932)
American actor SR
BARTENIEFF, George (b 1933)
German actor TW/3, 22-28
BARTET, Jeanne Julia (1854-1941)
French actress GRB/1-4,
WWT/1-4
BARTH, Alice (d 1910 [61]) singer
EA/11*
BARTH, Belle (d 1971 [59]) per-
former BP/55*
BARTH, Cecil [Cecil Walenn]
(d 1949 [84]) manager GRB/
1-3, WWT/4-7
BARTHELEMON, Master (fl 1783-
84) singer BD
BARTHELEMON, Cecilia Maria
[Mrs. Henslowe] (b 1770?)
singer, musician BD
BARTHELEMON, François Hippolyte
(1741-1808) French musician,
bandleader, composer BD,
DNB, ES, TD/1-2
BARTHELMESS, Richard Semler
(1895-1963) American actor
TW/20
BARTHOLDI, Fred (d 1961 [58])
manager BE*
BARTHOLOMAE, Phillip H. (1880-
1947) American dramatist,
librettist, manager SR, WWT/
5-9
BARTHOLOMEW, Mrs. (d 1891 [80])
composer, pianist EA/92*
BARTHOLOMEW, Anne Charlotte
[née Fayermann] (d 1862)
dramatist DD
BARTHOLOMEW, John (fl 1794)
dramatist CP/3
BARTHOLOMEW, John see Barty,
Jack
BARTHOLOMEW, William H. (1830-
1917) American actor, circus
performer CDP, SR
"BARTHOLOMEW FAIR MUSICIAN,
The" CDP
BARTHOLOMON, J. (fl 1786) actor
BD
BARTHROPE, Mr. (fl 1775-86)

house servant BD
BARTLE, Colin (d 1973 [58])
theatre club founder BP/
58*
BARTLE, Marion Elizabeth see
De Roos, Marie
BARTLE, Onye [?] (fl 1603)
actor DA
BARTLEMAN, James (1769-1821)
English singer BD, CDP,
DNB
BARTLEMAN, Thomas (d 1879)
singer EA/80*
BARTLET, Joseph (b 1763) Amer-
ican dramatist RJ
BARTLETT, Mr. (fl 1735-41)
musician? BD
BARTLETT, Mr. (fl 1794) Eng-
lish actor HAS
BARTLETT, Sir Basil (b 1905)
English actor ES, WWT/
8-13
BARTLETT, Bonnie (b 1929)
American actress TW/26
BARTLETT, Charles (b 1941)
American actor TW/29-30
BARTLETT, Clifford (1903-36)
Welsh actor WWT/8
BARTLETT, D'Jamin American
actress TW/30
BARTLETT, Elise [Elise Porter]
actress WWT/7-9
BARTLETT, Fred (d 1912)
actor, manager EA/13*
BARTLETT, Mme. Gordon (d
1894) singer EA/95*
BARTLETT, Homer Newton
(b 1845) American com-
poser WWA/4, WWM
BARTLETT, James J. (d 1880)
actor EA/81*
BARTLETT, J. J. English actor
GRB/1-3
BARTLETT, John (1820-1905)
American writer WWA/1
BARTLETT, Josephine (d 1910
[48]) American performer
BE*
BARTLETT, Lucinda (d 1904)
EA/05*
BARTLETT, Mrs. M. A. (d
1917) EA/18*
BARTLETT, Martine American
actress BE, TW/14
BARTLETT, Michael (b 1901)
American actor, singer
TW/27-29, WWT/9-10
BARTLETT, Peter (b 1942)

American actor TW/30
BARTLEY, Mr. (fl 1800-22) English
actor BS, TD/2
BARTLEY, Mrs. see Bartley,
Mrs. George
BARTLEY, George (1782-1858)
English actor CDP, DD,
DNB, ES, GT, HAS, OX, SR
BARTLEY, Mrs. George [née Wil-
liamson] (1783-1850) English
actress BS, CDP, DD, DNB,
HAS, SR
BARTLEY, Sarah see Bartley,
Mrs. George
BARTLEY, Sir William see
Berkley, Sir William
BARTOLETTI, Bruno (b 1926) Italian
conductor ES
BARTOLINI, Sig. (d 1894 [72])
singer EA/95*
BARTOLINI, Vincenzio (fl 1782-92)
singer BD
BARTOLOMEO, Noreen (b 1947)
American actress TW/28
BARTOLOMICI, Luigi (d 1800)
dancer BD
BARTOLOTTI, Girolamo (fl 1731)
trumpeter BD
BARTOLOZZI, Josephine see
Anderson, Josephine
BARTOLOZZI, Lucia Elizabeth see
Vestris, Mme.
BARTON, Mr. (fl 1721) dancer BD
BARTON, Mr. (fl 1736) actor BD
BARTON, Mr. (fl 1791-92) house
servant? actor? BD
BARTON, Mr. (d 1848) English
actor DD, HAS
BARTON, Andrew (fl 1767) Ameri-
can dramatist, librettist EAP,
WWA/H
BARTON, Charles (b 1902) American
actor ES
BARTON, Donald (b 1928) American
actor TW/15
BARTON, Dora [Dora Brockbank]
(d 1966) English actress GRB/
1-4, WWT/1-10
BARTON, Frances see Abington,
Mrs. James
BARTON, Gary (b 1947) American
actor TW/24
BARTON, Grace (fl 1900-06) Amer-
ican actress WWS
BARTON, H. Reyner (d 1966)
actor BP/50*, WWT/14*
BARTON, James (d 1848) English
actor, stage manager WWA/H

BARTON, James (1890-1962)
American actor ES, TW/
2-16, 18, WWT/8-13

BARTON, John (d 1875 [68])
actor EA/76*

BARTON, John (1870-1946)
American actor TW/3,
SR

BARTON, John (b 1928) English
director, dramatist AAS,
COC, WWT/14-16

BARTON, Julia see MacMillan,
Mrs.

BARTON, Lucy (b 1891) American costume designer, educator BE

BARTON, Margaret (b 1926)
English actress ES, WWT/
10-13

BARTON, Mary [Mrs. J. B.
Brockbank] (d 1970) English
actress ES, GRB/1-2,
WWT/4-10

BARTON, Onesiphorus (d 1608)
actor DA

BARTON, Reyner see Barton,
H. Reyner

BARTON, Sam (d 1941 [46])
performer BE*

BARTON, Susan (fl 1849) fat
woman CDP

BARTON, Ward J. (d 1963
[87]) performer BE*

BARTON, William (d 1778?)
musician, pleasure garden
proprietor BD

BARTON, William (d 1900 [71])
EA/01*

BARTON, Gen. William B. (d
1891) American actor EA/
92*

BARTON, Arthur (b 1935) American actor TW/27

BARTSCH, Hans (d 1952 [68])
German producer, literary
representative BE*

BARTY, Jack [John Bartholo-
mew] (1888-1942) English
actor WWT/9

BARWELL, Thomas (fl 1677-
1700) trumpeter BD

BARWICK, Edwin (d 1928 [70])
singer, comedian, composer
CDP

BARWICK, Mary Ann (d 1904
[69]) EA/05*

BARYSHNIKOV, Mikhail (b 1948)
Russian dancer CB

BARZELL, Wolfe (d 1969 [72])
performer BP/53*

BARZIN, Leon Eugene (b 1900)
Belgian/American conductor
CB

BASCOMB, Henry (b 1833) American actor HAS

BASCOMB, Mrs. Henry L. see
Skerrett, Mrs. George

BASECU, Elinor (b 1927) American
actress TW/30

BASEHART, Richard (b 1914/19)
American actor BE, ES, TW/
1-2, 14-18, 24, WWT/15-16

BASELEON, Michael American actor
TW/20, 22-23, 26

BASHALL, James A. (d 1905 [68])
EA/06*

BASHALL, Joseph (d 1883) singer
EA/84*

BASIL, Mr. (fl 1778) fair booth
proprietor BD

BASIL, Arthur John (d 1873 [25])
composer, author EA/74*

BASIL, George (d 1873 [26]) comedian EA/74*

BASING, S. Herberte (d 1898 [40])
actor, manager WWT/14*

BASKCOMB, A. W. (1880-1939)
English actor GRB/2-4, WWT/
1-9

BASKCOMB, Lawrence (1883-1962)
English actor WWT/7-11

BASKER, Thomas (fl 1620) English
dramatist CP/1-2

BASQUETTE, Lina (b 1909) American dancer ES

BASRIER, Mr. (fl 1675) violinist
BD

BASS, Mr. (fl 1778-84) actor BD

BASS, Alfred (b 1921) English actor
WWT/11-16

BASS, Charles (1803-63) English
actor CDP, DD, HAS

BASS, Mrs. Charles [Miss Ball]
(d 1852) Canadian actress
HAS

BASS, Emory American actor
TW/23, 25-26, 29-30

BASS, Helen Kennedy (d 1973) performer BP/58*

BASS, Kate (d 1894 [36]) EA/95*

BASS, Rochelle see Owens,
Rochelle

BASS, Tom (d 1913) singer, composer CDP

BASS, Will (d 1917) EA/18*

BASSAN, Mr. (fl 1766-84) house

servant BD
BASSAN, Miss (fl 1773-80)
dancer BD
BASSANO, Henry (d 1665) musician BD
BASSE, Joe (d 1972 [71]) performer BP/56*
BASSE, Thomas (fl 1611-19) actor DA
BASSERMAN, Albert (1867-1952) German actor COC, OC/1-3, TW/1, 8
BASSERMAN, Else (d 1961 [83]) actress TW/1
BASSERMANN, Dr. August (1848-1931) German manager COC, GRB/4, OC/1-3, WWT/1-2
BASSET, Serge (d 1917) dramatist, critic BE*
BASSETT, Mr. (fl 1794) bass viol player BD
BASSETT, Adelaide (d 1895) parachutist EA/96*
BASSETT, James see Bertram, Charles
BASSETT, John (d 1787) instrumentalist BD
BASSETT, Leon (b 1870) English musical director GRB/1
BASSETT, Russell (d 1918 [72]) American actor BE*
BASSETT, W. S. (d 1910 [38]) conductor EA/11*
BASSHE, Emjo (c. 1899-1939) American dramatist MD
BASSI, Amedeo (1874/76-1949) Italian singer ES, WWA/5, WWM
BASSIE, Joan (b 1939) American actress TW/23, 27-29
BASSINGWHITE, [John?] (fl 1779) actor BD
BASSMAN, George (b 1914) American musical director, composer, conductor, actor BE
BASTAR, Mrs. [née Green] (fl 1800) actress TD/1-2
BASTEE (d 1747) dancer BD
BASTER, Mrs. John [née Eleanor Green] (fl 1799-1809?) actress, singer BD
BASTIANINI, Ettore (d 1967) Italian singer WWA/4
BASTON, Mrs. (fl 1735-36) dresser BD
BASTON, Miss (fl 1732-35) dancer, harpsichordist BD

BASTON, John (fl 1709-39) flutist, composer BD
BASTON, Robert dramatist CP/3
BASTON, Thomas (fl 1709-20) musician BD
BASTOW, George (fl late 19th cent) actor, singer CDP
BASTOW, Louis (d 1886) advance agent EA/87*
BATAGLIO, Matteo (fl 1662?-70) musician BD
BATAILLE, Henry (d 1922 [49]) dramatist WWT/14*
BATCHELDER, Marjorie [Mrs. Paul McPharlin] (b 1903) American marionettist ES
BATCHELLER, Jennie (d 1966 [70]) performer BP/51*
BATCHELLER, Joseph D. (b 1915) American educator, director BE
BATCHELOR, Miss (fl 1750-54) dancer BD
BATCHELOR, Mrs. D. S. (d 1884) EA/85*
BATCHELOR, Nelly [Nelly Ethair] (d 1882) characteristic singer EA/83*
BATE, Mr. (fl 1779) actor BD
BATE, Henry see Dudley, Sir Henry Bate
BATEMAN, Mr. (fl 1782) actor BD
BATEMAN, Mrs. (fl 1730) actress? BD
BATEMAN, Ellen Douglas (1844-1936) American actress CDP, COC, DD, ES, HAS, OC/1-3, SR
BATEMAN, Frank (d 1906 [42]) actor EA/07*
BATEMAN, Harold L. (d 1878 [28]) EA/79*
BATEMAN, Hezekiah Linthicum (1812-75) American manager COC, DD, DNB, ES, OC/1-3, SR
BATEMAN, Isabel Emilie (1854-1934) American actress CDP, COC, DD, ES, OAA/1-2, OC/1-3
BATEMAN, Jessie (b 1877) actress GRB/3-4, WWT/1-9
BATEMAN, John (fl 1667) actor? BD
BATEMAN, Kate Josephine [Mrs. Crowe] (1843-1917) American actress CDP, COC, DAB, DD, ES, GRB/1-4, HAS, OAA/1-2,

OC/1-3, SR, WWT/1-3
BATEMAN, Leah [Leah Bateman-
Hunter] (b 1892) English
actress WWT/1-8
BATEMAN, Mrs. [Mary?] (1765?-
1829) actress, fencer, singer
BD
BATEMAN, Richard (d 1874)
actor EA/75*
BATEMAN, Sidney Frances
Cowell (1823-81) American
actress, dramatist COC,
DAB, DD, DNB, ES, HJD,
NTH, OC/1-3, WWA/H
BATEMAN, Thomas (fl 1660-69)
actor BD
BATEMAN, Mrs. Thomas (d
1900) EA/01*
BATEMAN, Victory (1866-1926)
American actress SR,
WWM, WWS
BATEMAN, Virginia Frances
[Mrs. Edward Compton]
(1853-1940) American actress,
manager DD, ES, GRB/1-4,
OAA/1-2, OC/1-3, WWT/
1-8
BATEMAN, Zillah (1900-70)
English actress WWT/7-8
BATEMAN-HUNTER, Leah see
Bateman, Leah
BATES, Mr. (fl 1749) actor BD
BATES, Mrs. (fl 1678) actress
BD
BATES, Miss [Mrs. Barfoot]
(fl 1793-1820?) dancer,
singer BD
BATES, Alan Arthur (b 1934)
English actor AAS, BE,
CB, COC, ES, TW/14, 18,
21, 29, WWT/13-16
BATES, Barbara (d 1969 [43])
performer BP/53*
BATES, Blanche (1873-1941)
American actress CB,
COC, DAB, ES, GRB/2-4,
NTH, OC/1-3, SR, WWA/
1-2, WWM, WWS, WWT/
1-9
BATES, Florence (1888-1954)
American actress BE*
BATES, F. M. (d 1879) Aus-
tralian actor EA/80*
BATES, Mrs. F. M. (d 1908)
actress SR
BATES, Frank M. (fl 1858-68)
actor, manager HAS
BATES, Guy (d 1968 [92])

performer BP/52*
BATES, J. (fl 1722) actor? BD
BATES, J. (fl 1794) singer BD
BATES, Jacob (fl 1760?-70?) Eng-
lish equestrian BD, CDP, ES
BATES, James (d 1784) actor BD
BATES, Mrs. James [née Patty Ann
Scrase] (d 1787) actress BD
BATES, James W. (d 1853) manager
HAS
BATES, Joah (1740-99) conductor,
organist BD
BATES, Mrs. Joah [née Sarah Har-
rop] (d 1811) English singer,
actress BD
BATES, John (fl 1685) singer BD
BATES, John (fl 1846-56) theatre
owner WWA/H
BATES, Jonathan (d 1967 [42])
dramatist BP/52*
BATES, Lulu American singer,
actress BE
BATES, Marie (d 1923 [70]) Amer-
ican actress CDP, SR
BATES, Mary see Dibdin, Mrs.
Charles Isaac Mungo
BATES, Michael (b 1920) Indian/
English actor AAS, WWT/15-
16
BATES, Cpt. M. V. giant CDP
BATES, Mrs. M. V. giant CDP
BATES, Robert (d 1786) actor BD
BATES, Sally (b 1907) American
actress WWT/8-9
BATES, Sarah (d 1811) singer
CDP, DNB
BATES, Thomas (d 1679) violist,
teacher BD
BATES, Thorpe (1883-1958) English
actor, singer WWT/4-11,
WWW/5
BATES, Wilbur M. (b 1861) Amer-
ican representative GRB/3-4
BATES, William (d 1813?) actor,
dancer, singer, machinist,
manager BD, DD, HAS
BATES, William Joseph (d 1901
[44]) proprietor EA/02*
BATES, William Oscar (1852-1924)
American dramatist WWA/1
BATESON, Timothy (b 1926) English
actor AAS, WWT/15-16
BATESSEN, [Mr. ?] (fl 1783-84)
performer? BD
BATH, Albert J. (d 1964 [85])
performer BE*
BATH, Hubert (b 1883) English
composer, conductor ES,

WWT/4-9

BATH, James (d 1909 [73]) publisher EA/10*

BATHURST, Charles Bradsworth (d 1889 [43]) music-hall performer EA/90*

BATIE, Frank (d 1949 [69]) American actor BE*, BP/34*

BATIERE, Mrs. (fl 1784) actress BD

BATIST, John (d 1875 [56]) proprietor EA/76*

BATIST, Mrs. John (d 1875) EA/76*

BATLEY, Dorothy (b 1902) English actress WWT/5-10

BATLEY, Mrs. Ernest G. [Ethel Gordon Mussay] (d 1917 [38]) EA/18*

BATLEY, Isaac see Hicken, Isaac George

BATLEY, Ralph Cecil (d 1917) EA/18*

BATLEY, Mrs. Ralph Cecil see Terry-Lewis, Mabel

BATSON, Mr. (fl 1774) actor BD

BATSON, Mrs. (fl 1774) actress BD

BATSON, George (b 1918) American dramatist BE

BATT, Mr. (fl 1734) actor BD

BATT, Madeline (d 1975 [80]) BP/60*

BATTALINI, Luis (fl 1847) singer HAS

BATTEN, Mrs. Louis see Wilton, Jenny

BATTERSBY, Harry (d 1917) proprietor EA/18*

BATTERSBY, Mrs. Henry (d 1902 [45]) manager EA/03*

BATTIS, Emery (b 1915) American actor TW/25

BATTISHILL, Jonathan (1738-1801) instrumentalist, singer, composer BD

BATTISHILL, Mrs. Jonathan see Davies, Elizabeth

BATTLE, Ralph (1649-1713) organist BD

BATTLE, Robert C. (d 1965 [34]) performer BP/50*

BATTLE, William (fl 1691-1711) singer BD

BATTLES, John (b 1921) American actor, singer BE, TW/1, 4, WWT/11-12

BATTLES, Marjorie (b 1939) American actress TW/22-24

BATTLEY, Thomas (d 1880 [26]) gymnast EA/81*

BATTY, Archibald (1887-1961) English actor WWT/8-13

BATTY, George (d 1867 [64]) proprietor ES

BATTY, Thomas (d 1903 [71]) equestrian, circus manager CDP, ES

BATTY, Mrs. Thomas (d 1875) EA/76*

BATTY, William (d 1868 [67]) equestrian manager, proprietor ES

BATTY, Mrs. William (d 1879 [69]) EA/80*

BAU, Gordon R. (d 1975 [68]) make up artist BP/60*

BAUCARDE, Carlo (1825-83) Italian singer ES, HAS

BAUDOUIN, Mons. (fl 1734-45) dancer BD

BAUEMANN, E. O. see Royelle, Charles

BAUER, David (d 1973 [55]) performer BP/57*

BAUERSMITH, Paula (b 1909) American actress BE, TW/14-20, 23-24, WWT/14-16

BAUGH, Mrs. Fred see Harvey, Alice

BAUGHAN, Edward Algernon (1865-1938) English critic GRB/2-4, WWT/1-8, WWW/3

BAUGHMAN, Eliza (d 1901 [49]) gunman EA/02*

BAUM, Harry (d 1974 [58]) performer BP/58*

BAUM, Mrs. H. William (d 1970 [88]) performer BP/54*

BAUM, Kurt (b 1908) Czech singer CB, ES

BAUM, Lyman Frank (1856-1919) American dramatist DAB, ES, HJD, SR, WWA/1, WWM, WWS

BAUM, Martin (b 1924) American talent representative BE

BAUM, Morton (d 1968 [62]) lawyer BP/52*

BAUM, Vicki (1898-1960) Austrian dramatist, librettist ES, NTH, WWA/4, WWW/5

BAUMANN, Kathryn (b 1946) American actress TW/26, 30

BAUMGARTEN, Karl Friedrich

(1740-1824) musician, com-
poser, teacher BD
BAUMGARTEN, Samuel (fl 1752-
92) bassoonist BD
BAUMGARTNER, Mr. (fl 1742)
actor? BD
BAUMGARTNER, Bertha (d 1888)
wild animal trainer EA/90*
BAUR, Franklyn (d 1950 [46])
singer TW/6
BAUSMAN, Nellie Dutton (d 1974
[85]) performer BP/58*
BAUX, Julien (b c.1789) violinist
BD
BAVAAR, Tony (b 1921) American
actor, singer TW/7, 9-14
BAVAN, Yolande (b 1942) Cey-
lonese actress TW/24, 26-
28
BAVIER, Frances (b 1905) Amer-
ican actress TW/1, 3-9
BAWCOMBE, Fred (d 1895)
comedian EA/96*
BAWCOMBE, Maria (d 1892)
EA/93*
BAWN, Harry (fl late 18th cent)
singer CDP
BAWTREE, Arthur actor GRB/1
BAWTREE, Charles Frederick
(d 1911) manager EA/12*
BAX, Clifford (1886-1962) Eng-
lish dramatist COC, ES,
MH, NTH, OC/3, WWT/
5-13, WWW/6
BAXLEY, Barbara (b 1925/27)
American actress BE, TW/
9-12, 19-21, 23, 25-26,
WWT/14-16
BAXTER, Mrs. (fl 1706-11)
actress BD
BAXTER, Mrs. (fl 1741) actress
BD
BAXTER, Sir A. Beverley (1891-
1964) Canadian critic WWT/
10-13
BAXTER, Alan (1908-76) Ameri-
can actor BE, ES, TW/2-
15, WWT/11-15
BAXTER, Anne (b 1923) Ameri-
can actress BE, CB, ES,
TW/14, 28, 30, WWT/16
BAXTER, Barry (1894-1922)
Welsh actor WWT/4
BAXTER, Beryl (b 1926) Eng-
lish actress WWT/12-15
BAXTER, Sir Beverley see
Baxter, Sir A. Beverley
BAXTER, Charles (b 1924)

American actor TW/20, 24
BAXTER, Eleanor (fl 1799-1801)
performer BD
BAXTER, Frank (b 1922) American
actor TW/2-3, 5-11
BAXTER, Gladys (d 1972) performer
BP/56*
BAXTER, Jane (b 1909) German/
English actress AAS, ES,
TW/3, WWT/7-16
BAXTER, Mrs. J. Emmett see
Corcoran, Jane
BAXTER, John (fl 1663-70) scene-
keeper BD
BAXTER, Keith [née Baxter-Wright]
(b 1933/35) Welsh actor BE,
TW/18-19, 24, 27-29, WWT/
15-16
BAXTER, Lora (d 1955 [47]) per-
former BE*, BP/40*
BAXTER, Phil (d 1972 [75]) com-
poser/lyricist BP/57*
BAXTER, Richard (1593-1666?)
English actor DA, OC/1-3
BAXTER, Richard (1618-c.1666)
English actor BD, OC/3
BAXTER, Richard (d 1747) English
dancer BD
BAXTER, Robert (fl 1600-13) actor
DA
BAXTER, Stanley (b 1926) Scottish
actor WWT/13-16
BAXTER, Warner (1893-1951) Amer-
ican actor ES, TW/7, WWA/3
BAXTER, William J. (d 1873 [31])
singer, actor EA/74*
BAXTER-DILLON, F. (b 1880)
English actor GRB/1
BAXTER-WRIGHT, Keith see
Baxter, Keith
BAY, Mr. (fl 1724) gallery keeper
BD
BAY, Howard (b 1912) American
designer BE, ES, TW/2, 5-8,
WWT/10-16
BAYES, Nora [Dora Goldberg] (1880-
1928) American actress, singer
CDP, ES, SR, WWT/4-5
BAYFIELD, St. Clair [J. St. Clair
Roberts] (1875-1967) English
actor GRB/1, TW/1, 5-6, 23
BAYLEY, Mr. (fl 1749) house ser-
vant BD
BAYLEY, Mr. (fl 1783-85) box and
lobby keeper BD
BAYLEY, Mrs. (fl 1780-81) singer
BD
BAYLEY, Caroline (b 1890) Irish

actress WWT/2-5

BAYLEY, Eric (fl 1882) actor
CDP

BAYLEY, George (fl 1662) actor,
manager BD

BAYLEY, Hilda (d 1971) English
actress WWT/3-13

BAYLEY, James G. (d 1887
[37]) actor EA/88*

BAYLEY, John (fl 1798) dramatist CP/3

BAYLIES, Edmund (b 1904)
American actor, stage manager, director BE

BAYLIS, Christina (d 1898 [70])
music-hall proprietor EA/
99*

BAYLIS, Donald (d 1920) business
manager WWT/14*

BAYLIS, James S. (d 1870) proprietor EA/71*

BAYLIS, John (fl 1804) translator
CP/3

BAYLIS, Lilian Mary (1874-1937)
English manager, impresario
AAS, COC, DNB, ES, OC/
1-3, PDT, WWT/4-8, WWW/3

BAYLIS, Mary (d 1902) EA/03*

BAYLISS, Jacob (d 1901) EA/02*

BAYLISS, John (d 1906 [59])
musical director EA/07*

BAYLISS, Peter actor WWT/
15-16

BAYLY, Ada Ellen see Lyall,
Edna

BAYLY, Caroline English actress
WWT/9-10

BAYLY, Edward (fl 1628) actor
DA

BAYLY, Thomas (fl 1581) actor
DA

BAYLY, Thomas Haines (1797-
1839) English dramatist
CDP, DD, HP

BAYLYE (fl 1582) actor DA

BAYMAN, Annie see Bayman,
Mary Anne

BAYMAN, Mary Anne [Annie
Bayman] (d 1882 [37])
EA/83*

BAYNE, Mr. (fl 1777-90) house
servant BD

BAYNE, Beverly (b 1896) American actress TW/2-11

BAYNE, Mrs. Milton H. see
Dubois, Gene

BAYNE, Robert actor GRB/1

BAYNE, Walter McPherson (d

1859 [64]) scene artist, actor
HAS

BAYNES, Mr. (fl 1797-1800) actor,
singer BD

BAYNHAM, Thomas (d 1882 [87])
EA/83*

BAYNHAM, Walter (fl 1853-92)
actor, critic DD

BAYNHAM, Mrs. Walter [Fanny
Maskell] (d 1919 [90]) actress
DD

BAYNTON, Henry (1892-1951) English actor, manager WWT/4-10

BAYZAND, William (d 1802)
dancer, actor BD

BAYZAND, Mrs. William [née
Elizabeth Taylor] (fl 1792-96)
singer BD

BAZON, [Mr. ?] (fl 1784-85) house
servant? BD

BAZZINI, Antonio (d 1897 [78])
Italian composer EA/98*

BEACH, Ann (b 1938) English
actress WWT/14-16

BEACH, Charles E. (fl 1854) American actor HAS

BEACH, Gary (b 1947) American
actor TW/29-30

BEACH, George B. (fl 1856-63)
actor HAS

BEACH, Hugh D. (d 1975 [61])
producer/director/choreographer
BP/59*

BEACH, Lewis (c.1807-27) American dramatist EAP, RJ, SR

BEACH, Rex (1877-1949) American
dramatist WWA/2

BEACH, W. E. (fl 1890) actor
SR

BEACH, William (1874-1926) actor
SR

BEACH AND BOWERS (fl 1892)
minstrels, managers SR

BEACHNER, Louis (b 1923) American actor TW/26, 29

BEADEMORE, Mr. (fl 1786?-94)
singer BD

BEADON, Phyllis (b 1889) Indian/
English actress GRB/1-2

BEAGLE, G. H. (d 1908) manager
EA/09*

BEAL, Jerry (b 1946) American
actor TW/30

BEAL, John (b 1909) American
actor, director BE, ES, TW/
2-20, 23, 25-28, WWT/8-16

BEAL, Royal (1899-1969) American
actor BE, TW/1-8, 12-14,

25, WWA/5

BEAL, Scott (d 1973 [83]) performer BP/58*

BEALBY, George [George Edward Wright] (1877-1931) English actor GRB/1-3, WWT/4-6

BEALE, Mr. (fl 1796-1815?) instrumentalist BD

BEALE, Charles (d 1905 [85]) EA/06*

BEALE, Charles James (d 1882 [63]) chorus master EA/83*

BEALE, Elizabeth (d 1891 [70]) actress EA/92*

BEALE, Felix C. (d 1879 [36]) violinist EA/80*

BEALE, Franklin Parkes (1874-1947) vaudevillian SR

BEALE, Harold G. W. (d 1911 [27]) variety manager EA/12*

BEALE, Simon (d c.1695) trumpeter BD

BEALE, Thomas Willert ["Walter Maynard"] (1831-94) musician DD

BEALE, Thurley (d 1897) singer EA/98*

BEALL, Thomas (fl 1794-1803?) singer BD

BEALS, Margaret American actress TW/23

BEAN, Joseph (d 1881 [74]) musician EA/82*

BEAN, Orson (b 1928) American actor BE, CB, TW/8, 10-15, 18-21, 23-24, 26, WWT/14-16

BEAN, Reathel (b 1942) American actor TW/25, 27-28, 30

BEANE, Fanny (b 1853) dancer, singer, actress CDP

BEANE, George A., Sr. (d 1893) American actor SR

BEANLAND, Mrs. R. W. (d 1875) EA/76*

BEARD, Charles (b 1945) American actor TW/26

BEARD, James American actor TW/25-27

BEARD, John (c.1716-91) English singer, actor, manager, patentee BD, CDP, DD, DNB, ES, GT, OC/1-3, TD/1-2

BEARD, Dr. Thomas (fl 1631)

dramatist CP/3

BEARD, Mrs. Thomas, Jr. see Conquest, Lizzie

BEARDA, T. (fl 1794) violinist BD

BEARDSLEY, Alice (b 1927) American actress TW/25, 28-29

BEARDWELL, John (fl 1671) musician BD

BEARNES, Hugh (fl 1794) bass viol player BD

BEART, Rudolf (fl 1608) actor DA

BEASLEY, Byron (1872-1927) actor SR

BEASLEY, Edward [Richard de Freyne Jones] (d 1899) actor EA/00*

BEASLEY, Harry (d 1890 [27]) music-hall performer EA/91*

BEASLEY, William Manton (d 1908) EA/09*

BEATON, Sir Cecil (b 1904) English designer AAS, BE, CB, ES, PDT, TW/3, WWT/10-16

BEATRICE, Mlle. [Marie Beatrice Binda] (1839-78) Italian actress CDP, DD, OAA/1-2

BEATTIE, Dorothy American actress TW/5-6

BEATTIE, Nancy (d 1908 [61]) lessee EA/09*

BEATTY, Bessie (1886-1947) American dramatist WWA/2

BEATTY, George (d 1971 [76]) performer BP/56*

BEATTY, Harcourt actor WWT/4-5

BEATTY, May (d 1945 [64]) New Zealand actress, singer WWT/4-9

BEATTY, Raymond (d 1973 [70]) performer BP/58*

BEATTY, Robert (b 1909) Canadian actor ES, WWT/10-16

BEATTY, Roberta (b 1891) American actress WWT/8-9

BEATTY, Sophia Elizabeth (d 1900 [73]) EA/01*

BEATTY, Warren (b 1937) American actor BE, CB, ES

BEATTY-KINGSTON, W. (fl 1884-92) librettist DD

BEAUCARDE, Carlo see Baucardé, Carlo

BEAUCHAMP, George [né Patrick Sarsfield Beauchamp] (d 1900 [38]) music-hall comedian CDP

BEAUCHAMP, Mrs. George
see Lingard, Nellie
BEAUCHAMP, John (d 1921 [70])
actor DD, EA/95, GRB/
3-4, WWT/1-3
BEAUCHAMP, Patrick Sarsfield
see Beauchamp, George
BEAUCHAMP, Richard John (d
1898 [21]) actor EA/00*
BEAUCHENE BEAUDOIN, Louise
(1817-94) French actress ES
BEAUDET, Louise (1865-1948)
French/Spanish actress,
singer CDP, DD, TW/4
BEAUFIELD, Mrs. (fl 1784)
actress BD
BEAUFORD, Mr. (fl 1741) actor
BD
BEAUFORT, [Miss?] (fl 1794-
95) singer BD
BEAUFORT, G. H. (d 1885 [41])
actor EA/86*
BEAUFORT, Grace [Mrs. Frank
Lister] (d 1896 [27]) actress
EA/97*
BEAUFORT, John (b 1912) Cana-
dian critic WWT/13-16
BEAUFORT, Leslie [T. Smyth
Nicolson] English actor
GRB/1
BEAULIEU, Mrs. (fl 1783-85)
figure dancer BD
BEAULIEU, Miss (fl 1785) figure
dancer BD
BEAUMONT, Dr. (fl 1777) actor
HAS
BEAUMONT, Mr. (fl 1731-47)
dancer, actor BD
BEAUMONT, Mr. (fl 1794) stage
door-keeper BD
BEAUMONT, Mrs. (fl 1769-73?)
singer BD
BEAUMONT, Mrs. [Mrs. Ixon]
(fl 1800-02) actress BD
BEAUMONT, Mrs. (fl 1810)
actress HAS
BEAUMONT, Allen (fl 1880)
actor DD, OAA/2
BEAUMONT, Alma see Odiva
BEAUMONT, Annie (d 1882)
actress, singer CDP
BEAUMONT, Arthur [A. B.
Collins] (d 1890 [28]) EA/91*
BEAUMONT, Cyril William
(1891-1976) English critic
WWT/12-14
BEAUMONT, Mrs. De Jersey
(fl 1810-14) actress DD

BEAUMONT, Diana (1909-64) Eng-
lish actress WWT/7-13
BEAUMONT, E. R. (b 1865) English
producer, stage manager, actor
GRB/1
BEAUMONT, Sir Francis (c. 1584-
1616) English dramatist CDP,
COC, CP/1-3, DD, DNB,
ES, FGF, HP, MH, NTH,
OC/1-3, PDT, RE
BEAUMONT, Harry (b 1888) Amer-
ican actor ES
BEAUMONT, Henry (d 1791) violin-
ist? BD
BEAUMONT, Hugh (1908-73) mana-
ger AAS, TW/29, WWT/8-15
BEAUMONT, John (b 1902) English
manager WWT/11-15
BEAUMONT, Mrs. M. R. (d 1878
[56]) housekeeper EA/79*
BEAUMONT, Muriel [Mrs. Gerald
du Maurier] (1881-1957) actress
COC, GRB/1-4, OC/3, WWT/
1-6
BEAUMONT, Nellie (d 1938 [68])
actress, singer CDP
BEAUMONT, Ralph (b 1926) Amer-
ican choreographer, dancer
BE
BEAUMONT, Roma (b 1914) English
actress, dancer WWT/9-11
BEAUMONT, Rose (d 1938) actress
BE*
BEAUMONT, Walter [Walter Bret-
tell] (1872-1910) English actor
GRB/1-2
BEAUMONT, William Alexander
(d 1895 [26]) Negro lion tamer
EA/97*
BEAUPINS, Mons. (fl 1672-75)
singer BD
BEAUPRE, Mons. (fl 1788-89)
dancer BD
BEAVEN, Mrs. (d 1905) EA/06*
BEAVERS, Louise (d 1962 [60])
actress BE*, BP/47*
BEAW, Mr. (fl 1730-35) box-keeper
BD
BEAZLEY, Samuel (1786-1851)
English architect, designer
COC, DD, OC/1-3
BEAZLEY, Samuel, Jr. (fl 1811)
dramatist CP/3
BEBAN, George (1873-1928) English
actor, producer ES, SR,
WWA/1
BECCELEY, Mrs. (fl 1753) actress
DD, HAS

BECHER, Lady see O'Neill, Eliza

BECHER, Albert J. see Bechervaire, Albert J.

BECHER, John C. (b 1915) American actor BE, TW/25-26

BECHER, Martin (fl 1870) dramatist DD

BECHER, Thomas costume designer BE

BECHER, Ulrich (b 1910) German dramatist CH, MD

BECHERVAIRE, Albert J. (d 1883 [28]) EA/84*

BECHET, Sidney (1897-1959) American musician WWA/4

BECHI, Gino (b 1913) Italian singer ES

BECHTEL, William (1858-1930) German/American actor SR

BECK, Don (d 1967 [31]) performer BP/52*

BECK, Gordon (b 1929) American educator, editor, director BE

BECK, James (d 1973 [41]) performer BP/58*

BECK, Julian (b 1925) American director, scene designer, actor, producer BE, COC, ES, WWT/15-16

BECK, Lethbridge (d 1897 [86]) actor EA/98*

BECK, Martin (1869-1940) Czech/American producer, manager, actor CB, DAB, NTH, SR, WWA/4

BECK, Mrs. Martin (b 1889) American executive BE

BECK, Philip (d 1889 [35]) actor EA/91*

BECK, Rolly (b 1918) American actor TW/3

BECK, Stanley (b 1936) American actor TW/19, 21, 29

BECK, Thomas (b 1909) American actor TW/3

BECK, William (1869-1925) Hungarian singer WWA/1

BECKER, Bruce (b 1925) American producer, theatre owner BE

BECKER, Edward American actor TW/24-27

BECKER, John C. (d 1963 [81]) scene designer BE*

BECKER, Nan Brennan (d 1965) performer BP/50*

BECKER, Ned M. (d 1975 [82]) performer BP/60*

BECKER, Pierre (d 1893) circus performer EA/94*

BECKER, Ray (b 1934) American actor TW/26-28

BECKER, William (b 1927) American theatre executive, actor, director BE

BECKERMAN, Bernard (b 1921) American educator, director BE

BECKER-THEODORE, Lee (b 1933) American choreographer, dancer, actress BE

BECKET, Andrew (fl 1806) writer CP/3, DD

BECKETT, Clara Bates (d 1869) EA/70*

BECKETT, Fred (d 1892 [46]) EA/94*

BECKETT, George (d 1876 [37]) comedian EA/77*

BECKETT, G. F. (d 1891) EA/92*

BECKETT, Harry (1839-80) English actor, comedian CDP, DD

BECKETT, J.G. (1839-87) English actor HAS

BECKETT, Mrs. J. G. see Desmond, Maggie

BECKETT, Mary (d 1886) EA/87*

BECKETT, May Ada Ivy (d 1917 [3]) EA/18*

BECKETT, Phillip (fl 1660-74) instrumentalist BD

BECKETT, Samuel Barclay (b 1906) Irish dramatist, director AAS, BE, CB, CD, CH, COC, ES, HP, MD, MH, MWD, NTH, OC/3, PDT, RE, WWT/13-16

BECKETT, Scotty (d 1968 [38]) performer BP/52*

BECKETT, Thomas William (d 1874 [61]) actor, pantomimist EA/75*

BECKETT, Walter (d 1887 [33]) bandmaster EA/88*

BECKHAM, Mr. (fl 1731-49) actor, prompter BD

BECKHAM, Mrs. (fl 1735-49) actress BD

BECKHAM, Mrs. (fl 1776-77) candle woman BD

BECKHAM, Willard (b 1948) American actor TW/30

BECKHARD, Arthur J. producer, manager WWT/8

BECKINGHAM, Charles (1699-1731)

English dramatist CP/1-3,
DD, DNB, GT, TD/1-2
BECKINGTON, Miss (fl 1734)
actress BD
BECKLEY, Beatrice Mary (b
1885) English actress WWT/
4-6
BECKMAN, David (b 1944) Amer-
ican actor TW/28
BECKMAN, Henry (b 1921) Cana-
dian actor TW/7
BECKWITH, Charles Alfred (d
1898 [33]) tank performer
EA/99*
BECKWITH, Frederick E. (d
1898 [76]) swimmer EA/99*
BECKWITH, J. W. (d 1908)
business manager GRB/4
BECKWITH, Linden [Mrs. Spencer
J. Johnson, Jr.] (b 1885)
American singer, vaude-
villian WWM
BECKWITH, Lizzie (d 1905)
swimmer EA/06*
BECKWITH, Reginald (1908-65)
English actor, dramatist
ES, WWT/10-13
BECKWITH, William (d 1892 [36])
swimmer EA/94*
BEDDOE, Alfred (d 1892 [45])
actor, manager EA/93*
BEDDOES, Thomas Lovell
(1803-49) English dramatic
poet DD, DNB, ES, HP,
NTH
BEDELIA, Bonnie (b 1948) Amer-
ican actress TW/22-23
BEDELLS, James actor DD
BEDELLS, Phyllis (b 1893)
English dancer, choreog-
rapher ES, WWT/4-10
BEDFORD, Arthur George Sharpe
(d 1899 [22]) actor EA/00*
BEDFORD, Brian (b 1935) Eng-
lish actor AAS, BE, TW/
19-21, 23-30, WWT/14-16
BEDFORD, Charles John Abbott
(d 1879 [37]) stage manager
EA/81*
BEDFORD, E. A. see Vasco
BEDFORD, Edward (fl 1667-71)
manager BD
BEDFORD, Harry singer, com-
poser CDP [see also next
two entries]
BEDFORD, Harry (d 1870 [70])
singer EA/71*
BEDFORD, Harry (d 1939 [66])

comedian BE*
BEDFORD, Henry (d 1923 [77])
actor, dramatist DD, DP
BEDFORD, Herbert (1867-1945)
English composer WWW/3
BEDFORD, Mrs. Herbert see
Lehmann, Liza
BEDFORD, Mary Anne (d 1875 [52])
box-office keeper EA/76*
BEDFORD, Mary Sophia (d 1886)
EA/87*
BEDFORD, Patrick (b 1932) Irish
actor TW/22, 26, 29
BEDFORD, Paul John (c.1792-1871)
English actor, singer CDP,
DD, DNB, ES, OC/1-3
BEDFORD, Mrs. Paul John see
Greene, Elizabeth
BEDINI, Signora (fl 1787-88) dancer
BD
BEDINI, Mlle. (fl 1793) dancer BD
BEDINI, Jean (d 1956 [85]) producer
BE*, BP/41*
BEDLOE, Cpt. William (d 1680)
English dramatist CP/1-2,
DD, GT
BEDOUIN ARABS (fl 1838) CDP
BEDOWE, Elis (fl 1635) actor DA
BEDSMORE, Thomas (d 1881) actor?
organist EA/82*
BEDWELL, Mr. (fl 1726-27) house
servant? BD
BEDWELL, Stanley (d 1916) EA/17*
BEE, William (fl 1599-1624) actor
DA
BEEBE, Henrietta (b 1844) singer
CDP
BEEBE, Lucius (d 1966 [63]) jour-
nalist BP/50*
BEEBE, Mary (fl 1885) singer
CDP
BEECHAM, Charles (d 1912 [41])
music-hall manager EA/13*
BEECHAM, E. T. (d 1901 [30])
singer EA/02*
BEECHAM, Sir Joseph (d 1916 [68])
producer BE*, WWT/14*
BEECHAM, Sir Thomas (1879-1961)
English conductor, composer
CB, ES, TW/17, WWW/6
BEECHER, Janet (1884-1955) Amer-
ican actress TW/1-3, 5-7,
12, WWM, WWT/4-11
BEECHER, William G., Jr. (d
1973 [69]) composer/lyricist
BP/58*
BEECHEY, A. B. (fl 1850) actor
HAS

BEECROFT, G. A. (d 1873)
composer EA/74*

BEEHLER, Dave (d 1968 [87])
agent BP/52*

BEEKMAN, John K. (fl 1802-21)
American? theatre owner
WWA/H

BEELAND, Ambrose (fl 1624-72)
violinist BD

BEEMS, Patricia Jane (d 1973
[46]) performer BP/57*

BEER, Henry see Henry, Basil

BEERBOHM, Clarence Evelyn
(d 1917 [32]) English actor
WWT/1-3

BEERBOHM, Julius (d 1906 [53])
EA/07*, GRB/2*

BEERBOHM, Sir Max (1872-1956)
English critic, dramatist
COC, DD, DNB, ES, GRB/
1-4, HP, MD, MWD, NTH,
OC/1-3, TW/12, WWA/3,
WWT/1-11, WWW/5

BEERBOHM, W. Julius Ewald
(d 1892 [82]) EA/93*

BEERE, Mrs. Bernard [Mrs.
H. C. S. Olivier] (1856-
1915) English actress CDP,
DD, DP, GRB/1-4, OAA/2,
WWT/1-2

BEERS, Francine American
actress TW/29

BEERS, Robert (d 1972 [51])
performer BP/56*

BEERY, Lee [or Leigh] American
actress TW/26, 29-30

BEERY, Noah (1882-1946) American actor TW/1-2

BEERY, Wallace (1885-1949)
American actor DAB, ES,
SR, WWA/2, WWW/4

BEESLEY, Mr. (fl 1780) actor
BD

BEESON, Mr. (fl 1729-31) house
servant? BD

BEESTON, (fl 1560-61) actor
DA

BEESTON, Mr. (fl 1708-12) violinist BD

BEESTON, Mr. (fl 1782-84)
house servant? BD

BEESTON, Christopher (1570?-
1638) English actor, manager COC, DA, ES, OC/1-3

BEESTON, George (fl 1660?-75)
actor BD

BEESTON, Robert (fl 1603-17)
actor DA

BEESTON, William (1606?-82) English actor, manager BD, COC,
DA, DD, OC/1-3

BEET, Alice (d 1931) English actress GRB/1-4, WWT/1-6

BEET, Fanny (d 1886 [40]) EA/87*

BEETLESTONE, W. M. actor CDP

BEETON, Mr. (fl 1794-1803)
house servant BD

BEFUS, Roy (d 1973 [44]) stage
manager BP/58*

BEGG, Mrs. William see Bentley,
Florence

BEGGARS THEATRE theatre collective CD

BEGGS, Lee (1870-1943) actor SR

BEGLEY, Ed (1901-70) American
actor BE, CB, TW/3-8, 11-
18, 25-26, WWA/5, WWT/14

BEHAN, Brendan (1923-64) Irish
dramatist AAS, BE, CB, CD,
CH, COC, ES, MD, MH,
MWD, PDT, RE, TW/20,
WWA/4, WWT/13, WWW/6

BEHEL, Jacob see Pedel, Jacob

BEHIN (d 1843 [36]) Belgian giant
EA/72*

BEHMANN, Edward (d 1888 [28])
manager EA/89*

BEHN, Mrs. Aphra (1640-89) Eng-
lish dramatist CDP, COC,
CP/1-3, DD, DNB, ES, GT,
HP, MH, NTH, OC/1-3

BEHN, Harry (d 1973 [74]) dramatist BP/58*

BEHN, Noel (b 1928) American
producer BE

BEHNKE, Emil (d 1892) teacher,
writer EA/93*

BEHREND, Henrietta (d 1859)
singer HAS

BEHRMAN, Samuel Nathaniel (1893-
1973) American dramatist
AAS, BE, CB, CH, COC, ES,
HJD, MD, MH, MWD, NTH,
OC/1-3, PDT, RE, SR, TW/
30, WWT/6-15

BEHYMER, Lynden Ellsworth
(1862-1947) American impresario WWA/2

BEHYMER, Minetta S. (d 1958 [93])
impresario BE*

BEILBY, Mr. (fl 1784-94) musician
BD

BEIN, Albert (b 1902) Rumanian/
American dramatist BE, ES,
HJD, MD, MWD

BEINHORN, Nat (d 1974 [55])

investor BP/58*
BEITH, John Hay see Hay, Ian
BEJARD, Mons. (fl 1675) musician BD
BEJART, Maurice (b 1927)
French choreographer CB,
ES
BELA, Nicholas (d 1963 [63])
Hungarian dramatist BE*,
BP/48*
BELAFONTE, Harry (b 1924/27)
American singer, actor BE,
CB, ES, TW/10-16
BELANGER, Joanne (b 1945)
American actress TW/30
BELARSKY, Sidor (d 1975 [77])
performer BP/60*
BELASCO, Anne Margaret (d
1895) EA/96*
BELASCO, David [né Valasco]
(1853-1931) American manager, dramatist COC, DAB,
DD, ES, GRB/2-4, HJD,
MH, MWD, NTH, OC/1-3,
PDT, RE, SR, WWA/1,
WWM, WWS, WWT/1-6,
WWW/3
BELASCO, Edward (1874-1937)
American producer SR
BELASCO, Frederick (d 1920
[59]) manager, producer
SR
BELASCO, Genevieve (d 1956
[84]) English actress BE*,
BP/41*
BELASCO, George (d 1896 [60])
EA/97*
BELASCO, Jacques (d 1973 [56])
composer/lyricist BP/58*
BELASCO, Juliet Crosby (d
1907 [30]) American actress
GRB/3*
BELASCO, Leon (b 1902) Russian/American actor BE
BELASCO, Ruby Hamilton actress, singer GRB/1-2
BELASCO, Will [né Sutherland]
(d 1911) music-hall performer
EA/12*
BELASCO, William (d 1976 [41])
producer/director/choreographer BP/60*
BELCHAM, Henry (d 1917 [67])
journalist EA/18*
BELCHER, Frank (1869-1947)
actor, singer SR
BELCHER, Marjorie Celeste
see Champion, Madge

BELCHIER, Dawbridge-Court (1580?-
1621) English dramatist CP/1-
3, DD, DNB, FGF
BELCOUR, Mrs. (fl 1830) actress
HAS
BELDEN, N. B. see Clarke,
N. B.
BELDING, Henry (d 1908) actor
EA/09*, GRB/4*
BELDING, Mrs. Henry see King,
Lottie
BELDON, Edwin (fl 1899) American
actor WWS
BELDON, Eileen (b 1901) English
actress AAS, WWT/4-16
BELENGER, Mr. (fl 1794-95) scene
designer BD
BELFIELD, Mrs. see Barrett,
Mrs. Giles Linnett
BELFIELD, Frederick H. (b 1901)
American executive BE
BELFILLE, Mrs. [Mrs. Arnold;
née Burdett] (d 1789) English
actress BD, DD
BELFORD, Mr. (fl 1849) actor
HAS
BELFORD, Mrs. (d 1887) EA/88*
BELFORD, William Rowles (1824-
81) English actor DD, OAA/2
BELFORT, Mrs. (fl 1760-61)
dancer BD
BELFOUR, Hugo John (1802-27)
dramatist DD
BELFRAGE, Bruce (1901-74) English actor BTR/74, WWT/11-
12
BELFRY, May (d 1902 [25]) actress
EA/03*
BELFRY, Venie [Mrs. C. Foster
Marner] (d 1910) comedienne
EA/11*
BELGADO, Mario (d 1969 [63])
performer BP/54*
BEL GEDDES, Barbara see
Geddes, Barbara Bel
BEL GEDDES, Edith Lutyens (b
1916) costume designer, costumier, producer BE
BEL GEDDES, Norman see
Geddes, Norman Bel
BELKNAP, Edwin Star (fl 1883-94)
American dramatist WWA/1,
WWM
BELL, Mr. (fl 1750-51) singer,
actor? BD
BELL, Mr. (fl 1785-91) equestrian,
dancer, tumbler BD
BELL, Mrs. (fl 1791) dancer BD

BELL, Master (fl 1785-86)
tumbler BD
BELL, Ann (b 1939) English
actress WWT/15-16
BELL, Archie (d 1943 [65])
critic, dramatist BE*
BELL, Armstrong (d 1910) act-
ing manager EA/11*
BELL, Benjamin John see
Dashwood, Harry
BELL, Brian see Murray,
Brian
BELL, Mr. C. (d 1888) EA/89*
BELL, Dr. Campton (d 1963
[58]) educator BE*
BELL, Christopher (fl 1628-61)
musician BD
BELL, Clarence F. (d 1963
[66]) press representative
BE*
BELL, Daniel W. (b 1891)
American executive BE
BELL, Diana (d 1964) performer
BP/49*
BELL, Mrs. Digby see Joyce,
Laura
BELL, Digby Valentine (1851-
1917) American actor, singer
CDP, GRB/2-4, SR, WWA/
1, WWM, WWS, WWT/1-3
BELL, D. V. (fl 1829) Ameri-
can dramatist EAP
BELL, Mrs. Edward M. see
Harrison, Maud
BELL, Eliza [Mrs. Robert Bell]
(d 1879) EA/80*
BELL, Emil (d 1902 [19]) circus
performer EA/03*
BELL, Enid (b 1888) English
actress WWT/2-5
BELL, Eva [Mrs. Charles Rod-
ney] (d 1901 [34]) actress,
singer CDP
BELL, Dame Florence Evelyn
Eleanore (1851-1930) drama-
tist NTH
BELL, Frank (b 1843) dancer,
minstrel CDP
BELL, Frank Eddington (d 1882
[52]) manager EA/83*
BELL, Gaston (1877-1963)
American actor WWS
BELL, Mrs. George Hamilton
see Hamilton, Georgina
BELL, Hillary (1857-1903) Irish
critic WWA/1
BELL, Mrs. Hugh (1851-1930)
French dramatist DD

BELL, Isabell (d 1870) EA/71*
BELL, J. (d 1884 [43]) circus
clown EA/84*
BELL, James (d 1917) lessee EA/
18*
BELL, James (b 1891) American
actor BE, WWT/8-11
BELL, Mrs. James (d 1891) EA/
92*
BELL, John (1745-1831) English
publisher, bookseller COC,
DNB, OC/1-3
BELL, John Joy (1871-1938) Scot-
tish dramatist OC/1-3, WWW/3
BELL, John Keble see Howard,
Keble
BELL, Joseph (d 1918) EA/19*
BELL, Joseph Henry (d 1890 [35])
EA/91*
BELL, Kittie English actress,
dancer GRB/1
BELL, Laura Joyce (1858-1904)
English comic opera singer
WWA/1
BELL, Leslie R. (d 1962 [55])
conductor, composer BE*
BELL, Louisa (d 1891) EA/92*
BELL, Mrs. M. (d 1873 [37]) EA/
74*
BELL, Marie (b 1905) French act-
ress TW/20
BELL, Marion American singer
TW/3-7
BELL, Mary (b 1904) American
actress TW/14, 19, 24, 28-
29
BELL, Mary Hayley (b 1914)
Chinese/English actress,
dramatist BE, WWT/10-14
BELL, Minnie (fl 1881-92) actress,
dramatist DD
BELL, Nolan D. (d 1976 [55]) per-
former BP/60*
BELL, Percy (1848-1913) English
actor OAA/1-2
BELL, Rex (d 1962 [58]) American
actor BE*
BELL, Richard (d 1672) actor BD
BELL, Richard (d 1881?) circus
proprietor EA/82*
BELL, Robert (1800-67) Irish
dramatist DD
BELL, Robert (d 1902 [66]) music-
hall proprietor EA/03*
BELL, Mrs. Robert see Bell,
Eliza
BELL, Robert Stanley Warren (1871-
1921) English dramatist WWW/2

BELL, Rose see Saroni, Rose

BELL, Stanley (1881-1952) English director, actor TW/1, 12-13, WWT/4-11

BELL, Stuart Henry (d 1896) scene painter, manager EA/97*

BELL, Thomas (d 1743) singer BD

BELL, Thomas (d 1815) actor, dancer BD

BELL, William (d 1874 [21]) Negro artist EA/75*

BELL, William (d 1891) EA/92*

BELL, William Henry (1873-1946) English composer ES

BELLA, Rose see Vining, Mrs. A.

BELLAIR, Ellen Amelia Frances (d 1880) actress, singer EA/81*

BELLAIR, Jenny see Warden, Mrs. J. F.

BELLAIR, John (d 1879 [76]) actor EA/80*

BELLAIR, Mary Ann [Mrs. Collie] (d 1881) actress EA/82*

BELLAM, [Mr. ?] (fl 1730) dancer BD

BELLAMY, Mr. (fl 1761) singer BD

BELLAMY, Mrs. [Mrs. Walter; née Seal] (d 1771) English actress BD

BELLAMY, Ada [Mrs. Howard Talbot] (d 1895) actress EA/96*

BELLAMY, B. P. (fl 1797) actor BD

BELLAMY, Daniel, Sr. (b 1687) English dramatist CP/1-3, DD

BELLAMY, Daniel, Jr. (d 1788) English dramatist CP/1-3, DD

BELLAMY, Frank see Denton, Frank

BELLAMY, Franklyn (b 1886) English actor WWT/5-9

BELLAMY, George Anne (c. 1727-88) English actress BD, CDP, COC, DD, DNB, ES, GT, NTH, OC/1-3, TD/1-2

BELLAMY, George E. (1866-1944) English actor GRB/1-2

BELLAMY, Henry Ernest (d 1932 [70]) English producer BE*, WWT/14*

BELLAMY, Ralph (b 1904) American actor BE, CB, ES, SR, TW/2-19, WWT/10-14

BELLAMY, Richard (1743?-1813) chorus master, composer BD, DNB

BELLAMY, Somers (fl 1877-89) dramatist DD

BELLAMY, Thomas (1745-1800) English dramatist CP/3, DD

BELLAMY, Thomas Ludford (1771-1843) singer, proprietor, choir master BD, CDP, DNB, GT

BELLAMY, William (d 1843 [74]) singer EA/72*

BELLAMY, William Hoare (1800-66) Irish actor DD, HAS, SR

BELLAMY, Mrs. William Hoare [Mrs. A. W. Penson] (d 1857) Scottish actress HAS

BELLANI, Mons. (fl 1794) dancer HAS

BELLARINA, Bella (d 1969 [72]) performer BP/53*

BELLAVER, Harry (b 1905) American actor BE, TW/22-23, 29-30

BELLE, Marjorie (b 1921) American actress TW/1

BELLERS, Fettiplace (1687-1750?) English dramatist CP/2-3, DD, DNB, GT

BELLETTI, Giovanni (b 1813) singer CDP

BELLEVERE see Hill, Mrs. George

BELLEW, Alfred (d 1932) director WWT/14*

BELLEW, Eugenie (d 1903) actress EA/04*

BELLEW, Harold Kyrle (1855-1911) English actor, dramatist DD, DNB, DP, ES, GRB/1-4, OAA/2, OC/1-3, SR, WWA/1, WWM, WWS

BELLEW, John Chippendale Mortesquieu (1824-74) English dramatic reader CDP

BELLEW, Kyrle (1887/90-1948) English actress TW/4, WWT/4-9

BELLEW, Mrs. Kyrle see Legrande, Eugénie

BELLEZZA, Vincenzo (1888-1964) Italian conductor WWA/4

BELLGUARD, Mr. (fl 1738)
actor BD

BELLIN, Mr. (fl 1794) bass
viol player BD

BELLIN, Olga [née Bielinski]
(b 1932/25) American
actress BE, TW/12-13,
18-20

BELLING, Tom (fl 1850-77)
American clown ES

BELLINGHAM, Mr. (fl 1775)
actor BD

BELLINGHAM, Henry (fl 1864-
95) dramatist DD

BELLINI, Cal American actor
TW/22-25

BELLINI, Laura (d 1975 [73])
performer BP/59*

BELLINI, Vincenzio (1802-35)
Italian composer CDP

BELLMORE, Bertha (b 1882)
English actress TW/3,
WWT/8

BELLOC, Teresa (1784-1855)
singer CDP

BELLOLI, Marianna (fl 1793)
singer BD

BELLOMO, Joe (b 1938) American actor TW/28-30

BELLONINI, Edna (b 1903)
English actress, singer
WWT/6

BELLONINI, Walter (d 1943 [87])
comedian BE*

BELLOW, Alexander (d 1976
[63]) composer/lyricist
BP/60*

BELLOW, Saul (b 1915) Cana-
dian/American dramatist
CD, HJD

BELLOWS, Henry Whitney (b
1814) American writer DD

BELLOWS, Jean American
actress TW/3

BELLOWS, Johnson McClure
(1870-1949) American im-
presario, critic WWA/2

BELLOWS, Phyllis (b 1934)
American literary agent
BE

BELL-PORTER, Lillian (b 1874)
English singer GRB/1

BELL-PORTER, W. E. (b
1868) English musical
director, composer GRB/1

BELLUGI, Piero (b 1924) Italian
conductor ES

BELLWOOD, Bessie [Elizabeth
Ann Katherine Mahoney] (1847-
96) English music-hall performer CDP, COC, OC/1-3

BELLWOOD, George (d 1894) comedian EA/95*

BELMAS, Mons. (d 1878) trapezist
EA/79*

BELMONT, Mr. (fl 1792) actor BD

BELMONT, Frances see Ashburton, Lady

BELMONT, Mrs. George (d 1900)
EA/01*

BELMONT, Harry (d 1888) music-
hall performer EA/89*

BELMONTE, Herman (d 1975 [84])
performer BP/60*

BELMORE, Alfred (d 1918) EA/19*

BELMORE, Alice (d 1919 [29])
actress WWT/14*

BELMORE, Alice (1870?-1943) English actress CB, DD, SR

BELMORE, Bertha (1882-1953)
English actress ES, TW/1-2,
5-10, WWT/9-11

BELMORE, Daisy (d 1954 [80])
English actress TW/1, 11

BELMORE, Edward (d 1918) EA/
19*

BELMORE, George [George Benjamin Garstin] (d 1875 [47])
actor CDP, DD

BELMORE, George (d 1898 [35])
actor EA/99*

BELMORE, George (d 1956) actor
BE*, WWT/14*

BELMORE, Mrs. George (d 1911)
EA/12*

BELMORE, Herbert (d 1952 [77])
actor BE*, WWT/14*

BELMORE, Lily [or Lillie; Mrs.
Claude Wallace] (d 1901 [29])
actress DD, EA/96

BELMORE, Lionel (d 1953 [86])
English actor, stage manager
BE*, BP/37*

BELMORE, Paul (d 1907 [34]) actor
EA/08*, GRB/3*

BELOID, Mme. (1803-56) actress
SR

BELON, Peter (fl 1690) dramatist
CP/1-3, GT

BELOT, Adolph French dramatist
SR

BELSON, Edward (d 1975 [77])
performer BP/60*

BELT, Elmer (b 1893) American
curator BE

BELT, T. (fl 1590) actor DA

BELT AND BRACES ROADSHOW
CO. LTD. theatre collective
CD
BELTON, F. Elizabeth (d 1867)
EA/68*
BELTON, Phoebe [Mrs. Charles
Rider-Noble] (d 1899) EA/
00*
BELTRAM, Sydney [né Bustin]
(d 1911 [60]) actor EA/12*
BELTRAM, Mrs. Sydney see
Engel, Nina
BELVERSTONE, Sarah (d 1867
[80]) EA/68*
BELVERSTONE, Mr. W. (d 1867
[71]) EA/68*
BELVISO, Thomas Henry (1896-
1967) American composer,
conductor WWA/4
BELWIN, Alma (d 1924 [29])
performer BE*, BP/8*
BELZONI, Antonio (b 1780)
Italian actor ES
BELZONI, Giovanni Baptista
(1778-1823) Italian actor
DNB, ES
BEN, Miss (fl 1720) actress BD
BENADERET, Bea (d 1968 [62])
performer BP/53*
BEN-AMI, Jacob (1890-1977)
Russian/American actor,
director, producer BE,
ES, NTH, TW/3, 5-7, 13-
16, 24, 29, WWT/5-10
BENARDIN, Estelle (fl 1828)
French dancer HAS
BENATZKY, Ralph (d 1957 [73])
Moravian composer BP/42*
BENAVENTA, Jacinto (1866-
1954) Spanish dramatist CB,
ES, OC/1-3, RE, WWT/
2-4, WWW/5
BENBROOK, E. J. (d 1888 [43])
business manager EA/89*
BENCE, Mr. (fl 1750-57) fair
booth operator BD
BENCHLEY, Marie Bucklin
singer CDP
BENCHLEY, Nathaniel (b 1915)
American writer BE, CB
BENCHLEY, Robert Charles
(1889-1945) American critic,
actor CB, DAB, ES, HJD,
NTH, OC/1-3, SR, TW/2
WWA/2, WWT/8-9
BENCKI, Mr. (fl 1751) violon-
cellist BD
BENCRAFT, James (d 1765)

actor, dancer, singer BD
BENDA, Mme. (fl 1790-92) singer
BD
BENDA, Georges K. [Georges
Kugelmann] French scene de-
signer ES
BENDA, Wladyslaw Theodor (d
1948 [75]) Polish artist BE*,
BP/33*
BENDALL, Ernest Alfred (1846-
1924) English critic, examiner
of plays DD, GRB/2-4,
WWT/1-4, WWW/2
BENDER, Mr. (fl c.1839) actor
CDP
BENDER, Charles (d 1857 [44])
call boy EA/72*
BENDER, Dr. Milton (d 1964 [69])
actors' business manager BE*
BENDER, Paul (1875-1947) German
singer ES
BENDER, Russell (d 1969 [59])
performer BP/54*
BENDIX, Doreen (d 1931 [25])
actress BE*
BENDIX, Max (1866-1945) American
conductor WWA/2, WWM
BENDIX, William (1906-64) Ameri-
can actor BE, CB, ES, TW/
21, WWA/4
BENDLER, Salomon (1683-1724)
German singer BD
BENDON, Bert (d 1964) Scottish
performer, writer BE*
BENECH, Rudolf F. (d 1975 [59])
producer/director/choreographer
BP/59*
BENEDETTI, Sesto (fl 1848-50)
Italian singer CDP, HAS
BENEDICT, Sir Julius (1804-85)
English conductor, composer
CDP, DD, DNB, ES
BENEDICT, Leon (b 1926) Ameri-
can actor TW/25
BENEDICT, Lew (1839-1920) Amer-
ican actor, minstrel CDP,
HAS, SR
BENEDICTUS, David (b 1938) Eng-
lish director, dramatist WWT/
15-16
BENEDIX, Roderick German drama-
tist DD
BENELLI, Antonio Peregrino (1771-
1830) Italian singer, composer
BD
BENELLI, Sem (1875-1949) Italian
dramatist MWD, OC/1-3,
TW/6, WWT/4

BENESH, Joan Dorothy [née
Rothwell] (b 1920) English
choreographer CB
BENESH, Rudolf Frank (1916-
75) English musician CB
BENET, Harry (d 1948 [71])
producer, director BE*
BENET, Stephen Vincent (1898-
1943) American dramatist,
librettist ES, HJD, HP
BENEUX, L. R. (1842-69)
American actor HAS
BENEVENTANO, G. F. (b 1824)
Italian singer CDP
BENFIELD, Robert (d 1649)
English actor DA, ES,
GT, OC/1-3
BENFORD, Austin (fl 1674-85)
singer BD
BENGE, Mr. (fl 1794) eques-
trian? BD
BENGOUGH, Henry (d 1825)
actor CDP, TD/2
BENHAM, Arthur (d 1895 [23])
dramatist DD
BENHAM, Earl (d 1976 [89])
performer BP/60*
BENHAM, Emily [Mrs. George
Benham] (d 1910 [50])
EA/12*
BENHAM, George (d 1911 [64])
clown EA/12*
BENHAM, Mrs. George see
Benham, Emily
BENHAM, Mrs. George see
Benham, Margaret
BENHAM, Margaret [Mrs.
George Benham] (d 1882)
EA/83*
BENIADES, Ted American actor
TW/26
BENIGNI, Guiseppe (fl 1790-91)
singer BD
BENINI, Anna [Signora Bernardo
Mengozzi] (fl 1784-c.1791)
Italian singer BD
BENION, John (fl 1661-77)
actor BD
BENJAMIN, Arthur (b 1893)
Australian composer ES
BENJAMIN, C. B. (d 1951 [65])
manager BE*
BENJAMIN, Fred (b 1944) Amer-
ican actor TW/26-28
BENJAMIN, Julius (d 1888 [60])
pianist EA/89*
BENJAMIN, Morris Edgar (b
1881) English manager

WWT/7-9
BENJAMIN, Park (b 1809) American
writer DD, RJ
BENJAMIN, Richard (b 1938) Amer-
ican actor TW/23-24, 28
BENLINE, Arthur J. (b 1902)
American architect, engineer
BE
BENNALD, Mr. (fl 1736) actor BD
BENNEE, William Jacob (d 1888
[46]) actor EA/89*
BENNELL, Peter (d c.1775) musi-
cian BD
BENNET, Mr. (fl 1749-51) house
servant BD
BENNET, Mr. (fl 1784-89) actor
BD
BENNET, Mrs. (fl 1783-85) dresser
BD
BENNET, Master (fl 1748) actor
BD
BENNET, Clarissa Ann see
Conquest, Mrs. Benjamin Oliver
BENNET, Elizabeth (1714-91)
actress, singer BD
BENNET, John (fl 1744?-72?) in-
strumentalist BD
BENNET, Philip (d c.1752) drama-
tist CP/1-3, DD, GT
BENNETT, Mr. (fl 1795-1816?)
box-keeper BD
BENNETT, Mr. (fl 1823) English
actor BS
BENNETT, Mr. (fl 1831) Scottish
actor HAS
BENNETT, Mrs. (fl 1883) actress
DD
BENNETT, Miss see Esten, Mrs.
BENNETT, Alan (b 1934) English
dramatist, actor AAS, BE,
CD, WWT/15-16
BENNETT, Annie Maria (d 1893
[24]) EA/95*
BENNETT, Arnold (1867-1931)
English dramatist, manager
DNB, ES, HP, MD, MH,
MWD, NTH, OC/1-3, SR,
WWM, WWT/1-6, WWW/3
BENNETT, Barbara (d 1958 [52])
American actress BE*, BP/43*
BENNETT, Belle (1883-1932)
American actress SR
BENNETT, Billy (d 1942) comedian
WWT/14*
BENNETT, Charles (d 1892 [48])
manager EA/94*
BENNETT, Charles (b 1889/99)
English dramatist ES, WWT/

7-10

BENNETT, Charles H. (d 1889 [36]) musical director EA/90*

BENNETT, Clarence (1858-1930) actor, dramatist, manager SR

BENNETT, Compton (d 1974 [74]) producer/director/choreographer BP/59*

BENNETT, Constance (1905-65) American actress, producer, director BE, ES, TW/22, WWA/4

BENNETT, Edward (d 1880) manager EA/81*

BENNETT, Eliza Frances see Foster, Eliza Frances

BENNETT, [Ellis?] see Bennett, James

BENNETT, Enid (1895-1969) Australian actress ES

BENNETT, Faith [Margaret Riddick] actress WWT/8

BENNETT, Fanny [Mrs. Cull] (d 1874 [22]) actress EA/76*

BENNETT, Fran (b 1935) American actress TW/25

BENNETT, George (d 1970 [53]) publicist BP/55*

BENNETT, George John (1800-79) English actor, dramatist CDP, DD, DNB

BENNETT, Mrs. Harry (d 1905) EA/06*

BENNETT, H. G. Dudley (d 1918 [52]) EA/19*

BENNETT, Hywel (b 1944) Welsh actor WWT/15-16

BENNETT, James [or Ellis?] (fl 1799) box-keeper BD

BENNETT, James (d 1885) actor CDP, DD

BENNETT, Jane (fl 1850) actress BD

BENNETT, Jane Sperry see Connell, Jane

BENNETT, Jill (b 1931) English actress AAS, WWT/14-16

BENNETT, Joan (b 1910) American actress BE, ES, SR, TW/14-15, WWT/15-16

BENNETT, Joe (d 1967 [78]) vaudevillian TW/24

BENNETT, John (fl 1665) scene-keeper BD

BENNETT, Johnstone (1870-1906)

actor WWA/1

BENNETT, Mrs. Johnstone American actress SR

BENNETT, Joseph (d 1911 [79]) dramatist, librettist DD

BENNETT, Mrs. Joseph (d 1943 [84]) actress BE*, WWT/14*

BENNETT, Julia (d 1903 [79]) English actress DD, SR

BENNETT, Kate (d 1917) EA/18*

BENNETT, Leila actress WWT/6-7

BENNETT, Lily [Mrs. Paddy Wood] (d 1879) music-hall performer EA/80*

BENNETT, Linda (b 1942) American actress TW/21, 23-24

BENNETT, Maria (fl 1752) singer BD

BENNETT, Meg (b 1948) American actress TW/29-30

BENNETT, Michael choreographer, director CD, WWT/16

BENNETT, Peter (b 1917) English actor TW/3, WWT/10-16

BENNETT, Raymond (d 1969 [68]) performer BP/53*

BENNETT, Richard (1870/72/73/75-1944) American actor CB, DAB, ES, GRB/3-4, SR, TW/1, WWA/2, WWM, WWS, WWT/1-9

BENNETT, R. M. (d 1886 [52]) journalist EA/87*

BENNETT, Robert Russell (b 1894) American composer, conductor BE, CB, ES

BENNETT, Rosa (fl 1852) actress DD

BENNETT, Stellar English actress TW/26

BENNETT, Stephen (fl 1825) actor CDP

BENNETT, Thomas (d 1872) actor WWT/14*

BENNETT, Vivienne (b 1905) English actress AAS, ES, WWT/8-16

BENNETT, Warner (fl 1741-68?) dancer, singer, actor BD

BENNETT, Wilda (1894-1967) American actress TW/24, WWT/4-8

BENNETT, Will A. (b 1874) Canadian press representative GRB/1-2

BENNETT, William (d 1875) actor, secretary EA/76*

BENNETT, William (d 1911 [76])

proprietor EA/12*

BENNETT, Mrs. William (d 1907) EA/08*, GRB/3*

BENNETT, William Mineard (1778-1858) singer CDP

BENNETT, William Sterndale (1816-75) English composer CDP, DNB

BENNETTS, R. T. (d 1888) EA/89*

BENNIE, Mr. (fl 1841) actor HAS

BENNISON, Louis (d 1929 [46]) American actor BE*, BP/ 13*

BENNY, Jack (1894-1974) American comedian BTR/74, CB, SR

BENOIS, Nadia (1896-1974) Russian scene designer, costume designer ES

BENOIT see Tourniaire, Benoit

BENOIT, Denise (d 1973 [53]) performer BP/58*

BENOIT, Patricia (b 1927) American actress TW/8-9, 12-16

BENONE, Alfred (d 1908) music-hall manager EA/09*

BENONVILLE, Mr. (fl 1774) machinist? BD

BENRIMO, Joseph Henry McAlpin (1871/74-1942) American dramatist, director CB, SR, WWA/1, WWT/4-9

BENSER, John Daniel (d 1785) instrumentalist, composer BD

BENSLEY, Robert (1742-1817) English actor BD, CDP, DD, DNB, ES, GT, OC/ 1-3, TD/1-2

BENSON, Mr. (fl 1735) actor BD

BENSON, Mr. (fl 1776-86) actor BD

BENSON, Mrs. (fl 1675) singer BD

BENSON, Mrs. (fl 1728-31) actress BD

BENSON, Mrs. (fl 1784-86) actress, singer BD

BENSON, Alex (d 1974 [46]) producer/director/choreographer BP/58*

BENSON, Arthur (d 1917) EA/ 18*

BENSON, Chris (d 1889 [39]) singer EA/90*

BENSON, Ellen see Yates, Ellen

BENSON, Eric William (d 1916 [29]) EA/17*

BENSON, Sir F[rank] R[obert] (1858-1939) English actor, manager AAS, DD, DNB, DP, ES, GRB/1-4, OC/1-3, PDT, WWM, WWT/1-9, WWW/3

BENSON, Lady F[rank] R[obert; Constance Featherstonhaugh] (1860-1946) actress GRB/2-4, OC/1-3, WWT/1-9

BENSON, George (d 1908 [83]) actor GRB/4*

BENSON, George (b 1911) Welsh actor AAS, BE, TW/4, WWT/ 9-16

BENSON, G. H. (d 1885 [23]) actor EA/87*

BENSON, Harry (d 1916) EA/17*

BENSON, Harry A. (d 1902 [36]) EA/04*

BENSON, Robby (b 1956) American actor TW/25, 27-28

BENSON, Robert (1765-96) English actor, dramatist BD, CP/3, DD, TD/1-2

BENSON, Mrs. Robert [née Susanna Satchell] (1758-1814) English actress BD

BENSON, Ruth [Mrs. Holbrook Blinn] (1873-1948) American actress GRB/3-4, WWT/1-5

BENSON, Sally (1897/1900-1972) American dramatist BE, CD, HJD, TW/29, WWA/5

BENSON, Tony (d 1891) music-hall artist EA/92*

BENSON, Mrs. T. W. see Weston, Emmeline Montague Falconer

BENSON, William (d 1869) wardrobe keeper EA/70*

BENSON, William (d 1887) EA/88*

BENSTEAD, Fabbie (d 1970) performer BP/55*

BENT, Mr. (fl 1793-1805) gallery doorkeeper BD

BENT, Buena (1890-1957) English actress WWT/4-12

BENT, Georgia (fl c.1874) singer CDP

BENT, Horace (d 1907 [70]) comedian EA/08*, GRB/3*

BENT, Marion [Mrs. Pat Rooney] (1879-1940) American performer SR

BENT, William Richard (d 1913)

EA/14*

BENTHALL, Michael Pickersgill
(1919-74) English director
AAS, BE, BTR/74, ES,
PDT, WWT/11-15

BENTHAM, Frederick (b 1911)
lighting designer, inventor
WWT/15-16

BENTHAM, Josephine American
dramatist BE

BENTHAM, Samuel (c.1653-c.
1730) English singer BD

BENTINCK, A. Gow (d 1902)
actor EA/03*

BENTLEY, Mrs. (d 1916 [63])
EA/18*

BENTLEY, Mrs. Arthur [Clara
Hayward] (d 1868 [21])
dancer EA/69*

BENTLEY, Dave (d 1912 [30])
comedian EA/13*

BENTLEY, Doris (d 1944)
actress BE*, WWT/14*

BENTLEY, Eric (b 1916)
English/American critic,
director, dramatist AAS,
BE, CD, ES, NTH, PDT,
WWT/14-16

BENTLEY, Florence [Mrs. William Begg] (b 1862) Italian/
English actress GRB/1-2

BENTLEY, Grendon (1877-1956)
English actor WWT/2-3

BENTLEY, Herschel American
actor TW/5-6

BENTLEY, Irene [Mrs. Henry
B. Smith] (d 1940 [70])
American actress, singer
GRB/3-4, WWA/1, WWS,
WWT/1-5

BENTLEY, John (c.1553-85)
actor DA

BENTLEY, John (fl 1803) dramatist CP/3, DD

BENTLEY, Joseph (d 1912)
EA/13*

BENTLEY, Laura see Linden,
Mrs.Henry

BENTLEY, Muriel (b 1922)
American dancer ES

BENTLEY, Richard (1708-82)
dramatist CP/1-3, DD,
GT, TD/1-2

BENTLEY, Spencer (d 1963)
actor BE*

BENTLEY, Thomas see
Bentley, Richard

BENTLEY, Walter (1849-1927)

Scottish actor DD, OAA/1-2

BENTON, Charles (d 1758) musician BD

BENTON, Mrs. Fred see Harrison-Tate, A.

BENTONELLI, Joseph (d 1975 [74])
performer BP/59*

BENUCCI, Francesco [Pietro?]
(c.1745-1824) Italian singer BD

BENUCCI, [Pietro?] see Benucci,
Francesco

BENWELL, Archibald (d 1918)
EA/19*

BEN-ZALI, Sidney (b 1945) Brazilian actor TW/27-28

BENZELL, Mimi (1924-70) American singer, actress BE,
TW/27

BENZON, Otto (1856-1927) dramatist BE*

BERARD, Christian (1902-49)
French designer ES, TW/5

BERARD, Peter (fl 1808) dramatist CP/3

BERARDI, Signor (fl 1763-65)
dancer BD

BERBERIAN, Cathy (b 1925) American singer ES

BERCHER, Jean see D'Auberval,
Jean

BERDEEN, Robert American actor
TW/26-28

BERDESHEVSKY, Margo Ann (b
1945) American actress TW/
23, 25, 28-29

BERECLOTH, Mr. (fl 1788-1814)
door-keeper BD

BERECLOTH, Mrs. (fl 1794-95)
dresser BD

BEREK, Augustus see Burt,
Frank A.

BERENDT, Rachel [Monique Arkell]
(d 1957) French actress WWT/
8-9

BERENSTADT, Gaetano (fl 1717-24)
singer BD

BERENY, Mrs. Henry see Wiehe,
Charlotte

BERESFORD, Bernard (d 1893)
singer EA/94*

BERESFORD, Blanche (d 1874 [20])
actress EA/75*

BERESFORD, George singer CDP

BERESFORD, Harry (1867-1944)
English actor TW/1, WWA/2,
WWT/5-8

BERESFORD, Hugh (d 1905 [21])
EA/06*

BERESFORD, J. Cooke (b 1870)
actor GRB/1-2
BERG, Dale (b 1931) American
actress TW/26
BERG, Ellen [Mrs. Robert Ede-
son] (d 1906 [32]) actress
BE*, WWT/14*
BERG, George (fl 1753-71)
instrumentalist, composer
BD
BERG, Gertrude (1899-1966)
American actress, dramatist
BE, CB, TW/23, WWA/4,
WWT/13-14
BERG, Harold C. (d 1973 [73])
composer/lyricist BP/58*
BERG, Nancy (b 1931) American
actress BE, TW/13
BERGAN, Harry (d 1917 [48])
actor EA/18*
BERGANZA, Teresa (b 1934)
Spanish singer ES
BERGE, Irénée (1870-1926)
French director, composer
WWA/1
BERGEL, John Graham (1902-41)
English critic WWT/7-9
BERGEN, Betty (d 1964 [34])
aerialist BE*
BERGEN, Edgar John (b 1903)
American ventriloquist
CB, ES
BERGEN, Fanny Dickerson (b
1846) American dramatist
WWA/4
BERGEN, Nella [Mrs. De Wolf
Hopper] (1873-1919) Amer-
ican singer, actress GRB/
3-4, WWM, WWS, WWT/
2-3
BERGEN, Polly (b 1930) Amer-
ican actress, singer BE,
CB, TW/11-13
BERGER, Anna (fl c.1873)
singer, musician CDP
BERGER, Augustin (b 1861)
Czech ballet master WWA/4
BERGER, Bob (b 1922) Ameri-
can actor TW/24-25
BERGER, Bill (b 1928) Aus-
trian/American actor,
director BE
BERGER, Henning (b 1872)
Swedish dramatist WWT/
3-4
BERGER, Henrietta Newman
(1856-1943) American act-
ress, bell-ringer SR

BERGER, Herbert L. (d 1968)
executive BP/52*
BERGER, Rosetta Jane (d 1911)
EA/12*
BERGER, Sam (d 1972 [63]) mana-
ger BP/57*
BERGER, Victoria Sherry (d 1975
[67]) performer BP/60*
BERGER, William (fl 1840) Amer-
ican dramatist RJ
BERGERAC, Savinien de Cyrano de
(1619-55) French dramatist
OC/1-3
BERGERE, Lee American actor
TW/29
BERGERE, Ouida [Mrs. Louis
Weadock] (b 1887) Spanish
actress WWM
BERGERE, Valerie (1872-1938)
French actress WWM, WWS,
WWT/7-8
BERGER FAMILY (fl 1850s) per-
formers SR
BERGERSEN, Baldwin (b 1914)
Australian/American composer,
musical director, musician
BE
BERGH, Arthur (d 1962) American
composer WWA/4
BERGHOF, Herbert (b 1900/09)
Austrian/American actor, di-
rector BE, TW/1, 3-17,
25-26, WWT/11-16
BERGIN, Pat (d 1893) music-hall
artist EA/94*
BERGLUND, Joel (b 1903) Swedish
singer ES
BERGMAN, Benedict (fl 1792-94)
violinist BD
BERGMAN, Carl see Bergmann,
Carl
BERGMAN, Gladys (d 1965 [82])
performer BP/49*
BERGMAN, Henry (d 1962 [75])
performer BE*
BERGMAN, Hjalmar Frederik
(1883-1931) Swedish dramatist
COC, ES, MH
BERGMAN, Ingrid (b 1917) Swedish
actress BE, SR, TW/3-6,
24, 28, WWT/11-16
BERGMANN, Alan American actor
TW/22, 26
BERGMANN, Carl (1821-76) Ger-
man conductor DAB
BERGMANN, Eugene J. (d 1975
[77]) performer BP/59*
BERGNER, Elisabeth (b 1900)

Austrian actress AAS, BE,
NTH, SR, TW/1-7, WWT/
8-16

BERGONZI, Carlo (b 1924) Italian
singer ES

BERGSON, Michael (d 1898) composer EA/99*

BERINGER, Esmé (1875-1972)
English actress COC, DD,
EA/96-97, GRB/1-4, OC/3,
WWT/1-14

BERINGER, Mrs. Oscar [Aimée
Daniell] (1856-1936) American
dramatist DD, GRB/1-4,
WWT/1-8, WWW/3

BERINGER, Vera (1879-1964)
English actress COC, DD,
DP, EA/97, GRB/2-4, OC/
3, WWT/1-13

BERIO, Luciano (b 1925) Italian
composer CB, ES

BERIOSOVA, Svetlana (b 1932)
Lithuanian/English dancer
CB, ES

BERK, Ernest (b 1909) English
choreographer, dancer ES

BERKELEY, Mrs. (fl 1765)
house servant? BD

BERKELEY, Miss (fl 1761-76)
house servant BD

BERKELEY, Arthur (d 1962
[66]) actor BE*

BERKELEY, Ballard (b 1904)
English actor ES, WWT/
9-13

BERKELEY, Busby [né Busby
Berkeley William Enos]
(1895-1976) American director, producer, actor BE,
CB, ES, WWT/15-16

BERKELEY, George Monck
(1763-93) English dramatist
CP/3, DD

BERKELEY, Gertrude [Mrs.
Wilson Enos] (fl 1900-08)
American actress WWS

BERKELEY, Lennox (b 1903)
English composer ES

BERKELEY, Reginald Cheyne
(1890-1935) English dramatist ES, WWT/4-7

BERKELEY, Sir William see
Berkley, Sir William

BERKELEY, Wilma Australian
actress, singer WWT/7-8

BERKELY, Mr. (fl 1766-67)
property man BD

BERKELY, Miss (fl 1776-77)

actress BD

BERKEY, Ralph (b 1912) American
dramatist BE

BERKLEY [or Barclay, or Bartley],
Sir William (d 1677) English
dramatist CP/1-3, DD, FGF

BERKOWITZ, Sol (b 1922) American
composer, writer BE

BERKOWSKY, Paul B. (b 1932)
American manager BE

BERKSON, Michael (b 1939) American actor TW/23

BERLE, Frank (d 1973 [70]) manager BP/57*

BERLE, Milton [né Berlinger] (b
1908) American actor, producer,
lyricist, writer BE, CB, ES,
TW/1-2, 5-8, 25, WWT/10-16

BERLEIN, Annie Mack (1850-1935)
Irish actress SR

BERLIN, Alexandra American actress
TW/24

BERLIN, Elaine see May, Elaine

BERLIN, Irving (b 1888) Russian/
American composer, lyricist
AAS, BE, CB, ES, HJD, MH,
NTH, PDT, WWT/4-16

BERLIN, J. Norman (d 1943 [67])
actor BE*

BERLINGER, Milton see Berle,
Milton

BERLINGER, Warren (b 1937)
American actor BE, TW/10-19,
WWT/14-16

BERLYN, Alfred (1860-1936) English
dramatist GRB/2-4, WWT/1-8,
WWW/3

BERLYN, Mrs. Alfred (d 1943)
critic, journalist WWW/4

BERLYN, Ivan [Ivan Emanuel
Julian von Berlin] (1874-1934)
English actor GRB/1-4

BERMAN, A. L. (1890-1975) American attorney BE

BERMAN, Eugene (1899-1972) Russian scene designer CB, ES

BERMAN, Harry (d 1974 [76]) performer BP/58*

BERMAN, Max (d 1972 [88]) costumier BP/57*, WWT/16*

BERMAN, Shelley (b 1926) American
comedian, actor BE

BERMANGE, Barry (b 1933) English
dramatist CD

BERN, Chris V. [Robinson Byrne]
(b 1872) English variety artist
GRB/1

BERN, Paul (1889-1932) American

actor, director ES, WWA/1

BERNACCHI, Antonio Maria (1685-1756) Italian singer BD

BERNAGE, George [né Burnidge] (d 1903 [47]) actor EA/04*

BERNAL, Mr. (fl 1796) puppeteer BD

BERNARD, Mr. (fl 1750) actor BD

BERNARD, Mrs. (fl 1824) actress CDP

BERNARD, Mons. (fl 1790-93) machinist BD

BERNARD, Mrs. Albert see Stafford, Emily

BERNARD, Anthony (1891-1963) English conductor, composer ES, WWW/6

BERNARD, Anthony W. (d 1879 [61]) American musician EA/80*

BERNARD, Barney (1877-1924) American actor SR, WWT/4

BERNARD, Caroline E. (fl 1853-62) actress HAS

BERNARD, Charles minstrel CDP

BERNARD, Charles (d 1895) actor, singer, manager, dramatist DD, SR

BERNARD, Mrs. Charles see Alleyn, Annie

BERNARD, Mrs. Charles [née Tilden] (d c.1870) actress DD, HAS

BERNARD, Charles S. (1816-74) American actor, secretary of the American Dramatic Fund CDP, HAS

BERNARD, Charles W. (d 1917) performer? SR

BERNARD, Dick (d 1925 [60]) actor BE*, WWT/14*

BERNARD, Dorothy [Mrs. A. H. Van Beuren] (1890-1955) actress TW/1, 12

BERNARD, Ed (b 1939) American actor TW/26

BERNARD, James (d 1973 [43]) performer BP/57*

BERNARD, Jean-Jacques (b 1888) French dramatist COC, OC/1-3

BERNARD, John (1756-1828) English actor, manager, author BD, CDP, DAB, DD, DNB, ES, HAS,

OC/3, SR, TD/2, WWA/H

BERNARD, Mrs. John, I [Mrs. Cooper; née Roberts] (1750-92) actress BD, DD, TD/1-2

BERNARD, Mrs. John, II [née Fisher] (d 1805) actress DD

BERNARD, Kenneth (b 1930) American dramatist, director CD

BERNARD, Kitty (d 1962) performer BE*

BERNARD, Leon (d 1935 [58]) actor BE*, WWT/14*

BERNARD, Lionel (1818-62) American actor DD, HAS

BERNARD, Paul see Bernard, Tristan

BERNARD, Richard (1566/67-1641) dramatist CP/1-3, DD

BERNARD, Sallie (d 1878 [12]) actress EA/79*

BERNARD, Sam (1863-1927) English actor GRB/2-4, SR, WWA/1, WWS, WWT/1-5

BERNARD, Sam (d 1950 [61]) actor BE*

BERNARD, Mrs. S. E. see Stanley, Laura

BERNARD, Tristan [Paul Bernard] (1866-1947) French dramatist COC, OC/1-3, WWT/3-4

BERNARD, Vivian (d 1913) actress SR

BERNARD, William Bayle (1807-75) American dramatist DAB, DD, DNB, EA/68, ES, HJD, SR, WWA/H

BERNARD, William H. (1833-90) American minstrel HAS, SR

BERNARDI, Signora (fl 1720) singer BD

BERNARDI, Master (fl 1783-85) call boy BD

BERNARDI, Boris (d 1974 [70]) manager BP/59*

BERNARDI, Helen (d 1971 [89]) performer BP/57*

BERNARDI, Herschel (b 1923) American actor TW/25-26

BERNARDO, [Mr.?] (fl 1688) musician BD

"BERNARDO" (d 1880) female impersonator, minstrel CDP

BERNASCHINA, Antonio (d 1876 [62]) ballet master EA/77*

BERNASCHINA, Marianna (d 1870) actress EA/71*

BERNASCONI, Antonia (b c.1740) German singer BD, ES

BERNAT, Julie see Judith,
Mlle.
BERNATO, Mlle. [Mrs. Charles
Romaine] (d 1877) pantomim-
ist? EA/78*
BERNAUER, Rudolph (d 1953
[73]) Hungarian dramatist,
librettist, producer BE*,
WWT/14*
BERNERS, Lord see Bourchier,
John
BERNERS, Lord [Gerald Hugh
Tyrwhitt Wilson Berners]
(1883-1950) English composer,
painter, writer ES, WWW/
4
BERNERS, Gerald Hugh Tyrwhitt
Wilson see Berners, Lord
BERNES, Mark (d 1969 [57])
performer BP/54*
BERNET, Mr. (fl 1797) scene
painter BD
BERNEY, William (d 1961 [40])
dramatist BE*, BP/46*
BERNEYOSKI, Hans (fl 1661-68)
drummer BD
BERNHARDT, Mrs. Curtis see
Argyle, Pearl
BERNHARDT, Maurice (d 1928
[65]) producer, manager
BE*, WWT/14*
BERNHARDT, Melvin American
director WWT/15-16
BERNHARDT, Sarah Henriette
Rosine (1845-1923) French
actress, manager CDP,
COC, DP, ES, GRB/1-4,
HP, NTH, OC/1-3, PDT,
SR, WWA/1, WWM, WWS,
WWT/1-4
BERNHEIM, Shirl (b 1921) Amer-
ican actress TW/27-38
BERNICAT, Firmin (d 1883 [33])
composer EA/84*
BERNIE, Ben (1891?-1943) Amer-
ican actor, musician CB,
SR
BERNIE, Dick (d 1971 [60]) per-
former BP/55*
BERNSTEIN, Aline [née Frankhau]
(1881/82-1955) American
designer COC, ES, NTH,
OC/1-3, TW/3, 5-8, 12,
WWT/7-12
BERNSTEIN, Henri (1876-1953)
French dramatist MWD,
TW/10
BERNSTEIN, Herman (d 1963

[58]) American executive, pro-
duction manager BE*, BP/
48*, WWT/14*
BERNSTEIN, Karl American press
representative BE
BERNSTEIN, Leonard (b 1918)
American composer, conductor
AAS, BE, ES, HJD, MH,
NTH, PDT, WWT/13-16
BERNSTEIN, Sidney (d 1966 [56])
producer TW/23
BERNSTEIN, Stephen (b 1944)
American actor TW/24
BEROLZHEIMER, Hobart F. (b
1921) American librettist BE
BERR, Georges (d 1942 [74]) actor,
dramatist BE*, WWT/14*
BERR DU TURIQUE, Julien (d
1923 [60]) dramatist BE*,
WWT/14*
BERRIAN, Bill see Berrian, Wil-
liam
BERRIAN, William (b 1929) Ameri-
can actor TW/5, 25, 29
BERRIDGE, Mr. (fl 1794) bass
viol player BD
BERRIMAN, Joseph (d 1730) actor
BD
BERRINGTON, Mary (d 1888) EA/
89*
BERRISFORD, [Robert?] (fl 1745-
77) house servant BD
BERRY, Aline (d 1967 [62]) actress
TW/23
BERRY, [Ann?] (fl 1749) actress
BD
BERRY, Bill see Berry, William
Henry
BERRY, Catherine see D'Egville,
Mrs. James Harvey
BERRY, Mrs. Charles see Dar-
ling, Bessie
BERRY, Charles W. (fl 1870-90)
actor, dramatist SR
BERRY, C[hristopher?] (fl 1776-81)
actor BD
BERRY, Edward (1697-1750) actor
CDP
BERRY, Edward (1706-60) actor,
singer, dancer BD, DD
BERRY, Eric (b 1913) English actor
AAS, BE, TW/11, 16-18, 20,
22, 27-30, WWT/11-16
BERRY, James (1883-1918) English
actor WWT/2
BERRY, James J. (d 1969 [54])
performer BP/53*
BERRY, John (d 1821) actor BD

BERRY, John American actor
TW/28
BERRY, Ken (b 1933) American
actor TW/16-17
BERRY, Mary (1763-1852)
dramatist DD
BERRY, Sidney N. (d 1975 [66])
producer/director/choreog-
rapher BP/59*
BERRY, Thomas (d 1701?) actor
BD
BERRY, Thomas (fl 1737) actor
BD
BERRY, Wallace (d 1949 [60])
actor TW/5
BERRY, Mrs. W. H. see
Hanson, Kitty
BERRY, William Henry (1872-
1951) English actor, singer
ES, GRB/4, WWT/1-11
BERSELLI, Matteo (fl 1719-21)
singer BD
BERSON, William (d 1916)
EA/17*
BERT, Frederic (1844-1911)
American minstrel, manager
SR
BERTE, Charles [Grant Bryant]
(1875-1908) English drama-
tist GRB/1-4
BERTEAU, Mons. (fl 1675)
dancer BD
BERTENSHAW, Betty Jane (d
1975) performer BP/60*
BERTHIER, Jacques (b 1916)
French actor ES
BERTI, Ettore (1870-1940)
Italian actor ES
BERTIE, Mr. (fl 1708) manager?
BD
BERTIN, Mr. (fl 1793) pianist
BD
BERTIN, Emile (b 1878) French
scene designer ES
BERTIN, Josephine (fl 1849)
dancer CDP, HAS
BERTIN, Pierre (b 1895) French
actor TW/9
BERTINI, Ambrose (d 1894 [28])
composer, pianist EA/96*
BERTLES, Miss see Dighton,
Mrs. Robert
BERTOLDI, Ena [Beatrice Mary
Spink] (d 1906 [28]) gymnast
EA/07*
BERTOLLI, Francesca (fl 1729-
37) singer BD
BERTON, Pierre (d 1912 [70])

actor, dramatist BE*, WWT/
14*
BERTONI, Ferdinando Giuseppe
(1725-1813) Italian composer
BD, ES
BERTRAM, Alexander Brown (d
1867) actor? EA/68*
BERTRAM, Arthur (1860-1955)
English business manager
GRB/1-4, WWT/1-5
BERTRAM, Bert (b 1893) Australian
actor TW/25
BERTRAM, Charles (fl 1794) horn
player BD
BERTRAM, Charles [James Bas-
sett] (d 1907 [53]) conjuror
EA/08*, GRB/3*
BERTRAM, Ellen see Walters,
Mrs. W. H.
BERTRAM, Eugene (1872-1941)
English business manager
WWT/4-6
BERTRAM, Eva [Ethel Brierley]
English actress GRB/1-2
BERTRAM, Frank (d 1941 [70])
actor BE*, WWT/14*
BERTRAM, Helen [née Lulu May
Burt; Mrs. E. J. Morgan] (b
1869) American actress, singer
WWA/5, WWS
BERTRAM, Henry (d 1898) actor
EA/99*
BERTRAM, Lily [Mrs. T. W. Raw-
son] English actress GRB/1
BERTRAM, Lucy see Hadaway,
Mrs. Thomas H.
BERTRAM, William [Benjamin
Switzer] (b 1880) Canadian
actor, director ES
BERTRAND (d 1883) singer EA/84*
"BERTRAND" see Dove, Mark
BERTRAND, E. C. (c.1842-87)
English dramatist, manager
DD, NYM
BERTRAND, Henry (d 1898) circus
manager EA/99*
BERTRAND, Kate Emma (d 1889
[33]) EA/90*
BERUH, Joseph (b 1924) American
producer, company manager,
general manager, director
BE, WWT/16
BERWICK, Mrs. (fl 1765) dresser
BD
BERYL, H. Cecil (d 1931) manager
WWT/14*
BERYL, Mrs. H. Cecil see
Eversfield, Miss

BERYL, Sara (d 1897) singer,
actress EA/98*

BERYL, William (d 1903 [22])
EA/04*

BESANT, Sonya (d 1970 [40])
performer BP/55*

BESANT, Sir Walter (1836-1901)
writer, dramatist DD

BESEMERES, John see Daly,
John

BESFORD, Mr. (fl 1759) messenger BD

BESFORD, Mr. (fl 1766-68)
actor BD

BESFORD, Mr. (1767-89) lamp
man BD

BESFORD, Esther (b c.1757)
English actress, dancer BD

BESFORD, Joseph (d 1789)
property man BD

BESFORD, Mrs. [Joseph?] (fl
1767-68) dancer BD

BESFORD, Samuel (fl 1763-91)
actor, dancer BD

BESIER, Rudolf (1878-1942)
Dutch/English dramatist
ES, MH, MWD, NTH, SR,
WWT/2-9, WWW/4

BESLEY, Henry (d 1902) actor,
dramatist EA/03*

BESOYAN, Rick (1924-70)
American composer, lyricist,
librettist, director, producer
BE

BESOZZI, Antonio (1714-81)
oboist BD

BESOZZI, Carlo (b c.1738)
Italian oboist BD

BESOZZI, Gaetano (1727-98)
Italian oboist BD

BESSIN, Henrietta (d 1850 [26])
singer HAS

BESSLE, Elizabeth (d 1906)
actress, dramatist DD

BESSMERTNOVA, Natalija (b
1941) Russian dancer ES

BESSON, George (d 1905 [47])
EA/06*

BEST, Mr. (fl 1779-85) actor
BD

BEST, Mrs. Charles see
Lalo, Louise Dorothy

BEST, Edna (1900-74) English
actress BE, BTR/74,
CB, ES, TW/8-16, WWT/
4-13

BEST, Paul (b 1908) German
actor TW/1-3

BEST, William (fl 1862-95) dramatist DD

BEST, Willie (d 1962 [46]) actor
BE*

BEST, W. T. (d 1897 [71]) organist EA/98*

BESTIC, Charles M. (d 1909) actor
EA/10*

BESTOR, Don (d 1970 [80]) com-
poser/lyricist BP/54*

BESTOW, William (d 1873 [84])
EA/74*

BESTRY, Harry (d 1969 [80]) agent
BP/54*

BESWICK, Mrs. (fl 1787) dancer
BD

BESWICK, Miss (fl 1726) house servant? BD

BESWICK, Miss (fl 1787) dancer
BD

BESWICK, Harriette Emily see
Everard, Harriette Emily

BESWICK, William [William Cres-
wick] (d 1883 [54]) EA/84*

BESWICKE, Mrs. Darley see
Everard, Harriette Emily

BESWORTH, [Mr.?] (fl 1761) wardrobe assistant BD

BETHELL, William (fl 1784-c.94)
singer BD

BETHEN, Charles (d 1876 [56])
actor? EA/77*

BETHENCOURT, Francis (b 1924/
26) English actor, writer BE,
TW/13, 18, 22-23, 26, 29

BETHUN, Mr. (fl 1733-38) dancer
BD

BETHUNE, Mr. (fl 1746) house
servant? BD

BETJEMANN, George Stanley (d
1899 [63]) EA/00*

BETJEMANN, Gilbert R. (d 1896
[31]) musician EA/97*

BETON, Miss (fl 1798) actress
BD

BETTANY, F. G. (d 1942 [73])
critic BE*, WWT/14*

BETTELHEIM, Edwin Sumner (1865-
1938) American critic WWM,
WWT/2-5

BETTENHAM, George (d 1694)
singer BD

BETTERTON, John (d 1816) actor
BD

BETTERTON, Julia see Glover,
Julia

BETTERTON, Mary see Betterton,
Mrs. Thomas

BETTERTON, Thomas (1635?-
1710) English actor, mana-
ger, dramatist BD, CDP,
COC, CP/1-3, DD, DNB,
ES, GT, HP, NTH, PDT,
OC/1-3, TD/1-2
BETTERTON, Mrs. Thomas [née
Mary Saunderson] (b c.1637-
1712) English actress BD,
COC, CP/1-3, DD, DNB,
ES, HP, NTH, OC/1-3
BETTERTON, Thomas William
(d 1834) Irish actor BD,
HAS, SR, TD/1-2
BETTERTON, William (1644-61)
English actor BD, DD
BETTGER, Lyle (b 1915) Amer-
ican actor TW/2-6
BETTI, Ugo (1892-1953) Italian
dramatist COC, MWD,
NTH, PDT, OC/2-3
BETTINI, Signor (fl 1850-52)
singer HAS
BETTINI, Signora (fl 1744-45)
dancer BD
BETTINI, Geremia (1823-65)
Italian singer CDP
BETTIS, Valerie Elizabeth
(b 1919) American dancer,
choreographer, actress,
director BE, CB, ES, TW/
4-9, WWT/15-16
BETTMANN, Otto L. (b 1903)
German/American archivist
BE
BETTON, George (d 1969) per-
former BP/54*
BETTS, Mr. (fl 1748) actor BD
BETTS, Mr. (fl 1797-99) actor,
singer BD
BETTS, Arthur (1776-1847) Eng-
lish violinist, composer BD
BETTS, Edward (c.1773?-c.1806)
English musician, instrument
maker BD
BETTS, Edward William (b 1881)
English journalist, critic
WWT/5, 9-11
BETTS, Ernest (1896-1975?)
English critic ES, WWT/
10-11
BETTS, John [Edward?] (1755-
1823) English violin maker,
teacher, musician BD
BETTS, Richard (fl 1669) musi-
cian? BD
BETTY, Mrs. (d 1872 [80])
EA/74*

BETTY, Ann Starkie (d 1904 [60])
EA/05*
BETTY, Henry (1819-97) English
actor CDP, DD
BETTY, William Henry West (1791-
1874) English actor CDP,
COC, DD, DNB, ES, GT, HP,
NTH, OC/1-3, OX, TD/2
BEUF, Augusto (b 1887) Italian
singer ES
BEULER, Jacob (d 1873) comic song
writer EA/74*
BEVAN, Billy (d 1957 [70]) Aus-
tralian actor BE*
BEVAN, Donald (b 1920) American
dramatist BE
BEVAN, Faith (b 1896) Welsh act-
ress, singer WWT/4-7
BEVAN, Frank (b 1903) American
educator, costume designer BE
BEVAN, Fred (d 1893) music-hall
artist EA/94*
BEVAN, Isla (b 1910) English act-
ress WWT/7-8
BEVANS, Lionel (d 1965 [81]) per-
former BP/49*
BEVANS, Philippa (1916/17-68)
English actress BE, TW/9-16,
24
BEVAN-SLATOR, Mrs. see
Crawford, Amy
BEVERIDGE, Mrs. (d 1887) EA/
88*
BEVERIDGE, Charles (d 1884)
EA/85*
BEVERIDGE, Mrs. Charles see
Clarke, Fanny M.
BEVERIDGE, Glen (1886-1947)
American actor SR
BEVERIDGE, J[ames] D. (1844-
1926) Irish actor DD, DP,
EA/97, GRB/1-4, OAA/1-2,
WWS, WWT/1-5
BEVERIDGE, Mrs. James D. see
Beveridge, Jenny
BEVERIDGE, Jenny (d 1898) EA/
99*
BEVERIDGE, Kuhne American act-
ress WWM
BEVERIDGE, Ray [Mrs. Madison
Seliger] (b 1887) American
actress WWM
BEVERLEY, E. D. (d 1880 [42])
singer EA/81*
BEVERLEY, George Augustus (d
1890) EA/91*
BEVERLEY, Henry (fl 1800-26)
English actor DD, GT, TD/1

BEVERLEY, Mrs. Henry (fl 1801) actress DD

BEVERLEY, Henry Roxby (1796-1863) comedian CDP, DD, DNB

BEVERLEY, Hilda (d 1942) actress BE*, WWT/14*

BEVERLEY, Maude (fl c. 1885) singer CDP

BEVERLEY, Percy Charles (d 1903 [54]) actor EA/04*

BEVERLEY, W. G. (d 1867 [86]) actor EA/68*

BEVERLEY, William [Roxby] (d 1842 [69]) manager, producer DD

BEVERLEY, William Roxby (c. 1814-89) English scene painter CDP, COC, DD, DNB, OC/1-3

BEVERLEY, Mrs. William Roxby (d 1851 [75]) actress, manager BE*, WWT/14*

BEVERLY, Henry Roxby (d 1873) author, actor EA/74*

BEVERLY, John (fl 1794?) double-bass player BD

BEVIGNANI, Enrico (1841-1903) Italian conductor, composer ES

BEVIL, Mr. (fl 1729-31) box keeper BD

BEW, Charles (fl 1791-1837) actor BD

BEWES, Rodney (b 1937) English actor WWT/15-16

BEWLEY, Mr. (fl 1715) housekeeper BD

BEWLEY, Elizabeth (fl 1716-21) house servant? BD

BEWLEY, John (fl 1724-36) stage doorkeeper BD

BEWLEY, William (fl 1724-36) gallerykeeper, boxkeeper BD

BEY, Rafic (b 1948) Moroccan actor TW/29-30

BEYER, Elsie manager WWT/11-13

BEZANSON, Philip (d 1975 [59]) composer/lyricist BP/59*

BHASKAR [Roy Chowhury] (b 1930) Indian actor, dancer, choreographer, singer BE, TW/16-17

BIAGGINI, Sig. (fl 1783) exhibitor BD

BIAL, Rudolf (1834-81) violinist, conductor, composer CDP

BIANCARDI, Sig. (fl 1720) musician? BD

BIANCHI, Sig. (fl 1769-70) singer BD

BIANCHI, Francesco (fl 1748-49) singer BD

BIANCHI, Francesco (c. 1751-1810) Italian composer, musician BD, ES, TD/1

BIANCHI, Mrs. Francesco [née Jane Jackson; Mrs. John Lacy] (1776-1858) English singer BD

BIANCHI, Giovanni Battista (fl 1780-82) Italian conductor, composer BD

BIANCHI, John C. M. (1775-1802) violinist, composer BD

BIANCHINI, Mr. (fl 1743-47) house servant BD

BIBB, Joe (d 1893 [48]) clown EA/95*

BIBBY, Mr. (fl 1746) actor, singer BD

BIBBY, Mr. (fl 1815-16) actor DD

BIBBY, Charles (1878-1917) English actor WWT/1-3

BIBERMAN, Herbert (d 1971 [71]) director TW/28

BIBO, Irving (d 1962 [72]) composer BE*

BIBSON, Miss (fl 1781) actress BD

BICK, James (d 1712?) ventriloquist, imitator BD, CDP

BICKEL, Frederick McIntyre see March, Fredric

BICKEL, George L. (1863?-1941) American comedian CB

BICKERDIKE, A. W. (d 1889 [39]) pianist EA/90*

BICKERDIKE, Mary (d 1882) EA/83*

BICKERSTAFF, Miss (d c. 1724) actress BD

BICKERSTAFF, Agnes (d 1893 [66]) EA/94*

BICKERSTAFF, Isaac (1735-1812) Irish dramatist COC, CP/1-3, DD, DNB, ES, GT, HP, MH, OC/1-3, PDT, TD/1-2

BICKERSTAFF, John (d c. 1724) English actor BD

BICKERSTAFFE, Henry (d 1873 [50]) scene artist EA/74*

BICKERTON, Joseph P., Jr. (d 1936 [58]) manager, producer WWT/14*

BICKFORD, Charles A. (1891-1967)

American actor BE, ES,
TW/24, WWT/7-9
BICKFORD, Melville G. T. (d
1913) EA/14*
BICKHAM, Mr. (fl 1733) actor?
BD
BICKHAM, Mrs. (fl 1779)
candle-woman BD
BICKLEY, Mrs. Harry see
Bickley, Thirza
BICKLEY, Thirza [Mrs. Harry
Bickley] (d 1916) EA/17*
BICKLEY, Tony American actor
TW/3-6
BICKNELL, Mr. (fl 1794) bas-
soonist BD
BICKNELL, Mrs. (fl 1755) singer
BD
BICKNELL, Alexander (fl 1788)
dramatist CP/3, DD
BICKNELL, George James (d
1874 [35]) pianist EA/75*
BICKNELL, Margaret [née
Younger] (c.1680-1723)
Scottish actress, dancer
BD, DD, DNB
BIDDALL, George Freeman (d
1909) illusionist EA/10*
BIDDALL, Mrs. William (d
1892) EA/93*
BIDDLE, Barnaby American
dramatist RJ
BIDDLE, Edward (fl 1717) drama-
tist CP/3, DD
BIDDLE, George see Edgar,
George
BIDDLE, Mrs. Harry see
Onzalo, Elise
BIDDLES, Mrs. Adelaide see
Calvert, Mrs. Charles
BIDDLES, Clara S. [Mrs.
Thomas Barry] (fl 1854-84)
English actress HAS, PP/1,
SR
BIDDLES, J. (fl 1856) actor HAS
BIDDY, Mrs. (fl 1728-29)
dancer BD
BIDEAUX, Gustave (b 1830)
French minstrel HAS
BIDLAKE, Rev. John (fl 1800)
dramatist CP/3, DD
BIDOTTI, Mons. (fl 1788-94)
dancer, actor BD
BIDOU, Henri (d 1943 [70])
critic BE*, WWT/14*
BIDWELL, Mr. (fl 1778-79)
actor BD
BIDWELL, Barnabas (1763-1833)

American dramatist EAP
BIDWELL, Charles E. (b 1831)
American actor HAS
BIDWELL, Mrs. Charles E. see
Bidwell, Dollie
BIDWELL, David (1820-89) Ameri-
can manager SR
BIDWELL, Dollie [Mrs. Charles E.
Bidwell] (b 1843) American
actress CDP, HAS
BIEBER, Margarete (b 1879) Ger-
man/American educator, writer
BE, ES
BIEL, Jacob see Pedel, Jacob
BIELINSKI, Olga see Bellin, Olga
BIEN, Robert Taylor see War-
wick, Robert
BIENFAIT, Mons. (fl 1756) dancer
BD
BIERDEMANN, Augustino (d 1880)
musician EA/81*
BIERDT, Burchart (fl 1612) English
actor DA
BIFFIN, Miss (d 1850 [66]) freak
EA/72*
BIGARI, Francesco (fl 1766-72)
scene painter, machinist BD
BIGELOW, Charles A. (1862-1912)
American actor SR, WWS
BIGELOW, Joe (d 1976 [66])
dramatist BP/60*
BIGELOW, Otis (b 1920) American
actor TW/18
BIGFORD, Mary (fl 1727) candle-
woman BD
BIGG, John (b 1777) English musi-
cian, teacher BD
BIGGERS, Earl Derr (1884-1933)
American dramatist DAB, ES,
SR, WWA/1, WWT/4-7
BIGGS, Mr. (fl 1737) actor BD
BIGGS, Mr. (fl 1794-97) singer
BD
BIGGS, Mrs. (fl 1719-20) actress
BD
BIGGS, Miss (fl 1798) BD
BIGGS, Anne [Mrs. Samuel Young]
(1775-1825) English actress,
singer BD, TD/1
[B]IGGS, James (fl 1669) scene
keeper BD
BIGGS, James (1771-98) English
actor, singer BD, TD/1-2
BIGGS, John (fl 1667?-89) actor
BD
BIGGS, John (fl 1731-39) violon-
cellist? BD
BIGI, Giacinta (fl 1791-96) Italian

singer BD

BIGLEY, Isabel (b 1928) American actress, singer BE, TW/7-12

BIGNAL, Mr. (fl 1732) actor BD

BIGNAL, Mrs. (fl 1732) actress BD

BIGNARDI, Sig. (fl 1857) singer CDP, HAS

BIGNELL, Mr. (fl 1830-31) prompter HAS

BIGNELL, Charles (fl late 19th cent) singer CDP

BIGNELL, Robert Richard (d 1888 [76]) proprietor EA/ 89*

BIGNEY, Mrs. Dibden see Bigney, Edith

BIGNEY, Edith [Mrs. Dibden Bigney] (d 1890 [24]) actress EA/91*

BIGNY, George (d 1889) property master EA/90*

BIGONZI, Sig. (fl 1724) singer BD

BIGWOOD, George Barnes (d 1913 [84]) actor BE*, EA/ 14*, WWT/14*

BIGWOOD, Mrs. G[eorge] B[arnes] (d 1893) EA/95*

BIHIN, Mons. (b 1808) Belgian giant CDP

BIJOU, Bert (fl c.1903) singer, comedian CDP

BIJOU, Mrs. Peter (d 1911) performer EA/12*

BIKEL, Theodore (b 1924) Austrian actor, musician, singer BE, CB, TW/11-17, 22-23, WWT/14-16

BILBROOKE, Lydia (b 1888) English actress WWT/1-6

BILETTA, Emanuele (1825-90) Italian composer ES

BILKINS, Taylor (fl 1871) dramatist DD

BILL-BELOTSERKOVSKY, Vladimir Naumovich (1884-1970) Russian dramatist COC, MWD, OC/3

BILLERS, William dramatist CP/1

BILLETDOUX, François (b 1927) French dramatist PDT

BILLING, H. Chiswell (1881-1934) Welsh business manager

WWT/4-7

BILLINGESLEY, John (fl 1572) payee DA

BILLINGS, A. D. (d 1882 [36]) actor EA/83*

BILLINGS, "Josh" [Henry W. Shaw] (1818-85) writer SR

BILLINGS, Mary [Mrs. G. Robinson] (d 1877) actress EA/78*

BILLINGS, William (1746-1800) American composer BE*

BILLINGTON, Adeline (1825-1917) actress DD, GRB/2-4, OAA/ 2, WWT/1-3

BILLINGTON, Elizabeth see Billington, Mrs. James

BILLINGTON, Fred (d 1917 [63]) actor, singer BE*, EA/18*, WWT/14*

BILLINGTON, James (1756-94) English double-bass player BD

BILLINGTON, Mrs. James [née Elizabeth Weichsel] (1765/68-1818) English singer, actress, composer BD, CDP, DD, DNB, ES, GT, OX, TD/1-2

BILLINGTON, John (1830-1904) actor CDP, DD, DP, OAA/ 1-2

BILLINGTON, Mrs. John see Billington, Adeline

BILLINGTON, Lee (b 1932) American actress TW/25

BILLINGTON, Michael (b 1939) English critic, actor, author WWT/16

BILLINGTON, Thomas (c.1754-1832) English musician, singer, teacher, composer BD, DNB

BILLIONI, Mons. (fl 1749-51) dancer BD

BILLOE, Miss (fl 1741) actress BD

BILLSBURY, John H. (d 1964 [78]) producer, theatre operator, agent, singer BE*

BILLY-HADEN (fl 19th cent) English clown ES

BILOWIT, Ira J. (b 1925) American producer BE

BILSINGHAM, Miss (fl 1786) dancer BD

BILTON, Belle see Clancarty, Countess of

BILTON, Florence actress CDP

BIMBONI, Alberto (b 1888) Italian conductor, composer ES

BIMKO, Fiszl [or Fishel]

(1890-1965) Polish/American
dramatist ES

BIMOLLE, Arcangelo (fl 1763)
Italian violinist BD

BINCKS, Mrs. (fl 1735-c.1740)
dresser BD

BINDA, Marie Beatrice see
Beatrice, Mlle.

BINDER, Fred (d 1963) American
performer BE*

BINDER, Marguerite (d 1870)
singer EA/71*

BINDIGER, Emily (b 1955) American actress TW/30

BINDLEY, (b 1869) actress,
musician CDP, SR

BINETY, Anna (fl 1761-63) dancer
BD

BINETY, Giorgio (fl 1761-63)
dancer BD

BING, Gus (d 1967 [74]) performer BP/52*

BING, Herman (d 1947 [57])
German actor BE*

BING, Rudolf (b 1902) Austrian
impresario CB, ES

BING, Suzanne (b 1885) French
actress, translator ES

BINGE, John (d 1878 [74]) singer
EA/79*

BINGHAM, Mr. (fl 1778) actor
BD

BINGHAM, Amelia [Mrs. Lloyd
Bingham] (1869-1927) Amer-
ican actress DAB, ES,
GRB/2-4, SR, WWA/1,
WWM, WWS, WWT/1-5

BINGHAM, Bob (b 1946) American actor TW/28-29

BINGHAM, Clifton (b 1859)
English librettist GRB/1

BINGHAM, Ernest (d 1907) business manager EA/08*,
GRB/3*

BINGHAM, George (fl 1689-97)
violinist? BD

BINGHAM, George (d 1967 [74])
actor, singer TW/24

BINGHAM, J. Clarke (d 1962
[65]) English actor BE*

BINGHAM, Leslie [Mrs. Joseph
Byton Totten] (d 1945 [61])
American actress TW/1

BINGHAM, Lionel John (1878-
1911) English critic, journalist WWW/2

BINGHAM, Lloyd (d 1915) press
agent, manager SR

BINGHAM, Mrs. Lloyd see
Bingham, Amelia

BINGHAM, Mark Albert see Albert, Mark

BINGHAM, Ralph (b 1870) American
performer WWM

BINGHAM, Tom (d 1892) Yankee
comedian EA/93*

BINGLEY, Isaac Charles see
Durand, Charles

BINGLEY, Vason I. (d 1898 [32])
circus musical director EA/
99*

BINGNER, Mr. (fl 1766-67) lobby
doorkeeper BD

BINKS, Maria (d 1894) EA/95*

BINLEY, [Mr.?] (fl 1792) singer
BD

BINNER, Margery (b 1908) English
actress WWT/8-9

BINNEY, Constance (b 1900) American actress ES, WWT/5-8

BINNEY, Frank singer, composer
CDP

BINNS, Edward (b 1916) American
actor TW/4-6, 16

BINNS, Jennie (d 1900) music-hall
artist EA/01*

BINT, Sidney W. (d 1910) EA/11*

BINT, Mrs. W. see Leamar, Kate

BINT, William singer CDP

BINYON, Laurence (1869-1946) English dramatist DNB, ES, GRB/
3-4, NTH, OC/1-3, WWA/2,
WWT/1-9, WWW/4

BIOLETTI, Mrs. (d 1899 [84])
EA/01*

BION, Victor (d 1908 [66]) variety
performer EA/09*

BIOW, Milton R. (d 1976 [83]) advertising agency executive
BP/60*

BIRABEAU, André (b 1890) French
dramatist MWD

BIRCH, Mr. (fl 1737) actor BD

BIRCH, Mr. (fl 1766) actor BD

BIRCH, Mr. (fl 1794) singer? BD

BIRCH, Emma (d 1891) EA/92*

BIRCH, Frank (1889-1956) English
producer, actor ES, WWT/
6-10

BIRCH, George (b c.1498) court
interluder DA

BIRCH, George (fl 1619-24) actor
DA

BIRCH, John (fl 1547-56) court
interluder DA

BIRCH, Joseph (d 1879) actor?

EA/80*

BIRCH, Patricia choreographer, director WWT/16

BIRCH, Paul (b 1912) American actor TW/10-11

BIRCH, Peter (b 1922) American actor TW/1-3, 6-9

BIRCH, Samuel (1757-1841) English dramatist CDP, CP/3, DD, DNB, GT, TD/1-2

BIRCH, Walter (d 1892 [41]) minstrel EA/94*

BIRCH, William (1831-97) American minstrel CDP, HAS, SR

BIRCH, William Alfred (d 1887) EA/88*

BIRCHALL, Miss actress TD/2

BIRCHALL, Robert (d 1819) publisher, impresario BD

BIRCHALL, William John [W. J. Seymour] (d 1871) comedian EA/72*

BIRCHENOUGH, Agnes [Mrs. Fawcett Lomax] (d 1891) actress EA/92*

BIRCHENOUGH, Bella [Mrs. George Blythe] (d 1891) music-hall artist EA/93*

BIRCHENOUGH, Mrs. Ellen (d 1874) EA/75*

BIRCHENSHA, John (d 1681) theorist, teacher, violist BD

BIRCHILL, Miss see Vincent, Mrs.

BIRCH-PFEIFFER, Mme. (d 1867) dramatist EA/68*

BIRD, Mr. (fl 1732-34) actor BD

BIRD, Miss [Mrs. W. Jukes] (d 1885 [49]) actress EA/85*

BIRD, Miss (fl 1784-85) actress BD

BIRD, Charles A. (d 1925 [70]) American manager BE*, BP/10*

BIRD, David (b 1907) English actor WWT/10-16

BIRD, James (1788-1839) English dramatist DNB

BIRD, John (fl 1702) mountebank BD

BIRD, John (b 1936) English actor, dramatist WWT/16

BIRD, John Woodall (d 1917 [25]) actor WWT/14*

BIRD, Joseph (b 1926) American actor TW/22-25

BIRD, Rhymus (fl 1702) mountebank BD

BIRD, Richard (b 1894) English actor AAS, ES, WWT/5-15

BIRD, Robert Montgomery (1806-54) American dramatist CDP, COC, DAB, DD, ES, HJD, MH, OC/1-3, RE, RJ, SR, WWA/H

BIRD, Theophilus (1608-64) English actor BD, COC, DD, ES, OC/1-3

BIRD [or Bourne], Theophilus (d 1682?) actor BD, DA

BIRD, Will (d 1910 [28]) music-hall stage manager EA/12*

BIRD [or Bourne], William (d 1624) English actor COC, DA, ES, FGF, OC/1-3

BIRIMISA, George (b 1924) American dramatist, director, actor CD

BIRKETT, Viva (1887-1934) English actress WWT/1-7

BIRKHEAD, Matthew (d 1722) singer, dancer BD

BIRMINGHAM, George A. [Rev. J. O. Hannay] (1865-1950) Irish dramatist WWT/2-10

BIRNEY, David (b 1939) American actor TW/24-29

BIRNIE, Mr. (fl 1796-97) house servant BD

BIRO, Lajos (d 1948 [68]) Hungarian dramatist BE*, WWT/14*

BIRON, Gerald (d 1906) actor EA/07*

BIRREL, Andrew (fl 1802) dramatist CP/3, DD

BIRRELL, Francis (d 1935 [44]) critic, dramatist BE*, WWT/14*

BIRT, [Mr. ?] (fl 1791-92) house servant? BD

BIRT, Miss S. [Mme. Frederic] (fl 1791-1813) dancer BD

BIRTCHNELL, Arthur J. (d 1869 [31]) professor of music EA/70*

BISBEE, Noah, Sr. (fl 1808) American dramatist EAP

BISCACCIANTI, Elise (1824?-96) American singer, actress CDP, ES, HAS

BISCARDI, Luigi (d 1876) composer, organist EA/77*

BISCHOF, Maria Anna see
Brandt, Marianne

BISHOP, Mr. (fl 1735) singer
BD

BISHOP, Mr. (fl 1738-44) gallery
keeper BD

BISHOP, Mr. (fl 1741) actor BD

BISHOP, Mr. (fl 1776-77) dancer
BD

BISHOP, Mr. (fl 1797-1803) box
keeper BD

BISHOP, Mr. (d 1871) actor
EA/72*

BISHOP, Mrs. (fl 1741-42)
dancer, actress, singer BD

BISHOP, Mrs. (fl 1776-78?)
actress BD

BISHOP, Mrs. (d 1886) EA/87*

BISHOP, A. C. (d 1893 [29])
EA/94*

BISHOP, Alfred (d 1910 [44])
comedian EA/11*

BISHOP, Alfred (1841/43/45-
1928) English actor DD,
GRB/1-4, WWT/1-5

BISHOP, Ann [Mrs. John Bishop]
(d 1892) EA/93*

BISHOP, Ann[a]; née Rivière]
(1814-84) English singer,
actress CDP, DD, DNB,
ES, HAS, SR

BISHOP, Arthur (d 1904 [26])
actor EA/05*

BISHOP, Charles B. (1833-89)
American actor, manager
CDP, SR

BISHOP, Charles E. (d 1889)
actor EA/90*

BISHOP, Charlotte (d 1883)
EA/84*

BISHOP, David (1857-1921) singer
SR

BISHOP, Mrs. George E. (d
1891) EA/92*

BISHOP, George Walter (1886-
1965) English critic COC,
OC/3, WWT/6-13, WWW/6

BISHOP, Harry W. see Robinson, Harry

BISHOP, Henry (fl 1784-90)
violinist, dancing master,
dancer? BD

BISHOP, Sir Henry Rowley
(1786-1855) English com-
poser CDP, DD, DNB,
ES, SR

BISHOP, James (d 1881 [88])
showman EA/82*

BISHOP, Jane (d 1969) performer
BP/53*

BISHOP, Jane Mary (d 1900) EA/
01*

BISHOP, Joe (b 1931) American
actor TW/13-16

BISHOP, Joey [Joseph Abraham
Gottlieb] (b 1919) American
comedian CB

BISHOP, Mrs. John see Bishop,
Ann

BISHOP, Kate (1847-1923) actress
DD, GRB/3-4, OAA/2, WWT/
1-4

BISHOP, Laura S. (fl 1859) dramatic reader HAS

BISHOP, Lilian (d 1917) EA/18*

BISHOP, Louisa (fl 1863-64) actress HAS

BISHOP, Richard (1898-1956)
American actor TW/1-3, 12

BISHOP, Robert (fl 1677) trumpeter
BD

BISHOP, Robert H., III (1916-63)
American producer, attorney
BE

BISHOP, Ronald (b 1923) American
actor TW/23-24, 27, 30

BISHOP, Rose see Egan, Rose

BISHOP, Sallie American actress
HAS

BISHOP, Samuel (1731-95) English
dramatist CP/3, DD

BISHOP, T. Brigham CDP

BISHOP, Thomas (fl 1837-52) English singer CDP, DD, HAS,
SR

BISHOP, Tom (d 1872) singer EA/
73*

BISHOP, Ward (d 1966 [66]) stage
manager TW/23

BISHOP, Washington Irving (d 1889
[41]) mind reader CDP

BISHOP, Will (1867-1944) English
dancer, ballet master, producer
GRB/1-4, WWT/1-5

BISHOP, William (1918-59) American actor BE*

BISPHAM, David Scull (1857-1921)
American singer DAB, DD,
ES, GRB/1-4, SR, WWA/1,
WWM, WWS, WWW/2

BISSELL, Richard (1913-77) American dramatist BE

BISSETT, Mr. (fl 1791) actor HAS

BISSETT, Donald J. (b 1930) American educator BE

BISSHOPP, Mrs. C. H. (d 1916)

EA/17*

BISSON, Mary Ann (d 1877 [64])
actress EA/78*
BISTEGHI, Achille Scipione see
Brizzi, Sig.
BITHMERE, Mme. (fl 1784-87)
French dancer BD
BITHMERE, A[ugustin?] (fl 1783)
French dancer BD
BITHMERE, Augustine Louis (fl
1784-87) French dancer BD
BITHMERE, Marie Françoise
(fl 1784-88) French dancer,
actress BD
BITTI, Alexander (fl 1715-30)
violinist BD
BITTLESTONE, George (d 1869
[50]) machinist EA/70*
BITTNER, Jack (b 1938) Amer-
ican actor TW/4-5, 29
BIVENS, Burke (d 1967 [64])
composer/lyricist BP/52*
BIXBY, Bill (b 1934) American
actor TW/23
BIXBY, Frank (fl 1890s) drama-
tist SR
BIZET, Georges (1838-75)
French composer ES
BJOERLING, Jussi (1911-60)
Swedish singer CB, ES,
WWA/4, WWW/5
BJÖNER, Ingrid (b 1932) Nor-
wegian singer ES
BJORKMAN, Edwin August
(1866-1951) critic, trans-
lator BE*
BJÖRLING, Sigurd (b 1907)
Swedish singer ES
BJÖRNSON, Björnstjerne (1832-
1910) Norwegian dramatist
COC, GRB/1-4, OC/1-3
BLACHER, Boris (d 1975 [72])
composer/lyricist BP/59*
BLACK, Alfred (b 1913) Eng-
lish manager WWT/11-15
BLACK, Arthur John (1855-
1936) English painter
WWW/3
BLACK, David (b 1931) Amer-
ican producer BE, WWT/
15-16
BLACK, Donna Olivia (b 1948)
American actress TW/27
BLACK, Dorothy (b 1899) South
African actress ES,
WWT/6-13
BLACK, Eugene R. (b 1898)
American executive BE

BLACK, George (1890-1945) English
manager, producer COC, ES,
OC/1-3, WWT/9
BLACK, George (1911-70) English
manager WWT/11-14
BLACK, Jean Ferguson (d 1969
[68]) dramatist BP/54*
BLACK, Jessica (b 1884) English
actress GRB/1-2
BLACK, J. Moreton (d 1892 [31])
dramatist EA/93*
BLACK, Karen (b 1942) American
actress CB
BLACK, Kenneth (b 1856) Scottish
actor GRB/1-2
BLACK, Mrs. Kenneth see Kirk,
Jessie
BLACK, Kitty (b 1914) South African
dramatist WWT/11-16
BLACK, Lew (d 1971 [60]) performer
BP/55*
BLACK, Maggie (d 1898) EA/99*
BLACKBURN, Mr. (fl 1780) actor
BD
BLACKBURN, Aubrey (d 1974 [74])
agent BTR/74
BLACKBURN, Clarice American
actress TW/12, 21
BLACKBURN, Dorothy American
actress BE, TW/30
BLACKBURN, John ["Cleo"] (d
1887 [34]) EA/88*
BLACKBURN, Joseph (d 1841)
American clown HAS, SR
BLACKBURN, Robert (b 1925)
American actor TW/13-18, 28
"BLACK DICK" (fl 1597) actor DA
BLACKER, Mr. (fl 1773) English
actor HAS
BLACKER, Henry (b 1724) giant
BD, CDP
BLACKET, Joseph (d 1810 [c. 24])
dramatist CP/3
BLACKFORD, Mr. (fl 1791-92)
house servant? BD
BLACKHAM, Olive English marion-
ettist ES
BLACKIE, Gregory Watt ["G. W.
Blake"] (d 1868 [39]) stage
manager EA/69*
BLACKLER, Betty (b 1929) English
actress WWT/10-14
BLACKLOCK, Dr. Thomas (1721-
91) Scottish dramatist CP/3
BLACKLY, Mr. (fl 1715) singer
BD
BLACKMAN, Eugene J. (b 1932)
American educator BE

BLACKMAN, Fred J. (1879-
1951) English producer
WWT/5-9
BLACKMAN, Honor actress
WWT/15-16
BLACKMER, Sidney (1894/95/
98-1973) American actor,
producer, director BE,
TW/1-17, 20, 30, WWT/
6-15
BLACKMERE, Sydney see
Blackmer, Sidney
BLACKMORE, Mr. (fl 1786-1804)
scene painter BD
BLACKMORE, Mr. (fl 1790)
puppeteer BD
BLACKMORE (d 1838) tight-rope
dancer EA/72*
BLACKMORE, Mrs. (fl 1791)
rope dancer BD
BLACKMORE, Master (fl 1798-
1807?) dancer, rope dancer,
actor, singer, esquestrian BD
BLACKMORE, Arthur (d 1894
[30]) agent EA/95*
BLACKMORE, Herbert (d 1938
[77]) agent WWT/14*
BLACKMORE, Peter (b 1909)
English dramatist WWT/
12-15
BLACKMORE, Robert (d 1879
[45]) agent EA/80*
BLACKMORE, Master T. (fl
1798-1807) dancer, rope
dancer, actor, singer,
equestrian BD
BLACKMORE, William (fl 1754-
70) tailor BD
"BLACK PRINCE, The" (fl 1700)
dwarf BD
"BLACK STORM, The" see
Collins, W. J.
BLACKTON, Jack (b 1938)
American actor TW/25-28,
30
BLACKTON, Jay (b 1909) Amer-
ican musical director, con-
ductor, composer BE
BLACKWAGE, William (fl 1594)
actor? servant? DA
BLACKWELL, Carlyle (1888-
1955) American actor ES,
TW/12
BLACKWELL, Carlyle, Jr. (d
1974 [61]) performer BP/
59*
BLACKWELL, Earl (b 1914)
American publisher BE

BLACKWELL, Henry (fl 1698)
fencing master? BD
BLACKWELL, Henry see Court-
ney, Baron
BLACKWOOD, George (b 1904)
American actor TW/3-6
BLACKWOOD, Thomas (fl 1592-
1603) actor DA
"BLADDERBRIDGE, Mr." (fl 1774)
musician BD
BLADEN, Martin (d 1746) English
dramatist CP/1-3, DD, GT
BLAGDEN, Mr. (fl 1760-67?)
dancer BD
BLAGDEN, Mr. (fl 1765-77) dresser
BD
BLAGDEN, [Mr. ?] (fl 1776-77)
dresser BD
BLAGDEN, Master (fl 1755-59)
dancer BD
BLAGDEN, Miss (fl 1759-62)
dancer BD
BLAGDEN, Nicholas (fl 1660-68)
actor BD
BLAGOI, George (d 1971 [73])
performer BP/56*
BLAGRAVE, John (fl 1683-94)
musician BD
BLAGRAVE, Robert (fl 1660-69)
instrumentalist BD
BLAGRAVE, Thomas (d 1688)
English instrumentalist, singer
BD, DNB
BLAGROVE, Henry Gamble (d 1872
[61]) violinist EA/74*
BLAGROVE, Richard Manning (d
1895 [69]) musician EA/96*
BLAGROVE, Thomas master of
the Revels COC, OC/3
BLAGROVE, William (fl 1624-35)
deputy to the master of the
Revels DA
BLAIKE, Ben (fl 1826) actor CDP,
HAS
BLAINE, Jimmy (d 1967 [42]) pro-
ducer, writer, actor TW/23
BLAINE, Vivian [née Stapleton]
(b 1923) American actress,
singer AAS, BE, TW/7-16,
19, 23, 28, WWT/12-16
BLAIR, Mr. (fl 1772-91) actor
BD
BLAIR, Mr. (d 1823) actor HAS
BLAIR, Barbara (b 1944) American
actress TW/30
BLAIR, Betsy (b 1923) American
actress BE, ES
BLAIR, David (1932-76) English

dancer, choreographer CB, ES

BLAIR, Eugenie (d 1922 [54]) American actress SR, WWA/5

BLAIR, George (d 1970 [64]) producer/director/choreographer BP/54*

BLAIR, Helen Bowen (d 1972 [82]) patron BP/57*

BLAIR, Isla (b 1944) Indian/English actress WWT/16

BLAIR, Janet American actress, singer, dancer BE

BLAIR, Joan [Mrs. A. S. Homewood] English actress GRB/1-2

BLAIR, John (d 1948 [73]) actor WWT/14*

BLAIR, Joyce [née Ogus] (b 1932) English actress, dancer WWT/15-16

BLAIR, Lionel [né Ogus] (b 1931) Canadian/English dancer, choreographer, actor WWT/15-16

BLAIR, Mary (d 1947 [52]) American actress TW/4

BLAIR, Phyllis [Mrs. J. E. Vedrenne] English actress GRB/1-4

BLAIR, William (d 1891) actor EA/92*

BLAIR, William (b 1896) American house manager, press representative BE

BLAISDELL, John W. (1840-1911) American actor, manager SR

BLAISDELL, William (1867-1930) actor SR

BLAK, John (fl 1624) lessee DA

BLAKE, Mr. (fl 1753?-98?) dancer, ballet master BD

BLAKE, Mr. (fl 1760-61) dancer BD

BLAKE, Mrs. (fl 1761) dancer BD

BLAKE, Miss (fl 1821) singer DD

BLAKE, Annie (b 1849) American actress HAS

BLAKE, Benjamin (1751-1827) English musician, composer, teacher BD

BLAKE, Betty (b 1920)

American publisher BE

BLAKE, Brandon English actor, dramatist, general manager GRB/2

BLAKE, Caroline (1798-1881) actress CDP

BLAKE, Charles (fl 1868) writer DD

BLAKE, Eubie (b 1883) American composer, lyricist CB

BLAKE, F. J. (d 1874) treasurer EA/76*

BLAKE, Flora [Mrs. Harry Blake] (d 1910) EA/11*

BLAKE, George see Redmond, Charles

"BLAKE, G. W." see Blackie, Gregory Watt

BLAKE, Mrs. Harry see Blake, Flora

BLAKE, James (fl 1794-1802?) singer BD

BLAKE, Joanna [Mrs. Adam Alexander] (d 1895) actress, singer EA/96*

BLAKE, John (d 1849 [58]) American? treasurer CDP

BLAKE, John (d 1878 [26]) actor EA/79*

BLAKE, Madge (d 1969) performer BP/53*

BLAKE, Maria Louisa Aylmer (d 1876) EA/77*

BLAKE, Minnie (d 1908) EA/09*

BLAKE, Orlando (b 1832) American actor HAS

BLAKE, Mrs. Orlando [Julia Weston] (b 1840) American actress HAS

BLAKE, Robert (b 1933) American actor CB

BLAKE, Robert (d 1975) manager BP/59*

BLAKE, Sydney (b 1951) Italian/American actor TW/30

BLAKE, Thomas (fl 1798) musician BD

BLAKE, Thomas G. dramatist DD

BLAKE, Violet Fisher (d 1967 [70]) performer BP/51*

BLAKE, William (1757-1827) English dramatist CP/3

BLAKE, William (d 1866) gymnast HAS

BLAKE, William Rufus (1805-63) Canadian actor, impresario CDP, DAB, DD, ES, GC, HAS, SR, WWA/H

BLAKE, Mrs. William Rufus
[Caroline Placide] (1798-
1881) American actress DD,
HAS
BLAKELEY, James (1873-1915)
English actor GRB/1-4,
WWS, WWT/1-3
BLAKELEY, Thomas see
Blakely, Thomas H.
BLAKELEY, Tom S. (b 1790)
actor, composer SR
BLAKELEY, William S. (1830-
97) actor DD, DNB, DP
BLAKELOCK, Denys (1901-70)
English actor WWT/6-14,
WWW/6
BLAKELY, Colin (b 1930) Irish
actor AAS, WWT/14-16
BLAKELY, Don F. (d 1976
[49]) producer/director/
choreographer BP/60*
BLAKELY, Gene (b 1922)
American actor BE, TW/
2-3, 6-8, 11-19, 24
BLAKELY, Thomas H. (fl 1782-
1840) American actor DD,
HAS
BLAKELY, William see
Blakeley, William
BLAKEMORE, Michael (b
1928) Australian actor,
director AAS, WWT/15-16
BLAKENEY, Olive (b 1899)
American actress WWT/
7-12
BLAKES, Mr. (fl 1698) actor?
booth operator BD
BLAKES, Mr. (fl 1761) fire
eater BD
BLAKES, Charles (d 1763)
actor, singer BD, CDP,
TD/2
BLAKEY, Mr. (fl 1743-63)
actor BD
BLAKISTON, Clarence (1864-
1943) English actor GRB/
1-4, WWT/1-9
BLAKISTON, Sydney (d 1917
[47]) professor of music
EA/18*
BLAMAUER, Karoline see
Lenya, Lottie
BLAME, Mr. (fl 1794) singer
BD
BLAMEY, Frederick (d 1944
[58]) actor, singer WWT/14*
BLAMIRE, William (d 1868)
scene artist, property man

EA/69*
BLAMPHIN, Charles (d 1895 [64])
harpist, composer EA/96*
BLANC, Ernest (b 1923) French
singer ES
BLANCH, Rev. John (b 1650?)
dramatist CP/1-3, DD, GT
BLANCH, William see Woodhull,
Fred
BLANCHAR, Pierre (d 1963 [67])
performer BP/48*
BLANCHARD, Mr. (fl 1819) actor
CDP
BLANCHARD, The Misses (fl 1789-
91) dancers BD
BLANCHARD, Amy (d 1910 [66])
burlesque artist EA/11*
BLANCHARD, Ann [Mrs. S. B.
Blanchard] (d 1874) EA/75*
BLANCHARD, Blanche (d 1893 [17])
trapezist EA/94*
BLANCHARD, Cecilia [Mrs. William
Blanchard] (d 1869 [89]) actress
HAS
BLANCHARD, Edward Leman (1820-
89) English dramatist, critic
CDP, COC, DD, EA/68, ES,
OC/1-3
BLANCHARD, Mrs. Edward Leman
(d 1907 [86]) GRB/3*
BLANCHARD, Edwin H. (d 1973
[78]) journalist, publicist BP/58*
BLANCHARD, Elizabeth Walker
see Charles, Elizabeth Walker
BLANCHARD, Jane (d 1903) EA/
05*
BLANCHARD, Jean-Pierre (b 1753)
French balloonist, exhibitor BD,
CDP
BLANCHARD, J. H. S. (d 1874
[43]) comic singer EA/75*
BLANCHARD, Kitty [Mrs. Arthur
McKee Rankin] (1847-1911)
American actress CDP, COC,
OC/2-3, PP/3
BLANCHARD, Lillian (d 1966 [91])
performer BP/50*
BLANCHARD, Mari (d 1970) per-
former BP/54*
BLANCHARD, Sarah (d 1875 [89])
EA/76*
BLANCHARD, Mrs. S. B. see
Blanchard, Ann
BLANCHARD, Thomas (fl 1766-87)
actor BD
BLANCHARD, Thomas (1760-97)
English actor BD, COC, DD,
OC/1-3, TD/1-2

BLANCHARD, Thomas (d 1859 [72]) actor CDP, COC, OC/1-3

BLANCHARD, Mrs. Thomas [Charlotte Wright] (b 1761) English singer, actress BD

BLANCHARD, William (1769-1835) English actor BS, CDP, COC, DD, DNB, ES, HAS, OC/1-3, OX, SR, TD/1-2

BLANCHARD, Mrs. William see Blanchard, Cecilia

BLANCHE, Mme. [Millie Catherine Nelson] (d 1896 [64]) circus performer EA/97*

BLANCHE, Mlle. (d 1892) rope dancer EA/93*

BLANCHE, Ada (1862/68-1953) English actress, singer CDP, DD, GRB/1-4, WWT/1-6

BLANCHE, Belle [Blanche Minzesheimer] (1891-1963) American actress, mimic WWS

BLANCHE, Edith (d 1929 [63]) actress WWT/14*

BLANCHE, Marie (b 1893) English actress, singer WWT/3-9

BLANCHFIELD, Charles E. (d 1971 [83]) performer BP/56*

BLANCK, Nicholas (d 1778) musician BD

BLAND, Mr. (fl 1790) actor CDP

BLAND, Mr. see Welson, Mr.

BLAND, Alan (1897-1946) English press representative WWT/7-9

BLAND, Charles (fl 1826-34) singer DD

BLAND, George (d 1753) actor BD

BLAND, George (d 1807) English actor BD, COC, OC/1-3, TD/1-2

BLAND, Mrs. George [née Maria Theresa Catherine Tersi; sometimes called Romani, Romanzini] (1770-1838) singer, actress BD, CDP, DD, DNB, EA/92, GT, OC/1-3, OX, TD/1-2

BLAND, Georgina (d 1881 [78])

EA/83*

BLAND, Harcourt (d 1875 [64]) actor BE*, EA/76*, WWT/14*

BLAND, Harry [Henry Clifford] (d 1888) actor EA/89*

BLAND, Humphrey (1812-69) English actor HAS

BLAND, Mrs. Humphrey [née Emily Lewis] (d 1880 [41]) American actress HAS

BLAND, Mrs. Humphrey see Faucit, Harriet

BLAND, James (fl 1784-1815) Scottish actor BD

BLAND, James (1798-1861) English actor, singer CDP, DD, OC/1-3

BLAND, James A. (1854-1911) American composer, minstrel HJD, SR

BLAND, John (d 1788) dramatist CP/2-3, DD, DNB

BLAND, Joyce (1906-63) Welsh actress ES, WWT/7-10

BLAND, Maria Theresa Romanzini see Bland, Mrs. George

BLAND, Robert Henderson (d 1941) actor, dramatist GRB/1-2

BLAND, Thomas Beckford (d 1870 [51]) duologue artist EA/71*

BLAND, W. Humphrey see Bland, Humphrey

BLAND, Zoe (d 1883) actress EA/84*

BLANDE, Edith (d 1923 [64]) actress DD

BLANDE, Sarah Ann (d 1901 [76]) EA/02*

BLANDFORD, Mr. (fl 1789) actor BD

BLANDFORD, F. W. (d 1879 [24]) actor EA/80*

BLANDFORD, Margaret (d 1884) EA/85*

BLANDFORD, Percy (fl 1880s) singer, actor OAA/2

BLANDWICK, Clara (d 1962 [81]) American actress WWM

BLANDY, Mr. (fl 1781-87) constable BD

BLANE, Elizabeth Bridget see Armstead, Mrs.

BLANE, Ralph [né Hunsecker] (b 1914) American composer, actor, singer, producer, director, dramatist BE

BLANEY, Miss (fl 1781-82) actress BD

BLANEY, Charles Edward (1868-1944) American manager, dramatist GRB/2-4, SR, WWT/1-6

BLANEY, Harry Clay (b 1874/78) American actor WWM, WWS

BLANEY, H. Clay (1908-64) American producer BE

BLANEY, John (fl 1609-26) actor DA

BLANEY, Norah (b 1896) English actress, composer, pianist WWT/5-8, 14-15

BLANFIELD, Mr. (fl 1767) pyrotechnist BD

BLANGY, Hermine (fl 1846) dancer CDP, HAS

BLANK, William Alexander (fl 1605) Scottish dancer DA

BLANKENSHIP, Vicki (b 1941) American actress TW/23

BLANKFORT, Michael (b 1907) American dramatist BE

BLANKSHINE, Robert (b 1948) American actor TW/29

BLANT, Mr. (fl 1788) house servant? BD

BLASINI, Elisa (b 1848) Austrian dancer HAS

BLASIS, Carlo (1795-1878) Italian dancer, choreographer, ballet master ES

BLASS, Robert (b 1867) American singer WWM

BLASTOCK, Mr. (fl 1735-36) actor BD

BLATCHLEY, W. E. (d 1889) actor EA/91*

BLATT, Edward A. (b 1905) American producer, director, manager BE

BLAU, Bela (d 1940 [44]) Hungarian producer BE*, BP/25*

BLAU, Herbert (b 1926) American director, educator, producer, dramatist BE, ES

BLAUVELT, Lilian [Mrs. William F. Pendleton] (1874-1947) American singer GRB/1, WWA/2, WWM, WWS

BLAVIS, Joseph Henry (d 1894 [55]) EA/95*

BLAYNEY, May (1875-1953) English actress TW/9, WWT/1-6

BLECHMAN, Marcus (d 1975 [67]) producer/director/choreographer BP/60*

BLECKNER, Jeff American director WWT/16

BLEDSOE, Earl (d 1962) performer BE*

BLEDSOE, Jules C. (1898-1943) American singer, actor, composer CB

BLEECK, John (d 1963 [83]) restaurateur BP/47*

BLEEZARDE, Gloria (b 1940) American actress TW/20, 23-24, 26

BLENDEL, Mr. (fl 1772) actor BD

BLENKINSOP-COULSON, H. B. see Conway, H. B.

BLENNOW, Alexandre (d 1892) horse trainer EA/93*

BLESSINGTON, Murrough Boyle, Lord (d 1702 [93]) dramatist CP/1-3, GT

BLEWITT, C. (fl 1785-88) singer BD

BLEWITT, Jonas (d 1805) organist, composer BD

BLEWITT, Jonathan (1782-1853) English musician, writer, composer, musical director CDP, DNB

BLEWITT, William (d 1884 [43]) music-hall performer EA/85*

BLEY, Maurice (b 1910) American community theatre director, producer BE

BLICK, Newton (1899-1965) actor WWT/14

BLIEDEN, Ivan Lawrence see Blyden, Larry

BLIGHT, John J. T. (d 1876 [75]) musician EA/77*

BLINCOE, Edward (d 1967 [28]) performer BP/51*

BLIND, Eric (d 1916) actor EA/18*

BLINK, George (fl 1837) dramatist DD

BLINN, Holbrook (1872-1928) American actor DAB, ES, GRB/1-4, SR, WWA/1, WWM, WWS, WWT/1-5

BLINN, Mrs. Holbrook see Benson, Ruth

BLINN, Nellie Holbrook (d 1909) actress BE*, WWT/14*

BLISS, Mr. (fl 1757) actor BD

BLISS, Anthony A. (b 1913) American lawyer BE
BLISS, Sir Arthur (1891-1975) English composer ES
BLISS, Hebe (d 1956 [79]) actress BE*, WWT/14*
BLISS, Helena [née Helen Louise Lipp] (b 1917/19) American actress, singer BE, TW/1-6, 10-13, WWT/11-16
BLISS, Herbert (b 1923) American dancer ES
BLISS, Imogene (b 1918) American actress TW/23-26, 30
BLISSET, Francis (1773-1850) actor CDP
BLISSETT, Mr. (fl 1797-1821) actor DD, TD/2
BLISSETT, Francis (1742?-1824) English actor BD, CDP, SR
BLITZ, Antonio (1810-77) English magician CDP, SR, WWA/H
BLITZSTEIN, Marc (1905-64) American composer, librettist AAS, BE, ES, MD, MH, MWD, NTH, TW/20, WWA/4
BLOCH, Bertram (b 1892) American dramatist BE
BLOCH, Ernest (1880-1959) Swiss/American composer ES
BLOCH, Rosine (d 1891 [41]) singer EA/92*
BLOCK, Chad (b 1938) American actor TW/23-24, 26-29
BLOCK, Larry (b 1942) American actor TW/28
BLOCK, Ralph (d 1974 [84]) dramatist BP/58*
BLOCK, Sheridan (fl 1900s) American actor WWS
BLOCK, Steven (b 1928) American talent representative BE
BLOCK, William Norris see Norris, William
BLOCK, William J. (d 1932 [63]) American manager WWS
BLOCKER, Dan (d 1972 [43]) performer BP/56*
BLODGET, Alden S. (d 1964 [80]) American producer, manager BE*
BLOFSON, Richard (b 1933)

American stage manager, producer, lighting designer BE
BLOGG, Mr. (fl 1739-48) singer BD
BLOIS, Eustace (d 1933 [52]) impresario WWT/14*
BLOMFIELD, Charles William see Marlow, Harry
BLOMFIELD, Derek (1920-64) English actor WWT/10-13
BLOMQUIST, Allen (b 1928) American director, educator BE
BLONDEL, Mons. (fl 1742) dancer BD
BLONDELL, Joan (b 1909/12) American actress BE, ES, TW/28, WWT/15-16
BLONDIN, Charles [Emile Gravele] (1824-97) tight-rope walker, acrobat CDP
BLONDIN, Charlotte Lawrence (d 1888) EA/90*
BLOOD, Adele [Mrs. Edward Davis] (1886-1936) American actress WWM
BLOOD, J. J. (fl 1885-91) dramatist DD
BLOODGOOD, Clara Sutton (1870-1907) American actress GRB/2-3, SR, WWA/1
BLOODGOOD, Harry [Carlos Mauran] (d 1886 [41]) comedian, minstrel CDP
BLOOM, Claire (b 1931) English actress AAS, BE, CB, ES, TW/13-16, 27-28, WWT/11-16
BLOOM, Norton L. (d 1972 [45]) producer/director/choreographer BP/57*
BLOOM, Rube (d 1976 [73]) composer/lyricist BP/60*
BLOOM, Sol (b 1870) American actor, songwriter SR
BLOOM, Verna American actress TW/23, 28
BLOOMER, Mr. (fl 1784) singer BD
BLOOMFIELD, Mr. (fl 1787-92) actor BD
BLOOMGARDEN, Kermit (1904-76) American producer, manager BE, CB, WWT/11-16
BLORE, Eric (1887-1959) English actor ES, TW/15, WWT/5-10
BLOSSOM, Henry Martyr, Jr. (1866-1919) American dramatist GRB/3-4, SR, WWA/1, WWS, WWT/1-3
BLOUNT, Arthur (b 1877) English

actor GRB/1

BLOUNT, Helon (b 1929) American actress, singer TW/29, WWT/16

BLOW, John (1649-1708) English composer, organist, teacher BD, CDP, DNB, ES

BLOW, Mark (d 1921 [49]) English actor, manager GRB/2

BLOW, Sydney [Jellings-Blow] (1878-1961) English actor, dramatist GRB/1-2, WWT/2-11, WWW/6

BLOWER, Mr. (fl 1777?-91) puppeteer, actor? BD

BLOWER, Miss A. (fl 1782) actress? BD

BLOWER, Elizabeth (b 1763) actress, singer BD

BLOWITZ, William F. (d 1964 [48]) American press representative BE*

BLUDRICK, Mr. (fl 1780) actor BD

BLUE, Ben (d 1975 [73]) actor, comedian BP/59*, WWT/16*

BLUE, Monte (d 1963 [73]) American actor, press representative BE*, BP/47*

BLUE, Rita Hassan (d 1973 [68]) actress, producer, critic TW/30

BLUETT, Gus (d 1936 [32]) actor, singer WWT/14*

BLUM, Daniel (1900-65) American writer, producer BE, ES, TW/21, WWA/4

BLUM, Edward (b 1928) American casting director BE

BLUM, Gustav (d 1963 [76]) producer TW/20

BLUM, Martin A. (d 1972 [36]) publicist BP/57*

BLUM, William (b 1901) American manager BE

BLUM, William David see Darrid, William

BLUMB, Mr. (fl 1792) imitator, pianist BD

BLUMBERG, Harold D. (b 1922) American costumier BE

BLUME, Mr. (fl 1783-85) box keeper BD

BLUME, Mrs. (fl 1783-85) dresser BD

BLUME, Heinrich (1788-1856) German singer ES

BLUMENFELD, Robert [Robert Fields] (b 1943) American actor, singer TW/27

BLUMENTHAL, George (1863?-1943) producer, manager CB

BLUMENTHAL, Jacques (1829-1908) German/English songwriter DNB

BLUMENTHAL, Oscar (1852-1917) German dramatist GRB/4, WWT/1-2

BLUMENTHAL, Richard M. (d 1962 [55]) French producer BE*

BLUMENTHAL-TAMARINA, Maria (d 1938 [79]) actress BE*, WWT/14*

BLUNDELL, James (d 1786) violoncellist, composer, singer BD

BLUNDIVILLE, John (fl 1665) singer BD

BLUNKALL, Ervin (1875-1943) actor SR

BLUNT, Mr. (fl 1689) actor BD

BLUNT, Mr. (fl 1744) actor BD

BLUNT, Mrs. (fl 1729-30) actress BD

BLUNT, Arthur Cecil see Cecil, Arthur

BLUNT, T. (fl 1794) violinist BD

BLURTON, James (b 1756) dancer, actor, singer BD

BLURTON, Mrs. James [Mary] (fl 1793-1800) actress, singer BD

BLY, Dan (d 1973 [37]) stage manager TW/29

BLYDE, Frederick (d 1887) EA/88*

BLYDEN, Larry [né Ivan Lawrence Blieden] (1925-75) American actor, director, producer BE, TW/23-25, 28-29, WWT/15-16

BLYTHE, Betty (d 1972 [72]) actress BP/56*, WWT/16*

BLYTHE, Bobby (b 1894) Australian actor, singer WWT/5-7

BLYTHE, Charles M. (d 1886 [58]) actor EA/87*

BLYTHE, Coralie (1880-1928) actress GRB/1-4, WWT/1-5

BLYTHE, Mrs. G. see Blythe, M.

BLYTHE, George (d 1892 [56]) EA/93*

BLYTHE, Mrs. George see Birchenough, Bella

BLYTHE, Herman see Barrymore, Maurice

BLYTHE, Mrs. James S. see

Hodson, Sylvia
BLYTHE, John (b 1921) English
   actor   WWT/16
BLYTHE, Mrs. John S.   see
   Hodson, Sylvia
BLYTHE, J. S. (d 1918)   EA/
   19*
BLYTHE, M. [Mrs. G. Blythe]
   (d 1875 [32])   EA/76*
BLYTHE, Stephen (d 1889)
   musical director   EA/90*
BLYTHE, T. Gordon (d 1974
   [85])   actor   BTR/74
BLYTHE, Violet   actress, singer
   WWT/4-13
BLYTH-PRATT, Violet   actress
   WWT/5-6
BOADEN, James (1762-1839)
   English dramatist, critic
   CDP, COC, CP/3, DD, ES,
   GT, OC/1-3, TD/1-2
BOAG, William (d 1939 [72])
   American actor, manager
   BP/23*
BOAK, Alfred Brydone   see
   Brydone, Alfred
BOAK, Eliza Brydone (d 1913
   [76])   EA/14*
BOARDMAN, Lillian [Mrs. Lil-
   lian Boardman Smith] (d
   1953 [60])   actress   BE*,
   BP/38*
BOARDMAN, Virginia True (d
   1971 [82])   performer   BP/
   56*
BOARER, Beatrice (d 1954)
   actress   WWT/14*
BOAZ, Charles (b 1919) Amer-
   ican actor   TW/8-10, 21
BOBADILLA, Pepita [née Nelly
   Burton] Ecuadorian actress
   WWT/4-5
BOBBIE, Walter (b 1945)
   American actor   TW/28-30
BOCCHINI, Sig. (fl 1773-74)
   dancer   BD
BOCHERT, Charles G. (d 1971
   [92])   publicist   BP/56*
BOCHSA, Robert-Nicholas-
   Charles (1789-1856) French
   harpist, composer   ES
BOCK, Jerry (b 1928) American
   composer   AAS, BE, WWT/
   15-16
BOCKELMANN, Rudolf (b 1892)
   German singer   ES
BODANZKY, Arthur (1877-1939)
   Austrian conductor   DAB,

ES, WWA/1
BODDA, Louisa Fanny   see   Pyne,
   Louisa Fanny
BODDAPYNE, Louisa Fanny   see
   Pyne, Louisa Fanny
BODDEN, James (d 1885) advance
   agent   EA/86*
BODDINGTON, Ernest Fearby (b
   1873) English/American dramatist
   WWA/5
BODDY, Edward (d 1918)   EA/19*
BODE, Allan (d 1975 [69]) performer
   BP/60*
BODE, Milton (1860/63-1938) Eng-
   lish manager, actor   GRB/4,
   WWT/1-8
BODEL, Burman (d 1969 [58]) per-
   former   BP/54*
BODEN, Rosa Augusta (d 1888 [78])
   actress   EA/89*
BODENHAM, Mr. (fl 1672) musician
   BD
BODENHAM, Estelle D'Arcy   see
   Yelland, Estelle D'Arcy
BODENHEIM, Maxwell (1893-1954)
   American performer   BE*
BODENS, Cpt. Charles (fl 1732-60)
   dramatist   CP/1-3, GT, TD/2
BODIE, Jack [Pat Murphy] (d 1917)
   comedian, dancer   EA/18*
BODIE, Jeannie (d 1909)   EA/10*
BODIN, Mr. (fl 1742) rope dancer,
   tumbler   BD
BODKIN, Thomas V. (d 1974 [87])
   manager   BP/58*
BODLEY, Ellen (d 1969) dramatist
   BP/54*
BODOM, Borghild (b 1908) Norwegian
   actress, singer   WWT/7
BODWIN, Mr. (fl 1784) bassoonist
   BD
BODY, W. (fl 1742-45) proprietor
   BD
BOEHM, Gustav (b 1854) Austrian/
   American dramatist   WWM
BOEHNEL, Molly (d 1963 [56])
   dramatist   BP/47*
BOESE, Joachim (d 1971 [38])
   performer   BP/55*
BOESEN, William (d 1972 [48])
   performer   BP/56*
BOETTCHER, Henry F. (b 1903)
   American educator, director   BE
BOGAERDE, Derek van den   see
   Bogarde, Dirk
BOGARD, Travis (b 1918) American
   educator   BE
BOGARDE, Dirk [Derek van den

Bogaerde] (b 1920/21) English
actor CB, ES, WWT/11-14
BOGARDUS, Cpt. A. N. (d 1913)
American marksman SR
BOGART, Andrew (b 1874)
American actor WWS
BOGART, David (d 1964 [81])
singer, actor BE*
BOGART, Humphrey DeForest (1899-
1957) American actor, producer
CB, ES, SR, TW/13, WWA/3,
WWT/8-10, WWW/5
BOGDANOFF, Leonard (d 1975
[50]) financier BP/60*
BOGDANOFF, Rose (d 1957
[53]) American designer BE*
BOGEL, Alexandra (d 1879 [35])
singer EA/80*
BOGERT, William (b 1936) Ameri-
can actor TW/24-25, 28-30
BOGGETTI, Victor (b 1895)
English actor WWT/10-12
BOGGS, Gail (b 1951) American
actress TW/29
BOHAM, Mr. (fl 1741) actor BD
BOHEE, George B. (b 1857) Can-
adian variety artist GRB/1
BOHEE, James Douglas (d 1897
[53]) comedian EA/99*
BOHEME, Anthony (d 1731)
actor BD, DD
BOHEME, Mrs. Anthony, II
(fl 1730) actress BD
BOHM, Joseph (1795-1876)
violinist, composer CDP
BOHM, Karl (b 1894) Austrian
conductor CB
BOHNEN, Michael (b 1888)
German ES
BOHNEN, Roman (1901-49) Amer-
ican actor ES, TW/5, WWT/10
BOIELDIEU, Adrien (d 1883
[67]) composer EA/84*
BOIMAISON, Mr. (fl 1788-96)
actor BD
BOIMAISON, Mrs. (fl 1793-96)
actress, singer BD
BOISEY, Michael see Boissy,
Michael
BOISGERARD, Mons. (fl 1791-1820)
dancer, choreographer BD
BOISGERARD, Mme. (fl 1791)
dancer BD
BOISSET (d 1901 [34]) gymnast,
pantomimist EA/03*
BOISSET, Fred (d 1895 [32]) gym-
nast, pantomimist EA/96*
BOISSY [or Boisey], Michael (fl 1752)

French dramatist CP/2-3, GT
BOITAR, Beatrice (fl 1729) actress
BD
BOITO, Arrigo (1842-1919) Italian
composer, librettist ES
BOKER, George Henry (1823-90)
American dramatist CDP, COC,
DAB, DD, ES, HJD, MH, OC/
1-3, RE
BOKOR, Margit (b 1909) Hungarian
singer WWA/3
BOLADO, Maria Margharita see
Margo
BOLAM, F. W. (d 1913 [50]) EA/14*
BOLAM, James (b 1938) English
actor WWT/15-16
BOLAN, Jeanne (d 1976 [49]) per-
former BP/60*
BOLAND, Bridget (b 1913) English
dramatist CD, PDT
BOLAND, Clay A. (d 1963 [59])
composer BP/48*
BOLAND, Eddie (b 1885) American
actor ES
BOLAND, Mary (1885-1965) Ameri-
can actress BE, ES, GRB/3-4,
TW/2-16, 22, WWA/4, WWM,
WWT/1-13
BOLAND, William (d 1953 [69])
singer WWT/14*
BOLASNI, Saul (b 1923) American
costume designer BE
BOLENDER, Todd (b 1914) American
dancer, choreographer, ballet
master ES
BOLENO, Emma (d 1867 [35])
actress EA/68*
BOLENO, Gardiner (d 1891) EA/92*
BOLENO, Harry (d 1875) clown CDP
BOLENO, Mrs. H. G. (d 1875) EA/
76*
BOLENO, Mrs. H. G. (d 1888) EA/
89*
BOLENO, Samson (d 1872) music-
hall performer EA/73*
BOLENO MARSH see Tolkein,
Alfred
BOLERO [Wilson Storey] (d 1910
[33]) acrobat, clown EA/12*
BOLES, Athena Lorde (d 1973
[57]) performer BP/58*
BOLES, John (1900-69) American
actor, singer BE, ES, TW/1,
25, WWT/7-12
BOLESLAVSKY, Richard (1889-1937)
Polish producer, director ES,
NTH, WWT/6-8
BOLEY, May (d 1963 [81]) musical

comedy actress TW/19

BOLEYN, Richard Smith (fl 1870-
80) English actor OAA/1-2

BOLEYN, Mrs. Richard Smith
see Brough, Fanny Whiteside

BOLGER, Ray[mond Wallace] (b
1904/06) American actor, dancer
AAS, BE, CB, ES, TW/2-20,
25, WWT/9-16

BOLGER, Robert (d 1969 [32])
performer BP/54*

BOLIN, Shannon (b 1917)
American actress, singer
BE, TW/20, 22, 26

BOLINGBROKE, Mrs. (fl 1777)
actress BD

BOLINI, Horace (d 1892)
singer EA/93*

BOLITHO, W. (d 1892) EA/93*

BOLLA, Maria (fl 1799-1804)
Italian singer, actress BD

BOLLAERT, James (d 1869
[57]) costumier EA/70*

BOLLARD, Robert Gordon (d 1964
[44]) musical director BP/49*

BOLLER, Robert O., Sr. (d
1962 [75]) architect BE*

BOLLINGER, Anne (d 1962
[39]) singer TW/19

BOLM, Adolph (1884/87-1951)
Russian dancer, choreog-
rapher ES, TW/7, WWT/
4, 9-11

BOLOGNA, Sig. (fl 1662-88)
puppeteer BD

BOLOGNA, Barbara (fl 1786-
1804) dancer BD

BOLOGNA, John Peter (1775-
1846) Italian harlequin,
dancer, tumbler, machinist
BD, CDP

BOLOGNA, Louis (d 1808) Italian
tumbler, clown, dancer, singer
BD

BOLOGNA, Mrs. Louis (fl 1799-
1800) dancer BD

BOLOGNA, Pietro (fl 1786-1814)
Italian clown, rope dancer BD

BOLOGNA, Mrs. Pietro (fl 1786-
98?) Italian tumbler, dancer,
singer BD

BOLSTER, Anita (b 1900) Irish
actress TW/2-6

BOLSTER, Stephen (b 1933) American actor TW/24, 27

BOLT, Carol (b 1941) Canadian
dramatist CD

BOLT, H. P. (d 1884 [68]) pro-

prietor EA/85*

BOLT, Robert Oxton (b 1924) Eng-
lish dramatist AAS, BE, CB,
CD, CH, COC, ES, MH, MWD,
OC/3, PDT, RE, WWT/13-16

BOLTON, Mr. (fl 1730-31) house
servant? BD

BOLTON, Mr. (fl 1773) actor BD

BOLTON, Mrs. (fl 1789-1801)
house servant BD

BOLTON, Mrs. (d 1913) EA/14*

BOLTON, A. J. (d 1917) manager
EA/18*

BOLTON, Caroline (d 1871 [28])
actress? EA/72*

BOLTON, Edwin L. (d 1971 [53])
critic BP/56*

BOLTON, Eliza (fl 1809) actress
CDP

BOLTON, G. Benson (d 1917 [27])
musician EA/18*

BOLTON, George (d 1868 [43]) actor,
manager EA/69*, WWT/14*

BOLTON, Guy Reginald (b 1881/
84/86) English dramatist, librettist AAS, BE, CD, ES, MWD,
PDT, SR, WWT/4-16

BOLTON, Jack (d 1962 [60]) talent
representative BE*

BOLTON, Lavinia, Duchess of
(1708-60) actress CDP, GT

BOLTON, Mary [Lady Thurlow]
(1790-1830) actress CDP, EA/79

BOLTON, Sam (d 1879 [32]) pantomimist EA/80*

BOLTON, Sarah (d 1893) writer
EA/94*

BOLTON, Thomas (d 1895) actor
EA/96*

BOLTON, Whitney (1900-69) American
critic BE, NTH, TW/26

BOMAN, Mr. (b c. 1695?) English
actor BD

BOMAN, Mrs. (fl 1716-56) singer,
dancer, actress BD

BOMAN [or Bowman], John (c. 1651?-
1739) English actor, singer BD,
DD

BOMAN, Mrs. John [née Elizabeth
Watson] (1677?-1707?) English
actress, singer BD

BOMBARDIN, Mr. (fl 1751) bassoonist BD

"BOMBASTINI, Sig." (fl 1759)
musician BD

"BOMBASTINI, Signora" (fl 1759)
dancer? BD

"BOMBASTO, Sig." (fl 1751-60)

singer, musician, dancer BD

"BOMBAZEENO, Sig. " (fl 1752-54) dancer BD

BONACCI, Anna (fl 20th cent) Italian dramatist ES

BONACICH, Walter Adey (d 1892 [44]) agent EA/93*

BONANOVA, Fortunio (d 1969 [73]) performer BP/53*

BONARELLI DELLA ROVERE, Guidobaldo (1563-1608) Italian dramatist COC, OC/1-3

BONARIUS, Harold (d 1917) musician EA/18*

BONASERA, Eftichios (1865-1928) Greek actor ES

BONCI, Alessandro (1870-1940) Italian singer ES, WWA/5

BOND, Mr. (fl 1784) singer BD

BOND, Professor (fl c. 1849) musician CDP

BOND, Acton (d 1941 [80]) Canadian actor, dramatist DD, GRB/1-4, WWT/1-6

BOND, Bert [Herbert Rowley] (d 1964 [81]) performer BE*

BOND, Carrie Jacobs (1862-1946) American composer BE*

BOND, C[hristopher] G[odfrey] (b 1945) English dramatist, actor CD

BOND, Edward (b 1935) English dramatist AAS, CD, CH, COC, PDT, WWT/15-16

BOND, Emmanuel (d 1874) music-hall performer EA/75*

BOND, Frederic Drew (1859/61-1914) American actor PP/1, WWS, WWT/1-2

BOND, Mrs. Frederick see Rose, Annie

BOND, Gary (b 1940) English actor TW/20, WWT/15-16

BOND, Henry Charles (d 1873 [41]) prompter EA/74*

BOND, Herbert (d 1869 [31]) singer EA/70*

BOND, Jean see Guillemen, Louis Charles

BOND, Jessie (1853-1942) English actress, singer CB, DD, DP, EA/95, OAA/2, SR, WWT/6-9

BOND, John (fl 1784-1807?) singer BD

BOND, Lilian (b 1910) English actress WWT/8-9

BOND, Ridge (b 1923) American actor TW/8

BOND, Rudy (b 1913/15) American actor, director BE, TW/4, 8, 23-25, 28-30

BOND, Sheila (b 1928) American actress, dancer, singer BE, TW/3-16, WWT/11-14

BOND, Sudie (b 1928) American actress, dancer BE, TW/22-27, 29-30, WWT/15-16

BOND, Thomas (d 1635) English actor CDP, DA, OC/1-3

BOND, Ward (d 1960 [c. 56]) American actor BE*

BOND, William (d 1735) English dramatist, actor CP/2-3, DD, DNB, GT, TD/1-2

BONDI, Beulah (b 1892) American actress BE, ES, WWT/7-9

BONDS, Margaret (d 1972 [59]) composer/lyricist BP/56*

BOND-SAYERS, Arthur (d 1912) musical director EA/13*

BONDY, Ed (b 1932) American talent representative BE

BONEFACE, George C. see Boniface, George C.

BONEFACE, George C., Jr. (d 1917) actor SR

BONEHILL, Mrs. (d 1904) EA/06*

BONEHILL, Bessie (d 1902) English actress, singer, music-hall comedienne CDP, SR

BONEHILL, Elias (d 1900 [75]) EA/02*

BONEHILL, Henry (d 1877 [30]) EA/88*

BONEHILL, Jane (d 1886 [35]) EA/87*

BONEHILL, Jessie (d 1884 [23]) singer, dancer EA/85*

BONEHILL, Marian (d 1874 [25]) singer EA/75*

BONELLE, Dick (b 1936) American actor TW/26, 28-30

BONELLI, William actor, dramatist SR

BONEMAN, Frederick (1833-1911) German singer SR

BONEN, William (fl 1623) English dramatist FGF

BONERZ, Peter (b 1938) American actor TW/27

BONEWAY, Mlle. (fl 1746) actress BD

BONFANTI, Luigi (fl 1794-98) singer BD

BONFANTI, Marietta (1847-1921) Italian/American dancer CDP, ES

BONFILS, Helen (d 1972 [82]) American producer, actress, publisher BE, TW/29, WWT/15

BONGARD, Hal (d 1967 [61]) executive BP/52*

BONHAM, Melville (d 1876) dramatic reader EA/78*

BONI, Daniela (b 1942) Italian actress TW/10

BONIFACE, George C. (1833-1912) American actor CDP, PP/1, SR

BONIFACE, Mrs. George C. (d 1883) actress BE*, WWT/14*

BONIFACE, George C., Jr. see Boneface, George C., Jr.

BONIME, Abby (b 1932) American actress TW/4

BONINSEGNA, Celestina (1877-1947) Italian singer ES

BONITA [Mrs. Lew Hearn] (b 1885) American comedienne WWM, WWS

BONN, Ferdinand (d 1933 [71]) actor WWT/14*

BONNAIRE, Mme. (d 1863 [28]) trapezist EA/69*

BONNAIRE, Henri (b 1869) French composer, journalist WWT/4

BONNELL, Jay (b 1932) American actor TW/27

BONNER, [Mrs.?] (fl 1791) actress BD

BONNER, Geraldine (fl 1887) American critic, dramatist WWM

BONNER, Isabel (d 1955 [47]) American actress TW/8, 12

BONNET, [Mr.?] (fl 1757-58) house servant? BD

BONNET, Eliza F. see White, Mrs. Cool

BONNET, James (b 1938) American actor TW/14-16

BONNEVAL, Mlle. (fl 1741-44) French dancer BD

BONNHEIM, Byron A. (d 1972 [54]) publicist BP/56*

BONNIE, Beatrice (d 1918 [35]) EA/19*

BONNOR, Charles (fl 1777-1829?) English actor, dramatist BD, CP/3, DD, DNB

BONOMI, Giac[inta?] (fl 1757-59) dancer BD

BONOCINI, Giovanni (1670-1747) Italian violoncellist, composer BD, CP/1, ES

BONSALL, Bessie (d 1963 [92]) performer BE*

BONSOR, Mr. (fl 1793-1810) doorkeeper BD

BONSTELLE, Jessie (1872-1932) American actress, manager, producer DAB, ES, NTH, OC/1-3, SR

BONTEMPS, Arna (d 1973 [70]) dramatist BP/58*

BONUS, Ben producer, dramatist, actor WWT/16

BONVILLE, Mr. [E. N. Morgan] (fl 1787-89) actor, singer BD

BONWICK, Miss (fl 1794) organist, singer BD

BONYNGE, Leta (b 1917) American actress TW/25-26

BOOKE, Sorrell (b 1930) American actor TW/23, 25, WWT/16

BOOKER, George [né Dingle] (d 1908 [49]) American comedian EA/09*

BOOKMAN, Leo (b 1932) American talent representative BE

BOOMAR, Mr. (fl 1719) singer BD

BOON, "Blind" Negro musician SR

BOONE, Lizzie [Mrs. P. L. Rose] (d 1897) actress, singer EA/98*

BOONE, Richard (b 1917) American actor, director BE, CB

BOONE, William (d 1891) EA/92*

BOOR, Frank (d 1938 [73]) Brazilian/English agent, manager GRB/1-2, WWT/4-8

BOORDE, Andrew (1490?-1549) English actor CDP

BOORN, Alfred (d 1886 [25]) equestrian EA/87*

BOORN, Benjamin, Jr. (d 1876 [25]) equestrian EA/77*

BOORN, James (d 1893 [73]) circus proprietor EA/94*

BOORNE, George (d 1893) equestrian EA/94*

BOOSE, Mr. C. (d 1868 [53]) bandmaster EA/69*

BOOSEY, Charles (d 1905 [78]) publisher EA/06*

BOOSEY, John (d 1893) concert organiser EA/94*

BOOSEY, Philip Harold see Cuningham, Philip

BOOSEY, William (d 1933 [69]) producer, publisher BE*, WWT/14*

BOOT, Gladys (d 1964 [74]) English actress WWT/13

BOOTE, Rosie [Marchioness of Headfort] (1878-1958) English actress COC, GRB/1, OC/3

BOOTH, Mr. (fl 1762-71) actor BD
BOOTH, Mr. (fl 1780-82) actor BD
BOOTH, Mr. (fl 1784) singer BD
BOOTH, Mrs. (fl 1740-41) actress
  BD
BOOTH, Mrs. (fl 1778) actress,
  dramatist CP/3
BOOTH, Miss (fl 1715) singer BD
BOOTH, Agnes [Marian Agnes Land
  Rookes] (1846-1910) Australian/
  American actress CDP, DAB,
  DD, ES, PP/1, SR, WWA/1
BOOTH, Arthur E. (d 1898 [29])
  gymnast EA/99*
BOOTH, Barton (1679?/81-1733)
  English actor, manager, dramatist
  BD, CDP, COC, CP/1-3, DD,
  DNB, ES, GT, OC/1-3, TD/1-2
BOOTH, Mrs. Barton, II [née
  Hester Santlow] (c. 1690-1773)
  English actress, dancer BD,
  CDP, DNB
BOOTH, Blanche de Bar (d 1930
  [86]) actress BE*, WWT/14*
BOOTH, Carol (b 1941) English
  actress TW/21
BOOTH, Charles (fl 1660?-82?)
  prompter BD
BOOTH, Cockran Joseph (d
  1789) actor, singer BD
BOOTH, Mrs. Cockran Joseph
  (fl 1774-91) actress BD
BOOTH, Edwin Thomas (1833-
  93) American actor CDP,
  COC, DAB, DD, DP, ES,
  HAS, HJD, NTH, OC/1-3,
  PDT, SR, WWA/H
BOOTH, Mrs. Edwin Thomas
  [Mary Devlin] (1840-62)
  American dancer HAS
BOOTH, Helen (d 1971) per-
  former BP/55*
BOOTH, Hope [Mrs. Rennold Wolf]
  (1872-1933) Canadian actress
  WWS
BOOTH, James [né Geeves-
  Booth] (b 1933) English actor
  AAS, WWT/14-16
BOOTH, J. H. English actor GRB/1
BOOTH, John (d 1779) perform-
  er? BD
BOOTH, John (fl 1780-96) tailor BD
BOOTH, Mrs. John [Ursula Agnes]
  (1740-1803) actress, singer BD
BOOTH, John E. (b 1919) Amer-
  ican writer BE
BOOTH, John Hunter (d 1971
  [85]) dramatist TW/28

BOOTH, John Wilkes (1838-65) Amer-
  ican actor CDP, COC, DAB, DD,
  ES, HAS, HJD, NTH, OC/1-3,
  PDT, SR, WWA/H
BOOTH, Joseph [né Martin] (d 1797)
  English actor, exhibitor BD
BOOTH, J. S. (1821-58) comedian
  HAS
BOOTH, Junius (d 1912 [c. 45])
  American actor GRB/1-2
BOOTH, Junius Brutus (1796-1852)
  English actor CDP, COC, DAB,
  DD, DNB, ES, HAS, HJD, NTH,
  OC/1-3, OX, PDT, RJ, SR,
  WWA/H
BOOTH, Junius Brutus, Jr. (1821-
  83) actor CDP, COC, DD, ES,
  HAS, OC/1-3, PDT, SR
BOOTH, Junius Brutus, III (b 1868)
  American actor SR
BOOTH, Mrs. Junius Brutus, Jr., I
  [née DeBar] (b 1810) Irish actress
  HAS
BOOTH, Mrs. Junius Brutus, Jr.,
  II [née Harriet Mace] (d 1859)
  actress HAS
BOOTH, Mrs. Junius Brutus, Jr.,
  III HAS
BOOTH, Mary (1840-62) actress
  CDP
BOOTH, Mary (d 1881) actress
  CDP
BOOTH, Nellie (d 1973 [84]) per-
  former BP/57*
BOOTH, Nesdon (d 1964 [45]) actor
  BE*
BOOTH, Rachel (d 1868 [55]) EA/69*
BOOTH, Rita (d 1892) actress SR
BOOTH, Rosalie Ann (d 1889 [65])
  EA/90*
BOOTH, Miss S. (b 1794) English
  actress BS
BOOTH, Sallie (d 1902 [63]) actress
  BE*, EA/03*, WWT/14*
BOOTH, Sarah (1793-1867) English
  actress CDP, DD, DNB, EA/92,
  OX
BOOTH, Shirley [née Thelma Booth]
  (b 1907) American actress AAS,
  BE, CB, ES, NTH, SR, TW/1-
  3, 5-19, 26-28, WWT/9-16
BOOTH, Sydney Barton (1873-1937)
  actor CDP, COC, OC/1-3, WWM
BOOTH, T. G. (d 1855) actor
  CDP, HAS
BOOTH, Thelma see Booth, Shirley
BOOTH, T[homas] B[ennett] (d 1872)
  actor SR

BOOTH, Webster (b 1902) English actor, singer WWT/10-13

BOOTHBY, Mr. (fl 1735-36) actor BD

BOOTHSBY, Sir Brooke (1743-1824) English dramatist CP/3, DD

BOOTHBY, Mrs. Frances (fl c. 1665) dramatist CP/1-3, GT

BOOTHE, Clare (b 1902/03) American dramatist CB, ES, HJD, MH, MWD, NTH, ST, WWT/9-12

BOQUET, Louis-René (1717-1814) French designer, decorator BD

BORAH, Leo Arthur (1889-1959) American editor WWA/4

BORANI, Charles [Henry Charles Moss] (d 1900 [37]) pantomimist EA/01*

BORCH, Gaston (b 1871) French composer, conductor WWM

BORCHARD, Mme. Comte (d 1866) singer, pianist HAS

BORCHERS, Gladys (b 1891) American educator BE

BORDEN, Olive (1907-47) American actress BE*

BORDO, Ed (b 1931) American actor TW/26, 28

BORDOGNI, Louisa (fl 1833) Italian singer CDP, ES

BORDONI, Irene (1895-1953) French actress, singer SR, TW/3, 5-9, WWT/4-11

BORDONI-HASSE, Faustina (1693-1781) Italian singer ES

BOREE, Albert (d 1910) German comedian EA/11*

BOREL, Louis see Borell, Louis

BORELL [or Borel], Louis (1906-73) Dutch actor TW/3, 29, WWT/9-14

BORELLA, Arthur James (1868-1947) American circus clown SR

BOREO, Emile (d 1951 [66]) Polish performer BE*, BP/36*

BORETZ, Allen (b 1900) American dramatist, composer BE

BORG, Veda Ann (d 1973 [58]) actress BP/58*, WWT/16*

BORGE, Victor (b 1909) Danish/American performer BE, CB

BORGHESA, Eufrasia (fl 1841-44) Italian singer CDP, HAS

BORGHI, Luigi (fl 1772-94) violinist, composer, manager BD

BORGHI, Signora Luigi [née Anna Casentini] (fl 1790-97) singer BD

BORGHI-MAMO, Adelaide (1829-1901) Italian singer CDP, ES

BORGIOLI, Dino (b 1891) Italian singer ES

BORGNINE, Ernest (b 1917) American actor CB, ES

BORI, Lucrezia (1889-1960) Spanish singer ES, TW/16, WWA/4

BORIS, Ruthanna (b 1918) American dancer, choreographer BE

BORLIN, Jean (1893-1930) Swedish dancer, choreographer ES

BORNAL, Mr. (fl 1796) puppeteer BD

BORNE, Constantine (fl 1768) freak BD

BORNE, Theophilus see Bird, Theophilus

BORNE, William see Bird, William

BOROMEO, Sig. (fl 1742-43) dancer BD

BOROSINI, Francesco (b c. 1690) Italian singer BD

BOROWSKY, Marvin S. (b 1907) American educator, writer BE

BORRANI, Sig. (fl 1854) singer CDP, HAS

BORRELLI, Jim (b 1948) American actor TW/27-30

BORRI, Pasquale (1820-84) Italian dancer, choreographer ES

BORROW, Sarah (d 1875 [76]) EA/76*

BORROW, William (d 1872 [74]) EA/73*

BORSELLI, Elisabetta see Borselli, Signora Fausto

BORSELLI, Fausto (fl 1789-90) singer BD

BORSELLI, Signora Fausto [Elisabetta] (fl 1789-90) singer BD

BORTHWICK, A. T. (d 1943 [65]) critic, journalist BE*, WWT/14*

BORUFF, John (b 1910) American actor, dramatist BE

BORUP, Doan (1875-1944) actor SR

BORUWLASKI, Joseph (1739-1837) Polish dwarf, musician BD, CDP, DNB

BORWELL, Montague (b 1866) English singer GRB/1

BORWICK, A. F. (d 1917?) EA/18*

BORZAGE, Daniel (d 1975 [78]) performer BP/60*

BORZAGE, Lew (d 1974 [71]) producer/director/choreographer BP/59*

BOSAN, Alonzo (b 1886) American actor TW/8

BOSANECK, Herr (d 1871)
musical director EA/72*
BOSCAWEN, Mr. (fl 1735)
actor BD
BOSCAWEN, Hon. Kathleen
Pamela see Carme,
Pamela
BOSCH, Frederick (fl 1739-43)
musician BD
BOSCHETTI, Leonilda (fl 1866)
French singer HAS
BOSCHETTI, Signora Mengis
(fl 1770-72) singer BD
BOSCHI, Giuseppe Maria (fl
1710-28) Italian singer
BD, ES
BOSCHI, Signora Giuseppe
Maria [née Francesca Vanini]
(fl 1710-11) Italian singer
BD
BOSCO (d 1906 [72]) magician
EA/07*
BOSCO, Leotard (d 1895 [45])
manager EA/96*
BOSCO, Mrs. Leotard see
Bosco, Mary
BOSCO, Mary (d 1897 [46])
EA/99*
BOSCO, Philip (b 1930) Amer-
ican actor AAS, BE, TW/
23-30, WWT/15-16
BOSEGRAVE, George (fl 1623-
24) lessee DA
BOSGRAVE, George see
Bosegrave, George
BOSILLO, Nick (d 1964 [80])
performer BE*
BOSIO, Angiolina (1830-59)
Italian singer CDP, ES,
HAS, SR
BOSKOTIN, Mr. (fl 1732) actor
BD
BOSLEY, Tom (b 1927) Ameri-
can actor BE, TW/21-24,
WWT/15-16
BOSSERT, Mr. magician CDP
BOSSI, Cesare (d 1802) com-
poser, instrumentalist BD
BOSSI, Mme. Cesare see
Del Caro, Mlle.
BOSSICK, Bernard B. (d 1975
[57]) performer BP/60*
BOSSY, Frederick (fl 1794)
violinist BD
BOSTOCK, Mr. (fl 1742-50)
actor BD
BOSTOCK, Mrs. [née Wombell]
(d 1904 [70]) EA/06*

BOSTOCK, Edward H. (d 1940 [81])
circus proprietor BE*, WWT/
14*
BOSTOCK, Frank (d 1898) conductor
EA/99*
BOSTOCK, Frank C. (1866-1912)
English circus and show propri-
etor ES, SR
BOSTOCK, Harry (d 1917) EA/18*
BOSTOCK, James (d 1878 [63])
proprietor EA/79*
BOSTOCK, N. C. ["The Comic
King"] (d 1916 [66]) EA/18*
BOSTOCK, Thomas H. (b 1899)
English manager WWT/9-10
BOSTOCK, Mrs. W. B. [née Kloet]
(d 1907) EA/08*
BOSTON, Nelroy Buck (d 1962
[51]) actress BE*
"BOSTON GEORGE" see Pablo
BOSTWICK, Barry (b 1945) Ameri-
can actor TW/25-30
BOSTWICK, Emma Gillingham (fl
1850s) singer CDP
BOSTWICK, Harold American actor,
pianist TW/3
BOSWELL, Mr. (fl 1788-95) house
servant? BD
BOSWELL, Mrs. (d 1898 [84])
circus performer? EA/99*
BOSWELL, A. P. [Arthur A.
Palmer] (d 1912 [55]) comedian
EA/13*
BOSWELL, Mrs. A. P. see
Hayes, Florence
BOSWELL, David (d 1865 [34])
actor HAS
BOSWELL, Edith [Mrs. Henry Luigi
Boswell] (d 1902) circus per-
former EA/04*
BOSWELL, Mrs. Henry Luigi see
Boswell, Edith
BOSWELL, James (fl 1821) scholar
DD
BOSWELL, James Clement (1826-
59) English clown ES
BOSWELL, Joseph H. (fl 1835-43)
American actor HAS
BOSWORTH, Agnes Ellinor [Nelly
Danvers] (d 1883 [31]) EA/84*
BOSWORTH, Henry Alexander (d
1893) scene artist, athlete
EA/84*
BOSWORTH, Hobart Van Zandt
(1867-1943) American actor CB,
ES, WWA/2
BOSWORTH, Patricia (b 1933)
American actress TW/13

BOSWORTH, Robart (1867-1943) American actor, dramatist, director SR

BOTARELLI, Mrs. (fl 1778-84) singer BD

BOTELLI, Sig. (fl 1717) Italian singer BD

BOTHAM, Benjamin William (d 1877) proprietor EA/79*

BOTHAM, Clayton (d 1907) music-hall director EA/08*, GRB/3*

BOTHAM, Ellen (d 1882 [51]) proprietor EA/83*

BOTHAM, William (fl 1663) actor? BD

BOTHMAN, Fay (d 1975) agent BP/59*

BOTHMAR, Mr. [Baron?] (fl 1734) oboist BD

BOTHNER, Gustave (1858-1933) manager SR

BOTLY, Mrs. [née Fanny Chapman] (d 1874 [29]) pianist EA/75*

BOTSFORD, Mrs. (fl 1830) American dramatist EAP

BOTT, Alan (b 1894) English critic WWT/8-9

BOTT, Mrs. Barrington (d 1894) EA/95*

BOTT, [Richard?] (fl 1785-87) house servant? BD

BOTT, William (d 1882 [56]) performer? manager? EA/83*

BOTTERO, Alessandro (1831-92) Italian singer ES

BOTTESINI, Giovanni (1822-89) Italian singer, composer, conductor ES

BOTTESINI, Pietro (d 1874) musician EA/75*

BOTTING, Mr. (d 1887) EA/88*

BOTTING, Robert F. (d 1892) proprietor EA/94*

BOTTOMLEY, Gordon (1874-1948) English dramatist COC, DNB, OC/1-3, WWT/5-10, WWW/4

BOTTOMLEY, Robert Maude (1886-1968) English actor GRB/1-2

BOTTOMLEY, Roland (1879-1947) English actor GRB/1-2, SR, TW/3

BOUCHELLE, Mme. Wallace

singer CDP

BOUCHER, Anthony (fl 1689-96) actor BD

BOUCHER, F. T. (d 1913) EA/14*

BOUCHER, Thomas (d 1755) dancer, prompter, boxkeeper, sub-treasurer BD

BOUCHEZ, Arthur (d 1965 [77]) performer BP/49*

BOUCHIER, Chili [née Dorothy Bouchier] (b 1909) English actress WWT/10-16

BOUCHIER, Dorothy see Bouchier, Chili

BOUCHIER, Josias (d 1695) English singer BD

BOUCICAULT, Aubrey (1869-1913) English actor, dramatist DD, DP, ES, GRB/1-4, OC/3, SR, WWM, WWS, WWT/1-2

BOUCICAULT, Mrs. Aubrey see Boucicault, Ruth Baldwin Holt

BOUCICAULT, Dion Clayton (1878-1937) dramatist ES, OC/3

BOUCICAULT, Dion George (1859-1929) American actor, manager COC, DD, DNB, ES, GRB/1-4, OC/1-3, WWA/1, WWT/1-5, WWW/3

BOUCICAULT, Mrs. Dion George see Vanbrugh, Irene

BOUCICAULT, Dion Lardner (1820/22-90) Irish dramatist, actor CDP, COC, DAB, DD, DNB, EA/68, ES, HAS, HJD, HP, MH, NTH, OAA/1-2, OC/1-3, PDT, RE, SR, WWA/H

BOUCICAULT, Mrs. Dion Lardner [Agnes Kelly Robertson] (1833-1916) Scottish actress CDP, COC, DD, EA/97, ES, GRB/1-4, HAS, OAA/1-2, OC/1-3, PP/3, WWT/1-3

BOUCICAULT, Mrs. Dion Lardner, II see Thorndyke, Louise

BOUCICAULT, Dion William (d 1876 [22]) EA/77*

BOUCICAULT, Donald (1888-1940) actor ES, OC/3

BOUCICAULT, Eva [Mrs. John Clayton] actress ES, OC/3

BOUCICAULT, Nina [Mrs. E. H. Kelly] (1867-1950) English actress COC, DD, ES, GRB/1-4, OC/2-3, SR, TW/7, WWT/1-10

BOUCICAULT, Ruth Baldwin Holt [Mrs. Aubrey Boucicault] (fl 1895-1920) American actress WWA/5

BOUCICAULT, W. S. (d 1881
[62]) EA/82*
BOUDET, Mons. (fl 1726) French
dancer BD
BOUDET, Mme. (fl 1726) French
dancer BD
BOUDET, Mlle. (fl 1726) French
dancer BD
BOUDINOT, Annie [Annie Sendel-
beck] (d 1887 [50]) actress
NYM
BOUDINOT, Frank B. (d 1864)
minstrel HAS
BOUDROW, Joseph Hart see
Hart, Joseph
BOUFFE, Hugues-Marie-Désiré
(1800-88) French actor ES
BOUGH, Sam (d 1878 [57]) scene
painter EA/79*
BOUGHNER, Daniel E. (d 1974
[65]) historian BP/58*
BOUGHTON, J. W. (d 1914)
manager WWT/14*
BOUGHTON, Rutland (1878-1960)
English composer DNB, ES,
WWT/5-11, WWW/5
BOUGHTON, Walter (b 1918)
American educator, director
BE
BOUGIER, Mlle. (fl 1791) dancer
BD
BOUHY, Jacques-Joseph-André
(1848-1929) Belgian singer ES
BOULAN, Alice (d 1877) EA/78*
BOULANGER, Mr. actor CDP
BOULARD, Sig. (fl 1840-51)
American actor, singer HAS
BOULARD, Sig. (fl 1848) singer
HAS
BOULARD, James M. singer
CDP
BOULD, Beckett (b 1880) English
actor WWT/11-13
BOULDING, J. W. (fl 1882-97)
dramatist DD
BOULE, Philip [Jean Philippe?]
(1697?-1744?) French?
scene painter BD
BOULLIMIER, Tony (d 1917)
manager EA/18*
BOULOINGE, Mr. (fl 1799)
house servant? BD
BOULT, Sir Adrian [Cedric]
(b 1889) English conductor
CB
BOULT, Mrs. Charles see
Boult, Gertrude
BOULT, Ernest (d 1909 [71])

manager EA/10*
BOULT, Gertrude [Mrs. Charles
Boult] (d 1903 [32]) EA/04*
BOULTBY, Mrs. (fl 1740-41)
actress BD
BOULTER, Rosalyn (b 1916) English
actress WWT/9-12
BOULTER, Stanley (d 1917) EA/18*
BOULTING, Sydney see Cotes,
Peter
BOULTON, Mr. (fl 1794) house
servant BD
BOULTON, Christian Harold Ernest
(d 1917 [20]) dramatist, writer
EA/18*
BOULTON, Guy Pelham (b 1890)
English actor WWT/7-10
BOULTON, Thomas (fl 1768) English
dramatist CP/2-3, GT
BOUNDY, Alice (d 1897) dancer
EA/98*
BOUNTY, William (d 1687?)
trumpeter BD
BOUQUET, James (fl 1794) violinist
BD
BOUQUETON, Mons. (fl 1775-76)
ballet master BD
BOURBON, Ray (d 1971 [78]) Amer-
ican actor TW/1, 28
BOURBONNEL, Jules Alphonse (d
1897) circus manager EA/98*
BOURCHIER, Arthur (1863-1927)
English actor, manager, drama-
tist COC, DD, DNB, EA/95,
ES, GRB/1-4, OC/2-3, SR,
WWM, WWT/1-5, WWW/2
BOURCHIER, Mrs. Arthur see
Vanbrugh, Violet
BOURCHIER, John, Lord Berners
(d 1532 [63]) English dramatist
CP/2-3, DD
BOURDET, Edouard (1877-1945)
French dramatist MH, OC/1-3
BOURDIN, Roger (b 1900) French
singer ES
BOURDON, Mr. [Gabriel?] (fl 1700-
37?) singer BD
BOURGEOIS, Mlle. (fl 1793) dancer
BD
BOURGEOIS, Benjamin (fl 1765)
dramatist CP/2-3, GT
BOURGEOIS, Jeanne see Mistin-
guett
BOURGET, Paul (1852-1935) drama-
tist, critic BE*, WWT/14*
BOURK, William (fl 1780-97) dancer
BD
BOURK, Mrs. William [née

Elizabeth Bradshaw] (fl 1779-93) dancer BD

BOURKE, E. (d 1869) actor EA/70*

BOURKE, George Arlington (d 1908 [48]) EA/09*

BOURN, Emma (d 1907) circus performer EA/08*

BOURNE, Adeline (d 1965 [92]) Indian/English actress WWT/1-5

BOURNE, [Barnard?] (fl 1733-60) actor BD

BOURNE, Barnard (b c.1745) musician BD

BOURNE, Joseph H. (d 1877 [50]) actor EA/78*

BOURNE, Nettie see Arlington, Mrs. Eddie

BOURNE, Reuben (fl 1692) dramatist CP/1-3, DNB, GT

BOURNE, Theophilus see Bird, Theophilus

BOURNE, Thomas (fl 1635) actor DA

BOURNE, William see Bird, William

BOURNE, William Payne (d 1972 [36]) performer BP/57*

BOURNEUF, Philip (b 1912) American actor BE, TW/2-14, 16, WWT/11-16

BOURNONVILLE, Antoine (1760-1843) French dancer BD

BOURRELIER, Mr. (fl 1785-90) house servant BD

BOURSKAYA, Ina (1888-1955) Russian singer WWA/3

BOURVIL (d 1970 [57]) performer BP/55*

BOUSET, John see Sackville, Thomas

BOUSFIELD, Elizabeth Hudson (d 1876) EA/77*

BOUTEL, Mrs. (fl 1663-96) actress DD, DNB

BOUTELL, Henry (fl 1687-89) actor BD

BOUTET, [Mons.?] (fl 1675) instrumentalist BD

BOUTFLOWER, Mr. (fl 1784) violinist BD

BOUTON, Miss (fl 1784) actress BD

BOUVERIE, Mark (d 1895) music-hall director EA/96*

BOUVET, Maximilien-Nicolas (1854-1943) French singer ES

BOUVIER, Corinne (d 1973 [31]) performer BP/58*

BOUWMEESTER, Louis (1842-1925) Dutch actor ES, WWT/3-4

BOUWMEESTER, Theo (b 1873) Dutch actor GRB/1

BOUXARY, Mons. (fl 1848) dancer HAS

BOVA, Joseph (b 1924) American actor BE, TW/20, 23-26, 28-30, WWT/15-16

BOVAL, [Mons.?] (fl 1714-70?) French dancer BD

BOVAL, William (fl 1739) musician BD

BOVASSO, Julie (b 1930) American actress, director, dramatist, producer AAS, BE, CD, TW/12-14, 22, 26, 28, WWT/15-16

BOVETT, La Petite (fl 1854) actress HAS

BOVEY, Mrs. A. (d 1882) costumier EA/83*

BOVILL, Charles H. (1878-1918) Indian/English lyricist, librettist WWT/2-3

BOWAN, Mr. (fl 1780) actor BD

BOWAN, Sibyl American actress TW/25-26

BOWATER, Mr. actor CDP

BOWDEN, Mrs. (fl 1699-1704) actress BD

BOWDEN, Charles (b 1913) American producer, director, actor BE, WWT/15-16

BOWDEN, Wright (1752-1823) English singer, actor BD, CDP, TD/1-2

BOWDLER, Thomas (1754-1825) English editor DNB, HP

BOWDOIN, Harriet S. (d 1965 [60]) critic BP/49*

BOWEN, Mr. (fl 1734-35) actor BD

BOWEN, Mr. (fl 1784) singer BD

BOWEN, Cyril see Moncrieff, R. Scott

BOWEN, Daniel (c.1760-1856) American? showman WWA/H

BOWEN, Frances C. (b 1905) American educator BE

BOWEN, Jemmy (b c.1685) singer BD

BOWEN, John (b 1924) Indian/English dramatist, director, actor AAS, CD, CH, WWT/15-16

BOWEN, Mr. W. (d 1886)
EA/87*
BOWEN, William (1666-1718)
Irish actor BD, DD
BOWER, Mrs. (fl 1721) singer
BD
BOWER, Miss E. [Mrs. Saphrini]
(d 1891) EA/92*
BOWER, Henry (fl 1664-67)
wardrobe keeper BD
BOWER, Marian (d 1945) drama-
tist WWT/4-9
BOWER, Richard (fl 1545-61)
master of the Chapel Royal
DA [see also B., R.]
BOWERING, Adelaide [Mrs. J.
B. Steele] (d 1899) actress
EA/00*
BOWERS, Mr. (fl 1757-73)
boxkeeper BD
BOWERS, Charles (b 1847) actor
SR
BOWERS, David P. (1822-57)
American actor HAS
BOWERS, Mrs. David P. see
Bowers, Elizabeth Crocker
BOWERS, Dun (d 1859) singer
HAS
BOWERS, Edward (d 1865 [38])
minstrel HAS
BOWERS, Elizabeth Crocker
(1830-95) American actress,
manager CDP, DAB, DD,
ES, HAS, SR, WWA/H
BOWERS, Faubion (b 1917)
American author BE
BOWERS, George Vining (1835-
78) American comedian DD,
HAS
BOWERS, John Valentine (fl
1834-50) English actor HAS
BOWERS, Kathleen see Bowers,
Lally
BOWERS, Kenny (b 1923) Amer-
ican actor TW/2-4
BOWERS, Lally [née Kathleen
Bowers] (b 1917) English
actress AAS, TW/23,
WWT/12-16
BOWERS, Richard (fl 1636)
actor DA
BOWERS, Robert Hood (1877-
1941) American composer
WWA/1, WWT/5-7
BOWERS, Viola [Mrs. Viola
Bowers Simmons] (d 1962
[79]) American performer
BE*

BOWES, Alice (d 1969 [79]) English
actress WWT/4-9
BOWES, Mjr. Edward E. (1874-
1946) American manager, pro-
moter SR
BOWES, Mary Eleanor, Countess
of Strathmore (d 1800) dramatist
CP/3
BOWFORD, Mr. (fl 1733) dancer
BD
BOWICK, Ellen reciter GRB/1-2
BOWINGTON, Mr. (fl 1737) actor
BD
BOWKETT, Sidney (d 1937 [69])
dramatist BE*
BOWLER, Annie Kemp (d 1876)
singer EA/77*
BOWLES, Miss (fl 1779) actress
BD
BOWLES, George (d 1968 [78])
composer/lyricist BP/52*
BOWLES, Mrs. George see
Rodney, Babette
BOWLES, Mrs. Henry Robert see
Aickin, Mrs. Graves
BOWLES, Jane (1917-73) American
dramatist BE
BOWLES, Paul Frederic (b 1910)
American composer, writer
BE, ES, HJD
BOWLES, Robert (1748-1806) English
actor, singer BD
BOWLEY, Mr. (fl 1792-1820) box-
keeper, officekeeper BD
BOWLEY, Mrs. (fl 1746-47) house
servant? BD
BOWLEY, Flora Juliet (fl 1900s)
American actress WWS
BOWLEY, Robert Kanzow (d 1870
[57]) manager EA/71*
BOWLING, J. P. (d 1886 [35])
principal EA/87*
BOWLING, Tom (d 1889 [72]) EA/
91*
BOWMAN, Mr. (fl 1792-94) actor
BD, TD/2
BOWMAN, Althea Olive see West,
Olive
BOWMAN, Empsie English actress
GRB/1-2
BOWMAN, Helen see Bowman,
Nellie
BOWMAN, Isa [Mrs. Reginald Bac-
chus] English actor GRB/1-3
BOWMAN, John see Boman, John
BOWMAN, John (b 1816) actor HAS
BOWMAN, John J. (d 1966 [57])
treasurer BP/50*

BOWMAN, Laura (d 1957 [76])
actress TW/13
BOWMAN, Lee (b 1914) Ameri-
can actor BE, ES
BOWMAN, Maggie [Mrs. Tom
J. Morton] English actor
GRB/1-2
BOWMAN, Mattie (d 1947 [68])
actress WWT/14
BOWMAN, Nellie [Helen Bow-
man] (b 1878) English actress
GRB/1-4, WWT/1-4
BOWMAN, Ross (d 1926) Amer-
ican stage manager BE
BOWMAN, Sarah (d 1892)
EA/93*
BOWMAN, T. C. (d 1907 [65])
actor EA/08*, GRB/3*
BOWMAN, Walter P. (b 1910)
American educator, writer
BE
BOWMAN, Wayne (b 1914)
American educator, writer,
director, designer ES
BOWMER, Angus L. (b 1904)
American producer, director,
educator BE
BOWN, Mrs. Clifford see
Cross, Jessie
BOWN, George (d 1910 [90])
actor EA/11*
BOWN, William Paul (d 1889
[35]) American singer,
comedian EA/90*
BOWNE, Owen O. (d 1963 [84])
dancer BE*
BOWRING, George (fl 1574)
actor DA
BOWRINGE, Gregory (fl 1582)
actor DA
BOWRON, William A. actor
GRB/1
BOWSKILL, Jack (d 1904) actor
EA/05*
BOWTELL, Mrs. Barnaby [née
Elizabeth Ridley] (fl 1662?-
97) actress BD
BOWYER, Mrs. (fl 1798-99)
singer BD
BOWYER, Frederick (d 1936
[87]) dramatist, songwriter
BE*, WWT/14*
BOWYER, Michael (d 1645)
English actor DA, OC/1-3
BOX, Muriel (b 1905) English
dramatist ES
BOX, Sidney (b 1907) English
dramatist ES

BOXER, John (b 1909) English actor
WWT/9-16
BOXHORN, Jerome (d 1975 [55])
designer BP/60*
BOXLEY, Edward (fl 1773) musician
BD
BOYACK, Mr. (fl 1766-76) actor,
singer BD
BOYAR, Ben A. (1895-1964) Ameri-
can producer, general manager
BE
BOYAR, Monica Dominican Republi-
can actress, singer BE
BOYCE, Miss (fl 1807) English
actress BS, CDP, GT
BOYCE, Mrs. Charles (d 1864 [44])
actress EA/72*
BOYCE, Frank (d 1904 [47]) lessee
EA/05*
BOYCE, John (fl 1701-10) actor
BD
BOYCE, John T. (1829-67) Ameri-
can minstrel HAS
BOYCE, Samuel (d 1775) dramatist
CP/2-3, DNB, GT
BOYCE, Thomas (d 1793) English
dramatist CP/3, DNB
BOYCE, Thomas (d 1794) English
dancer, actor BD
BOYCE, Mrs. Thomas (fl 1790-96)
dancer BD
BOYCE, William (1710-79) English
composer, organist, teacher,
conductor BD, CDP, DNB, ES
BOYCE, William (1764-1823?) Eng-
lish double-bass player BD
BOYD, Alastair (d 1970 [50]) pub-
licist BP/55*
BOYD, Alexander (d 1883 [53])
proprietor EA/84*
BOYD, Anna (d 1916) actress
WWT/14*
BOYD, Archie (1852-1914) American
actor SR, WWM
BOYD, Belle (1843-1900) American
actress SR, WWA/H
BOYD, Billie (1831-69) American
imitator HAS
BOYD, Charles A. (b 1864) actor
SR
BOYD, Mrs. Edwin (d 1913) EA/
14*
BOYD, Elisse American lyricist,
composer BE
BOYD, Elizabeth (fl 1739) dramatist
CP/2-3, GT
BOYD, Ernest (1887-1946) Irish
dramatist WWW/4

BOYD, Frank M. (b 1863) Scottish critic GRB/1-4, WWT/1-5

BOYD, Mrs. Frank M. see Hewitt, Agnes

BOYD, Harold E. (d 1965 [72]) performer BP/50*

BOYD, Harry Hutcheson (b 1869) Irish dramatist WWA/5, WWM

BOYD, Henry (fl 1793) Irish dramatist CP/3

BOYD, Jeanne (d 1968 [78]) composer/lyricist BP/53*

BOYD, J. M. (d 1887) EA/88*

BOYD, Richard (b 1937) American community theatre administrator BE

BOYD, Sam, Jr. (b 1915) American educator BE

BOYD, Stephen [William Millar] (1928-77) Irish/American actor CB

BOYD, Sydney (b 1901) Scottish actor TW/2-3

BOYD, William (d 1972 [74]) performer BP/57*

BOYD, William Henry (d 1935 [45]) American actor ES, SR

BOYDE, Edwin (d 1909 [39]) comedian EA/10*

BOYDE, Elizabeth dramatist CP/1

BOYDE, Hesther see Colles, Mrs. Joseph

BOYD-JONES, Ernest (d 1904) actor EA/05*, WWT/14*

BOYDSTON, Hazel Allen (d 1969) performer BP/54*

BOYER, Mr. (fl 1789-94?) singer BD

BOYER, Mrs. [Miss Percy Lorraine] (d 1888 [29]) American actress EA/89*

BOYER, Abel (1667-1729) French dramatist CP/1-3, GT

BOYER, Charles (b 1899) French actor BE, CB, ES, SR, TW/6, 8-11, 15, 19-20, WWT/15

BOYER, Ken (b 1934) American actor TW/14-15

BOYER, Rachel (d 1935 [70]) actress BE*, WWT/14*

BOYES, Mr. (d 1791) actor BD

BOYLAN, Mary American

actress TW/2-4, 28-30

BOYLE, Anna (b 1862) actress CDP

BOYLE, Billy (b 1945) Irish actor WWT/16

BOYLE, Charles, Earl of Orrery (1676-1731) English dramatist CP/2-3, GT

BOYLE, E. Roger (b 1907) American educator, director BE

BOYLE, Frank (d 1892) singer EA/93*

BOYLE, Herbert (d 1908) EA/09*

BOYLE, John Francis (1863-1918) singer SR

BOYLE, Murrough see Blessington, Murrough Boyle, Lord

BOYLE, Ray (b 1925) American director, producer, actor BE, TW/7

BOYLE, Roger see Orrery, Lord

BOYLE, William (fl 1529) dramatist CP/3

BOYLE, William (1853-1923) Irish dramatist COC, ES, MH, NTH, OC/1-3, WWT/2-4

BOYNE, Clifton (1874-1945) actor WWT/4-5

BOYNE, Eva Leonard (d 1960 [74]) English actress TW/16

BOYNE, Leonard (1853-1920) Irish actor DD, DP, EA/96, GRB/1-4, SR, WWT/1-3

BOYT, John (b 1921) American designer, producer, writer BE

BOYTLER, Arcadu (b 1895) Russian choreographer, dancer, actor ES

BOZ, Sig. [John Weston] (d 1880) conjurer EA/81*

BOZEMAN, Beverly (b 1927) American actress TW/12

BOZYK, Max (1900-70) Polish actor TW/23, 26

BOZYK, Rose (b 1914) Polish actress TW/23, 26-27

BRABAN, Harvey (b 1883) English actor WWT/7-9

BRABANT, Francis (fl 1669-90) kettledrummer BD

BRABAZON, T. B. English actor GRB/1

BRABAZON, Mrs. T. B. see Murray, Lillian

BRABOURNE, John (d 1908) actor EA/10*, GRB/4*

BRACCO, Roberto (1861-1943) Italian dramatist MH

BRACEGIRDLE, Anne (1663?-1748)

English actress BD, CDP, COC, DD, DNB, ES, GT, HP, NTH, OC/1-3, PDT, TD/1-2

BRACEWELL, Ethel Australian actress GRB/1

BRACEWELL, Joe (d 1909 [71]) English actor GRB/1

BRACKEN, Eddie (b 1920) American actor, director, writer, singer BE, CB, ES, TW/22-25, WWT/15-16

BRACKENBURY, Richard (fl 1598) actor DA

BRACKENRIDGE, Hugh Henry (1748-1816) American dramatist ES, OC/1-3

BRACKER, Milton (d 1964 [54]) critic BP/48*

BRACKETT, Charles (d 1969 [76]) critic BP/53*

BRACKMAN, Marie L. (d 1963 [90]) singer BE*

BRACY, Mr. (fl 1677) gallery-keeper BD

BRACY, Henry (d 1917) actor, singer DD

BRADA, Ede (b 1879) Austrian dancer, choreographer, ballet teacher ES

BRADA, Rezso (b 1906) Hungarian dancer, choreographer ES

BRADBURY, Mr. C. (d 1869 [65]) equestrian EA/70*

BRADBURY, Charles W. (d 1905) music-hall artist EA/06*

BRADBURY, James H. (1857-1940) American actor WWM, WWT/4-8

BRADBURY, John W. (fl 1879-84) actor DD

BRADBURY, Ray (b 1920) American dramatist HJD

BRADBURY, Robert (1774-1831) English clown CDP, DD

BRADDOCK, Edward (d 1708) singer BD

BRADDOCK, Hugh (fl 1679) singer BD

BRADDON, Mary Elizabeth (1837-1915) dramatist DD, EA/69, HP, WWW/1

BRADE, James (d 1870 [27]) actor EA/71*

BRADEL, John F. (d 1962 [79]) stage manager, union executive

BE*

BRADEN, Bernard (b 1916) Canadian actor, producer, director WWT/12-15

BRADEN, Frank (d 1962 [76]) press representative BE*

BRADEN, Waldo W. (b 1911) American educator BE

BRADFIELD, Axford (fl 1794) singer BD

BRADFIELD, W. Louis (1866-1919) English actor, singer GRB/1-4, WWT/1-3

BRADFORD, Mrs. (fl 1775) singer? BD

BRADFORD, Dora see Stuart, Dora

BRADFORD, Edith [Mrs. Charles Meakins] (b 1884) American singer WWM

BRADFORD, Gamaliel (1863-1932) American dramatist DAB

BRADFORD, Dr. Jacob (d 1897) music-hall director EA/98*

BRADFORD, James M. (d 1933 [89]) American performer BE*, BP/17*

BRADFORD, Joseph (1843-86) American actor, dramatist DAB, ES, WWA/H

BRADFORD, Lane (d 1973 [50]) performer BP/58*

BRADFORD, Marshall (d 1971 [75]) performer BP/55*

BRADFORD, Reuben A. (d 1975 [82]) performer BP/60*

BRADFORD, Roark (1896-1948) American dramatist WWA/2

BRADFORD, [Thomas?] (fl 1778-84?) violoncellist BD

BRADFORD, Thomas (d 1908 [63]) music-hall proprietor EA/09*, GRB/4*

BRADIE, Pat (d 1888 [22]) EA/89*

BRADLEY, Mrs. A. see Alexander, Annie Emma

BRADLEY, Albert Davis (fl 1849) American actor HAS

BRADLEY, Alice M. (fl 1915) dramatist SR

BRADLEY, Andrew Cecil (1851-1935) English critic DNB, ES, HP, WWW/3

BRADLEY, Buddy (1913-72) American choreographer, dancer, director, producer BE, WWT/10-12

BRADLEY, Mrs. Campbell see

Armytage, Grace
BRADLEY, Mrs. Dave see
Bradley, Mary Ann
BRADLEY, E. Campbell (d 1889)
EA/90*
BRADLEY, Harry C. [H. B.
Cockrill] (fl 1886-1912) Amer-
ican actor WWM
BRADLEY, Herbert Davies (1878-
1934) dramatist WWW/3
BRADLEY, James Knott (d 1896)
comedian EA/97*
BRADLEY, J. Kenneth (d 1969
[66]) trustee of the American
Shakespeare Festival BP/54*
BRADLEY, John (fl 1673) tailor
BD
BRADLEY, John (b 1829) Amer-
ican actor HAS
BRADLEY, John (d 1910 [46])
proprietor EA/11*
BRADLEY, J. W. (d 1887) act-
ing manager EA/88*
BRADLEY, Leonora (d 1935
[80]) American actress BE*,
BP/19*
BRADLEY, Lilian Trimble (b
1875) American dramatist,
producer WWT/6-11
BRADLEY, Lovyss (d 1969 [63])
performer BP/54*
BRADLEY, Mrs. M. (fl 1772-
77) singer BD
BRADLEY, Mary Ann [Mrs.
Dave Bradley] (d 1881) EA/
82*
BRADLEY, Michael J. (d 1888
[29]) American comedian,
dancer EA/89*
BRADLEY, Oscar (d 1948 [55])
English conductor BE*,
BP/33*
BRADLEY, Richard (fl 1694-
1700) musician BD
BRADLEY, Thomas (d 1829)
actor CDP
BRADLEY, Truman (d 1974 [69])
performer BP/59*
BRADLEY, Will (b 1868) Ameri-
can dramatist WWA/4
BRADNEY, Mr. (fl 1775) actor
BD
BRADNUM, Frederick dramatist
CD
BRADS, Charles (fl 1794) vio-
linist BD
BRADSHAW, Mr. (fl 1680s?)
boxkeeper BD

BRADSHAW, Mrs. (fl 1785) per-
former BD
BRADSHAW, Mrs. [Mrs. Hauton-
ville; Mrs. Cross] (fl 1831-52)
actress HAS
BRADSHAW, Ann Maria [née Tree]
(1801-62) English actress, singer
BS, CDP, DNB, OX
BRADSHAW, Elizabeth see Bowk,
Mrs. William
BRADSHAW, Fanny (1900-73) Amer-
ican director, teacher BE,
TW/30
BRADSHAW, John (1812-76) actor
CDP, DD
BRADSHAW, John J. (d 1855)
American actor HAS
BRADSHAW, Justin (d 1974 [59])
performer BP/59*
BRADSHAW, Leslie Havergal (d
1950) English manager WWA/3
BRADSHAW, Lucretia [Mrs. Martin
Folkes] (d c.1755) actress, singer
BD, DNB
BRADSHAW, Mary see Bradshaw,
Mrs. [William?]
BRADSHAW, Richard (fl 1595-1633)
actor DA
BRADSHAW, [William?] (fl 1735-45)
boxkeeper, box bookkeeper BD
BRADSHAW, Mrs. [William?;
Mary] (d 1780) actress BD
BRADSHAW, Mrs. William see
Abbott, Mrs. William
BRADSTREET, John (d 1618) actor
DA
BRADT, Clifton E. (d 1961 [62])
American critic BE*
BRADWELL, Edmund (d 1871 [72])
decorator EA/72*
BRADWELL, William (d 1849) ma-
chinist DD
BRADY, Mr. (fl 1774-75?) actor
BD
BRADY, Mr. (fl 1795) actor BD
BRADY, Master (fl 1785) dancer
BD
BRADY, Alice (1892-1939) American
actress, singer DAB, ES, NTH,
OC/1-3, SR, WWA/1, WWT/4-9
BRADY, Barbara (b 1927) American
actress TW/6-7
BRADY, Charles (fl 1783-85) stage
doorkeeper BD
BRADY, E. F. (d 1893 [58]) EA/
94*
BRADY, Eleanor (d 1971 [73])
actress TW/27

BRADY, Grace George see George, Grace
BRADY, Hugh (d 1921 [40]) actor BE*, BP/5*
BRADY, Mrs. James [Marie France] (d 1900) variety artist EA/01*
BRADY, John Albert (d 1913) EA/14*
BRADY, Kenneth Darryl (d 1974 [27]) performer BP/58*
BRADY, Leo B. (b 1917) American educator, dramatist, director BE
BRADY, Mary (d 1968) performer BP/53*
BRADY, Dr. Nicholas (1659-1726) Irish dramatist CP/1-3, GT
BRADY, Pat (d 1972 [57]) performer BP/56*
BRADY, Patrick (fl 1779-1816) barber, hair dresser BD
BRADY, Terence (b 1939) English actor, dramatist WWT/15-16
BRADY, Thomas (fl 1686) kettledrummer BD
BRADY, Veronica (1890-1964) Irish actress, singer WWT/5-11
BRADY, William Aloysius (1863-1950) American manager, actor COC, DAB, ES, GRB/2-4, NTH, OC/1-3, SR, TW/6, WWA/2, WWM, WWS, WWT/1-10
BRADY, William A[loysius], Jr. (1900-35) American producer, manager SR, WWT/6-7
BRADY, Mrs. William A[loysius] see George, Grace
BRAE, June (b 1918) English dancer ES, WWT/10-12
BRAGAGLIA, Marinella Italian actress WWT/2-3
BRAGDON, Claude Fayette (d 1946 [80]) American designer, architect BE*, BP/31*
BRAGG, Bernard (b 1928) American actor TW/25-26
BRAGHETTI, Prospero (fl 1793-1810) singer BD
BRAGNOLI, Sig. (fl 1856) singer SR
BRAHA, Herb [Herb Simon] (b 1946) American actor TW/

28-30
BRAHAM, Albert (fl 1861) English actor HAS
BRAHAM, Amelia Georgina [Mrs. Carl Robarts] (d 1903 [50]) EA/05*
BRAHAM, Augustus (fl 1850) English singer CDP, HAS
BRAHAM, Charles (d 1884) singer CDP
BRAHAM, David (1838-1905) English/American composer ES
BRAHAM, Hamilton (d 1862) singer EA/72*
BRAHAM, Harry (d 1923 [73]) English actor CDP, SR
BRAHAM, Horace (1896-1955) English actor TW/2-3, 12, WWT/7-11
BRAHAM, John (1777-1856) English singer, composer, manager BD, BS, CDP, DD, DNB, ES, GT, HAS, OX, SR, TD/2
BRAHAM, Josef (d 1877 [50]) musician EA/78*
BRAHAM, Leonora (1853-1931) actress, singer DD, DP, EA/97, WWT/6
BRAHAM, Lionel (d 1947 [68]) English actor TW/4, WWT/7-10
BRAHAM, Philip (1881-1934) English composer, conductor WWT/4-7
BRAHAM, Sarah (d 1883 [96]) EA/84*
BRAHAM, Cpt. W. (d 1877) amateur actor EA/78*
BRAHM, Otto [né Abrahamsohn] (1856-1912) performer, manager BE*, WWT/14*
BRAHMS, Caryl dramatist, critic, librettist CD, WWT/15-16
BRAID, George Ross (1812-78) actor DD
BRAIDWOOD, Margaret (b 1924) English actress TW/27
BRAINERD, Anna see Granger, Maude
BRAINERD, Maria S. (fl c. 1886) singer CDP
BRAITHWAITE, Mr. (d 1773) master tailor BD
BRAITHWAITE, Mr. (fl 1776-77) dresser BD
BRAITHWAITE, Ann (fl 1775-90) actress, dancer BD
BRAITHWAITE, Dame Lilian [Mrs. Gerald Lawrence] (1873-1948) English actress AAS, COC, DD,

DNB, ES, GRB/1-4, OC/
1-3, SR, TW/5, WWT/
1-10, WWW/4
BRAITHWAITE, Richard (1588-
1673) English dramatist
CP/3, FGF
BRAITHWAITE, Warwick (1898-
1971) New Zealand composer,
conductor ES
BRAMAH, Miss see McCor-
mack, Mrs. M.
BRAMAH, Marie [Mrs. John
Hudspeth] (d 1908 [64])
EA/09*, GRB/4*
BRAMALL, Eric (b 1922) English
marionettist ES
BRAMBELL, Wilfrid (b 1912)
Irish actor WWT/15-16
BRAMBILLA, Linda CDP
BRAMBILLA, Marietta (1807-75)
Italian singer CDP, ES
BRAMBILLA, Veronica Graziella
(d 1894) singer EA/95*
BRAMBLE, Mrs. actress TD/2
BRAME, Henry W. (d 1906 [46])
actor EA/07*
BRAMHALL, Mrs. (d 1886 [46])
EA/87*
BRAMHALL, Mrs. Walter [née
Tilly Wilbraham] (d 1878 [22])
actress EA/80*
BRAMHALL, William (d 1890
[61]) comedian EA/91*
BRAMLEY, Raymond (b 1891)
American actor BE, TW/3,
5-6, 8, 13
BRAMMER, Lily English singer
GRB/1
BRAMPTON, Lady [Miss Rey-
nolds] (d 1907) actress
GRB/3
BRAMPTON, John (fl 1423)
actor DA
BRAMSBOTTOM, Abraham (fl
1794) musician BD
BRAMSON, Karen (d 1936)
dramatist BE*, WWT/14*
BRAMSON, Sam (d 1962 [60])
American talent representative
BE*
BRAMSTON, Mr. (fl 1752)
actor? BD
BRAMWELL, Mr. (fl 1794-1804)
singer BD
BRAMWELL, Georgiana (fl
1791-1804) singer, actress
BD
BRAN, Mary (d 1972 [73])

producer/director/choreographer
BP/57*
BRANCA, Guglielmo (1849-1928)
Italian conductor, composer
ES
BRANCH, Eileen (b 1911) English
actress WWT/7-8
BRANCH, Phyllis (d 1972 [48])
performer BP/57*
BRAND, Miss (fl 1780) actress
BD
BRAND, Barbarina, Lady Dacre
(1768-1854) English dramatist
DNB
BRAND, Deane (d 1899 [39])
singer, actor DD
BRAND, George (d 1898 [50])
singer? EA/99*
BRAND, Hannah (d 1821) English
actress, dramatist BD, CP/3,
DD, DNB, GT, TD/1-2
BRAND, Mike (d 1975 [27]) per-
former BP/59*
BRAND, Neville (1895-1951) Eng-
lish dramatist WWW/5
BRAND, Oswald (d 1909 [52])
dramatist, manager DD
BRAND, Phoebe (b 1907) American
actress, director, teacher BE
BRAND, Tita English actress
GRB/1-3
BRANDANE, John [John MacIntyre]
(1869-1947) Scottish dramatist
ES, OC/1-3
BRANDE, Thomas (fl 1574) actor
DA
BRANDEAUX, Palmere (d 1965
[64]) choreographer BP/49*
BRANDEIS, Frederic (1835-91)
Austrian musician WWA/H
BRANDEIS, Ruth (b 1942) Ameri-
can actress TW/24
BRANDES, Marthe (1862-1930)
French actress GRB/1-4
BRANDFON, Martin (b 1949)
American actor TW/28
BRANDI, Gaetano (fl 1784-1818?)
musician? BD
BRANDIES, Bob (d 1973 [71])
performer BP/58*
BRANDO, Jocelyn (b 1919) Amer-
ican actor TW/4-8, 29-30
BRANDO, Marlon (b 1924) Amer-
ican actor, director, producer
BE, CB, ES, TW/1-14
BRANDON, Mr. (fl 1848) actor
HAS
BRANDON, Arthur F. (d 1975

[50]) composer/lyricist BP/
60*

BRANDON, Bella see Forge,
Mrs. R.

BRANDON, Bill (b 1944) American actor TW/24-25

BRANDON, Daisy (d 1899 [20])
actress EA/00*

BRANDON, Dorothy dramatist
WWT/5-11

BRANDON, Edith actress CDP

BRANDON, Florence [Mrs.
Harold Perry] (d 1961 [82])
English actress GRB/1

BRANDON, Henry (b 1912)
German/American actor
TW/6-9, 13-15

BRANDON, Isaac (fl 1808)
dramatist CP/3

BRANDON, James W. treasurer
CDP

BRANDON, James William
(1754-1825) English box book-
keeper, housekeeper BD

BRANDON, Jocelyn (d 1948
[82]) dramatist BE*, WWT/
14*

BRANDON, John (fl 1789-1813)
treasurer BD

BRANDON, [Martha?] (1727?-
98) concessionaire BD

BRANDON, Michael (b 1945)
American actor TW/25

BRANDON, Olga (1865-1906)
Australian actress CDP,
DD, DP

BRANDON, Peter (b 1926)
German/American actor
BE, TW/8-15, 18-20, 23, 29

BRANDON, Samuel (fl 1598)
English dramatist CP/1-3,
FGF

BRANDON, Violet [née Barling]
(d 1903 [26]) actress EA/04*

BRANDON-THOMAS, Amy Mar-
guerite (1890-1974) English
actress BTR/74, WWT/
1-11

BRANDON-THOMAS, Jevan
(b 1898) English actor,
dramatist WWT/6-15

BRANDRAM, Julia (d 1907 [77])
actress, singer WWT/14*

BRANDRAM, Rosina [Moult]
(d 1907) English actress,
singer DD, EA/95, GRB/
1-3, WWW/1

BRANDRAM, Samuel (d 1892

[68]) reciter EA/93*, WWT/
14*

BRANDRAM, Mrs. Samuel see
Murray, Julia

BRANDRETH, H. B. (d 1921)
manager WWT/14*

BRANDT, Alvin (b 1922) American
executive, editor, writer BE

BRANDT, George (1916-63) American producer BE*, BP/48*

BRANDT, Mrs. Harry N. (d 1973
[68]) co-chairman of the American Theatre Wing Club BP/
57*

BRANDT, Ivan [Roy Francis Cook]
(b 1903) English actor ES,
WWT/8-12

BRANDT, Lou (d 1971 [56]) pro-
ducer/director/choreographer
BP/56*

BRANDT, Marianne [Maria Anna
Bischof] (1842-1921) Austrian
singer ES

BRANDT, Martin (b 1908) German
actor TW/3

BRANDT, Max (b 1925) German
actor TW/30

BRANGIN, Mr. (fl 1781-91) house
servant? BD

BRANGIN, Rhoda [Mrs. James
Spriggs] (fl 1779-91) actress
BD

BRANMAN, Mr. (fl 1795) watchman BD

BRANNAN, Miss E. C. (fl 1866)
singer HAS

BRANNIGAN, Bob (d 1973 [75])
stagehand BP/57*

BRANNIGAN, Desmond (d 1918)
EA/19*

BRANNIGAN, Owen (1908-73) English singer ES

BRANNUM, Tom (b 1941) American actor TW/25-26, 29

BRANON, John (b 1939) American
actor TW/24, 26, 29

BRANSBY, Astley (d 1789) actor
BD, TD/2

BRANSCOMB, J. (d c.1815) machinist BD

BRANSCOMBE, Mrs. (d 1891)
EA/92*

BRANSCOMBE, Arthur (d 1924)
dramatist DD

BRANSCOMBE, Maud (fl 1876)
actress CDP

BRANSON, Mr. (fl 1767-84) house
servant? BD

BRANSON, Mrs. (fl 1767-84)
actress BD
BRANSON, Margaret (d 1868
[38]) EA/69*
BRANSON, May (b 1867) act-
ress, singer CDP
BRANSON, William Scholes
(d 1884 [74]) actor, manager
EA/85*
BRANT, Luke (d 1888 [35])
American vaudevillian EA/89*
BRANTON, Fred (d 1890) music-
hall stage manager EA/91*
BRANZELL, Karin Maria (1891-
1974) Swedish singer CB,
ES
BRAS, Hermans (fl c. 1819)
Prussian fat boy CDP
BRASINGTON, Alan American
actor TW/25-26, 30
BRASLAU, Sophie (1892-1935)
American singer DAB,
WWA/1, WWW/3
BRASMER, William (b 1921)
American educator, director
BE
BRASSELL, Peter minstrel
CDP
BRASSEUR, Albert Jules (1862-
1932) French actor WWT/
2-4
BRASSEUR, Jules (d 1890 [61])
actor, producer BE*,
WWT/14*
BRASSEUR, Pierre (d 1972
[66]) actor, dramatist BP/
57*, WWT/16*
BRASSEY, Mr. (fl 1728-48)
actor BD
BRASSINGTON, William Salt
(1859-1939) English curator
WWW/3
BRASWELL, Charles (d 1974
[49]) American actor TW/
23-24, 26-28, 30
BRATT, William (d 1871 [55])
proprietor EA/72*
BRATTON, John Walter (1867-
1947) American lyricist,
dramatist, manager SR,
WWA/4, WWS
BRAUN, Carl (1888-1946) German singer ES
BRAUN, Eric (d 1970 [46])
performer BP/55*
BRAUN, Eugene (d 1965 [77])
electrician, lighting designer
BP/49*

BRAUN, Felix (b 1885) Austrian
dramatist CH
BRAUN, Roger (b 1941) American
actor TW/26
BRAUNSTEIN, Alan (b 1947) Amer-
ican actor TW/27-29
BRAVILLE, Mr. (fl 1776-77) pup-
peteer BD
BRAVO, Nino (d 1973 [28]) per-
former BP/57*
BRAWN, John P. (1872-1943) pro-
ducer SR
BRAY, Mr. (fl 1689-85) dancer,
dancing master BD
BRAY, Mrs. (d 1752) proprietor,
actress BD
BRAY, Alice [Mrs. Charles Fan-
shawe Everest] (d 1889) actress
EA/90*
BRAY, Antony (fl 1635) actor DA
BRAY, John (1782-1822) dramatist,
actor, composer EAP, HAS,
RJ
BRAY, Walter [né Baker] (d 1891)
minstrel CDP
BRAY, Will H. actor CDP
BRAYBROOK, Marie see Hender-
son, Marie
BRAYFIELD, George W. (d 1968)
secretary, treasurer BP/52*
BRAYNE, Harry (b 1865) English
actor GRB/1
BRAYTON, Lily [Mrs. Oscar
Asche] (1876-1953) English
actress ES, GRB/1-4, OC/1-3,
WWT/1-11
BRAZONG, Mr. (fl 1691) musician
BD
BREAD AND PUPPET THEATRE
theatre collective CD
BREAKSTON, George P. (d 1972
[65]) performer BP/57*
BREARLEY, Mr. (fl 1783-85)
boxkeeper, lobby keeper BD
BRECHER, Egon (1885-1946)
Czech actor, producer SR,
TW/3, WWT/7-9
BRECHT, Bertolt Friedrich (1898-
1956) German dramatist CH,
COC, ES, MH, MWD, NTH,
OC/2-3, PDT, RE, WWA/4
BRECHT, George dramatist CD
BRECK, Charles (1782-1822) Amer-
ican dramatist EAP, RJ
BRECKENRIDGE, Hugh Henry
(1748-1816) Scottish/American
dramatist EAP
BREEDING, Guinevare (b 1939)

American actress TW/23
BREEN, Helen (b 1902/05)
English actress, singer
WWT/7-11
BREEN, May Singhi (d 1970
[76]) performer BP/55*
BREEN, Robert (b 1914) American director, actor, producer BE
BREEN, T. D. (d 1882) Irish?
prompter EA/83*
BREESE, Edmund (1871-1936)
American actor ES, GRB/
3-4, SR, WWA/1, WWM,
WWS, WWT/1-8
BREEZE, Mabel [Mrs. W. Percival] (d 1896 [31]) music-hall artist EA/97*
BREIL, Joseph Carl (1870-1926)
American composer ES,
WWA/1, WWM
BREILLAT, George (fl 1794)
singer BD
BREIT, Harvey (1913-68) American dramatist, editor BE,
TW/24
BREL, Jacques (b 1929) Belgian
composer, lyricist, singer
CB
BRELSFORD, Joseph P. (d 1854)
American actor HAS
BREMA, Marie (1856-1925)
English singer ES, WWW/2
BREMAN, Edward (d 1870 [33])
scene artist EA/71*
BREMAURE, Mrs. Gabriel see
Kiralfy, Amalia
BREMERS, Beverly Ann (b
1950) American actress
TW/26-28
BREMS, Else (b 1908) Danish
singer ES
BREMSETH, Lloyd (b 1948)
American actor TW/27, 30
BRENAN, Mr. (fl 1756) Irish?
dramatist CP/2-3, GT
BRENDEL, El (d 1964 [73])
American actor TW/20
BRENDERS, Stan (d 1969 [65])
composer/lyricist BP/54*
BRENLIN, George (b 1930)
American actor TW/14
BRENNAN, Mrs. (d 1891)
EA/92*
BRENNAN, Denis (b 1927)
Irish actor TW/4
BRENNAN, Eileen (b 1935)
American actress BE

BRENNAN, Frederick Hazlitt (d
1962 [60]) dramatist BP/47*
BRENNAN, James J. (d 1965 [80])
executive BE/49*
BRENNAN, Jay (d 1961 [78]) performer TW/17
BRENNAN, J. Keirn (d 1948 [74])
composer BE, BP/32*
BRENNAN, Maggie (d 1913 [74])
actress DD, OAA/1-2
BRENNAN, Maude (1855-1915)
English actress DD, OAA/1-2
BRENNAN, Maureen (b 1952)
American actress TW/30
BRENNAN, Walter (d 1974 [80])
performer BP/59*
BRENNEN, Anna American actress
TW/28-29
BRENNER, A. minstrel CDP
BRENNER, Paul see Baratow
Ben-Zwi
BRENON, Edward St. John (d
1917) EA/18*
BRENON, Mrs. Hettie St. John
see Alva, Mme.
BRENT, Mr. (fl 1797) actor BD
BRENT, Mrs. (fl 1787-97) actress
BD
BRENT, Bessie [Eliza Travers]
(d 1871) actress EA/72*
BRENT, Charles (1693-1770)
singer, fencing master BD
BRENT, Charlotte [Mrs. Pinto]
(d 1802) English singer, actress
DD, DNB, ES, TD/1-2
BRENT, Evelyn [Elizabeth Riggs]
(1899-1975) American actress
ES
BRENT, George (b 1904) Irish
actor ES
BRENT, Mabel [Mrs. Knight Aston]
(d 1874 [25]) actress EA/75*
BRENT, Marian [Mary Wentworth
Elroy] (1853-1887) American
actress NYM
BRENT, Romney [Rómulo Larralde]
(1902-76) Mexican actor, dramatist, director BE, ES, TW/
1-9, WWT/8-15
BRENTANO, Felix (d 1961 [52])
Austrian producer BE*, BP/
46*
BRENTANO, Lowell (d 1950 [55])
American dramatist BE*,
BP/35*
BRENTON, Howard (b 1942) English dramatist, actor CD,
WWT/16

BREON, Edmond (1882-1951)
Scottish actor WWT/5-10

BRERELY, Mr. (fl 1777) actor
BD

BRERETON, Mr. (fl 1771-88)
house servant BD

BRERETON, Alice (d 1896 [19])
singer EA/97*

BRERETON, Austin (1862-1922)
English critic, manager DD,
GRB/1-4, WWT/1-4, WWW/2

BRERETON, Stella (fl 1879-88)
actress DD

BRERETON, Thomas (1691-1722)
English dramatist CP/1-3,
DD, DNB, GT

BRERETON, William (fl 18th
cent) master of ceremonies
CDP

BRERETON, William (1751-87)
English actor BD, CDP,
DD, TD/1-2

BRESCHARD (fl 1809-12) equestrian, circus manager
WWA/H

BRESIL, Marguerite (b 1880)
French actress GRB/4,
WWT/1-4

BRESLAW, Philip (1726-1803)
German conjurer BD, CDP

BRESLIN, Tommy (b 1946)
American actor TW/24,
26-27, 29-30

BRESLOW, Rosalind American
actress TW/27

BREST, George see Arthur,
George K.

BRETHERTON, Dorothea (d
1976 [79]) performer BP/60*

BRETON, Cecil (d 1916) business manager WWT/14*

BRETON, Nicholas (fl 1605)
dramatist CP/1-3, FGF

BRETT, Mr. (fl 1740-50)
singer, actor BD

BRETT, Master (fl 1750) actor?
BD

BRETT, Mrs. (fl 1795-1803)
actress HAS

BRETT, Miss see King, Mrs.

BRETT, Anne [Mrs. F. Brett]
(d 1899 [71]) EA/91*

BRETT, Anne see Chetwood,
Mrs. William Rufus, II

BRETT, Arabella (d 1803)
actress BE* [?= Mrs. John
Hodgkinson, q. v.]

BRETT, Mrs. Dawson [née

Elizabeth Cibber] (b 1701) English dancer, actress BD

BRETT, Edwin J. (b 1867) English
actor GRB/1

BRETT, Mrs. F. see Brett,
Anne

BRETT, Frances R. see Chapman, Mrs. George

BRETT, Hannah see Brett, Mrs.
William

BRETT, Harry (d 1918) EA/19*

BRETT, Mrs. Harry J. (d 1916)
EA/17*

BRETT, Jeremy [né Huggins] (b
1933/35) English actor AAS,
TW/13, 20, WWT/14-16

BRETT, John G. (d 1899 [33])
actor EA/00*, WWT/14*

BRETT, Stanley (1879-1923) English actor GRB/1-4, WWT/1-4

BRETT, William (d 1789) singer,
actor BD

BRETT, William (fl 1773-82)
singer BD

BRETT, Mrs. William [Hannah]
(d c. 1804) actress, singer BD

BRETTELL, Walter see Beaumont, Walter

BRETTEN, William (fl 1546) member of the Chapel Royal DA

BRETTINGHAM, Elsa English
actress GRB/1

BREVAL, Cpt. John Durant (d
1738/39) English dramatist
CP/1-3, GT, TD/1-2

BREVAL, Lucienne [Berthe-Agnès-
Lisette Schilling] (1869-1935)
German singer ES, GRB/1-4

BREW, Anthony (fl 1619-22) actor
DA [see also: Brewer,
Anthony]

BREWER, Anthony (fl 1630-55)
English dramatist CP/1-3,
DD, DNB, FGF

BREWER, George (b 1766) English
dramatist CP/3, DD, GT,
TD/1-2

BREWER, George (d 1907 [50])
showman EA/08*

BREWER, George, Jr. (1899-1968)
American dramatist, producer,
director, executive BE

BREWER, Joseph W. (d 1860 [38])
gymnast HAS

BREWER, Sherri "Peaches"
American actress TW/24

BREWER-MOORE, Cathy (b 1948)
American actress TW/30

BREWERTON, Alice (d 1875
[24]) actress EA/76*
BREWMAN, Mr. (fl 1789)
actor BD
BREWSTER, Charles H. (d
1893) EA/94*
BREWSTER, Henry (c1747-88)
musician, singer, composer
BD
BREWSTER, John E. (d 1912
[58]) banjo troupe proprietor
EA/13*
BREYER, Mrs. J. E. [née
Eliza Walsh] (d 1864 [67])
actress HAS
BREYER, John F. (fl 1857-68)
Scottish actor HAS
BREYER, M. V. (fl 1851)
Scottish actor HAS
BREZANY, Eugene (b 1945)
American actor TW/28
BRIAN, Donald (1877-1948)
Canadian actor, singer CDP,
ES, SR, TW/2-3, 5, WWA/
2, WWM, WWS, WWT/1-10
BRIAN, J. F. (d 1890) singer,
dancer EA/91*
BRIAN, Mrs. J. F. singer
CDP
BRIAN, Mrs. J. F. (d 1895
[56]) actress EA/96*
BRIANSKY, Oleg (b 1929) Bel-
gian dancer, choreographer
ES
BRIANT, August W. (d 1970
[82]) performer BP/54*
BRIANT, Gertrude see Davies,
Gertrude
BRICE, Mr. (fl 1793-1801)
house servant BD
BRICE, Miss (fl 1782) actress
BD
BRICE, Elizabeth (d 1965)
singer, dancer TW/21
BRICE, Fanny (1891-1951)
American actress, singer
CB, ES, NTH, TW/7,
WWA/3, WWT/7-11
BRICE, Monte (d 1962 [71])
American producer, director
BE*
BRICHTA, Mme. (fl 1831)
singer HAS
BRICKELL, Susan (b 1950)
American actress TW/28
BRICKER, Hershel (b 1905)
American educator, director,
writer BE

BRICKLAYER, Miss (fl 1756-57)
singer BD
BRICKLER, Miss (fl 1758-67)
singer BD
BRICKWELL, H. T. (1858-1928)
English manager GRB/1
BRICKWELL, William (d 1893 [33])
manager, director EA/94*
BRIDA, Luigi (fl 1794-95) singer
BD
BRIDA, Marie Catherine see
Dorival à Corifet
BRIDE, Mr. (fl 1741?-61) scene
shifter BD
BRIDE, Mrs. (fl 1765) dresser
BD
BRIDE, Elizabeth [Mrs. Lefevre;
Mrs. Samworth?] (d 1826)
actress, dancer BD, DD, TD/
1-2
BRIDEKIRK, John (d 1879 [63])
actor? EA/80*
BRIDEL, Edmund Philip (fl 1807)
dramatist CP/3
BRIDER, Miss (fl 1765) dancer
BD
BRIDGE, John (d 1893 [72]) EA/
94*
BRIDGE, Peter (b 1925) English
producer WWT/14-16
BRIDGE, Thomas (d 1872) singer
EA/73*
BRIDGE, William see Agoust
BRIDGEMAN, Mr. (fl 1794) house
servant? BD
BRIDGEMAN, John V. (fl 1860-64)
dramatist DD [see also:
Bridgman, John V.]
BRIDGES, Mr. (fl 1690-92) actor
BD
BRIDGES, Mr. (fl 1728?-51) actor
BD
BRIDGES, Mr. (fl 1752-61) actor
BD
BRIDGES, Mrs. equestrienne
CDP
BRIDGES, Mrs. (fl 1744-49)
actress, singer BD
BRIDGES, Anthony O'Neil (d 1879)
equestrian EA/80*
BRIDGES, Beau (b 1941) American
actor TW/22
BRIDGES, Eloise (fl 1853) Amer-
ican actress CDP, HAS
BRIDGES, Gertrude Agnes [Mrs.
Charles Wincott] (d 1881 [41])
EA/89*
BRIDGES, Lloyd (b 1913) American

actor TW/10, 24
BRIDGES, Paul Francis (fl
1660-73) musician BD
BRIDGES, Robert Seymour (1844-
1930) English dramatist DD,
DNB, HP, WWW/3
BRIDGES, Mrs. Selim see
Organ, Harriet
BRIDGES, Thomas (fl 1759-75)
English dramatist CP/2-3,
DD, DNB, GT, TD/1-2
BRIDGES-ADAMS, William
(1889-1965) English director,
designer, author BE, COC,
ES, WWT/4-13, WWW/6
BRIDGETOWER, George Augustus
Polgreen (1778-1860) violinist
BD
BRIDGEWATER, John William
Stevenson see Kove, Kenneth
BRIDGEWATER, Leslie (1893-
1974) English composer, con-
ductor WWT/9-15
BRIDGEWATER, Mr. R. (d
1869 [55]) singer EA/70*
BRIDGMAN, Mr. (fl 1742) actor
BD
BRIDGMAN, Mrs. (fl 1794)
actress BD
BRIDGMAN, Cunningham (fl
1873-92) dramatist, libret-
tist DD
BRIDGMAN, F. W. (d 1892)
EA/94*
BRIDGMAN, John V. (d 1889
[69]) journalist, librettist
EA/90* [see also: Bridgman,
John V.]
BRIDGMAN, Louisa (d 1909)
EA/10*
BRIDGMAN, William (fl 1684)
musician? BD
BRIDGMAN, William (d 1903)
variety artist EA/04*
BRIDGWATER, Roger (d 1754)
actor, dancer BD, DD
BRIDIE, James [Osborne
Henry Mavor] (1888-1951)
Scottish dramatist AAS,
CH, COC, DNB, ES, HP,
MD, MH, MWD, NTH,
OC/1-3, PDT, RE, TW/7,
WWT/7-11, WWW/5
BRIEF, [Mr. ?] (fl 1734) actor
BD
BRIEN, Alan (b 1925) English
critic WWT/14-16
BRIERCLIFFE, Nellie (d 1966)

actress, singer WWT/4-8
BRIERLEY, Alfred (d 1916) EA/
17*
BRIERLEY, David (b 1936) English
general manager WWT/16
BRIERLEY, Ethel see Bertram,
Eva
BRIERLEY, Jack (d 1900) comedian
EA/01*
BRIERS, Richard (b 1934) English
actor AAS, WWT/14-16
BRIESEMEISTER, Otto (1866-1910)
German singer ES
BRIEUX, Eugène (1858-1932)
French dramatist COC, GRB/
1-4, HP, MD, MWD, OC/1-3,
RE, SR, WWT/1
BRIGG, Mr. (fl 1781-1803) dancer
BD
BRIGG, Mrs. (fl 1790-1802) dancer
BD
BRIGGS, Mr. (fl 1776-77) door-
keeper BD
BRIGGS, Mr. (fl 1781) actor BD
BRIGGS, Mr. (fl 1784) singer BD
BRIGGS, Bunny (b 1923) American
actress TW/2
BRIGGS, Don (b 1911) American
actor TW/8
BRIGGS, Harlan (d 1952 [72])
American actor BE*, BP/36*
BRIGGS, Hedley (1907-68) English
actor, producer, designer,
dancer WWT/9-12
BRIGGS, Matt (d 1962 [79]) Amer-
ican actor TW/1, 19
BRIGGS, Millard (d 1967 [59])
performer BP/51*
BRIGGS, Oceana (b 1928) vaude-
villian, actress TW/24
BRIGGS, Wallace Neal (b 1914)
American educator, director
BE
BRIGGS, William A. (b 1915)
American architect BE
BRIGHAM, William Stanhope (b
1938) American manufacturer
BE
BRIGHOUSE, Harold (1882-1958)
English dramatist AAS, COC,
ES, MD, MH, MWD, NTH,
OC/3, PDT, WWT/2-11, WWW/5
BRIGHT, Mr. (fl 1711) musician?
BD
BRIGHT, Mr. (fl 1733) actor,
singer BD
BRIGHT, Mrs. (fl 1750) actress
BD

BRIGHT, Addison (d 1906)
critic EA/07*, WWT/14*
BRIGHT, Mrs. Augustus (d
1906) dramatist DD
BRIGHT, Bella actress CDP
BRIGHT, Edward (1721-50)
English fat man CDP
BRIGHT, George (fl c. 1677-
1707) actor BD
BRIGHT, John Holloway see
Sargano
BRIGHT, Molly (fl 1783-85)
wardrobe keeper BD
BRIGHT, R. Golding (d 1941
[67]) agent WWT/14*
BRIGHT, Mrs. R. Golding
see Egerton, George
BRIGHT, Richard (b 1937) Amer-
ican actor TW/24, 27-28
BRIGHT, William (fl 1794)
singer? BD
BRIGHTEN, Charles R. (d 1899)
music-hall manager EA/00*
BRIGHTLING, Lotta see
Wynne, Evelyne
BRIGHTMAN, Stanley (1888-1961)
English producing manager,
dramatist WWT/7-13
BRIGHTON Charles (d 1896 [29])
actor, singer, composer CDP
BRIGHTSTAIN, Annie singer
CDP
BRIGHTWELL, Peter (fl 1689)
actor BD
BRIGNOLI, Mlle. (b 1844) Amer-
ican musician HAS
BRIGNOLI, Ortolani (d 1884)
singer HAS
BRIGNOLI, Pasquale (1823-84)
Italian singer CDP, HAS
BRILA, Mons. (fl 1742) acrobat
BD
BRILA, Mme. (fl 1742) acrobat
BD
BRILA, Fils (b c. 1739) acrobat
BD
BRILL, Daniel (d 1898 [81])
EA/99*
BRILL, Fran (b 1946) American
actress TW/25
BRILL, Gene (d 1970 [38])
executive BP/55*
BRILLIANSO, Charles (d 1896
[29]) circus performer EA/97*
BRILLIANT, Marie [Jeanne Le
Maignen] (1724-67) French
actress ES
BRILLIANT, Paul (c. 1824-64)

French dancer, ballet master
CDP, HAS, SR
BRINCKERHOFF, Burt (b 1936)
American actor, producer
BE, TW/24
BRINDLEY, Madge (d 1968) per-
former BP/53*
BRINDLEY, Thomas Tait (d 1892
[48]) actor? EA/93*
BRINK, Robert (b 1944) American
actor TW/26-27
BRINKEROFF, Clara M. (b 1828)
singer CDP
BRINKLEY, John D. (d 1972 [65])
performer BP/57*
BRINLEY, Matthew (fl 1671-77)
scenekeeper BD
BRINSLEY, Mr. (fl 1781-82) actor
BD
BRINSMEAD, John (d 1908 [93])
piano maker EA/09*
BRIQUET, Jean (1864-1936) Ger-
man composer, dramatist,
actor BE*
BRISCOE, Herbert (d 1902 [26])
actor, stage manager EA/03*
BRISCOE, Johnson (d 1969 [86])
agent, historian BP/53*
BRISCOE, Lottie [Mrs. Harry
Mountford] (d 1950 [67]) Amer-
ican actress TW/6
BRISCOE, Olive (b 1887) American
vaudevillian WWM
BRISMAN, Chaim (d 1970 [67])
performer BP/55*
BRISSON, Carl (1895-1958) Danish
actor ES, TW/2-3, 15, WWT/
5-12
BRISSON, Cleo (d 1975 [81]) per-
former BP/60*
BRISSON, Frederick (b 1913)
Danish producer BE, WWT/15-
16
BRISTOL, Earl of see Digby,
George
BRISTOW, Mr. (d 1848) English
actor HAS
BRISTOW, Miss (fl 1807) actress,
dancer CDP
BRISTOW, Mrs. [Mrs. Robert
Skinner] (fl 1797-1804) singer
BD
BRISTOW, Charles (b 1928) Eng-
lish lighting designer WWT/
15-16
BRISTOW, George (fl 1671) actor
BD
BRISTOW, George Frederick

(1825-98) American violinist,
composer, conductor, or-
ganist CDP, DAB, ES,
WWA/H

BRISTOW, James (fl 1597-1603)
actor DA

BRISTOWE, Agnes (d 1898)
actress EA/99*

BRISTOWE, Francis (fl 1635)
translator CP/3

BRITAIN, Mr. (fl 1675-78) pit
keeper BD

BRITEN, Mr. (fl 1661-64) actor
BD

BRITT, Elton (d 1972 [59]) com-
poser/lyricst BP/57*

BRITT, Jacqueline (d 1974 [29])
actress, singer TW/30

BRITTEN, Benjamin (1913-76)
English composer, conductor
CB, ES, HP, NTH

BRITTENHAM, Robert (fl 1838-
39) American actor HAS

BRITTENHAM, Mrs. Robert (fl
1839) actress HAS

BRITTINGHAM, Miss (fl 1852)
American actress HAS

BRITTLEBANK, Mrs. (d 1891
[60]) EA/92*

BRITTLEBANK, William (d
1897 [66]) lessee EA/98*

BRITTON, Mrs. (fl 1729-31)
actress, dancer BD

BRITTON, Clifton (d 1963 [52])
director BE*

BRITTON, Don (b 1937) American actor TW/13-14

BRITTON, Ethel (d 1972 [57])
performer BP/56*

BRITTON, Gary (b 1943)
American actor TW/23-24

BRITTON, George (b 1910)
American actor TW/8-9

BRITTON, Hutin [Mrs. Matheson Lang] (1876-1965) English actress COC, ES,
OC/1-3, WWT/1-11

BRITTON, Leonhard (b 1942)
American actor TW/25

BRITTON, Lillian [Mrs. Jefferson Egan] (fl 1900s)
American singer WWS

BRITTON, Pamela (d 1974 [51])
actress BP/59*, WWT/16*

BRITTON, Mrs. Robert see
Weber, Liza

BRITTON, Thomas (1644-1714)
English instrumentalist,

impresario BD, CDP

BRITTON, Tony (b 1924) English
actor AAS, WWT/15-16

BRITTON, Wallace (d 1872) actor
EA/73*

BRIZZI, Sig. [Achille Scipione
Bisteghi] (d 1884 [74]) singer
EA/85*

BROAD, Mr. (fl 1754-69) boxkeeper BD

BROAD, Mr. (fl 1760-61) doorkeeper BD

BROAD, Mrs. (fl 1735-36) house
servant BD

BROAD, George (b 1777) English
musician, composer BD

BROADBENT, Amanda see
Barrie, Amanda

BROADBENT, Dora see Bryan,
Dora

BROADBENT, Olive Ormond (d
1899 [17]) dancer EA/00*

BROADBRIDGE, Grace (d 1898
[23]) EA/99*

BROADFOOT, Alexander (d 1847)
actor, stage manager EA/72*

BROADFOOT, William (d 1852)
performer? EA/72*

BROADHEAD, W. H. (d 1931 [81])
manager WWT/14*

BROADHEAD, William Birch (d
1907 [34]) proprietor GRB/3

BROADHURST, Mr. (fl 1811)
singer BS

BROADHURST, Miss (fl 1773-96)
actress, singer CDP, HAS,
TD/1-2

BROADHURST, Miss (b c. 1775)
singer, actress BD

BROADHURST, George Howells
(1866-1952) English/American
dramatist DD, ES, GRB/2-4,
MWD, NTH, OC/1-3, SR, TW/
9, WWA/3, WWM, WWT/1-11,
WWW/5

BROADHURST, Kent (b 1940)
American actor TW/25, 30

BROADHURST, Thomas W. (1858-
1936) English dramatist SR

BROADHURST, William (d 1869
[82]) actor CDP

BROADLEY, Edward (d 1947) English actor, stage manager
SR

BROADWAY, James (d 1889) bill-
poster SR

BROADWOOD, Henry Fowler (d
1893 [82]) instrument maker

EA/94*
BROBSTON, Miss see Wilson, Mrs. Alexander
BROCAS, Mr. (fl 1755) actor BD
BROCHU, James (b 1946) American actor TW/26-27
BROCK, Mr. equestrian CDP
BROCK, Adam see Williams, E. B.
BROCK, Eliza (d 1893 [74]) EA/95*
BROCK, Fanny (d 1883 [30]) EA/84*
BROCK, James (b 1727) pyrotechnist BD
BROCK, John (d 1720) pyrotechnist BD
BROCK, John (b 1700) pyrotechnist BD
BROCK, Thomas (1756-1819) English pyrotechnist BD
BROCK, William (b 1752) English pyrotechnist BD
BROCK, William (1779-1849) pyrotechnist BD
BROCKBANK, Dora see Barton, Dora
BROCKBANK, Harrison (1867-1947) English actor, singer GRB/1-4
BROCKBANK, Mrs. Harrison (d 1894) EA/95*
BROCKBANK, Mrs. J. B. see Barton, Mary
BROCKBANK, John Benn (d 1896) EA/97*
BROCKETT, O. G. (b 1923) American educator, writer BE
BROCKIN, Mr. (fl 1776-90) dresser BD
BROCKIN, Mrs. (fl 1765) dresser BD
BROCKMAN, James (d 1967 [80]) performer BP/51*
BROCKSMITH, Roy (b 1945) American actor TW/28-30
BROCKWELL, Benjamin (fl 1665) musician BD
BROCKWELL, Henry (fl 1661-88) violinist BD
BRODAS, Mr. (fl 1750) tailor BD
BRODER, Jane talent representative BE
BRODERICK, Mr. (fl 1771-76) actor, singer BD

BRODERICK, Emma (1864-1948) singer SR
BRODERICK, Helen (1891-1959) American actress, singer ES, TW/16, WWT/7-10
BRODERICK, James (b 1928) American actor TW/22, 24, 26-27, 29
BRODIE, Matthew (1863-1908) Scottish actor DD, EA/95, GRB/1, 4
BRODIE, Mrs. Matthew see Rees, Alice
BRODIE, Steve singer CDP
BRODIE, Mrs. William (d 1886) EA/88*
BRODKIN, Herbert scene designer TW/4-5
BRODRIBB, John Henry see Irving, Sir Henry
BRODSZKY, Nicholas (b 1905) Russian/English composer ES
BRODY, Estelle (b 1904) Canadian actress ES
BROEDER, Ray (b 1898) Austro-Hungarian manager BE
BROEKMAN, David Hendrines (1899-1958) Dutch composer, conductor WWA/3
BROGDEN, Mr. (fl 1730) actor BD
BROGDEN, Mrs. Arthur, Sr. see Brogden, Dorothy
BROGDEN, Mrs. Arthur see LeButt, Ada
BROGDEN, Dorothy [Mrs. Arthur Brogden, Sr.] (d 1911 [34]) singer EA/12*
BROGDEN, Gwendoline (b 1891) English actress, singer WWT/3-6
BROGDEN, Paddy (d 1878) Irish singer EA/79*
BROHAN, Madeleine (d 1900 [66]) actress WWT/14*
BROHAN, Suzanne (d 1887 [80]) actress WWT/14*
"BROILEAU, The Mlles. " (fl 1753) performers BD
BROKAW, Charles (d 1975 [77]) actor BP/60*, WWT/16*
BROKE, Charles Frederick Tucker see Brooke, Charles Frederick Tucker
BROMBERG, J. Edward (1904-51) Hungarian actor ES, TW/3, 5-8, WWT/8-11
BROME, Alexander (1620-66)

English dramatist CP/1-3,
DD, DNB, FGF
BROME, Richard (c. 1590-1653)
English dramatist CP/1-3,
DD, DNB, ES, FGF, HP,
MH, NTH, OC/1-3, RE
BROME, Richard (fl 1628)
actor DA
BROMEFILD, Richard (fl 1628)
actor DA
BROMEHAM (fl 1582) actor DA
BROMELOW, John see Little
Gulliver
BROMFIELD, Louis (1896-1956)
American dramatist ES,
NTH, WWA/3, WWW/5
BROMFIELD, William (fl 1755)
dramatist CP/3
BROMHEAD, H. H. (d 1889
[29]) acting manager EA/91*
BROMLEY, Master (fl 1763-82)
harpist BD
BROMLEY, Charles (d 1902)
proprietor EA/03*
BROMLEY, Emily (d 1860 [31])
actress, singer WWT/14*
BROMLEY, John (fl 1778-1802)
scene painter BD
BROMLEY, Nelly (d 1939 [89])
actress DD, OAA/2
BROMLEY, Thomas (fl 1603)
lessee DA
BROMLEY Thomas (d 1841
[68]) actor EA/72*
BROMLEY, William (fl 1780-
1803) scene painter BD
BROMLEY, William (d 1887)
property master EA/88*
BROMLEY, Mrs. William
(d 1880 [51]) EA/81*
BROMLEY-DAVENPORT, Arthur
(1867-1946) English actor
WWT/4-10
BROMWICH, Frederick Dudman
(1873-1942) English actor,
manager GRB/1
BRON, Eleanor English actress
WWT/16
BRONNER, Edwin (b 1926)
American dramatist, his-
torian BE
BRONSON, Betty (d 1971 [64])
actress BP/56*, WWT/
16*
BRONSON, Charles (b 1922?)
American actor CB
BRONSON, James (b 1921)
American actor TW/8

BRONSON, Lillian (b 1902) Amer-
ican actress TW/4
BRONSON-HOWARD, George (b
1884) American critic WWM
BROOK, Clive (1887-1974) English
actor AAS, BTR/74, ES,
TW/7, WWT/5-15
BROOK, Edward Harcourt see
Brooke, Edward James Mac-
donald
BROOK, Faith (b 1922) English
actress TW/4, WWT/11-16
BROOK, Sir Fulk Greville (1554-
1628) English dramatist CP/1
BROOK, J. (fl 1722-23) house
servant? BD
BROOK, Joseph (d 1868 [65])
singer EA/69*
BROOK, Lesley (b 1917) English
actress WWT/10-11
BROOK, Lyndon (b 1927) American
actor TW/8
BROOK, Peter Stephen Paul (b
1925) English producer, direc-
tor, designer AAS, BE, CB,
CH, COC, ES, OC/2-3, PDT,
WWT/11-16
BROOK, Sara costume designer
WWT/16
BROOK, Thomas Graven Hodgkin-
son (d 1889 [36]) actor EA/90*
BROOKAM, Mrs. (fl 1779) dresser
BD
BROOKE, Mr. (fl 1788-89) actor
BD
BROOKE, Miss (fl 1781-89)
actress BD
BROOKE, Miss (fl 1789) dramatist
CP/3
BROOKE, Arthur (d 1563) writer
DD
BROOKE, C. [Mrs. Richard
Brooke] (d 1874 [32]) EA/75*
BROOKE, C. (d 1889) scene artist
EA/90*
BROOKE, Charles Frederick Tuck-
er (1883-1946) American scholar
DAB
BROOKE, Cynthia [Mrs. F. G.
Latham] (1875-1949) Australian
actress GRB/1, WWT/3-6
BROOKE, Edward James Mac-
donald [Edward Harcourt Brook]
(d 1884 [41]) actor EA/85*
BROOKE, E. H. (1843-84) actor
DD
BROOKE, E. H. (d 1929 [53])
English actor, stage manager

GRB/1-4

BROOKE, Mrs. E. H. (d 1915
[80]) actress DD, GRB/
3-4, WWT/1-3

BROOKE, Emily (d 1953) actress
WWT/4-5

BROOKE, Fergus (d 1882)
secretary EA/83*

BROOKE, Frances [née Moore]
(1724-89) English dramatist,
proprietor, actress BD,
CP/2-3, DD, DNB, GT,
TD/1-2

BROOKE, Frederick G. (d 1909)
sketch producer EA/10*

BROOKE, Gustavus Vaughan
(1818-66) English actor CDP,
COC, DD, DNB, ES, HAS,
OC/1-3

BROOKE, Mrs. Gustavus Vaughan
see Jones, Avonia

BROOKE, Harold (b 1910) English dramatist WWT/15-16

BROOKE, Harry (fl 1898-1913)
English scene designer ES

BROOKE, Henry (1703?-83)
Irish dramatist CDP, CP/
1-3, DD, ES, GT, HP,
NTH, TD/1-2

BROOKE, H. Sullivan (d 1923)
composer, conductor BE*,
WWT/14*

BROOKE, Iris (b 1908) English
educator, writer, costume
designer BE

BROOKE, James (fl 1773-84)
proprietor BD

BROOKE, James (d 1872 [36])
proprietor EA/73*

BROOKE, Mrs. John see
Brooke, Frances

BROOKE, Marie [Mrs. D.
Scott-Dalgleish] (d 1907)
composer EA/08*, GRB/3*

BROOKE, Paul (b 1944) English actor TW/30

BROOKE, Ralph (b 1920)
American actor TW/1, 3

BROOKE, Richard (fl 1672-73)
actor BD

BROOKE, Mrs. Richard see
Brooke, C.

BROOKE, Sarah (b 1875)
Indian/English actress
GRB/1-4, WWT/1-6

BROOKE, Walter American actor
TW/5, 8-9

BROOKES, Mr. (fl 1778) actor

BD

BROOKES, Mrs. [née Moore]
dramatist CP/1

BROOKES, Miss (fl 1774-75?)
dancer BD

BROOKES, George (1834-69) English actor HAS

BROOKES, George (d 1967 [68])
performer BP/51*

BROOKES, George see Verlino,
Charles

BROOKES, Mrs. George (fl 1861)
American actress HAS

BROOKES, Harriet Morton (d 1868
[55]) actress WWT/14*

BROOKES, Jacqueline (b 1930)
American actress AAS, BE,
TW/11-20, 22-23, 26-30, WWT/
15-16

BROOKES, L. DeGarmo American
actor, choreographer CDP

BROOKES, Mrs. Moreton (d 1868
[55]) actress EA/68*

BROOKES, R. (fl 1737) English
dramatist CP/2-3, GT

BROOKES, Robert (fl 1702) actor
BD

BROOKES, Dr. Samuel (fl 1613-15)
dramatist CP/3, FGF

BROOKFIELD, Mrs. (d 1895)
EA/97*

BROOKFIELD, Charles Hallam
Elton (1857-1913) English actor,
examiner of plays, dramatist
COC, DD, DP, GRB/1-4, SR,
WWT/1-2, WWW/1

BROOKFIELD, Sydney F. (d 1916)
journalist EA/17*, WWT/14*

BROOKHOUSER, Frank (d 1975
[63]) journalist BP/60*

BROOKING, Cecil (d 1940) actor
WWT/14*

BROOK-JONES, Elwyn (1911-62)
English actor WWT/10-13

BROOKLYN, Jessie (d 1886)
EA/87*

BROOKLYN, May English actress
SR

BROOKS, The Masters (fl 1737-
39) dancers BD

BROOKS, Mr. (d 1750) house servant, actor? BD

BROOKS, Mr. (fl 1774) animal
trainer? BD

BROOKS, Mr. (fl 1783-85) constable BD

BROOKS, [Mr.?] (fl 1794) actor?
BD

BROOKS, Mr. (fl 1839-40) actor, dancer HAS

BROOKS, Mrs. (fl 1760-67) charwoman BD

BROOKS, Mrs. [Miss Watson] (fl 1786-94) actress BD, DD, TD/1-2

BROOKS, Mrs. (fl 1798) actress BD

BROOKS, Mrs. (fl 1840) actress HAS

BROOKS, Miss see Pickup, Mrs.

BROOKS, Anita (fl c. 1855) singer CDP

BROOKS, Arreline (d 1879) dancer EA/80*

BROOKS, Beatrice (b 1925) American actress TW/23

BROOKS, Charles William Shirley (1815-74) dramatist DD, EA/68

BROOKS, Constance Ida (d 1901 [36]) EA/02*

BROOKS, David (b 1917-20) American actor, singer, director, producer BE, TW/1-6, 19-20, 26, 28

BROOKS, Donald (b 1928) American costume designer BE, CB

BROOKS, Edgar Oswald (b 1880) English manager GRB/1

BROOKS, Edith (d 1902) parachute proprietor EA/03*

BROOKS, Fred Emerson (1850-1923) American dramatist WWA/1

BROOKS, George singer, actor CDP

BROOKS, Geraldine (1925-77) American actress BE, ES, TW/3, 9-12, 26

BROOKS, Harvey O. (d 1968 [69]) composer/lyricist BP/53*

BROOKS, Helen (d 1971 [60]) actress TW/27

BROOKS, Helen M. (d 1912) EA/13*

BROOKS, Hugh (d 1974 [67]) impresario BP/59*

BROOKS, Mrs. Irving see Von Hatzfeldt, Olga

BROOKS, Jack (d 1971 [59]) performer BP/56*

BROOKS, James (fl 1749) house servant? BD

BROOKS, James (1760-1809) English band leader BD

BROOKS, James (d 1911 [49]) actor EA/12*

BROOKS, Joseph (d 1916 [68]) American manager SR

BROOKS, Lawrence (b 1912) American actor, singer BE, TW/1-3, 5-6, 22

BROOKS, Louise (b 1900) American dancer, actress ES

BROOKS, Maria Gowen (c. 1794-1845) American dramatist HJD

BROOKS, Martin (b 1925) American actor TW/7-18, 20

BROOKS, Maude (d 1971 [92]) theatre owner BP/56*

BROOKS, May K. (d 1963 [68]) performer BE*

BROOKS, Mel (b 1926?) American dramatist, writer BE, CB

BROOKS, Nat (d 1877 [39]) singer EA/78*

BROOKS, Neil (d 1975 [62]) general manager BP/60*

BROOKS, Phyllis (b 1914) American actress TW/1

BROOKS, Quintus H. (d 1916 [58]) manager WWT/14*

BROOKS, Ralph Turner (d 1963 [43]) producer, director BE*

BROOKS, Shelton L. (d 1975 [89]) composer/lyricist BP/60*

BROOKS, Shirley see Brooks, Charles William Shirley

BROOKS, Thomas (d 1878 [83]) cashier EA/79*

BROOKS, Virginia Fox see Vernon, Virginia

BROOKS, Mrs. Watson (fl 1786) actress CDP

BROOKS, Wilson (1914-66) American actor TW/6-7, 23

BROOKSBANK, Miss (fl 1785) actress BD

BROOKYN, May [Mrs. King] (d 1894 [35]) actress EA/95*

BROOM, Frank (d 1899 [29]) comedian, acrobat EA/00*

"BROOMSTICKADO, Mynheer Von Poop-Poop" (fl 1757-60) bassoonist BD

BROONES, Martin (b 1892) American composer WWT/8-11

BROPHY, Annie [Mrs. A. K. Thomas] (d 1910 [51]) actress EA/11*

BROPHY, Bridget (b 1929) English

dramatist CD

BROPHY, Edward (d 1960 [65])
American actor BE*

BROTHERSON, Eric (b 1911)
American actor TW/2-3,
6-12, WWT/11-16

BROTHERTON, Thomas J. R.
(d 1969 [77]) treasurer
BP/54*

BROUETT, Albert French actor
WWT/7

BROUGH, Mrs. Barnabas see
Brough, Fanny

BROUGH, Fanny [Mrs. Barnabas
Brough] (d 1897 [94]) EA/98*

BROUGH, Fanny Whiteside [Mrs.
Richard Smith Boleyn] (1854-
1914) French/English actress
COC, DD, DP, EA/95, ES,
GRB/1-4, OAA/1-2, OC/1-3,
WWT/1-2

BROUGH, Lionel (1836-1900)
Welsh actor CDP, COC, DD,
DNB, DP, ES, GRB/1-4,
OAA/1-2, OC/1-3, WWW/1

BROUGH, Mrs. Lionel see
Brough, Margaret Rose

BROUGH, Margaret (d 1901)
actress EA/02*

BROUGH, Margaret Rose [Mrs.
Lionel Brough] (d 1901 [60])
EA/02*

BROUGH, Mary Bessie (1863-
1934) English actress AAS,
COC, ES, GRB/4, OC/1-3,
WWT/1-7, WWW/3

BROUGH, Robert (d 1906 [49])
actor, manager, singer
CDP, DD

BROUGH, Mrs. Robert [Florence
Trevelyan] (d 1932 [73])
actress WWT/4-5

BROUGH, Robert Barnabas (1828-
60) English dramatist COC,
DD, DNB, ES, OC/1-3

BROUGH, Sarah Ann (d 1877)
pianist EA/78*

BROUGH, Sydney (1868-1911)
English actor DD, DP,
EA/95, ES, GRB/1-4,
OC/1-3

BROUGH, William (1826-70)
English dramatist COC, DD,
DNB, EA/68, ES, OC/1-3

BROUGH, Mrs. William see
Romer, Anne

BROUGH, William Francis (1798-
1867) Irish actor, singer

CDP, HAS, SR

BROUGHAM, Emma see Robertson, Emma

BROUGHAM, John (1810-80) Irish/
American dramatist, actor,
manager CDP, COC, DAB,
DD, DNB, EA/68, ES, GC,
HAS, HJD, NTH, OAA/1-2,
OC/1-3, SR, WWA/H

BROUGHAM, Mrs. John, I [Ann-
ette Nelson; Mrs. Coppleson
Hodges] (fl 1828-37) actress
HAS

BROUGHAM, Mrs. John, II [née
Williams] (fl 1836-42) actress
HAS

BROUGHAM, W. (d 1885 [48])
conjuror, singer EA/86*

BROUGHAM, W. H. (d 1916 [65])
actor EA/18*

BROUGHTON, Emma (d 1926)
actress, dancer WWT/14*

BROUGHTON, Frederick W. (1851-
94) dramatist DD

BROUGHTON, Henry James (d
1876 [29]) actor EA/77*

BROUGHTON, James (d 1887 [52])
musician EA/88*

BROUGHTON, Jessie (b 1885)
English vocalist GRB/1-4,
WWT/1-2

BROUGHTON, John (1705-89) English? pugilist DNB

BROUGHTON, Mrs. John, I (d
1870) actress CDP

BROUGHTON, Phyllis (d 1926 [64])
actress, dancer, singer DD,
DP, EA/96, GRB/2-4, WWT/
1-5

BROUGHTON, Simon J. (d 1964
[80]) performer BE*

BROUGHTON, Thomas (1704-74)
English dramatist CP/2-3,
DD, GT

BROUN, Heywood Campbell (1888-
1939) American critic NTH,
WWT/5-9

BROUN, Heywood Hale (b 1918)
American actor BE, TW/10-12,
22-23

BROUNOFF, Platon (1863-1924)
Russian composer WWA/1

BROUS, Mr. (fl 1708) tailor BD

BROUSIL, Alois (d 1888 [42])
musical director, violinist
EA/89*

BROUWENSTIJN, Gré (b 1915)
Dutch singer ES

BROWER, Frank (1820-74)
American comedian CDP,
HAS

BROWER, Mrs. Frank [Louisa
Banks] (fl 1851) performer
HAS

BROWN, Mr. (fl 1708) box-
keeper BD

BROWN, Mr. (fl 1718) dramatist CP/2-3

BROWN, Mr. (fl 1719-29) boxkeeper or officekeeper BD

BROWN, Mr. (fl 1724) actor
BD

BROWN, Mr. (fl 1748-51)
actor, dancer, singer BD

BROWN, Mr. (fl 1763-64)
actor BD

BROWN, Mr. (fl 1768?-1817?)
singer BD

BROWN, Mr. (fl 1770?-1808?)
actor BD

BROWN, Mr. (fl 1771) equestrian
BD

BROWN, Mr. (fl 1776-77)
dresser BD

BROWN, [Mr. ?] (fl 1776-77)
performer BD

BROWN, Mr. (fl 1791) exhibitor
BD

BROWN, Mr. (fl 1794) singer?
BD

BROWN, Mr. (fl 1796) CP/3

BROWN, Mr. (fl 1798-99) actor
BD

BROWN, Mr. ["Big Brown"] (d
1836) actor HAS

BROWN, Mrs. (fl 1662) actress
BD

BROWN, Mrs. (fl 1707) actress
BD

BROWN, Mrs. (fl 1708) dresser
BD

BROWN, Mrs. (fl 1736-51)
actress BD

BROWN, Mrs. (fl 1764) actress
BD

BROWN, Mrs. (fl 1776-78)
dresser BD

BROWN, Mrs. (fl 1786) performer? BD

BROWN, Mrs. (fl c. 1786-87)
singer BD

BROWN, Mrs. (fl 1790-97)
actress, singer BD

BROWN, Mrs. [née Biggs] (fl
1798-1801) actress BD

BROWN, Miss (fl 1767-78)
dancer, actress BD

BROWN, Miss (fl 1782) actress
BD

BROWN, Miss (fl 1791) actress
BD

BROWN, Abraham (fl 1739-68)
violinist, composer BD

BROWN, Mrs. A. H. see
Robson, May

BROWN, Albert O. (d 1945 [73])
American producer BE*, BP/
29*

BROWN, Alice (1857-1948) American dramatist WWA/2

BROWN, Ann see Cargill, Mrs.
R.

BROWN, Anthony (fl 1739) dramatist CP/1-3, DD, GT, TD/1-2

BROWN, Archibald (d 1916) EA/
18*

BROWN, Bertrand (d 1964 [75])
American songwriter, press
representative BE*

BROWN, Bessie Greenwood (d
1973 [92]) performer BP/57*

BROWN, Buster see Ansley,
Edmond

BROWN, Carrie Clarke Ward
(1862-1926) American performer
SR

BROWN, Chamberlain (d 1955 [67])
agent TW/12

BROWN, Charles Armitage (fl
1814) librettist DD

BROWN, Charles Brockden (1771-
1810) American dramatist
EAP

BROWN, Charles D. (d 1948 [60])
American actor TW/5

BROWN, Charles E. (1862-1947)
magician, ventriloquist SR

BROWN, Clark (1877-1943) American manager SR

BROWN, Dan (d 1875 [39]) minstrel
EA/76*

BROWN, Daniel (b 1947) American
actor TW/29

BROWN, Danny (d 1976 [63]) pro-
ducer/director/choreographer
BP/60*

BROWN, David Paul (1795-1875)
American dramatist CDP,
DAB, EAP, NTH, RJ

BROWN, DeMarcus (b 1900) American educator, director BE

BROWN, Dennis (d 1969 [55])
producer/director/choreographer
BP/54*

BROWN, Miss E. (fl 1797-98) actress BD

BROWN, Edith Ann see Heron-Brown, Edith

BROWN, Mrs. Edwin see Kelly, Kate

BROWN, Elizabeth (d 1885 [84]) EA/86*

BROWN, Elizabeth (d 1906) EA/07*

BROWN, Elizabeth American actress TW/26

BROWN, Ellen (d 1895) EA/97*

BROWN, Fanny (b 1837) American actress HAS

BROWN, Firman H. , Jr. (b 1926) American educator, director BE

BROWN, Florrie (d 1892 [19]) EA/93*

BROWN, Fred (d 1899) musician EA/01*

BROWN, Frederick (d 1871) pianist EA/72*

BROWN, Frederick (d 1901 [51]) entrepreneur EA/03*

BROWN, Master Frederick (fl 1805) juvenile prodigy CDP

BROWN, Frederick Charles see Seel, Charles

BROWN, George Anderson (d 1920 [81]) actor BE*, BP/5*

BROWN, Georgia [née Klot] (b 1933) English actress, singer AAS, BE, WWT/14-16

BROWN, G. H. (d 1881 [26]) musician EA/82*

BROWN, Gilmor (d 1960 [73]) American producer, director CB, ES, TW/16

BROWN, Graham (b 1924) American actor TW/24-27, 29-30

BROWN, Harry singer CDP

BROWN, Harry Joe (d 1972 [78]) producer/director/choreographer BP/56*

BROWN, Helen (b 1902) American community theatre director BE

BROWN, Helen see Hayes, Helen

BROWN, Henry (d 1720) actor BD

BROWN, Henry (d 1902 [87]) jester EA/03*

BROWN, Henry C. (d 1970 [44]) agent BP/54*

BROWN, Hubert Sydney (1898-

1949) English composer, writer WWW/4

BROWN, I. H. actor CDP

BROWN, Irene (d 1965 [72]) performer BP/50*

BROWN, Irving (b 1922) American educator, director BE

BROWN, Ivor (1891-1974) English critic, dramatist AAS, BE, BTR/74, OC/1-3, PDT, WWT/6-15

BROWN, J. (d 1818) actor, acrobat, singer BD

BROWN, J. (fl 1819) writer DD

BROWN, Mrs. J. [Mrs. William Ross; née Mills] (d 1823) actress, singer BD, CDP, DD

BROWN, James (fl 1783) dramatist CP/3

BROWN, James (fl 1794) trumpeter BD

BROWN, James H. (d 1930) actor, manager SR

BROWN, James Henry (d 1873 [66]) secretary EA/74*

BROWN, J. B. elocution teacher CDP

BROWN, Jessie (d 1892) actress EA/93*

BROWN, Joe (d 1883) minstrel CDP

BROWN, Joe (b 1830) American dancer, comedian HAS

BROWN, Joe E. (1892-1973) American actor, comedian BE, CB, ES, SR, TW/2-8, 30, WWA/5, WWT/7-15

BROWN, Dr. John (1715-66) English dramatist CP/3, DD

BROWN, John (fl 1732-36) singer, actor BD

BROWN, John Mason (1900-69) American critic AAS, BE, CB, COC, ES, HJD, NTH, OC/1-3, PDT, TW/25, WWT/6-14, WWW/6

BROWN, John Mills (d 1859 [77]) English actor CDP, HAS

BROWN, Johnnie ["Lord Tom Doddy"] (d 1898 [16]) comedian EA/00*

BROWN, Johnny Mack (d 1974 [70]) actor BP/59*, WWT/16*

BROWN, John Russell (b 1923) English director, scholar WWT/15-16

BROWN, Josephine actress TW/1, 13-14

BROWN, J. Purdy (d 1834)
manager HAS
BROWN, Kay (b 1902) American
talent representative, pro-
ducer BE
BROWN, Kelly (b 1928) American
dancer BE, TW/15-16
BROWN, Kenneth H. (b 1936)
American dramatist CD
BROWN, Kermit (b 1937) Amer-
ican actor TW/24-25, 28
BROWN, Lawrence (d 1972 [79])
composer/lyricist BP/57*
BROWN, Lew (1893/99-1958)
American lyricist, librettist,
producer, manager WWT/
8-11
BROWN, Lillian actress CDP
BROWN, Lillian (d 1969 [83])
actress, singer, male im-
personator TW/26
BROWN, Lionel (1888-1964)
Irish dramatist WWT/9-13
BROWN, Louise actress, singer
WWT/6-7
BROWN, L. Slade (b 1922)
American producer BE
BROWN, Lyman C. (d 1961
[60]) American talent repre-
sentative BE*
BROWN, Martin (d 1891 [50])
proprietor EA/92*
BROWN, Martin (1885-1936)
Canadian dramatist, dancer,
actor SR, WWT/5-8
BROWN, Mollie equestrienne
CDP
BROWN, Nacio Herb (d 1964
[68]) composer/lyricist BP/
49*
BROWN, Nella F. reader CDP
BROWN, Nellie [Mrs. Ellen
Alice Holt] (d 1892 [31])
music-hall artist EA/93*
BROWN, [Owen?] (fl 1794)
actor BD
BROWN, Pamela Mary (1917-75)
English actress AAS, BE,
ES, TW/3, 6-8, 14-16,
WWT/10-14
BROWN, Pendleton (b 1948)
American actor TW/28
BROWN, Percy (1883-1918) actor
SR
BROWN, R. see Persivani
BROWN, Reed, Jr. (d 1962 [63])
American actor TW/19
BROWN, R. G. (b 1933)

American actor TW/18, 25-27
BROWN, Robert ["Buster"] see
Ansley, Edmond
BROWN, Rose M. (d 1965 [61])
performer BP/49*
BROWN, Rowland C. (d 1963 [62])
director BE*
BROWN, Russ (d 1964 [72]) singer,
actor TW/21
BROWN, Russ (d 1971 [56]) com-
poser/lyricist BP/55*
BROWN, Samuel (d 1917) EA/18*
BROWN, Samuel Edwin (1826-69)
American actor HAS
BROWN, Sarah (1757-1806) dancer
BD
BROWN, Sedley (1856-1928) Amer-
ican director WWM
BROWN, Susan (d 1932) American
actress TW/23
BROWN, Tally (b 1934) American
actress TW/25-26, 28-29
BROWN, Thomas (1663-1704) Eng-
lish dramatist CP/3, DD, GT
BROWN, Thomas (fl 1715-40)
violinist, composer BD
BROWN, Thomas (fl 1794) singer
BD
BROWN, Thomas (d 1865) property
man HAS
BROWN, Thomas Allston (1836-
1918) American historian, agent,
manager CDP, DD, SR, WWA/
4, WWM
BROWN, Tom (b 1913) American
actor ES
BROWN, Vincent (fl 1901) drama-
tist DD
BROWN, Wally (d 1961 [57]) actor
BE*, BP/46*
BROWN, Walter P. (b 1926)
American actor TW/22, 24, 30
BROWN, William (fl 1789-94)
violoncellist BD
BROWN, William (d 1870 [31])
singer? EA/71*
BROWN, William B. singer,
humorist, composer, comedian
CDP
BROWN, William F. dramatist
CD
BROWN, William Ruddle (b 1868)
English actor GRB/1
BROWN, Mrs. William Ruddle
see Howitt, Nellie
BROWN, Winifred Colleano (d 1973
[75]) performer BP/57*
BROWNBILL, Thomas Robson see

Robson, Frederick
BROWNE (fl 1596) actor DA
BROWNE, Mr. (fl 1749-56)
house servant? BD
BROWNE, Mr. (fl 1787) Amer-
ican? actor TD/1-2
BROWNE, Mr. (fl 1823) actor
BS
BROWNE, Brineta (b 1885)
English actress GRB/1-2
BROWNE, Campbell (d 1903 [39])
singer EA/04*
BROWNE, Charles (fl 1739)
musician BD
BROWNE, Charles Farrar ["Art-
emus Ward"] (1834-67) Amer-
ican entertainer, comedian
CDP, HAS, SR
BROWNE, Mrs. Chris see
Browne, Leonora Mary
BROWNE, Coral (b 1913)
Australian actress AAS,
BE, CB, TW/12, 20, 22,
WWT/9-16
BROWNE, David (d 1871 [28])
actor EA/72*
BROWNE, Edward (fl 1584-1603)
actor DA
BROWNE, Edward (d 1916 [69])
circus musician EA/17*
BROWNE, E. Martin (b 1900)
English producer, actor,
director AAS, BE, COC,
ES, OC/1-3, PDT, WWT/9-16
BROWNE, Frederick (d 1838)
English actor, manager HAS
BROWNE, Mrs. Frederick [née
De Camp] see De Camp,
Sophia
BROWNE, George F. (b 1833)
American actor HAS
BROWNE, G. H. (d 1877 [51])
proprietor EA/78*
BROWNE, Mrs. Graham see
McIntosh, Madge
BROWNE, G. Walter (b 1856)
actor, singer, dramatist DD
BROWNE, Henry (fl 1583) actor
DA
BROWNE, Irene (1896-1965)
English actress BE, ES,
TW/22, WWT/4-13
BROWNE, James S. (1791-1869)
English actor HAS
BROWNE, John (fl 1551-63) court
interluder DA
BROWNE, John (fl 1608) actor
DA

BROWNE, Dr. John (1715-66)
English dramatist CP/1-2, GT,
TD/1-2
BROWNE, K. R. G. (d 1940 [45])
librettist WWT/14*
BROWNE, Laidman (1896-1961)
English actor ES, WWT/9-10
BROWNE, Leonora Mary [Mrs.
Chris Browne] (d 1905) EA/06*
BROWNE, Lewis Allen (1876-1937)
American dramatist WWA/1
BROWNE, Louise American act-
ress, singer, dancer WWT/8-9
BROWNE, Marjorie (b 1913) Eng-
lish actress, singer WWT/9-13
BROWNE, Matthew Campbell (fl
1778-1806) actor BD
BROWNE, Maurice (1881-1955)
English actor, manager, drama-
tist COC, ES, MWD, NTH,
OC/3, WWA/3, WWT/6-11,
WWW/5
BROWNE, Moses (1703-87) drama-
tist CP/1-3, DD
BROWNE, Nellie see Taylor,
Mrs. C. R.
BROWNE, Old (fl 1602) actor DA
BROWNE, Pattie (b 1869) Australian
actress GRB/1-4, WWT/1-5
BROWNE, Porter Emerson (1879-
1934) American dramatist SR,
WWA/1, WWM, WWT/1-7
BROWNE, Rachell (fl 1666-70)
tirewoman BD
BROWNE, Richard (fl 1670-75)
violinist BD
BROWNE, Robert (fl 1583-1620/40)
English actor COC, DA, ES,
OC/1-3
BROWNE, Roscoe Lee (b 1925)
American actor BE, WWT/15-
16
BROWNE, Solomon James (1791-
1869) English actor CDP, DD,
OX
BROWNE, Stella (b 1906) English
actress, singer WWT/7-9
BROWNE, Thomas (d 1704) English
dramatist CP/2
BROWNE, Thomas (fl 1675-83)
violinist BD
BROWNE, Thomas (b 1906) English
dramatist WWT/10-14
BROWNE, Tom (d 1884) musician,
composer EA/85*
BROWNE, Tom (d 1899) songwriter
EA/00*
BROWNE, Walter (1856-1911)

English actor, dramatist,
singer WWS
BROWNE, Walter E. dramatist
SR
BROWNE, W. Graham (1870/75-
1937) Irish actor COC, GRB/
1-4, WWT/1-8
BROWNE, William (fl c. 1600-32)
actor DA
BROWNE, William (1590-1645)
English writer CP/3, DD,
FGF
BROWNE, Wynyard Barry (1911-
64) English dramatist AAS,
PDT, WWT/11-13
BROWNELL, Mabel (b 1888)
American actress WWM
BROWNING, Mr. (fl 1785-86)
house servant? bassoonist?
BD
BROWNING, Miss (fl 1785-86)
singer, dancer BD
BROWNING, Bonnie (d 1918)
EA/19*
BROWNING, Edith (d 1926 [51])
actress, singer BE*, BP/
10*
BROWNING, Harry G. (b c. 1863)
actor SR
BROWNING, Robert (1812-89)
English dramatist DD, DNB,
ES, HP, NTH, OC/1-3,
PDT, RE
BROWNING, Robert (b 1942)
American actor TW/26, 29
BROWNING, Rod (b 1942) Amer-
ican actor TW/29
BROWNING, Susan (b 1941)
American actress, singer
TW/24, 26-30, WWT/16
BROWNING, Tod (d 1962 [82])
director BP/47*
BROWNLEE, Brian American
actor TW/29-30
BROWNLEE, Dell French/
American actor TW/27-29
BROWNLEE, John Donald Mac-
kenzie (1901-69) Australian
executive, singer BE, ES,
WWW/6
BROWNLOW, Wallace (d 1919)
actor, singer WWT/14*
BROWN-POTTER, Cora Urquhart
see Potter, Cora Urquhart
BROWNSMITH, John (fl 1751-79)
prompter, actor BD, DD
BROWNSTONE, Joseph (1920-70)
American stage manager,

director, producer BE
BROXUP, Katherine [née Studt]
(d 1906) EA/07*
BRUBACH, Gary (b 1950) Ameri-
can actor TW/30
BRUCATO, Jimmy (d 1973 [55])
producer/director/choreographer
BP/57*
BRUCE, Mr. actor CDP
BRUCE, Mr. (fl 1794-95) door-
keeper BD
BRUCE, Mrs. (fl 1705-06) dancer
BD
BRUCE, Allan (b 1930) Scottish
actor TW/22
BRUCE, Betty (1921/25-74) Amer-
ican dancer, singer, comedienne
BE, TW/1-7, WWT/10-11
BRUCE, Brenda (b 1918) English
actress AAS, ES, WWT/10-16
BRUCE, Carol (b 1919) American
actress, singer BE, TW/1,
5-7, 21-22, 24, WWT/10-16
BRUCE, Charles (d 1877 [32])
minstrel EA/78*
BRUCE, Charley (d 1890 [35])
EA/91*
BRUCE, Clifford [Clifford B.
Scott] (b 1884) Canadian actor
WWM
BRUCE, David (d 1976 [60]) per-
former BP/60*
BRUCE, Edgar (d 1901 [56]) actor,
manager, proprietor DD, DP,
OAA/2
BRUCE, Mrs. Edgar see Bruce,
Lucy Sybil
BRUCE, Edgar K. (1893-1971)
English actor WWT/8-15
BRUCE, Edith (d 1925) actress
DD, OAA/2
BRUCE, Geraldine (d 1953 [72])
actress TW/10
BRUCE, Mrs. H. A. see
Bruce, Mary Ann
BRUCE, Harry actor, producer,
stage manager, manager GRB/1
BRUCE, Henry Alexander (d 1901
[69]) managing director EA/02*,
WWT/14*
BRUCE, Katherine (b 1941) Amer-
ican actress TW/23, 29
BRUCE, Lucy Sybil [Mrs. Edgar
Bruce] (d 1901 [28]) EA/02*
BRUCE, Hon. Mrs. Lyndhurst
Henry see Clifford, Camille
BRUCE, Mary Ann [Mrs. H. A.
Bruce] (d 1908) EA/09*,

GRB/4*

BRUCE, Nigel (1895-1953)
American actor ES, TW/
10, WWT/5-11

BRUCE, Paul (d 1971) performer
BP/55*

BRUCE, Samuel (b 1936) Canadian actor TW/28

BRUCE, Sybil Etonia see
Bruce, Tonie Edgar

BRUCE, Tonie Edgar [Sybil
Etonia Bruce] (1892-1966)
English actress WWT/5-11

BRUCE, Tony (d 1937 [27])
actor BE*, WWT/14*

BRUCE, William (fl 1730-51)
musician BD

BRUCE-POTTER, Hilda (b 1888)
English actress WWT/2-12

BRUCKER, Mr. (fl 1795) house
servant? BD

BRUCKNER, Ferdinand [Theodor
Tagger] (1891-1958) Austrian/
American dramatist, director
CH, MH, MWD, OC/3

BRUDNAL, Mr. (fl 1753) actor
BD

BRUFORD, Rose Elizabeth (b
1904) English college principal WWT/14-16

BRUGNER, Mr. (fl 1766-67)
lobby doorkeeper BD

BRUGUIER, Anthony (fl 1786-
98) dancing master BD

BRUGUIER, Sophia (fl 1798-99)
dancer BD

BRUGUIER, Susan (fl 1798-99)
dancer BD

BRUHN, Erik Belton Evers (b
1928) Danish dancer,
choreographer CB, ES

BRUKERWICH, Mrs. see Stoll,
Blanche

BRULE, André (1879-1953)
French actor, manager ES,
WWT/4, 10

BRULL, Anton (d 1911 [74])
EA/12*

BRULL, Joseph [Pepi] (d 1908
36]) EA/10

BRUMEN, Miss (fl 1794) singer
BD

BRUMMEL, David (b 1942)
American actor TW/30

BRUMMELL, William (fl 1785?)
performer? BD

BRUNATTI, Antonio (fl 1663-67)
scene keeper BD

BRUNDAGE, John Herbert see
Herbert, John

BRUNDAGE, Mary Anne (fl 1815-
20) actress HAS

BRUNDIN, Bo (b 1937) Swedish
actor TW/23

BRUNE, Adrienne [Phyllis Caroline Brune] (b 1892/97)
Australian actress, singer
WWT/5-11

BRUNE, Clarence M. (b 1870)
Scottish actor WWT/1

BRUNE, Gabrielle (b 1912) English actress, singer WWT/10-
12

BRUNE, Minnie Tittell (b 1883)
American actress WWT/1-5

BRUNE, Phyllis Caroline see
Brune, Adrienne

BRUNEAU, Alfred (1857-1934)
French composer GRB/1-4,
WWM

BRUNEL, Adrian (b 1892) English
actor ES

BRUNETTE, Miss (fl 1734-42)
actress, dancer BD

BRUNETTI, Gaetano (d 1758)
scene painter BD

BRUNETTS, Mons. (fl 1675)
manager? BD

BRUNI, Domenico (fl 1793) singer
BD

BRUNING, Albert (1863-1929)
German actor WWM

BRUNING, Francesca (b 1907)
American actress BE, TW/3,
WWT/8-14

BRUNN, Mr. (fl 1775-78) puppeteer, dancer BD

BRUNO, Anthony J. (d 1976 [82])
photographer BP/60*

BRUNO, Giordano (1548-1600)
Italian dramatist COC, OC/
1-3

BRUNO, Jean (b 1926) American
actress TW/27-30

BRUNO, Mrs. W. Lee see
Garratt, Jessie

BRUNORO, Sig. (fl 1742) dancer
BD

BRUNOT, Andre (d 1973 [93])
performer BP/58*

BRUNS, Edna (d 1960 [80]) performer BE*, BP/45*

BRUNS, Julia (1895-1927) American actress WWT/4-5

BRUNS, Mona American actress
TW/2-3

BRUNS, Philip (b 1931) American actor TW/23, 25-27, 29

BRUNSDON, John (fl 1774-81) actor BD, CDP

BRUNSWICK, Mark (d 1971 [69]) composer/lyricist BP/55*

BRUNTON, Anna (b 1773) dramatist CP/3, DD

BRUNTON, Ann[e; Anne Merry; Mrs. Robert Merry] (1768-1808) English actress CDP, COC, DAB, ES, HAS, OC/1-3, SR, TD/1-2, WWA/H

BRUNTON, Annie (fl 1880) actress DD

BRUNTON, Dorothy (1893-1977) Australian actress, singer WWT/4-10

BRUNTON, Miss E. [Mrs. Diver] (d 1893] actress EA/94*

BRUNTON, Elizabeth [Mrs. Peter Columbine] (c. 1772-99) English actress BD, TD/1-2

BRUNTON, Elizabeth (d 1893) actress WWT/14*

BRUNTON, Elizabeth see Yates, Elizabeth

BRUNTON, Garland Lewis (d 1975 [72]) performer BP/60*

BRUNTON, John (1741-1822) English actor, manager BD, DD, ES, OC/1-3, TD/1-2

BRUNTON, John (1775-1848) English actor CDP, DD, GT, OC/1-3, TD/1-2

BRUNTON, John (d 1909 [62]) scene artist EA/10*

BRUNTON, Mrs. John [Anna Ross] (b 1773) English actress, dramatist BD

BRUNTON, Louisa [Countess Craven] (1779-1860) English actress CDP, COC, DD, ES, GT, OC/1-3

BRUNTON, Watty (d 1904 [76]) comedian EA/05*, WWT/14*

BRUNTON, Mrs. Watty, Sr. (d 1893 [57]) singer, actress EA/94*

BRUNTON, W. H. (fl 1836) English actor HAS

BRUNTON, Mrs. W. H. [née Helen Matthews] (b 1827) Irish actress HAS, SR

BRUODIN, Mr. (fl 1749) actor BD

BRUSCANTINI, Sesto (b 1919)

Italian singer ES

BRUSH, Clinton E., III (b 1911) American architect BE

BRUSH, Mrs. Clinton E. [née Martha Hughes Stockton] (b 1911) American actress, educator BE

BRUSKIN, Perry (b 1916) American producer, director, stage manager, actor BE

BRUSTEIN, Robert Sanford (b 1927) American actor, director, critic AAS, BE, CB, WWT/15-16

BRUTON, James (d 1867 [52]) writer EA/68*

BRUYLANTS, Francine (d 1974 [75]) performer BP/59*

BRYAN, Mr. (fl 1713?-26) musician BD

BRYAN, Mr. (fl 1750) actor? BD

BRYAN, Mr. (fl 1784) singer BD

BRYAN, Daniel (fl 1670) scene keeper BD

BRYAN, Dora [née Broadbent] (b 1924) English actress AAS, WWT/12-16

BRYAN, [Frederick?] (d 1770?) prompter BD

BRYAN, George (fl 1586-1613) English actor DA, GT, NTH

BRYAN, Hal [Johnson Clark] (1891-1948) English actor WWT/10

BRYAN, Herbert George (d 1948) English producer WWT/9-10

BRYAN, Jackson L. (d 1964 [55]) performer BP/49*

BRYAN, John (d 1769) musician BD

BRYAN, John (d 1969 [58]) producer/director/choreographer BP/54*

BRYAN, Julien H. (d 1974 [75]) producer/director/choreographer BP/59*

BRYAN, Marian Knighton (d 1974 [74]) dance teacher BP/59*

BRYAN, Mary (fl 1624) lessee DA

BRYAN, Peggy (b 1916) English actress WWT/9-11

BRYANT, Billy (1888-1948) actor, showboat manager SR

BRYANT, Cpt. Billy (d 1968 [79]) showboat captain BP/52* [?=preceding entry, q.v.]

BRYANT, Charles E. (1879-1948) English actor ES, TW/5, WWT/1-10

BRYANT, Dan [Daniel Webster O'Bryan] (1833-75) American comedian, minstrel, manager CDP, HAS, SR

BRYANT, George (d 1889) marionette proprietor EA/90*

BRYANT, Grant see Berte, Charles

BRYANT, Jerry [né O'Brien] (1828-61) American minstrel CDP, HAS

BRYANT, John (d 1868 [30]) singer EA/69*

BRYANT, John (b 1916) American actor TW/2

BRYANT, J. V. (1889-1924) English actress WWT/2-4

BRYANT, Mardi (b 1924) American actress TW/2

BRYANT, Margaret C. (b 1908) American educator BE

BRYANT, Marshall F. (d 1971 [79]) critic BP/56*

BRYANT, Mary (b 1936) American press representative, actress BE

BRYANT, Michael (b 1928) English actor AAS, WWT/14-16

BRYANT, Nana (d 1955 [67]) American actress TW/3, 12

BRYANT, Neil [Cornelius A. O'Brien] (1835-1902) minstrel CDP

BRYANT, Robin (d 1976 [50]) performer BP/60*

BRYANT, Sam (1855-1948) actor, showboat manager SR

BRYANT, Mrs. W. see Barlette, Sophie

BRYANT, Willie (d 1964 [56]) actor BE*, BP/48*

BRYARS, Mr. (fl 1723-24) boxkeeper BD

BRYCE, Edward (b 1921) American actor TW/4-16

BRYDEN, Bill (b 1942) Scottish director, dramatist WWT/16

BRYDEN, Ronald (b 1927) English critic AAS, WWT/15-16

BRYDGE, Matilda [Mrs. T. B. Brydge] (d 1882) EA/83*

BRYDGE, T. B. (d 1917) music-hall performer EA/18*

BRYDGE, Mrs. T. B. see Brydge, Matilda

BRYDON, W. B. (b 1933) English actor TW/24-25, 29-30

BRYDONE, Alfred [Alfred Brydone Boak] (1863-1920) Scottish actor GRB/1-4, WWT/1-3

BRYER, Vera (1905-67) English actress, singer TW/24, WWT/7-9

BRYER, William Frederick see Edouin, Willie

BRYERS, Mr. (fl 1716) boxkeeper BD

BRYGGMAN, Larry (b 1938) American actor TW/25-27, 30

BRYLAWSKI, Fulton (d 1973 [88]) lawyer BP/58*

BRYNING, John (b 1913) English actor WWT/10-14

BRYNNER, Yul (b 1917) Japanese/Swiss actor, director CB, ES, TW/7-15

BRYSON, Lyman Lloyd (b 1888) American dramatist CB

BRYTON, Frederick (d 1902) American actor CDP, SR

BUBB, [Elizabeth?] (fl 1723-27) dresser BD

BUBB, George (d 1878 [55]) EA/79*

BUBBLES, John (b 1902) American performer, actor TW/24

BUCALOSSI, Brigata (d 1924) composer, conductor BE*, WWT/14*

BUCALOSSI, Ernest (d 1933 [69]) composer, conductor BE*, WWT/14*

BUCALOSSI, Procida (d 1918 [86]) composer, conductor BE*, WWT/14*

BUCHAN, Mr. (d 1800) watchman, sweeper BD

BUCHAN, Mrs. (fl 1789-94) dresser BD

BUCHAN, Annabelle Whitford (d 1961 [83]) performer BE*

BUCHAN, D. B. see Young, D. B.

BUCHANAN, Mr. (fl 1724) actor BD

BUCHANAN, Mrs. Charles [Elizabeth] (d 1736) actress BD, DD

BUCHANAN, Charles L. (d 1962 [77]) critic BE*

BUCHANAN, Elizabeth see Buchanan, Mrs. Charles

BUCHANAN, George (1506-82) Scottish dramatist ES

BUCHANAN, Mrs. J. [née Sarah Vivash] (d 1871) actress EA/72*

BUCHANAN, Jack (1890-1957) Scottish actor, producer, manager AAS, DNB, ES, TW/4-7, 14, WWT/4-12, WWW/5

BUCHANAN, McKean (1823-72) American actor CDP, DD, HAS, SR

BUCHANAN, Margaret (d 1970) performer BP/55*

BUCHANAN, Maud actress WWT/4-5

BUCHANAN, Robert actor, manager SR

BUCHANAN, Robert Williams (1841-1901) English dramatist DD, DNB, HP, SR, WWW/1

BUCHANAN, Thompson (1877-1937) American dramatist SR, WWM, WWT/1-8

BUCHANAN, Virginia Ellen (1846/66-1931) American actress CDP, HAS

BUCHANAN, Walter John see Buchanan, Jack

BUCHANAN, William Insco (1852-1909) American manager DAB

BUCHHOLZ, Horst (b 1933) German actor BE, CB, TW/16-19

BUCHINGER, Mr. (fl 1735) flutist BD

BUCHINGER, Mathew see Buckinger, Matthew

BUCHMAN, Sidney (d 1975 [73]) dramatist BP/60*

BUCHNER, Georg (1813-37) German dramatist COC, NTH, OC/1-3, PDT

BUCHS, Julio (d 1973 [46]) producer/director/choreographer BP/57*

BUCHTRUP, Bjarne (b 1942) Danish actor TW/30

BUCHWALD, Julius (d 1970 [61]) composer/lyricist BP/55*

BUCK, [Mr. ?] (fl 1760-61) doorkeeper BD

BUCK, [Mr. ?] (fl 1761) property man BD

BUCK, David (b 1936) English actor WWT/15-16

BUCK, Dudley (d 1909) composer, organist EA/10*

BUCK, Mrs. Frank Pacey see Sale, Sara

BUCK, Gene (1885-1957) American librettist, producer, songwriter NTH, SR, TW/13

BUCK, Sir George (d 1622) master of the Revels COC, DD, OC/3

BUCK, Henry (d 1879) master of ceremonies EA/81*

BUCK, Inez (d 1957 [67]) actress TW/14

BUCK, Paul (fl 1592) dramatist CP/2-3 [see also: Bucke, Paul]

BUCK, Pearl S. (1892-1973) American writer BE

BUCK, Timothy (d 1741) swordsman, actor BD

BUCK, William (d 1777) actor BD

BUCKE, Charles (1781-1846) English dramatist DD, DNB

BUCKE, Paul (fl 1580-99) actor DA [see also; Buck, Paul]

BUCKEREDGE, Edward (fl 1594) actor DA

BUCKHAM, Bernard (1882-1963) English critic WWT/7-11, WWW/6

BUCKHAM, William (d 1887 [35]) drummer EA/88*

BUCKHOLTZ, Mr. (fl 1791-1801) music copyist BD

BUCKHURST, Lord see Sackville, Thomas

BUCKINGER, Miss (fl 1761-69) dancer BD

BUCKINGER, Joseph (fl 1784-1805) musician BD

BUCKINGER, Matthew (b 1674) German musician, painter, inventor, freak BD, CDP

BUCKINGHAM, Fannie Louise (fl 1877) actress CDP, SR

BUCKINGHAM, George Villiers, 2nd Duke of (1628-87) English dramatist CDP, COC, CP/1-3, DD, DNB, ES, GT, HP, OC/1-3, PDT

BUCKINGHAM, James (fl 1784-94) singer BD

BUCKINGHAM, John Sheffield, Duke of (1648-1721) English dramatist CP/1-3, DD, DNB, MH

BUCKINGHAM, Leicester Silk (1825-67) English dramatist DD, DNB

BUCKINGHAM, Robert (d 1895) box office keeper EA/96*

BUCKINGHAM, Thomas (d 1847 [52]) actor, singer CDP

BUCKLAND, George singer CDP

BUCKLAND, George (fl 1773) musician BD

BUCKLAND, George (d 1884 [63]) musical entertainer EA/85*

BUCKLAND, Mrs. John W. [Kate Horn] (c. 1826-96) actress CDP, HAS, SR

BUCKLAW, Alfred actor DD, EA/95, WWT/2-6

BUCKLER, Mrs. (fl 1789-97) actress BD

BUCKLER, Augustin (fl 1682) trumpeter BD

BUCKLER, Edward (fl c. 1677?) singer BD

BUCKLER, Hugh C. (d 1936 [66]) English actor WWT/ 4-8

BUCKLER, John (d 1936 [40]) English actor BE*, BP/ 21*

BUCKLER, Percy (d 1897) actor EA/98*

BUCKLER, Mrs. Sidney see Fairbrother, Sydney

BUCKLES, Ann American actress TW/8, 30

BUCKLEY, Mr. (fl 1742) door- keeper BD

BUCKLEY, Annie (1872-1916) American actress SR, WWS

BUCKLEY, Betty (b 1947) Amer- ican actress TW/25-27, 29-30

BUCKLEY, Charles T. (d 1920) manager BE*, BP/5*

BUCKLEY, E. J. (fl 1870s) actor SR

BUCKLEY, Elizabeth see Buckley, Mrs. Richard

BUCKLEY, Floyd (d 1956 [82]) American actor TW/13

BUCKLEY, Frank (d 1909) musical clown EA/10*

BUCKLEY, F. Rawson (1866- 1943) English actor GRB/1

BUCKLEY, Frederick [Master Ole Bull] (1833-64) English minstrel, composer, violin- ist CDP, HAS

BUCKLEY, George (d 1884 [37])

minstrel EA/85*

BUCKLEY, George Swayne ["Young Sweeney"] (1829-79) English minstrel, banjoist CDP, HAS

BUCKLEY, Hal (b 1937) American actor TW/23

BUCKLEY, J. (d 1867 [27]) comic singer EA/68*

BUCKLEY, James K. [James Burke] (1803-72) minstrel CDP

BUCKLEY, Joe [Timothy Clancy] (1835-84) minstrel CDP

BUCKLEY, Joe (d 1897) minstrel comedian EA/98*

BUCKLEY, John (d 1805) musician BD

BUCKLEY, John William (d 1869 [45]) box bookkeeper EA/70*

BUCKLEY, Kay (b 1921) American actress TW/4

BUCKLEY, May [May Uhl] (b 1875) American actress GRB/4, WWS, WWA/5, WWT/1-11

BUCKLEY, R. Bishop [J. C. Rainer] (1826-67) American minstrel CDP, HAS

BUCKLEY, Richard (fl 1694-1716) actor BD

BUCKLEY, Mrs. Richard [Eliza- beth] (fl 1694-1700) actress BD

BUCKLEY, [Thomas?] (fl 1784?- 94) violoncellist BD

BUCKLEY, Tim (d 1975 [28]) per- former BP/60*

BUCKLEY, Mrs. W. H. [née Fanny Moore] (d 1879 [34]) actress? EA/80*

BUCKLEY, William (d 1875 [35]) musician EA/76*

BUCKLEY, William ["Billy"] (d 1894) minstrel CDP

BUCKMAN, Rosina (d 1948) New Zealand singer WWW/4

BUCKMASTER, John (b 1915) English actor TW/3-8, WWT/ 9-12

BUCKNALL, H. W. (d 1895 [33]) circus manager EA/96*

BUCKNALL, Thomas (fl 1739-46?) musician BD

BUCKSTONE, Isabella see Copeland, Isabella

BUCKSTONE, John Baldwin (1802- 79) English dramatist, actor, manager CDP, COC, DD, DNB, EA/68, ES, HAS,

OAA/1-2, OC/1-3, OX, SR,
WWA/H
BUCKSTONE, Mrs. John Bald-
win see Copeland, Isabella
BUCKSTONE, John Copeland
(1858-1924) English actor
DD, EA/96, GRB/3-4, OAA/
2, WWT/1-4
BUCKSTONE, Lucy Isabella
(1859-93) actress CDP,
DD, DP, OAA/1-2
BUCKSTONE, Rowland (1860-
1922) English actor GRB/
3-4, WWS, WWT/1-4
BUCKTON, Florence (b 1893)
English actress WWT/5-8
BUCKY, Frida Sarsen (d 1974)
composer/lyricist BP/59*
BUD, Mrs. (fl 1697-1701)
actress BD
BUDD, Mrs. (d 1894) EA/95*
BUDD, Master (fl c. 1745-50)
singer BD
BUDD, Benjamin Richard (fl
1794) violinist, composer
BD
BUDD, George see Langley,
Charles
BUDD, Herbert (d 1913 [51])
EA/14*
BUDD, Jake (d 1888) American
actor EA/89*
BUDD, Nelson H. (d 1974 [74])
critic BP/59*
BUDD, Norman (b 1914) English
actor TW/24
BUDD, Thomas (b c. 1751)
English musician BD
BUDD, Thomas (c. 1761-89)
musician BD
BUDD, Thomas (fl 1774-94?)
musician BD
BUDGELL, Anne Eustace
(c. 1726-c. 55) actress,
singer BD
BUDWORTH, James H. (b 1831)
American minstrel HAS
BUEHLER, Arthur (d 1962 [68])
actor BE*
BUER, Minnie (d 1883 [25])
EA/84*
BUETT, Hugh (fl 1651-62)
musician BD
BUFANO, Remo (1894-1948)
Italian/American marionettist
ES
"BUFFALO BILL" see Cody,
William Frederick

BUFFETT, Kenny (b 1926) Amer-
ican actor TW/4
BUFFINGTON, Adele (d 1973 [73])
dramatist BP/58*
BUFFON, [Mons. ?] (fl 1734-35)
actor BD
BUFMAN, Zev (b 1930) Israeli
producer, actor BE, WWT/
15-16
BUFTON, Eleanor [Mrs. Arthur
Swanborough] (1840-93) Welsh
actress CDP, DD, DNB, ES,
OAA/1-2
BUFTON, Esther (d 1883 [71])
EA/84*
BUGBY, John (fl 1401) grammar
master of the children of the
Chapel Royal DA
"BUG-NOSE" (fl 1754) dancer BD
BUGIANI, Sig. (fl 1753-54) dancer
BD
BUGIANI, Elizabetta (fl 1752-57)
dancer BD
BUHER, Mr. (fl 1683) actor BD
BUHLER, Richard (d 1925 [48])
American actor BE*, BP/9*
BUISLAY FAMILY, The gymnasts,
pantomimists HAS
BUIST, W[alter] Scott (b 1860)
English actor DD, EA/97,
GRB/3-4, WWT/1-3
BUJONES, Fernando (b 1955)
American dancer CB
BUKA, Donald (b 1921) American
actor TW/1-6, 22-23, 27
BUKLANK, Alexander (fl 1624)
musician? DA
BULFINCH, Charles (1763-1844)
architect BE*
BULGAKOV, Barbara Russian
actress BE
BULGAKOV, Leo (1889-1948)
Russian actor, producer NTH,
TW/5, WWT/7-10
BULGAKOV, Mikhael Afanaseyev
(1891-1940) Russian dramatist
COC, OC/1-3
BULGER, Harry (1872-1926) actor,
singer CDP, SR
BULIFANT, Joyce (b 1938) Ameri-
can actress TW/15-18, 23
BULING, Hans (fl 1670) Dutch
mountebank, actor BD, CDP
BULKELEY, Mrs. (fl 1769) eques-
trienne BD
BULKELY, Mr. (fl 1742-43) actor
BD
BULKLEY, Mr. (fl 1709) musician

BD
BULKLEY, Mr. (fl 1713)
  musician? BD
BULKLEY, George (d 1784)
  violinist BD
BULKLEY, Mrs. George [Mary
  Wilford; Mrs. Ebenezer Bar-
  risford] (1748-92) English
  actress, dancer BD, CDP,
  DD, TD/1-2
BULL, Mr. (fl 1797) actor BD
BULL, Charles (d 1890) drama-
  tist EA/91*
BULL, George (d 1916) jour-
  nalist EA/17*, WWT/14*
BULL, John (fl 1572-86) actor,
  musician DA
BULL, Master Ole see Buck-
  ley, Frederick
BULL, Ole Bornemann (1810-
  80) Norwegian violinist CDP,
  ES, HAS, HJD, SR
BULL, Peter (b 1912) English
  actor, producer AAS, BE,
  TW/20, 22-24, WWT/11-15
BULL, Thomas (fl 1579-80)
  actor DA
BULL, Thomas (fl 1794) musi-
  cian BD
BULL, William (fl 1666-1700)
  trumpeter, instrument maker
  BD
BULLARD, John (fl 1690-92)
  kettledrummer BD
BULLBRICK, George (fl 1750-57)
  actor, dancer BD
BULLEN, Arthur Henry (fl
  1881-87) scholar DD
BULLEN, Julia [Mrs. George
  Lewis] (d 1891) burlesque
  and music-hall artist EA/93*
BULLER, Lady Yarde eques-
  trienne CDP
BULLEY, Moses (d 1880 [22])
  trapezist EA/81*
BULLIN, G. W. (d 1890 [38])
  advance agent EA/91*
BULLINS, Ed. (b 1935) Ameri-
  can dramatist CD, CH, WWT/
  16
BULLOCH, John (1805-82)
  scholar DNB
BULLOCH, John Malcolm (1867-
  1938) Scottish critic GRB/
  1-4, WWT/1-8, WWW/3
BULLOCK, Mrs. (d 1890) EA/91*
BULLOCK, Miss (fl 1777-78)
  dancer BD

BULLOCK, Christopher (c. 1690-
  1722) English actor, dramatist
  BD, CP/1-3, DD, DNB, TD/
  1-2
BULLOCK, Mrs. Christopher
  [Jane Rogers] (d 1739) English
  actress BD, DD, TD/2
BULLOCK, Elizabeth Villiers see
  Villiers, Lizzie
BULLOCK, Harriet see Dyer,
  Mrs. Michael
BULLOCK, Henrietta Maria [Mrs.
  John Ogden] (fl 1719-48?)
  dancer, actress BD
BULLOCK, Henry C. (d 1893 [37])
  EA/94*
BULLOCK, Hildebrand (d 1733)
  English actor BD
BULLOCK, Mrs. Hildebrand [Ann
  Russell] (fl 1714-48) dancer
  BD
BULLOCK, Phoebe (d 1888) EA/
  89*
BULLOCK, W. (d 1882) marionet-
  tist EA/83*
BULLOCK, William (c. 1667-1742)
  English actor, booth manager
  BD, CDP, DD, DNB
BULLOCK, William (d 1733 [c. 83])
  English actor BD
BULLOUGH, Mrs. John see
  Darrell, Maudi
BULLS, Mr. (fl 1782) actor BD
"BULL SPEAKER" see Amner,
  Ralph
BULMER, Mr. (fl 1772-74)
  scourer BD
BULOFF, Joseph (b 1907) Lithuan-
  ian actor, director BE, TW/
  1-3, 6-8, 15, 29, WWT/12-16
BULOID, Elizabeth see Abbott,
  Mrs. William
BULOS, Yusef (b 1940) Palestinian
  actor TW/28
BULTEEL, John (d 1669) dramatist
  GT
BULWER-LYTTON, Edward see
  Lytton, Edward George Earle
  Lytton Bulwer-Lytton, Lord
BUMBRY, Grace Ann (b 1937)
  American singer CB
BUNCE, Alan (d 1965 [62]) Amer-
  ican actor BE, TW/14-15,
  18, 21, WWT/8-10
BUNCE, Oliver Bell (1828-90)
  American dramatist HJD
BUNCH, Boyd (d 1969) composer/
  lyricist BP/53*

BUNDY, Robert M. (d 1974)
   agent BP/59*
BUNKER, Ralph (d 1966 [77])
   actor TW/22
BUNN, Alfred (1798-1860)
   English manager CDP,
   DD, DNB, ES, HAS, OC/
   1-3
BUNN, Margaret Agnes Somer-
   ville (1799-1883) English
   actress BS, CDP, DD,
   DNB, OC/2-3, OX
BUNNAGE, Avis English actress
   AAS, WWT/14-16
BUNNING, Herbert (1863-1937)
   English composer, conductor
   GRB/1-4, WWW/3
BUNNY, John (1863-1915) Amer-
   ican actor ES, SR
BUNSBY, Jack see Vanden-
   burgh, Theodore H.
BUNSTON, Herbert (1870-1935)
   English actor WWT/4-7
BUNT, George (b 1942) Ameri-
   can actor TW/25
BUNTEN, Margaret Edith see
   Aitken, Margaret Edith
BUNTH, H. see Sutton, Charles
BUNTING, Emma actress SR
BUNTLINE, Ned actor, drama-
   tist, manager SR
BUNYAN, John (1628-88) English
   writer ES, NTH
BUR, Mr. (fl 1742) actor BD
BURANI, Michelette (d 1957
   [73]) actress TW/14
BURBAGE, Mr. (fl 1794) singer
   BD
BURBAGE, Cuthbert (c. 1566-
   1636) English actor DA, ES,
   NTH, OC/1-3
BURBAGE, James (c. 1530-97)
   English actor COC, DA, DD,
   DNB, ES, HP, NTH, OC/
   1-3
BURBAGE, Richard (c. 1567-
   1619) English actor CDP,
   COC, DA, DD, DNB, ES,
   GT, HP, NTH, OC/1-3, PDT
BURBECK, Frank (1857-1930)
   American actor SR, WWM
BURBIDGE, Douglas (1895-1959)
   English actor WWT/5-10
BURBRIDGE, Edward scene de-
   signer WWT/16
BURCH, Mr. (fl 1708) dresser
   BD
BURCH, John George (d 1886

[24]) gymnast EA/87*
BURCHARD, Pepin (b 1775) Amer-
   ican circus performer & mana-
   ger SR
BURCHELL, Clara [Mrs. J. C.
   Smith] (d 1911 [78]) actress
   EA/12*
BURCHETT, Mr. (fl 1794) singer?
   BD
BURCHILL, William (d 1930) Eng-
   lish actor, business manager,
   producer GRB/1-2, WWT/2-6
BURDE, John (fl 1554) actor DA
BURDE, Simon (fl 1554) actor
   DA
BURDEN, Hugh (b 1913) English
   actor, dramatist AAS, WWT/
   10-16
BURDEN, Jahaziel (fl 1794) singer
   BD
BURDEN, John Jabez (fl 1794)
   singer BD
BURDEN, Kitty [née White] (fl
   1757-83) actress, singer BD,
   GT, TD/1-2
BURDEN, W. (fl 1768-94) actor,
   singer BD
BURDETT, Miss see Belfille,
   Mrs.
BURDETT, A. H. (d 1910) mana-
   ger EA/11*
BURDETT, Frank (d 1903 [62])
   property master EA/04*
BURDETT, James (fl 1794) instru-
   mentalist, singer? BD
BURDETT, Osbert (1885-1936)
   English dramatist WWW/3
BURDETTE, Harry (d 1918) EA/
   19*
BURDETTE, Henry (d 1903 [36])
   actor? EA/04*
BURDON, Mr. (fl 1795-1806?)
   singer BD
BURDON, Albert (b 1900) English
   actor WWT/8-11
BUREAU, Joseph Grégoir (fl 1749)
   musician BD
BURELL, Mr. (fl 1778) pit & box
   office keeper BD
BURETTE, Pauline see Nanton,
   Mrs. Lewis
BURFORD, Mr. (fl 1670-72)
   actor, dancer BD
BURFORD, Charles Henry (d 1899
   [77]) actor EA/00*
BURFORD, Robert (d 1861 [70])
   artist, proprietor EA/72*
BURGANI, Mr. (fl 1786-87) house

servant? BD

BURGE, James (b 1943) American actor TW/26

BURGE, Robert (d 1901 [55]) proprietor, manager EA/02*

BURGE, Mrs. S. A. (d 1901 [56]) proprietor EA/02*

BURGE, Stuart (b 1918) English actor, director WWT/14-16

BURGEN, Henry (fl 1667-70) scene keeper BD

BURGES, Sir James Bland (b 1752) English dramatist CP/3

BURGES, Robert (d 1559) actor DA

BURGESS, Mr. (fl 1852-65) actor HAS

BURGESS, Col. minstrel, manager SR

BURGESS, Master (fl 1738-39) actor BD

BURGESS, Master (fl 1789-90) house servant BD

BURGESS, Mrs. (fl 1780) dramatist CP/2-3, DD, GT, TD/1-2

BURGESS, Anthony (b 1917) English writer CB

BURGESS, Charles Frederick see Almonte, Charlie

BURGESS, Colin ["Cool Burgess"] (1840-1905) minstrel, manager CDP

BURGESS, Earl actor, manager SR

BURGESS, [Elizabeth?] (fl 1735-42) actress BD

BURGESS, Fred (d 1893 [66]) minstrel CDP

BURGESS, Mrs. Frederick (d 1882) EA/83*

BURGESS, Hazel (d 1973 [63]) performer BP/58*

BURGESS, Henry (d 1765) musician BD

BURGESS, Henry (fl 1738-65) musician, composer BD

BURGESS, Mr. J. (d 1868 [40]) proprietor EA/69*

BURGESS, John (fl 1794) singer BD

BURGESS, Lydia (d 1887 [81]) EA/88*

BURGESS, Neil (1846/51?-1910) American actor CDP, DAB, DD, PP/1, SR, WWS

BURGESS, Walter (b 1934) Canadian actor TW/15

BURGESS, William (d 1871 [35]) comedian EA/72*

BURGESS, William see Almonte, William

BURGESSE, Charles (fl 1686) trumpeter BD

BURGESSE, Robert (fl 1662-69) trumpeter BD

BURGETTE, William L. (d 1976 [64]) performer BP/60*

BURGHALL, J. E. (fl 1778-97) actor, fencing & dancing master BD

BURGHCLERE, Lord see Gardner, Herbert

BURGHER, Fairfax (1895/1908-1965) American actor TW/11-13

BURGHERSH, Lord (1784-1859) English composer ES

BURGHOFF, Gary (b 1943) American actor TW/23-24

BURGIS, Mrs. (fl 1740-47?) house servant? BD

BURGIS, Kathleen (b 1907) English actress, singer WWT/7-9

BURGOYNE, Mr. (d 1895) EA/96*

BURGOYNE, Mrs. E. A. (d 1916) EA/17*

BURGOYNE, John (1722-92) English dramatist CDP, CP/2-3, DD, DNB, EAP, ES, GT, HJD, HP, TD/1-2

BURGOYNE, Virginia see Rizareli, Virginia

BURIAN, Jarka M. (b 1927) American educator, director, actor BE

BURK, Amy (b 1944) American actress TW/26

BURK, John Daly (c. 1775-1808) Irish/American dramatist DAB, EAP, ES, HJD, RJ

BURKE, Mr. (fl 1751-52) house servant? BD

BURKE, Mr. (fl 1765-77) dresser BD

BURKE, Mr. (fl 1797-1807) house servant? BD

BURKE, Miss (fl 1793) Irish dramatist CP/3

BURKE, Alfred (b 1918) English actor WWT/16

BURKE, Billie (1885-1970) American actress AAS, BE, COC, ES, GRB/1-4, SR, TW/2-16,

26, WWA/5, WWM, WWS, WWT/1-14

BURKE, Bonnie (d 1971 [71]) performer BP/56*

BURKE, Charles A. (1822?-54?) American singer, composer CDP, HAS

BURKE, Mrs. Charles A. [Margaret Murcoyne] (1818-49) American actress HAS

BURKE, Mrs. Charles A., II actress HAS

BURKE, Charles Saint Thomas (1822-54) American actor, dramatist CDP, COC, DAB, DD, HAS, OC/3, SR, WWA/H

BURKE, Cornelius G. (d 1973 [70]) critic BP/57*

BURKE, Daniel (1867-1943) dancer SR

BURKE, David (b 1934) English actor WWT/16

BURKE, Edwin (b 1889) American dramatist, actor ES, SR

BURKE, Georgia (b 1906/08) American actress BE, TW/1-3, 6-9, 22

BURKE, Ione (fl 1870) actress CDP, DD, HAS

BURKE, James (d 1968) performer BP/52*

BURKE, James see Buckley, James K.

BURKE, John D. (fl 1797) writer DD

BURKE, John J. (fl c. 1895) actor, singer CDP, SR

BURKE, John M. (d 1880 [30]) Irish actor, singer, composer CDP

BURKE, Johnny (1908-64) American composer, lyricist, producer, publisher BE

BURKE, Joseph ["The Irish Roscius"] (b 1818) Irish actor, violinist CDP, DD, HAS, SR

BURKE, Kevin (d 1969 [25]) composer/lyricist BP/54*

BURKE, Margaret (1818-49) actress CDP

BURKE, Marie (b 1894) English actress, singer AAS, WWT/6-15

BURKE, Maurice (b 1902) American actor, singer TW/1-3

BURKE, Myra (d 1944 [79])

actress BE*, WWT/14*

BURKE, Patricia (b 1917) Italian actress WWT/8-16

BURKE, Thomas (d 1825) English actor CDP, DD, HAS

BURKE, Mrs. Thomas see Jefferson, Mrs. Joseph

BURKE, Tobias John (d 1878 [30]) actor EA/79*

BURKE, Tom (1890-1969) English actor, singer WWT/6-11

BURKE, W. (fl 1806) dramatist CP/3

BURKE, W. (fl 1832) actor? HAS

BURKE, Walter actor TW/1-3, 7-8, 13

BURKE, W. E. (d 1906 [63]) music-hall performer EA/07*

BURKE, William (d 1970 [74]) executive BP/54*

BURKE, William E. clown CDP

BURKE, William J. (1856-1915) minstrel SR

BURKHARDT, Adison (fl 1911) dramatist SR

BURKHEAD, Henry (fl 1641) English dramatist CP/1-3, GT

BURKITT, Thomas (fl 1776-90) singer BD

BURKS, Donnie [or Donny] American actor TW/24-26, 30

BURLEIGH, John (fl 1729) performer? BD

BURLES, W. J. (d 1873) actor EA/74*

BURLEY, Johnny see Butterly, John Thomas

BURLING, Mr. (fl 1785-88) singer BD

BURLINGHAME, Lloyd designer WWT/16

BURLINGTON, Mr. (fl 1784) singer BD

BURMAN, Borah Z. (d 1964 [34]) critic BP/49*

BURMAN, S. D. (d 1975 [76]) composer/lyricist BP/60*

BURME, Jef Van (d 1965 [58]) composer/lyricist BP/49*

BURN, Miss (fl 1759) actress, dancer BD

BURNABY, Charles (fl 1700-03) dramatist CP/1-3, GT

BURNABY, G. Davy (1881-1949) English actor, dramatist COC, WWT/4-10, WWW/4

BURNAND, Sir Francis Cowley (1836-1917) English dramatist,

actor CDP, DD, DNB,
EA/68, ES, GRB/1-4, HP,
OC/1-3, PDT, SR, WWM,
WWT/1-3, WWW/2

BURNAND, Mrs. F[rancis]
C[owley; Cecilia Ranoe] (d
1870 [27]) EA/71*

BURNAND, Lily (fl 1893) singer
CDP

BURNARD, Fred (d 1912) EA/
13*

BURNARD, Joseph (fl 1794)
singer? BD

BURNARD, Thomas (fl 1739)
musician BD

BURNE, Arthur (1873-1945)
English actor GRB/1,
WWT/9

BURNE, Nancy (1912-54) English
actress, dancer, singer
WWT/9-11

BURNEL, Henry (fl 1641) Irish?
dramatist CP/1-3, DNB,
FGF, GT

BURNELL, Mr. (fl 1719) boxkeeper BD

BURNELL, Buster (d 1964 [41])
dancer, choreographer BE*

BURNELL, Harry [Henry Williams Jee] (d 1906 [24])
music-hall performer EA/
07*

BURNELL, Henry see Burnel,
Henry

BURNELL, William see Arlington, William

BURNET, Mrs. (fl 1749) actress
BD

BURNET, Dana (d 1962 [74])
dramatist BE*

BURNET, [Richard?] (fl 1728-
55?) actor, dancer BD

BURNET, Mrs. Walter
Randall, Pollie

BURNETT, Mr. (fl 1772-81)
actor BD

BURNETT, Mrs. (fl 1772)
actress BD

BURNETT, Miss (fl 1783-1822)
singer, actress BD

BURNETT, Ada singer, actress
CDP

BURNETT, Al (d 1973 [67])
performer BP/57*

BURNETT, Alfred (1824-84)
American humorist CDP,
HAS

BURNETT, Mrs. Arnold see

Pearce, Lizzie

BURNETT, Carol (b 1935) American actress, comedienne, singer
BE, CB, ES, TW/16-21, WWT/
14-16

BURNETT, Charles A. (d 1974
[86]) performer BP/59*

BURNETT, Chester A. (d 1976
[65]) performer BP/60*

BURNETT, Elizabeth (d 1903)
EA/04*

BURNETT, Frances Hodgson [Mrs.
Stephen Townsend] (1849-1924)
English dramatist DD, ES,
GRB/2-4, HJD, HP, SR,
WWA/1, WWM, WWS, WWT/
1-4, WWW/2

BURNETT, Gertrude actress
GRB/1-4

BURNETT, Mr. H. (d 1893 [81])
singer EA/94*

BURNETT, Henry (fl 1607) actor
DA

BURNETT, James G. (1819-70)
comedian CDP

BURNETT, J. N. (d 1916) EA/17*

BURNETT, Joan (d 1908) English
actress GRB/1-4

BURNETT, J. P. (d 1917 [71])
dramatist, actor DD

BURNETT, Mrs. J. P. see
Lee, Jennie

BURNETT, Olive American actress
TW/25

BURNETT, Sally [Sarah A. John-
son] (d 1868) actress? HAS

BURNETT, William (c. 1742-c. 97)
kettledrummer BD

BURNETT, Mrs. [William?] (d
c. 1822?) actress, singer BD

BURNETTE, Amy (fl 1871-80)
English actress OAA/1-2

BURNETTE, Clarence (d 1906)
actor EA/07*, WWT/14*

BURNETTE, George Charles see
Byrne, Gerald

BURNEY, Mr. (fl 1718-31) actor
BD

BURNEY, Mr. (fl 1730) harpsichordist BD

BURNEY, Miss [Mrs. W. Holman]
(d 1903) actress EA/04*

BURNEY, Charles (1726-1814)
English organist, composer,
historian BD, CDP, CP/2-3,
ES, GT

BURNEY, Charles Rousseau (1747-
1819) English harpsichordist BD

BURNEY, Mrs. Charles Rousseau [Esther Burney] (1749-1832) English harpsichordist BD

BURNEY, Estelle (fl 1891) actress, dramatist CDP, DD

BURNEY, Esther see Burney, Mrs. Charles Rousseau

BURNEY, Fanny [Mme. D'Arblay] (1752-1840) English dramatist CP/3, DD

BURNEY, Thomas (fl 1726-32) dancer, dancing master BD

BURNHAM, Lord (d 1916 [82]) newspaper proprietor EA/17*

BURNHAM, Barbara (b 1900) English dramatist WWT/9-11

BURNHAM, Charles C. (1858-1938) American manager, producer WWM, SR

BURNHAM, John Price see Barnes, Price

BURNIDGE, George see Bernage, George

BURNLEIGH, Lena actress WWT/2-4

BURNLEY, Mr. (fl 1725-32) house servant? BD

BURNLEY, Curtis [Mrs. Christian E. Railing] (b 1880) American impersonator WWM

BURNLEY, Fred (d 1975 [41]) producer/director/choreographer BP/60*

BURNOT, Agnes (d 1893 [51]) EA/94*

BURNOT, Walter (d 1905) dramatist, songwriter EA/06*

BURNS, Alfred (d 1874 [34]) actor? EA/75*

BURNS, Anne K. (d 1968 [82]) dramatist BP/53*

BURNS, Bart (b 1918) American actor TW/8

BURNS, Bob (1890-1956) American comedian TW/12, WWA/3

BURNS, Catherine (b 1945) American actress TW/24, 26

"BURNS, Corrie" see Righton, Edward

BURNS, David (1902-71) American actor AAS, BE, TW/5-9,

13-27, WWA/5, WWT/9-15

BURNS, Edward (d 1970) performer BP/55*

BURNS, Eileen American actress TW/29

BURNS, George (b 1896) American comedian CB, ES

BURNS, Georgina (fl 1878) singer CDP

BURNS, James (d 1796) ventriloquist BD, CDP

BURNS, J. C. (d 1889) American singer, dancer EA/90*

BURNS, Jerry (d 1962 [73]) performer BE*

BURNS, John (d 1894 [35]) manager EA/95*

BURNS, Nat (d 1962 [75]) American actor TW/19

BURNS, Noel (d 1966 [67]) singer TW/23

BURNS, Orney (d 1838) circus performer HAS

BURNS, Ralph (b 1922) American orchestrator BE

BURNS, Robert Emmett (d 1974 [62]) agent BP/59*

BURNS, Thomas (d 1893 [31]) high diver EA/98*

BURNSIDE, Jean (fl 1873) actress, dramatist, manager CDP

BURNSIDE, Mortimer B. (d 1971 [81]) investor BP/56*

BURNSIDE, R. H. (1870-1952) English/American dramatist, director NTH, SR, WWT/4-12

BURNSIDE, Tom (d 1899) manager EA/00*

BURNSIDE, William, Jr. (d 1976 [49]) performer BP/60*

BURNUM, Mr. (fl 1729) actor BD

BURONI, Signora (fl 1777) singer BD

BURR, Mrs. (fl 1694) singer BD

BURR, Ann[e] (b 1920) American actress TW/1-3, 9, WWT/11-13

BURR, Bessie Fisher (d 1974 [82]) performer BP/59*

BURR, Courtney (d 1961 [70]) producer TW/18

BURR, Courtney (b 1948) American actor TW/30

BURR, Donald (b 1907) American actor, director BE

BURR, Lonnie (b 1943) American

actor TW/30

BURR, Marion (d 1976 [67]) performer BP/60*

BURR, Raymond William Stacy (b 1917) Canadian actor CB, ES

BURR, Robert American actor TW/20-24, 27-28, WWT/16

BURR, Simon (fl 1654-71) musician BD

BURRA, Edward (b 1905) English scene designer ES

BURRAGE, Alfred McLelland (1889-1956) English dramatist WWW/5

BURRELL, Miss (b 1795) singer, actress CDP

BURRELL, Daisy (b 1893) English actress, singer WWT/4-6

BURRELL, Fred (b 1936) American actor TW/23-24

BURRELL, John (1910-72) English director, producer AAS, ES, TW/29, WWT/10-13

BURRELL, Pamela (b 1945) American actress TW/24

BURRELL, Sheila (b 1922) English actress AAS, WWT/11-16

BURRELL, Sophia, Lady (1750?-1882) English dramatist CP/3, DNB

BURRILL, Ena (b 1908) Uruguayan actress WWT/8-13

BURRIS, Robert (d 1907) scene artist EA/08*, GRB/3*

BURRIS-MEYER, Harold (b 1902) American director, educator, consultant BE

BURROUGHES, Mr. (fl 1646) dramatist CP/2-3, FGF, GT

BURROUGHS, Mr. (fl 1771-81) house servant BD

BURROUGHS, Mrs. (fl 1671-73) actress BD

BURROUGHS, Mrs. see Emery, Miss

BURROUGHS, Claud de Blenau (1848-76) American actor CDP, HAS

BURROUGHS, John (d 1878 [69]) actor EA/80*

BURROUGHS, Judyth (b 1940) American actress TW/5

BURROUGHS, Marie [Little Arrington] (1866-1926) American actress DD, SR, WWA/4, WWM, WWS

BURROUGHS, Robert C. (b 1923) American educator BE

BURROUGHS, Watkins (1790?-1869) English actor, stage manager, manager CDP, HAS, SR

BURROUGHS, William F. (d 1898 [58]) actor CDP

BURROW, Robert Samuel see Faulkner, Robert

BURROWES, James (d 1926 [84]) actor BE*

BURROWS, Mr. (fl 1746) house servant? BD

BURROWS, Abe (b 1910) American dramatist, director BE, CB, CD, ES, HJD, MWD, PDT, WWT/12-16

BURROWS, Charles (1864-1947) actor SR

BURROWS, Mrs. Harriett see Palmerston, Minnie

BURROWS, James (fl 1796-1825) singer, actor, instrumentalist? BD

BURROWS, James (1842-1926) actor SR

BURROWS, John (b 1945) English dramatist, director, actor CD

BURROWS, Robert (fl 1794) singer? BD

BURROWS, Tom (d 1917) EA/18*

BURROWS, Vinie (b 1928) American actress TW/12, 25, 28-29

BURROWS, William Frederick (d 1894 [34]) music-hall artist EA/96*

BURRUS, Ron (b 1944) American actor TW/26

BURRY, Solen (1902-53) Russian actor TW/2

BURSLEM, Ashworth (d 1969 [55]) critic BP/54*

BURSLEM, Charles (d 1886 [28]) dramatist, journalist EA/87*

BURSTEIN, Mike (b 1945) American actor TW/25-26

BURSTON, Reginald (d 1968) producer/director/choreographer BP/52*

BURSTYN, Ellen (b 1932) American actress CB

BURT, Mr. (fl 1745) actor BD

BURT, Mr. (fl 1777-85) clown
BD
BURT, Benjamin Hapgood (b
1876) American composer,
lyricist WWM
BURT, Cecil (d 1916 [64])
EA/17*
BURT, Frank (b 1862) American
manager WWA/4
BURT, Frank A. [Augustus
Berek] (d 1964 [82]) performer
BE*
BURT, Frederick (d 1943 [67])
American actor BE*,
WWT/14*
BURT, Harriet (1885-1935)
American actress WWS
BURT, J. Norman (d 1888)
EA/89*
BURT, Laura [Mrs. H. B. Stan-
ford] (1875-1952) English
actress GRB/3-4, WWM,
WWS, WWT/1-7
BURT, Lulu May see Bertram,
Helen
BURT, Nicholas (fl c. 1635-90)
actor BD, DA, DD
BURT, William P. (d 1955 [88])
actor, director BE*, BP/
39*
BURTOFT, [William?] (fl 1781-
87) housekeeper, box book-
keeper BD
BURTON, Mr. (fl 1722-27)
numberer BD
BURTON, Mr. (fl 1792-94)
singer BD
BURTON, Mrs. (fl 1722-30)
boxkeeper BD
BURTON, Miss (d 1771?) actress
BD
BURTON, Anthony (fl 1628)
actor DA
BURTON, Charles (d 1897 [64])
transformation dancer EA/
98*
BURTON, David (1890-1963)
Russian/American director
ES
BURTON, Edmund (d 1772) actor
BD
BURTON, Edward (d 1896 [72])
actor EA/97*
BURTON, Elizabeth (1751-71)
English actress BD
BURTON, F. D. (d 1894 [69])
manager EA/95*
BURTON, Frederick (b 1871)

American actor GRB/3-4,
WWT/1-9
BURTON, Frederick Charles (d
1917 [95]) actor EA/18*
BURTON, Frederick Russell (1861-
1909) American composer DAB
BURTON, George (d 1784) singer
BD
BURTON, Henry D. (d 1895 [52])
comedian EA/96*
BURTON, Mrs. Henry D. see
Williams, Emma
BURTON, Henry K. (1886-1947)
actor SR
BURTON, Herschell American
actor TW/26
BURTON, Jessie singer CDP
BURTON, John English actor
GRB/1
BURTON, John (1730-82) English
musician, composer BD
BURTON, John (1763-97?) English
actor BD, CDP, TD/1-2
BURTON, John (d 1872 [38]) con-
ductor EA/73*
BURTON, Lancelot (fl 1776-86?)
actor? house servant? BD
BURTON, Langhorne (1872-1949)
English actor GRB/1, WWT/
3-7
BURTON, Maud [née Rankin] (d
1911 [49]) actress EA/12*
BURTON, Nellie (d 1868 [19])
actress EA/69*
BURTON, Nelly see Bobadilla,
Pepita
BURTON, Percy (1878-1948) Eng-
lish manager, business manager
WWT/2-10
BURTON, Philip (b 1904) Welsh
director, teacher BE
BURTON, Philippina [Mrs. Hill?]
(fl 1770-88?) actress, drama-
tist BD, CP/2-3
BURTON, Polly [née Kiddie] (d
1911 [42]) actress EA/13*
BURTON, Richard [né Richard
Walter Jenkins] (b 1925) Welsh
actor AAS, BE, CB, COC,
ES, PDT, TW/7-21, WWT/11-
16
BURTON, Richard P. see Bur-
ton, Percy
BURTON, Robert (fl 1784-1800)
proprietor BD
BURTON, Robert (d 1878 [62])
proprietor EA/79*
BURTON, Robert (d 1879 [30])

proprietor EA/80*
BURTON, Robert (d 1955 [46])
actor TW/12
BURTON, Robert J. (d 1965
[51]) executive BP/49*
BURTON, Sarah [Mrs. T. D.
Burton] (d 1882 [41]) EA/83*
BURTON, Sarah (b 1912) Eng-
lish actress TW/3-5
BURTON, Mrs. T. D. see
Burton, Sarah
BURTON, Thomas Bowman (d
1899) EA/00*
BURTON, W. minstrel CDP
BURTON, W. (d 1774) English
comedian CDP
BURTON, Warren (b 1944)
American actor TW/24-26
BURTON, William (fl 1596)
dramatist FGF
BURTON, William (1575-1645)
English dramatist CP/3
BURTON, William (d 1813?)
actor BD
BURTON, Mrs. William E.
see Hill, Jane
BURTON, William Evans (1804-
60) English/American actor,
manager, dramatist CDP,
COC, DAB, DD, DNB, ES,
HAS, HJD, OC/1-3, SR,
WWA/H
BURTON, William H. (1843?-
1926) English actor SR
BURTONYA, Clee (b 1932)
American actor TW/25
BURTT, Mr. (fl 1784) actor
BD
BURTWELL, Frederick (d 1948)
actor BE*, WWT/14*
BURVILLE, Alice (fl 1874-80)
actress, singer DD, OAA/2
BURY, Mons. (fl 1675) musi-
cian BD
BURY, Mr. (fl 1720-21) per-
former? BD
BURY, Miss (fl 1783-89) dancer
BD
BURY, John (b 1925) Welsh de-
signer AAS, ES, WWT/14-16
BURY, Samuel L. (d 1909)
variety agent EA/10*
BUSBY, Amy (d 1957 [85])
American actress TW/14,
SR
BUSBY, James (d 1871 [45])
comic singer EA/72*
BUSBY, John (1755-1838)

English composer, musician,
singer BD
BUSCH, Constance (d 1898 [48])
EA/99*
BUSCH, Fritz (1890-1951) German
conductor CB, WWA/3
BUSCH, Lydia English actress
GRB/2-4
BUSCH, Mae [Mrs. Thomas C.
Tate] (1897-1946) Australian
actress ES, TW/2
BUSH, Mr. (fl 1779) actor, singer
BD
BUSH, Alan Dudley (b 1900) Eng-
lish composer, conductor ES
BUSH, Amyas (fl 1758) dramatist
CP/1-3, GT
BUSH, Anita (d 1974) performer,
theatre company founder BP/
58*
BUSH, Mrs. Charles see
Charles, Florence
BUSH, Frances Cleveland (d 1967
[78]) musical-comedy singer
TW/24
BUSH, Frank (d 1927 [71]) mono-
logist BE*, BP/12*
BUSH, Fred [né Frederick Taylor]
(d 1903/04) variety artist EA/
04*, EA/05*
BUSH, Norman (b 1933) American
actor TW/26-28
BUSHBY, Mr. (fl 1784) singer
BD
BUSHE, Amyas see Bush, Amyas
BUSHEL, Robert (fl 1766-94)
gallerykeeper, treasurer BD
BUSHELL, Anthony (b 1904) Eng-
lish actor ES, WWT/6-13
BUSHELL, Frederick (d 1872 [38])
EA/73*
BUSHELL, Leonard O. (d 1976
[78]) voice teacher BP/60*
BUSH-FEKETE, Leslie (b 1896)
Hungarian dramatist BE
BUSHMAN, Francis X. (b 1885)
American actor ES
BUSHNELL, Arthur (d 1967 [50])
performer BP/52*
BUSHNELL, Catherine Hayes (d
1861 [36]) EA/72*
BUSLEY, Jessie [Mrs. Ernest
Joy] (1869-1950) American
actress GRB/3-4, SR, TW/
2-3, 5-6, WWT/1-10
BUSNACH, William (d 1907 [75])
dramatist BE*, WWT/14*
BUSS, Harry (b 1874) English

actor GRB/1

BUSS, Mary Ann (d 1907)
comedian EA/08*

BUSS, Robert William (1804-
75) theatrical portrait painter
DNB

BUSSE, Margaret [Margaret
Bussey] actress GRB/3-4,
WWT/1-5

BUSSELL, Jan (b 1909) English
marionettist ES

BUSSER, Henri (d 1973 [101])
composer/lyricist BP/58*

BUSSEY, Hank (d 1971 [80])
performer BP/55*

BUSSEY, Margaret see
Bussé, Margaret

BUSSLEY, Oliver James see
Cox, Harry

BUSSY, René (b 1879) French
actor GRB/4, WWT/1-3

BUSTIN, Sydney see Beltram,
Sydney

BUSTLER, Mr. (fl 1742-43)
actor BD

BUSWELL, John (1733-63) English musician, composer
BD

BUTCHER, Master (fl 1746)
singer BD

BUTCHER, Mr. (fl 1724-28)
actor BD

BUTCHER, Mrs. (fl 1724-25)
actress BD

BUTCHER, Mrs. (fl 1746-48)
house servant? BD

BUTCHER, Ernest (b 1885)
English actor, singer WWT/
9-10

BUTCHER, Harry (d 1895 [23])
dog trainer EA/96*

BUTCHER, John (d 1869 [36])
musician EA/70*

BUTCHER, Robert see Butler,
Robert

BUTE, Henry (d 1917 [50])
EA/18*

BUTE, Olive (d 1900) actress
EA/01*

BUTLER, Mr. (fl 1720) house
servant? BD

BUTLER, Mr. (fl 1734-48) actor
BD

BUTLER, Mr. (fl 1770-79)
actor BD

BUTLER, Mr. (fl c. 1772) organist BD

BUTLER, Mrs. (fl 1746-50)

actress BD

BUTLER, Albert W. (d 1973 [84])
publicist BP/58*

BUTLER, Alfred Joline see
Butler, Fred J.

BUTLER, Alice [Mrs. Charles W.
Butler] (1868-1919) English
actress WWS

BUTLER, Gen. Benjamin F.
(1818-93) American agent SR

BUTLER, Benjamin H. (d 1888
[41]) American manager EA/
89*

BUTLER, Charles (d 1920 [64])
actor BE*, BP/5*

BUTLER, Mrs. Charles see
Long, Harriet C.

BUTLER, Mrs. Charles W. see
Butler, Alice

BUTLER, Charlotte (fl 1673-95)
actress, singer, dancer BD

BUTLER, David (b 1894) American
actor ES

BUTLER, Edward (1882-1947)
actor SR

BUTLER, E. H. (fl 1839) actor
CDP

BUTLER, Elizabeth (d 1748) actress BD, DD

BUTLER, Mrs. Fanny see
Kemble, Fanny

BUTLER, Fred J. [Alfred Joline
Butler] (b 1867) American actor
WWS

BUTLER, Henry J. (d 1909 [63])
stage manager EA/10*

BUTLER, Mrs. Henry J. see
Tremayne, Bella

BUTLER, Horace (d 1906) proprietor EA/07*

BUTLER, James (fl 1732-39)
singer BD

BUTLER, James (d 1892) stage
manager EA/93*

BUTLER, James H. (b 1908)
American educator BE

BUTLER, John (fl 1773-88) gallery
office keeper BD

BUTLER, John (fl 1840) dramatist
RJ

BUTLER, John (d 1864) minstrel
HAS

BUTLER, John (b 1920) American
choreographer, director, dancer
BE, CB, ES, TW/2-3

BUTLER, John Dale (d 1882 [52])
manager EA/83*

BUTLER, John Davies see

Gaunt, David

BUTLER, John Pearce (d 1906 [54]) circus advance agent EA/07*

BUTLER, Michael see Esmond, Wilfred

BUTLER, Nellie [née Chute] (fl 1894-1912) American actress WWM

BUTLER, Philip (d 1786) master carpenter BD

BUTLER, Pierce CDP

BUTLER, Pierce J. [?= Pierce Butler] (d 1868 [74]) actor EA/69*

BUTLER, Rachel Barton (d 1920) dramatist BE*, BP/5*

BUTLER, Ralph (d 1969 [82]) composer/lyricist BP/53*

BUTLER, Rhoda (b 1949) American actress TW/30

BUTLER, Richard William (1844-1928) English dramatist, critic DD, GRB/3-4, WWT/1-5

BUTLER, Robert [né Butcher] (b 1832) clown CDP, HAS

BUTLER, Mrs. Robert [Amelia Wells] (b 1833) American circus performer, singer, actress, dancer HAS

BUTLER, Royal (d 1973 [80]) performer BP/58*

BUTLER, Sam actor, manager TD/2

BUTLER, Samuel (1612-80) English dramatist CP/3

BUTLER, Samuel (d 1812) theatre builder COC

BUTLER, Samuel (d 1945 [48]) actor WWT/14*

BUTLER, Samuel S. W. (1797-1845) English actor CDP, COC, DD, HAS, SR

BUTLER, Mrs. Samuel S. W. (fl 1841) actress HAS

BUTLER, Thomas Hamley (d 1823) composer DD

BUTLER, Todd (b 1936) American actor TW/25

BUTLER, W. actor TD/2

BUTLER, W. George (d 1882) comedian, pantomimist EA/83*

BUTLER, William (fl 1780-1817?) dancer, house servant? BD

BUTLER, William see Clancent,

William

BUTLER, Mrs. William (fl 1789-1812) singer BD

BUTLER, Mrs. William (d 1872) EA/73*

BUTLIN, Jan (b 1940) English director, dramatist WWT/16

BUTSOVA, Hilda (d 1976 [78]) performer BP/60*

BUTT, Sir Alfred (1878-1962) English manager, producer COC, GRB/3-4, NTH, WWT/1-9

BUTT, Dame Clara [Mrs. Kennerley Rumford] (1873-1936) English singer DNB, GRB/1, WWW/3

BUTT, George (1741-95) English dramatist CP/3

BUTTERFIELD, Everett (d 1925 [40]) American actor BE*, BP/9*

BUTTERFIELD, Isabel (d 1870) singer EA/71*

BUTTERFIELD, Walter S. (fl 1900s) American actor, dramatist, manager SR

BUTTERFIELD, Walton (d 1966 [68]) performer BP/51*

BUTTERLY, John Thomas [Johnny Burley] (d 1888 [32]) clown, comedian EA/89*

BUTTERSBY, Mrs. [Mrs. Stickney] (fl 1823-35) actress HAS

BUTTERWORTH, Annie (d 1885) singer EA/87*

BUTTERWORTH, Charles E. (1896-1946) American actor ES, SR, TW/2-3, WWT/8-9

BUTTERWORTH, Clara English singer, actress WWT/4-7

BUTTERWORTH, Walter T. (d 1962 [69]) actor BE*

BUTTERWORTH, William (d 1896 [72]) minstrel manager EA/98*

BUTTERY, Miss see Cleland, Miss

BUTTERY, Henry (d 1876 [30]) property master EA/77*

BUTTON, Dick (b 1929) American producer, actor BE, TW/13-15

BUTTONS, Red [Aaron Chwatt] (b 1919) American actor CB, TW/3-6

BUTTRAM, Jan (b 1946) American actress TW/30

BUXTON, Mr. (fl 1782) actor BD

BUXTON, Mr. (fl c. 1812) actor

CDP
BUXTON, Bertha (d 1881) act-
ress EA/82*
BUXTON, Charles Henry (d
1894 [49]) EA/95*
BUXTON, Frederick F. (d
1858) English actor HAS,
SR
BUXTON, Jedidiah (1707-72)
illiterate calculating genius
CDP, DNB
BUXTON, John see Zambra
BUXTON, Maria (fl 1837-52)
American dancer HAS
BUZARGLO, Mr. (fl 1792-97)
scene painter BD
BUZARGLO, Louis (fl 1793-95)
scene painter BD
BUZILARICO, Sig. (fl 1786)
ventriloquist BD
BUZO, Alexander (b 1944)
Australian dramatist, direc-
tor, actor CD, WWT/16
BUZZARD, Henry Thomas
see Ashley, J. B.
BUZZELL, Edward [Edie] (b
1897) American actor ES,
WWT/7-10
BUZZELL, Eugene (d 1973 [68])
public relations director
BP/57*
BUZZI, Ruth (b 1936) American
actress TW/22-24
BYAL, Carl (d 1972 [83]) per-
former BP/57*
BYARS, Thomas (d 1896) music-
hall stage manager EA/97*
BYATT, Henry (fl 1877-94)
dramatist DD
BYDE, Alfred J. (d 1916) actor
EA/17*
BYERLEY, John Scott ["John
Scott Ripon"] (fl 1803) English
dramatist CP/3
BYERLEY, Vivienne English
press representative WWT/
11-16
BYERLY, Mr. (fl 1769) actor
HAS
BYERS, Catherine American
actress TW/30
BYERS, Charles A. (d 1975
[72]) producer/director/
choreographer BP/60*
BYFIELD, Miss (fl 1828) actress
CDP
BYFORD, George actor, singer,
composer CDP

BYFORD, Roy (1873-1939) English
actor WWT/4-8
BYFORD, Mrs. Roy see Hunt,
Doris
BYINGTON, Spring (1893-1971)
American actress BE, CB,
ES, TW/28, WWA/5, WWT/
8-11
BYLAND, Ambrose (fl 1624) actor
DA
BYLES, Bobby (d 1969 [38]) per-
former BP/54*
BYNAM, Mr. J. (fl 1797-1820)
house servant BD
BYNG, David (d 1881 [72]) EA/
83*
BYNG, Mrs. David B. see
Byng, Jane Buckley
BYNG, Douglas (b 1893) English
actor, entertainer AAS, BTR/
74, TW/13, WWT/8-16
BYNG, George W. conductor,
composer WWT/4-7
BYNG, Jane Buckley [Mrs. David
B. Byng] (d 1881) EA/82*
BYNNER, Witter (1881-1968)
American dramatist WWA/5,
WWM, WWW/6
BYRAM, John (1901-77) American
press representative, editor,
producer BE
BYRAM, Marian (b 1904) American
press representative BE
BYRD, Carl (b 1935) American
actor TW/27
BYRD, Sam[uel Armanie] (1908-55)
American actor, producer CB,
TW/3, 12, WWT/9-11
BYRN, [Mrs. ?] (fl 1760-66) char-
woman BD
BYRN, James (1756-1845) dancer,
choreographer BD, DD
BYRN, John (fl 1794) singer? BD
BYRN, Oscar (c. 1795-1867) dancer
BD
BYRNE, Mr. (d 1780) dancer BD
BYRNE, Mr. (fl 1783-90) box-
keeper, lobby keeper BD
BYRNE, Mrs. (d 1782) dancer BD
BYRNE, Mrs. (fl c. 1785-1800)
singer, dancer, actress BD
BYRNE, Miss (fl 1784-87) dancer
BD
BYRNE, Cecily English actress
WWT/4-12
BYRNE, Charles (1761-83) giant
BD
BYRNE, Charles (d 1871 [27])

actor   EA/72*
BYRNE, Charles Alfred (1848-
1909) English/American
dramatist DD, WWA/1
BYRNE, Eleanor (fl 1817)
actress CDP
BYRNE, Francis M. (1875-1923)
American actor WWM, WWS
BYRNE, Gaylea American act-
ress   TW/25-29
BYRNE, George J. (d 1966 [62])
performer BP/51*
BYRNE, Gerald [George Charles
Burnette] (d 1917) actor
EA/18*
BYRNE, James see Byrn,
James
BYRNE, James A. (1868-1927)
American actor, acrobat,
dramatist SR
BYRNE, John J. (d 1968) drama-
tist BP/53*
BYRNE, John Keyes see Leonard,
Hugh
BYRNE, Kate Oscar English act-
ress, singer GRB/1
BYRNE, Oscar (1795-1867)
ballet master DD, DNB,
GT, HAS
BYRNE, Mrs. Oscar (fl 1793)
English actress HAS
BYRNE, Patsy (b 1933) English
actress WWT/14-16
BYRNE, Peter (b 1928) English
actor WWT/15-16
BYRNE, Peter C. (d 1867 [44])
actor HAS
BYRNE, Robinson see Bern,
Chris V.
BYRNE, [William?] (1743-1805?)
scene painter BD
BYRNE, William (d 1916 [21])
EA/17*
BYRNES, Mrs. [Mrs. Ferrers]
(fl 1836) English actress
HAS
BYRNES, Burke (b 1937) Amer-
ican actor TW/25-26
BYRNES, Maureen (b 1944)
American actress TW/26-29
BYRON, Alfred (d 1891) EA/
92*
BYRON, Arthur W[illiam] (1872-
1943) American actor CB,
ES, GRB/3-4, NTH, SR,
WWS, WWT/1-9
BYRON, Mrs. Arthur see
Mapleson, Laura

BYRON, Mrs. E. M. [Mrs. Henry
James Byron] (d 1889 [40])
actress EA/90*
BYRON, Fred (fl c. 1876) singer
CDP
BYRON, George Gordon, Lord
(1788-1824) English dramatist
COC, DD, DNB, ES, HP, MH,
OC/1-3, PDT, RE, SR
BYRON, H. (d 1884 [80]) EA/85*
BYRON, Henrietta [Mrs. Barney
Fagan] (d 1924) performer
BE*, BP/8*
BYRON, Mrs. Henry (d 1876 [44])
EA/77*
BYRON, Henry James (1834-84)
English dramatist, actor CDP,
COC, DD, DNB, EA/68, ES,
NTH, OAA/1-2, OC/1-3
BYRON, Mrs. Henry James see
Byron, Mrs. E. M.
BYRON, John (b 1912) Chinese/
English actor, dancer WWT/
10-12
BYRON, Kate see Byron, Mrs.
Oliver Doud
BYRON, Marie Josephine (d 1900
[70]) EA/01*
BYRON, Oliver Doud (1842-1920)
American actor CDP, NTH,
PP/1, SR, WWM, WWS
BYRON, Mrs. Oliver Doud [Kate
Crehan] (1846-1920) Irish act-
ress PP/1, SR
BYRON, Paul (b 1888) American
actor TW/2
BYRON, Terence (d 1936 [49])
actor, manager WWT/14*
BYRT, Wilfred Clarence (d 1908
[32]) music-hall performer?
EA/09*

- C -

C., J. (fl 1620) dramatist CP/1-3
C., J. (fl 1739) dramatist CP/3
C., R. (fl 1621) dramatist CP/
1-3, FGF
CAAN, James (b 1939) American
actor CB
CABAL, Alan (b 1953) American
actor TW/23
CABALLE, Montserrat (b 1933)
Spanish singer CB
CABAN, Rose Evangeline (d 1902)
circus performer EA/04*
CABANEL, Mons. (fl 1789-1804?)

dancer? actor? pyrotechnist
BD
CABANEL, Eliza (fl 1792-1800)
dancer BD
CABANEL, Harriot [later Mrs.
Helme] (fl 1791-1806) dancer
BD
CABANEL, Rudolphe (1763-
1839) French architect, ma-
chinist, inventor, pyrotechnist
BD
CABANEL, Victoire (fl 1792-93)
dancer BD
CABANES, Mr. (fl 1784) violinist
BD
CABEL, Marie (d 1885 [48])
singer EA/86*
CABELL, Mr. (fl 1760) dresser
BD
CABLE, Mrs. (d 1767) house
servant? BD
CABLE, Christopher (b 1930)
American actor TW/27
CABOT, Bruce (d 1972 [67/68])
performer BP/56*, WWT/
16*
CABOT, Eliot (1899-1938) Amer-
ican actor SR, WWT/7-8
CACCIALANZA, Gisella (b 1914)
American dancer ES
CACEY, Dorothy (b 1882) Eng-
lish actress GRB/1
CACOYANNIS, Michael (b 1922)
Cypriot director CB
CADDICK, Thomas (d 1877 [37])
comedian EA/78*
CADELL, Jean (1884-1967)
Scottish actress AAS, TW/3,
24, WWT/3-14
CADEMAN, Philip (b c. 1643)
actor BD
CADET, Mr. (fl 1707-11) musi-
cian BD
CADET, Mr. (fl 1708) house
servant BD
CADLE, Albert Henry (d 1907
[34]) agent EA/08*
CADLE, Ernest (b 1871) English
agent GRB/1
CADLE, Henry (b 1873) English
agent GRB/1
CADMAN, Charles Wakefield
(1881-1946) American com-
poser DAB, ES, HJD,
WWA/2
CADMAN, Ethel (b 1886) Eng-
lish actress, singer WWM,
WWT/2-8

CADMAN, Robert (d 1740) rope-
walker BD
CADWALADER, Jessica [Mrs.
Robert Ryan] (d 1972 [57]) per-
former BP/56*
CADWALADR, Llewelyn (1860-
1909) Welsh singer GRB/1
CADWELL, Mr. (fl 1776-77)
dresser BD
CADY, Mr. (fl 1773) hairdresser
BD
CAEDES, Auguste (d 1884) com-
poser EA/85*
CAESAR, Irving (b 1895) American
lyricist, librettist BE, WWT/
6-16
CAESAR, Sid (b 1922) American
actor, comedian, musician
BE, CB, ES, TW/19, 27,
WWT/15-16
CAFFARELLI, Sig. [Gaetano
Maiorano] (1710-83) Italian
singer BD
CAFFREY, Stephen (d 1902 [54])
actor EA/03*, WWT/14*
CAFFRY, John [Frank Fleming]
(d 1883) actor? EA/84*
CAGE, John (b 1912) American
composer CD, ES
CAGE, Ruth (b 1923) American
press representative BE
CAGNEY, James (b 1904) American
actor BE, CB, ES, WWT/7-10
CAGNEY, Jeanne (b 1919) Ameri-
can actress BE, TW/1, 3,
WWT/11-13
CAHILL, Albert Joseph Simmons
(d 1916) EA/17*
CAHILL, James (b 1940) American
actor TW/23, 25-26, 28, 30
CAHILL, Lily (1885/91-1955) Amer-
ican actress TW/2-6, 12,
WWT/6-11
CAHILL, Marie [Mrs. Daniel V.
Arthur] (1870-1933) American
actress, singer ES, GRB/2-4,
NTH, SR, WWA/1, WWS,
WWT/1-7
CAHILL, Paul (d 1974 [42]) pro-
ducer/director/choreographer
BP/59*
CAHILL, William B. (d 1906 [77])
manager WWT/14*
CAHLMAN, Robert (b 1924) Amer-
ican director, producer, lectur-
er, publicist BE
CAHN, Julius (d 1921) manager
BE*, BP/5*

CAHN, Sammy (b 1913) American actor, songwriter CB, TW/30, WWT/16

CAHUSAC, William Maurice (fl 1794-1829) musician, publisher, instrument maker, singer? BD

CAIL, Harold J. (d 1968 [66]) critic BP/53*

CAILLOT, François (fl 1771-93) pyrotechnist BD

CAIN, Mr. (fl 1799) English actor HAS

CAIN, Andrew (fl 1620-44) English actor COC, ES, OC/1-3

CAIN, James Mallahan (1892-1977) American dramatist BE, CB, ES, HJD

CAIN, Patrick J. (d 1949 [70]) American scenery warehouse operator BE*, BP/33*

CAIN, Perry (d 1975 [49]) performer BP/59*

CAIN, Robert (d 1954 [67]) actor BE*

CAINE, Derwent Hall (b 1892) English actor, manager WWT/2-5

CAINE, Georgia (d 1964 [88]) actress BE*

CAINE, Henry (1888-1962) English actor WWT/4-13

CAINE, John (d 1904 [83]) EA/05*

CAINE, Lily Hall (d 1914) actress DD, GRB/2-4, WWT/1-2

CAINE, Michael (b 1933) English actor CB

CAINE, Richard (b 1940) American actor TW/27

CAINE, Sir Thomas Henry Hall (1853-1931) English dramatist DD, ES, GRB/2-4, HP, SR, WWM, WWS, WWT/1-6, WWW/3

CAIRD, Mr. see D'Arcy, Mr.

CAIRD, Dora [Mrs. Graham Good] (d 1910) actress EA/11*

CAIRD, Laurence (d 1955 [88]) actor WWT/14*

CAIRNS, Angus (1910-75) American actor TW/26-27

CAIRNS, Fred (d 1896) music-hall comedian EA/97*

CAIRNS, Mrs. William see Achmet, Mrs.

CAIRNS-JAMES, Lewis Scottish actor GRB/1-4

CAJANUS, Mynheer (fl 1734) actor BD

CAJANUS, Daniel (1703-49) German giant BD

CALBES, Eleanor (b 1940) Filipino actress TW/24, 27

CALCAGNI, Mr. (fl 1790) singer BD

CALCOTT, John F. (d 1895) conductor EA/96*

CALCRAFT, Granby (d 1855) actor, manager EA/72*, WWT/14*

CALCRAFT, Mrs. Grandby see Love, Emma Sarah

CALCRAFT, John William [né Cole] (d 1870) actor, dramatist CDP, DD

CALDARA, Orme (1875-1925) American actor SR, WWM

CALDER, John Richard (d 1875 [25]) comedian EA/76*

CALDER, King (d 1964 [65]) American actor TW/8, 21

CALDERISI, David (b 1940) Canadian actor, director, producer WWT/15-16

CALDER-MARSHALL, Anna (b 1947) English actress WWT/15-16

CALDERON, George (1868-1915) English dramatist DNB, ES, HP, WWT/2-3, WWW/1

CALDERON DE LA BARCA, Pedro (1600-81) Spanish dramatist DD, OC/1-3, PDT

CALDICOT, Jonas (fl 1661) singer BD

CALDICOT, Richard (b 1908) English actor WWT/16

CALDICOTT, Alfred James (1842-97) musician, conductor DD, DNB

CALDUCCI, Sig. (fl 1781-82) singer BD

CALDWELL, Anne (1869-1936) American dramatist, composer SR, WWT/4-8

CALDWELL, Bryan (d 1969 [54]) public relations BP/54*

CALDWELL, Erskine (b 1903) American writer CB

CALDWELL, Gisela American actress TW/30

CALDWELL, Henry (d 1961 [42])

producer, actor BE*
CALDWELL, J. (d 1880) lessee,
proprietor EA/81*
CALDWELL, James H. (1793-
1863) English actor, manager,
dramatist CDP, DD, ES,
HAS, RJ, SR, WWA/H
CALDWELL, Marianne [Mari-
anne Lipsett] (d 1933 [67])
West Indian/English actress
GRB/1-4, WWT/1-5
CALDWELL, Orville (1896-1967)
American actor BE, TW/24
CALDWELL, Sarah (b 1928)
American conductor CB
CALDWELL, Zoe (b 1933/34)
Australian actress AAS,
CB, TW/23-26, 29-30,
WWT/14-16
CALEF, Jennie [née Murphy]
dancer, actress CDP
CALEF, Lillian [née Murphy]
actress, singer CDP
CALFHILL, James (d 1570)
English dramatist CP/3,
FGF
CALHAEM, Emilie (d 1943 [73])
actress WWT/14*
CALHAEM, Mrs. Francis Emily
[Mrs. Stanislaus Calhaem]
(d 1911 [68]) actress EA/
12*, WWT/14*
CALHAEM, Stanislaus (d 1901
[78]) actor DD, OAA/2
CALHAEM, Mrs. Stanislaus
see Calhaem, Francis Emily
CALHERN, Louis (1895-1956)
American actor AAS, CB,
ES, TW/1-8, 12, WWA/3,
WWT/7-11
CALHOUN, Eleanor (1862-1957)
American actress DD
CALHOUN, Mrs. Fred G. see
Thorndyke, Louise
CALHOUN, Robert (b 1930)
American technical director,
production supervisor, stage
manager BE
CALICE, Myron (d 1908 [61])
actor CDP
"CALIFORNIA DIAMOND, The"
see Dauvray, Helen
CALIN, Mickey (b 1935) Ameri-
can actor TW/12, 15-16
CALKIN, Mr. (fl 1790-1817)
gallery doorkeeper BD
CALKIN, Arthur (d 1974 [80s])
performer BP/60*

CALKIN, Joseph (fl 1781-1815)
musician BD
CALKIN, Joseph (1781-1846) Eng-
lish musician, bookseller BD
CALKINS, Michael (b 1948) Amer-
ican actor TW/30
CALL, John (1915-73) American
actor TW/1, 3, 16, 22-24,
27, 29
CALLADINE, C. (1822-61) actor
HAS, SR
CALLADINE, Mrs. C. see
Calladine, Eliza
CALLADINE, Eliza [née Eberle]
(1834-54) American actress
HAS, SR
CALLAGHAN, J. (d 1910 [39])
musical director EA/11*
CALLAGHAN, J. Dorsey (d 1975
[80]) critic BP/60*
CALLAGHAN, T. C. (d 1917 [64])
comedian EA/18*
CALLAHAN, Bill (b 1926) Ameri-
can actor TW/2-10
CALLAHAN, Billy (d 1964 [53])
performer BE*
CALLAHAN, Charles E. (1843-1917)
actor, dramatist SR
CALLAHAN, Charles S. (d 1964
[73]) performer BP/49*
CALLAHAN, Emmett (d 1965 [72])
performer BP/50*
CALLAHAN, James T. (b 1930)
American actor TW/30
CALLAHAN, Kristina American
actress TW/26
CALLAHAN, T. C. singer CDP
CALLAN, Chris (b 1944) American
actor TW/30
CALLAN, Henry J. (d 1905 [34])
English acting manager GRB/1
CALLAN, John (d 1909) minstrel
comedian EA/11*
CALLAN, William (b 1918) Amer-
ican actor TW/22
CALLAND, S. (d 1877) pianist
EA/78*
CALLAS, Maria (1923-77) Ameri-
can singer CB
CALLAWAY, Paul (b 1909) Ameri-
can conductor, musician, edu-
cator BE
CALLAWAY, Tod singer CDP
CALLCOTT, Albert (d 1888 [53])
scene artist EA/89*
CALLCOTT, Albert W. (d 1901
[30]) scene artist EA/02*
CALLCOTT, Augustus Wall

(1779-1844) English painter, singer BD

CALLCOTT, John Wall (1766-1821) English musician, composer, singer, teacher BD, DNB

CALLCOTT, William (fl 1790-1800) English musician BD

CALLCOTT, William (d 1878 [78]) musician, composer EA/79*

CALLCOTT, William John (d 1900 [77]) scene painter EA/01*

CALLEAR, Herbert (d 1917) EA/18*

CALLEGA, Joseph (d 1975 [78]) performer BP/60*

CALLEIA, Joseph [né Spurin-Calleia] (b 1897) Maltese actor BE, WWT/11-13

CALLENDER, Charles (d 1897 [70]) manager CDP, SR

CALLENDER, E. Romaine (fl 1875-82) actor, dramatist DD

CALLENDER, Mrs. E. Romaine (d 1890) actress EA/91*

CALLIGAN, Edward O. (d 1962 [64]) talent representative BE*

CALLOWAY, Cab (b 1907) American actor, musician, composer ES, TW/30, WWT/16

CALMOUR, Alfred Cecil (d 1912 [55]) dramatist, actor DD, GRB/2-4, WWT/1

CALORI, Angiola (1732-c. 90) Italian singer BD

CALTHROP, Dion Clayton (1878-1937) English dramatist, designer WWT/2-8, WWW/3

CALTHROP, Donald (1888-1940) English actor ES, WWT/2-9

CALTHROP, Gladys E. English designer ES, WWT/8-14

CALTHROP, John Alfred Clayton see Clayton, John

CALVE, Emma (1858/64-1942) Spanish singer CB, ES, GRB/1, 4, SR, WWA/1, WWS, WWW/4

CALVERLEY, Thomas (fl 1665-67) actor? BD

CALVERLY, Joseph (fl 1794) singer BD

CALVERT, Mrs. (fl 1772) singer BD

CALVERT, Adelaide Helen (1837-1921) English actress CDP,

OC/1-3

CALVERT, Alexander (d 1917) English actor GRB/1-4

CALVERT, Catherine (1890-1971) American actress TW/27, WWM, WWT/5-6

CALVERT, Cecil G. (b 1871) English actor GRB/3-4, WWT/1-5

CALVERT, [Charles?] (fl 1784-86) actor BD

CALVERT, Charles Alexander (1828-79) English actor, manager CDP, DD, DNB, ES, OC/1-3

CALVERT, Mrs. Charles Alexander [Adelaide Biddles] (1837-1921) English actress DD, GRB/1-4, HAS, WWT/1-3, WWW/2

CALVERT, E. H. (fl 1900-36) American actor ES

CALVERT, Frank (d 1913) EA/14*

CALVERT, Frederick Baltimore (1793-1877) actor DNB

CALVERT, George Henry (1803-89) American dramatist HJD

CALVERT, Henry (b 1920) American actor TW/23, 25-27

CALVERT, Leonard Charles English actor GRB/1-4

CALVERT, Louis (1859-1923) English actor COC, DD, GRB/1-4, OC/1-3, SR, WWT/1-4

CALVERT, Mrs. Louis see Roberts, Rose

CALVERT, Patricia (b 1908) English actress WWT/8-11

CALVERT, Phyllis (b 1915) English actress AAS, ES, WWT/10-16

CALVERT, Thomas (d 1901 [67]) professor of music EA/01*

CALVERT, William (fl 1877-92) director, actor, dramatist DD, EA/95

CALVERTO, J[ames] F[erguson] English agent GRB/1

CALVESI, Vincenzo (fl 1786-88) singer BD

CALVESI, Teresa (fl 1783-92) singer BD

CALVIN, Henry (1918-75) American actor TW/3-5, 10-12, 22

CALZOLARI, Enrico (1823-88) singer CDP

CAMANO, Mrs. (fl 1733) actress BD

CAMARGO, Marie Anne de Cupis

de (1710-70) dancer BD,
CDP, ES, OC/1-2
CAMBELL, Mr. dramatist CP/
2-3
CAMBER, Susan (b 1947) Amer-
ican dancer TW/24
CAMBERT, Robert (c. 1628-77)
French composer, impresario,
band leader BD
CAMBLOS, Charles S. (d 1887)
actor NYM
CAMBLOS, Mrs. Charles S.
see Conway, Lillian
CAMBRIA, Frank (d 1966 [83])
designer BP/51*
CAMBRIDGE, Mr. (fl 1827)
actor HAS
CAMBRIDGE, Arthur (b c. 1840)
manager, agent, dramatist?
SR
CAMBRIDGE, Godfrey (b 1933)
American actor, comedian
CB
CAMBRIDGE, Harry (d 1892)
vocal comedian EA/94*
CAMBURINI, Sig. singer CDP
CAMEL, Tom (fl 1785) eques-
trian BD
CAMELINAT, Hermine see
French, Hermene
CAMEO, Frank (d 1902 [27])
music-hall performer EA/
03*
CAMERON, Mr. (fl 1797) actor
BD
CAMERON, Mr. (d 1800) box-
keeper BD
CAMERON, Beatrice see
Mansfield, Beatrice
CAMERON, Charles E. F. (d
1917 [45]) EA/18*
CAMERON, Donald (d 1868)
musician EA/69*
CAMERON, Donald (d 1955 [66])
actor TW/12, WWT/7-11
CAMERON, Ewin (d 1892 [82])
EA/93*
CAMERON, Frances (b 1886)
American singer WWM
CAMERON, Hugh (1879-1941)
American actor CB, SR
CAMERON, Kathryn (d 1954
[71]) actress TW/1, 10
CAMERON, Marlene (b 1935)
American actress TW/6-7
CAMERON, Mary Agnes (b 1838)
Irish? actress HAS, SR
CAMERON, Retta (d 1975 [49])

performer BP/60*
CAMERON, Sylvia (b 1881) English
singer GRB/1
CAMERON, Violet [Mrs. De Ben-
saude] (1862-1919) actress,
singer CDP, DD, DP, GRB/
1-4, OAA/2, WWT/1-3
CAMERON, Walter M. (d 1909
[53]) EA/10*
CAMERY, Mr. (fl 1777-78) actor
BD
CAMILLE, Master (fl 1712) dancer
BD
CAMILLO, Mary (fl 1796-97)
posture maker BD
CAMMANS, Jan (d 1976 [84])
performer BP/60*
CAMP, Frank E. (1870-1943)
musician, dramatist? SR
CAMP, Harry Squire see Godfrey,
H. S.
CAMP, Jack (d 1907 [40]) comic
singer EA/08*
CAMP, Richard (b 1923) American
actor TW/2-3
CAMP, Sheppard (b 1876) Ameri-
can composer, actor WWM
CAMPAGNOLI, Bartolommeo (1751-
1827) violinist, musical direc-
tor, composer CDP
CAMPANA, Fabio (1819-82) Italian
composer, singing master ES
CAMPANARI, Giuseppe (1858-1927)
Italian singer CDP, WWA/1
CAMPANELLA, Joseph (b 1925/27)
American actor BE, TW/19
CAMPANELLA, Philip (b 1948)
American actor TW/28-30
CAMPANINI, Barbarina (1721-99)
Italian dancer BD, ES
CAMPANINI, Cleofonte (1860-1919)
Italian musical director ES,
WWA/1
CAMPANINI, Italio (1845-96)
Italian singer CDP, ES, SR
CAMPANINI, Miriamne see
Domitilla, Miriamne
CAMPBELL, Mr. (fl 1732-36)
actor BD
CAMPBELL, Mr. (fl 1804) actor
TD/2
CAMPBELL, Mr. (fl early 19th
cent) actor CDP
CAMPBELL, Mr. (d 1882 [67])
EA/83*
CAMPBELL, [Mrs. ? Miss?] (fl
1722-24) actress BD
CAMPBELL, Mrs. (fl 1751) singer,

actress BD

CAMPBELL, Mrs. [née Wallis]
(fl 1789-1814) English actress
CDP, DNB, GT, TD/1-2

CAMPBELL, Miss (fl 1779)
actress BD

CAMPBELL, Miss [Mrs. J.
Gunning] (fl 1799-1806?)
actress BD, TD/1-2

CAMPBELL, A. H. (1826-65)
English actor HAS, SR

CAMPBELL, Alan (d 1917)
dramatist EA/18*

CAMPBELL, Alan (d 1963 [58])
actor TW/20

CAMPBELL, Lady Archibald
Scottish dramatist GRB/1-3

CAMPBELL, A. V. see
Voullaire, Andrew Leonard

CAMPBELL, Bartley (1843-88)
American dramatist, manager
CDP, COC, DAB, DD, ES,
HJD, OC/1-3, SR, WWA/H

CAMPBELL, Charles (1905-64)
American actor TW/6-7

CAMPBELL, Clifford [Frederick
Hankins] (d 1901 [41]) actor
EA/03*

CAMPBELL, Colin Scottish
actor ES

CAMPBELL, Colin see Carleton, Royce

CAMPBELL, Craig (b 1884)
Canadian actor, singer WWM

CAMPBELL, Denis (d 1909 [48])
Irish comedian EA/10*

CAMPBELL, Douglas (b 1922)
Scottish actor, director AAS,
BE, CB, WWT/12-16

CAMPBELL, Duncan (d 1898
[46]) actor EA/99*

CAMPBELL, Mrs. Edmund V.
see Campbell, Mary

CAMPBELL, Edmund Vaullaire
(d 1910 [75]) actor EA/11*,
WWT/14*

CAMPBELL, Ellen (fl 1810)
actress CDP

CAMPBELL, Eric (d c. 1917)
Scottish actor ES

CAMPBELL, E. V. see
Campbell, Edmund Vaullaire

CAMPBELL, Flora American
actress TW/1, 20

CAMPBELL, Frances (d 1948)
actress BE*, WWT/14*

CAMPBELL, Sir Francis J.
(1832-1914) American musician

SR

CAMPBELL, Frank singer, composer CDP

CAMPBELL, Gabrielle Margaret
Vere see Preedy, George R.

CAMPBELL, Gary (b 1938) American actor TW/23

CAMPBELL, Herbert (1844-1904)
English actor, music-hall per-
former CDP, COC, DD, DP,
GRB/1, OC/1-3

CAMPBELL, Mrs. Herbert (d
1891 [33]) EA/92*

CAMPBELL, Mrs. Herbert see
Campbell, Lizzie

CAMPBELL, Howard (d 1896 [42])
comedian EA/97*

CAMPBELL, J. (d 1802) actor
BD

CAMPBELL, Mrs. J. A. see
Fulton, Mary

CAMPBELL, James (d 1893)
singer EA/94*

CAMPBELL, J. C. [né George
Keller St. John] (d 1875 [31])
comedian, minstrel CDP

CAMPBELL, John (fl 1868) American carpenter HAS

CAMPBELL, John actor TW/1,
23

CAMPBELL, Judy (b 1916) English
actress AAS, ES, WWT/10-16

CAMPBELL, Katherine Roger
see Fawcett, Marion

CAMPBELL, Lily Bess (1883-1967)
American scholar BE, WWA/4

CAMPBELL, Lizzie [Mrs. Herbert
Campbell] (d 1884) EA/85*

CAMPBELL, Margaret (b 1894)
English actress, singer WWT/
4-8

CAMPBELL, Mary [Mrs. Edmund
V. Campbell] (d 1896) EA/97*

CAMPBELL, Mary see Law-
rence, Mrs. Arthur

CAMPBELL, Maurice (d 1942 [74])
manager WWT/14*

CAMPBELL, Oscar James, Jr.
(d 1970 [90]) scholar BP/55*

CAMPBELL, Mrs. Patrick [Bea-
trice Stella Tanner] (1865-1940)
English actress COC, DD,
DNB, EA/95-96, ES, GRB/1-4,
NTH, OC/1-3, PDT, SR, WWA/
1, WWM, WWS, WWT/1-9,
WWW/3

CAMPBELL, Patton (b 1926) American designer BE, WWT/15-16

CAMPBELL, Sandy (b 1924)
American actor TW/2, 4
CAMPBELL, S. C. [né Sherwood A. Coan] (1829-74)
singer, minstrel CDP, HAS
CAMPBELL, Stella Patrick
(b 1886) English actress
GRB/3-4, WWT/1-9
CAMPBELL, Thomas (1777-1844) writer BD
CAMPBELL, Violet (1892-1970)
English actress WWT/4-8
CAMPBELL, Walter George
see Lucy, Arnold
CAMPBELL, Webster (d 1972
[79]) performer BP/57*
CAMPBELL, William (fl 1784-1810?) musician BD
CAMPBELL, William (d 1870
[48]) comedian EA/71*
CAMPBELL, William (d 1878
[26]) Scottish giant EA/79*
CAMPEAU, Frank (1864-1943)
American actor SR
CAMPEAU, Jane Harrison (d 1974
[48]) performer BP/58*
CAMPIAN, Edmund (1540-81)
English dramatist CP/3
CAMPINA, Fidela (b 1897)
Spanish singer ES
"CAMPIOLI" [Antonio Gualandi]
(fl 1708-32) German singer
BD
CAMPION, Alfred (d 1896 [25])
EA/97*
CAMPION, Cyril (1894-1961)
English dramatist WWT/6-13
CAMPION, Edmond (fl 1654)
dramatist FGF
CAMPION, Maria Ann [Mrs.
Alexander Pope] (1775/77-1803) Irish actress DD,
DNB, ES, GT, TD/1-2
CAMPION, Mary Anne (c. 1687-1706) singer, dancer, harpsichordist BD
CAMPION, Thomas (1567-1620)
English musician COC, CP/
2-3, DD, DNB, ES, FGF,
HP, OC/1-3
CAMPION, Thomas (d 1905)
EA/06*
CAMPION, William E. (d 1973
[61]) musician BP/58*
CAMPIONI, Sig. (fl 1744-70?)
dancer, ballet master BD
CAMPIONI, Signora (fl 1744-54?)
dancer BD

CAMPKIN, Reginald E. (d 1918)
EA/19*
CAMPLOS, Lilian Conway (d 1891
[32]) EA/92*
CAMPOLINI, Signora (fl 1767-68)
singer BD
CAMPORA, Giuseppe (b 1923)
Italian singer CB
CAMPORESE, Violante (1785-1839)
Italian singer, actress CDP,
ES
CAMPTON, David (b 1924) English
dramatist, director, actor CD,
CH, ES, MH, PDT
CAMRYN, Walter American dancer,
choreographer ES
CAMUS, Albert (1913-60) French
dramatist OC/3, WWW/5
CAN, Betty (b 1933) American
actress TW/15
CANADINA (fl 1761-66) house servant, constable BD
CANAVAN, Eliza Louisa see
Plunkett, Mrs. Charles
CANBY, Albert H. (1860-1940)
American manager CB, CDP,
GRB/2-4
CANDELIN, Susan Mary Charlotte
see Vaughan, Susie
CANDELON, Catherine see
Vaughan, Kate
CANDIDES, William (1840-1910)
singer CDP
CANDLER, James (fl 1569) actor
DA
CANDLER, Peter (b 1926) American general manager, educator,
lighting designer BE
CANDRIX, Fud (d 1974 [65]) musician BP/58*
CANE, Andrew (fl 1622-54?) actor
DA, DD
CANE, Harry (b 1849) actor DD
CANEGATA, Leonard Lionel
Cornelius see Lee, Canada
CANEMAKER, John (b 1943)
American actor TW/25, 29
CANETTI, Elias (b 1905) Austrian
dramatist CH
CANFIELD, Curtis (b 1903) American educator, director BE
CANFIELD, Eugene (1851-1904)
comedian, minstrel CDP
CANFIELD, Mary Grace (b 1926)
American actress TW/21
CANFIELD, William F. (d 1925
[64]) performer BE*, BP/9*
CANGALOVIC, Miroslav (b 1921)

Yugoslavian singer ES
CANIGLIA, Maria (b 1906)
Italian singer ES
CANLETS, Master (fl 1785)
actor BD
CANNAN, Denis (b 1919) English
dramatist, actor AAS, CD,
CH, PDT, WWT/11-16
CANNAN, Gilbert (1884-1955)
English dramatist ES, WWT/
2-7, WWW/5
CANNELL, William (d 1882 [32])
administrator EA/84*
CANNING, Effie J. composer
CDP
CANNING, Mrs. George [née
Mary Ann Costello; Mrs.
Samuel Reddish, II; Mrs.
Richard Hunn] (1747?-1827)
English actress BD, DD
CANNING, James J. (b 1946)
American actor TW/28-30
CANNINGE, George (b 1846)
actor DD
CANNON, Anthony see Hart,
Tony
CANNON, Charles James (1800-
60) American dramatist
CDP, HJD, WWA/H
CANNON, Esma (d 1972) Aus-
tralian actress WWT/10
CANNON, Frances Ann see
Dougherty, Frances Ann
CANNON, Hughie (1840-1912)
minstrel, composer SR
CANNON, J. D. (b 1922) Amer-
ican actor BE
CANNON, Jimmy (d 1973 [63])
journalist BP/58*
CANNON, Maureen (b 1926)
American actress TW/1-3
CANNON, Nicholas (fl 1662-65)
drummer BD
CANNON, Raymond American
actor ES
CANOLL, James (1817-67) Amer-
ican actor HAS
CANONGE, Louis Placide (1822-
93) American dramatist DAB
CANSINO, Eduardo, Jr. (d 1974
[54]) performer BP/58*
CANSINO, Gabriel (d 1963 [50])
dancer, teacher BE*
CANTELO, H. (d 1797) musician?
BD
CANTELO, Hezekiah (d 1811)
instrumentalist BD
CANTELO, Thomas (1774-1807)

instrumentalist, teacher BD
CANTER, Mr. (fl 1773-74) dancer
BD
CANTER, James (fl 1768-83) scene
painter, machinist, landscape
painter BD
CANTOR, Mrs. (fl 1838-48) Eng-
lish actress HAS
CANTOR, Arthur (b 1920) Ameri-
can producer, press representa-
tive BE, WWT/15-16
CANTOR, David L. (d 1968 [68])
publicist BP/52*
CANTOR, Eddie (1892-1964) Amer-
ican actor, singer, producer
BE, CB, ES, NTH, SR, TW/
2-8, 21, WWA/4, WWT/5-13,
WWW/6
CANTOR, Mrs. Eddie see
Cantor, Ida
CANTOR, Ida (d 1962 [70]) BP/
47*
CANTOR, Moss see Cinders,
Ettie
CANTOR, Nat (d 1956 [59]) actor
TW/12
CANTRELL, Mrs. (fl 1716-37)
actress, singer BD
CANTRELL, Miss (fl 1736-39)
dancer, actress BD
CANTRELL, Miss (fl 1766?-71)
singer BD
CANTRELL, Miss [Mrs. John
Morris] (d 1876) singer EA/77*
CANTRELL, Nick (b 1943) Ameri-
can actor TW/26
CANZI, Caterina (1805-40) Italian
singer ES
CAPALBO, Carmen (b 1925) Amer-
ican director, producer BE
CAPDEVILLE, Miss (fl 1762)
dancer BD
CAPDEVILLE, Mlle. (fl 1754-71)
dancer, proprietor BD
CAPE, Mr. (fl 1758-73) dresser
BD
CAPE, Fred (d 1893 [44]) comedian
EA/94*, WWT/14*
CAPE, Frederick Damer (d 1882
[52]) journalist, lecturer EA/
83*
CAPE, T. Ireby (b 1873) English
actor, stage manager GRB/1
CAPEK, Josef (1887-1945) Czech
dramatist COC
CAPEK, Josef Horymír (1860-1932)
musical director ES
CAPEK, Karel (1890-1938) Czech

dramatist COC, OC/2-3
CAPELL, Edward (1713-81)
English scholar CDP, CP/
2-3, DD, DNB, GT, HP,
TD/1-2
CAPERON, Nicholas (fl 1660-68)
trumpeter BD
CAPERS, Virginia (b 1925)
American actress TW/30
CAPET, Helen actress CDP
CAPITANI, Master (fl 1760)
dancer BD
CAPITANI, [John?] (fl 1743-63)
singer BD
CAPITANI, Polly (fl 1759-66)
dancer BD
CAPLE, [John?] (d 1860 [40])
actor, manager CDP, EA/
72*
CAPLIN, Gertrude (b 1921)
American producer BE
CAPO, Bobby, Jr. (b 1950)
Puerto Rican actor TW/25
CAPOCCI, Guerino C. (d 1973
[79]) musician BP/57*
CAPODILUPO, Tony (b 1940)
American actor TW/23-25
CAPON, Mr. (fl 1789) actor BD
CAPON, William (1757-1827)
English architect, scene de-
signer, artist BD, CDP,
COC, DNB, ES, OC/1-3
CAPORALE, Andrea Francisca
(d c. 1757) violoncellist,
composer BD
CAPOTE, Truman (b 1924)
American dramatist BE,
CB, CD, ES, HJD, MD,
MWD
CAPOUL, Joseph Amédée Victor
(b 1839) singer, actor CDP
CAPOUL, Victor (1839-1924)
French singer ES
CAPPELL, Mrs. (fl 1847)
actress HAS
CAPPELL, Cordelia (fl 1850)
actress HAS
CAPPELLETTI, [Petronio?
Giuseppe?] (fl 1791-96?) sing-
er, composer BD
CAPPELLETTI, Theresa Poggi (fl
1791) singer BD
CAPPER, Miss (fl 1798-1810?)
singer BD
CAPPERVILLA, Ellen see
Coppervilla, Ellen
CAPPONI, Sig. (d 1880) singer
EA/81*

CAPPY, Ted American choreog-
rapher, director BE
CAPRICE, June (1899-1936) Amer-
ican actress BE*
CAPTAIN EDDIE [Edward Henry
Knipschield] (d 1964 [57])
aerialist BE*
"CAPUCHINO, Sig. " (fl 1746)
dancer BD
"CAPUCHINO, Signora" (fl 1746)
dancer BD
CAPURRO, Alfred see Drake,
Alfred
CAPUS, Alfred (1858-1922) French
dramatist GRB/1-4
CAPUZZI, Giuseppe Antonio (1755-
1818) Italian violinist, composer
BD
CARA, Irene (b 1959) American
actress TW/26-30
CARABALDI, Sig. (fl 1773-74?)
singer BD
CARABO, Jacques (fl 1796-97)
posture maker BD
CARACOL, Manolo (d 1973 [62])
performer BP/57*
CARADIMAS, Lana (b 1945) Amer-
ican actress TW/29-30
CARADORI, Anna (b 1822) singer
HAS, SR
CARADORI-ALLEN, Maria Caterina
Rosalbina (1800-65) Italian singer
CDP, DNB
CARAFA, Sig. (d 1872 [85]) com-
poser EA/73*
CARANTI, Signora Luigia (fl 1857)
singer HAS
CARARA, Signora Antonio (fl
1768?-78) singer BD
CARATHA, Mahomet (fl 1819)
Turkish equilibrist CDP
CARATTA, Mahomet (fl 1747-51)
Turkish equilibrist, manager
BD
CARAVEN, Nora (d 1894 [24])
actress EA/95*
CARAVOGLIA, Charles [Charles
F. Caravoglia-Buckmaster]
(b 1868) English actor, stage
manager GRB/1-2
CARAVOGLIA-BUCKMASTER,
Charles F. see Caravoglia,
Charles
CARBERRY, Joseph (b 1948) Amer-
ican actor TW/30
CARBONE, Bobby (d 1964 [77])
performer BP/49*
CARBONELLI, Giovanni Steffano

(c. 1700-72) Italian violinist,
bandleader, composer BD
CARBREY, John (d 1962 [77])
performer BE*
CARCARES, Ernie (d 1971 [69])
musician BP/55*
CARD, Andrew (fl 1683-1707)
concessionaire BD
CARD, Kathryn (d 1964 [71])
actress BE*
CARDARELLI, Sig. (fl 1775-
76) singer BD
CARDEN, James (b 1837) Irish
actor HAS, SR
CARDEN, Mrs. James see
Leigh, Miss Marston
CARDEN, William (b 1947)
American actor TW/30
CARDER, Emmeline (d 1961)
actress BE*
CARDI, Signora (fl 1773-74)
singer BD
CARDINALE, Mr. (fl 1789)
singer BD
CARDON, Louis (1747-1805)
French harpist BD
CARDOW, Charles composer,
author CDP
CARDOWNIE, J. W. (d 1900)
dancer EA/01*
CARDUS, Sir Neville (d 1975
[85]) critic BP/59*
CARDWELL, Carolyn Y. (b
1938) American actress TW/
24
CARELESS, Elizabeth (d 1752)
singer BD
CARELL, Annette (d 1967) per-
former BP/52*
CARELL, John see Caryl,
John
CARESTINI, Giovanni (1705-60)
Italian singer BD, CDP,
ES
CAREW, Lady Elizabeth (fl 1613)
dramatist CP/1-3, FGF
CAREW, Helen American actress
BE, TW/11-12
CAREW, James (1875-1938)
American actor COC, GRB/
2-4, SR, WWA/1, WWM,
WWS, WWT/1-8
CAREW, John (fl 1660-63) house
servant BD
CAREW, Margaret Felicité Anne
(b 1799) actress, singer
CDP, OX
CAREW, Ora (d 1955 [62])

actress BE*
CAREW, Peter (b 1922) American
actor TW/27-28
CAREW, Thomas (1595?-1639?)
English masque writer, lyricist
CP/1-3, DD, DNB, FGF, HP
CAREWE, Edwin (1883-1940)
American actor ES
CAREY, Mr. (fl 1714-16) singer
BD
CAREY, Mr. (fl 1754) violinist
BD
CAREY, Miss (fl 1755-62) actress
BD
CAREY, Ann (d 1833) CDP
CAREY, Charles (d 1901) comedian
EA/03*
CAREY, Charles English actor,
manager GRB/1
CAREY, David (b 1945) American
actor TW/27
CAREY, Denis (b 1909) English
director, actor AAS, BE,
WWT/12-16
CAREY, Edna actress CDP
CAREY, Eleanor (1852-1915)
Chilean actress CDP, WWS
CAREY, Elizabeth [Mrs. Tom
Carey] (d 1876) EA/77*
CAREY, Francis Clive Savill (b
1883) English singer, director
ES
CAREY, Frank (b 1934) American
actor TW/26, 28-30
CAREY, George Saville (1743-1807)
English actor, monologuist,
dramatist BD, CDP, CP/3,
DD, DNB, GT, TD/1-2
CAREY, Mrs. George Saville [née
Gillo] (fl 1789-98) BD
CAREY, Giles (fl 1609-13) actor
DA
CAREY, Harriett [Mrs. Tom
Carey] (d 1868) EA/69*
CAREY, Harry (1878-1947) Amer-
ican actor ES, TW/4
CAREY, Henry (1690-1743) English
musician, dramatist CDP,
CP/1-3, DD, DNB, ES, GT,
HP, NTH, TD/1-2
CAREY, Henry Lucius, Lord Vis-
count Falkland (d 1663) drama-
tist CP/1-3, DD
CAREY, Joseph A. (d 1964 [81])
actor BE*
CAREY, Joseph P. actor, singer
CDP
CAREY, Joyce (b 1898) English

actress, dramatist BE,
COC, ES, WWT/4-16
CAREY, Macdonald (b 1913)
American actor BE, ES,
TW/10
CAREY, May (d 1966) producer,
director BP/50*
CAREY, Pat (d 1912 [53]) Irish
comedian EA/13*
CAREY, Mrs. Pat see Howard,
Lizzie
CAREY, Ron (b 1935) American
actor TW/25
CAREY, Rev. Thomas F. (1904-
72) American director, pro-
ducer BE, TW/28
CAREY, Mrs. Tom see Carey,
Elizabeth
CAREY, Mrs. Tom see Carey,
Harriett
CAREY, T. P. (fl 1865) Irish
singer HAS
CARFAX, Bruce (1905-70) Eng-
lish actor, singer WWT/
7-13
CARGILL, Ann see Cargill,
Mrs. R.
CARGILL, Judith American
actress TW/3
CARGILL, Patrick (b 1918)
English actor, dramatist
WWT/14-16
CARGILL, Mrs. R. [née Ann
Brown] (c. 1759-84) English
actress, singer BD, CDP,
DNB, TD/1-2
CARHART, Georgiana (d 1959
[93]) singer TW/15
CARHART, James L. (1843-
1937) American actor WWS
CARINGTON, Dorothy (b 1872)
English actress GRB/1
CARIOLI, Claudine (fl 1857-58)
singer HAS
CARIOU, Leonard (b 1939)
Canadian actor AAS, TW/
25-30, WWT/15-16
CARLE, Alice actress, singer
CDP
CARLE, Pietro (d 1899) bird
performer EA/00*
CARLE, Richard [Charles
Nicholas Carleton] (1871-
1941) American actor, drama-
tist CB, CDP, GRB/2-4,
SR, WWA/1, WWM, WWS,
WWT/1-9
CARLELL, Lodowick (fl 1629-

64) dramatist CP/1-3, DD,
DNB, FGF, GT
CARLES, Mr. actor GT, TD/2
CARLES, Henry (d 1858 [48])
actor, singer WWT/14*
CARLETON, Mr. (d 1783) house
servant BD
CARLETON, Mr. (fl 1765-90)
lobby doorkeeper BD
CARLETON, Miss (fl 1785) actress
BD
CARLETON, Billie [Florence
Lenora Stewart] (d 1918 [22])
actress EA/19*, WWT/14*
CARLETON, Charles Nicholas
see Carle, Richard
CARLETON, Claire [or Clare] (b
1913) American actress TW/
6-7, WWT/9-13
CARLETON, Henry Guy (1856?-
1910) American dramatist DAB,
DD, GRB/2-4, HJD, SR,
WWA/1, WWS
CARLETON, John (fl 1662-64)
actor? BD
CARLETON, Laurie (d 1899)
EA/00*
CARLETON, Lloyd B. American
actor, director ES
CARLETON, Marjorie (d 1964)
dramatist BE*
CARLETON, Nicholas (fl c. 1580)
actor DA
CARLETON, Royce [Colin Camp-
bell] (1860-95) Scottish actor
DD, DP
CARLETON, William (1827-85)
Irish actor, dramatist, singer
CDP, DD, HAS
CARLETON, William P. (d 1947
[74]) actor, singer WWT/14*
CARLETON, William T. (fl 1873)
singer, manager CDP
CARLETON, William T. (d 1930)
producer WWT/14*
CARLETON, W. T. (d 1922)
actor, singer WWT/14*
CARLI, Miss (fl 1762-70) singer
BD
CARLIER, Madeleine (d 1935 [57])
actress WWT/14*
CARLILE, Mrs. Frank see
Gerard, Ethel
CARLILE, James (d 1691) English
dramatist, actor CP/3, DD,
DNB
CARLIN, Charles (d 1908 [49])
performer? EA/09*

CARLIN, Chet (b 1918) American actor TW/28-30
CARLIN, Cynthia (d 1973) actress TW/28
CARLIN, Herbert (d 1967 [70]) press agent BP/51*
CARLIN, Roger (d 1974 [62]) producer/director/choreographer BP/58*
CARLIN, Thomas (b 1928) American actor TW/12-13, 15-16, 20
CARLINI, Rosa (fl 1758-59) dancer BD
CARLINO, Lewis John (b 1932) American dramatist CD
CARLINO, Sieur (fl 1777) tumbler BD
CARLISLE, Earl of see Howard, Frederic
CARLISLE, Mrs. (fl 1745) actress BD
CARLISLE, Miss (fl 1869-80) actress DD
CARLISLE, Alexandra [Alexandra Swift] (1886-1936) English actress GRB/3-4, SR, WWT/1-8
CARLISLE, Frank (d 1918) EA/19*
CARLISLE, Frederic Howard, Earl of see Howard, Frederic
CARLISLE, James (d 1691) English actor, dramatist BD, CP/1-2, GT
CARLISLE, James (d 1864) circus performer HAS
CARLISLE, Joseph (d 1896 [66]) comedian EA/97*
CARLISLE, Kitty (b 1914/15) American actress, singer BE, TW/5-13, 15-16, WWT/9-16
CARLISLE, Margaret (b 1905) American actress, singer WWT/7-10
CARLISLE, Sybil (b 1871) South African/English actress DD, GRB/1-4, WWT/1-8
CARLO (fl 1803) performing dog CDP
CARLO, Mr. (fl 1785-86) singer BD
CARLO, Harry acrobat CDP
CARLO, Monte (1883-1967) Danish lyricist, composer, publisher BE, TW/24
CARLO, Phoebe (fl 1883-86) actress CDP, DD
CARLO FAMILY, The (fl 1850) HAS
CARLOMAN, Mrs. (d 1875 [44]) EA/77*
CARLOS, Fred (d 1904) actor EA/05*, WWT/14*
CARLOS, Mrs. Fred see D'Lonra, Annie
CARLSBERG, Gotthold (1838-81) musician, orchestra leader CDP
CARLSEN, John A. (1915-75) Canadian representative WWT/11-14
CARLSON, Keith (d 1975 [34]) producer/director/choreographer BP/59*
CARLSON, Ken (d 1973 [53]) performer BP/57*
CARLSON, Leslie (b 1933) American actor TW/25-26
CARLSON, Richard (1912-77) American actor ES
CARLTON, Mr. (fl 1729) dancer BD
CARLTON, Sir Arthur Roscoe (1865-1931) English actor, manager, proprietor GRB/1-4
CARLTON, Mrs. Charles see Carlton, Lizzie
CARLTON, Henry singer CDP
CARLTON, Henry see Cavendish, Henry Frederick Compton
CARLTON, Henry F. (d 1973 [80]) dramatist BP/57*
CARLTON, James (d 1890) circus performer EA/91*
CARLTON, Kathleen (d 1964 [65]) actress BE*
CARLTON, Lizzie [Mrs. Charles Carlton] (d 1906) EA/07*
CARLTON, Louis H. (b 1863) English dramatist, manager GRB/1
CARLTON, Neil (d 1912 [58]) actor? EA/13*
CARLTON, Peter (fl 1673-77) actor BD
CARLTON, T. S. (d 1892 [45]) manager EA/93*
CARLTON, William (d 1973 [50]) musician BP/58*
CARLTON, William T. (fl 1870s) English singer SR
CARLYLE, Francis (d 1916 [48])

actor WWT/14*
CARLYLE, Richard (b 1920)
Canadian actor TW/6-8,
11-12
CARLYON, Eunice Nowlan (d
1904 [81]) EA/05*
CARLYON, Frank (d 1908 [36])
manager EA/09*
CARLYON, Kate (d 1924 [75])
actress WWT/14*
CARMAN, Mrs. [née Conway]
(fl 1848) actress HAS
CARMAN, Miss dancer HAS
CARMAN, Allan (d 1969 [72])
performer BP/54*
CARMAN, Jerry (d 1975 [75])
agent BP/60*
CARME, Pamela [Hon. Kathleen
Pamela Boscawen] (b 1902)
English actress WWT/6-8
CARMEL, Eddie (d 1972 [36])
circus giant BP/57*
CARMENCITA Spanish dancer
SR
CARMICHAEL, Ian (b 1920)
English actor AAS, WWT/
12-16
CARMICHAEL, Thomas (fl
1737-79) prompter BD
CARMICHAEL, Thomas Percy
see Percy, A. C.
CARMIGNANI, Giovanni (fl
1762-63) singer BD
CARMIGNANI, Signora Giovanni?
(fl 1763) singer? BD
CARMINATI, Tullio (1894-1971)
Italian actor ES, TW/27,
WWT/7-10
CARMINES, Al composer, lyri-
cist, performer, director,
producer WWT/16
CARMODY, Jay (d 1973 [72])
American critic BE
CARNABY, James (fl 1701?-13)
actor BD
CARNCROSS, John L. (b c. 1834)
American minstrel, singer
CDP
CARNE, Mrs. (fl 1793-95)
actress BD
CARNE, Miss (fl 1781-82)
actress BD
CARNE, Miss (fl 1799-1802)
dancer BD
CARNE, Elizabeth see Carne,
Mrs. John
CARNE, John (fl 1740-68) house
servant BD

CARNE, Mrs. John [Elizabeth]
(fl c. 1762-83) house servant
BD
CARNE, Joseph (fl 1877-96) actor
DD, EA/97
CARNE, Judy (b 1939) English
actress TW/26
CARNEGIE, Douglas John (d 1913)
EA/14*
CARNEGIE, Gordon (d 1916) EA/
17*
CARNELIA, Craig (b 1949) Amer-
ican actor TW/25-26
CARNEVALE, Pietro (fl 1782?-91)
Italian? musician, deputy mana-
ger, proprietor BD
CARNEVALE, Signora Pietro (fl
1783-92) singer, actress BD
CARNEY, Mr. (fl 1733-45) dancer,
actor BD
CARNEY, Alan (d 1973 [63])
entertainer TW/29
CARNEY, Annie [Mrs. Tom Car-
ney] (d 1910 [52]) EA/11*
CARNEY, Art (b 1918) American
performer, actor BE, CB,
TW/15-16, 19, 21-22, 25, 28-
30, WWT/15-16
CARNEY, Frank (b 1904) Irish
dramatist, actor, producer BE
CARNEY, George (1887-1947)
English actor WWT/9-10
CARNEY, Kate (1868-1950) English
music-hall artist CDP, COC,
ES, OC/1-3
CARNEY, Kay American actress
TW/26
CARNEY, Pat [James Sullivan]
(d 1893) music-hall artist
EA/94*
CARNEY, Tom [Henry Penny] (d
1911 [52]) Irish comedian EA/
13*
CARNEY, Mrs. Tom see
Carney, Annie
CARNEY, William (d 1972 [73])
journalist BP/56*
CARNEY, "Yankee" Henri (d 1902)
music-hall performer EA/03*
CARNOVSKY, Morris (b 1897/98)
American actor AAS, BE, ES,
TW/4-8, 12-18, WWT/9-16
CARO, Warren (b 1907) American
executive, actor BE, WWT/16
CAROL, J. C. (d 1899) manager
EA/00*
CAROL, John (d 1968 [58]) per-
former BP/53*

CAROLA, Mme. (d 1900 [37])
circus performer EA/01*

CAROLINA TWINS freaks CDP

CAROLINE, Mlle. (fl 1842)
equestrienne CDP

CARON, Leon (d 1905 [55])
composer, conductor EA/
06*

CARON, Leslie (b 1931) French
dancer, actress CB, COC,
ES, WWT/13-14

CAROZZI, Carlotta (fl 1864)
Italian singer HAS

CARPENTER, Mr. (fl 1736)
actor BD

CARPENTER, Mr. (fl 1838)
actor HAS

CARPENTER, Mrs. (fl 1851)
actress HAS

CARPENTER, Carleton [or
Carlton] (b 1926) American
actor, composer BE, TW/
10-17, 22-23, 26, 30,
WWT/16

CARPENTER, Claude E. (d
1976 [71]) designer BP/60*

CARPENTER, Constance (b
1906) English actress, singer
BE, WWT/7-16

CARPENTER, Edward Childs
(1871/72-1950) American
dramatist TW/7, WWA/5,
WWT/4-10

CARPENTER, Mrs. E. J.
see Evans, Millicent

CARPENTER, Ernest (1868-1909)
manager GRB/3-4

CARPENTER, Freddie (b 1908)
Australian dancer, director
WWT/10-16

CARPENTER, Frederick (d
1904 [63]) lessee EA/05*

CARPENTER, John Alden
(1876-1951) American com-
poser CB, ES, HJD,
WWA/3

CARPENTER, Joseph Edwards
(1813-85) English dramatist
DD, EA/68

CARPENTER, Louisa d'A. (d
1976 [68]) producer/director/
choreographer BP/60*

CARPENTER, Mary Ann (d
1877 [29]) EA/78*

CARPENTER, Maud (d 1967)
manager WWT/8-10

CARPENTER, Paul (d 1964 [43])
Canadian actor BE*

CARPENTER, Richard (fl 1623-70)
dramatist CP/1-3, DD

CARPENTER, Robert (1748-85)
actor, singer BD

CARPENTER, Thelma (b 1922)
American singer BE, TW/11,
25-26

CARPENTER, Tyler (b 1917)
American actor TW/4

CARPENTER, William (fl 1611-25)
actor DA

"CARPENTIER, Mr." (fl 1754)
actor? BD

CARR (fl 1805) actor? dramatist
CP/3

CARR, Mr. (d 1797) actor, equestrian, tumbler BD

CARR, Mr. (fl 1797) watchman
BD

CARR, Mrs. (fl 1741) dancer BD

CARR, Mrs. (fl 1789) American
dramatist EAP

CARR, Alexander (1878-1946)
Russian/American actor CB,
ES, GRB/3-4, SR, TW/3,
WWA/2, WWM, WWS, WWT/
1-9

CARR, Anthony (b 1924) American
actor TW/2-3

CARR, A. Selby (d 1974 [70])
agent BP/59*

CARR, Ben (d 1916) EA/17*

CARR, Benjamin (1768-1831) English composer, publisher, musician, singer BD, CDP, DAB,
ES, HAS, WWA/H

CARR, Eric Marcus (d 1916 [20])
EA/17*

CARR, F. Osmond (1858-1916)
English composer DD, ES,
GRB/3-4, WWT/1-3

CARR, George actor, singer CDP

CARR, George (d 1962 [69]) actor
WWT/6-9

CARR, Georgia (d 1971 [46]) performer BP/56*

CARR, Gina (d 1972 [35]) actress
TW/29

CARR, Howard (1880-1960) English
composer, conductor WWT/
4-7, WWW/5

CARR, I. N. (d 1866) pantomimist
HAS

CARR, Isabella (d 1867 [49])
actress? HAS

CARR, Jane [Rita Brunström]
(1909-57) English actress
WWT/9-12

CARR, John (fl 1631) actor
DA
CARR, Sir John (b 1772) English
dramatist CP/3
CARR, Rev. Dr. John (d 1807
[76]) dramatist CP/2-3, GT
CARR, Sir John (fl 1804) drama-
tist CP/3, DD
CARR, Joseph W. Comyns (1849-
1916) English dramatist,
critic, manager DD, ES,
GRB/1-4, NTH, WWT/1-3,
WWW/2
CARR, Kenneth (b 1943) Ameri-
can actor TW/22-26, 30
CARR, Lawrence (1916-69)
American producer BE,
TW/25, WWA/5, WWT/
14-15
CARR, Leon (d 1976 [65])
composer/lyricist BP/60*
CARR, Louisa [Mrs. Peach]
(fl 1821-23) actress CDP
CARR, Lucy (d 1897) English
equestrienne EA/98*
CARR, Mary (fl 1856) actress
HAS
CARR, Mary (d 1973 [99]) per-
former BP/58*
CARR, Mickey (d 1973) musi-
cian BP/58*
CARR, Mildred [Mrs. James
Willard] Welsh actress
GRB/1
CARR, Oliver (fl 1741-69)
actor, manager BD
CARR, Philip (1874-1957) Eng-
lish dramatist, critic, jour-
nalist DD, WWT/11-12
CARR, Philip (d 1969 [38])
performer BP/54*
CARR, Richard (fl 1684) musi-
cian, publisher BD
CARR, Robert (fl 1674-96)
violist BD
CARR, Robert (fl 1766) drama-
tist CP/3, DD
CARR, R. P. (d 1872) agent
EA/73*
CARR, Samuel (fl 1770) drama-
tist CP/2, GT
CARR, Sarah (d 1907 [70])
EA/08*
CARR, Tom (d 1906 [58]) musi-
cian EA/07*
CARRA, Lawrence (b 1909)
Italian director, educator
BE

CARRADINE, David (b 1940)
American actor TW/22-23,
25, 27
CARRADINE, John (b 1906) Amer-
ican actor AAS, BE, ES, TW/
5-7, WWT/11-16
CARR-COOK, Madge (1856-1933)
English actress GRB/3-4,
NTH, WWT/1-7
CARRE, Ada [Mrs. Oscar Carré]
(d 1897 [27]) EA/98*
CARRE, Adolph (d 1881 [31])
EA/82*
CARRE, Mrs. Adolf see Carré,
Mrs. M. P.
CARRE, Albert (1852-1938) French
dramatist GRB/1, 3-4, WWT/
1
CARRE, Anthony see Fawcett,
Anthony
CARRE, Marguerite (d 1947 [75])
singer WWT/14*
CARRE, Marie-Thérèse (b 1757)
French dancer BD
CARRE, Mrs. M. P. [Mrs. Adolf
Carré] (d 1877) EA/78*
CARRE, Mrs. Oscar see Carré,
Ada
CARREIRE, Victor (d 1966 [70])
performer BP/50*
CARRENO, Teresa (1853-1917)
pianist, composer, singer,
conductor CDP
CARRICK, Edward [Edward
Anthony Craig] (b 1905) English
designer ES, OC/1-2, WWT/
8-14
CARRICK, Hartley (1881-1929)
dramatist WWT/3-6
CARRICK, Tom [Alban Thomas
Steet] (b 1868) English actor
GRB/1
CARRIDEN, William (d 1911) actor
EA/12*
CARRIER, Mrs. (fl 1743) actress
BD
CARRIGAN, Thomas J. (d 1941
[55]) American actor BE*,
WWT/14*
CARRILLO, Leo (1881-1961)
American actor ES, TW/18,
WWT/7-10
CARRINGTON, Abbie Beeson (fl
1880) singer CDP
CARRINGTON, A. R. drummer,
composer CDP
CARRINGTON, Ethel (1889-1962)
English actress WWT/4-7

CARRINGTON, Eva see De Clifford, Lady

CARRINGTON, Evelyn (d 1942 [66]) actress BE*, WWT/ 14*

CARRINGTON, Frank (1901-75) American producer, director BE

CARRINGTON, Helen (d 1963 [68]) performer BP/48*

CARRINGTON, Katherine (d 1953 [43]) American actress BE*, BP/37*

CARRINGTON, Murray (1885-1941) English actor WWT/ 4-9

CARRODUS, John Tiplady (1836-95) English musician DNB

CARROLL, Adam (d 1974 [76]) composer TW/30

CARROLL, Albert (1898-1956) American actor TW/1, 3, 6-7, 13

CARROLL, Clifford A. (d 1970 [69]) journalist BP/54*

CARROLL, Daniel Patrick see La Rue, Danny

CARROLL, Danny (b 1940) American actor TW/21-25

CARROLL, Diahann (b 1935) American singer, actress BE, CB, TW/11, 18-20

CARROLL, Earl (1892/93-1948) American manager, producer, dramatist COC, DAB, ES, NTH, OC/3, SR, TW/5, WWA/2, WWT/5-10

CARROLL, Edward (d 1869 [27]) equestrian EA/70*

CARROLL, Edward (d 1879 [37]) prompter EA/80*

CARROLL, Edward Linus (d 1975 [68]) producer/director/ choreographer BP/60*

CARROLL, E. J. (d 1931 [62]) manager WWT/14*

CARROLL, Frederick (d 1889 [67]) novelty traveller EA/90*

CARROLL, Garnet H. (d 1964 [61]) producer, theatre owner, actor BE*, WWT/14*

CARROLL, Gene (d 1972 [74]) performer BP/56*

CARROLL, Harry (d 1962 [70]) composer BE*, BP/47*

CARROLL, Helena Scottish actress, producer BE, TW/ 22-24, 26-30

CARROLL, James (b 1817) American actor SR

CARROLL, Jean (d 1972 [63]) performer BP/57*

CARROLL, Jimmy (d 1972 [59]) composer/lyricist BP/56*

CARROLL, John actor, singer CDP

CARROLL, John (d 1880 [39]) comedian, dancer EA/81*

CARROLL, John Edward (d 1916) EA/17*

CARROLL, John W. (1837-81) American actor CDP, HAS

CARROLL, June American singer, actress, lyricist BE, TW/8-10

CARROLL, Mrs. J. W. [nee Jennie Melville] (b 1843) American actress HAS

CARROLL, Katie actress, singer CDP

CARROLL, Lawrence W. (d 1963 [65]) manager BE*

CARROLL, Leo G. (1892-1972) English actor AAS, BE, ES, TW/1-17, 29, WWA/5, WWT/ 5-14

CARROLL, Louise (d 1975) performer BP/60*

CARROLL, Madeleine (b 1906) English actress BE, CB, ES, TW/5-6, WWT/6-12

CARROLL, Marie Elise equestrienne CDP

CARROLL, Nancy [Ann La Hiff] (1906-65) American actress BE, ES, TW/5-6, 22, WWT/ 7-10

CARROLL, Nicholas Cahill (d 1871) comedian, pantaloon EA/72*

CARROLL, Pat (b 1927) American actress BE

CARROLL, Patrick (1902-65) American librarian BE

CARROLL, Paul Vincent (1900-68) Irish dramatist AAS, BE, COC, ES, MD, MH, MWD, NTH, OC/1-3, PDT, RE, SR, TW/25, WWA/5, WWT/9-14, WWW/6

CARROLL, Richard actor CDP

CARROLL, Richard Field (1864-1925) American actor CDP, SR, WWS

CARROLL, R. M. (1831-69) minstrel, female impersonator CDP

CARROLL, Robert (b 1920)

American actor TW/4-8,
10-13, 15

CARROLL, Sydney W. [George
Frederick Carl Whiteman]
(1877-1958) Australian critic,
dramatist, manager COC,
OC/3, WWT/7-11

CARROLL, Vinette (b 1922)
American actress, director,
administrator AAS, BE,
TW/18, WWT/15-16

CARROLL, William B. (d 1889
[74]) American circus performer EA/90*

CARROLL, William J. (1853-96)
minstrel, banjoist CDP

CARRON, George (d 1970 [40])
performer BP/54*

CARRUTH, Richard (d 1973
[53]) producer/director/
choreographer BP/58*

CARRUTHERS, James (b 1931)
American actor TW/29

CARRY, George D. (d 1970 [57])
musician BP/55*

CARSELL, Susette (d 1946)
musician SR

CARSEY, Mary (d 1973 [35])
performer BP/58*

CARSOIN, Mrs. (d 1893) EA/
95*

CARSON, Charles (b 1885) English actor TW/13, WWT/5-16

CARSON, Charles L. (d 1901)
publisher BE*, WWT/14*

CARSON, Mrs. Charles L.
[Kittie Claremont] (1879-1919)
English actress GRB/1-4,
WWT/1-3

CARSON, Cora Youngblood (1886-
1943) American entertainer,
bandleader SR

CARSON, Cyrus (fl 1850) American actor HAS

CARSON, David (b 1837) American? actor HAS, SR

CARSON, Doris (b 1910) actress,
singer WWT/9

CARSON, Emma actress CDP

CARSON, Frances (b 1895) American actress BE, TW/1-3,
WWT/4-13

CARSON, Jack (1910-63) Canadian actor ES, TW/8

CARSON, Jeannie (b 1925/29)
English actress, singer BE,
TW/5-8, 10-19, WWT/12-16

CARSON, J. Harold (b 1885)

English actor GRB/1

CARSON, John (b 1927) Ceylonese
actor TW/24

CARSON, Kate (fl 1857-65) actress
DD

CARSON, Lionel [Lionel Courtier-
Dutton] (1873-1937) editor
GRB/3-4, WWT/1-7, WWW/3

CARSON, Mindy (b 1926) American
actress, singer BE

CARSON, Murray (1865-1917) English actor, dramatist DD,
EA/95, GRB/1-4, WWS, WWT/
1-3, WWW/2

CARSON, William G. B. (b 1891)
American educator, dramatist
BE

CARSONI, Marie [Mrs. Walter
Thompson] (d 1898 [44]) musician EA/99*

CARSWELL, Mr. (d 1905 [68])
EA/06*

CARTE, Blanche [Mrs. Richard
D'Oyly Carte] (d 1885 [70])
EA/86*

CARTE, Charles (b 1870) actor,
manager GRB/1

CARTE, Lucas D'Oyly (d 1906)
EA/08*

CARTE, Richard (d 1891 [83])
composer, musician EA/92*

CARTE, Richard D'Oyly see
D'Oyly Carte, Richard

CARTE, Mrs. Richard D'Oyly
see Carte, Blanche

CARTE, Mrs. Richard D'Oyly
see D'Oyly Carte, Mrs.
Richard

CARTE, Rupert D'Oyly see
D'Oyly Carte, Rupert

CARTEN, Audrey (b 1900) English
actress WWT/5-9

CARTER, [Mr. ?] (fl c. 1661-62)
performer BD

CARTER, Mr. (fl 1746) actor BD

CARTER, Mr. (fl 1760-61) candle-
man BD

CARTER, Mr. (fl 1800) puppeteer
BD

CARTER, "Little" (d 1850 [81])
treasurer EA/72*

CARTER, Mrs. (fl 1719-26)
dresser BD

CARTER, Mrs. (fl 1728-36)
singer BD

CARTER, Mrs. (d 1910) EA/11*

CARTER, Miss (fl 1741-42) actress,
singer BD

CARTER, Miss (fl 1759-65)
singer BD
CARTER, Amanda see Fyffe,
Kitty
CARTER, Andrew (d 1669)
singer BD
CARTER, Mrs. B. (d 1887)
EA/88*
CARTER, Bere (d 1917) EA/18*
CARTER, Billy (b 1834) min-
strel, banjoist CDP
CARTER, Caroline Louise Dud-
ley see Carter, Mrs.
Leslie
CARTER, Carvel (d 1967 [31])
performer BP/51*
CARTER, Charles Thomas
(c. 1735-1804) Irish musician,
composer BD, DD, DNB,
TD/1-2
CARTER, Charlton see
Heston, Charlton
CARTER, Desmond (d 1939)
English lyricist, dramatist
WWT/6-8, WWW/3
CARTER, Don (b 1933) American
actor TW/30
CARTER, Elizabeth (d 1916
[52]) EA/17*
CARTER, Elizabeth Clegg (d
1890 [65]) EA/91*
CARTER, Elliott (b 1908) Amer-
ican composer ES
CARTER, Ernest (b 1886) Amer-
ican composer ES
CARTER, Frank (d 1920 [32])
comedian BE*, BP/4*
CARTER, Frederick (d 1970
[70]) English manager WWT/
14
CARTER, Helen E. H. (fl 1881)
singer CDP
CARTER, Henry Lee (d 1862
[37]) EA/72*
CARTER, Herbert (d 1918)
EA/19*
CARTER, Hubert Edward (d
1934 [65]) English actor
WWT/1-7
CARTER, Huntly (b 1874) Eng-
lish actor GRB/1
CARTER, J. (fl 1787) dramatist
CP/3, DD
CARTER, J. (fl 1794) singer
BD
CARTER, Jack (1917-67) Eng-
lish choreographer, dancer
ES

CARTER, James (1812/14-47)
English actor ES, HAS
CARTER, James (d 1899) wax-
works proprietor EA/00*
CARTER, Janis American actress
ES
CARTER, J. Heneage (b 1826)
English lecturer, singer, actor
HAS
CARTER, John (d 1871 [35])
musician EA/72*
CARTER, John (d 1907 [87]) actor
DD, GRB/3
CARTER, Mrs. John (d 1891)
actress DD
CARTER, Mrs. John (d 1908 [53])
actress GRB/4*
CARTER, John Richard (d 1885
[34]) manager EA/86*
CARTER, J. P. (fl 1843) minstrel,
banjoist CDP
CARTER, Leslie (d 1921 [48])
actor BE*, WWT/14*
CARTER, Mrs. Leslie [Caroline
Louise Dudley] (1862-1937)
American actress COC, DAB,
DD, ES, GRB/1-4, NTH, OC/
1-3, PP/1, SR, WWA/1,
WWM, WWS, WWT/1-8
CARTER, Lincoln J. (1865-1926)
dramatist SR
CARTER, Lloyd (b 1935) American
actor TW/25
CARTER, Lonnie (b 1942) Ameri-
can dramatist CD
CARTER, Margaret English actress
WWT/5-9
CARTER, Myra (b 1930) American
actress TW/29
CARTER, Nell (1894-1965) actress
WWT/2-13
CARTER, Ralph (b 1961) American
actor TW/29-30
CARTER, Richard (fl 1728-43)
musician BD
CARTER, Thomas (1768-1800)
singer BD
CARTER, Thomas see Carter,
Charles Thomas
CARTER-BROWN, T. (d 1893 [44])
manager EA/94*
CARTER-EDWARDS, James [James
Edwards] (1840-1930) English
actor DD, OAA/2, WWT/2-6
CARTERET, Anna [née Wilkinson]
(b 1942) Indian/English actress
WWT/15-16
CARTINI, Albert [Albert Ware]

(d 1894) equestrian comedian EA/95*

CARTINI, Fred (d 1899 [29]) circus performer EA/00*

CARTLITCH, John G. (1793-1875) actor, manager CDP, HAS

CARTON, James E. (d 1879 [25]) American comedian EA/80*

CARTON, R[ichard] C[laude; né Critchett] (1856-1928) English actor, dramatist COC, DD, EA/97, ES, GRB/1-4, NTH, OAA/1-2, OC/1-3, WWS, WWT/1-5, WWW/2

CARTOON ARCHETYPICAL SLOGAN THEATRE theatre collective CD

CARTWRIGHT, Mr. (fl 1710) doorkeeper BD

CARTWRIGHT, Mr. (fl 1740-51?) actor BD

CARTWRIGHT, Mr. (fl 1785) actor BD

CARTWRIGHT, Mrs. (fl 1671) actress BD

CARTWRIGHT, Mrs. (fl 1772) singer BD

CARTWRIGHT, Mrs. (fl 1785) actress BD

CARTWRIGHT, Mrs. (d 1792) actress BD

CARTWRIGHT, Master (b c. 1750) dancer BD

CARTWRIGHT, Miss (fl 1800) musical glasses player BD

CARTWRIGHT, Charles [Charles Morley] (1855-1916) actor DD, EA/96, GRB/2-4, SR, WWS, WWT/1-2

CARTWRIGHT, George (fl 1661) dramatist CP/1-3, DD, DNB, FGF, GT

CARTWRIGHT, John (1756-1824) musical glasses player BD, TD/1

CARTWRIGHT, Peggy (b 1912) Canadian actress, dancer WWT/7

CARTWRIGHT, Thomas (d 1875) musician EA/76*

CARTWRIGHT, William (d 1650?) actor DA, DD, OC/3

CARTWRIGHT, William (c. 1606-86) actor BD, CDP, COC, DA, DD, DNB, ES, OC/1-3

CARTWRIGHT, William (1611-43) English dramatist CDP, COC, CP/1-3, DD, DNB, ES, FGF, GT, HP, RE

CARTWRIGHT, William (d 1869) musician EA/70*

CARUS, Emma [Mrs. Harry James Everall] (1879-1927) German singer, actress CDP, WWA/1, WWS, WWT/4-5

CARUSO, Mr. (fl 1748-56) musician BD

CARUSO, Enrico (1873-1921) Italian singer CDP, DAB, ES, HP, SR, WWA/1

CARVALHO-MIOLAN, Caroline Marie Felix (1827-95) singer CDP

CARVER, Kathryn (d 1947 [41]) actress BE*

CARVER, Louise (d 1956 [87]) actress TW/12

CARVER, Lynne (d 1955 [38]) actress BE*

CARVER, Norman (b 1899) American manager BE

CARVER, Robert (d 1791) scene painter, artist BD

CARVER, Robert (d 1971) performer BP/56*

CARVER, W. F. ["Doctor"] champion rifle shot CDP

CARVER, William (fl 1624) actor DA

CARVIL, Bert Forrest (b 1880) Canadian actor WWS

CARVIL, Harry (b 1880) Canadian actor WWS

CARVILL, Henry J. (d 1941 [74]) English actor GRB/1-4

CARVILLE, Frederick (d 1881 [28]) EA/82*

CARY, Annie Louise (1841/42-1921) American singer CDP, DAB, ES, WWA/1, WWM

CARY, Falkland L. (b 1897) Irish dramatist WWT/11-16

CARY, Mary (fl 1865) actress CDP

CARYL, John (fl 1667-1717) English? dramatist CP/1-3, GT

CARYLL, Ivan [John or Felix Tilkin] (1861-1921) Belgian composer, conductor DD, ES, GRB/1-4, SR, WWT/1-3, WWW/2

CARYLL, John (1625-1711) dramatist DD

CARYLLON, Ethel L. [Mrs. Ralph Roberts] English actress GRB/1

CARYSFORT, Earl of see Proby, John Joshua

CASADESUS, Mathilde (d 1965 [44]) performer BP/50*

CASAIA, Miss (fl 1766-67) dancer BD

CASALI, Luigi (fl 1791) dancer BD

CASALIS, Jeanne de (1898-1966) actress, dramatist WWW/6

CASANOVA, Gaetano Giuseppe Giacomo (fl c. 1719-27) actor BD

CASANOVA, Signora Gaetano Giuseppe Giacomo [née Zanetta Farusi] (fl c. 1719-27) actress BD

CASARINI, Signora (fl 1746-48) Italian singer BD

CASARTELLI, Gabrielle (b 1910) English actress WWT/5-10

CASAUBON, Frances Anne (d 1885 [37]) performer? EA/86*

CASAZZA, Elvira (b 1887) Italian singer ES

CASE, Master (fl 1737-39) dancer BD

CASE, Allen American actor TW/14, 16, 22-23

CASE, Charley (d 1916) monologist SR

CASE, Ethel L. (d 1971 [87]) founder of Long Beach Community Players BP/56*

CASE, Nelson (d 1976 [66]) performer BP/60*

CASELLI, Signora (fl 1743-44) singer BD

CASELLI, T. (d 1883) comedian EA/84*

CASENTINI, Anna see Borghi, Signora Luigi

CASEY [Master] (fl 18th cent) squinting beggar boy CDP

CASEY, Mr. (fl 1748) actor BD

CASEY, Mrs. (fl 1783-85) actress BD

CASEY, Ethel (d 1971 [49]) performer BP/55*

CASEY, John (d c. 1792) actor BD

CASEY, Kenneth (d 1965 [66]) composer/lyricist BP/50*

CASEY, Pat (d 1962 [87])

American talent representative BE*

CASEY, Polly (fl 1741) singer BD

CASEY, Rosemary (1904-76) American dramatist BE

CASEY, William Francis (b 1884) Irish dramatist ES

CASH, Dan (d 1973 [53]) producer/director/choreographer BP/57*

CASH, Edith May [Mrs. George Cash] (d 1917) EA/18*

CASH, Mrs. George see Cash, Edith May

CASH, Morny singer CDP

CASH, Rosalind (b 1938) American actress TW/24-28, 30, WWT/16

CASH, William F. (d 1963) performer BE*

CASHAN, Patrick Martin (d 1899 [56]) music-hall singer EA/00*

CASHELL, Oliver (d 1747) actor BD

CASHMAN, Betty American actress, director, coach BE

CASHMORE, John Garrett (d 1876) harpist EA/77*

CASHMORE, Thomas Isaac (d 1886) equestrian clown EA/87*

CASIMERE, Mons. (fl 1785-87) tumbler, ropedancer BD

CASIMERE, Mme. (fl 1787) dancer BD

CASIMERE, Fils (fl 1785-87) tumbler BD

CASON, Mr. (fl 1726?-61) dresser BD

CASON, Barbara (b 1933) American actress TW/25, 27-30

CASPARY, Vera (b 1904) American dramatist BE, CB

CASPER, Richard (b 1949) American actor TW/29

CASS, Frank singer CDP

CASS, Henry (b 1902) English actor, producer AAS, WWT/8-16

CASS, H. Marie (d 1969 [77]) BP/54*

CASS, John (d 1890 [60]) performer? EA/91*

CASS, Peggy (b 1924/26) American actress BE, TW/13-20, 24-27, WWT/14-16

CASS, Ronald (b 1923) Welsh composer WWT/14-16

CASSANI, Giuseppe (fl 1708-12) singer BD

CASSAVETES, John (b 1929)
American actor CB
CASSEL, Irwin (d 1971 [84])
composer/lyricist BP/56*
CASSEL, Rita Allen (d 1968
[56]) director? choreographer?
BP/53*
CASSICK, Jack (d 1918) EA/
19*
CASSIDAY, Rose (fl 1851) actress
HAS
CASSIDY, Claudia American
critic BE, CB
CASSIDY, G. W. (d 1887)
manager, architect EA/88*
CASSIDY, Jack (1927-76)
American actor, singer,
dancer BE, TW/12-13,
15-16, 19-22, 26, WWT/
14-16
CASSIDY, James (d 1869) musi-
cian EA/70*
CASSIDY, John (d 1907 [40])
manager EA/08*
CASSIDY, J. Rice (d 1927 [66])
actor BE*, WWT/14*
CASSIM, James (d 1879 [28])
American clown EA/80*
CASSMORE, Judy (b 1942)
American actress TW/21
CASSON, Ann (b 1915) English
actress WWT/6-14
CASSON, Charles Henry (d
1886) EA/87*
CASSON, Christopher (b 1912)
English actor WWT/11-14
CASSON, Ezra (d 1887) EA/
88*
CASSON, John (b 1909) Eng-
lish actor, producer WWT/
11-12
CASSON, Sir Lewis Thomas
(1875-1969) English actor,
director AAS, BE, COC,
ES, OC/1-3, TW/13, 15,
25, WWT/2-14, WWW/6
CASSON, Louis (d 1950) actor,
producer, manager BE*,
WWT/14*
CASSON, Margaret (b c. 1775)
harpsichordist BD
CASSON, Mary (b 1914) Eng-
lish actress WWT/6-9
CASSON, Walter (d 1905 [44])
actor EA/06*
CASTANET, Mons. (d 1888)
gymnast EA/89*
CASTANG, Veronica (b 1938)

English actress TW/30
CASTANOS, Luz (b 1935) Ameri-
can actor TW/28-29
CASTEL, Albert R. (d 1972 [67])
musician BP/57*
CASTELL, Thomas (d 1730) door-
keeper BD
CASTELLAN, Anaide see Cas-
tellan-Giampietro, Jeanne
Anais
CASTELLAN-GIAMPIETRO, Jeanne
Anais (b 1819) French singer
CDP, HAS
CASTELLANO, Richard (b 1933)
American actor TW/23-26
CASTELLE, Mrs. [Mrs. Castelli]
(fl 1787-1804) singer BD
CASTELLI, Mr. (fl 1783-84) dog
trainer BD
CASTELLI, Mrs. see Castelle,
Mrs.
CASTELLI, Anna (fl 1754-55)
Italian singer BD
CASTELLO, Mr. (fl 1793-1803)
doorkeeper BD
CASTELLO, John (b 1924) Amer-
ican actor TW/4
CASTELMARY, Armand see
Castlemary, Armand
CASTIGLIONE, Master (fl 1771)
dancer BD
CASTIGLIONE, Mr. (fl 1734-36)
dancer BD
CASTILE, Lynn (d 1975 [77])
singer, actress BP/59*,
WWT/16*
CASTLE, Mrs. (fl 1734) actress
BD
CASTLE, Betty (d 1962 [47])
performer BE*
CASTLE, Egerton (1858-1920)
French/English dramatist
WWM, WWW/2
CASTLE, Harry Gilbert singer,
composer, minstrel CDP
CASTLE, Irene (d 1969 [75])
American dancer ES, SR,
TW/25
CASTLE, John (b 1940) English
actor WWT/15-16
CASTLE, Nick (d 1968 [56]) pro-
ducer, director BP/53*
CASTLE, Peggy (d 1973 [47])
performer BP/58*
CASTLE, Richard (d 1779) actor
BD
CASTLE, Roy (b 1932) English
actor, singer, dancer TW/22

CASTLE, Thomas (fl 1608-10) actor DA

CASTLE, Vernon Blythe (1887-1918) English actor, dancer CDP, DAB, ES, SR, WWA/4, WWM

CASTLE, William (1836-1909) English singer CDP, WWA/1

CASTLEMAN, Richard (fl 1711-39) treasurer BD

CASTLEMARY, Armand (1834-97) Italian singer CDP, ES

CASTLES, Mr. (fl 1734) house servant? BD

CASTLES, Amy (b 1884) Australian singer GRB/1

CASTLETON, Kate (d 1892 [35]) actress SR

CASTLETON, Robert [Robert Ellis] (b 1872) Mauritian actor, dramatist GRB/1

CASTLING, Will (d 1876) comedian EA/78*

CASTO, Jean actress TW/1, 3, 6-7

CASTON, George (d 1893) bandmaster EA/94*

CASTRUCCI, Pietro (1679-1752) Italian violinist, composer, bandleader BD

CASTRUCCI, Prospero (d 1760) violinist BD

CATALANI, Angelica (1779?/82-1849) Italian singer CDP, GT

CATANEO, Sig. (fl c. 1735-62) musician, teacher BD

CATCHPOLE, Mr. (fl 1799) puppeteer BD

CATENACCI, Maria (fl 1783-86) singer BD

CATER, Percy (d 1971 [73]) critic BP/55*

CATERINA, Signora (fl 1756) wire dancer BD

CATES, Mr. (fl 1746) actor BD

CATES, Frank (d 1896 [43]) actor EA/97*

CATES, Gilbert (b 1934) American producer, director BE

CATES, Gordon (d 1970 [63]) musician BP/55*

CATES, Joseph (b 1924) American producer, director BE

CATES, Madlyn (b 1925) American actress TW/26

CATESBY, Mr. (fl 1741)

actor BD

CATHCART, Charles (d 1912 [56]) actor EA/14*, WWT/14*

CATHCART, Mrs. Charles (d 1884) EA/85*

CATHCART, Mrs. Jack see Gumm, Suzanne

CATHCART, James Faucit (1828-1902) actor DD

CATHCART, James Leander (d 1865 [65]) actor WWT/14*

CATHCART, Jane (d 1875) actress EA/76*

CATHCART, Maud (fl 1878) English actress DD, OAA/1-2

CATHCART, Mrs. R. (d 1875) EA/76*

CATHCART, Rolleston William George (d 1896 [64]) actor EA/97*

CATHCART, Rowley (1832-96) English dramatist, actor DD, OAA/1

CATHERWOOD, Caroline (d 1889) EA/90*

CATHIE, Mrs. Leslie Roy see Cathie, Nina

CATHIE, Nina [Mrs. Leslie Cathie] (d 1904 [20]) EA/04*

CATLETT, Mary Jo (b 1938) American actress TW/23-30

CATLETT, Walter (1889-1960) American actor TW/17, WWT/4-11

CATLEY, Ann [Mrs. Francis Lascelles] (1745-89) English actress, singer, dancer BD, CDP, DD, DNB, ES, GT, TD/1-2

CATLIN, Edward N. musician, composer CDP

CATLIN, Faith (b 1949) American actress TW/29-30

CATLING, Thomas (1838-1920) English critic GRB/2-4, WWT/1-3

CATLING, Thomas Thurgood (1863-1939) English critic GRB/2-4

CATMUR, Caroline (d 1916) EA/18*

CATON, Mr. (fl 1796-1804) box keeper BD

CATON, Edward (b c. 1900) American dancer, choreographer ES

CATRANI, Catrano (d 1974 [61]) producer/director/choreographer BP/59*

CATT, Mrs. S. H. (d 1916 [39])

EA/17*
CATTANES (fl 1602-03) actor?
DA
CATTANI, Joseph (fl 1739)
musician BD
CATTLEY, Cyril (1876-1937)
English actor, stage manager
WWT/8
CATTO, John (d 1902 [40])
acrobat EA/03*
CATTO, Max (b 1907) English
dramatist WWT/9-14
CATTON, Charles (1728-98)
English artist, decorator,
scene painter? BD
CATTON, Charles (1756-1819)
English artist, scene painter
BD
CAUBAYE-BERNHARDT, Suzanne
(b 1897) French actress
TW/1
CAUBISENS, Henri stage manager
BE
CAUFFMAN, Frank Guernsey
(b 1850) American musician
WWA/4
CAUFIELD, Betty (b 1925)
American actress TW/1
CAULFIELD, James (1764-1826)
print seller, author CDP
CAULFIELD, Joan (b 1922)
actress CB
CAULFIELD, John (fl 1794-1819)
singer BD
CAULFIELD, John (d 1879)
musical director EA/80*
CAULFIELD, John see Caul-
field, Thomas
CAULFIELD, Mrs. John see
Caulfield, Louisa
CAULFIELD, Mrs. John see
Loseby, Constance
CAULFIELD, Louisa [Mrs.
John Caulfield] (1822-70)
actress DD
CAULFIELD, Thomas [or John]
(1766-1815) English actor
BD, CDP, DD, HAS,
TD/1-2
CAUN, Susanna (fl 1729) actress
BD
CAUSE, Miss H. see Fiddes,
Harriet Catherine
CAUSTON, Mr. (fl 1720-46)
house servant? BD
CAUTE, David (b 1936)
Egyptian/English dramatist
CD

CAUTHERLEY, Samuel (d 1805)
actor BD, DD, TD/1-2
CAUTLEY, Lawrence (d 1899 [37])
actor DD, DP, EA/95
CAUX, Marquis de (d 1889) EA/
91*
CAVALHO, Sylvia actress GRB/2
CAVALIERI, Lina (1874-1944)
Italian singer ES, WWA/5
CAVALLAZI-MAPLESON, Mme.
Italian ballet director GRB/
1-4
CAVALLERIZZO, Claudio (fl 1576)
Italian actor DA
CAVAN, Jack (d 1972 [64]) musi-
cian BP/57*
CAVAN, Marie (1889-1968) Amer-
ican singer WWA/5, WWM
CAVANA, Mr. (fl 1789-92) singer
BD
CAVANAGH, Elizabeth (d 1884)
EA/85*
CAVANAGH, James actor, singer
CDP
CAVANAGH, Lilian (d 1932) Eng-
lish actress WWT/3-7
CAVANAGH, Paul (b 1895) English
actor ES, WWT/6-10
CAVANAGH, W. B. (b 1833) Irish
actor HAS
CAVANAH, John (d 1901) manager
EA/02*
CAVANAUGH, Fannie (d 1975 [83])
performer BP/59*
CAVANAUGH, Hobart (d 1950 [63])
American actor TW/6
CAVANAUGH, James (d 1967 [75])
composer/lyricist BP/52*
CAVANAUGH, Michael American
actor TW/26-29
CAVANIA, Margaret [Mrs. Basil
Gill] English actress GRB/1-3
CAVANNA, Elise [Mrs. James
Welton] (d 1963 [61]) actress
BE*
CAVE, George (d 1877 [49]) treas-
urer EA/78*
CAVE, Mrs. Henry see Cave,
Marie Louise
CAVE, J. H. minstrel, banjoist
CDP
CAVE, John (d 1664) singer BD
CAVE, Joseph Arnold (1823-1912)
English actor, manager, pro-
prietor, music-hall performer
CDP, COC, DD, GRB/1-4,
OC/1-3
CAVE, Marie Louise [Mrs. Henry

Cave] (d 1891) EA/92*

CAVELL, Will (fl 1671-72) performer BD

CAVELLA, Harry singer, composer CDP

CAVENDER, Glenn W. (d 1962 [78]) performer BE*

CAVENDER, Leona (fl 1869) actress CDP

CAVENDISH, Ada [Mrs. Frank Marshall] (1847-95) English actress CDP, DD, DNB, DP, ES, OAA/1-2

CAVENDISH, Harry (d 1888) music-hall artist EA/89*

CAVENDISH, Henry Frederick Compton [Henry Carlton] (d 1886) actor EA/87*

CAVENDISH, Mrs. H. S. H. see Jay, Isabel

CAVENDISH, June (d 1976) performer BP/60*

CAVENDISH, Margaret, Duchess of Newcastle (d 1673) English dramatist CP/1-3, GT, HP

CAVENDISH, Milly (d 1867) English singer HAS

CAVENDISH, Rose [Mrs. Leopold Cohen] (d 1897 [32]) actress EA/98*

CAVENDISH, William, Duke of Newcastle (1592-1676) English dramatist CP/1-3, FGF, GT

CAVENS, Albert (b 1921) Belgian actor TW/24

CAVETT, Dick (b 1936) American actor CB

CAVETT, Dick (d 1973 [67]) dramatist BP/57*

CAVRAN, Georgia (fl 1880-82) actress CDP

CAWARDEN, Sir Thomas (fl 1545) master of the Revels COC, OC/2-3

CAWBRAEST, Walter (fl 1665) drummer BD

CAWDELL, James (d 1800) dramatist, manager, comedian CP/3, DD, DNB

CAWDER, Jo (fl 1760-61) sweeper BD

CAWDERY, George (d 1898 [68]) carpenter EA/99*

CAWLEY, Master (fl 1757-59) dancer, actor BD

CAWOOD, Martin (d 1867) secretary EA/68*

CAWSE, Harriet (fl 1832) singer, actress CDP

CAWSTON, Mr. (fl 1789-97) house servant BD

CAWTHORN, Joseph (1867/68-1949) American actor CDP, GRB/3-4, SR, TW/5, WWA/2, WWS, WWT/1-10

CAWTHORN, Lily [Mrs. Arthur Waller] (d 1894 [28]) actress EA/95*

CAXTON, Mr. (fl 1747) painter BD

CAYFORD, Mr. (fl 1735) house servant? BD

CAYVAN, Georgia (c. 1858-1906) American actress DAB, PP/1, SR, WWA/1

CAYWORTH, John (fl 1636) dramatist FGF

CAZALY, James (d 1904 [48]) EA/06*

CAZAURAN, Augustus R. (1820-89) French/American dramatist DD, SR

CAZENEUVE, Bernard Marius (b 1839) magician CDP

CAZMAN, Henri (d 1917) conjurer, illusionist EA/18*

CEBALLOS, Larry actor, singer CDP

CECCHETTI, Enrico (1847-1928) Italian dancer, maître de ballet ES, WWT/4-5

CECIL (fl 1614-15) dramatist CP/3, FGF

CECIL, Arthur [Arthur Cecil Blunt] (1843-96) English actor CDP, DD, DNB, DP, OAA/1-2

CECIL, Henry [né Henry Cecil Leon] (1902-76) dramatist WWT/15-16

CECIL, Mrs. John see Leslie, Minnie

CECIL, Mary (1885-1940) actress CB

CECIL, Phyllis [Phyllis Ponsford] English actress GRB/1

CECIL, Sylvia (b 1906) English actress, singer WWT/11-12

CECIL, Tom English actor GRB/1

CECILL see Cecil

CEDA, William (d 1873 [47]) minstrel EA/73*

CEDAR, Hugh (d 1916) music-hall comedian EA/17*

CEDERSTROM, Baroness see Patti, Adelina

CEDRIC, Mrs. (d 1917) EA/
18*
CEFALO, Pietro (fl 1670)
musician BD
"CELEBRATED GRIMACIER,
The" (fl c. 1790) clown BD
CELESIA, Dorothea (1738-90)
English dramatist DNB
CELESTE, Céline (1814-82)
French actress, dancer
CDP, COC, DD, DNB, ES,
HAS, OAA/1-2, OC/1-3,
SR
CELESTE, La Petite (fl 1837-
40) dancer HAS
CELESTE, Rosa (b 1848) Amer-
ican tight-rope performer
HAS
CELESTIN, Jack (b 1894) Irish
dramatist WWT/7-9
CELESTINO, Eligio (c. 1737-
1812) Italian violinist, com-
poser BD
CELESTINO, Signora Eligio (fl
1780-92) singer BD
CELISIA, Mrs. (d 1790) drama-
tist CP/2-3, DD, GT
CELLARIUS, Sig. dancer CDP
CELLI, Faith (1888-1942) Eng-
lish actress WWT/4-7
CELLI, Frank H. (d 1904 [63])
singer, actor, dramatist
DD
CELLI, Mrs. Frank H. see
Pyne, Susan
CELLI, Vincenzo (b 1905) Italian
dancer, choreographer, teacher
ES
CELLIER, Alfred (1844-91)
English composer, conductor
CDP, DD, DNB, ES
CELLIER, Antoinette (b 1913)
English actress WWT/8-13
CELLIER, Francois (1850-1914)
French musical director,
composer DD, SR
CELLIER, Frank (1872/84-1948)
English actor, manager ES,
GRB/2, TW/5, WWT/3-10
CELLIER, Marguerite (b 1880)
English actress GRB/1-2
CELLINI, Mme. singer CDP
CELLINI, Renato (1912-67)
Italian conductor WWA/4
CELOTTI, Ziuliana (fl 1705-
14) singer BD
CELSON, Miss (fl 1798) singer
BD

CEMMITT, Miss (fl 1785-91)
singer BD
CENTLIVRE, Joseph (fl 1715-39)
organist BD
CENTLIVRE, Susannah (1667-1723)
English actress, dramatist
CDP, COC, CP/1-3, DD, DNB,
ES, GT, HP, MH, NTH, OC/
1-3, TD/1-2
CERAIL, Mlle. (d 1723) French?
dancer, singer BD
CERISSA, Mlle. (d 1871 [21])
trapezist EA/72*
CERITO, Ada singer CDP
CERRITO, Fanny (1817/21-c. 1899/
1909) Italian dancer CDP, ES,
OC/2
CERVANTES SAAVEDRA, Miguel
de (1547-1616) Spanish drama-
tist COC
CERVETTO, Giacobbe (1682-1783)
Italian violoncellist, composer
BD, TD/1-2
CERVETTO, James (1749-1837)
English violoncellist, composer
BD, DNB
CERVI, Gino (d 1974 [72]) per-
former BP/58*, WWT/16*
CESANA, Renzo (d 1970) performer
BP/55*
CHABERT, Ivan Ivanetz (fl c. 1818?)
"fire king phenomenon" CDP
CHABERT, Julien Xavier (1791-
1859) French "fire king"
CDP, HAS, SR
CHABOT, Marie-Louise see
De Verneuil, Mme. Louis
François Joseph
CHABOUD, Pietro (fl 1707-25)
instrumentalist, composer BD
CHABRAN, Charles (b c. 1723)
Italian violinist BD
CHABRAN, Francesco [Felice?]
(c. 1757-1829) English? musi-
cian, composer BD
CHACE, Dorothy American actress
TW/24, 26, 28-30
CHADAL, Georges (b 1875) French
singer WWM
CHADBON, Tom (b 1946) English
actor WWT/15-16
CHADWICK (d 1889 [46]) English
clown EA/90*
CHADWICK, George Whitefield
(1854-1931) American composer
ES, HJD
CHADWICK, James see Olmar,
Mons.

CHADWICK, John (d 1972 [65])
performer BP/57*
CHADWICK, John Henry (d
1917 [60]) EA/18*
CHADWICK, Sophia [Mrs. H.
Valdo; "Avolina"] (d 1886)
performer? EA/87*
CHADWICK, Thomas (d 1908)
EA/09*
CHADWICK, William Thorpe
(d 1908 [57]) EA/09*
CHAFFE, Christopher (fl 1794)
musician BD
CHAGRIN, Francis (d 1972 [67])
conductor BP/57*
CHAGRIN, Julian (b 1940) Eng-
lish actor, mimist WWT/
15-16
CHAIGNEAU, William (1709-81)
Irish dramatist DNB
CHAIKIN, Joseph (b 1935) Amer-
ican actor, director, pro-
ducer WWT/16
CHAIKIN, Shami (b 1931) Amer-
ican actress TW/29-30
CHALBAUD, Esteban (b 1945)
Venezuelan actor TW/29
CHALET, William (d 1868 [38])
manager EA/89*
CHALIAPIN, Feodor (1873-
1938) Russian singer ES,
WWA/1
CHALIF, Frances Robinson (d
1971) performer BP/56*
CHALKLEY, Ann (b 1922)
English actress TW/3
CHALLENGER, Rudy (b 1928)
American actor TW/24,
26
CHALLENOR, Bromley (1884-
1935) English actor, manager
WWT/6-7
CHALLIS, Edith (d 1883) actress
OAA/2
CHALLIS, Emma [Mrs. Rass
Challis] (d 1892) EA/93*
CHALLIS, Mrs. Rass see
Challis, Emma
CHALLONER, Neville Butler
(b 1784) English instru-
mentalist, bandleader,
teacher, composer, music
seller BD
CHALMERS, Alexander (1759-
1834) writer DD
CHALMERS, F. S. (d 1806)
English actor SR
CHALMERS, James (d 1810)

actor, dancer BD, CDP, HAS,
TD/1-2
CHALMERS, Mrs. James [née
Eleanor Mills] (d 1792) actress,
singer BD
CHALMERS, [Mrs. James, Sarah?]
(fl 1754-85?) actress BD
CHALMERS, [Sarah?] see
Chalmers, [Mrs. James, Sarah?]
CHALMERS, Thomas Hardie (1884-
1966) American singer, actor
BE, TW/3, 5-7, 10-13, 15-16,
23, WWA/4
CHALMERS, William (d c. 1806)
scene painter BD
CHALONER, William (d 1868 [38])
performer? EA/69*
CHALZEL, Leo (d 1953 [52])
American actor WWT/10-11
CHAMBERLAIN, Charlie (d 1972
[61]) performer BP/57*
CHAMBERLAIN, George (1891-
1976) English manager WWT/
10-14
CHAMBERLAIN, John S. (d 1916)
actor, producer, comedian
EA/17*, WWT/14*
CHAMBERLAIN, Mrs. J. S. see
Chamberlain, Lizzie
CHAMBERLAIN, Lizzie [Mrs. J.
S. Chamberlain] (d 1884 [32])
EA/85*
CHAMBERLAIN, Richard (b 1935)
American actor AAS, CB,
WWT/16
CHAMBERLAIN, Robert (b 1607)
English dramatist CP/1-3,
DD, FGF
CHAMBERLAINE, Frances see
Sheridan, Frances
CHAMBERLAINE, Robert see
Chamberlain, Robert
CHAMBERLAYNE, Mr. (fl 1674)
performer? BD
CHAMBERLAYNE, William (1619-
89) dramatist CP/1-3, DD,
DNB, GT, HP
CHAMBERLIN, Ione (b 1880)
American actress WWS
CHAMBERLIN, Riley (b 1854)
American actor WWM
CHAMBERS, Mr. (fl 1758) stage-
hand? BD
CHAMBERS, Mr. (fl 1777-79)
actor BD
CHAMBERS, Mr. actor TD/2
CHAMBERS, Miss (fl 1805) drama-
tist CP/3, DD

CHAMBERS, A. A. (fl 1785-97) actor, singer BD

CHAMBERS, Charles (fl 1771) actor BD

CHAMBERS, Charles Haddon (1860-1921) Australian dramatist DD, GRB/1-4, SR, WWM, WWS, WWT/1-3, WWW/2

CHAMBERS, Sir Edmund Kercheever (1866-1954) English historian DNB, ES, HP

CHAMBERS, Emma (d 1933 [85]) actress, singer CDP, DD, OAA/2, WWT/1-3

CHAMBERS, Harriet [née Harriet Dyer; Mrs. William Taplin] (d 1804) actress BD

CHAMBERS, H. Kellett (1867-1935) Australian dramatist GRB/3-4, WWM, WWS, WWT/1-5

CHAMBERS, Isabella (fl 1722-41) singer, actress BD

CHAMBERS, James (d 1871 [44]) actor? EA/72*

CHAMBERS, John (fl 1702) mountebank BD

CHAMBERS, John (d 1880 [62]) actor EA/81*

CHAMBERS, Lucy (d 1894) Australian singer EA/95*

CHAMBERS, Lyster (1876-1947) American actor SR

CHAMBERS, McCall singer, actor CDP

CHAMBERS, Margaret (d 1880) actress EA/81*

CHAMBERS, Mary (d 1903 [71]) EA/04*

CHAMBERS, Mary see Kean, Mrs. Edmund

CHAMBERS, Norma (d 1953) American actress BE*, BP/37*

CHAMBERS, Ralph (d 1968 [76]) actor TW/24

CHAMBERS, Robert W. (1865-1933) American dramatist HJD

CHAMBERS, Mrs. Stephen see Corelli, Cecilia

CHAMBERS, Sydney (d 1871) comedian EA/72*

CHAMBERS, Thomas (d 1883 [59]) actor EA/84*

CHAMBERS, William (fl 1624) actor DA

CHAMBERS, William (b 1910) American stage manager, director, actor BE

CHAMBERS, Mrs. William [née Elizabeth Davis?] (d 1792) singer, actress BD

CHAMLEE, Mario (1892-1966) American singer WWA/4

"CHAMPION, Mr." (fl 1738) actor BD

CHAMPION, Ada Welsh actress GRB/1

CHAMPION, George (d 1871 [60]) professor of music EA/72*

CHAMPION, Gower (b 1920/21) American choreographer, director AAS, BE, CB, ES, TW/5-8, WWT/14-16

CHAMPION, Harry (1866-1942) English music-hall performer CDP, COC, OC/1-3, PDT

CHAMPION, Madge [née Marjorie Celeste Belcher] (b 1923/25) American actress, dancer BE, CB, ES

CHAMPION, William [William Rooles Lonnen] (d 1890 [57]) EA/91*

CHAMPNESS, Masters (fl 1794) singers BD

CHAMPNESS, Samuel Thomas (d 1803) singer, actor BD

CHAMPNESS, Thomas Weldon (fl 1794-1803) singer BD

CHAMPNESS, Weldon (fl 1758-98) singer BD

CHAMPVILLE, Gabriel-Léonard Hervé de Bus de (fl 1748-89) French actor BD

CHAN, Peter (d 1969 [68]) actor, entertainer TW/25

CHANCELLOR, Betty Irish actress WWT/9-10

CHANCELLOR, Joyce (b 1906) Irish actress WWT/7-10

CHANDLER, Christine (d 1975 [30]) performer BP/60*

CHANDLER, Douglas (1917-70) American actor TW/1

CHANDLER, George W. see Garrison, George W.

CHANDLER, Helen (1906/09-65) American actress BE, TW/21, WWT/6-11

CHANDLER, Jeff (d 1961 [42]) American actor BE*

CHANDLER, Joan actress TW/1

CHANDLER, Leah (b 1950)

American actress TW/29-30

CHANDLER, Lennox (d 1905 [30]) singer EA/06*

CHANDLER, Mildred (b 1902) American actress TW/24

CHANDLER, Thelma (d 1968 [64]) stage manager TW/25

CHANDLER, Thomas (d 1893 [36]) stage manager EA/94*

CHANDLER, W. Aubrey (d 1909 [72]) actor EA/10*

CHANDLER, Mrs. W. Aubrey see Aubrey, Mrs. W.

CHANDOS, Alice actress CDP

CHANEY, John (d 1895) music-hall proprietor EA/96*

CHANEY, Lon (1883-1930) American actor DAB, ES, SR, WWA/4

CHANEY, Lon, Jr. (d 1973 [67]) performer BP/58*, WWT/16*

CHANEY, Stewart (1905/10-69) American scene designer BE, ES, TW/2-8, 26, WWT/ 10-14

CHANFRAU, Francis S. (1824-84) American actor CDP, COC, DAB, DD, ES, HAS, OC/1-3, SR, WWA/H

CHANFRAU, Mrs. Francis S. see Chanfrau, Henrietta

CHANFRAU, Henrietta [Henrietta Baker; Jeanette Davis] (1837-1909) American actress CDP, COC, DAB, DD, HAS, OC/1-3, SR

CHANFRAU, Henry Trenchard (1858-1901) actor CDP

CHANG (d 1893 [46]) Chinese giant CDP

CHANG, Tisa Chinese actress TW/27-28

CHANIN, Henry (d 1973 [79]) theatre builder BP/57*

CHANLER, Mrs. William Astor see Ashley, Minnie

CHANNEL, Luke (fl 1653-91?) dancing master BD

CHANNING, Carol (b 1921) American actress, singer AAS, BE, CB, ES, TW/ 5-8, 10-24, 27, 29-30, WWT/11-16

CHANNING, William (d 1877) scene artist EA/78*

CHANNOUVEAU, Jean (fl 1661-67) actor, manager BD

CHANTRELL, Prof. (d 1879) acrobat EA/80*

CHANTRELL, Annie (d 1888) EA/89*

CHANTRELL, Clara [Mrs. H. J. Charlton] (d 1887) EA/88*

CHAPEL, Eugenia (d 1964 [52]) actress, executive BE*

CHAPENDER, Martin (d 1905) conjurer, illusionist EA/06*

CHAPIN, Alice (d 1934 [76]) American actress GRB/1-2

CHAPIN, Anne Morrison (d 1967) actress, dramatist TW/23

CHAPIN, Benjamin Chester (1874-1918) American dramatist WWA/ 1

CHAPIN, Harold (1886-1915) American actor, stage manager, dramatist ES, GRB/2-3, MD, MWD, NTH, WWT/2-3, WWW/1

CHAPIN, Louis Le Bourgeois (b 1918) American critic WWT/ 14-16

CHAPIN, Schuyler G. (b 1923) American manager CB

CHAPIN, Victor actor TW/1

CHAPLIN, Amelia [Mrs. G. H. Chaplin; Milly Arden] (d 1887 [47]) EA/88*

CHAPLIN, Charles (d 1901) music-hall comedian EA/02*

CHAPLIN, Charles, Jr. (1925-68) American actor TW/6-7

CHAPLIN, Sir Charles Spencer (1889-1977) English actor CDP, CB, ES, GRB/1, HJD, NTH, SR, WWT/4-11

CHAPLIN, Ellen see Fitzwilliam, Mrs. Edward Francis

CHAPLIN, George (d 1881) lessee EA/82*

CHAPLIN, George D. [né Inglis] (b 1837) actor CDP

CHAPLIN, Geraldine (b 1944) American actress TW/24

CHAPLIN, Mrs. G. H. see Chaplin, Amelia

CHAPLIN, Henry (d 1789) actor, singer BD

CHAPLIN, Sydney (1885-1965) South African actor ES

CHAPLIN, Sydney (b 1926) American actor BE, TW/13-22

CHAPMAN, Mr. (fl 1674) actor BD

CHAPMAN, Mr. (fl 1756-72) musician BD

CHAPMAN, Mr. (fl 1775) actor
BD
CHAPMAN, Mr. (fl 1776-1817?)
house servant BD
CHAPMAN, Mr. (fl 1794) vio-
linist BD
CHAPMAN, Mr. (fl 1799-1804?)
dancer? BD
CHAPMAN, Mr. (fl 1805) actor
TD/2
CHAPMAN, Mr. (fl 1805) actor
BS, GT
CHAPMAN, Mr. actor CDP
CHAPMAN, Miss (d 1805) Amer-
ican actress CDP, TD/1-2
CHAPMAN, Ada Blanche (b
1820) English actress SR
CHAPMAN, Ada Blanche (1851-
1941) American actress
CB, CDP, HAS
CHAPMAN, Addie see Adiny-
Millet, Ada
CHAPMAN, Alonzo see Parks,
Alonzo
CHAPMAN, Barnet [Charles
Robinson] (d 1870 [31]) actor
EA/71*
CHAPMAN, Blanche see
Chapman, Ada Blanche
CHAPMAN, Caroline (1818-76)
actress CDP, ES, HAS
CHAPMAN, Caroline (fl 1864)
actress HAS
CHAPMAN, Catherine [Mrs. John
Chapman] (d 1906) EA/07*
CHAPMAN, Mrs. Charles E.
see Chapman, Harriet Ethel
CHAPMAN, Charlotte Jane [Mrs.
Morton] (1762-1805) Ameri-
can/English actress, singer
BD
CHAPMAN, Christopher (d 1681)
singer BD
CHAPMAN, Constance (b 1912)
English actress WWT/15-16
CHAPMAN, David (d 1904 [39])
proprietor EA/05*
CHAPMAN, Edward (b 1901)
English actor AAS, ES,
WWT/7-15
CHAPMAN, Edythe [Mrs. James
Neill] (1863-1948) actress
SR, TW/5
CHAPMAN, Elizabeth [née Jeffer-
son; Mrs. Samuel Chapman;
Mrs. Augustus Richardson;
Mrs. Charles J. B. Fisher]
(1810-90) American actress

CDP, ES, SR
CHAPMAN, Ella (fl 1876-90) act-
ress, singer, musician CDP,
DD
CHAPMAN, Fanny see Botly,
Mrs.
CHAPMAN, Frank (d 1966 [66])
singer TW/23
CHAPMAN, Frank M. manager
CDP
CHAPMAN, George (c. 1560-1634)
English dramatist CDP, COC,
CP/1-3, DD, DNB, ES, FGF,
HP, MH, NTH, OC/1-3, PDT,
RE
CHAPMAN, [George?] (fl 1792-
1804?) exhibitor, treasurer
BD
CHAPMAN, George (fl 1830-51)
actor ES, HAS
CHAPMAN, George (d 1896 [64])
music-hall performer, manager
EA/97*
CHAPMAN, George (d 1902 [62])
musical director EA/04*
CHAPMAN, Mrs. George [née
Frances R. Brett] (d 1804)
actress, singer BD, TD/1-2
CHAPMAN, Mrs. George (d 1894)
EA/95*
CHAPMAN, Mrs. George see
Mandlebert, Kate
CHAPMAN, Gilbert W. (b 1902)
American executive BE
CHAPMAN, Hannah see Chap-
man, Mrs. Thomas
CHAPMAN, Harriet Ethel [Mrs.
Charles E. Chapman] (d 1904
[27]) EA/05*
CHAPMAN, Harry (1822-65) Eng-
lish actor HAS, SR
CHAPMAN, Harry (d 1888 [84])
showman EA/89*
CHAPMAN, Henry (b 1910) English
dramatist PDT
CHAPMAN, James Fitzjames Rock
(d 1876 [69]) actor EA/77*
CHAPMAN, J. M. (d 1906 [70])
EA/07*
CHAPMAN, John (d 1895 [59])
Negro comedian EA/96*
CHAPMAN, John (1900-72) Ameri-
can critic BE, NTH, TW/28,
WWT/10-15
CHAPMAN, Mrs. John see
Chapman, Catherine
CHAPMAN, John Jay (1862-1933)
American dramatist HJD

CHAPMAN, John Kemble (d
1852 [47/57[) manager
EA/72*, WWT/14*
CHAPMAN, John R. (b 1927)
English dramatist, actor
AAS, WWT/14-16
CHAPMAN, Mrs. J. W. see
Chapman, Martha
CHAPMAN, Lina (d 1967 [37])
performer BP/51*
CHAPMAN, Lonny (b 1920)
American actor, director,
dramatist BE
CHAPMAN, Martha [Mrs. T.
W. Chapman] (d 1906 [48])
EA/07*
CHAPMAN, Nathan (d 1871)
boxkeeper EA/72*
CHAPMAN, Pattie (d 1912 [82])
actress WWT/14*
CHAPMAN, Richard (fl 1787-
c. 1795?) instrumentalist,
composer BD
CHAPMAN, Robert (fl 1796)
violinist BD
CHAPMAN, Robert H. (b 1919)
American director, drama-
tist, educator BE
CHAPMAN, Mrs. Robert W.
see Desmond, Maggie
CHAPMAN, Mrs. Samuel see
Chapman, Elizabeth
CHAPMAN, Samuel Henry (1799-
1830) English/American actor,
dramatist EAP, ES, HAS,
RJ, SR
CHAPMAN, Thomas (c. 1683-
1747) actor BD
CHAPMAN, Mrs. Thomas
[Hannah] (d c. 1756) actress,
dancer BD
CHAPMAN, Mr. W. (d 1868
[68]) actor EA/69*
CHAPMAN, Mrs. W. H. (d
1879 [62]) American actress
EA/80*
CHAPMAN, William (1764-1839)
American showboat manager
COC, ES, HAS, OC/1-3
CHAPMAN, [William?] (fl 1770?-
1820?) actor, singer BD
CHAPMAN, William (fl 1829)
actor DD
CHAPMAN, William (d 1871
[41]) musical director EA/
72*
CHAPMAN, William (b 1923)
American actor TW/17

CHAPMAN, William A. (d 1857)
English actor ES, HAS, SR
CHAPMAN, Mrs. William A.
[Mrs. Trowbridge; Mrs. Josiah
Silsbee] (d 1880 [67]) English
actress HAS, SR
CHAPMAN, William Adams (fl
1839) actor CDP
CHAPMAN, William B. (1799-1857)
English actor, manager HAS,
SR
CHAPMAN, William S. (1769-1839)
English actor SR
CHAPMAN-HUSTON, W. M. see
Raleigh, Desmond Mountjoy
CHAPPELL, Mr. (fl 1690-91)
actor BD
CHAPPELL, Charles (b 1860)
English business manager
GRB/1
CHAPPELL, Fred (b 1943) Ameri-
can actor TW/25
CHAPPELL, James (d 1899 [61])
manager EA/00*
CHAPPELL, James (d 1907 [78])
clown, music-hall manager
EA/08*
CHAPPELL, John (fl 1600-01)
member of the Chapel Royal
DA
CHAPPELL, William (d 1888 [78])
antiquarian society founder
EA/89*
CHAPPELL, William (b 1908)
English dancer, designer, direc-
tor ES, WWT/9-16
CHAPPELL, William Francis (d
1886 [67]) equestrian clown
EA/87*
CHAPPELLE, Frederick W. (b
1895) English composer WWT/
4-9
CHAPPIEL, Richard (1774-1830)
English musician BD
CHAPPINGTON, Mr. (fl 1735-36)
constable BD
CHAPUY, Leonard Louis (d 1906
[41]) actor? EA/07*
CHAPUY, Louis (d 1908 [72])
professor of elocution EA/09*
CHARD, Kate (d 1942 [80]) Eng-
lish actress, singer CDP, DD,
DP, EA/96
CHARDIN, Mr. (fl 1729) actor
BD
CHARELL, Erik (1895-1974) Ger-
man producer WWT/7-9
CHARIG, Phil (d 1960 [58])

composer BE*

CHARINI, Mr. (fl 1786) equestrian? BD

CHARISSE, Zan (b 1951) American actress TW/28

CHARKE, Catharine Maria [Mrs. Harman] (1730-73) actress BD

CHARKE, Charlotte see Charke, Mrs. Richard

CHARKE, Richard (d c. 1738) violinist, singer, composer, actor, dancer BD

CHARKE, Mrs. Richard [née Charlotte Cibber; Mrs. John Sacheverell] (1713-60) English actress, manager, puppeteer, author BD, CDP, COC, CP/1-3, DD, DNB, ES, OC/1-3, TD/1-2

CHARLAP, Mark ["Moose"] (d 1974 [45]) composer BE

CHARLES, Mons. (fl 1733-56) musician BD

CHARLES, Mr. (fl 1740-41) dancer BD

CHARLES, Mr. (fl 1744-55) actor BD

CHARLES, Mr. (fl 1784-85) stage door keeper BD

CHARLES, Prof. (d 1917) EA/18*

CHARLES, Master (fl 1748) BD

CHARLES, Master (fl 1780) actor BD

CHARLES, Elizabeth Walker [née Blanchard; Mrs. Thomas S. Hamblin] (d 1849) actress CDP, HAS

CHARLES, Florence [Mrs. Charles Bush] (d 1907) EA/08*

CHARLES, Fred (d 1904 [75]) actor DD

CHARLES, G. C. (fl 1855) Irish comedian HAS

CHARLES, G. F. [George Imbert] (d 1891 [69]) lessee, manager EA/92*

CHARLES, H. R. (d 1876 [25]) actor EA/78*

CHARLES, Jacques (d 1971 [89]) talent scout, producer, dramatist BP/56*, WWT/16*

CHARLES, James S. (1808-65) American actor HAS, SR

CHARLES, John (fl 1671-72) scene keeper BD

CHARLES, Leonard (d 1886 [43]) music-hall artist EA/87*

CHARLES, Lucile (d 1965 [64]) performer BP/49*

CHARLES, Marie (d 1864) columbine EA/72*

CHARLES, Mary Ann (fl 1855-58) actress CDP, HAS

CHARLES, Meroe actress CDP

CHARLES, Michael (d 1967 [26]) performer BP/51*

CHARLES, Pamela [née Foster] (b 1932) English actress, singer WWT/15-16

CHARLES, Paul (b 1947) American actor TW/23, 26

CHARLES, Thomas W. (d 1895) manager, musician, conductor DD

CHARLES, Walter (b 1945) American actor TW/30

CHARLES, William (d 1910) scene artist EA/11*

CHARLES, Zachary A. (b 1943) American actor TW/2

CHARLESON, Mary (d 1961 [76]) actress BE*

"CHARLES THE MERRY TRUMPETER" (fl 1729-33?) horn player, dancer, actor BD

CHARLESWORTH, Dr. G. H. (d 1916) EA/17*

CHARLIP, Morris I. (d 1974 [45]) composer WWT/16*

CHARLOT, André Eugene Maurice (1882-1956) French/English manager AAS, COC, DNB, PDT, TW/12, WWT/4-11, WWW/5

CHARLOT, Mrs. André see Gladman, Florence

CHARLTON, Mr. (fl 1729-31) box keeper BD

CHARLTON, Mr. (fl 1794-98) violinist BD

CHARLTON, Alethea (d 1976 [43]) performer BP/60*

CHARLTON, Archer (d 1880) assistant acting manager EA/81*

CHARLTON, Harold C. (d 1954) actor BE*, WWT/14*

CHARLTON, Henry (d 1888 [25]) circus performer EA/89*

CHARLTON, Mrs. H. J. see Chantrell, Clara

CHARLTON, Loudon (b 1869)
American impresario WWM
CHARLTON, Nathaniel Daniel
(d 1889) equestrian clown
EA/90*
CHARLTON, Randal (d 1931)
critic WWT/14*
CHARLTON, Mrs. Richard see
Charlton, Sarah
CHARLTON, Sarah (d 1879)
EA/80*
CHARLTON, Will (d 1916)
EA/17*
CHARMAN, W., Jr. (d 1870
[18]) actor EA/71*
CHARNEY, Jordan American
actor TW/22-24, 26-30
CHARNIN, Martin (b 1934)
American lyricist, actor,
director, producer BE,
WWT/15-16
CHARNLEY, Lucy (d 1905 [64])
EA/06*
CHARNOCK, John (1756-1807)
dramatist CP/3, DD
CHARON, Mme. (fl 1755-56)
dancer BD
CHARON, Jacques (d 1975 [55])
actor, director BP/60*,
WWT/16*
CHARPENTIER, Mme. (fl 1734-
35) dancer? BD
CHARPENTIER, Suzanne Georg-
ette see Annabella
CHARREL, Erik (d 1974 [80])
producer/director/choreog-
rapher BP/59*
CHARRINGTON, Charles (d 1926)
actor, lessee, dramatist DD
CHARRINGTON, Mrs. Charles
see Achurch, Janet
CHARSTONE, W. (d 1886) con-
ductor EA/88*
CHART, Mr. (fl 1794-95) car-
penter BD
CHART, Ellen Elizabeth [née
Rollason] (d 1892) actress?
EA/93*
CHART, F. B. (d 1878 [49])
treasurer, acting manager
EA/79*
CHART, Henry Nye (1822-76)
lessee, actor, manager DD,
ES
CHART, Henry Nye (1868-1934)
English actor DD, ES, WWT/
3-5
CHART, Mrs. Henry Nye

(d 1892) manager ES
CHART, Thomas (d 1875) treasurer
EA/76*
CHART, William (d 1910 [78]) re-
freshment contractor EA/11*
CHARTERS, John (d 1917 [53])
EA/18*
CHARTERS, Spencer (1864-1943)
American actor CB, SR
CHARTOFF, Melanie (b 1948)
American actress TW/29
CHARVAY, Robert [Adrien Lefort]
(1858-1926) French dramatist
GRB/4, WWT/3
CHASE, Cleveland B. (d 1975 [71])
producer/director/choreographer
BP/59*
CHASE, Edna (b 1888) American
actress WWS
CHASE, Ilka (1900/05-78) Ameri-
can actress BE, CB, ES,
TW/1-8, 22-23, WWT/8-16
CHASE, Jo Flores American actor
TW/24
CHASE, Lucia dancer, ballet com-
pany manager CB
CHASE, Mary Coyle (b 1907) Amer-
ican dramatist BE, CB, CD,
ES, HJD, MD, MH, MWD,
WWT/16
CHASE, Pauline (1885-1962) Amer-
ican actress, dancer ES,
GRB/1-4, WWM, WWS, WWT/
1-9
CHASE, Sallie Marshall (d 1965
[55]) performer BP/50*
CHASE, Stanley (b 1928) American
producer BE
CHASE, Stephen (b 1902) Ameri-
can actor TW/2-4, 6-7, 10-12
CHASE, Tommy (d 1969 [62])
musician BP/54*
CHASE, William comedian, min-
strel CDP
CHASE, William B. (d 1948 [76])
American critic BE*, BP/33*,
WWT/14*
CHASEN, Dave (d 1973 [74])
vaudevillian, actor TW/30
CHASEN, Heather (b 1927) English
actress WWT/15-16
CHATEAUNEUF, Mons. (fl 1748-49)
dancer, manager BD
CHATEAUNEUF, Marie (b 1721)
French dancer, singer, mana-
ger BD
CHATER, Geoffrey [né Robinson]
(b 1921) English actor

WWT/15-16
CHATHAM, Pitt (d 1923 [37])
actor, singer BE*, WWT/
14*
CHATILLION, Mons. (fl 1735)
dancer BD
CHATIN, Marienne (d 1972 [68])
executive BP/56*
CHATRIEN, Louis Gratien
Charles Alexandre see
Erckmann-Chatrian
CHATTAWAY, Miss M. (d 1891
[77]) custodian of Shake-
speare's birthplace EA/92*
CHATTAWAY, Thurland com-
poser CDP
CHATTERLEY, Mr. (fl c.
1812?) actor CDP
CHATTERLEY, Mrs. see
Chatterley, Louisa
CHATTERLEY, Miss (fl 1791-
98) actress, singer BD
CHATTERLEY, J. (fl 1795?-
1803?) dancer, actor BD
CHATTERLEY, Louisa [Mrs.
William Simmonds Chatterley;
née Simeon] (1797-1866)
English actress BS, CDP,
DD, OX
CHATTERLEY, Robert E. (fl
1792-1818) messenger,
prompter, actor BD
CHATTERLEY, Mrs. Robert
E. (1795-1819) actress BD
CHATTERLEY, William Sim-
monds (1787-1821) English
actor, dancer BD, CDP,
DD, DNB
CHATTERLEY, Mrs. William
Simmonds see Chatterley,
Louisa
CHATTERS, Frank (d 1868)
Negro artist EA/69*
CHATTERS, Kate [Mrs. Flower-
day] (d 1897) variety per-
former EA/98*
CHATTERTON, Mrs. Balsir
see Kinton, Swaine
CHATTERTON, Charles (d 1894)
secretary EA/95*
CHATTERTON, E. A. (d 1875
[65]) EA/77*
CHATTERTON, Edward Keble
English critic GRB/2-3
CHATTERTON, Eliza D. [Mrs.
John Balsir Chatterton] (d
1877 [70]) EA/78*
CHATTERTON, Frederick Balsir

(1834-86) manager, actor
CDP, DD
CHATTERTON, Mrs. Frederick
Balsir see Chatterton, Mary
Ann
CHATTERTON, Lady Georgiana
(d 1876) dramatist DD
CHATTERTON, John Balsir (d
1871 [66]) musician EA/72*
CHATTERTON, Mrs. John Balsir
see Chatterton, Eliza D.
CHATTERTON, Mary (d 1899 [42])
musician EA/00*
CHATTERTON, Mary Ann [Mrs.
Frederick Balsir Chatterton]
(d 1909 [77]) EA/10*
CHATTERTON, Ruth (1893-1961)
American actress ES, SR,
TW/2-8, 10-16, 18, WWA/4,
WWT/4-13
CHATTERTON, Thomas (1752-70)
English dramatist CDP, CP/
2-3, DNB, GT, HP, TD/1-2
CHATTERTON, Vivienne (d 1974)
actress BTR/74
CHATTON, Sydney (d 1966 [48])
performer BP/51*
CHATWIN, Margaret (d 1937 [56])
English actress WWT/5-8
CHAUCHOIN, Lily see Colbert,
Claudette
CHAUNDLER, George (fl 1669)
manager? BD
CHAUVENET, Virginia (d 1949
[65]) American actress TW/5
CHAVCHAVADZE, Paul (d 1971
[72]) actor BP/56*
CHAVES, A. (fl 1705) dramatist
CP/1-3, DD
CHAVEZ, Carlos (b 1899) Mexi-
can composer, conductor ES
CHAVIGNY, Mons. (fl 1720-21)
actor BD
CHAVIGNY, Mme. (fl 1720-21)
actress BD
CHAYEFSKY, Paddy [Sidney] (b
1923) American dramatist,
producer, director AAS, BE,
CB, CD, CH, COC, ES, HJD,
MD, MH, MWD, PDT, WWT/
14-16
CHAZAL, Mrs. see De Gam-
barini, Elisabetta
CHAZEL, Leo (d 1953 [52]) actor
TW/10
CHEATHAM, Kitty (1864?-1946)
American actress CB, WWM,
WWS

CHECCHI, Andrea (d 1974 [57])
performer BP/58*
CHECCO, Al (b 1922) American
actor TW/5-6
CHEEKE, Henry (fl 1561) drama-
tist CP/1-3, FGF
CHEER, Miss (fl 1767-93) actress
CDP, HAS, WWA/H
CHEESE, Mr. (fl 1784) singer
BD
CHEESEMAN, Peter (b 1932)
English director WWT/15-16
CHEESMAN, William (1860-
1907) English actor EA/96,
GRB/1, 3
CHEETHAM, Leonard see
Mudie, Leonard
CHEEVERS, Joseph E. (b 1848)
dancer, minstrel CDP
CHEKHOV, Anton Pavlovich
(1860-1904) Russian dramatist
COC, MD, OC/1-3
CHEKHOV, Michael [Alexandro-
vich] (1891-1955) Russian
actor, director ES, NTH,
OC/3, WWT/10-11
CHEKINI, Mr. English dancer
HAS
CHELLERI, Sig. (fl 1725) bass
viol player BD
CHELSUM, James (c. 1700-43)
singer BD
CHELTNAM, Charles Smith (b
1823) English dramatist,
critic DD, EA/68
CHELTON, Nick (b 1946) Eng-
lish lighting designer WWT/
16
CHEMBINI, Mr. (fl 1784-85)
singer? BD
CHEMONT, Mons. (fl 1742)
dancer BD
CHEN, Kitty Chinese actress
TW/30
CHEN, Tina Chinese actress
TW/28, 30
CHENAL, Marthe (d 1947 [62])
actress, singer WWT/14*
CHENERY, Arthur English actor,
variety artist GRB/1
CHENERY, Herbert (d 1928)
business manager WWT/14*
CHENERY, James William (d
1907 [28]) EA/08*
CHENEY, Master (fl 1770)
singer BD
CHENEY, Miss see Gardiner,
Mrs.

CHENEY, Arthur (1837-78) mana-
ger CDP
CHENEY, Mrs. B. P., Jr. see
Arthur, Julia
CHENEY, Sheldon (b 1886) Ameri-
can writer BE, ES, WWT/10-
11
CHENG, Stephen Chinese actor
TW/28
CHENOWETH, Emily [Emily
Ernest] (d 1881 [20]) actress
EA/82*
CHERB, George W. (d 1974 [50])
musician BP/58*
CHERENSI, B. Frere (fl 1796)
French dramatist CP/3
CHERI, Rose [Rose-Marie Cizos]
(1824-61) French actress OC/
1-3
CHERIE, Adelaide actress CDP
CHERIN, Robert (b 1936) American
house manager BE
CHERINGTON, Richard (fl 1678-
85) singer BD
CHERITON, David (c. 1707-58)
singer BD
CHERKASOV, Nicolai (d 1966 [63])
actor WWT/14
CHERNUCK, Dorothy American
producer, director, educator
BE
CHERRELL, Gwen (b 1926) English
actress AAS, WWT/11-16
CHERRIER, Miss (fl 1708) dancer
BD
CHERRIER, René (fl 1699-1708)
dancer, choreographer BD
CHERRINGTON, Harriet Eastman
(d 1965 [81]) performer BP/
49*
CHERRINGTON, John (fl 1676)
singer BD
CHERRY, Miss (fl 1814) actress
CDP
CHERRY, Addie (1859?-1942)
American performer CB, ES
CHERRY, Andrew (1762-1812)
Irish actor CDP, CP/3, DD,
DNB, ES, GT, TD/1-2
CHERRY, Charles (1872/74-1931)
English actor WWA/5, WWS,
WWT/1-6
CHERRY, Effie (d 1944 [66])
American actress, singer TW/1
CHERRY, Elizabeth [Mrs. J. W.
Cherry] (d 1886) EA/87*
CHERRY, Fred English actor
GRB/1

CHERRY, Harriet (d 1880 [84])
actress? EA/81*

CHERRY, Helen (b 1915) English actress WWT/10-11

CHERRY, Jessie (d 1903 [67])
American performer ES

CHERRY, John (d 1968 [80])
actor TW/1, 24

CHERRY, J. W. (d 1889)
songwriter EA/90*

CHERRY, Mrs. J. W. see
Cherry, Elizabeth

CHERRY, Lizzie (d 1936 [67])
American performer ES

CHERRY, Malcolm (1878-1925)
English actor, dramatist
WWT/1-5

CHERRY, V. Ewing (d 1969
[76]) performer BP/53*

CHERRY, Wal (b 1932) Australian
director, educator WWT/16

CHERRYMAN, Rex (d 1928 [30])
American actor BE*, BP/
13*, WWT/14*

CHERRY SISTERS ES

CHESKIN, Irving (b 1915) American executive BE, WWT/16

CHESLOCK, Louis (b 1899)
English/American composer
ES

CHESNEY, Arthur (d 1949 [67])
English actor WWT/3-10

CHESSMAN, Edward (d 1891)
comedian EA/92*

CHESSON, Thomas (fl 1580?)
actor DA

CHESTER, Mrs. Alfred see
Chester, Marie

CHESTER, Betty (1895/96-1943)
English actress WWT/4-7

CHESTER, Eddie (d 1964 [67])
performer BP/49*

CHESTER, Edith (d 1894 [33])
actress DD

CHESTER, Elsie (d 1937)
actress WWT/14*

CHESTER, Eliza (b 1799) English actress BS, CDP, DD,
OX

CHESTER, Francis (d 1881 [70])
architect EA/83*

CHESTER, George Randolph
(1869-1924) American dramatist WWA/1

CHESTER, Harry (d 1869) comedian EA/70*

CHESTER, John (d 1878) actor
EA/79*

CHESTER, Kate actress CDP

CHESTER, Marie [Mrs. Maitland;
Mrs. Alfred Chester] (d 1889)
music-hall artist EA/90*

CHESTER, Roland (d 1916) EA/
17*

CHESTER, Mrs. Sam (d 1918)
American actress SR

CHESTER, S. K. [S. C. Knapp]
(1836-1921) American actor
HAS

CHESTER, Mrs. S. K. (b 1843)
American actress HAS

CHESTERTON, Gilbert K. (1874-
1936) English dramatist ES

CHESTNEY, Josephine (fl 1861)
American actress HAS

CHETHAM-STRODE, Warren
(1897-1974) English dramatist
WWT/9-14

CHETTLE, Mr. (fl 1740-48?)
actor, dancer, singer BD

CHETTLE, Henry (c. 1560-1607)
English dramatist COC, CP/3,
DD, DNB, ES, FGF, HP,
NTH, OC/1-3, RE

CHETWOOD, Richabella [Mrs.
Tobias Gemea] (fl 1738-71)
actress BD

CHETWOOD, William Rufus (d
1766) prompter, dramatist,
actor BD, CDP, CP/1-3, DD,
DNB, GT, TD/1-2

CHETWYN, Robert [né Suckling]
(b 1933) English actor, director
WWT/15-16

CHEVALIER, Mons. (fl 1784) exhibitor BD

CHEVALIER, Albert (1861-1923)
English actor, music-hall performer CDP, COC, DD, DNB,
DP, ES, GRB/1-4, OC/1-3,
PDT, SR, WWS, WWT/1-4,
WWW/2

CHEVALIER, Albert (d 1959 [60])
actor WWT/14*

CHEVALIER, Gus (d 1947 [56])
performer BE*, WWT/14*

CHEVALIER, Marcelle actress
WWT/2-4

CHEVALIER, Maurice (1888-1972)
French actor, singer BE, CB,
COC, ES, NTH, OC/3, SR,
TW/3, 5-7, 21, 28, WWA/5,
WWT/7-15

CHEVALIER, May (d 1940) actress
BE*, WWT/14*

CHEVALIER, Pierre (fl 1780-88)

dancer, choreographer BD
CHEVALIER, Thomas (fl 1694-99)
oboist BD
CHEVALLIER, Zara dancer CDP
CHEVIGNY, Mr. (fl 1797-98)
dancer? BD
CHEVRIER, [Mons. ?] (fl 1726-
27) dancer BD
CHEW, Virgilia R. (b 1905)
American actress TW/23,
25-26
CHEYNE, Mr. (fl 1794-1806)
carpenter, machinist BD
CHIARELL, Luigi (1880/84-
1947) Italian dramatist
COC, MWD, OC/3
CHIARINA, Sig. (d 1897 [82])
circus proprietor EA/98*
CHIARINI, Mme. (fl 1854)
equestrienne HAS
CHICHESTER, Henry [Henry
Chichester Baker] (1864-
1908) English actor GRB/1
CHICKINGHAM, Mr. (fl 1799)
actor BD
CHICOINE, Randal (b 1944)
actor TW/30
CHIDLEY, Mrs. Sidney (d 1889)
EA/90*
CHIESI, Amy [Mrs. Arthur
Chiesi] (d 1888) EA/89*
CHIESI, Mrs. Arthur see
Chiesi, Amy
CHIESI, Giuseppe (d 1887)
proprietor EA/88*
CHILD, Mr. (fl 1732) actor BD
CHILD, Mr. (fl 1794-95) dresser
BD
CHILD, Mrs. (fl 1773?-82) ac-
tress BD
CHILD, Miss see Webb, Mrs.
CHILD, Ann see Seguin, Mrs.
Arthur Edward Shelden
CHILD, Anne (fl 1666-68)
actress? BD
CHILD, Harold Hannyngton
(1869-1945) English critic
DNB, ES, WWT/2-9, WWW/4
CHILD, Marilyn American
actress TW/24, 27, 30
CHILD, Thomas (fl 1714) actor
BD
CHILD, Rev. Thomas (d 1906
[66]) EA/07*
CHILD, William (1606-97) singer,
composer, instrumentalist
BD, DNB
CHILDE, Henry Langdon (d

1874 [92]) inventor EA/75*
CHILDERS, Naomi (d 1964 [71])
actress BE*
CHILDRESS, Alice (b 1920) Amer-
ican actress, dramatist, direc-
tor CD, TW/1
CHILDS, Gilbert (d 1931) actor
WWT/4-6
CHILIBY (fl 1783) performing horse
BD
CHIMENTI, Margherita (fl 1736-
38) singer BD
CHINA, Mr. (fl 1724) horn player
BD
CHING LING LOO [Will E. Robin-
son] magician SR
CHINN, Lori American actress
TW/29
CHINNALL, Mr. (fl 1764-75)
doorkeeper, checktaker BD
CHINOY, Helen Krich (b 1922)
American educator, director
BE
CHIPCHASE, Elizabeth (d 1892)
EA/93*
CHIPP, Mr. (fl 1822) actor HAS
CHIPP, Mrs. (fl 1822) actress
HAS
CHIPP, Dr. Edmund Thomas (d
1886 [63]) organist EA/88*
CHIPP, Thomas Paul (1793-1870)
English musician DNB
CHIPPENDALE, Alfreda [née
Schoolcraft] (d 1887 [42])
American actress DD, NYM
CHIPPENDALE, Arthur A. see
Lynn
CHIPPENDALE, Henry (d 1878
[29]) agent EA/79*
CHIPPENDALE, Johann (d 1910)
actor EA/12*
CHIPPENDALE, Mary Jane [Mary
J. Snowdon] (1837?-88) English
actress CDP, DD, DNB,
OAA/1-2
CHIPPENDALE, Thomas (1782-99)
callboy BD
CHIPPENDALE, Mrs. W. B. (fl
1863) actress HAS
CHIPPENDALE, William (fl 1793-
1835?) actor BD
CHIPPENDALE, Mrs. William (fl
1797-1820?) singer BD
CHIPPENDALE, William Henry
(1801-88) English actor CDP,
DD, DNB, ES, HAS, OAA/1-2,
SR
CHIPPENDALE, Mrs. William

Henry see Chippendale,
Mary Jane
CHIRGWIN, Edward (d 1882 [72])
EA/83*
CHIRGWIN, George H. (1854-
1922) English variety artist
CDP, COC, GRB/1-4,
OC/1-3
CHIRGWIN, Mrs. George H. (d
1892 [37]) EA/93*
CHIRGWIN, John (d 1882) EA/
83*
CHIRINGHELLI, Signora (fl
1774) dancer BD
CHISE, Mme. (fl 1757) dancer
BD
CHISHOLM, Eric (b 1904) Scot-
tish musical director, com-
poser ES
CHISHOLM, James D. (d 1907
[75]) EA/08*
CHISHOLM, Robert (1898-1960)
Australian actor, singer
TW/1-4, 6-7, WWT/7-12
CHISHOLM, Samuel Robertson
(d 1900 [67]) proprietor
EA/01*
CHISHOLM, Mrs. S. R. (d
1886 [53]) EA/87*
CHISNEL, John (d 1867) circus
performer? EA/68*
CHISWELL, Melville (d 1918
[32]) EA/19*
CHISWICK, William (b 1813)
English actor SR
CHITTLE, Samuel (fl 1715-20)
singer BD
CHIVERS, Thomas Holley
(1809-58) American drama-
tist HJD, WWA/H
CHLUMBERG, Hans (1897-1930)
Austrian dramatist MWD
CHOATE, Edward (1908-75)
American manager, producer
BE
CHOBANIAN, Haig (b 1937)
American actor TW/24, 26
CHOBER, Cora Lena [Mrs. M.
E. Coudelle] (d 1877) singer
NYM
CHOCA, Mrs. (fl 1734) actress
BD
CHOCK, Alexander (fl 1666-67)
scene keeper BD
CHOCK, Dennis (b c. 1689)
actress BD
CHOCKE, George (fl 1698-99)
musician BD

CHODOROV, Edward (b 1904)
American dramatist, director,
producer, scenarist BE, CB,
ES, HJD, MD, MWD, WWT/
10-14
CHODOROV, Jerome (b 1911)
American dramatist, director
BE, CD, COC, ES, HJD, MH,
MWD, WWT/10-16
CHOFE, Robert (fl 1554) actor
DA
CHOLLET, Mons. (d 1892 [95])
singer EA/93*
CHOLLET, Constance (fl 1771)
dancer BD
CHORLEY, Henry Fothergill (1808-
72) English dramatist, critic
DD, DNB
CHORLEY, John Rutter (1807?-67)
English scholar, dramatist
DNB
CHORPENNING, Ruth (b 1905)
American actress WWT/8-10
CHOSE, Mr. (fl 1734-35) dancer
BD
CHOTZINOFF, Samuel (d 1964 [74])
Russian/American dramatist,
critic BE*, BP/48*
CHOW, Caryn Ann (b 1957) Amer-
ican actress TW/24
CHOWHURY, Roy see Bhaskar
CHRIS, Marilyn (b 1939) American
actress TW/27-30
CHRISMAN, Carolyn American
actress TW/27, 29
CHRISTENSEN, Harold (b 1902)
American dancer, teacher ES
CHRISTENSEN, Lew (b 1906/09)
American choreographer, dancer
BE, ES
CHRISTENSEN, William F. (b
1902) American choreographer,
dancer, educator BE, ES
CHRISTI, Vito (b 1924) American
actor TW/1-7
CHRISTIAN, Mr. (fl 1750-53)
dancer BD
CHRISTIAN, Mrs. [née Vaughan]
(fl 1730-33) actress BD
CHRISTIAN, Miss (fl 1784) actress
BD
CHRISTIAN, Benjamin (fl 1794)
violinist BD
CHRISTIAN, Charles (fl c. 1700)
singer BD
CHRISTIAN, Edward (fl 1784?-94)
singer BD
CHRISTIAN, Frances Ann [née

Fanny Waldron] (d 1874 [83])
EA/76*

CHRISTIAN, Frank J. (d 1973
[86]) musician BP/58*

CHRISTIAN, Robert (b 1939)
American actor TW/23,
25-28, 30

CHRISTIAN, Thomas (1810-67)
minstrel HAS, SR

CHRISTIAN, Thomas see
Christmas, Thomas

CHRISTIAN, Thomas Berry (d
1874 [90]) EA/76*

CHRISTIAN, Mrs. Thomas
Berry see Christian,
Frances Ann

CHRISTIAN, Lieut. T. P. (fl
1790-91) dramatist CP/3,
DD

CHRISTIAN, William (d 1699)
singer BD

CHRISTIANS, Mady (1900-51)
Austrian actress CB, ES,
TW/1-8, WWT/8-11

CHRISTIANS, Rudolf (1869-
1921) German actor, manager
WWT/2

CHRISTIE, Dame Agatha Mary
Clarissa [née Miller] (1890/
91-1976) English dramatist
AAS, BE, CB, CD, COC,
ES, HP, PDT, WWT/10-16

CHRISTIE, Al (1886-1951)
Canadian producer, director,
actor ES

CHRISTIE, Audrey (b 1911/12)
American actress BE,
TW/1-19, WWT/9-16

CHRISTIE, Campbell (1893-1963)
Indian/English dramatist
AAS, WWT/12-13

CHRISTIE, Charles H. (d 1955
[75]) producer BE*

CHRISTIE, Dorothy [née Dorothy
Casson Walker] (b 1896) English dramatist AAS, WWT/
12-14

CHRISTIE, George (1873-1949)
American actor WWT/8-10

CHRISTIE, John (d 1962 [80])
impresario BE*

CHRISTIE, Julie (b 1941) Indian/
English actress CB, TW/
29-30

CHRISTMAS, Mrs. (fl c. 1673-
75) actress? BD

CHRISTMAS, David (b 1942)
American actor TW/25-26

CHRISTMAS, John (d c. 1677)
trumpeter BD

CHRISTMAS, Thomas (fl 1663)
trumpeter BD

CHRISTMAS, Thomas (fl 1692-96)
singer BD

CHRISTOFF, George see Christopher, George

CHRISTOPHER, George [George
Christoff] (d 1881 [c. 55]) tight-
rope artist EA/82*

CHRISTOPHER, Jordan (b 1940)
American actor TW/29

CHRISTOPHER, Thom (b 1940)
American actor TW/29-30

CHRISTOPHERSON, John (fl 1546)
dramatist CP/3

CHRISTY, Dave (1853-1926) minstrel SR

CHRISTY, E. Byron (d 1866 [28])
minstrel? HAS

CHRISTY, Edwin P. (1815-62)
singer, banjoist, founder of
Christy's Minstrels CDP, HAS,
HJD, SR, WWA/H

CHRISTY, Floyd (d 1962 [55])
performer BE*

CHRISTY, George N. [né Harring-
ton] (1827-68) American minstrel CDP, HAS, SR

CHRISTY, George Washington (d
1975 [86]) circus owner BP/
60*

CHRISTY, Ken (d 1962 [67]) actor
BE*

CHRISTY, William A. (d 1862
[23]) minstrel HAS

CHRONEGK, Ludwig (1837-91)
actor COC

CHUDLEIGH, Arthur (1858-1932)
English manager GRB/4,
WWT/1-6

CHUDLEIGH, John (fl 1669-74)
actor? BD

CHUJOY, Anatole (d 1969 [74])
critic BP/53*

CHUMBLEY, Mr. (fl 1797-1802)
boxkeeper BD

CHUNG LING SOO [Williams Ellsworth Robinson] (d 1918 [56])
EA/19*

CHURCH, Mr. (fl 1744) house servant? BD

CHURCH, Mr. (fl 1752-53) musician BD

CHURCH, Mr. (fl 1770) actor,
singer BD

CHURCH, Mrs. (d 1877 [74])

actress? EA/78*
CHURCH, Charles (d 1872 [69])
actor? EA/73*
CHURCH, Esmé (1893-1972)
English actress, director
AAS, ES, WWT/7-14
CHURCH, George (d 1871)
musician EA/72*
CHURCH, George (b 1912)
American actor TW/11-
12, 20
CHURCH, Harry (d 1890 [58])
chairman EA/91*
CHURCH, John (1675-1741)
English singer, composer
BD, DNB
CHURCH, Maria (d 1887)
EA/88*
CHURCH, Samuel (fl 1792) per-
former BD
CHURCH, Samuel Harden
(1858-1943) dramatist CB
CHURCH, Sandra American
actress BE
CHURCH, Tom (d 1872 [37])
pianist EA/73*
CHURCH, Tony (b 1930) English
actor AAS, TW/24, WWT/
15-16
CHURCH, William (fl 1666-70)
scenekeeper BD
CHURCHILL, Miss (fl 1782)
actress BD
CHURCHILL, Allen (b 1911)
American writer BE
CHURCHILL, Berton (1876-1940)
Canadian actor CB, ES, SR,
WWT/7-9
CHURCHILL, Caryl (b 1938)
English dramatist CD
CHURCHILL, Charles (1731-64)
poet CDP
CHURCHILL, Diana (b 1913)
American actress AAS,
ES, WWT/8-15
CHURCHILL, Donald dramatist
CD
CHURCHILL, Prof. J. Edwin
American actor HAS
CHURCHILL, John (fl 1699-
1700) carpenter BD
CHURCHILL, J. W. singer
CDP
CHURCHILL, Marguerite (b
1910) American actress ES,
WWT/7-9
CHURCHILL, Sarah (b 1914)
English actress CB, ES,

TW/7-8, WWT/10-16
CHURCHILL, William (1760?-1812)
musician BD
CHURCHILL, William James (d
1893 [49]) music-hall artist
EA/94*
CHURCHILL, Winston (1871-1947)
American dramatist GRB/2-4,
WWT/1-3
CHURCHMAN, Mr. (fl 1715) actor
BD
CHURTON, Mr. (fl 1796) manager?
actor? BD
CHURTON, Mrs. (fl 1792) actress
BD
CHUTE, Charles Kean (d 1905
[46]) actor EA/06*
CHUTE, George Macready (d 1888
[37]) manager EA/89*, WWT/
14*
CHUTE, James H. (d 1878 [68])
proprietor, manager EA/79*,
WWT/14*
CHUTE, Mrs. James H. (d 1878
[54]) EA/79*
CHUTE, James Macready (d 1912
[55]) manager, proprietor EA/
13*, WWT/14*
CHUTE, John Coleman (d 1913
[94]) manager WWT/14*
CHUTE, Marchette (b 1909) Amer-
ican dramatist BE
CHUTE, Stephen Macready (d 1899
[47]) EA/00*
CHUTE, William Charles Macready
(d 1908 [25]) EA/09*
CHWATT, Aaron see Buttons,
Red
CIACCHI, Sig. (fl 1746-48) singer
BD
CIANCHETTINI, Pio ["Mozart
Britannicus"] (1799-1851) Eng-
lish composer CDP
CIANELLI, Alma (d 1968 [76])
performer BP/53*
CIANNELI, Eduardo (1889-1969)
Italian/American actor ES,
TW/26
CIAPARELLI, Gina (fl 1897-1911)
Italian singer WWM
CIARDINI, Domenico (fl 1763)
singer BD
"CIAVARTINO, Sig." (fl 1754)
musical performer? BD
CIBBER, Charlotte see Charke,
Mrs. Richard
CIBBER, Colley (1671-1757) Eng-
lish actor, manager, dramatist

BD, CDP, COC, CP/1-3,
DD, DNB, ES, GT, HP,
MH, NTH, OC/1-3, PDT,
SR, TD/1-2
CIBBER, Mrs. Colley [née
Katherine Shore] (c. 1669-
1734) singer, actress BD
CIBBER, Elizabeth see
Brett, Mrs. Dawson
CIBBER, Jane (b 1730) English
actress BD
CIBBER, Susanna Maria see
Cibber, Mrs. Theophilus, II
CIBBER, Theophilus (1703-58)
English actor, dancer,
dramatist, manager BD,
CDP, COC, CP/1-3, DD,
DNB, ES, GT, OC/1-3,
TD/1-2
CIBBER, Mrs. Theophilus, I
[née Jane Johnson] (1706-33)
actress, singer BD
CIBBER, Mrs. Theophilus, II
[née Susanna Maria] (1714-66)
English actress, singer,
dramatist BD, CDP, CP/
1-3, DD, DNB, ES, GT,
NTH, OC/1-3, TD/1-2
CICERI, Charles (fl 1793-1800)
Italian scene painter, ma-
chinist BD
CICERI, Leo (1928-70) Canadian
actor TW/12, 27
CIECA, Io (1710-11) singer BD
CIEPLINSKI, Jan (d 1972 [71])
producer/director/choreog-
rapher BP/56*
CIGADA, Francesco (b 1878)
Italian singer ES
CIGNA, Gina Italian singer ES
CILENTO, Diane (b 1933)
Australian actress AAS,
BE, TW/12-15, WWT/14-16
CIMA, Victoria Gamez see
Angeles, Victoria de los
CIMADOR, Giovanni Battista
(1761-1805) Italian musician,
composer BD, ES
CIMADORI, Giovanni Andrea
(d c. 1684) Italian actor BD
CIMBER, Matt (b 1936) Ameri-
can producer, director BE
CIMINI, Pietro (d 1971 [97])
conductor BP/56*
CINDERS, Ettie [Miss Cantor]
English actress GRB/1
CINKO, Paula (b 1950) actress
TW/29-30

CINQUEVALLI, Adelina [Mrs.
Paul Cinquevalli] (d 1908)
EA/09*
CINQUEVALLI, Paul (1859-1918)
Polish juggler OC/1-3
CINQUEVALLI, Mrs. Paul see
Cinquevalli, Adelina
CINTI, Mlle. see Damoreau,
Laure Cinthie
CIOCCA, Signora (fl 1847) dancer
HAS
CIOFFI, Charles (b 1935) American
actor TW/25-27
CIOLLI, Augusta (d 1967 [65])
actress TW/23
"CIPERINI, Sig. " (fl 1759) singer
BD
CIPRANDI, Ercole (fl 1754-91?)
singer BD
CIPRIANI, Giovanni Battista (1727-
85) Italian scene painter, en-
graver, historical painter BD
CIPRIANI, Lorenzo Angelo (fl 1791-
96) singer BD, CDP
CIPRICO, George M. (b 1847)
American actor CDP, DD,
HAS
CIRKER, Mitchell (d 1953 [70])
American set designer BE*,
BP/37*
CIRRI, Giovanni Battista (b c. 1740)
Italian violoncellist, composer
BD
CISNEROS, Eleanora de (1878-
1934) American singer ES
CISNEY, Marcella [Marcella
Ruth Abels] American adminis-
trator, director, actress BE
CISSEL, Chuck (b 1948) American
actor TW/29-30
CITKOWITZ, Israel (d 1974 [65])
composer/lyricist BP/58*
CIZO, Mr. (fl 1790) singer BD
CIZOS, Rose-Marie see Chéri,
Rose
CLABBURN, Mr. (fl 1794) singer
BD
CLACY, Frederick (d 1874 [30])
dwarf pantomimist EA/75*
CLAGGET, Charles (1740?-1820?)
Irish violinist, inventor, com-
poser BD, DNB
CLAGGET, Walter (1742-98) Irish
instrumentalist, composer,
proprietor BD
CLAGGETT, Crispus (fl 1795-97)
impresario, lessee BD
CLAIR, Cissie [Mrs. H. Buckstone

Clair] (d 1901) EA/02*

CLAIR, Mrs. H. Buckstone
see Clair, Cissie

CLAIR, Lionel (d 1891) actor
EA/92*

CLAIR, Lucy [Mrs. Watty Clair]
(d 1882) EA/83*

CLAIR, Mavis (b 1916) English
actress WWT/8-10

CLAIR, Richard (b 1935)
American actor TW/14,
17-18

CLAIR, Mrs. Watty see
Clair, Lucy

CLAIRBERT, Clara (b 1899)
Belgian singer ES

CLAIRE, Attalie (fl 1890-97)
Canadian singer, actress
DD, DP

CLAIRE, Helen (1911-74) American actress BE, TW/1,
30, WWT/9-11

CLAIRE, Ina (b 1892/95) Amer-
ican actress, singer AAS,
BE, CB, ES, NTH, SR,
TW/2-8, 10-16, WWT/3-14

CLAIRE, Ludi [née Edilou
Bailhé] (b 1922) American
actress BE, TW/14-17,
27, 30

CLAIRVILLE, Charles (d 1918
[63]) librettist WWT/14*

CLAMAKIN, Mrs. (fl 1731)
dancer BD

CLAMAN, Julian (d 1969 [51])
dramatist BP/53*

CLAMP, John (d 1907 [74])
banjo maker EA/08*

CLANCARTY, Countess of
[Belle Bilton; Lady Dunlo]
(d 1906 [38]) English actress
CDP, GRB/1

CLANCENT, William [William
Butler] (d 1893 [53]) EA/95*

CLANCEY, Jean (d 1893) sand
dancer EA/94*

CLANCY, Deirdre (b 1943)
English designer WWT/16

CLANCY, James (b 1912) American director, educator BE

CLANCY, Laura (d 1884) actress
CDP

CLANCY, Michael (fl c. 1700-
c. 50) Irish? dramatist, actor
CP/1-3, DD, GT

CLANCY, Timothy see Buck-
ley, Joe

CLANCY, Tom (b 1926) Irish

actor TW/16, 29-30

CLANCY, Venie (d 1882) actress
CDP

CLANFIELD, Mr. (fl 1775-76)
boxkeeper BD

CLANFIELD, Mr. (fl 1794) singer?
musician BD

CLANFIELD, Samuel (fl 1750-
1800) pyrotechnist, proprietor
BD

CLANTON, Ralph (b 1914) American actor TW/1-8, 10-12,
24, 28-29, WWT/12-13, 16

CLAPHAM, Mrs. (fl 1786) actress
BD

CLAPHAM, Charles (d 1959 [65])
performer BE*, WWT/14*

CLAPP, C. C. (fl 1856) actor
HAS

CLAPP, Charles (d 1962 [63])
American songwriter BE*

CLAPP, Charles Edwin, Jr. (d
1957 [57]) American producer
BE*, BP/41*

CLAPP, Henry Austin (d 1904
[62]) critic WWT/14*

CLAPP, Philip Greeley (1888-
1954) American composer
WWA/3

CLAPP, William W. (1826-91)
journalist CDP

CLAPTON, John (d 1872) proprietor EA/73*

CLARA, Mlle. equestrienne CDP

CLARA, Mlle. (fl 1828) dancer
HAS

CLARANCE, Lloyd (d 1939 [90])
actor, manager WWT/14*

CLARE, Ada actress EA/97

CLARE, Ada [née Jane McEthenrey;
Mrs. Frank P. Noyes; Agnes
Stansfield] (1836-74) actress
CDP, HAS

CLARE, Bridget [Mrs. Edward
Clare] (d 1887 [46]) EA/88*

CLARE, Dickie [Richard Clare
Robinson] (b 1871) English actor
GRB/1

CLARE, Edward (d 1869 [51])
professor of music EA/70*

CLARE, Mrs. Edward see
Clare, Bridget

CLARE, Mary (1892/94-1970)
English actress AAS, ES,
WWT/3-14, WWW/6

CLARE, Phyllis (d 1947 [42/62])
English actress BE*, WWT/
14*

CLAREMONT, Kittie see
Carson, Mrs. Charles L.
CLAREMONT, Lizzie [Mrs.
Henry Spry] (d 1904 [62])
actress EA/05*, WWT/
14*
CLAREMONT, William (d 1832)
English actor BD, BS
CLARENCE, George D. (d
1904 [60]) actor EA/06*
CLARENCE, James (d 1906
[35]) performer? EA/07*
CLARENCE, O[liver] B. (1870-
1955) English actor ES,
GRB/3-4, WWT/1-11
CLARENCE, Nellie actress
GRB/1-2
CLARENDON, Miss (fl 1742)
actress BD
CLARENDON, Miss (fl 1841)
actress, manager HAS
CLARENDON, Charles (d 1899
[34]) comic singer EA/00*
CLARENDON, J. Hayden (b
1879) Irish actor WWS
CLARENS, Elsie (d 1917)
actress EA/18*
CLAREY, H. O. (d 1906)
comedian EA/07*
CLARGES, Verner (d 1911 [65])
English actor PP/1, SR
CLARIDGE, John (fl 1766-90)
lobby doorkeeper, supernum-
erary BD
CLARIDGE, Norman (b 1903/05)
English actor WWT/8-16
CLARISSA (b 1924) American
actress TW/2-3
CLARK, Mr. (fl 1731) actor
BD
CLARK, Mr. (fl 1792-1819?)
singer BD
CLARK, Mr. (fl 1800) puppeteer
BD
CLARK, Mr. (fl 1800-06) scene
painter BD
CLARK, Mr. (d 1812) waxworks
exhibitor BD
CLARK, Mr. (d 1881) EA/83*
CLARK, Mrs. (fl 1695-1723?)
actress, singer, dancer BD
CLARK, Mrs. (fl 1760-1814?)
waxworks exhibitor? BD
CLARK, Mrs. (fl 1789) singer
BD
CLARK, Mrs. ["Naneys Gown"]
(d 1884 [70]) giant EA/85*
CLARK, Master (fl 1724-30)

dancer BD
CLARK, Miss (fl 1736) actress,
singer BD
CLARK, Miss (fl 1736-47?) act-
ress, singer BD
CLARK, Miss (fl 1787) actress
BD
CLARK, Miss see Isherwood,
Mrs.
CLARK, Alexander (d 1932 [66])
American comedian BE*,
BP/17*
CLARK, Alexander (b 1901/04)
American actor BE, TW/8,
19, 21, 23-26
CLARK, Alfred Indian/English
actor WWT/4-9
CLARK, Allan (d 1908) bandmaster
EA/09*
CLARK, Barrett H. (1890-1953)
Canadian critic, actor, director
ES, HJD, NTH, WWA/3, WWT/
7-13
CLARK, Bobby (1888-1960) Amer-
ican actor CB, ES, SR, TW/
1-8, 10-13, 15-16, WWA/3,
WWT/7-12
CLARK, Brian dramatist CD
CLARK, Buddy (1911-49) American
singer TW/6
CLARK, Mrs. C. [Mrs. T. G.
Clark] (d 1890) EA/91*
CLARK, Charles (d 1919 [64])
manager WWT/14*
CLARK, Charles Dow (d 1959
[89]) actor TW/15
CLARK, Charles William (1865-
1925) American singer WWA/1
CLARK, Cuthbert (1869-1953)
English musical director, com-
poser BE*
CLARK, D. (fl 1784?-94) violinist
BD
CLARK, Dane (b 1913) American
actor ES
CLARK, Dorothy L. English act-
ress, singer GRB/1
CLARK, Dort (b 1917) American
actor BE, TW/1, 3-8, 10-18,
26
CLARK, Edward (d 1789) singer,
organist BD
CLARK, Edward (d 1894 [62])
architect EA/95*
CLARK, Edwin A. (b 1871) Amer-
ican actor WWS
CLARK, E. Holman (1864-1925)
English actor DD, EA/96,

GRB/2-4, WWT/1-5

CLARK, Elsie (d 1966 [67])
performer BP/50*

CLARK, Ernest (b 1912) English actor AAS, TW/6, 11,
WWT/12-16

CLARK, Ethel Schneider (d
1964 [48]) actress BE*

CLARK, F. Donald (b 1913)
American educator BE

CLARK, Mrs. Frank Pierce
see Hughes, Lizzie

CLARK, Fred (1914-68) American actor BE, TW/13-16,
25, WWA/5, WWT/14

CLARK, Mrs. Fred (d 1909)
EA/10*

CLARK, Frederick (d 1916)
stage manager EA/17*

CLARK, Garner (d 1971 [56])
musician BP/56*

CLARK, Harry (d 1956 [45])
actor TW/12

CLARK, Henri (d 1905 [65])
music-hall comedian CDP

CLARK, Mrs. Henri (d 1881)
EA/82*

CLARK, Herbert F. (d 1920
[60]) dramatist WWT/14*

CLARK, Hugh (d 1653) English
actor DA, OC/1-3

CLARK, Israel see De Luré

CLARK, Jerman (d 1705)
dancing master BD

CLARK, Jerry American actor
TW/28

CLARK, John (fl 1793-1803)
scene painter BD

CLARK, John (fl 1794) violinist
BD

CLARK, Johnny (d 1967) performer BP/52*

CLARK, John Pepper (b 1935)
Nigerian dramatist CD

CLARK, John Richard (b 1932)
Australian director WWT/16

CLARK, John Sleeper see
Clarke, John Sleeper

CLARK, Johnson see Bryan,
Hal

CLARK, Joseph (d 1696?) posture
maker BD, CDP, DNB

CLARK, Kendall (b 1912) American actor BE, TW/3, 8,
10-16

CLARK, Lillian actress CDP

CLARK, Louise Hamilton (d
1900 [26]) comedienne EA/01*

CLARK [or Clarke], Marguerite
(1882/87-1940) American singer,
actress CB, ES, GRB/3-4,
SR, WWA/1, WWM, WWS,
WWT/1-6

CLARK, Marilyn American actress
TW/23

CLARK, Marjory (b 1900) English
actress WWT/7-10

CLARK, Norman (b 1887) American critic BE

CLARK, Oliver (b 1939) American
actor TW/23-27

CLARK, Peggy (b 1915) American
designer BE

CLARK, Phillip (b 1941) American
actor TW/23, 26

CLARK, Richard (b 1780) singer,
pianist, violinist BD

CLARK, Roger actor TW/1, 3, 5

CLARK, Rose Francis Langdon
(d 1962 [80]) performer BE*

CLARK, Rosie Amy (d 1897)
EA/98*

CLARK, Sill (fl 1600-41?) actor?
stage-attendant? DA

CLARK, Sylvia (d 1970) performer
BP/54*

CLARK, T. G. (d 1894) actor?
EA/95*

CLARK, Mrs. T. G. see Clark,
Mrs. C.

CLARK, Thomas (fl 1670-91?)
actor BD

"CLARK, Thornton" see Carson,
Murray

CLARK, T. Sealey (d 1909 [59])
publisher BE*, EA/10*, WWT/
14*

CLARK, Wallis (1888/89-1961)
English actor TW/2-3, 17,
WWT/7-11

CLARK, W. H. (c. 1863-1913)
Canadian singer SR

CLARK, William (fl 1784-88)
singer BD

CLARK, William (fl 1794) singer
BD

CLARK, William (1816-87) actor,
musician DD, NYM

CLARK, William (d 1899 [65])
EA/00*

CLARK, William (d 1909) showman
EA/10*

CLARK, William (d 1917) actor
EA/18*

CLARK, William George (1821-78)
English? scholar DNB

CLARK, William H. (d 1887
[71]) actor WWT/14*

CLARK, William T. (d 1925
[62]) actor BE*, BP/10*

CLARK, Willis Gaylord (1810-
41) American author CDP

CLARK, Wyndham (d 1872 [35])
Scottish singer EA/73*

CLARKE, Mr. (fl 1675) French?
dancer BD

CLARKE, Mr. (fl 1724-26)
dancer? BD

CLARKE, Mr. (fl 1726-28)
dancer BD

CLARKE, Mr. (fl 1729) singer
BD

CLARKE, Mr. (fl 1743) actor
BD

CLARKE, Mr. (fl 1760-62)
house servant BD

CLARKE, Mr. (fl 1765) singer
BD

CLARKE, Mr. (fl 1778-79)
actor BD

CLARKE, Mr. (fl 1786-90?)
actor BD

CLARKE, Mr. (fl 1793-95)
doorkeeper BD

CLARKE (fl 1797) actor BD

CLARKE, Mr. actor CDP

CLARKE, Mrs. (fl 1765) singer
BD

CLARKE, Mrs. (fl 1786) actress
BD

CLARKE, Mrs. [Mrs. W. S.
Forrest] (1831-52) actress
HAS

CLARKE, Mrs. (d 1879) EA/
81*

CLARKE, Master (fl 1781-83)
dancer BD

CLARKE, Miss (fl 1829) tight-
rope performer CDP

CLARKE, Miss (fl 1847)
actress HAS

CLARKE, A. (d 1889) manager
EA/90*

CLARKE, Adele (fl 1868)
actress HAS

CLARKE, Albert (d 1971 [73])
performer BP/55*

CLARKE, Albert H. (b 1851)
English actor GRB/1

CLARKE, Mrs. Albert H.
see Barley-Clarke, Marion

CLARKE, Alfred (d 1883)
scene artist EA/84*

CLARKE, Alfred Claude (d

1899 [48]) manager EA/00*

CLARKE, Algernon (b 1864) English musical director, composer
GRB/1

CLARKE, Annie M. (1845-1902)
American actress CDP, PP/1,
SR

CLARKE, Mrs. Asia Booth [Mrs.
John Sleeper Clarke] (1838-88)
writer DD

CLARKE, Austin (1896-1974) Irish
dramatist ES, MD

CLARKE, Bryan see Forbes,
Bryan

CLARKE, Burt G. (1847-1913)
actor SR

CLARKE, C. A. (fl 1875-94)
dramatist DD

CLARKE, Mrs. C. A. (d 1900
[66]) EA/01*

CLARKE, Sir Campbell (1835-
1902) dramatist DD, WWW/1

CLARKE, Celenia [Mrs. George
Clarke] (d 1901) EA/02*

CLARKE, Charles (d 1875 [55])
box book-keeper EA/76*

CLARKE, Charles A. (d 1876
[48]) manager EA/77*

CLARKE, Charles A. (d 1913)
EA/14*

CLARKE, Charles Cowden (1787-
1877) writer DD

CLARKE, Mrs. Charles Cowden
see Clarke, Mary Cowden

CLARKE, Conrad B. (d 1859)
actor HAS

CLARKE, Constantia (1825-53)
English actress HAS

CLARKE, Corson W. (1814-67)
American actor CDP, HAS

CLARKE, Creston (1865-1910)
American actor DD, GRB/3-4,
PP/1, WWA/1, WWS

CLARKE, Mrs. Creston see
Prince, Adelaide

CLARKE, Cuthbert (1869-1953)
English musical director, composer GRB/4, WWT/1-6

CLARKE, David (b 1908) American
actor BE, TW/26

CLARKE, Della [Mrs. J. F. Sulli-
van] (b 1878) American actress,
dramatist WWM

CLARKE, Eden (d 1869 [26])
comic singer EA/70*

CLARKE, Edward see Clarke,
Nathaniel

CLARKE, E. Holman see

Clark, E. Holman

CLARKE, Ellen (d 1903) EA/04*

CLARKE, Elsie (d 1917 [19]) actress EA/18*

CLARKE, Ernie [Tommy Dodd] (d 1898 [62]) comedian EA/99*

CLARKE, Eugene singer, singing teacher CDP

CLARKE, Fanny M. [Mrs. Charles Beveridge] (d 1890) EA/92*

CLARKE, Florence [Mrs. L. S. Dewar] (d 1890 [28]) EA/91*

CLARKE, Francis (d 1907 [31]) EA/08*

CLARKE, Frederick (fl 1851) actor HAS

CLARKE, Frederick see Victor, Frederick

CLARKE, Gage (1905-64) American actor TW/6-7, 21

CLARKE, George (1886-1946) English actor WWT/6-10

CLARKE, Mrs. George see Clarke, Celenia

CLARKE, George H. (1840-1906?) American actor CDP, DD, HAS, PP/1

CLARKE, George P. (1824-60) American actor HAS

CLARKE, George Somers (fl 1790) dramatist CP/3, DD

CLARKE, Gordon B. (1906-72) American actor TW/23, 28

CLARKE, Hamilton (1840-1912) composer, conductor DD

CLARKE, Harry Corson (d 1923 [62]) American comedian, agent WWS

CLARKE, Henry Savile (1841-93) dramatist, critic DD

CLARKE, Holman see Clark, E. Holman

CLARKE, Isaac (fl 1660-64) musician BD

CLARKE, James W. (d 1880 [40]) dancer EA/81*

CLARKE, Jeremiah (1673?-1707) English singer, organist, composer BD, DNB, ES

CLARKE, J. Hamilton see Clarke, Hamilton

CLARKE, J. I. C. see Clarke, Joseph Ignatius Constantine

CLARKE, J. L. (fl 1784?-1811?) musician BD

CLARKE, John (fl 1608) member of the Chapel Royal DA

CLARKE, John (fl 1671-1701) theatre keeper BD

CLARKE, [John?] (fl 1770-1836?) singer BD

CLARKE, John (d 1879 [c. 50]) actor DD, DNB, OAA/1-2

CLARKE, John (d 1974 [69]) performer BP/59*

CLARKE, Mrs. John see Furtado, Terese Elizabeth

CLARKE, John H. (1788-1838) English actor DD, HAS, SR

CLARKE, John H. (d 1910) actor? EA/11*

CLARKE, John Sleeper (1833-99) American actor, manager CDP, COC, DAB, DD, DNB, ES, HAS, OAA/1-2, OC/1-3, PP/1, SR, WWA/1

CLARKE, Mrs. John Sleeper see Clarke, Mrs. Asia Booth

CLARKE, John Woodruff (fl 1794-1800) actor BD

CLARKE, Joseph Ignatius Constantine (1846-1925) Irish/American dramatist DAB, GRB/3-4, WWA/1, WWM

CLARKE, Josiah (d 1907 [70]) EA/08*

CLARKE, Lydia (b 1923) American actress TW/6-8, 10-11

CLARKE, Mae (b 1907/10) American actress, dancer ES, WWT/8-9

CLARKE, Marcus Andrew Hislop (1846-81) English dramatist DNB, HP

CLARKE, Marion [Mrs. Fred Pollard] (d 1898 [32]) actress EA/99*

CLARKE, Marlande (d 1892 [34]) actor EA/93*

CLARKE, Mary [alias Wood] (fl 1603) actress? DA

CLARKE, Mary Anne (1776-1852) English actress? DNB

CLARKE, Mary Bayard Devereux (1827-86) American librettist WWA/H

CLARKE, Mary Victoria Cowden (1809-98) English scholar DD, DNB, HP

CLARKE, Matthew (d 1786) actor BD, CDP, DD

CLARKE, Nathaniel (1699-1783) actor, dancer BD

CLARKE, Mrs. [Nathaniel?] (fl 1727-47) actress, singer BD

CLARKE, N. B. [né Belden] (b 1810) American actor, stage manager, dramatist HAS, SR

CLARKE, Nigel (1895-1976) English actor WWT/10-12

CLARKE, Philip (b 1904) English actor TW/2

CLARKE, Richard (fl 1730-60?) violinist BD

CLARKE, Richard (fl 1889-95) singer, actor, dramatist DD

CLARKE, Richard (b 1933) English actor TW/24, 27

CLARKE, Robert (fl 1617-24) actor DA

CLARKE, Robert (1777-1853) dancer BD

CLARKE, Robert (fl 1844) acting manager CDP

CLARKE, Sir Rupert (1865-1926) manager WWT/1-5

CLARKE, Stephen (fl 1809) dramatist CP/3, DD

CLARKE, Thomas (fl 1572) actor DA

CLARKE, Thomas (d 1866 [24]) comedian HAS

CLARKE, Thomas [Tom Griffiths] (d 1904 [32]) comedian EA/05*

CLARKE, Walter (d 1903 [27]) circus performer EA/04*

CLARKE, Mrs. W. H. see Leatitia, Mme.

CLARKE, Wilfred (1867-1945) American actor DD, SR, WWM

CLARKE, William Hutchinson (b 1865) Canadian actor, singer WWS

CLARKE-JERVOISE, Lady Florence (d 1912) dramatist EA/13*

CLARKE-SMITH, Douglas A. (1888-1959) Scottish actor WWT/5-12

CLARKE-TRAVERS, Sarah Ada (d 1916) EA/17*

CLARKSON, Mr. (fl 1723-28) pit office keeper BD

CLARKSON, Mr. (fl 1750-65) actor BD, HAS

CLARKSON, Mr. (fl 1778) booth proprietor BD

CLARKSON, Mrs. (fl 1752-53) actress HAS

CLARKSON, George (d 1908) manager EA/09*

CLARKSON, Joan (b 1903) actress WWT/6-10

CLARKSON, John (b 1932) English actor TW/28-30

CLARKSON, Louisa see Wall, Mrs. Harry

CLARKSON, W. H. (d 1878 [58]) perruquier EA/79*

CLARKSON, William (1865-1934) English costumier, perruquier GRB/1, WWT/2-7

CLARY, Mr. (fl 1791-95) costume designer BD

CLARY, Mme. (fl 1757-58) dancer BD

CLARY, Robert [né Widerman] (b 1926) French actor, singer BE

CLARY, Roy (b 1939) Canadian actor TW/24

CLASON, Mr. (d 1830 [32]) actor HAS

CLATTEN, Lilian see Mayo, Margaret

"CLATTERBANE" (fl 1774) musician BD

CLAUDE, Mrs. [Miss Hogg] (fl 1798) American actress HAS

CLAUDE, Angelina (fl 1873-76) actress DD

CLAUDE, John (fl 1804) actor HAS

CLAUDEL, Paul (1868-1955) French dramatist COC, OC/1-3

CLAUGHTON, Susan English actress WWT/4-5

CLAUSEN, Constance (b 1925) American actress TW/9

CLAUSSEN, Johanna (b 1842) German actress HAS

CLAUSSEN, Joy (b 1938) American actress, singer BE

CLAUSSEN, Julia (1879-1941) Swedish singer CB, WWA/1

CLAVERDON, Jennie (d 1900) music-hall performer EA/01*

CLAVERING, Marie (b 1869) actress GRB/2

CLAVERING-WARDELL, Anna Maria [née Kelly] (d 1875) EA/76*

CLAWOOD, Robert (fl 1765)

musician BD

CLAWSON, Mrs. Isaac S. see
Holman, Mrs. Joseph George

CLAXTON, Mr. (fl 1703-07)
dancer BD

CLAXTON, Mr. (fl 1703-07)
dancer, composer BD

CLAXTON, Kate (1848-1924)
American actress CDP,
COC, DAB, DD, ES, OC/
1-3, PP/1, SR, WWA/1,
WWM

CLAXTON, Tom (d 1916) variety agent EA/18*

CLAY, Cecil (d 1920 [73])
dramatist BE*, WWT/14*

CLAY, Mrs. Cecil see
Vokes, Rosina

CLAY, Edwin (d 1908 [56])
EA/09*

CLAY, Frederick (1839-89)
French/English musician,
composer DD, DNB, ES

CLAY, Henry (fl 1624-26?)
actor DA

CLAY, Joseph (fl 1709-10)
musician BD

CLAY, Lila (d 1899) actress,
composer, director EA/00*

CLAY, Louise (b 1938) American actress TW/26, 29-30

CLAY, Nathaniel (fl 1618-29)
actor DA

CLAY, Samuel (fl 1784?-94)
singer? instrumentalist?
music copyist BD

CLAY, Tom [né Thomas
Lindsay Clay] (d 1892) song
& pantomime writer EA/93*

CLAY, William (fl 1784-94)
singer BD

CLAYBURGH, Alma (d 1958 [77])
singer TW/15

CLAYBURGH, Jill (b 1944)
American actress TW/25-
27, 29-30

CLAYDEN, Pauline (b 1922)
English dancer ES

CLAYSACK, S. (fl 1794) musician BD

CLAYTON, Master (fl 1763)
dancer BD

CLAYTON, Bessie (1870-1948)
American vaudevillian ES,
TW/5

CLAYTON, Dorine (d 1917 [4])
EA/18*

CLAYTON, Ella see Tannyhill,

Mrs. Francis A.

CLAYTON, Estelle (1867-1917)
American actress, dramatist
CDP, DD, SR

CLAYTON, Ethel (d 1966 [82])
American actress ES, TW/23

CLAYTON, Frank H. composer
CDP

CLAYTON, Harold (d 1971 [68])
producer, director BP/56*

CLAYTON, Hazel [Mrs. Mack
Hilliard] (d 1963 [77]) actress
BE*

CLAYTON, Herbert (1876-1931)
English actor, singer, producer,
manager GRB/1-4, WWT/5-6

CLAYTON, Jan (b 1917) American
actress, singer BE, TW/1-2,
12-16, 29

CLAYTON, John (fl 1762-78) scene
painter BD

CLAYTON, John [John Alfred Clayton Calthrop] (1845-88) English
actor CDP, COC, DD, DNB,
ES, OAA/1-2

CLAYTON, Mrs. John see
Boucicault, Eva

CLAYTON, Lou (d 1950 [63])
actor, manager TW/7

CLAYTON, Thomas (1673-1725?)
English composer, impresario,
violinist? BD, CP/1, DD,
DNB, ES

CLAYTON, Una (d 1968 [92])
actress WWS

CLAYTON, William (c. 1636-97)
instrumentalist, singer BD

CLAYTON, William (d 1867 [21])
musician EA/68*

CLAYTONE, Richard (fl 1623)
actor DA

CLEAR, Richard (fl 1659-62)
carver BD

CLEARY, Mr. (fl 1811) actor HAS

CLEARY, Edwin (d 1922 [64])
actor, manager, journalist
WWT/14*

CLEARY, Maurice G. (d 1973
[78]) actors' business manager
BP/57*

CLEARY, Peggy (d 1972 [80]) performer BP/56*

CLEATER, Mrs. (fl 1745-65)
dresser BD

CLEATHER, Gordon (b 1872)
Italian/English actor, singer
GRB/3-4, WWT/1-5

CLEAVE, Arthur (b 1884) English

actor WWT/4-5
CLEAVELY [or Clevly], Price
(fl 1732) singer BD
CLEETER, Mr. (fl 1708) bill
carrier BD
CLEGG, Miss see Davis, Mrs.
CLEGG, Charles Albert (d 1893
[29]) actor? EA/94*
CLEGG, John (1714-50?) Irish
violinist BD, DNB
CLEGG, Joseph (d 1880 [35])
actor? EA/81*
CLEGG, Marie [Mrs. Hodgkin-
son] (d 1893 [34]) actress?
EA/94*
CLEGG, Sarah (d 1890 [54])
actress? EA/91*
CLEGG, Tom (d 1897 [48]) Negro
comedian EA/98*
CLEGG, William (fl 1784?-94) singer,
actor? BD
CLEGHORN, William see
Yates, George
CLEIN, Ed (b 1944) American
actor TW/25-26
CLELAND, Miss [Miss Buttery]
(b 1762) actress BD, TD/2
CLELAND, John (1709-89) Eng-
lish dramatist CP/1-3, DD,
DNB
CLEMENS, Henry Cameron (d
1932 [66]) actor SR
CLEMENS, Le Roy (b 1889)
American dramatist WWT/
6-9
CLEMENT, Clay (1863-1910)
American actor, dramatist
WWA/1
CLEMENT, Clay (1888/89-1956)
American actor SR, TW/
13, WWT/6-7
CLEMENT, Donald (d 1970 [29])
American actor TW/26-27
CLEMENT, Dora actress TW/1
CLEMENT, Edmond (1871-1928)
French singer WWA/1, WWM
CLEMENT, Elfrida English actress
GRB/1-4, WWT/1-2
CLEMENT, Frank (d 1937)
critic BE*, WWT/14*
CLEMENT, Franz (1780-1842)
Austrian violinist, composer,
conductor BD
CLEMENT, John (fl 1660-88?)
singer, therbo player BD
CLEMENT, John Maurice (d
1912 [71]) proprietor EA/13*

CLEMENT, Tom Henri (d 1872)
skater, singer EA/73*
CLEMENT, William (fl 1550)
actor DA
CLEMENTI, Sig. (fl 1739) singer
BD
CLEMENTI, Muzio (1752-1832)
Italian musician, composer,
conductor BD
CLEMENTINA, Sobieska (fl 1772)
equestrienne BD
CLEMENTINE, Sig. (fl 1699)
singer BD
CLEMENTS, Arthur (fl 1876-84)
dramatist DD
CLEMENTS, Charles see Rix,
John
CLEMENTS, Colin (1894-1948)
American dramatist SR, TW/
4, WWA/2
CLEMENTS, Dudley (d 1947 [58])
actor TW/4
CLEMENTS, Florence Ryerson (d
1965 [70]) dramatist BP/50*
CLEMENTS, Frank (1844-86?)
Scottish actor OAA/1-2
CLEMENTS, Harry (d 1970) musi-
cian BP/55*
CLEMENTS, H. C. (b 1880) Eng-
lish manager GRB/1
CLEMENTS, Sir John Selby (b
1910) English actor, manager,
producer AAS, COC, ES,
PDT, WWT/9-16
CLEMENTS, Larry (d 1916) EA/
17*
CLEMENTS, Miriam actress GRB/
3-4, WWT/1-6
CLEMENTS, Neva West (d 1965)
performer BP/50*
CLEMENTS, William (d 1906)
fireman EA/07*
CLEMENT-SCOTT, Joan (1907-69)
English actress WWT/5-7
CLEMMENTS, George (d 1907
[67]) circus musical director
EA/08*
CLEMSON, Charles (d 1909 [41])
variety performer? EA/10*
CLENDINING, Miss (fl 1798)
actress BD
CLENDINING, Mrs. William [née
Elizabeth Arnold] (1768-99)
English actress, singer BD,
TD/1-2
CLENDON, Elizabeth see
Baker, Mrs. David Lionel

Erskine

"CLEO" see Blackburn, John

CLERC, Elise (d 1925) dancer WWT/14*

CLERICI, Roberto (fl 1711-48) scene painter BD

CLERICUS, Joseph see Clark, Joseph

CLERK, Mr. (fl 1784) singer BD

CLERKE, Shadwell see Hamund, St. John

CLERKE, William (fl 1662-63) actor, dramatist CP/3, DD

CLERKE, William (d 1663) musician BD

CLEUGH, Dennis (b 1881) actor GRB/1

CLEVA, Fausto (1902-71) Italian conductor WWA/5

CLEVELAND, Mr. (fl 1728) dancer BD

CLEVELAND, Mr. (fl 1796) actor HAS

CLEVELAND, Mrs. (fl 1796) actress HAS

CLEVELAND, Miss see Stirling, Mrs. Arthur

CLEVELAND, Anna (fl 1900s) American actress WWM

CLEVELAND, Charles Edward (1864-1914) minstrel, circus manager, agent SR

CLEVELAND, George (d 1957 [71]) actor BE*

CLEVELAND, Jean (b 1903) American actress TW/2

CLEVELAND, Louie (d 1899) actress EA/00*

CLEVELAND, Thomas (fl 1792-99) actor BD

CLEVERE, Amy singer CDP

CLEVERMAN, M. (d 1875 [45]) conjuror EA/76*

CLEVLY, Price see Cleavely, Price

CLEWES, Winston (1906-57) dramatist WWW/5

CLEWLOW, F. D. (d 1957 [72]) director BE*, WWT/14*

CLEY, Henry see Clay, Henry

CLEZY, Cool (d 1893) comedian EA/94*

CLIBURN, Mrs. J. F. see Ware, Irene

CLIFF, Laddie (1891/92-1937) English actor, manager, dancer ES, SR, WWM,

WWT/4-8

CLIFF, Oliver (b 1918) American actor TW/2-8

CLIFFE, Alice Belmore see Belmore, Alice

CLIFFE, H. Cooper (1862-1939) English actor DD, EA/97, GRB/2-4, WWS, WWT/1-8

CLIFFORD, Mr. (fl 1781-94?) actor BD

CLIFFORD, Mr. (fl 1792-93) singer BD

CLIFFORD, Mr. (fl 1796) actor BD

CLIFFORD, Mr. (fl 1799) manager BD

CLIFFORD, Mrs. [née Robins; Mrs. George Sims] (fl 1779-1809?) actress BD

CLIFFORD, Mrs. (fl 1799) actress BD

CLIFFORD, Mrs. see Price, Mrs.

CLIFFORD, Lady see De La Pasture, Mrs. Henry

CLIFFORD, Miss see Harrison, Mrs.

CLIFFORD, B. (d 1884) actor EA/85*

CLIFFORD, Bessie (d 1967) performer BP/51*

CLIFFORD, Billy "Single" (1869-1930) American minstrel, circus performer SR

CLIFFORD, Camille [Hon. Mrs. Lyndhurst Henry Bruce] Danish/American actress GRB/1, 3-4, WWT/1-6

CLIFFORD, Charles (d 1908 [39]) actor GRB/4*

CLIFFORD, Charles [Sir Charles William Woolfe Clifton-Browne] (1867-1943) English actor, manager GRB/1

CLIFFORD, Mrs. Charles (d 1877) actress EA/78*

CLIFFORD, Miss E. [Mrs. Talbot] (d 1891) actress EA/92*

CLIFFORD, Ed (1845-95) American actor SR

CLIFFORD, Edmund see Junot, W. E. D.

CLIFFORD, Edwin (fl 1867-76) English actor OAA/1-2

CLIFFORD, Elizabeth [Miss McGinty] (d 1889) actress, ballet mistress EA/90*

CLIFFORD, Ellen actress CDP

CLIFFORD, Frank see Watts, Francis Walter
CLIFFORD, Gervan (d 1886) actor EA/87*
CLIFFORD, Gordon (d 1968 [65]) composer BP/53*
CLIFFORD, Harry (d 1897 [65]) actor CDP
CLIFFORD, Harry singer CDP
CLIFFORD, Henry see Bland, Harry
CLIFFORD, Mrs. Henry Marston see Clifford, Rose
CLIFFORD, Herbert (d 1874) actor? EA/76*
CLIFFORD, Jack (d 1956 [76]) dancer, actor TW/13
CLIFFORD, John (b 1947) American dancer, choreographer CB
CLIFFORD, Kathleen (1887-1962) American actress, singer TW/19, WWT/4-6
CLIFFORD, Margaret Ellen (1908-71) American director, actress, educator BE
CLIFFORD, Maria (1794?-1850) actress CDP
CLIFFORD, Marie [Mrs. R. J. Seaton] (d 1906) entertainer EA/07*
CLIFFORD, Martin (fl 1671-77) writer DD
CLIFFORD, Nat singer, composer CDP
CLIFFORD, Rose [Mrs. Henry Marston Clifford] (d 1909) EA/10*
CLIFFORD, Thomas E. singer CDP
CLIFFORD, Mrs. William (1791-1850) English actress DD
CLIFFORD, Mrs. W. K. (d 1929) dramatist DD, GRB/3-4, WWM, WWT/1-5, WWW/3
CLIFT, Ernest Paul (1881-1963) English manager, dramatist WWT/4-13
CLIFT, Montgomery (1920-66) American actor BE, CB, ES, TW/1-7, 10-13, 23, WWA/4, WWT/10-11
CLIFTON, Mr. (fl 1852) actor HAS
CLIFTON, Ada (fl 1855-67) English actress CDP, HAS

CLIFTON, Augusta (d 1882 [55]) actress EA/83*
CLIFTON, Bernard (1902-70) actor, singer WWT/10-14
CLIFTON, Elmer (d 1949 [59]) actor, director BE*
CLIFTON, Mrs. Ernest see Adams, Isabel
CLIFTON, Ethel [Mrs. Herbert Ralland] (d 1897) actress EA/98*
CLIFTON, Fanny see Stirling, Mrs.
CLIFTON, Frederic (b 1844) actor OAA/1-2
CLIFTON, George (d 1876 [35]) comic singer EA/77*
CLIFTON, Harriett (d 1910 [63]) actress EA/11*, WWT/14*
CLIFTON, Harry (1832-72) English music-hall performer CDP, OC/1-3
CLIFTON, Howard singer, composer CDP
CLIFTON, John (d 1880 [40]) actor EA/81*
CLIFTON, Joseph [né Dilks] (b 1858) American dramatist, actor SR
CLIFTON, Josephine [née Miller; Mrs. Robert Place] (1813-47) American actress CDP, DAB, ES, HAS, SR, WWA/H
CLIFTON, Lina [Miss P. Weldon] (d 1890 [27]) American singer EA/91*
CLIFTON, Marion P. (1833-1917) English actress SR
CLIFTON, Thomas (fl 1600) actor DA
CLIFTON, W. (d 1875) stage manager EA/76*
CLIFTON, William Rumball (d 1877) actor, stage manager EA/79*
CLIFTON-BROWNE, Sir Charles William Woolfe see Clifford, Charles
CLIMENHAGA, Joel Ray (b 1922) South African educator BE
CLINCH, Mr. (c. 1663-1734) imitator BD
CLINCH, Charles Powell (1797-1880) American dramatist CDP, EAP, RJ, WWA/H
CLINCH, Herbert (fl 1697) musician BD
CLINCH, J. H. (d 1916) EA/17*

CLINCH, Lawrence (d 1812)
Irish actor BD, CDP, DD,
TD/1-2
CLINE, Andre (fl 1828-62)
English tight-rope dancer
HAS
CLINE, John (d 1886) tight-rope
performer CDP
CLINE, Maggie (1857-1934)
American actress, singer
CDP, NTH, SR
CLINE, Rose see Merryfield,
Rose
CLINE, Thomas S. (fl 1835)
English actor HAS
CLINETOP, Lucie (b 1849)
American dancer CDP, HAS
CLINETOP, Sallie (b 1851)
American dancer CDP, HAS
CLINFORD, Mr. (fl 1792) actor
BD
CLINGO, Mr. (fl 1759-63) pit
doorkeeper BD
CLINTON, Mr. [né Hamblin]
(fl 1856) actor HAS
CLINTON, Master (fl 1763-65)
dancer BD
CLINTON, Arthur (d 1869)
prompter EA/70*
CLINTON, Dudley [Ernest Gil-
lame] (1868-1908) English
actor GRB/4
CLINTON, Edward (b 1948)
American actor TW/26
CLINTON, Ella [Mrs. Frances
H. France] (d 1898) actress
EA/99*
CLINTON, Henry see Gilligan,
Joseph
CLINTON, James (d 1897 [43])
musician EA/98*
CLINTON, J. W. (d 1880)
actor EA/81*
CLINTON, Kate (d 1935) actress
BE*, WWT/14*
CLINTON, Kitty CDP
CLINTON-BADDELEY, Constance
(d 1901) EA/02*
CLINTON-BADDELEY, Victor
Clinton (1900-70) English
actor ES
CLITHEROE, Jimmy (d 1973
[50s] performer BP/58*
CLITHEROW, Benjamin (fl c.
1740-74) pyrotechnist BD
CLITHEROW, W. F. (b 1848)
English actor GRB/1-2
CLIUTMAS, Harry F. (d 1964

[83]) performer BE*
CLIVE, Colin (1900-37) French/
English actor ES, SR, WWT/
6-8
CLIVE, David J. (b 1923) Ameri-
can stage manager, producer,
director BE
CLIVE, Edward E. (1876-1940)
English actor, producer CB,
SR
CLIVE, Franklin (d 1924) singer
WWT/14*
CLIVE, F. Wybert [Frederic W.
Maclachlan] (b 1879) English
dramatist, actor GRB/1-2
CLIVE, Mrs. George see
Clive, Kitty
CLIVE, Kitty [née Catherine
Raftor; Mrs. George Clive]
(1711-85) English actress,
singer BD, CDP, COC, CP/
1-3, DD, DNB, ES, GT, HP,
OC/1-3, TD/1-2
CLIVE, Vincent (d 1943) English
actor WWT/1-7
CLIVE, Wybert (d 1892 [32])
actor, dramatist EA/93*
CLODOCHE, Mons. (fl 1869)
dancer CDP
CLOFULLIA, Josephine [née
Rebecca Westgate] (1824-80)
bearded lady CDP
CLOGG, Hallye (d 1965 [86])
chorus girl TW/22
CLOSE, Elizabeth (d 1869) EA/
70*
CLOSE, Ivy (d 1968 [78]) perform-
er BP/53*
CLOSE, W. R. (d 1875 [39])
lessee EA/76*
CLOSS, William F. (d 1908)
musical director EA/09*
CLOSSER, Louise see Hale,
Louise
CLOSSON, Mr. (fl 1738-55) actor,
dancer, animal imitator BD
CLOSSON, Mlle. (fl 1740) dancer
BD
CLOTHIER, Devereux (fl 1662-99)
drummer BD
CLOTHIER, John (d 1753) drum-
mer BD
CLOUGH, Mrs. (fl 1670-73) act-
ress BD
CLOUGH, Miss (fl 1748) actress
BD
CLOUGH, Thomas (d 1770) actor
BD, CDP

CLOVELLY, Cecil (d 1965 [74])
English actor TW/21
CLOW, William E. , II (d 1970
[40]) production assistant
BP/54*
CLOWES, Louisa Jane (d 1884)
marionettist? EA/86*
CLOWES, Richard (b 1900)
English representative, mana-
ger WWT/8, 10
CLOZEL, Mlle. (fl 1828) act-
ress? HAS
CLUBLEY, John Sherwood (d
1964) actor, director BE*
CLUCAS, Charles (d 1905 [39])
manager GRB/1
CLUCHEY, Rich (b 1933) Amer-
ican dramatist, director,
actor CD
CLUN, Walter (d 1664) actor
BD, DA, DD
CLUNES, Alec S. (1912-70)
English actor AAS, COC,
ES, WWT/9-14, WWW/6
CLURMAN, Edith (d 1973 [55])
dancer BP/57*
CLURMAN, Harold Edgar (b
1901) American director,
manager, critic AAS, BE,
CB, COC, ES, OC/3, PDT,
TW/2-8, WWT/10-16
CLUTSAM, George H. (1866-
1951) Australian composer
ES, WWW/5
CLYDE, Amy [Mrs. J. Dobson
Clyde] (d 1917) EA/18*
CLYDE, Mrs. J. Dobson see
Clyde, Amy
CLYDE, Jean (d 1962 [73])
actress BE*, WWT/14*
CLYDE, Jeremy (b 1941) Eng-
lish actor TW/27
CLYDE, John (d 1917) EA/18*
CLYDE, June (b 1909) American
actress WWT/8-11
CLYNDES, J. H. (d 1927 [86])
actor DD
CO, Ja. (fl 17th cent?) drama-
tist FGF
COAD, Emily (fl 1839-51)
English singer CDP
COAD, Harry (1825-87) actor
NYM
COAD, Oral Sumner (b 1887)
American historian, educator
ES
COAKLEY, Marion actress
WWT/7

COAN, Caryll [Crickett] American
actress TW/28, 30
COAN, John (1728-64) English
dwarf BD
COAN, Sherwood A. see Camp-
bell, S. C.
COATES, Mr. (fl 1793-1803)
doorkeeper BD
COATES, Mr. (fl 1799) proprietor
BD
COATES, Mrs. (fl 1797-1822?)
singer, actress BD
COATES, Albert (1882-1953)
Russian/English composer,
conductor ES, WWW/5
COATES, Arthur see Coates,
Fred
COATES, Carolyn (b 1930) Ameri-
can actress TW/22-28, WWT/
15-16
COATES, Edith (b 1908) English
singer ES
COATES, Elizabeth (fl 1788?-
1830) actress BD
COATES, Emma Anne [Mrs.
Robert Coates] (fl c. 1830?)
CDP
COATES, Fred [Arthur Coates]
(b 1867) English actor GRB/1
COATES, Mrs. James S. (d 1875
[28]) EA/76*
COATES, John (1865-1941) English
actor, singer CB, DD, EA/96
COATES, Robert ["Romeo"] (1772-
1848) English actor CDP, COC,
DD, DNB, OC/1-3
COATES, Mrs. Robert see
Coates, Emma Anne
COATES, Mrs. W. H. (d 1870
[65]) actress EA/71*
COATS, Mrs. (fl 1796) actress
TD/1-2
COATS, Miss (fl 1779-80) singer
BD
COBB, Charles Edward see
Ross, Charles
COBB, Edmund (d 1974 [82]) per-
former BP/59*
COBB, George (d 1877 [90]) pro-
prietor EA/79*
COBB, Gerard Francis (d 1904)
composer EA/05*
COBB, Gladys (b 1892) English
costumier ES
COBB, Irvin S. (1876/77-1944)
American actor, dramatist
CB, SR, WWM
COBB, James (d 1697) singer,

composer BD

COBB, James (1756-1818)
dramatist CDP, CP/2-3,
DD, DNB, ES, GT, TD/1-2

COBB, John S. (d 1969 [37])
producer, director BP/53*

COBB, Lee J. (1911-76)
American actor AAS, BE,
ES, TW/5, 25-26, WWT/
10-13

COBB, Richard see Temple,
Richard

COBB, Tiger (d 1965) performer
BP/49*

COBBE, John (d 1891) acting
manager EA/92*

COBHAM, Mr. (fl 1769) performer? BD

COBHAM, Charles (1774-1819)
English violinist, violist BD

COBHAM, Thomas (1779/86-
1842) English actor CDP,
DD, DNB, OX

COBORN, Mr. (d 1886 [87])
EA/88*

COBORN, Mrs. (d 1905 [93])
EA/06*

COBORN, Charles [Colin Whitton
McCallum] (1852-1945) Eng-
lish actor, singer, librettist
CDP, COC, ES, GRB/1-3,
OC/1-3

COBORNE, Edward (fl 1616)
actor DA

COBRA, Frederic Walter (d
1886 [25]) acrobat EA/87*

COBURN, Mrs. Charles D.
see Coburn, Ivah

COBURN, Charles Douville
(1877-1961) American actor,
manager CB, COC, ES,
NTH, OC/1-3, SR, TW/1,
3, 5-7, 18, WWA/4, WWM,
WWT/4-13

COBURN, Ivah [Ivah Wills]
(1882-1937) American act-
ress, manager NTH, OC/
1-3, WWM

COBURN, Joan actress TW/11

COBURN, John Arthur (1869-
1943) minstrel SR

COCA, Imogene (b 1908/09)
American actress BE,
CB, ES, TW/2-3, 5-7, 30,
WWT/15-16

COCCHI, Gioacchino (1715-
1804) Italian composer,
musical director, conductor BD

"COCHININO, Sig. " (fl 1754)
musician BD

COCHOIS, Francis H. (fl 1734-35)
dancer, actor BD

COCHOIS, Michel (fl 1719-35)
actor BD

COCHOIS, Mme. Michel [née
Moylin] (fl 1719-35) actress
BD

COCHOY, Michel see Cochois,
Michel

COCHRAN, Sir Charles Blake
(1873-1951) English manager,
agent AAS, CB, COC, DNB,
ES, GRB/1-2, NTH, OC/1-3,
PDT, TW/7, WWT/2-11,
WWW/5

COCHRAN, Eddie (d 1975) performer BP/60*

COCHRAN, Mrs. Howard see
Jenoure, Aida

COCHRAN, Steve (1917-65) American actor, director, producer
BE, ES, TW/22

COCHRANE, Frank (1882-1962)
English actor WWT/4-11

COCHRANE, George (d 1917)
EA/18*

COCHRANE, Howard (b 1873)
English actor GRB/2

COCHRANE, Jeanetta (b 1883)
English costumier ES

COCHRANE, June (d 1967 [64])
actress TW/24

COCK, J. Lamborn (d 1891 [82])
publisher, treasurer EA/92*

COCKAIN, Sir Aston see
Cokayne, Sir Aston

COCKBURN, Mr. (fl 1784-85)
actor BD

COCKBURN, Catharine [née Trot-
ter] (1679-1749) English dramatist CP/1-3, DD, DNB, GT,
TD/1-2

COCKBURN, George W. (b 1869)
English actor GRB/1

COCKBURN, John M. (d 1964
[66]) critic BE*, BP/49*

COCKBURN, Mrs. Peter see
Dyer, Lizzie

COCKERILLE, Lili American
actress TW/29

COCKETTES, The theatre collective CD

COCKING, Robert (d 1837) aeronaut CDP

COCKINGS, George (d 1802) English dramatist CP/2-3, DNB,

EAP, GT
COCKLIN, Mr. (fl 1764-65)
  violinist BD
COCKRAM, Master (d 1878)
  musician EA/79*
COCKRAM, William Edward
  [Leigh Wilson] (d 1870 [34])
  singer EA/71*
COCKRILL, H. B. see Brad-
  ley, Harry C.
COCKRILL, Helen (d 1880)
  EA/81*
COCKSHUTT, Stanislaus (d
  1969 [66]) performer BP/
  55*
COCKYE, Miss (fl 1685-91)
  actress BD
COCO [Thomas Cox] (d 1899)
  music-hall performer EA/
  01*
COCO, Antony (fl 1796) acro-
  bat? BD
COCO, Concetto (fl 1796-97)
  posture maker BD
COCO, James (b 1929/30)
  American actor CB, TW/
  22-27, WWT/15-16
COCROFT, Thoda (1893-1943)
  American actress, agent
  SR
COCTEAU, Jean Maurice (1889-
  1963) French dramatist COC
CODBOLT, Lightfoot (fl 1607)
  actor DA
CODBOLT, Thomas (fl 1607)
  actor DA
CODE, Grant (1896-1974)
  American actor, dramatist
  TW/28
CODE, Reginald F. (d 1975
  [78]) producer/director/
  choreographer BP/60*
CODECASA, Mme. Giovanni
  (d 1869) singer EA/70*
CODESACA, Mme. [Saporiti]
  (d 1870 [101]) singer EA/
  71*
"CODGERINO, Sig. " (fl 1752)
  dancer BD
"CODGERINO, Signora" (fl 1752)
  dancer BD
CODMAN, Louie (d 1947 [84])
  actress WWT/14*
CODONA, W. (d 1873 [27])
  circus performer EA/74*
CODRINGTON, Ann (b 1895)
  Indian/English actress
  WWT/9-13

CODRINGTON, Robert (1601-65?)
  English dramatist CP/1-3, DD
CODRON, Michael (b 1930) Eng-
  lish manager, producer WWT/
  13-16
CODY, Ethel (d 1957 [62]) Ameri-
  can actress, singer TW/14
CODY, Frank (d 1917) EA/18*
CODY, Lew (1887-1934) American
  actor ES
CODY, William Frederick (1846-
  1917) American showman CDP,
  DAB, ES, HP, HJD, NTH,
  OC/1-3, SR
COE, Mr. (fl 1719-23) pit office
  keeper BD
COE, Mr. (fl 1855-64) actor DD
COE, Fred H. (b 1914) American
  producer, director BE, CB,
  WWT/15-16
COE, Isabelle (d 1919) actress
  SR
COE, John (b 1925) American
  actor TW/24-26, 28-29
COE, Peter (b 1929) English direc-
  tor AAS, BE, WWT/14-16
COE, Richard L. (b 1916) Ameri-
  can critic BE
COE, Thomas (d 1886) actor,
  stage manager EA/87*
COERNE, Louis Adolphe (1870-
  1922) American composer DAB,
  ES
COFFEE, Andrew J. (d 1975 [74])
  performer BP/60*
COFFEE, Lenore J. (b 1895)
  American dramatist ES
COFFEY, Charles (d 1745) Irish
  dramatist CP/1-3, DD, DNB,
  ES, GT, TD/1-2
COFFEY, Denise (b 1936) English
  actress WWT/15-16
COFFIELD, Peter (b 1945) Ameri-
  can actor TW/25-29
COFFIN, C. Hayden (1862-1935)
  English actor, singer CDP,
  DD, DP, ES, GRB/1-4, WWT/
  1-7, WWW/3
COFFIN, Emily (fl 1887-92)
  dramatist DD
COFFIN, Francis (fl 1595-1602)
  actor DA
COFFIN, Frederick (b 1943)
  American actor TW/27-30
COGAN, David J. (b 1923) Amer-
  ican producer, theatre owner,
  representative BE
COGAN, Jane [Mrs. William R.

Cogan] (d 1886) EA/87*

COGAN, John (d c. 1673) actor BD

COGAN, Mrs. William R. see Cogan, Jane

COGERT, Jed (d 1961 [80]) actor BE*

COGGIN, Barbara American actress TW/28, 30

COGHILL, Nevill Henry Kendal Aylmer (b 1899) Irish producer, director, adapter CD, COC, WWT/15-16

COGHLAN, Charles F. (1842-99) English actor CDP, DD, ES, NTH, OAA/2, OC/1-3, PP/1, SR, WWA/1

COGHLAN, Charles F. (d 1972 [25]) director? choreographer? BP/56*

COGHLAN, Eily (d 1900) actress EA/01*, WWT/14*

COGHLAN, Gertrude [Mrs. Augustus Pitou, Jr.] (1879-1952) English actress GRB/2-4, TW/9, WWS, WWT/1-6

COGHLAN, Lewis (d 1888 [30]) actor EA/89*

COGHLAN, Rosalind (d 1937 [51]) American actress WWM

COGHLAN, Rose (1851?-1932) English actress CDP, COC, DAB, DD, GRB/2-4, NTH, OAA/2, OC/1-3, PP/1, SR, WWA/1, WWM, WWS, WWT/1-6

COGILL, Charles W. (d 1903 [53]) actor, dancer CDP

COGILL, Harry (d 1903) minstrel EA/04*

COGNIARD, Hippolyte (d 1882 [74]) dramatist, director EA/83*

COHAN, Cal (1859-1944) minstrel SR

COHAN, George Michael (1878-1942) American actor, dramatist, composer, manager AAS, CB, COC, DAB, ES, GRB/2-4, HJD, MD, MH, MWD, NTH, OC/1-3, PDT, SR, WWA/1, WWM, WWS, WWT/1-9, WWW/4

COHAN, Mrs. George Michael (d 1972 [89]) dancer BP/57*

COHAN, Georgette (b 1900) American actress SR, WWT/4-7

COHAN, Helen Frances Costigan (1854-1928) actress BE*, BP/13*, WWT/14*

COHAN, Henry (d 1975 [75]) manager, agent BP/59*

COHAN, Jere J. (1848-1917) American actor SR

COHAN, Josephine (1876-1916) American performer BE*, WWT/14*

COHAN, Robert (b 1929) American dancer TW/13

COHAN, Timothy (1846-1914) Irish actor SR

COHAN, William (d 1976 [66]) producer/director/choreographer BP/60*

COHEN, Mr. (fl 1770) musician BD

COHEN, Abe (d 1974 [76]) company manager BP/58*

COHEN, Al (b 1939) American actor TW/25-26

COHEN, Alexander (b 1920) American producer AAS, BE, CB, WWT/14-16

COHEN, Alfred J. see Dale, Alan

COHEN, Angelina (d 1893) EA/94*

COHEN, Betty see Comden, Betty

COHEN, Frederick (1904-67) German/American director, composer, actor, musical director, producer, educator BE, TW/23

COHEN, Gustave (1879-1958) French scholar COC, OC/1-3

COHEN, Harold (d 1969 [63]) critic BP/54*

COHEN, Harry I. (b 1891) New Zealand manager WWT/6

COHEN, Isaac (d 1910 [77]) manager, producer EA/11*, WWT/14*

COHEN, Mrs. Isaac see Harrison, Fanny

COHEN, Katie (d 1946 [82]) actress BE*, WWT/14*

COHEN, Kip (b 1940) American casting director, production associate BE

COHEN, Mrs. Leopold see Cavendish, Rose

COHEN, Margery (b 1947) American actress TW/26-30

COHEN, Martin B. (b 1923)
American producer, director
BE

COHEN, Max (d 1968) manager
BP/52*

COHEN, Max A. (d 1971 [75])
theatre owner BP/56*

COHEN, Morris (d 1973 [66])
performer BP/57*

COHEN, Nathan (1923-71)
Australian critic BE

COHEN, Octavus Roy (1891-
1959) American dramatist
BE*, BP/43*

COHEN, Sammy (b 1902) American actor ES

COHEN, Sara B. (d 1963 [82])
performer BE*

COHEN, Selma Jeanne (b 1920)
American writer, editor BE

COHEN, Sidney I. (d 1973 [64])
consultant BP/58*

COHN, Harry (1891-1958) performer, producer BE*

COHN, Janet American literary
representative BE

COINDE, Mr. (fl 1788-89)
ballet master BD

COIT, Dorothy (b 1889) American dramatist, educator
ES

COKAIN, Sir Aston see
Cokayne, Sir Aston

COKAYNE, Sir Aston (1608-84)
English poet CDP, CP/1-3,
DD, FGF

COKAYNE, Mary (fl 1753-75)
actress BD

COKE, Mr. (fl 1784) singer
BD

COKE, Peter (b 1913) English
actor, dramatist WWT/9-15

COKE, Richard (fl 1547-56)
actor DA

COKE, Richard (d 1955 [63])
actor BE*, WWT/14*

COKER, Mr. (fl 1715-21) actor
BD

COKER, Mr. (fl 1733) dancer
BD

COKER, Mrs. (fl 1731-39)
actress BD

COKER, Master Richard CDP

COLAS, Stella (d 1913 [65])
French actress CDP, DD

COLBERT, Claudette [née Lily
Chauchoin] (b 1905/07)
French actress AAS, BE,

CB, ES, SR, TW/14, 16, 20,
30, WWT/6-16

COLBIN, Rod (b 1923) American
actor, fencing master BE

COLBORNE, John (fl 1775-84)
boxkeeper BD

COLBOURNE, Maurice (1894-1965)
English actor, manager WWT/
7-14

COLBRAN, Isabella (1785-1845)
Spanish singer ES

COLBRAND, Edward (fl 1610-13)
actor DA

COLBRON, Grace Isabel (d 1943)
American dramatist GRB/3-4,
WWT/1

COLBY, Barbara (1940-75) American actress TW/22, 28

COLBY, Ethel [née Duckman] (b
1908) American actress, singer,
critic BE, NTH

COLBY, Marion (b 1923) American
actress TW/3

COLBY, Sidney J. (d 1970 [42])
manager BP/55*

COLCHESTER, Enrique (d 1896)
proprietor EA/97*

COLCLOUGH, Mr. musician CDP

COLE, Mr. (d 1730) harpsichordist
BD

COLE, Mr. (fl 1749) house servant? BD

COLE, Mr. (fl 1760-61) billsticker
BD

COLE, Mr. (fl 1761) dresser BD

COLE, Mr. (fl 1784) violinist BD

COLE, Mr. (fl 1785?-94) violist
BD

COLE, Mr. (fl 1795-99) boxkeeper
BD

COLE, Mrs. (fl 1696) actress BD

COLE, Mrs. (fl 1838) actress
HAS

COLE, Miss (b 1729) English actress, dancer, singer BD

COLE, Alonzo Deen (d 1971 [74])
producer, director BP/55*

COLE, Belle (d 1905 [60]) American singer CDP, GRB/1

COLE, Blanche (d 1888) singer,
actress CDP, DD

COLE, Bob (1869-1912) librettist,
lyricist BE*

COLE, Brian (d 1972 [28]) musician BP/57*

COLE, Charles H. (d 1916) EA/
17*

COLE, David (b 1936) English

actor TW/13

COLE, Dennis (b 1943) American actor TW/28

COLE, E. D. (fl 1707-41) actor, dancer, prompter BD

COLE, Eddie (d 1969 [59]) performer BP/55*

COLE, Edith (1870-1927) actress WWT/2-5

COLE, Edward C. (b 1904) American educator BE

COLE, Elizabeth see Ashley, Elizabeth

COLE, George (b 1925) English actor AAS, WWT/10-16

COLE, Hazel B. (d 1974 [79]) business manager BP/59*

COLE, Horace (d 1916 [41]) manager EA/17*

COLE, Mr. J. (fl 1785?-94) singer BD

COLE, Jack (1914-74) American choreographer, dancer, director BE, TW/30

COLE, Jacob (d 1868 [73]) comic songwriter EA/69*

COLE, Mrs. James (d 1881 [73]) EA/82*

COLE, Janet see Hunter, Kim

COLE, Jennie (d 1908) EA/09*

COLE, Jessie (d 1877 [28]) EA/78*

COLE, John (d 1901 [85]) EA/02*

COLE, John William see Calcraft, John William

COLE, Kay (b 1948) American actress TW/28-30

COLE, Laurence (d 1883 [32]) comedian EA/84*

COLE, Maggie Porter (1857-1942) singer SR

COLE, Mary Keith (d 1975 [61]) performer BP/59*

COLE, Maurice (d 1965 [72]) performer BP/50*

COLE, Owen Blayney (d 1886 [78]) EA/87*

COLE, Robert (1865-1911) American comedian SR

COLE, Rose C. [Mrs. Walter Cole] (d 1890 [35]) EA/91*

COLE, Toby (b 1916) American talent & literary representative BE

COLE, Walter ventriloquist, entertainer CDP

COLE, Mrs. Walter see

Cole, Rose C.

COLE, Wendall (b 1914) American educator BE

COLE, William Washington (b 1847) American manager SR

COLE, W. J. (d 1870) manager, actor EA/71*

COLEBY, Wilfred T. (b 1865) dramatist WWT/2-3

COLEMAN, Mr. (fl 1670s?) impresario BD

COLEMAN, Mr. (fl 1749-50) actor BD

COLEMAN, Alexander see Sandy, Little

COLEMAN, Alice performer CDP

COLEMAN, Amy English actress GRB/1

COLEMAN, Carole (d 1964 [42]) American performer BE*

COLEMAN, Charles (c. 1595-1664) English instrumentalist, singer, composer BD, DNB, ES

COLEMAN, Charles (d 1694) musician BD

COLEMAN, Clara performer CDP

COLEMAN, Cornelius J. (d 1973 [44]) musician BP/57*

COLEMAN, Cy composer BE

COLEMAN, David (d 1882) variety agent EA/83*

COLEMAN, Deborah (b 1919) American representative BE

COLEMAN, E. B. [E. Coles] (b 1838) English actor HAS, SR

COLEMAN, Edward (d 1669) singer, composer BD, DNB

COLEMAN, Edward (b 1840) English actor HAS

COLEMAN, Emil (d 1965 [72]) conductor BP/49*

COLEMAN, Fanny (1840-1919) actress DD, GRB/2-4, WWT/1-3

COLEMAN, Fay R. (b 1918) American puppeteer BE

COLEMAN, Frank, III (d 1970 [35]) singer, actor TW/27

COLEMAN, Frank J. American actor ES

COLEMAN, Helen (b 1843) American actress HAS, SR

COLEMAN, Irene see Murdock, Ann

COLEMAN, James (d 1868) scene artist EA/69*

COLEMAN, Jane (b 1810) American actress HAS

COLEMAN, J. J. (b 1860) American actor, agent, manager SR

COLEMAN, John (fl 1668) musician BD

COLEMAN, John (1831-1904) actor, manager, dramatist CDP, DD

COLEMAN, Mrs. John see Davies, Maria Jane

COLEMAN, John A. CDP

COLEMAN, Laurina [Mrs. Sandy Coleman] (d 1882 [30]) EA/83*

COLEMAN, Leo (b 1919) American actor TW/3

COLEMAN, Lonnie (b 1920) American dramatist BE

COLEMAN, Louie performer CDP

COLEMAN, Maggie [Mrs. J. O'Gorman] (d 1898 [30]) dancer? EA/99*

COLEMAN, Maria Jane see Davies, Maria Jane

COLEMAN, Millicent American actress TW/1

COLEMAN, Nancy (b 1914) American actress BE, ES, TW/12-13, 25-26

COLEMAN, Robert, Jr. (1900-74) American critic BE, NTH, WWT/11-14

COLEMAN, Sam (d 1883 [36]) comedian EA/84*

COLEMAN, Mrs. Sandy see Coleman, Laurina

COLEMAN, Shepard (b 1924) American musical director BE

COLEMAN, Warren R. (d 1968 [67]) actor TW/24

COLEMAN, William (1766-1829) American journalist, author CDP

COLEMAN, William (fl 1794) violinist BD

COLEMAN, William (d 1885) equestrian EA/86*

COLENO, Florrie (d 1889 [18]) male impersonator EA/90*

COLENO, Mrs. Tom (d 1894 [41]) EA/95*

COLERIDGE, Amy (d 1951 [85]) actress CDP

COLERIDGE, Ethel (1883-1976) English actress WWT/5-11

COLERIDGE, Samuel Taylor (1772-1834) English critic, dramatist COC, CP/3, DD, DNB, ES, HP, NTH, OC/1-3

COLERIDGE, Sylvia (b 1909/12) Indian/English actress WWT/9-16

COLERIDGE-TAYLOR, Samuel (1875-1912) English composer DNB

COLES, A. J. see Stewer, Jan

COLES, Charles (fl 1760-70) house servant? BD

COLES, C. Mortimer (d 1896) actor EA/97*

COLES, E. see Coleman, E. B.

COLES, John (d 1800) violinist BD

COLES, Robert (fl 1598-99) actor DA

COLES, William (fl 1784-94) oboist BD

COLES, Zaida (b 1933) American actress TW/24-27, 29

COLETTI, Ferdinand (d 1876 [32]) pianist EA/77*

COLETTI, Filippo (1811-94) Italian singer CDP, ES

COLETTI, Frank (d 1968 [68]) actor, singer, stage manager TW/25

COLEY, John (d 1870 [25]) comic singer EA/71*

COLEY, Thomas (b 1917/18) American actor TW/3, 26-27

COLGAN, Michael (d 1870 [35]) musician EA/71*

COLICOS, John (b 1928) Canadian actor AAS, TW/22, 24, WWT/16

COLIN, Jean (b 1905) English actress, singer WWT/6-12

COLIN, Saul (d 1967 [58]) director, critic TW/23

COLINA, Fernando (d 1969 [37]) producer, director BP/53*

COLL, Owen (b 1887) Canadian actor TW/3

COLLA, Mme. Giuseppe see Aguiari, Lucrezia

COLLARD, Mr. (fl 1736) dancer BD

COLLARD, Archangello Corelli (b 1772) musician BD

COLLARD, Henry ["Pocket Sims Reeves"] (d 1888) singer EA/89*

COLLEANO, Bonar, Sr. (d 1957 [60+]) performer BE*,

WWT/14*

COLLEANO, Bonar, Jr. (1923-58) American actor WWT/10-12

COLLEANO, Con (d 1973 [73]) performer BP/58*

COLLENS, Gina American actress TW/23

COLLES, Mrs. Joseph [née Hesther Boyde] (fl 1776-80) actress, singer BD

COLLET, Mr. (fl 1729-34) actor BD

COLLET, Mr. (fl 1770-71) actor BD

COLLET, Mr. (fl 1785-1822?) dancer, singer, equestrian, machinist? BD

COLLET, Mrs. [Ann?] (fl 1765-71) actress, singer BD

COLLET, Catherine [Mrs. Tetherington] (fl 1767-1800) dancer, actress BD

COLLET, John (fl 1754?-70) violinist BD

COLLET, Osmond (d 1881 [78]) proprietor EA/82*

COLLET, Richard (fl 1737-67) violinist BD

COLLET, Richard (1885-1946) English manager NTH, SR, WWT/4-9

COLLET, Thomas (fl 1739-43) musician BD

COLLETT, Catherine see Collet, Catherine

COLLETT, Dan (d 1904) music-hall performer EA/05*

COLLETT, John (fl 1806) dramatist CP/3

COLLETT, John (d 1888 [77]) actor EA/89*

COLLETT, Thomas George [Wilfred Roxby] (d 1887 [42]) music-hall artist EA/88*

COLLETTE, Charles Henry (1842-1924) English actor, singer CDP, DD, DP, GRB/1-4, OAA/1-2, WWT/1-4, WWW/2

COLLETTE, Mary (fl 1889-91) actress DD

COLLETTI, Sig. (b 1820) Italian singer HAS, SR

COLLEWELL, Richard (fl 1633) actor DA

COLLEY, Mr. (fl 1774-84) house servant BD

COLLEY, Edward (d 1883 [45])

EA/84*

COLLEY, Edward (d 1890 [31]) music-hall agent EA/91*

COLLEY, Mrs. Edward see Leonie, Annie

COLLIE, Mrs. see Bellair, Mary Ann

COLLIER, Mr. (fl 1725?-31) actor, dancer BD

COLLIER, Cecil (d 1975 [67]) performer BP/60*

COLLIER, Constance (1878-1955) English actress CB, COC, DD, EA/97, ES, GRB/1-4, NTH, OC/1-3, SR, TW/11, WWM, WWT/1-11, WWW/5

COLLIER, Freddie (d 1965 [70]) performer BP/49*

COLLIER, Gaylan Jane (b 1924) American educator BE

COLLIER, Sir George (fl 1762-84) dramatist CP/2-3, GT

COLLIER, Hal (1859-1931) English actor GRB/1

COLLIER, Isabel M. Field (b 1881) English actress GRB/1-4

COLLIER, J. (fl 1702) orator BD

COLLIER, James Walter (1836-98) American actor, manager CDP, HAS, SR

COLLIER, Mrs. James W[alter] dancer CDP

COLLIER, Jeremy (1656-1726) English writer CDP, COC, DD, HP, NTH, OC/1-3, PDT

COLLIER, Joel [George Veal] (fl 18th cent) musician DNB

COLLIER, John Payne (1789-1883) English critic COC, DD, DNB, ES, HP, OC/1-3

COLLIER, J. W. (d 1868) panto-mimist EA/69*

COLLIER, J. Walter (d 1920 [60]) manager BP/5*

COLLIER, Lizzie (d 1914) actress WWT/14*

COLLIER, Lizzie Hudson (d 1924 [60]) actress BE*, WWT/14*

COLLIER, Luiza Leopoldina (d 1891 [70]) EA/92*

COLLIER, Marie Elizabeth (1927-71) Australian singer WWA/5

COLLIER, Patience [née Rene Ritcher] (b 1910) English actress AAS, WWT/13-16

COLLIER, William (fl 1709-14) proprietor, manager BD, TD/1-2

COLLIER, William (1866-1944)
American actor, dramatist
CB, DD, ES, GRB/2-4,
NTH, SR, WWA/2, WWM,
WWS, WWT/1-9

COLLIER, Mrs. William see
Allen, Louise

COLLIER, William C. (b 1903)
American dramatist ES

COLLIGAN, James (d 1974 [70])
producer/director/choreog-
rapher BP/58*

COLLINGBOURNE, Mr. (fl
1824) actor HAS

COLLINGBOURNE, Miss (fl
1840) actress HAS

COLLINGBOURNE, Florence
English actress GRB/1-2

COLLINGBOURNE, William E.
(d 1862) American? prompter
HAS

COLLINGE, Patricia (1894-1974)
Irish actress BE, ES, NTH,
SR, TW/2-19, 30, WWT/4-14

COLLINGHAM, G. G. (d 1923)
dramatist BE*, WWT/14*

COLLINGS, Mr. (fl 1792-1804)
actor, scene painter BD

COLLINGS, W. H. (d 1890
[63]) English/American actor,
stage manager EA/91*

COLLINGS, W. Jesse (b 1887)
English critic WWT/7-8

COLLINGWOOD, Dr. dramatist
CP/3

COLLINGWOOD, Lawrence
Arthur (b 1887) English composer, conductor ES

COLLINGWOOD, Lester (d
1910 [54]) actor, manager,
dramatist, proprietor EA/
11*, WWT/14*

COLLINGWOOD, S. (fl 1794)
singer BD

COLLINGWOOD, William (fl
1793-94) singer BD

COLLINI, Signora (fl early 19th
cent) singer CDP

COLLINS, Mr. (fl 1771) actor
BD

COLLINS, Mr. (fl 1774-81)
doorkeeper, supernumerary
BD

COLLINS, Mr. (fl 1794) actor
HAS

COLLINS, Mrs. (fl 1771) actress
BD

COLLINS, Mrs. (fl 1794)

actress HAS

COLLINS, A. B. see Beaumont,
Arthur

COLLINS, A. Greville (b 1896)
English manager WWT/5-7

COLLINS, Allen Frederick (b
1915) American stage manager,
actor, bookseller BE

COLLINS, Anthony (b 1893) English
conductor, composer ES

COLLINS, Mrs. Arthur see
Collins, Elizabeth

COLLINS, Arthur Pelham (1863-
1932) English manager DD,
ES, GRB/1-4, SR, WWM,
WWT/1-6, WWW/3

COLLINS, Barry (b 1941) English
dramatist CD

COLLINS, Bert (d 1962 [63]) performer BE*

COLLINS, Bill (b 1935) American
actor TW/30

COLLINS, Blanche (b 1918) American actress TW/2-6, 22-23,
25-26

COLLINS, C. E. (fl 1868) dancer
HAS, SR

COLLINS, Cecil A[rthur] (b 1874)
English actor GRB/1-2

COLLINS, Charles (fl 1667-70)
scene keeper BD

COLLINS, Charles (b 1880) American actor CDP, SR

COLLINS, Charles (d 1964 [83])
critic BE*, BP/48*

COLLINS, Charles (b 1904) American actor TW/2, WWT/8-11

COLLINS, Charles (b 1942) American actor TW/29

COLLINS, Charles James (1820-
64) dramatist DNB

COLLINS, Clementina [née Hayward?; Mrs. Thomas Woodfall]
(fl 1776-1837) actress BD

COLLINS, Dan W. actor, singer
CDP

COLLINS, David (d 1917) manager
EA/18*

COLLINS, Dorothy (b 1927) Canadian actress TW/28-29

COLLINS, Mrs. E. [Mrs. William
Collins] (d 1874) EA/75*

COLLINS, Edward (fl 1636) actor
DA

COLLINS, Edwin J. (b 1875) English actor GRB/1

COLLINS, Eli Whitney (b 1880)
American actor, dramatist SR

COLLINS, Elizabeth [Mrs. Arthur Collins] (d 1898 [30]) EA/99*

COLLINS, Elizabeth see Ripon, Mrs. George

COLLINS, Elizabeth Eayrs see Larkelle, Lillie

COLLINS, Emma (fl 1853) singer HAS

COLLINS, Ernest H. (d 1948 [89]) business manager WWT/14*

COLLINS, Ernest S. (d 1975 [84]) producer/director/choreographer BP/60*

COLLINS, Frank (d 1917 [20]) EA/18*

COLLINS, Frank (1878-1957) English actor, producer GRB/3-4, WWT/5-12

COLLINS, Fred (d 1916) EA/17*

COLLINS, Grace (d 1892) EA/93*

COLLINS, Dr. G. T. (d 1866) treasurer HAS

COLLINS, Horace (1875-1964) English secretary of the Society of West-end Theatre Managers WWT/10-13

COLLINS, Hubert (d 1868) comedian, pantomimist EA/69*

COLLINS, Isaac (1797-1871) violinist CDP

COLLINS, J. (fl 1763-92) actor, carpenter BD, TD/2

COLLINS, Mrs. J. (fl 1770-96) actress BD

COLLINS, Janet (b 1923) American dancer ES

COLLINS, Jeffery (fl 1624) actor DA

COLLINS, Jem see Lennox, James

COLLINS, Jennie Higham [Mrs. Wildon Collins] (d 1917) EA/18*

COLLINS, Jerry (d 1976 [50]) performer BP/60*

COLLINS, John (c. 1725-c. 57) scene painter BD, DNB

COLLINS, John (1741-97) English scholar DNB

COLLINS, John (1742-1808) English monologuist, actor, singer, poet, publisher BD, DD, DNB, TD/1-2

COLLINS, John (1811-74)

Irish comedian CDP, HAS, SR

COLLINS, John Churton (1848-1908) critic HP

COLLINS, John H. (d 1860) singer, minstrel CDP

COLLINS, John J. (d 1903 [37]) showman EA/04*

COLLINS, John R. (b 1878) English actor GRB/1

COLLINS, José (1887-1958) English actress, singer DNB, OC/1-3, TW/15, WWT/4-11

COLLINS, Joshua (fl 1819-20) theatre builder, manager WWA/H

COLLINS, Laura (d 1868) actress EA/69*

COLLINS, Lewis D. (b 1899) American actor ES

COLLINS, Lottie (1866-1910) English music-hall performer CDP, COC, DD, OC/1-3, PDT

COLLINS, Marie actress, singer CDP

COLLINS, Marty (d 1968 [72]) performer BP/53*

COLLINS, May (d 1955 [49]) actress TW/11

COLLINS, O. B. (b 1830) American actor CDP

COLLINS, Mrs. O. B. see Raymond, Kate

COLLINS, Olive (c. 1871-87) American actress NYM

COLLINS, Patrick (1859-1943) English showman WWW/4

COLLINS, Paul (b 1937) English actor TW/22-24

COLLINS, Pauline (b 1940) English actress WWT/15-16

COLLINS, Peter (d 1973) musician BP/58*

COLLINS, Ray (d 1965 [75]) actor TW/22

COLLINS, Rosina (fl 1853) singer HAS

COLLINS, Russell (1897-1965) American actor BE, ES, TW/1-20, 22, WWT/9-14

COLLINS, Sam [né Vagg] (1826-65) Irish music-hall performer CDP, COC, OC/2-3

COLLINS, Sewell (1876-1934) American producer, dramatist NTH, WWM, WWT/5-7

COLLINS, Stephen (b 1947) American actor TW/28-30

COLLINS, Strangways Churton

see Lesmere, Henry
COLLINS, Ted (d 1964 [64])
personal manager BP/48*
COLLINS, Thomas (1775-1806)
actor CDP, DD, TD/2
COLLINS, Thomas (d 1877)
musician EA/78*
COLLINS, Thomas Francis (d
1904 [40]) music-hall per-
former EA/05*
COLLINS, Thomas W. (fl 1836)
dramatist RJ
COLLINS, Una (d 1964 [45])
actress BE*
COLLINS, Viotti (d 1899 [77])
musician EA/00*
COLLINS, Walter E. (d 1917
[31]) conductor EA/18*
COLLINS, W. H. (fl 1863)
actor HAS
COLLINS, Mrs. Wildon see
Collins, Jennie Higham
COLLINS, Wilkie (1824-89)
English dramatist CDP,
COC, DD, DNB, EA/69, ES
COLLINS, William (d 1763)
actor, dancer BD
COLLINS, William (d 1898 [39])
variety performer EA/99*
COLLINS, Mrs. William see
Collins, Mrs. E.
COLLINS, William P. see
Pearson, William C.
COLLINS, Winnie (b 1896)
English actress, singer
WWT/6-9
COLLINS, W. J. ["The
Black Storm"] (d 1876)
comedian EA/77*
COLLINSON, Annie (d 1869)
actress EA/70*
COLLINSON, Laurence (b 1925)
English dramatist CD
COLLIS, [Francis?] (fl 1777-
84?) house servant? super-
numerary? BD
COLLIS, Mrs. [Francis? née
Susanna Richardson] (fl
1777-84) house servant? BD
COLLIS, John (fl 1672) musician
BD
COLLIS, Thomas W. (d 1873)
musician EA/74*
COLLISON, Wilson (1892/93-
1941) American dramatist
CB, SR, WWA/1, WWT/4-8
COLLOM, Ida M. (d 1879)
singer EA/80*

COLLS, J. H. (fl 1795-1805)
dramatist, actor CP/3
COLLUM, John (d 1962 [36]) actor
BE*
COLLYER, Bud (d 1969 [61]) actor
TW/26
COLLYER, Dan (d 1918) performer
BE*
COLLYER, Eve (b 1927) American
actress TW/22
COLLYER, June (d 1968 [61]) per-
former BP/52*
COLMACK, John (fl 1699) musi-
cian BD
COLMAN, Mr. (fl 1749) actor,
singer BD
COLMAN, Benjamin (1673-1747)
American dramatist EAP
COLMAN, Booth (b 1923) American
actor TW/2-6
COLMAN, George, the Elder
(1732-94) English dramatist,
manager BD, CDP, COC,
CP/1-3, DD, DNB, ES, GT,
HP, MH, NTH, OC/1-3, PDT,
SR, TD/1-2
COLMAN, George, the Younger
(1762-1836) English dramatist,
manager, examiner of plays
BD, CDP, COC, CP/3, DD,
DNB, ES, GT, HP, NTH,
OC/1-3, PDT, SR, TD/1-2
COLMAN, Mrs. George, the
Younger see Colman, Mary
COLMAN, Mary [née Logan; Mrs.
Gibbs] (1770-1844) English act-
ress BS, CDP, DD, DNB,
GT, OC/1-3, OX, TD/1-2
COLMAN, Ronald (1891-1958)
English actor CB, ES, SR,
TW/14, WWT/6-11, WWW/5
COLMAN, William (fl 1509-26?)
member of the Chapel Royal
DA
COLMER, Albert Ernest (d 1906)
music-hall assistant manager
EA/07*
COLMER, Graham John see
John, Graham
COLNAGHI, C. P. (fl 1891) actor,
dramatist DD
COLOMBA, Giovanni Battista Inno-
cenzo (1717-93) Italian scene
painter, machinist, costume de-
signer BD
COLOMBATI, Elisabetta (fl 1791-
1811) Italian singer BD
COLOMBE, Emilie (fl 1788-89)

COLOMBIER

dancer BD
COLOMBIER, Marie (c. 1842-
1910) French actress OC/
1-3
COLOMBO, Vera (b 1931) Italian
dancer ES
COLON, Alex (b 1941) Puerto
Rican actor TW/27
COLON, Jenny (1808-42) French
actress OC/3
COLON, Miriam (b 1945) Puerto
Rican actress, producer,
director TW/28-29, WWT/
16
COLONA, Edgardo (d 1904 [58])
actor EA/05*
COLONNE, Edouard (d 1910)
conductor EA/11*
COLONY, Alfred T. (d 1964)
actor BE*
"COLOSSUS" (fl 1745) giant
BD
COLPI, Sig. (fl 1764-89)
posture maker, ropedancer
BD
COLPI, Signora (fl 1777) rope-
dancer BD
COLPI, Signorino (fl 1767-77)
ropedancer BD
COLQUHOUN, Jessie [Mrs. R.
M. Colquhoun] (d 1899) EA/
00*
COLQUHOUN, Mrs. R. M. see
Colquhoun, Jessie
COLRIEN, Harriet (d 1909)
EA/10*
COLSON, C. David (b 1941)
American actor TW/26-
29
COLSON, Lizzie [née Richmond]
(1861-1887) American actress
NYM
COLSON, Pauline (1833-84)
singer CDP, HAS, SR
COLSTON, C. I. (d 1932 [95])
secretary of the Actors'
Benevolent Fund WWT/14*
COLT, Alvin (b 1915/16)
American designer BE, ES,
TW/8, WWT/13-16
COLT, Phyllis (d 1971 [52])
performer BP/55*
COLTMAN, Mr. (fl 1794)
organist BD
COLTON, Cheri American actor
TW/25-30
COLTON, Jacque Lynn (b 1939)
American actress TW/25

COLTON, John B. (1889-1946)
English/American dramatist
ES, HJD, MH, TW/3, WWT/
6-11
COLUM, Padraic (1881-1972) Irish
dramatist COC, ES, MD, MH,
MWD, OC/1-3, RE, WWA/5
COLUMBINE, Mrs. Peter see
Brunton, Elizabeth
COLUMBUS, Tobie (b 1951)
American actress TW/30
COLVERD, Edward Fred (d 1910
[37]) EA/11*
COLVERD, Joseph (d 1903) comic
singer EA/04*
COLVILL (fl 1779) singer BD
COLVILLE, Samuel (1825-86)
Irish manager, actor CDP,
SR
COLWELL, Claire [Mrs. Wedg-
wood Nowell] (b 1882) American
actress WWM
COLYER, Austin (b 1935) Ameri-
can actor TW/24-26, 30
COMANNI, Mr. (fl 1734) dancer
BD
COMBE, Mrs. George (d 1868)
EA/69*
COMBER, Mrs. (d 1908) EA/09*
COMBER, Bobbie [né Edmund]
(1886-1942) English actor WWT/
8-9
COMBER, Edmund see Comber,
Bobbie
COMBERMERE, Edward (b 1888)
English actor WWT/4-5
COMBES, William (fl 1594) actor
DA
COMDEN, Betty [née Cohen] (b
1918/19) American librettist,
lyricist, dramatist, actress
AAS, BE, CB, CD, ES, TW/
1-3, WWT/14-16
COMEGYS, Kathleen (b 1895) Amer-
ican actress BE, TW/3, 11-12
COMELATI, Mr. (fl 1735-41)
singer? BD
COMELLI, Attilio (1858-1925)
Italian/English designer ES
COMER, Mr. (fl 1813-19) actor
DD
COMER, Amelia (fl 1861) English
actress HAS
COMER, Bobbie see Comber,
Bobbie
COMER, Charles A. (d 1971 [73])
community theatre founder
BP/56*

COMER, George (fl 1865-99)
dramatist DD
COMER, Henry (fl 1660-76)
violinist BD
COMER, John (d 1886 [86])
singer EA/87*
COMER, Samuel M. (d 1974
[81]) designer BP/59*
COMER, Thomas (1790-1862)
English actor, musician
CDP, HAS, SR
COMERFORD, Mr. (fl 1789-94)
prompter's assistant, actor
BD
COMERFORD, Henry (d 1718)
actor BD
COMERFORD, Maurice (d 1903
[49]) publisher, editor EA/
04*, BE*, WWT/14*
"COMIC KING, The" see
Bostock, N. C.
COMINGORE, Dorothy (d 1971)
performer BP/56*
COMINS, Mr. (fl 1784) singer
BD
COMMANO, Giovanni Giuseppe
(fl 1730-32) singer BD
COMO, Professor [Percy James
Harley] (d 1892) sleight-of-
hand performer EA/93*
COMO, Antonio (fl 1770-76)
dancer, ballet master BD
COMO, Signora Antonio (fl 1775)
dancer BD
COMORN, Mlle. dancer CDP
COMPANY OF FOUR, The
producing managers WWT/
11
COMPANY THEATRE, The
theatre collective CD
COMPSON, Betty (1897-1974)
American actress ES
COMPTON, Betty (d 1944 [37])
actress SR, TW/1
COMPTON, Charles (d 1897 [37])
music-hall comedian EA/
98*
COMPTON, Charles G. (d 1911)
dramatist, critic, writer DD
COMPTON, Edward (1854-1918)
English actor COC, DD,
EA/96, GRB/1-4, OAA/2,
OC/1-3, WWT/1-3
COMPTON, Mrs. Edward see
Bateman, Virginia
COMPTON, Elizabeth [Mrs.
Henry Compton] (d 1881 [34])
EA/83*

COMPTON, Emmeline Catherine
[Mrs. Henry Compton] (d 1910)
EA/12*
COMPTON, Fay (b 1894) English
actress, singer AAS, BE,
COC, ES, OC/1-3, WWT/3-15
COMPTON, Francis (b 1885/90-
1964) English actor BE, TW/
8-16, 19-21
COMPTON, Henry [né Charles
Mackenzie] (1805-77) English
actor CDP, COC, DD, DNB,
ES, OC/1-3
COMPTON, Mrs. Henry see
Compton, Elizabeth
COMPTON, Mrs. Henry see
Compton, Emmeline Catherine
COMPTON, H. L. (d 1916 [54])
EA/17*
COMPTON, John (b 1923) Ameri-
can actor TW/2
COMPTON, June-Lynn (b 1942)
American actress TW/23
COMPTON, Katharine Mackenzie
(1853-1928) English actress
DD, ES, GRB/1-4, OAA/1-2,
OC/1-3, WWT/1-5
COMPTON, Madge (d 1970) actress
WWT/4-14
COMPTON, Percy (d 1910) actor
DD
COMPTON, Rouse (fl 1784-94)
violinist BD
COMPTON, Sydney (d 1938) English
actor GRB/1-4
COMPTON, Mrs. Sydney see
Osborne, Theresa
COMPTON, Viola (1886-1971) Eng-
lish actress GRB/3-4, WWT/
1-9
COMPTON, W. H. (b 1843) Eng-
lish actor SR
COMPTON, Wilfred (b 1877) Eng-
lish actor GRB/1
COMSTOCK, Anthony (1844-1915)
American reformer NTH
COMSTOCK, F. Ray (1880-1949)
American manager TW/6,
WWA/2, WWT/4-10
COMSTOCK, Mrs. F. Ray (d 1970
[80]) manager BP/55*
COMSTOCK, Martin (b 1864)
American manager GRB/1
COMSTOCK, Nanette [Mrs. Frank
Burbeck] (1871/73-1942) Amer-
ican actress DD, GRB/2-4,
SR, WWM, WWS, WWT/1-6
COMYN, Henry (d 1880 [46])

actor? EA/81*

CON, Jim see Gillespy, James

CONAWAY, Donald F. union
executive BE

CONAWAY, Jeff (b 1950) American actor TW/30

CONCANEN, Edward (d 1879
[32]) actor EA/80*

CONCANEN, Matthew (1701-49)
Irish dramatist CP/1-3,
DNB

CONCEPCION, Cesar (d 1974
[64]) musician BP/58*

CONCHAS, Paul (d 1916) EA/
17*

CONCHITA (d 1940 [79]) actress
BE*, WWT/14*

CONDELL, Charlotte (d 1759)
actress BD

CONDELL, Henry (d 1627) Eng-
lish actor COC, DA, DD,
DNB, ES, NTH, OC/1-3,
PDT

CONDELL, Henry (c. 1757-1824)
English musician, composer
BD, DD, DNB

CONDELL, John (d 1779) boxkeeper, concessionaire BD

CONDELL, John (fl 1779-84)
boxkeeper BD

CONDELL, T. (d 1876) manager
EA/77*

CONDO, Alice Maud (d 1901)
"Japanese performer" EA/
02*

CONDON, Eddie (1905-73)
musician CB

CONDON, Eva actress TW/1,
11

CONDOS, Dimo (b 1932) American actor TW/25-28

CONDUIT, Mrs. Mauvaise [née
Ribbon; Mrs. DeBar] (1805-
41) English actress HAS,
SR

CONE, Thomas George (d 1976
[85]) performer BP/60*

CONE, Spencer Houghton (1785-
1855) actor CDP, HAS, SR

CONEGLIANO, Emanuele see
Da Ponte, Lorenzo

CONELLY, Patrick C. (1842-
74) actor CDP

CONFORTI, Gino (b 1932) American actor TW/22-24

CONFREY, Zez (d 1971 [76])
composer/lyricist BP/56*

CONGDON, David (b 1943)

American actor TW/25

CONGO, William (d 1908) equestrian EA/09*

CONGOR, Pauline (fl 1867) actress
HAS

CONGREVE, William (1670-1729) English dramatist CDP, COC, CP/1-
3, DD, DNB, ES, GT, HP, MH,
NTH, OC/1-3, PDT, RE, SR

CONGREVE, W. La Touche (d
1916) EA/17*

CONHEIM, Mrs. Hermann see
Morton, Martha

CONIBEAR, Elizabeth Jenkins (d
1965 [86]) performer BP/49*

CONINGHAM, Mr. (fl 1768-72)
equestrian BD

CONINGSBY, Gilbert (fl 1674-82)
singer BD

CONINX, Louis Joseph (d 1876
[72]) flautist EA/77*

CONKEY, Thomas (1882-1927) singer
SR

CONKLE, E[llsworth] P[routy]
(b 1899) American dramatist,
educator BE, ES, HJD, MD,
MWD, NTH, SR

CONKLIN, Chester (1888-1971)
American circus clown ES

CONKLIN, George circus performer, animal trainer SR

CONKLIN, James (d 1971 [71])
theatre owner BP/56*

CONKLIN, John (d 1838) American
circus performer HAS

CONKLIN, Peggy (b 1912) American actress BE, SR, TW/1-9,
WWT/8-15

CONKLIN, Peter (b 1842) American
minstrel, tumbler HAS, SR

CONKLING, Charles A. (d 1964
[57]) dancer BE*

CONLAN, Frank (d 1955 [81])
actor TW/12

CONLEY, Eugene (b 1908/18)
American singer CB, ES

CONLEY, Harry J. (d 1975 [90])
performer BP/60*

CONLEY, Tom (d 1903 [31])
music-hall comedian EA/04*

CONLIN, Bernard see Florence,
William Jermyn

CONLIN, Jimmy (d 1962 [77])
actor BE*

CONLIN, Ray, Sr. (d 1964 [73])
performer BE*

CONLON, Edward Jerrold (d 1912
[61]) secretary EA/13*

CONLOW, Peter (b 1929)
American actor TW/8-20
CONLY, George A. (1845-82)
singer CDP
CONN, Maurice H. (d 1973
[67]) producer/director/
choreographer BP/58*
CONN, Stewart (b 1936) Scot-
tish dramatist, director CD
CONNARD, Miss (fl 1794)
actress, singer BD
CONNEAUX, Arthur F. (d 1902
[16]) EA/03*
CONNEL, Henry (fl 1668-69)
barber BD
CONNELL, David (b 1935)
American actor TW/25-26,
28-30
CONNELL, E. (d 1801) singer,
actor BD
CONNELL, Mrs. E. [Maria]
(fl 1785-93?) ticket seller,
boxkeeper, actress BD
CONNELL, F. Norreys (1874-
1948) Irish dramatist WWT/
2-10
CONNELL, Gordon (b 1923)
American actor, musician,
coach BE, TW/23-24, 28-29
CONNELL, Horatio (b 1876)
American singer WWM
CONNELL, James W. (d 1969
[56]) musician BP/54*
CONNELL, Jane [née Jane
Sperry Bennett] (b 1925)
American actress BE, TW/
13, 22-25, 27-29, WWT/
15-16
CONNELL, John (b 1923) Amer-
ican actor TW/12-13
CONNELL, Leigh (b 1926)
American producer BE
CONNELLY, Mr. (fl 1793-95)
doorkeeper BD
CONNELLY, [Miss?] (fl 1724)
house servant? BD
CONNELLY, Miss (fl 1799)
dancer BD
CONNELLY, Celia Logan (1837-
1904) American dramatist
WWA/1
CONNELLY, Edward J. (d 1928
[73]) American actor GRB/
3-4, WWM, WWT/1-2
CONNELLY, Fanny [Mrs.
Michael Connelly] (d 1888)
EA/89*
CONNELLY, Marc[us Cook]

(b 1890) American dramatist,
director, actor, educator, pro-
ducer AAS, BE, CB, CD,
COC, ES, HJD, MD, MH,
MWD, NTH, PDT, RE, SR,
WWT/5-16
CONNELLY, Michael (d 1911)
musical director EA/12*
CONNELLY, Mrs. Michael see
Connelly, Fanny
CONNER, Charlotte Mary Sanford
Barnes [Mrs. Edmon S. Con-
ner] (d 1863) actress CDP
CONNER, Edmon S. (1809-91)
American actor CDP, SR
CONNER, Mrs. Edmon S. see
Conner, Charlotte Mary San-
ford Barnes
CONNER, Nadine (b 1913) Ameri-
can singer CB
CONNERS, Barry (1883-1933)
American dramatist, actor
WWT/6-7
CONNERS, James L. (d 1970 [72])
journalist BP/55*
CONNERY, Sean (b 1930) Scottish
actor CB, ES
CONNESS, Robert (1867?-1941)
American actor CB
CONNIFORD, T. P. (d 1900 [38])
actor EA/01*
CONNOLLEY, Denise (b 1951)
American actress TW/30
CONNOLLY, Mr. (fl 1736) drama-
tist GT
CONNOLLY, Bobby (d 1944 [49])
dance director BE*, WWT/14*
CONNOLLY, Charles (d 1969 [90])
manager of the Players BP/
54*
CONNOLLY, George (b 1944)
American actor TW/25-26, 29
CONNOLLY, Gus (d 1900) Irish
comedian EA/01*
CONNOLLY, J. (fl 1847) Irish
actor HAS
CONNOLLY, James Smith (d 1874)
singer EA/75*
CONNOLLY, Maria [Mrs. Mary
Anne Lowrey] (d 1890 [26])
EA/91*
CONNOLLY, Michael (d 1911 [80])
composer BE*, WWT/14*
CONNOLLY, Patricia (b 1933)
actress TW/24-25, 29-30
CONNOLLY, Patrick (b 1842)
English/American fight arranger,
actor, gas boy, engineer HAS

CONNOLLY, Sadie (fl 1875-1906) American actress WWS

CONNOLLY, T. (d 1884) musical director EA/85*

CONNOLLY, Thomas American actor TW/22-23, 27

CONNOLLY, Walter (1887-1940) American actor CB, ES, SR, WWT/7-9

CONNOR, Mr. (fl 1741?-50) house servant? BD

CONNOR, Mr. (fl 1788) actor BD

CONNOR, Allen (d 1973 [75]) talent agent BP/58*

CONNOR, Charles (d 1826) Irish actor BS, CDP, DD, DNB, OX

CONNOR, Edmund Sheppard (1809-91) American actor, manager HAS

CONNOR, Mrs. Edmund Sheppard (d 1863) actress HAS

CONNOR, Frank J. (d 1902) manager EA/03*

CONNOR, H. (d 1887) EA/88*

CONNOR, James (1824-67) Irish actor HAS, SR

CONNOR, John, Sr. (d 1880 [86]) scene artist EA/81*

CONNOR, John (d 1911 [78]) scene artist EA/12*

CONNOR, Kaye (b 1925) Canadian actress TW/3

CONNOR, Patrick (d 1897) Irish comedian EA/98*

CONNOR, Thomas L. (d 1878) American actor EA/79*

CONNOR, Whitfield (b 1916) Irish actor BE, TW/4-19, 24-26

CONOLLY, Mr. (fl 1736) Irish dramatist CP/1-3

CONOLLY, Patricia see Connolly, Patricia

CONOR, Harry (d 1931 [75]) performer BE*, BP/15*

CONOVER, Anna (fl 1886) actress, lessee, manager CDP, DD

CONQUEST, Mr. (fl 1830) singer CDP

CONQUEST, Arthur (1875-1945) English actor, gymnast ES, GRB/1-4, OC/2-3, WWT/1-9

CONQUEST, Benjamin Oliver

(1805-72) English actor, proprietor DD, ES, OC/1-3

CONQUEST, Mrs. Benjamin Oliver [Clarissa Ann Bennett] (1802-67) ballet mistress, dancer ES

CONQUEST, Clara see Dillon, Mrs. Charles

CONQUEST, Daisy (d 1889 [16]) EA/91*

CONQUEST, Elizabeth Oliver (d 1890 [50]) EA/92*

CONQUEST, Fred (1871-1941) English actor, gymnast ES, GRB/2-4, OC/2-3, WWT/1-9

CONQUEST, George (d 1901 [64]) proprietor, pantomimist EA/02*

CONQUEST, George (1858-1926) English actor, manager, dramatist CDP, DD, DP, ES, GRB/1-4, OAA/2, OC/2-3, WWT/1-5

CONQUEST, Mrs. George (d 1890 [50]) ballet mistress, dancer WWT/14*

CONQUEST, George Augustus (1837-1901) English actor, manager, acrobat COC, DD, DNB, OAA/2, OC/1-3

CONQUEST, Ida (1870/76-1937) American actress GRB/2-4, WWA/1, WWS, WWT/1-6

CONQUEST, Lizzie [Mrs. Thomas Beard, Jr.] (d 1876 [17/18]) actress EA/77*, WWT/14*

CONRAD, Barbara see Hoffe, Barbara

CONRAD, Con (1890/91-1938) American composer ES, WWT/6-8

CONRAD, Eugene J. (d 1964 [69]) American dramatist BE*, BP/48*

CONRAD, John (d 1888 [58]) musician EA/90*

CONRAD, Joseph (1857-1924) Polish/English writer MD, MWD

CONRAD, Robert Taylor (1810-58) American dramatist CDP, DAB, ES, HJD, MH, NTH, RJ

CONRAD, William (d 1891) German clown CDP

CONRAN, William Sansfield (d 1867 [56]) musician EA/68*

CONRIED, Hans (b 1917) actor WWT/16

CONRIED, Heinrich (1855-1909) Austrian manager DAB, ES, GRB/3-4, WWS

CONROY, Constance (d 1888
[25]) actress EA/89*
CONROY, Frank (1890-1964)
English actor, manager
ES, SR, TW/1-20, WWT/
5-13
CONROY, Jean (d 1964 [29])
performer BP/49*
CONROY, Mrs. Peter S. (d
1879) EA/80*
CONROY, Thom (d 1971 [60])
performer BP/56*
CONS, Emma (d 1912 [74])
manager WWT/14*
CONSIDINE, Bob (d 1975 [68])
journalist BP/60*
CONSIDINE, Mrs. George
see Angeles, Aimee
CONSIDINE, John (1862-1943)
American showman SR
CONSTABLE, Mr. (fl 1749-
1803) house servant BD
CONSTABLE, Francis editor
CP/1
CONSTABLE, Mrs. Fred H.
see Stanley, Rose
CONSTABLE, James M. (d
1974 [68]) producer/director/
choreographer BP/59*
CONSTANCE, Mlle. (fl 1784-
87) dancer BD
CONSTANDUROS, Mabel (d
1957 [77]) English actress
WWT/8-12, WWW/5
CONSTANT, Yvonne [née
Coronakis] (b 1935) French
actress, singer, dancer
BE, TW/23
CONSTANTINE, Michael (b 1927)
American actor BE, TW/15
CONSTANTINI, Sig. (fl 1741-
42) dancer BD
CONSTANTINI, Signora (fl 1726-
27) dancer BD
CONSTANTIN-WEYER, Maurice
(d 1964 [83]) dramatist
BP/49*
CONTANDIN, Ferdinand Joseph
Desire see Fernandel
CONTAT, Louise (d 1813 [52])
actress WWT/14*
CONTE, John (b 1915) American
actor, singer BE, WWT/
11-12
CONTE, Richard (d 1975 [65])
actor WWT/16*, BP/59*
CONTI, Anna (fl 1754-55)
dancer BD

CONTI, Italia (1874-1946) English
actress, teacher COC, ES,
GRB/1-3, OC/1-3, PDT, WWT/
4-9, WWW/4
CONTI, Vincenzo (fl 1766-96) scene
painter BD
CONTINI, Giovanna (fl 1742-43)
singer BD
CONVERSE, Frank B. (b 1837)
American banjoist, minstrel
HAS, SR
CONVERSE, Frederick S[hepherd]
(1871-1940) American composer
CB, DAB, HJD, WWM
CONVILLE, Mrs. Alec (d 1900 [27])
actress EA/01*
CONVILLE, David (b 1929) English
actor, director AAS, WWT/15-
16
CONVY, Bert (b 1936) American
actor BE, TW/14, 20-26,
WWT/15-16
CONWAY, Mr. Irish piper, dancer
CDP
CONWAY, Miss see Carman, Mrs.
CONWAY, Bert (d 1910) EA/11*
CONWAY, Billy (d 1892 [38])
comedian, minstrel CDP
CONWAY, Curt (1915-74) American
actor, director, teacher BE,
TW/16, 30
CONWAY, Diane (b 1944) American
actress TW/24-26
CONWAY, E. H. (fl 1825-32) Eng-
lish dancer, ballet master, teach-
er CDP, HAS
CONWAY, Mrs. E. H. (fl 1825-55)
English dancer CDP, HAS
CONWAY, Frederick Bartlett (1819-
74) English actor, manager
CDP, DAB, HAS, OC/1-3, SR,
WWA/H
CONWAY, Mrs. Frederick Bartlett
see Conway, Sarah G.
CONWAY, George [John Foot] (d
1908 [27]) musical director
EA/09*
CONWAY, George W. (d 1919)
actor SR
CONWAY, Harold (b 1906) English
press representative, critic
WWT/8-14
CONWAY, Harry (d 1905) Negro
comedian EA/06*
CONWAY, H. B. [Blenkinsop-Coul-
son] (1850-1909) English actor
CDP, DD, DP, GRB/1, OAA/
1-2

CONWAY, Helen [Mrs. Herbert H. Spencer] (d 1901) EA/02*
CONWAY, Henry Seymour (1720-95) dramatist CP/3, GT, TD/1-2
CONWAY, H. J. (1800-60) English prompter HAS, SR
CONWAY, Mrs. H. J. (d 1839) English actress HAS, SR
CONWAY, Hugh [F. J. Fargus] (1848-85) dramatist DD
CONWAY, Jack (1887-1952) American actor, director ES
CONWAY, J. H. dramatist RJ
CONWAY, John American actor TW/1, 3
CONWAY, John (b 1922) Canadian marionettist ES
CONWAY, John Ashby (b 1905) American educator BE
CONWAY, J. Rudolph (d 1973 [80]) associated with circuses BP/58*
CONWAY, Kevin Bryan (b 1942) American actor TW/26-30
CONWAY, Lillian [Mrs. Charles S. Camblos] (d 1891) actress CDP
CONWAY, Lizzie (d 1916) actress WWT/14*
CONWAY, Marianne see Tearle, Marianne
CONWAY, Minnie see Tearle, Marianne
CONWAY, Neal (d 1888 [36]) American acrobat EA/89*
CONWAY, Norbert (d 1965 [76]) executive BP/50*
CONWAY, Russ (b 1913) Canadian actor TW/12
CONWAY, Sarah [née Crocker; Mrs. Frederick B. Conway] (1834-75) English actress CDP, HAS, OC/1-3, SR, WWA/H
CONWAY, Shirl [née Shirley Elizabeth Crosman] (b 1916) American actress BE, TW/11-13
CONWAY, Tom (d 1916) music-hall performer EA/17*
CONWAY, W. (fl 1836) English actor HAS
CONWAY, William (d 1950 [36]) manager WWT/14*
CONWAY, William Augustus

[né Rugg] (1789-1828) English actor CDP, COC, DD, DNB, ES, HAS, OC/1-3, SR
CONWY, Mr. (fl 1797) actor BD
CONY, Barkham ["The Dog Star"] (1802-58) English actor, performer CDP, HAS, SR
CONY, B. B. (d 1867) actor HAS
CONY, Thomas (d 1866) actor HAS
CONYERS, Mr. (fl 1744-52) singer, actor BD
CONYERS, Addie (fl 1884-88) actress DD
CONYERS, Charles (d 1896 [35]) singer EA/97*, WWT/14*
CONYERS, Charles Harold (d 1905 [21]) EA/06*
CONYERS, Joseph (d 1920 [60]) actor BE*, BP/5*
CONYNGHAM, Fred (b 1909) Australian actor WWT/7-11
COOGAN, Richard actor TW/1, 11-12
COOGRAN, Gene B. (d 1972) performer BP/56*
COOK, Mr. (fl 1694-1718) singer, violinist? BD
COOK, Mr. (fl 1716-32) dancer BD
COOK, Mr. (fl 1718-50?) dancer BD
COOK, Mr. (d 1731) boxkeeper BD
COOK, Mr. (fl 1735) musician BD
COOK, Mr. (fl 1765) singer BD
COOK, Mr. (fl 1785) tumbler BD
COOK, Mr. (fl 1793-1800) singer BD
COOK, Mr. (fl 1794) singer BD
COOK, Mr. (fl 1795) costumier BD
COOK, Mr. (fl 1829) actor HAS
COOK, Mrs. (fl 1718) performer BD
COOK, Mrs. (fl 1726-37) boxkeeper BD
COOK, Mrs. (fl 1730) actress BD
COOK, Mrs. (fl 1740-41) dancer BD
COOK, Mrs. (fl 1748) actress BD
COOK, Mrs. (fl 1763) actress BD
COOK, Master (fl 1737) singer, harpsichordist BD
COOK, Alice Aynsley (fl 1873) actress, singer DD
COOK, Alton F. (d 1967 [62]) critic BP/52*
COOK, Arthur (fl 1794) violinist BD
COOK, Augustus (1859-1904)

Scottish actor SR

COOK, Mrs. Aynsley (d 1880
[48]) actress, singer EA/81*

COOK, Barbara (b 1927) Amer-
ican actress, singer BE,
CB, TW/8, 11-23, 28-29,
WWT/14-16

COOK, Charles Emerson (d 1941
[71]) American agent, producer, director BE*, BP/
25*, WWT/14*

COOK, Dan (d 1894) singer, clown
EA/95*

COOK, Dan (1901-61) American
actor CB, ES, TW/1-16,
18, WWA/4, WWT/10-13

COOK, Edward Dutton (1829-83)
English critic COC, DD,
DNB, ES, OC/1-3

COOK, Elisha, Jr. (b 1902/06)
American actor BE, WWT/
8-11

COOK, Francis Edward ["Zeno"]
(d 1881 [22]) gymnast EA/82*

COOK, Furneaux see Cook,
John Furneaux

COOK, George (fl 1830) actor
HAS

COOK, George Cram (1873-
1924) American dramatist,
producer ES, HJD, MD,
MWD, NTH

COOK, James (fl 1863) see
Cooke, James

COOK, James (b 1937) American
actor TW/24-25, 27, 29

COOK, James A. (d 1908)
EA/09*

COOK, James M. (b 1825)
English actor HAS, SR

COOK, Jean Lawrence (d 1976
[76]) composer/lyricist
BP/60*

COOK, Joe (1890-1959) American
actor ES, SR, TW/15,
WWT/6-11

COOK, John (fl 1599-1604)
see Cooke, John

COOK, John (fl 1767-1801)
puppeteer, exhibitor BD

COOK, John (d 1881) equestrian
EA/82*

COOK, John Furneaux (d 1903
[63]) actor, singer DD

COOK, John Russell (1911-64)
American theatre librarian BE*

COOK, Joseph (fl 1702) performer BD

COOK, Kattie (d 1890) EA/92*

COOK, Ken (d 1963 [49]) actor
BE*

COOK, Layton (fl 1794) singer BD

COOK, Madge Carr see Carr-
Cook, Madge

COOK, Michael (b 1933) English/
Canadian dramatist CD

COOK, Patrick (b 1949) American
actor TW/26

COOK, Peter (b 1937) English
actor, writer BE, TW/30,
WWT/16

COOK, Roderick (b 1932) English
actor TW/26, 29-30

COOK, Roy Francis see Brandt,
Ivan

COOK, Mr. [S?] (fl 1797-1819)
doorkeeper? BD

COOK, Sarah see Cooke, Sarah

COOK, Thomas (fl 1766-68) house
servant BD

COOK, Thomas Aynsley (1832-94)
actor, singer DD

COOK, William (d 1824) Irish
dramatist, writer CDP, CP/3,
DD, DNB

COOK, William Henry (d 1891 [27])
EA/92*

COOK, Will Marion (1869-1944)
American composer DAB

COOKE, Mr. actor CDP

COOKE, Mr. (fl 1719) musician BD

COOKE, Mr. (fl 1751-70) equilibrist
BD

COOKE, Mr. (fl 1758) harpsichordist
BD

COOKE, Mr. (fl 1761-62) actor BD

COOKE, Mr. (fl 1782-84) actor BD

COOKE, Mr. (fl 1796-97) singer
BD

COOKE, Mrs. (fl 1735-36) dresser
BD

COOKE, Mrs. (d 1745) see
Cooke, Mary

COOKE, Mrs. (fl 1756-57) actress?
BD

COOKE, Mrs. (fl 1852) actress
HAS

COOKE, Abell (fl 1606-07) actor
DA

COOKE, A[dam] M[oses] E[manuel;
né Thomas] (fl 1762-71) English
dramatist CP/2-3, GT

COOKE, Alexander (d 1614) English
actor DA, ES, GT, NTH

COOKE, Arthur (fl 1669) musician
BD

COOKE, Benjamin (d c.1743) musician, music seller, publisher BD

COOKE, Benjamin (1734-93) English organist, composer, choirmaster, conductor BD, CDP, DNB

COOKE, Charles (d 1900 [70]) actor EA/01*

COOKE, Mrs. Charles (d 1881) EA/82*

COOKE, Charles J. (b 1857) English scene painter, property man GRB/1

COOKE, Mrs. Charles P. see Cooke, Emma

COOKE, Eddie (1869-1942) American manager, press agent SR

COOKE, Edward (fl 1509-11) member of the Chapel Royal DA

COOKE, Edward (fl 1678) dramatist CP/1-3, DD, DNB

COOKE, Ellen equestrienne CDP

COOKE, Emma [Mrs. Charles P. Cooke] (d 1904) EA/05*

COOKE, Mrs. Eugene see Cooke, Helena

COOKE, Frank (d 1869 [67]) actor? EA/70*

COOKE, Fred (d 1905 [59]) actor EA/06*

COOKE, G. A. (d 1905) illusionist GRB/1

COOKE, George (1807/11-63) English actor CDP, DD, DNB

COOKE, Mrs. George (d 1877 [74]) EA/78*

COOKE, George A. (d 1905 [79]) vaudevillian? EA/06*, WWT/14*

COOKE, George Frederick (1756-1812) English actor BD, CDP, COC, DD, DNB, ES, GT, HAS, NTH, OC/1-3, OX, SR, TD/1-2

COOKE, Mrs. George Frederick, II see Daniels, Alicia

COOKE, Harry (d 1958 [56]) American performer BE*, BP/42*

COOKE, Harry Welby (d 1882) circus proprietor EA/83*

COOKE, Helena [Mrs. Eugene Cooke] (d 1890 [43]) EA/91*

COOKE, Henry (c.1616-72) English singer, composer, teacher BD, DNB, ES

COOKE, Henry (d 1898 [71]) actor EA/99*

COOKE, H. Michael Angelo Gratton (d 1889) musician EA/90*

COOKE, James (fl 1791-1825) singer, actor BD

COOKE, James (fl 1863) English clown, manager CDP, ES, HAS

COOKE, James (d 1869) equestrian EA/70*

COOKE, James (d 1899) actor EA/00*

COOKE, Mrs. James (d 1875 [61]) EA/76*

COOKE, Mrs. James [Bessie Walters] (d 1887) actress? EA/88*

COOKE, James Henry (d 1879 [43]) actor EA/80*

COOKE, Jemima (d 1882 [74]) EA/83*

COOKE, J. M. see Maguire, James

COOKE, Mrs. J. M. see Jones, Mrs. W. G.

COOKE, Jo (fl 1614) dramatist DNB

COOKE, John (fl 1599-1604) dramatist CP/1-3, DD, FGF

COOKE, John (d 1887 [66]) EA/88*

COOKE, John (d 1900 [40]) music-hall agent, songwriter EA/01*

COOKE, John Corbet (d 1879) manager EA/80*

COOKE, John Esten (1830-86) American writer OC/1-2

COOKE, John Henry (d 1901 [87]) proprietor EA/02*

COOKE, John Henry (d 1917 [80]?) equestrian CDP

COOKE, John P. (1820-65) English composer, conductor HAS, SR

COOKE, Mrs. John P. see Weston, Lottie

COOKE, Julia CDP

COOKE, J. Y. F. (d 1918) EA/19*

COOKE, Kate equestrienne CDP

COOKE, Lionel (fl 1583-88) actor DA

COOKE, Mrs. M. A. (d 1868 [85]) EA/69*

COOKE, Marjorie Benton (d 1920 [44]) monologist BE*, BP/4*

COOKE, Mary (1666?-1745) actress, singer BD

COOKE, Mary Anne equestrienne

HAS

COOKE, Matthew (fl 1780-1800?) instrumentalist, singer, composer BD

COOKE, Philip (fl 1739-55) dancing master BD

COOKE, Philip (d 1755) dancer BD

COOKE, Richard P. (b 1904) American critic BE, NTH

COOKE, Robert (1768-1814) English organist, composer, singer BD

COOKE, Rosa actress, singer CDP

COOKE, Sander (d 1614) actor WWT/14*

COOKE, Sarah (d 1688) actress BD

COOKE, Stanley (1868-1931) English actor WWT/2-5

COOKE, Steve (d 1909 [47]) music-hall comedian EA/10*

COOKE, Thomas (fl 1583-84) actor DA

COOKE, Thomas (c.1702-56) English dramatist CP/1-3, DD, GT

COOKE, Thomas (1722-83) English dramatist DNB

COOKE, Thomas (b c.1752) English circus performer ES

COOKE, Thomas (d 1939 [65]) American actor BE*

COOKE, Thomas Coffin (d 1939 [65]) actor BP/23*

COOKE, Thomas Edwin circus performer ES

COOKE, Thomas Potter (1786-1864) English actor BS, CDP, COC, DD, DNB, ES, OC/1-3, OX

COOKE, Thomas Simpson (1782-1848) Irish actor, singer, composer BS, CDP, DD, DNB, ES, OX

COOKE, Thomas Taplin (1782-1866) English circus performer ES

COOKE, Cpt. Tom (d 1901) musical performer EA/02*

COOKE, William (fl 1608-35) share-holder, actor DA

COOKE, William (fl 1763-1800) deputy treasurer BD

COOKE, William (d 1824) see Cook, William

COOKE, William (fl 19th cent?) circus manager CDP

COOKE, William (d 1886) equestrian manager, clown ES

COOKE, William (d 1895 [45]) conductor EA/96*

COOKE, Mrs. William (d 1874) EA/75*

COOKMAN, Anthony Victor (1894-1962) English critic AAS, COC, ES, OC/1-3, WWT/10-13, WWW/6

COOKSEY, Curtis (1892-1962) American actor TW/3-4, 6

COOKSON, Georgina (b 1918) English actress TW/3, WWT/12-15

COOKSON, Peter (b 1913/15) American actor, producer BE, TW/3-16

COOKSON, S. A. (d 1947 [78]) actor BE*, WWT/14*

COOLEY, Dennis (b 1948) American actor TW/29

COOLEY, Hollis Eli (1859-1918) American manager WWA/1, WWM

COOLEY, Spade (d 1969 [59]) musician BP/54*

COOLIDGE, Philip (1908-67) American actor BE, TW/1, 3, 5-13, 15-16, 23

COOLING, John (fl 1640?) actor DA

COOMBE, Carol [Gwendoline Alice Coombe] (1911-66) Australian actress WWT/8-12

COOMBE, Gwendoline Alice see Coombe, Carol

COOMBES, Mr. (fl 1789-1805) property man, actor, singer BD

COOMBES, Miss (fl 1795-1802) dancer BD

COOMBS, Arthur actor, singer CDP

COOMBS, Jane (b 1842) actress CDP, HAS, SR

COOMBS, Martin B. (fl 1852) actor HAS

COON, Gene L. (d 1973 [48]) producer/director/choreographer BP/58*

COONAN, Sheila (b 1922) Canadian actress TW/25-28

COONEY, Dennis (b 1938) American actor TW/18-20, 22, 24, 29

COONEY, Laurette see Taylor,

Laurette
COONEY, Ray (b 1932) English
dramatist, actor, director
WWT/15-16
COONS, Johnny (d 1975 [58])
performer BP/60*
COOP, Colin (d 1937) actor
BE*, WWT/14*
COOPE, James E. (d 1892)
circus proprietor EA/93*
COOPER, Mr. (fl 1695-1701)
singer BD
COOPER, Mr. (fl 1729-46)
boxkeeper BD
COOPER, Mr. (fl 1749) actor
BD
COOPER, Mr. (fl 1767) per-
former BD
COOPER, Mr. (fl 1781) dancer
BD
COOPER, Mr. (fl 1795) scene
painter, machinist BD
COOPER, Mr. (fl 1795-1803)
actor TD/1-2
COOPER, Mr. (fl 1798) actor
BD
COOPER, Mr. (d 1809) actor
BD
COOPER, Dr. (fl 1822) drama-
tist EAP
COOPER, Mrs. (fl 1722-34)
actress BD
COOPER, Mrs. (fl 1775-77?)
wardrobe assistant? BD
COOPER, Mrs. (d 1868)
EA/69*
COOPER, Mrs. see Bernard,
Mrs. John, I
COOPER, Mrs. (d 1906) see
Lina, Mme.
COOPER, Master (fl 1795) actor
BD
COOPER, Miss (fl 1785-87?)
dancer BD
COOPER, Miss (fl 1793) singer,
actress BD
COOPER, Mrs. A. M. Garratt
(d 1916) EA/17*
COOPER, Anna (fl 1851) actress
HAS
COOPER, Anthony Kemble (b
1908) English actor BE,
TW/1-3, 6, 8, 20, 22-23,
WWT/7-15
COOPER, Ashley (d 1952 [70])
Australian actor BE*, BP/36*
COOPER, Charles (d 1876 [56])
organist EA/77*

COOPER, Charles Kemble (d 1923
[69]) actor BE*, WWT/14*
COOPER, Christine (b 1946) Amer-
ican actress TW/26
COOPER, Clancy (d 1975 [68])
actor BP/60*, WWT/16*
COOPER, Clarence (d 1974 [53])
performer BP/59*
COOPER, Clifford (d 1895 [76])
actor BE*, EA/96*, WWT/14*
COOPER, Mrs. Clifford [Agnes
Kemble] (1823-95) actress BE*,
EA/96*, WWT/14*
COOPER, Dulcie (b 1907) American
actress TW/2-3
COOPER, Edward (d 1956) actor
BE*, WWT/14*
COOPER, Edward W. (d 1912)
variety performer EA/13*
COOPER, Elizabeth (fl 1737) drama-
tist CP/1-3, DD, DNB, GT
COOPER, Emil (b 1877) English/
Russian conductor ES
COOPER, Enid (b 1902) English
actress WWT/7
COOPER, Ernest George (d 1894
[40]) EA/95*
COOPER, Evelyne Love (d 1968)
composer/lyricist BP/53*
COOPER, Eward (d 1945 [40])
actor, entertainer WWT/14*
COOPER, Fannie [Mrs. Sidney
Cooper] (d 1909) EA/10*
COOPER, Fanny see Cooper,
Frances
COOPER, F. Fox see Cooper,
Frederick Fox
COOPER, F. Harwood (d 1905 [78])
actor WWT/14*
COOPER, Frances [Mrs. Thomas
Haines Lacy] (1819-72) actress
CDP, DD, DNB
COOPER, Francis (fl 1671) musi-
cian BD
COOPER, Frank talent representative
BE
COOPER, Frank J. (d 1875 [35])
proprietor EA/76*
COOPER, Frank Kemble (1857-1918)
English actor DD, EA/96, GRB/
1-4, OAA/2, WWT/1-3
COOPER, Frank Staunton (d 1885
[30]) actor EA/86*
COOPER, Fred actor, dancer CDP
COOPER, Fred (d 1909 [50]) humor-
ist EA/10*
COOPER, Frederick (1890/97-1945)
English actor WWT/5-8

COOPER, Frederick Fox (1806-79) dramatist, manager DD

COOPER, Frederick Harwood (d 1905 [78]) actor EA/06*

COOPER, George (fl 1794) musician BD

COOPER, George A. (d 1889) proprietor EA/90*

COOPER, Giles (1918-66) English dramatist AAS, CD, CH, WWT/14, WWW/6

COOPER, Dame Gladys (1888-1971) English actress AAS, BE, CB, COC, ES, TW/2-8, 12-16, 28, WWA/4, WWT/1-15

COOPER, G. Melville (1896-1973) English actor AAS, BE, ES, TW/1-10, 22-23, 27, 29, WWT/7-15

COOPER, Greta Kemble actress WWT/7-8

COOPER, Harwood (d 1943 [74]) actor DD, OAA/2

COOPER, Henry (fl 1790?-1819?) musician BD

COOPER, Henry C. (1807/19-81) English musician, manager HAS, SR

COOPER, Herbert B. see Treherne, Bernard

COOPER, Herman E. lawyer BE

COOPER, Jackie (b 1922) American actor, producer, director BE, ES, TW/5-16

COOPER, James (d 1882 [83]) EA/83*

COOPER, John (1790-1870) actor BS, CDP, DD, DNB, EA/92, OX

COOPER, John Wilbye (d 1885) singer EA/86*

COOPER, Joseph (fl 1794) singer? BD

COOPER, Joseph (d 1886) music-hall artist EA/87*

COOPER, Lillian Kemble (1891-1977) actress WWT/6-8

COOPER, Lizzie (b 1844) American actress HAS

COOPER, Margaret (d 1922) performer BE*, WWT/14*

COOPER, Marian (fl 1940s) American actress SR

COOPER, Marilyn (b 1935) American singer, actress, dancer BE, TW/18, 23-24, 26-28

COOPER, Melville see Cooper, G. Melville

COOPER, Merian C. (d 1973 [78]) producer/director/choreographer BP/57*

COOPER, Milroy (d 1917 [69]) actor EA/18*

COOPER, Peggy (b 1931) American actress TW/27-28

COOPER, Priscilla Elizabeth (d 1889) actress HAS, SR

COOPER, Ralph (fl 1763) singer BD

COOPER, Ray (b 1930) English actor TW/24-25

COOPER, Reynaud (d 1892 [35]) actor EA/93*

COOPER, Richard (fl 1794) singer? BD

COOPER, Richard (1893-1947) English actor WWT/7-8

COOPER, Mrs. Sidney see Cooper, Fannie

COOPER, Thomas Abthorpe (1776-1849) English actor, manager BD, CDP, COC, DAB, DD, ES, HAS, OC/1-3, SR, WWA/H

COOPER, Thomas Clifford (1819-95) English actor DD, OAA/2

COOPER, Violet Kemble (1886/89-1961) English actress NTH, TW/18, WWT/4-9

COOPER, Wilbye (d 1907 [47]) musician, music-hall manager EA/09*

COOPER, William (d 1868) actor EA/69*

COOPER, Wyatt (b 1927) American actor TW/16

COOPER-CLIFFE, Henry see Cliffe, H. Cooper

COOTE, Bert (1868-1949) English manager, actor COC, GRB/1-2, SR, WWT/4-8

COOTE, Carrie see Pearce, Lady

COOTE, Charles (d 1880 [71]) musician EA/81*

COOTE, Charles (1858-97) actor CDP, DD

COOTE, Lizzie (1862-86) actress CDP, DD

COOTE, Louie see Mills, Mary Louisa

COOTE, Robert (d 1888 [54]) musical director, composer CDP

COOTE, Robert (b 1909) English actor BE, TW/9, 12-16,

WWT/13-16
COOTON, Mrs. Frank see
Spence, Beatrice
COOTS, J. Fred (b 1897) Amer-
ican composer BE
COPE, Mrs. (fl 1770-71) dancer
BD
COPE, Patricia (b 1943) Ameri-
can actress TW/26, 29
COPEAU, Jacques (1878-1949)
French actor, manager, pro-
ducer COC, MWD, NTH,
OC/1-3, PDT, WWT/9-10,
WWW/4
COPELAN, Sheila (d 1966 [30])
performer BP/50*
COPELAND, Mrs. (fl 1729)
dancer BD
COPELAND, Miss (b 1801)
actress EA/92
COPELAND, Alfred (d 1872)
harpist EA/73*
COPELAND, Bella see Cope-
land, Isabella
COPELAND, Fanny Elizabeth
see Fitzwilliam, Mrs. Ed-
ward
COPELAND, Mrs. Harry see
Copeland, Margaret
COPELAND, Isabella [Mrs. J.
B. Buckstone] (d 1912 [73])
actress DD
COPELAND, Joan [née Joan
Maxine Miller] (b 1922)
American actress, singer
BE, TW/5-7, 21, 25, 27-28,
WWT/15-16
COPELAND, J. T. (d 1882)
journalist EA/83*
COPELAND, Margaret [Mrs.
Harry Copeland] (d 1894)
EA/95*
COPELAND, Mary Dowell (d
1963 [48]) American per-
former BE*, BP/47*
COPELAND, William R. (1799-
1867) manager, actor, lessee
DD
COPELAND, Mrs. William R.
(d 1863) actress WWT/14*
COPEN, Elizabeth see Copin,
Mrs. Roger
COPERARIO, Giovanni (d 1626)
composer DNB
COPIN, Mrs. Roger [Elizabeth]
(fl 1733-73) actress, singer
BD
COPINGER, May Irene see

Howard, Kathryn
COPLAND, Mr. (fl 1756) boxkeeper
BD
COPLAND, Mr. (fl 1789-91) house
servant BD
COPLAND, Aaron (b 1900) American
composer CB, ES, HJD
COPLAND, Charles (fl 1891) singer
DD
COPLAND, H. (fl 1859) actor HAS
COPLANDE, Robert (fl 16th cent)
English writer ES
COPLEY, Ada Mary see Morgan,
Ada
COPLEY, Joan (d 1969 [69]) per-
former BP/53*
COPLEY, Peter (b 1915) English
actor AAS, WWT/11-16
COPLEY, Mrs. Walter see
Morgan, Ada
COPLEY, Mrs. Walter see
Oakley, Ada
COPPEE, François (1842-1908)
French dramatist GRB/1-4
COPPEL, Alec (d 1972) Australian
dramatist BE, WWT/11
COPPEN, Hazel (d 1975 [50])
performer BP/59*
"COPPER CAPTAIN" see Brown,
Henry
COPPERVILLA, Ellen (d 1852)
dancer HAS
COPPIN, Elizabeth J. (d 1873 [85])
EA/74*
COPPIN, Hon. George Selth (1818/
19-1906) Australian actor, mana-
ger DNB, GRB/1, HAS
COPPING, Bernard (b 1871) English
actor GRB/1
COPPINGER, Matthew (d 1685)
actor BD
COPPINI, Ettore (d 1935 [91])
maître de ballet WWT/14*
COPPOLA, Anton (b 1918) American
musical director BE
COPPOLA, Frank (b 1944) American
actor TW/28, 30
COPPOLA, Giuseppe (fl 1777-79)
singer BD
COPPOLA, Nora American actress
TW/27
COPPOLA, Sam J. (b 1935) Amer-
ican actor TW/27, 29
COPRARIO, Giovanni see Coper-
ario, Giovanni
COQUELIN, Constant-Benoît (1841-
1909) French actor CDP, GRB/
1-4, OC/3, WWA/4

COQUELIN, Ernest-Alexandre-
Honoré [cadet] (1848-1909)
French actor GRB/1-4
COQUELIN, Jean (1865-1944)
French actor, manager GRB/
1-4, OC/3, WWT/1-4
CORADINI, Sig. (fl 1767-68?)
dancer BD
CORADINI, Mlle. see Kruger,
Annie
"CORALLINA" see Costantini,
Domenica
CORBALLY, Miss (fl 1732)
actress BD
CORBET, Hamilton (d 1885)
Scottish singer EA/86*
CORBET, [Neeves?] (d 1761?)
singer BD
CORBET, Symon (b 1675?)
singer BD
CORBETT, Mr. (fl 1780) actor
BD
CORBETT, Gretchen (b 1947)
American actress TW/25-
29, WWT/16
CORBETT, Harry H. (b 1925)
Burmese/English actor WWT/
14-16
CORBETT, James John (1866-
1933) American actor, fighter
DAB, SR, WWS
CORBETT, Leonora (1908-1960)
English actress TW/2-7,
17, WWT/7-11
CORBETT, Mary (fl 1670?-82?)
actress BD
CORBETT, Mary (d 1974 [48])
performer BP/58*
CORBETT, Thalberg see Thal-
berg, T. B.
CORBETT, William (1680-1748)
English violinist, composer
BD, DNB
CORBETTA, Francesco (c.1620-
81) guitar player BD
CORBIN, Barry (b 1940) Amer-
ican actor TW/26, 28-29
CORBIN, John (1870-1959)
American critic GRB/2-4,
WWT/1-9, WWW/5
CORBY, Mr. (fl 1847) dancer
CDP
CORBY, Mlle. (fl 1828-35)
actress HAS
CORBYN, Master (fl 1785) dancer
BD
CORBYN, H. W. (d 1880) agent
EA/81*

CORBYN, Wardle (d 1880) agent
EA/81*
CORCORAN, Jane [Mrs. J. Em-
mett Baxter] American actress
GRB/3-4, WWM, WWT/1-9
CORCORAN, Katharine see
Herne, Mrs. James A.
CORCORAN, Leslie (d 1891) EA/
92*
CORCY, Diancinto (fl 1669-71)
scene keeper BD
CORDELL, Cathleen [née Kelly]
(b 1916/17) American actress
BE, TW/4, WWT/9-13
CORDELL, Thomas (fl 1663-70)
scene keeper BD
CORDEN, George (fl 1640) actor
DA
CORDER, Bruce English manager
BE
CORDER, Frederick (1852-1932)
English composer ES, WWW/3
CORDIER, Angiolina (fl 1862)
French singer CDP, HAS
CORDNER, Blaine (b 1901) Ameri-
can actor TW/1, 3-10, 27
CORDNER, W. J. (d 1870) musi-
cian EA/71*
CORDON, Norman (d 1964 [60])
American singer, teacher BE*
CORDONA, Cpt. Thomas Bridgman
(d 1891) lion tamer EA/92*
CORDONI, Sig. (fl 1760) violinist
BD
CORELLI, Sig. (fl 1849) musician?
HAS
CORELLI, Alfonso (d 1970 [70])
conductor BP/55*
CORELLI, Blanche singer, actress
CDP
CORELLI, Cecilia [Mrs. Stephen
Chambers] (d 1886) EA/87*
CORELLI, Franco (b 1924?) Italian
singer CB
CORELLI, Kathryn (d 1970 [70])
performer BP/54*
COREN, Leo (d 1974 [73]) talent
booker BP/59*
COREY, John (fl c.1699-1735)
actor, dramatist CP/1-3,
DD, DNB, GT, TD/2
COREY, John (d c.1721) dramatist
CP/1-3, GT, TD/1
COREY, Mrs. John [née Katherine
Mitchell] (b c.1635) actress BD
COREY, Joseph (d 1972 [45]) per-
former BP/57*
COREY, Madison (b 1873) American

manager WWM
COREY, Mrs. Madison see
Wilber, Mabel
COREY, Sidney A. actor CDP
COREY, Mrs. W. E. see
Gillman, Mabelle
COREY, Wendell (1914-68) Amer-
ican actor BE, ES, TW/2-3,
6, 13, 25, WWA/5, WWT/
11-14
COREY, William (d c. 1664?)
actor BD
CORFE, Mr. (b 1718) singer BD
CORFE, Arthur Thomas (1773-
1863) English musician, sing-
er, composer BD
CORFE, James (fl 1735-50)
musician, composer BD
CORFE, John (b 1769) musician
BD
CORFE, Joseph (1740-1820)
English singer, organist,
composer BD
CORI, Angelo Italian musician,
composer CP/1 [see also:
Corri, Angelo]
CORINNE [Corinne Belle De
Brion] (1873-1937) American
actress CDP, WWM, WWS
CORKE, Norman (d 1889 [20])
actor EA/90*
CORKERY, Daniel (1878-1964)
Irish dramatist ES
CORLESSE, Mrs. E. C. see
Taylor, Annie
CORLEY, Robert A. (d 1971)
performer BP/56*
CORMACK, Mr. actor CDP
CORMACK, John (d 1890) ballet
master EA/91*
CORN, Alfred Jacob see
Ryder, Alfred
CORNACCHINI, Emanuele (fl
1759-60) singer BD
CORNE, Mr. (fl 1782) actor BD
CORNEILLE, [Mons. ?] (fl 1675)
harpsichordist BD
CORNEILLE, Mons. (fl 1735-
36) acrobat BD
CORNEILLE, Pierre (1606-84)
French dramatist DD, OC/
1-3
CORNEL, Master (fl 1745-47)
singer BD
CORNELIUS, Mr. (fl 1675)
violinist BD
CORNELIUS, Peter (1865-1934)
Danish singer ES

CORNELL, John (1913-69) American
stage manager BE, TW/25
CORNELL, Katharine (1893/98-
1974) German/American actress
AAS, BE, BTR/74, CB, ES,
HJD, NTH, OC/2-3, PDT, SR,
TW/1-21, WWT/4-15
CORNELYS, Mrs. (fl 1781) actress,
dramatist CP/3
CORNELYS, Miss (fl 1791-1801)
actress BD
CORNELYS, John (1735-1818)
Irish? actor, singer BD,
CDP, TD/1-2
CORNELYS, Mrs. John [Margaret]
(1723-97) actress BD
CORNELYS, Margaret see
Cornelys, Mrs. John
CORNELYS, Teresa [née Imer]
(1723-97) Italian singer, entre-
preneur BD, DNB
CORNER, Julia (1798-1875) English
dramatist DNB
CORNES, James (d 1874) musician
EA/76*
CORNET, Sig. (fl 1726-27) dancer
BD
CORNEWALL-WALKER, Thomas
James Raglan see Raglan,
James
CORNEY, Mr. (fl 1661) singer BD
CORNEY, Arthur singer, composer
CDP
CORNILLE, Marguerite CDP
CORNISH, James (d 1804) oboist
BD
CORNISH, James John (1767-1803)
musician BD
CORNISH, John (fl 1501) gentleman
of the Chapel Royal, pageant-
master DA
CORNISH, Kit (fl 1508) actor DA
CORNISH, Thomas (fl 1794-1818)
oboist BD
CORNISH, William (fl 1479-80)
master of song school DA
CORNISH, William (fl 1509-23)
master of the Chapel Royal
DA, ES
CORNOCK, J. R. see Crauford,
J. R.
CORNUE, Virginia (b 1945) Ameri-
can actress TW/30
CORNWALL, Mr. (d c. 1724) scene
painter BD
CORNWALL, Anna (d 1872 [93])
pianist EA/73*
CORNWALL, Barry see Proctor,

Bryan Walter

CORNWALL, Mr. H. (d 1869 [59]) equestrian? EA/70*

CORNWELL, David (fl c.1700-13?) acrobat, conjurer, exhibitor BD

CORNWELL, Judy (b 1942) English actress WWT/15-16

CORNYSSHE, William (d 1524?) musician DNB

CORONA SABOLINI, Teresa see Costantini, Signora Giovanni Battista

CORONAKIS, Yvonne see Constant, Yvonne

CORPORA, Sig. (fl 1722) violinist BD

CORRE, Joseph (fl 1800) manager WWA/H

CORREL, Gladis (d 1962 [70]) performer BE*

CORRELL, Charles J. (1890-1972) actor CB, TW/29

CORRER, Mrs. Vittorio see Angelelli, Augusta

CORREY, Elizabeth (d 1912 [63]) EA/13*

CORRI, Adrienne (b 1932) Scottish actress TW/8

CORRI, Angelo (fl 1739) manager? BD

CORRI, Charles Montague (b 1861) English conductor WWT/5-9

CORRI, Clarence (fl 1899) composer, musical director DD

CORRI, Domenico (1746-1825) Italian composer DNB, ES

CORRI, Signora Domenico [née Bacchelli] (fl 1771-1810) Italian singer BD

CORRI, Dussek (d 1870) actor, singer DD

CORRI, Mrs. E. Dussek see Thirlwall, Annie

CORRI, Francesca (b 1795) actress, singer ES

CORRI, Ghita [Mrs. Neville Lynn] Scottish singer GRB/1

CORRI, Haydn (1785-1860) musician DD

CORRI, Haydn (1842-76) actor, singer DD, ES

CORRI, Mrs. Haydn (d 1867 [67]) singer EA/68*

CORRI, Henry (1824-88) actor, singer DD, ES

CORRI, Ida Gillies (d 1908 [67]) singer EA/09*

CORRI, Kathleen (fl 1880) actress, singer DD

CORRI, Monte (1784-1849) composer, musical director DD

CORRI, Pat (1820-76) actor, singer CDP, DD, ES

CORRI, Rupert (d 1876) scene artist EA/77*

CORRI, Sophia see Dussek, Mrs. Jan Ladislav

CORRI, Mrs. V. [née Annie Parker] (d 1870 [29]) actress EA/71*

CORRI, William (d 1932 [73]) musician WWT/14*

CORRIE, D. T. actor, singer, composer CDP

CORRIE, Joe (1894-1968) Scottish dramatist OC/1-3

CORRIGAN, Charles (d 1966 [72]) performer BP/50*

CORRIGAN, Emmett (1868/71-1932) Dutch/American actor SR, WWS, WWT/4-6

CORRIGAN, Helen (d 1887) EA/88*

CORRIGAN, Lloyd (d 1969 [69]) performer BP/54*

CORRIGAN, Robert W. (b 1927) American educator BE

CORRUCCINI, Roberto (1859-1926) Italian singer WWA/1

CORRY, A. D. (d 1902 [43]) manager EA/03*

CORRY, Eliza (d 1877) EA/79*

CORRY, Mrs. T. C. S. see Corry, Eliza

CORRY, Walter Frederick Stewart (d 1893) singer EA/94*

CORSARO, Frank (b 1924) American director, dramatist, actor, teacher BE, CB, WWT/14-16

CORSETTI, Guiseppe (fl 1833) singer HAS

"CORSICAN FAMILY, The" see Teresia, Mme.

CORSON, Richard American actor, writer, educator BE

CORSON, Robert Frederick see Artell, R. F.

CORT, Alex (b 1939) American dancer TW/23-24

CORT, Harry Linsley (d 1937 [44]) producer, author BE*, BP/21*

CORT, John (1859-1929) American manager SR

CORTES, Mr. (fl 1790-91) rope walker, dancer, tumbler BD

CORTESI, Adelaide (1828-89)
Italian singer CDP, ES,
HAS
CORTESI, Antonio (1796-1879)
Italian dancer, choreographer
ES
CORTEZ, Leon (d 1970 [72])
performer BP/55*
CORTHELL, Herbert (1875/78-
1947) American actor SR,
TW/3, WWM, WWS
CORTIS, Antonio (1892-1952)
Italian singer ES
CORTO, Diana (b 1942) Ameri-
can actress TW/25
CORUM, Paul (b 1943) Ameri-
can actor TW/27
CORWIN, Norman [Lewis] (b
1910) American dramatist,
director, producer BE,
CB, HJD
CORY, Mr. (fl 1675) actor BD
CORY, Kenneth (b 1941) Ameri-
can actor TW/28-29
CORY, Thomas (fl 1791-1808?)
actor BD, TD/1-2
CORY-THOMAS, Lambert (d
1908) English actor GRB/1
CORZATTE, Clayton (b 1927)
American actor TW/22-25
COSBY, Bill (b 1938) American
comedian CB
COSBY, Thomas (fl 1663-70)
rope dancer, booth operator
BD
COSBY, Mrs. Thomas (fl 1663-
64) rope dancer BD
COSGROVE, Marie [Mrs. Charles
Pateman] (d 1892 [34]) actress
EA/93*
COSHAM, Ernest (d 1910 [44])
actor GRB/3-4
COSIO, Rosita (b 1933) Puerto
Rican actress TW/2
COSLOW, Jacqueline (b 1943)
American actress TW/28
COSMAN, Lydia (d 1900)
music-hall singer EA/01*
COSNETT, T. (d 1871 [27])
comic singer EA/72*
COSSA, Sig. (fl 1785) tumbler
BD
COSSART, Ernest (1876-1951)
English actor TW/2-7,
WWT/7-11
COSSART, Valerie (b 1910)
English actress WWT/9-12
COSSINS, W. (fl 1734-35)

boxkeeper BD
COSSIRA, Emile (1857-1923) French
singer ES
COSTA, Carlo (d 1888 [62]) music
teacher EA/89*
COSTA, Davide (fl 1843-64) Italian
dancer, choreographer ES
COSTA, Gioacchino (fl 1790) singer
BD
COSTA, Sir Michael (1810-84)
Italian/English composer, con-
ductor CDP, DNB, ES
COSTA, Raphael (d 1892 [76])
EA/93*
COSTAIN, Mr. (fl 1764-95) dresser,
caller, concessionaire? BD
COSTANTINI, Signora (fl 1726)
singer BD
COSTANTINI, Costantino (b c.1634)
Italian actor, musician BD
COSTANTINI, Domenica (fl 1674-
86) Italian actress BD
COSTANTINI, Giovanni Battista
(d 1720) Italian actor, musician
BD
COSTANTINI, Signora Giovanni
Battista [née Teresa Corona
Sabolini] (d 1730) Italian actress
BD
COSTANZA, Signora (fl 1742-43)
dancer BD
COSTELL, Mary Anne see Can-
ning, Mrs. George
COSTELLA, Michael (d 1896)
"jester" EA/97*
COSTELLO, Miss (fl 1780) actress
BD
COSTELLO, Charles (d 1973 [83])
stage manager BP/58*
COSTELLO, Helene (d 1957 [53])
American actress BE*
COSTELLO, Joseph (d 1888 [56])
musical director EA/89*
COSTELLO, Lou (1906-59) Ameri-
can vaudevillian ES, TW/15,
WWA/3
COSTELLO, Mariclare American
actress TW/25-26, 29
COSTELLO, Mary Anne see
Canning, Mrs. George
COSTELLO, Maurice (1877-1950)
American actor ES, TW/7
COSTELLO, Michael (d 1883 [39])
music-hall artist EA/84*
COSTELLO, Philip (d 1901) EA/02*
COSTELLO, Tom (1863-1945) Eng-
lish music-hall performer CDP,
COC, OC/1-3

COSTELLO, Mrs. Tom (d 1912 [49]) EA/13*

COSTELLO, William A. (d 1971 [73]) performer BP/56*

COSTELLOW, Thomas (fl 1775-1815?) composer, singer, teacher BD

COSTENTENUS, Cpt. Greek/ Albanian tattoed man CDP

COSTER, Nicholas (b 1934) English actor TW/18-20, 24-25, 27-30

COSTETOMEPOLITAN, Mr. (fl 1772-82) Greek acrobat, slack-rope walker, clown, equestrian BD

COSTIGAN, James (b 1926/28) American dramatist, actor BE, ES

COSTIGAN, Josephine see Pardey, Mrs. George

COSTIL, William, Jr. (d 1976 [63]) producer/director/ choreographer BP/60*

COSTIN, Mr. (fl 1746-72) box-keeper BD

COSTOLLO, Patrick (d 1766) actor BD

COTA, Keith (b 1931) American actor TW/25

COTES, Mr. (fl 1767) singer BD

COTES, Charles Greville (d 1905 [31]) songwriter EA/07*

COTES, Peter [né Sydney Boulting] (b 1912) English actor, manager, producer, director AAS, WWT/10-16

COTON, A. V. (d 1969 [63]) critic BP/54*

COTOPOULI, Marika (d 1954 [68]) Greek actress TW/11

COTSHALL, Mr. (fl 1758) actor BD

COTSOPOULOS, Thanos (b 1911) Greek actor TW/9

COTSWORTH, Staats (b 1908) American actor BE, TW/ 10-11, 21-24, 26, 28, WWT/ 14-16

COTT, Ted (d 1973 [55]) direc-tor/producer/choreographer BP/58*

COTTAM, Kent (b 1935) actor TW/30

COTTE, Edward (d 1906 [70]) singer, actor DD

COTTELL, Lansdowne (d 1909

[73]?) singer GRB/1

COTTELL, Victor Lansdowne (d 1912) professor of music EA/ 13*

COTTEN, Joseph (b 1905) American actor AAS, BE, ES, TW/14, 16, 19, WWT/14-16

COTTER, George Sackville (1755-1831) translator, writer DD

COTTER, Jayne see Meadows, Jayne

COTTER, Patrick [alias O'Brien] (1761?-1806) Irish giant CDP, DNB

COTTEREAU, Symon (fl 1670) musician BD

COTTEREL, Miss (fl 1750) singer BD

COTTIN, Mr. (fl 1700-06) dancer BD

COTTINET, Edmond (d 1895 [71]) dramatist EA/96*

COTTON, Mr. (fl 1782) actor BD

COTTON, Mrs. (fl 1708) dresser BD

COTTON, A. Benjamin (1829-1908) American minstrel manager and performer CDP, HAS

COTTON, Charles (1630-87) English dramatist CP/1-3, DD, GT

COTTON, Fred Ayres (d 1964 [57]) American actor, executive TW/ 2-3, 20

COTTON, George (d 1975 [72]) performer BP/60*

COTTON, John (fl 1794-1800) vio-linist BD

COTTON, John (1886-1946) Ameri-can dramatist SR

COTTON, Lucy (d 1948 [57]) act-ress TW/5

COTTON, Robert F. English actor BE*

COTTON, Wilfred (b 1873) English actor, manager GRB/1-4, WWT/1-6

COTTON, Mrs. Wilfred see Reeve, Ada

COTTRELL, Miss (d 1866 [25]) actress, singer EA/72*

COTTRELL, Cherry (b 1909) Eng-lish actress WWT/9-12

COTTRELL, Richard (b 1936) Eng-lish director, manager, drama-tist AAS, WWT/15-16

COTTRELL, Richard (b 1944) American actor TW/25-26

COTTRELL, Thomas (d 1867 [52])

musician EA/68*

COTTRELL, William (b 1918) American actor TW/25-26

COTTRELLY, Mathilde (1851-1933) German singer, actress CDP, SR

COTTS, Campbell (1902-64) South African actor TW/9

COTZ, Peter (fl 1818-29) equestrian HAS

COUCH, Mr. (fl 1710-21?) impresario, dancing master? violinist? BD

COUDELLE, Mrs. M. E. see Chober, Cora Lena

COUGHLIN, Bill T. (d 1974 [81]) performer BP/59*

COUGHLIN, Kevin (1945-76) American actor TW/15

COUGHTREE, Rosa Ann [Marie Leslie] (d 1882) actress EA/83*

COULDOCK, Charles Walter (1815-98) English/American actor CDP, DAB, DD, ES, HAS, OC/1-3, SR, WWA/H

COULDOCK, Eliza (fl 1853) actress HAS

COULDOCK, Louisa (d 1877 [60]) English actress HAS

COULON, Anne Jacqueline [Mme. Pierre Gabriel Gardel, I] (fl 1787-92) French dancer BD

COULON, Eugene (fl 1787-1830) dancing master CDP

COULOURIS, George (b 1903) English actor AAS, BE, ES, TW/2-7, 21-22, WWT/9-16

COULSEY, Charles (d 1881 [13]) performer EA/82*

COULSON, Robert F. (d 1909 [35]) lessee EA/10*

COULSONE, Harry (d 1887 [40]) variety entertainer EA/88*

COULSON-MAYNE, E. W. (d 1917 [20]) EA/18*

COULTER, Frazer (1848-1937) Canadian actor CDP, WWM, WWS

COULTER, Kay actress TW/1

COULTER, Philip Frazer see Coulter, Frazer

COULTER, Mrs. Robert Porter see Millard, Evelyn

COULTON, Mr. (fl 1789-90)

house servant? BD

COUNCIL, Richard (b 1947) American actor TW/30

COUNSELL, John (b 1905) English director, manager, actor AAS, COC, OC/3, WWT/10-16

COUNTER, Frederick Stanhope see Stanhope, Frederick

COUNTISS, Cathrine (fl 1900s) American actress WWM, WWS

COUNTS, Mr. (fl 1794) musician BD

COUP, William Cameron (1833-95) American circus & theatrical manager CDP, ES

COUPE, Diane (b 1939) English actress TW/23-26

COUPER, Barbara (b 1903) English actress WWT/8-14

COURCO, Mr. see Curco, Mr.

COURT, Beatrice K. see Arkinstall, Beatrice K.

COURT, Bob (d 1970 [68]) performer BP/55*

COURT, Geraldine (b 1942) American actress TW/29

COURTAINE, Harry (d 1899) actor CDP

COURTE, Mrs. Henry see Courte, Louisa

COURTE, Louisa [Mrs. Henry Courte] (d 1906 [82]) EA/07*

"COURTE, S. X." (fl 1894-98) dramatist DD

COURTELINE, Georges [Georges Moinaux] (1858-1929) French dramatist MWD, WWT/3

COURTENAY, Mr. (fl late 18th cent) actor CDP

COURTENAY, Miss [Miss Crawley] (fl 1777) actress, singer BD

COURTENAY, Denis (1760-94) Irish piper BD

COURTENAY, Edward (d 1884) EA/85*

COURTENAY, Eliza [Mrs. Lindo Courtenay] (d 1906 [64]) EA/08*

COURTENAY, Eveline [Mrs. John Hay] (d 1898) actress EA/00*

COURTENAY, Foster (d 1909) actor EA/11*

COURTENAY, Dr. Fred (d 1910) proprietor? EA/11*

COURTENAY, Lindo (d 1896 [65]) lessee, manager EA/97*

COURTENAY, Mrs. Lindo (d 1885) EA/86*

COURTENAY, Mrs. Lindo see

Courtenay, Eliza
COURTENAY, Tom (b 1937)
English actor AAS, CB,
ES, WWT/14-16
COURTENAY, Vera (fl 1900s)
American singer WWM
COURTENAY, William (1875-
1933) American actor WWS,
WWT/1-7
COURTENAY, William J. (d
1908) EA/09*
COURTENEY, Fay (d 1943 [65])
American actress BE*,
BP/28*
COURTEVILLE, Raphael (d
1675) singer BD
COURTEVILLE, Raphael (d
c.1735) organist, composer,
singer BD, DNB
COURTEVILLE, Raphael (d
1772) organist BD
COURTICE, Thomas [Sydney
W. Curtiss] (b 1872) Eng-
lish business manager
GRB/1-2
COURTICE, Mrs. Thomas
see Curtiss, Alice May
COURTIER-DUTTON, Lionel
see Carson, Lionel
COURTLEIGH, Edna (d 1962 [77])
actress BE*
COURTLEIGH, William Louis
(1869-1930) Canadian actor
ES, GRB/2-4, SR, WWA/1,
WWS, WWT/1-6
COURTLY, Thomas J. (d 1934
[67]) business manager
WWT/14*
COURTNAY, Denis see Cour-
tenay, Denis
COURTNEIDGE, Charles (d 1935)
actor BE*, WWT/14*
COURTNEIDGE, Dame Cicely
(b 1893) Australian actress
AAS, COC, NTH, TW/4-11,
WWT/1-16
COURTNEIDGE, Robert (1859-
1939) Scottish manager,
dramatist GRB/4, WWT/
1-8
COURTNEIDGE, Mrs. Robert
[Rosie Nott] (d 1914 [46])
actress BE*, WWT/14*
COURTNEIDGE, Rosaline (1903-
26) English actress WWT/5
COURTNEY, Mr. (fl 1749-62)
singer BD
COURTNEY, Mr. (fl 1773-75)

actor, singer BD
COURTNEY, Alexander (b 1940)
American actor TW/24-26
COURTNEY, Baron [Henry Black-
well] (d 1901 [66]) music-hall
chairman EA/02*
COURTNEY, C. C. librettist CD
COURTNEY, Denis see Courtenay,
Denis
COURTNEY, Elizabeth (d 1974 [69])
designer BP/59*
COURTNEY, Fay (1868-1943) Amer-
ican actress SR
COURTNEY, F. C. (d 1890) actor
EA/91*
COURTNEY, Gordon (1895-1964)
English composer, producer,
manager, press representative,
business manager WWT/9-10
COURTNEY, Harry (d 1872) pianist
EA/73*
COURTNEY, Inez (d 1975 [67])
performer BP/59*
COURTNEY, James (b 1924) Amer-
ican actor TW/6
COURTNEY, James J. (d 1888
[43]) proprietor EA/89*
COURTNEY, John (1813-65) actor,
dramatist DD
COURTNEY, Mary (d 1874 [65])
EA/76*
COURTNEY, Maud actress, singer
CDP
COURTNEY, Oscar W. (d 1963 [85])
performer BE*
COURTNEY, Paul (d 1906) comedian,
sketch artist EA/08*
COURTNEY, William (1876-1933)
American actor SR
COURTNEY, William Leonard
(1850-1928) Indian/English
dramatist, critic DD, ES,
GRB/2-4, WWT/1-5, WWW/2
COURTRIGHT, Clyde (d 1967 [82])
performer BP/52*
COURTS, Mr. (fl 1760-61) singer
BD
COURVILLE, Albert de see De
Courville, Albert
COUSENS, Robert (1818-67) English
actor HAS
COUSINS, Mr. (fl 1748) fair booth
proprietor BD
COUSINS, Charles (d 1890) musical
director EA/91*
COUSINS, Rosie [Mrs. Fred Street]
(d 1908 [31]) EA/09*
COUSTOS, Mr. (fl 1747-50) singer

BD

COUSTUP, George (fl 1785-99) musician BD

COUTCHEE, Noyai (fl 1795-96) performer BD

COUTTS, Miss (fl 1779) actress BD

COUTTS, Compton (d 1910 [60]) actor EA/11*, WWT/14*

COUTTS, Harriot see Mellon, Harriot

COUTTS, Henri (d 1910 [42]) quick-change artist EA/11*

COVE, Augusta (d 1903) actress? EA/04*

COVENEY, George (d 1918 [60]) EA/19*

COVENEY, H. (1790-1881) actor CDP, DD

COVENEY, Mrs. H. (d 1854 [67]) actress WWT/14*

COVENEY, Harriett [Mrs. Charles A. Jecks] (1828-92) actress DD, DP, OAA/2

COVENEY, Jane [Mrs. Larkins] (1824-1900) actress CDP, DD

COVENTRY, Rev. Francis (d c.1759) dramatist CP/3

COVENTRY, Lucy (d 1918) EA/19*

COVER, Franklin Edward (b 1928) American actor TW/23, 25-27, 30

COVERDALE, Ernest Charles see Prescott, Walter

COVERT, Mr. singer CDP

COVILL, Mr. (fl 1786-94) singer, dancer? BD

COWAN, Adam (d 1908) manager EA/09*

COWAN, Clara (d 1907) EA/08*

COWAN, Grant (b 1935) Canadian actor TW/27-28

COWAN, Irene (b 1914) American actress TW/8

COWAN, Jerome (1897-1972) American actor BE, TW/28

COWAN, John F. actor CDP

COWAN, Lynn F. (d 1973) musician BP/58*

COWAN, Maurice A. (b 1891) English manager WWT/6

COWARD, Edward Fales (1862-1933) American dramatist WWA/1, WWM

COWARD, James (1824-80) English musician DNB

COWARD, Sir Noel Pierce (1899-1973) English actor, dramatist, composer, producer AAS, BE, CB, CH, COC, ES, HP, MD, MH, MWD, NTH, OC/1-3, PDT, RE, SR, TW/15-16, 29, WWA/5, WWT/4-15

COWCHER, Mr. (fl 1781) actor BD

COWDEN, Irene (d 1961) actress BE*

COWDERY, Mrs. [née Bessie Edwards] (d 1878) actress EA/79*

COWDERY, Charles (d 1878) actor EA/79*

COWE, Charlotte (d 1905) EA/06*

COWELL, Mrs. [née Sheppard] (b 1801) English actress HAS

COWELL, Anna [née Cruise] (b 1824) Irish singer, actress HAS, SR

COWELL, Emilie Marguerite [Mrs. Sam Cowell] (d 1899 [80]) EA/00*

COWELL, Florence see Tapping, Mrs. Alfred B.

COWELL, Henry Dixon (b 1897) American composer ES

COWELL, Joseph (d before 1870) English scene painter ES, HAS

COWELL, Joseph Leathley [Hawkins Witchett] (1792-1863) English actor CDP, COC, DD, DNB, ES, HAS, OC/1-3, SR, WWA/H

COWELL, Lydia (fl 1876-91) actress DD

COWELL, Mrs. Sam see Cowell, Emilie Marguerite

COWELL, Samuel Houghton (1820-64) English/American music-hall performer CDP, COC, DD, DNB, ES, HAS, OC/1-3

COWELL, Sidney Frances see Bateman, Sidney Frances

COWELL, Sydney (1846-1925) English actress CDP, ES, OC/1-3, PP/1

COWELL, Sydney (1872-1941) see Fairbrother, Sydney

COWELL, William (1820-68) Irish business manager, writer, actor? HAS, SR

COWELS, Charles O. (1861-1916) actor SR

COWELS, Eugene (1860-1948) Canadian composer, actor SR

COWEN, Emily (d 1910 [89]) EA/11*

COWEN, Sir Frederick Hymen (1852-1935) Jamaican/English composer, conductor DD, DNB, ES, GRB/1, WWW/3
COWEN, Henrietta (fl 1891-99) actress DD
COWEN, Lawrence (1865-1942) English dramatist WWW/2-7
COWEN, Louis (d 1925 [69]) critic, dramatist BE*, WWT/14*
COWEN, Ron (b 1944) American dramatist CD
COWEN, William Joyce (d 1964 [76]) dramatist BE*
COWIE, Laura (1892-1969) Scottish actress ES, WWT/1-11
COWIE, Robert, Sr. (d 1877 [67]) proprietor EA/78*
COWIE, Robert G. W. (d 1963 [49]) press officer BP/48*
COWL, Jane (1884/90-1950) American actress, dramatist COC, DAB, ES, NTH, SR, TW/2-7, WWA/3, WWM, WWT/4-10
COWLE, William (d 1885 [84]) actor EA/86*
COWLES, Chandler (b 1917) American producer, actor BE, TW/2-6
COWLES, Eugene (1860-1948) Canadian singer, actor TW/5, WWA/4, WWS
COWLES, Matthew (b 1944) American actor TW/22, 24-26, 30
COWLES, M. B. (1843-87) American advance agent NYM
COWLEY, Abraham (1618-67) English dramatist COC, CP/1-3, DD, DNB, ES, FGF, GT, HP, OC/1-3
COWLEY, Albert (d 1876 [35]) singer EA/77*
COWLEY, Eric (1886-1948) English actor WWT/7-10
COWLEY, Francis Laurence (fl 1739) musician BD
COWLEY, Hannah [née Parkhouse] (1743-1809) English dramatist CDP, COC, CP/2-3, DD, DNB, ES, GT, HP, NTH, OC/1-3, TD/1-2
COWLEY, Richard (d 1619)

English actor COC, DA, GT, NTH, OC/1-3
COWLEY-POLHILL, R. (b 1844) English business manager, actor GRB/1
COWPER, Mr. (fl 1785-94) singer BD
COWPER, Mrs. (fl 1748-60) actress BD
COWPER, Miss (fl 1771-80?) singer BD
COWPER, Clara (d 1917) actress DD, EA/95
COWPER, Edward Alfred (d 1893) EA/94*
COWPER, John Curtis (1827-85) actor CDP, DD
COWRAN, Clay (d 1972 [58]) critic BP/56*
COWSLADE, Miss (fl 1755) actress BD
COX, Mr. (fl 1729-30) house servant BD
COX, Mr. (fl 1732-36) dancer BD
COX, Mr. (fl 1741) actor BD
COX, Mr. (fl 1761) actor BD
COX, Mr. (fl 1781-89) house servant BD
COX, Mr. (fl 1788-92) actor, singer BD
COX, Mrs. (fl 1760) singer BD
COX, Mrs. (fl 1781-82) singer, actress BD
COX, Mrs. (fl 1783-85) dresser BD
COX, Mrs. (fl 1798) dancer? BD
COX, Miss (fl 1795-1804) actress, dancer, singer? BD
COX, Brian (b 1946) Scottish actor WWT/16
COX, C. Douglas (d 1904 [60]) manager, actor EA/05*, WWT/14*
COX, Charles B. (d 1889 [48]) proprietor EA/90*
COX, Constance (b 1912) English dramatist AAS, WWT/11-16
COX, Dorothy Isobel see Wynyard, Diana
COX, Douglas see Cox, C. Douglas
COX, Elizabeth (c.1639?-88?) actress BD
COX, Faulkner (d 1906) actor EA/08*
COX, Gabriel (1747-92) master carpenter, machinist BD
COX, Garnet Wolseley (d 1904 [32])

composer EA/05*
COX, George William [George
Lupriel] (d 1886 [59]) circus
performer EA/88*
COX, Harry [Oliver James
Bussley] (1841-82) actor DD
COX, Henry Blackford (d 1880
[43]) EA/82*
COX, Hugh (1731-63) singer,
harpsichordist BD
COX, [John?] (fl 1751-64?)
singer, publisher, instrument
maker BD
COX, John George (d 1758)
oboist, dancing master BD
COX, Nellie singer CDP
COX, Ray (fl 1900s) American
actress, singer CDP, WWM
COX, Richard (b 1948) Ameri-
can actor TW/28, 30
COX, Robert (d 1655) English
actor, dramatist COC,
CP/1-3, DD, OC/1-3
COX, Robert (d 1974 [79])
performer BP/59*
COX, Susannah (fl 1702-15)
actress BD
COX, Thomas see Coco
COX, Wally (1924-73) American
actor CB, TW/29, WWA/5
COX, W. Herbert English
actor GRB/1
COXE, Louis O. (b 1918) Amer-
ican educator, dramatist
BE
COXER, Sarah see Anderton,
Sarah
COXEY, William Douglas (1883/
84-1943) American writer
SR, WWM
COX-IFE, William (d 1968)
producer/director BP/52*
COY, Walter (b 1913) American
actor TW/4-6
COYLE, Mr. (fl 1784) musician
BD
COYLE, Mr. (fl 1832) English/
American manager HAS
COYLE, Mrs. Frank see
Drew, Nelly
COYLE, George (d 1876) singer
EA/77*
COYLE, Mrs. George see
Coyle, Mary Ann
COYLE, Joe (d 1973 [56])
performer BP/58*
COYLE, John E. (d 1909 [40])
variety comedian EA/10*

COYLE, John E. (d 1964 [70])
singer, actor CDP
COYLE, Mary Ann [Mrs. George
Coyle] (d 1877) EA/78*
COYLE, Matilda (d 1889) EA/91*
COYLE, Miles (1714-96?) singer,
musician BD
COYLE, S. (d 1889) EA/90*
COYNE, Alice M. Rawlinson
[Mrs. Fred Coyne] (d 1884 [35])
EA/85*
COYNE, Anne [Mrs. Joseph Stirling
Coyne] (d 1880) EA/81*
COYNE, Edmund Stirling (d 1902
[52]) dramatist EA/03*
COYNE, Elizabeth [Mrs. J. Dennis
Coyne] (d 1892 [46]) EA/94*
COYNE, Frank singer, actor CDP
COYNE, Frank (d 1882) music-hall
artist EA/83*
COYNE, Frank (d 1906 [30]) variety
comedian EA/07*
COYNE, Fred singer, actor CDP
COYNE, Fred (d 1886 [39]) come-
dian EA/87*
COYNE, Mrs. Fred see Coyne,
Alice M. Rawlinson
COYNE, Gardiner [Henry Andrew
Gardiner] (d 1900) Irish actor
CDP, HAS
COYNE, Mrs. J. Dennis see
Coyne, Elizabeth
COYNE, Joseph (1867/70-1941)
American actor ES, GRB/2-4,
WWS, WWT/1-9
COYNE, Joseph Stirling (1803/05-
68) Irish dramatist CDP, DD,
DNB, EA/68, ES
COYNE, Mrs. Joseph Stirling see
Coyne, Anne
COYNE, Kathleen (b 1945) American
actress TW/26
[COYSH, Miss?] (fl 1682) actress
BD
COYSH, John (fl 1667-c. 97) actor,
manager BD
COYSH, Mrs. John [Dorothy?] (fl
1668-79) actress BD
CRABBE, Mrs. see Herbert,
Louisa
CRABTREE, Charles [Charles
Lestree] (d 1917) comedy juggler
EA/18*
CRABTREE, Charlotte see Lotta
CRABTREE, Don (b 1928) American
actor TW/26
CRABTREE, Paul (b 1918) American
director, actor, producer BE,

TW/1, 3, 6-8
CRACE, Mr. (fl 1789-1803)
scene painter BD
CRACRAFT, Tom Adrian (d
1963 [58]) scene designer
BP/48*
CRADDOCK, John (d 1873 [43])
actor? EA/74*
CRADDOCK, Joseph (fl 1771)
dramatist GT
CRADDOCK, Louisa see
Austin, Mrs. Noel
CRADOCK, Joseph (1742-1826)
English dramatist CDP,
CP/2-3, DD, DNB
CRADOCK, William (fl 1669)
musician BD
CRAFT, Roy (d 1965 [75])
performer BP/49*
CRAFT, Thomas (b 1937) Eng-
lish actor TW/26
CRAFTS, Charley (d 1974 [78])
performer BP/58*
CRAFTS, Griffin (d 1973 [73])
performer BP/58*
CRAFTS, William (1787-1826)
American critic, dramatist
EAP, HJD
CRAGEN, William (d 1972 [62])
actor, director TW/29
CRAGG, Amanda [Mrs. J. W.
Cragg] (d 1909) acrobat
EA/10*
CRAGG, Billy (d 1918) EA/19*
CRAGG, Mrs. J. W. [Alice
Daly] (d 1889) EA/90*
CRAGG, Mrs. J. W. see
Cragg, Amanda
CRAGGS, Mr. (fl 1744) actor
BD
CRAIG, Master (fl 1792) singer
BD
CRAIG, [Adam?] (d 1741) vio-
linist BD
CRAIG, Adam H. (d 1911)
EA/13*
CRAIG, Casey American actor
TW/29
CRAIG, Clavering [Graham
Daviss] (d 1916 [44]) actor,
musical director EA/17*
CRAIG, David (b 1923) American
lyricist, librettist, coach BE
CRAIG, Edith Geraldine Ailsa
(1869-1947) English actress,
director GRB/1-4, OC/1-3,
SR, TW/3, WWS, WWT/1-10
CRAIG, Edward Anthony see

Carrick, Edward
CRAIG, Edward Gordon (1872-1966)
English actor, producer, scene
designer BE, COC, DD, DP,
ES, GRB/1-4, NTH, OC/1-3,
PDT, TW/23, WWT/1-14
CRAIG, George Wymark (d 1898
[64]) manager EA/99*
CRAIG, Hardin (1875-1968) Ameri-
can scholar BE
CRAIG, Helen (b 1912/14) American
actress, teacher BE, ES, TW/
2-11, 22-24, WWT/10-16
CRAIG, Joel American actor TW/
29
CRAIG, John (d 1890 [62]) EA/91*
CRAIG, John (1868-1932) American
actor SR
CRAIG, Laura (1880-1947) American
actress SR
CRAIG, May (d 1972 [83]) Irish
actress TW/28
CRAIG, Michael [né Gregson] (b
1929) Indian/English actor
WWT/15-16
CRAIG, Miriam (d 1971 [54])
performer BP/55*
CRAIG, Noel American actor TW/
26-30
CRAIG, Phyllis (b 1936) English
actress TW/24-26
CRAIG, Robert H. (b 1842) Ameri-
can actor HAS
CRAIG, Walter (d 1972 [71]) singer,
dancer, actor TW/29
CRAIG, Walter James (d 1885)
EA/86*
CRAIG, Wendy (b 1934) English
actress WWT/14-16
CRAIG, William C. (b 1908) Amer-
ican educator, director BE
CRAIG, William James (1843-1906)
Irish scholar DNB
CRAIGIE, Mrs. Pearl Mary Teresa
see Hobbes, John Oliver
CRAIN, Harold (b 1911) American
educator BE
CRAMER, Miss [Mrs. Plumer] (fl
1828) actress CDP
CRAMER, Charles (d 1799) violinist
BD
CRAMER, Edd (d 1963 [39]) actor
BE*
CRAMER, Fanny [Mrs. William
Danvers; Mrs. Nagle] (fl 1852-
59) actress? HAS
CRAMER, Franz (1772-1848) German
violinist, impresario BD, CDP,

DNB
CRAMER, Mrs. H. [Miss M.
E. Poole] (1803-68) English
actress HAS
CRAMER, Henry (d 1877) musi-
cian EA/78*
CRAMER, Johann Baptist (1771-
1858) German musician,
composer, publisher BD,
CDP, DNB
CRAMER, M. E. (1803-68)
actress CDP
CRAMER, Wilhelm (1745-99)
German violinist, composer,
impresario BD, CDP, DNB
CRAMERER, Mlle. (fl 1779-80)
dancer BD
CRAMPTON, Charlotte (b 1816)
actress CDP, HAS, SR
CRAMPTON, Victoire, Lady
(1837-71) French/English
singer DNB
CRANDALL, Edward (1904-68)
American actor TW/1-3,
6, 24
CRANDALL, Jashf (b 1900)
American dancer, choreog-
rapher, maître de ballet ES
CRANDELL, David Miller (b
1914) American executive
BE
CRANDELL, R. F. (d 1974 [72])
journalist BP/59*
CRANE, Mrs. (fl 1761) actress
HAS
CRANE, Dean (b 1932) American
dancer, choreographer, direc-
tor, aerialist, costume de-
signer BE, TW/25-27
CRANE, D. H. see Howard,
Dan
CRANE, Edith (1865/75-1912)
American actress SR, WWS
CRANE, Edward (fl 1761) drama-
tist CP/2-3, GT
CRANE, Ellen (d 1963 [78])
performer BP/48*
CRANE, Emily (d 1901) actress
EA/02*
CRANE, Gardner (b 1874)
American vaudevillian WWM
CRANE, Mrs. Gardner (b 1875)
American vaudevillian WWM
CRANE, Harold (b 1975) English
actor, singer WWM
CRANE, Harry T. English actor
GRB/1
CRANE, Jessie [Mrs. Harry

J. Crane] (d 1908) EA/09*
CRANE, Mrs. Harry J. see
Crane, Jessie
CRANE, John (fl 1550) actor DA
CRANE, Lillian Marie (d 1916 [14])
EA/17*
CRANE, Norma (d 1973 [42]) act-
ress TW/30
CRANE, Ralph (c.1550/60-after
1621) English player copier DA,
OC/1-3
CRANE, Richard (b 1944) English
dramatist WWT/16
CRANE, William (fl 1523-45)
master of the Chapel Royal
DA, DNB
CRANE, William Henry (1845-1928)
American actor CDP, COC,
DAB, DD, ES, GRB/1-4, OC/
1-3, PP/1, SR, WWA/1, WWM,
WWS, WWT/1-5
CRANFIELD, Mr. (fl 1780-1800?)
dancer, actor BD
CRANFIELD, Mrs. (fl 1790-98)
dancer BD
CRANFIELD, T. (fl 1796-1805?)
dancer BD
CRANFORD, Miss (fl 1784-94)
singer, actress BD
CRANKE (d 1783) dramatist CP/3
CRANKO, John (1927-73) American
choreographer, ballet director
CB, ES
CRANMER, Arthur (d 1954 [69])
singer WWT/14*
CRANWIGGE, James (fl 1598)
actor? DA
CRAPEAU [or Crapo], Marion H.
[Mrs. W. W. Pearce] (fl 1859)
actress HAS
CRAPO, Marion H. see Crapeau,
Marion H.
CRASTON, Mrs. see Durant,
Marie
CRASTON, Annie [Mrs. W. Walton]
(d 1908) actress EA/09*
CRASTON, William (d 1902 [33])
manager EA/03*
CRATER, Allene (d 1957 [77])
singer, actress TW/14
CRATHORN, Mr. (fl 1776-94)
English violoncellist, composer
BD
CRAUFORD, Mrs. (fl 1765) dancer
BD
CRAUFORD, Ellen Elizabeth [Mrs.
W. R. Crauford] (d 1873) EA/
74*

CRAUFORD, J. R. [J. R.
Cornock] (1847/48/50-1930)
English actor   OAA/2,
WWT/1-6
CRAUFORD, Mrs. J. R.   see
Ingram, Alice
CRAUFORD, Lane (d 1928 [44])
historian, actor   WWT/14*
CRAUFORD, Louise (d 1892)
actress   EA/93*
CRAUFORD, W. R. (d 1874
[45]) actor?   EA/75*
CRAUFORD, Mrs. W. R.
see Crauford, Ellen Elizabeth
CRAUFURD, David (fl 1700-04)
Scottish dramatist   CP/1-3,
DD
CRAUFURD, Russell actor   EA/
96
CRAUFURD, Mrs. Russell   see
Poole, Annie
CRAVEN, Mr. (fl 1749) actor,
singer   BD
CRAVEN, Miss (fl 1771-73)
actress   BD
CRAVEN, Countess   see   Brun-
ton, Louisa
CRAVEN, Alicia singer   CDP
CRAVEN, Arthur [John Edward
Davies] (d 1894) clown, come-
dian   EA/95*
CRAVEN, Arthur Scott (d 1917)
actor, dramatist   GRB/3-4,
WWT/1-3
CRAVEN, Elise [Elise Barbara
Alleyne-Barrett] (b 1898)
English actress, dancer
WWT/1-7
CRAVEN, Lady Elizabeth (fl
1767-80) dramatist   CP/2
CRAVEN, Frank (1875-1945)
American actor, dramatist,
producer   CB, DAB, ES,
NTH, OC/1-3, SR, TW/2,
WWA/2, WWT/3-9
CRAVEN, Gemma (b 1950) Irish
actress   WWT/16
CRAVEN, Hawes [Henry Hawes
Craven Green] (1837-1910)
English scene painter   COC,
DD, DNB, ES, OC/1-3
CRAVEN, Henry Thornton (1818/
21-1905) English dramatist,
actor   CDP, DD, DNB, EA/
68, GRB/1, OAA/1-2
CRAVEN, Mrs. H[enry] T[horn-
ton]   see   Nelson, Eliza
CRAVEN, Jane [Mrs. Will Craven]

(d 1884)   EA/85*
CRAVEN, Robin (b 1906/10) Eng-
lish actor   BE, TW/3-16
CRAVEN, Ruby (d 1964 [76/77])
Australian actress   BE*, WWT/
14*
CRAVEN, Tom (1868-1919) English
actor, manager, dramatist   DD,
WWT/2-3
CRAVEN, Walter Stokes (fl 1894-
97) actor, singer, dramatist
DD, SR
CRAVEN, Mrs. Will   see   Craven,
Jane
CRAVEN, William (fl 1770-74)
proprietor   BD
CRAVES, H. (fl 1705) dramatist
GT
CRAWCOUR, David (d 1891 [43])
EA/92*
CRAWFORD, Mr. actor, manager
TD/1-2
CRAWFORD, Mrs. (fl 1760-61)
dancer   BD
CRAWFORD, Mrs. (fl 1857) actress
HAS
CRAWFORD, Miss (fl 1770-71)
actress   BD
CRAWFORD, Miss (fl 1785?-94?)
singer   BD
CRAWFORD, Adelaide actress?
singer?   CDP
CRAWFORD, Alice (b 1882) Aus-
tralian actress   GRB/3-4, WWT/
1-7
CRAWFORD, Amy [Mrs. Bevan-
Slator] (d 1898) actress   EA/99*
CRAWFORD, Anne (1920-56) Pales-
tinian/English actress   ES,
WWT/12
CRAWFORD, Anne   see   Barry,
Mrs. Spranger
CRAWFORD, Bertie actress, singer
CDP
CRAWFORD, Boyd (b 1914) American
actor   TW/4-6
CRAWFORD, Broderick (b 1911)
American actor   BE, CB, ES
CRAWFORD, Charles (d 1969 [44])
critic   BP/54*
CRAWFORD, Cheryl (b 1902) Amer-
ican producer, director, manager
AAS, BE, CB, COC, ES, TW/
2-8, WWT/10-16
CRAWFORD, Clifton (1870-1920)
Scottish actor   SR
CRAWFORD, Dorothy (d 1976 [90])
theatre founder   BP/60*

CRAWFORD, Dorothy Maude
[née Gabain] (b 1885) li-
brarian BE
CRAWFORD, F. Marion (1854-
1909) American writer,
dramatist DD, ES
CRAWFORD, Howard M. (d 1969
[55]) performer BP/54*
CRAWFORD, Jack Randall (b
1878) American educator BE
CRAWFORD, Joan (1908-77)
American actress CB
CRAWFORD, Mary (b 1940)
American actress TW/24
CRAWFORD, Michael (b 1942)
English actor TW/23,
WWT/16
CRAWFORD, Mimi (d 1966 [61])
English actress, singer,
dancer WWT/5-8
CRAWFORD, Nan (d 1975 [82])
actress BP/60*, WWT/16*
CRAWFORD, Peter (d 1793)
treasurer, manager BD
CRAWFORD, Thomas (1750-94)
English actor, musician,
manager BD, GT
CRAWFORD, Mrs. Thomas
see Barry, Mrs. Spranger
CRAWFORD, William (d 1916)
comedian EA/18*
CRAWLEY, Mr. (fl 1695-c.
1727) puppeteer BD
CRAWLEY, Mr. (fl 1784) singer
BD
CRAWLEY, Miss see Cour-
tenay, Miss
CRAWLEY, Dan (d 1912 [40])
Irish comedian CDP, EA/
13*
CRAWLEY, J. Sayre see
Crawley, Sayre
CRAWLEY, Robert (b 1917)
American actor TW/4-5, 23
CRAWLEY, Sayre (1870-1948)
English actor SR, TW/4
CRAWSHAW, John (d 1871 [35])
musician EA/72*
CRAWSHAW, William James
(d 1913 [43]) EA/14*
CRAYFORD, Mrs. see Thorne,
Alice
CRAYTHORNE, James ["Rus-
sell"] (d 1887 [37]) music-
hall artist EA/88*
CREAMER, Harry (d 1894)
minstrel EA/95*
CREAMER, Henry (d 1891)

EA/92*
CREAN, Mrs. John see Rogers,
Maggie
CREBER, Theophilus (d 1902) pro-
prietor EA/03*
CRECRAFT, Elizabeth (d 1917 [97])
travelling show-woman EA/18*
CREE, Mrs. Douglas see Rorke,
Kate
CREED, Mr. (fl 1794-95) singer
BD
CREED [or Creede], Thomas (d
1616?) stationer DNB
CREEDON, John Barry (d 1900)
comedian EA/01*
CREEK, Thomas (fl 1668-70?)
actor? BD
CREEL, Frances (d 1957 [43])
actress TW/13
CREESE, D. (d 1917 [33]) manager
EA/18*
CREESE, René see Ray, René
CREESE, T. A. (fl 1860-66) Amer-
ican actor HAS
CREESE, Mrs. T. A. [née Eliza-
beth Perry] (b 1843) American
dancer, singer, actress HAS
CREGAN, David (b 1931) English
dramatist CD, WWT/15-16
CREGAR, Samuel Laird (1916-44)
American actor TW/1
CREHAN, Ada see Rehan, Ada
CREHAN, Joseph (d 1966 [82])
performer BP/50*
CREHAN, Kate see Byron, Mrs.
Oliver Doud
CREIGHTON, Anthony (b 1923)
Scottish actor, dramatist PDT
CRELIN, Mrs. E. W. see
D'Arville, Camille
CRELLIN, Herbert see Standing,
Herbert
CREMLIN, F. Canadian actor
GRB/1
CREMONINI, Clementina (fl 1763-
66) Italian singer BD
CREMONINI, Domenico (fl 1784-87)
Italian singer BD
CREMONINI, Giuseppe (1866-1903)
Italian singer ES
CREPE, Mlle. see D'Auberval,
Mme. Jean
CRESCENTINI, Girolamo (1762-
1846) Italian singer BD
CRESCIMANO, Mlle. (fl 1859)
singer HAS
CRESPI, Signora (fl 1773-86)
dancer BD

CRESPIN, Régine (b 1927)
French singer ES
CRESPION, Stephen (c.1649-
1711) singer BD
CRESSALL, Maud (1886-1962)
English actress WWT/1-8
CRESSEA, Mrs. (fl 1698) im-
presario BD
CRESSETT, John (fl in Restora-
tion) impresario BD
CRESSON, James (b 1935)
American actor TW/18-19
CRESSWELL, Mr. (fl 1780-
1809?) actor BD
CRESSWELL, Helen (fl 1880)
actress DD
CRESSWELL, John (fl 1796-1814)
carpenter, scene painter,
machinist, chorus singer?
BD
CRESSWELL, Thomas (fl 1660-
79) trumpeter BD
CRESSY, Mrs. Will M. see
Dayne, Blanche
CRESSY, Will Martin (1863/65-
1930) American actor SR,
WWA/1, WWM, WWS
CREST, Robert (b 1938) Ameri-
can actor TW/28
CRESWELL, Helen (d 1949 [103])
actress BE*, WWT/14*
CRESWELL, Saylor (b 1939)
American actor TW/24, 30
CRESWICK, Charles Edward (d
1885 [35]) EA/86*
CRESWICK, Elizabeth [Mrs.
William Creswick] (d 1876
[67]) EA/77*
CRESWICK, Janette (d 1900)
EA/01*
CRESWICK, Mr. [W.?] (d 1792)
actor BD, TD/2
CRESWICK, William (1813-88)
English actor CDP, DD,
DNB, ES, HAS, OAA/1-2
CRESWICK, William see
Beswick, William
CRESWICK, Mrs. William see
Creswick, Elizabeth
CRETA, Joachim Frederic (fl
1729) horn player BD
CREVELLI, Signorina (fl 1825)
singer HAS
CREW, Mr. (d 1871) publisher
EA/72*
CREWE, Mr. (fl 1792) actor BD
CREWE, Bertie (d 1937 [74])
architect BE*, WWT/14*

CREWES, Jeremiah (fl 1630-65?)
drummer BD
CREWS, Laura Hope (1880-1942)
American actress CB, ES, SR,
WWS, WWT/1-9
CRIBARAI, Joe (d 1971 [51]) com-
poser/lyricist BP/56*
CRIBBINS, Bernard (b 1928) Eng-
lish actor WWT/15-16
CRICHTON, Haldane (d 1938 [85])
manager WWT/14*
CRICHTON, Kyle S. (1896-1960)
American dramatist BE*
CRICHTON, Madge (b 1881) English
actress GRB/1-4, WWS, WWT/
1-6
CRICK, Edmund (d 1886) EA/87*
CRIDER, Ethel Osborne (d 1975)
composer/lyricist BP/59*
CRIDLAND, Mr. (fl 1761-73)
boxkeeper BD
CRIDLAND, Howard (d 1917 [46])
EA/18*
CRIEVE, Mrs. (d 1787?) sweeper
BD
CRIGHTON, James (d 1902 [59])
steam circus proprietor EA/03*
CRIPPEN, Mr. (fl 1784) singer
BD
CRIPPEN, George [George Dele-
vanti] (d 1887 [39]) somersault
rider EA/88*
CRISAFULLI, Henri (d 1900 [72])
dramatist EA/01*
CRISCUOLO, Louis (b 1934) Amer-
ican actor TW/29
CRISHAM, Walter (b 1906) Ameri-
can actor, dancer WWT/9-14
CRISP, Mrs. (fl 1787) actress BD
CRISP, Miss (fl 1799) actress BD
CRISP, Charles (fl 1799-1821?)
actor, manager BD
CRISP, Donald (d 1974 [93]) per-
former BP/58*, WWT/16*
CRISP, Henry (fl 1754) dramatist
CP/1-3, GT, TD/1-2
CRISP, Henry (1844-82) actor CDP
CRISP, Henry (d 1906 [53]) actor
EA/07*, WWT/14*
CRISP, John (fl 1799-1819?) actor,
manager BD
CRISP, Samuel (1707-68) actor BD
CRISP, Samuel (d 1783 [76]) drama-
tist DD, DNB
CRISP, Mrs. Samuel [née Henrietta
Maria Tollett] (1709-80) actress,
dancer, singer BD
CRISP, W.H. (fl 1848) Irish actor

HAS, SR

CRISPE, Samuel see Crisp, Samuel

CRISPI, Signora see Crespi, Signora

CRISPI, Ida (fl 1900s) English actress, singer WWS

CRIST, Bainbridge (1883-1969) American composer WWA/5

CRISTIANI, Ernesto (d 1973 [91]) associated with circuses BP/58*

CRITCHETT, R. C. see Carton, R. C.

"CROAKER, Alley" (fl 1759) singer BD

CROCKER, Emerson (d 1971 [60]) producer/director/ choreographer BP/56*

CROCKER, Emily Viola see Barrett, Mrs. J. H.

CROCKER, Henry (d 1937 [62]) producer, manager BE*, WWT/14*

CROCKER, John (d 1853) American actor HAS

CROCKER, Mrs. John (d 1853) HAS

CROCKER, John Paul (d 1869 [35]) minstrel proprietor & performer CDP

CROCKER, Sarah see Conway, Sarah

CROCKETT, James (1835-65) English circus performer HAS

CROCKETT, Sarah (d 1901 [78]) EA/03*

CROFT, Annie [or Anne] (1896-1959) English actress, singer WWT/5-10

CROFT, Henry (fl 1771-72) actor BD

CROFT, Michael (b 1922) English actor, Founder of British National Youth Theatre, director COC, ES, WWT/ 15-16

CROFT, Nita (b 1902) English actress, singer WWT/10-14

CROFT, Paddy English actress TW/25-30, WWT/16

CROFT, William (1678-1727) English organist, composer BD, DNB

CROFTON, Cecil (d 1935 [76]) actor, dramatist DD

CROFTON, Charles (d 1883)

actor EA/84*

CROFTS, Mr. (fl 1740-57?) actor, dancer? BD

CROFTS, Mrs. (fl 1680-87) actress BD

CROFTS, Mrs. (d 1778) BD

CROFTS, Miss (fl 1786-90) equestrienne, dancer, actress, singer BD

CROFTS, Mary (fl 1740-41) lamp woman BD

CROISETTE, Sophie (d 1901 [54]) actress WWT/14*

CROKE, Wentworth (1871-1930) English manager GRB/4, WWT/1-6

CROKER, John Wilson (1780-1857) writer DD

CROKER, T. F. Dillon (1831-1912) English dramatic journalist GRB/3-4, WWT/1

CROKER, Thomas Crofton (1798-1854) dramatist DD

CROKER-KING, C. H. (1873-1951) English actor GRB/1, WWT/4-9

CROLL, Don (b 1947) American actor TW/28

CROLY, George (1780-1860) Irish critic, dramatist DD, DNB, HP, NTH

CROME, Mrs. Michael Sharp see Crome, Teresa

CROME, Robert (fl c.1745-c.65) violinist, composer BD

CROME, Teresa [Mrs. Michael Sharp Crome] (d 1881) EA/82*

CROMMELYNCK, Fernand (1888-1970) Belgian dramatist COC

CROMPTON, Reginald (d 1945 [75]) English actor, singer GRB/1-3

CROMPTON, William H. (1843-1909) English actor CDP, GRB/ 3-4, PP/1

CROMWELL, Mr. (fl 1799-c.1860) actor HAS

CROMWELL, Cecil [Miss Pym] (d 1913) English actress GRB/ 1-4

CROMWELL, George Reed (d 1899) lecturer CDP

CROMWELL, John (b 1887/88) American actor, producer, producing manager AAS, BE, ES, TW/8-12, 28, WWT/6-16

CROMWELL, J. T. (b 1935) American actor TW/27-28

CROMWELL, Richard (d 1960 [50]) actor TW/17

CROMWELL, William Oliver
(d 1890 [55]) actor, acting
manager EA/91*
CRONE, Adeline (d 1962 [70])
performer BE*
CRONIN, Jane (b 1936) Ameri-
can actress TW/22, 29-30
CRONIN, John (d 1898) circus
musical director EA/99*
CRONIN, William (d 1911)
actor, dancer CDP
CRONIN, William Francis (1905-
65) American executive
WWA/4
CRONIN-SMYTHE (d 1889 [29])
singer, writer EA/90*
CRONYN, Carrie [Mrs. Frank
Curzon] Irish actress GRB/1
CRONYN, George William
(1888-1969) American
dramatist WWA/5
CRONYN, Hume (b 1911) Cana-
dian actor, director, writer
AAS, BE, CB, ES, TW/8-
23, 26, 28-30, WWT/12-16
CRONYN, Lizzie singer CDP
CRONYN, Tandy (b 1945) Amer-
ican actress TW/26-27, 29
CROOK, Miss (fl 1747-48)
actress BD
CROOK, John (d 1922) com-
poser, conductor DD, GRB/
1-4, WWT/1-4
CROOKE, Miss see Mason,
Mrs.
CROOKE, C. (d 1882 [57])
proprietor EA/83*
CROOKE, John (d 1882) musi-
cal director EA/84*
CROOKS, Alexander Richard
(d 1972 [72]) American
singer WWA/5
CROOME, Mr. (fl 1667) booth
operator BD
CROPPER, Roy (1898-1954)
American actor, singer
TW/10, WWT/9-11
CROPPONI, Mr. (fl 1733-34)
dancer, actor BD
CROSBIE, Richard (fl 1793)
Irish aeronaut CDP
CROSBY, Mr. (fl 1786) house
servant BD
CROSBY, Miss (fl 1800) singer
BD
CROSBY, Bing (1904-77) Amer-
ican singer CB
CROSBY, Charles A. manager

CDP
CROSBY, Edward Harold (d 1934
[75]) American dramatist, critic
BE*, BP/19*, WWT/14*
CROSBY, Edward John (d 1973 [73])
publicist BP/58*
CROSBY, Hazel (d 1964 [74]) per-
former BE*
CROSBY, James (d 1930) minstrel
SR
CROSBY, J. H. (b 1830) American
manager SR
CROSBY, John (d 1724) actor BD
CROSBY, Joseph (b 1922) American
executive BE
CROSBY, Juliette (d 1969 [73])
actress TW/25
CROSBY, L. V. H. (d 1884 [60])
singer, composer, minstrel
CDP
CROSBY, Sir Richard (fl 1793)
Irish actor HAS
CROSBY, Wade (d 1975 [65]) per-
former BP/60*
CROSBY-BELASCO, Juliet (d 1907
[30]) actress WWT/14*
CROSDILL, John (1751?-1825)
English musician BD, DNB
CROSDILL, Richard (1698-70)
violoncellist BD
CROSE, Mr. (fl 1794) double-bass
player BD
CROSLAND, Mrs. W. H. see
Rutland, Ruth
CROSMAN, Mr. (fl 1762) viola
d'amore player BD
CROSMAN, Henrietta [Mrs. Maurice
Campbell] (1865-1944) American
actress ES, GRB/2-4, WWA/2,
WWM, WWS, WWT/1-9
CROSMAN, Shirley Elizabeth see
Conway, Shirl
CROSMOND, Hélène see Turner,
Helena
CROSS, Mr. (fl c. 1745?) animal
tamer BD
CROSS, Mr. (fl 1772-91?) actor
BD
CROSS, Mrs. see Bradshaw, Mrs.
CROSS, Miss (fl 1740-41) actress?
BD
CROSS, Alfred B. (d 1910 [56])
actor EA/96
CROSS, Mrs. Alfred B. see
Cross, Mary
CROSS, Mrs. A. W. see Gold,
Belle
CROSS, Benjamin (1786-1857) CDP

CROSS, Beverley (b 1931) English dramatist, director, actor   AAS, CD, WWT/14-16

CROSS, Douglas (d 1975 [54]) composer/lyricist   BP/59*

CROSS, Edward (d 1854 [81]) menagerie proprietor   EA/72*

CROSS, Emily (d 1884) actress   CDP

CROSS, Emily [Mrs. M. E. Jobling] (d 1904) actress, singer   DD

CROSS, George (d 1800?) violinist?   BD

CROSS. Jack (d 1904) comedian   EA/05*

CROSS, James C. (d c.1810) English actor, proprietor, acting manager, dramatist   CP/3, DD, ES, GT, TD/1-2

CROSS, Jessie [Mrs. Clifford Bown] (d 1903) actress   EA/04*

CROSS, Joan (b 1900) English singer, director   ES

CROSS, John Cartwright (d 1809) actor, dramatist, manager   BD

CROSS, Mrs. [John Cartwright? Mrs. Gilbert Hamilton] (fl 1790-93) singer, actress   BD

CROSS, Joseph C. (d 1877) singer   EA/78*

CROSS, Julian (1851-1925) English actor, dramatist   DD, GRB/1-4, WWT/1-5

CROSS, Mrs. Julian see Cross, Sophie

CROSS, Letitia (c.1677-1737) singer, dancer   BD

CROSS, Margaret (d 1913) EA/14*

CROSS, Marie ["George Eliot"] (d 1880 [57])   EA/82*

CROSS, Mary [Mrs. Alfred B. Cross] (d 1904)   EA/05*

CROSS, Max (d 1900) scene artist   EA/01*

CROSS, Richard (fl c.1695?-1725) actor   BD

CROSS, Richard (d 1760) prompter, actor, dancer   BD, TD/1-2

CROSS, Richard (fl 1748-60) actor, dancer, violinist   BD

CROSS, Mrs. Richard [née Frances Shireburn] (1707-81) actress, singer   BD

CROSS, Sophia (d 1884 [73]) actress   EA/85*

CROSS, Sophie [Mrs. Julian Cross] (d 1910)   EA/11*

CROSS, Thomas (b c.1630) treasurer   BD

CROSS, Thomas (d 1737) numberer   BD

CROSS, Wellington (d 1975 [88]) performer   BP/60*

CROSS, William (d 1900 [57]) wild animal importer   EA/01*

CROSS, Mrs. William (d 1891)   EA/92*

CROSSAN, Mrs. W. H. (d 1880) actress   EA/81*

CROSSARO, Signor (fl 1787-89) Italian dancer   BD

CROSSE, Edward (d 1907 [56]) musical director, composer   EA/08*

CROSSE, Mrs. Edward see Crosse, Mary

CROSSE, Gay S. (d 1971 [54]) musician   BP/55*

CROSSE, Mary [Mrs. Edward Crosse] (d 1911 [50])   EA/12*

CROSSE, Nicholas (fl 1607) actor   DA

CROSSE, Rupert (d 1973 [45]) performer   BP/57*

CROSSE, Samuel (fl 1594?-1623?) actor   DA, GT

CROSSFIELD, Mr. (fl 1698-99) singer   BD

CROSSLAND, Maggie [Mrs. Victor Gouriet] (d 1904)   EA/05*

CROSSLEY, Ada [Mrs. Muecke] Australian singer   GRB/1

CROSSLEY-TAYLOR, E. W. (d 1963 [68]) manager   BE*

CROSSLING, Tom (d 1873) Negro minstrel   EA/74*

CROSSMAN, Master (fl 1785-93) equestrian   BD

CROSSMAN, Harriet (d 1875 [35]) actress   EA/76*

CROSSMAN, Henrietta (1865-1944) American actress   SR, TW/1

CROSSMAN, John (fl 1787-1817) equestrian, dancer   BD

CROSWELL, Anne [née Mary Ann Pearson] American lyricist, writer   BE

CROSWELL, Joseph (fl 1802?) American? dramatist   EAP

CROTCH, William (1775-1847) English musician, composer, teacher BD, CDP, DNB

CROTHERS, Rachel (1878-1958) American dramatist, producing manager AAS, COC, ES, GRB/3-4, HJD, MD, MH, MWD, NTH, OC/2-3, RE, SR, TW/15, WWA/3, WWM, WWT/1-11

CROTTY, Leslie (d 1903 [50]) singer EA/04*, WWT/14*

CROUCH, Mr. (fl 1743) actor BD

CROUCH, Mrs. [née S. Phillips] (fl 1834) actress HAS

CROUCH, Anna Maria see Crouch, Mrs. Rawlings Edward

CROUCH, Frederick William Nichols (1808-96) English musician SR

CROUCH, Harry (d 1893) comedian EA/94*

CROUCH, Jack H. (b 1918) American educator BE

CROUCH, John (fl 1679-1710?) violinist, dancing master? BD

CROUCH, John (1762-93) instrumentalist BD

CROUCH, Mrs. Rawlings Edward [née Anna Maria Phillips] (1763-1805) English actress, singer BD, CDP, DD, DNB, OX, TD/1-2

CROUCH, William (1749-1833) instrumentalist BD

CROUESTE, Edwin (1841-91) English circus clown HAS

CROUESTE, George John Coney (d 1881 [18]) EA/82*

CROUESTE, Harry ["Queen's Jester"] (d 1891) circus clown EA/92*

CROUSE (fl 17th cent?) dramatist FGF

CROUSE, Russel (1893-1966) American dramatist, producer, writer BE, CB, COC, ES, HJD, MH, MWD, NTH, SR, TW/2-8, 22, WWT/10-14, WWW/6

CROUTA, Mr. (fl 1837) American actor HAS

CROW (fl 1740) Irish? porter CDP

CROWDEN, Graham (b 1922) Scottish actor AAS, WWT/15-16

CROWDEN, Roy see Royston, Roy

CROWDER, Charles (d 1887 [69]) EA/88*

CROWDER, Mrs. Charles (d 1893 [56]) EA/94*

CROWDER, Charles S. (d 1889) proprietor EA/90*

CROWDER, Jack (b 1939) American actor TW/24-26

CROWDER, John (d 1674) trumpeter BD

CROWDY, James (d 1909 [61]) proprietor EA/10*

CROWE, Mrs see Bateman, Mrs.

CROWE, Charles Henry (d 1900 [65]) EA/01*

CROWE, [Eleanor?] (fl 1796-1801) actress BD

CROWE, Ellen Beatrice (d 1974 [78]) performer BP/58*

CROWE, George (d 1889 [47]) EA/90*

CROWE, Gillian (b 1934) English executive BE

CROWE, Gwyllym (d 1894) conductor EA/95*

CROWE, Sidney (b 1871) English actress DD, EA/97, GRB/1-2

CROWE, William (fl 1792-96) dancer BD

CROWE, Mrs. William [née Jane Rowson] (fl 1791-99) dancer BD

CROWHURST, Alfred (d 1878 [33]) equestrian director EA/79*

CROWHURST, Charles (d 1891 [60]) EA/93*

CROWHURST, Charles (d 1892) EA/94*

CROWHURST, Mary (d 1886 [79]) EA/87*

CROWLEY, Mr. (fl 1845) actor HAS

CROWLEY, Alice (d 1972 [88]) co-founder of the Neighbourhood Playhouse BP/56*

CROWLEY, Ann (b 1929) American actress TW/3-11

CROWLEY, Dick (b 1929) American actor TW/26

CROWLEY, Edward (b 1926) American actor TW/24-26, 28, 30

CROWLEY, Mart (b 1935) American dramatist CD, MH, WWT/16

CROWLEY, Pat (b 1934) American actress TW/7-11

CROWNE, John (1640?-1703/04/

12/14) English dramatist
COC, CP/1-3, DAB, DD,
DNB, ES, GT, HP, MH,
OC/1-3, WWA/H
"CROWQUILL, Alfred" see For-
rester, Alfred Henry
CROWSON, Will (d 1905) EA/
06*
CROWTHER, Mr. (fl 1782) actor
BD
CROWTHER, Amelia Augusta
[Mrs. T. H. Crowther] (d
1890) EA/91*
CROWTHER, Mrs. Benjamin
see Vincent, Eliza
CROWTHER, F. C. (d 1884 [34])
journalist EA/85*
CROWTHER, John (d 1879 [37])
promoter EA/80*
CROWTHER, Leslie (b 1933)
English actor WWT/15-16
CROWTHER, Richard (d 1871
[21]) clog dancer EA/72*
CROWTHER, Mrs. T. H. see
Crowther, Amelia Augusta
CROX, Elvia [Mrs. T. Q.
Seabrooke] (d 1911) actress
WWT/14*
CROXALL, Dr. Samuel (d 1752)
English dramatist CP/2-3,
GT
CROXTON, Arthur (b 1868)
English manager WWT/4-5
CROXTON, Darryl (b 1946)
American actor TW/26
CROYDON, Joan (b 1908) Amer-
ican actress TW/11
CROZA, John Francis (fl 1748-
50) manager BD
CROZIER, Miss (fl 1742)
dancer, singer BD
CROZIER, Charles (b 1852)
English dramatist, actor,
acting manager GRB/1-2
CROZIER, Eric (b 1904) English
librettist, director ES
CROZIER, Robert American
actor TW/7
CROZIER, Temple Edgcumbe
(d 1896 [24]) actor EA/97*
CRUDDAS, Audrey (b 1914)
South African designer ES
CRUDGE, Alexander (d 1759)
doorkeeper, housekeeper BD
CRUFT, Mrs. (d 1858) English?
HAS
CRUICKSHANK, Andrew (b 1907)
Scottish actor AAS, TW/8,

WWT/9-16
CRUICKSHANK, Gladys (b 1902)
English actress, singer WWT/
6-7
CRUICKSHANK, Jessie [Mrs. Wil-
liam C. Cruickshank] (d 1892)
EA/93*
CRUICKSHANK, Mrs. William C.
see Cruickshank, Jessie
CRUIKSHANK, A. Stewart (1877-
1949) Scottish manager WWT/
7-10
CRUIKSHANK, Stewart (1908-66)
Scottish manager WWT/10-14
CRUIKSHANK, Victor (d 1882)
actor EA/83*
"CRUIKSHANK OF AMERICA, The"
see Johnson, David
CRUIKSHANKS, Charles (1844-1928)
actor WWT/3-5
CRUIKSHANKS, Charles C. (d 1904
[39]) actor EA/05*
CRUIKSHANKS, William C. (d 1902
[57]) clown, jester EA/03*
CRUISE, Anna see Cowell, Anna
CRUISE, Mrs. Henry (d 1884)
pianist EA/86*
CRUISE, John H. (d 1906 [46])
performer? EA/07*
CRUISE, Marie [Mrs. R. Barker]
(d 1887 [56]) actress EA/88*
CRUMMIT, Frank (1889-1943)
American actor, songwriter
CB, SR
CRUSE, Annie [née Dashwood] (d
1868 [23]) singer EA/69*
CRUTCHLEY, Rosalie (b 1921)
English actress WWT/10-15
CRUTCHLOW, F. E. [Mrs. Thomas
Crutchlow] (d 1899 [51]) EA/00*
CRUTCHLOW, Mrs. Thomas see
Crutchlow, F. E.
CRUTTWELL, Hugh (b 1918) Eng-
lish director, principal of the
Royal Academy of Dramatic Art
WWT/14-16
CRUVELLI, Mlle. (fl 1859) singer
HAS
CRUVELLI, Marie (d 1868) EA/69*
CRUYS, Francis (fl 1673-1700)
violinist BD
CRUYS, Samuel CDP
CRUZE, James (1884-1942) Ameri-
can actor ES
CRYER, Charles Henry [Vitelo] (d
1916 [24]) weight-lifter EA/17*
CRYER, David (b 1936) American
actor, singer TW/20, 24-30,

WWT/16

CRYER, Gretchen (b 1935)
American actress, librettist
CD, TW/24, 30

CSIRSCU, Eugene (d 1970 [53])
musician BP/55*

CUBAS, Isabella (1831-64)
Spanish dancer CDP, HAS

CUBIT, Mr. (fl 1794-1807)
musician BD

CUBITT, Miss see Jackson,
Charlotte

CUBITT, Marie Caroline (b
1800) actress BS, CDP, OX

CUBITT, William (fl 1775-1830?)
actor, singer, violinist,
dancer? BD, TD/1-2

CUCKOW, Mr. see Curco, Mr.

CUDD, Leslie (d 1916) EA/17*

CUDDY, Edward flautist CDP

CUDMORE, Richard (1787-1840)
English instrumentalist, composer BD, DNB

CUDWORTH, Mr. (fl c.1675-
91) actor BD

CUDWORTH, Mr. (fl 1794)
violinist BD

CUENCA, Pedro Fernandez (d
1940) actor BE*, WWT/14*

CUERTON, Mr. (fl 1800-04)
dancer, whistler BD

CUKA, Frances (b 1936) English
actress AAS, WWT/13-16

CUKOR, George (b 1899) American director BE, CB, ES,
SR

CULBERTSON, Ernest H. (d
1972 [86]) executive BP/57*

CULCUP, The Misses (fl 1797)
actresses BD

CULEEN, James Edward (d
1909 [29]) business manager
EA/10*

CULHANE, Will E. actor,
manager SR

CULL, Mrs. see Bennett,
Fanny

CULL, Cecil (d 1875 [33]) singer
EA/76*

CULLEN, Mr. (fl c.1810?)
actor CDP

CULLEN, Bernard (d 1883)
actor EA/84*

CULLEN, Edward L. (1899-
1964) American actor BE

CULLEN, Richard Limmere
(d 1900 [45]) scene artist
EA/02*

CULLEN, Rose [Mrs. Albert Tuck]
(d 1888) actress DD

CULLENFORD, George Everett (d
1881 [57]) actor EA/82*

CULLENFORD, Thomasin Catherine
[Mrs. William Cullenford] (d
1890 [82]) EA/91*

CULLENFORD, William (d 1874
[77]) secretary of the Royal
General Theatrical Fund EA/
75*, WWT/14*

CULLENFORD, Mrs. William see
Cullenford, Thomasin Catherine

CULLEY, Frederick (1879-1942)
English actor WWT/8-9

CULLEY, Jane (b 1943) American
actress TW/29

CULLIFORD, C. J. (d 1893) printer EA/94*

CULLINAN, Ralph (d 1950 [68])
actor TW/6

CULLING, Mrs. Greek/English
actress GRB/1

CULLING, Ada Clare [Mrs. Otto
C. Culling] (d 1903 [31]) EA/
05*

CULLING, Mrs. Otto C. see
Culling, Ada Clare

CULLIS, Brian (d 1969 [41]) performer BP/53*

CULLMAN, Howard S. (1891-1972)
American investor, executive
BE, TW/29

CULLMAN, Marguerite [née Sand-
ers] author, investor BE

CULLUM, Mrs. (fl 1775) dramatist
CP/3

CULLUM, Jim, Sr. (d 1973 [59])
musician BP/58*

CULLUM, John (b 1930) American
actor, singer TW/22-30,
WWT/16

CULMER, Lee (d 1965) performer
BP/50*

CULP, Robert (b 1930) American
actor TW/13

CULVER, Mr. (fl 1772-94) singer
BD

CULVER, D. Jay (1902-68) American journalist, photographer BE

CULVER, Roland (b 1900) English
actor AAS, BE, ES, TW/22-23,
WWT/9-16

CUMBER, John (fl 1616-23) actor
DA

CUMBERBIRCH, Lilian (d 1903 [20])
musician EA/05*

CUMBERLAND, Gerald (1879-1926)

English critic, dramatist
WWT/2-5, WWW/2
CUMBERLAND, John (1787-1866)
publisher DD
CUMBERLAND, John (b 1880)
Canadian actor WWT/4-8
CUMBERLAND, Richard (1732-
1811) English dramatist
CDP, COC, CP/1-3, DD,
DNB, ES, GT, HP, MH,
NTH, OC/1-3, SR, TD/1-2
CUMMENS, Ellen [Nellie] (d
1905 [54]) American actress
CDP
CUMMING, Gordon (d 1866
[47]) "lion hunter" EA/72*
CUMMING, Ruth (d 1967 [63])
actress, singer TW/24
CUMMINGS, Arthur see Cum-
mings, Richard
CUMMINGS, Bob (b 1910) Amer-
ican actor, producer BE
CUMMINGS, Clara (d 1894 [15])
singer EA/95*
CUMMINGS, Constance [née
Halverstadt] (b 1910) Amer-
ican actress AAS, BE, ES,
TW/1-7, 25-26, WWT/8-16
CUMMINGS, Cyril (d 1912 [39])
EA/13*
CUMMINGS, E. E. (1894-1962)
American dramatist HJD,
MD, MH, MWD
CUMMINGS, Irving (1889-1959)
American actor ES, TW/15
CUMMINGS, Jennie see Dreher,
Virginia
CUMMINGS, Minnie actress
CDP
CUMMINGS, Richard (d 1872)
singer EA/73*
CUMMINGS, Richard (d 1916)
EA/17*
CUMMINGS, Robert (b 1910)
American actor CB, ES,
TW/8, 22-23
CUMMINGS, Vicki (1913-69)
American actress BE, TW/
1-17, 23-24, 26, WWT/11-14
CUMMINS, Mr. actor TD/2
CUMMINS, Alexander (fl 1818)
manager WWA/H
CUMMINS, Geraldine Dorothy
(1890-1969) dramatist WWW/6
CUMMINS, Margaret (d 1879)
EA/80*
CUMMINS, Peggy (b 1925) Welsh
actress ES, WWT/10-11

CUNARD, Grace (d 1967 [73]) per-
former BP/51*
CUNARD, James (d 1912) perform-
er? EA/13*
CUNARD, Lance (b 1910) American
actor TW/22-23, 25-26
CUNDALL, Henry (d 1627) actor
GT
CUNDELL, Edric (d 1961 [67])
director WWT/14*
CUNINGHAM, Peter (d 1869 [53])
critic WWT/14*
CUNINGHAM, Philip [Philip Harold
Boosey] (1865-1928) English actor
GRB/1-4, WWT/1-5
CUNINGHAME, Charles [Charles
John Cuninghame Minney] (b
1850) English actor, agent
GRB/1
CUNLIFFE, Jerry (b 1935) Ameri-
can actor TW/28
CUNLIFFE, John William (1865-1946)
English scholar WWW/4
CUNNINGHAM, Annie (d 1916 [64])
EA/17*
CUNNINGHAM, Arthur (1869-1944)
Canadian singer SR
CUNNINGHAM, Arthur (d 1955 [67])
musical comedy actor TW/12
CUNNINGHAM, Claude (b 1880)
English singer WWM
CUNNINGHAM, Dan (b 1917) English
actor TW/8
CUNNINGHAM, Edward (d 1880)
comic vocalist EA/81*
CUNNINGHAM, Francis (1820-75)
scholar DNB
CUNNINGHAM, George (d 1962 [58])
actor, choreographer, director
BE*
CUNNINGHAM, Harry (d 1878) actor,
agent EA/79*
CUNNINGHAM, James see Sey-
mour, James
CUNNINGHAM, John (1729-73) Irish
actor, dramatist CDP, CP/2-3,
DD, DNB, GT, HP, TD/1-2
CUNNINGHAM, John (b 1932) Amer-
ican actor TW/24-28
CUNNINGHAM, Josias (fl 1765)
dramatist CP/2-3, GT
CUNNINGHAM, Merce (b 1922)
American choreographer, dancer
CB, CD, ES
CUNNINGHAM, Minnie (1853-1924)
actress CDP
CUNNINGHAM, Paul (1890-1960)
American composer WWA/4

CUNNINGHAM, Peter (fl c. 1852?) writer DD

CUNNINGHAM, Peter C. (fl 1836-60) Scottish actor CDP, HAS

CUNNINGHAM, Mrs. Peter C. see Cunningham, Virginia

CUNNINGHAM, Richard D. (fl 1861) American actor HAS

CUNNINGHAM, Robert (b 1866) Tasmanian actor, singer WWT/6-8

CUNNINGHAM, Robert (b 1921) American actor TW/6-8

CUNNINGHAM, Ronnie (b 1923) American actor TW/2-3, 23

CUNNINGHAM, Ruby Hale White (d 1971 [79]) performer BP/55*

CUNNINGHAM, Sarah (b 1918) American actress TW/22-23, 26, 29

CUNNINGHAM, [Thomas?] (fl 1795-1817?) actor BD

CUNNINGHAM, Virginia [Mrs. Peter C. Cunningham; Mrs. Charles Pope; Mrs. John D. German] (1834-74) actress CDP

CUNNINGHAM, W. (fl 1733-54?) dancer, singer, actor BD

CUNNINGHAM, Zamah (d 1967 [74]) American actress TW/1, 22, 24

CUNNINGTON, Phillis writer BE

CUOZZO, Alberta American actress TW/25-26

CUPER, Boyder (fl c.1691) proprietor BD

CUPER, John (fl 1717) proprietor BD

CURCO, Mr. (fl 1687-1700) singer BD

CURIONI, Rosa (fl 1754-62) Italian singer BD

CURKAW, Mr. see Curco, Mr.

CURLL, Edmund (d 1747 [72]) publisher WWT/14*

CURNOCK, Richard (b 1922) English actor TW/26, 28-29

CURNOW, Allen (b 1911) New Zealand dramatist CD

CURRAH, Brian (b 1929) English designer WWT/15-16

CURRAN, Homer F. (d 1952) American producer BE*, BP/37*

CURRAN, Paul (b 1913) English actor AAS

CURRANS, Mrs. J. W. (d 1904) EA/06*

CURRER, Elizabeth (fl 1673-1743?) actress BD

CURRIE, Clive (1877-1935) English actor, producer WWT/5-7

CURRIE, Finlay (1878-1968) Scottish actor ES, WWT/8-14

CURRIE, Thomas A. (b 1929) American talent representative BE

CURRIER, Frank (d 1928 [71]) actor BE*, BP/12*

CURRY, Mr. (fl 1708-16) boxkeeper BD

CURRY, Henry J. (d 1907 [61]) entertainment director EA/08*

CURRY, Mrs. Henry James see Curry, Selina

CURRY, Mason (b 1906/08) Canadian actor TW/2, 7-8

CURRY, Selina [Mrs. Henry James Curry] (d 1887 [39]) EA/88*

CURRY, Thomas (b 1855) English organist GRB/1

CURRY, Winnie Garland (d 1973) performer BP/57*

CURRYER, Mr. (fl 1744-47) office-keeper BD

CURTEEN, Mr. (fl 1772-95) box-keeper BD

CURTEN, Miss (fl 1791-95) house servant? performer? BD

CURTET, Pierre (fl 1762-74) dancer BD

CURTEYS, James (fl 1509-11) member of the Chapel Royal DA

CURTI, Carlos musical director, composer CDP

CURTIES, Mr. (fl 1794-1801) actor, singer BD

CURTIN, Phyllis (b 1922?) American singer CB

CURTIS, Alan (d 1953 [43]) American actor BE*

CURTIS, Allen (d 1861 [84]) actor BE*

CURTIS, Arthur John Powles (d 1916) actor EA/17*

CURTIS, Beatrice see White, Beatrice

CURTIS, Donald (b 1915) American actor TW/5-7

CURTIS, Donna (b 1938) American

actress TW/24, 29
CURTIS, G. W. P. (1824-92)
American dramatist SR
CURTIS, Jack (d 1970 [44])
performer BP/55*
CURTIS, Jackie (b 1947) American dramatist, director,
actor CD
CURTIS, Keene (b 1923) American actor, production stage
manager BE, TW/22-29,
WWT/15-16
CURTIS, King (d 1971 [37])
musician BP/56*
CURTIS, May singer CDP
CURTIS, M. B. (1851-1921?)
actor CDP, SR
CURTIS, Samuel (d 1906 [23])
singer? EA/07*
CURTIS, Samuel J. (b 1867)
American singer, vaudevillian
CDP, WWM
CURTIS, Tony (b 1925) American
actor CB
CURTIS, Walter (d 1910) entertainer EA/11*
CURTIS, W. H. (b 1809) American actor HAS
CURTISS, Alice May [Mrs.
Thomas Courtice] (d 1917)
EA/18*
CURTISS, Charles M. (d 1899)
EA/00*
CURTISS, George [Robert J. H.
de Courcy] English actor
GRB/1
CURTISS, Sydney (d 1916 [8])
EA/17*
CURTISS, Sydney W. see
Courtice, Thomas
CURTIZ, David (d 1962 [68])
Hungarian actor BE*
CURTO, Gregorio (1805-87)
Spanish singer, composer
NYM
CURTZ, Mlle. (fl 1769-76)
dancer BD
CURVIN, Jonathan W. (b 1911)
American educator BE
CURWEN, John Spencer (d
1916 [68]) EA/17*
CURWEN, Patric (1884-1949)
English actor WWT/6-10
CURZ, Mlle. see Curtz, Mlle.
CURZON, Frank A. (1868-1927)
English manager, lessee,
actor ES, GRB/1-4, WWT/
1-5, WWW/2

CURZON, Mrs. Frank [A.] see
Cronyn, Carrie
CURZON, George (1898-1976)
English actor TW/6, WWT/6-14
CUSACK, Cyril (b 1910) South
African/Irish actor, manager
AAS, BE, ES, WWT/11-16
CUSACK, Philip (b 1934) American
actor TW/23, 26, 28
CUSHING, Catherine Chisholm (d
1952) American dramatist SR,
WWT/4-10
CUSHING, Charles C. S. see
Cushing, Tom
CUSHING, Henry W. (d 1899 [56])
EA/00*
CUSHING, John (1719-90) actor BD
CUSHING, Mrs. John (fl 1743-51)
actress, singer BD
CUSHING, Mary W. (d 1974 [80s])
critic BP/59*
CUSHING, Peter (b 1913) English
actor AAS, ES, WWT/11-16
CUSHING, Tom (1879-1941) American dramatist CB, WWA/1,
WWT/5-9
CUSHING, Winnifred American actress TW/5-7
CUSHMAN, Alice (b 1861) American
actress HAS
CUSHMAN, Asa (b 1833) American
actress HAS
CUSHMAN, Charles Augustus (d
1896 [78]) EA/97*
CUSHMAN, Charlotte Saunders
(1816-76) American actress
CDP, COC, DAB, DD, ES, HAS,
HJD, NTH, OC/1-3, SR, WWA/H
CUSHMAN, Corlene [Mrs. Ike Jones]
(d 1894) singer EA/96*
CUSHMAN, Emma (fl 1856) English?
actress HAS
CUSHMAN, Frank (1853-1907) minstrel CDP
CUSHMAN, Nancy (b 1913) American
actress BE, TW/9, 21-23, 29
CUSHMAN, Major Pauline (1833-93)
American actress CDP, DAB,
HAS, WWA/H
CUSHMAN, Reuben Adcock (d 1906
[63]) Negro performer EA/07*
CUSHMAN, Sadie actress CDP
CUSHMAN, Susan Webb (1822-59)
American actress CDP, DAB,
HAS, OC/1-3, SR, WWA/H
CUSICK, Polly [Mrs. Charles
Rezene] (d 1903 [37]) seriocomic EA/04*

CUSINS, Sir William George (d 1893 [60]) master of the Queen's music EA/94*

CUSSANS, Mrs. [Mrs. Higginson; Mrs. Egerson] (fl 1797-1800) actress BD

CUSSANS, John P. (fl 1797-1803) actor, singer BD, TD/1-2

CUSSANS, William see Cussans, John P.

CUSTANCE, Richard L. (d 1873) musician EA/74*

CUSTIS, George Washington Parke (1781-1857) American dramatist DAB, EAP, ES, HJD, RJ, WWA/H

CUSTONELLI, Signora (fl 1752) singer BD

CUTHBERT, Mr. (fl 1743-55) actor BD

CUTHBERT, Mrs. (fl 1708-26) dresser BD

CUTHBERT, Mrs. (fl 1743-55) actress BD

CUTHBERT, Agnes [Mrs. Alfred Cuthbert] (d 1891) EA/92*

CUTHBERT, Mrs. Alfred see Cuthbert, Agnes

CUTHBERT, Edmund (d 1908) actor? EA/09*

CUTHBERT, Henry John (d 1888 [78]) scene artist EA/89*

CUTHBERT, Ian Holm see Holm, Ian

CUTHBERT, Maud see Robini, Mrs. Alf

CUTHBERT, Mrs. P. G. (d 1878 [83]) actress EA/79*

CUTHBERT, Robert Arthur (d 1903 [33]) EA/04*

CUTHBERT, Thomas (d 1737) violinist, copyist BD

CUTHBERTSON, Miss (fl 1793) dramatist CP/3

CUTHBERTSON, Iain (b 1930) Scottish actress, director WWT/15-16

CUTLER, James (fl c.1605) member of the Chapel Royal DA

CUTLER, James (fl 1678-83) singer BD

CUTLER, Kate [Mrs. Sydney Ellison] (1870-1955) English actress, singer DD, GRB/1-4, WWT/1-11

CUTLER, Lucy A. (fl 1849-54) American actress HAS

CUTLER, Peggy [Mrs. Douglas Furber] (d 1945) actress BE*, WWT/14*

CUTLER, Robert Frye (d 1976 [75]) producer/director/choreographer BP/60*

CUTLER, William Henry (b 1792) English musician DNB

CUTNER, Sidney B. (d 1971 [68]) composer/lyricist BP/56*

CUTTER, Mrs. George Albert (b 1873) American composer WWA/5

CUTTER, William F. (d 1866) comedian HAS

CUTTI, Bertha (1887-1948) Italian singer SR

CUTTING, Master (b 1718) singer BD

CUTTS, G. W. (d 1916) EA/17*

CUTTS, John (fl 1745) dramatist CP/1-3, GT

CUTTS, John English actor TW/28

CUTTS, Patricia (1931-74) English actress BE, TW/22-23

CUVILLIER, Charles (b 1879) French composer WWT/4

CUYLER, Margaret [Mrs. Dominic Rice] (1758-1814) English actress BD, CDP, TD/1-2

CUZZONI, Francesca [Signora Pietro Guiseppe Sandoni; Signora San-Antonio Ferre] (c. 1700-70) Italian singer BD, CDP

CWIKOWSKI, Bill (b 1945) American actor TW/29

CYMBER, Miss (fl 1747) actress BD

CYPHER, Jon (b 1932) American actor TW/22-23, 25-27, 30

CYPKIN, Diane (b 1948) German actress TW/27, 29-30

CZAJOWSKI, Maryan see Lester, The Great

CZAKO, Glenn R. (b 1949) American actor TW/27

CZETTEL, Ladislaus (1894/1904-1949) Hungarian/American costume designer CB, TW/2-5

CZILLAG, Rose (d 1892) singer EA/93*

CZINNER, Paul (d 1972 [82]) producer/director/choreographer BP/57*

- D -

D., Jr., Mr. (fl 1766-67) property man BD
D., D. (fl 1633) dramatist CP/1-3
D., I. dramatist CP/1-2
D., J. (fl 1640-74) dramatist CP/3, FGF
D., R. dramatist CP/1
D., T. dramatist CP/1
DAB see Dob
DABBS, Dr. G. H. R. (d 1913) dramatist DD
DABDOUB, Jack American actor TW/25-29
DABELL, Mr. (fl 1772) actor BD
DABNEY, Kathleen (b 1942) American actress TW/24, 28
DABOLL, William S. (d 1892) actor CDP
DABORNE, Robert (d 1628) dramatist, patentee CP/1-3, DA, DD, DNB, FGF
DABOVILLE, Mons. (d 1883) pianist EA/84*
DACE, Mr. (fl 1735) dancer BD
D'ACE, Annie [Mrs. Charles D'Ace] (d 1894 [39]) EA/95*
D'ACE, Mrs. Charles see D'Ace, Annie
DA COSTA, Mrs. [née Kent; Mrs. H. Knight] (fl 1837-52) English actress HAS
DACOSTA, Albert Lloyd (1928-67) American singer WWA/5
DA COSTA, Morton [né Morton Tecosky] (b 1914) American director, actor, producer BE, TW/2, 6-9, WWT/13-16
DACRE, Lady see Brand, Barbarina
DACRE, Arthur [né Culver James] (d 1895) actor CDP, DD, DP
DACRE, Mrs. Arthur see Roselle, Amy
DACRE, Harry composer CDP
DACRE, Helena actress EA/97
DACRE, H. S. (d 1918 [68]) EA/19*
DACRES, Mr. (fl 1661) actor BD
DACRES, Andrew (d 1669) painter BD
DACROY, Owen (b 1859) English

actor, acting manager GRB/1
DADSWELL, Pearl (d 1963 [47]) performer BE*
DAGGETT, Robert True (d 1975 [71]) performer BP/60*
DAGLISH, Master (fl 1790) actor BD
DAGLISH, Thomas (fl 1776-94) music copyist, house servant BD
DAGMAR, Anna Lang Wolseley (d 1917) EA/18*
DAGMAR, James (d 1903 [76]) circus performer EA/04*
DAGMAR, Marie (d 1925) actress EA/97
DAGNALL, Mr. (fl 1661) singer BD
DAGNALL, Ells (1863/68-1935) English actor, producer, stage manager GRB/1, WWT/1-7
DAGNALL, Thomas C. (d 1926 [46]) manager WWT/5
D'AGOSTINO, Albert (b 1893) American scene designer ES
D'AGUILAR, Rose (fl 1799?) translator CP/3
DAHL, Arlene American actress TW/10
DAHMEN, Hermanus (1755-1830) Dutch horn player BD
DAHMEN, Wilhelm (b 1769) Dutch horn player BD
DAHURON, [Francis?] (fl 1719-28) flutist, singer BD
DAI, Lin (d 1964 [33]) actress BE*
DAILEY, Dan (b 1915) American actor, singer, dancer TW/22-23, 25-26, WWT/16
DAILEY, Irene (b 1920) American actress, teacher BE, TW/19-22, 24, WWT/15-16
DAILEY, Jack (b 1883) American actor TW/2
DAILEY, J. W. (d 1976 [74]) publicist BP/60*
DAILEY, Peter (1868-1908) American actor NTH, WWS
DAILING, David American dramatist RJ
DAINE, Lois (b 1941) English actress TW/22
DAINTON, Marie (1877/80/81/83-1938) English actress GRB/1-4, WWT/1-8
DAIPER, H. W. (d 1911) EA/12*
DAIROLLES, Adrienne (fl 1888-97) actress DD

DALBERG, Camilla (b 1880) German actress, singer GRB/1-4

D'ALBERG, Rose singer CDP

DALBERG, Baron Wolfgang Heribert von (1750-1806) producer BE*

D'ALBERT, George (d 1884) comedian EA/86*

D'ALBERT, George (d 1949 [71]) singer, performer CDP

D'ALBERTE, Albert David (d 1903) high-rope walker EA/04*

D'ALBERTE, Julia (d 1912 [57]) operatic dancer EA/13*

D'ALBERTE, Theodore (d 1871) dancer EA/72*

DALBEY, Cynthia (b 1944) American actress TW/25-26

DALBY, Mr. (fl 1785-90) house servant BD

DALBY, Miss [Mrs. Hulme] (d 1906) gymnast EA/07*

DALBY, Louisa see Simpson, Mrs. (d 1872)

DALE, Mr. (fl 1784) singer BD

DALE, Mr. (fl 1794) violinist BD

DALE, Al. (d 1969 [48]) talent agent BP/54*

DALE, Alan [Alfred J. Cohen] (1861-1928) English dramatist, critic GRB/2-4, WWA/1, WWM, WWT/1-5

DALE, Brian (d 1907) comedian EA/08*

DALE, Charles (1883-1971) American variety artist ES, TW/28

DALE, E. J. (d 1900) magician CDP

DALE, Elise see Jones, Mrs. Herbert B.

DALE, Esther (d 1961 [75]) American actress TW/1, 18

"DALE, Felix" see Merivale, H. C.

DALE, Georgiana singer CDP

DALE, Gretchen [Mrs. Howard Estabrook] (b 1886) American actress WWS

DALE, Grover [né Grover Robert Aitken] (b 1935/36) American singer, dancer BE, TW/21-23

DALE, Harold S. (d 1974 [84])

performer BP/59*

DALE, Mrs. Harry see Monti, Gertie

DALE, James Littlewood (b 1886/87) English actor ES, WWT/4-14

DALE, J. Baldwin (d 1874 [37]) comedian EA/75*

DALE, Jim [né Smith] (b 1935/36) English actor AAS, TW/30, WWT/15-16

DALE, John (1803-72) actor CDP, EA/73*

DALE, Joseph (1750-1821) instrumentalist, music seller BD, ES

DALE, Margaret (1880-1972) American actress GRB/2-4, TW/2-7, 28, WWM, WWS, WWT/1-11

DALE, Margaret (b 1922) English dancer WWT/10-12

DALE, Margie [Mrs. Nicholas Rinaldo] (d 1962 [54]) performer BE*

DALE, Pat (d 1970 [57]) performer BP/55*

DALE, Thomas (fl c.1699) booth operator BD

DALE, Welton (b 1867/69) English actor GRB/2-4

DALE, William (fl 1774-1805?) box keeper BD

DALE, William (d 1807) boxkeeper BD

D'ALENCON, Emilienne [Emilie Andrée] French variety artist GRB/1

DALES, Harry (d 1903 [64]) Negro comedian EA/04*

DALES, John L. (b 1907) American lawyer, executive BE

DALEY, Miss actress CDP

DALEY, Cass (d 1975 [59]) actress BP/59*, WWT/16*

DALEY, Guilbert A. (b 1923) American educator BE

DALEY, Mary Patricia (b 1932) American educator, director BE

D'ALFREDS, Mrs. Edward see D'Alfreds, Jemima

D'ALFREDS, Jemima [Mrs. Edward D'Alfreds] (d 1883) EA/84*

DALL, Miss (fl 1776-94) singer, actress, composer BD, TD/1-2

DALL, John (1916-71) American actor TW/1, 5-7, 11-12, 27

DALL, Nicholas Thomas (d 1776) Dutch scene painter, painter BD

DALL' ABACO, Giuseppe Marie

Clement (1710-1805) Dutch violoncellist, composer BD

DALLA RIZZA, Gilda (d 1975 [82]) performer BP/60*

DALLAS, Mrs. E. S. see Dallas, Isabelle

DALLAS, George (d 1905) musical director EA/06*

DALLAS, Henry (d 1917 [51]) comedian, manager EA/18*

DALLAS, Isabelle see Glyn, Isabelle

DALLAS, Mrs. James see Varden, Dorothy

DALLAS, J. J. (1853-1915) actor, singer CDP, DD, DP, GRB/1-4, WWT/1-2

DALLAS, John (fl 1780-87) scene painter BD

DALLAS, Letitia Marion [Miss Darragh] (d 1917) actress EA/18*

DALLAS, Meredith (b 1916) American educator, actor, director BE

DALLAS, Mervyn (d 1911 [87]) English actor SR

DALLAS, Robert Charles (1754-1824) English dramatist CP/3, DD

DALLIMORE, Maurice (d 1973 [70s]) performer BP/57*

D'ALMAINE, Mrs. (d 1906) EA/07*

D'ALMAINE, Mrs. Ernest see D'Almaine, Mary

D'ALMAINE, Mary [Mrs. Ernest D'Almaine] (d 1909) singer EA/10*

D'ALMAINE, Maude see Barrassford, Mrs.

DAL MONTE, Toti (d 1975 [81]) performer BP/59*

DALMORES, Charles (1871-1939) French singer WWA/1, WWS

D'ALROY, Evelyn (d 1915 [33]) English actress WWT/1-2

DALRYMPLE, Mrs. (fl 1782-83) house servant? BD

DALRYMPLE, Jean (b 1910) American producer, director, publicist AAS, BE, CB, TW/3-8, WWT/11-16

DALTON, Mr. (fl 1759-63) ticket taker BD

DALTON, Mrs. (d 1891) EA/92*

DALTON, Miss (fl 1791) actress BD

DALTON, Amy (fl 1664-67) actress BD

DALTON, Charles (1864-1942) English actor CB, DD, EA/95, GRB/2, 4, SR, WWS, WWT/1-9

DALTON, Charles see Bethen, Charles

D'ALTON, Curtis (d 1911 [51]) singer EA/12*

D'ALTON, Mrs. Curtis see D'Alton, Emma

DALTON, Doris (b 1910/12) American actress TW/3-11, WWT/10-11

DALTON, Dorothy (1893/94-1972) American actress ES, TW/28, WWT/4-6

D'ALTON, Emma [Mrs. Curtis D'Alton] (d 1893) EA/95*

DALTON, Harry (d 1906) EA/07*

DALTON, Harry (d 1909) manager EA/10*

DALTON, Helen (d 1893) singer EA/94*

DALTON, Mrs. James T. [Sally Holman] (1852-88) American actress, singer CDP

D'ALTON, Jessie (d 1911) actress EA/12*

DALTON, John (1709-63) English dramatist CP/1-3, GT, TD/1-2

DALTON, John (fl 1775) dramatist CP/2-3, GT

DALTON, Kate [Mrs. George Ellison] (d 1912 [62]) singer EA/13*

D'ALTON, Marion [Mrs. Charles Sullivan] (d 1900 [36]) EA/01*

DALTON, Mrs. Sam (d 1895) EA/96*

DALTON, Shirley English actress GRB/1

DALTON, Test (1875-1945) American dramatist WWA/2

DALTON, Will singer CDP

DALTON, William see Eltinge, Julian

DALTRA, Marie [Mrs. Lionel Rignold] (d 1932 [84]) Welsh actress GRB/1

DALTRAY, Thomas (d 1889 [39]) gymnast EA/90*

D'ALTROY, Walter (d 1875) acrobat EA/76*

D'ALVERA, Marie (d 1902) actress EA/03*

D'ALVINI, William see

Armstrong, William
DALY, Mr. (fl 1732) actor   BD
DALY, Mr. (fl 1779) actor   BD
DALY, Mr. (fl 1856) actor   HAS
DALY, Mrs. (fl 1756?-63)
  actress   BD
DALY, Miss   CDP
DALY, Alice   see   Cragg, Mrs.
  J. W.
DALY, Arnold (1875-1927)
  American actor, producer
  COC, ES, GRB/2-4, NTH,
  OC/1-3, SR, WWA/1,
  WWM, WWS, WWT/1-5
DALY, Augustin (1839-99) Amer-
  ican dramatist, manager,
  critic   CDP, COC, DAB,
  DD, ES, HJD, MH, MWD,
  NTH, OC/1-3, RE, SR,
  WWA/1, WWW/1
DALY, Mrs. Augustin (d 1907
  [58])   GRB/3*
DALY, Cpt. Bill   see   Daly,
  William
DALY, Blyth (b 1902) American
  actress   WWT/6-8
DALY, Brian (d 1923 [60])
  actor, lyricist   WWT/14*
DALY, Carroll John (1889-
  1958) American manager
  WWA/3
DALY, Claude (d 1892) marks-
  man   EA/93*
DALY, Dan (1858-1904) actor
  BE*, BP/2*, WWT/14*
DALY, Dixie (d 1963 [66])
  performer   BE*
DALY, Ellen [Mrs. Frederick
  L. Phillips] (1815-90)
  actress   CDP
DALY, Miss H.   see   O'Grady,
  Mrs. F.
DALY, Henry F. (b 1828) actor
  SR
DALY, James (b 1918) American
  actor   BE, CB, TW/7-15,
  20, WWT/14-16
DALY, John (d 1867 [63]) actor
  EA/68*
DALY, John [John Besemeres]
  (fl 1850-74) dramatist   DD,
  EA/69
DALY, Julia [Mrs. Wayne Ol-
  wine; Mrs. Warren Edgarton]
  (1833-87) actress   CDP, HAS,
  NYM, SR
DALY, Lawrence (d 1900 [38])
  actor, producer, manager

BE*, EA/01*, WWT/14*
DALY, Lillian Moran (d 1894 [18])
  EA/95*
DALY, Lizzie Derious (1876-1913)
  actress, dancer, singer   CDP,
  SR
DALY, Mae (d 1962 [70]) performer
  BE*
DALY, Maria (d 1905 [75]) actress
  EA/06*, WWT/14*
DALY, Mark (1887-1957) Scottish
  actor   WWT/6-11
DALY, Mrs. Michael H.   see
  Nolan, Pattie
DALY, Peter Christopher Arnold
  (1875-1927) American actor
  DAB
DALY, Richard (1758-1813) Irish
  actor, manager   BD, CDP,
  DD, DNB, TD/1-2
DALY, Mrs. Richard   see   Bar-
  santi, Jane
DALY, Robert (d 1889) American
  actor   EA/90*
DALY, Tom (1855-92) minstrel
  CDP
DALY, Vinie dancer, singer   CDP
DALY, William ["Captain Bill"]
  minstrel   CDP
DALY, William (d 1857 [61]) actor
  WWT/14*
DALY, William, Jr. (d 1974 [67])
  performer   BP/59*
DALY, Mrs. William (d 1883 [79])
  actress   EA/84*, WWT/14*
DALYA, Jacqueline (b 1919) Amer-
  ican actress   TW/2, 6
DALZELL, Allan C. [né Allan
  Cameron Pfeifer] (1896-1972)
  American press representative,
  manager   BE
DALZELL, Davidson (b 1858) Eng-
  lish actor   SR
DALZELL, William (b 1917) Amer-
  ican actor   TW/4
DALZIEL, May (d 1969 [68]) per-
  former   BP/54*
DAM, Henry J. W. (d 1906 [48])
  American dramatist   DD, WWA/1
DAM, Mrs. Henry J. W.   see
  Dorr, Dorothy
DAMALA, Jacques (d 1889 [40])
  actor   BE*, WWT/14*
DAMASCENE, Alexander (d 1719)
  French singer, composer   BD,
  DNB
DAMASZEK, Marvin   see   Deems,
  Mickey

D'AMBOISE, Jacques (b 1934) American dancer, choreographer CB, ES

D'AMBROSIA, Angela American actress TW/24

DAME, Mr. (fl 1783) musician BD

D'AMELI, Eugene see Eugene, Master

DAMEN, Henry Alban (d 1891) EA/92*

DAMER, Frank [Edward F. Dawson] (d 1911) stage manager EA/12*

DAMEREL, George (d 1936 [57]) American singer BE*, BP/21*

DAMES, Harry L. (d 1971 [82]) performer BP/55*

DAMIANI, Vitale (fl 1799-1800) Italian singer BD

DAMON, Cathryn American actress TW/21-22, 25-30

DAMON, Les (d 1962 [53]) actor BE*

DAMON, Stuart [né Stuart Michael Zonis] (b 1937) American actor, singer BE, TW/16, 18-22, WWT/15-16

DAMOREAU, Laure Cinthie [Mlle. Cinti] (1801-63) singer CDP

DAMPIER, Alfred (b 1842) actor, manager DD, GRB/2-4

DAMPIER, Claude (d 1955 [76]) music-hall comedian WWT/14*

DAMPORT, Edward (fl 1633) actor DA

DAMROSCH, Frank Heino (1859-1937) German/American chorus master DAB

DAMROSCH, Walter Johannes (1862-1950) Prussian composer, conductor CB, DAB, ES, HJD, SR, WWA/3, WWM, WWW/4

DANA, Barbara (b 1940) American actress TW/22, 26, 30

DANA, Henry (1855-1921) English manager GRB/2-4, WWT/1-3

DANA, Leora (b 1923) American actress BE, TW/6-16, 20-26, 28-29, WWT/15-16

DANA, Marie Louise (d 1946 [70]) actress TW/3

DANA, Viola (b 1898) American actress ES

DANBURY, Ethel [Mrs. Harry Starr] (d 1905) actress EA/07*

DANBY, Master (fl 1792-1814?) singer BD

DANBY, Charles (fl 1776-1814?) actor, singer BD

DANBY, Charles (1857-1906) English actor, singer CDP, DD, GRB/1

DANBY, Frank (d 1912) actor EA/13*

DANBY, Humphrey (fl 1709-39) flutist BD

DANBY, John (1757-98) singer, composer BD, DNB

DANCE, Miss (fl 1821) actress CDP

DANCE, Charles (1794-1863) dramatist DD, DNB

DANCE, Sir George (1858/65-1932) English dramatist, manager COC, DD, ES, GRB/1-4, OC/1-3, SR, WWT/1-6, WWW/3

DANCE, James [alias Love] (1722-74) English? comedian, manager, dramatist CDP, CP/2-3, DD, DNB, GT, TD/1-2

DANCE, Reginald [Francis Reginald Dance Scroggs] (b 1867) English actor GRB/1

DANCE, William (1755-1840) musician, composer BD, DNB

DANCER, Mrs. (fl 1766) house servant? BD

DANCER, Miss (fl 1782-88) actress BD

DANCER, Ann see Barry, Mrs. Spranger

DANCER, John (fl 1660-75) Irish? dramatist CP/1-3, DD, DNB, GT

DANCER, John Wimperis (d 1790) actor, singer BD

DANCER, William (d 1759) actor BD

DANCER, Mrs. William see Barry, Mrs. Spranger

DANCEY, Mr. (fl 1734) dancer? BD

DANCEY, Mrs. (fl 1732-39) actress, dancer BD

DANCEY, Miss (fl 1731-40) actress, dancer BD

DANDO, Letitia see Aenea

DANDO, W[alter] P[feffer] (1852-1944) English theatrical

engineer GRB/1

DANDO, William (d 1878 [30]) comedian EA/79*

DANDRE, Victor (d 1944 [74]) ballet impresario WWT/14*

D'ANDRIA, Giorgio (d 1972 [72]) producer/director/choreographer BP/57*

DANDRIDGE, Dorothy (d 1965) singer, actress WWA/4

DANDY, Jess [Jesse A. Danzig] (1871-1923) American comedian WWM

DANE, Clemence [Winifred Ashton; Diana Portis] (1888-1965) English dramatist, actress AAS, BE, COC, ES, MD, MH, MWD, NTH, OC/3, SR, TW/21, WWA/4, WWT/5-13, WWW/6

DANE, Essex (d 1962 [96]) English actress GRB/1-4, WWS

DANE, Ethel actress WWT/2-5

DANE, Marjorie (b 1898) actress WWT/2-3

DANEEL, Sylvia [née Sylvia Jadviga Lakomska] (b 1930/31) Polish actress BE, TW/13-16, 30

DANEMAN, Paul (b 1925) English actor AAS, WWT/12-16

DANEMORE, A. [Augustus Yorke] (d 1891) EA/92*

DANESE, Connie American actress TW/29-30

DANEY, Mr. (fl 1766) house servant? BD

DANFORTH, Edward W. (d 1857) prompter HAS

DANFORTH, William (1867-1941) actor, singer CB, SR, WWT/7-9

D'ANFOY, Mr. (fl 1730) dancer BD

D'ANGELIS, Mr. American actor HAS

D'ANGELIS, Sally see Fulton, Sarah

D'ANGELO, Carlo (d 1973 [54]) performer BP/58*

DANGERFIELD, Mr. (fl 1791-1804) boxkeeper BD

DANGERFIELD, Frederick (d 1904 [53]) scene artist EA/05*

DANGEVILLE, Mons. (fl 1720)

dancer BD

DANGLE, Steven (fl 1794) violinist BD

DANGLER, Anita American actress TW/12, 23-24, 29-30

D'ANGRI, Eléna (b 1824) Italian singer CDP, HAS

DANIEL, Mr. (fl 1782-89) actor BD

DANIEL, Billy (d 1962 [50]) choreographer BE*

"DANIEL, Dapper" see "Dapper Daniel"

DANIEL, George (1789-1864) English critic, dramatist CDP, DD, DNB

DANIEL, John (fl 1615-24) musician, patentee DA, DNB

DANIEL, Mark (fl 1794-1802?) singer BD

DANIEL, Mary see Daniel, Mrs. William

DANIEL, Rita (d 1951) actress BE*, WWT/14*

DANIEL, Samuel (c.1563-1619) English dramatist CP/1-3, DA, DD, DNB, FGF, HP, NTH, OC/1-3, RE

DANIEL, William (fl 1621-37) actor DA

DANIEL, William (d 1755) actor BD

DANIEL, Mrs. William [Mrs. Charles Somerset Woodham] (fl 1742-56) actress, dancer BD

DANIELE, Graciela (b 1939) Brazilian actress TW/25-29

DANIELEWSKI, Tad (b 1921) Polish director, producer, scenarist BE

DANIELIAN, Leon (b 1920) American dancer ES

DANIELL, Aimée see Beringer, Mrs. Oscar

DANIELL, Henry (1894-1963) English actor ES, TW/2-11, 20, WWT/4-13

DANIELOVITCH, Issure see Douglas, Kirk

DANIELS, Mr. (fl 1850-60) American actor HAS

DANIELS, Miss singer? CDP

DANIELS, Alfred (d 1964 [81]) performer BP/49*

DANIELS, Alicia [Mrs. George Frederick Cooke, II. Mrs. Windsor] (d 1826) singer, actress

BD, CDP

DANIELS, Bebe (1901-71) American actress, singer ES, WWT/10-14

DANIELS, Becky [Mrs. E. Gaertner] (d 1907 [26]) circus performer EA/08*

DANIELS, Bill (b 1927) American actor TW/9

DANIELS, Carolan (b 1940) American actress TW/21-22

DANIELS, Carrie E. actress, musician CDP

DANIELS, Charlotte (d 1973 [44]) performer BP/57*

DANIELS, Danny (b 1924) American choreographer, dancer, director BE, TW/2-4, 6-8

DANIELS, David (b 1927) American singer, actor BE, TW/11-20, 25-26

DANIELS, Edgar (b 1932) American actor TW/19-20, 22-24

DANIELS, Frank Albert (1856/60-1935) American actor, singer DAB, GRB/2-4, OC/1-3, SR, WWA/1, WWS, WWT/1-7

DANIELS, Harold (d 1971 [68]) producer/director/choreographer BP/56*

DANIELS, Mo (d 1890 [60]) musical clown EA/92*

DANIELS, Mrs. Moses see Daniels, Rotana

DANIELS, Rotana [Mrs. Moses Daniels] (d 1881 [48]) EA/82*

DANIELS, Walker (b 1943) American actor TW/24-25

DANIELS, William (b 1927) American actor BE, TW/18-20, 22-28, 30

DANILOVA, Alexandra (b 1904/07) Russian dancer, choreographer BE, ES, TW/14, WWT/9-12

DANJURO, Ichikawa (d 1903) actor, manager WWT/14*

DANK, David [né Zweibelsharf] (b 1895) Russian actor BE

D'ANKA, Cornélie (fl 1871) actress, singer DD

DANKS, Hart Pease (1834-1903) American composer BE*

DANKS, John (fl 1723-24) violinist BD

DANNELL, Mr. (fl 1784) actor BD

DANNER, Blythe American actress TW/25-28, WWT/16

DANNER, John (fl 1629) actor DA

DANNREUTHER, Edward George (1844-1905) German pianist ES, GRB/1

D'ANNUNZIO, Gabriele (1864-1938) Italian dramatist GRB/3

D'ANNUNZIO, Lola (d 1956 [26]) actress TW/13

DANO, Royal (b 1922) American actor TW/8

DANOIGERS, Oscar (d 1976 [74]) producer/director/choreographer BP/60*

DANSEY, Herbert (1870-1917) Italian actor GRB/3-4, WWT/1-3

DANSON, George (d 1881 [82]) scene artist EA/82*

DANSON, Thomas (d 1893 [64]) scene artist EA/95*

DANTE (1883-1955) Danish magician TW/12

DANTE, Ethel (d 1954 [92]) actress BE*, WWT/14*

DANTE, Lionel (d 1974 [67]) performer BP/59*

DANTER, John (d 1908 [64]) showman EA/09*

DANTER, William (d 1902 [65]) amusement caterer EA/03*

DANTINE, Helmut (b 1918) Austrian actor TW/3

D'ANTONAKIS, Fleury (b 1939) Greek actress TW/21-22

D'ANTONIE, Elise dancer CDP

DANTZIG, Eli (d 1968 [70]) conductor BP/53*

DANVERS, Billy (d 1964) English actor BE*

DANVERS, Edward (d 1906) comedian EA/08*

DANVERS, Edwin (d 1906) actor DD

DANVERS, Frank B. (d 1896 [42]) actor EA/97*

DANVERS, Mrs. Fred see Rainbird, Marie

DANVERS, George (d 1917 [39]) comedian EA/18*

DANVERS, H. dramatist DD

DANVERS, John composer, lyricist, minstrel CDP

DANVERS, Johnny (1860/70-1939) English actor OC/1-3, WWT/4-7

DANVERS, Nelly see Bosworth,

Agnes Ellinor
DANVERS, Thomas Ramsay
(d 1895 [37]) actor EA/96*
DANVERS, Mrs. William
see Cramer, Fanny
DANVIL, Maud [Mrs. Dan
Leeson] (d 1898) music-hall
performer EA/00*
DANZI, Muriel Chapman (d 1973
[62]) performer BP/57*
DANZIG, Jesse A. see Dandy,
Jess
DANZIGER, Maia (b 1950) ac-
tress TW/30
D'APOLITO, Alfred (d 1965
[54]) executive, journalist
BP/50*
DA PONTE, Lorenzo [Emanuele
Conegliano] (1749-1838)
Italian librettist, impresario,
teacher BD, COC, EAP,
ES, WWA/H
DA PONTE, Lorenzo L. (d
1840) dramatist EAP
"DAPPER DANIEL" (fl 1699)
fencer BD
DARBIE, Richard (fl 1602) actor
DA
D'ARBLAY, Frances see
Burney, Fanny
DARBY, Mr. (fl 1760) house
servant? BD
DARBY, Mr. (fl 1769) actor
HAS
DARBY, Aaron (fl 1688-89)
actor BD
DARBY, Fred (d 1898 [37])
comic singer EA/99*
DARBY, Mary see Robinson,
Mary
DARBY, William [Pablo Fanque]
(d 1871 [67]) circus propri-
etor EA/72*
DARBYSHIRE, Iris (b 1905)
English actress WWT/8-9
DARBYSHIRE, Taylor (1875-
1943) English critic WWW/4
D'ARC, Lambert (d 1893 [69])
waxworks proprietor EA/
94*
D'ARC, Nellie (d 1901 [32])
marionettist EA/02*
D'ARCY, Mr. [Mr. Caird] (fl
1797-1802?) singer, actor
BD, TD/1-2
D'ARCY, Miss (fl 1770-71)
actress BD
D'ARCY, Belle (d 1936 [64])

American actress GRB/1,
WWM, WWS
D'ARCY, George see Yelland,
Willie
D'ARCY, Hugh Antoine (d 1925
[82]) French actor, manager
BE*, BP/10*
DARCY, James (fl 1732-49) Irish
dramatist CP/1-3, GT, TD/
1-2
D'ARCY, Roy (1894-1969) Ameri-
can actor ES, TW/26
DARCY, Stafford (fl 1660-62)
singer BD
DARDEN, Norma Jean American
actress TW/24, 27, 30
DARE, Cyrus singer, composer,
lyricist CDP
DARE, Daphne English designer
WWT/16
DARE, Dulcie [Mrs. Dan Thomas]
(d 1904) music-hall performer
EA/05*
DARE, Ernest (d 1969 [87]) per-
former BP/54*
DARE, Eva (d 1931) actress BE*,
WWT/14*
DARE, Frank H. acrobat CDP
DARE, Leona (1855-1922) trapezist
CDP
DARE, Phyllis (1890-1975) actress
GRB/2-4, WWT/1-12
DARE, Richard (d 1964 [41]) actor
BE*
DARE, Stuart (d 1902) gymnast,
athlete EA/03*
DARE, Thomas S. acrobat CDP
DARE, Virginia (d 1962) actress
BE*
DARE, Zena (1887-1975) English
actress ES, GRB/2-4, WWT/
1-14
DAREMONT, A. (b 1862) French
actor, dramatist SR
DAREWSKI, Herman (1883-1947)
Russian composer WWT/4-10,
WWW/4
DAREWSKI, Max (1894-1929) Eng-
lish composer, conductor, pian-
ist WWT/4-6
DARGAN, Olive Thomas (fl 1904-
47) dramatist HJD
DARGON, Augusta C. (d 1902) ac-
tress CDP
DARIMATE, Mlle. see Durancy,
Mme.
DARK, Christopher (d 1971) per-
former BP/56*

DARK, Frederick (d 1917) comedian EA/18*

DARK, Sidney (1874-1947) English critic GRB/2-4, WWT/1-4, WWW/4

DARK, Stanley (b 1874) English actor WWS

DARKE, Rebecca (b 1935) American actress TW/23

DARKIN, Joseph (fl 1794) singer BD

DARLEY, Mr. see Darley, John

DARLEY, Mrs. [née Ellen Westray] (d 1849) English actress HAS

DARLEY, Anne see Darley, Mrs. William [John?]

DARLEY, George (1795-1846) Irish critic, dramatist DD, DNB, HP

DARLEY, John (d 1819) English actor HAS, SR

DARLEY, John, Jr. (1775/79-1853) actor HAS, SR

DARLEY, John Edward (d 1878 [37]) master carpenter EA/79*

DARLEY, William [John?] (c. 1756-1809) English singer, actor BD, CDP, TD/1-2

DARLEY, Mrs. William [John?; Anne] (1758?-1838?) singer, actress BD, CDP

DARLING, Mr. (fl 1785) actor BD

DARLING, Bessie [Mrs. Charles Berry] actress CDP

DARLING, Candy (d 1974 [26]) American actress TW/30

DARLING, Daisy (d 1974 [67]) actress TW/30

DARLING, David dramatist EAP

DARLING, Jean [née Dorothy Jean LeVake] (b 1925) American singer, actress BE, TW/1-5

DARLING, Joan [née Kugell] (b 1935/40) American actress, director BE, TW/24

DARLING, May (d 1971 [83]) performer BP/55*

DARLING, William (fl 1794) singer BD

DARLINGTON, William Aubrey (b 1890) English critic,

dramatist AAS, BE, COC, OC/1-3, PDT, WWT/4-16

DARLOE, Richard see Darlowe, Richard

DARLOWE, Richard (fl c. 1590-1602) actor DA

DARMOND, Grace (d 1963 [65]) performer BP/48*

D'ARMOND, Isabell (b 1887) American actress, singer WWM

DARNEL, Hale (d 1969 [44]) producer/director/choreographer BP/53*

DARNELL, Linda (d 1965 [43]) performer BP/49*

DARNELL, Nellie (d 1905 [21]) EA/06*

DARNELL, Robert (b 1929) American actor TW/26, 28-29

DARNLEY, Alice [Mrs. J. H. Darnley] (d 1908) EA/09*

DARNLEY, Herbert (d 1947 [75]) English actor, dramatist GRB/1-3

DARNLEY, Herbert Blundell (d 1917) actor EA/18*

DARNLEY, J. H. (d 1938 [81]) actor, dramatist DD

DARNLEY, Mrs. J. H. see Darnley, Alice

DARNLEY, Wilfred (d 1916 [37]) EA/17*

DARNTON, Charles (d 1950 [80]) critic BE*, BP/34*, WWT/14*

DARRAGH, Miss see Dallas, Letitia Marion

DARRAGH, Miss F. (d 1917) actress GRB/3-4, WWT/1-3

DARRANT, Symon (fl 1672) violinist BD

DARRELL, Mr. (fl 1708) house servant BD

DARRELL, Bennett (d 1907) performer? EA/08*

DARRELL, Charles (1858-1932) English dramatist, actor GRB/1-3

DARRELL, Mrs. Charles see Tempest, Amy

DARRELL, Fred (d 1898) actor, variety agent EA/99*

DARRELL, Mrs. George see Peachey, Catherine

DARRELL, J. Stevan (d 1970 [65]) actor TW/27

DARRELL, Maisie (b 1901) English actress WWT/6-10

DARRELL, Maudi [Mrs. John

Bullough] (1882-1910) English
actress GRB/1-4
DARRELL, Peter (b 1929) Eng-
lish choreographer, dancer
ES
DARRID, William [né William
David Blum] (b 1923) Ameri-
can producer BE
DARRIEUX, Danielle (b 1917)
French actress TW/29
DARROCH, Joseph (d 1917)
EA/18*
DARROW, Richard American
actor TW/26
DARROW, Stephen (d 1892 [74])
Australian actor EA/93*
DARTON, Mrs. H. see
Sloman, Mrs. John
DARVAS, Lili (1902/06-74)
Hungarian/American actress
BE, ES, TW/1-7, 9-19,
24-25, 27, WWT/13-15
DARVI, Bella (d 1971 [44])
performer BP/56*
DARVILE, Mr. (fl 1784) singer
BD
DARVILE, Jr., Mr. (fl 1784)
singer BD
D'ARVILLE, Camille [Mrs. E.
W. Crelin] (1863-1932)
Dutch actress, singer CDP,
DD, DP, GRB/2-4, SR,
WWA/1, WWM, WWS, WWT/
1-5
DARWELL, Jane (d 1967 [87])
American actress ES, TW/24
DARYL, Julian (d 1880 [36])
actor EA/81*
DARZIN, Diana (b 1953) Amer-
ican actress TW/30
DASH, Pauly (d 1974 [55])
performer BP/58*
DASH, Thomas R. (b 1897)
Russian/American critic
NTH
DASHIELL, Willard (1868?-
1943) actor CB
DASHINGTON, James J. (d
1962 [84]) performer BE*
DASHWAY, Mrs. Charles (d
1886) EA/87*
DASHWOOD, Annie see
Cruse, Annie
DASHWOOD, Mrs. A. P. see
Delafield, E. M.
DASHWOOD, Edmée Elizabeth
Monica see Delafield, E. M.
DASHWOOD, Harry [Benjamin

John Bell] (d 1900 [35]) comic
singer EA/01*
DASHWOOD, [John?] (fl 1799-
1813) doorkeeper BD
DA SILVA, Howard [né Silverblatt]
(b 1909) American actor, di-
rector, producer BE, TW/25-
28, WWT/13-16
DASSIN, Jean [or Jules] (b 1911)
American director BE, ES
D'ASTE, Lottie (d 1878 [26])
gymnast EA/79*
DATE, Keshavrao (d 1971 [32])
performer BP/56*
D'AUBAN, Mrs. (d 1867 [47])
EA/68*
D'AUBAN, Emma (d 1910) dancer
EA/11*, WWT/14*
D'AUBAN, Ernest (d 1941 [67])
director BE*, WWT/14*
D'AUBAN, John (d 1922 [80]) stage
manager, dancer WWT/14*
D'AUBAN, Mariette (d 1906 [60])
ballet mistress EA/07*
DAUBENY, Sir Peter Lauderdale
(1921-75) English impresario,
manager AAS, COC, OC/3,
WWT/10-15
D'AUBERVAL, Jean [Jean Bercher]
(1742-1806) French dancer,
ballet master, choreographer
BD, ES
D'AUBERVAL, Mme. Jean [née
Crépé; Mme. Théodore] (d
1798) dancer BD
DAUBRAY, Mons. (d 1892 [55])
actor EA/93*
DAUFEL, Andre (d 1975 [56])
performer BP/59*
D'AUNAY, Josias? (fl 1635) French
actor DA
DAUNCEY, Sylvanus (1864-1912)
dramatist DD
DAUNT, William (1893-1938) Irish
actor WWT/8
DAUPHIN, Claude [né Claude Maria
Eugent LeGrand] (b 1903/04)
French actor, writer, director
BE, TW/3, 6-8, 12-16, 18,
WWT/12-16
DAUSE, Mrs. (fl 1760) dancer BD
D'AUVIGNE, Mons. (fl 1773) ballet
master BD
DAUVRY, Helen [née Nellie Wil-
liams; "Little Nell, the Cali-
ornia Diamond"] (b 1858) Eng-
lish actress, singer CDP, DD,
SR

DAVALOS, Richard (b 1930)
American actor   TW/12-16

DAVANT, Henrick (fl 1685-1716)
trumpeter BD

DAVENANT, Alexander (b c. 1658)
treasurer, proprietor BD

DAVENANT, Charles (1656-1714)
proprietor, producer, inspector of plays, dramatist BD,
CP/1-3, DD

DAVENANT, Henrietta Maria du
Tremblay (d 1691) French?
proprietor BD

DAVENANT, Nicholas (b c. 1665)
lessee BD

DAVENANT, Ralph (c. 1659-98)
treasurer BD

DAVENANT, Thomas (b 1664)
English manager BD

DAVENANT, W. (fl 1857) English actor HAS

DAVENANT, Sir William (1606-
68) English dramatist, manager BD, CDP, COC, CP/
1-3, DA, DD, DNB, ES,
FGF, HP, MH, NTH, OC/
1-3, PDT, RE

DAVENCOURT, Mons. (fl 1705)
dancer BD

DAVENPORT, Mr. (fl 1729-58?)
dancer, actor, dancing master
BD

DAVENPORT, Mr. (fl 1776?-79)
actor BD

DAVENPORT, Mr. (fl 1795-1803)
actor TD/1-2

DAVENPORT, Mrs. (fl 1733-41)
dancer, actress BD

DAVENPORT, Adolphus H. [né
Hoyt] (1828-73) American
actor CDP, DD, HAS, SR

DAVENPORT, Alice [Mrs. Harry
Bryant Davenport] (b 1864)
actress ES

DAVENPORT, Mrs. Arthur
Bromley (d 1917) actress
EA/18*

DAVENPORT, Blanche [Bianca
Lablanche] singer, actress
CDP

DAVENPORT, Butler (1871-
1958) American actor,
dramatist, producer NTH,
TW/14

DAVENPORT, Clara (d 1908
[68]) actress GRB/4*

DAVENPORT, Davis (d 1975 [42])
performer BP/60*

DAVENPORT, Dorothy (b 1895)
American actress ES

DAVENPORT, Edgar Longfellow
(1862-1918) American actor
COC, ES, OC/1-3, PP/1

DAVENPORT, Edward Loomis
(1815-77) American actor
CDP, COC, DAB, DD, ES,
HAS, NTH, OC/1-3, SR,
WWA/H

DAVENPORT, Mrs. Edward
Loomis see Davenport, Fanny
Elizabeth

DAVENPORT, Elizabeth (fl 1664?-
75?) actress BD

DAVENPORT, Eva [Mrs. Neil
O'Brien] (d 1932 [74]) English
actress WWS

DAVENPORT, Fanny Elizabeth
[née Vining; Mrs. Edward
Loomis Davenport] (1829-91)
English actress CDP, COC,
DD, ES, HAS, OC/1-3, SR

DAVENPORT, Fanny Lily Gipsy
(1850-98) English actress
CDP, COC, DAB, ES, HAS,
NTH, OC/1-3, WWA/H

DAVENPORT, Frances (fl 1664-68)
actress BD

DAVENPORT, George Gosling (c.
1758-1814) actor, manager BD,
DD, GT

DAVENPORT, Mrs. George Gosling [née Mary Ann Harvey]
(1759-1843) English actress,
singer BD, BS, CDP, DD,
DNB, GT, OX

DAVENPORT, G. Victor (d 1899
[30]) actor EA/00*

DAVENPORT, Mrs. Harry see
Rankin, Phyllis

DAVENPORT, Harry Bryant (1866-
1949) American actor COC,
ES, OC/1-3, TW/6, WWS,
WWT/7-10

DAVENPORT, Mrs. Harry Bryant
see Davenport, Alice

DAVENPORT, Henry (d 1880 [36])
manager, lessee EA/81*

DAVENPORT, Hester [Countess of
Oxford; Mrs. Peter Hoet] (1641?-
1717) actress BD

DAVENPORT, Ira (1839-1911)
American magician SR

DAVENPORT, Jane (fl 1667-68)
actress BD

DAVENPORT, Jean (1826-1903)
actress, dramatist SR

DAVENPORT, Jean Margaret
see Lander, Mrs. Frederick
W.
DAVENPORT, John (fl 1689)
musician BD
DAVENPORT, Julia [Mrs. Lewis
Davenport] (d 1909 [27]) EA/
11*
DAVENPORT, Mrs. Lewis see
Davenport, Julia
DAVENPORT, Lily (d 1878)
American actress EA/79*
DAVENPORT, Lizzie see
Mathews, Mrs. Charles
James
DAVENPORT, Louise see
Sheridan, Mrs. William Ed-
ward
DAVENPORT, Mary (d 1916?
[65]) actress CDP
DAVENPORT, Mary Ann see
Davenport, Mrs. George
Gosling
DAVENPORT, May (1856-1927)
American actress COC, ES,
OC/1-3, PP/1
DAVENPORT, Millia (b 1895)
American costume designer
BE
DAVENPORT, Nigel (b 1928)
English actor WWT/14-16
DAVENPORT, N. T. [né
Deven] (fl 1849-50) actor
HAS
DAVENPORT, Orrin B. (d 1962
[77]) equestrian BE*
DAVENPORT, Pembroke (b 1911)
American musical director,
composer, lyricist, actor
BE
DAVENPORT, Robert (fl 1623)
English dramatist CP/1-3,
DD, DNB, FGF, NTH
DAVENPORT, Ruth [Mrs. Wil-
son] actress, singer GRB/1
DAVENPORT, Thomas Donald
(1792-1851) English actor,
manager COC, DD, HAS
DAVENPORT, William Henry
Harrison (1841-77) Ameri-
can illusionist WWA/H
DAVENTRY, George (d 1904
[45]) actor EA/05*
DAVES, Delmer (1904-77)
American actor ES
DAVEY, George (d 1909 [71])
EA/10*
DAVEY, Leon G. (b 1904)

English scene designer ES
DAVEY, Nuna [née Margaret Sy-
monds] (b 1902) Indian/English
actress WWT/10-14
DAVEY, Peter (1857-1946) English
agent, manager GRB/1-4,
WWT/1-9
DAVEY, Richard (d 1870 [69])
property master EA/71*
DAVEY, Richard (fl 1886-93)
dramatist DD
DAVEY, Samuel (fl 1737-39) Irish
dramatist CP/1-3, GT
DAVEY, Thomas W. actor, manager SR
DAVID, Mr. (fl 1791) Czech musician BD
DAVID, Clifford (b 1932/33) American actor BE, TW/16-19,
22-23, 25-28
DAVID, Jean (b 1931) American
actress TW/26-27, 29-30
DAVID, Jeff (b 1940) American
actor TW/24, 26-28
DAVID, Mack (b 1912) American
composer, lyricist BE
DAVID, Pete (d 1974 [80]) per-
former BP/58*
DAVID, Ross singer CDP
DAVID, Thayer (b 1927) American
actor TW/12-13, 19-20, 22-
23, 27, 29-30
DAVID, Virginia (d 1973 [47]) per-
former BP/58*
DAVID, William (d 1965 [83]) per-
former BP/49*
DAVID, Worton (d 1940) dramatist,
composer WWT/4-9
DAVIDE, Giacomo (1750-1820)
Italian singer BD
DAVIDGE, Mr. (fl 1792) puppeteer
BD
DAVIDGE, George B. (1793-1842)
actor, manager CDP, DD, OX
DAVIDGE, J. H. (d 1874 [49])
property master EA/75*
DAVIDGE, William (d 1899) English
actor CDP, HAS
DAVIDGE, Mrs. William (d 1892
[74]) comedian HAS?, EA/93*
DAVIDGE, Mrs. William see
Harold, Maggie
DAVIDGE, William Pleater (1814-
88) English actor, dramatist
CDP, DAB, DD, ES, HAS, SR,
WWA/H
DAVIDOFF, Frances Mack (d 1967
[60]) performer BP/52*

DAVIDS, Joseph (fl 1783) house servant? BD

DAVIDSON, Mrs. (d 1870 [67]) equestrian EA/71*

DAVIDSON, Rev. Anthony (fl 1805) Scottish dramatist CP/3

DAVIDSON, Bill (b 1918) American writer BE

DAVIDSON, Cecil (d 1974 [69]) producer/director/choreographer BP/59*

DAVIDSON, Doré (1847-1930) actor, dramatist SR

DAVIDSON, Frederick Lewis Maitland (d 1936) critic WWW/3

DAVIDSON, Gordon (b 1933) American producer, director WWT/16

DAVIDSON, Jack (d 1903 [22]) actor? EA/04*

DAVIDSON, Jack (b 1936) American actor TW/25, 28

DAVIDSON, John (1857-1909) Scottish dramatist DD, DNB, GRB/1-4, HP, WWW/1

DAVIDSON, John (b 1941) American actor, singer CB, TW/20, 22

DAVIDSON, Lorraine (b 1945) American actress TW/30

DAVIDSON, Maitland (d 1936 [62]) critic BE*, WWT/14*

DAVIDSON, Margaret Miller (1823-38) American actress, dramatist WWA/H

DAVIDSON, Milton editor BE

DAVIDSON, Norris West (d 1975 [69]) producer/director/choreographer BP/60*

DAVIDSON, Richard (b 1918) American lawyer BE

DAVIES, Mr. (fl 1716-17) music copyist BD

DAVIES, Mr. (fl 1783-1817) constable BD

DAVIES, Mr. (fl 1796-99) dancer BD

DAVIES, Master (fl 1779) dancer BD

DAVIES, Miss (fl 1794-95) singer BD

DAVIES, Acton (1870-1916) Canadian critic GRB/2-4, WWA/1, WWM, WWT/1-3

DAVIES, A. Gardner (d 1939 [32]) producer WWT/14*

DAVIES, Alfred (b 1856) English stage manager, manager GRB/1

DAVIES, Anna [Mrs. Emanuel Samuel] (fl 1786-1836) actress BD

DAVIES, Ben[jamin Grey] (1858-1943) Welsh singer, actor DD, DP, ES, GRB/1-4, WWT/1-9, WWW/4

DAVIES, Betty-Ann (1910-55) English actress, singer TW/8, 11, WWT/10-11

DAVIES, Brian (b 1912) American actor, singer BE

DAVIES, Brian (b 1938/39) Welsh actor, singer BE, TW/30

DAVIES, Cecilia (1753?-1836) English singer BD, DNB, ES

DAVIES, Charles see Stirling, Charles

DAVIES, Charles J. (d 1910 [74]) secretary of the Royal General Theatrical Fund EA/11*

DAVIES, Denis (d 1900 [21]) actor EA/01*

DAVIES, D. R. (d 1870 [41]) proprietor EA/71*

DAVIES, E. D. (d 1896 [76]) ventriloquist CDP

DAVIES, Edna (b 1905) Welsh actress WWT/6-8

DAVIES, Elizabeth [Mrs. Jonathan Battishill; Mrs. Anthony Webster] (d 1777) actress, singer BD

DAVIES, Elizabeth see Davies, Mrs. William

DAVIES, George [George Smythe] (d 1885 [33]) EA/86*

DAVIES, Mrs. George see O'Malley, Alice Mary

DAVIES, Harry Parr (1914-55) Welsh composer WWT/10-11

DAVIES, Hubert Henry (1869-1917) English dramatist ES, GRB/1-4, NTH, WWT/1-3, WWW/2

DAVIES, Hugh (fl 1742-43?) actor BD

DAVIES, Jack (d 1946 [57]) manager, agent WWT/14*

DAVIES, Jessie Gordon (d 1913) EA/14*

DAVIES, John Edward see Craven, Arthur

DAVIES, Katie see Deane, Barbara

DAVIES, "Kiddy" see Davies, William

DAVIES, Lew (d 1968 [57])
composer/lyricist BP/53*
DAVIES, Lilian (d 1910) actress EA/12*
DAVIES, Lilian (1895-1932)
Welsh actress, singer WWT/5-6
DAVIES, Maria Jane [Mrs. John Coleman] (d 1893) actress EA/94*, WWT/14*
DAVIES, Marianne (1744-1816?)
singer, instrumentalist BD, DNB
DAVIES, Marion (1897-1961)
American actress ES, TW/18, WWA/4, WWT/7-10
DAVIES, Phoebe (d 1912) American actress WWM, WWS
DAVIES, Phoebe see Davis, Phoebe
DAVIES, Robert (d 1896 [65])
circus proprietor EA/97*
DAVIES, Robertson (b 1913)
Canadian dramatist, actor, educator CD, MH, RE
DAVIES, Susannah see Davies, Mrs. Thomas
DAVIES, Richard (d 1773) flutist, composer BD
DAVIES, Thomas (c. 1712-85)
Scottish? actor, bookseller, printer, proprietor BD, CDP, DD, DNB, ES, TD/1
DAVIES, Mrs. Thomas [née Susannah Yarrow] (1723-1801) actress BD
DAVIES, Thomas C. (d 1881 [33]) comedian EA/82*
DAVIES, Tudor (d 1958) Welsh singer WWW/5
DAVIES, Valentine (1905-61)
American dramatist WWA/4
DAVIES, W. G. (d 1909) EA/10*
DAVIES, W. H. (d 1883 [76])
EA/84*
DAVIES, William (1751-1809)
English singer BD
DAVIES, William (fl 1786) dramatist CP/3
DAVIES, William (d 1907 [47])
song composer, professor of music EA/08*
DAVIES, Mrs. William [Elizabeth] (d 1782) actress BD
DAVIES, Mrs. William (d 1873 [72]) EA/75*
DAVIES, William Cadwalader

(d 1905 [57]) EA/06*
DAVILA, Diana (b 1947) American actress TW/24-26, 28-29
DAVIN, John A. see Pell, Johnny
DAVIN-POWER, Maurice (d 1975 [66]) dramatist BP/60*
DAVIOT, Gordon [Elizabeth Mackintosh] (1896-1952) Scottish dramatist ES, WWT/8-11, WWW/5
DAVIS, Mr. (fl 1696) actor BD
DAVIS, Mr. (fl 1722-23) actor BD
DAVIS, Mr. (fl 1733-35) singer, actor BD
DAVIS, Mr. (fl 1736-52) dancer BD
DAVIS, Mr. (fl 1754-61) violinist BD
DAVIS, Mr. (fl 1780) actor BD
DAVIS, Mr. (fl 1787-95?) singer, dancer BD
DAVIS, Mr. (fl 1787-1803) costume designer BD
DAVIS, Mr. (fl 1794) singer BD
DAVIS, Mrs. [née Clegg] (fl 1726-45) singer BD
DAVIS, Mrs. (fl 1741) actress BD
DAVIS, [Mrs. ?] (fl 1793-1814) dresser BD
DAVIS, Mrs. (fl 1795) singer? dancer? BD
DAVIS, Mrs. (fl 1799?-1803) singer, actress BD
DAVIS, Mrs. [Miss Williams] (fl 1799-1803) costume designer BD
DAVIS, Master (fl 1792) dancer BD
DAVIS, Miss (b c. 1736) Irish harpsichordist BD
DAVIS, Miss (fl 1739-62?) actress, dancer, singer? BD
DAVIS, Miss (fl 1789-91) equestrienne BD
DAVIS, Miss (fl 1794) singer BD
DAVIS, Miss (fl 1799) actress BD
DAVIS, Prof. Alexander ventriloquist CDP
DAVIS, Alfred (d 1916 [88]) EA/17*
DAVIS, Mrs. Alfred (d 1869 [32]) EA/70*
DAVIS, Allan (b 1913) English producer, director WWT/11-16
DAVIS, Andrew Jackson (1826-

1910) lecturer CDP
DAVIS, Ann (d 1961 [68]) actress
TW/18
DAVIS, Arthur (d 1894 [67])
comedian, manager EA/95*
DAVIS, Bessie McCoy (d 1931)
actress, singer WWT/14*
DAVIS, Bette [Ruth Elizabeth]
(b 1908) American actress
BE, CB, ES, WWT/16
DAVIS, Blevins (d 1971 [68])
producer, dramatist TW/28
DAVIS, Bob (d 1971 [61]) stand-
in BP/56*
DAVIS, Boyd (1885-1963) Amer-
ican actor WWT/7-10
DAVIS, Buster [Carl Estes
Davis] (b 1920) American
arranger, musical director
BE
DAVIS, Carl (b 1936) American
composer WWT/16
DAVIS, Caroline (fl 1853) actress
HAS
DAVIS, Charles Belmont (d
1926 [60]) American critic
BE*, BP/11*, WWT/14*
DAVIS, Charles Lindsay (b 1849)
American producer SR
DAVIS, Cherry American actress
TW/27-29
DAVIS, Clatie Polk (d 1975)
performer BP/60*
DAVIS, Clifton American actor
TW/26-30
DAVIS, David (fl 1799-1815?)
musician, instrument maker
BD
DAVIS, Dibble see Davis,
Thomas Dibble
DAVIS, Dick ["Fixer"] (d 1892
[43]) sketch artist EA/93*
DAVIS, Donald (b 1928) Cana-
dian actor, director, producer
BE
DAVIS, Dora (d 1967 [92]) actress
WWT/15*
DAVIS, E. D. see Davies,
E. D.
DAVIS, Eddie (d 1958 [58]) Amer-
ican writer BE*, BP/43*
DAVIS, Edward Dean (1806-87)
English manager, lessee,
actor DD, NYM
DAVIS, Edwards (b 1873) Amer-
ican actor, dramatist, pro-
ducer WWM
[DAVIS?], Elizabeth see

Chambers, Mrs. William
DAVIS, Emma J. see Nichols,
Emma J.
DAVIS, Eugene C. (d 1969) pro-
ducer/director/choreographer
BP/54*
DAVIS, Evelyn (b 1906) American
actress TW/2-3, 11-12
DAVIS, F. (fl 1768) actor BD
DAVIS, Fay [Mrs. Gerald Law-
rence] (1872-1945) American
actress COC, DD, ES, GRB/
1-4, WWA/2, WWS, WWT/1-9
DAVIS, Fitzroy (b 1912) American
actor, writer, singer, director,
critic BE
DAVIS, Flora (b 1883) English
actress GRB/1
DAVIS, Florence (b 1876) American
actress WWM
DAVIS, Freeman (d 1974 [71])
performer BP/59*
DAVIS, Garry (b 1921) American
actor TW/7-8
DAVIS, Rev. Gary (d 1972 [76])
performer BP/56*
DAVIS, Gilbert (b 1899) South
African actor WWT/7-10
DAVIS, Gussie L. comedian, au-
thor CDP
DAVIS, Hallie Flanagan (1890-1969)
American director, educator
BE, COC, TW/26, WWA/5
DAVIS, Hannah [Mrs. J. W.
Davis] (d 1893) EA/94*
DAVIS, Harry composer CDP
DAVIS, Harry E. (b 1905) Amer-
ican educator, director BE
DAVIS, Henry (fl 1756) doorkeeper
BD
DAVIS, Henry (d 1865) American
Ethiopian performer HAS
DAVIS, Mrs. Henry [née Nash]
(d 1868 [30]) actress? EA/69*
DAVIS, Horace (d 1910) EA/11*
DAVIS, Hugh (fl 1594-1603) actor?
DA
DAVIS, Irving Kaye (d 1965 [65])
dramatist, press agent TW/22
DAVIS, J. (fl c. 1824?) actor CDP
DAVIS, J. (fl 1837) English actor
HAS
DAVIS, Mrs. J. (d 1894) EA/95*
DAVIS, James see Hall, Owen
DAVIS, Jeanette see Chanfrau,
Henrietta
DAVIS, Jed H. (b 1921) American
educator, director BE

DAVIS, Jessie Bartlett (1859/61-1905) American singer, actress CDP, SR

DAVIS, "Jew" (fl 1795?-1819) singer, actor BD

DAVIS, Joan (b 1906) English dancer, director, producer WWT/12-15

DAVIS, Joan (1912-61) American comedienne CB, TW/17, WWA/4

DAVIS, Joe (b 1912) English lighting designer WWT/15-16

DAVIS, John (fl 1700-05) singer BD

DAVIS, John (fl 1771-1813?) actor BD

DAVIS, John (d 1793) proprietor BD

DAVIS, John (c. 1780-c. 1838) French/American manager DAB, WWA/H

DAVIS, John (1821-75) English actor, manager CDP, HAS

DAVIS, John B. (d 1970 [76]) critic BP/54*

DAVIS, John Francis (fl c. 1730?-53) composer, flutist? BD

DAVIS, Josephine singer, actress CDP

DAVIS, Mrs. J. W. see Davis, Hannah

DAVIS, Mrs. K. (fl 1789-92) dancer BD

DAVIS, Katherine (fl 1681-91) actress BD

DAVIS, "Kiddy" see Davies, William

DAVIS, Lee (d 1973) performer BP/58*

DAVIS, Lew (d 1878) American minstrel, comedian EA/79*

DAVIS, Luther (b 1916) American dramatist, producer BE

DAVIS, Mary [Mrs. James Paisible] (fl 1660-98) actress, dancer, singer BD, CDP, DD, DNB

DAVIS, Meyer (1896-1976) American musician, actor, producer BE

DAVIS, Mildred (d 1969 [68]) performer BP/54*

DAVIS, "Moll" see Davis, Mary

DAVIS, Nancy (b 1921) American actress TW/2

DAVIS, Lieut. -Col. Newnham

see Newnham-Davis, Lieut. -Col. Nathaniel

DAVIS, Ossie (b 1917) American actor, dramatist, producer, director BE, CB, CD, ES, TW/22, 28, WWT/15-16

DAVIS, Owen (1874-1956) American dramatist COC, ES, MD, MH, MWD, NTH, OC/1-3, SR, TW/13, WWT/5-12

DAVIS, Owen, Jr. (1907-49) American actor TW/5, WWT/8-10

DAVIS, Peter (d 1974 [80]) producer/director/choreographer BP/59*

DAVIS, Peter (d 1974 [78]) general manager BP/59*

DAVIS, Phil (d 1974 [78]) performer BP/58*

DAVIS, Phoebe (b 1864/65) Welsh actress PP/1, WWT/1

DAVIS, Ray C. actor, dancer WWT/16

DAVIS, Richard (1697-1785) box office keeper BD

DAVIS, Richard American actor TW/1-3

DAVIS, Richard Harding (1864-1916) American dramatist ES, GRB/2-4, WWA/1, WWM, WWS, WWT/1-3, WWW/2

DAVIS, Mrs. Richard Harding see McCoy, Bessie

DAVIS, Robert (d 1906) actor? EA/07*

DAVIS, Mrs. Robert see Fernandez, Rose

DAVIS, Robert H[obart] (1869-1942) American dramatist CB, WWA/2, WWM

DAVIS, Rufe (d 1974 [66]) performer BP/59*

DAVIS, Sammy, Jr. (b 1925/26) American performer, dancer, singer, actor BE, CB, ES, TW/13, 21-22, WWT/14-16

DAVIS, Sarah see Davis, Mrs. William [Sarah]

DAVIS, Sidney (d 1883 [70]) actor EA/84*

DAVIS, Sidney [Alfred Earl Sidney Davis] (b 1867) English acting manager GRB/1

DAVIS, Solomon (fl 1785) musician BD

DAVIS, Thomas (fl 1702) stroller BD

DAVIS, Thomas (fl 1739-c. 1778)

composer, instrumentalist?
BD
DAVIS, Thomas (fl c. 1760-68)
watchman, dresser BD
DAVIS, Thomas (d 1874 [48])
minstrel EA/75*
DAVIS, Thomas Dibble (d 1795)
actor, manager BD
DAVIS, Mrs. [Thomas Dibble,
I?; Elizabeth] (fl 1758?-68)
actress BD
DAVIS, Mrs. Thomas Dibble,
V (fl 1785-1813?) actress
BD
DAVIS, Thomas H. (1859-1911)
American actor, manager SR
DAVIS, Tom Buffen (1867-1931)
English manager GRB/3-4,
WWT/1-6
DAVIS, Uriel (d 1971 [80]) com-
poser/lyricist BP/56*
DAVIS, W. (fl 1817-24) eques-
trian CDP
DAVIS, Mrs. W. A. see
Murray, Thomasina Pringle
DAVIS, Will (b 1914) American
actor TW/6
DAVIS, William (fl 1685) singer
BD
DAVIS, William (fl 1789-1824)
equestrian, manager BD
DAVIS, William (fl 1794) singer
BD
DAVIS, William (d 1868) Irish
actor HAS
DAVIS, Mrs. William [Sarah] (d
1797) actress, singer BD
DAVIS, William Boyd (b 1885)
American actor WWT/4-6
DAVIS, William G. (d 1889 [45])
American acting manager
EA/90*
DAVIS, Willis J. (d 1963 [76])
American manager BE*
DAVIS, Will J. (1844/47/54-
1919) American manager
SR, WWA/1, WWM, WWS
DAVISON, Mr. (fl 1788) actor
BD
DAVISON, Charles (d 1871) min-
strel, comedian EA/72*
DAVISON, James W. (d 1885
[71]) critic EA/86*
DAVISON, Maria Rebecca [née
Duncan] (1783-1858) English
actress BS, CDP, DD, DNB,
GT, OX
DAVISON, Mary (fl 1718?-25)

actress BD
DAVISON, Robert (b 1922) Ameri-
can designer ES, TW/2-4
DAVISON, Will (d 1905) EA/06*
DAVISS, Graham see Craig,
Clavering
DAVITS, Mary see Davis, Mary
DAVY, Master (fl 1741) dancer
BD
DAVY, Charles (d 1797 [75])
dramatist CP/3
DAVY, John (1763-1824) English
composer, instrumentalist BD,
CDP, DNB, ES, TD/1-2
DAVY, Samuel see Davey, Sam-
uel
DAVYS, Mary (fl 1725/56) Irish
dramatist CP/1-3, DNB, GT
DAW, Miss (fl 1760-68) dancer
BD
DAW, Evelyn (d 1970 [58]) per-
former BP/55*
DAWE, Carlton (d 1935 [69])
dramatist BE*, WWT/14*
DAWE, Thomas F. (1881-1928)
Irish manager WWT/4-5
DAWE, William (fl 1792-95) car-
penter, sceneman BD
DAWE, William Henry (d 1898
[51]) actor EA/99*
DAWES, Mr. (fl 1791-92) singer
BD
DAWES, Mrs. (fl 1777-79) actress
BD
DAWES, Mrs. (fl 1799) canvas
worker BD
DAWES, Miss see Daw, Miss
DAWES, Ezekiel H. (1817-50)
American actor HAS
DAWES, Gertrude [née Briant] (b
1835) American actress, dancer
HAS
DAWES, Robert (fl 1610-14) actor
DA
DAWES, Rufus (1803-59) American
dramatist HJD, RJ
DAWISON, Bogumil (fl 1866-67)
German actor HAS
DAWLEY, Herbert M. (d 1970
[90]) performer BP/55*
DAWLEY, J. Searle American ac-
tor ES
DAWN, Hazel (b 1891/94) American
actress, singer BE, ES, WWT/
3-8
DAWN, Hazel, Jr. (b 1929) Amer-
ican actress TW/5-8
DAWN, Isabel (d 1966 [62])

actress TW/23

DAWN, J. R. (d 1872 [23])
singer EA/73*

DAWSON, Mr. actor, manager
TD/1-2

DAWSON, Mr. (d 1748) actor
BD

DAWSON, Mr. (fl 1767) bill-
sticker BD

DAWSON, Mr. (fl 1776-82)
tumbler, ropedancer BD

DAWSON, Mr. (fl 1789-97)
actor BD

DAWSON, Miss (fl 1779-82)
actress, singer BD

DAWSON, Anna actress WWT/
16

DAWSON, Anthony (b 1916)
Scottish actor TW/9

DAWSON, Beatrice (1908-76)
English costume designer
WWT/15-16

DAWSON, Mrs. Charles see
Robins, Gertrude L.

DAWSON, Curt (b 1941) American actor TW/26-27, 30

DAWSON, Edward F. see
Damer, Frank

DAWSON, Elide Webb (d 1975
[79]) performer BP/59*

DAWSON, Forbes (b 1860) English actor, dramatist DD,
DP, GRB/1-4, WWT/1-8

DAWSON, Mrs. Forbes see
Harcourt, Lottie

DAWSON, George comedian,
dancer, ballet master TD/1

DAWSON, George (d 1876)
scholar EA/77*

DAWSON, Gladys (d 1969 [71])
performer BP/53*

DAWSON, Grattan (fl 1857)
actor HAS

DAWSON, Ivo (d 1934 [54]) actor
BE*, WWT/14*

DAWSON, James (d 1878 [79])
actor EA/79*

DAWSON, Jane [Mrs. Randal
Lingham] (d 1909 [86])
EA/10*

DAWSON, Jenny (d 1936) actress
EA/97

DAWSON, John (fl 1607) actor
DA

DAWSON, Jon (b 1910) American
actor TW/3-6

DAWSON, Joseph Morrison
(1818-67) English actor HAS

DAWSON, Mark (b 1920) American
actor, singer BE, TW/3-20,
23, 28-29

DAWSON, Nancy (c. 1730?-67)
English dancer BD, CDP, DD,
DNB, ES

DAWSON, Nancy (fl 1785) dancer
BD

DAWSON, Peter (1882-1961)
Australian singer WWW/6

DAWSON, Richard (fl 1739-66)
house servant BD

DAWSON, Stewart (d 1896) actor
EA/97*, WWT/14*

DAWSON, Mrs. William V. (d
1896) EA/97*

DAY, Mr. (fl 1742) dancer BD

DAY, Mr. (fl 1759-61) pyrotechnist BD

DAY, Mr. (fl 1852-53) actor HAS

DAY, Mr. (d 1873) carpenter
EA/75*

DAY, Mrs. (fl 1744) singer BD

DAY, Anna (b 1884) American
actress WWS

DAY, Charles (fl 1767) house servant? BD

DAY, Charles Ernest David (d
1911 [36]) EA/12*

DAY, Clarence [Shepard] (1874-
1935) writer HJD

DAY, Connie (b 1940) American
actress TW/28, 30

DAY, Cyrus L. (d 1968 [67])
teacher BP/53*

DAY, Dinah (b 1945) American
actress TW/28

DAY, Dorothy [née Ettlinger]
(1898-1975) American actress,
dramatist, critic BE

DAY, Edith (1896-1971) American
actress, singer TW/27, WWT/
4-11

DAY, Edmund (1860/66/67-1923)
American dramatist SR, WWA/
1, WWM

DAY, Ellen [Mrs. James Day] (d
1892) EA/93*

DAY, Frances [Frances Victoria
Schenk] (b 1908/12) American/
English actress, singer ES,
WWT/7-11

DAY, [George?] (fl 1762?-99?)
actor BD

DAY, Mrs. [George?] (fl 1770?-
1800?) actress BD

DAY, George D. (fl 1895-99)
dramatist DD

DAY, George D. (d 1911) manager EA/13*

DAY, Harry (d 1898) music-hall
proprietor EA/99*

DAY, Harry (d 1939 [59]) proprietor, manager WWT/14*

DAY, Mrs. Harry (d 1886 [38])
actress EA/87*

DAY, Harry T. (d 1900) acrobat, pantomimist EA/01*

DAY, James (d 1868 [18]) Canadian circus performer HAS

DAY, James (d 1876 [64]) proprietor EA/77*

DAY, James (d 1883 [47]) proprietor EA/84*

DAY, Mrs. James see Day,
Ellen

DAY, Jane [Mrs. John Day]
(d 1884 [52]) EA/85*

DAY, Janet (b 1938) American
actress TW/24

DAY, John (d 1584) dramatist
BE*, WWT/14*

DAY, John (c. 1574-c. 1640)
English dramatist, diarist
COC, CP/1-3, DD, DNB,
FGF, HP, NTH, OC/1-3,
RE

DAY, John (fl 1600-04) actor
DA

DAY, John (d 1888) menagerie
proprietor EA/89*

DAY, John (d 1905 [75]) musician
EA/06*

DAY, Mrs. John see Day,
Jane

DAY, John T. (fl 1897-98)
dramatist DD

DAY, Julietta (d 1957 [63])
actress TW/14

DAY, Laraine (b 1920) American
actress ES

DAY, Marie Elizabeth see
Santley, Marie

DAY, Marjorie (b 1889) New
Zealand actress WWT/2-6

DAY, May (b 1887) English
actress GRB/1

DAY, Nora [Mrs. Julian Royce]
(d 1898) actress EA/99*

DAY, Percy Leng English
journalist GRB/1-2

DAY, Philip (d 1887 [42]) actor
DD

DAY, Richard Digby (b 1940)
Welsh director WWT/15-16

DAY, Roy (d 1963 [75]) actor,

librarian BE*, BP/47*

DAY, Thomas (fl 1600-37) actor,
musician, organist, master of
the Chapel Royal DA

DAY, William (fl 1673) musician
BD

DAY, William (d 1894 [50]) lessee
EA/95*

DAY, William Charles (d 1895
[73]) actor EA/96*

DAY, William H. (1854-1927) English actor DD, EA/95

DAYKARHANOVA, Tamara (b 1892/
94) Russian actress, teacher
BE, TW/9-10

DAYLEY, Maggie (fl 1864) actress
HAS

DAYNE, Blanche [Mrs. Will M.
Cressy] (d 1944 [73]) American
vaudevillian WWM

DAYNES-GRASSOT, Brigitte (d
1926 [93]) actress WWT/14*

DAYRELL, Ada see Fowler,
Mrs. Montague

DAYTON, E. Mans (d 1907) acrobat EA/08*

DAYTON, June American actress
TW/3, 5-7

DAZEY, Charles Turner (1853-
1938) American dramatist ES,
GRB/2-4, SR, WWA/1, WWM,
WWS, WWT/1-8

DAZEY, Francis Mitchell (d 1970
[78]) dramatist BP/55*

DAZIE, Mlle. [née Daisy Peterkin]
(1882-1952) American dancer
TW/9, WWT/4-5, WWM, WWS

D'BAINVILLE, [Mons.] (fl 1733)
dancer BD

DEACON, James (d 1871 [68])
music-hall proprietor EA/72*

DEACON, James William (d 1896)
music-hall proprietor EA/97*

DEACON, Mrs. J. W. see
Deacon, Mary Ann

DEACON, Mary Ann [Mrs. J. W.
Deacon] (d 1879 [42]) EA/80*

DEACON, Richard (b 1922) American actor TW/26

DE ACOSTA, Mercedes (d 1968
[75]) dramatist BP/52*

DEACY, Jane talent representative
BE

DEADRICK, Louisa (fl 1864) actress HAS

DEAGON, Arthur (1873-1927)
Canadian actor WWS

DEAKIN, James (d 1879) EA/80*

DE ALBELA, Pedro (d 1877)
music teacher EA/78*
DEALY, James (d 1965 [85])
performer BP/50*
DE AMICIS, Domenico (fl 1759-
63) Italian singer BD
DE AMICIS, Signora Domenico,
Anna Lucia (fl c. 1755-89)
Italian singer, dancer BD, ES
DEAN, Mr. (fl 1761) trumpeter
BD
DEAN, Mr. (fl 1799) lamplighter
BD
DEAN, Alexander (1893-1939)
American director WWA/1
DEAN, Alfred (b 1830) SR
DEAN, Basil (1888-1971) Eng-
lish actor, director, drama-
tist, manager AAS, COC,
ES, MWD, OC/3, WWT/2-14
DEAN, Mrs. Benjamin F. see
Jones, Mrs. W. G.
DEAN, Benjamin John (d 1879)
musician EA/80*
DEAN, Doris (b 1889) English
actress, singer, dancer,
mimic GRB/1-4
DEAN, Edwin (b 1805) actor,
manager SR
DEAN, Fabian (d 1971 [41]) per-
former BP/55*
DEAN, Fanny [Mrs. Henry P.
Halsey] (d 1859) Canadian
actress CDP, HAS
DEAN, Georgie see Spaulding,
Georgie Dean
DEAN, Henry (fl 1794) musician
BD
DEAN, Isabel (b 1918) English
actress WWT/10-16
DEAN, Ivor (d 1974 [57]) per-
former BP/59*
DEAN, James (d 1867) Negro
delineator EA/68*
DEAN, James (1931-55) Ameri-
can actor ES, TW/10-12,
WWA/4
DEAN, John W. (d 1950 [75])
American actor BE*, BP/
35*, WWT/14*
DEAN, Joseph (d 1867) clown
EA/68*
DEAN, Joseph (d 1880 [29])
equestrian EA/81*
DEAN, Julia (1830-68) American
actress CDP, COC, DAB,
DD, ES, HAS, OC/1-3, SR,
WWA/H

DEAN, Julia (1880-1952) American
actress SR, TW/9, WWM,
WWT/4-6
DEAN, Kate singer CDP
DEAN, Laura (b 1963) American
actress TW/30
DEAN, Matthew (d 1878) singer,
banjoist EA/79*
DEAN, Milton (d 1962 [63]) press
agent BP/47*
DEAN, Priscilla (b 1896) American
actress ES
DEAN, Thomas (fl 1701-31) instru-
mentalist, composer BD, DNB
DEAN, Thomas (fl 1707-08) in-
strumentalist, singer, composer
BD
DEAN, Thomas ["The Royal Punch
Man"] (d 1887 [37]) EA/88*
DEAN, Thomas (d 1901) proprietor
EA/02*
DEAN, William (d 1885 [47]) con-
ductor EA/86*
DeANDA, Peter (b 1940) American
actor TW/22-24, 26
DEANE, Barbara [Katie Davies;
Mrs. Basil Loder] (b 1886)
Welsh actress, singer GRB/
1-4, WWT/5-7
DEANE, Charles (d 1910 [44])
variety comedian EA/11*
DEANE, Charles singer CDP
DEANE, Doris (d 1974 [73]) per-
former BP/58*
DEANE, Henry (d 1897) actor
EA/98*
DEANE, Henry (d 1917) EA/18*
DEANE, Julia A. see Jones,
Mrs. W. G.
DEANE, Lucie (b 1842) American
actress HAS
DEANE, Richard (fl 1661-73?)
trumpeter BD
DEANE, Tessa actress, singer
WWT/7-12
DEANE, Vivian (d 1893 [10]) actor
EA/94*
DEANE, William (d 1910 [45])
conductor EA/11*
DE ANGELIS, Mme. singer CDP
DE ANGELIS, Jefferson (1859-
1933) American actor, singer
DAB, DD, ES, GRB/2-4, OC/
1-3, SR, WWA/1, WWM, WWS,
WWT/1-7
DE ANGELO, Carlo (d 1962 [66])
actor, director BE*
DEANI, Herr (d 1888 [60]) con-

tortionist EA/89*

DEANS, Charlotte (1768-1859)
actress HAS

DEANS, F. Harris (1886-1961)
English critic, dramatist
WWT/4-13, WWW/6

DEAR, Peter see Dearing,
Peter

DEARBORN, Dalton (b 1930)
American actor TW/14-15, 23

DEARDEN, Audrey American
actress TW/9

DEARDEN, Basil (b 1911) English
dramatist, actor ES

DEARDEN, Harold (1882-1962)
English dramatist WWT/6-11

DEARDORFF, David (b 1947)
American actor TW/30

DEARING, Edgar (d 1974) performer BP/59*

DEARING, Peter [Peter Dear]
(b 1912) actor, producer
WWT/9-13

DEARING, Rose singer, actress
CDP

DEARING, William H. (d 1859)
actor HAS

DEARL, Mrs. (fl 1765) singer
BD

DEARLE, Mr. (fl c. 1755-c. 80)
singer BD

DEARLOVE, Charles Henry (d
1896 [63]) EA/97*

DEARLOVE, Mark William (d
1880 [78]) musician EA/81*

DEARLOVE, Mrs. Richard see
Dearlove, Sarah

DEARLOVE, Richard H. (d 1894)
musical director EA/95*

DEARLOVE, Sarah [Mrs. Richard
Dearlove] (d 1873) EA/74*

DEARLY, Max (1875-1943)
French actor, singer GRB/
4, WWT/1-4

DEARMER, Jessie Mabel see
Dearlove, Mrs. Percy

DEARMER, Mrs. Percy [Jessie
Mabel] (1872-1915) dramatist
WWW/1

DEARTH, Harry (1876-1933) English actor, singer WWT/2-7

DEASE, Mr. (fl 1732) actor BD

DEATH, Thomas (1739-1802)
English actor, lecturer BD,
CDP, TD/1-2

DE AUBRY, Diane (d 1969 [79])
performer BP/54*

DEAVEN, John Bruce (b 1947)

American actor TW/30

DEAVES, Mr. (fl 1848) actor HAS

DEAVES, Ada (d 1920 [64]) performer BE*, BP/5*

DEAVES, Walter Eugene (1854-
1919) American marionettist
ES

DE BANZIE, Brenda English actress BE, TW/13-14, WWT/
12-15

DeBAR, Mrs. see Conduit, Mrs.
Mauvaise

DEBAR, Miss see Booth, Mrs.
Junius Brutus, Jr., I

DEBAR, Benedict (1812-77) American actor, manager CDP,
HAS, SR

DE BAR, Mrs. Benedict [Henrietta
Vallee] (b 1828) American
dancer, actress HAS

DE BAR, Blanche Booth (b 1844)
American actress CDP, HAS

DE BASIL, Wassily (1880-1951)
Russian impresario ES, WWT/
9-11

DE BATHE, Lady see Langtry,
Lily

DE BAUDIN, Baptiste (fl c. 1787)
dancer BD

DE BEAR, Archibald (1889-1970)
English producer, manager,
critic WWT/5-13

DE BEER, Gerrit (b 1935) Dutch
actor TW/23-25, 30

DE BEGNIS, Claudine (1800-53)
singer CDP

DE BEGNIS, Giuseppe (1793-1849)
singer CDP

DE BEGNIS, Signora Giuseppe
see De Begnis, Claudine

DE BELLEVILLE, Frederick (1857-
1923) Belgian actor CDP, GRB/
2-4, WWA/1, WWM, WWS,
WWT/1-4

DE BELOCCA, Anna (b 1854)
Russian singer CDP

DEBENHAM, Cicely (1891-1955)
English actress, singer WWT/
4-8

DE BENSAUDE, Mrs. see
Cameron, Violet

DE BENSAUDE, David (d 1897)
EA/98*

DE BERIOT, Charles Auguste (d
1870 [68]) musician EA/71*

DEBIN, Nat[han] (b 1911) American
talent representative BE

DE BLASIO, Gene (d 1971 [30])

performer BP/56*

DE BLASIS, James (b 1931)
American educator, director
BE

DEBLIN, Miss (fl 1825) dancer
CDP

DE BLOIS, Mons. (fl 1732)
dancer BD

DE BOER VAN RIJK, Esther
(d 1937 [84]) actress WWT/
14*

DEBON, Mme. (fl 1742) performer BD

DEBONAY, John L. (b 1848)
actor HAS

DE BRAHAM, Miss see Greene,
Emma Marie

DE BRAY, Henry (1889-1965)
French actor, singer WWT/
4-8

DE BREAME, Maxent (fl 1675-
78) oboist BD

DE BRECOURT, Sieur [Guil-
laume Marcoureau] (fl 1674)
French manager BD

DE BRENNER, Harry (d 1903)
minstrel EA/04*

DE BRESMES, Maxent see
De Breame, Maxent

DE BRION, Corinne Belle see
Corinne

DEBROC, Mons. (fl 1720-43)
acrobat, dancer BD

DEBROKE, Mons. see Debroc,
Mons.

DEBUIN, Henry (fl 1794) singer
BD

DE BURGH, Aimée (d 1946)
Scottish actress WWT/2-6

DE BURGH, Frank (d 1909 [63])
tattooed man EA/10*

DEBUSKEY, Merle (b 1923)
American press representative
BE

DE CAMP, Mons. (fl 1727) dancer
BD

DECAMP, Anne Theresa actress,
dancer TD/1-2

DE CAMP, Adelaide (1780-1834)
French actress, dancer BD,
TD/2

DE CAMP, George Louis (1752-
87) flutist BD

DE CAMP, Sophia (fl 1776-77)
dancer BD

DE CAMP, Sophia [Mrs. Frederick Browne] (1785-1841)
English actress, dancer BD,

HAS

DE CAMP, Vincent (1779-1839)
English actor, singer BD,
CDP, GT, HAS, TD/1

DE CARLO, Yvonne (b 1922/24)
Canadian dancer ES, TW/27-29

DE CARMO, Pussy (d 1964 [63])
Portuguese performer BE*

DE'CARO see Del Caro

DE CASALIS, Jeanne (1897-1966)
South African actress ES,
WWT/5-13

DE CASTAN, Armand see
Castelmary, Armand

DE CASTREJON, Blanca (d 1969
[53]) performer BP/54*

DE CASTRO, Mrs. A. see De
Castro, Caroline

DE CASTRO, Caroline [Mrs. A.
De Castro] (d 1884) EA/85*

DE CASTRO, Frances (fl 1795)
equestrienne? BD

DE CASTRO, James (1758-1835)
English actor, monologist,
mimic, singer BD, CDP

DE CASTRO, Mrs. James (fl 1791-
95) singer, actress BD

DECASTRO, John (d 1758) actor
WWT/14*

DECATERS-LABLACHE, Mme.
La Baronne (d 1881) EA/82*

DECATUR, Emmett Daniel (1815-
1904) musician WWA/H

DECAYNE, Andrew see Cane,
Andrew

DE CISNEROS, Eleonora (1878-
1934) American singer WWA/
1, WWM

DECKARD, Diane American actress TW/28

DECKER, Nelson W. (b 1841)
American actor HAS

DE CLEVE, Vincent (d 1827)
treasurer BD

DE CLIFFORD, Lady [Eva Car-
rington] (b 1886) English actress
GRB/1

DE CORDOBA, Pedro (1881-1950)
American actor ES, TW/7,
WWM, WWT/4-10

DE CORDOVA, Mr. (fl 1824) West
Indian actor HAS

DE CORDOVA, Arturo (d 1973
[66]) performer BP/58*

DE CORDOVA, Rudolph (1860-
1941) Jamaican actor, dramatist DD, GRB/3-4, NTH,
WWM, WWT/1-9, WWW/4

DECOURCELLE, Adrien (d 1892
[69]) dramatist EA/93*
DECOURCELLE, Pierre (1856-
1926) French dramatist
GRB/1-4
DECOURCY, Ellie see Mack-
worth, Patti
DE COURCY, Robert J. H. see
Curtiss, George
DE COURCY, William (d 1917)
EA/18*
DECOURSEY, Nellie (d 1964 [95])
vaudevillian BE*, WWT/14*
DE COURVILLE, Albert P.
(1887-1960) English manager,
producer COC, ES, NTH,
OC/3, TW/2, WWT/4-12
DEE, Blanche (b 1936) American
actress TW/23, 26, 29
DEE, Danny (d 1970 [48]) per-
former BP/55*
DEE, Frances (b 1907) American
actress TW/2
DEE, Ruby [née Ruby Ann Wal-
lace] (b 1923) American ac-
tress BE, CB, ES, TW/26-
27, 29, WWT/15-16
DEEBANK, Felix (b 1920) Eng-
lish actor TW/9-10
DEEBLE, Mr. (fl 1767-94)
singer BD
DEEBLE, Deborah (b 1945)
American actress TW/25,
28-29
DEEKS, Barbara see Windsor,
Barbara
DEEMS, Mickey [né Marvin
Damaszek] (b 1925) American
actor, writer BE, TW/19,
30
DEEN, Nedra (d 1975) performer
BP/60*, WWT/16*
DEERING, Nathaniel (1791-1881)
American dramatist DAB,
EAP, ES, HJD
DEERING, Olive actress TW/
2-4, 20, 24, WWT/16
DEERING, Olly (d 1906) actor
EA/07*
DEERING, Rebekah [Mrs. Ernest
Stevens] (d 1906 [51]) EA/07*
DEERS, Harry (d 1906) minstrel
EA/07*
DEETER, Jasper (1893-1972)
American producer, director,
actor, teacher BE, ES, TW/
28
DEEVY, Teresa (d 1963 [60])

dramatist BE*
DE FABECK, Arthur Charles
Rock see Rock, Charles
DE FABEES, Richard (b 1947)
American actor TW/30
DE FAIBER, Ernestine (b 1843)
dancer HAS
DE FELICE, Aurelia American
actress TW/30
DE FERAUDY, Maurice (1859-
1932) French actor, dramatist
GRB/1, 3-4, WWT/1-3
DE FERRIS, Lola (d 1974 [81])
performer BP/59*
DE FESCH, William (1687-1761)
Dutch musician, composer BD
DE FESCH, Mrs. [William?] (fl
1732) singer BD
DEFFENBACH, F. (fl 1821?)
American dramatist EAP, RJ
DE FILIPPO, Eduardo (b 1900)
Italian actor, dramatist NTH,
OC/3
DE FILIPPO, Peppino (b 1903)
Italian actor, dramatist COC,
OC/3
DE FILIPPO, Titina (1898-1963)
Italian actress, dramatist OC/3
DE FIVAS, Sidney see Glover,
Augustus
DE FLERS, Robert (d 1927 [56])
dramatist BE*, WWT/14*
DE FLORENCE, Ferdinand (fl 1663-
65) musician BD
DEFOE, Alice (b 1883) English
actress GRB/1
DeFOE, Louis Vincent (1869-1922)
American critic WWA/1, WWM,
WWT/4
DE FOMPRE, Mons. (fl 1724-36)
Italian? actor, dancer BD
DE FOMPRE, Mme. (fl 1734-35)
actress, dancer BD
DE FORE, Don (b 1916/17) Amer-
ican actor, producer BE, ES
DE FOREST, Marian (d 1935 [70])
American dramatic editor WWM
DE FORRESTER, F. Claude see
De Haven, F. Claude
DE FRANCESCO, Giuseppe Venuto
(d 1892 [54]) ballet master
EA/93*
DE FRANCESCO, Louis (d 1974
[87]) composer/lyricist BP/59*
DE FRANO, Mlle. (fl 1737) dancer
BD
DE FRECE, Henry (d 1931 [96])
proprietor, manager WWT/14*

DE FRECE, Hettie [Mrs. Jack
De Frece] (d 1908 [33])
EA/10*
DE FRECE, Isaac (d 1902)
music-hall agent EA/03*
DE FRECE, Mrs. Jack see
De Frece, Hettie
DE FRECE, Lauri (1880-1921)
English actor GRB/2-4,
WWT/1-3
DE FRECE, Sir Walter (1870-
1935) English manager GRB/
2-4
DE FRECE, Mrs. Walter see
Tilley, Vesta
DEFRERE, Désiré (1888-1964)
Belgian singer, director BE*
DE FRIES, Mr. (fl 1859) actor
HAS
DEFRIES, Violet English singer
GRB/1
DeGAETANI, Thomas (b 1929)
American technician, educator
BE
DEGAMAR, Mr. (fl 1760s?) actor
BD
DE GAMBARINI, Elisabetta [Mrs.
Chazal] (b 1731?) singer, com-
poser, organist BD
DEGENER, Claire S. [née
Sweeney] (b 1928) American
literary representative BE
DeGHELDER, Stephan (b 1945)
American actor TW/25
DEGHELDERODE, Michel see
Ghelderode, Michel de
DE GIOVANNI, Pasquale (fl
1796-1820) Italian singer BD
DE GLORION, William [Watkin
Wyatt Wynne] (d 1898) circus
entrepreneur EA/99*
DE GOGORZA, Emilio Eduardo
(1874-1949) American singer
WWA/3
DEGOTTI, Mr. (fl 1797-98)
scene painter BD
DE GRAFT, Joe Ghanaian drama-
tist CD
DE GRANGER, Claude (fl 1663)
musician BD
DE GRASSE, Sam (d 1953 [78])
actor BE*
DE GREMONT, Mlle. (fl 1720)
performer? BD
DE GRESAC, Fred (d 1943 [75])
dramatist, librettist BE*,
WWT/14*
DE GREY, Marie [Ellen Wash-

ington Preston] (d 1897) actress
DD
DE GRIMBERGUE, Jean-Baptiste
(d 1722) Belgian manager BD
DE GROACH, Mrs. (fl 1852) ac-
tress HAS
DE GROOT, Gerry (d 1975) per-
former BP/60*
DE GROOT, Sara Irish actress
GRB/1-4
DE GROOT, Walter (b 1896) Eng-
lish press representative
WWT/9
DE GUERBEL, Countess see
Ward, Genevieve
D'EGVILLE, Master (fl 1794) singer
BD
D'EGVILLE, Miss (fl 1794) singer
BD
D'EGVILLE, Mons. (fl 1794) vio-
linist BD
D'EGVILLE, Fanny (fl 1779-1800)
dancer BD
D'EGVILLE, George (fl 1786-1806)
dancer, dancing master BD
D'EGVILLE, James Harvey (c.
1770-1836) dancer, choreograph-
er BD, CDP, GT, TD/1-2
D'EGVILLE, Mrs. James Harvey
[née Catherine Berry] (fl 1791-
1802) dancer BD
D'EGVILLE, Lewis (fl 1792-99)
dancer BD
D'EGVILLE, Peter (fl 1768-94)
dancer, ballet master, chore-
ographer BD
D'EGVILLE, Mme. Peter (fl 1772-
96) dancer BD
D'EGVILLE, Sophia (fl 1791-95)
dancer BD
DE HAGA, John (d 1872) singer
EA/73*
DEHALLE, Samuel (d 1887 [50])
EA/88*
DE HALSALLE, Henry (b 1872)
dramatist, critic GRB/1
DE HARTOG, Jan (b 1914) Dutch
dramatist BE, MD
DE HAVEN, Carter (1886-1977)
American actor ES, WWM
DE HAVEN, F. Claude [F. Claude
De Forrester] (b 1846) Ameri-
can banjoist, singer, ventrilo-
quist, magician, actor HAS
DE HAVEN, Gloria (b 1925) Amer-
ican actress, singer BE, TW/
24
DE HAVEN, Rose (d 1972 [91])

performer BP/57*

DE HAVILLAND, Olivia (b 1916) American actress BE, CB, ES, TW/7-9

DE HENNEY, [Mme. ?] (fl 1753) dancer BD

DeHETRE, Katherine (b 1946) American actress TW/28

DE HIGHTREHIGHT, Mr. (fl 1718) Swiss fire-eater BD

DEHN, Paul (1912-76) English dramatist, lyricist, critic WWT/12-16

DEIGHTON, Mr. actor TD/1-2

DEIGHTON, Marga Ann Indian/ English actress TW/5-11

DEITCH, Dan (b 1945) American actor TW/30

DE JACQUES, Eulallean see Lorraine, Lilian

DE JARDIN, Mons. (fl 1750-51) dancer BD

DEJAZET, Eugene (d 1880 [60]) composer EA/81*

DEJAZET, Pauline Virginie (1798-1875) French actress COC, OC/1-3

DE JONG, Frank (d 1903) manager EA/05*

DEKARO (d 1916 [86]) juggler EA/18*

DEKKER, Albert (1905-68) American actor, director BE, ES, TW/22, 24, WWA/5, WWT/13-14

DEKKER, Thomas (c. 1572-c. 1632) English dramatist CDP, COC, CP/1-3, DD, DNB, ES, FGF, HP, MH, NTH, OC/1-3, PDT, RE

DEKOLTA, Joseph B. (b 1845) French magician SR

DE KORPONAY, Gabriel (fl 1884) dancer CDP

DE KOVEN, Reginald (1859/61-1920) American conductor, composer DAB, DD, ES, GRB/3-4, HJD, SR, WWA/1, WWM, WWS, WWT/1-3

DeKOVEN, Roger (b 1907) American actor BE, TW/3, 22, 24, 26-27

DE KOWA, Victor (d 1973 [69]) performer BP/57*

DE KRUIF, Paul (1890-1971) American writer BE

DELACEY, Kate (fl 1852) singer HAS

DE LA CHAPELLE, Mons. (fl 1791-92) French dancer BD

DE LA COINTRIE, Mons. (fl 1751-53) dancer BD

DE LA COINTRIE, Mme. (fl 1749-52) dancer BD

DE LA COUR, W. (fl 1740-63) scene painter BD

DEL'ACQUA, Teresa (fl 1790) singer BD

DE LA CROIX, Mlle. (fl 1790-99) dancer BD

DE LACY, Valerie English actress, singer GRB/1-2

DE LACY, Walter (d 1874) musician EA/75*

DELAFIELD, E. M. [née Edmée Elizabeth de la Pasture; Mrs. A. P. Dashwood] (1890-1943) English dramatist DNB, WWT/8-9

DE LA FOINTE, Renée see Adoree, Renée

DE LA FOND, Mr. (fl 1716) impresario BD

DELAFORCE, Augustus Edward (d 1900 [86]) EA/02*

DELAGAR, Mr. (fl 1775) dancer BD

DELAGARDE, [Charles?] (fl 1705-36) dancer, choreographer, dancing master BD

DELAGARDE, Mrs. [Charles?] (fl 1710-11) dancer BD

DELAGARDE, Charles (fl 1718-34) dancer BD

DELAGARDE, J. (fl 1718-50) dancer BD

DELAGARDE, Mrs. J. [née Oates] (fl 1730-51) English actress, dancer BD

DE LA GRANGE, Mons. (fl 1738) dancer BD

DE LA GRANGE, Mlle. (fl 1738) dancer BD

DE LA GRANGE, Anna (b 1825) French singer HAS

DE LA GRANGE, Sophie (fl 1865) pianist HAS

DE LA HAY, Mons. (fl 1707) dancer BD

DE LA HAY, Mr. (fl 1736-38) dancer BD

DE LA HAYE, Ina (1906-72) Russian actress, singer WWT/10-15

DELAHOY, [Master?] (fl 1799) dancer BD

DELAHOYDE, Mr. (fl 1745-50)
    musician BD
DELAINE, Jack (d 1918) EA/19*
DELAIR, Paul (d 1894 [52])
    dramatist BE*, WWT/14*
DE LAITRE, Mons. (fl 1752-59)
    dancer BD
DELAMAINE, Henry (fl 1733-55?)
    dancer, choreographer BD
DELAMANO, William (fl 1850s)
    artist WWA/H
DE LA MARCA, Raffaello (b
    1871) Italian singer WWM
DELAMAYNE, Thomas (fl 1742)
    dramatist CP/2-3, GT
DE LA MOTTE, Marguerite
    (1902-50) actress BE*
DELAN, [B. ?] (fl 1797) house
    servant? BD
"DE LA NASH, Mme. " see
    Fielding, Henry
DELAND, Annie [Mrs. George
    Finnegan] (1842-93) American
    actress CDP, HAS
"DELANE" see Huntley, Thomas
    L.
DELANE, Dennis (d 1750) Irish
    actor BD, DD, DNB
DELANEY, Arthur (d 1899 [31])
    comic singer EA/00*
DELANEY, Charles (d 1959
    [67]) actor BE*
DELANEY, J. S. (d 1884) come-
    dian EA/86*
DELANEY, Maureen (d 1961
    [73]) Irish actress BE*, BP/
    45*, WWT/14*
DELANEY, Shelagh (b 1939)
    English dramatist AAS, BE,
    CB, CD, CH, ES, MD, MH,
    MWD, PDT, WWT/14-16
DELANEY, Tom (d 1905 [36])
    music-hall comedian EA/06*
DE LANGE, Herman (1851-1929)
    Dutch/English actor DD,
    WWT/2-5
DE LANGE, Mrs. Herman see
    Hill, Annie
DELANNOY, Edmond (d 1888
    [71]) actor WWT/14*
DELANO, Fanny actress CDP
DELANO, Jeppe actor CDP
DELANO, Paul tattooed man CDP
DELANOY, Edmond (d 1888 [71])
    actor BE*
DE LANTY, Virginia see
    Powys, Stephen
DELANY, Maureen (d 1961 [73])

Irish actress TW/17
DELANY, Richard see Guido,
    Frank
DELAP, John (1725-1812) English
    dramatist CP/1-3, DD, DNB,
    GT, TD/1-2
DE LA PASTURE, Edmée Eliza-
    beth Monica see Delafield,
    E. M.
DE LA PASTURE, Mrs. Henry
    [Lady Clifford] (1866-1945)
    Italian dramatist GRB/2-4,
    NTH, WWT/1-7, WWW/4
DELAPORTE, Agnes (fl 1886-90)
    actress, singer DD
DELAPORTE, Eleanor (d 1917)
    EA/18*
DE LA PORTE, [Gérard?] (fl
    1660s?) violinist BD
DE LA LAPPE, Gemze (b 1921/22/25)
    American dancer, actress,
    choreographer BE, ES, TW/
    8-9, 15, 21
DE LARA, Isidore (d 1935) com-
    poser WWW/3
DELARO, Elma singer, actress
    CDP
DE LA ROCHE, Mazo (d 1961
    [82]) dramatist WWT/14*
DELAROCHE, Suzanne see
    Avril, Suzanne
DE LA ROCHE-GUILHEN, Mme.
    (fl 1677) director, dramatist
    BD
DE LAROUX, Hugues (d 1925)
    dramatist WWT/14*
DE LA ROVERE, Luigi (fl 1790-
    91) scene painter BD
DELARUE, Mr. (fl 1827) actor
    HAS
DE LA SALLE, Michel Joseph
    ["Old Joe"] (d 1887) actor,
    critic NYM
DELASCEY, Mr. (fl 1757) dancer
    BD
DE LASCO, Maude singer CDP
DE LA TORRE, Claudio (d 1973
    [77]) dramatist BP/57*
DE LA TOUR, Alexander (fl 1689-
    1700) violinist? BD
DE LA TOUR, Frances (b 1944)
    English actress WWT/16
DELAUNAY, Louis (d 1903 [77])
    actor WWT/14*
DELAVAL, Frances actress EA/97
DE LAVALLADE, Carmen (b 1931)
    American dancer, actress BE,
    CB

DE LA VALLE, Mme. (fl 1790-
96) musician BD
DELAVANTI, Rose (d 1883 [47])
EA/84*
DE LA VOLEE, Jean (fl 1633)
French musician BD
DELAWN, Mr. (fl 1734) dancer
BD
DELBERT, Robert (b 1946) Amer-
ican actor TW/26, 30
DEL CAMPO, Thomazio Alegro
(fl 1718) Italian acrobat BD
DEL CARO, Mlle. [Mme. Cesare
Bossi] (fl 1794-1803) dancer
BD
DEL CARO, Mlle. (fl 1790-1815)
dancer BD
DELCY, Catharine (fl c. 1845)
English actress CDP, HAS
DELDERFIELD, R. F. (1912-72)
English dramatist AAS,
WWT/10-14
DELEGALL, Bob (b 1945) Amer-
ican actor TW/27-28
DE LEGH, Kitty (b 1887/95)
English actress WWT/7-11
DELEHANTY, Thornton W. (d
1971 [77]) critic BP/56*
DELEHANTY, William H. (1846-
80) American singer, com-
poser, choreographer, min-
strel CDP, HAS, SR
DE LEON, Jack (1897-1956)
Panamanian manager WWT/
6-12
DE LEON, Millie (d 1922 [52])
dancer BE*, BP/7*
DE LEON, Thomas Cooper
(1839-1914) American writer
WWA/1
DE LEON, Walter American
actor ES
DE LEPINE, Mr. (fl 1719)
machinist BD
DE L'EPINE, Francesca
Margherita [Mrs. John Chris-
topher Pepusch] (d 1746)
singer BD
DE LETRAZ, Jean (d 1954 [57])
dramatist WWT/14*
DELEVANTE, Frederick (d
1889) musical director EA/
90*
DELEVANTI, Cyril (d 1975 [86])
performer BP/60*
DELEVANTI, George see
Crippen, George
DELEVANTI, John (d 1908 [83])

acrobat, clown EA/09*
DELEVINE, Minnie (d 1911) per-
former? EA/12*
DELF, Harry (d 1964 [71]) come-
dian, dramatist, director TW/
20
DELF, Juliet (d 1962 [74]) vaude-
villian TW/18
DELFEVRE, Mme. (fl 1786-87)
dancer BD
DELFONT, Bernard [né Barnet
Winogradsky] (b 1909) Russian/
English producer, manager
BE, WWT/10-16
DELGADO, Roger (d 1973 [53])
performer BP/58*
DEL GRANDE, Gertrude (d 1894
[20]) singer EA/95*
DELIA, Mlle. French actress
CDP
DE LIAGRE, Alfred, Jr. (b 1904)
American producer, director,
manager BE, TW/2-8, WWT/
15-16
DE LIAS, R. J. (d 1883) manager
EA/84*
DELICATI, Luigi (fl 1789) singer
BD
DELICATI, Signora Luigi [Margher-
ita] (fl 1789) singer BD
DELICATI, Margherita see
Delicati, Signora Luigi
DELIGHT, June (d 1975 [77])
performer BP/60*
DELIGNY, Louise (fl 1791) dancer
BD
DELILLE, Octavia (fl 1851) French
singer CDP
DELIMA, Margaret Linley (d 1969
[67]) performer BP/54*
DE LISLE, Mons. (fl 1675)
dancer BD
DELISLE, Mons. (fl 1734-35)
French actor, dancer BD
DELISLE, Mlle. (c. 1684-1758)
French actress BD
DE L'ISLE, Mlle. (fl 1735-36)
dancer BD
DE LISSALE, Mr. (fl 1742) house
servant? BD
DE LIURY, Mlle. (fl 1720) per-
former? BD
DELL, Mr. (fl 1760-61) horn
player BD
DELL, African (d 1899 [37])
ventriloquist EA/00*
DELL, Floyd (1887-1969) Ameri-
can dramatist ES, WWT/7-9

DELL, Gabriel [né del Vecchio] (b 1923/30) West Indian actor TW/20-25, 28, 30, WWT/15-16

DELL, Henry (fl 1756-66) dramatist CP/2-3, DNB, GT, TD/1-2

DELL, James (d c. 1774) musician BD

DELL, Jeffrey (b 1899) English dramatist WWT/8-9

DELLA CASA, Lisa (b 1921) Swiss singer CB, ES

DELLA CHIESA, Vivian (b 1915) American singer CB

DELL AGATA, Michele (fl 1758-63) dancer BD

DELLA PORTA, Giambattista (1538-1613) Italian dramatist COC

DELLA ROVERE see De La Rovere

della SORTE, Joseph (b 1940) American actor TW/25, 27-28, 30

DELLENBAUGH, Harriet Rogers Otis (d 1930) American actress, dramatic reader WWA/1

DELLINGER, Miss (fl 1817) English actress HAS

DELLO JOIO, Norman (b 1913) American composer CB, ES

DELMAN, Mr. actor HAS

D'ELMAR, Camille [Mrs. Richard Baker] (d 1902) actress EA/03*

DELMAR, Emily (d 1881) EA/83*

DELMAR, Georgina [Mrs. H. Winsloe Hall] English actress, vocalist GRB/1-4

DEL MEDICO, Michael (b 1933) American actor TW/26-27, 30

DELMONTE, Jack (d 1973 [84]) actor TW/30

DELMORE, George E. (b 1874) American vaudevillian WWM

DELMORE, Ralph (1853-1923) American actor SR, WWM, WWS

DELNA, Marie (1875-1932) French singer ES

DELON, Jack (d 1970 [42]) actor, singer TW/27

DELONEY, The Messrs. (fl 1675) guitar players BD

DE LONG, Mons. dancing teacher CDP

DELORME, Mme. (fl 1730-37) dancer BD

DELORME, Mlle. (fl 1730-37) dancer, actress BD

DE LORNE, Blanche (d 1911) actress EA/12*

DE LOS ANGELES, Victoria see Angeles, Victoria de los

DE LOSSKING (d 1890) American comedian EA/91*

DELOTTO, Joseph (d 1899) circus clown, comedian EA/00*

DE LOUTHERBOURG, Philip James [Philippe Jacques] (1740-1812) German scene designer, painter BD, COC, ES, OC/1-3

DELPINI, Carlo Antonio (1740-1828) Italian actor, dancer, choreographer, singer BD, CDP, DNB, ES, TD/1-2

DELPINI, Signora Carlo Antonio (fl 1784-1828) actress, singer BD

DELPIT, Albert (b 1849) American/French dramatist DD

DEL PUENTE, Giuseppe (1843-1900) Italian singer ES

DELROY, Irene (b 1898) American actress, dancer WWT/7-8

DELROY, Maurice (d 1917) illusionist EA/18*

DE LUCA, Giuseppe (1876-1950) Italian singer CB, ES, WWA/3

DE LUCE, Virginia [née Virginia de Luce Wilson] (b 1921) American actress, singer, dancer BE, TW/8-19

De LUISE, Dom (b 1933) American actor TW/20

DE LUNGO, Tony (b 1892) Italian actor WWT/7-10

DE LURE [Israel Clark] (d 1900) illusionist EA/01*

DE LUSSAN, Zelie (c. 1865-1949) American singer CDP, GRB/1-4, WWS

DEL VAL, Jean (d 1975 [83]) performer BP/59*

DEL VECCHIO, Gabriel see Dell, Gabriel

DELVERD, Thomas ["Japanese Tommy"] (d 1887) minstrel EA/88*

D'ELVILLE, Rinallo (fl 1813) dramatist EAP

DELYLE, Alda (d 1927 [33]) prima donna BE*, BP/12*

DELYSIA, Alice (b 1885/89/91)
French actress, singer
COC, OC/1-3, WWT/4-12

DEMAIMBRAY [Stephen Triboudet?]
(fl 1735?-44) machinist BD

DeMAIO, Peter American actor
TW/26, 29-30

DE MAJO, Signor (fl 1766) singer?
BD

DEMAR, Mons. (fl 1736) dancer
BD

DE MAR, Carrie (d 1963 [87])
performer BE*

DE MARCHI, Emilio (1861-1917)
Italian singer ES

DEMARCO, Norman (b 1910)
American educator BE

DE MARCO, Tony (d 1965 [67])
dancer TW/22

DEMAREST, Rubin (d 1962 [76])
actor BE*

DEMAREST, William (b 1892)
American actor ES

DEMARIA, Mr. (fl 1773-75)
dancer? BD

DEMARIA, J. (fl 1793?-1814)
scene painter BD

DE MARNEY, Derrick (b 1906)
English actor ES, WWT/8-14

DE MARNEY, Terence (1909-71)
English actor WWT/8-14

DeMARTIN, Imelda [née Imelda
Italia deMartin di Fabbro]
(b 1936) Italian actress,
dancer, singer BE, TW/20-
21

DEMAS, Carole (b 1940) American actress TW/20, 24-25,
28-30

DE MATTOS, A. T. (1865-1921)
translator DD

DE MAX, Edouard (d 1924 [55])
actor WWT/14*

DeMAY, Sally (b 1922) American
actress TW/28

DEMEMBRAY see Demaimbray

DE MENDOZA, Don Fernando
Diaz (d 1930) actor, manager
WWT/14*

DEMERA, Signora (fl 1771)
singer BD

DEMEREST, G. W. minstrel
CDP

DE MERODE, Cléo French
dancer GRB/1-4

DE MEYER, Leopold pianist
CDP

DE MICHELI, Mr. (fl 1783-85)

boxkeeper BD

DE MICHELI, Leopoldo (fl 1761-
91) singer, music copyist BD

DE MICHELI, Signora Leopoldo
[Mary Ann] (fl 1775-78) singer
BD

DE MICHELI, Mary Ann see
De Micheli, Signora Leopoldo

DE MILLE, Agnes (b 1908) American dancer, choreographer,
director AAS, BE, CB, ES,
NTH, TW/2-8, WWT/10-16

DeMILLE, Beatrice M. (d 1923)
talent representative BE*,
BP/8*

DE MILLE, Mrs. Cecil [Constance
Adams] (d 1960 [87]) American
actress BE*

DE MILLE, Cecil Blount (1881-
1959) American actor, dramatist, producer ES, GRB/3-4,
NTH, SR, TW/15, WWA/5,
WWT/1-9, WWW/5

DE MILLE, Henry Churchill
(1850-93) American dramatist
CDP, DAB, DD, SR, WWA/H

DE MILLE, William Churchill
(1878/83-1955) American dramatist, actor ES, GRB/3-4,
NTH, SR, TW/11, WWA/3,
WWM, WWT/1-9

DEMING, Mrs. L. L. singer,
composer, lyricist CDP

DEMING, Will H. (1870/71-1926)
American actor SR, WWM

DE MINIL, Renée (d 1941) actress
BE*, WWT/14*

DE MIRA, Signora (fl 1793-1800)
singer BD

DE MIRAIL see Dumirail

DEMODORE, Mr. (fl 1715) flutist
BD

DE MOE, William (d 1874) musical director, composer EA/
75*

DE MOLAS, Nicholas (d 1944)
Russian/American scene designer ES

DE MOND, Willy (d 1976 [72])
hosier BP/60*

DE MONDION, Edmund [Edmund
Pilletts] (fl 1866-67) actor
HAS

DEMONT, Charles (d 1976 [84])
performer BP/60*

DE MONTI (d 1910 [42]) skater
EA/11*

DE MOOR, Teda (b 1915) South

African dancer, choreographer
ES
DEMOREST, Vienna singer,
composer CDP
DeMOTT, John A. (d 1975 [63])
performer BP/59*
DeMOTTE, Warren (d 1970
[60]) critic BP/55*
DEMOURIER, Mr. (fl 1774-75?)
dancer BD
DEMPSEY, Clifford (d 1938 [73])
American actor BE*, BP/23*
DEMPSEY, Jerome (b 1929)
American actor TW/28
DEMPSEY, Mark (b 1936) Amer-
ican actor TW/26-28
DEMPSEY, Mary Ellen (d 1905
[25]) EA/06*
DEMPSEY, W. P. singer CDP
DEMPSTER, Hugh (b 1900) Eng-
lish actor WWT/11-15
DEMPSTER, John Hugh (d 1901)
manager EA/02*
DEMPSTER, Robert (b 1883)
American actor WWM
DEMPSTER, William R. (1808-
71) composer CDP
DE MURSKA, Ilma (d 1889 [53])
singer EA/90*
DEMUTH, Norman (1898-1968)
English composer, conductor
ES
DE NAVARRO, Mary see
Anderson, Mary
DENBY, Mr. (fl 1784) violinist
BD
DENBY, Edwin (b 1903) Amer-
ican dancer, choreographer
ES
DENBY, William (fl 1842-46)
English actor HAS
DENCE, Marjorie (d 1966) ac-
tress WWT/15*
DENCH, Judi (b 1934/35) English
actress AAS, COC, WWT/
14-16
DENE, Dorothy (d 1899) actress
DD, DP, EA/96
DENE, Ruyston (d 1911 [52])
actor, sketch artist EA/12*
DE NEERGAARD, Beatrice [née
Flood] (b 1908/10) American
actress BE, TW/2-3
DENENHOLZ, Reginald (1913-73)
American press representative
BE, TW/30
DENES, Oscar (b 1893) Hungarian
actor, singer WWT/8-9

DENGEL, Jake (b 1933) American
actor TW/25, 27, 29-30
DENGEL, Roni (b 1942) American
actor TW/27
DENHAM, Mr. (d 1832) actor
CDP
DENHAM, Miss see Durham,
Miss
DENHAM, Fanny actress CDP
DENHAM, George W. (d 1907
[62]) American actor GRB/3*,
WWT/14*
DENHAM, Isolde (b 1920) English
actress WWT/10-11
DENHAM, Sir John (1615-68/69)
Irish/English dramatist CP/
1-3, DD, FGF, HP
DENHAM, June Catherine Church
see St. Denis, Teddie
DENHAM, Mary Anne (d 1855)
American actress HAS
DENHAM, Maurice (b 1909) Eng-
lish actor WWT/11-16
DENHAM, Reginald (b 1894) Eng-
lish actor, producer, director
AAS, BE, ES, TW/2-8, WWT/
5-16
DENHAM, Robert (c. 1723-82)
singer BD
DENIER, John (b 1838) American
pantomimist, gymnast, tight-
rope performer HAS
DENIER, Tony (1839-1917) clown,
manager CDP, SR
DENIN, Kate (1837-1907) Ameri-
can actress CDP, HAS, SR
DENIN, Susan (1835-75) American
actress CDP, HAS, SR
DE NIRO, Robert (b 1943) Amer-
ican actor CB, TW/27-28
DENIS, Charles (d c. 1772) drama-
tist CP/2-3, GT
DENIS, Ruth see St. Denis,
Ruth
DENISON, A. M. (d 1891) actor
EA/92*
DENISON, Merrill (b 1893) Cana-
dian dramatist MH, RE
DENISON, Michael (b 1915) Eng-
lish actor AAS, ES, WWT/
11-16
DENISON, Robert G. (b 1937)
American actor TW/29
DENKER, Henry (b 1912) Ameri-
can dramatist, director, pro-
ducer BE, ES, MD
DENLEY, Mrs. (d 1875) EA/76*
DENMAN, Edmund (c. 1754-1827)

English? instrumentalist
BD
DENMAN, Henry (1774-1816)
English singer, actor, in-
strumentalist BD
DENMAN, William (1766-1806)
actor, singer BD, GT, TD/
1-2
DENMARK, L. Kirk (b 1916)
American educator BE
DENNEN, Barry (b 1938) Amer-
ican actor TW/28-29
DENNER, Mr. (fl 1758) violinist
BD
D'ENNERY, Adolphe Philippe
(1812-99) French dramatist
DD
DENNET, Mr. (fl 1753) actor
BD
DENNETT, Miss B. (fl 1799?-
1820?) dancer, actress?
BD, DD
DENNETT, Eliza [Mrs. Robert
O'Neill] (fl 1799?-1820?)
dancer, actress? BD, DD
DENNETT, Miss F. (fl 1799?-
1820?) dancer, actress?
BD, DD
DENNING, Thomas (1790-1821)
actor CDP
DENNING, Will H. (d 1926 [55])
actor BE*
DENNIS, Mr. (fl 1725-31) per-
former? BD
DENNIS, Mr. (fl 1752-80?)
singer, dancer BD
DENNIS, Mr. (fl 1779) actor BD
DENNIS, Mrs. (fl 1720) singer
BD
DENNIS, Mrs. (fl 1752-70?)
singer, dancer BD
DENNIS, Arthur (b 1870) English
actor GRB/1-2
DENNIS, Dorian (d 1970 [47])
performer BP/55*
DENNIS, John (1657-1733/34)
English critic, dramatist
CDP, CP/1-3, DD, ES, GT,
HP, NTH, TD/1-2
DENNIS, Nick actor TW/4
DENNIS, Nigel (b 1912) English
dramatist, critic AAS, CD,
MD, MWD, PDT
DENNIS, Roland (b 1944) Amer-
ican actor TW/25, 27, 29
DENNIS, Dr. Russell (d 1964
[48]) actor BE*
DENNIS, Sandy (b 1937) American

actress AAS, BE, CB, TW/24,
27, 29, WWT/15-16
DENNIS, Will [Stephen Townesend]
(1859-1914) English actor DD,
EA/95, GRB/1-4
DENNISON, Mr. (d 1756) dancer
BD
DENNISON, Mr. Irish actor HAS
DENNISON, Mrs. (fl 1752) singer,
dancer BD
DENNISON, Frank (d 1964 [63])
English actor, conductor BE*
DENNISTON, Reynolds (1881-1943)
New Zealand actor CB, SR
DENNISTOUN, J. (d 1898 [39])
manager EA/99*
DENNON, T. J. (d 1889 [28])
business manager EA/90*
DENNY, Mr. (fl 1757-68) door-
keeper BD
DENNY, Mr. (fl 1784) violoncellist
BD
DENNY, Mrs. (fl 1783-85) dresser
BD
DENNY, Ernest (1869-1943) Eng-
lish dramatist GRB/4, WWT/
1-9
DENNY, Frances Ann (1798-1875)
actress COC
DENNY, George V. (b 1899) actor
SR
DENNY, Henry (fl 1783-91) car-
penter BD
DENNY, Reginald (1891-1967)
English actor, singer BE, ES,
TW/24, WWA/4, WWT/7-14
DENNY, Mrs. W. H. (d 1902
[41]) EA/03*
DENNY, William Henry [William
Henry Dugmore] (1853-1915)
English actor DD, DP, EA/
97, GRB/1-4, WWM, WWS,
WWT/1-2
DENNY, W. R. (d 1896 [32])
dramatist EA/97*
DENOYE see Denoyer
DENOYER, [G. ? Philip?] (d 1788)
dancer, choreographer BD
DENT, Alan (b 1905) Scottish
critic ES, WWT/9-16
DENT, Bert music-hall manager
GRB/1
DENT, G. Calvert (d 1904 [51])
acting manager EA/05*
DENT, John (fl 1782-95) dramatist
CP/3, GT, TD/1-2
DENT, Lizzie [Mrs. Jack Seebold]
(d 1897) EA/99*

DENT, Richard (fl c. 1714-28)
barber BD

DENTON, Mrs. (fl 1749-67?)
actress BD

DENTON, Crahan (d 1966 [52])
American actor BE, TW/23

DENTON, C. St. John see
Denton, St. John C.

DENTON, Frank [Frank Bellamy]
(1878-1945) English actor
WWT/1-6

DENTON, John see Denton,
"Thomas"

DENTON, Percy singer CDP

DENTON, St. John C. (d 1933
[76]) English agent, manager
GRB/1-4

DENTON, "Thomas" [John] (d
1789) English artificer, exhibitor BD

DENTS, [Master?] (fl 1723)
dancer BD

DENTS, [Miss?] (fl 1723) dancer
BD

DENTS, De Long (fl 1723)
dancer BD

DENVIL, Alice (d 1908) actress
EA/09*, WWT/14*

DENVIL, Clara (d 1867 [18])
EA/68*, WWT/14*

DENVIL, Mrs. Henry see
Denvil, Marianne

DENVIL, Henry Gaskell (1804-66)
English actor CDP, DD,
HAS

DENVIL, Horace Gaskin (d 1878
[25]) actor EA/79*

DENVIL, Marianne [Mrs. Henry
Denvil] (d 1889 [79]) EA/91*

DENVIL, Rachel [Mrs. Rachel
Finney Troy] (d 1885) actress
CDP

DENVILLE, Alfred (1876-1955)
English actor, manager WWT/
7-11

DENVILLE, Charles (d 1876 [25])
actor EA/77*

DENYER, James (d 1972 [46])
publicist BP/57*

DENYGTEN, Thomas see Dow-
ton, Thomas

DENZER, Jacob (d 1863) gymnast
HAS

DENZIL, Madge [Mrs. Alec F.
Frank] (d 1897) actress EA/
98*

DEODORE, Peter (fl 1674) performer? BD

D'EON DE BEAUMONT, Charles
Geneviève Louis Auguste André
Timothée (1728-1810) French
swordsman, impresario, diplo-
matist BD, CDP

DE ORDUNA, Juan (d 1974 [67])
producer/director/choreographer
BP/58*

DE OSTA, Mrs. John (d 1891
[37]) EA/92*

DE PAOLI, Gaetano (fl 1795)
singer BD

DE PAOLIS, Alessio (1893-1964)
Italian singer ES, WWA/4

"DE PARIS, Mlle. à la mode" (fl
1731) dancer BD

DE PARRAVICINI, S. A. (d 1893)
agent EA/94*

DE PASQUALI, Bernice (d 1925)
American singer WWM

DE PAUL, Gene (b 1919) American composer, pianist BE

DE PINNA, David (d 1908) manager EA/09*

DEPORT, Mr. (fl 1749) wigmaker
BD

DE POUGY, Liane (b 1873) French
variety artist GRB/1-4

DEPPE, Hans (d 1969 [71]) pro-
ducer/director/choreographer
BP/54*

DER ABRAHMIAN, Arousiak (d
1973 [82]) performer BP/58*

DERBY, Mr. (fl 1757-62) office
keeper BD

DERBY, Countess of see Farren,
Elizabeth

DERBY, Edward Smith-Stanley
(1752-1834) CDP

DE REEDER, Louis (d 1910)
musical director EA/12*

DE REES, James (d 1908) fit-up
proprietor EA/10*

DE RENZIE, Leonard (d 1974
[73]) manager BP/58*

DE RESZKE, Edouard (1853-1917)
Polish singer ES, SR, WWA/1

DE RESZKE, Jean (1850-1925)
Polish singer ES, SR, WWA/2

DE RETZSKE, Josefina (1855-91)
singer ES

DE REYES, Consuelo (1893-1948)
English director, dramatist
WWT/8-10

DERHAM, Miss see Durham,
Miss

D'ERINA, Rosa singer CDP

DERIOUS, Lizzie singer CDP

DERIVIS, Maria (fl 1882) singer CDP

D'ERLANGER, Frederic A. (1868-1943) composer WWW/4

DERLE see Dearle

DERMAN, Lou (d 1976 [61]) dramatist BP/60*

DERMONT, Paul (d 1970 [54]) performer BP/55*

DERMOT, Garrett (1830-63) comedian HAS

DERN, Bruce (b 1936) American actor TW/15

D'ERNE, Frances Mabel see Newcombe, Mabel

DeROCHER, L. E. (b 1912) Canadian manager BE

DEROISEY, Lucien (d 1972 [60]) producer/director/choreographer BP/57*

DEROISSI, Miss (fl 1763) dancer BD

DE ROOS, Marie [Marion Elizabeth Battle] English actress GRB/1

DE ROSA, Sig. (d 1871 [90]) singer EA/72*

DE ROSA, Mlle. (fl 1868) dancer CDP

DE ROSE, Peter (1896-1953) American songwriter BE*, BP/37*

DE ROSSENAW, Ninetta (fl 1754-55) actress BD

DERR, Richard (b 1917) American actor BE, TW/5-19, WWT/12-14

DERRICK, Joseph (fl 1880-86) dramatist DD

DERRICK, Samuel (1724-69) Irish translator CP/1-3, GT, TD/1-2

DE RUSSO, Richard (b 1946) American actor TW/29

DERWENT, Clarence (1884-1959) English actor, producer, dramatist CB, COC, OC/3, TW/1-8, 12-16, WWA/3, WWT/8-12

DERWENT, Elfrida (d 1958 [80+]) English actress BE*, BP/43*

DERWOOD, Mrs. Charles E. see Wynter, Florrie

DE SABATA, Victor (b 1892) Italian conductor ES

DESABAYE, Mr. (fl 1687-1711) musician BD

DESAGULIERS, [Dr. ?] (fl 1740) pyrotechnist BD

DE ST. LEU, Mr. (fl 1794) flutist BD

DeSAL, Frank (b 1943) American actor TW/25

DE SANCTIS, Alfredo Italian actor WWT/2-4

DE SANTIS, Joe (b 1909) American actor TW/9

DESBARQUES, Mons. (fl 1705-08) dancer BD

DESBARQUES, Mme. (fl 1708) dancer BD

DESBARQUES, Mlle. (fl 1707) dancer BD

DESBOROUGH, Juliet [Mrs. F. W. Irish] (d 1892 [54]) actress EA/93*, WWT/14*

DESBOROUGH, Philip (b 1883) English actor WWT/5-6

DESCHALLIEZ, Louise [Louise Deschalliez de Vaurenville] (fl 1720-22) dancer BD

DESCHAMPS, Emile (d 1871 [79]) composer EA/72*

DESCOATE, John (fl 1695) trumpeter BD

DESCOMBES, Mrs. [Fraulein Laura] (d 1904 [73]) high-wire performer EA/05*

DESDECHINA, Signora (fl 1749) dancer BD

DE SELINCOURT, Hugh (1878-1951) English critic WWT/1-5

DE SHADE, Mons. (fl 1743) dancer BD

DESHALN, Mr. (fl 1737) house servant? BD

DES HAYES, André J. J. (fl 1797?-1811) dancer, choreographer BD

DESHAYES [Jean Baptiste François] (1705-79?) actor, choreographer? BD

DESHAYES, Paul (d 1891 [57]) actor BE*, WWT/14*

DE SHIELDS, Andre (b 1946) American actor TW/29-30

DE SICA, Vittorio (d 1974 [73]) performer BP/59*

DE SILVA, David (b 1936) American talent representative BE

DE SILVA, Frank (d 1968 [78]) actor TW/24

DE SILVA, Nina [Angelita Helena] (1868/69-1949) actress COC, WWT/1-10

DeSIMONE, B. J. (b 1939)
American actor TW/24-27
DE SISLEY, Mme. (fl 1794)
singer BD
DESJARDINS, Pauline (fl 1844)
dancer CDP, HAS
DESKINS, Mervyn (b 1937) Amer-
ican actor TW/30
DESLANDES, Raymond (d 1890
[64]) manager WWT/14*
DESLYS, Gaby (1881/84-1920)
French actress, dancer ES,
OC/1-3, SR, WWT/3
DESMOND, Bob (d 1901 [42])
Negro comedian EA/01*
DESMOND, Florence (b 1905/07)
English actress, singer AAS,
ES, WWT/7-14
DESMOND, Maggie [Mrs. J. G.
Beckett; Mrs. Robert W.
Chapman] (1848-72) Irish
actress CDP, HAS
DESMOND, Mona actress, singer
CDP
DESMOND, Patrick American
actor TW/25-26
DESMOND, Shaw (1877-1960)
Irish dramatist WWW/6
DESMOND, William (1878-1949)
Irish/American actor ES,
TW/6
DESMOULINS, John (fl 1778)
house servant? BD
DESMOULINS, Mrs. [John?]
(fl 1778) house servant? BD
DESNOYE see Denoyer
DESNOYER see Denoyer
DE SOLLA, Barton (d 1899 [66])
actor EA/00*
DE SOLLA, B. M. (d 1894 [77])
professor of music EA/95*
DE SOLLA, Rachel (d 1920)
actress BE*, WWT/14*
DESORMES, Mons. (fl 1749)
actor BD
DE SOUSA, May (1887-1948)
American actress, singer
GRB/2-4, TW/5, WWT/1-5
DESPLACES, Henri (d 1877
[53]) singer EA/78*
DESPO (b 1922) Greek performer
TW/23, 27-30
DESPREAUX, Louise Rosalie
see Allan, Louise Rosalie
DESPRES, Suzanne (1875-1951)
French actress GRB/4,
WWT/1-3
DESPREZ, Frank (1853-1916)

English dramatist, critic DD,
WWT/1-3
DESSE, Mons. (fl 1735-61) dancer
BD
DESSE, Mr. (fl 1761) dancer BD
D'ESSER, Mr. (fl 1748) dancer
BD
DESSESSARS, Mons. (fl 1734-35)
actor BD
DESSESSARS, Mme. (fl 1734-35)
actress BD
"DES SINGES, Le Chevalier" (fl
1767-68) performing monkey
BD
DESSUSLEFOUR, Françoise-Marie
see Durancy, Mme. Jean-
François
DE STAINER, Marguerite [Mrs.
James Guidery] (d 1911 [25])
EA/12*
D'ESTE, Emmie see Warner,
Mrs. H.
DESTINN, Emmy (1878-1930)
Bohemian singer WWA/1
DESTOUCHES, Philippe Néricault
(1680-1754) French dramatist
OC/1-3
DESTRADE, [Francis?] (d 1754)
dancer, actor BD
DE SURLIS, Jean (fl 1663-1707)
actor, manager BD
DE SWIRSKY, Countess Thamara
(b 1888) Russian dancer WWM
DE SYLVA, Brown G. (1896-1950)
American librettist, lyricist
AAS, CB, DAB, ES, TW/7,
WWA/3, WWT/6-10
DE SYLVA, Buddy see De Sylva,
Brown G.
DE SYLVA, Henderson American
librettist, lyricist AAS
DETCHON, Adelaide actress CDP
DE TOLLY, Deena (d 1976) per-
former BP/60*
DETOY, Charles (b 1897) Ameri-
can executive BE
DE TREVILLE, Yvonne (1881-
1954) American singer WWA/
3, WWM
DETTEY, Miss (fl 1794) singer
BD
DETTMAR, Lottie (d 1902) ac-
tress, dancer EA/03*
DETTMER, Roger (b 1927) Amer-
ican critic BE
DE TURA, Gennaro (1880-1939)
Italian singer ES
DEULIN, Herr [Isaac Dowling] (d

1860 [43]) EA/72*
DEULIN, Paul (d 1878 [37])
comedian EA/79*
DEULIN, Mrs. Paul (d 1879
[38]) EA/80*
DEUSTER, Joseph see Anthony,
Joseph
DEUTSCH, Ernst (1890-1969)
Austrian actor ES, TW/25
DEUTSCH, Milt (d 1974 [56])
manager, agent BP/58*
DEVAL, Jacques (1890-1972)
French dramatist BE, MWD,
WWT/9
DE VALOIS, Dame Ninette [Edris
Stannus] (b 1898) Irish dancer
CB, ES, OC/1-2, WWT/5-12
DEVANT, Anthony (fl 1669) musi-
cian? BD
DEVANT, David [David Wighton]
(1863-1941) English illusionist
GRB/1-4
DE VASCO, Mlle. (d 1886)
trapezist EA/87*
DE VAURENVILLE, Louise
Deschalliez see Deschalliez,
Louise
DE VAUX, Renée (d 1961 [80])
actress WWT/14*
D'EVELYN, Miss (fl 1797-98)
actress, singer BD
DEVEN, N. T. see Davenport,
N. T.
DE VERA, Cris (d 1974 [49])
performer BP/59*
DE VERE, Charles (1823-68)
American circus performer
HAS
DE VERE, Clementine Duchene
(d 1954 [89]) singer WWT/14*
DE VERE, Mrs. E. see De
Vere, Stella
DEVERE, Francesca (d 1952
[61]) American actress BE*,
BP/37*
DE VERE, Frederick (d 1910)
EA/11*
DE VERE, George F. (d 1910
[75]) actor BE*, WWT/14*
DE VERE, Nellie see Bailey,
Mary
DE VERE, Nora (d 1905) serio-
comic EA/06*
DEVERE, Sam (d 1907 [65])
minstrel, banjoist CDP
DE VERE, Stella [Mrs. E. De
Vere] (d 1893) music-hall
performer EA/94*

DEVEREAUX, Jack (d 1958 [76])
actor TW/14
DEVEREAUX, Mrs. Jack see
Drew, Louise
DEVEREAUX, Louise Drew see
Drew, Louise
DEVERELL, John W. (1880-1965)
actor WWT/3-13
DEVERELL, Mrs. M. (fl 1792)
English? dramatist CP/3
DEVEREUX, Ernest (d 1908 [29])
actor EA/10*
DEVEREUX, John (d 1890) musical
director EA/91*
DEVEREUX, John Drew (b 1918)
American actor TW/5-11
DEVEREUX, Robert, Earl of Es-
sex (1566-1601) English masque
writer DNB
DEVEREUX, William (d 1945 [75])
actor, dramatist GRB/3-4,
WWT/1-9
DE VERNEUIL, [Louis François
Joseph?] (fl 1718-35) actor
BD
DE VERNEUIL, [Mme. Louis
François Joseph; née Marie-
Louise Chabot] (fl 1718-35)
actress BD
DE VERNEUIL, Mimi (fl 1733-35)
dancer, actress? BD
DEVIENNE, Mr. (fl 1797-98)
flutist BD
DE VILLABOS, Guadeloupe Velez
see Velez, Lupe
DEVIN, William (d 1917 [50])
musician EA/18*
DEVINE, Claire (d 1973 [82])
singer, actress TW/29
DEVINE, George Alexander (1910-
66) English actor, producer,
manager AAS, BE, CH, COC,
ES, OC/2-3, PDT, WWT/9-14,
WWW/6
DEVINE, William M. see
Armstrong, William
DEVINGUT, Gertrude F. see
Argyle, Gertrude
DEVISSE, Mons. (fl 1750-54)
dancer BD
DEVLIN, Jay (b 1929) American
actor TW/26
DEVLIN, John (b 1937) American
actor TW/21, 23, 25, 28-29
DEVLIN, Mary see Booth, Mrs.
Edwin Thomas
DEVLIN, William (b 1911) Scottish
actor AAS, TW/4, WWT/8-14

DEVNEY, Mrs. M. A. (d
1890 [61]) EA/91*

DE VOLA, Robert (d 1886 [37])
acrobat EA/87*

"DE VOLTORE, Mons. " (fl 1734)
acrobat BD

DEVON, Pru (d 1973) performer
BP/57*

DEVONO, Prof. (d 1909) conjurer EA/10*

DEVONSHIRE, Mr. (fl 1795)
exhibitor BD

DEVOTO, Mr. (fl 1778-84)
house servant? BD

DEVOTO, Anthony (fl c. 1662-67)
puppeteer BD

DEVOTO, John (fl 1672-76)
property man, manager BD

DEVOTO, John (fl 1708-52)
scene painter BD

DE VOY, Mrs. Albert see
De Voy, Sarah

DE VOY, George (d 1896) EA/97*

DE VOY, Sam (d 1907 [64])
Negro comedian EA/08*

DE VOY, Sarah [Mrs. Albert
De Voy] (d 1893) EA/94*

DE VOYE, James (d 1906) animal trainer EA/08*

DEVRIENT, Eduard (1801-77)
producer, actor BE*, WWT/
14*

DEVRIENT, Emil (1803-72)
German actor OC/1-3

DEVRIENT, Karl (1797-1872)
actor BE*

DEVRIENT, Ludwig (d 1832 [48])
actor, manager WWT/14*

DEVRIENT, Max (1857-1929)
actor BE*, WWT/14*

DE VRIES, Peter (b 1910) American dramatist BE

DE VRIES, Rosa (fl 1850) singer
CDP, HAS

DEW, Edward (b 1909) American
actor TW/2-3

DEW, John Henry see Drew,
Harry

DE WALDEN, T. B. (b 1811)
English actor, dramatist DD,
HAS, SR

DEWAR, Fred (fl 1860-77) actor
DD

DEWAR, Frederick C. (d 1878
[46]) actor EA/79*, WWT/
14*

DEWAR, J. A. (d 1897 [64])
actor WWT/14*

DEWAR, Mrs. James see
Dewar, Rose Eliza

DEWAR, John A. (d 1897 [60])
actor EA/98*

DEWAR, L. S. (d 1885) actor
EA/86*

DEWAR, Mrs. L. S. see
Clarke, Florence

DEWAR, Rose Eliza [Mrs. James
Dewar] (d 1867 [70]) EA/68*

DE WARFAZ, George (1889-1959)
actor WWT/4-10

DE WEERTH, Ernest (d 1967 [62])
designer TW/23

DEWELL, Michael (b 1931) American producer BE, WWT/16

DEWELL, Nicholas (fl 1689-99)
trumpeter BD

DEWEY, James G. (d 1964 [86])
composer/lyricist BP/49*

DEWEY, Kenneth S. G. (d 1972
[37]) theatre founder BP/57*

DEWEY, Pat (d 1892 [34]) EA/
93*

DEWEY, Rufus Hosmer (b 1881)
American press representative
WWM

DeWHARTON, Barbara Lee (d
1972 [48]) performer BP/56*

DEWHURST, Colleen (b 1926?)
Canadian actress AAS, BE,
CB, TW/14-20, 24, 26-30,
WWT/14-16

DEWHURST, Elizabeth [Mrs. J.
Dewhurst] (d 1885 [36]) EA/86*

DEWHURST, Frances Clara [Mrs.
Jonathan Dewhurst] (d 1912
[50]) EA/13*

DEWHURST, J. (fl 1871-84) actor
DD

DEWHURST, Mrs. J. see
Dewhurst, Elizabeth

DEWHURST, Mrs. J. D. see
Dewhurst, Mrs. M. M.

DEWHURST, Jonathan (d 1913)
actor BE*, EA/14*, WWT/14*

DEWHURST, Mrs. Jonathan see
Dewhurst, Frances Clara

DEWHURST, Keith (b 1931) English dramatist CD

DEWHURST, Mrs. M. M. [Mrs.
J. D. Dewhurst] (d 1874 [33])
EA/75*

DEWICK, Dawson English actor
GRB/1

DE WILD, Gene (b 1929) American educator, director, actor
BE

DE WILDE, Brandon (1942-72)
American actor TW/9, 21,
29, WWA/5
DE WILDE, Frederic (b 1914)
American stage manager,
actor, director BE
DE WILHORST, Cora (fl 1857)
singer · CDP
DeWINDT, Hal (b 1933) Ameri-
can actor TW/18
DEWINNE, Henri (d 1897 [64])
ballet master EA/98*
DE WINTON, Alice English ac-
tress DD, EA/96, GRB/1-4,
WWT/1-5
DE WINTON, Stewart (b 1879)
Scottish actor GRB/1
DE WITT, Fay (b 1935) Ameri-
can actress, singer BE
DEWITZ, Ursula (d 1975 [60])
theatre owner BP/60*
DE WOLFE, Billy [né William
Andrew Jones] (1907-74)
American actor BE, BTR/
74, TW/10-11, 13, 30, WWT/
14-15
DE WOLFE, Elsie (1865-1950)
American actress DAB,
GRB/2-4, SR, TW/7, WWM,
WWS, WWT/1-4
DEWS, Peter (b 1929) English
director AAS, WWT/16
DE WYNNE, Charles (d 1902)
juggler EA/03*
DEXTER, Aubrey [Douglas Peter
Jonas] (1898-1958) English
actor WWT/9-12
DEXTER, Brad (b 1917) Ameri-
can actor TW/5-6
DEXTER, Elliott (1870-1941)
American actor ES
DEXTER, John (1726-64) Irish
actor BD
DEXTER, John (b 1925) English
director AAS, CB, ES,
PDT, WWT/14-16
DEYMAN, Mrs. (fl 1714) actress
BD
DeYOUNG, Cliff (b 1945) Amer-
ican actor TW/28-29
D'FERROU VILLE, Mons. (fl
1732) dancer BD
D'HERBAGE, Mons. (fl 1736)
actor BD
D'HERVIGNI, Mlle. (fl 1735-36)
dancer BD
DHERY, Robert [né Fourrey] (b
1921) actor, director BE

D'HIVER, Marian (d 1882) EA/
83*
DHOTRE, Damoo (d 1973 [72])
performer BP/57*
DIACOFF, Mrs. Tom see
Shelton, Laura Blanche
DIAGHILEV, Serge (1872-1929)
Russian impresario COC, ES,
OC/1-3, WWT/4-5
DIAMOND, Mr. (fl 1660) acrobat
BD
DIAMOND, Mr. (fl 1784-90) actor
BD
DIAMOND, Alf (d 1917 [24]) come-
dian EA/18*
DIAMOND, Charles singer, min-
strel CDP
DIAMOND, David (b 1915) Ameri-
can composer CB
DIAMOND, Frank (d 1888) minstrel
EA/89*
DIAMOND, Harry (d 1906 [40])
EA/07*
DIAMOND, Mrs. Harry see
Stanley, Nelly
DIAMOND, John (1823-57) Ameri-
can dancer HAS
DIAMOND, Lillian (d 1962 [73])
performer, wardrobe mistress
BE*
DIAMOND, Margaret (b 1916)
English actress WWT/11-16
DIAMOND, Matthew (b 1951)
American actor TW/28
DIAMOND, Michael (b 1945) Amer-
ican actor TW/27-29
DIAMOND, Neil (b 1941) American
singer TW/29
DIAMOND, William see Dimond,
William Wyatt
DIAMOND, Zelda see Fichandler,
Zelda
"DIANA" see Constantini, Signora
Giovanni Battista
"DIANA, Signora" (fl 1726-27)
actress BD
DIANI, Ermissilde (b 1848) Italian
dancer HAS
DIANTA [Auguste Offroy] (d 1900
[41]) acrobat EA/01*
DI ASPINO, Diego (fl 1744-45)
singer BD
"DIAVOLINO, Signor" (fl 1754)
musician BD
DIBBLE, Robert (fl 1793-1817)
singer BD
DIBBLE, Thomas see Davis,
Thomas Dibble

DIBDIN, Miss (fl 1799-1804) dancer BD

DIBDIN, Ann see Dibdin, Mrs. Thomas John

DIBDIN, Anne CDP

DIBDIN, Charles (1745-1814) English dramatist, actor, lyricist, singer, pianist BD, CDP, COC, CP/2-3, DD, DNB, ES, GT, HP, OC/1-3, PDT, SR, TD/1-2

DIBDIN, Charles Isaac Mungo [né Pitt] (1768-1833) English dramatist, actor, singer, manager BD, CDP, COC, CP/3, DD, DNB, ES, OC/1-3

DIBDIN, Mrs. Charles Isaac Mungo [née May Bates] (1782-1816) actress, singer BD, CDP

DIBDIN, Henry Edward (1813-66) English musician DNB

DIBDIN, Mary see Dibdin, Mrs. Charles Isaac Mungo

DIBDIN, Thomas John [né Pitt] (1771-1841) English actor, scene painter, dramatist, manager BD, CDP, COC, CP/3, DD, DNB, ES, GT, OC/1-3, TD/1-2

DIBDIN, Mrs. Thomas John [née Ann Hilliar] (1775-1828) actress, singer BD, CDP

Di BLASIO, Joe (d 1973 [62]) producer/director/choreographer BP/58*

DICK, Mr. (fl 1790-1805) tailor BD

DICK, Mrs. (fl 1797) house servant? BD

DICK, C. G. Cotsford (1846-1911) English composer, dramatist DD, GRB/1-4, WWW/1

DICK, E. [Dutton's Boy] (fl 1597) actor DA

DICKENS, Miss (fl 1855) actress HAS

DICKENS, Charles (1812-70) English writer CDP, COC, DD, DNB, EA/69, ES, OC/1-3

DICKENS, Charles (d 1896 [59]) EA/97*

DICKENS, C. Stafford (1896-1967) English dramatist, producer, actor TW/24, WWT/8-14

DICKENS, Edward Buller Lytton (d 1902 [50]) EA/03*

DICKENS, Fanny (d 1895) actress EA/96*

DICKENS, Mary (fl 1883-86) actress DD

DICKENSON, Mrs. (fl 1746-65) boxkeeper BD

DICKENSON, G. K. (d 1863) actor WWT/14*

DICKENSON, [Samuel?] (fl 1784-1810) oboist BD

DICKER, Maitland (1858-1917) English actor, stage manager, manager GRB/4

DICKERSON, Mr. (fl 1794) violinist BD

DICKERSON, Maude see Bartelle, Jennie Dickerson

DICKESON, Herbert (b 1875) English actor GRB/1

DICKEY, Anna Mary actress TW/1

DICKEY, Paul (1884/85-1933) American dramatist WWT/6-7

DICKINS, Mr. (fl 1705-06) actor BD

DICKINS, Mrs. see Barnett, Alice

DICKINS, John Thanet (d 1896 [61]) EA/97*

DICKINSON, Albert (d 1908) performer? EA/09*

DICKINSON, Anna Elizabeth (1842-1932) American actress, lecturer, dramatist CDP, DAB

DICKINSON, Genevieve [née Giesen] (b 1909) American educator, director BE

DICKINSON, George acting manager GRB/1

DICKINSON, G. K. (d 1863) English actor HAS

DICKINSON, Isabel (fl 1848) actress DD

DICKINSON, John (fl 1745-79) gallery office keeper BD

DICKINSON, Maggie (d 1949) actress, singer BE*, WWT/14*

DICKINSON, Thomas Herbert (b 1877) American critic ES

DICKONS, Maria [née Poole] (1770?-1833) English singer, actress CDP, DD, DNB

DICKSON, Charles (1862-1927) American actor, dramatist, manager SR

DICKSON, Donald (d 1972 [61]) performer BP/57*

DICKSON, Dorothy (b 1896)
American actress, dancer
AAS, BE, ES, WWT/4-13
DICKSON, Gloria (d 1945 [28])
actress BE*
DICKSON, James (b 1949) Amer-
ican actor TW/29
DICKSON, James A. (1774-1853)
English actor HAS
DICKSON, J. W. (fl 1858) actor
HAS
DICKSON, Lamont (d 1944)
actor BE*, WWT/14*
DICKSON, Lydia (d 1928 [40])
comedienne BE*, BP/12*
DICKSON, Walter (d 1918)
EA/19*
"DICK WHITTINGTON" see
Colman, George, the Elder
DIDCOTT, Hugh Jay (d 1909
[73]) variety agent EA/10*
DIDDEAR, Charles Bannister
(1801-59) actor CDP, DD
DIDDEAR, Harriet Elizabeth
[Mrs. John Saville Faucit;
Mrs. William Farren, the
Younger] (1789-1857) English
actress BD, BS, DD, OX
DIDDEAR, [John? Charles?]
(1761-1841) manager, actor
BD
DIDELOT, Charles-Louis (1767-
1837) Swedish dancer, chore-
ographer BD
DIDELOT, Mme. Charles-Louis
[née Marie-Rose Paul] (d
1803) dancer BD
DIDIEE, Nantier (fl 1855) singer
CDP, HAS
DIDIER, Abraham J. (1739-1823)
actor BD, TD/1-2
DIDIER, Mrs. Abraham J. [née
Margaret Evans] (1741-1829)
actress, singer BD
DIDIER, Kate (d 1901) EA/02*
DIDO, Mrs. Tony see James,
Lil
DIDRING, Ernest (1868-1931)
Swedish dramatist WWT/2-3
DIDSBURY, Robert (fl 1787-94)
singer BD
DIEG, Alfred (d 1901) music-
hall producer EA/02*
DIENER, Joan (b 1934) Ameri-
can actress, singer BE,
TW/10-12, 22-24, 26, 28-29,
WWT/15-16
DIERKES, John (d 1975 [69])

performer BP/59*
DIERLAM, Robert J. (b 1917)
American educator, director
BE
DIERS, Eugene (d 1970 [70s])
performer BP/55*
DIERS, Hank (b 1931) American
educator BE
DIESEL, Leota American critic
BE
DIESEY, Mr. (fl 1767) dancer
BD
DIETERLE, Charlotte (d 1968
[72]) performer BP/52*
DIETERLE, William (d 1972 [79])
producer/director/choreographer
BP/57*
DIETRICH, Christian (d 1760)
bass player BD
DIETRICH, Dena (b 1928) Ameri-
can actress TW/23-24, 28-30
DIETRICH, John E. (b 1913)
American educator BE
DIETRICH, Marlene (b 1900/04)
German performer TW/24-25,
WWT/16
DIETRICH, Rene (b 1886) Ameri-
can singer WWM
DIETRICHSTEIN, Leo (fl 1893)
actor, dramatist DD
DIETZ, Claude see Garry,
Claude
DIETZ, Eileen American actress
TW/27-28, 30
DIETZ, Ella (fl 1872) actress
CDP
DIETZ, Howard (b 1896) American
lyricist, librettist, dramatist
CB, CD, MWD, NTH, WWT/
8-16
DIETZ, Linda (d 1920) American
actress, singer CDP, DD,
OAA/2
DIEUPART, Charles (d c. 1740)
French musician, composer,
impresario BD
DIEY, Mrs. Alf see Diey, Annie
DIEY, Annie [Mrs. Alf Diey] (d
1874) EA/75*
DI FABBRO, Imelda Italia de
Martin see DeMartin, Imelda
D'IFFANGER, Thomas Howard
Paul ["Valentine"] (d 1886 [42])
comedian EA/87*
DIFFEN, Ray (b 1922) English
costume designer, costumier
BE
DIFILIPPI, Arturo (d 1972 [78])

performer BP/57*

DIGBY, Mr. (fl 1781) actor, singer BD

DIGBY, George, Earl of Bristol (d 1676) dramatist CP/1-3, GT

DIGBY, Maude English actress EA/97, GRB/1

DIGBY, Robert (d 1963 [50]) manager WWT/14*

DIGGES, Dudley (1879/80-1947) Irish actor, producer, director COC, DAB, NTH, OC/1-3, SR, TW/1-4, WWA/2, WWT/6-10

DIGGES, Mrs. Dudley see Digges, Mary

DIGGES, Dudley West (1720-86) English actor, singer, manager BD, CDP, COC, DD, DNB, ES, OC/1-3, TD/1-2

DIGGES, Ernest (d 1970) performer BP/55*

DIGGES, Mary [Mrs. Dudley Digges; née Mary Quinn] (d 1947) Irish actress SR

DIGGES, Richard Evered (d 1889) EA/91*

DIGGORY, William Thomas (d 1882 [27]) actor EA/84*

DIGGS, Richard (d 1727) actor BD

DIGHTON, Mr. (fl 1733-48) actor BD

DIGHTON, John (b 1909) English dramatist AAS, WWT/12-16

DIGHTON, Robert (c. 1752-1814) actor, singer, dramatist, scene painter BD, CDP

DIGHTON, Mrs. Robert [Miss Bertles] (fl 1787-94) singer BD

DIGNAM, Mr. (fl 1743) house servant? BD

DIGNAM, Mark (b 1909) English actor AAS, WWT/9-16

DIGNUM, Charles (c. 1765-1827) English singer, actor, composer BD, CDP, DD, DNB, GT, TD/2

DI GRAZIO, Randy (b 1952) American actor TW/30

DIL, Mr. (fl 1796) house servant? BD

DILBERGLUE, Mrs. see Anderton, Sarah

DILKE, Charles Wentworth (1789-1864) critic DNB

DILKE, Thomas (d c. 1698) English dramatist CP/1-3, DD, GT

DILKS, Joseph see Clifton, Joseph

DILL, Max M. (d 1949 [71]) comedian TW/6

DILLER, Mons. (fl 1788) pyrotechnist BD

DILLER, Phyllis (b 1917) American actress, comedienne CB, TW/26

DILLEY, Joseph J. (b 1838) dramatist DD, EA/69

DILLIGH, Avni (d 1971 [62]) performer BP/56*

DILLINGHAM, Anna E. (fl 1859-68) actress HAS

DILLINGHAM, Charles Bancroft (1868-1934) American manager DAB, NTH, OC/1-3, SR, WWA/1, WWM, WWT/2-7

DILLMAN, Bradford (b 1930) American actor BE, CB, ES, TW/13-19

DILLON, Alexander see Macindoe, Alexander

DILLON, Baron (fl 1784) singer BD

DILLON, Charles (1819-81) English actor, manager CDP, DD, ES, HAS, OAA/1-2

DILLON, Mrs. Charles [Clara Conquest] (d 1888 [63]) actress DD

DILLON, Charles E. (d 1964 [76]) actor BE*

DILLON, Clara (d 1898 [53]) dramatist, actress DD

DILLON, Enrica Clay (b 1780) singer SR

DILLON, Fanny (1881-1947) American composer WWA/2

DILLON, Frances (d 1947 [75]) actress GRB/3-4, WWT/1-7

DILLON, James (d 1889) actor EA/90*

DILLON, John [né John Daily Marum] (1831-1913) Irish actor CDP, SR

DILLON, Melinda (b 1939) American actress BE, TW/19-20, 23-27

DILLON, Thomas Patrick (d 1962 [66]) performer BE*

DILLON, Tom see Spence, Tom

DILLON, Will (d 1966 [89]) composer/lyricist BP/50*

DILMEN, Güngör (b 1930) Turkish

dramatist RE

DI LORENZO, Tina (d 1930 [57])
actress BE*, WWT/14*

DILWORTH, Gordon (b 1913)
American actor, singer BE,
TW/22-23

DIMITRIEW, Vladimir (d 1964
[78]) ballet school founder
BP/49*

DIMKNELL, Mr. (fl 1799) house
servant BD

DIMMOCK, Mr. (fl 1758-62)
doorkeeper, billsticker BD

DIMMOCK, Master (fl 1739)
actor BD

DIMOND, William H. (1832-57)
American actor? HAS

DIMOND, William Wyatt (d 1812
[62]) actor, manager, dramatist BD, CDP, CP/3, DD,
GT, TD/1-2

DI MURSKA, Ilma (1843-89)
singer CDP

DIN, Dulce S. (d 1975 [39])
performer BP/60*

DINE, Jim painter CD

DINEHART, Alan (1890-1944)
American actor, producer
CB, SR, TW/1, WWA/2,
WWT/5-9

DING----, Mr. (fl 1661-62)
actor BD

"DINGDONG" (fl 1774) musician
BD

DINGEON, Helen actress CDP

DINGLE, Charles (1887-1956)
American actor TW/10-12

DINGLE, George see Booker,
George

DINGLE, Tom (d 1925 [38])
dancer BE*, BP/10*

DINGLEY, Joseph (fl 1766)
proprietor BD

DINGWALL, Alexander W. (d
1918 [60]) producer BE*,
WWT/14*

DINNEFORD, William (d 1852)
English actor, manager HAS

DINSMORE, O. A. (b 1849)
American actor HAS

DIPAOLA, Earlamae (d 1972 [44])
performer BP/57*

DIPLOCK, Dr. (d 1892) EA/93*

DIPLOCK, F. Bramah (d 1898)
acting manager EA/99*

DIPPEL, Andreas (1866-1932)
German singer, manager ES,
SR, WWA/1, WWM

DIPPLE, George (d 1909) pantomimist EA/10*

DIRCKS, Rudolf (b 1875) English
dramatist, critic GRB/2-4

DI RHIGINI, Countess see
Russell, Ella

DI RHONA, Albina (fl 1860) actress, dancer CDP

DIRKENS, Annie (1870-1942) German actress, singer ES

DISHER, Maurice Willson (1893-
1969) English critic AAS, ES,
WWT/4-14, WWW/6

DISHLEY see Distle

DISHY, Bob actor WWT/16

DISKIN, Marshall (d 1975 [62])
producer/director/choreographer
BP/60*

DISNEY, Thomas (fl 1671-98)
actor BD

DISTIN, John (d 1863 [74]?) musician CDP

DISTIN, Theodore (d 1893 [69])
singer, composer EA/94*

DISTIN, Mrs. Theodore [Sarah
Connor] (d 1863 [33]) singer
EA/72*

DISTIN FAMILY musicians CDP

DISTLE (fl 1610-36?) actor DA

DISTLEY see Distle

DISWELL, Mr. (fl 1794-95) puppeteer BD

DITCHER, Mr. (fl 1797-1813)
doorkeeper BD

DITHMAR, Edward Augustus (1854-
1917) American critic WWM

DITRICHSTEIN, Leo (1858/65-
1928) Austrian actor, dramatist DAB, ES, GRB/2-4, SR,
WWA/1, WWM, WWS, WWT/
1-5

DITSON, Lenny (d 1975 [63]) performer BP/60*

DITTINI, Mme. (d 1904 [45])
actress EA/05*

DITTMAR, Heinrich (d 1910)
musician EA/11*

DIVENY, Mary American actress
TW/5

DIVER, Mrs. see Brunton,
Miss E.

DIX, Beulah Marie (1876-1970)
American dramatist GRB/2-4,
WWM, WWS, WWT/1-3

DIX, Dorothy (1892-1970) English
actress WWT/1-10

DIX, Frank (d 1949 [78]) pantomime author BE*, WWT/14*

DIX, J. Airlie (d 1911) song composer EA/13*

DIX, Lillian (d 1922 [58]) actress BE*, BP/7*

DIX, Richard (1894-1949) American actor ES, TW/6

DIXEY, E. Freeman (1833-1904) minstrel CDP

DIXEY, Henry E. (1859-1943) American actor CB, CDP, GRB/2-4, NTH, PP/1, SR, WWA/2, WWS, WWT/1-9

DIXEY, Phyllis (d 1964 [50]) performer BE*

DIXON, Mr. (fl 1762-71) doorkeeper BD

DIXON, Adèle (b 1908) English actress WWT/6-14

DIXON, Aland (d 1976 [65]) performer BP/60*

DIXON, Mrs. B. [Mme. Purcell] (d 1869 [30]) singer EA/70*

DIXON, Campbell (1895-1960) Tasmanian dramatist, critic WWT/9-12, WWW/5

DIXON, Charlotte [Mrs. G. H. Dixon] (d 1891) EA/93*

DIXON, Clara Ann [Mrs. Smith; Mrs. Sterling] (fl 1795-1822) singer, actress BD, CDP, TD/1-2

DIXON, Cliff (d 1968 [79]) performer BP/52*

DIXON, Conway (d 1943 [69]) actor BE*, WWT/14*

DIXON, Cornelius (fl 1770-1821) scene painter, architect BD

DIXON, Mrs. [Cornelius?] (fl 1787) dancer BD

DIXON, Denver (d 1972 [82]) performer BP/57*

DIXON, Dorothy (1875-1947) actress SR

DIXON, Edwin (d 1871 [42]) comedian EA/72*

DIXON, George Washington (1795-1861) American actor, blackface performer CDP, HAS, SR

DIXON, Gerald (d 1879) dramatist DD

DIXON, Mrs. G. H. see Dixon, Charlotte

DIXON, Harland (d 1969 [83]) vaudevillian TW/26

DIXON, James (fl 1660-62) actor BD

DIXON, Jean (b 1896/1905) American actress BE, TW/1-9, 14-17, WWT/8-14

DIXON, J. L. (d 1888 [47]) comedian EA/89*

DIXON, Lee (1914-53) American actor, dancer TW/1, 9

DIXON, Lillian B. (d 1962 [69]) performer BE*

DIXON, MacIntyre (b 1931) American actor TW/22, 25, 27-30

DIXON, Madelyn (d 1975 [81]) performer BP/60*

DIXON, Paul (d 1974 [53]) performer BP/59*

DIXON, Mrs. Robert (d 1911) EA/12*

DIXON, Thomas (fl 1794) violinist BD

DIXON, Thomas (1864-1946) American actor, dramatist, manager SR, WWA/2, WWM, WWS

DIXON, W. (d 1872) singer? EA/73*

DIXON, William (fl 1792-96?) singer, music engraver, copyist BD

DIXON, William Jerrold (d 1879) dramatist EA/80*

DIZENZO, Charles (b 1938) American dramatist CD

D'JALMA, Prince Sadi (d 1891) "fire king" CDP

DJURY, Vladimir (d 1972 [60]) specialist BP/57*

D'LEGARD, [Charles?] see Delagarde, [Charles?]

D'LONRA, Annie [Mrs. Fred Carlos] (d 1900) serio-comic? EA/01*

DMITRI, Richard American actor TW/25, 29

DOANE, Joseph (fl 1793-94) singer BD

DOANE, Samantha (b 1946) American actress TW/27

DOB (fl 1598-1601) actor DA

DOBBIN, Mrs. Francis Le Fanu (d 1895) EA/96*

DOBBS, Mr. actor CDP

DOBBS, Francis (fl 1774) Irish dramatist, producer CP/2-3, GT, TD/1-2

DOBBS, Mattiwilda (b 1925) American singer CB, ES

DOBE see Dob

DOBELL, Elizabeth Rothwell [Mrs. Frederic Dobell] (d 1877 [24]) EA/78*

DOBELL, Mrs. Frederic see
Dobell, Elizabeth Rothwell
DOBELL, William L. (d 1932)
manager, actor WWT/14*
DOBIE, Alan English actor
AAS, WWT/14-16
DOBLE, Frances (1902-69) Cana-
dian actress WWT/5-9
DOBLER, Herr (d 1904 [65])
wizard EA/05*
DOBNEY, Ann (c. 1670-1760)
proprietor BD
DOBREE, Hugh Leslie (b 1884)
English actor GRB/1-2
DOBRITSCH, Al (d 1971 [60])
performer BP/55*
DOBSON, Mr. (fl 1728-34)
violoncellist BD
DOBSON, Mr. (fl 1792) actor
BD
DOBSON, Benjamin (fl 1664-69)
fencing master, manager?
BD
DOBSON, Franklin B. (1838-87)
manager, banjoist NYM
DOBSON, James (b 1923) Amer-
ican actor TW/2, 5-9
DOBSON, John (fl 1626) actor
DA
DOBSON, John (d 1904) comedian
EA/05*
DOBSON, Marjorie (d 1911 [43])
actress EA/12*
DOBSON, Oswald Harry (d 1917
[24]) actor EA/18*
DOCKRILL, Eliza [Mrs. R. H.
Dockrill] equestrienne CDP
DOCKRILL, R. H. equestrian
CDP
DOCKRILL, Mrs. R. H. see
Dockrill, Eliza
DOCKSTADER, Lew (1856-1924)
American minstrel, manager
CDP, DAB, ES, OC/3, SR
DOCTOR, Joseph (fl 1787-1800)
clown, equilibrist, tumbler,
actor BD, HAS
DOCTOR, Mrs. [Joseph] (fl
1799) actress HAS
DODD, Alice (d 1869) actress
EA/70*
DODD, Alice singer, actress
CDP
DODD, Claire (d 1973 [50+])
actress TW/30
DODD, Emily (d 1944) actress
TW/1
DODD, Henry (d 1867 [53])

EA/68*
DODD, James Solas (1721-1805)
English actor, lecturer BD,
CP/2-3, DNB, GT, TD/1-2
DODD, James William (1734-96)
English actor, singer, manager
BD, CDP, COC, DD, ES, GT,
OC/1-3, SR, WWA/1, WWM,
WWT/4-7
DODD, Mrs. James William (d
1769) actress, singer BD
DODD, John (fl 1784?-94) singer
BD
DODD, Ken (b 1929) English come-
dian WWT/14-16
DODD, Lee Wilson (1879-1933)
American dramatist DAB, OC/
1-3, SR, WWA/1, WWM,
WWT/4-7
DODD, Martha see Dodd, Mrs.
James William
DODD, Tommy see Clarke,
Ernie
DODD, William (1729-77) English
dramatist CP/3, GT
DODD, William (d 1908) circus
agent EA/09*
DODDRIDGE, Joseph (1769-1826)
American dramatist EAP
DODDS, Jack (d 1962 [35]) dancer
BE*
DODDS, Jamieson (1884-1942)
English actor, singer WWT/
4-9
DODDS, William American stage
manager BE
"DODDY, Lord Tom" see
Brown, Johnny
DODGE, Mrs. see Watson, Mrs.
DODGE, Henry Irving (1861-1934)
American critic, dramatist
WWT/4-6
DODGE, Jerry (1937-74) American
actor TW/24-25, 28-30
DODGE, Ossian E. (b 1820) Amer-
ican singer CDP
DODGE, Roger Pryor (d 1974
[76]) performer BP/59*
DODGE, Shirlee American chore-
ographer, teacher, director
BE
DODGE, Wendell P. (d 1976 [92])
producer/director/choreographer
BP/60*
DODGSON, Henry (d 1876 [39])
harpist EA/77*
DODIMEAD, David (b 1919) Eng-
lish actor WWT/15-16
DODIMEAR, Mr. (fl 1793)

dancer BD
DODSLEY, James (d 1797 [73])
publisher BE*, WWT/14*
DODSLEY, Robert (1703-64)
English dramatist CDP,
COC, CP/1-3, DD, DNB,
ES, GT, HP, OC/1-3, TD/
1-2
DODSON, Mr. (fl 1731-34) sing-
er, actor BD
DODSON, Mrs. (fl 1740-49)
actress, singer BD
DODSON, Miss (fl 1740-42)
actress, dancer BD
DODSON, Mrs. Alfred D. see
Dodson, Clare
DODSON, Clare [Mrs. Alfred
D. Dodson] (d 1908) EA/09*
DODSON, John E. (1857-1931)
English actor DD, GRB/2-4,
PP/1, SR, WWA/1, WWM,
WWS, WWT/1-5
DODSON, Mrs. John E. see
Irish, Annie
DODSON, Lamott (d 1975) per-
former BP/59*
DODSON, Owen (b 1914) Ameri-
can educator, dramatist,
director BE
DODSWORTH, Charles (d 1920)
actor DD
DODSWORTH, Mrs. Charles
see Aubrey, Lizzie
DODWORTH, Allen composer,
musician CDP
DODWORTH, Harvey B. (1822-
91) bandmaster CDP
DOE, Miss (fl 1772) actress BD
DOE, Edith (d 1905) EA/06*
DOE, John (fl 1766-1804) house
servant, actor BD
DOEL, James (1803/04-1902)
actor DD, WWW/1
"DOGE OF DRURY, The" see
Steele, Richard
DOGGET, Mr. (fl 1748) actor
BD
DOGGET, James (fl 1794) singer
BD
DOGGETT, Gertrude (fl 1866)
actress HAS
DOGGETT, Thomas (c. 1670-
1721) English actor, singer,
manager, dramatist BD,
CDP, COC, CP/1-3, DD,
DNB, ES, GT, HP, OC/1-3,
TD/1-2
DOGGETT, Thomas (fl 1791)

actor, dancer BD
"DOG STAR, The" see Cony,
Barkham
DOHERTY, Brian (d 1974 [68])
dramatist BP/59*
DOHERTY, Charlotte Ellen see
Grant, Nellie
DOHERTY, Chester (d 1975 [71])
performer BP/59*
DOHMAN, Dennis (b 1945) Ameri-
can actor TW/30
DOIGE, Mr. (fl 1810) actor HAS
DOILE, Ann (fl 1797) house ser-
vant? BD
DOILE, Margaret (fl 1797-1800)
house servant? BD
D'OISLY, Maurice (1882-1949)
English singer WWW/4
DOLAN, Mary [née Mary Rebecca
Goettling] (b 1919) American
talent representative BE
DOLAN, Michael J. (d 1954 [70])
actor BE*, WWT/14*
DOLAN, Robert Emmett (1908-72)
American composer, conductor
BE, TW/29, WWA/5
DOLARO, Hattie (d 1941 [80])
actress, singer BE*, WWT/
14*
DOLARO, Selina (1853-89) singer,
actress CDP, DD, OAA/2
DOLBIER, Maurice (b 1912) Amer-
ican actor CB
DOLBY, Charlotte Helen CDP
DOLBY, Henry Gray (d 1913 [59])
EA/14*
DOLENZ, George (d 1963 [55])
Italian actor BE*
DOLIN, Anton [Patrick Healey-
Kay] (b 1904) English dancer,
choreographer CB, ES, OC/2,
TW/3, WWT/6-13
DOLIVE, William (b 1943) Amer-
ican actor TW/24
DOLL, Bill (b 1910) American
press representative BE
DOLLAR, William (b 1907) Amer-
ican dancer, choreographer
ES
"DOLL COMMON" see Corey,
Mrs. John
DOLLY, Jennie (1892-1941) Hun-
garian dancer CB, ES, WWT/
4-9
DOLLY, Rosie (1892-1970) Hun-
garian dancer ES, TW/26,
WWT/4-9
DOLMAN, Frederick William see

Dolman, Richard
DOLMAN, John (1824/30?-95)
American actor, lawyer
CDP, HAS
DOLMAN, Richard [Frederick
William Dolman] (b 1895)
English actor WWT/7-12
DOMBRE, Barbara (d 1973 [28])
performer BP/57*
DOME, Mrs. Zoltan see
Nordica, Mme.
DOMINGO, Placido (b 1941)
Spanish singer CB
DOMINGUEZ, Alberto (d 1975
[73]) composer/lyricist BP/
60*
DOMINIC, Mr. (fl 1726) scene
painter BD
"DOMINICHINO" see Annibali,
Domenico
DOMINIQUE, Mons. (fl 1742-51)
actor, acrobat, manager BD
DOMINIQUE, Mme. (fl 1748)
singer, dancer BD
DOMINIQUE, Ivan (d 1973 [45])
performer BP/57*
DOMINIQUE, Polly (b 1741)
performer BD
DOMITILLA, Miriamne [née
Campanini] (fl 1741-48)
dancer BD
DON, Lady Emilia Eliza [née
Emily Saunders] (d 1875)
English actress HAS
DON, Laura actress, dramatist
CDP
DON, Sir William Henry (1826-
62) English actor CDP, DD,
DNB, HAS
DONADIEU, Miss (fl 1775) singer
BD
DONAGH, Emily (d 1891) chorister
EA/92*
DONAGHEY, Frederick (1870-1937)
American dramatist, manager
WWS
DONAHUE, Jack (1892-1930)
American actor, singer SR,
WWT/6
DONAHUE, Vincent (d 1976 [58])
executive BP/60*
DONALD, James (b 1917) Eng-
lish actor AAS, WWT/10-15
DONALD, John (b 1856) English
manager GRB/1-4
DONALD, Mrs. John see
Temple, Rose
DONALDSON, Mr. (fl 1772)

actor BD
DONALDSON, Alexander (d 1794)
printer, bookseller, treasurer
BD
DONALDSON, Anne Maria see
Faulkner, Anne Maria
DONALDSON, Arthur (1869-1955)
Swedish actor, singer TW/12,
WWS
DONALDSON, Donella see Hay-
don, Julie
DONALDSON, Jack (d 1975 [65])
performer BP/60*
DONALDSON, Muriel Pollock (d
1971) composer/lyricist BP/
56*
DONALDSON, Walter (1893-1947)
American songwriter BE*
DONALDSON, Walter A. (b 1832)
American actor HAS
DONALDSON, Walter Alexander
(d 1877 [84]) actor EA/79*,
WWT/14*
DONALDSON, William B. (1822-
73) minstrel CDP, HAS
DONALLAN, Mr. (fl 1798-1819)
sweeper, watchman BD
DONAT, Peter (b 1928) Canadian
actor BE, TW/13-20, 28
DONAT, Robert (1905-58) English
actor AAS, COC, DNB, ES,
OC/3, WWA/3, WWT/7-12
DONATH, Ludwig (1907-67) Aus-
trian actor, coach BE, TW/
24, WWT/14
DONATO (d 1865) dancer EA/72*,
WWT/14*
DONATO, Josephine Lucchese (d
1974 [78]) performer BP/59*
DONAVON, Lucy [Mrs. Thomas
Donavon] (d 1887) EA/88*
DONAVON, Mrs. Thomas see
Donavon, Lucy
DONDELL, Sprackling (fl 1712)
musician? BD
DONE, Dr. William (d 1895 [80])
conductor, musician EA/96*
DONEGAN, James E. (d 1916)
proprietor EA/17*
DONEGAN, Martin (b 1931) Irish
actor TW/25, 30
DONEHUE, Vincent J. (1916/20/
22-66) American director BE,
TW/22, WWA/4, WWT/13-14
DONELLY, Henry V. see
Donnelly, Henry V.
DONER, Maurice (d 1971 [66])
performer BP/55*

DONHOWE, Gwyda (b 1933)
American actress TW/26-28
DONISTHORPE, G. Sheila (1898-
1946) English dramatist WWT/
9
DONIZETTI, Gaetano (1797-1848)
composer CDP
DONLAN, Yolande (b 1920) Amer-
ican actress AAS, WWT/11-
16
DONLEAVY, J. P. (b 1926)
American dramatist AAS,
CD, HJD, MD, MWD, WWT/
14-16
DONLEVY, Brian (1903-72) Irish
actor BE, ES, TW/28,
WWT/9-10
DONMAN, Mr. (fl 1785-89) bas-
soonist BD
DONN, Marie (d 1973 [74]) per-
former BP/58*
DONNAHEY, Edith see Vaughan,
Ada
DONNAY, Maurice (1862-1945)
French dramatist GRB/1,
3-4
DONNE, Mary (d 1866) dancer
HAS
DONNE, William Bodham (1807-
82) English examiner of plays
DNB
DONNELL, E. T. (d 1879 [32])
actor? musician? EA/81*
DONNELL, Martin (d 1891 [35])
EA/93*
DONNELL, Patrick (b 1916)
Irish actor, administrator
WWT/14-16
DONNELLY, Charles (d 1875)
comedian EA/76*
DONNELLY, Mrs. Charles see
Donnelly, Mrs. R.
DONNELLY, Donal (b 1931)
English actor TW/23-24,
29, WWT/15-16
DONNELLY, Dorothy Agnes
(1880-1928) American actress,
dramatist. GRB/3-4, WWA/
1, WWM, WWS, WWT/1-5
DONNELLY, Henry V. (d 1910
[49]) actor, vaudevillian
CDP
DONNELLY, H. Grattan (fl 1898)
American? dramatist DD,
SR
DONNELLY, Jamie actress
TW/24
DONNELLY, Leo (1878-1935)

American actor, dramatist SR
DONNELLY, Michael (d 1882)
stage manager EA/84*
DONNELLY, Mrs. R. [Mrs.
Charles Donnelly] (d 1898)
EA/00*
DONNELLY, Ruth (b 1896) Amer-
ican actress BE, TW/29
DONNELLY, Thomas Lester (1832-
80) actor, manager CDP
DONNELLY, Tom (d 1976 [57])
critic BP/60*
DONNER, Clive (b 1926) English
director WWT/16
DONNOLLY, R. J. (d 1908 [45])
American critic GRB/4*
DONOGHUE, William (d 1872 [30])
singer EA/72*
DONOHUE, Jack (b 1908) Ameri-
can actor, dancer, director,
choreographer BE, WWT/9-16
DONOVAN, Master (fl 1739-41)
actor BD
DONOVAN, Alice Dougan (d 1971
[90]) dramatist BP/55*
DONOVAN, Frank R. (d 1975 [69])
producer/director/choreographer
BP/60*
DONOVAN, Josephine [Mrs. W.
H. Donovan] (d 1894 [25]) EA/
95*
DONOVAN, Walter (d 1964 [75])
American performer, composer
BE*
DONOVAN, Warde (b 1919) Amer-
ican actor, singer TW/3-4
DONOVAN, Mrs. W. H. see
Donovan, Josephine
DONSTALL, James see Tun-
stall, James
DONSTONE, James see Tun-
stall, James
DONWALT, Mr. (fl 1767) musi-
cian BD
DONZELLI, Domenico (1790-1873)
Italian singer ES
DOOLEY, Gordon (d 1930 [31])
comedian BE*, BP/14*
DOOLEY, James (d 1949 [69])
vaudevillian TW/5
DOOLEY, Jed (d 1973 [89]) per-
former BP/58*
DOOLEY, Johnny (d 1928 [41])
Scottish comedian BE*, BP/
12*, WWT/14*
DOOLEY, Paul (b 1928) American
actor TW/25-26
DOOLEY, Ray [Rachel Rice

Dooley] (b 1896/1903) Scottish actress, singer, dancer BE, TW/4-7, WWT/6-9

DOOLEY, Robert (d 1922 [52]) comedian BE*, BP/7*

DOOLEY, William (d 1921 [39]) acrobatic comedian BE*, BP/6*

DOOLEY, Willian G. (d 1975 [70]) critic BP/59*

DOOLITTLE, James (b 1914) American executive, producer BE

DOONAN, George (d 1973 [76]) performer BP/57*

DOONAN, J. P. (d 1900) Irish comedian EA/01*

DOONE, Neville (fl 1891-98) actor, dramatist DD

DOONE, Rupert (1904-66) director COC

DOONER, James (d 1910 [70]) showman EA/11*

DOORESCOURT, John (fl 1689-99) trumpeter BD

DOORLEY, Frank M. (d 1966 [80]) performer BP/50*

DOORSMING, Mr. (fl 1748) singer BD

DORAN, Charles (1877-1964) Irish actor, manager WWT/3-13

DORAN, James see Vane, W. H.

DORAN, John (1807-78) English writer CDP, DD, DNB, ES

DORATI, Antal (b 1906) Hungarian conductor CB

DORCASE, Mr. (fl 1675) singer BD

DORE, Mrs. (fl 1785) actress BD

DORE, Alexander (b 1923) English director, actor WWT/15-16

DORE, Hezekiah (d 1874 [34]) manager EA/75*

DOREE, Ada (fl 1888) actress, singer DP

DORELL, Miss (fl 1797) actress BD

DORELLI, Signor (fl 1791-95) singer BD

DOREMUS, Mrs. C. A. American? dramatist DD

DOREMUS, Mrs. Thomas C. see Wilton, Ellie

DORFMAN, Irvin (b 1924)

American press representative, producer BE

DORFMAN, Nat (b 1895) American press representative, dramatist BE

DORGERE, Arlette French actress, singer WWT/4

DORI, Alison (d 1909) EA/10*

DORIA, Clara see Rogers, Clara Kathleen

DORIEN, Mr. (fl 1773) actor BD

DORIN, Phoebe (b 1940) American actress TW/26, 29-30

DORIN, Rube (d 1965 [48]) critic BP/49*

DORION, Mr. (fl 1784-95) singer BD

DORIS, John B. (fl 1863-86) circus performer SR

DORIS, Lily (d 1906) performer? EA/07*

DORIVAL, Anne Marguerite (d 1788) dancer BD

DORIVAL, Georges (d 1939 [78]) actor BE*, WWT/14*

DORIVAL A CORIFET [Marie Catherine Brida] (b c. 1754) French dancer BD

DORKIN, Jack (d 1975 [81]) performer BP/60*

DORKIN, Millie Morgan (d 1972 [77]) performer BP/57*

DORLAG, Arthur H. (b 1922) American educator, director BE

DORMAN, Mr. (fl 1740) dramatist CP/1-3

DORMAN, Mr. (fl 1740-41) house servant? BD

DORMAN, John (b 1922) American actor TW/15, 22-23, 25

DORMAN, Ridley (fl 1752-73?) violinist BD

DORMAN, Mrs. Ridley [née Elizabeth Young] (d 1773) singer, actress BD

D'ORME, Aileen (1877-1939) English actress, singer WWT/4-7

D'ORME, Josephine [née Ordz] (1830-81) singer CDP

DORMER, Mr. (fl 1805) actor CDP

DORMER, Daisy (d 1947 [64]) singer CDP

D'ORMY, Martini (fl 1854) singer HAS

DORN, Dolores [née Dorn-Heft] (b 1935) American actress BE

DORN, Lily Austrian singer
WWM

DORN, Philip (d 1975 [75])
Dutch actor TW/3

DORNAN, John (d 1918 [71])
EA/19*

DORNEY, Louis (1876-1940)
singer CB

DORNEY, Richard (1620-81)
violinist BD

DORNEY, Richard (d 1921 [79])
manager BE*, BP/5*

DORN-HEFT, Dolores (b 1936)
American actress TW/25

DORNTON, Agnes (d 1901)
EA/02*

DORNTON, Charles (d 1900)
actor, manager DD

DORNTON, Mrs. Charles see
Dornton, Louisa

DORNTON, Harold (d 1891)
EA/92*

DORNTON, Louisa [Mrs. Charles
Dornton; née Louisa Robertson]
(d 1881) EA/82*

DORO, Marie (1882-1956) American actress ES, GRB/2-4,
TW/13, WWM, WWS, WWT/
1-6

DORR, Dorothy [Mrs. H. J.
W. Dam] (b 1867) American
actress DD, GRB/2-4,
WWM, WWS, WWT/1-5

DORREE, Bobbie (d 1974 [68])
performer BP/58*

DORRELL, William (d 1896
[86]) composer, musician
EA/98*

DORRILL, Charles C. (d 1912
[51]) manager, director EA/
13*

DORRILL, John (d 1974 [44])
managing director BTR/74

D'ORSAY, Fifi (b 1904) Canadian actress TW/27-29

D'ORSAY, Lawrance [Dorset
William Lawrence] (1853/60-
1931) actor DD, EA/95,
GRB/1-4, SR, WWM, WWS,
WWT/1-6

DORSET, Earl of see Sack-
ville, Thomas

DORSEY, Sandra [Sandy Ellen]
(b 1939) American actress
TW/29

DORSION, Mlle. (fl 1792) dancer
BD

D'ORTA, Rachele [Signora

Giorgi] (fl 1784-85) singer BD

D'ORTA, Rosina (fl 1784) singer
BD

DORTOR, Joseph see Doctor,
Joseph

DORUS-GRAS, Julie Aimée Josèphe
(1805-96) singer CDP

DORVAL, Max (d 1902) manager
WWT/14*

D'ORVAL-VALENTIONO, E. L.
(d 1885 [32]) singer EA/86*

DORZIAT, Gabrielle French actress GRB/4, WWT/1-4

DOSEL, [William?] (fl 1788-96)
doorkeeper BD

DOSER, Mr. (fl 1789) house servant? BD

DOS PASSOS, John (1896-1970)
American dramatist BE, CB,
ES, HJD, HP, MD, MWD,
WWW/6

DOSSIE, Robert (d 1777) dramatist
CP/2-3, GT, TD/1-2

DOSTOIEVSKY, Feodor Milhailovich
(1821-81) Russian writer COC,
OC/2-3

DOT, Doreen (d 1969 [70]) performer BP/54*

DOTHWAIT, Mr. (fl 1794) flutist
BD

DOTRICE, Roy (b 1923/25) English
actor AAS, COC, TW/24,
WWT/14-16

DOTTI, Anna (fl 1724-27) singer
BD

DOTTRIDGE, Mrs. (d 1886) EA/
87*

DOTTRIDGE, Dolly [Mrs. C. H.
Longden] (d 1909 [47]) EA/10*

DOTTRIDGE, Joseph William (d
1896 [78]) EA/98*

DOUBLEDAY, Richard (d 1975
[52]) producer/director/chore-
ographer BP/59*

DOUBLEDAY, Thomas (1790-1870)
English dramatist DNB

DOUBTON, Thomas see Down-
ton, Thomas

DOUCE, Francis (1775-1834)
writer DD

DOUCET, Catherine Calhoun (d
1958 [83]) American actress
TW/1-3, 14, WWT/8-9

DOUGHARTY, Hougline (1844-1919)
minstrel SR

DOUGHERTY, Mr. (fl c.1870)
actor HAS

DOUGHERTY, Frances Ann [née

Cannon] American producer
BE

DOUGHERTY, Hughey (b 1844)
American minstrel CDP,
HAS

DOUGHERTY, M. J. (fl 1854)
actor HAS

DOUGHERTY, Walter Hampden
see Hampden, Walter

DOUGHTON, Thomas (fl 1628-34)
actor DA

DOUGHTY, Charles Montagu
(1843-1926) dramatist HP

DOUGHTY, Henry actor GRB/1

DOUGHTY, James (1819-1913)
clown DD

DOUGLAS, Mr. (fl 1770) actor
BD

DOUGLAS, Mr. (fl 1776-1817)
house servant BD

DOUGLAS, Rev. (fl 1784?)
dramatist CP/3

DOUGLAS, Miss (fl 1777) actress
BD

DOUGLAS, Alexander (fl 1672-
73) actor? BD

DOUGLAS, Belle [Emma Ducklin]
(d 1907) actress EA/08*

DOUGLAS, Byron (d 1935 [70])
actor BE*, BP/19*, WWT/
14*

DOUGLAS, Daphne (d 1917)
EA/18*

DOUGLAS, David (b c. 1730)
English actor, theatre builder
HAS, SR

DOUGLAS, Mrs. David see
Hallam, Mrs. Lewis

DOUGLAS, Dorothea (d 1962 [79])
performer BE*

DOUGLAS, Felicity [née Tomlin]
(b 1910) English dramatist
WWT/15-16

DOUGLAS, Fred (d 1892 [42])
actor EA/93*

DOUGLAS, G. R. [G. Douglas
Robertson] (d 1882) dramatist
DD

DOUGLAS, Helen Gahagan see
Gahagan, Helen

DOUGLAS, Mrs. Jack (d 1911)
EA/12*

DOUGLAS, Jeff (d 1975 [32])
critic BP/60*

DOUGLAS, Johanna (b 1917)
American actress TW/23-26

DOUGLAS, John (d 1872) proprietor EA/73*

DOUGLAS, Kenneth [Kenneth
Savory] (d 1923 [49/52]) English
actor GRB/3-4, WWT/1-4

DOUGLAS, Mrs. Kenneth see
Lane, Grace

DOUGLAS, Kirk [né Issure Daniel-
ovitch] (b 1916/20) American
actor BE, CB, ES, TW/1-3

DOUGLAS, Larry (b 1914) American actor, singer BE, TW/
4-12, 25-26

DOUGLAS, Lewis W. (b 1894)
American executive BE

DOUGLAS, Maggie St. Clair see
Hampton, Mrs. Henry

DOUGLAS, Marie Booth (d 1932
[75]) actress BE*, WWT/14*

DOUGLAS, Melvyn [Melvyn Hes-
selberg] (b 1901) American
actor, director, producer
AAS, BE, CB, ES, SR, TW/
5-19, 24, WWT/7-16

DOUGLAS, Michael (b 1944) American actor TW/27

DOUGLAS, Milton (1901-70) American actor TW/2-3

DOUGLAS, Paul (1907-59) American actor ES, TW/2-5, 13-14,
16

DOUGLAS, R. H. (d 1935) actor
BE*, WWT/14*

DOUGLAS, Richard see Douglass, Richard

DOUGLAS, Robert (b 1909/10)
English actor AAS, BE, ES,
WWT/8-13

DOUGLAS, Mrs. Stephen A. see
Shattuck, Truly

DOUGLAS, Susan (b 1926) Hun-
garian/English actress TW/2-5

DOUGLAS, T. B. (fl 1851) American actor HAS

DOUGLAS, Tom (b 1903) American
actor WWT/5-9

DOUGLAS, Torrington (b 1901)
English press representative
WWT/11-16

DOUGLAS, Valerie (d 1969 [31])
performer BP/53*

DOUGLAS, Wallace (b 1911) Canadian producer, director WWT/
11-16

DOUGLAS, William (fl 1720-45)
trumpeter BD

DOUGLAS, William Budd (d 1867)
actor HAS

DOUGLAS-BARBOR, Dorothy English actress GRB/1

DOUGLASS, Albert (1864-1940) manager WWT/7-9

DOUGLASS, Amy (b 1902) American actress TW/5-6

DOUGLASS, Bertie Richard (d 1904 [26]) EA/05*

DOUGLASS, Bill Henry (b 1951) American actor TW/29-30

DOUGLASS, Mrs. Byron (d 1905) EA/06*

DOUGLASS, David (d 1786) American actor, manager COC, ES, NTH, OC/1-3

DOUGLASS, Edwin Herbert (b 1867) American singer WWA/4

DOUGLASS, George Samuel (1853-1909) English music-hall manager GRB/1

DOUGLASS, Jane Isabella [Mrs. John Douglass] (d 1881 [65]) EA/82*

DOUGLASS, John (1814-74) proprietor, actor, manager DD

DOUGLASS, John (d 1917 [76]) manager, dramatist, producer DD

DOUGLASS, Mrs. John see Douglass, Jane Isabella

DOUGLASS, Margaret (d 1949 [53]) American actress TW/1-6

DOUGLASS, P. American actor TW/28

DOUGLASS, R. H. (d 1935?) actor, monologist GRB/1-4

DOUGLASS, Richard (d 1911 [67]) scene artist BE*, EA/12*, WWT/14*

DOUGLASS, Stephen [né Fitch] (b 1921) American actor, singer, director AAS, BE, TW/7-8, 10-17, 20, 22-23, WWT/11-16

DOUGLASS, Thomas Mace (d 1906 [83]) EA/07*

DOUGLASS, Vincent (1900-26) English dramatist WWT/5

DOULENS, Roger B. (d 1972 [57]) publicist BP/57*

DOURIF, Brad (b 1950) American actor TW/30

D'OUVILLY, George Gerbier (fl 1661) Dutch? dramatist CP/1-3, DNB

DOVA, Nina (b 1926) English actress TW/11, 25, 27-29

DOVE, Elizabeth see Dove, Mrs. Michael

DOVE, Henry (fl 1674-78?) violinist BD

DOVE, Mark ["Bertrand"] (d 1867 [18]) gymnast EA/68*

DOVE, Michael (d 1747) actor, dancer BD

DOVE, Mrs. Michael (fl 1731-47) actress, dancer BD

DOVE, Owen (d 1893 [48]) dramatist, actor EA/94*

DOVER, Antony (fl 1635) actor DA

DOVER, John (d 1725) dramatist CP/1-3, DNB, GT

DOVEY, Mr. (fl 1724-27) house servant BD

DOVEY, Alice (1885-1969) American actress, singer WWT/4-6

DOW, Ada (d 1926 [79]) actress BE*, BP/10*, WWT/14*

DOW, Alexander (d 1779) Scottish dramatist CDP, CP/2-3, DNB, GT, TD/1-2

DOW, Clara (1883-1969) English actress, singer GRB/4, WWT/1-3

DOW, Emily (fl 1854) singer HAS

DOW, R. A. (b 1941) American actor TW/27, 29-30

DOWD, Harrison (b 1897) American actor BE

DOWD, M'el American actress BE, TW/22-29, WWT/15-16

DOWDELL, Mr. (fl c. 1710) bass player BD

DOWDELL, Robert (b 1932) American actor TW/14

DOWDEN, Edward (1843-1913) Irish critic DD, DNB

DOWDING, Mr. (fl 1784) singer BD

DOWELL, Anthony (b 1943) English dancer CB

DOWELL, Horace (d 1974 [70]) composer/lyricist BP/59*

DOWER, E. (fl 1738) dramatist CP/1-3, GT

DOWGHTON, Thomas see Downton, Thomas

DOWLAND, Robert see Dulandt, Robert

DOWLE, Rowland (fl 1636) actor DA

DOWLER, Mrs. (fl 1794-95) dresser BD

DOWLING, Mr. prompter HAS

DOWLING, Constance (d 1969 [49]) actress TW/26

DOWLING, Eddie [né Joseph
Nelson Goucher] (1894?-1976)
American actor, dramatist,
producer AAS, CB, ES,
NTH, SR, TW/1-9, WWT/7-15
DOWLING, Edward Duryea (d
1967 [63]) director, producer
TW/24
DOWLING, Isaac see Deulin,
Herr
DOWLING, Joan (1928-54) Eng-
lish actress WWT/11
DOWLING, Joseph (b 1850)
dramatist, actor SR
DOWLING, Maurice G. (fl 1834-
37) dramatist DD
DOWLING, Richard (1846-98)
dramatist DD
DOWLING, Robert W. (1895-1973)
American theatre owner, execu-
tive BE, TW/30
DOWLING, Vincent (b 1922)
American actor TW/24
DOWN, Mr. (fl 1731) house ser-
vant? BD
DOWN, Mrs. (d 1881 [90])
EA/82*
DOWN, Oliphant (d 1917) drama-
tist EA/18*
DOWNER, Alan S. (1912-70)
American scholar BE, WWA/5
DOWNER, J. W. (d 1893 [56])
manager EA/94*
DOWNES, Mr. (fl 1729) actor
BD
DOWNES, Cpt. (fl 1733) drama-
tist CP/3
DOWNES, Edward Ray (d 1968
[63]) stage manager BP/52*
DOWNES, John (fl 1661-1719)
English writer, prompter,
actor BD, COC, DD, DNB,
ES, OC/1-3
DOWNES, W. H. singer CDP
DOWNES, Wilhelmina [Mrs.
William Downes] (d 1917 [34])
EA/18*
DOWNES, Mrs. William see
Downes, Wilhelmina
DOWNEY, Morton (b 1902)
American singer CB
DOWNHAM, Hugh (fl 1779)
dramatist CP/2, GT, TD/1-2
DOWNIE, Alex (b 1806) Ameri-
can clown, equestrian, trampo-
linist HAS
DOWNIE, Louise (b 1841) Amer-
ican? drummer girl HAS

DOWNIE, William M. (d 1911)
EA/12*
DOWNING, Adelaide see Lewis,
Mrs. G.
DOWNING, David (b 1943) Ameri-
can actor TW/24-29
DOWNING, George (d 1780) actor,
dramatist BD, CP/2-3, DD,
GT, TD/1-2
DOWNING, Joe (b 1904) American
actor TW/2-3
DOWNING, Robert (1914-75) Amer-
ican actor, stage manager,
director, dramatist, historian
BE, TW/23
DOWNING, Robert L. (1857-1944)
American actor GRB/2-3,
PP/1, SR, WWA/2, WWM,
WWS
DOWNING, Russell (d 1968 [67])
executive BP/53*
DOWNING, Sam (d 1967 [82])
performer BP/52*
DOWNING, Virginia American ac-
tress TW/26, 29
DOWNMAN, Mr. (fl 1788) scene
painter BD
DOWNMAN, Hugh (d 1809) English
dramatist CP/3, DD
DOWNES, Johnny see Downs,
Johnny
DOWNS, Jane English actress
WWT/14-16
DOWNS, Johnny American actor
TW/2-6
DOWNS, Margaret see Rogers,
Mrs. Ben G.
DOWNS, Will (d 1918) EA/19*
DOWNTON, Thomas (fl 1593?-
1622?) actor, dramatist CP/
3, DA
DOWNTON'S BOY (fl 1600-02)
actor DA
DOWSE, Mr. (d 1783) singer BD
DOWSE, Thomas Edward Fugion
(d 1897 [44]) actor EA/98*
DOWSETT, Ellen [Mrs. Vernon
Dowsett] (d 1907 [45]) EA/08*
DOWSETT, Mrs. Vernon see
Dowsett, Ellen
DOWSING, Emma Ada [Mrs.
Thomas C. Howitt] (d 1884)
EA/85*
DOWSING, John (fl 1678) singer
BD
DOWSON, Mr. (fl 1777) actor BD
DOWSON, Mrs. H. M. (fl
1680) see Filippi, Rosina

DOWSON, Ann (fl c. 1765-74)
   singer BD
DOWSON, John (fl 1680) dancing
   master BD
DOWTEN, Thomas see Down-
   ton, Thomas
DOWTON, Emily (d 1924 [84])
   actress BE*, WWT/14*
DOWTON, Harry (d 1889 [29])
   singer EA/90*
DOWTON, Henry (b 1798) actor
   DNB
DOWTON, Thomas see Down-
   ton, Thomas
DOWTON, William (1764-1851)
   English actor, manager BD,
   BS, CDP, COC, DD, DNB,
   ES, GT, HAS, OC/1-3, OX,
   SR, TD/1-2
DOWTON, William Paton (d
   1883 [88]) actor DNB
DOYLE, Mr. (fl 1800-09) house
   servant? BD
DOYLE, Mr. English actor
   HAS
DOYLE, Mrs. (fl 1789-1801)
   house servant? BD
DOYLE, Sir Arthur Conan (1859-
   1930) Scottish dramatist DD,
   DNB, ES, GRB/2-4, WWM,
   WWT/1-6, WWW/3
DOYLE, C. W. (d 1901 [79])
   musician EA/02*
DOYLE, Edward (d 1905) EA/
   06*
DOYLE, Frank Q. (b 1872)
   American singer, actor, agent
   WWM
DOYLE, Gene [né Eugene Tauben-
   haus] (b 1909) American actor,
   lyricist BE
DOYLE, James (fl 1794) singer?
   BD
DOYLE, James (d 1927 [38])
   American dancer BE*,
   BP/11*
DOYLE, John (d 1794) singer,
   actor BD
DOYLE, John T. (d 1935 [62])
   American actor BE*, BP/20*
DOYLE, Kathleen (b 1947) Amer-
   ican actress TW/27
DOYLE, Len (d 1959 [66]) actor
   TW/16
DOYLE, Lila [Mrs. Harry Mills]
   (d 1908) EA/09*
DOYLE, Margaret (d 1793) BD
DOYLE, Michael (d 1890 [45])

manager EA/91*
DOYLE, Miriam (d 1962) actress,
   producer BE*
DOYLE, Moya see Mannering,
   Moya
DOYLE, Paddy (d 1873) comic
   singer EA/74*
DOYLE, Paddy (d 1895) Irish
   comedian EA/96*
D'OYLY CARTE, Richard (1844-
   1901) English impresario COC,
   DD, DNB, ES, NTH, OC/1-3,
   PDT, SR, WWW/1
D'OYLY CARTE, Mrs. Richard
   [née Couper Black] (d 1913)
   manager GRB/2-4, ES, WWT/1
D'OYLY CARTE, Rupert (1876-
   1948) English manager CB,
   NTH, TW/5, WWT/4-10, WWW/
   4
DOYNE, Jennie [Mrs. John Henry
   Doyne] (d 1894) EA/95*
DOYNE, John H. (d 1893) stage
   manager EA/94*
DOYNE, Mrs. J[ohn?] H. (d 1879)
   EA/80*
DOYNE, Mrs. John Henry see
   Doyne, Jennie
DRACO, Mrs. Pan E. (d 1906
   [24]) EA/07*
DRAGHI, Giovanni Battista (b c.
   1640) Italian musician, com-
   poser, librettist BD, DNB
DRAGO, Cathleen (d 1938) actress
   BE*, WWT/14*
"DRAGON" (fl 1775) performing
   dog BD
DRAGONETTI, Domenico (1763-
   1846) double-bass player, com-
   poser BD, DNB
DRAKE, Mr. (fl 1799-1802) dancer
   BD
DRAKE, Mrs. (fl 1799) dancer
   BD
DRAKE, Miss (fl 1798-1801)
   dancer, singer BD
DRAKE, Alexander (1800-93) Eng-
   lish actor, manager HAS, SR
DRAKE, Mrs. Alexander see
   Drake, Frances Ann
DRAKE, Alfred [né Capurro] (b
   1914) American actor, singer,
   director AAS, BE, CB, ES,
   TW/1-24, 30, WWT/10-16
DRAKE, Christopher (b 1929)
   American actor TW/15-18
DRAKE, Fabia (b 1904) English
   actress WWT/6-11

DRAKE, Frances Ann [Mrs. Alexander Drake] (1797-1875) American actress CDP, DAB, DD, HAS, WWA/4

DRAKE, Harry (d 1971 [70]) agent BP/56*

DRAKE, Dr. James (1667-1706/07) English dramatist CP/1-3, DD, GT

DRAKE, Jonas Hardcastle (d 1901 [66]) Diorama proprietor EA/02*

DRAKE, Mrs. Jonas Hardcastle see Drake, Rebecca

DRAKE, Julia (fl 1800-15) English actress DD, HAS, SR

DRAKE, Julia [Mrs. George Edwards?] (d 1888 [32]) actress SR

DRAKE, Rebecca [Mrs. Jonas Hardcastle Drake] (d 1901 [67]) EA/02*

DRAKE, Robert (fl 1550) actor DA

DRAKE, Ronald (b 1928) English actor BE

DRAKE, Samuel (1768/69-1854) English actor COC, DAB, DD, ES, OC/2, SR, WWA/4

DRAKE, Tom (b 1915) American actor ES

DRAKE, William A. (1899-1965) American dramatist WWT/9-13

DRAKEUP, Daniel (d 1879 [44]) musician EA/80*

DRANGE, Emily (d 1961 [63]) performer BE*

DRANSFIELD, Jane (b 1875) American dramatist, actress WWA/5

DRAPER, Mr. (fl 1776) singer BD

DRAPER, Miss (fl 1776-82) singer BD

DRAPER, Anne (b 1938) American actress BE, TW/24

DRAPER, Don (b 1929) American actor TW/28

DRAPER, J. F. (d 1876) burlesque writer EA/77*

DRAPER, Joseph (d 1962 [55]) performer BE*

DRAPER, Marcus (d 1917 [32]) actor, manager WWT/14*

DRAPER, Margaret (b 1922) American actress TW/5

DRAPER, Mark Denman (d 1917

[32]) actor, manager EA/18*

DRAPER, Matthew (fl 1731) dramatist CP/2-3, DD, GT

DRAPER, Paul (b 1913) Italian dancer BE, CB

DRAPER, Ruth (1884-1956) American monologist COC, ES, HP, NTH, OC/3, PDT, TW/13, WWA/3, WWT/8-12, WWW/5

DRASIN, Tamara see Tamara

DRATLER, Jay (d 1968 [57]) dramatist BP/53*

DRAYCOTT, Charles (d 1917 [44]) lessee EA/18*

DRAYCOTT, Wilfred (b 1848) actor GRB/1-4, WWT/4-6

DRAYLIN, Paul (d 1970 [56]) performer BP/55*

DRAYSON, Edith (d 1926 [37]) actress BE*, WWT/14*

DRAYTON, Alfred (1881-1949) English actor AAS, ES, WWT/4-10

DRAYTON, Edwin (d 1885) actor EA/86*

DRAYTON, Henry (d 1871) American singer CDP, HAS

DRAYTON, Mrs. Henry [née Susanna Lowe] (fl 1853) singer HAS

DRAYTON, Michael (1563-1631) English dramatist, share-holder CP/1-3, DA, DD, ES, FGF, MH

DRAYTON, W. H. (d 1874 [38]) actor EA/75*

DRAZ, Francis K. (d 1974 [79]) designer BP/59*

DREGHORN, Lord see MacLaurin, John

DREHER, Konrad (b 1859) German actor, manager WWT/2

DREHER, Mrs. Paul see Dreher, Virginia

DREHER, Virginia [née Jennie Cummings; Mrs. Paul Dreher] (d 1898) actress CDP

DREHER, Walter Arthur (d 1962 [61]) Argentinian/American actor BE*

DREIER, John T. (b 1913) American designer, director, educator BE

DREISER, Edward M. (d 1958 [84]) actor BE*, BP/42*

DREISER, Theodore (1871-1945)

American dramatist ES, MD,
MWD, NTH, WWT/6-9
DREMAK, W. P. American actor
TW/24, 29
DRENCH, Master (fl 1795) actor
BD
DRESDEL, Sonia [née Lois Obee]
(1909-76) English actress
AAS, ES, WWT/10-16
DRESSER, Louise (1882-1965)
American actress ES, TW/
21, WWA/4, WWT/1-8
DRESSER, Paul (1857-1911) Amer-
ican composer, lyricist, actor,
manager CDP, SR
DRESSLER, Eric (b 1896/1900)
American actor BE, ES,
WWT/7-10
DRESSLER, John (fl 1777-1808)
musician, composer BD
DRESSLER, Marie [Lelia Koerber]
(1869/71-1934) Canadian ac-
tress, singer DAB, ES,
GRB/3-4, NTH, OC/1-3, SR,
WWA/1, WWM, WWS, WWT/
1-7
DREUSSART, Mr. (fl 1707) pro-
prietor? BD
DREVER, Constance (d 1948 [68])
Indian singer, actress GRB/
1-4, WWT/1-7
DREW, Mr. (fl 1722-23) actor
BD
DREW, Adine (d 1888) American
actress EA/89*
DREW, Frank Nelson (1831-1903)
Irish actor CDP, HAS, SR
DREW, Mrs. Frank Nelson
[Fanny Gribbles; Mrs. C. L.
Stone] (b 1831) American ac-
tress HAS
DREW, George (b 1929) Ameri-
can actor TW/8
DREW, Georgiana (1856-93)
actress DD, ES
DREW, Harry [John Henry Dew]
(b 1865) Welsh singer GRB/1
DREW, James H. see Sum-
merville, Hamilton S.
DREW, John (1827-62) Irish/
American actor CDP, DAB,
DD, ES, HAS, HJD, NTH,
OC/1-3, SR, WWA/H
DREW, John (1853-1927) Ameri-
can actor CDP, COC, DAB,
DD, DP, ES, GRB/1-4,
NTH, OC/1-3, PP/1, SR,
WWA/1, WWM, WWS,

WWT/1-5
DREW, Mrs. John [Louisa Lane]
(1820-97) English/American
actress CDP, COC, DD, ES,
HAS, NTH, OC/1-3, WWA/H
DREW, Louisa D. (1846-94?) ac-
tress ES, HAS
DREW, Louise (d 1954 [72]) Amer-
ican actress TW/10, WWM
DREW, Lucille McVey (d 1925
[35]) actress BE*, BP/10*
DREW, Nelly [Mrs. Frank Coyle]
(d 1892 [29]) comedian, dancer
EA/93*
DREW, Sidney [Sidney White]
(1868-1919/20) American actor
ES, OC/1-3, SR
DREW, Thomas Henry (d 1891)
costumier EA/92*
DREW, William (d 1871) singer
EA/72*
DREWE, Bartholomew (fl 1614)
actor DA
DREWE, Thomas (fl 1616-53?)
actor, dramatist CP/2-3, DA,
DD, DNB, FGF
DREWITT, Stanley (b 1874/78)
English actor, director GRB/
2, WWT/2-11
DREYFUSS, Henry (1904-72) Amer-
ican designer WWT/7-12
DREYFUSS, Jane [née Jane Dever-
eux Philbin] (b 1924) American
talent representative BE
DREYFUSS, Michael (d 1960 [32])
actor TW/16
DREYFUSS, Richard (b 1947) Amer-
ican actor CB
DREYSCHOCK, Alexander (1818-69)
pianist CDP
DRIDGE, Mr. (fl 1740) dancer?
BD
DRIESBACH, Jacob (d 1877) lion
tamer CDP
DRINKWATER, Albert Edwin (d
1923 [71]) English actor, drama-
tist, manager EA/96, GRB/1-4,
WWT/2-4
DRINKWATER, John (1882-1937)
English dramatist, actor AAS,
COC, DNB, ES, HP, MD,
MH, MWD, NTH, OC/1-3,
PDT, SR, WWT/4-8, WWW/3
DRISCHELL, Ralph (b 1927) Amer-
ican actor TW/24-27, 30
DRISCOLL, Mr. (fl 1745-56) house
servant BD
DRISCOLL, Arthur F. (d 1967 [82])

lawyer BP/51*

DRISCOLL, H. C. D. (d 1917)
EA/18*

DRISCOLL, Lawrason (b 1946)
American actress TW/30

DRIVAS, Robert (b 1938) American actor, director BE,
TW/14-15, 19-21, 25, 28,
30, WWT/16

DRIVER, Donald actor, director,
dramatist CD, WWT/16

DRIVER, Harry (d 1973 [46])
dramatist BP/58*

DRIVER, John (b 1947) American
actor TW/30

DRIVER, Tom F. (b 1925) American critic, educator BE

DRIVER, W. (d 1870) clown
EA/71*

DROESHOUT, Martin (fl 1620-51)
English engraver NTH

"DROGHIERINA, La" see
Chimenti, Margherita

DROHAN, Benjamin V. (d 1972
[77]) composer/lyricist BP/56*

"DROLLELO, Mynheer" (fl 1746)
dancer BD

DROM, Thomas (fl 1600-01) actor
DA

DROMAT, [Marianne?] (fl 1792-
95) dancer BD

DROMGOOLE, Patrick (b 1930)
Chilean director WWT/15-16

DROUET, Mlle. (fl 1852) French
dancer CDP, HAS

DROUET, Louis (d 1873 [81])
flautist EA/74*

DROUET, Robert (1870-1914)
American actor, dramatist
GRB/3-4, WWA/1, WWS,
WWT/1-2

DROUVILLE, Mons. (fl 1771-73)
dancer BD

DROY, Frank (d 1973 [64])
performer BP/57*

DROZ, Henri Louis Jaquet
(1752-91) exhibitor, mechani-
cian BD

DRUCE, Duncan (d 1916 [37])
actor, stage manager, producer EA/17*

DRUCE, Herbert (1870-1931)
English actor, producer
GRB/4, WWT/1-6

DRUCKER, Frances (d 1970 [69])
producer TW/26

DRUE, Thomas see Drewe,
Thomas

DRULIE, Sylvia (b 1928) American
producer, executive BE

DRUM, Leonard American actor
TW/23

DRUMMOND, Mr. (fl 1738-69)
proprietor BD

DRUMMOND, Mr. (fl 1756) actor
BD

DRUMMOND, Mrs. see Barrett,
Mrs. George Horton

DRUMMOND, Alexander M. (1884-
1956) American educator BE*

DRUMMOND, Alice (b 1929) American actress TW/21-23, 26-
28, 30

DRUMMOND, Dolores [Mrs.
Sprague] (1834/38/40-1926)
English actress DD, GRB/1-4,
OAA/1-2, WWT/1-5

DRUMMOND, Mary (d 1837 [77])
actress HAS

DRUMMOND, Thomas George (d
1873) actor EA/74*

DRUMMOND, W. C. (fl 1810-50)
English actor, stage manager,
dancing master HAS

DRURY, John (d 1916) EA/17*

DRURY, Robert (fl 1732-41) dramatist, actor BD, CP/1-3,
DD, GT

DRURY, Thomas see Drury,
Robert

DRURY, William (fl 1618-41)
dramatist CP/3, DNB, FGF

DRURY, William Henry (d 1896
[48]) scene artist EA/97*

DRURY, Lieut.-Col. William
Price (1861-1949) dramatist
GRB/4, WWT/1-9, WWW/4

DRUSIANO see Martinelli

DRY, Mr. actor CDP

DRYCE, John Pete (d 1892) comedian EA/93*

DRYDEN, James (d 1913) EA/14*

DRYDEN, John (1631-1700) English
dramatist, critic CDP, COC,
CP/1-3, DD, DNB, ES, GT,
HP, MH, NTH, OC/1-3, PDT,
RE

DRYDEN, John, Jr. (1667/68-
1701) English dramatist CP/
1-3, DD, GT

DRYDEN, J. P. (d 1911) actor,
sketch proprietor EA/12*

DRYDEN, Leo singer, composer
CDP

DRYDEN, Mrs. Leo see Tyler,
Marie

DRYDEN, Vaughan (b 1875) English critic, dramatist WWT/6

DRYE, John W. , Jr. (b 1900) American lawyer BE

DRYSDALE, Learmont (1866-1909) Scottish composer DNB, ES

DUANE, Frank [né Frank Duane Rosengren] (b 1926) American dramatist BE

DUBAS, Marie (d 1972 [78]) performer BP/56*

DUBE, Marcel (b 1930) Canadian dramatist MH

DUBELLAMY, Charles Clementine [John Evans] (d 1793) actor, singer BD, CDP, TD/1-2

DUBELLAMY, Mrs. Charles Clementine, I [Frances Maria] (d 1773) actress, singer BD

DUBELLAMY, Margaret see Didier, Mrs. Abraham J.

DUBERMAN, Martin B. (b 1930) American historian, dramatist CD, CH

DUBEY, Matt [né Matthew David Dubinsky] (b 1928) American lyricist BE

DUBIN, Al (d 1945 [54]) Swiss lyricist BE*

DUBINSKY, Matthew David see Dubey, Matt

DU BOIS, [Mons. ?] (fl 1730) dancer? BD

DUBOIS, Mr. (fl 1859-60) actor HAS

DUBOIS, Baptiste see Dubois, Jean Baptiste

DUBOIS, Camille (fl 1875) actress DD

DU BOIS, Charles (fl 1792-1807) dancer BD

DUBOIS, Dorothea (d 1774) dramatist CP/2-3, DD, GT, TD/1-2

DUBOIS, Frank (fl 1696) actor BD

DUBOIS, Gene [Mrs. Milton H. Bayne] (d 1962 [61]) actress BE*

DUBOIS, Jack (d 1908 [16]) EA/09*

DUBOIS, James [Alfonso Maillard] (d 1907 [36]) animal impersonator EA/08*

DUBOIS, Jean Baptiste (1762-1817) clown, acrobat, dancer, actor, singer BD, TD/1-2

DUBOIS, M. (fl 1796) dancer HAS

DUBOIS, P. B. (fl 1726) translator CP/3

DU BOIS, Raoul Pene (b 1914) American designer WWT/10-16

DUBOISON, Mr. (fl 1795) performer? BD

DUBOSC, Gaston (d 1941 [81]) actor WWT/14*

DUBOURG, Augustus W. (d 1910 [80]) dramatist DD

DUBOURG, Matthew (1703-67) English violinist, composer BD, DNB

DUBRAWSKI, Frank (d 1972 [46]) BP/57*

DU BREIL, Mons. (fl 1711) dancer BD

DUBREUIL, Mons. (fl 1721-22) actor? dancer? BD

DUBREUIL, Mme. (fl 1721-22) actress? dancer? BD

DUBREUIL, Ernest (d 1886 [55]) librettist EA/87*

DUBREUL, Sig. (fl 1848) singer HAS

DU BROCQ, Mons. see Debroc, Mons.

DUBRUCQ, Jean Batiste (d 1893 [63]) musician EA/94*

DUBUISSON, Mons. (fl 1734-42) dancer, actor BD

DU CANE, Augusta (d 1909 [69]) EA/10*

DUCE, R. W. (d 1916) music-hall manager EA/17*

DUCHEMIN, [Mlle. ?] (fl 1789) dancer BD

DUCHESNE, Mons. (fl 1791-92) dancer BD

DUCHESNE, Mme. (fl 1791) dancer BD

DUCK, Mr. (fl 1735-44) doorkeeper BD

DUCK, William (d 1892 [72]) manager EA/93*, WWT/14*

DUCKENFIELD, Mrs. George (d 1878) EA/79*

DUCKENFIELD, John (d 1875) proprietor EA/76*

DUCKLIN, Emma see Douglas, Belle

DUCKMAN, Ethel see Colby, Ethel

DUCKWORTH, Mr. (fl 1792-93) manager BD

DUCKWORTH, Mr. (fl 1794)

violinist BD
DUCKWORTH, Mrs. W. M. (d
1912 [67]) actress EA/13*
DUCRAST, Mme. (fl 1794) singer
BD
DUCROW, Miss equestrienne
CDP
DUCROW, Andrew (1793-1842)
English equestrian, ropedancer,
equilibrist, manager BD,
CDP, DD, DNB, ES, HP, OX
DUCROW, Mrs. Andrew see
Woolford, Miss
DUCROW, John (d 1834) eques-
trian, clown BD, CDP
DUCROW, Peter (d 1814) strong
man, acrobat, manager BD
DUCY-BARRE, Louise (fl 1850)
French dancer CDP
DUDA, Andrea (b 1945) American
actress TW/29-30
DUDDY, John (fl 1794) singer BD
DUDDY, Thomas (fl 1794) instru-
mentalist BD
DUDGEON, Thomas (d 1880)
scene artist EA/81*
DUDLAY, Adeline (1859-1934)
actress CDP
DUDLEY, Mr. (fl 1794) singer
BD
DUDLEY, Mr. (fl 1800-12) house
servant BD
DUDLEY, Miss (fl 1778-83) ac-
tress, dancer BD
DUDLEY, Arthur F. (d 1916
[37]) EA/17*
DUDLEY, Arthur W. see
Ward, Henry
DUDLEY, Bide (1877-1944) Amer-
ican critic, dramatist CB,
WWA/2, WWT/6-9
DUDLEY, Carl (d 1973 [63])
producer/director/choreograph-
er BP/58*
DUDLEY, Caroline Louise see
Carter, Mrs. Leslie
DUDLEY, Ethel M. (d 1968 [76])
performer BP/52*
DUDLEY, Henry (d 1873) actor
EA/74*
DUDLEY, Sir Henry Bate (1745-
1814) English dramatist CP/
2-3, DD, DNB, GT, TD/1-2
DUDLEY, J. (fl 1794) singer BD
DUDLEY, John S. (d 1966 [72])
lawyer BP/50*
DUDLEY, Raymond see Turner,
Montague

DUDLEY, S. (fl 1794) singer BD
DUDLEY, Mrs. Sam (d 1876)
EA/78*
DUDLEY, Samuel (d 1882 [36])
music-hall artist EA/83*
DUDLEY, Sara English actress
GRB/1
DUDLEY, William (b 1947) English
designer WWT/16
DUDLEY-BENNETT, H. G. (d
1918 [52]) manager WWT/14*
DUEL, Mr. (fl 1724-27) house
servant BD
DUEL, Peter (d 1971 [31]) per-
former BP/56*
DUELL, William (b 1923) Ameri-
can actor TW/23-28
DUERR, Edwin (b 1906) American
director, educator BE
DUERRENMATT, Friedrich see
Dürrenmatt, Friedrich
DUFAINANAS, Miss (fl 1799)
house servant? BD
DUFF, Charles St. Lawrence
(1894-1966) Scottish dramatist
WWW/6
DUFF, Gordon (d 1975 [66]) pro-
ducer/director/choreographer
BP/60*
DUFF, Harry (d 1890 [85]) actor?
EA/91*
DUFF, J. C. (d 1928 [73]) mana-
ger WWT/14*
DUFF, John A. (d 1889) American
actor, manager EA/90*, WWT/
14*
DUFF, John R. (1787-1831) Irish
actor CDP, COC, DD, HAS,
SR
DUFF, Mrs. John R. see
Duff, Mary Ann
DUFF, Mary [Mrs. A. A. Adams;
Mrs. Joseph Gilbert; Mrs. J.
G. Porter] (d 1852) Irish ac-
tress HAS, SR
DUFF, Mary Ann [née Dyke; Mrs.
John R. Duff] (1794-1857) Eng-
lish/American actress CDP,
COC, DAB, DD, HAS, OC/1-3,
SR, WWA/H
DUFF, Sarah see Halliday, Mrs.
Andrew
DUFF, Thomas (d 1892 [69])
American actor HAS
DUFF, William (b 1927) American
actor TW/6-7
DUFFEE, F. Harold American
dramatist RJ

DUFFELL, Bee (d 1974) Irish
actress BTR/74
DUFFET, Thomas (fl 1678)
dramatist CP/1-3, DD, DNB,
ES, GT
DUFFEY, Peter (fl 1768-1805)
singer, actor BD, TD/1-2
DUFFIELD, Mrs. (d 1854) ac-
tress HAS
DUFFIELD, Caesar (fl 1669-
1707) violinist BD
DUFFIELD, Harry S. actor CDP
DUFFIELD, John (fl 1720-22)
dancer BD
DUFFIELD, Kate [Kate Wemyss]
(b 1821) American actress
HAS
DUFFIELD, Kenneth (b 1885)
Australian composer, pro-
ducing manager WWT/8-11
DUFFIELD, Saunders B. (d 1879)
actor, manager EA/80*
DUFF-MacCORMICK, Cara Cana-
dian actress TW/26, 28-30
DUFFOUR, Mr. (fl 1777-97)
property man? BD
DUFFRY, Thomas (d 1889 [45])
musician EA/90*
DUFFY, Anne (d 1913 [60])
EA/14*
DUFFY, Barney (d 1906) per-
former? EA/07*
DUFFY, Bernard (d 1858) actor
HAS
DUFFY, Henry (d 1961 [71])
producer, actor, theatre
owner TW/18
DUFFY, Herbert (d 1952) actor
BE*, BP/37*
DUFFY, James (d 1972 [56])
circus manager BP/57*
DUFFY, John (d 1909 [55]) cir-
cus proprietor EA/10*
DUFFY, Maureen (b 1933) Eng-
lish dramatist CD
DUFFY, Patrick James (d 1890
[63]) gymnast EA/91*
DUFFY, William (1801-36)
American actor, manager
HAS
DUFLOS, Raphael (d 1946 [88])
actor BE*, WWT/14*
DUFOUR, Mr. (fl 1760-63)
dancer BD
DUFOUR, Camilla [Mrs. Jacob
Henry Sarratt] (fl 1796-1809)
singer, actress BD, TD/2
DUFOUR, Val (b 1928) American

actress TW/8-14
DUFRANNE, Hector French singer
WWM
DUGAN, Dennis (b 1946) American
actor TW/28
DUGAN, Johnny (d 1972 [50]) per-
former BP/56*
DUGANNE, Augustine Joseph Hick-
ey (1823-84) dramatist HJD
DUGARD, Mark John (d 1882 [40])
performer EA/84*
DUGAY, Mons. (fl 1741-48)
dancer, slackrope dancer BD
DUGDALE, Mr. (fl 1779) actor
BD
DUGGAN, Andrew (b 1923) Ameri-
can actor BE, TW/10-13
DUGGAN, Edmund (d 1938 [72])
producer, actor BE*, WWT/
14*
DUGGAN, Maggie (d 1919 [59])
actress, singer CDP
DUGGAN, Mary (fl 1886-92) ac-
tress, singer DD
DUGGAN, Tom (d 1903) EA/04*
DUGMORE, William Henry see
Denny, William Henry
DUGRANDE, Mons. (fl 1743)
dancer BD
DUIGNAN, Thomas (d 1910) music-
hall manager EA/12*
DUILL, Mrs. John Lewis [née
Catherine Mary Satchell; Mrs.
John Taylor, I] (d 1789) ac-
tress BD
DUJONCEL, Mons. (fl 1749-62?)
French dancer BD
DUKAS, James (b 1926) American
actor TW/22-24, 26
DUKE, Mr. see Dyke, Mr.
DUKE, Ivy (b 1896) English actress
WWT/6-7
DUKE, John (fl 1590-1617) actor
DA
DUKE, N. see Dukes, N.
DUKE, Patty (b 1946) American
actress BE, CB, TW/18-19
DUKE, Robert (b 1917) American
actor BE, TW/7-20
DUKE, Vernon [Vladimir Dukelsky]
(1903-69) Russian composer,
lyricist BE, CB, TW/25,
WWA/5, WWT/6-11
DUKES, Ashley (1885-1959) Eng-
lish dramatist, manager, critic
COC, DNB, ES, NTH, OC/1-3,
PDT, WWT/4-12, WWW/5
DUKES, Mrs. Ashley see Ram-

bert, Marie

DUKES, Charles William [Charles Wilford] (d 1887 [42]) performer? EA/88*

DUKES, N. (fl 1730-55) dancer BD

DUKINFIELD, William Claude see Fields, W[illiam] C[laude]

DULAC, Arthur (d 1962 [52]) French actor BE*

DULAC, Odette [Jeanne Latrilhe] singer GRB/1-4

DULANDT, Robert (fl 1623) musician DA

DULCKEN, Louise (1811-50) pianist CDP

DULEY, John Henry (1835-64) American comedian HAS

DULIN, [Mons.] (fl 1767) dancer BD

DULISSE, Mme. (fl 1757-58) dancer BD

DULISSE, Mlle. (fl 1757-59) dancer BD

DULLEA, Keir (b 1936?) American actor CB, TW/15, 24, 26, WWT/16

DULLIN, Charles (1885-1949) French actor, producer OC/1-3

DULLZELL, Paul (1879-1961) American actor, director, administrator WWT/10-13

DULO, Jane (b 1918) American actress TW/2

DULONDEL, Mons. (fl 1720) actor BD

DUMAI, D. (fl 1756-83) dancer BD

DUMAS, Alexandre (1803-70) French dramatist SR

DU MAURIER, Daphne (b 1907) English dramatist BE, COC, ES, OC/3, WWT/10-14

DU MAURIER, George Louis Palmella Busson (1834-96) English artist, writer DNB, NTH, OC/1-3

DU MAURIER, Sir Gerald Hubert Edward Busson (1873-1934) English actor AAS, COC, DD, DNB, ES, GRB/1-4, NTH, OC/1-3, PDT, SR, WWT/1-7, WWW/3

DU MAURIER, Mrs. Gerald see Beaumont, Muriel

DU MAURIER, Guy (1865-1916) English dramatist OC/1-3

DU MAURIER, Muriel see Beaumont, Muriel

DUMAYNE, Norma (d 1910) EA/11*

DUMBRILLE, Douglass (d 1974 [84]) Canadian actor TW/30

DUMENEY, Mrs. (fl 1709-17?) actress BD

DUMENY, Camille (d 1920 [62]) actor BE*, WWT/14*

DUMILATRE, Adele (fl c. 1840?) dancer CDP

DU MINIL, Renée (b 1868) French actress GRB/4, WWT/1-4

DUMIRAIL, Mons. (fl 1674-1716) French dancer BD

DUMIRAIL, fils (fl 1716) French dancer BD

DUMKE, Ralph (d 1964 [64]) comedian TW/20

DUMONT, Mons. (fl 1734-35) scene keeper BD

DUMONT, Mons. (fl 1737-50) dancer BD

DUMONT, Mme. (fl 1724-25) actress BD

DUMONT, Mme. (fl 1738-48) dancer BD

DUMONT, Mrs. (fl 1799-1800) singer BD

DUMONT, Mlle. (fl 1748) dancer BD

DUMONT, Mlle. (fl 1781) dancer BD

DUMONT, Frank (d 1918) American minstrel, dramatist, actor, manager CDP, SR

DUMONT, J. B. (fl 1824) American dramatist EAP, RJ

DUMONT, Louise (d 1932) actress BE*, WWT/14*

DUMONT, Margaret (d 1965 [75]) actress, singer TW/21

DUMORIER, Mr. (fl 1792-93) scene painter? BD

DUMPHEY, Mrs. (d 1782) actress BD

DUNANT, Mr. (fl 1799) actor BD

DUNAWAY, Faye (b 1941) American actress CB, TW/22-23, WWT/16

DUNBAR, Mr. (d c. 1762) boxkeeper BD

DUNBAR, E. C. actor, singer CDP [see also following]

DUNBAR, Edward Charles (d 1900 [58]) actor, singer, musician EA/01* [see also previous

entry]
DUNBAR, Erroll (fl 1905) American actor WWA/1, WWS
DUNBAR, George (d 1887) actor EA/88*
DUNBAR, Joan Pauline (d 1913) EA/14*
DUNBAR, Joe (d 1894) EA/96*
DUNBAR, John (b 1877) English actor, business manager GRB/1
DUNCA, Kenney (d 1972 [69]) performer BP/56*
DUNCALFE, Henry (fl 1732-39) musician BD
DUNCAN, Angus (b 1912) American executive BE, WWT/13-16
DUNCAN, Archie (b 1914) Scottish actor WWT/15-16
DUNCAN, Augustin (1873-1954) American actor, producer ES, TW/2-4, 10, WWT/7-11
DUNCAN, Charles H. see Keston, C. B.
DUNCAN, David (d 1874 [48]) musician EA/75*
DUNCAN, Emily (d 1889) actress CDP, DD
DUNCAN, Ged (fl 1798) dramatist CP/3
DUNCAN, Isadora (1878-1927) American dancer DAB, ES, HJD, NTH, OC/1-2, PDT, WWA/4, WWT/4-5
DUNCAN, Lisa (d 1976 [76]) performer BP/60*
DUNCAN, Malcolm (1881-1942) American actor CB, WWS, WWT/7-9
DUNCAN, Maria Rebecca see Davison, Maria Rebecca
DUNCAN, Mary (b 1903/05) American actress ES, WWT/5-8
DUNCAN, Pamela (b 1934) American actress TW/25
DUNCAN, Raymond (d 1966 [91]) actor, dancer TW/23
DUNCAN, Ronald (b 1914) English dramatist, director AAS, CD, CH, ES, MD, MWD, PDT, WWT/11-16
DUNCAN, Rosetta (d 1959 [63]) American actress TW/16, WWT/6-11
DUNCAN, Sandy (b 1946) American actress TW/23-27,

WWT/16
DUNCAN, Sophie (d 1894 [28]) American? variety performer EA/95*
DUNCAN, Thomas R. (d 1865) actor HAS
DUNCAN, Thomas W. (b 1905) American dramatist CB
DUNCAN, Timothy (d 1801) Irish? actor BD
DUNCAN, Mrs. Timothy [née Legg] (fl 1778-1801) actress BD
DUNCAN, Todd (b 1900/03) American actor, singer BE, CB, WWT/10-11
DUNCAN, Vivian American actress WWT/6-11
DUNCAN, William (d 1961 [81]) actor BE*
DUNCAN, William see Rowley, Cpt.
DUNCAN, William Cary (1874-1945) American librettist WWT/5-11
DUNCAN, William H. American actor ES
DUNCAN, William James (d 1917) EA/18*
DUNCOMB, Mr. (fl 1784-94) singer BD
DUNCOMBE, John (fl 1710-16) singer BD
DUNCOMBE, William (d 1769 [80]) dramatist CP/1-3, DD
DUNCOMBE, Mrs. William see Eldéf, Lilian
DUNDAS, Henry [Arthur Harrison] (d 1907 [47]) manager, actor GRB/3
DUNDAS, Lilian (d 1911) actress EA/12*
DUNDAS-SLATER, Charles (d 1912) music-hall manager EA/13*
DUNDY, Elmer S. (d 1907 [45]) American manager GRB/3*, WWT/14*
DUNEMBRAY see Demaimbray
DUNFEE, Ethelyne (b 1937) American actress TW/23-24
DUNFEE, Jack (b 1901) manager, agent WWT/9-15
DUNFEE, Katharine (b 1948) American actress TW/27
DUNGAN, Andrew (d 1887) journalist EA/88*
DUNHAM, Joanna (b 1936) English

actress TW/18, WWT/15-16

DUNHAM, Katherine (b 1910/12) American dancer, choreographer, producer, actress BE, CB, ES, TW/2-8, WWT/11-16

DUNHAM, S. S. (b 1819?) American actor, singer HAS

DUNHILL, Thomas Frederick (1877-1946) English composer DNB, ES

DUNKEL, Eugene (d 1972 [81]) designer BP/56*

DUNKELS, Dorothy (b 1907) English actress WWT/7-10

DUNKELS, Marjorie (b 1916) English actress, impersonator WWT/12-13

DUNKLEY, Theophilus (d 1909 [65]) theatrical undertaker EA/10*

DUNLAP, Louis M. (d 1976 [64]) composer, lyricist BP/60*

DUNLAP, William (1766-1839) American dramatist, manager CDP, COC, CP/3, DAB, DD, EAP, ES, HAS, HJD, MH, NTH, OC/1-3, RE, RJ, SR, WWA/H

DUNLO, Lady see Clancarty, Countess of

DUNLOP (fl 1789) dramatist CP/3

DUNLOP, Frank (b 1927) English director AAS, WWT/15-16

DUNLOP, John see Langtry, Paul

DUNN, Arthur (1866-1932) American comedian WWM

DUNN, Dick (d 1903 [55]) comic singer EA/04*

DUNN, Edwin Wallace (d 1931 [73]) American press representative WWM

DUNN, Emma (1875-1966) English actress SR, TW/23, WWT/4-10

DUNN, Geoffrey (b 1903) English actor, singer, producer, director ES, WWT/10-16

DUNN, Gregg (d 1964 [48]) actor BE*

DUNN, Henry (d 1876 [21]) violinist EA/77*

DUNN, James (1905/06-67) American actor BE, ES, TW/24

DUNN, James Colgan (1818-91)

actor, singer CDP

DUNN, James Phillip (1884-1936) American composer WWA/1

DUNN, J. Malcolm (d 1946 [70]) actor TW/3

DUNN, [John?] (fl 1745-62?) violinist, composer? BD

DUNN, John (fl 1844) actor CDP, DD, HAS, SR

DUNN, John (d 1875) comedian EA/76*

DUNN, John Benjamin (b 1812) actor CDP

DUNN, Joseph (d 1851) comedian HAS

DUNN, Joseph Barrington (d 1920 [58]) American actor BE*

DUNN, Liam (d 1976 [59]) performer BP/60*

DUNN, Michael [né Gary Neil Miller] (1934-73) American actor, singer BE, TW/25, 28, 30

DUNN, Ralph (b 1900/02) American actor BE, TW/15

DUNN, Sinclair (d 1911 [64]) Scottish singer EA/12*

DUNN, William Nathaniel (1782-1855) treasurer BD

DUNNE, Eithne Irish? actress TW/3

DUNNE, Irene (b 1904) American actress, singer BE, CB, ES, WWT/7-11

DUNNETT, Walter A., III (b 1941) American actor TW/23

DUNNING, Mr. (fl 1747-48) actor BD

DUNNING, Alice (b 1847) English singer HAS, SR

DUNNING, A. T. (d 1886) Australian manager EA/87*

DUNNING, Harriet Sarah see Lingard, Dickey

DUNNING, Philip Hart (1890-1968) American actor, dramatist, producer, director BE, ES, MD, MH, MWD, NTH, SR, WWA/5, WWT/6-11

DUNNING, Ruth (b 1911) Welsh actress WWT/9-16

DUNNINGER, Joseph (1892-1975) American magician CB

DUNNOCK, Mildred (b 1900) American actress AAS, BE, CB, TW/1-13, 20-23, 26-27, WWT/11-16

DUNOYER see Denoyer

DUNPHIE, Charles J. (d 1908 [87]) critic BE*, WWT/14*

DUNROBIN, L. Race [Lionel Claude Race Procter] Madagascan/English? actor GRB/1-4

DUNSANY, Lord [Edward John Moreton Drax Plunkett] (1878-1957) Irish dramatist AAS, COC, ES, HP, MD, MH, MWD, NTH, OC/1-3, RE, WWT/1-11, WWW/5

DUNSTALL, John (1717-78) actor, singer BD, CDP, DD

DUNSTALL, Mrs. John [Mary] (d 1758) actress, singer BD

DUNSTALL, Mary see Dunstall, Mrs. John

DUNSTER, Charles (fl 1785) translator CP/3, DD

DUNSTONE, Mrs. (fl 1735) actress BD

DUNTHORNE, Henry (d 1883) singer EA/84*

DUNVILLE, Mrs. Fred see Rehan, Meg

DUNVILLE, T. E. [T. E. Wallon] (c. 1870-1924) English music-hall performer CDP, COC, OC/1-3

"DUODECIMO" see Dodd, James William

DU PAIN, [Mlle. ?] (fl 1789) dancer BD

DU PARK, Miss (fl 1800) harpist BD

DUPEE, William (fl 1794) music porter BD

DU PERIER, François du Mouriez (c. 1650-1723) French manager, actor BD

DUPIN, Mons. (fl 1661-63) actor BD

DUPLAISIR, Lewis see Duplessis, Lewis

DUPLANY, Claude Marius see Marius, Claude

DUPLESSEY, Lewis see Duplessis, Lewis

DUPLESSIS, Lewis (fl 1724-76?) dancer BD

DUPLISSY, Lewis see Duplessis, Lewis

DUPONT, Charlotte Louise (b 1791) French actress CDP

DU PONT, Paul (d 1957 [51]) American costume designer BE*, BP/41*

DUPORT, Miss (fl 1770) singer BD

DUPORT, Jean Pierre (1741-1818) French violoncellist, composer BD

DUPRATO, Jules (d 1892 [65]) composer EA/93*

DUPRE, Mons. (fl 1679-1705) lutenist BD

DUPRE, Mons. (fl 1715-1717) dancer BD

DUPRE, Mons. (d c. 1735) dancer, choreographer BD

DUPRE, Mr. (fl 1754) singer BD

DUPRE, Mme. (fl 1735-55) dancer? BD

DUPRE, Eléonore [Caroline?] (fl 1776-87) dancer BD

DUPRE, James (fl 1725-51) dancer BD

DUPRE, Louis (c. 1690/95-c. 1774) French dancer, choreographer ES

DUPREE, Miss (fl 1797) harpist BD

DUPREE, Josie see Zanfretta, Josephine

DUPREE, Minnie (1873/75-1947) American actress GRB/3-4, SR, TW/1-3, WWM, WWS, WWT/1-10

DUPRES, Mr. (fl 1761) dancer BD

DUPRET, Mr. (fl 1800) choreographer BD

DUPREZ, Mr. (fl 1776-82) dancer BD

DUPREZ, Charles H. minstrel manager HAS

DUPREZ, Fred (1884-1938) American actor WWT/4-8

DUPREZ, John Louis Philippe (d 1899 [54]) illusionist EA/00*

DUPREZ, June (b 1918) English actress ES, TW/3, WWT/11

DUPREZ, Louis Gilbert (1806-96) singer CDP

DUPREZ, May Moore (d 1946 [57]) music-hall performer BE*, WWT/14*

DUPREZ-VANDEN HEUVEL, Mme. (d 1876) singer EA/76*

DUPUIS, Mons. (fl 1757-59) dancer BD

DUPUIS, Mr. (fl 1797-1800) watchman BD

DUPUIS, Adolphe (d 1891 [67]) actor BE*, WWT/14*

DUPUIS, Charles (fl 1794-1804)
organist, singer? BD
DUPUIS, Thomas Sanders (1733-
96) English organist, com-
poser BD
DUPUIS, Thomas Skelton (fl
1789) dramatist CP/3
DUPUY, Louis T. see Leyton,
Edgar
DU QUA, Mrs. (fl 1697) actress
BD
DUQUESNE, Edmond [Edmond
Lockard] (b 1855) French actor
GRB/4, WWT/1-3
DUQUESNEY, Mons. (fl 1784-86)
dancer BD
DUQUESNEY, Jacques Alexandre
(fl 1756?-91) dancer BD
DUQUETTE, Tony (b 1918) Amer-
ican designer BE
DURANCI, Mr. (d 1793) actor,
swordsman? BD
DURANCY, Mons. [Jean-Fran-
çois Fienzal] (fl 1746-66)
actor BD
DURANCY, Mme. [Mme. Jean-
François Fienzal; née Fran-
çoise-Marie Dessuslefour]
(fl 1746-62) actress BD
DURAND, Mlle. (fl 1791) dancer
BD
DURAND, Charles [Isaac Charles
Bingley] (1827-1904) singer,
manager DD
DURAND, Charles [né Spring-
meyer] (b 1912) American
stage manager, director, actor
BE
DURAND, Edouard (d 1926 [55])
French actor BE*, BP/11*
DURAND, Rosalie [née Durang]
(1829-66) American singer,
actress CDP, HAS
DURANDEAU, Augustus E. (d
1893) songwriter EA/94*
DURANG, Augustus F. (b 1800)
American actor HAS, SR
DURANG, Caroline (fl 1785)
dancer ES
DURANG, Catharine American
actress HAS, SR
DURANG, Charles (b 1794)
American actor, stage mana-
ger, prompter, ballet master
ES, HAS
DURANG, Charles (1796-1870)
historian BE*
DURANG, Mrs. Charles [née

Mary White] (b 1802) English
actress ES, HAS
DURANG, Charlotte (1803-24)
American actress ES, HAS,
SR
DURANG, Mrs. F. [née Plane]
actress HAS
DURANG, Ferdinand (1796-1831)
American actor CDP, HAS,
SR
DURANG, John (1786-1822) Amer-
ican dancer ES, HAS, SR
DURANG, Juliet Catharine see
Godey, Mrs.
DURANG, Mary (fl c. 1812) dancer
ES
DURANG, Richard F. (1796-1831)
American actor SR
DURANG, Rosalie see Durand,
Rosalie
DURANT, Marie [Mrs. Craston]
(d 1900) actress EA/01*
DURANTE, Jimmy (b 1893) Amer-
ican actor, singer BE, CB,
SR, WWT/9-11
DURAS, Marguerite [née Donna-
dieu] (b 1914) French dramatist
COC, MWD, WWT/15-16
DURASTANTI, Margherita [Signora
Casimiro Avelloni] (b c. 1685)
Italian singer BD
DURBIN, Maud [Mrs. Otis Skinner]
(d 1936 [66]) American actress
BE*, BP/21*, WWT/14*
DURBRIDGE, Mr. (fl 1783-85)
box & lobby keeper BD
DU REE, Meurisse (d 1970 [37])
producer/director/choreographer
BP/55*
DURET, Marie (d 1881) actress
CDP, DD, HAS
DUREVIDGE, J. E. (1813-61)
American actor, dramatist SR
D'URFEY, Thomas (1653-1723)
English dramatist, lyricist,
singer, composer, actor? BD,
CDP, COC, CP/1-3, DD,
DNB, ES, GT, HP, NTH, OC/
1-3
DURGIN, Cyrus W. (1907-62)
American critic, editor BE*,
BP/47*
DURHAM, Mr. (fl 1714) actor
BD
DURHAM, Miss (fl 1757-58) dancer
BD
DURHAM, Edward P. (b 1881)
English actor GRB/1

DURHAM, Richard (d 1969 [80])
composer/lyricist BP/54*
DURIE, Mrs. [neé Hanna] (fl
1827) actress HAS
DURIEUX, Tilla (d 1971 [90])
German actress TW/27
DURIUSSEL, Mons. (fl 1828)
French dancer HAS
DURIVAGE, Francis Alexander
(1814-81) American dramatist
DAB
DURIVAGE, John (d 1869) actor
HAS
DURIVAGE, O. E. American
dramatist, actor HAS
DURKIN, James (1876-1934)
Canadian actor WWM
DURLAND, Sig. (d 1916 [82])
proprietor, caterer EA/17*
DURNING, Charles (b 1933)
American actor TW/24-28,
30
DURRANT, John Rowland (d 1853)
founder of Garrick Club EA/
72*
DURRAVAN, Malachy (fl 1772-
83) actor BD
DURRELL, Lawrence (b 1912)
English dramatist CD, MD,
MWD
DURRELL, Michael actor TW/
24-25, 29-30
DÜRRENMATT, Friedrich (b
1921) Swiss dramatist BE,
CB, COC, MH, MWD, OC/3,
WWT/14-16
DURRIVAGE, John E. (1813-
61) American actor HAS
DURSTON, Zoe singer CDP
DURU, Alfred (d 1889 [60])
dramatist BE*, WWT/14*
DU RUEL, Mons. (fl 1703-06)
dancer BD
DU RUEL, Mme. (fl 1704-06)
dancer BD
DURUSET, Mr. (b 1776) English
actor BS
DURUSET, John (1796-1843)
singer CDP, DD
DURYEA, Dan (1907-68) Amer-
ican actor ES, TW/25,
WWA/5
DURYEA, George (b 1904) Amer-
ican actor ES
DURYEA, May (d 1949 [80])
actress TW/6
DURYEA, Mrs. Peter see
Allen, Viola

DUSCHNITZ, Marco (1827-87)
Hungarian singer NYM
DUSE, Eleonora (1859-1924) Italian
actress COC, ES, GRB/1-4,
NTH, OC/1-3, SR, WWA/4,
WWM, WWS, WWT/1-4
DUSER, Mons. (fl 1775?-90?)
clown, tumbler BD
DUSONI, George (d 1895 [70])
animal trainer EA/96*
DU SOUCHET, H. A. (1852-1922)
American dramatist DD, GRB/
2-4, SR, WWM, WWT/1-4
DUSSAULT, Nancy (b 1936) Amer-
ican singer, actress BE, TW/
17-23, 27, 29, WWT/15-16
D'USSEAU, Arnaud (b 1916) Amer-
ican dramatist BE, CB, ES,
WWT/10-14
DUSSEAU, Joanne (b 1942) Amer-
ican actress TW/27
DUSSEK, Jan Ladislav (1760-1812)
Bohemian musician, composer
BD, ES
DUSSEK, Mrs. Jan Ladislav [neé
Sophia Giustina Corri; Mrs.
John Alvis Moralt] (1775-c.
1830) Scottish singer, harpist,
pianist, composer BD, DNB,
ES
DUTAC, Mons. (fl 1724-25) actor
BD
DU TERREAUX, Louis Henry
(1841-78) dramatist DD
DUTFIELD, William Rochez (d
1905 [70]) EA/06*
DUTNALL, Martin (d 1867 [29])
pantomime writer EA/68*
DUTTON, Mr. (fl 1730) actor BD
DUTTON, Mrs. (fl 1730) actress
BD
DUTTON, Alice (b 1851) American
pianist HAS
DUTTON, Dolie dwarf CDP
DUTTON, Edward (fl 1597-1600)
actor DA
DUTTON, Frederick (fl 1768-85)
actor BD
DUTTON, John (fl 1575-91) actor
DA
DUTTON, Lawrence (fl 1561-92)
actor DA
DUTTON, Thomas (fl c. 1799)
dramatist CP/3
DUTTON, Thomas (d 1893 [67])
managing director EA/94*
DUVAL, Mr. (fl 1742) dancer BD
DUVAL, Mr. (fl 1764-67) dancer

BD
DUVAL, Mme. (fl 1741-45)
dancer BD
DUVAL, Mlle. (fl 1740-44)
dancer BD
DU VAL, Charles (d 1889)
monologuist EA/90*
DU VAL, Charles H. composer,
mimic, singer CDP
DUVAL, Charles Henry see
Scholes, Charles Henry
DUVAL, Clifton gymnast CDP
DUVAL, Elizabeth (d 1904)
EA/05*
DUVAL, Eugene gymnast CDP
DUVAL, Frederick James (d
1913 [27]) EA/14*
DUVAL, Georges (d 1919 [72])
dramatist BE*, WWT/14*
DUVAL, Heaton (d 1888) ventrilo-
quist EA/89*
DUVAL. Livingston gymnast
CDP
DuVAL, John (fl 1730) dancer
BD
DUVAL, Marie Nina de Harven
see Stella, Nina
DuVAL, Paul (d 1900 [53]) actor
EA/01*
DUVARD, Mrs. Primogene (d
1877 [53]) dramatist EA/78*
DUVERNAY, C. B. (d 1873)
EA/74*
DUVERNAY, Pauline Yolande
Marie Louise [Mrs. Lyne
Stephens] (1813-94) dancer
CDP
DUX, Emilienne (b 1874) French
actress WWT/2-3
DUXBURY, Elspeth (1909-67)
Indian/English actress WWT/
8-10
DVONCH, Frederick (b 1914)
American conductor, musical
director BE
DWIGHT, Mrs. (d 1892) EA/93*
DWIGHT, Christine (d 1889)
music-hall performer EA/90*
DWIGHT, Henry Charles (d
1889 [60]) proprietor EA/90*
DWIGHT, Henry James (d 1875
[27]) Negro artist EA/76*
DWIGHT, Mrs. J. see St.
John, Miss J.
DWIGHT, James (d 1892) EA/93*
DWIGHT, John (d 1903 [40])
comic acrobat EA/04*
DWIGHT, Ogden G. (d 1970 [55])

critic BP/55*
DWORSHAK, Mr. (fl 1791) musi-
cian BD
DWYER, Mr. (d 1817) actor CDP,
DD, TD/2
DWYER, Ada [Mrs. Harold Rus-
sell] (d 1952 [89]) American
actress GRB/3-4, TW/9,
WWM, WWS, WWT/1-6
DWYER, Frank (b 1945) American
actor TW/29-30
DWYER, James (d 1888 [60])
EA/89*
DWYER, Jimmy (d 1965 [72]) per-
former BP/50*
DWYER, John Hambury (d 1843)
Irish singer, actor CDP, HAS
DWYER, Leslie (b 1906) English
actor WWT/11-15
DWYER, Michael (d 1926 [72])
actor, singer DD
DWYER, P. W. dramatist CP/3,
DD
DWYER, Tim (d 1903 [42]) actor
EA/04*
DYALL, Franklin (1874-1950)
English actor, producer ES,
GRB/2-4, WWT/1-10, WWW/4
DYALL, Valentine (b 1908) English
actor WWT/11-16
DYAS, Ada (1843-1908) English
actress CDP, DD, GRB/4,
OAA/2, WWA/4
DYAS, Ann Ada [Mrs. E. Dyas]
(d 1871 [48]) EA/72*, WWT/
14*
DYAS, Mrs. E. see Dyas, Ann
Ada
DYAS, Edward (1815-77) actor
DD
DYBAS, James (b 1944) American
actor TW/21-22, 24-25, 29
DYBLE, Richard (fl 1672) musi-
cian BD
DYCE, Rev. Alexander (1798-1869)
editor, critic DD
DYCKE, Marjorie L. [née Platt]
(b 1916) American educator
BE
DYE, Carol Finch (d 1962 [31])
American actress BE*
DYELL, Mr. (fl 1776) actor BD
DYER, Mr. (fl 1716?-20?) singer
BD
DYER, Mr. (fl 1732-34) actor BD
DYER, Mr. (fl c. 1752) actor
TD/1
DYER, Mrs. (fl 1692-93) singer

BD
DYER, Mrs. (fl 1733-34) actress
BD
DYER, Arthur Edwin (d 1902
[58]) composer, musician
EA/03*
DYER, [Benjamin? John?] (fl
1675) dancer BD
DYER, Charles Raymond (b 1928)
English dramatist, actor,
director AAS, BE, CD, CH,
WWT/14-16
DYER, Deb (d 1973 [69]) per-
former BP/57*
DYER, Edward (fl 1672-86) vio-
linist, composer BD
DYER, Harriet see Chambers,
Harriet
DYER, James (fl 1770) dancer
BD
DYER, Jane (d 1881 [82]) actress
EA/82*
DYER, Lizzie [Mrs. Peter Cock-
burn] (d 1906) singer EA/07*
DYER, Michael (d 1774) actor,
singer BD
DYER, Mrs. Michael [née Harriet
Bullock] (b 1721?) actress,
dancer BD
DYER, Robert (fl 1833) writer
DD
DYER, Teddy (d 1912 [67])
gymnast EA/13*
DYER, William (fl 1726?-39)
musician BD
DYETT, Walter Fairman (b 1873)
American actor WWS
DYKE, Mr. (fl c. 1661-62) actor
BD
DYKE, Mr. (fl 1754) bassoonist
BD
DYKE, Mr. (fl 1819) actor HAS
DYKE, John (fl 1789?-1814?)
actor, singer, dancer BD
DYKE, Mary Ann see Duff,
Mary Ann
DYKE, Winifred Hart English
actress, dancer GRB/1-4
DYKES, Mr. (fl 1710-25) box
keeper BD
"DYKWYNKYN". see Keene,
Richard Wynne
DYMOCK (fl c. 1602-c. 33) trans-
lator CP/3
DYMOV, Ossip (1878-1959) Rus-
sian dramatist COC, MWD
DYNE, John (d 1788) singer,
composer BD

DYNE, Richard (fl c. 1760-76)
singer BD
DYNELEY, Peter English actor
TW/9
DYOTT, John (d 1876) Irish actor
CDP, DD, HAS
DYOTT, Mrs. John (d 1876) ac-
tress HAS
DYRENFORTH, James (d 1973)
American actor, dramatist
WWT/6-8
DYSART, Florence (fl 1886-91)
actress, singer DD
DYSART, Richard A. actor WWT/
16
DYSON, Sir George (d 1964 [81])
composer/lyricist BP/49*
DYSON, Joshua (d 1910 [58]) per-
former? EA/11*
DYSON, Laura (d 1950 [80]) ac-
tress BE*, WWT/14*

- E -

EACHARD, Lawrence see Echard,
Lawrence
EADEN, Henry (d 1880) actor
EA/81*
EADES, Dr. Richard (1571-1604)
English dramatist FGF
EADIE, Dennis (1869/75-1928)
Scottish actor, manager ES,
WWT/1-5, WWW/2
EAGAN, Louis (d 1919) American?
actor, stage manager SR
EAGELS, Jeanne (1894-1929) Amer-
ican actress DAB, ES, NTH,
SR, WWA/1, WWT/4-6
EAGER, Edward (d 1964 [53])
composer/lyricist BP/49*
EAGER, Helen (d 1952) American
critic WWA/3
EAGER, Johnny (d 1963 [38]) per-
former BP/48*
EAGLE, George Barnardo (d 1858
[41]) "Wizard of the South"
EA/72*
EAGLE, Jeff (b 1947) American
actor TW/28
EAGLESFIELD, Tom (d 1874)
music-hall performer? EA/76*
EAGLESON, Thomas Wallace see
Keene, Thomas Wallace
EAGON, Joel (b 1941) American
actor TW/29
EAKER, Ira (b 1922) American
publisher BE

EAMES, Clare (1896-1930)
American actress ES, WWT/
5-6

EAMES, Emma [Mrs. Julian
Story] (1867-1949) American
singer ES, GRB/1, SR,
WWA/3

EAMES, Ethelbert Richard (d
1897 [22]) singer EA/98*

EARDLEY-WILMOT, May (d
1970 [86]) composer/lyricist
BP/55*

EARL, Donna (d 1965 [63])
performer BP/50*

EARL, Josephine (d 1972) pro-
ducer/director/choreographer
BP/56*

EARLE [Richard Williams] (d
1906) musician EA/08*

EARLE, Clara [Mrs. George
Howard] English actress
GRB/1

EARLE, Edward Canadian actor
ES

EARLE, Evalyn [née Emerson]
American actress WWA/5

EARLE, Fred actor, singer
CDP

EARLE, J. (d 1917 [19]) EA/18*

EARLE, Jackson (d 1971 [69])
performer BP/55*

EARLE, John (fl 1640) actor
DA

EARLE, Lilias [Mrs. Nevill
Graham] (d 1935 [62]) English
actress GRB/1

EARLE, Mattie actress CDP

EARLE, Mrs. Robert see
Johnstone, Clara

EARLE, Virginia (1875-1937)
American actress, singer
GRB/2-4, SR, WWS, WWT/
1-5

EARLE, William, Jr. (fl 1799)
dramatist CP/3

EARLESMERE, Florence Helena
see Evers, Adeline

EARNFRED, Thomas (b 1915)
American press representative
BE

EASON, Myles (b 1915) Australian
actor WWT/11-16

EAST, Mr. (d 1880) Negro performer EA/81*

EAST, Charles A. (d 1914 [51])
actor, producer WWT/14*

EAST, James Gully (d 1900 [37])
actor EA/01*, WWT/14*

EAST, John M. (d 1924 [63]) actor
BE*, WWT/14*

EAST, Joseph Samuel (d 1896)
singer EA/97*

EAST, Patrick (d 1969 [48]) agent,
publicist BP/54*

EASTCOTT, Mrs. (fl 1848?) singer
CDP

EASTLAKE, Mary (d 1911 [55])
actress DD, DP

EASTLAKE, Wallace (d 1909 [35])
actor EA/10*

EASTMAN, Barrett (1869-1910)
American critic WWA/1

EASTMAN, Carl (d 1970 [61/62])
press agent TW/26

EASTMAN, Frederick (1859-1920)
English actor GRB/2-4, WWT/
1-3

EASTMAN, Helen (fl 1864) American actress HAS

EASTMAN, Jimmy (d 1904 [19])
acrobat EA/05*

EASTMAN, Joan (d 1969 [32])
performer BP/54*

EASTON, Edward (b 1942) American actor TW/23, 28-29

EASTON, Florence (1884-1955)
English singer ES, TW/12

EASTON, Richard (b 1933) Canadian actor AAS, BE, TW/24-
25, 28, WWT/14-16

EASTWOOD, F. (d 1909 [34])
musical director EA/10*

EASTWOOD, Irene Frances see
Ziegler, Anne

EASTWOOD, Lillian (d 1917)
EA/18*

EATON, Miss (fl 1837) actress
HAS

EATON, Charles (d 1903 [45])
actor EA/04*

EATON, Charles Henry (1813-43)
American actor CDP, HAS,
SR, WWA/H

EATON, Dorothy actress TW/3

EATON, Edwin (d 1890) EA/91*

EATON, Jack (d 1903 [24]) actor?
singer? EA/04*

EATON, Mary (1902-48) American
actress, singer, dancer SR,
TW/5, WWT/6-8

EATON, N. W. (fl 1809?) American? dramatist EAP

EATON, Sally (b 1947) American
actress TW/27

EATON, Thomas Davis see
Vose, Val

EATON, Wallas (b 1917) English actor WWT/11-16
EATON, Walter Prichard (1878-1957) American critic ES, WWT/10-12
EATON, Will D. (fl 1878-97) American dramatist SR
EATON, William (fl 1622) actor DA
EAVES, George (d 1899) proprietor EA/90*
EAVES, Hilary (b 1914) English actress WWT/9-10
EBB, Fred (b 1933) American lyricist CD, WWT/15-16
EBERG, Victor (d 1972 [47]) performer BP/56*
EBERHART, Constance American singer BE
EBERHART, Richard (b 1904) American dramatist, educator BE
EBERLE, Annie see Sefton, Mrs. Joseph
EBERLE, Charles (d 1840) American actor HAS
EBERLE, David (1804-64) American actor HAS
EBERLE, Eliza see Calladine, Eliza
EBERLE, Elizabeth see Kent, Mrs. William
EBERLE, Eugene A. (1840-1917) American actor WWS
EBERLE, Henry (d 1842) American actor HAS
EBERLE, Mrs. Henry (fl 1840) actress HAS
EBERLE, Robert M. (1840-1912) American actor, manager SR
EBERLE, Sophia see La Forrest, Mrs.
EBERS, John (1785?-1830?) English manager DNB
EBERT, Joyce [née Womack] (b 1933) American actress BE, TW/28, WWT/16
EBI, Earl (d 1973 [69]) producer/director/choreographer BP/57*
EBOR, Little see Silbon, Fred
EBSEN, Buddy actor TW/2-3
EBSWORTH, Joseph (1788-1868) dramatist DD
EBSWORTH, Mrs. Joseph see Ebsworth, Mary Emma
EBSWORTH, Mary Emma [Mrs. Joseph Ebsworth] (1794-1881)

English dramatist DD, DNB
EBURNE, Margaret see Eburne, Mrs. W[illiam?] H[awthorne?]
EBURNE, Maude (d 1960 [85]) actress TW/17
EBURNE, William Hawthorne (d 1874) actor EA/75*, WWT/14*
EBURNE, Mrs. W[illiam?] H[awthorne?] (d 1903 [73]) actress WWT/14*
ECCLES, Ambrose (d 1809) Irish dramatist, scholar CP/3, DD, DNB
ECCLES, Donald (b 1908) English actor WWT/12-16
ECCLES, Janet (1895-1966) English actress TW/13, WWT/6-8
ECCLES, John (c. 1668-1735) English composer DD, DNB, ES
ECCLES, Joseph Bruce (d 1882 [37]) scene artist EA/83*
ECCLESHALL, James (d 1875 [37]) stage manager EA/76*
ECCLESTON, William (fl 1625/52?) English actor DA, DNB, ES, GT, NTH, OC/1-3
ECCLESTONE, Edward (fl 1679) dramatist CP/1-3, GT
ECHARD, Lawrence (1671-1730) English dramatist CP/1-3, DD, GT
ECHEGARAY, José (1832/33-1916) Spanish dramatist COC, GRB/1-4, NTH, OC/1-3, WWT/1
ECKART, Jean [née Jean Levy] (b 1921) American designer, producer BE, ES, WWT/12-16
ECKART, William Joseph (b 1920) American designer, producer BE, ES, WWT/12-16
ECKER, I. Elmer (d 1975 [77]) lawyer BP/60*
ECKERLIN, Fanny actress CDP
ECKERT, George (b 1927) American stage manager, director BE
ECKERT, Johanna see Holm, Hanya
ECKERT, Karl Anton Florian (1820-79) composer CDP
ECKLES, Robert (d 1975 [55]) performer BP/60*
ECKSTEIN, Louis (d 1935 [70]) American patron BP/20*
ECKSTEIN, Maxwell (d 1974 [69]) composer/lyricist BP/58*
eda-YOUNG, Barbara (b 1945) American actress TW/26, 28-30

EDDIE, El Nino (b 1855) American rope dancer HAS

EDDINGER, Wallace (1881-1929) American actor WWA/1, WWM, WWT/2-5

EDDINGTON, Paul (b 1927) English actor WWT/14-16

EDDISON, Robert (b 1908) Japanese/English actor AAS, ES, WWT/9-16

EDDLEMAN, Jack (b 1933) American actor TW/22

EDDOWES, Geraldine see Allestree, Mary

EDDY, Edward (1822-75) American actor CDP, COC, HAS, OC/1-3, SR

EDDY, Jim (d 1975 [50]) publicist BP/60*

EDDY, Nelson (1901-67) American actor, singer CB, ES, SR, WWA/4, WWT/9-10

EDE, Mr. actor CDP

EDE, George (b 1931) American actor TW/29-30

EDELMAN, Louis F. (d 1976 [75]) producer/director/choreographer BP/60*

EDELSTEIN, Gertrude see Berg, Gertrude

EDELSTEIN, Ray (b 1937) American actor TW/27-29

EDELSTEIN, Rose (d 1969) production manager BP/54*

EDELSTEN, Mrs. E. H. see Edelsten, Eliza

EDELSTEN, Eliza [Mrs. E. H. Edelsten] (d 1897) EA/98*

EDEN, Guy E. Morton (d 1954) dramatist WWW/5

EDEN, Tony (b 1927) American actress TW/1-3, 5

EDENS, Roger (d 1970 [64]) producer/director/choreographer BP/55*

EDESON, Robert (1868-1931) American actor COC, DAB, GRB/2-4, OC/1-3, SR, WWA/1, WWM, WWS, WWT/1-6

EDESON, Mrs. Robert see Berg, Ellen

EDGAR, Alfred (d 1881) EA/82*

EDGAR, Alice [Mrs. J. Thorp] (d 1907) actress EA/08*

EDGAR, Alice see Marriott, Alice

EDGAR, Charles (d 1905 [44]) music-hall comedian EA/06*

EDGAR, David (b 1948) English dramatist CD

EDGAR, Edward Fisher (d 1884 [56]) actor, manager, lessee CDP, DD, OAA/2

EDGAR, Mrs. Edward Fisher see Edgar, Eliza

EDGAR, Eliza [Mrs. Edward Fisher Edgar] (d 1901 [87]) EA/02*

EDGAR, George [né Biddle] (d 1899 [68]) actor CDP

EDGAR, Howard Tripp (d 1927) English actor GRB/1

EDGAR, John W. (d 1909 [67]) music-hall manager EA/10*

EDGAR, Marriott (1880-1951) Scottish actor, dramatist WWT/8-10

EDGAR, Maud (d 1890 [21]) EA/91*

EDGAR, Mrs. R. see Marriott, Alice

EDGAR, Mrs. Richard [Jennie Taylor] (d 1937 [81]) actress BE*, WWT/14*

EDGAR, Richard Horatio (1848-94) actor, manager DD

EDGAR, Robert (d 1870) manager, lessee DD

EDGAR, Stuart (d 1903) actor EA/04*

EDGAR, Thomas (d 1874 [62]) musician EA/75*

EDGARTON, Mrs. Warren see Daly, Julia

EDGCUMBE, Richard (1764-1839) English composer, writer DNB, ES

EDGE, Mrs. T. A. see Tuplin, Lily

EDGETT, Edwin Francis (1867-1946) American historian, critic WWT/9

EDGEWORTH, Jane (b 1922) English actress, administrator WWT/14-16

EDGINTON, May (1883-1957) dramatist WWT/5-11

EDISON, Thomas Alva (1847-1931) American lighting designer BE*

EDISS, Connie (1871/77-1934) English actress CDP, ES, GRB/1-4, WWM, WWS, WWT/1-7

EDLIN, Tubby [Henry] (b 1882) English actor WWT/5-7

EDLOE (b 1943) American ac-
tress TW/26, 29
EDMEAD, Miss (fl 1795) drama-
tist CP/3
EDMISTON, Miss (b 1801) Irish
actress BS, CDP
EDMONDS, Mrs. see Yeomans,
Mrs. Thomas
EDMONDS, Charles (fl 1855-65)
Irish actor HAS
EDMONDS, Mrs. Charles (fl
1852-68) Canadian actress
HAS
EDMONDS, Connie [Priscilla
Mary Grant] (d 1897 [29])
actress EA/98*
EDMONDS, E. (d 1907 [70])
stage manager EA/08*
EDMONDS, Emma (fl 1854)
singer? HAS
EDMONDS, Georgie (d 1883
[27]) singer EA/84*
EDMONDS, Mrs. H. [Mrs. J.
Edmonds] (d 1890) EA/92*
EDMONDS, Mrs. J. see Ed-
monds, Mrs. H.
EDMONDS, James (d 1871 [66])
menagerie proprietor EA/73*
EDMONDS, Mrs. Joe see
Robina, Lilian
EDMONDS, John (d 1634?) actor
DA
EDMONDS, Lily (d 1902 [17])
EA/03*
EDMONDS, Louis (b 1923) Amer-
ican actor TW/13-19, 25, 30
EDMONDS, Mitchell (b 1940)
American actor TW/25, 29
EDMONDS, T. W. [Thomas Ed-
mond Wharton] (d 1874)
prompter EA/75*
EDMONDSON, Edward E. (d
1976 [65]) performer BP/60*
EDMONSTON, R. S. (d 1917)
EA/18*
EDMONSTON, W. S. (d 1917)
EA/18*
EDMUNDA, Prof. (d 1904)
ventriloquist EA/05*
EDMUNDS, Edmund (d 1872)
comedian EA/73*
EDMUNDS, Mrs. Edmund see
Macready, Caroline
EDMUNDS, Lydia (d 1889) EA/
90*
EDMUNDS-HEMINGWAY, Clara
(1878-1958) American singer,
composer, dramatist WWA/3

EDNEY, Florence (1879-1950)
English actress TW/2-3, 7,
WWT/8-10
EDOUARD, Louis (d 1887 [43])
scene artist EA/88*
EDOUIN, May (d 1944) actress
BE*, WWT/14*
EDOUIN, Rose (1844-1925) English
actress WWT/4-5
EDOUIN, Willie [William Frederick
Bryer] (1841/46-1908) English
actor, manager, dramatist
CDP, COC, DD, DNB, DP,
GRB/1-4, OC/1-3
EDOUIN, Mrs. Willie see
Atherton, Alice
EDRIAN, Fanny [née Parks] (d
1867) actress HAS
EDROFF, William (d 1870) musi-
cal director EA/71*
EDSON, Calvin ["The Living
Skeleton"] (1789-1833) American
freak HAS
EDSON, Elie (d 1971 [89]) publi-
cist BP/56*
EDSON, Marjory (b 1943) Ameri-
can actress TW/26
EDSTROM, Katherine (d 1973 [72])
performer BP/58*
EDVINA, Marie Louise Lucienne
Juliette (1885?-1948) Canadian
singer ES, WWW/4
EDWARD, Georgiana see
Pauncefort, Mrs. George
EDWARD, John (d 1882 [76])
actor? EA/83*
EDWARDES, Conway Theodore
Marriott (d 1880) dramatist DD
EDWARDES, Mjr. D'Arcy (d 1916)
EA/17*
EDWARDES, Felix (d 1954 [83])
English producer WWT/6-11
EDWARDES, George (1852-1915)
English manager COC, ES,
GRB/1-4, OC/1-3, PDT, WWS,
WWT/1-3, WWW/1
EDWARDES, George D'Arcy (d
1917) EA/18*
EDWARDES, Olga (b 1917) South
African actress WWT/11-13
EDWARDES, Paula (b 1878) Amer-
ican actress, singer GRB/2-4,
WWS, WWT/1-5
EDWARDES, Richard (c. 1523-66)
English dramatist DD, FGF
EDWARDS, Mrs. (fl 1780-89)
actress CDP, TD/1-2
EDWARDS, Miss (fl 1781) drama-

tist CP/3

EDWARDS, A. C. (b 1909) American educator, publisher BE

EDWARDS, Alan (d 1954 [61]) actor TW/10

EDWARDS, Arthur (d 1910) singer? EA/11*

EDWARDS, Ben [né George Benjamin] (b 1916) American designer BE, WWT/15-16

EDWARDS, Bessie see Cowdery, Mrs.

EDWARDS, Bruce (d 1927 [54]) Scottish manager BE*, BP/11*

EDWARDS, Clara (d 1974 [95]) composer/lyricist BP/58*

EDWARDS, Cliff (d 1971 [76]) actor, singer, vaudevillian TW/28

EDWARDS, Darrell Darwin (d 1975 [56]) composer/lyricist BP/60*

EDWARDS, David (d 1900) music-hall comedian EA/01*

EDWARDS, Emily Frances [Mrs. George Edwards] (d 1885) EA/87*

EDWARDS, E. W. (fl 1854) actor HAS

EDWARDS, Fanny actress CDP

EDWARDS, Fred (b 1860) English actor, stage manager WWS

EDWARDS, George actor? CDP

EDWARDS, Mrs. George see Drake, Julia

EDWARDS, Mrs. George see Edwards, Emily Frances

EDWARDS, George Henry (d 1908 [81]) actor EA/09*

EDWARDS, G. Spencer (d 1916 [79]) English critic CDP, DD, GRB/1-4, WWT/1-3

EDWARDS, Gus (1881?-1945) German/American actor, producer, songwriter CB, NTH, SR, TW/2

EDWARDS, Harry (d 1891 [66]) actor EA/92*

EDWARDS, Harry (d 1917) stage manager EA/18*

EDWARDS, Harry D. (d 1969 [82]) producer/director/choreographer BP/54*

EDWARDS, Henry (1824/30-91) English actor, manager CDP, HAS

EDWARDS, Henry (1882/83-1952) English actor, dramatist, manager ES, WWT/6-11

EDWARDS, Henry Sutherland (1829-1906) English writer, dramatist DD, ES

EDWARDS, Hilton (b 1903) English actor, producer, director COC, ES, OC/3, TW/4-7, WWT/8-16

EDWARDS, James (d 1970 [48]) actor TW/26

EDWARDS, James see Carter-Edwards, James

EDWARDS, J. Gordon (d 1925) Canadian actor, director ES

EDWARDS, Joan (b 1919) American singer, songwriter CB

EDWARDS, John actor, singer TD/2

EDWARDS, John (fl 1808) Irish dramatist CP/3

EDWARDS, John (d 1911 [67]) actor EA/12*

EDWARDS, J. P. see Swinburne, John

EDWARDS, Julia (d 1976 [93]) performer BP/60*

EDWARDS, Julian (1855-1910) English composer, actor, manager DAB, DD, ES, GRB/2-4, SR, WWS

EDWARDS, Margaret (d 1891 [69]) actress? EA/92*

EDWARDS, Nate (d 1972 [70]) producing manager BP/57*

EDWARDS, Neely (d 1965 [82]) performer BP/50*

EDWARDS, Osman (1864-1936) English critic, translator DD, GRB/2-4, WWT/1-6

EDWARDS, P. H. (fl 1808) dramatist CP/3

EDWARDS, Richard (1523-66) English dramatist, master of the Chapel Royal CP/1-3, DA, DNB, ES, HP

EDWARDS, Richard (d 1604 [81]) dramatist BE*, WWT/14*

EDWARDS, Ronnie Claire (b 1933) American actor TW/27-29

EDWARDS, Sarah (d 1965 [82]) performer BP/49*

EDWARDS, Sarah Ann (d 1870) EA/71*

EDWARDS, Sherman (b 1919) American composer, lyricist AAS, WWT/15-16

EDWARDS, Susie (d 1963 [65])

performer BE*, BP/48*

EDWARDS, T. Mills see Mills, T. E.

EDWARDS, Tommy (d 1969 [47]) composer/lyricist BP/54*

EDWARDS, Prof. Vaughan (d 1891) musician EA/92*

EDWARDS, Vincent (b 1928) American actor CB

EDWARDS, Virginia [Mrs. William Hunter] (d 1964) actress, dramatist BE*

EDWARDS, Welsh [né Edward Welsh] (1832-83) actor CDP

EDWARDS, W. H. (d 1891 [59]) panoramist EA/92*

EDWARDS, Mrs. W. H. see Edwards, Sarah Anne

EDWARDS, Will actor, singer CDP

EDWARDS-MINOR, George English acting manager GRB/1-2

EDWARD THE SIXTH English dramatist CP/2-3

EDWIN, Mr. (d 1842) English actor HAS

EDWIN, Benjamin W. [né Huggins] (b 1794) English actor CDP, OX

EDWIN, Elizabeth Rebecca [Elizabeth Rebecca Richards] (c. 1771-1854) English actress CDP, DD, DNB, OC/1-3, OX, TD/1-2

EDWIN, Grace English actress GRB/1

EDWIN, J. H. [De Vere Hayes] (b 1878) Irish actor GRB/1

EDWIN, John, the Elder (1749-90) English actor CDP, COC, DD, DNB, ES, GT, OC/1-3, TD/1-2

EDWIN, Mrs. John, the Elder (d 1794) actress WWT/14*

EDWIN, John, the Younger (1768-1803) English actor CDP, DD, DNB, ES, OC/1-3, TD/1-2

EDWIN, Mrs. John, the Younger (d 1805 [37]) actress WWT/14*

EDWIN, Lina (d 1883) actress, manager CDP, DD

EDWIN, Ruth (d 1909) actress EA/10*

EDWIN, Sophie (b c. 1838) Australian actress HAS

EDWIN, T. Emery (d 1951 [79]) actor BE*

EDWIN, Walter (d 1899 [61]) stage manager EA/00*

EDWIN, William (fl 1836) actor CDP

EDZARD, George (d 1885) EA/86*

EEDES, Richard (d 1604) English dramatist CP/2-3

EEKHOFF, Isaac (d 1874 [64]) musician EA/75*

EFFRAT, John (1908-65) American stage manager, producer, director, actor BE, TW/2, 21

EGAN, Catherine Ann see Achmet, Mrs.

EGAN, F. B. (1818-77) actor, manager DD

EGAN, Frank C. (d 1927 [55]) American producer BE*, BP/11*

EGAN, Jane (d 1893) EA/94*

EGAN, Jefferson (fl 1902-06) American actor, singer WWS

EGAN, Mrs. Jefferson see Britton, Lillian

EGAN, Jenny American actress TW/25

EGAN, Michael (1896-1956) Irish dramatist ES, WWT/8-12

EGAN, Miska (d 1964 [73]) actor BE*

EGAN, Pierce (1772-1849) English journalist, dramatist COC, OC/1-3

EGAN, Rose [Rose Bishop] (fl 1870s) English actress DD, OAA/2

EGAN, Mrs. Thomas W. see Gordon, Marie

EGAN, William (d 1785) actor TD/1-2

EGAN, William, the Younger (d 1822 [60]) actor WWT/14*

EGBERT, Albert (d 1942) comedian BE*, WWT/14*

EGBERT, Tom E. see Tennyck, Egbert Fairchild

EGBUNA, Obi (b 1938) Nigerian dramatist CD

EGERSON, Mrs. see Cussans, Mrs.

EGERTON, Mrs. see Ambrose, Miss

EGERTON, Daniel (1772-1835) English actor, manager BS, CDP, DD, DNB, OX, TD/1-2

EGERTON, Mrs. Daniel see Egerton, Sarah

EGERTON, Frank composer CDP

EGERTON, Frank [W. F. Hughes] (d 1905) music-hall agent & manager EA/06*

EGERTON, Mrs. Frank [Leonora Grey] (d 1887) EA/88*

EGERTON, George (d 1880) acting manager EA/81*

EGERTON, George [Mrs. R. Golding Bright] (d 1945 [86]) Australian dramatist WWT/3-7

EGERTON, Percy (d 1905 [31]) musician EA/06*

EGERTON, Sarah [née Fisher] (1782-1847) English actress BS, CDP, DD, DNB, OX

EGERTON, Mrs. Walter see Scott, Frances Emily

EGGAR, Jack (b 1904) South African manager WWT/9-10

EGGERTH, Marta (b 1912/15/16) Hungarian actress, singer BE, CB, ES, TW/2, WWT/10

EGGINGTON, Arthur Gostling see Willerby, Arthur

EGGINTON, R. (d 1917) EA/18*

EGINTON, Walter see Lilo, Toby

EGLETON, Mrs. actress CDP

EGLEVSKY, André (1917-77) Russian dancer CB

EGLI, Joseph E. (d 1974 [74]) producer/director/choreographer BP/59*

EHRENBERG, Alexandra (d 1896 [33]) musician, singer EA/97*

EHRENSPERGER, Harold (b 1897) American educator BE

EICHBERG, Julius (1824-93) German musician, composer CDP, DAB, WWA/H

EICHBERGER, Wilhelm see Esmond, Carl

EICHELBAUM, Stanley (b 1926) American critic BE

EICHELIN (fl 1604) actor DA

EICHLER, C. H. musician CDP

EIGSTI, Karl (b 1938) American designer WWT/16

EINFELD, S. Charles (d 1974 [73]) producer/director/ choreographer BP/59*

EINSTEIN, Harry (d 1958 [54]) performer BE*

EISELE, Lou (b 1912) American costume designer TW/2-5

EISEN, Max American press representative BE

EISENSTAT, Jacob (d 1975 [33]) producer/director/choreographer BP/60*

EISFELDT, Mrs. Kurt see Irwin, May

EISINGER, Irene (b 1906) Austrian actress, singer WWT/9-11

EISLER, Hanns (1898-1962) German composer CB

EISLEY, Fred (b 1925) American actor TW/12

EKHOF, Conrad (d 1778 [58]) actor WWT/14*

EKINS, John R. W. (d 1917 [18]) actor EA/18*

ELBA [Albert Edward Fenton] (d 1900 [34]) trapezist EA/01*

ELBIN, Thomas (d 1907 [64]) acrobat EA/08*

ELCAR, Dana (b 1927) American actress BE, TW/23

ELCOCK, Mary (d 1908 [53]) EA/09*

ELDEE, Lilian (d 1904 [34]) singer, dramatist WWT/14*

ELDEF, Lilian [Mrs. William Duncombe] (d 1904 [34]) actress EA/05*

ELDER, Eldon (b 1924) American designer BE, WWT/12-16

ELDER, Lonne, III (b 1931) American dramatist, actor CD, WWT/15-16

ELDERSHAW, Albert (d 1917) EA/18*

ELDERTON, Joseph (fl 1746) dramatist CP/3

ELDERTON, William (d 1592?) actor, dramatist DA, DNB, FGF

ELDON, Bob (d 1916) EA/17*

ELDRED, Arthur (d 1942 [66]) English actor GRB/3-4, WWT/1-2

ELDRED, Gill (d 1885 [72]) animal trainer, equestrian EA/86*

ELDRED, Ida (d 1918) EA/19*

ELDRED, Joseph (1843-84) English actor CDP, DD, OAA/2

ELDRED, Mrs. Joseph (d 1883) actress EA/84*

ELDRIDGE, Elaine American actress TW/27

ELDRIDGE, Florence (b 1901) American actress BE, CB, TW/3-9, 13-16, WWT/7-15

ELDRIDGE, Lillie (b 1852) American actress HAS

ELDRIDGE, Louisa [née Harwood] (d 1905 [76]) American actress DD, HAS, PP/1

ELDRIDGE, Preston W. (d 1925 [71]) American minstrel BE*, BP/10*

ELEN, Ernest Augustus see Elen, Gus

ELEN, Gus [Ernest Augustus Elen] (1862-1940) English actor CDP, COC, GRB/1-3, OC/1-3 WWS

ELEN, Mercy (d 1896 [65]) EA/97*

ELENA, Signorina (fl 1861) singer HAS

ELEY, Douglas N. (d 1911 [44]) EA/12*

ELFORD, Richard (d 1714) singer DNB

ELGAR, Avril [née Williams] (b 1932) English actress WWT/15-16

ELGAR, Sir Edward (1857-1934) English composer ES

ELGAR, Henry (d 1917 [84]) musician EA/18*

ELIAS, Ellen (b 1950) American actress TW/26

ELIAS, Hector Argentinian actor TW/28-29, WWT/16

ELIAS, Rosalind (b 1931) American singer CB

ELIC, Josip (b 1921) American actor TW/27

ELINORE, Kate [Mrs. Samuel Goldberg] (1876-1924) American actress WWM

ELINORE, May [Mrs. Robert Franckin] (fl 1912-13) American vaudevillian WWM

ELIOT, Arthur (d 1936 [62]) dramatist, producer BE*, WWT/14*

"ELIOT, George" see Cross, Marie

ELIOT, Max [Mrs. Granville Alden Ellis] (d 1911) American critic GRB/2-4

ELIOT, T[homas] S[tearns] (1888-1965) American/English dramatist AAS, BE, CB, CH, COC, ES, HJD, HP, MD, MH, MWD, NTH, OC/1-3, PDT, RE, TW/21, WWA/4, WWT/9-13, WWW/6

ELISCU, Fernanda (1878/82-1968) Rumanian actress WWM, WWT/1-11

ELISE, Mlle. (fl 1867?) dancer CDP

ELITZ, Jenny see Van Zandt, Mrs.

ELIZABETH, Mrs. see Mason, Mrs.

ELIZABETH, Queen see Queen Elizabeth I

ELIZONDO, Hector (b 1936) American actor TW/25-27, 29-30, WWT/16

ELKAN, Emil (d 1917) EA/18*

ELKINS, Edward B. see Fielding, Edward

ELKINS, Flora American actress TW/24, 30

ELKINS, Hillard (b 1929) American producer WWT/15-16

ELKINS, Marie Louise (d 1961 [71]) producer BE*

ELLA, Miss [Petronella Jensen] (b 1870) German lion tamer & trainer GRB/1

ELLA, John (1802-88) Scottish musician, musical director DNB, ES

ELLABY, J. N. (d 1895 [45]) reciter EA/96*

ELLAR, Thomas (1782-1842) harlequin CDP

ELLA ZOYARA, Miss [Olmaz or Omar Kingsley] (1830-79) American equestrian CDP, ES

ELLEN, Sany see Dorsey, Sandra

ELLERBE, Harry (b 1905) American actor, director BE, TW/1-17

ELLERTON, Alfred, Jr. (d 1910 [20]) composer EA/11*

ELLERTON, J. L. (d 1873) composer EA/74*

ELLERTON, John A. (d 1911) EA/12*

ELLERTON, William (fl 1858-69) English actor HAS

ELLERY, John English actor, business manager, stage manager GRB/1

ELLIN, David (b 1925) Canadian actor TW/2, 24, 26-27, 29-30

ELLINGER, Désirée (1893/95-1951) English actress, singer TW/7, WWT/4-10

ELLINGTON, Duke (1899-1974) American composer, musician BE, CB, TW/30

ELLINGTON, Evie Ellis (d 1976

346

[64]) performer BP/60*

ELLIOT, Miss actress TD/2

ELLIOT, Arthur (d 1936 [78]) Indian/English? actor BE*, BP/20*

ELLIOT, Drew American actor TW/23

ELLIOT, George [Anderson Mc-Dowell] (b 1899) English press representative WWT/9-11

ELLIOT, Jane (b 1947) American actress TW/22-24

ELLIOT, Samuel (fl 1800) American? dramatist EAP

ELLIOT, Stephanie (b 1931) American actress TW/25-26

ELLIOT, W. G. (fl 1882-1900) actor DD, EA/95

ELLIOT, William (d 1931 [52]) actor, manager BE*

ELLIOT, Mr. actor CDP

ELLIOTT (d 1883 [63]) acrobat EA/84*

ELLIOTT, Alonzo (d 1964 [73]) American composer, lyricist BE*

ELLIOTT, Ann (1743-69) actress CDP

ELLIOTT, Ann [Mrs. Will Elliott] (d 1886 [27]) EA/87*

ELLIOTT, Augustus (d 1904) acrobat EA/06*

ELLIOTT, Bob (b 1923) American actor TW/27

ELLIOTT, Cecil (b 1900) American actor TW/2

ELLIOTT, Charles (d 1881) acrobat EA/82*

ELLIOTT, Charlotte [Mrs. Tom E. Smale] (d 1906) comedienne EA/07*, WWT/14*

ELLIOTT, Denholm (b 1922) English actor AAS, BE, ES, TW/23, WWT/11-16

ELLIOTT, Dick (d 1961 [75]) actor BE*

ELLIOTT, Don (b 1926) American musician, composer, singer, actor BE

ELLIOTT, E. P. [E. Green] (d 1874 [60]) actor? EA/75*

ELLIOTT, George (d 1903) comic singer EA/04*

ELLIOTT, Mrs. George see Scott, Nellie

ELLIOTT, George Henry (1884-1962) English/American music-hall performer COC, OC/1-3

ELLIOTT, Gertrude [Mrs. J. Forbes-Robertson] (1874-1950) American actress COC, DD, GRB/1-4, OC/1-3, TW/7, WWA/3, WWM, WWS, WWT/1-10

ELLIOTT, G. H. (d 1962 [78]) English performer BE*, WWT/14*

ELLIOTT, Gus (d 1910 [30]) comic acrobatic juggler EA/11*

ELLIOTT, James (d 1876 [35]) actor EA/77*

ELLIOTT, Mme. James (d 1888) EA/89*

ELLIOTT, James B. (d 1906) EA/07*

ELLIOTT, James S. (b 1924) American actor, producer TW/1-4

ELLIOTT, Jeannie see Venoi, Jeannie

ELLIOTT, John H. (d 1889 [34]) manager EA/90*

ELLIOTT, John Tiffany (d 1963 [48]) literary representative BE*

ELLIOTT, Julia (fl 1858-60) actress HAS

ELLIOTT, Lizzie (d 1889 [33]) dancer EA/91*

ELLIOTT, Louie (d 1886 [26]) transformation dancer EA/87*

ELLIOTT, Madge (1896/98-1955) English actress, dancer TW/12, WWT/6-11

ELLIOTT, Maxine [Mrs. Nat Goodwin] (1868/71/73-1940) American actress CB, COC, DAB, DD, ES, GRB/1-4, NTH, OC/1-3, SR, WWA/1, WWM, WWS, WWT/1-9

ELLIOTT, Michael (b 1931) English director AAS, WWT/14-16

ELLIOTT, Otto (d 1895) acrobatic comedian EA/96*

ELLIOTT, Patricia (b 1942) American actress, singer TW/25-30, WWT/16

ELLIOTT, Paul (b 1941) English producing manager WWT/16

ELLIOTT, Percy (b 1870) English violinist, composer, conductor GRB/1

ELLIOTT, Ralph (d 1909 [68]) EA/10*

ELLIOTT, Ruth (d 1971 [81]) performer BP/55*

ELLIOTT, Sarah Barnwell (1848-1928) American dramatist DAB

ELLIOTT, Stephen actor WWT/16
ELLIOTT, Sumner Locke (b 1917) Australian dramatist, actor BE
ELLIOTT, Thomas (d 1889) agent EA/90*
ELLIOTT, Timothy James (d 1877 [28]) clown EA/78*
ELLIOTT, Topsy (d 1902) dancer EA/03*
ELLIOTT, Mrs. Will see Elliott, Ann
ELLIOTT, William (1885-1932) American actor, producer WWT/4-6
ELLIOTT, William A. (d 1905) actor EA/07*, WWT/14*
ELLIOTT, Zo (d 1964 [73]) composer/lyricist BP/49*
ELLIS, Mrs. (fl 1809?) American? dramatist EAP, RJ
ELLIS, Amy (d 1911) music-hall comedienne EA/12*
ELLIS, Anita (b 1926) Canadian singer, actress BE
ELLIS, Anthony Louis (1873-1944) English critic, manager GRB/2-4, WWT/1-9, WWW/4
ELLIS, Sir Arthur E. (d 1907) comptroller of the Lord Chamberlain's department EA/08*
ELLIS, Bert (d 1917) EA/18*
ELLIS, Brandon (d 1916 [87]) dramatist BE*, EA/17, WWT/14*
ELLIS, Carrie [Mrs. Leslie Beaufort] English actress GRB/1
ELLIS, Charles (d 1976 [83]) performer BP/60*
ELLIS, Charles T. actor, singer, composer CDP
ELLIS, Clara (d 1850) English actress CDP, HAS
ELLIS, Edith (d 1960 [86]) American dramatist TW/17, WWT/6-11
ELLIS, Edward (1872-1952) American actor, dramatist TW/9, WWM, WWT/7-9
ELLIS, Edwin (1844-78) musician, musical director, composer DNB
ELLIS, Evelyn (1894?/1900-1958) American actress TW/9, 14
ELLIS, George (d 1871 [54]) professor of music EA/72*
ELLIS, George (d 1900 [59])

music-hall comedian EA/01*
ELLIS, George see Raeburn, Sam
ELLIS, George Cressall [or Cresswell] (d 1875 [65]) manager, director EA/76*, WWT/14*
ELLIS, Mrs. Granville Alden see Eliot, Max
ELLIS, Harold dramatist DD
ELLIS, Harvey (fl 1850) actor HAS
ELLIS, Havelock (1859-1939) English writer DD, HP
ELLIS, Mrs. Havelock (d 1916) writer EA/17*
ELLIS, James (d 1874 [61]) manager EA/75*
ELLIS, James R. (d 1895 [65]) manager EA/96*
ELLIS, John B. (d 1873 [34]) musician EA/74*
ELLIS, John Somerville (b 1870) Scottish musical director GRB/1
ELLIS, Larry (b 1939) American actor TW/28-29
ELLIS, Lionel English manager, actor GRB/1
ELLIS, Lottie see Langlois, Caroline
ELLIS, Louis (d 1887) pantomimist EA/88*
ELLIS, Marie English actress GRB/1
ELLIS, Marion (b 1942) American actress TW/29
ELLIS, Mary (d 1884 [41]) EA/85*
ELLIS, Mary (b 1900) American actress, singer AAS, BE, ES, WWT/6-16
ELLIS, Maurice (b 1905) American actor TW/11
ELLIS, Max (d 1964 [50]) production executive BE*
ELLIS, Michael (b 1917) American producer BE
ELLIS, Patricia (d 1970 [49]) performer BP/54*
ELLIS, Percy (d 1905 [29]) acting manager GRB/1
ELLIS, Richard George (d 1868) comic singer EA/69*
ELLIS, Robert see Castleton, Robert
ELLIS, Vivian (b 1904) English composer, lyricist AAS, ES, WWT/6-16
ELLIS, Walter L. G. dramatist, critic DD
ELLIS, Walter W. (1874-1956) English dramatist WWT/4-11

ELLIS, Will (d 1896 [43]) music-
hall chairman EA/97*
ELLIS, William (fl 1839) actor,
theatre builder HAS
ELLIS, William (d 1858) American
actor HAS
ELLIS, William Henry (d 1869
[43]) actor EA/70*
ELLIS-FERMOR, Una (1894-1958)
critic BE*
ELLISON, Ada (d 1969) production
manager BP/54*
ELLISON, Mrs. George see
Dalton, Kate
ELLISON, James (fl 1812?) Amer-
ican? dramatist EAP, RJ
ELLISON, James (b 1910) Amer-
ican actor TW/1
ELLISON, Joseph Roy (b 1875)
American manager WWA/5
ELLISON, Sydney (d 1930 [61])
director BE*, WWT/14*
ELLISON, William (d 1903 [60])
circus musical director EA/
04*
ELLISSEN, Isabel see Raleigh,
Mrs. Cecil
ELLISTON, Charles (d 1909 [44])
manager EA/10*
ELLISTON, Daisy (b 1894) Eng-
lish actress, dancer WWT/
4-7
ELLISTON, Grace [Grace Rutter]
(1881-1950) American actress
GRB/3-4, TW/7, WWA/3,
WWM, WWS, WWT/1-6
ELLISTON, Louise [Sarah Stone]
(d 1899) EA/00*
ELLISTON, Robert William (1774-
1831) English actor, lessee,
manager BS, CDP, COC,
CP/3, DD, DNB, ES, GT,
OC/1-3, OX, TD/1-2
ELLISTON, W. (d 1893) manager
EA/94*
ELLISTON, William Henry (d
1901 [66]) EA/02*
ELLMENREICH, Franziska (1850-
1931) German actress WWT/2
ELLMORE, Thomas see Saxon,
Thomas A.
ELLSLER, Effie see Ellsler,
Mrs. John A.
ELLSLER, Effie (1858-1942)
American actress CDP, SR,
WWA/1
ELLSLER, John A. (1821/22-
1903) American actor, manager

CDP, HAS, PP/1
ELLSLER, Mrs. John A. [née
Euphemia Murray] (1824-1918)
American actress HAS
ELLSLER, Therese see Elssler,
Therese
ELLSTEIN, Abraham (d 1963 [56])
composer, conductor BE*,
BP/47*
ELLSWORTH, Arley B. (d 1971
[74]) performer BP/56*
ELLSWORTH, Elinor American
actress TW/28
ELMER, Bessie English actress
GRB/1
ELMO, Cloe (b 1910) Italian singer
ES
ELMORE, Mrs. actress CDP
ELMORE, Miss (fl 1850) actress
HAS
ELMORE, Annie [Mrs. James El-
more] (d 1898) EA/00*
ELMORE, James (d 1901 [61]) actor
EA/02*, WWT/14*
ELMORE, Mrs. James see El-
more, Annie
ELMORE, Marcus (d 1872) Eng-
lish? actress HAS
ELMORE, Mrs. Marcus (d 1899)
actress HAS
ELMORE, Marion [Mrs. Frank
Losee] actress CDP
ELMORE, Mary Hannah see El-
more, Mrs. Marcus
ELMORE, Maud actress CDP
ELMORE, Steve (b 1936) American
actor TW/30
ELMORE-FRITH, Mrs. H. see
Liston, Effie
"ELM ORTON" see Pomeroy,
Louise
ELMY, Mary (1712-92) English
actress ES, TD/2
ELPHICK, Michael (b 1946) English
actor TW/25
ELPHINSTONE, Mr. actor CDP
ELPHINSTONE, Miss (fl 1834-36)
English actress HAS
ELPHINSTONE, Annie [Mrs. James
Elphinstone] (d 1900) EA/01*
ELPHINSTONE, Mrs. Charles G.
(d 1904) EA/06*
ELPHINSTONE, Douglas (d 1909
[26]) manager EA/10*
ELPHINSTONE, Emma Marian
Maria [Mrs. James Sheridan
Knowles] (d 1888 [81]) actress
CDP

ELPHINSTONE, Mrs. James see
Elphinstone, Annie
ELPHINSTONE, James H. (d 1892)
manager EA/93*
ELPHINSTONE, Montague (b 1880)
English actor GRB/1-4
ELRINGTON, Francis (d 1746
[54]) actor WWT/14*
ELRINGTON, Thomas (1688-1732)
English actor, manager DD,
DNB, ES
ELROY, Mary Wentworth see
Brent, Marian
ELSER, Frank B. (d 1935 [50])
American dramatist BE*,
BP/19*
ELSGOOD, Mr. (fl 1839?) actor
CDP
ELSIE, Lily (1886-1962) English
actress ES, GRB/1-4, TW/19,
WWT/1-11
ELSIE, Marie actress, singer
CDP
ELSLER, Herminie (fl 1838)
dancer CDP
ELSNER, Marie E. (b 1856)
American singer HAS
ELSOM, Isobel (b 1893) English
actress, singer BE, ES, TW/
1, 6-11, 13-15, WWT/3-14
ELSON, Anita (b 1898) English
actress WWT/5-7
ELSSLER, Fanny (1810-84) Aus-
trian dancer CDP, ES, HAS,
OC/1-2, SR
ELSSLER, Theodore dancer CDP
ELSSLER, Therese (d 1878 [70])
dancer CDP
ELSTON, Robert (b 1934) Amer-
ican actor BE, TW/20, 23-
25, 28-29
ELSWORTH, Thomas (d 1895 [55])
lessee EA/96*
ELSWORTHY, Agnes (fl 1850-56)
English actress CDP, HAS
ELSWORTHY, Maria [Mrs. Arche-
deckne] (1825-79) actress DD
ELTINGE, Julian [William Dalton]
(1883-1941) American actor
CB, COC, ES, OC/3, SR,
WWA/1, WWT/3-9
ELTON, Miss (fl 1836) actress
HAS
ELTON, Caroline (d 1901/02
[68]) actress EA/03*, WWT/
14*
ELTON, Edward S. (d 1884 [53])
actor EA/85*

ELTON, Edward William (1794-
1843) English actor CDP, DD,
DNB, OC/1-3
ELTON, Frank (d 1874) comic song-
writer EA/75*
ELTON, Frank (d 1954 [73]) actor
BE*, WWT/14*
ELTON, Fred (fl 1904?) composer
CDP
ELTON, George (1875-1942) English
actor WWT/4-9
ELTON, Henry (d 1874 [32]) actor
EA/75*
ELTON, Jenny see Lane, Jane
ELTON, William (d 1843 [49]) actor
WWT/14*
ELTON, William (1850-1903) actor
DD
ELVEY, Gwladys (d 1972) perform-
er BP/56*
ELVEY, Maurice [William Seward
Folkard] (1887-1967) English ac-
tor, director ES, WWT/2-11,
WWW/6
ELVIDGE, June (d 1965 [59]) per-
former BP/49*
ELVIN, Mrs. [Charlotte Elizabeth
Keegan] (d 1916) actress EA/
17*
ELVIN, Joe (1862-1935) English
music-hall performer OC/1-3
ELVIN, Violetta (b 1925) Russian/
English dancer ES, WWT/12
ELVIN, Will (d 1893) music-hall
performer EA/94*
ELWELL, Herbert (d 1974 [75])
critic BP/58*
ELWELL, Isaac (d 1890) circus
clown EA/92*
ELWELL, Joe (d 1910 [80]) clown,
animal trainer EA/11*
ELWOOD, Arthur (d 1903 [53]) ac-
tor DD
ELY, Lyn American producer BE
ELZE, Karl critic DD
ELZY, Ruby (1910?-43) singer CB
EMANUEL, Lauren (d 1887) EA/
88*
EMANUEL, Samuel (d 1887) music-
hall performer? EA/88*
EMCH, George (b 1927) Polish ac-
tor TW/29
EMDEN, Henry (1852-1930) English
scene designer ES
EMDEN, Margaret (d 1946) actress
BE*, WWT/14*
EMDEN, T. Walter L. (b 1847)
architect DD

EMDEN, William Samuel (d 1872 [71]) manager, dramatist DD

EMDEN, Mrs. William Samuel actress DD

EMERALD, Connie (d 1959 [68]) actress WWT/6-9

EMERICK, Robert (d 1973 [57]) performer BP/58*

EMERSON, Mr. singer, variety performer CDP

EMERSON, Billy [ne Redmond] (1846-1902) singer, minstrel CDP

EMERSON, Edward (d 1975 [65]) performer BP/59*

EMERSON, Evalyn see Earle, Evalyn

EMERSON, Faye (b 1917) American actress BE, CB, TW/4-19, WWT/14-15

EMERSON, George A. (d 1963 [59]) animal trainer BE*

EMERSON, Hope (d 1960 [62]) American actress TW/1, 3-4, 16

EMERSON, James Curtis (d 1904) manager, actor EA/05*

EMERSON, John (1874-1956) American actor, dramatist, director ES, NTH, TW/12, WWM, WWT/5-11

EMERSON, Mary (d 1921) actress BE*, BP/5*

EMERSON, Mort (b 1853) singer, dancer, minstrel CDP

EMERSON, Walter actor, singer CDP

EMERSON, Walter (d 1893) American musician CDP

EMERSON, William P. [ne William E. Redman] (1836/46-1932) Irish minstrel HAS, SR

EMERTON, Roy [Hugh Fitzroy Emerton] (1892-1944) English actor WWT/9

EMERY, Miss [Mrs. Burroughs] (d 1832) English actress CDP, HAS

EMERY, Ann [Mrs. John Emery] (d 1870 [89]) EA/71*, WWT/14*

EMERY, Edward (1861-1938) English actor ES, WWS

EMERY, Mrs. Edward see Farr, Florence

EMERY, Mrs. Edward see Waldron, Georgia

EMERY, Edwin T. (d 1951 [79])

actor TW/8

EMERY, Frances A. (fl 1846) actress HAS

EMERY, Frank (d 1910) actor EA/11*, WWT/14*

EMERY, Frederick (d 1930 [65]) actor BE*, WWT/14*

EMERY, Gilbert [Gilbert Emery Bensley Pottle] (1875-1945) American actor, dramatist HJD, WWT/5-9

EMERY, Isabella Mackle (d 1827 [72]) actress WWT/14*

EMERY, John (1777-1822) English actor CDP, COC, DD, DNB, ES, GT, OC/1-3, OX, TD/1-2

EMERY, John (d 1874) comedian EA/75*

EMERY, John (c. 1905-64) actor BE, ES, TW/21, WWT/9-13

EMERY, Mrs. John see Emery, Ann

EMERY, Katherine (b 1908) American actress BE, WWT/9-11

EMERY, Louise [or Louie] (d 1943) actress BE*, WWT/14*

EMERY, Mackle (d 1825 [85]) actor DD

EMERY, Philip (d 1859 [44]) actor WWT/14*

EMERY, Pollie (1875-1958) English actress GRB/1-4, WWT/1, 4-11

EMERY, Rose (d 1912 [61]) EA/14*

EMERY, Rose (d 1934 [89]) actress BE*, WWT/14*

EMERY, Mrs. S. A. see Meates, Mrs. Arthur E.

EMERY, Mrs. Samuel (d 1886) EA/87*, WWT/14*

EMERY, Samuel Anderson (1817-81) English actor CDP, COC, DD, DNB, ES, HAS, OAA/1-2, OC/1-3

EMERY, Winifred [Mrs. Cyril Maude] (1862-1924) English actress CDP, COC, DD, DP, EA/95-96, ES, GRB/1-4, OC/1-3, WWT/1-4, WWW/2

EMHARDT, Robert (b 1916) American actor, director BE, TW/5-8, 12-16, WWT/14

EMIL-BEHNKE, Kate (d 1957 [86]) drama instructor BE*, WWT/14*

EMILE, Robert (d 1889) clown EA/90*

EMMERSON, Aggie [Mrs. Frederick Renad] (d 1894) EA/95*

EMMERSON, Alfred T. (d 1917) musical director EA/18*

EMMERSON, Dorothy L. Japanese/American actress TW/26

EMMET, Alfred (b 1908) English director WWT/15-16

EMMET, Katherine (d 1960 [78]) actress TW/17

EMMETT, Bessie [Mrs. Richard Temple] (d 1875 [28]) EA/76*

EMMETT, Bobbie [W. J. McNeill] (d 1898 [37]) music-hall performer EA/00*

EMMETT, Daniel Decatur (1815-1904) American minstrel, composer CDP, DAB, HJD, SR, WWA/H

EMMETT, Joseph Kline (1841-91) American actor, manager CDP, DD, HAS, SR

EMMETT, Nat (d 1910) variety artist EA/11*

EMMETT, Robert (b 1921) American actor TW/9-10

EMMONS, Lizzie (d 1863) actress HAS

EMMOTT, Mrs. Elizabeth see Herbert, Miss Emmott

EMNEY, Fred (1865-1917) English actor COC, GRB/1-4, OC/1-3, WWT/1-3

EMNEY, Fred (b 1900) English actor COC, OC/1-3, WWT/8-16

EMNEY, Joan Fred actress WWT/9-10

EMORY, Carl (d 1966 [59]) actor TW/23

EMPY, Cleo see Mayfield, Cleo

EMPY, Guy (d 1963 [79]) songwriter, actor, director BE*

EMSON, Mr. singer, minstrel CDP

ENDERSBY, Paul (d 1968 [69]) performer BP/53*

ENDERSON, Carrie see Barker, Carrie

ENDERSSOHN, Harry (d 1877 [49]) clown EA/78*

ENDORE, Guy (d 1970 [69]) dramatist BP/54*

ENDRES, Augusta actress? CDP

ENDREY, Eugene (d 1967 [76]) producer/director/choreographer BP/52*

ENGEL, Carl (d 1893) EA/94*

ENGEL, Jennie (fl 1858?) actress CDP

ENGEL, Josephine [Mrs. Leo Engel] (d 1888 [31]) EA/89*

ENGEL, Lehman (b 1910) American composer, conductor BE

ENGEL, Mrs. Leo see Engel, Josephine

ENGEL, Nina [Mrs. Sidney Beltram] (d 1917) EA/18*

ENGEL, Robert (b 1948) American actor TW/27

ENGEL, Susan (b 1935) Austrian actress WWT/15-16

ENGELBACH, E. C. (d 1916 [69]) lessee EA/17*, WWT/14*

ENGELHARDT, Wallace (b 1923) American actor TW/26

ENGELS, George (d 1907 [61]) dramatist, actor BE*, WWT/14*

ENGELS, M. (fl 1838) musician CDP

ENGLAND, Barry (b 1934) English dramatist CD

ENGLAND, Daisy (d 1943 [81]) actress EA/97

ENGLAND, James Sharp (fl 1809?) performer? CDP

ENGLAND, Paul (1893-1968) English actor, singer WWT/6-7

ENGLANDER, Ludwig (1859/82-1914) Austrian conductor, composer DD, GRB/3-4, SR, WWS, WWT/1-2

ENGLE, Billy (d 1966 [77]) performer BP/51*

ENGLEFIELD, Violet (d 1946 [60]) actress BE*, WWT/14*

ENGLER, Alvina (d 1913) EA/14*

ENGLISH, Mr. (d 1875 [39]) agent, manager EA/76*

ENGLISH, D. G. (d 1893) EA/94*

ENGLISH, George (d 1911) music-hall proprietor EA/12*

ENGLISH, Mrs. George (d 1894 [40]) EA/95*

ENGLISH, George Griffiths (d 1907 [38]) EA/08*

ENGLISH, Granville (d 1968 [73]) composer/lyricist BP/53*

ENGLISH, John (fl 1494-1531) actor DA

ENGLISH, Paul Allen (d 1972 [44]) performer BP/57*

ENGLISH, Ralph (d 1970 [59]) performer BP/55*

ENGLISH, Thomas Dunn (1819-1902)

American dramatist DAB, RJ
ENGLISH, William B. (d 1864
[52]) manager HAS
ENGLISH DWARF (b 1709) CDP
ENGLISH STAGE COMPANY LTD.
producing managers WWT/
13-14
ENGLUND, George (b 1926) Amer-
ican actor TW/8
ENGLUND, Maude Beatrice Gal-
braith (d 1962 [71]) singer BE*
ENGSTROM, Arthur Hamilton
see Revelle, Arthur Hamilton
ENKE, Edith see Adams, Edith
ENLOE, William G. (d 1972 [70])
manager BP/57*
ENNIS, Charles (b 1917) American
choirmaster BE
ENOCH, Frederick (d 1905) lyricist
GRB/1
ENOS, Busby Berkeley William
see Berkeley, Busby
ENOS, Mrs. Wilson see Berkeley,
Gertrude
ENRIGHT, Josephine (d 1976 [72])
performer BP/60*
ENRIGHT, Sara (d 1963 [75]) ac-
tress, talent representative
BE*, BP/47*
ENSERRO, Michael (b 1918) Amer-
ican actor TW/20-24, 26, 28-
29
ENSON, Fanny (d 1897) actress
DD
ENSSLEN, Dick (b 1926) American
actor TW/24-25, 30
ENTEN, Boni (b 1947) American
actress TW/25-26, 28-29
ENTERS, Angna (b 1907) American
mime actress BE, CB, COC,
ES, OC/3
ENTERS, Warren (b 1927) Amer-
ican director BE
ENTHOVEN, Gabrielle (1868-
1950) English historian, drama-
tist COC, ES, OC/1-3, WWT/
6-10, WWW/4
ENTWISTLE, Mr. (fl 1804-14)
actor HAS
ENTWISTLE, Mrs. see Mason,
Mrs.
ENTWISTLE, Ethel (d 1918)
EA/19*
ENTWISTLE, Lillian Millicent
(d 1932) actress BE*
ENTWISTLE, William (d 1869
[35]) music-hall proprietor
EA/71*

ENZER, Jack (d 1917) performer?
EA/18*
EPAILLY, Jules (d 1967 [80s])
performer BP/51*
EPHRAIM, Lee (1877-1953) Ameri-
can manager WWT/6-11
EPHRON, Henry (b 1912) American
dramatist BE
EPHRON, Phoebe [née Wolkind]
(1916-71) American dramatist
BE, TW/28
EPITAUX, Fred (d 1913) actor
WWT/14*
EPLETT, Kate (d 1905) EA/06*
EPLETT, Tom (d 1905) EA/06*
EPPERSON, Don (d 1973 [35])
performer BP/57*
EPSTEIN, Alvin (b 1925) American
actor AAS, BE, ES, TW/15-
16, 18-20, 22-23, 26-27, WWT/
14-16
EPSTEIN, Brian (d 1967 [32]) pro-
ducing manager WWT/15*
EPSTEIN, Howard (d 1969 [51])
lawyer BP/54*
EPSTEIN, Julius (b 1909) American
dramatist, producer BE
EPSTEIN, Philip G. (d 1952 [42])
American dramatist BE*, BP/
36*
EPSTEIN, Pierre (b 1930) French
actor TW/28, 30
ERANION, Henry E. (d 1905) con-
jurer EA/06*
ERATO, Carl John Bergstrom (d
1885 [52]) Swedish gymnast
EA/86*
ERB, George see Allen, Johnny
ERCKMANN, Emile see Erck-
mann-Chatrian
ERCKMANN-CHATRIAN [Emile
Erckmann (1822-99), & Louis
Gratien Charles Alexandre
Chatrian (1826-90) French
dramatists COC, ES, HP,
NTH, OC/1-3
ERDMAN, Jean (b 1917) Hawaiian
dancer, choreographer CB,
TW/23, 29
ERDMAN, Nikolai R. (d 1970 [68])
dramatist BP/55*
ERHARDT, Thomas (b 1928) Amer-
ican literary & talent repre-
sentative BE
ERIC, Elspeth American actress
TW/1
ERIC, Fred (d 1935 [61]) American
actor WWT/1-7

ERICHS, Harold (d 1976 [74])
editor BP/60*
ERICKSON, Ed (b 1931) Ameri-
can actor TW/24
ERICKSON, John (d 1972 [74])
composer/lyricist BP/57*
ERICKSON, Leif (b 1911) Ameri-
can actor BE
ERICSON, John (b 1926) German/
American actor BE, TW/9
ERIVEN, Stuart (d 1967 [64])
actor WWT/15*
ERK, Ludwig (d 1883 [77])
musical director EA/84*
ERLANGER, Abraham Lincoln
(1860-1930) American manager
DAB, ES, GRB/2-4, NTH,
SR, WWA/1, WWM, WWT/1-6
ERLANGER, Frederic [Ferdinand
Regnal] (1868-1943) French/
English composer ES
ERLE, T. W. (fl 1880) writer
DD
ERMINIE, Mlle. (fl 1857) singer?
HAS
ERMOLIEFF, Joseph N. (d 1962
[72]) Russian producer BE*
ERNE, Vincent (b 1884) English
actor WWT/5-7
ERNEST, Charles (d 1897) sing-
er, minstrel CDP
ERNEST, Emily see Chenoweth,
Emily
ERNEST, Lily see Mansel, Lady
ERNESTINE, Mme. (d 1890)
dancer EA/91*
ERNO, George (d 1905) EA/06*
ERNO, Harry (d 1890 [35]) music-
hall performer EA/91*
ERNST, Earle (b 1911) American
educator, director BE
ERNST, Leila (b 1922) American
actress TW/3-4
ERNST, Phillip (1792-1868)
German musician HAS
ERNSTONE, Helena Cecile [née
Schott] (fl 1863-79) German
actress DD, OAA/2
ERON, Kate (d 1885 [24]) EA/86*
ERRANI, Achille (d 1897 [73])
singer CDP, HAS
ERRINGTON, Bertha (d 1889)
actress? EA/90*
ERRINGTON, Richard (fl 1622-
36) manager, actor DA
ERRIS, Fanny actress GRB/1
ERROL, Leon (1881-1951) Aus-
tralian actor ES, SR, TW/8,

WWT/4-11
ERROLLE, Ralph [né Ralph Errolle
Smith] (1887-1973) American
singer WWM
ERSKIN, Chester (b 1903) Austrian
producer, manager, actor
WWT/7-11
ERSKINE, Hon. Andrew (fl 1764)
dramatist CP/3
ERSKINE, Sir David (1772-1837)
dramatist DD, DNB
ERSKINE, Howard (b 1926) Ameri-
can producer, director, actor
BE, WWT/14-16
ERSKINE, James see Rosslyn,
Earl of
ERSKINE, John (1879-1951) Amer-
ican librettist WWW/5
ERSKINE, Mrs. Steuart (d 1948)
dramatist WWW/4
ERSKINE, Wallace (d 1943 [81])
English actor WWM, WWS
ERVINE, St. John Greer (1883-
1971) Irish dramatist, critic
AAS, COC, ES, MD, MH,
MWD, NTH, OC/1-3, PDT, RE,
SR, TW/27, WWA/5, WWT/2-14
ERWIN, Barbara (b 1937) American
dancer TW/29-30
ERWIN, Stuart (1902/03-67) Ameri-
can actor BE, ES, TW/24
ESCAMO [Charles Waldon] (d 1901
[35]) conjuror EA/03*
ESCANDE, Maurice (d 1973 [80])
actor WWT/16*
ESCOTT, Lucy (fl 1858-60) singer,
dancer CDP, HAS
ESCOTT, Thomas Hay Sweet (d
1924) writer WWW/2
ESDAIL, Arthur (b 1857) actor
GRB/1
ESDAILE, Florence (b 1875) Aus-
tralian singer GRB/1-3
ESDEN, Alice English actress
GRB/1
ESHER, Lord (d 1963 [82]) chair-
man of London Theatre Council
WWT/14*
ESKENAS, Linda (b 1950) American
actress TW/30
ESLER, Lemist (1888-1960) drama-
tist, actor, educator BE*
ESMOND, Annie (1873-1945) actress
WWT/6-9
ESMOND, Carl [Wilhelm Eichberg-
er] (b 1905/08) Austrian actor
TW/14, WWT/9-10
ESMOND, Henry Vernon [H. V.

Jack] (1869-1922) English actor,
dramatist COC, DD, DNB,
EA/95, ES, GRB/1-4, OC/1-3,
WWS, WWT/1-4, WWW/2

ESMOND, Mrs. Henry Vernon
see Moore, Eva

ESMOND, Jill (b 1908) English
actress WWT/6-12

ESMOND, Wilfred [Michael Butler]
(1849-1913) Irish singer, manager GRB/1

ESMONDE, Lewis (d 1877 [32])
lessee EA/78*

ESMONDE, Teresa (fl 1853) actress HAS

ESMOND-MOORE, Jill see
Esmond, Jill

ESPINDA, David (d 1975 [61])
performer BP/60*

ESPINOSA, Mme. (d 1933 [84])
dancer WWT/14*

ESPINOSA, Clarence (b 1961)
American actor TW/25

ESPINOSA, Edouard (1872-1950)
English dancer, maître de
ballet, choreographer ES,
WWT/6-10

ESPINOSA, Judith (d 1949 [72])
dancer BE*, WWT/14*

ESPINOSA, Leon (fl 1850-51)
dancer CDP, HAS

ESPLA, Oscar (d 1976 [96])
composer/lyricist BP/60*

ESPOSITO, Giancarlo (b 1958)
Danish actor TW/29-30

ESPOSITO, Michele (1855-1929)
Italian composer WWW/3

ESSEN, Viola (b 1925) American
dancer TW/1, 5-6

ESSER, Peter (d 1970 [84])
performer BP/55*

ESSEX, Dowager Countess of
see Stephens, Catherine

ESSEX, Earl of see Devereux,
Robert

ESSEX, George, Sr. (d 1871 [55])
singer EA/72*

ESSEX, Harcourt see Algeranoff,
Harcourt

ESSEX, Harold (d 1973 [68])
performer BP/57*

ESSEX, John (d 1744) English
dancer, choreographer ES

ESSEX, Tony (d 1975 [49])
producer/director/choreographer
BP/60*

ESSLER, Fred (d 1973 [77]) performer BP/57*

ESSLIN, Martin (b 1918) Hungarian
critic BE, WWT/16

ESSMAN, Manuel (b 1898) American
scene designer ES

ESTABROOK, Howard (b 1884)
American actor ES, WWM,
WWT/4-8

ESTABROOK, Mrs. Howard see
Dale, Gretchen

ESTCOURT, Dick (1668-1712) English actor COC, CP/1-3, DD,
DNB, GT, OC/1-3, TD/1-2

ESTCOURT, Frank (d 1893 [46])
music-hall chairman? EA/94*

ESTCOURT, Richard see Estcourt, Dick

ESTELLE, Mr. (d 1829) American
actor HAS

ESTELLE, Caroline (d 1874) dancer
EA/75*

ESTEN, Harriet Pye [née Bennett;
Mrs. Scott-Waring] (1768?-1868)
actress CDP, GT, TD/1-2

ESTERMAN, Laura (b 1945) American actress TW/26-27, 29-30

ESTEVEZ, Ramon see Sheen,
Martin

ESTEY, Suellen American actress
TW/28-30

ESTHER, Mlle. (b 1816) French
dancer HAS

ESTOTEVILLE, George (fl 1640)
actor DA

ESTY, Alice (d 1935 [71]) American singer DD, GRB/1-4

ESTY, Annah B. (d 1912) EA/13*

ETCHELLS, Will (d 1878) comic
singer EA/79*

ETHAIR, Emily [Mrs. A. Scott]
(d 1878 [27]) singer, actress
EA/79*

ETHAIR, Nelly see Batchelor,
Nelly

ETHAIR, Rose (d 1870) equestrienne EA/71*

ETHAIR, Uncle Steve [Stephen
Etheridge] (d 1891 [72]) EA/92*

ETHARDO, Steve (d 1911 [76])
spiral ascensionist EA/12*

ETHEL, Agnes (1852-1903) American? actress, manager? CDP,
DD, HAS, WWA/H

ETHERDO [John Johnson] (d 1916
[82]) clown, pantomimist EA/
17*

ETHERDO, Mary Ann [Emily Man-
fred] (d 1882) EA/83*

ETHERDO, Thomas (d 1902 [49])

acrobat EA/03*

ETHERDO, William (d 1893) gymnast EA/95*

ETHEREGE, Sir George (1634-91) English dramatist COC, CP/ 1-3, DD, DNB, ES, GT, HP, MH, NTH, OC/1-3, PDT, RE

ETHERIDGE, May (d 1935) actress WWT/14*

ETHERIDGE, Stephen see Ethair, Uncle Steve

ETHERINGTON, James (d 1877 [46]) pantomimist EA/78*

ETHERINGTON, James (1902-48) English actor, singer WWT/10

ETHLO, Maggie [Mrs. Fred Stokes] (d 1897 [20]) dancer EA/98*

ETLER, Alvin D. (d 1973 [60]) composer/lyricist BP/58*

ETTING, Ruth (b 1907) American actress, singer WWT/7-9

ETTLINGER, Dorothy see Day, Dorothy

EUGENE, Marvellous [Alfred Eugene Godolphin Cooke] (d 1900 [55]) equestrian EA/01*

EUGENE, Master [Eugene D'Ameli] (1836-1907) female impersonator, minstrel CDP

EUGENE, Max (d 1917) singer EA/18*

EUGENE, Thomas (d 1911 [52]) acrobat, gymnast EA/12*

EUNSON, Dale (b 1904) American dramatist BE

EUNSON, Katherine Albert (d 1970 [68]) dramatist BP/55*

EURARDO, Sig. see Rowley, Joseph

EURIPIDES (480-406 B.C.) Greek dramatist ES

EUSTACE, Edward J. (d 1971) dramatist BP/56*

EUSTACE, Jennie A. (1865/66-1936) American actress WWM, WWS

EUSTAPHIEVE, Alexis (fl 1814?) American? dramatist EAP

EUSTREL, Antony (b 1904) English actor WWT/10-13

EVAIN, W. H. (fl 1850) actor HAS

EVANKO, Ed Canadian actor TW/25-26, 28, 30

EVANS, Mr. actor, singer CDP

EVANS, Alice (b 1939) American actress TW/24

EVANS, Alison Ridley (b 1929) English producer BE

EVANS, Amy Rosalind [Mrs. Fred Evans] (d 1885) EA/86*

EVANS, Anne [Mrs. George Evans] (d 1877 [26]) EA/78*

EVANS, Bob (d 1903 [34]) one-legged singer, dancer EA/04*

EVANS, Caradoc (d 1945 [70]) Welsh dramatist WWT/6-9, WWW/4

EVANS, Charles E. (1856/57-1945) American actor, manager CDP, SR, WWS

EVANS, Charles Smart (1778-1849) singer DNB

EVANS, Clifford (b 1912) Welsh actor ES, WWT/9-10, 14

EVANS, Damon [Dickie Evans] (b 1950) American actor TW/27-30

EVANS, Dickie see Evans, Damon

EVANS, Dillon (b 1921) English actor TW/28-29

EVANS, Douglas (d 1968 [64]) performer BP/52*

EVANS, Dame Edith Mary (1888-1976) English actress AAS, CB, COC, ES, OC/1-3, PDT, TW/7-15, WWT/4-16

EVANS, Edwin, Jr. (1874-1945) English critic ES

EVANS, Eliza (d 1908) EA/09*

EVANS, Evan E. (d 1962 [73]) performer BE*

EVANS, Frank J. (fl 1865) actor CDP

EVANS, Fred comedian CDP

EVANS, Fred (d 1909 [69]) clown BE*, EA/10*, WWT/14*

EVANS, Mrs. Fred (d 1904 [83]) EA/05*

EVANS, Mrs. Fred see Albert, Rose

EVANS, Mrs. Fred see Evans, Amy Rosalind

EVANS, George (1870-1915) Welsh minstrel BE*

EVANS, Mrs. George see Evans, Anne

EVANS, George F. actor HAS

EVANS, George S. (d 1911) scene artist EA/12*

EVANS, Geraint (b 1922) Welsh singer ES

EVANS, Gouldwais (fl 1629) musician DA

EVANS, Greek Harry (d 1967 [77]) singer TW/23

EVANS, Harry (d 1905) comedian
EA/06*

EVANS, Harvey (b 1941) American actor TW/26-30

EVANS, Helen Hartz (d 1974 [77]) performer BP/58*

EVANS, Henry (fl 1582-1603) Welsh lessee DA

EVANS, J. (d 1879) minstrel? EA/80*

EVANS, Jane (d 1898) EA/99*

EVANS, Jessie (b 1918) Welsh actress AAS, WWT/10-16

EVANS, J. H. (d 1865) dramatist HAS

EVANS, Joe (d 1973 [57]) performer BP/58*

EVANS, John (1693?-1734?) Irish? actor, manager DNB

EVANS, John (d 1878) gymnast EA/79*

EVANS, John see Dubellamy, Charles Clementine

EVANS, John see Pasco

EVANS, John D. (d 1887) circus performer NYM

EVANS, Johnny (b 1946) American actor TW/25

EVANS, Judith American actress TW/29

EVANS, Julia [Mrs. Thomas Evans] (d 1910 [83]) EA/11*

EVANS, Madge (b 1909) American actress BE, ES, TW/5-7, WWT/7-11

EVANS, Margaret see Didier, Mrs. Abraham J.

EVANS, Mary (d 1892 [49]) EA/93*

EVANS, Mary Jane (b 1923) American educator BE

EVANS, Maurice Herbert (b 1901) English actor, producer AAS, BE, CB, COC, ES, NTH, OC/1-3, SR, TW/2-21, WWT/7-16

EVANS, May [Mrs. W. Horne] (d 1911) music-hall comedian EA/12*

EVANS, Michael (b 1922/26) English actor BE, TW/8, WWT/14-15

EVANS, Michele (b 1942) American actress TW/23

EVANS, Millicent [Mrs. E. J. Carpenter] (fl 1900s) American actress WWM

EVANS, Nancy (b 1915) English actress, singer WWT/10-14

EVANS, Nathaniel (1742-67) American dramatist EAP

EVANS, Norman (d 1962 [61]) performer BE*

EVANS, Pat (b 1940) American actress TW/28

EVANS, Ray (b 1915) American songwriter BE

EVANS, Redd L. (d 1972 [60]) composer/lyricist BP/57*

EVANS, Renee (d 1971 [63]) performer BP/56*

EVANS, Rex (1903-69) English actor TW/3, 5-9, 25

EVANS, Reynolds (d 1967 [72]) actor TW/1, 8, 10-15, 20, 24

EVANS, Rose (d 1875 [25]) actress EA/76*

EVANS, Ross (d 1967 [51]) dramatist BP/52*

EVANS, Rothbury (d 1944 [81]) actor BE*, WWT/14*

EVANS, Susan (d 1888) EA/89*

EVANS, T. E. (d 1894) lessee EA/95*

EVANS, Tenniel (b 1926) Kenyan actor WWT/15-16

EVANS, T. F. (d 1876 [58]) music-hall proprietor EA/77*

EVANS, Thomas (d 1881) singer EA/82*

EVANS, Thomas (d 1887 [62]) animal impersonator EA/88*

EVANS, Mrs. Thomas see Evans, Julia

EVANS, Tom (d 1903) scene artist EA/04*

EVANS, Wilbur (b 1905/08) American singer, actor, director BE, TW/1-6, 10-12, 23-24

EVANS, Will (1873/75-1931) English actor CDP, COC, GRB/1-3 OC/1-3, WWT/4-6

EVANS, Mrs. Will see Luxmore, Ada

EVANS, William C. (fl 1822) actor CDP

EVANS, Winifred (b 1890) English actress WWT/7-14

EVARART, E. (d 1889) deputy manager EA/90*

EVARD, Mr. (fl 1842-50) actor, manager HAS

EVARTS, William H. (1867-1940) American actor SR

EVATT, Mr. (fl 1798-99) actor TD/1-2

EVELEIGH, Corp. Harold West-
lake (d 1916 [19]) EA/17*
EVELEIGH, Lawrence Westlake
(d 1917 [21]) EA/18*
EVELING, Stanley (b 1925) Eng-
lish dramatist CD, WWT/
15-16
EVELYN, Clara (b 1886) English
actress, singer WWT/1-7
EVELYN, Ernest Evelyn (d 1892)
EA/93*
EVELYN, John (1620-1706) drama-
tist DD
EVELYN, Judith (1913-67) Amer-
ican actress BE, TW/2-18,
23, WWA/4, WWT/10-14
EVELYN, T. H. (d 1879) lessee
EA/80*
EVELYNE, Alma [Mrs. G. L.
Bannerman] English actress
GRB/1
EVENNETT, Wallace (b 1888)
English actor WWT/6-10
EVERALL, Mrs. Harry James
see Carus, Emma
EVERARD, Miss see Everard,
Harriette Emily
EVERARD, Edward Cape (b
1755) actor DD
EVERARD, George (d 1907 [34])
songwriter EA/08*
EVERARD, H. (fl 1870s) actress
OAA/2
EVERARD, Harriette Emily [Mrs.
Darley Beswicke] (1844-82)
actress, singer DD
EVERARD, James E. (d 1879
[38]) stage hand? EA/80*
EVERARD, Margaret Ada Clegg
see Lundberg, Ada
EVERARD, Tom L. (d 1896)
music-hall singer EA/97*
EVERARD, W. (d 1884) EA/85*
EVERARD, Walter (d 1924 [74])
actor BE*, WWT/14*
EVEREST, Barbara (1890-1968)
English actress TW/2-6,
WWT/3-14
EVEREST, Mrs. Charles Fan-
shawe see Bray, Alice
EVERETT, David (1770-1813)
American dramatist EAP
EVERETT, Ethel (d 1973 [63])
performer BP/56*
EVERETT, George (d 1881 [57])
actor WWT/14*
EVERETT, Jake (b 1946) Amer-
ican actor TW/30

EVERETT, Sophie (d 1963 [88])
performer BE*
EVERETT, Timmy (b 1938/39)
American actor, dancer, direc-
tor, choreographer BE, TW/
14-17, 20
EVERETTE, Lily (d 1891) skater
EA/92*
EVERHART, Rex (b 1920) American
actor AAS, BE, TW/22-28, 30,
WWT/15-16
EVERILL, Frederick Augustus
(1829-1900) English actor DD,
OAA/1-2
EVERITT (1779-80) gigantic infant
CDP
EVERLEIGH, Kate (d 1926 [62])
actress BE*, WWT/14*
EVERS, Adeline [Florence Helena
Earlesmere] (d 1896) actress
EA/97*
EVERS, Herbert (b 1922) American
actor TW/5-11, 14-15
EVERSFIELD, Miss [Mrs. H. Cecil
Beryl] (d 1885) EA/86*
EVERSFIELD, Harry (d 1896) actor
DD, EA/95
EVERSLEIGH, Clara (d 1918) EA/
19*
EVERSLEIGH, Flo [Mrs. Harry
Kirk] (d 1910) actress EA/12*
EVERSLEIGH, Harry (d 1906) actor
EA/07*
EVERSLEY, H. A. [C. H. James]
(d 1899) professor of music
EA/00*
EVERSMAN, Alice M. (d 1974 [88])
critic BP/58*
EVERTON, Paul (1868/70-1948)
American actor TW/4, WWM,
WWS
EVESEED, Henry (d 1614?) member
of the Chapel Royal DA
EVESSON, Isabelle [Mensing] (1863-
1914) American actress DD,
GRB/3-4, SR, WWS
EVETT, Robert (1874-1949) English
actor, singer, manager GRB/
1-4, WWT/1-10
EVETT, Robert (d 1974 [52]) com-
poser/lyricist BP/59*
EVILL, Henry (d 1916 [91]) director
of the Royal General Theatrical
Fund EA/17*
EVISON, Fred G. (b 1871) English
actor GRB/1
EWART, Stephen T. (b 1869) English
actor WWT/4-5

EWELL, Caroline Elizabeth (d 1909 [69]) actress BE*, EA/ 10*, WWT/14*

EWELL, Lois (b 1885) American singer WWM

EWELL, Tom (b 1909) American actor AAS, BE, CB, TW/ 3-6, 14-17, 22, WWT/11-16

EWER, Donald (b 1923) English actor TW/27-28

EWING, Aileen see Grey, Anne

EWING, Frederick Baxter see Albini, Lieut.

EWING, Cpt. Peter (fl 1792?) dramatist CP/3

EWING, Robert W. (fl 1825-26) dramatist, critic EAP, RJ

EWING, Sherman (d 1975 [73]) producer/director/choreographer BP/59*

EWINS, Harry (d 1901 [39]) clown, pantomimist EA/02*

EWINS, Mrs. Harry see Tyrrell, Kittie

EXTON, Clive (b 1930) English dramatist CD, PDT

EXTON, Florence see Alix, Mina

EXTON, Winifred see Fraser, Winifred

EYDTWARTT, John (fl 1627) actor DA

EYEN, Tom (b 1941) American dramatist, director CD, WWT/15-16

EYLAND, Henry (d 1881 [78]) composer EA/82*

EYRE, Edmund John (1767-1816) English actor, dramatist CP/ 3, GT, TD/1-2

EYRE, Gerald (d 1885) actor BE*, EA/86*, WWT/14*

EYRE, John Edmund (d 1816 [48]) dramatist BE*, WWT/ 14*

EYRE, Laurence (1881-1959) American dramatist, actor ES, WWA/3, WWT/4-11

EYRE, Lyttleton (d 1902 [26]) actor EA/04*

EYRE, Peter (b 1942) American actor WWT/16

EYRE, Richard (b 1943) English director WWT/16

EYRE, Ronald (b 1929) English director, dramatist AAS, WWT/15-16

EYRE, Sophie [née Ryan] (1853-92) Irish actress CDP, DD, DP

EYSSELINCK, Walter (b 1931) Belgian director, dramatist WWT/ 15-16

EYTHE, William (1918-57) American actor, producer TW/5-9, 13, WWT/11-12

EYTINGE, Harry (1822-1902) actor CDP

EYTINGE, Rose [Mrs. Cyril Searle] (1835/38-1911) American actress DAB, DD, ES, HAS, PP/1, WWA/1, WWM, WWS

EYTINGE, Samuel D. (d 1859) American actor HAS

EYTON, Frank (1894-1962) English lyricist, dramatist WWT/9-13, WWW/6

- F -

FABBRI, Diego (b 1911) Italian dramatist OC/3

FABBRI, Flora dancer CDP

FABBRI, Guerrina (1868-1946) Italian singer ES

FABBRI, Inez (fl 1860) German singer CDP, HAS

FABELL, Peter (fl 15th cent) magician DNB

FABER, Beryl [Mrs. Cosmo Hamilton] (d 1912) English actress GRB/1-4, WWT/1

FABER, Leslie (1879-1929) English actor ES, GRB/3-4, WWT/1-5

FABER, Mrs. Leslie see Arthur-Jones, Winifred

FABER, Myrtie Bedell (d 1896) actress EA/97*

FABIAN, Mons. (d 1876) equestrian clown EA/77*

FABIAN, Madge (b 1880) English actress WWT/1-7

FABIAN, Olga Austrian actress TW/3, 6, 8-9

FABIAN, Simon (d 1970 [71]) theatre builder BP/55*

FABIAN, Thomas (fl 1735) dramatist CP/1-3, GT

FABIAN, Thomas (d 1896) circus performer? EA/97*

FABIANI, Aurelio (1895-1973) Italian manager WWA/5

FABRAY, Nanette (b 1920/22) American actress, singer BE, CB, TW/2-13, 19-20, 29, WWT/11-16

FABRE, Emil (d 1955 [86])
French dramatist BP/40*
FABRI, Annibale Pio (1697-1760)
Italian singer, composer ES
FABRICUS, Jan (d 1964 [93])
dramatist BP/49*
FABRIS, Armanda (fl 1886) singer
CDP
FABRIZI, Mario (d 1963 [38])
performer BE*
FACCIO, Franco (d 1891 [51])
conductor, composer EA/92*
FADEL, Yvan (d 1971 [78]) per-
former BP/56*
FAGAN, Barney (d 1937 [87])
American actor BE*, BP/21*
FAGAN, Mrs. Barney see
Byron, Henrietta
FAGAN, Irene (d 1971 [86])
costumier BP/55*
FAGAN, James Bernard (1873-
1933) English dramatist, pro-
ducer, manager, actor COC,
DNB, ES, GRB/3-4, OC/1-3,
WWT/1-7, WWW/3
FAGAN, Mrs. James Bernard
see Kirby, Elisabeth
FAGAN, Joan (b 1934) American
singer, actress BE
FAGAN, Myron C. dramatist,
producer, manager WWT/
6-13
FAHEY, Myrna (d 1973 [34])
performer BP/57*
FAIN, Sammy (b 1902) American
composer BE
FAINE, Hy (b 1910) Russian/
American executive BE
FAIR, Adrah (b 1897) American
actress, singer WWT/6-7
FAIR, Elinor (b 1904) American
actress ES
FAIR, May (d 1971 [67]) per-
former BP/55*
FAIR, William B. (1851-1909)
music-hall performer CDP,
COC, OC/1-3
FAIR, Mrs. William D. (fl 1863)
actress HAS
FAIRBANKS, Albert L. (d 1971
[65]) performer BP/56*
FAIRBANKS, Douglas, Sr. (1883-
1939) American actor DAB,
ES, SR, WWA/1, WWM,
WWT/3-9, WWW/3
FAIRBANKS, Douglas, Jr. (b
1909) American actor CB,
ES, SR, WWT/8-11, 16

FAIRBANKS, Robert (d 1908) actor?
singer? EA/09*
FAIRBROTHER, Benjamin Smith (d
1878 [74]) actor? EA/79*
FAIRBROTHER, Louisa [Mrs. Fitz-
George] (1816-90) actress
CDP, DD
FAIRBROTHER, Robert (d 1841
[72]) prompter CDP
FAIRBROTHER, Sydney [Sydney
Cowell; Mrs. Sidney Buckler]
(1872-1941) actress COC, DD,
EA/97, GRB/2-4, OC/1-3,
WWT/1-9
FAIRBURN, George (d 1918 [54])
EA/19*
FAIRCHILD, Mr. (d 1852) comedian
HAS
FAIRCHILD, Charlotte (b 1930)
American actress TW/28-30
FAIRCHILD, Edgar (d 1975 [76])
composer/lyricist BP/59*
FAIRCHILD, J. L. (fl 1826) actor
HAS
FAIRCLOUGH, Boothroyd (d 1911
[86]) American actor CDP, HAS
FAIRFAX, Lance (1899-1974) New
Zealand actor, singer BTR/74,
WWT/8-10
FAIRFAX, Lettice (1876-1948) ac-
tress DD, GRB/3-4, WWT/1-8
FAIRFAX, Marion [Mrs. Tully
Marshall] (b 1879) American
dramatist WWM, WWT/3-7
FAIRFIELD, Miss see McClean,
Mrs.
FAIRFIELD, Sumner Lincoln (1803-
44) American dramatist, actor
EAP, HJD, WWA/H
FAIRHURST, Edwin (d 1973) per-
former BP/57*
FAIRHURST, James (d 1907 [87])
music-hall proprietor EA/08*
FAIRLAMB, James Remington
(1838-1908) American composer
DAB
FAIRLEIGH, Paget [Arthur Paget
Ford] (d 1885) EA/86*
FAIRLEY, Dorothy [Mrs. Charles
Locke] (d 1907) actress EA/08*
FAIRLEY, Mrs. M. A. [Mrs. P.
G. Fairley] (d 1916) EA/17*
FAIRLEY, Mrs. P. G. see
Fairley, Mrs. M. A.
FAIRMAN, Austin (1892-1964) Eng-
lish actor WWT/8-11
FAIRMAN, Michael (b 1934) Amer-
ican actor TW/22-24

FAIRS, Gilbert see Hare, Gilbert

FAIRS, John see Hare, John

FAIRWEATHER, David Carnegy (b 1899) English editor, press representative WWT/9-16

FAIRWEATHER, Virginia (b 1922) English press representative WWT/14-16

FAIRY QUEEN [Eliza Nestel] CDP

FAITHFULL, Emily (d 1895 [60]) dramatic reader EA/96*

FAITHFULL, Marianne (b 1946) English actress WWT/15-16

FALASCO, Donald (d 1965 [38]) performer BP/50*

FALCK, Lionel (1889-1971) English manager WWT/11

FALCON, Cornélie see Falcon, Marie Cornélie

FALCON, Marie Cornélie (1812-97) singer CDP

FALCONER, Mrs. see Lambert, E. A.

FALCONER, Edmund (1813/14/25-79) Irish actor, manager, dramatist DNB, EA/68, HAS, OAA/1-2, SR

FALCONER, Mrs. Edmund (d 1864) actress WWT/14*

FALCONER, Helen (d 1968) actress TW/25

FALGI, Nick (d 1973 [40+]) performer BP/58*

FALK, Peter (b 1927) American actor BE, CB, TW/20, 28-30

FALK, Richard (b 1912) American press representative, producer BE

FALK, Sawyer (1898-1961) American educator BE*

FALKENHAIN, Patricia (b 1926) American actress BE

FALKLAND, Lord Viscount see Carey, Henry Lucius

FALKLAND, Amelia, Lady actress CDP

FALLON, Richard (b 1923) American educator, director BE

FALLS, Gregory A. (b 1922) American educator, director, actor BE

FANCHETTE, Amy [Amy Vaile] (b 1861) English actress GRB/1

FANCHETTE, Kate [Mrs. John Russell] (d 1896) EA/97*

FANCK, Arnold (d 1974 [85]) producer/director/choreographer BP/59*

FANCOURT, Darrell (1888-1953) English actor, singer TW/4, 10, WWT/5-11

FANCOURT, Mrs. Tom see Rubie, Jennie

FANCY, Richard (b 1943) American actor TW/30

FANE, Blanche (d 1858) actress CDP, DD

FANE, Sir Francis, Jr. (d 1689?) English dramatist CP/1-3, DNB, GT

FANN, Albert (b 1933) American actor TW/27

FANNIN, Joseph T. (fl 1850) actor HAS

FANNIN, Paddy (d 1888 [48]) comic singer CDP

FANNING, James Francis (d 1883) professor of music EA/84*

FANNING, Lillie (d 1892 [39]) EA/94*

FANNING, Win (b 1918) American journalist BE

FANQUE, Pablo see Darby, William

FANSHAW, Sir Richard (1607-66) English dramatist CP/1-3

FANSHAWE, H. A. W. (d 1917) EA/18*

FANT, Lou (d 1931) American actor TW/25-26

FANT, Roy actor TW/1

FANTI, Clementina (fl 1833) singer CDP

FARADAY, Philip Michael (1875-1944) English manager, composer WWT/1-8

FARAGOH, Francis Edwards (d 1966 [71]) dramatist TW/23

FARBAR, Bernard (b 1935) American actor TW/23

FAREBROTHER, Miss see Fairbrother, Louisa

FAREBROTHER, Violet (1888-1969) English actress TW/3, WWT/4-14

FARENTINO, James (b 1938) American actor TW/29-30

FARGUS, R. J. see Conway, Hugh

FARIA, Arthur (b 1944) American actor TW/28-29

FARINI ["Lulu"] (fl 1871-86) female impersonator CDP

FARJEON, Benjamin Leopold (d 1903 [65]) dramatist BE*, EA/04*, WWT/14*

FARJEON, Eleanor (1881-1965) English dramatist NTH, WWW/6

FARJEON, Herbert (1887-1945) English critic, dramatist NTH, OC/1-3, WWT/6-9, WWW/4

FARJEON, Joseph Jefferson (1883-1955) dramatist NTH, WWT/6-11, WWW/5

FARKAS, Karl (d 1971 [77]) performer BP/55*

FARKOA, Maurice (1864/67-1916) Egyptian/English? actor, singer GRB/1-4, WWS, WWT/1-3

FARLEIGH, Lynn (b 1942) English actress WWT/15-16

FARLEY, Mr. (fl 1797-1801) actor, prompter TD/1-2

FARLEY, Charles (1771-1859) English actor, dramatist, machinist BS, CDP, DD, DNB, GT

FARLEY, James (d 1887 [46]) musical director EA/88*

FARLEY, Mary Ann see Vincent, Mrs. James R.

FARLEY, Morgan (b 1901) American actor WWT/6-10

FARLOW, Mary Ann see Vincent, Mrs. James R.

FARMER, Elizabeth (d 1890 [78]) EA/91*

FARMER, Frances (d 1970 [56]) actress TW/27

FARMER, Henry (d 1891) composer EA/92*

FARMER, John (fl 1554) actor DA

FARMER, John (d 1874 [83]) singer EA/75*

FARMER, John (1835-1901) composer DNB

FARMER, Lucia Eliza [Mrs. James Harwood] (d 1898 [62]) actress EA/00*

FARNABY, Richard (fl 1623-24) musician DA

FARNELL, Jack (d 1976 [61]) producer/director/choreographer BP/60*

FARNIE, Henry Brougham (d 1899) Scottish dramatist, journalist DD

FARNOL, Lynn (d 1963 [63]) American press representative BE*, BP/47*

FARNSWORTH, Harry (d 1916) EA/17*

FARNUM, Dustin (1871/74/75/76-1929) American actor DAB, ES, GRB/3-4, SR, WWA/1, WWM, WWS, WWT/1-3

FARNUM, Franklyn (d 1961 [83]) American actor BE*

FARNUM, G. Dustin (d 1912 [65]) actor WWT/14*

FARNUM, William (1875-1953) American actor ES, SR, TW/10, WWT/3-9

FARQUHAR, George (1678-1707) English dramatist CDP, COC, CP/1-3, DD, DNB, ES, GT, HP, MH, NTH, OC/1-3, PDT, RE, SR

FARQUHAR, Gilbert (1850-1920) English actor DD, DP, EA/97, GRB/1-4, WWW/2

FARQUHAR, Malcolm (b 1924) Welsh director, actor WWT/15-16

FARQUHAR, Robroy (b 1916) English director, actor, manager BE

FARQUHARSON, Alexander (d 1904 [43]) actor EA/05*

FARQUHARSON, Robert (d 1880 [59]) singer EA/80*

FARQUHARSON, Robert (1877-1966) English actor WWT/5-9

FARQUHARSON, Wilfred (d 1916) EA/17*

FARR, "Chick" (d 1948) comedian BE*, WWT/14*

FARR, Derek (b 1912) English actor WWT/11-16

FARR, Florence [Mrs. Edward Emery] (1860-1917) English actress, producer, manager COC, DD, OC/3, WWT/1-3

FARR, Kimberly (b 1948) American actress TW/29-30

FARRAH, Abd'Elkader (b 1926) Algerian designer AAS, WWT/15-16

FARRANT, Richard (fl 1564-80) master of the Children of Windsor, lessee DA

FARRAR, Geraldine (1882-1967) American singer ES, SR, TW/23, WWA/4, WWW/6

FARRAR, Gwen (1879-1944)

English actress, singer WWT/
5-9
FARREL, Charles (d c.1795
[c.97] actor TD/2
FARRELL, Alfred (d 1907) variety
comedian EA/08*
FARRELL, Anthony B. (1899-
1970) producer, investor BE
FARRELL, Brian American actor
TW/29-30
FARRELL, Catherine F. (d 1964
[73]) performer BE*
FARRELL, Charles (d 1970 [78])
producer/director/choreograph-
er BP/55*
FARRELL, Charles (b 1901/02/
06) Irish actor ES, WWT/
8-16
FARRELL, Eileen (b 1920) Amer-
ican singer CB
FARRELL, Eve (d 1972) per-
former BP/56*
FARRELL, Glenda (1904-71)
American actress BE, TW/1,
5-7, 11-16, 25, 27, WWA/5,
WWT/8-15
FARRELL, Henry (d 1878 [43])
actor EA/79*
FARRELL, John (d 1848 [57])
actor, dramatist, manager
CDP
FARRELL, John J. (fl 1884)
American actor WWS
FARRELL, Josephine (d 1972
[87]) performer BP/56*
FARRELL, Margaret [Mrs. Ken-
nedy] (d 1793) actress CDP
FARRELL, Marguerite (d 1951
[62]) actress TW/7
FARRELL, Mary (b 1912) Amer-
ican actress, director BE,
TW/13
FARRELL, M. J. [née Mary
Nesta Skrine] (b 1905) drama-
tist WWT/10-14
FARRELL, Nellie [or Nelly]
(d 1889) singer CDP
FARRELL, Paul (1893-1975)
Irish actor WWT/8-14
FARRELL, Sarah Ann (d 1906)
show girl EA/08*
FARRELL, Suzanne (b 1945)
American dancer CB, ES
FARREN, Miss see Knight,
Mrs. Thomas
FARREN, Babs [Clara Bianca
Rouhan Farren] (b 1904)
actress WWT/4-5, 7

FARREN, Clara Bianca Rouhan
see Farren, Babs
FARREN, Elizabeth (1759-1829)
English actress CDP, COC,
DD, DNB, GT, OC/1-3, TD/1-2
FARREN, Ellen [Mrs. Robert
Soutar; Nellie Farren] (1848-1904)
English actress CDP, COC,
DD, DNB, DP, ES, OAA/1-2,
OC/1-3
FARREN, Fanny Fitz (fl 1859)
actress HAS
FARREN, Florence (d 1878 [25])
actress EA/79*, WWT/14*
FARREN, Fred (d 1956 [82]) Eng-
lish actor, dancer WWT/2-8
FARREN, George Francis (d 1935
[74]) American actor BE*,
BP/19*
FARREN, George Percy (d 1861
[53]) Irish actor CDP, HAS,
WWA/H
FARREN, Mrs. George Percy [née
Mary Ann Russell] (d 1894 [76])
actress CDP, HAS, WWA/H
FARREN, Mrs. Harry see Win-
slow, Kate
FARREN, Henry (1826-60) English
actor DD, DNB, ES, HAS,
OC/1-3
FARREN, Mary Ann see Farren,
Mrs. George Percy
FARREN, Nellie see Farren,
Ellen
FARREN, Percival (1784-1843)
English actor DD, ES, OC/1-3
FARREN, William (1725-95) English
actor CDP, DD, ES, OC/1-3,
TD/1-2
FARREN, William (1786-1861) Eng-
lish actor, manager BS, CDP,
DD, DNB, ES, OC/1-3, OX
FARREN, William, Sr. (1825-1908)
English actor CDP, DD, DNB,
DP, ES, GRB/1-4, OAA/1-2,
OC/1-3
FARREN, William, Jr. (1853-1937)
English actor, dramatist DD,
DP, ES, GRB/1-4, OC/1-3,
WWT/1-6, WWW/3
FARREN, Mrs. William, the
Younger see Diddear, Harriet
Elizabeth
FARRER, Mr. (fl 1790) dramatist
CP/3
FARRER, Ann (b 1916) English ac-
tress WWT/11-14
FARRISSEY, Dan (d 1880) Irish

comedian EA/80*

FARRON, Thomas J. actor CDP

FARROW, John (b 1904) Australian dramatist ES

FARROW, Mia (b 1946) American actress CB, WWT/16

FARTHING, Maud [Mrs. Christie Simonsens] (d 1907) singer EA/08*

FARUSI, Zanetta see Casanova, Signora Gaetano Giuseppe Giacomo

FASCIANO, Richard (b 1943) American actor TW/27-29

FASCIOTTI, Signorina (fl 1849) singer HAS

FASSETT, Jay (b 1889) American actor BE, TW/3-6

FATTY ARBUCKLE see Arbuckle, Roscoe

FAUCIT, Mrs. (fl 1811) dramatist CP/3

FAUCIT, Edmund Saville (1811-57) actor DD

FAUCIT, Harriet [Mrs. Humphrey Bland] (1789/99-1847/57) actress CDP, DD

FAUCIT, Helen [Helena Saville; Mrs. Theodore Martin] (1817-98) English actress CDP, COC, DD, DNB, ES, OAA/1-2, OC/1-3, WWW/1

FAUCIT, John Saville (d 1853 [70]) actor, dramatist, manager DD

FAUCIT, Mrs. John Saville see Diddear, Harriet Elizabeth

FAUE, Mrs. James see Faue, Mary Anne

FAUE, Mary Anne [Mrs. James Faue] (d 1907) EA/08*

FAUGERES, Margaretta Bleecker (1771-1801) American dramatist EAP, RJ

FAUGHMAN, Richard (d 1962 [29]) acrobat BE*

FAULKLAND, Mary [née Fielding] (d 1879 [48]) actress EA/80*

FAULKNER, Mr. (fl 1800s?) actor TD/2

FAULKNER, Anne Maria [Mrs. Donaldson] (fl 18th cent) singer CDP

FAULKNER, Edith Jane (d 1975 [81]) performer BP/60*

FAULKNER, Fanny (d 1871) actress EA/72*

FAULKNER, Robert [Robert Samuel Burrow] (b 1879) English actor GRB/1

FAULKNER, Seldon (b 1929) American educator BE

FAULKNER, Thomas (1775-1847) Irish actor HAS

FAULKNER, William (1897-1962) American dramatist CH, ES, MD, MWD, WWW/6

FAUST, Edwin (d 1910 [69]) EA/11*

FAUST, Lotta [Mrs. Richie Ling] (1880/81-1910) American actress GRB/3-4, WWS

FAVANTI, Rita (d 1867) singer EA/68*

FAVART, Mme. (d 1772 [44]) actress WWT/14*

FAVART, Edmée (d 1941) actress, singer WWT/14*

FAVART, Maria (d 1908 [75]) actress WWT/14*

FAVERO, Mafalda (b 1905) Italian singer ES

FAVERSHAM, Edith Campbell (d 1945 [61]) actress TW/1

FAVERSHAM, Julie Opp see Opp, Julie

FAVERSHAM, William (1868-1940) English/American actor, manager CB, COC, DAB, ES, GRB/2-4, NTH, OC/1-3, SR, WWA/1, WWM, WWS, WWT/1-9

FAVERSHAM, Mrs. William see Opp, Julie

FAVORITE, Harriet Leaf (d 1972 [76]) patron BP/57*

FAVRE, John (d 1876 [36]) property master EA/77*

FAWCETT, Mr. (fl 1760-92) actor TD/1-2

FAWCETT, Mr. (fl 1795) English actor HAS

FAWCETT, Mrs. [Miss Miles] (d 1797) actress WWT/14*

FAWCETT, Anthony [Carré] (b 1869) English actor GRB/1

FAWCETT, Charles (d 1867) English actor, dramatist HAS

FAWCETT, Charles S. (1855-1922) actor, dramatist DD, DP, WWT/4

FAWCETT, Edgar (1847-1904) American dramatist DD, HJD

FAWCETT, Eric (1904-72) English actor, singer WWT/9-10

FAWCETT, George (1860/61-1939)

American actor, manager
GRB/3-4, WWA/1, WWM,
WWT/1-8

FAWCETT, Mrs. George see
Haswell, Percy

FAWCETT, John (d 1793) actor,
singer, musician DD, DNB

FAWCETT, John (1768/69-1837)
English actor, dramatist,
singer BS, CDP, CP/3,
DNB, GT, OX, TD/1-2

FAWCETT, Mrs. John [née
Moore] (d 1797) English actress TD/1-2

FAWCETT, L'estrange English
critic WWT/7-9

FAWCETT, Marion [Katherine
Roger Campbell] (1886-1957)
Scottish actress, producer
WWT/8-12

FAWCETT, Owen S. (1838-1904)
English actor CDP, HAS,
PP/1, WWA/1

FAWCETT, William (d 1916)
EA/17*

FAWDON, Walter see Vokes,
Walter

FAWKES, Mr. (fl early 18th
cent) conjuror CDP

FAWN, James (1850-1923) actor,
singer CDP, DD, WWT/4

FAWSITT, Amy [Mrs. Menzies]
(d 1876 [30]) American? actress CDP, DD

FAX, Max [Fred C. Wilson] (b
1867) English actor, dramatist
GRB/1

FAX, Reuben (d 1908 [46]) actor
GRB/4*

FAY, Abby (fl 1858?) singer
CDP

FAY, Anna Eva (1863-1927)
American mind reader SR

FAY, Bertha singer CDP

FAY, Brendan (d 1975 [54])
American actor TW/24-26,
28-30

FAY, Edward M. (d 1964 [88])
theatre owner, manager BE*

FAY, Frank (1897-1961) American actor, singer CB, SR,
TW/1-8, 18, WWT/7-12

FAY, Frank J. [or G.] (1870-
1931) Irish actor COC, OC/
1-3

FAY, Hugh (d 1895 [43]) actor
CDP

FAY, Léontine CDP

FAY, Maude (fl 1900s) American
singer WWM

FAY, Terry American casting director BE

FAY, William George (1872-1949)
Irish actor, manager COC,
DNB, ES, GRB/4, OC/1-3,
TW/4, WWT/1-10

FAYE, Irma (d 1976 [63]) performer
BP/60*

FAYE, Joey [né Joseph Antony Pal-
ladino] (b 1910) American actor,
comedian BE, TW/8, 11, 25-
27, 30, WWT/15-16

FAYERMANN, Anne Charlotte see
Bartholomew, Anne Charlotte

FAYME, T. B. (d 1906) comedian
EA/07*

FAYNE, Greta actress, singer
WWT/6-11

FAYNE, Kate [Mrs. Richard Bain-
bridge] (d 1903) actress EA/04*

FAYOLLE, Berthe (d 1934 [68])
actress BE*, WWT/14*

FAYRE, Eleanor [née Eleanor Mary
Tydfil Smith-Thomas] (b 1910)
Welsh actress WWT/10

FAZAN, Eleanor (b 1930) Kenyan
director, choreographer, actress
WWT/14-16

FAZENDA, Louise [Mrs. Hal Wal-
lis] (d 1962 [67]) American actress BE*

FEALY, Maude [Mrs. Louis F.
Sherwin] (1883-1971) American
actress GRB/2-4, WWM, WWS,
WWT/1-8

FEARL, Clifford American actor
TW/25-26

FEARNLEY, John (b 1914) American
director BE

FEARON, Mr. (fl 1803) actor TD/2

FEARON, George Edward (b 1901)
English press representative
WWT/9-15

FEARON, James (d 1789 [43])
actor CDP, TD/1-2

FEATHER, Ike (b 1949) American
actor TW/28

FEATHER, Lorraine (b 1948) American actress TW/25

FEATHER, Ruth (d 1965 [77]) performer BP/49*

FEATHERSTON, Eddie (d 1965)
performer BP/50*

FEATHERSTON, Vane (1864-1948)
English actress DD, EA/95,
GRB/1-4, WWT/1-9

FEATHERSTONE, Miss actress
CDP
FEATHERSTONE, Bessie (d 1907)
variety comedian, actress
GRB/3
FEATHERSTONE, Edward George
(d 1893) music-hall proprietor
EA/94*
FEATHERSTONE, Edward George,
Jr. (d 1893) musician EA/94*
FEATHERSTONE, Isabella see
Paul, Mrs. Howard
FEATHERSTONE, Kevin (b 1958)
American actor TW/23
FEATHERSTONE, Mrs. S. (d
1889 [78]) EA/90*
FEATHERSTONHAUGH, Constance
see Benson, Mrs. F. R.
FECHTER, Mrs. Charles (d
1894 [74]) EA/96*
FECHTER, Charles Albert (1824-
79) English actor, dramatist
CDP, COC, DAB, DD, DNB,
ES, NTH, OAA/1-2, OC/1-3,
SR, WWA/H
FECHTER, Paul (d 1888) EA/89*
FECTOR, William (b 1764) actor
CDP
FEDER, Abe (b 1909) American
lighting & scene designer,
producer BE, WWT/16
FEDER, A. H. see Feder, Abe
FEDER, Joseph (d 1970 [69])
business manager BP/55*
FEDER, Sabina (d 1975) per-
former BP/59*
FEDERICI, Frederick (d 1888)
singer WWT/14*
FEDOROVA, Alexandra (d 1972
[83]) dancer, choreographer
BP/57*, WWT/1*
FEDOROVITCH, Sophie (1893-
1953) designer COC, OC/3
FEELEY, Clara (d 1889) acrobat
EA/90*
FEELEY, Mattie [Mrs. Michael
Feeley] (d 1887) EA/88*
FEELEY, Michael (d 1889 [49])
EA/90*
FEELEY, Mrs. Michael see
Feeley, Mattie
FEELY, Terence John (b 1928)
English dramatist WWT/15-
16
FEENEY, Emma [Mrs. Patrick
Feeney] (d 1888) EA/89*
FEENEY, Patrick (d 1883 [82])
showman EA/84*

FEENEY, Patrick (d 1889 [38])
Irish comedian, singer EA/90*
FEENEY, Mrs. Patrick see
Feeney, Emma
FEIFFER, Jules (b 1929) American
dramatist AAS, CD, CH, MH,
WWT/15-16
FEIGAY, Paul (b 1920) American
producer BE, TW/2-5
FEILD, Edward A. (d 1891) singer,
musician EA/93*
FEILDE, Matthew (d 1796) drama-
tist CP/3, DD
FEILER, Herta (d 1970 [54]) per-
former BP/55*
FEIN, Maria (d 1965 [73]) actress
WWT/14*
FEINBERG, Abe I. (d 1962 [71])
talent representative BE*
FEINBERG, Joe (d 1975 [73]) agent
BP/60*
FEINER, Marjorie Lynne (b 1948)
American actress TW/27
FEINMAN, Sigmund (d 1909 [52])
actor BE*, WWT/14*
FEINSTEIN, Alan (b 1941) American
actor TW/22, 25, 30
FEINSTEIN, Laurence [Alan Yorke]
see Feinstein, Alan
FEIST, Catherine (d 1876 [78])
actress EA/77*
FEIST, Gene (b 1930) American
director, producer WWT/15-16
FELD, Eliot (b 1942) American
dancer, choreographer CB
FELD, Israel S. (d 1972 [61]) cir-
cus owner BP/57*
FELD, Leo (d 1896 [39]) conductor
EA/97*
FELDARY, Eric (d 1968 [48]) per-
former BP/52*
FELDER, Clarence (b 1938) Amer-
ican actor TW/30
FELDMAN, Andrea (d 1972) per-
former BP/57*
FELDMAN, David (d 1895 [17])
acrobat EA/96*
FELDMAN, Edythe A. (d 1971 [58])
performer BP/55*
FELDMAN, Erwin (d 1972 [67])
lawyer BP/56*
FELDMAN, Gladys (1899-1974)
actress BE, TW/30
FELDMAN, Laurence (1926-67)
American producer, director
BE, TW/23
FELDMAN, Maurice (d 1976 [66])
publicist BP/60*

FELDMAN, Shellie American
actress TW/23-24

FELDSTEIN, Robert D. (d 1969
[42]) producer/director/
choreographer BP/54*

FELEKY, Leslie (d 1971 [59])
composer/lyricist BP/56*

FELGATE, Peter (b 1919) English actor, dancer, singer
WWT/12-15

FELIX, Adeline M. [Mrs. Tony
Felix] (d 1908) EA/09*

FELIX, Charlotte [Mrs. Fred
Felix] (d 1890) EA/91*

FELIX, Elisa see Rachel

FELIX, Mrs. Fred see Felix,
Charlotte

FELIX, George (b 1866) American vaudevillian WWM

FELIX, Mrs. George see
Barry, Lydia

FELIX, Hugo (1866-1934) composer WWT/2-7

FELIX, Lena [Mrs. Tony Toney
Felix] (d 1891) EA/92*

FELIX, Raphael (d 1872 [46])
director EA/73*

FELIX, Sarah (d 1877 [59]) actress BE*, WWT/14*

FELIX, Mrs. Toney see Felix,
Lena

FELIX, Tony [Thomas Green]
(d 1911) clown EA/12*

FELIX, Mrs. Tony see Felix,
Adeline M.

FELL, C. C. (d 1907 [64])
museum proprietor EA/08*

FELL, Charles Tasker (d 1894
[58]) acting manager EA/95*

FELL, Talbot (d 1898 [24]) actor
EA/99*

FELLMAN, Mons. (fl 1828)
French dancer HAS

FELLOWES, Amy [Mrs. William
Terriss] (d 1898) actress
COC

FELLOWES, Rockcliffe (d 1950
[65]) Canadian actor BE*

FELLOWES-ROBINSON, Dora
(d 1946) Mauritian/English
business manager, producer
WWT/4-5

FELLOWS, Dexter William (d
1937 [66]) American press
representative BE*, BP/22*

FELLOWS, Don (b 1922) American actor TW/6-8, 21-23,
27-28

FELLOWS, Edith (b 1923) American
actress TW/2-7, 13

FELLOWS, Frances Ethel (d 1882)
actress EA/83*

FELLOWS, J. B. (fl 1852?) minstrel manager CDP

FELSENSTEIN, Walter (d 1975
[74]) producer/director/chore-
ographer BP/60*

FELSTED, Beatrice English actress
GRB/1

FELTON, Happy (d 1964 [56]) performer BP/49*

FELYNE, Renée (d 1910 [26]) actress BE*, WWT/14*

FENDALL, Percy (d 1917) dramatist DD

FENDER, Doris (d 1975 [75]) performer BP/60*

FENELON, E. (d 1863) musical
director HAS

FENN, Ezekiel (b 1620) English
actor DA, COC, OC/1-3

FENN, Frederick (1868-1924)
English dramatist DD, GRB/
2-4, WWT/1-4, WWW/2

FENN, George Manville (d 1909
[78]) dramatist DD

FENN, Peggy American actress
BE

FENNELL, James (1766-1816) Eng-
lish actor, dramatist CDP,
COC, CP/3, DAB, DD, DNB,
EAP, HAS, OC/1-3, RJ, SR,
TD/1-2, WWA/H

FENNELL, James, Jr. (fl 1812)
actor HAS

FENNER, H. Wolcott (d 1972 [61])
circus executive BP/57*

FENNESSY, John (b 1946) American
actor TW/27

FENNO, Ada V. (d 1975 [90]) pro-
ducer/director/choreographer
BP/60*

FENNO, Richard F. (d 1967 [40])
composer/lyricist BP/52*

FENNO, Will (b 1948) American
actor TW/28

FENNO, William Augustus (b 1814)
American actor, lecturer, dramatist HAS, RJ

FENTON, Albert Edward see
Elba

FENTON, Mrs. C. H. see
Hodson, Kate

FENTON, Charles (d 1877 [56])
actor, scene artist DD

FENTON, Mrs. Charles [Caroline

Parkes] (d 1887) actress EA/
88*

FENTON, Mrs. Charles <u>see</u>
Hodson, Kate

FENTON, Elijah (1683-1730) English dramatist CP/1-3, DD,
GT, TD/1-2

FENTON, Elizabeth [Mrs. John
Fenton] (d 1874 [32]) EA/76*

FENTON, Frank (b 1868) English
actor, manager GRB/1-4

FENTON, Frank (d 1957 [51])
American actor BE*, BP/42*

FENTON, Frederick Gill (1817-
98) English scene designer
ES

FENTON, Harry (d 1868 [33])
actor? EA/69*

FENTON, James Gill (d 1877
[83]) actor? EA/78*

FENTON, Mrs. John T. <u>see</u>
Fenton, Rosina Ruth

FENTON, Kitty [Mrs. Harry
Roxbury] (d 1902 [32]) actress
EA/03*

FENTON, Lavinia (1708-60) English actress CDP, COC, DD,
DNB, ES, OC/1-3

FENTON, Lucille (d 1966 [50s])
performer BP/51*

FENTON, Mabel (1872-1931)
American actress SR, WWS

FENTON, Ralph D. (b 1883)
English assistant manager
GRB/1

FENTON, Rosina Ruth [Mrs.
John T. Fenton] (d 1892)
EA/93*

FENTUM, John (d 1879) performer? EA/81*

FENTUM, Jonathan (fl 1784?)
musician? CDP

FENWICK, Harry <u>see</u> Hardie,
W. R.

FENWICK, Irene (1887-1936)
American actress CDP,
WWT/4-8

FENWICK, John (fl 1800) dramatist CP/3

FENWICKE, Arthur (d 1895)
actor EA/96*

FENZL, Franz dancer CDP

FENZL, John dancer, acrobat
CDP

FENZL, Sophie dancer CDP

FEODOROVNA, Vera (d 1910)
actress WWT/14*

FERAL, Roger (d 1964 [60])

dramatist BP/49*

FERBER, Bernie (d 1965 [59])
manager BP/50*

FERBER, Edna (1887-1968) Ameri-
can dramatist AAS, BE, COC,
HJD, MD, MH, MWD, NTH,
OC/3, TW/24, WWT/6-14,
WWW/6

FERDINAND, Annie [Mrs. George
Ferdinand] (d 1872 [37]) EA/73*

FERDINAND, Mrs. George <u>see</u>
Ferdinand, Annie

FERGUSON, Miss actress CDP

FERGUSON, Anna E. (fl 1858) actress HAS

FERGUSON, Barney (d 1924 [71])
performer BE*, BP/9*

FERGUSON, Catherine (b 1895)
English actress, singer WWT/
5-7

FERGUSON, Elizabeth [Mrs. R.
Ferguson] (d 1876) EA/77*

FERGUSON, Elsie (1883/85/86-
1961) American actress CB,
SR, TW/2-6, 18, WWA/4,
WWM, WWT/1-11

FERGUSON, Frank (d 1937 [74])
American dramatist, actor
WWM

FERGUSON, Howard (d 1974 [78])
performer BP/58*

FERGUSON, John (d 1867 [70])
comedian EA/68*

FERGUSON, John (d 1887 [70])
music-hall performer? EA/88*

FERGUSON, Mrs. R. <u>see</u> Ferguson, Elizabeth

FERGUSON, Rachel (1893-1957)
English dramatist WWW/5

FERGUSON, Robert V. (c.1860-
1913) Scottish actor SR, WWS

FERGUSON, William Jason (1849-
1930) American actor DAB,
PP/1, SR, WWA/1, WWM,
WWS

FERGUSSON, Francis (b 1904)
American critic BE

FERLINGHETTI, Lawrence (b 1911)
American dramatist CD, CH

FERN, Sable (d 1942 [66]) comedienne, singer WWT/14*

FERNALD, Chester Bailey (1869-
1938) American dramatist
GRB/3-4, HJD, NTH, WWA/1,
WWT/1-8, WWW/3

FERNALD, John Bailey (b 1905)
American producer, principal of
the Royal Academy of Dramatic

Art, director AAS, OC/2-3, WWT/7-16

FERNANDEL [Ferdinand Joseph Desire Contandin] (1903-71) French actor WWA/5

FERNANDEZ, Mrs. (d 1880 [76]) EA/81*

FERNANDEZ, A. B. (d 1909 [68]) EA/10*

FERNANDEZ, Bijou [Mrs. W. L. Abingdon] (1877-1961) American actress GRB/3-4, TW/10-11, 18, WWM, WWS, WWT/1-5

FERNANDEZ, James (1835-1915) Russian/English actor DD, GRB/1-4, OAA/1-2, WWT/1-2

FERNANDEZ, Jose (b 1948) Cuban actor TW/26-28, 30

FERNANDEZ, Rose [Mrs. Robert Davis] (d 1900 [30]) equestrian EA/01*

FERNE, Fred (d 1953 [61]) manager WWT/14*

FERNLEY, Henry (d 1918) EA/19*

FERNS, Katie (d 1900 [34]) actress EA/01*

FERON, Elizabeth (1793/97-1853) English singer, actress CDP, DD, HAS, WWA/H

FERRABOSCO, Alfonso (fl 1562-78) Italian actor DA

FERRAND, Henry (d 1892) actor EA/93*

FERRANI, Frederick (d 1888) singer EA/89*

FERRANTI, Pietro (d 1896) composer, singer CDP

FERRAR, Ada (1867-1951) English actress DD, GRB/2-4

FERRAR, Beatrice (d 1958 [82]) English actress DD, GRB/3-4, WWT/1-6

FERRAR, John (fl 1765) Irish? dramatist CP/3

FERRAR, Thomas H. (d 1917) EA/18*

FERRARD, Grace (d 1965 [100]) performer BP/49*

FERRARI-FONTANA, Edoardo (1878-1936) Italian singer WWA/1

FERRARIS, Amalia (1828-1904) Italian dancer ES

FERRE, Signora San-Antonio see Cuzzoni, Francesca

FERRELL, Conchata (b 1943) American actress TW/29-30

FERRER, José (b 1909/12) Puerto Rican actor, producer, director AAS, BE, CB, ES, NTH, TW/1-21, 23-26, WWT/10-16

FERRER, Mel (b 1917) American actor, director, producer BE, ES, TW/10

FERRER, Melchior singer TW/2

FERRERS, Mr. (d 1841) Scottish prompter HAS

FERRERS, Mrs. see Byrnes, Mrs.

FERRERS, Edward (d c.1564) dramatist CP/2-3

FERRERS, George (1500?-79) dramatist, Master of the King's Pastimes DD, FGF

FERRERS, Helen (d 1943 [77]) English actress EA/96, GRB/1-4, WWT/1-8

FERRET, James (fl 1635) actor DA

FERRI, Gaetano (1816-81) singer CDP, HAS

FERRIAR, Dr. John (fl 1788) dramatist CP/3, DD

FERRIER, Jessie see Lindon, Louie

FERRIER, Kathleen (1912-53) English singer CB, DNB, ES, WWA/4, WWW/5

FERRIER, Paul (d 1920 [77]) dramatist WWT/14*

FERRIS, Barbara (b 1943) English actress TW/24, WWT/15-16

FERRIS, David (fl 1629) actor DA

FERRIS, John (b 1839) American actor HAS

FERRISS, Joseph (d 1885) comedian EA/86*

FERRO, Beth H. (d 1974 [49]) producer/director/choreographer BP/59*

FERRUGIO, Richard (b 1949) American actor TW/29

FERRUSAC, La Comtesse de (fl 1859) American singer HAS

FERRY, Robert (d 1890 [70]) musician EA/91*

FESCO, Michael (b 1936) American actor TW/16-19

FESSENDEN, William H. (fl 1879?) singer CDP

FEST, J. (fl 1845) actor HAS

FETHERSON, William (fl 1612) actor DA

FETTER, Selena see Royle,
Selena Fetter
FEUCHTWANGER, Lion (1884-
1958) German dramatist
MWD, NTH
FEUER, Cy (b 1911) American
producer, director BE, WWT/
14-16
FEUILLERE, Edwige (b 1907)
French actress OC/3, TW/
13-14
FEUILLET, Octave (1821-90)
French dramatist DD
FEUSSNER, Alfred (d 1969 [33])
performer BP/54*
FEYDEAU, Georges (1862-1921)
French dramatist COC, MD,
MWD, OC/3, PDT
FEYGHINE, Julie (d 1882) ac-
tress EA/83*
FFOLKES, David (b 1912) Eng-
lish designer ES, TW/3-8,
WWT/11-13
FFOLLIOTT, Gladys (d 1928
[69]) Irish actress WWT/4-5
FFRANGCON-DAVIES, David
(1850-1918) Welsh singer
WWW/2
FFRANGCON-DAVIES, Gwen (b
1896) English actress, singer
AAS, ES, WWT/5-16
FIAN, Robbee (b 1951) American
dancer TW/30
"FIBBER McGEE" see Jordan,
James E.
FICE, E. S. (d 1875) musician
EA/76*
FICHANDLER, Zelda [née Dia-
mond] (b 1924) American pro-
ducer, director AAS, BE,
WWT/15-16
FICKETT, Mary American actress
BE, TW/14-17, 20
FIDDES, Harriet Catherine [Miss
H. Cause] (d 1889 [77]) EA/
90*
FIDDES, Josephine (d 1923 [85])
English actress HAS
FIDGE, William (fl 1571) actor
DA
FIEDLER, John (b 1925) Ameri-
can actor BE, TW/10, 21-
23, 26
FIELD dramatist EAP
FIELD, Mrs. (d 1881 [61]) drama
coach? EA/82*
FIELD, Miss (fl 1777) actress
CDP

FIELD, Alexander (1892-1971) Eng-
lish actor WWT/7-13
FIELD, Al. G. (d 1921 [72]) Amer-
ican minstrel BE*, WWT/14*
FIELD, Barron (d 1846 [59]) critic
WWT/14*
FIELD, Ben (d 1939 [61]) actor
WWT/4-9
FIELD, Benjamin (d 1897) manager
EA/98*
FIELD, Mrs. Benjamin see
Field, Sarah Fawcett
FIELD, Betty (1918-73) American
actress AAS, BE, CB, TW/1-
20, 22, 27, 30, WWT/9-16
FIELD, Edward Salisbury (d 1936
[56]) American dramatist WWT/
4-8
FIELD, Francis (d 1968 [75])
dramatist BP/52*
FIELD, Henry (fl 1635) actor DA
FIELD, Henry (d 1889) EA/90*
FIELD, Jean see Kent, Jean
FIELD, J. K. (d 1842) Irish actor
HAS
FIELD, John (b 1921) English
dancer, ballet master ES
FIELD, Jonathan (b 1912) English
actor, producer, composer
WWT/11-14
FIELD, Joseph M. (1810-56) Eng-
lish/American actor, editor,
manager, dramatist CDP, DAB,
HAS, HJD, RJ, WWA/H
FIELD, Julian dramatist DD
FIELD, Kate see Field, Mary
Katherine Kemble
FIELD, Leonard (b 1908) American
producer, director BE
FIELD, Lila (d 1954) dramatist
BE*, WWT/14*
FIELD, Margaret St. John see
Field, Virginia
FIELD, Mary Katherine Kemble
(1838-96) American actress,
dramatist, singer CDP, DAB,
DD, WWA/H
FIELD, Matthew see Feilde,
Matthew
"FIELD, Michael" dramatist DD,
HP, WWW/1
FIELD, Nathaniel (1587-1620) Eng-
lish actor, dramatist CDP,
COC, CP/1-3, DA, DNB, ES,
FGF, GT, HP, NTH, OC/1-3,
RE
FIELD, Rachel Lyman (1894-1942)
children's dramatist CB, HJD,

WWA/2

FIELD, Richard Montgomery (1834-1902) manager CDP

FIELD, Robert (b 1916) American actor TW/1-3

FIELD, Robin (b 1947) American actor TW/28-29

FIELD, Ron choreographer, director WWT/16

FIELD, Roswell Martin (1851-1919) critic HJD

FIELD, Sarah Fawcett [Mrs. Benjamin Field] (d 1883 [40]) EA/80*

FIELD, Shirley Ann (b 1936) English actress ES

FIELD, Sid (1904-50) English comedian TW/6, WWT/10

FIELD, Sylvia [Harriett Johnson] (b 1901/02) American actress BE, TW/5-8, WWT/7-13

FIELD, T. M. American writer DD

FIELD, Virginia [née Margaret St. John Field] (b 1917) English actress TW/5, WWT/10-12

FIELD, William H. (d 1971 [56]) producer/director/choreographer BP/56*

FIELDE, Matthew see Feilde, Matthew

FIELDEN, Lionel (d 1974 [78]) producer/director/choreographer BP/59*

FIELDHOUSE, Harry (d 1909 [43]) musician EA/11*

FIELDING, Mr. (fl 1825) English actor HAS

FIELDING, Anne (b 1936) American actress TW/15

FIELDING, Anne (b 1943) American actress TW/26

FIELDING, Ben (d 1893 [44]) singer, actor CDP

FIELDING, Mrs. C. (d 1886) EA/87*

FIELDING, Dora (d 1898) seriocomic EA/99*

FIELDING, Edward [Edward B. Elkins] (1875-1945) American actor WWM

FIELDING, Fenella (b 1934) English actress WWT/14-16

FIELDING, Harold English producer WWT/15-16

FIELDING, Henry (1707-54) English dramatist, writer CDP,

COC, CP/1-3, DD, DNB, ES, GT, HP, MH, NTH, OC/1-3, RE, SR, TD/1-2

FIELDING, John actor CDP

FIELDING, Maggie actress CDP

FIELDING, Marjorie (1892-1956) English actress WWT/8-12, WWW/5

FIELDING, Mary see Faulkland, Mary

FIELDING, Sarah (1710/14-68) English dramatist CP/2-3, GT, HP

FIELDING, Timothy (d 1738) actor COC, OC/3

FIELDING, William J. (d 1874 [48]) singer EA/75*

FIELDING, W. J. actor? CDP

FIELDS, A. G. (b 1851) circus manager, actor, singer, minstrel SR

FIELDS, Benny (d 1959 [65]) American vaudevillian TW/16

FIELDS, Dorothy (1905-74) American librettist, lyricist BE, CB, COC, NTH, TW/30, WWT/10-15

FIELDS, Frank (d 1869) equestrian EA/70*

FIELDS, Frank Gaskin (d 1969 [59]) composer/lyricist BP/53*

FIELDS, Gracie [née Stansfield] (b 1898) English actress, singer CB, COC, ES, OC/3, SR, WWT/5-11

FIELDS, Harry D. (d 1961 [65]) performer BE*

FIELDS, Herbert (1897/98-1958) American librettist CB, COC, NTH, TW/14, WWT/7-12

FIELDS, John F. (b 1853) minstrel CDP

FIELDS, Joseph (1895-1966) American dramatist AAS, BE, COC, MD, MH, MWD, NTH, TW/22, WWT/10-14

FIELDS, Joseph H. (1798-1856) English/American actor, manager, dramatist SR

FIELDS, Judy American actress TW/29

FIELDS, Kate (d 1896) American actress SR

FIELDS, Lew [Lewis Maurice Fields] (1867-1941) American actor, manager CB, COC, ES, GRB/3-4, NTH, SR, WWA/1, WWM, WWS, WWT/1-9

FIELDS, Robert (b 1938) American

actor TW/23

FIELDS, Robert see Blumenfeld, Robert

FIELDS, Sid (d 1975 [77]) comedian, dramatist BP/60*, WWT/16*

FIELDS, Stanley (1884?-1941) actor CB

FIELDS, William (d 1961 [62]) press agent TW/17

FIELDS, W[illiam] C[laude; né Dukinfield] (1879/80-1946) American actor COC, DAB, ES, OC/3, SR, TW/3, WWA/2, WWM, WWT/7-10

FIENNES, Sydney [Cowley Polhill] (b 1877) English actor GRB/1

FIENZAL, Jean-François see Durancy, Mons.

FIENZAL, Mme. Jean-François see Durancy, Mme. Jean-François

FIFE, Bobby (d 1972 [70]) performer BP/56*

FIFE, Evelyn Henderson (d 1969 [81]) performer BP/53*

FIFE, George (d 1902) manager EA/03*

FIFIELD, Elaine (b 1930) Australian dancer WWT/12

FIGETTE, Ada (d 1904 [21]) EA/05*

FIGG, James (d 1734) English pugilist DNB

FIGGINS, Jane see Wenham, Jane

FIGMAN, Max (1868-1952) Austrian actor, director WWS, WWT/1-2

FIGMAN, Oscar (d 1930 [48]) actor BE*, BP/15*, WWT/14*

FIGNER, Nikolai Nikolaevich (1857-1918) Russian singer ES

FIGUERORA, Laura (b 1948) Puerto Rican actress TW/26

FILDES, Audrey (b 1922) English actress WWT/10-13

FILIPPI, Rosina [Mrs. H. M. Dowson] (1866-1930) Italian actress, dramatist DD, GRB/1-4, WWT/1-6

FILKINS, Grace (d 1962 [97]) American actress TW/19, WWS, WWT/2-7

FILLIS, Annie (b 1866) English circus performer ES

FILLIS, Annie (1869-1951) English acrobat, circus performer ES

FILLIS, Charles (b 1839) English acrobat, equestrian ES

FILLIS, Frank (d 1927) English equestrian ES

FILLIS, Mrs. Frank E. see Fillis, Lizzie

FILLIS, Harry (d 1873 [23]) equestrian EA/74*

FILLIS, Henry (d 1869 [41]) EA/70*

FILLIS, James (1834-1913) English circus performer ES

FILLIS, Lizzie [Mrs. Frank E. Fillis] (d 1890) EA/91*

FILLIS, Thomas (d 1876 [45]) equestrian EA/77*

FILLIS, Thomas English equestrian, clown ES

FILMER, A. E. producer, actor WWT/6-10

FILMER, Edward (fl 1675-1707) dramatist CP/1-3, DNB, GT

FILMORE, Lewis (fl 1841-82) dramatist, translator DD

FILOMENA, Josefina (b 1853) Chilean pianist HAS

FIMBERG, Harold A. (d 1974 [67]) dramatist BP/58*

FINA, Jack (d 1970) composer/lyricist BP/54*

FINCH, Anne, Countess of Winchilsea (d 1720) English dramatist CP/1-3, GT

FINCH, Flora (1869-1940) English actress ES

FINCH, Henry (d 1901 [62]) lessee EA/02*

FINCH, John dramatist CD

FINCH, Mrs. Jones see Finch, Sarah

FINCH, Peter (1916-77) English actor AAS, CB, ES, WWT/11-15

FINCH, Sarah [Mrs. Jones Finch] (d 1877) EA/78*

FINCK, Herman [Herman von der Finck] (1869/72-1939) English conductor, composer GRB/1, WWT/4-8, WWW/3

FINDLATER, Adam S. (d 1911) music-hall director EA/12*

FINDLATER, Richard (b 1921) critic AAS

FINDLAY, Ruth (d 1949 [45]) actress TW/6

FINDLAY, Thomas B. (1871-1941) Canadian actor WWM

FINDON, B. W. (1859-1943)
English dramatist, critic DD,
GRB/2-4, WWT/1-8, WWW/4

FINE, Aaron (d 1963 [46]) dramatist BE*

FINE, Hank (d 1975 [72]) publicist BP/60*

FINE, Larry (d 1975 [73]) comedian BP/59*, WWT/16*

FINE, Marshall H. (d 1975
[48]) executive BP/59*

FINE, Max (d 1974 [74]) theatrical display creator BP/59*

FINEBERG, Isaac (d 1903 [85])
music-hall proprietor EA/
04*

FINEGAN, James (d 1916 [49])
agent EA/18*

FINEMAN, Vivian (b 1951) American actress TW/30

FINGER, Godfrey (c.1685-1717)
Moravian composer DD, DNB

FINGER, Simeon Woolfe (d 1916
[42]) musician EA/17*

FINKELSTEIN, Sidney (d 1974
[64]) critic BP/58*

FINKELSTONE, George N. (d
1966 [74]) performer BP/50*

FINKLEHOFFE, Fred F. (1911-
77) American producer,
dramatist BE

FINLAY, Edward J. (d 1912)
actor EA/13*

FINLAY, Frank (b 1926) English
actor AAS, WWT/14-16

FINLAY, P. (d 1875) scene
artist EA/76*

FINLEY, Patte American actress
TW/22-23

FINN, Arthur actor WWT/8-9

FINN, Frank S. (fl 1857) actor
HAS

FINN, George H. (d 1854) American actor HAS

FINN, Henry James (1785/87/
90-1840) American actor,
dramatist CDP, COC, DAB,
EAP, HAS, OC/1-3, RJ, SR,
WWA/H

FINN, H. W. (fl 1850) actor HAS

FINN, Jonathan (d 1971 [87])
dramatist BP/56*

FINNEGAN, Edward (d 1971 [72])
performer BP/55*

FINNEGAN, Mrs. George see
Deland, Annie

FINNEGAN, James F. (d 1972
[64]) publicist BP/57*

FINNELL, Carrie (d 1963 [70])
American performer BE*, BP/
48*

FINNERTY, Warren (d 1974 [40/49])
actor BP/59*, WWT/16*

FINNEY (fl 1783) dramatist CP/3

FINNEY, Albert (b 1936) English
actor AAS, BE, CB, COC, ES,
PDT, TW/20, 24, WWT/13-16

FINNEY, Jameson Lee (1863/68-
1911) American actor GRB/3-4,
WWS

FINNEY, Martha (d 1889) EA/90*

FINNEY, Mary (1906-73) American
actress BE, TW/9-15, 29

FINNEY, May see Fortescue,
May

FINNEY, William (d 1903) diver
EA/04*

FIORE, Frank (b 1953) American
actor TW/26-27

FIORENTINI, Claudina (fl 1853)
singer CDP

FIORILLO, Tiberio (1608-94) Italian
actor OC/1-3

FIRE, Richard (b 1945) American
actor TW/29

FIREHOUSE THEATRE, The theatre
collective CD

FIRESTONE, Eddie (b 1920) American actor, director BE, TW/
10-11

FIRESTONE, Scott (b 1962) American actor TW/29

FIRMIN, Dorothy (b 1888) English
actress, singer, dancer GRB/1

FIRTH, Anne (b 1918) English actress WWT/9-11

FIRTH, Edwin (b 1869) English actor GRB/1

FIRTH, Elizabeth (b 1884) American
actress, singer GRB/4, WWT/
1-5

FIRTH, Henry (d 1884 [58]) musician EA/85*

FIRTH, Henry Redfern (d 1916 [1])
EA/17*

FIRTH, Tazeena (b 1935) English
designer WWT/16

FISCALL, Martha (d 1880) equestrian EA/81*

FISCHER, Alice [Mrs. William Har-
court] (1869-1947) American actress GRB/2-4, TW/4, WWM,
WWS, WWT/1-9

FISCHER, Bob (d 1972 [36]) performer BP/57*

FISCHER, Charlotte Andrews (d

1968 [58]) performer BP/53*
FISCHER, Clifford C. (d 1951
[69]) Belgian producer BE*,
BP/36*
FISCHER, Emil Friedrich August
(1838-1914) German singer
DAB, ES
FISCHER, Harry (d 1908) actor
EA/09*, WWT/14*
FISCHER, Mrs. Harry see
Searle, Kate
FISCHER, Jane (b 1930) American
dancer TW/4
FISCHER, Max (d 1974 [65]) per-
former BP/59*
FISCHER, Robert E. (b 1923)
American architect BE
FISCHER, Ruth (b 1895) Rumani-
an/American press representa-
tive BE
FISCHER, Ruth (b 1919) American
press representative BE
FISH, Mrs. A. F. see Fish,
Eliza Rachel
FISH, Charles W. (fl 1877)
equestrian CDP
FISH, Eliza Rachel [Mrs. A. F.
Fish] (d 1910) EA/11*
FISH, Fred C. (d 1900 [43])
variety comedian EA/02*
FISH, Jenny (b 1852) actress,
dancer CDP
FISH, Marguerite [Mrs. Charles
Warren; "Baby Benson"] (d
1903 [34]) actress CDP
FISHBOURNE, Mr. dramatist
CP/1-3
FISHER (fl 1798?) dramatist
CP/3
FISHER, Miss see Bernard,
Mrs. John, II
FISHER, A. (d 1875) acting
manager EA/76*
FISHER, Alexander (d 1893 [71])
American actor EA/94*,
WWT/14*
FISHER, Alexina CDP
FISHER, Alfred (d 1975 [68])
performer BP/59*
FISHER, Mrs. Alice see Rams-
dale, Alice
FISHER, Allan (d 1917 [23]) ac-
tor EA/18*
FISHER, Amelia (fl 1827-29)
English actress HAS
FISHER, Carl (1909-74) American
business manager, general
manager BE

FISHER, Charles (1795-1869) actor,
manager, musician DD
FISHER, Charles (1815/16-91)
English actor CDP, DD, ES,
GC, HAS, WWA/H
FISHER, Charles (d 1916) actor
WWT/14*
FISHER, Charles J. B. (1804-59)
actor HAS
FISHER, Mrs. Charles J. B. see
Chapman, Elizabeth
FISHER, Clara (1811-98) English
actress, singer BS, CDP,
COC, DAB, DD, HAS, OC/1-3,
WWA/H
FISHER, Clara, Little (b 1853)
American actress HAS
FISHER, David (1760/61-1832)
English singer, manager DD,
ES
FISHER, David, the Elder (1788-
1858) English actor CDP, DD,
DNB, ES
FISHER, David, the Younger (1816-
87) English actor DD, DNB,
ES, NYM, OAA/1-2
FISHER, Mrs. David see Fisher,
Mary
FISHER, Douglas (b 1934) American
actor TW/27, 29-30
FISHER, Fred (d 1875) scene painter
EA/76*
FISHER, Fred (1875-1942) German
composer BE*
FISHER, Gail (b 1939) American
actress TW/22
FISHER, George (d 1864) agent
EA/72*
FISHER, Harry E. (d 1923 [55])
English performer BE*, BP/7*
FISHER, Irving (d 1959 [73]) actor,
singer TW/15
FISHER, Irving (d 1964 [60]) per-
former BP/49*
FISHER, James B. (d 1887) Amer-
ican journalist, dramatist EA/
88*
FISHER, Jane [Mrs. George Ver-
non] (d 1869) actress BE*
FISHER, Dr. Jasper (fl 1607-31)
English dramatist CP/2-3,
FGF
FISHER, J. B. (fl 1808) dramatist
CP/3
FISHER, J. B. S. (1804-59) English
actor, manager SR
FISHER, John (fl 1622) lessee DA
FISHER, John (d 1848) English

actor HAS

FISHER, John (d 1885) lessee
EA/86*

FISHER, John Abraham (1744-
1806) English musician, composer DNB

FISHER, John C. (d 1921 [67])
American manager, producer
BE*, BP/6*, WWT/14*

FISHER, John R. (d 1868) actor
HAS

FISHER, Jules (b 1937) American
lighting designer BE, WWT/
16

FISHER, Kate (1823/40-1918)
American actress CDP, HAS

FISHER, Lewis T. (b 1915)
American producer, actor BE

FISHER, Lilian May see Ramsdale, Lilian

FISHER, Lola (1896-1926) American actress SR, WWT/5

FISHER, Lola American singer,
actress BE

FISHER, Mary [Mrs. David Fish-
er] (d 1879) EA/80*

FISHER, Nelle (b 1914) American
dancer, choreographer, director
BE, TW/1, 4

FISHER, Oceana (fl 1838-68) actress HAS

FISHER, Palmer (d 1827) English
actor HAS

FISHER, Mrs. Palmer see
Thayer, Mrs. Edward

FISHER, Perkins D. (1860-1930)
American actor, manager SR

FISHER, Ruth H. (d 1974 [60s])
performer BP/59*

FISHER, Sallie (d 1950 [69])
American actress TW/7,
WWM

FISHER, Sarah see Egerton,
Sarah

FISHER, Mrs. Thomas see
Abrams, Theodosia

FISHER, Thomas Alexander [né
Thomas Smith] (fl 1847) actor
HAS

FISHER, Walter David (1845-89)
English actor, manager ES

FISHER, Walter H. (fl 1873-
79) English actor DD, OAA/2

FISHMAN, Henry (d 1964 [76])
Russian/American actor BE*

FISHMAN, Melvin A. (d 1976
[46]) producer/director/
choreographer BP/60*

FISK, Edith (d 1976 [67]) performer
BP/60*

FISK, James, Jr. (d 1872) manager
WWT/14*

FISKE, Harrison Grey (1861-1942)
American dramatist, manager
DAB, DD, GRB/2-4, SR, WWA/
2, WWM, WWS, WWT/1-9

FISKE, Mrs. Harrison Grey see
Fiske, Minnie Maddern

FISKE, James B. (1835-72) American manager, impresario CDP,
HAS, SR

FISKE, Marian [Mrs. Thomas J.
Martin] (d 1896) actress CDP

FISKE, Mary H. (d 1889) American
dramatist, journalist EA/90*

FISKE, Minnie Maddern [Mrs. Har-
rison Grey Fiske] (1865-1932)
American actress CDP, COC,
DAB, ES, GRB/2-4, HJD, NTH,
OC/1-3, PP/1, SR, WWA/1,
WWM, WWS, WWT/1-6

FISKE, Moses W. (1830-87) American actor, manager CDP,
HAS, NYM

FISKE, Stephen (1840-1916) Amer-
ican dramatist, critic CDP,
DAB, GRB/2-4, WWA/1, WWM,
WWT/1-3

FITCH, Clyde (1865-1909) American
dramatist COC, DAB, DD, ES,
GRB/2-4, HJD, MD, MH,
MWD, NTH, OC/1-3, RE, WWA/
1, WWS, WWW/1

FITCH, Haidee (b 1892) English actress, dancer GRB/1

FITCH, Joseph (b 1921) American
educator, director BE

FITCH, Robert (b 1934) American
actor TW/30

FITCH, Stephen see Douglass,
Stephen

FITCH, William Clyde see Fitch,
Clyde

FITCHETT, Henry (d 1877 [40])
musician EA/78*

FITCHETT, H. W. (d 1877) musician EA/78*

FITE, Mrs. E. M. S. (fl 1890s-
1900s) American agent WWM

FITT, Mrs. (d 1892 [53]) EA/93*

FITTS, Dudley (1903-68) American
educator, translator BE

FITTS, Harry Atkinson see Atkinson, Harry

FITZ, Charles E. (d 1920) actor
BE*, BP/5*

FITZ, Erica (b 1942) American
actress TW/24
FITZBALL, Edward (1792-1873)
English dramatist CDP,
COC, DD, DNB, EA/68, OC/
1-3
FITZGEORGE, Mrs. see Fair-
brother, Louisa
FITZGERALD, Mr. actor CDP
FITZGERALD, Alexander (fl
1858-68) actor HAS
FITZGERALD, Aubrey Whitestone
(b 1876) Irish actor GRB/1,
WWT/1-5
FITZGERALD, Barry [né William
Joseph Shields] (1888-1961)
Irish actor CB, ES, TW/17,
WWA/4, WWT/10-11
FITZGERALD, Cissy (1873?-1941)
English actress CB
FITZGERALD, Daniel (d 1906
[46]) circus proprietor EA/07*
FITZGERALD, Dorothy (d 1899)
EA/01*
FITZGERALD, Eddie see Foy,
Eddie
FITZGERALD, Edith (d 1968
[75]) dramatist BP/52*
FITZGERALD, Edward (1809-83)
translator, dramatist DD, HP
FITZGERALD, Edward (b 1876)
Irish actor, business manager
GRB/1-4, WWS, WWT/3-4
FITZGERALD, Ellie Teresa
[Mrs. John G. Fitzgerald]
(d 1886 [28]) EA/87*
FITZGERALD, Florence Irene
(d 1962 [72]) actress BE*
FITZGERALD, F. Scott (1896-
1940) American dramatist
MD
FITZGERALD, Geraldine (b 1914)
Irish actress BE, CB, TW/
27-28, WWT/15-16
FITZGERALD, John (d 1912 [74])
musical director EA/13*
FITZGERALD, Mrs. John G.
see Fitzgerald, Ellie Teresa
FITZGERALD, Leo William (d
1968 [78]) agent BP/52*
FITZGERALD, Lillian (d 1947)
actress, singer TW/4
FITZGERALD, M. (fl 1792)
dramatist CP/3
FITZGERALD, Michael see
Robinson, James
FITZGERALD, Neil (b 1898)
Irish actor TW/9, 19, 23,

25-28, 30, WWT/16
FITZGERALD, Percy Hetherington
(1834-1925) Irish historian,
dramatist DD, WWT/1-5
FITZGERALD, Randle Hannaford
(d 1890 [26]) actor EA/91*
FITZGERALD, Richard (d 1889)
American agent EA/90*
FITZGERALD, S. J. Adair (1859-
1925) dramatist DD, WWT/3-5,
WWW/2
FITZGERALD, Thomas (1819-91)
American dramatist DAB,
WWA/H
FITZGERALD, Tom (d 1910) EA/
11*
FITZGERALD, Walter (1896-1976)
English actor AAS, BE, TW/
12, WWT/9-15
FITZGERALD, William C. (d 1969
[53]) critic BP/53*
FITZGIBBON, Gerald singer CDP
FITZGIBBON, H. B. see Gibbon,
H. B.
FITZGIBBON, Louis A. (d 1961
[81]) performer BE*
FITZGIBBONS, John Joseph (1890-
1966) American executive WWA/4
FITZHARRIS, Coralie (d 1973 [74])
performer BP/58*
FITZHARRIS, Edward (d 1974 [84])
performer BP/59*
FITZHENRY, Mrs. [née Flannigan]
(d 1790) actress CDP, DNB,
GT, TD/1-2
FITZHUGH, Mrs. (d 1905) EA/06*
FITZJAMES, Louise dancer CDP
FITZ-JAMES, Nathalie (fl 1851)
dancer CDP
FITZMAURICE, Mrs. see Hip-
pisley, E.
FITZMAURICE, George (1877-1963)
Irish dramatist MH, MWD, RE
FITZMAURICE, Michael T. (d 1967
[59]) performer BP/52*
FITZPATRICK, Emma (d 1868)
English actress CDP, DD, HAS
FITZPATRICK, Mrs. J.H. see
Josephs, Patti
FITZPATRICK, Kelly (b 1937)
American actor TW/27, 30
FITZPATRICK, P. (d 1884 [42])
musician EA/85*
FITZPATRICK, Thomas J. (d 1971
[89]) publicist BP/56*
FITZ-RENHARD, Mr. (d 1880)
ventriloquist EA/81*
FITZROY, F. R. (d 1888) actor

EA/89*
FITZROY, J. B. (d 1879 [72])
actor EA/80*
FITZROY, Kate [Mrs. A. R.
Fitzroy] (d 1887) actor EA/88*
FITZROY, Thomas (d 1918)
EA/19*
FITZSIMMONS, Robert Prometheus
(1862-1917) English pugilist,
actor DAB
FITZWARREN, Fanny (fl 1859)
actress CDP
FITZWILLIAM, Mr. (fl 1821)
actor EA/92
FITZWILLIAM, Edward (1788-
1852) English actor BS, CDP,
DD, DNB, OX
FITZWILLIAM, Mrs. Edward
[Fanny Elizabeth Copeland]
(1802-54) English actress BS,
CDP, DD, DNB, HAS, OX,
WWA/H
FITZWILLIAM, Edward Francis
(1824-57) English composer,
musical director DD, DNB
FITZWILLIAM, Mrs. Edward
Francis [Ellen Chaplin] (1822-
80) actress DD, DNB
FITZWILLIAM, Fanny Elizabeth
see Fitzwilliam, Mrs. Edward
FITZWILLIAM, Kathleen Mary
[Mrs. C. Withall] (1826-94)
actress, singer CDP, DD,
OAA/1-2
FITZWILLIAMS, Edwin (d 1857)
composer HAS [? = Fitzwil-
liam, Edward Francis, q.v.]
FITZWILLIAMS, Fanny see
Fitzwilliam, Mrs. Edward
FIX, Ress Jenkins (d 1975 [81])
performer BP/59*
"FIXER" see Davis, Dick
FLACK, Nanette (d 1971) per-
former BP/56*
FLACKS, Niki (b 1943) American
actress TW/23
FLAGEOLET, Mons. (fl 1869)
dancer CDP
FLAGSTAD, Kirsten (1895-1962)
Norwegian singer CB, ES,
TW/19, WWA/4, WWW/6
FLAHERTY, Pat. J., Sr. (d
1970) performer BP/55*
FLAKEY, James (d 1907) acrobat
EA/08*
FLAMM, Donald (b 1899) Ameri-
can producer BE
FLANAGAN, Ann (d 1975 [60s])

performer BP/60*
FLANAGAN, Bud [né Robert Winth-
rop] (1896-1968) English comedian
COC, WWT/10-14
FLANAGAN, Charles [Charles
Knowles] (d 1887 [65]) musician
EA/89*
FLANAGAN, Dick (d 1970 [56])
publicist BP/55*
FLANAGAN, Fionnuala (b 1941)
Irish actress TW/25, 28, 30
FLANAGAN, Florence see Forde,
Florrie
FLANAGAN, Hallie (1890-1969)
American director of Federal
Theatre Project of America
W.P.A., historian COC, NTH,
OC/1-3, WWT/9-14
FLANAGAN, Neil (b 1934) American
actor TW/29-30
FLANAGAN, Pauline (b 1925) Irish
actress TW/27-29
FLANAGAN, Richard (d 1917 [68])
manager WWT/2-3
FLANAGAN, Walter (b 1928) Amer-
ican actor TW/24-26, 29-30
FLANAGAN, William, Jr. (d 1969
[46]) composer/lyricist BP/54*
FLANDERS, Christian (b 1929)
Dutch actor TW/15
FLANDERS, Ed (b 1934) American
actor TW/30
FLANDERS, Michael Henry (1922-
75) English actor, lyricist, en-
tertainer BE, CB, COC, ES,
OC/3, TW/23, WWT/13-15
FLANGE, Dora [Mrs. George Vil-
liers] (d 1901) actress EA/02*
FLANNIGAN, Miss see Fitzhenry,
Mrs.
FLASTER, Karl (d 1965 [59]) com-
poser/lyricist BP/49*
FLAVIN, James (d 1976 [69]) per-
former BP/60*
FLAVIN, Martin (1883-1967) Amer-
ican dramatist BE, CB, HJD,
MD, MH, MWD, NTH, TW/24,
WWA/4, WWT/7-13
FLAWS, Mary (d 1888 [60]) EA/89*
FLEAY, F. Gard (1831-1909) his-
torian DD, DNB
FLEBBE, Beulah Marie Dix (b
1876) American dramatist
WWA/5
FLECKER, James Elroy (1884-1915)
English dramatist COC, DNB,
ES, HP, MH, OC/1-3, PDT
FLECKNOE, Richard (fl 1654-67)

dramatist CP/1-3, DD, GT
FLEET, Mrs. George see
Gillette, Florence .
FLEET, George Rutland see
Barrington, Rutland
FLEETWOOD, Charles (d c.1745)
English manager CDP, COC,
OC/1-3, TD/1-2
FLEETWOOD, John Gerard (d
1776) actor WWT/14*
FLEETWOOD, Susan (b 1944)
Scottish actress AAS, WWT/
16
FLEISCHMAN, Mark (b 1935)
American actor TW/15-20
FLEISCHMAN, Maurice L. (d
1963 [79]) theatre owner BE*
FLEISCHMANN, Julius (1900-68)
producer BE
FLEMING, Miss [Mrs. Stanley]
(1796?-1861) actress DNB
FLEMING, Alice (d 1952 [70])
actress TW/9
FLEMING, Brandon (b 1889)
English dramatist WWT/6-10
FLEMING, Eric (1924-66) Amer-
ican actor TW/9, 11, 23
FLEMING, Frank see Caffry,
John
"FLEMING, George" see
Fletcher, Constance
FLEMING, Ian (1888-1969) Aus-
tralian actor WWT/5-13
FLEMING, Lucy (b 1947) English
actress WWT/15-16
FLEMING, Nita (d 1876 [15])
singer EA/77*
FLEMING, Noel (d 1950 [67])
actor BE*, WWT/14*
FLEMING, Rhonda (b 1922) Amer-
ican actress TW/29
FLEMING, Robert, Jr. (fl 1691)
dramatist CP/3
FLEMING, Tom (b 1927) Scottish
actor, director AAS, WWT/
14-16
FLEMING, William J. [W. J.
Baker] (1839-1921) American
actor HAS
FLEMING, William Maybury
(1817-66) American actor,
manager CDP, DAB, HAS,
WWA/H
FLEMING, Mrs. William M[ay-
bury?] (d 1859) actress HAS
FLEMMING, Claude (1884-1952)
Australian actor, singer
WWT/2-9

FLEMMING, Herbert (1856-1908)
actor, manager DD, EA/97
FLEMYNG, Robert (b 1912) English
actor AAS, BE, TW/3-4, 6-9,
11-17, WWT/8-16
FLERS, P. L. (d 1932 [65]) drama-
tist BE*, WWT/14*
FLERS, Robert de (1872-1927)
French dramatist MWD
FLESCH, Ella (d 1957 [55]) Hun-
garian singer TW/13
FLETCHER, Mr. (fl 1856) American
actor HAS
FLETCHER (d 1893) waxworks pro-
prietor EA/94*
FLETCHER, Mrs. [née Greer] (fl
1826) actress HAS
FLETCHER, Allen (b 1922) Ameri-
can director AAS, BE, WWT/
15-16
FLETCHER, Bramwell (b 1904/06)
English actor BE, TW/1, 3-16,
19, 22, WWT/8-16
FLETCHER, C. C. (b 1833) scene
artist CDP
FLETCHER, Constance ["George
Fleming"] (b 1858) dramatist
DD, GRB/2-4, WWA/4, WWT/
1-8, WWW/3
FLETCHER, Mrs. E. (d 1890)
EA/91*
FLETCHER, Edward (d 1896 [59])
proprietor EA/97*
FLETCHER, Mrs. Edward see
Fletcher, Elizabeth
FLETCHER, Elizabeth [Mrs. Ed-
ward Fletcher] (d 1899) EA/00*
FLETCHER, Emily Payne [Mrs.
Payne Fletcher] (d 1895 [46])
EA/96*
FLETCHER, George (fl 1847)
critic DD
FLETCHER, Ifan Kyrle (d 1969)
historian WWT/15*
FLETCHER, Jack (b 1921) Ameri-
can actor TW/7, 22-26, 29-30
FLETCHER, John (1579-1625) Eng-
lish dramatist CDP, COC, CP/
1-3, DD, DNB, ES, FGF, HP,
MH, NTH, OC/1-3, PDT, RE
FLETCHER, John (b 1809) English
actor HAS
FLETCHER, John C. (d 1886 [45])
property master EA/87*
FLETCHER, Lawrence (d 1608?)
actor DA, GT
FLETCHER, Lawrence (1902/04-70)
American actor TW/1-7, 13-15,

26
FLETCHER, Payne (d 1916 [69])
EA/18*
FLETCHER, Mrs. Payne see
Fletcher, Emily Payne
FLETCHER, Percy (1879-1932)
English composer, conductor
WWT/4-6
FLETCHER, Phineas (1582-1650)
English dramatist CP/1-3,
DD, DNB, FGF, HP
FLETCHER, Robert (d 1972 [87])
composer/lyricist BP/57*
FLETCHER, Robert [né Robert
Fletcher Wyckoff] (b 1923)
American designer AAS, BE,
WWT/15-16
FLETCHER, W. (d 1873 [29])
comic singer EA/74*
FLEXMORE, Ann (d 1869 [88])
EA/71*
FLEXMORE, Richard [R. F.
Geater] (1824-60) English
pantomimist CDP, DD, DNB
FLEXNER, Anne Crawford (1874-
1955) American dramatist
WWA/3, WWT/5-10
FLICKER, Theodore (b 1930)
American director, dramatist,
actor, producer BE
FLINDT, Flemming (b 1936)
Danish dancer, choreographer
ES
FLINN, Kate Irish singer GRB/1
FLINT, Ettie (d 1904) music-hall
performer EA/05*
FLINT, Helen (d 1967 [69]) ac-
tress TW/24
FLINT-SHIPMAN, Veronica (b
1931) English producing mana-
ger WWT/16
FLIPPEN, Jay C. (d 1971 [70])
actor TW/27
FLIPPIN, Lucy Lee (b 1943)
American actress TW/27, 30
FLOCKTON, Mr. conjuror CDP
FLOCKTON, Charles P. (d 1904
[76]) actor DD, OAA/2
FLOOD, Ann (b 1932) American
actress TW/13
FLOOD, Beatrice see De Neer-
gaard, Beatrice
FLOOD, Brean Stewart (d 1917)
EA/18*
FLOOD, John (d 1865) actor?
HAS
FLOOD, John (d 1924) actor
BE*, BP/9*

FLOOD, Susan (d 1879 [40]) Amer-
ican actress EA/80*
FLOOD, W. H. (d 1900) musical
director EA/01*
FLOOD-PORTER, Gertrude Mary
(d 1911) EA/12*
FLOOD-PORTER, Matilda Grace
(d 1911) EA/12*
FLOOK, Richard actor CDP
FLORADOR, Minnie (d 1902) bur-
lesque artiste EA/03*
FLORANCE, Cassius (d 1975 [65])
producer/director/choreographer
BP/59*
FLORENCE, Katherine (fl 1890s)
English actress PP/1, WWS
FLORENCE, Tom (d 1908) showman
EA/10*
FLORENCE, William Jermyn [né
Bernard Conlin] (1831-91) Amer-
ican actor CDP, COC, DAB,
DD, HAS, NTH, OC/1-3, SR,
WWA/H
FLORENCE, Mrs. William Jermyn
[Mrs. Joseph Littell; née Malvina
Pray] (1834-1906) actress, mana-
ger, dancer CDP, COC, HAS,
NTH, SR, WWA/1
FLORENE, Nellie (d 1904) EA/
05*
FLORIDA, Pietro (b 1860) Italian
composer WWA/1, WWM
FLORIDOR [Josias de Soulas, Sieur
de Primefosse] (1608-72) French
actor DA, OC/1-3
FLORIDOR, Josias see Lau,
Hurfries de
FLORINGTON, Jane Hinton [Mrs.
John Hinton Florington] (d 1886
[73]) EA/87*
FLORIO, C. M. (fl 1800-01) English
composer TD/1-2
FLORY, Julia McClune (d 1971
[89]) designer BP/55*
FLORY, Regine (1894-1926) actress,
dancer WWT/4-5
FLORY, Mrs. Walter (d 1971 [89])
theatre founder BP/55*
FLOSSOW, Al (d 1976 [80]) per-
former BP/60*
FLOTOW, Frederich (1812-88) Ger-
man composer SR
FLOURY, Antoine (d 1894 [59])
manager EA/95*
FLOWER, (fl 1600) actor DA
FLOWER, Sir Archibald (d 1950
[85]) English executive BE*,
WWT/14*

FLOWER, Charles E. (d 1892) founder of Shakespeare Memorial EA/93*

FLOWER, Sir Fordham (d 1966 [62]) patron, executive BP/51*, WWT/15*

FLOWER, Sara (d 1865) actress, singer EA/72*, WWT/14*

FLOWER, Thomas (d 1839) actor CDP

FLOWERDAY, Mrs. see Chatters, Kate

FLOWERTON, Consuelo (d 1965 [65]) actress, singer TW/22

FLOYD, Carlisle (b 1926) American composer CB

FLOYD, Gwendoline (d 1950 [80]) actress WWT/4-10

FLOYD, Sara (d 1972 [78]) actress TW/29

FLOYD, William Rudolph (1832-80) American actor, manager CDP, HAS

"FLYING PIEMAN, The" see England, James Sharp

FLYNN, Miss (fl 19th cent) actress HAS

FLYNN, Errol (1909-59) actor TW/16

FLYNN, George H. (d 1854) actor? HAS

FLYNN, Harry (d 1905) actor EA/06*

FLYNN, Hazel (d 1964 [65]) journalist, press representative BE*, BP/48*

FLYNN, J. D. [John Phelton, Jr.] (d 1889 [40]) comedian EA/90*

FLYNN, Joe (d 1974 [49]) performer BP/59*

FLYNN, Thomas (1798-1849) English actor, stage manager, manager HAS, WWA/H

FLYNN, Mrs. Thomas [née Twybell] (d 1851) American actress HAS

FLYNN, Thomas F. (b 1946) American actor TW/27-28

FOCH, Dirk (d 1973 [87]) composer/lyricist BP/57*

FOCH, Nina (b 1924) Dutch actress BE, TW/3-4, 6-9, 13-14, 16, WWT/11-16

FODOR, Joleen (b 1939) American actress TW/21-22, 26

FODOR, Josephine (1793-1870) singer CDP

FODOR, Ladislaus (b 1898) Hungarian dramatist WWT/8-14

FOGARTY, Frank (d 1925 [50]) vaudevillian BP/9*

FOGARTY, Jan (d 1969 [65]) performer BP/54*

FOGARTY, Dr. J. S. (d 1893 [34]) EA/94*

FOGERTY, Elsie (1866-1945) English founder of Central School of Speech Training and Dramatic Art, actress COC, DNB, OC/1-3, WWT/7-9, WWW/4

FOGERTY, Joseph (d 1887 [83]) proprietor EA/88*

FOGERTY, Mrs. Joseph (d 1888) EA/89*

FOGERTY, Robert (d 1907 [63]) proprietor EA/08*

FOGLER, Gertrude (d 1970 [91]) diction coach BP/55*

FOKINA, Vera (d 1958 [69]) dancer TW/15

FOKINE, Alexander Russian/American dancer, choreographer ES

FOKINE, Leon (d 1973 [68]) performer BP/58*

FOKINE, Michel (1880-1942) Russian dancer, choreographer, maître de ballet CB, DAB, ES, NTH, WWA/2, WWT/4-9

FOLEY, Allen James see Foli, Allen James

FOLEY, Michael (b 1848) American comedian HAS

FOLEY, Paul A. (b 1905) American stage manager, director, actor BE

FOLEY, Red (d 1968 [58]) performer BP/53*

FOLGER, Henry Clay (1857-1930) American philanthropist COC, OC/1-3

FOLGER, Mrs. John H. see Macmillan, Violet

FOLI, Allen James [né Foley] (1842-99) singer CDP

FOLKARD, William Seward see Elvey, Maurice

FOLKES, Mrs. Martin see Bradshaw, Lucretia

FOLLAND, Mr. (d 1856) agent HAS

FOLLAND, Minnie see Montez, Minnie

FOLLET, John (d 1799 [32]) actor CDP, TD/1-2

FOLLIS, Dorothy (1892-1923)

American actress BE*, BP/8*

FOLLOWS, John (d 1888) actor?
EA/89*

FOLTZ, Jane (d 1975) performer
BP/60*

FOLWELL, Denis (d 1971 [66])
performer BP/55*

FONDA, Henry (b 1905) American
actor AAS, BE, CB, ES, SR,
TW/4-20, 22-23, 26, 30,
WWT/9-16

FONDA, Jane (b 1937) American
actress BE, CB, ES, TW/
16-20, WWT/14-16

FONDA, Peter (b 1939) American
actor TW/18-20

FONSECA, Joseph (d 1974 [49])
performer BP/59*

FONTAINE, Joan (b 1917) American actress BE, ES, TW/13

FONTAINE, Lillian (d 1975 [88])
performer BP/59*

FONTAINE, Tony (d 1974) performer BP/59*

FONTANNE, Lynn (b 1887?)
English actress BE, CB,
COC, ES, HJD, NTH, OC/
1-3, PDT, SR, TW/2-21,
WWT/3-16

FONTENELLE, Miss see Wil-
liamson, Mrs. J. Brown

FONTEYN, Margot [née Margaret
Hookham] (b 1919) English
dancer CB, ES, WWT/9-12

FOOT, Jesse (fl 1811) dramatist
CP/3

FOOT, John see Conway,
George

FOOT, John Forester dramatist
EAP, RJ

FOOTE, Mr. (fl 1802) actor
TD/2

FOOTE, Commodore [Charles W.
Nestel] (b 1848) dwarf CDP

FOOTE, Mr. (d 1882) actor EA/
83*

FOOTE, Miss see Harrington,
Maria, Dowager Countess of

FOOTE, Miss see Lytton, Miss

FOOTE, Barrington see Foote,
Vere Cecil

FOOTE, Gene (b 1936) American
actor TW/29-30

FOOTE, Horton (b 1916) American dramatist BE, ES, PDT,
WWT/14-16

FOOTE, John Forrester (fl 1822)
actor CDP, HAS

FOOTE, John S. (d 1882) comedian,
proprietor, actor, manager,
lessee DD

FOOTE, John Taintor (1881-1950)
American dramatist WWA/2

FOOTE, Lydia Alice (1844-92) English actress DD, DNB, OAA/
1-2, OC/1-3

FOOTE, Maria (c.1797-1867) English actress BS, CDP, COC,
DD, DNB, OC/1-3, OX

FOOTE, Samuel (1720-77) English
actor, dramatist CDP, COC,
CP/1-3, DD, DNB, ES, GT,
HP, MH, NTH, OC/1-3, SR,
TD/1-2

FOOTE, Samuel (fl 1796-98) actor,
manager TD/1-2

FOOTE, Vere Cecil [Barrington
Foote] (d 1910) singer EA/11*

FOOTE, W. S. (d 1882) actor
EA/82*

FOOTIT, George (b 1864) English
clown GRB/1

FOOTTIT, George (d 1875) circus
proprietor EA/76*

FORAN, Anna E. (d 1969 [77])
dancer BP/54*

FORAN, Arthur F. (d 1967 [55])
performer BP/51*

FORAN, Thomas F. (d 1970 [79])
performer BP/55*

"FORBES, Athol" see Phillips,
Rev. Forbes Alexander

FORBES, Billy see Randall, W.

FORBES, Brenda (b 1908/09) English actress AAS, BE, TW/1-4,
13-14, 23-24, 30, WWT/10-16

FORBES, Bryan [né Clarke] (b
1926) English actor WWT/13-14

FORBES, Donna Liggitt (b 1947)
American actress TW/29

FORBES, Earle (d 1970 [73]) performer BP/55*

FORBES, Edward (1889-1969?)
American actor TW/2

FORBES, Fred (d 1899 [35]) music-
hall acting manager EA/00*

FORBES, Freddie (1895-1952) English actor WWT/7-9

FORBES, James (1871/72-1938)
Canadian manager, dramatist,
actor GRB/3-4, HJD, MWD,
SR, WWA/1, WWM, WWT/1-8

FORBES, Kenneth (b 1920) American actor TW/5-7

FORBES, Mary (1880-1964?) actress TW/21, WWT/2-9

FORBES, Meriel (b 1913) English actress BE, WWT/8-16

FORBES, Norman [Forbes-Robertson] (1858/59-1936) Scottish actor DD, GRB/1-4, OC/1-3, WWT/1-6

FORBES, Ralph (1902/05-51) English actor TW/1-7, WWT/6-11

FORBES, Scott (b 1921) English actor TW/9-12

FORBES, William C. (d 1868 [61]) actor, manager HAS, WWA/H

FORBES, Mrs. William C. [née Fannie Marie Gee] (d 1865) actress HAS

FORBES, William Nathaniel (d 1900 [75]) EA/01*

FORBES-ROBERTSON, Beatrice (1883-1967) English actress GRB/3-4, WWT/1-8

FORBES-ROBERTSON, Eric (1865-1935) English actor OC/1-3

FORBES-ROBERTSON, Frances (d 1902 [75]) EA/04*

FORBES-ROBERTSON, Frank (1885-1947) actor WWT/6-10

FORBES-ROBERTSON, Ian see Robertson, Ian

FORBES-ROBERTSON, J., Sr. (d 1903 [81]) EA/04*

FORBES-ROBERTSON, Jean (1905-62) English actress AAS, COC, OC/1-3, TW/19, WWT/6-13, WWW/6

FORBES-ROBERTSON, Sir Johnston (1853-1937) English actor, manager CDP, COC, DNB, DP, EA/97, ES, GRB/1-4, NTH, OAA/1-2, OC/1-3, PDT, SR, WWA/1, WWM, WWS, WWT/1-8, WWW/3

FORBES-ROBERTSON, Mrs. Johnston see Elliott, Gertrude

FORBES-ROBERTSON, Norman see Forbes, Norman

FORCE, Joan American actress TW/23

FORCER, Francis, the Elder (1650?-1705?) composer, lessee DNB

FORD, Miss see Johnson, Mrs.

FORD, Arthur Paget see Fairleigh, Paget

FORD, Audrey [Mrs. James Welch] English actress GRB/3-4, WWT/1-6

FORD, Constance American actress BE, TW/22, 30

FORD, Corey (d 1969 [67]) performer BP/54*

FORD, David (b 1929) American actor TW/11, 21, 25-28

FORD, Edward H. (d 1970 [82]) vaudevillian TW/26

FORD, Ernest (1858-1919) composer, conductor DD, WWW/2

FORD, Francis (d 1953 [71]) actor BE*

FORD, Frank (b 1916) American producer BE

FORD, George D. (d 1974 [94]) producer/director/choreographer BP/59*

FORD, Gipsy (d 1907) variety performer EA/09*

FORD, Glenn (b 1916) Canadian/American actor CB, ES

FORD, Harriet (d 1949 [86]) American dramatist TW/6, WWA/3, WWT/4-9

FORD, Harrison (d 1957 [73]) actor TW/14

FORD, Harry (d 1883 [36]) musician EA/84*

FORD, Harry (d 1894) comedian, singer CDP

FORD, Helen American actress, singer BE, WWT/6-11

FORD, Hugh (fl 1898-1917) American actor, manager WWA/5

FORD, Mrs. Jack see Morgan, Violet

FORD, John (1586-1639) English dramatist COC, CP/1-3, DD, DNB, ES, FGF, HP, MH, NTH, OC/1-3, PDT, RE

FORD, John (d 1963 [81]) performer BE*

FORD, John (d 1973 [78]) producer/director/choreographer BP/58*

FORD, Mrs. John see Gehrue, Mayme

FORD, John Thomson (1829-94) American manager, actor? CDP, COC, DAB, DD, HAS, OC/1-3, SR, WWA/H

FORD, Julia Ellsworth (b 1859) American dramatist WWA/5

FORD, Mrs. Martin [Jeannie Scott] (d 1874) actress EA/75*

FORD, Millie (d 1911 [32]) actress EA/12*

FORD, Olivia (d 1884) EA/85*

FORD, Paul [né Paul Ford Weaver] (1901-76) American actor BE, TW/2-4, 10-12, 15-17, 19-22, 24, 26, 28, WWT/14-16

FORD, Philip (d 1976 [73]) producer/director/choreographer BP/60*

FORD, Rosetta (d 1912 [56]) EA/13*

FORD, Ruth (b 1920) American actress, dramatist AAS, BE, TW/4-9, 12, 15, 23-24, 28-30, WWT/14-16

FORD, Sydney (b 1938) English actor TW/27

FORD, Thomas (fl 1660) English dramatist CP/1-3, GT

FORD, Thomas W. (d 1909) EA/10*

FORD, W. (d 1890) EA/91*

FORD, Wallace (1898-1966) English actor BE, TW/23, WWT/9-11

FORD, Wilton (d 1908 [57]) variety manager EA/09*

FORDE, Master (fl 1837?) actor CDP

FORDE, Blanche see Sennett, Mrs. Thomas

FORDE, Brownlow (fl 1771) actor, dramatist CP/2-3, GT

FORDE, Catherine Maria (b 1805) actress, singer CDP

FORDE, Emmie [Mrs. Edward A. Ryleston] (d 1889) actress EA/90*

FORDE, Florrie [Florence Flanagan] (1876-1940) Australian music-hall performer CDP, COC, OC/1-3

FORDE, George (d 1872 [60]) singer EA/73*

FORDE, Hal (d 1955 [78]) Irish actor, singer TW/12

FORDE, H. Athol actor EA/96

FORDE, Mrs. H. Athol see Forde, Kathleen

FORDE, Mrs. H. Athol see Protheroe, May

FORDE, J. G. (d 1873 [42]) patter singer, actor CDP

FORDE, Kathleen [Mrs. H. Athol Forde] (d 1908) EA/09*

FORDE, Stanley Hamilton (b 1878) American actor WWS

FORDE, Thomas (fl 1660) drama-

tist FGF

FORDHAM, Edward King (b 1881) English actor GRB/1-4

FORDHAM, Fred (d 1909 [55]) music-hall manager EA/10*

FORDIN, Hugh G. (b 1935) American producer BE

FORDRED, Dorice (b 1902) South African actress WWT/8-13

FORDYCE, Marie D. (d 1976 [83]) performer BP/60*

FORDYCE, Vera actress GRB/1

FOREMAN, Elliot S. (d 1971 [87]) advance man BP/55*

FOREMAN, Richard (b 1937) American dramatist, director CD

FOREPAUGH, Adam (1831-90) American circus manager CDP, DAB, SR, WWA/H

FOREPAUGH, John A. (d 1895) producer BE*, WWT/14*

FOREST, Charles (d 1871) actor EA/72*

FOREST, Lillian (d 1887) actress NYM

FOREST, Lucy (d 1903 [34]) variety performer EA/04*

FOREST, Theophilus see Forrest, Theophilus

FORGE, Mrs. R. [née Bella Brandon] (d 1868 [19]) singer EA/69*

FORGEOT, Eliza (fl 1845) French actress CDP

FORIOSE, The Sisters (fl 1829) tight-rope performers HAS

FORLOW, Ted (b 1931) American actor TW/25-29

FORMAN, Arthur Edmund (b 1918) American actor TW/27, 30

FORMAN, George Frederick (1811-52) actor CDP

FORMAN, Justus Miles (1875-1915) American dramatist WWW/1

FORMAN, Simon (1552-1611) writer DD

FORMBY, George (1905-61) English comedian, performer CDP, COC, ES, OC/3, WWW/6

FORMES, Carl [or Karl] (1810/16/18-89) German singer CDP, HAS, ES, WWA/H

FORMES, Theodor (d 1874) singer EA/75*

FORMIDO, Sir Cornelius (fl 1653) dramatist CP/3, FGF

FORNASARI, Luciano (fl 1833) singer CDP, HAS

FORNES, Maria Irene (b 1930)

Cuban/American dramatist, director CD

FORNIA, Rita (1876-1922) American singer WWA/1

FORREST, Anne (b 1897) Danish actress WWT/7-8

FORREST, Arthur (d 1908 [50]) music-hall comedian CDP

FORREST, Arthur (d 1933 [74]) German actor BE*, BP/17*

FORREST, Mrs. Arthur see Rhodes, Pollie

FORREST, Catharine Norton [Mrs. Edwin Forrest] (1818-91) actress CDP

FORREST, Edwin (1806-72) American actor CDP, COC, DAB, DD, ES, HAS, HJD, NTH, OC/1-3, SR, WWA/H

FORREST, Mrs. Edwin see Forrest, Catharine Norton

FORREST, Mrs. Edwin see Sinclair, Caroline N.

FORREST, Ella [Mrs. John Soden] (d 1908) performer EA/09*

FORREST, Fred (b 1936) American actor TW/26

FORREST, George (b 1915) American lyricist, composer BE

FORREST, Milton Earl (b 1946) American actor TW/27

FORREST, Paul (b 1923) American actor TW/26

FORREST, Rebecca CDP

FORREST, Sam (1870-1944) American producer, dramatist, actor SR, WWT/6-9

FORREST, Theodosius [or Theophilus] (1728-84) English dramatist CP/2-3, DNB, GT, TD/1-2

FORREST, Col. Thomas (1747-1825) American? dramatist EAP, ES [see also Barton, Andrew]

FORREST, William (b 1800) American actor, manager SR

FORREST, W. S. (d 1868 [62]) actor, manager HAS

FORREST, Mrs. W. S. see Clarke, Mrs.

FORRESTAL, Josephine Ogden (d 1976 [76]) investor BP/60*

FORRESTER, Alfred Henry ["Alfred Crowquill"] (d 1872 [67]) EA/73*

FORRESTER, Frederick C. (d 1952 [80]) actor TW/9

FORRESTER, Henry (1797-1840) actor CDP, DD

FORRESTER, Henry [Henry Frost] (1827-82) English actor DD

FORRESTER, Jack (d 1963 [59]) performer BE*

FORRESTER, Maude actress CDP

FORRESTER, N. C. (fl 1848) actor HAS

FORRESTER, Mrs. N. C. (fl 1850) actress HAS

FORRESTER, William (d 1885) actor EA/86*

FORSLUND, Connie (b 1950) American actress TW/29-30

FORSTER, Mrs. (d 1873) EA/75*

FORSTER, Mrs. Edwin (d 1893 [67]) EA/94*

FORSTER, E. M. (1879-1970) English librettist, dramatist WWA/5, WWW/6

FORSTER, Emily Rachel see Hinton, Mary

FORSTER, Harry (d 1885) comic singer EA/87*

FORSTER, John (1812-76) English historian CDP, DD, DNB, GT, OC/1-3

FORSTER, Robert (d 1888 [64]) manager EA/89*

FORSTER, Robert (b 1941) American actor TW/22, 29-30

FORSTER, Rudolf (d 1968 [84]) performer BP/53*

FORSTER, Wilfred (1872-1924) English actor GRB/2-4, WWT/1-4

FORSTER, William Pateman (d 1917) EA/18*

FORSTER, W. R. (d 1887) musician EA/88*

FORSTER-BOVILL, W. B. (b 1871) Welsh business manager WWT/5

FORSYTH, Bertram (d 1927 [40]) actor, dramatist BE*, WWT/14*

FORSYTH, Bruce [né Bruce Forsyth Johnson] (b 1928) English actor WWT/15-16

FORSYTH, Clara Fisher [Mrs. Francis Forsyth] (d 1884) EA/85*

FORSYTH, Mrs. Francis see Forsyth, Clara Fisher

FORSYTH, Gerald (d 1971 [90]) designer BP/55*

FORSYTH, Helen (d 1901) actress CDP, DD, EA/95

FORSYTH, James (b 1913) Scottish dramatist BE, CD, MD, MWD, PDT

FORSYTH, Lina Dalrymple [Mrs. Robert Forsyth] (d 1886) EA/87*

FORSYTH, Matthew (1896-1954) English actor, producer WWT/8-11

FORSYTH, Neil (1866-1915) manager GRB/1-3, WWT/1-2, WWW/1

FORSYTH, Mrs. Robert see Forsyth, Lina Dalrymple

FORSYTHE, Charles (b 1928) American stage manager, director, actor BE

FORSYTHE, Henderson (b 1917) American actor, director BE, TW/14, 21-24, 26-30, WWT/15-16

FORSYTHE, John [né John Lincoln Freund] (b 1918) American actor BE, CB, TW/10-12, WWT/12-13, 15-16

FORT, Hank (d 1973 [59]) composer/lyricist BP/57*

FORT, Robert (d 1901) proprietor EA/02*

FORT, Syvilla (d 1975 [58]) performer BP/60*

FORTENBERRY, Beth (b 1948) American actress TW/28

FORTESCUE, Florence (d 1917 [63]) EA/18*

FORTESCUE, George K. (1846?-1914) actor CDP

FORTESCUE, Gulia H. (fl 19th cent) singer CDP

FORTESCUE, Julia [Lady Gardner] (d 1899) actress DD

FORTESCUE, May [May Finney] (1862-1950) English actress CDP, DD, DP, GRB/1-4, WWT/1-9

FORTESCUE, Viola (d 1953 [78]) American actress TW/10

FORTH, Eric [Fred Osterstock] (d 1908) EA/09*

FORTI, Giuseppe (fl 1849) singer CDP

FORTI, Marietta dancer CDP

FORTIER, Frank (d 1974) showman BP/58*

FORTUNE, Henry (d 1877 [55]) actor EA/78*

FORTUNE, Richard (d 1880) musician EA/81*

FORTUS, Daniel (b 1953) American actor TW/30

FORWOOD, Harry (d 1967 [62]) press agent TW/23

FOSBERG, Harold (d 1888) American actor EA/89*

FOSBROOKE, Sophia Louisa actress CDP

FOSBROOKE, Thomas Leopold (d 1871) pantomimist EA/72*

FOSBROOKE, William (1835-98) actor DD

FOSS, Charles see Fulton, Charles

FOSS, George R. (1859-1938) English producer, actor GRB/1-4, WWT/5-7

FOSS, Mrs. George R. see Fraser, Winifred

FOSS, Lukas (b 1922) German/American composer ES

FOSSE, Bob (b 1927) American director, choreographer, dancer, actor BE, CB, CD, TW/6, WWT/15-16

FOSSETT, Alfred Francis (d 1896 [33]) circus performer EA/97*

FOSSETT, Emma (d 1912 [84]) circus proprietor EA/13*

FOSTER dramatist EAP, RJ

FOSTER, Mr. (fl 1831?) actor CDP

FOSTER, Miss see Young, Mrs. Charles

FOSTER, Alexander (fl 1611-29) actor DA

FOSTER, Barry (b 1927) American actor AAS, TW/20, WWT/14-16

FOSTER, Basil S. (1882-1959) English actor, singer WWT/2-10

FOSTER, Betty (d 1970) performer BP/55*

FOSTER, Charles American actor, dramatist DD

FOSTER, Charles B. (d 1887) actor? NYM

FOSTER, Charles Hubbs (d 1895 [61]) American dramatist EA/96*

FOSTER, Charles J. (1827-64) English dancer? actor CDP, HAS

FOSTER, Claiborne (b 1896/98/1900) American actress TW/13, WWT/6-8

FOSTER, Donald (1894?-1969) American actor TW/1, 4, 8-9, 26

FOSTER, Dudley (d 1973 [48])

actor BP/57*
FOSTER, Edward (1876-1927) Irish manager, actor GRB/1, WWT/4-5
FOSTER, Eliza Frances [née Bennett] (b 1829) American actress HAS
FOSTER, Fanny (fl 1872) actress CDP
FOSTER, F. Carlton (d 1912 [29]) singer EA/13*
FOSTER, Frances American actress TW/25-30
FOSTER, Fred (d 1880 [30]) music-hall performer, actor CDP, EA/81*
FOSTER, Gloria (b 1936) American actress TW/22-23, 28-29, WWT/16
FOSTER, Gus (d 1901 [53]) music-hall manager EA/02*
FOSTER, Herbert (b 1936) Canadian actor TW/25-27
FOSTER, John (b 1830) American clown HAS
FOSTER, John (d 1917) actor EA/18*
FOSTER, Joseph (d 1974 [69]) critic BP/59*
FOSTER, Julia (b 1942) English actress WWT/15-16
FOSTER, Lewis R. (d 1974 [75]) producer/director/choreographer BP/59*
FOSTER, Lillian (d 1949 [63]) actress TW/5
FOSTER, Marie (b 1927) American actress TW/4
FOSTER, Matthew (d 1868 [43]) musician EA/69*
FOSTER, M. P. (d 1882 [49]) actor? EA/83*
FOSTER, Norman (1900/03-76) American actor WWT/7-10
FOSTER, Pamela see Charles, Pamela
FOSTER, Paul (b 1931) American dramatist CD, WWT/16
FOSTER, Phoebe (b 1896) American actress WWT/7-11
FOSTER, Preston (d 1970 [69]) performer BP/55*
FOSTER, S. actor CDP
FOSTER, Sidney (d 1870) equestrian? actor? EA/71*
FOSTER, Stephen Collins (1826-64) American composer CDP, DAB, HAS, HJD, WWA/H

FOSTER, Thomas Cooke (d 1891 [78]) critic, journalist EA/92*
FOSTER, Vivian [Foster Hall] English humorist, ventriloquist, conjuror GRB/1
FOSTER, Mrs. W. see Lauri, Charlotte
FOSTER, William Miles (b 1811) American actor HAS
FOSTER, W. M. (d 1872) conductor EA/74*
FOSTER, Mrs. W. M. (d 1869) EA/70*
FOSTER, Mrs. W. M. see White, Mrs. Cool
FOTHERGILL, Edwin Frederick (d 1903 [64]) music-hall comedian EA/04*
FOTTERAL, James Irish actor TD/1-2
FOUCART, M. (d 1896) balloonist EA/97*
FOUCH, Richard (fl 1631) actor DA
FOULDS, J. E. (d 1892) musician EA/93*
FOULGER, Byron (d 1970 [70]) performer BP/54*
FOULKROD, Emily Virginia (fl 1852-57) American dancer HAS
FOUNTAIN, John (d c. 1669) English? dramatist CP/1-3, GT
FOUNTAIN, Joseph (d 1887 [60]) scene artist EA/88*
FOURREY, Robert see Dhery, Robert
FOWKES, Conrad (b 1933) American actor TW/23-24, 26-28
FOWLER, Bruce (d 1973 [80]) producer/director/choreographer BP/58*
FOWLER, Edward (d 1883) actor EA/85*
FOWLER, Eliza (d 1896) EA/98*
FOWLER, Elsie (d 1916) performer? EA/17*
FOWLER, Emily [Mrs. John C. Pemberton] (1849-96) English actress CDP, DD, OAA/1-2
FOWLER, Gene (1890-1960) American dramatist BE*
FOWLER, Gertrude (d 1935 [42]) actress BE*, BP/19*
FOWLER, Henry J. (d 1899) actor? EA/00*
FOWLER, Manly B. (fl 1821?) American? dramatist EAP, RJ
FOWLER, Mrs. Montague [Ada

Dayrell] (d 1911) dramatist EA/12*

FOWLER, Richard (d 1643) English actor DA, OC/1-3

FOWLER, William (d 1871 [25]) musician EA/72*

FOWLES, Derek (b 1937) English actor TW/20

FOWLIE, Wallace (b 1908) American educator, writer BE

FOX, Mr. (fl 1797-99) actor HAS

FOX, Mr. (d 1803) actor TD/2

FOX, Adèle [Mrs. C. H. Fox] (d 1896 [33]) EA/97*

FOX, Caroline see Howard, Mrs. George Cunnibell

FOX, Mrs. C. H. see Fox, Adèle

FOX, Charles, Sr. (d 1882) scene artist EA/83*

FOX, Charles (d 1888) music-hall artist EA/89*

FOX, Charles (d 1893) manager EA/94*

FOX, Charles H. (1828-64) American comedian, musician CDP, HAS

FOX, Charles H. (d 1893 [35]) perruquier EA/94*, WWT/14*

FOX, Mrs. Charles James see Armstead, Mrs.

FOX, Charles Kemble (1833-75) American actor, manager CDP, DAB, HAS, OC/1-3, SR, WWA/H

FOX, Colin (b 1938) Canadian actor TW/25

FOX, Della [Mrs. J. Levy] (1871/72-1913) American actress, singer GRB/2-4, SR, WWA/1, WWS, WWT/1

FOX, Eddie (b 1848) minstrel, composer CDP

FOX, Eleanor Byrne see Allenby, Peggy

FOX, Emma [Mrs. Thompson] (d 1893) EA/94*

FOX, Ernest singer, minstrel CDP

FOX, Franklyn (d 1967 [73]) actor TW/24

FOX, Fred (d 1913 [51]) EA/14*

FOX, Frederick (b 1910) American designer BE, ES, TW/3-8, WWT/10-15

FOX, George (d 1902 [54]) com-

poser, singer DD

FOX, George Washington Lafayette (1825-77) American actor CDP, COC, DAB, DD, HAS, OC/1-3, WWA/H

FOX, Gilbert (1776-1807?) English actor, singer DAB, WWA/H

FOX, Harry (d 1876) music-hall chairman EA/77*

FOX, Harry (d 1959 [77]) vaudevillian TW/16

FOX, Mrs. Harry (d 1872) EA/73*

FOX, Herbert Henry (d 1916) EA/17*

FOX, Imro (d 1910 [60]) EA/11*

FOX, James (1843-87) American comedian NYM

FOX, James A. (b 1827) American actor HAS

FOX, Janet American actress TW/6, 23

FOX, John, Jr. (fl 1890s-1900s) writer WWM

FOX, John S. (d 1881) comedian EA/82*

FOX, Joseph (b 1852) comedian, minstrel CDP

FOX, Mary H. [née Mary Hewins] (b 1842) American actress HAS

FOX, Melvin J. (d 1968 [53]) theatre owner BP/52*

FOX, Phil (d 1972) performer BP/56*

FOX, Mrs. Polly see Phillips, Mabel

FOX, Robin (1913-71) English producer WWT/14

FOX, Sidney (1910-42) American actress CB, WWT/7-9

FOX, Stuart (d 1951 [57]) American performer BE*, BP/36*

FOX, W. (d 1891) athlete EA/92*

FOX, Will H. (b 1858) American vaudevillian WWM

FOX, Mrs. Will H. (d 1902 [33]) EA/03*

FOX, William (b 1911) Philippino/ English actor WWT/8-16

FOXWORTH, Robert (b 1941) American actor TW/28

FOY, Bertha variety artist CDP

FOY, Eddie [Eddie Fitzgerald] (1854/56-1928) American actor COC, DAB, GRB/3, OC/1-3, SR, WWA/1, WWM, WWS, WWT/1-5

FOY, Eddie, Jr. (b 1905) Ameri-

can actor, dancer BE, TW/2-
19, WWT/15-16
FOY, Ida variety artist CDP
FOY, Richard (d 1947 [42]) vaude-
villian, manager TW/3
FOY, Tom (d 1917 [51]) comedian
EA/18*
FOY SISTERS see Foy, Bertha;
Foy, Ida
FRACCI, Carla (b 1936) Italian
dancer CB, ES
FRAGANZA, Trixie see Friganza,
Trixie
FRAGSON, Harry [Harry Potts]
(1869-1913) English variety
artist, composer COC, ES,
GRB/1-4, OC/1-3
FRAINE, Mr. CDP
FRAME, Mrs. W. F. (d 1890)
EA/91*
FRAMPTON, Charles H. (d 1911
[63]) scene artist EA/12*
FRAMPTON, Eleanor (d 1973
[77]) performer BP/58*
FRAMPTON, Mrs. F. see
Frampton, M. K. P.
FRAMPTON, Fred (d 1884 [68])
manager, pantomimist, ballet
master, dancer EA/85*,
WWT/14*
FRAMPTON, M. K. P. [Mrs. F.
Frampton] (d 1896 [83]) EA/
97*
FRANCA, Celia (b 1921) English
dancer, choreographer CB,
ES
FRANCE, Mrs. (fl 1853) actress
HAS
FRANCE, Abbie (d 1907) EA/08*
FRANCE, Alexis (b 1906) Rhode-
sian actress WWT/8-14
FRANCE, Alf (d 1917) EA/18*
FRANCE, Anna see Wheelock,
Mrs. J. F.
FRANCE, Caesar (d 1890 [67])
professor of music EA/91*
FRANCE, Charles Vernon (1868-
1949) English actor GRB/3-4,
WWT/1-10
FRANCE, Charlotte see Hale,
Mrs. Charles B.
FRANCE, Mrs. Frank H. see
Clinton, Ella
FRANCE, Marie see Brady,
Mrs. James
FRANCE, Richard (b 1930) Amer-
ican actor, singer, dancer,
choreographer BE, TW/10,

12, 20-23, 25
FRANCE, Shirley Henry (1839-79)
English actor, prompter HAS
FRANCE, Sidney C. (1838-95)
actor, dramatist CDP
FRANCE, Thomas (d 1909 [77])
EA/10*
FRANCI, Benvenuto (b 1891)
Italian singer ES
FRANCIA, Leopoldo (b 1875)
Italian singer GRB/1
FRANCINE, Anne (b 1917) Ameri-
can actress, singer BE, TW/
2, 10-11, 25-26
FRANCIOSA, Anthony [né Papaleo]
(b 1928) American actor BE,
CB, ES, TW/12-15
FRANCIS (fl 1792) dramatist
CP/3, GT, TD/1-2
FRANCIS, Mrs. (d 1911 [78])
circus proprietor EA/12*
FRANCIS, Alfred (b 1909) English
manager WWT/15-16
FRANCIS, Ann (d 1800) translator
CP/3
FRANCIS, Arlene (b 1908) Ameri-
can actress BE, CB, TW/1-7,
10-16, 21-23, 30, WWT/10-16
FRANCIS, Dick (d 1949 [59])
comedian BE*, WWT/14*
FRANCIS, Doris (b 1903) English
actress, singer WWT/10
FRANCIS, Edmonstone (d 1880
[41]) actor, acting manager
EA/81*
FRANCIS, Emma (d 1889 [15])
EA/90*
FRANCIS, Gerald G. (b 1950)
American actor TW/28-30
FRANCIS, Harry (d 1901) Negro
comedian EA/02*
FRANCIS, Ivor (b 1918) Canadian
actor TW/23
FRANCIS, Jack (d 1917) EA/18*
FRANCIS, James (d 1886 [46])
minstrel proprietor, singer
CDP
FRANCIS, James (d 1897 [67])
actor EA/98*
FRANCIS, Mrs. James see
Francis, Mary Ann
FRANCIS, Mrs. James A. see
Francis, Louisa
FRANCIS, Jane F. (d 1876 [41])
actress? EA/77*
FRANCIS, Jean (b 1923) American
actress TW/25
FRANCIS, J. O. (d 1956 [74])

Welsh dramatist BE*, WWT/14*

FRANCIS, John (d 1893) musician EA/94*

FRANCIS, Kay (1899/1905-1968) American actress ES, TW/2-7, 25, WWA/5, WWT/7-13

FRANCIS, Louisa [Mrs. James A. Francis] (d 1894 [27]) EA/95*

FRANCIS, Mary Ann [Mrs. James Francis] (d 1881 [40]) EA/82*

FRANCIS, M. E. (d 1930 [72]) Irish dramatist WWT/1-6

FRANCIS, Nelson (b 1852) English manager GRB/1-2

FRANCIS, Philip (d 1773) Irish dramatist CP/2-3, DD, GT, TD/1-2

FRANCIS, Robert (d 1955 [25]) actor BE*

FRANCIS, Virginia see Bateman, Virginia Francis

FRANCIS, W. (d 1892) aerial performer EA/93*

FRANCIS, William (d 1826 [69]) English dancer, circus performer? actor CDP, HAS

FRANCIS, William (d 1908 [62]) performer? EA/09*

FRANCIS, Mrs. William (d 1834) English actress? circus performer? CDP, HAS

FRANCIS, Mrs. William (d 1888) EA/89*

FRANCISQUY, Mons. (fl 1796) French dancer HAS

FRANCK, C. Harry (b 1844) American actor HAS

FRANCK, Celestine (fl 1850-51) dancer HAS

FRANCK, Henry (d 1880 [28]) actor? EA/81*

FRANCK, Victorine (fl 1850-51) dancer HAS

FRANCKIN, Mrs. Robert see Elinore, May

FRANCKLIN, Dr. Thomas (1721-84) dramatist CP/2-3, DD, GT, TD/1-2

FRANCKS, Don (b 1932) Canadian actor TW/22, 25

FRANCOIS, Annie (d 1878) tightrope artist EA/79*

FRANCONI [John Measey] (d 1894) EA/95*

FRANCONI, Henri Adolphe (b 1801) equestrian CDP

FRANCONI, Laurent (1776-1849) circus owner, equestrian CDP

FRANK, Mrs. Alec F. see Denzil, Madge

FRANK, Arlyne (b 1930) American singer, actress BE

FRANK, Bruno (1887-1945) German dramatist COC, OC/1-3, WWT/8

FRANK, Carl (d 1972 [63]) actor TW/29

FRANK, Dorothy [or Dottie] (b 1942) American actress TW/26, 28, 30

FRANK, Jim American actor TW/28

FRANK, John C. (d 1910) EA/11*

FRANK, Judy (b 1936) American actress TW/24

FRANK, Marvin (d 1974 [48]) publicist BP/58*

FRANK, Mary K. (b 1911) American producer BE

FRANKAU, Aline see Bernstein, Aline

FRANKAU, Ronald (1894-1951) English actor, entertainer WWT/10-11

FRANKEL, Benjamin (d 1973 [67]) composer/lyricist BP/57*

FRANKEL, Gene (b 1923) American director ES, WWT/15-16

FRANKEL, Kenneth (b 1941) American actor TW/23

FRANKEL, Lou (d 1974 [63]) journalist BP/59*

FRANKEN, Rose (b 1895/98) American dramatist, producer CB, MD, MWD, WWT/10-11

FRANKENBERG, Lloyd F. (d 1975 [67]) critic BP/59*

FRANKENHEIMER, John (b 1930) American director CB

FRANKFORT MOORE, Grace (d 1901) EA/02*

FRANKISS, Betty (b 1912) English actress, singer WWT/9-13

FRANKLEIN, Lucy (d 1903 [59]) singer EA/04*

FRANKLIN, Mr. actor CDP

FRANKLIN, Alberta (d 1976 [79]) performer BP/60*

FRANKLIN, Andrew (fl 1785-1804) Irish dramatist CP/3, DD, GT, TD/1

FRANKLIN, Benjamin F. (d 1963 [88]) minstrel BE*

FRANKLIN, Bonnie (b 1944)

American actress TW/26-30

FRANKLIN, Clara (fl 1889?)
singer CDP

FRANKLIN, Daniel (b 1940) American actor TW/23, 25

FRANKLIN, Frederic (b 1914) English dancer CB, ES

FRANKLIN, Gertrude singer CDP

FRANKLIN, Mrs. H. (d 1874 [43]) EA/75*

FRANKLIN, Harold B. (1890-1941) American manager WWT/8

FRANKLIN, Henry (d 1877 [62]) advance agent EA/78*

FRANKLIN, Hugh (b 1916) American actor TW/4, 22-24, 26, 28-29

FRANKLIN, Irene (1876-1941) American actress CB, SR, WWT/7-9

FRANKLIN, J. C. (d 1879) American pantomimist EA/80*

FRANKLIN, Lidija (b 1922) Russian actress TW/3-4

FRANKLIN, Nancy American actress TW/26-27

FRANKLIN, Nony (d 1965 [40]) performer BP/50*

FRANKLIN, Roger American actor TW/25

FRANKLIN, William (b 1906) American actor TW/2

FRANKLYN, Beth (d 1956 [83]) actress TW/12

FRANKLYN, Charles (d 1891 [39]) stage manager EA/92*

FRANKLYN, Irwin (d 1966 [62]) publicist, actor TW/23

FRANKLYN, Leo (1897-1975) English actor AAS, WWT/9-15

FRANKLYN-LYNCH, Grace (fl 1893-1907) American actress WWS

FRANKS, Mrs. Arthur B. see Hunt, Maggie

FRANKS, Hannah Louisa (d 1892 [28]) EA/93*

FRANKS, Jerry (d 1971 [63]) producer/director/choreographer BP/56*

FRANKS, Laurie (b 1929) American actress TW/25-26

FRANKS, Leo W. (d 1968 [62]) performer BP/52*

FRANKS, Lorraine (d 1976 [58]) producer/director/choreographer BP/60*

FRANKS, Ollie (d 1976 [56]) performer BP/60*

FRANKS, Percy (d 1976 [83]) performer BP/60*

FRANKS, Sydney [Frank Sylvester] (d 1900 [58]) actor, singer CDP

FRANKS, Wilfred (b 1872) English manager, business manager, stage manager GRB/1-4

FRANMORE, Ida (d 1913) EA/14*

FRANZ, Adele American literary representative BE

FRANZ, Eduard (b 1902) American actor TW/1-4, 14-15, 23, 25-26, WWT/16

FRANZ, Joy (b 1944) American actress TW/29-30

FRARY, Mrs. (fl 1848) English actress HAS

FRASCA, Mary (d 1973) performer BP/58*

FRASCHINI, Gaetano (d 1887 [72]) singer EA/88*

FRASER, Agnes [Mrs. Walter Passmore] (d 1968 [90]) Scottish actress GRB/1-4, WWT/1-6

FRASER, Alec (1884-1956) Scottish actor, singer WWT/4-9

FRASER, Bill (b 1908) Scottish actor WWT/11-16

FRASER, Claude Lovat (1890-1921) English artist, stage designer COC, DNB, ES, OC/1-3, PDT

FRASER, Constance (d 1973 [63]) performer BP/57*

FRASER, Eddie (d 1972 [61]) producer/director/choreographer BP/56*

FRASER, Fred (d 1879 [63]) actor, scene artist EA/80*

FRASER, Mrs. John see Vincent, Ruth

FRASER, John James see Frazer, John James

FRASER, Kate [The Little Wonder] (d 1868 [18]) EA/69*

FRASER, Keith (d 1915 [41]) actor WWT/14*

FRASER, Lovat (b 1908) Scottish manager WWT/11-13

FRASER, Lydia [Lydia Bashall] (d 1898) actress EA/99*

FRASER, Margaret Campbell actress GRB/1-2

FRASER, Marie (fl 1886-91) actress DD

FRASER, Moyra (b 1923) Australian actress, dancer WWT/ 12-16

FRASER, Robert (d 1878 [45]) singer EA/79*

FRASER, Robert (1842-96) actor, dramatist CDP, SR

FRASER, Shelagh English actress WWT/15-16

FRASER, Winifred [Mrs. George R. Foss; née Exton] (b 1868/ 72) English actress DD, GRB/ 2-4, WWT/1-7

FRASER-BRUNNER, Queenie [Lizzie Webb] English actress GRB/1

FRASER-SIMSON, Harold (1878-1944) English composer WWT/ 4-9

FRATELLINI, Paul (d 1940) clown CB

FRATTI, Mario (b 1927) Italian/ American dramatist, educator CD, MWD

FRAUNCE, Abraham (fl 1590-91) dramatist CP/1-3

FRAWLEY, T. Daniel (1864-1936) American actor, manager SR

FRAWLEY, William (1893-1966) American actor, singer, dancer TW/22, WWA/4

FRAYN, Michael (b 1933) English dramatist AAS, CD, WWT/16

FRAYNE, Frank (fl 1870-90) dramatist, manager SR

FRAYNE, Frankie marksman CDP

FRAYNE, Frank Ives (1836-91) actor, marksman CDP

FRAYNE, Mrs. Frank Ives markswoman CDP

FRAYNE, Matthew (d 1887) actor EA/88*

FRAYNE, Viola actress TW/1

FRAZEE, Harry Herbert (1880-1929) American manager WWA/1, WWT/4-5

FRAZER, E. see Rogers, E.

FRAZER, Henry (d 1892 [70]) actor EA/93*

FRAZER, I. J. (fl 1844) singer CDP

FRAZER, John J[ames] (d 1863 [59]) actor, singer CDP

FRAZIER, Charlotte (b 1939) American actress TW/27

FRAZIER, Mattie see Herndon, Agnes

FREAR, "Billy" (d 1888) American minstrel EA/90*

FREAR, Fred (fl 1879-1908) American actor WWS

FREDA, Mlle. (d 1917) EA/18*

FREDERIC, Mme. see Birt, Miss S.

FREDERICI, Blanche (d 1933 [55]) actress BE*, WWT/14*

FREDERICI, Mme. Himmer (fl 1864) singer HAS

FREDERICK [Antoine-Louis-Prosper Lemaître] (1800-76) French actor COC

FREDERICK, Helena (d 1926 [44]) prima donna BE*, BP/11*

FREDERICK, James (d 1888) EA/ 89*

FREDERICK, Pauline (1884/85-1938) American actress, singer ES, GRB/3-4, SR, WWA/1, WWM, WWS, WWT/1-8

FREDERICK, Walter (d 1885) actor EA/86*

FREDERICKS, Mons. (fl 1845) dancer HAS

FREDERICKS, Albert (d 1901 [61]) proprietor BE*, EA/02*, WWT/14*

FREDERICKS, Charles (1918-70) American actor, singer TW/2, 4-8, 26

FREDERICKS, Emily [Mrs. Fred Fredericks] (d 1901 [61]) EA/ 02*

FREDERICKS, Mrs. F. see Vaul, Polly

FREDERICKS, Fred [F. L. O'Leary] (d 1894) actor? EA/ 95*

FREDERICKS, Fred (d 1939 [75]) producer, manager BE*, WWT/14*

FREDERICKS, Mrs. Fred see Fredericks, Emily

FREDERICKS, George (d 1891 [45]) music-hall performer EA/92*

FREDERICKS, Louise (d 1870) dancer EA/71*

FREDERICKS, Sam (d 1922 [46]) producer, manager BE*, WWT/14*

FREDERICKS, W. H. (d 1897) manager EA/98*

FREDERICKS, William Hamlet (d 1897 [27]) actor? EA/98*

FREDERICKS, William Sheridan

(1799-1878) Irish actor CDP, HAS

FREDMAN, Alice (d 1950 [71]) founder of theatre societies BE*, WWT/14*

FREDRIK, Burry (b 1925) American producer, stage manager, director BE

FREDRO, Aleksander (1793-1876) Polish dramatist COC, OC/3

FREE, John (fl 1757) dramatist CP/3

FREEAR, Albert (d 1905) minstrel comedian EA/06*

FREEAR, Charles Thomas Wood (d 1906 [59]) entertainer EA/07*

FREEAR, Harriett [Mrs. Charles T. W. Freear] (d 1893) EA/94*

FREEAR, Louie (1871/73-1939) English actress CDP, COC, DD, GRB/1-4, WWT/1-8

FREEBERTHYSER, Dora (d 1867) dancer HAS

FREEBORN, Cassius (d 1954 [76]) composer, musical director BE*

FREECE, Mrs. de (d 1881 [78]) EA/82*

FREED, Mr. dramatist RJ

FREED, Arthur (d 1973 [78]) composer/lyricist, producer/director/choreographer BP/57*

FREED, Barboura M. (d 1975 [43]) performer BP/60*

FREED, Bert (b 1919) American actor TW/2, 4

FREED, Fred (d 1974 [53]) producer/director/choreographer BP/58*

FREED, Isadore (1900-60) Russian/American composer WWA/4

FREED, Sam (b 1948) American actor TW/30

FREEDLEY, George Reynolds (1904-67) American historian AAS, BE, CB, COC, ES, NTH, OC/2-3, WWT/10-14

FREEDLEY, Vinton (1891-1969) American managing producer, actor BE, NTH, TW/3-8, 26, WWA/5, WWT/6-14

FREEDMAN, Bill (b 1929) Canadian producing manager WWT/16

FREEDMAN, Gerald (b 1927) American director, producer, composer, dramatist WWT/16

FREEDMAN, Harold (d 1966 [69]) Scottish literary representative BE

FREEDMAN, Leonore (d 1964) actress BE*

FREEDMAN, Zac (d 1968 [61]) publicist BP/52*

FREEHOLD, The theatre collective CD

FREEL, Alira (d 1935 [28]) American actress BE*, BP/20*

FREELAND, Frank [Joseph Mulligan] (b 1847) English actor, singer GRB/1

FREELAND, Joseph (d 1909 [61]) manager EA/10*

FREELAND, Louie (d 1910) actress EA/11*

FREEMAN, Al, Jr. (b 1934) American actor TW/25-26, 29-30, WWT/16

FREEMAN, Ann [Mrs. Harry Freeman] (d 1885 [25]) EA/86*

FREEMAN, Ann English actress TW/24, 27

FREEMAN, Arny (b 1908) American actor TW/22-24, 26, 28-30, WWT/16

FREEMAN, Charles (d 1881) proprietor EA/82*

FREEMAN, Charles J. (d 1964 [82]) agent BE*

FREEMAN, Charles K. (b 1900/05) English critic, director BE, TW/2, 4

FREEMAN, David (b 1945) Canadian dramatist CD

FREEMAN, Edward Urquhart (d 1902) musical director EA/03*

FREEMAN, Elijah (d 1887 [70]) lion-tamer EA/88*

FREEMAN, Frances (b 1923) American actress TW/5

FREEMAN, Frank (1892-1962) English actor WWT/6-7

FREEMAN, H. A. (d 1929) producer, manager BE*, WWT/14*

FREEMAN, Harry actor, singer CDP

FREEMAN, Mrs. Harry see Freeman, Ann

FREEMAN, Henry Charles (d 1887) scene artist EA/88*

FREEMAN, Howard (d 1967) American actor, director BE,

TW/24

FREEMAN, Isabella (fl 1860)
American actress, reader
HAS

FREEMAN, Leonard (d 1974 [53])
producer/director/choreographer
BP/58*

FREEMAN, Mark (fl 1733) English dramatist CP/2-3

FREEMAN, Max (d 1912) German
actor, stage manager WWS

FREEMAN, Morgan (b 1937)
American actor TW/24, 26, 28

FREEMAN, Ralph (d 1655) dramatist CP/1-3, DD, FGF

FREEMAN, Stella (1910-36) English actress WWT/6-8

FREEMAN, Thomas (d 1874 [60])
costumier EA/75*

FREEMAN, Valdo Lee (d 1972
[72]) producer/director/choreographer BP/57*

FREEMANTLE, George (d 1894)
musical director EA/95*

FREER, Charles (d 1857 [55])
Maltese actor CDP, DD, HAS

FREER, John Charles see
Freer, Charles

FREESE, Marie (d 1905) EA/06*

FREE SOUTHERN THEATRE, The
theatre collective CD

FREEZER, Herbert J. (d 1963
[61]) investor BE*

FREGOLI, Leopold (d 1936 [69])
Protean artist BE*, WWT/
14*

FREIMAN, Louis (d 1967 [75])
actor, dramatist TW/23

FREITAG, Dorothea (b 1914)
American composer, arranger,
musical director BE

FREMAN, Maurice (d 1912)
German/American actor, stage
manager, director SR

FREMSTAD, Olive (d 1951 [83])
Swedish singer CDP, TW/7,
WWA/3, WWM

FRENCH, Col. see French,
Mjr.

FRENCH, Mjr. (fl 18th cent) actor
CDP

FRENCH, Anne Warner see
Warner, Anne

FRENCH, Arthur American actor
TW/24-30

FRENCH, Arthur W., III (b 1965)
American actor TW/28

FRENCH, Bruce (b 1945) American actor TW/28

FRENCH, David (b 1939) Canadian
dramatist, actor CD

FRENCH, Edie [Mrs. Edith Smith]
(d 1902) music-hall performer
EA/03*

FRENCH, Eleanor (d 1975 [59])
performer BP/59*

FRENCH, Elizabeth (d 1913) EA/
14*

FRENCH, Elizabeth English actress, singer WWT/10-13

FRENCH, Elsie actress WWT/7-
12

FRENCH, Eva (fl 1883?) actress
CDP

FRENCH, Fred (d 1899 [68])
comic singer, actor CDP

FRENCH, Mrs. Fred see
French, Mary Ann

FRENCH, George (d 1911 [65])
proprietor EA/12*

FRENCH, G. H. (d 1873) actor
EA/74*

FRENCH, Harold (b 1897/1900)
English actor, producer, director AAS, WWT/4-16

FRENCH, Henri, the Great (b
1876) Belgian vaudevillian
WWM

FRENCH, Herbert C. (d 1924
[33]) dancer, director BE*,
BP/8*

FRENCH, Hermene [née Hermine
Camelinat] (b 1924) English actress, dancer, singer WWT/
11-13

FRENCH, Hugh (b 1910) English
actor, singer WWT/10-11

FRENCH, James Murphy (d 1758)
dramatist CP/3

FRENCH, La Verne (b 1923) American actor TW/6-7

FRENCH, Lena G. actress CDP

FRENCH, Leslie (b 1904) English
actor, singer, dancer, director
AAS, WWT/7-16

FRENCH, Lizzie (d 1911) EA/12*

FRENCH, Marie (d 1918) EA/19*

FRENCH, Mary Amelia [Mrs.
Samuel French] (d 1887 [60])
EA/88*

FRENCH, Mary Ann [Mrs. Fred
French] (d 1904 [75]) EA/05*

FRENCH, Minnie (d 1899) actress
CDP

FRENCH, Park M. (d 1974 [93])
designer BP/58*

FRENCH, Pauline American actress GRB/1, WWS
FRENCH, Samuel (d 1898 [76]) publisher DD
FRENCH, Mrs. Samuel see French, Mary Amelia
FRENCH, Stanley J. (1908-64) English business manager, producing manager WWT/ 10-13
FRENCH, Sydney (d 1878 [42]?) dramatist, critic DD
FRENCH, T. Henry (d 1902) producer, publisher, manager BE*, WWT/14*
FRENCH, Tom see Leak, Thomas
FRENCH, Valerie [née Harrison] (b 1932) English actress TW/ 22-23, 25, 27, 30, WWT/15-16
FRENCH, Windsor B., II (d 1973 [68]) critic BP/57*
FRENCH GIANT (b 1800?) CDP
FRENCH OPERA TROUPE (fl 1845) HAS
FRENI, Mirella (b 1935) Italian singer ES
FRERE, Gladys Bartle English actress GRB/1
FRERE, John Hookham (1769-1846) translator DA
FRESNAY, Pierre [Pierre Laudenbach] (1897-1975) French actor, director BE, CB, PDT, WWT/ 8-14
FREUD, Sigmund (1856-1939) Austrian psychologist NTH
FREUND, John C. (b 1848) English dramatist WWM
FREUND, John Lincoln see Forsythe, John
FREUND, Kim (b 1955) American actress TW/24
FREY, Leonard (b 1938) American actor TW/28, 30
FREY, Nathaniel (1913-70) American actor BE, TW/8-13, 15, 19, 21-24, 27, WWT/14-15
FREYERBOTT, Bartholomeus (fl 1615) actor DA
FREZZOLINI, Ermine (1818-84) Italian singer CDP, ES, HAS
FRIAS, Duchess de see Balfe, Victoria
FRIEBUS, Florida (b 1909) American actress, dramatist BE, TW/5, 22

FRIED, Walter (1910-75) American producer, manager BE, TW/ 3, 6-7
FRIEDBERG, Dr. Charles K. (d 1972 [64]) dramatist BP/57*
FRIEDERICH, W. J. (b 1916) American educator, director BE
FRIEDLAND, Anatole (1888-1938) Russian composer, performer BE*
FRIEDLANDER, Jane (b 1939) American producer BE
FRIEDLANDER, William B. (d 1968 [83]) dramatist, composer, producing manager TW/24, WWT/6-11
FRIEDMAN, Bruce Jay (b 1930) American dramatist, director CD
FRIEDMAN, Leo B. producer BE
FRIEDMAN, Leon (b 1872) American agent WWM
FRIEDMAN, Lillian see Weber, Mrs. Joe
FRIEDMAN, Max (d 1964 [76]) songwriter, performer BE*, BP/49*
FRIEDMAN, Phil (d 1974 [83]) producer/director/choreographer BP/58*
FRIEDMAN, Phil (b 1921) American business manager BE
FRIEDMAN, Samuel J. (1912-74) American press representative BE, TW/30
FRIEDMANN, Shraga (d 1970 [47]) performer BP/55*
FRIEL, Brian (b 1929) Irish dramatist CB, CD, MWD, RE, WWT/15-16
FRIEND, Cliff (d 1974 [80]) composer/lyricist BP/59*
FRIEND, Philip (b 1915) English actor TW/8
FRIEND, Violet (d 1906) actress, singer, manager CDP
FRIEND, Wilton (d 1912 [76]) music-hall manager EA/13*, WWT/14*
FRIENDLY, Dan (d 1972 [59]) treasurer BP/56*
FRIERSON, Monte L. (b 1930) American manager, producer BE
FRIES, Helen Warnow (d 1970 [44]) performer BP/55*
FRIES, Mrs. Wulf [née Gann]

(d 1853) actress? HAS
FRIESEN, Norman actor TW/23
FRIGANZA, Trixie [Delia O'Cal-
laghan] (1870-1955) American
actress, singer GRB/2-4,
TW/11, WWM, WWS, WWT/
1-9
FRIMBLEY, Frederick (d 1871)
actor? EA/72*
FRIMBLY, Mr. actor CDP
FRIML, Charles Rudolf (1879/
81/84-1972) Czech composer
AAS, BE, PDT, TW/29,
WWA/5, WWT/4-14
FRINGS, Ketti [née Katherine
Hartley] American dramatist
BE
FRINK, Robert (b 1937) American
actor TW/25
FRISBIE, Noah, Jr. (b 1758)
American dramatist EAP
FRISBY, Terence (b 1932) Eng-
lish actor, director, dramatist
AAS, CD, WWT/15-16
FRISCH, Albert (d 1976 [60])
composer/lyricist BP/60*
FRISCH, Max Rudolf (b 1911)
Swiss dramatist BE, CB,
COC, MWD, OC/3, WWT/
14-16
FRISCO, Joe (d 1958 [68]) vaude-
villian TW/15
FRISWELL, Hain (d 1878) co-
founder of Urban Club EA/79*
FRITCH, Letitia Louise singer
CDP
FRITH, Edward (d 1875 [38])
music-hall lessee EA/76*
FRITH, J. Leslie (1889-1961)
English actor, dramatist
WWT/10-13
FRITH, Mary (fl 1610) DA
FRITH, Walter (d 1941) English
dramatist DD, WWW/4
FRITSCH, Willy (d 1973 [72])
performer BP/58*
FRITSCHY, Walter A. (d 1972
[91]) producer/director/chore-
ographer BP/57*
FRITZ, Mrs. Edward (d 1883
[36]) EA/85*
FRITZ, Jack (d 1901) music-hall
performer EA/02*
FRIZZELL, William Orville (d
1975 [47]) performer BP/60*
FRODSHAM, Bridge (1734-68)
English actor CDP, DD,
DNB

FROELICH, William J. (d 1963
[60]) American performer BE*
FROGGATT, R. H. (d 1877 [45])
musician EA/78*
FROHMAN, Bert (d 1974 [74])
performer BP/59*
FROHMAN, Charles (1860-1915)
American manager CDP, COC,
DAB, DD, ES, GRB/1-4, HJD,
NTH, OC/1-3, SR, WWA/1,
WWM, WWS, WWT/1-2, WWW/1
FROHMAN, Daniel (1850/51/53-
1940) American manager CB,
CDP, COC, DAB, DD, ES,
GRB/2-4, HJD, NTH, OC/1-3,
SR, WWA/1, WWM, WWS,
WWT/1-9
FROHMAN, Gustave (1855-1930)
American manager COC, OC/
1-3
FROME, Barbara (d 1976 [54])
performer BP/60*
FROME, Lawrence (d 1916) EA/
17*
FROME, Samuel Blake (fl 1809)
dramatist? librettist? lyricist?
CP/3
FRONANI, Angelo (d 1918 [44])
EA/19*
FROSCH, Aaron R. (b 1924) Amer-
ican lawyer BE
FROST, Alice American actress
TW/12-13
FROST, Edith [Mrs. H. L. War-
ren] American actress WWM
FROST, Henry see Forrester,
Henry
FROST, Mrs. J. C. (fl 1852) ac-
tress HAS
FROST, John (fl 1600) actor DA
FROWDE, Philip (d 1738) drama-
tist CP/1-3, DD, DNB, GT,
TD/1-2
FRUIN, J. J. (d 1907 [44]) secre-
tary of Music Hall Home EA/
08*
FRY, Charles (d 1928 [83]) per-
former, director BE*, WWT/
14*
FRY, Christopher [né Harris] (b
1907) English dramatist, direc-
tor, actor AAS, BE, CB, CD,
CH, COC, ES, GT, MD, MH,
MWD, NTH, OC/1-3, PDT,
WWT/11-16
FRY, Horace (d 1942 [67]) business
manager WWT/14*
FRY, Ray (b 1923) American actor

TW/24-30

FRY, Roy H. (d 1905) actor EA/
06*

FRY, William Henry (1815-64)
American composer DAB,
WWA/H

FRYER, J. C. manager CDP

FRYER, Peg (fl late 17th &
early 18th cents) actress DD

FRYER, Robert (b 1920) American
producer BE, WWT/14-16

FRYERS, Austin (fl 1883-99)
dramatist DD

FUCHS, Dick (b 1944) American
actor TW/28-29

FUCHS, Leo (b 1911) Polish actor
BE, TW/30

FUCHS, Theodore (b 1904) American educator BE

FUDGE, Alan (b 1944) American
actor TW/24-25

FUE, Charles (d 1965 [80]) dramatist BP/50*

FUELL, Emelia [Milly Seymour;
Mrs. J. C. Fuell] (d 1878) actress EA/79*

FUELL, J. C. (d 1882) EA/83*

FUELL, Mrs. J. C. see Fuell,
Emelia

FUERHEERD, Josephine B. (d
1976 [84]) performer BP/60*

FUERTES, Dolores Adios see
Menken, Adah Isaacs

FUGARD, Athol (b 1932) South
African dramatist, actor, director AAS, CB, CD, WWT/
15-16

FUJI-KO (1883-1912) Japanese
dancer, pantomimist WWM

FULCHER, Florence (d 1917 [25])
singer EA/18*

FULDA, Dr. Ludwig (1862-1939)
German dramatist DD, GRB/
1, 3-4

FULFORD, David (b 1925) American director, actor, producer
BE

FULLAM, Michael (d 1825) actor
CDP

FULLER, Mr. (fl 1838) American
actor HAS

FULLER, Alfred (d 1844 [37])
clown EA/72*

FULLER, Ben (d 1894) diver
EA/95*

FULLER, Sir Benjamin John (b
1875) English manager WWT/
5-9

FULLER, Caroline Macomber (b
1873) American dramatist
WWA/5

FULLER, Dean (b 1922) American
composer, dramatist BE

FULLER, Frances (b 1907/08)
American actress BE, WWT/
9-10

FULLER, Frank (d 1908 [64]) actor EA/09*

FULLER, Mrs. Frank see
Howard, Constance

FULLER, Isaac (1606-72) English
scene painter COC, OC/1-3

FULLER, John, Sr. (d 1909 [60])
EA/10*

FULLER, John G. (b 1913) American dramatist BE

FULLER, Leslie (d 1948 [57])
comedian BE*, WWT/14*

FULLER, Loie (1870-1928) Amer-
ican actress, dancer CDP,
DAB, DD, ES, GRB/1-4,
WWA/1, WWS, WWT/1-5

FULLER, Margaret Hastings (d
1916 [40]) EA/17*

FULLER, Mollie (d 1933 [68])
American actress BE*

FULLER, Penny (b 1940) American
actress TW/26-28

FULLER, Rosalinde (b 1901) English actress COC, OC/3,
WWT/6-16

FULLERTON, Richard (d 1802)
actor HAS

FULLERTON, William (d 1888)
composer DD

FULLFORD, Mrs. Robert see
Pixley, Annie

FULMER, Ray (b 1933) American
actor TW/14-15

FULTON, Charles J. [Charles
Foss] (1857-1938) English actor
GRB/2-4, WWT/1-5

FULTON, Eileen American actress, singer BE

FULTON, Mary [Mrs. J. A.
Campbell] actress GRB/1

FULTON, Maude (1881-1950)
American dramatist, actress
TW/7, WWT/5-9

FULTON, Reuben (d 1891 [55])
proprietor EA/92*

FULTON, Richard S. (d 1916)
EA/17*

FULTON, Sarah [Sally D'Angelis]
(d 1882) actress EA/83*

FULWEL, Ulpian (b 1556) English

dramatist CP/1-3, DD, FGF
FUNKE, Lewis (b 1912) American
editor BE
FUQUA, Charles (d 1971 [60])
performer BP/56*
FURBER, Douglas (1885-1961)
English actor, dramatist
WWT/5-13, WWW/6
FURBER, Mrs. Douglas see
Cutler, Peggy
FURBISH, Charles E. (1846-81)
American manager CDP
FURLEY, Shelagh (d 1951) ac-
tress BE*, WWT/14*
FURNESS, Betty (b 1916) Ameri-
can actress CB
FURNESS, Horace Howard (1833-
1912) American critic DD,
HJD, WWA/1, WWM
FURNISS, Grace Livingstone (d
1938 [74]) American dramatist
GRB/3-4, WWM, WWT/1-2
FURNIVAL, Henry [W. Henry
Parr] (b 1862) English actor,
manager GRB/1
FURNIVALL, Frederick James
(1825-1910) English critic DD,
HP, WWW/1
FURR, James (d 1897) equestrian
EA/98*
FURRER, Urs B. (d 1975 [41])
producer/director/choreographer
BP/60*
FURRY, Edna see Hopper,
Hedda
FURSCH-MADI, Amy (d 1894
[46]) singer CDP
FURSE, Douglas (b 1903) English
designer WWT/9
FURSE, Jill (d 1944 [28]) actress
BE*, WWT/14*
FURSE, Judith (1912-74) English
actress, producer WWT/10-14
FURSE, Margaret (d 1974 [63])
designer BP/59*
FURSE, Roger (1903-73) English
designer AAS, ES, WWT/
10-15
FURST, William American drama-
tist DD
FURST, William Wallace (d 1917
[65]) composer BE*
FURTADO, Charles Knox (d 1891)
acting manager EA/92*
FURTADO, Teresa Elizabeth
[Mrs. John Clarke] (1845-77)
actress CDP, DD
FURTH, George actor, dramatist

CD, WWT/16
FURTWANGLER, Wilhelm (1886-
1954) German conductor ES,
WWA/3
FUSSELLE, Kate (d 1911 [50])
singer EA/12*
FYFE, Alexander (fl 1705-09)
dramatist CP/1-3, GT
FYFE, H. Hamilton (1869-1951)
English critic CB, DNB,
GRB/2-4, WWT/1-6, WWW/5
FYFE, Isaac (d 1964) performer
BP/49*
FYFFE, Charles J. (1830-1910)
American actor HAS
FYFFE, Kitty [Amanda Carter]
(fl 1865) comedienne HAS
FYFFE, Will (1885-1947) Scottish
music-hall performer TW/4,
OC/1-3
FYLES, Franklin (1847-1911)
American critic, dramatist
DD, GRB/2-4, SR
FYNE, Elizabeth (d 1913) EA/14*
FYNES, Richard (d 1892) propri-
etor, manager EA/93*

- G -

GABAIN, Dorothy Maude see
Crawford, Dorothy Maude
GABEL, June (b 1945) American
actress TW/25-30
GABEL, Martin (b 1912) American
actor AAS, BE, TW/12-15,
19, 26, WWT/9-16
GABLE, Christopher (b 1940) Eng-
lish dancer ES
GABLE, Clark (1901-60) American
actor CB, ES, TW/17, WWA/
4, WWT/7-10, WWW/5
GABLER, Carl (b 1932) American
actor TW/23
GABOR, Eva (b 1925/26) Hungarian
actress BE, CB, TW/12-14
GABOR, Zsa Zsa (b 1923) Hun-
garian actress TW/27
GABRIEL, Ethel (d 1967 [78])
actress WWT/15*
GABRIEL, Gilbert W. (1890-1952)
American critic NTH, TW/9,
WWT/6-9
GABRIEL, Gus (d 1973 [63]) show-
man BP/58*
GABRIEL, Virginia [Mary Ann
Virginia March] (1825-77) Eng-
lish composer CDP, DD, DNB

GABRIELLI, Caterina (1730-96)
Italian singer ES

GABUSSI, Vincenzo (1800-46)
Italian singer, singing teacher
ES

GACHET, Alice (d 1960) actress,
director, teacher BE*, WWT/
14*

GADD, Renée (b 1908) Argentinian
actress, dancer WWT/7-11

GADEMANN, Elsa (b 1881) German actress GRB/4, WWT/
1-2

GADES, Antonio (b 1936) Spanish
dancer, choreographer CB

GADSBY, C. Rivers (d 1961
[73]) actor WWT/14*

GADSBY, Henry R. (d 1907)
composer EA/08*

GADSDEN, Lionel (d 1965 [86])
actor WWT/14*

GADSKI, Bertha (d 1907) actress
WWT/14*

GADSKI, Johanna (1871-1932)
German singer CDP, ES,
WWA/1

GAERTNER, Mrs. E. see
Daniels, Becky

GAERTNER, Jenny (d 1894)
EA/95*

GAFFIGAN, Catherine American
actress TW/23

GAFFNEY, Mrs. John see
Gaffney, Laura

GAFFNEY, Laura [Mrs. John
Gaffney] (d 1903) EA/04*

GAFFNEY, Liam (b 1911) Irish
actor WWT/11-14

GAGE, Richard N. (1905-72)
American director BE

GAGER, William (fl 1574-1610)
dramatist CP/1-3, DD, FGF

GAGLIANO, Frank (b 1931)
American dramatist CD,
WWT/15-16

GAHAGAN, Helen (b 1900) American actress, singer BE,
CB, SR, WWT/5-13

GAIGE, Crosby (1882-1949)
American producing manager
NTH, TW/5, WWA/2, WWT/
6-10

GAIGE, Truman [né Stanley Ruh-
land] American actor BE

GAIL, Zoë [née Zoë Margaret
Stapleton] (b 1920) South African actress, dancer WWT/
10-13

GAINES, Richard American actor
TW/9

GAINSBOROUGH, Monta (fl 1869-
78) English actress DD, OAA/
1-2

GAITES, Joseph M. (d 1940 [67])
American producer, director
BE*, BP/25*, WWT/14*

GALA, Frank (d 1911 [37]) performer? EA/12*

GALARNO, Bill (b 1938) American
actor TW/20

GALDOS, Benito Pedro (b 1845)
Spanish dramatist GRB/1, 3-4

GALE, Lieut. (d 1850 [54]) aeronaut EA/72*

GALE, Adeona (1842-61) Irish
dancer CDP, HAS

GALE, Chet W. (d 1970 [52])
performer BP/55*

GALE, Florence (b 1881) American
actress WWM

GALE, Fred (d 1902 [43]) music-
hall performer EA/03*

GALE, George (1800-50) English/
American actor CDP, HAS,
SR

GALE, George (fl 1890s?) singer
CDP

GALE, Mrs. George (fl 1831-61)
actress HAS

GALE, Hannah (1839-61) Irish
dancer CDP, HAS

GALE, John (b 1929) English producer WWT/14-16

GALE, Joseph T. (d 1976 [70])
entertainment pioneer BP/60*

GALE, Mrs. J. W. (d 1892) EA/
93*

GALE, Matilda (d 1880 [75]) EA/
81*

GALE, Minna [Minna Gale Haynes;
Mrs. Archibald C. Haynes]
(1867/69-1944?) American actress PP/1, SR, WWA/5,
WWM

GALE, Moe (d 1964 [65]) agent
BP/49*

GALE, Richard (b 1921) English
actor TW/7

GALE, Ruth (b 1846) English
dancer HAS

GALE, Sarah Ann see Rouse,
Mrs.

GALE, Mrs. William Charles
see Rouse, Mrs.

GALE, Zelia (b 1844) English
equestrienne, tight-rope per-

former HAS

GALE, Zona (1874-1938) American dramatist MD, MH, MWD, NTH, WWT/6-8, WWW/3

GALEFFI, Carlo (b 1885) Italian singer ES

GALEOTTI, Vincenzo (1733-1916) Italian/Danish dancer, choreographer ES

GALER, Mrs. Elliot see Reeves, Fanny

GALER, Elliot John Norman (1828-1901) proprietor, singer, manager, dramatist DD

GALE SISTERS, The HAS

GALICI, Vincent Michael (b 1945) American actor TW/28

GALIK, Denise (b 1951) American actress TW/29

GALINDO, Mrs. [née Gough] actress CDP, TD/1-2

GALIPAUX, Felix (1860-1931) French dramatist, actor WWT/1

GALLACHER, Tom Scottish dramatist CD

GALLAGHER, Mr. (fl 1846) actor HAS

GALLAGHER, Dan (d 1973) performer BP/58*

GALLAGHER, Helen (b 1926) American actress, singer BE, TW/22-29, WWT/14-16

GALLAGHER, Jack singer, actor CDP

GALLAGHER, James Lancaster (1817-87) American actor, stage manager NYM

GALLAGHER, John (d 1879 [39]) equestrian director EA/80*

GALLAGHER, Mjr. John (d 1912 [79]) manager EA/13*

GALLAGHER, John (b 1947) American actor TW/27

GALLAGHER, Mrs. John see Gallagher, Mary

GALLAGHER, Mary [Mrs. John Gallagher] (d 1904 [71]) EA/06*

GALLAGHER, Richard (1896/1900-55) American actor WWT/6-10

GALLAGHER, Robert (b 1920) American actor TW/10

GALLAGHER, Skeets (1896-1955) American actor TW/1, 3, 11

GALLAHER, Donald (b 1895) Irish actor WWT/7-10

GALLAND, Bertha (1876/77-1932) American actress GRB/2-4, WWM, WWS, WWT/1-3

GALLATIN, Alberta (d 1948 [87]) American actress TW/5

GALLAWAY, Marian (b 1903) American educator, director BE

GALLET, Sébastien (b c.1750) French dancer, choreographer ES

GALLETTI, Annetti (fl 1858-69) French dancer CDP, HAS

GALLETTI GIANOLI, Isabella (1835-1901) Italian singer ES

GALLEY, Arthur English giant CDP

GALLI, Richard (b 1942) American actor TW/30

GALLI, Rosina (d 1940 [45]) dancer BE*, BP/24*, WWT/14*

GALLIARD, John Ernest (1687?-1749) composer DD, DNB

GALLI-CURCI, Amelita (1889-1963) Italian singer ES, SR, TW/20, WWA/4, WWW/6

GALLIER, Charles H. (b 1878) English actress GRB/1

GALLIER, Elizabeth (d 1894) EA/95*

GALLI-MARIE DE L'ISLE, Célestine (1840-1905) French singer ES

GALLIMORE, Catherine (d 1962 [57]) performer BE*, BP/47*

GALLIMORE, Florrie singer CDP

GALLIMORE, Henry (d 1885) EA/86*

GALLIMORE, Mary (d 1898) EA/99*

GALLINI, Giovanni Andrea Battista (1728-1805) dancing master CDP

GALLISON, Joseph (b 1939) American actor TW/24-26

GALLO, Alberto (d 1964 [75]) choreographer, teacher BE*

GALLO, Fortune (1878-1970) Italian impresario CB, NTH, WWA/5

GALLO, Lew (b 1928) American actor TW/12

GALLO, Sofia (1888-1948) American singer SR

GALLON, Nellie Tom (d 1938) actress BE*, WWT/14*

GALLON, Tom (1866-1914) English dramatist WWW/1

GALLONE, Carmine (d 1973 [87]) producer/director/choreographer BP/57*

GALLOP, Sammy (d 1971 [55]) composer/lyricist BP/55*

GALLOTT, John (d 1852) English actor CDP, HAS

GALLOWAY, B. T. (d 1916) EA/17*

GALLOWAY, Don (b 1937) American actor TW/18-19

GALLOWAY, Mrs. F. see Le Grand, Mlle.

GALLOWAY, George (fl 1802-06) dramatist CP/3

GALLOWAY, George (b 1834) American actor, singer HAS

GALLOWAY, Hunter (d 1969 [59]) performer BP/53*

GALLOWAY, Louise (d 1949 [70]) American actress TW/6

GALLUP, Bonnie (b 1945) American actress TW/29-30

GALMAN, Peter W. (b 1945) American actor TW/26

GALPHIN, Martha American actress TW/26

GALSWORTHY, John (1867-1933) English dramatist AAS, COC, DNB, GRB/3-4, ES, HP, MD, MH, MWD, NTH, OC/1-3, PDT, RE, SR, WWM, WWT/1-7, WWW/3

GALT, John (d 1839 [59]) writer BE*, WWT/14*

GALT, William R. (d 1972 [91]) vaudeville agent BP/57*

GALTON, Blanche (fl 1868) actress? CDP, HAS

GALTON, Mary Pyne (fl 1868) actress? HAS

GALTON, Susan (b 1849) English singer, actress CDP, HAS

GALVANI, Dino (1890-1960) Italian actor WWT/6-10

GALVIN, Gene (b 1917) American actor TW/24-25

GALVIN, George see Leon, Dan

GALVIN, James (b 1933) American actor TW/29

GALVIN, Sydney Paul [Dan Leno, Jr.] (1892-1962) dancer, comedian COC, OC/3

GAM, Rita (b 1928) American actress BE, TW/24, 29

GAMBLE, Ralph (d 1966 [64]) performer BP/50*

GAMBLE, Theodore Roosevelt (1906-61) American executive WWA/4

GAMBLE, Tom (1898-1946) English comedian WWT/10

GAMBLE, Warburton (d 1945 [62]) actor BE*, WWT/14*

GAMBLING, John B. (d 1974 [77]) performer BP/59*

GAMBOA, Marcelo (b 1939) Argentinian actor TW/25-26, 28

GAMBOLD, John (d 1771) Welsh dramatist CP/2-3, DD, GT

GAMBON, Michael (b 1940) Irish actor WWT/16

GAMLIN, Lionel James (1903-67) actor WWW/6

GAMMON, Percy (d 1917) EA/18*

GAMMON, William (b 1943) American actor TW/30

GAMPEL, Chris see Gampel, C. M.

GAMPEL, C. M. (b 1921) Canadian actor TW/14, 25-26, 30

GAMPEL, Morison see Gampel, C. M.

GANDY, Sidney (d 1912 [47]) ventriloquist EA/13*

GANEY, David J. (d 1887) actor NYM

GANIMAN, Charles "Chick" (b 1926) American actor TW/26

GANN, Miss see Fries, Mrs. Wulf

GANN, James (fl 1844) English actor HAS

GANN, Louisa M. A. (b 1826) actress, singer CDP, HAS

GANNE, Louis (b 1862) French composer GRB/1

GANNON, Charles A. (d 1972 [78]) performer BP/57*

GANNON, Elenor [Mrs. T. R. Gannon] (d 1893) EA/94*

GANNON, James (d 1974 [73]) composer/lyricist BP/56*

GANNON, Liam Irish actress TW/26

GANNON, Martha Ann (d 1906) EA/07*

GANNON, Mary (1829-68) American actress CDP, DD, HAS, SR

GANNON, Thomas (d 1917) variety agent EA/18*

GANNON, Mrs. T. R. see Gannon, Elenor

GANNON, W. (d 1891) EA/92*

GANON, James American actor
TW/1, 3

GANS, Sidney (d 1972 [60])
critic BP/57*

GANT, William George (d 1881)
EA/82*

GANT, William George see
Ross, Charlie

GANTHONY, Nellie [Mrs. Arthur
Sykes] English entertainer
GRB/1-4

GANTHONY, Richard (d 1924
[67]) dramatist, actor BE*,
WWT/14*

GANTHONY, Robert (d 1931 [82])
dramatist, performer BE*,
WWT/14*

GANTILLON, Simon (1887-1961)
French dramatist COC

GANTRY, Donald (b 1936) American actor TW/28, 30

GANTY, Little singer, actor
CDP

GANZ, Herr (d 1869 [74]) musician EA/70*

GANZ, Moritz (d 1868 [64])
musician EA/69*

GANZ, Wilhelm (1833-1914)
Austrian conductor, composer,
musician GRB/1, WWW/1

GAPPER, H. B. M. see
Gascoigne, Henry

GARBANATI, Mr. (fl 1850) actor
HAS

GARBER, Victor (b 1949) Canadian actor TW/29

GARBIN, Eduardo (1865-1943)
Italian singer ES

GARBOIS, Sophie Charlotte
see Neville, Charlotte

GARBOIS, Mrs. W. H. see
Neville, Charlotte

GARCIA, Sig. (1778-1836) Spanish
singer HAS

GARCIA, Edward (d 1893) lessee
EA/94*

GARCIA, Henry (d 1970 [66])
performer BP/55*

GARCIA, Manuel (1805-1906)
Spanish singer, singing teacher
ES

GARD, Robert E. (b 1910) American educator, director BE

GARDE, Betty (b 1905) American
actress BE, TW/5-8, 23-24,
WWT/10-11, 15-16

GARDEL, Mme. Pierre Gabriel,
I see Coulon, Anne Jacqueline

GARDELLA, Tess (d 1950 [52])
American singer, comedienne
TW/6

GARDEN, David (b 1932) American actor TW/2

GARDEN, Edmund (1822-80) actor
DD

GARDEN, E[dmund] W[illiam]
(1845-1939) English actor DD,
DP, GRB/1-4, OAA/1-2, WWT/
1-9

GARDEN, Mary (1874/76/77-1967)
Scottish singer ES, GRB/1,
SR, TW/23, WWA/4, WWW/6

GARDENER, Julian see Royce,
Julian

GARDENER, Shayle (b 1890) New
Zealand actor WWT/5-6

GARDENIA, Vincent [né Scogna-
miglio] (b 1922/23) Italian/
American actor BE, TW/25-
30, WWT/16

GARDER, Ann American actress
TW/25

GARDIE, Mme. (d 1798) actress
HAS

GARDIN, Vladimir (1877-1965)
Russian actor OC/3

GARDINER, Mrs. [née Cheney]
(fl 1763-82) actress, dramatist
CP/2, GT, TD/1-2

GARDINER, Cyril (b 1897) English
actor WWT/10

GARDINER, E. W. (d 1899 [37])
actor DD, DP, EA/96

GARDINER, Henry Andrew see
Coyne, Gardiner

GARDINER, John (d 1884 [46])
actor EA/86*

GARDINER, John (d 1889 [24])
EA/90*

GARDINER, John (d 1897 [74])
circus manager EA/99*

GARDINER, Matthew (fl 1740-41)
Irish? dramatist CP/1-3, GT

GARDINER, Patrick (d 1970 [44])
performer BP/55*

GARDINER, Reginald (b 1903) English actor BE, TW/12, WWT/
7-10

GARDINER, William (fl 1806)
dramatist CP/3

GARDINER, Willie Elslice (d
1917 [7]) EA/18*

GARDNER, Lady see Fortesque,
Julia

GARDNER, Mrs. [Miss Cheney] (d
1790) actress, dramatist CDP,

CP/3, DD, DNB
GARDNER, Master CDP
GARDNER, Archibald M. (d 1972
[65]) critic BP/57*
GARDNER, Cecil (d 1901 [25])
variety manager EA/02*
GARDNER, Charles A. (c. 1848-
1924) actor, composer, singer
CDP, SR
GARDNER, David (b 1928) Cana-
dian actor TW/12
GARDNER, Ed (1905-63) Ameri-
can producer, writer CB,
WWA/4
GARDNER, Eliza (d 1911) EA/12*
GARDNER, Godfrey Derman (d
1916 [34]) EA/17*
GARDNER, Harry (d 1917) clown
EA/18*
GARDNER, Helen Louise (d
1968) performer BP/53*
GARDNER, Herb (b 1934) drama-
tist BE
GARDNER, Herbert [Lord Burgh-
clere] (fl 1875-85) dramatist
DD
GARDNER, Jack (d 1950 [77])
singer, actor CDP, TW/7
GARDNER, John (d 1851 [49])
actor EA/72*
GARDNER, Mrs. John see
Gardner, Ruth
GARDNER, Katie see Sawin,
Mrs. George Arthur
GARDNER, Peter H. (d 1917)
actor EA/18*
GARDNER, Renée (d 1973 [43])
performer BP/58*
GARDNER, Rita actress, singer
BE
GARDNER, Ruth [Mrs. John
Gardner] (d 1892) EA/93*
GARDNER, Shayle (1890-1945)
New Zealand actor WWT/7-9
GARDNER, Thomas (d 1867 [55])
proprietor EA/68*
GARDNER, William (d 1870)
actor EA/71*
GARDNER, William Henry (1865-
1932) American composer
WWA/1
GARDNER, William John (d 1912
[41]) EA/14*
GARDONI, Sig. (d 1882 [61])
singer EA/83*
GAREY, James R. (1861-1947)
actor, dramatist SR
GAREY, Peter (b 1917) American

actor TW/6-7
GARFEIN, Jack (b 1930) Czech/
American director BE, ES
GARFIELD, Allen (b 1939) Ameri-
can actor TW/26
GARFIELD, Benjamin dramatist
CP/3, FGF
GARFIELD, David (b 1941) Amer-
ican actor TW/26-29
GARFIELD, John [né Julius Gar-
finkle] (1913-53) American ac-
tor AAS, CB, ES, TW/5-8,
WWT/11
GARFIELD, Julie (b 1946) Ameri-
can actress TW/25, 27, 30
GARFIELD, Kurt (b 1931) Ameri-
can actor TW/26, 28
GARFINKLE, Julius see Gar-
field, John
GARGAN, Edward F. (d 1964 [62])
actor BE*, BP/48*
GARGAN, William (b 1905) Amer-
ican actor WWT/8-10
GARLAND, Geoff (b 1932) English
actor TW/23, 25-29
GARLAND, Hamlin (1860-1940)
American dramatist WWA/1
GARLAND, Mrs. Herbert see
McKenzie, Florence
GARLAND, Herbert Theodore see
Trevor, Theodore
GARLAND, John (fl 1583-1616)
actor DA
GARLAND, Judy [née Gumm]
(1922-69) American actress,
singer, dancer CB, TW/26,
WWA/5
GARLAND, Patrick director,
dramatist AAS, WWT/15-16
GARLAND, Robert (1895-1955)
American critic NTH, TW/12,
WWT/8-12
GARLICK (fl c. 1610) actor DA
GARMAN, Mr. G. (d 1867 [48])
singer EA/68*
GARNER, Mr. (d 1843) singer
HAS
GARNER, Arthur (b 1851) English
actor DD, OAA/1-2
GARNER, Mrs. Arthur [Blanche
Stammers] (d 1883) actress
EA/84*
GARNER, James (b 1928) Ameri-
can actor CB
GARNER, Martin (b 1927) Ameri-
can actor TW/28, 30
GARNER, Peggy Ann (b 1932)
American actress TW/6-8,

11-12

GARNER, William Henry (d 1916
[74]) EA/17*

GARNERIN, André Jae (1769-1823)
French aeronaut CDP

GARNETT, Constance (1862-1948)
translator NTH

GARNETT, Edward (1868-1937)
dramatist NTH, WWT/1-8,
WWW/3

GARNETT, Louise Ayres (d 1937)
American composer WWA/1

GARNIER, Mr. (d 1884) EA/85*

GARNIER, Leon (d 1905 [49])
French songwriter GRB/1

GARON, Norm (d 1975 [41]) performer BP/59*

GAROZZO, Nella (d 1972 [50+])
publicist BP/57*

GARR, Eddie (d 1940) comedian
WWT/14*

GARR, Eddie (d 1956 [56]) American vaudevillian TW/13

GARRARD, Mr. (d 1878 [46])
musician EA/79*

GARRATT, Adah (d 1898) actress
EA/00*

GARRATT, Jessie [Mrs. W. Lee
Bruno] (d 1896 [44]) actress
EA/97*

GARRATT, John (d 1871) clown
EA/72*

GARRATT, Mary Annie (d 1886
[90]) EA/87*

GARRETT, Arthur (1869-1941)
English manager WWT/2-9

GARRETT, Betty (b 1919/20)
American actress, singer
BE, TW/1-6, 20-21, WWT/
11, 14-16

GARRETT, Bob (b 1947) American actor TW/29-30

GARRETT, George (d 1878 [46])
musician EA/79*

GARRETT, John (fl 1619) actor
DA

GARRETT, Joy (b 1945) American
actress TW/26-28

GARRETT, Kelly (b 1948) American actress TW/29-30

GARRETT, Oliver H. P. (d
1952 [54]) American dramatist BE*, BP/36*

GARRETT, William H. (d 1888
[49]) actor, manager EA/89*

GARRICK, Mrs. [née Gray]
(d c.1844) actress CDP

GARRICK, Beulah (b 1921) Eng-

lish actress TW/27, 30

GARRICK, David (1717-79) English
actor, dramatist, manager
CDP, COC, CP/1-3, DD, DNB,
ES, GT, HP, MH, NTH, OC/
1-3, OX, PDT, SR, TD/1-3

GARRICK, Mrs. David see Violetti, Eva Maria

GARRICK, Eva Marie see Violetti, Eva Maria

GARRICK, Gus (fl 1890s?) singer,
actor CDP

GARRICK, Helen Collier (d 1954
[87]) actress TW/11

GARRICK, Henry Walter (b 1871)
English press manager GRB/
1-3

GARRICK, Jack (d 1917 [19])
comedian EA/18*

GARRICK, John (b 1902) English
actor, singer WWT/7-11

GARRICK, Nathan David (d 1876
[67]) EA/77*

GARRICK, P. CDP

GARRICK, Richard T. (d 1962
[83]) actor BE*

GARRICK, Sarah Jane (d 1859
[76]) actress EA/72*

GARRISON, George W. [né
Chandler] (fl 1867) actor HAS

GARRISON, Mabel (d 1963 [77])
American singer TW/20, WWA/
4

GARRISON, Michael (d 1966 [43])
performer BP/51*

GARRISON, Sean (b 1937) American
actor TW/16, 18-20, 22

GARROD, W[alter] V[incent] (b
1879) Irish actor, manager
GRB/1

GARROW, Mrs. Joseph see
Abrams, Theodosia

GARRY, Charles (d 1939 [68]) actor BE*, WWT/14*

GARRY, Claude [Claude Dietz]
(1877-1918) French actor WWT/
3

GARSI, Ginlia (b 1822) Italian
singer SR

GARSIDE, John (1887-1958) English
actor, designer WWT/6-12

GARSIDE, Thomas (d 1881 [44])
conductor EA/82*

GARSON, Greer (b 1908) Irish actress CB, ES, SR, WWT/8-11

GARSON, T. E. (fl 1838) American actor HAS

GARSTIN, George Benjamin see

Belmore, George

GARSTONE, Kate (d 1885) music-
hall performer EA/86*

GARTEN, H. F. [né Koenigsgar-
ten] (b 1904) Austrian librettist,
educator BE

GARTER, Thomas (fl 1578) dramatist CP/1-3, FGF

GARTHORNE, C. W. [Charles
Warlhouse Grimston] (d 1900
[54]) actor DD, OAA/2

GARTON, Flo [Mrs. F. Heath]
(d 1907) variety performer
EA/08*

GARTSIDE, Henry see Neville,
Henry

GARTSIDE-NEVILLE, Mrs.
George see Neville, Mary
C. H.

GARVEY, Miss (fl 1849) actress
HAS

GARVICE, Charles (d 1920)
dramatist WWW/2

GARVIE, Edward (1870-1939)
American actor WWM

GARY, David (b 1946) American
actor TW/26

GARY, Harold (b 1910) American
actor TW/3, 23-25, 28-30

GARY, Sid (d 1973 [72]) performer BP/57*

GASCOIGNE, Bamber (b 1935)
English critic, lyricist AAS,
WWT/14-16

GASCOIGNE, Charles [Charles
Sullivan] (d 1887 [39]) Irish
comedian EA/88*

GASCOIGNE, George (c. 1535-
77) English scholar, dramatist
CDP, COC, CP/1-3, DD,
DNB, ES, FGF, HP, MH,
OC/1-3, PDT, RE

GASCOIGNE, George (d 1916)
assistant manager EA/17*

GASCOIGNE, Henry [H. B. M.
Gapper] (d 1894 [44]) actor,
manager, dramatist, lessee
DD

GASCOIGNE, William (fl 1589)
actor DA

GASCON, Edward E. (d 1965
[93]) performer BP/49*

GASCON, Jean (b 1921) Canadian
actor, director AAS, WWT/
13-16

GASCOYNE, William (fl 1624-31)
actor DA

GASELLI, Silva see Gassell,

Sylvia

GASKELL, Clarence (1892-1948)
composer, musical director
SR

GASKILL, William (b 1930) English
director, stage manager, actor
AAS, COC, ES, PDT, WWT/
14-16

GASNIER, Louis (d 1963 [87])
French actor, director BE*

GASPARONI, Sig. (fl 1856) singer
HAS

GASPARRE, Dick (d 1971 [72])
composer/lyricist BP/56*

GASPER, Edd K. (b 1937) American actor TW/25-26

GASSELL, Sylvia [Silva Gaselli]
(b 1923) American actress
TW/9, 20, 24-27

GASSIER, Louis Edward (1822-71)
singer CDP, HAS

GASSIER, Mme. Louis Edward (fl
1855-58) singer CDP, HAS

GASSIER, Pepita see Gassier,
Mme. Louis Edward

GASSMAN, Josephine (d 1962 [82])
performer BE*

GASSNER, John (1903-67) Hungari-
an/American critic, historian,
dramatist BE, CB, COC, ES,
NTH, TW/23, WWT/11-14

GASTELLE, Stella (d 1936) actress, singer BE*, WWT/14*

GASTON, E. B. (d 1858 [35]) actor WWT/14*

GASTON, George (1843-1937)
American actor BE*, WWT/14*

GASTON, Penny (b 1942) Canadian
actress TW/23

GATAKER, Thomas (fl 1730)
dramatist CP/3

GATES, Mrs. (d 1870 [72]) actress EA/71*

GATES, Eleanor (1875-1951) American dramatist TW/7, WWT/
4-9

GATES, James (d 1868 [39]) scene
artist EA/69*

GATES, Larry (b 1915) American
actor BE, TW/8-12, 20, 24,
WWT/12-16

GATES, Ruth (1888-1966) American
actress BE, TW/1, 22

GATES, William F. (d 1843) American actor CDP, HAS

GATES AND MORANGE American
scene designer ES

GATESON, Marjorie (1891/97-

1977) American actress, singer BE, TW/3-7, 10-14, WWT/11-14

GATHERCOLE, John (d 1895 [42]) manager EA/96*

GATLEY, T. (d 1886) proprietor EA/87*

GATTI, Agostino (d 1897 [55]) proprietor EA/98*, WWT/14*

GATTI, Carlo (d 1878 [61]) music-hall proprietor EA/79*, WWT/14*

GATTI, Sir John Maria (1872-1929) English manager WWT/1-6

GATTI, Rocco J. S. (d 1950 [76]) proprietor WWT/14*

GATTI, Stefano (d 1906 [61]) proprietor, manager EA/07*, GRB/2*

GATTI-CASAZZA, Giulio (1869-1940) Italian impresario DAB, ES, WWA/1, WWM

GATTIE, A. W. (d 1925 [69]) dramatist BE*, WWT/14*

GATTIE, Henry (1774-1844) English actor, singer BS, CDP, DD, DNB, EA/92, OX

GATTY, Alfred Scott singer, composer CDP

GATTY, Nicholas Comyn (1874-1946) composer WWW/4

GAUDIN, Thomas (d 1889 [78]) EA/90*

GAUDRY, Joseph actor TD/1-2

GAUDSCHMIDT, Max (d 1972 [83]) performer BP/56*

GAUDY, Miss (b c. 1780) actress TD/2

GAUGE, Alexander (1914-60) Chinese/English actor TW/3

GAUGIN, Lorraine (d 1974 [50]) performer BP/59*

GAUL, George (1885-1939) American actor WWT/7-8

GAUL, Patricia American actress TW/29

GAUNT, David [John Davies Butler] (d 1883 [20]) actor EA/84*

GAUNT, Elsie (d 1910) actress EA/11*

GAUNT, Percy (1852-96) American songwriter BE*

GAUNT, Picton see Roxborough, Picton

GAUNT, William Clifford (d

1942 [69]) proprietor WWT/14*

GAUNTIER, Gene (d 1966 [80s]) performer BP/51*

GAUNTLETT, Dr. (d 1876) musician EA/77*

GAUNTLETT, Hilary Sebastian (d 1911 [24]) musician EA/12*

GAUTHIER, Eva (1885-1958) Canadian singer WWA/3

GAUTIER, Eugene (d 1878 [56]) composer EA/79*

GAUTIER, Leonard (d 1948 [56]) dog trainer TW/4

GAVER, Jack (1906-74) American editor, critic BE, NTH

GAVIN, John (b 1935) American actor TW/30

GAVON, Igors (b 1937) Latvian actor TW/23-29

GAWTHORNE, Peter A. (1884-1962) Irish actor WWT/4-10

GAXIOLA, Arturo see Gaxton, William

GAXTON, William [Arturo Gaxiola] (1893-1963) American actor AAS, TW/1-14, 19, WWT/7-11

GAY, Mr. (fl 1831-33) English actor HAS

GAY, Mrs. (d 1889) EA/91*

GAY, John (1685-1732) English dramatist CDP, COC, CP/1-3, DNB, ES, GT, HP, MH, NTH, OC/1-3, PDT, RE, SR, TD/1-2

GAY, Joseph see Breval, Cpt. John Durant

GAY, Maisie (1883-1945) English actress, singer TW/2, WWT/4-9, WWW/4

GAY, Maria (1879-1943) Spanish singer ES

GAY, Noel [R. M. Armitage] (1898-1954) English composer WWT/6-11

GAY, Ralph George (d 1890 [27]) EA/91*

GAY, Walter (d 1936 [73]) actor BE*, WWT/14*

GAYARRE, Julian (1844-90) Spanish singer ES

GAYE, Albie (d 1965) performer BP/50*

GAYE, Freda (b 1907) English actress, editor, curator BE, WWT/13-15

GAYER, Echlin (1878-1926) actor SR

GAYLE, Tim (d 1970 [57]) publicist BP/55*

GAYLER, Charles (1820-92)
American dramatist, actor
CDP, DAB, SR, WWA/H

GAYLOR, Bobbie (b c. 1861)
actor, dramatist, producer
SR

GAYLORD, Julia (d 1894) actress,
singer CDP

GAYLORD, Lowrenzo (1836-78)
minstrel, manager CDP

GAYNES, Edmund (b 1947) American actor TW/25-28

GAYNES, George [George Jon-
geyans] (b 1917) Finnish actor,
singer BE, TW/7, 9-15, 19-
23, 30, WWT/16

GAYNOR, Charles (1909-75) American lyricist, composer BE

GAYTHORNE, Pamela (b 1882)
actress WWT/2-6

GAYTIE, Fred A. [Frederick
Augustus Hetherington] (b 1862)
English actor GRB/1

GAYTON, Edmund dramatist
CP/3

GAZE, George (d 1904 [72]) proprietor EA/05*

GAZE, Mrs. Leslie see Gorton, Belle

GAZZANIGA, Marietta (c. 1824-
84) Sardinian singer CDP,
HAS

GAZZARA, Ben (b 1930) American actor AAS, BE, CB, ES,
TW/10-21, WWT/12-16

GAZZO, Michael V. (b 1923)
American dramatist, actor,
director BE, MH

GAZZOLO, Frank A. P. (b 1873)
American manager, producer,
agent SR

GEAR, Luella (b 1897/99) American actress BE, TW/1-8,
10-15, WWT/5-15

GEAR, Robert (d 1893 [73]) performer? EA/94*

GEARY, Sam see Arthur, Sam

GEARY, Samuel (d 1889 [46])
EA/90*

GEATER, R. F. see Flexmore,
Richard

GeBAUER, Gene (b 1934) American actor TW/27-30

GEBERT, Ernst (d 1961 [59])
German conductor BE*

GECKS, Mr. (d 1888) bandmaster
EA/89*

GEDDA, Nicolai (b 1925) Swedish

singer CB, ES

GEDDES, Dr. (fl 1582?) dramatist
FGF

GEDDES, Barbara Bel (b 1922/23)
American actress AAS, BE,
CB, COC, ES, OC/3, TW/2-20,
22-24, 29-30, WWT/11-16

GEDDES, George E. (d 1973 [68])
theatre founder BP/58*

GEDDES, Norman Bel (1893-1958)
American scene designer, pro-
ducer, director CB, COC,
ES, NTH, OC/1-3, PDT, SR,
TW/14, WWA/3, WWT/7-11,
WWW/5

GEDGE, John Kerr (d 1876) singer
EA/77*

GEE, Caroline Eliza [Mrs. Palm-
er] (d 1887 [71]) actress? EA/
88*

GEE, Caroline Eliza Palmer (d
1871 [19]) actress EA/72*

GEE, Fannie Marie see Forbes,
Mrs. W. C.

GEE, George (d 1959 [64]) actor
WWT/6-12

GEE, Jack (d 1973 [84]) manager
BP/58*

GEE, John (d 1902) actor? EA/
03*

GEER, Ellen (b 1941) American
actress BE

GEER, Seth (d 1866) actor HAS

GEER, Will (b 1902/05) American
actor AAS, BE, TW/1-6, 10-
14, 22-23, 25, 27, WWT/10-16

GEEVES-BOOTH, James see
Booth, James

GEFFREY, John dramatist CP/2-3

GEHMAN, Richard (1921-72)
American writer BE

GEHRI, Alfred (d 1972 [76]) performer, dramatist BP/56*,
WWT/16*

GEHRUE, Mayme [Mrs. John
Ford] (b 1883) American actress
WWM

GEIRINGER, Jean (d 1962 [62])
Austrian librettist, lyricist
BE*

GEIS, Wayne (b 1945) American
actor TW/26

GEIST, Irving (d 1970 [70]) backer
BP/55*

GEISTINGER, Marie (1836-1903)
German singer, actress CDP,
ES

GEISWEILER, Maria (fl 1799)

translator CP/3

GEIWITZ, Emma C. (c. 1820-1915)
German actress SR

GELB, Arthur (b 1924) American
editor, critic BE

GELB, James stage manager,
director BE

GELBART, Larry S. (b 1923)
American librettist BE

GELBER, Eugene (d 1974 [46])
producer/director/choreographer
BP/58*

GELBERT, Jack Allen (b 1932)
American dramatist, director
AAS, BE, CD, CH, COC,
ES, MD, MH, MWD, PDT,
RE, WWT/15-16

GEL'CER, Ekaterina Vasil'evna
(b 1876) Russian dancer ES

GELDARD, Mrs. R. see Gel-
dard, Sarah Ann

GELDARD, Sarah Ann [Mrs. R.
Geldard] (d 1878) EA/79*

GELDERD, James (d 1918) EA/
19*

GELFAND, Carol (b 1937) American actress TW/26-28

GELLMAN, Jacob see Gilford,
Jack

GELLNER, Julius (b 1899)
Bohemian director, actor
WWT/15-16

GELTZER, Catherine (fl 1871-
1914) dancer OC/1-2

GEMEA, Mrs. Tobias see
Chetwood, Richabella

GEMIER, Firmin (d 1933 [68])
French actor, producer BP/
18*

GEMIGNANI, Rhoda (b 1940)
American actress TW/25, 30

GEMMELL, Don (b 1903) Scottish
director, manager, actor
WWT/14-16

GEMMILL, William D. (d 1882
[37]) manager CDP

GENDRON, Pierre (d 1956 [60])
actor BE*

GENEE, Dame Adeline (1878-
1970) Danish dancer CDP, ES,
GRB/1-4, OC/1-2, WWM,
WWS, WWT/1-12, WWW/6

GENEE, Alexander (d 1938 [88])
dancer, director BE*, WWT/
14*

GENEE, Ottilie (fl 1865) German
actress CDP

GENEST, Edmond (b 1943) Amer-

ican actor TW/28-29

GENEST, John (1764-1839) scholar
HP

GENET, Jean (b 1909/10) French
dramatist CB, COC, OC/3,
PDT, WWT/14-16

GENET, Pauline (d 1856) English
dancer HAS

GENEVIEVE [née Genevieve Auger]
(b 1930) French singer, actress
BE

GENGE, George (d 1863 [42])
singer EA/72*

GENIAT, Marcelle [née Eugenie
Martin] (d 1959 [80]) Russian/
French actress WWT/4, 10

GENIN, John H. (d 1878 [59])
American? merchant CDP

GENISE, Livia (b 1949) American
actress TW/29-30

GENN, Edward P. (d 1947 [50])
producer BE*, WWT/14*

GENN, Leo (1905-78) English actor AAS, BE, ES, TW/3-6,
13-14, 20, 24, WWT/9-16

GENNARO, Peter (b 1924?) American choreographer, dancer
BE, CB, ES, TW/13-15

GENT, George (d 1974 [49]) journalist BP/59*

GENTELE, Goeran (1917-72)
Swedish manager, director CB,
WWA/5

GENTILE, Gerard L. (d 1973
[62]) designer BP/58*

GENTLE, Alice (1885-1958) American singer TW/14, WWA/3,
WWM

GENTLEMAN, Francis (1728-84)
Irish critic, actor, dramatist
COC, CP/1-3, DNB, GT, OC/
1-3, TD/1-2

GENTLES, Avril (b 1929) American actress TW/25-27, 29-30

GENTRY, Amelia (d 1963 [40])
performer BE*

GENTRY, Bob (b 1940) American
actor TW/17-20

GENZMER, Hertha (d 1971 [74])
performer BP/55*

GEOFFREY, Mr. dramatist CP/3

GEOGHEGAN, Frederick (d 1868
[28]) professor of music EA/
69*

GEOGHEGAN, J. B. (d 1889)
music-hall manager, songwriter
EA/90*

GEOGHEGAN, Mrs. J. B. (d 1889)

EA/90*

GEOLY, Andrew (b 1907) costumier BE

GEORGE, Mr. (fl 1800s) actor TD/2

GEORGE, Miss (d c. 1803?) actress TD/1-2

GEORGE, Mlle. [Marguerite-Josephine Weymer] (1787-1867) French actress COC

GEORGE, Miss see Tuson, Isabella

GEORGE, A. E. (1869-1920) English actor GRB/1-4, WWT/1-3

GEORGE, Alfred (d 1906) music-hall comedian EA/07*

GEORGE, Amelia Angelica (b 1803) English singer, actress CDP, HAS, OX

GEORGE, Collin (b 1929) Welsh director, actor WWT/15-16

GEORGE, Mrs. E. [née Lottie Moreton] (d 1873 [28]) actress EA/74*

GEORGE, Mrs. Edward J. see George, Emily

GEORGE, Edward John (b 1842) English actor OAA/2

GEORGE, Emily [Mrs. Edward J. George] (d 1901 [45]) actress EA/02*

GEORGE, G. H. (d 1875) dramatist, actor? EA/76*

GEORGE, Mrs. G. H. see Hadwin, Ann

GEORGE, Gladys (1904-54) American actress TW/5-6, 11, WWT/8-11

GEORGE, Gorgeous (d 1963 [48]) performer BP/48*

GEORGE, Grace [Mrs. William A. Brady] (1879-1961) American actress COC, GRB/2-4, OC/1-3, SR, TW/2-9, 17, WWM, WWS, WWT/1-12

GEORGE, Harry (d 1904) EA/05*

GEORGE, Henry (d 1908 [60]) actor, manager GRB/4

GEORGE, Joseph H. (fl 1851) American actor HAS

GEORGE, Marie (1879-1955) American actress GRB/1-4, WWS, WWT/1-8

GEORGE, Muriel (1883-1965) English actress WWT/9-12

GEORGE, Sam J. (d 1969) manager BP/54*

GEORGE, William (d 1896 [50]) hosier EA/97*

"GEORGE FLEMING" see Fletcher, Constance

GEORGER, Alfred M. (d 1974 [85]) treasurer BP/59*

GEORGES, Katherine (d 1973) performer BP/58*

GEORGI, Yvonne (d 1975 [77]) dancer, choreographer BP/59*, WWT/16*

"GEORGIA MAGNET, The" see Abbott, Annie

GERACI, Robert (b 1939) American actor TW/26, 28-30

GERAGHTY, Pat (d 1898) Irish comedian EA/99*

GERALD, Ara (1900-57) Australian actress WWT/8-10

GERALD, Florence (d 1942 [84]) American actress BE*, WWT/14*

GERALD, Frank (1855-1942) English actor BE*, WWT/14*

GERARD, Dorothy (d 1908) EA/09*

GERARD, Florence (fl 1878-83) actress DD

GERARD, John (d 1886) circus performer? EA/87*

GERARD, Linda (b 1938) American actress TW/28

GERARD, Manny (d 1973 [47]) designer BP/58*

GERARD, Richard see Husch, Richard J.

GERARD, Teddie (b 1892) Argentinian actress WWT/4-7

GERAY, Steve (b 1904) Hungarian actor WWT/8-10

GERBER, Alex (d 1969 [74]) composer/lyricist BP/53*

GERBER, Ella (b 1916) American director, actress BE

GERBER, Henry W. (d 1967 [85]) producer/director/choreographer BP/52*

GERBER, Jay (b 1929) American actor TW/24

GERBER, Morton (d 1975 [60]) executive? BP/59*

GERDLER, Adam (fl 1635) actor DA

GERHARD, Karl (d 1964 [73]) performer BP/48*

GERLACH, Robert American actor TW/25-26

GERLE, Theodolinda (fl 1847)

singer HAS
GERMAN, Sir Edward (1862-1936)
English composer DD, DNB,
ES, GRB/1-4, WWS, WWT/
1-8, WWW/3
GERMANOVA, Maria Nikolaevna
(1884-1940) Russian actress
COC, OC/3
GERMAN-REED, Mrs. Alfred
(d 1916) EA/18*
GERMON, Euphemia [Effie]
(1845/47-1914) American ac-
tress CDP, HAS, PP/1, SR,
WWS
GERMON, Francis (fl 1844) min-
strel CDP
GERMON, Greene C. (d 1854)
actor CDP, HAS
GERMON, Mrs. Greene C. [Jane
Anderson or Andrews] (fl
1839-58) actress DD, HAS,
SR
GERMON, Jane (d 1909 [87])
actress WWT/14*
GERMON, John (fl 1857) actor
HAS
GERMON, Mrs. John D. see
Cunningham, Virginia
GEROLD, Arthur (b 1923) Amer-
ican costumier, producer,
manager BE
GERRARD, Ethel [Mrs. Frank
Carlile] (d 1903) actress
EA/04*
GERRARD, Gene (1892-1971)
English actor WWT/5-11
GERRARD, John Francis (d
1907 [54]) actor GRB/2*
GERRARD, Teddie (1892-1942)
Argentinian actress BE*
GERRING, Mrs. Charles (d 1887)
EA/88*
GERRINGER, Robert (b 1926)
American actor BE
GERRISH, Sylvia (d 1906 [48])
American actress, singer CDP
GERRY (fl 1607) actor DA
GERSHWIN, George (1898-1937)
American composer AAS,
DAB, ES, HJD, MH, NTH,
PDT, SR, WWA/1, WWT/5-8,
WWW/3
GERSHWIN, Ira (b 1896) American
lyricist BE, CB, ES, HJD,
WWT/7-14
GERSTAD, John [né Gjerstad] (b
1924/25) American actor, pro-
ducer, director, dramatist

BE, TW/1, 24-28, WWT/13-16
GERSTEN, Bernard (b 1923) Amer-
ican producer, director, stage
manager BE, WWT/16
GERSTEN, Berta (d 1972 [78])
Polish actress TW/29
GERSTER, Etelka (1855/57-1920)
Hungarian singer CDP, ES
GERSTLE, Frank (d 1970 [53])
performer BP/54*
GERSTMAN, Felix G. Austrian
impresario, producer BE
GERUSSI, Bruno actor WWT/14-15
GERVASE, Charles (d 1901) actor
EA/02*
GERVILLE-REACHE, Jeanne
[Mme. George Gibier Rambaud]
(fl 1900s) French singer WWM
GESENSWAY, Louis (d 1976 [70])
composer/lyricist BP/60*
GESSNER, Adrienne Austrian ac-
tress TW/1, 24
GEST, Morris (1881-1942) Russian
manager CB, DAB, NTH, SR,
WWA/2, WWT/4-9
GETCHELL, Dr. Charles Munro
(1909-63) American educator
BE*
GETCHELL, Franklin (b 1947)
American actor TW/30
GETHING, William Henry (d 1904
[45]) musical director EA/06*
GETTY, Talitha Pol (d 1971)
performer BP/56*
GETZ, Johnnie G. (d 1964 [84])
American performer BE*
GEVA, Tamara (b 1907) Russian
actress, dancer BE, TW/9,
11, 21, WWT/9-15
GEW (fl late 16th cent) actor? DA
GHELDERODE, Michel de (1898-
1962) Belgian dramatist OC/3,
PDT
GHEON, Henri (1875-1943) French
dramatist COC, OC/1-3
GHEUSI, Pierre B. (b 1865)
French dramatist GRB/4
GHIONI, Mlle. (fl 1858) singer
HAS
GHOSTLEY, Alice (b 1926) Amer-
ican actress TW/9-19, 21-22,
WWT/14-16
GIACHETTI, Fosco (d 1974 [70])
performer BP/59*
GIACOMINO (1884-1956) Italian
clown ES
GIACOSA, Giuseppe (1847-1906)
Italian dramatist OC/1-3, RE

GIANNINI, Olga Italian actress WWT/3-4

GIBB, Margaret (d 1967 [54]) performer BP/51*

GIBB, Mary (d 1967 [54]) performer BP/51*

GIBBERSON, William (b 1919) American actor BE

GIBBES, George (fl 1628) actor DA

GIBBON, Charles (d 1917) acting manager EA/18*

GIBBON, H. B. [FitzGibbon] (b 1873) English actor, producer, business manager GRB/1-2

GIBBON, James Deverell (1779-1852) actor CDP

GIBBONS, Mr. (fl 1845) actor HAS

GIBBONS, Mrs. (fl 1845) actress HAS

GIBBONS, Alfred (d 1900) EA/01*

GIBBONS, Mrs. Alfred see Mario, Dot

GIBBONS, Arthur (1871-1935) English actor, manager WWT/6-7

GIBBONS, Barney (d 1876 [46]) Irish singer EA/77*

GIBBONS, Carroll (d 1954 [51]) musician WWT/14*

GIBBONS, Edyth (fl 1899-1904) English vaudevillian WWM

GIBBONS, Frank A. trapezist CDP

GIBBONS, Irene (1907-62) American costume designer BE*

GIBBONS, Nellie Isabella [Mrs. Walter Gibbons] (d 1911 [28]) EA/12*

GIBBONS, Rod (b 1949) American actor TW/29

GIBBONS, Rose (d 1964 [78]) actress BE*, BP/49*

GIBBONS, Mrs. Walter see Gibbons, Nellie Isabella

GIBBORNE, Thomas (fl 1624) lessee DA

GIBBS (fl 1602) actor DA

GIBBS, Mrs. see Colman, Mary Logan

GIBBS, Mrs. see Gibbs, P.

GIBBS, Abigail (d 1907 [80]) EA/08*

GIBBS, Mrs. Alexander see Gibbs, P.

GIBBS, Andrew (d 1873) comedian EA/74*

GIBBS, Ann American actress TW/26-27

GIBBS, Charles (d 1910) coon artist EA/11*

GIBBS, Cora (d 1966 [65]) treasurer BP/50*

GIBBS, Cosmo see Hamilton, Cosmo

GIBBS, John (d 1870) property master EA/71*

GIBBS, John see Gilbert, John

GIBBS, Maria see Colman, Mary

GIBBS, Nancy (d 1956 [63]) Welsh singer, actress WWT/4-7

GIBBS, P. [Mrs. Alexander Gibbs; née Graddon] (1804-54?) English actress CDP, DD, DNB, HAS, OX

GIBBS, Robert Paton (d 1940 [81]) American actor BE*, BP/25*

GIBBS, Robert Weston (d 1891 [51]) circus agent EA/92*

GIBBS, Robert Wilkes (d 1871 [51]) pantomimist EA/72*

GIBBS, Robert Wilkes see Harrison, Robert

GIBBS, Sheila (b 1947) American actress TW/29

GIBBS, Thomas (d 1869) singer EA/70*

GIBBS, Wolcott (1902-58) American critic COC, NTH, OC/1-3, TW/15, WWA/3

GIBES, Antony (fl 1628) actor DA

GIBNEY, Frank (b 1924) American journalist BE

GIBSON, Mr. (d 1771) actor TD/1-2

GIBSON, Alfred (d 1920 [60]) actor, singer CDP

GIBSON, Brenda (b 1870) actress WWT/1-5

GIBSON, Chloë (b 1899) English producer WWT/11-15

GIBSON, Clara (d 1882) actress EA/83*

GIBSON, Don (b 1917) American actor TW/1-3

GIBSON, Edward see Lyle, Lyston

GIBSON, Ernest (d 1917) EA/18*

GIBSON, Florrie (d 1917) EA/18*

GIBSON, Francis (fl 1800) dramatist CP/3

GIBSON, Frank (1853-87) American agent NYM

GIBSON, H. (fl c. 1620) actor DA

GIBSON, Hoot (1892-1962) American actor BE*, BP/47*

GIBSON, James Rhind (1842-87) Scottish actor DD, OAA/1-2

GIBSON, Judy (b 1947) American actress TW/27-30

GIBSON, Mrs. L. (d 1866) actress HAS

GIBSON, Madeline (b 1909) English actress WWT/8-10

GIBSON, Preston (1879-1937) American dramatist WWA/1

GIBSON, Richard (fl 1494-1508) actor DA

GIBSON, Virginia American actress TW/13-14

GIBSON, William (b 1914) American dramatist AAS, BE, CD, ES, MD, MWD, PDT, WWT/14-16

GIBSON, Wynne (b 1905) American actress, singer BE, WWT/7-10

GIDDENS, George (1845-1920) English actor CDP, DD, DP, EA/95, GRB/1-4, OAA/2, WWS, WWT/1-3, WWW/2

GIDE, André (1871-1951) French dramatist OC/3

GIDEON (fl 1602) actor DA

GIDEON, Johnny (d 1901 [78]) dramatist, historian BE*, EA/02*, WWT/14*

GIDEON, Melville J. (1884-1933) American composer WWT/4-7

GIEHSE, Therese (d 1975 [76]) performer BP/59*

GIELGUD, Sir John (b 1904) English actor, producer AAS, BE, CB, COC, ES, NTH, OC/1-3, PDT, TW/3-23, 27, WWT/5-16

GIELGUD, Val (b 1900) English dramatist, producer ES, WWT/9-14

GIERASCH, Stefan (b 1926) American actor TW/15, 23, 26-27, 29-30

GIESEN, Genevieve see Dickinson, Genevieve

GIESLER, Jerry (d 1962 [75]) American lawyer BE*

GIFFARD, Mrs. (fl 1786) English actress CDP, HAS

GIFFARD, Henry (1694-1772) English actor, manager CP/3, OC/1-3, TD/1-2

GIFFARD, Mary Agnes (fl 1871-83) actress DD

GIFFEN, Robert Lawrence (d 1946 [73]) American producer, director, authors' representative BE*, BP/30*

GIFFORD, Elizabeth (d 1893) EA/94*

GIFFORD, Frances [Mrs. S. L. Gifford] (d 1892 [64]) EA/94*

GIFFORD, Gordon (d 1962 [48]) performer BE*

GIFFORD, Hazen (b 1928) Canadian actor TW/23

GIFFORD, John actor TW/1

GIFFORD, Samuel L. (d 1896) manager EA/97*

GIFFORD, Mrs. S. L. see Gifford, Frances

GIFFORD, William (1756/57-1826) English dramatist CP/3, DD

GIFFORD, William (d 1886) EA/87*

GIFTOS, Elaine (b 1945) American actress TW/24

GIGLI, Benjamino (1890-1957) Italian singer ES, TW/14, WWW/5

GIGLIO, A. Gino American manager BE

GILBART, Eleanor [Ena Graham] (d 1909) English actress GRB/1

GILBERT, Mr. dancer CDP

GILBERT, Miss see Norton, Mrs.

GILBERT, Anne Jane see Gilbert, Mrs. George Henry

GILBERT, Barbara American actress TW/29

GILBERT, Benjamin A. (1904-72) American physician BE, TW/29

GILBERT, Billy (1894-1971) American actor, director BE, TW/3, 28

GILBERT, Bobby (d 1973 [75]) performer BP/58*

GILBERT, Edmond (d 1869) proprietor EA/70*

GILBERT, Eliza M. (d 1873) dancer, ballet mistress EA/74*

GILBERT, Fred (d 1903) songwriter EA/04*

GILBERT, George Hartley (d 1878 [28]) American actor EA/79*

GILBERT, George Henry (1821-66) English dancer, stage manager CDP, HAS

GILBERT, Mrs. George Henry [Ann Hartley] (1821-1904) American actress CDP, COC, DAB, DD, HAS, NTH, OC/1-3,

PP/1, SR, WWA/1

GILBERT, Henry (d 1868 [47])
scene artist EA/69*

GILBERT, Henry Franklin Belknap
(1868-1928) American composer
DAB, WWA/1

GILBERT, H. Pomeroy (d 1891
[54]) actor EA/92*

GILBERT, Jean [M. Winterfield]
(1879-1943) German composer
WWT/5-9

GILBERT, Jody (b 1916) American actress TW/3

GILBERT, John [John Gibbs]
(1810-89) American actor
CDP, COC, DAB, DD, HAS,
NTH, OC/1-3, WWA/H

GILBERT, John (1897/98-1936)
American actor SR, WWA/1

GILBERT, Mrs. John (1806-66)
American actress CDP, HAS

GILBERT, Mrs. Joseph see
Duff, Mary

GILBERT, Kate actress CDP

GILBERT, Lizzie [Mrs. E. G.
Savage] (d 1904 [75]) ballet
mistress EA/04*

GILBERT, Lou [né Gitlitz] (b
1909) American actor AAS,
BE, TW/5-8, 10-14, 23,
25-27, 29-30, WWT/15-16

GILBERT, Louis Wolfe (1886-
1970) Russian/American
vaudevillian, songwriter,
journalist WWA/5

GILBERT, Maria (d 1904 [73])
EA/05*

GILBERT, Marian (d 1872)
dancer EA/73*

GILBERT, Mercedes (d 1952
[58]) American actress TW/2,
8

GILBERT, Michael George (d
1908 [77]) EA/09*

GILBERT, Olive Welsh actress,
singer AAS, WWT/9-16

GILBERT, Paul (d 1976 [58])
performer BP/60*

GILBERT, Ray (d 1976 [63])
composer/lyricist BP/60*

GILBERT, Ronnie American actor
TW/25

GILBERT, Vivian (b 1881) English actor GRB/1

GILBERT, Walter (d 1947 [60])
American actor TW/3

GILBERT, William (d 1871 [23])
musician EA/72*

GILBERT, William (1804-90)
dramatist, librettist DD

GILBERT, William G. (d 1868
[25]) comedian EA/69*

GILBERT, Sir William Schwenck
(1836-1911) English dramatist
CDP, COC, DD, DNB, EA/69,
ES, GRB/1-4, HP, MH, MWD,
NTH, OC/1-3, PDT, RE, SR,
WWS, WWW/1

GILBERT, Willie (b 1916) American dramatist BE

GILBERT, Mrs. W. J. see
Mostyn, Annie

GILBEY, George singer, actor
CDP

GILBEY, Tom [Tom J. Kildare]
(d 1916) music-hall performer
EA/17*

GILBIRT, Bert singer, actor CDP

GILBURNE, Samuel (fl 1605) actor
DA, GT, NTH

GILCHRIST, Connie [Countess of
Orkney] (1865-1946) English ac-
tress CDP, COC, DD, GRB/1,
OC/1-3

GILCHRIST, James (d 1894 [62])
musician EA/95*

GILCHRIST, James Walt see
Kelvin, James

GILCHRIST, Rubina (d 1956) actress BE*, WWT/14*

GILDAY, Charles (1859-89) actor,
minstrel CDP

GILDEA, Mary (d 1957 [70]) actress TW/13

GILDER, Jeanette (d 1916 [66])
critic, dramatist BE*, WWT/
14*

GILDER, Rosamond (b 1900)
American critic BE, CB,
COC, ES, NTH, OC/1-3, WWT/
9-11, 14-16

GILDON, Charles (1665-1724)
English dramatist CP/1-3,
DD, GT, TD/1-2

GILES, Arthur (d 1904 [48])
manager EA/05*

GILES, Harriet Gilleno see Onra

GILES, John (d 1868) conductor
EA/69*

GILES, John S. (1799-1881) theatre
owner CDP

GILES, Nathaniel (fl 1595-1634)
master of the Children of the
Chapel Royal DA

GILES, Paul Kirk (1895-1976)
American actor, executive BE

GILES, Thomas (fl 1585-1613) master of the Children of Paul's DA

GILES'S BOY (fl 1602) actor DA

GILFERT, Charles (1787-1829) German/American manager, composer, conductor DD, HAS, SR

GILFERT, Mrs. Charles [née Agnes Holman] (1793-1833) English actress CDP, HAS

GILFORD, Jack [né Jacob Gellman] American actor AAS, BE, TW/13-18, 23-24, 26-30, WWT/15-16

GILKES, William (d 1868) scene artist EA/69*

GILKEY, Stanley (b 1900) American producer BE

GILL, Basil (1877-1955) English actor GRB/1-4, TW/11, WWT/1-11

GILL, Mrs. Basil see Cavania, Margaret

GILL, Brendan (b 1914) American critic, dramatist BE, WWT/15-16

GILL, Mr. C. (d 1869 [72]) lessee EA/70*

GILL, Mrs. C. (d 1869) EA/70*

GILL, Harry (d 1893 [42]) comic singer EA/94*

GILL, Henry (d 1954 [55]) singer WWT/14*

GILL, Mrs. J. B. see Gill, Mary

GILL, John (d 1868 [50]) singer? EA/69*

GILL, John (d 1971 [41]) comic singer EA/72*

GILL, Joseph (d 1870) music-hall manager EA/71*

GILL, Mary [Mrs. J. B. Gill] (d 1911) EA/12*

GILL, Paul (d 1934) actor WWT/6-7

GILL, Peter (b 1939) Welsh director, dramatist, actor CD, WWT/15-16

GILL, Thomas (d 1894) EA/96*

GILL, Tom (b 1916) English actor WWT/10-16

GILL, William Fearing (1844-1917) American dramatist DD, WWA/1

GILLAIN, Maurice (d 1971 [80]) actor WWT/16*

GILLAME, Ernest see Clinton, Dudley

GILLARS, Mildred E. (b 1900) American actress SR

GILLEASE, Elizabeth Ellen see Allen, Elizabeth

GILLENO, Albert Edward (d 1899) clown EA/00*

GILLENO, Henry William (d 1874) circus proprietor EA/75*

GILLENO, Janet (d 1894) EA/95*

GILLENO, Tom (d 1905) EA/06*

GILLESPIE, Jean (b 1923) American actress TW/4-5

GILLESPIE, Joseph (fl 1897) singer, actor CDP

GILLESPIE, Marie (d 1969) performer BP/54*

GILLESPIE, Richard Henry (1878-1952) English manager WWT/4-11

GILLESPIE, T. (d 1883) actor EA/84*

GILLESPIE, W. F. (b 1830) American actor HAS

GILLESPY, James [Jim Con] (d 1898) proprietor EA/99*

GILLETT, Eric (b 1893) English critic WWT/14

GILLETT, Margaret (d 1876 [61]) dramatist EA/77*

GILLETTE, Anita [née Luebben] (b 1936) American actress, singer BE, TW/19-21, 23-27, WWT/14-16

GILLETTE, A. S. (b 1904) American educator, scene designer BE

GILLETTE, Florence [Mrs. George Fleet] (d 1900) actress CDP

GILLETTE, Priscilla (b 1925) American actress TW/6-16

GILLETTE, Ruth (b 1907) American singer, actress BE, TW/27

GILLETTE, Viola (fl 1898-1912) American singer, actress WWM, WWS

GILLETTE, William (1855-1937) American actor, dramatist CDP, COC, DAB, DD, ES, HJD, GRB/2-4, MH, MWD, NTH, OC/1-3, PP/1, SR, WWA/1, WWM, WWS, WWT/1-8, WWW/3

GILLETTE, Mrs. William (d 1888) EA/89*

GILLIAN, Kay (b 1932) American actress TW/29

GILLIAN, Maurice (d 1971 [80])
performer BP/56*
GILLIE, Jean (1915-49) English
actress, singer WWT/9-10
GILLIES, Robert (d 1876 [24])
musician EA/77*
GILLIES, Robert Pearse (1788-
1858) translator DD
GILLIGAN, Joseph [Henry Clinton]
(d 1871) comedian EA/73*
GILLILAND, Helen (1897-1942)
Irish actress, singer WWT/
5-9
GILLILAND, Thomas (d c. 1816)
historian CDP, DD, DNB
GILLIN, Delia (d 1908) ventrilo-
quist EA/09*
GILLINGHAM, Miss E. singer
CDP
GILLINGHAM, George (fl 1797)
musician CDP
GILLIS, Thomas C. (d 1972
[58]) fund raiser BP/56*
GILLMAN, Mabelle [Mrs. W. E.
Corey] (b 1880) American
actress, singer CDP, GRB/
2-4, WWM, WWS, WWT/1-6
GILLMORE, Frank (1867-1943)
American actor CB, CDP,
DD, EA/96, GRB/2-4, NTH,
SR, WWA/2, WWM, WWS,
WWT/1-9
GILLMORE, Mrs. Frank see
McGilvray, Laura
GILLMORE, Margalo (b 1897)
English actress AAS, BE,
TW/2-16, WWT/5-14
GILLO, Miss see Carey, Mrs.
George Saville
GILLUM, William (d 1797)
dramatist CP/3
GILMAN, Ada (d 1921 [67]) ac-
tress CDP, PP/1
GILMAN, Henry (d 1902 [59])
manager EA/04*
GILMAN, Larry (b 1950) Ameri-
can actor TW/30
GILMAN, Lawrence (1878-1939)
American critic WWA/1
GILMAN, Mabelle see Gillman,
Mabelle
GILMER, Mlle. (d 1903 [79])
dancer EA/04*
GILMER, Albert (d 1917 [56])
manager GRB/2-4
GILMER, Albert Hatton (1878-
1950) American dramatist,
educator WWA/3

GILMER, William J. (d 1899 [72])
EA/01*
GILMORE, Barney (b 1867) Amer-
ican singer, comedian WWS
GILMORE, Douglas (d 1950 [47])
actor TW/7
GILMORE, Edward G. (d 1908
[69]) American manager CDP,
GRB/4
GILMORE, Mrs. Harry (d 1912
[41]) EA/13*
GILMORE, Janette (b 1905) ac-
tress, singer WWT/6-8
GILMORE, Patrick Sarsfield
(1829-92) Irish bandmaster
CDP, DAB, SR
GILMORE, Paul (fl 1896) actor
SR
GILMORE, Peter (b 1931) actor,
singer WWT/15-16
GILMORE, Ruth (d 1976) perform-
er BP/60*
GILMORE, Thomas (d 1892 [35])
scene artist EA/93*
GILMORE, Virginia (b 1919)
American actress BE, TW/1-4,
WWT/10-14
GILMORE, W. H. producer, actor
WWT/6-7
GILMOUR, Brian (1894-1954) actor
WWT/6-8
GILMOUR, Gordon (d 1962 [48])
actor, dramatist BE*
GILMOUR, J. H. (d 1922 [65])
Canadian actor, producer
WWS
GILPIN, Charles Sidney (1878-
1930) American actor COC,
DAB, ES, OC/1-3, SR, WWA/
1, WWT/5-6
GILPIN, John (b 1930) English
dancer ES
GILROY, Frank D. (b 1925)
American dramatist CB, CD,
CH, ES, HJD, MH, MWD,
WWT/15-16
GILSON, Lottie (1867-1912) ac-
tress CDP, SR
GILTINAN, Donal (d 1976 [67])
dramatist BP/60*
GILTON, Miss (d 1880) music-
hall performer EA/81*
GIM, Asa (b 1945) Korean actress
TW/28-29
GIMBEL, Norman (b 1927) Amer-
ican lyricist, composer BE
GINASTERA, Alberto (b 1916)
Argentinian composer CB

GINGOLD, Hermione Ferdinanda
(b 1897) English actress AAS,
BE, CB, COC, ES, TW/10-
21, 29-30, WWT/9-16
GINISTY, Paul (d 1932 [66])
dramatist, critic BE*, WWT/
14*
GINNER, Ruby (b 1886) French
dancer WWT/5-9
GINNES, Abram S. (b 1914)
dramatist BE
GINNETT, Albert George (d 1894)
EA/95*
GINNETT, Amelia [Mrs. Claude
Ginnett] (d 1896 [31]) EA/97*
GINNETT, Claude (d 1911 [54])
circus proprietor EA/13*
GINNETT, Mrs. Claude see
Ginnett, Amelia
GINNETT, Ellen [Mrs. William
Ginnett] (d 1910 [67]) EA/11*
GINNETT, Florence [Mrs. Fred
Ginnett] (d 1898) circus pro-
prietor EA/99*
GINNETT, Mrs. Fred see
Ginnett, Florence
GINNETT, George (d 1907) circus
proprietor EA/08*
GINNETT, John Frederick (d
1892) circus proprietor EA/
93*
GINNETT, Mrs. J. P. (d 1877
[75]) EA/78*
GINNETT, William (d 1888 [49])
circus proprietor EA/89*
GINNETT, Mrs. William see
Ginnett, Ellen
GINSBERG, Ernest (d 1964 [61])
performer BP/49*
GINSBERG, Sol see Violinsky
GINSBURG, Allen (b 1926) Amer-
ican actor TW/29
GINSBURY, Norman (b 1903)
English dramatist BE, WWT/
9-16
GINTY, Elizabeth Beall (d 1949
[86]) American dramatist
BE*, BP/34*
GINTY, Robert (b 1948) American
actor TW/29
GINZLER, Robert (d 1962 [53])
orchestrator BP/47*
GIOI, Vivi (d 1975 [58]) per-
former BP/60*
GIONI, J. M. (fl 1854) actor
HAS
GIORDANI, Thomaso (fl 1783-1804)
composer, manager TD/1-2

GIORDANO, Frank American actor
TW/26, 30
GIORDMAINE, John (d 1974 [75])
performer BP/58*
GIORGI, Signora see D'Orta,
Rachele
GIORGI, Leonard (d 1871 [30])
musician EA/72*
GIORZA, Paolo (1832-1914) Italian
composer ES
GIOVANELLI, Edward (d 1881
[57]) manager WWT/14*
GIPSON, Fred (d 1973 [65])
dramatist BP/58*
GIRARD, Donald (b 1953) Ameri-
can actor TW/25-26
GIRARD, Eddie (b 1858) minstrel,
vaudevillian CDP
GIRARD, Mrs. Emile see
Girard, Kate
GIRARD, Florence [Mrs. Henry
E. Abbey] (fl 1877) actress
CDP
GIRARD, Kate [Mrs. George Faw-
cett Rowe] (d 1885) actress
CDP
GIRARD, Kate [Mrs. Emile Gir-
ard] (d 1897 [36]) pantomimist
EA/99*
GIRARD, Oscar (d 1899) Ameri-
can comedian EA/00*
GIRARDEAU, Frank (b 1942)
American actor TW/29
GIRARDELLI, Josephine (fl 1820)
fire-eater CDP
GIRARDOT, Mlle. (fl 1829)
French actress HAS
GIRARDOT, Etienne (1856-1939)
English/American actor SR,
WWM, WWS
GIRARDOT, Isabelle English ac-
tress WWS
GIRAUDOUX, Jean (1882-1944)
French dramatist COC, MD,
OC/1-3
GIRDLESTONE, Amy [née Emma
Ames] (fl 1868) actress HAS
GIRDLESTONE, Madge English
actress GRB/1-2
GIROFLI, Mme. John (d 1893)
ballet mistress EA/94*
GISH, Dorothy (1898-1968) Amer-
ican actress BE, CB, ES,
NTH, SR, TW/2-21, 25, WWT/
6-14
GISH, Lillian (b 1896/99) Ameri-
can actress BE, CB, ES,
NTH, SR, TW/2-22, 24, 29-30,

WWT/7-16

GISH, Mary R. (c. 1860-1948)
actress SR

GITANA, Gertie [Gertrude Mary
Ross] (1889-1957) American
music-hall performer COC,
OC/3

GITLITZ, Lou see Gilbert, Lou

GITTINS, Mary (d 1906) EA/07*

GIUBELEI, Mr. (d 1851) singer
HAS

GIUBILEI, Augustine (d 1848)
dancer CDP, HAS

GIUBILEI, Theodore Victor (1801-
45) English actor, singer CDP,
HAS

GIUGLINI, Antonio (1827-65)
Italian singer ES

GIULINI, Carlo Maria (b 1914)
Italian conductor ES

GIVENS, Jimmie (d 1964 [47])
performer BE*

GIVLER, Mary Louise [Mrs.
Oscar Shaw] (d 1964 [77])
American performer BE*

GIVNEY, Kathryn American actress TW/1-4

GJERSTAD, John see Gerstad,
John

GLADDING, R. H. (fl 1858)
actor HAS

GLADHILL, John (d 1874) actor,
scene painter EA/75*

GLADMAN, Florence [Mrs.
André Charlot] (d 1956 [66])
performer, producer BE*,
WWT/14*

GLADSTANE, Mary (b 1830)
English actress CDP, HAS

GLADSTONE, W. H. (d 1900
[80]) actor EA/01*, WWT/14*

GLAGOLIN, Boris (d 1948 [70])
actor BE*, WWT/14*

GLANVILLE, Maxwell (b 1918)
West Indian actor TW/25-26,
29-30

GLAPTHORNE, Henry (fl 1634-
40) dramatist CP/1-3, DD,
DNB, FGF

GLASER, Darrel (b 1957) American actor TW/25-26

GLASER, Joseph G. (d 1969
[72]) agent BP/54*

GLASER, Lulu [Mrs. R. C.
Herz] (1874/76-1958) Amer-
ican actress, singer CDP,
DD, GRB/2-4, SR, TW/15,
WWA/3, WWS, WWT/1-7

GLASER, Paul (d 1974 [50]) executive BP/57*

GLASER, Vaughan actor TW/2

GLASKIN, T. J. (d 1890) EA/91*

GLASPELL, Susan (1882-1948)
American dramatist COC,
DAB, ES, HJD, MD, MH,
MWD, NTH, OC/1-3, TW/5,
WWT/5-10, WWW/4

GLASS, Dudley (b 1899) Australian
composer WWT/9-14

GLASS, Montague (1877-1934)
English dramatist NTH, WWT/
4-7

GLASSER, Lulu see Glaser,
Lulu

GLASSFORD, Andrew L. (d 1918)
actor, manager SR

GLASSFORD, David (1866-1935)
Australian actor SR, WWM,
WWT/7

GLASSINGTON, Mr. prompter
TD/2

GLASSMAN, William (b 1945)
American actor TW/25

GLAUM, Louise (d 1970 [70])
performer BP/55*

GLAZER, Barney (d 1975 [66])
columnist BP/59*

GLAZER, Benjamin (1887-1956)
Irish/American dramatist ES

GLAZER, Maurice (d 1971 [51])
producer/director/choreographer
BP/56*

GLAZIER, Marie (b 1881) American actress, vaudevillian
WWM

GLEASON, Frederic Grant (1848-
1903) American composer
DAB, WWA/1

GLEASON, Jackie (b 1916) American comedian, composer BE,
ES, TW/1, 5-6

GLEASON, James (1886-1959)
American actor, dramatist,
manager TW/15, WWA/3,
WWT/6-10

GLEASON, John (b 1941) American
lighting designer WWT/16

GLEASON, Lucille Webster (1888-
1947) American actress SR,
TW/3

GLEASON, Ralph J. (d 1975 [58])
critic BP/60*

GLEASON, Russell (d 1945 [36])
actor TW/2

GLEASON, Thomas (b 1915)
American actor TW/5-10

GLEN, Archie (d 1966 [77])
performer BP/50*
GLENDINNING, Ernest (1884-
1936) English actor SR,
WWM, WWT/4-8
GLENDINNING, Ethel (b 1910)
Scottish actress WWT/7, 9
GLENDINNING, John (1857-1916)
English actor GRB/3-4,
WWS, WWT/1-3
GLENDINNING, Mrs. John see
Millward, Jessie
GLENGALL, Lord dramatist DD
GLENISTER, Frank (1860-1945)
manager WWT/4-9
GLENN, Alice (b 1941) American
actress TW/23
GLENN, Bette (b 1946) American
actress TW/27
GLENN, Cynda (d 1968 [59]) per-
former BP/53*
GLENN, Frederick (b 1939)
American actor TW/26
GLENN, Raymond [Bob Custer]
(d 1974 [76]) performer BP/
59*
GLENN, Roy, Sr. (d 1971 [56])
performer BP/55*
GLENN, Samuel W. (1828-1903)
American actor CDP, HAS
GLENN, Scott (b 1942) American
actor TW/22-24
GLENNEY, Bessie [Elizabeth
Alice Graham] (d 1903) ac-
tress EA/04*
GLENNEY, Charles see Glenny,
Charles H.
GLENNEY, Thomas H. see
Glenny, Thomas H.
GLENNIE, Brian (b 1912) Eng-
lish actor WWT/6-8
GLENNIE, Dora English actress
GRB/1-2
GLENNIE, Miss G. (d 1876
[23]) actress EA/77*
GLENNIE, Herbert [George
Holiday] (d 1890) EA/91*
GLENN-SMITH, Michael (b 1945)
American actor TW/25-26,
30
GLENNY [or Glenney], Charles
H. (1857-1922) Scottish actor
DD, DP, EA/95, GRB/1-4,
OAA/2, WWT/1-4
GLENNY, Mrs. Charles see
Abingdon, Marie
GLENNY, Mrs. Charles Hall
see Glenny, Isabella Jane

GLENNY, Isabella Jane [Mrs.
Charles Hall Glenny] (d 1891
[32]) EA/93*
GLENNY, Thomas H. (d 1891
[60]) actor CDP, DD
GLENROY, William Cruikshanks
(d 1911) manager EA/12*
GLENVILLE, Harry (d 1910 [62])
actor EA/11*
GLENVILLE, Peter (b 1913) Eng-
lish actor, director, producer,
dramatist BE, COC, ES,
PDT, TW/7-8, WWT/8-16
GLENVILLE, Philip Irish actor
TD/1-2
GLENVILLE, Shaun (1884-1968)
Irish actor COC, WWT/4-13
GLICK, Carl (1889-1971) Ameri-
can dramatist, director NTH,
WWA/5
GLICK, Joseph (1880-1943) Amer-
ican actor, manager SR
GLICKMAN, Will (b 1910) Amer-
ican librettist BE
GLINDON, Mr. singer, songwrit-
er CDP
GLOSE, Augusta [Mrs. Charles
S. Leeds] (fl 1900s) American
vaudevillian WWM
GLOSSOP, Mme. Feron (d 1853)
singer EA/72*
GLOSSOP, Joseph (d 1835) actor,
producer BE*, WWT/14*
GLOSSOP, Mrs. Joseph see
Feron, Elizabeth
GLOSSOP, Maria Elizabeth see
Harris, Maria
GLOSSOP, Mary Ann see
Harris, Mary Ann
GLOSSOP-HARRIS, Florence
(1883-1931) English actress,
producer BE*, WWT/14*
GLOUCHEVITCH, Barbara (d 1974
[46]) performer BP/59*
GLOVER, Mrs. (d 1871) EA/72*
GLOVER, Mrs. see Glover,
Julia
GLOVER, Annie (d 1910) EA/11*
GLOVER, Augustus [Sidney De
Fivas] (1846-1903) Scottish
actor DD, OAA/1-2
GLOVER, Bessie (d 1911 [50])
actress EA/12*
GLOVER, Bruce (b 1932) American
actor TW/17-20
GLOVER, Carrie (d 1976 [49])
performer BP/60*
GLOVER, Charles William (1806-

63) English composer, musician DD, DNB

GLOVER, David (b 1927) English actor TW/26

GLOVER, Edmund (1813-60) English manager, actor DD, DNB, OC/1-3

GLOVER, Edmund Samuel (d 1884 [24]) property master EA/85*

GLOVER, Eleanor [Mrs. George Harvey] (d 1908 [25]) actress EA/09*

GLOVER, Ferdinand (d 1859 [23]) singer EA/72*

GLOVER, Frederick (fl 1869-74) actor DD

GLOVER, Halcott (1877-1949) English dramatist WWT/8-9, WWW/4

GLOVER, Howard W. (d 1875) composer EA/76*

GLOVER, James Mackey (1861-1931) Irish conductor, composer, managing director DD, GRB/1-4, WWT/1-6, WWW/3

GLOVER, John (b 1944) American actor TW/27-30

GLOVER, Mrs. John (d 1881) EA/82*

GLOVER, Julia [née Betterton] (1779/81/83-1850) English actress BS, CDP, DD, DNB, ES, GT, OC/1-3, OX

GLOVER, Julian (b 1935) English actor WWT/15-16

GLOVER, Lyman Beecher (1846-1915) American manager WWA/1, WWM

GLOVER, Phillis Frances Agnes (1807-31) actress CDP, OX

GLOVER, Phyllis (fl 1870) actress DD

GLOVER, Richard (1712-85) dramatist CP/1-3, DD, TD/1-2

GLOVER, Stephen (d 1869 [58]) composer EA/71*

GLOVER, Thomas J. (d 1971) performer BP/55*

GLOVER, William (d 1916 [83]) manager, scene artist, lessee DD

GLOVER, William (b 1911) American critic BE

GLOVER, William Howard (1819-75) English composer, con-

ductor, musician DD, DNB, WWA/H

GLUCK, Alma (1884-1938) Rumanian singer DAB, WWA/1

GLUCK, Arnold Jack see Arnold, Jack

GLUCKMAN, Leon (b 1922) South African actor, director, producing manager WWT/16

GLYN, Gertrude (d 1908 [52]) composer EA/09*

GLYN, Isabella [Mrs. E. S. Dallas] (1823-89) Scottish actress CDP, DD, DNB, ES, OAA/1-2

GLYN, Neva Carr (d 1975) performer BP/60*

GLYNN, Golly see Green (d 1916)

GLYNNE, Angela (b 1933) English actress WWT/10-12

GLYNNE, Ella Florentia (d 1904 [20]) EA/06*

GLYNNE, Howell (d 1969 [64]) performer BP/54*

GLYNNE, Mary (1898-1954) Welsh actress WWT/2-11

GLYNNE, Olivia (b 1888) English actress GRB/2

GNATT, Poul (b 1923) Danish dancer, dancing teacher ES

GNONE, Sig. (fl 1859) actor HAS

GOAD, Christopher (fl 1629-35) actor DA

GOBBI, Tito (b 1913/15) Italian singer CB, ES

GOBERMAN, Max (d 1962 [51]) American conductor BE*

GOBLE, Diana (b 1946) American actress TW/26

GODARD, Benjamin (d 1895) composer EA/96*

GODD, Barbara (d 1944) actress BE*

GODDARD, Mrs. [Katie Hamilton] (d 1883 [42]) Scottish singer EA/84*

GODDARD, Miss (fl 1850) actress CDP

GODDARD, Alfred (d 1908 [57]) proprietor EA/09*

GODDARD, Arabella (b 1836) pianist CDP

GODDARD, Charles W. (1879-1951) American dramatist WWA/3, WWT/5-11

GODDARD, Percy (d 1917 [33])

musician EA/18*
GODDARD, Willoughby (b 1926)
English actor WWT/14-16
GODDEN, Jimmy (1879-1956)
English actor WWT/5-11
GODDERIS, Albert (d 1971 [89])
performer BP/55*
GODEFROID, Felix (d 1897 [79])
musician, composer EA/98*
GODEY, Mrs. [née Juliet Cath-
erine Durang] (1804-49) Amer-
ican dancer, actress HAS
GODEY, Howard (d 1894 [29])
EA/95*
GODFREY, Charles [Paul Lacey]
(1851-1900) English music-
hall singer CDP, OC/1-3
GODFREY, Mrs. Charles see
Godfrey, Maude
GODFREY, Mrs. Daniel God-
frey (d 1890) EA/92*
GODFREY, Derek (b 1924) Eng-
lish actor AAS, WWT/14-16
GODFREY, Frederick (d 1882)
bandmaster EA/83*
GODFREY, Fred W. (d 1912
[43]) EA/13*
GODFREY, George (d 1974
[80+]) talent scout BP/58*
GODFREY, George William (1844-
97) dramatist DD
GODFREY, Henry (d 1879 [43])
equestrian EA/80*
GODFREY, H. S. [Harry Squire
Camp] (b 1877) English vari-
ety artist GRB/1
GODFREY, Maude [Mrs. Charles
Godfrey] (d 1897 [30]) EA/
98*
GODFREY, Peter (1899-1970)
English actor, manager, pro-
ducer COC, WWT/6-11
GODFREY, Renee Haal (d 1964
[44]) performer BE*
GODFREY, Thomas (1736-63)
American dramatist COC,
CP/3, DAB, DD, DNB, EAP,
ES, NTH, OC/1-3, RJ,
WWA/H
GODFREY-TURNER, L. [Leopold
McClintock Turner] English
critic WWT/1-4
GODKIN, Paul (b 1918) American
actor TW/4
GODMOND, Christopher (fl 1836-
40?) dramatist DD
GODOWSKY, Dagmar (d 1975
[78]) actress WWT/16*

GODREAU, Miguel (b 1946) Puerto
Rican actor TW/25
GODRICH, Thomas (d 1887 [50])
music-hall proprietor EA/88*
GODWIN, Arthur J. (d 1892 [39])
musician, musical director
EA/93*
GODWIN, Edward William (1833-
86) English architect, designer
COC, DD, OC/1-3
GODWIN, Harold (d 1917 [42])
EA/18*
GODWIN, Harry (d 1902) manager
EA/03*
GODWIN, Richard (fl 1631) actor
DA
GODWIN, Will (fl 1890s?) singer,
composer CDP
GODWIN, William (1756-1836)
dramatist CP/3, DD
GOEKEL, Fred (b 1936) American
actor TW/23
GOETHE, Johann Wolfgang von
(1749-1832) German dramatist
COC
GOETTLING, Mary Rebecca see
Dolan, Mary
GOETZ, Augustus (d 1957 [56])
American dramatist BE*,
BP/42*, WWT/14*
GOETZ, E. Ray (d 1954 [68])
English producer, songwriter
TW/11
GOETZ, Ruth Goodman (b 1912)
American dramatist WWT/13-
16
GOETZ, Theo (d 1972 [78]) Austri-
an actor TW/29
GOETZL, Dr. Anselm (d 1923
[44]) composer BP/7*
GOFF, Mr. actor CDP
GOFF, Mr. see Goiffee, Mons.
GOFF, Lewin (b 1919) American
educator BE
GOFFE, Alexander see Goughe,
Alexander
GOFFE, Robert see Goughe,
Robert
GOFFE, Thomas (1591-1629) Eng-
lish dramatist CP/1-3, DD,
FGF
GOFFIN, Cora (b 1901/02) actress
WWT/3-11
GOFFIN, Peter (1906-74) English
designer BTR/74, WWT/9-14
GOFORTH, Frances American
actress, dramatist BE, TW/1
GOFTON, E. Story (d 1939 [92])

actor BE*, WWT/14*

GOGOL, Nikolai Vasilievich
(1809-52) Russian dramatist
COC, OC/2-3

GOIFFEE, Mons. [né Goff] (fl
1831) English actor, pantomimist HAS

GOIFFEE, Mme. (fl 1832) English? actress HAS

GOIMBAULT, Odette (b 1901)
French actress WWT/3

GOING, Frederica American actress TW/1

GOLD, Belle [Mrs. A. W.
Cross] (b 1882) American
actress WWM, WWS

GOLD, Ben (d 1918) EA/19*

GOLD, David (b 1929) American
dancer TW/24

GOLD, Jimmy (d 1967 [81/87])
comedian BP/52*, WWT/
15*

GOLD, Joey (d 1966) ticket broker
BP/51*

GOLD, Michael (1893-1967) American dramatist HJD, MD,
MWD

GOLD, Sid (d 1974 [67]) performer BP/58*

GOLD, Zisha (b 1910) American
actress TW/25

GOLDBECK, Robert (1839-1908)
Prussian composer DAB

GOLDBERG, Dora see Bayes,
Nora

GOLDBERG, Isaac (1887-1938)
American writer WWA/1

GOLDBERG, J. P. (d 1890 [65])
professor of music EA/92*

GOLDBERG, Marcus see Lyle,
Kenyon

"GOLDBERG, Max" (fl 1895-98)
dramatist DD

GOLDBERG, Miles M. (b 1882)
American critic WWM

GOLDBERG, Nathan (d 1961
[74]) Austrian actor, producer
BE*

GOLDBERG, Rose (d 1966 [78])
actress TW/23

GOLDBERG, R[ubin?] L. (1883-
1974?) American vaudevillian
WWM

GOLDBERG, Mrs. Samuel see
Elinore, Kate

GOLDBLATT, Charles see
Vance, Charles

GOLDBLATT, Harold M. (d 1966

[75]) lawyer BP/51*

GOLDBLATT, Martin (d 1968
[43]) publicist BP/52*

GOLDBOGEN, Michael see
Todd, Michael

GOLDEN, Bartholomew (d 1897
[54]) proprietor EA/99*

GOLDEN, Edward (b 1917) Irish
actor TW/4

GOLDEN, Edward J., Jr. (b 1934)
American director, actor, educator BE

GOLDEN, George Fuller (1868-
1912) American singer, dancer,
monologist CDP

GOLDEN, Grace (fl 1889) American actress WWA/5

GOLDEN, John (1874/75-1955)
American dramatist, composer,
producer CB, COC, NTH,
SR, TW/2-8, 12, WWA/3,
WWT/5-11

GOLDEN, John (d 1972 [68]) com-
poser/lyricist BP/57*

GOLDEN, Joseph (b 1928) American educator, dramatist BE

GOLDEN, Michael (b 1913) Irish
actor WWT/10-16

GOLDEN, Richard (1853/54-1909)
American actor, singer DD,
GRB/3-4, SR, WWA/1, WWS

GOLDEN, Mrs. Richard see
Wiley, Dora

GOLDER, Jennie (d 1928 [34])
actress BE*, WWT/14*

GOLDER, Lew (d 1962 [78]) producer BE*

GOLDFADEN, Abraham (1840-
1908) Russian dramatist COC,
ES, MWD, OC/1-3, RE

GOLDGRAN, Henry (d 1972 [58])
producer/director/choreographer
BP/57*

GOLDHARDT, William (d 1967
[72]) treasurer BP/52*

GOLDIE, F. Wyndham (1897/98-
1957) English actor WWT/8-12

GOLDIE, Horace (d 1939 [65])
magician BE*

GOLDIE, Hugh (b 1919) English
director, actor WWT/15-16

GOLDIE, Sydney E. (d 1974 [73])
journalist BP/59*

GOLDIN, Elias (d 1972 [59]) pro-
ducer/director/choreographer
BP/56*

GOLDIN, Horace (1873-1939)
Russian/American illusionist

DAB, GRB/1-3, SR
GOLDINA, Miriam (b 1898) Russian actress, director, translator BE
GOLDING (fl 1640?) actor DA
GOLDING, Arthur (d 1570) dramatist CP/2-3, DD
GOLDING, George (d 1907 [47]) comedian EA/08*
GOLDING, William (b 1911) English dramatist CB, MWD
GOLDINGHAM, William dramatist CP/3, FGF
GOLDMAN, Edwin Franks (1878-1956) American conductor, composer BE*
GOLDMAN, Irving (b 1909) American executive BE
GOLDMAN, Isaac (d 1973 [80]) performer BP/58*
GOLDMAN, James (b 1927) American dramatist, lyricist BE, CD, MH
GOLDMAN, Milton (b 1914) American talent representative BE
GOLDMAN, Nannie English actress GRB/1
GOLDMAN, Theodore see Mann, Theodore
GOLDMAN, William (b 1931) American dramatist BE, CD
GOLDMANN, Max see Reinhardt, Max
GOLDNER, Charles (1900-65) Austrian actor, producer WWT/10-11
GOLDONI, Carlo (1707-93) Italian dramatist OC/1-3
GOLDOVSKY, Boris (b 1908) Russian director, conductor CB
GOLDOWSKY, Dagmar (d 1975 [78]) performer BP/59*
GOLDRICH, Fred (b 1947) American actor TW/29
GOLDSACK, Daisy (fl 1900?) singer CDP
GOLDSCHMID, Otto (fl 1851) actor? singer? HAS
GOLDSCHMIDT, Otto (d 1907 [77]) composer EA/08*
GOLDSMID, Lionel (fl 1856) English actor HAS
GOLDSMITH, Edith see Oliver, Edith
GOLDSMITH, Eleanor (b 1923) American costume designer

TW/5
GOLDSMITH, Francis (d 1655) dramatist CP/1-3, DD
GOLDSMITH, George American talent representative BE
GOLDSMITH, Ina (d 1915 [56]) actress EA/96
GOLDSMITH, Mary (fl 1803-04) dramatist CP/3
GOLDSMITH, Merwin (b 1937) American actor TW/24, 26, 28-30
GOLDSMITH, Oliver (1730-74) English dramatist CDP, COC, CP/2-3, DD, DNB, ES, GT, HP, MH, NTH, OC/1-3, PDT, RE, SR, TD/1-2
GOLDSMITH, R. G. (d 1887 [67]) manager EA/88*
GOLDSMITH, Ted (b 1909) American press representative BE
GOLDSON, Belinda see Groshon, Belinda
GOLDSTEIN, Becky (d 1971 [94]) actress BP/55*, WWT/16*
GOLDSTEIN, Braham see Murray, Braham
GOLDSTEIN, Elliott see Gould, Elliott
GOLDSTEIN, Jennie (1899-1960) American actress TW/9-11, 16
GOLDSTEIN, Robert (d 1974 [70]) producer/director/choreographer BP/58*
GOLDSTON, James Mayer see Mokana
GOLDSTONE, Nat (d 1966 [62]) producer/director/choreographer BP/51*
GOLDTHWAIT, Jennie (fl 1887) American actress SR
GOLDTWAITE, Dora (d 1922) actress CDP
GOLENPAUL, Dan (d 1974 [73]) producer/director/choreographer BP/58*
GOLLANCZ, Israel scholar DD
GOLLICKER, James G. see Ashmer, James G.
GOLLMER, Benjamin (1865-1947) circus manager SR
GOLONKA, Arlene (b 1936) American actress BE
GOLSWORTHY, Arnold (1865-1939) dramatist, writer WWW/3
GOLTERMANN, Julius (d 1876) composer, musician EA/77*

GOLUB, Harry (d 1970 [74])
performer BP/55*
GOMBELL, Minna (1893-1973)
American actress TW/29,
WWT/7-10
GOMERSAL, Mr. (fl 1850s) actor
DD
GOMERSAL, Alexander Edward
(1788-1862) English actor,
manager CDP, DD
GOMERSAL, Amy [Mrs. William
Gomersal] (d 1903 [43]) EA/
04*
GOMERSAL, Maria [Mrs. Wil-
liam Gomersal] (d 1871 [26])
EA/72*
GOMERSAL, Robert (1600-46?)
English dramatist CP/1-3,
DD, DNB, FGF
GOMERSAL, William (d 1902
[70]) lessee EA/03*
GOMERSAL, Mrs. William
see Gomersal, Amy
GOMERSAL, Mrs. William
see Gomersal, Maria
GOMERSALL, E. W. (d 1863)
English actor, lessee, mana-
ger HAS
GOMERSALL, William (fl 1863-
68) English actor, singer
HAS
GOMERSALL, Mrs. William
(fl 1863-68) English actress,
singer HAS
GOMEZ, Alice (d 1922) Indian
singer WWW/2
GOMEZ, Gene (fl 1910?) singer
CDP
GOMEZ, Jerry (d 1974 [73])
producer/director/choreographer
BP/59*
GOMEZ, Thomas (1905-71) Amer-
ican actor BE, TW/28
GOMPERTZ, Mrs. (d 1878 [63])
EA/79*
GONCHAROV, George (d 1954
[50]) ballet master WWT/14*
GONCHAROVA, Nathalie (1881-
1962) Russian scene designer
COC
GONDOLFO, Lucia Rosita (d
1891 [19]) lion tamer EA/92*
GONNE, Lillian (fl 1910?)
singer CDP
GONZALES, Mary F. (fl 1854)
actress HAS
GONZALEZ, Nilda (b 1929)
Puerto Rican educator BE

GOOCH, Harriet (d 1895 [79])
proprietor EA/96*
GOOCH, Henry (d 1873 [62])
music-hall proprietor EA/74*
GOOCH, Steve (b 1945) English
dramatist, director CD
GOOD, Mrs. Graham see Caird,
Dora
GOOD, Karen (b 1948) American
actress TW/29
GOOD, Kip (d 1964 [45]) actor,
production assistant BE*,
BP/48*
GOOD, William (d 1911) manager,
journalist EA/12*
GOODALE, Baptiste (fl 1589) actor
DA
GOODALE, George Pomeroy (1843-
1919) American critic WWA/1
GOODALE, Thomas (fl 1581-93)
actor DA
GOODALL, Mrs. [née Stanton]
see Goodall, Charlotte
GOODALL, Miss (b 1801?) singer
CDP
GOODALL, Anne (1847-77) actress
DD
GOODALL, Bella (1852-84) actress
DD
GOODALL, Charlotte [née Stanton]
(1765-1830) actress CDP, DD,
DNB, GT, TD/1-2
GOODALL, Edyth (1886-1929)
Scottish actress WWT/2-5
GOODALL, Elizabeth (d 1884
[75]) EA/85*
GOODALL, Isabella (b 1851) Eng-
lish actress OAA/1-2
GOODALL, James see Goodhall,
James
GOODALL, M. A. [Mrs. Maltheus
Goodall] (d 1889) EA/90*
GOODALL, Mrs. Maltheus see
Goodall, M. A.
GOODALL, Rose (fl 1879) actress
CDP
GOODALL, Thomas (b 1767) Eng-
lish dramatist CP/3
GOODALL, Thomas (d 1881) mu-
sician EA/82*
GOODALL, William (fl 1740)
dramatist CP/2-3, GT
GOODALL, William R. (1831-56)
American actor CDP, HAS
GOODALL, Mrs. William R. [née
Fanny L. Riley] (1834-58)
American actress HAS
GOODBODY, Buzz (d 1975 [28])

director BP/59*, WWT/16*

GOODCHILD, Edward (d 1878 [63]) proprietor EA/79*

GOODCHILD, George (1888-1969) English dramatist WWW/6

GOODE, Jack (d 1971 [63]) actor, singer TW/28

GOODENOUGH, Richard Josceline (d 1781) dramatist CP/2-3, GT

GOODENOW, Miriam C. see Robb, Mariam G.

GOODES, Cpt. (d 1916) reciter, teacher EA/17*

GOODFRIEND, Lynda (b 1950) American actress TW/28

GOODHALL, James (fl c. 1754-72) English? dramatist CP/2-3, GT

GOODHALL, Mathew (d 1897) music-hall performer EA/98*

GOODHART, Charles (d 1910 [41]) actor EA/12*

GOODING, R. A. (d 1881) spiritualist EA/82*

GOODLIFFE, John Herbert [Sig. Trippello] (d 1917) EA/18*

GOODLIFFE, Michael (1914-76) English actor AAS, WWT/12-16

GOODMAN, Mr. (fl 18th cent) American actor NTH

GOODMAN, Mr. (fl 1772) English? actor HAS

GOODMAN, Alfred (1890-1972) Russian musical director, composer BE, TW/28

GOODMAN, Arthur (d 1965 [74]) dramatist BP/49*

GOODMAN, Bernard R. (d 1975 [64]) producer/director/choreographer BP/60*

GOODMAN, Cardell [or Cardonnel] (c. 1649-99) English actor COC, DD, OC/1-3

GOODMAN, Dody American actress BE, TW/22, 25-26, 29-30, WWT/15-16

GOODMAN, Edward (d 1962 [74]) American dramatist, producer, director TW/19

GOODMAN, Frank (d 1897) business manager EA/98*

GOODMAN, Frank (b 1916) American press representative BE

GOODMAN, Gladys B. see Unger, Gladys B.

GOODMAN, Harry (d 1970) composer/lyricist BP/55*

GOODMAN, John Spellman (1838-68) American actor HAS

GOODMAN, Jules Eckert (1876-1962) American dramatist MH, NTH, WWA/4, WWM, WWT/4-11

GOODMAN, Kenneth Sawyer (1883-1918) American dramatist DAB

GOODMAN, Lillian Rosedale (d 1972 [84]) performer BP/56*

GOODMAN, Paul (1911-72) American dramatist WWA/5

GOODMAN, Philip (d 1940 [55]) American producer, manager WWT/6-7

GOODMAN, Randolph (b 1908) American educator, dramatist BE

GOODMAN, Richard (d 1881) actor, scene artist EA/82*

GOODMAN, Robyn (b 1947) American actress TW/30

GOODNER, Carol (b 1904) American actress BE, TW/2-11, 18, WWT/6-14

GOODRICH, Arthur F. (1878-1941) American dramatist CB, WWA/1, WWT/5-9

GOODRICH, Edna [Mrs. Nat C. Goodwin] (b 1883) American actress GRB/3-4, SR, WWM, WWS, WWT/1-7

GOODRICH, Frances (b 1891?) American dramatist BE, MH

GOODRICH, Frank Boott (1826-94) American dramatist DAB

GOODRICH, Louis [L. G. Abbot Anderson] (d 1945 [72]) English actor GRB/1-4, WWT/4-9

GOODRICH, Sallie B. (fl 1863-68) actress, lecturer HAS

GOODROW, Garry (b 1938) American actor TW/29-30

GOODSELL, Comfort (d 1868 [40]) comedian HAS

GOODSELL, G. Dean (b 1907) American educator, director, choreographer BE

GOODSON, Lennie (d 1917 [15]) EA/18*

GOODWIN, Bonnie (d 1907) coon impersonator EA/08*

GOODWIN, Clara (d 1903 [85]) dancer EA/04*

GOODWIN, Ewart (b 1907) American executive BE

GOODWIN, George K. (1830-82) manager CDP

GOODWIN, J. Cheever (1850-1912) American dramatist DD, GRB/3-4, SR, WWA/1, WWS, WWT/1

GOODWIN, John (d 1883) EA/84*

GOODWIN, John (b 1921) English press representative WWT/11-16

GOODWIN, Louise (d 1968 [86]) performer BP/52*

GOODWIN, Michael American actor TW/29

GOODWIN, Myra (1867-92) American actress CDP

GOODWIN, Nat Carl (1857-1919) American actor CDP, COC, DAB, GRB/2-4, OC/3, PP/1, SR, WWA/1, WWM, WWS, WWT/1-3, WWW/2

GOODWIN, Mrs. Nat Carl see Elliott, Maxine

GOODWIN, Mrs. Nat Carl see Goodrich, Edna

GOODWIN, Mrs. Nat Carl see Weathersby, Eliza

GOODWIN, T. (fl 1779) dramatist CP/2-3, GT

GOODWIN, W. R. see Linyard, W. K.

GOODYER, Percy R. (b 1884) English actor GRB/1

GOOLD, Charles (d 1907 [53]) actor EA/08*

GOOLD, William (d 1889) EA/90*

GOOLDEN, Richard (b 1891/95) English actor AAS, WWT/8-16

GOOSSENS, Eugene (d 1906 [60]) conductor EA/08*

GOOSSENS, Sir Eugene (1893-1962) English conductor CB, ES, WWA/4, WWW/6

GOOSTRY, Mrs. Charles see Sedgwick, Amy

GOPAL, Ram (b 1917) Indian dancer, choreographer WWT/11-12

GORALL, Leslie (d 1971 [54]) producer/director/choreographer BP/55*

GORBEA, Carlos (b 1938) Puerto Rican actor TW/30

GORCEY, Bernard (d 1955 [67]) actor BE*, BP/40*

GORCEY, Leo (d 1969 [52]) actor TW/26

GORCHAKOV, Nicolai Mikhailovich (1899-1958) Russian producer COC

GORDANI, Nina (d 1966 [64]) performer BP/50*

GORDIN, Jacob (1853-1909) Ukranian dramatist COC, DAB, ES, MWD, OC/1-3, RE

GORDON, Mr. (fl 1752) translator CP/2-3

GORDON, Miss actress CDP

GORDON, Alexander (fl 1731) dramatist CP/3

GORDON, Amy actress? CDP

GORDON, Archibald D. (1835-95) Ceylonese dramatist WWA/H

GORDON, Barry (b 1948) American singer, actor BE

GORDON, Bernard (d 1912 [39]) singer? EA/13*

GORDON, Bert (d 1974 [76]) performer BP/59*

GORDON, Bobby (d 1973 [69]) performer BP/57*

GORDON, Bruce (b 1916) American actor BE, TW/8

GORDON, Carl (b 1932) American actor TW/28-30

GORDON, Cecil [Thomas Johnstone] (d 1902) minstrel EA/03*

GORDON, Charles Kilbourn (b 1888) American producer, manager, dramatist WWT/6-9

GORDON, Cliff (b 1880) Austrian/American actor, manager WWM

GORDON, Cliff (d 1964 [44]) performer BP/49*

GORDON, Colin (1911-72) Ceylonese actor AAS, WWT/12-15

GORDON, Douglas (1871-1935) English actor, producer GRB/1, 3-4, WWT/1-7

GORDON, Edith Althoff (d 1970 [65]) performer BP/55*

GORDON, Fanny (fl 1850) actress HAS

GORDON, Frank Odell (d 1973 [95]) performer BP/58*

GORDON, Gavin (1901-70) Scottish actor, singer, composer TW/4-8, 27, WWT/9-14

GORDON, George G. (d 1917) singer? EA/18*

GORDON, George Lash (1851-95) English actor, dramatist DD, OAA/2

GORDON, George W. W. (d
1887 [32]) EA/88*
GORDON, Gloria (d 1962) actress
BE*
GORDON, Grant (d 1972 [64])
performer BP/57*
GORDON, G. Swayne (d 1949
[69]) American actor   BE*,
BP/34*
GORDON, Harriett (d 1869 [35])
actress DD
GORDON, Hayes (b 1920) Amer-
ican director, producer, actor
BE, TW/6-8, WWT/16
GORDON, Huntley (d 1956 [69])
actor BE*
GORDON, James M. (d 1944
[86]) actor, director BE*,
WWT/14*
GORDON, J. B. (d 1914) actor
WWT/14*
GORDON, Mrs. J. B. see
Scobie, Lizzie
GORDON, Joseph William (d
1893) lessee EA/94*
GORDON, Mrs. J. W. (d 1884)
actress EA/85*
GORDON, Kitty [Hon. Mrs. W.
W. Horsley-Beresford] (1878-
1974) English actress, singer
CDP, GRB/3-4, TW/30,
WWM, WWT/1-7
GORDON, Leon (1884-1960) Eng-
lish actor, dramatist WWT/
5-11
GORDON, Lizzie (d 1866) actress
HAS
GORDON, L. S. dramatist DD
GORDON, Mack (d 1959 [54])
Polish lyricist, performer
BE*
GORDON, Mrs. M. A. M.
[Mrs. T. Gordon] (d 1875)
EA/76*
GORDON, Marie [née Marie
Eugenie Phillips; Mrs. Thomas
W. Egan; Mrs. John T. Ray-
mond] (d 1891) actress CDP
GORDON, Marjorie (b 1893)
English actress, singer WWT/
4-10
GORDON, Mark American actor
TW/22
GORDON, Martha (d 1909) EA/
10*
GORDON, Max (b 1892) American
manager, producer BE, CB,
NTH, SR, TW/2-8, WWT/8-14

GORDON, Michael (b 1909) Amer-
ican director, actor BE, TW/2
GORDON, Nellie English actress
GRB/1
GORDON, Nelly see Gourlay,
Helen Lawson
GORDON, Noele (b 1923) English
actress, singer WWT/11-13
GORDON, Oliver (d 1970 [67])
performer BP/55*
GORDON, Pamela (b 1918) English
actress TW/3
GORDON, Paul (d 1929 [43])
American actor BE*, BP/13*
GORDON, Paul Vincent (d 1965
[45]) drama coach BP/50*
GORDON, Peggy (b 1949) Ameri-
can actress TW/27-30
GORDON, Riki (d 1973 [38]) per-
former BP/57*
GORDON, Robert (d 1971 [76])
performer BP/56*
GORDON, Robert H. (d 1963 [58])
director BP/48*
GORDON, Rose M. (d 1973) per-
former BP/58*
GORDON, Ruth (b 1896) American
actress, dramatist AAS, BE,
CB, ES, NTH, SR, TW/1-23,
WWT/7-16
GORDON, Scott (b 1951) American
actor TW/30
GORDON, Stanley S. (b 1870) Eng-
lish actor GRB/1
GORDON, Mrs. T. see Gordon,
Mrs. M. A. M.
GORDON, Vera (1886-1948) Rus-
sian actress TW/4
GORDON, Walter [William Aylmer
Gowing] (1823-92) English actor
DD, EA/69
GORDON, Walter (d 1901 [30])
variety comedian EA/03*
GORDON, Walter Lewis (d 1888)
musician EA/89*
GORDON, William (fl 1731) drama-
tist CP/2, GT
GORDON, William (d 1874 [73])
scene artist EA/76*
GORDONA, Adelaide equestrienne
CDP
GORDONE, Charles (b 1925/27)
American dramatist, actor,
director CD, MH, TW/26,
WWT/16
GORDON-LEE, Kathleen English
actress WWT/4-6
GORDON-LENNOX, Mrs. C.

Cosmo see Tempest, Marie Susan

GORDON-LENNOX, Cosmo Stuart Charles see Stuart, Cosmo

GORDON-MADDICK, Frank (d 1906 [48]) EA/07*

GORE, Catherine Grace Frances [née Moody] (1799-1861) English dramatist DD, DNB, HP

GORE, Ivan Pat [Robert T. G. de Vaux Balbirnie] English actor GRB/1

GORE, Larry (d 1973 [50]) publicist BP/58*

GORE, Walter (b 1910) English dancer, choreographer ES

GORE-BROWNE, Robert (b 1893) English dramatist WWT/9-14

GOREE, Frederick [Frank Musgrave] (d 1876 [28]) musician EA/77*

GOREE, George, Sr. (d 1876) musician EA/77*

GORELIK, Mordecai (b 1899) Russian/American designer, director, educator BE, ES, NTH, TW/3-4, WWT/15-16

GORHAM, Maurice (d 1975 [73]) producer/director/choreographer BP/60*

GORIN, G. T. (d 1889) EA/90*

GORIN, Igor (b 1909) Russian/American singer CB

GORING, Charles (fl 1687?-1708) dramatist CP/1-3, GT

GORING, Marius (b 1912) English actor AAS, ES, WWT/9-16

GORKY, Maxim (1868-1936) Russian dramatist COC, MWD, OC/1-3

GORMAN, Bob (b 1928) American actor TW/24, 26

GORMAN, Cliff (b 1936) American actor TW/24, 27-29, WWT/16

GORMAN, Edward (d 1915) American actor SR

GORMAN, Eric (d 1971 [85]) actor BP/56*, WWT/16*

GORMAN, Frederick E. (d 1972 [89]) performer BP/56*

GORMAN, Mari (b 1944) American actress TW/29-30

GORMAN, Tom (d 1971 [63]) actor TW/28

GORME, Eydie American actress, singer TW/24

GORNEY, Jay (b 1896) Russian composer, director, producer, executive BE

GORNEY, Karen (b 1945) American actress TW/28

GORNO, Jimmy (d 1969 [65]) designer BP/54*

GORR, Rita (b 1926) Belgian singer ES

GORSKI, Virginia (b 1926) American actress TW/4-5

GORST, Mrs. Harold (1869-1926) dramatist WWW/2

GORST, Richard (d 1896 [65]) executive EA/97*

GORTON, Belle [Mrs. Leslie Gaze] (d 1912 [28]) actress EA/13*

GORTON, Francis G. (d 1894) music-hall director EA/96*

GORTON, Joseph (fl 1880s-1890s) American minstrel SR

GORWIN, Peter (b 1948) American actor TW/28

GOSCH, Martin A. (d 1973 [62]) producer/director/choreographer BP/58*

GOSDEN, Charles Freeman ["Amos" of "Amos & Andy"] actor SR

GOSE, Carl see McKay, Scott

GOSFIELD, Maurice (1913-64) American actor TW/7, 21

GOSHEN, Col. Ruth (d 1889) giant CDP

GOSLING, Harold (b 1897) English business manager WWT/7-13

GOSNAY, Francis (d 1899) acting manager EA/00*

GOSS, Barry (b 1961) American actor TW/30

GOSS, Sir John (d 1880 [79]) composer, musician EA/81*

GOSS, Joseph (d 1892) EA/93*

GOSSE, Edmund (1849-1928) English writer DD, NTH

GOSSETT, Louis (b 1936) American actor, singer BE, TW/10, 12, 20, 22-24, 28

GOSSIN, Harry W. (1832-66) actor HAS

GOSSIN, John American clown HAS

GOSSMAN, Irving (d 1964 [63]) American actor, producer BE*

GOSSON, Stephen (1554-1623) English dramatist, actor CP/2-3, DA, DD, FGF, HP, NTH

GOTH, Trudy (d 1974) performer
BP/58*
GOTHIE, Bob (b 1930) American
actor TW/13
GOTT, Barbara (d 1944) actress
WWT/4-9
GOTTESFELD, Chone (d 1964
[73]) Russian dramatist BE*,
BP/48*
GOTTFRIED, Martin (b 1933)
American critic BE
GOTTHOLD, J. Newton (d 1888)
American actor CDP, HAS
GOTTLIEB, Arthur (d 1962
[63]) American producer BE*
GOTTLIEB, David (d 1962 [81])
costumier BE*
GOTTLIEB, Joseph Abraham
see Bishop, Joey
GOTTLIEB, Morton (b 1921)
American producer, manager
BE, WWT/15-16
GOTTLIEB, Polly Rose (d 1971)
performer BP/55*
GOTTSCHALK, Ferdinand (1858/
69-1944) English actor, drama-
tist, producer GRB/3-4,
PP/1, SR, TW/1, WWM,
WWT/1-9
GOTTSCHALK, Louis Moreau
(1829-69) American pianist,
composer CDP, DAB, HAS,
WWA/H
GOUDGE, Elizabeth (b 1900)
English dramatist CB
GOUFFE, Mons. (fl 1831) actor
CDP
GOUGENHEIM, Adelaide (b 1828)
English actress CDP, HAS,
SR
GOUGENHEIM, Josephine (fl
1850-60) American actress
CDP, DD, HAS
GOUGH, Miss see Galindo,
Mrs.
GOUGH, Alexander (b 1614)
English actor DA, OC/1-3
GOUGH, J. G. (fl 1640) drama-
tist CP/2-3, FGF
GOUGH, John (d 1968 [74]) per-
former BP/53*
GOUGH, John Robert (d 1899
[64]) musician EA/00*
GOUGH, Lloyd actor TW/2-3,
10, 14
GOUGH, Michael (b 1917)
Malaysian/English actor
AAS, WWT/11-16

GOUGH, Minnie (d 1891) music-
hall performer CDP
GOUGH, Robert (d 1625) English
actor COC, DA, DD, GT,
NTH, OC/1-3
GOUGH, Thomas (d 1879 [37])
actor? EA/80*
GOUGHE, Alexander see Gough,
Alexander
GOUGHE, Robert see Gough,
Robert
GOUGHE, Thomas (fl 1572) actor
DA
GOULD, Mr. (fl 1737) dramatist
CP/1
GOULD, Mrs. Irish actress HAS
GOULD, Bernard [né Partridge]
(1861-1945) English actor DD,
GRB/1-4
GOULD, Billy (d 1950 [81]) actor
TW/6
GOULD, Dave (d 1969 [70]) dance
director BP/54*
GOULD, Diana (b 1913) actress,
dancer WWT/10-11
GOULD, Edith (c. 1861-1921) ac-
tress SR
GOULD, Edward (d 1893) manager
EA/95*
GOULD, Elliott [né Goldstein] (b
1938) American actor BE,
CB, TW/18, 22-24, WWT/15-16
GOULD, Fred (d 1902) EA/03*
GOULD, Fred (d 1917 [75/76])
actor, dramatist, producer
BE*, EA/18*, WWT/14*
GOULD, Fred (d 1918) EA/19*
GOULD, Mrs. George J. see
Kingdon, Edith
GOULD, Gordon (b 1930) American
actor TW/22-25, 27, 30
GOULD, Gypsy (d 1966 [64]) per-
former BP/50*
GOULD, Harold (d 1952 [78])
American performer BE*, BP/
36*
GOULD, Harold (b 1923) American
actor TW/26-27
GOULD, Harry E., Sr. (d 1971
[72]) showman, theatre owner
BP/55*
GOULD, Howard (1863/67-1938)
American actor PP/1, SR,
WWA/1, WWM, WWS
GOULD, James Nutcombe see
Gould, Nutcombe
GOULD, John (d 1974 [37]) drama-
tist BP/59*

GOULD, John (b 1940) English composer, performer WWT/16

GOULD, Julia (1824/27-93) English actress CDP, HAS

GOULD, Lita singer CDP

GOULD, Marguerite (b 1923) American actress TW/8

GOULD, Morton (b 1913) American composer, conductor BE

GOULD, Napoleon W. (fl 1819-81) singer, composer, musician CDP

GOULD, Nutcombe (1849-99) actor DD, EA/95, WWW/1

GOULD, Prissie (d 1892 [22]) EA/93*

GOULD, Robert (fl 1696-1737) dramatist CP/1-3, DNB, GT

GOULD, Mrs. S. M. (d 1880) EA/81*

GOULD, William (fl 1900?) comedian, singer CDP

GOULDEN, Mrs. Edmund B. see Goulden, Mary

GOULDEN, Mary [Mrs. Edmund B. Goulden] (d 1895) EA/96*

GOULDING, Alfred (d 1972 [76]) performer BP/56*

GOULDING, Edmund (1891/92-1959) English actor, dramatist, composer ES, WWT/5-10

GOULET, Robert (b 1933) Canadian/American actor, singer BE, CB, TW/17-20, 24, WWT/16

GOULSTONE, James (d 1852) balloonist EA/72*

GOURIET, Mrs. Victor see Crossland, Maggie

GOURLAY, Corbet Ryder (d 1897 [50]) advertiser, entrepreneur EA/98*

GOURLAY, Haggie see Gourlay, Maggie

GOURLAY, Helen Lawson [Nelly Gordon] (d 1872 [26]) actress EA/73*, WWT/14*

GOURLAY, Jenny (fl 1858-68) actress HAS

GOURLAY, John actor CDP

GOURLAY, Maggie (1847-68) Scottish actress HAS, SR

GOURLAY, Minnie (d 1889) actress EA/90*

GOURLAY, William (d 1882) actor DD

GOURLAY, William Cameron (d 1883 [65]) Scottish comedian EA/84*

GOURRON, Albert Raymond see Alvarez

GOUVY, Ludwig Theodore (d 1898 [79]) composer EA/99*

GOVELL, R. dramatist CP/3, FGF

GOVER, Mrs. Charles see Hanbury, Pattie

GOVEY, Alfred (d 1889 [67]) actor EA/90*

GOW, James (d 1879 [85]) Scottish actor EA/80*

GOW, James (1907-52) American dramatist CB, ES, TW/8, WWT/10

GOW, Ronald (b 1897) English dramatist AAS, CD, WWT/8-16

GOWARD, Miss see Keeley, Mary Ann

GOWARD, Annie [Mrs. Charles Fawcett] (d 1907 [48]) actress GRB/3

GOWARD, Mary Ann see Keeley, Mary Ann

GOWER, James (d 1917 [67]) EA/18*

GOWER, Rose (d 1891) music-hall performer EA/93*

GOWING, Emilia Julia [Mrs. William Aylmer Gowing] (d 1905) EA/06*

GOWING, William Aylmer see Gordon, Walter

GOWING, Mrs. William Aylmer see Gowing, Emilia Julia

GOZ, Harry G. (b 1932) American actor TW/27-30

GOZZI, Carlo (1720-1806) Italian dramatist COC, NTH, OC/2-3

GRABLE, Betty (1916-73) American actress, singer, dancer TW/22-24, 30, WWA/5, WWT/15

GRACE, Amy [Mrs. Leonard Rayne] (1876-1945) English actress GRB/1-4

GRACE, Carol actress BE, TW/15

GRACE, Charity (d 1965 [86]) actress TW/22

GRACE, Edmund (d 1908 [62]) actor EA/10*

GRACE, Francis (fl 1610-23) actor DA

GRACE, James Delmon (1827-76) American actor CDP, HAS

GRACE, Jean (d 1972 [85]) agent BP/56*

GRACE, Jessica (fl 1900?) singer, actress CDP

GRACE, Richard (d 1627?) actor DA

GRACIE, Sally American actress BE, TW/12-14, 25, 30

GRADDON, Miss see Gibbs, P.

GRADWELL, Henry (fl 1631) actor DA

GRADY, Alfred (d 1918) EA/19*

GRAEVER, Madeline (fl 1858) pianist HAS

GRAF, Herbert (1903-73) Austrian director CB, WWA/5

GRAFF, Edward (d 1893 [46]) variety agent EA/94*

GRAFF, George (d 1973 [86]) composer/lyricist BP/57*

GRAFF, Wilton (1903-69) American actor BE, TW/25

GRAFTON, Cecil [Constance M. Smith] (d 1904) actress EA/05*

GRAFTON, Jane [Mrs. Stafford Grafton] actress CDP

GRAFTON, Mrs. Stafford see Grafton, Jane

GRAHAM, Alma (d 1884) EA/85*

GRAHAM, Annie (fl 1855) American actress CDP, HAS

GRAHAM, Caroline (d 1910 [74]) EA/11*

GRAHAM, Colin (b 1931) English director ES

GRAHAM, Daphne see Sheridan, Mary

GRAHAM, Elizabeth Alice see Glenney, Bessie

GRAHAM, Ena see Gilbart, Eleanor

GRAHAM, Ernest (d 1945 [67]) actor BE*, WWT/14*

GRAHAM, Frank (d 1862 [32]) actor? HAS

GRAHAM, Frank (d 1867 [26]) comedian EA/68*

GRAHAM, Mrs. Frank (b 1842) English actress HAS

GRAHAM, Mrs. Fred see Graham, Lucinda

GRAHAM, Fred W. (d 1916 [42]) comedian EA/17*

GRAHAM, Genine (b 1925) English actress TW/9

GRAHAM, George (d 1767) dramatist CP/2-3, DNB

GRAHAM, George (d 1847) English actor HAS, SR

GRAHAM, George (d 1869) property man EA/70*

GRAHAM, George (1875-1939) English actor SR

GRAHAM, Mrs. George see George, Mary Stuart

GRAHAM, George St. Casse (d 1893 [28]) scene artist EA/94*

GRAHAM, Gertrude [Mrs. Fred Temple] (d 1908) actress EA/09*

GRAHAM, Harry (1874-1936) English dramatist NTH, WWT/4-8

GRAHAM, Irvin (b 1909) American composer, lyricist BE

GRAHAM, J. F. (d 1933 [82]) actor, producer BE*, WWT/14*

GRAHAM, John (fl 1812-17) American actor HAS

GRAHAM, John [née G. Monro] (d 1863 [46]) actor CDP

GRAHAM, John Somerville (d 1907) EA/08*

GRAHAM, Joseph (d 1976 [83]) performer BP/60*

GRAHAM, J. P. (d 1904) music-hall performer EA/05*

GRAHAM, June F. American actress TW/25, 27

GRAHAM, Kenneth L. (b 1915) American educator BE

GRAHAM, Lillie (fl 1855) American actress HAS

GRAHAM, Lionel (d 1893 [42]) actor EA/94*

GRAHAM, Lucinda [Mrs. Fred Graham] (d 1906) EA/07*

GRAHAM, Ly [Graham Lobb] (d 1883 [27]) actor EA/84*

GRAHAM, Malcolm Harry (d 1889 [24]) actor EA/90*

GRAHAM, Martha (b 1900/02) American dancer, choreographer BE, CB, ES, NTH, WWT/11-12

GRAHAM, Mary Ann see Yates, Mary Ann

GRAHAM, Mary Anne (fl 1856) actress HAS

GRAHAM, Mary Stuart [Mrs. George Graham] (d 1880) EA/81*

GRAHAM, Morland (1891-1949)

Scottish actor WWT/8-10

GRAHAM, Nevill English actor, stage manager, business manager GRB/1

GRAHAM, Mrs. Nevill see Earle, Lilias

GRAHAM, Richard (b 1915) American actor TW/26, 30

GRAHAM, Richard Elliott (fl 1850) actor CDP

GRAHAM, Richard L. (d 1851) Scottish actor HAS

GRAHAM, Robert Emmet (b 1858) American actor CDP, WWM, WWS

GRAHAM, Ronald (1913-50) Scottish actor TW/1, 3, 7

GRAHAM, Ronny (b 1919) American actor, director, lyricist, composer BE, TW/8-19, 21, WWT/15-16

GRAHAM, Shad E. (d 1969 [72]) designer BP/53*

GRAHAM, Tom (d 1897 [28]) music-hall comedian, composer CDP

GRAHAM, Violet (1890-1967) actress WWT/4-8

GRAHAM, Virginia (d 1964 [45]) actress BE*

GRAHAM, Mrs. Walter (d 1867) EA/68*

GRAHAM, William (d 1974 [74]) producer/director/choreographer BP/59*

GRAHAME, Cissy [Mrs. James Allen] (b 1862) English actress, manager DD, DP, EA/95, GRB/1, OAA/2

GRAHAME, Emmie [Mrs. Kerbey D. Bowen] (d 1917) EA/18*

GRAHAME, Gloria (b 1925) American actress ES

GRAHAME, Gracie actress, singer CDP

GRAHAME, James (fl 1807) dramatist CP/3

GRAHAME, J. G. (d 1907) actor DD, GRB/3, OAA/2

GRAHAME, J. Lynward (b 1881) Irish actor GRB/1

GRAHAME, Margot (b 1911) English actress WWT/7-11

GRAHN, Lucile (1819/25-1907) Danish dancer CDP, ES

GRAHN, Mary (b 1901) librarian BE

GRAIN, Richard Corney (1844-95)

English actor, composer, singer CDP, DD

GRAINER, Ron (b 1922) Australian composer WWT/15-16

GRAINGER, Gawn (b 1940) Irish actor TW/23-24, WWT/16

GRAINGER, George Pugh (d 1879 [64]) actor EA/80*

GRAINGER, Mrs. W. P. (d 1886) actress EA/87*

GRAJALES, Fernando Felix (d 1975 [32]) producer/director/choreographer BP/60*

GRAMM, Donald (b 1927) American singer CB

GRAMMANI, W. H. (d 1855 [55]) pantomimist CDP

GRANACH, Alexander (1890-1945) Russian actor BE*

GRANBY, Cornelius W. (d 1886 [82]) actor, producer BE*, WWT/14*

GRANBY, Joseph (d 1965 [80]) performer BP/50*

GRANDIN, Elmer (d 1933 [72]) actor BE*

GRANDJEAN, Louise (d 1934 [64]) actress BE*, WWT/14*

GRANDY, Fred (b 1948) American actor TW/29-30

GRANGER, Miss see Jones, Mrs.

GRANGER, Farley (b 1925) American actor BE, TW/15-18, 20

GRANGER, John (b 1924) American actor TW/10-13, 28

GRANGER, Maude [Anna Brainerd] (b 1851?) actress CDP

GRANGER, Stewart [né James Lablache Stewart] (b 1913) English actor ES, WWT/10-12

GRANIER, Jeanne (d 1939 [88]) French actress GRB/1-4, WWT/1-4

GRANLUND, Nils T. (d 1957 [65]) Finnish? producer BP/41*

GRANNELL, Denis (d 1896) manager, lessee EA/97*

GRANNELL, William (b 1929) American actor TW/25

GRANT, Mr. see Raymond, Mr.

GRANT, Prof. (d 1900 [48]) ventriloquist EA/01*

GRANT, Miss see Saville, Mrs. E. F.

GRANT, Alexander (b 1925) New Zealand/English dancer ES

GRANT, Barney (d 1962 [50])

performer BE*
GRANT, Billy (d 1971) performer
BP/55*
GRANT, Bob (b 1932) English ac-
tor, dramatist WWT/15-16
GRANT, Burt (fl 1893?) dancer
CDP
GRANT, Cary (b 1904) English/
American actor CB, ES, SR
GRANT, Charles (b 1865) Eng-
lish actor GRB/1
GRANT, Earl (d 1970) performer
BP/55*
GRANT, Elspeth (d 1975 [60s])
critic BP/60*
GRANT, Francis Thomas Hope
(d 1887) EA/88*
GRANT, James Edward (d 1966
[61]) dramatist BP/50*
GRANT, James M. (fl 1805)
dramatist CP/3
GRANT, Lee (b 1927/29?) Amer-
ican actress BE, CB, TW/
5-9, 13-15, 28-30
GRANT, Maxwell (d 1961 [39])
sketch writer BE*
GRANT, Micki American actress
TW/22, 26-30
GRANT, Neil (b 1882) Scottish
dramatist WWT/6-14
GRANT, Nellie [Charlotte Ellen
Doherty] (d 1911 [31]) actress
EA/12*
GRANT, Pauline (b 1915) Eng-
lish dancer, choreographer,
director WWT/10-16
GRANT, Priscilla Mary see
Edmonds, Connie
GRANT, Sydney (1873-1953)
American vaudevillian TW/10,
WWM
GRANT, Thomas (d 1881 [25])
EA/82*
GRANT, Mrs. W. Christie (d
1910) EA/11*
GRANT, W. F. (d 1923) actor
BE*, WWT/14*
GRANTHAM, John (d 1882) actor
EA/83*
GRANTHAM, Louisa (d 1884)
EA/85*
GRANTHAM, Wilfred (b 1898)
English actor WWT/9-14
GRANTZOW, Adele (d 1877 [36])
dancer EA/78*
GRANVAL, Jean-Pierre (b 1923)
French actor TW/9
GRANVILLE, Audrey (d 1972

[62]) performer BP/56*
GRANVILLE, Bernard (1886-1936)
American actor, dancer WWT/
4-8
GRANVILLE, Charlotte [née Stu-
art; Mrs. Synge] (b 1863) ac-
tress DD, EA/96, GRB/2-4,
WWM, WWT/1-9
GRANVILLE, Edgar (d 1909 [54])
music-hall comedian, composer
CDP
GRANVILLE, Edward (d 1917)
EA/18*
GRANVILLE, Fred [Ralph Haines
Watson] (d 1894 [35]) singer
EA/95*
GRANVILLE, George, Lord Lans-
down (1667-1735) English drama-
tist CP/1-3
GRANVILLE, H. Such (fl 1868-80)
dramatist DD
GRANVILLE, Louise (d 1968 [73])
performer BP/53*
GRANVILLE, Millicent [Millicent
Granville Smith] (b 1884) Eng-
lish actress GRB/1
GRANVILLE, Sydney (d 1959 [79])
English actor, singer TW/16,
WWT/5-11
GRANVILLE-BARKER, Harley
(1877-1946) English actor,
dramatist, manager AAS,
COC, DD, DNB, ES, GRB/1-4,
HP, MD, MH, MWD, NTH,
OC/1-3, PDT, RE, SR, WWS,
WWT/1-9, WWW/4
GRANVILLE-BARKER, Helen (d
1950) dramatist WWT/6-8,
WWW/4
GRAPEWIN, Charles (1869-1956)
American vaudevillian, actor
TW/12
GRASS, Gunter (b 1927) German
dramatist COC
GRASSAN, Adeline see Hind,
Mrs. Thomas James
GRASSINI, Giuseppina (1773-1850)
Italian singer ES
GRASSLE, Karen American actress
TW/25, 28-29
GRASSMAN, Daniel see Mason,
Dan
GRASSO, Giovanni (1875-1930)
Italian actor COC, OC/1-3,
WWT/3
GRASSOT, Paul (d 1860 [59])
actor WWT/14*
GRATTAN, Miss see Harris,

Mrs.

GRATTAN, Emily (fl 1875-77)
actress CDP

GRATTAN, Emma (fl 1854-69)
English actress CDP, HAS

GRATTAN, Harry (1867?-1951)
English actor, dramatist
CDP, DD, GRB/1-4, WWT/
3-9

GRATTAN, Henry Plunkett (1808-
89) Irish actor, dramatist
CDP, DD, HAS

GRATTAN, Mrs. Henry P[lunkett;
Mrs. Barker; Mrs. Madison]
(1810-76) English actress
CDP, HAS

GRATTAN, Kittie [Mrs. Edward
Lytton] (b 1874) English actress GRB/1-4

GRATTAN, Lawrence (d 1941
[71]) American actor, dramatist SR

GRATTON, Fred (1894-1966)
English press representative
WWT/11-14

GRAU, Jacob F. (1817-77) Austrian impresario CDP, SR

GRAU, Maurice (1849-1907)
Austrian manager DAB, ES,
GRB/2-3, WWA/1, WWW/1

GRAU, Robert (d 1916) writer,
producer, manager BE*,
WWT/14*

GRAUMAN, Sid (1879-1950)
American executive BE*

GRAUNGER, John (fl 1509-11)
member of the Chapel Royal
DA

GRAUPNER, Mr. (fl 1796) actor
HAS

GRAUPNER, Mrs. [Miss Heelyer]
(fl 1794) actress HAS

GRAVELE, Emile see Blondin,
Charles

GRAVENSTEIN, Wynand (d 1886)
musician EA/87*

GRAVER, J. Adams (b 1835)
American actor HAS

GRAVES, Mr. (d 1869) scene
artist EA/70*

GRAVES, Alfred Percival (b
1846) dramatist DD

GRAVES, Clotilde Inez Mary
(1863-1932) Irish dramatist
DD, GRB/2-4, WWT/1-6,
WWW/3

GRAVES, Elsie Elizabeth (d 1969
[78]) performer BP/54*

GRAVES, Ernest (b 1919) American actor TW/3-4, 22, 24

GRAVES, George (1876-1949) English actor DNB, GRB/1-4,
TW/5, WWT/1-10

GRAVES, J. (d 1869) scene artist
WWT/14*

GRAVES, Kate (d 1898 [24]) actress EA/00*

GRAVES, Laura (d 1925 [55])
actress BE*, WWT/14*

GRAVES, Maud actress CDP

GRAVES, Peter (b 1911) English
actor, singer AAS, WWT/10-16

GRAVES, Richard (1715-1804)
English dramatist CP/3

GRAVET, Fernand (1905-70) Belgian actor TW/21, 27

GRAVEUR, Emma (d 1899) EA/00*

GRAVEY, Fernand see Gravet,
Fernand

GRAY, Mr. (fl 1798) singer, actor
TD/1-2

GRAY, Dr. (fl 1822) dramatist
EAP

GRAY, Mrs. (fl 1791) actress
HAS

GRAY, Mrs. see Garrick, Mrs.

GRAY, Ada [Mrs. Charles A.
Watkins; Mrs. Charles S. Tin-
gay] (1834-1902) actress CDP

GRAY, Alice (b 1833) American
actress HAS

GRAY, Beatrice (b 1924) American
actress TW/4

GRAY, Charles [né Donald Marshall Gray] (b 1928) English
actor BE, TW/13, 21-22,
WWT/15-16

GRAY, Dolores (b 1924) American
actress, singer AAS, BE,
TW/2-3, 6-11, 15-18, 23,
WWT/11-16

GRAY, Donald Marshall see
Gray, Charles

GRAY, Dora English actress
GRB/2

GRAY, Dulcie (b 1919) Malaysian/
English actress WWT/10-16

GRAY, Duncan (d 1969 [76]) performer BP/54*

GRAY, Edith (d 1898) actress
EA/99*

GRAY, Mrs. Edward (d 1905
[27]) EA/06*

GRAY, Edward Earl ["Monsewer
Eddie Gray"] (d 1969 [71])
performer BP/54*

GRAY, Elaine (d 1969) performer BP/54*

GRAY, Elspet (b 1929) Scottish actress WWT/15-16

GRAY, Eve (b 1904) English actress, singer WWT/6-9

GRAY, Florence [Mrs. David Collins] (d 1904) EA/06*

GRAY, Gilda (d 1959 [60]) Polish actress, singer TW/16

GRAY, Ida M. (d 1942 [84]) actress BE*, WWT/14*

GRAY, Jack (b 1927) American/Canadian dramatist, director CD

GRAY, Jackson (1796-1837) American actor HAS

GRAY, James see Stuart, Edward Patrick

GRAY, Jennifer (1916-62) Chinese/English actress WWT/10-13

GRAY, Joan American actress TW/5, 10-11

GRAY, John (d 1873 [56]) scene artist EA/74*

GRAY, John (fl 1890) dramatist DD

GRAY, John (d 1903) actor? EA/04*

GRAY, Lawrence (d 1970 [71]) performer BP/54*

GRAY, Leonard (d 1964 [50]) performer BE*

GRAY, Leslie A. (d 1916 [25]) EA/17*

GRAY, Linda (b 1910) English actress, singer WWT/10-16

GRAY, Madge (d 1965 [58]) performer BP/49*

GRAY, Margaret (fl 1623-24) lessee DA

GRAY, Margery American actress, singer, dancer BE

GRAY, Nicholas Stuart (b 1919) Scottish dramatist, actor, director WWT/13-16

GRAY, Paul (b 1930) American educator, director, editor BE

GRAY, Richard (b 1896) English actor WWT/9

GRAY, Robert (b 1940) American actor TW/24

GRAY, Robert S. (b 1911) American educator BE

GRAY, Sally [née Constance

Vera Stevens] (b 1916) English actress WWT/10-11

GRAY, Simon (b 1936) English dramatist AAS, CD, WWT/15-16

GRAY, Terence (b 1895) English producer COC, ES, OC/3, WWT/6-10

GRAY, Thomas (d 1768 [100+]) clown EA/72*

GRAY, Thomas (1716-72) English dramatist CP/2-3

GRAY, Thomas J. (1888-1924) American writer WWM

GRAY, Timothy American performer, director BE

GRAY, William (d 1875) lessee EA/76*

GRAY, William (d 1896 [60]) actor EA/97*

GRAY, William (d 1943 [83]) actor, dramatist BE*

GRAY, Winifred see Russell, Countess

GRAYDON, J. L. music-hall proprietor & manager GRB/1-3

GRAYSON, Bette [Mrs. Clifford Odets] (d 1954 [32]) actress BE*

GRAYSON, Helen singer CDP

GRAYSON, Richard (b 1925) American manager, stage manager, actor, director BE

GREANEY, Mary (b 1944) Irish actress TW/23

GREASLEY, Alice Georgina [Mrs. T. H. Greasley] (d 1892) EA/94*

GREASLEY, Emily [Mrs. T. G. Greasley] (d 1888 [25]) EA/89*

GREASLEY, Mrs. T. G. see Greasley, Emily

GREASLEY, Mrs. T. H. see Greasley, Alice Georgina

GREATHEED, Bertie (1759-1826) English dramatist CP/3, DNB, TD/1-2

GREATOREX, George (d 1916 [28]) magician EA/18*

"GREAT RAYMOND, The" see Raymond, Maurice

GREAVES, John (fl 1572) actor DA

GREAVES, Thomas (d 1877 [37]) secretary, treasurer EA/78*

GREAVES, Thomas (d 1908 [71]) musical director EA/09*

GREAZA, Walter N. (1897/1900-

1973) American actor BE,
TW/1-6, 29, WWT/9-11
GREBANIER, Bernard (b 1903)
American educator, director,
writer BE
GREBER, Giacomo dramatist
CP/1
GRECO, Francis (d 1909) EA/10*
GRECO, José (b 1918) Italian
dancer, choreographer CB
GREDULE, Mons. (fl 1850)
dancer HAS
GREE, Mrs. (fl 1845) actress
HAS
GREEN, Gen. dwarf CDP
GREEN (d 1916 [27]) EA/17*
GREEN, Miss see Bastar, Mrs.
GREEN, Mrs. [Jane Hippisley]
see Green, Jane
GREEN, Abel (1900-73) American
editor, writer NTH, TW/29,
WWT/15
GREEN, Adolph (b 1915/18)
American librettist, lyricist,
entertainer AAS, BE, CB,
ES, TW/1, WWT/14-16
GREEN, Alexander (fl 1663)
dramatist CP/1-3, GT
GREEN, Amelia see Bannister,
Mrs. Nathaniel Harrington
GREEN, Anna Katherine [Anna
K. G. Rohlfs] (b 1846)
American dramatist WWA/1,
WWM
GREEN, Belle (b 1881) Indian/
English entertainer GRB/1
GREEN, Bernard (d 1975 [66])
composer BP/60*, WWT/
16*
GREEN, Dr. Carleton (d 1962
[52]) educator BE*
GREEN, Charles (1785-1870)
aeronaut CDP
GREEN, Daniel Harding (d 1877
[70]) actor EA/78*
GREEN, Del (b 1938) American
actress TW/23, 28
GREEN, Denis (1903-54) English
actor, dramatist TW/5-6
GREEN, Dorothy (1886-1961)
English actress AAS, ES,
WWT/4-13
GREEN, Dorothy [Mrs. Norman
November] (d 1963 [71]) ac-
tress BE*
GREEN, E. see Elliott, E. P.
GREEN, Eleanor see Baster,
Mrs. John

GREEN, Elizabeth (d 1909) EA/
10*
GREEN, Frank (d 1891) actor
EA/93*
GREEN, Frank W. (d 1884) drama-
tist CDP, DD
GREEN, George (d 1876 [38])
clown EA/77*
GREEN, George Smith (d 1762)
English? dramatist CP/1-3
GREEN, George Thomas (d 1877)
musical director EA/78*
GREEN, Gladys see Arthur, Jean
GREEN, Harry (1892-1958) Amer-
ican actor TW/14, WWT/4-12
GREEN, Henry Hawes Craven
see Craven, Hawes
GREEN, Hernandez (d 1902 [73])
acrobat EA/03*
GREEN, H. J. see Kemble,
H. J.
GREEN, Howard (b 1936) American
actor TW/24, 27, 29
GREEN, Isadore (d 1963 [59])
journalist BE*
GREEN, J. (d 1910 [47]) stage
manager EA/11*
GREEN, James Burton (d 1922
[48]) songwriter, musician BE*
GREEN, Jane [née Hippisley] (d
1791) actress CDP, DD, DNB
GREEN, Janet (b 1914) English
dramatist, actress BE, WWT/
12-14
GREEN, Jeanette F. (d 1970 [71])
artists' representative BP/55*
GREEN, J. Edwin (b 1834) Amer-
ican singer, proprietor, imi-
tator HAS
GREEN, John musician CDP
GREEN, John? (fl 1606-27) Eng-
lish actor COC, DA, OC/1-3
GREEN, John (1801-74) American
actor, manager, singer DNB,
SR
GREEN, John H. (b 1915) Ameri-
can educator BE
GREEN, Johnny (b 1908) American
composer, musical director
BE
GREEN, Julien (b 1900) American
dramatist MD, MH, MWD
GREEN, Leonard (d 1917 [2])
EA/18*
GREEN, Lizzie (d 1906) actress
EA/07*
GREEN, Mabel (b 1887/90) English
actress GRB/1-3, WWT/5-7

GREEN, Marion (1890-1956)
American actor, singer TW/1,
12, WWT/8-11

GREEN, Martyn [William Martyn-
Green] (1899-1975) English actor, singer BE, CB, TW/4-9,
12-19, 23-25, 27-28, WWT/8-
16

GREEN, Mary-Pat (b 1951) American actress TW/30

GREEN, Mitzi (1920-69) American
actress TW/2-6, 25, WWT/
9-11

GREEN, Morris (d 1963 [73])
producer BE*, BP/47*

GREEN, Paul Eliot (b 1894)
American dramatist AAS,
BE, CD, COC, ES, HJD,
MD, MH, MWD, NTH, OC/
1-3, RE, SR, WWT/6-11,
15-16

GREEN, Richard (d 1884 [52])
comic singer EA/85*

GREEN, Richard (d 1914 [49])
English singer, actor DD,
GRB/1-4

GREEN, Robert musician CDP

GREEN, Robert (d 1882) singer
CDP

GREEN, Rupert (fl 1777) dramatist CP/2-3, GT

GREEN, Ruth (d 1976 [72])
executive BE

GREEN, Stanley (b 1923) American publicist, writer BE

GREEN, Thomas (1786-1859)
actor DD

GREEN, Thomas (fl 1847?) scene
painter CDP

GREEN, Thomas see Felix,
Tony

GREEN, Thomas C. (1832-66)
American actor HAS

GREEN, Tom (b 1852) English
actor, stage manager GRB/1

GREEN, William (d 1816) actor,
manager CDP

GREEN, William A. (d 1917)
EA/18*

GREENBANK, Harry Hewetson
(1866-99) dramatist, librettist,
lyricist DD

GREENBANK, Percy (1878-1968)
English librettist, lyricist
WWT/5-14, WWW/6

GREENBANK, T. K. (fl 1832)
actor HAS

GREENBAUM, Hyam (b 1910)

English conductor, composer
WWT/8

GREENBERG, Ben (d 1972 [70])
manager BP/56*

GREENE, Mr. (d 1816) actor
HAS

GREENE, Mrs. [Miss Willems]
(d 1827) actress HAS

GREENE, Billy M. (d 1973 [76])
performer BP/58*

GREENE, Charles (d 1849) American actor HAS

GREENE, Mrs. Charles (d 1838)
American actress HAS

GREENE, Mrs. Charles C. see
Tiffany, Annie Ward

GREENE, Clay M. (1850-1933)
American dramatist DD, GRB/
2-4, SR, WWA/1, WWM,
WWS, WWT/1-7

GREENE, Edith Elizabeth see
Greene, Eric

GREENE, Elizabeth [Mrs. Paul
John Bedford] (d 1833) actress
CDP

GREENE, Emma Marie [Miss De
Braham] (d 1889) actress EA/
90*

GREENE, Eric [née Edith Eliza-
beth] (1876-1917) English actress
BE*

GREENE, Ethel Frances (b 1887)
English actress GRB/1

GREENE, Evie [Mrs. Richard
Temple, Jr.] (1876/87-1917)
English actress, singer CDP,
DD, GRB/1-4, WWS, WWT/1-3

GREENE, Gene (b 1881) American
vaudevillian WWM

GREENE, Mrs. Gene (d 1913)
EA/14*

GREENE, Graham (b 1904) English
dramatist AAS, BE, CB, CD,
COC, ES, HP, MD, MH,
MWD, OC/3, PDT, WWT/13-16

GREENE, G. W. (fl 1848) American actor HAS

GREENE, Herbert (b 1921) American producer, conductor, composer, actor BE

GREENE, H. Plunket (1865-1936)
Irish singer CDP, DNB, GRB/
1, WWW/3

GREENE, James (b 1926) American actor TW/22-25, 27-30

GREENE, Jeanne (d 1975 [69])
actress BP/59*, WWT/16*

GREENE, John (d 1860) American

actor, manager HAS

GREENE, Mrs. John [Anne Nuskay] (1800-62) American actress HAS

GREENE, Lorne (b 1915) Canadian actor BE, CB

GREENE, Marty (b 1909) American actor TW/25, 27

GREENE, Mary (d 1970) producer/director/choreographer BP/55*

GREENE, Maxine (b 1945) American actress TW/24

GREENE, Milton American musical director, actor, composer BE

GREENE, Norman (d 1945 [66]) actor, singer BE*, WWT/14*

GREENE, Patterson (1898-1968) American critic, dramatist BE, WWA/5

GREENE, Reuben (b 1938) American actor TW/24-27

GREENE, Richard (b 1946) American actor TW/28

GREENE, Robert (c. 1560-92) English dramatist COC, CP/1-3, DA, DD, DNB, ES, FGF, HP, MH, NTH, OC/1-3, PDT, RE

GREENE, Thomas (d c. 1612/14) comedian CDP, DA

GREENE, Walter (d 1963 [69]) journalist BE*

GREENE, William (d 1970 [43]) actor, executive TW/26

GREENER, Dorothy (1917-71) English actress BE, TW/16-19, 25, 28, WWT/15

GREENFIELD (fl 1790) dramatist CP/3

GREENFIELD, Elizabeth T. (1826-76) singer CDP, HAS

GREENFIELD, Felix (d 1974 [57]) performer BP/59*

GREENHILL, Mrs. Thomas see Richards, Mrs.

GREENHOUSE, Martha American actress TW/17-21, 25, 27-29

GREENLAW, Nora (d 1909) actress EA/10*

GREENLEAF, Raymond (1892-1963) American actor BE*

GREENLEES, Leslie M. (d 1975 [68]) critic BP/60*

GREENSHIELDS, Charles (d 1907 [61]) EA/08*

GREENSTREET, Sydney (1879/80-1954) English actor CB, SR, TW/10, WWM, WWT/9-11

GREENWALD, Joseph (c. 1878-1938) American actor SR, WWT/6-8

GREENWALD, Milton see Kidd, Michael

GREENWALL, Henry W. (1832-1913) manager SR

GREENWAY, Teresa [Mrs. George Prestwich] (d 1876) singer EA/77*

GREENWOOD, Anne [Mrs. Thomas Greenwood] (d 1882 [31]) actress EA/83*

GREENWOOD, Charlotte (b 1893) American actress BE, ES, TW/5-9, WWT/7-13

GREENWOOD, Ethel (d 1970 [72]) performer BP/55*

GREENWOOD, Jane (b 1934) English designer WWT/15-16

GREENWOOD, Joan (b 1919/21) English actress AAS, BE, CB, ES, TW/10-12, 23, WWT/11-16

GREENWOOD, Lyndon (b 1873) English actor, business manager GRB/1

GREENWOOD, Reginald Charles see Payne, Reginald

GREENWOOD, Thomas, Sr. (d 1797) English scene designer ES

GREENWOOD, Thomas (1779-1822) English scene artist DD, ES

GREENWOOD, Mrs. Thomas see Greenwood, Anne

GREENWOOD, Thomas Longdon (1806-79) manager, dramatist DD, ES

GREENWOOD, Tom (d 1909 [71]) showman EA/10*

GREENWOOD, Walter (1903-74) English dramatist AAS, BTR/74, WWT/10-15

GREENWOOD, William see McCoy, W.

GREER, Miss see Fletcher, Mrs.

GREER, Howard (d 1974 [78]) designer BP/58*

GREER, Michael (b 1943) American actor TW/26

GREET, Ben see Greet, Sir Philip Ben

GREET, Clare (1871-1939) actress

WWT/4-8

GREET, Maurice (d 1951 [70])
English actor BE*, BP/35*

GREET, Mildred C. (d 1964
[64]) actress BE*, BP/49*

GREET, Sir Philip Ben (1857-
1936) English actor, manager
AAS, COC, DD, DNB, EA/
96, ES, GRB/1-4, NTH,
OC/3, SR, WWS, WWT/1-8,
WWW/3

GREET, William (d 1914 [63])
manager WWT/14*

GREET, Mrs. William (fl 1890s)
dramatist DD

GREEVEN, Alix Augusta see
Greveen, Alice Augusta

GREEY, E. (d 1888 [52]) dramatist, manager EA/89*

GREG, Sir Walter Wilson (1875-
1959) English scholar DNB,
ES, HP, WWW/5

GREGG, Everley (1903-59)
English actress WWT/9-12

GREGG, Hubert (b 1914/16)
English actor, lyricist, composer WWT/8-16

GREGG, Julie (b 1944) American
actress TW/24

GREGG, Mitchell (b 1921) American actor TW/16-20

GREGG, Peter (b 1913) American
actor TW/2

GREGG, Robert (d 1909 [88])
EA/10*

GREGOR, Nora (d 1949) actress
BE*, WWT/14*

GREGORI, Mercia (b 1901) South
African actress WWT/6

GREGORY, Andre producer,
director WWT/16

GREGORY, Arthur William (d
1887) EA/88*

GREGORY, Lady Augusta (1852-
1932) Irish dramatist, director
COC, DNB, ES, HP, MH,
MWD, NTH, OC/1-3, PDT,
RE, WWT/1-4, WWW/3

GREGORY, Barnard (1796-1852)
actor, journalist DD

GREGORY, Bobby (d 1971 [71])
composer/lyricist BP/55*

GREGORY, Lady Charles see
Stirling, Mrs.

GREGORY, Dora (1872-1954)
English actress WWT/5-11

GREGORY, Elizabeth [Mrs. J.
C. Gregory] (d 1872 [42])

EA/73*

GREGORY, Fanny [Mrs. Thomas
Gregory] (d 1894) EA/95*

GREGORY, Frank (b 1884) English
manager WWT/7-10

GREGORY, George (d 1808) Irish
dramatist CP/3

GREGORY, Hilda (d 1917) actress
EA/18*

GREGORY, Jack (fl 1602) actor
DA

GREGORY, James (d 1912 [76])
manager EA/13*

GREGORY, James (b 1911) American actor BE, TW/6-12

GREGORY, Jay (b 1939) American
actor TW/23, 26

GREGORY, Mrs. J. C. see
Gregory, Elizabeth

GREGORY, John (d 1907 [61])
musical director EA/09*

GREGORY, Joseph (d 1882) proprietor EA/83*

GREGORY, Paul (b 1920) American producer, actor, talent
representative BE

GREGORY, Sara (b 1921) Australian actress, singer WWT/11-14

GREGORY, Susan (d 1970 [25])
assistant stage manager BP/
54*

GREGORY, Thomas (d 1899 [80])
showman EA/01*

GREGORY, Mrs. Thomas see
Gregory, Fanny

GREGORY, W. A. (b 1923)
American producer, director
BE

GREGORY, Walner (d 1911 [43])
manager EA/11*

GREGORY, Will (b 1928) Scottish
actor TW/23, 25-26

GREGSON, Frederick Holgate (d
1895) actor EA/97*

GREGSON, James R. (b 1889)
English dramatist, producer,
actor WWT/5-14

GREGSON, John (d 1975 [55])
actor BP/59*, WWT/16*

GREGSON, Michael see Craig,
Michael

GREHAN, Samuel (d 1880 [44])
comic singer EA/81*

GREIG, Andrew (d 1887) secretary
EA/88*

GREIG, Florence see St. John,
Florence

GREIG, George Taffey (d 1913

[34]) EA/14*

GREIN, J[acob] T[homas] (1862-
1935) Dutch critic COC, DD,
ES, GRB/1-4, NTH, OC/1-3,
WWT/1-7, WWW/3

GREIN, Mrs. J[acob] T[homas]
see Greveen, Alice Augusta

GRENE, David (b 1913) American educator BE

GRENEKER, Claude P. (d 1949
[68]) American press agent
TW/5

GRENFELL, Joyce Irene (b 1910)
English diseuse, actress AAS,
BE, CB, COC, OC/3, PDT,
TW/12, WWT/10-16

GRENICH, B. (fl 1840) dancer
HAS

GRENVILLE, Mr. (fl 1767)
actor HAS

GRENVILLE, Arthur actor EA/96

GRESAC, Mme. Fred French
dramatist WWT/1, 6-7

GRESHAM, Alfred (d 1912 [49])
actor EA/13*

GRESHAM, Edith American actress TW/4

GRESHAM, Herbert (d 1921 [68])
English actor, director BE*,
BP/5*, WWT/14*

GREVE, Dora singer CDP

GREVEEN, Alice Augusta
["Michael Orme"; Mrs. J.
T. Grein; Alix Augusta
Greeven] dramatist, producer,
translator GRB/2-4, WWT/
4-9

GREVILLE, Mr. (fl 1767) actor
WWA/H

GREVILLE, Mrs. (d 1802) actress CDP

GREVILLE, Mrs. Arthur see
Oram, Mona K.

GREVILLE, Clara (b 1792)
actress CDP

GREVILLE, Curtis (fl 1622-34)
actor DA

GREVILLE, Eden (fl 1891)
dramatist DD

GREVILLE, Sir Fulke, Lord
Brooke (1554-1628) English
dramatist CP/2-3, DD,
DNB, FGF, HP, RE

GREVILLE, Isabella (d 1882)
EA/83*

GREVILLE, Mabel [Mrs. W. H.
Webster] (b 1882) English
actress, singer GRB/1

GREVILLE, Lady Mercy see
Parson, Nancie

GREVILLE, Lady Violet (fl 1890-
94) dramatist DD

GREW, Mary (1902-71) English
actress WWT/6-15

GREY, Mr. (d 1884) EA/85*

GREY, Alice (1833-90) actress
CDP

GREY, Anne [née Aileen Ewing]
(b 1907) English actress WWT/8

GREY, Beryl (b 1925/27) English
dancer ES, WWT/11-12

GREY, Caroline Edith [Mrs. Lytton Grey] (d 1887) EA/88*

GREY, Charles Oscar (d 1885
[25]) EA/86*

GREY, Christian (b 1938) American
actor TW/29-30

GREY, Clifford (1887-1941) English
lyricist, dramatist, actor CB,
WWT/4-9, WWW/4

GREY, Edwin (d 1873 [39]) actor
EA/74*

GREY, Elise (d 1889 [32]) actress
EA/90*

GREY, Ellen Martha Colfield (d
1884) EA/85*

GREY, Eve English actress, singer
WWT/5

GREY, Frank Herbert (d 1951
[67]) composer, conductor BE*,
WWT/14*

GREY, Jane (1883-1944) American
actress SR, TW/1, WWM,
WWT/4-9

GREY, Jane Susan Mary (d 1899
[61]) actress EA/00*

GREY, Joel (b 1932) American
actor, singer, entertainer CB,
TW/12, 23-26, WWT/15-16

GREY, Katherine (1873-1950)
American actress GRB/3-4,
SR, TW/6, WWM, WWS, WWT/
1-10

GREY, Leonora see Egerton,
Mrs. Frank

GREY, Lily (d 1898) actress EA/
99*

GREY, Lytton (d 1931 [80]) actor
BE*, WWT/14*

GREY, Mrs. Lytton see Grey,
Caroline Edith

GREY, Marie de [Ellen Washington
Preston] (d 1897) actress BE*,
EA/98*, WWT/14*

GREY, Marion (d 1949 [74]) actress BE*

GREY, Mary (d 1974 [96]) actress BTR/74, WWT/4-11
GREY, Nina (d 1905 [25]) actress EA/06*
GREY, Stanley (fl 1891) singer, actor CDP
GREY, Sylvia (d 1958 [92]) actress, dancer DD, DP
GREY, William (d 1877) musician EA/78*
GRIBBIN, Daniel (d 1884) musical director, composer EA/85*
GRIBBLE, George Dunning (1882-1956) dramatist WWT/6-10
GRIBBLE, Harry Wagstaff (b 1896) English dramatist, producer, actor BE, CB, TW/2, 5, WWT/6-11
GRIBBLES, Fanny see Drew, Mrs. Frank Nelson
GRIBBON, Eddie T. (d 1965 [75]) performer BP/50*
GRIBBON, Harry (d 1961 [75]) American actor TW/1
GRIBOV, Alexei Nikolaevich (b 1902) Russian actor WWT/13-14
GRICE, C. E. (fl 1816?) American? dramatist EAP, RJ
GRICE, Wayne (b 1942) American actor TW/24
GRICE, W. H. (d 1896) singer EA/97*
GRIDLEY, James Lawrence (d 1901 [42]) actor, manager EA/03*
GRIEBLING, Otto (d 1972 [75]) performer BP/56*
GRIEG, Florence see St. John, Florence
GRIEG, Nordahl (1902-43) dramatist BE*
GRIERSON, Robert (b 1810) American actor HAS
GRIERSON, Thomas (fl 1827-28) English actor HAS
GRIESBACH, George Adolphus (d 1875 [74]) musician EA/76*
GRIESBACH, John Henry (d 1875) composer EA/76*
GRIEVE, John Henderson (1770-1845) English scene painter COC, DD, ES, OC/1-3
GRIEVE, Thomas (1799-1882) English scene artist COC, DD, DNB, ES, OC/1-3

GRIEVE, Thomas Walford (1841-82) English scene artist COC, ES, OC/1-3
GRIEVE, William (1800-44) English scene painter COC, DD, DNB, ES, OC/1-3
GRIFF [Henry Hadden Griffiths] (b 1864) English juggler, ventriloquist GRB/1
GRIFF, George (d 1916) EA/17*
GRIFFEN, Dr. Hamilton (d 1893) EA/94*
GRIFFIES, Ethel (1878-1975) English actress BE, CB, TW/4-7, 22-23, WWT/11-15
GRIFFIN (fl 1597) actor DA
GRIFFIN, Mr. (fl 17th cent) actor CDP
GRIFFIN, Arbid (d 1974 [60]) producer/director/choreographer BP/59*
GRIFFIN, Arthur (d 1953 [75]) American actor BE*, BP/37*
GRIFFIN, Benjamin (1680-1740) English actor, dramatist CDP, CP/1-3, DD, DNB, GT, TD/1-2
GRIFFIN, Elsie English actress, singer WWT/5-9
GRIFFIN, Fred Seeley (d 1904 [32]) music-hall comedian EA/05*
GRIFFIN, George (d 1875 [62]) equestrian tent maker EA/76*
GRIFFIN, Gerald (1803-40) Irish dramatist CDP, DD, DNB, HP
GRIFFIN, Gerald (d 1962 [70]) American actor, singer, songwriter BE*
GRIFFIN, G. W. H. (1829-79) American minstrel, manager CDP, HAS
GRIFFIN, Hayden (b 1930) American talent & literary representative BE
GRIFFIN, Hayden (b 1943) South African designer WWT/16
GRIFFIN, James Warren (d 1903) musician EA/04*
GRIFFIN, John David (d 1973 [45]) critic BP/58*
GRIFFIN, Norman (b 1887) Welsh actor, singer WWT/5-7
GRIFFIN, Mrs. Tony see Ralf, Emily
GRIFFIS, William (b 1917) American actor TW/22-23, 26, 30

GRIFFITH, Andy (b 1926) American actor BE, CB, ES, TW/12-17

GRIFFITH, David Wark (1875/ 80-1948) American director, dramatist ES, NTH, WWA/2, WWT/4-10

GRIFFITH, Donald M. (b 1947) American actor TW/29-30

GRIFFITH, Ed (b 1938) American actor TW/19

GRIFFITH, Elizabeth (1720?-93) dramatist, actress CDP, CP/2-3, DD

GRIFFITH, Frank Carlos (1851-1939) American actor, manager CDP, WWA/ 1

GRIFFITH, George H. (b 1822) English actor HAS

GRIFFITH, Mrs. George H. (fl 1854) actress HAS

GRIFFITH, Hubert (1896-1953) English critic, dramatist COC, OC/1-3, WWT/5-11

GRIFFITH, Hugh (b 1912) Welsh actor AAS, BE, TW/8, 19, WWT/11-16

GRIFFITH, John (b 1868/69) Canadian actor SR, WWA/5

GRIFFITH, Linda (d 1949 [65]) actress BE*

GRIFFITH, Lydia Elizabeth (1832-97) actress COC

GRIFFITH, Peter (b 1933) American actor TW/3

GRIFFITH, Raymond (d 1957 [70]) actor, producer BE*

GRIFFITH, Richard (d 1788) dramatist CP/3, DD

GRIFFITH, Richard (d 1969 [57]) critic BP/54*

GRIFFITH, Robert E. (d 1961 [54]) American producer, stage manager, actor TW/18

GRIFFITH, Samuel (d 1883) equestrian EA/84*

GRIFFITH, Thomas (d 1744 [63]) actor WWT/14*

GRIFFITHS, Mr. (d c. 1804) prompter, actor TD/1-2

GRIFFITHS, Mrs. (d 1895 [75]) EA/96*

GRIFFITHS, Derek (b 1946) English actor WWT/16

GRIFFITHS, Doris (b 1970 [68]) performer BP/54*

GRIFFITHS, Dorothy see Scott, Dorothy

GRIFFITHS, Elizabeth (fl 1765-79) dramatist GT, TD/1-2

GRIFFITHS, George H. (d 1888 [65]) actor EA/89*

GRIFFITHS, Henry Hadden see Griff

GRIFFITHS, James (d 1850) actor HAS

GRIFFITHS, Jane (b 1930) English actress WWT/12-15

GRIFFITHS, Joe (d 1901 [49]) music-hall acrobat, clown EA/02*

GRIFFITHS, John (d 1880 [59]) equestrian clown EA/81*

GRIFFITHS, R. (d 1877) music-hall musical director EA/79*

GRIFFITHS, Robert (d 1881 [69]) musician EA/82*

GRIFFITHS, Tom see Clarke, Thomas

GRIFFITHS, Trevor (b 1935) English dramatist WWT/16

GRIFFITHS, W. H. (d 1923) manager WWT/14*

GRIFFITHS, William (d 1908 [77]) musician EA/09*

GRIGAS, John (b 1930) American actor TW/27-29

GRIGGS, John (1908-58) American actor TW/9, 23

GRILLO, John (b 1942) English dramatist, actor CD

GRIMALD, Nicholas (1519-62) English dramatist CP/3, DD

GRIMALDI, Denis (b 1947) American actor TW/27

GRIMALDI, George H. (d 1951 [58]) dramatist BE*, WWT/14*

GRIMALDI, Giuseppe (1713-88) ballet master COC, DD

GRIMALDI, Joseph (1778-1837) English clown BS, CDP, COC, DD, DNB, ES, HP, NTH, OC/1-3, OX, PDT, TD/1-2

GRIMALDI, Joseph Samuel (1802-63) clown CDP, COC, DD, DNB, ES, GT

GRIMALDI, Marion (b 1926) English actress, singer WWT/15-16

GRIMALDI, Nicolini Italian composer, director? CP/1

GRIMANI, Miss (fl 1803) actress TD/2

GRIMANI, Cecilia (fl 1822?) actress CDP

GRIMANI, Julia [Mrs. Charles Wayne Young] (d 1806 [21])

actress BE*, WWT/14*

GRIMBALL, Elizabeth Berkeley
(d 1953) American producer
WWA/3

GRIME, Edward (d 1907 [50])
proprietor EA/08*

GRIMES, Mr. (fl 1712) dramatist CP/2-3

GRIMES, Arthur (fl 1625-26)
actor DA

GRIMES, Daryl (b 1931) American actor TW/12

GRIMES, Frank (b 1947) Irish
actor TW/26

GRIMES, Margaret (d 1912) EA/
13*

GRIMES, Tammy (b 1934) Amer-
ican actress, singer AAS,
BE, CB, TW/12-21, 24, 26,
WWT/14-16

GRIMM, Harry E. (d 1970 [72])
performer BP/55*

GRIMSHAW, Nicholas (d 1970
[69]) performer BP/55*

GRIMSTON, Charles W. see
Garthorne, C. W.

GRIMSTON, Dorothy May English
actress GRB/3-4, WWT/1-5

GRIMSTON, Harold Robertson
(d 1930) conductor WWT/14*

GRIMSTON, William, Lord
Viscount (c. 1692-1756) Irish?
dramatist CP/1-3, GT

GRIMSTON, William Hunter
see Kendal, William Hunter

GRIMWOOD, Herbert (1875-1929)
English actor GRB/2-4,
WWT/1-7

GRINDALL, Annie Elizabeth
[Mrs. Harry E. Grindall]
(d 1883) EA/84*

GRINDALL, Mrs. Harry E.
see Grindall, Annie Elizabeth

GRINDALL, Henry Rupert (d
1905 [57]) EA/06*

GRINDALL, William (d 1879
[74]) costumier EA/80*

GRINER, Barbara (b 1934)
American producer, theatre
owner BE

GRINER, Geunie (d 1975 [47])
performer BP/60*

GRINGLE, Arthur E. (fl 1900s)
American actor, editor,
reader, lecturer WWM

GRISDALE, Walter (d 1883 [59])
actor EA/84*

GRISEL, Louis Racine (b 1849)

American actor WWS

GRISI, Carlotta (1819-99) Italian
dancer, singer CDP, ES,
OC/1-2

GRISI, Giuditta (1805-40) Italian
singer ES

GRISI, Guilia (1811-69) Italian
singer CDP, ES, HAS, SR

GRISMAN, Sam H. producer,
manager WWT/9-11

GRISMER, Joseph Rhode (1849-
1922) American actor, dramatist, manager CDP, GRB/3-4,
SR, WWA/1, WWM, WWS,
WWT/1-4

GRIST, Mr. actor TD/1-2

GRIST, Harriet (fl 1792) actress
CDP

GRIST, Thomas (fl 18th cent)
author CDP

GRIST, William (1840-96) librettist, dramatist DD

GRISWOLD, Gertrude (c. 1860-
1912) American singer SR

GRISWOLD, Grace (d 1927 [55])
American actress, dramatist
GRB/4, WWM, WWT/1-5

GRIZZARD, George (b 1928)
American actor AAS, BE,
CB, TW/11-26, 28-30, WWT/
14-16

GROCE, [Catherine?] see
Barre, Mrs. [Joseph?]

GROCK [Adrien Wettach] (1880-
1959) Swiss clown COC,
NTH, OC/2-3, PDT, TW/16

GRODIN, Charles (b 1935) American actor, director TW/19,
27, WWT/16

GROENINGS, Franz (d 1902 [63])
musical director EA/03*

GROH, David (b 1939) American
actor TW/30

GROODY, Louise (1897-1961)
American actress, singer TW/
18, WWT/6-11

GROOM, Philip (d 1917 [26])
dancer, ballet master EA/18*

GROOME, Reginald (b 1861) Irish
singer GRB/1

GROOME, Mrs. Samuel W. see
Haslam, Maud

GROOMS, Red painter CD

GROPPER, Milton Herbert (1896/
97-1955) American dramatist
WWT/6-11

GROS, Edward (d 1901 [19]) EA/
02*

GROS, Eugene (d 1902 [23])
EA/03*

GROS, Henri (d 1910 [60])
music-hall managing director
EA/11*

GROS, Mrs. Henri see Gros,
Isabella

GROS, Isabella [Mrs. Henri Gros]
(d 1909 [61]) EA/10*

GROS, Louise (d 1902 [81])
EA/03*

GROSBARD, Ulu (b 1929) Belgian director BE, WWT/
15-16

GROSBAYNE, Benjamin (d 1976
[82]) critic BP/60*

GROSETTE, Henry William (fl
1810) dramatist CP/3

GROSHON, Belinda (d 1822) English actress HAS

GROSS, Edward (b 1897) American producer TW/2

GROSS, Edwin (d 1866) comedian
HAS

GROSS, Gene (b 1920) American
actor TW/24-26

GROSS, Jesse (b 1929) American
theatre reporter BE

GROSS, Seymour (d 1970 [56])
stage manager, actor BP/54*

GROSS, Shelly (b 1921) American
producer BE, WWT/16

GROSSI, Mlle. (d 1873) singer
EA/75*

GROSSI, Enrico (1828-66) Italian
singer HAS

GROSSKURTH, Kurt (d 1975 [66])
performer BP/60*

GROSSMAN, George (d 1972 [67])
publicist BP/56*

GROSSMAN, Suzanne Swiss actress TW/22, 24-26

GROSSMITH, Mrs. (d 1882)
EA/83*

GROSSMITH, Ena (1896-1944)
English actress WWT/4-9

GROSSMITH, George (d 1880)
reader, entertainer, dramatist
DD

GROSSMITH, George, Sr. (1847-
1912) English actor CDP,
COC, DD, DNB, DP, EA/95,
ES, GRB/1-4, OC/1-3, OAA/
2, PDT, SR, WWM, WWT/1,
WWW/1

GROSSMITH, George, Jr. (1874-
1935) English actor, dramatist
CDP, COC, DD, DNB, ES,

GRB/1-4, OC/1-3, PDT, WWS,
WWT/1-7, WWW/3

GROSSMITH, Mrs. George see
Astor, Adelaide

GROSSMITH, Mrs. George see
Grossmith, Rosa

GROSSMITH, Lawrence (1877-1944)
English actor COC, ES, GRB/
1-4, OC/1-3, WWS, WWT/1-9

GROSSMITH, Rosa [Mrs. George
Grossmith] (d 1905 [57]) EA/06*

GROSSMITH, Weedon (1852-1919)
English actor COC, DD, DNB,
DP, EA/95, GRB/1-4, OC/1-3,
PDT, WWM, WWS, WWT/1-3,
WWW/2

GROSSMITH, Mrs. Weedon see
Palfrey, May Lever

GROSSMITH, William Robert (b
c. 1827) actor CDP

GROSVENOR, Annie (d 1891) music-
hall performer EA/92*

GROSVENOR, Henry (d 1892) EA/
93*

GROSVENOR, Joseph (fl 1840-57)
English actor HAS

GROSVENOR, Laura (d 1879)
singer EA/80*

GROSVENOR, William H. see
Hamilton, William Henry

GROTO, Luigi (1541-85) Italian
dramatist COC

GROTOWSKI, Jerzy (b 1933) Polish
director CB, COC

GROUT, James David (b 1927)
English actor, director TW/21,
30, WWT/15-16

GROUT, Philip (b 1930) English
director WWT/15-16

GROVE, Mr. (fl 1793-1803) actor
CDP, GT, TD/2

GROVE, Miss (fl 1837) Scottish
actress HAS

GROVE, Miss see Yarnold, Mrs.
Edwin

GROVE, Florence C. (d 1902)
dramatist DD

GROVE, Fred [F. Grove Palmer]
(1851-1927) English actor
GRB/1, 4, WWT/1-5

GROVE, Sir George (d 1900 [80])
director of the Royal College of
Music EA/01*

GROVE, Joseph (d 1764) publisher
CP/2-3

GROVE, W. (fl 1782) dramatist
CP/3

GROVER, Edward (b 1932) American actor TW/22

GROVER, J. Holmes (b 1838)
American dramatist, actor
DD

GROVER, Leonard (1835-1926)
American actor, manager,
dramatist CDP, HAS, SR

GROVER, Leonard, Jr. (1859-
1947) actor SR

GROVER, Myrtle (d 1970) performer BP/55*

GROVER, Russell singer, actor
CDP

GROVER, Stanley (b 1926) American actor, singer BE, TW/
17-20, 23-24, 26-28, 30

GROVES, Charles (1843-1909)
Irish actor DD, GRB/1-4,
OAA/2

GROVES, Charles (1875-1955)
English actor WWT/5-11

GROVES, Eliza [née Smith] (fl
1834) American actress HAS

GROVES, Fred (1880-1955) English actor WWT/6-11

GROVES, John (d 1887 [70])
property master EA/88*

GROVES, Johnny (d 1912) comedian EA/13*

GROVES, Richard (d 1879 [21])
property master EA/80*

GROVES, Walter (d 1906 [41])
comedian EA/07*

GRUBB, John (fl 1795) share-
holder TD/1-2

GRUBB, Lily (d 1890) American
actress, singer CDP

GRUBE, Carl (b 1866) German
actor, stage manager GRB/4,
WWT/1-2

GRUBE, Max (d 1934 [80]) actor,
dramatist BE*, WWT/14*

GRUENBERG, Louis (1884-1964)
Russian/American composer
HJD

GRUET, Allan (b 1945) American
actor TW/27-28

GRUN, Bernard (1901-72) Czech
composer, conductor WWT/
10-14

GRÜNDGENS, Gustaf (1899-1963)
German actor, producer COC,
OC/3

GRUNDMAN, Clare (b 1913)
American composer, actor
BE

GRUNDY, Lily English actress
GRB/3-4, WWT/1-5

GRUNDY, Sydney (1848-1914) Eng-
lish dramatist COC, DD, ES,
GRB/1-4, MH, NTH, OC/1-3,
SR, WWM, WWS, WWT/1-2,
WWW/1

GRUNEISEN, Charles Lewis (1806-
79) English critic, director
DNB

GRUNWALD, Alfred (d 1951 [67])
Austrian librettist BE*, BP/35*

GRUSKIN, George (d 1975 [65])
agent BP/60*

GRUVER, Elbert A. (d 1962 [57])
stage manager BE*

GRYMES, Anthony (fl 1628) actor
DA

GRYMES, Thomas (fl 1600-01)
member of the Chapel Royal
DA

GRYMMESBY, John (fl 1423)
member of the Chapel Royal
DA

GRYNES (fl 1633) actor DA

GRYZBOWSKI, Walter (d 1976
[58]) personal manager BP/60*

GUALANDI, Antonio see "Campioli"

GUARALDI, Vince (d 1976 [47])
composer/lyricist BP/60*

GUARD, Kit (d 1961 [67]) actor
BE*

GUARD, William J. (d 1932 [70])
Irish press representative BE*,
BP/16*

GUARDINO, Harry (b 1925) American actor BE, ES, TW/20,
23-24

GUARE, John (b 1938) American
dramatist AAS, CD, WWT/16

GUARINI, Giovanni Battista (1537-
1612) Italian dramatist OC/1-3

GUARRINO, Sig. (d 1876) ballet
master EA/77*

GUBER, Lee (b 1920) American
producer BE, WWT/16

GUEDALLA, Mrs. Herbert see
Hanbury, Lily

GUEDEN, Hilde (b 1923) Austrian
singer CB

GUENTHER, Dorothee (d 1975
[79]) producer/director/chore-
ographer BP/60*

GUENTHER, Ruth (d 1974 [64])
performer BP/59*

GUERIN, Michael (d 1884) agent
EA/85*

GUERINT, Sebastian Francis (d
1870 [79]) acting manager

EA/71*

GUERITE, Laura (fl 1900?) singer, actress CDP

GUERRABELLA, Mme. (fl 1859-62) singer HAS

GUERRERO, Danny (b 1945) American actor TW/24, 27-29

GUERRERO, Maria (1868-1928) Spanish actress GRB/2-4

GUEST, Christopher Haden (b 1948) American actor TW/26, 28-30

GUEST, Ellis (fl 1625-34) actor DA

GUEST, James W. (d 1879) American? prompter EA/80*

GUEST, Jean H. (b 1921) American executive BE

GUEST, Rosa Annie (d 1908 [58]) EA/09*

GUETARY, Georges [né Lambros Worloou] (b 1917) Egyptian actor, singer WWT/11-15

GUETTEL, Henry (b 1928) American producer BE

GUGGISBERG, Mrs. see Moore, Decima

GUHLKE, Antoinette (b 1925) American actress TW/5

GUIDERY, Mrs. James see De Stainer, Marguerite

GUIDI, Sig. (d 1857) singer HAS

GUIDI, Clementina Noel (b 1841) Italian singer HAS

GUIDO, Frank [Richard Delany] (d 1893) musician EA/94*

GUILBERT, Ann (b 1928) American actress TW/16

GUILBERT, Yvette [Mrs. Max Schiller] (1868/69-1944) French singer CDP, COC, GRB/1-4, NTH, OC/1-3, SR, WWA/4, WWM, WWS, WWT/1-9, WWW/4

GUILFORD, Earl of see North, Francis

GUILFOYLE, Paul (d 1961 [58]) American actor, director BE*

GUILLAMORE, Joseph (d 1890) EA/91*

GUILLAUME, Robert (b 1937) American actor TW/29-30

GUILLAUME, Umberto see Antonet

GUILLEMEN, Louis Charles [Jean Bond] (d 1870) antipodean artist EA/71*

GUILMAN, Robert (fl 1628-29)

actor DA

GUILMETTE, Charles (fl 1856) singer CDP

GUINAN, Texas (d 1933) American actress BE*, BP/18*

GUINARD, John [Henry Barnard] (d 1883 [26]) singer EA/84*

GUINNESS, Sir Alec (b 1914) English actor AAS, BE, CB, COC, ES, OC/2-3, PDT, TW/6-9, 20-21, WWT/9-16

GUINNESS, Arthur D'Esterre (d 1893) actor EA/94*

GUION, Daniel (d 1896 [39]) EA/97*

GUION, John (d 1906) EA/08*

GUION, Netta (fl 1892) actress CDP

GUION, Raymond see Raymond, Gene

GUITERMAN, Arthur (1871-1943) dramatist CB

GUITRY, Lucien-Germain (1860-1925) French actor GRB/1-4, NTH, WWT/2, 4

GUITRY, Sacha (1885-1957) Russian dramatist, actor, manager COC, NTH, OC/1-3, TW/14, WWT/8-12

GUITRY, Yvonne Printemps (b 1895) French actress OC/2-3

GUITTARD, Laurence (b 1939) American actor TW/29-30

GUITTON, Frances Eleanor [Mrs. Jules Guitton] (d 1881 [48]) EA/82*

GUITTON, Jean (d 1973 [86]) dramatist BP/57*

GUITTON, Mrs. Jules see Guitton, Frances Eleanor

GUIVER, James (d 1894) actor EA/96*

GULBRANDSEN, Charles (d 1974 [83]) designer BP/58*

GULLAN, Campbell (d 1939) Scottish actor, producer WWT/3-9

GULLIFER, A. F. (d 1916) EA/17*

GULLIVER, Charles (1882-1961) English manager WWT/4-10

GULLIVER, Joseph Henry (d 1884) Negro comedian EA/86*

GULLY, John (1783-1863) boxer CDP

GUMBERT, Ferdinand (d 1896 [78]) composer, critic EA/97*

GUMM, Mary Jane see Gumm, Suzanne

GUMM, Suzanne [Mrs. Jack Cathcart; née Mary Jane Gumm] (d 1964 [48]) performer BE*

GUNDUNAS, Lewis (b 1930) American actor TW/25

GUNDY, George (d 1880) manager EA/81*

GUNG'L, Josef (d 1889 [78]) composer, conductor EA/90*

GUNN, Miss see Wulfries, Mrs.

GUNN, Archie (b 1863) English artist, designer WWM

GUNN, Haidee (1882/83-1961) English actress GRB/1-4, WWT/1-7

GUNN, James (d 1895) EA/96*

GUNN, John (d 1878 [46]) actor? EA/79*

GUNN, John (d 1909 [38]) proprietor, manager EA/10*, WWT/14*

GUNN, Mrs. John see Gunn, Mary Frances

GUNN, Judy (b 1914) English actress WWT/8-11

GUNN, Mary Frances [Mrs. John Gunn] (d 1894) EA/95*

GUNN, Mary Louise see Arnot, Louise

GUNN, Michael (d 1901 [61]) proprietor, manager EA/02*, WWT/14*

GUNN, Michael Louis (d 1886 [19]) EA/87*

GUNN, Moses (b 1929) American actor, director TW/23-28, WWT/15-16

GUNN, Vincenetta (b 1944) American actress TW/29

GUNNELL, John (b 1911) American educator, director BE

GUNNELL, Richard (d 1634) English actor, dramatist, manager DA, FGF, OC/1-3

GUNNING, Miss (fl 1803) dramatist CP/3

GUNNING, Mrs. J. see Campbell, Miss

GUNNING, Louise (1879-1960) actress, singer TW/17, WWT/1-5

GUNTER, Archibald Clavering (1847-1907) English dramatist CDP, DAB, DD, GRB/3, HJD, SR, WWA/1, WWW/1

GURIE, Sigrid (d 1969 [58])

performer BP/54*

GURIN, Ellen (d 1972 [24]) performer BP/57*

GURN, James C. see Marlowe, James C.

GURNER, Mrs. (fl 1834-37) English actress SR

GURNETT, Ursula (fl 1890s?) singer CDP

GURNEY, A. R., Jr. (b 1930) American dramatist CD

GURNEY, Claud (1897-1946) English producer WWT/9

GURNEY, Dennis (b 1897) English actor, director BE

GURNEY, Edmund (d 1925 [73]) actor BE*, BP/9*, WWT/14*

GURNEY, Rachel English actress WWT/13-16

GURTLER, Arnold B., Jr. executive BE

GUSS, Louis (b 1918) American actor BE, TW/18-19, 24-25, 27-28

GUSTAFSON, Carol (b 1925) American actress BE

GUSTAFSON, William (b 1887) American singer WWA/1

GUSTAVE, George (d 1896) Ethiopian minstrel EA/97*

GUTHERIE, Thomas Anstey see Anstey, F.

GUTHRIE, Lady (d 1972 [67]) dramatist BP/57*

GUTHRIE, Robert Graham (d 1898) EA/99*

GUTHRIE, Thomas J. (d 1899 [32]) actor, sketch artist EA/00*

GUTHRIE, Sir Tyrone (1900-71) English producer, actor, director, dramatist AAS, BE, CB, COC, ES, NTH, OC/1-3, PDT, TW/27, WWA/5, WWT/7-15

GUTHRIE, William (d 1885 [53]) acting manager EA/86*

GUTSKOW, Karl (d 1878 [67]) dramatist, singer EA/80*

GUTTMANN, Jean see Babilée, Jean

GUTZKOW, Karl Ferdinand (1811-78) German dramatist OC/2-3

GUY, Cooper (d 1887 [34]) EA/88*

GUY, George G. (d 1872 [33]) box-keeper EA/73*

GUY, Horace (d 1900 [34]) actor EA/01*

GUY, John William (d 1902 [32])

music-hall stage manager
EA/03*

GUY, W. E. (d 1876 [65]) actor
EA/77*

GUYNES, Charles (d 1971 [37])
dramatist BP/56*

GUYON, Albert (d 1913 [45])
EA/14*

GUZMAN, Richard (d 1972 [29])
performer BP/57*

GWALTER, William (fl 1622-23)
lessee DA

GWENN, Edmund (1875-1959)
Welsh actor CB, ES, GRB/
4, NTH, TW/2-7, 16, WWT/
1-11

GWENN, Mrs. Edmund see
Terry, Minnie

GWENT, Gwilym (d 1891) composer CDP

GWILLIM, Jack (b 1915) English
actor TW/28, 30

GWILYM, Mike (b 1949) Welsh
actor WWT/16

GWINNE, Matthew (d 1627/39)
dramatist CP/2-3, FGF

GWINNET, Richard (d 1717) English dramatist CP/2-3, GT

GWYNN, Michael (1916-76) English actor WWT/12-16

GWYNN, Nell (1650-87) English
actress CDP, COC, DD,
DNB, ES, GT, NTH, OC/
1-3, PDT

GWYNNE, Emma [Mrs. Edward
Sass] actress CDP

GWYNNE, Fanny (fl 1864-71)
actress DD

GWYNNE, Fred (b 1926) American actor TW/8, 29-30,
WWT/16

GWYNNE, Jack (d 1969 [74])
performer BP/54*

GWYNNE, Jennie [Mrs. Arthur
Rodney] (d 1889) actress
EA/90*

GWYNNE, Julia (d 1934 [78])
actress DD

GWYNNE, Nell (d 1903 [34])
serio-comic CDP

GWYTHER, Geoffrey Matheson
(1890-1944) actor, singer,
composer WWT/6-9

GYDE, Margaret (d 1909) EA/
10*

GYE, Frederick (d 1869 [88])
manager WWT/14*

GYE, Frederick (1810-78) English

proprietor, director CDP, DNB

GYLLOME, Foke (fl 1581) actor
DA

GYNGELL, G. ? (d 1833) magician
CDP

GYNT, Greta (b 1916) Norwegian
actress, dancer WWT/9-13

GYRDLER, Russell (fl 1598) member of the Children of Paul's
DA

GYRKE, Richard (fl 1550) actor
DA

- H -

H. , C. (fl 1800) dramatist CP/3

H. , Eleanor (fl 1803) dramatist
CP/3

H. , W. (fl 1737) dramatist CP/3

HAAGA, Agnes (b 1916) American
educator BE

HAAS, Dolly (b 1910) German actress BE

HAAS, Hugo (b 1902) Czech actor
TW/5

HAAS, Mabel (fl 1885?) singer
CDP

HABBERTON, John (1842-1921)
American? dramatist WWW/2

HABELMANN, Theodore (fl 1864)
German singer CDP

HABERFIELD, Graham (d 1975
[34]) performer BP/60*

HABERSTROTH, Alex (d 1973 [67])
producer/director/choreographer
BP/58*

HABINGTON, William (1605-54)
English dramatist CP/1-3,
DNB, FGF, HP

HACHE, Mlle. [Julia Wideman]
(d 1892) actress EA/93*

HACK, Signe (d 1973 [74]) performer BP/57*

HACKER, Maria (d 1963) actress
BE*

HACKET, Dr. John (1592-1670)
English dramatist CP/2-3,
FGF

HACKETT, Albert (b 1900) American dramatist, actor BE,
HJD, MWD

HACKETT, Arthur (1884-1969)
American singer WWA/5

HACKETT, Buddy (b 1924) American actor BE, CB, TW/21-22,
24

HACKETT, Charles (1889-1942)

American singer CB, WWA/1
HACKETT, Charles M. (d 1970 [61]) journalist BP/55*
HACKETT, Clara C. [Mrs. James Henry Hackett, II] (1834-1909) actress CDP
HACKETT, Florence (d 1954 [72]) actress BE*
HACKETT, Hal (1924-67) American actor TW/13-16, 24
HACKETT, James Henry (1800-71) American actor, manager CDP, COC, DAB, ES, HAS, NTH, OC/1-3, SR, WWA/H
HACKETT, Mrs. James Henry [Catharine Lee Sugg] (1797-1848) actress CDP, COC, HAS, OC/3
HACKETT, Mrs. James Henry, II see Hackett, Clara C.
HACKETT, James Ketelas (1869-1926) Canadian actor, manager CDP, COC, DAB, GRB/2-4, OC/1-3, PP/1, SR, WWA/1, WWM, WWS, WWT/1-5
HACKETT, Mrs. James Ketelas see Mannering, Mary
HACKETT, Joan American actress BE, TW/17-21, 26, 28-29
HACKETT, Lillian (d 1973) performer BP/57*
HACKETT, Maria (d 1874 [91]) EA/75*
HACKETT, Norman Honore (b 1874) Canadian actor GRB/3-4, WWT/1-6
HACKETT, Raymond (1902-57) American actor TW/2, 15, WWT/6-9
HACKETT, Walter (1876-1944) American dramatist COC, SR, WWT/3-9, WWW/4
HACKMAN, Gene (b 1931) American actor CB, TW/24
HACKMAN, William H. (d 1973 [62]) performer BP/58*
HACKNEY, Mabel [Mrs. Laurence Irving] (d 1914) actress GRB/3-4, WWT/1-2
HACKURT, Mr. (fl 1844) actor HAS
HACKURT, Mrs. (fl 1846) actress HAS
HACON, Harry (d 1892) sketch artist EA/93*
HADAWAY, Polly (fl 1836) actress HAS

HADAWAY, Mrs. Thomas [Lucy Bertram] (d 1834) actress, singer HAS, SR
HADAWAY, Thomas H. (1801-92) English actor CDP, HAS, SR
HADDOCK, J. (d 1887 [65]) treasurer EA/88*
HADDON, Archibald (1871-1942) English critic WWT/4-9, WWW/4
HADDON, Peter (1898-1962) English actor WWT/5-13
HADDRICK, Ron (b 1929) Australian actor AAS, WWT/14-16
HADFIELD, Annie [Mrs. Samuel Hadfield] (d 1912 [58]) EA/13*
HADFIELD, James (1772-1841) lunatic/assassin CDP
HADFIELD, Mrs. Samuel see Hadfield, Annie
HADGE, Michael (b 1932) American actor TW/22-24, 26, 28-29
HADING, Jane [Jeanette Hadingue] (1859-1933) French actress CDP, GRB/1, 3-4, SR, WWA/4, WWT/1-3
HADING, Jane [Jeanne Alfredine Trefouret] (d 1941 [81]) French actress BE*, WWT/14*
HADINGUE, Jeanette see Hading, Jane
HADLEY, Henry Kimball (1871-1937) American composer, conductor DAB, ES
HADLEY, Reed (d 1974 [63]) performer BP/59*
HADWIN, Ann [Mrs. G. H. George] (d 1877 [58]) actress EA/78*
HAEMANN, F. W. (d 1899) conjuror EA/00*
HAERTING, Edward (fl 1866) manager CDP
HAFFNER, Frank see Heywood, Charles
HAGAN, James B. (1888-1947) American actor, dramatist, manager SR
HAGAN, John (d 1887 [28]) music-hall proprietor EA/89*
HAGEMAN, Larry see Hagman, Larry
HAGEMAN, Richard (1882-1966) Dutch composer, conductor WWA/4
HAGEN, Reigh (b 1936) American actor TW/26
HAGEN, Uta (b 1919) German actress AAS, BE, CB, ES, TW/1, 3-17, 19-20, 24, WWT/10-16

HAGEN, Mrs. Warner see
Woodward, Grace
HAGENBECK, Carl (d 1887 [78])
EA/88*
HAGGAR, Charles (d 1904 [87])
lion tamer EA/05*
HAGGAR, Sarah [Mrs. W. Hag-
gar] (d 1909 [58]) EA/10*
HAGGAR, Mrs. W. see Haggar,
Sarah
HAGGARD, Stephen (1911-43)
Guatemalan actor AAS, COC,
WWT/8-9
HAGGIN, Ben Ali (1882-1951)
American scene designer
NTH, TW/8
HAGGITT, Rev. John (fl 1794)
dramatist CP/3
HAGGOTT, John Cecil (d 1964
[50]) American producer,
director BE*, BP/49*
HAGLEY, Miss (fl 1788) actress
TD/1-2
HAGMAN, Larry [Hageman] (b
1931) American actor TW/
7-8, 15-20
HAGUE, Albert (b 1920) German
composer BE, WWT/15-16
HAGUE, Charles (1769-1821)
music professor CDP
HAGUE, Clarence [James M.
Hague] Welsh actor GRB/1-3
HAGUE, James M. see Hague,
Clarence
HAGUE, Mary (d 1894) EA/95*
HAGUE, Pauline (b 1884) English
actress, singer GRB/1
HAGUE, Mrs. Sam (d 1879)
EA/80*
HAGUE, Samuel (1829-1901) Eng-
lish clog dancer, manager,
minstrel CDP, HAS
HAID, Charles (b 1943) American
actor TW/28
HAIG, Emma (1898-1939) Amer-
ican actress, singer WWT/
6-8
HAIG, Peter (b 1939) American
actor TW/26
HAIGH, Mme. (d 1899) singer
EA/00*
HAIGH, Henry (b 1832) English
singer CDP, HAS, SR
HAIGH, Kenneth (b 1932) English
actor AAS, BE, TW/14-17,
24, PDT, WWT/13-16
HAIGH, Winter singer, minstrel
CDP

HAIGH, Mrs. Winter (d 1890 [53])
EA/91*
HAIGHT, George (b 1905) American
producer, dramatist BE, WWT/
9
HAILES, Lord (1726-92) Scottish
dramatist CP/3
HAILEY, Marion (b 1941) Ameri-
can actress TW/23-24, 26-29
HAILEY, Oliver (b 1932) American
dramatist CD, WWT/15-16
HAIM, Matti (d 1967 [56]) per-
former BP/52*
HAINES, A. Larry (b 1917) Amer-
ican actor TW/22-23, 25-29
HAINES, Edmund (d 1974 [59])
composer/lyricist BP/59*
HAINES, Herbert E. (1880-1923)
English composer, conductor
WWT/2-4
HAINES, John Thomas (1799?-
1843) actor, dramatist CDP,
DNB
HAINES, Joseph (d 1701) English
actor CDP, COC, CP/1-3,
DNB, ES, GT, OC/1-3
HAINES, Mervyn, Jr. (b 1933)
American actor TW/25-27
HAINES, Rhea (d 1964 [69])
actress BE*
HAINES, Robert Terrel (1870-1943)
American actor GRB/3-4, SR,
WWA/5, WWM, WWS, WWT/1-9
HAINES, William (d 1973 [73])
performer BP/58*
HAINES, Mrs. William see
Austa, Amber
HAINES, William Wister (b 1908)
American dramatist BE, MWD
HAIRE, Wilson John (b 1932) Irish
dramatist CD
HAITE, J. J. (d 1874) composer
EA/75*
HAIZINGER, Amalie (1800-84)
German singer, actress ES
HAJOS, Mitzi (b 1891) Hungarian
actress CDP, TW/2-3, WWM,
WWT/9-11
HALASZ, Laszlo (b 1905) Hungarian
musical director CB
HALDON, Lady English actress
GRB/1
HALE (fl 17th cent) piper CDP
HALE, Mr. (d 1746?) actor TD/
1-2
HALE, Alan (1892-1950) American
actor TW/6
HALE, Barnaby (d 1964 [37])

performer BP/49*

HALE, Binnie [Beatrice Mary Hale-Munro] (b 1899) English actress, singer WWT/4-14

HALE, Charles B. (1819-76) English actor CDP, HAS

HALE, Mrs. Charles B. (1830-65) English actress HAS

HALE, Dorothy (d 1938 [33]) American actress BE*, BP/23*

HALE, Edward Everett, III (d 1953 [46]) American actor BE*

HALE, Frank (d 1972 [72]) theatre owner BP/57*

HALE, George (d 1956 [55]) American choreographer TW/13

HALE, Helen (fl 1902-07) American actress WWS

HALE, John (fl 1852) actor HAS

HALE, John (d 1947 [88]) actor, manager SR, TW/3

HALE, John (b 1926) English dramatist, director CD

HALE, J. Robert (1874-1940) English actor, singer CDP, WWT/2-9

HALE, Lionel (b 1909) English critic, dramatist WWT/8-16

HALE, Louise [née Closser; Mrs. Walter Hale] (1872-1933) American actress, dramatist DAB, GRB/3-4, NTH, OC/1-3, WWA/1, WWM, WWT/1-7

HALE, Malcolm (d 1968 [27]) performer BP/53*

HALE, Mary Beale (fl 1860) actress HAS

HALE, Norman (d 1916 [26]) entertainer EA/17*

HALE, Philip (1854-1934) American critic DAB, WWA/1

HALE, Randolph (d 1974 [65]) performer BP/59*

HALE, Ruth (d 1934 [48]) American critic, press representative BE*, BP/19*

HALE, Sarah Josepha (1788-1879) dramatist HJD

HALE, Sonnie [John Robert Hale-Munro] (1902-59) English actor TW/15, WWT/5-12

HALE, S. T. (b 1899) English press representative WWT/7-10

HALE, Walter (b 1869) American actor GRB/3, WWM

HALE, Mrs. Walter see Hale, Louise

HALE, William Palmer (d 1871 [46]) burlesque writer EA/72*

HALE-MUNRO, Beatrice Mary see Hale, Binnie

HALE-MUNRO, John Robert see Hale, Sonnie

HALES, Charles (1810-65) English actor SR

HALES, F. David (d 1976 [55]) publicist BP/60*

HALES, Henry (d 1874 [52]) costumier EA/75*

HALES, John (d 1873) singer, comedian EA/74*

HALES, Jonathan (b 1937) English dramatist, director WWT/16

HALES, Martha [Mrs. T. Gardiner Hales] (d 1909 [65]) EA/10*

HALES, Richard (d 1892 [48]) actor? EA/93*

HALES, Richard King (d 1887 [65]) EA/88*

HALES, Robert (d 1863 [43]) giant HAS

HALES, Rose [Mrs. Fred Hibernia] (d 1895) variety performer, singer EA/96*

HALES, T. Gardiner (d 1913) EA/14*

HALES, Mrs. T. Gardiner see Hales, Martha

HALES, Thomas (1740?-80) English/French dramatist DNB, NTH

HALEVY, Ludovic (1834-1908) French dramatist GRB/1-4

HALEY, Jack (b 1901/02) American actor BE, TW/2-8, WWT/8-11

HALFORD, J. actor CDP

HALFORD, John (d 1904 [84]) actor EA/05*

HALFPENNY, Tony (b 1913) English actor WWT/7-10

HALIWELL, Edward (fl 1532) dramatist CP/3

HALL, Abraham Oakey (1826-98) dramatist, actor CDP

HALL, Adelaide (b 1910) American actress, singer BE

HALL, Adrian (b 1928) American director BE

HALL, Albert (d 1907 [43]) songwriter EA/08*

HALL, Albert (b 1937) American

actor TW/27-30

HALL, Alfred (d 1917 [79]) comedian, entertainer EA/18*

HALL, Anmer [Alderson Burrell
Horne] (1863-1953) English
producer, manager, actor
COC, WWT/6-11, WWW/5

HALL, Artie [Mrs. Robert Ful-
gora] (fl 1890?) singer, actress CDP

HALL, Benjamin M. , III (d 1970
[46]) editor BP/55*

HALL, Bettina (b 1906) American
actress, singer WWT/7-10

HALL, Bob (d 1970 [83]) performer BP/55*

HALL, Bob (b 1907) American
theatre owner, manager, producer BE

HALL, Brian (b 1959) American
actor TW/28

HALL, Bruce (b 1919) American
actor TW/25-26, 29

HALL, Charles (d 1867) scene
artist EA/68*

HALL, Charles (d 1874 [58])
conductor EA/75*

HALL, Charles (d 1907 [69])
Australian actor EA/08*

HALL, Charles King (d 1895
[50]) musician EA/96*

HALL, Clay (b 1940) American
actor TW/11

HALL, Cliff (d 1972 [78])
vaudevillian TW/29

HALL, Clinton (d 1880 [63])
lessee EA/81*

HALL, David (b 1929) English
producer, actor WWT/14-15

HALL, David S. (d 1965 [76])
performer BP/49*

HALL, Dorothy (d 1953 [47])
American actress TW/9,
WWT/7-10

HALL, Ed (b 1931) American actor
TW/20, 22, 26

HALL, Edward dramatist RJ

HALL, Edwin S. (d 1973 [54])
sound technician BP/58*

HALL, Emma (fl 1856) actress
HAS

HALL, Everard American? dramatist EAP

HALL, Foster see Foster, Vivian

HALL, Frank singer, song composer CDP

HALL, Frank (d 1898 [62]) comedian EA/99*

HALL, Frederick (d 1898) manager
EA/99*

HALL, George (d 1893) EA/94*

HALL, George (b 1907/16) Canadian actor TW/2-3, 5-7, 24,
26, 28, 30

HALL, Mrs. George see Kelton,
Aggie

HALL, George D. (d 1894 [28])
EA/95*

HALL, Geraldine (d 1970 [65])
performer BP/55*

HALL, Grayson actress WWT/16

HALL, Harry [or Henry] (1804-58)
Irish actor, stage manager
CDP, HAS

HALL, Henry (d 1893 [55]) steam
circus proprietor EA/94*

HALL, Henry Tudor (d 1887 [46])
EA/88*

HALL, Mrs. H. Winsloe see
Delmar, Georgina

HALL, Jacob (fl 1668) rope dancer
CDP, DNB

HALL, James (fl 1834) American
actor HAS

HALL, James (1900-40) American
actor CB

HALL, J. Clinton (1840-89) actor,
manager CDP

HALL, Jeanette F. (d 1976 [77])
performer BP/60*

HALL, J. H. (d 1850) actor HAS

HALL, J. M. (d 1877 [36]) actor
EA/78*

HALL, John actor TD/2

HALL, John C. , Jr. (b 1929)
American union representative
BE

HALL, Josephine (d 1920) American actress WWA/1

HALL, Juanita [née Long] (d 1968
[66]) American actress, singer
BE, TW/5-9, 11-18, 24, WWA/4

HALL, J. W. (fl c. 1900?) actor,
singer, song composer CDP

HALL, Laura Nelson [Mrs. Frederick Truesdell] (b 1876) American actress GRB/3-4, WWM,
WWT/1-6

HALL, Lillian (b 1850) American
actress HAS

HALL, Lois Ann (b 1947) American actress TW/28

HALL, Margaret American actress
TW/19-20, 22-26

HALL, Mark (b 1955) American
actor TW/26-27

HALL, Michael (b 1927) American actor TW/4

HALL, Natalie (b 1904) American actress, singer WWT/7-11

HALL, Owen [James Davis] (1853-1907) English dramatist, librettist GRB/1-3, WWS, WWW/1

HALL, Pamela (b 1946/47) American actress TW/25, 27-30

HALL, Pauline (1860-1919) American actress, singer CDP, SR, WWA/1, WWM, WWS, WWT/1-3

HALL, Sir Peter Reginald Frederick (b 1930) English producer, manager, director AAS, BE, CB, COC, ES, OC/3, PDT, WWT/13-16

HALL, Porter (d 1953 [65]) actor TW/10

HALL, Richard (b 1938) American actor TW/25

HALL, Mrs. R. J. see Hayes, Mabel

HALL, Robert (fl 1779) dramatist CP/3

HALL, Robert (d 1901 [56]) music-hall lessee EA/02*

HALL, Mrs. S. C. (d 1881 [81]) dramatist BE*, WWT/14*

HALL, Thurston (1882-1958) American actor TW/14, WWS, WWT/5-10

HALL, Mrs. Tom (d 1899 [37]) EA/00*

HALL, William (fl 1632) actor DA

HALL, Willis (b 1929) English dramatist AAS, CD, CH, MD, MWD, PDT, WWT/14-16

HALLAM, Mrs. (fl 1752-53) actress HAS

HALLAM, Mrs. [née Hattie Sheppard] (d 1874) actress EA/75*

HALLAM, A. (fl 1750) translator CP/3

HALLAM, A. (fl 1752-95) actor HAS

HALLAM, Adam (d 1738) actor BE*, WWT/14*

HALLAM, Ann (d 1740) actress BE*, WWT/14*

HALLAM, Ann see Barrington, Mrs. John

HALLAM, Basil (1889-1916)

English actor, singer WWT/3

HALLAM, Frederick (d 1920 [60]) Canadian comedian BE*, BP/4*

HALLAM, Isabella (1746-1826) English actress OC/1-3

HALLAM, John (d 1829) English actor HAS

HALLAM, Mrs. John [née Stannard] (d 1838) English actress HAS

HALLAM, Lewis, Sr. (1714-56) English actor, manager COC, HAS, OC/1-3, SR

HALLAM, Lewis, Jr. (1740-1808) English/American actor, manager CDP, COC, DAB, HAS, ES, OC/1-3, SR, WWA/H

HALLAM, Mrs. Lewis [Mrs. David Douglas] (d 1773) English actress CDP, HAS

HALLAM, Mrs. Lewis, II [née Tuke] (fl 1785) actress CDP, HAS

HALLAM, Mirvan (1771-1811) West Indian actor HAS

HALLAM, Nancy (fl 1759-61) actress BE*

HALLAM, Sarah (fl 1770-75) actress BE*

HALLAM, Thomas (d 1735) actor CDP

HALLAM, William (d 1758 [46]?) actor, manager HAS, SR

HALLANDE, Miss (d 1832) English actress BS, CDP

HALLARD, Charles Maitland (1865-1942) Scottish actor GRB/3-4, WWT/1-9

HALLATT, Henry (1888-1952) English actor WWT/6-11

HALLATT, May (b 1878) English actress TW/13

HALLATT, W. H. (d 1927 [80]) actor, producer BE*, WWT/14*

HALLATT, Mrs. W. H. see Hope, Carrie Sydney

HALLAWAIE, "The Younger" (fl 1580) actor DA

HALL-CAINE, Lily see Caine, Lily Hall

HALLE, C. (fl 1859) pantomimist, comedian HAS

HALLE, Sir Charles (1819-95) conductor, musician CDP

HALLE, Lady Charles (d 1911 [72]) EA/12*

HALLE, Cliff (d 1976 [57]) performer BP/60*

HALLEAN, Mme. American?
bearded lady CDP
HALLECK, Daniel (b 1946)
American actor TW/25
HALLEN, Mrs. Fred [Enid Hart]
(d 1889 [32]) American actress
EA/90*
HALLEN, Molly Fuller (fl 1894?)
singer, actress CDP
HALLER, Tobias (b 1951) Amer-
ican actor TW/29
HALLET, Benjamin (b 1744?)
musician CDP
HALLETT, Jack (b 1948) Ameri-
can actor TW/28
HALLETT, Louis (b 1870) Amer-
ican manager, agent WWM
HALLETT, Mrs. W. H. see
Hope, Carrie Sydney
HALLEWELL, F. J. (d 1899 [53])
singer EA/00*
HALLEY, Mandane Phillips (d
1967 [87]) performer BP/51*
HALLEY, Richard (fl 1636) actor
DA
HALLIDAY, Andrew (1830/31-77)
Scottish dramatist CDP, DNB,
EA/68
HALLIDAY, Mrs. Andrew [Sarah
Duff] (d 1879) EA/80*
HALLIDAY, Charles (d 1886
[34]) musician EA/87*
HALLIDAY, Charles (d 1901 [58])
musical director EA/02*
HALLIDAY, Gardner (b 1966 [56])
performer BP/51*
HALLIDAY, Hildegarde (1907-77)
American actress TW/1, 3,
5-9
HALLIDAY, James (d 1917)
EA/18*
HALLIDAY, John (1880-1947)
American actor TW/4,
WWT/6-10
HALLIDAY, Lena (d 1937) actress
WWT/1-8
HALLIDAY, Richard (1905-73)
American producer BE, TW/29
HALLIDAY, Robert (b 1893) Scot-
tish actor, singer TW/8,
WWT/6-10
HALLING, Daisy (b 1881) English
actress GRB/1
HALLING, Sydney (d 1904 [49])
actor EA/05*
HALLIWELL, David (b 1936/37)
English dramatist, producer
AAS, CD, CH, WWT/15-16

HALLIWELL, Edward (fl 1532)
dramatist FGF
HALLIWELL-PHILLIPS, James
Orchard (1820-89) writer CDP,
DNB, HP
HALLOR, Edith (d 1971 [75])
performer BP/56*
HALLORAN, L. H. ["Philo-Nauti-
cus"] (fl 1801) dramatist CP/3
HALLOW, John (b 1924) American
actor TW/23-26
HALLOWS, Edward Noble (d 1887)
actor EA/88*
HALLOWS, Mrs. Sydney L. see
Rigden, Maud
HALLS, William (d 1893 [35])
"A Jackley Wonder" EA/94*
HALMAN, Ella (b 1906) English
actress TW/4
HALPERIN, Michael (d 1974 [71])
lawyer BP/58*
HALPERIN, Nan (d 1963 [65])
performer BE*, BP/48*,
WWT/14*
HALPERN, Leivick see Leivick,
H.
HALPERN, Morty stage manager,
actor BE
HALPIN, Frank (d 1917) EA/18*
HALPIN, John (d 1916 [41]) EA/
17*
HALPRIN, Ann choreographer CD
HALSEY, Mrs. Henry P. see
Dean, Fanny
HALSTAN, Margaret [Mrs. John
Hartman Morgan] (b 1879/80)
English actress GRB/1-4,
WWT/1-14
HALSTEAD, Byron C. (d 1963
[62]) performer BP/48*
HALSTEAD, David (d 1890 [51])
EA/91*
HALSTEAD, William P. (b 1906)
American educator BE
HALTINER, Fred (d 1973 [37])
Swiss actor BP/58*, WWT/16*
HALTON, Charles American actor
TW/6
HALTON, Mrs. P. W. (d 1894)
EA/95*
HALVERSTADT, Constance see
Cummings, Constance
HAM, Isabella C. (d 1910) EA/11*
HAMAN, Catharine Maria (d 1773)
English actress HAS
HAMAR, Clifford E. (b 1914)
American educator, director
BE

HAMBLETON, Mrs. (d 1851)
Australian actress HAS
HAMBLETON, Anne B. C. (d
1962 [24]) BE*, BP/46*
HAMBLETON, T. Edward (b
1911) American producer,
director BE, WWT/13-16
HAMBLETON, William (d 1879
[81]) actor EA/80*
HAMBLIN, Mr. see Clinton,
Mr.
HAMBLIN, Bessie (fl 1838-57)
English actress HAS
HAMBLIN, Thomas Sowerby
(1800-53) American actor,
manager CDP, COC, DAB,
HAS, OC/1-3, SR, WWA/H
HAMBLIN, Mrs. Thomas Sowerby
see Charles, Elizabeth Walker
HAMBLIN, Mrs. Thomas Sowerby,
IV see Shaw, Mrs.
HAMBLIN, Mrs. Thomas Sowerby
see Shaw, Mary
HAMBLIN, William H. (b 1827)
American actor HAS
HAMBLIN, Mrs. William H.
(b 1833) American dancer,
actress HAS
HAMBLING, Arthur (b 1888) Eng-
lish actor WWT/9-13
HAMELIN, Clement (d 1957)
actor BE*, WWT/14*
HAMER, Gerald (d 1972 [86])
performer BP/57*
HAMER, Joseph (b 1932) Amer-
ican actor TW/25-26, 30
HAMER, Mrs. R. J. see
Pearce, Lottie
HAMER, Robert (d 1963 [52])
director BE*
HAMERTON, Henry (fl 1635)
groom DA
HAMES, Jack (b 1880) English
actor GRB/1
HAMID, George Abou (1896-1971)
Lebanese circus executive
WWA/5
HAMILL, Mary (b 1943) American
actress TW/25, 27, 29-30
HAMILTON, Col. (fl 1823?)
American? dramatist EAP,
RJ
HAMILTON, Mrs. (fl 1745-72)
actress DNB, GT, TD/1-2
HAMILTON, Mrs. [née Peters]
(fl 1800) actress TD/1-2
HAMILTON, Mrs. (d 1834) ac-
tress HAS

HAMILTON, Mrs. (d 1907) EA/08*
HAMILTON, Miss (fl 1830) actress
HAS
HAMILTON, Alfred H. (d 1906)
EA/07*
HAMILTON, Allen (b 1935) Amer-
ican actor TW/25
HAMILTON, Caroline [Mrs. Josiah
Hamilton] (d 1904 [70]) EA/05*
HAMILTON, Charles (fl 1784?)
translator CP/3
HAMILTON, Cicely [née Cicely
Mary Hammill] (1872-1952)
dramatist, actress GRB/4,
NTH, WWT/1-11, WWW/5
HAMILTON, Claude (b 1831) Amer-
ican actor HAS
HAMILTON, Mrs. Claude [Hattie]
(fl 1862-64) English actress
HAS
HAMILTON, Clayton (1881-1946)
American critic, dramatist
CB, DAB, SR, WWA/2, WWT/
7-9
HAMILTON, Cosmo [Cosmo Gibbs]
(1872?-1942) dramatist CB,
GRB/3-4, NTH, WWT/1-9,
WWW/4
HAMILTON, Mrs. Cosmo see
Faber, Beryl
HAMILTON, David (d 1908) EA/
09*
HAMILTON, Diana (1898/1900-
1951) English actress WWT/
5-11
HAMILTON, Dorothy (b 1897) Eng-
lish actress WWT/7-11
HAMILTON, Edward H. (d 1837)
English actor HAS
HAMILTON, Eric (b 1954) Ameri-
can actor TW/25
HAMILTON, Fanny see Addie,
Mrs.
HAMILTON, Gavin J. (d 1911 [58])
actor EA/12*
HAMILTON, George Sinclair (d
1899) EA/00*
HAMILTON, Georgina [Mrs.
George Hamilton Bell] (b 1869)
English actress GRB/1
[HAMILTON, Mrs. Gilbert?] see
Cross, Mrs. [John Cartwright?]
HAMILTON, Gloria American ac-
tress TW/8
HAMILTON, Grace see Russell,
Mrs.
HAMILTON, Grosvenor Herbert (d
1916) EA/17*

HAMILTON, Hale [Hale Rice Hamilton] (1880-1942) American actor CB, SR, WWT/2-9

HAMILTON, Hale Rice see Hamilton, Hale

HAMILTON, Hattie see Hamilton, Mrs. Claude

HAMILTON, Henry (d 1918 [65]) English dramatist, actor GRB/3-4, OAA/1-2, WWT/1-3, WWW/2

HAMILTON, Henry Bishop (b 1810) English actor, manager SR

HAMILTON, Jeffrey (b 1957) American actor TW/26

HAMILTON, John (b 1940) American actor TW/27

HAMILTON, John Angus (d 1913) EA/14*

HAMILTON, John F. (1893-1967) American actor BE, TW/24

HAMILTON, Joseph (d 1892) panorama exhibitor EA/93*

HAMILTON, Joseph (d 1894) EA/95*

HAMILTON, Mrs. Josiah see Hamilton, Caroline

HAMILTON, Karen Sue (d 1969 [23]) performer BP/54*

HAMILTON, Kate (d 1893) dancer, dancing teacher EA/94*

HAMILTON, Katie see Goddard, Mrs.

HAMILTON, Lance producer BE

HAMILTON, Lindisfarne (b 1910) English actress WWT/9-10

HAMILTON, Mahlon (d 1960 [77]) actor BE*

HAMILTON, Margaret (d 1963 [95]) critic BP/47*

HAMILTON, Margaret (b 1902) American actress BE, TW/8, 13-17, 22-23, 25-26, 30, WWT/14-16

HAMILTON, Murray American actor BE, TW/25-26

HAMILTON, Myron actor TD/2

HAMILTON, Nancy (b 1908) American dramatist, lyricist, actress, producer BE

HAMILTON, Neil (b 1897/99) American actor BE, ES, TW/1-8, 10-12, WWT/11-14

HAMILTON, Newburgh (fl 1715-43) dramatist CP/1-3, GT, TD/1-2

HAMILTON, Patrick (1904-62)

English dramatist MD, PDT, WWT/7-13

HAMILTON, Peter (b 1915) American actor TW/4-8

HAMILTON, Robert (fl 1836-49) Scottish actor CDP, HAS

HAMILTON, Mrs. Robert [née Sarah Johannot; Mrs. Rowbotham] (d 1838) English actress HAS

HAMILTON, Roger (b 1928) American actor TW/24, 27-30

HAMILTON, Rose (d 1897) actress, singer EA/98*

HAMILTON, Roy (d 1969 [40]) performer BP/54*

HAMILTON, R. P. (b 1874) English actor GRB/1

HAMILTON, Sidney [Percy T. F. Kingsmill] (b 1885) English entertainer GRB/1

HAMILTON, Sidney (d 1974 [78]) performer BP/59*

HAMILTON, Theodore (1830/36-1916) American actor CDP, HAS, PP/1, SR, WWS

HAMILTON, William actor TD/2

HAMILTON, William (d 1907 [69]) proprietor EA/08*

HAMILTON, William Bishop (1810-68) English actor, lessee, manager HAS

HAMILTON, William Henry [William H. Grosvenor] (1829-64) English actor HAS

HAMILTON, Willie (d 1894 [22]) EA/95*

HAMLET, T. (d 1853 [84]) theatre builder EA/72*

HAMLETT, Dilys (b 1928) English actress WWT/15-16

HAMLETT, Robert (fl 1611-25) actor DA

HAMLEY-CLIFFORD, Molly (d 1956) actress BE*, WWT/14*

HAMLIN, George (d 1923) American singer BE*, BP/7*

HAMLIN, George (b 1920) American director, producer, educator, actor BE

HAMLIN, Mrs. George Wright (d 1964 [93]) dramatist BE*, BP/49*

HAMLIN, John A. (d 1908 [73]) manager GRB/4*, WWT/14*

HAMLUC, W. (fl c. 1625) actor DA

HAMMER, Ben (b 1925) American

actor TW/22-23, 28
HAMMER, Mark (b 1937) American
actor TW/29
HAMMER, Will (d 1957 [69])
impresario BE*, WWT/14*
HAMMERLEE, Patricia (b 1929)
American actress TW/9,
12-13
HAMMERSLEY, Mrs. (d 1906)
EA/07*
HAMMERSLEY, Miss (fl 1818-24)
English actress BS, CDP
HAMMERSLY, Robert (d 1964
[29]) magician BE*
HAMMERSTEIN, Arthur (1872/
73/76-1955) American manager
ES, NTH, TW/12, WWT/6-11
HAMMERSTEIN, Elaine (1898-
1948) actress TW/5
HAMMERSTEIN, James (b 1931)
American producer, director,
stage manager BE, WWT/16
HAMMERSTEIN, Oscar (1847-
1919) German manager, drama-
tist, composer, theatre de-
signer CDP, COC, ES, GRB/
2-4, HJD, NTH, SR, WWA/1,
WWS, WWT/1-3, WWW/2
HAMMERSTEIN, Oscar, II (1895-
1960) American librettist,
lyricist AAS, CB, COC,
DAB, ES, HJD, MH, MWD,
NTH, OC/3, PDT, TW/2-8,
17, WWA/4, WWT/5-12,
WWW/5
HAMMERSTEIN, Theodore M.
(d 1973 [72]) producer/direc-
tor/choreographer BP/58*
HAMMERSTEIN, William (1874-
1914) American impresario
ES
HAMMERTON, Mr. Irish actor
TD/1-2
HAMMERTON, Stephen (fl 1630-
47) English actor DA, OC/
1-3
HAMMIL, John (b 1948) American
actor TW/30
HAMMILL, Cicely Mary see
Hamilton, Cicely
HAMMOND, Mr. (fl 1791) actor
HAS
HAMMOND, Mr. (fl 1800) Welsh
actor HAS
HAMMOND, Aubrey (1893-1940)
English designer ES, WWT/
6-9, WWW/3
HAMMOND, Bert E. (b 1880)

English business manager WWT/
4-12
HAMMOND, Caroline [Mrs. W.
Hammond] (d 1894) EA/95*
HAMMOND, Dorothy (d 1950 [76])
English actress WWT/4-5
HAMMOND, Edward (d 1895) actor
EA/96*
HAMMOND, Felix (d 1885) actor
EA/86*
HAMMOND, Jessie (d 1868 [33])
musician EA/69*
HAMMOND, John (fl 1494) actor
DA
HAMMOND, Kay [Dorothy Katherine
Standing] (b 1909) English ac-
tress AAS, COC, ES, WWT/7-
14
HAMMOND, Percy (1873-1936)
American critic AAS, COC,
DAB, NTH, OC/3, WWA/1,
WWT/5-8
HAMMOND, Peter (b 1923) English
actor WWT/11-14
HAMMOND, Ruth (b 1905) actress
TW/1, 3, 5-7
HAMMOND, Mrs. T. see Ham-
mond, Caroline
HAMMOND, Virginia (d 1972 [82])
American actress BE, TW/28
HAMMOND, William (fl 1740)
dramatist CP/1-3, GT
HAMMOND, William James (1797-
1848) actor, manager CDP
HAMMONDE, Frank (d 1909) actor
EA/11*
HAMOND (fl 1565) actor DA
HAMPDEN, Walter [Walter Hamp-
den Dougherty] (1879-1956)
American actor CB, COC, ES,
GRB/1-4, NTH, OC/1-3, SR,
TW/1-12, WWA/3, WWM, WWS,
WWT/1-11
HAMPER, Genevieve (d 1971 [82])
actress TW/27
HAMPSHIRE, Susan (b 1941?/42)
English actress, stage manager
CB, WWT/14-16
HAMPSON, Ernie (d 1909 [35])
EA/10*
HAMPSON, Harry (d 1906 [30])
EA/07*
HAMPSON, Oscar (d 1906) come-
dian EA/08*
HAMPTON, Mr. (d 1871 [72])
aeronaut EA/72*
HAMPTON, Christopher (b 1946)
English dramatist AAS, CD,

CH, COC, WWT/15-16
HAMPTON, Henry (d 1895 [45])
actor EA/96*
HAMPTON, Mrs. Henry [Maggie
St. Clair Douglas] (d 1902)
actress EA/03*
HAMPTON, Louise (1876-1954)
English actress WWT/5-11
HAMPTON, Mary (d 1931 [63])
American actress BE*,
BP/15*
HAMPTON, Myra (d 1945 [44])
actress BE*, WWT/14*
HAMPTON, Wade skeleton CDP
HAMRICK, Burwell (d 1970
[64]) designer BP/55*
HAMUND, St. John [Shadwell
Clerke] (1869-1929) English
actor GRB/1
HANAKO, Mme. (b 1882) Japanese
actress GRB/4, WWT/1-4
HANAU, Stella (d 1972 [81])
publicist BP/56*
HANBURY, Elizabeth (d 1916)
EA/17*
HANBURY, Lily [Mrs. Herbert
Guedalla] (1874-1908) English
actress EA/96, GRB/1-4,
WWW/1
HANBURY, Pattie [Mrs. Charles
Gover] (d 1908) actress EA/
09*
HANCHETT, David (b 1823)
American actor, manager
HAS, SR
HANCHETT, Emma (d 1879 [60])
American actress EA/80*
HANCOCK, Christopher (b 1928)
English actor WWT/15-16
HANCOCK, Myrtle J. (d 1948
[65]) American minstrel BE*,
BP/33*
HANCOCK, Sheila (b 1933) Eng-
lish actress AAS, TW/22,
WWT/14-16
HANCOCK, Tony (1924-68) Eng-
lish actor WWW/6
HANCOX, Daisy (b 1898) Eng-
lish actress, singer WWT/4-5
HANDEL, George Frederick
(1685-1759) German composer
CDP, DNB, ES, HP, TD/1-2
HANDFORD, Henry (d 1888 [64])
EA/89*
HANDKE, Peter (b 1942) Austrian
dramatist CB
HANDL, Irene (b 1901/12) Eng-
lish actress AAS, WWT/9-16

HANDLEY, J. W. actor EA/97
HANDLEY, Tommy (1896-1949)
English performer WWW/4
HANDMAN, Wynn (b 1922) director,
producer, teacher BE, WWT/
15-16
HANDS, Terry (b 1941) English
director AAS, WWT/15-16
HANDWERKER, Nathan (d 1974
[83]) BP/58*
HANDY, William Christopher
(1873-1958) American composer
BE*, BP/42*
HANDYSIDE, Clarence (d 1931
[77]) Canadian actor BE*,
BP/16*, WWT/14*
HANDZIC, Jean (d 1963 [41])
singer TW/20
HANEY, Carol (1924-64) American
actress TW/10-20, WWA/4
HANEY, Felix (b 1861) American
actor WWM
HANEY, J. Francis (d 1964) per-
former BE*
HANEY, Sonja (b 1943) American
actress TW/28-29
HANFORD, Charles Barnum (1859/
64-1926) American actor,
manager PP/1, SR, WWA/1,
WWM
HANFORD, Edwin (fl 1889?) sing-
er, actor, song composer CDP
HANKIN, St. John (1869-1909)
English dramatist COC, DNB,
ES, GRB/2-4, MD, MH, MWD,
NTH, OC/1-3, RE, WWW/1
HANKINS, Frederick see Camp-
bell, Clifford
HANKINSON, James B. (d 1873
[35]) musician EA/74*
HANKS, Charles (d 1870) comedian
EA/71*
HANKS, John singer, song com-
poser, minstrel CDP
HANLEY, Ellen (b 1926) American
actress TW/3-20, 26-28
HANLEY, Jack (d 1973 [50]) per-
former BP/58*
HANLEY, James (1892-1942) com-
poser CB
HANLEY, James (b 1901) Irish
dramatist CD
HANLEY, J. G. (1822?-1869)
American actor, manager,
stage manager HAS, SR
HANLEY, Jimmy (1918-70) actor
WWT/13-14
HANLEY, Katie (b 1949) American

actress TW/28-30
HANLEY, Martin (b 1820) Irish
actor, manager SR
HANLEY, Martin W. (d 1905)
manager WWT/14*
HANLEY, Ted (fl 1898?) singer,
actor CDP
HANLEY, William (b 1931)
American dramatist BE,
CD, CH, ES, MWD, WWT/
15-16
HANLON, Bert (d 1972) com-
poser/lyricist BP/56*
HANLON, Bob (d 1907 [46])
gymnast GRB/3
HANLON, Daniel E. (b 1877)
American actor WWM
HANLON, Dick (d 1905) acrobat
EA/06*
HANLON, Frederick (b 1848)
acrobat, pantomimist CDP,
ES
HANLON, Jane [Mrs. Thomas
Hanlon] (d 1894) EA/95*
HANLON, Thomas (d 1880 [69])
EA/81*
HANLON, Mrs. Thomas see
Hanlon, Jane
HANLON, William A. (d 1969)
performer BP/54*
HANLON BROTHERS, The HAS
HANLON-LEES, Alfred (b 1844)
acrobat CDP, ES, HAS
HANLON-LEES, Edward (1854-
1931) English acrobat CDP,
COC, ES, OC/1-3
HANLON-LEES, George (1839-
1926) English acrobat CDP,
COC, ES, HAS, OC/1-3, SR
HANLON-LEES, Thomas (1838-
68) English acrobat CDP, SR
HANLON-LEES, William (1844-
1923) English acrobat CDP,
COC, ES, HAS, OC/1-3, SR
HANLY, Richard (fl 1628) actor
DA
HANMER, Don (b 1919) American
actor TW/5-9, 12-13
HANMER, Sir Thomas (1677-
1746) writer CDP
HANN, Charles R. (b 1868) Eng-
lish actor GRB/1
HANN, Thomas R. (d 1878 [57])
English actor HAS
HANN, Walter (1838-1922) English
scene artist WWT/1-3
HANNA, Mrs. (fl 1821) actress
HAS

HANNA, Miss see Durie, Mrs.
HANNAFIN, Daniel P. (b 1933)
American actor TW/22, 24
HANNAH, Rose Ann (d 1887)
EA/89*
HANNAN, Philip see Phillips,
Frederick
HANNAY, Rev. J. O. see
Birmingham, George
HANNEFORD, Mr. (d 1889) cir-
cus performer EA/90*
HANNEFORD, Mrs. (d 1889) cir-
cus performer EA/90*
HANNEN, Hermione (b 1913)
English actress WWT/9-10,
12-13
HANNEN, Nicholas James (1881-
1972) English actor, producer
AAS, NTH, TW/2, WWT/4-14
HANNING, Geraldine American
actress TW/28
HANNOCH, Dan (d 1974 [69])
performer BP/58*
HANRAY, Lawrence (1874-1947)
English actor WWT/4-10
HANSARD, J. B. (d 1908 [68])
actor, scene artist EA/09*
WWT/14*
HANSBERRY, Lorraine (1930-65)
American dramatist AAS, BE,
CB, CD, CH, ES, MH, MWD,
PDT, TW/21, WWA/4
HANSELL, Thomas (d 1895 [41])
acting manager EA/96*
HANSEN, Al painter CD
HANSEN, Hans (d 1962 [76]) Ger-
man actor TW/19
HANSEN, Harold I. (b 1914)
American educator BE
HANSEN, Juanita (d 1961 [66])
actress BE*
HANSEN, Laura (d 1914) English
actress GRB/1
HANSEN, Lawrence William (d
1968) composer/lyricist BP/
52*
HANSEN, Ronn (b 1939) American
actor TW/26, 28
HANSEN, William (1911-75) Amer-
ican actor TW/3, 8, 10-12,
19
HANSON, Gladys (1887-1973)
American actress TW/29,
WWT/4-10
HANSON, Harry (1895-1972) South
African actor, manager AAS,
WWT/10-13
HANSON, Harry L. [Harry L.

Parker] (b 1856) American minstrel, vaudevillian WWM

HANSON, Howard (b 1896) American composer CB, HJD

HANSON, Isadora (fl 1847) American actress HAS

HANSON, John [né Watts] (b 1922) Canadian singer, actor AAS, WWT/15-16

HANSON, Johnny (d 1907 [64]) clown, comedian BE*, EA/08*, WWT/14*

HANSON, Kitty [Mrs. W. H. Berry] (d 1947 [76]) actress BE*, WWT/14*

HANSON, Lars (d 1965 [78]) Swedish actor TW/21

HANSON, M. H. (b 1864) Danish impresario WWM

HANSON, Nicholas (fl 1623-28) actor DA

HANSON, Peter (b 1921) American actor TW/9

HANSON, Philip (b 1924) American actor TW/27

HANSON, Preston (b 1921) American actor TW/7-9

HANSON, Mr. T. (d 1868 [29]) stage manager EA/69*

HANSON, Winnie see Lightner, Winnie

HANTON, John Dee (d 1906 [18]) EA/07*

HANZEL, Carol (b 1945) American actress TW/29

HAPGOOD, Elizabeth Reynolds (1894-1974) American translator BE

HAPGOOD, Hutchins (1869-1944) American critic WWA/2

HAPGOOD, Norman (1868-1937) American critic GRB/2-3, NTH

HARA, Mary American actress TW/26, 30

HARARI, Ezra (d 1970 [76]) producer/director/choreographer BP/54*

HARBACH, Otto A. (1873-1963) American dramatist, librettist, lyricist CB, TW/19, WWA/4, WWT/4-11, WWW/6

HARBACH, William (fl c. 1785) dramatist CP/3

HARBAGE, Alfred (1901-76) American scholar BE

HARBEN, Hubert (1878-1941) English actor WWT/3-9

HARBEN, Joan (1909-53) English actress WWT/7-11

HARBON, William James (d 1884) EA/85*

HARBORD, Carl English actor WWT/7-9

HARBORD, Gordon (b 1901) English manager WWT/8-10

HARBURG, Edgar Y. (b 1898) American lyricist, dramatist BE, CD, WWT/15-16

HARBURY, Charles (d 1928 [85]) actor BE*, BP/12*, WWT/14*

HARBY, George Washington dramatist RJ

HARBY, Isaac (1788-1828) American dramatist DAB, EAP, RJ, WWA/H

HARCOURT, Charles (d 1880 [42]) actor OAA/1-2

HARCOURT, Cissie (d 1916) comedian EA/18*

HARCOURT, Cyril (d 1924 [52]) actor, dramatist WWT/3-4

HARCOURT, Francis (d 1884 [35]) actor EA/85*

HARCOURT, Fred (d 1906) magician EA/07*

HARCOURT, G. Bees (fl 1871?) singer, song composer, minstrel CDP

HARCOURT, Mrs. George see Harcourt, Mrs. M.

HARCOURT, James (1873-1951) English actor WWT/8-11

HARCOURT, Leonard (d 1880) actor EA/81*

HARCOURT, Leslie (b 1890) English actor, producer WWT/8-9

HARCOURT, Lottie [Mrs. Forbes Dawson] (d 1893) actress EA/94*

HARCOURT, Mrs. M. [Mrs. George Harcourt] (d 1888 [31]) EA/89*

HARCOURT, Marie [Miss Hart] Scottish actress GRB/1

HARCOURT, Robert Vernon (1878-1962) English dramatist GRB/1-4, WWT/1-4

HARCOURT, Sidney (d 1905 [49]) comedian EA/06*

HARCOURT, Mrs. William see Fischer, Alice

HARDACRE, Agnes Denby (d 1911 [39]) actress EA/12*

HARDACRE, Esther (d 1896 [60]) EA/97*

HARDACRE, John Pitt (1855-1933)

English actor, manager WWT/ 3-7

HARDENBERG, Frank (1829-89) American actor CDP

HARDHAM, John (d 1772) English dramatist CP/1-3, GT

HARDIE, A. C. (d 1939) actor BE*, WWT/14*

HARDIE, Mrs. J. M. see Von Ler, Sarah

HARDIE, James M. (d 1905) managing director EA/06*

HARDIE, James W. (d 1912) actor, manager SR

HARDIE, Russell (1904/06-73) American actor BE, TW/1-20, 30, WWT/10-14

HARDIE, Sarah Blanche (d 1884) EA/85*

HARDIE, W. R. [Harry Fenwick] (d 1884) actor? EA/85*

HARDIMAN, Terrence (b 1937) English actor WWT/15-16

HARDIN, John A. (d 1976 [88]) theatre supply company executive BP/60*

HARDING, Mr. (fl 1839?) actor CDP

HARDING, Miss see Marshall, Mrs. G.

HARDING, Alfred (d 1945) English actor GRB/1

HARDING, Alfred (d 1969 [77]) editor BP/54*

HARDING, Ann (b 1902/04) American actress BE, ES, WWT/6-15

HARDING, Bert (d 1917 [31]) musician, composer EA/18*

HARDING, Charles (d 1895 [50]) singer EA/96*

HARDING, Mrs. Charles see Sutherland, Annie

HARDING, D. Lyn [David Llewellyn Harding] (1867-1952) Welsh actor GRB/2-4, TW/9, WWM, WWT/1-11

HARDING, Florence R. (d 1913 [26]) EA/14*

HARDING, Frank (d 1911 [47]) actor EA/12*

HARDING, John (b 1948) English actor, dramatist CD, WWT/16

HARDING, Joseph (d 1881 [51]) proprietor EA/82*

HARDING, Joseph R. W. (d 1880 [58]) EA/81*

HARDING, June (b 1940) American actress TW/17-20

HARDING, Nannie Welsh singer GRB/1

HARDING, Rudge (d 1932 [70]) English actor EA/97, GRB/1-4, WWT/1-4

HARDING, Samuel (1618-c. 40) English dramatist CP/2-3, DNB, FGF

HARDING, W. (d 1909) actor? EA/10*

HARDINGE, Mr. (fl 1797-1802) English actor HAS, TD/2

HARDINGE, Mrs. actress HAS

HARDINGE, Emma (fl 1855) actress CDP, HAS

HARDINGE, Fanny (fl 1854) actress HAS

HARDINGE, H. C. M. dramatist WWT/4-7

HARDMAN, W. H. (d 1886) comedian EA/87*

HARDMUTH, Paul (d 1962 [73]) German actor BE*

HARDS, Ira (1872-1938) American producer WWT/6-8

HARDWICK, James (d 1886 [71]) comic songwriter EA/87*

HARDWICK, Paul (b 1918) English actor AAS, WWT/14-16

HARDWICKE, Sir Cedric Webster (1893-1964) English actor, director AAS, BE, CB, COC, ES, NTH, OC/1-3, TW/2-16, 18-19, 21, WWA/4, WWT/5-13, WWW/6

HARDWICKE, Clarice (b 1900) Australian actress WWT/5-10

HARDWICKE, Edward (b 1932) English actor WWT/15-16

HARDY, Prof. (d 1899 [30]) ventriloquist EA/00*

HARDY, Arthur F. (b 1870) English manager WWT/1-11

HARDY, A. S. (d 1901) Negro comedian EA/02*

HARDY, Betty (b 1904) English actress WWT/7-10

HARDY, Charles Edward (d 1906 [50]) manager EA/07*

HARDY, Cherry (1897-1963) English actress TW/4-6

HARDY, James (d 1877) musician EA/78*

HARDY, Joseph (b 1918) American actor TW/28, 30

HARDY, Joseph (b 1929) American

director WWT/15-16
HARDY, Nelson (b 1861) English
ventriloquist GRB/1
HARDY, Oliver (1892-1957)
vaudevillian, actor TW/14
HARDY, Robert (b 1925) English
actor AAS, TW/14, WWT/
14-16
HARDY, Sam B. (1883-1935)
American actor WWS
HARDY, Sarah (b 1940) American
actress TW/30
HARDY, Silva giantess CDP
HARDY, Thomas (1840-1928)
English dramatist DNB, ES,
HP, MWD, NTH, PDT,
WWW/2
HARE, Betty (b 1900) English ac-
tress, singer WWT/8-15
HARE, David (b 1947) English
dramatist AAS, CD, WWT/16
HARE, Doris (b 1905) Welsh
actress, singer WWT/8-16
HARE, Ernest Dudley (b 1900)
English actor AAS, WWT/9-16
HARE, Francis Lumsden see
Hare, Lumsden
HARE, Mrs. Francis Lumsden
see Ruttledge, Frances
HARE, Gilbert [Fairs] (1869-
1951) English actor ES, GRB/
1-3, WWT/4-8
HARE, J. (d 1909 [87]) agent
EA/10*
HARE, Sir John [Fairs] (1844-
1921) English actor, manager
CDP, COC, DNB, DP, ES,
GRB/1-4, NTH, OAA/1-2,
OC/1-3, SR, WWS, WWT/1-3,
WWW/2
HARE, J. Robertson (b 1891)
English actor COC, WWT/
6-16
HARE, Kate (d 1957 [83]) actress
BE*, WWT/14*
HARE, Lumsden (1875-1964) Irish
actor BE, GRB/1-2, TW/21
HARE, Mrs. Lumsden see
Ruttledge, Frances
HARE, Mollie (d 1971) performer
BP/55*
HARE, Reginald (d 1888) acting
manager EA/89*
HARE, Rene Vivian (d 1969 [72])
performer BP/54*
HARE, Will (b 1919) American
actor TW/1-7, 10-14, 20,
23-24, 28-30, WWT/16

HARE, Winifred (b 1875) English
actress, singer CDP, GRB/
3-4, WWT/1-8
HARENS, Dean (b 1921) American
actor TW/3-7, 9-11
HAREWOOD, Earl of (b 1923)
English director, executive
CB
HARFORD, Miss see Hoper,
Mrs.
HARFORD, W. scene artist WWT/
1-7
HARGRAVE, Mr. (fl 1796-1804)
actor TD/1-2
HARGRAVE, Roy (b 1908) Ameri-
can actor, director, dramatist
WWT/10-13
HARGREAVES, Mrs. Albert [Kitty
Page] (d 1916 [35]) EA/17*
HARGREAVES, Anthony (d 1969)
composer/lyricist BP/54*
HARGREAVES, Frank (d 1886)
music-hall manager EA/87*
HARGREAVES, Mrs. J. (d 1908)
EA/09*
HARGREAVES, William (1841-1919)
English actor GRB/1
HARKER, Mrs. (d 1916 [90]) EA/
17*
HARKER, Mrs. Allen (d 1933)
English dramatist WWW/3
HARKER, Frederick (d 1941 [79])
actor BE*, WWT/14*
HARKER, George (d 1875) prompter
EA/76*
HARKER, Mrs. George see
Wynter, Amy
HARKER, George H. English actor
EA/96
HARKER, Gordon (1885-1967) Eng-
lish actor ES, WWT/6-14,
WWW/6
HARKER, Joseph (b 1892) English
scene artist WWT/9-12
HARKER, Joseph C. (1855-1927)
English scene artist ES,
WWT/1-5, WWW/2
HARKEY, James (b 1934) Ameri-
can actor TW/28
HARKINS, Daniel H. (1835/36-1902)
American actor, manager
CDP, HAS, PP/1, SR
HARKINS, Jim (d 1970 [82]) per-
former BP/55*
HARKINS, Marion (d 1962 [68])
performer BE*
HARKINS, William S. (1856-1945)
manager SR

HARKNESS, Rebekah (b 1915)
American dance patron, com-
poser CB
HARLAM, Macey (d 1924) actor
BP/8*
HARLAN, Otis (1865-1940)
American actor CB, GRB/
3-4, WWA/1, WWM, WWS,
WWT/1-9
HARLAN, Russell B. (d 1974
[70]) performer BP/58*
HARLAND, Ada (b 1847) English
actress CDP, HAS
HARLAND, Alec (d 1965) per-
former BP/50*
HARLAND, Fred [William R.
Russ] (d 1912) actor EA/13*
HARLAND, Julia [née Wallack;
Mrs. W. Haskins] actress,
singer CDP
HARLEY, Charles (d 1916) Eng-
lish actor GRB/1
HARLEY, Mrs. Charles see
Barron, Madge Douglas
HARLEY, Edwin (fl 1885) sing-
er, minstrel CDP
HARLEY, Frederick (d 1867)
comic singer, composer CDP
HARLEY, George Davies (1762-
1811) English actor CDP,
DNB, GT, TD/1-2
HARLEY, Henry (d 1891) musi-
cian EA/92*
HARLEY, John Pritt (1786/90?-
1858) English actor, singer
BS, CDP, DNB, OX
HARLEY, Kate singer, actress
CDP
HARLEY, Percy James see
Como, Professor
HARLEY, Rex [Reginald Ernest
Page] (d 1909 [40]) mimic
EA/10*
HARLEY, Violet (d 1903 [35])
serio-comic, singer EA/04*
HARLEY, Violet M. English
actress GRB/1
HARLEY, Walter (d 1909 [63])
magician, showman EA/11*
HARLING, William Franke
(1887-1958) English composer
WWA/3
HARLINGTON, Grace [Mrs. F.
R. Gwyn Richardson] (b 1883)
English actress GRB/1
HARLOW, Edward (d 1890 [35])
circus clown EA/91*
HARLOW, Elizabeth (fl 1789)

dramatist CP/3
HARLOW, Gertrude (d 1947 [73])
actress BE*, WWT/14*
HARLOW, Richard (1872-1920)
comedian BE*, BP/4*
HARLOW, Tom (d 1901) comedian
EA/02*
HARLOWE, Mrs. see Harlowe,
Sarah
HARLOWE, Sarah [Mrs. Francis
G. Waldron] (1765-1852) English
actress BS, CDP, DNB, GT,
OX, TD/1-2
HARMAN, Mrs. see Clarke,
Catharine Maria
HARMAN, Billy (d 1913) EA/14*
HARMAN, Homer H. (d 1971) pub-
licity director BP/55*
HARMAN, Lindsay (b 1865) English
actor, singer, stage manager
GRB/1
HARMAN, W. (d 1888) music-hall
performer EA/89*
HARMER, Dolly (d 1956 [89]) Eng-
lish actress, variety artist
CDP, GRB/1
HARMER, Margaret (d 1902) ac-
tress EA/03*
HARMER, Peter (d 1894 [68])
EA/95*
HARMON, Charlotte American pro-
ducer, editor BE
HARMON, Irving (d 1973 [66]) ac-
tor, singer TW/29
HARMON, Jennifer (b 1943) Ameri-
can actress TW/28, 30
HARMON, Jill (b 1949) American
actress TW/27-29
HARMON, Joy (b 1940) American
actress TW/15
HARMON, Lee (d 1972 [41]) per-
former BP/57*
HARMON, Lewis (b 1911) American
press representative, producer,
manager BE
HARMSTON, W. (d 1881 [71]) cir-
cus manager, architect EA/82*
HARMSTON, William Batty (d 1893
[49]) circus proprietor EA/94*
HARNED, Virginia [Mrs. E. H.
Sothern] (1872-1946) American
actress CDP, GRB/2-4, TW/2,
WWA/2, WWM, WWS, WWT/1-6
HARNEY, Ben (b 1952) American
actor TW/28-30
HARNEY, Benjamin Robertson
(1872-1938) composer, performer
BE*

HARNICK, Jay (b 1928) American director, producer BE
HARNICK, Sheldon (b 1924) American lyricist, composer BE
HAROLD, Henry (d 1871 [44]) actor EA/72*
HAROLD, John Danvers (d 1868) musician EA/69*
HAROLD, Lizzie (fl 1872) singer, actress CDP
HAROLD, Maggie [Mrs. William Davidge] (1852-1907) singer, actress CDP
HAROLDE, Ralf (d 1974 [75]) performer BP/59*
HARPER, Mr. (fl 1733-34) actor GT, TD/1-2
HARPER, Mr. (d 1813) West Indian actor HAS
HARPER, Mrs. actress HAS
HARPER, David H. (d 1969 [41]) union executive BP/54*
HARPER, Elizabeth see Bannister, Mrs. John
HARPER, Fanny (d 1875 [22]) statue performer EA/76*
HARPER, Fred (d 1963 [60]) performer BE*
HARPER, George T. (d 1974 [72]) performer BP/59*
HARPER, Gerald (b 1929) English actor WWT/15-16
HARPER, John (d 1742) actor CDP, DNB
HARPER, Ron (b 1936) American actor TW/29
HARPER, Samuel (fl 1737) dramatist CP/2-3, GT
HARPER, Thomas (1787-1853) English musician DNB
HARPER, Thomas (d 1892) EA/93*
HARPER, Valerie (b 1940?) American actress, dancer CB
HARPLEY, T. (fl 1790) dramatist CP/3
HARRADINE, Archie (d 1974 [76]) actor BTR/74
HARRIGAN, Edward (1845-1911) American actor, dramatist, manager CDP, COC, DAB, GRB/2-4, HJD, MH, MWD, NTH, OC/1-3, PP/1, RE, SR, WWA/1, WWS
HARRIGAN, Nedda [Grace Harrigan] (b 1902) American actress BE, WWT/8-11
HARRIGAN, William (1893/94-

1966) American actor BE, OC/1-3, TW/1-8, 11-15, 22, WWT/6-13
HARRINGTON, Mr. actor TD/1-2
HARRINGTON, Mr. (fl 1837-41) English actor HAS
HARRINGTON, Mrs. (fl 1837) actress HAS
HARRINGTON, Dowager Countess of see Foote, Maria
HARRINGTON, Alice (d 1954 [81]) American actress BE*, BP/39*
HARRINGTON, Charles English actor, manager GRB/1
HARRINGTON, Charles Stanhope (1780-1851) CDP
HARRINGTON, Donal (b 1905) American educator BE
HARRINGTON, Florence (d 1942 [80]) actress BE*, WWT/14*
HARRINGTON, George A. (d 1859) minstrel CDP
HARRINGTON, George N. see Christy, George N.
HARRINGTON, Herschel R. (d 1975 [75]) producer/director/choreographer BP/59*
HARRINGTON, James (d 1906 [22]) stage manager EA/07*
HARRINGTON, James A. (d 1908 [88]) actor GRB/4*
HARRINGTON, John Patrick (b 1865) English composer, dramatist GRB/1-3
HARRINGTON, Prof. Jonathan (b 1809) American ventriloquist HAS
HARRINGTON, Kate American actress TW/19, 23, 30
HARRINGTON, Maria see Foote, Maria
HARRINGTON, Pat, Sr. (1900-64) Canadian actor BE, TW/22
HARRINGTON, William (1804-35) American equestrian CDP, HAS
HARRIOTT, Mrs. F. C. see Morris, Clara
HARRIS, Mrs. [Miss Grattan] (d 1856) actress? HAS
HARRIS, Alexander (b 1927) English actor TW/7
HARRIS, Audrey Sophia (1901-66) English designer WWT/8-14 [see also: Motley]
HARRIS, Augustus Glossop (1825-73) English manager, actor COC, DNB, OC/1-3
HARRIS, Sir Augustus Henry Glossop

(1852-96) French/English actor, manager, producer, dramatist CDP, DNB, NTH, OAA/1-2, OC/1-3

HARRIS, Averell (d 1966) actor TW/23

HARRIS, Bagnall (b 1907) Canadian/English designer ES

HARRIS, Barbara (b 1935/37) American actress BE, CB, ES, TW/22-24, 26, WWT/15-16

HARRIS, Bennie Michel (d 1975 [54]) performer BP/59*

HARRIS, Charlene (b 1925) American actress TW/7

HARRIS, Charles (d 1897 [42]) stage manager, producer EA/98*, WWT/14*

HARRIS, Charles A. "Honey" (d 1962 [75]) performer BE*

HARRIS, Charles Kassell (1865-1930) American songwriter DAB, WWS

HARRIS, Charles L. (1854-92) actor CDP

HARRIS, Christopher see Fry, Christopher

HARRIS, Clare (d 1949 [59]) actress WWT/5-10

HARRIS, Cynthia American actress TW/28-30

HARRIS, Dru (b 1952) American actress TW/30

HARRIS, Mrs. E. see Rose, Mlle.

HARRIS, Elmer Blaney (1878-1966) dramatist TW/23, WWT/4-11

HARRIS, Mrs. F. J. (d 1893) EA/95*

HARRIS, Flora [Mrs. Sheridan Moore] (d 1910 [80]) Australian actress EA/11*

HARRIS, Florence Glossop (b 1883) English actress GRB/3-4, WWT/1-6

HARRIS, Frank (1855-1931) Irish writer MD, NTH, WWW/3

HARRIS, Fred Orrin (b 1901) American educator BE

HARRIS, George, II American actor TW/25-26

HARRIS, George W. (d 1895 [63]) actor, manager EA/96*

HARRIS, George W. (d 1929 [49]) scene designer & artist BE*, WWT/14*

HARRIS, Georgiana see Kenny, Mrs. George

HARRIS, G. F. (d 1867 [70]) professor of music EA/68*

HARRIS, Gus (fl 1914?) singer CDP

HARRIS, Mrs. G. W. (d 1869) EA/70*

HARRIS, Mrs. G. W. (d 1873) EA/74*

HARRIS, Henry (c. 1634-1704) English actor COC, OC/1-3

HARRIS, Henry B. (1866-1912) American manager GRB/2-4, SR, WWA/1, WWM, WWS, WWT/1

HARRIS, Herbert H. (c. 1896-1948) American producer TW/3-5

HARRIS, Hildred (1898-1944) actress SR

HARRIS, Howard (d 1878) music-hall chairman EA/79*

HARRIS, James (1709-80) English dramatist CP/2-3, GT

HARRIS, Jed [Jed Horowitz] (b 1899/1900) American producing manager BE, NTH, TW/2-8, WWT/6-14

HARRIS, John (fl 1635) actor DA

HARRIS, John (d 1874) lessee EA/75*

HARRIS, John H. (d 1969 [70]) showman BP/53*

HARRIS, Jonathan (b 1914) American actor TW/6-9

HARRIS, Joseph? (fl 1661-81) actor DNB

HARRIS, Joseph (fl 1661-1702) actor, dramatist CDP, CP/1-3, DNB

HARRIS, Joseph manager BE

HARRIS, Julie (b 1925) American actress AAS, BE, CB, ES, NTH, TW/5-23, 25-30, WWT/14-16

HARRIS, Leland B. (b 1912) American union executive BE

HARRIS, Leonore (d 1953 [74]) American actress TW/3-7, 10

HARRIS, Leslie (fl 1895?) singer, musician, actor CDP

HARRIS, Lizzie (fl 1864) actress HAS

HARRIS, Margaret F. (b 1904) English designer WWT/9-16 [see also: Motley]

HARRIS, Maria [Maria Elizabeth Glossop] (1851-1904) English

actress CDP, OAA/1-2

HARRIS, Mary Ann [née Glossop] (d 1892) EA/93*

HARRIS, Mary Ann (d 1900 [25]) EA/01*

HARRIS, Mildred (1901-44) American actress BE*

HARRIS, Mitchell (d 1948 [65]) performer BE*

HARRIS, Morris O. (d 1974 [59]) performer BP/59*

HARRIS, Nelly [Mrs. Horace Sedger] (d 1897) actress CDP

HARRIS, Patience Glossop (d 1901 [44]) EA/03*

HARRIS, Raymond (d 1971 [86]) dramatist BP/55*

HARRIS, Renée (d 1969 [93]) producer TW/26

HARRIS, Richard (b 1933) Irish actor CB, ES, WWT/14-15

HARRIS, Robert (b 1900) actor AAS, WWT/5-16

HARRIS, Robert H. (b 1911) American actor TW/22

HARRIS, Rosemary (b 1930) English actress AAS, BE, CB, TW/9, 15-23, 28-30, WWT/ 12-16

HARRIS, Sadie (b 1888) American actress WWS

HARRIS, Sam H. (1872-1941) American manager, producer CB, DAB, NTH, SR, WWA/1, WWM, WWS, WWT/1-9

HARRIS, Samuel E. [S. Wesley Barmore] (1825-58) actor CDP, HAS

HARRIS, Stacy (d 1973 [54]) performer BP/57*

HARRIS, Sylvia (d 1966 [60]) producer TW/23

HARRIS, T. C. see O'Callan, Thomas

HARRIS, Thomas (d 1820 [82]) proprietor TD/1-2

HARRIS, William (1839/42-1916) American actor, manager, producer CDP, HAS, SR, WWM

HARRIS, William, Jr. (1884-1946) American producer, manager CB, TW/3, WWA/2, WWT/6-9

HARRIS, Will J. (d 1967 [73]) producer/director/choreographer BP/52*

HARRISBURG, J. C. M. dramatist RJ

HARRISON, Mr. (fl 1824) actor? CDP

HARRISON, Mrs. [née Clifford] (d 1842) English actress HAS

HARRISON, Mrs. see Allegranti, Teresa Maddalena

HARRISON, Miss see Powell, Mrs. Snelling

HARRISON, Mrs. A. [Mrs. C. Harrison] (d 1875) EA/77*

HARRISON, Agnes (d 1868 [87]) EA/69*

HARRISON, Alice Maud (1849/50-96) American actress CDP, HAS, SR

HARRISON, Arthur see Dundas, Henry

HARRISON, Austin (1873-1928) critic, dramatist WWT/1-5

HARRISON, Bob [Bayard Patterson] (1842-1912) minstrel CDP

HARRISON, Mrs. C. see Harrison, Mrs. A.

HARRISON, C. B. (d 1862) actor? HAS

HARRISON, Charles (d 1870) actor? EA/71*

HARRISON, Charles Lancelot (d 1917) EA/18*

HARRISON, Charles Samuel (d 1891 [37]) singer EA/93*

HARRISON, Clifford (d 1903) elocutionist EA/05*

HARRISON, Cyril (b 1866) English actor GRB/1

HARRISON, Dennis see Patrick, Dennis

HARRISON, Duncan (d 1934 [72]) Canadian dramatist, manager BE*, BP/18*

HARRISON, Mjr. Duncan B. dramatist, song composer CDP

HARRISON, Mrs. E. C. [Mrs. William Harrison] (d 1889) EA/90*

HARRISON, Edward (d 1912 [44]) music-hall manager EA/13*

HARRISON, Elizabeth (fl 1756) dramatist CP/3

HARRISON, E. T. (d 1889 [70]) circus architect EA/90*

HARRISON, Evelyn [Mrs. Walter Maxwell] (d 1903 [28]) actress EA/04*

HARRISON, Fanny [Mrs. Isaac Cohen] (d 1909 [70]) actress, singer BE*, EA/10*, WWT/14*

HARRISON, Frances actress
CDP

HARRISON, Frank (b 1869) English stage manager, producer
GRB/1-3

HARRISON, Mrs. Frank see
Kay, Ethel

HARRISON, Frederick (d 1904)
variety performer EA/05*

HARRISON, Frederick (d 1926
[72]) English lessee, manager
GRB/1-4, WWT/1-5, WWW/2

HARRISON, Gabriel (1818-1902)
American actor, dramatist,
manager CDP, DAB

HARRISON, George (d 1886)
EA/87*

HARRISON, George (d 1887) costumier EA/88*

HARRISON, George (d 1887)
manager EA/88*

HARRISON, Mrs. Gulielma
[Mrs. Robert Harrison] (d
1870 [31]) EA/71*

HARRISON, Harriet (d 1881 [62])
costumier EA/82*

HARRISON, Harry P. (1878-
1968) American manager
WWA/5

HARRISON, H. T. (d 1899)
singer EA/00*

HARRISON, James G. (d 1890)
EA/91*

HARRISON, Jay S. (d 1974 [47])
critic BP/59*

HARRISON, J. N. (d 1870 [79])
president of the Sacred Harmonic Society EA/71*

HARRISON, John (fl 1602) actor
DA

HARRISON, John (d 1878 [59])
costumier EA/79*

HARRISON, John (b 1924) English director, dramatist,
actor CD, WWT/16

HARRISON, Kathleen (b 1898)
English actress AAS, WWT/
7-16

HARRISON, Lee (d 1916 [50])
singer, actor CDP

HARRISON, Leo (1850-1916)
actor SR

HARRISON, Louis (1859-1936)
American actor, dramatist,
manager CDP, SR

HARRISON, Maud [Mrs. Edward
M. Bell] (1854-1907) American actress CDP, WWS

HARRISON, Michael (b 1945) American actor TW/25

HARRISON, Mona (d 1957) Scottish
actress GRB/2-4, WWT/1-12

HARRISON, Nell (d 1973 [93])
American actress TW/1, 30

HARRISON, Lieut. Nicholas Bacon
(fl 1789) dramatist CP/3

HARRISON, Percy (d 1917 [71])
concert director EA/18*

HARRISON, Peter Basil see
Markham, David

HARRISON, Ray American actor
TW/1

HARRISON, Rex (b 1908) English
actor AAS, BE, CB, ES, TW/
5-18, 29, WWT/9-16

HARRISON, Richard (fl 1617) actor
DA

HARRISON, Richard Berry (1864-
1935) American actor, lecturer
COC, DAB, OC/1-3, SR, WWA/1

HARRISON, Robert [Robert Wilkes
Gibbs] (d 1885 [22]) acrobat
EA/86*

HARRISON, Robert (d 1953 [68])
American actor BE*, BP/37*

HARRISON, Mrs. Robert see
Harrison, Gulielma

HARRISON, Rowley (d 1898) comedian EA/99*

HARRISON, Samuel (1760-1812)
singer CDP

HARRISON, Susan (b 1938) American actress TW/14

HARRISON, Thomas (fl 1727-29)
dramatist CP/2-3, GT

HARRISON, Thomas (d 1879 [34])
musician EA/80*

HARRISON, Valerie see French,
Valerie

HARRISON, W. (d 1847) English
actor HAS

HARRISON, Mrs. W. see Majilton, Flo

HARRISON, W[ilbur] Vernon (1879-
1929) American manager WWA/1

HARRISON, William (fl 1583) licensee, actor? DA

HARRISON, William (fl 1701) dramatist CP/1-3, GT

HARRISON, William (1813-68) English actor, singer, manager
CDP, DNB, HAS, SR

HARRISON, Mrs. William see
Harrison, Mrs. E. C.

HARRISON, William Bristow (1812-
81) English actor, manager

CDP, HAS, SR
HARRISON-TATE, A. [Mrs.
Fred Benton] English actress
GRB/1
HARRISS, Sophie Australian
actress GRB/1
HARRITY, Richard (b 1907) Amer-
ican dramatist, actor BE
HARROD, W. (fl 1753-69) Eng-
lish dramatist CP/2-3, GT
HARROLD, J. (d 1908) EA/09*
HARROLD, Jack (b 1920) Amer-
ican actor TW/27
HARROLD, Orville (d 1933 [55])
American singer WWA/1
HARRON, Donald (b 1924) Cana-
dian actor BE, TW/11-20
HARRON, Robert (1894-1920)
actor BE*, BP/5*
HARROP, Sarah (d 1890 [85])
EA/91*
HARROP, Sarah see Bates,
Mrs. Joah
HARROWAY, John (d 1857 [47])
composer, musical director
EA/72*
HARRY (fl 1710) raree showman
CDP
HART, Mrs. actress TD/2
HART, Miss see Harcourt,
Marie
HART, Annie [Mrs. William
Lester] (d 1947 [87]) singer,
actress CDP, TW/4
HART, Arthur (d 1911 [54])
dramatic agent EA/12*
HART, Bernard (1911-64) Amer-
ican producing manager, stage
manager BE, TW/2-8, 21,
WWT/11-13
HART, Billy (b 1864) American
vaudevillian WWM
HART, Mrs. Billy see Marie,
La Belle
HART, Charles (d 1683) English
actor COC, DA, DNB, ES,
NTH, OC/1-3
HART, Charles (fl 1754) Scottish
dramatist CP/2-3, GT
HART, Diane (b 1926) English
actress WWT/15-16
HART, Dolores (b 1930) Ameri-
can actress TW/15-16
HART, Dora Jane (d 1890 [66])
EA/91*
HART, E. A. actor, singer,
song composer CDP
HART, Enid see Hallen, Mrs.

Fred
HART, Everett L. (d 1973 [51])
producer/director/choreographer
BP/57*
HART, Fred (d 1894) manager
EA/95*
HART, Gabriel (d 1905) EA/06*
HART, George (d 1891 [52]) musi-
cian EA/92*
HART, Henry (d 1909 [81]) music-
hall proprietor CDP
HART, Henry (b 1917) American
actor TW/6-7
HART, Jack (d 1974 [102]) performer
BP/59*
HART, Jerry (d 1908 [23]) EA/09*
HART, John (1833-1904) comedian,
minstrel manager, performer
CDP
HART, John (d 1937) producer,
executive, manager BE*, WWT/
14*
HART, Joseph [Joseph Hart Boud-
row] (1858/62-1921) American
comedian, producer, manager
WWM, WWS
HART, Joseph Binns (1794-1844)
English composer, musician,
chorus-master DNB
HART, Josh [J. Jones] (b 1834)
American prop-man, actor HAS
HART, Leolyn (d 1911 [59]) scene
artist EA/12*
HART, Leonard (d 1917 [37]) musi-
cian EA/18*
HART, Lorenz (1895-1943) Ameri-
can lyricist AAS, CB, DAB,
ES, MH, PDT, WWA/4, WWT/6-9
HART, Marie see Marie, La Belle
HART, M. Blair (b 1907) American
educator, director BE
HART, Moss (1904-61) American
librettist, dramatist, director
AAS, CB, COC, ES, HJD, MD,
MH, MWD, NTH, OC/2-3,
PDT, RE, SR, TW/18, WWA/4,
WWT/8-13, WWW/6
HART, Nicholas (b 1684) the great
sleeper CDP
HART, Richard (1915-51) American
actor TW/1-7
HART, Teddy (1897-1971) American
actor BE, TW/27, WWT/10-11
HART, Tony [Anthony Cannon]
(1857-91) female impersonator
CDP, COC, NTH, OC/2-3, SR
HART, Vivian actress, singer
WWT/7-10

HART, Walter (d 1973 [67]) producer, director TW/30

HART, William (fl 1634-36) actor DA

HART, William Griffith see Melville, Harry

HART, William Matthew (d 1905 [42]) manager GRB/1

HART, William S. (1870?-1946) American actor CB, CDP, DAB, ES, SR, TW/3, WWM, WWT/4-9

HARTE, Francis Bret (1839-1902) American dramatist NTH

HARTFORD, Huntington (b 1911) American producer, publisher, patron BE, CB

HARTFORD, W. S. (b 1879) Scottish actor GRB/1

HARTIG, Mary (b 1935) American actress TW/9

HARTIG, Michael Frank (b 1936) American talent representative BE

HARTILL, Willie [Horrox] (b 1872) English stage manager GRB/1

HARTKE, Rev. Gilbert (b 1907) American educator BE

HARTLAND, Frank (1783-1852) actor CDP [see also following entry]

HARTLAND, Frederick (d 1852 [70]) pantomimist EA/72* [see also previous entry]

HARTLEY, Ann see Gilbert, Mrs. George

HARTLEY, Charles William see Harley, Charles

HARTLEY, Elizabeth [née White] (1751-1824) English actress CDP, COC, DNB, OC/1-3, OX

HARTLEY, Frederick Charles (d 1891 [28]) animal trainer EA/93*

HARTLEY, Henry (d 1868 [41]) professor of music EA/69*

HARTLEY, J. H. (d 1901 [49]) Negro comedian EA/02*

HARTLEY, Katherine see Frings, Ketti

HARTLEY, Neil (b 1919) American producer BE

HARTLEY, Randolph (b 1870) American dramatist, librettist WWM

HARTLEY, Mrs. Randolph see

Wakeman, Emily

HARTLEY, Vivian Mary see Leigh, Vivien

HARTLEY-MILBURN, Julie (1904-49) English actress WWT/5-7

HARTMAN, Elek (b 1922) American actor TW/24-25

HARTMAN, Ferris (fl 1894?) singer, actor CDP

HARTMAN, Grace (1907-55) American dancer CB, TW/4-7, 12

HARTMAN, Jonathan William (d 1965 [90]) performer BP/50*

HARTMAN, M. (d 1900 [95]) composer EA/01*

HARTMAN, Paul (1904-73) American dancer, actor, magician, singer BE, CB, TW/4-18, 30

HARTMANN, Helene (d 1898) Australian actress EA/99*

HARTNELL, William (1908-75) English actor WWT/11-15

HARTNOLL, Phyllis (b 1906) English scholar, historian, dramatist AAS, BE

HARTREE, Walter D. (d 1907 [49]) acting manager EA/08*

HARTSON, Hall (d 1773) Irish dramatist CP/2-3, GT, TD/1-2

HARTWIG, Brigitta see Zorina, Vera

HARTWIG, Walter (d 1941 [61]) American producer BE*, BP/25*

HARTY, Mrs. Hamilton see Nicholls, Agnes

HARTZ, Mr. (d 1903 [66]) ventriloquist, conjuror CDP

HARTZ, M. magician CDP

HARTZELL, Willard C. (d 1970 [60]) performer BP/55*

HARUM, Avind (b 1944) Norwegian actor TW/25

HARVEN, Jane (d 1969 [50]) performer BP/54*

HARVEY (fl 1597) actor DA

HARVEY, Mr. actor CDP

HARVEY, Miss see Lewis, Mrs. Henry

HARVEY, Alice [Mrs. Fred Baugh] (d 1908 [43]) comedian EA/09*

HARVEY, Catherine (d 1899) EA/01*

HARVEY, Dennis (d 1902) EA/03*

HARVEY, Don C. (d 1963 [51]) performer BE*

HARVEY, Edward (d 1906) music-hall performer EA/07*

HARVEY, Edward (d 1975 [82])
performer BP/60*
HARVEY, Mrs. E. M. [Mrs.
Frank Harvey] (d 1907) EA/
08*
HARVEY, Forrester (d 1945
[55]) actor BE*, WWT/14*
HARVEY, Frank (1842-1903)
English actor, dramatist
OAA/2
HARVEY, Frank (1885-1965)
English actor, dramatist
WWT/7-13
HARVEY, Mrs. Frank see
Harvey, Mrs. E. M.
HARVEY, Frank, Jr. (b 1912)
English actor, dramatist,
producer WWT/11-16
HARVEY, Fred (d 1895 [39])
singer, actor CDP
HARVEY, Mrs. George see
Glover, Eleanor
HARVEY, Georgette (d 1952 [69])
American actress TW/8
HARVEY, Georgia (d 1960 [85])
Canadian actress TW/16
HARVEY, Helen (b 1916) Amer-
ican literary representative
BE
HARVEY, James Clarence (b
1859) American dramatist
WWM
HARVEY, J. B. (d 1862 [70])
manager EA/72*
HARVEY, Joan (b 1935) Ameri-
can actress TW/17-18
HARVEY, John (d 1901) EA/02*
HARVEY, John (d 1908 [62])
EA/10*
HARVEY, John (d 1970 [53])
actor, talent representative
TW/27
HARVEY, John (b 1917) Ameri-
can talent representative BE
HARVEY, Mrs. John see
Zerbini, Carlotta
HARVEY, Sir John Martin (1863-
1944) English actor, manager
COC, DNB, GRB/1-4, NTH,
OC/1-3, WWT/1-9, WWW/4
HARVEY, Lady John Martin
see De Silva, Nina
HARVEY, Kenneth (b 1918) Cana-
dian actor TW/11-12
HARVEY, Laurence [né Skikne]
(1928-73) Lithuanian actor
AAS, BE, CB, ES, TW/12-
18, 30, WWT/13-15

HARVEY, Lilian (1906-68) English
actress, singer, dancer ES
HARVEY, Mary Ann see Daven-
port, Mrs. George Gosling
HARVEY, May [Mrs. Charles T.
H. Helmsley] (d 1930) English
actress GRB/1-4
HARVEY, Michael (b 1917) Ameri-
can actor TW/6-8
HARVEY, Morris (1877-1944) Eng-
lish actor WWT/4-9
HARVEY, Patsey J. (d 1890 [27])
EA/91*
HARVEY, Paul (d 1955 [71]) Amer-
ican actor TW/12
HARVEY, Peter (b 1933) Guate-
malan/American designer WWT/
15-16
HARVEY, Rose [Mrs. W. Lindsay]
(d 1899) actress? singer? EA/
00*
HARVEY, Rupert (1887-1954) Eng-
lish actor WWT/4-9
HARVEY, Susie [Susannah Elizabeth
Matthews; Mrs. Theodore Mat-
thews] (d 1893) EA/94*
HARVEY, Walter (d 1905) actor?
EA/06*
HARVEY, W. H. (d 1889 [56])
clown EA/90*
HARVEY, Mrs. Will see Holt,
Hettie
HARVEY, William (d 1856 [43])
harlequin EA/72*
HARVEY, William (d 1907) music-
hall comedian EA/08*
HARVEY, William François (d
1899 [49]) equestrian EA/00*
HARVUOT, Inez see Manning,
Irene
HARVYE, William (fl 1628) actor
DA
HARWOOD, Mr. (fl 1822?) actor
CDP
HARWOOD, Mrs. [née Julia Wade]
(d 1876) EA/77*
HARWOOD, Miss (d 1888) dramatist
EA/89*
HARWOOD, Florence actress
GRB/3-4
HARWOOD, George (d 1903 [61])
music-hall proprietor EA/04*
HARWOOD, George Julian (d 1909)
musical director EA/10*
HARWOOD, Harold Marsh (1874-
1959) English dramatist, mana-
ger COC, OC/3, WWT/4-12
HARWOOD, Harry (d 1926 [78])

American actor BE*, BP/11*

HARWOOD, H. R. (d 1898) Australian actor EA/99*

HARWOOD, Mrs. H. R. (d 1887) EA/88*

HARWOOD, Isabella (1840?-88) dramatist DNB

HARWOOD, Isabella see Neil, Ross

HARWOOD, James (d 1900 [83]) actor EA/01*, WWT/14*

HARWOOD, James see Farmer, Lucia Eliza

HARWOOD, John (1876-1944) English actor, stage manager, director GRB/4, WWT/1-9

HARWOOD, John Edmund (1771-1809) American actor CDP, COC, HAS, OC/1-3, SR, WWA/H

HARWOOD, Louisa see Eldridge, Louisa

HARWOOD, Lucia actress CDP

HARWOOD, Robb (d 1910 [40]) English actor GRB/1-4

HARWOOD, Thomas (fl 1787) dramatist CP/3

HASCALL, Lon (d 1932 [60]) American actor BE*, BP/17*, WWT/14*

HASELDEN, T. J. (d 1895) professor of music EA/96*

HASELMAYER, Louis (b 1839) Austrian magician HAS

HASHIM, Edmund (d 1974 [42]) performer BP/59*

HASKELL, Arnold Lionel (b 1903) English critic ES

HASKER, James John (d 1906 [88]) Australian actor EA/07*

HASKINS, Douglas N. (d 1973 [45]) performer BP/58*

HASKINS, Mrs. W. see Harland, Julia

HASLAM, James (d 1891 [33]) step-dancer EA/92*

HASLAM, John (d 1892 [37]) EA/94*

HASLAM, Maud [Mrs. Samuel W. Groome] (d 1899 [30]) actress CDP

HASLAM, Rene (d 1918) EA/19*

HASLEM, Bert (d 1903) actor, dancer BE*, EA/04*

HASSALL, Christopher (1912-63) English actor, dramatist, lyricist WWT/9-13, WWW/6

HASSAN, Prince (d 1908) wire-walker EA/09*

HASSELL, George (d 1937 [56]) English actor BE*, BP/21*, WWT/14*

HASSELMANS, Louis (1878-1957) French conductor WWA/3

HASSELQUIST, Jenny Swedish dancer WWT/4

HASSETT, Michael (d 1972) performer BP/56*

HASSLER, Simon (1832-1901) musician, composer WWA/1

HASSO, Signe [née Larssen] (b 1910/15/18) Swedish actress BE, TW/12-16, 24, WWT/11-16

HASTINGS, Alice [Mrs. Roland Reed] (d 1888 [32]) American actress EA/90*

HASTINGS, Annie [née Wilmot] (d 1891 [45]) EA/92*

HASTINGS, Basil Mcdonald (1881-1928) English dramatist WWT/2-5

HASTINGS, Christopher (b 1948) American actor TW/30

HASTINGS, Fred (d 1891) comedian, stage manager EA/92*

HASTINGS, Mrs. Frederick (d 1880 [51]) actress EA/82*

HASTINGS, Gilbert see MacDermott, The Great

HASTINGS, H. (d 1894 [41]) manager EA/95*

HASTINGS, Harold (d 1973 [56]) musical director, composer BE, TW/29

HASTINGS, Helen [Mrs. T. H. Smith] (d 1895 [28]) actress CDP

HASTINGS, Hugh (b 1917) Australian actor, dramatist TW/30, WWT/11-16

HASTINGS, Kate [Mrs. W. C. Phillips] (d 1890) actress EA/91*

HASTINGS, Michael (b 1938) English dramatist AAS, CD, PDT

HASTINGS, Mortimer S. (d 1899 [53]) actor EA/00*

HASTINGS, Sir Patrick (1880-1952) dramatist WWT/7-11

HASTINGS, William T. (d 1972 [65]) manager BP/57*

HASWELL, Percy [Mrs. George Fawcett] (d 1945 [74]) American actress GRB/3-4, PP/1, TW/2, WWM, WWS, WWT/1-8

HATCH, Eric (d 1973 [71]) drama-

tist BP/58*
HATCH, Frank (d 1938 [74])
American actor, dramatist,
director BE*, BP/23*
HATCH, Henry (d 1885 [69])
proprietor EA/86*
HATCH, Ike (d 1961 [69]) Amer-
ican performer BE*
HATCH, James V. (b 1928)
American dramatist, educator
BE
HATCHER, Tom (b 1933) Amer-
ican actor TW/13-15
HATCHETT, William (fl 1730-41)
dramatist, actor CP/1-3,
GT, TD/1-2
HATCHMAN, Emily (d 1903)
EA/04*
HATCHMAN, Henry C. (d 1903)
EA/04*
HATCHMAN, Henry William (d
1916) actor EA/17*
HATFIELD, Hurd (b 1920) Amer-
ican actor BE
HATFIELD, Lansing (d 1954)
American singer TW/1,
WWA/3
HATHAWAY, Miss actress HAS
HATHERTON, Arthur (d 1924)
actor WWT/4
HATHOL (d 1890) boy acrobat
EA/91*
HATHWAY, Richard (fl 1598-
1602) dramatist CP/2-3,
DNB, FGF
HATHWELL, Mr. English actor
HAS
HATHWELL, Henrietta American
actress HAS
HATHWELL, Louisa (fl 1822)
American actress HAS
HATHWELL, Matilda English
dancer, actress HAS
HATLEN, Theodore (b 1911)
American educator BE
HATT, W. [W. Rousillion] (d
1887) trapezist EA/88*
HATTON, Mr. (fl 1801-03)
actor TD/1-2
HATTON, A. C. (d 1883 [34])
actor EA/84*
HATTON, Adele Bradford (d
1957 [76]) actress BE*,
WWT/14*
HATTON, Alfred (d 1917) musi-
cian EA/18*
HATTON, Ann Julia (fl 1794)
dramatist EAP, RJ

HATTON, Bessie English actress
CDP, DP, GRB/1-3
HATTON, Fanny [Fanny Locke] (d
1939 [69]) American dramatist
WWT/4-9
HATTON, Frederick H. (1879-1946)
American dramatist, critic
WWT/4-9
HATTON, John Liptrot (1809-86)
English composer, conductor
DNB
HATTON, Joseph (b 1801) American
dramatist SR
HATTON, Joseph (1841-1907) Eng-
lish dramatist DNB, GRB/1-3,
WWW/1
HATTON, Louisa (d 1901 [56])
actress EA/02*
HATTON, Raymond (d 1971 [84])
actor BP/56*, WWT/16*
HATTON, Walter [Thomas Spurway]
(d 1903 [54]) lessee EA/04*
HATTON, William (d 1916) EA/17*
HATTORI, Raymond (d 1973 [65])
composer/lyricist BP/58*
HAUCK, Minnie see Hauk, Minnie
HAUERBACH, Otto (b 1873) Amer-
ican dramatist WWM
HAUGER, George (b 1921) English
educator BE
HAUGHTON, Miss actress TD/1-2
HAUGHTON, Hugh (fl 1634) actor
DA
HAUGHTON, William (1578-1603)
dramatist CP/3, DNB, FGF
HAUK, Minnie (1852?-1929) Amer-
ican singer CDP, DAB, ES,
HAS, SR, WWA/2, WWM
HAUPT, William A. (fl 1863) actor
HAS
HAUPT, William Ayers see
Mestayer, William A.
HAUPTMAN, Laurent (d 1870)
musician, composer EA/71*
HAUPTMANN, Carl (d 1921) drama-
tist BE*, WWT/14*
HAUPTMANN, Gerhart (1862-1946)
German dramatist COC, GRB/
1-4, OC/3, WWM, WWT/1-2
HAUPTMANN, John (fl 1815) dwarf
CDP
HAUSER, Frank (b 1922) Welsh
director AAS, COC, WWT/13-
16
HAUSER, Miska (1822-87) musician
CDP
HAUSMAN, Howard L. (b 1914)
American talent representative

BE

HAUSTED, Peter (d 1645) English dramatist CP/1-3, DNB, FGF

HAUTONVILLE, Mrs. see Bradshaw, Mrs.

HAVANA ITALIAN OPERA TROUPE HAS

HAVARD, William (d 1778 [68]) actor, dramatist CDP, CP/1-3, DNB, GT, TD/1-2

HAVEL, Arthur (d 1965 [68]) performer BP/49*

HAVENS, John F. (b 1912) American attorney BE

HAVER, Phyllis (d 1960 [60]) American actress BE*

HAVERGAL, Giles (b 1938) Scottish director WWT/15-16

HAVERLAND, Anna (fl 1892) singer CDP

HAVERLY, Jack H. (1837-1901) American manager CDP, DAB, SR, WWA/H

HAVESON, Jimmy (b 1924) American actor TW/26

HAVEZ, Jean (d 1925 [55]) songwriter BE*, BP/9*

HAVILAND, Augusta (d 1925) actress BE*, WWT/14*

HAVILAND, William (1860-1917) English actor, manager GRB/2-4, WWT/1-3

HAVILAND, Mrs. William see Latimer, Edyth

HAVLIN, John H. (d 1924 [77]) American manager, treasurer SR

HAVOC, June [née Hovick] (b 1916) American actress, singer, director AAS, BE, TW/1-19, 23, WWT/10-16

HAWES, David (b 1919) American educator, director BE

HAWES, Maria B. [Mrs. J. D. Merest] (d 1886) singer EA/87*

HAWES, William (1785-1846) English singer, composer, manager DNB

HAWK, Harry (1837-1916) actor CDP

HAWK, Jeremy (b 1916) South African actor WWT/15-16

HAWKER, Essex (fl 1729) actor, performer CP/2-3, GT, TD/1-2

HAWKES, John (b 1925) American

dramatist, educator CD, CH

HAWKES, Kirkby (d 1970 [67]) dramatist BP/54*

HAWKES, Thomas (d 1902) music-hall manager EA/03*

HAWKESWORTH (fl 1636) dramatist CP/3, FGF

HAWKESWORTH, John (1716-73) dramatist CP/1-3, DNB, GT, TD/1-2

HAWKESWORTH, Walter (d 1606) dramatist DNB

HAWKINS, Alexander (fl 1601) lessee, patentee DA

HAWKINS, Anthony Hope (1863-1933) English dramatist DNB, GRB/1, 4, HP, WWW/3

HAWKINS, Erick (b 1915/17) American dancer, choreographer CB, ES

HAWKINS, Erskine (b 1914) American musician CB

HAWKINS, Etta (d 1945 [80]) actress BE*, WWT/14*

HAWKINS, Harry Stuart see Stuart, Harry

HAWKINS, Henry (d 1878 [52]) musician EA/79*

HAWKINS, Iris (b 1893) English actress GRB/2-4, WWT/1-6

HAWKINS, Jack (1910-73) English actor AAS, CB, ES, TW/7-15, 30, WWA/5, WWT/7-14

HAWKINS, Micah (fl 1825?) dramatist EAP, RJ

HAWKINS, Michael American actor TW/24, 26

HAWKINS, Robert (d 1875) actor EA/76*

HAWKINS, Stockwell (1874-1927) Welsh actor WWT/5

HAWKINS, Trish (b 1945) American actress TW/29-30

HAWKINS, W. (fl 1780-86) dramatist CP/3

HAWKINS, William (fl 1627-34) dramatist CP/1-3, FGF

HAWKINS, William (d 1801) dramatist CP/2-3, GT

HAWKINS, William see Roselle, W. H.

HAWKS, Mr. dramatist CP/1

HAWKS, Wells (1870-1941) American theatrical representative GRB/3-4, WWM

HAWLEY, Dudley (d 1941 [62]) English actor BE*, BP/25*, WWT/14*

HAWLEY, Emma Cox [Mrs. Fred
Hawley] (d 1898 [67]) EA/99*
HAWLEY, Esther (d 1968 [62])
performer BP/53*
HAWLEY, Mrs. Fred see Haw-
ley, Emma Cox
HAWLEY, Frederick (1827-89)
English scholar, actor, drama-
tist DNB, OAA/2
HAWLEY, H. Dudley (1879?-1941)
English actor CB
HAWLEY, Ida (fl 1897-1908)
Canadian actress WWS
HAWLEY, Richard (fl 1636) actor
DA
HAWLEY, Stanley (d 1916) EA/
17*
HAWLEY, Thomas (b 1935) Amer-
ican actor TW/19
HAWLING, Francis (fl 1723-51)
dramatist CP/2-3, GT
HAWORTH, Don dramatist CD
HAWORTH, Joseph (1855/58-1903)
American actor CDP, DAB,
PP/1, SR, WWA/1
HAWORTH, Lawrence (d 1868
[25]) manager EA/69*
HAWTHORNE, Alice (fl 1855?)
song composer CDP
HAWTHORNE, Charles J. (1809-
87) scene artist NYM
HAWTHORNE, David (d 1942)
actor WWT/8-9
HAWTHORNE, Georgiana (b 1811)
English dancer, singer? ac-
tress? HAS
HAWTHORNE, Grace (d 1922
[62]) actress, lessee, pro-
ducer CDP, DP
HAWTHORNE, Lil American vari-
ety artist CDP, GRB/1-2
HAWTHORNE, Lola singer, ac-
tress CDP
HAWTHORNE, Louise [née Mary
Timmons; Mrs. George Mor-
ton] (d 1876 [29]) actress
CDP
HAWTHORNE, Nellie actress,
singer CDP
HAWTHORNE, Nigel (b 1929)
English actor WWT/15-16
HAWTIN, Miss (fl 1770) freak
CDP
HAWTREY, Anthony (1909-54)
English actor, manager
WWT/9-11
HAWTREY, Charles (b 1914)
English actor WWT/9-13

HAWTREY, Mrs. Charles see
Hawtrey, Madeline Harriet
HAWTREY, Sir Charles Henry
(1858-1923) English actor, mana-
ger CDP, COC, DNB, DP,
EA/97, ES, GRB/1-4, NTH,
OC/1-3, SR, WWA/1, WWM,
WWS, WWT/1-4, WWW/2
HAWTREY, Edward M. (d 1916)
EA/17*
HAWTREY, George P[roctor] (d
1910 [64]) actor, dramatist
BE*, EA/11*, WWT/14*
HAWTREY, Madeline Harriet [Mrs.
Charles Hawtrey] (d 1905 [47])
EA/06*
HAWTREY, Marjory (b 1900) Eng-
lish actress WWT/11-14
HAWTREY, William Francis (1856-
1914) English actor DP, WWM
HAWTRY, Anthony see Hawtrey,
Anthony
HAY, Mrs. Charles see Saker,
Rose
HAY, Harriett see Litchfield,
Harriett
HAY, Ian [John Hay Beith] (1876-
1952) English dramatist COC,
DNB, NTH, OC/3, WWT/4-11
HAY, Joan (b 1894) actress, singer
WWT/5-9
HAY, Mrs. John see Courtenay,
Eveline
HAY, John M. (b 1868) English ac-
tor, singer GRB/1
HAY, Mary (1901-57) American
actress, singer TW/13, WWT/
6-7
HAY, Valerie (b 1910) English ac-
tress, singer WWT/8-11
HAY, Will (1888-1949) actor
WWW/4
HAYAKAWA, Sessue (1890-1973)
Japanese actor CB
HAYDEN, Bob (d 1974 [49]) per-
former BP/59*
HAYDEN, Louis (d 1971 [56]) per-
former BP/55*
HAYDEN, Madoline Mary (d 1908
[34]) EA/09*
HAYDEN, Martin (fl 1892) actor
CDP
HAYDEN, Maud [Mrs. Heath
Saunders] (d 1910 [38]) EA/11*
HAYDEN, Melissa (b 1922/28)
Canadian dancer CB, ES
HAYDEN, Terese (b 1921) American
producer, director, actress

BE, WWT/15-16

HAYDOCK, George see Bandurria, George

HAYDON, Ethel [Mrs. George Robey] (1876/78-1954) Australian actress CDP, GRB/1-4, WWT/1-6

HAYDON, Florence (d 1918 [80]) English actress WWT/1-3

HAYDON, John S. (d 1907 [70]) actor BE*, EA/08*, WWT/14*

HAYDON, Mrs. J[ohn] S. see Haydon, Mary Ann

HAYDON, Julie [Donella Donaldson] (b 1910) American actress BE, NTH, TW/1-12, WWT/8-12

HAYDON, Mary Ann [Mrs. John S. Haydon] (d 1887) EA/88*

HAYE, Helen (1874-1957) Indian/English actress COC, ES, GRB/1, OC/3, TW/14, WWT/1-12

HAYES, Miss (d 1881) actress EA/82*

HAYES, Ada (d 1962 [87]) performer BE*

HAYES, Barbara American actress TW/24-25

HAYES, Ben American actor TW/19-20

HAYES, Benjamin (b 1842) American comedian, minstrel HAS

HAYES, Bernadene American actress TW/1

HAYES, Beverly (b 1940) American actress TW/25

HAYES, Bill (b 1925) American actor, singer BE, TW/9-10, 24

HAYES, Blanche [Mrs. Fred Rutt] (d 1889 [38]) actress EA/90*

HAYES, Catharine (1825-61) Irish singer CDP, DNB, ES, HAS

HAYES, Clarence E. singer CDP

HAYES, De Vere see Edwin, J. H.

HAYES, Elton (d 1917) performer? EA/18*

HAYES, Florence [Mrs. A. P. Boswell] (d 1908 [52]) music-hall performer EA/09*

HAYES, Frank (fl 1907?) actor, singer CDP

HAYES, F. W. (d 1918 [70])

dramatist BE*, WWT/14*

HAYES, George (1888-1967) English actor AAS, BE, TW/3, WWT/4-13

HAYES, Mrs. George see May, Eva

HAYES, Helen [née Brown] (b 1900) American actress AAS, BE, CB, COC, ES, NTH, OC/1-3, PDT, SR, TW/1-26, WWT/4-16

HAYES, Henry (d 1891) singer EA/92*

HAYES, Henry J. (d 1905) music-hall manager EA/06*

HAYES, Hubert (d 1964) dramatist BE*, BP/49*

HAYES, James (d 1975 [60]) producer/director/choreographer BP/59*

HAYES, Joseph (b 1918) American dramatist, producer, director BE

HAYES, Laurence C. (d 1974 [71]) performer BP/59*

HAYES, Louis [Louis de Vere Hayes] American actor GRB/1

HAYES, Mabel [Mrs. R. J. Hall] (d 1892 [43]) actress EA/93*

HAYES, Margaret [Maggie] (1924-77) American actress BE, TW/1-3, 20

HAYES, Maurice (fl 1900?) singer, actor CDP

HAYES, Milton (d 1940 [56]) performer BE*, WWT/14*

HAYES, Patricia (b 1909) English actress WWT/9-10

HAYES, Paul (d 1969 [86]) performer BP/54*

HAYES, Percy (d 1908 [42]) music-hall manager EA/09*

HAYES, Peter Lind (b 1915) American actor BE, CB, TW/25

HAYES, Reginald (d 1953) actor, singer BE*, WWT/14*

HAYES, Samuel (b 1749) dramatist CP/2-3, GT

HAYES, Samuel (d 1892) entrepreneur EA/93*

HAYES, Sydney see Page, James Augustus

HAYES, Tim (1841-77) Irish clog dancer HAS

HAYESON, Jimmy (b 1924) American actor TW/28-29

HAYLE, Douglas (b 1942) American actor TW/25, 27, 30

HAYLEY, George see Stayley,

George
HAYLEY, William (1745-1820)
English dramatist CDP, CP/
3, GT, TD/1-2
HAYM, Nicholas dramatist CP/1
HAYMAN, Alf (1865-1921) Amer-
ican producer BE*, BP/5*,
WWT/14*
HAYMAN, Alfred (d 1917 [67])
American manager GRB/2-4,
WWA/1, WWT/1-3
HAYMAN, Arthur (d 1901 [39])
actor EA/02*
HAYMAN, Leonard (d 1962 [61])
English performer BE*
HAYMAN, Lillian (b 1922) Amer-
ican actress, singer WWT/16
HAYMEN, Helen Violet Carolyn
see Lynne, Carole
HAYMES, Thomas (fl 1789-1800)
English actor TD/1-2
HAYNES, Alfred W. (d 1924
[63]) American performer
BE*, BP/9*
HAYNES, Mrs. Archibald C.
see Gale, Minna
HAYNES, F. (fl 1830s) dramatist
RJ
HAYNES, Henry D. (d 1971
[51]) performer BP/56*
HAYNES, Henry S. (d 1885 [45])
comedian EA/86*
HAYNES, Mrs. Henry S. (d
1885) actor EA/86*
HAYNES, Hilda American actress
TW/29-30
HAYNES, Jennie [Mrs. Harry
Wenburn] (d 1904/06) EA/05*,
EA/07*
HAYNES, Mrs. Joe see Haynes,
Louisa
HAYNES, Joseph (d 1909 [59])
music-hall manager EA/10*
HAYNES, Joseph see Haines,
Joseph
HAYNES, Joseph see Stanley,
Jean
HAYNES, Louisa [Mrs. Joe
Haynes] (d 1907 [53]) music-
hall manager EA/08*
HAYNES, Mel (b 1921) American
actor TW/21
HAYNES, Michael (d 1879 [26])
Irish comic singer EA/81*
HAYNES, Minna Gale see
Gale, Minna
HAYNES, Rosetta [Mrs. T. P.
Haynes] (d 1908) actress

GRB/4*
HAYNES, T[homas] P[ercival] (d
1915 [65]) English actor EA/96,
OAA/1-2
HAYNES, Mrs. T[homas] P[ercival]
see Haynes, Rosetta
HAYNES, Tiger (b 1907) actor
TW/23, 30
HAYS, Mr. (fl 1821) actor HAS
HAYS, Alfred (d 1899 [61]) librarian
EA/00*
HAYS, Bill (b 1938) English director
WWT/15-16
HAYS, David (b 1930) American
designer BE, ES, WWT/15-16
HAYS, Jack (d 1975 [76]) producer/
director/choreographer BP/60*
HAYS, William Shakespeare (1837-
1907) American songwriter,
journalist BE*
HAYSELL, George (fl 1583-84)
actor DA
HAYTER, James (b 1907) Indian/
English actor WWT/9-16
HAYTER, William (d 1904 [67])
EA/06*
HAYTHORNE, Joan (b 1915) English
actress WWT/10-16
HAYTON, Lennie (d 1971 [63])
composer, lyricist BP/55*
HAYTOR, Arthur (d 1909) variety
comedian EA/10*
HAYWARD, Mr. (d 1860) American
actor HAS
HAYWARD, Beatrice Herford (d
1952 [84]) actress WWT/14*
HAYWARD, Caroline Mary see
Rignold, Kate
HAYWARD, Clara see Bentley,
Mrs. Arthur
[HAYWARD?], Clementina see
Collins, Clementina
HAYWARD, Mrs. E. (d 1888 [26])
EA/89*
HAYWARD, George (d 1869 [52])
musical director EA/70*
HAYWARD, Henry (d 1884) musi-
cian EA/85*
HAYWARD, Leland (1902-71) Amer-
ican manager, agent BE, CB,
TW/2-8, 27, WWT/10-15
HAYWARD, William (d 1896) music-
hall chairman EA/97*
HAYWELL, Frederick see Haw-
ley, Frederick
HAYWOOD, Eliza (1693?-1756)
actress, dramatist CP/1-3,
GT, HP, TD/1-2

HAYWOOD, Hetty (fl 1896?)
singer, actress CDP
HAYWORTH, Vinton (d 1970 [64])
performer BP/54*
HAZARD, Mr. (d 1831) actor
HAS
HAZARD, Mrs. (fl 1839) actress
HAS
HAZARD, Joseph (fl 1767) drama-
tist CP/2-3, GT
HAZELL, Francis Nalder (d 1913
[59]) EA/14*
HAZELL, Hy (1922-70) English
actress WWT/12-14
HAZELTINE, William (b 1866)
American actor WWS
HAZLEHURST, Jack (d 1908 [19])
EA/09*
HAZLETON, George Cochrane
(1868-1921) American drama-
tist, actor DAB, SR, WWS
HAZLETON, Mrs. Victor (d
1883) EA/84*
HAZLEWOOD, Colin Henry (d
1875 [52]) dramatist EA/69
HAZLEWOOD, Eliza (d 1876)
dancer EA/77*
HAZLEWOOD, Henry Colin (d
1897 [59]) manager EA/98*
HAZLITT, William (1778-1830)
English critic CDP, COC,
DNB, ES, HP, NTH, OC/1-3,
PDT
HAZZARD, Alice Dovey (d 1969
[84]) performer BP/53*
HAZZARD, John E. (1881-1935)
American actor WWA/1,
WWM, WWT/4-7
HEAD, Charles (d 1889 [61])
proprietor EA/90*
HEAD, Henry C. S. see Henry,
S. Creagh
HEAD, Richard (d 1678) Irish
dramatist CP/1-3, GT
HEADFORT, Marchioness of
see Boote, Rosie
HEADLAM, Rev. Stewart Duck-
worth (b 1847) English minis-
ter GRB/2-4
HEADLAND, T. (d 1888 [82])
secretary EA/89*
HEAL, Joan (b 1922) English
actress, singer WWT/12-16
HEALEY, J. R. (d 1877 [45])
American actor EA/78*
HEALEY, Thomas A. (d 1872)
actor EA/73*
HEALEY-KAY, Patrick see

Dolin, Anton
HEALY, Dan (d 1969 [80]) actor,
singer TW/30
HEALY, Gerald (d 1963 [45]) per-
former, dramatist, producer
BE*, BP/47*
HEALY, Jack (d 1972 [68]) perform-
er BP/57*
HEALY, John see Le Hay, John
HEALY, Mary (b 1918/20) Ameri-
can actress, singer BE, TW/
1-3, 14-15
HEALY, Robert (b 1922) American
actor TW/2
HEAP, Swinnerton (d 1900 [53])
composer EA/01*
HEAPHY, Mr. Irish manager TD/
1-2
HEAPHY, Thomas M. (b 1891)
American actor TW/3
HEARD, Mr. (fl 1797) actor HAS
HEARD, Miss (fl 1801) actress
CP/3, TD/1-2
HEARD, Elizabeth (d 1797 [47])
actress CDP
HEARD, William (d c. 1776 [34])
dramatist, bookseller CP/2-3,
DNB, GT
HEARD, Mrs. William (d 1799) ac-
tress CP/3
HEARN, Bert (d 1898) music-hall
performer EA/99*
HEARN, Dennis (b 1949) American
actor TW/30
HEARN, George (b 1934) American
actor TW/25, 29
HEARN, James S. (1873-1913) Eng-
lish actor GRB/2-4, WWT/1-2
HEARN, Julia Knox (d 1976 [92])
performer BP/60*
HEARN, Lew (b 1882) Polish actor,
singer WWT/6-11
HEARN, Mrs. Lew see Bonita
HEARN, Sam (d 1964 [75]) per-
former BP/49*
HEARNE, George (d 1909 [78])
EA/10*
HEARNE, Mrs. George (d 1901
[45]) EA/02*
HEARNE, Richard (b 1909) English
actor WWT/8-14
HEARNE, Thomas (fl 1597) actor
DA
HEARTWELL, Henry (fl 1799)
dramatist CP/3, GT, TD/1-2
HEATH, Bob (b 1948) American
actor TW/29-30
HEATH, Boxley (d 1882) enter-

tainer EA/83*

HEATH, Caroline [Mrs. Wilson Barrett] (1837-87) actress CDP, NYM, OAA/1-2

HEATH, Dody (b 1928) American actress TW/7-8

HEATH, Eira (b 1940) English actress WWT/15-16

HEATH, Mrs. F. see Garton, Flo

HEATH, Frank (d 1908 [52]) treasurer EA/10*

HEATH, Frederic (d 1900 [43]) music-hall performer EA/01*

HEATH, Frederick (d 1874 [29]) musician EA/76*

HEATH, George (b 1852) American actor, minstrel WWS

HEATH, Gordon (b 1918) American actor, director BE, TW/2, 26

HEATH, Ida (d 1950 [77]) performer BE*, WWT/14*

HEATH, Lily (d 1913) EA/14*

HEATH, Marie (b 1866) singer, actress CDP

HEATH, Rosée singer, actress CDP

HEATH, Thomas (d 1889 [63]) scene artist EA/91*

HEATH, Thomas Kurton (1852/53-1938) American comedian, minstrel DAB, SR, WWM

HEATH, William (d 1868 [48]) actor? EA/69*

HEATH, Mrs. William (d 1898 [23]) EA/99*

HEATHCOTE, A. M. (d 1934 [87]) dramatist BE*, WWT/14*

HEATHCOTE, Ernest (fl 1895) actor, dancer, singer CDP

HEATHCOTE, Kate (fl 1871) actress CDP

HEATHER, Jerrold (b 1874) English actor GRB/1

HEATHERLEY, Clifford (1888-1937) English actor WWT/4-8

HEATHERTON, Ray (b 1910) American actor, singer BE

HEATON, Percy (1894-1971) American actor WWA/5

HEATON, Theodore (d 1880) conductor EA/81*

HEAVENS, Mrs. J. (d 1873) EA/74*

HEAVER, Mrs. W. (d 1910) EA/12*

HEAVER, William (d 1906) EA/07*

HEAVER, Rev. William (d 1912) EA/13*

HEBDEN, John (fl 1740) musician CDP

HEBDEN, Will (fl 1890?) singer, actor CDP

HEBERLE, Teresa dancer CDP

HEBERT, Fred (1911-72) American producer, director, manager BE, TW/28

HEBERTOT, Jacques (d 1970 [84]) producer/director/choreographer BP/55*

HECHT, Albert (b 1903) American actor TW/4-7

HECHT, Ben (1894-1964) American dramatist AAS, CB, ES, HJD, MD, MH, MWD, NTH, PDT, SR, TW/20, WWA/4, WWT/8-13

HECHT, Edward (d 1887 [54]) musician, conductor EA/88*

HECHT, Jenny (b 1943) American actress TW/9

HECHT, Paul (b 1941) English actor TW/23-29

HECHT, Ted (d 1969 [61]) actor TW/26

HECK, Howard (d 1969 [73]) treasurer BP/54*

HECKART, Eileen (b 1919) American actress AAS, BE, CB, TW/9-27, 30, WWT/12-16

HECKLE, Emma singer CDP

HECKROTH, Hein (d 1970 [69]) designer BP/55*

HECKSCHER, August (b 1913) American journalist, writer, executive BE

HECTOR, "Little" [Tom Hector Walsh] (d 1893) music-hall performer EA/94*

HEDGES BROTHERS (fl 1912?) variety artists CDP

HEDISON, Al (b 1929) American actor TW/12-15

HEDLEY, H. B. (d 1931 [41]) composer, lyricist WWT/6

HEDLEY, John (d 1890) lessee EA/91*

HEDMAN, Martha (b 1888) Swedish actress WWT/3-6, 10

HEDMONT, E. C. (1857-1940) American singer GRB/1-4

HEELEY, Desmond designer AAS, WWT/15-16

HEELEY, Frank (d 1895) clown EA/96*

HEELY, Mr. (fl 1794) actor HAS
HEELY, Mrs. (fl 1794) actress
HAS
HEELYER, Miss see Graupner,
Mrs.
HEENAN, Mrs. John C. see
Stevens, Sara
HEFFERNAN, John (b 1934) Amer-
ican actor BE, TW/22, 24-30,
WWT/15-16
HEFFERNAN, Mary (d 1908) EA/
09*
HEFFERNON, E. M. (d 1876 [64])
manager EA/77*
HEFFNER, Hubert (b 1901) Ameri-
can educator, writer BE
HEFFRON, J. C. singer, actor
CDP
HEFLIN, Emmet Evan see
Heflin, Van
HEFLIN, Frances (b 1922/24)
American actress BE, TW/1,
21, WWT/10-11
HEFLIN, Marta (b 1945) American
actress TW/24-29
HEFLIN, Martin (d 1972) publicist
BP/56*
HEFLIN, Nora (b 1950) American
actress TW/29
HEFLIN, Van [né Emmet Evan
Heflin] (1909/10-71) American
actor BE, TW/20, 28,
WWA/5, WWT/10
HEGGEN, Thomas O. (1919-49)
American writer MH, TW/5
HEGGIE, O. P. (1879-1936)
Australian actor WWT/1-8
HEGLON, Meyriane Belgian
singer GRB/1-2
HEGNER, Otto (b 1876) musi-
cian, composer CDP
HEHL, Walter (d 1890) manager,
treasurer EA/91*
HEIDEGGER, John James (1659?-
1749) Swiss manager CDP,
CP/1, DNB
HEIDT, Joseph (d 1962 [52])
American press representative
BE*, BP/47*
HEIGHLEY, Bruce (b 1939) Eng-
lish actor TW/26, 29
HEIGHT, Bob (d 1881) comedian
EA/82*
HEIJERMANS, Herman (1864-
1924) Dutch dramatist COC,
GRB/1-4, NTH, WWT/3
HEILBRONN, Marie (d 1886) ac-
tress, singer CDP

HEILBRONN, William (b 1879)
English actor WWT/9-11
HEIMAN, Marcus (b 1886) Ameri-
can executive SR
HEIMER, Mel (d 1971 [55]) critic
BP/55*
HEIN, Silvio (1879-1928) American
composer WWM, WWT/4-6
HEINE, Albert (1867-1949) German
actor, manager GRB/4, WWT/
1-2
HEINEL, Anne Frédérique (1752-
1808) German dancer OC/1-2
HEINEMAN, William (d 1974 [74])
producer/director/choreographer
BP/59*
HEINEMANN, Eda (b 1900) Japanese
actress BE, TW/1, 13-15, 19
HEINEMANN, William (1863-1920)
English publisher, dramatist
WWW/2
HEININGER, Francis (d 1973 [62])
dramatist BP/58*
HEINLEIN, Mary Virginia (d 1961
[58]) American educator BE*
HEINRICH JULIUS, Duke of Bruns-
wick (1564-1613) German drama-
tist OC/1-3
HEINRICH, Rudolf (d 1975 [49])
designer BP/60*
HEINZ, Gerard (1904-72) German
actor WWT/11-15
HEIR, Robert (d 1868) actor EA/
69*
HEISKELL, Josephine see Louis-
ette, Josephine
HEISS, John Stanger see Asche,
Oscar
HEISTER, George scene artist
CDP
HEIT, Michael (b 1943) American
actor TW/23-24
HELBURN, Theresa (1887-1959)
American dramatist, manager
CB, COC, TW/2-8, 16, WWA/3,
WWT/7-12
HELD, Anna [Mrs. Florenz Zieg-
feld] (1873-1918) French actress,
singer CDP, COC, ES, GRB/
2-4, NTH, SR, WWM, WWS,
WWT/1-3
HELD, Dan (b 1948) American ac-
tor TW/29-30
HELENA, Mme. see Sleap, Ellen
Caroline
HELENA, Edith (b 1876) American
actress, singer WWS
HELENE [Rose Hélène Winter] (d

1912) variety performer EA/13*

HELENE, Eily (fl 1902?) singer CDP

HELFEND, Dennis (b 1939) American actor TW/29-30

HELLE, John (fl 1597) clown DA

HELLER, Claire (b 1929) American producer BE

HELLER, Haidée performer CDP

HELLER, Jeanne (d 1908) actress BE*, WWT/14*

HELLER, Joseph (b 1923) American dramatist CB, CD

HELLER, Robert see Heller, Robert Palmer

HELLER, Robert see Palmer, William Henry

HELLER, Robert P. (d 1975 [60]) producer/director/ choreographer BP/60*

HELLER, Robert Palmer (1833-78) American magician, pianist CDP, HAS, SR

HELLER, Stephen (d 1888 [72]) musician, composer EA/89*

HELLINGER, Mark (1903/04-47) American writer SR

HELLIWELL, Hubert J. (d 1917) EA/18*

HELLMAN, Lillian (b 1905) American dramatist, director AAS, BE, CB, CD, CH, COC, ES, HJD, MD, MH, MWD, NTH, OC/1-3, PDT, RE, SR, WWT/9-16

HELLMER, Kurt (b 1909) German literary representative BE

HELM, Anne (b 1938) Canadian actress TW/14

HELM, Frances American actress BE

HELM, Peter (b 1941) Canadian actor TW/16

HELME, Mr. (fl 1801) actor CDP

HELME, Mrs. see Cabanel, Harriot

HELMERS, June (b 1941) American actress TW/23, 26-27, 29

HELMOND, Katherine American actress TW/27-29

HELMORE, Arthur (d 1941 [83]) actor EA/95

HELMORE, Tom (b 1912/16) English actor BE, TW/6-16,

22, 24

HELMS, Alan (b 1938) American actor TW/17-19

HELMSLEY, Charles Thomas Hunt (1865-1940) English manager, actor GRB/2-4, WWT/1-7

HELMSLEY, Mrs. Charles Thomas Hunt see Harvey, May

HELPMANN, Sir Robert Murray (b 1909) Australian actor, dancer, choreographer AAS, BE, CB, COC, ES, OC/1-3, TW/8, WWT/8-16

HELPS, Sir Arthur (1813-75) dramatist HP

HELSCHER, Fern (d 1974 [73]) publicist BP/58*

HELTAI, Jenö (1871-1957) Hungarian dramatist COC, OC/1-3

HELTON, Alf (d 1937 [78]) English actor BE*, BP/21*

HELTON, Mrs. George see Zaraza

HELTON, Percy (d 1971 [77]) vaudevillian, actor TW/28

HELY, R. W. (d 1881) EA/83*

HEMING, Fred (d 1908) actor EA/09*

HEMING, Percy (b 1885) English actor, singer WWT/5-11

HEMING, Violet (b 1893/95) English actress BE, TW/1-3, WWM, WWT/4-14

HEMINGE, John (1556-1630) English actor COC, DA, DNB, ES, GT, HP, NTH, OC/1-3, PDT

HEMINGE, William (b 1602) English dramatist CP/1-3, DNB, FGF, GT

HEMINGWAY, Ernest (1899-1961) American dramatist ES, HJD, MD, MWD

HEMINGWAY, Marie (1893-1939) English actress WWT/3-7

HEMLEY, Jesse (d 1970 [63]) lawyer BP/55*

HEMMERDE, Edward George (1871-1948) English dramatist WWT/ 1-10

HEMMING, Miss see Walton, Elsie

HEMMING, Alfred (d 1942 [91]) singer, composer, actor CDP

HEMMING, Henry (1805-49) actor CDP

HEMMING, Richard Walton (d 1909) comedian EA/10*

HEMMINGS, William (d 1874) circus

performer? EA/75*

HEMPEL, Frieda (1884-1955) German singer ES, TW/12, WWA/3, WWW/5

HEMPLE, Samuel (b 1833) American comedian HAS

HEMSLEY, Estelle (1892-1968) American actress BE, TW/25

HEMSLEY, Harry May (d 1951 [73]) child impersonator BE*, WWT/14*

HEMSLEY, Margaret (d 1918) EA/19*

HEMSLEY, Sherman (b 1938) American actor TW/25-29

HEMSLEY, Winston DeWitt (b 1947) American actor TW/28

HEMSLEY, W. T. (1850-1918) English scene artist WWT/1-3

HENABERY, Joseph E. (d 1976 [88]) producer/director/choreographer BP/60*

HENDERSON, A. see Henderson, Andrew

HENDERSON, Alexander (1823/29-86) manager CDP, COC

HENDERSON, Mrs. Alexander see Thompson, Lydia

HENDERSON, Alex F. (1866/68-1933) English manager WWT/2-7

HENDERSON, Andrew (fl 1752?) Scottish dramatist CP/1-3, GT

HENDERSON, Annie (d 1878 [27]) dancer EA/79*

HENDERSON, Archibald (b 1877) American critic NTH

HENDERSON, Bessie [Mrs. H. F. Young] (d 1885) actress EA/86*

HENDERSON, Mrs. C. E. T. see Horwood, Lena

HENDERSON, Charles (fl 1854) actor HAS

HENDERSON, David (1853-1908) Scottish manager, producer GRB/4, SR, WWS

HENDERSON, Del (d 1956 [79]) actor, director BE*

HENDERSON, Dickie (b 1922) American actor, music-hall comedian WWT/12-16

HENDERSON, Elvira (b 1903) Cuban actress WWT/7-10

HENDERSON, Ettie see Henderson, Mrs. William

HENDERSON, Florence (b 1934) American actress, singer BE, CB, WWT/15-16

HENDERSON, Frank (d 1907) musician? EA/08*

HENDERSON, Grace (d 1944 [84]) American actress BE*, WWT/14*

HENDERSON, Henrietta (d 1887) actress NYM

HENDERSON, J. (d 1916 [63]) dramatist, producer EA/18*

HENDERSON, Jack (d 1957 [79]) actor TW/13

HENDERSON, John (1747-85) English actor CDP, COC, DNB, ES, GT, NTH, OC/1-3, OX, TD/1-2

HENDERSON, John (d 1867 [45]) equestrian director CDP

HENDERSON, John Raymond (d 1937 [48]) American press representative BE*, BP/22*

HENDERSON, Laura (d 1944 [80]) producer BE*, WWT/14*

HENDERSON, Lizzie (d 1917) EA/18*

HENDERSON, Lucius (d 1947 [86]) American actor, producer TW/3

HENDERSON, Mrs. Lucius see Lyons, Gretchen

HENDERSON, Luther (b 1919) composer, musical director BE

HENDERSON, Marcia (b 1929) American actress TW/6-9

HENDERSON, Marie [Mrs. James Aubrey] (d 1882) actress EA/83*

HENDERSON, Marie [Mrs. George Rignold; Marie Braybrook] (d 1902 [58]) actress BE*, EA/03*, WWT/14*

HENDERSON, Melanie (b 1957) American actress TW/26-28

HENDERSON, Ray (d 1937 [48]) press representative WWT/14*

HENDERSON, Ray (1896-1970) American composer BE, TW/27, WWT/6-11

HENDERSON, Robert (b 1904) American producer, manager, director, actor WWT/11-16

HENDERSON, Thomas (d 1970 [81]) composer/lyricist BP/54*

HENDERSON, William (fl 1821-55) actor, manager HAS

HENDERSON, William (1824-89) actor, manager CDP

HENDERSON, William (d 1908)
manager EA/09*
HENDERSON, Mrs. William
[Henrietta Lewis] (1835-1909)
American? actress HAS
HENDERSON, Willie (b 1839)
American actor HAS
HENDL, Walter (b 1917) Amer-
ican conductor CB
HENDON, Agnes actress SR
HENDRICKS, Ben F. (1868-1930)
American actor WWM
HENDRIE, Ernest (1859-1929)
actor, dramatist WWT/2-5
HENDRY, Thomas (b 1929)
Canadian dramatist CD
HENDRY, Tiffany (b 1942)
American actress TW/26, 29
HENEKER, David (b 1906) Eng-
lish composer, lyricist
WWT/15-16
HENGLER, Herr see Severn, A.
HENGLER, Mrs. Charles see
Hengler, Mary Ann Frances
HENGLER, Edward Henry (d
1865 [45]) equestrian EA/72*
HENGLER, F. C. (d 1889 [34])
EA/90*
HENGLER, Frederick Charles
(d 1887 [67]) circus proprietor
BE*, EA/88*, WWT/14*
HENGLER, Julia Fanny (d 1879
[21]) EA/80*
HENGLER, Mary Ann Frances
[Mrs. Charles Hengler] (d
1902 [74]) EA/03*
HENGLER, T[homas] M. (1844/
45-88) American minstrel,
actor CDP, HAS
HENGST, Marilyn (b 1946) Amer-
ican actress TW/27
HENIE, Sonja (d 1969 [57]) per-
former BP/54*
HENKENS, Harry [né Hincken]
(1809-53) American actor
HAS
HENLEY, Anthony (d 1711) Eng-
lish? dramatist CP/2-3
HENLEY, Drewe English actor
TW/23
HENLEY, Edward J[ohn] (1861-
98) English actor CDP, SR
HENLEY, Herbert James (1882-
1937) English critic WWT/
5-7
HENLEY, Joan (b 1904) Irish
actress WWT/7-15
HENLEY, Josephine [Mrs.

Charles H. Reid] (d 1908) bur-
lesque artist EA/09*
HENLEY, William Ernest (1849-
1903) English dramatist DNB,
HP, WWW/1
HENNECART, Maria (fl 1859)
Italian dancer CDP, HAS
HENNEQUIN, F. C. (d 1917 [41])
monologist EA/18*
HENNESIER, Samuel (d 1870) min-
strel EA/71*
HENNESSEY, May (fl 1901?) singer,
actress CDP
HENNESSY, Roland Burke (1870-
1939) American critic GRB/2-4,
WWM, WWT/1-2
HENNIGER, Rolf (b 1925) German
actor WWT/14
HENNING, Doug (b 1947) Canadian
magician, actor CB, TW/30
HENNING, Pat (d 1973 [62]) per-
former BP/56*
HENNINGS, Betty (d 1939 [89])
actress BE*, WWT/14*
HENNIS, Bob (d 1893) comedian
EA/94*
HENO, Prof. (d 1907 [56]) conjuror
EA/08*
HENRADE, Mary (d 1876 [34])
actress EA/77*
HENREID, Paul (b 1908) Italian ac-
tor CB, TW/29
HENRI, Blanche see Macklin,
Mrs. Francis Mary
HENRI, Blanche Marian (fl 1870-
79) English actress OAA/1-2
HENRI, Charles [né Montague] (d
1865) actor HAS
HENRI, Mrs. Charles (d 1879
[48]) actress EA/80*
HENRI, Jack (d 1917) EA/18*
HENRI, Louie (d 1947 [84]) actress
BE*, WWT/14*
HENRIQUES, Madelaine (1841-1929)
American actress CDP, HAS
HENRITZE, Bette American actress
TW/23-30, WWT/16
HENRY, Mr. actor HAS
HENRY, Mr. performer CDP
HENRY, Mr. (fl 1820) conjuror
CDP
HENRY, Mrs. performer CDP
HENRY, Mrs. see Barrett, Mrs.
George Horton
HENRY, Annie K. (d 1907 [30])
EA/08*
HENRY, Basil [Henry Beer] (d
1893) actor EA/94*

HENRY, Chaplin singer CDP
HENRY, Charles (d 1910) performer EA/11*
HENRY, Charles (1890-1968) English dramatist, producer WWT/6-14
HENRY, Creagh see Henry, S. Creagh
HENRY, David (d 1903 [64]) EA/04*
HENRY, Mrs. David Skene (d 1912) EA/13*
HENRY, Dick (d 1971 [82]) agent BP/55*
HENRY, Mrs. E. Bayle (d 1871) actress EA/72*
HENRY, George B. (d 1869) actor HAS
HENRY, George H. (b 1903) American educator, director BE
HENRY, Hiram (d 1920 [76]) minstrel BE*, BP/4*
HENRY, Jo-Ann (d 1972 [49]) performer BP/56*
HENRY, John (1738-94) American actor, manager, dramatist CDP, COC, CP/3, DAB, EAP, HAS, OC/1-3, RJ, SR, WWA/H
HENRY, Mrs. John, I [Miss Storer] (fl 1765) actress HAS
HENRY, Mrs. John, II (fl 1786) actress HAS
HENRY, Little minstrel CDP
HENRY, Mabel (d 1904) actress EA/05*
HENRY, Martha (b 1938) American actress TW/27-28
HENRY, Martin (1872-1942) English manager, actor WWT/5-8
HENRY, Patrick, II (b 1935) American educator, director BE
HENRY, Roland (fl 1909?) singer, song composer CDP
HENRY, Sam H. (d 1968) performer BP/53*
HENRY, S. Creagh [Henry C. S. Head] (1863-1946) English actor, dramatist GRB/1-4
HENRY, Shirley (d 1972 [47]) composer/lyricist BP/56*
HENRY, Thomas (b 1815) actor CDP
HENRY, Victor (b 1943) English actor TW/23, WWT/15

HENRY, William (b c. 1800) English actor SR
HENRY, William (fl 1831-37) English actor HAS
HENRY, Mrs. William (b c. 1800) English actress HAS, SR
HENSCHEL, Sir Georg (1850-1934) composer, singer CDP, WWA/2, WWW/3
HENSCHEL, Mrs. Georg see Bailey, Lilian
HENSHAW, James Ene (b 1924) Nigerian dramatist CD
HENSHAW, Thomas E. (d 1914) actor SR
HENSHAW, Thomas H. (d 1868 [87]) professor of music EA/69*
HENSHAW, William (d 1879 [29]) bill poster EA/80*
HENSLER, Elise (1832-1929) actress, singer CDP, HAS
HENSLOWE, Mrs. see Barthélemon, Cecilia María
HENSLOWE, Francis (fl 1590) actor DA
HENSLOWE, Philip (d 1616) English proprietor, manager COC, DA, DNB, GT, HP, NTH, OC/1-3, PDT
HENSON, Gladys (b 1897) Irish actress WWT/9-16
HENSON, J. W. (d 1916) EA/17*
HENSON, Leslie (1891-1957) English actor, producing manager AAS, COC, DNB, ES, OC/3, TW/14, WWT/4-12, WWW/5
HENSON, Nicky (b 1945) English actor WWT/15-16
HENTON, Thomas (d 1883 [20]) equestrian? EA/84*
HENTSCHEL, Carl (d 1930 [65]) club founder BE*, WWT/14*
HENTSCHEL, Irene (b 1891) English producer WWT/8-14
HENTZ, Caroline Lee (fl 1833?) dramatist RJ
HENZE, Hans Werner (b 1926) German composer CB
HEPBURN, Audrey (b 1929) Belgian/English actress BE, CB, ES, TW/8-16
HEPBURN, Katharine Houghton (b 1909) American actress AAS, BE, CB, COC, ES, NTH, SR, TW/2-21, 26-27, WWT/8-16
HEPBURNE, George (d 1880) scene artist, property master EA/81*
HEPENSTALL, Hazel see

Hughes, Hazel

HEPPELL, Albert H. (d 1912) high diver EA/13*

HEPPLE, Jeanne (b 1936) English actress TW/22-23, 27-30, WWT/14-16

HEPPLE, Peter (b 1927) English editor WWT/16

HEPPNER, Rosa (b 1905) English press representative WWT/10-16

HEPTON, William Thomas [Frank Williams] (d 1872 [38]) EA/73*

HEPWORTH, Mrs. Cecil M. (d 1917) EA/18*

HEPWORTH, Joseph (d 1868) singer EA/69*

HEPWORTH, William Henry (d 1886 [24]) musician EA/87*

HERAUD, Mrs. (d 1867) EA/68*

HERAUD, Edith (fl 1851-70) English actress OAA/2

HERAUD, John A. (1799-1887) English dramatist EA/68, NYM

HERBECK, Johann (d 1877 [46]) composer EA/78*

HERBERT, Mr. (fl 1752) English actor HAS

HERBERT, Mr. (fl 1802-04) actor, dramatist CP/3

HERBERT, Mrs. [Helen Kent] (fl 1829-51) English actress HAS

HERBERT, Mrs. [Agnes Michell] (d 1877) actress EA/78*

HERBERT, Miss see Taylor, Mrs. Charles

HERBERT, Sir Alan Patrick (1890-1971) English dramatist AAS, PDT, WWT/6-15

HERBERT, Annie [Mrs. George Townway] (d 1885) singer EA/87*

HERBERT, Arthur (d 1906 [36]) EA/07*

HERBERT, Diana (b 1928) American actress TW/8-17

HERBERT, Don American producer BE

HERBERT, Eliza (d 1878) EA/79*

HERBERT, Miss Emmott [Elizabeth Emmott] (d 1895 [30]) actress EA/96*

HERBERT, Ethel (d 1904) actress EA/05*

HERBERT, Evelyn (b 1898) Amer-

ican actress, singer WWT/7-10

HERBERT, F. Hugh (1897-1958) English dramatist MH, TW/14, WWA/3, WWT/10-12

HERBERT, Fred (fl 1891?) singer CDP

HERBERT, Fred (d 1972 [60]) producer/director/choreographer BP/56*

HERBERT, Mrs. Fred see Herbert, Janie

HERBERT, Galwey English actor GRB/1

HERBERT, George (d 1891 [26]) EA/92*

HERBERT, Sir Henry (1596-1673) English Master of the Revels COC, OC/1-3

HERBERT, Henry (1879-1947) English actor SR, TW/3, WWT/6-10

HERBERT, Holmes (d 1956 [28]) actor BE*

HERBERT, Hugh (1887-1952) American actor TW/2

HERBERT, Janie [Mrs. Fred Herbert] (d 1890 [24]) EA/91*

HERBERT, Jocelyn (b 1917) English designer AAS, ES, WWT/14-16

HERBERT, John (d 1835) English actor HAS

HERBERT, John (d 1852 [38/40]) actor EA/72*, WWT/14*

HERBERT, John [John Herbert Brundage] (b 1926) Canadian dramatist, director, actor, dancer CD

HERBERT, John, Jr. (1803-64) English actor CDP, HAS

HERBERT, Joseph (d 1923 [56]) English comedian, librettist BE*, BP/7*, WWT/14*

HERBERT, Kate see Lewis, Mrs. W.

HERBERT, Lew (d 1968 [65]) performer BP/53*

HERBERT, Louisa [Mrs. Crabbe] (d 1921 [89]) actress OAA/1-2

HERBERT, Mary, Countess of Pembroke (d 1621) translator CP/1-3

HERBERT, Tim actor TW/1

HERBERT, Victor (1859-1924) Irish composer, conductor DAB, ES, GRB/3-4, HJD, MH, NTH, PDT, SR, WWA/1, WWS, WWT/1-4

HERBERT, William (1844-96) In-

dian/English actor CDP,
OAA/1-2

HERBERTE, Mrs. E. B. see
Herberte, Elizabeth

HERBERTE, Elizabeth [Mrs.
E. B. Herberte] (d 1883 [32])
EA/84*

HERBERTSON, John Anthony
see Anthony, Jack

HERCAT, Prof. (d 1913) EA/14*

HERCZEG, Geza (d 1954 [65])
Hungarian dramatist BP/38*

HERENDEEN, Fred (d 1962 [68])
dramatist BE*

HERFORD, Beatrice (d 1952 [84])
English actress, monologist
TW/9, WWA/5

HERGET, Bob (b 1924) American
choreographer, director, dancer
BE, TW/5

HERIAT, Philippe (d 1971 [73])
critic BP/56*

HERIG, Maria freak CDP

HERING, Doris American critic
BE

HERIOT, Henry (fl 1547-52) actor
DA

HERIOT, Wilton (d 1913) actor,
stage manager, dramatist EA/
14*

HERIOT, Mrs. Wilton [Flossie
Wilkinson] (d 1905) EA/06*

HERKO, Fred (d 1964 [29])
choreographer BP/49*

HERLEIN, Lillian (d 1971) performer BP/55*

HERLIE, Eileen (b 1920) Scottish
actress AAS, BE, TW/12-21,
24, 29, WWT/10-16

HERLIHY, Ed American actor
TW/24, 30

HERLIHY, James Leo (b 1927)
American dramatist, actor,
director BE, CB, CD

HERMAN, Al (d 1967 [84]) performer BP/52*

HERMAN, Cynthia (b 1947) American actress TW/30

HERMAN, Henry (1832-94) dramatist DNB

HERMAN, Jerry (b 1933) American composer, lyricist BE,
CB, WWT/16

HERMAN, John producer BE

HERMAN, La Rosa (d 1920 [79])
actress BP/5*

HERMAN, Lewis (b 1905) English
director, producer BE

HERMAN, Marguerite (b 1914)
American director, producer,
actress BE

HERMAN, Maxine (b 1948) American actress TW/26-27

HERMAN, Selma American actress
WWS

HERMAN, Tom (d 1972 [63]) performer BP/56*

HERMANN, Prof. (b 1821) German
magician HAS

HERMANN, Agnes M. [Mrs. Louis
Hermann] (d 1909) EA/10*

HERMANN, Alexander (d 1896 [52])
conjuror EA/98*

HERMANN, David (1876-1930) director, actor, producer COC

HERMANN, Leon (d 1909 [42])
conjuror EA/10*

HERMANN, Louis (d 1884 [73])
actor EA/85*

HERMANN, Mrs. Louis see
Hermann, Agnes M.

HERMANN, Phil (fl 1890?) singer,
actor CDP

HERMANN, Theodore (d 1874) conductor EA/75*

HERMANT, Abel (d 1950 [86])
dramatist, critic BE*, WWT/
14*

HERMES, Alice American speech
teacher BE

HERNANDEZ, Juano (d 1970 [74])
actor TW/27

HERNDON, Agnes [née Mattie
Frazier; Mrs. Joseph A. Jessel;
Mrs. Albert Andruss] (d 1920)
American actress CDP

HERNDON, Richard G. (d 1958
[85]) French producing manager
WWT/6-9

HERNDON, T. J. (b 1833) American actor HAS

HERNE, Chrystal see Herne,
Katherine Chrystal

HERNE, James A. (1839-1901)
American actor, dramatist
CDP, COC, DAB, ES, HAS,
HJD, MH, MWD, NTH, OC/1-3,
PP/1, RE, SR, WWA/1

HERNE, Mrs. James A. [Katharine
Corcoran] (1839-1901) actress
COC, PP/1, WWA/H

HERNE, John F. (d 1888 [41])
American actor EA/88*

HERNE, Julie (1881-1955) American
actress, dramatist TW/11,
WWM, WWS

HERNE, Katherine Chrystal
(1882/83-1950) American ac-
tress DAB, GRB/3-4, TW/7,
WWM, WWS, WWT/1-10
HERNE, Katherine Corcoran see
Herne, Mrs. James A.
HERO, Maria (b 1942) American
actress TW/25
HERON, Agnes see Natali, Agnes
HERON, Bijou see Miller, Mrs.
Henry
HERON, Dalziel (d 1911) actor
BE*, EA/12*, WWT/14*
HERON, Fanny see Natali, Fanny
HERON, James (d 1918) EA/19*
HERON, Joyce (b 1916) Egyptian/
English actress WWT/10-16
HERON, Mary Ann (fl 1848) ac-
tress HAS
HERON, Matilda Agnes (1830-77)
American actress CDP, COC,
DAB, HAS, OC/1-3, WWA/H
HERON, Philip (d 1911 [23]) actor
EA/12*
HERON, Robert (c. 1760-1807)
Scottish dramatist CP/3
HERON-BROWN, Edith [Edith
Anne Brown] English actress
GRB/1-2
HERR, Melvin (b 1916) American
administrator, business mana-
ger BE
HERRAND, Marcel (d 1953 [55])
actor, producer WWT/14*
HERRIDGE, Frances American
critic, editor BE
HERRING, Mrs. (fl 1836) actress
HAS
HERRING, Fanny (1832-1906)
English actress CDP, HAS
HERRING, Paul (d 1878 [78])
clown CDP
HERRMANN, Alexander (1844-
96) German magician CDP,
SR, WWA/H
HERRMANN, Bernard (d 1975
[64]) composer/lyricist BP/60*
HERRMANN, Prof. Carl (d
1887) conjurer EA/88*
HERRMANN, Compar (1815-87)
German magician NYM, SR
HERRMANN, Edward (b 1943)
American actor TW/27-28,
30
HERRMANN, Priscilla (d 1893)
EA/94*
HERRON, Mark (b 1930) Ameri-
can actor TW/13

HERRON, Randy (b 1946) American
actor TW/29
HERSCHER, Sylvia (b 1913) Ameri-
can literary representative, pro-
ducer, agent, manager BE
HERSEE, Henry (d 1896 [76]) libret-
tist EA/97*
HERSEE, Rose (fl 1867-69) singer
CDP, HAS
HERSEY, David (b 1939) American
lighting designer WWT/16
HERSHEY, Burnet (1896-1971)
Rumanian dramatist BE
HERSHOLT, Jean (1886-1956) Danish
actor BE*, BP/41*, WWT/14*
HERSKOVITS, Bela (d 1974 [54])
performer BP/58*
HERTER, William (b 1947) Ameri-
can actor TW/24
HERTZ, Alfred (1872-1942) German
conductor CB, DAB, WWA/2,
WWM, WWW/4
HERTZ, Carl (d 1924 [64]) magician
BE*, WWT/14*
HERTZ, Henrik (1798-1870) Danish
dramatist COC, OC/1-3
HERTZ, Ida (fl 1870-79) English
actress OAA/1-2
HERVEY, Miss (fl early 19th cent)
albino CDP
HERVEY, Arthur (1855-1922)
French/English? composer
WWW/2
HERVEY, Grizelda (b 1901) English
actress WWT/6-11
HERVEY, Irene American actress
TW/1
HERVEY, Joe (d 1899) singer EA/
00*
HERVEY, John, Lord (1696-1743)
English dramatist CP/2-3
HERVEY, Rose actress, singer
DP
HERVIEU, Paul (1857-1915) French
dramatist GRB/1-4
HERWYN, W. G. (d 1877 [32])
stage manager EA/78*
HERZ, Andrew (d 1972 [25]) drama-
tist BP/57*
HERZ, Ralph C. (1878-1921) French
actor CDP, GRB/3-4, WWM,
WWS, WWT/1-3
HERZ, Mrs. Ralph C. see
Glaser, Lulu
HESLEWOOD, Tom (1868-1959)
English actor, costume designer
GRB/1-4, WWT/1-7
HESLOP, Mr. (d 1854) actor CDP

HESLOP, Charles (1883-1966)
English actor, singer WWT/
8-14

HESS, Cort (b 1838) American
actor HAS

HESS, Jack J. (d 1970 [78]) publicist BP/55*

HESS, Rodger (b 1938) American
talent representative BE

HESSELTINE, Stark (b 1929)
American talent & literary
representative BE

HESSER, Jupiter Z. K. M. (fl
1851?) composer CDP

HESSLEGRAVE, Mrs. H. see
Riley, Eliza

HESTER, Sally American actress
TW/5

HESTON, Charlton [né Carter]
(b 1921/22/23/24) American
actor BE, CB, ES, TW/6-11,
13-16, WWT/13-16

HESTOR, George (1877-1925)
English actor WWT/2-5

HETHERINGTON, Frederick
Augustus see Gaytie, Fred A.

HETON, Robert (fl 1635-37)
manager, actor? DA

HEUER, George (d 1887) treasurer NYM

HEUMAN, Barbara (b 1944) American actress TW/28-29

HEWER, John (b 1922) English
actor TW/11

HEWERDINE, William (fl 1790)
singer CDP

HEWES, Henry (b 1917) American
critic, dramatist BE, COC,
NTH, OC/3, WWT/13-16

HEWETSON, W. B. (fl 1808)
dramatist CP/3

HEWETT, Christopher English
actor, director BE, WWT/
12-16

HEWETT, Dorothy (b 1923) Australian dramatist CD

HEWETT, J. H. (fl 1831?)
American? dramatist RJ

HEWETT, Molly (d 1970) performer BP/56*

HEWINS, Mary see Fox, Mary
H.

HEWITT, Agnes [Mrs. Frank M.
Boyd] (d 1924 [61]) Indian/
English actress DP, GRB/
3-4, WWT/1-4

HEWITT, Alan (b 1915) American
actor, director BE, TW/4-8,
10-13

HEWITT, Alice (d 1973 [102]) performer BP/58*

HEWITT, Barnard Wolcott (b 1906)
American educator BE

HEWITT, Henry C. (1885/86-1968)
English actor WWT/5-14

HEWITT, James (1770-1827) English composer, conductor DAB,
HJD

HEWITT, John (fl 1729-34) dramatist CP/1-3, GT, TD/1-2

HEWITT, John Hill (1801-90) American songwriter, journalist BE*

HEWITT, John Q. (b 1881) American actor TW/2

HEWITT, John S. (d 1881) actor
EA/82*

HEWITT, Robert (b 1922) Australian
actor TW/22, 25-27

HEWLETT, Mr. (fl 1821) actor
CDP

HEWLETT, Maurice (1861-1923)
English dramatist GRB/2-4,
WWT/1-4

HEWSE, Richard (fl 1554) actor
DA

HEWSON, J. James (d 1923 [71])
dramatist, journalist BE*,
WWT/14*

HEWSON, John Thomas (d 1880
[26]) comic singer EA/81*

HEY, Richard (fl 1782-96) dramatist CP/3

HEYBURN, Weldon (d 1951 [46])
actor TW/7

HEYDT, Louis Jean (1905-60)
American actor TW/1, 3-6,
16, WWT/10-12

HEYES, Herbert (1889-1958) American actor TW/2

HEYL, Lewis J. (d 1839) American
actor HAS

HEYLIN, Peter (1599-1662) English
dramatist CP/2-3, FGF

HEYMAN, Barton (b 1937) American actor TW/26-30

HEYSE, Paul Johann Ludwig (1830-
1914) German dramatist GRB/
1-4

HEYSHAM, William Sayre American? dramatist RJ

HEYWARD, Dorothy (1890-1961)
American dramatist ES, MWD,
TW/18, WWA/4, WWT/9-13

HEYWARD, Du Bose (1885-1940)
American dramatist DAB, ES,
HJD, MD, MH, MWD, NTH,

WWT/9, WWW/3-4

HEYWOOD, Charles [né Frank Haffner] (b 1848) singer, female impersonator CDP

HEYWOOD, Eliza see Haywood, Eliza

HEYWOOD, Frank (d 1874) actor EA/75*

HEYWOOD, Jasper (1535-98) English dramatist CP/1-3

HEYWOOD, John (c. 1497-1580) English dramatist COC, CP/1-3, DA, DNB, ES, HP, MH, OC/1-3, PDT, RE

HEYWOOD, Joseph (d 1877 [44]) equestrian clown EA/78*

HEYWOOD, Matthew dramatist CP/1-3

HEYWOOD, Thomas (c. 1570-1641) English actor, dramatist COC, CP/1-3, DA, DNB, ES, FGF, HP, MH, NTH, OC/1-3, PDT, RE

HIAM, Frank (d 1899 [58]) conjuring apparatus manufacturer EA/01*

HIAM, Henry (d 1900 [35]) conjuring apparatus manufacturer EA/01*

HIBBARD, Edna (1895-1942) American actress CB, WWT/7-9

HIBBERD, Jack (b 1940) Australian dramatist, director CD

HIBBERT, Geoffrey (d 1969 [48]) performer BP/53*

HIBBERT, Henry George (1862-1924) English critic GRB/2-3, WWT/4

HIBBERT, Louise (b 1855) Spanish/English actress OAA/1-2

HIBBS, Elizabeth (d 1896) music-hall performer EA/97*

HIBBS, Thomas (d 1894) music-hall performer EA/95*

HIBERNIA, Fred (d 1893) music-hall performer? EA/94*

HIBERNIA, Mrs. Fred see Hales, Rose

HICHENS, Robert Smythe (1864-1950) English dramatist GRB/1-4, NTH, SR, WWT/1-10, WWW/4

HICHINS, H. J. (d 1911 [67]) manager GRB/1

HICKEN, Edward (d 1887 [85]) equestrian EA/88*

HICKEN, Isaac George [Isaac Batley] (d 1890 [34]) EA/91*

HICKEN, Thomas see Battley, Thomas

HICKEY, Hiram Phineas (b 1824) American actor HAS

HICKEY, William American actor, director BE, TW/27-30

HICKIN, Jacques (d 1904 [49]) acrobat EA/05*

HICKLEY, Richard Barkley (d 1904) EA/06*

HICKLIN, Margery (b 1904) English actress WWT/5-8

HICKLIN, Ralph (d 1970 [48]) critic BP/54*

HICKMAN, Alfred (d 1931 [57]) actor CDP

HICKMAN, Charles (b 1905) English actor, director AAS, WWT/7-16

HICKMAN, Howard (d 1949 [69]) actor TW/6

HICKMAN, James (b 1932) American actor TW/12

HICKMAN, J. Hampton (b 1937) American theatre owner, producer BE

HICKS, Agnes Rosa (d 1886 [36]) singer EA/87*

HICKS, Annie [Mrs. W. R. Hicks] (d 1873 [28]) EA/74*

HICKS, Betty Seymour (b 1905) English actress WWT/6-7

HICKS, C. Carroll (fl 1858) actor HAS

HICKS, Cecil (d 1888) musician EA/89*

HICKS, Sir Edward Seymour (1871-1949) English actor, manager, dramatist AAS, CDP, COC, DNB, EA/96, ES, GRB/1-4, NTH, OC/1-3, SR, TW/5, WWS, WWT/1-10, WWW/4

HICKS, Mrs. Edward Seymour see Terriss, Ellaline

HICKS, Henry Douglas (d 1902 [60]) actor EA/03*

HICKS, Jack (d 1974 [60]) producer/director/choreographer BP/59*

HICKS, Julian (d 1882) scene artist EA/84*, WWT/14*

HICKS, Julian (1858-1941) English scene artist WWT/1-6

HICKS, Leonard M. (d 1971 [53]) actor TW/28

HICKS, Newton Tree (d 1873 [62]) actor CDP

HICKS, Patricia (b 1921) English

actress TW/7

HICKS, Richard (d 1900) Irish
comedian EA/02*

HICKS, Russell (1895-1957)
American actor TW/10-11, 13

HICKS, Thomas Reid Strachan
see Trelawney, R. S.

HICKS, Tommy see Steele,
Tommy

HICKS, Walter (d 1917 [28])
comedian EA/18*

HICKS, Mrs. W. R. see Hicks,
Annie

HICKSON, Henry (d 1887) EA/88*

HICKSON, Joan (b 1906) English
actress WWT/9-16

HICKWORTH, John (1815-58) actor,
manager HAS

HIDALGO, Elvira de (b 1892?)
Spanish singer ES

HIELD, Mrs. (fl 1836) English
actress SR

HIELD, Anne [née Scholey] (fl
1832-55) English actress HAS

HIELD, C. W. (fl 1834-38)
actor HAS

HIELD, Mrs. C. W. (fl 1834-38)
actress HAS

HIELD, William (d 1877 [71])
actor EA/78*

HIELD, William, Jr. (d 1858)
English actor HAS

HIFFERNAN, Paul (1719-77) Irish
dramatist CP/1-3, GT, TD/
1-2

HIFFERT, Caroline (fl 1844)
German singer, actress CDP

HIFFERT, Catherine (fl 1849-58)
German actress, singer HAS

HIGDEN, Henry (fl 1693) dramatist CP/1-3, GT

HIGDEN, Ralph (fl 1328) dramatist CP/3

HIGGIE, Thomas Henry (d 1893
[85]) actor, dramatist BE*,
EA/94*, WWT/14*

HIGGINBOTTOM, Frances Ann
[Fanny Smith] (d 1868 [22])
dancer EA/69*

HIGGINS, Prof. (d 1891 [34])
aeronaut EA/92*

HIGGINS, Albert (d 1975 [32])
performer BP/59*

HIGGINS, David (d 1936 [78])
American actor, dramatist
BE*, BP/21*

HIGGINS, Dennis (b 1942) American actor TW/27

HIGGINS, Dick performer? CD

HIGGINS, Frederick Robert (1896-
1941) Irish manager, dramatist
CB

HIGGINS, Michael (b 1922) American actor, director BE, TW/
2-3, 7, 13-15, 21, 28-30

HIGGINS, Norman (1898-1974) English manager BTR/74, WWT/
11-15

HIGGINS, Robert (b 1932) American
actor TW/13-14

HIGGINSON, Mrs. see Cussans,
Mrs.

HIGGONS, Bevil (c. 1670-1735)
dramatist CP/1-3, GT

HIGH, Bolen (b 1945) American actor TW/26-28

HIGHAM, Fred (d 1918 [63]) EA/
19*

HIGHLAND, George A. (d 1954)
producer, director BE*, WWT/
14*

HIGHLEY, Reginald (1884-1942)
English manager WWT/6-7

HIGHMORE, John (fl 1731) manager
CDP, TD/1-2

HIGHT, Mrs. B. F. see Hight,
Lizzie

HIGHT, Fred (fl 1853) American
actor HAS

HIGHT, Lizzie [Mrs. T. M. Hunter; Mrs. B. F. Hight] (1843-
1927) actress CDP

HIGHTOWER, Marilyn (b 1923)
American dancer WWT/11-13

HIGHTOWER, Rosella (b 1920)
American dancer, choreographer
ES

HIGNELL, Rose (b 1896) English
actress, singer WWT/6-9

HIGNETT, H. R. (1870-1959) English actor GRB/4, WWT/1-11

HIKEN, Gerald (b 1927) American
actor, director BE, TW/14,
21, 29, WWT/14-16

HIKEN, Nat (1914-68) American
dramatist, director BE

HILARIOT, Antonia see Hilariot,
Mrs. Charles

HILARIOT, Charles (fl 1851) French
dancer HAS

HILARIOT, Mrs. Charles (fl 1851)
dancer CDP, HAS

HILARY, Jennifer (b 1942) English
actress TW/23-24, WWT/14-16

HILARY, Ruth (d 1968 [61]) performer BP/53*

HILDEBRANDT, F. (d 1870)
pantomimist EA/71*

HILDON, Chester see Hildon,
Rochester L.

HILDON, Rochester L. [Chester
Hildon] (d 1886) acting manager
EA/87*

HILDRETH, Mr. (fl 1851) actor
HAS

HILDRETH, Miss (d 1847) actress
HAS

HILDRETH, Albert (d 1969 [64])
box office treasurer BP/53*

HILDRETH, Sarah (b 1810) American actress HAS, SR

HILDYARD, Walter (d 1901 [78])
clown EA/02*

HILL, Mrs. (fl 1724-34) BD

HILL, Mrs. [Mrs. Stanley] (d
1834) English actress HAS

HILL, Mrs. (d 1906) EA/07*

HILL, Mrs. see Atkins, Mrs.
William

HILL, Mrs. see Burton,
Philippina

HILL, Aaron (1685-1750) English
dramatist CDP, COC, CP/
1-3, DNB, GT, HP, NTH,
OC/3, TD/1-2

HILL, Abram (b 1911) American
director, dramatist CB

HILL, Ann (b 1921) American
children's theatre executive
BE

HILL, Anne Russell (fl 1840-52)
English actress HAS

HILL, Annie [Mrs. Herman de
Lange] (d 1943) actress CDP,
DP

HILL, Arthur (b 1922) Canadian
actor AAS, BE, ES, TW/14-
15, 19-22, 24, WWT/14-16

HILL, Barton (d 1911 [82]) actor
WWT/14*

HILL, Benson (d 1845 [49]) actor,
dramatist BE*, EA/72*,
WWT/14*

HILL, Billie English actress,
singer WWT/6-8

HILL, Billy (1899-1940) American songwriter BE*

HILL, Brownlow (d 1872) actor
EA/73*

HILL, Caroline L. Brook English
actress OAA/1-2

HILL, Charles John (1805-74)
actor CDP

HILL, Charles John Barton

(1828/30-1911) English actor
CDP, HAS, PP/1

HILL, Mrs. Charles John Barton
(fl 1851) actress HAS

HILL, Charles Walter Blencoe (d
1869 [31]) actor? EA/70*

HILL, Charlotte (d 1872 [40]) performer? EA/73*

HILL, Ellen (d 1866 [63]) actress
EA/72*

HILL, Emily Caroline [Mrs. Frank
Hill] (d 1912) EA/13*

HILL, Errol (b 1921) Trinidadian
dramatist, director, educator
CD

HILL, Mrs. Frank see Hill,
Emily Caroline

HILL, Frederic Stanhope (1805-51)
American actor, dramatist
DAB, HAS, RJ, WWA/H

HILL, Mrs. F. Wilbur see
Whitaker, Willette

HILL, George (d 1878 [35]) musician EA/79*

HILL, Mrs. George [Bellevere] (d
1879 [25]) actress? EA/80*

HILL, George Handel ["Yankee"]
(1798-1849) American actor
CDP, DAB, HAS, HJD, SR,
WWA/H

HILL, George Ray (b 1922) American director BE, ES, WWT/
14-16

HILL, Gus (1860-1940) American
actor, dramatist, manager SR,
WWM

HILL, Hamilton (fl 1900?) Australian
singer CDP

HILL, Harriet [Mrs. T. Hill] (fl
early 19th cent) actress, singer
CDP

HILL, Helen Oursler (d 1968) performer BP/52*

HILL, Holly American actress
TW/24

HILL, Miss J. (fl 1847-52) actress
HAS

HILL, James (d 1817) English actor, singer CDP, DNB, GT,
TD/1-2

HILL, Jane [Mrs. William E. Bur-
ton] (d 1863 [39]) actress CDP

HILL, Jane (d 1975 [95]) performer
BP/60*

HILL, Jenny [Jane Woodley] (1851-
96) English music-hall performer
CDP, COC, OC/1-3

HILL, Jerome (d 1972 [67]) pro-

ducer/director/choreographer
BP/57*

HILL, J. M. (d 1912) manager
SR

HILL, Sir John (c. 1716/17-75)
dramatist CDP, CP/1-3,
GT, TD/1-2

HILL, John Henry [John Wilson]
(d 1887 [31]) property man
EA/88*

HILL, John Henry (d 1893 [35])
conductor EA/94*

HILL, John J. (d 1962 [70]) press
representative BE*

HILL, John T. (d 1900) music-
hall proprietor EA/01*

HILL, June (d 1975 [95]) actress
WWT/16*

HILL, Lawrence (b 1912) American producer BE

HILL, Lucienne [née Palmer]
English dramatist BE, WWT/
14-16

HILL, Martha American educator
BE

HILL, Percy (d 1912 [34]) acrobat EA/13*

HILL, Peter Murray (b 1908)
English actor WWT/9-11

HILL, Phyllis (b 1925) American
actress TW/9-12

HILL, Ralston (b 1927) American
actor TW/25-28

HILL, Reuben (fl 1899?) singer,
actor CDP

HILL, Richard (fl 1778) dramatist CP/2-3, GT

HILL, Richard (d 1890) actor
EA/91*

HILL, Ronnie (b 1911) English
composer, lyricist, journalist
WWT/12-16

HILL, Rose (b 1914) English actress, singer WWT/12-16

HILL, Ruby (b 1922) American
actress TW/2

HILL, Sinclair [Gerard Arthur
Lewin Sinclair-Hill] (1896-
1945) English producer WWT/
8-9

HILL, Mrs. Stephen see Hoban,
Lilian

HILL, Steven (b 1922) American
actor TW/4-11, 17-19

HILL, Mrs. T. see Hill, Harriet

HILL, Thomas see Hill, Tom

HILL, Thomas see Hilson,
Thomas

HILL, Thomas Bentley Lilwall (d
1902 [21]) actor EA/03*

HILL, Thomas Henry Weist (d 1891
[63]) principal of Guildhall
School of Music EA/93*

HILL, Tom (d 1851 [57]) clown
CDP

HILL, Walter (d 1879) comedian
EA/80*

HILL, Walter Osborn (d 1963 [87])
actor BE*

HILL, Wesley (d 1930 [55]) American actor BE*, BP/15*

HILL, William see Maynard,
Ambrose

HILL, William J. (1834-88) actor
CDP

HILLARY, Ann (b 1931) American
actress BE

HILLER, Ferdinand (d 1885 [74])
composer EA/86*

HILLER, Dame Wendy (b 1912)
English actress AAS, BE, CB,
ES, TW/4-8, 18, WWT/8-16

HILLERY, Mable (d 1976 [46]) performer BP/60*

HILLHOUSE, James Abraham (1789-
1841) American dramatist EAP,
HJD, RJ

HILLIAR, Ann see Dibdin, Mrs.
Thomas John

HILLIARD, Bob (1918-71) American
songwriter, producer, publisher
BE

HILLIARD, Harry (d 1890) sketch
artist EA/91*

HILLIARD, Harry S. (d 1895 [34])
actor EA/96*

HILLIARD, Harry S. (d 1966) performer BP/50*

HILLIARD, Hazel (d 1971 [83])
performer BP/56*

HILLIARD, Kathlyn (1896-1933)
Scottish actress, singer WWT/
6-7

HILLIARD, Mack C. (d 1965 [89])
producer/director BP/50*

HILLIARD, Patricia (b 1916) Indian/
English actress WWT/8-13

HILLIARD, Peter (d 1974 [37])
performer BP/59*

HILLIARD, Robert C. (1857-1927)
American actor, dramatist
CDP, GRB/2-4, SR, WWA/1,
WWM, WWS, WWT/1-5

HILLIAS, Peg (b 1914) American
actress TW/6-7

HILLIE, Edward (d 1975 [56])
producer/director/choreographer
BP/60*
HILLIER, Alice May (d 1873 [19])
actress EA/74*
HILLIER, Emily [Mrs. William
Hillier] (d 1917) EA/18*
HILLIER, James (d 1874 [34])
actor, comic singer CDP
HILLIER, Mrs. William see
Hillier, Emily
HILLIGSBERG, Mme. (fl 1801)
dancer CDP
HILLIS, Margaret (b 1921) Amer-
ican conductor CB
HILLMAN, George (b 1906) Amer-
ican actor TW/24-25
HILLMAN, Lori (b 1951) Ameri-
can actress TW/29
HILLMAN, Michael (1902-41)
South African actor, manager
WWT/9
HILLYARD, Mr. actor, manager
TD/2
HILSON, Ellen see Hilson,
Mrs. Thomas
HILSON, Thomas [né Hill] (1784-
1834) English actor CDP,
HAS
HILSON, Mrs. Thomas [Ellen
Augusta Johnson] (1801-37)
actress CDP, HAS
HILTON, A. T. (d 1908 [67])
EA/09*
HILTON, Daisy (d 1969 [60])
performer BP/53*
HILTON, Hilda (d 1888 [35])
actress EA/89*, WWT/14*
HILTON, James (d 1954 [54])
English writer BE*, BP/39*
HILTON, J. W. (d 1871 [35])
Negro minstrel EA/72*
HILTON, Marie American singer
SR
HILTON, Tessy [Mrs. Widdell]
(d 1879 [25]) actress EA/80*
HILTON, Violet (d 1969 [60])
performer BP/53*
HILTON, William (fl 1776) drama-
tist CP/3
HILYARD, Maud (d 1926) actress
BE*, WWT/14*
HIME, Edward Lawrence (d 1900
[77]) composer EA/01*
HINCHMAN, Mr. (fl 1849) actor
HAS
HINCKEN, Harry see Henkens,
Harry

HINCKLEY, Alfred (b 1920) Amer-
ican actor TW/23, 25, 27
HINCKLEY, Allen (1877-1954)
American singer WWA/3,
WWM
HINCKLEY, Dorothy (d 1972) ac-
tress TW/29
HINCKLEY, Isabella (1840-62)
American singer CDP, HAS
HINCKLEY, Sallie A. (b 1841)
American actress HAS
HIND, Adeline see Hind, Mrs.
Thomas James
HIND, Benjamin Nash (d 1873 [40])
singer EA/74*
HIND, Horace (d 1917 [21]) EA/18*
HIND, Thomas James (b 1815)
English actor CDP, HAS
HIND, Mrs. Thomas James [née
Adeline Grassan; Mrs. Stephen
Knight] (b 1813) American ac-
tress CDP, HAS
HINDELL, Gus singer CDP
HINDERER, Mrs. (d 1893) EA/94*
HINDES, Mr. manager TD/2
HINDLE, Annie (fl 1869?) singer,
male impersonator CDP
HINDLE, James A. (d 1917) EA/
18*
HINDLE, Winifred (d 1969) per-
former BP/54*
HINDLEY, John (d 1867 [47]) pro-
fessor of music EA/68*
HINDLEY, John W. (d 1878 [26])
musician EA/79*
HINDS, Michael (d 1892 [66]) cir-
cus performer? EA/93*
HINE, Frederick (d 1879 [70])
treasurer EA/80*
HINE, Hubert (d 1950 [59]) actor,
director, stage manager BE*,
WWT/14*
HINE, Jack (d 1899 [40]) actor?
EA/00*
HINES, Dixie (d 1928 [56]) press
representative BE*, BP/13*
HINES, Elizabeth (1899-1971)
American actress, singer TW/
27, WWT/5-7
HINES, Harry (d 1967 [78]) per-
former BP/51*
HINES, Jerome (b 1921) American
singer CB, ES
HINES, Mimi (b 1933) Canadian
actress TW/22-23
HINES, Patrick (b 1930) American
actor, director BE, TW/22,
29-30, WWT/15-16

HINES, Timothy Edwin see Hines, William E.

HINES, William (d 1889 [22]) American clog dancer EA/90*

HINES, William E. [Timothy Edwin Hines] (b 1859) American actor WWM

HINGLE, Pat (b 1923) American actor BE, CB, TW/11-22, 24-28, 30, WWT/13-16

HINGSTON, Edward Peron (d 1876 [52]) acting manager EA/77*

HINGSTON, Hannah [Mrs. P. Hingston] (d 1895 [77]) EA/96*

HINGSTON, James (d 1902 [75]) EA/03*

HINGSTON, Lilian actress CDP

HINGSTON, Mrs. P. see Hingston, Hannah

HINKEL, Cecil E. (b 1913) American educator BE

HINKLEY, Del (b 1930) American actor TW/23, 25, 27

HINKSON, Mary (b 1930) American dancer BE

HINNANT, Bill (b 1935) American actor TW/18-19, 23-24, 26-30

HINNANT, Skip (b 1940) American actor TW/23-25

HINRICHS, Gustav (1850-1942) German conductor CB

HINSHAW, William W. (1867-1947) American singer, conductor, producer SR, WWA/2, WWM

HINSON, Bonnie (b 1946) American actress TW/26-27, 30

HINSTOCK, Robert (fl 1538-51) actor DA

HINT, Robert (fl 1629) actor DA

HINTON, Charles (d 1917) EA/18*

HINTON, Henry L. (b 1840) American actor HAS

HINTON, Mary [Emily Rachel Forster] (b 1896) actress WWT/9-14

HIPPISLEY, E. [Mrs. Fitzmaurice] (fl 1741-66) actress DNB

HIPPISLEY, Jane see Green, Jane

HIPPISLEY, John (d 1748) actor, dramatist CDP, CP/1-3, DNB, GT, TD/1-2

HIPPISLEY, John (d 1767) actor, dramatist DNB

HIPPLE, Hugh see Marlowe, Hugh

HIPWORTH, Mr. (d 1795) actor HAS

HIRD, James William (d 1871 [43]) musician EA/72*

HIRD, Thora (b 1916) English actress WWT/11-16

HIROSE, George (d 1974 [75]) performer BP/59*

HIRSCH, John Stephan (b 1930) Hungarian director AAS, WWT/15-16

HIRSCH, Judd (b 1935) American actor TW/24-25, 29-30

HIRSCH, Louis Achille (1881/87-1924) American composer WWT/4

HIRSCH, Max (d 1925 [61]) executive BE*, BP/10*

HIRSCH, Samuel (b 1917) American educator, director, actor BE

HIRSCHBEIN, Peretz (1880-1948) Russian dramatist DAB, MH, MWD, NTH, RE

HIRSCHFELD, Al (b 1903) American artist BE

HIRSCHFELD, Guido (d 1889) manager EA/90*

HIRSCHFELD, Kurt (d 1964 [62]) producer/director BP/49*

HIRSON, Alice (b 1929) American actress TW/23, 30

HISHIN, Bernard (d 1944 [59]) manager WWT/14*

HISLOP, Joseph (b 1887) Scottish actor, singer WWT/8-10

HISSAM-DEMOSS, Mary (fl 1890-1910) American singer WWM

HITCHCOCK, Edward (1793-1864) American dramatist EAP

HITCHCOCK, Flora Zabelle (d 1968 [88]) performer BP/53*

HITCHCOCK, Fordyce (fl 1844-48) manager CDP

HITCHCOCK, Pat (b 1930) English actress TW/1

HITCHCOCK, Raymond (1865-1929) American actor CDP, DAB, GRB/3-4, SR, WWM, WWS, WWT/1-6

HITCHCOCK, Robert (d 1809) actor, prompter, dramatist CP/2-3, DNB, GT, TD/1-2

HITCHENER, W. H. (fl 1808) dramatist CP/3

HITCHINS, Harry J. (d 1911)

EA/12*

HITCHINS, H. J. manager GRB/
2-4

HITE, Mabel (1883/85-1912)
American actress CDP, SR,
WWS

HIVNOR, Robert (b 1916) American dramatist CD, CH

HIX, Don (d 1964) performer
BP/49*

HIXON, Frank G. (d 1973 [82])
promoter BP/57*

HO, Wai Ching (b 1943) British
actor TW/25, 27

HOADLY, Benjamin (1706-57)
English dramatist COC, CP/
1-3, DNB, GT, HP, OC/1-3,
SR, TD/1-2

HOADLY, Dr. John (1711-76)
English dramatist CP/2-3,
DNB, GT, TD/1-2

HOAG, Mitzi (b 1932) American
actress TW/15

HOAGLAND, Harland (d 1971 [75])
performer BP/55*

HOARE, Miss see Ward, Mrs.

HOARE, Douglas (b 1875) English
dramatist WWT/3-11

HOARE, Prince (1755-1834) English dramatist CDP, CP/3,
DNB, GT, TD/1-2

HOARE, Ryton (d 1908 [24])
EA/09*

HOBAN, Agnes E. (d 1962 [73])
performer BE*

HOBAN, Lilian [Mrs. Stephen
Hill] (d 1890) EA/91*

HOBAN, Michael see Hoban,
James Brown

HOBART, Doty (d 1958 [72])
dramatist BE*, BP/43*

HOBART, George V. (1867-1926)
Canadian/American dramatist
GRB/2-4, SR, WWA/1, WWS,
WWT/1-5

HOBART, Rose (b 1906) American
actress BE, WWT/7-11

HOBBES, Halliwell, Jr. English
actor TW/4

HOBBES, Herbert Halliwell (1877-
1962) English actor GRB/1,
TW/1, 3-4, 11-12, 18, WWT/
1-13

HOBBES, John Oliver [Mrs.
Craigie] (1867-1906) American
dramatist DNB, GRB/1, HP,
WWA/1, WWW/1

HOBBES, Thomas (fl 1610-31)

actor DA

HOBBS, Mr. (d 1877) singer EA/
78*

HOBBS, Billy (d 1917) actor, singer CDP

HOBBS, Carleton (b 1898) English
actor WWT/7-8

HOBBS, Frederick (1880-1942)
New Zealand actor, singer
WWT/4-9

HOBBS, Jack (1893-1968) English
actor WWT/3-12

HOBBS, William (b 1939) English
fight arranger, actor WWT/15-16

HOBGOOD, Burnet (b 1922) American educator, director BE

HOBIN, Thomas (d 1911) singer
EA/12*

HOBSON, Cpt. A. P. (d 1885)
manager EA/86*

HOBSON, Fred see Leslie, Fred

HOBSON, Harold (b 1904) English
critic AAS, BE, CH, COC,
PDT, WWT/11-16

HOBSON, James (b 1938) Canadian
actor TW/27

HOBSON, John (d 1887) musical
director EA/88*

HOBSON, Joseph (d 1892 [69]) proprietor EA/93*

HOBSON, Mrs. Joseph (d 1886)
EA/87*

HOBSON, Martin (d 1880 [47])
conductor EA/82*

HOBSON, Maud (d 1913) actress
BE*, WWT/14*

HOBSON, May (b 1889) English actress, singer WWT/4-6

HOBSON, Valerie (b 1917) Irish
actress ES

HOBY, Mrs. Charles J. see
Lynde, Flo

HOCHHUTH, Rolf (b 1931) German
dramatist CB, CH, COC, ES,
MH, MWD, PDT, RE, WWT/14-
16

HOCHULI, Paul (d 1964 [60]) journalist BE*

HOCHWÄLDER, Fritz (b 1911)
Austrian/Swiss dramatist COC,
PDT

HOCKENHULL, John Charles (d
1892 [41]) musician EA/93*

HOCKER, David (b 1911) American
talent representative BE

HOCKRIDGE, Edmund (b 1919)
Canadian actor, singer WWT/
12-15

HOCTOR, Harriet (b 1907) American dancer BE, WWT/8-10

HOCTOR, Robin (b 1953) American actor TW/29

HODAPP, Ann (b 1946) American actress TW/26-30

HODGDON, Samuel K. (d 1922 [69]) American vaudeville manager BE*, BP/6*

HODGE, Francis Richard (b 1915) American educator, director BE

HODGE, Merton [Horace Emerton Hodge] (1904-58) New Zealand dramatist WWT/8-11

HODGE, William Thomas (1874-1932) American actor, dramatist COC, DAB, OC/1-3, SR, WWA/1, WWM, WWT/3-6

HODGES, Ann American actress TW/28

HODGES, Ann Elizabeth (d 1871 [29]) singer EA/72*

HODGES, Mrs. Coppleson see Brougham, Mrs. John, I

HODGES, Eddie (b 1947) American actor, singer BE

HODGES, Horace (1865-1951) actor WWT/1-11

HODGES, J. A. (fl 1856) Canadian actor HAS

HODGES, Mrs. J. A. English actress HAS

HODGES, James (d 1881 [38]) journalist EA/82*

HODGES, Joy American actress TW/1-6, 29

HODGES, Nicholas (d 1884 [56]) manager EA/85*

HODGES, Thomas see Hogini, T.

HODGINS, Earle (d 1964 [65]) actor BE*

HODGKINSON, Frances see Hodgkinson, Mrs. John

HODGKINSON, John (c. 1765-1805) English actor, dramatist CDP, COC, DAB, EAP, HAS, OC/1-3, RJ, SR, WWA/H

HODGKINSON, Mrs. John [née Brett; ?= Arabella Brett, q.v.] (d 1803 [32]) English actress CDP, HAS

HODGKINSON, Marie see Clegg, Marie

HODGSON, Albert (d 1897) music-hall stage manager EA/98*

HODGSON, Alfred G. P. see

Paumier, Alfred

HODGSON, A. R. (d 1896 [47]) actor EA/98*

HODGSON, E. Miles (b 1889) English actor GRB/1

HODGSON, John (d 1888 [71]) EA/89*

HODGSON, William Wilson (d 1904) EA/05*

HODIAK, John (1914-55) American actor TW/8-10, 12

HODSON, Charles Henry see Stanley, Hodson

HODSON, George A. (d 1869 [47]) comedian, singer CDP

HODSON, Georgina Rosa (b 1830) Irish actress, singer CDP, HAS

HODSON, Henrietta [Mrs. Henry Labouchere] (1841-1910) English actress CDP, COC, DNB, OC/1-3, OAA/2

HODSON, James Landsdale (d 1956 [65]) English dramatist BE*, WWT/14*

HODSON, Kate [Mrs. Charles Fenton] (d 1917) actress OAA/2

HODSON, Nellie (d 1940) actress BE*, WWT/14*

HODSON, Sylvia [Mrs. John S. Blythe] (d 1893) actress BE*, EA/94*, WWT/14*

HODSON, William (fl 1775-83) dramatist CP/2, GT, TD/1-2

HOELBURG, Franz (d 1965 [79]) performer BP/49*

HOENY, A. Winfield American actor TW/1

HOERLE, Helen (d 1966 [65]) press agent BP/50*

HOET, Mrs. Peter see Davenport, Hester

HOEY, Dennis [Samuel David Hyams] (1893-1960) English actor, singer WWT/8-12

HOEY, Iris (b 1885) English actress WWT/1-13

HOEY, James F. (1851-1924) actor, minstrel CDP

HOEY, Mrs. John [Josephine Shaw] (1822/24-96) English actress CDP, HAS, SR

HOEY, Josephine see Hoey, Mrs. John

HOEY, W. H. (d 1970 [76]) performer BP/55*

HOEY, William F. (1855-97) actor, performer CDP, SR

HOFER, Chris (d 1964 [44]) American press representative, actor BE*

HOFF, Louise (b 1921) American actress, singer, dancer BE

HOFF, Robin (b 1952) American actress TW/30

HOFFE, Barbara [Barbara Conrad] actress WWT/4-9

HOFFE, Monckton [Reaney Monckton Hoffe-Miles] (1880-1951) Irish dramatist, actor WWT/2-11, WWW/5

HOFFE-MILES, Reaney Monckton see Hoffe, Monckton

HOFFMAN, Aaron (1880-1924) American dramatist WWM, WWT/4

HOFFMAN, Bill (d 1962 [44]) American dramatist BE*

HOFFMAN, Charles H. (d 1972 [60]) producer/director/ choreographer BP/56*

HOFFMAN, Dustin (b 1937) American actor AAS, CB, TW/23, 25, WWT/15-16

HOFFMAN, Ferdi actor TW/1, 4, 18, 21, 23

HOFFMAN, Frederick (d 1887) music-hall proprietor EA/88*

HOFFMAN, Gertrude (d 1966 [80]) Canadian dancer TW/23

HOFFMAN, Howard R. (d 1969 [76]) performer BP/54*

HOFFMAN, Irving (d 1968 [59]) critic BP/53*

HOFFMAN, Jane American actress BE, TW/2, 13, 19-21, 25-29, WWT/15-16

HOFFMAN, Lloyd (d 1973 [62]) publicist BP/57*

HOFFMAN, Maud American actress GRB/1-4, WWS, WWT/1-5

HOFFMAN, Max (d 1963 [88]) German musical director TW/19

HOFFMAN, Max, Jr. (d 1945 [c. 42]) American actor TW/1

HOFFMAN, Theodore (b 1922) American educator, dramatist BE

HOFFMAN, William M. (b 1939) American dramatist, director, actor CD

HOFFMANN, Hermine H. (d 1971 [47]) performer BP/56*

HOFFMANN, Mrs. Maurice H. see Irving, Sydney

HOFLICH, Lucie (d 1956 [73]) actress BE*, WWT/14*

HOFMAN, Elsbeth (b 1918) American actress TW/2

HOFMANN, Josef (b 1877) musician CDP

HOFMEISTER, Caroline CDP

HOFPAUER, Max (fl 1890) German actor CDP

HOGAN, Babette Hilda see Warren, Betty

HOGAN, Charlie (d 1970 [67]) agent BP/55*

HOGAN, John P. (b 1847) dancer, minstrel CDP

HOGAN, Jonathan (b 1951) American actor TW/29-30

HOGAN, Michael (b 1898) English actor WWT/7-10

HOGARTH, George (d 1870 [86]) writer EA/71*

HOGARTH, Lionel (1874-1946) American actor TW/2

HOGARTH, Vladimir [A. E. Moore] (b 1876) English singer GRB/1

HOGARTH, William (d 1899 [55]) singer, manager BE*, EA/00*, WWT/14*

HOGG, Miss see Claude, Mrs.

HOGG, Curly (d 1974 [57]) performer BP/59*

HOGG, Ian (b 1937) English actor AAS, WWT/15-16

HOGG, John (1770-1813) English actor HAS

HOGG, Mrs. John [Ann Storer] (d 1816 [67]) actress HAS

HOGG, Mary Anne [Mrs. Wentworth Hogg] (d 1907 [58]) EA/08*

HOGG, Mrs. Wentworth see Hogg, Mary Anne

HOGGAN-ARMADALE, E. (d 1917) actor, dramatist EA/18*

HOGGETT, Henry (d 1881 [55]) acrobat EA/82*

HOGINI, Mrs. Harry (d 1895) EA/96*

HOGINI, T. [Thomas Hodges] (d 1893) acrobat EA/94*

HOHLER, Thomas Theobald (d 1892) singer EA/93*

HOHNSTOCK, Adele (fl 1849) actress HAS

HOHNSTOCK, Charles (fl 1849) actor HAS

HOIER, Thomas P. (d 1951 [74]) Danish performer BE*, BP/36*

HOKER, John (d c. 1548) dramatist

CP/2-3

HOLBERG, Ludvig (1684-1754)
Norwegian dramatist COC

HOLBROOK, Ann Catherine (1780-
1837) actress DNB

HOLBROOK, E. G. C. (d 1943)
business manager WWT/14*

HOLBROOK, Hal (b 1916/25)
American actor AAS, BE,
CB, TW/18-25, 28, WWT/15-16

HOLBROOK, Joseph Charles (d
1870 [41]) circus proprietor
EA/71*

HOLBROOK, Louise actress
WWT/1-7

HOLBROOK, Ruby (d 1975 [63])
performer BP/60*

HOLBROOK, William (d 1971
[70s]) performer BP/56*

HOLBROOKE, Josef (1878-1958)
English musician WWW/5

HOLCOMB, Marion actress,
singer HAS

HOLCOMBE, Herbert (d 1908)
singer, vaudevillian CDP

HOLCOMBE, Ray Edward (b 1898)
American educator, director,
dramatist BE

HOLCOMBE, Thomas (d 1625?)
actor DA

HOLCROFT, Thomas (1744-1809)
English dramatist, actor
CDP, COC, CP/2-3, DNB,
ES, GT, HP, NTH, OC/1-3,
TD/1-2

HOLDEN, Mr. (fl 1662-65) dramatist CP/2-3

HOLDEN, Mr. (fl 1799) dramatist
CP/3

HOLDEN, Fay (d 1973 [79]) performer BP/58*, WWT/16*

HOLDEN, Hal (b 1938) American
actor TW/25

HOLDEN, James (b 1923) American actor TW/4, 10-12

HOLDEN, Jan [née Wilkinson] (b
1931) English actress WWT/
15-16

HOLDEN, John (d 1879 [63])
marionette exhibitor EA/80*

HOLDEN, John (d 1899 [58])
marionette proprietor EA/00*

HOLDEN, John (d 1967) pro-
ducer/director/choreographer
BP/52*

HOLDEN, Mrs. John see
Holden, Louisa

HOLDEN, Louisa [Mrs. John

Holden] (d 1891) EA/92*

HOLDER, G. B. see Howard,
Rollin

HOLDER, Geoffrey (b 1930/31)
West Indian dancer, choreographer, singer BE, CB, WWT/
16

HOLDER, Henry (d 1880 [69])
music-hall proprietor EA/81*

HOLDER, Owen (b 1921) English
actor TW/4, WWT/12-16

HOLDRIDGE, Barbara (b 1929)
American producer BE

HOLDSWORTH, Camilla (d 1897
[43]) sketch artist EA/98*

HOLE, Rev. Donald (d 1947 [79])
WWT/14*

HOLE, Richard (fl 1526-30) actor
DA

HOLFORD, Mrs. M. (fl 1799)
dramatist CP/3

HOLGATE, Ronald (b 1937) American actor TW/17, 22-23, 25-28

HOLGMAN, Benjamin (d 1963 [72])
press agent BP/47*

HOLIDAY, Dr. Barten (d 1661)
English dramatist CP/1-3, FGF

HOLIDAY, Billie (d 1959 [44])
American singer BE*

HOLIDAY, George see Glennie,
Herbert

HOLL, Henry (d 1884 [73]) actor,
dramatist CDP

HOLLAND, Mr. actor TD/2

HOLLAND, Mr. (fl early 19th
cent) actor CDP

HOLLAND, Aaron (fl 1605) theatre
builder DA

HOLLAND, Alice (fl 1868?) CDP

HOLLAND, Anthony (b 1912) English designer WWT/14-16

HOLLAND, Anthony (b 1933) American actor BE, TW/25-28

HOLLAND, Betty Lou (b 1931)
American actress BE, TW/2-4

HOLLAND, Charles (1733-69) English actor CDP, DNB, GT,
TD/1-2

HOLLAND, Charles (1768-1849?)
English actor DNB, GT, TD/1

HOLLAND, C. Maurice (d 1974)
producer/director/choreographer
BP/59*

HOLLAND, Edmund Milton (1848-
1913) English actor CDP, DAB,
GRB/2-4, OC/1-3, PP/1,
WWA/1, WWM, WWS, WWT/
1-2

HOLLAND, Edwin Clifford (1794-1824) American dramatist EAP, RJ

HOLLAND, Mrs. E. M. see Seward, Emily

HOLLAND, Fanny [Mrs. Arthur Law] (1847-1931) English actress, singer CDP, GRB/1-3, WWW/3

HOLLAND, George (1791-1870) English actor, promoter CDP, COC, DAB, GC, HAS, OC/1-3, SR, WWA/H

HOLLAND, George (d 1910 [63/64]) American actor BE*, EA/11*, WWT/14*

HOLLAND, John (fl 1590) actor DA

HOLLAND, Joseph Jefferson (1860-1926) English actor DAB, OC/1-3, SR, WWA/1

HOLLAND, J. Talbot (b 1928) American actor TW/12

HOLLAND, Mildred (1869-1944) actress CDP, GRB/3-4, SR, WWM, WWT/1-3

HOLLAND, R. V. (b 1916) American educator BE

HOLLAND, Samuel (fl 1656) dramatist CP/2-3

HOLLAND, Theodore (1878-1947) composer WWW/4

HOLLAND, Vyvyan (d 1967 [80]) dramatist BP/52*

HOLLAND, W. A. (fl 1806) dramatist CP/3

HOLLAND, William (d 1895 [58]) manager, caterer EA/97*, WWT/14*

HOLLANDER, Frederick (d 1976 [79]) composer BP/60*

HOLLANDER, Jack (b 1918) American actor TW/22-26, 29-30

HOLLENDER, Count Max (d 1906 [51]) director EA/07*

HOLLES, Antony (1901-50) English actor WWT/4-10

HOLLES, Robert dramatist CD

HOLLES, William (1867-1947) English actor, producer, manager GRB/1-3, WWT/4-8

HOLLICK, W. F. (d 1899) music-hall stage manager EA/00*

HOLLIDAY, Bob (b 1932) American actor TW/22-23

HOLLIDAY, David (b 1937) American actor TW/25-28

HOLLIDAY, Judy (1921/22/23-65) American actress, singer BE, CB, ES, TW/1-20, 22, WWA/4, WWT/11-13

HOLLIDAY, Marjorie (d 1969 [49]) performer BP/54*

HOLLIDAY, Polly American actress TW/29

HOLLINGSHEAD, Austin (d 1941 [64]) business manager WWT/14*

HOLLINGSHEAD, Bessie (d 1915) actress CDP

HOLLINGSHEAD, John (1827-1904) English dramatist, manager CDP, COC, DNB, EA/69, GRB/1, OC/1-3, WWW/1

HOLLINGSHEAD, Mrs. John see Hollingshead, Mrs. M.

HOLLINGSHEAD, John Edward (d 1902 [44]) acting manager, treasurer, business manager EA/03*

HOLLINGSHEAD, Mrs. M. [Mrs. John Hollingshead] (d 1890 [67]) EA/91*

HOLLINGSWORTH, Mr. (fl 1788) actor TD/1-2

HOLLINGSWORTH, Alfred (d 1926 [52]) actor BE*, BP/11*

HOLLINGSWORTH, Mrs. C. S. [Mrs. T. R. Hollingsworth] (d 1875) EA/76*

HOLLINGSWORTH, George (d 1892 [63]) EA/93*

HOLLINGSWORTH, Mrs. T. R. see Hollingsworth, Mrs. C. S.

HOLLINS, Henry Harrison (d 1882 [50]) bandmaster EA/83*

HOLLINS, Mabel (b 1887) English actress WWS

HOLLIS, John (d 1878) Negro comedian EA/79*

HOLLISTER, Louis (b 1921) American actor TW/5-7

HOLLISTER, Paul M. (d 1970 [79]) publicist BP/55*

HOLLISTER, Walter (d 1905 [44]) acting manager GRB/1

HOLLMAN, Carl (d 1879 [23]) musician, composer EA/81*

HOLLOWAY, Miss (fl 1804) actress TD/2

HOLLOWAY, Baliol (1883-1967) English actor AAS, WWT/4-11, WWW/6

HOLLOWAY, Catherine [Mrs. Henry Holloway] (d 1880 [34]) EA/81*

HOLLOWAY, Edmund (d 1906 [85])

Australian actor EA/07*

HOLLOWAY, Mrs. Edmund (d 1887) Australian actress EA/88*

HOLLOWAY, Mrs. Henry see Holloway, Catherine

HOLLOWAY, James (d 1879 [60]) actor CDP

HOLLOWAY, Jean (b 1929) American actress TW/13-14

HOLLOWAY, John (d 1871) actor EA/72*

HOLLOWAY, John (d 1878 [24]) clown, vaulter EA/79*

HOLLOWAY, John J. (d 1890 [22]) EA/91*

HOLLOWAY, Stanley (b 1890) English actor, singer AAS, BE, CB, ES, TW/12-14, WWT/6-16

HOLLOWAY, Sterling American actor BE

HOLLOWAY, W. E. (1885-1952) Australian actor WWT/9-11

HOLLOWAY, William (d 1893) clown EA/94*

HOLLOWAY, William Edward (d 1903 [37]) circus performer EA/04*

HOLLOWAY, W. J. (d 1913) English actor, producer GRB/1-4

HOLLY, Ellen (b 1931) American actress BE, TW/29-30

HOLLY, John (b 1944) American actor TW/30

HOLLYWOOD, Daniel (b 1914) Irish producer, literary representative BE

HOLM, Cecil (b 1904) American actor, dramatist WWT/9-11

HOLM, Celeste (b 1919) American actress, singer AAS, BE, TW/1-20, 24-26, WWT/10-16

HOLM, Dolores (d 1976 [69]) designer BP/60*

HOLM, Hanya [née Johanna Eckert] (b 1898) German/American dancer, choreographer, director BE, CB, ES, TW/5-8, WWT/15-16

HOLM, Ian [né Ian Holm Cuthbert] (b 1931) English actor AAS, WWT/14-16

HOLM, John Cecil (b 1904) American actor, dramatist, director BE, MD, MWD,

TW/20, 22-23, 25-27, WWT/12-16

HOLM, Klaus (b 1920) German designer BE

HOLMAN, Agnes see Gilfert, Mrs. Charles

HOLMAN, Benjamin (d 1864 [22]) comedian HAS

HOLMAN, George (fl 1836) American singer HAS

HOLMAN, Mrs. George [Harriet Phillips] (fl 1838) American singer HAS

HOLMAN, Gertrude [Mrs. Sydney Smith] (d 1912) EA/13*

HOLMAN, Joseph George (1764-1817) English actor, dramatist CDP, CP/3, DNB, GT, HAS, TD/1-2

HOLMAN, Mrs. Joseph George [Miss Lattimer] (d 1859) English actress CDP, HAS

HOLMAN, Julia (d 1879 [31]) American singer, actress CDP

HOLMAN, Libby (1906-71) American actress, singer BE, TW/2-3, 28, WWT/9-11

HOLMAN, Mary see Holman, Mrs. Joseph George

HOLMAN, Sally see Dalton, Mrs. James T.

HOLMAN, Sandra (b 1928) American actress TW/2

HOLMAN, Sonja (b 1949) American actress TW/25

HOLMAN, Thomas (fl 1629) actor DA

HOLMAN, Mrs. W. see Burney, Miss

HOLME, Constance (d 1955) dramatist WWW/5

HOLME, Myra [Lady A. W. Pinero] (d 1919) actress OAA/2

HOLME, Stanford (b 1904) French actor, producer WWT/8-13

HOLME, Thea (b 1907) English actress WWT/7-16

HOLMES, Alfred (d 1876) composer EA/77*

HOLMES, Alfred Miles (d 1917) door-keeper EA/18*

HOLMES, Basil Ralph Gardiner (d 1917) actor EA/18*

HOLMES, Brenda (b 1954) American actress TW/30

HOLMES, Burton (1870-1958) American lecturer TW/15

HOLMES, Charles W. (b 1846)

American actor HAS

HOLMES, E. B. (b 1840) American actor HAS

HOLMES, Edward (d 1885 [48]) music-hall manager EA/86*

HOLMES, Florence (d 1917) EA/18*

HOLMES, Helen (1892-1950) American actress WWT/4-7

HOLMES, Henry (d 1883) music-hall performer? EA/85*

HOLMES, Jack (b 1932) American composer, lyricist, musical director, conductor, singer BE

HOLMES, Jerry (b 1938) American actor TW/23

HOLMES, Mrs. John see Holmes, Sarah Eliza

HOLMES, Mjr. Know (d 1893 [85]) actor EA/94*

HOLMES, Morrice [James Morrice Orr] (d 1909 [59]) EA/10*

HOLMES, Phillips (1909-42) American actor CB, WWA/2

HOLMES, Ralph (d 1945 [30]) American actor TW/2

HOLMES, Robert (1899-1945) English actor WWT/6-9

HOLMES, Sarah Eliza [Mrs. John Holmes] (d 1890 [54]) EA/91*

HOLMES, S. F. R. (d 1847) actor HAS

HOLMES, Stuart (d 1971 [87]) performer BP/56*

HOLMES, Taylor (1872/78-1959) American actor TW/2-7, 16, WWM, WWT/6-11

HOLMES, Thomas (b 1816) actor CDP

HOLMES, Mrs. Thomas (d 1893 [69]) EA/94*

HOLMES, T. W. (d 1887 [28]) EA/88*

HOLMES, Wendell (d 1962 [47]) actor BE*

HOLMES, William (1840-66) American comic singer HAS

HOLMES, W. M. (d 1888 [72]) EA/90*

HOLMES-GORE, Arthur (1871-1915) English actor WWT/1-3

HOLMES-GORE, Dorothy (1896-1977) English actress WWT/4-9

HOLSTON, William (d 1876 [45]) English actor HAS

HOLT, Abe (d 1904 [42]) comedian EA/05*

HOLT, Alice [Mrs. Clarance H.] (d 1895 [44]) actress EA/96*

HOLT, Clarance (1826-1903) English actor OAA/2

HOLT, Mrs. Clarance (d 1878) actress EA/79*

HOLT, Mrs. Clarance H. see Holt, Alice

HOLT, Clarence (d 1920) actor BE*, BP/5*

HOLT, Elise (1847-73) English dancer, actress CDP, HAS

HOLT, Elizabeth Ruth (d 1912) actress? EA/13*

HOLT, Ellen Alice see Brown, Nellie

HOLT, Francis Ludlow (fl 1805-10) dramatist CP/3

HOLT, Harold (d 1953 [67]) impresario BE*, WWT/14*

HOLT, Hettie [Mrs. Will Harvey] (d 1911 [34]) EA/12*

HOLT, Issy [Mrs. H. F. Tyrrell] (d 1893 [26]) music-hall performer EA/94*

HOLT, Jack (1888-1951) American actor BE*

HOLT, James (fl 1603-19) actor DA

HOLT, John (fl 1561) actor DA

HOLT, John (d 1901 [57]) director EA/02*

HOLT, Marshall (d 1917) performer EA/18*

HOLT, Maud see Tree, Maud Beerbohm

HOLT, Nat (d 1971 [78]) manager BP/56*

HOLT, Richard (d 1867 [41]) professor of music EA/68*

HOLT, Richard (1867-1931) American critic WWA/1

HOLT, Stella (d 1967 [50]) American producer, manager BE, TW/24

HOLT, Tim (d 1973 [54]) performer BP/57*

HOLTUM (fl 1875?) cannon-ball catcher CDP

HOLTZ, Lou (b 1898) American actor BE, WWT/9-11

HOLTZMANN, David Marshall (1908-65) American producer, lawyer BE

HOLZAGER, Toni Ward (d 1973 [66]) designer BP/58*

HOLZER, Adela producer WWT/ 16

HOLZHEW, Behrendt (fl 1614-15) actor DA

HOLZMAN, Benjamin F. (d 1963 [72]) talent representative, press representative BE*

HOLZMAN, Samuel (d 1972 [80]) amusement park operator BP/57*

HOMAN, David (b 1907) Norwegian designer WWT/9-13

HOMAN, Gertrude (d 1951 [71]) actress TW/8

HOME, Rev. John (1722-1808) Scottish dramatist CDP, COC, CP/1-3, DNB, ES, GT, HP, OC/1-3, SR, TD/1-2

HOME, North Dalrymple (d 1887 [30]) singer EA/88*

HOME, William Douglas (b 1912) Scottish dramatist, actor AAS, BE, CD, CH, COC, ES, MD, MWD, PDT, WWT/ 11-16

HOMER, Benjamin (d 1975 [57]) composer/lyricist BP/59*

HOMER, Louise Dilworth Beatty (1871-1947) American singer DAB, TW/3, WWA/2, WWW/4

HOMEWOOD, A[shley] S[pencer] (b 1869) English actor GRB/ 1-2

HOMEWOOD, Mrs. A[shley] S[pencer] see Blair, Joan

HOMFRAY, Emma Sophia see Sterling, Ella

HOMFREY, Gladys (d 1932 [83]) actress WWT/2-5

HOMOLKA, Oscar (b 1898/1903) Austrian actor BE, TW/1-6, WWT/8-14

HONE, Mary (d 1909) EA/10*

HONE, Mary (b 1904) American actress WWT/7-10

HONER, Mary (b 1914) English dancer WWT/9-11

HONEY, George (d 1905 [40]) actor GRB/1, OAA/1-2

HONEY, George Alfred (1822/ 23-80) actor, singer CDP, DNB

HONEY, Laura (1816?-43) actress, singer CDP, DNB

HONEY, Laura (fl 1858) English actress HAS

HONEY, Sam see Sherar, John

HONIG, Edwin (b 1919) American educator, translator, critic BE

HONIG, Gale (b 1956) American actress TW/24

HONNAN, Richard (fl 1640) actor DA

HONNER, Adele (fl 1852?) singer CDP

HONNER, Maria see Honer, Mrs. Robert William

HONNER, Robert William (1809-52) English actor CDP

HONNER, Mrs. Robert William (1808/12-70) Irish actress CDP, DNB

HONNOR, Mrs. R. see Morton, Mrs. F.

HONRI, Percy [Percy Harry Thompson] (1874-1953) English musical entertainer CDP, GRB/1

HONYMAN, John (1613-36) English actor DA, OC/1-3

HONYMAN, Richard (b 1618) English actor OC/1-3

HOOD, Cpt. Basil (1864-1917) English dramatist GRB/1-4, WWT/ 1-3, WWW/2

HOOD, Henry Lionel (d 1879 [45]) actor EA/80*

HOOD, John (b 1831) American actor HAS

HOOD, John D. (fl 1900) singer, minstrel CDP

HOOD, Marion (d 1912 [59]) actress, singer DP

HOOD, Sydney Paxton see Paxton, Sydney

HOOK, Miss (fl 1782) actress TD/1-2

HOOK, Alfred H. (b 1879) English acting manager GRB/1

HOOK, Mrs. Alfred H. see Kearns, Rosie

HOOK, James (1746-1827) English musician, composer, musical director CDP, ES

HOOK, Rev. Dr. James (fl 1795-97) dramatist CP/3, GT, TD/ 1-2

HOOK, Mrs. James [née Madden] (d 1805) dramatist CP/3

HOOK, Nellie (d 1966 [80]) performer BP/50*

HOOK, Theodore Edward (1788-1842) dramatist CDP, CP/3, GT

HOOKER, Brian (1880-1946) American actor, librettist HJD, TW/3, WWM

HOOKHAM, Margaret see Fonteyn, Margot
HOOKS, David (b 1920) American actor, director BE, TW/28-29
HOOKS, Robert (b 1937) American actor, producer, director CB, TW/22-24, 26, 30, WWT/16
HOOLE, Charles (1610-66) English dramatist CP/2-3
HOOLE, John (1727-1803) English dramatist CP/2-3, GT, TD/1-2
HOOLEY, Richard M. (1822-93) Irish musician, manager CDP, HAS, SR
HOOPE, Richard (fl 1595?) actor? DA
HOOPER, Edward (d 1865 [70]) actor, lessee, manager CDP
HOOPER, Ewan (b 1935) Scottish actor, director, manager AAS, WWT/15-16
HOOPER, F. Pitman (d 1892 [31]) EA/93*
HOOVER, Richard A. (d 1973 [59]) BP/58*
HOPE, Adele Blood (d 1936 [50]) actress, promoter BE*, BP/21*
HOPE, Anthony [Anthony Hawkins] (1863-1933) English dramatist GRB/2, WWM, WWT/1-7
HOPE, Bob (b 1903) English/American actor, producer BE, CB, ES, SR, WWT/9-10
HOPE, Carrie Sydney [Mrs. W. H. Hallatt] (d 1887) actress NYM
HOPE, Charlotte [Charlotte Elizabeth Young] (d 1891 [26]) EA/92*
HOPE, Douglas (d 1975 [82]) performer BP/60*
HOPE, Eric see Yarmouth, Earl of
HOPE, Ethel [Mrs. E. B. Norman] (d 1899 [49]) actress CDP
HOPE, Evelyn (d 1966) English actress WWT/6-9
HOPE, Francis James (d 1975 [84]) performer BP/60*
HOPE, Henry Jenner (d 1897 [55]) musician EA/98*
HOPE, Mabel Ellams (d 1937) dramatist BE*, WWT/14*
HOPE, Maidie (1881-1937) English actress WWT/2-8

HOPE, Mrs. Stanley see Thearle, Nellie
HOPE, Vida (1918-63) English actress, singer WWT/11-13
HOPER, Mrs. [née Harford] (fl 1748-49) dramatist CP/1-3, GT, TD/1-2
HOPE-WALLACE, Philip A. (b 1911) critic AAS, WWT/11-16
HOPKINS, Mr. (fl 1799) actor HAS
HOPKINS, Mrs. (d 1801) actress CDP, TD/1-2
HOPKINS, Miss (fl 1771?) actress CDP, TD/1-2
HOPKINS, Miss see Kemble, Mrs. John Philip
HOPKINS, Albert (d 1889 [35]) gymnast EA/90*
HOPKINS, Anthony (b 1937) Welsh actor AAS, WWT/15-16
HOPKINS, Arthur (1878-1950) American manager, dramatist, producer CB, NTH, TW/2-6, WWT/4-10
HOPKINS, Bob (d 1962 [44]) actor BE*
HOPKINS, Bruce (b 1948) American actor TW/30
HOPKINS, Charles (d c. 1700) English dramatist CP/1-3, GT
HOPKINS, Charles (1884-1953) American actor, producing manager TW/9, WWT/6-11
HOPKINS, Cherry Preisser (d 1964 [46]) performer BP/49*
HOPKINS, Henry C. (d 1876 [32]) equestrian agent EA/77*
HOPKINS, Joan (b 1915) English actress WWT/11
HOPKINS, John (b 1931) English dramatist CD
HOPKINS, Miriam (1902/04-72) American actress BE, ES, NTH, TW/1-8, 29, WWA/5, WWT/6-14
HOPKINS, Richard (d 1881) actor EA/82*
HOPKINSON, Francis (1737-91) American dramatist EAP
HOPKINSON, Thomas (1709-51) English/American dramatist EAP
HOPPER, Bernhard (d 1877) composer EA/78*
HOPPER, Charles H. (d 1916 [53]) actor, singer CDP
HOPPER, De Wolf (1858-1938)

American actor, singer CDP, COC, DAB, GRB/2-4, NTH, OC/1-3, SR, WWA/1, WWM, WWS, WWT/1-7

HOPPER, Mrs. De Wolf see Bergen, Nella

HOPPER, Edna Wallace (1864/74-1959) American actress, singer CDP, GRB/2-4, NTH, TW/16, WWA/3, WWM, WWS, WWT/1-7

HOPPER, E. Mason (d 1967 [82]) performer BP/51*

HOPPER, Hedda [née Edna Furry] (1890-1966) American actress, singer SR, TW/22

HOPPER, Rika (d 1963 [86]) actress BE*

HOPPER, Victoria (b 1909) Canadian actress, singer WWT/8-14

HOPPER, William (d 1970 [55]) performer BP/54*

HOPWOOD, Avery (1882-1928) American dramatist DAB, GRB/3-4, HJD, MH, MWD, WWA/1, WWM, WWT/1-5, WWW/2

HORAN, Edward (b 1898) American composer WWT/10-13

HORD, John (d 1876 [64]) actor, manager EA/77*

HORDE, Thomas, Jr. (fl 1769-84) dramatist CP/2-3, GT

HORDEN, Hildebrand (d 1696) actor, dramatist CP/1-3, GT, WWT/11-16

HORDERN, Michael (b 1911) English actor AAS, WWT/11-16

HOREN, Bob (b 1925) American actor TW/25-26

HOREN, Leah (b 1942) American actress TW/25, 28

HORGAN, Patrick (b 1929) English actor TW/30

HORINE, Kathryn Kunkel (d 1965 [56]) performer BP/50*

HORITZ, Joseph F. (d 1961 [87]) performer BE*

HORKHEIMER, Herbert M. (d 1962 [80]) producer BE*

HORMAN, Nora (d 1916) EA/17*

HORMAN, W. E. (d 1875 [48]) EA/76*

HORMANN, Nicholas (b 1944) American actor TW/30

HORN, Charles Edward (1786-1849) English actor, singer, composer BS, CDP, HAS, OX, WWA/H

HORN, Mrs. Charles Edward, I see Horn, Matilda

HORN, Mrs. Charles E[dward], II [Miss Horton] (d 1887 [76]?) English actress CDP, HAS

HORN, Eph (1818-77) American minstrel CDP, HAS, SR

HORN, H. C. (fl 1842) composer, conductor SR

HORN, James (fl 1625) actor DA

HORN, Mrs. James see Reeve, Joey

HORN, Kate see Buckland, Mrs. John W.

HORN, Leonard (d 1975 [48]) producer/director/choreographer BP/60*

HORN, Mary (b 1916) Scottish actress WWT/11-12

HORN, Mary Ann see Horn, Mrs. Charles Edward

HORN, Matilda [Mrs. Charles Edward Horn, I] (b 1790) English actress CDP, OX

HORNBLOW, Arthur (1865/68-1942) English writer CB, ES, GRB/3, SR, WWA/2

HORNBLOW, Juliette Crosby (d 1969 [73]) performer BP/53*

HORNBY, Kate see Phillips, Harriett

HORNCASTLE, Henry see Horncastle, James Henry

HORNCASTLE, James Henry (1801-69) English actor, singer CDP, HAS

HORNE, Alderson Burrell see Hall, Anmer

HORNE, A. P. business manager, actor WWT/6-8

HORNE, David (d 1869 [27]) scene artist EA/70*

HORNE, David (1898-1970) English actor WWT/6-14

HORNE, F. Lennox (d 1874 [67]) dramatist EA/75*

HORNE, Geoffrey (b 1933) Argentinian/American actor BE

HORNE, John (fl 1677) dramatist CP/3

HORNE, Kenneth (1900-75) English dramatist AAS, WWT/8-15

HORNE, Lena (b 1917) American performer BE, CB

HORNE, Marilyn (b 1934) American singer CB, ES

HORNE, Richard Hengist (1803-84) English dramatist CDP, HP

HORNE, Rev. Thomas (d 1918 [68]) EA/19*

HORNE, Mrs. W. see Evans, May

HORNE, William actor TW/1

HORNER, Harry (d 1917 [44]) EA/18*

HORNER, Harry (b 1910/12) Czech/American director, scene designer BE, ES, TW/3-5

HORNER, James (d 1892 [43]) EA/93*

HORNER, Jed (b 1922) American director BE

HORNER, Lottie (d 1964) talent representative BE*

HORNER, Richard (b 1920) American manager, producer BE, WWT/16

HORNIMAN, Annie Elizabeth Fredericka (1860-1937) English manager AAS, COC, DNB, ES, GRB/4, HP, NTH, OC/1-3, PDT, WWT/1-8, WWW/3

HORNIMAN, Roy (1872-1930) English dramatist GRB/4, WWT/1-6, WWW/3

HORNSBY, Nancy (1910-58) English actress WWT/8-11

HORNUNG, E. W. (b 1866) English dramatist WWM

HOROVITZ, Israel (b 1939) American dramatist, director CD, CH, WWT/15-16

HORREY, Frederick (b 1921) English actor TW/3

HORRIGAN, John P. (d 1973 [47]) publicist BP/58*

HORROCKS, Joseph R. (d 1912 [45]) scene artist EA/13*

HORROX, John (d 1868 [47]) proprietor EA/69*

HORROX, Willie see Hartill, Willie

HORSFALL, John Thomas (d 1902 [52]) musician, composer EA/03*

HORSFORD, Anna Maria (b 1947) American actress TW/26, 30

HORSFORD, Arthur J. (d 1877) scene artist EA/78*

HORSLEY, Charles Edward (d 1876 [51]) musician EA/77*

HORSLEY, William (1774-1858) musician, composer CDP

HORSLEY-BERESFORD, Hon. Mrs. W. W. see Gordon, Kitty

HORSMAN, Charles (1825-86) Welsh actor OAA/1-2

HORSMAN, Mrs. Charles see Horsman, Charlotte

HORSMAN, Charlotte [Mrs. Charles Horsman] (d 1878 [50]) actress EA/79*

HORSNELL, Horace (1882/83-1949) English critic, dramatist WWT/9-10, WWW/4

HORSPOOL, J. (b 1856) English composer GRB/1-3

HORST, Louis (1884-1964) American composer, dance teacher WWA/4

HORTON, Mrs. (fl 1713) actress TD/2

HORTON, Miss see Horn, Mrs. Charles E[dward], II

HORTON, Bessie see Love, Bessie

HORTON, Christiana (1696?-1756?) actress DNB

HORTON, Claude English actor TW/8, 28

HORTON, Edward (fl 1630) actor DA

HORTON, Edward Everett (1886/87-1970) American actor, manager, producer BE, CB, TW/7-8, 22, 27, WWA/5, WWT/7-14

HORTON, F. C. (d 1867 [52]) musical librarian EA/68*

HORTON, George (d 1888 [66]) professor of music EA/89*

HORTON, George (d 1908 [83]) professor of music EA/09*

HORTON, James (d 1879 [25]) advance agent EA/80*

HORTON, Jane [Mrs. Walter Horton] (d 1892) EA/93*

HORTON, J. W. (d 1889 [49]) librarian EA/90*

HORTON, Lester (1906-53) American dancer, choreographer ES

HORTON, Priscilla see Reed, Priscilla

HORTON, Robert (b 1870/76) English actor WWT/5-8

HORTON, Russell (b 1941) American actor TW/24, 27

HORTON, Mrs. Walter see Horton, Jane

HORTON, W. F. (1817-87) singer NYM

HORTON, William (d 1892 [39])

musical director EA/93*

HORTON, William Charles (d 1894 [73]) actor EA/95*

HORTOP, Jack (d 1970 [57]) tour manager BP/55*

HORWIN, C. Jerome (d 1954 [49]) American dramatist BE*, BP/38*

HORWITT, Arnold B. (b 1918) American lyricist, sketch writer BE

HORWITZ, Charles (b 1864) American dramatist WWM

HORWOOD, Lena [Mrs. C. E. T. Henderson] (d 1905 [27]) EA/06*

HORWOOD, Thomas (d 1878) musical black clown EA/79*

HOSKING, Arthur (d 1970 [96]) composer/lyricist BP/55*

HOSKINS, Ben (d 1876 [36]) comic singer EA/77*

HOSKINS, Bob (b 1942) English actor WWT/16

HOSKINS, Maurice (d 1917) musician EA/18*

HOSKINS, William (d 1886 [70]) actor CDP

HOSKWITH, Arnold K. (b 1917) American talent representative BE

HOSMER, Adele (fl 1852?) singer CDP

HOSMER, Jean [Jean Stanley] (1842-90) American actress CDP, HAS

HOSMER, William Henry Cuyler (1814-77) American dramatist EAP

HOTCHKISS, Mrs. Sterne (fl 1859) actress HAS

HOTINE, Mrs. (d 1890 [99]) EA/92*

HOTINE, John (d 1904 [64]) animal trainer EA/05*

HOTINE, Mary (d 1890) EA/91*

HOTTENTOT VENUS exhibit CDP

HOTVEDT, Phyllis Shaw (d 1964 [53]) actress BE*

HOTZ, Mr. (fl 1829) American singer HAS

HOUDIN, Robert (d 1871 [66]) conjuror EA/72*

HOUDINI, Harry (1872-1926) American magician NTH, SR, WWA/1

HOUGH, Mrs. G. A. (d 1854

[36]) actress? HAS

HOUGH, J. (fl 1778) dramatist CP/2-3, GT

HOUGH, Lotty (fl 1862-63) actress, singer HAS

HOUGH, W. actor, prompter TD/2

HOUGH, Mrs. W. H. (b 1833) American actress HAS

HOUGH, William (fl 1806?) tutor CDP

HOUGH, Will M. (d 1962 [80]) librettist, lyricist BE*, BP/47*

HOUGHTON, Belle (d 1964 [95]) performer BE*

HOUGHTON, Charles G. (d 1869) manager EA/70*

HOUGHTON, Genevieve (d 1974 [78]) actress, singer, vaudevillian BP/59*, WWT/16*

HOUGHTON, Rev. George C. (d 1923) BP/7*

HOUGHTON, Katharine (b 1945) American actress TW/22, 25-26

HOUGHTON, Mary Anne (d 1916 [86]) EA/18*

HOUGHTON, Norris (b 1909) American director, producer, designer AAS, BE, WWT/13-16

HOUGHTON, Robert (fl 1633) actor DA

HOUGHTON, Stanley (1881-1913) English dramatist COC, DNB, HP, MD, MH, MWD, OC/1-3, PDT, WWT/2, WWW/1

HOUGHTON, T. C. see Howard, T. Charles

HOUK, Norman C. (d 1970 [73]) critic BP/54*

HOULTON, Robert (fl 1784-1800) English composer, lyricist, dramatist CP/3, DNB, GT, TD/1-2

HOUPT, Charles J. (d 1851) American actor HAS

HOUPT, Mrs. Charles J. [Emily Mestayer] (fl 1822) American actress HAS

HOUSE, Billy (d 1961 [71]) comedian TW/18

HOUSE, Eric Canadian actor AAS, WWT/14-16

HOUSE, Jane (b 1946) Panamanian actress TW/28-29

HOUSE, Ron American actor TW/29-30

HOUSEHOLDER, Cyril (d 1969 [73]) performer BP/54*

HOUSEMAN, John (b 1902) Rumanian/American manager, director, producer AAS, BE, COC, TW/2, WWT/13-16

HOUSER, Mervin (d 1976 [65]) performer BP/60*

HOUSLEY, Gracie (d 1902 [24]) actress EA/03*

HOUSMAN, Laurence (1865-1959) English dramatist AAS, COC, DNB, ES, GRB/2-4, HP, MD, MH, MWD, NTH, OC/3, WWA/3, WWT/1-12, WWW/5

HOUSSEIN, Lassar (d 1917) acrobat EA/18*

HOUSTON, Billie (d 1972 [66]) performer BP/57*

HOUSTON, Donald (b 1923) Welsh actor WWT/11-16

HOUSTON, George F. (d 1944 [45]) American actor TW/1

HOUSTON, Grace (b 1916) American costume designer TW/2-3, 6-7

HOUSTON, Jane American actress WWT/4-7

HOUSTON, Josephine (b 1911) American actress, singer WWT/9-10

HOUSTON, Renée (b 1902) Scottish actress WWT/11-16

HOUSTON, T. (fl 1803) dramatist CP/3

HOUSTON, Lady Thomas (d 1780) dramatist CP/3

HOVELER, Audrey (d 1974 [48]) producer/director/choreographer BP/59*

HOVELL, William (fl 1615) actor DA

HOVEY, Richard (1864-1900) American dramatist HJD

HOVHANESS, Alan (b 1911) American composer CB

HOVICK, June see Havoc, June

HOVICK, Rose Louise see Lee, Gypsy Rose

HOVIS, Joan (b 1932) American actress TW/14-16

HOWARD, Mme. (d 1890 [52]) costumier EA/91*

HOWARD, Alan (b 1937) English actor AAS, WWT/15-16

HOWARD, Alan (b 1951) American actor TW/22, 24, 28

HOWARD, Andrée (1910-68) English dancer, choreographer ES, WWT/10-12, WWW/6

HOWARD, Anne [née Addison; Mrs. Welmhurst] English actress HAS

HOWARD, Art (d 1963 [71]) performer BE*

HOWARD, Bart (b 1915) American composer, lyricist BE

HOWARD, Bella (d 1886) actress EA/87*

HOWARD, Bronson (1842-1908) American dramatist CDP, COC, DAB, ES, GRB/2-4, HJD, MH, MWD, NTH, OC/1-3, RE, SR, WWA/1, WWS, WWW/1

HOWARD, Bruce (b 1963) American actor TW/30

HOWARD, Carrie [Mrs. H. Sweet] (d 1883) performer? EA/85*

HOWARD, Cecil (d 1895 [59]) critic, historian BE*, EA/96*, WWT/14*

HOWARD, Charles (d 1898) lecturer EA/99*

HOWARD, Charles actor TW/1

HOWARD, Mrs. Charles see Watkins, Mrs. Henry

HOWARD, Charles D. A. (1855-87) actor NYM

HOWARD, Charles D. S. (1800/05-53/58) English actor CDP, HAS, SR

HOWARD, Charles Thomas see Williams, Charles

HOWARD, Constance [Mrs. Frank Fuller] (d 1881) actress EA/82*

HOWARD, Cordelia (1848-1941) American actress CDP, HAS

HOWARD, Dan [D. H. Crane] (d 1877) American banjoist EA/78*

HOWARD, David S. (b 1928) American actor TW/23

HOWARD, Eddy (d 1963 [54]) composer/lyricist BP/47*

HOWARD, Edward (fl 1668-78) dramatist CP/1-3, DNB

HOWARD, Edward (d 1900 [55]) ghost illusion proprietor EA/01*

HOWARD, Emma (d 1900 [62]) EA/01*

HOWARD, Esther (d 1965 [72]) performer BP/49*

HOWARD, Eugene (1880/81-1965) American actor, singer BE, TW/22, WWT/7-11

HOWARD, Florence (b 1879) American actress WWS

HOWARD, Florence Emily (d 1907) actress EA/08*

HOWARD, Francis (b 1835) Canadian actress HAS

HOWARD, Francis see Howerd, Frankie

HOWARD, Frank (fl 1870?) song composer CDP

HOWARD, Frank (1850-1915) American minstrel SR

HOWARD, Frederic, Earl of Carlisle (1748-1826) dramatist CP/3, DD

HOWARD, Frederick (d 1882 [26]) comedian EA/83*

HOWARD, Mrs. G. C. (d 1908 [79]) actress GRB/4*

HOWARD, Sir George dramatist FGF

HOWARD, George (d 1921 [55]) English actor, manager GRB/1

HOWARD, Mrs. George see Earle, Clara

HOWARD, George Bronson (1884-1922) American dramatist WWA/1

HOWARD, George Cunnibell (1820-87) Canadian actor CDP, HAS, NYM, WWA/H

HOWARD, Mrs. George Cunnibell [née Caroline Fox] (1829-1908) American actress CDP, GRB/4, HAS

HOWARD, George Edmund (d 1786) dramatist CP/2-3, GT, TD/1-2

HOWARD, G. W. (fl 1851) American actor HAS

HOWARD, Harold (b 1875) American actor WWS

HOWARD, Henry [Henry Howard Moffatt] (d 1890 [42]) diorama proprietor EA/91*

HOWARD, Henry John (1812-53) English actor HAS

HOWARD, Inez [Harriette Adye] (d 1901) EA/02*

HOWARD, Jack (b 1889) American actor TW/2

HOWARD, James (fl 1672-74) dramatist CP/1-3, DNB

HOWARD, James (1808-48) English actor HAS

HOWARD, James Brown [Michael Hoban] (d 1895 [54]) actor, producer, proprietor BE*, EA/96*, WWT/14*

HOWARD, J. B. (d 1879 [35]) American comedian EA/80*

HOWARD, Mrs. J. B. see

Howard, Sarah

HOWARD, J. Bannister (1867-1946) English manager WWT/3-9

HOWARD, J. C. (d 1892 [58]) actor EA/93*

HOWARD, Johnny (d 1976 [70s]) performer BP/60*

HOWARD, Joseph (1868-1961) American composer, vaudevillian SR, TW/17

HOWARD, Joseph E. (fl 1890s?) singer, vaudevillian CDP

HOWARD, Kathleen (d 1956 [77]) Canadian/American singer TW/13, WWA/3

HOWARD, Kathryn [May Irene Copinger] American dramatic editor WWM

HOWARD, Keble [John Keble Bell] (1875-1928) English dramatist GRB/2-4, WWT/1-5, WWW/2

HOWARD, Ken (b 1944) American actor TW/25-27, 29-30, WWT/15-16

HOWARD, Leslie (1893-1943) English actor AAS, CB, DAB, DNB, ES, NTH, SR, WWT/4-9, WWW/4

HOWARD, Lionel G. (d 1917) EA/18*

HOWARD, Lisa (b 1930) American actress TW/15

HOWARD, Lizzie [Mrs. Pat Carey] (d 1901 [37]) singer, actress CDP

HOWARD, Louisa (fl 1854) English actress HAS

HOWARD, Mabel (b 1884) American actress WWS

HOWARD, May C. (b 1845) American actress CDP, HAS, SR

HOWARD, Milly actress, singer CDP

HOWARD, Moe (d 1975 [78]) comedian BP/59*, WWT/16*

HOWARD, Norah (1901-68) English actress TW/4, 9, WWT/6-14

HOWARD, Paul Mason (d 1975 [84]) composer/lyricist BP/59*

HOWARD, Peter (b 1927) American conductor, composer, musician BE

HOWARD, Rance (b 1928) American actor TW/13

HOWARD, Sir Robert (1626-98) dramatist CP/1-3, DNB

HOWARD, Roger (b 1938) English dramatist CD

HOWARD, Rollin [G. B. Holder] (1840-79) female impersonator CDP, HAS

HOWARD, Russell (b 1918) English actor TW/8

HOWARD, Sam (d 1877 [32]) Negro comedian EA/78*

HOWARD, Sam (d 1964 [61]) talent representative, performer BE*

HOWARD, Sam (d 1972 [88]) performer BP/57*

HOWARD, Sarah [Mrs. J. B. Howard] (d 1912 [84]) EA/13*, WWT/14*

HOWARD, Sarah Martin (d 1902 [83]) EA/03*

HOWARD, Selby (b 1874) English actor GRB/1

HOWARD, Seth C. (d 1860 [38]) minstrel HAS

HOWARD, Shemp (d 1955 [60]) comedian TW/12

HOWARD, Sidney Coe (1891-1939) American dramatist AAS, COC, ES, HJD, MD, MH, MWD, NTH, OC/1-3, PDT, RE, WWT/6-8

HOWARD, Sydney (1885-1946) English actor TW/3, WWT/6-9

HOWARD, Sydney Lester (d 1908) EA/09*

HOWARD, T. Charles [T. C. Houghton] (b 1845) American actor HAS

HOWARD, Thomas (fl 1598) actor DA

HOWARD, Thomas (d 1894) circus performer? EA/95*

HOWARD, Thomas Martin (b 1859) English entertainer, illusionist GRB/1

HOWARD, Tom (1885-1955) Irish comedian TW/11

HOWARD, Trevor (b 1916) English actor AAS, CB, ES, WWT/10-16

HOWARD, Virginia (b 1834) American actress HAS

HOWARD, Walter (d 1905 [58]) singer, minstrel CDP

HOWARD, Walter (1866-1922) English actor, manager, dramatist WWT/3-4, WWW/2

HOWARD, Mrs. Walter (d 1903) EA/04*

HOWARD, William Chouet (d 1871 [65]) actor EA/72*

HOWARD, William Jason (d 1871 [62]) actor EA/72*

HOWARD, William W. (d 1963 [65]) American executive BE*

HOWARD, Willie (1883/86-1949) American actor, singer CDP, DAB, NTH, TW/2-5, WWA/3, WWT/7-10

HOWARD, Wilson actor GRB/1

HOWARD, Mrs. Wilson see Anson, Carlotta

HOWARTH, Donald (b 1931) English dramatist, director, actor AAS, CD, WWT/15-16

HOWE, Elizabeth [Mrs. H. Howe] (d 1875) EA/76*

HOWE, Elizabeth Sophia (d 1886) EA/87*

HOWE, Fred (d 1885) music-hall performer EA/86*

HOWE, George (b 1900) Chilean actor, director AAS, BE, TW/9, WWT/7-16

HOWE, Mrs. H. see Howe, Elizabeth

HOWE, Harry (b 1866) English actor, singer, dancer GRB/1

HOWE, Helen (1905-75) American monologist CB

HOWE, Henry [Henry Howe Hutchinson] (1812-96) English actor CDP, DNB, DP, OAA/1-2, OC/1-3, SR

HOWE, Henry A. H. (d 1894 [61]) critic EA/95*

HOWE, Illa Cameron (b 1948) American actress TW/28

HOWE, J. Burdette (1828-1908) English actor, manager CDP, GRB/4, HAS, SR

HOWE, Julia Ward (1819-1910) American dramatist WWW/1

HOWE, Katharine B. (fl 1889?) singer CDP

HOWE, Leonard (b 1875) English actor, business manager GRB/1

HOWE, Lizzie (d 1902) actress EA/03*

HOWE, Mary (fl 1891?) singer CDP

HOWE, Molly (d 1890 [15]) music-hall performer EA/91*

HOWE, Walter (b 1860) English actor, manager GRB/1

HOWE, Willard American actor WWS

HOWELL, Mr. singer CDP

HOWELL, Mr. (fl 1811-12) actor

CDP
HOWELL, Alfred (d 1862 [53])
costumier HAS
HOWELL, Arthur (d 1885 [49])
musician EA/86*
HOWELL, Edward (d 1898 [54])
musician EA/99*
HOWELL, Eric American actor
TW/28.
HOWELL, Miss F. (fl 1800)
singer TD/1-2
HOWELL, Fred A. (d 1886 [46])
singer EA/87*
HOWELL, J. A. (d 1895) actor
EA/96*
HOWELL, James (1594-1666)
Welsh dramatist CP/1-3
HOWELL, James (d 1877) min-
strel EA/78*
HOWELL, Jane director WWT/
15-16
HOWELL, John (1888-1928)
Welsh actor WWT/4-5
HOWELL, John Daggett (b 1911)
American director BE
HOWELL, Margaret (b 1947)
American actress TW/26,
28
HOWELL, Matthew (d 1873 [76])
harlequin EA/74*
HOWELL, Miriam American
literary representative BE
HOWELL, Stephanus (fl 1423)
actor DA
HOWELL-POOLE, William (d
1894 [37]) actor, dramatist
EA/95*
HOWELLS, Fanny (fl 1800) ac-
tress CDP
HOWELLS, Ursula (b 1922) Eng-
lish actress TW/7, WWT/
11-16
HOWELLS, William Dean (1837-
1920) American dramatist,
critic ES, HJD, HP, MH,
MWD, NTH, SR, WWA/1,
WWW/2
HOWERD, Frankie [né Francis
Howard] (b 1921) English actor
TW/25, WWT/14-16
HOWERTON, Clarence (d 1975
[62]) performer BP/60*
HOWES, Basil (b 1901) English
actor, singer WWT/6-8
HOWES, Bobby (1895-1972) Eng-
lish actor AAS, WWT/6-15
HOWES, Frank (d 1974 [82])
critic BP/59*

HOWES, John F. (d 1968 [54]) per-
former BP/52*
HOWES, Oliver (fl 1628) actor DA
HOWES, Sally Ann (b 1930) English
actress, singer BE, TW/20-21,
WWT/12-16
HOWES, Seth B. (1815-1901) Amer-
ican circus manager SR
HOWITT, Belle (fl 1869) actress
CDP
HOWITT, Nellie [Mrs. W. Ruddle
Brown] Scottish actress GRB/1
HOWITT, T. C. (d 1886) EA/88*
HOWITT, Mrs. Thomas C. see
Dowsing, Emma Ada
HOWLAND, Alan (d 1946 [47])
actor BE*, WWT/14*
HOWLAND, Beth (b 1941) American
actress TW/26-28
HOWLAND, Jobyna (1880-1936)
American actress WWT/6-8
HOWLAND, Olin (d 1959 [63]) actor
TW/16
HOWLE, William J. (d 1907) EA/
08*
HOWLETT, Carl (d 1907 [48])
marionette proprietor EA/08*
HOWLETT, Noel (b 1901) English
actor WWT/9-16
HOWROYDE, Mrs. (d 1911) EA/12*
HOWS, J. W. S. (fl 1834) actor
HAS
HOWSON, Albert S. (b 1881) Amer-
ican actor WWM
HOWSON, Charles Edwin (d 1907
[59]) treasurer EA/08*
HOWSON, Charles Edwin (d 1916)
actor SR
HOWSON, Emma (1844-1928) Tas-
manian singer, actress CDP,
OAA/2
HOWSON, Emma see Albertazzi,
Emma
HOWSON, Frank (1817-69) English
singer, musician, manager,
director, producer HAS
HOWSON, Frank A. (d 1945 [66])
actor BE*, WWT/14*
HOWSON, John (1844-87) Tasmanian
actor, singer CDP, NYM,
OAA/2
HOY, Mr. manager TD/1-2
HOYLE, Edgar (d 1917) manager
EA/18*
HOYLE, Fanny (d 1874) singer?
EA/75*
HOYM, Eliza actress CDP
HOYM, Otto (fl 1854) manager CDP

HOYT, Adolphus H. see Davenport, Adolphus H.

HOYT, Caroline Miskel [Mrs. Charles H. Hoyt] (d 1898 [25]) American actress BE*, EA/99*, WWT/14*

HOYT, Mrs. Charles H. see Hoyt, Caroline Miskel

HOYT, Charles Hale (1860-1900) American dramatist CDP, COC, DAB, HJD, MWD, NTH, OC/1-3, RE, WWA/1

HOYT, Mrs. Charles Hale [Flora Walsh] (d 1893) actress BE*, WWT/14*

HOYT, Edward N. (b 1859) American actor WWS

HOYT, Eileen (d 1970 [67]) performer BP/55*

HOYT, Harlowe R. (d 1970) critic BP/55*

HOYT, Howard (1913-71) American producer, manager, artists' representative BE

HOYT, Julia (d 1955 [58]) American actress TW/12

HROSWITHA (fl 10th cent) German dramatist COC

HRUBY, Norbert J. (b 1918) American producer, educator, director BE

HSIUNG, Shih I. (b 1902) Chinese dramatist BE, WWT/9-14

HUBAN, Eileen (1895-1935) Irish actress WWT/4-7

HUBBARD, Christiana (d 1893) EA/94*

HUBBARD, Didrikke (d 1974) performer BP/58*

HUBBARD, Elbert (b 1856) American dramatist, entertainer, lecturer WWM

HUBBARD, Elizabeth American actress TW/24, 28

HUBBARD, Frances Virginia American composer WWA/5

HUBBARD, Lilian (fl 1880?) singer CDP

HUBBARD, Lorna (b 1910) actress, singer WWT/7-10

HUBBARD, Lulu Mae (d 1966 [59]) actress TW/23

HUBBARD, Robert F. (d 1909 [72]) EA/10*

HUBBELL, Kyra Deakin (d 1965 [63]) performer BP/50*

HUBBELL, Raymond (1879-1954) American composer WWA/3,

WWT/4-11

HUBER, Ann Elizabeth (d 1905) EA/06*

HUBER, Gusti (b 1914) Austrian actress BE, TW/8-15, WWT/12-13

HUBER, Harold (d 1959 [49]) American actor BE*, BP/44*

HUBER, Paul (b 1895) American actor TW/10

HUBER, Richard M. (d 1965 [84]) publisher BP/49*

HUBERT (fl 1631) actor DA

HUBERT, George (d 1963 [82]) performer BE*

HUBERT, Marcie Japanese/American actress TW/23

HUBY, John, Jr. (d 1880) master carpenter EA/81*

HUBY, Roberta actress, singer WWT/10-14

HUDD, Walter (1898-1963) English actor, producer AAS, WWT/8-13, WWW/6

HUDDART, Mr. (fl 1798) actor TD/1-2

HUDDART, Fanny [Mrs. John Russell] (d 1880) singer, actress CDP

HUDDART, John F. (fl 1869?) song composer CDP

HUDDART, Mary Amelia see Warner, Mary Amelia

HUDDART, Thomas (d 1831) actor WWT/14*

HUDDLE, Elizabeth (b 1940) American actress TW/22-23, 27

HUDMAN, Wesley (d 1964 [48]) actor BE*

HUDSMITH, William Henry (d 1889) music-hall chairman EA/90*

HUDSON, Mr. (fl 1849-50) Irish comedian HAS

HUDSON, Alfred (1879-1914) actor SR

HUDSON, Charles (d 1897) actor, dramatist BE*, EA/98*, WWT/14*

HUDSON, Charles (b 1931) American actor TW/22, 27, 30

HUDSON, Edward (b 1924) American actor TW/2

HUDSON, Eric (1861-1918) English actor GRB/1

HUDSON, Harry B. [né Hunter] (b 1839) Canadian actor CDP, HAS

HUDSON, James (1811-78) Irish

comedian CDP

HUDSON, Jeffrey (1619-82) dwarf
CDP

HUDSON, John (b 1921) American
actor TW/3

HUDSON, Leo (1839-73) English
equestrienne CDP, HAS

HUDSON, Richard (fl 1612) actor
DA

HUDSON, Rochelle (d 1972 [57])
performer BP/56*, WWT/16*

HUDSON, Thomas (d 1844 [50])
comic songwriter & singer
EA/72*

HUDSON, T. P. (d 1909 [57]) performer EA/10*

HUDSPETH, Henrietta [Mrs. Edmund Phelps] (fl 1859) actress
OAA/2

HUDSPETH, John (d 1866 [59])
actor CDP

HUDSPETH, Mrs. John (d 1891
[84]) EA/93*

HUDSPETH, Mrs. John see
Bramah, Marie

HUDSPETH, John Henry (d 1903
[63]) comedian EA/04*

HUESTON, John (d 1865) American actor HAS

HUFF, Alexander F. (d 1965
[70]) performer BP/49*

HUFF, Forrest (1876-1947) actor,
singer SR, TW/4

HUFF, Louise (d 1973 [77]) performer BP/58*

HUFFMAN, David (b 1945) American actor TW/28-30

HUFFMAN, Jessie C. (d 1935
[66]) director, producer BE*,
WWT/14*

HUGGINS, Mr. (d 1800) actor
HAS

HUGGINS, Benjamin W. see
Edwin, Benjamin W.

HUGGINS, Jeremy see Brett,
Jeremy

HUGGINS, William (d 1761)
dramatist CP/2-3

HUGHES, Mr. (fl 1794-1824)
actor HAS

HUGHES, Mr. (fl 1794) actor
CDP

HUGHES, Mr. (fl 1834) actor
CDP

HUGHES, Mrs. (fl 1784-90)
dramatist CP/3

HUGHES, Mrs. (fl 1794) actress
CDP

HUGHES, Mrs. (fl 1794-1824) actress HAS

HUGHES, Mrs. [Mrs. Young] (fl
1846) actress HAS

HUGHES, Miss (fl 1831) actress
HAS

HUGHES, Adelaide (d 1937 [20])
American performer BE*

HUGHES, Adelaide (d 1960 [70])
dancer TW/16

HUGHES, Andy actor, song composer CDP

HUGHES, Anna May (b 1918) American educator BE

HUGHES, Annie [Mrs. Edmund
Maurice] (1869-1954) English actress CDP, DP, EA/95, GRB/
1-4, WWS, WWT/1-11

HUGHES, Archie (d 1860?) actor
NTH

HUGHES, Barnard (b 1915) American actor TW/24-30, WWT/16

HUGHES, Beaumont (d 1906 [76])
actor EA/07*

HUGHES, Mrs. Beaumont see
Hughes, Margaret Hackett

HUGHES, Mrs. C. H. see
Hughes, Mary

HUGHES, Daisy (d 1893) serio-
comic EA/94*

HUGHES, David (d 1973 [43]) performer BP/57*

HUGHES, Del American stage
manager, director, actor BE

HUGHES, Edwin (d 1867 [54])
equestrian EA/68*

HUGHES, Elinor (b 1906) American
critic BE, NTH

HUGHES, Elizabeth (fl 1831) actress, singer CDP

HUGHES, Ernest (d 1962 [82]) performer, historian BE*

HUGHES, Esther (fl 1812) actress
CDP

HUGHES, Fanny [Mrs. Julio Henry
Hughes] (d 1880 [66]) EA/81*

HUGHES, Fanny (d 1888 [45]) actress BE*, WWT/14*

HUGHES, Fanny see Swanborough,
Fanny

HUGHES, Mrs. Frederic see
Hughes, Sarah Jane

HUGHES, Frederick (d 1883 [41])
comedian EA/84*

HUGHES, Gareth (d 1965 [71])
Welsh actor TW/22

HUGHES, Glenn (1894-1964) American educator, dramatist BE

HUGHES, Gordon (fl 1894?)
singer CDP
HUGHES, Harry (d 1897) come-
dian EA/98*
HUGHES, Hatcher (1883-1945)
American dramatist CB,
HJD, MD, MWD, NTH, SR,
WWA/2, WWT/8-11
HUGHES, Hazel [née Hepenstall]
(1913-74) South African ac-
tress BTR/74, WWT/15]
HUGHES, Henry (d 1872 [62])
actor CDP
HUGHES, Henry (1828-1914)
American minstrel SR
HUGHES, James American press
representative, manager BE
HUGHES, Jennie (fl 1873) ac-
tress, singer CDP
HUGHES, J. J. see Albert,
Frank
HUGHES, John (1677-1719) Eng-
lish dramatist CDP, CP/
1-3, GT, SR, TD/1-2
HUGHES, John (d 1887) Welsh
writer EA/88*
HUGHES, John Charles (1789-
1840) actor CDP
HUGHES, Julio Henry (d 1872
[62]) actor EA/73*
HUGHES, Mrs. Julio Henry
see Hughes, Fanny (d 1880)
HUGHES, Langston (1902-67)
American dramatist BE,
CB, CH, ES, MD, MH,
MWD, TW/23, WWA/4
HUGHES, Lizzie [Mrs. Frank
Pierce Clark] actress CDP
HUGHES, Lloyd (d 1958 [61])
actor BE*
HUGHES, Margaret (1643?-1719)
English actress CDP, DNB,
NTH
HUGHES, Margaret Hackett [Mrs.
Beaumont Hughes] (d 1877)
EA/79*
HUGHES, Mary [Mrs. C. H.
Hughes] (d 1876 [35]) EA/77*
HUGHES, Matt (d 1882 [61])
scene artist EA/83*
HUGHES, Morfa [Ethel Margaret
Morfa-Hughes] (b 1876) Eng-
lish actress, singer GRB/1
HUGHES, R. see Newcomb,
Bobby
HUGHES, Richard (1789-1814)
English actor, manager BS,
TD/1-2

HUGHES, Richard (1900-76) dramatist HP
HUGHES, Roddy (b 1891) Welsh
actor WWT/10-13
HUGHES, R. S. (d 1893) Welsh
song composer EA/94*
HUGHES, Ruey (d 1871 [23]) dancer,
minstrel CDP
HUGHES, Rupert (1872-1956) American dramatist GRB/3-4, HJD,
WWA/3, WWM, WWS, WWT/1-
11
HUGHES, Sarah Jane [Jennie Kel-
sey; Mrs. Frederic Hughes]
(d 1880) EA/82*
HUGHES, T. Harris (1806-91)
magician SR
HUGHES, Thomas (fl 1587) drama-
tist CP/3, DNB, FGF
HUGHES, Thomas (d 1857 [49])
actor EA/72*, WWT/14*
HUGHES, Tom (b 1932) American
producer BE
HUGHES, Tresa (b 1929) American
actress TW/17, 21-30
HUGHES, W. F. see Egerton,
Frank
HUGHES, W. H. (d 1905 [58])
manager EA/06*
HUGHES, William (b 1924) Ameri-
can actor TW/21
"HUGH MORTON" see McLellan,
C. M. S.
HUGHSON, Matthew (d 1879 [28])
Negro comedian EA/80*
"HUGO see Oxford, Mr.
HUGO, Emil (b 1836) German actor
HAS
HUGO, Lawrence (b 1917) American
actor BE, TW/24, 27, 30
HUGO, Mauritz (d 1974 [65]) per-
former BP/59*
HUGO, Victor (1802-85) French
dramatist SR
HUGO, William (d 1896) minstrel
EA/97*
HUGUENET, Felix (1858-1926)
French actor WWT/1-2
HUGUES, Clovis (d 1907 [56])
dramatist EA/08*
HUISH, Robert (fl 1809) translator
CP/3
HULBERT, Claude (1900-64) Eng-
lish actor WWT/5-13, WWW/6
HULBERT, Jack (b 1892) English
actor, dramatist, manager,
producer AAS, ES, WWT/3-16
HULBURD, H. L. (d 1973) per-

former BP/57*

HULBURT, John W. (b 1907) American educator BE

HULET, Charles (1701-36) actor DNB

HULETT, Mr. (fl 1753) English dancer, violinist HAS

HULEY, Pete (d 1973 [80]) performer BP/57*

HULINE, James (d 1890 [74]) pantomimist, clown BE*, EA/91*, WWT/14*

HULINE, James (d 1904 [54]) EA/06*

HULINE, John Alfred (d 1904 [35]) EA/06*

HULINE, W. (d 1890 [74]) actor, clown CDP

HULL, Charles (b 1936) Austrian/ American actor TW/24-25

HULL, Henry (1890-1977) American actor, dramatist BE, TW/1-16, WWT/5-14

HULL, John (fl 1600) actor DA

HULL, Josephine [née Sherwood] (1886-1957) American actress CB, TW/1-13, WWA/3, WWT/10-12

HULL, Maryann (d 1970 [39]) performer BP/54*

HULL, Shelley (d 1919 [35]) American actor WWM

HULL, Thomas (1728-1808) English actor, manager, dramatist CDP, CP/2-3, DNB, GT, TD/1-2

HULL, Tom American actor TW/26

HULL, Warren (d 1974 [71]) performer BP/59*

HULLEY, Bernard (d 1917 [49]) musical director EA/18*

HULLEY, Will (d 1878 [28]) comic singer EA/79*

HULLIN, Mme. (fl 1820s?) dancer CDP

HULL TRUCK theatre collective CD

HULME, Mrs. see Dalby, Miss

HULSKAMP, Victoria S. (fl 1885?) singer CDP

HULTMAN, Robert L. (b 1927) American actor TW/29

HUMBY, Anne (fl 1818-49) actress CDP, DNB

HUME, Benita (1906-68) English actress WWT/6-10

HUME, Ernest (d 1910) singer? EA/11*

HUME, Fergus (d 1932 [73]) dramatist BE*, WWT/14*

HUME, J. (d 1892) Negro comedian EA/94*

HUME, Kenneth (d 1967 [41]) dramatist BP/52*

HUMIERES, Robert D' (d 1916) dramatist WWT/14*

HUMISTON, William Henry (1869-1923) American musician, conductor, composer DAB

HUMMERT, James (b 1944) American actor TW/29-30

HUMPERDINCK, Engelbert (1854-1921) German composer WWM

HUMPHREY, Cavada American actress BE, TW/22-24, 26, 29, WWT/14-16

HUMPHREY, Doris (1895-1958) American dancer, choreographer CB, ES, TW/15, WWA/3

HUMPHREYS, Mr. (d c.1738 [c. 40]) dramatist CP/2-3

HUMPHREYS, Mrs. (fl 1803) actress CDP

HUMPHREYS, Cecil (1883-1947) English actor TW/2-4, WWT/4-10

HUMPHREYS, Col. David (1753-1818) American dramatist CP/3, EAP, RJ

HUMPHREYS, George (d 1911 [32]) variety acting manager EA/12*

HUMPHREYS, Griffith (fl 1895?) singer, song composer CDP

HUMPHREYS, John D. (d 1906) circus advance agent EA/07*

HUMPHREYS, Rex (d 1911 [28]) actor EA/12*

HUMPHRIES, Mr. (d 1867) musician EA/68*

HUMPHRIES, Miss (fl 1797) actress TD/1-2

HUMPHRIES, John (d 1927 [63]) actor WWT/4-5

HUMPHRIES, Mrs. John see Innes, Isabel

HUMPHRIS, Gordon (b 1921) English actor, dancer WWT/11

HUNDON, Mrs. T. J. [Clara Goldsby Wilton] (d 1889) American actress EA/90*

HUNEKER, Erick H. (d 1971 [77]) designer BP/55*

HUNEKER, James Gibbons (1857/60-1921) American critic COC,

DAB, ES, HJD, NTH, OC/1-3, WWA/1, WWM, WWW/2

HUNN, Richard see Canning, Mrs. George

HUNNICUTT, Arthur American actor TW/1-3

HUNNIS, William (fl 1566-97) master of the Chapel Royal DA, FGF

HUNSECKER, Ralph Uriah see Blane, Ralph

HUNT, Al (d 1964 [45]) press representative BE*

HUNT, Arabella (d 1705) singer CDP

HUNT, Betty Lee (b 1920) American press representative BE

HUNT, Carl (b 1941) American actor TW/27-28

HUNT, Mrs. Charles [née Ann Jeannette Kerr] (b 1816) English actress HAS

HUNT, Charles Henry (d 1879 [33]) music-hall proprietor EA/80*

HUNT, Charles W. (d 1855) actor HAS

HUNT, Doris [Mrs. Roy Byford] (d 1911 [39]) actress EA/12*

HUNT, Miss E. (d 1893) EA/94*

HUNT, Eliza (d 1889) EA/90*

HUNT, George W. "Jingo" (d 1904) composer EA/05*

HUNT, Henry B. (d 1854 [60]) English actor, singer CDP, HAS

HUNT, Hugh Sydney (b 1911) English producer, director, critic AAS, COC, WWT/8-16

HUNT, John (d 1894) EA/95*

HUNT, Mrs. John see Hunt, Mary Ann

HUNT, Julia A. (fl 1881?) singer, actress CDP

HUNT, Leigh (1784-1859) English critic COC, ES, HP, OC/1-3

HUNT, Maggie [Mrs. Arthur B. Franks] (d 1904 [44]) actress EA/05*

HUNT, Marsha (b 1917) American actress BE, TW/5-8, 23, WWT/11

HUNT, Martita (1900-69) Argentinian/English actress AAS, BE, COC, ES, TW/5-6, 26, WWT/6-14, WWW/6

HUNT, Mary Ann [Mrs. John Hunt] (d 1875) EA/76*

HUNT, Nathaniel (d 1891) manager EA/92*

HUNT, Peter (b 1938) American director, lighting designer WWT/15-16

HUNT, Peter H. (d 1970 [55]) producer/director/choreographer BP/55*

HUNT, Phil (b 1868) American manager, actor WWS

HUNT, Ralph (d 1900) minstrel? EA/01*

HUNT, Reginald (d 1916 [19]) actor? EA/17*

HUNT, Robert (fl 1631) actor DA

HUNT, Thomas (fl 1597-1611) actor DA

HUNT, William (fl 1713) dramatist CP/1-3, GT

HUNT, William (d 1827) gymnast HAS

HUNT, William E. (b 1923) American producer, director, actor BE

HUNT, William Henry (d 1894 [42]) composer EA/96*

HUNTEN, Franz (1793-1878) composer CDP

HUNTER, Mr. (fl 1829-39) equestrian HAS

HUNTER, Agnes Emma (d 1908 [52]) actress EA/09*

HUNTER, Frederick J. (b 1916) American educator BE

HUNTER, George M. (fl 1794) dramatist CP/3

HUNTER, Glenn (1896-1945) American actor CB, TW/2, WWT/5-9

HUNTER, Govenor see Hunter, [Robert]

HUNTER, Harriet see Seymour, Mrs. Guilfoyle

HUNTER, Harrison (d 1923) English actor BE*, BP/7*, WWT/14*

HUNTER, Harry (d 1881) actor CDP

HUNTER, Harry (d 1906 [65]) minstrel EA/07*

HUNTER, Harry B. see Hudson, Harry B.

HUNTER, Ian (1900-75) South African actor AAS, ES, TW/5-6, WWT/5-14

HUNTER, Ivory Joe (d 1974 [63]) composer/lyricist BP/59*

HUNTER, Jackie (d 1951 [50]) Canadian actor BE*, WWT/14*

HUNTER, James (d 1887) EA/88*

HUNTER, James (d 1890) circus
custodian EA/91*
HUNTER, James (b 1943) English
actor TW/24
HUNTER, J. D. (d 1916) come-
dian, pantomime director EA/
18*
HUNTER, Jeffrey (d 1969 [42])
performer BP/54*
HUNTER, John (1763-1801) Eng-
lish dramatist CP/3
HUNTER, Kenneth (b 1882) South
African actor WWT/7-10
HUNTER, Kermit (b 1910) Amer-
ican dramatist, educator BE,
CB, MWD
HUNTER, Kim [née Janet Cole]
(b 1922) American actress
BE, CB, TW/7-15, 23-24, 26,
29-30, WWT/12-16
HUNTER, Lavinia Ernestine (d
1909 [59]) dramatist EA/10*
HUNTER, Maria (fl 1782) actress
CDP
HUNTER, Mary American director
TW/5-6
HUNTER, Mary see Austin,
Mary
HUNTER, Norman Charles (1908-
71) English dramatist AAS,
CD, CH, COC, MD, PDT,
WWT/9-15
HUNTER, Mrs. Parke see
Price, Lillah
HUNTER, Richard (fl 1699-1702)
actor WWA/H
HUNTER, Richard (d 1962 [87])
actor BE*
HUNTER, [Robert] (d 1734) Eng-
lish dramatist CP/1-3, EAP,
GT
HUNTER, Ruth (d 1976 [74]) ward-
robe supervisor BP/60*
HUNTER, Susan (d 1976 [39])
performer BP/60*
HUNTER, Mrs. T. M. see
Hight, Lizzie
HUNTER, T. Marvin (fl 1860)
actor HAS
HUNTER, Victor William (b 1910)
English manager WWT/15-16
HUNTER, William (d 1886 [42])
Ethiopian comedian EA/87*
HUNTINGDON, Mr. (fl 1807)
actor HAS
HUNTINGTON, Agnes (fl 1889)
singer, actress DP
HUNTINGTON, Catharine (b 1889)

American actress, director,
producer BE
HUNTINGTON, Harry (1832-60)
American agent, circus per-
former? HAS
HUNTINGTON, Nathaniel (d 1970
[87]) performer BP/54*
HUNTLEY, Mr. (b 1787) English
actor BS
HUNTLEY, Dick (fl 1592) actor?
prompter? DA
HUNTLEY, Francis (1787-1831)
English actor CDP, DNB, OX
HUNTLEY, Francis Walter [Frank
Huntley] (d 1885 [56]) actor
EA/86*, WWT/14*
HUNTLEY, Frank see Huntley,
Francis Walter
HUNTLEY, Mrs. Frank (d 1895)
actress EA/96*, WWT/14*
HUNTLEY, George (b 1826) actor
CDP
HUNTLEY, George Frederick (d
1913 [54]) EA/14*
HUNTLEY, George Patrick (1868-
1927) Irish actor GRB/1-4,
WWT/1-5
HUNTLEY, Mrs. George Patrick
see Kelly, Eve
HUNTLEY, G[eorge] P[atrick], Jr.
(b 1904) American actor WWT/
7-9
HUNTLEY, Grace (d 1896) actress
BE*, EA/97*, WWT/14*
HUNTLEY, Mrs. James H. see
Kennedy, Florence
HUNTLEY, John (b 1805) English
prompter, actor, manager HAS
HUNTLEY, Marion (d 1899 [36])
actress EA/00*
HUNTLEY, Raymond (b 1904) Eng-
lish actor AAS, TW/7, WWT/
9-16
HUNTLEY, Thomas L. ["Delane"]
(d 1865) tight-rope walker HAS
HUNTLEY, Tim (b 1904) American
actor WWT/10
HUNTLEY-WRIGHT, Betty (b 1911)
actress, singer WWT/10-15
HUNTLEY-WRIGHT, José (b 1918)
English actress WWT/10-11
HUOT, Denise (b 1936) American
actress TW/23-25
HUPFELD, Herman (d 1951 [57])
American songwriter BE*, BP/
36*
HUPPELER, Cindia (b 1951) Amer-
ican actress TW/29

HURDLE, Jack (d 1971 [62])
producer/director/choreographer
BP/56*

HURGINI, Herr (d 1900) juggler
EA/01*

HURGON, Austen A. (d 1942
[74]) actor, dramatist, producer WWT/3-7

HURLBUT, W. J. (b 1883) American dramatist SR, WWT/1-11

HURLEY, Alec (1863/71-1913)
English actor GRB/1-3, OC/
1-3, WWS

HURLEY, Dunlea (d 1973 [64])
dramatist BP/58*

HURLEY, Jerry (d 1901 [38])
gymnast EA/02*

HURLEY, Laurel (b 1927) American singer CB, TW/10

HURLEY, Michael (d 1879) American scene artist EA/80*

HURLSTONE, Thomas (fl 1792-
94) dramatist CP/3, TD/1-2

HURN, Douglas (d 1974 [49])
performer BP/59*

HURNDALL, Richard (b 1910)
English actor WWT/15-16

HURNEY, Kate American actress
TW/23, 29

HUROK, Sol (1888-1974) Russian/
American impresario AAS,
BE, CB, ES, TW/30, WWT/
13-15

HURRAN, Dick (b 1911) English
director WWT/12-16

HURRELL, John D. (b 1924)
English educator BE

HURRY, Leslie (b 1909) English
designer AAS, COC, ES,
OC/3, PDT, WWT/11-16

HURST, Mr. actor TD/1-2

HURST, Agnes (d 1869 [75])
EA/70*

HURST, Brandon (d 1947 [81])
English actor BE*, BP/32*,
WWT/14*

HURST, David (b 1926) German
actor, director BE

HURST, Fannie (1889-1968) American dramatist HJD, WWT/
5-10

HURST, J. H. (d 1905) comic
singer, mimic EA/06*

HURST, Joseph (d 1899 [66])
box office manager EA/00*

HURST, Lew (d 1975 [57]) designer BP/59*

HURST, Robert (fl 1725) drama-

tist CP/1-3, GT, TD/1-2

HURST, Will (d 1911) Negro comedian EA/12*

HURST, Mrs. William (d 1887)
actress EA/88*

HURST, William George (d 1905
[47]) acrobat EA/06*

HURSTBOURNE, Walter (d 1917)
EA/18*

HURT, Helen see Ashley, Helen

HURT, John (b 1940) English actor
WWT/15-16

HURTIG, Mrs. Joseph see Austin,
Jennie

HURTIG, Louis (d 1924 [53]) producer BE*, BP/9*

HURWITCH, Moses (1844-1910)
dramatist BE*

HURWITZ, Mr. B. (d 1868) decorator EA/69*

HUSBANDS, J. W. (d 1917) critic
EA/18*

HUSCH, Richard J. [Richard Ger-
ard] (d 1948 [72]) American
lyricist BE*, BP/33*

HUSK, James (d 1879 [68]) singer
EA/80*

HUSMANN, Ron (b 1937) American
actor, singer BE, TW/17-20,
27-30, WWT/16

HUSSEY, Dyneley (d 1972 [79])
critic BP/57*

HUSSEY, Frank (b 1834) comedian,
minstrel CDP

HUSSEY, Jimmy (1891-1930) American actor WWT/5-6

HUSSEY, John George (d 1881)
EA/82*

HUSSEY, Ruth (b 1914) American
actress BE, TW/2-7, WWT/
10-11

HUSTING, Lucille (d 1972 [70s])
performer BP/57*

HUSTON, James (b 1941) American
actor TW/30

HUSTON, John (b 1906) American
actor, dramatist CB, ES

HUSTON, Martin (b 1941) American
actor TW/22-23, 26

HUSTON, Philip (b 1908/10) American actor, director BE, TW/
1-12, 27

HUSTON, Walter (1884-1950) Cana-
dian actor AAS, CB, DAB, ES,
NTH, SR, TW/2-6, WWA/4,
WWT/6-10

HUTCHESON, David (1905-76)
Scottish actor WWT/8-16

HUTCHESON, LaVerne American
actor, singer BE
HUTCHINGS, William (fl 1827)
English actor HAS
HUTCHINGS, W. S. ["The Light-
ning Calculator"] (b 1832)
American actor HAS
HUTCHINS, Fred B. (b 1911)
American educator BE
HUTCHINS, G. T. (d 1917) musi-
cal director EA/18*
HUTCHINSON, Abby J. (1829-92)
singer CDP
HUTCHINSON, Ann [Mrs. David
Hutchinson] (d 1878 [66]) EA/
79*
HUTCHINSON, Mrs. David see
Hutchinson, Ann
HUTCHINSON, Dorothy (d 1962
[80]) American singer BE*
HUTCHINSON, Emma (d 1917
[72]) actress, manager WWT/3
HUTCHINSON, George H. (d
1869) actor HAS
HUTCHINSON, George P. (d 1898
[70]) circus proprietor EA/99*
HUTCHINSON, Gerald (d 1897
[29]) actor EA/98*
HUTCHINSON, Harry (b 1892)
Irish actor WWT/9-16
HUTCHINSON, Henry Howe see
Howe, Henry
HUTCHINSON, Jessie singer
CDP
HUTCHINSON, Jody (d 1973 [57])
composer/lyricist BP/58*
HUTCHINSON, John W. singer
CDP
HUTCHINSON, Joseph (d 1871
[44]) proprietor EA/72*
HUTCHINSON, Joseph (d 1890)
circus proprietor EA/91*
HUTCHINSON, Josephine (b 1904)
American actress BE, WWT/
6-9
HUTCHINSON, Kathryn (fl 1900s)
American actress WWS
HUTCHINSON, Laurie (b 1945)
American actress TW/27
HUTCHINSON, Leslie (d 1969
[69]) performer BP/54*
HUTCHINSON, Mary (d 1887)
EA/88*
HUTCHINSON, Willie A. (d 1887
[18]) EA/88*
HUTCHINSON BROTHERS acro-
bats CDP, SR
HUTCHINSON SCOTT, Jay (b

1924) English designer WWT/
13-14
HUTCHISON, Emma see Hutchi-
son, Mrs. James George
HUTCHISON, Mrs. James George
[Emma Hutchison] (d 1917) ac-
tress, manager EA/18*
HUTCHISON, Muriel (d 1975 [60])
American actress WWT/10-11
HUTCHISON, Percy (1875-1945)
English actor, manager WWT/
1-9
HUTCHISON, Ronald Macdonald
see Tate, Henry
HUTH, Mrs. Frank see Moore,
Bertha
HUTH, Harold (1892-1967) English
actor WWT/7-9
HUTT, William (b 1920) Canadian
actor, director AAS, TW/24,
WWT/13-16
HUTTO, Jack (b 1928) American
literary representative BE
HUTTON, Mons. (fl 1827) French
dancer HAS
HUTTON, Mme. (fl 1827) French
dancer HAS
HUTTON, Betty (b 1921) American
singer, actress BE, CB, ES
HUTTON, Joseph (1787-1828)
American dramatist EAP, NTH,
RJ
HUTTON, Joseph (fl 1812) actor
HAS
HUTTON, June (d 1973) performer
BP/57*
HUTTON, Lawrence (1843-1904)
American? critic CDP, HJD
HUTTON, Mary (d 1898 [37]) singer
EA/99*
HUXLEY, Aldous (1894-1963) Eng-
lish dramatist ES, MD, MWD
HUY, John (d 1891 [57]) acting
manager EA/92*
HYACINTH, Mlle. (fl 1828) dancer
HAS
HYAMS, Barry (b 1911) American
press representative, producer,
critic BE
HYAMS, Harry (d 1965 [84]) pro-
ducer/director BP/50*
HYAMS, Samuel David see Hoey,
Dennis
HYATT, George F. (fl 1825-32)
actor CDP, HAS
HYATT, Herman (d 1968 [62]) per-
former BP/52*
HYDE, A. J. (d 1917) EA/18*

HYDE, Bruce (b 1941) American
actor TW/23, 25
HYDE, Douglas (1860-1949) Irish
dramatist COC, MWD, WWW/4
HYDE, Florence Mary (d 1879
[18]) singer EA/80*
HYDE, Henry, Lord Hyde &
Cornbury (d 1758) dramatist
CP/2-3, GT
HYDE, Herman (d 1967 [69])
performer BP/52*
HYDE, Mariette English actress
GRB/1
HYDE, Marion [Mrs. M. J.
White] (d 1911) actress EA/
12*
HYDE, Tom (d 1893) actor EA/
94*
HYDE, Walter (d 1951) English
singer WWW/5
HYDES, J. P. (fl 1859) Aus-
tralian comedian HAS
HYDES, Marcus John (d 1902)
manager EA/03*
HYDE-WHITE, Wilfrid (b 1903)
English actor AAS, BE, TW/
29, WWT/14-16
HYEM, Constance Ethel (1874-
1928) English actress, singer
GRB/4, WWT/1-5
HYER, W. G. (fl c. 1820?) drama-
tist EAP, RJ
HYETT, Robert (b 1873) English
actor, singer GRB/2
HYLAN, Donald (d 1968 [69])
performer BP/53*
HYLAND, Augustin Allen (d 1963
[58]) performer BE*
HYLAND, Diana (1936-77) Amer-
ican actress BE
HYLAND, Frances (b 1927)
Canadian actress WWT/12-16
HYLAND, William (fl 1746) drama-
tist CP/2-3, GT
HYLES, Ann (d 1884 [61]) music-
hall proprietor EA/85*
HYLES, Edwin Charles (d 1885
[35]) music-hall proprietor
EA/86*
HYLES, George (d 1879) music-
hall proprietor EA/80*
HYLES, William (d 1878 [35])
music-hall proprietor EA/79*
HYLL, Nicholas (fl 1423) mem-
ber of the Chapel Royal DA
HYLTON, C. Barry (d 1916)
performer? EA/17*
HYLTON, Jack (1892-1965) Eng-

lish conductor, composer, mana-
ger TW/21, WWT/9-13, WWW/6
HYLTON, Millie (1868-1920) Eng-
lish actress CDP, WWT/3
HYLTON, Richard (1920-62) Amer-
ican actor TW/1, 4-7, 18,
WWT/11
HYMAN, Earle (b 1926) American
actor AAS, BE, TW/1, 9-16,
18-20, 22, 24, 27, 29-30,
WWT/14-16
HYMAN, Elaine American actress
TW/23, 27-28
HYMAN, Joseph M. (1901-77?)
American producing manager
BE, TW/3-6, WWT/11
HYMAN, Maurice A. (d 1907
[63]) music-hall director EA/08*
HYMAN, Prudence English dancer
WWT/12
HYMAN, Walter A. (d 1973 [51])
producer/director/choreographer
BP/58*
HYMER, John B. (d 1953 [77])
American dramatist WWT/6-11
HYMER, Warren (d 1948 [42]) actor
BE*
HYND, Colin (d 1970 [84]) performer
BP/55*
HYNES, Katherine English? actress
TW/13
HYNICKA, Rudolph Kelker (1859-
1927) American executive
WWA/1
HYSLOP, Alfred (b 1925) American
actor TW/5
HYSON, Dorothy (b 1915/16) Amer-
ican actress WWT/8-11
HYTOWN, Noel (d 1965 [66]) per-
former BP/50*

- I -

IACANGELO, Peter (b 1948) Amer-
ican actor TW/30
IBBOT, Miss (fl 1760-87) actress
TD/1-2
IBRAHIM, Ada (d 1893) equilibrist
EA/94*
IBSEN, Henrik (1828-1906) Nor-
wegian dramatist COC, ES,
GRB/1, OC/1-3, RE
IDA, Mr. acrobat CDP
IDALENE actress, singer CDP
IDE, Patrick (b 1916) English
manager WWT/11-16
IDEN, Rosalind (b 1911) English

actress TW/3-4, WWT/10-14

IDZIKOWSKI, Stanislas (d 1977)
Polish dancer WWT/9-11

IFERD, Alice (d 1868) dancer
HAS

IGLESIAS, Roberto (b 1927)
Guatemalan dancer, choreographer CB

IGNATOV, Johnna (b 1941) American actress TW/30

IHNAT, Steve (d 1972 [37]) performer BP/56*

IKELHEIMER, Desire (fl 1848)
Belgian singer? HAS

ILES, Samuel (d 1872 [27]) musician EA/73*

ILIFF, Edward Henry (fl 1788)
actor TD/1-2

ILIFF, Mrs. Edward Henry actress TD/1-2

ILLING, Meta (d 1909 [37]) actress EA/11*, WWT/14*

ILLING, Peter (1905-66) Austrian
actor WWT/13-14

ILLINGTON, Margaret [Mrs.
Daniel Frohman] (1879/81-
1934) American actress DAB,
GRB/2-4, OC/1-3, SR, WWA/1,
WWM, WWS, WWT/1-7

ILLINGTON, Marie [Mrs. Gordon
Maddick] (d 1927 [71]) English
actress CDP, GRB/1-3,
OAA/2, WWT/1-5

ILLINGWORTH, Elsie (d 1973
[87]) performer BP/58*

ILLINGWORTH, Prunella see
Scales, Prunella

IMANO, Gertrude [Mrs. H. M.
Imano] (d 1899) singer EA/
00*

IMANO, Mrs. H. M. see
Imano, Gertrude

IMBERT, George see Charles,
G. F.

IMBODEN, David C. (d 1974
[87]) performer BP/58*

IMER, Teresa see Cornelys,
Teresa

IMESON, George L. (d 1918 [65])
EA/19*

IMESON, John (d 1885 [61])
manager EA/86*

IMHOF, Roger (d 1958 [83])
American vaudevillian TW/14

IMPERT, Margaret (b 1946)
American actress TW/30

IMRIE, Cuthbert (d 1908 [27])
actor? EA/09*

INCE, Alexander (1892-1966) Hungarian producer, publisher BE,
TW/22

INCE, Annette (fl 1849-57) dancer,
actress HAS

INCE, Edith see Melvin, Mrs.
A. Douglas

INCE, Emma (b 1828) American
dancer HAS

INCE, John E. (d 1909 [68]) comedian EA/10*

INCE, Ralph W. (d 1935 [50])
American actor, director BE*,
BP/21*

INCE, Thomas Harper (1882-1924)
American actor ES

INCH, William (d 1888 [44]) musician EA/90*

INCHBALD, Elizabeth [née Simpson]
(1753-1821) English actress,
dramatist CDP, COC, CP/3,
DNB, ES, GT, HP, OC/1-3,
SR, TD/1-2

INCHBALD, Joseph (d 1779) actor
BE*, WWT/14*

INCHINDI, Sig. (d 1876 [78]) singer
EA/77*

INCLEDON, Benjamin Charles
(1757/63-1826) English singer,
actor? CDP, DNB, GT, HAS,
OX, TD/1-2

INCLEDON, Charles (d 1826 [63])
WWT/14*

INCLEDON, Charles (1791-1865)
actor, singer DNB

INCLEDON, John (d 1826 [69])
singer EA/72*

INESCORT, Elaine (d 1964 [86])
English actress GRB/3-4,
WWT/1-8

INESCORT, Frieda (1901/05-76)
Scottish actress TW/1-7,
WWT/6-11

INFANT LYRA, The (fl 1825?)
musician CDP

ING, Alvin (b 1938) American actor
TW/27-28, 30

INGALS, Miles (d 1974 [71]) agent
BP/58*

INGE, Benson (d 1970 [61]) dramatist BP/54*

INGE, William (1913-73) American
dramatist AAS, CB, CD, CH,
COC, HJD, MD, MH, MWD,
NTH, OC/3, PDT, RE, TW/30,
WWA/5, WWT/12-15

INGELAND, Thomas (fl 1560s)
dramatist CP/1-2, FGF

INGERSOLL, Charles Jared (1782-
1862) American dramatist
EAP, RJ, SR
INGERSOLL, David (d 1847) Amer-
ican actor CDP, HAS, SR
INGERSOLL, William (d 1936
[76]) actor BP/20*, WWT/14*
INGHAM, Barrie (b 1932/42) Eng-
lish actor AAS, WWT/15-16
INGHAM, John dramatist EAP,
RJ
INGHRAM, Rose American actress
TW/2
INGLE, Charles (d 1940 [77])
composer WWT/14*
INGLEBY, Clement Mansfield
(d 1886 [63]) Shakespearean
commentator EA/87*
INGLESBY, Mona (b 1918) Eng-
lish dancer, choreographer
WWT/10-12
INGLIS, George D. see Chaplin,
George D.
INGLIS, Phil (d 1917) EA/18*
INGRAHAM, Prentiss (1843-1904)
dramatist HJD
INGRAM, Alice [Mrs. J. R.
Crauford] actress OAA/2
INGRAM, Beatrice [Mrs. Charles
Borland] (fl 1890-1900) Amer-
ican actress WWM
INGRAM, Mrs. Clyde Rapp (d
1974 [75]) designer BP/58*
INGRAM, Fred (d 1916) comedian
EA/17*
INGRAM, Gwladys (d 1911 [24])
actress EA/12*
INGRAM, Jack (d 1969 [66]) per-
former BP/53*
INGRAM, James (d 1890) "Late
of Wall's Phantoscope Com-
pany" EA/91*
INGRAM, Rex (1896-1969) Ameri-
can actor BE, TW/2-6, 26,
WWT/9-11
INKERSALL, J. G. (d 1867 [44])
singer EA/68*
INMAN, Bessie (d 1907) EA/08*
INMAN, Edward Frederick (d
1898 [69]) EA/99*
INMAN, Mary (d 1892) EA/93*
INNES, Isabel [Mrs. John
Humphries] English actress
GRB/1
INNESS-BROWN, Virginia Royall
(b 1901) American executive
BE
INTER-ACTION TRUST theatre

collective CD
INTROPODI, Ethel (d 1946 [50])
American actress SR, TW/3
INTROPODI, Josie (d 1941 [75])
American actress BE*, BP/26*,
WWT/14*
INVERARITY, Elizabeth see
Martyn, Mrs. Charles
IONESCO, Eugène (b 1912) Rumani-
an/French dramatist BE, CB,
COC, OC/3
IOOR, William (c. 1780-c. 1830)
American dramatist DAB, EAP,
HJD, RJ, WWA/H
IRELAND, Anthony (1902-57) Peru-
vian/English actor TW/7-8, 14,
WWT/7-12
IRELAND, John (b 1916) Canadian
actor, director BE
IRELAND, Joseph Norton (1817-98)
American writer CDP, WWA/H
IRELAND, Kenneth (b 1920) Scottish
administrator WWT/14-16
IRELAND, Thomas (d 1873 [65])
actor? EA/75*
IRELAND, William Henry (1775-
1835) English forger, dramatist
CDP, COC, CP/3, DNB, HP,
OC/1-3, TD/1-2
IRISH, Annie [Mrs. J. E. Dodson]
(1862/65-1947) English actress
DP, GRB/2-4, WWS, WWT/1-5
IRISH, Frederick William (b 1835)
English actor OAA/1-2
IRISH, Mrs. Frederick William
see Desborough, Juliet
"IRISH ROSCIUS, The" see
Burke, Joseph
IRMA, Mlle. (fl 1868) French ac-
tress CDP
IRSCHICH, Magda (fl 1866) German
actress CDP
IRTON, Mrs. see Russell, Edith
IRVIN, John (d 1918) EA/19*
IRVINE, Harry (d 1951 [77]) Eng-
lish actor TW/1, 4, 8
IRVINE, John (d 1968 [55]) per-
former BP/52*
IRVINE, Richard F. (d 1976 [65])
designer BP/60*
IRVINE, Robin (1901-33) English
actor WWT/7
IRVING, Ben (1919-68) American
union executive BE
IRVING, Daisy (d 1938) Irish ac-
tress, singer WWT/3-7
IRVING, Elizabeth (b 1904) English
actress WWT/4-6

IRVING, Ellis (b 1902) Australian
actor WWT/9-16
IRVING, Ernest (d 1953 [75])
composer, conductor WWT/14*
IRVING, Ethel [Mrs. Gilbert Por-
teous] (1869-1963) actress
GRB/1-4, WWT/1-11
IRVING, Frederick R. (d 1969
[75]) performer BP/54*
IRVING, George (1874-1914)
American actor WWA/1, WWS
IRVING, George S. [né George
Irving Shelasky] (b 1922)
American actor, singer BE,
TW/5-6, 9-10, 13-14, 16,
19-30, WWT/15-16
IRVING, Henrietta (1855-91)
American actress CDP, HAS,
SR
IRVING, Sir Henry [John Henry
Brodribb] (1838-1905) English
actor, manager CDP, COC,
DNB, DP, ES, GRB/1, HP,
NTH, OAA/1-2, OC/1-3,
PDT, SR, WWA/1, WWW/1
IRVING, H[enry] B[rodribb] (1870-
1919) English actor CDP,
COC, EA/97, ES, GRB/1-4,
NTH, OC/1-3, SR, WWS,
WWT/1-3, WWW/2
IRVING, Mrs. H[enry] B[rodribb]
see Baird, Dorothea
IRVING, Isabel [Mrs. W. H.
Thompson] (1871-1944) Amer-
ican actress GRB/2-4, PP/2,
SR, TW/1, WWA/2, WWM,
WWS, WWT/1-8
IRVING, John (d 1867 [63]) pro-
fessor of music EA/68*
IRVING, John (b 1927) English
actor TW/17
IRVING, Mrs. Joseph (d 1925
[80]) actress BE*, WWT/14*
IRVING, Joseph Henry (d 1870
[31]) English comedian HAS
IRVING, Jules [né Jules Israel]
(b 1925) American director,
producer BE, CB, WWT/
15-16
IRVING, K. Ernest (1878-1953)
English composer, conductor
WWT/9-11
IRVING, Laurence Henry Forster
(b 1897) English designer,
writer AAS, COC, ES,
OC/3, WWT/6-14
IRVING, Laurence Sidney Brod-
ribb (1871-1914) English actor,

dramatist COC, ES, GRB/1-4,
NTH, OC/1-3, SR, WWT/1-2,
WWW/1
IRVING, Mrs. Laurence Sidney
Brodribb see Hackney, Mabel
IRVING, Roy (b 1911) English actor
TW/4, 9
IRVING, Sydney [Mrs. Maurice H.
Hoffmann] (d 1900) EA/01*
IRVING, Washington (1783-1859)
American dramatist COC, ES,
OC/3
IRWIN, Charles Irish actor TW/1
IRWIN, Edward (1867-1937) English
actor, dramatist WWT/5-8
IRWIN, Eyles (b 1751) Indian/Irish
dramatist CP/3
IRWIN, Felix (d 1950 [57]) actor
BE*, WWT/14*
IRWIN, Flo (d 1930 [71]) Canadian
actress BE*, BP/15*
IRWIN, Kathleen (fl 1868-77) Eng-
lish actress, singer OAA/1-2
IRWIN, Margaret (d 1967) writer
WWW/6
IRWIN, Max (d 1864) American
comedian HAS
IRWIN, May [Mrs. Kurt Eisfeldt]
(1862-1938) Canadian actress
DAB, GRB/2-4, PP/2, SR,
WWA/1, WWM, WWS, WWT/1-8
IRWIN, Percy G. (d 1917) actor?
EA/18*
IRWIN, Selden (b 1833) American
actor HAS, SR
IRWIN, Mrs. Seldon (b 1834)
American actress HAS
IRWIN, Wallace (1875-1959) Amer-
ican dramatist WWA/3
IRWIN, Will (b 1907) American
musician, musical director,
composer BE
IRWIN, William Henry (1873-1948)
American dramatist WWA/2
ISAAC (c. 1655-c. 1720) English bal-
let master ES
ISAAC, Arthur (d 1890) actor EA/
91*
ISAAC, John (1791-1839) actor
CDP
ISAACS, Mr. (b 1791) singer BS
ISAACS, Miss see Millar, Mrs.
S. A.
ISAACS, A. see Andrews, A.
ISAACS, Edith J. R. (1878-1956)
American theatrical journalist,
critic, historian AAS, COC,
ES, NTH, OC/1-3, TW/12,

WWA/3, WWT/7-11

ISAACS, P. B. (1831-65) English minstrel HAS, SR

ISAACS, Rebecca [Mrs. Thomas Roberts] (d 1877 [47]) actress, singer CDP

ISAACSON, Carl L. (b 1920) American educator BE

ISDELL, Miss (fl 1811) Irish dramatist CP/3

ISHAM, Frederick S. (d 1922 [57]) dramatist BE*, BP/7*

ISHAM, Sir Gyles (1903-76) English actor WWT/6-11

ISHERWOOD, Mr. American actor HAS

ISHERWOOD, Mrs. [Miss Clark] (d 1841) American actress HAS

ISHERWOOD, Christopher (b 1904) English dramatist CB, CD, HJD, HP, MD, MH, MWD, NTH, PDT, WWT/9-11

ISHERWOOD, Harry (d 1840) actor, scene painter SR

ISHERWOOD, William (d 1841) American actor HAS

ISHII, Kan (d 1972 [71]) performer BP/56*

ISIDORA, Don (d 1876) actor EA/77*

ISLIPP, Adam (fl 1622) shareholder DA

ISOLA, Emile (d 1945 [85]) manager BE*, WWT/14*

ISOLA, Vincent (d 1947 [85]) manager BE*, WWT/14*

ISRAEL, Jules see Irving, Jules

ITALIANO, Anne see Bancroft, Anne

ITKIN, Bella (b 1920) Russian director BE

ITO, Yuji (d 1963 [66]) scene designer BP/48*

IT'S ALL RIGHT TO BE WOMAN THEATRE theatre collective CD

IVAN, Rosalind (d 1959 [75]) English actress TW/15

IVANOFF, Nicholas (1809-80) singer CDP

IVANS, Elaine (b 1900) American actress TW/2-3

IVERS, Miss see Orger, Mrs. Thomas

IVES, Alice E. (1883-1930) American dramatist SR, WWM

IVES, Anne American actress TW/27-30

IVES, Burl (b 1909) American actor, singer BE, CB, ES, TW/1, 6-7, 10-13, 24, WWT/15-16

IVES, George (b 1922) American actor TW/6-7

IVES, G. H. (d 1862) Irish magician HAS, SR

IVES, Joe (d 1917) EA/18*

IVES, Robert (d 1879) singer EA/80*

IVO, Alexander actor TW/1

IVOR, Frances Scottish actress EA/96, GRB/3-4, WWT/1-7

IVORY, Thomas (1709-79) architect DNB

IXON, Mrs. see Beaumont, Mrs.

IZANT, Robert J. (d 1971 [84]) critic BP/56*

IZARD, Alfred E. (d 1910 [47]) musician EA/11*

IZENOUR, George (b 1912) American theatre designer BE

IZON, Ada (d 1889) EA/90*

IZON, Thomas (d 1900 [55]) music-hall comedian EA/01*

IZUMI, Edward I. (d 1975 [63]) performer BP/60*

- J -

J., B. (fl 1661) dramatist CP/1-3

J., T. (fl 1654) dramatist CP/3

JACCHIA, Agide (1875-1932) Italian musical director WWA/1

JACK, Edwin Booth (b 1863) actor HAS

JACK, H. V. see Esmond, Henry V.

JACK, John Henry (b 1836) American actor, manager CDP, HAS, PP/2

JACK, Rosalie (b 1855) American actress HAS

JACK, Sam T. (d 1899 [46]) manager CDP

JACK, Walter C. (d 1888 [27]) American actor EA/89*

JACKLEY, George (d 1950 [65]) comedian BE*, WWT/14*

JACKMAN, H. (d 1873) musician EA/74*

JACKMAN, Henry Wilson (d 1879) treasurer EA/80*

JACKMAN, Isaac (fl 1777-95) Irish dramatist CP/2-3, DNB,

GT, TD/1
JACKMAN, W. (d 1852 [70])
manager EA/72*
JACKSON (fl c. 1629) actor DA
JACKSON, Mr. (fl 1714) trans-
lator CP/2-3
JACKSON, Miss (fl 1775) actress
CDP
JACKSON, Abram Wilbur (1806-
66) American actor, theatre
builder, manager CDP, HAS
JACKSON, Al (d 1975 [39]) com-
poser/lyricist BP/60*
JACKSON, Albert (d 1913) Eng-
lish actor SR
JACKSON, Alfred Graham (d
1965 [72]) dramatist BP/50*
JACKSON, Ann see Jackson,
Anne (b 1926)
JACKSON, Anne (1782-1869)
actress COC
JACKSON, Anne (b 1926) Amer-
ican actress BE, ES, TW/
5-24, 26-28, 30, WWT/11-16
JACKSON, Sir Barry Vincent
(1879-1961) English manager,
dramatist AAS, COC, ES,
OC/1-3, PDT, WWT/4-13,
WWW/6
JACKSON, C. D. (b 1902) Amer-
ican publisher BE
JACKSON, Charles (fl 1857)
American actor HAS
JACKSON, Charles (d 1873)
music-hall chairman EA/74*
JACKSON, Charles (d 1968 [65])
dramatist BP/53*
JACKSON, Charlotte [Miss Cubitt]
(d 1870) singer? musician?
EA/71*
JACKSON, Dorothea American
actress TW/3
JACKSON, Edward (fl 1622) les-
see DA
JACKSON, Ella (fl 1862) actress
HAS
JACKSON, Ernestine American
actress TW/30
JACKSON, Ethel (1877-1957)
American actress, singer
TW/14, WWT/1-10
JACKSON, Freda (b 1909) Eng-
lish actress AAS, WWT/9-16
JACKSON, Frederic (1886-1953)
American dramatist WWT/
4-11
JACKSON, George (d 1871 [24])
music-hall chairman EA/72*

JACKSON, George James William
(d 1896) professor of music
EA/98*
JACKSON, Glenda (b 1936) English
actress AAS, CB, WWT/15-16
JACKSON, Gordon (b 1923) Scottish
actor WWT/15-16
JACKSON, Harry (fl 1865) Australian
actor, circus clown HAS, SR
JACKSON, Harry (d 1885 [49]) ac-
tor, stage manager EA/86*,
WWT/14*
JACKSON, Harry (b 1923) American
actor TW/10-12
JACKSON, Mrs. Harry [Annie Lock-
hart] (fl c. 1865) actress HAS,
SR
JACKSON, Mrs. Harry see
Jackson, Marie Louise
JACKSON, Hart (d 1882 [47]) drama-
tist, manager CDP
JACKSON, Henry Conrad (d 1973
[46]) performer BP/58*
JACKSON, Horace Bertie (d 1908)
showman EA/09*
JACKSON, Isabella [Mrs. T. Jack-
son] (d 1871 [26]) EA/72*
JACKSON, James (fl 1789?) singer
CDP
JACKSON, Jane see Bianchi,
Mrs. Francesco
JACKSON, Jennie (d 1976 [54]) per-
former BP/60*
JACKSON, Jenny (d 1899 [27])
male impersonator EA/00*
JACKSON, Joe (d 1942 [62]) Austrian
comedian CB
JACKSON, John (1742-1806) English
actor, manager, dramatist CDP,
CP/2-3, DNB, GT
JACKSON, John (1769-1845) English
pugilist CDP, DNB
JACKSON, John [né McIllway] (d
1843) American slack-rope per-
former HAS
JACKSON, John (d 1892) music-hall
proprietor EA/94*
JACKSON, John Enderby (d 1903
[76]) manager EA/04*
JACKSON, John George (d 1879
[35]) professor of music EA/81*
JACKSON, John Sidney (d 1859)
HAS
JACKSON, Leonard [L. Errol
Jaye] (b 1928) American actor
TW/26-29
JACKSON, Lizzie see Mathews,
Mrs. Charles James

JACKSON, Marie Louise [Mrs. Harry Jackson] (d 1903) EA/04*

JACKSON, Mary (b 1915) American actress TW/26

JACKSON, Minnie (fl 1859-69) actress HAS

JACKSON, Nelson (b 1870) English entertainer GRB/1-3

JACKSON, Phebe (d 1891) EA/92*

JACKSON, Mrs. T. see Jackson, Isabella

JACKSON, Theodore (b 1838) American actor, minstrel HAS, SR

JACKSON, Theodore John (d 1891 [58]) musical director EA/92*

JACKSON, Thomas (d 1798) actor TD/2

JACKSON, Thomas (d 1967 [81]) performer BP/52*

JACKSON, W. F. (d 1896 [63]) singer EA/97*

JACKSON, William (1730-1803) English dramatist, composer, performer CDP, CP/3, GT, TD/1-2

JACKSON, William (d 1876) musician EA/77*

JACOB, Giles (1686-1744) dramatist CP/1-3, GT

JACOB, Sir Hildebrand (fl 1664) English dramatist CP/1-3, GT

JACOB, Naomi (1889-1964) English actress WWT/10-11

JACOBI, Derek (b 1938) English actor AAS, WWT/15-16

JACOBI, Frederick (1891-1952) American composer WWA/3

JACOBI, Georges (1840-1906) German composer, conductor GRB/1, WWW/1

JACOBI, Lou (b 1913) Canadian actor BE, TW/23-26, 28, 30, WWT/15-16

JACOBI, Maurice (d 1939) musical director BE*, WWT/14*

JACOBI, Victor (1883-1921) Hungarian composer BE*, BP/6*, WWT/14*

JACOBS, Mr. (d 1870) wizard EA/71*

JACOBS, Miss (fl 1792) singer TD/1-2

JACOBS, Arthur P. (d 1973 [51]) producer/director/choreographer BP/58*

JACOBS, Austin Lewis see Parker, Lew

JACOBS, Carl (b 1916) American actor TW/24

JACOBS, Charles (fl 1857) singer HAS

JACOBS, E. M. (d 1966 [85]) booking agent BP/51*

JACOBS, G. W. musician CDP

JACOBS, Helen (d 1974 [53]) producer/director/choreographer BP/59*

JACOBS, Jim (b 1942) American actor, librettist CD, TW/28

JACOBS, Max William (b 1937) American actor TW/22

JACOBS, Morris (b 1906) American business manager BE

JACOBS, Sally [née Rich] (b 1932) English designer AAS, WWT/15-16

JACOBS, Steven (d 1969 [32]) talent scout BP/54*

JACOBS, Thomas (d 1976 [73]) stand in BP/60*

JACOBS, Will (b 1945) American actor TW/29

JACOBS, William Wymark (1863-1943) English dramatist WWM, WWT/1-9

JACOBSEN, L. H. (d 1941 [81]) critic BE*

JACOBSON, Mr. singer, musician CDP

JACOBSON, Barbara Scott (d 1972 [57]) performer BP/56*

JACOBSON, Clarence (d 1971 [84]) manager BP/56*

JACOBSON, Irving (b 1905) American actor, producer BE

JACOBSON, Lisa Japanese/American actress TW/30

JACOBSON, Sam (d 1964 [89]) performer BE*

JACOBSON, Sol (b 1912) American press representative BE

JACOBY, Scott (b 1955) American actor TW/24, 26

JACQUEMOT, Ray American actor TW/3-7

JACQUES, Mrs. Edgar F. see Jacques, Fanny Lavinia

JACQUES, Fanny Lavinia [Mrs. Edgar F. Jacques] (d 1911 [81]) EA/12*

JACQUES, Frederic (b 1864) English actor GRB/1

JACQUES, Mrs. Frederic see
Rayner, Minnie Gray
JACQUES, Hattie [née Josephine
Edwina] (b 1924) English ac-
tress WWT/13-16
JACQUES, Josephine Edwina see
Jacques, Hattie
JACQUES, Rosa (d 1857) singer
HAS
JACQUIN, Maurice (d 1974 [74])
producer/director/choreographer
BP/59*
JADEN, Donna Mae see Paige,
Janis
JAELL, Alfred (1832-82) musician,
composer CDP
JAFFE, Carl (d 1974 [72]) actor,
producer BP/58*, WWT/16*
JAFFE, Herb literary representa-
tive BE
JAFFE, Michael (d 1976 [71])
performer BP/60*
JAFFE, Sam (b 1893/97/98)
American actor AAS, BE,
TW/2-8, 10-15, WWT/8-16
JAFFE, Teri (d 1975 [58]) charity
organiser BP/60*
JAGGARD, William (1568-1623)
English printer, publisher
NTH
JAGGER, Dean (b 1904) American
actor TW/4-6, WWT/10-11
JAGO, Richard (1715-81) English
dramatist CP/3
JAHN, Marie Léonie Eugénie
see Yahne, Mlle.
JAKEWAY, Samuel John (d 1887)
singer EA/88*
JALKIO, Maj-Lis (b 1945) actress
TW/30
JALLAND, Henry (1861-1928)
English business manager
WWT/2-4
JAMES, Albert (fl 1868-90) actor,
singer CDP, DP
JAMES, Amelia Jane see Smyth-
son, Miss Montague
JAMES, Aphie [Mrs. Louis James]
(b 1875) American actress
WWA/5, WWM
JAMES, C. (fl 1787) translator
CP/3
JAMES, Cairns see James,
Lewis Cairns
JAMES, Mrs. Cairns see Moore,
Jessie
JAMES, C. H. see Eversley,
H. A.

JAMES, Mrs. Charles see James,
Sarah
JAMES, Charles A. (d 1917) pro-
prietor EA/18*
JAMES, Charles James (d 1888
[83/84]) scene artist, producer,
lessee BE*, EA/89*, WWT/14*
JAMES, Charles S. (d 1868 [35])
scene artist EA/69*
JAMES, Charlotte Varian (fl 1859)
American singer? HAS
JAMES, Clifton (d 1963 [65]) actor
BE*
JAMES, Clifton (b 1921) American
actor BE, TW/14, 19, 21-22,
24
JAMES, C. Stanfield (d 1868 [35])
scene artist, manager WWT/14*
JAMES, Culver see Dacre, Arthur
JAMES, Cyril (d 1975 [63]) pro-
ducer/director/choreographer
BP/60*
JAMES, David (1839-93) English
actor CDP, COC, DNB, DP,
OAA/1-2, OC/1-3
JAMES, Mrs. David (d 1881 [38])
EA/82*
JAMES, David, Jr. (d 1917) actor,
director BE*, WWT/14*
JAMES, Dorothy Dorian American
actress TW/28
JAMES, Edwin F. (fl 1865) actor
HAS
JAMES, Emrys (b 1930) Welsh ac-
tor AAS, WWT/15-16
JAMES, Eric (b 1943) American
actor TW/25-26
JAMES, Mrs. E. W. see James,
Florrie
JAMES, Florence (1857-1929) Eng-
lish dramatist WWW/3
JAMES, Florrie [Mrs. E. W.
James] (d 1911 [28]) EA/12*
JAMES, Francesca American ac-
tress TW/30
JAMES, Francis (b 1907) Australian
actor WWT/7-10
JAMES, Frankie (d 1974 [72]) ac-
tress, singer TW/30
JAMES, Frazer singer CDP
JAMES, George (d 1898 [76]) come-
dian EA/99*
JAMES, Gerald (d 1964 [77]) actor,
manager BE*, WWT/14*
JAMES, Gerald (b 1917) Welsh ac-
tor AAS, WWT/15-16
JAMES, Hal (d 1971 [58]) producer
TW/28

JAMES, Hattie (1845-61) English dancer HAS

JAMES, Haydn (d 1916) musical director, composer EA/17*

JAMES, Henry (1843-1916) American dramatist COC, DNB, ES, HJD, HP, MD, MWD, OC/1-3, PDT, RE

JAMES, Horace D. (d 1925 [72]) actor BE*, BP/10*

JAMES, Jessie (d 1974 [38]) performer BP/59*

JAMES, John (d 1900) acrobat EA/01*

JAMES, John Albert (d 1906 [33]) minstrel, comedian EA/07*

JAMES, John Edward (d 1885 [54]) EA/86*

JAMES, Johnny Painter (d 1881) step-dancer EA/82*

JAMES, Julia (1890-1964) English actress WWT/2-5

JAMES, Kate (d 1913 [57]) actress CDP

JAMES, Lewis Cairns (1865-1946) Scottish actor, singer, stage manager, producer WWW/4

JAMES, Lil [Mrs. Tony Dido] (d 1904) music-hall performer EA/05*

JAMES, Lithgow (d 1900) singer EA/01*, WWT/14*

JAMES, Louis (1842-1910) American actor COC, DAB, GRB/2-4, OC/1-3, PP/2, SR, WWA/1, WWS

JAMES, Mrs. Louis see James, Aphie

JAMES, Mary American actress TW/2-7, 9

JAMES, Michael see Jayston, Michael

JAMES, Millie [Mrs. Edgar Seidenberg] (b 1876) actress GRB/2, WWS

JAMES, Peter (b 1940) English director WWT/16

JAMES, Philip (d 1975 [85]) composer/lyricist BP/60*

JAMES, Polly English actress (b 1941) English actress TW/21, WWT/16

JAMES, Mrs. P. R. see Smythson, Miss Montague

JAMES, Rian (d 1953 [53]) dramatist BE*, BP/37*

JAMES, Richard Jones's Boy (fl 1599) actor? DA

JAMES, Sarah [Mrs. Charles James] (d 1905 [47]) EA/06*

JAMES, Sidney (d 1976 [62]) actor BP/60*

JAMES, Skip (d 1969 [67]) performer BP/54*

JAMES, William (b 1938) American actor TW/29

JAMESON, House (1902-71) American actor BE, TW/15, 19-20, 22-24, 27

JAMESON, Jo Anne (b 1944) American actress TW/23

JAMESON, Joyce (b 1932) American actress BE

JAMESON, Pauline (b 1920) English actress AAS, WWT/11-16

JAMES-TAYLOR, Jeremy (b 1948) English actor TW/30

JAMIESON, Carrie (d 1892) American actress EA/93*

JAMIESON, George (1812-68) American actor, dramatist CDP, HAS, RJ

JAMIESON, William L. (1835-68) American actor HAS

JAMIN, Georges (d 1971 [64]) performer BP/55*

JAMIN-BARTLETT, D. (b 1948) American actress TW/29

JAMISON, Alexander (d 1880 [84]) musician EA/81*

JAMISON, Bob (1799-1868) English actor HAS

JAMISON, Judith (b 1944) American dancer CB

JAMISON, Marshall (b 1918) American producer, director, actor BE

JAMROG, Joe (b 1932) American actor TW/30

JANAUSCHEK, Francesca Romana Magdalena (1830-1904) Czech actress CDP, COC, DAB, HAS, OC/1-3, PP/2, WWA/1

JANCOWSKI, Elizabeth (d 1904) EA/05*

JANES, Kenneth H. English educator, director, actor, dramatist BE

JANIS, Chelle (d 1974 [71]) performer BP/59*

JANIS, Conrad (b 1928) American actor, musician BE, TW/1-2, 8-16, 18-20, 25-26, 29, WWT/15-16

JANIS, Elsie (1889-1956) American actress, mimic COC, GRB/3-4,

NTH, SR, TW/12, WWA/3,
WWS, WWT/1-11

JANIS, Percy (d 1907) American
actor GRB/3*

JANISCH, Antonie (fl 1868) Austrian actress CDP

JANNEY, Ben (b 1927) American
director, stage manager BE

JANNEY, Leon (b 1917) American
actor BE, TW/5-6, 10-16,
18, 20-21, 26

JANNEY, Russell (1884-1963)
American manager CB, TW/
20, WWA/3, WWT/6-9

JANNINGS, Emil (1886-1950)
American/German actor NTH

JANNINGS, Orin (d 1966 [48])
actor, dramatist TW/23

JANS, Harry (d 1962 [62]) performer BE*

JANSEN, Jim (b 1945) American
actor TW/30

JANSEN, Marie (1864-1914) American actress, singer CDP, SR,
WWA/1, WWS

JANSSEN, Herbert (b 1895) German singer ES

JANVIER, Emma (d 1924) comedienne BE*, BP/9*, WWT/14*

"JAPANESE TOMMY" see
Delverd, Thomas

JAQUES, Eliza (d 1893 [71])
EA/94*

JAQUES, Francis (fl 1642) dramatist CP/2-3, FGF

JAQUET, Catharine (b 1760)
actress CDP

JARBEAU, Vernona (d 1914 [53])
actress CDP

JARDINE, Betty [Elizabeth Mc-
Kittrick Jardine] (d 1945) English actress WWT/9

JARDON, Dorothy (d 1966 [83])
performer BP/51*

JARKOWSKY, Andrew American
actor TW/30

JARMAN, Anthony (fl 1622)
lessee DA

JARMAN, Frances Eleanor
see Ternan, Mrs. Thomas

JARMAN, Herbert (1871-1919)
actor GRB/3-4, WWT/1-3

JARMAN, Peter (d 1969) critic
BP/54*

JARNAC, Dorothy American actress TW/2, 5-7, 10

JARRATT, Edward (d 1885 [86])
EA/86*

JARRELL, Randall (d 1965 [51])
dramatist BP/50*

JARRETT, Asbury Bond (d 1894
[62]) American manager EA/95*

JARRETT, Bella (b 1931) American
actress TW/29

JARRETT, Henry C. (d 1886)
manager BE*

JARRETT, Henry C. (1827/28-1903)
American actor, manager CDP,
HAS, SR

JARRETT, Jerry (b 1918) American
actor TW/25-29

JARRY, Alfred (1873-1907) French
dramatist COC, OC/3

JARVICE (fl 1635) musician DA

JARVIS, Ernest Herbert (d 1908)
showman's manager EA/09*

JARVIS, Graham (b 1930) Canadian
actor TW/23-25, 30

JARVIS, Henry (d 1871 [44]) actor
EA/72*

JARVIS, J. H. (1845-87) English
actor NYM

JARVIS, Robert C. (d 1971 [79])
director, actor, singer TW/28

JASLOW, Annette Schein (d 1967
[79]) publicity agent BP/51*

JASON, Harvey (b 1940) English
actor TW/22-23

JASON, Rick (b 1926) American actor TW/6-9

JASON, Will (d 1970 [69]) com-
poser/lyricist BP/54*

JASPER, Zina (b 1939) American
actress TW/24, 26-27

JAY, David (b 1961) American actor
TW/28, 30

JAY, Don American actor TW/30

JAY, Dorothy (b 1897) English actress, singer WWT/4-5

JAY, Ernest (1893-1957) English
actor WWT/9-12

JAY, Harriett (1863-1932) English
dramatist DP, GRB/4, WWT/
1-6, WWW/3

JAY, Isabel [Mrs. H. S. H. Caven-
dish] (1879-1927) English actress,
singer GRB/1-4, WWT/1-5

JAY, John Herbert (1871-1942)
English business manager,
manager WWT/1-9

JAY, William (b 1935) American
actor TW/24-29

JAYE, L. Errol see Jackson,
Leonard

JAYSTON, Michael [né James] (b
1936) English actor WWT/15-16

JEAKINS, Dorothy (b 1914) American costume designer BE

JEAN, Jess [John William Quick] (d 1908 [55]) EA/09*

JEANMAIRE, Zizi [Renée] (b 1924) French dancer, singer, actress BE, CB, ES, TW/10-11, 21

JEANNETTE, Gertrude (b 1918) American actress TW/25-26

JEANS, Frederick see Lennox, Fred J.

JEANS, Isabel (b 1891) English actress AAS, NTH, WWT/5-16

JEANS, Ronald (1887-1973) English dramatist AAS, WWT/4-14

JEANS, Ursula (1906-73) Indian/English actress AAS, NTH, TW/29, WWT/6-15

JEAYES, Allan (1885-1963) English actor WWT/4-13

JECKS, Mrs. Charles A. see Coveney, Harriett

JECKS, Charles Albert (d 1895) business manager, manager EA/96*, WWT/14*

JECKS, Clara (d 1951 [94]) actress DP, EA/97, GRB/3-4, OAA/2, WWT/1-6

JEDD, Gerry (d 1962 [37]) American actor TW/16, 19

JEE, Mrs. Albert (d 1906 [24]) EA/07*

JEE, Henry Williams see Burnell, Harry

JEE, James Henry (d 1906 [57]) acrobat, circus proprietor EA/07*

JEE, Joseph (d 1890 [49]) musical performer? EA/91*

JEE, Joseph (d 1911) music-hall performer EA/12*

JEE, Mrs. Joseph, Sr. (d 1887) EA/88*

JEE, William (d 1885 [40]) musical grotesque EA/86*

JEFF (d 1899) music-hall performer EA/00*

JEFFERIES, Mr. dramatist CP/1

JEFFERIES, Mr. (fl 1812) actor CDP

JEFFERIES, Douglas (1884-1959) English actor WWT/5-12

JEFFERIMI, Mr. (fl 1835) actor CDP

JEFFERS, Doug (b 1942) American actor TW/29

JEFFERS, John Robinson (1887-1962) American dramatist ES, HJD, HP, MD, MH, MWD, TW/18

JEFFERSON, Mr. actor TD/2

JEFFERSON, Mrs. Arthur see Metcalfe, Madge

JEFFERSON, Charles Burke (1851-1908) American actor, manager OC/1-3

JEFFERSON, Cornelia (b 1835) American actress HAS, SR

JEFFERSON, Cornelia Frances [Cornelia Frances Thomas] (1796-1849) actress, singer CDP, HAS, OC/1-3, SR, WWA/H

JEFFERSON, Elizabeth see Chapman, Elizabeth

JEFFERSON, Euphemia American? actress? ES

JEFFERSON, Herbert, Jr. (b 1946) American actor TW/29

JEFFERSON, Hester (d c.1845) American? actress? ES

JEFFERSON, John (d 1831) American actor ES, HAS, SR

JEFFERSON, Joseph (1774-1832) English/American actor CDP, DAB, ES, HAS, OC/1-3, SR, WWA/H

JEFFERSON, Joseph (1804-42) American actor, scene painter CDP, ES, HAS, OC/1-3, SR

JEFFERSON, Joseph (1829-1905) American actor CDP, COC, DAB, GRB/1, HAS, HJD, NTH, OAA/1-2, OC/1-3, PP/2, SR, WWA/1, WWW/1

JEFFERSON, Joseph (1869-1919) American actor WWA/1

JEFFERSON, Mrs. Joseph [née Thomas; Mrs. Thomas Burke] (1796-1850) American singer, actress? ES, HAS

JEFFERSON, Mrs. Joseph, I [Miss Lockyer] (1832-61) English actress HAS

JEFFERSON, Mary Anne American? actress? ES

JEFFERSON, Maude [Mrs. Edward P. Durham] (b 1885) American actress GRB/1

JEFFERSON, Thomas (1732-1807) English actor, manager CDP, ES, OC/1-3

JEFFERSON, Thomas (d 1824) American actor ES, HAS

JEFFERSON, Thomas (d 1932 [76]) actor BE*, BP/16*, WWT/14*

JEFFERSON, William Winter (d 1946 [70]) English actor BE*, BP/30*, WWT/14*

JEFFERY, Daniel Smith (d 1904 [44]) singer EA/05*

JEFFERYE, William (d 1889 [60]) proprietor EA/90*

JEFFES, Anthony (fl 1597-1612) actor DA

JEFFES, Humphrey (d 1618) actor DA

JEFFORD, Barbara (b 1930) English actress AAS, BE, WWT/11-16

JEFFREY, John dramatist? FGF

JEFFREY, Peter (b 1929) English actor WWT/16

JEFFREY, Robert (b 1934) Canadian actor TW/18-19

JEFFREYS, Ann (b 1923/28) American actress, singer BE, TW/3-11, 22, WWT/11-16

JEFFREYS, Ellis [Mrs. Herbert Sleath Skelton] (1868/72-1943) Irish actress GRB/1-4, SR, WWS, WWT/1-9

JEFFREYS, George (1678-1755) English dramatist CP/2-3, DNB, GT, TD/1-2

JEFFREYS, Hilda Irish actress GRB/1

JEFFREYS, Ida (d 1926 [70]) actress BE*, BP/10*, WWT/14*

JEFFREYS-GOODFRIEND, Ida see Jeffreys, Ida

JEFFRIES, Emblem Ann (d 1892 [82]) EA/93*

JEFFRIES, Maud (1869-1946) American actress GRB/1-4, SR, PP/2, WWS, WWT/1-8

JEFFRIES, W. W. (d 1867) actor HAS

JEFFRYS, George (d 1755 [77]) dramatist BE*, WWT/14*

JEFFS, Charles William (d 1886 [55]) music-hall singer EA/87*

JEFFS, Elizabeth Walker [Mrs. Waller Jeffs] (d 1909 [43]) EA/10*

JEFFS, Mrs. Waller see Jeffs, Elizabeth Walker

JEFTON, J. O. (d 1881) comedian EA/82*

JEHLINGER, Charles (1866-1952) American teacher TW/9

JELLICOE, Anne (b 1927) English dramatist, director AAS, CD, CH, ES, MH, MWD, PDT, RE, WWT/14-16

JELLIFFE, Rowena Woodham (b 1892) American executive, director BE

JELLINECK, Frances see Williams, Frances

JELLINGS-BLOW, Sydney see Blow, Sydney

JENKINS, Allen (d 1974 [74]) actor BP/59*, WWT/16*

JENKINS, Billy (d 1880 [34]) equestrian clown EA/81*

JENKINS, Claude (d 1967 [88]) producer/director/choreographer BP/52*

JENKINS, David (d 1883 [31]) proprietor EA/84*

JENKINS, Emma (d 1909) EA/10*

JENKINS, George (b 1910) American designer BE, ES, TW/5-8, WWT/15-16

JENKINS, James George (d 1878 [21]) musician EA/79*

JENKINS, Megs (b 1917) English actress AAS, WWT/10-16

JENKINS, Patricia American actress TW/13-14

JENKINS, R. Claud (1878-1967) English producer, manager WWT/9-11

JENKINS, Richard Walter see Burton, Richard

JENKINS, Warren E. C. (b 1905) English actor, director WWT/8-16

JENKINS, William K. (d 1968 [77]) executive BP/52*

JENKS, Frank (d 1962) American actor BE*

JENKS, Fred (1874-1947) American clown SR

JENKS, Si (d 1970 [93]) performer BP/54*

JENNENS, Charles (d 1773) editor, composer CP/2-3, GT, TD/1-2

JENNER, Caryl [Pamela Penelope Ripman] (1917-73) English director, manager COC, WWT/12-15

JENNER, Charles (1737-74) dramatist CP/2-3, GT

JENNER, Edwin (d 1909) EA/10*

JENNINGS, Mr. (d 1880 [32]) EA/82*

JENNINGS, Mrs. (fl 1863) English actress HAS

JENNINGS, Mrs. Charles Herrick

see Auckland, Marie

JENNINGS, Dewitt C. (d 1937) American actor BE*, BP/21*

JENNINGS, Frederick (1890-1947) actor, banjoist SR

JENNINGS, Frederick Summers (b 1872) English manager GRB/1

JENNINGS, George (d 1912) EA/14*

JENNINGS, Gertrude E. (d 1958 [81]) dramatist WWT/3-12, WWW/5

JENNINGS, Hargrave (d 1890) singer? EA/91*

JENNINGS, Harry (d 1910) comic singer, clog dancer EA/11*

JENNINGS, Mrs. J. H. (d 1893) singer EA/94*

JENNINGS, John Charles (d 1887 [27]) equestrian EA/88*

JENNINGS, John Henry (d 1902 [78]) singer, manager CDP

JENNINGS, Thomas (d 1880 [70]) musician EA/81*

JENNINGS, Toney (d 1878 [80]) musician EA/79*

JENNION, Tom (d 1901) EA/02*

JENNISON, John (d 1869 [80]) proprietor EA/70*

JENNYNGES, Giles (fl 1594) actor DA

JENOURE, Aida [Mrs. Howard Cochran] English actress, singer GRB/1-4, WWT/1-7

JENS, Salome (b 1935/36) American actress BE, TW/19-21, 23-26, 28, WWT/15-16

JENSEN, Adolf (d 1879 [41]) composer EA/80*

JENSEN, Howard C. (d 1972 [58]) producer/director/choreographer BP/57*

JENSEN, Petronella see Ella, Miss

JENSEN, Sterling (b 1925) American actor TW/27-28

JEPHSON, Robert (1736-1803?) Irish? dramatist CDP, CP/2-3, DNB, GT, SR, TD/1-2

JEPPE, Mr. (fl 1874?) singer CDP

JEREMY, James (d 1899) musician EA/00*

JERITZA, Maria (b 1887) Czech singer ES

JERNINGHAM, Edward (1727-1812) English dramatist CDP, CP/

2-3, DNB, GT, TD/1-2

JEROME, Ben M. (d 1938 [c. 55]) American composer BE*

JEROME, Mrs. Charles [Ella Jerome] (d 1889 [35]) vaudevillian EA/90*

JEROME, Daisy American actress, variety artist GRB/1-4

JEROME, Edwin (d 1959 [73]) actor BE*, BP/44*

JEROME, Ella see Jerome, Mrs. Charles

JEROME, Helen (b 1883) English dramatist WWT/9-11

JEROME, Jerome K[lapka] (1859-1927) English dramatist COC, DNB, ES, GRB/1-4, HP, MH, MWD, OC/1-3, PDT, WWM, WWS, WWT/1-5, WWW/2

JEROME, Peter (d 1967 [74]) dramatist BP/52*

JEROME, Rowena (b 1889/90) actress WWT/2-5

JEROME, Sadie (1876-1950) American actress GRB/2-4, WWT/1-5

JEROME, William (d 1932 [67]) American lyricist BE*

JERRARD, John Francis (d 1906 [54]) actor EA/07*, WWT/14*

JERROLD, Douglas William (1803-57) English dramatist CDP, COC, DNB, ES, HP, MH, OC/1-3

JERROLD, Evelyn Douglas (d 1885 [34]) EA/86*

JERROLD, Mary (1877-1955) English actress ES, WWT/1-11, WWW/5

JERROLD, Mary Ann (d 1910 [78]) EA/11*

JERROLD, Robert (c. 1755-c. 1818) English actor ES

JERROLD, Samuel (d 1820) English actor, impresario ES

JERROLD, William Blanchard (1826-84) English dramatist DNB, ES, OC/1-3

JERVIS, George F. (1784-1851) English singer, actor HAS

JERVIS, Mrs. St. Vincent see Wadman, Miss

JERWOOD, T. J. (d 1866) lawyer EA/72*

JESON, Thomas (d 1688) actor, dancing master, dramatist GT

JESSE, Fryn[iwyd] Tennyson (1889-1958) dramatist COC, WWT/

4-12, WWW/5

JESSE, Stella (b 1897) English actress WWT/4-6

JESSEL, George (b 1898) American actor, dramatist, producer BE, CB, SR, WWT/6-16

JESSEL, Joseph (b 1859) American dramatist SR

JESSEL, Mrs. Joseph A. see Herndon, Agnes

JESSEL, Patricia (1920-68) English actress BE, TW/11-12, WWT/10-14

JESSEMAN, Caroline (d 1888) EA/90*

JESSEMAN, Tom (d 1873 [29]) EA/74*

JESSNER, Leopold (1878-1945) German director, producer BE*

JESSOP, George H. (d 1915) Irish dramatist SR

JESSOP, Mrs. Henry see Jessop, Maria

JESSOP, Maria [Mrs. Henry Jessop] (d 1880) EA/82*

JESSUP, Stanley (d 1945 [67]) American actor BE*, BP/30*

JETHRO, Phil (b 1947) American actor TW/28-29

JEVON, Thomas (1652-88) English actor, dancer, dramatist COC, CP/1-3, DNB, OC/1-3

JEVONS, Shirley Byron (d 1928) English critic WWW/2

JEWEL, Mr. treasurer TD/1-2

JEWELL, Mrs. (d 1798) actress WWT/14*

JEWELL, Isabel (d 1972 [62]) actress BP/56*, WWT/16*

JEWELL, Izetta [Izetta Kenney] (b 1883) American actress WWS, WWT/1-6

JEWELL, Jacob (d 1884) showman EA/85*

JEWELL, James (d 1975 [69]) producer/director/choreographer BP/60*

JEWELL, James (b 1925) American actor TW/10

JEWELL, James (b 1929) American educator, lighting designer, engineer BE

JEWELL, Jennie (fl 1857) reader HAS

JEWELL, Jesse (d 1909 [62]) performer? EA/10*

JEWETT, Henry (d 1930 [68])

Australian actor PP/2, WWS

JEWETT, Sara (d 1899 [c. 52]) actress CDP

JEWKES, Penny (d 1972 [22]) performer BP/57*

JEWSON, Frederick Bowen (d 1891 [68]) composer, professor of music EA/92*

JEWSON, Solomon (d 1877 [77]) professor of music EA/78*

JILLSON, Franklin F. (d 1892) EA/93*

JILLSON, Joyce (b 1946) American actress TW/22

JIMSON, J. C. (d 1910 [47]) animal trainer EA/11*

JOACHIM, Amelie (d 1899 [60]) singer EA/00*

JOACHIM, Josef (d 1907 [76]) musician, composer EA/08*

JOB, Thomas (1900-47) Welsh dramatist TW/4, WWA/2, WWT/10

JOBIN, Peter (b 1944) Canadian actor TW/25-26

JOBLING, Mrs. M. E. see Cross, Emily

JOCELYN, Mary [Mrs. Calvert Routledge] English actress GRB/1-3

JOCKO, The Brazilian Ape see Magilton, Henry M.

JODRELL, Sir Paul (d 1803) English dramatist CP/2-3, GT

JODRELL, Sir Richard Paul (1745-1831) English dramatist CP/3, DNB

JOE, Nicholas (fl 1509-11) actor DA

JOEL, Clara (b 1890) American actress WWT/5-9

JOEL, Hettie (d 1896) singer EA/97*

JOEL, Michael Joseph (d 1893 [63]) EA/94*

JOFFREY, Robert (b 1930) American choreographer, director, dancer CB

JOHANN, Dalla (b 1944) American actor TW/24-25

JOHANN, John (b 1942) American actor TW/23, 25-26, 28-29

JOHANN, Zita (b 1904) Hungarian actress WWT/7-9

JOHANNET, Miss see Vining, Mrs.

JOHANNOT, Sarah see Hamilton, Mrs. Robert

JOHANNOT, Tony (d 1825) actor
CDP

JOHANSEN, Mme. (fl 1856) English singer HAS

JOHANSEN, Aud (b 1930) Norwegian actress, dancer, singer
WWT/12

JOHN, Alice (d 1956 [75]) Welsh
actress TW/13

JOHN, Errol (b 1924) West Indian
dramatist, actor CD, MD,
MWD, PDT

JOHN, Evan (1901-53) English actor, dramatist, producer WWT/
9-10

JOHN, Graham [Graham John
Colmer] (b 1887/89) English
dramatist, lyricist WWT/8-11

JOHN, Rosamund [née Nora Rosamund Jones] (b 1913) English
actress WWT/11-14

JOHN, Samuel see Johnson,
Samuel

JOHN BULL PUNCTURE REPAIR
KIT theatre collective CD

JOHNS, Andrew (b 1935) American actor TW/24

JOHNS, Clay (b 1934) American
actor TW/26-28

JOHNS, Eric (1907-75) English
critic AAS, WWT/11-15

JOHNS, Glynis (b 1923) South
African actress AAS, BE,
CB, ES, TW/8, 13-15, 19,
29-30, WWT/9-16

JOHNS, Harriette (b 1921) Scottish actress WWT/11-16

JOHNS, John (d 1963 [54]) performer BP/48*

JOHNS, Johnny see Thorogood,
John

JOHNS, Mervyn (b 1899) Welsh
actor ES, WWT/9-16

JOHNS, William (b c. 1644)
dramatist CP/2-3, GT

JOHNSON, Mr. actor CDP

JOHNSON, Mr. (fl 1735) translator CP/2-3, GT

JOHNSON, Mr. (fl 1772) American? actor HAS, SR

JOHNSON, Mr. (fl 1847) singer?
actor? HAS

JOHNSON, Prof (d 1877 [38])
"The African Hercules" EA/78*

JOHNSON, Mrs. [née Ford] (fl
1798) English actress TD/1-2

JOHNSON, Adelaide (b 1844)
American music-hall performer

HAS

JOHNSON, A. E. (d 1909 [35])
musician EA/10*

JOHNSON, Albert (1910-67) American designer, architect, producer, director BE, ES, TW/2,
5-8, 24

JOHNSON, Albert E. (b 1912)
American educator, director
BE

JOHNSON, Amelia [Mrs. J. G.
Johnson] (d 1905) EA/06*

JOHNSON, Arte (b 1931) American
actor TW/11

JOHNSON, Bayn (b 1958) American
actor TW/24

JOHNSON, Ben (b 1866) American
actor WWM

JOHNSON, Benjamin (1665?-1742)
actor CDP, DNB

JOHNSON, Bess (d 1975 [73]) performer BP/59*

JOHNSON, Bill (1918-57) American
actor, singer TW/2-4, 13,
WWT/11

JOHNSON, Bobby (b 1946) American
actor TW/26, 29-30

JOHNSON, Bruce Forsyth see
Forsyth, Bruce

JOHNSON, Carroll (b 1851) singer,
minstrel CDP

JOHNSON, Celia (b 1908) English
actress AAS, ES, WWT/7-16

JOHNSON, Charles (1679-1748)
dramatist CP/1-3, DNB, GT,
TD/1-2

JOHNSON, Charles (d 1865) circus
performer HAS

JOHNSON, Charles (d 1879 [68])
music-hall chairman EA/80*

JOHNSON, Charles F. (b 1865)
English actor, manager GRB/1

JOHNSON, Chic [né Harold Ogden
Johnson] (1891-1962) American
actor CB, TW/1-8, 18, WWT/
10-13

JOHNSON, Choo Choo American
actress TW/1

JOHNSON, Christine actress TW/1

JOHNSON, Clara [Mrs. Frank
Johnson] (d 1880) EA/81*

JOHNSON, Clara (d 1912 [55])
equestrienne EA/13*

JOHNSON, Clint (d 1975 [60])
dramatist BP/60*

JOHNSON, David ["The Cruikshank
of America"] (fl 1825) American
actor? HAS

JOHNSON, Dotts American actor
TW/29

JOHNSON, Edith (d 1901) tank
performer? EA/02*

JOHNSON, Edna (d 1971 [83])
performer BP/56*

JOHNSON, Edward (1880-1959)
Canadian singer, impresario
CB, SR, TW/15

JOHNSON, Elijah (d 1885) circus
proprietor EA/86*

JOHNSON, Elizabeth (fl 1790-1810)
American actress COC, OC/
1-3, WWA/H

JOHNSON, Ellen Augusta see
Hilson, Mrs. Thomas

JOHNSON, Emory (d 1960 [66])
actor, director BE*

JOHNSON, Ethel May (d 1964
[76]) performer, composer
BE*

JOHNSON, Florence (b 1902)
American critic BE

JOHNSON, Florence Osbeck (d
1971 [63]) performer BP/56*

JOHNSON, Frank (fl 1846?) musician CDP

JOHNSON, Mrs. Frank see
Johnson, Clara

JOHNSON, Fred (b 1899) Irish
actor TW/3

JOHNSON, George (b 1835) American actor HAS

JOHNSON, Gertrude (d 1973
[78]) performer BP/57*

JOHNSON, Gladys (d 1974 [40s])
performer BP/59*

JOHNSON, Greer (d 1974 [54])
dramatist BP/59*

JOHNSON, Hall (1888-1970)
American musician, composer
CB, TW/26

JOHNSON, Harold Ogden see
Johnson, Chic

JOHNSON, Harriet see Field,
Sylvia

JOHNSON, Harry (d 1878) musician EA/79*

JOHNSON, Harry Whitmarsh
see Meddows, Kenny

JOHNSON, Henry (fl 1576-86)
gatherer DA

JOHNSON, Henry (d 1760) English? translator CP/2-3, GT

JOHNSON, Henry (d 1910 [103])
acrobat EA/11*

JOHNSON, Henry Erskine (d 1840)
Scottish actor HAS

JOHNSON, Howard E. (1888?-1941)
songwriter, musician CB

JOHNSON, Isa (d 1941) actress
BE*, WWT/14*

JOHNSON, Jacob A. (b 1794)
American carpenter HAS

JOHNSON, James Weldon (1871-
1938) American dramatist HJD

JOHNSON, Jane see Cibber,
Mrs. Theophilus, I

JOHNSON, Janet (b 1915) Australian
actress WWT/9-10

JOHNSON, J. E. (fl 1853) comic
singer, actor HAS

JOHNSON, Mrs. J. G. see
Johnson, Amelia

JOHNSON, Mrs. J. H. see
Johnson, Margaret Jane

JOHNSON, John (1759-1819) English
actor HAS, SR

JOHNSON, John (d 1871 [47]) comedian EA/72*

JOHNSON, John (d 1894 [59]) proprietor EA/95*

JOHNSON, John see Etherdo

JOHNSON, Mrs. John (d 1830)
English actress HAS, SR

JOHNSON, Joseph Towers (d 1891
[76]) actor WWT/14*

JOHNSON, J. Rosamond (1873-
1954) American actress, composer BE*

JOHNSON, J. T. (b 1815) actor
CDP

JOHNSON, J. W. (d 1917) variety
agent EA/18*

JOHNSON, Karen (b 1939) American actress TW/26-27

JOHNSON, Katie (d 1957 [78])
English actress TW/13

JOHNSON, Kay American actress
TW/2, WWT/7-9

JOHNSON, Kennedy (d 1906 [38])
music-hall assistant manager
EA/07*

JOHNSON, Lamont (b 1922) American director, actor, producer
BE

JOHNSON, Laurence see Naismith, Laurence

JOHNSON, Lilian Clara see St.
John, Lily

JOHNSON, Lonnie (d 1970 [70])
performer BP/55*

JOHNSON, Louisa (fl 1830s) English actress, dancer CDP,
HAS, SR

JOHNSON, Lydia (b 1896) Russian

dancer, singer ES
JOHNSON, Margaret Jane [Mrs.
J. H. Johnson] (d 1905) EA/
06*
JOHNSON, Marguerite see
Angelou, Maya
JOHNSON, Marion Pollock (fl
1900s) American actress WWS
JOHNSON, Mark see Mitchell,
John W.
JOHNSON, Mrs. Mark (d 1887)
music-hall performer EA/88*
JOHNSON, Mary Ann (d 1902
[65]) proprietor EA/03*
JOHNSON, Molly (b 1903) Eng-
lish actress, singer WWT/
10-11
JOHNSON, Nicholas (d 1857)
circus ringmaster HAS, SR
JOHNSON, Olga [Mrs. Richard
Johnson] (d 1886 [42]) EA/87*
JOHNSON, Onni (b 1949) Ameri-
can actress TW/28-29
JOHNSON, Orrin American actor
GRB/3-4, WWT/1-8
JOHNSON, Ottilie (d 1908) per-
former? EA/09*
JOHNSON, Owen (b 1878) Amer-
ican dramatist WWS
JOHNSON, Page (b 1927/30)
American actor TW/9-16,
21-30
JOHNSON, Pamela Hansford (b
1912) English dramatist CB
JOHNSON, Peter (d 1890) swim-
mer EA/91*
JOHNSON, Philip (b 1900) Eng-
lish dramatist WWT/8-11
JOHNSON, Rachel (b 1845)
American actress HAS, SR
JOHNSON, Richard (fl 1633)
actor DA
JOHNSON, Richard (d 1901 [62])
music-hall performer EA/02*
JOHNSON, Richard (b 1927)
English actor AAS, BE, ES,
WWT/12-16
JOHNSON, Mrs. Richard see
Johnson, Olga
JOHNSON, Robert (fl 1626)
musician DNB
JOHNSON, Robert (b 1827)
American actor HAS, SR
JOHNSON, Robert (d 1892)
scene artist EA/94*
JOHNSON, Roma Burton (d 1976)
publicist BP/60*
JOHNSON, Roy L. (1867-1943)

minstrel SR
JOHNSON, Sam (d 1900 [69]) actor
WWT/14*
JOHNSON, Samuel (d 1773) English
dramatist, actor CP/2, GT,
TD/1-2
JOHNSON, Dr. Samuel (1709-84)
English dramatist CDP, COC,
CP/1-3, ES, HP, GT, OC/1-3,
TD/1-2
JOHNSON, Samuel (1821-63) Irish
actor HAS, SR
JOHNSON, Samuel (fl 1853-79)
Scottish actor, manager OAA/2
JOHNSON, Samuel (d 1900 [69])
comedian EA/01*
JOHNSON, Mrs. Samuel (d 1884)
EA/85*
JOHNSON, Samuel D. (1813-63)
American actor HAS, SR
JOHNSON, Sarah A. see Burnett,
Sally
JOHNSON, S. Kenneth, II (d 1974
[62]) performer BP/59*
JOHNSON, Mrs. Spencer J., Jr.
see Beckwith, Linden
JOHNSON, Susan (b 1927) American
singer, actress BE, TW/9,
12-19
JOHNSON, Suzanne American ac-
tress TW/29
JOHNSON, Thomas (fl 1574) actor
DA
JOHNSON, Thomas Baldwin (d 1917)
manager EA/18*
JOHNSON, Travis (d 1970 [64])
performer BP/55*
JOHNSON, Van (b 1916) American
actor BE, CB, TW/19-20, 22-
23, WWT/16
JOHNSON, Virginia (d 1969 [59])
producer/director/choreographer
BP/53*
JOHNSON, Mrs. W. see Martini,
Laura
JOHNSON, Walter (d 1964 [80])
producer/director BP/49*
JOHNSON, W. F. (d 1859) Ameri-
can? actor CDP, HAS, SR
JOHNSON, Dr. W. Gerald (d 1963
[51]) dramatist, director, actor
BE
JOHNSON, William (fl 1572-88)
actor DA
JOHNSON, William (fl 1638?)
dramatist FGF
JOHNSON, William (fl 1640) actor
DA

JOHNSON, William (d 1882)
music-hall proprietor EA/83*

JOHNSON, William (d 1902 [52])
proprietor EA/04*

JOHNSON, William (d 1905) EA/
06*

JOHNSON, William (d 1957 [41])
American actor TW/11-12

JOHNSON, Mrs. William (d 1905)
EA/06*

JOHNSON, Mrs. William (d 1910)
EA/11*

JOHNSON, William Octavius
(1819-58) American actor
HAS, SR

JOHNSRUD, Harold (d 1939 [35])
American actor BE*, BP/24*

JOHNSTON, Arthur James (d
1954 [56]) composer BE*,
WWT/14*

JOHNSTON, Audre (b 1939) American actress TW/18, 29-30

JOHNSTON, Daisy B. (d 1974
[94]) performer BP/58*

JOHNSTON, David Claypoole
(1799-1865) American actor
DAB

JOHNSTON, Denis (b 1901) Irish
dramatist, educator, director,
actor AAS, BE, CD, COC,
ES, MD, MH, MWD, OC/1-3,
PDT, RE, WWT/8-11, 14

JOHNSTON, Gail (b 1943) American actress TW/23, 29

JOHNSTON, Henry Erskine
(1777-1845) Scottish actor
CDP, COC, DNB, GT, OC/
1-3, SR, TD/1-2

JOHNSTON, Mrs. Henry Erskine
[née Parker] (b 1782) English
actress CDP, OX, TD/1-2

JOHNSTON, Jane A. (b 1934)
American actress TW/28

JOHNSTON, Johnny (b 1918)
American actor TW/7-8

JOHNSTON, Justine (b 1899)
American actress, singer
BE, TW/21-22, 27-30, WWT/
4-8

JOHNSTON, Lyell (b 1875) English singer GRB/1

JOHNSTON, Margaret (b 1917/
18) Australian actress WWT/
10-16

JOHNSTON, Moffat (1886-1935)
Scottish actor WWT/7

JOHNSTON, Oliver (d 1966 [78])
actor WWT/15*

JOHNSTON, T. B. (1815-61)
American actor CDP, HAS, SR

JOHNSTON, Mrs. T. B. [Annie
Lee; Mrs. C. L. Stone] (d
1858) actress HAS, SR

JOHNSTONE, Mrs. (fl 1797-1804)
actress TD/1-2

JOHNSTONE, Anna Hill (b 1913)
American costume designer BE

JOHNSTONE, A. S. (d 1917 [83])
EA/18*

JOHNSTONE, Clara [Mrs. Robert
Earle] (d 1902) actress EA/03*

JOHNSTONE, Clarence (d 1953)
performer BE*, WWT/14*

JOHNSTONE, Edward F. (d 1919)
composer SR

JOHNSTONE, Eliza (d 1899) actress EA/00*, WWT/14*

JOHNSTONE, Elizabeth [Mrs.
Owen Johnstone] (d 1876) EA/
77*

JOHNSTONE, Jack (d 1828 [78])
Irish actor EA/72*, WWT/14*

JOHNSTONE, James (fl 1786)
dramatist CP/3

JOHNSTONE, James (b 1817) English actor, stage manager
OAA/1-2

JOHNSTONE, John (d 1874 [41])
gymnast EA/75*

JOHNSTONE, John Beer (d 1891
[88]) dramatist, actor EA/68

JOHNSTONE, John Henry (1749-
1828) Irish actor, singer CDP,
DNB, GT, OX, TD/1-2

JOHNSTONE, Mrs. John Henry
[née Poctier] (d c. 1785) actress
TD/2

JOHNSTONE, Justine see Johnston, Justine

JOHNSTONE, Keith English dramatist, director CD

JOHNSTONE, Madge (d 1913) actress BE*, WWT/14*

JOHNSTONE, Owen (d 1908) EA/
09*

JOHNSTONE, Mrs. Owen see
Johnstone, Elizabeth

JOHNSTONE, Paul (d 1976 [55])
producer/director/choreographer
BP/60*

JOHNSTONE, Susan [Mrs. James
W. Wallack] (d 1850) actress
CDP

JOHNSTONE, Thomas (d 1970 [81])
composer/lyricist BP/54*

JOHNSTONE, Thomas see Gordon, Cecil

JOHNSTONE, W. H. (d 1890 [68]) musical & variety agent EA/92*

JOHNSTONE-SMITH, George (d 1963 [81]) actor, producer BE*

JOINER, Barbara (d 1961 [61]) performer BE*

JO JO (d 1904) "dog-faced man" EA/05*

JOLIVET, Andre (d 1974 [69]) composer/lyricist BP/59*

JOLIVET, Rita American actress WWT/3-5

JOLLY, Edward (b 1876) American vaudevillian WWM

JOLLY, George (fl 1640-73) English actor COC, OC/1-3

JOLLY, John (d 1864 [74]) composer, conductor EA/72*

JOLSON, Al[bert; Asa Yoelson] (1886-1950) American actor CB, CDP, DAB, ES, NTH, SR, TW/3-7, WWA/3, WWT/4-10

JOLSON, Harry (d 1953 [71]) Polish vaudevillian TW/9

JONA, Mrs. see Ambrose, Mrs.

JONAS, Douglas Peter see Dexter, Aubrey

JONAS, Elizabeth (fl 1832) musician CDP

JONAY, Roberta (d 1976 [50s]) performer BP/60*

JONES, Mr. (d 1806) English actor HAS

JONES, Mr. (d 1868 [22]) conductor EA/69*

JONES, Mrs. [née Granger] (1782-1806) English singer HAS, SR

JONES, Mrs. [née Wallack] (d 1860) English actress HAS, SR

JONES, Mrs. (d 1864) see Stickney, Mrs. E. M.

JONES, Miss see Simpson, Mrs. E.

JONES, Al (b 1909) American manager BE

JONES, Ann Courtney [Mrs. M. Jones] (d 1875) EA/76*

JONES, Anne see Moreland, Mrs. Harry

JONES, Avonia Stanhope [Mrs. Gustavus Vaughan Brooke]

(1839-67) American actress CDP, COC, DNB, HAS, SR

JONES, Bambi (b 1961) American actress TW/25

JONES, Barry (b 1893/94) English actor, manager BE, CB, TW/8-15, WWT/7-14

JONES, Bartholomew (fl 1633) actor DA

JONES, Benjamin (d 1878 [41]) musician EA/79*

JONES, Mrs. Benjamin see Jones, Maria B.

JONES, Benjamin M. (fl 1858) American actor? HAS

JONES, B. N. (d 1890) Australian actor EA/91*

JONES, Brooks (b 1934) American producer, director, composer, singer BE

JONES, Buck (d 1942 [53]) American actor BE*

JONES, Carolyn (b 1933) American actress CB

JONES, Carrie B. (d 1904 [21]) music-hall performer EA/05*

JONES, Mrs. Charles F. (1796-1866) English actress CDP, OX

JONES, Charlotte [Mrs. George Jones] (d 1872 [86]) EA/73*

JONES, Charlotte American actress TW/22-30

JONES, Clingan (d 1874) comedian EA/76*

JONES, C. S. actor, manager TD/2

JONES, David (b 1934) English director AAS, WWT/15-16

JONES, Mrs. David H. [Lizzie Mandlebert] (d 1883 [49]) actress EA/84*

JONES, Dean (b 1930/35) American actor BE, TW/16-17, 26

JONES, D. H. (d 1867) actor EA/68*

JONES, Disley (b 1926) English designer WWT/14-16

JONES, Douglas P., Jr. (d 1964 [38]) actor, director BE*

JONES, Dudley (b 1914) English actor WWT/14-16

JONES, Edmund R. (d 1873 [67]) pantomime writer EA/74*

JONES, Edward (d 1917) conductor, composer, musical director WWT/3

JONES, Edward H. (d 1905 [53])

manager EA/06*

JONES, Mrs. E. J. see Jones, Ellen E.

JONES, Elizabeth (fl early 19th cent) actress CDP

JONES, Ellen [Mrs. George Jones] (d 1881) EA/82*

JONES, Ellen E. [Mrs. E. J. Jones] (d 1916 [75]) EA/17*

JONES, Emrys (1915-72) English actor AAS, WWT/10-15

JONES, Ersser (d 1877 [71]) actor EA/78*, WWT/14*

JONES, Mrs. Evan see Jones, Henrietta

JONES, Fanny [Mrs. Samuel Jones] (d 1878) EA/79*

JONES, Francis (d 1888) scene artist EA/90*

JONES, Frederick (d 1891 [31]) actor EA/92*

JONES, Frederick Edward (1759-1834) Irish patentee, manager DNB, TD/1-2

JONES, Gemma (b 1942) English actress WWT/15-16

JONES, George (d 1872 [77]) proprietor EA/73*

JONES, George (1810-79) English actor CDP, HAS, SR

JONES, Mrs. George see Jones, Charlotte

JONES, Mrs. George see Jones, Ellen

JONES, Griffith (b 1910) English actor AAS, WWT/8-16

JONES, Hazel (1896-1974) English actress TW/2, 25, WWT/4-6

JONES, Henrietta [Miss H. Simms; Mrs. Evan Jones] (d 1887 [45]) actress EA/88*

JONES, Henry (1721-70) Irish dramatist CP/2-3, DNB, GT

JONES, Henry (fl 18th cent) dramatist, shoemaker CP/1-3, TD/1-2

JONES, Henry (d 1890 [86]) dramatic curiosity collector EA/91*

JONES, Henry (b 1912) American actor BE, TW/5-8, 10-16

JONES, Henry Arthur (1851-1929) English dramatist COC, DNB, ES, GRB/1-4, HP, MH, MWD, NTH, OC/1-3, PDT, RE, SR, WWM, WWS, WWT/1-5, WWW/3

JONES, Mrs. Herbert B. [Elise Dale] (d 1917) EA/18*

JONES, Howard Mumford (b 1892) dramatist HJD

JONES, Ifano (1865-1955) Welsh dramatist WWW/5

JONES, Mrs. Ike see Cushman, Corlene

JONES, Inigo (1573-1652) English architect, artist COC, ES, FGF, HP, NTH, OC/1-3, PDT

JONES, Isham (1894-1956) American composer, musician BE*

JONES, J. see Hart, Josh

JONES, Jack (fl 1602) actor? DA

JONES, James (fl 1623) actor DA

JONES, James (fl 1818) theatre founder CDP

JONES, James Earl (b 1931) American actor AAS, BE, CB, TW/18-23, 25-30, WWT/15-16

JONES, Jeff see Warren, Jeff

JONES, Jeffrey Duncan (b 1947) American actor TW/30

JONES, Cpt. Jenkin (fl 1801) dramatist CP/3

JONES, Jennifer (b 1919) American actress BE, CB, ES, SR, TW/23

JONES, J. Matheson (d 1931 [83]) clown, director BE*, WWT/14*

JONES, Joan Granville (d 1974) performer BP/58*

JONES, John (fl 1615) actor DA

JONES, John (fl 1635) dramatist CP/1-3, FGF

JONES, John (1796-1861) English singer HAS, SR

JONES, John (d 1881 [75]) EA/82*

JONES, John (b 1917) American educator, designer, director BE

JONES, Johnny (d 1971 [71]) manager BP/55*

JONES, John Price (d 1961 [70]) actor, singer TW/17

JONES, Joseph Stevens (1809-77) American dramatist, actor COC, DAB, HJD, NTH, OC/1-3, RJ, SR, WWA/H

JONES, J. S. (fl 1857) actor, manager HAS

JONES, Julia (d 1847) actress HAS

JONES, Julia A. see Jones, Mrs. W. G.

JONES, Julian (d 1930 [57]) conductor WWT/14*

JONES, J. Wilton (d 1897 [43])
dramatist BE*, EA/98*,
WWT/14*

JONES, Mrs. J. Wilton (d 1886
[31]) EA/87*

JONES, Lauren (b 1942) American actress TW/24-25, 28

JONES, Lena Beatrice (d 1895
[15]) variety performer EA/
96*

JONES, Leroi see Baraka,
Imamu Amiri

JONES, Leslie Julian (b 1910)
English composer, librettist
WWT/10-12

JONES, Lillian B. (d 1962 [80])
Canadian monologist BE*

JONES, Lindesius (fl 1755)
dramatist CP/3

JONES, Louise M. (d 1912 [81])
EA/13*

JONES, Mrs. M. see Jones,
Ann Courtney

JONES, Margo (1913-55) American director, producer COC,
ES, NTH, OC/2-3, TW/3-8,
12, WWT/11

JONES, Maria (d 1893) actress
EA/95*, WWT/14*

JONES, Maria B. [Mrs. Francis
Phillips] (d 1873 [27]) actress,
dramatist BE*, EA/74*,
WWT/14*

JONES, Marie [Mrs. Ernest
Munro] English actress GRB/1

JONES, Marjorie Dunn (d 1974
[86]) performer BP/59*

JONES, Mary (b 1915) Welsh
actress WWT/9-16

JONES, Mary Kay (b 1925)
American actress TW/4

JONES, Mary Tupper (d 1964
[86]) performer BP/49*

JONES, Melinda [née Topping]
(1815-75) American actress
CDP, HAS, SR

JONES, Neil (b 1942) American
actor TW/20-28

JONES, Nora Rosamund see
John, Rosamund

JONES, Patty see Astley, Mrs.
Philip

JONES, Paul [né Pond] (b 1942)
English actor TW/27, WWT/
15-16

JONES, Peter (b 1920) English
actor, dramatist WWT/12-16

JONES, Phyllis Ann (d 1962
[24]) performer BE*

JONES, Richard (fl 1590-1615)
English actor DA, OC/1-3

JONES, Richard (1779-1851) English actor, dramatist BS, CDP,
DNB, OX

JONES, Richard de Freyne see
Beasley, Edward

JONES, Richard P. (1826-69)
American minstrel, actor HAS

JONES, Richard William Cattlin
(d 1889 [49]) pantomimist EA/
90*

JONES, Robert (fl 1602) actor DA

JONES, Robert (b 1819) English
actor, prompter HAS

JONES, Robert Edmond (1887-1954)
American designer, producer,
manager AAS, CB, COC, ES,
HJD, NTH, OC/1-3, TW/2-8,
11, WWT/5-11, WWW/5

JONES, Lady Roderick see
Bagnold, Enid

JONES, Rozene Kemper (d 1964
[74]) actress BE*, BP/49*

JONES, Rupel J. (b 1895) American educator BE

JONES, Mrs. Samuel see Jones,
Fanny

JONES, S[amuel] Major (1863-
1952) English actor, stage
manager GRB/1, 3-4, WWT/
3-9

JONES, Mrs. S[amuel] Major see
Stanley, Blanche

JONES, Shirley (b 1934) American
actress, singer BE, CB, ES,
TW/25

JONES, Stanley D. (d 1963 [49])
songwriter, actor BE*

JONES, Stephen (d 1827 [64]) historian WWT/14*

JONES, Sydney (1861/69-1946)
English composer, conductor
GRB/1-4, DNB, ES, WWT/1-9

JONES, T. (fl 1803-05) dramatist
CP/3

JONES, T. (fl 1809) dramatist
CP/3

JONES, T. singer CDP

JONES, T. actor CDP

JONES, T. C. (1920-71) American
female impersonator, actor,
dancer BE, TW/13-15, 28

JONES, Mrs. Theodore see
Mansfield, Ada

JONES, Thomas (d 1893 [77])
EA/94*

JONES, Tom (d 1905 [37]) actor?
EA/06*

JONES, Tom (b 1928) American
dramatist, lyricist, librettist
BE, CD

JONES, Tom Lee (b 1946) American actor TW/26-27, 29-30

JONES, Trefor (1902-65) Welsh
actor, singer WWT/8-13

JONES, W. A. see Oliver,
Roland

JONES, Walter (1868/72-1922)
American actor SR, WWS

JONES, W. G. (1817-53) American actor CDP, HAS, SR

JONES, Mrs. W. G. [Julia A.
Deane] (1829-1907) American
actress CDP, GRB/3, HAS,
PP/2, SR

JONES, Whitworth (b 1873) English actor WWT/4

JONES, Sir William (1746-94)
English dramatist CP/3

JONES, William (d 1828) Canadian clown HAS

JONES, William (1781-1841)
American manager, actor
HAS

JONES, William Andrew see
De Wolfe, Billy

JONES, William H. (d 1883 [39])
lessee EA/84*

JONES, Mrs. Wilton see Warden, Gertrude

JONES, Winifred Arthur see
Faber, Mrs. Leslie

JONES, W. O. (d 1890 [29])
actor EA/91*

JONES, Dr. W. T. (d 1871
[42]) actor EA/72*

JONES, "Young" (fl 1818-19)
actor CDP

JONG, Frank de (d 1903) manager
WWT/14*

JONGEYANS, George see
Gaynes, George

JONGHMANS, Edward (d 1902)
musical director, composer
EA/03*

JONGMANS, F. (d 1887 [65])
singer CDP

JONNS, Daniel (fl 1586) actor?
DA

JONSON, Ben (1572-1637) Eng-
lish dramatist, actor CDP,
COC, CP/1-3, DA, DNB,
ES, FGF, HP, MH, NTH,
OC/1-3, PDT, RE

JONSON, Benjamin, Jr. (d 1635)
dramatist CP/3, FGF

JONSON, William (d 1972 [51])
producer/director/choreographer
BP/57*

JONSTON, Alexander (d 1775) actor
CDP

JOOSS, Kurt (b 1901) German
dancer, choreographer ES, OC/
2, WWT/9-12

JOPE-SLADE, Christine (d 1942
[49]) dramatist BE*, WWT/14*

JORDAN, Annie see Jordan,
Mrs. George Clifford

JORDAN, Bernard (d 1962 [77])
English performer BE*

JORDAN, Clifford, Jr. (b 1931)
American actor TW/29

JORDAN, Dorothy (1761-1816) Eng-
lish actress CDP, COC, DNB,
ES, GT, HP, NTH, OC/1-3,
OX, TD/1-2

JORDAN, Dorothy (b 1908) American actress WWT/7-8

JORDAN, Elizabeth (1867-1947)
American dramatist WWA/2,
WWM

JORDAN, Frances (b 1890) American actress WWM

JORDAN, George (d 1873 [43])
actor EA/74*

JORDAN, George C. (b 1847)
American actor HAS

JORDAN, George Clifford (1825-73)
English actor CDP, HAS, SR

JORDAN, Mrs. George Clifford
[Annie Walters] (fl 1848-67)
actress CDP, HAS, SR

JORDAN, Glenn R. (d 1975 [56])
producer/director/choreographer
BP/60*

JORDAN, Henry Charles (b 1821)
American actor HAS, SR

JORDAN, Mrs. Henry Charles (fl
1846) English actress HAS, SR

JORDAN, James E. ["Fibber Mc-
Gee"] (b 1898) actor SR

JORDAN, Mrs. James E. [Molly
Driscoll Jordan] actress SR

JORDAN, Joe (d 1971 [89]) com-
poser/lyricist BP/56*

JORDAN, John (b 1923) American
actor TW/3-7

JORDAN, Jules (1850-1927) American singer, composer, conductor CDP, WWA/1

JORDAN, Kate (1862-1926) Irish
dramatist DAB

JORDAN, Louis (d 1975 [66])
performer BP/59*
JORDAN, Mabel (fl 1877) actress
CDP
JORDAN, Marian (1898-1961)
American performer BE*
JORDAN, Marion Driscoll see
Jordan, Mrs. James E.
JORDAN, Richard (b 1938) Amer-
ican actor TW/18, 20-23,
26-27
JORDAN, Thomas (d 1685?) actor,
dramatist CP/2-3, DA, FGF
JORDAN, Walter C. (d 1951
[74]) American literary repre-
sentative, producer BE*,
BP/35*
JORDAN, Dr. Warwick (d 1909
[68]) professor of music
EA/10*
JORDAN, William (fl 1611) Eng-
lish dramatist DNB
JORDAN, William dramatist
CP/3
JORDIN, Russ (d 1972 [43]) per-
former BP/57*
JORDISON, Mrs. H. A. [Nellie
Jordison] (d 1901) EA/02*
JORDISON, Nellie see Jordi-
son, Mrs. H. A.
JORDON, Gaye American ac-
tress TW/15
JORGENSEN, Robert (b 1903)
Danish press representative,
journalist WWT/8-9
JORY, Victor (b 1902) Alaskan
actor, producer BE, TW/
1-3, 6, WWT/10-16
JOSE, Richard J. (b 1869/70)
English actor, singer CDP,
WWM
JOSEFFY, Rafael (b 1853) musi-
cian, composer CDP
JOSEPH, Harry (fl 1867-69)
Scottish actor SR
JOSEPH, Harry (d 1962 [64])
English theatre owner BE*
JOSEPH, Jackie (b 1936) Amer-
ican actress TW/16
JOSEPH, John Charles (d 1871)
patentee, lessee EA/72*
JOSEPH, Marilyn (b 1948) English
actress TW/26
JOSEPH, Robert L. (b 1924)
American producer BE
JOSEPH, Stephen (1921-67) Eng-
lish actor, producer COC,
OC/3

JOSEPH, Will C. (d 1973 [88])
designer BP/58*
JOSEPHS, Fanny (d 1890 [48]) ac-
tress CDP, OAA/1-2
JOSEPHS, Harry (b 1845) Scottish
actor HAS
JOSEPHS, Henry (d 1880) comedian
EA/81*
JOSEPHS, Patti [Mrs. J. H. Fitz-
patrick] (d 1876) actress, singer
EA/77*, WWT/14*
JOSLIN, Howard (d 1975 [67])
performer BP/60*
JOSLYN, Allyn (b 1905) American
actor WWT/9-10
JOSSET, Alfred (d 1878) dancer,
pantomimist EA/79*
JOURDAN, Mons. (d 1879) singer
EA/80*
JOURDAN, Alecia actress, singer
CDP
JOURDAN, Louis (b 1920) French
actor BE, CB, TW/10-15
JOURNET, Marcel (1870-1933)
French singer WWA/1
JOUVET, Louis (1887-1951) French
actor, manager, director CB,
COC, ES, NTH, TW/8, WWT/11
JOWSEY, John Edward (d 1916)
variety agent, director EA/18*
JOY, Mrs. Ernest see Busley,
Jessie
JOY, Job (d 1869) proprietor EA/
70*
JOY, John (b 1937) American actor
TW/24-25
JOY, Leonard W. (d 1961 [65])
producer BE*, BP/46*
JOY, Nicholas (1889-1964) French/
English actor TW/1-9, 13-15,
20, WWT/10-13
JOY, Signa (b 1947) American ac-
tress TW/29
JOY, William (1675?-1734) "Eng-
lish Sampson" CDP, DNB
JOYCE, Alice (1890-1955) Ameri-
can actress TW/12
JOYCE, Archibald (d 1963) com-
poser BE*
JOYCE, Barbara American actress
TW/3
JOYCE, Billy (d 1970 [73]) agent
BP/54*
JOYCE, Elaine (b 1945) American
actress TW/28-29
JOYCE, James (1882-1941) Irish
dramatist AAS, DNB, ES, HP,
MD, MWD, WWW/4

JOYCE, James (d 1974 [53])
performer BP/58*
JOYCE, Laura [née Maskell;
Mrs. James V. Taylor; Mrs.
Digby Bell] (b 1856) actress,
singer CDP
JOYCE, Lind (d 1971 [51]) per-
former BP/55*
JOYCE, Peggy Hopkins (d 1957
[64]) American showgirl
TW/13
JOYCE, Sarah [Mrs. Walter
Joyce] (d 1907 [75]) EA/08*
JOYCE, Stephen (b 1931/33)
American actor TW/22, 24,
26-27, WWT/15-16
JOYCE, Thomas (fl 1849) Cana-
dian actor HAS
JOYCE, Walter (d 1916 [79/81])
actor, manager BE*, EA/
17*, WWT/14*
JOYCE, Mrs. Walter see Joyce,
Sarah
JOYNER, William (d 1706) Eng-
lish dramatist CP/1-3
JOYNSON-POWELL, Queenie (d
1907) actress EA/09*
JUANA [Johanna Jurgens] (b
1916) English/American
dancer ES
JUBA (fl 1848) dancer CDP
JUBY, Edward (fl 1602) drama-
tist, actor CP/3, DA
JUBY, Richard (fl 1600-02)
actor DA
JUBY, [William?] (fl 1599-1602)
sharer DA
JUCH, Emma [Mrs. Francis L.
Wellman] (1863/65-1939)
Austrian/American singer
CDP, WWA/1, WWM
JUDAH, Emanuel (fl 1832) Amer-
ican actor HAS, SR
JUDAH, Mrs. Emanuel see
Judah, Sophia
JUDAH, Samuel Benjamin Hel-
bert (c. 1799-1876) American
actor, dramatist DAB, EAP,
RJ, SR
JUDAH, Sophia (1829-83) Ameri-
can actress CDP, HAS, SR
JUDD-GREEM, Richard A. (d
1909 [32]) music-hall manager
EA/10*
JUDE, Patrick (b 1951) American
actor TW/29
JUDELL, Maxson F. (d 1972
[74]) publicist BP/57*

JUDELS, Charles (b 1881) Dutch
actor TW/3-4
JUDGE, Arline (d 1974 [61])
dancer, actress TW/30
JUDGE, John (d 1917) EA/18*
JUDGE, Lily (d 1911) music-hall
performer EA/13*
JUDGE, William James (d 1903
[54]) animal trainer EA/04*
JUDIC, Anne Marie Louise (1849-
1911) French actress CDP,
GRB/4
JUDITH, Mlle. [Julie Bernat] (d
1912 [85]) actress BE*, WWT/
14*
JUDSON, Edward Z. C. (d 1886
[64]) actor, dramatist CDP
JUGLER, Richard (fl 1550) actor
DA
JUKES, Mrs. W. see Bird,
Miss
JULEENE, H. F. [John Parsons]
(d 1905 [59]) performer? EA/
06*
JULIA, Raul (b 1940) Puerto Rican
actor TW/24-30, WWT/16
JULIAN, Henry (d 1878 [30])
gymnast EA/79*
JULIAN, W. R. (d 1886 [59])
music-hall performer EA/87*
JULIE, Lillian (d 1966) performer
BP/51*
JULIEN, Jay (b 1919) American
producer, attorney BE
JULIEN, Louis Antoine (1812-60)
French composer, conductor
CDP, DNB
JULIEN, Paul [Gus Vaughan] (d
1877 [31]) comic singer EA/78*
JULIET [Juliet Rosenfeld] (1889-
1962?) American impersonator
WWM
JULLIEN, Louis George (1812-60)
actor? HAS
JULLIEN, Paul (fl 1851) violinist
HAS
JULVES, Encarnación López see
Argentinita
JUNCA, Marcel (d 1878) singer
CDP
JUNDELIN, Robert American actor
TW/29
JUNE [June Howard Tripp] (b
1900/01) English actress, singer
WWT/5-11
JUNE, Lewis (d 1888) circus
manager SR
JUNG, Carl (d 1893) musician

EA/94*
JUNG, Paul (d 1965 [65]) per-
former BP/49*
JUNOT, W. E. D. [Edmund
Clifford] (d 1872 [21]) harle-
quin EA/73*
JURGENS, Johanna see Juana
JURMANN, Walter (d 1971 [67])
composer/lyricist BP/56*
JUSTICE, Barry (b 1940) Indian/
English actor TW/20
JUSTICE, James Robertson (d
1975 [70]) actor BP/60*,
WWT/16*
JUSTICE, Jimmy (b 1941) Amer-
ican actor TW/26
JUSTIN, John (b 1917) English
actor WWT/11-16
JUSTIN, Morgan (d 1974 [47])
performer BP/59*
JUVENEAU, John J. (d 1973
[57]) performer BP/57*

- K -

K., F. [Francis Kirkman] (fl
1661) dramatist CP/1-3, GT
KAELRED, Katherine (b 1882)
English actress WWT/2-6
KAESTNER, Erich (d 1974 [75])
dramatist BP/59*
KAFKA, John H. (d 1974 [71])
dramatist BP/58*
KAGAN, Diane American actress
TW/24, 29-30
KAGEN, Sergius (d 1964 [55])
Russian composer BE*
KAHAN, Evelyn K. (d 1976 [72])
performer BP/60*
KAHAN, Judy (b 1948) American
actress TW/29-30
KAHANU, Archie (d 1975 [69])
performer BP/60*
KAHL, Howard (b 1930) Ameri-
can actor TW/23-24, 26-28
KAHN, Carolyn Sally see
Teitel, Carol
KAHN, Florence (1877/78-1951)
American actress COC, OC/
3, WWS, WWT/1-2
KAHN, Gilbert W. (d 1975 [72])
patron BP/60*
KAHN, Gustav Gerson (1886-
1941) German lyricist DAB
KAHN, L. Stanley (d 1964 [66])
American producer BE*,
BP/49*

KAHN, Madeline (b 1942) Ameri-
can actress TW/24, 26-28, 30
KAHN, Marvin (d 1969 [54]) com-
poser/lyricist BP/53*
KAHN, Michael American director
AAS, WWT/15-16
KAHN, Otto Hermann (d 1962
[68]) German/American? patron
BE*, BP/18*
KAIFFER, Mons. (fl 1840) dancer
HAS
KAINZ, Josef (1858-1910) German
actor GRB/2
KAISER, Ardyth American actress
TW/27, 30
KALB, Marie (d 1930 [76]) actress
BE*, WWT/14*
KALCHEIM, Harry (d 1974 [73])
agent BP/59*
KALCHEIM, Lee (b 1938) Ameri-
can dramatist CD
KALEM, Theodore (b 1919) Amer-
ican critic BE
KALICH, Bertha (1874-1939)
Galician actress GRB/3-4,
SR, WWT/1-8
KALICH, Jacob (1891-1975) Polish
director, actor, producer,
dramatist BE
KALIDASA (373-415) dramatist
COC
KALISCH, Alfred (1863-1933) Eng-
lish librettist WWW/3
KALIZ, Armand (d 1941 [49]) ac-
tor, songwriter, singer BE*,
WWT/14*
KALKOVEN, Frederick D'Alton
(d 1894 [70]) music-hall chair-
man EA/95*
KALLAN, Randi (b 1950) American
actress TW/29
KALLESSER, Michael (d 1975
[89]) dramatist BP/59*
KALLMAN, Chester (d 1975 [53])
composer/lyricist BP/59*
KALLMAN, Dick (b 1933) Ameri-
can actor, singer, dancer BE,
TW/8-12, 23
KALMAN, Emmerich (1882-1953)
Hungarian composer TW/10,
WWT/6-11
KALMANOVTICH, Harry (d 1966
[80]) dramatist BP/51*
KALMAR, Bert (d 1947 [66])
American lyricist, librettist,
composer TW/4, WWT/6-10
KALTHOUM, Um (d 1975 [77])
performer BP/59*

KAMINSKA, Ida (b 1899) American actress, producer, director CB, TW/24, 26, WWT/15-16

KAMLOT, Robert (b 1926) Austrian/American actor, manager TW/25-26

KAMMANS, Louise-Philippe (d 1972 [60]) performer BP/57*

KAMMER, Klaus (d 1964 [35]) performer BP/48*

KAMMERER, Mr. (d 1879) musician EA/80*

KAMSLER, Ben (b 1905) American producer, director, actor BE

KANDER, John (b 1927) American composer, musician BE, WWT/15-16

KANE, Charles S. (b 1822) American actor HAS

KANE, Gail (1887-1966) English actress WWT/6-7

KANE, Helen (d 1966 [62]) singer, actress TW/23

KANE, Irving (d 1972 [68]) performer BP/56*

KANE, John Irish actor TD/1-2

KANE, John (b 1920) American actor TW/22

KANE, Joseph (d 1975 [81]) producer/director/choreographer BP/60*

KANE, Richard (b 1938) English actor WWT/16

KANE, Whitford (1881/82-1956) Irish actor TW/1-13, WWM, WWT/4-12

KANER, Ruth (d 1964) American producer, actress BE*

KANIN, Fay American dramatist, actress BE

KANIN, Garson (b 1912) American actor, dramatist, director AAS, BE, CB, CD, ES, HJD, MD, MWD, PDT, SR, TW/2-8, WWT/10-16

KANIN, Michael (b 1910) American dramatist, producer, director BE

KANN, Lily German actress WWT/11-14

KANNER, Alexis (b 1942) French actor WWT/15-16

KANNON, Jackie (d 1974 [54]) performer BP/58*

KANTER, Mitchell (d 1972 [68]) treasurer BP/57*

KAPEC, Michael (b 1944) American actor TW/24

KAPEN, Ben (b 1928) American actor TW/25-26

KAPLAN, Dewitte (fl 1903-10) American dramatist WWM

KAPLAN, Eddie (d 1964 [57]) talent representative BE*

KAPLAN, Harriet (1917-69) American talent representative BE

KAPLAN, Jeanne American actress TW/24-26, 28

KAPLAN, Saul (b 1898) American manager BE

KAPLAN, Sol (b 1919) American composer, musician BE

KAPPEL, Gertrude (1884/93-1971) German singer ES, WWA/5

KAPPELER, Alfred (d 1945 [69]) Swiss actor BE*, BP/30*

KAPP-YOUNG, Louise (fl 1867) singer CDP

KAPRAL, Janet Czech actress TW/27, 30

KAPROW, Allan painter CD

KAPS, Arthur (d 1974 [66]) producer/director/choreographer BP/58*

KARATY, Tommy (b 1940) American actor TW/23-26

KAREN, James (b 1923) American actor TW/26, 28, 30

KARGER, Ann (d 1975 [89]) performer BP/60*

KARISBALIS, Curt (b 1947) American actor TW/29-30

KARIN, Rita (b 1919) Polish actress TW/24-28

KARINSKA, Barbara (b 1886) Russian costume designer BE, CB

KARL, Theodore O. H. (b 1912) American educator, producer, director BE

KARL, Tom (1846-1916) Irish singer CDP, WWA/4

KARLAN, Richard (b 1919) American actor TW/2

KARLIN, Miriam (b 1925) English actress WWT/12-16

KARLOFF, Boris [né William Henry Pratt] (1887-1969) English actor BE, CB, ES, SR, TW/4-8, 12-14, 25, WWA/5, WWT/11-14, WWW/6

KARLWEIS, Oscar (d 1956 [60]) Austrian actor, singer TW/2-8, 12, WWT/10-11

KARM, Michael (b 1941) American

actor TW/27-28

KARNILOVA, Maria (b 1920) American dancer, actress BE, TW/19, 21-25, 30, WWT/ 15-16

KARNO, Fred (1866-1941) English manager, producer CB, GRB/ 2-3, OC/1-3

KARNO, Mrs. Ted (d 1917) EA/ 18*

KARNS, Roscoe (1893-1970) American actor TW/1

KAROLY, Mons. (d 1879) snake trainer EA/80*

KARR, Harold (b 1921) American composer BE

KARR, Patti (b 1932) American singer, dancer, actress BE, TW/25-26, 28-30

KARSAVINA, Tamara (b 1885) Russian dancer ES, WWT/ 4-11

KARSON, Kit (d 1940 [65]) performer BE*

KARSON, Nat (1910-54) American scene designer NTH, TW/11

KASCHMANN, Giuseppe (1850-1925) Italian singer ES

KASE, C. Robert (b 1905) American educator BE

KASHA, Lawrence N. (b 1933) American producer, director BE, WWT/15-16

KASON, Corinne American actress TW/26-30

KASS, Alan (b 1928) American actor TW/28-29

KASSABIAN, Jack (b 1934) American actor TW/23

KASZNAR, Kurt S. (b 1913) Austrian actor BE, TW/4-9, 12-22, WWT/14-16

KATAYEV, Valentin Petrovich (b 1897) Russian dramatist COC, OC/1-3

KATES, Bernard (b 1922) American actor TW/7-8, 15, 22

KATOW, Helen De (fl 1865) musician HAS

KATSELAS, Milton (b 1933) American director WWT/15-16

KATSMAN, Sam (d 1973 [72]) producer/director/choreographer BP/58*

KATTERFELTO, Gustavus (d 1799) conjurer DNB

KATZ, Herman (d 1973 [73]) performer BP/58*

KATZ, Raymond American talent representative BE

KATZELL, William R. (d 1974 [68]) producer TW/5-7

KATZENELSON, Isaac (1886-c. 1941) producer BE*

KATZKA, Emil (d 1966 [69]) backer BP/50*

KAUFFMAN, Abraham (d 1911 [74]) performer EA/12*

KAUFFMAN, Archie E. (d 1899) manager EA/00*

KAUFMAN, Alvin S. (d 1973) composer/lyricist BP/58*

KAUFMAN, George Simon (1889-1961) American dramatist, producer AAS, CB, ES, HJD, MD, MH, MWD, NTH, OC/1-3, PDT, RE, SR, TW/18, WWT/ 5-13, WWW/6

KAUFMAN, Harry A. (d 1944 [57]) director BE*, WWT/14*

KAUFMAN, Irving (d 1976 [85]) performer BP/60*

KAUFMAN, S. Jay (1886-1957) dramatist, press representative BE*, BP/42*

KAUFMAN, Wolfe (d 1970 [65]) critic, press agent TW/27

KAUL, Avtar (d 1974 [34]) producer/director/choreographer BP/59*

KAUSER, Alice (d 1945 [73]) Hungarian play broker, agent WWM

KAVANAGH, J. H. (d 1907) variety performer EA/08*

KAVANAGH, Mary (d 1887) EA/ 88*

KAVANAGH, Mike (d 1967 [80]) manager BP/51*

KAVANAGH, Patrick (d 1967 [62]) dramatist BP/52*

KAVANAGH, Seamus (d 1964 [53]) performer BP/48*

KAVANAUGH, Dorrie American actress TW/27-28

KAY, Arthur composer, musical director BE

KAY, Beatrice (b c. 1912) comedienne CB

KAY, Charles [né Piff] (b 1930) English actor AAS, WWT/15-16

KAY, Ethel [Mrs. Frank Harrison] (b 1877) English actress GRB/1

KAY, Hershey (b 1919) American composer BE, CB

KAY, Jay (d 1970 [48]) dramatist

BP/55*

KAY, Katherine E. (d 1967 [44]) performer BP/52*

KAY, Mary see Barrington, Pattie

KAY, Richard (b 1937) English actor WWT/15-16

KAY, Sidney (b 1927) American actor TW/13

KAY, Virginia (d 1969 [42]) columnist BP/53*

KAYE, Albert Patrick (1878-1946) English actor SR, TW/3, WWT/9

KAYE, Alma (b 1925) American actress TW/1

KAYE, Anne (b 1942) American actress TW/24-26, 30

KAYE, Benjamin (d 1970 [86]) dramatist BP/54*

KAYE, Carmen (d 1962) performer BE*

KAYE, Danny [né Daniel Kominski] (b 1913) American performer, actor BE, CB, COC, ES, SR, OC/3, TW/27-28, WWT/10-16

KAYE, Deborah (d 1976 [83]) performer BP/60*

KAYE, Frederick (d 1913 [58]) actor DP, WWT/1

KAYE, Mrs. Frederick see Kaye, Lucy

KAYE, Gloria (b 1944) American actress TW/24

KAYE, Joseph (d 1975 [77]?) journalist BE

KAYE, Lucy [Mrs. Frederick Kaye] (d 1917) EA/18*

KAYE, Nora (b 1920) American dancer CB, ES, TW/9

KAYE, Sparky (d 1971 [65]) performer BP/56*

KAYE, Stubby (b 1918) American comedian, singer BE, TW/14-15, 30, WWT/16

KAYSER, Kathryn E. (b 1896) American educator BE

KAZAN, Elia (b 1909) Turkish/American actor, director AAS, BE, CB, COC, ES, HJD, OC/3, PDT, TW/2-8, WWT/10-15

KAZAN, Molly (1906-63) American dramatist BE, TW/20

KAZNAR, Kurt see Kaszar, Kurt S.

KCHESSINSKA, Mathilde (d 1971

[99]) dancer BP/56*, WWT/16*

KEACH, Edward F. (1824-63) American actor HAS

KEACH, Stacy (b 1941) American actor, director AAS, CB, TW/25-28, WWT/15-16

KEAL, Anita American actress TW/29-30

KEALY, Thomas J. (1874-1949) Irish business manager WWT/5-10

KEAN (fl 1811) dramatist CP/3

KEAN, Betty (b 1920) American actress, comedienne BE

KEAN, Charles John (1811-68) English actor, manager CDP, COC, DNB, ES, HAS, HP, NTH, OC/1-3, WWA/H

KEAN, Mrs. Charles John [Ellen Tree] (1805-80) English actress CDP, COC, DNB, ES, HAS, OAA/1-2, OC/1-3, OX, SR

KEAN, Edmund (1787-1833) English actor BS, CDP, COC, DNB, ES, HAS, HP, NTH, OC/1-3, OX, PDT, SR, WWA/H

KEAN, Mrs. Edmund [Mary Chambers] (c. 1780-1844) actress COC

KEAN, Ellen see Kean, Mrs. Charles John

KEAN, Jane (b 1924/28) American actress, singer BE, TW/2-4

KEAN, J. Harold (d 1975 [79]) critic BP/60*

KEAN, Marie (b 1922) Irish actress WWT/15-16

KEAN, Moses (fl 1789) imitator CDP, TD/1-2

KEAN, Norman (b 1934) American manager, producer, stage manager BE, WWT/16

KEAN, Thomas (fl mid 18th cent) English manager, actor COC, OC/1-3, SR, WWA/H

KEAND, Mrs. Arthur see Talbot, Evelyn

KEANE, Claire Whitney (d 1969 [79]) performer BP/54*

KEANE, Doris (b 1881/85-1945) American actress CB, COC, GRB/3-4, NTH, SR, TW/2, WWA/2, WWM, WWT/1-9

KEANE, George (b 1917) American actor TW/2-7

KEANE, John B. (b 1928) Irish dramatist CD

KEANE, Joseph H. (d 1890 [45])

actor CDP

KEANE, Robert Emmett (b 1883)
American actor WWT/4-9

KEANEY, Patrick (d 1933)
dramatist SR

KEARNEY, Mr. (fl 1875?) comedian, singer CDP

KEARNEY, John Joseph (d 1875)
property man EA/76*

KEARNEY, Kate (d 1926 [85])
actress BE*, WWT/14*

KEARNEY, Mary Agnes (d 1881)
EA/82*

KEARNEY, Michael (b 1955) American actor TW/25

KEARNEY, Patrick (d 1933 [36])
American dramatist BE*,
BP/17*

KEARNS, Allen (1893-1956)
Canadian actor TW/1, 12,
WWT/6-9

KEARNS, Elsie Herndon (b 1884)
American actress WWM

KEARNS, Joseph (d 1962 [55])
American actor BE*, BP/46*

KEARNS, Red (d 1971 [64]) performer BP/56*

KEARNS, Rosie [Mrs. Alfred H.
Hook] (1878-1917) Irish actress, singer GRB/1

KEARNS, William Henry (1794-
1846) Irish composer DNB

KEAST, G. V. (d 1905 [56])
pantomime writer EA/06*

KEATE, George (1729/30-97)
English dramatist CP/2-3

KEATHLEY, George (b 1925)
American director BE

KEATING, Charles (b 1941)
English actor WWT/16

KEATING, Dan actor CDP

KEATING, Fred (d 1961 [64])
American magician, actor
TW/18

KEATING, John (1919-68) American critic NTH

KEATING, Joseph (1871-1934)
Welsh dramatist WWW/3

KEATING, Larry (d 1963 [67])
American performer BE*

KEATING, Michael see Shandy,
Tristram

KEATING, Nicholas (d 1903)
music-hall manager EA/04*

KEATON, Buster (1895/96-1966)
American variety performer
ES, WWA/4

KEATON, Georgia (d 1975 [65])

performer BP/60*

KEATS, John (1795-1821) English
dramatist DNB, ES, HP

KEATS, Sydney Carl (d 1908 [24])
EA/09*

KEATS, Thomas (d 1889 [92])
singer EA/90*

KEATS, Viola (b 1911) Scottish
actress WWT/8-16

KEAY, Arthur (d 1895 [32]) music-
hall performer EA/96*

KEBBLE, Nora (d 1917 [37]) comedian EA/18*

KECK, Edith see King, Edith

KEDOBRA, Maurice (d 1973 [88])
dramatist BP/58*

KEDROV, Mikhail Nikolayevich
(1893-1972) Russian actor, director, producer COC, OC/3

KEEBLE, G. Walter (fl 1854-69)
actor HAS

KEEDICK, Lee (1879-1959) American manager WWA/4

KEEDICK, Mabel Ferris (d 1973
[89]) performer BP/57*

KEEFE, Adam (b 1931) American
actor TW/26

KEEFE, Jim (d 1881 [24]) Negro
comedian EA/82*

KEEFE, John (fl 1779-81) actor,
dramatist CP/2

KEEFER, Don (b 1916) American
actor TW/5-9

KEEGAN, Joseph (d 1901 [60])
music-hall comedian EA/02*

KEEL, Howard (b 1919) American
actor, singer BE, TW/29,
WWT/15-16

KEELER, Charles D. (1820-59)
American actor HAS

KEELER, Jane (d 1974 [93]) educator BP/58*

KEELER, Ralph (1840-73) actor
CDP

KEELER, Ruby (b 1909/10) Canadian actress, dancer AAS, BE,
CB, TW/27-29, WWT/8-10,
15-16

KEELEY, Edward Montague (d
1872 [37]) actor EA/73*

KEELEY, Mrs. E. M. (d 1896
[69]) EA/97*

KEELEY, Louise (1833-77) actress
CDP, OC/3

KEELEY, Louise see Williams,
Mrs. Montague

KEELEY, Mary Ann [Mary Ann
Goward; Mrs. Robert Keeley]

(1806-99) English actress
CDP, COC, DNB, ES, HAS,
OAA/1-2, OC/1-3, OX
KEELEY, Robert (1793-1869)
English actor BS, CDP, COC,
DNB, ES, HAS, OC/1-3, OX,
SR
KEELEY, Mrs. Robert see
Keeley, Mary Ann
KEEN, Elsie (d 1973) actress
TW/30
KEEN, Frederick Grinham see
Kerr, Frederick
KEEN, Geoffrey (b 1916/18)
English actor BE, WWT/9-16
KEEN, Malcolm (1887-1970)
English actor AAS, BE, NTH,
TW/4, 6-9, WWT/4-14
KEENAN, Frank [né James Fran-
cis] (1858-1929) American actor
DAB, WWA/1, WWT/4-5
KEENAN, James Francis see
Keenan, Frank
KEENAN, Sam (d 1895) minstrel
comedian EA/96*
KEENAN, Mrs. Tom (d 1899)
EA/00*
KEENE, Arthur (d 1845) Irish
actor CDP, HAS
KEENE, Donald (b 1922) trans-
lator BE
KEENE, Laura [Mary Moss]
(c. 1820-73) American actress,
manager CDP, COC, DAB,
ES, HAS, NTH, OC/1-3,
SR, WWA/H
KEENE, Richard Wynne ["Dy
Kwynkyn"] (d 1887 [76]) the-
atrical modeller, mask de-
signer EA/88*
KEENE, Theophilus (d 1718)
actor WWT/14*
KEENE, Thomas Wallace [né
Eagleson] (1840-98) American
actor CDP, DAB, HAS,
OC/1-3, SR, WWA/H
KEENE, Tom (d 1963 [65]) Amer-
ican performer BE*
KEES, John David American
actor TW/28-29
KEESE, William Linn (1835-1904)
American writer WWA/1
KEGLEY, Kermit (1918-74)
American director, stage
manager, actor BE, TW/30
KEHL, Mary Anne see Stir-
ling, Fanny
KEIGHLEY, William (b 1893)

American actor, director ES
KEIGHTLEY, Cyril (1875-1929)
Australian actor GRB/2-4,
WWM, WWT/1-5
KEIGWIN, John (1641-1716) English
dramatist CP/3, DNB
KEILING, John (fl 1720) musician
CDP
KEIM, Adelaide (b 1880/85) Amer-
ican actress WWS, WWT/1-2
KEIM, Betty Lou (b 1938/39)
American actress BE, TW/12
KEIM, Buster C. (d 1974 [68])
producer/director/choreographer
BP/59*
KEIPER, Robert (b 1935) American
actor TW/29
KEISER, Kris American actor
TW/24
KEITH, Benjamin Franklin (1846-
1914) American manager COC,
DAB, GRB/3-4, NTH, OC/1-3,
SR, WWA/1, WWS
KEITH, Caroline [Mrs. J. L
Keith] (d 1900) EA/01*
KEITH, Charles Henry (d 1895 [57])
circus proprietor EA/96*
KEITH, Eliane Muriel (d 1910 [24])
EA/11*
KEITH, Mrs. H. (d 1917) EA/18*
KEITH, Ian (1899-1960) American
actor TW/5-9, 16, WWT/6-12
KEITH, James (d 1970 [68]) per-
former BP/55*
KEITH, J. I. (d 1905) scene artist
EA/06*
KEITH, Mrs. J. I. see Keith,
Caroline
KEITH, Mrs. J. I. see Keith,
Susannah
KEITH, Lawrence (b 1931) Ameri-
can actor TW/28, 30
KEITH, Leslie (d 1908 [32]) actor
EA/09*
KEITH, Maxine (d 1966 [50]) press
agent, critic TW/22
KEITH, Penelope English actress
WWT/16
KEITH, Robert (1898-1966) Ameri-
can dramatist, actor, director,
producer BE, TW/1-8, WWT/
8-12
KEITH, Robert, Jr. (b 1921) Amer-
ican actor TW/7-8
KEITH, Sherwood (d 1972 [59])
performer BP/56*
KEITH, Susannah [Mrs. J. L
Keith] (d 1873 [30]) EA/74*

KEITH-JOHNSTON, Colin (b 1896)
English actor BE, TW/2-15,
WWT/6-14
KEL[B]Y, Lydia (fl 1824-31) ac-
tress HAS
KELCEY, Herbert (1855/56-1917)
English actor GRB/2-4, PP/
2, WWA/1, WWM, WWS,
WWT/1-3
KELCEY, Mrs. Herbert see
Shannon, Effie
KELETY, Julia (d 1972 [85]) ac-
tress, singer TW/28
KELF, Mrs. see Ambrose,
Miss
KELHAM, Avice (b 1892) English
actress, singer WWT/4-5
KELK, Jackie (b 1923) American
actor TW/3-4, 9
KELL, Michael (b 1944) American
actor TW/30
KELLAR, Harry (1849-1922)
American magician CDP,
SR, WWA/1, WWM
KELLARD, Ralph (1884/85-1955)
American actor TW/11,
WWM, WWS
KELLAWAY, Cecil (d 1973 [79])
actor TW/29
KELLEHER, Charles (d 1878 [25])
singer EA/79*
KELLEHER, Louis (1858-98)
actor EA/97
KELLER, Mr. (fl 1854) actor
HAS
KELLER, Jeff (b 1947) American
actor TW/30
KELLER, Jules (d 1906) acrobat,
equilibrist EA/07*
KELLER, Lewis (fl 1856) Polish
actor CDP, HAS
KELLER, Mrs. Lewis (d 1860)
actress CDP, HAS
KELLER, Nan (d 1975) performer
BP/60*
KELLER, Nell Clark (d 1965
[89]) performer BP/50*
KELLER, Nina (d 1974 [43])
originator of mini-theatre
BP/59*
KELLER, Wilhelmina see
Keller, Mrs. Lewis
KELLERD, John E. (1863/66-
1929) English actor PP/2,
WWM, WWS
KELLEY, Edgar Stillman (1857-
1944) American composer
DAB

KELLEY, John T. (1852-1922)
American minstrel, comedian
SR
KELLEY, Lloyd (d 1972 [69]) elec-
trician BP/57*
KELLEY, Peter (b 1925) American
actor TW/9-15
KELLEY, Robert F. (d 1975 [75])
publicist BP/60*
KELLIE, Lawrence (1862-1932)
English singer WWW/3
KELLIN, Mike (b 1922) American
actor BE, TW/5, 9, 12-15,
19, 23-24, 30
KELLIN, Nina C. (d 1963 [44])
performer BP/47*
KELLING, Alfred (d 1893 [68])
clown EA/94*
KELLING, Thomas (d 1886 [49])
acrobat, pantomimist EA/87*
KELLINO, Pamela (b 1917) English
actress TW/3
KELLOGG, Mr. (d 1850) actor
HAS
KELLOGG, Clara Louise (1842-
1916) American singer CDP,
DAB, ES, HAS, WWA/1
KELLOGG, Fannie (fl 1881?) ac-
tress, singer CDP
KELLOGG, Gertrude reader CDP
KELLOGG, Lynn American actress
TW/24
KELLOGG, Nelly (b c. 1855) ac-
tress HAS
KELLOGG, Riley (b 1961) American
actor TW/28-29
KELLOGG, Shirley (b 1888) actress,
singer WWT/4-7
KELLSTROM, Gail (b 1944) Amer-
ican actress TW/27, 29
KELLY, Mr. (fl 1792-1803) English
actor TD/2
KELLY, Mr. (d 1876) Negro come-
dian EA/77*
KELLY, Al (d 1966 [67]) performer
BP/51*
KELLY, Alfred Cain (d 1911) vari-
ety acting manager EA/12*
KELLY, Miss A. M. see Clav-
ering-Wardell, Anna Maria
KELLY, Ann (d 1852 [103]) actress
BE*, WWT/14*
KELLY, Anthony Paul (d 1932
[37]) American dramatist BE*,
BP/17*
KELLY, Bob (b 1923) American
perruquier, make-up artist
BE

KELLY, Cathleen see Cordell, Cathleen

KELLY, Charles [Charles Clavering Wardell] (1839-85) actor CDP, COC, OAA/2

KELLY, Charles D. (d 1859) American actor? HAS

KELLY, Charlotte actress CDP

KELLY, Desmond (b 1884) American actress WWM

KELLY, Dorothy H. (d 1969 [51]) performer BP/54*

KELLY, Edward (fl 1860s) minstrel SR

KELLY, Edwin (1835-98) Irish singer, actor CDP, HAS

KELLY, E. H. Irish actor GRB/1-2, WWT/3-4

KELLY, Mrs. E. H. see Boucicault, Nina

KELLY, Emmett (b 1898) American clown CB

KELLY, Eva [Mrs. G. P. Huntley] (1880-1948) American actress, singer GRB/1-4, WWT/1-5

KELLY, Fanny see Kelly, Frances Maria

KELLY, Flo (d 1972 [68]) performer BP/57*

KELLY, Francis Harriet (b 1800/03/05) English actress BS, CDP, OX

KELLY, Frances Maria (1790-1882) English actress, singer BS, CDP, COC, DNB, ES, OC/1-3, OX

KELLY, Fred (d 1902) pantomimist, acrobat EA/03*

KELLY, Gene (b 1912) American actor, dancer, choreographer BE, CB, ES, WWT/10-11

KELLY, George (b 1872) Canadian actor SR

KELLY, George (1887-1974) American actor, producer, dramatist BE, COC, ES, HJD, MD, MH, MWD, NTH, OC/1-3, SR, WWT/5-11

KELLY, G. M. (b 1841) American acrobat HAS

KELLY, Grace (b 1928/29) American actress BE, CB, ES, TW/6-11

KELLY, Grace see Arundale, Grace

KELLY, Gregory (d 1927 [36]) American actor BE*, BP/12*,

WWT/14*

KELLY, Harry (d 1936 [63]) American comedian WWS

KELLY, Herb (d 1970 [71]) critic BP/55*

KELLY, Hugh (1739-77) English dramatist CDP, COC, CP/2-3, DNB, GT, OC/1-3, SR, TD/1-2

KELLY, Jack American actor TW/19, 21

KELLY, James (d 1964 [49]) performer BE*

KELLY, James T. (b 1855) actor, singer CDP

KELLY, Jno (d 1856) HAS

KELLY, John (d 1751 [71]) dramatist CP/1-3, DNB, GT, TD/1-2

KELLY, John T. (1855-1922) American comedian CDP, WWS

KELLY, Judy (b 1913) Australian actress WWT/9-11

KELLY, J. W. (1857-96/97) American actor EA/97*, SR

KELLY, Kate [Mrs. Edwin Brown] (d 1899) variety comedian EA/01*

KELLY, Mrs. K. B. (d 1904 [78]) manager EA/05*

KELLY, Kevin (b 1930) American critic BE

KELLY, Kitty (d 1968 [66]) performer BP/53*

KELLY, Lawrence (d 1974 [46]) impresario BP/59*

KELLY, Lew (d 1944 [65]) American actor TW/1

KELLY, Lydia (b 1795) English actress BS, CDP

KELLY, Margot (d 1976 [82]) performer BP/60*

KELLY, Maurice (d 1974 [59]) performer BP/59*

KELLY, Michael (1764?-1826) Irish singer, composer, actor CDP, DNB, ES, GT, TD/1-2

KELLY, Nancy (b 1921) American actress BE, CB, TW/7-9, 11-20, 25, WWT/14-16

KELLY, Nolan (d 1893 [34]) American song & dance artist EA/94*

KELLY, Pat (b 1908 [50]) songwriter EA/09*

KELLY, Patsy (b 1910) American actress, singer TW/27-30, WWT/16

KELLY, Paul (1899-1956) American actor ES, TW/2-8, 13, WWA/3, WWT/9-12

KELLY, Renée (1888-1965) English actress WWT/2-12

KELLY, Robert (d 1949 [74]) American actor BE*, BP/34*

KELLY, Sybil see Arundale, Sybil

KELLY, Toney (d 1883) comic singer EA/84*

KELLY, Walter C. (1873-1939) American actor WWT/8

KELLY, William J. (1875-1949) American actor TW/5

KELLY, W. W. (1853-1933) American manager WWT/1-7

KELLY AND LEON see Kelly, Edward, & Leon, Mr.

KELMAR, Fred (d 1901) ventriloquist EA/02*

KELSEY, Emily [Mrs. Charles R. Stone] (b 1860) English actress GRB/1

KELSEY, Herbert (fl 1880s) English actor SR

KELSEY, Jennie see Hughes, Sarah Jane

KELSEY, Lizzie (d 1888 [36]) actress CDP

KELSEY, Matilda (d 1916) EA/17*

KELSO, Vernon (b 1893) English actor WWT/10-11

KELT, John (d 1935 [70]) actor BE*, WWT/14*

KELTON, Aggie [Mrs. George Hall] (d 1910) singer EA/11*

KELTON, Dorrit American actress TW/19

KELTON, Gene (b 1938) American actor TW/26-29

KELTON, Pert (d 1968 [61]) American actress BE, TW/24-25

KELVIN, James [James Watt Gilchrist] (d 1905 [37]) EA/06*

KEMBLE, Adelaide [Mrs. E. T. Sartoris] (c. 1816/17-79) actress, singer CDP, DNB, ES, NTH, OAA/1-2

KEMBLE, Agnes see Cooper, Mrs. Clifford

KEMBLE, Blanche see Shea, Mrs.

KEMBLE, Charles (1775-1854) English actor, dramatist BS, CDP, CP/3, DNB, ES, GT, HAS, HP, NTH, OC/1-3, OX, SR, TD/1-2

KEMBLE, Eliza [Mrs. Thomas Kemble] (d 1855) HAS

KEMBLE, Elizabeth [Elizabeth Whitlock] (1761-1836) English actress HAS, OC/1-3, SR, TD/1-2

KEMBLE, Elizabeth [Mrs. Stephen Kemble] (1763?-1841) actress CDP, DNB, ES, TD/1, WWA/H

KEMBLE, Eugenie [Miss Stevens] English actress GRB/1

KEMBLE, Fanny [Fanny Butler] (1809-93) English actress CDP, COC, DAB, DNB, ES, HAS, HJD, HP, NTH, OAA/1-2, OC/1-3, SR, WWA/H

KEMBLE, Frances [Mrs. Twiss] (d 1822 [62]) actress BE*, WWT/14*

KEMBLE, Frances "Frankie" actress CDP

KEMBLE, Frances Anne see Kemble, Fanny

KEMBLE, "Frankie" see Kemble, Frances

KEMBLE, Henry (1848-1907) English actor DNB, EA/96, ES, GRB/1-3, OAA/1-2, OC/1-3

KEMBLE, Mrs. Henry see Kemble, Nina

KEMBLE, Henry Stephen (1789-1836) English actor BS, CDP, DNB, ES, OX

KEMBLE, H. J. [H. J. Green] (b 1861) English actor GRB/1

KEMBLE, John (d 1908) performer EA/09*

KEMBLE, John Mitchell (d 1857 [49]) examiner of plays BE*, WWT/14*

KEMBLE, John Philip (1757-1823) English actor, dramatist, adapter CDP, COC, CP/3, DNB, ES, GT, HP, NTH, OC/1-3, OX, TD/1-2

KEMBLE, Mrs. John Philip [née Hopkins] (1756-1845) actress CDP, DNB, ES, TD/1-2

KEMBLE, Marie-Therese see Kemble, Theresa

KEMBLE, Myra [Mrs. James H. White] (d 1906) Australian actress DP

KEMBLE, Nina [Mrs. Henry Kemble] (d 1904 [33]) EA/05*

KEMBLE, Priscilla see Kemble, Mrs. John Philip

KEMBLE, Roger (1721-1802) English actor, manager CDP,

COC, DNB, ES, GT, NTH,
OC/1-3, TD/1-2
KEMBLE, Mrs. Roger see
Kemble, Sarah
KEMBLE, Sarah (1735-1807)
actress CDP, ES, NTH
KEMBLE, Stephen (1758-1822)
English actor, dramatist
CDP, CP/3, ES, GT, OC/
1-3, OX, TD/1-2
KEMBLE, Mrs. Stephen see
Kemble, Elizabeth (d 1841)
KEMBLE, T. D. (fl 1846) HAS
KEMBLE, Mrs. T. D. (d 1855)
HAS
KEMBLE, Theresa (1773-1838)
English actress, dancer,
dramatist CDP, CP/3, DNB,
ES, GT, OC/1-3
KEMBLE, Mrs. Thomas see
Kemble, Eliza
KEMBLE-BARNETT, Harry (d
1913) EA/14*
KEMP, Annie (fl 1860s) Ameri-
can singer, actress HAS
KEMP, Beatriz [Beatriz Phipps;
Mrs. Maurice F. Kemp] (d
1887) EA/88*
KEMP, Cornelius (d 1887) ad-
vance agent EA/88*
KEMP, Everett (b 1873) Ameri-
can monologist WWA/5
KEMP, Isaac (d 1889) music-
hall proprietor EA/90*
KEMP, Mrs. I. T. (d 1874)
EA/75*
KEMP, Jeremy [né Walker] (b
1935) English actor WWT/
15-16
KEMP, John (fl 1601) actor DA
KEMP, John (d 1867 [33])
pantomimist EA/68*
KEMP, Joseph (fl 1809-10)
dramatist CP/3
KEMP, Mrs. Maurice F. see
Kemp, Beatriz
KEMP, Robert (d 1959 [73])
French critic BE*, WWT/14*
KEMP, Roger (b 1931) English
actor TW/24
KEMP, Sally (b 1933) American
actress BE
KEMP, T[homas] C[harles] (1891-
1955) English critic, dramatist
COC, OC/3, WWT/11
KEMPE, William (d 1603) English
clown, actor, dancer, drama-
tist CDP, COC, CP/3, DA,

DNB, ES, FGF, GT, HP, NTH,
OC/1-3
KEMPER, Colin (1870-1955) Amer-
ican manager GRB/2-4, WWS,
WWT/1-7
KEMPER, Dolly [Charlotte Keogh]
(d 1943) actress SR
KEMPSON, Rachel (b 1910) English
actress COC, WWT/8-16
KEMPSTER, Frederick (d 1881)
actor, elocutionist EA/82*
KEMP-WELCH, Joan (b 1906) Eng-
lish actress, director WWT/
10-16
KENDAL, Doris actress WWT/5-6
KENDAL, Felicity (b 1946) English
actress WWT/15-16
KENDAL, Dame Madge [Margaret]
(1848-1935) English actress,
manager CDP, COC, DNB,
DP, ES, GRB/1-4, NTH, OAA/
1-2, OC/1-3, SR, WWA/4,
WWS, WWT/1-7, WWW/3
KENDAL, William Hunter [Grim-
ston] (1843-1917) English actor,
manager CDP, COC, DNB,
DP, ES, GRB/1-4, OAA/1-2,
OC/1-3, SR, WWA/1, WWS,
WWT/1-3, WWW/2
KENDALL, Mrs. (d 1906 [54])
EA/07*
KENDALL, A. A. (d 1916 [20])
EA/18*
KENDALL, Cricket E. (d 1972
[65]) publicity director BP/56*
KENDALL, Edward P. (1834-75)
American actor, manager, agent
HAS
KENDALL, Ezra Fremont (1861-
1910) American actor, dramatist
GRB/3-4, SR, WWA/1, WWS
KENDALL, Henry (1897-1962)
English actor AAS, WWT/4-13,
WWW/6
KENDALL, Jennie (fl 1858) Amer-
ican actress HAS
KENDALL, John (b 1869) English
dramatist WWT/2-7
KENDALL, Kay (1926-59) English
actress TW/16
KENDALL, Lizzie (fl 1858) Amer-
ican actress HAS
KENDALL, Marie (d 1964 [90])
singer CDP
KENDALL, Richard (fl 1635) actor
DA
KENDALL, Richard (b 1945) Cana-
dian actor TW/25-26

KENDALL, Thomas (d 1608) patentee, manager DA

KENDALL, Will (d 1892) Negro comedian EA/94*

KENDALL, William (fl 1597-1614) actor DA

KENDALL, William (b 1903) English actor WWT/8-16

KENDRICK, Alfred (b 1869) English actor GRB/1-4, WWT/1-7

KENDRICK, Brian (d 1970 [40]) performer BP/54*

KENDRICK, Jackie (d 1917) EA/18*

KENDRICK, Merle T. (d 1968 [71]) composer/lyricist BP/53*

KENDRICK, Richard (b 1910) American actor TW/5-7

KENEDE, Richard (fl 1607) actor DA

KENLEY, John (b 1907) American producer BE

KENMORE, Eddie (b 1940) American actor TW/19-20

KENNA (fl 1785) actor HAS

KENNA, Mrs. (fl 1785) actress HAS

KENNA, Peter (b 1930) Australian dramatist CD

KENNARD, Jane see Kennark, Jane

KENNARD, Willie (d 1910) EA/11*

KENNARK [Or Kennard], Jane (d 1938 [75]) American actress BE*, BP/22*

KENNAWAY, James (d 1968 [40]) dramatist BP/53*

KENNEALLY, Michael (d 1972 [80]) performer BP/56*

KENNEDY, Mr. (d 1786 [66]) actor TD/1-2

KENNEDY, Mrs. (d c.1788) actress GT, TD/1-2

KENNEDY, Miss (d 1888) actress EA/89*

KENNEDY, Adrienne (b 1931) American dramatist CD, CH

KENNEDY, Anne G. (d 1974 [38]) performer BP/58*

KENNEDY, Arthur (b 1914) American actor AAS, BE, CB, TW/3-15, 24-25, 30, WWT/11-16

KENNEDY, Beulah (d 1964 [71]) American performer BE*

KENNEDY, Bob (d 1974 [41])

performer BP/59*

KENNEDY, Charles E. (b 1867) American actor WWS

KENNEDY, Charles Rann (1871-1950) English dramatist, actor GRB/4, HJD, TW/6, WWA/2, WWT/1-9, WWW/4

KENNEDY, Mrs. Charles Rann see Matthison, Edith Wynne

KENNEDY, Cheryl (b 1947) English actress, singer WWT/15-16

KENNEDY, David (1825-86) Scottish singer CDP, DNB

KENNEDY, Edgar (d 1948 [58]) American actor BE*

KENNEDY, Edmund F. (b 1873) English actor GRB/1-4, WWT/1-5

KENNEDY, Edward J. (b 1844) dancer, minstrel CDP

KENNEDY, Mrs. E. J. (d 1899 [51]) EA/00*

KENNEDY, Elise Marie Dalton (d 1876) actress EA/77*

KENNEDY, Florence [Mrs. James H. Huntley] (c.1849-87) American actress NYM

KENNEDY, Mrs. H. A. see Lovel, Gertrude

KENNEDY, Harold J. actor, director, dramatist WWT/16

KENNEDY, Harry see Kennedy, William Henry

KENNEDY, Hugh Arthur (d 1905 [50]) dramatist, critic GRB/1

KENNEDY, Mrs. Hugh Arthur see Lovel, Gertrude

KENNEDY, Joe (d 1969 [80]) performer BP/54*

KENNEDY, John (d 1898 [34]) proprietor EA/99*

KENNEDY, John (b 1902) American director BE, TW/3

KENNEDY, Joyce (1898/1900-1943) English actress WWT/5-9

KENNEDY, J. T. (d 1896) actor EA/97*

KENNEDY, Kathleen M. (d 1975 [28]) publicist BP/60*

KENNEDY, Lila (b 1903) American executive, director, actress BE

KENNEDY, Madge (b 1890) American actress TW/22, WWT/4-9

KENNEDY, Margaret (1896-1967) English dramatist ES, MH, MWD, NTH, WWA/4, WWT/8-13, WWW/6

KENNEDY, Margaret see Farrell, Margaret

KENNEDY, Mary (d 1887 [57]) EA/88*

KENNEDY, Mary American actress, dramatist WWT/7-9

KENNEDY, Maurice (d 1962 [51]) manager BE*

KENNEDY, Merna (d 1944 [35]) actress TW/1

KENNEDY, Patricia (b 1917) Australian actress WWT/16

KENNEDY, Mrs. T. (fl 1773) actress CDP

KENNEDY, Thomas (d 1898 [32]) actor EA/99*

KENNEDY, Walter (d 1886) EA/87*

KENNEDY, Warder Howard (1880-1943) actor SR

KENNEDY, William Henry (1855-91) ventriloquist, singer, composer CDP

KENNEDY, Zona American actress TW/23

KENNER, Chris (d 1976 [46]) performer BP/60*

KENNER, Hugh (b 1923) Canadian critic BE

KENNETT, Amelia Sevenoaks (d 1907) actress? EA/09*

KENNETTE (d 1906) aerial wonder EA/07*

KENNEY, Charles Horace (d 1909 [52]) actor EA/10*

KENNEY, Charles Lamb (1821-81) French/English dramatist DNB

KENNEY, Mrs. Charles Lamb see Kenney, Rosa

KENNEY, Ed (b 1933) American actor TW/15

KENNEY, Horace (d 1955 [65]) music-hall performer WWT/14*

KENNEY, Izetta see Jewell, Izetta

KENNEY, Jack (d 1964 [76]) actor BE*

KENNEY, James (1780-1849) Irish dramatist CDP, CP/3, DNB, GT, TD/2

KENNEY, James (b 1930) English actor WWT/12-16

KENNEY, Rosa [Mrs. Charles Lamb Kenney] (d 1900) EA/01*

KENNEY, Rose (d 1905) actress

GRB/1, OAA/2

KENNICOTT, James H. (fl 1830) American dramatist EAP, RJ

KENNINGHAM, Charles (d 1925) actor BE*, WWT/14*

KENNINGTON, Anne (d 1962 [77]) dramatist WWT/14*

KENNION, Rose (d 1912) actress EA/13*

KENNIS, Stanley (d 1897) EA/99*

KENNY, Mr. (fl 1794) actor HAS

KENNY, Mrs. George [Georgiana Harris] (d 1883 [27]) EA/84*

KENNY, James see Kenney, James

KENNY, Nick (d 1975 [80]) songwriter, columnist BP/60*, WWT/16*

KENNY, Sean (1932-73) Irish designer AAS, BE, ES, PDT, WWT/14-15

KENRICK, William (1725?-79) English dramatist CDP, CP/2-3, GT, TD/1-2

KENT, Miss see Da Costa, Mrs.

KENT, Allegra (b 1938) American dancer CB, ES

KENT, Barbara (b 1921) English actress TW/1

KENT, Barry [né Sautereau] (b 1932) English actor WWT/15-16

KENT, Beatrice E. English lyricist GRB/1

KENT, Carl (b 1918) American designer TW/3-5

KENT, Charles (d 1923 [69]) English actor BE*, BP/7*

KENT, Crawford (d 1953 [72]) actor BE*

KENT, Eleanor (b 1879) American singer WWM

KENT, Frederick M. (1829-57) American actor CDP, HAS

KENT, Fred S. American actor HAS

KENT, Mrs. Fred S. [Josephine Tyson] (d 1869 [30]) actress HAS

KENT, Georgia Tyler (1848-1914) actress HAS

KENT, Harry (fl 1897?) singer CDP

KENT, Helen see Herbert, Mrs.

KENT, Herbert (d 1973 [96]) English actor TW/29

KENT, Imogene (b 1838) American actress HAS

KENT, Jean [née Field] (b 1921)

English actress WWT/12-16

KENT, John (d 1830) English
actor HAS

KENT, John, Jr. (d 1833) English actor HAS

KENT, Mrs. John [née Yardley]
(fl 1824-33) English actress
HAS

KENT, Keneth (1892-1963) English actor, producer AAS,
WWT/5-13

KENT, Sidney Miller (c. 1861-
1948) actor SR

KENT, Thomas M. (d 1898 [58])
actor EA/99*

KENT, Walter composer BE

KENT, Walter Speakman (d
1887 [18]) EA/88*

KENT, Willard (d 1968 [85])
performer BP/53*

KENT, William (b 1811) Scottish dancer HAS

KENT, William (1886-1945)
American actor SR, TW/2,
WWT/6-9

KENT, Mrs. William [Elizabeth
Eberle] (d 1850) American
actress, singer HAS

KENTISH, Agatha (b 1897) English actress WWT/5-8

KENTON, Godfrey (b 1902)
English actor AAS, WWT/
8-16

"KENTUCKY GIANT, The" see
Porter, Mr. (fl 1838)

KENWARD, Edith (d 1905) actress, dramatist CDP, GRB/1

KENWAY, George (d 1909 [73])
EA/10*

KENWAY, Rebecca (d 1912 [89])
EA/13*

KENYON, Charles (1878-1961)
English actor WWT/2-7

KENYON, Doris (b 1897) American actress WWT/5-9

KENYON, Harry (d 1907 [37])
performer? EA/08*

KENYON, Laura (b 1947) American actress TW/28

KENYON, Neil [Neil McKinnon]
(d 1946 [73]) Scottish actor
WWT/4-7

KENYON, Taldo (b 1936) American actor TW/23

KEOGH, Mrs. Arthur H. see
Keogh, Leah

KEOGH, Charlotte see Kemper,
Dolly

KEOGH, John see Stables, Harry

KEOGH, Joseph Augustus (1884-
1942) Irish actor, manager
GRB/1, SR

KEOGH, Leah [Mrs. Arthur H.
Keogh] (d 1876 [24]) EA/77*

KEOGH, William T. (d 1947 [87])
producer, manager BE*, WWT/
14*

KEOUGH, Emma (b 1829) English
actress, singer HAS

KEOWN, Eric (1904-63) English
critic WWT/12-13

KEPLER, Constance (fl 1838)
dancer HAS

KEPPELL, W. H. (fl 1880s) actor
SR

KER, Paul (d c. 1929 [54]) German
singer, actor BP/13*

KERBY, Marion (d 1956 [79]) American actress, singer TW/13

KERCHEVAL, Ken (b 1935) American actor TW/24-29

KERIN, Nora [Mrs. Cyril Michael]
(b 1883) English actress GRB/4,
WWT/1-7

KERKER, Gustave Adolph (1857-
1923) German composer, conductor GRB/3-4, SR, WWA/1,
WWM, WWS, WWT/1-4

KERKOW, Herbert (d 1972 [68])
producer/director/choreographer
BP/57*

KERMOYAN, Michael (b 1925)
American actor, singer BE,
TW/22-24, 30

KERN, Jerome David (1885-1945)
American composer AAS, CB,
DAB, ES, HJD, MH, NTH,
PDT, SR, TW/2, WWA/2,
WWT/4-9, WWW/4

KERNAN, David (b 1939) English
actor WWT/15-16

KERNAN, Joseph Lewis (d 1964
[83]) manager, talent representative BE*

KERNELL, Harry (1853-93) Irish
comedian, minstrel CDP

KERNELL, Harry (b 1888) American actor WWM

KERNODLE, George R. (b 1907)
American educator, director BE

KERNWOOD, Grace (1863-1943)
singer SR

KERR, Miss (fl 1839) actress HAS

KERR, Alexander (d 1876 [50])
scene artist EA/77*

KERR, Dr. Alfred (d 1948 [80])

critic BE*, WWT/14*
KERR, Anne (d 1973 [48]) per-
former BP/58*
KERR, Ann Jeannette see Hunt,
Mrs. Charles
KERR, Bill actor WWT/16
KERR, Charles see Arnold,
Mat
KERR, Deborah (b 1921) Scottish
actress BE, CB, ES, WWT/
10-14, 16
KERR, Elaine (b 1942) American
actress TW/28-29
KERR, Frederick [Frederick
Grinham Keen] (1858-1933)
English actor DP, EA/95,
GRB/1-4, NTH, WWM, WWT/
1-7
KERR, Geoffrey (b 1895) English
actor, dramatist BE, TW/6-
7, WWT/4-14
KERR, Jean (b 1923/24) Ameri-
can dramatist BE, CB, ES,
WWT/14-16
KERR, John (fl 1830?) drama-
tist EAP
KERR, John (b 1931) American
actor BE, TW/9-18, 24
KERR, John George (b 1814)
English actor, dancer HAS
KERR, Marge American talent
representative BE
KERR, Molly (b 1904) English
actress WWT/5-6
KERR, Philip (b 1940) American
actor TW/26-27, 29
KERR, Sophie (1880-1965) Amer-
ican dramatist WWA/4
KERR, Walter F. (b 1913)
American critic, director,
dramatist AAS, BE, CB,
COC, HJD, NTH, WWT/13-16
KERRIDGE, Donald (d 1874)
musical director EA/75*
KERRIDGE, Mary (b 1914) Eng-
lish actress COC, WWT/
11-16
KERRIGAN, J. M. (1885-1964)
Irish actor TW/3, WWT/
2-11
KERRIGAN, J. Warren (1880-
1947) actor BE*
KERRIGAN, T. F. musician,
composer, dancer CDP
KERRY, Norman (d 1956 [66])
actor BE*
KERSANDS, "Billy" actor CDP
KERSHAW, Elinor (d 1971 [86])

performer BP/56*
KERSHAW, Willette (1890-1960)
American actress TW/16,
WWT/4-10
KERT, Larry [né Frederick Law-
rence] (b 1930) American actor,
singer AAS, BE, TW/18-20,
23, 25-30, WWT/15-16
KERZ, Leo (1912-76) German de-
signer, director, producer BE
KESHAN, Fred (d 1890) music-hall
performer EA/91*
KESHAN, John (d 1877) instrument
maker EA/78*
KESSELRING, Charlotte E. (d
1971) dramatist BP/56*
KESSELRING, Joseph D. (1902-67)
American dramatist BE, ES,
MH, MWD, TW/24, WWA/4,
WWT/10-14
KESSLER, David (1860-1920) Rus-
sian dramatist ES
KESSLER, Ferdinand Mozart (d
1888 [38]) conductor EA/89*
KESSLER, Joseph (d 1933 [51])
actor BE*, WWT/14*
KESSLER, Mabel (b 1873) English
singer, musician GRB/1
KESSLER, Phillip (d 1878 [55])
musician EA/79*
KESTELMAN, Sara (b 1944) Eng-
lish actress TW/27, 30,
WWT/16
KESTER, Paul (1870-1933) Ameri-
can dramatist COC, DAB,
GRB/2-4, OC/1-3, WWA/1,
WWM, WWT/1-7
KESTON, C. B. [Charles H. Dun-
can] English actor CDP, GRB/1
KETCHUM, George F. (1837-80)
American actor, stage manager
CDP, HAS
KETCHUM, Robyna Neilson (d
1972) performer BP/57*
KETHRO, Frank (d 1910) musical
director EA/11*
KETTEN, Henry (d 1883 [35]) com-
poser, musician EA/84*
KEY, Kathleen (d 1954 [57]) actress
BE*
KEY, Pat Ann (d 1962) performer
BE*
KEYES, Daniel (b 1914) American
actor TW/22-27, 29-30
KEYMER, Mrs. (d 1882) EA/83*
KEYS, Miss see Lee, Mrs.
KEYS, Miss see Mills, Mrs.
KEYS, Nelson (1886-1939) English

actor WWT/3-8
KEYS, Simon actor TD/1-2
KEYS, Mrs. Simon (fl 1803)
actress TD/2
KEYSAR, Robert (fl 1605-08)
lessee DA
KEZER, Glenn (b 1923) American
actor TW/24-26
KHACIDOVITCH, Tamara see
Toumanova, Tamara
KHOURY, Edith Leslie (d 1973)
performer BP/57*
KIALLMARK [or Kilmark],
George (1781-1835) English
composer, musician DNB
KIBBEE, Guy (1882-1956) Amer-
ican actor TW/12
KIDD, Kathleen (d 1961) Cana-
dian actress BE*, BP/45*,
WWT/14*
KIDD, Michael [né Milton Green-
wald] (b 1918/19) American
dancer, choreographer, di-
rector AAS, BE, CB, ES,
WWT/14-16
KIDD, Robert (b 1943) Scottish
director WWT/15-16
KIDDER, E. E. American
dramatist SR
KIDDER, Kathryn [Mrs. Louis
Kaufman Anspacher] (1867-
1939) American actress CDP,
GRB/2-4, PP/2, SR, WWA/1,
WWM, WWS, WWT/1-4
KIDDIE, Polly see Burton, Polly
KIDGER, Mrs. John see
Kidger, Mary
KIDGER, Mary [Mrs. John Kid-
ger] (d 1887) acting manager
EA/88*
KIDWELL, Gene (b 1946) Amer-
ican actor TW/25-27
KIENZL, Florian (d 1972 [77])
critic BP/56*
KIEPURA, Jan (1904-66) Polish
singer, actor BE, CB, SR,
TW/2-3, 23, WWA/4, WWT/
10-14
KIERNAN, James (1939-75)
American actor TW/30
KIESLER, Frederick J. (b 1896)
Austrian scene designer BE
KIKUME, Al (d 1972 [78]) per-
former BP/56*
KILBRIDE, Percy (d 1964 [76])
American actor TW/2-3, 21
KILBURN, Eliza (d 1891) EA/92*
KILBURN, Harry (d 1908 [42])

comedian EA/09*
KILBURN, Terrance (b 1928) Eng-
lish actor TW/8, 10-14
KILDARE, Tom J. see Gilbey,
Tom
KILEY, Richard (b 1922) American
actor, singer BE, CB, TW/9-
25, 28-30, WWT/14-16
KILFOIL, Thomas F. (b 1922)
American librarian, curator BE
KILFOY, Tam (d 1874) musician
EA/75*
KILGALLEN, Dorothy (d 1965 [52])
journalist BP/50*
KILGOUR, Joseph (1863/72-1933)
Canadian actor SR, WWM
KILIAN, Victor (b 1891) American
actor BE, TW/14-15
KILLIAN, Phil American actor
TW/29-30
KILLICK, C. Egerton (1891/92-
1967) English manager WWT/5-
14
KILLIGREW, Charles (1665-1725)
English manager, Master of the
Revels DNB, OC/1-3
KILLIGREW, Dr. Henry (1612-1700)
English dramatist CP/1-3,
FGF, HP
KILLIGREW, Thomas (1612-83)
English dramatist, manager,
Master of the Revels CDP,
COC, CP/1-3, DNB, FGF, HP,
NTH, OC/1-3, RE
KILLIGREW, Thomas (1657-1719)
English dramatist CP/1-3,
DNB, HP, OC/1-3
KILLIGREW, Sir William (1606-95)
English dramatist CP/1-3,
DNB, ES, HP, OC/1-3
KILLINGER, Marion (b 1941) Amer-
ican actress TW/29
KILLMER, Nancy (b 1936) Ameri-
can actress TW/26
KILMARK, George see Kiallmark,
George
KILMOREY, Earl of (d 1915 [73])
producer, dramatist, manager
BE*, WWT/14*
KILNER, Naomi (d 1900 [64])
EA/01*
KILNER, Thomas (1777-1862) Eng-
lish actor CDP, HAS
KILPACK, Bennett (d 1962 [79])
English actor BE*
KILPACK, Frank (d 1889 [51])
acting manager EA/90*
KILPATRICK, Mrs. Edwin E. see

Kilpatrick, Kintchie

KILPATRICK, Jack Frederick (b 1915) American composer, educator BE

KILPATRICK, Kintchie [Mrs. Edwin E. Kilpatrick] (d 1917) EA/18*

KILPATRICK, Thomas (b 1902) American producer, manager, publicist BE

KILTY, Jerome (b 1922) American actor, director, dramatist BE, COC, ES, WWT/14-16

KIM, Christal (b 1916) American actress TW/27-28

KIMBALL, Grace [Mrs. Laurence McGuire] (b 1870) American actress GRB/2-4, SR, WWS, WWT/1-2

KIMBALL, Jennie (1848-96) American actress, manager CDP, HAS, SR

KIMBALL, Louis (1889-1936) American actor WWT/6-7

KIMBALL, Moses (1810-95) manager CDP

KIMBER, J. W. (d 1884) manager EA/86*

KIMBER, Mrs. J. W. (d 1879) EA/80*

KIMBERLEY, Mrs. F. G. (d 1939 [62]) dramatist, producer BE*, WWT/14*

KIMBERLY, E. (fl 1849) actress, reader CDP

KIMBRELL, Marketa (b 1928) Czech actress TW/23

KIMBROUGH, Charles (b 1936) American actor TW/25-28, 30

KIMBROUGH, Clinton (b 1935/36) American actor BE, TW/18-21

KIMM, Anne (d 1911) EA/12*

KIMM, H. Val (b 1873) English business manager GRB/1

KIMMIE, Miss (fl 1851) actress HAS

KIMMINS, Anthony (1901-64) English dramatist AAS, WWT/8-13

KIMMINS, Grace (b 1942) American actress TW/27

KIMMINS, Kenneth (b 1941) American actor TW/28-29

KIMPTON, Robert (fl 1629-32) actor DA

KINDLE, Tom (b 1948) American actor TW/29

KING, Mr. (fl 1801-04) actor, dancer, equestrian TD/1-2

KING, Mrs. see Brookyn, May

KING, Mrs. [née Brett] (fl 1793) actress HAS

KING, Ada (d 1940 [78]) actress WWT/2-8

KING, Adah (fl 1850s) English actress HAS

KING, Alan (b 1927) American actor, producer CB

KING, Alfred George (d 1907) EA/08*

KING, Amelia (d 1900) EA/01*

KING, Archer American talent representative, producer BE

KING, Arthur (fl 1581) actor DA

KING, Bob Brown (d 1970 [33]) performer BP/54*

KING, Cecil (d 1958 [83]) Irish actor, stage manager WWT/4-10

KING, Charles (d 1881) acting manager EA/83*

KING, Charles (1887/89-1944) American actor, singer SR, WWT/7-8

KING, Mrs. Charles see King, Martha

KING, Charles A. (1823-57) American actor? HAS

KING, Clara (d 1879 [29]) actress EA/80*

KING, Clara (d 1884 [46]) ballet mistress, dancer EA/85*

KING, Claude (1876-1941) English actor WWT/2-9

KING, Dennis (1897-1971) English actor, singer, director AAS, BE, TW/1-24, 26-27, WWT/6-15

KING, Dennis, Jr. English actor TW/1, 3-5

KING, Donald W. (d 1886 [74]) actor, singer WWT/14*

KING, Edith (d 1975 [91]) BP/59*

KING, Edith [née Keck] (b 1896/97) American actress BE, TW/1-3, 8, 10-18, 20, WWT/10-15

KING, Ellen Langley (d 1916 [79]) EA/17*

KING, Emmett C. (d 1953 [87]) American actor BE*, BP/37*

KING, George (d 1909 [36]) proprietor EA/10*

KING, Gerard James (d 1889 [53]) comedian EA/90*

KING, Harry (d 1870 [19]) duologue artist EA/71*

KING, Harry (d 1886 [39]) Negro comedian, panorama proprietor EA/87*

KING, Henry (b 1888) American actor ES

KING, Henry James see Martley, Bob

KING, Herbert G. (d 1975 [73]) director of opera club BP/60*

KING, Hetty (d 1972 [89]) music-hall performer BP/57*, WWT/16*

KING, Howard (d 1975 [91]) circus executive BP/60*

KING, James (d 1909 [81]) music-hall manager EA/10*

KING, James Joyce (d 1971 [61]) publicist BP/56*

KING, Jane (d 1971 [75]) vaudevillian, actress TW/27

KING, John-Michael (b 1926/29) American actor, singer BE, TW/12-16, 22-24

KING, Karl L. (d 1971 [80]) composer/lyricist BP/55*

KING, Katty [Mrs. Arthur Lloyd] (d 1891 [39]) actress EA/92*

KING, Lottie [Mrs. Henry Belding] (d 1899) actress EA/00*

KING, Marie see Sutherland, Marie

KING, Martha [Mrs. Charles King] (d 1876) EA/78*

KING, Mary [Mrs. Tom King] (fl 1772?) dancer CDP

KING, Matthias (fl early 19th cent) clown, actor CDP

KING, Murray (b 1874) English actor, manager GRB/2

KING, Nosmo (d 1949 [63]) performer BE*, WWT/14*

KING, Omega J. (d 1973 [81]) performer BP/58*

KING, P. (fl 1805) English composer TD/2

KING, Philip (b 1904) dramatist, actor WWT/10-16

KING, Robert (b 1936) American actor TW/28

KING, Robert A. (1862-1932) American composer BE*

KING, Robert M. (d 1974 [54]) producer/director/choreographer BP/58*

KING, Mrs. T. C. (d 1878) EA/79*

KING, Mrs. T. G. see Richardson, Nell

KING, Thomas (fl 1586-87) actor DA

KING, Thomas (d 1903 [68]) proprietor EA/04*

KING, T[homas] C. (1825-93) English actor CDP, OAA/1-2

KING, Tom (1730-1804) English actor, dramatist CDP, COC, CP/2-3, DNB, GT, OC/1-3, TD/1-2

KING, Tom (b 1835) singer CDP

KING, Mrs. Tom see King, Mary

KING, Vicki Kernan (d 1975 [49]) performer BP/59*

KING, Victor (d 1964 [72]) performer BE*

KING, Walter (d 1911 [44]) comic singer EA/12*

KING, Walter Woolf (b 1899) American actor, singer WWT/8-9

KING, Dr. William (1663-1712) English dramatist CP/2-3, GT

KING, William (d 1796) actor HAS

KING, William A. (d 1968 [41]) stage manager BP/53*

KING, Woodie, Jr. (b 1937) American actor TW/25-26

KING, Wright (b 1927) American actor TW/6-8

KING-COBURN, S. (d 1892 [39]) American actor EA/93*

KINGDOM, John M. (d 1876) dramatist WWT/14*

KINGDON, Edith [Mrs. George J. Gould] (1862-1921) American actress CDP

KINGDON, Frank (d 1937 [72]) American actor BE*, BP/21*

KINGDON, John M. (d 1876) dramatist BE*

KINGDON, W. (d 1878 [46]) musician, singer EA/79*

KINGDON-GOULD, Edith Maughan see Kingdon, Edith

KING-HALL, Sir Stephen (1893-1966) dramatist WWT/7-14

KINGHORNE, Mark Alexander Mackenzie (1850/51-1906) English actor DP, EA/96, GRB/1

KING-LLOYD, Mrs. Harry see Lloyd, Margaret Leah

KINGSBURY, Alice (fl 1859-69) American actress HAS

KINGSBURY, Frederick (d 1892 [76]) conductor EA/93*

KINGSFORD, Walter (1881-1959) English actor TW/1-3, 15

KINGSLEY, A. F. actor HAS

KINGSLEY, Mrs. A. F. [née Kate Thornton] actress HAS

KINGSLEY, Cecil (b 1876) Canadian actor GRB/1

KINGSLEY, Edith see Loraine, Mrs. Henry

KINGSLEY, Grace (d 1962 [89]) journalist BE*

KINGSLEY, Mary (d 1936 [74]) actress CDP

KINGSLEY, Omar see Ella Zoyara, Miss

KINGSLEY, Rex (d 1974 [73]) performer BP/59*

KINGSLEY, Sidney (b 1906) American dramatist, actor, director AAS, BE, CB, CD, CH, COC, ES, HJD, MD, MH, MWD, NTH, OC/1-3, PDT, RE, SR, WWT/8-16

KINGSLEY, Walter J. (1878-1929) American press representative WWM

KINGSMAN, Philip (fl 1596-1615) actor DA

KINGSMAN, Robert (fl 1599-1618) actor DA

KINGSMILL, Percy T. F. see Hamilton, Sidney

KINGSTON, Al (d 1975 [72]) agent BP/59*

KINGSTON, Bertha English actress GRB/1

KINGSTON, Gertrude [Mrs. Silver] (1866/68-1937) English actress, manager, producer CDP, COC, DP, EA/95, GRB/1-4, NTH, OC/1-3, WWT/1-8, WWW/3

KINGSTON, Kaye (b 1924) American actress TW/24, 30

KINGSTON, Sam F. (c. 1866-1929) Irish manager SR

KINGSTON, Thomas (1870-1911) actor EA/96

KING-WOOD, David actor TW/13

KINHARVIE, Frances (d 1892) EA/93*

KINKEAD, Cleves (1882-1955) American dramatist WWA/3

KINLOCH, John (d 1873 [63]) acting manager EA/74*

KINLOCK, Eliza (1796-1887) English actress HAS, NYM, SR

KINLOCK, Georgiana (d 1864) actress HAS

KINNAIRD, David (d 1971 [45]) performer BP/55*

KINNAIRD, Helen English actress GRB/2

KINNEAR, De Leon (d 1870 [55]) circus manager EA/71*

KINNEAR, Roy (b 1934) English actor WWT/14-16

KINNELL, Murray (d 1954 [65]) English actor BE*, BP/39*

KINNEY, Ray (d 1972 [71]) performer BP/56*

KINNIAD, Annie singer CDP

KINO, Walter (d 1901 [34]) music-hall comedian CDP

KINROSS, Charles (d 1905 [21]) actor EA/06*

KINSELLA, Kathleen (d 1961 [83]) English actress TW/17

KINSELLA, Polly (d 1910) actress EA/11*

KINSELLA, Walter (d 1975 [74]) performer BP/59*

KINSOLVING, Lee (d 1974 [36]) performer BP/59*

KINTON, Swaine [Mrs. Balsir Chatterton] (d 1897 [32]) actress EA/98*

KINWELLMARSHE, Francis (fl 1575) translator CP/3

KINZIE, Elizabeth Miller (1875-1947) actress SR

KIPNESS, Joseph producer BE, WWT/16

KIPNIS, Alexander (b 1891) Russian/American singer CB, ES

KIRALFY, Amalia [Mrs. Gabriel Bremaure] (d 1917) actress SR

KIRALFY, Arnold (d 1908) dancer GRB/4*

KIRALFY, Bolossy (d 1932 [84]) Hungarian dancer, manager CDP

KIRALFY, Haniola [Mrs. A. L. Parkes] (d 1889) Hungarian dancer CDP

KIRALFY, Imre (1845-1919) Hungarian producer, dramatist CDP, GRB/1-4, SR

KIRALYFY, Johana (fl 1861?) dancer CDP

KIRBY, Mrs. see Stark, Mrs. James

KIRBY, Miss (fl 1844) actress HAS

KIRBY, Elisabeth [Mrs. James Bernard Fagan] English actress GRB/1-2

KIRBY, Hartwell J. (d 1910) EA/11*

KIRBY, Helen DuVall (d 1973 [81]) performer BP/58*

KIRBY, Hudson (1819-48) American actor CDP, DAB, HAS, SR, WWA/H

KIRBY, Mrs. Hudson (d 1896 [74]) actress HAS

KIRBY, James (d 1826) English clown CDP, HAS

KIRBY, J. Hudson see Kirby, Hudson

KIRBY, John (1894-1930) New Zealand actor WWT/6

KIRBY, John (d 1973 [41]) performer BP/58*

KIRBY, Mae Elaine (d 1968 [87]) performer BP/53*

KIRBY, Norman (d 1905 [71]) singer EA/06*

KIRBY, Thomas, Jr. (d 1876 [21]) musical director EA/77*

KIRBY, Tom (d 1884) comic singer EA/85*

KIRCHMAYER, Thomas (1511-63) German dramatist OC/2-3

KIRCHNER, Simplicieus (d 1879) musician EA/80*

KIRCK, John (fl 1579-80) actor DA

KIRK, George (d 1912) actor EA/13*

KIRK, Mrs. Harry see Eversleigh, Flo

KIRK, Helen (d 1871) Scottish singer EA/72*

KIRK, James (fl 1858) actor HAS

KIRK, Jessie [Mrs. Kenneth Black] (d 1905) EA/06*

KIRK, John (d 1948 [86]) American actor, producer, director TW/4

KIRK, Joseph (d 1975 [71]) performer BP/59*

KIRK, Lisa (b 1925) American actress, singer, dancer TW/5-9, 20, WWT/16

KIRK, Neil (d 1972 [79]) booking agent BP/57*

KIRK, Samuel (d 1883 [64]) musician EA/84*

KIRK, Sarah (d 1879) EA/80*

KIRK, William (d 1887 [78]) supermaster EA/88*

KIRK, William T. (d 1974 [65]) producer/director/choreographer

BP/58*

KIRKE, John (d 1643) English actor, dramatist CP/1-3, DA, DNB, FGF, OC/1-3

KIRKHAM, Miss singer CDP

KIRKHAM, Edward (fl 1602-06) yeoman of the Revels DA

KIRKHAM, Sam (1923-70) American actor TW/23-24, 26-27

KIRKLAND, Alexander (b 1903/08) Mexican/American actor, director, dramatist BE, NTH, TW/1-6, WWT/8-11

KIRKLAND, Gelsey (b 1952) American dancer CB

KIRKLAND, Hardee (b 1868) American actor WWM

KIRKLAND, Jack (1901-69) American dramatist, producer BE, MD, MH, MWD, TW/25, WWT/9-14

KIRKLAND, Muriel (1903/04-71) American actress BE, TW/25, 28, WWT/7-15

KIRKLAND, Patricia (b 1925) American actress TW/1, 3-4, WWT/11-12

KIRKLAND, Sally (b 1944) American actress TW/24-25, 27-28, WWT/16

KIRKMAN, Francis see K., F.

KIRKWOOD, Gertrude Robinson (d 1962 [71]) actress BE*

KIRKWOOD, Jack (1894-1964) Scottish performer BE*, BP/49*

KIRKWOOD, James (d 1879) proprietor EA/80*

KIRKWOOD, James (d 1963 [80]) performer BP/48*

KIRKWOOD, Mrs. James see Kirkwood, Martha

KIRKWOOD, Jim (b 1925) American actor TW/6-7

KIRKWOOD, Martha [Mrs. James Kirkwood] (d 1879) EA/80*

KIRKWOOD, Pat (b 1921) English actress, singer AAS, WWT/10-16

KIRKWOOD-HACKETT, Eva (d 1968 [91]) performer BP/52*

KIRSCH, Carolyn (b 1942) American actress TW/26-27, 30

KIRSHON, Vladimir Mikhailovich (1902-38) Russian dramatist COC

KIRSTEIN, Lincoln (b 1907) American director CB, ES

KIRSTEN, Dorothy (b 1917) American singer CB

KIRTLAND, Louise (b 1905/10) American actress BE, TW/5, 30, WWT/8-16

KIRTLEY, Mrs. Thomas (d 1897) EA/98*

KIRTLEY, Thomas H. (d 1900) proprietor EA/01*

KIRWAN, Patrick (d 1929 [67]) Irish actor, manager GRB/2-4, WWT/1-5

KISER, Terry (b 1939) American actor TW/23-30

KISER, Virginia (b 1939) American actress TW/25

KISKADDEN, Maude see Adams, Maude

KISSEL, Herman (d 1964 [53]) critic BP/49*

KISSOCK, James Mills (d 1917) manager EA/18*

KISTEMAECHERS, Henry (1872-1938) dramatist BE*, WWT/14*

KITCHELL, Iva (b 1912) American dancer CB

KITCHEN, Dick (d 1907 [47]) EA/08*

KITCHEN, Fred (d 1951 [77]) performer BE*, WWT/14*

KITCHEN, R. H. (d 1910 [80/81]) clown BE*, EA/11*, WWT/14*

KITCHIN, Laurence (b 1913) English critic, actor WWT/16

KITE, Mrs. see Thomas, Mrs.

KITE, John (fl 1508) actor DA

KITT, Eartha (b 1930) American singer, actress, dancer BE, CB, TW/8-9, WWT/15-16

KITTREDGE, George Lyman (1860-1941) American scholar CB, DAB, HJD

KIVER, Hubert W. (d 1917 [23]) performer? EA/18*

KLAFSKY, Katharina (1855-96) Hungarian singer CDP, ES

KLANERT, Mr. (fl 1798) actor TD/1-2

KLANWELL, Marie (d 1911 [58]) singer EA/12*

KLATT, Mme. (fl 1845) equestrienne CDP

KLAUBER, Adolph (1879-1933) American producer, manager, critic WWA/1, WWM, WWT/4-7

KLAUSNER, Margot (d 1975 [70]) dramatist BP/60*

KLAVUN, Walter (b 1906) American actor, director BE, TW/6, 28-29

KLAW, Alonzo (1886-1944) manager, producer SR

KLAW, Marc (1858-1936) American manager, agent, producer DAB, GRB/2-4, WWA/1, WWS, WWT/1-8

KLEIN, Adelaide (b 1904) American actress BE

KLEIN, Alfred (1864-1904) actor, singer CDP

KLEIN, Arthur (d 1964 [79]) producer/director BP/49*

KLEIN, Cecil (b 1875) American actor GRB/1-2

KLEIN, Charles (1867-1915) English dramatist COC, DAB, GRB/2-4, HJD, OC/1-3, SR, WWA/1, WWM, WWS, WWT/1-2

KLEIN, Deanne A. (d 1975 [40]) critic BP/59*

KLEIN, Gordon D. (d 1972 [58]) performer BP/57*

KLEIN, Jacob (d 1973 [94]) lawyer BP/57*

KLEIN, Joseph (d 1970 [62]) journalist BP/55*

KLEIN, Manuel (1876-1919) English composer, conductor WWA/1, WWM

KLEIN, Miriam Lillian (d 1973 [78]) performer BP/58*

KLEIN, Paul (d 1964 [61]) press representative BE*

KLEIN, Reid (b 1938) American actor TW/24

KLEIN, Robert (b 1942) American actor TW/24-25

KLEIN, Sadie (d 1974 [91]) performer BP/59*

KLENOSKY, William J. (b 1922) American actor TW/24

KLEPER, Sidney H. (d 1974 [58]) manager BP/59*

KLETT, Mr. (d 1834) actor HAS

KLEWER, Leonore N. (b 1912) American manager BE

KLIBAN, Terry (b 1942) American actor TW/26

KLIEGL, Herbert (b 1904) American executive BE

KLIETZ, Valesca (fl 1848) German singer? HAS

KLIMT, George (1861-1942)
American actor SR

KLINE, James C. (1850-1934)
actor SR

KLINE, Kevin (b 1947) American actor TW/29-30

KLINE, Richard (b 1944) American actor TW/28-29

KLINE, Tiny (d 1964 [74]) Hungarian acrobat BE*

KLING, Irene Frances (b 1947)
American actress TW/29

KLIPSTEIN, Abner D. (b 1912)
American press representative
BE

KLOET, Miss see Bostock,
Mrs. W. B.

KLOT, Georgia see Brown,
Georgia

KLOTZ, Florence American designer WWT/15-16

KLUGMAN, Jack (b 1922) American actor BE, TW/22-23,
25, WWT/15-16

KLUNIS, Tom American actor
TW/22, 24, 26, 29

KNAGGES, Richard (fl 1612)
actor DA

KNAIZ, Judy (b 1940) American actress TW/28

KNAPP, Betty (d 1973 [72])
performer BP/57*

KNAPP, Edward Lee (d 1896
[59]) EA/97*

KNAPP, Eleanore American actress TW/29

KNAPP, Fred L. (d 1962 [67])
performer BE*

KNAPP, Harry L. (b 1863)
American editor, singer,
stage manager, actor WWM

KNAPP, Henry (fl 1780-84)
dramatist CP/2-3, TD/1-2

KNAPP, S. C. see Chester,
S. K.

KNAR, Henry see Knapp, Henry

KNAUB, Richard K. (b 1928)
American educator BE

KNEALE, Patricia (b 1925)
English actress WWT/11-16

KNEASS, Mrs. [née Sharpe]
(d 1857) singer HAS

KNEASS, Nelson (d 1869) American actor CDP, HAS

KNECHT, Karl Kae (d 1972
[88]) journalist BP/57*

KNELL, William? (fl 1580s)
actor DA, DNB

KNELLER, James (fl 1623) actor
DA

KNEPP, Mary (d 1677) English actress COC, DNB, OC/1-3

KNEVET, Ralph (fl 1631) English?
dramatist CP/1-3, FGF

KNICKERBOCKER, Paine (b 1912)
American critic BE

KNIGHT (fl 1628) actor DA

KNIGHT (fl 1633) book-keeper DA

KNIGHT, Mr. (fl 1803-09), actor,
dramatist CP/3, EA/92

KNIGHT, Mrs. (fl 1749) singer
CDP

KNIGHT, Mrs. [née Annie Manton]
(d 1876) musician EA/77*

KNIGHT, Anthony (fl 1624) musician? DA

KNIGHT, Augustine (1868-1910)
English actor GRB/1

KNIGHT, David [né Mintz] (b 1927)
American actor WWT/14-16

KNIGHT, Mrs. E. [née Eliza
Povey] (1804-61) English singer,
actress HAS

KNIGHT, Edward (fl 1624) musician? DA

KNIGHT, Edward (1774-1826) English actor BS, CDP, DNB, OX

KNIGHT, Mrs. Edward see
Knight, Susan

KNIGHT, Esmond (b 1906) English
actor, singer AAS, BE, TW/9,
WWT/7-16

KNIGHT, Frank (d 1973 [79]) actor
TW/30

KNIGHT, Fuzzy (d 1976 [74]) performer BP/60*

KNIGHT, George S. (1850-92) actor
CDP

KNIGHT, Mrs. George S. [Sophie
Worrell] (d 1917) actress CDP,
SR

KNIGHT, G. Wilson (b 1897) English educator BE

KNIGHT, H. (d 1839) English actor
HAS

KNIGHT, Mrs. H. see Da
Costa, Mrs.

KNIGHT, Irene (d 1966) performer
BP/50*

KNIGHT, John (d 1964 [64]) American actor BE*

KNIGHT, Joseph (1829-1907) English critic DNB, GRB/1-3,
OC/1-3, WWW/1

KNIGHT, Joseph Philip (d 1887
[75]) composer EA/88*

KNIGHT, Julius (1863-1941) Scottish actor GRB/3-4, WWT/1-6

KNIGHT, June [née Margaret Rose Valliquietto] (b 1911) American actress TW/2-3, WWT/8-11

KNIGHT, Lloyd (b 1922) American actor TW/8

KNIGHT, Percival (d 1923 [50]) comedian, dramatist BE*, BP/8*, WWT/14*

KNIGHT, Robert (fl 1574) actor DA

KNIGHT, Shirley (b 1937) American actress TW/22-23, 25, WWT/16

KNIGHT, Mrs. Stephen see Hind, Mrs. Thomas James

KNIGHT, Susan [Mrs. Edward Knight] (1788-1859) actress CDP

KNIGHT, Thomas (d 1820) actor, dramatist BE*, WWT/14*

KNIGHT, Thomas (1759-1838) English actor, proprietor, dramatist CDP, CP/3, DNB, GT, TD/1-2

KNIGHT, Mrs. Thomas [née Farren] (d 1804) actress TD/1-2

KNIGHT, William (b 1934) American actor TW/27-28, 30

KNIGHTLEY, Winifred Welsh singer GRB/1

KNILL, C. Edwin manager BE

KNIPE, Charles (fl 1715) dramatist CP/1-3

KNIPP, Mrs. (fl 1664-77) actress WWT/14*

KNIPSCHIELD, Edward Henry see Captain Eddie

KNITTEL, John Herman Emanuel (1891-1970) Indian/English dramatist WWW/6

KNIVETON, Mrs. actress TD/2

KNOBLAUCH [or Knoblock], Edward (1874-1945) American dramatist CB, COC, ES, MWD, NTH, OC/1-3, PDT, TW/2, WWM, WWT/1-9

KNORR, Ludwig (d 1871) actor EA/72*

KNOTT, Else (d 1975 [63]) performer BP/60*

KNOTT, Frederick English dramatist AAS, BE

KNOTT, John (d 1878 [61]) musi-

cian EA/79*

KNOTT, Roselle [Agnes Roselle] (1870-1948) Canadian actress GRB/3-4, WWM, WWS, WWT/1-4

KNOTT, W. Frederick (d 1889 [35]) EA/90*

KNOWLES, Alex (1850-1917) Scottish critic, press representative WWT/1-3

KNOWLES, Charles see Flanagan, Charles

KNOWLES, Christopher W. (d 1889 [56]) actor EA/90*

KNOWLES, David (d 1974 [27]) performer BP/59*

KNOWLES, Mrs. E. M. A. M. see Elphinstone, Emma Marian Maria

KNOWLES, Mrs. Forrest [née Annie Manners] (d 1876 [40]) actress EA/77*

KNOWLES, Frederick Milton (b 1877) American dramatist WWA/5

KNOWLES, George H. (d 1905 [32]) acting manager EA/06*

KNOWLES, James Sheridan (1784-1862) English dramatist, actor CDP, COC, DNB, ES, HAS, HP, MH, OC/1-3, SR

KNOWLES, Mrs. James Sheridan see Elphinstone, Emma Marian Maria

KNOWLES, John (d 1880 [69]) manager, lessee EA/81*, WWT/14*

KNOWLES, Nellie actress HAS

KNOWLES, Richard Brinsley (1820-82) Scottish dramatist DNB

KNOWLES, Richard George (1858-1919) Canadian variety artist CDP, COC, GRB/4, OC/1-3

KNOWLTON, Maude (fl 1900s) American actress WWS

KNOX, Alexander (b 1907) Canadian actor AAS, BE, TW/6-8, WWT/9-16

KNOX, Henry (fl 1781-84) dramatist GT

KNOX, Mabel [Mrs. Philip F. Knox] (d 1905 [25]) EA/06*

KNOX, Mrs. Philip F. see Knox, Mabel

KNUDSEN, Hans (d 1971 [84]) critic BP/55*

KNUST, Valli see Valli, Valli

KNUTSON, Wayne S. (b 1926)

American educator, director
BE

KNYVETT, Mrs. (d 1876) singer
CDP

KNYVETT, Charles, Sr. (1752-1822) musician CDP

KNYVETT, William (1779-1856)
English singer, composer
CDP, DNB

KOBART, Ruth [née Ruth Maxine
Kohn] (b 1924) American actress, singer BE, TW/22,
26, WWT/15-16

KOBBE, Gustave (b 1857) American writer WWM

KOBER, Arthur (1900-75) American dramatist, press representative, producer BE, MWD

KOBRIN, Leon (1873-1946) Rus-
sian/American dramatist ES

KOCH, Fred, Jr. (b 1911) American educator, director BE

KOCH, Frederick Henry (1877-
1944) American scholar CB,
DAB, ES, OC/1-3

KOCH, Howard dramatist CD

KOCH, Kenneth (b 1925) American dramatist, director CD

KOEHLER, Ted (d 1973 [83])
lyricist WWT/16*

KOENIG, John (1910-63) German
designer BE*, BP/47*

KOENIGSGARTEN, H. F. see
Garten, H. F.

KOERBER, Hilde (d 1969 [63])
performer BP/54*

KOERBER, Lelia see Dres-
sler, Marie

KOETTER, Paul (d 1974 [76])
performer BP/59*

KOHL, John Y. (d 1974 [79])
critic BP/59*

KOHLER, Charles (d 1888 [39])
American actor EA/89*

KOHLER, Donald American actor
TW/1

KOHLER, Estelle (b 1940) South
African actress AAS, WWT/
15-16

KOHLMAR, Lee (d 1946 [73])
actor TW/2

KOHN, Ruth Maxine see Kobart,
Ruth

KOHNER, Susan (b 1936) American actress BE, TW/14

KOLAS, Mary Lynn (b 1950)
American actress TW/28

KOLB, Clarence (d 1964 [90])

vaudevillian TW/21

KOLB, Matt B., Sr. (d 1947)
American producer, actor SR

KOLKER, Henry (1874-1947) German actor SR, TW/4, WWM,
WWT/4-9

KOLLMAR, Richard (1910-71)
American actor, manager, pro-
ducer BE, CB, TW/2, 27,
WWT/10-14

KOLTAI, Ralph (b 1924) German
designer AAS, WWT/15-16

KOMEDA, Christopher (d 1969 [36])
composer/lyricist BP/53*

KOMINSKI, Daniel see Kaye,
Danny

KOMISARJEVSKAYA, Vera Fedorovna
(1864-1910) Russian actress,
manager COC, NTH, OC/3

KOMISARJEVSKY, Theodore (1882-
1954) Russian producer, designer
AAS, COC, DNB, NTH, OC/1-3,
PDT, TW/10, WWT/6-11, WWW/
5

KONDOR, R. W. (b 1937) American
producer, business manager BE

KONER, Pauline (b 1912?) American dancer, choreographer CB

KONIG, Marie (fl 1880) German
actress CDP

KONING, Fred Wittop see Wittop,
Freddy

KONOW, Charles (d 1890) variety
proprietor EA/91*

KONSTAM, Anna (b 1914) English
actress WWT/10-11

KONSTAM, Phyllis (1907-76) English actress WWT/6-10

KONSTANTINOV, Vladimir (d 1972
[67]) producer/director/chore-
ographer BP/56*

KONTSKI, Herr (d 1879) musician
EA/80*

KOOK, Edward (b 1903) American
executive, designer of lighting
equipment BE

KOOP, Mary Jane (d 1975 [57])
performer BP/60*

KOOY, Pete (d 1963) actor BE*

KOP, Mila (d 1973 [68]) performer
BP/57*

KOPF, Jack (d 1973 [79]) costumier
BP/57*

KOPIT, Arthur (b 1937/38) Ameri-
can dramatist AAS, BE, CB,
CH, COC, ES, HJD, MD, MH,
MWD, PDT, WWT/15-16

KOPLAN, Harry (d 1973 [53]) pro-

ducer/director/choreographer
BP/57*
KOPP, Rudolph G. (d 1972 [84])
composer/lyricist BP/56*
KOPS, Bernard (b 1920/26/28)
English dramatist AAS, BE,
CD, CH, ES, MD, MWD,
PDT, WWT/15-16
KOPSKI (b 1870) English musician
GRB/1-2
KORALLI, Vera (d 1972 [81])
performer BP/57*
KORDA, Zoltan (1895-1961) Hun-
garian producer, director BE*
KORFF, Arnold (1870-1944) Aus-
trian actor SR, TW/1
KORMAN, Murray (d 1961 [59])
Russian photographer BE*,
BP/46*
KORMAN, Sey (d 1971 [60]) critic
BP/55*
KORNGOLD, Erich Wolfgang (1897-
1957) Moravian composer CB,
WWA/3
KORNMAN, Mary (d 1973 [56])
performer BP/58*
KORNZWEIG, Ben (d 1969 [59])
American press representative
BE, TW/26
KORRIE, Edith [Mrs. Ernest
Korrie] (d 1896) music-hall
performer EA/98*
KORRIE, Mrs. Ernest see
Korrie, Edith
KORRIS, Harry (d 1971 [79]) per-
former BP/56*
KORSINSKI, Mlle. M. (fl 1847)
singer HAS
KORTNER, Fritz (d 1970 [78])
performer BP/55*
KORVIN, Charles (b 1912) Hun-
garian actor, director BE,
TW/22
KOSARIN, Oscar (b 1918) Ger-
man musical director, com-
poser BE
KOSLECK, Martin (b 1914) Ger-
man actor TW/15-16
KOSLOFF, Theodore (d 1956
[74]) Russian dancer, actor
TW/13
KOSMA, Joseph (d 1969 [63])
composer/lyricist BP/54*
KOSOW, Sophia see Sidney,
Sylvia
KOSSOFF, David (b 1919) English
actor WWT/12-16
KOSTA, Tessa (b 1893) American

actress, singer WWT/5-8
KOSTELANETZ, André (b 1901)
Russian/American conductor,
musician CB
KOSTER, John (d 1895) American?
proprietor EA/96*
KOSTRESSEN, Johan (fl 1623) mu-
sician DA
KOTT, Jan (b 1914) Polish critic
CB, COC
KOTTAUN, Anny [Mrs. Celian
Kottaun] (d 1910) EA/11*
KOTTAUN, Mrs. Ceclian see
Kottaun, Anny
KOTTAUN, Mrs. M. M. [Mrs.
Thomas Kottaun] (d 1888) EA/
89*
KOTTAUN, Thomas (d 1885 [57])
musician EA/86*
KOTTAUN, Mrs. Thomas see
Kottaun, Mrs. M. M.
KOTTO, Yaphet (b 1937) American
actor TW/22, 26
KOTZEBUE, August Friedrich
Ferdinand (1761-1819) German
dramatist COC, OC/1-3, SR
KOUN, Karolos (b 1908) Greek
director COC, WWT/14
KOURKOULOS, Nikos (b 1934)
Greek actor TW/23-24
KOUTOUKAS, H. M. Greek/Ameri-
can dramatist, director CD
KOVACS, Ernie (1919-62) American
comedian CB
KOVAL, Francis W. (d 1971 [62])
critic BP/55*
KOVAL, Rene (d 1936 [50]) actor,
singer BE*, WWT/14*
KOVE, Kenneth [John William
Stevenson Bridgewater] (b 1893)
English actor WWT/7-10
KOVENS, Edward (b 1934) Ameri-
can actor TW/27, 29
KOWAL, Mitchell (d 1971 [56])
performer BP/56*
KOZELKA, Paul (b 1909) American
educator BE
KRABER, Karl (b 1935) American
actor TW/25
KRAFFT, John (fl 1579-80) actor
DA
KRAFT, Beatrice American actress
TW/1
KRAFT, Gil (b 1926) American
publisher BE
KRAFT, Hy (1899-1975) American
dramatist BE
KRAFT, Jill (1930-70) American

actress BE, TW/27

KRAFT, Leonard (b 1932) American executive BE

KRAFT, Martin (b 1919) American actor TW/2

KRAKOWER, Arnold (d 1969 [53]) lawyer BP/53*

KRAMER, Amelia (d 1905 [66]) EA/06*

KRAMER, A. Walter (d 1969 [79]) composer/lyricist BP/53*

KRAMER, Joel (b 1943) American actor TW/30

KRAMER, John (b 1938) American actor TW/25-26

KRAMER, Lawrence (d 1975 [66]) performer BP/60*

KRAMER, Lloyd (b 1947) American actor TW/26-27

KRAMER, Marsha (b 1945) American actress TW/29

KRAMER, Phil (d 1972 [72]) performer BP/56*

KRAMER, Wright (d 1941 [71]) American actor BE*, BP/26*, WWT/14*

KRAMM, Joseph (b 1907/08) American dramatist, director, actor BE, CB, HJD, MD, MWD, WWT/12-16

KRANSKE, Violet [Mrs. Ambrose Thorne] (d 1897 [28]) EA/98*

KRANTZ, Milton (b 1912) American executive BE

KRAPP, Herbert J. (d 1973 [86]) architect BP/57*

KRASNA, Norman (b 1909) American dramatist BE, CB, MH, WWT/11-16

KRATOCHVIL, Frantisek (b 1934) Czech actor TW/23

KRATON, Harry (d 1912 [30]) music-hall performer EA/13*

KRATZ, Karl L. (d 1974 [74]) critic BP/59*

KRAUS, Philip (b 1949) American actor TW/29

KRAUS, Ted M. (b 1923) American publisher, editor BE

KRAUSS, Ruth (b 1911) American dramatist CD

KRAUSS, Werner (1884-1959) German actor OC/3, TW/16, WWT/8-11

KRAWFORD, Gary (b 1941) American actor TW/24, 27, 29

KRAWITZ, Seymour (b 1923)

American press representative BE

KRELLING, Joseph (1855-87) proprietor, manager NYM

KREMBSER, Frangott (d 1889 [55]) circus director EA/90*

KREMER, Theodore (b 1873) German dramatist GRB/3-4, WWT/1-2

KRESS, Gladys (d 1969 [67]) performer BP/54*

KRESSEN, Samuel (b 1918) American actor TW/24

KRETLOW, Arthur (d 1968 [73]) producer/director/choreographer BP/53*

KRETZMER, Herbert (b 1925) South African critic, dramatist WWT/15-16

KREUTZER, Leon (d 1868) composer EA/69*

KREYMBORG, Alfred (1883-1966) American dramatist HJD

KRIEGER, Lee (1919-67) American actor TW/4-5, 24

KRIEGER, Lester (d 1975 [71]) executive BP/59*

KRIMSKY, John (b 1906) American producer BE

KRIPS, Josef (1902-74) Austrian conductor CB

KRISS, Fred (d 1964 [76]) magician BE*

KRISTEN, Erik (b 1921) Danish actor TW/4

KRISTEV, George (d 1974 [32]) performer BP/59*

KRISTIN, Karen (b 1939) American actress TW/25

KRITZ, Karl (d 1969) conductor WWA/5

KRIZA, John (1919-75) Czech/American dancer ES

KRIZMAN, Lynne Allen (d 1972 [48]) performer BP/57*

KROEGER, Berry (b 1912) American actor TW/2-3, 7-8

KROLL, Lucy American literary & talent representative BE

KROLLMAN, Gustave (d 1857) musician HAS

KRONE, Gerald (b 1933) American producer, director, actor BE

KRONEMANN, Ludwig (d 1899) acrobat EA/00*

KRONENBERGER, Louis (b 1904) American critic BE, CB, HJD, NTH, WWT/10-16

KROSCHELL, Joan American actress TW/22, 25

KROSS, Ronald (b 1936) American actor TW/25-28

KROT, William (d 1971 [45]) stage manager TW/28

KRUEGER, Bum (d 1971 [65]) performer BP/55*

KRUEGER, Emmy (d 1976 [89]) performer BP/60*

KRUG, Karl (d 1963 [65]) critic BP/48*

KRUGER, Alma (d 1960 [88]) American actress GRB/3-4, TW/16, WWT/1-10

KRUGER, Annie [Mlle. Coradini] German/American actress HAS

KRUGER, Daniel D. (b 1942) American actor TW/30

KRUGER, Fred H. (d 1961 [48]) actor BE*

KRUGER, Hardy (b 1928) German actor TW/22

KRUGER, Hugo German actor, singer CDP

KRUGER, Jaques (d 1910 [69]) actor CDP

KRUGER, Ottilie (b 1926) American actress TW/2-3, 5

KRUGER, Otto (1885-1974) American actor BE, TW/2-7, WWT/4-11

KRUMSCHMIDT, E. A. (b 1904) German actor TW/3-4

KRUPSKA, Dania (b 1923) American dancer, choreographer BE, WWT/15-16

KRUSCHEN, Jack (b 1922) Canadian actor BE, TW/18

KRUTCH, Joseph Wood (1893-1970) American critic BE, CB, COC, ES, HJD, NTH, OC/1-3, WWA/5, WWT/10-14

KUBIAK, Thomas J. (b 1936) American actor TW/26, 30

KUGELL, Joan see Darling, Joan

KUGELMANN, Georges see Benda, Georges K.

KUHL, H. Calvin (d 1973 [66]) producer/director/choreographer BP/58*

KUHN, Sophie Gimber (1838-67) English actress HAS

KUHNER, John (b 1942) American actor TW/24, 26-29

KULUKUNDIS, Eddie (b 1932) English producing manager WWT/15-16

KULUVA, Will (b 1917) American actor TW/7-9, 15

KUMARI, Meena (d 1972 [40]) performer BP/56*

KUMMER, Clare [Clare Rodman Beecher] (d 1958 [85]) American dramatist HJD, SR, WWT/4-12

KUMMER, Frederic Arnold (1873-1943) American dramatist WWT/5-9

KUN, Magda (1912-45) Hungarian actress WWT/8-9

KUNKEL, George (d 1885 [62]) actor, manager CDP

KUNKEL, Jacob composer, publisher CDP

KUNNEKE, Eduard (b 1885) composer WWT/6-9

KUNZ, Raoul de Dreux (d 1906 [37]) EA/07*

KUPCINET, Karyn (d 1963 [22]) performer BP/48*

KUPPERMAN, Alvin (b 1945) American actor TW/26-28

KURENKO, Maria Russian singer CB

KURKAMP, John (d 1914) American actor SR

KURNITZ, Harry (1908-68) American dramatist BE

KURNITZ, Julie (b 1942) American actress TW/30

KURT, Melanie (1880-1941) Austrian singer ES

KURTON, Peggy actress, singer WWT/4-7

KURTY, Hella (d 1954 [48]) Austrian actress, singer WWT/8-10

KURTZ, Efrem (b 1900) Russian conductor CB

KURTZ, Marcia Jean American actress TW/29

KURTZ, Swoosie (b 1944) American actress TW/25-28

KURZ, Laura singer CDP

KURZ, Selma (1874-1933) Austrian singer ES

KUSCHER, Marion North (d 1971 [54]) performer BP/56*

KUSELL, Mrs. Harold (d 1971 [68]) performer BP/55*

KUSS, Richard (b 1927) American actor TW/29

KUSSACK, Elaine American actress TW/26-29

KYASHT, Lydia (1886-1959) Russian

dancer ES, WWT/4-11
KYD, Thomas (1558-94) English
dramatist COC, CP/1-3,
DNB, ES, FGF, HP, MH,
NTH, OC/1-3, PDT, RE
KYDD, Samuel (d 1892 [78])
lawyer EA/94*
KYFFIN, Maurice (fl 1588) trans-
lator CP/1-3
KYLE, Edward musician CDP
KYLE, Howard [Howard Anderson
Vandergrift] (1861-1950) Amer-
ican actor TW/7, WWM
KYNASTON, Edward (c. 1640-
1706) English actor CDP,
DNB, OC/1-3
KYNDER, Philip dramatist FGF
KYRLE, Judith (d 1922) actress
BE*, WWT/14*

- L -

L., G. (fl 1778) dramatist CP/3
LABAN, Rudolf von (1879-1958)
Hungarian choreographer,
dancer ES
LABATE, Bruno (d 1968 [85])
composer/lyricist BP/53*
LaBELLE, Rupert (d 1972
[72]) performer BP/57*
LABICHE, Eugène (1815-88)
French dramatist COC, NTH,
OC/1-3
LABIS, Attilio (b 1936) French
dancer, choreographer ES
LABLACHE, Fanny (d 1897)
singer WWT/14*
LABLACHE, Fanny Rose Louise
(d 1885) EA/86*
LABLACHE, Frederick (1815-87)
singer DNB
LABLACHE, Louise (fl 1886)
singer CDP
LABLACHE, Luigi (1794-1858)
Italian singer CDP, DNB, ES
LABLACHE, Luigi (d 1914 [64])
actor DP, GRB/3-4, WWT/
1-2
LABLANCHE, Bianca see Daven-
port, Blanche
LABOCHETTA, Sig. D. (fl 1857)
singer CDP
LABORDE, Mons. (fl 1848)
singer HAS
LABORDE, Mme. (fl 1848) singer
HAS
LABOUCHERE, Henry (d 1912

[81]) producer, manager BE*,
WWT/14*
LABOUCHERE, Mrs. Henry see
Hodson, Henrietta
LABOUSE, Charles (d 1889) Amer-
ican aeronaut EA/90*
LABROCA, Mario (d 1973 [76])
composer/lyricist BP/58*
LABURNUM, Walter singer, song-
writer CDP
LACEBY, Arthur (b 1879) English
actor WWM
LACEY, Catherine (b 1904) English
actress AAS, WWT/8-16
LACEY, Charles (d 1909) EA/11*
LACEY, Franklin (b 1917) Canadian
dramatist, lyricist BE
LACEY, Fred (d 1904 [39]) music-
hall performer EA/05*
LACEY, George (d 1896) comic
singer EA/97*
LACEY, Henry see Lacy, Henry
LACEY, Marion (d 1915 [95]) ac-
tress BE*, WWT/14*
LACEY, Paul see Godfrey,
Charles
LACEY, Willoughby (fl 1774-1801)
proprietor GT, TD/1-2
LACHMAN, Harry (d 1975 [88])
producer/director/choreographer
BP/59*
LACHNER, Ignaz (d 1895 [87])
composer, musician EA/96*
LACK, Simon [né Macalpine] (b
1917) Scottish actor WWT/12-16
LACKAYE, Helene [Mrs. H. J.
Ridings] (b 1883) American ac-
tress WWM
LACKAYE, James (1867-1919)
American actor SR
LACKAYE, Wilton (1862-1932)
American actor COC, DAB,
GRB/2-4, OC/1-3, PP/2, SR,
WWA/1, WWS, WWT/1-6
LACKET, Dr. John see Hacket,
Dr. John
LACKEY, Kenneth (d 1976 [74])
performer BP/60*
LACOMBE, Mrs. see Allen,
Clarissa
LA COMPTE, Mons. (fl 1840)
dancer HAS
LA COMPTE, Mme. (fl 1838)
dancer HAS
LA COOMB, Mrs. see Allen,
Clarissa
LACOSTE, Anna (1848-68) Amer-
ican actress, reader HAS

LACY, Mr. (fl 1850) actor HAS

LACY, Mrs. (fl 1850) actress HAS

LACY, Miss (fl 1822) actress BS

LACY, Ernest (1863-1916) American dramatist DAB, HJD

LACY, Frances see Cooper, Frances

LACY, Frank (b 1842) English actor, aeronaut, dancer, tightrope dancer HAS

LACY, Frank (d 1870 [28]) harlequin EA/71*

LACY, Frank (1867-1937) English actor GRB/1-4, WWM, WWT/1-7

LACY, George (b 1904) English actor WWT/10

LACY, Harriette Deborah (1807-74) English actress DNB

LACY, Henry (fl 1586) dramatist CP/3, FGF

LACY, James (1696-1774) patentee CDP

LACY, Jerry (b 1936) American actor TW/25-26

LACY, John (1622-81) English actor, dramatist, dancing master CDP, COC, CP/1-3, DA, DNB, GT, NTH, OC/1-3

LACY, Mrs. John see Bianchi, Mrs. Francesco

LACY, Maria Anne see Lovell, Maria Anne

LACY, Michael Rophino (1795-1867) Spanish musician, composer, actor CDP, DNB, SR

LACY, Robin T. (b 1920) American educator, scene designer BE

LACY, Rophino see Lacy, Michael Rophino

LACY, Sara see Roberts, Sara

LACY, Sarah (d 1868) EA/69*

LACY, Mrs. Sidney see Stalman, Julia

LACY, Thomas Haines (1809-73) actor, dramatist, publisher DNB, SR

LACY, Mrs. Thomas Haines see Cooper, Frances

LACY, Tom (b 1933) American actor TW/23-26, 28-30

LACY, Walter (1809-98) actor CDP, DNB, OAA/2

LACY, Mrs. Walter (d 1874 [67]) actress EA/75*, WWT/14*

LACY, William (1788-1871) singer DNB

LACY, Willoughby (d 1831 [62]) actor, manager WWT/14*

LADD, Alan (1913-64) American actor WWA/4

LADD, Hank American actor TW/4-5, 23

LADD, Margaret (b 1942) American actress TW/22-23, 26

LAFAYETTE [Sigmund Neuburger] (d 1911 [38]) German illusionist SR

LA FEUILLADE, Sarah Elizabeth (d 1887) EA/88*

LAFFAN, Kevin Barry (b 1922) English dramatist CD, WWT/15-16

LAFFAN, Patricia (b 1919) English actress WWT/10-15

LAFFAN, Mrs. Robert Stuart de Courcy (d 1912) English dramatist WWW/1

LAFFAR, Mrs. (d 1885 [73]) EA/87*

LAFFAR, Mrs. William (d 1871) EA/72*

LAFFAR, William Joseph (d 1900 [65]) scene artist EA/01*

LAFFERTY, Wilson (d 1962) performer BE*

LAFFIN, Charles (b 1922) American actor TW/2

LA FOLLE, Mrs. [Mrs. Placide; née Pownall] (d 1823) actress HAS

LA FOLLETTE, Fola (1882-1970) American actress BE, TW/26, WWA/5

LA FOND, Florence (b 1845) American actress HAS

LAFONTAINE, Anna [Mrs. John Lafontaine] (d 1890) EA/91*

LAFONTAINE, Mrs. John see Lafontaine, Anna

LA FORREST, Mr. (fl 1823-30) American actor, circus performer HAS

LA FORREST, Mrs. [Sophia Eberle] (fl 1824) American actress HAS

LA FORREST, Sophia (d 1888 [76]) American actress EA/89*

LAGERFELT, Carolyn French actress TW/27, 29

LAGIER, Suzanne (1833-93) French actress, singer ES

LAGIOIA, John P. (b 1937) Amer-

ican actor TW/26-27
LAGRANGE, Anne-Caroline de
(1824-1905) French singer
ES
LAGRANGE, Felix (d 1901 [75])
actor BE*, WWT/14*
LAGUERRE, John (d 1748) Eng-
lish scene painter, actor DNB
LA HIFF, Ann see Carroll,
Nancy
LAHR, Bert [Irving Lahrheim]
(1895-1967) American actor
AAS, BE, CB, COC, TW/1-
21, 24, WWA/4, WWT/7-14
LAHR, John (b 1941) American
critic WWT/16
LAHR, Mercedes (d 1965 [67])
performer BP/49*
LAHRHEIM, Irving see Lahr,
Bert
LAHTINEN, Warner H. (d 1968
[58]) performer BP/53*
LAIDLAW, Alexander Hamilton,
Jr. (1869-1908) American
dramatist WWA/1
LAIDLAW, Clara see Lloyd,
Clara
LAIDLAW, Louise (d 1871) ac-
tress WWT/14*
LAIDLAW, Louise Caroline
see Weston, Louise Caroline
LAIDLER, Francis (1870-1955)
English manager WWT/8-11
LAIDMAN, C. H. (d 1874) ac-
tor? EA/75*
LAINE, Vicki (d 1972 [41]) per-
former BP/56*
LAING, Alexander (d 1873 [28])
musician EA/74*
LAING, Hugh (b 1914) West In-
dian dancer CB, ES
LAING, Peggy (b 1899) English
press representative WWT/9
LAIRD, Gus (b 1881) English
actor, singer GRB/1
LAIRD, Jenny (b 1917) English
actress TW/26, WWT/10-16
LAIRD, Landon (d 1970 [75])
critic BP/55*
LAIRE, Judson actor TW/1, 15
LAISON (fl 1796) circus manager,
equestrian HAS
LAIT, Jack (1883-1954) American
critic BE*, BP/38*
LAIT, Sarah (d 1917 [68]) EA/18*
LAKE, Mr. (fl 1785) actor HAS
LAKE, Charles H. F. (d 1905
[18]) EA/06*

LAKE, Emma (d 1911) circus per-
former CDP, SR
LAKE, Ethel Mae (d 1975 [73])
actress, singer BP/59*, WWT/
16*
LAKE, Fanny [Mrs. J. Lake, Sr.]
(d 1876 [52]) EA/78*
LAKE, Harriette see Sothern,
Anne
LAKE, Mrs. J., Sr. see Lake,
Fanny
LAKE, Lew (d 1939 [65]) perform-
er, producer BE*, WWT/14*
LAKE, Samuel (d 1859) English
dancer, pantomimist, actor
HAS
LAKE, Sue (d 1970) performer
BP/55*
LAKE, Veronica (d 1973 [53]) ac-
tress BP/58*, WWT/16*
LAKE, William (1835-69) circus
performer & manager SR
LAKOMSKA, Sylvia Jadviga see
Daneel, Sylvia
LaKOTA, Jewel (d 1968 [60]) per-
former BP/52*
LALLY, Gwen (d 1963 [81]) Eng-
lish actress, producer, pageant
master WWT/8-9, WWW/6
LALO, Louise Dorothy [Mrs.
Charles Best] (d 1905 [35])
EA/06*
LALOR, Frank (1869-1932) Amer-
ican actor WWT/4-6
LA MAMA EXPERIMENTAL THE-
ATRE CLUB theatre collective
CD
LAMAREUX, Augusta (b 1845)
American dancer, actress HAS
LAMAREUX, Edith (d 1868) music-
hall performer HAS
LA MARR, Barbara (d 1926 [30])
actress BE*
LA MARR, Harry (fl 1887?) sing-
er, songwriter CDP
LAMAS, Fernando (b 1920/23)
Argentinian actor, director BE,
TW/13
LAMASH, Philip (d 1800) actor
TD/1-2
LAMB, Alexander (d 1871) come-
dian EA/73*
LAMB, Beatrice (b 1866) actress
CDP, EA/95, GRB/3-4, WWT/
1-5
LAMB, Charles (1775-1834) Eng-
lish critic, dramatist COC,
CP/3, DNB, ES, HP, NTH,

OC/1-3

LAMB, Edward (1829-87) American actor CDP, HAS, NYM

LAMB, Florence (d 1966 [82]) performer BP/50*

LAMB, Frank E. (d 1918) actor, director SR

LAMB, George (1784-1834) dramatist DNB

LAMB, Mr. H. (d 1869 [88]) president of the Dover Catch Club EA/70*

LAMB, Henry (d 1888 [77]) music-hall performer? EA/89*

LAMB, Shirley (b 1939) American actress TW/30

LAMB, Sybil (b 1932) American actress TW/14

LAMB, T. (d 1875) pantomimist EA/76*

LAMB, Thomas see Melrose, Tom

LAMBART, Ernest (d 1945 [71]) Irish actor, singer BE*, BP/30*, WWT/14*

LAMBART, Ernest O. C. (1876-1924) English actor SR

LAMBART, Richard (d 1924) actor BE*, WWT/14*

LAMBART, Mrs. Richard F. L. see Spencer-Brunton, Enid

LAMBDIN, John O. (d 1923 [50]) critic BE*, BP/7*

LAMBE, George (fl 1807) dramatist CP/3

LAMBELET, Napoleon (1864-1932) composer, musical director WWT/4-6

LAMBERT, Mr. (b 1816) English actor HAS

LAMBERT, Mrs. (fl 1838-41) English? actress HAS

LAMBERT, Barrowdale (fl 1747) dramatist CP/2-3, GT

LAMBERT, Charles Edward (d 1910) EA/11*

LAMBERT, Constant (1905-51) English composer, conductor, critic DNB, ES, WWT/8-11, WWW/5

LAMBERT, Daniel (1770-1809) fat man CDP

LAMBERT, Daniel, Jr. fat giant CDP

LAMBERT, David (d 1873) singer EA/74*

LAMBERT, E. A. [Mrs. Fal-

coner] (d 1901) singer EA/02*

LAMBERT, Edward see Stirling, Edward

LAMBERT, George (1710-65) English scene designer & painter ES

LAMBERT, Harry (d 1879 [38]) Negro comedian EA/80*

LAMBERT, H. S. (d 1935 [68]) treasurer WWT/14*

LAMBERT, Hugh choreographer, dancer BE

LAMBERT, Jack (b 1899) Scottish actor WWT/8-16

LAMBERT, James (d 1880) Negro comedian EA/81*

LAMBERT, John (d 1871 [56]) proprietor EA/72*

LAMBERT, J. W. (b 1917) English critic WWT/14-16

LAMBERT, Lawson (1870-1944) Indian/English business manager GRB/1-3, WWT/6-9

LAMBERT, Louie [Mrs. Walter Lambert] (d 1902) EA/03*

LAMBERT, Mabel [Mrs. John Terry] American actress GRB/1-2

LAMBERT, Richard (b 1870) Irish manager, press representative WWM

LAMBERT, Sammy (b 1907) Russian/American producer TW/4-8

LAMBERT, Spencer (d 1872 [45]) treasurer EA/73*

LAMBERT, Mrs. Walter see Lambert, Louie

LAMBERTI, Prof. (d 1950 [58]) comedian TW/6

LAMBLE, T. B. (d 1917) EA/18*

LAMBORN, Amy English actress GRB/1-2

LAMBOURNE, Harry (d 1891 [31]) musician EA/92*

LAMER, Mrs. (d 1851) HAS

LA MERI (b 1903) American dancer, choreographer ES

LAMOND, Stella (d 1973 [62]) performer BP/58*

LAMONT, Forrest (1885-1937) Canadian singer WWA/1

LAMONT, Robin (b 1950) American actor TW/27-30

LAMOS, Mark (b 1946) American actor TW/28-29

LaMOTTA, Johnny (b 1939) American actor TW/24-26, 28

LAMOURET, Robert (1916-59) French performer ES

LAMOUREUX, Louise (fl 1857) dancer CDP

LAMPARD, Edward James (d 1896 [34]) EA/97*

LAMPE, Gus (d 1975 [74]) producer/director/choreographer BP/60*

LAMPE, Isabella (d 1795) singer, actress WWT/14*

LAMPE, John Frederick (1703?-51) German? composer DNB

LAMPELL, Millard (b 1919) American dramatist BE

LAMPERT, Zohra (b 1936) American actress BE, TW/14, 18-20, 22-23, 25-26, 28

LAMSLEY (d 1891) conductor EA/92*

LAMSON, Ernest (d 1908) American actor, dramatist WWS

LAMSON, Gardner American singer WWM

LAMSON, Gertrude see O'Neill, Nance

LAMY, Marcel (d 1970 [52]) producer/director/choreographer BP/55*

LAN, David (b 1952) South African dramatist CD

LANA, Agustin (d 1970 [70]) composer/lyricist BP/55*

LANAGAN, Michael J. (d 1879 [45]) American actress EA/80*

LANCASHIRE BELL RINGERS (fl 1850) HAS

LANCASTER, Ann (d 1970 [50]) performer BP/55*

LANCASTER, Burt (b 1913) American actor, vaudevillian, acrobat CB, ES, TW/2-3

LANCASTER, Henry John (d 1892 [72]) scene artist EA/93*

LANCASTER, John (d 1896) manager, proprietor EA/97*, WWT/14*

LANCASTER, John (d 1970 [67]) performer BP/54*

LANCASTER, Lucie (b 1907) American actress TW/24, 26-27, 29-30

LANCASTER, Nora (b 1877/82) English actress GRB/1-4, WWT/1-5

LANCASTER, Sylvester (fl 1640) actor DA

LANCASTER, William (d 1889)

EA/90*

LANCASTER-WALLIS, Ellen (d 1940 [86]) actress, producer, manager BE*, WWT/14*

LANCE, Leon O. (d 1973 [76]) agent BP/58*

LANCHESTER, Elsa (b 1902) English actress BE, CB, ES, NTH, WWT/6-11

LANCHESTER, Robert (b 1941) American actor TW/26-27, 30

LAND, Charles (d 1883 [28]) EA/84*

LAND, Robert E. (b 1948) Canadian actor TW/26

LANDAU, David (d 1935 [57]) American actor WWT/7

LANDAU, Jack (1925-67) American director, producer, designer BE, TW/23

LANDAU, Marty W. (d 1973 [74]) artists' manager BP/57*

LANDEAU, Cecil (b 1906) actor, producing manager WWT/11-13

LANDECK, Ben (1864-1928) English dramatist WWT/4-5

LANDEN, Dinsdale (b 1932) English actor WWT/15-16

LANDER, Charles Oram (1866-1934) English actor GRB/2-4

LANDER, Mrs. Frederick W. see Lander, Jean Margaret Davenport

LANDER, Harald (d 1972 [66]) producer/director/choreographer BP/56*

LANDER, Jean Margaret Davenport (1829-1903) English actress CDP, COC, DAB, HAS, OC/1-3, PP/2, WWA/1

LANDESMAN, Jay (b 1919) American producer, dramatist BE

LANDI, Elissa (1904-48) Italian actress ES, SR, TW/1, 5, WWT/6-10

LANDI, Erberto (d 1971 [63]) producer, publicist BP/56*

LANDICK, Olin (d 1972 [77]) performer BP/56*

LANDIN, Hope (d 1973 [80]) actress BP/57*, WWT/16*

LANDIS, Carole (1919-48) American actress TW/1, 5

LANDIS, Cullen (d 1975 [79]) performer BP/60*

LANDIS, Jeanette English actress TW/28

LANDIS, Jessie Royce (1900/04-

72) American actress BE,
TW/1-15, 21, 24, 28, WWA/
5, WWT/7-15

LANDIS, Joe (d 1966) performer
BP/51*

LANDIS, John (d 1863) minstrel
HAS

LANDIS, William (b 1921) American producer, actor, director
BE

LANDON, Avice (1908/10-76) Indian/English actress AAS,
WWT/10-16

LANDRETH, Gertrude Griffith
(d 1969 [72]) performer BP/
54*

LANDSMAN, Jenny (fl 1866-67)
Hungarian/American singer
HAS

LANDSTONE, Charles (b 1891/
97) Austrian business manager, dramatist, administrator
WWT/7-15

LANDWEST, Tom (d 1878 [26])
Negro comedian EA/79*

LANE, Alfred (d 1881) actor?
EA/82*

LANE, Allan (d 1973 [64]) performer BP/57*

LANE, Burton [né Burton Levy]
(b 1912) American composer
BE, CB, WWT/15-16

LANE, Clara [Mrs. J. K. Murray] (fl 1884-95) American
actress, singer WWS

LANE, Dorothy (b 1889/90)
English actress WWT/4-11

LANE, Genette (b 1940) American actress TW/27

LANE, Grace [Mrs. Kenneth
Douglas] (1876-1956) actress
GRB/1-2, 4, WWT/1-11

LANE, Horace English actor
GRB/2

LANE, Jane (d 1882 [78]) EA/
83*

LANE, Jane [Jenny Elton; Mrs.
W. E. Lane] (d 1883) actress?
EA/84*

LANE, Louisa see Drew, Mrs.
John

LANE, Lucie (d 1901 [20]) burlesque actress EA/02*

LANE, Lupino (1892-1959) English actor, dancer, manager
AAS, COC, DNB, ES, OC/
1-3, TW/16, WWT/4-12,
WWW/5

LANE, Montague (b 1882) English
actor GRB/1

LANE, Pete (d 1858) jig dancer
HAS

LANE, Rosemary (d 1974 [64])
performer BP/59*

LANE, Russell (d 1918) EA/19*

LANE, Rusty (b 1899) American
actor, educator TW/3-6, 11-12

LANE, Sam (1804-71) manager
COC

LANE, Sara (1823-99) English actress, manager CDP, COC,
OC/2-3

LANE, Sherry (d 1974 [55]) performer BP/59*

LANE, Sylvia (b 1934) American
actress TW/3

LANE, Mrs. W. E. see Lane,
Jane

LANE, Willie (b 1879) English actor GRB/1

LANEHAM, John (fl 1572-91) actor
DA

LANERGAN, James W. (1828-86)
actor CDP

LAN-FANG, Mei see Mei Lan-Fang

LANFIELD, Sidney (d 1972 [74])
performer BP/57*

LANG, Alois (d 1971 [80]) performer BP/56*

LANG, Benjamin Johnson (1837-
1909) American conductor, composer DAB

LANG, Charles (b 1915) American
actor TW/1-6

LANG, Doreen (b 1918) New Zealand actress TW/6-8

LANG, Eva Clara (d 1933 [48])
American actress BE*

LANG, Gertrude (d 1941 [42])
performer BE*

LANG, Gertrude (d 1942) actress
BE*, WWT/14*

LANG, Gertrude (d 1971 [73]) performer BP/56*

LANG, Harold (d 1970) performer
BP/55*

LANG, Harold (b 1920/23) American dancer, actor, singer BE,
TW/2-3, 5-16, 18, 21, WWT/
14-16

LANG, Harry (d 1953 [58]) actor
BE*, WWT/14*

LANG, Howard (d 1941 [65]) actor
WWT/7-8

LANG, Ione (fl 1873?) singer CDP

LANG, Jimmy (d 1970) performer BP/55*

LANG, Matheson (1879-1948) Canadian actor, manager, dramatist AAS, COC, DNB, ES, GRB/1-4, NTH, OC/1-3, PDT, TW/4, WWT/1-10, WWW/4

LANG, Mrs. Matheson see Britton, Hutin

LANG, Pearl (b 1922/25) American choreographer, dancer, educator BE, CB, TW/6

LANG, Peter (d 1932 [73]) actor, singer BE*, BP/17*

LANG, Philip J. (b 1911) American composer, educator, musician BE

LANG, Robert (b 1934) English actor, director AAS, WWT/15-16

LANGAN, Glenn (b 1917) American actor TW/5-9

LANGBAINE, Garard (d 1692 [35]) historian WWT/14*

LANGDON, George C. (d 1859) HAS

LANGDON, Harry (1884-1944) American actor, vaudevillian CB, DAB, ES, SR, TW/1

LANGDON, Henry A. (fl 1849-57) American actor HAS

LANGDON, Mrs. Henry A., I [Emily Rosalie Reed] (1832-57) American dancer, singer, actress HAS

LANGDON, Mrs. Henry A., II [Annie Senter] (1836-67) American actress HAS

LANGDON, Sue Ann American actress TW/24

LANGE, Barbara Pearson (b 1910) American educator BE

LANGE, Mary (d 1973 [60]) actress TW/29

LANGE, Sven (d 1930 [62]) dramatist BE*, WWT/14*

LANGELLA, Frank (b 1940) American actor TW/22-23, 25-26, WWT/16

LANGER, Anton (d 1879 [56]) dramatist EA/81*

LANGFORD, Abraham (1711-74) English dramatist CP/1-3, DNB, GT, TD/1-2

LANGFORD, Joseph Munt (d 1884 [75]) dramatist, critic EA/85*

LANGFORD, William (d 1955 [35]) Canadian actor BE*, BP/40*

LANGHAM, Michael (b 1919) English director AAS, BE, CB, WWT/13-16

LANGHAM, Mrs. W. Clement see Langham, Winnifred

LANGHAM, Winnifred [Mrs. W. Clement Langham] (d 1917) EA/18*

LANGHANS, Edward A. (b 1923) American director, designer, historian, educator BE

LANGHORNE, John (d 1779) English dramatist CP/2-3, GT

LANGLEY, Charles [George Budd] (d 1911) actor EA/12*

LANGLEY, Francis (d 1601) theatre builder DA

LANGLEY, Frank (d 1879) American actor EA/80*

LANGLEY, Georgianna (b 1845) American actress, dancer HAS

LANGLEY, Kate (d 1886) actress EA/87*

LANGLEY, Noel (b 1911) South African dramatist AAS, BE, WWT/8-15

LANGLEY, Stuart (d 1970 [60]) actor, singer TW/26

LANGLEY, Mrs. Will (d 1897 [53]) music-hall performer EA/98*

LANGLEY, William (d 1849) circus performer HAS

LANGLOIS, Caroline [Lottie Ellis; Mrs. H. A. Langlois] (d 1882 [30]) EA/83*

LANGLOIS, Mrs. H. A. see Langlois, Caroline

LANGNER, Herbert B. (d 1965 [73]) patron BP/50*

LANGNER, Lawrence (1890-1962) Welsh/American dramatist, director CB, COC, ES, MWD, NTH, OC/3, TW/2-8, 19, WWT/6-13

LANGNER, Philip (b 1926) American producer BE, WWT/16

LANGRISH, John S. (1830-95) Irish actor, manager SR

LANGSTAFFE, Arthur (d 1904) musical director EA/05*

LANGTON, Basil C. (b 1912) English actor, manager, producer TW/24, WWT/10-11

LANGTON, Fred (d 1903 [31])

variety comedian EA/04*

LANGTON, J. D. (d 1918 [60])
EA/19*

LANGTON, Polly (d 1896) music-
hall performer EA/98*

LANGTRY, Edward (d 1897)
EA/98*

LANGTRY, Lily [or Lillie;
Lady de Bathe] (1852-1929)
English actress CDP, COC,
DP, ES, GRB/1-4, HP, NTH,
OC/1-3, PDT, WWA/2, WWS,
WWT/1-5

LANGTRY, Paul [John Dunlop]
(d 1903 [32]) Negro comedian
EA/05*

LANIER, Nicholas (1588-1666)
English composer DNB

LANIER, Thomas see Williams,
Tennessee

LANING, Robert E. (d 1974
[56]) dramatist BP/59*

LANNER, Katti (1831-1908) Austrian dancer CDP, ES, GRB/
1-4

LANNIER, Minnie (fl 1866) actress HAS

LANNING, Jerry (b 1943) American actor TW/23-24, 28-30

LANPHIER, James F. (d 1969
[48]) actor TW/25

LANSBURY, Angela (b 1925)
English actress AAS, BE,
CB, TW/20, 22-26, WWT/15-16

LANSBURY, Edgar (b 1930) English producer, designer BE,
WWT/15-16

LANSCAR, Christine (d 1907
[22]) performer? EA/08*

LANSDALE, Harry Nelson (d
1964 [49]) critic BP/49*

LANSDOWN, Lord see Gran-
ville, George

LANSING, Mr. (fl 1831) actor
HAS

LANSING, Loi (d 1972 [37]) performer BP/57*

LANSING, Robert American actor
BE, TW/29-30

LANTEAU, William (b 1922)
American actor TW/8, 13-
14

LANTZ, Robert (b 1914) German/
American literary & talent
representative, producer,
dramatist BE

LAPARCERIE, Cora [Mme. La-
parcerie-Richepin] French

actress GRB/1, 3-4, WWT/1-3

LAPARCERIE-RICHEPIN, Mme.
see Laparcerie, Cora

LA PLANTE, Laura (b 1904) American actress WWT/8

LAPOINTE, Doris Lilian (d 1917
[19]) EA/18*

LAPORTE, Mons. (fl 1827) actor
CDP

LAPORTE, Miss (d 1880) actress
EA/81*

LAPOTAIRE, Jane (b 1944) English
actress WWT/16

LA PRADE, Ernest (d 1969 [79])
performer BP/53*

LARABEE, Louise American actress TW/9, 22-23

LARDNER, Ring (1885-1933) American dramatist NTH, PDT, SR

LARGAY, Raymond J. (d 1974
[88]) performer BP/59*

LARIMORE, Earle (1899-1947)
American actor TW/4, WWT/7-
10

LARK, Kingsley (d 1948 [58]) actor,
singer WWT/14*

LARKELLE, Lillie [Elizabeth
Eayrs Collins] (d 1898 [26])
burlesque actress EA/99*

LARKELLE, Nellie (fl 1ο77) actress CDP

LARKIN, Bob (b 1929) American
actor TW/26

LARKIN, John (d 1965) dramatist
BP/49*

LARKIN, Joseph (d 1908) variety
manager EA/09*

LARKIN, Peter (b 1926) American
designer BE, ES, WWT/14-16

LARKIN, Rhoda actress EA/97

LARKIN, Sophie (d 1903 [70]) actress OAA/2

LARKINS, Mr. (fl 1840) English
actor HAS

LARKINS, Mrs. (d 1880) EA/81*

LARKINS, Mrs. see Coveney,
Jane

LARNED, Mel (1925-55) American
singer TW/11-12

LAROCHE, James (fl 1696-1713)
singer CDP, DNB

LA ROCQUE, Rod (1898-1969)
American actor ES, TW/26

LaROSA, Julius (b 1930) American
actor TW/21

LaROSE, Rose (d 1972 [59]) performer BP/57*

LARPENT, John (1741-1824) in-

spector of plays DNB
LARRALDE, Rômulo see Brent,
Romney
LARRIMORE, Francine (1898-1975)
French actress BE, NTH, TW/
2-8, WWT/4-11
LARSEN, Darrell D. (d 1965 [68])
producer/director BP/50*
LARSEN, Niels (d 1975 [49])
producer/director/choreographer
BP/60*
LARSEN, William (b 1927) Amer-
ican actor TW/24-26, 28-29
LARSON, John (b 1914) American
actor TW/3-4
LARSON, Paul (b 1918) American
actor TW/6, 23, 29
LARSON, Philip (b 1942) American
actor TW/28
LARSSEN, Signe see Hasso,
Signe
LA RUE, Danny [Daniel Patrick
Carroll] (b 1928) Irish female
impersonator COC
LA RUE, Grace (1882-1956) Amer-
ican actress, singer TW/12,
WWT/4-7
LASCELLES, Miss (fl 1800) ac-
tress TD/1-2
LASCELLES, Ernita (d 1972
[87]) English actress, drama-
tist TW/29
LASCELLES, Mrs. Francis see
Catley, Ann
LASCELLES, Frank (d 1934 [58])
English actor, pageant master
GRB/1-4
LASCELLES, Vera see Las-
celles-Scott, Mrs.
LASCELLES-SCOTT, Mrs. [Vera
Lascelles] (d 1885) actress
EA/86*
LASCOE, Henry (d 1964 [50])
actor TW/21
LASHANSKA, Hulda (d 1974 [80])
performer BP/58*
LA SHELLE, Kirke (1863-1905)
manager BP/2*, WWT/14*
LASHWOOD, George (d 1942
[79]) singer, composer, actor
CDP
LASHWOOD, Mrs. George see
Williams, Lottie
LASK, George Edwin (b 1865)
American director, manager,
actor WWM
LASKY, Jesse L. (1880-1958)
American manager, producer

WWM, WWW/5
LASKY, Zane (b 1953) American
actor TW/29-30
LASLEY, David (b 1947) American
actor TW/29
LASLO, Alexander (d 1970 [75])
composer/lyricist BP/55*
LASSALLE, Jean-Louis (1845-1909)
French singer ES
LASSER, Louise (b 1940?) Ameri-
can actress CB
LASTFOGEL, Abe (b 1898) Amer-
ican talent representative BE
LASZLO, Miklos (d 1973 [69])
dramatist BP/57*
LATCHAW, Paul (b 1945) American
actor TW/29
LATEINER, Joseph (1853-1935)
Rumanian dramatist MWD, OC/
2-3
LATELLE, Cornelius (d 1910 [63])
EA/11*
LATEWARE, Dr. Richard (1560-
1601) English writer CP/3
LATHAM, Mr. (fl 1834) actor
HAS
LATHAM, Alfred Henry (d 1899
[32]) EA/00*
LATHAM, Cynthia (b 1897) English
actress TW/14-15, 26
LATHAM, Daniel (d 1885 [24])
actor, manager EA/86*
LATHAM, Frederick G. (d 1943
[90]) English producer, director,
manager SR, WWT/7-9
LATHAM, Mrs. Frederick G.
see Brooke, Cynthia
LATHAM, Hope (d 1951 [79]) ac-
tress TW/7
LATHAM, Joseph W., Sr. (d 1970
[80]) actor TW/27
LATHAM, W. H. (d 1844) actor,
singer CDP
LATHBURY, Stanley (b 1873) Eng-
lish actor GRB/1-2, WWT/5-11
LATHOM, Earl of see Wilbra-
ham, Edward
LATHOM, Francis (1777-1832)
English dramatist CP/3
LA THORNE, John (fl 1845-69)
American actor, athlete, circus
performer, stage manager
HAS
LATHRAM, Elizabeth (b 1947)
American actress TW/29-30
LATHROP, Elise (fl 1901-07)
American translator WWM
LATHROP, George Parsons (1851-

98) Hawaiian composer, writer
WWA/H

LATHROP, Sam American clown
CDP

LATHY, Thomas Pike (b 1771)
English dramatist CP/3,
DNB, EAP

LATIMAR, Mrs. (d 1894) EA/95*

LATIMER, Edyth [Mrs. William
Haviland] (1883-1967) Australian
actress GRB/3-4, WWT/1-5

LATIMER, Henry (d 1963 [86])
performer BE*

LATIMER, Hugh (b 1913) English
actor WWT/11-16

LATIMER, Sally (b 1910) English
actress, producer, manager
WWT/10-14

LATONA, Jen (fl 1911?) singer,
actress CDP

LATOUCHE, John Treville (1917-
56) American dramatist, lyricist CB, MH, TW/13

LATOUR, M. (d 1854) aeronaut
EA/72*

LaTOUR, Babe (d 1973 [79]) performer BP/57*

LATOUR, William (b 1845) Ger-
man/American actor HAS

LATRILHE, Jeanne see Dulac,
Odette

LA TROBE, Charles (1879-1967)
English director, producer
WWT/7-14

LA TROBE, Mrs. Charles see
Addison, Carlotta

LA TROBE, Charles Albert (d
1909 [63]) EA/10*

LATTER, Mary (1725-77) English dramatist CP/2-3, GT

LATTIMER, Miss see Holman,
Mrs. Joseph George

LATTIMORE, Richmond (b 1906)
American educator, translator
BE

LAU, Hurfries de [Josias Flor-
idor] (fl 1635) French actor
DA

LAUB, Ferdinand (d 1875) musician EA/76*

LAUCHLAN, Agnes (b 1905) English actress WWT/8-16

LAUCK, Pierre Ham (d 1899
[42]) gymnast EA/00*

LAUDENBACH, Pierre see
Fresnay, Pierre

LAUDER, Mrs. (d 1905) EA/06*

LAUDER, Sir Harry (1870-1950)

English singer, actor CDP,
COC, DNB, ES, NTH, OC/1-3,
PDT, SR, TW/6, WWA/4,
WWT/4-10

LAUDER, John C. (d 1916) EA/18*

LAUDICINA, Dino (b 1939) American actor TW/24, 26

LAUGHLIN, Anna [Mrs. Dwight
Van Monroe] (1885-1937) American actress CDP, WWS

LAUGHLIN, Sharon actress TW/
26-28, 30

LAUGHTON, Charles (1899-1962)
English actor, director AAS,
CB, ES, NTH, PDT, TW/8-9,
13-15, 19, WWA/4, WWT/6-13,
WWW/6

LAUHER, Bob (d 1973 [42]) performer BP/58*

LAUNDON, Mrs. John Crossley (d
1909 [61]) EA/10*

LAURA, Fraulein see Descombes,
Mrs.

LAUREL, Jane (fl 1900-12) actress
WWM

LAUREL, Lily (d 1897) serio-
comic EA/98*

LAUREL, Mrs. Sid (d 1912 [27])
performer? EA/13*

LAUREL, Stan (b 1890) English
performer ES

LAUREN, Jane (d 1974 [56]) performer BP/59*

LAURENCE, Baby (d 1974 [53])
performer BP/58*

LAURENCE, Charles (d 1896 [62])
property master EA/97*

LAURENCE, Larry (b 1920) Italian
actor TW/2

LAURENCE, Paula (b 1916) American actress, singer BE, TW/
1-16, 20, 22-23, 26, WWT/11-
16

LAURENS, William B. (d 1879
[42]) American actor EA/80*

LAURENT, Mr. (fl 1808) comedian,
harlequin CDP

LAURENT, Ada (fl 1860s) English
actress HAS

LAURENT, Charles Emile (d 1857)
musician EA/72*

LAURENT, Edwin (d 1877) singer?
EA/78*

LAURENT, Henry (d 1861 [26])
musician EA/72*

LAURENT, Marie (d 1904 [78])
actress WWT/14*

LAURENTI, Mario (d 1922) Italian

singer WWA/1

LAURENTS, Arthur (b 1918/20) American dramatist, director AAS, BE, CD, ES, GT, MD, MH, MWD, PDT, WWT/12-16

LAURET, Laryssa (b 1939) Polish actress TW/26

LAUREYS, Simon W. (c. 1827-87) Belgian costumier NYM

LAURI, Charles (1833-89) pantomimist, clown CDP

LAURI, Charles, Jr. (d 1904 [56]) pantomimist, animal mimic CDP, DP

LAURI, Charlotte [Mrs. W. Foster] (d 1878) singer EA/79*

LAURI, Edward (d 1919) actor, manager CDP

LAURI, Mrs. Edward (d 1907) actress EA/08*

LAURI, Ernest (d 1904 [26]) EA/05*

LAURI, George (d 1909) actor WWT/14*

LAURI, Harry see Lowe, Albert Henry

LAURI, Joe, Jr. (1892-1954) American actor BE*

LAURI, John (d 1881 [52]) pantomimist EA/82*

LAURI, Lelia [Mrs. Fred H. Lowerre] (1856-84) singer CDP

LAURI, Stella [Mrs. Harry Ulph] (d 1907 [44]) dancer EA/08*

LAURI, Ted (d 1893) pantomimist EA/94*

LAURI BROTHERS (fl 1869) English pantomimists HAS

LAURIA, Larri (d 1965 [64]) performer BP/50*

LAURIE, Fannie (d 1885 [37]) performer? EA/86*

LAURIE, Joe, Jr. (1892-1954) American vaudevillian NTH, TW/10

LAURIE, John (b 1897) Scottish actor AAS, WWT/6-16

LAURIE, William Pitcairn (d 1871 [28]) actor EA/72*

LAURIEN, Fanny [Mrs. James G. Laurien] (d 1884 [34]) EA/86*

LAURIEN, Mrs. James G. see Laurien, Fanny

LAURIER, Jay (1879-1969) English actor WWT/7-11

LAURILLARD, Edward (b 1870)

Dutch manager WWT/4-8

LAURI-VOLPI, Giacomo (b 1893) Italian singer ES

LAUTNER, Joe (b 1924) American actor TW/10

LaVALLEE, Bill (b 1943) American actor TW/27-30

LAVALLIERE, Eve (d 1929 [61]) Italian/French actress WWT/3-4

LAVENU, E. singer, actress CDP

LAVER, James (1899-1975) English dramatist, historian BE, COC, OC/1-3, WWT/8-14

LAVER, Mrs. James H. see Laverne, Pattie

LA VERE, Earl (d 1962 [71]) performer BE*

LAVERICK, Beryl (b 1919) English actress WWT/8-9

LA VERNE, Lucille (1875-1945) American actress TW/1, WWT/5-9

LAVERNE, Pattie [Mrs. James H. Laver] (d 1916) English actress OAA/1-2

LAVERTON, Vyvian see Thomas, Vyvian

LAVERY, Emmet (b 1902) American writer, dramatist BE, CB, MD, MWD

LAVERY, Richard (d 1962 [79]) Australian equestrian BE*

LAVIGNE, Mlle. (fl 1852) dancer HAS

LAVIGNE, Joseph (d 1875) ballet master, pantomimist EA/76*

LAVIN, Linda (b 1937/39) American actress TW/21-27, 29, WWT/15-16

LAVINA [Mrs. Joseph Miller] (d 1909 [47]) performer? EA/10*

LAVINE, Miss see Simmons, Lavinia

LAVIZZO, Valcour (b 1953) American actor TW/28

LAVREN, Christine (b 1944) American actress TW/27

LAW, Arthur (1844-1913) English dramatist, actor GRB/1-4, SR, WWT/1, WWW/1

LAW, Fred (d 1902 [57]) singer, actor, manager CDP

LAW, Mrs. Fred (d 1892) EA/93*

LAW, Jenny Lou (d 1961 [39]) actress TW/17

LAW, John Phillip (b 1937) American actor TW/21

LAW, Mouzon (b 1922) American

educator, director BE

LAWDER, Wallace actor TW/1

LAWES, Henry (1596-1662) English composer CDP, DNB

LAWES, William (d 1645) English composer DNB

LAWFORD, Betty (1910-60) English actress WWT/10-11

LAWFORD, Ernest (1870-1940) English actor CB, WWT/8-9

LAWLER, D. (fl 1808) dramatist CP/3

LAWLER, Frank (b 1835) American actor, manager HAS, SR

LAWLER, John William (d 1869) actor EA/70*

LAWLER, Kate (fl 1878) actress OAA/2

LAWLER, Mike (1828-65) Irish actor HAS

LAWLER, Ray (b 1921/22) Australian actor, dramatist AAS, BE, CD, COC, MD, MH, MWD, OC/3, PDT, RE

LAWLER, Richard H., Sr. (d 1969 [67]) designer BP/54*

LAWLER, William (d 1916) musician EA/17*

LAWLESS, Sue American actress TW/23, 25-26, 29

LAWLOR, Mr. (fl 1888?) singer, actor CDP

LAWLOR, Charles B. (d 1925 [73]) Irish performer BE*, BP/9*

LAWLOR, Mary American actress, singer WWT/6-8

LAWRENCE, Mrs. (d 1890) EA/91*

LAWRENCE, Adrian (d 1953 [79]) actor, producer, manager BE*, WWT/14*

LAWRENCE, Mrs. Arthur [Mary Campbell] (d 1889) EA/90*

LAWRENCE, Bert (d 1971 [47]) performer BP/56*

LAWRENCE, Boyle (1869-1951) English dramatist, critic, lyricist GRB/1-4, WWT/1-9, WWW/5

LAWRENCE, Carol (b 1932/35) American dancer, singer, actress CB, TW/18-19, WWT/16

LAWRENCE, C. E. (d 1940 [69]) dramatist BE*, WWT/14*

LAWRENCE, Charles (b 1896) American actor WWT/5-9

LAWRENCE, Delphi (b 1932) English actress TW/28-29

LAWRENCE, D. H. (1885-1930) English dramatist AAS, COC, MD, MWD, WWT/6, WWW/3

LAWRENCE, Dorset William see D'Orsay, Lawrence

LAWRENCE, Eddie (b 1919) American actor TW/23

LAWRENCE, Elaine (d 1971 [28]) performer BP/55*

LAWRENCE, Eliza Jane [Mrs. Sidney Lawrence] (d 1869) musician EA/70*

LAWRENCE, Elliot (b 1926) American musical director, composer BE

LAWRENCE, Emma [Mrs. Joe Lawrence] (d 1916 [66]) EA/17*

LAWRENCE, Florence (1888-1938) actress BE*

LAWRENCE, Frederick see Kert, Larry

LAWRENCE, George A., Jr. (d 1894) musician EA/95*

LAWRENCE, Georgia (d 1923 [46]) actress BE*, BP/7*

LAWRENCE, Gerald (1873-1957) English actor COC, GRB/1-4, OC/3, WWS, WWT/1-11

LAWRENCE, Mrs. Gerald see Davis, Fay

LAWRENCE, Mrs. Gerald see Braithwaite, Lilian

LAWRENCE, Gertrude (1898-1952) English actress AAS, CB, COC, DNB, ES, NTH, OC/3, SR, TW/2-9, WWA/3, WWT/5-11, WWW/5

LAWRENCE, Jack (b 1912) American lyricist, composer, producer BE

LAWRENCE, James (fl 1799) dramatist CP/3

LAWRENCE, Jennie (d 1894) gymnast, trapezist EA/95*

LAWRENCE, Jerome (b 1915) American dramatist, director BE, CD, MWD, WWT/13-16

LAWRENCE, Joe (d 1909 [60]) singer, actor CDP

LAWRENCE, Mrs. Joe see Lawrence, Emma

LAWRENCE, J. W. (d 1900 [70]) clown, pantaloon EA/01*

LAWRENCE, J. W. (d 1916 [83]) actor EA/17*

LAWRENCE, Katie (fl 1890s?) singer, actress CDP

LAWRENCE, Lawrence Shubert (1894-1965) American executive BE, TW/21

LAWRENCE, Lawrence Shubert, Jr. (b 1916) American executive BE

LAWRENCE, Lillian (fl 1892-1908) American actress WWS

LAWRENCE, Margaret (1889-1929) American actress HAS, WWA/1, WWT/4

LAWRENCE, Marjorie (b 1908) Australian singer CB

LAWRENCE, Nellie [Mrs. Harry McClelland] (d 1912 [51]) EA/13*

LAWRENCE, Pauline (d 1971 [70]) designer BP/56*

LAWRENCE, Reginald (1900-67) American dramatist BE, TW/24

LAWRENCE, Mrs. Sidney see Lawrence, Eliza Jane

"LAWRENCE, Slingsby" see Lewes, George Henry

LAWRENCE, Stan make-up artist BE

LAWRENCE, Steve (b 1935) American actor, singer BE, CB, TW/24

LAWRENCE, Sydney Boyle see Lawrence, Boyle

LAWRENCE, Thomas (d 1896 [78]) portable theatre manager EA/97*

LAWRENCE, Vincent (b 1896) English press representative WWT/6-8

LAWRENCE, Vincent S. (1890-1946) American dramatist TW/3, WWT/6-10

LAWRENCE, Walter N. (d 1920 [62]) manager BE*, BP/4*, WWT/14*

LAWRENCE, William (d 1921) actor BE*, BP/5*

LAWRENCE, William John (1862-1940) Irish historian, critic GRB/4, WWT/1-9

LAWRENCE, Wingold (b 1874) English actor GRB/1

LAWRIE, Charles singer, actor CDP

LAWRIE, Ted (b 1923) American actor TW/4, 28

LAWRIE, T. T. V. (d 1868 [22]) actor? EA/69*

LAWS, Edmund (d 1852 [48]) actor WWT/14*

LAWS, Mrs. Edmund (d 1880 [69]) actress WWT/14*

LAWS, Frederick (d 1976 [65]) dramatist BP/60*

LAWS, Jane (d 1880 [69]) actress EA/81*

LAWS, Jerry (b 1912) American actor TW/25-26

LAWS, Steve (b 1937) American actor TW/30

LAWSON, Charles (d 1879 [30]) American musician EA/80*

LAWSON, Lady Edward see Lawson, Henrietta

LAWSON, Ennis (d 1888 [52]) actor EA/89*

LAWSON, Henrietta [Lady Edward Lawson] (d 1897) EA/98*

LAWSON, James (1799-1880) Scottish? American dramatist CDP, EAP, HJD, RJ

LAWSON, John (d 1920 [55]?) English variety artist GRB/1-3

LAWSON, John Howard (1895-1977) American dramatist AAS, BE, CD, HJD, MD, MH, MWD, NTH, WWT/8-11

LAWSON, Kate (b 1894) American designer, executive BE

LAWSON, Lee (b 1941) American actress TW/24-25, 27-30

LAWSON, Lionel (d 1879) proprietor EA/80*

LAWSON, Mary (1910-41) English actress, singer CB, WWT/6-9

LAWSON, Robb (d 1947 [74]) critic BE*, WWT/14*

LAWSON, Roger (b 1942) American actor TW/25-26, 29-30

LAWSON, Wilfred (1900-66) English actor AAS, WWT/7-14

LAWSON, William E. (d 1897) musical director EA/98*

LAWSON, Winifred (1894-1961) English actress, singer WWT/5-10

LAWTON, Elizabeth Ann (d 1917) EA/18*

LAWTON, Frank (d 1914) actor, whistler CDP

LAWTON, Frank (1904-69) English actor COC, TW/26, WWT/6-14, WWW/6

LAWTON, Thais (1881/82-1956) American actress TW/13,

WWM, WWT/1-11

LAWTON, Thomas (d 1913 [42])
EA/14*

LAX, Percy (d 1909 [44]) musical director EA/10*

LAY, Dilys see Laye, Dilys

LAYE, Dilys [née Lay] (b 1934) English actress WWT/15-16

LAYE, Evelyn (b 1900) English actress, singer AAS, BE, COC, ES, WWT/4-16

LAYFIELD, James (d 1877) comic singer EA/79*

LAYLAND, Edward [E. Westbourne] (d 1882 [28]) actor? EA/83*

LAYTON, Joe [né Lichtman] (b 1931) American choreographer, director BE, CB, WWT/14-16

LAYTON, Thomas (d 1893) conductor EA/94*

LAYTON, William (b 1917) American actor TW/4-6

LAZAR, Irving (b 1907) American literary representative BE

LAZARUS, Emma (1849-87) American dramatist WWA/H

LAZARUS, Henry (d 1895) musician EA/96*

LAZELLO, Bob (d 1909) gymnast, acrobat EA/10*

LAZER, Peter (b 1946) American actor BE, TW/13-14, 26-27

LAZZARI, Carolina (1891-1946) American singer TW/3, WWA/2

LEA, Albert (d 1863) HAS

LEA, Bruce (b 1949) American actor TW/29-30

LEA, Fanny Heaslip (1884-1955) American dramatist WWA/3

LEA, Marion see Mitchell, Mrs. Langdon Elwyn

LEABO, Loi (b 1938) American actress TW/22

LEACH, Arthur (d 1887 [22]) advance agent EA/88*

LEACH, Emily Sarah [Mrs. Gus Leach] (d 1895 [48]) EA/96*

LEACH, Gus (d 1903) comedian, music-hall manager EA/04*

LEACH, Gus see Leach, Emily Sarah

LEACH, Harvey (1804-47) American performer CDP, HAS

LEACH, Mrs. Harvey (fl 1841) actress HAS

LEACH, Hervey [Sig. Hervio Nano] (1804-47) dwarf CDP

LEACH, Marjorie (b 1902) American actress TW/27

LEACH, Stephen W. (d 1895 [75]) singer, actor, composer HAS

LEACH, Wilford (b 1929) American educator, dramatist, director BE

LEACHMAN, Cloris (b 1926?) American actress CB, TW/8-19

LEACHMAN, Cloris W. (d 1967 [66]) little theatre pioneer BP/52*

LEACOCK, John (fl c. 1776) dramatist EAP

LEADER, John (d 1897) choir secretary EA/98*

LEADLAY, Edward O. (1884-1951) Canadian press representative WWT/5-9

LEAHY, Christine Dobbins (d 1974 [82]) performer BP/59*

LEAHY, Eugene (1883-1967) Irish actor WWT/6-14

LEAK, Miss (fl 1792) English singer GT, TD/1-2

LEAK, Elizabeth (b 1777) actress CDP

LEAK, Thomas [Tom French] (d 1888 [25]) pantomimist EA/89*

LEAKE, James (d 1791 [76]) patentee BE*, WWT/14*

LEAKE, W. H. (b 1832) English actor, manager HAS

LEAL, Milagros (d 1975 [73]) performer BP/59*

LEAMAN, Felix (d 1899 [36]) musical director EA/00*

LEAMAN, Samuel B. (d 1857 [27]) American actor HAS

LEAMAR, Alice (d 1950 [81]) performer BE*, WWT/14*

LEAMAR, Kate [Mrs. W. Bint] (d 1893) music-hall singer EA/94*

LEAMAR SISTERS singers CDP

LEAMING, Chet (b 1925) American actor TW/12-15, 18, 25

LEAMORE, Florence [Florrie Palmer; Mrs. Tom Leamore] (d 1895) EA/96*

LEAMORE, Tom (d 1939 [73]) actor, songwriter, dancer CDP

LEAMORE, Mrs. Tom see Leamore, Florence

LEAN, Cecil (1878-1935) Canadian actor WWT/4-7

LEAN, Mrs. Francis see Marryat, Florence

LEANDER, Harry (d 1909 [50]) comedian EA/10*

LEANDER, Thomas S. (d 1890 [48]) music-hall performer EA/91*

LEANERD, John (fl 1679-78) dramatist CP/1-3, DNB, GT

LEAPOR, Mary (1722-46) English dramatist CP/2-3, GT

LEAR, Evelyn (b 1929?) American singer CB

LEAR, Joyce (b 1926) American actress TW/7

LEARMONT, John (fl 1791) dramatist CP/3

LEARMOUTH, Mary (d 1913 [46]) EA/14*

LEARY, Miss (fl late 18th cent) singer CDP

LEARY, David (b 1939) American actor TW/25, 27, 29

LEARY, Gilda (d 1927 [31]) English actress BE*, BP/11*

LEASK, George Alfred (1878-1950) English dramatist WWW/4

LEATHEM, Barclay (b 1900) American educator, director BE

LEATHERBEE, Mary American educator BE

LEATHES, Edmund (1847-91) actor DP, OAA/2

LEATITIA, Mme. [Mrs. W. H. Clarke] (d 1880 [27]) equestrienne EA/81*

LEAVER, Philip (b 1903/04) English actor, dramatist WWT/7-14

LEAVETT, Marie see Rose, Marie

LEAVITT, Charles [Max] (b 1905) American actor TW/2

LEAVITT, Michael B. (1843-1935) German/American actor, manager CDP, COC, SR

LE BARGY, Charles Gustave Antoine (1858-1936) French actor GRB/1, 3-4, WWT/1-4

LE BARGY, Simone see Simone, Mme.

LeBARON, Louise (fl 1904-10) American singer, actress

WWM, WWS

LE BARON, William (1883-1958) American dramatist, producer WWA/3, WWT/4-12

LE BARR, Fanny [Mrs. Henry Le Barr] (d 1897) EA/98*

LE BARR, Mrs. Henry see Le Barr, Fanny

LEBEDEFF, Ivan (d 1953 [58]) Russian actor BE*, BP/37*

LEBERWURST, Hans (fl 1613) actor DA

LEBLANC-MAETERLINCK, Georgette (1876-1941) French actress, singer WWT/3-4

LE BLOND, Mr. (fl 1820) French dancer CDP, EA/92

LEBOWSKY, Stanley (b 1926) American conductor, composer, musician BE, TW/28-29

LE BOZEC, Marcel see Varnel, Marcel

LE BRETON, Flora (b 1898) English actress WWT/6-9

LE BRETON, Rev. William Corbet (d 1888 [73]) EA/89*

LEBRUN-DANZI, Franziska (1756-91) German singer ES

LE BRUNN, George (1863-1905) English composer GRB/1

LE BRUNN, Thomas (b 1864) English songwriter GRB/1

LE BUTT, Ada [Mrs. Arthur Brogden] (d 1902) singer EA/03*

LECKIE, William Lloyd (d 1916 [30]) EA/17*

LECKY, Eleazer (b 1903) American educator BE

LeCLAIR, Henry American actor TW/25-28

LE CLAIR, Maggie (d 1923 [65]) American comedienne BE*, BP/7*

LE CLAIR, Shedrach see Smith, Shedrach

LE CLAIR, William (d 1910) dog trainer EA/11*

LE CLERCK, Mme. (fl 1822) dancer CDP

LECLERCQ, Arthur (d 1890) pantomimist, dancer, acting manager EA/91*, WWT/14*

LECLERCQ, Carlotta [Mrs. John Nelson] (1836-93) English actress CDP, DNB, DP, OAA/1-2

LECLERCQ, Charles (1797-1861)

dancer, ballet master CDP
LECLERCQ, Charles (d 1895)
pantomimist, ballet master
EA/96*, WWT/14*
LECLERCQ, Louise (d 1898)
dancer, actress EA/99*,
WWT/14*
LECLERCQ, Pierre (d 1932)
dramatist BE*, WWT/14*
LECLERCQ, Rose (1845?-99)
actress CDP, DNB, DP,
EA/95, OAA/1-2
LE CLERCQ, Tanaquil (b 1929)
American dancer CB, ES
LECLERQ, Mrs. (d 1889 [77])
actress EA/90*
LE CLERQ, Florence (d 1960 [89])
actress BE*, WWT/14*
LE CLERQ, George (1855-1911?)
Irish actor GRB/1
LECOCQ, Charles (d 1918 [86])
EA/19*
LECOMTE, Mons. (fl 1838)
singer CDP
LECOMTE, Mme. (fl 1837)
dancer CDP
LEDBETTER, Robert (fl 1597-
1606) actor DA
LEDERER, Charles (1911-76)
American dramatist, producer,
director BE
LEDERER, Francis (b 1906)
Czech actor, director BE,
NTH, TW/2-9, WWT/7-14
LEDERER, George W. (1861-
1938) American manager
GRB/2-4, SR, WWA/1,
WWT/1-8
LEDERER, George W., Jr. (d
1924 [33]) talent representative
BE*, BP/9*
LEDERER, Gretchen (d 1955
[64]) actress BE*
LEDFORD, Harrison C. (d 1970
[69]) performer BP/55*
LEDGER, Mr. ["Honest Ledger"]
actor TD/1-2
LEDGER, Edward (d 1921) jour-
nalist WWW/1
LEDGER, Frederick (d 1874
[58]) editor, publisher BE*,
EA/75*, WWT/14*
LEDIARD, Thomas (d 1759)
dramatist CP/2-3, GT,
TD/1-2
LEDUC, Claudine (d 1969) BP/
53*
LEE (fl 1798) actor, dramatist

CP/3, GT
LEE, Mr. (fl 1795-98) manager,
actor TD/1-2
LEE, Mr. (fl c. 1850) actor CDP
LEE, Mrs. [née Keys] (fl 1793)
actress TD/1-2
LEE, Ada (d 1902 [35]) actress
EA/03*
LEE, Albert (d 1888) minstrel
EA/90*
LEE, Alexander (d 1851) composer
EA/72*
LEE, Mrs. Alexander (d 1851
[51]) EA/72*
LEE, Alfred (d 1906) composer
EA/07*
LEE, Annie see Johnston, Mrs.
T. B.
LEE, Auriol (1880-1941) English
actress, producer CB, GRB/
3-4, WWT/1-9
LEE, Belinda (d 1961 [26]) English
actress BE*, WWT/14*
LEE, Bernard (b 1908) English ac-
tor AAS, WWT/8-16
LEE, Bert (1880-1946) English
dramatist, composer WWT/7-9
LEE, Bessie [Mrs. F. Cumminger]
(d 1904 [31]) "Coloured Patti"
EA/05*
LEE, Bessie (d 1972 [66]) perform-
er BP/57*
LEE, Big (b 1939) American actor
TW/27
LEE, Bruce (d 1973 [32]) performer
BP/58*
LEE, Bryarly (b 1934/35) American
actress BE, TW/13-15, 30
LEE, Canada [né Leonard Lionel
Cornelius Canegata] (1907-52)
American actor CB, COC, TW/
1-8, WWA/3, WWT/10-11
LEE, Charles (d 1947 [71]) per-
former BE*, WWT/14*
LEE, Clara (d 1899 [74]) actress
EA/00*
LEE, Edgar [William Tasker] (d
1908 [58]) journalist EA/10*
LEE, Elizabeth (d 1905) EA/06*
LEE, Esmé (fl 1881) singer CDP
LEE, Florence (d 1962 [74]) ac-
tress BE*
LEE, Fred (d 1890) comedian
EA/91*
LEE, Mrs. Fred (d 1889) EA/91*
LEE, George (d 1871 [47]) come-
dian EA/72*
LEE, George Alexander (1802-51)

English composer, singer,
conductor DNB

LEE, George B. (b 1866) American business manager GRB/1

LEE, George Vandeleur (d 1886 [55]) composer EA/87*

LEE, Gypsy Rose [née Rose Louise Hovick] (1914-70) American actress BE, CB, COC, SR, TW/26, WWA/5, WWT/10-11

LEE, Harriet (1757-1851) English dramatist CP/2-3, DNB, GT

LEE, Harriett [Mrs. Richard Austin Lee] (d 1883 [50]) EA/84*

LEE, Harry A. (d 1919 [76]) American manager BE*, BP/4*

LEE, Henry (1765-1836) English manager, dramatist, actor CP/3, DNB

LEE, Henry (d 1910 [53]) performer BE*, WWT/14*

LEE, Mrs. Henry (d 1874 [63]) actress EA/75*

LEE, Hettie de (b 1849) American actress HAS

LEE, Ida (d 1867) music-hall performer HAS

LEE, James (b 1923) American dramatist BE

LEE, James E. (d 1965 [58]) critic BP/50*

LEE, Jane (d 1957 [45]) performer BE*

LEE, Jean (d 1963) performer BE*

LEE, Jennie (d 1925 [75]) actress BE*, BP/10*, WWT/14*

LEE, Jennie [Mrs. J. P. Burnett] (d 1930 [84]) English actress CDP, DP, GRB/1-4, OAA/1-2, WWT/1-6

LEE, Jenny [Mrs. E. S. Vincent] (d 1893) actress EA/94*

LEE, Jim (d 1866) minstrel HAS

LEE, John (d 1781) actor, dramatist, manager CDP, CP/2-3, DNB, TD/1-2

LEE, John (1795-1881) actor, stage manager CDP

LEE, Johnny see Wardroper, John

LEE, J. Stacey (d 1868 [42])

comic songwriter EA/69*

LEE, Kathryn (b 1926) American actress TW/4-6

LEE, Katie [Mrs. C. Stuart] (d 1916) actress EA/17*

LEE, Lavater (d 1891 [73]) EA/92*

LEE, Lavater (d 1899) performing dog proprietor EA/00*

LEE, Lila (d 1973 [68]) actress TW/30

LEE, Lillie (d 1941 [81]) actress, dancer BE*, WWT/14*

LEE, Madaline (d 1974) performer BP/58*

LEE, Marion (d 1864 [24]) American actress HAS

LEE, Mary Ann see Vanhook, Mrs. W. F.

LEE, Mary Anne (fl 1837-45) American dancer HAS

LEE, Michele (b 1942) American actress, singer, dancer BE, TW/18-19, 29-30

LEE, Ming Cho (b 1930) Chinese designer BE, WWT/15-16

LEE, Moe (d 1966 [81]) performer BP/50*

LEE, Nathaniel (c. 1653-92) English dramatist CDP, COC, CP/1-3, DNB, ES, GT, HP, MH, NTH, OC/1-3, RE

LEE, Nelson (1806-72) English dramatist, manager CDP, EA/68

LEE, Olga (b 1899) American talent representative BE

LEE, Raymond (d 1974 [64]) performer BP/59*

LEE, R. G. (fl 1793) dramatist CP/3

LEE, Richard (d 1905) EA/06*

LEE, Richard Austin (d 1883 [63]) actor EA/84*

LEE, Mrs. Richard Austin see Lee, Harriett

LEE, Richard L. (b 1872) American actor WWS

LEE, Richard Nelson (1806-72) English actor, dramatist DNB

LEE, Robert (fl 1590-1622) dramatist, actor, lessee CP/3, DA

LEE, Robert E. (b 1918) American dramatist, producer, director BE, CD, MWD, WWT/13-16

LEE, Rosa (fl 1872?) actress, singer CDP

LEE, Rowland V. (d 1975 [84]) producer/director/choreographer

BP/60*

LEE, Sammy (d 1968 [78]) producer/director/choreographer BP/52*

LEE, S. L. (d 1906 [49]) proprietor EA/07*

LEE, Sondra (b 1930) American actress, dancer BE, TW/ 11, 13, 20-24

LEE, Sophia (1750-1824) English dramatist CDP, CP/3, DNB, TD/1-2

LEE, Thomas (1810-56) Irish actor CDP

LEE, Tom (d 1971 [61]) designer BP/56*

LEE, Valerie (d 1975 [52]) American actress TW/26

LEE, Vanessa [née Winifred Ruby Moule] (b 1920) English actress, singer WWT/11-16

LEE, Cpt. W. H. (d 1874 [33]) business manager EA/76*

LEE, Will (b 1908) American actor, teacher, director BE, TW/23, 29

LEE, William (d 1907 [52]) music-hall performer EA/08*

LEE, William A. (b 1890) American actor, vaudevillian TW/ 2-4, 8-9

LEE, William T. (fl 1850) actor HAS

LEECH, Dempster (b 1942) American actor TW/29

LEECH, Richard [né Richard Leeper McClelland] (b 1922) Irish actor AAS, WWT/11-16

LEECHMAN, Kate [Mrs. Harry Walker] (d 1909) comedian EA/10*

LEEDER, Mlle. (fl 1852) dancer HAS

LEEDS, Mrs. Charles S. see Glose, Augusta

LEEDS, Florence (d 1970 [75]) performer BP/55*

LEEDS, Phil American actor BE, TW/23, 26, 29-30

LEEDS, Strelsa (b 1920) American actress TW/2

LEEDY, Harry (d 1975 [67]) artists' manager BP/59*

LEEKE, David (fl 1571) actor DA

LEE LEWIS, Charles (d 1803 [63]) actor GT, TD/1-2

LEEMAN, Walter H. (d 1903)

business manager EA/04*

LEES, C. Lowell (b 1904) American educator BE

LEES, Mrs. M. (d 1875) EA/76*

LEES, Noah (d 1905 [69]) music-hall performer? EA/06*

LEES, Thomas (d 1908) variety performer EA/09*

LEES, Tom (d 1878 [57]) equestrian, gymnast EA/79*

LEESON, Dan (d 1903 [42]) variety performer EA/04*

LEESON, Mrs. Dan see Danvil, Maud

LEESON, Dan W. (fl 1859-61) actor HAS

LEESON, Henrietta [Mrs. William Thomas Lewis] (1751-1826) English actress COC, TD/1-2

LEE-THOMPSON, Jack (b 1914) English dramatist ES

LE FANU, Alicia (1753-1817) dramatist DNB

LEFANU, Peter (fl 1778) dramatist CP/3, DNB

LE FANU, Sheridan (1814-73) dramatist HP

LEFEAUX, Charles (b 1909) English actor, director WWT/9-15

LE FEUVRE, Guy (1883-1950) Canadian actor, singer, composer WWT/10

LEFEVRE, Mrs. see Bride, Elizabeth

LEFFINGWELL, Miron [or Myron] Winslow (1828-79) American actor HAS, CDP

LEFFINGWELL, Mrs. Miron [Winslow] (b 1836) American actress HAS

LEFFLER, Adam (1805-57) English singer CDP, HAS

LEFFLER, Adam (d 1905 [76]) actor EA/06*, WWT/14*

LEFFLER, George (d 1951 [77]) American producer BE*, BP/36*

LEFFLER, John (1875-1947) manager, producer SR

LEFKOWITZ, Nat (b 1905) American executive, talent representative BE

LEFORT, Adrien see Charvay, Robert

Le FRE, Albert (d 1970 [99]) performer BP/54*

LE FRE, Albert William (d 1905 [13]) EA/05*

LE FRE, Elizabeth [Mrs. James Le Fre] (d 1903 [47]) EA/04*

LE FRE, Mrs. James see Le Fre, Elizabeth

LE FRE, William (d 1894 [34]) performer? EA/95*

LEFTLY, Charles (fl 1802) dramatist CP/3

LEFTWICH, Alexander (d 1947 [63]) producer TW/3, WWT/6-9

LEFTWICH, Alexander (d 1974 [66]) producer/director/choreographer BP/59*

LEGA, Mons. (d 1868) circus performer? EA/69*

LE GALLIENNE, Eva (b 1899) English actress, producer, director, translator AAS, BE, CB, COC, ES, GT, NTH, OC/1-3, SR, TW/2-22, 24, WWT/4-16

LEGARD, [Charles?] see Delagarde, [Charles?]

LEGARDE, Millie actress, singer CDP, GRB/3-4, WWT/1-5

LEGAT, Nadine (d 1971 [81]) performer BP/55*

LEGAT, Nikolai (1869-1937) Russian dancer, choreographer ES

LEGE, Mr. (fl 1796) actor HAS

LEGE, Mrs. (fl 1796) actress HAS

LEGG, Miss see Duncan, Mrs. Timothy

LEGGATT, Alison Joy (b 1904) English actress AAS, WWT/6-16

LEGGATT, Steve (d 1896) music-hall songwriter EA/97*

LEGGE, Lydia Alice see Foote, Lydia

LEGGE, R. G. (b 1864) English manager GRB/1

LEGGE, Thomas (d 1607 [72]) English dramatist CP/1-3, FGF

LEGGETT, Mr. (fl 1826) actor HAS

LEGGETT, Emma Elizabeth [Mrs. R. Leggett] (d 1901) burlesque actress EA/03*

LEGGETT, Mrs. R. see Leggett, Emma Elizabeth

LEGGETT, Richard (d 1906) music-hall comedian EA/07*

LEGHERE, Mrs. Leopold see

Naroni, Mlle.

LEGIONAIRE, Robert (b 1926) American actor TW/27

LEGLERE, Alice [Mrs. George Leglere] (d 1896 [35]) acrobat EA/97*

LEGLERE, Artois Leopold (d 1886 [55]) pantomimist EA/87*

LEGLERE, Mrs. George see Leglere, Alice

LEGLERE, Louis (d 1885) EA/86*

LE GRAND, Mlle. [Mrs. F. Galloway] (d 1898) tank performer EA/99*

LEGRAND, Claude Maria Eugent see Dauphin, Claude

LEGRAND, Eugénie [Mrs. Kyrle Bellew] (fl 1882-84) actress CDP

LE GRAND, Phyllis actress, singer WWT/2-7

LE GRYS, Sir Robert (fl 1629-60) dramatist CP/2-3, FGF

LE GUERE, George (d 1947 [66]) American actor TW/4

LEHAR, Franz (1870-1948) Austrian composer GRB/3-4, WWS, WWT/1-2, 9-10

LE HAY, Daisy (b 1883) actress, singer WWT/2-5

LE HAY, John [John Healy] (1854-1926) Irish actor DP, EA/97, GRB/1-4, WWT/1-5

LEHMAN, Adelaide HAS

LEHMAN, Andrew (d 1863 [30]) pantomimist HAS

LEHMAN, Anna (d 1868 [32]) HAS

LEHMAN, Christian (d 1868 [73]) HAS

LEHMAN, Moriz (d 1877 [58]) scene painter EA/78*

LEHMAN, Susan (b 1940) American actress TW/27

LEHMAN, Walter M. (fl 1827-56) American actor, call boy HAS

LEHMAN FAMILY, The HAS

LEHMANN, Beatrix (b 1903) English actress AAS, WWT/7-16

LEHMANN, Carla (b 1917) Canadian actress WWT/10-11

LEHMANN, Caroline (fl 1847) CDP

LEHMANN, Lilli (1848-1929) German singer ES

LEHMANN, Liza [Mrs. Herbert Bedford] (d 1918) singer, composer CDP

LEHMANN, Lotte (1888-1976)

German singer CB, ES

LEHMANN, Maurice (d 1974 [79]) producer/director/ choreographer BP/58*

LEHN, Norma American actress TW/2

LEHR, Harry (1830-81) minstrel CDP

LEHR, Wilson (b 1913) American educator BE

LEHRER, George (d 1966 [77]) performer BP/51*

LEIBER, Fritz (1882/83/84- 1949) American actor DAB, NTH, TW/6, WWM, WWT/ 7-10

LEIBMAN, Ron (b 1937) American actor TW/25-26, WWT/ 15-16

LEIBOWITZ, Rene (d 1972 [59]) composer/lyricist BP/57*

LEICESTER, Mr. (fl 1830-37) American actor, singer CDP, HAS

LEICESTER, Charles (d 1907) actor EA/08*

LEICESTER, Ernest (1866-1939) actor EA/97, GRB/3-4, WWT/1-6

LEICESTER, George F. (d 1916 [72]) actor BE*, EA/17*, WWT/14*

LEICESTER, Lillie (d 1884) singer EA/85*

LEICHNER, Ludwig (b 1836) singer, inventor of grease paint COC

LEIDER, Frida (1888-1975) German singer ES

LEIGH, Adèle (b 1928) English singer ES

LEIGH, Andrew George (1887- 1957) English actor, producer WWT/5-11

LEIGH, Anthony (d 1692) English actor CDP, COC, DNB, OC/1-3

LEIGH, Carol (b 1933) American actress TW/10

LEIGH, Carolyn American lyricist BE

LEIGH, Charlotte (b 1907) English actress, singer WWT/ 9-10

LEIGH, Dorma (b 1893) English actress, dancer WWT/4-8

LEIGH, George (d 1909 [76]) actor EA/10*

LEIGH, Georgie (d 1884) singer EA/85*

LEIGH, Gracie [Mrs. Lionel Mackinder] (d 1950 [75]) actress GRB/1-4, WWT/1-10

LEIGH, Henry (d 1881 [63]) actor EA/82*, WWT/14*

LEIGH, Mrs. Henry (d 1915 [90]) actress WWT/14*

LEIGH, Henry Sambrooke (1837- 83) English dramatist DNB

LEIGH, J. H. (d 1934 [75]) producer, actor, scholar BE*, WWT/14*

LEIGH, John (d 1726 [37]) Irish actor, dramatist CP/1-3, GT, TD/1-2

LEIGH, Miss Marston [Mrs. James Carden] (d 1897) actress EA/98*

LEIGH, Mary (1904-43) English actress, singer WWT/5-7

LEIGH, Philip (d 1935 [55]) actor BE*, BP/20*, WWT/14*

LEIGH, Richard (fl 1809) dramatist CP/3

LEIGH, Rowland (1902-63) dramatist, lyricist WWT/7-13

LEIGH, Stella [Mrs. George Mallett] English actress GRB/1

LEIGH, Vivien [Vivian Mary Hartley] (1913-67) Indian/English actress AAS, BE, CB, COC, ES, OC/2-3, PDT, TW/8-24, WWA/4, WWT/8-14, WWW/6

LEIGH, Walter (b 1905) English composer WWT/9

LEIGH-HUNT, Barbara (b 1935) English actress TW/24

LEIGHTON, Alexes (d 1926) actress BE*, WWT/14*

LEIGHTON, Bert (d 1964 [87]) performer, songwriter BE*

LEIGHTON, Betty (b 1920) English actress TW/29

LEIGHTON, Clara [Mrs. E. Lewis] (d 1913) EA/14*

LEIGHTON, Frank (1908-62) Australian actor WWT/10-13

LEIGHTON, Harry (d 1913 [42]) EA/14*

LEIGHTON, Harry (1866-1926) American actor WWM

LEIGHTON, Margaret [Mrs. Margaret Alcott] (d 1908 [56]) Welsh actress CDP, OAA/1-2

LEIGHTON, Margaret (1922-76) English actress AAS, BE, CB, COC, ES, OC/3, PDT, TW/2,

13-20, 22, 24, WWT/10-16
LEIGHTON, Queenie (1872-1943)
actress, singer GRB/1-4,
WWT/4-6
LEIGHTON, Mrs. W. H. actress
HAS
LEINSDORF, Erich (b 1912)
Austrian conductor CB
LEIPZIG, Nate (1873-1939) Swed-
ish magician DAB
LEISEN, Mitchell (d 1972 [74])
producer/director/choreographer
BP/57*
LEISH, Kenneth William (b 1936)
American critic BE
LEISTER, Frederick (1885-1970)
English actor WWT/6-14
LEITCH, George (d 1907) actor,
dramatist EA/08*
LEITCH, William Leighton (1804-
83) Scottish scene painter
DNB
LEITZEL, Lillian (1891/93-1931)
German aerial performer SR
LEIVICK, H. [Leivick Halpern]
(1888-1962) Russian/American
dramatist MH, MWD, RE
LEJARS, Mme. (d 1899) eques-
trienne CDP
LEJEUNE, C. A. (d 1973 [76])
critic BP/57*
LEKAIN, Henri Louis Cain
(1728-78) French actor CDP
LELAND, Aaron W. (1761-1833)
American dramatist EAP
LELAND, Rosa M. [Mrs. Rosa
St. Clair] (d 1889) actress,
manager EA/90*
LELOIR, Louis (d 1909 [49])
actor WWT/14*
LELY, Durward (d 1944 [91])
actor DP
LE MAIGNEN, Jeanne see
Brillant, Marie
LEMAIRE, Fred (d 1896) music-
hall singer EA/97*
LE MAIRE, George (d 1930
[46]) comedian BE*
LEMAIRE, Harry (d 1896) music-
hall singer EA/97*
LeMAIRE, Rufus (d 1950 [55])
American producer BP/35*
LEMAITRE, Antoine-Louis-
Prosper see Frédérick
LEMAITRE, Frédérick (1800-
76) French actor ES
LEMAITRE, Jules (1853-1914)
French dramatist GRB/1, 3-4

LEMARE, Edwin Henry (1866-
1934) English composer WWA/1
LE MASSENA, William (b 1916)
American actor BE, TW/6-17,
19-20, 22, 24-26, 28, WWT/
15-16
LEMBECK, Harvey (b 1923) Amer-
ican actor BE, TW/4-8
LEMMENS-SHERRINGTON, Helen
(1834-1906) singer DNB
LEMMON, Harry see Warde,
George Henry
LEMMON, Jack (b 1925) American
actor BE, CB, ES
LEMMON, Priscilla see Warde,
Mrs. George
LEMMON, Shirley (b 1948) Amer-
ican actress TW/30
LEMON, Mark (1809-70) English
dramatist CDP, COC, DNB,
EA/68, HP, OC/1-3
LEMON, Mrs. Mark (d 1890)
EA/91*
LEMONT, John (d 1888) American
acrobat EA/89*
LEMORE, Clara [Mrs. Clara
Lemore Roberts] (d 1898 [48])
actress EA/99*
LEMORE, Harry (d 1898) music-
hall singer EA/99*
LE MOYNE, Sarah Cowell (1859-
1915) American actress CDP,
PP/2, WWS, WWT/1-2
LE MOYNE, William J. (1831-
1905) American actor CDP,
DAB, PP/2, WWA/1
LENA, Lily [Mrs. Alice Lily New-
house] (b 1879) English come-
dian CDP, WWM
LENARD, Mark (b 1927) American
actor BE
LENDER, Marcelle (d 1926 [64])
actress BE*, WWT/14*
LE NEVE, Marion (d 1897) music-
hall performer EA/98*
LENG, Fred G. (d 1878) musical
director EA/79*
LENGEL, Elijah (fl 1848-68) Amer-
ican animal tamer CDP, HAS
LENGEL, William C. (d 1965
[77]) dramatist BP/50*
LENGYEL, Menyhert (1880-1974?)
Hungarian dramatist NTH
LENIER, A. W. (fl 1855) actor
HAS
LENIHAN, Brigid (d 1970 [41])
performer BP/55*
LENIHAN, Burton (d 1974 [96])

performer BP/59*

LENIHAN, Wilfred T. (d 1972 [89]) manager BP/57*

LENIHAN, Winifred (1898-1964) American actress TW/21, WWT/5-11

LENN, Robert (b 1914) American actor TW/4, 24-25

LENNARD, Arthur (d 1954 [86]) singer, actor CDP

LENNARD, Mrs. Arthur T. see Lennard, Sophia

LENNARD, Horace (d 1920) dramatist, lyricist BE*, WWT/14*

LENNARD, Sophia [Mrs. Arthur T. Lennard] (d 1909 [21]) EA/10*

LENNART, Isobel (d 1971 [55]) dramatist BP/55*

LENNON, John (d 1908) EA/09*

LENNON, Mathilde singer CDP

LENNON, Nestor Forbes Richardson (b 1863) American actor WWS

LENNON, Tom (d 1963 [67]) journalist BE*

LENNON, William (d 1898 [44]) manager EA/99*

LENNOX (d 1889) aeronaut EA/90*

LENNOX, Charlotte (1720-1804) American dramatist CDP, CP/1-3, DAB, GT, HP, NTH, TD/1-2, WWA/H

LENNOX, Cosmo Gordon see Stuart, Cosmo

LENNOX, Fred (fl 1878) comedian, singer CDP

LENNOX, Frederick (d 1884) EA/85*

LENNOX, Fred J. [Frederick Jeans] (d 1916) EA/17*

LENNOX, James [Jem Collins] (d 1879) comedian EA/80*

LENNOX, Lottie (d 1947 [61]) actress, singer CDP

LENNOX, Thomas F. (d 1849) Scottish actor HAS

LENNOX, Vera (b 1904) English actress, singer WWT/5-11

LENNOX, Walter S. (fl 1867) American actor HAS

LENNOX, Will (d 1884 [24]) comic singer EA/85*

LENNY, Jack American talent representative, casting director, producer BE

LENO, Dan [George Galvin] (1860-1904) English variety artist, actor CDP, COC, DNB, ES, GRB/1, OC/1-3, PDT

LENO, Dan, Jr. see Galvin, Sydney Paul

LE NOIRE, Rosetta [née Burton] (b 1911) American actress, singer, dancer BE, TW/1, 15-23, 25, 28-30, WWT/14-16

LENON, Edmund Fitz-Maurice see Maurice, Edmund

LENORE, Fred [Frederick Smith] (d 1903) music-hall performer EA/05*

LENORMAND, Henri-René (1882-1951) French dramatist COC, MWD

LENS, Patricia (b 1947) American actress TW/25-29

LENSCHOW, Charles (d 1890) conductor CDP

LENT, Lewis B. (1813/14-87) American circus manager CDP, HAS, NYM, SR

LENTHALL, David (b 1948) American actor TW/29

LENTHALL, Franklyn (b 1919) American director, producer, theatre owner, actor BE

LENTO, Mrs. E. [Mrs. Harry Lento] (d 1891) EA/92*

LENTO, Harry (d 1900 [54]) pantomimist EA/01*

LENTO, Mrs. Harry see Lento, Mrs. E.

LENTON, Harry (d 1884) singer EA/85*

LENTON, J. (d 1895) ventriloquist EA/96*

LENTON, Lance (d 1900) variety performer EA/01*

LENTON, Thomas (d 1878 [47]) gymnast, acrobat, clown, ceiling walker EA/79*

LENTZ, Abraham (d 1975 [64]) writer BP/60*

LENYA, Lotte [née Karoline Blamauer] (b 1900) Austrian actress, singer BE, CB, PDT, TW/1, 10-12, 23-25, WWT/15-16

LENZ, Rick (b 1939) American actor TW/23-24, 26

LEO, Beatrice (fl 1884?) singer CDP

LEO, Frank (d 1940 [66]) composer CDP

LEO, Tom (b 1936) American
actor TW/30
LEON, Mr. (d 1844) minstrel
SR
LEON, Anne (b 1925) English
actress WWT/11-14
LEON, Dan (1826-63) minstrel
HAS
LEON, Francis (b 1840/44)
American dancer, singer,
minstrel manager CDP, HAS
LEON, Frank (d 1909) variety
dancer EA/10*
LEON, Geoff American actor
TW/28-29
LEON, Henry Cecil see Cecil,
Henry
LEON, John see Standing,
John
LEON, Joseph (d 1917 [63])
proprietor, musician EA/18*
LEON, Joseph (b 1923) American
actor TW/28, 30
LEON, W. D. (d 1964 [78]) per-
former, theatre operator BE*
LEON, William Henry (d 1901
[34]) variety performer
EA/03*
LEONARD, Agnes (d 1890 [38])
actress CDP
LEONARD, Billy (1892/95-1974)
Irish actor BTR/74, WWT/
4-13
LEONARD, Denis (d 1878 [78])
Irish comedian EA/79*
LEONARD, Eddie (1871?/75-
1941) American minstrel,
vaudevillian, comedian, song-
writer CB, CDP
LEONARD, Frank (d 1904 [28])
acrobat EA/05*
LEONARD, Frederick see
Lonsdale, Frederick
LEONARD, Georgina (fl 1900s?)
actress, singer CDP
LEONARD, Hugh [né John Keyes
Byrne] (b 1926) Irish drama-
tist AAS, CD, CH, WWT/
14-16
LEONARD, Mrs. J. A. see
Sefton, Mrs. Joseph
LEONARD, Jack E. (d 1973
[61]) comedian WWT/16*
LEONARD, Joseph A. (b 1830)
American actor HAS
LEONARD, Julie (b 1923) Amer-
ican talent representative,
casting consultant BE

LEONARD, Louise see Russell,
Lillian
LEONARD, Mabel (fl 1876) actress
CDP
LEONARD, Marion (d 1956 [75])
actress BE*
LEONARD, Murray (d 1970 [72])
performer BP/55*
LEONARD, Patricia (b 1916) Eng-
lish actress, singer WWT/9-11
LEONARD, Patrick A. (d 1971
[82]) performer BP/55*
LEONARD, Robert (1889-1948)
actor ES, TW/4, WWT/4-10
LEONARD, Tom (d 1878 [27])
comic singer EA/79*
LEONARD, William Ellery (1876-
1944) American writer HJD
LEONARD-BOYNE, Eva (1883/85-
1960) English actress TW/1,
3, 8, 12-13, WWT/4-12
LEONARDO, Harry (d 1964 [61])
performer BP/49*
LEONARDOS, Urylee American
actress TW/25-26, 30
LEONCAVALLO, Ruggero (1858-
1919) Italian composer ES
LEONE, Henry (d 1922 [64]) actor,
singer BE*, BP/6*
LEONE, Leonard (b 1914) American
educator BE
LEONE, Maude (d 1930 [45]) ac-
tress BE*, WWT/14*
LEONI, Mr. (d 1797) singer, actor
CDP, GT, TD/1-2
LEONI, Henri actor, singer CDP
LEONIDOFF, Leon (b 1895) Ru-
manian producer CB
LEONIE, Annie [Mrs. Edward
Colley] (d 1899) serio-comic
EA/00*
LEONOV, Leonid Maximovich (b
1899) Russian dramatist COC,
OC/3
LEONTINE, Countess (b 1881)
French singer WWM
LEONTOVITCH, Eugenie (b 1894/
1900) Russian actress, director,
dramatist AAS, BE, NTH,
TW/3-8, 14-15, 28-29, WWT/
7-16
LEOPOLD, Bertha (d 1905 [26])
EA/06*
LEOPOLD, George (d 1895) gym-
nast EA/96*
LEOPOLD, Harry (d 1904) acrobat
EA/05*
LEOPOLD, Lydia [Mrs. William

Leopold] (d 1899 [53]) EA/00*
LEOPOLD, Sid (d 1897 [23])
pantomimist EA/98*
LEOPOLD, William (d 1888) per-
former? EA/89*
LEOPOLD, Mrs. William see
Leopold, Lydia
LEOTARD, Jules (1830-70) French
gymnast HAS, OC/3
LEOTI, Mr. (fl 1848) actor?
HAS
LEOTI, Mrs. (fl 1848) actress?
HAS
LEPIN, Emanuel (d 1972 [55])
composer/lyricist BP/57*
LEPORSKA, Zoya (b 1920) Rus-
sian actress TW/28
LEPRIS, Sig. (d 1893) ballet
master EA/94*
LE RAE, Grace (d 1956 [75])
actress BE*, WWT/14*
LERIGO, Charles (d 1907 [71])
actor EA/08*
LERMAN, Omar K. (b 1927)
American producer, theatre
consultant BE
LERNER, Alan Jay (b 1918)
American dramatist, lyricist
AAS, BE, CB, CD, ES,
HJD, MWD, PDT, WWT/14-16
LERNER, Carl (d 1973 [61])
performer BP/58*
LERNER, Robert (b 1921) Amer-
ican producer BE
LEROUX, Camille (fl 1843)
French equestrienne CDP
LeROUX, Madeleine (b 1946)
American actress TW/27-30
LEROY, Ernie (d 1917) come-
dian EA/18*
LeROY, Gloria American actress
TW/25, 27
LeROY, Ken (b 1927) American
actor, dancer BE, TW/14,
25-29
LeROY, Loretta (d 1975 [77])
performer BP/60*
LE ROY, Warner (b 1935) Amer-
ican producer, director, actor
BE
LESAGE (d 1882) singer EA/83*
LE SAGE, Geraldine (d 1913
[25]) EA/14*
LE SAGE, Stanley (1880-1932)
English business manager
WWT/2-5
LESAN, David E. (d 1974 [64])
producer/director/choreographer

BP/58*
LESBOROUGH, Violet (d 1910) per-
former? EA/11*
LESDERNIER, Emily (fl 1851-54)
reader, actress HAS
LESLEY, Brenda American actress
TW/23
LESLEY, Carole (d 1974 [38])
performer BP/58*
LESLEY, George (fl 1675-76) Scot-
tish? dramatist CP/2-3
LESLIE, Mrs. (d 1887) EA/88*
LESLIE, Alfred (d 1876) comedian
EA/77*
LESLIE, Alfred (b 1875) English
actor GRB/1
LESLIE, Alfred see Lester,
Alfred
LESLIE, Amy (1860-1939) American
critic, actress WWA/4
LESLIE, Arthur (d 1894 [30]) drama-
tist EA/95*
LESLIE, Arthur (d 1970 [68]) per-
former BP/55*
LESLIE, Bethel (b 1929) American
actress TW/7-9, 21-22, 25
LESLIE, Charlotte Jane [Mrs. T.
N. Leslie] (d 1878) EA/79*
LESLIE, Coss (d 1890) musician,
comedian EA/91*
LESLIE, Edgar (d 1976 [90]) lyri-
cist BP/60*, WWT/16*
LESLIE, Edwin (b 1867) English
manager GRB/1
LESLIE, Elsie [Mrs. W. J. Winter]
(1880/81-1966) American actress
PP/1, WWM, WWS
LESLIE, Enid (d 1890 [34]) actress
CDP
LESLIE, Enid (b 1888) English ac-
tress WWT/2-5
LESLIE, Fannie [or Fanny] (1856-
1935) actress, singer CDP
LESLIE, Frank (b 1926) American
actor TW/8-9
LESLIE, Fred [Fred Hobson] (b
1881) English actor WWT/2-7
LESLIE, Fred[erick] (1855-92)
English actor, dramatist, singer
CDP, DNB, DP, NTH
LESLIE, Mrs. Fred (d 1891 [33])
EA/92*
LESLIE, George W. (d 1911 [48])
actor WWT/14*
LESLIE, Grace [Mrs. George S.
Tutton] (1861-87) actress, singer
NYM
LESLIE, Harry (1837-76) American

tight-rope performer, proprietor, minstrel CDP, HAS
LESLIE, Henry (1830-81) English dramatist, actor EA/68
LESLIE, Henry David (d 1896 [74]) composer EA/97*
LESLIE, Henry J. (d 1900) manager, composer CDP
LESLIE, H. L. [Leslie Lovell] (d 1916) singer EA/17*
LESLIE, Ida (b 1844) American actress HAS
LESLIE, James Orr (d 1907 [70]) singer EA/08*
LESLIE, Lew (1886-1963) composer, producer TW/19, WWT/8-10
LESLIE, Lillian (fl 1895?) singer, actress CDP
LESLIE, Marguerite (1884-1958) Swedish actress GRB/4, WWT/1-6
LESLIE, Marie see Coughtrie, Rosa Ann
LESLIE, Mary (d 1945) English actress SR
LESLIE, May (d 1965 [84]) performer BP/50*
LESLIE, Minnie [Mrs. John Cecil] (d 1907 [38]) actress, dancer GRB/3
LESLIE, Noel (1888-1974) English actor TW/4, 15, 30
LESLIE, Scott (d 1975) performer BP/60*
LESLIE, Sid [Leslie Talford Munford] (b 1882) English actor, singer GRB/1
LESLIE, Sylvia (b 1900) English actress, singer WWT/5-11
LESLIE, Mrs. T. N. see Leslie, Charlotte Jane
LESLIE, Tom (d 1964 [68]) performer BE*
LESLIE, Vera actress GRB/1-2
LESLIE, Will [W. W. Pigott] (d 1911 [39]) EA/12*
LESLIE, William minstrel CDP
LESLIE-STUART, May English actress WWT/2-7
LESMERE, Henry [Strangways Churton Collins] (b 1876) English actor GRB/1
LESSAC, Arthur (b 1910) Palestinian voice teacher & therapist BE
LESSANE, Leroy (b 1942) American actor TW/28

LESSER, Amy (fl 1899-1911) American actress WWM
LESSEY, Mrs. George see Abbey, May Evers
LESSEY, Percy (d 1890) actor EA/91*
LESSING, Doris (b 1919/21) South African dramatist CB, CD, CH, MD, MWD, PDT
LESSING, Gotthold Ephraim (1729-81) German dramatist, critic COC, OC/1-3
LESSING, Madge [Mrs. McClellan] English actress, singer GRB/1-4, WWS, WWT/1-8
LESSINGHAM, Jane (d 1774) actress CDP
LESTER, Ada (d 1881) actress EA/82*
LESTER, Alfred [Alfred Leslie] (1872/74-1925) English actor GRB/4, WWT/1-5
LESTER, Annie [Mrs. Leo Lester] (d 1906) EA/07*
LESTER, Barbara (b 1928) English actress TW/26-29
LESTER, Charles H. English actor GRB/1
LESTER, Edwin American producer, executive BE
LESTER, The Great [Maryan Czajowski] (b 1880) Polish ventriloquist WWM
LESTER, Harry (d 1908) secretary EA/09*
LESTER, Kate English actress WWS
LESTER, Keith (b 1904) English dancer, choreographer ES
LESTER, Ketty (b 1938) American actress TW/20
LESTER, Mrs. Leo see Lester, Annie
LESTER, Mark (b 1876) English actor WWT/4-11
LESTER, William (1889-1956) English composer, musician WWA/3
LESTER, Mrs. William see Hart, Annie
LESTOCK, Charles (d 1900) acting manager EA/01*
LESTOCQ, George (d 1924) actor, director BE*, WWT/14*
LESTOCQ, William [Lestocq Boileau Woolridge] (d 1920 [69]) actor, manager DP, GRB/1-4, WWT/1-3
L'ESTRANGE, Mr. (fl 1796) English

actor HAS

L'ESTRANGE, Mrs. (fl 1796)
English actress HAS

L'ESTRANGE, Jules [or Julian]
(1878-1918) actor GRB/3-4,
WWT/1-3

L'ESTRANGE, Mary (d 1885 [25])
EA/86*

L'ESTRANGE, Nellie singer,
actress CDP

LeSTRANGE, Philip (b 1942)
American actor TW/26, 30

LESTREE, Charles (d 1917)
manager EA/18*

LE SUEUR, Charles (b 1879)
English singer GRB/1-3

LeSUEUR, Hal (d 1963 [59])
actor BE*

LETCHFORD, John (d 1874) actor
EA/76*

LETHBRIDGE, J. W. English
acting manager GRB/3-4,
WWT/1-2

LETHCOURT, H. J. [J. H.
Lorimer] (d 1897 [41]) actor
EA/98*, WWT/14*

LE THIERE, Roma Guillon (d
1903) Italian actress OAA/
1-2

LETTERI, Al (d 1975 [47]) performer BP/60*

LETTERS, Will (d 1910 [33])
singer, composer CDP

LETTON, Francis (b 1912)
American dramatist, director,
actor BE

LETTS, Pauline (b 1917) English
actress WWT/10-16

LETTY, Frances (d 1918) EA/19*

LeVAKE, Dorothy Jean see
Darling, Jean

LEVAN, Harry (d 1963 [61])
performer BE*

LEVANI, Henry (d 1870 [20])
trapezist EA/71*

LEVANT, Oscar (1906-72) American composer, musician CB

LEVANTINE, Frederick F. (fl
1866) equilibrist CDP

LEVASSEUR, Mons. (d 1871)
singer EA/73*

LEVE, Samuel (b 1910) scene
designer TW/2-4, 6-8

LEVEAUX, Montagu V. (b 1875)
English manager WWT/2-3

L'EVEILLE, Auguste (d 1882
[52]) composer EA/83*

LEVENE, Mrs. George see

Levene, Madeline A.

LEVENE, Madeline A. [Mrs. George
Levene] (d 1890 [31]) EA/91*

LEVENE, Samuel (b 1905/07) American actor BE, TW/2-24, 26-27,
29-30, WWT/9-16

LEVENS, Chrissy see Wardell,
Chrystabel Elizabeth

LEVENS, Eva (d 1900 [30]) singer,
dancer EA/01*

LEVENSTON, Michael (d 1904
[48]) manager EA/05*, WWT/
14*

LE VENT, J. (d 1871) gymnast
EA/72*

LEVENTHAL, Jules (1889-1949)
Russian producer TW/5

LEVER, Lady Arthur Levy (d 1917)
dramatist EA/18*

LEVER, J. W. (d 1975 [62]) dramatist BP/60*

LEVERE, Mr. American actor
HAS

LEVERIDGE, Lynn Ann (b 1948)
American actress TW/28-30

LEVERIDGE, Richard (c. 1670-1758)
English dramatist, singer, composer CDP, CP/2-3, DNB

LEVERING, Annie (b 1830) American actress HAS

LEVERSEE, Loretta (b 1928) American actress TW/10-16, 18-19

LEVERTON, George [or Garrett]
H. (d 1949 [52]) American educator, editor BE*, BP/34*

LEVERTON, Henry Fergus (d 1876
[35]) musical director EA/77*

LEVERTON, W. H. (d 1941 [75])
box-office keeper WWT/14*

LEVESON, John (d 1905 [75]) singer
EA/06*

LEVESON, Robert (fl 1580) actor
DA

LEVETT, George (d 1901 [21])
acrobat EA/03*

LEVETTEZ, Edward Ernest (d
1894) EA/95*

LEVEY, Adèle (fl 1900s?) singer,
actress CDP

LEVEY, Carlotta (fl 1900s?) singer, actress CDP

LEVEY, Charles (b 1877) English
actor GRB/1

LEVEY, Ethel (1881-1955) American actress, singer TW/2-4,
11, WWS, WWT/1-11

LEVEY, Florence (fl 1895) dancer,
singer CDP

LEVEY, Harold A. (d 1967 [73])
composer TW/24
LEVEY, John (d 1891) dramatist,
actor EA/92*
LEVEY, Joseph (d 1899 [44])
circus manager EA/00*
LEVEY, Jules (d 1903) musician
EA/04*
LEVEY, Jules (d 1975 [78]) pro-
ducer/director/choreographer
BP/59*
LEVEY, May Lilian singer CDP
LEVEY, Nellie [Mrs. J. H.
Anderson] (d 1916) EA/17*
LEVEY, R. M. (d 1899) con-
ductor EA/00*
LEVEY, W. C. (d 1894 [57])
composer, conductor EA/95*
LEVI, A. actor? HAS
LEVI, Baruk (b 1947) American
actor TW/28-29
LEVICK, Gustavus (1854-1909)
actor CDP
LEVICK, Halper (1888-1962)
dramatist OC/1-3
LEVICK, Milnes (1825/27-97)
English actor CDP, SR
LEVILLY, Jacques (d 1893)
EA/94*
LEVIN, Bernard critic BE
LEVIN, David (b 1932) American
actor TW/12-15
LEVIN, Harry (d 1972 [68])
ticket broker BP/56*
LEVIN, Herman (b 1907) Amer-
ican producing manager BE,
WWT/11-16
LEVIN, Ira (b 1929) American
dramatist BE
LEVIN, Meyer (b 1905) Ameri-
can dramatist BE, HJD, MD
LEVIN, Michael (b 1932) Amer-
ican actor TW/22-23, 26-27
LEVIN, Philip J. (d 1971 [62])
executive BP/56*
LEVINE, Charles B. (d 1974
[75]) creator of Broadway
displays BP/59*
LEVINE, Elliot (b 1924) American
actor TW/23
LEVINE, James (b 1943) Amer-
ican conductor CB
LEVINE, Joseph (d 1964 [68])
lawyer BE*
LEVINE, Joseph E. (b 1905)
American producer BE
LEVINE, Joseph L (b 1926)
American producer, lawyer BE

LeVINESS, Carl (d 1964 [79]) per-
former BP/49*
LEVINSON, Barry (b 1932) Ameri-
can talent representative BE
LEVINSON, Leonard Louis (d 1974
[69]) dramatist BP/58*
LEVIS, Dora actress GRB/1
LEVISON, Alfred (d 1907 [46])
circus manager EA/09*
LEVI-TANAI, Sara Israeli director,
composer, choreographer CB
LEVITE, Jessie Nina (d 1883)
EA/85*
LEVITE, Katie (d 1903) EA/04*
LEVITON, Stewart (b 1939) English
lighting designer WWT/16
LEVITT, Paul (b 1926) American
producer BE
LEVITT, Sanford (b 1947) American
actor TW/30
LEVITT, Saul (b 1913) American
dramatist BE
LEVOY, Albert E. (d 1972 [70])
producer/director/choreographer
BP/57*
LEVY, Benn W. (1900-73) English
dramatist AAS, BE, MD, MH,
MWD, NTH, TW/30, WWT/6-15
LEVY, Burton see Lane, Burton
LEVY, Edwin L. (b 1917) American
educator, director BE
LEVY, Helen Marsh (d 1962) Amer-
ican journalist BE*
LEVY, Mrs. J. see Fox, Della
LEVY, Jacques (b 1935) American
director WWT/15-16
LEVY, Jean see Eckart, Jean
LEVY, J. Langley (d 1945 [74])
critic, journalist BE*, WWT/
14*
LEVY, Jonas (d 1894) lawyer EA/
95*
LEVY, José G. (1884-1936) English
manager, dramatist WWT/3-8
LEVY, Leon Ralph (d 1975 [75])
designer BP/60*
LEVY, Marianne see Tearle,
Marianne
LEVY, Sylvan (d 1962 [56]) per-
former BE*
LEWELLEN, Mr. English actor
HAS
LEWELLEN, Mrs. actress HAS
LEWELLEN, Hester (b 1946)
American actress TW/30
LEWES, Charles Lee (1740-1803)
English actor CDP, DNB,
OC/1-3

LEWES, Charles Lee (d 1891)
EA/92*

LEWES, Mrs. Charles Lee (fl
1792) actress CDP

LEWES, George Henry (1817-78)
English dramatist, critic COC,
DNB, EA/69, ES, OC/1-3,
PDT

LEWES, Miriam Russian/English
actress GRB/2-4, WWT/1-9

LEWESTEIN, Oscar (b 1917) English manager WWT/14-16

LEWIN, Thomas Herbert F.
see Terriss, Tom

LEWINE, Irving I. (d 1965 [84])
theatre owner BP/49*

LEWINE, Richard (b 1910)
American composer, producer
BE

LEWINSKY, Josef (d 1907 [72])
actor WWT/14*

LEWIS, Abby (b 1910) American
actress BE, TW/24, 27

LEWIS, Ada (c. 1875-1925) American actress CDP, SR, WWM,
WWS, WWT/4-5

LEWIS, Allan (b 1908) American
educator, critic, director BE

LEWIS, Alwyn (d 1893 [29])
acting manager EA/94*

LEWIS, Ann (d 1975 [76]) journalist? BP/59*

LEWIS, Arthur (1846-1930)
English actor, manager DAB,
SR, WWT/1-6

LEWIS, Arthur (b 1916) American
producer, director WWT/14-
16

LEWIS, Mrs. Arthur see Terry,
Kate

LEWIS, Arthur James (d 1901
[76]) EA/02*

LEWIS, Bertha (b 1831) English
actress HAS

LEWIS, Bertha (1887-1931) English actress, singer WWT/
4-6

LEWIS, Brenda (b 1921) American singer, actress BE,
TW/11

LEWIS, Carole Ann (b 1939)
American actress TW/23-24

LEWIS, Catherine (1856-1942)
actress, singer CDP

LEWIS, Cathy (d 1968 [50])
performer BP/53*

LEWIS, Charles Bertrand (1842-
1924) American dramatist

DAB

LEWIS, Charles M. (b 1836) American actor HAS

LEWIS, Curigwen Welsh actress
WWT/9-11

LEWIS, Curtis R. (d 1969 [50])
composer/lyricist BP/54*

LEWIS, Dan (fl 1890?) songwriter
CDP

LEWIS, Darrelene (d 1975 [18])
performer BP/59*

LEWIS, Dave (1870-1924) American
actor WWA/5

LEWIS, David (fl 1727-47) dramatist CP/1-3, GT

LEWIS, David (b 1916) American
actor TW/8, 10

LEWIS, Mrs. E. see Leighton,
Clara

LEWIS, Edward (fl 1754-69) dramatist CP/2-3, GT

LEWIS, Edward (1866-1922) English
actor CDP? EA/97

LEWIS, Emily see Bland, Mrs.
Humphrey

LEWIS, Emory (b 1919) American
critic BE

LEWIS, Eric [Tuffley] (1855-1935)
English actor DP, EA/95,
GRB/1-4, WWT/1-7

LEWIS, Estelle Anna Blanche
Robinson (1824-80) American
dramatist WWA/H

LEWIS, Frank (fl 1850?) minstrel
CDP

LEWIS, Frank A. (d 1963 [71])
director BE*

LEWIS, Fred (1860-1927) English
actor WWT/1-5

LEWIS, Frederick G. (1873-1946)
American actor GRB/3-4,
TW/2, WWM, WWS, WWT/1-8

LEWIS, Fred Irving actor TW/1

LEWIS, Mrs. G. [Adelaide Down-
ing] (d 1870) actress EA/72*

LEWIS, George (d 1893) music-
hall performer CDP

LEWIS, Mrs. George see Bullen,
Julia

LEWIS, George W. (1827-53)
American actor, prompter,
agent HAS

LEWIS, Gilbert (b 1941) American
actor TW/26, 28, 30

LEWIS, Mrs. H. see Terry,
Eliza

LEWIS, Hal (d 1934 [61]) business
manager WWT/14*

LEWIS, Henrietta see Henderson, Mrs. William

LEWIS, Henry singer, actor CDP

LEWIS, Henry (1803-92) English actor CDP, HAS

LEWIS, Henry (b 1932) American conductor CB

LEWIS, Mrs. Henry [née Harvey] (d 1855) English actress CDP, HAS

LEWIS, Henry Naish (d 1862 [46]) actor WWT/14*

LEWIS, Horace (fl 1869-1900) American actor PP/2

LEWIS, Ida (d 1935 [86]) actress BE*, WWT/14*

LEWIS, Ida T. (d 1879 [24]) dancer EA/80*

LEWIS, James (1837/40-96) American actor CDP, DAB, SR, WWA/H

LEWIS, Jane (d 1907) EA/08*

LEWIS, Jeffreys (c. 1857-1926) English actress CDP, SR

LEWIS, Jerry (b 1926) American comedian CB

LEWIS, Mrs. Joe see Ward, Fanny

LEWIS, Joe E. (d 1971 [69]) performer BP/56*

LEWIS, John (d 1873 [29]) actor EA/74*

LEWIS, John (d 1892) music-hall performer EA/93*

LEWIS, Mrs. John see Baker, Alexina

LEWIS, Larry (d 1974 [106]) performer BP/58*

LEWIS, Leopold David (1828-90) English dramatist DNB

LEWIS, Lillian [Mrs. Lawrence Marsden] (d 1899) American actress WWA/1

LEWIS, Lloyd Downs (1891-1949) American critic, historian, dramatist BE*, BP/33*

LEWIS, Mabel Terry see Terry-Lewis, Mabel

LEWIS, Marcia (b 1938) American actress TW/25-26, 28-29

LEWIS, Martin (1888-1970) English actor WWT/4-13

LEWIS, Mary Sybil (1900-41) American singer CB, WWA/1

LEWIS, Matthew Gregory (1775-1818) English dramatist CDP, COC, CP/3, DNB, GT, HP, OC/1-3, PDT, TD/1-2

LEWIS, Mel (d 1973 [53]) critic BP/58*

LEWIS, Michael (1930-75) American actor TW/22-24

LEWIS, Mitchell (d 1956 [76]) actor TW/13

LEWIS, Morgan (d 1968 [63]) composer TW/25

LEWIS, Percy (d 1890 [27]) actor EA/92*

LEWIS, Philip (d 1931) musical director BE*, WWT/14*

LEWIS, R. B. (d 1897 [44]) manager EA/98*

LEWIS, Ripple (d 1969 [45]) performer BP/54*

LEWIS, Robert (b 1909) American director, producer, actor BE, TW/3-8, WWT/13-16

LEWIS, Rosie see Haynes, Rosetta

LEWIS, Rudolph (d 1917) actor? singer? EA/18*

LEWIS, Russell (b 1908) American producer BE, TW/3-5, 7

LEWIS, Sam (d 1964) performer BE*

LEWIS, Sarah [Mrs. William Lewis] (d 1886 [68]) EA/87*

LEWIS, Sheldon (1869-1958) American actor TW/14, WWM

LEWIS, Sinclair (1885-1951) American dramatist HJD, MWD, NTH, WWA/3, WWW/5

LEWIS, Sue American actress GRB/1

LEWIS, Susan L. (b 1847) American actress HAS

LEWIS, Ted (1891-1971) American vaudevillian, musician WWA/5

LEWIS, Tim (d 1893 [28]) performer? EA/94*

LEWIS, Tom (d 1927 [63]) Canadian comedian BE*, BP/12*

LEWIS, Tommy (d 1912 [29]) Welsh comedian EA/13*

LEWIS, Violet (b 1885) English actress GRB/1-2

LEWIS, Mrs. W. [Kate Herbert] (d 1873 [21]) EA/74*

LEWIS, Walter (d 1881) EA/82*

LEWIS, William (d 1891 [63]) EA/93*

LEWIS, William (d 1900 [68]) lessee EA/01*

LEWIS, Mrs. William see Lewis, Sarah

LEWIS, William Thomas (1749-

1811) English actor CDP,
COC, DNB, GT, OC/1-3,
TD/1-2

LEWIS, Mrs. William Thomas
see Leeson, Henrietta

LEWIS, Willie (b 1910) American
actor TW/7

LEWIS, Windsor (1918-72) American director, producer BE,
TW/28

LEWISOHN, Alice (fl 1915-59)
American designer, choreog-
rapher, director BE, COC,
OC/3

LEWISOHN, Irene (d 1944) designer, choreographer, director COC, OC/3

LEWISOHN, Oscar (d 1917)
EA/18*

LEWISOHN, Mrs. Oscar see
May, Edna

LEWISOHN, Victor Max (1897-
1934) English actor WWT/
6-7

LEWITAN, Joseph (d 1976 [82])
critic BP/60*

LEWNS, R. (d 1916) EA/17*

LEXY, Edward (b 1897) English
actor WWT/9-10

LEY, Marie actress COC

LEYBOURNE, George [Joe
Saunders] (1842-84) English
music-hall performer CDP,
COC, OC/1-3

LEYDEN, Leo (b 1929) Irish
actor TW/24, 26-29

LEYEL, Carl F. (1875-1925)
English manager WWT/5

LEYERLE, William American
actor TW/30

LEYRITZ, Mr. G. (d 1869 [48])
professor of music EA/70*

LEYSSAC, Paul (d 1946) Danish
actor, lecturer SR, TW/1, 3

LEYTON, Edgar [Louis T.
Dupuy] (d 1902 [33]) singer
EA/03*

LEYTON, George (d 1948 [84])
performer BE*, WWT/14*

LEYTON, Harry (d 1889) music-
hall performer EA/91*

LEYTON, Helen (d 1913) actress EA/96

LEYTON, H. Lawrence actor
GRB/1

LEYTON, Sydney (d 1909 [43])
actor EA/10*

LIAGRE, Alfred de, Jr. (b 1904)

American producer, manager
WWT/9-14

LIBBEY, J. Aldrich (1864-1925)
singer, actor CDP

LIBBY, George A. (d 1973 [86])
performer BP/57*

LIBERTO, Don (b 1915) American
actor TW/4, 28

LIBIN, Paul (b 1930) American
producer, theatre operator BE,
WWT/16

LIBOTT, Robert Y. dramatist,
director, producer BE

LIBUSE, Frank American actor
TW/1

LICHINE, David (1909-72) Russian/
American dancer, choreographer
ES, WWT/9-12

LICHNIAVSKAIA, Alexandra (d
1973 [24]) performer BP/57*

LICHT, David (d 1975 [71]) actor,
director BP/60*, WWT/16*

LICHTENSTEIN, Miss (fl 1847)
singer HAS

LICHTENSTEIN, Ethel [Mrs. Frederick Rosse] (d 1908) EA/09*

LICHTENSTEIN, George (d 1893
[70]) musician EA/94*

LICHTERMAN, Marvin (b 1938)
American actor TW/24-27

LICHTMAN, Joe see Layton, Joe

LICKFOLD, Charles see Warner,
Charles

LICKFOLD, James (d 1888) actor
EA/89*

LIDDELL, John (d 1899 [69]) EA/
00*

LIDDELL, Mrs. John see Markham, Agnes

LIDDON, Amy (d 1896 [52]) actress
EA/97*

LIDDY, Thomas (d 1903 [76]) EA/
04*

LIDEL, Joseph (d 1878) singer,
musician EA/79*

LIDGETT, Dr. Scott (d 1953 [98])
administrator BE*, WWT/14*

LIDINGTON, Alva (d 1917) EA/18*

LIEB, Herman (d 1966 [93]) performer BP/50*

LIEBENAU, Henry (fl 1826) artist
CDP

LIEBHART, Louise (1828-99) singer, actress CDP

LIEBLER, Theodore A. (1852/53?-
1941) American manager, producer CB, WWM

LIEBLER, Theodore A., Jr. (b

1886) American press representative WWM

LIEBLING, George (b 1865)
German composer WWA/4

LIEBLING, Leonard (1874-1945)
American librettist, composer
CB

LIEBLING, William (1895-1969)
Polish/American talent representative BE, TW/26

LIEBMAN, Marvin (b 1923)
American producing manager
WWT/15-16

LIEBMAN, Max (b 1902) American
producer, director BE, CB

LIEBOVITZ, David (d 1968 [76])
dramatist BP/52*

LIEURANCE, Thurlow (1878-1963)
American composer WWA/4

LIEVAN, Albert (1906-65) German actor WWT/10-11

LIEVEN, Tatiana (b 1910) Russian actress WWT/10-11

LIFAR, Serge (b 1905) Russian
dancer, choreographer ES,
WWT/9-12

LIFF, Samuel (b 1919) American stage manager, director,
producer BE

LIGERO, Miguel (d 1968 [71])
performer BP/52*

LIGHT, James (d 1964 [69])
American director BE*,
BP/48*

LIGHT, Norman (d 1970 [70])
manager TW/26

LIGHTFOOT, T. R. (d 1893
[48]) comedian EA/94*

LIGHTNER, Rosella (d 1974
[66]) performer BP/59*

LIGHTNER, Winnie [Winnie
Hanson] (1901-71) American
actress, singer TW/27,
WWT/7-8

"LIGHTNING CALCULATOR, The"
see Hutchings, W. S.

LIGON, Tom (b 1945) American
actor TW/26, 28

LIKELEY, Patricia (d 1976
[52]) performer BP/60*

LILBURN, Charles (fl c. 1900?)
singer, actor CDP

LILIAN, Mme. see Pitt, Mrs.
H. M.

LILLEY, Edward Clarke (d 1974
[86]) actor, director TW/30

LILLEY, Mrs. John (d 1887)
EA/88*

LILLEY, Joseph J. (d 1971 [56])
composer/lyricist BP/55*

LILLIBRIDGE, Gardner R. (fl
1824?) dramatist EAP, RJ

LILLIE, Miss [Lizzie Swindlehurst]
(fl 1863) actress CDP, HAS

LILLIE, Beatrice (b 1898) Canadian
actress AAS, BE, CB, COC,
ES, NTH, PDT, TW/1-2, 4-21,
WWT/4-16

LILLIE, George (fl 1628) actor DA

LILLIE, John (fl 1628) actor DA

LILLIE, Muriel (d 1973 [81]) com-
poser/lyricist BP/58*

LILLIES, Leonard (1860-1923)
English business manager GRB/
4, WWT/1-3

LILLO, George (1693-1739) English
dramatist COC, CP/1-3, DNB,
ES, GT, HP, MH, NTH, OC/
1-3, PDT, RE, TD/1-2

LILLY, A. C. (d 1916 [75]) actor
WWT/14*

LILO, Toby [Walter Eginton] (d
1902 [22]) bicyclist EA/03*

LIMBERT, Roy (1893-1954) English
manager, producer WWT/7-11,
WWW/5

LIMERICK, Mona South American
actress COC, WWT/1-8

LIMON, José (1908-72) Mexican
dancer, choreographer CB, ES,
WWA/5

LIMPUS, Alban Brownlow (1878-
1941) English producer, manager
WWT/6-9

LINA, Mme. [Mrs. Cooper] (d
1906) musician EA/08*

LINCOLN, Alpheus (d 1970 [78])
performer BP/54*

LINCOLN, Ann American actress
TW/1

LINCOLN, Elmo (1889-1952) actor
BE*, BP/37*

LINCOLN, Frank (d 1912 [33])
actor EA/13*

LINCOLN, Jean (d 1969 [34]) agent
BP/54*

LINCOLN, Pattie see Wise,
Mrs. John

LIND, Bertha (fl 1870) dancer
CDP

LIND, Eliza see Zilla, Mme.

LIND, Gillian (b 1904) Indian/Eng-
lish actress WWT/6-16

LIND, Jenny (1820-87) Swedish actress, singer CDP, DNB, ES,
HAS, HP, NTH, NYM, SR,

WWA/H

LIND, Karl acrobat CDP

LIND, Letty [Rudge] (1862-1923) actress, dancer, singer CDP, DP, EA/96, GRB/1-4, WWT/1-4

LIND, Marion English actress GRB/1-2

LINDELHEIM, Johanna Maria see "Baroness, The"

LINDEN, Eric (b 1909) American actor TW/2-3, WWT/8-10

LINDEN, Frank (d 1911) actor, manager SR

LINDEN, Hal [né Harold Lipshitz] (b 1931) American actor, singer BE, TW/19, 21, 24, 27-28, 30, WWT/15-16

LINDEN, Harry (1831-87) American actor CDP, HAS, NYM

LINDEN, Henry see Linden, Harry

LINDEN, Mrs. Henry [Laura Bentley] (fl 1860s) actress HAS

LINDEN, Laura (d 1906 [49]) actress, singer CDP, EA/95

LINDEN, Marie (b 1862) English actress EA/95, WWT/1-9

LINDEN, Marta (b 1910) American actress TW/3-4, 6-9

LINDEN, Robert (b 1912) American stage manager, producer BE

LINDEN, Tommy (d 1969) performer BP/54*

LINDER, Cec (b 1921) Polish actor TW/25-26

LINDER, Jack (b 1896) American producer BE

LINDER, Max (d 1925 [41]) actor BE*, WWT/14*

LINDERMAN, Ed (b 1947) American actor TW/29

LINDFORS, Viveca (b 1920/21) Swedish actress BE, CB, TW/9, 22, 24-25, 27, 30, WWT/15-16

LINDIG, Jillian (b 1944) American actress TW/26-27

LINDLEY, Audra (b 1918) American actress TW/4-5, 22, 24-25, WWT/11

LINDLEY, Henrietta actress EA/96

LINDLEY, Henry (b 1836) Irish actor HAS

LINDLEY, Robert (1776-1855) English musician CDP, DNB

LINDO, Frank (d 1933 [68]) actor, producer, dramatist BE*, WWT/14*

LINDO, Olga (1898-1968) English actress WWT/5-14

LINDOE (fl 1804) actor, dramatist CP/3

LINDON, Agnes (d 1886) singer EA/87*

LINDON, Clarence (d 1862 [37]) actor, manager EA/72*

LINDON, George (d 1883 [28]) EA/84*

LINDON, Isabel (d 1897) music-hall performer EA/98*

LINDON, Louie [Jessie Ferrier] (d 1907 [20]) actress EA/08*

LINDON, Millie (fl 1900s?) singer, actress CDP

LINDON, Tom (d 1888) songwriter EA/89*

LINDROTH, Walter (d 1889 [27]) actor EA/90*

LINDSAY, Mr. (fl 1808) English actor HAS

LINDSAY, Mr. (fl 1836) actor HAS

LINDSAY, Bertha Goulding [Mrs. Charles Mildare] (d 1901) EA/02*

LINDSAY, Sir David (1490-1553/55) Scottish dramatist CP/2-3, HP, PDT

LINDSAY, Howard (1889-1968) American actor, dramatist, producer AAS, BE, CB, COC, ES, MD, MH, MWD, OC/1-3, SR, TW/2-8, 24, WWA/4, WWT/8-14, WWW/6

LINDSAY, Hugh ["Old Hontz, the Clown"] (b 1804) American circus performer HAS

LINDSAY, Jack Graham see Tracy, Douglas

LINDSAY, James (1869-1928) English actor WWT/4-5

LINDSAY, John V. (b 1921) American lawyer BE

LINDSAY, Kevin (d 1975 [51]) performer BP/59*

LINDSAY, Kevin-John (b 1957) American actor TW/26-28

LINDSAY, Lex (d 1971 [69]) actor TW/27

LINDSAY, Philip (b 1924) American actor TW/25-26

LINDSAY, T. (d 1877) Negro
comedian EA/78*
LINDSAY, Vera [Vera Poliakoff]
(b 1911) Russian actress
WWT/9-10
LINDSAY, Mrs. W. see Harvey,
Rose
LINDSEY, Gene (b 1936) American
actor TW/23, 25, 30
LINDSEY, William (1858-1922)
American dramatist DAB
LINDSLEY, A. B. (fl 1809?)
dramatist EAP, RJ
LINDSLEY, Guy (d 1923) Amer-
ican actor BE*, BP/7*
LINDSTROM, Carl (b 1938)
American actor TW/28-29
LINDSTROM, Erik (d 1974 [68])
performer BP/59*
LING, Ritchie (d 1937 [70])
English actor, singer BE*,
BP/21*, WWT/14*
LING, Mrs. Richie see Faust,
Lotta
LINGARD, Alice [Mrs. William
Horace Lingard] (1847-97) ac-
tress CDP, DP
LINGARD, Dickey [Harriet Sarah
Dunning] (b 1850) English ac-
tress CDP, HAS
LINGARD, George A. (d 1876)
actor EA/77*, WWT/14*
LINGARD, George Alexander
(d 1871 [32]) minstrel? EA/72*
LINGARD, Horace (d 1927 [89])
producer, actor, singer BE*,
WWT/14*
LINGARD, James W. (1823-70)
English actor, manager CDP,
HAS, WWA/H
LINGARD, Nellie [Mrs. George
Beauchamp] (d 1899) serio-
comic, actress DP
LINGARD, William Horace (b
c. 1840) English actor, manager
CDP, HAS, SR
LINGARD, Mrs. William Horace
see Lingard, Alice
LINGHAM, Matthew W. (1832-
81) American actor CDP, HAS
LINGHAM, Mrs. Randal see
Dawson, Jane
LINGRAM, Randall Hopley (d
1907 [83]) actor EA/08*
LINJERIS, George (b 1942)
American actor TW/23, 25
LINK, Adolf (d 1933 [81]) Hun-
garian actor BE*, BP/18*

LINK, Peter (b 1944) American
composer WWT/16
LINKLATER, Eric (1899-1974)
Scottish dramatist AAS, MD,
MWD, PDT
LINLEY, Betty (d 1951 [61]) Eng-
lish actress WWT/7-11
LINLEY, Elizabeth Ann [Mrs. R.
B. Sheridan] (1754-92) English
singer COC, ES
LINLEY, George (1798-1865) Eng-
lish composer CDP, DNB
LINLEY, Mrs. George (d 1872)
EA/74*
LINLEY, Margaret (d 1969 [65])
casting director BP/54*
LINLEY, Maria (1763-84) singer
CDP
LINLEY, Thomas, Sr. (1733-95)
English musician, composer
ES
LINLEY, Thomas (1756-78) English
composer, dramatist CDP,
DNB, ES, TD/1-2
LINLEY, William (1771-1835) Eng-
lish dramatist, composer CP/
3, DNB, ES
LINN, Bambi (b 1926) American
dancer, actress BE, TW/1-15,
18-19, WWT/11-15
LINN, Mrs. George (d 1875) EA/
77*
LINN, Harry (d 1890 [44]) Scottish
singer, songwriter CDP
LINN, John Blair (1777-1804)
American dramatist CDP,
EAP, RJ
LINN, Margaret (1934-73) Ameri-
can actress TW/24-30
LINNECAR, Richard (fl 1789)
dramatist CP/3
LINNET, Mrs. Alfred see
North, Ada
LINNEY, Daniel A. (b 1930) Amer-
ican educator BE
LINNIT, S. E. (d 1956 [58]) mana-
ger, business manager, agent
WWT/9-12
LINNIT AND DUNFEE LTD. pro-
ducing managers WWT/13-16
LINTON, Mr. (d c. 1802) singer
TD/1-2
LINTON, Betty Hyatt (b 1930)
American actress TW/25
LINTON, Fred (d 1917 [50]) music-
hall proprietor EA/18*
LINTON, William (b 1935) Scottish
actor TW/28

LINTOTT, Bernard (d 1903)
stage manager EA/04*
LINUS, Ludwig (d 1900) contor-
tionist EA/02*
LINVILLE, Lawrence (b 1939)
American actor TW/24
LINWOOD, Miss (d 1845 [90])
EA/72*
LINYARD, W. K. [W. R.
Goodwin] (b 1837) English
actor HAS
LION, Leon M. (1879-1947)
English actor, dramatist,
manager GRB/1-4, WWT/
1-10
LIONEL, George A. (d 1898)
actor EA/99*
LIONEL, Jerome (d 1887) clown,
pantomimist EA/88*
LIONEL, Mme. Jerome (d
1869) EA/70*
"LION QUEEN" see Moore,
Eliza
LiPARI, Marjorie (b 1945)
American actress TW/25-28,
30
LIPMAN, Mrs. actress HAS
LIPMAN, Alvah S. (1884-1911)
actor, dramatist CDP, SR
LIPMAN, Ann (d 1972 [32])
publicist BP/57*
LIPMAN, Clara [Mrs. Louis
Mann] (1869-1952) American
actress, dramatist GRB/2-4,
TW/9, WWA/3, WWM, WWS,
WWT/1-9
LIPMAN, Mike (fl 1858) clown,
actor HAS
LIPMAN, Sol J. clown HAS
LIPP, Helen Louise see
Bliss, Helena
LIPPARD, George dramatist RJ
LIPPARD, John B. (b 1919)
American theatre designer
BE
LIPPIN, Renee (b 1946) Ameri-
can actress TW/28
LIPPMAN, Monroe (b 1905)
American educator, director
BE
LIPPMANN, Julie Mathilde
(1864-1952) American drama-
tist, critic WWA/3, WWM
LIPPMANN, Zilla American
executive BE
LIPSCOMB, William Percy (1887-
1958) English dramatist
WWT/8-10

LIPSETT, Marianne see Cald-
well, Marianne
LIPSHITZ, Harold see Linden,
Hal
LIPSIS, Elias (d 1879) stage mana-
ger EA/80*
LIPSKY, David (b 1907) American
press representative BE
LIPSON, Clifford (b 1947) Ameri-
can actor TW/26-29
LIPSON, Paul (b 1913) American
actor TW/26-30
LIPTON, Celia (b 1923) Scottish
actress, singer WWT/10-13
LIPTON, Dan English songwriter
GRB/1
LIPTON, George (d 1962 [45])
singer, actor BE*, BP/46*
LIPTON, James (b 1926) American
actor TW/7-8
LIPTON, Michael (b 1925) Ameri-
can actor TW/11, 22-23, 25-
26, 28
LIPZIN, Kenny (1856-1918) Rus-
sian actor ES
LISA, Luba (d 1972 [31]) American
actress TW/21-22, 26, 28-29
LISBOURNE, John (d 1899 [34])
comedian EA/00*
LISBOURNE, Mrs. John see
Priestly, Kate
LISITZKY, Prof. Ephram E. (d
1962 [77]) Russian educator,
scholar BE*
LISLE, Herbert (d 1917) EA/18*
LISLE, Lucille Australian actress
WWT/8-11
LISLE, Rose (d 1891) actress EA/
92*
LISLEY, Mrs. see Barsanti,
Jane
LIST, Emanuel (1891-1967) Austrian
singer WWA/4
LIST, Kurt (d 1970 [57]) producer/
director/choreographer BP/55*
LISTER, Edward (fl 1612) actor
DA
LISTER, Eve (b 1918) English ac-
tress, singer WWT/11-14
LISTER, Francis (1899-1951) Eng-
lish actor TW/8, WWT/4-11
LISTER, Frank (1868-1917) Eng-
lish actor GRB/1, WWT/1-3
LISTER, Mrs. Frank see
Beaufort, Grace
LISTER, George (d 1893) comedian,
manager EA/95*
LISTER, Lance [Solomon Lancelot

Inglis Watson] (b 1901) actor
WWT/4-10
LISTER, Laurier (b 1904/07)
English actor, manager,
director WWT/9-16
LISTER, Moira (b 1923) South
African actress AAS, WWT/
11-16
LISTER, Thomas Henry (1800-
42) English dramatist DNB
LISTMAN, Ryan (b 1939) Amer-
ican actor TW/24-25
LISTON, Mr. actor TD/2
LISTON, Alice [Mrs. Victor
Liston] (d 1880 [23]) EA/81*
LISTON, Mrs. Andrew (d 1899
[27]) actress EA/00*
LISTON, Effie [Mrs. H. Elmore-
Frith] (d 1904 [42]) actress
EA/05*
LISTON, Eleanor [Mrs. Harry
Liston] (d 1890) EA/91*
LISTON, Harry actor, singer,
songwriter CDP
LISTON, Mrs. Harry see
Liston, Eleanor
LISTON, John (1776-1846) Eng-
lish actor BS, CDP, COC,
DNB, ES, GT, OC/1-3, OX
LISTON, Mrs. John [née Sarah
Tyrer] (c. 1780-1854) English
actress BS, CDP, ES
LISTON, Mary Ann (d 1882
[68]) EA/83*
LISTON, Sarah see Liston,
Mrs. John
LISTON, Victor (1838-1913)
English music-hall comedian
CDP, COC, OC/1-3
LISTON, Mrs. Victor see
Liston, Alice
LISTON, William Henry (d 1876
[46]) acting manager EA/77*,
WWT/14*
LISTON, Mrs. W. H. [Maria
Simpson] (d 1879 [45]) actress,
manager EA/80*, WWT/14*
LITCHFIELD, Edward Carr
(d 1894 [57]) manager EA/95*
LITCHFIELD, Mrs. E[dward]
C[arr] (d 1905 [71]) EA/96*
LITCHFIELD, Harriett [née
Hay] (1777-1854) English ac-
tress CDP, DNB, GT, TD/
1-2
LITEL, John (d 1972 [77]) actor
TW/28
LITHGOW, Arthur W. (b 1915)

actor, director, administrator
BE
LITHGOW, John American actor
TW/30
LITOLFF, Henry (d 1891 [72])
composer EA/92*
LITONIUS, Marian (d 1971 [62])
performer BP/56*
LITT, Isaac (d 1887) manager
NYM
LITT, Jacob (1860-1905) American
manager WWA/1
LITT, Sol (d 1913) American
manager SR
LITTA, Marie (1850-83) singer
CDP
LITTELL, Joseph (1821-56) actor
HAS
LITTELL, Mrs. Joseph see
Florence, Mrs. William Jermyn
LITTELL, Robert (1896-1963)
American critic, dramatist
WWA/4, WWT/6-11
LITTLE, Betty Green (b 1898)
American actress TW/5
LITTLE, Cleavon (b 1939) Ameri-
can actor TW/26-28, 30,
WWT/16
LITTLE, C. P. (d 1914) actor,
journalist BE*, WWT/14*
LITTLE, Mrs. Fred J. (d 1894)
EA/95*
LITTLE, George W. (d 1863 [41])
HAS
LITTLE, Guy S. , Jr. (b 1935)
American producer, director,
manager BE
LITTLE, James F. (d 1969 [62])
performer BP/54*
LITTLE, Lillian (d 1972 [66]) ac-
tress TW/29
LITTLE, Ron Paul (b 1949) Amer-
ican actor TW/29-30
LITTLE, Rose Amelia [Mrs. Tom
E. Little] (d 1910 [33]) EA/11*
LITTLE, Stuart W. (b 1921)
American theatre reporter BE
LITTLE, Terence (b 1920) Amer-
ican stage manager, actor BE
LITTLE, Mrs. Tom E. see
Little, Rose Amelia
"LITTLE CORINNE" see Corinne
LITTLEDALE, Richard (d 1951
[47]) actor BE*, WWT/14*
LITTLEFIELD, Catherine (1904/
05-51) American dancer, chore-
ographer ES, WWT/10-11
LITTLEFIELD, Emma [Mrs. Victor

Frederick Moore] (1883-1934)
American actress WWS

LITTLEFIELD, Lucien (d 1960
[64]) American actor BE*

LITTLE GULLIVER [John
Bromelow] (d 1906 [29]) dwarf
comedian EA/07*

"LITTLE MAC" (1844-90) comedian, minstrel CDP

"LITTLE NELL" see Dauvray,
Helen

LITTLER, Blanche (b 1899) English manager OC/1-2, WWT/
8-13

LITTLER, Emile (b 1903) English manager, producer OC/
1-2, WWT/7-16

LITTLER, F. R. (d 1940 [60])
manager BE*, WWT/14*

LITTLER, Prince (1901-73)
English manager, proprietor
OC/1-2, WWT/7-15

LITTLE SIMMY [William Arthur
Simmons] (d 1908) circus
performer EA/09*

LITTLE TICH see Tich, Little

LITTLEWOOD, Joan (b 1914)
English director, manager
BE, CH, COC, ES, OC/3,
PDT, WWT/13-16

LITTLEWOOD, S[amuel] R[ob-
inson] (1875-1963) English
critic GRB/2-4, OC/1-2,
WWT/1-13, WWW/6

LITTON, Marie [Mrs. Whybrow
Robertson] (1847-84) English
actress CDP, DNB, OAA/2

LITVINNE, Félia (1860-1936)
Russian/French singer ES

LIVANOV, Boris N. (d 1972
[68]) performer BP/57*

LIVELY, William E. (d 1973
[66]) dramatist BP/58*

LIVERIGHT, Horace Brisbin
(1886-1933) American manager, producer, publisher
DAB, OC/2-3, WWT/6-7

LIVERMORE, Charles John (d
1906 [61]) variety theatre
director EA/07*

LIVERMORE, Louis (d 1891)
performer? EA/92*

LIVERT, Richard (b 1944)
American actor TW/30

LIVESEY, Barrie (b 1904) actor
ES, WWT/8-12

LIVESEY, Gustavus Carter (d
1905 [34]) EA/06*

LIVESEY, Jack (1901-61) Welsh
actor ES, TW/14-15, WWT/7-
13

LIVESEY, Joseph (d 1911 [31])
actor EA/12*

LIVESEY, Maggie (d 1913) EA/14*

LIVESEY, Roger (1906-76) Welsh
actor AAS, ES, WWT/8-16

LIVESEY, Sam (1873-1936) Welsh
actor ES, WWT/4-8

LIVESEY, Thomas Carter (d 1890)
EA/91*

LIVINGS, Henry (b 1929) English
dramatist, actor AAS, CD,
CH, ES, MH, MWD, PDT, RE,
WWT/14-16

"LIVING SKELETON, The" see
Edson, Calvin

LIVINGSTON, Deacon (d 1963 [c.
75]) performer BE*

LIVINGSTON, Jay (b 1915) American songwriter, composer BE

LIVINGSTONE, Kay (d 1975 [55])
performer BP/60*

LIVING THEATRE, The theatre
collective CD

LIVIUS, Charles Barham (d 1865
[80]) dramatist EA/72*

LJUNGBERG, Göta (d 1955) Swedish
singer WWW/5

LLEWELYN, Alfred H. (d 1964)
actor BE*

LLEWELLYN, Fewlass (1866-1941)
English actor, manager, pro-
ducer, dramatist GRB/1-4,
WWT/1-9

LLEWELLYN, Richard Welsh
dramatist CB

LLOYD (d c. 1807) actor, dramatist
CP/3

LLOYD, Al (d 1964 [80]) performer
BE*, BP/49*

LLOYD, Alfred (d 1916) EA/17*

LLOYD, Alice [Mrs. T. McNaugh-
ton] (d 1949 [76]) singer, actress CDP, TW/6

LLOYD, Alice Marie (d 1891)
music-hall performer EA/92*

LLOYD, Arthur (1840-1904) English
music-hall performer CDP,
OC/1-2

LLOYD, Mrs. Arthur see King,
Katty

LLOYD, Arthur Watson see
Rigby, Arthur

LLOYD, Charles (d 1889) advance
agent EA/90*

LLOYD, Mrs. Charles F. see

Stafford Smith, Mary

LLOYD, Clara [Clara Laidlaw; Mrs. F. W. Lloyd] (d 1887) actress EA/88*

LLOYD, Delarue (d 1899) comedian EA/00*

LLOYD, Doris (d 1968 [68]) English actress WWT/5-9

LLOYD, Eddie (d 1974 [83]) performer BP/59*

LLOYD, Edward (d 1909 [74]) EA/10*

LLOYD, Eliza [Mrs. F. H. Lloyd] (d 1870 [60]) EA/71*

LLOYD, Mrs. F. H. see Lloyd, Eliza

LLOYD, Florence (b 1876) Welsh actress, singer GRB/4, WWT/1-5

LLOYD, Frederick (d 1962 [75]) manager WWT/14*

LLOYD, Frederick William (1880-1949) English actor WWT/6-10

LLOYD, Fred W. (d 1884) acting manager EA/85*

LLOYD, Mrs. F. W. see Lloyd, Clara

LLOYD, George American actor TW/1

LLOYD, Grace (d 1961 [86]) performer BE*

LLOYD, Hannibal Evans (fl 1799) translator CP/3

LLOYD, Harold (1894-1971) American actor, producer CB

LLOYD, Horatio F. (d 1889) actor, singer CDP

LLOYD, Jack (d 1976 [53]) performer BP/60*

LLOYD, James William (d 1909) performer? EA/10*

LLOYD, John (d 1873 [56]) actor? EA/74*

LLOYD, John (d 1944 [74]) actor BE*, WWT/14*

LLOYD, John (d 1976 [38]) dramatist BP/60*

LLOYD, Mrs. John (d 1886 [40]) EA/87*

LLOYD, John Robert (b 1920) American designer BE, TW/7-8

LLOYD, Margaret Leah [Mrs. Harry King-Lloyd] (d 1904 [30]) EA/05*

LLOYD, Marie [Wood] (1870-1922) English variety artist CDP, COC, ES, GRB/1-4, OC/1-3, PDT, WWT/4

LLOYD, Mildred Davis (d 1969 [68]) performer BP/54*

LLOYD, Morris (d 1974 [83]) actor, vaudevillian BP/58*, WWT/16*

LLOYD, Myra Mackenzie see Rosalind, Myra

LLOYD, Norman (b 1914) American producer, director, actor BE, TW/10, 13

LLOYD, Ramsey Percy R. (d 1910 [23]) EA/11*

LLOYD, Robert (d 1764) dramatist CP/1-3, GT, TD/1-2

LLOYD, Robert (d 1881 [44]) Scottish comedian EA/83*

LLOYD, Roderick (d 1945 [39]) singer WWT/14*

LLOYD, Rosie (d 1944 [64]) singer, actress CDP

LLOYD, Sam (d 1883 [37]) comedian EA/84*

LLOYD, Theodore (d 1907) showman EA/08*

LLOYD, Tom singer, actor CDP

LLOYD, Violet (b 1879) English actress GRB/1-4, WWT/1-5

LLOYD, William Watkiss (1813-93) scholar DNB

LLOYD-JAMES, Mrs. (d 1911 [28]) actress EA/12*

LLOYDS, Frederick (d 1894) scene artist WWT/14*

LLOYD-WEBBER, Andrew (b 1948) English composer AAS, WWT/16

LOADER, A. McLeod (b 1869) English manager, dramatist WWT/3

LOANE, Mary American actress TW/27

LOBB, Graham see Graham, Ly

LoBIANCO, Tony (b 1936) American actor TW/24-26

LOBLEY, William (d 1883 [65]) mechanist, modeller EA/84*

LOCATILI, Louisa (d 1857) singer HAS

LOCHER, Felix (d 1969 [87]) performer BP/53*

LOCK, J. H. (d 1888) agent EA/89*

LOCK, Mrs. J. H. [Mme. Ramsden] (d 1883 [55]) EA/84*

LOCKARD, Edmond see Duquesne,

Edmond
LOCKE, Mrs. C. H. (d 1910)
EA/11*
LOCKE, Edward (1869-1945)
English dramatist, actor
WWA/2, WWM, WWT/3-7
LOCKE, Fanny see Hatton,
Fanny
LOCKE, Fred (d 1907 [55]) ac-
tor, manager, pantomime
writer GRB/3
LOCKE, George E. (1817-80)
American actor CDP, HAS,
SR
LOCKE, Mrs. George E. (b
1828) American actress
HAS
LOCKE, Katherine (b 1910)
American actress WWT/9-11
LOCKE, Matthew (1632?-77)
English composer CDP,
DNB, ES
LOCKE, Robinson (1856-1920)
American critic NTH
LOCKE, Sam (b 1917) American
dramatist BE
LOCKE, Vivia (b 1917) American
educator BE
LOCKE, Will H. (d 1950 [82])
dramatist BE*, WWT/14*
LOCKE, William John (1863-
1930) West Indian dramatist
GRB/2-4, WWM, WWT/1-6
LOCKE, Yankee (d 1880) Ameri-
can actor EA/81*
LOCKER, Jody (b 1944) Ameri-
can actor TW/24
LOCKERBIE, Beth (d 1968 [53])
performer BP/53*
LOCKETT, Louis (d 1964 [71])
American performer, dancer
BE*, BP/49*
LOCKHART, Alice [Mrs. Sam
Lockhart] (d 1897 [41]) EA/
98*
LOCKHART, Annie see Jack-
son, Mrs. Harry
LOCKHART, Gene (1891/92-
1957) Canadian actor CB,
TW/1, 6-7, 13, WWA/3,
WWT/9-12
LOCKHART, George (d 1904
[54]) animal trainer EA/05*
LOCKHART, June (b 1925)
American actress BE, TW/
4-8, 11-13
LOCKHART, Kathleen actress
TW/1

LOCKHART, Mrs. Sam see
Lockhart, Alice
LOCKHART, Samuel (d 1894 [69])
EA/95*
LOCKMAN, John (d 1771) dramatist
CP/2-3
LOCKRIDGE, Frances D. (d 1963
[66]) dramatist BP/47*
LOCKRIDGE, Richard (b 1898)
American critic, dramatist
CB, NTH, WWT/10-11
LOCKTON, Joan (b 1901) English
actress, singer WWT/6-7
LOCKWOOD, Adolphus (d 1885)
musician EA/86*
LOCKWOOD, Carolyn (b 1932)
American educator, director
BE
LOCKWOOD, Edmund E. P. (d
1911 [55]) manager EA/12*,
WWT/14*
LOCKWOOD, Ernest Raven (d 1897
[57]) singer? EA/98*
LOCKWOOD, Mrs. Fred see
Lockwood, Harriet
LOCKWOOD, Harold (1887-1918)
actor BE*
LOCKWOOD, Harriet [Mrs. Fred
Lockwood] (d 1889) EA/91*
LOCKWOOD, John (d 1891 [61])
bandmaster EA/92*
LOCKWOOD, King (d 1971 [73])
performer BP/55*
LOCKWOOD, Margaret (b 1916)
Indian/English actress AAS,
CB, ES, WWT/8-16
LOCKWOOD, Robert (d 1885 [89])
comedian EA/86*
LOCKYER, Miss see Jefferson,
Mrs. Joseph, I
LODEN, Barbara American actress
BE, TW/15, 20-21, 24
LODER, Basil (b 1885) English
actor WWT/6-8
LODER, Mrs. Basil see Deane,
Barbara
LODER, Charles A. (1858-1949)
actor SR
LODER, Edward James (1813-65)
English conductor, composer
CDP, DNB, HAS
LODER, Mrs. [Edward James]
(d 1855) actress HAS
LODER, Mrs. [Edward James],
II [Emily Neville] (d 1867) HAS
LODER, Mrs. E. J. (d 1880 [67])
singer EA/81*
LODER, George (1816?-68) English

composer DNB
LODER, John (d 1853 [41]) musician EA/72*
LODER, Kathryn (b 1940) American actress TW/30
LODGE, John Davis (b 1903) American actor BE
LODGE, Ruth (b 1914) English actress WWT/7-9
LODGE, Thomas (c. 1558-1625) English dramatist CP/1-3, FGF, HP, NTH, PDT
LODS, Jean (d 1974 [71]) producer/director/choreographer BP/58*
LOEB, John Jacob (d 1970 [60]) composer/lyricist BP/54*
LOEB, Philip (1892/94-1955) American actor, producer TW/1-6, 8-9, 12, WWT/9-11
LOESSER, Frank (1910-69) American composer, lyricist AAS, BE, CB, ES, NTH, TW/26, WWT/14
LOESSER, Lynn producer BE
LOEW, David L. (d 1973 [75]) producer/director/choreographer BP/57*
LOEW, Marcus (1870-1927) American manager DAB, NTH, SR, WWA/1
LOEWE, Frederick (b 1901/04) Austrian/American composer AAS, BE, CB, ES, HJD, PDT, WWT/16
LOEWE, Sophie (1815-66) singer CDP
LOFTHOUSE, Mrs. (d 1872 [29]) music-hall performer? EA/73*
LOFTHOUSE, John Steel (d 1883 [54]) equestrian & variety agent EA/85*
LOFTING, Kitty actress GRB/2
LOFTUS, Cissie [Cissy] see Loftus, Marie Cecilia
LOFTUS, Edgar (d 1891) EA/92*
LOFTUS, John (d 1896) EA/97*
LOFTUS, Kitty [Mrs. P. Warren-Smith] (1867-1927) English actress, singer CDP, GRB/1-4, WWT/1-5
LOFTUS, Marie (d 1940 [83]) singer, actress CDP
LOFTUS, Marie Cecilia [Cissie] (1876-1943) Scottish actress CB, CDP, EA/94, GRB/1-4, NTH, OC/1-3, SR, WWS,

WWT/1-9, WWW/4
LOFTUS-LEYTON, Rosie [Mrs. A. G. Spry] (d 1902 [27]) actress EA/03*, WWT/14*
LOGAN, Miss see Colman, Mary
LOGAN, Celia (fl 1852-68) American actress HAS
LOGAN, Cornelius A. (1806-53) American actor, manager, dramatist CDP, DAB, HAS, HJD, RJ, WWA/H
LOGAN, Eliza (1829/30-72) American actress, lessee CDP, HAS
LOGAN, Ella (1910/13-69) Scottish actress, singer BE, TW/3-15, 25, WWT/11
LOGAN, John (1748-85) Scottish dramatist CP/3
LOGAN, John (d 1972 [48]) performer BP/57*
LOGAN, Joshua (b 1908) American producing manager, dramatist AAS, BE, CB, CD, ES, MWD, PDT, TW/2-8, WWT/11-16
LOGAN, Mary see Colman, Mary
LOGAN, Nedda Harrigan (b c. 1900) American actress BE
LOGAN, Olive (1839/41-1909) American actress CDP, DAB, HAS, WWA/1
LOGAN, Stanley (1885-1953) English actor, producer WWT/4-10
LOGAN, T. D. (d 1854) HAS
LOGGIA, Robert (b 1930) American actor TW/13-15, 21, 25-26, 29-30
LOGIE, Charles Harry Gordon (d 1897 [20]) EA/98*
LoGRIPPO, Joe (b 1939) American actor TW/30
LOGUE, Christopher (b 1926) English dramatist MD, MWD
LOGUE, Mary see Nagle, Mrs. Joseph E.
LOHMAN, Dorothy (d 1973) agent BP/57*
LOHMANN, Otto (b 1921) American actor TW/18
LOHN, Anna (1830-1902) actress CDP
LOHR, Marie (1890-1975) Australian/English actress AAS, ES, GRB/3-4, WWT/1-15
LOHSE, Frau (d 1906 [30]) singer EA/07*
LOISSET, Mr. (fl 1847) acrobat CDP
LOISSET, Emilie (d 1882 [25])

equestrian CDP

LOKER, William A. (d 1965
[74]) performer BP/50*

LOLA, Little (b c. 1854) actress
HAS

LOLKES, Mynheer Wylrand (fl
1799) dwarf CDP

LOLLER, Charles P. (d 1908
[28]) conductor EA/09*

LOM, Herbert (b 1917) Czech
actor WWT/12-13

LOMAN, Hal (b 1929) American
actor TW/12

LOMAS, Mr. (fl 1851) actor
HAS

LOMAS, Bert (d 1898) music-
hall performer EA/99*

LOMAS, Herbert (1887-1961)
English actor WWT/3-13,
WWW/6

LOMAS, Richard (b 1877) English animal impersonator
GRB/1

LOMAS, William (d 1881) scene
painter EA/82*

LOMATH, Stuart Scottish actor
GRB/1

LOMATH, Mrs. Stuart see
Owen, Ellen

LOMAX, Dick (d 1889 [36])
comedian EA/90*

LOMAX, Elizabeth [Mrs. Robert
Lomax] (d 1887) EA/88*

LOMAX, Mrs. Fawcett see
Birchenough, Agnes

LOMAX, Felix (b 1858) English
actor GRB/1

LOMAX, John (d 1895 [71]) actor,
manager EA/96*

LOMAX, Mrs. John (d 1891
[80]) actress EA/92*

LOMAX, John A. (d 1974 [67])
performer BP/59*

LOMAX, Mrs. Robert see
Lomax, Elizabeth

LOMAX, Robert Charles (d
1890 [47]) EA/91*

LOMBARD, Harry (d 1963 [74])
performer BE*

LOMBARD, Michael (b 1934)
American actor TW/22-23,
26-27, 30

LOMBARD, Pat (d 1974 [61])
producer/director/choreographer
BP/59*

LOMBARD, Peter (b 1935) American actor TW/28-29

LOMBARDO, Carmen (d 1971

[67]) performer BP/55*

LOMBARDO, Guy (1902-77) Canadian producer, musical director
BE

LOMIER, Charles (fl 1894) singer
CDP

LONDON, Chet (b 1931) American
actor TW/22

LONDON, Ernest A. (d 1964 [85])
performer BE*, BP/49*

LONDON, George (b 1920/21) Cana-
dian/American singer CB, ES

LONDON, Jack (d 1916 [40])
dramatist WWT/14*

LONDON, Marc (b 1930) American
actor TW/21

LONDON, Tom (d 1963 [81]) actor
BE*

LONERGAN, Leonore (b 1928)
American actress TW/1-9

LONERGAN, Lester (d 1931 [62])
Irish actor, director BE*, BP/
16*

LONERGAN, Lester, Jr. (d 1959
[65]) actor BE*, BP/44*

LONERGAN, Mrs. Lester see
Ricard, Amy

LONG, Avon (b 1910) American
actor, singer, dancer, songwriter BE, TW/2-5, 28-29,
WWT/16

LONG, Charles (d 1906 [49])
architect EA/07*

LONG, Gabrielle (1888-1952)
English dramatist WWW/5

LONG, Harriet C. [Mrs. J. H.
Long; Mrs. Charles Butler]
(1830-98) singer CDP

LONG, Mrs. J. H. see Long,
Harriet C.

LONG, John (d 1897) manager
EA/98*

LONG, John Luther (1861-1927)
American dramatist COC,
DAB, GRB/2-4, HJD, MWD,
OC/3, WWS, WWT/1-5, WWW/2

LONG, Mrs. Johnny see Long,
Norah

LONG, Joseph Sidney (d 1904 [56])
writer EA/05*

LONG, J. P. singer, songwriter
CDP

LONG, Juanita see Hall, Juanita

LONG, Lily Augusta (d 1927)
American writer WWA/1

LONG, Lois (d 1974 [73]) journalist
EA/59*

LONG, Mary Elitch (d 1936 [86])

American theatre owner & manager BE*, BP/21*

LONG, Nicholas (d 1622) actor, manager DA

LONG, Nick, Jr. (d 1949 [43]) dancer TW/6

LONG, Norah [Mrs. Johnny Long] (d 1916) EA/18*

LONG, Ray American actor TW/6

LONG, Richard (d 1974 [47]) performer BP/59*

LONG, Sam, Big (d 1863) HAS

LONG, Shorty (b 1923) American actor TW/12-13

LONG, Sumner Arthur (b 1921) American dramatist BE

LONG, Susan (b 1947) American actress TW/27

LONG, Tamara (b 1941) American actress TW/25-26, 29-30

LONG, Mrs. V. C. (d 1870 [36]) EA/71*

LONG, Walter (b 1889) American actor TW/1

LONG, W. Bethell, Jr. (d 1969 [53]) actor TW/26

LONG, Wesley (d 1973 [72]) performer BP/57*

LONGDEN, C. H. (d 1918 [60]) EA/19*

LONGDEN, Mrs. C. H. see Dottridge, Dolly

LONGDEN, John (b 1900) West Indian actor WWT/7-9

LONGDON, Terence (b 1922) English actor WWT/15-16

LONGE, Jeffery (d 1974 [51]) stage manager BP/59*

LONGFELLOW, H. W. American dramatist RJ

LONGFELLOW, Stephanie (fl 1906-08) actress WWS

LONGFORD, Earl of (1902-61) English dramatist, manager COC, MH, OC/1-3, WWT/9-13

LONGFORD, Lady see Trew, Christine Patti

LONGO, Peggy (b 1943) American actress TW/26-29

LONGO, Peggy see Atkinson, Peggy

LONGSTREET, Stephen (b 1907) American dramatist BE, CD

LONGSTRETH, Marian (b 1906) executive BE

"LONG TOM COFFIN" see Scott, John M.

LONGVILLE, Emily Kate (d 1886 [31]) music-hall performer EA/88*

LONGWORTH, Theresa (d 1881) public reader & lecturer EA/82*

LONGWORTH, Thomas Frederick [Teddy O'Lynn] (d 1883 [31]) performer? EA/84*

LONNEN, Beatrice Helen see Lonnen, Jessie

LONNEN, Edward Jesse (d 1863-1901) singer, actor CDP, CP

LONNEN, Ellen Farren see Lonnen, Nellie

LONNEN, Harriett [Mrs. William Rooles Lonnen] (d 1892 [67]) EA/93*

LONNEN, Jessie [Beatrice Helen Lonnen] (b 1886) English actress GRB/2-4, WWT/1-5

LONNEN, Nellie [Ellen Farren Lonnen] (b 1887) English actress GRB/2-4, WWT/1-5

LONNEN, Walter (d 1903) actor EA/05*, WWT/14*

LONNEN, William Rooles see Champion, William

LONNEN, Mrs. William Rooles see Lonnen, Harriett

LONNON, Alice (b 1872) American actress GRB/3-4, WWS, WWT/1-5

LONSDALE, Ada (d 1889 [16]) variety performer EA/90*

LONSDALE, Annie (fl 1852) English actress CDP, HAS

LONSDALE, Frederick [Frederick Leonard] (1881-1954) English dramatist AAS, COC, DNB, ES, MD, MH, MWD, NTH, OC/1-3, PDT, TW/10, WWT/1-11, WWW/5

LONSDALE, H. G. (d 1923) actor BE*, WWT/14*

LONSDALE, Lillie (d 1880 [39]) actress EA/81*

LONSDALE, M. (fl 1784-94) machinist, dramatist CP/3

LONSDALE, Thomas J. (d 1928) lyricist BE*, WWT/14*

LONSDALE, T. W. S. (d 1910 [28]) EA/11*

LOOFBOURROW, John G. (d 1964 [61]) American actor BE*

LOOMIS, Deborah (b 1945) American actress TW/29

LOOMIS, Harvey Worthington (1865-1930) American composer WWA/1, WWM

LOOMIS, Rod (b 1942) American actor TW/28-30

LOONE, Mrs. E. [Mrs. Samuel Loone] (d 1870) actress? EA/71*

LOONE, Samuel (d 1878 [59]) portable theatre manager EA/79*

LOONE, Mrs. Samuel see Loone, Mrs. E.

LOOS, Anita (b 1893) American dramatist AAS, BE, CB, ES, HJD, WWT/6-16

LOPER, Don (d 1972 [66]) choreographer, dancer BP/57*, WWT/16*

LOPEZ, Miss (fl 1828-50) American actress, dancer HAS

LOPEZ, Eddie (d 1971 [31]) journalist BP/56*

LOPEZ, Gerald (d 1905 [27]) coloured comedian EA/06*

LOPEZ, Jesus M. (d 1962 [85]) Mexican magician BE*

LOPEZ-CEPERO, Luis American actor TW/26

LOPOKOVA, Lydia (b 1892) Russian dancer, actress WWT/4-12

LOPUKHOV, Fyodor (d 1973 [86]) performer BP/57*

LOQUASTO, Santo designer WWT/16

LORAINE, A. S. English actor, manager GRB/1

LORAINE, Henry (d c. 1857) English actor HAS

LORAINE, Henry (d 1899 [80]) actor BE*, EA/00*, WWT/14*

LORAINE, Mrs. Henry [Edith Kingsley] (d 1895) EA/96*

LORAINE, Robert (1876-1935) English actor, manager AAS, COC, ES, GRB/2-4, OC/1-3, WWM, WWS, WWT/1-7

LORAINE, Violet (1886/87-1956) English actress, singer CDP, DNB, WWT/4-11

LORCA, Federico García (1898-1936) Spanish dramatist COC, NTH, OC/1-3

LORD, Barbara (b 1937) American actress BE

LORD, Basil (b 1913) English actor WWT/12-16

LORD, Charles minstrel CDP

LORD, Jack American actor TW/11-16

LORD, James A. (fl 1860) American actor HAS

LORD, Lucy (d 1969 [70]) performer BP/53*

LORD, Pauline (1890-1950) American actress AAS, DAB, ES, NTH, TW/1-7, WWA/3, WWT/5-10

LORD, Philip (d 1968 [89]) performer BP/53*

LORD, Phillips H. (d 1975 [73]) dramatist BP/60*

LORD, Robert New Zealand dramatist CD

LORD, William (d 1868) pianist EA/69*

LORD, Wilson (d 1880 [41]) musical director EA/81*

LORDE, Athena (d 1973 [57]) performer BP/57*

LORENGAR, Pilar (b 1930) Spanish singer ES

LORENZ, George (d 1972 [52]) performer BP/57*

LORENZ, John A. (d 1972 [85]) performer BP/57*

LORENZ, Max (d 1975 [72]) performer BP/59*

LORENZI, Frank (d 1906) performer? EA/07*

LORENZO, Ange (d 1971 [77]) composer, lyricist BP/55*

LORENZO, Will (d 1880) music-hall performer EA/81*

LORIMER, Jack [John G.] (b 1883) Scottish actor, dancer, entertainer CDP, GRB/1

LORIMER, J. H. see Lethcourt, H. J.

LORIMER, Maxwell George see Wall, Max

LORIMER, Wright (1874-1911) American actor, dramatist GRB/3-4, SR, WWA/1, WWS

LORING, Master (b 1790) American actor HAS

LORING, Estelle (b 1925) American actress TW/4-9

LORING, Eugene (b 1914) American choreographer, dancer BE, CB, ES

LORING, Kay (b 1913) American actress TW/2

LORING, Norman (1888-1967) English producer, manager, actor WWT/6-10

LORINI, Sig. Domenico Bragioni (fl 1847-50) singer CDP, HAS

LORINI, Virginia (d 1865 [31]) singer CDP

LORNE, Constable (d 1969 [55]) performer BP/54*

LORNE, Constance (b 1914) Scottish actress WWT/11-16

LORNE, Marion (1888-1968) American actress BE, SR, TW/24, WWA/5, WWT/4-12, WWW/6

LOROS, George (b 1944) American actor TW/24, 27, 29-30

LORRAINE, Emily (d 1944 [66]) English actress TW/1

LORRAINE, Ettie (d 1884) music-hall performer EA/86*

LORRAINE, Lilian [Eulallean de Jacques] (1892-1955) American actress CDP, TW/11, WWT/4-6

LORRAINE, Miss Percy see Boyer, Mrs.

LORREANO, Harry (b 1861) English actor GRB/1

LORRING, Joan (b 1931) actress BE, TW/26

LORTEL, Lucille American producer, actress BE, WWT/15-16

LORTON, John T. (1824-60) American actor, manager HAS

LOS ANGELES, Victoria de (b 1923) Spanish singer ES

LOSCH, Tilly (1907?-75) Austrian dancer, choreographer, actress BE, CB, WWT/7-12

LOSEBY, Constance [Mrs. John Caulfield] (d 1906 [55]) actress, singer OAA/2

LOSEBY, Elizabeth (d 1888 [69]) EA/90*

LOSEE, Frank (1856-1937) American actor PP/2

LOSEE, Mrs. Frank see Elmore, Marion

LOSEY, Joseph (b 1909) American director ES

LOTHAR, Rudolph (b 1865) German dramatist, critic GRB/3-4, WWT/1

LOTINGA, Ernest (1876-1951) English actor WWT/8-11

LOTITO, Louis A. (b 1900) American manager BE

LOTTA [Charlotte Crabtree] (1847-1924) American actress CDP, COC, DAB, ES, HAS, GRB/3-4, HJD, NTH, OC/1-3, PP/1, SR, WWA/1, WWS, WWT/1-4

LOTTO, Alf (d 1912 [34]) trick cyclist EA/13*

LOTTO, Mrs. Jack (d 1904) EA/05*

LOUCHLAMN, Gearold O. (d 1970 [78]) performer BP/55*

LOUDON, Dorothy (b 1933) American actress WWT/15-16

LOUGHEAD, Flora Haines (b 1855) American dramatist WWA/4

LOUIS, Mons. (fl 1826?) French giant CDP

LOUIS, Miss (fl 1829) actress CDP

LOUIS, Anita (d 1970 [53]) performer BP/54*

LOUIS, Murray (b 1926) American dancer, choreographer CB

LOUISE, Mme. [Louise Miller] (d 1892 [81]) dancer EA/93*

LOUISE, Mlle. (fl 1828) French dancer HAS

LOUISE, Tina (b 1937) American actress BE

LOUISETTE, Josephine [Mrs. Josephine Heiskell] (1837-60) American performer HAS

LOU-TELLEGEN (b 1881/85) Dutch/French actor WWT/3-7

LOUTHER, Henry (d 1887) actor EA/88*

LOUTHERBOURG, Philip James de see De Loutherbourg, Philip James

LOUW, Allan (b 1915) American actor TW/23

LOVAT, Nancie (1900-46) English actress, singer WWT/4-8

LOVE, Mr. (fl 1753) actor HAS

LOVE, Mrs. (fl 1753) actress HAS

LOVE, Miss see Love, Emma Sarah

LOVE, Bessie [née Horton] (b 1891/98) American actress BE, ES, WWT/13-16

LOVE, Ellen American actress TW/2-3

LOVE, Emma Sarah [Mrs. Grandby Calcraft] (b 1801) English actress, singer BS, CDP, OX

LOVE, James see Dance, James

LOVE, John James magician, ventriloquist CDP

LOVE, Mabel (1874-1953) English actress, dancer DP, EA/94, GRB/1-4, WWT/1-10

LOVE, Montagu (1877-1943) English actor WWT/7-9

LOVE, Phyllis (b 1925/29) American actress BE, TW/10-17

LOVE, Valentine (fl 1869) performer HAS

LOVE, Mrs. Valentine (fl 1869) performer HAS

LOVE, William Edward (1806-67) polyphonist CDP

LOVECRAFT, Frederick A. (d 1893 [42]) manager CDP

LOVEDAY, Mrs. Ely (d 1892 [92]) actress EA/93*

LOVEDAY, George (d 1887 [54]) acting manager EA/89*

LOVEDAY, George B. (d 1887) manager NYM

LOVEDAY, Henry Joseph (d 1910 [71]) stage manager GRB/1-4

LOVEDAY, Thomas (fl 1635-67?) actor DA

LOVEGROVE, Jane (d 1905 [95]) actress EA/06*

LOVEGROVE, William (1778-1816) actor CDP

LOVEGROVE, William (d 1879 [63]) actor, manager EA/80*

LOVEJOY, Alexander Frederick (d 1896) music-hall proprietor EA/97*

LOVEJOY, Mrs. Alexander Frederick see Lovejoy, Louisa

LOVEJOY, Alfred (d 1891 [41]) music-hall manager EA/92*

LOVEJOY, Edith (d 1891) EA/92*

LOVEJOY, Frank (1914-62) American actor TW/19

LOVEJOY, Louisa [Mrs. Alexander Frederick Lovejoy] (d 1895) EA/97*

LOVEJOY, Robin (b 1923) Fijian director WWT/16

LOVEKYN, Arthur (fl 1509-13) member of the Chapel Royal DA

LOVEL, Gertrude [Mrs. H. A. Kennedy] (1868-1908) English actress GRB/1

LOVELACE, Richard (1618-58)

English dramatist CP/2-3, FGF

LOVELL, Florence (d 1972 [50]) critic BP/57*

LOVELL, George William (1804-78) dramatist DNB, EA/69

LOVELL, Mrs. George William see Lovell, Maria Anne

LOVELL, Harold C. (d 1969 [82]) founder of American Shakespeare Festival BP/53*

LOVELL, Henry V. (fl 1853) actor HAS

LOVELL, Mrs. Henry V. (fl 1853) actress HAS

LOVELL, James (d 1972 [59]) producer/director/choreographer BP/57*

LOVELL, Leslie see Leslie, H. L.

LOVELL, Maria Anne [née Lacy] (1803-77) English actress, dramatist CDP, DNB, OX

LOVELL, Raymond (1900-53) Canadian actor WWT/8-11

LOVELL, Thomas (fl 1635) actor DA

LOVELL, Tom (d 1909) clown EA/10*, WWT/14*

LOVELL, W. T. actor GRB/3-4, WWT/1-6

LOVELY, Joseph (d 1882 [35]) minstrel CDP

LOVER, Mr. (fl 1848) actor HAS

LOVER, Samuel (1797-1868) Irish dramatist, actor CDP, EA/68, SR

LOVESEY, Alfred Frank (d 1908 [33]) music-hall manager EA/09*

LOVETT, Beresford (b 1878) English actor GRB/1

LOVETT, Robert Irish dramatist CP/2-3

LOVETT, Robert Morss (1870-1956) American dramatist HJD

LOVETT-JANISON, P. W. (d 1916) EA/17*

LOW, Carl (b 1916) American actor, designer, director BE

LOW, Samuel (fl 1788) American dramatist EAP, RJ

LOWANDE, Martinho equestrian CDP

LOWDEN, George D. (d 1876) singer EA/77*

LOWE, Albert Henry [Harry Lauri] (d 1886 [44]) EA/87*

LOWE, Alva Hovery (d 1972 [80])

agent BP/57*

LOWE, Arthur (b 1915) English actor WWT/15-16

LOWE, Caroline (1865-1947) actress SR

LOWE, Christopher (d 1801) English bill distributor TD/1-2

LOWE, David (b 1913) American producer, director TW/6

LOWE, Douglas (b 1882) English business manager WWT/4

LOWE, Edmund (1892-1971) American actor ES, TW/2-3, 27, WWT/7-11

LOWE, Enid (b 1908) English actress, singer WWT/11-15

LOWE, Jane (d 1883 [75]) EA/84*

LOWE, J. J. M. (d 1876 [24]) musician EA/77*

LOWE, John Francis (d 1887 [77]) EA/88*

LOWE, Joshua (d 1945 [72]) journalist BE*, WWT/14*

LOWE, K. Elmo (1899-1971) American executive, director, actor BE, TW/27

LOWE, Nicholas (fl 1628) actor DA

LOWE, Robert (d 1939 [64]) American actor BE*, BP/24*

LOWE, Sophie (d 1903) EA/04*

LOWE, Susanna see Drayton, Mrs. Henry

LOWE, Thomas (d 1783) singer, actor, lessee, manager CDP, DNB, GT, TD/1-2

LOWE, Trevor (d 1910 [32]) actor EA/11*, WWT/14*

LOWE, Mrs. William [Fanny Wallis] (d 1916) actress EA/17*

LOWELL, Cal (d 1967 [45]) stage manager BP/52*

LOWELL, Helen [Helen Lowell Robb] (1866-1937) American actress WWT/7-8

LOWELL, Joan (1902-67) American actress WWA/4

LOWELL, Molly [or Mollie] English actress GRB/1-4, WWT/1-5

LOWELL, Robert (b 1917) American dramatist AAS, CB, CD, CH, ES, MWD

LOWENFELD, Henry (d 1931 [72]) producer, manager BE*,

WWT/14*

LOWENS, Curt (b 1925) German actor TW/22

LOWER, Sir William (1600?-62) English dramatist CDP, DNB, CP/1-3, FGF

LOWERRE, Mrs. Fred H. see Lauri, Lelia

LOWERY, Marcella (b 1945/46) American actress TW/25, 28-30

LOWERY, Robert (d 1971 [57]) performer BP/56*

LOWIN, G. (fl 1619) actor DA

LOWIN, John (1576-1653) English actor CDP, COC, DA, DNB, ES, GT, NTH, OC/1-3

LOWN, Bert (d 1962 [59]) composer/lyricist BP/47*

LOWNE, C[harles] M[acready] (d 1941 [78]) actor EA/97, GRB/2-4, WWT/1-8

LOWREY, Annie [Mrs. D. Lowrey] (d 1889 [24]) EA/90*

LOWREY, Mrs. D. see Lowrey, Annie

LOWREY, Dan, Sr. (d 1889 [66]) music-hall proprietor EA/90*

LOWREY, Mrs. Dan (d 1882) EA/83*

LOWREY, Mrs. Dan, Jr. (d 1887 [49]) EA/88*

LOWREY, Daniel (d 1897 [56]) music-hall proprietor EA/98*

LOWREY, Mrs. Mary Anne see Connolly, Maria

LOWREY, W. H. (d 1885 [26]) musical director EA/86*

LOWRIE, Edward (d 1965 [72]) performer BP/50*

LOWRIE, Jeanette [Mrs. Thomas Q. Seabrooke] Welsh/American actress WWS

LOWRY, C. H. equestrian CDP

LOWRY, John (d 1962 [79]) executive BE*

LOWRY, Judith (1890-1976) American actress TW/26-28

LOWRY, Philip W. (d 1969 [75]) lawyer BP/53*

LOWRY, Robert (d 1840) clown HAS

LOWRY, Rudd (d 1965 [73]) performer BP/50*

LOWRY, W. McNeil (b 1913) American executive, journalist BE

LOWTHER, George F. (d 1975 [62]) producer/director/chore-

ographer BP/59*
LOWTHER, J. G. (d 1917) EA/
18*
LOXLEY, Violet (b 1914) English
actress WWT/9-10
LOY, Myrna (b 1905) American
actress TW/22, 29
LOYAL, Leopold (d 1889) circus
ringmaster EA/91*
LOYALE, Mme. (d 1863) English
equestrienne HAS
LOYO, Caroline (fl 1851) eques-
trienne CDP
LOZANO, Roy (b 1943) American
actor TW/24
LUBBOCK, Sydney Reginald (d
1905) EA/07*
LUBIN, Frederick (fl 1856)
magician HAS
LUBIN BROTHERS jugglers CDP
LUBINOFF, A. Russian actor
CDP
LUBOTSKY, Charlotte see Rae,
Charlotte
LUBY, Edna (b 1884) American
actress, mimic WWS
LUCAN, Arthur (d 1954 [67])
performer BE*, WWT/14*
LUCAS, Mr. (d 1824) actor HAS
LUCAS, Arthur Melville (1881-
1943) American manager
WWA/2
LUCAS, Charles (1808-69) Eng-
lish composer DNB
LUCAS, Mrs. Edward H. see
Lucas, May
LUCAS, Henry (fl 1776-95)
Irish? dramatist CP/2-3, GT
LUCAS, J. Frank American
actor TW/30
LUCAS, John T. (d 1880 [45])
dramatist EA/81*
LUCAS, Jonathan (b 1922) Amer-
ican director, choreographer,
producer, actor BE, TW/
5-13
LUCAS, Karl (b 1919) American
actor TW/8
LUCAS, Louisa (d 1885 [72])
EA/87*
LUCAS, May [Mrs. Edward H.
Lucas] (d 1911 [39]) EA/12*
LUCAS, Nellie [Nellie Heitzman]
(b 1884) English actress
GRB/1
LUCAS, Paul (b 1908) actor SR
LUCAS, Rupert (d 1953 [57])
actor BE*, WWT/14*

LUCAS, Samuel (fl 1878?) song-
writer, minstrel CDP
LUCAS, Thomas (d 1917 [78])
EA/18*
LUCAS, William (fl 1809) dramatist
CP/3
LUCCA, Helen (d 1895 [29]) ac-
tress EA/96*, WWT/14*
LUCCA, Pauline (1841-1908) singer
CDP
LUCCHESE, Josephine (d 1974
[78]) performer BP/59*
LUCE, Claire (b 1901/03) American
actress BE, NTH, TW/3-20,
WWT/6-16
LUCE, Claire Boothe (b 1903)
American dramatist BE, CB,
HJD
LUCE, Polly [Pauline Marion
Luce] (1905-73) American ac-
tress WWT/7-9
LUCELLE, Fannie (fl 1869) dancer
CDP
LUCELLE, Rose dancer CDP
LUCETTE, Catherine [Mrs.
Charles Medwin] (d 1892) Eng-
lish actress CDP, HAS
LUCETTE, Madeline singer CDP
LUCK, Booth P. (d 1962 [52])
actor BE*
LUCKETT, Edith (b 1891) Ameri-
can actress WWM
LUCKHAM, Cyril (b 1907) English
actor AAS, WWT/12-16
LUCKINBILL, Laurence George
(b 1934/38) American actor
TW/21, 24-26, 29, WWT/16
LUCY, Arnold [Walter George
Campbell] (1865-1945) English
actor GRB/1, 3-4
LUDECUS, Louisa (fl 1860) Amer-
ican actress? singer? HAS
LUDERS, Gustav (1865-1913)
German composer GRB/3-4,
WWA/1, WWM, WWT/1
LUDGER, C. (fl 1799) translator
CP/3
LUDLAM, Charles (b 1943) Amer-
ican actor, dramatist, director,
producer CD, WWT/16
LUDLAM, Christine see Zavis-
towski, Christine
LUDLOW, Charles Lyon (d 1911)
actor EA/12*
LUDLOW, Henry (b 1879) English
actor GRB/1-2
LUDLOW, Kate (fl 1846) actress
HAS

LUDLOW, Noah Miller (1795-1886) American actor, manager CDP, COC, DAB, ES, HAS, OC/1-3, SR, WWA/H

LUDLOW, Patrick (b 1903) English actor WWT/4-16

LUDLUM, Robert (b 1927) American producer, actor BE

LUDWIG, Christa (b 1932?) German singer CB, ES

LUDWIG, Karen (b 1942) American actress TW/22, 25

LUDWIG, Salem (b 1915) American actor, director TW/22-23, 25-26, 28, 30, WWT/15-16

LUDWIG, W. (fl 1890) actor DP

LUEBBEN, Anita see Gillette, Anita

LUELLA, Marie (fl 1887) actress CDP

LUFF, William (b 1872) actor GRB/1-4

LUFTIG, Charles (d 1975) personal manager BP/60*

LUGG, Alfred (b 1889) English actor, executive WWT/4

LUGG, William (1852-1940) English actor GRB/3-4, WWT/1-7

LUGNE-POË, Aurélien-Marie (1869/70-1940) French actor, manager COC, GRB/1, 3-4, OC/1-3, WWT/1-4

LUGOSI, Bela (1883-1956) Hungarian actor TW/13, WWT/9-11

LUGUET, André (b 1892) French actor WWT/10

LUHDE, Henry (d 1866) German musician HAS

LUISI, James (b 1928) American actor TW/22-25

LUKA, Milo (b 1890) Czech singer WWA/3

LUKAS, Paul (1891/94/95-1971) Hungarian actor BE, CB, ES, TW/28, WWA/5, WWT/10-13

LUKASHOK, E. David (d 1974 [34]) producer/director/choreographer BP/59*

LUKE, Peter (b 1919) English dramatist, director AAS, CD

LUKOS, Alex (d 1918) EA/19*

LULLI, Folco (d 1970 [58]) performer BP/55*

"LULU" see Farini

LUM, Alvin (b 1931) American actor TW/28-30

LUM, Charles N. (d 1966 [88]) performer BP/50*

LUMB, Geoffrey (b 1905) English actor BE, TW/5-6, 10-15

LUMBARD, Jules G. (fl 1896?) singer CDP

LUMBY, Ilah R. (b 1911) American executive BE

LUMET, Baruch (b 1898) Polish actor, dramatist BE

LUMET, Sidney (b 1924) American director BE, ES, TW/4

LUMIERE, La Belle (d 1917) electrical dancer EA/18*

LUMIERE AND SON theatre collective CD

LUMLEY, Benjamin (1811-75) manager CDP, DNB

LUMLEY, Eliza (fl 1868) English singer HAS

LUMLEY, Ralph Robert (d 1900 [35]) dramatist BE*, EA/01*, WWT/14*

LUMLEY, Reginald Hope (d 1917) dramatist EA/18*

LUMLEY, Terry (b 1945) American actor TW/28

LUMSDEN, Alexander (d 1890 [35]) singer EA/91*

LUMSDEN, Geoffrey (b 1914) English actor TW/22-23

LUNA, Edelberta (d 1964 [27]) Cuban circus performer BE*

LUND, Art (b 1920) American actor, singer BE, TW/22-23, WWT/14-16

LUND, Arthur (d 1917) EA/18*

LUND, Joe (d 1894) Negro comedian EA/95*

LUND, Mrs. Joe see Lund, Rebecca

LUND, John (fl 1777) dramatist CP/3

LUND, John (b 1913) American actor TW/1-14

LUND, Rebecca [Mrs. Joe Lund] (d 1876 [28]) EA/77*

LUNDBERG, Ada [Margaret Ada Clegg Everard] (d 1899 [49]) music-hall comedian EA/00*

LUNDEL, Kert Fritjof (b 1936) Swedish designer WWT/16

LUNDELL, Ludovic (d 1867 [48]) equestrian EA/68*

LUNDIGAN, William (d 1975 [61]) actor BP/60*, WWT/16*

LUNDY, Harry (d 1908 [45])
music-hall manager GRB/4
LUNN, Henry C. (d 1894 [76])
professor of music EA/95*
LUNN, Joseph (1784-1863)
dramatist DNB
LUNN, Louise Kirkby (1873-
1930) English singer ES,
WWW/3
LUNN, William Arthur Brown (d
1879) composer EA/80*
LUNNY, Robert (b 1942) American
actor TW/30
LUNT, Alfred (1892/93-1977)
American actor AAS, BE,
CB, COC, ES, HJD, NTH,
OC/1-3, PDT, SR, TW/2-21,
WWT/5-16
LUNT, Mrs. Alfred see Fon-
tanne, Lynn
LUNT, Eleanor (d 1900) EA/01*
LUNT, James (d 1879 [65])
actor EA/80*
LUPINO, Arthur (d 1908 [44])
pantomimist, animal imper-
sonator EA/09*
LUPINO, Barry (1882/84-1962)
English actor, pantomimist,
dancer COC, OC/1-3, TW/
19, WWT/7-13
LUPINO, Florence [Mrs. George
Lupino] (d 1899 [38]) EA/00*
LUPINO, George (d 1903) clown,
pantomimist EA/04*
LUPINO, George (1853-1932)
English pantomimist COC
LUPINO, Mrs. George see
Lupino, Florence
LUPINO, Harry (d 1896 [68])
pantomimist EA/97*
LUPINO, Henry George see
Lane, Lupino
LUPINO, Ida (b 1918) English
actress SR
LUPINO, Lily (d 1912 [20])
EA/13*
LUPINO, Mark (d 1930 [36]) actor
BE*, WWT/14*
LUPINO, Pandora Bronson Amer-
ican actress TW/27
LUPINO, Richard (b 1929) Amer-
ican actor TW/27
LUPINO, Stanley (1893/94-1942)
English actor, dancer CB,
COC, OC/2-3, SR, WWT/
4-9
LUPINO, Wallace (1897-1961)
Scottish actor WWT/7-12

LUPINO FAMILY ES
LUPO, George G. (d 1973 [49])
performer BP/58*
LUPO, Giovanni Batista (d 1868)
dancer HAS
LuPONE, Patti (b 1949) American
actress TW/29-30
LUPRIEL, George see Cox,
George William
LUPTON, Thomas (fl 1578) drama-
tist CP/1-3, FGF
LURIE, Louis (d 1972 [84]) "Broad-
way angel" BP/57*
LURIE, Samuel press representative
BE
LUSBY, William (d 1907) proprietor
EA/08*
LUSBY, Mrs. William (d 1889)
EA/90*
LUSTIK, Marlena (b 1944) American
actress TW/28
LUTHER, Anna (d 1960 [67]) ac-
tress BE*
LUTHER, Lester (d 1962 [74]) actor
BE*
LUTZ, E. O. (b 1919) American
educator, executive BE
LUTZ, H. B. American producer,
dramatist BE
LUTZ, William Aynesley (d 1898)
EA/99*
LUTZ, W. Meyer (1829-1903)
Bavarian composer, conductor
DNB
LUTZER, Jenny (d 1877 [51])
singer EA/78*
LUXMORE, Ada [Mrs. Will Evans]
(d 1897) music-hall performer
EA/98*
LYALL, Charles (d 1911) singer
EA/12*
LYALL, Edna [Ada Ellen Bayly]
(d 1903 [45]) dramatist EA/04*
LYDGATE, John (c. 1370-c. 1451)
English dramatist ES
LYDIARD, Bob (b 1944) American
actor TW/25-27, 30
LYEL, Viola (1900-72) English ac-
tress AAS, WWT/7-15
LYLE, Arthur (d 1903) English ac-
tor OAA/2
LYLE, Cecil (d 1955 [63]) magician
BE*, WWT/14*
LYLE, Kenyon [Marcus Goldberg]
(d 1902 [35]) actor EA/04*
LYLE, Lyston [Edward Gibson]
(1856-1920) actor, manager
GRB/1-4, WWT/1-3

LYLY, John (c. 1554-1606) English dramatist, lessee COC, CP/1-3, DA, DNB, ES, FGF, HP, MH, NTH, OC/1-3, PDT, RE

LYMAN, Debra (b 1940) American actress TW/23, 28-29

LYMAN, Dorothy (b 1947) American actress TW/26

LYMAN, George (1869-1943) actor SR

LYMAN, Peggy (b 1950) American actress TW/28-29

LYMAN, Rose Blaine (d 1974) performer BP/59*

LYMAN, Tommy (d 1964 [73]) singer BE*, BP/48*

LYNCH, Brid (d 1969 [55]) performer BP/54*

LYNCH, Edward D. (b 1880) American actor WWM

LYNCH, Francis (fl 1737) dramatist CP/1-3

LYNCH, Francis composer, minstrel CDP

LYNCH, Fred (d 1968 [59]) publicist BP/52*

LYNCH, Harry (d 1890 [34]) Negro comedian EA/91*

LYNCH, Nell (d 1910) markswoman EA/11*

LYNCH, Richard (b 1940) American actor TW/22, 27, 29

LYNCH, William (d 1861 [78]) pantaloon EA/72*

LYND, Rosa (1884-1922) American actress WWT/4

LYNDE, Flo [Mrs. Charles J. Hoby] (d 1898 [22]) actress EA/99*

LYNDE, Janice (b 1947) American actress TW/26, 28-29

LYNDE, Joseph (d 1905) singer EA/06*

LYNDE, Paul (b 1926) American actor, director BE, CB, TW/8-9

LYNDECK, Edmund (b 1925) American actor TW/25-29

LYNDON, Barré (b 1896) English dramatist WWT/9-11

LYNDON, Harry (d 1916) EA/18*

LYNDSAY, Sir David (1490-c. 1554) Scottish dramatist COC, ES

LYNE, Thomas A. (b 1806) American actor HAS

LYNHAM, William (d 1881 [42]) lessee EA/82*

LYNILL, Harry (d 1878) actor EA/79*

LYNLEY, Carol (b 1942) American actress ES, TW/13-16

LYNN [Arthur A. Chippendale] American actor, singer GRB/1

LYNN, Charlotte (d 1974) performer BP/58*

LYNN, Dane W. (d 1975 [56]) producer/director/choreographer BP/60*

LYNN, Diana (1926-71) American actress BE, CB, TW/8-12, 28

LYNN, Eleanor (b 1925) American actress TW/6-7

LYNN, Harry (d 1918) EA/19*

LYNN, Iola (b 1922) Welsh actress TW/14

LYNN, Jeffrey (b 1909) American actor BE, TW/8, 23

LYNN, John Westley Symonds (d 1899 [63]) conjuror EA/00*

LYNN, J. Wellesley (b 1875) English actor, entertainer GRB/1

LYNN, Mara (b 1929) American dancer, actress, choreographer BE

LYNN, Natalie (d 1964) performer BP/49*

LYNN, Mrs. Neville see Corri, Ghita

LYNN, Ralph (1882-1962) English actor COC, OC/3, WWT/4-13, WWW/6

LYNN, Regina (b 1938) American actress TW/24

LYNN, Sharon (d 1963 [53]) performer BP/47*

LYNN, William H. (d 1952 [63]) American dancer, actor TW/8

LYNNE, Ada (b 1928) American actress TW/4

LYNNE, Carole [née Helen Violet Carolyn Haymen] (b 1918) English actress, singer WWT/10-12

LYNNE, Frank (d 1916) singer, actor CDP

LYNNE, Gillian English director, choreographer, dancer WWT/16

LYNTON, Ethel (fl 1881?) actress, singer CDP

LYNTON, Mayne (b 1885) English actor WWT/7

LYON, Ben (b 1901) American actor ES, WWT/7-14

LYON, Frank (b 1905) American
actor TW/3
LYON, Herb (d 1968 [49]) jour-
nalist BP/53*
LYON, James S. (d 1897 [72])
theatrical furnisher EA/98*
LYON, John Henry Hobart (d
1961 [83]) scholar BE*,
BP/46*
LYON, Louis see Aldrich, Louis
LYON, Sarah see Allen, Mrs.
C. Leslie
LYON, Thomas (1812-69) actor,
dramatist CDP
LYON, Wanda (b 1897) American
actress WWT/7-8
LYON, William (d 1748) actor,
dramatist CP/2-3, GT, TD/
1-2
LYONNET, William [or Henry]
(d 1933 [80]) historian BE*,
WWT/14*
LYONS, A. Neil (1880-1940)
South African dramatist WWT/
6-7
LYONS, Arthur S. (d 1963 [62])
talent agent BP/48*
LYONS, Edmund (d 1867 [39])
actor WWT/14*
LYONS, E. D. (d 1867 [39])
lessee EA/68*
LYONS, E. D. (d 1880) giant
EA/81*
LYONS, Edmund D. (1851-1906)
Scottish actor OAA/1-2
LYONS, Edward (d 1905 [77])
actor EA/07*
LYONS, Frederick (d 1887)
singer, actor NYM
LYONS, George (d 1911 [38])
dancer EA/12*
LYONS, Gretchen [Mrs. Lucius
Henderson] (fl 1890) English
actress WWS
LYONS, Harry (d 1975) dramatist
BP/59*
LYONS, Sir Joseph (d 1917)
actor, dramatist EA/18*
LYONS, Katharine (1889-1933)
American critic WWA/1
LYONS, Robert (d 1908) actor
GRB/4*
LYONS, Robert Charles (1853-
92) Scottish actor OAA/1-2
LYRIC, Dora (d 1962 [83])
performer BE*
LYSLE, Cora (1861-87) actress
NYM

LYSTER, Frederick (b 1822) Irish
singer HAS
LYSTER, Mrs. Frederick see
Walton, Minnie
LYSTER, Mrs. John Richard Kir-
wan see Barsanti, Jane
LYTELL, Bert (1885/87/90-1954)
American actor TW/2-8, 11,
WWA/3, WWT/7-11
LYTELL, Wilfred (d 1954 [62])
actor TW/11
LYTTLETON, Dame Edith (d 1948
[83]) dramatist WWT/2-7
LYTTON, Miss [née Foote] (d 1890
[27]) EA/91*
LYTTON, Bart (d 1969 [56]) drama-
tist BP/54*
LYTTON, Doris (1893-1953) Eng-
lish actress WWT/2-10
LYTTON, Edward English business
manager, actor GRB/1-4
LYTTON, Mrs. Edward see
Grattan, Kittie
LYTTON, Edward George Earle
Lytton Bulwer-Lytton, Lord
(1803-73) English dramatist
CDP, COC, DNB, EA/68, ES,
HP, MH, NTH, OC/1-3, SR
LYTTON, Elsie Keith [Mrs. Wil-
liam Henry Hart] actress GRB/1
LYTTON, Henry, Jr. [Lord Alva
Lytton] (1904-65) English singer,
actor WWT/6-8
LYTTON, Sir Henry A. (1860/65/
67-1936) English actor DNB,
GRB/1-4, NTH, WWT/1-7,
WWW/3
LYUS, James (d 1885) music-hall
chairman EA/86*
LYVEDEN, Lord [Percy Vernon]
(1857-1926) English actor GRB/1

- M -

M., E. dramatist CP/1-3
M., J. C. (fl 1801?) dramatist
CP/3
M., W. (fl 1697?) dramatist CP/
1-3, FGF
MAARTENS, Maarten [Joost Marius
Willem Van der Poorten-
Schwartz] (b 1858) Dutch drama-
tist WWM
MAAS, Audrey Gellen (d 1975 [40])
dramatist BP/60*
MAAS, Joseph (1847-86) English
singer CDP, DNB

MABBE, James (1569-c. 1642) English dramatist CP/2-3, FGF, HP

MABBETT, Ambrose (d 1916) musical director EA/18*

MABLEY, Edward (b 1906) American dramatist, educator BE

MABLEY, Moms (d 1975 [75]) performer BP/59*

MABOU MINES theatre collective CD

MacADAM, William (b 1943) American actor TW/24

McADAMS, Stanley (b 1938) American actor TW/25, 28-29

McADOO, Orpheus M. (d 1900) minstrel, proprietor EA/01*

McAFEE, Diane (b 1943) American actress TW/25

MACAFERRI, Sig. (fl 1857) singer CDP

McALEER, Mr. (fl 1851) actor HAS

McALINNEY, Patrick (d 1913) Irish actor TW/12

MACALLAME, Anna (b 1615) bearded woman CDP

MACALLAN, Patrick Robert see Robertson, Robert

MACALLISTER, Andrew (d 1856) magician CDP, HAS

MacALLISTER, Mme. L. A. de (d 1859 [27]) magician CDP, HAS

McALLISTER, Alister P. see Wharton, Anthony P.

McALLISTER, William (b 1843) minstrel, manager CDP

McALLON, Andrew see Mack, Andrew

MacALPINE, Miss (fl 1815) actress CDP

MACALPINE, Simon see Lack, Simon

McANALLY, Ray (b 1926) Irish actor AAS, WWT/14-16

McANDREWS, J. W. (1835-99) minstrel SR

McARDLE, Arthur (d 1898) EA/99*

McARDLE, James (d 1881 [38]) EA/82*

McARDLE, J. F. American actor WWT/1-5

McARDLE, John F. songwriter CDP

McARDLE, John Francis (d 1883 [41]) dramatist EA/84*

MACARTE, Adelaide (d 1908) variety performer EA/09*

MACARTE, Dan (d 1873) equestrian EA/74*

MACARTE, Regina (d 1892) equestrian EA/93*

MACARTHUR, Charles (1895?-1956) American dramatist AAS, ES, HJD, MH, MWD, NTH, TW/12, WWA/3, WWT/6-11

MacARTHUR, Harry (d 1973 [62]) critic BP/58*

MacARTHUR, James (b 1937) American actor BE

MacARTHUR, Mary (1930-49) American actress TW/6

McARTHUR, Molly (1900-72) English designer WWT/8-12

MACARTHUR, Samuel (fl 1780) dramatist CP/3

MACARTHY, Mr. (fl 1848) actor CDP

MACARTHY, Harry (fl 1869?) singer, songwriter CDP

MacARTHY, Harry B. (b 1834) English actor HAS

MacARTHY, Huntley May (d 1866 [51]) manager EA/72*

MacARTHY, Marion (1838-63) English actress, singer CDP, HAS

MACARTNEY, C. L. (fl 1800) actor, dramatist CP/3, TD/1-2

McASKILL, Angus (d 1863) giant HAS

McATEE, Ben (d 1961 [58]) actor BE*

MACAULAY, John (fl 1785) dramatist CP/3

MACAULAY, Joseph (d 1967 [76]) American actor, singer WWT/9-14

MACAULAY, Rose Kathleen (d 1900) EA/01*

MACAULEY, Mrs. (d 1837 [52]) actress WWT/14*

MACAULEY, Bernard (1837-86) American actor, manager CDP, HAS, SR

MACAULEY, Mrs. Bernard see Macauley, Rachel

MACAULEY, Elizabeth Wright (1785-1837) English? actress CDP, OX

MACAULEY, John T. (d 1915 [69]) manager WWT/14*

MACAULEY, Rachel [Mrs. Bernard

Macauley] (1845-98) actress
CDP
MCAULL, John A. (d 1894) mana-
ger WWT/14*
McBAN, Patrick (d 1906) juggler
EA/07*
MACBETH, Allan (d 1910 [54])
composer, conductor EA/11*
MACBETH, Florence (1891-
1966) American singer WWA/4
MACBETH, Helen [Mrs. Frank
Mills] American actress
GRB/1-4, WWT/1-5
McBRIDE, Alex (fl 1853-58) actor
HAS
McBRIDE, Claude E. (d 1973
[36]) composer/lyricist BP/57*
MacBRIDE, Donald (d 1957
[63]) actor BE*
McBRIDE, James (d 1917 [75])
doorkeeper EA/18*
McBRIDE, Jinnie (d 1916) EA/
17*
McBRIDE, John S. (d 1961 [84])
ticket agent BE*
McBRIDE, Mary Margaret (d
1976 [76]) performer BP/60*
McBRIDE, Miss M. C[ecelia]
(d 1846) American dancer
CDP, HAS
McBRIDE, Patricia (b 1942)
American dancer CB, ES
MacBRYDE, John N. (d 1966
[84]) performer BP/51*
McCABE, D. W. (d 1907 [47])
minstrel, manager CDP
MACCABE, Frederick (1831-
1904) ventriloquist, mimic,
musician CDP
MacCABE, James (d 1918) EA/
19*
McCABE, Mary (d 1975 [73])
performer BP/60*
McCABE, May North (d 1949
[76]) actress BE*, BP/34*
MACCABE, Michael (d 1883)
EA/84*
MACCABE, Mike (d 1894 [39])
Irish comedian EA/95*
MACCABE, Joseph (d 1893)
music-hall performer EA/94*
McCAFFREY, Edward (d 1911
[85]) musician EA/12*
MacCAFFREY, George (1870-
1939) Irish critic WWT/8
McCAHEN, Col. J. (fl 1828)
American actor HAS
McCALL, Angela (d 1965 [90])

performer BP/50*
McCALL, Janet (b 1935) American
actress TW/28-30
McCALL, Joan (b 1943) American
actress TW/21
McCALL, Lizzie (d 1942 [84])
actress BE*, WWT/14*
McCALL, Monica English literary
representative BE
McCALLA, Dolly (b 1891) American
actress GRB/1
McCALLIN, Clement (b 1913) Eng-
lish actor AAS, WWT/9-16
McCALLUM, Colin Whitton see
Coborn, Charles
McCALLUM, David (b 1933) Scot-
tish actor TW/25
McCALLUM, John (b 1914/18)
Australian actor, director
WWT/12-16
McCALLUM, Neil (d 1976 [46])
performer BP/60*
McCALMON, George A. (b 1909)
American educator BE
McCAMBRIDGE, Mercedes (b 1918)
American actress BE, CB,
TW/28
McCAMMON, Bessie J. (d 1964
[80]) American actress BE*
McCANDLESS, Stanley (1897-1967)
American educator, lighting de-
signer BE
McCANE, Mabel (fl 1906-12) Amer-
ican actress WWM
MACCANN, Mrs. (d 1896 [59])
musician EA/97*
McCANN, Alfred W., Jr. (d 1972
[64]) performer BP/57*
McCANN, Dora (d 1975 [60]) per-
former BP/60*
McCANN, Frances actress TW/3
McCANN, Mrs. J. H. see Mc-
Cann, Mary Jane
McCANN, Harrison (d 1962 [82])
advertising executive BE*
McCANN, Mary Jane [Mrs. J. H.
McCann] (d 1908) EA/10*
McCANN, Walter E. (fl 1890-1912)
American editor WWM
McCAREY, Leo (d 1969 [71]) pro-
ducer/director/choreographer
BP/54*
McCARROLL, Alexander (d 1876)
musician EA/78*
McCARROLL, James (1814-92)
Irish/Canadian dramatist DAB
McCARTEN, John (1916-74) Amer-
ican critic BE

McCARTHER, Avis (b 1947)
American actress TW/26, 28
McCARTHY, Mrs. (d 1872)
EA/74*
McCARTHY, Bartlett singer,
songwriter CDP
McCARTHY, Charles singer,
songwriter CDP
MACCARTHY, Charlotte (fl
1765?) dramatist CP/2-3
McCARTHY, Daniel musician,
composer, dancer CDP
McCARTHY, Daniel (b 1869)
English actor GRB/4, WWT/
1-5
MacCARTHY, Sir Desmond (1877-
1952) English critic COC,
DNB, ES, GRB/2-4, OC/1-3,
PDT, WWT/1-11, WWW/5
McCARTHY, John (d 1888) circus
rider EA/89*
McCARTHY, Joseph A. (d 1975
[53]) dramatist BP/60*
McCARTHY, Justin (d 1912 [81])
EA/13*
McCARTHY, Justin Huntly (1860-
1936) English dramatist GRB/
1-4, MWD, WWM, WWT/1-7,
WWW/3
McCARTHY, Kevin (b 1914)
American actor BE, TW/2-
12, 14-15, 18, 21, 23, 30,
WWT/11-16
McCARTHY, Lillah (1875-1960)
English actress COC, DNB,
ES, GRB/1-4, NTH, OC/3,
TW/16, WWT/1-11
McCARTHY, Lin American actor
TW/13
McCARTHY, Mary (b 1912)
American critic BE
McCARTHY, Neil S. (d 1972
[84]) lawyer BP/57*
McCARTHY, Mrs. W. H. see
MacNally, Jessie
McCARTY, E. Clayton (b 1901)
American educator, dramatist
BE
McCARTY, Eddie (b 1940) Amer-
ican actor TW/24
McCARTY, Mary (b 1923) Amer-
ican actress, singer TW/5-7,
20, 27-29, WWT/15-16
MacCAULAY, Joseph (d 1967
[76]) actor, singer TW/24
McCAULEY, Jack (b 1900) Amer-
ican actor TW/4-7
McCAULEY, Judith American

actress TW/29-30
MacCAULEY, Mark (b 1948)
American actor TW/26, 28-
30
McCAULL, John A. (d 1894) Amer-
ican manager EA/95*
McCAWLEY, Charles H. (b 1928)
American actor TW/9
McCAY, Peggy (b 1931) American
actress TW/12-13
McCHLERY, Grace (d 1975 [77])
performer BP/59*
McCLAIN, John (1904-67) Amer-
ican critic BE, NTH, TW/
23
McCLANAHAN, Rue American ac-
tress TW/23, 25-26, 28-29,
WWT/16
McCLANE, John E. (d 1972 [50])
publicist BP/57*
McCLANNIN, Robert F. (b 1832)
American actor HAS
McCLARNEY, Pat (b 1925) Amer-
ican actress TW/2
McCLEAN, Mrs. [née Fairfield]
(fl 1828-62) actress HAS
McCLEAN, Jessie (fl 1856-62)
actress HAS
McCLEERY, Albert (d 1972 [60])
producer/director/choreographer
BP/56*
McCLEERY, R. C. (d 1927) scene
artist WWT/14*
McCLELLAN, Mrs. see Les-
sing, Madge
McCLELLAN, John Jasper (1874-
1926) American conductor
WWA/1
McCLELLAND, Allan (b 1917) Irish
actor WWT/12-16
McCLELLAND, Charles actor
TW/1
McCLELLAND, Donald (1903-55)
American actor TW/2, 12
McCLELLAND, Evelyn A. (d 1972
[79]) performer BP/57*
McCLELLAND, Mrs. Harry see
Lawrence, Nellie
McCLELLAND, Richard Leeper
see Leech, Richard
McCLENDON, Ernestine (b 1918)
American actress BE
McCLENDON, Rose (1885-1936)
American actress NTH
McCLINTIC, Guthrie (1893-1961)
American actor, producing
manager, director AAS, CB,
COC, ES, NTH, OC/1-3, SR,

TW/2-8, 18, WWA/4, WWT/
6-12

McCLOSKEY, James R. (b 1918)
American educator, director
BE

McCLOSKY, J. J. (1826-1913)
dramatist, manager, actor
SR

McCLURE, Mrs. (fl 1832-54)
actress HAS

McCLURE, Linda (b 1947) American actress TW/30

McCLURE, Michael (b 1932)
American dramatist CD

MacCLURE, Victor (1887-1963)
Scottish dramatist WWW/6

McCOLE, John (d 1874) actor?
EA/75*

McCOLL, Ewan theatre group
founder COC

MACCOLL, James (d 1956 [44])
actor TW/12

MacCOLL, Virginia Lenore (b
1951) American actress TW/29

McCOLLOM, James [or John]
C. (1838-83) American actor
CDP, HAS

McCOLLOUGH, John (1832-85)
Irish actor, manager SR

McCOLLUM, Thomas (d 1872
[44]) equestrian, circus proprietor CDP

McCOLLUM, Mrs. Thomas (d
1906) EA/08*

McCOMAS, Carroll (1891/94-1962)
American actress TW/6-8,
19, WWT/6-7

McCOMB, H. (d 1971 [90]) performer BP/56*

McCOMB, Kate (d 1959 [87])
actress BE*, BP/43*

MACCOMO, Martini (d 1871 [32])
lion tamer EA/72*

McCONNELL, Anna (d 1891
[21]) music-hall performer
EA/93*

McCONNELL, Charles (d 1916)
EA/17*

McCONNELL, C. J. (d 1895
[52]) music-hall singer EA/96*

McCONNELL, Mrs. C. J. see
McConnell, Mary

McCONNELL, Forrest W. (d
1962 [51]) American performer
BE*

McCONNELL, Lulu (d 1962 [80])
American actress TW/19

McCONNELL, Mary [Mrs. C.

J. McConnell] (d 1893 [53])
EA/94*

McCONNELL, Ty (b 1940) American actor TW/25-26, 29-30

McCONNELL, Mr. W. (d 1867
[36]) artist EA/68*

McCORD, J. C. (b 1920) American
actor TW/8

McCORD, Nancy American actress,
singer WWT/8-10

McCORMAC, Esther see Ashley,
Esther Potter

McCORMACK, Benjamin (d 1871)
clown EA/72*

McCORMACK, Frank (d 1941 [65])
American actor BP/25*

MacCORMACK, Franklyn (d 1971
[63]) performer BP/56*

McCORMACK, John (1884-1945)
Irish/American singer CB,
DAB, ES, WWA/2, WWW/4

McCORMACK, Mrs. M. [née
Bramah] (d 1871) ballet mistress
EA/72*

McCORMACK, Patty (b 1945)
American actress BE

McCORMICK, Arthur Langdon (d
1954 [81]) American dramatist
WWM, WWT/4-8

McCORMICK, F. J. (d 1947 [c.
50]) Irish actor TW/3

McCORMICK, John (d 1945 [61])
singer TW/2

McCORMICK, John (d 1975 [82])
theatrical store owner BP/60*

McCORMICK, Langdon (d 1954)
American dramatist WWA/3

McCORMICK, Myron (1906/07/08-
62) American actor CB, TW/
1-15, 19, WWA/4, WWT/9-13

McCORMICK, Nancy (b 1946)
American actress TW/25

McCORMICK, Ruth (b 1913) American actress TW/29

McCORRY, Marion (b 1945) American actress TW/30

McCOURT, Joseph (d 1876 [52])
musician EA/78*

McCOWEN, Alec (b 1925) English
actor AAS, CB, COC, TW/24-
27, WWT/12-16

McCOY, Bessie [Mrs. Richard
Harding Davis] (d 1931 [45])
comedienne BE*, BP/16*,
WWT/14*

McCOY, Frank (d 1947 [58]) producer BE*, BP/31*

McCOY, W. [William Greenwood]

(d 1885 [26]) music-hall performer EA/86*

McCRACKEN, Esther (1902-71)
English dramatist, actress
AAS, PDT, WWT/10-14

McCRACKEN, James (b 1926)
American singer CB

McCRACKEN, Joan (1922-61)
American actress, singer,
dancer CB, TW/1-15, 18,
WWT/10-13

McCREE, Junie (b 1866) American actress, writer WWM

McCREERY, Bud (b 1925) American composer, lyricist, performer BE

McCULLERS, Carson (1917-67)
American dramatist AAS,
BE, MD, MH, MWD, PDT,
TW/24

McCULLEY, Johnston (1883-1958)
American dramatist WWA/3

McCULLOCH, Andrew [Albert
Macolla] (d 1889) musician
EA/90*

McCULLOCH, Arthur (b 1860)
Scottish actor GRB/1

McCULLOCH, Rose (d 1886)
EA/87*

McCULLOUGH, Brien (d 1911)
actor, dramatist EA/12*

McCULLOUGH, John (1832-85)
Irish/American actor CDP,
DAB, ES, HAS, NTH, OC/
1-3, WWA/H

McCULLOUGH, Mrs. John see
McCullough, Letitia

McCULLOUGH, Letitia [Mrs.
John McCullough] (d 1888)
EA/89*

McCULLOUGH, Paul (1883-1936)
American actor WWT/7-8

McCULLOUGH, Russell H. (d
1972 [76]) director of theatre
construction BP/57*

MACCUNN, Hamish (1868-1916)
Scottish composer, conductor
DNB, GRB/1-4, WWW/2

MacCURDY, James Kyrle (fl
1894) American actor WWS

McCURRY, Jack Howard (d 1970
[94]) performer BP/55*

McCUTCHEON, George Barr
(b 1866) American dramatist
WWM

McCUTCHEON, Thomas (d 1847)
American actor HAS

McCUTCHEON, Wallace (d 1928

[47]) actor BE*, BP/12*

McDANIEL, Hattie (1898-1952)
American actress CB

MacDERMOT, Galt composer AAS,
WWT/16

MacDERMOT, Robert [Robert Mac-
Dermot Barbour] (1910-64) In-
dian/English dramatist WWT/9-
13

MacDERMOTT, The Great [Gilbert
Hastings] (1845-1901) actor,
stage manager, manager, agent,
singer CDP, DNB, OC/1-3

McDERMOTT, Aline (d 1951 [70])
actress TW/7

MacDERMOTT, Gilbert Hastings
see MacDermott, The Great

McDERMOTT, Hugh (1908-72)
Scottish actor WWT/10-14

McDERMOTT, James (d 1869 [30])
actor? EA/70*

MacDERMOTT, Norman (b 1890)
Scottish producer, manager,
director COC, OC/3, WWT/4-
13

McDERMOTT, Robert Joseph (d
1917 [55]) musical director,
composer EA/18*

McDERMOTT, William F. (1891-
1958) American critic TW/15,
WWA/3

McDEVITT, Ruth [née Shoecraft]
(1895-1976) American actress
BE, WWT/14-16

MACDONA, Charles (d 1946 [86])
Irish manager WWT/5-10

MACDONA, Henry Edwin (d 1900)
EA/01*

MACDONA, William (d 1892) EA/
93*

MacDONAGH, Donagh (d 1968 [55])
dramatist BP/52*

McDONALD, Mr. (fl 1802) actor
HAS

McDONALD, Mr. (d 1832) clown
HAS

McDONALD, Mrs. (d 1883) EA/84*

McDONALD, Albert (d 1900) music-
hall manager EA/01*

McDONALD, Andrew (1755?-90)
Scottish dramatist CP/3, DNB,
GT, TD/1-2

MACDONALD, Ballard (d 1935
[52]) American songwriter BE*,
BP/20*

McDONALD, Bella (d 1892) EA/93*

MacDONALD, Brian (b 1928) Canadian choreographer, ballet

director CB

McDONALD, Charles (fl 1818-19)
clown HAS

MACDONALD, Mrs. Charles
[Mrs. James Macdonald] (d
1877 [47]) EA/78*

McDONALD, Christie (1875-1962)
Canadian actress, singer TW/
19, WWM, WWS, WWT/1-6

MacDONALD, Cordelia Howard
(1848-1941) American actress
CB

MacDONALD, Donald (1898-1959)
American actor TW/2-3, 16,
WWT/8-12

MacDONALD, Duncan (fl 1753?)
Scottish equilibrist CDP

McDONALD, Earl (b 1905) American actor TW/21, 24

MACDONALD, Emily (d 1889
[19]) actress? singer? EA/90*

McDONALD, Estelle [Estelle
Potter] (fl 1842-59) American
actress HAS

MACDONALD, Eva (b 1886) Australian actress WWM

MacDONALD, Eve March (d 1974)
performer BP/59*

McDONALD, Flora see Spencer,
Mrs. George Preston

McDONALD, Francis (d 1968
[77]) performer BP/53*

McDONALD, Gordon (b 1921)
American actor TW/2

McDONALD, James (d 1889 [60])
comedian, lessee EA/90*

McDONALD, James American
actor TW/24, 27-29

MACDONALD, Mrs. James see
Macdonald, Mrs. Charles

MacDONALD, James Weatherby
(d 1962 [63]) actor BE*

MACDONALD, J. C. (d 1895
[45]) Scottish comedian, singer
EA/96*

MacDONALD, J. Carlisle (d 1974
[80]) publicist, journalist BP/
59*

MacDONALD, Jeanette (1907-65)
American actress, singer BE,
TW/21, WWA/4, WWT/7-12

MacDONALD, Jet (b 1927) American actor TW/3-4

McDONALD, John G. (d 1888)
American comedian EA/89*

MacDONALD, Katherine (d 1956
[c. 64]) actress BE*

MACDONALD, Lily see Morelli,

Mrs. Charles

MacDONALD, McGregor (d 1856)
actor HAS

McDONALD, Marie (d 1965 [42])
performer BP/50*

McDONALD, Marvin (d 1973 [78])
producer/director/choreographer
BP/57*

MacDONALD, Michael Alan (b 1941)
American actor TW/23

MacDONALD, Murray [Walter Mac-
Donald Honeyman] (b 1899)
Scottish producer, director,
manager, actor AAS, WWT/9-16

McDONALD, Ray (d 1959 [38])
American dancer TW/15

MACDONALD, Robert (d 1887)
music-hall Irish comedian EA/
88*

MacDONALD, Robert (d 1964 [91])
producer/director BP/49*

MACDONALD, Ronald (1860-1933)
dramatist WWW/3

McDONALD, Sadie (d 1896) actress
EA/97*

McDONALD, Samuel ["Big Sam"]
(1762-1802) giant CDP

McDONALD, Tanny (b 1939) American actress TW/23, 28-30

MACDONALD, William H. (d 1906)
American singer WWA/1

MacDONELL, Kathlene (b 1890)
Canadian actress WWT/7-8

McDONNELL, Frank (d 1905 [49])
actor EA/06*

MacDONNELL, Rev. George Alcock
(d 1899 [69]) dramatic reader
EA/00*

MACDONNELL, Leslie A. (b 1903)
Welsh manager, producer
WWT/14-15

MacDONOUGH, Glen (d 1924 [57])
librettist WWT/4

MACDONOUGH, Glen librettist,
dramatist GRB/3-4, WWT/1-8

MACDONOUGH, Harry (fl 1880-
1913) American actor WWM

MACDONOUGH, Harry, Jr. (fl
1908-13) American actor, banjoist WWM

McDONOUGH, John Edwin (1825-
82) American actor CDP, HAS,
SR

MacDONOUGH, Thomas B. (b 1835)
American actor, business manager, manager HAS

McDOUGALL, Gordon (b 1941)
Scottish director WWT/16

MacDOUGALL, Roger (b 1910) Scottish dramatist, director AAS, BE, CD, PDT, WWT/11-16

MacDOUGALL, Ronald (d 1973 [58]) dramatist BP/58*

McDOUGALL, R. W. (b 1819) American actor HAS

MacDOUGALL, Sally (d 1973 [97]) critic BP/57*

McDOWALL, George (d 1879 [35]) EA/80*

McDOWALL, Roddy (b 1928) English actor AAS, BE, CB, TW/9-20, WWT/13-16

McDOWELL, Anderson see Elliot, George

McDOWELL, Claire (d 1966 [88]) performer BP/51*

MACDOWELL, Edward (d 1908 [47]) composer EA/09*

McDOWELL, Fred (d 1972 [68]) performer BP/57*

McDOWELL, J. (fl 1839) actor HAS

McDOWELL, J. (d 1883) manager EA/84*

McDOWELL, John H. (b 1903) American educator BE

McDOWELL, Joseph (d 1888 [44]) comic singer EA/89*

MacDOWELL, Melbourne (1856-1941) American actor PP/2, WWS

McDOWELL, Norman (b 1931) Irish dancer, choreographer, director ES

McDOWELL, Roddy see McDowall, Roddy

MacDOWELL, William Melbourne (d 1941 [84]) American actor BP/25*

MACE, Harriet see Booth, Mrs. Junius Brutus, Jr., II

MACE, James (1831-1910) circus performer, showman DNB

MACE, Louis L. (d 1965 [71]) critic BP/50*

McEARCHAN, Malcolm (d 1945 [61]) performer BE*, WWT/14*

McELHANY, Thomas J. (d 1966 [75]) performer BP/51*

McELHONE, Eloise (d 1974 [53]) performer BP/59*

McENERY, Peter (b 1940) English actor AAS, WWT/14-16

McENROE, Robert E. dramatist BE

McENTEE, Millicent Evison (d

1970 [93]) performer BP/54*

McETHENREY, Jane see Clare, Ada

McEVOY, Arthur Thompson (d 1891) composer EA/92*

MacEVOY, Charles (fl 1871?) comedian, song composer CDP

McEVOY, Charles (1875/79-1929) English dramatist GRB/4, WWT/1-5, WWW/3

MacEVOY, John lecturer, manager CDP

McEVOY, J. P. (1894/95/97-1958) American dramatist, librettist WWA/3, WWT/7-11

MacEVOY, Mary musician CDP

McEVOY, Nellie [Mrs. Neil Soloman] (d 1882) EA/83*

MacEVOY, Master Spaulding (fl 1868?) singer CDP

McEWAN, Geraldine [née McKeown] (b 1932) English actress AAS, BE, COC, TW/20, WWT/12-16

MacFADDEN, Gertrude (d 1967 [67]) performer BP/52*

McFADYEN, Louisa (d 1870) actress? EA/71*

MacFARLAND, Mr. (fl 1851) actor HAS

McFARLAND, Mr. (fl 1848) vaulter HAS

MCFARLAND, Mrs. see Woodbury, Miss S.

McFARLAND, Beulah (d 1964 [67]) American showgirl BE*, BP/49*

MacFARLAND, Dorothea American actress TW/3-6, 30

McFARLAND, Edith Agnes (d 1892 [17]) EA/93*

McFARLAND, Gary (d 1971 [38]) composer/lyricist BP/56*

McFARLAND, Nan (1916-74) American actress TW/8-9, 12

McFARLAND, Mrs. W. (d 1882 [36]) EA/83*

McFARLAND, William (d 1888) actor SR

McFARLAND, William (d 1898 [61]) lessee EA/99*

MacFARLANE, Bruce (d 1967 [57]) actor TW/1, 24, WWT/9-11

MacFARLANE, Elsa (b 1899) English actress, singer WWT/5-9

McFARLANE, George (d 1932 [55]) Canadian singer BE*, BP/16*

McFARLANE, Lillian C. (d 1975

[73]) producer/director/choreographer BP/59*

McFARLIN, Julius R. (d 1973 [85]) performer BP/57*

MACFARREN, Alice [Mrs. Henry Anderson] (d 1879 [26]) actress EA/80*

MACFARREN, Clarina Thalia, Lady (fl 1849?) singer CDP

MacFARREN, Mme. G. A. (fl 1847) singer HAS

MacFARREN, George (1788-1843) English dramatist, manager DNB

MACFARREN, Sir George Alexander (1813-87) English musician, composer, conductor CDP, DNB, NYM

MACFARREN, John (d 1901 [83]) EA/02*

MACFARREN, Walter Cecil (d 1905 [79]) composer EA/06*

McFAYDEN, Charles D. (d 1894) actor EA/95*

McGAVIN, Darren (b 1922) American actor BE, TW/9-15, 23

McGAW, Charles (b 1910) American educator, director BE

MacGEACHEY, Charles (d 1921 [62]) manager BE*, BP/6*

McGEE, Fibber (b 1896) actor CB

McGEE, Harold (1899-1955) American actor TW/2

McGEE, Molly (b 1898) actress CB

McGHEE, Paul A. (d 1964 [64]) educator BE*

McGILL, Everett (b 1945) American actor TW/29

MacGILL, Moyna [Chattie McIldowie] (d 1975 [80]) Irish actress TW/11-12, WWT/4-8

McGILL, R. C. (d 1918) EA/19*

McGILL, Wallace Read (d 1973 [67]) performer BP/58*

McGILVRAY, Laura [Mrs. Frank Gillmore] American actress WWS

MAGINLEY, Benjamin R. (d 1888 [51]) American actor EA/89*

McGINLEY, Laurence Joseph (b 1905) American educator BE

MacGINNIS, Niall (b 1913) Irish actor WWT/9-13

McGINTY, Miss see Clifford, Elizabeth

McGIVENEY, Owen (d 1967 [83]) performer BP/52*

McGIVER, John (1913-75) American actor BE, TW/14, 24-26, WWT/15-16

McGLATHERY, Mr. (fl 1831) American actor HAS

McGLYNN, Frank (1866-1951) American actor TW/7, WWA/3, WWT/5-8

McGOLRIC, Kate (d 1858) actress HAS

McGONAGILL, Gerald (b 1925) American actor TW/20, 23

McGONICLE, Margaret (d 1975 [66]) performer BP/60*

McGOOHAN, Patrick (b 1928) American actor WWT/12-14

McGOVERN, John actor BE

McGOWAN, J. D. (d 1866) actor HAS

McGOWAN, John [Jack] (b 1892) American dramatist, director, actor BE

McGOWAN, John P. (d 1952 [72]) Australian dramatist, librettist WWT/7-9

McGOWAN, John W. American dramatist, librettist WWT/10

MacGOWAN, Kenneth (1888-1963) American critic, producer, manager, director COC, ES, NTH, OC/1-3, TW/19, WWT/5-11

McGOWAN, Oliver (1907-71) American actor, director BE, TW/28

MacGOWRAN, Jack (1918-73) Irish actor AAS, TW/27-29, WWT/14-15

McGRAIL, Walter B. (d 1970 [81]) performer BP/54*

McGRATH, Don (b 1940) American actor TW/28, 30

McGRATH, Frank (d 1976 [72]) dramatist BP/60*, WWT/16*

MacGRATH, Harold (1871-1932) American librettist WWA/1

McGRATH, James W. see Mack, James W.

McGRATH, John (b 1935) English dramatist, director AAS, CD, PDT, WWT/15-16

MCGRATH, Katherine (b 1944) American actress TW/27, 29

MacGRATH, Leueen (b 1914/19) English actress AAS, BE, TW/5-16, WWT/10-16

McGRATH, Michael (d 1976) performer BP/60*

McGRATH, Paul (b 1904) American actor BE, TW/1, 3-5, 8-12, 21, 26, WWT/9-16

McGRATH, William P. (d 1971 [45]) performer BP/56*

McGRAW, Bill (b 1920) American actor TW/4

McGRAW, William Ralph (b 1930) American educator BE

McGREEVEY, Annie American actress TW/28, 30

MacGREGOR, Barry (b 1936) Scottish actor TW/26

MacGREGOR, Jock (d 1971 [56]) journalist BP/56*

McGREGOR, Joseph (d 1871) Jacobite singer EA/72*

MacGREGOR, Lynn (b 1945) American actress TW/29

McGREGOR, Malcolm (1892-1945) actor BE*

McGREGOR, Parke (d 1962 [55]) actor BE*

MacGREGOR, Robert M. (1911-74) American editor, publisher BE

McGREW, James (b 1917) American actor TW/2

McGROARTY, John Steven (1862-1944) American dramatist CB

McGUCKIN, Barton (1852/53-1913) Irish singer GRB/1, WWW/1

MACGUFFIE, W. M. see Raymond, Mat

McGUINN, Joseph Ford (d 1971 [67]) performer BP/56*

McGUINNESS, Edward (d 1869 [42]) duologist EA/70*

McGUINNESS, Jack [John D. Cowie] (d 1889 [30]) Irish comedian EA/90*

McGUIRE, Barry (b 1930) American actor TW/12

McGUIRE, Biff [né William J. McGuire] (b 1926) American actor, dramatist BE, TW/6, 12-16, 26-30, WWT/12-16

McGUIRE, Dorothy (b 1918) American actress BE, CB, ES, WWT/10-16

McGUIRE, Mrs. Laurence see Kimball, Grace

McGUIRE, Lavinia (d 1971 [56]) performer BP/56*

McGUIRE, Maeve American actress TW/24-25

McGUIRE, Michael see McGuire, Mitchell

McGUIRE, Mitchell [né Michael] (b 1936) American actor TW/24-29

McGUIRE, William Anthony (1885/87-1940) American dramatist, producing manager CB, WWM, WWT/6-9

McGUIRE, William J. see McGuire, Biff

McGURK, Harriet (d 1975 [72]) performer BP/60*

MACHADO, Lena (d 1974 [70]) performer BP/58*

McHAFFIE, Amelia (d 1868) EA/69*

McHALE, Rosemary (b 1944) English? actress WWT/16

McHATTIE, Stephen [Stephen Smith] Canadian actor TW/25-30

MACHATY, Gustav (d 1963 [63]) director BP/48*

McHENRY, Carrie (d 1881) actress CDP

McHENRY, Don (b 1908) American actor BE, TW/4, 15, 19, 23, 25, 27-28, 30

McHENRY, James (1785-1845) Irish dramatist EAP, RJ

McHENRY, Nellie [Mrs. John Webster] (d 1935 [82]) actress CDP

McHENRY, Tillie actress CDP

MACHIAVELLI, Niccolo di Bernardo dei (1469-1527) Italian writer COC, OC/1-3

MACHIN, Mr. (d 1870 [72]) singer EA/71*

MACHIN, Mrs. Charles E. (d 1898) EA/99*

MACHIN, Lewis (fl 1608) dramatist CP/1-3, FGF

MACHIN, Richard (fl 1600-06) actor DA

MACHIZ, Herbert (1923-76) American director BE, WWT/14-16

MACHRAY, Robert (b 1945) American actor TW/29

MacHUGH, Augustin dramatist, actor WWT/4-7

McHUGH, Edward A. (d 1973 [81]) stage manager BP/58*

McHUGH, Florence (b 1906) Canadian actress, singer WWT/6-8

McHUGH, Frank (b 1898) American actor BE, TW/23

MCHUGH, James Francis (1896-
1967) American composer BE,
TW/25

McHUGH, Mathew (d 1971 [77])
performer BP/55*

McHUGH, Therese Irish press
representative WWT/10-13

McIAN, R. (d 1856 [51]) actor,
artist EA/72*

McILDOWIE, Chattie see Mac-
Gill, Moyna

McILLWAY, John see Jackson,
John

McILRATH, Patricia (b 1917)
American educator, director
BE

MACINDOE, Alexander [Alexander
Dillon] (d 1878 [30]) actor?
EA/79*

McINERNEY, Bernie (b 1936)
American actor TW/30

McINNES, Mrs. (d 1869 [30])
Scottish? singer EA/70*

McINNES, Donald (d 1889) proprietor EA/90*

McINTIRE, Janet (b 1945) American actress TW/26

McINTOSH, Burr (1862-1942)
American actor, dramatist
SR, WWA/2, WWM, WWS

McINTOSH, Madge [Mrs. Graham
Browne] (1875-1950) Indian/
English actress, producer
EA/97, GRB/1-4, WWT/1-9

McINTOSH, Nancy (fl 1895) actress, singer CDP

McINTYRE, Bill (b 1935) American actor TW/29

McINTYRE, Rev. Duncan (d 1892)
EA/93*

McINTYRE, Duncan (d 1973 [66])
performer BP/58*

McINTYRE, Frank J. (1879-1949)
American actor SR, TW/6,
WWM, WWT/4-10

McINTYRE, James (1857-1937)
American minstrel, comedian
DAB, NTH, SR, WWM, WWS

MacINTYRE, Dr. John see
Brandane, John

McINTYRE, John T. (1871-1951)
American dramatist WWA/3,
WWM

McINTYRE, Leila (d 1953 [71])
actress TW/9

McINTYRE, Marion (d 1975 [90])
performer BP/60*

McINTYRE, Mark Walton (d 1970

[53]) composer/lyricist BP/55*

McINTYRE, Molly (d 1952 [65])
actress TW/8

McINTYRE, William (d 1885) actor
EA/86*, WWT/14*

McINTYRE AND HEATH see
McIntyre, James & Heath, Thomas

McIVER, William (b 1942) American
actor TW/9

MACK, Andrew [Andrew McAloon]
(1863-1931) American actor,
singer CDP, GRB/3-4, SR,
WWA/1, WWS, WWT/1-6

MACK, Annie (d 1935 [85]) actress
BE*, WWT/14*

MACK, Charles E. (d 1934 [46])
American actor SR

MACK, George E. (d 1948 [82])
comedian TW/4

MACK, Harry (d 1909 [69]) variety
performer EA/10*

MACK, Herbert J. (1856-1947)
actor, manager SR

MACK, James W. [né McGrath]
(d 1889 [41]) actor CDP

MACK, John (d 1891 [38]) minstrel
CDP

MACK, Joseph H. (1849-92) manager CDP

MACK, Lester (d 1972 [66]) actor
TW/29

MACK, Nila (d 1953 [62]) American
actress, producer, director
BE*, BP/37*

MACK, Russell (d 1972 [79]) performer BP/57*

MACK, Vantile giant baby CDP

MACK, Wilbur (d 1964 [91]) performer BE*, BP/48*

MACK, Willard (1873/78-1934)
American actor, dramatist,
manager SR, WWT/4-7

MACK, William B. (fl 1902-12)
American actor WWM

MACKARNESS, George Fleming
(b 1884) English actor GRB/2

MACKARNESS, Mrs. Henry (d 1881)
writer EA/82*

McKASSON, Molly (b 1947) American actress TW/30

MacKAY, Barry (b 1906) English
actor WWT/8-13

MACKAY, Charles (c. 1785-1857)
Scottish actor CDP, COC, OC/3

MacKAY, Colin (d 1905 [29])
dramatist, actor GRB/1

McKAY, David (d 1884) acting
manager EA/85*

McKAY, David actor TW/1

MacKAY, Elsie (b 1894) Australian actress WWT/4-7

MACKAY, Eric Colin (d 1905 [29]) actor EA/06*

MACKAY, Fenton (d 1929) dramatist BE*, WWT/14*

MacKAY, Frank Findley (1832-1923) Canadian/American actor CDP, PP/2, WWM

McKAY, Frederick E. (1874-1944) agent, manager, critic, producer SR

McKAY, Mrs. Frederick E. see Ring, Blanche

MACKAY, Fulton (b 1922) Scottish actor WWT/15-16

MACKAY, J. L. (b 1867) English actor GRB/3-4, WWT/1-5

MacKAY, John actor TW/26

MACKAY, John A. (d 1891 [c. 40]) American actor CDP

MACKAY, Joseph (d 1889 [39]) dramatist EA/91*

MACKAY, Leonard (d 1929 [53]) actor BE*, WWT/14*

MACKAY, Phoebe (b 1890) English actress TW/11-12

MacKAY, Ruth English actress GRB/1-4, WWT/1-6

McKAY, Scott [Carl Gose] (b 1915/17) American actor BE, TW/2-3, 6-15, 21, 24, 30, WWT/16

McKAY, Mrs. Scott see Morgan, Joan

McKAY, Ted (d 1973 [55]) dramatist BP/58*

McKAY, Tony actor TW/26

MACKAY, W. Gayer (d 1920) actor, dramatist BE*, WWT/14*

MacKAY, Mrs. W. Gayer see "Ord, Robert"

MacKAYE, James Morrison Steele (1842-94) American theatre designer, dramatist, actor, manager CDP, COC, DAB, ES, HJD, MH, NTH, OC/1-3, SR, WWA/H

MacKAYE, Norman (d 1968 [62]) performer BP/52*

MacKAYE, Percy Wallace (1875-1956) American dramatist CDP, COC, ES, GRB/3-4, HJD, MD, MH, MWD, NTH, OC/1-3, RE, TW/13, WWA/3, WWM, WWS, WWT/1-12

MacKAYE, Steel see MacKaye, James Morrison Steele

MACKAYE, W. Payson (d 1889 [21]) actor EA/90*

McKAYLE, Donald (b 1930) American choreographer, dancer BE, CB

McKEAN, R. (d 1885 [36]) music-hall proprietor EA/86*

McKEAN, Thomas (1869-1942) American dramatist WWA/1

McKEAND, Emily (d 1891) actress EA/92*

McKECHNIE, Donna (b 1940/44) American actress, dancer, singer TW/25-28, 30, WWT/16

McKECHNIE, James (1911-64) Scottish actor WWW/6

McKEE, Andy (b 1844) dancer, minstrel CDP

McKEE, Clive R. (b 1883) Canadian manager WWT/4-7

McKEE, Donald (1898-1968) American actor TW/10, 25

McKEE, James W. (fl 1874?) singer, actor CDP

McKEE, John (d 1953 [80+]) Irish actor, director BE*, BP/38*

MACKEEN, Mr. (fl 1821?) actor CDP

McKEEVER, Jacquelyn (b 1934) American actress TW/14-15

McKELLAN, Ian (b 1939) English actor AAS, TW/24, WWT/15-16

MacKELLAR, Helen (b 1891/95) American actress BE, TW/2-7, WWT/4-13

McKELLEN, Ian see McKellan, Ian

MACKEN, Walter (1915-67) Irish actor, dramatist MD, TW/7, 11, 23

McKENNA, Edwin (d 1969 [68]) producer/director/choreographer BP/53*

MACKENNA, John (d 1873) secretary, agent EA/74*

MacKENNA, Kenneth (1899-1962) American actor TW/18, WWT/7-11

McKENNA, Rose (d 1886) EA/87*

McKENNA, Siobhan (b 1922/23) Irish actress AAS, BE, CB, ES, PDT, TW/12-16, 27, 29, WWT/11-16

McKENNA, T. P. (b 1929) Irish actor WWT/15-16

McKENNA, Virginia (b 1931) Eng-

lish actress AAS, ES, WWT/
12-16

McKENNA, William J. (d 1950
[69]) American songwriter
BE*, BP/34*

MACKENZIE (d 1896 [60]) proprietor EA/97*

MacKENZIE, Sir Alexander Campbell (1847-1935) Scottish composer, conductor ES

McKENZIE, Alexander James
see Moore, Alec

MacKENZIE, Charles see Compton, Henry

MacKENZIE, Compton (d 1972
[89]) dramatist BP/57*

MACKENZIE, Mrs. Compton see
Oliffe, Geraldine

McKENZIE, D. (fl 1811) Scottish
actor HAS

MACKENZIE, Donald (d 1972
[92]) performer BP/57*

McKENZIE, Florence [Mrs. Herbert Garland] (d 1909 [35])
actress EA/10*

MacKENZIE, Francis Sidney see
Compton, Francis

MACKENZIE, George (d 1975
[74]) performer BP/60*

MACKENZIE, Hector Kenneth
Leslie (d 1878 [38]) actor
EA/79*

MacKENZIE, Henry (fl 1771-93)
Scottish dramatist CP/2-3

MACKENZIE, Herbert (d 1918
[35]) EA/19*

MacKENZIE, Hetty (d 1845) American actress HAS

McKENZIE, James B. (b 1926)
American producer, manager,
actor BE, WWT/16

MacKENZIE, J. H. (fl 1777-89)
Scottish dramatist GT, TD/1-2

McKENZIE, Joseph (d 1969 [62])
critic BP/54*

MACKENZIE, Katharine see
Compton, Miss

MACKENZIE, Mary (b 1922)
English actress WWT/11-14

MacKENZIE, May (b 1883) American actress WWM

MACKENZIE, Sir Morell (d 1892
[55]) EA/93*

McKENZIE, Richard (b 1930)
American actor TW/26, 29-30

MACKENZIE, Ronald (d 1932
[29]) dramatist BE*, WWT/14*

MACKENZIE, Tandy (1892-1963)

Hawaiian singer WWA/4

MACKENZIE, Will (b 1938) American actor TW/20-24, 26-27,
29-30

McKEON, Thomas [né Blackburn]
(fl 1833-65) English actor, manager HAS

McKEOWN, Geraldine see Mc-
Ewan, Geraldine

McKERN, Leo (b 1920) Australian
actor, director AAS, WWT/13-
16

McKESSON, Molly (b 1947) American actress TW/27

MACKETT, John (fl 179-) dramatist
CP/3

MACKEY, Colin singer, song composer CDP

MACKEY, F. F. American actor
SR

MACKEY, George William Reay (d
1883 [35]) manager EA/84*

MACKEY, Julie (fl 1896?) singer,
actress CDP

MACKEY, Keith (b 1918) American
actor TW/26

MACKIE, Charles (d 1940) journalist WWW/3-4

MACKIE, Philip dramatist CD

MacKILLOP, T. H. see Ramsay,
Scott

McKIM, Robert Stewart (d 1904
[33]) lessee EA/05*

MacKINDER, Lionel (d 1915 [46])
actor WWT/1-2

MacKINDER, Mrs. Lionel see
Leigh, Gracie

MacKINLAY, Jean Sterling (1882-
1958) English actress COC,
GRB/1-4, OC/1-3, WWT/1-9,
WWW/5

MacKINLAY, Malcolm Sterling (b
1876) actress, singer GRB/1-4

McKINLEY, John (d 1893) EA/94*

McKINLEY, Mrs. W. J. [née
Florence Wilson] (d 1870) music-
hall performer EA/71*

McKINNEL, Norman (1870-1932)
Scottish actor GRB/1-4, WWT/
1-6

McKINNELL, Mrs. Norman see
Scott, Gertrude

McKINNEY, Mr. (fl 1835) actor,
manager HAS

McKINNEY, George W. (b 1923)
American educator, designer
BE

McKINNEY, Mrs. Glennford see

Webster, Jean
McKINNON, Neil see Kenyon,
Neil
MACKINTOSH, Mrs. (d 1886 [72])
EA/87*
MACKINTOSH, Elizabeth see
Daviot, Gordon
MACKINTOSH, Robert (b 1925)
costume designer BE
MacKINTOSH, William (1855-1929)
Australian actor DP, GRB/
1-4, OAA/2, WWT/1-5
McKINZIE, Alexander (fl 1830s)
American manager, actor? SR
McKISSOCK, John Lawrence (d
1964 [94]) American magician
BE*
MACKLIN, Mr. (fl 1846) actor
HAS
MACKLIN, Charles (c. 1700-97)
Irish actor, dramatist CDP,
COC, CP/1-3, DNB, ES, GT,
HP, NTH, OC/1-3, OX, TD/
1-2
MACKLIN, Francis Henry (1848-
1903) English actor DP, OAA/
1-2
MACKLIN, Mrs. Francis Henry
[Blanche Henri] (d 1904 [55])
actress BE*, EA/05*, WWT/
14*
MACKLIN, Maria (d 1781) actress
CDP, DNB
MACKNEY, C. H. (d 1886 [65])
theatrical leader EA/87*
MACKNEY, Mrs. C. H. see
Mackney, Eliza
MACKNEY, Eliza [Mrs. C. H.
Mackney] (d 1867) EA/68*
MACKNEY, E. W. (1824/35-
1909) music-hall performer
CDP, OC/1-3
McKNIGHT, Mrs. S. C. see
Randolph, Louise
McKNIGHT, Tom (d 1963 [62])
producer BE*
MacKRIS, Orestes (d 1975 [75])
performer BP/59*
MACKWORTH, Patti [Ellie De-
Courcy] (b 1851) Scottish ac-
tress HAS
MACLACHLAN, Agnes Bruce
[Mrs. B. G. Maclachlan] (d
1911) EA/12*
MACLACHLAN, Mrs. B. G.
see Maclachlan, Agnes Bruce
MACLACHLAN, Frederic W.
see Clive, F. Wybert

MACLAGAN, Thomas (d 1902 [75])
actor, singer CDP
MACLAGAN, Tom, Jr. (d 1889)
singer, musician EA/90*
MACLAGHLAN, B. G. (d 1916)
manager EA/17* [see also:
Maclachlan]
McLAGLEN, Victor (1886-1959)
English actor BE*, BP/44*
McLAIN, Oscar see Willis, Oscar
MacLAINE, Shirley (b 1934) Amer-
ican actress, dancer CB, ES
MACLANE, Barton (d 1969 [66])
actor TW/25
McLANE, Robert (b 1944) American
actor TW/26, 29
McLANEY, Celestine (d 1894)
coloured artist EA/95*
McLAREN, Archibald (1755-1826)
Scottish actor, dramatist CP/
3, DNB, RJ
MacLAREN, Ian (b 1879) English
actor WWM, WWT/7-10
MacLAREN, Ivor (d 1962 [58])
English performer, producer
BE*
McLAREN, Mary [Mrs. Tom Dil-
lon] (d 1882) Negro artist EA/
83*
McLAREN, Neil (d 1889) actor
EA/90*
MacLARNIE, Thomas (d 1931 [60])
American actor BE*, BP/16*
McLAUGHLIN, Emily Louisa (d
1898) elocution teacher EA/99*
McLAUGHLIN, John (d 1968 [71])
composer/lyricist BP/53*
McLAUGHLIN, Leonard B. (1892-
1970) American manager BE
McLAUGHLIN, Michael (d 1916)
EA/17*
McLAUGHLIN, Millicent English
actress GRB/1-2, WWS
McLAUGHLIN, Robert (d 1973
[65]) dramatist BP/58*
MacLAURIN, John, Lord Dreghorn
(1734-96) Scottish dramatist
CP/3
McLAURIN, Kate (b 1885) Ameri-
can actress WWS
McLEAN, Miss actress CDP
McLEAN, A. G. (d 1879 [27]) actor
EA/80*
MacLEAN, Alick Scottish composer,
conductor GRB/1
MacLEAN, Douglas (d 1967 [77])
performer BP/52*
MacLEAN, John (1835?-90) English

actor OAA/1-2

McLEAN, Lex (d 1975 [67]) performer BP/59*

MacLEAN, Peter (b 1936) American actor TW/25-27

McLEAN, R. D. [R. D. Shepherd] (1859-1948) American actor SR, WWM, WWT/3-6

McLEAN, Mrs. R. D. see Tyler, Odette

McLEAN, Mrs. Robert D. see Prescott, Marie Victor

MACLEAN, Tom (d 1892 [47]) singer EA/94*

McLEARN, Frank C. (d 1969 [67]) executive BP/53*

McLEAY, Franklin (d 1900) actor EA/01*, WWT/14*

McLEAY, Mrs. Franklin see Warner, Grace

MacLEISH, Archibald (b 1892) American dramatist AAS, BE, CB, CD, CH, COC, ES, HJD, HP, MD, MH, MWD, NTH, OC/3, PDT, WWT/13-16

McLELLAN, C. M. S. ["Hugh Morton"] (1865-1916) American dramatist GRB/1-4, WWS, WWT/1-3, WWW/2

McLELLAN, G. B. (d 1932 [65]) producer BE*, WWT/14*

McLELLAN, R. C. (fl 1839?) dramatist RJ

MACLENNAN, Francis (1879-1935) American singer WWA/1

McLENNAN, K. J. (d 1917 [64]) scene artist EA/18*

McLENNAN, Rodney Australian actor TW/1

MACLEOD, Alexander Burgess (d 1889 [22]) acting manager EA/90*

MacLEOD, Angus (d 1962 [82]) producer, manager BE*, WWT/14*

McLEOD, Archibald (b 1906) Scottish educator, director, producer BE

McLEOD, Helen (d 1964 [40]) actress BE*

MacLEOD, Mary Canadian actress TW/5-6

MACLEOD, Norman (d 1903) manager EA/04*

McLEOD, Norman Z. (d 1964 [68]) director BP/48*

McLEOD, Tex (d 1973 [83]) performer BP/57*

MacLEOD, W. Angus (b 1874) English manager GRB/2-4, WWT/2-13

McLERIE, Allyn Ann (b 1926) Canadian actress, singer, dancer BE, TW/5-20, 23, WWT/15-16

McLIAM, John (b 1920) Canadian actor, dramatist BE

MacLIAMMOIR, Micheál (b 1899) Irish actor, designer, producer, director AAS, BE, COC, ES, MD, MH, MWD, OC/1-3, PDT, TW/4-7, WWT/8-16

MAC LOW, Jackson (b 1922) American dramatist, actor CD

MacMAHON, Aline (b 1899) American actress BE, TW/2-7, 10-18, 23-25, 27-28, WWT/7-16

McMAHON, Charles (d 1917 [55]) Australian executive EA/18*

McMAHON, Charles W., Sr. (d 1973 [93]) agent BP/58*

McMAHON, David (d 1972 [63]) performer BP/56*

McMAHON, Mrs. [Dennis] (fl 1857) actress CDP, HAS

MACMAHON, George (d 1908) boy actor-singer EA/09*

McMAHON, Horace (1907-71) American actor BE, TW/28

McMAHON, Jere dancer TW/1

McMAHON, Tim (d 1916) music-hall comedian EA/17*

McMANNS, Charles A. (d 1888 [59]) American actor EA/90*

McMANUS, C. A. (fl 1865) actor HAS

MacMANUS, Clive (d 1953) English critic, journalist WWT/9

McMANUS, John L. (d 1963 [71]) musical director BE*

MacMANUS, Patrick F. (d 1965 [56]) dramatist BP/50*

MacMANUS, Seumas (1869-1960) Irish dramatist WWA/4, WWW/5

McMARTIN, John American actor TW/22-24, 27-30, WWT/16

McMASTER, Anew (1894-1962) Irish actor, director AAS, COC, OC/3, WWT/8-9

McMATH, Virginia Katherine see Rogers, Ginger

MacMICHAEL, Florence actress TW/1

McMILLAN, Mr. (b 1813) English actor HAS

McMILLAN, Mrs. [Julia Barton] (fl 1847) singer HAS

MACMILLAN, Alick (d 1908 [21])
EA/09*
McMILLAN, Dan (d 1860) actor
HAS
MacMILLAN, Duncan (d 1866
[49]) ventriloquist EA/72*
MacMILLAN, J. T. Scottish actor
GRB/1
MacMILLAN, Kenneth (b 1929)
Scottish dancer, choreographer
ES
McMILLAN, Kenneth (b 1934)
American actor TW/26, 30
McMILLAN, Lida (d 1940 [71])
American actress WWM
McMILLAN, Roddy (b 1923) Scot-
tish actor, dramatist WWT/16
MACMILLAN, Violet [Mrs. John
H. Folger] (1885-1953) Amer-
ican actress TW/10, WWM,
WWS
McMULLAN, Frank (b 1907)
American educator, director
BE
MacMULLEN, Charles see
Munro, C. K.
McMULLEN, Susan (b 1944)
American actress TW/24
McMURDIE, Joseph (d 1878 [85])
EA/80*
McMURRAY, J. S. (fl 1881)
minstrel CDP
McNAIR, Barbara (b 1939) Amer-
ican singer, actress BE, CB
MACNALLY, Jessie (d 1886)
EA/87*
MACNALLY, Jessie [Mrs. W.
H. McCarthy] (d 1903 [35])
serio-comic EA/04*
McNALLY, John J. (d 1931 [76])
American critic, dramatist
BE*, BP/15*, WWT/14*
MacNALLY, J. J. (d 1918) EA/
19*
MACNALLY, J. P. (d 1908 [49])
performer? EA/09*
MacNALLY, Mrs. J. P. see
O'Beirne, Tessie
MacNALLY, Leonard (1752-1820)
Irish dramatist CP/3, GT,
TD/1-2
McNALLY, Terrence (b 1930/39)
American dramatist CD, CH,
MH, WWT/15-16
MACNAMARA, Mrs. (d 1862
[84]) actress EA/72*, WWT/
14*
MACNAMARA, Brinsley [John

Weldon] (1890/91-1963) Irish ac-
tor, dramatist COC, MD, MH,
MWD, OC/3
McNAMARA, Daniel I. (d 1962
[76]) press representative, editor
BE*
McNAMARA, Dermot (b 1925) Irish
actor TW/18, 22-23, 26-27
McNAMARA, Edward (1887-1944)
English actor, singer SR, TW/1
McNAMARA, Maggie (b 1928)
American actress TW/7-9
McNAMARA, Rosemary (b 1943)
American actress TW/23
McNAMARA, Tom (d 1964 [78])
performer BE*
McNATTY, Ted (d 1904) music-hall
performer EA/05*
MacNAUGHTON, Alan (b 1920)
Scottish actor AAS, WWT/12-16
MCNAUGHTON, Anne (b 1943)
American actress TW/29
McNAUGHTON, Gus (1884-1969)
English actor WWT/10-11
McNAUGHTON, Harry (d 1967 [70])
actor TW/23
McNAUGHTON, Mrs. T. see
Lloyd, Alice
McNAUGHTON, Tom (1867-1923)
English actor WWT/4
McNAY, Evelyn [Mrs. William Mol-
lison] (d 1944 [73]) actress
BE*, WWT/14*
McNEAR, Howard (d 1969 [64])
performer BP/53*
MACNEE, Patrick (b 1922) English
actor TW/29-30
McNEELEY, Gale (b 1946) American
actress TW/28
MacNEICE, Louis (1907-65) Irish
dramatist NTH, PDT
McNEIL, Claudia (b 1917) American
actress BE, TW/14-20, 24-26,
WWT/14-16
MacNEIL, Cornell (b 1922) Ameri-
can singer CB
McNEILE, Lt.-Col. Cyril see
"Sapper"
McNEILL, Mrs. A. D. see
Ryder, Jessie Henry
McNEILL, Alexander Duncan (d
1884 [55]) lessee EA/85*
McNEILL, Amy New Zealand ac-
tress EA/96
McNEILL, Robert Stuart (d 1887
[70]) manager? EA/88*
McNEILL, W. J. see Emmett,
Bobbie

McNICHOL, Eileen American
executive BE

McNISH, Francis Edward (1853-
1924) American manager,
minstrel CDP

McNUTT, Patterson (d 1948 [52])
American producer, dramatist
TW/5

MACOLLA, Albert see McCulloch, Andrew

MACOLLUM, Barry Irish actor
TW/1, 24

MACOMB, General (fl 1838?)
dramatist RJ

MACOSKO, Greg (b 1947) American actor TW/30

MacOWAN, Michael (b 1906) English producer, actor AAS,
COC, OC/3, WWT/9-16

MacOWAN, Norman (1877-1961)
Scottish actor, dramatist
COC, WWT/5-13

McPETERS, Taylor (d 1962 [62])
actor BE*

McPHAIL, Lindsay (d 1965 [70])
composer/lyricist BP/49*

McPHARLIN, Paul (1903-48)
puppeteer CB

McPHARLIN, Mrs. Paul see
Batchelder, Marjorie

McPHERRIN, John W. (d 1974
[77]) investor BP/59*

McPHERSON, Mr. (fl 1787) actor
HAS

McPHERSON, Alexander (d 1883
[36]) actor EA/84*

MACPHERSON, Andrew (d 1913)
EA/14*

MACPHERSON, J. (fl 1771)
dramatist EAP

McPHERSON, Mervyn (b 1892)
English press representative
WWT/6-10

MACPHERSON, Quinton (d 1940
[69]) actor BE*, WWT/14*

McPHILLIPS, Edward (b 1925)
English actor TW/24-25, 29

McQUADE, Arlene (b 1936) American actress TW/5

McQUEEN, Annie (d 1890) EA/91*

McQUEEN, Butterfly (b 1911)
American actress TW/24,
26, WWT/15-16

McQUEEN, Steve (b 1930?) American actor CB, ES

McQUEENEY, Robert American
actor TW/11-12

MacQUEEN-POPE, W. James

(1888-1960) English business
manager, dramatist, press-
manager, historian, manager
AAS, COC, DNB, OC/3, WWT/
4-12, WWW/5

McQUIGGAN, Jack (b 1935) American producer, actor BE

McQUINN, Robert (d 1975 [92])
designer BP/60*

McQUIRE, Christopher (d 1893
[52]) EA/94*

McQUOID, Percy (1852-1925) designer, painter WWT/4, WWW/2

McQUOID, Rose Lee (d 1962 [75])
actress BE*

McRAE, Anne Buchanan (d 1889
[61]) EA/90*

MacRAE, Arthur (1908-62) English
actor, dramatist AAS, WWT/
7-13

McRAE, Bruce (1867-1927) Indian/
English actor GRB/3-4, WWA/
1, WWM, WWS, WWT/1-5

McRAE, Duncan (d 1931) actor,
director BE*, WWT/14*

MACRAE, Duncan (1905-67) Scottish actor COC, WWT/14

MACREADY, Mrs. (d 1873) actress
CDP, HAS

MACREADY, Caroline [Mrs. Edmund Edmunds] (d 1867 [27])
EA/68*

MACREADY, Cécile Louisa [Mrs.
W. C. Macready] (d 1908 [81])
EA/09*

MACREADY, George (d 1973 [63/
73]) actor TW/30

MACREADY, Mrs. W. C. see
Macready, Cécile Louisa

MacREADY, William (1755-1829)
Irish actor, manager, dramatist
CDP, CP/3, ES, GT, TD/1-2

MACREADY, William Charles
(1793-1873) English actor, manager BS, CDP, COC, DNB, ES,
HAS, HJD, HP, NTH, OC/1-3,
OX, PDT, SR

MacROE (fl 1784) dramatist CP/3

MacSARIN, Kenneth (d 1967 [55])
press agent BP/51*

McSHANE, Ian (b 1942) English
actor WWT/15-16

McSHANE, Kitty (d 1964 [66])
actress BE*

McSORLEY, Lars Michael (d 1972
[41]) publicist BP/56*

McSPADDEN, Joseph W. (b 1874)
American writer WWM

McSTAY, Robert (d 1964 [60])
journalist BP/48*
MacSWINEY, Owen (d 1754)
manager WWT/14*
MacTAGGART, James (d 1974
[46]) performer BP/59*
McTERNAN, Agnes M. (d 1974
[56]) editor BP/59*
McTURK, David Harvey (d 1972
[67]) performer BP/57*
McVEY, Patrick (1913-73) Amer-
ican actor TW/11-12, 21-22,
25-27, 30
MacVICARS, Frank (d 1907) actor
GRB/3*
McVICKER, Horace (d 1931 [75])
American manager BE*, BP/
16*, WWT/14*
McVICKER, James Hubert [or
Horace] (1822/24-76) American
actor, manager CDP, DAB,
HAS, SR, WWA/H
McVICKER, Sara (fl 1880s) ac-
tress SR
McWADE, Robert (1835-1913)
Canadian actor CDP, HAS,
SR
McWADE, Robert (d 1938 [56])
American actor WWT/7-8
McWATTERS, Arthur J. (d 1963
[92]) performer BP/48*
McWHINNEY, Michael (d 1970
[39]) composer/lyricist BP/
55*
McWHINNIE, Donald (b 1920) Eng-
lish director AAS, BE, WWT/
14-16
McWILLIAMS, Caroline American
actress TW/28
McWILLIAMS, James (fl 1852)
actor HAS
MACY, Carleton (d 1946 [85])
actor, vaudevillian TW/3
MACY, Gertrude (b 1904) Amer-
ican manager, producer BE,
TW/2, 5-8
MACY, William (b 1922) American
actor TW/23-27
MADACH, Imre (1823-64) Hun-
garian dramatist OC/1
MADDEN, Miss see Hook,
Mrs. James
MADDEN, Archibald American
clown HAS
MADDEN, Cecil (b 1902) English
dramatist WWT/9-14
MADDEN, Ciaran (b 1945) ac-
tress WWT/15-16

MADDEN, Donald (b 1933) Ameri-
can actor BE, TW/16-21, 23-
25, 27, WWT/14-16
MADDEN, Richard (d 1951 [71])
American literary representative
BE*, BP/35*
MADDEN, Dr. Samuel (1686-1765)
Irish dramatist CP/2-3, GT
MADDERN, Emma (fl 1842-69)
American actress HAS
MADDERN, Merle (b 1887) Ameri-
can actress TW/1-7
MADDICK, Mrs. Gordon see
Illington, Marie
MADDOCK, C. B. (d 1974 [93])
producer/director/choreographer
BP/59*
MADDOCKS (fl 1829?) dramatist
EAP
MADDOX, Mrs. (fl 1854) actress
HAS
MADDOX, Anthony (d 1758) equili-
brist CDP
MADDOX, Diana (b 1926) English
actress TW/14
MADDOX, J. M. (d 1861 [72])
manager EA/72*, WWT/14*
MADDOX, Thomas (d 1880) propri-
etor EA/81*
MADEIRA, Humberto (d 1971 [50])
performer BP/56*
MADEIRA, Jean (1924-72) American
singer CB, WWA/5
MADELAINE, Marion (d 1865) ac-
tress HAS
MADELLE-STONE, Charles R.
see Stone, Charles R.
MADERNA, Bruno (d 1973 [53])
composer/lyricist BP/58*
MADIGAN, Eggie (d 1892 [34])
equestrian EA/93*
MADIGAN, Henry P. (1820-62)
American circus manager,
vaulter, equestrian HAS
MADISON, Mrs. see Grattan,
Mrs. Henry P.
MADISON, Cleo (d 1964 [81]) ac-
tress BE*
MADISON, Nathaniel J. (d 1968
[72]) performer BP/52*
MADISON, Noel (d 1975 [77])
performer BP/59*
MAEDER, Frank manager CDP
MAEDER, Frederick G. (d 1891
[50]) American actor, dramatist
HAS, SR
MAEDER, Mrs. Frederick G.
see Maeder, Rena

MAEDER, Mrs. James see
Fisher, Clara
MAEDER, James Gaspard (d 1876
[67]) musician, composer,
director, manager CDP
MAEDER, Maria A. (c. 1839-1916)
actress SR
MAEDER, Rena [Mrs. Frederick
G. Maeder] actress CDP
MAEKEY, James (d 1882) EA/83*
MAETERLINCK, Maurice (1862-
1949) Belgian dramatist COC,
ES, GRB/1-4, MH, NTH,
OC/1-3, RE, WWM, WWT/
1-3, 10, WWW/4
MAETZKER-MERITT, Mrs. (d
1887 [72]) EA/88*
MAFFEI, Scipione (1675-1755)
Italian dramatist OC/1-3
MAFFITT, James Strawbridge
(1832-97) actor, pantomimist
CDP
MAFLIN, Alfred W. (b 1840) Eng-
lish actor WWS
MAGALLANES, Nicholas (1919-77)
Mexican/American dancer CB,
ES
MAGAN, James see Middleton,
James
MAGARSHACK, David (b 1899)
Latvian translator BE
MAGEE, Patrick Irish actor
AAS, WWT/15-16
MAGENON, Mrs. actress CDP
MAGET, Stephen (fl 1596) actor
DA
MAGGART, Brandon (b 1933)
American actor TW/18-20,
24, 26-30
MAGGIORE, Charles (b 1936)
American actor TW/24, 29
MAGILTON, Henry M. [Jocko,
The Brazilian Ape] (d 1901)
acrobat CDP
MAGINLEY, Benjamin R. (1832-
88) American actor, circus
manager, clown CDP, HAS
MAGINN, Bonnie (fl 1903-04)
American actress, dancer
WWS
MAGINN, Dr. William (d 1842
[49]) critic BE*, EA/72*,
WWT/14*
MAGLEY, Guy (d 1971 [79]) per-
former BP/55*
MAGNANI, Anna (d 1973 [65])
actress BP/58*, WWT/16*
MAGNAY, Sir William (d 1917)

dramatist EA/18*
MAGO, William (fl 1624-31) actor
DA
MAGOWAN, Mrs. (fl 1847) actress
HAS
MAGRANE, Thais (d 1957 [79])
American actress WWM
MAGRATH, Charles [Charles Ryland
Magrath] (b 1865) Irish singer
GRB/1-2
MAGUINNIS, Daniel J. (1834-89)
American actor CDP
MAGUIRE, James [J. M. Cooke]
(d 1880) actor? EA/81*
MAGUIRE, James (d 1899) perform-
er EA/00*
MAGUIRE, J. R. (d 1883 [44])
actor EA/84*
MAGUIRE, Kathleen American ac-
tress BE, TW/14, 25
MAHARAM, Joseph (b 1898) Amer-
ican executive BE
MAHARIS, George (b 1928/33)
American actor, singer BE,
TW/15-20
MAHER, James P. (d 1973 [78])
critic BP/57*
MAHER, Joseph (b 1933) Irish actor
TW/23-24, 26, 28, 30
MAHIEU, Charles (d 1964 [70])
performer BP/49*
MAHLER, Gustav (1860-1911) Ger-
man conductor, composer ES,
WWA/4
MAHON, Mrs. (fl 1781?) actress
CDP
MAHON, Miss (fl 1770-89) see
Ambrose, Mrs.
MAHON, Robert (fl 1775) singer
TD/1-2
MAHON, Thomas Raleigh (1827-59)
American actor? singer? musi-
cian? HAS
MAHONEY, Elizabeth Ann Katherine
see Bellwood, Bessie
MAHONEY, Trish (b 1946) Egyptian/
American actress TW/28-29
MAHONEY, Will (1896-1967) Amer-
ican actor TW/23, WWT/7-14
MAHR, Herman Carl (d 1964 [62])
composer BE*
MAIDMAN, Irving (b 1897) Russian/
American theatre owner BE
MAIDWELL, L. (fl 1680) dramatist
CP/1-3, GT
MAILLARD, Alfonso see Dubois,
James
MAILLY, William (1871-1912)

American critic DAB

MAIN, Ann (d 1894) EA/95*

MAIN, Marjorie (1890-1975) actress CB

MAINBOCHER (b 1890) American costumier, costume designer BE

MAINE, Bruno (1896-1962) Finish designer BE*, BP/47*

MAINSTONE, Gracie (d 1891) music-hall performer EA/92*

MAINWARING, Ernest (1876-1941) English actor WWT/2-9

MAIORANO, Gaetano see Caffarelli, Sig.

MAIR, George Herbert (1887-1926) critic WWT/5

MAIRVIN (fl 1635) actor DA

MAIS, Stuart Petre Brodie (1885-1975) critic WWT/5

MAISELL, Joe (b 1939) American actor TW/26

MAISEY, E. J. (d 1890) lessee EA/91*

MAISEY, Elise (fl 1875-78) actress OAA/2

MAISON, René (d 1962 [67]) Belgian singer TW/19

MAITLAND, Mrs. see Chester, Marie

MAITLAND, Ada (d 1871) singer EA/72*

MAITLAND, Charles (d 1892) actor EA/93*

MAITLAND, Lauderdale (d 1929 [52]) English actor WWT/2-5

MAITLAND, Mrs. Lauderdale see Valentine, Gertrude

MAITLAND, Mary Ann (d 1875 [59]) actress EA/76*

MAITLAND, Michael (d 1956) American actor TW/27-28

MAITLAND, Ruth (1880/83-1961) English actress GRB/2, WWT/5-13

MAITLAND, Ruth (b 1926) American actress TW/28-29

MAJERONI, Edward (d 1892) actor CDP

MAJERONI, Mario (d 1931 [61]) actor BE*

MAJILTON, Charles (1849-1931) pantomimist, dancer CDP

MAJILTON, Flo [Mrs. W. Harrison] (d 1906) actress EA/07*

MAJILTON, Frank (fl late 19th cent) performer CDP

MAJILTON, Marie actress, dancer

CDP

MAJOR, Bessie actress WWT/3-5

MAJOR, Charles (1856-1913) American dramatist WWM

MAJOR, Clare Tree (d 1954 [74]) English producer TW/11

MAJOR, Elizabeth [Mrs. Thomas Major] (d 1892 [44]) music-hall singer EA/93*

MAJOR, Frank A. (b 1925) American executive BE

MAJOR, H. A. (d 1902) dramatist EA/03*

MAJOR, Hannah [Mrs. Tom Major] (d 1886) EA/87*

MAJOR, H. Lance (d 1876 [25]) songwriter EA/77*

MAJOR, Mrs. Thomas see Major, Elizabeth

MAJOR, Tom (d 1896) property master EA/98*

MAJOR, Mrs. Tom see Major, Hannah

MAKAROVA, Natalia (b 1940) Russian dancer CB

MAKEATH, Miss see Vandenhoff, Mrs. George

MAKEHAM, Eliot (1882-1956) English actor TW/12, WWT/6-11

MAKEHAM, Gladys (b 1891) English actress GRB/1-2

MAKGILL-MAITLAND, Maisie (b 1871) American actress GRB/1

MAKIN, Mrs. (fl 1806) English actress GT

MAKLETZOVA, Xenia (d 1974 [81]) performer BP/58*

MALBIN, Elaine (b 1932) American singer CB

MALCOLM, Edith Fisk (d 1976 [67]) performer BP/60*

MALCOLM, John (1906-69) English actor TW/22-23, 26

MALCOLM, Reginald (d 1966 [82]) performer BP/50*

MALDEN, Herbert John (1882-1966) English business manager WWT/9-12

MALDEN, Karl (b 1914) American actor, director BE, CB, ES, TW/2-9, 11-15

MALEKOS, Nick (b 1935) Greek actor TW/25

MALET, Arthur (b 1927) English actor TW/13-16

MALEY, Denman (d 1927 [50]) American comedian BE*, BP/11*

MALEY, Peggy American actress TW/4-6

MALIANDI, Paula (b 1949) American actress TW/29

MALIBRAN, Maria Felicita (1808-36) French singer, actress CDP, ES, HAS, HP

MALIGNY, Félix Bernier de see Aristippe

MALINA, Judith (b 1926) German director, producer, actress BE, COC, WWT/15-16

MALINA, Luba Russian actress TW/3, 14-15

MALINOFSKY, Max (d 1963 [70]) performer, manager BE*

MALIPIERO, Gian Francesco (d 1973 [91]) composer/lyricist BP/58*

MALIPIERO, Luigi (d 1975 [74]) producer/director/choreographer BP/59*

MALIS, Claire (b 1944) American actress TW/25

MALKIN, Beata (d 1973 [82]) performer BP/58*

MALKIN, Benjamin Heath (fl 1804) dramatist CP/3

MALL, Dr. Richard (d 1973 [54]) performer BP/58*

MALLAH, Vivian (b 1924) American actress TW/2

MALLALIEU, Aubrey (1873-1948) English actor WWT/8-10

MALLALIEU, William (d 1927 [81]) actor BE*, WWT/14*

MALLANDAINE, J. (d 1886) musician, conductor EA/87*

MALLESON, Miles (1888-1969) English actor, dramatist AAS, COC, ES, OC/3, PDT, WWT/4-14, WWW/6

MALLET, David (d 1765) Scottish dramatist CP/1-3, GT, TD/1-2

MALLETT, George English actor, stage manager, manager GRB/1-2

MALLETT, Mrs. George see Leigh, Stella

MALLETT, Richard (d 1972 [62]) critic BP/57*

MALLIN, Tom dramatist CD

MALLINGER, Mathilde (b 1847) singer CDP

MALLINSON, Joseph (fl 1811) actor CDP

MALLISON, Marvin Morton see Ward, William H.

MALLORY, Ben (1829-59) American minstrel, equestrian HAS

MALLORY, Boots (d 1958 [45]) American actress BE*, BP/43*

MALLORY, Burton (d 1962 [79]) performer BE*

MALLORY, Rene (d 1931 [24]) actress BE*, WWT/14*

MALLORY, Victoria (b 1948) American actress TW/25, 27-30

MALLOY, Marie Louise American critic WWM

MALO, Gina (1909-63) American actress, singer TW/20, WWT/7-10

MALONE, Andrew E. (d 1939) critic BE*, WWT/14*

MALONE, Dudley Field (b 1931) American talent representative BE

MALONE, Edmond (1741-1812) Irish scholar COC, DNB, GT, HP, NTH, OC/1-3, TD/1-2

MALONE, Elizabeth (d 1955 [75]) actress BE*, WWT/14*

MALONE, J. A. E. (d 1929 [69]) Indian/English manager, producer WWT/2-5

MALONE, Mrs. J. A. E. see Moody, Hilda

MALONE, John (b 1854) American actor PP/2

MALONE, Mary (b 1924) American actress TW/5-7

MALONE, Nancy (b 1935) American actress TW/13-15, 27-28

MALONE, Patricia (b 1899) English actress, singer WWT/6-8

MALONE, Pick (d 1962 [69]) performer BE*

MALONE, Ray (d 1970 [44]) actor, dancer TW/26

MALONE, Richard see Raymond, Malone

MALONEY, J. W. (d 1897) manager EA/98*

MALONY, Mrs. (d 1894 [52]) EA/95*

MALTBY, Alfred (d 1901 [59]) actor, dramatist CDP

MALTBY, Harold Constable (d 1892) actor EA/93*

MALTBY, Henry Francis W. (1880-1963) South African actor, dramatist GRB/1-2, WWT/4-13, WWW/6

MALTBY, Mara English actress

GRB/2
MALTBY, Tom (d 1918 [75])
EA/18*
MALTEN, Therese (b 1855)
singer CDP
MALTEN, William (b 1902) actor
TW/2
MALTZ, Albert (b 1908) American
dramatist BE, CB, CD, ES,
HJD, MD, MWD, NTH
MALVERN, Emma (d 1877) ac-
tress EA/78*
MALVERN, J. H. (d 1901 [73])
actor EA/02*
MALVERN, Louisa Maud (d 1901
[25]) EA/02*
MALVEY, Harold (d 1975 [70])
performer BP/59*
MAMOULIAN, Rouben (b 1897/98)
Russian/American director
AAS, BE, CB, COC, ES,
NTH, TW/2-8, WWT/7-14
MAN, Henry (1747-99) English
dramatist CP/3
MANA, Archibald (d 1878 [43])
singer EA/80*
MANAHAN, Anna Irish actress
TW/25
MANBY, Dr. Fred (d 1891)
director EA/92*
MANCHESTER, Hannah see Al-
bertine, Hannah
MANCHESTER, Thomas (d 1897
[34]) acting manager EA/99*
MANCINELLI, Luigi (1848-1921)
Italian conductor, composer
ES, WWW/2
MANCINELLI, Marino (d 1894
[52]) composer, conductor
EA/95*
MANCINI, Ric (b 1933) American
actor TW/27-28
MANDAN, Robert (b 1932) Amer-
ican actor TW/13, 25-28
MANDEL, Bebe (d 1975 [50])
booking agent BP/60*
MANDEL, Frank (1884-1958)
American dramatist, librettist,
producer, manager TW/14,
WWT/5-11
MANDEL, Loring (b 1928) Amer-
ican dramatist BE
MANDEL, Mike (d 1963 [69])
stage manager BE*
MANDELL, Israel (d 1962 [60])
performer BE*
MANDELSTAM, Abraham (d 1969
[86]) dramatist BP/54*

MANDERS, Mr. (d 1871) menagerie
proprietor EA/72*
MANDERS, James (d 1907 [74])
menagerie proprietor EA/08*
MANDERS, Louisa (d 1880 [79])
actress EA/81*
MANDERS, Lucy [Mrs. G. Howard
Watson] (d 1894) actress EA/95*
MANDERS, Thomas (d 1859 [61])
actor EA/72*, WWT/14*
MANDEVILLE, Alicia (fl 1859-67)
actress HAS
MANDEVILLE, Frank N. (d 1921)
American conductor BE*, BP/6*
MANDIA, Joe (d 1970 [45]) per-
former BP/55*
MANDLEBERT, Kate [Mrs. George
Chapman] (d 1899) EA/00*
MANDLEBERT, Lizzie see Jones,
Mrs. David H.
MANEY, Richard (1891-1968) Amer-
ican press representative BE,
CB, TW/25
MANFIELD, A. B. (d 1901) mana-
ger EA/02*
MANFRE, Blaise de (b c. 1579)
juggler CDP
MANFRED, Emily see Etherdo,
Mary Ann
MANGAN, Francis A. (d 1971 [86])
producer/director/choreographer
BP/55*
MANGEON, Mrs. (fl 1826-32) Eng-
lish actress HAS
MANGEON, Miss (fl 1816) singer,
actress CDP
MANGER, Itzik (d 1969 [67]) mana-
ger BP/53*
MANGES, Carl (d 1874) proprietor
EA/75*
MANGES, John (d 1878 [59]) musi-
cian EA/79*
MANGIN, Edward (fl 1810) trans-
lator CP/3
MANHILL, James (d 1899 [51])
comedian EA/00*
MANHOFF, Arnold (d 1965 [50])
dramatist BP/49*
MANHOFF, Wilton (d 1974 [54])
dramatist BP/59*
MANIS, James (b 1939) American
actor TW/25
MANKIEWICZ, Herman J. (d 1953
[56]) American dramatist, critic
BE*, BP/37*, WWT/14*
MANKOWITZ, Wolf (b 1924) English
dramatist, producer CD, PDT,
WWT/13-16

MANLEY, Alfred (d 1869) equestrian EA/70*

MANLEY, Beatrice (b 1921) American actress TW/4, 23

MANLEY, Prof. E. (d 1880 [59]) scene artist EA/81*

MANLEY, Mrs. H. see Manley, Martha

MANLEY, Henry (d 1887) circus proprietor EA/88*

MANLEY, Mrs. Henry (d 1874 [44]) actress EA/75*

MANLEY, Henry Christian (d 1891 [72]) EA/92*

MANLEY, J. H. (d 1917 [78]) actor EA/18*

MANLEY, John (d 1892 [76]) stage manager EA/93*

MANLEY, Martha [Mrs. H. Manley] (d 1872 [55]) EA/74*

MANLEY, Mary de la Riviere (1663-1724) English dramatist CP/1-3, DNB, GT

MANLEY, Oliver (d 1878 [38]) musician, composer EA/79*

"MAN MONKEY, The" see Gouffe, Mons.

MANN, Alice Placide (fl 1855-61) actress CDP, HAS

MANN, Anthony (1906-67) American director, actor TW/23, WWA/4

MANN, Billy (d 1974) performer BP/58*

MANN, Caroline (d 1907 [80]) GRB/3*

MANN, Charlton (1876-1958) English manager, dramatist WWT/4-8

MANN, Christopher (b 1903) English press representative WWT/6-13

MANN, Daniel (b 1912) American director BE, ES

MANN, David (d 1908) managing director EA/09*

MANN, Eliza (d 1874) actress CDP

MANN, Erika (d 1969 [63]) performer BP/54*

MANN, Frances (d 1969 [68]) dancer, play doctor BP/54*

MANN, Mrs. H. (d 1878 [70]) EA/80*

MANN, Hannah (d 1881) EA/82*

MANN, Harry (d 1901) manager EA/02*

MANN, Henry John see Montague, F. J.

MANN, Iris (b 1939) American actress TW/9

MANN, Louis (1865-1931) American actor, dramatist DAB, GRB/2-4, WWA/1, WWM, WWS, WWT/1-6

MANN, Mrs. Louis see Lipman, Clara

MANN, Paul (b 1913/15) American actor, director BE, TW/8, 13, 21-23

MANN, Ralph (b 1922) American talent representative BE

MANN, Sam (d 1965 [77]) performer BP/50*

MANN, Mrs. Sheridan [née Eliza Placide] (fl 1814-69) actress HAS

MANN, Theodore [né Goldman] (b 1924) American producer, director BE, WWT/15-16

MANN, Winifred American actress TW/24

MANNA, Charlie (1925-71) comedian CB

MANNERING, Doré Lewin (1879-1932) Polish/English actor WWT/4-6

MANNERING, Mary [Mrs. J. K. Hackett] (1876-1953) English actress CDP, GRB/2-4, NTH, PP/2, SR, TW/9, WWM, WWS, WWT/1-7

MANNERING, Moya [Moya Doyle] (b 1888) actress, singer WWT/3-8

MANNERS, Mr. (fl 1839-50) English singer HAS

MANNERS, Annie see Knowles, Mrs. Forrest

MANNERS, Catherine (d 1890) EA/91*

MANNERS, Charles [Mansergh] (1857/58-1935) English singer, manager GRB/1-4, WWW/3

MANNERS, Mrs. Charles see Moody, Fanny

MANNERS, David (b 1900/05) Canadian actor SR, TW/2-7, WWT/11

MANNERS, George (fl 1806) dramatist CP/3

MANNERS, Jayne English actress, manager BE

MANNERS, John Hartley (1870-1928) Irish/American dramatist, actor COC, DAB, ES, HJD,

MWD, NTH, OC/1-3, SR, WWA/1, WWM, WWT/1-5, WWW/2

MANNERS, Josephine (fl 1856) English actress HAS

MANNERY, Samuel (fl 1631) actor DA

MANNES, Florence V. (d 1964 [68]) performer BP/49*

MANNEY, Charles Fonteyn (b 1872) American composer WWM

MANNHARDT, Renata German actress TW/27

MANNHEIM, Albert (d 1972 [58]) dramatist BP/58*

MANNHEIM, Lucie (1899/1905-1976) German actress ES, WWT/8-14

MANNING, Mrs. (d 1891) EA/92*

MANNING, Ambrose (d 1940 [79]) actor GRB/1-4, WWT/1-9

MANNING, Billy (d 1876) minstrel SR

MANNING, David (b 1958) American actor TW/24

MANNING, Edward Betts (1874-1948) Canadian composer WWA/2

MANNING, Francis (fl 1688-1716) dramatist CP/1-3

MANNING, Frank (d 1899 [34]) actor EA/00*

MANNING, Hugh Gardner (b 1920) English actor WWT/15-16

MANNING, Irene [née Inez Harvuot] (b 1916/17/18) American actress, singer BE, TW/2-3, WWT/11-14

MANNING, Jack (b 1916) American actor, director BE, TW/1-4, 7-9, 11-16, 21-22, 27

MANNING, John (1850-87) American actor, performer NYM

MANNING, John (d 1890 [64]) actor EA/91*, WWT/14*

MANNING, Marty (d 1971 [55]) actor BP/56*

MANNING, Maybelle (d 1968 [74]) costumier BP/52*

MANNING, Otis (d 1963 [50]) American performer BE*

MANNING, Riccardo (d 1954 [40]) singer WWT/14*

MANNION, Moira (d 1964 [46]) actress BE*

MANNO, Anthony P. (d 1973 [34]) composer/lyricist BP/58*

MANNOCK, Patrick L. (b 1887) English critic WWT/7-13

MANNON, C. H. (d 1918) EA/19*

MANNS, Mrs. A. (d 1893) EA/94*

MANNS, Sir August (d 1907 [81]) conductor EA/08*

MANNS, Otto, Jr. (b 1873) German musical director, composer GRB/1

MANNY, Charles (d 1962 [71]) performer BE*

MANOLA, Adelaide [Mrs. Rupert Hughes] (b 1885) Canadian actress WWM

MANOLA, Marion (d 1914 [48]) performer BE*, WWT/14*

MANON, Sylvia (d 1966 [56]) performer BP/51*

MANSEL, Lady [Lily Ernest] (d 1916) comedian EA/17*

MANSEL, Eliza [Mrs. Frederic Reynolds] (fl 1795-96?) actress CDP

MANSEL, Sir Richard (d 1892) EA/93*

MANSELL, Mrs. Ernest see Wright, Maudie

MANSELL, John (fl 1607) actor DA

MANSELL, Richard (d 1907) manager, actor GRB/1-3

MANSELL, William (fl 1784) dramatist CP/3

MANSELL, W. L. (d 1893 [48]) EA/94*

MANSERGH, Charles see Manners, Charles

MANSFIELD, Ada [Mrs. Theodore Jones] (d 1906) actress EA/08*

MANSFIELD, Alfred F. (d 1938 [60]) actor, director BE*, WWT/14*

MANSFIELD, Alice (d 1938 [80]) actress WWT/4-7

MANSFIELD, Beatrice [Beatrice Cameron] (1868-1940) American actress COC, DD, OC/1-3, SR, WWA/4

MANSFIELD, Fred see Martin, F. W.

MANSFIELD, Jayne (1933-67) American actress ES, TW/12-15, 22, WWA/4

MANSFIELD, Josephine (b c. 1840) actress SR

MANSFIELD, Portia (b 1887) American educator BE

MANSFIELD, Richard (1854/57-1907) American actor, manager, dramatist CDP, COC, DAB, DP, ES, GRB/1-3, HJD, NTH, OC/1-3, PP/2, SR, WWA/1, WWS, WWW/1

MANSFIELD, Scott (b 1949) American actor TW/30

MANSON, Alan American actor TW/24, 26-27, 29

MANSON, Eddy (b 1919) American actor TW/3

MANSON, Edward (d 1969 [77]) public relations BP/54*

MANSOUR, George P., Jr. (b 1949) American actor TW/29

MANTELL, Bruce (d 1933 [24]) American actor BE*

MANTELL, Marianne (b 1929) German/American executive BE

MANTELL, Robert Bruce (1854-1928) Scottish/American actor, manager COC, DAB, ES, GRB/2-4, NTH, OC/1-3, PP/2, SR, WWA/1, WWM, WWS, WWT/1-5

MANTELL, Mrs. Robert Bruce see Russell, Marie Booth

MANTELL, Mrs. R[obert] B[ruce] see Sheldon, Marie

MANTIA, Charles (d 1974 [85]) actor TW/30

MANTIN, Sig. (fl 1847) dancer HAS

MANTLE, George Hunter (d 1886) EA/87*

MANTLE, Robert Burns (1873-1948) American critic CB, COC, DAB, NTH, OC/1-3, SR, TW/4, WWT/5-10

MANTON, Annie see Knight, Mrs.

MANTON, Maria (b 1924) German actress TW/1

MANTON, Mme. T. (d 1886) singer EA/87*

MANUCHE, Cosmo (fl 1650-52) Italian? dramatist CP/1-3, DNB, FGF

MANUEL, Dean (d 1964 [30]) conductor, manager, musician BE*

MANUTI, Alfred Joseph (b 1909) American union executive, musician BE

MANVERS, Charles W. (d 1874) singer CDP

MANVERS, Louise [Mrs. David Honeysett] (d 1891) EA/93*

MANZ, Julia Chandler American editor WWM

MANZINI, Constanza (fl 1853-54) singer CDP, HAS

MANZOTTI, Luigi (1835-1905) Italian choreographer, mimist ES

MAPES, Victor (1870-1943) American dramatist, manager, director CB, GRB/3-4, WWA/5, WWM, WWS, WWT/1-9

MAPHOON and MOUNG-PHOSET (fl 1886?) hairy family CDP

MAPLE, Audrey (d 1971 [72]) actress TW/27

MAPLESON, Agnes [Mrs. Harry Mapleson] (d 1892) EA/93*

MAPLESON, Charles (d 1893) acting manager EA/94*

MAPLESON, Mrs. Harry see Mapleson, Agnes

MAPLESON, Henry (b 1851) English impresario WWM

MAPLESON, James Henry, Sr. (d 1869) manager EA/70*, WWT/14*

MAPLESON, James Henry (1830-1901) singer, musician, manager CDP, DNB

MAPLESON, Mrs. James Henry see Mapleson, Laura

MAPLESON, Laura [Mrs. Arthur Byron; Mrs. James Henry Mapleson] (1862-94) singer CDP

MARA, Mr. (fl 1806-07) Irish GT

MARA, Gertrude Elizabeth [née Scheneling] (1749-1833) Austrian singer CDP, DNB, ES, GT, TD/1-2

MARALTI, E. (fl 1850) singer CDP

MARAND, Patricia (b 1934) American actress TW/9, 22-23

MARANO, Charles (d 1964 [61]) talent representative BE*

MARASCO, Robert (b 1936) American dramatist WWT/15-16

MARATIER, Florence Tanner (d 1970) performer BP/55*

MARAVAN, Lila (d 1950 [54]) actress WWT/5-8

MARBECK, Thomas (fl 1602-03) actor DA

MARBERG, Lili (d 1962 [84]) performer BP/46*

MARBLE, Anna [Mrs. Channing Pollock] American press representative WWM

MARBLE, Danforth (1810-49) American actor CDP, COC, DAB, HAS, HJD, OC/1-3, WWA/H

MARBLE, Mrs. Danforth [née Anna Warren] (b 1815) American actress HAS

MARBLE, Emma (1848-1930) American actress SR

MARBLE, John S. (b 1844) actor HAS

MARBLE, Mary (1873-1965) American actress SR, TW/21, WWM, WWS

MARBLE, Scott (fl 1865) actor, dramatist SR

MARBLE, William (d 1912) actor SR

MARBURY, Elizabeth (1856-1933) American agent DAB, OC/1-3

MARCEAU, Felicien (b 1913) Belgian dramatist BE

MARCEAU, Marcel (b 1923) French mimist BE, CB, PDT

MARCEL, Gabriel (d 1973 [83]) dramatist BP/58*

MARCELINE (1873-1927) Spanish clown BE*, WWT/14*

MARCELLA, Marco (d 1962 [53]) performer BE*

MARCELLUS, George W. (d 1921 [80]) actor BE*

MARCH, Ellen (b 1948) American actress TW/30

MARCH, Elspeth English actress WWT/10-16

MARCH, Frederic [Frederick McIntyre Bickel] (1897-1975) American actor AAS, BE, CB, ES, SR, TW/1-21, WWT/7-15

MARCH, Hal (1920-70) American actor BE, TW/26, WWA/5

MARCH, Kendall American actor TW/25-26

MARCH, Lori American actress TW/10

MARCH, Mary Ann Virginia see Gabriel, Virginia

MARCH, Nadine (1898-1944) English actress WWT/5-9

MARCH, Virginia see Gabriel, Virginia

MARCHAND, Alida (d 1876 [107]) dancer EA/78*

MARCHAND, Colette (b 1925) French dancer, actress ES, TW/8

MARCHAND, Floram juggler CDP

MARCHAND, Leopold (d 1952) dramatist WWT/14*

MARCHAND, Nancy (b 1928) American actress AAS, BE, TW/14-18, 22-30, WWT/14-16

MARCHANT, Beatie (d 1892 [19]) music-hall performer EA/93*

MARCHANT, Frank (d 1878 [41]) dramatist BE*, WWT/14*

MARCHANT, Frederick (d 1878 [41]) dramatist, actor EA/80*

MARCHANT, G. F. (fl 1851) English actor HAS

MARCHANT, Mrs. G. F. [née Emeline Raymond] (b 1831) English actress HAS

MARCHANT, Will (d 1885 [38]) sketch artist EA/86*

MARCHANT, William (b 1923) American dramatist BE

MARCHESI, Blanche (fl 1895-1903) French singer WWM

MARCHESI, Mathilde (d 1913) EA/14*

MARCHESI, Salvatore (d 1908) singer EA/08*

MARCHESIO, Antonio (d 1875) musician, composer EA/76*

MARCHINGTON, Maria F. singer CDP

MARCHISO, Barbara (fl 1860) singer CDP

MARCHISO, Carlotta (fl 1860) singer CDP

MARCIN, Max (1879-1948) German/American dramatist, producing manager SR, TW/4, WWT/4-10

MARCIONA, Anthony (b 1961) American actor TW/25

MARCIONA, Suzan (b 1959) American actress TW/25

MARCKWALD, F. V. (fl 1874?) singer CDP

MARCO, Caterina singer CDP

MARCONI, Francesco (d 1916 [60]) EA/17*

MARCOTTE, Don (d 1964 [58]) composer/lyricist BP/49*

MARCUPP, Samuel (fl 1598) actor DA

MARCUS, Albert (d 1873) music-hall chairman EA/74*

MARCUS, Frank (b 1928) German/English dramatist, critic, director, actor AAS, CD, CH, COC, MH, WWT/14-16

MARCUS, Sol (d 1976 [63]) composer/lyricist BP/60*

MARCUSE, Theodore (d 1967 [47]) performer BP/52*

MARCY, George (b 1930) American actor TW/12-13, 23, 25

MARCY, Helen (b 1920) American actress TW/2-3, 8

MARDEN, Mr. (b 1833) American actor HAS

MARDEN, Ben (d 1973 [77]) showman, theatre owner BP/57*

MARDEN, Emma see Morella, Mrs. William

MARDEN, Lillie (fl 1868) English actress HAS

MARDEN, Mary (d 1892 [29]) EA/93*

MARDO, Charles (d 1976 [80]) performer BP/60*

MARDYN, Charlotte (b 1789) Irish actress CDP, OX

MARECHAL, Judith Rutherford (b 1937) American producer BE

MARETZEK, Bertucca (fl 1849-51) singer CDP, HAS

MARETZEK, Max (1821-97) Moravian manager, composer, musical director, conductor CDP, DAB, HAS, WWA/H

MAREY, Jacques (b 1877) French actor GRB/4, WWT/1-3

MARFIELD, Dwight American actor TW/2

MARGETSON, Arthur (1887/97-1951) English actor, singer TW/1-8, WWT/5-11

MARGO [Maria Margharita Bolado] (b 1917/18/19/20) Mexican actress, dancer BE, TW/1, WWT/9-11

MARGOLIN, Janet (b 1943) American actress TW/18-19

MARGOLIS, Henry (b 1909) American producer BE

MARGOT, John David (d 1886 [57]) EA/87*

MARGOT, John David see Mildmay, Frank

MARGUERITES, Julie de (d 1866) French singer, actress? HAS

MARGUERITES, Noemie de (fl 1865) actress, critic HAS

MARGULIES, Virginia M. (d 1969 [53]) performer BP/53*

MARIA, Lisa (b 1948) Polish actress TW/24

MARIAN (d 1884 [48]) Amazon queen EA/85*

MARIAN, Miss (fl 1854) actress HAS

MARIANO, Patti (b 1945) American actress TW/24-26

MARIASSEY, Felix (d 1975 [55]) producer/director/choreographer BP/59*

MARICLE, Leona (b 1905) American actress BE

MARICLE, Marijane (b 1922) American actress TW/8-9, 24

MARIE, Mlle. [Marie Rabineau] (d 1863 [18]) dancer HAS

MARIE, La Belle [Marie Hart; Mrs. Billy Hart] (b 1881) American vaudevillian WWM

MARIE, Julienne (b 1943) American actress TW/20-23

MARIE, Paola (b 1851/52) American dancer, singer CDP, HAS

MARIE-JEANNE (b 1921) American dancer ES

MARIEMMA (b 1912) Spanish dancer, choreographer ES

MARIES, Nance (d 1910) music-hall comedian EA/11*

MARIETTA, Miss (fl 1853-67) American dancer HAS

MARIMON, Marie Ernestine (b 1835) singer CDP

MARINELLI, H. B. (1864-1924) German vaudeville agent BE*, BP/8*

MARINELLI, Mrs. H. B. (d 1908) GRB/4*

MARINI, Ignazio (1811-73) Italian singer CDP, ES, HAS

MARINI, Sofia (fl 1847) singer HAS

MARINO, Louis (d 1965 [75]) costumier BP/50*

MARINOFF, Fania (1890-1971) Russian actress BE, TW/2-8, 28, WWT/5-11

MARIO, Dot [Mrs. Alfred Gibbons] (d 1898) burlesque actress EA/99*

MARIO, Giuseppe (1810-83) Sardinian singer CDP, ES, HAS

MARIO, Minnie (d 1905 [46]) actress, singer CDP, GRB/1

MARIO, Queena (1896-1951) American singer TW/7, WWA/3

MARION, Miss (fl 1848) actress

HAS

MARION, Charles (d 1889 [23]) American vaudevillian EA/90*

MARION, Dave (d 1934 [73]) American dramatist, manager, actor BE*, BP/19*

MARION, Frances (d 1973 [86]) performer BP/57*

MARION, George (1860-1945) American actor, producer CB, WWT/5-9

MARION, George, Jr. (d 1968 [68]) librettist, actor BE, TW/24, WWT/10-12

MARION, Joan (b 1908) Tasmanian actress WWT/8-13

MARION, Millie (fl 1889) actress CDP

MARION, Sid (d 1965 [65]) performer BP/50*

MARIUS, Claude [Claude Marius Duplany] (1850-96) French actor, singer, stage manager CDP, DP, OAA/1-2

MARK, Dr. (d 1868 [52]) proprietor EA/69*

MARK, Donald (b 1944) American actor TW/26

MARK, Michael (d 1975 [88]) performer BP/59*

MARKAS, Gary (d 1972 [42]) producer/director/choreographer BP/57*

MARKBY, Robert Bremner (d 1908 [66]) actor OAA/2

MARKERT, Gladys (d 1975 [71]) publicist BP/59*

MARKEY, Enid American actress BE, TW/1-21, 24, WWT/15-16

MARKEY, Melinda (b 1934) American actress TW/9

MARKHAM, Agnes [Mrs. John Liddell] (d 1889) actress EA/90*

MARKHAM, Daisy (b 1886) Indian/English actress WWT/1-8

MARKHAM, David [Peter Basil Harrison] (b 1913) English actor WWT/9-16

MARKHAM, Gervase (1568-1637) dramatist CP/1-3, FGF, HP

MARKHAM, Monte (b 1935) American actor TW/29

MARKHAM, Pauline (1847-1919) English actress CDP, HAS, SR

MARKLIN, Peter (b 1939) American actor TW/26-29

MARKOE, Peter (c. 1752-92) West Indian dramatist DAB, EAP, HJD, RJ, WWA/H

MARKOVA, Alicia [Alicia Marks] (b 1910) English dancer CB, ES, OC/1-2, TW/1, 3, WWT/8-12

MARKS, Alfred (b 1921) English actor WWT/12-16

MARKS, Alicia see Markova, Alicia

MARKS, Ben (d 1970 [72]) performer BP/55*

MARKS, Fred (b 1884) English actor GRB/1

MARKS, Jeannette (1875-1964) American dramatist WWA/4

MARKS, Joe E. (1891-1973) American actor TW/6-7, 13-15, 19, 23-24, 30

MARKS, Josephine Preston Peabody see Peabody, Josephine

MARKS, Mrs. Lionel see Peabody, Josephine

MARKS, Sherman (d 1975) producer/director/choreographer BP/59*

MARKUS, Thomas B. (b 1934) American actor TW/27

MARLATT, Donald (b 1940) American actor TW/23

MARLBOROUGH, Leah (d 1953/54 [85]) actress BE*, WWT/14*

MARLE, Arnold (d 1970 [82]) performer BP/54*

MARLER, George F. (d 1902 [68]) singer, manager EA/03*

MARLER, Mrs. George F. (d 1894) EA/95*

MARLER, Maitland (b 1863) English actor EA/97, GRB/1-2

MARLER, Mrs. Maitland see Maitland, Mary

MARLER, Mrs. Maitland see Rawlings, Mabel

MARLER, Mary [Mrs. Maitland Marler] (d 1898) EA/99*

MARLEY, John (b 1914) American actor TW/11, 14, 23

MARLIN, Max composer BE

MARLIN, Paul (b 1925) American actor TW/3

MARLING, Ilse see Marvenga, Ilse

MARLO, Micki (b 1932) American actress TW/13

MARLOW, David (b 1945) American actor TW/29

MARLOW, George (d 1939 [62])
actor BE*, WWT/14*
MARLOW, Harry [Charles William Blomfield] (1880-1957)
English actor GRB/1
MARLOW, John Horatio (d 1893)
marionettist EA/94*
MARLOWE, Alan (d 1975 [40])
performer BP/59*
MARLOWE, Anthony (b 1913)
English actor WWT/11-16
MARLOWE, Christopher (1564-
93) English dramatist COC,
CP/3, DNB, ES, FGF, HP,
MH, NTH, OC/1-3, PDT,
RE, SR
MARLOWE, Ethel (d 1898) actress CDP
MARLOWE, Frank (d 1964 [60])
actor BE*
MARLOWE, Frederick (d 1964
[61]) producer WWT/14*
MARLOWE, Gloria American
actress TW/9-14
MARLOWE, Hugh [né Hipple]
(b 1911/14) American actor
BE, TW/3-6, 22-25, WWT/
11-12, 15-16
MARLOWE, James C. [né Gurn]
(b 1866) American comedian
WWM
MARLOWE, Joan (b 1920) American publisher, writer BE
MARLOWE, Julia (1866-1950)
English actress CDP, COC,
DAB, ES, GRB/2-4, HJD,
NTH, OC/1-3, PP/2, SR,
TW/7, WWM, WWS, WWT/
1-10
MARLOWE, Marion (b 1930)
American singer, actress,
dancer BE, TW/23-24
MARLOWE, Owen (1830-76) English/American actor CDP,
HAS
MARLOWE, Mrs. Owen [Virginia
Nickinson] (fl 1853-66) American actress HAS
MARMION, Emily M. [née
Trewren; Mrs. Thomas Marmion] (d 1906 [56]) EA/07*
MARMION, Shackerley (c. 1602-
39) English dramatist CP/
1-3, DNB, FGF, HP
MARMION, Thomas (d 1903)
manager EA/05*
MARMION, Mrs. Thomas see
Marmion, Emily M.

MARMONT, Patricia (b 1921/22)
American actress TW/4, 7
MARMONT, Percy (b 1883) English
actor WWT/7-14
MARNAY, Carol E. (b 1942/43)
American actress TW/25, 30
MARNER, Mrs. C. Foster see
Belfry, Venie
MARNEY, Frank (d 1909) comedian,
dancer EA/10*
MARNEY, Lily (fl 1898?) singer
CDP
MAROFF, Robert (b 1934) American actor TW/30
MAROWITZ, Charles (b 1934)
American director, dramatist,
critic AAS, COC, WWT/15-16
MAROZZI, Lorenza (fl 1833) singer
HAS
MARQUERIE, Alfredo (d 1974 [67])
critic BP/59*
MARQUES, René (b 1919) Puerto
Rican dramatist MWD, RE
MARQUET, Louise (d 1890 [58])
dancer, ballet mistress EA/92*
MARQUIS, Don (1878-1937) American dramatist WWA/1, WWT/
6-8
MARQUIS, Marjorie Vonnegut (d
1936 [44]) American actress
BE*, BP/21*
MARR, Joe (b 1916) American actor TW/4-6
MARR, Paul (d 1976 [71]) booking
agent BP/60*
MARR, Paula American actress
WWT/1-5
MARR, Richard (b 1928) American
actor TW/25-26, 29-30
MARRANT, Edward theatre owner
DA
MARRAS, Giacinto (1810-83) Italian
singer, composer DNB
MARRE, Albert (b 1925) American
director, producer BE, WWT/
15-16
MARRIOT, Mr. (fl 1794) Scottish
actor HAS
MARRIOT, Mrs. (fl 1794) Scottish
actress HAS
MARRIOTT, Miss (fl 1802) actress
CDP, GT, TD/2
MARRIOTT, Miss (fl 1854) actress
EA/96
MARRIOTT, Miss (fl 1850-69) English actress HAS
MARRIOTT, Alice [Mrs. R. Edgar]
(1824-1900) actress CDP, COC,

DP, OAA/1-2

MARRIOTT, Frank (d 1888 [42])
minstrell proprietor EA/89*

MARRIOTT, G. M. (d 1940 [81])
actor BE*, WWT/14*

MARRIOTT, J. H. (d 1886 [87])
EA/87*

MARRIOTT, John (1900-77) American actor TW/4, 12, 15, 24

MARRIOTT, Moore (d 1949 [64])
actor BE*, WWT/14*

MARRIOTT, Raymond Bowler (b
1911) English critic WWT/16

MARRIOTT, Sarah (d 1885) EA/
86*

MARRIOTT, Thomas Arthur
see Picardo, Arthur

MARRIOTT-WATSON, Nan (b
1899) actress, dramatist
WWT/5-8

MARRIS, Samuel Arthur (d 1906
[63]) EA/07*

MARRONEY, Peter R. (b 1913)
American educator, director
BE

MARRYAT, Florence [Mrs. Francis Lean] (1837-99) dramatist,
actress BE*, EA/00*, WWT/
14*

MARS, Mons. (d 1892) menagerie
proprietor EA/93*

MARS, Mme. (d 1892) EA/93*

MARS, Leo (fl 1896-1901) pantomimist, singer WWS

MARS, Marjorie (b 1903) English
actress WWT/6-13

MARS, Severin (d 1921 [43]) actor WWT/14*

MARSDEN, Betty (b 1919) English actress WWT/12-16

MARSDEN, Fred (d 1888) actor,
dramatist SR

MARSDEN, Mrs. Lawrence see
Lewis, Lillian

MARSDENE, Beatrice [Miles]
Welsh actress GRB/1

MARSDIN, Dorothy Chiffon English actress GRB/1

MARSH, Mr. (fl 1846-55) actor
HAS

MARSH, Alec (b 1860) English
singer DP

MARSH, Alexander (d 1947) actor, producer BE*, WWT/14*

MARSH, Alphonso (1648?-92)
musician DNB

MARSH, Mrs. Arthur H. see
Marsh, Juliana Phillis

MARSH, Charles (d 1782) dramatist
CP/1-3, GT

MARSH, Daisy (d 1887) EA/88*

MARSH, Della (d 1973) performer
BP/57*

MARSH, Ernest W. (d 1917) EA/
18*

MARSH, Garry (b 1902) English
actor WWT/7-15

MARSH, George W. (b 1848) actor
CDP

MARSH, Henry see Marston,
Henry

MARSH, Howard (d 1969) actor,
singer TW/26

MARSH, Juliana Phillis [Mrs.
Arthur H. Marsh] (d 1878 [34])
EA/79*

MARSH, Leo A. (d 1936 [42]) journalist BE*, WWT/14*

MARSH, Linda American actress
TW/20

MARSH, Lucille (b 1921) American
actress TW/1-15

MARSH, Mae (d 1968 [72]) performer BP/52*

MARSH, Maria (d 1907 [76]) EA/
08*

MARSH, Mary (b 1847) actress
CDP

MARSH, Muriel see Alexander,
Muriel

MARSH, Richard Henry see
Marston, Henry

MARSH, Risley Halsey (d 1965
[38]) performer BP/49*

MARSH, William Henry the infant
drummer CDP

MARSH, W. Ward (d 1971 [77])
critic BP/56*

MARSHAK, Samuel (d 1964 [77])
performer BP/49*

MARSHAL, Alan (d 1961 [52]) actor
TW/18

MARSHALL, Mr. (fl 1790) dramatist CP/3

MARSHALL, Mr. (fl 1781-90) English actor TD/1-2

MARSHALL, Mr. (d 1816) English
actor CDP, HAS

MARSHALL, Mrs. see Wilmot,
Mrs.

MARSHALL, Miss (fl 1841) singer
HAS

MARSHALL, Miss see Yeomans,
Mrs. Thomas

MARSHALL, Alan (d 1961 [52])
Australian actor BE*

MARSHALL, Armina (b 1900)
American producer, actress
BE, WWT/16

MARSHALL, Charles (fl 1613-16)
actor DA

MARSHALL, Charles (1806-90)
scene painter DNB

MARSHALL, Charles E. (d 1975
[76]) performer BP/59*

MARSHALL, Charles Frederick
(d 1879 [84]) comedian EA/80*

MARSHALL, David (d 1917) electrician EA/18*

MARSHALL, Edward (d 1904 [78])
actor BE*, WWT/14*

MARSHALL, Edward (b 1869)
American dramatist WWM

MARSHALL, Edward (d 1884)
EA/85*

MARSHALL, Edward (d 1904 [78])
comedian EA/05*

MARSHALL, E. G. (b 1910)
American actor BE, ES,
TW/2-6, 9-13, 22, 24-25, 29,
WWT/16

MARSHALL, Ethelbert A. (fl
1838-57) manager HAS

MARSHALL, Everett (b 1901)
American actor, singer WWT/
10

MARSHALL, F. Elmer (d 1971
[89]) performer BP/55*

MARSHALL, Francis Albert
(1840-89) English dramatist
DNB

MARSHALL, Frank (d 1889 [34])
actor EA/90*

MARSHALL, Frank (d 1939
[81]) critic WWT/14*

MARSHALL, Mrs. Frank see
Cavendish, Ada

MARSHALL, Mrs. Frank see
Marshall, Imogene

MARSHALL, Mrs. Fred (d 1884)
EA/85*

MARSHALL, Frederick (1848-86)
Scottish actor OAA/1-2

MARSHALL, Mrs. G. [née
Harding] actress HAS

MARSHALL, George (d 1975 [84])
producer/director/choreographer
BP/59*

MARSHALL, Harry (d 1895)
comedian EA/96*

MARSHALL, Henry (d 1895 [71])
comedian EA/96*

MARSHALL, Herbert (1890-1966)
English actor BE, ES, NTH,

TW/22, WWA/4, WWT/4-11

MARSHALL, Horace (d 1976 [73])
performer BP/60*

MARSHALL, Imogene [Mrs. Frank
Marshall] (d 1885) EA/86*

MARSHALL, Mrs. James see
Marshall, Margaret

MARSHALL, Jane (fl 1772) dramatist CP/3

MARSHALL, Joseph (d 1873) ballet
master EA/74*

MARSHALL, Julian J. (d 1889 [27])
actor EA/90*

MARSHALL, Lois (b 1924) Canadian
singer CB

MARSHALL, Louisa (d 1896 [70])
actress EA/97*

MARSHALL, Margaret [Mrs. James
Marshall] (d 1889 [43]) EA/90*

MARSHALL, Mary see St. Clair,
Mme.

MARSHALL, Mort (b 1918) American actor BE, TW/28-29

MARSHALL, Norman (b 1901) In-
dian/English producer, director,
manager AAS, COC, ES, PDT,
WWT/8-16

MARSHALL, Norman Thomas (b
1939) American actor TW/25,
28, 30

MARSHALL, O. (b 1822) American
actor HAS

MARSHALL, Oriana (d 1867) actress HAS

MARSHALL, Patricia American actress TW/2-3, 12-15

MARSHALL, Percy F. (1861-1927)
English actor EA/95, GRB/1-4

MARSHALL, Peter L. (b 1930)
American actor TW/22-23

MARSHALL, Polly [Mrs. Zerman]
(1813-78) English actress,
dancer HAS

MARSHALL, Cpt. Robert (1863-
1910) Scottish dramatist GRB/
1-4, WWW/1

MARSHALL, Sarah (b 1933) American actress BE, TW/9-19

MARSHALL, Sid (b 1941) American
actor TW/26, 28

MARSHALL, Tully (1864-1943)
American actor, director CB,
SR, WWA/2, WWM, WWT/1-9

MARSHALL, Mrs. Tully see
Fairfax, Marion

MARSHALL, William (d 1875 [69])
EA/76*

MARSHALL, William (b 1924)

American actor, singer, director BE, TW/23
MARSHALL, Will Sharpe (b 1947) American actor TW/29-30
MARSHALL, Wyzeman (1815-96) actor, manager CDP
MARSHALOV, Boris (d 1967 [65]) Russian/American actor TW/24
MARSH TROUPE, The (fl 1855) HAS
MARSON, Aileen (1912-39) Egyptian/English actress WWT/8
MARSON, Frederick C. (d 1889 [21]) Negro minstrel EA/90*
MARSTON, Beatrice (d 1868 [17]) actress EA/72*
MARSTON, Eleanor Jane [Mrs. Westland Marston] (d 1870) EA/71*
MARSTON, E. W. (b 1836) American actor, manager HAS
MARSTON, H. E. (d 1901 [56]) acting manager EA/02*
MARSTON, Henry [Richard Henry Marsh] (d 1883 [79]) English actor CDP, OAA/2
MARSTON, Mrs. Henry (1809-87) English actress CDP, NYM
MARSTON, Jenny actress CDP
MARSTON, Joel (b 1922) American actor TW/1-3
MARSTON, John (c. 1575-1634) English dramatist COC, CP/1-3, DA, DNB, ES, FGF, HP, MH, NTH, OC/1-3, PDT, RE
MARSTON, John (d 1962 [72]) actor TW/19
MARSTON, John Westland (1819-90) English dramatist CDP, DNB, EA/68, HP, OC/1-3
MARSTON, Philip Bourke (d 1887 [35]) EA/88*
MARSTON, Richard (d 1917 [75]) scene artist WWT/14*
MARSTON, Mrs. Westland see Marston, Eleanor Jane
MARTAIN, A. J. (fl 1861) American actor HAS
MARTEL, Flora American executive BE
MARTEL, Tom (b 1949) American actor TW/28
MARTEL, William (b 1916) American actor TW/25
MARTELL, Gillian (b 1936) English actress WWT/15-16
MARTELL, Mrs. Harry see Martell, May
MARTELL, May [Mrs. Harry Martell] (d 1890) EA/91*
MARTENS, The (fl 1882) vaudevillians CDP
MARTERSTEIG, Dr. Max (b 1853) German manager GRB/4, WWT/1-2
MARTIN, Mr. see Booth, Joseph
MARTIN, Mons. (fl 1831) French animal trainer, actor CDP
MARTIN, Mons. (fl 1839) dancer HAS
MARTIN, Ada Beatrice [Mrs. William Martin] (d 1905) EA/06*
MARTIN, Allen (b 1936) American actor TW/6
MARTIN, Angela actress TW/24
MARTIN, Boyd (d 1963 [76]) critic, director, educator BE*, BP/47*, WWT/14*
MARTIN, Charles G. (b 1912) American actor TW/6
MARTIN, Christina (d 1973) dresser BP/57*
MARTIN, Cye (d 1972 [56]) performer BP/56*
MARTIN, Dolphe (d 1974 [81]) composer/lyricist BP/59*
MARTIN, E. (d 1881) secretary EA/82*
MARTIN, Edgar (d 1900) music-hall performer EA/01*
MARTIN, Edie (1880-1964) English actress WWT/9-13
MARTIN, Edward (d 1897) manager EA/98*
MARTIN, Elliot (b 1924) American producer, stage manager BE, WWT/16
MARTIN, Ernest (b 1862) English actor, dramatist GRB/1
MARTIN, Ernest H. (b 1919) American manager, producer, dramatist BE, WWT/12-16
MARTIN, Eugene see Geniat, Marcelle
MARTIN, Frank (d 1974 [84]) composer/lyricist BP/59*
MARTIN, F. W. [Fred Mansfield] (d 1881) EA/82*
MARTIN, George William (d 1881 [53]) musician EA/82*
MARTIN, Harry (d 1970 [67]) performer BP/54*
MARTIN, Harry J. (d 1975 [82])

promoter, manager BP/60*
MARTIN, Helen American actress BE, TW/26, 29-30
MARTIN, H. Sherwood (b 1877) English manager GRB/1
MARTIN, Hugh composer, lyricist BE
MARTIN, Hugh Whitfield see Martin, Riccardo
MARTIN, Ian (b 1912) Scottish actor TW/29-30
MARTIN, Mrs. Jacques (1863-1936) American actress BE*, BP/21*
MARTIN, James (b 1825) Canadian actor HAS
MARTIN, Jared (b 1943) American actor TW/24
MARTIN, John (d 1764) actor WWT/14*
MARTIN, John E. (1768-1807) American actor CDP, HAS, NTH
MARTIN, John F. X. (d 1973 [46]) performer BP/57*
MARTIN, Joy (b 1944) American actress TW/24
MARTIN, Laura (d 1898 [57]) EA/99*
MARTIN, Leila (b 1932/36) American actress, singer BE, TW/11, 13, 16, 27-29
MARTIN, Lewis (1898-1969) American actor TW/3, 25
MARTIN, Miss M. (d 1889) EA/90*
MARTIN, Martin Adams (d 1878 [38]) professor of music EA/79*
MARTIN, Mary (b 1913/14) American actress, singer AAS, BE, CB, ES, PDT, TW/1-25, WWT/10-16
MARTIN, Mildred Palmer (d 1962 [59]) critic BE*
MARTIN, Millicent (b 1934) English actress, singer AAS, WWT/14-16
MARTIN, Nan (b 1927) American actress BE, TW/8, 16, 21, 23
MARTIN, Nicholas (b 1938) American actor TW/23-25
MARTIN, Owen (d 1960 [71]) actor TW/16
MARTIN, Pam American actress TW/28
MARTIN, Pete (b 1901) journalist

BE
MARTIN, Philip dramatist CD
MARTIN, Philip, Jr. (d 1974 [57]) producer/director/choreographer BP/58*
MARTIN, Riccardo [Hugh Whitfield Martin] (1879-1952) American singer WWA/3, WWM
MARTIN, Robert Jasper (d 1905 [62]) songwriter, journalist EA/06*
MARTIN, Ron (b 1947) American actor TW/27-29
MARTIN, Sarah (d 1879 [71]) EA/80*
MARTIN, T. (d 1890) stage manager EA/91*
MARTIN, Mrs. Theodore see Faucit, Helen
MARTIN, Thomas J. (1842-87) American actor NYM
MARTIN, Mrs. Thomas J. see Fiske, Marian
MARTIN, Tom (d 1962 [58]) artists' representative BE*
MARTIN, Townsend (d 1951 [55]) American writer BE*, BP/36*
MARTIN, Virginia (b 1932) American actress, singer BE, TW/13, 19, 28
MARTIN, Vivian (b 1893) American actress WWT/6-7
MARTIN, Vivienne (b 1936) New Zealand actress WWT/15-16
MARTIN, Walter (d 1916 [19]) actor EA/17*
MARTIN, William (1767-1810) English actor DNB
MARTIN, William (d 1917) EA/18*
MARTIN, Mrs. William see Martin, Ada Beatrice
MARTIN, William Richard see Minton, William Richard
MARTIN, W. T. (b 1947) American actor TW/29-30
MARTINDEL, Edward (d 1955 [80]) actor TW/11
MARTINE, Stella (d 1961 [81]) actress BE*
MARTINEAU, Francis (d 1886 [29]) actor EA/87*
MARTINEC, Lee A. (d 1975 [49]) performer BP/60*
MARTINELLI [?], Angelica (fl 1580?) Italian actress DA
MARTINELLI, Drusiano (d 1606/08) Italian actor COC, DA, OC/2-3
MARTINELLI, Giovanni (1885-1969)

Italian singer CB, ES, TW/
25, WWA/5
MARTINETTE, Albert (d 1898
[33]) variety performer EA/99*
MARTINETTI, Clara (d 1945)
pantomimist BE*, WWT/14*
MARTINETTI, Ignacio actor CDP
MARTINETTI, Julian (1821-84)
acrobat, pantomimist, clown
CDP
MARTINETTI, Paul (d 1924 [73])
American pantomimist, mana-
ger CDP, GRB/2-4
MARTINETTI, Pauline (d 1927
[82]) pantomimist BE*,
WWT/14*
MARTINEZ SIERRA, Gregorio
(1881-1947) Spanish dramatist
COC, OC/1-3
MARTIN-HARVEY, John see
Harvey, John Martin
MARTIN-HARVEY, Muriel (b
1891) English actress WWT/
2-9
MARTINI, Fausto Maria (1886-
1931) Italian dramatist MWD
MARTINI, Laura [Mrs. W. John-
son] (d 1909) variety performer
EA/10*
MARTINO, Mrs. Fred see
Martino, Lydia
MARTINO, Lydia [Mrs. Fred
Martino] (d 1898) circus per-
former EA/99*
MARTINOT, Sadie [Mrs. Louis
F. Nethersole] (1861-1923)
American actress, singer
CDP, GRB/2-4, SR, WWA/4,
WWM, WWS, WWT/1-4
MARTINSON, Joseph B. (b 1911)
American executive BE
MARTLEW, Mary (b 1919) Eng-
lish actress WWT/10-12
MARTLEY, Bob [Henry James
King] (d 1895) performer?
EA/96*
MARTON, Thomas (fl 1601) actor
DA
MARTSON, Beatrice (d 1868 [17])
actress EA/69*
MARTYN, Mr. (fl 1839-40) ac-
tor? singer? HAS
MARTYN, Benjamin (d 1763 [64])
dramatist CP/1-3, GT
MARTYN, Mrs. Charles [Miss
Inverarity] (1813-47) actress?
singer? CDP, DNB, HAS
MARTYN, Edward (1859-1924)

Irish dramatist COC, HP, MD,
MWD, OC/2-3, RE, WWW/2
MARTYN, Eliza (d 1846 [33]) ac-
tress BE*, WWT/14*
MARTYN, Katherine (d 1893 [17])
EA/94*
MARTYN, May [Mrs. Nigel Play-
fair] (1880-1948) English actress
GRB/2-3
MARTYN, William (fl 1569-72) ac-
tor DA
MARTYN-GREEN, William see
Green, Martyn
MARTYR, Margaret [née Thornton]
(d 1807) actress, singer CDP,
GT, TD/1-2
MARUM, John Daily see Dillon,
John
MARUM, Marilyn Harvey (d 1973
[44]) performer BP/57*
MARUNAS, P. Raymond (b 1939)
Lithuanian actor TW/26
MARVEL, Pauline [Pauline Anton]
(b 1918) American actress TW/
24
MARVENGA, Ilse [Ilse Marling]
German actress, singer WWT/
7-9
MARVIN, Charles see Mervin,
Fred
MARVIN, Lee (b 1924) American
actor CB, ES
MARWIG, Carl (fl 1879) CDP
MARX, Chico (1891-1961) American
comedian CB, TW/18
MARX, Groucho (1895-1977) Amer-
ican actor BE, CB
MARX, Gummo (1894-1977) Ameri-
can comedian BE
MARX, Harpo (1893-1964) American
comedian, musician BE, CB,
TW/21
MARX, Marie Simard (d 1974) per-
former BP/58*
MARX, Marvin (d 1975 [50]) drama-
tist BP/60*
MARX, Milton (d 1973 [75]) car-
toonist BP/57*
MARX, Zeppo (b 1901) American
comedian BE
MARY ANGELITA, Sister (b 1912)
American educator BE
MARYE, Donald (b 1905) American
actor TW/22-23, 28
MARY IMMACULATE, Sister
executive BE
MARYON, Alice (d 1883) actress?
EA/84*

MARYOTT, Susan (d 1963 [30])
performer BP/48*
MARZETTI, Joseph (d 1864)
pantomimist CDP, HAS
MARZETTI, Mathilde actress,
dancer CDP
MASCAGNI, Pietro (1863-1945)
Italian composer, conductor
ES, GRB/1, WWM
MASCHWITZ, Eric (1901-69)
English dramatist, composer
AAS, WWT/9-14
MASCOLO, Joseph (b 1935) Amer-
ican actor TW/23, 26-30
MASEFIELD, John (1878-1967)
English dramatist COC, ES,
HP, MH, MWD, NTH, OC/
1-3, WWT/1-14, WWW/6
MASFIRI, Sidi-El-Hadjali-Ben-
Mahomed (d 1895 [80]) acrobat
EA/96*
MASIELL, Joe (b 1939) American
actor TW/25, 27-30
MASINI, Angelo (1844-1926) Italian
singer ES
MASKELL, Mr. (fl 1855) English
actor HAS
MASKELL, Fanny see Baynham,
Mrs. Walter
MASKELL, George K. (d 1881)
comedian EA/82*
MASKELL, Laura see Joyce,
Laura
MASKELL, Virginia (d 1968
[31]) performer BP/52*
MASKELYNE, Elizabeth [Mrs.
John Nevil Maskelyne] (d 1911
[70]) EA/12*
MASKELYNE, John Nevil (1839-
1917) English mechanical &
optical illusionist GRB/1-4
MASKELYNE, Mrs. John Nevil
see Maskelyne, Elizabeth
MASKOVA, Hana (d 1972) per-
former BP/56*
MASKY, Jeanne (b 1926) Amer-
ican actress TW/3
MASON (fl 1515) actor DA
MASON, Mrs. [née Barber]
English actress HAS
MASON, Mrs. [Mrs. Elizabeth;
Mrs. Crooke; Mrs. Entwistle]
(1780-1835) English actress
CDP, HAS
MASON, Miss (fl 1836) Scottish
actress HAS
MASON, Alfred Edward Woodley
(1865-1948) English dramatist,

actor DNB, GRB/4, MH,
WWT/1-10, WWW/4
MASON, Ann (d 1948 [50]) Ameri-
can actress TW/4
MASON, Beryl (b 1921) English ac-
tress WWT/10-16
MASON, Brewster (b 1922) English
actor AAS, WWT/14-16
MASON, Bruce (b 1921) New Zea-
land dramatist CD
MASON, Charles Kemble (1805-75)
English actor CDP, HAS, SR
MASON, Colin (d 1971 [47]) critic
BP/55*
MASON, Dan [Daniel Grassman]
(b 1855) American comedian
WWM
MASON, David (d 1888 [74]) musi-
cian EA/89*
MASON, Edith (d 1973 [80]) per-
former BP/58*
MASON, Edward (d 1916) singer,
songwriter CDP
MASON, Elliot C. (d 1949 [52])
Scottish actress WWT/9-10
MASON, F. R. (d 1904) acting
manager EA/05*
MASON, Fred (d 1895 [27]) comic
singer EA/97*
MASON, Mrs. Fred (d 1899 [34])
EA/00*
MASON, Gladys (b 1886) English
actress GRB/4, WWT/1-8
MASON, Henry J. (d 1901 [38])
music-hall manager EA/02*
MASON, Herbert producer WWT/
5-9
MASON, Homer B. (d 1959 [80])
actor, vaudevillian TW/16
MASON, James (fl 1805) dramatist
CP/3
MASON, James (b 1909) English
actor CB, ES, TW/3, WWT/9-
14
MASON, Mrs. James see
Wheatley, Emma
MASON, Jane (d 1874) singer EA/
75*
MASON, Jennie (d 1909 [72]) EA/
10*
MASON, Mrs. J. J. (d 1881) pro-
prietor EA/82*
MASON, J. M. (d 1871 [27])
musician EA/71*
MASON, John (fl 1606-10) drama-
tist, lessee CP/1-3, DA
MASON, John B. (1857/58-1919)
American actor CDP, DAB,

ES, GRB/2-4, PP/2, WWA/1, WWM, WWS, WWT/1-3

MASON, John Kemble (fl 1831-32) Scottish actor CDP, HAS

MASON, John Monck (1726-1809) Irish scholar DNB

MASON, Joseph B. (d 1897 [67]) actor EA/98*

MASON, Mrs. J. W. see Mason, Theresa

MASON, Kitty [Mrs. W. E. Aspinall] (b 1882) English dancer GRB/1-4, WWT/1-3

MASON, Lawrence (d 1939 [57]) American critic, educator BE*, WWT/14*

MASON, LeRoy (d 1947 [44]) actor BE*

MASON, Lesley (d 1964 [76]) American press representative, journalist BE*

MASON, Marjorie (d 1968) performer BP/53*

MASON, Marlyn (b 1940) American actress TW/24

MASON, Marsha (b 1942) American actress TW/23-24, 27, 30

MASON, Mary (d 1867 [79]) EA/68*

MASON, Reginald (1882-1962) American actor TW/1, 4, 9-10, 19, WWT/7-13

MASON, Richard (d 1970 [24]) actor TW/26

MASON, Ruth Fitch (d 1974 [84]) agent, author BP/59*

MASON, Theresa [Mrs. J. W. Mason] (d 1897 [44]) EA/98*

MASON, Thomas Monk (d 1889 [86]) entrepreneur, musician, aeronaut EA/90*

MASON, William (1725-77) English dramatist CP/2-3, GT, TD/1-2

MASS, Joseph E. (d 1974 [62]) performer BP/58*

MASSARIK, Friederike see Massary, Fritzi

MASSARY, Fritzi [Friederike Massarik] (1882-1969) Austrian actress, singer ES, WWT/9-10

MASSEN, Louis F. (d 1925 [67]) French/American actor, director BE*, BP/9*, WWT/14*

MASSENET, Jules (1842-1912) French composer GRB/1,

SR, WWM

MASSET, Stephen C. (1820-98) English actor, singer CDP, HAS, SR

MASSEY, Mrs. (fl 1778?) actress CDP

MASSEY, Anna (b 1937) English actress BE, ES, TW/13-14, WWT/13-16

MASSEY, Blanche (d 1929 [51]) actress BE*, WWT/14*

MASSEY, Charles (d 1625) English actor, dramatist CP/3, DA, OC/1-3

MASSEY, Daniel (b 1933) English actor BE, TW/14, 19, 30, WWT/13-16

MASSEY, George (fl 1622) lessee DA

MASSEY, Ilona (d 1974 [60/62]) actress, singer BP/59*, WWT/16*

MASSEY, Mary (d 1902 [79]) EA/03*

MASSEY, Raymond (b 1896) Canadian actor, producer, director AAS, BE, CB, ES, NTH, TW/2-16, WWT/6-16

MASSEY, Rose (d 1883 [32]) English actress HAS, OAA/2

MASSI, Bernice American actress BE, TW/20-22, 24-27, 30, WWT/15-16

MASSINE, Leonide (b 1896) Russian/American dancer, choreographer, maître de ballet CB, ES, WWT/8-12

MASSINGER, Philip (1583-1640) English dramatist CDP, COC, CP/1-3, DNB, ES, FGF, HP, MH, NTH, OC/1-3, PDT, RE

MASSINGHAM, Dorothy (1889-1933) English actress, dramatist WWT/5-7

MASSINK, Mr. (d 1789) machinist, pantomime inventor TD/1-2

MASSOT, Pierre (d 1868) ballet master EA/69*

MASTEROFF, Joe (b 1919) American dramatist, librettist BE, CD

MASTERS, Amos (d 1917 [67]) stage manager, carpenter EA/18*

MASTERS, Benjamin (b 1947) American actor TW/27-28

MASTERS, E. H. Frank (d 1917) comedian, manager EA/18*

MASTERS, Harry (d 1974 [79])
performer BP/58*
MASTERS, M. K. (fl 1811)
dramatist CP/3
MASTERS, Ruth (d 1969 [75])
performer TW/26
MASTERSON, C. (fl 180-) drama-
tist CP/3
MASTERSON, Carroll (b 1913)
American producer BE
MASTERSON, Harris (b 1914)
American producer BE
MASTERSON, Peter (b 1936)
American actor TW/24-26
MASUR, Richard (b 1948) Amer-
ican actor TW/29-30
MATACHENA, Oreste (b 1941)
Cuban actor TW/25
MATALON, Vivian (b 1929) Eng-
lish director WWT/14-16
MATALON, Zack (b 1928) English
actor, singer, dancer, pro-
ducer, director BE, TW/18
MATE, Charles (b 1776) actor
TD/2
MATERNA, Amalie (1844-1918)
Austrian singer CDP, ES
MATHER, Aubrey (1885-1958)
English actor TW/1, 3, 6-7,
14, WWT/6-12
MATHER, Donald (b 1900) Eng-
lish actor, singer WWT/7-9
MATHER, Margaret (1859-98)
actress CDP
MATHER, Sydney (d 1925 [49])
English actor BE*, BP/9*
MATHERS, Arthur (d 1878 [34])
musician EA/79*
MATHERS, Edward Powys (1892-
1939) dramatist WWW/3
MATHESON, Murray (b 1912)
Australian actor BE, TW/
10-16
MATHEW, Ann (d 1976 [65])
dancer WWT/16*
MATHEW, Ray (b 1929) Aus-
tralian dramatist CD
MATHEWS, Mr. actor CDP
MATHEWS, Anne (d 1869) writer
CDP
MATHEWS, Carmen (b 1914/18)
American actress BE, TW/
2-9, 13-20, 22-25, 28-29,
WWT/11-16
MATHEWS, Carole (b 1922)
American actress TW/6
MATHEWS, Charles (1776-1835)
English actor BS, CDP,

COC, DNB, ES, GT, HAS,
NTH, OC/1-3, OX, TD/2
MATHEWS, Mrs. Charles (d 1869
[87]) EA/70*
MATHEWS, Mrs. Charles see
Mathews, Eliza Kirkland
MATHEWS, Charles James (1803-
78) English actor, dramatist
CDP, COC, DNB, EA/68, ES,
HAS, NTH, OAA/1-2, OC/1-3,
SR
MATHEWS, Mrs. Charles James
see Vestris, Mme.
MATHEWS, Mrs. Charles James,
II [Lizzie Weston; née Jackson;
Lizzie Davenport] (d 1899)
American actress CDP, HAS,
OAA/1-2, SR
MATHEWS, Chris ["Comical
Chris"] (d 1916) ventriloquist
EA/17*
MATHEWS, Cicely (d 1975 [65])
producer/director/choreographer
BP/60*
MATHEWS, Cornelius (1817-89)
dramatist CDP
MATHEWS, Elizabeth see Math-
ews, Mrs. Charles James, II
MATHEWS, Eliza Kirkland (d 1802)
CDP
MATHEWS, Frances Aymar (d
1923) American dramatist
GRB/3-4, WWA/2, WWM,
WWT/1-2
MATHEWS, George (b 1911) Amer-
ican actor BE, TW/1, 3-9,
11-16, 21-23, 25-26, WWT/11-
16
MATHEWS, Helen (d 1890) actress
EA/91*
MATHEWS, James W. (d 1920
[56]) New Zealand business
manager GRB/3-4, WWT/1-3
MATHEWS, Joyce actress TW/1
MATHEWS, Julia (d 1876 [34]) ac-
tress, singer CDP
MATHEWS, Lizzie Weston see
Mathews, Mrs. Charles James,
II
MATHEWS, Mark (b 1943) Ameri-
can actor TW/27
MATHEWS, Norman American ac-
tor TW/25
MATHEWS, Richard (b 1823) Amer-
ican actor HAS
MATHEWS, Sarah (d 1876 [74])
EA/77*
MATHIAS, Yrca (fl 1853) dancer

CDP

MATHIESEN, Jack (b 1924) American actor TW/3

MATHIS, June (1890/92-1927) American actress ES, WWM

MATHIS, Sherry (b 1949) American actress TW/29-30

MATINEZ, Joseph J. (d 1975 [82]) performer BP/59*

MATLAW, Myron (b 1924) German/American educator, historian BE

MATRON, Miss see Second, Mrs.

MATSON, Norman (d 1965 [72]) dramatist BP/50*

MATSUI, Suisei (d 1973 [73]) performer BP/58*

MATSUSAKA, Tom American actor TW/24, 30

MATT, John (d 1910 [66]) professor of music EA/11*

MATTEI, Tito (1841-1914) Italian conductor, composer WWW/1

MATTESON, Ruth (1909-75) American actress BE, TW/1-3, 6-9, 14-16, WWT/11-15

MATTFELD, Julius (b 1893) American composer BE

MATTFELD, Marie (fl 1890-1912) German singer WWA/5, WWM

MATTHAEI, Konrad American actor TW/25-26, 28-29

MATTHAU, Walter [né Matthow] (b 1920) American actor BE, CB, ES, TW/21, WWT/14-16

MATTHEW, Sir Robert (d 1975 [68]) designer BP/60*

MATTHEW, Ross actor TW/1

MATTHEWS, Miss actress CDP

MATTHEWS, Adelaide (b 1886) dramatist WWT/6-11

MATTHEWS, A[lfred] E[dward] (1869-1960) English actor AAS, COC, DNB, ES, GRB/3-4, OC/3, TW/17, WWM, WWT/1-12, WWW/5

MATTHEWS, Ann (d 1891 [58]) EA/92*

MATTHEWS, Art American actor TW/18, 22-27

MATTHEWS, Bache (1876-1948) English director WWT/6-9

MATTHEWS, Billy (b 1922) American director, stage manager, actor BE

MATTHEWS, Brander see Matthews, James Brander

MATTHEWS, Charles Eli (d 1897 [60]) actor EA/98*

MATTHEWS, Cornelius (d 1889 [71]) American dramatist EA/90*

MATTHEWS, Dakin (b 1940) American actor TW/29

MATTHEWS, Dan (b 1922) American actor TW/8

MATTHEWS, Eliza (d 1879) EA/80*

MATTHEWS, Emma (d 1890) EA/91*

MATTHEWS, Emma Louisa (d 1917) EA/18*

MATTHEWS, Ethel (b 1870) actress DP, GRB/1-4, WWT/1-5

MATTHEWS, Fanny Marie [Mrs. Tom Matthews] (d 1871) EA/72*

MATTHEWS, Frances Aymar see Mathews, Frances Aymar

MATTHEWS, Francis (b 1933) English actor TW/23

MATTHEWS, Frank (d 1871 [64]) actor CDP

MATTHEWS, Mrs. Frank (d 1873 [66]) actress EA/74*, WWT/14*

MATTHEWS, George see Mathews, George

MATTHEWS, Gerry (b 1936) American actor TW/23-24

MATTHEWS, Harry (d 1896) minstrel? EA/97*

MATTHEWS, Helen see Brunton, Mrs. W. H.

MATTHEWS, H. P. singer CDP

MATTHEWS, Inez (b 1917) American singer, actress BE

MATTHEWS, James (d 1879 [55]) actor EA/80*

MATTHEWS, James (d 1880 [60]) prestidigitateur EA/81*

MATTHEWS, James Brander (1852-1929) American dramatist, critic CDP, COC, ES, GRB/3-4, HJD, NTH, OC/1-3, SR, WWA/1, WWM, WWT/1-5, WWW/3

MATTHEWS, Mrs. J. C. see Matthews, Sarah Elizabeth

MATTHEWS, Jessie (b 1907) English actress, dancer AAS, BE, ES, WWT/6-16

MATTHEWS, John Thomas (1805-89) clown CDP

MATTHEWS, Lacy (d 1902) actor EA/04*

MATTHEWS, Lester (b 1900)

English actor WWT/6-9
MATTHEWS, Mary Frances (d
1906 [45]) actress EA/07*
MATTHEWS, Sant (d 1896) actor
EA/97*, WWT/14*
MATTHEWS, Sarah Blanche (b
1794) actress CDP
MATTHEWS, Sarah E. [Mrs.
Fred Matthews] (d 1891 [31])
EA/92*
MATTHEWS, Sarah Elizabeth
[Mrs. J. C. Matthews] (d
1876) EA/77*
MATTHEWS, Sherrie (1868-1921)
comedian SR
MATTHEWS, Susannah Elizabeth
see Harvey, Susie
MATTHEWS, Theodore (d 1888
[32]) performer? EA/89*
MATTHEWS, Mrs. Theodore
see Harvey, Susie
MATTHEWS, Thomas (1805-89)
actor, pantomimist DNB
MATTHEWS, Thomas F. (d
1904 [26]) music-hall per-
former EA/05*
MATTHEWS, Mrs. Tom see
Matthews, Fanny Marie
MATTHEWS, Will (d 1892) come-
dian EA/94*
MATTHEWS, William (d 1906
[70]) minstrel EA/07*
MATTHEWS, William S. (d 1907)
dramatic student EA/08*
MATTHEWSON, John (d 1871)
actor EA/72*
MATTHISON, Arthur (d 1883
[57]) dramatist, actor BE*,
EA/84*, WWT/14*
MATTHISON, Edith Wynne [Mrs.
Charles Rann Kennedy] (1875-
1955) English actress GRB/
1-4, SR, TW/12, WWA/3,
WWS, WWT/1-11
MATTHISON, Mrs. H. [Kate
Wynne] (d 1912) singer EA/
13*
MATTHISON, Henry (d 1905)
singer GRB/1
MATTHOW, Walter see Matthau,
Walter
MATTIOLI, Lino (b 1853) Italian
musician WWA/4
MATTOCKS, George (d 1804) ac-
tor CDP
MATTOCKS, Isabella (1746-1826)
English actress CDP, COC,
DNB, GT, HAS, OC/1-3,

TD/1-2
MATTOX, Matt (b 1921) American
dancer, actor, singer, chore-
ographer BE, TW/12-15
MATTSON, Eric (b 1908) American
producer, director BE, TW/1
MATURA, Mustapha (b 1939) West
Indian dramatist CD, WWT/16
MATURE, Victor (b 1915) American
actor ES
MATURIN, Charles Robert (1782-
1824) Irish dramatist CDP,
DNB
MATURIN, Eric (1883-1957) Indian/
English actor WWT/1-12
MATYAS, Maria (d 1963 [57]) singer
BE*
MATZ, Walter J. (d 1975 [81])
performer BP/60*
MATZENAUER, Margarete (1881-
1963) Hungarian singer ES,
TW/19, WWA/4
MAUDAUNT, Frank (b 1841) Amer-
ican actor SR
MAUDE, Charles Raymond (1882-
1943) actor COC, GRB/3-4,
WWT/1-5
MAUDE, Mrs. Charles Raymond
see Price, Nancy
MAUDE, Cyril (1862-1951) English
actor, manager CDP, COC,
DP, EA/95, ES, GRB/1-4, OC/
1-3, SR, TW/7, WWA/3, WWT/
1-11, WWW/5
MAUDE, Mrs. Cyril see Emery,
Winifred
MAUDE, Elizabeth (b 1912) actress
WWT/7-10
MAUDE, Gillian actress WWT/9-10
MAUDE, Joan (b 1908) English ac-
tress WWT/5-11
MAUDE, Margery (b 1889) English
actress BE, TW/2-3, 8, 25,
WWT/1-16
MAUDE, Maude Amy Mannakay (d
1896 [20]) acrobat EA/97*
MAUDE, Robert Henry Ernest (d
1916 [26]) actor EA/17*
MAUDE-ROXBY, Roddy (b 1930)
English actor WWT/15-16
MAUDSLEY, Mrs. H. (d 1872 [37])
EA/74*
MAUGHAM, Augustus Freshwater
(d 1871 [41]) Negro minstrel
EA/72*
MAUGHAM, William Somerset
(1874-1965) French/English
dramatist AAS, BE, CB, COC,

ES, GRB/2-4, HP, MD, MH,
MWD, NTH, OC/1-3, PDT,
RE, TW/22, WWM, WWT/
1-14, WWW/6

MAUGHAN, Fanny Amelia [Mrs.
John Sheffield Maughan] (d
1879) EA/80*

MAUGHAN, John Sheffield see
Maughan, Fanny Amelia

MAUGIN, Emile (fl 1856) pantomimist CDP

MAULE, Annabel (b 1922/23)
English actress WWT/9-16

MAULE, Donovan (b 1899) English director, manager WWT/
14-16

MAULE, Herbert (b 1873) English actor GRB/1

MAULE, Robin (1924-42) English
actor WWT/9

MAUNDER, Edith (fl 1889) actress CDP

MAUNDER, Henry J. (d 1897
[30]) actor EA/98*

MAUNDY-GREGORY, J. English
manager, dramatist GRB/1-4

MAUNSELL, Charles (d 1968)
performer BP/53*

MAURAN, Carlos see Blood-
good, Harry

MAUREL, Victor (1848-1923)
French singer, actor CDP,
ES, GRB/1-4

MAURER, Peggy (b 1931) American actress TW/13

MAUREY, Max (d 1947 [76])
manager WWT/14*

MAURICE (d 1927 [41]) dancer
BE*, WWT/14*

MAURICE, Edmund [Edmund
Fitz-Maurice Lenon] (d 1928
[65]) actor GRB/1-4, WWT/
1-5

MAURICE, Mrs. Edmund see
Hughes, Annie

MAURICE, George (d 1903)
music-hall comedian EA/04*

MAURICE, Mary (1844-1918)
American actress BE*

MAURICE, Newman (d 1920)
actor, producer BE*, WWT/
14*

MAURICE, Mrs. Newman see
Moncrieff, Rose

MAURICE, Thomas (fl 1779-
1812) dramatist CP/2-3, GT

MAUS, Herr (d 1869 [57]) circus
proprietor EA/70*

MAUS, Arthur (d 1975 [70]) performer BP/60*

MAUS, Louisa (d 1869 [49]) EA/
70*

MAUS DAYTON, Mary [Mrs. O.
Maus Dayton] (d 1910 [31])
EA/11*

MAUS DAYTON, Mrs. O. see
Maus Dayton, Mary

MAVIUS, Arthur Henry (d 1887
[28]) actor EA/88*

MAVOR, Osborne Henry see
Bridie, James

MAWDESLEY, Robert (d 1953 [53])
actor BE*, WWT/14*

MAWER, Irene (d 1962) teacher of
mime & dance WWT/14*

MAWSON, Edward R. (d 1917 [55])
actor BE*, WWT/14*

MAWSON, Harry P. (b 1853) American dramatist WWM

MAX, Edouard Alexandre de (1869-
1925) French actor GRB/1-4,
WWT/1-4

MAXAM, Clara [Mrs. Harry Max-
am] (d 1907 [38]) comic singer
EA/08*

MAXAM, Mrs. Harry see Maxam,
Clara

MAXAM, Louella Modie (d 1970
[74]) performer BP/55*

MAXE, William (fl 1509-13) actor
DA

MAXEY, Paul (d 1963 [55]) American actor BE*

MAXSEY, Gilbert (fl 1554) actor
DA

MAXTONE-GRAHAM, John (b 1929)
American stage manager BE

MAXWELL, Arthur (b 1919) American actor TW/5-10

MAXWELL, Barry (b 1848), actor,
minstrel CDP

MAXWELL, Edwin (d 1948 [58])
Irish actor BE*, BP/33*

MAXWELL, Elsa (1883-1963)
American actress CB, SR

MAXWELL, Frank (b 1916) American actor TW/8

MAXWELL, Gary (b 1939) American actor TW/25

MAXWELL, George (b 1837) American actor, manager HAS

MAXWELL, Gerald (1862-1930)
English actor, critic EA/96,
WWT/3-6

MAXWELL, Guy (d 1918) EA/19*

MAXWELL, John (fl 1740-61)

English dramatist CP/2-3

MAXWELL, Margery (1895-1966) American singer WWA/4

MAXWELL, Marilyn (d 1972 [49]) actress, singer WWT/16*

MAXWELL, Meg (d 1955) actress BE*, WWT/14*

MAXWELL, Robert (d 1971 [61]) producer/director/choreographer BP/55*

MAXWELL, Vera (d 1950 [58]) actress, dancer TW/6

MAXWELL, Walter (b 1877) English business manager, manager GRB/4, WWT/1-5

MAXWELL, Mrs. Walter see Silver, Christine

MAXWELL, Mrs. Walter see Harrison, Evelyn

MAXWELL, Wayne (b 1939) American actor TW/23

MAY, Miss actress CDP

MAY, Ada (b 1900) actress, dancer WWT/7-10

MAY, Akerman (1869-1933) English actor GRB/1-4, WWT/1-7

MAY, Alice [Mrs. Louis Raymond] (1847-87) English singer, actress NYM

MAY, Alice English actress GRB/2

MAY, Charles F. (d 1911 [67]) costumier EA/12*

MAY, Edna [Edna Pettie; Mrs. Oscar Lewisohn] (1878-1948) American actress, singer GRB/1-4, SR, TW/4, WWA/1, WWS, WWT/1-10

MAY, Edward (fl 1494-1503) actor DA

MAY, Edward (fl 1631-35) actor DA

MAY, Elaine [née Berlin] (b 1932) actress, dramatist, director BE, CB, CD, WWT/15-16

MAY, Eva [Mrs. George Hayes] (d 1908) EA/09*

MAY, Frances [Mrs. Samuel May, Jr.] (d 1873) EA/74*

MAY, Frank (1829-96) American actor, manager SR

MAY, Hans (1891-1959) Austrian composer, musical director WWT/11-12

MAY, Harold R. (d 1973 [70])

performer BP/58*

MAY, H. Gomer (b 1865) English actor GRB/1

MAY, Jack (b 1922) English actor WWT/16

MAY, Jane French actress, singer WWT/1-4

MAY, Joe (d 1964 [60]) performer BP/49*

MAY, John (1816-54) American circus performer, actor HAS

MAY, Juliana (fl 1857-58) American singer CDP, HAS

MAY, Martha (d 1868) EA/69*

MAY, Marty (d 1975 [77]) comedian, singer BP/60*, WWT/16*

MAY, Nathan (fl 1615) actor DA

MAY, Olive [Mrs. John W. Albaugh, Jr.] (d 1938 [65]) American actress WWS

MAY, Olive [Countess of Drogheda] (d 1947) actress WWT/14*

MAY, Pamela (b 1917) West Indian/English dancer WWT/10-12

MAY, Randolph (b c. 1540) stage-attendant? DA

MAY, Rose (fl 1851) English singer? HAS

MAY, Samuel (d 1876 [54]) costumier EA/77*, WWT/14*

MAY, Samuel, Jr. (d 1875 [30]) costumier EA/76*

MAY, Mrs. Samuel, Jr. see May, Frances

MAY, Thomas (1595-1650) English dramatist CP/1-3, FGF

MAY, Val[entine] (b 1927) English director WWT/14-16

MAY, Winston (b 1937) American actor TW/27-29

MAYAKOVSKY, Vladimir Vladimirovich (1894-1930) Russian dramatist COC, OC/3

MAYBRICK, Michael [Stephen Adams] (1844-1913) singer, composer CDP

MAYCOCK, John Henry (d 1907 [89]) musician EA/08*

MAYCOCKE, William (fl 1594) actor DA

MAYDESTON, John (fl 1423) actor DA

MAYE, Bernyce (d 1962 [52]) American performer BE*

MAYE, Geraldine (fl 1875) actress CDP

MAYEHOFF, Eddie (b 1914) actor BE

MAYER, Mrs. (fl 1847) actress
HAS
MAYER, Bertie Alexander English
business manager GRB/1
MAYER, Charles (b 1904) actor
TW/30
MAYER, Daniel (1856-1928) agent,
impresario WWT/3-5
MAYER, Dot (d 1964 [68]) per-
former BE*
MAYER, Edwin Justus (1896/97-
1960) American dramatist
MD, MH, MWD, WWT/7-11
MAYER, Gaston (1869-1923) Eng-
lish manager, director GRB/
1-4, WWT/1-4
MAYER, Mrs. Gaston see The-
cla, Maud
MAYER, Jack W. (d 1971 [77])
theatre owner BP/55*
MAYER, Jerome (d 1965 [55])
producer, director TW/21
MAYER, Jerry (b 1941) American
actor TW/24, 27, 29-30
MAYER, Marcus (d 1918 [77])
producer, manager BE*,
WWT/14*
MAYER, Marcus L. (d 1903 [71])
French manager EA/04*,
WWT/14*
MAYER, Renée (b 1900) English
actress, dancer WWT/2-7
MAYER, Sylvain (d 1948 [85])
dramatist BE*, WWT/14*
MAYER, Therese (fl 1885) ac-
tress CDP
MAYER-BOERCKEL, Ferdy
see Mayne, Ferdy
MAYERL, Billy [Joseph W.
Meyer] (1902-59) English con-
ductor, composer WWT/9-12
MAYERS, Wilmette K. (d 1964)
singer BE*
MAYEUR, Eugene F. (1866-1919)
English actor GRB/3-4, WWT/
1-3
MAYFIELD, Cleo [Cleo Empy]
(d 1954 [59]) actress TW/11,
WWT/4-9
MAYHALL, Jerome (d 1964 [70])
musical director BE*
MAYHEW, Augustus S. (d 1875
[49]) dramatist EA/77*
MAYHEW, Charles (b 1908) Eng-
lish actor, singer WWT/8-9
MAYHEW, Edward (d 1868)
manager, actor EA/69*
MAYHEW, H. (d 1834) manager

WWT/14*
MAYHEW, Henry (1812-87) English
dramatist DNB, HP, NYM
MAYHEW, Henry (d 1900 [54])
proprietor EA/01*
MAYHEW, Horace (d 1872 [53])
dramatist BE*, EA/73*, WWT/
14*
MAYHEW, Kate (1853-1944) Amer-
ican actress SR, TW/1
MAYHEW, Stella [née Sadler; Mrs.
Billee Taylor] (1871-1934) Amer-
ican actress SR, WWM
MAYLEAS, Ruth (b 1925) American
executive BE
MAYLER, George (fl 1526-40) actor
DA
MAYNARD, Ambrose [William Hill]
(d 1888 [66]) agent EA/89*
MAYNARD, George (d 1851 [40])
actor EA/72*, WWT/14*
MAYNARD, Gertrude (d 1953 [48])
Canadian actress BE*, BP/37*
MAYNARD, Sir John (fl 1619-24)
dancer, masque writer FGF
MAYNARD, Ken (d 1973 [77]) per-
former BP/57*
MAYNARD, Kermit (d 1971 [73])
performer BP/55*
MAYNARD, Lizzie [Mrs. Henry
Wilson] (b 1865) English dancer,
singer GRB/1
MAYNARD, Richard (d 1944 [70])
business manager WWT/14*
MAYNARD, Ruth (b 1913) American
actress BE
"MAYNARD, Walter" see Beale,
Thomas Willert
MAYNE, Clarice (1886-1966) Eng-
lish actress, singer OC/1-3,
WWT/5-8
MAYNE, Eric (d 1947 [81]) Irish
actor BE*
MAYNE, Ernest (1872-1937) Eng-
lish actor, singer CDP, GRB/1
MAYNE, Ferdy [né Mayer-Boerckel]
(b 1920) actor WWT/15-16
MAYNE, Jasper (1604-72) English
dramatist CP/1-3, FGF
MAYNE, Rutherford (1878-1967)
Irish dramatist COC, OC/1-3,
RE
MAYNE, Will (d 1918 [41]) EA/19*
MAYO, Archie (b 1898) American
actor ES
MAYO, Ella (1862-81) singer CDP
MAYO, Frank (1839-96) American
actor CDP, DAB, HAS, HJD,

WWA/H

MAYO, Frank (d 1963 [74]) actor
BE*, BP/48*

MAYO, Mrs. Frank (d 1896) actress BE*

MAYO, Harry (d 1964 [65]) actor
BE*

MAYO, Joseph Anthony (d 1966
[36]) performer BP/51*

MAYO, Margaret [Lilian Clatten]
(1882-1951) American dramatist, actress NTH, TW/7,
WWM, WWS, WWT/1-9

MAYO, Nannie Nye (fl 1850?)
singer CDP

MAYO, Nick (b 1922) American
producer, director BE

MAYO, Paul (b 1918) English
scene designer ES

MAYO, Sam (d 1938 [63]) comedian, songwriter BE*, WWT/
14*

MAYON, Amy [Mrs. Edwin Mayon]
(d 1904) EA/05*

MAYON, Mrs. Edwin see Mayon, Amy

MAYOR, George (d 1890) property
man EA/91*

MAYORGA, Margaret (b 1894)
American editor, writer BE

MAYR, Richard (b 1877) Austrian
singer ES

MAYRO, Jacqueline (b 1948)
American actress TW/24-25,
27

MAYRSEIDL, Caroline see
Seidl, Lea

MAYVILLE, Harry (d 1912 [37])
marionettist EA/13*

MAYWOOD, Augusta (1825-76?)
American actress CDP, ES,
HAS

MAYWOOD, Martha (1793-c. 1855)
English actress HAS

MAYWOOD, Mary Elizabeth (b
1822) Irish actress, lessee
HAS

MAYWOOD, Robert Campbell
(1786/90-1856) Scottish actor
CDP, HAS, SR

MAZURIER, Mons. (d 1828)
French dancer, pantomimist
CDP

MAZZA, Alfred (b 1946) American actor TW/27

MAZZINGHI, Joseph (1765-1844)
English composer DNB, TD/
1-2

MAZZO, Kay (b 1947) American
dancer CB

MAZZOLA, John W. (b 1928)
American executive BE

MEACHAM, Anne (b 1925) American actress BE, TW/16, 18-20,
23-25, WWT/14-16

MEACHUM, James H. (d 1963 [70])
American performer BE*

MEAD (fl 1819?) dramatist EAP

MEAD, Charles (d 1894 [41])
chairman EA/95*

MEAD, Charlotte (d 1906) actress
EA/07*

MEAD, Jessie (d 1901 [18]) actress
EA/02*

MEAD, Robert (1616-52) English
dramatist CP/1-3, FGF

MEAD, Thomas (1819/21-89) English actor, dramatist CDP,
OAA/1-2

MEADE, Gerald (d 1965) performer
BP/49*

MEADE, Mrs. Henry (d 1874 [26])
EA/75*

MEADE, Jacob (fl 1599-1619)
manager? DA

MEADE, James H. (d 1898 [c. 65])
manager CDP

MEADE, Julia (b 1928) American
actress BE, TW/13, 25-26

MEADER, George (1888/90-1963)
American actor, singer BE,
TW/2-3, WWT/8-10

MEADOW, Walter (d 1879 [33])
actor EA/80*

MEADOWS, Mr. (fl 1821) actor
BS

MEADOWS, Connie [Miss Wood]
English actress GRB/1

MEADOWS, Drinkwater (1799-1869)
English actor CDP, DNB, OX

MEADOWS, James (d 1863 [64])
scene artist EA/72*

MEADOWS, Jayne [Jayne Cotter]
(b 1920?/23/26) American actress BE, CB, TW/1-3

MEADOWS, Joseph R. (d 1964 [65])
clown BE*

MEADOWS, Kate see Ryner,
Mrs. H.

MEADOWS, T. (fl 1805) actor,
dramatist CDP, CP/3

MEAGHERSON, Henry George (d
1895) actor EA/96*

MEAKINS, Charles (d 1951 [70])
actor TW/7

MEAKINS, Mrs. Charles see

Bradford, Edith
MEARA, Anne (b 1929) American
    actress TW/12
MEARES, Thomas Charles see
    Melville, Charles
MEARNS, T. (d 1879) actor?
    EA/80*
MEARS, DeAnn American actress
    TW/26-27, 30
MEARS, George (d 1879) actor?
    EA/80*
MEARS, J. H. (d 1956 [78])
    director, lyricist BE*, WWT/
    14*
MEARS, Marion (d 1970 [71])
    performer BP/54*
MEARS, William (d 1902 [67])
    master carpenter EA/03*
MEASE, Peter (fl c. 1618-27)
    dramatist FGF
MEASEY, John see Franconi
MEASOR, Adela (1860/65-1933)
    Irish actress EA/96, GRB/
    2-4, WWT/1-7
MEASOR, Beryl (1908-65) English
    actress TW/13, WWT/9-13
MEATES, Mrs. Arthur E. [Mrs.
    S. A. Emery] (d 1889) EA/91*
MECHANIC, Emaline (d 1971)
    production assistant BP/55*
MEDBOURNE, Matthew (d 1679)
    actor, dramatist CP/1-3,
    DNB, GT
MEDCRAFT, Russell Graham
    (d 1962 [65]) dramatist BE*
MEDDOWS, Kenny [Harry Whit-
    marsh Johnson] (d 1904 [36])
    EA/05*
MEDEIROS, John (b 1944) Amer-
    ican actor TW/25
MEDFORD, Kay [née Regan] (b
    1920) American actress BE,
    TW/12-24, WWT/14-16
MEDICA, Miss (fl 1850) actress
    HAS
MEDINA, Louisa (c. 1795-1838)
    American? dramatist RJ,
    SR
MEDINA, Patricia (b 1923) Eng-
    lish actress BE
MEDLEY, George (d 1898 [44])
    music-hall mimic EA/99*
MEDLEY, Matthew see Aston,
    Anthony
MEDNICK, Murray (b 1939)
    American dramatist, director
    CD
MEDOFF, Mark (b 1940) Amer-

ican dramatist, actor, director
    CD
MEDWALL, Henry (c. 1462-1500)
    English dramatist COC, CP/2-
    3, DNB, ES, MH, OC/1-3
MEDWIN, Mrs. Charles see
    Lucette, Catherine
MEE, Charles Louis, Jr. (b 1938)
    American dramatist BE
MEECH, John H. (1842-1902) Amer-
    ican manager SR
MEEHAN, Danny (b 1933) American
    actor TW/20, 22, 30
MEEHAN, William E. (d 1920 [35])
    American comedian BE*, BP/4*
MEEK, Donald (1880-1946) Scottish
    actor SR, TW/3, WWT/7-10
MEEK, Francis dramatist CP/3
MEEK, John Robert (d 1882) circus
    performer EA/83*
MEEK, Kate (c. 1838-1925) actress
    SR
MEEKER, Ralph [née Rathgeber]
    (b 1920) American actor BE,
    TW/4-16, 18-20, 22, 28, WWT/
    12-16
MEEKER, W. H. (fl 1845-48)
    American actor HAS
MEEN, George (d 1887 [34]) comic
    singer EA/88*
MEES, Arthur (1850-1923) American
    musical director WWA/1
MEGGAS, Joseph J. (d 1971 [53])
    performer BP/55*
MEGGS, Mary (d 1691) English ac-
    tress COC, OC/1-3
MEGIA, F. (fl 1824-25?) dramatist
    EAP
MEGLEY, Macklin (d 1965 [74])
    producer/director BP/49*
MEGNA, John (b 1952) American
    actor BE
MEGRUE, Roi Cooper (1882/83-
    1927) American dramatist DAB,
    SR, WWA/1, WWM, WWT/4-5
MEHAFFEY, Harry (d 1963 [56])
    American actor TW/3
MEHARRY, Houston (d 1911) actor
    EA/12*
MEHTA, Zubin (b 1936) Indian
    conductor CB
MEIER, Dave (d 1912 [35]) music-
    hall performer EA/13*
MEIGHAM, Thaddeus W. (b 1821)
    American actor HAS
MEIGHAN, James E., Jr. (d 1970
    [66]) actor TW/27
MEIGHAN, Thomas (1879-1936)

American actor ES, WWA/1,
WWT/4-8

MEIGHAN, Mrs. Thomas see
Ring, Frances

MEIKLE, Pat (d 1973 [49]) performer BP/57*

MEILAN, Mark Anthony (fl 1771)
dramatist CP/3

MEI LAN-FANG (1894-1961)
Chinese actor COC, NTH,
OC/3, RE, TW/18

MEISER, Edith (b 1898) American
actress, dramatist, director,
producer BE, TW/4-8, 10-
15, 29, WWT/16

MEISLE, Kathryn (1899-1970)
American singer WWA/5

MEISNER, Sanford (b 1905) American teacher, actor, director
BE

MEISSNER, Alfred Austin (d 1885
[63]) dramatist EA/86*

MEISTER, Barbara Ann American
actress, singer BE

MELANCON, Louis (d 1974 [73])
photographer BP/59*

MELBA, Dame, Nellie [Mrs.
Charles Armstrong] (1859/61/
63/66-1931) Australian singer
CDP, DNB, ES, GRB/1-4,
HP, SR, WWA/1, WWS, WWW/3

MELBOURNE, Mr. (fl 1844) actor
CDP

MELBOURNE, Miss (fl 1796)
actress HAS

MELBOURNE, Arthur E. (b 1867)
English acting manager, business manager GRB/1

MELBOURNE, Robert Rivers (d
1869 [57]) actor? EA/70*

MELBOURNE, Mrs. Walter [Nina
Anato] (d 1889) EA/90*

MELCHIOR, Lauritz (1890-1973)
Danish singer CB, ES, TW/
29, WWA/5

MELDON, H. Percy (b 1856)
Irish director WWM

MELFI, Leonard (b 1935) American dramatist, actor CD,
WWT/15-16

MELFORD, Austin (1855/60-1908)
English actor, manager EA/
96, GRB/1-4

MELFORD, Austin (1884-1971)
English actor, dramatist, producer WWT/2-14

MELFORD, Jack (1899-1972)
English actor WWT/5-14

MELFORD, Jill (b 1934) English
actress WWT/15-16

MELFORD, Mark (d 1914) actor,
producer, dramatist BE*,
WWT/14*

MELHADO, William Henry Hunter
(d 1906) EA/07*

MELIA, Joe English actor WWT/16

MELINGUE, Etienne Marin (1808-
75) French actor CDP

MELLER, Harro (d 1963 [56])
German dramatist, actor BE*

MELLER, Raquel (d 1962 [74])
Spanish diseuse TW/19

MELLING, James Alfred (d 1870)
musician EA/71*

MELLING, T. (d 1878) musical
director EA/79*

MELLISH, Fuller (1865-1936) English actor DP, GRB/2-4,
WWM, WWS, WWT/1-8

MELLISH, Fuller, Jr. (d 1930
[35]) actor BE*, BP/14*,
WWT/14*

MELLISH, Mary (b 1890) American
singer WWA/3

MELLISON, Sarah Ann (d 1878 [64])
performer? EA/79*

MELLON, Ada (d 1914) actress
EA/96

MELLON, Alfred (1820-67) English
composer, conductor, musician
CDP, DNB

MELLON, Alfred (d 1904) EA/05*

MELLON, Mrs. Alfred [Sarah Jane
Woolgar] (1824-1909) English
actress CDP, COC, DNB,
OAA/1-2, OC/1-3

MELLON, Emily (d 1899 [51])
music-hall performer EA/00*

MELLON, Harriot (1777-1837)
English actress CDP, COC,
DNB, GT, OC/1-3, OX, TD/1-2

MELLON, Henry (d 1876) actor
EA/77*

MELLON, Sarah Jane see Mellon, Mrs. Alfred

MELLOR, Henry (d 1889) performer
EA/90*

MELLOR, Mark Moss (d 1897) actor EA/98*

MELLORS, Arthur (d 1899) acrobat, gymnast EA/00*

MELLY, Andrée (b 1932) English
actress WWT/14-16

MELMOTH, Charlotte (1749-1823)
American actress CDP, COC,
HAS, OC/1-3, TD/1-2

MELMOTH, Courtney see Pratt,
S. J.
MELNIKER, William (d 1976 [80])
lawyer BP/60*
MELNITZ, William W. (b 1900)
German educator, director
BE
MELNOTTE, Violet (1856-1935)
English actress, manager
COC, GRB/3-4, OC/1-3,
WWT/1-7
MELONEY, William Brown (d
1971 [69]) producer/director/
choreographer BP/55*
MELROSE, Mr. (b 1799) English
actor CDP, OX
MELROSE, Doris [Mrs. Ernie
Vincent] (d 1916) EA/18*
MELROSE, Tom [Thomas Lamb]
(d 1895 [44]) Negro comedian
EA/96*
MELROY, Clara (d 1966 [68])
performer BP/51*
MELROYD, Frank (b 1879) Eng-
lish actor, dancer GRB/1
MELTON, Miss (fl 1840-61)
English actress HAS
MELTON, Charles (d 1869) music-
hall performer EA/70*
MELTON, Fred (d 1917 [47])
performer? EA/18*
MELTON, James (1904-61)
American singer CB, TW/
17, WWA/4
MELTON, J. Rexton [Francis
Michael Thompson] (d 1900)
actor EA/02*
MELTZER, Charles Henry (d
1936 [83]) English critic,
dramatist GRB/2-4, WWA/1,
WWM, WWS, WWT/1-7
MELVILLE, Miss (fl 1810?)
CDP
MELVILLE, Alan (b 1910) Eng-
lish lyricist, dramatist AAS,
BE, WWT/10-16
MELVILLE, Alice (d 1906 [39])
variety performer EA/07*
MELVILLE, Andrew (d 1896
[43]) manager, proprietor
EA/97*, WWT/14*
MELVILLE, Andrew (d 1938 [52])
producer, director, actor,
dramatist BE*, WWT/14*
MELVILLE, Andrew (b 1912)
English producing manager
WWT/11-14
MELVILLE, Mrs. Andrew (d 1904

[54]) actress EA/05*, WWT/14*
MELVILLE, Mrs. Andrew (d 1927
[46]) actress WWT/14*
MELVILLE, Charles (d 1862) actor
WWT/14*
MELVILLE, Charles [Thomas
Charles Meares] (d 1896 [38])
actor EA/97*
MELVILLE, Charles (d 1901 [65])
manager, agent, minstrel CDP
MELVILLE, Mrs. Charles (d 1893)
EA/94*
MELVILLE, Daisy (d 1895) actress
EA/96*
MELVILLE, Eliza (d 1892 [86])
actress EA/93*
MELVILLE, Emilie (d 1932 [82])
actress BE*, WWT/14*
MELVILLE, Emily (fl 1855-68)
American actress CDP, HAS
MELVILLE, Frederick (1876/79-
1938) Welsh actor, proprietor,
dramatist, manager COC, OC/
1-3, WWT/3-8
MELVILLE, George (d 1898 [74])
actor EA/00*, WWT/14*
MELVILLE, George (d 1900) Aus-
tralian actor EA/01*
MELVILLE, Harry [William Grif-
fith Hart] (d 1898) Irish come-
dian CDP
MELVILLE, James (b 1837) Aus-
tralian equestrian HAS
MELVILLE, Jean-Pierre (d 1973
[55]) producer/director/chore-
ographer BP/58*
MELVILLE, Jennie see Carroll,
Mrs. J. W.
MELVILLE, John (d 1908) EA/09*
MELVILLE, June (1915-70) English
actress, manager OC/1, WWT/
9-13
MELVILLE, M. A. (d 1900) ac-
tress EA/01*
MELVILLE, Nina (d 1966 [56])
performer BP/51*
MELVILLE, Pearl (d 1917) actress
SR
MELVILLE, Richard (d 1873 [35])
composer EA/74*
MELVILLE, Rose (1873-1946)
American actress TW/3, WWA/
2, WWM, WWS, WWT/1-5
MELVILLE, Violet (d 1911 [25])
actress EA/12*
MELVILLE, Walter (1874/75-1937)
English actor, manager COC,
GRB/2-4, OC/1-3, WWT/1-8

MELVILLE, Winifred (d 1950
[40]) actress BE*, WWT/14*
MELVILLE, Winnie (d 1937 [42])
actress, singer WWT/4-8
MELVIN, Mr. (fl 1806) actor
CDP, GT, TD/2
MELVIN, Mrs. A. Douglas [Edith
Ince] (d 1917) EA/18*
MELVIN, Donnie (b 1955) Ameri-
can actor TW/24-25
MELVIN, Duncan (b 1913) Scot-
tish press representative
WWT/13-14
MELVIN, George J. (d 1911 [47])
Scottish entertainer EA/13*
MELVIN, G. S. (d 1946 [69])
comedian BE*, WWT/14*
MELVIN, Murray English actor
WWT/14-16
MELYONEK, John (fl 1483-85)
master of the Chapel Royal?
DA
MEMBRIVES, Lola (d 1969 [86])
performer BP/54*
MEMINGER, Edward Lynn (d
1975 [70]) performer BP/59*
MENAGE, Master (fl 1801)
pantomimist CDP
MENAGE, Bella actress TD/1-2
[see also: Sharp, Mrs. W.]
MENCKEN, Helen actress SR
MENCKEN, Henry Louis (1880-
1956) American critic, drama-
tist ES, HP, NTH, WWA/3
MENDEL, Mr. (d 1905) EA/06*
MENDEL, Hugo S. (b 1877)
manager GRB/1
MENDEL, [James Samuel Smith]
(b 1875) English pianist
GRB/1
MENDELSSOHN, Eleonora (d 1951
[51]) German actress TW/2-
3, 7
MENDES, Catulle (1841-1909)
French dramatist, critic
GRB/1, 3-4
MENDES, Lothar (d 1974 [79])
producer/director/choreographer
BP/58*
MENDEZ, Moses (d 1758) drama-
tist CP/1-3, DNB, GT, TD/
1-2
MENDHAM, James, Jr. (fl 1811)
dramatist CP/3
MENDUM, Georgie Drew (d 1957
[82]) American actress TW/
14, WWM
MENELLY, Lilian (d 1900 [27])

actress EA/01*
MENG, Constance (b 1939) Ameri-
can actress TW/24
MENGES, Herbert (1902-72) English
composer, conductor WWT/8-15
MENGOZZI, Signora Bernardo see
Benimi, Anna
MENJOU, Adolphe Jean (1890-1963)
American actor WWA/4
MENKE, Cpt. Bill (d 1968 [88])
river showboat owner BP/53*
MENKEN, Adah Isaacs [Dolores
Adios Fuertes] (1835-68) Amer-
ican actress CDP, COC, DAB,
DNB, ES, HAS, HJD, NTH,
OC/1-3, SR, WWA/H
MENKEN, Faye (b 1947) American
actress TW/26-29
MENKEN, Helen (1901-66) Ameri-
can actress, producer, executive
BE, NTH, TW/2-3, 22, WWT/
6-14
MENNIN, Peter (b 1923) American
composer BE
MENNINGER, Marion K. (d 1973)
performer BP/57*
MENOTTI, Gian Carlo (b 1911)
Italian composer, librettist BE,
CB, ES, HJD, MH, NTH
MENZIES, Amy see Fawsitt,
Amy
MENZIES, Archie (b 1904) English
dramatist WWT/9-14
MERANDE, Doro (d 1975 [70s])
American actress BE, TW/1,
3-16, 25-26, 29, WWT/15
MERANTE, Louis (d 1887 [58])
dancer, choreographer BE*,
WWT/14*
MERCE, Antonia see Argentina
MERCEDES, Joe (d 1966 [77]) per-
former BP/51*
MERCER, Amelia (d 1890) actress
EA/91*
MERCER, Ben J. (d 1906 [22])
Negro comedian EA/07*
MERCER, Beryl (1882-1939)
Spanish/English actress GRB/4,
WWT/1-8
MERCER, David (b 1928) English
dramatist AAS, CD, CH, COC,
PDT, WWT/15-16
MERCER, Ernestine American ac-
tress TW/25
MERCER, J. (b 1820) actor HAS
MERCER, Johnny (1909-76) Amer-
ican composer, lyricist BE,
CB, WWT/15-16

MERCER, Marian (b 1935) American actress, singer BE, TW/18-19, 22, 24-27, WWT/15-16

MERCER, Thomas, Sr. (b 1796) English actor HAS

MERCER, Thomas, Jr. (b 1817) English actor HAS

MERCER, Tom (d 1916) music-hall singer EA/17*

MERCER, Tony (d 1973 [51]) performer BP/58*

MERCHANT, Thomas see Dibdon, Thomas

MERCHANT, Vivien [né Thomson; Mrs. Harold Pinter] (b 1929) English actress AAS, WWT/14-16

MERCIER, Louis Sébastien (1740-1814) French dramatist OC/1-3

MERCOURI, Melina Greek actress TW/29

MERCUR, William (d 1972 [74]) publicist BP/57*

MEREDITH, Mr. (d 1810) singer CDP

MEREDITH, Burgess (b 1907/08/09) American actor, director AAS, BE, CB, ES, NTH, SR, TW/2-16, 21, WWT/9-16

MEREDITH, Charles H. (d 1964 [70]) performer BP/49*

MEREDITH, George (1828-1909) English dramatist DNB

MEREDITH, Harry C. (d 1898 [68]) actor CDP

MEREDITH, Lee (b 1947) American actor TW/29-30

MERENSKY, John (b 1943) American actor TW/26, 28

MERER, Frederick (d 1911 [61]) actor, manager EA/12*

MERES, Francis (1565-1647) English writer NTH

MEREST, Mrs. J. D. see Hawes, Maria B.

MERETZEK, Max (fl 1848) conductor, impresario SR

MERIC-LALANDE, Mme. (d 1867 [69]) singer EA/68*

MERIN, Eda Reiss American actress TW/25, 27

MERINGTON, Marguerite (d 1951) dramatist WWA/3, WWM

MERITON, Thomas (fl 1658) dramatist CP/1-3, DNB

MERIVALE, Bernard (1882-1939) English dramatist WWT/6-8

MERIVALE, Herman (1839-1906) English dramatist DNB, HP, GRB/1, WWW/1

MERIVALE, Mrs. Herman (d 1932 [85]) dramatist BE*, WWT/14*

MERIVALE, John (b 1917) Canadian actor BE, TW/4-14, 16, 22-23

MERIVALE, Philip (1886-1946) Indian/English actor CB, ES, NTH, TW/2, WWA/2, WWT/2-9

MERKEL, Una (b 1903) American actress BE, WWT/6-14

MERLI, Francesco (b 1887) Italian singer ES

MERLIN, Clarence de (fl 1850) American singer, actress HAS

MERLIN, Frank (d 1968 [76]) Irish/American actor, director, producer TW/24

MERLIN, Joanna (b 1931) American actress BE

MERLIN, Mrs. Max see Merlin, Ray

MERLIN, Ray [Mrs. Max Merlin] (d 1901 [24]) EA/02*

MERLINI (d 1971 [64]) performer BP/55*

MERMAN, Ethel (b 1908/09) American actress, singer AAS, BE, CB, ES, PDT, SR, TW/2-20, 22-23, 26-27, WWT/8-16

MERRALL, Mary (1889/90-1973) English actress AAS, WWT/4-15

MERRICK, David (b 1912) American producing manager AAS, CB, WWT/13-16

MERRICK, Leonard (1864-1939) English dramatist GRB/2-4, WWT/1-8, WWW/3

MERRIDEW, T. J. (d 1895) actor EA/96*

MERRIE, Cecil actor, singer CDP

MERRIGE-ABRAMS, Salway (d 1973 [43]) performer BP/58*

MERRILEES, Andrew (d 1892 [79]) EA/93*

MERRILEES, Andy (d 1904 [63]) comedian EA/05*

MERRILEES, Mrs. Andy see Merrilees, Jessie

MERRILEES, Jane [Mrs. Andy Merrilees] (d 1879) EA/80*

MERRILEES, Jessie [Mrs. Andy Merrilees] (d 1900 [37]) Scottish comedian EA/01*

MERRILL, Alfa (fl 1878) actress

CDP

MERRILL, Beth actress TW/
3-4, 6, WWT/6-7, 10-11

MERRILL, Bob (b 1920) American composer, lyricist BE,
WWT/15-16

MERRILL, Fred R. (d 1976 [87])
performer BP/60*

MERRILL, Gary (b 1915) American actor BE, TW/2-3,
5-6, 23

MERRILL, Louis (d 1963 [52])
performer BE*

MERRILL, Robert (b 1919) American singer CB

MERRILL, Scott (b 1922) American actor TW/10-20

MERRIMAN, Dan (b 1929) American actor TW/23-24, 28

MERRIMAN, Richard (d 1917 [34])
performer? EA/18*

MERRINGTON, Margaret dramatist SR

MERRITON, Annie see Richardson, Annie

MERRITT, Alice see Oates,
Mrs. James A.

MERRITT, George (b 1890) English actor WWT/6-16

MERRITT, Grace (b 1881) actress
WWT/1-5

MERRITT, Guy E. (d 1975 [49])
designer BP/60*

MERRITT, James (d 1908 [57])
music-hall chairman, singer
EA/09*

MERRITT, Kate (fl 1861) actress
HAS

MERRITT, Larry (b 1937) American actor TW/28

MERRITT, Lillie (d 1971 [90])
performer BP/55*

MERRITT, Paul (d 1895) dramatist BE*, WWT/14*

MERRITT, William (1852-87)
American actor NYM

MERRY, Anne see Brunton,
Ann[e]

MERRY, Lydia Ellen (fl 1816)
singer, actress CDP

MERRY, Robert (1755-98) English dramatist CDP, CP/3,
EAP, GT, RJ, TD/1-2

MERRY, Mrs. Robert see
Brunton, Ann[e]

MERRYFIELD, Jerry (1820-62)
English actor HAS

MERRYFIELD, Rose [Rose Cline]

(fl 1850) actress CDP, HAS

MERRYLEES, James (d 1902 [33])
variety comedian EA/03*

MERSON, Billy [William Henry
Thompson] (1881-1947) English
actor, singer COC, OC/1-3,
WWT/4-10

MERSON, Fred (d 1875) comedian,
singer EA/76*

MERTON, Annie [Mrs. Charles
Sennett] (d 1912 [67]) EA/13*

MERTON, Charlie (d 1892) performer? EA/93*

MERTON, Collette (d 1968 [61])
performer BP/53*

MERVIN, Frederick [Charles Mar-
vin] (d 1897) English actor
OAA/2

MERVIN, Will (d 1886 [32]) comic
singer EA/87*

MERVYN, Lee (d 1962 [34]) performer BE*

MERVYN, William [né Pickwoad]
(1912-76) Kenyan/English actor
WWT/15-16

MERWIN, W. S. (b 1927) American
dramatist HJD

MERYELL, Henry (fl 1509-11)
member of the Chapel Royal
DA

MESERVEY, Robert see Preston,
Robert

MESSAGER, André (1853-1929)
French composer, conductor,
manager GRB/4, WWT/1,
WWW/3

MESSEL, Oliver (b 1905) English
designer AAS, BE, COC, ES,
OC/3, PDT, TW/6-8, WWT/7-16

MESSITER, Eric (d 1960 [68]) actor
BE*, WWT/14*

MESTAYER, Anna Maria see
Thorne, Mrs. Charles Robert,
Sr.

MESTAYER, Charles (c. 1820-49)
actor HAS, SR

MESTAYER, Emily see Houpt,
Mrs. Charles J.

MESTAYER, Harry musician HAS

MESTAYER, Henry (fl 1716) dramatist CP/2-3

MESTAYER, John actor HAS

MESTAYER, Mrs. John (d 1860
[74]) actress HAS

MESTAYER, Louis J. (d 1880 [60])
American actor EA/81*

MESTAYER, Louis Joseph (1818-80)
American actor CDP, HAS

MESTAYER, Maria Ann see Thorne, Mrs. Charles Robert, Sr.

MESTAYER, William A. [né William Ayers Haupt] (1844-96) American actor CDP, HAS, SR

MESTAYER, Mrs. William H. see Vaughn, Theresa

MESTEL, Jacob (d 1958 [74]) Polish actor, director BE*, BP/43*

METASTASIO, Abbé (fl 18th cent) dramatist CP/1

METAXA, Georges (1899-1950) Rumanian actor, singer TW/7, WWT/6-9

METCALF, A. (d 1892 [29]) conductor EA/93*

METCALF, Mark American actor TW/30

METCALF, S. (d 1900 [66]) director EA/01*

METCALF, Thomas Edmund see Rosenthal, Edmund

METCALFE, Catharine (d c. 1790?) dramatist CP/3

METCALFE, Ernest (b 1869) English acting manager GRB/1

METCALFE, George Taylor (d 1908 [24]) manager EA/09*

METCALFE, James Stetson (1858-1927) American critic GRB/2-4, WWA/1, WWM, WWT/1-5

METCALFE, Madge [Mrs. Arthur Jefferson] (d 1908) actress EA/10*

METCALFE, Mrs. P. A. see Rochester, Jenny

METEYARD, Eliza (d 1879 [63]) writer EA/80*

METHOT, Mayo (d 1951 [47]) American actress TW/8

METRA, Olivier (d 1889 [58]) composer, conductor EA/90*

METZ, E. (fl 1827) actor HAS

METZ, Lucius Wells (d 1969 [71]) performer BP/53*

METZ, Theodore (1848-1936) German songwriter BE*

METZLER, George Richard (d 1893 [24]) EA/95*

MEURICE, Paul (d 1905 [85]) dramatist WWT/14*

MEUX, Lady [Valerie Reece] actress GRB/1

MEWBURN, Hugh (d 1909 [31]) actor EA/10*

MEWE, Mr. dramatist CP/3, FGF

MEWHA, Sam A. (d 1917) actor EA/18*

MEYER, Mr. actor HAS

MEYER, Bertie Alexander (1877-1967) English business manager GRB/2-4, WWT/1-14

MEYER, Charles (d 1881 [59]) musician EA/82*

MEYER, Ernest (d 1927 [50]) literary representative BE*, WWT/14*

MEYER, Frederic E. (d 1973 [63]) actor, director, stage manager TW/30

MEYER, George W. (1884-1959) American composer BE*

MEYER, Jean (b 1914) French actor, director CB

MEYER, Johannes (d 1976) producer/director/choreographer BP/60*

MEYER, Kerstin (b 1928) Swedish singer ES

MEYER, Leopold de (1816-83) pianist, composer CDP, HAS

MEYER, Lester (d 1965 [91]) producer/director BP/50*

MEYER, Louis (1871-1915) English manager, lessee WWT/2, WWW/1

MEYER, Rudy (d 1969 [67]) producer/director/choreographer BP/54*

MEYER, Torben (d 1975 [90]) performer BP/59*

MEYER, Yale (d 1966 [49]) acting teacher BP/51*

MEYER-FORSTER, Wilhelm (d 1934 [72]) dramatist WWT/14*

MEYERL, Joseph W. see Mayerl, Billy

MEYERS (fl 1792) translator CP/3

MEYERS, Louisa (fl 1865) American actress, singer CDP, HAS

MEYERS, Marsha (b 1946) American actress TW/29

MEYERS, Martin (b 1934) American actor TW/24-25, 27

MEYN, Robert (d 1972 [76]) performer BP/56*

MEYNALL, Percy (d 1900) actor EA/01*

MEYNELL, Claude (1867-1934) English manager, actor WWT/1-7

MEYRICK, Ellen (fl 1874-79)

actress OAA/2

MEYRICK, George (d 1868) EA/69*

MICHAEL, Mrs. Cyril see Kerin, Nora

MICHAEL, Edward (d 1950 [97]) business manager GRB/1-3

MICHAEL, Gertrude (1910-64/65) American actress WWT/8-9

MICHAEL, Kathleen (b 1917) English actress WWT/11-16

MICHAEL, Mary American actress TW/4, 8

MICHAEL, Meyers (b 1960) American actor TW/27

MICHAEL, Mickie (d 1973 [30]) performer BP/58*

MICHAEL, Ralph [né Ralph Champion Shotter] (b 1907) English actor AAS, WWT/10-16

MICHAELIS, Robert (1882/84-1965) French actor, singer WWT/2-7

MICHAELS, Bert (b 1943) American actor TW/30

MICHAELS, Frankie (b 1955) American actor TW/23

MICHAELS, Laura (b 1953) American actress TW/26-29

MICHAELS, Max (d 1968 [70]) manager BP/52*

MICHAELS, Patricia American actress TW/25

MICHAELS, Raf (b 1928) American actor TW/29

MICHAELS, Sidney (b 1927) American dramatist MWD

MICHAELS, Stuart (b 1940) American actor TW/28

MICHAELS, Sully (d 1966 [49]) performer BP/50*

MICHAELS, Timmy (b 1963) American actor TW/26

MICHALESCO, Michael (d 1957 [72]) Russian actor BE*, WWT/14*

MICHELBORNE, John (fl 1688-89) dramatist CP/2-3, GT

MICHELENA, Vera (d 1961 [77]) actress, singer TW/18

MICHELL, Agnes see Herbert, Mrs.

MICHELL, Keith (b 1926/28) Australian actor AAS, BE, TW/17, 20, 26-27, WWT/13-16

MICHLIN, Barry (b 1941) American actor TW/30

MICHOT, M. (d 1896 [66]) singer

EA/97*

MICKEY, Jered (b 1934) American actor TW/27-28

MICKLE, William Julius (1735-88) Scottish dramatist CP/3

MICKMAN, Mrs. James T. (d 1882) EA/83*

MIDDLEMAS, Henry (d 1918) EA/19*

MIDDLETON, Alfred (d 1887 [53]) marionettist EA/88*

MIDDLETON, Arthur D. (1880-1929) American singer WWA/1

MIDDLETON, Edgar (1894-1939) English dramatist WWT/6-8, WWW/3

MIDDLETON, Edwin (d 1887 [47]) marionettist EA/88*

MIDDLETON, George (c. 1845-1926) American manager SR

MIDDLETON, George (1880-1967) American dramatist BE, WWA/4, WWM, WWT/4-11

MIDDLETON, Guy (1907-73) English actor WWT/9-11, 13-14

MIDDLETON, Herman D. (b 1925) American educator BE

MIDDLETON, James [né Magan] (c. 1768-99) Irish actor CDP, GT, TD/1-2

MIDDLETON, James (d 1880 [76]) marionettist EA/81*

MIDDLETON, Mrs. James Alfred see Middleton, Mary

MIDDLETON, John F. (d 1912 [27]) musician EA/13*

MIDDLETON, Josephine (1886-1971) American actress WWT/10-14

MIDDLETON, Mary [Mrs. James Alfred Middleton] (d 1877 [72]) EA/78*

MIDDLETON, Olive (d 1974 [83]) performer BP/59*

MIDDLETON, Ray (b 1907) American actor, singer BE, TW/22-27, WWT/11-16

MIDDLETON, Robert (1911-77) American actor TW/10

MIDDLETON, Thomas (c. 1570-1627) English dramatist CDP, COC, CP/1-3, DNB, ES, FGF, GT, HP, MH, NTH, OC/1-3, PDT, RE

MIDGLEY, Robin (b 1934) English director WWT/16

MIELL, William (d c. 1796) English actor TD/2

MIELZINER, Jo (1901-76) French/

American designer AAS, BE,
CB, COC, ES, NTH, OC/1-3,
PDT, TW/2-8, WWT/7-16)

MIERS, Charles J. (fl 1869?)
singer, song composer CDP

MIERS, Virgil (d 1967 [42]) critic
BP/52*

MIGATZ, Marshall (d 1973) pro-
ducer/director/choreographer
BP/57*

MIGAUX, Frank (d 1891) singer
EA/92*

MIGDEN, Chester L. (b 1921)
American executive, lawyer
BE

MIGHEL (fl 1619) actor DA

MIGNON, Sara [Mrs. Rollo Bal-
main] English actress GRB/
1-3

MIGNOT, Flore French actress
WWT/2-3

MIHAIL, Alexandra (d 1975 [28])
performer BP/60*

MIHALYI, Judith (b 1944) American actress TW/25

MILAN, Frank American actor
TW/12-16

MILANA, Vincent (b 1939) American actor TW/25, 27, 29-30

MILANO, Mrs. see Sidney,
Minnie

MILANO, Frank (d 1962) American
performer BE*

MILANO, John (d 1874 [49]) harlequin, ballet master EA/75*

MILANOV, Zinka (b 1906) Yugoslavian singer CB

MILBANK, George (1853-1902)
manager CDP

MILBANK, Mrs. George see
Paine, Lizzie

MILBERT, Seymour (b 1915)
American stage manager BE

MILBURN, J. H. (d 1941 [73])
comedian, singer CDP

MILDARE, Mrs. Charles see
Lindsay, Bertha Goulding

MILDMAY, Frank [John David
Margot] (d 1894 [38]) music-
hall manager EA/95*

MILES, Miss see Fawcett,
Mrs.

MILES, Allan (b 1929) American
dancer notator BE

MILES, Beatrice see Marsdene,
Beatrice

MILES, Sir Bernard (b 1907)
English actor, director,

manager AAS, COC, ES, OC/3,
PDT, WWT/10-16

MILES, Lady Bernard see Wilson, Josephine

MILES, Bridget [Mrs. Paddy
Miles] (d 1878 [27]) EA/79*

MILES, Carlton (d 1954 [70+])
American dramatist, talent
representative, critic BE*,
BP/39*

MILES, Edward (1814-1906) English
actor EA/07*, GRB/2*

MILES, Eugene (b 1928) American
actor TW/15

MILES, George (d 1911 [49]) musician EA/12*

MILES, George Henry (1824-71)
American dramatist DAB, HJD

MILES, Helen Clark (d 1976)
treasurer BP/60*

MILES, Jackie (d 1968 [54]) performer BP/52*

MILES, James (d 1882) music-hall
performer EA/83*

MILES, Joanna (b 1940) French/
American actress TW/28

MILES, Joseph (d 1874) musician
EA/75*

MILES, Julia (b 1829) American
actress HAS

MILES, Kate see Munroe, Kate

MILES, Maralyn Canadian actress
TW/25

MILES, Mrs. Paddy see Miles,
Bridget

MILES, Mrs. Patrick see Miles,
Susannah

MILES, Pliny (d 1865) American
lecturer HAS

MILES, Robert E. J. (1834/35-94)
American actor, manager CDP,
HAS, SR

MILES, Sarah actress WWT/15-16

MILES, Sophie [Mrs. S. Shorey]
(d 1891) actress EA/92*, WWT/
14*

MILES, Susannah [Mrs. Patrick
Miles] (d 1886) EA/87*

MILES, Sylvia (b 1932/34) American
actress BE, TW/28-30

MILES, William Augustus (fl 1779-
1812) dramatist CP/2-3, GT,
TD/1-2

MILFORD, Mary see Waller,
Mary

MILGRIM, Lynn (b 1944) American
actress TW/25-27, 29

MILIAN, Tomas (b 1937) Cuban

actor ES

MILJAN, John (d 1960 [67]) American actor BE*

MILL, Paul ["The Whistling Comedian"] (d 1916 [53]) entertainer, singer, composer GRB/1-2

MILL, Robert Reid (d 1906) EA/08*

MILLAIS, Helena (b 1887) English actress, singer GRB/1-2

MILLAND, Ray (b 1908) Welsh actor TW/22-23

MILLAR, Douglas (1875-1943) Scottish manager WWT/4-7

MILLAR, Gertie [Mrs. Lionel Monckton] (1879-1952) English actress COC, DNB, ES, GRB/1-4, OC/3, TW/8, WWT/1-11

MILLAR, Mack (d 1962 [57]) press representative BE*

MILLAR, Mary [née Wetton] (b 1936) English actress, singer WWT/15-16

MILLAR, Robins (1889-1968) Canadian dramatist, journalist OC/1-2, WWT/8-10

MILLAR, Ronald (b 1919) English actor, dramatist AAS, CD, COC, WWT/10-16

MILLAR, Mrs. S. A. [Miss Isaacs] (d 1878 [41]) EA/79*

MILLAR, William see Boyd, Stephen

MILLARD, Edward R. (d 1963) performer BE*

MILLARD, Evelyn [Mrs. Robert Porter Coulter] (1869-1941) English actress, manager EA/95, GRB/1-4, WWT/1-9, WWW/4

MILLARD, Harry W. (d 1969 [41]) performer BP/54*

MILLARD, J. (d 1893) professor of elocution & music EA/94*

MILLARD, Ursula (b 1901) English actress WWT/5-6

MILLAUD, Albert (d 1892 [47]) dramatist EA/93*

MILLAY, Edna St. Vincent (1892-1950) American dramatist MD, MH, MWD

MILLAY, George (d 1901) gymnast EA/02*

MILLER, Mr. (fl 1806?) actor, singer CDP

MILLER, Mr. (d 1879 [60]) musician EA/80*

MILLER, Miss (fl 1795?) actress CDP, TD/1-2

MILLER, Agatha Mary Clarissa see Christie, Dame Agatha

MILLER, Agnes English actress WWT/2-5

MILLER, Alice Duer (1874-1942) American dramatist CB

MILLER, Allan (b 1929) American actor TW/30

MILLER, Andrew Kennedy (d 1906 [45]) manager EA/07*

MILLER, Ann (b 1919) American actress, dancer, singer TW/25-26, WWT/16

MILLER, Art (d 1971 [67]) performer BP/55*

MILLER, Arthur (d 1935) dramatist BE*, WWT/14*

MILLER, Arthur (b 1915) American dramatist, director AAS, BE, CB, CD, CH, COC, ES, HJD, HP, MD, MH, MWD, OC/2-3, PDT, RE, WWT/11-16

MILLER, Arthur H. (d 1975 [81]) critic BP/59*

MILLER, Ashley (b 1877) American actor WWS

MILLER, Barbara (d 1972 [86]) performer BP/56*

MILLER, Benjamin (b 1923) American actor TW/3

MILLER, Betty (b 1925) American actress TW/22-25, 27, 29

MILLER, Bob (b 1929) American actor TW/11

MILLER, Buzz (b 1928) American dancer, actor, choreographer BE, TW/19-23

MILLER, Clarence (d 1963 [67]) stagehand BE*

MILLER, Clementine (d 1905) EA/06*

MILLER, David (1871-1933) Scottish actor, director WWT/4-7

MILLER, David Prince (d 1873 [65]) producer, manager, showman BE*, EA/74*, WWT/14*

MILLER, Drout (b 1942) American actor TW/26, 28

MILLER, Dutch (b 1927) American actor TW/24

MILLER, Eddie (d 1971 [80]) performer BP/55*

MILLER, Edith (d 1903) singer, actress EA/04*, WWT/14*

MILLER, Edward (1735-1807) composer CDP

MILLER, Elizabeth see Baker, Mrs. Thomas

MILLER, Emily (d 1902 [62]) actress WWT/14*

MILLER, Flournoy (d 1971 [84]) comedian TW/27

MILLER, Gary Neil see Dunn, Michael

MILLER, Mr. G. H. (d 1868) EA/69*

MILLER, Gilbert Heron (1884-1969) American producing manager, producer BE, CB, NTH, OC/2-3, TW/2-8, 25, WWA/5, WWT/4-14, WWW/6

MILLER, Harold (b 1935) American actor TW/25, 28

MILLER, Harry M. (b 1934) New Zealand producing manager WWT/16

MILLER, Hattie Brown (fl 1861?) singer CDP

MILLER, Henry (1860-1926) English actor, manager COC, DAB, ES, GRB/2-4, OC/1-3, PP/2, SR, WWA/1, WWM, WWS, WWT/1-5

MILLER, Mrs. Henry [Bijou Heron] (1863-1937) American actress CDP, PP/2

MILLER, Hugh (1889-1976) English actor WWT/8-14

MILLER, Irene Bliss (d 1962 [86]) publicity representative BE*

MILLER, James (1703-44) English dramatist CP/1-3, DNB, GT, TD/1-2

MILLER, James see Wilmot, Fred

MILLER, James Hull (b 1916) American theatre design consultant, scene designer BE

MILLER, Jason (b 1932/39?/40) American dramatist, actor AAS, CB, CD, TW/28-30, WWT/16

MILLER, Mrs. J. Ellis see Mason, Katherine Jane

MILLER, Jennie [Mrs. Kennedy Miller] (d 1899) EA/00*

MILLER, Joan (b 1910) Canadian actress AAS, WWT/11-16

MILLER, Joan Maxine see Copeland, Joan

MILLER, Joaquin (1841-1913) American dramatist SR

MILLER, John D. (b 1771) American actor HAS

MILLER, Jonathan (b 1934) English actor, director, dramatist AAS, BE, CB, COC, ES, WWT/ 14-16

MILLER, Joseph ["Joe"] (1684-1738) English actor CDP, NTH

MILLER, Mrs. Joseph see Lavina

MILLER, Josephine see Clifton, Josephine

MILLER, June (b 1934) American actress TW/24

MILLER, Katherine Jane [Mrs. J. Ellis Miller] (d 1917) EA/18*

MILLER, Kathleen (b 1945) American actress TW/27-29

MILLER, Mrs. Kennedy see Miller, Jennie

MILLER, Leon C. (b 1902) American executive, editor BE

MILLER, Llewellyn (d 1971 [72]) critic BP/56*

MILLER, Louisa Missouri see Missouri, Miss

MILLER, Louise see Louise, Mme.

MILLER, Madeline (b 1945) American actress TW/26

MILLER, Malcolm E. (d 1963 [40]) critic BE*, BP/47*

MILLER, Marilyn (1898-1936) American actress, dancer, singer AAS, ES, NTH, SR, WWT/ 4-8

MILLER, Martin (1899-1969) Czech actor WWT/10-14

MILLER, Marty (b 1934) American actor TW/2

MILLER, Mary Beth (b 1942) American actress TW/26

MILLER, Max (d 1963 [68]) performer BE*, BP/47*, WWT/14*

MILLER, Maximillian Christopher (1674-1734) German giant CDP

MILLER, Michael (b 1931) American actor TW/27-30

MILLER, Mildred (b 1924) American singer CB

MILLER, Morris (b 1927) American actor TW/9-10, 13

MILLER, Page (b 1947) American actor TW/28

MILLER, Paul Eduard (d 1972 [64]) critic BP/57*

MILLER, R. Mack (b 1937) American actor TW/30

MILLER, Ruby (1889-1976) English actress WWT/4-10

MILLER, Seton I. (d 1974 [71])
dramatist BP/58*
MILLER, Seymour (d 1971 [63])
composer/lyricist BP/56*
MILLER, Sharron (b 1948) American actress TW/29
MILLER, Skedge (b 1918) American actor TW/9-19
MILLER, Sonny (d 1969 [64])
composer/lyricist BP/54*
MILLER, Tod (b 1944) American actor TW/25, 27
MILLER, Tom (d 1917) secretary EA/18*
MILLER, Truman (d 1963 [39])
stage manager, actor BE*
MILLER, Walter (1892-1940)
BE*
MILLER, W. Christie (b 1842)
American actor HAS
MILLER, Mrs. W. Christie [née Towell] (b 1847) Irish actress HAS
MILLER, William (fl 1819?) impersonator CDP
MILLER, Wyn (d 1932 [85]) producer, dramatist, manager BE*, WWT/14*
MILLER, Wynne (b 1930/35) American actress, singer BE, TW/14-19
MILLET, Albert (d 1891) composer EA/92*
MILLETT, Maude [Mrs. Tennant] (1867-1920) Indian/English actress DP, GRB/1-4, WWT/1-3
MILLI, Robert (b 1933) American actor TW/20, 25-26
MILLICAN, Jane (b 1902) American actress WWT/7-10
MILLIGAN, John Canadian actor TW/17, 22
MILLIGAN, Spike [Terence Alan] (b 1918) Indian/English actor, director, dramatist WWT/14-16
MILLIKEN, Mr. (fl 1835) American actor HAS
MILLIKEN, Col. James Foster (d 1917) manager, agent SR
MILLIKEN, J. Edwin (d 1884 [35]) actor CDP
MILLIKEN, Sandol [Mrs. Carlos French Stoddard] (fl 1900-04) American actress WWS
MILLINGEN (fl 1811) dramatist CP/3
MILLINGHEN, J. (d 1874 [95])

EA/75*
MILLINGTON, Miss (fl 1850) actress HAS
MILLINGTON, Rodney (b 1905)
English actor, publisher BE, WWT/8-16
MILLIS, Fred W. (d 1913 [55])
EA/14*
MILLONS, Thomas (d 1853) Scottish actor? HAS
MILLS, Mr. (fl 1806) English actor HAS
MILLS, Mr. (fl 1830-39) English actor HAS
MILLS, Mrs. [née Keys] (fl 1798-1804) actress TD/1-2
MILLS, Mrs. (fl 1830-39) English actress HAS
MILLS, Miss (b c. 1787) actress TD/2
MILLS, Miss see Brown, Mrs. J.
MILLS, Annette (d 1955 [60]) performer, actress BE*, WWT/14*
MILLS, A. W. (d 1889 [22]) music-hall performer EA/90*
MILLS, Bertram Wagstaff (1873-1938) English circus proprietor DNB, ES, WWW/3
MILLS, Carley (d 1962 [65]) composer BE*, BP/47*
MILLS, Mrs. Clifford (d 1933 [70])
dramatist WWT/4-7
MILLS, Donna (b 1943) American actress TW/23-24
MILLS, Eleanor see Chalmers, Mrs. James
MILLS, Eliza (d 1857) singer HAS
MILLS, Florence (1895/1901-1927) American actress, singer WWT/5
MILLS, Frank [Frank Ransom] (1870-1921) American actor GRB/1-4, WWT/1-3
MILLS, Mrs. Frank see Macbeth, Helen
MILLS, Frederick see Norton, Fleming
MILLS, Grant (d 1973) actor TW/30
MILLS, Guy (d 1962 [64]) performer BE*
MILLS, Mrs. Harry see Doyle, Lila
MILLS, Hayley (b 1946) English actress WWT/16
MILLS, Horace (1864-1941) English actor, dramatist CDP, WWT/2-5
MILLS, Hugh Travers (d 1971)

dramatist BP/56*

MILLS, Jack (d 1974 [88]) circus owner BP/59*

MILLS, Jake (d 1975 [65]) circus owner BP/60*

MILLS, James (d 1870 [58]) agent, stage manager EA/71*

MILLS, James (d 1908) EA/09*

MILLS, John, Sr. (1670-1736) actor CDP, DNB

MILLS, John (d 1872 [35]) musician, singer EA/73*

MILLS, Sir John (b 1908) English actor, singer AAS, BE, CB, ES, TW/18-19, WWT/8-16

MILLS, Juliet (b 1941) English actress BE, WWT/14-16

MILLS, Kerry (1869-1948) American composer BE*

MILLS, Martha Norman (d 1906 [78]) EA/07*

MILLS, Mary Louisa [Louie Coote] (d 1905 [30]) EA/06*

MILLS, Oscar see Barry, Bob

MILLS, R. J. (d 1889 [46]) music-hall chairman EA/90*

MILLS, Steve (b 1895) American actor TW/26-27

MILLS, Stratton (d 1916 [45]) actor EA/17*

MILLS, T. E. [T. Mills Edwards] (fl 1857) English actor CDP, HAS

MILLS, Tom Norman (d 1917 [55]) clown, comedian EA/18*

MILLS, William (d 1750) actor TD/1-2

MILLS, Win (d 1971 [63]) columnist BP/56*

MILLSTEIN, Gilbert writer BE

MILLWARD, Augusta (d 1892) EA/94*

MILLWARD, Charles (d 1892 [62]) dramatist BE*, EA/93*, WWT/14*

MILLWARD, F. Aubrey (b 1879) English actor, singer GRB/2

MILLWARD, Jessie [Mrs. John Glendinning] (1861-1932) English actress CDP, DP, EA/95, GRB/1-4, PP/2, SR, WWM, WWS, WWT/1-6

MILLWARD, John (d 1890) actor EA/91*

MILMAN, Dean (d 1868 [77]) dramatist BE*, WWT/14*

MILMAN, Rev. Henry Hart (d 1868 [77]) dramatist EA/69*

MILN, Mrs. W. S. see Richards, Cicely

MILNE (fl 1798) dramatist EAP

MILNE, A[lan] A[lexander] (1882-1956) English dramatist AAS, DNB, ES, HP, MD, MH, MWD, NTH, PDT, TW/12, WWT/4-11, WWW/5

MILNE, George C. actor CDP

MILNE, Lennox Scottish actor TW/24

MILNER, Mr. (fl 1839) Canadian actor HAS

MILNER, Lieut.-Col. (d 1917 [70]) EA/18*

MILNER, Alfred (d 1887 [63]) music-hall proprietor EA/89*

MILNER, Annie (b 1836) Scottish singer HAS

MILNER, Prof. George (d 1907 [84]) performer? EA/08*

MILNER, Martin (b 1931) American actor TW/24

MILNER, Ron (b 1938) American dramatist CD

MILNES, Sherrill (b 1935) American singer CB

MILO, Vic (d 1965 [80]) performer BP/50*

MILORADOVICH, Milo (d 1972 [71]) performer BP/57*

MILS, Tobias (fl 1583-94?) actor DA

MILTERN, John E. (d 1937 [67]) American actor WWT/4-8

MILTON, Arthur (d 1918 [61]) EA/19*

MILTON, Mrs. Arthur (d 1936) actress BE*, WWT/14*

MILTON, Betty Rea (d 1969) performer BP/54*

MILTON, Billy (b 1905) English actor, dancer, lyricist WWT/7-15

MILTON, Charles [Charles Hooper Wilson] (d 1900 [35]) actor EA/01*

MILTON, E. C. (d 1906) gymnast EA/08*

MILTON, Ernest (1890-1974) American actor AAS, BTR/74, WWT/4-15

MILTON, Frank (b 1918) American actor TW/3

MILTON, Mrs. Hal (d 1908 [21]) EA/09*

MILTON, Harry (1900-65) English actor, singer WWT/7-11

MILTON, John (1606-74) English

dramatist CP/1-3, DNB, ES,
FGF, GT, HP, NTH, PDT,
RE, SR

MILTON, Mark (fl 1896?) actor,
singer CDP

MILTON, Maud (1859-1945) English actress CDP, GRB/1-4,
WWT/1-9

MILTON, Percy (d 1898) comedian
EA/00*

MILTON, Mrs. Percy see
Pigot, Elizabeth

MILTON, Robert (d 1956 [70])
Russian producer, director
TW/12, WWT/6-10

MILWARD, Dawson (1862/70-1926)
English actor GRB/1-4, WWT/
1-5

MILWARD, John (d 1742 [40])
actor WWT/14*

MILWARD, William (d 1742) actor
WWT/14*

MINCIOTTI, Esther (d 1962 [74])
Italian actress BE*, BP/46*

MINDIL, Philip (b 1874) American
press agent, editor WWM

MINELLI, Liza (b 1946) American
actress BE, CB, WWT/16

MINELLI, Vincente (b 1908) American designer, director ES

MINEO, Sal (d 1976 [37]) performer BP/60*

MINER, Henry Clay (d 1950 [84])
American manager SR

MINER, Jan (b 1917/19) American
actress BE, TW/25, 27-30,
WWT/16

MINER, Worthington C. (b 1900)
American producer, director
BE, WWT/8-10

MINETTI, Maria (d 1971) actress
WWT/7-8

MINEVITCH, Borrah (d 1955
[52]) Russian performer TW/12

MINIL, Renée du see Du Minil,
Renée

MINION, Samuel (fl 1634) actor
DA

MINNER, Kathryn (d 1969 [77])
performer BP/54*

MINNEY, Charles John Cuninghame see Cuninghame,
Charles

MINNEY, Rubeigh James (b 1895)
Indian/English critic WWT/
6-10

MINOR, Philip (b 1927) American
actor TW/25

MINOTIS, Alexis (b 1902/06) Greek
actor, director BE, COC, OC/
3, TW/9

MINOTTA, Duchess of see
Sorma, Agnes

MINSHULL, Mrs. George see
Minshull, Mary Jane

MINSHULL, George T. (d 1943
[87]) actor, producer, manager
DP

MINSHULL, John (fl 1801-05)
dramatist EAP

MINSHULL, Mary Jane [Mrs.
George Minshull] (d 1879) EA/
80*

MINSKY, Abraham Bennet (1881-
1949) American producer BE*,
BP/34*, WWT/14*

MINSKY, Jack (d 1973 [85]) manager BP/58*

MINSKY, Mollie (d 1964 [69]) American executive BE*

MINSTER, Jack (1901-66) English
actor WWT/8-14

MINSTER, Mrs. Robert see
Minster, Sybil

MINSTER, Sybil [Mrs. Robert Min-
ster] (d 1909) EA/10*

MINTER, Mary Miles (b 1902)
American actress WWT/4-7

MINTO, Dorothy [Mrs. Shiel Barry]
(b 1891) English actress GRB/
3-4, WWT/1-9

MINTON, William Richard [William
Richard Martin] (d 1916) actor?
EA/17*

MINTUN, John (b 1941) American
actor TW/26, 30

MINTURN, Harry L. (d 1963 [79])
producer, actor BE*

MINTZ, David see Knight, David

MINTZ, Eli (b 1904) Polish actor
TW/21-22, 25, 30

MINZESHEIMER, Blanche see
Blanche, Belle

MINZEY, Frank (d 1949 [70])
American actor BE*, BP/34*

MIRAMOVA, Elena Russian actress
WWT/7-11

MIRAN, Miss actress, singer CDP

MIRANDA, Carmen (1913-55) Brazilian singer, actress CB, TW/
12

MIRANDA, David Myers (d 1886
[50]) singer EA/87*

MIRANDOLA, Sig. (fl 1860) singer
HAS

MIRATO, Sig. (d 1885) singer

EA/87*

MIRBEAU, Octave (1848-1917)
French dramatist COC, GRB/
1-4, WWT/1-3

MIRREN, Helen (b 1946) actress
HAS, WWT/15-16

MISHIMA, Masao (d 1973 [67])
performer BP/58*

MISITA, Michael (b 1947) actor
TW/26-30

MISKEL, Caroline [née Scales]
(b 1873) actress SR

MISSA, Edmond (d 1910) composer
WWT/14*

MISSOURI, Miss [Louisa Missouri
Miller] (1821-38) American actress CDP, HAS

MISTALE (fl 1635) actor DA

MISTINGUETT [née Jeanne Bour-
geois] (1875-1956) French actress, dancer COC, TW/12,
WWT/10-11, WWW/5

MISTRAL, Jorge (d 1972 [49])
performer BP/56*

MITCHEL, Thomas (d 1894 [57])
musician EA/95*

MITCHELHILL, J. P. (1879-1966)
English manager, proprietor
WWT/9-11

MITCHELL, Abbie (d 1960 [76])
actress, singer TW/16

MITCHELL, Ada (b 1880) American actress WWS

MITCHELL, Adrian (b 1932) English dramatist CD

MITCHELL, Ann American actress TW/20, 28-29

MITCHELL, Arthur (b 1934)
American dancer, choreographer
CB, ES, TW/25

MITCHELL, Cameron (b 1918)
American actor BE, TW/5-9,
27

MITCHELL, Charles, Jr. (d
1917) EA/18*

MITCHELL, Charlotte (fl 1840)
English actress HAS

MITCHELL, Colin (d c. 1800)
Scottish actor TD/1-2

MITCHELL, Cooper (d 1918 [37])
EA/19*

MITCHELL, David designer
WWT/16

MITCHELL, Dodson (1868-1939)
American actor, dramatist
WWT/7-9

MITCHELL, Doris (fl 1907-13)
American actress WWM

MITCHELL, Earle (d 1946 [64])
American actor TW/2

MITCHELL, Edith (1834-68) English
actress HAS

MITCHELL, Elihu (b 1861) English
singer GRB/1

MITCHELL, Emma (fl 1853-58)
actress HAS

MITCHELL, Esther (d 1953 [56])
Australian actress TW/2-3, 10

MITCHELL, Fred (d 1890) comedian
EA/91*

MITCHELL, Gary (b 1938) Canadian
actor TW/25-27

MITCHELL, George (1905-72)
American actor BE, TW/28

MITCHELL, Grant (1874-1957)
American actor SR, TW/13,
WWM, WWT/5-11

MITCHELL, Grover E. (d 1969 [60])
critic BP/54*

MITCHELL, G. W. (b 1840) American actor HAS

MITCHELL, Ian Priestley (d 1969
[77]) performer BP/54*

MITCHELL, James (b 1920) American actor, dancer BE, TW/3-
20, 30

MITCHELL, James I. (d 1969 [78])
performer BP/54*

MITCHELL, Jan (b 1916) Swedish
investor, backer BE

MITCHELL, J. F. (d 1888) songwriter EA/89*

MITCHELL, John (d 1856 [57]) actor, manager EA/72*, WWT/14*

MITCHELL, John (d 1874 [68])
manager EA/76*, WWT/14*

MITCHELL, John D. (b 1917)
American executive, director
BE

MITCHELL, John W. [Mark John-
son] (d 1887) professor of living
statuary EA/88*

MITCHELL, Joseph (c. 1684-1738)
Scottish? dramatist CP/1-3,
GT, TD/1-2

MITCHELL, Julian (d 1926 [72])
director, producer BE*, BP/
11*, WWT/14*

MITCHELL, Julien (1888-1954)
English actor, director SR,
WWT/9-11

MITCHELL, Katherine see
Corey, Mrs. John

MITCHELL, Ken (b 1944) American
actor TW/26, 30

MITCHELL, Kittie (b 1868) American actress SR

MITCHELL, Langdon Elwyn (1862-1933) American dramatist DAB, ES, GRB/3-4, HJD, MD, MH, MWD, OC/1-3, WWA/1, WWM, WWT/1-7

MITCHELL, Mrs. Langdon Elwyn [née Marion Lea] (1864-1944) English actress DP, SR, TW/1

MITCHELL, Lathrop (b 1907) American actor TW/6-14

MITCHELL, Lee (b 1906) American educator BE

MITCHELL, Leonard (d 1905) musician EA/06*

MITCHELL, Les (d 1975 [70]) performer BP/59*

MITCHELL, Loften (b 1919) American dramatist, actor BE, CD

MITCHELL, Mae (d 1963 [52]) performer BE*

MITCHELL, Maggie [Margaret Julia] (1832/37-1918) American actress CDP, COC, DAB, HAS, OC/1-3, PP/2, SR, WWA/1, WWM

MITCHELL, Margaret Julia see Mitchell, Maggie

MITCHELL, Mary (b 1831) American actress HAS

MITCHELL, Mason (b 1859) American actor WWM

MITCHELL, Maurine American educator, costume designer BE

MITCHELL, Millard (1903-53) Cuban actor TW/1, 3-5, 10

MITCHELL, Norma (d 1967) dramatist BP/51*

MITCHELL, Mrs. Percival J. see Van Buskirk, June

MITCHELL, Rhea (d 1957 [63]) actress BE*

MITCHELL, Ronald E. (b 1905) English educator, director BE

MITCHELL, Ruth (b 1919) American stage manager, producer, director BE, WWT/16

MITCHELL, Sam (d 1965 [90]) performer BP/49*

MITCHELL, Stephen (b 1901/07) Scottish manager WWT/10-16

MITCHELL, Theodore (d 1938 [63]) American press representative, critic BE*, BP/22*

MITCHELL, Thomas (1895-1962) American actor, dramatist ES, SR, TW/4-9, 19, WWA/4,

WWT/7-13

MITCHELL, Victoria (d 1911) EA/12*

MITCHELL, Warren (b 1926) English actor WWT/15-16

MITCHELL, William (1798-1856) English/American manager, actor CDP, COC, DAB, HAS, OC/1-3, SR, WWA/H

MITCHELL, William (d 1870 [53]) circus clown EA/71*

MITCHELL, William see Revolti, Felix

MITCHELL, William C. manager CDP

MITCHELL, William Henry (d 1901 [51]) manager EA/02*

MITCHELL, Yvonne (b 1925) English actress ES, WWT/11-16

MITCHENSON, William (d 1870 [49]) pantomimist EA/71*

MITE, Mjr. [John Dempster Simpson] (d 1902 [30]) midget performer EA/03*

MITE, General Tiny (b 1864) dwarf CDP

MITFORD, Mary Russell (1787-1855) English dramatist CDP, DNB

MITTERWURZER, Friedrich (1844-97) German actor CDP

MITTLER, William H. (d 1976 [70s]) manager BP/60*

MITTY, Nomi (b 1939) American actress TW/8

MITZI (b 1891) Hungarian actress WWT/4-11

MIX, Tom (1880-1940) American actor DAB, ES

MIXON, Alan (b 1933) American actor TW/22-24, 28-29

MIZNER, Wilson (1875/76-1933) American dramatist SR, WWA/1, WWM

MOBERG, Vilhelm (d 1973 [74]) dramatist BP/58*

MOBERLY, Robert (b 1939) American actor TW/25-26, 28

MOCEK, Henry K. (d 1973) producer/director/choreographer BP/59*

MOCKERITZ, Arnold (d 1857) freak child HAS

MODENA, Gustavo (1803-61) Italian actor OC/1-3

MODJESKA, Helena (1844-1909) Polish actress CDP, COC, DAB, DP, ES, GRB/1-4, HJD,

NTH, OC/1-3, PDT, PP/2,
SR, WWA/1, WWS, WWW/1

MODLEY, Sidney Allen (d 1976
[73]) performer BP/60*

MOE, Christian H. (b 1929) American dramatist, educator BE

MOELLER, Philip (1880-1958)
American dramatist, producer,
director ES, HJD, MWD,
NTH, TW/14, WWA/3, WWT/
5-10

MOFFAT, Dickson (d 1916) performer EA/17*

MOFFAT, Donald (b 1930) English
actor, director AAS, BE,
TW/22-25, 27, WWT/15-16

MOFFAT, Graham (1866-1951)
Scottish actor, dramatist
WWT/2-11, WWW/5

MOFFAT, Mrs. Graham (1873-
1943) Scottish actress WWT/
6-9

MOFFAT, Kate Scottish actress
WWT/2-8

MOFFAT, Margaret (1882-1942)
Scottish actress WWT/5-9

MOFFAT, Winifred (b 1902) Scottish actress WWT/5-8

MOFFATT, Alice (b 1894/90)
German/Scottish actress
WWT/4-7

MOFFATT, Edward (d 1876) equestrian, gymnast EA/77*

MOFFATT, Mrs. Edward see
Moffatt, Rebecca

MOFFATT, Henry Howard see
Howard, Henry

MOFFATT, John (b 1922) English actor AAS, BE, TW/14,
WWT/14-16

MOFFATT, Rebecca [Mrs. Edward Moffatt] (d 1872 [22])
equestrienne EA/73*

MOFFATT, Richard (d 1883 [72])
equestrian EA/84*

MOFFATT, Sanderson (d 1918)
actor BE*, EA/19*, WWT/14*

MOFFET, Harold (b 1892) American actor WWT/8

MOFFET, Sally (b 1931) American actress TW/5

MOFFETT, Cleveland (1863-1926)
American dramatist WWM

MOFFETT, Harold (1892-1938)
American actor BE*, WWT/14*

MOFFIT, James W. (1830-95)
American actor, manager SR

MOFFITT, Harry see Walton,

H. B.

MOFFO, Anna (b 1935?) American
singer CB, ES

MOGUY, Leonide (d 1976 [77]) producer/director/choreographer
BP/60*

MOHR, Gerald (d 1968 [54]) performer BP/53*

MOHR, Marcia (b 1935) American
actress TW/23, 28

MOHUN, Michael (c. 1620-84) English actor CDP, COC, DA,
DNB, OC/1-3

MOHYEDDIN, Zia (b 1931/33)
Pakistani actor TW/24, WWT/
15-16

MOINAUX, Georges see Courteline, Georges

MOIR, Frank L. (d 1904 [53])
composer EA/05*

MOIR, William Wallace (d 1901)
actor EA/02*

MOISEIWITSCH, Tanya (b 1914)
English designer AAS, BE, CB,
COC, ES, PDT, WWT/10-16

MOISEYEV, Igor (b 1906) Russian
choreographer, dancer CB, ES

MOISSI, Alexander (1880-1935)
German actor COC, NTH, OC/
1-3

MOJICA, Jose (d 1974 [78]) performer BP/59*

MOK, Michel (d 1961 [72]) Dutch
press agent TW/17

MOKANA [James Mayer Goldston]
(d 1905 [23]) handcuff performer
EA/06*

MOLASSO, Giovanni (1870-1928)
Italian choreographer, dancer,
impresario ES

MOLESWORTH, Ida (d 1951) Indian/
English actress, manager GRB/
2-4, WWT/1-8

MOLIERE (1622-73) French dramatist COC, ES, OC/3

MOLIQUE, Bernhardt (d 1869 [75])
musician EA/70*

MOLLENHAUER, Henrietta singer
CDP

MOLLIEN, Roger (b 1931) French
actor TW/15

MOLLISON, Clifford (b 1896/97)
English actor AAS, WWT/5-16

MOLLISON, Henry (b 1905) Scottish
actor WWT/7-13

MOLLISON, William (1862-1911)
Scottish actor GRB/1-4

MOLLISON, William (1893-1955)

MOLLISON 674

English producer WWT/6-11
MOLLISON, Mrs. William see
McNay, Evelyn
MOLLOY, Charles (d 1767) Irish
dramatist CP/1-3, GT, TD/
1-2
MOLLOY, James Lynam (1837-
1909) Irish composer DNB
MOLLOY, Joseph Fitzgerald (d
1908) author EA/09*
MOLLOY, Michael (b 1917) Irish
dramatist CD
MOLNAR, Ferenc (1878-1952)
Hungarian dramatist COC,
ES, MH, MWD, NTH, OC/
1-3, PDT, SR, TW/8, WWA/
3, WWT/10-11
MOLNAR, Lily (d 1950) actress
BE*, WWT/14*
MOLYNEUX, Eileen (1893-1962)
South African actress WWT/
4-6
MOMBACH, J. L. (d 1880 [66])
professor of music EA/81*
MOMBER, Harry (d 1917) actor
EA/18*
MONACO, Jimmy (1885-1945)
Italian composer BE*
MONACO, Mario del (b 1915)
Italian singer CB
MONAGHAN, George (d 1889)
music-hall performer EA/90*
MONAHAN, Kaspar J. (b 1900)
American critic BE
MONCION, Francisco (b c. 1922)
American dancer ES
MONCK, Matthews (d 1907 [57])
actor, manager GRB/3*,
WWT/14*
MONCK, Nugent (1877-1958)
English actor, producer COC,
OC/1-3, WWT/5-12, WWW/5
MONCKTON, Lady (d 1920 [83])
English actress CDP, GRB/
1-4
MONCKTON, Fanny (d 1912 [35])
performer? EA/13*
MONCKTON, Lionel (1862-1924)
English composer GRB/1-4,
WWT/1-4, WWW/2
MONCKTON, Mrs. Lionel see
Millar, Gertie
MONCKTON, Lady Louisa (fl
1858-90) actress DP
MONCRIEFF, Gladys (1893-
1976) Australian actress,
singer WWT/6-11
MONCRIEFF, John (d c. 1767)

Scottish dramatist CP/1-3, GT,
TD/1-2
MONCRIEFF, Murri (d 1949) actor
BE*, WWT/14*
MONCRIEFF, Richard (1840-1915)
American actor SR
MONCRIEFF, Rose [Mrs. Newman
Maurice] (d 1916) actress, sing-
er CDP
MONCRIEFF, R. Scott [Cyril
Bowen] (d 1882 [28]) dramatist,
acting manager EA/83*
MONCRIEFF, William George
Thomas (1794-1857) English
dramatist, manager CDP, COC,
OC/1-3, SR
MONDOSE, Alex (d 1972 [78]) per-
former BP/56*
MONEAN, Thomas P. (d 1875
[69]) actor EA/76*
MONEY, Henry (d 1877) musician
EA/78*
MONGINI, Sig. (d 1874) singer
EA/75*
MONIER, Virginia (fl 1834-41)
West Indian actress HAS, SR
MONK, Ada (d 1898 [53]) actress
CDP
MONK, Albert P. (d 1905 [30])
musician EA/06*
MONK, C. W. Montague (d 1895)
circus performer EA/96*
MONK, John (d 1880) musician
EA/81*
MONKE, William (fl 1619) musician
DA
MONKHOUSE, Allan (1858-1936)
English dramatist, critic, jour-
nalist COC, MWD, OC/3,
WWT/5-8
MONKHOUSE, Harry (1854-1901)
English actor DP, EA/95
MONKMAN, Phyllis (1892-1976)
English actress, dancer WWT/
4-11
MONKS, James (b 1917) American
actor TW/3, 5, 13-15, WWT/10
MONKS, John, Jr. (b 1910) Ameri-
can dramatist BE
MONNAI, Mme. singer CDP
MONNIER, Marguerite (d 1883 [19])
dancer EA/84*
MONNOT, Marguerite (d 1961 [58])
composer BP/46*, WWT/14*
MONPLAISIR, Adele (fl 1847)
French dancer CDP
MONPLAISIR, Hyppolyte (1821-77)
French dancer, choreographer

ES
MONPLAISIR TROUPE see Mont-
plaisir Troupe
MONRO, G. see Graham, John
MONROE, Ann Swinburne (d 1973
[87]) performer BP/58*
MONROE, Dale (b 1930) American
actor TW/16
MONROE, Mrs. Dwight Van see
Laughlin, Anne
MONROE, Frank (d 1937 [73])
American actor BE*, BP/22*
MONROE, George W. (d 1932 [75])
American actor BE*, WWT/
14*
MONROE, Lucy American singer
CB
MONROE, Shirley American ac-
tress TW/29
MONRO-MORTIMER, Rosa Susan-
nah (d 1913) EA/14*
MONTA, Rudolph (d 1963 [62])
lawyer BE*
MONTAGNANI, William Francis
Montague (d 1885) EA/86*
MONTAGU, Arthur (d 1909 [36])
actor EA/10*
MONTAGU, Elizabeth (b 1909)
English actress WWT/8-9
MONTAGU, Jane A. [Mrs. Will
Montagu] (d 1911) EA/13*
MONTAGU, Mrs. Will see
Montagu, Jane A.
MONTAGUE, Mr. see Talbot,
Mr.
MONTAGUE, Alicia [Mrs. William
Montague] (d 1877) EA/78*
MONTAGUE, Bertram (b 1892)
English manager WWT/11-13
MONTAGUE, Charles see
Henri, Charles
MONTAGUE, Charles Edward
(1867-1928) English journalist,
critic ES, OC/1-3, WWT/5
MONTAGUE, Daisy (d 1893 [25])
singer EA/94*
MONTAGUE, Edward John Bruce
(d 1876 [25]) actor EA/77*
MONTAGUE, Emmeline (d 1910)
actress BE*, WWT/14*
MONTAGUE, F. J. [Henry John
Mann] (1843-78) actor SR
MONTAGUE, G. H. (d 1887)
marionette manager EA/88*
MONTAGUE, G. L. (d 1901)
comedian EA/02*
MONTAGUE, H. (d 1888) min-
strel EA/89*

MONTAGUE, Harold [Harold Mon-
tague Smith] (b 1874) English ac-
tor, entertainer, producer
GRB/1-3
MONTAGUE, Harry (d 1927 [83])
actor, songwriter BE*, BP/11*
MONTAGUE, Mrs. Harry see
Montague, Margaret Elizabeth
MONTAGUE, Henry (d 1869) actor?
EA/70*
MONTAGUE, Henry James (1843/
44-78) American actor CDP,
COC, DAB, DNB, OC/1-3,
WWA/H
MONTAGUE, Lee (b 1927) English
actor TW/9, 22, WWT/15-16
MONTAGUE, Louise (1871-1906)
performer BE*
MONTAGUE, Louise (1859-1910)
actress CDP
MONTAGUE, Margaret Elizabeth
[Mrs. Harry Montague] (d 1884)
EA/85*
MONTAGUE, Rita (d 1962 [78]) ac-
tress, dramatist BE*
MONTAGUE, Susie [Mrs. Walter
Lewis] (d 1905) actress EA/07*
MONTAGUE, Walter (d 1669) Eng-
lish dramatist CP/1-3, FGF
MONTAGUE, William (d 1869 [73])
actor WWT/14*
MONTAGUE, William (d 1885) les-
see EA/86*
MONTAGUE, William (d 1900 [75])
actor EA/01*
MONTAGUE, Mrs. William see
Montague, Alicia
MONTAGUE, Winnetta [Mrs. Walter
Montgomery] (d 1877 [26]) Amer-
ican actress EA/78*
MONTAGU-SMITHSON, Mr. (d 1891
[64]) actor EA/92*
MONTAIGNE, Frank (d 1896) EA/
97*
MONTALBAN, Ricardo (b 1920)
Mexican actor BE, TW/14-15,
29
MONTANO, Delhi (d 1892) lion tam-
er EA/93*
MONTCHRETIEN, Antoine de (c.
1575-1621) French dramatist
COC, OC/1-3
MONTCRIEFF, W. T. (d 1857 [63])
dramatist WWT/14*
MONTEFIORE, Eade (1866-1944)
English manager, producer,
press representative WWT/2-4,
8-9

MONTEFIORE, Thomas Cecil
(d 1939 [29]) press-representative, manager WWT/14*
MONTEITH, Benjamin (d 1908)
musician EA/09*
MONTEREY, Carlotta (d 1970
[82]) actress TW/27
MONTEROSSO, Emily Jan Madson
(d 1971 [29]) performer BP/
56*
MONTESOLE, Max (d 1942 [52])
dramatist, director BE*,
WWT/14*
MONTEUX, Pierre (1875-1964)
French conductor ES
MONTEZ, Lola (1818/24-61) Irish
dancer, actress CDP, ES,
HAS, HJD, SR, WWA/H
MONTEZ, Minnie [née Folland]
(fl 1857) actress HAS
MONTFORT, Stanley W. (d 1970
[67]) performer BP/55*
MONTGOMERY, Mr. (fl 1807)
actor CDP
MONTGOMERY, Alfred Augustus
(d 1911 [66]) variety agent
EA/12*
MONTGOMERY, Charles (fl 1850)
actor HAS
MONTGOMERY, Charles (d 1866
[56]) clown EA/72*
MONTGOMERY, Charles (d 1871
[30]) singer EA/72*
MONTGOMERY, Christopher (d
1902 [33]) EA/03*
MONTGOMERY, David Craig
(1870-1917) American actor,
producer BE*, BP/3*, EA/
18*
MONTGOMERY, Douglass (1909-66)
American actor BE, TW/23,
WWT/8-14
MONTGOMERY, Earl (b 1921)
American actor BE, TW/10,
12-13, 15, 19-20, 22-25, 30,
WWT/15-16
MONTGOMERY, Elizabeth (b
1902) English designer BE,
WWT/9-16 [see also: "Motley"]
MONTGOMERY, Elizabeth (b 1933)
American actress ES, TW/
10-15
MONTGOMERY, Florence [Mrs.
George Arliss] (d 1950 [77])
actress BE*, WWT/14*
MONTGOMERY, Harry "Scamp"
(1868-1911) American actor
SR

MONTGOMERY, Henry W. (1842-
1908) actor CDP
MONTGOMERY, Hugh Welsh actor
GRB/1
MONTGOMERY, Jack (d 1962 [70])
actor BE*
MONTGOMERY, James H. (1882-
1966) dramatist, actor SR,
TW/23, WWT/2-11
MONTGOMERY, Marshall (d 1942
[55]) American ventriloquist
BE*, BP/27*
MONTGOMERY, Matthew (d 1906
[61]) proprietor EA/07*
MONTGOMERY, Monty (b 1945)
American actor TW/25
MONTGOMERY, Robert (b 1904)
American actor BE, CB, ES,
WWT/7-10
MONTGOMERY, Robert Humphrey,
Jr. (b 1923) American lawyer
BE
MONTGOMERY, Rose (d 1912) actress EA/13*
MONTGOMERY, Walter (1827-71)
American/English actor DNB
MONTGOMERY, Mrs. Walter see
Montgomery, Winnetta
MONTGOMERY, William Henry (d
1886 [76]) composer, conductor
EA/87*
MONTGOMMERY, David Craig
(1870-1917) American actor
GRB/3-4, WWT/1-3
MONTHERLANT, Henri de (b 1896)
French dramatist COC, OC/3
MONTI, Mlle. (fl 1851) actress
CDP
MONTI, Gertie [Mrs. Harry Dale]
(d 1910 [45]) variety performer
EA/11*
MONTPLAISIR, Ippolito see
Monplaisir, Hyppolyte
MONTPLAISIR TROUPE, The (fl
1848) HAS
MONTRESOR, Beni (b 1926) Italian
designer CB
MONTRESSOR, George B. (fl 1833)
singer HAS
MONTRESSOR, Giovanni Batta (fl
1832) singer CDP
MONTROSE, Jack [John Thacker]
(d 1916) EA/18*
MONTROSE, Kate (fl 1873?) singer
CDP
MONTROSE, Marie actress EA/96
MONTROSE, Muriel English actress, dancer WWT/10-11

MONTT, Cristina (d 1969 [72])
performer BP/53*

MOODIE, Douglas (d 1973 [64])
performer BP/58*

MOODIE, George (d 1894) pantomimist EA/95*

MOODIE, Louise M. R. (d 1934
[88]) actress CDP, EA/97,
GRB/1-4, OAA/2

MOODNICK, Ronald see Moody,
Ron

MOODY, Catherine Grace Frances
see Gore, Catherine Grace
Frances

MOODY, Fanny [Mrs. Charles
Manners] (1864/66-1945) English
singer CDP, ES, GRB/1-4,
WWW/4

MOODY, Hilda [Mrs. J. A. E.
Malone] English actress GRB/
1-2

MOODY, John (c 1724?-1813)
Irish? actor CDP, DNB, GT,
SR, TD/1-2

MOODY, John (d 1852 [38]) comic
singer EA/72*

MOODY, Mrs. John, II see
Armstrong, Elizabeth

MOODY, Mary [Mrs. Charles
Williams] (d 1910) EA/11*

MOODY, Michaux (d 1970 [78])
manager BP/54*

MOODY, Ralph (d 1971 [84]) performer BP/56*

MOODY, Richard (b 1911) American educator, historian BE

MOODY, Ron [né Ronald Mood-
nick] (b 1924) English actor
AAS, WWT/14-16

MOODY, William Vaughn (1869-
1910) American dramatist
COC, DAB, ES, GRB/2-4,
HJD, MH, MWD, NTH, OC/
1-3, RE, SR, WWA/1, WWS

MOON, Nellie (d 1907) music-
hall artist CDP, GRB/3

MOON, Peter (fl 1562) actor
DA

MOON, William H. (d 1889 [27])
EA/90*

MOONEY, Harry (d 1972 [83])
vaudevillian WWT/16*

MOONEY, Rita (d 1973 [69]) actress, director BP/57*,
WWT/16*

MOONEY, William American actor TW/23, 26, 29-30

MOOR, Bill (b 1931) American

actor TW/23-26, 29-30

MOORA, Robert L. (d 1971 [58])
critic BP/55*

MOORE, A. C. singer, songwriter
CDP

MOORE, Ada American singer BE

MOORE, Adelaide (b 1865) Irish
actress DP

MOORE, A. E. see Hogarth,
Vladimir

MOORE, Alec [Alexander James
McKenzie] (d 1896 [35]) comic
singer CDP

MOORE, A. P. (b 1906) Irish
manager WWT/9

MOORE, Augustus G. M. (d 1910
[54]) stage manager, dramatist,
journalist EA/12*, WWT/14*

MOORE, Bella (fl 1870) actress,
song composer CDP

MOORE, Bertha [Mrs. Frank Huth]
English singer, actress GRB/
1-4

MOORE, Carlyle (b 1875) American
actor, stage manager WWS

MOORE, Carrie (1882/83-1956)
Australian actress GRB/1-4,
WWT/1-5

MOORE, Carrie Augusta (b 1843)
American actress HAS

MOORE, Carroll (b 1913) American
dramatist BE

MOORE, Charles American actor
TW/24, 26-27

MOORE, Charles J. (d 1962 [84])
American performer BE*

MOORE, Charles Werner (b 1920)
American educator, actor, director BE

MOORE, Chris (d 1975 [55]) performer BP/60*

MOORE, Cleo (d 1973 [44]) performer BP/58*

MOORE, Colleen (b 1900) American
actress ES

MOORE, Cornelius (d 1916) carpenter EA/17*

MOORE, Cullen (d 1975) writer
BP/59*

MOORE, C. W. (d 1895 [32]) scene
artist EA/96*

MOORE, Daniel (d 1873 [54]) comedian EA/74*

MOORE, Daniel (d 1874 [27])
Negro artist EA/75*

MOORE, Decima [Mrs. Guggisberg]
(1871-1964) English actress,
singer CDP, DP, EA/94,

GRB/1-4, WWS, WWT/1-8

MOORE, Del (d 1970 [53]) performer BP/55*

MOORE, Dennie (b 1907) American actress BE, TW/1, 12, WWT/10-11

MOORE, Diane (b 1948) American actress TW/25

MOORE, Dick (b 1925) American actor, director, editor BE

MOORE, Douglas (1893-1969) American composer HJD

MOORE, Dudley (b 1935) English actor, composer BE, WWT/15-16

MOORE, Edith (d 1907) singer EA/08*

MOORE, Edward (1712-57) English dramatist CDP, COC, CP/1-3, GT, HP, OC/1-3, TD/1-2

MOORE, Edward (b 1935) American actor TW/24, 26

MOORE, Eileen (d 1902 [22]) actress EA/03*

MOORE, Eleanora [Nelly] (d 1869 [24]) actress DNB

MOORE, Eliza ["Lion Queen"] (fl 1836) dancer, performer HAS

MOORE, Elizabeth [Mrs. G. W. Moore] (d 1882 [50]) EA/84*

MOORE, Elizabeth (d 1904 [80]) EA/05*

MOORE, Elsie actress, singer CDP, WWS

MOORE, Eulabelle (d 1964 [61]) American actress BE, TW/21

MOORE, Eunice singer CDP

MOORE, Eva [Mrs. H. V. Esmond] (1870-1955) English actress COC, EA/95, GRB/1-4, WWT/1-11, WWW/5

MOORE, Fanny see Buckley, Mrs. W. H.

MOORE, F. Frankfort (d 1931 [75]) dramatist BE*, WWT/14*

MOORE, Flora (fl 1893?) actress, singer CDP

MOORE, Florence (d 1935 [49]) actress WWT/4-7

MOORE, Frances see Brooke, Frances

MOORE, Frank F. (b 1880) American comedian WWM

MOORE, Gar (b 1920) American actor TW/4

MOORE, George (fl 1804) dramatist CP/3, TD/2

MOORE, George (1852-1933) Irish dramatist COC, DNB, HP, MWD, NTH, OC/3, RE, WWT/2-7, WWW/3

MOORE, George A. E. (d 1906 [27]) EA/07*

MOORE, George Austin (b 1876) American vaudevillian WWM

MOORE, George F. (d 1890) music-hall performer EA/91*

MOORE, George Washington, Jr. (1820/25-1909) American comedian, manager CDP, HAS

MOORE, Gerald (d 1897) actor EA/96

MOORE, Grace (1901-47) American actress, singer CB, DAB, SR, TW/3, WWA/2, WWT/7-10

MOORE, Mrs. G. W. see Moore, Elizabeth

MOORE, Mrs. G. W., Jr. see Moore, Mrs. Louie

MOORE, Hattie (d 1898) actress CDP

MOORE, Henrietta (d 1973 [50]) performer BP/58*

MOORE, Hilda (d 1929 [42]) actress WWT/2-5

MOORE, Horatio Newton (b 1820?) dramatist RJ

MOORE, Ioma Mae [Dennie Graves] (d 1974 [73]) performer BP/59*

MOORE, Irene (b 1890) American actress WWS

MOORE, Irene (b 1928) French/American actress TW/6

MOORE, Jack (b 1930) American dancer TW/12-14

MOORE, Jennifer (b 1944) South African actress TW/27

MOORE, Jenny (d 1973 [50]) dramatist BP/58*

MOORE, Jessie [Mrs. Cairns James] (d 1910) English actress GRB/2-4

MOORE, John (b 1814) English actor HAS

MOORE, John (fl 1818-25) American actor HAS

MOORE, John Cecil (1907-67) dramatist WWW/6

MOORE, Jonathan (b 1923) American actor TW/25-28

MOORE, Joseph (fl 1st half of 17th cent) English actor DA, OC/1-3

MOORE, Mrs. J. Warwick (d 1893)

EA/94*
MOORE, Laura singer CDP
MOORE, Laurens (b 1919) American actor TW/24
MOORE, Leon (b 1926) American actor TW/9-11
MOORE, Lillian (1911/17-67) American dancer ES, WWA/4
MOORE, Mrs. Louie [Mrs. G. W. Moore, Jr.] (d 1891) EA/92*
MOORE, Louisa (d 1898) English actress HAS
MOORE, Maggie (1847-1926) American actress, singer WWT/5
MOORE, Marshall (b 1861) Scottish director GRB/2-4
MOORE, Mary [Lady Wyndham] (1861/62-1931) English actress CDP, COC, DNB, DP, EA/96, ES, GRB/1-4, OC/1-3, SR, WWT/1-6, WWW/3
MOORE, Mary Alice (b 1923) American actress TW/3, 10
MOORE, Mary Tyler (b 1937) American actress CB
MOORE, Matt (1890-1960) Irish actor BE*
MOORE, Mavor (b 1919) Canadian dramatist, critic, educator, director, actor CD
MOORE, Melba (b 1945) American singer, actress CB, TW/26-27
MOORE, Michael (b 1942) American actor TW/24
MOORE, Monette (d 1961 [50]) performer BE*
MOORE, Nelly see Moore, Eleanora
MOORE, Owen (1886-1939) Irish actor, producer BE*, BP/23*, WWT/14*
MOORE, Patti (d 1972 [71]) performer BP/57*
MOORE, Percy (d 1945 [67]) Canadian actor TW/1
MOORE, Raymond (1897-1940) theatre founder CB
MOORE, Reginald (d 1880 [41]) actor EA/81*
MOORE, Robert (b 1927/30) American actor, director TW/22-24, WWT/15-16
MOORE, Robert Francis (d 1964 [69]) American critic BE*, BP/48*
MOORE, Roger (b 1927?) English

actor CB
MOORE, Mrs. Sheridan see Harris, Flora
MOORE, Sonia Russian/American producer, director BE
MOORE, Stephen (b 1937) English actor WWT/15-16
MOORE, Sir Thomas (d 1735) dramatist CP/1-3, GT
MOORE, Thomas (fl 1801) dramatist CP/3, GT
MOORE, Tom (d 1955 [71]) Irish actor BE*, BP/39*
MOORE, Victor Frederick (1876-1962) American actor AAS, GRB/3-4, SR, TW/1-16, 19, WWA/4-5, WWM, WWS, WWT/1-13
MOORE, Mrs. Victor Frederick see Littlefield, Emma
MOORE, William A. (b 1825) English singer, prompter, business manager, stage manager, manager HAS
MOORE, William Henry (d 1890 [30]) scene artist EA/92*
MOORE, Wyke (d 1884) actor EA/85*
MOOREHEAD, Agnes (1906-74) American actress BE, BTR/74, CB, ES, TW/8, 19, 29-30, WWT/14-16
MOOREHEAD, John (d 1804) Irish composer, musician DNB, TD/1-2
MOORES, Franklin T. (d 1909 [32]) singer EA/10*
MOOREY, Stefa (d 1972 [38]) performer BP/56*
MOORHEAD, Jean (d 1953 [39]) American actress BE*, BP/38*
MOORHOUSE, Mrs. Charles see Wallack, Fanny
MOOR-JONES, Edna (d 1975 [84]) performer BP/60*
MORA [Richard Price] (d 1901 [25]) gymnast EA/02*
MORA, Thomas (d 1908 [37]) performer? EA/09*
MORAHAN, Christopher (b 1929) English director, producing manager WWT/15-16
MORALES, Santos (b 1935) actor TW/30
MORALT, Mrs. John Alvis see Dussek, Mrs. Jan Ladislav
MORAN, Dominick see Murray, Dominick

MORAN, Don American actor
TW/24

MORAN, F. H. J. (d 1916) musical director, composer
EA/17*

MORAN, George (d 1949 [67])
American performer BE*

MORAN, James (d 1866) musician
HAS

MORAN, Jim (b 1909) American
press representative, performer BE

MORAN, Lee (d 1961 [73]) actor
BE*

MORAN, Lois (b 1907) American
actress, singer WWT/7-9

MORAN, Pat (d 1965 [64]) performer BP/50*

MORAN, Patsy (d 1968 [63])
performer BP/53*

MORAN, Polly (1885-1952) American actress BE*

MORAND, Mary Catharine (d 1894
[56]) EA/95*

MORAND, M. R. (1860-1922)
English actor GRB/1-4,
WWT/2-4

MORANT, C. Ellen (fl 1857) actress HAS

MORANT, Fanny (1821-1900)
English actress CDP, HAS

MORATH, Max (b 1927) American
actor TW/25

MORCHEN, Horace (d 1905) black
& white artist, actor EA/06*

MORDANT, Edwin (d 1942 [74])
American actor WWM

MORDANT, Mrs. Edwin see
Atwell, Grace

MORDAUNT, Mrs. Charles see
Peterborough, Anastasia,
Countess of

MORDAUNT, Frank (d 1891 [40])
ventriloquist EA/92*

MORDAUNT, Frank (1841-1906)
American actor CDP, HAS,
PP/2

MORDAUNT, Mrs. Frank (d
1878) American actress HAS

MORDAUNT, George (d 1890)
comedian EA/91*

MORDAUNT, John (d 1871) actor
EA/72*

MORDAUNT, Louisa Cranstoun
see Nisbett, Louisa Cranstoun

MORDAUNT, Marian actress
CDP

MORDAUNT, Plessy (fl 1871) actress CDP

MORDE, Gertie (d 1902) variety
singer EA/04*

MORDEN, Roger (b 1939) American
actor TW/27, 29

MORDEY, Mrs. George, Sr. see
Mordey, Rachel

MORDEY, Rachel [Mrs. George
Mordey, Sr.] (d 1881 [53])
EA/82*

MORDKIN, Mikhail H. (1881?-1944)
Russian? dancer, ballet master
CB, SR

MORE, Miss see Fawcett, Mrs.
John

MORE, George (fl 1554) actor DA

MORE, Hannah (1745-1833) English
dramatist CDP, CP/2-3, DNB,
GT, HP, TD/1-2

MORE, Kenneth (b 1914) English
actor AAS, ES, WWT/12-16

MORE, Roger (fl 1640) actor DA

MORE, Unity (b 1894) Irish actress, dancer, singer WWT/3-6

MOREAU, Emile (b 1852) French
dramatist WWT/2

MOREHEN, Horace (d 1905) actor
GRB/1

MOREHOUSE, Ward (1897/98/1900-
1966) American critic, dramatist BE, CB, COC, NTH, OC/
1-3, TW/23, WWT/10-14

MORELAND, Mr. (fl 1848) actor
CDP

MORELAND, Abraham (d 1875)
actor EA/76*

MORELAND, Frank (d 1884 [62])
actor EA/85*

MORELAND, George Harry (d 1832)
English actor HAS

MORELAND, Harry actor HAS

MORELAND, Mrs. Harry [née Anne
Jones] (d 1866) actress HAS

MORELAND, Mantan (d 1973) performer BP/58*

MORELAND, Marjorie (b 1896)
American actress SR

MORELAND, Peg Leg (d 1973 [84])
performer BP/57*

MORELL, André (b 1909) English
actor AAS, WWT/9-16

MORELL, Dollie [Mrs. Bond-Sayers]
(d 1908) comedian EA/09*

MORELL, H. H. see Morrell,
H. H.

MORELL, Dr. Thomas (1701-84)
dramatist CP/2-3

MORELLA, Mrs. William [Emma Marden] (d 1889) vaudevillian EA/90*

MORELLI, Sig. (fl 1856) singer CDP, HAS

MORELLI, Antonio (d 1974 [69]) producer/director/choreographer BP/59*

MORELLI, Carlo (d 1970 [72]) singer TW/26

MORELLI, Mrs. Charles [née Lily Macdonald] (d 1876 [29]) actress EA/77*

MORELLI, Charles Francis (d 1882 [81]) pantomimist, scene painter EA/83*

MORELLI, Fanny [Mrs. Henry Rivers] (d 1901 [75]) actress EA/02*

MORELLI, Giovanni (fl 1790s) singer CDP

MORENO, Antonio (d 1967 [78]) actor TW/23

MORENO, Ascension (d 1972 [86]) performer BP/57*

MORENO, Rita (b 1931) Puerto Rican actress, dancer TW/27, 29, WWT/16

MORETON, J. C. (d 1888) phatoscopic entertainer EA/89*

MORETON, John Pollard [né Pollard] (d 1798) American actor CDP, HAS

MORETON, Lottie see George, Mrs. E.

MORETON, Lydia [Elizabeth Harriman Potier] (d 1897) burlesque actress EA/98*

MORETON, Ursula (b 1903) English dancer ES, WWT/9-12

MORETTI, Eleanor English actress WWS

MOREY, Arthur (b 1941) American actor TW/27, 30

MORFA-HUGHES, Ethel Margaret see Hughes, Morfa

MORFITT, Ada (d 1889) performer? EA/90*

MORFOGEN, George (b 1933) American actor TW/30

MORFORD, Henry (1823-81) American dramatist HJD

MORGAN, Lady (fl 1803?) dwarf CDP

MORGAN, Mrs. [Lizzie Rayner] (d 1882 [35]) actress EA/83*

MORGAN, Miss (fl 1836) actress HAS

MORGAN, Miss (fl 1849) actress HAS

MORGAN, Ada [Ada Mary Copley; Mrs. Walter Copley] (d 1893 [25]) actress EA/94*

MORGAN, Agnes American director BE

MORGAN, Al (b 1920) American dramatist BE

MORGAN, Appleton (1845-1928) American scholar WWA/1, WWM

MORGAN, Armel (d 1898) limelight contractor EA/99*

MORGAN, Beatrice (fl 1895-1913) American actress WWM

MORGAN, Charles (d 1917) EA/18*

MORGAN, Mrs. Charles (d 1903) EA/04*

MORGAN, Charles Langbridge (1894-1958) English critic, dramatist AAS, CH, COC, DNB, ES, HP, MD, MWD, OC/1-3, PDT, WWA/3, WWT/5-12, WWW/5

MORGAN, Charles S., Jr. (d 1950 [75]) American producer, director BE*, BP/35*

MORGAN, Clara (d 1882) dancer EA/83*

MORGAN, Claudia [Claudia Wuppermann] (1912-74) American actress BE, TW/1-3, 8-9, 13-16, WWT/8-15

MORGAN, Clifford (d 1908) advertising manager EA/09*

MORGAN, Mrs. Clifford see Morgan, Norah Louise

MORGAN, Diana (b 1910/13) Welsh dramatist, actress WWT/9-16

MORGAN, Mrs. Edmund Nash (b 1857) American dramatist WWM

MORGAN, Edward (b 1866) English actor GRB/1-2

MORGAN, Edward J. (1871-1906) English actor PP/2

MORGAN, Mrs. Edward J. see Bertram, Helen

MORGAN, E. N. see Bonville, Mr.

MORGAN, Etta singer CDP

MORGAN, Fitzroy (d 1912 [50]) actor EA/13*, WWT/14*

MORGAN, Fluellen (fl 1633) actor? puppeteer? DA

MORGAN, Frank (1890/93-1949) American actor ES, TW/6, WWT/7-10

MORGAN, Gareth (b 1940) Welsh
director, actor WWT/15-16
MORGAN, George (d 1949 [67])
performer TW/6
MORGAN, George (d 1975 [50])
performer BP/60*
MORGAN, Helen (1900-41) American actress, singer DAB,
SR, WWT/7-9
MORGAN, Henry (d 1884 [36])
limelight contractor EA/85*
MORGAN, Henry (d 1906) EA/07*
MORGAN, Jane (d 1972 [91]) performer BP/56*
MORGAN, Joan [Mrs. Scott McKay] (d 1962 [43]) American
actress BE*, BP/47*
MORGAN, Joan (b 1905) English
actress, dramatist WWT/5-7,
10-16
MORGAN, Mrs. John Hartman
see Halstan, Margaret
MORGAN, Kay Summersby (d
1975 [66]) designer BP/59*
MORGAN, Laura (d 1884) EA/85*
MORGAN, McNamara (d 1762)
Irish dramatist CP/1-3,
DNB, GT, TD/1-2
MORGAN, Matt (d 1890 [54])
scene artist CDP
MORGAN, Merlin (d 1924 [47])
conductor, composer BE*,
WWT/14*
MORGAN, Netty (d 1881) EA/82*
MORGAN, Norah Louise [Mrs.
Clifford Morgan] (d 1905)
EA/06*
MORGAN, Rachel [Mrs. Walter
Morgan] (d 1868 [38]) EA/69*
MORGAN, Ralph (1887/88-1956)
American actor ES, TW/2-4,
6-8, 12, WWT/6-12
MORGAN, Ray (d 1974) performer
BP/59*
MORGAN, Rebekah (d 1898 [69])
EA/99*
MORGAN, R. J. (fl 1863) actor
HAS
MORGAN, Roger (b 1938) American lighting designer, theatre
consultant WWT/16
MORGAN, Swifty (d 1975 [90])
Broadway character BP/60*
MORGAN, Sydney (1885-1931)
Irish actor WWT/6
MORGAN, Thomas (fl 1817-18)
actor WWA/H
MORGAN, Violet [Mrs. Jack

Ford] (d 1909) mimic EA/10*
MORGAN, Walter (d 1885) pantomimist EA/86*
MORGAN, Mrs. Walter see
Morgan, Rachel
MORGAN, Wilford (fl 1879) singer
OAA/2
MORGAN, Wilfred R. (d 1912)
singer EA/13*
MORGAN, William (1829-1907)
English manager GRB/3
MORGAN, William (d 1944 [92])
actor BE*, WWT/14*
MORGAN, William A. (d 1888 [33])
American singer EA/89*
MORGAN, William Alton (d 1898
[73]) circus performer EA/99*
MORGANTHAU, Rita Wallach (1880-
1964) American educator BE
MORIARTY, Mr. (fl 1847) actor
HAS
MORIARTY, Joanne (d 1964 [25])
actress BE*
MORIARTY, Michael (b 1941) American actor CB, TW/30, WWT/
16
MORISON, Bradley (b 1924) American press representative BE
MORISON, David (fl 1790) dramatist CP/3
MORISON, Patricia (b 1915/19)
American actress, singer AAS,
BE, TW/5-13, 15, 21, WWT/
11-15
MORITZ, Edward (d 1974 [83])
composer/lyricist BP/59*
MORLACCHI, Josephine (d 1886)
dancer CDP, HAS
MORLAY, Gaby (d 1964 [71]) actress BE*, BP/49*, WWT/14*
MORLEY, Mr. (fl 1839) actor
CDP, HAS
MORLEY, Mrs. actress CDP
MORLEY, Charles (b 1938) American actor TW/23
MORLEY, Charles see Cartwright, Charles
MORLEY, Charlotte [Mrs. Joe G.
Scott] (d 1911) EA/12*
MORLEY, Christopher designer
AAS, WWT/15-16
MORLEY, Christopher Darlington
(1890-1957) American dramatist,
manager HJD, WWA/3
MORLEY, D. (d 1894 [72]) journalist EA/95*
MORLEY, Harry William (d 1953
[82]) actor BE*, WWT/14*

MORLEY, Henry (1822-94) English critic OC/1-3
MORLEY, John (b 1914) Canadian actor TW/6-7
MORLEY, Malcolm (1890-1966) English actor, manager, producer WWT/6-14
MORLEY, Robert (b 1908) English actor, dramatist AAS, BE, CB, COC, OC/3, PDT, TW/5-6, WWT/9-16
MORLEY, Ruth costume designer BE
MORLEY, Thomas (fl 1574) actor DA
MORLEY, Victor (d 1953 [82]) English vaudevillian, actor TW/10
MORNINGSTAR, Carter (d 1964 [53]) American scene designer BE*
MORON, Carmen Unda Y prima donna CDP
MOROSCO, Oliver (1875/76-1945) American manager SR, TW/2, WWA/5, WWM, WWT/3-9
MOROSS, Jerome (b 1913) American composer BE
MOROZOV, Mikhail Mikolaevich (1897-1952) Russian scholar OC/3
MORRA, Sig. (fl 1847) dancer HAS
MORREL (fl 1596?) dramatist FGF
MORRELL, Mr. (fl 1810) actor HAS
MORRELL, H. H. (d 1916) producer, actor DP
MORRELL, Millie [Mrs. Walter Scott] (d 1904) serio-comic EA/05*
MORRELL, Thomas (fl 1722-73) dramatist, translator GT
MORRICE, Norman (b 1931) dancer, choreographer ES
MORRILL, Priscilla (b 1927) American actress BE, TW/23
MORRIS, Miss (fl 1797) actress TD/2
MORRIS, Alfred J. (d 1905 [44]) songwriter, librettist EA/06*
MORRIS, Mrs. Allen see Morris, Madge
MORRIS, Annie (d 1880) trapezist EA/81*
MORRIS, Austin W. (d 1887) American advance agent,

manager NYM
MORRIS, Chauncey (d 1917 [42]) English actor, stage manager, manager GRB/1
MORRIS, Chester (1901-70) American actor BE, TW/17-19, 22, 27, WWT/7-9
MORRIS, Clara [Mrs. F. C. Harriott] (1846/48/49-1925) Canadian actress CDP, COC, DAB, ES, GRB/2-4, NTH, OC/1-3, PP/2, SR, WWA/1, WWM, WWT/1-5
MORRIS, Mrs. Cleze Gill (d 1963 [78]) performer BE*
MORRIS, David E. (d 1842 [72]) manager, proprietor EA/72*, WWT/14*
MORRIS, David L. (d 1879) comedian CDP
MORRIS, Edward (fl 1790-99) dramatist CP/3, GT, TD/1-2
MORRIS, Elizabeth see Morris, Mrs. Owen, II
MORRIS, Felice (fl 1903-13) American actress WWM
MORRIS, Felix (1850-1900) English actor SR, WWA/1
MORRIS, Mrs. Felix (d 1954) American actress BE*, BP/38*
MORRIS, Frederick [Frederick Laroche] (d 1881) actor? EA/82*
MORRIS, F. S. (d 1847) actor HAS
MORRIS, Garrett (b 1944) American actor TW/26-30
MORRIS, George Pope (1802-64) American dramatist CDP, EAP, RJ
MORRIS, Howard (b 1919) American actor TW/2
MORRIS, Ida (b 1895) serio-comic EA/96*
MORRIS, J. (d 1870) actor EA/71*
MORRIS, J. actor, singer CDP
MORRIS, Jack (d 1948 [61]) actor WWT/10
MORRIS, John (b 1926) American composer, conductor BE
MORRIS, Mrs. John see Cantrell, Miss
MORRIS, Johnny (d 1969 [83]) performer BP/54*
MORRIS, Joseph M. (d 1882 [70]) proprietor EA/83*
MORRIS, Leigh E. (b 1934) American community theatre leader BE
MORRIS, Lily (d 1952 [68]) per-

former BE*, WWT/14*

MORRIS, Lon (1830-82) minstrel manager & performer CDP

MORRIS, Lorena A. Adee (d 1967 [83]) performer BP/52*

MORRIS, McKay (1890/91-1955) American actor TW/1-4, 7, 12, WWT/8-11

MORRIS, Madge [Mrs. Allen Morris] (d 1896) EA/97*

MORRIS, Mrs. Maesmore [Gertrude Wilmot] English actress GRB/1-3

MORRIS, Margaret (b 1891) English dancer WWT/4-9

MORRIS, Marty [or Marti] (b 1949) American actress TW/29-30

MORRIS, Mary (1895-1970) American actress AAS, BE, TW/26, WWT/8-14

MORRIS, Mary (b 1915) Fijian/English actress AAS, WWT/10-16

MORRIS, Mathias (fl early 17th cent) actor DA

MORRIS, Maynard (d 1964 [65]) agent TW/20

MORRIS, Mrs. M. C. see Ralph, Julia

MORRIS, Mildred (fl 1902-11) English actress WWM, WWS

MORRIS, Mowbray (d 1911 [63]) critic BE*, WWT/14*

MORRIS, Nat (b 1951) American actor TW/29

MORRIS, Newbold (d 1966) executive BP/50*

MORRIS, Owen (1719-1809) American actor HAS, OC/1-3

MORRIS, Mrs. Owen, I (d 1767) actress HAS

MORRIS, Mrs. Owen, II (1753-1826) American actress CDP, COC, DAB, HAS, OC/1-3, WWA/H

MORRIS, Peter (b 1821) American comic singer CDP, HAS

MORRIS, Phyllis (b 1894) English dramatist, actress WWT/6-16

MORRIS, Richard (b 1924) American dramatist, director BE

MORRIS, Robert (fl 1742) dramatist CP/2-3

MORRIS, Theodore (d 1892 [c. 63]) manager, proprietor CDP

MORRIS, Thomas (d 1894) musician EA/95*

MORRIS, Thomas E. (b 1829) American actor, manager, agent HAS

MORRIS, Wayne (1914-59) American actor TW/14-16

MORRIS, William (1873-1932) German/American manager, agent SR

MORRIS, William (1861-1936) American actor GRB/3-4, WWA/1, WWM, WWS, WWT/1-8

MORRIS, Mrs. William see Terry, Florence

MORRIS, William, Jr. (b 1899) American executive BE

MORRIS, William E. (1831/32-78) American minstrel, manager CDP, HAS

MORRISON, Mr. (fl early 19th cent) actor CDP

MORRISON, Mrs. (d 1917 [79]) EA/18*

MORRISON, Adrienne (1889-1940) American actress CB

MORRISON, Allan (d 1968 [51]) critic BP/52*

MORRISON, Anna Marie (d 1972 [88]) performer BP/57*

MORRISON, Arthur (1863-1945) dramatist WWW/4

MORRISON, Bill dramatist CD

MORRISON, Charles P. (fl 1899?) music-hall singer CDP

MORRISON, Effie (d 1974 [57]) performer BP/59*

MORRISON, George E. (1860-1930) English critic, dramatist, journalist WWT/1-6

MORRISON, George Pete (d 1973 [82]) performer BP/57*

MORRISON, Henrietta Lee (d 1948 [79]) actress BE*, WWT/14*

MORRISON, Hobe (b 1904) American critic BE, WWT/15-16

MORRISON, Howard Priestly (d 1938 [66]) American actor, director, producer BE*, BP/22*

MORRISON, Jack (1887-1948) English actor, singer WWT/4-10

MORRISON, Jack (b 1912) American educator BE

MORRISON, James W. (d 1974 [86]) performer BP/59*

MORRISON, Jim (1944-71) American singer, lyricist WWA/5

MORRISON, John (d 1903 [102]) clown EA/05*

MORRISON, John Clark (1828-87)

American actor NYM
MORRISON, Leo (d 1974 [75])
publicist BP/58*
MORRISON, Lewis (1844/45-1906)
West Indian actor, manager
CDP, HAS, PP/2, SR, WWA/1
MORRISON, Mrs. Lewis see
Roberts, Florence
MORRISON, Mrs. Lewis see
Wood, Rose
MORRISON, Paul (b 1906) American designer BE
MORRISON, Priestly (1871-1938)
American producer WWT/8
MORRISON, Rosabel (1869-1911)
American actress SR
MORRISON, Talmadge H. (d
1974 [82]) photographer BP/59*
MORRISON, William James (d
1901) EA/02*
MORRISS, Mary Ann [Mrs. William Morriss] (d 1885) EA/
86*
MORRISS, Mrs. William see
Morriss, Mary Ann
MORRISSEY, Eamon (b 1943) Irish
actor TW/22-23, 25
MORRISSEY, James W. (d 1917)
Irish dramatist? manager SR,
WWM
MORRISSEY, John F. (d 1941
[58]) actor BE*, WWT/14*
MORRISSEY, John J. (c. 1855-
1925) American actor SR
MORRISSEY, Marguerite (b 1920)
American actress TW/5
MORRISSEY, Will (d 1957 [72])
actor, songwriter, producer
TW/14
MORROS, Boris (d 1963 [c. 70])
Russian musical director, producer BE*
MORROW, Mr. (d 1867) singer
EA/68*
MORROW, Doretta (1928-68)
American actress, singer BE,
TW/5-13, 24, WWT/12-13
MORROW, Karen (b 1936) American actress TW/18-25, 28,
30
MORSE, Mr. (b 1784) American
actor HAS
MORSE, Barry (b 1919) English
actor WWT/10-11
MORSE, Hayward (b 1947) English
actor TW/29
MORSE, John M. (b 1911) American architect BE

MORSE, Richard (b 1927) American
actor TW/11-15, 18-20, 24-30
MORSE, Robert (b 1931) American
actor, singer BE, CB, ES,
TW/12-20, 28-29, WWT/16
MORSE, Salmi (1826?-84) dramatist, manager CDP
MORSE, Theodore F. (1873-1924)
American composer BE*
MORSE, Woolson (1858-97) American composer BE*
MORSELL, Fred A. (b 1940)
American actor TW/27, 29-30
MORSELL, Herndon (fl 1882?) actor, songwriter CDP
MORTIMER, Mr. (fl early 19th
cent) actor CDP
MORTIMER, Miss (fl 1803) actress
TD/2
MORTIMER, Miss (d 1874) musichall performer EA/76*
MORTIMER, Allie (d 1866 [8])
actress HAS
MORTIMER, Bella [Mrs. Charles
Dillon] (d 1886 [40]) actress
EA/87*
MORTIMER, C. H. (fl 1852) actor
HAS
MORTIMER, Charles (d 1913 [82])
actor BE*, WWT/14*
MORTIMER, Charles (1885-1964)
actor WWT/9-11
MORTIMER, Mrs. Charles (d 1881)
EA/82*
MORTIMER, Charles Neil (d 1913)
EA/14*
MORTIMER, Dorothy (d 1950 [52])
actress TW/6
MORTIMER, Ellen see Smith,
Mrs.
MORTIMER, Estelle (d 1904 [52])
actress CDP
MORTIMER, George Charles (d
1912 [87]) singer EA/13*
MORTIMER, Henry (b 1882) Canadian actor WWM
MORTIMER, James (1833-1911)
French dramatist GRB/2-4
MORTIMER, John (b 1923) English
dramatist, critic AAS, CD,
CH, COC, MD, MH, MWD,
PDT, RE, WWT/13-16
MORTIMER, John K. (d 1878 [48])
American actor CDP
MORTIMER, John K. (b 1862)
American actor HAS
MORTIMER, Joseph H. (d 1880
[38]) manager EA/81*

MORTIMER, Joseph Parker
Hopwood (d 1884 [36]) EA/86*
MORTIMER, Miss L. (fl 1850)
actress HAS
MORTIMER, Lee (d 1963 [58])
American journalist BE*
MORTIMER, Lillian (d 1941) ac-
tress, dramatist, producer
SR
MORTIMER, Mrs. T. G. see
Saker, Maria
MORTLOCK, Charles Bernard
(1888-1967) English critic
WWT/7-14
MORTON, Mrs. see Chapman,
Charlotte Jane
MORTON, Alfred H. (d 1974
[76]) producer/director/chore-
ographer BP/58*
MORTON, Brooks (b 1932) Amer-
ican actor TW/25-27, 29
MORTON, Charles (1819-1904)
English manager CDP, COC,
OC/1-3, WWW/1
MORTON, Mrs. Charles see
Temple, Henrietta
MORTON, Charles H. (1832-82)
Scottish actor, manager CDP,
HAS
MORTON, Clara (d 1948 [66])
performer TW/4
MORTON, Clive (1904-75) Eng-
lish actor AAS, WWT/8-15
MORTON, E. (fl 1758) dramatist
CP/2-3, GT
MORTON, Mrs. E. see Morton,
Rosamond
MORTON, Edward (d 1922) drama-
tist, critic GRB/1-4, WWT/
1-4, WWW/2
MORTON, E. M. (d 1856) Eng-
lish actor? HAS
MORTON, Mrs. F. [Mrs. R.
Honnor] (d 1870 [61]) actress
EA/71*
MORTON, George (1849-1917)
American actor HAS, SR
MORTON, Mrs. George see
Hawthorne, Louise
MORTON, George W. actor CDP
MORTON, Gregory (b 1911) Amer-
ican actor TW/11
MORTON, Guy Mainwaring see
Traill, Peter
MORTON, Harry K. (d 1956
[67]) vaudevillian, actor TW/
12
"MORTON, Hugh" see McLellan,

C. M. S.
MORTON, James C. (b 1884)
American comedian WWM
MORTON, James J. (1861-1938)
American vaudevillian WWM
MORTON, Jennie (fl 1865) actress
CDP, HAS
MORTON, Joe (b 1947) American
actor TW/30
MORTON, John (d 1907) Negro
comedian EA/08*
MORTON, John (d 1974 [84]) actor
BP/58*, WWT/16*
MORTON, John Henry (d 1911
[62]) proprietor EA/12*
MORTON, John Maddison (1811-91)
English dramatist CDP, DNB,
EA/68, HP, OC/1-3
MORTON, Joseph (d 1884 [29])
actor, minstrel CDP
MORTON, Kitty (d 1927 [65])
American actress BE*, BP/11*
MORTON, Leon (d 1941) actor
WWT/4
MORTON, Louis Russell (d 1917
[68]) advertising agent EA/18*
MORTON, Maggie (d 1939 [82])
actress, producer BE*, WWT/
14*
MORTON, Margaret [Mrs. W. H.
Morton] (d 1899) EA/00*
MORTON, Martha [Mrs. Herman
Conheim] (1870-1925) American
dramatist GRB/2-4, WWM,
WWT/1-5
MORTON, Michael (c. 1863-1931)
English dramatist GRB/2-4,
SR, WWT/1-6, WWW/3
MORTON, Rosamund [Mrs. E.
Morton] (d 1905) dramatist,
critic EA/06*
MORTON, Rosco (d 1887 [42])
conjurer EA/88*
MORTON, Sam (d 1941 [79])
American actor BE*, BP/26*
MORTON, Thomas (c. 1764-1838)
English dramatist CDP, COC,
CP/3, DNB, GT, HP, OC/1-3,
SR, TD/1-2
MORTON, Thomas (d 1879 [76])
dramatist BE*, EA/80*,
WWT/14*
MORTON, Tom J. English actor
GRB/1
MORTON, Mrs. Tom J. see
Bowman, Maggie
MORTON, Tommy (b 1926) Amer-
ican actor TW/5-6, 12

MORTON, W. H. (d 1894 [62])
actor EA/95*

MORTON, Mrs. W. H. see
Morton, Margaret

MORTON, Will H. (d 1895) singer,
minstrel CDP

MORTON, William (b 1829) English actor HAS

MORTON, William (1838-1938)
producer, manager BE*,
WWT/14*

MOSCONA, Nicola (d 1975 [68])
performer BP/60*

MOSCONI, Charlie (d 1975 [84])
performer BP/59*

MOSCONI, Louis (d 1969 [74])
dancer TW/26

MOSCOVITCH, Maurice (1871-1940)
Russian actor CB, WWT/4-9

MOSCOWITZ, Jennie (d 1953 [85])
Rumanian actress TW/10

MOSEDALE, Edward (d 1908
[70]) music-hall performer
CDP

MOSEL, Tad (b 1922) American
dramatist BE, CB, CD, ES,
HJD, MH, MWD

MOSELEY, Hannah (d 1905 [82])
EA/06*

MOSELEY, Thomas W. (d 1971
[93]) actor TW/28

MOSELEY, W. B. (d 1907 [50])
impersonator EA/08*

MOSENTHAL, Solomon Hermann
(d 1877 [66]) dramatist WWT/
14*

MOSER, Hans (d 1964 [84]) performer BP/49*

MOSER, Joseph (b 1748) English
dramatist CP/3

MOSER, Margot (b 1930) American actress, singer BE,
TW/24

MOSES, Gilbert, III (b 1942)
American director WWT/16

MOSES, Harry (d 1937 [64])
American producer BE*,
BP/22*, WWT/14*

MOSES, John (d 1967 [60]) agent,
producer TW/23

MOSES, Montrose Jonas (1878-
1934) American critic DAB,
ES, HJD, NTH, OC/1-3,
WWT/7

MOSES, Robert (b 1888) American
executive BE

MOSHEIM, Grete (b 1907) German
actress TW/1, WWT/8-10

MOSKOWITZ, Dr. Henry (d 1936
[57]) lawyer BE*, WWT/14*

MOSKVIN, Ivan M. (d 1946 [72])
Russian actor TW/2

MOSLEY, John (d 1869 [62]) manager EA/70*

MOSS, Mr. (fl 1786-91) Irish actor
TD/1-2

MOSS, Amelia Hogue Burgess [Mrs.
Joseph L. S. Moss] (d 1916)
EA/17*

MOSS, Arnold (b 1910) American
actor, director, producer, executive BE, TW/1, 3-4, 6-8, 28-
29, WWT/11-16

MOSS, Clarence H. (d 1975 [75])
executive BP/60*

MOSS, Sir Edward see Moss,
Sir Horace Edward

MOSS, Mrs. H. E. (d 1892) EA/
94*

MOSS, Henry (1729-73) Irish actor
GT

MOSS, Henry Charles see Borani,
Charles

MOSS, Sir [Horace] Edward (1852/
54-1912) English director GRB/
1-4, OC/1-3, WWT/1

MOSS, Hugh (1855-1926) Indian/
English stage manager, producer,
dramatist GRB/1-4

MOSS, Mrs. Hugh see Wallis,
Bella

MOSS, James (d 1882 [49]) proprietor, comic singer EA/83*

MOSS, James Edward (d 1904 [23])
EA/05*

MOSS, Joseph Lewis (d 1917 [55])
proprietor EA/18*

MOSS, Mrs. Joseph L. S. see
Moss, Amelia Hogue Burgess

MOSS, Little Dot (b 1890) English
actress GRB/1

MOSS, Mrs. M. (d 1908) EA/09*

MOSS, Maitland (d 1967 [66]) performer BP/52*

MOSS, Marty (d 1973) producer/
director/choreographer BP/58*

MOSS, Mary see Keene, Laura

MOSS, Paul (d 1950 [70]) American
producer BE*, BP/34*

MOSS, Sydney (d 1902 [48]) musician EA/03*

MOSS, Theophilus (fl 1749) dramatist CP/1-3

MOSS, W. (d 1817) actor CDP

MOSS, W. F. actor, singer CDP

MOSS, W. Keith (1892-1935) English producer, director, journalist WWT/7

MOSSENSON, Yig'al (b 1917) Israeli dramatist RE

MOSSETTI, Carlotta (b 1890) English dancer, ballet mistress WWT/5-8

MOSSOLOVA, Vera (d 1949 [74]) dancer WWT/14*

MOSSOP, George (1814-49) Irish actor, singer HAS, SR

MOSSOP, Henry (1729-74) Irish actor, manager CDP, DNB, OC/1-3, TD/1-2

MOSTEL, Samuel Joel see Mostel, Zero

MOSTEL, Zero [né Samuel Joel] (1915-77) American actor AAS, BE, CB, COC, ES, WWT/14-16

MOSTYN, Annie [Mrs. W. J. Gilbert] (d 1877) actress EA/78*

MOSTYN, George H. (d 1885 [26]) business manager EA/86*

MOSTYN, Hallen actor, singer CDP

MOTE, John Hurden (d 1898) lawyer EA/99*

MOTLEY designers AAS, ES, PDT, TW/2-3, 5-8, WWT/8-16

MOTT, Charles (d 1918) EA/19*

MOTTE, Adelina Sophia (1855-96) American singer SR

MOTTER, Charlotte Kay (b 1922) American educator, director BE

MOTTERAM, John (fl 1600-01) member of the Chapel Royal DA

MOTTEUX, Peter Anthony (1660-1718) French dramatist CP/1-3, DNB, GT

MOTTL, Felix (1856-1911) Austrian conductor, composer ES

MOTTLEY, John (1692-1750) English dramatist CP/1-3, DNB, GT, HP, TD/1-2

MOTYLEFF, Ilya (d 1970 [76]) producer/director/choreographer BP/55*

MOUBRAY, Mr. (fl 1798) dramatist CP/3

MOUBREY, Lilian (d 1970 [95]) performer BP/55*

MOUILLOT, Frederick (1864-1911)

Irish proprietor GRB/1-4

MOUILLOT, Mrs. Frederick see Mouillot, Gertrude

MOUILLOT, Gertrude [Mrs. Frederick Mouillot] (d 1961 [91]) actress GRB/1-4, WWT/1-7

MOUL, Alfred (d 1924) managing director WWT/14*

MOULAN, Frank (1875-1939) American actor, singer WWS, WWT/7-8

MOULAND, Florence (d 1897 [19]) performer? EA/98*

MOULD, Raymond Wesley (b 1905) English press representative WWT/10-11

MOULDER, Walter (1935-67) American actor TW/19-20, 24

MOULE, Winifred Ruby see Lee, Vanessa

MOULT, Rosina see Brandram, Rosina

MOULTON, Arthur E. (fl 1891?) actor, singer CDP

MOULTON, Mrs. Charles (fl 1870s?) singer CDP

MOULTON, Robert (b 1922) American educator, dancer, choreographer, director BE

MOULTRIE, Arthur (d 1893) Negro singer, musician EA/94*

MOULTRU, Rev. (fl 1798) dramatist CP/3

MOUNET-SULLY, Jean (1841-1922) French actor GRB/1-4, WWT/1

MOUNFELD, John (fl 1538) actor DA

MOUNT, Peggy (b 1916) English actress AAS, WWT/12-16

MOUNTAIN, Earl B. (d 1962 [74]) performer BE*

MOUNTAIN, Mrs. Rosoman [née Wilkinson] (c. 1770-1841) English actress, singer CDP, DNB, GT, OX, TD/1-2

MOUNTCASTLE, Fanny [Mrs. Charles H. Thorpe] (d 1887) English actress NYM

MOUNTFIELD, Reginald (d 1911) conductor EA/13*

MOUNTFORD, Mrs. see Vanbruggen, Mrs.

MOUNTFORD, Harry (d 1950 [79]) Irish actor, dramatist BE*, BP/35*

MOUNTFORD, Mrs. Harry see Briscoe, Lottie

MOUNTFORT, Susanna Percival

(1667-1703) English actress
COC, DNB, ES, OC/1-3
MOUNTFORT, William (1664-92)
English actor, dramatist
COC, CP/1-3, DNB, ES,
GT, OC/1-3
MOUNTFORT, Mrs. William see
Mountfort, Susanna Percival
MOUNTIER, Thomas (fl 1719-33)
singer DNB
MOURAVIEF, Mme. (d 1868)
Russian dancer EA/69*
MOUVET, Maurice (d 1927 [40])
Swiss dancer BP/11*
MOVAR, Dunja (d 1963 [23]) per-
former BP/47*
MOVING BEING, The theatre
collective CD
MOWAT, David (b 1943) Egyptian/
English dramatist CD
MOWATT, Anna Cora [Anna Cora
Ogden; Mrs. Ritchie] (1819-70)
American dramatist, actress
CDP, COC, DAB, ES, HAS,
HJD, MH, NTH, OC/1-3, RJ,
SR, WWA/H
MOWBRAY, Mrs. (fl 1854) actress
HAS
MOWBRAY, Alan (d 1969 [72])
English actor, dramatist, di-
rector BE, TW/25
MOWBRAY, Charles (d 1909)
EA/10*
MOWBRAY, Fanny (fl 1849) dancer
HAS
MOWBRAY, Laura (fl 1854) ac-
tress HAS
MOWBRAY, Thomas (d 1900 [77])
actor, dramatist BE*, WWT/
14*
MOWBRAY, Mrs. Thomas (d 1885)
manager EA/86*
MOXON, Constance (fl 1888-91)
actress, singer CDP
MOYA, Natalie (b 1900) Irish
actress WWT/6-11
MOYER, Dot (d 1964 [68]) per-
former BP/49*
MOYER, Irene (d 1975) performer
BP/59*
MOYES, Patricia (b 1923) Irish
dramatist BE
MOYLAN, Mrs. Cecil see
Moylan, Edith Mary
MOYLAN, Edith Mary [Mrs.
Cecil Moylan] (d 1916 [35])
EA/17*
MOYLAN, Mary Ellen (b 1926)

American dancer CB, TW/2
MOYLIN, Mlle. see Cochois,
Mme. Michel
MOZART, George (d 1947 [83])
English performer BE*, WWT/
14*
"MOZART BRITANNICUS" see
Cianchettini, Pio
MOZEEN, Thomas (d 1768) actor,
dramatist CP/1-3, DNB, GT,
TD/1-2
MOZLEY, William Orford [William
Orford] (d 1886) EA/87*
MROZEK, Slawomir (b 1930) Polish
dramatist MH
MUCK, Carl (1859-1940) German
conductor ES
MUDIE, Mrs. (fl 1808) actress
CDP
MUDIE, A. S. (b 1798?) actress
CDP
MUDIE, George (d 1918 [59]) actor
BE*, EA/19*, WWT/14*
MUDIE, Mrs. George see Newton,
Adelaide
MUDIE, Leonard [Leonard Cheetham]
(1883/84-1965) English actor
TW/5, WWT/4-11
MUDIE, T. M. (d 1876) composer,
musician EA/77*
MUECKE, Mrs. see Crossley,
Ada
MUELLER, Mrs. (fl 1848) actress
HAS
MUFFORD, John (fl 1590) actor
DA
MUHLMANN, Adolf (b 1867) Rus-
sian singer WWA/4
MUIR, Emily Margaret (d 1883)
singer EA/84*
MUIR, Florabel (d 1970 [81]) jour-
nalist BP/54*
MUIR, Gavin (d 1972 [62]) performer
BP/56*
MUIR, Jean (b 1911) American ac-
tress WWT/9-10
MUIR, Kenneth (b 1907) English
scholar BE
MULCAHY, Cara (d 1901 [24])
EA/02*
MULCASTER, G. H. (1891-1964)
English actor WWT/4-11
MULCASTER, Richard (fl 1561-
1608) headmaster DA, DNB
MULDENER, Louise (d 1938 [84])
American actress BE*, BP/22*
MULDOON, William (1852-1933)
American wrestler DAB

MULHARE, Edward (b 1923) Irish actor BE, TW/29

MULHERN, Harry (b 1897) manager BE

MULHOLLAND, J. B. (1858-1925) manager GRB/3-4, WWT/1-5

MULHOLLAND, Mrs. J. B. see Nunn, Annette

MULLALLY, Don (d 1933 [48]) American actor, dramatist, director BE*, BP/17*, WWT/14*

MULLANEY, Jack (b 1932) American actor TW/11

MULLE, Ida (1863-1934) American actress SR

MULLEN, Barbara (b 1914) American actress WWT/10-16

MULLEN, Jack (d 1972 [54]) publicist BP/57*

MULLEN, Margaret (b 1910) American actress TW/22

MULLER, Harrison (b 1926) American actor TW/8

MULLER, Maxmillian Christopher (1674-1734) German giant CDP

MULLETT, Ann (d 1906 [77]) EA/07*

MULLETT, C. (d 1888 [46]) waxwork proprietor EA/89*

MULLETT, James (d 1909 [70]) manager EA/10*

MULLIGAN, Eugene (d 1976 [47]) dramatist BP/60*

MULLIGAN, John (1827-73) minstrel, circus performer CDP, HAS

MULLIGAN, Joseph see Freeland, Frank

MULLIGAN, Richard (b 1932) American actor TW/22-23, 27-28, 30, WWT/16

MULLIKIN, Bill (b 1927) American actor TW/8-9, 26

MULLINS, Michael (b 1951) American actor TW/30

MULLIS, George (d 1910 [81]) bootmaker EA/11*

MULREAN, Linda (b 1950) American actress TW/30

MULROY, Steve (d 1972 [80]) performer BP/57*

MULVANEY, Constance (d 1918) EA/19*

MULVANEY, John (d 1976 [45]) performer BP/60*

MULVEY, Walter (d 1899 [30])

actor EA/00*

MUMFORD, Mr. (fl 1826-27) actor HAS

MUMFORD, Dora A. (fl 1847?) dancer CDP

MUMFORD, Ethel Watts (d 1940) dramatist CB

MUNCK, Mme. E. de (d 1889 [49]) singer EA/90*

MUNDAY, Anthony (c. 1553-1633) English actor, dramatist COC, CP/2-3, DA, DNB, ES, FGF, HP, NTH, OC/1-3

MUNDAY, Penelope (b 1926) English actress TW/9

MUNDEN, Joseph Shepherd (1758-1832) English actor BS, CDP, COC, DNB, ES, GT, NTH, OC/1-3, OX, TD/1-2

MUNDIN, Herbert (1898-1939) English actor WWT/5-8

MUNDY, Frank (d 1974 [65]) manager BP/58*

MUNDY, John (d 1971 [85]) composer/lyricist BP/56*

MUNDY, Meg English actress, singer BE, TW/4-16, WWT/11-14

MUNFORD, Leslie Talfourd see Leslie, Sid

MUNFORD, Robert (d 1784) American dramatist DAB, EAP

MUNFORD, William (1775-1825) American dramatist EAP

MUNI, Paul (1895-1967) Austrian/American actor BE, CB, ES, NTH, PDT, TW/5-7, 24, WWT/7-14, WWW/6

MUNK, Kaj (d 1944 [45]) dramatist WWT/14*

MUNKITTRICK, Howard see Talbot, Howard

MUNNINGS, Hilda see Sokolova, Lydia

MUNNINGS, J. S. (fl 1803) dramatist CP/3

MUNOZ, Morayma (d 1975 [30]) performer BP/59*

MUNRO, Billy (d 1969 [76]) composer/lyricist BP/54*

MUNRO, C. K. (1889-1973) Irish dramatist MD, MH, NTH, WWT/5-11

MUNRO, Donald (d 1911) manager EA/12*

MUNRO, Douglas English actor GRB/1-3

MUNRO, Ernest Overton (b 1865)

English actor GRB/1

MUNRO, Mrs. Ernest see
Jones, Marie

MUNRO, George (d 1968 [66])
dramatist BP/52*

MUNRO, James (d 1916) EA/17*

MUNRO, Janet (d 1972 [38]) performer BP/57*

MUNRO, Nan (b 1905) South African actress AAS, WWT/9-16

MUNROE, Elizabeth Emma [Mrs.
Walter Munroe] (d 1902 [39])
EA/03*

MUNROE, Harry (d 1875 [32])
comic singer EA/76*

MUNROE, J. L. (d 1856?) American actor HAS

MUNROE, Kate [Mrs. Miles]
(1848-87) American singer,
actress CDP, NYM, OAA/
1-2

MUNROE, Katherine see Munroe,
Kate

MUNROE, Walter actor, singer
CDP

MUNSAL, F. A. (b 1822) American actor HAS

MUNSEL, Patrice (b 1925) American actress, singer BE, CB

MUNSELL, J. (b 1825) American
actor HAS

MUNSELL, Jeanette (d 1974 [84])
performer BP/60*

MUNSELL, Warren P. (b 1889)
American executive, director,
manager, actor BE

MUNSELL, Warren P., Jr. (d
1952 [37]) American dramatist,
manager BE*, BP/37*

MUNSHIN, Jules (1915-70) American actor BE, TW/2-3, 7-13,
16-18, 22-23, 26

MUNSON, Ona (1906-55) American
actress, singer TW/11, WWT/
6-11

MUNTO, Mr. (fl 1793) actor HAS

MUNYARD, James Henry (d 1850
[35]) comedian CDP

MURA, Corinna (d 1965 [55]) performer BP/50*

MURATORE, Lucien (d 1954)
French singer WWA/3

MURCELL, George (b 1925)
Italian actor, director WWT/
15-16

MURCH, Robert G. (b 1935)
American actor TW/26-30

MURCOYNE, Margaret see

Burke, Mrs. Charles A.

MURDOCH, Daisy Adele (d 1887
[18]) actress, singer CDP

MURDOCH, Frank actor CDP

MURDOCH, Frank Hitchcock (1843-
72) American actor, dramatist
DAB, HJD, OC/1-3

MURDOCH, Harry Stark (1845-76)
actor CDP

MURDOCH, Irene actress CDP

MURDOCH, Iris (b 1919) Irish
dramatist CD

MURDOCH, James Edward (1811-93)
American actor CDP, COC,
DAB, HAS, OC/1-3, SR, WWA/H

MURDOCH, John (fl 1783) dramatist
CP/3

MURDOCH, Mortimer (d 1908 [86])
actor, dramatist GRB/4

MURDOCH, Richard (b 1907) English actor WWT/10-16

MURDOCH, Samuel K. (b 1821)
American actor HAS

MURDOCK, Ann [Irene Coleman]
(b 1890) American actress
WWM, WWT/4-6

MURDOCK, Henry (1902-71) American critic BE, WWA/5

MURDOCK, J. (fl 1795?) dramatist
EAP

MURDOCK, John J. (1865-1949)
American manager SR

MURDOCK, Kermit (b 1908) American actor TW/24

MURDOCK, Mortimer (b 1815) English actor, dramatist SR

MURFIN, Jane (d 1955 [62]) American dramatist WWT/7-8

MURIEL, Will (d 1909 [52]) performer? EA/10*

MURIELLE, Constance (d 1887) actress NYM

MURILLA, Edith actress, singer
CDP

MURPHY, Arthur (1727-1805) Irish
actor, dramatist CDP, COC,
CP/1-3, DNB, GT, HP, OC/1-3,
SR, TD/1-2

MURPHY, Arthur Lister (b 1906)
Canadian dramatist CD

MURPHY, Audie (d 1971 [46]) performer BP/55*

MURPHY, Christopher (b 1944)
American actor TW/28

MURPHY, C. W. (d 1913 [38])
English composer GRB/1

MURPHY, Danny (d 1966 [75]) performer BP/51*

MURPHY, Delia (d 1971 [68])
performer BP/55*
MURPHY, Donald (b 1920)
American actor TW/1-13
MURPHY, Eliza [Mrs. Bill
Powell] (d 1900 [88]) EA/01*
MURPHY, Ella [Mrs. P. Murphy]
(d 1891 [38]) actress, music-
hall performer CDP
MURPHY, Frank M. (d 1970 [59])
executive BP/55*
MURPHY, Gerry (b 1934) Amer-
ican actor TW/27-28
MURPHY, Guffer (d 1964 [64])
performer BP/49*
MURPHY, James (1725-59) Irish
dramatist DNB
MURPHY, Jennie see Calef,
Jennie
MURPHY, John Daly (1873-1934)
Irish actor SR, WWM
MURPHY, John E. (b 1855)
actor, minstrel CDP
MURPHY, John T. (d 1964 [64])
performer BE*
MURPHY, Joseph (d 1916 [83])
American minstrel, actor,
manager CDP, SR
MURPHY, Juliette (d 1973 [71])
performer BP/58*
MURPHY, Lillian see Calef,
Lillian
MURPHY, Mark (1855-1917)
actor SR
MURPHY, Mary (d 1887) EA/89*
MURPHY, Mrs. P. see Murphy,
Ella
MURPHY, Paddy (d 1917) come-
dian, dancer CDP
MURPHY, Pat (d 1917) comedian,
dancer EA/18*
MURPHY, Pat see Bodie, Jack
MURPHY, Rosemary (b 1927)
German/American actress
AAS, BE, TW/20-21, 23-25,
27, WWT/15-16
MURPHY, Seamus American actor
TW/25
MURPHY, Thomas (b 1935) Irish
dramatist CD
MURPHY, Tim (d 1928 [67])
American actor WWM
MURPHY, W. H. (d 1912 [60])
musician, singer EA/13*
MURRAY, Mrs. [nee Parker]
English actress HAS
MURRAY, Mrs. see Nicholls,
Elizabeth

MURRAY, Miss see Siddons,
Mrs. Henry
MURRAY, Miss (fl 1860?) actress
CDP
MURRAY, Miss (d 1905) EA/06*
MURRAY, Ada (d 1913 [74]) actress
WWT/14*
MURRAY, Alma (1854/55/56-1945)
English actress COC, DP,
GRB/1-4, OAA/1-2, OC/3,
WWT/1-9, WWW/4
MURRAY, Arthur (d 1918 [24])
EA/19*
MURRAY, Arthur B. actor EA/96
MURRAY, Barbara (b 1929) English
actress WWT/15-16
MURRAY, Braham [né Goldstein]
(b 1943) English director WWT/
15-16
MURRAY, Brian [né Bell] (b 1937/
39) South African actor AAS,
TW/25-26, 28-30, WWT/14-16
MURRAY, Charles (1754-1821)
English dramatist, actor CDP,
CP/2-3, DNB, GT, TD/1-2
MURRAY, Mrs. Charles see
Victor, Ethel
MURRAY, Charlie (1872-1941)
American comedian CB
MURRAY, David Christie (1847-
1907) English actor GRB/3,
WWW/1
MURRAY, Dominick [né Moran] (fl
1853-69) Irish actor CDP, HAS,
OAA/2
MURRAY, Don (b 1929) American
actor CB, TW/7-13
MURRAY, Douglas (d 1936 [73])
dramatist WWT/4-8
MURRAY, Edward (d 1878 [49])
acting manager EA/79*
MURRAY, Elizabeth [Mrs. Leigh
Murray] (d 1892 [77]) actress
CDP, DNB, OAA/2
MURRAY, Elizabeth M. (d 1946
[75]) comedienne TW/2
MURRAY, Emma (d 1843) actress
CDP
MURRAY, Esther Jane (d 1875)
actress CDP
MURRAY, Euphemia see Ellsler,
Mrs. John A.
MURRAY, Fanny see Murray,
Mary Frances
MURRAY, Gaston [Garstin Parker
Wilson] (1826-89) English actor
CDP, DNB, OAA/1-2
MURRAY, Mrs. Gaston see

Murray, Mary Frances
MURRAY, George Cecil (b 1851)
Scottish actor GRB/1
MURRAY, George Gilbert Aimé
(1866-1957) Australian drama-
tist, scholar COC, DNB, ES,
GRB/2-4, HP, NTH, OC/3,
WWA/3, WWT/1-12, WWW/5
MURRAY, Gladys (d 1967 [65])
performer BP/52*
MURRAY, G. W. [George Barker]
(d 1878) comic singer EA/80*
MURRAY, Henry Leigh (1820-70)
English actor CDP, DNB
MURRAY, Henry Valentine (d
1963 [71]) performer BE*
MURRAY, Isabel (d 1879) dancer
EA/80*
MURRAY, James (d 1878 [42])
minstrel? EA/79*
MURRAY, J. Harold (1891-1940)
American actor, singer CB,
WWT/7-9
MURRAY, J. K. [George Edward
Sykes] (d 1905 [64]) English
actor, dramatist, manager,
singer GRB/1, WWS
MURRAY, Mrs. J. K. see
Lane, Clara
MURRAY, John (d 1889 [70])
American actor EA/90*
MURRAY, John (b 1906) American
dramatist, lyricist, composer
BE
MURRAY, John H. (1829-81)
circus manager CDP
MURRAY, John J. (d 1924)
clown, manager, performer
BE*, BP/8*
MURRAY, John W. (d 1868 [30])
actor? EA/69*
MURRAY, Julia [Mrs. Samuel
Brandram] (d 1907) actress
WWT/14*
MURRAY, Katherine (d 1974
[80]) performer BP/60*
MURRAY, Kathleen (1932-69)
American actress TW/16, 26
MURRAY, Mrs. Leigh see
Murray, Elizabeth
MURRAY, Lillian [Mrs. T. B.
Brabazon] English actress
GRB/1
MURRAY, Lucy [Finette Raymur]
(d 1880) acrobat EA/81*
MURRAY, Mae (1889-1965)
American actress, dancer
ES, TW/21

MURRAY, Mary Frances [Mrs.
Gaston Murray] (d 1891 [61])
German/English actress DNB,
DP, OAA/1-2
MURRAY, Michael (b 1932) Ameri-
can director BE
MURRAY, Montague (d 1880) Aus-
tralian actor EA/81*
MURRAY, Paul (1885-1949) Irish
manager WWT/6-7
MURRAY, Peg American actress
TW/23-30, WWT/16
MURRAY, Percy [Percival H. T.
Sykes] (b 1870) English actor
GRB/1
MURRAY, Peter (b 1925) English
actor TW/4, WWT/11
MURRAY, Slade actor, singer CDP
MURRAY, Stephen (b 1912) English
actor AAS, WWT/8-16
MURRAY, T[homas] C[ornelius]
(1873-1959) Irish dramatist
COC, MD, MWD, OC/1-3, RE,
WWT/2-10, WWW/5
MURRAY, Thomasina Pringle [Mrs.
W. A. Davies] (d 1896 [27])
EA/98*
MURRAY, Tom (d 1895 [40]) whistler
EA/96*
MURRAY, Walter (fl 18th cent) ac-
tor, manager COC, OC/3, SR
MURRAY, Will (d 1955 [77]) actor,
director, producer BE*, WWT/
14*
MURRAY, William Henry (d 1852
[62]) actor, manager CDP
MURRAY, Wynn (d 1957 [35])
American actress, singer TW/
13
MURREL, Roger E. (d 1973 [86])
vaudeville agent BP/57*
MURTAGH, Thomas (d 1886) EA/
87*
MURTAUGH, James (b 1942) Amer-
ican actor TW/25
MURTON, Henry (d 1876 [34]) actor
EA/77*
MUSANTE, Mrs. John Wilson see
Waring, Bertha
MUSANTE, Tony (b 1936) American
actor TW/23, 28
MUSAPHIA, Joseph (b 1935) New
Zealand dramatist CD
MUSGRAVE, Frank (d 1888 [54])
composer, conductor EA/89*
MUSGRAVE, Frank see Goree,
Frederick
MUSGRAVE, Will (fl 1900?) actor,

singer CDP
MUSGROVE, Cpt. Forbes (d
1906) EA/07*
MUSGROVE, George (1854-1916)
Australian manager GRB/1-3
MUSGROVE, Mrs. George see
Stewart, Nellie
MUSGROVE, Gertrude (b 1912)
English actress, singer WWT/
9-10
MUSGROVE, Stuart (d 1916 [28])
EA/17*
MUSKERRY, William (d 1918)
dramatist BE*, WWT/14*
MUSKERRY-TILSON, W. (d 1918)
EA/19*
MUSSAY, Ethel Gordon see
Batley, Mrs. Ernest G.
MUSSER, Tharon (b 1925) Amer-
ican lighting designer BE,
WWT/16
MUSSET, Alfred de (1810-57)
French dramatist COC, OC/3
MUSSIERE, Lucien (d 1972 [82])
performer BP/57*
MUSSULMO, Mahomet Achmed
Vizaro (fl 1637) Turkish tight-
rope walker CDP
MUTCH, James E. (d 1974 [84])
performer BP/58*
MUZIO, Sig. (fl 1865) musician
HAS
MUZIO, Claudia (1889/92-1936)
Italian singer ES, WWA/1
MUZIO, Emanuele (d 1890 [65])
conductor EA/91*
MUZZY, Charles (d 1852) actor
HAS
MUZZY, Mrs. Charles actress
HAS
MUZZY, Helen see Muzzy,
Mrs. Charles
MUZZY, William American actor?
HAS
MYDELL, Joseph (b 1945) Amer-
ican actor TW/29
MYERBERG, Michael (1906-74)
American producer, agent
BE, TW/30
MYERS, Mr. (d 1859 [85]) actor
HAS
MYERS, Mrs. (d 1853) actress?
HAS
MYERS, Annie see Phillips,
Mrs. J. B.
MYERS, Bessie Allen (d 1964)
American performer BE*
MYERS, Beverly H. (d 1976 [49])

performer BP/60*
MYERS, Cecilia Dora [Mrs. Wil-
liam Myers] (d 1889) EA/90*
MYERS, Frederick S. (1816-48)
American actor HAS
MYERS, Harry C. (1882-1938)
American actor BE*
MYERS, James (d 1855) clown
HAS
MYERS, Mrs. James see Myers,
Rosaltha
MYERS, James Washington (d 1892
[69]) circus proprietor EA/94*
MYERS, John Edgar (d 1885) actor
EA/86*
MYERS, Joseph C. (b 1818) Amer-
ican actor, manager CDP, HAS,
SR
MYERS, J. R. (b 1810) American
minstrel HAS
MYERS, Louis (d 1916 [53]) EA/
17*
MYERS, Louise (fl 1866?) singer
CDP
MYERS, Michaele (d 1974 [49])
American actress TW/25-26
MYERS, Pamela (b 1947) American
actress TW/26-28
MYERS, Paul (b 1917) American
librarian, stage manager, actor
BE
MYERS, Pauline American actress
TW/2, 10
MYERS, Peter (b 1923) English
lyricist, dramatist AAS, WWT/
12-16
MYERS, Richard (b 1901) American
producing manager, composer
BE, TW/2, 4-8, WWT/10-15
MYERS, Rosaltha [Mrs. James
Myers] (d 1907 [63]) EA/08*
MYERS, Samuel (fl 1849) American
actor HAS
MYERS, William (d 1856) American
clown CDP, HAS
MYERS, William (d 1892) actor,
journalist EA/93*
MYERS, Mrs. William see
Myers, Cecilia Dora
MYERS, William H. (d 1860)
American actor HAS
MYHERS, John (b 1924) American
actor, singer, director BE,
TW/16
MYLDEVALE, Thomas (fl 1423)
member of the Chapel Royal
DA
MYLES, Lynda actress TW/24-28

MYLNE, James (1737-c. 90) Scottish dramatist CP/3
MYLONG, John (d 1975 [82]) performer BP/60*
MYNOTT, Mrs. (d 1890 [81]) EA/91*
MYRON, D. (b 1828) American actor HAS
MYRTIL, Odette (b 1898) French actress, violinist BE, TW/2-4, WWT/4-14

- N -

N. , L. (fl 1735) dramatist CP/3
N. , M. (fl 1706) dramatist CP/1-3
N. , N. (fl 1681) dramatist CP/3
NABBES, Thomas (fl 1637-40) dramatist CP/1-3, DNB, FGF
NADAJAN (d 1974) performer BP/59*
NADEL, Norman (b 1915) American critic BE, WWT/15-16
NADIR, Moses (1885-1943) American dramatist OC/1-3
NAGEL, Claire (d 1921 [25]) American actress BE*, BP/6*
NAGEL, Conrad (1897-1970) American actor, director BE, ES, SR, TW/1-20, 26, WWA/5, WWT/8-14
NAGIAH, V. (d 1973 [70]) performer BP/58*
NAGLE, Mrs. see Cramer, Fanny
NAGLE, Archibald (d 1899) director EA/00*
NAGLE, Joseph E. (b 1828) actor CDP
NAGLE, Joseph E. (b 1828) American actor HAS
NAGLE, Mrs. Joseph E. [Mary Logue] (fl 1847) actress HAS
NAGLE, Kate (fl 1858-59) Irish actress HAS
NAGLE, Rev. Urban (d 1965 [59]) dramatist BP/49*
NAGLER, A. M. (b 1907) Austrian educator, historian BE
NAGRIN, Daniel (b 1921) American actor TW/6-8, 11-14
NAGY, Bill (d 1973) performer BP/57*
NAGY, Dr. Elmer (d 1972 [65]) producer/director/choreographer BP/56*

NAIDOO, Bobby (d 1967 [40]) performer BP/52*
NAIL, Joanne (b 1947) American actress TW/27, 29-30
NAIL, John (d 1905) EA/07*
NAILER, Miss (fl 1770?) CDP
NAILL, Mahlon (b 1912) American actor TW/2
NAINBY, Robert (1869-1948) Irish actor GRB/1-2, WWT/4-9
NAIRN, Ralph (d 1934 [61]) Scottish comedian BE*, BP/19*
NAISH, J. Carrol (1901-73) American actor BE, CB, TW/29
NAISMITH, Laurence [né Johnson] (b 1908) English actor BE, TW/20, 22-23, 25, WWT/12-16
NALDI, Giuseppe (1765-1820) singer, actor CDP
NALDI, Nita (1899/1900-1961) American actress ES, TW/9-14, 17
NALOD, Edward (1857-1919) American actor SR
"NANEYS GOWN" see Clark, Mrs.
NANKEVILLE, William (d 1911) manager WWT/14*
NANNETTI, Romano (c. 1845-1910) Italian singer ES
NANO, Sig. Hervio see Leach, Hervey
NANSEN, Betty (d 1943 [67]) actress BE*, WWT/14*
NANTON, Lewis (d 1871 [31]) dramatist, actor EA/72*
NANTON, Mrs. Lewis [Pauline Burette] (d 1888) actress EA/89*
NAPHTALI, Israel (d 1886 [86]) EA/87*
NAPIER, Alan (b 1903) English actor TW/10, 13, WWT/7-13
NAPIER, Frank (d 1949 [45]) actor, director BE*, WWT/14*
NAPIER, Mrs. Frederick Craig (d 1912) EA/13*
NAPIER, John (b 1926) American actor TW/17-19
NAPIER, John (b 1944) English designer WWT/16
NAPIERKOWSKA, Stanislawa Turkish dancer WWT/4
NAPOLI, Joseph (b 1940) American actor TW/27-29
NARDINO, Gary (b 1935) American talent & literary representative BE

NARELLE, Marie (1874?-1941) Australian singer CB

NARES, Geoffrey (1917-42) English actor, designer WWT/9

NARES, Owen (1888-1943) English actor, producer AAS, CB, COC, ES, OC/1-3, WWT/2-9, WWW/4

NARONI, Mlle. [Mrs. Leopold Leghere] (d 1911 [48]) EA/12*

NARPIER, Mrs. A. B. see Theodore, Mlle.

NASH, Miss (b 1797) singer CDP

NASH, Miss see Davis, Mrs. Henry

NASH, Florence (1888-1950) American actress TW/6, WWT/4-8

NASH, George Frederick (1866-1944) American actor SR, TW/1, WWT/4-9

NASH, Harry (d 1894 [41]) proprietor EA/95*

NASH, John (1828-1901) English music-hall artist CDP, OC/1-2

NASH, Louis Joseph (d 1901 [40]) EA/02*

NASH, Mary (1885-1965?) American actress BE, WWT/4-9

NASH, N. Richard (b 1913/16) American dramatist AAS, BE, MD, MH, MWD, PDT, WWT/16

NASH, Ogden (1902-71) American lyricist BE, CB, HJD, WWA/5

NASHE, Thomas (1567-1601) English dramatist COC, CP/1-3, DNB, FGF, HP, NTH, OC/1-3

NASON, Emma (d 1916 [80]) EA/17*

NASSAU, Paul (b 1930) American composer, lyricist BE

NASSOUR, Edward (d 1962 [45]) American producer, inventor BE*

NASTASI, Frank (b 1923) American actor TW/24, 27

NATALI, Agnes [née Heron] (fl 1848-60) American actress, singer CDP, HAS

NATALI, Fanny [née Heron] (fl 1848-60) American actress, singer CDP, HAS

NATANSON, Jacques dramatist WWT/9

NATHAN, Baron (d 1856 [63]) master of ceremonies EA/72*

NATHAN, Ben (1857/59-1919) Scottish agent GRB/1-3

NATHAN, Benjamin (d 1892) American manager EA/93*

NATHAN, George Jean (1882-1958) American critic AAS, CB, COC, ES, HJD, HP, NTH, OC/1-3, PDT, TW/14, WWA/3, WWT/4-12, WWW/5

NATHAN, Rose (d 1872 [43]) actress EA/73*

NATHAN, Vivian (b 1921) American actress BE, TW/23, 25, 30

NATION, Henry (fl 1574) actor DA

NATION, W. H. C. (1843-1914) English manager, composer, dramatist GRB/2-4, WWT/1-2

NATION, William, Jr. (fl 1789) dramatist CP/3

NATIONAL THEATRE CO. producing manager WWT/14-15

NATURAL THEATRE, The theatre collective CD

NATWICK, Mildred (b 1908) American actress AAS, BE, TW/2-21, 26-27, WWT/9-16

NAU, Dolores (1818-91) actress, singer HAS

NAUDAIN, May (1880-1923) American actress WWS

NAUDIN, Emilio (1823-90) Italian singer ES

NAUGHTON, Bill (b 1910) Irish dramatist AAS, CD, CH, RE, WWT/14-16

NAUGHTON, Charles (d 1976 [89]) performer BP/60*

NAUGHTON, James (b 1945) American actor TW/27-28

NAVARRO, Mrs. see Zulima, Mme.

NAVARRO, Carlos (d 1969 [47]) performer BP/53*

NAVARRO, Emilio (d 1903 [57]) circus performer EA/04*

NAVARRO, John (fl 1635) actor DA

NAVARRO, Mary de see Anderson, Mary

NAYLOR, Henry (d 1879 [61]) actor, pantomimist, prompter EA/80*

NAYLOR, John (d 1898) showman EA/99*

NAYLOR, Robert (b 1899) English actor, singer WWT/7-10

NAYLOR, Sidney (d 1893 [52]) musician EA/94*

NAYLOR, William (d 1888 [76])

stage manager EA/89*

NAYLOR, William Frederick (d 1878 [60]) EA/79*

NAZIMOVA, Alla (1878/79-1945) Russian/American actress AAS, CB, COC, DAB, ES, GRB/3-4, NTH, OC/1-3, PDT, SR, TW/2, WWA/2, WWM, WWS, WWT/1-9

NAZZO, Angelo (b 1939) Indian actor TW/25-26

NEAFIE, Andrew Jacksòn (1815-92) American actor CDP, HAS

NEAGLE, Dame Anna [Marjorie Robertson] (b 1904) English actress, singer, dancer AAS, BE, CB, COC, ES, WWT/7-16

NEAL, Charles Edward (d 1917) carpenter EA/18*

NEAL, John (1793-1876) American dramatist EAP

NEAL, Patricia (b 1926) American actress BE, CB, ES, TW/3-4, 6, 9-19, WWT/13-14

NEAL, Tom (d 1972 [58/59]) actor BP/57*, WWT/16*

NEAL, Walter (b 1920) American stage manager, actor BE

NEALE, Frederick (d 1856) producer, dramatist, manager BE*, WWT/14*

NEALE, Lille Dillon (d 1889 [4]) gymnast EA/90*

NEALE, Thomas (fl 1637?) dramatist FGF

NEALE, W. Vaughan Greek stage flyer GRB/1

NEALIE, Mary (b 1949) American actress TW/30

NEARY, Sime (d 1971 [77]) performer BP/56*

NEATE, Charles (d 1877 [93]) musician EA/78*

NEATT, Fred see Weston, Harold

NEBIOL, Gary (b 1943) American actor TW/29

NED (fl 1590) actor DA

NED (fl 1592) clown DA

NEDD, Stuart (b 1915) American actor TW/2

NEDELL, Bernard (1897-1972) American actor, producer, director BE, WWT/7-13

NEDERLANDER, David T. (d 1967 [81]) executive BP/52*

NEDERLANDER, James (b 1922)

American theatre owner, producer BE, WWT/16

NEDHAM, Marchmont (1620-78) English dramatist CP/2-3

NEEBE, Fred E. H. (d 1897 [54]) manager EA/98*

NEEDHAM, Vincent Loraine (d 1916) musician EA/17*

NEEDHAM, William (d 1903 [41]) conductor EA/04*

NEEL, Mr. (fl 1851) actor HAS

NEELY, Henry M. (d 1963 [84]) actor, director BE*

NEGRO, Mary-Joan (b 1948) American actress TW/30

NEGRO ENSEMBLE CO. theatre collective CD

NEHRER, John W. (d 1972 [61]) performer BP/56*

NEIDLINGER, William Harold (1863-1924) American composer WWA/1

NEIGHBORS, George American actor TW/17-19

NEIL, Jimmy (d 1976 [58]) performer BP/60*

NEIL, Ross [Isabella Harwood] (d 1888 [48]) dramatist BE*, WWT/14*

NEILAN, Marshall (1891-1958) American director, actor BE*

NEILD, Samuel (d 1873 [54]) comic dwarf EA/74*

NEILE, Rufus W. singer CDP

NEILE, William Cyrus (d 1874 [25]) singer, minstrel EA/75*

NEILL, James (d 1931 [70]) actor BE*, BP/15*

NEILL, James (d 1962 [65]) American actor BE*

NEILL, Mrs. James see Chapman, Edythe

NEILL, Richard R. (d 1970 [94]) performer BP/54*

NEILSON, Ada [Mrs. Allen Thomas] (1846-1905) actress GRB/1

NEILSON, Adelaide (1846-80) English actress CDP, COC, DNB, ES, NTH, OAA/1-2, OC/1-3, SR

NEILSON, Francis (1867-1961) English/American dramatist, director WWT/1-3, WWW/6

NEILSON, Harold V. (1874-1956) English actor, manager WWT/5-10

NEILSON, James Gardner (d 1872 [44]) comedian EA/73*

NEILSON, Julia [Mrs. Fred
Terry] (1868/69-1957) English
actress COC, DNB, DP,
EA/94, GRB/1-4, OC/
1-3, WWM, WWT/1-11,
WWW/5
NEILSON, Perlita [née Margaret
Sowden] (b 1933) English ac-
tress WWT/13-16
NEILSON-TERRY, Dennis (1895-
1932) English actor ES,
WWT/2-6
NEILSON-TERRY, Julia (1868-
1957) English actress TW/13
NEILSON-TERRY, Phyllis (1892-
1977) English actress AAS,
BE, ES, TW/13-15, WWT/
1-14
NEIMAN, Adolf (d 1902) EA/03*
NEIMAN, Fred (d 1910 [50])
ventriloquist, variety agent
EA/12*
NEIMAN, John M. (b 1935) Eng-
lish press representative
WWT/13-14
NeJAME, George (b 1953) Amer-
ican actor TW/24
NELIGAN, Donal (d 1975 [27])
performer BP/60*
NELLIGAN, Kate (b 1951) English
actress WWT/16
NELLIS, S. K. G. (1817-65)
American freak CDP, HAS
NELMS, Henning (b 1900) Amer-
ican director BE
NELSON, Mr. (fl 1850) Ameri-
can actor HAS
NELSON, Alfred (d 1894 [64])
professor of elocution EA/
95*
NELSON, Alice Brainerd (d 1963
[79]) director BE*
NELSON, Annette see Brougham,
Mrs. John, I
NELSON, Arthur (d 1860 [49])
clown EA/72*
NELSON, Barry [né Robert Niel-
son] (b 1925) American actor
AAS, BE, TW/6-15, 22-26,
29, WWT/12-16
NELSON, Carrie (d 1916 [80])
actress, singer HAS
NELSON, Christopher (b 1944)
American actor TW/28-29
NELSON, Ed (d 1969 [84]) com-
poser/lyricist BP/53*
NELSON, Edith (d 1970 [78]) per-
former BP/55*

NELSON, Eliza [Mrs. H. T. Crav-
en] (d 1908 [81]) actress GRB/4
NELSON, Florence [Mrs. John A.
Atkin] English actress GRB/1
NELSON, Francis Arthur St. George
(d 1916 [24]) EA/17*
NELSON, Gail American actress
TW/27, 30
NELSON, Gene (b 1920) American
actor, dancer, singer, director
TW/5-9, 27-30, WWT/16
NELSON, Gordon (d 1956 [58])
actor TW/12
NELSON, Harold (d 1901 [35])
manager EA/02*
NELSON, Mrs. Harry Adair see
Nelson, Nellie
NELSON, Harry G. (d 1908) actor
EA/09*, WWT/14*
NELSON, Haywood, Jr. (b 1960)
American actor TW/30
NELSON, Henry (b 1843) English
actor, stage manager GRB/1
NELSON, Herbert (b 1913) Ameri-
can actor TW/29
NELSON, James (d 1794 [83]) Eng-
lish dramatist CP/3
NELSON, Joan (b 1943) American
actress TW/28-29
NELSON, John (d 1879 [49]) actor
EA/80*, WWT/14*
NELSON, John (d 1972 [74]) per-
former BP/56*
NELSON, Mrs. John see Le-
clercq, Carlotta
NELSON, Kenneth (b 1930) Ameri-
can actor BE, TW/8-9, 23-25,
27, WWT/15-16
NELSON, Millie Catherine see
Blanche, Mme.
NELSON, Nellie [Mrs. Harry Adair
Nelson] (d 1898) manager EA/99*
NELSON, Oliver (d 1975 [43]) per-
former BP/60*
NELSON, Ozzie (d 1975 [69]) actor
BP/60*, WWT/16*
NELSON, Peggy (b 1930) American
actress TW/8
NELSON, Raymond (b 1898) Amer-
ican manager, treasurer BE
NELSON, Ruth (b 1905) American
actress TW/26, 28, WWT/15-16
NELSON, Sarah (fl 1860-62) ac-
tress, singer HAS
NELSON, Sidney (d 1862 [62]) com-
poser EA/72*
NELSON, Mrs. Sidney (d 1880)
EA/81*

NELSON, Skip (d 1974 [53]) performer BP/58*

NELSON, Tom (d 1918) EA/19*

NELSON, Violet actress, singer CDP

NELSON, Virginia Tallent (d 1968 [57]) performer BP/53*

NELSON SISTERS, The (fl 1860-62) HAS

NELTHORPE, Mrs. A. R. (d 1917) EA/18*

NEMCHINOVA, Vera dancer WWT/9-11

NEMETZ, Lee (d 1963) producer BP/47*

NEMIROFF, Robert librettist CD

NEMIROVITCH-DANTCHENKO, Vladimir Ivanovich (d 1943 [85]) Russian actor, producer BP/27*

NENO, George singer, actor CDP

NERI, Gaetano (1821-52) Italian actor HAS

NERI, Mme. Gaetano (fl c. 1850) dancer? actress? HAS

NERINA, Nadia (b 1927) South African dancer CB, ES

NERREY, Jessie (d 1906) EA/08*

NERVO, Jimmy (d 1975 [78]) music-hall performer BP/60*, WWT/16*

NESBIT, G. (fl 1733) Scottish dramatist CP/2-3, GT

NESBITT, Cathleen (b 1888/89) English actress AAS, BE, CB, ES, TW/6-19, 29-30, WWT/2-16

NESBITT, Max (d 1966 [63]) performer BP/50*

NESBITT, Miriam Anne (b 1879/80) American actress GRB/3-4, WWM, WWS, WWT/1-5

NESBITT, Robert (b 1906) English dramatist, producer AAS, WWT/9-16

NESBITT, Tom (1890-1927) English actor BE*, WWT/14*

NESMITH, Ottola (b 1893) American actress WWT/4-5

NESTEL, Charles W. see Foote, Commodore

NESTEL, Eliza see Fairy Queen

NESTOR, Mrs. (b 1824) American dancer HAS

NESTOR, Al (b 1920) American actor TW/26

NESTOR, George (b 1935) American actor TW/25

NESTROY, Johann Nepomuk (1801-62) Austrian actor, dramatist COC

NESVILLE, Juliette (d 1900 [30]) actress, singer EA/01*, WWT/14*

NETCHER, Roszika (d 1970 [71]) performer BP/54*

NETHE, John (fl 1550) actor DA

NETHERSALL, John (fl 1550) actor DA

NETHERSOLE, Louis (d 1936 [71]) producer, press representative, manager BE*, WWT/14*

NETHERSOLE, Mrs. Louis F. see Martinot, Sadie

NETHERSOLE, Olga Isabel (1863/70-1951) English actress DP, ES, GRB/1-4, OC/3, TW/7, WWA/3, WWM, WWS, WWT/1-11, WWW/5

NETTLEFOLD, Archibald (1870-1944) English manager WWT/6-8

NETTLEFOLD, Frederick John (1867-1949) English actor, manager WWT/4-8

NETTLETON, John (b 1929) English actor WWT/15-16

NETTLETON, Lois American actress BE, TW/29-30, WWT/16

NEUBURGER, Sigmund see Lafayette

NEUENDORF, Mme. (1850-1914) German singer SR

NEUENDORFF, Adolph Heinrich Anton Magnus (1843-97) German musician, conductor, impresario DAB, WWA/H

NEUMAN, H. (fl 1798-99) translator CP/3

NEUMANN, Elisabeth (b 1906) Austrian actress TW/3

NEUMANN, F. Wight (1851-1924) German impresario WWA/1

NEVADA, Aimée (d 1903) actress EA/04*

NEVADA, Emma (1861-1940) American singer CDP, DAB, WWA/5

NEVERE, Norah (d 1891 [21]) music-hall performer EA/92*

NEVERIST, Kate [Mrs. J. C. Shepherd] (d 1896) actress, singer EA/97*

NEVILE, Robert (d 1694) dramatist CP/1-3, DNB, FGF, GT

NEVILL, Alexander (1544-1614)

English dramatist CP/1-3

NEVILLE (fl 1779) dramatist
CP/2-3, GT

NEVILLE, Mr. (fl 1840?) actor
CDP

NEVILLE, Charlotte [Sophie Charlotte Garbois; Mrs. W. H.
Garbois] (d 1891) EA/92*

NEVILLE, Emily see Loder,
Mrs., II

NEVILLE, Fred (d 1899) minstrel
EA/00*

NEVILLE, Harry (d 1945 [77])
actor TW/1

NEVILLE, Henry (d 1694) English
dramatist CP/2-3

NEVILLE, Henry [Henry Gart-
side] (1837-1910) English actor
CDP, DNB, DP, GRB/1-4,
OAA/1-2, OC/1-3, WWW/1

NEVILLE, John (b 1925) English
actor, director, manager AAS,
BE, CB, COC, ES, TW/13-15,
WWT/12-16

NEVILLE, John Gartside (d 1874
[87]) actor, manager EA/75*,
WWT/14*

NEVILLE, Katie (d 1964 [94])
performer BP/49*

NEVILLE, Mary C. H. [Mrs.
George Gartside-Neville] (d
1899 [67]) EA/00*

NEVIN, Arthur Finley (1871-1943)
American composer HJD,
WWA/2, WWM

NEVIN, Gordon Balch (1892-1943)
American composer WWA/2

NEVIN, Hardwick (d 1965 [68])
dramatist BP/50*

NEVIN, P. J. (d 1893) stage
manager EA/94*

NEVINS, Claudette American actress TW/24-26

NEVIS, Ben (fl 1890s?) actor,
singer CDP

NEVIT, Thomas (d 1873 [36])
chairman EA/74*

NEWALL, Guy (1885-1937) English actor WWT/6-8

NEWARK, William (fl 1493-1509)
master of the Chapel Royal
DA

NEWAY, Patricia (b 1919) American singer, actress AAS,
BE, WWT/15-16

NEWBERRY, Barbara (b 1910)
American actress, dancer
WWT/8

NEWBORN, Abe (b 1920) American
talent representative BE

NEWBURG, Frank (d 1969 [83])
performer BP/54*

NEWBURN, George (d 1918) EA/19*

NEWBURY, Pollie [Mrs. Frederick
Wolstenholme] (d 1891 [27])
music-hall performer EA/92*

NEWBY, John J. (d 1876 [23]) musician EA/77*

NEWCASTLE, Duchess of see
Cavendish, Margaret

NEWCASTLE, Duke of see Cavendish, William

NEWCOMB, Bobby (1847-88) minstrel CDP

NEWCOMB, George (d 1890 [54])
lion tamer EA/91*

NEWCOMB, Mary (1897-1966)
American actress TW/23, WWT/
6-12

NEWCOMB, William W. (1823/30-
77) American comedian, manager
CDP, HAS

NEWCOMBE, Albert (d 1881 [48])
acting manager, treasurer EA/
82*

NEWCOMBE, Arthur (d 1883 [34])
business manager EA/84*

NEWCOMBE, Caroline (d 1941 [69])
actress BE*, WWT/14*

NEWCOMBE, Effie singer CDP

NEWCOMBE, Jessamine (d 1961)
actress WWT/14*

NEWCOMBE, John Reilly (d 1887
[84]) lessee EA/86*

NEWCOMBE, Mabel [Frances Mabel
D'Erne] (d 1890 [25]) actress
EA/91*

NEWELL, Frank (b 1946) American
actor TW/25

NEWELL, Joan (b 1921) English
actress TW/4

NEWELL, Michael (b 1931) English
actor TW/4

NEWELL, Raymond (b 1894) English actor, singer WWT/7-11

NEWELL, Thomas (d 1899 [61])
actor EA/00*

NEWELL, Tom D. (d 1935 [45])
actor BE*, WWT/14*

NEWELL, William (d 1967 [73])
performer BP/51*

NEWES, Tilly (1886-1970) actress
COC

NEWHALL, Patricia American actress, director, producer BE

NEWHAM, Rose [Mrs. A. M.

Stuart] (d 1905) actress GRB/1
NEWHAM, Mrs. W. H. (d 1883)
EA/84*
NEWHAM, William (d 1870) come-
dian, pantaloon EA/71*
NEWHOUSE, Alice Lily see
Lena, Lily
NEWHOUSE, Willie (d 1911) trick
bicyclist EA/12*
NEWLAND, David (d 1879) property
master EA/80*
NEWLAND, Mary [Lilian Oldfield]
(b 1905) English actress WWT/
7-8
NEWLAND, Samuel (d 1867) Negro
comedian EA/68*
NEW LAYFAYETTE THEATRE
theatre collective CD
NEWLEY, Anthony (b 1931) Eng-
lish actor, director, composer,
writer, singer AAS, BE, CB,
CD, TW/19, 21-22, WWT/14-
16
NEWMAN, Mjr. A. A. (d 1908)
EA/09*
NEWMAN, Alfred (d 1970 [68])
composer/lyricist BP/54*
NEWMAN, Benjamin (d 1875)
carpenter EA/76*
NEWMAN, Claude (1903/08-74)
English dancer WWT/9-12
NEWMAN, Ellen (b 1950) Amer-
ican actress TW/29-30
NEWMAN, George (d 1871 [48])
comic singer EA/72*
NEWMAN, Greatrex (b 1892) Eng-
lish lyricist, librettist, drama-
tist BE, WWT/6-15
NEWMAN, Joseph J. (d 1967 [80])
ticket broker BP/52*
NEWMAN, Martin (b 1924) Amer-
ican actor TW/8-9, 27
NEWMAN, Paul (b 1925) Ameri-
can actor AAS, BE, CB,
ES, TW/9-21, WWT/13-15
NEWMAN, Phyllis (b 1935)
American actress, singer
BE, TW/15, 18-19, 23-24,
28-30, WWT/16
NEWMAN, Stephen D. (b 1943)
American actor TW/27-30
NEWMAN, Stuart see Ander-
son, Stuart
NEWMAN, Thomas (fl 1627)
translator CP/1-3
NEWMAN, Thomas Edmund see
Wenman, Thomas Edmund
NEWMAN, Mrs. W. see

Ormonde, Nelly
NEWMAN, Will (d 1905 [36]) actor,
singer CDP
NEWMAN, W. S. (d 1897) music-
hall comedian EA/98*
NEWMAR, Julie (b 1935) American
actress, singer, dancer BE,
TW/15
NEWNHAM-DAVIS, Lieut. -Col.
Nathaniel (1854-1917) English
critic, producer, dramatist
GRB/1-4, WWT/1-3
NEWSHAM, Mrs. (fl 1790) white
negress CDP
NEWSOM, Earl (d 1973 [75]) pub-
licist BP/57*
NEWSOME, Carman (d 1974 [62])
performer BP/59*
NEWSOME, James (d 1912 [87])
circus proprietor EA/13*
NEWSOME, Mrs. James see
Newsome, Pauline
NEWSOME, Pauline [Mrs. James
Newsome] (d 1904 [78]) EA/05*
NEWSOME, W. H. (d 1917 [73])
EA/18*
NEWSON-SMITH, Elizabeth [Mrs.
Henry Newson-Smith] (d 1898
[43]) EA/99*
NEWSON-SMITH, Henry (d 1898
[43]) music-hall director EA/99*
NEWSON-SMITH, Mrs. Henry see
Newson-Smith, Elizabeth
NEWTE, Horace Wykeham (d 1949
[80]) dramatist WWW/4
NEWTON, Adelaide [Mrs. George
Mudie] (d 1900) singer, actress
EA/01*, WWT/14*
NEWTON, Amelia [Mrs. Thomas
Thorne] (d 1884) actress WWT/
14*
NEWTON, Eliza (d 1882) Scottish
actress CDP, HAS
NEWTON, Elizabeth Blanche [Mrs.
Charles J. Barber] (d 1893)
EA/94*
NEWTON, George (d 1880) actor
EA/81*
NEWTON, Henry Chance (1854-
1931) English critic, dramatist,
lyricist GRB/1-4, WWT/1-6,
WWW/3
NEWTON, James (fl 1722) drama-
tist CP/2-3
NEWTON, John (d 1625) English
actor DA, OC/1-3
NEWTON, John (d 1872) comedian,
singer EA/73*

NEWTON, John (b 1925) American actor TW/29-30

NEWTON, Kate (1842-73) actress CDP, HAS

NEWTON, Kate (d 1940 [94]) actress BE*, WWT/14*

NEWTON, Richard (b 1911) Canadian actor TW/3, 10

NEWTON, Robert (1905-56) English actor ES, TW/12, WWT/9-11, WWW/5

NEWTON, Theodore (1904-63) American actor TW/5-7, 19

NEWTON, Thomas (d 1607) English translator CP/1-3

NEY, Marie (b 1895) English actress AAS, WWT/5-14

NEYLIN, James (b 1920) Irish actor TW/12-15

NGUGI, James T. (b 1938) Nigerian dramatist CD

NIBLO, Fred (1874-1948) American actor, entertainer ES, TW/5, WWM

NIBLO, William (1789-1878) Irish/American manager CDP, DAB, WWA/H

NICANDER, Edwin (1876-1951) American actor TW/7, WWT/7

NICCOLS, [Richard] (b 1584) dramatist CP/2-3, FGF

NICHOL, Charles (d 1894) actor EA/95*

NICHOLAS (fl 1626-31) actor DA

NICHOLAS, Denise (d 1944) American actress TW/24

NICHOLAS, Fayard performer TW/2

NICHOLAS, Harold performer TW/2

NICHOLAS, Harry (fl 1574?) dramatist CP/3

NICHOLL, William (d 1902 [50]) singer EA/03*

NICHOLLS, Agnes [Mrs. Hamilton Harty] English singer GRB/1

NICHOLLS, Allan (b 1945) Canadian actor TW/28-29

NICHOLLS, Anne (1891/96-1966) American dramatist, producing manager, actress BE, MH, MWD, NTH, TW/23, WWA/4, WWT/5-11

NICHOLLS, Anthony (b 1907) English actor AAS, WWT/14-16

NICHOLLS, Bernhard Downs (d 1886) musician EA/87*

NICHOLLS, Elizabeth [Mrs. Mur-

ray] (d 1887 [55]) actress EA/88*

NICHOLLS, Harry (1852-1926) English actor CDP, DP, GRB/1-4, WWT/1-5, WWW/2

NICHOLLS, Richard (b 1900) English actor TW/25-26

NICHOLLS, W. Dutton (d 1917) EA/18*

NICHOLS, Anne see Nicholls, Anne

NICHOLS, Beatrice (d 1970 [78]) actress TW/27

NICHOLS, Beverley (b 1898/99) composer, critic WWT/6-14

NICHOLS, Emma J. [née Davis] (b 1841) American singer HAS

NICHOLS, George A. (b 1872) American musical director WWM

NICHOLS, Guy (d 1928 [65]) actor BE*, BP/12*

NICHOLS, Master Horace circus performer CDP

NICHOLS, Mrs. Horace F. [née Barker; Mrs. Preston] (fl 1828) American actress HAS

NICHOLS, Joseph V. (b 1846) glass blower CDP

NICHOLS, Les (d 1964 [63]) performer BP/49*

NICHOLS, Lewis (b 1903) American critic WWT/10-11

NICHOLS, Marjorie J. (d 1970) performer BP/55*

NICHOLS, Mike (b 1931) German/American actor, director AAS, BE, CB, ES, WWT/14-16

NICHOLS, Noreen (b 1945) American actress TW/26

NICHOLS, Peter (b 1927) English dramatist, director AAS, CD, COC, MH, PDT, WWT/15-16

NICHOLS, Robert Malise Bowyer (1893-1944) English dramatist WWW/4

NICHOLS, William American actor TW/4

NICHOLSON, Alfred (d 1870 [48]) musician EA/71*

NICHOLSON, Alfred C. (d 1909 [60]) professor of music EA/10*

NICHOLSON, Anne P. (b 1920) American manager, dramatist BE

NICHOLSON, Arthur W. (d 1882) EA/83*

NICHOLSON, Charles (1795-1837)

musician, composer CDP
NICHOLSON, George (d 1907 [73])
proprietor EA/08*
NICHOLSON, G. W. singer, actor
CDP
NICHOLSON, Henry (d 1907 [83])
musician EA/08*
NICHOLSON, H. O. (b 1868)
Swedish actor WWT/4-9
NICHOLSON, Jack (d 1917) EA/
18*
NICHOLSON, James (d 1972 [56])
producer/director/choreographer
BP/57*
NICHOLSON, John (d 1916) come-
dian EA/17*
NICHOLSON, John (d 1934 [61])
American actor BE*, BP/19*
NICHOLSON, Kenyon (b 1894)
American dramatist BE,
NTH, WWT/6-13
NICHOLSON, Nora (1889/92-1973)
English actress AAS, WWT/
11-15
NICHOLSON, Norman (b 1914)
English dramatist CH
NICHOLSON, Renton (d 1861 [52])
EA/72*
NICHOLSON, Val (d 1898) musi-
cian EA/00*
NICHOLSON, Sir William (d 1949
[77]) designer, artist BE*,
WWT/14*
NICHOLSON, William Henry (d
1875 [28]) musician EA/76*
NICHTERN, Claire (b 1920)
American producer BE
NICK (fl 1590-1603) actor DA
NICKEL, Paul (d 1975 [35]) per-
former BP/60*
NICKERSON, Emily H. (d 1889)
American actress EA/90*
NICKERSON, Shane (b 1964)
American actor TW/29-30
NICKINSON, Charlotte (fl 1858-
64) actress CDP, HAS
NICKINSON, Isabella (1847-1906)
actress BE*
NICKINSON, John (1808-64) Eng-
lish actor, stage manager
CDP, HAS, SR
NICKINSON, Isabella see Wal-
cot, Isabella
NICKINSON, Virginia see
Marlowe, Mrs. Owen
NICKLE, Robert (b 1842) Ameri-
can magician CDP, HAS
NICKLIN, Horace Montgomery

(d 1880 [34]) actor, musician
EA/81*
NICKOLE, Leonidas (b 1929) Amer-
ican educator BE
NICOL, Mrs. (fl 1834) actress
CDP, DNB
NICOL, Alex (b 1919) American
actor, director BE
NICOL, Emma (1801-77) actress
DNB
NICOL, Lesslie Scottish actress
TW/23, 30
NICOLINI, Ernesto (1834-98) French
singer ES
NICOLL, Allardyce (1894-1976)
Scottish historian BE, COC,
ES, NTH, OC/1-3, PDT, WWT/
6-16
NICOLL, Basilius sharer DA
NICOLL, Harry N. (d 1962 [73])
vaudeville agent BE*
NICOLL, Oliver H. (d 1971 [67])
manager BP/56*
NICOLSON, T. Smyth see Beau-
fort, Leslie
NIDORF, Mike (d 1975 [60s]) agent
BP/60*
NIELSEN, Alice [Mrs. Benjamin
Wentwig] (1870/76-1943) Ameri-
can singer CDP, DAB, GRB/
1-4, PP/2, SR, WWA/2, WWM,
WWS, WWT/2-7
NIELSEN, Asta (d 1972 [90]) per-
former BP/57*
NIELSEN, Karl (d 1975 [85]?)
American stage manager BE
NIELSEN, Leslie (b 1926) Canadian
actor TW/9-10
NIELSON, Robert see Nelson,
Barry
NIEMEYER, Joseph H. (d 1965
[78]) performer BP/50*
NIESEN, Claire (d 1963 [40]) per-
former BP/48*
NIESEN, Gertrude (1910/17-75)
American actress, singer TW/
1-8, WWT/9-11
NIGHTINGALE, Alfred (d 1957
[67]) general manager BE*,
WWT/14*
NIGHTINGALE, Joe actor WWT/
4-6
NIGHTINGALE, John William (d
1911 [60]) proprietor EA/12*
NIGHTINGALE, W. H. (d 1841)
imitator EA/72*
NIJINSKA, Bronislava (1891-1972)
Russian dancer, choreographer

ES, WWT/9-11
NIJINSKY, Vaslav (1890-1950)
Russian dancer, choreographer
CB, ES, TW/6, WWA/4,
WWT/4, 10
NIKI, Mariko Japanese actor
TW/10-12
NIKITA, Louise (b 1872) singer
CDP
NIKITINA, Alice (b 1909) Russian
dancer ES, WWT/7-10
NIKOLA, Louis (b 1878) English
prestidigitateur & shadowgraphist
GRB/1
NIKOLAIS, Alwin (b 1912) Amer-
ican choreographer, composer,
designer CB, CD
NILES, Mary Ann (b 1933) Amer-
ican actress TW/21-30
NILES, P. James (1851-82)
singer, dancer CDP
NILL, John (fl 1601) actor DA
NILLO, David (b 1918) American
actor TW/2-3, 15-16, 24
NILLSON, Anna Q. (d 1974 [85])
actress BP/58*, WWT/16*
NILLSON, Carlotta (c. 1878-1951)
Swedish/American actress
GRB/3-4, TW/8, WWS, WWT/
1-5
NILSON, Einar (d 1964 [83]) com-
poser, conductor BE*
NILSON, Loy (b 1918) American
actor TW/2
NILSSON, Anna Q. see Nillson,
Anna Q.
NILSSON, Birgit (b 1918) Swedish
singer CB, ES
NILSSON, Christine (1843-1921)
Swedish singer CDP, ES,
WWW/2
NIMMO, Andrew (d 1872 [54])
agent EA/73*
NIMMO, Derek (b 1932) English
actor AAS, WWT/15-16
NIMS, Letha (b 1917) American
executive BE
NIRDLINGER, Charles Frederic
(d 1940 [77]) dramatist, critic
BE*, WWT/14*
NIRDLINGER, Jane Nixon (d 1971
[80]) performer BP/56*
NISBET, John Ferguson (1851-99)
Scottish critic WWW/1
NISBETT, Louisa Cranstoun
[Louisa Cranstoun Mordaunt]
(1812?-58) actress CDP, DNB
NISBETT, William Walker (d

1905 [83]) EA/06*
NISH, Antony (d 1874 [43]) musical
director EA/75*
NISITA, Giovanni (d 1962 [66])
singer BE*
NISSEN, Brian (b 1927) English ac-
tor WWT/10-13
NISSEN, Greta [Grethe Ruzt-Nissen]
(b 1906) Norwegian dancer, ac-
tress WWT/8-10
NISSEN, Peter (b 1964) American
actor TW/29
NISSEN-SALOMAN, Henrietta (d
1879 [58]) singer EA/80*
NIXEN, Gilbert S. (b 1795) Ameri-
can actor HAS
NIXON, Adelaide (1848-75) Ameri-
can singer, equestrienne, dancer
CDP, HAS
NIXON, Caroline L. (d 1864) Amer-
ican equestrienne HAS
NIXON, Charles Elston (b 1860)
American editor, dramatist
WWA/4
NIXON, Hugh (d 1921 [62]) actor
BE*, BP/5*
NIXON, Rebecca see Sinclair,
Rebecca
NIXON, Samuel F. (b 1848) Amer-
ican manager WWA/4, WWM
NIXON, Thomas (d 1896 [34]) mu-
sic-hall performer EA/97*
NIXON, William Joseph (d 1902
[43]) marionettist EA/03*
NIXON-NIRDLINGER, Fred G. (d
1931 [54]) theatre owner BE*,
BP/15*, WWT/14*
NIX-WEBBER, G. (b 1872) English
actor GRB/1-2
NIZER, Louis (b 1902) English
lawyer, writer BE
NKOSI, Lewis (b 1936) South Afri-
can/English dramatist CD
NOAH, Moredecai Manuel (1785-
1851) American dramatist
CDP, COC, DAB, EAP, HJD,
OC/1-3, RJ, SR
NOAH, Rachel Adine (b 1845)
American actress HAS
NOAKES, Frances [Mrs. J. Noakes]
(d 1895 [56]) EA/96*
NOAKES, Mrs. J. see Noakes,
Frances
NOAKES, Richard John (d 1908
[33]) EA/09*
NOBLE, Mr. (fl 1803-05) actor
GT, TD/2
NOBLE, Monsieur le (fl 1718?)

French dramatist CP/1-3, GT
NOBLE, Dennis (1898-1966) English actor, singer WWT/7-11, WWW/6
NOBLE, Florence (fl 1866-67) actress HAS
NOBLE, James (b 1922) American actor TW/6-8, 23, 25-28
NOBLE, John (d 1875) circus tent master EA/76*
NOBLE, Milner (b 1878) English actor GRB/1
NOBLE, Milton American actor, dramatist SR
NOBLE, Tim (b 1945) American actor TW/28
NOBLE, Vernon (d 1909 [28]) performer? EA/10*
NOBLE, William (b 1921) American dramatist BE
NOBLES, Dolly (d 1930 [67]) American actress BE*, BP/15*
NOBLES, Milton (1847-1924) American actor, dramatist CDP, WWA/1, WWM, WWS
NOBLES, Milton, Jr. (d 1925 [32]) American actor BE*, BP/9*
NOBLET, Lise (fl 1821) French dancer CDP
NOEHDEN, N. H. (fl 1798) translator CP/3
NOEL, Craig R. (b 1915) American producer, director BE
NOEL, Nancy actress CDP
NOEL, Nestor (d 1874 [37]) manager EA/74*
NOEL, Tom (b 1911) American actor TW/23
NOEL, W. H. actor, singer CDP
NOEMI, Lea (d 1973 [90]) actress TW/30
NOKES, James (d 1696) English actor COC, DNB, OC/1-3
NOLA, Mina (fl 1837) musician CDP
NOLAN, Doris (b 1915/16) American actress TW/6-7, WWT/10-12
NOLAN, John Francis (d 1908) actor EA/09*
NOLAN, Kathy [or Kathleen] (b 1933) American actress TW/11-12, 23
NOLAN, Lloyd (b 1902/03) American actor AAS, BE, CB,

ES, TW/10-13, WWT/8-10, 13-14
NOLAN, Mary (d 1904 [68]) EA/05*
NOLAN, Mary (1906-48) actress TW/5
NOLAN, Michael Patrick (d 1909/10 [42]) Irish musician, actor, comedian EA/11*
NOLAN, Pattie [Mrs. Michael H. Daly; Mrs. Pat Rooney] (d 1907) EA/08*
NOLAN, Robin (b 1945) American actor TW/30
NOLAND, Nancy (b 1912) American actress TW/1
NOLEN, Joyce (b 1949) American actress TW/24, 28
NOLTE, Charles (b 1926) American actor, dramatist BE, TW/6-21
NONELL, Mrs. (fl 1850) actress HAS
NOONAN, Billy performer CDP
NOONAN, John Ford (b 1943) American dramatist, actor, director CD
NOONAN, Tommy (d 1968 [46]) performer BP/52*
NOONE, Bill E. (b 1944) American actor TW/29
NORCROSS, Frank (d 1926 [70]) actor BE*, BP/11*
NORCROSS, Hale (d 1947 [70]) American actor TW/4
NORCROSS, Joseph M. (d 1925 [84]) performer BE*, BP/9*
NORD, Betty (d 1976 [69]) performer BP/60*
NORDICA, Lillian [Mrs. Zoltan Dome] (1859-1914) American singer CDP, DAB, ES, GRB/1, SR, WWA/1, WWS, WWW/1
NORDLI, Ernie (d 1968 [55]) designer BP/52*
NORDSTROM, Clarence (d 1968 [75]) American actor TW/21, 23
NORDSTROM, Frances dramatist WWT/4-7
NORDSTROM, Marie (b 1886) American actress WWS
NORELLI, Jennie Swedish singer WWM
NORFLEET, Cecelia (b 1949) American actress TW/28-30
NORFOLK, Edgar (b 1893) English actor WWT/7-13
NORGATE, W. Matthew (b 1900/01)

English critic WWT/6, 9-16

NORINS, Leslie H. (d 1975 [59])
performer BP/60*

NORMA, Bebe (d 1975 [49]) performer BP/59*

NORMA, Hettie [Janet MacIntyre
Mackenzie Stevenson] (d 1907)
EA/09*

NORMAN, Miss (fl 1850) actress
HAS

NORMAN, A. D. (d 1908) pier
manager EA/09*

NORMAN, Arthur W. (d 1896
[31]) actor EA/97*

NORMAN, Bruce (d 1976 [73])
performer BP/60*

NORMAN, E. B. (d 1930 [77])
actor, producer, director,
manager BE*, WWT/14*

NORMAN, Mrs. E. B. see
Hope, Ethel

NORMAN, Ethel (fl 1866-69) English actress HAS

NORMAN, Frank (b 1930/31)
English dramatist CD, CH,
MWD, PDT

NORMAN, Fred (d 1972 [78])
agent BP/56*

NORMAN, Gertrude (d 1961 [81])
actress WWT/14*

NORMAN, Harry (fl 1867?)
singer, minstrel CDP

NORMAN, Helen (d 1891) singer
EA/92*

NORMAN, Henry (b 1862) singer,
actor CDP

NORMAN, Horace singer CDP

NORMAN, Mrs. James see
Norman, Rhoda

NORMAN, Jessye (b 1945)
American singer CB

NORMAN, Karyl (d 1947 [51])
vaudevillian, female impersonator TW/4

NORMAN, Mabel (d 1930) actress
SR

NORMAN, Maurice (d 1969 [82])
performer BP/54*

NORMAN, May (d 1899 [25])
musician EA/00*

NORMAN, Norman J. (1870-1941)
American manager WWT/5-9

NORMAN, Norman V. (1864-
1943) English actor, manager
GRB/1-4, WWT/4-9

NORMAN, R. (d 1858 [70])
pantaloon CDP

NORMAN, Rhoda [Mrs. James

Norman] (d 1891 [50]) EA/92*

NORMAN, Thyrza (b 1884) English
actress WWT/2-5

NORMAN, Walter English actor
GRB/1

NORMAN-BURT, George Templeman (b 1872) English actor
GRB/1-3

NORMAND, Mabel (1894-1930)
Canadian actress BE*, BP/14*

NORMAUTON, Sara actress, singer
CDP

NORMINGTON, John (b 1937/38)
English actor TW/23, WWT/
15-16

NORREYS, Rose (d 1946 [84])
American/English actress DP

NORRIE, Anna (d 1957 [97]) actress
BE*, WWT/14*

NORRIE, James (fl 1899?) singer,
actor CDP

NORRIE, Russell English actor
GRB/1

NORRIS, Prof. (d 1904 [81]) conjuror EA/05*

NORRIS, Mrs. (fl 1759) actress
HAS

NORRIS, Charles (b 1846) Canadian
actor HAS

NORRIS, Ernest E. (1865-1935)
manager, actor, dramatist
GRB/1-4

MORRIS, Henry (d 1731) actor,
dramatist CP/1-3, GT, TD/1-2

MORRIS, Herbert (d 1950) costume
designer WWW/4

NORRIS, Ida [Ada Sennett] (d 1894
[24]) actress EA/95*

NORRIS, James W. (b 1849) American actor HAS

NORRIS, Jay (b 1917) American
actor TW/2-3

NORRIS, Kathleen (1880-1966)
American dramatist WWA/4

NORRIS, Lee (d 1964 [59]) actress
BE*

NORRIS, Percy (d 1889) actor
EA/90*

NORRIS, Thomas (1741-90) musician, singer CDP

NORRIS, W. H. (d 1910) actor
EA/11*

NORRIS, William [William Norris
Block] (1870/71/72-1929) Amer-
ican actor GRB/2-4, WWA/1,
WWM, WWS, WWT/1-5

NORSA, Hannah (d 1785) actress
CDP

NORTH, Ada [Mrs. Alfred Linnet] (d 1900) EA/02*

NORTH, Alan (b 1927) American actor TW/24

NORTH, Alex (b 1910) American composer BE

NORTH, Bobby (b 1884) American actor, manager WWM

NORTH, Charles see Smith, Charles Frederick

NORTH, Corinne F. (d 1966 [69]) performer BP/50*

NORTH, Francis, Earl of Guilford (b 1761) dramatist CP/3, GT, TD/1-2

NORTH, Heather (b 1945) American actress TW/24

NORTH, Henry Morley (d 1869 [58]) actor? EA/70*

NORTH, John (d 1891 [39]) conductor EA/92*

NORTH, Levi J. (1814-85) equestrian CDP

NORTH, Rex (d 1969 [52]) journalist BP/54*

NORTH, Sheree (b 1933) American actress TW/9-11, 18-19

NORTH, Wilfred [W. Northcroft] (fl 1882-1913) English actor, stage manager WWM

NORTHALL, Julia L. (d 1896) singer CDP

NORTHALL, William K. dramatist CDP

NORTHCOTE, Charles (d 1877) prompter EA/78*

NORTHCOTE, Thomas Price (d 1904) variety manager EA/05*

NORTHCOTT, John (d 1905 [62]) critic GRB/1

NORTHCOTT, Richard (1871-1931) English composer, critic, writer, archivist WWT/5-6

NORTHCROFT, W. see North, Wilfred

NORTHEN, Michael (b 1921) English lighting designer WWT/15-16

NORTHWAY, Alfred [Alfred Edward Robbins] (b 1876) English manager, actor GRB/1

NORTON (fl 1696?) dramatist CP/2-3

NORTON, Mrs. [Miss Gilbert] (fl 1796) actress TD/1-2

NORTON, Miss (fl 1808?) actress CDP

NORTON, Mrs. Alfred see Norton, Sophie

NORTON, Annie Burt actress CDP

NORTON, Barry (d 1956 [51]) Argentinian/American actor BE*

NORTON, Bruce (d 1861 [43]) actor EA/72*, WWT/14*

NORTON, C. W. (d 1875 [25]) actor EA/76*

NORTON, Dean (b 1914) American actor TW/4-8

NORTON, Elliot (b 1903) American critic BE, WWT/14-16

NORTON, Fleming [Frederick Mills] (d 1895 [59]) entertainer OAA/2

NORTON, Mrs. Fleming see Norton, Jeannie

NORTON, Frederic (d 1946) English composer WWT/4-10, WWW/4

NORTON, Frederick Naphtali (d 1882) EA/84*

NORTON, I. T. musician CDP

NORTON, Jack (d 1958 [69]) American actor BE*, BP/43*

NORTON, Jeannie [Mrs. Fleming Norton] (d 1880) EA/81*

NORTON, John (fl 1827) English actor HAS

NORTON, John W. (d 1895 [50]) actor, manager CDP, SR

NORTON, Ruby English actress GRB/1

NORTON, Sophie [Mrs. Alfred Norton] (d 1902 [44]) EA/03*

NORTON, Thomas (1532-84) English dramatist COC, CP/1-3, FGF, MH, OC/1-3

NORTON, Timothy W. (d 1862 [23]) minstrel HAS

NORTON, Washington (b 1839) American minstrel HAS

NORTON, William Henry (d 1876 [67]) English actor CDP, HAS

NORTON, William Henry [William Selmore] (d 1884) acrobat EA/85*

NORVAL, James (fl 1792) dramatist CP/3, EAP

NORWICK, Douglas American actor TW/29

NORWOOD, Edwin P. (1881-1940) American writer WWA/1

NORWOOD, Eille (1861-1948) English actor GRB/3-4, WWT/1-10

NORWOOD, John (fl 1598) actor DA

NORWORTH, Jack (1879-1959)

American actor CDP, COC, OC/3, SR, TW/16, WWT/4-11

NOSILLIE, Lucia (d 1886) singer EA/87*

NOSSECK, Max (d 1972 [70]) performer BP/57*

NOSSEN, Bram actor TW/1

NOSWORTHY, Frank (d 1892) actor EA/93*

NOTO, Lore (b 1923) American producer, actor BE

NOTT, Cicely [Sarah Ann Adams; Mrs. Sam Adams] (d 1900 [67]) actress, singer BE*, EA/01*, WWT/14*

NOTT, Rosie see Courtneidge, Mrs. Robert

NOTTEBOHM, Gustav (d 1882 [67]) historian EA/83*

NOURI, Michael (b 1945) American actor TW/27

NOVAK, Norma (b 1937) American actress TW/26

NOVARA, Franco (d 1899) professor of singing EA/00*

NOVARRO, Ramon (1899-1968) Mexican dancer, actor WWA/5

NOVELLI, Ermete (1851-1919) Italian actor COC, GRB/3-4, OC/1-3, WWS, WWT/1-3

NOVELLI, Pedro (fl 1847) singer HAS

NOVELLO, Clara Anastasia (1818-1908) singer CDP, DNB, ES

NOVELLO, Ivor (1893-1951) Welsh actor, manager, dramatist, composer AAS, COC, DNB, ES, MH, MWD, OC/1-3, PDT, TW/7, WWA/4, WWT/4-11, WWW/5

NOVELLO, Richard Italian actor TW/26

NOVELO, Ruben Z. (d 1974 [43]) performer BP/59*

NOVEMBER, Mrs. Norman see Green, Dorothy

NOVERRE, Jean Georges (1727-1810) French maître de ballet ES, OC/1-2

NOVIKOFF, Laurent (d 1956 [68]) Russian dancer TW/13

NOVIS, Donald (d 1966 [60]) singer TW/23

NOVOTNA, Jarmila (b 1911) Czech singer CB, TW/1

NOVY, Nita (b 1950) American actress TW/29

NOWAK, Adelaide (fl 1903-10)

American actress WWM

NOWELL, Mrs. Wedgwood see Colwell, Claire

NOWLAN, Patrick (d 1876) Irish singer, dancer EA/77*

NOYES, Mrs. Frank P. see Clare, Ada

NOYES, Mrs. J. F. (fl 1862) actress HAS

NOYES, Lilly (b 1944) American actress TW/29

NOYES, Thomas (b 1922) American producer, actor BE

NOYLE, Olga Kate (d 1899) actress EA/00*

"NUBIAN KING, The" see Sungham, Harry

NUCE, Thomas (fl 1581) dramatist CP/1-3

NUCHTERN, Jean (b 1939) American actress TW/27

NUDELL, Sam actor TW/24

NUGENT, Mr. (d 1880) EA/81*

NUGENT, Mrs. (d 1890 [81]) EA/91*

NUGENT, Charles (d 1876 [67]) actor EA/77*

NUGENT, Claud (d 1901 [33]) composer EA/02*

NUGENT, Eddie (b 1904) American actor TW/1-2

NUGENT, Elliott (b 1899/1900) American actor, dramatist, producer, director AAS, BE, CB, CD, ES, MD, MH, MWD, TW/1-8, WWT/6-15

NUGENT, George William (d 1884) music-hall proprietor EA/85*

NUGENT, James (d 1917) EA/18*

NUGENT, John Charles (1878-1947) American actor, dramatist SR, TW/1, 3, WWT/6-10

NUGENT, Moya (1901-54) actress WWT/4-11

NUGENT, Nancy (b 1933) American actress, producer BE

NUNN, Annette [Mrs. J. B. Mulholland] (d 1896) actress EA/97*

NUNN, Trevor (b 1940) English director AAS, COC, WWT/15-16

NUNO, Jaime (1824-1908) Spanish conductor, composer, impresario DAB, WWA/H

NUNS, Mr. (fl 1786) actor, manager TD/1-2

NUREYEV, Rudolf (b 1938) Russian/English dancer CB, ES

NUSKAY, Anne see Greene,
Mrs. John
NUTE, Don American actor
TW/29-30
NUTT, Commodore see Nutt,
George Washington M.
NUTT, Mrs. Commodore (d 1878)
dwarf EA/79*
NUTT, George Washington M.
(1844-81) dwarf CDP
NUTTALL, Thomas (d 1887)
singer EA/88*
NUTTER, Edna May see Oliver,
Edna May
NUYEN, France (b 1939) French
actress BE, TW/15
NYBERG, Peter (b 1939) Canadian
actor TW/23, 27
NYCOWLLES, Robert (fl 1595)
actor DA
NYE, Carrie actress BE, TW/
25, 28-29, WWT/15-16
NYE, Carroll (d 1974 [72]) per-
former BP/58*
NYE, Elizabeth Ann see Staun-
ton, Ella
NYE, Gene (b 1939) American
actor TW/23, 27
NYE, Henry (fl 1849) actor CDP
NYE, Mary (d 1879 [70]) EA/80*
NYE, Pat (b 1908) English ac-
tress WWT/11-16
NYE, Tom F. (d 1925 [78]) actor
BE*, WWT/14*
NYITRAY, Emil (d 1922) drama-
tist BE*, BP/6*, WWT/14*
NYLAND, Robert (d 1877) eques-
trian EA/78*
NYPE, Russell (b 1924) American
actor, singer BE, TW/7-8,
12-16, 23-24, 26-27, 29,
WWT/15-16
NYREN, David (d 1973 [47]) the-
atrical agency executive BP/
57*

- O -

OAKDEN, William (d 1876) musician EA/77*
OAKELEY, Sir Herbert Stanley
(d 1903 [73]) composer EA/
04*
OAKER, Jane [Minnie Dorothy
Peper] (b 1880) American
actress WWM, WWS, WWT/
4-7

OAKES, Betty (b 1930) American
actress TW/8, 30
OAKES, Gary (b 1936) American
actor TW/23, 27-28
OAKES, George (d 1966 [69]) per-
former BP/51*
OAKEY, Mr. (d 1845) dancer,
pantomimist HAS
OAKLAND, Si (b 1918) American
actor TW/4, 6, 11-15
OAKLAND, Simon (b 1920) Ameri-
can actor TW/26, 28-29
OAKLAND, Will (1883-1956) Amer-
ican entertainer TW/12
OAKLEY, Ada [Mrs. Walter Cop-
ley] English actress GRB/1
OAKMAN, Wheeler (d 1949 [59])
American actor BE*
OATES, Miss see Delagarde,
Mrs. J.
OATES, Alice see Oates, Mrs.
James A.
OATES, Cicely (d 1934 [45]) ac-
tress BE*, WWT/14*
OATES, James A. (b 1842) Irish
actor, manager HAS
OATES, Mrs. James A. [née
Alice Merritt] (1849-87) Ameri-
can actress, singer CDP, HAS,
NYM, SR
OATES, Henry see Austin, Henry
OATLEY, Julia (fl 1856-57) Amer-
ican actress HAS
OBEE, Lois see Dresdel, Sonia
O'BEIRNE, Calder (d 1917 [69])
singer EA/18*
O'BEIRNE, Tessie [Mrs. J. P.
Macnally] (d 1912) EA/13*
O'BEIRNE, Thomas Lewis (fl 1781)
Irish dramatist CP/2-3, GT,
TD/1-2
OBER, George (1849-1912) Ameri-
can actor SR
OBER, Harold (d 1959 [78]) liter-
ary representative BE*
OBER, Philip (b 1902) American
actor BE, TW/3-7, WWT/9-13
OBER, Robert (1881/89-1950)
American actor TW/2-3, 7,
WWS
OBERDING, Antoine (d 1974 [81])
costumier BP/59*
OBERLE, Thomas (d 1906) actor
BE*, WWT/14*
OBERLIN, Russell (b 1928) Ameri-
can singer CB
OBEY, André (b 1892) French
dramatist COC, MWD, OC/3

OBOLER, Arch (b 1907/09) American dramatist, director, producer BE, MD, MWD, NTH

OBORIN, Lev (d 1973 [66]) performer BP/58*

OBRAZTSOV, Sergei Vladimirovich (b 1901) Russian puppet-master COC

O'BRIAN, Hugh (b 1925/28) American actor, producer BE, CB, TW/18-19, 23-24, WWT/16

O'BRIAN, John Skenado (b 1753) American actor HAS

O'BRIEN, Barry (1893-1961) English producing manager, agent WWT/8-13

O'BRIEN, Charles (1848-1917) circus performer & manager SR

O'BRIEN, Chet (b 1911) stage manager, performer BE

O'BRIEN, Cornelius A. see Bryant, Neil

O'BRIEN, David (b 1930) English actor WWT/10-15

O'BRIEN, David (b 1935) American actor TW/22-26

O'BRIEN, Dennis (fl 1783) Irish dramatist GT, TD/1-2

O'BRIEN, Donnell (d 1970) actor, singer TW/27

O'BRIEN, E. C. (d 1916 [34]) comedian EA/17*

O'BRIEN, Edmond (b 1915) American actor ES

O'BRIEN, Edward ["Tennyson"] (d 1878 [24]) ventriloquist, music-hall proprietor EA/79*

O'BRIEN, Edward J. (1890-1941) dramatist HJD

O'BRIEN, Fitz-James (c. 1828-62) Irish/American dramatist HJD

O'BRIEN, Frank American actor TW/28-30

O'BRIEN, Havergal (d 1972 [96]) composer BP/57*

O'BRIEN, Henry (d 1878) marionette proprietor EA/79*

O'BRIEN, Jerry see Bryant, Jerry

O'BRIEN, John see Raymond, John T.

O'BRIEN, J. T. (fl 1854) actor HAS

O'BRIEN, Justin (d 1968 [62])

dramatist BP/53*

O'BRIEN, Kate (1897/98-1974) Irish dramatist WWT/6-7, 10-11

O'BRIEN, Liam (b 1913) American dramatist, producer BE

O'BRIEN, Marcia (b 1934) American actress TW/27, 29

O'BRIEN, Marie see Saker, Mrs. Edward

O'BRIEN, Maureen (b 1943) English actress WWT/15-16

O'BRIEN, M. Barry (b 1893) English producer, manager, agent WWT/6-7

O'BRIEN, Neil (d 1909 [55]) actor BE*, WWT/14*

O'BRIEN, Neil (d 1954 [85]) American minstrel performer & manager SR

O'BRIEN, Mrs. Neil see Davenport, Eva

O'BRIEN, Pat (b 1899) American actor BE, CB, ES

O'BRIEN, Patrick see Cotter, Patrick

O'BRIEN, Seamus (b 1932) English actor TW/29

O'BRIEN, Sylvia (b 1924) Irish actress TW/23, 25-27, 29

O'BRIEN, Terence (1887-1970) Irish actor WWT/5-12

O'BRIEN, Thomas Simon (d 1898 [40]) comedian, acrobat EA/99*

O'BRIEN, Timothy (b 1929) Indian/English designer AAS, WWT/15-16

O'BRIEN, Virginia (b 1896) American actress, singer WWT/7-8

O'BRIEN, William (d 1815 [79]) dramatist, actor CDP, CP/2-3, DNB, GT, TD/1-2

O'BRIEN-MOORE, Erin (b 1908) actress TW/3-8, WWT/7-11

O'BRYAN, Miss dancer CDP

O'BRYAN, Daniel Webster see Bryant, Dan

O'BRYAN, Pat (d 1912) comedian EA/13*

O'BRYEN, Dennis (1755-1832) dramatist CP/3, DNB

O'BRYEN, W[ilfrid] J[ames Wheeler] (b 1898) English manager, agent WWT/9-10

O'CALLAGHAN, Daniel J. (d 1900 [84]) EA/01*

O'CALLAGHAN, Delia see Friganza, Trixie

O'CALLAGHAN, Richard (b 1940)

English actor WWT/16

O'CALLAN, Thomas [T. C. Harris] (d 1897 [59]) actor EA/98*

O'CASEY, Sean (1880-1964) Irish dramatist AAS, BE, CB, CH, ES, HP, MD, MH, MWD, NTH, OC/1-3, PDT, RE, TW/21, WWA/4, WWT/6-13, WWW/6

OCASIO, Jose (b 1938) Puerto Rican actor TW/24, 29

OCEANA [Oceana Renz] (d 1895) wire walker EA/96*

OCEANA, La Belle (fl 1846-69) dancer HAS

OCHS, Al (d 1964 [70]) talent representative BE*

OCHS, Lillian (d 1964) talent representative BE*

OCHS, Phil (d 1975 [35]) performer BP/60*

O'CONNELL, Arthur (b 1908) American actor BE, TW/9-15, WWT/16

O'CONNELL, Gerald (b 1904) American manager BE

O'CONNELL, Hugh (1898-1943) American actor CB, SR, WWT/7-9

O'CONNELL, Jerry (d 1969 [64]) manager BP/54*

O'CONNELL, Patricia American actress TW/28, 30

O'CONNELL, Thomas (d 1970 [96]) publicist BP/55*

O'CONNER, James Owen (1839-94) actor CDP

O'CONNOR, Mrs. (d 1886) EA/87*

O'CONNOR, Mrs. (d 1917) EA/18*

O'CONNOR, Bill (b 1919) Canadian singer, actor WWT/12-13

O'CONNOR, Carroll (b 1924) American actor CB

O'CONNOR, Charles William (1878-1955) Irish press agent GRB/1-4, WWT/1-3

O'CONNOR, Donald (b 1925) American comedian, singer, dancer CB

O'CONNOR, Edwin (d 1968) dramatist BP/52*

O'CONNOR, Frank (1903-66) Irish dramatist, director HP, MD, WWA/4, WWW/6

O'CONNOR, Harry M. (d 1971

[98]) performer BP/56*

O'CONNOR, Mrs. J. see Willing, Bella

O'CONNOR, James Francis (1892-1963) American editor WWA/4

O'CONNOR, John [Harry Wilkinson] (d 1883 [29]) performer? EA/84*

O'CONNOR, John (d 1889 [57/59]) scene artist EA/90*, WWT/14*

O'CONNOR, John (d 1897 [58]) variety & circus manager EA/98*

O'CONNOR, John J. (b 1933) American critic WWT/15

O'CONNOR, Kathryn (d 1965 [71]) performer BP/50*

O'CONNOR, Kevin (b 1938) American actor, director, producer TW/23-26, 28-30, WWT/16

O'CONNOR, Richard (d 1975 [59]) performer BP/59*

O'CONNOR, Robert (d 1947) actor TW/3

O'CONNOR, Robert Emmett (d 1962 [77]) American actor BE*

O'CONNOR, Rod (d 1964 [51]) actor BE*

O'CONNOR, Thomas (d 1881 [25]) stage manager EA/82*

O'CONNOR, Thomas [Tom Wilkinson] (d 1881) Irish comedian EA/83*

O'CONNOR, Una (1880/93-1959) Irish actress TW/2-7, 11-13, 15, WWT/6-12

O'CONNOR, William (d 1955 [77]) press representative, journalist WWT/3

O'CONOLLY, Gerald (d 1909) executive? EA/10*

O'CONOR, Joseph (b 1916) Irish actor, dramatist AAS, MH, WWT/11-16

O'DALY, Cormac (d 1949 [55]) dramatist BE*, WWT/14*

O'DAY, Alice (d 1937) actress BE*, WWT/14*

ODDY, George (d 1888 [15]) aerial flight performer EA/89*

O'DEA, Denis (b 1905) Irish actor WWT/11-14

O'DEA, James (1871-1914) Canadian dramatist, librettist SR, WWA/1, WWM

O'DEA, Jimmy (d 1965 [66]) performer BP/49*

O'DEA, John (d 1972 [63]) dramatist

BP/56*
O'DELL, Dell (d 1962) magician
BE*
ODELL, E. J. (d 1928 [93]) actor
BE*, WWT/14*
ODELL, George C. D. (1866-
1949) American historian CB,
DAB, ES, HJD, NTH, WWT/
6-10
ODELL, Maude (d 1937 [65])
American actress BE*, BP/
21*, WWT/14*
ODELL, Thomas (1691-1749)
Master of the Revels, drama-
tist, proprietor CP/1-3,
DNB, GT, TD/1-2
O'DEMPSEY, Brigit (d 1952 [65])
actress BE*, WWT/14*
ODETS, Clifford (1906-63) Amer-
ican actor, dramatist AAS,
CB, CH, COC, ES, HJD, HP,
MD, MH, MWD, NTH, OC/
1-3, PDT, RE, TW/20, WWA/
4, WWT/8-13, WWW/6
ODETS, Mrs. Clifford see
Grayson, Bette
ODETTE, Mary (b 1901) French
actress WWT/4-7
ODINGSELS, Gabriel (1690-1734)
English dramatist CP/1-3,
DNB, GT
ODIVA [Alma Beaumont] (b 1883)
English aquatic entertainer
WWM
ODLUM, Drelincourt (b 1865)
Irish actor GRB/1
O'DOHERTY, Eileen [Anna Walk-
er] (b 1891) Irish actress
WWT/2-7
O'DOHERTY, Mignon (1890-1961)
Australian actress WWT/4-13
O'DONNELL, Anne American
actress TW/27
O'DONNELL, Cathy (d 1970 [45])
performer BP/54*
O'DONNELL, Charles H. (d 1962
[76]) performer BE*
O'DONNELL, Edwin P. (1895-
1943) dramatist CB
O'DONOVAN, Desmond (b 1933)
English director WWT/15-16
O'DONOVAN, Frank (d 1974
[74]) actor BP/59*, WWT/
16*
O'DONOVAN, Fred (1889-1952)
Irish actor WWT/2-11
O'DUFFY, Eimar Ultan (1893-
1935) Irish dramatist WWW/3

ODY, Mel (d 1976 [62]) performer
BP/60*
OELRICHS, Blanche (d 1950 [60])
actress BE*, WWT/14*
OENSLAGER, Donald (1902-75)
American designer BE, CB,
COC, ES, NTH, OC/1-3, TW/
2-8, WWT/8-15
OESTREICHER, Gerard (b 1916)
American producer BE
O'FARRELL, Mary (1892-1968)
English actress WWT/4-8
O'FARRELL, Talbot (d 1952 [72])
performer BE*, WWT/14*
OFFENBACH, Joseph (d 1971 [66])
performer BP/56*
OFFERMAN, George, Jr. (d 1963
[45]) American actor BE*
OFFIN, Phil (d 1974 [70]) agent
BP/58*
OFFLEY, Thomas (fl c. 1509-22)
actor DA
OFFNER, Mortimer (d 1965 [64])
producer/director BP/50*
OFFROY, Auguste see Dianta
OFFROY, Mrs. Auguste see
Offroy, Emily Jane
OFFROY, Emily Jane [Mrs. Au-
guste Offroy] (d 1899) EA/00*
O'FLYNN, Michael (d 1908 [60])
EA/09*
OGBORNE, David (fl 1765?) Eng-
lish dramatist CP/2-3, GT
OGDEN, Anna Cora see Mowatt,
Anna Cora
OGDEN, Grace [Mrs. Nat Ogden]
(d 1873 [37]) EA/74*
OGDEN, Mrs. John see Bullock,
Henrietta Maria
OGDEN, John H. (d 1864 [35])
English comic singer CDP,
HAS
OGDEN, Nat (d 1876 [43]) comic
singer EA/77*
OGDEN, Mrs. Nat see Ogden,
Grace
OGG, Marguerite (d 1972 [64])
agent BP/57*
OGILBY, John (1600-76) Scottish
dramatist CP/3
OGILVIE, Mrs. (fl 1823) actress
BS, CDP
OGILVIE, George (b 1931) Aus-
tralian director, actor WWT/
16
OGILVIE, Glencairn Stuart (1858-
1932) English dramatist GRB/
1-4, WWT/1-6

O'GORMAN, Dave (d 1964 [70])
performer BP/49*
O'GORMAN, Mrs. J. see Cole-
man, Maggie
O'GORMAN, Jane (d 1906 [84])
EA/07*
O'GORMAN, Jessie [Mrs. Joe
O'Gorman] (d 1908 [34]) gym-
nast EA/09*
O'GORMAN, Joe (d 1974 [85])
music-hall performer BTR/
74, CDP
O'GORMAN, Mrs. Joe see
O'Gorman, Jessie
O'GORMAN, William (d 1966
[63]) performer BP/51*
O'GRADY, Mrs. F. [Miss H.
Daly] (d 1889 [33]) actress
EA/90*
O'GRADY, Frank (d 1901) come-
dian EA/01*
O'GRADY, Hubert (d 1899 [58])
dramatist, actor EA/01*
O'GRADY, William (d 1893 [56])
EA/94*
O'GRATH, Mrs. (fl 1836) ac-
tress HAS
OGUS, Joyce see Blair, Joyce
OGUS, Lionel see Blair, Lionel
O'HAFFEY, Thom (d 1971 [53])
journalist BP/56*
O'HAGAN, Mrs. John D. (d 1969
[78]) performer BP/54*
O'HANLON, Redmond L. (d 1964
[48]) Shakespearean authority
BE*
O'HARA, Mrs. Dan Briggs (d
1876) singer EA/77*
O'HARA, Fiske [né George Fiske
Brenen] (1880-1945) American
actor, dramatist SR, TW/2
O'HARA, Frank (1926-66) Amer-
ican dramatist WWA/4
O'HARA, Geoffrey (1882-1967)
Canadian composer WWA/4
O'HARA, Hugh (d 1901) music-hall
comedian EA/02*
O'HARA, Jenny American actress
TW/26-30
O'HARA, Jill (b 1947) American
actress TW/24-28
O'HARA, John (d 1929 [70]) actor
BE*, BP/14*
O'HARA, John (1905-70) American
writer, dramatist BE, CB,
MD, WWW/6
O'HARA, Kane (1714?-82) Irish
dramatist CDP, CP/2-3, DNB,

GT, TD/1-2
O'HARA, Maureen (b 1921) Irish
actress CB
O'HARA, Neal (d 1962 [69]) jour-
nalist BP/47*
O'HARA, Terence (d 1917) EA/18*
O'HEARN, Robert (b 1921) Ameri-
can designer BE
O'HERLIHY, Daniel (b 1919) Irish
actor TW/5
O'HIGGINS, Harvey J. (1876-1929)
Canadian dramatist HJD, WWT/
4-5
OHNET, Georges (1848-1918)
French dramatist COC, GRB/1,
3, OC/1-3, WWT/1
O'HORGAN, Tom (b 1927) American
director, composer CB, WWT/
16
O'KEEFE, Anna American actress
WWA/5
O'KEEFE, Dennis (d 1968 [60])
performer BP/53*
O'KEEFFE, Mrs. actress CDP
O'KEEFFE, John (1747-1833) Irish
dramatist CDP, COC, CP/3,
DNB, ES, GT, HP, OC/1-3,
SR, TD/1-2
O'KELLY, Joseph (d 1885) French
composer EA/86*
O'KELLY, Seumas (1881-1918) Irish
dramatist RE
OKHLOPKOV, Nicolai (1900-67)
Russian actor, director WWT/
13-14
OLAF, Pierre [né Pierre-Olaf
Trivier] (b 1928) French actor
BE, TW/17-21, 23, 25, WWT/
15-16
OLAND, Warner (1880-1938) Swedish
actor WWT/7-8
OLCOTT, Chauncey (1860-1932)
American actor, singer CDP,
DAB, GRB/2-4, SR, WWA/1,
WWM, WWS, WWT/1-6
OLCOTT, Ida Lillian (d 1888 [c. 27])
actress CDP
OLCOTT, Sidney (d 1949 [76])
director, actor BE*
OLD, John (d 1892 [65]) composer
EA/93*
OLD, Mary Ann (d 1874 [83]) ac-
tress EA/75*
OLDAKER, Max (d 1972 [64]) per-
former BP/56*
OLDAKER, Thomas Norris (d 1918)
EA/19*
OLDALE, Marion (d 1876 [17])

dancer EA/77*

OLDENBURG, Claes sculptor CD

OLDFIELD, Miss (fl 1797) actress HAS

OLDFIELD, Anne (1683-1730) English actress CDP, COC, DNB, ES, GT, HP, NTH, OC/1-3, TD/1-2

OLDFIELD, Lilian see Newland, Mary

OLDFIELD, Nance (d 1904 [30]) EA/05*

OLDFIELD, Thomas J. (b 1809) English actor, musical director HAS

OLDHAM, Derek (1892-1968) English actor, singer AAS, WWT/4-14

"OLD JOE" see De La Salle, Michel Joseph

OLDLAND, Lilian (b 1905) English actress WWT/6

OLDLAND, Marion (d 1892) EA/93*

OLDMIXON, Mrs. [Georgina Sidus] (d 1835) English singer, actress CDP, COC, HAS, OC/1-3

OLDMIXON, John (1673-1742) English dramatist CP/1-3, DNB, GT

OLDMIXON, Sir John (d 1818) dramatist CDP, CP/3

OLDMIXON, Mrs. John see Oldmixon, Mrs.

O'LEARY, Bryan (d 1970 [36]) performer BP/54*

O'LEARY, F. L. see Fredericks, Fred

O'LEARY, John (b 1926) American actor TW/23, 29-30

O'LEARY, Kevin (b 1940) American actor TW/25, 30

O'LEARY, Miriam (fl c. 1890?) actress CDP

O'LEARY, Pat see Tollett, John

O'LEARY, Willie (d 1973 [69]) performer BP/58*

OLESEN, Oscar (b 1916) English manager BE

OLESEN, Otto K. (d 1964 [72]) Danish lighting equipment expert BE*

OLFSON, Ken (b 1937) American actor TW/24, 30

OLGINI, Olga (b 1846) Polish singer HAS

OLIFF, Mr. (fl 1810) actor, prompter HAS

OLIFFE, Geraldine [Mrs. Compton Mackenzie] actress GRB/1, WWT/2-5

OLIM, Dorothy (b 1934) American producer BE

OLINZA, Margaretta (fl 1854) tight-rope dancer HAS

OLIPHANT, Jack (b 1895) English press representative WWT/10-13

OLIPHANT, Julie (d 1969 [60]) performer BP/54*

OLIPHANT, Robert (d 1792) English dramatist CP/3

OLIPHANT, Thomas (1799-1873) Scottish composer DNB

OLITZKA, Rosa (d 1949 [76]) singer BE*, WWT/14*

OLIVARI, Francis (fl 1797) Italian dramatist CP/3

OLIVE, Edyth [Mrs. Arthur Applin] (d 1956 [84]) English actress GRB/1-4, WWT/1-6

OLIVE, Kittie [Mrs. Tom Pilbeam] (d 1913) EA/14*

OLIVE, Lily (d 1909 [34]) actress EA/10*

OLIVER, Mrs. A. E. (d 1890) EA/91*

OLIVER, Anthony (b 1923/24) Welsh actor TW/10, 24, WWT/12-16

OLIVER, Barrie (b 1900) American actor, dancer WWT/6-8

OLIVER, Bessie [Mrs. Henry Arlington Duncan] (d 1885) actress EA/86*

OLIVER, C. W. (d 1890) lessee EA/91*

OLIVER, Eddie (b 1894) American treasurer, manager BE

OLIVER, Edith [née Goldsmith] (b 1913) American critic BE, WWT/15-16

OLIVER, Edna May [Edna May Nutter] (1883/85-1942) American actress CB, ES, SR, WWA/2, WWT/7-9

OLIVER, Florence [Mrs. Will Oliver] (d 1902 [40]) EA/03*

OLIVER, Harry (d 1973 [85]) designer BP/58*

OLIVER, Henry (b 1921) American actor TW/23

OLIVER, J. (fl 1849) actor HAS

OLIVER, Jody (b 1954) American actor TW/28-29

OLIVER, Larry (d 1973 [93]) actor

10-11, 13-15, 19, 21, WWT/
9-15

OMAN, Julia Trevelyan (b 1930)
English designer WWT/15-16

OMAR, Jemela (b 1941) American
actress TW/25

O'MARA (d 1891 [67]) acrobat
EA/92*

O'MARA, Joseph Irish singer
GRB/1-4

O'MARA, Kate (b 1939) English
actress WWT/16

OMENS, Estelle (b 1928) American actress TW/26-28

OMOHUNDRO, John B. (d 1880)
actor CDP

O'MORRISON, Kevin (b 1916)
American actor TW/23

O'NEAL, Frederick (b 1905)
American actor, director,
administrator, lecturer BE,
CB, TW/1, 10-12, 20-23,
26, WWT/12-16

O'NEAL, Patrick (b 1927) American actor TW/18, WWT/14-16

O'NEAL, Ron (b 1937) American
actor TW/25-27

O'NEAL, Zelma (b 1907) American actress, singer WWT/
7-9

ONEGIN, Sigrid (1891-1943)
German singer ES

O'NEIL, Barbara actress TW/1,
3, 11-13

O'NEIL, Billy (b 1834) American
singer, dancer, actor HAS

O'NEIL, Charles (d 1863) comedian HAS

O'NEIL, Colette Scottish actress
WWT/16

O'NEIL, George (1898-1940)
American dramatist CB, MD

O'NEIL, J. H. (fl 1871) dancer
CDP

O'NEIL, Kathleen ["Kitty"] (1840-
93) Irish music-hall performer
CDP, HAS

O'NEIL, Nance see O'Neill,
Nance

O'NEIL, Nancy (b 1911) Australian
actress WWT/8-9

O'NEIL, Peggy (1898-1960) Irish
actress TW/16, WWT/4-10

O'NEIL, Standish (d 1969 [75])
producer/director/choreographer
BP/54*

O'NEIL, Tricia (b 1945) American
actress TW/27-28

O'NEIL, William (d 1868 [34])
comedian, singer EA/69*

O'NEILL, Annie (b 1872) Scottish
actress SR

O'NEILL, Carlotta Monterey (d
1970 [82]) performer BP/55*

O'NEILL, Dick (b 1928) American
actor TW/22-28, 30

O'NEILL, Eliza (1791-1872) English
actress CDP, COC, DNB, OC/
1-3, OX

O'NEILL, Eugene F. (d 1972 [84])
performer BP/57*

O'NEILL, Eugene Gladstone (1888-
1953) American dramatist AAS,
CH, COC, ES, HJD, HP, MD,
MH, MWD, NTH, OC/1-3, PDT,
RE, SR, TW/10, WWA/3,
WWT/4-11, WWW/5

O'NEILL, Frank B. (1869-1959)
English business manager
GRB/4, WWT/1-9

O'NEILL, Henry [or Harry] (1891-
1961) American actor TW/17,
WWT/8-10

O'NEILL, James (1849-1920) Irish
actor CDP, DAB, ES, HJD,
GRB/1-4, NTH, PP/2, SR,
WWA/1, WWM, WWS, WWT/1-3

O'NEILL, James, Jr. (d 1923
[43]) actor BE*, BP/8*

O'NEILL, James, Jr. (b 1920)
American critic BE

O'NEILL, Joseph J. (d 1962 [66])
performer BE*

O'NEILL, J. R. [Hugo Vamp] (d
1860 [37]) author EA/72*

O'NEILL, Maire (1887-1952) Irish
actress COC, ES, OC/2-3,
TW/9, WWT/2-11

O'NEILL, Michael English dramatist CD

O'NEILL, Nance [Gertrude Lamson]
(1874-1965) American actress
BE, COC, ES, GRB/2-4, WWM,
TW/4-7, 21, WWS, WWT/1-11

O'NEILL, Norman (1875-1934)
English composer, conductor
WWT/4-7, WWW/3

O'NEILL, Mrs. Robert see
Dennett, Eliza

O'NEILL, Sally (d 1968 [55]) performer BP/53*

O'NEILL, Sheila (b 1930) English
actress, dancer, choreographer
WWT/15-16

O'NEILL, T. H. (d 1907 [47])
American business manager

GRB/3*

ONETO, Richard (b 1925) American actor TW/11

ONGAR, Ivy (b 1883) English dancer GRB/1

O'NIEL, Colette [Lady Constance Annesley] (1896-1975) Irish actress WWT/4-8

ONODERA, Sho (d 1974 [59]) performer BP/59*

ONOE, Biacho (d 1965 [73]) performer BP/49*

ONRA [Harriet Gilleno Giles] (d 1909 [37]) acrobat EA/10*

ONZALO, Elise [Mrs. Harry Biddle] (d 1889) gymnast EA/90*

ONZALO, William (d 1900 [51]) gymnast, acrobat EA/01*

OPATOSHU, David (b 1918) American actor BE, TW/19, 25, 29

OPENSHAW, Charles Elton dramatist WWT/6-10

OPEN THEATRE theatre collective CD

OPERTI, Le Roi (1895-1971) American actor, singer, director BE, TW/1, 28

OPFERMANN, Arthur Edward (d 1909 [39]) variety acting manager EA/10*

OPIE, Mrs. (b c. 1772) English dramatist CP/3

OPP, Julie [Mrs. William Faversham] (1871-1921) American actress GRB/2-4, WWA/1, WWM, WWS, WWT/1-3

OPP, Paul F. (b 1894) American educator BE

OPPENHEIMER, George (1900-77) American critic, dramatist BE

ORAM, Mona K. [Mrs. Arthur Greville] English actress GRB/1, 3-4

O'RAMEY, Georgia (1886-1928) American actress WWM, WWT/4-5

ORBACH, Jerry (b 1935) American actor AAS, BE, CB, TW/21-27, 29, WWT/15-16

ORBASANY, Irma (d 1961 [95]) performer BE*

ORCHARD, Julian (b 1930) English actor TW/22, WWT/16

ORCZY, Baroness Emmusca (d 1947 [80]) Hungarian dramatist

WWT/4-10, WWW/4

ORD, Ralph Jerrold (b 1869) Irish actor GRB/1

"ORD, Robert" [Mrs. W. Gayer MacKay] dramatist WWT/4-7

ORD, Simon (1874-1944) Scottish manager WWT/6-7

ORDZ, Josephine see D'Orme, Josephine

O'REGAN, Kathleen (b 1903) Irish actress WWT/6-11

O'REILLY, General see O'Reilly, Eugene

O'REILLY, Emmie [Mrs. Austin-Leigh] actress GRB/1

O'REILLY, Eugene [General O'Reilly] (d 1873) actor EA/74*

O'REILLY, William see Bailey, William

O'REILLY, Mrs. William see Bailey, Mrs. William

O'REILY, William (fl 1792) Irish actor CDP, TD/1-2 [see also: O'Riley, Mr.]

ORFALY, Alexander (b 1935) American actor TW/24, 26-30

ORFORD, Earl of see Walpole, Horace

ORFORD, Emma Maria (d 1898) actress EA/99*

ORFORD, Emmeline English actress EA/96, GRB/1-2

ORFORD, William see Mozley, William Orford

ORFORD, William Henry (d 1906 [74]) EA/07*

ORGAN, Harriet [Mrs. Selim Bridges] (d 1888) EA/89*

ORGANIC THEATRE theatre collective CD

ORGER, Mrs. Thomas [née Ivers] (1788-1849) English actress BS, CDP, OX

O'RIADA, Sean (d 1971 [40]) Irish? musical director BP/56*

ORIENT, Milt H. (d 1975 [56]) composer/lyricist BP/59*

ORIGLIO, Tony (b 1948) American actor TW/30

O'RILEY, Mr. (fl 1792) Irish actor HAS [see also: O'Reily, William]

ORIN, Renee American actress TW/29

ORKIN, Harvey (d 1975 [57]) performer BP/60*

ORKNEY, Countess of see Gilchrist, Connie

ORLANDI, Felice (b 1925) Italian
actress TW/11-12, 21
ORLANDINI, Ernesto (fl 1833)
singer HAS
ORLENEV, Pavel Nikolayevich
(1869-1932) Russian actor
COC, OC/3
ORLOB, Harold (b 1885) American
composer, lyricist, dramatist,
producer BE
ORLOVA, Lyubov (d 1975) per-
former BP/59*
ORLOVITZ, Gil (d 1973 [55])
dramatist BP/58*
ORME, Denise [Hon. Mrs. John
Yarde-Buller] (1884-1960) ac-
tress, singer GRB/1-4,
WWT/1-5
ORME, Michael see Greveen,
Alice Augusta
ORMEROD, John (d 1896) lessee
EA/98*
ORMEROD, John (d 1906 [73])
director EA/07*
ORMISTON, George (b 1939)
American actor TW/24
ORMOND, Mr. (d 1870) music-
hall chairman EA/71*
ORMOND, Mme. (d 1863) eques-
trienne HAS
ORMONDE, Dr. (d 1902 [60])
conjuror EA/03*
ORMONDE, Florrie (d 1905 [30])
comedian, dancer EA/06*
ORMONDE, Mabel Irish actress
GRB/2
ORMONDE, Nelly [Mrs. W.
Newman] (d 1891) EA/92*
ORMONDE, Will (d 1904) music-
hall performer EA/05*
ORMS, Howard R. (b 1920)
American executive BE
ORMSBY, E. L. (d 1905) lessee
EA/06*
ORNBO, Robert (b 1931) English
lighting designer WWT/15-16
ORNELLAS, Norman (d 1975 [36])
performer BP/60*
ORNSTEIN, Honora (d 1975 [92])
performer BP/60*
O'RORKE, Brefni (1889-1946)
Irish actor WWT/10
O'RORKE, John (d 1899 [76])
actor? EA/00*
O'ROURKE, Edna (b 1925) Amer-
ican actress TW/4
O'ROURKE, Eugene (b 1863)
American actor CDP, WWM,

WWS
O'ROURKE, J. A. (d 1937 [55])
actor BE*, WWT/14*
O'ROURKE, Tex (d 1963 [77])
American performer BE*
ORR, Charles W. (d 1976 [82])
performer BP/60*
ORR, Christine Grant Millar (d
1963 [63]) dramatist WWW/6
ORR, Forrest (d 1963 [63]) Amer-
ican actor TW/1
ORR, James Morrice see
Holmes, Morrice
ORR, Margaret (d 1894 [78]) EA/
95*
ORR, Mary (b 1918) American ac-
tress, dramatist BE, TW/1-6,
WWT/15-16
ORR, William Amory (d 1892) mu-
sic-hall comedian EA/93*
ORRERY, Lord (1621-79) English
dramatist COC, CP/1-3, GT,
OC/1-3
ORRIDGE, Miss (d 1883 [26]) singer
EA/84*
ORRIN, Edward acrobat CDP
ORRIN, George acrobat CDP
ORRIN, George Frederick (d 1884
[68]) EA/85*
ORRIN, Mrs. George Frederick
see Orrin, Zilla Toncliffe
ORRIN, George W. (1846-92) cir-
cus manager CDP
ORRIN, Zilla Toncliffe [Mrs.
George Frederick Orrin] (d 1884
[58]) EA/85*
ORRY-KELLY (1897-1964) Australian
designer WWA/4
ORSKA, Marie (d 1930) actress
BE*, WWT/14*
ORT, Izzy (d 1975 [84]) performer
BP/60*
ORTEGA, Carlos M. (d 1965 [80])
dramatist BP/50*
ORTEGA, Santos (d 1976 [76]) per-
former BP/60*
ORTH, Frank (d 1962 [82]) actor
BE*
ORTH, Lizette Emma (1858-1913)
American composer WWA/1
ORTON, Joe (1933-67) English
dramatist AAS, CD, CH, COC,
MH, MWD, PDT, RE
ORTON, John Nicholas Colthurst
see Overton, Charles
ORTON, Josephine (1843-1926)
American actress CDP, HAS
ORY, Edward (d 1973 [86]) com-

poser/lyricist BP/57*
OSATO, Sona (b 1919) American
dancer, actress BE, CB,
TW/1, 3-5
OSBALDESTONE, Estelle M.
see Phelps, Stella
OSBALDISTON, David Webster
(1794-1850) actor CDP
OSBORN, E. W. (1860-1930)
American critic WWT/6
OSBORN, Laughton (c. 1809-78)
American dramatist DAB,
WWA/H
OSBORN, Paul (b 1901) American
dramatist BE, MD, MH,
MWD, NTH, WWT/9-15
OSBORN, Master R. W. dwarf
CDP
OSBORNE, Annie [Mrs. Fred
G. Latham] (d 1894) actress
CDP, EA/95*
OSBORNE, Charles (d 1908 [79])
dramatist EA/09*
OSBORNE, Charles (d 1911)
actor EA/12*
OSBORNE, Edward (d 1876 [33])
actor EA/77*
OSBORNE, Mrs. Elizabeth C.
Douglas (d 1890 [61]) EA/91*
OSBORNE, Fanny (d 1855) ac-
tress HAS
OSBORNE, Fred (d 1888 [35])
minstrel EA/89*
OSBORNE, George Alexander (d
1893 [87]) composer EA/94*
OSBORNE, Georgia Lund (d 1975
[57]) talent agent BP/60*
OSBORNE, Hubert (b 1881) Cana-
dian actor WWM
OSBORNE, James (d 1889 [51])
EA/90*
OSBORNE, Jane see Barry,
Mrs. William
OSBORNE, John (b 1929) English
dramatist, actor, director
AAS, BE, CB, CD, CH,
COC, ES, HP, MD, MH,
MWD, OC/3, PDT, RE,
WWT/14-16
OSBORNE, Kate actress GRB/1
OSBORNE, Kipp (b 1944) Ameri-
can actor TW/27-30, WWT/
16
OSBORNE, Lennie (d 1964 [69])
actor BE*
OSBORNE, Theresa [Mrs. Sydney
Compton] Indian/English ac-
tress GRB/1-2

OSBORNE, Vivienne (b 1900/05)
American actress WWT/6-10
OSBORNE, Walter (d 1900 [43])
performer? EA/01*
OSBORN-HANNAH, Jane (d 1943)
American singer WWA/3
OSBOURNE, Lloyd (1868-1947)
American dramatist HJD
OSCAR, [Mons. ?] (d 1879 [21])
trapezist EA/80*
OSCAR, Henry (1891-1969) English
actor, producer WWT/5-14
OSCARD, Fifi (b 1921) American
talent representative BE
OSGOOD, Charles (d 1922 [63])
manager BE*, BP/6*
OSGOOD, Helen (fl 1863) actress
HAS
OSGOOD, Mrs. J. M. (fl 1874?)
singer CDP
OSGOOD, Lawrence (b 1929) Amer-
ican dramatist, director CD
O'SHAUGHNESSY, John (b 1907)
American director, actor BE,
TW/4-8, 22
O'SHAUGHNESSY, Peter (d 1910)
proprietor EA/11*
O'SHEA, John (d 1908 [76]) EA/09*
O'SHEA, Julia (d 1974 [83]) per-
former BP/59*
O'SHEA, Kevin (b 1915) American
actor TW/2-3
O'SHEA, Michael (d 1973 [67])
actor TW/30
O'SHEA, Michael Sean (b 1922)
American press representative
BE
O'SHEA, Milo (b 1926) Irish actor
TW/24-25
O'SHEA, Tessie (b 1918) Welsh ac-
tress TW/20, 22-23
OSHEROWITCH, Mendel (d 1965
[78]) dramatist BP/49*
OSHINS, Julie (d 1956 [50]) Amer-
ican performer TW/12
OSHRIN, George (d 1972 [69])
manager BP/57*
OSMAN, Harry (d 1907 [46]) actor
EA/08*
OSMAN, William (d 1891) actor
EA/92*
OSMOND, Maude see Walton,
Mrs. J. K.
OSMONDE, Florrie (d 1905 [30])
English variety artist GRB/1
OSNATH-HALEVY, Sarah (d 1975
[62]) performer BP/60*
OSRANI, Jean (d 1908 [49]) acrobat

EA/09*

OSSORY, Bishop of see Bale, John

OSTERMAN, Jack (d 1939 [37]) American comedian BE*, BP/23*

OSTERMAN, Kathryn (d 1956 [73]) actress TW/13

OSTERMAN, Lester (b 1914) American producer BE, WWT/ 14-16

OSTERMAN, Rolfe A. (d 1969 [78]) performer BP/54*

OSTERSTOCK, Fred see Forth, Eric

OSTERTAG, Barna (b 1902) American agent, actress BE

OSTERWALD, Bibi (b 1920/21) American actress, singer BE, TW/1, 4-8, 10-15, 26-27, WWT/13-16

OSTLER, William (d 1614) English actor COC, DA, DNB, GT, NTH, OC/1-3

OSTRANDER, Albert A. (d 1964 [61]) designer TW/21

OSTRANDER, Clarence M. (d 1887) singer NYM

OSTRIN, Art (b 1937) American actor TW/22, 25-26

OSTROSKA, George (d 1969 [32]) performer BP/54*

OSTROVSKY, Alexander Nikolaivich (1823-86) Russian dramatist COC, NTH, OC/3

OSTROW, Stuart (b 1932) American producer WWT/15-16

O'SULLIVAN, Denis (1868-1908) American actor, singer GRB/ 1-4

O'SULLIVAN, James Joseph (d 1872 [37]) Irish comedian EA/73*

O'SULLIVAN, Mairin D. Irish actress TW/22-23, 26

O'SULLIVAN, Maureen (b 1911/ 17) Irish actress BE, TW/ 19-22, 26-27, 29, WWT/14-16

O'SULLIVAN, Michael (1934-71) American actor TW/21-24, 26, 28

O'SULLIVAN, Vincent (b 1872) American dramatist WWA/5

OSUNA, Jess (b 1933) American actor TW/23-25

OSWALD, Charlie [Charlie Oswald Young] (d 1898) music-hall comedian EA/99*

OSWALD, Frank (d 1896 [38]) actor EA/97*

OSWALD, Genevieve (b 1923) American librarian BE

OSWALD, John (fl 1783-89) Scottish dramatist CP/3

OSWALD, Virginia (b 1926) American singer, actress BE

OTERO, Caroline (1868/71-1965) Spanish dancer, variety artist GRB/1-4, WWS

OTIS, Elita Proctor (d 1927 [76]) American actress WWS

OTLEY, Charles (b 1850) English actor GRB/1

O'TOOLE, Peter (b 1932/33) Irish actor AAS, CB, ES, WWT/13-16

OTT, Alexander (d 1970 [82]) producer/director/choreographer BP/55*

OTTAWAY, Frank (d 1907) minstrel bone soloist EA/08*

OTTAWAY, James (b 1908) English actor WWT/15-16

OTTENHEIMER, Albert M. (b 1904) American actor TW/22, 29

OTTER, William (d 1896 [38]) Negro comedian EA/97*

OTTINGER, Maurice American actor TW/23

OTTO, Mme. (d 1860/75) actress, singer CDP, HAS, SR

OTTO, Liz American actress TW/ 26-28

OTTO-ALVSLEBEN, Melitta (1842-93) singer CDP

OTWAY, Grace (d 1935) actress BE*, WWT/14*

OTWAY, Rita (d 1972 [85]) performer BP/57*

OTWAY, Silvester see Oswald, John

OTWAY, Thomas (1652-85) English dramatist CDP, COC, CP/1-3, DNB, ES, GT, HP, MH, NTH, OC/1-3, PDT, RE, SR

OUELLETTE, Paul E. (b 1927) American educator BE

OUGHTERSON, Hugh George (d 1916) EA/17*

OUGHTON, Winifred (1890-1964) English actress WWT/9-13

OUKRAINSKY, Serge (d 1972 [86]) performer BP/57*

OULD, Hermon (1885/86-1951) English dramatist, journalist MD, MWD, WWT/6-11

OULTON, Brian (b 1908) English
actor WWT/12-16
OULTON, Walley Chamberlaine
(d 1820 [50]) Irish dramatist
CP/3, GT, TD/1-2
OUROUSSOW, Eugenie (d 1975
[66]) producer/director/chore-
ographer BP/59*
OURSLER, Fulton (1893-1952)
American dramatist CB
OUSPENSKAYA, Maria (1876-1949)
Russian actress TW/6, WWT/
10
OUSTER, Murray (d 1974 [67])
performer BP/59*
OUTRAM, Leonard S. (d 1901
[45]) actor, dramatist EA/01*,
WWT/14*
OUVILLY, George Gerbier D'
see D'Ouvilly, George Gerbier
OVEREND, Dorothy Australian
actress WWT/5-7
OVERMAN, Lynne (1887-1943)
American actor CB, SR,
WWT/5-9
OVERTON, Charles [John Nicholas
Colthurst Orton] (d 1898 [44])
actor, dramatist EA/99*
OVERTON, Frank (1918-67) Amer-
ican actor BE, TW/10, 14, 23
OVERTON, Hall (d 1972 [52])
composer/lyricist BP/57*
OVERTON, Robert (1859-1924)
dramatist WWW/2
OVETTE, Joseph (d 1946 [61])
Italian/American magician SR
OWEN, Mr. (d 1905 [61]) EA/06*
OWEN, Mrs. (d 1879 [44]) music-
hall proprietor EA/80*
OWEN, Mrs. (d 1905 [57]) EA/
06*
OWEN, Master actor CDP
OWEN, Alun (b 1925/26) Welsh
dramatist, actor, assistant
stage manager AAS, CD, CH,
ES, MH, PDT, WWT/14-16
OWEN, Bill (b 1916) English actor
TW/6, WWT/11-16
OWEN, Catherine Dale (1900-65)
American actress TW/22,
WWT/6-8
OWEN, Charles (d 1912 [38])
music-hall manager EA/13*
OWEN, Charles (d 1917) circus
& variety performer EA/18*
OWEN, Dave (d 1906) singer
EA/07*
OWEN, Ellen [Mrs. Stuart

Lomath] English actress GRB/1
OWEN, Emmie (d 1905 [33]) ac-
tress, singer CDP
OWEN, F. C. (d 1875 [53]) propri-
etor EA/76*
OWEN, Mrs. Fred see Robert-
son, Marie
OWEN, George (d 1882) actor,
manager EA/83*, WWT/14*
OWEN, Mrs. George (d 1907 [81])
EA/08*
OWEN, Harold (1872-1930) English
dramatist WWT/4-6
OWEN, Harrison (1890/91-1966)
Australian dramatist WWT/7-9,
WWW/6
OWEN, Henry C. (d 1916 [75])
EA/17*
OWEN, Jennie (d 1904 [28]) bur-
lesque actress EA/05*
OWEN, John (d 1883 [62]) composer
EA/84*
OWEN, John (d 1911 [64]) comedian
EA/12*
OWEN, Reginald (1887-1972) Eng-
lish actor, dramatist BE,
GRB/4, TW/7-8, 28-29, WWT/
1-14
OWEN, Rich (d 1884 [38]) master
carpenter EA/85*
OWEN, Robert (fl 1696) dramatist
CP/1-3, GT
OWEN, Robert Dale (1801-77) Eng-
lish/American dramatist CDP,
HJD
OWEN, T. James (d 1916) EA/17*
OWEN, Mrs. W. H. see Smith-
ers, Florence
OWEN, William (d 1975 [38]) edu-
cator BP/60*
OWEN, William Florence (1844-
1906) Irish actor CDP, DAB,
HAS, PP/2
OWENS, Elizabeth (b 1938) Ameri-
can actress TW/27-30
OWENS, John Edmond (1823-86)
English/American actor CDP,
COC, DAB, ES, HAS, OC/1-3,
SR, WWA/H
OWENS, John Lennergan Irish actor
TD/1-2
OWENS, Rochelle [née Rochelle
Bass] (b 1936) American drama-
tist CD, CH, WWT/15-16
OWENS, William (d 1926 [63]) actor
BE*, BP/11*
OWENS, William H. (b 1922)
American educator BE

OWENSON, Mr. (fl 1785-1804)
Irish actor TD/1-2
OWENSON, Miss (fl 1807) drama-
tist CP/3
OWENSON, Robert (1744-1812)
Irish actor DNB
OXBERRY, Vincent Wild (d 1881
[44]) acting manager EA/82*
OXBERRY, William (1784-1824)
English actor, publisher BS,
CDP, COC, DNB, OC/1-3
OXBERRY, William Henry (1808-
52) English actor COC, DNB,
OC/1-3
OXENFORD, Edward (d 1929
[82]) dramatist, librettist
BE*, WWT/14*
OXENFORD, John (1812-77) Eng-
lish dramatist CDP, DNB,
EA/68
OXFORD, Mr. ["Hugo"] (d 1871
[18]) trapezist EA/72*
OXFORD, Countess of see
Davenport, Hester
OXLEY, John E. (b c. 1800)
American actor, manager
CDP, HAS, SR
OYA, Ichijiro (d 1972 [78]) per-
former BP/57*
OYRA, Jan (b 1888) Polish
dancer WWT/4-6
OYSHER, Moishe (d 1958 [51])
Bessarabian composer, actor
TW/15
OYSTER, Jim (b 1930) American
actor TW/11-20, 23-25
OZELL, John (d 1743) English
translator CP/1-3, GT

- P -

P. , G. (fl 1742) dramatist CP/3
P. , P. , Mons. (fl 1674) drama-
tist CP/1-3
P. , R. (fl 1575) dramatist CP/1-3
P. , S. see Pordage, Samuel
P. , T. (fl 1663-78) dramatist
CP/1-3
PAAL, Alexander (d 1972 [60s])
producer/director/choreographer
BP/57*
PAALEN, Bella (d 1964 [82])
Austrian singer BE*
PAAP, Simon (fl 1820) Dutch
dwarf CDP
PABLO ["Boston George"] (d
1881) circus performer EA/

82*
PACCHIEROTTI, Gaspare (1740-
1821) Italian singer ES
PACEY, John (d 1873) scene artist,
stage manager EA/74*
PACEY, Tom (b 1863) English vari-
ety artist GRB/1
PACINI, Regina (b 1871) Portuguese
singer ES
PACINO, Al (b 1940) American ac-
tor CB, TW/24-26, WWT/16
PACK, George (fl 1700-24) actor
DNB
PACKARD, Miss see Wilks,
Mrs.
PACKARD, Albert (b 1909) Ameri-
can business manager BE
PACKARD, Edward G. (b 1843)
American actor HAS
PACKARD, Marie singer CDP
PACKER, John Hayman (1730-1806)
actor CDP, DNB, GT, TD/1-2
PACKER, Netta (d 1962 [65]) per-
former BE*
PACKWOOD, Harry (b 1944) Amer-
ican actor TW/25
PACUVIO, Giulio (b 1910) Italian
director ES
PADDOCK, Robert Rowe (b 1914)
American scene designer BE
PADUANI, Virginia (fl 1847) singer
HAS
PADULA, Edward (b 1916) Ameri-
can producer, director BE
PAEZ, Cecelia de [née Saeman]
(fl 1857) French singer HAS
PAGAN, Anna (b 1946) American
actress TW/25
PAGAN, Peter (b 1921) Australian
actor TW/13-15, 22-23
PAGANINI, Niccolo (1784-1840)
musician CDP
PAGDEN, Emma Tanner (d 1899)
EA/00*
PAGDEN, Harry [or Henry] (d
1907) actor EA/08*, WWT/14*
PAGDEN, Leonard (d 1928 [66])
English actor GRB/1-2
PAGE, Ambrose (d 1887 [74])
EA/88*
PAGE, Anthony (b 1935) Indian/
English director AAS, WWT/
15-16
PAGE, Ashley (d 1934 [67]) actor
BE*, WWT/14*
PAGE, Augusta (fl 1862) actress
HAS
PAGE, Austin dramatist WWT/7-11

PAGE, Dr. Byrd (d 1916) con-
jurer EA/17*
PAGE, Charles (d 1898) music-
hall manager EA/99*
PAGE, Mrs. Charles see Tal-
bot, Mrs.
PAGE, Curtis C. (b 1914) Amer-
ican educator BE
PAGE, E. V. manager, song
composer CDP
PAGE, Mrs. E. V. see Page,
Sarah Florence
PAGE, Evelyn American actress
TW/25, 28
PAGE, Geraldine (b 1924) Amer-
ican actress AAS, BE, CB,
ES, TW/9-24, 26-27, 29,
WWT/12-16
PAGE, Henry C. (b 1825) Ameri-
can actor, manager, agent HAS
PAGE, James Augustus [Sydney
Hayes] (d 1888 [30]) actor
EA/89*
PAGE, John (fl c. 1626) actor
DA
PAGE, Kitty see Hargreaves,
Mrs. Albert
PAGE, Nathaniel Clifford (b
1866) American composer
WWA/4, WWM
PAGE, Norman (d 1935 [59])
English actor, stage manager,
producer GRB/2-3, WWT/1-7
PAGE, Oliver (fl 1550) actor
DA
PAGE, Patti (b 1927) American
singer CB
PAGE, Paul (d 1974 [70]) per-
former BP/58*
PAGE, Philip (d 1968 [80]) actor
WWT/15*
PAGE, Philip P. (b 1884/89)
English critic, dramatist
WWT/5-13
PAGE, Reginald Ernest see
Harley, Rex
PAGE, Rita (1906-54) English ac-
tress, singer WWT/7-8
PAGE, Ruth (b 1903?/05) Amer-
ican dancer, choreographer
CB, ES
PAGE, Sarah Florence [Mrs. E.
V. Page] (d 1902 [50]) EA/03*
PAGE, Tilsa (b 1926) English
actress WWT/11-12
PAGE, Will A. (d 1928 [55])
press representative BE*,
BP/13*

PAGE, William J. (d 1870) music-
hall chairman EA/71*
PAGENT, Robert (b 1917) American
actor TW/1-3
PAGE-PHILLIPS, Percy see An-
stey, Percy
PAGET, Lord Alfred (d 1888 [72])
EA/89*
PAGET, Cecil (d 1955) manager
WWT/6-9
PAGET, Mrs. F. M. see Paget,
Martha E.
PAGET, Frederick Maurice (d 1911
[62]) actor EA/12*
PAGET, Martha E. [Mrs. F. M.
Paget] (d 1912 [82]) EA/13*
PAGET, Rose Vernon English ac-
tress GRB/1-2
PAGET, Violet [Vernon Lee] (1856-
1935) dramatist WWW/3
PAGET-BOWMAN, Cicely (b 1910)
English actress WWT/10-16
PAGETT, Nicola (b 1945) Egyptian/
English actress WWT/16
PAGLIA, Gina (b 1955) American
actress TW/28
PAGNOL, Marcel (1895-1974)
French dramatist, director, pro-
ducer BE, CB, ES, MD, MWD,
NTH
PAIGE, Autris (b 1941) American
actor TW/28
PAIGE, Janis [née Donna Mae Jaden]
(b 1922) American actress, singer
BE, CB, TW/8, 10-15, 24-25,
WWT/15-16
PAIGE, Mabel (d 1954 [74]) Ameri-
can actress TW/10
PAIGE, Raymond North (1900-65)
American conductor WWA/4
PAIN, Mr. (fl 1857?) actor CDP
PAINE, Albert Bigelow (1861-1937)
dramatist HJD
PAINE, Ira (d 1889 [53]) marksman
EA/90*
PAINE, John Knowles (1839-1906)
American composer DAB, HJD
PAINE, Lizzie [Mrs. George Mil-
bank] (fl 1888?) songwriter CDP
PAINTER, Eleanor (1890-1947)
American actress, singer TW/
4, WWT/4-7
PAISNER, Dina (b 1963) American
actress TW/27, 29
PAKENHAM, Essie [Mrs. R. J.
Pakenham] (d 1893) EA/94*
PAKENHAM, Henry (d 1875) actor
EA/76*

PAKENHAM 724

PAKENHAM, Mrs. R. J. see
Pakenham, Essie
PALANCE, Jack (b 1920) Ameri-
can actor ES, TW/7-14
PALERME, Gina actress, dancer
WWT/4-5
PALERMO, Alex (b 1929) Ameri-
can director, choreographer,
actor BE
PALETTE, Billy (d 1963) English
performer BE*
PALEY, John (d 1918) EA/19*
PALFREY, May Lever [Mrs.
Weedon Grossmith] (1867/73-
1929) English actress CDP,
EA/96, GRB/1-4, WWT/1-6
PALFREYMAN, Thomas (d 1589?)
member of the Chapel Royal
DNB
PALITZ, Morty (d 1962 [53])
composer/lyricist BP/47*
PALLADINO, Emma (1861-1922)
Italian dancer ES
PALLADINO, Joseph Antony see
Faye, Joey
PALLADIO, Andrea (1518-80)
Italian architect COC, OC/
1-3
PALLANT, Robert (fl 1590-1616)
actor DA
PALLANT, Robert, the Younger
(fl 1620s) actor DA
PALLANT, Walter (d 1904 [45])
dramatist, theatre chairman
BE*, EA/05*, WWT/14*
PALLENBERG, Max (d 1934 [57])
actor WWT/14*
PALLERINI, Antonia (1790-1870)
Italian dancer, mimist ES
PALLES, Joseph (d 1895 [45])
music-hall comedian EA/96*
PALLETTE, Eugene (d 1954 [65])
American actor BE*, BP/39*
PALLING, Arthur (d 1916) actor
EA/17*
PALLING, Mrs. Arthur see
Palling, Laura
PALLING, Laura [Mrs. Arthur
Palling] (d 1896) EA/97*
PALLING, Walter (d 1896) actor
EA/97*
PALLISER, Esther (b 1872) ac-
tress, singer CDP, DP
PALMER, Mr. (fl 19th cent)
actor CDP
PALMER, Mr. (d 1833) American
actor CDP, HAS
PALMER, Mrs. see Gee,

Caroline Eliza
PALMER, Miss (fl 1752-53) actress
HAS
PALMER, Ada English actress
GRB/1
PALMER, Albert Marshman (1838-
1905) American manager CDP,
COC, DAB, ES, NTH, OC/1-3,
SR, WWA/1
PALMER, Alexander (d 1888 [74])
comic singer EA/90*
PALMER, Mrs. A. M. (d 1923)
president of the Professional
Women's League BP/7*
PALMER, Anthony (b 1934) Ameri-
can actor TW/26, 29-30
PALMER, Arthur A. see Boswell,
A. P.
PALMER, Barbara (b 1911) English
actress WWT/9
PALMER, Bessie (d 1910 [79])
singer EA/11*
PALMER, Betsy (b 1929) American
actress BE, TW/12, WWT/16
PALMER, Byron (b 1921) American
actor TW/5-16
PALMER, Charles (1869-1920)
critic WWT/2-3
PALMER, Charles (d 1976 [46])
performer BP/60*
PALMER, Charles Edward (d 1878
[75]) actor EA/79*
PALMER, David S. (1826-57) Amer-
ican actor HAS
PALMER, Mrs. David S. [Lizzie
Steele] (1832-58) American ac-
tress HAS
PALMER, Dawson (d 1972 [35]) per-
former BP/57*
PALMER, E. Blanchard (d 1877)
caterer EA/78*
PALMER, Ethelyn (b 1879) Ameri-
can actress WWS
PALMER, F. C. (d 1917) EA/18*
PALMER, F. Grove see Grove,
Fred
PALMER, Florrie see Leamore,
Florence
PALMER, Henry [Harry Siddons]
(d 1886 [41]) actor? EA/87*
PALMER, Henry David (1832-79)
American manager CDP
PALMER, Herbert Edward (1880-
1961) English dramatist WWW/6
PALMER, Jack (d 1976 [75]) com-
poser/lyricist BP/60*
PALMER, James (d 1882 [52])
ceiling walker EA/84*

PALMER, Jay (d 1970 [71]) performer BP/55*

PALMER, John (1728-68) English actor COC, DNB, GT, OC/1-3, TD/1-2

PALMER, John (1742/45/47-98) English actor CDP, COC, DNB, GT, OC/1-3, OX, TD/1-2

PALMER, John (fl 1791) actor CDP

PALMER, John (d 1868 [86]) wardrobe keeper EA/69*

PALMER, John (1885-1944) English critic, dramatist CB, NTH, WWT/2-9, WWW/4

PALMER, Langford H. (d 1894 [28]) comedian EA/96*

PALMER, Leland (b 1945) American actor TW/28-30

PALMER, Lilli (b 1914) Austrian actress AAS, CB, ES, TW/5-15, WWT/9-16

PALMER, Lucienne see Hill, Lucienne

PALMER, Mary see Adcock, Mrs. William

PALMER, Millicent see Bandmann-Palmer, Mrs.

PALMER, Minnie (1857/60-1936) American actress, singer CDP, DP, GRB/2-4, PP/2, WWS, WWT/1-8

PALMER, Peter (b 1931) American actor, singer BE, TW/13-16, 21, 29-30

PALMER, Reginald (d 1964 [74]) performer BP/49*

PALMER, Robert (1754-1817) English actor COC, GT, OC/3, TD/2

PALMER, Robert (1757-1805) actor CDP

PALMER, Samuel (d 1869 [42]) pantomimist EA/70*

PALMER, Samuel S. (fl 1848) American actor HAS

PALMER, Sarah Annie [Mrs. William Palmer] (d 1883 [35]) EA/84*

PALMER, Stacy (b 1930) American actor TW/28, 30

PALMER, Thomas (d 1868 [41]) costumier EA/69*

PALMER, Thomas (b 1914) Canadian actor TW/6-7

PALMER, William (d 1797) actor COC, OC/3, TD/2

PALMER, William (d 1887) music-hall manager EA/88*

PALMER, Mrs. William see Palmer, Sarah Annie

PALMER, William Henry [Robert Heller] (c. 1830-78) English entertainer DAB, WWA/H

PALMERSTON, Minnie [Mrs. Harriett Burrows] (d 1904) music-hall performer EA/05*

PALMERTON, Guy (d 1975 [61]) producer/director/choreographer BP/59*

PALMIERI, Joseph (b 1939) American actor TW/23-24, 26, 28-30

PALMIERI, Maria (fl 1876) singer CDP

PALMO, Ferdinand (1785-1869) Italian manager, singer? CDP, HAS

PALOTTA, Grace Austrian actress GRB/2

PALSEN, Mlle. (fl 1852) English dancer HAS

PALSGRAVE, John (fl 1514-31) translator CP/1-3

PAMPANINI, Rosetta (1900-73) Italian singer ES

PANAIEFF, Michel (b 1913) Russian/American dancer, choreographer ES

PANAMA, Norman (b 1914) American dramatist, producer, director BE

PANASSIE, Hugues (d 1974 [62]) critic BP/59*

PANDELAKIS, Beatrice (d 1973 [52]) performer BP/58*

PANDOLFI, Frank (d 1975 [73]) performer BP/59*

PANDOLFINI, Francesco (1836-1916) Italian singer ES

PANE-GASSER, John (1897-1964) Italian singer WWA/4

PANETTA, George (1915-69) American dramatist BE

PANGBORN, Franklyn (1889-1958) American actor TW/15, WWM

PANKEY, Aubrey (d 1971 [65]) performer BP/55*

PANKHURST, Frank (fl 1869?) minstrel CDP

PANKIN, Stuart (b 1946) American actor TW/28-29

PANT, Thomas (fl 1607-10) actor DA

PANTALEONI, Adriano (1837-1908) Italian singer ES

PANTER, Joan (b 1909) English
actress WWT/9-10

PANTHULU, B. R. (d 1974 [64])
producer/director/choreographer
BP/59*

PANVINI, Ron (b 1945) American
actor TW/28

PANZER, Paul W. (d 1958 [86])
actor BE*

PAOLIS, Alessio de (d 1964 [71])
Italian singer BE*

PAONE, Marion American actress
TW/28

PAPALEO, Anthony see Franciosa, Anthony

PAPANTI, Sig. (fl 1827) actress?
singer? HAS

PAPAS, Irene (b 1929) Greek actress TW/29

PAPE, Herr (d 1874) musician
EA/75*

PAPE, Joan (b 1944) American
actress TW/27, 29-30

PAPE, Willie Barnesmore (b
1854) American pianist CDP,
HAS

PAPENDICK, George (fl 1798)
translator CP/3

PAPI, Gennaro (1886-1941) Italian
conductor CB, WWA/1

PAPINI, Guido (d 1912 [65]) musician EA/13*

PAPIROFSKY, Joseph see Papp,
Joseph

PAPP, Joseph [né Papirofsky]
(b 1921) American producer,
director AAS, BE, CB, COC,
ES, OC/3, WWT/14-16

PAPPENHEIM, Eugenie singer
CDP

PAQUE, Mons. C. (d 1876 [50])
musician EA/77*

PARADISE, Sophia (d 1906 [63])
EA/07*

PARADO, Eleanore (d 1974) wardrobe mistress BP/58*

PARDAVE, Jose (d 1970 [68])
performer BP/55*

PARDEE, Chester F. (d 1974
[58]) producer/director/chore-
ographer BP/59*

PARDEE, C. W. (d 1975 [90])
performer BP/60*

PARDEY, George (b 1835) English
actor HAS

PARDEY, Mrs. George [Josephine
Costigan] (b 1852) American
actress HAS

PARDEY, H. O. (1808-65) English
actor, dramatist HAS, SR

PARDINI, Gaetano (fl 1849) singer
CDP

PARDOLL, David (b 1908) American
stage manager, production supervisor BE

PARDUE, Henry (d 1917 [34]) EA/
18*

PARDY, Laurie Athey (d 1916
[42]) EA/18*

PAREEZER, Barnett (d 1918 [59])
EA/19*

PARELLA, Anthony (b 1915) American producer, director BE

PARENTEAU, Zoel (d 1972 [89])
composer/lyricist BP/57*

PAREPA, Euphrosyne see Rosa,
Parepa

PAREPA-ROSA, Euphrosyne see
Rosa, Parepa

PARERA, Grace Moore (d 1947)
singer WWW/4

PARFITT, Judy English actress
AAS, WWT/15-16

PARFRE, Ihan (fl 1512?) dramatist
CP/2-3

PARIS, Jackie (b 1961) American
actress TW/29

PARIS, Robert Graham (d 1974
[68]) drama coach BP/58*

PARISH, James (1904-74) English
dramatist, actor WWT/9-15

PARISH, Michael J. American actor
TW/26

PARISH, William (d 1917 [74]) circus proprietor EA/18*

PARISOT, Mlle. (fl 1796-99?)
dancer CDP

PARK, Merle (b 1937) Rhodesian
dancer CB, ES

PARK, R. (d 1894 [56]) EA/95*

PARK, Tom (d 1891 [32]) actor
EA/93*

PARKE, James H. (d 1970) educator BP/55*

PARKE, John (b c. 1750) American
dramatist EAP

PARKE, Walter (d 1922) dramatist
BE*, WWT/14

PARKE, William (1873?-1941) actor, manager CB

PARKER, Mr. (fl 1769) actor HAS

PARKER, Mrs. (fl 1700) singer
CDP

PARKER, Mrs. (fl 1798) actress
TD/1-2

PARKER, Mrs. (d 1893) EA/94*

PARKER, Miss (fl 1863) American singer HAS
PARKER, Miss see Johnston, Mrs. Henry Erskine
PARKER, Miss see Murray, Mrs.
PARKER, Ada see Stetson, Ada
PARKER, Adam (fl 1849) American actor HAS
PARKER, Albert (d 1974 [87]) producer/director/choreographer BP/59*
PARKER, Amelia (1827-59) American actress HAS
PARKER, Annie [Mrs. Edwin Drew] (d 1913) EA/14*
PARKER, Annie see Corri, Mrs. V.
PARKER, Anthony (b 1912) English producer, manager WWT/11-14
PARKER, Barnett (1889?-1941) English comedian CB
PARKER, Bob (d 1975) performer BP/60*
PARKER, Cecil (1897-1971) English actor TW/7, 27, WWT/7-14
PARKER, Charles (d 1889) American actor, dancer EA/90*
PARKER, Charles (d 1898) scene artist EA/99*
PARKER, Clementina (d 1888 [85]) actress EA/89*
PARKER, Dorothy (fl 1910-13) English actress WWM
PARKER, Dorothy (1893-1967) American lyricist, dramatist, critic HJD, WWW/6
PARKER, Eleanor (b 1922) American actress ES
PARKER, Flora (d 1950 [67]) actress, singer TW/7
PARKER, Frank (d 1919) EA/19*
PARKER, Frank (1858/62/64-1926) stage manager, producer GRB/1-4, WWT/1-5
PARKER, George (1732-1800) actor DNB
PARKER, George (d 1910) fireman EA/11*
PARKER, George D. (d 1937 [64]) producer, director BE*, WWT/14*
PARKER, Sir Gilbert (1862-1932) Canadian dramatist WWW/3
PARKER, Gilbert (b 1927) American talent representative BE
PARKER, Harry L. see Hanson, Harry L.
PARKER, Henry, Lord Morley (d 1556 [80]) dramatist CP/2-3
PARKER, Henry Taylor (1867-1934) American critic DAB, NTH, OC/1-3, WWA/1
PARKER, Horatio William (1863-1919) American composer DAB, HJD, WWM, WWA/1
PARKER, Jane (fl 1827) dancer CDP
PARKER, Jane (d 1908 [74]) EA/09*
PARKER, Jean (b 1918) American actress TW/3-8
PARKER, John (d 1858) clown, ballet master HAS
PARKER, John (d 1892 [31]) proprietor EA/93*
PARKER, John (1875-1952) American critic, historian COC, DNB, GRB/2-4, OC/1-3, WWA/3, WWT/1-11, WWW/5
PARKER, Mrs. John (fl 1798-1818) actress, dancer CDP
PARKER, John Barry (d 1917) scene artist EA/18*
PARKER, Johnny (d 1893) variety owner EA/94*
PARKER, John William (b 1909) American educator BE
PARKER, Joseph (fl 1832-41) English actor HAS
PARKER, Joseph S. (d 1970 [57]) producer/director/choreographer BP/54*
PARKER, Joy (b 1924) English actress WWT/11-14
PARKER, Lara (b 1942) American actress TW/25-26, 28
PARKER, Leonard (b 1932) American actor TW/29
PARKER, Lester (d 1975 [43]) performer BP/60*
PARKER, Lew [né Austin Lewis Jacobs] (1906/10-72) American actor BE, TW/2-3, 6-7, 11-15, 20, 29, WWT/11-15
PARKER, Lizzie (fl 1861?) singer CDP
PARKER, Lottie Blair (1858-1937) American dramatist GRB/3-4, SR, WWA/1, WWM, WWT/1-8
PARKER, Louise Little (d 1857) child actress CDP, HAS
PARKER, Louis Napoleon (1852-1944) French/English dramatist CB, COC, DNB, ES, GRB/1-4,

MWD, OC/1-3, SR, WWM,
WWS, WWT/1-9, WWW/4
PARKER, Margaret (fl 1850s)
actress HAS
PARKER, Martha Marian (d 1868
[37]) singer EA/69*
PARKER, Mary [Mrs. Stafford
Smith] (d 1910) EA/11*
PARKER, Mary Jennie (fl 1838-
67) American actress HAS
PARKER, Murray (d 1965 [69])
performer BP/50*
PARKER, Rachel (d 1904 [80])
EA/05*
PARKER, Richard (d 1892 [39])
scene artist EA/93*
PARKER, Roger (d 1917) come-
dian EA/18*
PARKER, Ross (d 1974 [59])
composer/lyricist BP/59*
PARKER, Sarah (fl 1827) dancer
CDP
PARKER, Sarah Naomi Jane
[Mrs. Will Parker] (d 1876)
EA/77*
PARKER, Thane (1907-75) English
manager WWT/9-14
PARKER, T. W. (d 1892) actor
EA/93*
PARKER, Warren (b 1909) Amer-
ican actor TW/3
PARKER, W. E. (d 1875 [52])
pantaloon EA/76*
PARKER, Will (d 1886) Negro
comedian EA/87*
PARKER, Mrs. Will see Parker,
Sarah Naomi Jane
PARKER, William (d 1886) sing-
er, composer CDP
PARKER, W. Oren (b 1911) Amer-
ican educator, designer BE
PARKER SISTERS singers,
dancers CDP
PARKES, Mrs. A. L. see Kiral-
fy, Haniola
PARKES, Caroline see Fenton,
Mrs. Charles
PARKES, George (d 1894) actor
CDP
PARKES, George (d 1895 [68])
lessee EA/96*
PARKES, Mrs. George Richmond
see Robins, Elisabeth
PARKES, W. S. (d 1908) EA/09*
PARKHILL, Dale (b 1925) Amer-
ican actor TW/8-10
PARKHIRST, Douglass (1921-64)
American actor TW/13-14, 20

PARKHOUSE, Miss see Cowley,
Mrs. Abraham
PARKHOUSE, Hannah see Cowley,
Hannah
PARKHURST, Edwin R. (b 1848)
English critic WWM
PARKHURST, George A. (d 1890)
American comedian EA/91*
PARKIN, Mrs. Thomas P. (d 1868)
actress? EA/69*
PARKINA, Elizabeth (b 1882) Amer-
ican singer GRB/1-4
PARKINSON, James (d 1894 [46])
actor EA/95*
PARKINSON, Thomas (fl 1769-89)
portrait-painter DNB
PARKINSON, William (d 1891)
cornopean player EA/92*
PARKS, Alonzo [Alonzo Chapman]
(d 1863 [31]) American actor?
HAS
PARKS, Bernice actress TW/3
PARKS, Fanny see Edrian, Fanny
PARKS, George R. (d 1887) actor
NYM
PARKS, Hildy (b 1926) American
actress BE, TW/8-9
PARKS, J. C. (d 1888 [30]) "circus
leader" EA/90*
PARKS, John Gower (1904-55) Eng-
lish designer ES
PARKS, Larry (1914-75) American
actor BE, WWT/15
PARKS, Trina American actress
TW/28
PARLO, Dita (d 1972 [65]) per-
former BP/56*
PARLOWE, Richard see Par-
rowe, Richard
PARMALEE, Barbara (d 1965 [24])
performer BP/50*
PARMALEE, Charles (d 1965 [37])
performer BP/50*
PARNELL, James (1923-61) Amer-
ican actor TW/2-6
PARNELL, Thomas Frederick see
Russell, Fred
PARNELL, Val (1894-1972) English
manager COC, WWT/10-14
PARNES, Nathan (d 1964 [69])
producer/director BP/49*
PARODI, Teresa (b 1827) singer
CDP, HAS
PAROSSI, Napoleon (fl 1848) actor?
singer? HAS
PARR, Miss see Smith, Mrs.
PARR, W. Henry see Furnival,
Henry

PARR, William (fl 1602-20) actor
DA
PARRIS, George John (d 1910
[79]) actor? EA/11*
PARRIS, Steve Greek/American?
actor TW/25
PARRISH, Helen (d 1959 [35])
American actress BE*
PARRISH, Judy (b 1916) American
artists' representative, actress
BE
PARROCK, Eliza (b 1806) actress
CDP
PARROCK, Isabella [Mrs. William
Parrock] (d 1891) EA/92*
PARROCK, Mrs. William see
Parrock, Isabella
PARROWE, Richard (fl 1538-45)
actor DA
PARRY, Alfred (d 1892) EA/93*
PARRY, Alfred W. English drama-
tist GRB/1
PARRY, Sir Edward Abbott (d
1943 [80]) dramatist GRB/1-4,
WWT/1-7
PARRY, Henry (d 1886 [43]) ac-
tor? EA/87*
PARRY, John (1776-1851) musi-
cian, composer, dramatist
CDP, DNB
PARRY, John (d 1877 [67]) actor
EA/78*
PARRY, John (d 1881) comedian,
pantomimist EA/82*
PARRY, Mrs. John actress CDP
PARRY, John Orlando (1810-79)
English actor, singer CDP,
DNB, OAA/1-2
PARRY, Joseph (1841-1903) com-
poser DNB
PARRY, Katharine (b 1880) Eng-
lish actress GRB/1-2
PARRY, Robert (d 1869) musician
EA/70*
PARRY, R. W. (d 1905 [31])
actor EA/06*
PARRY, Sefton Henry (1822-87)
manager, actor DNB, NYM
PARRY, Stella (d 1906) burlesque
actress EA/07*
PARRY, Tom (d 1862 [56]) actor,
dramatist BE*, EA/72*,
WWT/14*
PARRY, W. Haydn (d 1894 [29])
composer EA/95*
PARRY, William (b 1856) English
manager, actor, stage manager
WWS

PARSELLE, John (1820-85) actor
CDP
PARSLEY, Daniel (d 1890) EA/91*
PARSLEY, William (d 1880 [95])
EA/81*
PARSLOE, Charles Thomas (1804-
70) English actor, agent CDP,
HAS
PARSLOE, Charles Thomas, Jr.
(1836-98) American actor CDP,
HAS, SR
PARSLOE, Edmond John (d 1832
[31]) actor, pantomimist CDP,
HAS
PARSLOE, James (d 1847 [48])
actor, prompter EA/72*, WWT/
14*
PARSONAGE, Mr. J. (d 1868 [34])
proprietor EA/69*
PARSONS, Mrs. [née Phelps] (d
1811) dramatist CP/3
PARSONS, Alan (1888-1933) English
critic, journalist COC, WWT/
6-7
PARSONS, Charles Booth (b 1805)
American actor CDP, HAS
PARSONS, Donovan (b 1888) lyricist
WWT/6-9
PARSONS, Eliza (d 1811) dramatist
DNB
PARSONS, Estelle (b 1927) Ameri-
can actress BE, CB, TW/19-28,
30, WWT/15-16
PARSONS, George (b 1873) Ameri-
can actor WWM
PARSONS, Gram (d 1973 [27]) per-
former BP/58*
PARSONS, John see Juleene, H.
F.
PARSONS, Louella (d 1972 [91])
critic BP/57*
PARSONS, Milton (b 1904) American
actor TW/6
PARSONS, Nancie [Lady Mercy
Greville] (b 1904) actress WWT/
6-7
PARSONS, Percy (1878-1944) Amer-
ican actor, singer WWT/5-9
PARSONS, Philip dramatist FGF
PARSONS, Thomas (fl 1599-1602)
actor DA
PARSONS, Thomas A. (1822-57)
American actor HAS
PARSONS, Tom (d 1874 [60]) comic
singer, pantomimist EA/75*
PARSONS, William (1736-95) English
actor CDP, DNB, GT, TD/1-2
PARSONS, Sir William (1746?-

1817) professor of music CDP
PARSONS, William C. (d 1973
[49]) union representative
BP/57*
PARTCH, Harry (d 1974 [73])
composer/lyricist BP/59*
PARTINGTON, Mary (fl 1853)
dancer HAS
PARTINGTON, Sally (fl 1865)
actress CDP
PARTLETON, Henry (d 1893)
actor EA/94*
PARTRIDGE, Bernard see
Gould, Bernard
PARTRIDGE, William see Tit-
bits, Mjr.
PARVER, Michael (b 1936) Amer-
ican producer BE
PASCAL, Ernest (d 1966 [70])
dramatist BP/51*
PASCAL, Gabriel (1894-1954)
Hungarian director BE*
PASCO [John Evans] (d 1902)
music-hall performer EA/03*
PASCO, Richard (b 1926) English
actor AAS, TW/23, WWT/
14-16
PASCOE, Charles Eyre (d 1912
[70]) editor BE*, WWT/14*
PASCOE, James (d 1910 [34])
EA/11*
PASERO, Tancredi (b 1893) Italian
singer ES
PASLE-GREEN, Jeanne American
actress TW/26
PASO, Alfonso (b 1926) Spanish
dramatist MWD
PASQUA, Giuseppina (1855-1930)
Italian singer ES
PASQUIN, Antony see Williams,
John
PASSANTINO, Anthony (b 1945)
American actor TW/26-27
PASSELTINER, Bernie (b 1931)
American actor TW/27-29
PASSEUR, Steve (d 1966 [67])
dramatist BP/51*, WWT/15*
PASSMORE, Mr. (fl 1848) actor
HAS
PASSMORE, Alfred (d 1889)
EA/90*
PASSMORE, James (d 1889)
EA/90*
PASSMORE, Walter (1867-1946)
English actor, singer GRB/
1-4, WWT/1-9
PASSMORE, Mrs. Walter see
Fraser, Agnes

PASTA, Guiditta (1797/98/99-1865)
Italian singer CDP, ES, OX
PASTA, Johnny [John Wilson Wood-
ley] (d 1890) EA/91*
PASTENE, Robert (b 1918) Ameri-
can actor TW/7-9, 19-20, 25
PASTON, Adelaide Clotilda (d
1898 [46]) equestrienne EA/99*
PASTON, George [Emily Morse
Symonds] (d 1936) dramatist
WWT/1-8
PASTOR, Antonio [Tony] (1837-
1908) American manager CDP,
COC, DAB, HAS, HJD, GRB/
3-4, NTH, OC/3, SR, WWS
PASTOR, Billy (fl 1860s) American
vaulter, equestrian, comic singer
HAS
PASTOR, Frank (b 1837) American
equestrian CDP, HAS
PASTOR, G. W. (d 1918) EA/19*
PASTOR, Lizzie (d 1891) circus
performer EA/92*
PASTOR, Stuart (d 1881 [34]) clown
EA/82*
PASTOR, Tony see Pastor, An-
tonio
PASTOR, William H. (1840-77)
actor, acrobat, singer, manager
CDP
PASTRANA, Julia (d 1860) freak
CDP, HAS
PATANIA, Deolia (fl 1855) singer
HAS
PATANIA, Elise (fl 1855) singer
CDP
PATCH, Blanche (d 1966 [87])
secretary BP/51*
PATCH, Julia (d 1872) actress
EA/73*
PATCH, W. (d 1895) actor? EA/
96*
PATCH, Wally (1888-1970) English
actor WWT/10-14
PATE, Emma (d 1884) EA/85*
PATEGG, Max (b 1855) German
actor, manager WWT/2
PATEMAN, Bella [Mrs. Robert
Pateman] (1843-1908) English
actress CDP, GRB/3-4, OAA/
1-2
PATEMAN, Mrs. Charles see
Cosgrove, Marie
PATEMAN, Isabella see Pateman,
Bella
PATEMAN, Robbie (d 1910 [24])
EA/11*
PATEMAN, Robert (1840-1924)

actor GRB/3-4, OAA/1-2,
WWT/1-4
PATEMAN, Mrs. Robert see
Pateman, Bella
PATERSON, William (fl 1740)
Scottish dramatist CP/1-3, GT
PATERSON, William (b 1919)
American actor, director BE,
TW/26
PATESON, William (fl 1584) actor
DA
PATEY, George (d 1893) actor?
EA/95*
PATEY, Janet Monach [Mrs.
John G. Patey] (1842-94) Eng-
lish singer CDP, DNB
PATEY, Mrs. John G. see
Patey, Janet Monach
PATEY, John George (d 1902 [66])
singer EA/03*
PATI, Pramod (d 1975 [42]) pro-
ducer/director/choreographer
BP/59*
PATIERNO, Sig. (d 1877) singer
EA/78*
PATON, Mr. (fl 1780) Scottish
dramatist CP/2-3, GT
PATON, Miss see Paton, Mary
Ann
PATON, Eliza (fl 1829-34?) ac-
tress CDP
PATON, Isabella (fl 1827?) singer
CDP
PATON, Mary Ann (1802-64)
Scottish singer, actress BS,
DNB, OX
PATRICK, Benilde (b 1927)
American educator BE
PATRICK, Dennis [Dennis Har-
rison] (b 1918) American actor
TW/6-15, 23, 28
PATRICK, Edward John Harley
(d 1898) EA/99*
PATRICK, Jerome (d 1923 [40])
New Zealand actor BE*,
BP/8*
PATRICK, John (b 1902/05/06/
07/10) American dramatist
AAS, BE, CD, HJD, MD, MH,
MWD, WWT/11-16
PATRICK, Lee American actress
BE
PATRICK, Leonard stage manager,
actor BE
PATRICK, Nigel (b 1913) English
actor, director AAS, WWT/
9-16
PATRICK, Richard (fl 1607) actor

DA
PATRICK, Robert (b 1937) Ameri-
can dramatist, director, actor
CD
PATRICK, Dr. Samuel (d 1748)
dramatist CP/1-3
PATRICOLA, Tom (1891-1950)
American actor, singer TW/6,
WWT/7-8
PATRICOLO, Angelo Italian com-
poser CDP
PATRIZIO, Count Ernest (fl 1878)
strong man CDP
PATSALL (fl 1773) dramatist CP/3
PATSTON [Or Patson], Doris (1908-
57) English actress, singer
TW/1, 5-6, 8, 13
PATTEN, Dorothy (d 1975 [70])
actress BP/59*, WWT/16*
PATTERSON, Ada (d 1939) Ameri-
can writer, critic WWM
PATTERSON, Albert (b 1911) Amer-
ican actor TW/3
PATTERSON, Bayard see Harri-
son, Bob
PATTERSON, Benjamin performer?
CD
PATTERSON, Burdella (d 1973 [90])
performer BP/57*
PATTERSON, Dick American actor
TW/21
PATTERSON, Elizabeth (1874/82-
1966) American actress BE,
TW/10, 22
PATTERSON, Elma C. (d 1975
[86]) performer BP/60*
PATTERSON, James (1932-72)
American actor TW/22, 24-26,
29
PATTERSON, James Henry see
Sutton, Sambo
PATTERSON, John (d 1889) circus
clown EA/90*
PATTERSON, Mrs. Johnny (d 1886)
EA/87*
PATTERSON, Joseph Medill (1879-
1946) American dramatist WWM
PATTERSON, Lee (d 1967 [49])
critic BP/52*
PATTERSON, Marjorie (d 1948
[61]) actress BE*, WWT/14*
PATTERSON, Neva (b 1922) Amer-
ican actress BE, TW/4-16,
WWT/14
PATTERSON, Phil (b 1952) Ameri-
can actor TW/27
PATTERSON, Tom (b 1920) Cana-
dian journalist, founder of

Stratford Shakespearian festival of Canada AAS, WWT/13-16

PATTERSON, Troy (d 1975 [49]) performer BP/60*

PATTERSON, Wilbur, Jr. (b 1946) American actor TW/27-29

PATTERSON, William (d 1907 [76]) marksman EA/08*

PATTERSON, Mrs. William see Templeton, Fay

PATTI, Adelina [Baroness Cederstrom] (1843-1919) Spanish singer CDP, GRB/1-4, ES, HAS, HP, SR, WWA/1, WWS, WWW/2

PATTI, Amalia see Strakosch, Mme.

PATTI, Signora Barilli (fl 1848) singer HAS

PATTI, Carlotta (1840-89) singer CDP, DNB, HAS

PATTI, Caterina singer CDP

PATTI, Salvatore (d 1869) Italian singer CDP, HAS

PATTISON, Mr. see Paterson, William

PATTISON, Emma (fl 1892?) singer CDP

PATTISON, Kate (fl 1877-79) English actress OAA/1-2

PATTMIE? Edward (fl 1574) actor DA

PATTON, Fred (1888-1951) American singer WWA/3

PATTON, Lucille American actress TW/23, 25-26, 28-29

PATTON, Phil (d 1972 [61]) producer/director/choreographer BP/57*

PATTON, Willard (1853-1924) American composer WWA/1

PATTRICK, William (fl 1624-36) actor DA

PATZAK, Julius (d 1974 [75]) performer BP/58*

PAUKER, Dr. Edmond (d 1962 [74]) Hungarian literary representative BE*, BP/46*

PAUL, Ann [Mrs. W. Paul] (d 1891 [71]) EA/92*

PAUL, Betty (b 1921) English actress BE, WWT/11-14

PAUL, Elliot (b 1942) American actor TW/24

PAUL, George (fl 1755) dramatist CP/3

PAUL, Howard (1830-1905) American entertainer, dramatist,

actor CDP, EA/69, GRB/1, HAS

PAUL, Mrs. Howard [Isabella Featherstone] (1833-79) English actress, singer CDP, DNB, HAS, OAA/1-2

PAUL, James (d 1891) music-hall proprietor EA/92*

PAUL, Marie-Rose see Didelot, Mme. Charles-Louis

PAUL, Rene (b 1914) Swiss actor TW/6, 13

PAUL, Steven (b 1959) American actor TW/26-27

PAUL, Mrs. W. see Paul, Ann

PAUL, Wauna (d 1973 [61]) actress, producer TW/29

PAUL, W. H. (d 1865 [32]) agent HAS

PAUL, William (d 1882) music-hall proprietor EA/83*

PAULDING, Frederick (1859-1937) American actor, dramatist CDP

PAULDING, James Kirke (1779-1860) American dramatist CDP, EAP, RJ

PAULETTE, Larry (b 1949) American actor TW/30

PAULINA, Princess (d 1895 [19]) music-hall performer EA/96*

PAULL, Harry Major (1854-1934) English dramatist GRB/4, WWT/1-7, WWW/3

PAULLIN, Mr. (fl 1854-64) actor HAS

PAULLIN, Miss (fl 1864) actress HAS

PAULLIN, Louise [Mrs. H. B. Warner] (d 1910) actress, singer CDP

PAULO, Sig. (d 1835 [48]) clown CDP

PAULO, James (d 1883) clown, pantomimist BE*, EA/84*, WWT/14*

PAULO, Mrs. James see Paulo, Matilda

PAULO, Matilda [Mrs. James Paulo] (d 1880 [64]) EA/81*

PAULSEN, Albert (b 1927) actor TW/28

PAULSEN, Arno (d 1969 [69]) performer BP/54*

PAULTON, Edward Antonio (d 1939 [73]) Scottish dramatist, lyricist BE*, WWT/14*

PAULTON, Harry (1842-1917) English actor, dramatist CDP,

GRB/1-4, OAA/2, WWT/1-3
PAULTON, Joseph (d 1875) actor
EA/76*
PAULTON, Tom (d 1914 [76])
English actor, dramatist
GRB/1-3
PAULY, Rose (b 1894) Austrian
singer ES
PAUMGARTNER, Bernhard (d
1971 [83]) producer/director/
choreographer BP/56*
PAUMIER, Alfred [Alfred G. P.
Hodgson] (1870-1951) English
actor, manager GRB/1,
WWT/4-7
PAUMIER, M. N. (d 1876) actor,
lessee EA/77*
PAUNCEFORT, Claire (d 1924)
actress BE*, WWT/14*
PAUNCEFORT, George (fl 1854-
62) actor HAS
PAUNCEFORT, George (d 1942
[72]) actor BE*, WWT/14*
PAUNCEFORT, Mrs. George
[née Georgiana Edward] (d 1895
[70]) actress HAS, OAA/2
PAUNCEFORT, Georgiana see
Pauncefort, Mrs. George
PAUR, Emil (1855-1932) con-
ductor WWW/3
PAVAROTTI, Luciano (b 1935)
Italian singer CB
PAVEK, Janet (b 1936) American
singer, actress BE
PAVILLIO, Tom (d 1906) acrobat
EA/07*
PAVLOS, Anthony E. (d 1975
[44]) performer BP/60*
PAVLOVA, Anna (1882-1932)
Russian dancer ES, OC/2,
WWT/4-6
PAVLOW, Muriel (b 1921) English
actress WWT/10-16
PAVY, Salathiel [or Salmon]
(1590-1603) English actor
DA, OC/2-3
PAVYE, William (fl 1597-1608)
actor DA
PAWLE, J. Lennox (1872-1936)
English actor GRB/1-4,
WWT/1-8
PAWLEY, Edward (b 1901) Amer-
ican actor CB
PAWLEY, Eric (b 1907) American
educator, architect BE
PAWLEY, Nancy (b 1901) English
actress WWT/9-10
PAWLEY, William (d 1952 [47])

American actor BE*
PAWNEE, Bill [Gordon W. Lily]
(1866-1942) American performer
SR
PAWSON, Hargrave (1902-45) Eng-
lish actor WWT/9
PAXINOU, Katina (1900-73) Greek
actress BE, CB, COC, OC/3,
PDT, TW/1, 3, 9-10, 29,
WWT/10-15
PAXTON, Glenn (b 1931) American
composer BE
PAXTON, Sydney [Sydney Paxton
Hood] (1860-1930) English actor,
manager GRB/1-4, WWT/1-6
PAXTON-HOOD, Lavinia (d 1903)
EA/04*
PAYE, Mrs. Edmund see Paxton,
Emily Saxon
PAYE, Emily Saxon [Mrs. Edmund
Paye] (d 1899) EA/01*
PAYN, Graham (b 1918) South Afri-
can actor, singer TW/4, WWT/
10-16
PAYNE, Ben Iden (1881-1976) Eng-
lish actor, manager, director
AAS, BE, COC, GRB/4, NTH,
OC/3, WWT/1-15
PAYNE, Edmund (1865-1914) actor
GRB/1-4, WWT/1-2
PAYNE, F[anny] Ursula (fl 1894-
1928) American dramatist WWA/
5
PAYNE, Frederick (d 1880 [39])
pantomimist EA/81*, WWT/14*
PAYNE, Mrs. G. A. see Payne,
Mary Ann Misterson
PAYNE, George Adney (1846-1907)
Irish music-hall proprietor,
manager GRB/1-3
PAYNE, George Henry (1876-1945)
American dramatist WWA/2
PAYNE, Harry (d 1895 [63/64])
clown, pantomimist CDP, DP
PAYNE, Henry Neville (fl 1672-
1700) dramatist DNB
PAYNE, John (b 1912) American
actor ES
PAYNE, John Howard (1791-1852)
American actor, dramatist
CDP, COC, DAB, EAP, ES,
HAS, HJD, HP, OC/1-3, RJ,
SR, WWA/H
PAYNE, Laurence (b 1919) English
actor WWT/11-13
PAYNE, Leon (d 1969 [52]) per-
former BP/54*
PAYNE, Louisa (d 1887) actress

EA/88*

PAYNE, Mary Ann Misterson [Mrs. G. A. Payne] (d 1897 [47]) EA/98*

PAYNE, Millie (d 1917) EA/18*

PAYNE, Nevil (fl 1673-75) dramatist CP/2-3, GT

PAYNE, Reginald [Reginald Charles Greenwood] (b 1883) English actor GRB/1

PAYNE, Robert (fl 1604) patentee DA

PAYNE, Walter (d 1949 [76]) English director, manager WWT/5-10

PAYNE, William Henry (1804-78) actor, pantomimist CDP, DNB

PAYNE, William J. (d 1900 [33]) bellringer EA/01*

PAYNE, William Louis (d 1953 [80]) American actor TW/10, WWM, WWS

PAYNE, Willie (d 1889 [23]) skater EA/90*

PAYNE, W. Reuben (d 1909) actor EA/10*

PAYNE-JENNINGS, Victor (1900-62) English manager TW/19, WWT/9-10

PAYNE-TOWNSHEND, Charlotte Frances see Shaw, Mrs. George Bernard

PAYNTER, David William (1791-1823) English dramatist DNB

PAYNTON, Harry (d 1964 [74]) performer BE*, BP/49*

PAYSON, Blanche (d 1964 [83]) actress BE*

PAYSON, William Farquhar (1876-1939) American dramatist WWA/1

PAYTON, Adelaide (d 1901 [61]) EA/02*

PAYTON, Adelaide (d 1904) EA/05*

PAYTON, Corse (1867-1934) American actor, manager WWS

PAYTON-WRIGHT, Pamela (b 1941) American actress TW/1, 24-29, WWT/16

PEABODY, Josephine [Mrs. Lionel Marks] (1874-1922) American dramatist DAB, HJD, MWD, WWA/1, WWM

PEACH, Mrs. see Carr, Louisa Maria

PEACH, George R. (d 1908 [52]) actor EA/09*

PEACH, Lawrence Du Garde (d 1974 [94]) dramatist BTR/74

PEACH, Louisa actress EA/97

PEACHEY, Catherine [Mrs. George Darrell] (d 1892) actress EA/93*

PEACOCK, Bertram (d 1963 [70/79]) American actor, singer TW/19

PEACOCK, Kim (1901-66) English actor WWT/8-11

PEACOCK, Trevor (b 1931) English actor, composer, dramatist WWT/15-16

PEACOCKE, Robert (fl 1550) actor DA

PEADON, Pamela (b 1947) American actress TW/30

PEAKE, Lewis (d 1917) EA/18*

PEAKE, Mervyn (1911-68) Chinese/English dramatist WWW/6

PEAKE, Richard Brinsley (1792-1847) English dramatist DNB

PEAKES, Henry C. actor, singer CDP

PEAK FAMILY (fl 1850s) bell ringers SR

PEAL, Gilbert (d 1964 [76]) Lithuanian performer BE*

PEAPS, William dramatist CP/1-3, FGF

PEARCE, Lady [Carrie Coote] (1870-1907) actress DD, DP, GRB/3

PEARCE, Alice (1917-66) American actress BE, TW/6-8, 14-18, 22, WWT/14

PEARCE, Edward (fl 1598-1609) master of the Children of Paul's DA

PEARCE, Mrs. G. J. (d 1880) performer? EA/81*

PEARCE, H. Edward (d 1901 [40]) treasurer EA/02*

PEARCE, James (d 1884 [53]) property master EA/86*

PEARCE, John (b 1931) American actor TW/15, 20

PEARCE, Lizzie [Mrs. Arnold Burnett] (d 1890) serio-comic singer EA/92*

PEARCE, Lottie [Mrs. R. J. Hamer] (d 1916) EA/17*

PEARCE, Sam (1909-71) American curator BE

PEARCE, S. T. (d 1917 [66]) actor EA/18*

PEARCE, Vera (d 1966 [70])
Australian actress, singer
WWT/6-13

PEARCE, Walter (b 1878) English
actor GRB/3-4

PEARCE, Mrs. Will see Renetti, Lilian

PEARCE, William (fl 1785-96)
dramatist CP/3, GT, TD/1-2

PEARCE, W. W. (d 1864 [26])
comedian HAS

PEARCE, Mrs. W. W. see
Crapeau, Marion H.

PEARCE, Wynn (b 1929) American
actor TW/14

PEARL, Cora (d 1886) EA/87*

PEARL, Hal (d 1975 [61]) dramatist BP/60*

PEARL, Irwin (b 1945) American
actor TW/24-26

PEARL, Jack (b 1895) American
actor BE, WWT/8-11

PEARLMAN, Steve [or Stephen]
(b 1935) American actor TW/
23, 26, 30

PEARMAN, William (1792-1837)
English singer, actor CDP,
HAS, OX

PEARS, Peter (b 1910) English
singer CB

PEARSON, Alfred (d 1868 [34])
comedian EA/69*

PEARSON, Anne (b 1931) American actress TW/13

PEARSON, Beatrice (b 1920)
American actress TW/1-14,
WWT/11-12

PEARSON, Elizabeth (d 1896 [67])
EA/97*

PEARSON, Harry (1824-84) English actor CDP, HAS

PEARSON, Henry (fl 1826) American actor HAS

PEARSON, Hesketh (1887-1964)
English writer, actor AAS,
WWW/6

PEARSON, James (d 1910) carpenter EA/11*

PEARSON, John Henry (d 1887)
equestrian ring-master EA/
88*

PEARSON, Joshua (d 1870 [42])
stage carpenter EA/71*

PEARSON, Leon Morris (1899-
1963) American critic BE*,
BP/47*

PEARSON, Lloyd (1897-1966)
English actor WWT/9-14

PEARSON, Mary Ann see Croswell, Anne

PEARSON, Molly (d 1959 [83])
Scottish actress TW/15, WWM,
WWT/4-10

PEARSON, Richard (b 1918) Welsh
actor AAS, WWT/15-16

PEARSON, Scott (b 1941) American
actor TW/23, 25-28

PEARSON, Sidney (fl 1836) actor
HAS

PEARSON, Susan G. (b 1941)
American actress TW/26-28

PEARSON, Virginia (1886-1958)
American actress WWM

PEARSON, William C. [William P.
Collins] (d 1881) Negro minstrel
EA/82*

PEARSONS, Lyle (b 1947) American
actor TW/27

PEART, Prof. (d 1896 [23]) high
diver EA/97*

PEASE, Alfred Humphries (1838-
82) musician, composer CDP

PEASE, Charles H. (fl 1866?)
singer, songwriter CDP

PECHEY, Archibald Thomas see
Valentine

PECHNER, Gerhard (d 1969 [66])
singer TW/26

PECK, Mrs. (fl 1797) actress HAS

PECK, Francis (1692-1743) English
dramatist CP/2-3, GT

PECK, Gregory (b 1916) American
actor BE, CB, ES, WWT/10-11

PECK, Jack (d 1974 [72]) performer
BP/58*

PECK, Jon (b 1938) American actor
TW/30

PECKHAM, John (d 1974 [45]) pro-
ducer/director/choreographer
BP/59*

PECKOVER, J. W. (d 1888) music-
hall proprietor EA/89*

PECON, John J. (d 1975 [60]) performer BP/59*

PEDEL, Abraham (fl 1614-23) actor
DA

PEDEL, Jacob (fl 1597-1615) actor
DA

PEDEL, William (fl 1608-39?)
pantomimist, dancer DA

PEDEN, Emily (b 1944) American
actress TW/24

PEDERSON, Michael (b 1947)
American actor TW/24, 30

PEDGRIFT, Frederic Henchman
journalist GRB/2-4, WWT/1

PEDI, Tom (b 1913) American
actor BE, TW/23-24
PEDICORD, Harry W. (b 1912)
American educator BE
PEDINA, Gustave (d 1901 [28])
acrobat EA/02*
PEDRICK, Gale (1905-70) English
critic, journalist WWT/9-11
PEDRO, Little Dick (d 1894)
performer? EA/95*
PEDROTTI, Sig. (fl 1833) singer
HAS
PEDROTTI, Adelaide Varese (fl
1832-33) singer CDP, HAS
PEEL, David (b 1920) English
actor WWT/11
PEEL, Eileen (b 1909) English
actress AAS, WWT/6-16
PEEL, Matt (1830-59) American
minstrel, manager CDP,
HAS
PEEL, Tommy [Thomas Riley]
(d 1869) American jig dancer
HAS
PEELE, George (c. 1558-97) Eng-
lish dramatist COC, CP/1-3,
DNB, ES, FGF, HP, MH,
NTH, OC/1-3, PDT, RE, SR
PEER, William (d 1713) actor
DNB
PEERCE, Jan (b 1904) American
singer, actor CB, TW/28-29
PEERS, Donald (d 1973 [64])
performer BP/58*
PEERS, Edward see Pearce,
Edward
PEERS, Thomas (fl 1607) actor
DA
PEFFER, Crawford A. (d 1961
[94]) booking agent BE*
PEIL, Charles Edward (d 1962
[54]) actor BE*
PEIL, Edward J. (d 1958 [70])
actor BE*
PEILE, Frederick Kinsey (1862-
1934) Indian/English dramatist,
actor GRB/4, WWT/1-7
PEISLEY, Frederick (b 1904)
English actor WWT/5-16
PELBY, Julia see Thomas,
Mrs. Jacob Wonderly, II
PELBY, Ophelia see Anderson,
Ophelia
PELBY, Rosalie see Pelby,
Mrs. William
PELBY, William (1793-1850)
American manager, actor
CDP, HAS

PELBY, Mrs. William (1793-1857)
American actress CDP, HAS
PELHAM, Miss (fl 1834-36) Eng-
lish actress HAS
PELHAM, Dick (1815-76) minstrel
CDP
PELHAM, Harriet (fl 1863?) ac-
tress CDP
PELHAM, Jimmy American actor
TW/25-26, 28, 30
PELHAM, Meta (d 1948 [98]) ac-
tress BE*, WWT/14*
PELHAM, Paul (fl 1899?) singer,
songwriter CDP
PELHAM, Richard Ward (d 1876
[60]) minstrel manager EA/77*
PELHAM, Walter (d 1907 [72])
American actor GRB/3*, WWT/
14*
PELISSIER, Harry Gabriel (1874-
1913) English composer, enter-
tainer COC, DNB, GRB/3-4,
OC/1-3, WWT/1-2
PELL, Abner W. (d 1865 [45])
circus advertiser HAS
PELL, Gilbert Ward (d 1872 [47])
minstrel CDP
PELL, Harry (d 1866) Ethiopian
performer HAS
PELL, Johnny [John A. Davin]
(d 1866 [33]) Ethiopian comedian
HAS
PELLET, Ida (1838-63) actress
CDP
PELLETIER, Gilles (b 1925) Cana-
dian actor TW/21
PELLETIER, Wilfred (b 1896)
Canadian conductor CB
PELLICER, Pina (d 1964 [24])
performer BP/49*
PELLOW, Clifford (b 1928) Amer-
ican actor TW/23-25
PELLY, Ellen (d 1873 [20]) dancer
EA/74*
PELLY, Farrell (d 1963 [72]) Irish
performer BE*, BP/47*
PELMAN, Paul (d 1971 [81]) com-
poser/lyricist BP/55*
PELTON, Walter (d 1887) actor
NYM
PELTZER, William (c. 1832-87)
German actor NYM
PELZER, Catherina Josepha see
Pratten, Mme. Sydney
PEMBER, Ron (b 1934) English
actor WWT/15-16
PEMBERTON, Mr. (fl 1824) Eng-
lish actor HAS

PEMBERTON, Mrs. see Tatnall, Mrs.
PEMBERTON, Brock (1885-1950) American producing manager CB, DAB, NTH, TW/2-6, WWA/2, WWT/6-10
PEMBERTON, Charles Reece (1790-1840) Welsh/English actor DNB
PEMBERTON, Henry W. (d 1952 [77]) actor BE*, BP/37*
PEMBERTON, Mrs. John C. see Fowler, Emily
PEMBERTON, John Wyndham (1883-1947) Indian/English manager WWT/9-10
PEMBERTON, Madge (d 1970 [85]) dramatist BP/55*
PEMBERTON, Sir Max (1863-1950) English dramatist WWT/3-10
PEMBERTON, Reece (b 1913/14) English designer ES, WWT/15-16
PEMBERTON, Thomas Edgar (1849-1905) English dramatist, historian DNB, GRB/1, OC/1-3, WWW/1
PEMBERTON, William (d 1879 [37]) music-hall performer EA/81*
PEMBERTON-BILLING, Robin (b 1929) English director, dramatist WWT/15-16
PEMBROKE, Countess of see Herbert, Mary
PEMBROKE, George see Prud'homme, George
PEMBROKE, Wilson (d 1916) singer EA/17*
PENA, Julio (d 1972 [70]) performer BP/57*
PENBERTHY, Beverly American actress TW/25
PENCO, Rosina (1823/30-94) Italian singer CDP, ES
PENDENNIS, Rose (d 1943) actress BE*, WWT/14*
PENDERED, Mary Lucy (1858-1940) English dramatist WWW/4
PENDLETON, Austin (b 1940) American actor TW/23-24, 26-27, 30, WWT/16
PENDLETON, David (b 1937) American actor TW/30
PENDLETON, Marc J. (d 1892 [43]) actor CDP
PENDLETON, Nat (d 1967 [72])

performer BP/52*
PENDLETON, Mrs. William F. see Blauvett, Lilian
PENDLETON, Wyman (b 1916) American actor TW/22-23, 25-28, WWT/15-16
PENDRY, Charles (fl 1598) actor DA
PENE du BOIS, Raoul (b 1914) American designer BE
PENFOLD, George (d 1896 [40]) actor EA/97*
PENKETHMAN, William (d 1725) English actor COC, OC/1-3, TD/1-2
PENLEY, Mr. (fl 1807-08) actor GT
PENLEY, Mr. (fl 1815) actor BS
PENLEY, Arthur (1881-1954) English business manager WWT/2-7
PENLEY, Belville (d 1893 [84]) actor, manager EA/94*, WWT/14*
PENLEY, Belville S. (d 1940) producer, manager, author BE*, WWT/14*
PENLEY, Sampson (d 1838) actor, dramatist CDP
PENLEY, William (d 1838) actor WWT/14*
PENLEY, William Sydney (1851/52-1912) English actor, manager CDP, COC, DNB, DP, GRB/1-4, OC/1-3, WWT/1, WWW/1
PENLEY, Mrs. W[illiam] S[ydney] (d 1916) EA/17*
PENMAN, Charles (d 1912) carpenter EA/13*
PENMAN, Lea (d 1962 [67]) American actress BE*
PENN, Arthur (b 1922) American director, actor AAS, BE, CB, ES, WWT/13-16
PENN, Arthur A. (1880-1941) English composer, musician CB, WWA/1
PENN, Bill (b 1931) American actor, producer, director TW/12-20, WWT/15
PENN, Edward American actor TW/28-30
PENN, John (fl 1792) dramatist CP/3
PENN, Leo (b 1921) American actor TW/8-18
PENN, William (b c. 1592/98) English actor DA, OC/1-3

PENNA, Catherine (d 1879)
singer EA/81*
PENNA, Susanna Elizabeth [Mrs.
William Penna] (d 1885 [25])
EA/86*
PENNA, William (d 1889 [38])
music-hall singer EA/90*
PENNA, Mrs. William see
Penna, Susanna Elizabeth
PENNECUIK, Alexander (fl 1723)
dramatist CP/3
PENNER, Joe (1904-41) Hungarian
comedian CB
PENNER, Ralph (b 1947) American
actor TW/29
PENNICK, Ronald (d 1964 [69])
American actor BE*
PENNIE, John Fitzgerald (1782-
1848) English dramatist DNB
PENNIKET, Thomas (d 1877
[63]) comic singer EA/78*
PENNINGTON, Ann (1892/93/98-
1971) American dancer, ac-
tress BE, TW/28, WWT/6-11
PENNINGTON, Michael (b 1943)
English actor TW/25
PENNINGTON, W. E. actor,
minstrel CDP
PENNINGTON, W. H. (d 1923
[91]) actor BE*, WWT/14*
PENNOCK, Christopher (b 1944)
American actor TW/26-27
PENNOYER, Augustus S. (b
1829) American property man,
carpenter, actor, prompter,
stage manager, treasurer,
manager, business manager,
agent HAS
PENNOYER, Kate (fl 1855) Amer-
ican dancer, pantomimist HAS
PENNY, Anne (d 1784 [53])
dramatist CP/2-3, GT
PENNY, Henry see Carney,
Tom
PENNYCUICKE, Andrew (b 1620)
English dramatist, actor DA,
OC/1-3
"PENNY SHOWMAN, The" see
Richardson, Mr.
PENROSE, Charles (d 1952 [76])
comedian BE*, WWT/14*
PENROSE, Edith (fl 1888) actress
CDP
PENROSE, John (b 1917) English
actor WWT/11-13
PENROSE, John H. R. see
Able, Frank
PENROSE, Mrs. John H. R.

see Anson, Cecile E.
PENROSE, Pearl singer, actress
CDP
PENSON, Mrs. A. W. see Bel-
lamy, Mrs. William Hoare
PENSON, George (d 1833) singer,
actor CDP
PENSON, John Cranmer (d 1874
[73]) actor EA/75*
PENTECOST, George (b 1939)
American actor TW/23, 25-30
PENTITH, Mrs. (d 1900) actress?
EA/01*
PENTLAND, Joseph (fl 1841-68)
clown CDP, HAS
PENTLAND, Nicol actor EA/97
PENTLAND, Young (d 1906) EA/
07*
PENTLAND, Mrs. Young (d 1905)
EA/06*
PENTON, Fabian (fl 1602) actor
DA
PENZNER, Seymour (b 1915) Amer-
ican actor TW/26-29
PEOPLE SHOW, The theatre col-
lective CD
PEPER, Minnie Dorothy see
Oaker, Jane
PEPEREL, Giles (fl c. 1564-65?)
actor DA
PEPI see Brull, Joseph
PEPITA, Señorita (fl 1863) Spanish
dancer HAS
PEPLE, Edward H. (b 1867/69)
American dramatist GRB/2-4,
WWM, WWS, WWT/1-7
PEPOLI, Countess see Alboni,
Marietta
PEPPARD, George (b 1933) Amer-
ican actor CB, TW/13-16
PEPPER, Barbara (d 1969 [57])
performer BP/54*
PEPPER, George (fl 1830-31?)
American? dramatist EAP, RJ
PEPPER, Harry (fl 1890) actor,
songwriter CDP
PEPPER, Harry S. (d 1970 [79])
composer/lyricist BP/55*
PEPPER, Herman (d 1975 [77])
theatregoer BP/59*
PEPPER, John Henry (d 1900 [79])
EA/01*
PEPPIN, Henry Bedford (d 1916)
EA/17*
PEPPIN AND BURSCHARD (fl 1806)
French circus performers HAS
PEPUSCH, John Christopher (1667-
1752) German/English composer

ES
PEPUSCH, Mrs. John Christopher
  see De L'Epine, Francesca
  Margherita
PEPYS, Samuel (1633-1703) Eng-
  lish diarist COC, ES, NTH,
  OC/1-3
PERCASSI, Don American actor
  TW/30
PERCEVAL-CLARK, Perceval
  (1881-1938) English actor
  WWT/4-8
PERCIE, Norman (d 1885 [27])
  author, composer EA/86*
PERCIVAL, A. E. (d 1898 [39])
  actor EA/99*
PERCIVAL, Mrs. A. E. see
  Percival, Emily
PERCIVAL, Emily [Mrs. A. E.
  Percival] (d 1890 [25]) EA/91*
PERCIVAL, Horace (d 1961 [73/
  75]) actor BE*, WWT/14*
PERCIVAL, James Gates (1795-
  1856) American dramatist
  EAP
PERCIVAL, Percy (d 1909 [58])
  music-hall manager EA/10*
PERCIVAL, Susanna see Mount-
  fort, Susanna Percival
PERCIVAL, Thomas Purcell (d
  1904) actor EA/05*
PERCIVAL, Mrs. W. see
  Breeze, Mabel
PERCIVAL, Walter C. (d 1934
  [46]) American actor, drama-
  tist BE*, BP/18*
PERCIVAL, William (d 1871 [37])
  Negro singer & dancer EA/
  72*
PERCY, A. C. [Thomas Percy
  Carmichael] (d 1905 [45]) actor
  GRB/1
PERCY, Arthur Cecil [Thomas
  Percy Carmichael] (d 1905
  [43]) actor EA/06*
PERCY, Edward (1891-1968)
  English dramatist AAS, BE,
  WWT/5-14
PERCY, Eileen (d 1973 [72]) per-
  former BP/58*
PERCY, Ernest (d 1912 [44])
  actor EA/13*
PERCY, Esmé (1887-1957) Eng-
  lish actor, producer COC,
  ES, GRB/4, OC/3, TW/13,
  WWT/1-12, WWW/5
PERCY, George (d 1962 [90])
  performer BE*

PERCY, Mrs. H. (d 1875) singer
  EA/76*
PERCY, Harry (d 1874 [50]) comic
  singer EA/75*
PERCY, Henry (d 1880 [31]) singer,
  composer EA/81*
PERCY, Madeleine see Richard-
  son, Mrs. L. A.
PERCY, Rita (b 1840) English
  singer HAS
PERCY, Robert (fl 1586-87) actor
  DA
PERCY, S. Esmé see Percy,
  Esmé
PERCY, Thomas (d 1811 [83])
  dramatist CP/2-3, GT
PERCY, Thomas (d 1878 [35])
  actor EA/79*
PERCY, William (fl 1602) dramatist
  FGF
PERCY, William Stratford (1872-
  1946) Australian actor WWT/4-5
PERCYVAL, T. Wigney (b 1865)
  English actor, dramatist EA/
  96, GRB/1-4, WWT/4-9
PEREIRA, Louisa see Slater,
  Mrs. J. H.
PERELLI, Natole (d 1867) singer
  HAS
PERELMAN, Laura (d 1970 [58])
  dramatist BP/54*
PERELMAN, S. J. (b 1904) Amer-
  ican dramatist, writer BE,
  CB, CD, HJD, MH
PEREZ, Lazaro (b 1945) Cuban ac-
  tor TW/25, 29
PEREZ, Pepito (d 1975 [79]) per-
  former BP/60*
PERFECT, J. R. (d 1912 [77])
  manager WWT/14*
PERFECT, William (1740-1809)
  English dramatist CP/3
PERFITT, Frank (b 1880) English
  actor, singer GRB/1-2
PERFITT, Samuel (d 1872) actor
  EA/73*
PERFORMANCE GROUP, The
  theatre collective CD
PERHACS, Marylou (b 1944) Amer-
  ican actress TW/29
PERHAM, Josiah (1803-68) Ameri-
  can showman DAB
PERIER, Jean-Alexis (1869-1954)
  French actor, singer ES
PERKIN, John (fl 1572) actor DA
PERKINS, Anthony (b 1932) Amer-
  ican actor, director BE, CB,
  ES, TW/11-20, 23-24, 27,

WWT/13-16
PERKINS, Berkley (d 1904) actor
EA/05*
PERKINS, Charles (d 1869 [66])
actor? EA/70*
PERKINS, David Fessenden (d
1962 [77]) actor, dramatist
BE*, BP/47*, WWT/14*
PERKINS, Don (b 1928) American
actor TW/26-27
PERKINS, Francis D. (d 1970
[72]) critic BP/55*
PERKINS, Giulio (d 1875) singer
EA/76*
PERKINS, John (b 1927) Ameri-
can actor TW/9, 30
PERKINS, Julius Edson (1845-
75) singer CDP
PERKINS, Osgood (1892-1937)
American actor ES, WWT/
7-8
PERKINS, Richard (1585?-1650)
English actor CDP, DA, OC/
1-3
PERKINS, Rodney Croskey see
Rodney, Frank
PERKINS, Walter Eugene (d 1925
[55]) American actor WWA/5
PERKINS, Will (fl c. 1599?)
actor DA
PERKS, George [George Edward
Reed] (d 1893 [62]) EA/94*
PERKS, John (d 1874) actor?
performer? equestrian? EA/
75*
PERL, Arnold (1914-71) Ameri-
can producer, writer BE
PERL, Lothar (d 1975 [64]) com-
poser/lyricist BP/59*
PERLET, Herman (b 1864)
American conductor, composer
WWM
PERLEY, Frank Lee (b 1859)
American designer GRB/3
PERLMAN, Phyllis American
press representative BE
PERLMAN, William J. (d 1954
[72]) dramatist, director,
producer BE*, BP/39*,
WWT/14*
PERMAIN, Fred W. (d 1933)
actor EA/96
PERONI, Carlo (1889?-1944)
Italian conductor CB
PEROZZI, Luigi (fl 1844) singer
HAS
PERPER, Bob (d 1972) com-
poser/lyricist BP/57*

PERREN, George (1823-1909)
singer, director CDP
PERRETT, Francis L. (d 1972
[73]) publicist BP/57*
PERREY, Mireille French actress,
singer WWT/7-8
PERRIE, Ernestine (b 1912) Amer-
ican director BE
PERRIN, Mrs. [née J. B. Wood-
bury] actress HAS
PERRIN, Ceci (b 1945) American
actress TW/25
PERRINE, Valerie (b 1943) Ameri-
can actress, dancer CB
PERRINER, J. (fl 1839) actor
HAS
PERRING, James Ernest (d 1889
[66]) EA/90*
PERRINI, Signorina (fl 1850) sing-
er? HAS
PERRINI, Alfred Edward (d 1899
[38]) musician EA/00*
PERRINS, Leslie (d 1962 [60])
English actor WWT/5-11
PERRUCCHINI, Sig. (d 1870) com-
poser EA/71*
PERRY, Albert H. (d 1933 [63])
American actor BE*, BP/17*
PERRY, Alf [Alfred Thomas Allan]
(d 1902) minstrel comedian
EA/03*
PERRY, Antoinette (1888-1946)
American actress, manager,
producer, director CB, DAB,
NTH, TW/3, WWA/2, WWT/8-9
PERRY, Charles (d 1969) performer
BP/54*
PERRY, Charlotte (b 1890) Ameri-
can educator, director BE
PERRY, Clara [Mrs. Ben Davies]
(d 1944 [86]) singer BE*,
WWT/14*
PERRY, Elaine (b 1921) American
actress, producer, director BE
PERRY, Elizabeth see Creese,
Mrs. T. A.
PERRY, Florence (d 1949 [80])
actress BE*, WWT/14*
PERRY, Frederick William (d 1917
[81]) musician EA/18*
PERRY, Mrs. Harold see Bran-
don, Florence
PERRY, Harry A. (1826-62) Amer-
ican actor CDP, HAS
PERRY, Mrs. Harry A., I ac-
tress HAS
PERRY, Mrs. Harry A., II [née
Marian Agnes Land Rookes] (b

1843) Australian actress HAS

PERRY, Harry H. (d 1965 [84])
performer BP/50*

PERRY, Henry (d 1877 [36]) actor
EA/78*

PERRY, Horatio (d 1876 [29])
singer EA/77*

PERRY, Irma (d 1955 [79]) actress BE*, WWT/14*

PERRY, Joe (d 1904) minstrel?
EA/05*

PERRY, John (b 1906) Irish
dramatist, actor WWT/10-14

PERRY, John Bennett (b 1941)
American actor TW/24-25,
27, 29

PERRY, Margaret (b 1913) American actress, director, dramatist BE, WWT/7-11

PERRY, Martha American administrator BE

PERRY, Mary (d 1971 [83])
American actress TW/12-15

PERRY, Robert E. (d 1962 [83])
actor, director BE*

PERRY, Ronald (d 1963 [53])
performer BE*

PERRY, Ty (b 1918) American
actor TW/5

PERRY, Vic (d 1974 [54]) performer BP/59*

PERRY, William (fl 1615-42)
actor, manager DA

PERRYMAN, Daniel (d 1878 [68])
manager EA/80*

PERRYMAN, Jill (b 1933) Australian actress WWT/16

PERSIAN DWARF (fl 18th cent)
CDP

PERSIANI, Sig. (d 1869 [65])
composer EA/70*

PERSIANI, Fanny (1812-67)
singer CDP

PERSIAN TWIN SISTERS CDP

PERSINI, Elise singer CDP

PERSIVANI [R. Brown] (d 1890
[48]) clown, contortionist
EA/91*

PERSJ, Rupert see Percy,
Robert

PERSKE, Betty see Bacall,
Lauren

PERSOFF, Nehemiah (b 1920)
Israeli actor BE, WWT/14-16

PERSONN, Johann (fl 1579-80)
actor DA

PERSSON, Frederic J. (d 1966
[74]) actor, singer TW/23

PERSTEN, Rupert see Percy,
Robert

PERTOLDI, Ermina (d 1907 [52])
dancer GRB/3

PERTWEE, Jon (b 1919) English actor TW/24, WWT/15-16

PERTWEE, Michael (b 1916) English dramatist WWT/15-16

PERTWEE, Roland (1885/86-1963)
English dramatist WWT/5-13,
WWW/6

PERUGINI, Sig. [John Chatterton]
(d 1914 [59]) English actor BE*,
WWT/14*

PERY, Robert (fl 1529-31) member
of the Chapel Royal DA

PERY, William (fl 1530) member
of the Chapel Royal DA

PESCHKA-LEUTNER, Minna (1839-
90) singer CDP

PESSINA, Arturo (1858-1926) Italian
singer ES

PESTELL, Thomas (fl 1631-45)
dramatist CP/3, FGF

PETE [Herbert Williams] (d 1909
[38]) minstrel? EA/10*

"PETER?" (fl early 17th cent) actor? DA

PETERBOROUGH, Anastasia, Countess of [Mrs. Charles Mordaunt]
(d 1755) singer CDP, DNB

PETERKIN, Daisy see Dazie,
Mlle.

PETERS, Miss see Hamilton,
Mrs.

PETERS, Bernadette (b 1948) American actress, singer TW/24-28,
WWT/15-16

PETERS, Brandon (d 1956 [63])
American actor TW/12

PETERS, Brock (b 1927) American
actor, singer BE, TW/22-23,
28

PETERS, Charles (1825-70) English
actor CDP, HAS

PETERS, Fred (d 1963 [78]) actor
BE*

PETERS, F. W. (fl 1859) actor
HAS

PETERS, Gunnar (d 1974) performer
BP/58*

PETERS, Holly (b 1946) German/
American? actress TW/27

PETERS, Kay (b 1942) American
actress TW/25

PETERS, Roberta (b 1930) American
singer CB, ES

PETERS, Rollo (1892-1967) French

actor, designer, director, producer BE, TW/23, WWT/5-11

PETERS, Stephen [or Stefan] (b 1944) American actor TW/23, 28, 30

PETERS, Susan (d 1952 [31]) American actress BE*, BP/37*

PETERS, Werner (d 1971 [52]) performer BP/55*

PETERS, William (d 1975 [51]) performer BP/59*

PETERSEN, Alfred (d 1911) musical director EA/12*

PETERSEN, Erika (b 1949) American actress TW/26, 28

PETERSEN, Karen (d 1940 [37]) actress BE*, WWT/14*

PETERSILEA, Franz musician CDP

PETERSON, Daniel McCloud (d 1974 [57]) performer BP/59*

PETERSON, Eloise Kimball Walton (d 1971 [69]) publicist BP/56*

PETERSON, Joe (d 1964 [63]) performer BP/49*

PETERSON, Joseph (d 1798) actor, dramatist CP/2-3, GT, TD/1-2

PETERSON, Kurt (b 1948) American actor TW/25-29

PETERSON, Lenka (b 1925) American actress BE, TW/4, 8, 30

PETERSON, Louis (b 1922) American dramatist, actor BE

PETERSON, Margaret (1883-1933) dramatist WWW/2

PETERSON, Marjorie (d 1974 [68]) American actress TW/6-14

PETERSON, May (1889-1952) American singer WWA/3

PETERSON, Wally (b 1919) American actor TW/23

PETHERBRIDGE, Edward (b 1936) English actor AAS, WWT/15-16

PETIE, Mary Ann (d 1884 [30]) EA/85*

PETINA, Irra (b 1900/14) Russian actress, singer BE, TW/1-3, 5-7, 13-15, 22

PETIPA, Marius (1822-1910) dancer, choreographer BE*, WWT/14*

PETIT, Roland (b 1924) French

dancer, choreographer CB, ES, WWT/11-12

PETLEY, E. S. (d 1945 [69]) actor BE*, WWT/14*

PETLEY, Frank E. (1872-1945) English actor WWT/4-9

PETRASS, Sari (1890-1930) Austrian actress, singer WWT/2-6

PETRICOFF, Elaine American actress TW/28-30

PETRIE, Daniel M. (b 1920) Canadian director, actor BE

PETRIE, David Hay (1895-1948) Scottish actor WWT/5-10

PETRIE, Eliza Place (d 1865) actress HAS

PETRIE, George (b 1915) American actor TW/2-3

PETRIE, Howard A. (d 1968 [61]) performer BP/52*

PETRO, Michael (b 1944) American actor TW/27-29

PETRONE, Susan (d 1963 [32]) performer BP/48*

PETRONJ, Egidio [Bernard Sylvester] (d 1882) actor, pantomimist EA/84*

PETROVA, Olga (1886-1977) English actress, dramatist WWT/5-7

PETT dramatist FGF

PETTEBONE, Jean (d 1970 [56]) publicist BP/55*

PETTENGILL, Charlie (d 1870 [27]) minstrel manager & performer CDP

PETTET, Edwin Burr (b 1913) American educator, director BE

PETTET, Joanna (b 1944) English actress TW/21

PETTIE, Edna see May, Edna

PETTIFER, Mary Ann [Mrs. John Bond Ratcliffe] (d 1892 [70]) actress CDP

PETTIGROVE, Richard (d 1902 [70]) showman EA/03*

PETTINGELL, Frank (1891-1966) English actor WWT/7-14

PETTINGTON, Henry (fl 1636) actor DA

PETTIT, Paul Bruce (b 1920) American educator, director BE

PETTITT, Annette [Mrs. Henry Pettitt] (d 1916) EA/17*

PETTITT, Henry (1848-93) English dramatist DNB

PETTITT, Henry (b 1881) Eng-
lish actor, manager, drama-
tist GRB/1-2
PETTITT, Mrs. Henry see
Pettitt, Annette
PETTMAN, Julia (d 1896 [28])
actress EA/97*
PEVERIL, C. H. (d 1875) actor
EA/76*
PEW, John (d 1890) conductor
EA/91*
PEYRANI, Giovanni (d 1901)
animal trainer EA/02*
PFEIFER, Allan Cameron see
Dalzell, Allan C.
PFEIFER, Sidney B. (d 1967 [73])
critic BP/52*
PFEIFFER, Oscar (b 1830) Aus-
trian pianist HAS
PFLUGBEIL, August (fl 1614-15)
actor DA
PHALEN, Robert (b 1937) Ameri-
can actor TW/23-30
PHARAR, Renée (d 1962 [83])
actress BE*
PHELAN, John A. (b 1842) Amer-
ican actor HAS
PHELPS, Miss see Parsons,
Mrs.
PHELPS, A. R. (b 1824) Ameri-
can actor HAS
PHELPS, Charles H. (d 1910)
actor EA/11*
PHELPS, Dodie (d 1963 [65]) per-
former BE*
PHELPS, Edmund (d 1870 [32])
actor EA/71*
PHELPS, Edmund actor OAA/1
PHELPS, Mrs. Edmund (d 1907
[67]) actress GRB/3
PHELPS, Eleanor (d 1882) EA/
83*
PHELPS, Eleanor American ac-
tress TW/26, 30
PHELPS, Fanny Morgan (fl 1854-
67) Irish actress HAS
PHELPS, Frederick (d 1912)
music-hall manager EA/13*
PHELPS, George Turner (1867-
1920) American writer WWA/1
PHELPS, Leonard P. (d 1924
[73]) American manager BE*,
BP/8*
PHELPS, Lucian (d 1973 [65])
performer BP/57*
PHELPS, Lyon (b 1923) American
dramatist BE
PHELPS, Pauline (fl 1908-13)

American dramatist WWM
PHELPS, Rev. Robert (d 1890
[84]) EA/91*
PHELPS, Samuel (1804-78) English
actor CDP, COC, DNB, ES,
OAA/1-2, OC/1-3
PHELPS, Mrs. Samuel (d 1867)
EA/68*
PHELPS, Stella [Estelle M. Os-
baldestone] (d 1918) EA/19*
PHELPS, William Robert (d 1867)
EA/68*
PHELPS-LEO, Arthur [Louis H. T.
Phelps-Payne] (b 1882) English
actor, singer GRB/1
PHELPS-PAYNE, Louis H. T.
see Phelps-Leo, Arthur
PHELTON, John, Jr. see Flynn,
J. D.
PHETHEAN, David (b 1918) English
director, actor WWT/15-16
PHILBIN, Jane Devereux see
Dreyfuss, Jane
PHILBRICK, Norman (b 1913)
American educator BE
PHILIP (fl 1599?) dramatist FGF
PHILIP, James E. (d 1910 [42])
actor, composer BE*
PHILIP, Robert (fl 1514) member
of the Chapel Royal DA
PHILIPE, Gérard (1922-59) French
actor COC, OC/3, TW/16
PHILIPP, Adolf (1867-1936) German
dramatist, composer, actor,
manager, singer WWM
PHILIPPS, Thomas (1774-1881)
English singer CDP, DNB
PHILIPS, Ambrose (c. 1671/74-
1749) English dramatist CDP,
COC, CP/1-3, GT, OC/3, TD/
1-2
PHILIPS, Augustus (b 1873) Ameri-
can actor WWS
PHILIPS, F. C. (1849-1921) English
dramatist GRB/1-4, WWT/1-3,
WWW/2
PHILIPS, John (fl 1716-17) drama-
tist CP/1-3, GT
PHILIPS, Katherine (1631-64) Eng-
lish dramatist CP/1-3, GT
PHILIPS, Lee (b 1927) American
actor, director, writer BE,
TW/12-14
PHILIPS, Marie L. (b 1925) Amer-
ican director, administrator,
actress BE
PHILIPS, Marvin James (b 1923)
American educator BE

PHILIPS, Mary (1901-75) American actress WWT/8-13

PHILIPS, Robert (fl 1543-59?) musician DNB

PHILIPS, William see Phillips, William

PHILLIMORE, Mr. actor TD/1-2

PHILLIPP, Peter (fl 1574) actor DA

PHILLIPPE, Robert (fl 1559) actor DA

PHILLIPS, Mr. (fl 1797) singer TD/1-2

PHILLIPS, Mr. ["Harlequin Phillips"] (fl 1748-49?) actor CDP

PHILLIPS, Mrs. (d 1906 [65]) EA/07*

PHILLIPS, Mrs. see Rogers, Mrs.

PHILLIPS, Aaron J. (d 1846) American actor, manager HAS

PHILLIPS, Acton (d 1899 [69]) proprietor, manager EA/00*, WWT/14*

PHILLIPS, Acton (d 1940 [86]) producer, manager BE*, WWT/14*

PHILLIPS, Adelaide (b 1822) American actress SR

PHILLIPS, Adelaide (1833-82) English actress, singer CDP, HAS

PHILLIPS, Albert (1875-1940) American actor CB

PHILLIPS, Mrs. Alfred (d 1876 [54]) dramatist, actress BE*, EA/77*, WWT/14*

PHILLIPS, Alfred S. (d 1888 [34]) comedian EA/89*

PHILLIPS, Andrew (d 1871 [70]) scene artist EA/72*

PHILLIPS, Anna Maria see Crouch, Mrs. Rawlings Edward

PHILLIPS, Ann Eliza see Stone, Ann Eliza

PHILLIPS, Augustine (d 1605) English actor COC, DA, NTH, OC/1-3

PHILLIPS, Augustus G. (1838-93) actor CDP

PHILLIPS, Benjamin Woolf (d 1899 [74]) actor? EA/00*

PHILLIPS, Catherine see Philips, Katherine

PHILLIPS, Charles (1880-1933) American dramatist WWA/1

PHILLIPS, Charles (d 1974 [25]) performer BP/59*

PHILLIPS, Cyril L. (b 1894) English manager WWT/8-9

PHILLIPS, David Graham (1867-1911) American dramatist HJD

PHILLIPS, Diane (b 1945) American actress TW/26

PHILLIPS, Eddie (b 1928) American actor TW/13-14, 23, 30

PHILLIPS, Edward (fl 1730-39) dramatist CP/1-3, DNB, GT, TD/1-2

PHILLIPS, Edwin (b 1911) American actor TW/14-15

PHILLIPS, Eleanor Hyde (d 1975 [94]) performer BP/60*

PHILLIPS, Eliza (fl 1837) actress CDP

PHILLIPS, Elizabeth [Mrs. Philip Phillips] (d 1887 [76]) EA/88*

PHILLIPS, Emily (d 1894 [59]) EA/95*

PHILLIPS, Rev. Forbes Alexander ["Athol Forbes"] (b 1866) English dramatist GRB/1-4

PHILLIPS, Mrs. F. R. (d 1899 [70]) music-hall performer EA/01*

PHILLIPS, Mrs. Francis see Jones, Maria B.

PHILLIPS, Frederick [Philip Hannan] (d 1871) lessee, manager EA/72*

PHILLIPS, Mrs. Frederick L. see Daly, Ellen

PHILLIPS, Harriet [née Kate Hornby] (d 1873 [24]) singer EA/74*

PHILLIPS, Harriet see Holman, Mrs. George

PHILLIPS, Harry (d 1891 [58]) showman EA/92*

PHILLIPS, H. B. (b 1819) American actor, stage manager, manager HAS

PHILLIPS, H. B. (d 1950 [83]) impresario BE*, WWT/14*

PHILLIPS, Mrs. H. B. (d 1867) English dancer HAS

PHILLIPS, Henry (1801-76) English singer, actor, musician CDP, DNB

PHILLIPS, H. I. (d 1965 [75]) dramatist BP/49*

PHILLIPS, Ida English actress GRB/1

PHILLIPS, Irna (d 1973 [72]) dramatist BP/58*

PHILLIPS, Jack (d 1956 [55]) stage manager, director BE*, WWT/14*

PHILLIPS, J. B. (d 1862) stage

manager HAS

PHILLIPS, Mrs. J. B. [Annie Myers] (1833-68) American actress HAS

PHILLIPS, J. O. (fl 1828-30?) dramatist EAP

PHILLIPS, Joe (d 1966 [78]) performer BP/51*

PHILLIPS, Jonas B. (fl 1820s?) dramatist RJ, SR

PHILLIPS, Kate (1856-1931) English actress DP, EA/97, GRB/1-4, OAA/2, WWT/1-6

PHILLIPS, Leslie (b 1924) English actor, director AAS, WWT/12-16

PHILLIPS, Louisa Anne see Salzberg, Mrs.

PHILLIPS, Mabel [Mrs. Polly Fox] (d 1912 [29]) variety performer EA/13*

PHILLIPS, Margaret (b 1923) Welsh actress BE, TW/1, 3-20, 23-24, WWT/11-16

PHILLIPS, Marie Eugenie see Gordon, Marie

PHILLIPS, Mary Bracken (b 1946) American actress TW/26-29

PHILLIPS, Mathilde (1841-1915) actress, singer SR

PHILLIPS, Matilda see Stoddart, Mrs. James Henry

PHILLIPS, Minna (d 1963 [91]) Australian actress TW/19

PHILLIPS, Montague Fawcett (1885-1969) composer WWW/6

PHILLIPS, Norma (1893-1931) American actress BE*, BP/16*

PHILLIPS, Mr. P. (d 1869) music-hall performer EA/70*

PHILLIPS, Paul (b 1947) American actor TW/30

PHILLIPS, Philip (d 1864 [62]) scene artist EA/72*

PHILLIPS, Mrs. Philip see Phillips, Elizabeth

PHILLIPS, R. (fl 1683) dramatist CP/1-3, GT

PHILLIPS, Randy (b 1926) American actor TW/24-26, 29

PHILLIPS, Richard Empson (d 1872 [51]) actor EA/73*

PHILLIPS, Robin (b 1942) English director, actor AAS, WWT/15-16

PHILLIPS, Miss S. see Crouch, Mrs.

PHILLIPS, Sian Welsh actress WWT/14-16

PHILLIPS, Sid (d 1973 [65]) composer/lyricist BP/58*

PHILLIPS, Sidney (d 1973 [82]) producer/director/choreographer BP/58*

PHILLIPS, Sophia (fl 1828) singer CDP

PHILLIPS, Stephen (1864-1915) English dramatist, actor COC, DNB, ES, GRB/1-4, MH, MWD, NTH, OC/1-3, PDT, WWT/1-3, WWW/1

PHILLIPS, T. (1802-41) English actor HAS

PHILLIPS, Thomas (d 1739) dramatist CP/2-3, GT, TD/1-2

PHILLIPS, Mrs. W. A. (d 1867) actor? EA/68*

PHILLIPS, Watts (1825/29-74) English dramatist DNB, EA/68

PHILLIPS, Mrs. Watts (d 1899 [68]) EA/00*

PHILLIPS, Mrs. W. C. see Hastings, Kate

PHILLIPS, Mrs. W. C. see Oliver, Martha

PHILLIPS, Wendell K. (b 1907) American actor, director, designer, dramatist BE, TW/23, 28-29

PHILLIPS, W. H. (d 1887 [28]) comedian EA/88*

PHILLIPS, William (d 1734) Irish? actor, dramatist CDP, CP/1-3, DNB, GT

PHILLIPS, William Lovell (d 1860 [43]) composer EA/72*

PHILLPOTTS, Adelaide (b 1896) dramatist WWT/6-14

PHILLPOTTS, Ambrosine (b 1912) English actress WWT/10-16

PHILLPOTTS, Eden (1862-1960) Indian/English dramatist COC, DNB, ES, OC/1-3, PDT, WWT/3-12, WWW/5

"PHILO-NAUTICUS" see Halloran, L. H.

PHILP, Elizabeth (d 1885) author, composer EA/86*

PHILP, James East (d 1910 [42]) conductor, composer EA/11*, WWT/14*

PHILP, Rowline [Harry Proctor] (d 1887) actor EA/88*

PHINN, C. Mort (d 1965 [75]) performer BP/50*

PHIPP, Sophia Matilda (d 1906
[74]) EA/08*

PHIPP, W. Scott (b 1870) English manager, dramatist, lyricist, composer GRB/1

PHIPPS, Beatriz see Kemp,
Beatriz

PHIPPS, Charles John (d 1897
[62]) architect EA/98*

PHIPPS, Nicholas (b 1913) English actor WWT/11-16

PHIPPS, William Henry (d 1877
[69]) EA/78*

PHISTER, Montgomery (b 1852)
American critic WWA/4

PHOENIX, Walter (fl 1880?)
dancer, singer, songcomposer
CDP

PHYDORA, Joe (d 1896) pantomimist EA/97*

PHYDORA, William (d 1909) performer? EA/10*

PHYSIOC, Joseph Allen (d 1951
[86]) American scene artist
BE*, BP/36*

PIACENTINI, Anne American actress TW/27

PIAF, Edith (1915-63) French
singer, actress CB, OC/3,
TW/20

PIATOV, Sascha (1890-1947)
dancer, director SR

PIATTI, Alfredo (d 1901 [79])
musician, composer EA/02*

PIAZZA, Ben (b 1934) American
actor BE, TW/15-20, 24-25,
WWT/14-16

PIAZZA, Dario (d 1974 [70])
costumier BP/59*

PICARD, Louis Baptiste (1769-
1828) French dramatist COC,
OC/2-3

PICARDO, Arthur [Thomas Arthur
Marriott] (d 1900 [31]) music-
hall performer EA/01*

PICAUD, Mrs. (d 1905) EA/06*

PICCAVER, Alfred (1884-1958)
Anglo-Austrian singer ES

PICCOLOMINI, Henry Pontent
(d 1902) composer EA/03*

PICCOLOMINI, Maria (1834-99)
Italian singer CDP, ES, HAS

PICHEL, Irving (d 1954 [63])
American actor, director BE*,
BP/39*, WWT/14*

PICKARD, Helena (1899-1959)
English actress COC, OC/
2-3, WWT/6-12

PICKARD, James (d 1874 [34]) comic
singer EA/75*

PICKARD, Mae (d 1946) actress
BE*, WWT/14*

PICKARD, Margery (b 1911) English
actress WWT/8-11

PICKENS, Miss see Abbott,
Bessie

PICKENS, Jane American singer
CB, TW/8

PICKER, Mlle. (fl 1856) German
singer HAS

PICKERING, Alexander L. (fl 1839)
actor CDP

PICKERING, Andrew (fl 1839) actor
HAS

PICKERING, Mrs. Andrew (d 1837
[19]) actress HAS

PICKERING, Edward A. (b 1871/73)
English actor, acting manager,
business manager GRB/3-4,
WWT/1, 4-7

PICKERING, James (fl 1612) actor
DA

PICKERING, John (fl 1567?) dramatist FGF

PICKERING, J. Russell (d 1947
[67]) producer, manager BE*,
WWT/14*

PICKERT, Willis clog dancer CDP

PICKETT, Ingram B. (d 1963 [64])
actor BE*

PICKETT, Jack (b 1935) American
actor TW/23

PICKFORD, Jack (d 1933 [36])
Canadian actor, producer BE*

PICKFORD, James (d 1872) music-
hall proprietor EA/73*

PICKFORD, Lottie (1895-1936)
Canadian actress BE*, BP/21*

PICKFORD, Mary [Gladys Mary
Smith] (b 1893) Canadian actress
CB, ES, NTH, SR, WWT/4-11

PICKLES, Little [John Scott] (d
1895 [32]) circus clown EA/96*

PICKLES, David Joseph (d 1891
[42]) manager EA/92*

PICKLES, James (d 1872 [63])
musician EA/73*

PICKULS, Sarah [Mrs. Stephen
Pickuls] (d 1874) EA/75*

PICKULS, Mrs. Stephen see
Pickuls, Sarah

PICKUP, Mrs. [née Miss Brooks]
(d 1874) actress EA/75*

PICKUP, Ronald (b 1941) English
actor AAS, WWT/15-16

PICKWOAD, William see Mervyn, William

PICO, Rosina (fl 1844) singer
CDP

PICON, Molly (b 1898) American
actress, manager BE, CB,
NTH, TW/5-8, 23-24, 26,
WWT/10-16

PICTON, George (d 1882) EA/84*

PICTON, Sam (d 1893 [34]) comic
singer, manager EA/94*

PIDCOCK, Richard (d 1894 [74])
director EA/95*

PIDDOCK, J. C. (d 1919 [56])
actor, singer BE*, WWT/14*

PIDGEON, Edward Everett (1869-
1941) American editor, critic
WWM

PIDGEON, Walter (b 1897) Canadian actor BE, CB, ES, SR,
TW/23, WWT/15-16

PIDGIN, Charles Felton (1844-
1923) American dramatist
WWA/1, WWM

PIEL, David (b 1946) American
actor TW/25

PIERCE, Earl Horton (1823-59)
American minstrel CDP, HAS

PIERCE, Edward (d 1974 [80])
performer BP/59*

PIERCE, Frank (d 1897) proprietor EA/98*

PIERCE, George (d 1964 [70])
performer BP/49*

PIERCE, Grace Adele (d 1923)
American writer WWA/1

PIERCE, Mrs. H. (d 1883 [34])
EA/89*

PIERCE, Jane [Mrs. J. H.
Pierce] (d 1888) EA/89*

PIERCE, J. H. [James Hart
Glen] (d 1895) music-hall performer EA/96*

PIERCE, Mrs. J. H. see
Pierce, Jane

PIERCE, Randolph (b 1940)
American actor TW/23

PIERCE, Rik (b 1939) American
actor TW/24

PIERCE, William E. (b 1847)
American actor HAS

PIERCEY, William Edgar see
Austin, Edgar

PIERCY, Samuel W. (1849-82)
actor CDP

PIERLOT, Francis (d 1955 [79])
actor BE*

PIERPOINT, Joseph Charles
Garland (d 1887 [40]) singer
EA/88*

PIERPOINT, Laura (1890-1972)
American actress TW/5-7, 9-
12, 29

PIERRO, Annie (d 1884) EA/85*

PIERS, Edward see Pearce, Edward

PIERSON, Arthur (d 1975 [73])
actor, director, writer WWT/
16*

PIERSON, Blanche (b 1840) actress
CDP

PIERSON, Ethel [Mrs. Frank E.
Randell] (d 1892) singer, actress
EA/93*

PIERSON, Henry Hugh (d 1873
[58]) composer EA/74*

PIERSON, Rennie (d 1973 [75])
performer BP/58*

PIERSON, Thomas (d 1791) dramatist CP/3

PIESEN, Margery Korman (d 1968
[62]) performer BP/53*

PIETER, Ruth Yingling (d 1974
[80]) critic BP/59*

PIETRACK, Irving (d 1972 [70])
composer/lyricist BP/57*

PIETRO, Paul see Tarrant,
George

PIFF, Charles see Kay, Charles

PIFFARD, Frederick (1902-75) In-
dian/English manager WWT/11-
15

PIG, John (fl 1593-99) actor DA

PIGEON, Richard Walter (d 1887
[56]) EA/88*

PIGNIERES, Rene (d 1973 [68])
producer/director/choreographer
BP/58*

PIGOT, Elizabeth [Mrs. Percy
Milton] (d 1899 [44]) EA/00*

PIGOTT, A. S. English business
manager WWT/2-5

PIGOTT, Edward Frederick Smyth
(d 1895 [71]) examiner of plays
EA/96*, WWT/14*

PIGOTT, Howard H. (d 1974 [76])
performer BP/59*

PIGOTT, Tempe (d 1962 [78]) performer BE*

PIGOTT, W. W. see Leslie, Will

PIGUE, William W. (d 1970 [62])
journalist, publicist BP/54*

PIGUENIT, D. J. (fl 1774) dramatist CP/3

PIHODNA, Gottlieb (d 1969 [61])
critic BP/53*

PIKE, Marshall S. (1818-1901)

American female impersonator CDP, HAS

PIKE, Maurice B. (b 1837) American actor HAS

PIKE, Richard Jarvis (d 1905) bandmaster EA/06*

PIKE, Robert (d 1974 [56]) manager, press agent BP/59*

PIKE, Samuel N. theatre builder CDP

PIKET, Frederick (d 1974 [71]) composer/lyricist BP/58*

PILARCZYK, Helga (b 1925) German singer ES

PILAR-MORIN, Mme. (fl 1900s) Spanish actress, pantomimist WWM

PILBEAM, Nova (b 1919) English actress WWT/8-11

PILBEAM, Mrs. Tom see Olive, Kittie

PILBROW, Richard (b 1933) English lighting designer, managing director, producer WWT/14-16

PILCER, Harry (d 1961 [75]) American dancer, actor TW/17, WWT/4-7

PILGRIM, James (1825-79) actor, dramatist, manager CDP, HAS

PILKINGTON, Laetitia (1712-50) Irish dramatist CP/1-3, GT

PILLANS, R. S. (d 1878 [34]) Scottish comedian EA/79*

PILLETTS, Edmund see De Mondion, Edmund

PILLING, Mr. (d 1907) musical director EA/08*

PILLING, Harry (d 1910) EA/11*

PILON, Frederick (1750-88) Irish actor, dramatist CP/2-3, DNB, GT, TD/1-2

PILOTTI, Alessandro (d 1875) professor of music EA/76*

PIM, Sgt. (d 1917) EA/18*

PIMBURY, Martha (d 1878 [77]) EA/79*

PIMLEY, John (d 1972 [53]) performer BP/57*

PIMM, Harry S. (d 1965 [75]) performer BP/50*

PIM-PIM [Charles Stuart Hall] (d 1905) circus clown EA/07*

PINACCI, Giovanni Battista see Bagnolesi, Anna

PINANSKI, Sam (d 1971 [77]) pioneer in developing theatres BP/56*

PINANSKY, Sam (d 1966 [77]) performer BP/50*

PINAUD, Charles Phoite (d 1906) performer? EA/07*

PINCHOT, Rosamond (1904-38) American actress BE*, BP/22*

PINCUS, Warren (b 1938) American actor TW/24, 27-29

PINDAR, Peter see Wolcot, John

PINDER, Mrs. (fl 1826-31) English actress HAS

PINDER, Emma (d 1890) performer? EA/91*

PINDER, George (d 1906 [75]) circus proprietor EA/07*

PINDER, Mrs. George see Pinder, Louisa

PINDER, George Ord (d 1912 [43]) circus manager EA/13*

PINDER, James (d 1886 [32]) performer? EA/88*

PINDER, Louisa [Mrs. George Pinder] (d 1892 [57]) EA/93*

PINDER, Powis (d 1941 [68]) actor GRB/3

PINDER, Rebecca [Mrs. William Pinder] (d 1901) EA/02*

PINDER, Mrs. W. (d 1870) EA/71*

PINDER, William (d 1876) carpenter EA/77*

PINDER, Mrs. William see Pinder, Rebecca

PINDER, William Olman (d 1906 [38]) circus director EA/07*

PINE, Phillip (b 1925) American actor TW/8-12

PINERO, Sir Arthur Wing (1855-1934) English dramatist, actor CDP, COC, DNB, ES, GRB/1-4, HP, MH, MWD, NTH, OAA/1-2, OC/1-3, PDT, RE, SR, WWM, WWS, WWT/1-7, WWW/3

PINERO, Lady Arthur Wing see Holme, Myra

PINERO, Lucy (d 1905 [69]) EA/06*

PINI CORSI, Antonio (1858-1918) Italian singer ES

PINK, Wal (d 1922 [60]) English actor, singer, dramatist, writer WWT/4

PINKARD, Maceo (d 1962 [65]) composer BE*, BP/47*

PINKERT, Regina (1869-1931) Polish/Italian singer ES

PINKES, Elijah see Potter, Stanley

PINKETHMAN, William (d 1725)
actor CDP, DNB
PINKETT, Willis (d 1975 [55])
performer BP/59*
PINNER, David (b 1940) English
dramatist, actor CD
PINSKI, David (1872-1959) Rus-
sian dramatist MH, MWD,
RE, WWA/5
PINTER, Emily (d 1965 [65])
performer BP/50*
PINTER, Harold (b 1930) English
dramatist, director, actor
AAS, BE, CB, CD, CH,
COC, ES, MD, MH, MWD,
OC/3, PDT, RE, WWT/13-16
PINTER, Mrs. Harold see
Merchant, Vivien
PINTO, Mrs. see Brent, Char-
lotte
PINTO, Charlotte (d 1802) ac-
tress, singer WWT/14*
PINTO, Effingham (b 1886) Amer-
ican actor WWM
PINTO, Thomas (1710?-73) Eng-
lish musician DNB
PINZA, Carla (b 1942) Puerto
Rican actress TW/28-29
PINZA, Ezio (1892-1957) Italian
singer, actor AAS, CB, ES,
TW/5-8, 11-13, WWA/3
PIPER, John (b 1903) English
scene designer ES
PIPER, Walter H. (d 1903 [28])
proprietor EA/04*
PIPO (d 1970 [68]) performer
BP/55*
PIP SIMMONS THEATRE GROUP
theatre collective CD
PIRANDELLO, Luigi (1867-1936)
Italian dramatist COC, ES,
OC/2-3, RE, WWT/8
PIRANDELLO, Stefano (d 1972
[76]) dramatist BP/56*
PIRO, Phillip (b 1943) American
actor TW/25
PIRSSON, J. P. (fl 19th cent)
dramatist EAP
PISANI, Mme. (fl 1879?) singer
CDP
PISARONI, Benedetta Rosmunda
(1793-1872) Italian singer ES
PISCATOR, Erwin (1893-1966)
German producer, director
BE, CB, CH, COC, ES, OC/
1-3, PDT, TW/22, WWA/4
PISCATOR, Maria Ley [Maria
Ley] Austrian director BE

PISHOU, Jane (d 1864) "fat lady"
HAS
PISTONI, Mario (b 1933) Italian
dancer ES
PITCAIRNE, Dr. Archibald (1652-
1713) Scottish dramatist CP/
2-3, GT
PITHEY, Wensley (b 1914) South
African actor WWT/15-16
PITKIN, William (b 1925) American
designer BE, WWT/15-16
PITMAN, Richard (d 1941 [67])
American actor, talent repre-
sentative BE*, BP/26*
PITOËFF, Georges (1886/87-1939)
Russian actor, manager OC/1-
3, WWT/8-9
PITOËFF, Ludmilla (1896-1951)
Russian actress COC, OC/1-3,
WWT/8-11
PITOT, Genevieve American com-
poser BE
PITOU, Augustus (1843-1915)
American manager, dramatist
GRB/3-4, SR, WWA/1, WWM,
WWT/1-3
PITOU, Mrs. Augustus, Jr. see
Coghlan, Gertrude
PITROT, Antoine Bonaventure (fl
1744-84) French dancer, chore-
ographer ES
PITT, Mrs. (d 1800) English ac-
tress TD/1-2
PITT, Miss actress CDP
PITT, Addison (d 1968 [91]) per-
former BP/52*
PITT, Ann (1720?-99) English ac-
tress CDP, DNB
PITT, Annie [Mrs. Henry Pitt]
(d 1870 [39]) EA/71*
PITT, Archie (1885-1940) actor,
manager COC, WWT/6-9
PITT, Cecil (d 1879 [53]) actor
CDP
PITT, Charles (d 1871) actor EA/
72*
PITT, Mrs. Charles see Pitt,
Ellen
PITT, Charles Dibdin (d 1866 [47])
actor, manager CDP, HAS
PITT, Mrs. Charles Dibdin (fl
1849-50) actress HAS
PITT, Charles Isaac Mungo see
Dibdin, Charles Isaac Mungo
PITT, Dibdin (d 1855 [56]) actor,
dramatist CDP
PITT, Ellen [Mrs. Charles Pitt]
(d 1897 [76]) EA/98*

PITT, Emily Lavinia (fl 1863-68) singer HAS

PITT, Fanny (d 1898) actress EA/99*

PITT, Fanny Addison (d 1937 [93]) English actress BE*, BP/21*, WWT/14*

PITT, Felix (d 1922) actor EA/96

PITT, Mrs. Felix see Armstrong, Clara

PITT, Frank J. (b 1878) English actor GRB/1

PITT, George Dibdin see Pitt, Dibdin

PITT, Harriet (d 1814) dancer DNB

PITT, Mrs. Harry see Pitt, Annie

PITT, Henry Mader (1850-98) American actor, stage manager CDP, OAA/1-2

PITT, Mrs. H. M. [Mme. Lilian] (d 1873) actress EA/75*

PITT, John (d 1871 [46]) proprietor EA/72*

PITT, Lottie (d 1885) actress EA/87*

PITT, Mary (fl 1863-68) English singer HAS

PITT, Percy (1870-1932) English composer, conductor WWW/3

PITT, Rose Ellen Dibdin (d 1912 [40]) actress EA/13*

PITT, Samuel (d 1897 [65]) showman EA/99*

PITT, Thomas Henry (d 1873 [70]) scene artist EA/74*

PITT, Thomas John see Dibdin, Thomas John

PITT, Tom (d 1924 [68]) English business manager WWT/2-4

PITT, W. H. (d 1879 [44]) actor EA/80*

PITT-HARDACRE, Mrs. J. see Pitt-Hardacre, Kate Adelaide

PITT-HARDACRE, Kate Adelaide [Mrs. J. Pitt-Hardacre] (d 1916) EA/17*

PITTMAN, Frank (d 1973 [50s]) producer/director/choreographer BP/58*

PITTMAN, Josiah (1816-66) musician, librettist DNB

PITTMAN, W. E. [Will Harris] (d 1873 [19]) Negro comedian EA/74*

PITTS, Eliza Susan see Pitts, ZaSu

PITTS, ZaSu [née Eliza Susan] (1898/1900-1963) American actress ES, TW/9, 20, WWT/10-13

PIX, Mary (1666-1720?) English dramatist CP/1-3, DNB, GT

PIXERECOURT, René Charles Guilbert de (1773-1844) French dramatist COC, OC/1-3

PIXLEY, Annie [Mrs. Robert Fullford] (1858-93) American actress CDP, SR

PIXLEY, Frank (1867-1919) American librettist GRB/3-4, SR, WWA/1, WWM, WWT/1-3

PIXLEY, Gus (d 1923 [58]) comedian BE*, WWT/14*

PIZZI, Donna (b 1945) American actress TW/27

PLACE, Mrs. Robert see Clifton, Josephine

PLACIDE, Mrs. see La Folle, Mrs.

PLACIDE, Alexandre (d 1812) French dancer ES, HAS, OC/1-3, WWA/H

PLACIDE, Mrs. Alexandre (d 1823 [50]) singer, dancer, actress HAS

PLACIDE, Caroline see Blake, Mrs. William Rufus

PLACIDE, Eliza see Mann, Mrs. Sheridan

PLACIDE, Henry (1799-1870) American actor, manager CDP, COC, DAB, ES, GC, HAS, OC/1-3, SR, WWA/H

PLACIDE, Jane (1804-35) American actress HAS

PLACIDE, Thomas (1808-77) American actor, manager CDP, HAS

PLACKETT, Mrs. Isaac see Plackett, Nellie

PLACKETT, Nellie [Mrs. Isaac Plackett] (d 1916) EA/17*

PLANCHE, James Robinson (1796-1880) English dramatist CDP, COC, DNB, EA/68, ES, HP, OC/1-3, PDT

PLANCHON, Roger (b 1931) French producer, actor, dramatist COC, OC/3, WWT/14

PLANÇON, Paul Henry (1853-1914) French singer ES

PLANE, Miss see Durang, Mrs. F.

PLANK, Thomas C. (d 1962 [34]) performer BE*

PLANQUETTE, Robert (d 1903 [54]) composer EA/04*
PLANQUETTE, Mrs. Robert (d 1903) EA/04*
PLANT, Jack (d 1973 [77]) performer BP/58*
PLANT, Jimmy (d 1964 [66]) performer BP/49*
PLANTOU, Mr. (fl 1827) actor HAS
PLATER, Alan (b 1935) English dramatist AAS, CD, WWT/15-16
PLATT, Agnes English journalist WWT/4-6
PLATT, Batt (d 1758) actor CDP
PLATT, Edward (1916-74) American actor TW/14
PLATT, Livingston designer WWT/8-9
PLATT, Louise (b 1915) American actress TW/5-7
PLATT, Marjorie L. see Dycke, Marjorie L.
PLATTEZ, Louisa (d 1890 [68]) EA/91*
PLATTS, Mr. (d 1872) bandmaster EA/73*
PLATTS, William (d 1875 [33]) perruquier EA/76*
PLATZER, Joseph (d 1877 [36]) composer EA/78*
PLAYFAIR, Arthur (1869-1918) Indian/English actor GRB/2-4, WWT/1-3, WWW/2
PLAYFAIR, Mrs. Arthur see Ashwell, Lena
PLAYFAIR, Sir Nigel (1874-1934) English actor AAS, COC, DNB, ES, GRB/2-4, OC/1-3, PDT, WWT/1-7, WWW/3
PLAYFAIR, Mrs. Nigel see Martyn, May
PLAY-HOUSE OF THE RIDICULOUS, The theatre collective CD
PLAYTEN, Alice (b 1947) American actress, singer TW/24-27, 29-30
PLAYWRIGHTS' COMPANY producers TW/2-8
PLEASANT, Richard (d 1962 [52]) American press representative BE*, BP/46*
PLEASENCE, Angela English actress WWT/15-16
PLEASENCE, Donald (b 1919/20/

21) English actor AAS, BE, CB, TW/18, 21, 28, WWT/12-16
PLEGE, Nicolo (d 1877 [47]) equestrian EA/78*
PLEON, Harry (d 1911) actor, singer, composer CDP
PLEON, Harry, Jr. (d 1911 [19]) EA/12*
PLEON, Joseph (d 1884) EA/85*
PLEON, Percy (d 1900 [31]) music-hall comedian EA/01*
PLEON, Tom (d 1892 [30]) actor, music-hall performer EA/93*
PLESCHETTE, Suzanne (b 1937) American actress BE, TW/15
PLESHETTE, John (b 1942) American actor TW/22-24, 27, 29-30
PLEWS, Arthur Gordon Lane see Poulton, A. G.
PLEYDELL, George [George P. Bancroft] (1868-1956) English dramatist DD, GRB/2-4, WWT/1-6, WWW/3
PLEYELL, Mme. (d 1875 [64]) musician EA/76*
PLIMMER, Annie [Mrs. James Yuill, Jr.] (d 1892) EA/94*
PLIMMER, Edward (d 1878 [50]) Negro artist EA/79*
PLIMMER, Walter J. (d 1968 [67]) performer BP/53*
PLIMPTON, C. F. (d 1870 [66]) actor? EA/71*
PLIMPTON, Shelley (b 1947) American actress TW/27
"PLINGE, Walter" actor WWT/12
PLISETSKAYA, Maya (b 1925) Russian dancer CB
PLOUGHMAN, Miss see Sloan, Mrs. John T. K.
PLOUX, Edith [Mme. Theisen] (d 1892 [34]) singer EA/93*
PLOWDEN, Florence [Mrs. Vyner Robinson] (d 1890 [38]) actress EA/91*
PLOWDEN, Mrs. Frances (fl 1800) dramatist GT, TD/1-2
PLOWMAN, Joseph John (d 1898) lessee EA/99*
PLOWRIGHT, Joan (b 1929) English actress AAS, BE, CB, COC, ES, OC/3, PDT, TW/14-18, WWT/13-16
PLUGGE, Mary Lou (b 1906) American educator BE
PLUMER, Mr. (fl 1828) singer

CDP
PLUMER, Mrs. see Cramer, Miss
PLUMFIELD, Thomas (fl 1632) actor DA
PLUMLEY, Don (b 1934) American actor TW/26-29
PLUMMER, Christopher (b 1927/29) Canadian actor AAS, BE, CB, COC, TW/11-23, 29-30, WWT/13-16
PLUMMER, John (fl 1444-55) master of the Chapel Royal DA
PLUMPTON, Alfred Thomas (d 1902 [61]) musical director EA/03*
PLUMPTON, Mrs. Alfred Thomas see Plumpton, Charlotte E.
PLUMPTON, Charlotte E. [Mrs. Alfred Thomas Plumpton] (d 1902 [54]) EA/03*
PLUMPTON, Josiah singer, song composer CDP
PLUMPTRE, Anne (1760-1818) translator CP/3, DNB
PLUMPTRE, Bell (fl 1799) translator CP/3
PLUMPTRE, James (1770-1832) dramatist CP/3, DNB
PLUNKETT, Adeline see Plunkett, Marie Adeline
PLUNKETT, Charles (b 1822) English actor HAS
PLUNKETT, Mrs. Charles [Eliza Louisa Canavan] (1835-67) actress HAS
PLUNKETT, Edward John Moreton Drax see Dunsany, Lord
PLUNKETT, Marie Adeline (1824-1910) Belgian dancer CDP, ES
PLUNKETT, Patricia (b 1926) English actress WWT/11-13
PLYMPTON, Eben (1853-1915) American actor CDP, GRB/3-4, PP/2, WWA/1, WWS, WWT/1-2
POBER, Leon (d 1971 [51]) composer/lyricist BP/56*
"POCKET SIMS REEVES" see Collard, Henry
POCKETT, James G. (d 1950 [69]) business manager WWT/14*
POCKRISS, Lee (b 1927) American composer BE
POCOCK, Isaac (1782-1835) English dramatist COC, DNB, OC/1-3
POCOCK, J. (fl 1809-10) dramatist CP/3
POCTIER, Miss see Johnstone, Mrs. John
PODELL, Rick (b 1946) American actor TW/28-29
PODGLAZE, Roderick (d 1884) showman EA/85*
PODMORE, Frederick Vere see Vere, Fred R.
PODMORE, William (b 1888) English actor TW/11
POE, Aileen (d 1973 [79]) actress TW/30
POE, David (b 1773) actor SR
POE, Elizabeth Arnold (d 1811) English actress CDP, WWA/H
POE, Gary (b 1947) American actor TW/25, 27
POEL, William [Pole] (1852-1934) English actor, producer COC, DNB, ES, GRB/1-4, NTH, OC/1-3, PDT, WWT/1-7, WWW/3
POGANY, Willy (d 1955 [72]) Hungarian designer BE*
POGGI, Antonio (1808-75) Italian singer ES
POGODIN, Nikolai Fedorovich (1900-62) Russian dramatist COC, OC/1-3
POHLMAN, Max Edward (d 1971) dramatist BP/56*
POINTER, Priscilla American actress TW/22-30
POINTER, Sidney (d 1955) actor, singer BE*, WWT/14*
POITIER, Sidney (b 1924) American actor BE, CB, ES, WWT/15-16
POKELEY, Richard (fl 1550) actor DA
POL, Talitha (d 1971 [31]) performer BP/56*
POLACCO, Giorgi (1875-1960) Italian conductor WWA/4
POLACEK, Louis Vask (1920-63) American performer BE*, BP/47*
POLAIRE, Mlle. [Emilie Zouzé] (1879-1939) French actress WWT/2-4
POLAK, Jeanie Gertrude (d 1888) EA/89*
POLAK, John Michael (d 1887 [54]) EA/88*
POLAK, Marie (d 1966 [70]) per-

former BP/50*

POLAN, Barron (b 1914) American talent representative BE

POLAN, Lou (1904/05-76) Russian/American actor BE, TW/4, 11-13, 24, 29, WWT/15-16

POLANSKI, Eugen (d 1912 [62]) musician EA/13*

POLDEN, T. E. (d 1916) theatre chairman EA/17*

POLE (fl 1582) gatekeeper DA

POLE, William see Poel, William

POLERI, David Samuel (1927-67) American singer WWA/4

POLGAR, Alfred (d 1955 [81]) Austrian/American dramatist BP/39*

POLHILL, Cowley see Fiennes, Sydney

POLIAKOFF, David (b 1953) dramatist CD

POLIAKOFF, Nikolai [Coco the Clown] (d 1974 [78]) clown BP/59*

POLIAKOFF, Vera see Lindsay, Vera

POLIKOFF, Benet, Sr. (d 1970 [72]) lawyer BP/55*

POLINI, Emilie (d 1927) English actress GRB/1-2

POLINI, G[iovanni] M[aria] (d 1914 [63]) Italian manager GRB/1-3

POLINI, Marie (d 1960) English actress GRB/1-2, WWT/2-6

POLINI, Mary Ann (d 1886 [58]) EA/87*

POLITO, Philip (b 1944) American actor TW/25-28, 30

POLK, Joseph B. (d 1902 [61]) actor CDP

POLLACK, Lew (d 1946 [50]) American songwriter TW/2

POLLAND, Elizabeth (d 1975 [82]) acting teacher BP/60*

POLLARD, Daphne (b 1890) Australian actress WWT/4-9

POLLARD, Fred (b 1862) English actor GRB/1

POLLARD, Mrs. Fred see Clarke, Marion

POLLARD, Harry (d 1934 [55]) American director, actor BE*

POLLARD, Harry (d 1962 [72]) Australian performer BE*

POLLARD, John (d 1880) box

attendant EA/81*

POLLARD, John see Moreton, John Pollard

POLLARD, Michael J. (b 1939) actor BE

POLLARD, Percival (1869-1911/12) German/English dramatist, critic DAB, WWM

POLLARD, Thomas (fl first half of 17th cent) English actor DA, COC, OC/1-3

POLLER, Rosa Cash (b 1842) Hungarian singer HAS

POLLEY, Mr. minstrel CDP

POLLICK, Teno (b 1935) American actor TW/26-27

POLLINI, Bianca Charitas Bianchi (1858-1947) German singer ES

POLLINI, Hograth (d 1897 [57]) manager EA/98*

POLLITZER, Adolphe (d 1900 [68]) musician EA/01*

POLLOCK, Mrs. (d 1875 [73]) actress, manager EA/76*

POLLOCK, Allan (d 1942 [64]) English actor CB, WWM

POLLOCK, Anna (d 1946 [65]) American press representative, dramatist BE*, BP/30*

POLLOCK, Arthur (b 1886) American critic WWT/9-13

POLLOCK, Channing (1880-1946) American dramatist CB, DAB, GRB/2-4, HJD, MWD, NTH, SR, TW/3, WWA/2, WWM, WWS, WWT/1-9

POLLOCK, Mrs. Channing see Marble, Anna

POLLOCK, Elizabeth (1898-1970) English actress WWT/5-9

POLLOCK, Ellen (b 1903) German/English actress AAS, WWT/7-16

POLLOCK, Frank (b 1878) American singer WWM

POLLOCK, Gordon W. (d 1956 [28]) producer BE*

POLLOCK, Sir John (1878-1963) dramatist WWT/4-7

POLLOCK, Nancy R. [née Reiben] (b 1905/07) American actress BE, TW/12, 20, 24-26, WWT/15-16

POLLOCK, W. H. (d 1877) actor EA/78*

POLLOCK, William (1881-1944) English journalist WWT/5-8

POLO, Eddie (d 1961 [86]) actor,

acrobat BE*

POLONSKY, Joe (d 1974 [81])
publicist BP/59*

POLSON, Edith Mary [Mrs.
George P. Polson] (d 1892)
EA/93*

POLSON, Mrs. George P. see
Polson, Edith Mary

POLUSKI, Miss (d 1888) EA/89*

POLWORTH, Lewis actor CDP

POMERANZ, Joseph see Pom-
eroy, Jay

POMEROY, Jay [né Joseph Pom-
eranz] (1895-1955) Russian director WWT/10-11

POMEROY, Louise ["Elm Orton"]
(d 1893) actress, dramatist
CDP

PONAZECKI, Joe (b 1934) American actor TW/22-28, 30

PONCHARD, Mme. (d 1873 [81])
singer EA/74*

PONCIN, Marcel (d 1953) actor
BE*, WWT/14*

PONCIONE, John P., Jr. (d 1890
[57]) lawyer EA/92*

PONCIONE, Mrs. John Paul see
Poncione, Sophia

PONCIONE, Sophia [Mrs. John
Paul Poncione] (d 1898 [89])
actress EA/99*

POND, Anson Phelps (1856-1920)
American dramatist WWA/4

POND, Charles Glover (d 1880)
musician, composer EA/81*

POND, Christopher (d 1881 [54])
EA/82*

POND, Helen (b 1924) American
designer WWT/16

POND, John (d 1975 [72]) designer
BP/60*

POND, Paul see Jones, Paul

PONGER, Fred (b 1922) American
actor TW/30

PONIATOWSKI, Prince (d 1873
[56]) composer EA/74*

PONISI, Elizabeth (1818-99) English actress CDP

PONISI, James (fl 1850) English
actor HAS

PONISI, Mrs. James (fl 1848-69)
English actress HAS

PONS, Helene (b 1898) Russian
costume designer BE, ES

PONS, Lily (1904-76) French
singer CB, ES

PONSELLE, Rosa (b 1897) American singer ES

PONSFORD, Phyllis see Cecil,
Phyllis

PONSONBY, Eustace (d 1924) composer, actor BE*, WWT/14*

PONTE, Lorenzo da see Da
Ponte, Lorenzo

PONTERIO, Robin (b 1957) American actor TW/24

PONTOPPIDAN, Clara (d 1975
[80s]) performer BP/59*

POOL, F. C. (d 1944 [69]) business
manager BE*, WWT/14*

POOLE, Mr. (fl 1851) actor HAS

POOLE, Mrs. (d 1883) EA/85*

POOLE, Miss (fl 1839) English actress HAS

POOLE, Annie [Mrs. Russell Crau-
furd] (d 1895) actress, singer
EA/96*

POOLE, Charles (b 1815) English
actor, manager HAS

POOLE, Charles (d 1877 [54]) EA/
78*

POOLE, C. W. (d 1918 [60]) EA/
19*

POOLE, Elizabeth (1820-1906) actress, singer CDP

POOLE, Ellen [Mrs. J. J. Poole]
(d 1895 [49]) proprietor EA/96*

POOLE, Ernest (1880-1950) American dramatist WWA/2, WWM

POOLE, Flora (d 1896) music-hall
performer EA/97*

POOLE, Frederick (d 1907) proprietor EA/08*

POOLE, George (d 1898 [25])
myriorama manager EA/99*

POOLE, George Walter (d 1878)
panorama proprietor EA/79*

POOLE, Mrs. Harry (d 1893 [38])
EA/94*

POOLE, Harry Herbert (d 1905
[26]) EA/06*

POOLE, J. J. (d 1882) proprietor
EA/83*

POOLE, Mrs. J. J. see Poole,
Ellen

POOLE, John (1786?/92-1872)
English dramatist CDP, DNB,
EA/69, HP

POOLE, John (d 1889 [71]) EA/90*

POOLE, John Peter (d 1899 [64])
actor EA/00*

POOLE, Joseph (d 1906 [59]) myriorama proprietor? EA/07*

POOLE, Joseph J. (d 1895) EA/97*

POOLE, Maria see Dickons,
Maria

POOLE, Matilda (d 1899 [75])
EA/01*
POOLE, Miss M. E. see
Cramer, Mrs. H.
POOLE, Richard Edward (d 1901
[48]) minstrel? EA/02*
POOLE, Roy (b 1924) American
actor TW/14, 19, 21, 25-27
POOLE, Sidney G. E. (d 1905
[28]) EA/06*
POOLE, Sivori (d 1896) EA/97*
POOLE, Tilly see Warde, Mrs.
G. F.
POOLE, Vivien (d 1897 [14])
EA/98*
POOLEY, Olaf English actor,
director WWT/12-15
POORTEN-SCHWARTZ, Joost
Marius Willem van der see
Maartens, Maarten
POPE, Alexander (1688-1744)
English dramatist CDP, CP/
3, HP
POPE, Alexander (1763-1835)
Irish actor, dramatist BS,
CDP, CP/3, DNB, ES, GT,
TD/1-2
POPE, Mrs. Alexander, I [née
Young] (1740-97) English ac-
tress CDP, DNB, ES, GT,
TD/2
POPE, Mrs. Alexander, II see
Campion, Maria Ann
POPE, Charles R. (1829/32-99)
German/American actor,
manager CDP, HAS, SR
POPE, Mrs. Charles R. see
Cunningham, Virginia
POPE, Coleman (d 1868) actor
HAS
POPE, Mrs. Coleman (b 1809)
English actress HAS
POPE, Curtis L. (b 1919) Amer-
ican educator BE
POPE, Elizabeth see Pope,
Mrs. Alexander, I
POPE, Jane (1742-1818) English
actress, dramatist CDP,
COC, CP/3, DNB, ES, GT,
OC/1-3, TD/1-2
POPE, Johanna [Mrs. William
Coleman Pope] (1809-80) ac-
tress CDP
POPE, John (d 1874 [64]) actor
EA/75*
POPE, Dr. Joseph (d 1885 [49])
surgeon EA/86*
POPE, Maria Ann see Campion,

Maria Ann
POPE, Muriel Indian/English ac-
tress WWT/4-7
POPE, Peggy (b 1929) American
actress TW/13, 23-24, 26-28
POPE, Robert (b 1911) American
actor, singer TW/2
POPE, Susan (b 1797) English ac-
tress CDP, OX
POPE, Thomas (d 1604) English
actor DA, COC, GT, OC/1-3
POPE, T. Michael (d 1930 [55])
critic, journalist BE*, WWT/
14*
POPE, William Coleman (d 1868)
actor BE*, WWT/14*
POPE, Mrs. William Coleman see
Pope, Johanna
POPOV, Alexei Dmitrevich (1892-
1961) Russian producer OC/3
POPOV, Oleg (b 1930) Russian
clown CB
POPPER, Hermine I. (d 1968 [53])
editor BP/53*
POPPLE, William (1701-64) English
dramatist CP/1-3, DNB, GT
POPPLEWELL, Jack (b 1911) Eng-
lish dramatist WWT/13-16
PORDAGE, Samuel [P., S.] (1633-
91?) English dramatist CP/1-3,
DNB
POREL, Paul (d 1917 [73]) manager
WWT/14*
PORRET, Robert (fl 1788) dramatist
CP/3
PORSON, Richard (1759-1808) Eng-
lish translator CP/3
PORT, George (d 1887) musician
EA/88*
PORTAL, Abraham (fl 1758-96)
boxkeeper, dramatist CP/1-3,
DNB, GT
PORTANS, Miss see Shaw, Mrs.
Alfred
PORTEOUS, Gilbert (1868-1928)
English actor GRB/4, WWT/1-5
PORTEOUS, Mrs. Gilbert see
Irving, Ethel
PORTER, Mr. ["Kentucky Giant"]
(fl 1838) actor HAS
PORTER, Mrs. (fl first half of 18th
cent) actress TD/1-2
PORTER, Miss see Baker, Mrs.
J. S.
PORTER, Alexander W. (d 1975
[94]) performer BP/59*
PORTER, Anna Maria (fl 1803)
dramatist CP/3

PORTER, Benjamin C. (1839-79)
actor, stage manager CDP

PORTER, Caleb (1867-1940) English actor WWT/5-9

PORTER, Charles S. (1797-1867) American actor HAS

PORTER, Cole (1892-1964) American composer AAS, BE, CB, ES, MH, NTH, PDT, TW/21, WWA/4, WWT/6-13, WWW/6

PORTER, Don (b 1912) American actor TW/21, 25-26, WWT/15-16

PORTER, Elise see Bartlett, Elise

PORTER, Eric (b 1928) English actor AAS, COC, WWT/13-16

PORTER, Hal (b 1911) Australian dramatist CD

PORTER, Harry A. (d 1920 [52]) actor BE*, BP/5*

PORTER, Henry (fl 1596-99) English dramatist CP/1-3, DNB, FGF, OC/1-3, RE

PORTER, Henry (d 1876 [40]) agent EA/77*

PORTER, James S. (d 1863) actor HAS

PORTER, Jane (1776-1850) dramatist HP

PORTER, J. G. (fl 1834) actor HAS

PORTER, Mrs. J. G. see Duff, Mary

PORTER, Joshua (fl 1837) American actor HAS

PORTER, Mabel Butterworth (d 1970 [85]) performer BP/55*

PORTER, Mary Ann (d 1765) English actress DNB, GT, OC/1-3

PORTER, Neil (1895-1944) English actor, producer WWT/7-9

PORTER, Stan (b 1928) American actor TW/25-28, 30

PORTER, Stephen (fl 1798) translator CP/3

PORTER, Stephen (b 1925) American director, producer WWT/15-16

PORTER, Thomas (1636-80) dramatist CP/1-3, DNB

PORTER, Walsh (d 1809) dramatist CP/3

PORTERFIELD, Robert (1905-71) American actor, director, manager BE, TW/28, WWA/5,

WWT/13-15

PORTIS, Diana see Dane, Clemence

PORTMAN, Eric (1903-69) English actor AAS, BE, CB, COC, ES, TW/15-16, 26, WWA/5, WWT/7-14, WWW/6

POSER, Linda American actress TW/30

POSFORD, George (b 1906) English composer WWT/9-14

POSSART, Ernst Ritter von see Von Possart, Ernest Ritter

POST, Guy Bates (1875-1968) American actor GRB/3-4, NTH, TW/24, WWS, WWT/1-11

POST, Lily (d 1890) actress, singer WWT/14*

POST, Lu Ann (b 1947) American actress TW/29

POST, William, Jr. actor TW/1, 3, 10-11

POST, Wilmarth H. (1867-1930) American dramatist SR

POSTLETHWAITE, Frank (d 1910 [37]) variety agent EA/11*

POSTON, Richard (b 1922) American actor TW/8

POSTON, Tom (b 1921/27) American actor BE, CB, TW/11-12, 25-26, 29, WWT/15-16

POTEL, Victor (d 1947 [57]) comedian TW/3

POTIER, Elizabeth Harriman see Moreton, Lydia

POTT, Joseph Holden (fl 1782) dramatist CP/3

POTTER, Andrew (b 1944) American actor TW/28

POTTER, Mrs. Brown see Potter, Cora Urquhart

POTTER, Cora Urquhart [Mrs. Brown Potter] (1859-1936) American actress CDP, DP, GRB/1-4, NTH, OC/1-3, SR, WWA/1, WWS, WWT/1-8, WWW/3

POTTER, Dennis (b 1935) English dramatist CD, WWT/16

POTTER, Don (b 1932) American actor TW/26-27

POTTER, Elizabeth (d 1887) EA/88*

POTTER, Estelle see McDonald, Estelle

POTTER, Gillie (d 1975 [87]) performer BP/59*

POTTER, H. C. (1904-77) American director, producer BE,

TW/5-8, WWT/11-13

POTTER, Helen impersonator, reader CDP

POTTER, Henry (fl 1733) dramatist CP/2-3, GT

POTTER, John (b 1734) English composer, critic, dramatist CP/2-3, DNB, GT

POTTER, John H. (d 1966 [78]) talent manager BP/51*

POTTER, John Hindley (d 1892 [53]) EA/93*

POTTER, John S. (1809-69) American actor, manager HAS

POTTER, Joseph (d 1908 [64]) proprietor EA/09*

POTTER, Paul American actor TW/1

POTTER, Paul Meredith (1853-1921) English/American dramatist DAB, GRB/2-4, HJD, SR, WWA/1, WWM, WWS, WWT/1-3

POTTER, Philip Cipriani (d 1871 [78]) principal of the Royal Academy of Music EA/72*

POTTER, Reuben (fl 1825?) dramatist EAP, RJ

POTTER, Robert (1721-1804) English translator CP/2-3, DNB

POTTER, Stanley [Elijah Pinkes] (d 1894 [75]) singer? EA/96*

POTTER, T. H. (d 1887) stage manager EA/88*

POTTINGER, Israel (fl 1759-61) dramatist CP/2-3, DNB, GT

POTTLE, Gilbert Emery Bensley see Emery, Gilbert

POTTS, Harry see Fragson, Harry

POTTS, Nancy costume designer WWT/16

POTTS, Sidney (d 1968 [62]) producer/director/choreographer BP/52*

POTTS, William J. (d 1888 [36]) American manager EA/89*

POUGARD, Leontine (fl 1852) French dancer CDP, HAS

POUGIN, Arthur (d 1921 [78]) historian, critic BE*, WWT/14*

POULAIN, Bernard (b 1934) French actor TW/24-25

POULTNEY, George (d 1972) union representative BP/57*

POULTON, A. G. [Arthur Gordon Lane Plews] (b 1867) English actor WWT/2-8

POUNDS, Courtice (1862-1927) English actor, singer CDP, DP, GRB/1-4, WWT/2-5, WWW/2

POUNDS, Louie English actress GRB/1-4, WWT/1-8

POVAH, Phyllis American actress BE, TW/1, 3, 5, 10-12, WWT/6-13

POVEY, Miss see Povey, Mary Ann

POVEY, Eliza see Knight, Mrs. E.

POVEY, John (d 1867 [68]) actor, agent CDP

POVEY, Mary Ann (1804-61) English singer, actress BS, CDP, OX

POWEL, Eldred (d 1903) music-hall comedian EA/04*

POWELL, Mr. (b c.1768?) actor BS

POWELL, Mr. (fl 1788-1800) actor GT, TD/1-2

POWELL, Mr. (fl 1798-1804) actor TD/1-2

POWELL, Mrs. (fl 1787-94) actress GT, TD/1-2

POWELL, Alfred Henry (d 1882 [26]) scene artist EA/83*

POWELL, Alfred Thomas (d 1902 [61]) circus manager EA/03*

POWELL, Alma Webster (1874-1930) American singer DAB

POWELL, Anthony James (d 1882 [52]) circus proprietor EA/83*

POWELL, Arthur W. (d 1885 [63]) prompter EA/86*

POWELL, Bertha T. (b 1895) American actress TW/3

POWELL, Mrs. B. H. (d 1894) EA/95*

POWELL, Mrs. Bill see Murphy, Eliza

POWELL, Charles Anthony (d 1887 [17]) EA/88*

POWELL, Charles Stuart (d 1811 [62]) English actor, manager HAS, WWA/H

POWELL, Mrs. Charles Stuart (fl 1794) actress HAS

POWELL, Clara (d 1897) actress EA/98*

POWELL, Mrs. Edward (d 1891)

EA/92*

POWELL, Edward Soldene (b 1865) English actor, stage manager WWS

POWELL, Eleanor (b 1912) American actress, dancer BE, ES, WWT/9-11

POWELL, Eliza Ann [Mrs. William Powell] (d 1885 [70]) EA/87*

POWELL, Elizabeth Jane [Mrs. T. Morton Powell] (d 1891 [24]) EA/92*

POWELL, Ellis (d 1963 [57]) actress BE*

POWELL, Fanny (d 1877) serio-comic, singer EA/79*

POWELL, George (1668-1714) English actor, dramatist CP/1-3, DNB, GT, OC/1-3

POWELL, George Frederick (d 1887 [75]) EA/88*

POWELL, Henry (d 1878) equestrian actor EA/79*

POWELL, J. (d 1836 [82]) actor EA/72*, WWT/14*

POWELL, Jack (d 1976 [75]) performer BP/60*

POWELL, James (fl 1787?) dramatist CP/3

POWELL, James (fl 1805) dramatist CP/3

POWELL, James, Sr. (d 1894 [63]) EA/95*

POWELL, Jane (b 1929) American actress, singer CB

POWELL, John (fl 1798) actor CDP

POWELL, John (d 1873 [22]) EA/74*

POWELL, John (d 1893 [67]) circus performer EA/94*

POWELL, Johnny (d 1897) music-hall performer EA/98*

POWELL, Ken (d 1976 [61]) performer BP/60*

POWELL, Martin (fl 1709-29) English puppeteer, dramatist CP/2-3, DNB, OC/2-3

POWELL, Mary Ann (1761-1831) actress CDP, DNB

POWELL, Maude (d 1920 [51]) musician BE*, BP/4*

POWELL, Maud Morton (d 1969) performer BP/53*

POWELL, Peggy (d 1970 [56]) performer BP/55*

POWELL, Peter (b 1908) English

producer, director WWT/11-14

POWELL, Rebecca (d 1870) EA/71*

POWELL, Robert (fl 18th cent) fire-eater CDP

POWELL, Robert (fl 1710-15) English puppeteer OC/2

POWELL, Robert (b 1944) English actor WWT/16

POWELL, S. Morgan (d 1962 [95]) critic BP/47*

POWELL, Snelling (1758-1821) Welsh actor DAB, HAS, WWA/H

POWELL, Mrs. Snelling [née Harrison] (1774-1843) English actress HAS

POWELL, Thomas (1809-87) English dramatist DAB, WWA/H

POWELL, Mrs. T. Morton see Powell, Elizabeth Jane

POWELL, Tom (d 1961 [79]) minstrel BE*

POWELL, Walter Templer (d 1949) actor, producer, manager BE*, WWT/14*

POWELL, William (1735-69) English actor, manager CDP, DNB, ES, GT, OC/1-3, TD/1-2

POWELL, William (b 1892) American actor CB, ES, WWT/9-10

POWELL, Mrs. William, Sr. see Powell, Eliza Ann

POWELL, William H. (d 1888 [47]) circus manager EA/89*

POWER, Agnes (d 1894) EA/95*

POWER, Alexander (d 1901 [54]) minstrel manager EA/02*

POWER, Caroline Amelia [Mrs. Clavering Power] (d 1911 [71]) EA/12*

POWER, Clavering (1842-1931) English actor OAA/1-2

POWER, Mrs. Clavering see Power, Caroline Amelia

POWER, Mrs. Fred [Maggie Smith] (d 1878 [31]) EA/79*

POWER, Sir George (1848-1928) Irish actor OAA/2

POWER, Harry (d 1898) comedian EA/99*

POWER, Hartley (1894-1966) American actor BE, WWT/6-13

POWER, Henrietta Maria (d 1895 [66]) EA/96*

POWER, James (d 1890 [64]) singer, songcomposer CDP

POWER, John (fl 1846) singer CDP

POWER, Maurice (d 1849) Irish actor COC, HAS

POWER, Nelly (d 1887 [32]) English music-hall singer CDP

POWER, R. J. (d 1884) box office keeper EA/85*

POWER, Robert (d 1875 [36]) pantomimist EA/76*

POWER, Rosine (1840-1932) English singer, actress BE*, WWT/14*

POWER, Mrs. S. (d 1909) EA/10*

POWER, Tyrone (1795-1841) Irish actor BS, CDP, COC, DNB, ES, HAS, NTH, OC/1-3, OX, SR

POWER, Tyrone (1869-1931) English actor COC, DAB, ES, GRB/3-4, NTH, OC/1-3, WWM, WWS, WWT/1-6

POWER, Tyrone (1914-58) American actor CB, COC, ES, NTH, OC/1-3, TW/9-15, WWA/3, WWT/9-12

POWER, Mrs. Tyrone (d 1876 [81]) EA/77*

POWER, Mrs. Tyrone see Crane, Edith

POWERS, Arba Eugene (d 1935 [62]) American actor BE*, BP/19*

POWERS, Chris L. (d 1972 [82]) performer BP/57*

POWERS, Ed (b 1938) American actor TW/24

POWERS, Eugene (1872-1935) American actor WWT/7

POWERS, Harry Joseph (1859-1941) Irish manager WWA/1-2

POWERS, James T. (1862-1943) American actor, singer GRB/2-4, SR, WWA/4, WWS, WWT/1-9

POWERS, John (b 1935) Australian dramatist WWT/16

POWERS, Leona (1896/1900-1967) American actress BE, TW/26, WWT/9-11

POWERS, Marie (1913?-73) American actress, singer BE, CB, TW/30

POWERS, Tom (1890-1955) American actor TW/2-4, 12, WWA/3, WWT/6-11

POWIER, Robert John (d 1884

[57]) EA/85*

POWLES, William Henry see Ball, Harry

POWLEY, Bryan (d 1962 [91]) actor WWT/14*

POWLTON, Thomas (fl 1584) actor DA

POWNALL, Mrs. (d 1796) English singer, actress HAS, WWA/H

POWNALL, Miss see La Folle, Mrs.

POWNALL, John (d 1910) singer EA/11*

POWRIE, Thomas (d 1868 [44]) actor EA/69*

POWYS, Stephen [Virginia de Lanty] (b 1907) American dramatist BE, WWT/9-15

POYNTER, Mrs. (d 1898 [81]) actress EA/99*, WWT/14*

POYNTER, Beulah (b 1886) American actress WWM

POYNTER, Richard (d 1882 [72]) actor EA/83*

POYNTON, Frank (d 1895) comic singer EA/96*

POZZOLINI, Gasparo (fl 1853) singer CDP

PRAEGER, Ferdinand (d 1891 [76]) musician EA/92*

PRAGER, Bernard (d 1969 [71]) executive BP/54*

PRAGER, Gerhard (d 1975 [55]) producer/director/choreographer BP/60*

PRAGER, Stanley (1917-72) American actor, director, producer BE, TW/28

PRATESI, Signorina (fl 1860) dancer HAS

PRATESI SISTERS (fl 1857) dancers CDP

PRATT, Mrs. (fl 1848) actress HAS

PRATT, Charles Edward James Blyth manager GRB/2-4

PRATT, G. (d 1881 [56]) EA/82*

PRATT, G. H. ["Yankee" Pratt] (d 1867) comedian HAS

PRATT, Judson (b 1916) American actor TW/11-12

PRATT, Mike (d 1976 [45]) actor WWT/16*

PRATT, Muriel (d 1945 [54]) English actress WWT/4-7

PRATT, Robert (fl 1774-90) actor, dramatist TD/1-2

PRATT, Silas Gamaliel (1846-1916)

American composer DAB, WWA/1, WWM

PRATT, S. J. [Courtney Melmoth] (1749-1814) English actor, dramatist CP/2-3, DNB, GT

PRATT, William Henry see Karloff, Boris

PRATT, W. W. (fl 1821-64) actor, dramatist, musician, manager, lecturer, preacher HAS

PRATTEN, R. Sidney (d 1868) musician EA/69*

PRATTEN, Mme. Sidney [Catherina Josepha Pelzer] (d 1895) musician EA/96*

PRAXY, Raoul (d 1967 [75]) dramatist BP/52*

PRAY, Anna (d 1878) EA/79*

PRAY, Anna M. (d 1971 [80]) performer BP/56*

PRAY, Isaac Clark (1813-69) American producer, dramatist, critic, actor, manager DAB, HAS, WWA/H

PRAY, Louisa (fl 1849) dancer HAS

PRAY, Malvina see Florence, Mrs. William Jermyn

PRAY, Maria see Williams, Mrs. Barney

PREBLE, Ed (b 1919) American actor TW/26

PREDOVIC, Dennis (b 1950) American actor TW/30

PREECE, Josephine (d 1909) actress EA/10*

PREECE, Richard (d 1918 [85]) EA/19*

PREECE, Tim (b 1938) English actor TW/23, WWT/15-16

PREEDY, George R. [Gabrielle Margaret Vere Campbell] (1888-1952) English dramatist WWT/8-11

PREISCH, J. Allen singer CDP

PREISSER, Cherry (d 1964 [46]) acrobatic dancer TW/21

PREMICE, Josephine (b 1926) American actress, dancer, singer BE, TW/12, 14-15, 23-24, 29-30

PREMINGER, Marion (d 1972 [58]) performer BP/56*

PREMINGER, Otto (b 1906) Austrian producer, director BE, CB, ES

PRENDERGAST, John (d 1869) comedian HAS

PRENDERGAST, Thomas B. (d 1869) minstrel CDP, HAS

PRENSKY, Lester American lawyer BE

PRENTICE, Aleck see Prentice, John

PRENTICE, Charles W. ["Jock"] (b 1898) Scottish musical director, composer WWT/9-14

PRENTICE, Herbert M. (b 1890) English producer, designer WWT/8-13

PRENTICE, John (1829-67) actor HAS

PRENTICE, Lena (fl 1866-68) actress HAS

PRENTISS, Alvin Stewart (1826-65) American agent HAS

PRENTISS, Lewis (d 1967 [62]) performer BP/52*

PRESANO, Rita (d 1935 [70]) actress BE*, WWT/14*

PRESBREY, Eugene Wyley (1853-1931) American dramatist DAB, GRB/2-4, WWA/1, WWM, WWT/3-6

PRESCOTT, Marie Victor [Mrs. Robert D. McLean] (1853-93) actress CDP

PRESCOTT, Norman (d 1973 [81]) performer BP/58*

PRESCOTT, Norman see Prescott-Davies, N.

PRESCOTT, Walter [Ernest Charles Coverdale] (d 1903 [50]) actor EA/05*

PRESCOTT-DAVIES, N. [Norman Prescott] (1862-1915) English dramatist WWW/1

PRESLEY-EMERY, Mary Jane (d 1905) EA/06*

PRESNELL, Harve (b 1933) American actor TW/17, 22

PRESSMAN, David (b 1913) Russian/American director, educator, actor BE

PRESSMAN, Lawrence (b 1939) American actor TW/20, 25

PRESTBURY, Sarah see Roberts, Sarah

PRESTIGE, Fanny (b 1846) English actress CDP, HAS

PRESTON, Mr. (fl 1750) actor, dramatist CP/3

PRESTON, Mrs. see Nichols, Mrs. Horace F.

PRESTON, Amy see Sheridan,

Amy
PRESTON, Barry (b 1945) American actor TW/23
PRESTON, Christopher (d 1902) EA/03*
PRESTON, Edna (b 1892) American actress TW/8-15
PRESTON, Ellen Washington see Grey, Marie de
PRESTON, Georgina actress, dancer, singer CDP
PRESTON, Henry W. (d 1859) actor, manager HAS
PRESTON, Isabella (fl 1845) actress HAS
PRESTON, J. B. (d 1886 [50]) actor EA/87*
PRESTON, Jessie (d 1928 [51]) actress, dancer, singer CDP
PRESTON, Robert [né Meservey] (b 1913/18) American actor BE, CB, TW/8-24, WWT/13-16
PRESTON, Thomas (1537-98) English dramatist COC, CP/1-3, FGF, HP, MH, OC/1-3
PRESTON, Tom (d 1899 [26]) comedian EA/00*
PRESTON, William (1753-1807) Irish dramatist CP/3, DNB
PRESTON, William (fl 1794?) American? dramatist EAP, RJ
PRESTON, William (b 1921) American actor TW/30
PRESTON, William C. (d 1963) HAS
PRESTWICH, Edmund (fl 1650-51) dramatist CP/1-3
PREVIN, André (b 1929) German/American composer, conductor CB, ES
PREVIN, Charles (d 1973 [86]) producer/director/choreographer BP/58*
PREVOST, Eugene-Prosper (1809-72) French conductor WWA/H
PREWETT, Eda Valerga (d 1964 [81]) singer, dancer BE*
PREY, Hermann (b 1929) German singer CB, ES
PRICE, Mr. equestrian CDP
PRICE, Mr. (d 1842) HAS
PRICE, Mrs. [née Warren; Mrs. Clifford] actress HAS
PRICE, Albert Guy (b 1885) Canadian editor WWM

PRICE, Annie (d 1889 [47]) fat woman EA/90*
PRICE, Dennis (1915-73) English actor BE, WWT/10-15
PRICE, E. D. (1849-1935) American manager, dramatist GRB/3, WWM
PRICE, Edward (b 1847) Canadian actor HAS
PRICE, Edward (d 1895 [55]) actor EA/96*
PRICE, Mrs. Edward see Ryder, Emma
PRICE, Edwin H. (d 1907) American manager GRB/3
PRICE, Eleazer D. (d 1935 [86]) American manager, press agent BP/19*
PRICE, Evadne [Helen Zenna Smith] (b 1896) actress WWT/9-11
PRICE, Fanny Bayard (b 1847) American actress HAS
PRICE, Frank (d 1885) scene artist EA/86*
PRICE, George (1900-64) American vaudevillian, actor TW/20
PRICE, George N. (d 1962 [86]) performer BE*
PRICE, Georgie see Price, George
PRICE, Gerald (b 1921) American actor TW/10-15
PRICE, Gilbert (b 1942) American actor TW/20-22, 26-28
PRICE, Graham (d 1916) English actor GRB/1-2
PRICE, H. E. (d 1892) American actor EA/93*
PRICE, Mrs. Henry Ernest see Price, Mary Ann
PRICE, Henry P. (d 1908) EA/09*
PRICE, James (1761-1805) English dancer ES
PRICE, James (1801-65) English dancer ES
PRICE, Mrs. James see Price, Jane
PRICE, Jane [Mrs. James Price] (d 1881 [66]) EA/82*
PRICE, J. B. (fl 1842) actor HAS
PRICE, Jesse (d 1974 [64]) performer BP/58*
PRICE, John (fl 1609-29) musician DA
PRICE, John (fl 1795) dramatist CP/3
PRICE, John Adolph (1805-90) dancer ES

PRICE, John Edward (d 1863 [45]) manager EA/72*

PRICE, John L. , Jr. (b 1920) American producer, actor, director BE

PRICE, Joseph Percy (b 1822) Irish actor HAS

PRICE, Kate (1873-1943) Irish actress BE*

PRICE, Leontyne (b 1927) American singer, actress BE, CB, ES

PRICE, Lillah [Mrs. Parke Hunter] (d 1910) performer? EA/11*

PRICE, Lizzie (b 1842) American actress CDP, HAS

PRICE, Lorain M. (d 1963 [53]) performer BE*

PRICE, Maire (d 1958) Irish actress COC, OC/3

PRICE, Mary Ann [Mrs. Henry Ernest Price] (d 1887) EA/88*

PRICE, Morton [Horton Rhys] (d 1876 [52]) actor, lessee CDP, HAS

PRICE, Nancy [Mrs. Charles Maude] (1880-1970) English actress, manager COC, GRB/2-4, OC/1-3, WWT/1-14, WWW/6

PRICE, Paul B. (b 1933) American actor TW/26-27, 29

PRICE, Richard (fl 1600) actor DA

PRICE, Richard (fl 1612-27) actor DA

PRICE, Richard see Mora

PRICE, Roger (b 1920) American actor TW/6-7

PRICE, Cpt. Spencer Cosby (d 1892 [72]) EA/93*

PRICE, Stanley (d 1955 [55]) actor TW/12

PRICE, Stephen (1782/83-1840) American manager CDP, COC, DAB, OC/1-3, WWA/H

PRICE, Stuart Banner (d 1917 [39]) EA/18*

PRICE, Thomas (d 1863 [52]) actor, prompter HAS

PRICE, Tom (d 1901) actor? EA/02*

PRICE, Vincent (b 1911) American actor BE, CB, TW/10-15, 24, WWT/8-16

PRICE, Will (d 1962 [49]) director BE*

PRICE, William (d 1873) actor EA/75*

PRICE, William Thompson (1846-1920) American dramatist DAB

PRICE-DRURY, Lt. -Col. W. (d 1949 [87]) dramatist BE*, WWT/14*

PRICKETT, Oliver B. (b 1905) American manager, producer, actor BE

PRIDE, Malcolm (b 1930) English designer AAS, ES, WWT/14-16

PRIDE, Sam (d 1871) musician EA/72*

PRIDE, Ted (d 1963) performer BE*

PRIDEAUX, Miss (fl 1789) actress TD/1-2

PRIDEAUX, James (d 1887 [44]) musician EA/89*

PRIDEAUX, Tom editor BE

PRIEST, Dan (b 1924) American actor TW/23-26

PRIEST, Janet (b 1881) American actress WWM, WWS

PRIEST, Josias (d 1734) dancer, choreographer ES

PRIEST, Sophia (d 1874 [32]) EA/75*

PRIESTLEY, J[ohn] B[oynton] (b 1894) English dramatist, director AAS, BE, CB, CD, CH, COC, ES, HP, MD, MH, MWD, NTH, OC/1-3, PDT, WWT/8-16

PRIESTLEY, Kate [Mrs. John Lisbourne] (d 1891) EA/92*

PRIEUR, Don (b 1942) American actor TW/26

PRIGMORE, Mrs. (fl 1793) English actress HAS

PRIMAVESI, Herbert (d 1917) EA/18*

PRIMROSE, "The Spotted Indian" (fl 1789) CDP

PRIMROSE, Alek (b 1934) American actor TW/25-26, 28-29

PRIMROSE, Dorothy (b 1916) Scottish actress WWT/11-16

PRIMROSE, George H. (1852-1919) Canadian minstrel CDP, WWM

PRIMROSE, Jenny [Mrs. J. E. Marshall] (d 1910) actress EA/12*

PRIMUS, Barry (b 1938) American actor TW/21, 25-26, 29-30

PRIMUS, Pearl (b 1919) West Indian dancer CB, ES

PRINCE, Adelaide [Mrs. Creston Clarke] (1866-1941) English

actress, dramatist CDP,
GRB/3-4, WWM, WWS, WWT/
1-7
PRINCE, Arthur (d 1948 [66])
ventriloquist BE*, WWT/14*
PRINCE, Mrs. Arthur (d 1904)
EA/06*
PRINCE, Elsie (b 1902) English
actress, singer WWT/6-9
PRINCE, Harold S. (b 1928)
American producer, director
AAS, BE, CB, WWT/14-16
PRINCE, Jessie (d 1903 [36])
serio-comic EA/04*
PRINCE, Lillian (d 1962 [68])
actress BE*
PRINCE, Rebecca (d 1886) EA/
87*
PRINCE, William (b 1913) Amer-
ican actor BE, TW/3-16,
18-19, 24, 26, 30, WWT/11-16
PRINCEP, Valentine Cameron
(d 1904) dramatist EA/05*
PRINDLE, Johnnie (fl 1880?)
comedian CDP
PRINE, Andrew American actor
BE
PRINELLA, Joe (d 1909 [31])
acrobat EA/10*
PRING, Edward H. (d 1887) Eng-
lish agent NYM
PRINGLE, Lemprière (d 1914)
actor, singer WWT/14*
PRINGLE, Thomas (d 1869 [28])
actor? EA/70*
PRINSEP, Anthony Leyland (1888-
1942) English manager WWT/
5-9, WWW/4
PRINSEP, Val (d 1904 [66])
dramatist WWT/14*
PRINTEMPS, Yvonne (1894/95-
1977) French actress, singer
BE, COC, ES, OC/3, WWT/
4, 8-14
PRIOLO, Susan (b 1957) American
actress TW/22
PRIOR, Allan actor, singer WWT/
6-9
PRIOR, Anna Louise (b 1854)
American actress HAS
PRIOR, George Bertram (d
1897 [39]) comedian EA/98*
PRIOR, James J. (1823-75)
English actor CDP, HAS
PRIOR, Mrs. James J. [Louisa
Young] (1830-83) American
actress CDP, HAS
PRIOR, Louisa see Prior, Mrs.

James J.
PRIOR, Lulu (b 1854) actress CDP
PRITCHARD, Mr. (fl 1736) drama-
tist CP/2-3
PRITCHARD, Mrs. (fl 1832-36)
English actress HAS
PRITCHARD, Miss (d 1781) actress
CDP
PRITCHARD, David actor TD/2
PRITCHARD, Dick (d 1963 [58])
manager BE*
PRITCHARD, Hannah (1711-68)
English actress CDP, COC,
DNB, ES, GT, OC/1-3, TD/1-2
PRITCHARD, Irving J. (d 1975
[93]) photographer BP/59*
PRITCHARD, James (d 1823) Eng-
lish actor HAS
PRITCHARD, Johanna actress
CDP
PRITCHARD, John (d 1868 [38])
actor EA/69*, WWT/14*
PRITCHARD, John Langford (1799-
1850) actor CDP, DNB
PRITCHARD, Maria (fl 1863) ac-
tress HAS
PRITCHARD, Marie [Mrs. Fred-
erick Archer] (d 1910) actress
EA/11*
PRITCHARD, R. (d 1876 [39]) mu-
sician EA/77*
PRITCHARD, Richard Valentine (d
1973 [79]) performer BP/58*
PRITCHARD, Ted (b 1936) Ameri-
can actor TW/30
PRITCHARD, Val (d 1898) Negro
comedian EA/99*
PRITCHARD, William (d 1763)
treasurer COC
PRITCHARD, William (d 1892 [35])
EA/93*
PRITCHETT, Lizabeth (b 1920)
American actress TW/28-29
PRITECA, B. Marcus (d 1971 [81])
architect BP/56*
PRITT, Stephen (b 1873) English
manager, dramatist GRB/1
PROBY, David (d 1964) actor BE*
PROBY, John Joshua, Earl of
Carysfort (b 1751) dramatist
CP/3
PROCTER, Arthur Wyman (1889-
1961) American dramatist
WWA/4
PROCTER, Ivis Goulding (d 1973
[67]) performer BP/57*
PROCTER, Lionel Claude Race
see Dunrobin, L. Race

PROCTOR (fl c. 1599?) actor?
DA

PROCTOR, Bryan Walter [Barry Cornwall] (1787-1874) dramatist CDP

PROCTOR, Catherine (b 1879) Canadian actress TW/1, WWS

PROCTOR, Cecil Vernon (b 1878) English actor GRB/1

PROCTOR, Charles (b 1925) American actor TW/8-14

PROCTOR, David (b 1878) American? actor WWS

PROCTOR, Frederick Francis (1851/56-1929) American actor, manager COC, DAB, GRB/3-4, OC/1-3, SR, WWS

PROCTOR, Harry see Philp, Rowline

PROCTOR, James D. (b 1907) American press representative BE

PROCTOR, Jessie (d 1975 [102]) performer BP/60*

PROCTOR, Joseph (b c. 1798) actor, manager HAS, SR

PROCTOR, Joseph (1816-97) American actor, manager CDP, DAB, WWA/H

PROCTOR, Mrs. Joseph [Hester Warren; Mrs. Willis] (1810-41) American actress HAS

PROCTOR, Maria [Mrs. Robert Proctor] (d 1906 [69]) EA/07*

PROCTOR, Philip (b 1940) American actor TW/20, 22-23

PROCTOR, Robert (d 1888 [56]) circus proprietor EA/89*

PROCTOR, Mrs. Robert see Proctor, Maria

PROFANATO, Gene (b 1964) American actor TW/27

PROFEIT, Leopold (d 1917) actor EA/18*, WWT/14*

PROKOFIEV, Serge (1891-1953) Russian composer, conductor CB, ES

PROSER, Monte (d 1973 [69]) English producer BE

PROSPER, Eugénie (fl 1844?) singer CDP

PROTHERO, May [Mrs. H. Athol Forde] (d 1900) actress EA/97

PROUT, Dr. Ebenezer (d 1909 [74]) professor of music EA/11*

PROUTY, Charles (d 1974 [64])

scholar BP/58*

PROUTY, Jed (d 1956 [77]) American actor TW/12

PROVAN, Lizzie (d 1867) tight-rope performer EA/68*

PROVO, Frank (d 1975 [62]) dramatist BP/60*

PROVOL [Nathan Provolsky] (b 1882) American vaudevillian WWM

PROVOLSKY, Nathan see Provol

PROVOST, Mary [Mrs. J. P. Addams] (b 1835) American actress CDP, HAS

PRUD'HOMME, Cameron (1892-1967) American actor, director BE, TW/13-15, 24

PRUD'HOMME, George [George Pembroke] (d 1972 [71]) actor TW/29

PRUD'HOMME, June American actress TW/26

PRUDOM, Miss (fl 1781?) actress, singer CDP

PRUETTE, William American actor, singer WWS

PRUN, Peter de (fl 1594) actor DA

PRUNIERE, M. (d 1878) contortionist EA/79*

PRUSSING, Louise (b 1897) American actress WWT/6-11

PRYCE, Catharine Gompertz [Kitty Turner] (d 1889 [15]) actress EA/90*

PRYCE, Richard (d 1942 [79]) French/English dramatist WWT/1-9, WWW/4

PRYCE-JONES, Alan (b 1908) English critic, dramatist BE

PRYDE, Peggy (fl 1891?) actress, dancer, singer CDP

PRYNCE, Richard (fl 1554) actor DA

PRYNNE, William (1600-69) writer CDP

PRYOR, Ainslie (b 1921) American actor TW/10-13

PRYOR, Arthur W. (1870-1942) American composer DAB

PRYOR, C. E. (fl 1862) American actor HAS

PRYOR, Maureen (b 1924) Irish actress TW/24

PRYOR, Nicholas (b 1935) American actor BE, TW/14-15, 23, 26, 30

PRYOR, Roger (1901/03-74) American actor TW/3, 30, WWT/7-11

PRYORE, Rychard see Price,
Richard
PRYSE, Hugh (1910-55) English
actor WWT/11
PRYTHERCH, Harriet [Mme.
Gerard Coventry] (d 1882 [33])
musician EA/83*
PSACHAROPOULOS, Nikos (b
1928) Greek educator, director
BE
PUCCINI, Giacomo (1858-1924)
Italian composer ES, GRB/1,
WWM
PUCCIO, Mae Crane (d 1969 [44])
performer BP/53*
PUCK, Harry (d 1964 [71]) per-
former, songwriter BE*
PUDSEY, Edward (fl 1628-40)
actor DA
PUENTE, Giuseppe del (1841-
1900) Italian singer WWA/H
PUGH, Mrs. J. (d 1887 [41])
wardrobe mistress EA/88*
PUGH, John (d 1886 [34]) eques-
trian EA/87*
PUGH, Ted (b 1937) American
actor TW/23-26, 29-30
PUGH, Winnifred (d 1881) EA/
82*
PUGLIA, Frank (d 1975 [83])
actor BP/60*, WWT/16*
PUGLIESE, Rudolph E. (b 1918)
American educator BE
PUGNANI, Gaetano (1728-98)
composer, musician CDP
PUGNI, Sig. (d 1869) composer
EA/70*
PULASKI, Jack (d 1948) Ameri-
can theatrical reporter, editor,
critic BE*, BP/33*, WWT/
14*
PULHAM, George (d c. 1612)
sharer DA
PULITZER, Margaret Leech (d
1974 [80]) dramatist BP/58*
PULLAN, Henry (d 1903 [86])
proprietor EA/04*
PULLAN, James (d 1894 [45])
music-hall lessee EA/95*
PULLEN, Master actor CDP
PULLY, B. S. (1910-72) Amer-
ican actor TW/28, WWA/5
PULOS, Virginia (b 1947) Amer-
ican actress TW/29-30
PUMA, Marie American actress
TW/26
PUMAREJO, Gaspar (d 1975
[61]) producer/director/chore-

ographer BP/59*
PURCELL, Charles (1883-1962)
American actor, singer TW/3-
4, 18, WWT/7-11
PURCELL, Gertrude (d 1963 [67])
performer, dramatist BE*,
BP/47*
PURCELL, Harold (b 1907) English
dramatist, librettist, lyricist
WWT/10-14
PURCELL, Henry (1658?-95) Eng-
lish composer CDP, DNB, ES,
HP
PURCELL, Irene (1903-72) Ameri-
can actress TW/29, WWT/7-10
PURCELL, Tom (d 1892) mimic,
entertainer EA/93*
PURCHASE, Andrew (d 1879 [78])
wax-work proprietor EA/81*
PURDELL, Reginald (1896-1953)
English actor WWT/8-11
PURDOM, C. B. (1883-1965) Eng-
lish critic, general secretary of
British actors' Equity BE,
WWT/9-13, WWW/6
PURDOM, Edmund (b 1926) English
actor ES
PURDY, Alexander H. (d 1862)
manager, proprietor CDP, HAS
PURDY, Richard American actor
TW/8-9
PURDY, Richard Augustus (1863-
1925) American dramatist, lec-
turer WWA/1, WWWM
PURDY, S. S. (b 1836) American
comedian HAS
PURKIS, J., Jr. (b 1781) musician
CDP
PURKISS, M. A. [Mrs. W. T.
Purkiss] (d 1905 [72]) EA/06*
PURKISS, William (d 1894) EA/95*
PURKISS, Cpt. W. S. (d 1899
[75]) music-hall proprietor EA/
01*
PURKISS, Mrs. W. T. see
Purkiss, M. A.
PURNELL, Louise (b 1942) English
actress AAS, WWT/15-16
PURNELL, Roger (b 1943) Ameri-
can actor TW/27-28
PURNELL, Thomas (d 1889) jour-
nalist EA/91*
PURSSORD, Walter (d 1896 [39])
conjurer EA/97*
PURTON, John C. (d 1876 [66])
musician EA/77*
PURVIANCE, Edna (1895-1958)
American actress BE*

PURVIS, Mrs. Billy (d 1880 [94]) EA/81*

PURVIS, Walter (b 1870) Welsh actor GRB/1

PURVIS, Walter (d 1912 [45]) actor EA/13*

PURVIS, William Frederick (b 1870) English critic GRB/2-4

PUSEY, Arthur actor WWT/4-11

PUSSER, Buford (d 1974 [36]) performer BP/59*

PUTNAM, Boyd (d 1908) actor GRB/4*

PUTNAM, Katie (b 1852) American actress, singer CDP, HAS

PUTNAM, William James (d 1897) musician EA/98*

PUTTENHAM, George (fl 1589) dramatist CP/2-3, FGF

PUZZI, Sig. (d 1876 [84]) musician EA/77*

PUZZI, Giacinta (d 1889 [81]) singer EA/90*

PYAT, Félix (d 1889 [79]) dramatist, singer EA/90*

PYE, Henry James (d 1813 [58]) English dramatist CP/3, GT, TD/1-2

PYE, Mrs. Henry James (d 1796) dramatist CP/3

PYE, John (fl 1559) actor DA

PYE, Merrill (d 1975 [73]) designer BP/60*

PYGE, John see Pig, John

PYK, John see Pig, John

PYKMAN, Phillip (fl 1600-01) member of the Chapel Royal DA

PYLE, Thomas F. (d 1976 [58]) performer BP/60*

PYM, Miss see Cromwell, Cecil

PYMER, James (d 1898 [79]) clown EA/00*

PYMER, Mrs. James see Pymer, Matilda

PYMER, Matilda [Mrs. James Pymer] (d 1881 [64]) EA/82*

PYNE, Mr. singer, actor BS

PYNE, George (d 1877 [87]) musician, singer EA/78*

PYNE, J. (d 1857) singer EA/72*

PYNE, Louisa Fanny [Louisa Fanny Bodda] (1835-1904) English singer CDP, DNB, HAS

PYNE, Rena (d 1889) music-hall singer EA/90*

PYNE, Susan [Mrs. F. H. Celli] (d 1886) singer EA/87*

PYNES, Thomas see Sanford, Jim

PYTCHER, Carolus (fl 1598) actor DA

- Q -

QUAGLIENI, Amalia Gasperini [Mrs. Antonio Quaglieni] (d 1882 [63]) EA/84*

QUAGLIENI, Antonio (d 1892) equestrian, circus director EA/93*

QUAGLIENI, Mrs. Antonio see Quaglieni, Amalia Gasperini

QUAGLIENI, Georgina [Mrs. Romeo Quaglieni] (d 1895 [47]) EA/96*

QUAGLIENI, Mrs. Romeo see Quaglieni, Georgina

QUALCH, Mr. (fl 1759-61) actor HAS

QUALTERS, Tot (d 1974 [79]) actress, singer TW/30

QUAM, Mylo (b 1942) American actor TW/22-24

QUARLES, Francis (1592-1665) English dramatist CP/1-3, DNB, FGF

QUARREL, William Thomas see Thomas, William

QUARRY, Richard (b 1944) American actor TW/26, 28-30

QUARRY, Robert (b 1924) American actor TW/6-9

QUARTERMAINE, Charles (1877-1958) English actor COC, GRB/4, OC/1-3, WWT/1-11

QUARTERMAINE, Leon (1876-1967) English actor BE, COC, OC/1-3, WWT/1-11, WWW/6

QUAYLE, Anna (b 1936/37) English actress BE, TW/19, WWT/15-16

QUAYLE, Anthony (b 1913) English actor, producer, director AAS, BE, CB, COC, ES, OC/1-3, PDT, TW/23-24, 27-30, WWT/9-16

QUAYLE, Calvin (b 1927) American educator, scene designer, director BE

QUAYLE, Charles (d 1901) Irish comedian EA/02*

QUAYLE, Peter (fl 1834-38) American singer HAS

QUEDENS, Eunice see Arden, Eve

QUEEN, Ellery (b 1905) American dramatist CB

QUEEN, John (1843-84) dancer, minstrel CDP

QUEEN, Richard (d 1870) EA/71*

QUEEN ELIZABETH I translator CP/1-3

"QUEEN'S JESTER" see Croueste, Harry

QUELER, Eve (b 1936) American conductor, musician CB

QUENOT, Mons. (fl 1794) French actor HAS

QUESTEL, Mae (b 1910) American actress BE

QUICK, Mrs. Charles (d 1887) EA/88*

QUICK, Charles E. (d 1888) actor EA/89*

QUICK, Charles M. (d 1886) scene artist EA/87*

QUICK, Gerard C. (1811-69) American circus proprietor HAS

QUICK, John (1748-1831) English actor CDP, COC, DNB, ES, GT, OC/1-3, TD/1-2

QUICK, John William see Jean, Jess

QUIDANT, Alfred (d 1893 [79]) composer, musician EA/94*

QUIGLEY, Jennie dwarf CDP

QUIGLEY, Thomas see Seabrooke, Thomas Q.

QUILLEY, Denis (b 1927) English actor, singer AAS, WWT/14-16

QUILTER, Roger (1877-1953) English composer WWW/5

QUIMBY, Harriet (1884-1938) American critic WWA/1

QUIN, Edward (fl 1790) Irish dramatist GT

QUIN, James (1693-1766) English actor CDP, COC, DNB, ES, GT, HP, OC/1-3, TD/1-2

QUIN, Thomas H. (d 1832) English actor HAS

QUINBY, George H. (b 1901) American educator, director BE

QUINE, Richard (b 1920) American actor ES

QUINLAN, Gertrude (1875-1963) American actress, singer GRB/4, WWM, WWS, WWT/1-5

QUINLAN, John C. (d 1954 [62]) New Zealand actor, singer TW/11

QUINLAN, Mark (b 1846) Irish actor HAS

QUINLIVAN, Charles (d 1974 [50]) performer BP/59*

QUINN, Anna Maria (b 1845) actress HAS

QUINN, Anthony (b 1915) Mexican actor BE, CB, ES, WWT/16

QUINN, Arthur Hobson (1875-1960) American critic, historian ES, HJD, NTH

QUINN, Billy (d 1863) Negro performer HAS

QUINN, Billy (b 1945) American actor TW/13

QUINN, Joe (d 1971 [54]) toastmaster, publicist BP/55*

QUINN, Joe (d 1974 [75]) actor TW/30

QUINN, Mary see Digges, Mary

QUINN, Miriam (d 1970 [71]) performer BP/55*

QUINN, Tony (1899-1967) Irish actor WWT/9-14

QUINNEY, Maureen (b 1931) English actress TW/15

QUINTERO, Joaquin Alvarez see Alvarez Quintero, Joaquin

QUINTERO, José (b 1924) Panamanian/American director AAS, BE, CB, COC, ES, PDT, WWT/14-16

QUINTERO, Lamar C. (b 1863) Mexican critic WWM

QUINTERO, Serafin Alvarez see Alvarez Quintero, Serafin

QUINTON, Mark (d 1891 [32]) dramatist, actor BE*, EA/92*, WWT/14*

QUIRK, Margaret C. (d 1971 [70]) performer BP/55*

QUITAK, Oscar (b 1926) English actor TW/22

QUITTNER, Joseph (d 1971 [83]) lawyer BP/55*

QUIVE, Grace see Van Studdiford, Grace

QUONG, Rose Lanu (d 1972 [93]) performer BP/57*

- R -

R., C. (fl 1769) dramatist CP/3

R., J. dramatist CP/1-3
R., T. dramatist CP/1-3
R., W. dramatist CP/1-2
RAB, Phyllis talent representative
BE
RABB, Ellis (b 1930) American
actor, director, producer
AAS, TW/15-16, 23-25,
WWT/15-16
RABE, David (b 1940) American
dramatist CB, CD, WWT/16
RABEL, A. dancing master
CDP
RABINEAU, Augusta see Au-
gusta, Mlle.
RABINEAU, Marie see Marie,
Mlle.
RABINOFF, Max (1877-1966)
Russian impresario WWA/4,
WWM
RABORN, George (d 1974 [50])
critic BP/59*
RABY, Roger Allan (b 1939)
American actor TW/25-26
RACHEL [Elisa Félix] (1820-
58) French actress CDP,
COC, ES, HAS, NTH, OC/
1-3, PDT, SR, WWA/H
RACHEL, Lydia (d 1915) actress
WWT/14*
RACHELLE, Bernie (b 1939)
American actor TW/24, 29
RACHINS, Alan (b 1942) Ameri-
can actor TW/24-29
RACIMO, Victoria (b 1945) Amer-
ican actress TW/28
RACINE, Jean (1639-99) French
dramatist COC, ES, OC/1-3
RACIOPPI, James (b 1946)
American actor TW/26
RACKERBY, Don (b 1926) Amer-
ican actor TW/11
RACKIN, Martin Lee (d 1976
[58]) producer/director/chore-
ographer BP/60*
RACKSTRAW, Mary J. (d 1907)
EA/08*
RADBOURNE, Caroline (d 1890
[80]) EA/91*
RADCLIFF, Ralph (1519?-59)
English dramatist CP/2-3,
DNB
RADCLIFFE, J. (d 1875) actor
EA/76*
RADCLIFFE, John (d 1917 [75])
musician EA/18*
RADCLIFFE, Mat (d 1874 [30])
actor EA/75*

RADCLIFFE, Minnie (d 1918) ac-
tress SR
RADCLIFFE, Thomas B. (1812-66)
English actor HAS
RADCLIFFE, Thornton (d 1909)
EA/10*
RADCLIFFE, Mrs. Walter Thorn-
ton see Watson, Henrietta
RADD, Ronald (1929-76) English
actor TW/22-23, 27, WWT/
15-16
RADECKE, Luise Moore (b 1847)
singer CDP
RADFORD, Basil (1897-1952) Eng-
lish actor WWT/9-11, WWW/5
RADFORD, Robert (1874-1933)
English singer WWW/3
RADICATI, Teresa (b 1778) singer
CDP
RADILAK, Charles H. (d 1972
[65]) performer BP/57*
RADO, James librettist CD
RADSTONE, John (fl 1550) actor
DA
RAE, Alexander (1782-1820) English
actor CDP, DNB, GT, OX
RAE, Bob (d 1899 [33]) singer
CDP
RAE, Charlotte [née Lubotsky] (b
1926) American actress, singer
BE, TW/8, 12-15, 19, 22, 25-
26, 29-30, WWT/15-16
RAE, Mrs. E. J. S. see Rae,
Finaretta
RAE, Eric (b 1899) English actor
WWT/2-3
RAE, Finarette [Mrs. E. J. S.
Rae] (d 1899) EA/00*
RAE, J. B. (d 1891) comedian
EA/92*
RAE, Kenneth (b 1901) English ad-
ministrator BE, WWT/14-15
RAE, Melba (d 1971 [49]) perform-
er BP/56*
RAE, Peter (d 1870 [70]) actor
EA/71*
RAE, Robert (d 1899 [33]) singer
EA/00*
RAE, Sheilah (b 1946) American
actress TW/28
RAEBURN, Henzie (1900-73) Eng-
lish actress COC, WWT/12-15
RAEBURN, Sam [George Ellis] (d
1890 [25]) minstrel? EA/91*
RAEDLER, Dorothy (b 1917) Amer-
ican director, producer, mana-
ger BE, CB, WWT/15-16
RAEVSKY, Iosif Moiseevich (b

1900) Russian director WWT/13-14

RAFAEL, Al (d 1897 [16]) acrobat EA/98*

RAFF, Joachim (d 1882 [58]) composer EA/83*

RAFFERTY, Chips (d 1971 [62]) performer BP/55*

RAFFERTY, Emily [Mrs. Pat Rafferty] (d 1906) music-hall singer EA/07*

RAFFERTY, Pat (d 1952 [91]) actor, songwriter, singer CDP

RAFFERTY, Mrs. Pat see Rafferty, Emily

RAFILLE, Mr. (fl 1834-41) actor HAS

RAFT, George (b 1903) American actor ES

RAFT, Tommy Moe (d 1974 [59]) performer BP/58*

RAFTERY, Edward C. (d 1967 [69]) lawyer BP/51*

RAGLAN, James [Thomas James Raglan Cornewall-Walker] (1901-61) English actor WWT/8-13

RAGLAND, Rags (1905?-46) American comedian CB, TW/3

RAGNI, Gerome librettist CD

RAGNO, Joseph (b 1936) American actor TW/28-30

RAGOTZY, Jack (b 1921) American director, producer, actor BE

RAHERE (d 1144) jester COC, OC/1-3

RAHN, Muriel (d 1961 [50]) American singer TW/18

RAHN, Patsy (b 1950) American actress TW/28

RAHT, Katharine (b 1904) American actress TW/4, 13-14, 20

RAIMUND, Ferdinand (d 1836 [46]) actor, manager WWT/14*

RAIN, Douglas Canadian actor AAS, WWT/13-16

RAINBIRD, Marie [Mrs. Fred Danvers] (d 1904 [30]) actress EA/05*

RAINBOW, Frank (b 1913) English press representative WWT/14-16

RAINBOW, J. G. (d 1893) proprietor EA/94*

RAINBOW, John (d 1892 [79]) EA/93*

RAINE, Bessie [Elizabeth Rowlands] (d 1901/02) actress EA/03*, EA/04*

RAINE, Gillian Ceylonese actress TW/20

RAINE, Jack (b 1897/98) English actor BE, WWT/6-15

RAINER, J. C. see Buckley, R. Bishop

RAINER, Luise (b 1912) Austrian actress WWT/9-11

RAINES, Walter (b 1940) American actor TW/24

RAINESCROFTE, Thomas (fl 1598) actor DA

RAINEY, Ford (b 1908) American actor BE

RAINEY, William S. (d 1964 [70]) producer/director BP/49*

RAINFORD, James H. (d 1900 [53]) actor, stage manager EA/01*

RAINFORD, Louis minstrel CDP

RAINFORD, Tom H. (d 1906 [75]) singer EA/07*

RAINFORTH, Elizabeth (1814-77) singer CDP, DNB

RAINFORTH, John (d 1888 [28]) actor EA/89*

RAINGER, Ralph (1901-42) American composer BE*

RAINIERT, Teresa (fl 1847) singer HAS

RAINOLDI, Paul pantomime master CDP

RAINS, Claude (1889-1967) English actor AAS, BE, CB, ES, NTH, TW/7-9, 13-16, 23, WWA/4, WWT/4-14

RAINS, Leon (1870-1954) American singer WWA/3, WWM

RAINSFORD, Louis (d 1873) singer EA/74*

RAISA, Rosa (1893-1963) Russian singer ES, TW/20, WWA/4

RAITT, John (b 1917) American actor, singer BE, TW/1-9, 12-16, 22-24, WWT/12-16

RAJAH, Raboid (d 1962) performer BE*

RAKE, J. (d 1876) comic singer EA/78*

RALEIGH, Cecil [Rowlands] (1856-1914) GRB/1-4, SR, WWT/1-2, WWW/1

RALEIGH, Mrs. Cecil [Isabel Ellissen] (1866-1923) actress GRB/1-4, WWT/1-4

RALEIGH, Desmond Mountjoy
[W. M. Chapman-Huston]
(b 1881) Irish manager, writer
GRB/2-3
RALEIGH, Saba see Raleigh,
Mrs. Cecil
RALF, Emily [Mrs. Tony Grif-
fin] (d 1892 [25]) EA/93*
RALL, Tommy (b 1929) Ameri-
can dancer, singer, actor,
choreographer BE, TW/26
RALLAND, Bertie (b 1883) Eng-
lish manager GRB/1
RALLAND, Clarissa (d 1899)
EA/01*
RALLAND, Herbert (d 1942 [82])
business manager WWT/14*
RALLAND, Mrs. Herbert see
Clifton, Ethel
RALLI, Richard (d 1913) EA/14*
RALPH, Francis (d 1887 [40])
musician EA/88*
RALPH, James (1695/c. 1705-
1762) American? dramatist
CP/1-3, GT, HJD, WWA/H
RALPH, Jessie (d 1944 [79])
American actress BE*, BP/
28*
RALPH, Julia [Mrs. M. C.
Morris] (b 1876) American
actress WWM
RALSTON, Teri (b 1943) Amer-
ican actress TW/26-30
RAM, Jerry (b 1946) Indian
actor TW/24
RAMAGE, Cecil B. (b 1895)
Scottish actor WWT/7-12
RAMA RAU, Santha (b 1923)
Indian dramatist BE, CB
RAMBAL, Enrique (d 1971
[47]) performer BP/56*
RAMBAUD, Mme. George Gibier
see Gerville-Reache, Jeanne
RAMBEAU, Marjorie (1889-
1970) American actress
TW/27, WWA/5, WWT/4-11
RAMBERT, Marie [Mrs. Ash-
ley Dukes] (b 1888) Polish
choreographer, ballet teacher
ES, OC/1-2, WWT/8-12
RAMIN, Sid (b 1924) American
composer, conductor BE
RAMIREZ, Ray (b 1939) Amer-
ican actor TW/23
RAMKINS, William (fl 1598-
1600) dramatist CP/3
RAMM, Matilde (d 1877) actress
EA/78*

RAMOS, Signorina (fl 1857) singer
HAS
RAMOS, Carlos (d 1969 [62]) per-
former BP/54*
RAMOS, Richard (b 1941) American
actor TW/25, 28, 30
RAMSAY, Allan (1686-1758) Scot-
tish dramatist CDP, COC,
CP/1-3, DNB, GT
RAMSAY, Ernest actor, composer
GRB/1
RAMSAY, John Nelson (d 1892
[53]) EA/93*
RAMSAY, Nelson (d 1929 [66])
actor WWT/14*
RAMSAY, Remak (b 1937) American
actor TW/26-30, WWT/16
RAMSAY, Scott [T. H. MacKillop]
(d 1871) actor EA/72*
RAMSAY, Thomas (d 1896) lessee
EA/97*
RAMSDALE, Alice [Alice Fisher]
(b 1877) English actress GRB/1
RAMSDALE, Edwin (d 1909 [40])
manager EA/10*
RAMSDALE, Fred (b 1879) English
actor GRB/1
RAMSDALE, Isabella Fisher (d
1911 [75]) EA/12*
RAMSDALE, James (d 1891 [69])
touring manager EA/92*
RAMSDALE, Lilian [Lilian May
Fisher] actress GRB/1
RAMSDALE, William N. (d 1909)
actor? EA/10*
RAMSDEN, Mme. see Lock,
Mrs. J. H.
RAMSDEN, Dennis (b 1918) English
actor, director WWT/15-16
RAMSDEN, Newton (d 1896 [43])
actor EA/97*
RAMSEL, Gina (b 1950) American
actress TW/30
RAMSEY, Alicia (d 1933) English
dramatist GRB/3-4, WWT/1-3,
6-7, WWW/3
RAMSEY, Cecil (d 1814) actor
WWT/14*
RAMSEY, Cecil actor EA/97
RAMSEY, Charles Ernest (d 1905
[33]) advance agent EA/06*
RAMSEY, James (b 1928) American
actor TW/6
RAMSEY, John (b 1940) American
actor TW/30
RAMSEY, Johnnie (d 1962 [86])
magician BE*
RAMSEY, Logan (b 1921) American

actor BE, TW/7-8, 13, 22

RAMSEY, Marion (b 1947) American actress TW/27-28, 30

RAMSEY, Mary E. (d 1972) performer BP/57*

RAMSEY, Nelson (d 1929 [66]) actor BE*

RAMSEY, Owen (d 1878) actor EA/79*

RAMZA, Frank W. (d 1889) minstrel comedian EA/90*

RANALLI, Ralph (d 1974 [53]) performer BP/59*

RANALOW, Frederick Baring (1873-1953) Irish actor, singer WWT/5-11, WWW/5

RAND, Bill (d 1961) performer BE*

RAND, L. F. (fl 1852-59) American actor HAS

RAND, Mrs. L. F. (fl 1855) American actress HAS

RAND, Olivia (fl 1867-69) American actress HAS

RAND, Rosa (fl 1868) American actress HAS

RAND, Mrs. William W., Jr. (b 1927) American director BE

RANDALL, Adelaide actress, singer CDP

RANDALL, Annie (d 1913) EA/14*

RANDALL, Beard (b 1880) English actor, stage manager GRB/1

RANDALL, Billy (d 1898) comedian EA/99*

RANDALL, Bob librettist CD

RANDALL, Brett (d 1963 [79]) Australian actor, director WWT/14*

RANDALL, Carl (d 1965 [67]) American dancer, producer WWT/8-10

RANDALL, Charles (b 1923) American actor TW/24, 28

RANDALL, Harry (1860-1932) English actor, music-hall performer CDP, COC, GRB/1-4, OC/1-3, WWW/3

RANDALL, Joe (d 1876 [31]) Negro comedian EA/77*

RANDALL, John (fl 1732) dramatist CP/2-3, GT

RANDALL, Leslie (b 1924) English actor, comedian WWT/13-15

RANDALL, Maria (d 1887 [29]) music-hall performer EA/88*

RANDALL, Martha American actress TW/9

RANDALL, Paul E. (b 1902) American educator, director, actor BE

RANDALL, Peter (d 1971 [55]) producer/director/choreographer BP/56*

RANDALL, Pollie [Mrs. Walter Burnet] (d 1910 [57]) burlesque performer CDP

RANDALL, Richard (1736-1828) singer CDP

RANDALL, Samuel (1778-1864) American dramatist DAB

RANDALL, Susann (b 1943) American actress TW/25

RANDALL, Thomas (fl 1660) dramatist CP/3

RANDALL, Tony (b 1920/24) American actor BE, CB, ES, TW/4, 6, 14-15, 22, WWT/16

RANDALL, W. [Billy Forbes] (d 1917) EA/18*

RANDALL, Mrs. W. (d 1888) EA/89*

RANDALL, William (fl 1584-1603) musician DNB

RANDALL, William (d 1917) actor, singer CDP

RANDALLE, Willie (d 1901) acrobat EA/02*

RANDEGGER, Alberto (1832-1911) Italian conductor, composer DNB, GRB/1, WWW/1

RANDEGGER, Giuseppe Aldo (b 1874) Italian composer WWM

RANDELL, Mrs. Frank E. see Pierson, Ethel

RANDELL, Ron (b 1920/23) Australian actor BE, TW/6-8, 15-16, WWT/14-16

RANDLE, Percy E. (d 1918) EA/19*

RANDOLPH, Amanda (d 1967 [65]) actress TW/24

RANDOLPH, Clemence (d 1970 [81]) dramatist BP/55*

RANDOLPH, Donald South African actor TW/3

RANDOLPH, Miss E. (d 1847) English actress HAS

RANDOLPH, Elsie (b 1904) English actress, singer WWT/6-16

RANDOLPH, Eva (d 1927 [64])

actress BE*, BP/12*

RANDOLPH, Isabel (d 1973 [83]) actress TW/29

RANDOLPH, John (b 1915) American actor, dramatist, producer BE, TW/4, 6-7, 9-10, 19, 22-24, 26-27, 29-30

RANDOLPH, Louise [Mrs. S. C. McKnight] (d 1953 [83]) American actress WWM, WWS

RANDOLPH, Mimi (b 1922) Canadian actress TW/27-29

RANDOLPH, Robert [or Thomas] (b 1926) American designer BE, WWT/15-16

RANDOLPH, Thomas (1605-35) English dramatist CP/1-3, DNB, FGF, RE

RANDOLPH, Thomas see Randolph, Robert

RANDOLPH, Virginia (b 1882) American actress WWS

RANDS, Harry actor, singer CDP

RANEVSKY, Boris (b 1891) Russian actor WWT/6-10

RANGER, Mr. (fl 1840) actor HAS

RANGER, George (d 1917) EA/18*

RANKEN, Frederick W. (d 1905 [36]) American librettist, lyricist BE*

RANKIN, Mrs. (fl 1791) actress HAS

RANKIN, Arthur (d 1947 [51]) American actor TW/3

RANKIN, Arthur McKee (1841-1914) Canadian actor, manager CDP, COC, DAB, GRB/2-4, OC/1-3, PP/3, SR, WWS, WWT/1-2

RANKIN, Mrs. Arthur McKee see Blanchard, Kitty

RANKIN, Doris [Mrs. Lionel Barrymore] (c. 1880-c. 1946) actress BE*

RANKIN, Gladys (d 1914 [40]) actress BE*, WWT/14*

RANKIN, Linda (b 1945) American actress TW/25

RANKIN, Maud see Burton, Maud

RANKIN, Molly Scottish actress WWT/9-10

RANKIN, Phyllis [Mrs. Harry Davenport] (1874-1934) Amer-

ican actress, singer GRB/2-4, WWS, WWT/1-6

RANKIN, Thomas (1862-1944) Canadian showman SR

RANKINS, William (fl 1587-1601) dramatist DNB, FGF

RANKL, Karl (1898-1968) conductor WWW/6

RANKLEY, Caroline (d 1846 [29]) actress WWT/14*

RANNEY, Frank (b 1863) American actor WWS

RANNIE, John (fl 1806) dramatist CP/3

RANOE, Miss see Barrett, Mrs. Giles Linnett

RANOE, Cecilia see Burnand, Mrs. F. C.

RANOE, James (d 1877 [69]) actor EA/78*

RANSFORD, Edwin (1805-76) English actor, singer CDP, DNB

RANSFORD, Mrs. Edwin see Ransford, Hannah

RANSFORD, George (d 1910) performer? EA/11*

RANSFORD, Hannah [Mrs. Edwin Ransford] (d 1876 [71]) EA/77*

RANSFORD, Mary Elizabeth CDP

RANSLEY, Peter (b 1931) English dramatist CD

RANSOM, Mrs. Charles B. (fl 1859?) CDP

RANSOM, Frank see Mills, Frank

RANSOME, John W. (1860-1929) actor CDP, SR

RANSON, Blanche [Mrs. Sam Ranson] (d 1892 [36]) music-hall performer EA/93*

RANSON, Herbert (1889-1970) English actor WWT/8-14

RANSON, Sam (d 1893) performer EA/94*

RANSON, Mrs. Sam see Ranson, Blanche

RANSONE, John W. see Ransome, John W.

RAPETTI, Michele (fl 1832) conductor, musician CDP

RAPHAEL, Miss see Ruskin, Sybil

RAPHAEL, Bette-Jane (b 1943) American actress TW/25

RAPHAEL, Enid (d 1964) actress BE*

RAPHAEL, Frederic dramatist CD

RAPHAEL, Gerrianne (b 1935) American actress TW/17, 22-24, 29

RAPHAEL, John N. (1868-1917) dramatist GRB/3-4, SR, WWT/1-3, WWW/2

RAPHAEL, William (b 1858) Scottish scene artist WWT/3-7

RAPHAELSON, Samson (b 1896/99) American dramatist, director BE, MH, WWT/8-13

RAPOPORT, Gene W. (d 1975 [36]) agent BP/60*

RAPP, Charles (d 1974 [71]) agent BP/59*

RAPP, William J. (1895-1942) American dramatist CB, WWA/2

RAPPOLD, Marie (d 1957 [80]) American singer TW/13, WWA/3

RAPPOPORT, Salomov see Ansky

RASBACH, Oscar (d 1975 [86]) performer BP/59*

RASCH, Albertina (1896-1967) Austrian maîtresse de ballet BE, TW/24, WWA/4, WWT/8-13

RASCOE, Burton (1892-1957) American critic WWT/10-12

RASKIN, Judith (b 1928) American singer CB

RASPE, R. E. (fl 1781) dramatist CP/2-3

RASTALL, John see Rastell, John

RASTELL, John (c. 1475-1536) English dramatist COC, CP/2-3, ES, OC/1-3

RASTELL, William (d 1608) manager DA

RASUMNY, Mikhail (1896-1956) Russian actor TW/10

RATCLIFFE, Annie (d 1899 [31]) EA/00*

RATCLIFFE, E. J. (fl 1860s) actor SR

RATCLIFFE, Mrs. John Bond see Pettifer, Mary Ann

RATCLIFFE, Samuel D. (b 1945) American actor TW/26-29

RATHBONE, Basil (1892-1967) South African actor AAS, BE, CB, ES, TW/3-16, 24, WWA/4, WWT/4-14, WWW/6

RATHBONE, George (d 1972 [77]) performer BP/56*

RATHBONE, Guy B. (1884-1916) English actor WWT/2-3

RATHBONE, Ouida (b 1887) Spanish/American dramatist,

designer BE

RATHBUN, Janet (d 1975) performer BP/59*

RATHBURN, Roger (b 1940) American actor TW/27-29

RATHGEBER, Ralph see Meeker, Ralph

RATNER, Anna (d 1967 [75]) performer BP/52*

RATNER, Herbert (b 1912) American actor TW/7

RATOFF, Gregory (1893/97-1960) Russian actor CB, SR, TW/17, WWA/4, WWT/7-12

RATTIGAN, Sir Terence (1911-77) English dramatist AAS, BE, CB, CD, CH, COC, ES, MD, MH, MWD, NTH, OC/2-3, PDT, WWT/9-16

RAUCH, Greta (d 1976 [74]) publicist BP/60*

RAUH, Ida (d 1970 [92]) founder of the Provincetown Players BP/54*

RAUSCHENBERG, Robert (b 1925) American designer CD, ES

RAUZZINI, Matteo (1754-91) singer DNB

RAUZZINI, Venanzio (1747-1810) Italian composer, singer CDP, DNB

RAVEL, Antoine (b 1812) French performer CDP, HAS

RAVEL, François (1823-81) actor CDP

RAVEL, Gabriel (1810-82) French acrobat CDP, HAS, SR

RAVEL, Jerome (1814-90) French performer CDP, HAS

RAVEL, Marietta (b 1847) French dancer, tight-rope performer, actress CDP, HAS

RAVEL FAMILY (fl 1832) HAS

RAVEN, David (d 1971 [58]) performer BP/56*

RAVEN, Elsa (b 1929) American actress TW/26, 28, 30

RAVENOT, Adrie (fl 1828) French dancer HAS

RAVENSCROFT, Edward (fl 1671-97) English dramatist COC, CP/1-3, DNB, GT, OC/1-3

RAVENSCROFT, Ernest (d 1897) acting manager EA/98*

RAVIK, Michael (d 1971 [40]) performer BP/56*

RAWLING, Sylvester (d 1921 [63]) English critic BE*, BP/5*

RAWLINGS, Francis (d 1887
[65]) lessee, manager EA/88*
RAWLINGS, Mabel [Mrs. Mait-
land Marler] (d 1894 [26])
EA/95*
RAWLINGS, Margaret (b 1906)
Japanese/English actress AAS,
WWT/7-16
RAWLINS, Lester (b 1924) Amer-
ican actor BE, TW/18, 21-
22, 25-26, 28, WWT/15-16
RAWLINS, Thomas (1620?-70)
dramatist CP/1-3, DNB,
FGF, GT
RAWLINS, W. H. (d 1927) actor
BE*, WWT/14*
RAWLINSON, A. R. (b 1894)
English dramatist WWT/11-14
RAWLINSON, Herbert (d 1953
[67]) English actor TW/10
RAWLINSON, John (d 1875 [36])
minstrel CDP
RAWLINSON, Priscilla see
Abbott, Annie
RAWLINSON, William (d 1884
[72]) EA/86*
RAWLS, Eugenia (b 1916) Amer-
ican actress BE, TW/1-2,
24, WWT/16
RAWLSTON, Zelma (d 1915)
German?/American? actress,
singer SR, WWS
RAWLYNS, John (fl 1550) actor
DA
RAWORTH, Mr. (fl 1767) English
actor HAS
RAWSON, Graham (1890-1955)
English dramatist WWT/8-11
RAWSON, Sarah Ellen (d 1916
[67]) EA/17*
RAWSON, Thomas William (b
1867) English actor GRB/1
RAWSON, Mrs. Thomas William
see Bertram, Lily
RAWSON, Tristan (1888-1974)
English actor, dramatist
AAS, BTR/74, WWT/5-14
RAY, Alfred (d 1868) actor EA/
69*
RAY, Andrew (b 1939) English
actor BE
RAY, Charles (1891-1943) Ameri-
can actor ES
RAY, Ellen American choreog-
rapher, dancer, singer, ac-
tress BE
RAY, Estelle Goulding (d 1970
[82]) performer BP/55*

RAY, Gabrielle (1883-1973) English
actress, dancer GRB/3-4,
WWT/1-6
RAY, Helen (d 1965 [86]) vaudevil-
lian, actress TW/22
RAY, Isaac (d 1876 [71]) minstrel?
EA/77*
RAY, Jack (d 1975 [58]) performer
BP/60*
RAY, James (d 1901 [36]) perform-
er? EA/02*
RAY, James (b 1932) American
actor BE, TW/25-27, WWT/15-16
RAY, J. H. (d 1875) actor EA/
76*, WWT/14*
RAY, John (d 1873 [42]) Negro
comedian EA/74*
RAY, John William (d 1871 [64])
actor, dramatist BE*, EA/72*,
WWT/14*
RAY, Johnny (d 1927 [68]) Welsh
comedian BE*, BP/12*
RAY, Martha (d 1779) singer DNB
RAY, Naomi (d 1966 [73]) perform-
er BP/50*
RAY, Nicholas (b 1911) American
actor, producer, director ES
RAY, Phil (d 1918 [46]?) singer,
composer CDP
RAY, René [René Creese] (b 1912)
English actress WWT/9-14
RAY, Ruby (fl 1905-07) Brazilian/
English? actress, dancer WWS
RAYBURN, Kittie (fl 1900?) ac-
tress, singer CDP
RAYE, Carol [née Kathleen Mary
Corkrey] (b 1923) English ac-
tress WWT/10-13
RAYE, Martha [née Margaret
Theresa Yvonne Reed] (b 1916)
American actress, singer BE,
CB, TW/23, 29, WWT/15-16
RAYE, Ralph (fl 1594) actor? DA
RAYE, Thelma (fl 1907-08) Bra-
zilian/English? actress WWS
RAYFIELD, Fred (d 1972 [49])
critic BP/57*
RAYM, Maxmilian E. (d 1974
[71]) publicist BP/58*
RAYMON, Rubee (d 1971 [77]) per-
former BP/56*
RAYMOND, Mr. actor CDP
RAYMOND, Mrs. (d 1875 [57])
actress CDP
RAYMOND, Agnes (fl 1850) actress
HAS
RAYMOND, Alfred G. (d 1888
[36]) EA/87*

RAYMOND, Charles (d 1911)
dramatist BE*, WWT/14*
RAYMOND, Charles Reeves (d
1903 [42]) dancer EA/04*
RAYMOND, Cyril (d 1973) actor
AAS, WWT/5-15
RAYMOND, Dorothy American
actress TW/22
RAYMOND, Emeline see Mar-
chant, Mrs. G. F.
RAYMOND, Florence (d 1886) EA/87*
RAYMOND, Gene [Raymond Guion]
(b 1908) American actor, pro-
ducer, director BE, ES,
TW/14-15, WWT/7-16
RAYMOND, Helen (d 1965 [76])
American actress BE, TW/
22, WWT/4-11
RAYMOND, James (d 1854) cir-
cus manager HAS
RAYMOND, James Grant (1771-1817)
Scottish?/Irish? actor CDP, GT,
TD/1-2
RAYMOND, John T. (1836-87) Amer-
ican actor CDP, COC, DAB, HAS,
NTH, NYM, OC/1-3, SR, WWA/H
RAYMOND, Mrs. John T. see
Gordon, Marie
RAYMOND, Kate [Mrs. O. B.
Collins] (1840/44-79) French/
American actress CDP, HAS
RAYMOND, Mrs. Louis see
May, Alice
RAYMOND, Malone [né Richard
Malone] (d 1862 [64]) Irish?
actor? HAS
RAYMOND, Mark (d 1875) per-
former? EA/76*
RAYMOND, Mat [W. M. Mac-
guffie] (d 1879) comedian,
stage manager EA/80*
RAYMOND, Maud (d 1961 [89])
American actress WWS
RAYMOND, Maurice (1878-1948)
magician SR, TW/4
RAYMOND, Moore (d 1965 [62])
critic BP/50*
RAYMOND, Ned (d c. 1827)
actor HAS
RAYMOND, O. B. (d 1851)
American actor HAS
RAYMOND, Richard Malone (d
1862 [62]) EA/72*
RAYMOND, Mrs. W. (d 1880)
EA/81*
RAYMOND, Walter (1852-1931)
English dramatist WWW/3
RAYMOND, William (fl 1900s)

American actor WWM
RAYMOND, William Giddens (d
1905) lessee EA/06*
RAYMONDE, Frankie (b 1874)
American actress WWS
RAYMUND, Carl (d 1966 [50]) editor
TW/22
RAYMUR, Finette see Murray,
Lucy
RAYNAUD, Fernand (d 1973) per-
former BP/59*
RAYNE, Mrs. Henry E. see
Rayne, Mary
RAYNE, John Charles Lin (d 1886
[47]) actor EA/87*
RAYNE, Leonard (1869-1925) actor,
manager WWT/4-5
RAYNE, Mrs. Leonard see
Grace, Amy
RAYNE, Lin (d 1886 [47]) Indian/
English actor OAA/2
RAYNE, Mary [Mrs. Henry E.
Rayne] (d 1911) EA/12*
RAYNER, Alfred (d 1898 [75]) actor
BE*, EA/99*, WWT/14*
RAYNER, Mrs. Alfred see Ray-
ner, Martha
RAYNER, Lionel Benjamin (1787/
88?-1855) English actor BS,
CDP, DNB, OX
RAYNER, Lizzie see Morgan,
Mrs.
RAYNER, Martha [Mrs. Alfred
Rayner] (d 1893 [55]) EA/94*
RAYNER, Minnie Gray [Mrs. Fred-
eric Jacques] (1869-1941) English
actress, singer GRB/1, WWT/
6-9
RAYNER, Sarah (d 1871 [50]) ac-
tress EA/72*
RAYNER, William John (d 1894
[50]) EA/95*
RAYNHAM, Miss (d 1871 [27]) ac-
tress EA/72*, WWT/14*
RAYNHAM, Carry (d 1874) dancer
EA/75*
RAYNHAM, Kate actress, singer
CDP
RAYNOR, Charles (d 1896 [47])
music-hall performer EA/97*
RAYNOR, Mrs. Charles (d 1896
[38]) EA/97*
RAYNOR, Mrs. Charles see St.
Ledger, Clara
RAYNOR, Clarice (b 1878) English
singer GRB/1
RAYNOR, George see Rea,
George James

RAYNOR, Harry (d 1890 [45])
Negro comedian, performer
EA/91*

RAYNOR, Mrs. Jack see
Simpson, Catherine Raynor

RAYNOR, Joseph Napoleon (d
1901 [81]) EA/02*

RAYNOR, J. W. (1823-1900) minstrel manager, performer
CDP

RAYNOR, Thomas (d 1873) comic
singer EA/74*

RAYNOR, William (d 1904 [30])
music-hall performer EA/05*

RAYNORE, Katherine (fl 1897-
1907) American actress WWS

RAYSON, Benjamin American
actor TW/29-30

RAYTON, Velma (d 1974 [81])
actress WWT/16*

RAZAF, Andy (d 1973 [77]) composer, lyricist TW/29

REA, Alec L. (1878-1953) English manager WWT/4-11

REA, Frank E. (1819-87) American actor, singer NYM

REA, George James [George
Raynor] (d 1864 [44]) minstrel
HAS

REA, Oliver (b 1923) American
executive, producer BE

REA, William J. (1884-1932)
Irish actor WWT/4-6

REACH, Angus B. (d 1856 [35])
dramatist BE*, EA/72*,
WWT/14*

REACH, James (d 1970 [60])
dramatist BP/54*

READ, Alvin A. (1830-64) American actor HAS

READ, Grace see Arthur,
Mrs. John, II

READ, Henrietta Fanning (fl 1848)
actress HAS

READ, Henry (d 1898 [57]) lessee
EA/99*

READ, John (fl 1885?) singer,
composer, chairman of Collins's Music Hall CDP

READ, Opie (b 1852) American
writer WWM

READ, Theophilus (d 1906 [59])
EA/07*

READE, Charles (1814-84) English dramatist CDP, COC,
DNB, EA/68, ES, HP, OC/
1-3

READE, Emanuel (fl 1613-20)
actor DA

READE, John (fl 1600-08) actor
DA

READE, Timothy (fl 1626-47) English actor COC, DA, OC/1-3

READER, Ralph (b 1903/04) English
actor, producer, director BE,
WWT/7-16

READING, Beatrice (b 1933) American actress TW/15

READING, Hazel (d 1966) performer
BP/51*

READING, William (d 1563) actor
DA

READY, Eddie (d 1974) performer
BP/59*

REAMS, Lee Roy (b 1942) American
actor TW/26-30

REANEY, James (b 1926) Canadian
dramatist, director, actor CD,
MH, RE

REANO, Archie (d 1903) acrobat,
gymnast EA/04*

REARDON, Catherine (d 1884 [49])
EA/85*

REARDON, Dennis J. (b 1944)
American dramatist CD

REARDON, Edward (d 1894) actor
EA/95*

REARDON, Mrs. Edward see
Reardon, Rosalind Becket

REARDON, Eleanor (d 1903) actress
EA/04*

REARDON, John (b 1930) American
actor, singer BE, CB, TW/17-
19

REARDON, Leo F. (d 1965 [73])
dramatist BP/50*

REARDON, Nancy (b 1942) American actress TW/24-25, 27

REARDON, Rosalind Becket [Mrs.
Edward Reardon] (d 1893) EA/
94*

REASON, Gilbert (fl 1610-25) actor
DA

REAY, George Campbell (d 1899
[28]) proprietor EA/00*

RECKORD, Barry (b 1952) Jamaican
dramatist, director CD

REDD, Cora (d 1968 [c. 70]) performer BP/52*

REDDEN, Eliza [Mrs. Sam Redden]
(d 1875) EA/77*

REDDEN, Mrs. Sam (d 1880) singer
EA/81*

REDDEN, Mrs. Sam see Redden,
Eliza

REDDICK, Walter (d 1971 [65])

performer BP/56*

REDDIN, Kenneth S. (d 1967 [72]) dramatist BP/52*

REDDING, Eugene (b 1870) Canadian actor WWS

REDDISH, Samuel (1735-85) English actor CDP, DNB, GT, TD/1-2

REDDISH, Mrs. Samuel, II see Canning, Mrs. George

REDDY, Max (d 1973 [59]) performer BP/58*

REDE, Leman Thomas Tertius (1799-1832) English actor COC, DNB, OC/1-3

REDE, William Leman (1802-47) English dramatist CDP, DNB, OC/1-3

REDFERN, Mrs. (d 1905 [49]) EA/06*

REDFERN, Lilian English singer GRB/1

REDFERN, Sam singer, composer CDP

REDFERN, W. B. (d 1923 [83]) producer, manager BE*, WWT/14*

REDFIELD, Billy see Redfield, William

REDFIELD, William (1927-76) American actor BE, TW/1, 3, 5-15, 18-19, 24, 28-29, WWT/14-16

REDFORD, George Alexander (d 1916) Lord Chamberlain's examiner of plays GRB/1-4, WWW/2

REDFORD, John (fl c. 1540) master of the Children of Paul's, dramatist DA, DNB

REDFORD, Leslie (b 1929) American actor TW/23-24

REDFORD, Robert (b 1937) American actor BE, CB, TW/20-21

RED FOX, Chief William (d 1976 [105]) performer BP/60*

REDGATE, William (d 1874 [66]) musician EA/75*

REDGRAVE, Corin (b 1939) English actor PDT, TW/20, WWT/15-16

REDGRAVE, Lynn (b 1943/44) English actress CB, PDT, TW/23, 30, WWT/14-16

REDGRAVE, Sir Michael Scudamore (b 1908) English actor, dramatist, director AAS, BE,

CB, COC, ES, OC/2-3, PDT, TW/4-7, 12-21, 30, WWT/9-16

REDGRAVE, Vanessa (b 1937) English actress AAS, CB, COC, ES, PDT, WWT/13-16

REDHEAD, Joseph William see Reed, Howard

RED LADDER THEATRE theatre collective CD

REDMAN, Mr. (fl 1751-55) actor CDP

REDMAN, Ben Ray (1896-1961/62) American critic BE*, BP/46*

REDMAN, John (d 1893) singer EA/94*

REDMAN, Joyce (b 1918/19) Irish actress AAS, BE, TW/2-8, WWT/9-16

REDMAN, William E. see Emerson, William P.

REDMOND, Billy see Emerson, Billy

REDMOND, Charles (fl 1880?) dancer, singer CDP

REDMOND, George E. (d 1893 [38]) actor? EA/95*

REDMOND, Liam (b 1913) Irish actor AAS, TW/23-24, WWT/11-16

REDMOND, Moira actress WWT/15-16

REDMOND, T. C. (d 1937 [80]) actor BE*, WWT/14*

REDMUND, Clara S. [Mrs. Thomas Barry; Mrs. William Redmund] (1840-1905) actress CDP

REDMUND, William (1850-1915) English actor CDP, OAA/2, PP/3

REDMUND, Mrs. William see Redmund, Clara S.

REDNER, Frederick August (d 1899 [61]) musical director EA/00*

REDPATH, James (1833-91) Scottish booking agent WWA/H

REDPATH, William Seyton (d 1881 [59]) dramatist EA/82*

REDSTONE, Willy (d 1949 [66]) composer, musical director BE*, WWT/14*

REDWOOD, Arthur (d 1887) comedian EA/88*

REDWOOD, John Henry (b 1942) American actor TW/27-28

REECE, Arthur (fl 1890s) music-hall singer CDP

REECE, Mrs. Arthur see Sullivan, Rose

REECE, Brian (1913-62) English actor WWT/11-13

REECE, Louisa [Mrs. Robert
Reece] (d 1900) EA/01*
REECE, Robert (1838-91) West
Indian/English dramatist DNB,
EA/68
REECE, Mrs. Robert see Reece,
Louisa
REECE, Valerie see Meux,
Lady
REED, Mr. (fl 1759-61) actor
HAS
REED (d 1891 [83]) actor, stage-
door keeper EA/92*
REED, Alexander (b 1916) Amer-
ican actor TW/28, 30
REED, Alfred German (1847-95)
actor DNB
REED, Billy (d 1974 [60]) dancer,
choreographer TW/30
REED, Carl D. (d 1962 [79])
producer BE*
REED, Carol (1906-70) English
actor, director WWT/7, 10-11
REED, Charles (d 1889) assistant
stage manager EA/90*
REED, Clara (b 1840) American
singer, actress HAS
REED, Dan[iel] (b 1892) American
actor TW/4, 6-9, 15
REED, Daniel (d 1836) American
actor HAS
REED, Dave (1830-1906) minstrel
manager & performer CDP
REED, E. dwarf CDP
REED, Emily Rosalie see Lang-
don, Mrs. Henry A. , I
REED, Flora [Florence Matilda
McNiven] (1844-68) Irish dancer,
music-hall performer HAS
REED, Florence (1883-1967)
American actress BE, TW/
1-17, 24, WWA/4, WWM,
WWT/4-14
REED, Frank Arthur (d 1912 [56])
musician EA/13*
REED, George Edward see
Perks, George
REED, Mrs. German see Reed,
Priscilla
REED, Gus (d 1965 [85]) perform-
er BP/50*
REED, Henry dramatist CD
REED, Henry Dore (d 1897 [56])
manager EA/98*
REED, Howard [Joseph William
Redhead] (d 1899) manager
EA/00*
REED, Isaac (1742-1807) English

critic, historian CDP, DNB
REED, Janet (b 1920) American
dancer ES
REED, Jared (d 1962 [38]) Amer-
ican actor, singer TW/19
REED, Jennings (d 1918) EA/19*
REED, Mrs. Jerrold E. (d 1916)
EA/17*
REED, John (d 1880 [74]) music-
hall manager EA/81*
REED, John (d 1898) manager
EA/99*
REED, John (d 1971 [66]) lawyer
BP/56*
REED, John Roland (1808-91)
American actor CDP, HAS
REED, Joseph (1723/25-87) English
dramatist CDP, CP/2-3, DNB,
GT, TD/1-2
REED, Joseph Verner, Sr. (1902-
73) French/American producer
BE, TW/30, WWT/15
REED, Julian (b 1860) American
actor, dancer HAS
REED, Laura (b 1850) actress?
HAS
REED, Lewis (d 1976 [80]) per-
former BP/60*
REED, Lydia (b 1944) American
actress TW/8-9
REED, Margaret Theresa Yvonne
see Raye, Martha
REED, Mark (b 1890/93) American
dramatist BE, MH, WWT/9-11
REED, Peter Hugh (d 1969 [77])
critic BP/54*
REED, Priscilla [née Horton; Mrs.
Thomas German Reed] (1818-95)
English actress CDP, DNB,
OAA/1-2
REED, Robert (d 1873) musician
EA/74*
REED, Mrs. Roland see Hastings,
Alice
REED, Roland Lewis (1852-1901)
American actor CDP, HAS,
PP/3, WWA/1
REED, T. (d 1871 [76]) musician
EA/72*
REED, Thomas German (1817-88)
English actor, singer, musician
CDP, DNB
REED, Mrs. Thomas German see
Reed, Priscilla
REED, Vernon minstrel CDP
REED, William (d 1889 [46]) musi-
cian EA/90*
REED, William Albert (d 1892 [38])

EA/93*

REED, William Francis (d 1898 [78]) EA/99*

REED, William Henry (1831-60) American dancer, prompter HAS

REED, Wilton (b 1866) English actor, business manager GRB/1

REEDER, George (b 1931) American actor TW/24

REEDER, Louisa (1837-59) American actress HAS

REEKIE, A. L. (d 1917) EA/18*

REES, Mr. actor, mimic TD/1-2

REES, Mr. (d 1843) English actor HAS

REES, Alice [Mrs. Matthew Brodie] (d 1906 [36]) EA/07*

REES, David (d 1843 [49]) comedian EA/72*, WWT/14*

REES, Edward (d 1976 [57]) producer/director/choreographer BP/60*

REES, Ernest (d 1916) actor, singer CDP

REES, James (1802-85) critic, dramatist CDP, RJ

REES, Les (d 1973 [84]) Variety stringer BP/57*

REES, Llewellyn (b 1901) English actor, executive, manager WWT/10-16

REES, Roger (b 1944) Welsh actor WWT/16

REES, Rosemary New Zealand actress GRB/1-2

REES, T. D. (fl 1795) dramatist CP/3

REESE, James W. (d 1960 [62]) American actor BE*, BP/44*

REESE, J. Mark (d 1974 [31]) agent BP/59*

REEVE, Ada [Mrs. Wilfred Cotton] (1876-1966) English actress CDP, GRB/1-4, WWT/1-14, WWW/6

REEVE, Alex (b 1900) English educator, director BE

REEVE, Charles (d 1906 [63]) actor EA/07*

REEVE, Emma Louisa [Mrs. Robert Wardell] (d 1868 [44]) EA/69*

REEVE, George (d 1871) musician EA/72*

REEVE, Mrs. James [née Seymour] (d 1825) actress HAS

REEVE, Joey [Mrs. James Horn] (d 1898) serio-comic EA/99*

REEVE, John (1799-1838) English actor BS, CDP, DNB, HAS, OX, SR

REEVE, Ralph (fl 1603-11) actor DA

REEVE, William (1757-1815) English composer, actor CDP, DNB, ES, TD/1-2

REEVE, Wybert (1831-1906) English actor, dramatist CDP, OAA/1-2

REEVES, Arnold [Aubrey Ruggles] (fl 1891-1913) Canadian dramatist WWM

REEVES, Emma [Mrs. Sims Reeves] (d 1895 [74]) EA/96*

REEVES, Fanny [Mrs. Elliot Galer] (d 1897) singer EA/98*

REEVES, Fanny (d 1917) actress SR

REEVES, Geoffrey (b 1939) English director WWT/15-16

REEVES, George (d 1959 [45]) American actor BE*

REEVES, Jackie (d 1917) EA/18*

REEVES, Jim (d 1959 [45]) American singer, actor BE*

REEVES, John (fl 1842) Irish actor HAS

REEVES, John (d 1890 [57]) acting manager EA/91*

REEVES, John Sims (1818/22-1900) English musician, singer CDP, DNB, ES, WWW/1

REEVES, Joseph (fl 1794) translator CP/3

REEVES, Kynaston (1893-1971/72) English actor AAS, WWT/9-15

REEVES, Mrs. Sims see Reeves, Emma

REEVES, Steve (b 1928) American actor TW/10-11

REEVES, Theodore (1910-73) dramatist BE

REEVES, W. H. (d 1857 [36]) singer CDP, HAS

REEVES, William Sheridan (d 1925 [40]) comedian BE*, BP/9*

REEVES-SMITH, Mrs. G. (d 1898 [57]) EA/99*

REEVES-SMITH, George (d 1897 [67]) manager EA/98*

REEVES-SMITH, H. see Smith, H. Reeves

REEVES-SMITH, Olive (1894-1972) English actress, singer BE,

TW/2-3, 12-17, 29
REGAN, Daniel T. (d 1975 [60s])
performer BP/60*
REGAN, Kay see Medford, Kay
REGAN, Sylvia (b 1908) Ameri-
can dramatist, actress BE
REGAS, Pedro (d 1974 [82])
performer BP/59*
REGENT, Ernest (d 1917) EA/
18*
REGNAL, Ferdinand see Er-
langer, Frederic
REGNIER, Martha (b 1880)
French actress WWT/1-4
REHAN, Ada [Ada Crehan]
(1860-1916) Irish/American
actress CDP, COC, DAB,
DP, ES, GRB/1-4, HJD,
NTH, OC/1-3, PP/3, SR,
WWA/1, WWM, WWS, WWT/
1-3, WWW/2
REHAN, Mary (d 1963 [76])
American actress BE*
REHAN, Meg [Mrs. Fred Dun-
ville] (d 1904) comedienne
EA/05*
REIBEN, Nancy R. see Pollock,
Nancy R.
REICH, George (b 1926) American
actor TW/10-14
REICH, John (b 1906) Austrian/
American director, producer,
educator BE
REICHARDT, Alexander (1825-85)
singer CDP
REICHER, Emmanuel (1849-1924)
actor, director BE*
REICHER, Frank (1875-1965) Ger-
man actor, producer WWM,
WWT/6-9
REICHER, Hedwig (b 1884) Ger-
man actress WWM
REICHER-KINDERMANN, Mme.
(d 1883 [30]) singer EA/84*
REICHMAN, Thomas (d 1974
[30]) producer/director/chore-
ographer BP/59*
REICHMANN, Theodore (1849-
1903) German singer ES
REID, Beryl (b 1920) English
actress AAS, WWT/14-16
REID, Carl Benton (1893-1973)
American actor TW/6, 29
REID, Mrs. Charles H. see
Henley, Josephine
REID, Elliott (b 1920) American
actor BE, TW/4-6, 8-9, 16
REID, Frances (b 1918) Ameri-

can actress BE, TW/2-3, 5-10,
WWT/11
REID, Francis Ellison (d 1933
[67]) American press representa-
tive BE*, BP/18*
REID, Hal (d 1920 [60]) American
dramatist GRB/2-4, WWT/1-4
REID, Henry (d 1868 [65]) armourer
EA/69*
REID, Henry E. (d 1910 [83]) pro-
prietor EA/11*
REID, Ian (d 1969 [51]) agent
BP/54*
REID, James Halleck actor SR
REID, James MacArthur (d 1970
[70]) critic BP/55*
REID, Kate (b 1930) English actress
BE, TW/22, 24-25, 30, WWT/
14-16
REID, Margaret (fl 1892) singer
CDP
REID, Marita (b 1895) Spanish ac-
tress TW/10
REID, Mayne (1818-83) Irish actor,
dramatist HJD
REID, Patricia see Stanley, Kim
REID, S. (d 1878 [70]) actor?
EA/79*
REID, Trevor (d 1965 [56]) per-
former BP/49*
REID, Wallace (b 1891) American
actor WWT/4
REIDY, Kitty (b 1902) Australian
actress, singer WWT/6-11
REIF, Keith (d 1976 [33]) performer
BP/60*
REIFFARTH, Jennie (b 1848) Amer-
ican actress WWS [see also:
Reiforth, Jennie]
REIFORTH, Jennie (1848-1913)
actress, singer SR [see also:
Reiffarth, Jennie]
REIFSNEIDER, Robert (b 1912)
American educator BE
REIGNOLDS, F. S. (fl 1858)
prompter HAS
REIGNOLDS, Kate (d 1911 [75])
English actress CDP, HAS,
PP/3
REILEY, Orrin (b 1946) American
actor TW/26-30
REILLY, Anastasia (d 1961 [58])
performer BE*
REILLY, Charles Nelson (b 1931)
American actor BE, TW/21-23,
WWT/15-16
REILLY, Daniel (b 1833) American
actor HAS

REILLY, Frederick Freame (d 1876 [70]) professor of singing EA/77*

REILLY, James F. (d 1967 [80]) executive BP/52*

REILLY, John (fl 1876?) actor, singer CDP

REILLY, William W. (d 1975 [53]) producer/director/choreographer BP/59*

REINAGLE, Alexander (1756-1809) American musician, impresario DAB, SR, WWA/H

REINAGLE, Hugh (d 1834) American actor? HAS

REINER, Carl (b 1922) American actor, producer BE, CB

REINER, Ethel Linder (d 1971 [65]) producer BE, TW/27

REINER, Fritz (1888-1963) Hungarian conductor CB, ES, WWA/4

REINHARDT, Lizzie (d 1872 [34]) actress EA/73*

REINHARDT, Max [né Goldmann] (1873-1943) German actor, manager, director CB, COC, ES, NTH, OC/1-3, PDT, SR, WWA/2, WWT/1-2, 7-9, WWW/4

REINHARDT, Mrs. Max see Thimig, Helene

REINHARDT, Stephen (b 1947) American actor TW/25-26

REINHEIMER, Howard E. (1899-1970) American lawyer BE

REINHOLD, Mr. (fl 1776-84) actor TD/1-2

REINHOLD, Charles Frederick (1737-1815) English singer, actor DNB

REINHOLD, Conny (d 1974 [42]) producer/director/choreographer BP/59*

REINHOLD, Thomas (1690?-1751) German singer DNB

REINHOLT, George (b 1940) American actor TW/24-25

REINKING, Ann (b 1949) American actress TW/30

REIS, Irving (d 1953 [47]) American director BE*

REISER, Robert (b 1946) American actor TW/26

REISNER, Robert (d 1974 [53]) critic BP/58*

REJANE, Gabrielle [Charlotte Reju] (1857-1920) French ac-

tress COC, GRB/1-4, NTH, OC/1-3, PDT, WWM, WWT/1-3

REJU, Charlotte see Réjane, Gabrielle

RELF, Robert S. (d 1905 [41]) EA/06*

RELPH, George (1888-1960) English actor AAS, TW/2, 16, WWT/3-12

RELPH, Harry see Tich, Little

RELPH, Michael (b 1915) English scene designer WWT/10-13

RELPH, Phyllis (b 1888) actress WWT/3-13

REMENYI, Eduard (1830-98) musician CDP

REMER, Helen see Ware, Helen

REMICK, Lee (b 1935) American actress BE, CB, TW/9, 22-23

REMINGTON, Earle American vaudevillian WWM

REMME, John (b 1935) American actor TW/28

REMMELSBURG, Betty (fl 1867) dancer CDP

REMMELSBURG, Sophie (fl 1867) dancer CDP

REMOND, Fritz (d 1976 [73]) producer/director/choreographer BP/60*

REMUS, Jorie (b 1929) American actress TW/18

REMUSAT, Jean (d 1880 [65]) musician EA/81*

RENAD, Mrs. Charles see Renad, Jeanne Juliette

RENAD, Frederick (d 1939 [73]) actor BE*, WWT/14*

RENAD, Mrs. Frederick see Emmerson, Aggie

RENAD, Jeanne Juliette [Mrs. Charles Renad] (d 1895 [34]) EA/96*

RENARD, David (d 1973 [52]) performer BP/58*

RENARD, Jules (1864-1910) French dramatist MWD

RENAUD, Madeleine (b 1900) French actress BE, WWT/14

RENAUD, Maurice (1862-1933) French singer ES

RENAUD, May (d 1910) actress EA/12*

RENAULT, Francis (d 1955 [62]) female impersonator TW/11

RENAULT, Paul (b 1945) actor TW/25

RENDER, Dr. William (fl 1798)

translator CP/3

RENDLE, John (d 1882 [66]) musical director EA/83*

RENDLE, Thomas McDonald (1856-1926) English critic WWT/4-5

RENDLE, William Edgecumbe (d 1881 [61]) lessee EA/82*

RENETTI, Lilian [Mrs. Will Pearce] (d 1904) serio-comic singer EA/05*

RENEVANT, Georges (d 1969 [75]) actor TW/25

RENFRO, Rennie (d 1962 [69]) animal trainer BE*

RENNELL, Charles (d 1882) actor EA/83*

RENNERT, Günther (b 1911) German director, producer, opera director CB

RENNIE, Hugh (d 1953 [50]) English actor, director TW/10

RENNIE, James (1890-1965) Canadian actor BE, TW/2-9, 14-15, 22, WWT/5-13

RENNIE, John (d 1952 [77]) actor BE*, WWT/14*

RENNIE, Margaret (d 1903 [84]) EA/04*

RENNIE, Michael (1909-71) English/American actor, director BE, TW/28

RENNON, "Tilda" (d 1916 [24]) EA/17*

RENO, Doris (d 1973) critic BP/57*

RENOUF, Henry (d 1913 [53]) actor BE*, EA/14*, WWT/14*

RENSHAW, Edyth (b 1901) American educator, director BE

RENTZ, Master (b 1844) American singer CDP, HAS

RENZ, Herr (d 1892) circus proprietor EA/93*

RENZ, Oceana see Oceana

REPP, Stafford (d 1974 [56]) performer BP/59*

REPTON, H. (fl 1804) dramatist CP/3

RESDAN, Rita [Flo Windsor] (d 1912) burlesque performer EA/13*

RESNICK, Muriel dramatist BE

RESNICK, Regina (b 1922) American singer CB

RESOR, Stanley Burnet (d 1962 [83]) American executive BE*

RESS, Regina American actress

TW/29

RESSLER, Benton Crews (d 1963) performer BE*

RESTER (fl c. 1602) actor DA

RESTIFO, Gary (b 1948) American actor TW/27

RESZKE, Josephine see De Retzske, Josefina

RETFORD, Ella (d 1962 [76]) Irish actress, singer WWT/5-13

RETHBERG, Elisabeth (1894-1976) German singer ES

RETTICH, Julie (b 1810) actress CDP

RETZSKE see De Retzske

REVAL, Rosie (d 1909 [19]) variety performer EA/10*

REVEL, Harry (1905-58) English composer BE*

REVELL, Dorothy (1879-1908) American actress WWS

REVELL, Lilian M. English actress GRB/1-2

REVELLE, Arthur Hamilton [Arthur Hamilton Engström] (1872-1958) English actor GRB/3-4, TW/15, WWS, WWT/1-6

REVERE, Anne (b 1903/06) American actress BE, TW/23, WWT/9-10

REVET, Edward (fl 1671) dramatist CP/1-3

REVILL, Clive (b 1930) New Zealand actor AAS, BE, TW/9, 19, 23, 28, WWT/13-16

REVILL, Frederick William (d 1892 [35]) EA/93*

REVILL, Juliet [Mrs. W. Revill] (d 1885) EA/86*

REVILL, Mrs. W. see Revill, Juliet

REVILL, Wallace (d 1898 [40]) proprietor, manager EA/00*

REVILL, Mrs. Wallace (d 1899 [36]) proprietor EA/00*

REVILL, Mrs. Wallace Ann [Mrs. William Revill] (d 1871 [35]) EA/72*

REVILL, Mrs. William see Revill, Mrs. Wallace Ann

REVILL, William John (d 1897) proprietor EA/98*

REVILL, William Wallace (d 1898 [16]) EA/00*

REVILLE, Robert [Robert Reville Barrett] (d 1893) actor BE*, EA/94*, WWT/14*

REVNER, Katherine Howard (d 1964)

performer BP/49*

REVOLTI, Felix [William Mitchell] (d 1879 [50]) equestrian director CDP

REVY, Aurelie Hungarian actress, singer GRB/1-3

REX, Charles (d 1903) actor EA/04*

REX, Harry (d 1917) EA/18*

REXROAD, David (b 1950) American actor TW/30

REXROTH, Kenneth (b 1905) American dramatist CD

REY, Antonia (b 1927) Cuban actress TW/25-30

REY, Roberto (d 1972 [67]) performer BP/57*

REYMOND, Charles Aguri (d 1902) actor EA/03*

REYMOND, Phil singer CDP

REYNOLDS (fl 1797) dramatist CP/3

REYNOLDS, Miss see Brampton, Lady

REYNOLDS, Adeline de Walt (1862-1961) American actress BE*

REYNOLDS, A. E. (d 1879 [81]) actor EA/80*

REYNOLDS, Alfred (d 1901) musician EA/02*

REYNOLDS, Alfred (1884-1969) English composer, conductor WWT/8-14, WWW/6

REYNOLDS, Alfred John (d 1895 [72]) waxworks exhibitor EA/96*

REYNOLDS, Barney actor CDP

REYNOLDS, Burt (b 1936) American actor CB, TW/18

REYNOLDS, Carrie [Mrs. Charles F. Tingay] (d 1893) EA/95*

REYNOLDS, Charles (d 1918 [69]) EA/19*

REYNOLDS, Charles H. (d 1874) acting manager EA/75*

REYNOLDS, Craig (1907-49) American actor BE*

REYNOLDS, Dale (b 1944) American actor TW/25

REYNOLDS, Debbie (b 1932) American actress TW/29-30

REYNOLDS, Dorothy (b 1913) English actress, dramatist AAS, WWT/13-16

REYNOLDS, Ellis (d 1868 [65]) musician EA/69*

REYNOLDS, Emma [Mrs. R. G. Reynolds] (d 1887 [35]) EA/88*

REYNOLDS, Eugene (b 1944) American actor TW/26

REYNOLDS, E. Vivian (1866-1952) English actor, stage manager GRB/2-4, WWT/1-9

REYNOLDS, Frank E. (d 1962 [57]) director, producer, actor BE*

REYNOLDS, Fred (d 1970) agent BP/55*

REYNOLDS, Frederic (1764-1841) English dramatist CDP, COC, CP/3, DNB, GT, OC/1-3, SR, TD/1-2

REYNOLDS, Mrs. Frederic see Mansel, Eliza

REYNOLDS, George (d 1897) comedian EA/99*

REYNOLDS, George Francis (b 1880) English manager WWT/7-12

REYNOLDS, Harold (d 1973 [76]) performer BP/57*

REYNOLDS, Howard (d 1898 [49]) musician EA/99*

REYNOLDS, James (1891-1957) American designer ES

REYNOLDS, James J. (d 1894 [46]) EA/95*

REYNOLDS, Jane (fl 1839-46) English actress HAS

REYNOLDS, Jane Louisa [Baroness Brampton] (1824-1907) actress, singer CDP

REYNOLDS, John (fl 1628) translator CP/2-3

REYNOLDS, John (d 1871 [29]) Irish comedian EA/72*

REYNOLDS, Jonathan (b 1942) American actor TW/24

REYNOLDS, Joseph (d 1887 [69]) actor EA/88*

REYNOLDS, Joseph (d 1917) musician EA/18*

REYNOLDS, Lydia (fl 1886) music-hall performer COC

REYNOLDS, Patrick J. (d 1972 [59]) director BP/57*

REYNOLDS, Mrs. R. G. see Reynolds, Emma

REYNOLDS, Robert (fl 1610-40) English actor COC, DA, OC/1-3

REYNOLDS, Thomas (d 1947 [67]) producer, director WWT/7-9

REYNOLDS, Tom (1866-1942) Eng-

lish actor, producer WWT/
4-9
REYNOLDS, Vera (d 1962 [61])
actress BE*
REYNOLDS, Walter (d 1941 [89])
dramatist, producer BE*,
WWT/14*
REYNOLDS, Mrs. Walter (d 1901)
EA/02*
REYNOLDS, Mrs. Walter see
Wallis, Ellen Lancaster
REYNOLDS, William (fl c. 1630)
actor DA
REYNOLDS, William H. (d 1863)
actor CDP, HAS
REYNOLDSON, T. H. (d 1883
[75]) dramatist, singer EA/84*
REYNOLDSON, T. H. (d 1888
[80]) actor, dramatist BE*,
WWT/14*
REYNOR, Tom (d 1893) musician,
singer, dancer EA/94*
REZENE, Mrs. Charles see
Cusick, Polly
REZZUTO, Tom (b 1929) Ameri-
can educator, designer, di-
rector BE
RHEA, Hortense (1844-99) Belgian
actress CDP, WWA/1
RHO, Stella (b 1886) English ac-
tress WWT/4-9
RHODES, Bill (d 1967 [72]) per-
former BP/52*
RHODES, Enoch (d 1880 [43])
actor EA/81*
RHODES, Erik (b 1906) American
actor, singer, director BE,
TW/9-15, 25, 27
RHODES, George Ambrose (fl
1806) dramatist CP/3
RHODES, Harrison (1871-1929)
American dramatist WWM,
WWT/4-6
RHODES, Helen (d 1936) French
singer WWW/3
RHODES, James (d 1904 [81])
proprietor EA/05*
RHODES, John (c. 1606-68?)
English bookseller, prompter,
manager COC, DA, NTH,
OC/1-3
RHODES, John (d 1850) proprietor
EA/72*
RHODES, Marie [Mrs. J. H.
Savile] (d 1891) actress EA/
92*
RHODES, Marjorie (b 1903) Eng-
lish actress WWT/10-16

RHODES, Percy William (d 1956
[85]) actor BE*, WWT/14*
RHODES, Pollie [Mrs. Arthur For-
rest] (d 1901 [43]) music-hall
singer EA/02*
RHODES, Raymond Crompton (1887-
1935) English critic, dramatist
WWT/6-7
RHODES, Richard (d 1668) English?
dramatist CP/1-3, DNB, GT
RHODES, Ruth (d 1975 [79]) per-
former BP/60*
RHODES, Thomas (fl 1789) drama-
tist CP/3
RHODES, Thomas Stanley (d 1911)
EA/12*
RHODES, William Barnes (1772-
1826) English dramatist CP/3,
DNB
RHYNSBURGER, H. Donovan (b
1903) American educator BE
RHYS, Horton see Price, Morton
RHYS, William (b 1945) American
actor TW/29-30
RHYS-JONES, Dilys see Watling,
Dilys
RIABOUCHINSKA, Tatiana (b 1916)
Russian dancer TW/2, WWT/
9-12
RIAL, Louise (d 1940 [90]) actress
BE*, BP/25*, WWT/14*
RIANO, Renie (d 1971) actress
TW/28
RIBAS, Mrs. (fl 1847) actress
HAS
RIBBON, Miss see Conduit,
Mrs. Mauvaise
RIBBON, William (d 1875 [29])
equestrian EA/77*
RIBMAN, Ronald (b 1932) American
dramatist CD, CH, WWT/15-16
RIBNER, Irving (1921-72) American
scholar BE
RICARD, Amy [Mrs. Lester Lon-
ergan] (b 1880) American ac-
tress WWM
RICARDEL, Molly (d 1963 [56])
dramatist, actress BE*
RICARDO, Henry (d 1886 [66])
acrobat, pantomimist EA/87*
RICCI, Nora (d 1976 [51]) per-
former BP/60*
RICCI, Rosalin (b 1948) American
actress TW/29
RICCOBONI, Antonio (fl 1675-95)
Italian actor OC/1-3
RICE, Alice Hegan [Mrs. Cale
Young Rice] (fl 1900s) American

dramatist WWM
RICE, Andy (d 1963 [82]) performer BE*
RICE, Cale Young (1872-1943) American dramatist WWA/2, WWM, WWW/4
RICE, Mrs. Cale Young see Rice, Alice Hegan
RICE, Charles (d 1880 [60]) actor, producer, manager BE*, EA/81*, WWT/14*
RICE, Mrs. Charles see Rice, Harriot
RICE, Charles P. (d 1944) dramatist SR
RICE, Charles William (d 1879) menagerie proprietor EA/80*
RICE, Cy (d 1971 [58]) writer BP/56*
RICE, Dan (d 1881) equestrian clown EA/82*
RICE, Dan (1822/23-1900) American clown, manager CDP, DAB, HAS, HJD, WWA/H
RICE, Decius (fl 1833) English actor HAS
RICE, Mrs. Dominic see Cuyler, Margaret
RICE, Edward Everett (1848-1924) American manager, dramatist, composer CDP, GRB/3-4, WWM, WWS, WWT/1-4
RICE, Elmer E. (1892-1967) American dramatist AAS, BE, CB, COC, ES, HJD, HP, MD, MH, MWD, NTH, OC/1-3, PDT, RE, SR, TW/23, WWA/4, WWT/4-14, WWW/6
RICE, Mrs. E. Roberts (d 1891) EA/92*
RICE, Fanny (d 1936 [77]) American actress BE*, BP/21*, WWT/14*
RICE, Felix (b 1946) American actor TW/25
RICE, Florence (d 1974 [67]) actress TW/30
RICE, Gitz (d 1947 [56]) songwriter TW/4
RICE, Harriot [Mrs. Charles Rice] (d 1887) EA/88*
RICE, John (b c. 1596) English actor COC, DA, GT, NTH, OC/1-3
RICE, John (d 1887) Negro comedian EA/88*
RICE, John B. (1809-74) American actor, manager CDP,

HAS, SR
RICE, Mrs. John B. [née Mary Ann Warren] (fl 1837-39) American actress HAS
RICE, J. R. (d 1860 [52]) performer EA/72*
RICE, Myron B. (b 1864) American manager WWS
RICE, Peter (b 1928) Indian/English designer AAS, ES, WWT/15-16
RICE, Roy (d 1966 [79]) performer BP/51*
RICE, Thomas Dartmouth (1808-60) American vaudevillian CDP, COC, HAS, HJD, OC/1-3, SR, WWA/H
RICE, Tim (b 1944) English lyricist CD, WWT/16
RICE, Vernon (d 1954 [46]) American editor TW/10
RICE-KNOX, Florence actress CDP
RICH, Charles J. (1855-1921) American manager BE*, BP/5*
RICH, Christopher (d 1714) English manager COC, DNB, NTH, OC/1-3
RICH, Doris (b 1905) American actress TW/4-7, 12, 21-23, 28
RICH, Eddie (b 1926) American producer BE
RICH, Helen (d 1963 [66]) performer BE*, BP/48*
RICH, Irene (b 1895) American actress TW/5-6
RICH, Isaac B. (1827-1908) American manager GRB/3-4, SR
RICH, J. C. actor, singer CDP
RICH, John (c. 1682-1761) English manager, actor CDP, COC, DNB, ES, GT, HP, OC/1-3, TD/1-2
RICH, Lillian (d 1954) actress BE*
RICH, Lucius C. [Bozo Kelly] (d 1975 [61]) performer BP/59*
RICH, Ron (b 1938) American actor TW/26
RICH, Roy (b 1909) English manager WWT/9-14
RICH, Sally see Jacobs, Sally
RICHARD, Charles (d 1888) singer EA/89*
RICHARD, Don (d 1967 [22]) performer BP/52*
RICHARD, George N. (b 1892) executive BE
RICHARD, Georges (d 1891 [60])

actor, producer, dramatist, manager BE*, WWT/14*

RICHARD, Houston (d 1965 [79]) performer BP/50*

RICHARDS (fl 1777) dramatist CP/2-3, GT

RICHARDS, Mr. actor CDP

RICHARDS, Mr. (fl 1794) Irish actor HAS

RICHARDS, Mrs. [Mrs. Thomas Greenhill] (d 1917) EA/18*

RICHARDS, Addison (d 1964 [61]) actor BE*

RICHARDS, Alfred Bate (1820-76) English dramatist, producer EA/69

RICHARDS, Angela (b 1944) actress WWT/16

RICHARDS, Archie (d 1901) music-hall serio EA/02*

RICHARDS, Beah American actress BE, TW/24

RICHARDS, Brinley (d 1885 [66]) composer, musician EA/86*

RICHARDS, Cicely [Mrs. W. S. Miln] (d 1933 [83]) English actress GRB/3-4, OAA/2, WWT/1-7

RICHARDS, Davis (d 1867) American equestrian HAS

RICHARDS, Donald (1919-53) American actor TW/3-7, 10, WWA/3

RICHARDS, Elizabeth Rebecca see Edwin, Elizabeth Rebecca

RICHARDS, Ernest H. (d 1917 [20]) EA/18*

RICHARDS, George (fl 1791-1804) dramatist CP/3

RICHARDS, George (fl 1854) comedian, minstrel CDP

RICHARDS, Gordon (1893-1964) English actor TW/7

RICHARDS, Grant (d 1963 [47]) performer BP/48*

RICHARDS, Huston (d 1965 [79]) actor TW/22

RICHARDS, Janet (d 1909) EA/10*

RICHARDS, Jean American actress TW/26

RICHARDS, Jennifer (b 1948) American actress TW/29-30

RICHARDS, Jess (b 1943) American actor TW/28-29

RICHARDS, John (d 1810) scene artist WWT/14*

RICHARDS, John Frederick (d

1884 [35]) music-hall performer EA/85*

RICHARDS, Johnny (d 1968 [56]) composer/lyricist BP/53*

RICHARDS, Jon American actor TW/27-29

RICHARDS, Kurt American actor TW/2, 9

RICHARDS, Lex American actor TW/4

RICHARDS, Lloyd Canadian director, educator, actor BE, TW/14

RICHARDS, Louis Arthur (d 1906) actor EA/07*

RICHARDS, Marie (d 1903 [60]) actress EA/04*

RICHARDS, Nathaniel (d 1652) dramatist CP/1-3, DNB, FGF

RICHARDS, Neil A. (b 1879) Welsh singer GRB/1

RICHARDS, Nellie actress, singer CDP

RICHARDS, Paul (d 1974 [50]) performer BP/59*

RICHARDS, Paul (b 1934) American actor TW/25-28

RICHARDS, Paul E. (b 1924) American actor TW/10-12, 15

RICHARDS, Penelope (b 1948) American actress TW/29

RICHARDS, Richard R. (d 1925 [52]) press representative BE*, BP/9*

RICHARDS, Sam (fl 1902?) song composer CDP

RICHARDS, Susan (b 1898) Welsh actress WWT/10-14

RICHARDS, Thomas (fl 1560?) dramatist FGF

RICHARDS, Tom (d 1893) songwriter EA/94*

RICHARDSON, Mr. (fl 1790) English actor, singer CDP, TD/1-2

RICHARDSON, Mr. ["Penny Showman"] (d 1836) American actor CDP, HAS

RICHARDSON, Mr. (d 1856) actor, property man HAS

RICHARDSON, Miss (fl 1852) actress HAS

RICHARDSON, Miss see Vickery, Mrs. J. G.

RICHARDSON, Annie [née Merriton] (d 1868 [30]) actress? EA/69*

RICHARDSON, Mrs. Augustus see Chapman, Elizabeth

RICHARDSON, Bella (d 1910 [56]) actress EA/11*

RICHARDSON, Billy (d 1913)
EA/14*
RICHARDSON, Mrs. Billy see
Richardson, Mary
RICHARDSON, Dorothy (d 1955)
American press representative
WWA/3
RICHARDSON, Elizabeth (d 1779)
dramatist CP/2-3, GT, TD/
1-2
RICHARDSON, Elizabeth (1813-
53) American singer, actress
HAS
RICHARDSON, Ernest (d 1917
[24]) EA/18*
RICHARDSON, Foster (d 1942
[52]) singer WWW/4
RICHARDSON, Frank (1871-1917)
English dramatist, critic
GRB/4, WWT/1-3
RICHARDSON, Frankie (d 1962
[63]) performer BE*
RICHARDSON, Mrs. F. R. Gwyn
see Harlington, Grace
RICHARDSON, Gwyn (b 1879)
English actor GRB/1
RICHARDSON, Harry (d 1910)
actor EA/12*
RICHARDSON, Mrs. Harry see
Richardson, Minnie
RICHARDSON, Henry Royston
(d 1873) circus manager EA/
74*
RICHARDSON, Howard (b 1917)
American dramatist, actor,
director, educator, producer
BE, MH
RICHARDSON, Ian (b 1934) Scot-
tish actor AAS, WWT/14-16
RICHARDSON, Jack (b 1935)
American dramatist, critic
BE, CD, CH, ES, MD, MH,
MWD, RE
RICHARDSON, John (d 1837 [76])
showman CDP
RICHARDSON, John (d 1889 [34])
musician EA/90*
RICHARDSON, Joseph (c. 1756-
1803) English dramatist CDP,
CP/3, GT, TD/1-2
RICHARDSON, Joseph (d 1862)
musician EA/72*
RICHARDSON, Mrs. Joseph
patentee, dramatist CP/3
RICHARDSON, Mrs. L. A. [née
Madeleine Percy] (d 1870)
actress EA/71*
RICHARDSON, Leander (1856-

1918) American dramatist, jour-
nalist GRB/3-4, WWM, WWT/
1-3
RICHARDSON, Leander B. (d 1852)
comedian HAS
RICHARDSON, Lee (b 1926) Amer-
ican actor BE
RICHARDSON, Mary [Mrs. Billy
Richardson] (d 1882) EA/83*
RICHARDSON, Minnie [Mrs. Harry
Richardson] (d 1916) EA/18*
RICHARDSON, Myrtle English ac-
tress WWT/9-10
RICHARDSON, Nell [Mrs. T. G.
King] (d 1908) actress, singer
EA/09*
RICHARDSON, Sir Ralph David
(b 1902) English actor AAS,
BE, CB, COC, ES, OC/1-3,
PDT, TW/2-17, 27, WWT/7-16
RICHARDSON, Susanna see
Collis, Mrs. [Francis?]
RICHARDSON, Tony (b 1928) Eng-
lish director, producer AAS,
BE, CB, COC, ES, PDT,
WWT/13-16
RICHARDSON, W. E. actor EA/97
RICHARDSON, Wells American ac-
tor TW/11-14
RICHARDSON, William (1743-1814)
Scottish dramatist, writer
CDP, CP/3
RICHARDSON, William (d 1890
[56]) EA/91*
RICHARDSON, William Thomas (d
1896 [53]) comedian EA/97*
RICHEPIN, Jean (1849-1926) Al-
gerian/French dramatist GRB/
1-4, WWT/1
RICHEUX, Jules (d 1911) lessee
EA/12*
RICHINGS, Caroline Mary (d 1882)
English pianist, actress, mana-
ger HAS
RICHINGS, Peter (1797/98-1871)
English singer, dancer, mana-
ger, actor CDP, DAB, HAS,
SR, WWA/H
RICHINGS-BERNARD, Caroline (d
1882) musician, singer CDP
RICHMAN, Arthur (1886-1944)
American dramatist NTH, SR,
WWA/2, WWT/5-9
RICHMAN, Charles J. (1870-1940)
American actor CB, GRB/2-4,
WWM, WWS, WWT/1-9
RICHMAN, Harry (1895-1972)
American actor, singer BE,

TW/29, WWT/7-11
RICHMAN, Henry John (d 1868
[39]) music-hall performer?
EA/69*
RICHMAN, Lou (d 1970 [84])
performer BP/55*
RICHMAN, Mark (b 1927) Amer-
ican actor BE, TW/10-12
RICHMOND, Mrs. (d 1883) EA/
85*
RICHMOND, Adah actress, singer
CDP
RICHMOND, Harry G. (d 1885)
actor, dancer, singer CDP
RICHMOND, Henry (d 1902) ac-
tor EA/03*
RICHMOND, Mrs. James see
Richmond, Winifred
RICHMOND, Jane (d 1962 [47])
performer BP/47*
RICHMOND, Lizzie see Col-
son, Lizzie
RICHMOND, Susan (1894-1959)
English actress WWT/8-12
RICHMOND, Winifred [Mrs.
James Richmond] (d 1881)
EA/82*
RICHMOND SISTERS dancers,
singers CDP
RICHTER, George (d 1905 [48])
EA/06*
RICHTER, Hans (1843-1916)
Austrian conductor ES
RICHTER, Hans (d 1976 [87])
producer/director/choreographer
BP/60*
RICKARD, Al (d 1962 [69]) talent
representative, performer BE*
RICKARD, Ellen (d 1917) EA/
18*
RICKARDS, Harry (d 1911 [63])
manager, singer CDP, GRB/
2-3
RICKARDS, J. H. (fl 1857) actor
CDP
RICKARDS, W. E. (d 1879 [50])
music-hall proprietor EA/80*
RICKER, Elswyth Thane see
Thane, Elswyth
RICKETS, J. (fl 1570?) drama-
tist FGF
RICKETTS, Arthur (b 1845)
American actor GRB/1
RICKETTS, Charles (1866-1931)
Swiss/English designer OC/
2-3, WWT/6
RICKETTS, Harry (d 1896 [45])
pantomimist EA/97*

RICKETTS, John (d 1873 [43]) pan-
tomimist EA/74*
RICKETTS, John (d 1899 [61]) the-
atre chairman EA/00*
RICKETTS, John Bill (fl 1793) cir-
cus manager & proprietor CDP
RICKETTS, Richard (d 1883 [29])
pantomimist EA/84*
RICKETTS, Mrs. Samuel see
Allingham, Maria Caroline
RICKS, James (d 1974 [49]) per-
former BP/59*
RICKS, Nellie [Mrs. Pat J. Ricks]
(d 1898 [31]) EA/99*
RICKS, Mrs. Pat J. see Ricks,
Nellie
RICKS, William R. (d 1880) treas-
urer EA/81*
RIDDELL, George (d 1944 [80])
actor BE*, WWT/14*
RIDDICK, Margaret see Bennett,
Faith
RIDDLE, Miss see Sedley-Smith,
Mrs. William Henry
RIDDLE, Cordelia (fl 1834) actress
HAS
RIDDLE, Eliza (fl 1835) American
actress HAS
RIDDLE, Fred (d 1892 [52]) con-
ductor, musician EA/93*
RIDDLE, George (1851/53-1910)
American actor, reader CDP,
DAB, PP/3
RIDDLE, George (b 1937) American
actor TW/25
RIDEOUT, Percy Rodney (1862-
1956) English composer WWW/5
RIDER, William (fl 1613) dramatist
CP/1-3, FGF
RIDER-KELSEY, Corinne (b 1881)
American singer WWM
RIDER-NOBLE, Mrs. Charles
see Belton, Phoebe
RIDGELY, John (d 1968 [59]) per-
former BP/52*
RIDGES, Stanley (d 1951 [59]) Eng-
lish actor TW/7
RIDGEWAY, Peter (d 1938 [44])
actor, producer BE*, WWT/14*
RIDGEWAY, Philip (1891-1954)
English producing manager
WWT/6-7
RIDGEWAY, Philip (b 1920) English
press-representative, producer,
writer WWT/12-14
RIDGEWELL, Audrey (d 1968 [64])
performer BP/53*
RIDGLEY, Cleo (d 1962 [68]) ac-

tress BE*

RIDGWAY, Charles (d 1893 [82])
actor CDP

RIDGWAY, Mrs. Charles (d 1881
[62]) EA/83*

RIDGWAY, Mrs. Charles see
Ridgway, Elizabeth

RIDGWAY, Elizabeth [Mrs. Charles
Ridgway] (d 1897) EA/98*

RIDGWAY, Graziella (fl 1872?)
singer CDP

RIDGWAY, John (d 1907 [62])
EA/08*

RIDGWAY, Nellie (d 1904 [51])
music-hall performer EA/05*

RIDGWAY, T. (fl 1829?) actor
CDP

RIDGWAY, Thomas (d 1880 [37])
acrobat EA/81*

RIDGWELL, Charles (d 1916)
writer EA/17*

RIDICULOUS THEATRE CO.
theatre collective CD

RIDINGS, Mrs. H. J. see
Lackaye, Helene

RIDLER, Anne (b 1912) English
dramatist CD

RIDLEY, Arnold (b 1896) English
dramatist WWT/6-16

RIDLEY, Elizabeth see Bowtell,
Mrs. Barnaby

RIDLEY, Dr. Gloster (1702-74)
English dramatist CP/2-3

RIDLEY, Mrs. James see Ridley, Mary Ann

RIDLEY, John (d 1899) comedian
EA/00*

RIDLEY, Joseph (d 1868) acrobat
EA/69*

RIDLEY, Mary Ann [Mrs. James
Ridley] (d 1882) EA/83*

RIDOUT, Mr. (d c. 1760/61) actor
TD/2

RIDYARD, William Henry (d 1879
[45]) comedian EA/80*

RIEDEL, Karl Heinrich (1879-
1946) Austrian conductor
WWA/2

RIEGER, W. H. songwriter CDP

RIESENFELD, Hugo (1884/85-
1939) Austrian conductor,
composer WWA/1, WWW/3

RIETTI, Victor (1888-1963)
Italian actor, producer, translator WWT/12-13

RIETTY, Robert (b 1923) English
actor, dramatist, translator,
director WWT/11-16

RIFFE, Bessie Tons (d 1976 [93])
wardrobe mistress BP/60*

RIFKIN, Ron (b 1939) American
actor TW/28

RIGA, Nadine (d 1968 [59]) performer BP/53*

RIGAUT, Mme. (d 1883 [86]) singer
EA/84*

RIGBY, Mr. (fl 1752-53) English?
actor HAS

RIGBY, Mrs. (fl 1752-53) English?
actress HAS

RIGBY, Arthur [Arthur Watson
Lloyd] (d 1894 [36]) actor EA/
96*

RIGBY, Arthur [William Turner]
(1870-1944) English dramatist,
actor, singer WWT/8-9

RIGBY, Arthur, Jr. [Arthur Turn-
er] (1900-71) English actor
WWT/8-16

RIGBY, Edward [Edward Coke]
(1879-1951) English actor GRB/
1-4, WWT/4-11

RIGBY, Frank J. (d 1963 [100])
musician BE*

RIGBY, Lionel (d 1891) actor EA/
92*

RIGDEN, Maud [Mrs. Sydney L.
Hallows] (d 1904) EA/05*

RIGER, John (d 1874 [40]) professor of music EA/75*

RIGG, Diana (b 1938) English actress AAS, CB, WWT/14-16

RIGGS, Elizabeth see Brent,
Evelyn

RIGGS, Mrs. George C. see
Wiggin, Kate Douglas

RIGGS, Glenn E. (d 1975 [68])
performer BP/60*

RIGGS, Katherine Witchie (d 1967
[80]) dancer, vaudevillian TW/
23

RIGGS, Lynn (1899-1954) American
dramatist AAS, HJD, MD,
MH, MWD, NTH, TW/11,
WWT/9-11

RIGGS, Ralph (d 1951 [66]) American actor, singer, dancer TW/8

RIGGS, Thomas Grattan (1835-99)
American actor CDP, HAS

RIGGS, Mrs. Thomas Grattan (fl
1866?) actress CDP

RIGHTON, Edward ["Corrie Burns"]
(1838-99) English actor, dramatist CDP, DP, HAS, OAA/2,
WWW/1

RIGHTON, J. H. (d 1873) musician

EA/74*

RIGHTON, Mary (d 1913) EA/14*

RIGL, Emily (fl 1866) actress, dancer CDP

RIGNALL, Lionel see Rignold, Lionel

RIGNALL, Walter Lionel see Rignold, Walter Lionel

RIGNOLD, Emily (d 1913) EA/14*

RIGNOLD, George (d 1912 [76]) English actor, manager CDP, GRB/3-4, OAA/2, WWT/1

RIGNOLD, Mrs. George see Henderson, Marie

RIGNOLD, Henry (1813?-73) actor CDP

RIGNOLD, Kate [Mrs. Caroline Mary Hayward] (d 1897) EA/98*

RIGNOLD, Lilian [Mrs. James Salter] (b 1883) English actress GRB/1

RIGNOLD, Lionel [Lionel Rignall] (d 1919 [69]) English actor DP, EA/95, GRB/1-4, WWT/1-3

RIGNOLD, Mrs. Lionel see Daltra, Marie

RIGNOLD, Marie see Daltra, Marie

RIGNOLD, Patience Blaxland (d 1888 [88]) actress EA/89*

RIGNOLD, Stanley (1868-1943) actor SR

RIGNOLD, Susan (d 1895) actress OAA/2

RIGNOLD, Walter Lionel [Rignall] (b 1875) English actor GRB/1-2

RIGNOLD, William (d 1904 [68]) actor BE*, EA/06*, WWT/14*

RIGNOLD, William Henry Rignall (1836/38-1910) English actor DP, OAA/2

RIGNOLD, William Ross (d 1883 [79]) actor EA/85*

RIKER, Franklin Wing (1876-1958) American singer WWA/3, WWM

RILEY, Ed (b 1933) American actor TW/25-26

RILEY, Edna Goldsmith (d 1962 [82]) dramatist BE*

RILEY, Eliza [Mrs. H. Hesslegrave] (d 1899) EA/00*

RILEY, Fanny L. see Goodall, Mrs. William R.

RILEY, Fred (d 1909 [55]) music-hall singer EA/10*

RILEY, George (d 1972 [72]) performer BP/57*

RILEY, Henry D. (d 1970 [71]) circus agent BP/55*

RILEY, Henry J. (1801-41) English actor HAS, SR

RILEY, James (d 1869 [52]) EA/70*

RILEY, Janet (b 1930) American actress TW/11-12

RILEY, John (d 1897 [47]) manager EA/98*

RILEY, Lawrence (1891-1975) American dramatist BE

RILEY, Madeline Lucette see Ryley, Madeleine Lucette

RILEY, Pat (d 1894 [37]) Irish comedian, dancer EA/95*

RILEY, Ritter William (d 1904 [31]) actor EA/05*

RILEY, Thomas see Peel, Tommy

RILEY, W. H. (1833-67) American actor HAS

RILEY, Mrs. W. H. [née Katie L. Woodbury] (fl 1856) actress HAS

RILEY, William (d 1897 [52]) manager, music-hall singer CDP

RILL, Eli (b 1926) American actor, director, dramatist BE

RILLEY, James (b 1947) American actor TW/27

RIMBAULT (d 1890) assistant stage manager EA/91*

RIMBAULT, Dr. E. F. (d 1876 [60]) antiquarian EA/77*

RIMINI, Giacomo (d 1952) Italian singer WWA/3

RIMMA, Fritz (d 1904 [44]) actor EA/05*, WWT/14*

RINALDI, Joy American actress TW/25, 30

RINALDINI, Sig. (d 1875) singer EA/76*

RINALDO, Mrs. Nicholas see Dale, Margie

RIND, Kathleen English actress GRB/1-2

RINDLER, Milton (b 1898) American accountant, treasurer BE

RINEHART, Mary Roberts (1876-1958) American dramatist MWD, NTH, WWA/3, WWM, WWT/4-11

RING, Barbara T. (1879-1941)

dramatist CB

RING, Blanche [Mrs. Frederick E. McKay] (1877-1961) American actress, singer GRB/2-4, SR, TW/2-3, 5-7, 17, WWA/4, WWS, WWT/1-11

RING, Cyril (d 1967 [74]) performer BP/52*

RING, Frances [Mrs. Thomas Meighan] (1882-1951) American actress GRB/3-4, TW/7, WWM, WWS, WWT/1-7

RING, James H. (fl 1848) English actor HAS

RINGGOLD, Benjamin T. (b 1835) American actor PP/3

RINGLE, Dave (d 1965 [71]) composer/lyricist BP/50*

RINGLING, Albert (1858-1916) American circus proprietor ES

RINGLING, Alfred (1861-1919) American circus proprietor ES

RINGLING, August (d 1918) American circus proprietor ES

RINGLING, Charles (1863-1926) American circus proprietor ES, WWA/H, 4

RINGLING, Henry (d 1918) American circus proprietor ES

RINGLING, John (1866-1936) American circus proprietor ES, WWA/1

RINGLING, Otto (1851-1911) actor, circus manager ES, SR

RINGLING, Robert E. (1897-1950) American circus executive, singer CB, WWA/2

RINGLING BROTHERS circus managers SR

RIORDAN, Naomi (b 1926) American actress TW/6-7

RIOS, Lalo (d 1973 [46]) performer BP/57*

"RIP" [George Thenon] (d 1941) revue author WWT/14*

RIPLEY, Gladys (1908-55) singer WWW/5

RIPLEY, Patricia see Ripley, Trescott

RIPLEY, Trescott [Patricia] (b 1926) American actress BE, TW/22-23

RIPMAN, Pamela Penelope see Jenner, Caryl

RIPON, George (d 1908) actor,

singer CDP

RIPON, Mrs. George [Elizabeth Collins] (d 1883) EA/84*

RIPON, John Scott see Byerley, John Scott

RIPPON, Mrs. S. A. (d 1892) EA/93*

RISCOE, Arthur (1896-1954) English actor WWT/7-11

RISDON, Elizabeth (1887-1958) English actress TW/15, WWT/6-10

RISKIN, Robert (1897-1955) American dramatist ES

RISLEY, Prof. (d 1874) manager, athlete, musician CDP

RISLEY, Miss L. (d 1892) singer EA/93*

RISQUE, W. H. (d 1916) librettist, lyricist BE*, EA/17*, WWT/14*

RISS, Dan (d 1970 [60]) performer BP/55*

RISTORI, Adelaide (1822-1906) Italian actress CDP, COC, ES, HAS, NTH, OC/1-3, SR, WWW/1

RITCHARD, Cyril (1898-1977) Australian actor, director AAS, BE, CB, TW/5-22, 25, 28-29, WWT/6-16

RITCHER, Rene see Collier, Patience

RITCHEY, Buck (d 1973 [58]) composer/lyricist BP/58*

RITCHIE, Mrs. see Mowatt, Anna Cora

RITCHIE, Adele (1874-1930) American actress, singer GRB/3-4, SR, WWA/1, WWM, WWS, WWT/1-6

RITCHIE, Alice Jane (d 1893) EA/94*

RITCHIE, Camilla (b 1945) American actress TW/26

RITCHIE, Carl (d 1974 [64]) performer BP/58*

RITCHIE, Estelle American actress TW/15

RITCHIE, June actress WWT/16

RITCHIE, Robert (d 1912 [24]) EA/13*

RITCHIE, Mrs. W. E. (d 1901 [21]) EA/02*

RITELLI, Harry (d 1901 [59]) pantomimist EA/03*

RITMAN, William designer WWT/16

RITT, Martin (b 1920) American
actor, director BE, ES
RITTENBERG, Arnold (d 1974
[78]) showman BP/58*
RITTENBERG, Barbara (d 1973
[42]) dramatist BP/58*
RITTENHOUSE, David (fl 1798?)
dramatist EAP, RJ
RITTENHOUSE, Florence (d 1929
[35]) American actress BE*,
BP/13*
RITTENHOUSE, Mae (d 1972 [88])
performer BP/57*
RITTER, Blake (d 1973 [58])
singer, actress TW/30
RITTER, John P. (d 1920 [62])
dramatist BE*, BP/5*
RITTER, Kathryn (b 1948) Amer-
ican actress TW/30
RITTER, Tex (d 1974 [67]) per-
former BP/58*
RITTER, Thelma (1905-1969)
American actress BE, CB,
TW/22, 25, WWA/5
RITTER, Theodore (1841-86) mu-
sician CDP
RITTMAN, Trude German com-
poser BE
RITWISE, John (fl 1507-22) Eng-
lish dramatist CP/2-3
RITZ, Al (d 1965 [62]) comedian
TW/22
RIVALLI [John Watkins] (d 1900)
"The Fire Prince" EA/01*
RIVE, Caroline (d 1882 [60])
singer CDP
RIVE-KING, Julie (b 1857) musi-
cian, composer CDP
RIVERA, Chita [née Concita del
Rivero] (b 1933/34) American
actress, singer, dancer AAS,
BE, TW/21-22, WWT/14-16
RIVERO, Julian (d 1976 [85])
performer BP/60*
RIVERS, Mr. (fl 1635) dramatist
CP/1-3, FGF
RIVERS, Mr. (d 1889) EA/90*
RIVERS, Mrs. see Barnett,
Mrs. Giles Linnett
RIVERS, Miss (fl 1827) actress
HAS
RIVERS, Albert singer CDP
RIVERS, Alfred (d 1955 [88])
actor BE*, WWT/14*
RIVERS, Basil George (d 1870
[54]) actor EA/71*
RIVERS, Harry (fl 1862) Ameri-
can actor, singer CDP, HAS

RIVERS, Henry (d 1901 [82]) actor
EA/03*
RIVERS, Mrs. Henry see Mor-
elli, Fanny
RIVERS, Joan (b 1935?) American
comedienne CB
RIVERS, Laurence see Stebbins,
Rowland
RIVERS, Pamela (b 1926) American
actress TW/2
RIVERS, R. (d 1889 [22]) advance
agent EA/90*
RIVES, Amélie (1863-1945) Amer-
ican dramatist HJD, WWW/4
RIVIERE, Anna see Bishop,
Anna
RIVINGTON, Reginald (b 1869)
English actor GRB/3-4
RIX, Brian (b 1924) English actor,
manager WWT/12-16
RIX, John [Charles Clements] (d
1874 [28]) comic singer EA/75*
RIZARELI, Virginia [Virginia Bur-
goyne] (d 1891 [26]) EA/93*
ROACH, James Conner actor CDP
ROACH, Thomas A. (d 1962 [51])
performer BE*
ROACHE, Viola (1885-1961) English
actress TW/1-7, 12-17, WWT/
9-13
ROAD, Michael (b 1915) American
actor TW/3
ROBARDS, Jason, Sr. (d 1963
[70]) American actor TW/19
ROBARDS, Jason, Jr. (b 1922)
American actor AAS, BE,
CB, ES, TW/13-22, 25, 28,
WWT/13-16
ROBARTS, Mrs. Carl see Bra-
ham, Amelia Georgina
ROBB, Helen Lowell see Lowell,
Helen
ROBB, Lotus (d 1969) actress
TW/1, 26
ROBB, Miriam G. [née Goodenow]
(d 1856) performer CDP, HAS
ROBBINS, Alfred Edward see
Northway, Alfred
ROBBINS, Sir Alfred Farthing
(1856-1931) English dramatist,
critic GRB/2-4, WWT/1-6
ROBBINS, Archie (d 1975 [62])
performer BP/60*
ROBBINS, Carrie Fishbein (b 1943)
American costume designer
WWT/16
ROBBINS, Edward E. (b 1930)
American talent representative

BE
ROBBINS, Herbert (d 1918) EA/
18*
ROBBINS, Jane Kiser (d 1974
[53]) performer BP/59*
ROBBINS, Jane Marla (b 1943)
American actress TW/24-25
ROBBINS, Jerome (b 1918) Amer-
ican director, choreographer,
dancer AAS, BE, CB, ES,
NTH, PDT, TW/2-8, WWT/
13-16
ROBBINS, Marla Jane (b 1944)
American actress TW/30
ROBBINS, Rex (b 1939) American
actor TW/26-27, 29
ROBBINS, Richard (d 1969 [50])
actor TW/26
ROBBINS, Rose J. [Mrs. Wal
Rose] (d 1908) EA/09*
ROBBINS, Mrs. Wal see Rob-
bins, Rose J.
ROBE, Annie (d 1922) actress
BE*, WWT/14*
ROBE, [Miss?] J. (fl 1723) dra-
matist CP/2-3, GT
ROBE, James Banks (d 1880
[38]) scene artist EA/81*
ROBER, Richard (1906-52) Amer-
ican actor TW/1-3, 8
ROBERDEAU, John Peter (d 1815
[60]) dramatist CP/3
ROBERT, Eugene (b 1877) Hun-
garian producer, manager
WWT/9
ROBERT-HOUDIN, Jean Eugène
(1805-71) magician CDP
ROBERTI, Lyda (1909-38) Polish
actress WWT/8
ROBERTS, Mr. (fl 1767) actor
HAS
ROBERTS, Miss see Bernard,
Mrs. John, I
ROBERTS, Anthony (b 1939)
American actor TW/23-27
ROBERTS, Arthur (1852-1933)
English actor CDP, COC,
DP, ES, GRB/1-4, OC/1-3,
WWS, WWT/1-7, WWW/3
ROBERTS, Arthur (b 1938) Amer-
ican actor TW/26, 28-29
ROBERTS, Beverly (b 1914/17)
American actress, director,
executive BE, TW/1
ROBERTS, Carrie (d 1895) serio-
comic EA/96*
ROBERTS, Charles (d 1869)
actor? EA/70*

ROBERTS, Charles (d 1897) agent
EA/98*
ROBERTS, Clara Lemore see
Lemore, Clara
ROBERTS, Cledge (d 1957 [52])
actor, director TW/13
ROBERTS, David (d 1864 [68])
scene artist EA/72*, WWT/14*
ROBERTS, Davis (b 1917) Ameri-
can actor TW/27-28
ROBERTS, Dennis (b 1950) Ameri-
can actor TW/29
ROBERTS, Doris (b 1930) American
actress TW/26-27, 29-30,
WWT/16
ROBERTS, Edward Barry (d 1972
[71]) performer BP/57*
ROBERTS, Ellis (d 1873) musician
EA/74*
ROBERTS, Mrs. Ellis see
Roberts, Isabel
ROBERTS, Evelyn (1886-1962) Eng-
lish actor WWT/7-13
ROBERTS, Ewan (b 1914) Scottish
actor WWT/11-16
ROBERTS, Florence [Mrs. Freder-
ick Vogeling] (d 1927 [56])
American actress BE*, BP/
12*, WWT/14*
ROBERTS, Florence [Mrs. Lewis
Morrison] (1871-1940) American
actress CB, GRB/3-4, WWA/
1, WWM, WWS, WWT/1-5
ROBERTS, Florence Smythe (d
1925 [47]) actress BE*
ROBERTS, Frank (d 1907 [58])
American actor GRB/3*
ROBERTS, Mrs. Franklyn see
Wainright, Marie
ROBERTS, George [Robert Walters]
(b 1832) English dramatist EA/
69
ROBERTS, Hans (d 1954 [80]) actor
TW/10
ROBERTS, H. R. Indian/English
actor GRB/2
ROBERTS, Isabel [Mrs. Ellis
Roberts] (d 1868 [41]) EA/69*
ROBERTS, Jack (d 1899 [25])
EA/01*
ROBERTS, James (fl 1564-1606)
printer DNB
ROBERTS, James (fl 1794) drama-
tist CP/3
ROBERTS, James (1798/99-1833)
Scottish actor, circus performer
CDP, HAS
ROBERTS, James (d 1892 [56])

scene artist EA/93*

ROBERTS, James Booth (1815/18-1901) American actor CDP, HAS, PP/3

ROBERTS, J. H. (fl 1867) English comedian, minstrel HAS

ROBERTS, J. H. (1884-1961) English actor WWT/4-13

ROBERTS, Jimmy (d 1962 [60]) American performer BE*

ROBERTS, Joan (b 1918/20/22) American actress, singer BE, TW/2-5, WWT/10-12

ROBERTS, John (1916-72) English producing manager, actor WWT/15-16

ROBERTS, Joseph L. (d 1970 [61]) public relations BP/54*

ROBERTS, J. St. Clair see Bayfield, St. Clair

ROBERTS, Marilyn (b 1939) American actress TW/24-26

ROBERTS, Mark (b 1921) American actor TW/8-9

ROBERTS, Meade (b 1930) American dramatist BE

ROBERTS, Morley (1857-1942) English dramatist WWW/4

ROBERTS, Nancy (d 1962 [70]) actress BE*

ROBERTS, N. D. manager CDP

ROBERTS, Owen (d 1911 [52]) singer EA/12*

ROBERTS, Paddy (d 1975 [65]) composer/lyricist BP/60*

ROBERTS, Peter editor AAS

ROBERTS, R. (d 1873) comedian EA/74*

ROBERTS, Miss R. (fl 1779) dramatist CP/2-3

ROBERTS, R. A. (b 1870) English actor GRB/1-3, WWM

ROBERTS, Rachel (b 1927) Welsh actress AAS, ES, TW/30, WWT/14-16

ROBERTS, Ralph (d 1944 [75]) Indian/English actor WWT/8-9

ROBERTS, Ralph (b 1918) American actor TW/4-16, 20, 28-29

ROBERTS, Mrs. Ralph see Caryllon, Ethel L.

ROBERTS, Sir Randall (d 1899 [62]) actor, producer, dramatist BE*, EA/00*, WWT/14*

ROBERTS, R. J. (d 1884 [34]) comedian EA/85*

ROBERTS, Robert (d 1888) minstrel EA/89*

ROBERTS, Rose [Mrs. Louis Calvert] English actress EA/96, GRB/1-3

ROBERTS, Roy (d 1975 [69]) performer BP/60*

ROBERTS, Sara [Sara Lacy; Mrs. Valentine Roberts] (d 1881 [59]) EA/82*

ROBERTS, Sarah [Sarah Prestbury] (d 1873) actress, singer EA/75*

ROBERTS, Sara Jane (d 1968 [44]) performer BP/53*

ROBERTS, Stephen (b 1917) American actor TW/3

ROBERTS, Theodore (1861-1928) American actor DAB, GRB/4, WWA/1, WWS, WWT/1-5

ROBERTS, Thomas (d 1876 [44]) acting manager EA/77*

ROBERTS, Mrs. Thomas see Isaacs, Rebecca

ROBERTS, T. M. (d 1885 [75]) scene artist EA/86*

ROBERTS, Tony (b 1939) American actor TW/28-29, WWT/16

ROBERTS, Mrs. Valentine see Roberts, Sara

ROBERTS, Vera Mowry (b 1918) American educator, director BE

ROBERTS, Wallace (d 1890) manager EA/91*

ROBERTS, Walter (d 1917 [83]) EA/18*

ROBERTS, William (fl 1770-82) dramatist CP/3

ROBERTS, William (fl 1791) dramatist CP/3

ROBERTS, William (d 1888) acting manager EA/89*

ROBERTSHAW, Jerrold (1866-1941) English actor GRB/1-4, WWT/1-9

ROBERTSON, Mr. (fl 1778-90) dramatist CP/3

ROBERTSON, Mrs. (fl 1800) actress, dramatist CP/3

ROBERTSON, Miss actress HAS

ROBERTSON, Agnes Kelly see Boucicault, Mrs. Dion

ROBERTSON, Alex (d 1964 [64]) Scottish dramatist BE*, BP/49*

ROBERTSON, Alexander (d 1885 [20]) scene artist EA/86*

ROBERTSON, Mrs. Brougham [née Tanner] (1820-65) English actress, manager CDP, HAS

ROBERTSON, Cliff (b 1925) American actor, director BE, CB, ES, TW/11-16

ROBERTSON, Craven (d 1879 [33]) actor, manager EA/80*, WWT/14*

ROBERTSON, Donald (1860-1926) Scottish actor SR, WWA/1, WWM, WWS

ROBERTSON, E. [Mrs. W. Robertson] (d 1876) EA/78*

ROBERTSON, East (d 1916) actress BE*, WWT/14*

ROBERTSON, Edward Shafto (d 1871 [27]) actor EA/72*

ROBERTSON, E. T. (d 1890 [30]) EA/91*

ROBERTSON, G. Douglas see Douglas, G. R.

ROBERTSON, Guy (b 1892) American actor, singer TW/2-3, 6-7, WWT/7-11

ROBERTSON, Hamish (b 1943) Scottish actor TW/28

ROBERTSON, Cpt. Henry (d 1885) EA/86*

ROBERTSON, Hermine (d 1962 [61]) actress BE*

ROBERTSON, Hopkins (d 1819 [40]) actor HAS

ROBERTSON, Ian [Ian Forbes-Robertson] (1858-1936) English actor, stage manager GRB/3-4, OC/1-3, WWT/1-8

ROBERTSON, Jack [J. G.] Peruvian/English actor, singer GRB/1-3

ROBERTSON, James (1714-95) actor CDP

ROBERTSON, Jane (b 1948) American actress TW/27-28

ROBERTSON, Jerome (d 1962 [62]) performer BE*

ROBERTSON, J. G. see Robertson, Jack

ROBERTSON, John (d 1908 [46]) variety agent EA/09*

ROBERTSON, John (d 1962 [35]) scene designer BE*

ROBERTSON, John S. (b 1878) Canadian actor ES

ROBERTSON, Johnston Forbes see Forbes-Robertson, Johnston

ROBERTSON, John Wylie see Watson, Wylie

ROBERTSON, Kate (d 1868) lessee EA/69*

ROBERTSON, Mrs. Lionel [née Edith Tinsley] (d 1876) EA/77*

ROBERTSON, Louisa see Dornton, Louisa

ROBERTSON, Malcolm (b 1933) Australian director, actor WWT/16

ROBERTSON, Margaret see Kendal, Mrs.

ROBERTSON, Maria (d 1892 [91]) EA/93*

ROBERTSON, Marie [Mrs. Fred Owen] (d 1889 [26]) actress EA/90*

ROBERTSON, Marjorie see Neagle, Anna

ROBERTSON, Maud (d 1930) actress BE*, WWT/14*

ROBERTSON, Orie O. (d 1964 [83]) actor, stunt man BE*

ROBERTSON, Pax (d 1948) actress, director BE*, WWT/14*

ROBERTSON, Peter (1847-1911) Scottish dramatist, critic WWA/1, WWM

ROBERTSON, Robert [Patrick Robert Macallan] (d 1894 [49]) actor EA/95*

ROBERTSON, Mrs. T. (fl 1796) dramatist CP/3

ROBERTSON, Mrs. Thomas (d 1855 [87]) actress, producer BE*, WWT/14*

ROBERTSON, Thomas William (1829-71) English dramatist, actor CDP, COC, DNB, EA/68, ES, HP, MH, NTH, OC/1-3, PDT

ROBERTSON, Thomas William Shafto (d 1895 [37]) actor, producer BE*, EA/96*, WWT/14*

ROBERTSON, Toby (b 1928) English director AAS, WWT/15-16

ROBERTSON, Tom (d 1916) EA/17*

ROBERTSON, Mrs. T. W. see Rodwell, Mrs. John

ROBERTSON, W. (d 1836) American actor HAS

ROBERTSON, Mrs. W. see Robertson, E.

ROBERTSON, W. Graham (1867-1948) English dramatist WWT/4-10, WWW/4

ROBERTSON, Mrs. Whybrow see Litton, Marie

ROBERTSON, William (d 1872 [73]) actor EA/74*, WWT/14*

ROBERTSON, William (b 1908)
American actor TW/26-27,
29-30

ROBERTSON, Mrs. William (d
1876 [71]) actress WWT/14*

ROBERTSON, Sir William Tindal
(d 1889) EA/90*

ROBESON, Paul (1898-1976) Amer-
ican actor, singer AAS, BE,
CB, COC, ES, HJD, NTH,
OC/1-3, PDT, SR, TW/1-3,
WWT/6-14

ROBEY, Don D. (d 1975 [71])
entertainment pioneer BP/60*

ROBEY, Sir George [George Ed-
ward Wade] (1869-1954) Eng-
lish variety artist AAS, CDP,
COC, DNB, GRB/1-4, OC/1-3,
PDT, TW/11, WWT/4-11,
WWW/5

ROBIN, Leo (b 1899) American
lyricist BE

ROBINA, Fanny (d 1927 [65]) actress, singer BE*, WWT/14*

ROBINA, Florrie (d 1953 [86])
actress, singer CDP

ROBINA, Lilian [Mrs. Joe Ed-
wards] (d 1903) serio-comic
EA/04*

ROBINI, Mrs. Alf [Maud Cuthbert]
(d 1905) EA/06*

ROBINS, Miss see Clifford,
Mrs.

ROBINS, Adolph (d 1950 [64])
Austrian/American comedian,
clown TW/7

ROBINS, Edward H. (1880/81-
1955) American actor TW/12,
WWT/5-11

ROBINS, Elisabeth [or Elizabeth;
Mrs. George Richmond Parkes]
(1862/65-1952) American ac-
tress COC, EA/95, GRB/1-4,
HJD, OC/1-3, WWT/1-8,
WWW/5

ROBINS, Gertrude L. [Mrs.
Charles Dawson] (d 1917 [30/
31]) actress, dramatist WWT/
2-3

ROBINS, J. F. (d 1890) EA/91*

ROBINS, Joseph (d 1878 [52])
actor CDP

ROBINS, Mrs. Joseph (d 1894)
comedian EA/95*

ROBINS, William (d 1645?) actor
DA

ROBINS, William A. (d 1948 [81])
Australian conductor, composer

GRB/1-4

ROBINS, William Robert (d 1911
[87]) actor EA/12*

ROBINSON, Mr. (fl 1738) dramatist
CP/3, GT

ROBINSON, Mr. (fl 1787) dramatist
CP/3

ROBINSON, Mr. (fl 1793) actor,
dramatist CP/3

ROBINSON, Mrs. [Polly Sinclair]
(d 1880 [28]) actress? EA/81*

ROBINSON, Alexander (c. 1812-87)
American circus manager NYM

ROBINSON, Anastasia see Peterborough, Anastasia, Countess of

ROBINSON, Andy (b 1942) American
actor TW/25-28

ROBINSON, Anna [Lady Rosslyn] (d
1917 [47]) American actress
GRB/1

ROBINSON, Bartlett (b 1912) American actor TW/3, 5, 8-10

ROBINSON, Bertrand (d 1959 [70])
American actor, dramatist BE*,
BP/43*

ROBINSON, Bill (1878-1949) American dancer, singer CB, DAB,
SR, TW/6, WWA/2, WWT/10

ROBINSON, Charles American actor
TW/16

ROBINSON, Charles (b 1909) American dramatist BE

ROBINSON, Charles see Chapman,
Barnet

ROBINSON, David (1868-1913)
American manager WWM

ROBINSON, Edward G. (1893-1973)
Rumanian/American actor BE,
CB, ES, TW/29, WWA/5,
WWT/7-14

ROBINSON, Edwin Arlington (1869-
1935) American dramatist HJD,
WWA/1

ROBINSON, Ethan M. (d 1919 [47])
vaudeville manager BE*, BP/4*

ROBINSON, Fayette Lodawick
["Yankee Robinson"] (1818-84)
American actor, circus propri-
etor CDP, HAS

ROBINSON, Forrest (1859-1924)
actor SR

ROBINSON, Dr. Francis (d 1872)
composer EA/73*

ROBINSON, Frederic C. P. (1832-
1912) English actor CDP, HAS,
PP/3

ROBINSON, Mrs. G. see Billings, Mary

ROBINSON, Gad (fl 1883?) song composer CDP

ROBINSON, Geoffrey see Chater, Geoffrey

ROBINSON, George (d 1857 [57]) singer CDP

ROBINSON, Gil circus performer SR

ROBINSON, Gladys L. (d 1971 [75]) performer BP/56*

ROBINSON, Hal American actor TW/30

ROBINSON, Harry [Harry W. Bishop] (d 1889 [55]) American minstrel manager EA/90*

ROBINSON, Henry (d 1879 [28]) dramatist EA/80*

ROBINSON, Horace (b 1909) American educator, director BE

ROBINSON, Hubbell (d 1974 [68]) producer/director/choreographer BP/59*

ROBINSON, J. (fl 1791-1806) English actor HAS

ROBINSON, J. (fl 1792?) actor, dramatist EAP, RJ

ROBINSON, Jack (d 1975 [65]) dramatist BP/60*

ROBINSON, James (fl 1600) manager DA

ROBINSON, James American circus performer SR

ROBINSON, James [Michael Fitzgerald] (b 1835) American equestrian CDP, HAS, SR

ROBINSON, James Hall (d 1862) American actor HAS

ROBINSON, Jay (b 1930) American actor BE, TW/8

ROBINSON, Jethro T. (d 1878) architect EA/79*

ROBINSON, John (d 1641) actor DA

ROBINSON, John (1801-88) American circus performer, manager CDP, SR

ROBINSON, John (b 1908) English actor AAS, WWT/11-16

ROBINSON, J. Russel (d 1963 [71]) American composer, lyricist, performer BE*, BP/48*

ROBINSON, Judith (b 1937) American actress TW/14

ROBINSON, Kathleen (b 1909) Australian actress, manager WWT/9-11

ROBINSON, Larry (b 1929) American actor TW/9

ROBINSON, Lennox (1886-1958) Irish manager, dramatist, producer, actor, critic COC, DNB, ES, HP, MD, MH, MWD, OC/1-3, PDT, RE, TW/15, WWA/3, WWT/2-12, WWW/5

ROBINSON, Leslie (b 1940) American actor TW/26

ROBINSON, Lily (d 1893 [21]) midget EA/94*

ROBINSON, Mrs. Lottie see Walton, Lottie

ROBINSON, Madeleine (b 1908) English actress WWT/4-6

ROBINSON, Marie (d 1903 [80]) lion tamer EA/04*

ROBINSON, Mary [Mary Darby; "Perdita"] (1758-1800) English actress, dramatist CDP, COC, CP/2-3, DNB, GT, OC/1-3, TD/1-2

ROBINSON, Matthew, Lord Rokeby (1713-1800) English dramatist CP/3

ROBINSON, Norah (b 1901) actress WWT/5-9

ROBINSON, Percy (1889-1967) Irish dramatist, actor WWT/6-14

ROBINSON, Perdita see Robinson, Mary

ROBINSON, Raisbeck Welford (d 1889 [42]) EA/90*

ROBINSON, Richard (d 1648) English actor COC, DA, GT, NTH, OC/1-3

ROBINSON, Richard Clare see Clare, Dickie

ROBINSON, Riddell (d 1913) EA/14*

ROBINSON, Cpt. Robert Dansey (d 1894) EA/95*

ROBINSON, Roger (b 1941) American actor TW/23-25, 28-29

ROBINSON, Stuart (b 1936) American literary representative BE

ROBINSON, Susan E. (d 1916) singer SR

ROBINSON, Thomas (fl 1627-28) actor DA

ROBINSON, Thomas (d 1891 [36]) EA/92*

ROBINSON, Tom (d 1875 [37]) musician EA/76*

ROBINSON, Mrs. Vyner see Plowden, Florence

ROBINSON, Walter W. (d 1974

[46]) writer, publicist BP/59*

ROBINSON, Wayne (b 1916) American editor BE

ROBINSON, Will E. see Ching Ling Loo

ROBINSON, William (d 1875 [58]) scene artist EA/77*

ROBINSON, William see Robins, William

ROBINSON, William Ellesworth see Chung Ling Soo

ROBINSON-DUFF, Frances (d 1951 [74]) American actress BE*, BP/36*

ROBLES, Rud (d 1970 [60]) performer BP/55*

ROBSON, Eleanor Elise (b 1879) English actress GRB/2-4, NTH, SR, WWS, WWT/2-8

ROBSON, E. M. (1855-1932) English actor GRB/4, OAA/1-2, WWT/1-6

ROBSON, Emily Maria [Mrs. Mat Robson] (d 1909) EA/10*

ROBSON, Ernest singer CDP

ROBSON, Evelyn Stuart [Mrs. W. S. Stevenson] (b 1874) English actress GRB/1

ROBSON, Dame Flora (b 1902) English actress AAS, BE, CB, COC, ES, OC/1-3, PDT, TW/2-19, WWT/7-16

ROBSON, Frederick [Thomas Robson Brownbill] (1821-64) English actor CDP, COC, DNB, ES, NTH, OC/1-3

ROBSON, Frederick (d 1919 [72]) actor BE*, WWT/14*

ROBSON, Mrs. Frederick see Robson, Rosetta Frances

ROBSON, Horatio (fl 1784-93) dramatist CP/3

ROBSON, John (d 1917) comedian, dancer EA/18*

ROBSON, June (d 1972 [50]) performer BP/56*

ROBSON, Mary (b 1893) English actress WWT/4-7

ROBSON, Mat (d 1899 [69]) actor, singer CDP

ROBSON, Mrs. Mat see Robson, Emily Maria

ROBSON, May [Mrs. A. H. Brown] (1858/65-1942) Australian actress CB, CDP, DAB, ES, GRB/3-4, PP/3, SR, WWA/1, WWM, WWS, WWT/1-9

ROBSON, Rosetta Frances [Mrs. Frederick Robson] (d 1899 [77]) EA/00*

ROBSON, Stuart [Henry Robson Stuart] (1836-1903) American actor COC, DAB, HAS, OC/1-3, PP/3, SR, WWA/1

ROBSON, Stuart, Jr. (d 1946) actor BE*

ROBSON, Mrs. Stuart [May Waldron] (d 1924 [56]) actress BE*, BP/9*, WWT/14*

ROBSON, Thomas (d 1893) musician EA/94*

ROBSON, Tom (d 1892 [50]) Negro comedian EA/93*

ROBSON, William (d 1863 [78]) writer EA/72*, WWT/14*

ROBSON, William see Robins, William

ROBY, Henry Greatrex (d 1875) comedian EA/76*

ROBY, Mrs. Henry Greatrex (d 1880) EA/81*

ROBYN (fl 1518) member of the Chapel Royal DA

ROBYN, Alfred George (1860-1935) American composer WWA/1, WWM

ROCCO, Luigi (fl 1853) singer CDP

ROCH, Madeleine (d 1930 [46]) French actress BE*, WWT/14*

ROCHE, Emeline American costume designer TW/4-8

ROCHE, Eugene (b 1928) American actor TW/24

ROCHE, Eugenius (fl 1808) dramatist CP/3

ROCHE, Mrs. R. (d 1874 [34]) EA/75*

ROCHEAD, Mrs. Charles J. see Rochead, Maggie

ROCHEAD, Maggie [Mrs. Charles J. Rochead] (d 1878) EA/80*

ROCHELLE, Edward (d 1908 [56]) actor BE*, EA/09*, WWT/14*

ROCHELLE, Lisa (b 1959) American actress TW/30

ROCHELLE, Sandy (b 1942) American actress TW/24

ROCHESTER, Jenny [Mrs. P. A. Metcalfe] (d 1900) EA/01*

ROCHESTER, John Wilmot, Earl of see Wilmot, John

ROCHETTE, J. B. (d 1866 [41]) clown, cannon-ball performer HAS

ROCHEZ, Mr. (fl 1846) bottle equilibrist CDP

ROCHIN, Paul (d 1964 [75]) actor BE*

ROCK, Mr. (fl 1790s-1800s) Irish actor GT, TD/1-2

ROCK, Charles [Arthur Charles Rock de Fabeck] (1866-1919) Indian/English actor GRB/1-4, WWT/1-3

ROCK, Mrs. Charles see Wynne, Cybel

ROCK, Edward Anthony (d 1815) actor CDP

ROCK, Mrs. Edward Anthony (fl 1785-91) actress CDP

ROCK, Mary (d 1883) actress CDP

ROCK, William (d 1922 [53]) comedian, dancer BE*, BP/7*

ROCKEFELLER, John D., III (b 1906) American executive BE

ROCKHILL, Mr. (fl 1838) actor HAS

ROCKMORE, Robert (d 1963 [60]) lawyer BP/47*

ROCKSTRO, William S. (d 1895) composer, musician EA/96*

ROCKWELL, Charles Henry (d 1883 [40]) actor CDP

ROCKWELL, Donald S. (d 1974 [75]) composer/lyricist BP/58*

ROCKWELL, Florence (1880/82-1964) American actress TW/20, WWM, WWS

ROCOMORA, Susanne (fl 1900s) German actress WWM

RODALE, J. I. (d 1971 [72]) dramatist BP/56*

RODD, Marcia (b 1940) American actress, singer TW/23-24, 26-27, 29, WWT/15-16

RODD, Thomas (fl 1800) translator CP/3

RODDICK, John (b 1944) Australian actor TW/30

RODEN, Eric John (b 1966) American actor TW/29

RODEN, Frank (d 1896 [45]) music-hall singer EA/97*

RODGER-REID, Paul (b 1938) American actor TW/26

RODGERS, Cpt. (d 1907) proprietor, manager EA/08*, WWT/14*

RODGERS, Anton (b 1933) English actor, director WWT/15-16

RODGERS, Bob (b 1924) American dramatist, actor, director BE

RODGERS, Carrie (d 1961 [59]) talent representative BE*

RODGERS, Eileen (b 1933) American actress, singer BE, TW/16-18

RODGERS, Enid (b 1924) English actress TW/26, 29-30

RODGERS, Gaby German/American? actress TW/12-19

RODGERS, James (d 1890 [74]) producer, proprietor, manager BE*, EA/91*, WWT/14*

RODGERS, Jerry (b 1941) American actor TW/27

RODGERS, Jimmy (1897-1933) American performer BE*

RODGERS, Katherine (d 1892) actress EA/93*

RODGERS, Lou (b 1935) actor TW/23-24, 26

RODGERS, Mary (b 1931) American composer BE

RODGERS, Richard (b 1902) American composer, producer, lyricist AAS, BE, CB, ES, HJD, MH, NTH, PDT, TW/2-8, WWT/6-16

RODGERS, Shev (b 1928) American actor TW/22-25, 28-30

RODGERS, Mrs. T. J. (d 1872 [35]) EA/73*

RODIN, Gil (d 1974 [64]) producer/director/choreographer BP/59*

RODNEY, Arthur (d 1918) EA/19*

RODNEY, Mrs. Arthur see Gwynne, Jennie

RODNEY, Babette [Mrs. George Bowles] actress CDP

RODNEY, Mrs. Charles see Bell, Eva

RODNEY, Mrs. C. M. see Settle, Nellie

RODNEY, Frank [Rodney Croskey Perkins] (d 1902 [43]) English actor EA/97

RODNEY, John (b 1914) American actor TW/8

RODNEY, Stratton (d 1932 [67]) actor BE*, WWT/14*

RODRIGUES, Diana (d 1968 [25]) performer BP/52*

RODRIGUEZ, Charlie J. (b 1944) Puerto Rican actor TW/29-30

RODRIQUEZ, Tito (d 1973 [50]) performer BP/57*

RODWAY, Norman (b 1929) Irish actor AAS, WWT/14-16

RODWAY, Philip (d 1932 [55])
producer, manager BE*,
WWT/14*

RODWELL, George Herbert Buon-
aparte (1800-52) English musical director, composer, proprietor DNB

RODWELL, Mrs. John [Mrs. T.
W. Robertson] (d 1912) EA/13*

ROE, Mrs. Alfred see Roe,
Mrs. R.

ROE, Bassett (1860-1934) English
actor DP, EA/95, GRB/1-4,
WWT/1-7

ROE, Dan F. (b 1879) actor
GRB/1

ROE, John E. (d 1871 [33]) pantomime writer EA/72*

ROE, Patricia (b 1932) American
actress BE, TW/18-20, 24-26

ROE, Mrs. R. (d 1871 [35])
EA/72*

ROE, William (fl 1640) actor DA

ROEBLING, Paul (b 1934) American actor BE, TW/11-20, 24,
WWT/15-16

ROEBUCK, Cpt. Disney (d 1885
[66]) actor, producer, manager
BE*, EA/86*, WWT/14*

ROEBUCK, Cpt. Francis Algernon
Disney see Roebuck, Cpt.
Disney

ROEBURT, John (d 1972 [63])
dramatist BP/56*

ROECKEL, Herr (d 1870) singer
EA/71*

ROECKER, Edward O. (d 1975
[65]) performer BP/59*

ROEDER, Benjamin F. (d 1943
[77]) American producer,
manager BE*, BP/27*,
WWT/14*

ROEHRICH, William see
Roerick, William

ROELAND, Augusta American actress TW/9-11

ROELS, Marcel (d 1973 [80])
performer BP/58*

ROERICK, William [né Roehrich]
(b 1912) American actor TW/
2-4, 10, 22-25, 27, 30, WWT/
15-16

ROEWADE, Paul (d 1976 [39])
producer/director/choreographer
BP/60*

ROFFMAN, Rose actress TW/25

ROGAN, Peter (b 1939) Irish
actor TW/28-29

ROGELL, Sid (d 1973 [73]) pro-
ducer/director/choreographer
BP/58*

ROGER BROTHERS (fl 1885) variety performers SR

ROGERS, Mr. (fl 1857) English
actor HAS

ROGERS, Mrs. [Mrs. Phillips]
(d 1850) English actress HAS

ROGERS, Miss (b 1821) actress
CDP

ROGERS, Alfred R. (d 1891) EA/
92*

ROGERS, Anne (b 1933) English actress, singer AAS, BE, TW/
23, WWT/13-16

ROGERS, Arthur (d 1894) EA/95*

ROGERS, Ben G. (d 1895 [75])
American actor CDP, HAS

ROGERS, Mrs. Ben G. [née Margaret Downs] (d 1852) actress
HAS

ROGERS, Bernard (1893-1968)
American composer WWA/5

ROGERS, Bob (d 1974) performer
BP/59*

ROGERS, Budd (d 1975 [84]) pro-
ducer/director/choreographer
BP/60*

ROGERS, Charles (d 1899) dramatist EA/00*

ROGERS, Charles J. (fl 1845)
equestrian manager, equestrian
HAS

ROGERS, Charles R. (d 1957 [64])
producer BE*

ROGERS, Charles S. (d 1888)
American actor EA/90*

ROGERS, Charles S. (1845-90)
actor CDP, HAS

ROGERS, Clara Kathleen ["Clara
Doria"] (1844-1931) English
singer DAB, WWA/1, WWM

ROGERS, Cynthia (1912-71) American actress TW/6, 27

ROGERS, Daniel (fl 1818?) dramatist EAP

ROGERS, E. [né Frazer] (fl 1850)
Scottish actor HAS

ROGERS, Edmund (d 1889 [33])
journalist EA/90*

ROGERS, Edward (fl 1626) actor
DA

ROGERS, Emmett (1915-65) American producer, director, actor
BE, TW/2-8, 22

ROGERS, E. W. (d 1913 [49])
EA/14*

ROGERS, Felix (fl 1863-69)
English comedian HAS
ROGERS, Genevieve (1859-89)
actress CDP
ROGERS, G. H. (d 1872 [54])
Australian comedian EA/73*
ROGERS, Gil (b 1934) American
actor TW/25-26, 29-30
ROGERS, Ginger [Virginia Kath-
erine McMath] (b 1911) Amer-
ican actress, dancer BE,
CB, ES, SR, TW/22-24,
WWT/8-10, 16
ROGERS, Gus (1869-1908) actor
GRB/3-4, WWS
ROGERS, H. (d 1909 [42])
manager EA/10*
ROGERS, Harry (d 1889 [40])
musician EA/90*
ROGERS, Helen Augusta (d 1890
[23]) actress EA/91*
ROGERS, Henry (d 1896) music-
hall chairman EA/97*
ROGERS, Herbert (d 1912 [33])
EA/13*
ROGERS, Mrs. J. [née Minne
Shemelds] (d 1878 [28]) serio-
comic EA/79*
ROGERS, James (d 1877 [78])
American? actor EA/78*
ROGERS, Mrs. James see
Rogers, Sarah Ann
ROGERS, James G. (1822-63)
English comedian, singer
CDP, HAS
ROGERS, Jane see Bullock,
Mrs. Christopher
ROGERS, John (d 1905 [65])
EA/06*
ROGERS, John R. (d 1932 [92])
American press representative,
manager BE*, BP/17*,
WWT/14*
ROGERS, Jonathan (d 1880 [68])
musician EA/81*
ROGERS, Katherine (d 1891)
actress CDP
ROGERS, Laura (d 1948 [74])
actress TW/5
ROGERS, Louise Mackintosh (d
1933 [68]) actress BE*,
BP/18*
ROGERS, Maggie [née Margaret
Stowell; Mrs. John Crean]
(1818-87) Canadian actress
NYM
ROGERS, Max [Max Solomon] (d
1932 [59]) American actor

GRB/3-4, WWA/1, WWS, WWT/
1-5
ROGERS, Mildred (d 1973 [74])
performer BP/57*
ROGERS, Oliver (b 1873) English
actor GRB/1
ROGERS, Paul (b 1917) English ac-
tor AAS, BE, CB, ES, TW/
24, 28-30, WWT/12-16
ROGERS, Robert (1727-98) Ameri-
can dramatist CP/2-3, EAP,
GT
ROGERS, Robert Emmons (1888-
1941) American dramatist
WWA/1
ROGERS, Robert John (d 1871
[34]) manager EA/72*
ROGERS, Sarah Ann [Mrs. James
Rogers] (d 1917 [68]) EA/18*
ROGERS, Stuart actor, impersona-
tor CDP
ROGERS, Suzanne (b 1947) Ameri-
can actress TW/26
ROGERS, W. actor, singer CDP
ROGERS, Will (1879-1935) Ameri-
can actor COC, DAB, ES,
OC/1-3, SR, WWT/7, WWW/3
ROGERS, William (fl 1628) actor
DA
ROGERS, William (d 1876 [70])
actor EA/77*, WWT/14*
ROGERSON, Anne [Mrs. J. Roger-
son] (d 1868 [58]) EA/69*
ROGERSON, Budd (b 1927) Ameri-
can actor TW/5-6
ROGERSON, Mrs. J. see Roger-
son, Anne
ROGERSON, James B. (d 1876
[68]) actor EA/77*
ROGERSON, J. B. (d 1879 [32])
actor EA/80*
ROGERSON, Tom W. (d 1889 [53])
EA/90*
ROGERSON, Whit (d 1906 [63])
comedian EA/07*
ROGERSON, Mrs. Whit [Edith
Sandford] (d 1889 [52]) eques-
trian actress EA/90*
ROGIER, Frank (b 1918) American
actor TW/3, 9
ROGNAN, Lorraine (d 1969 [57])
performer BP/54*
ROGOFF, Gordon (b 1931) Ameri-
can critic, educator, producer
BE
ROHLFS, Anna K. G. see
Green, Anna Katherine
ROHMER, Sax [Arthur Sarsfield

Ward] (1886-1959) English
dramatist, composer WWT/
6-11, WWW/5
ROKEBY, Lord see Robinson,
Matthew
ROLAND, Frank (d 1882 [42])
comedian EA/83*
ROLAND, Ida (1881-1951) Aus-
trian actress BE*, WWT/14*
ROLAND, Ruth (1893-1937)
American actress BE*
ROLAND, Will (d 1973 [63]) pro-
ducer/director/choreographer
BP/57*
ROLF, Frederick (b 1926) German
actor, director BE, TW/14-
15, 22-23
ROLFE, Arthur Collins actor
GRB/1
ROLFE, Fourness (d 1891 [69])
actor, singer EA/92*
ROLFE, William James (1827-
1910) American scholar WWA/1
ROLIN, Judi (b 1946) American
actress TW/26
ROLL, John (d 1539) actor DA
ROLLA, Kate (b 1865) singer
CDP
ROLLA, Theresa (b 1837) dancer
CDP, HAS
ROLLAND, Caroline (fl 1871)
equestrienne CDP
ROLLAND, Romain (d 1944 [78])
dramatist, critic, historian
WWT/14*
ROLLAND, William E. (d 1890)
clown EA/91*
ROLLAND, Little Willie (d 1879
[15]) equestrian, acrobat EA/
80*
ROLLASON, Ellen Elizabeth see
Chart, Ellen Elizabeth
ROLLASON, John (d 1879 [79])
EA/80*
ROLLE, Esther American actress
TW/22-23, 25-29, WWT/16
ROLLI, Paolo Antonio (fl 1744)
Italian dramatist? manager,
composer? CP/1
ROLLINE, Mr. (fl 1833) actor
HAS
ROLLINS, Jack personal manager,
producer BE
ROLLINS, Walter E. (d 1973
[66]) composer/lyricist BP/
57*
ROLLINSON (fl 1596?) dramatist
FGF

ROLLITT, Joe (d 1917 [38]) EA/
18*
ROLLO, Billy (d 1964 [40]) actor,
stage manager BE*
ROLLS, Mrs. Alexander see
Barry, Helen
ROLLY, Jeanne (d 1929 [70]) ac-
tress BE*, WWT/14*
ROLPH, Mr. (d 1917) EA/18*
ROLSTON, William (d 1964) actor,
director, stage manager BE*
ROLT, Bernard (1874-1937) com-
poser, lyricist WWW/3
ROLT, Richard (1724/25-70) Eng-
lish dramatist CP/2-3, GT,
TD/1-2
ROLYAT, Dan [Herbert Taylor]
(1872-1927) English actor GRB/
2-4, WWT/1-5
ROMA, Caro (b 1869) American
singer, composer WWM, WWS
ROMA, Willy (d 1902 [25]) acro-
bat, gymnast EA/03*
ROMAH, Lou (d 1918) EA/19*
ROMAINE, Annie (d 1893) EA/94*
ROMAINE, Charles (d 1896) panto-
mimist EA/97*
ROMAINE, Mrs. Charles see
Bernarto, Mlle.
ROMAINE, Claire (1873/77-1964)
English actress, singer WWT/
4-8
ROMAINE, Doug (d 1971 [56]) per-
former BP/56*
ROMAINE, Edith (d 1974 [87]) per-
former BP/59*
ROMAINE, Martin (d 1917) per-
former? EA/18*
ROMAINS, Jules (1885-1972)
French dramatist COC, OC/3
ROMAN, Joseph (b 1927) American
actor TW/8
ROMAN, Lawrence (b 1921) Amer-
ican dramatist BE
ROMANI, Maria Theresa Catherine
see Bland, Mrs. George
ROMANINI, Mme. (fl 1841) rope
dancer CDP
ROMANO, Charles (d 1937 [38])
English actor BE*, BP/22*
ROMANO, Jane (d 1962 [33])
American actress TW/19
ROMANO, Nicolino (d 1901 [56])
proprietor EA/02*
ROMANOV, Boris Georgievik (1891-
1957) Russian/American dancer,
choreographer ES
ROMANZINI, Maria Theresa see

Bland, Maria Theresa Roman-
zini
ROMANZINI, Maria Theresa
Catherine see Bland, Mrs.
George
ROMBERG, Bernard (1767-1841)
composer, conductor, musi-
cian CDP
ROMBERG, Sigmund (1887-1951)
Hungarian/American composer
AAS, CB, ES, NTH, PDT,
TW/8, WWA/3, WWT/4-11
ROME, Harold (b 1908) American
composer, lyricist AAS, BE,
CB
ROMEO, Gene (b 1944) American
actor TW/25
ROMER, Mr. (d 1886 [64]) min-
strel singer EA/87*
ROMER, Alec [Alex Haines
Woodman] (d 1909 [37]) EA/10*
ROMER, Anne [Mrs. William
Brough] (d 1852 [23]) actress
BE*, WWT/14*
ROMER, Carrie see Stokes,
Caroline Ann
ROMER, Emma see Almond,
Emma
ROMER, Frank (d 1889) composer
EA/90*
ROMER, Robert (d 1874 [66])
actor BE*, EA/75*, WWT/14*
ROMER, Tomi (d 1969 [45]) ac-
tress TW/26
ROMER, Violet (b 1895) American
dancer WWM
ROMEYN, Jane (d 1963 [62])
actress BE*
ROMNEY, Edana (b 1919) South
African actress WWT/9-10
ROMOFF, Woody (b 1918) Amer-
ican actor BE
ROMONDO, George eccentric
mimic CDP
RONALD, Sir Landon (1873-1938)
English composer
GRB/1-4, WWT/1-8, WWW/3
RONAN, Robert (b 1938) Ameri-
can actor TW/24-28
RONCA, Frank (d 1886) concert-
hall chairman EA/87*
RONCONI, Sig. (d 1875) com-
poser EA/76*
RONCONI, Giorgio (d 1890)
singer HAS
RONDIRIS, Dimitrios (b 1899)
Greek director BE, COC
RONELL, Ann composer, lyricist,

librettist BE
RONNER, John (fl 1550) actor DA
RONZANI, Domenico (1800-68)
Italian maître de ballet HAS
ROO, John see Roll, John
ROODS, John theatre owner DA
ROOKE, Arthur Leonard (d 1892)
singer EA/93*
ROOKE, Irene (1878-1958) English
actress COC, GRB/3-4, OC/3,
WWT/1-8
ROOKE, Valentine (b 1912) English
actor WWT/8-10
ROOKE, William Michael (1794-
1847) Irish composer, musician,
director? CDP, DNB
ROOKES, Marian Agnes Land see
Booth, Agnes, & Perry, Mrs.
Harry A., II
ROOME, Edward (d 1729) drama-
tist CP/1-3, DNB, GT
ROON, Al (d 1976 [73]) dance
trainer BP/60*
ROONEY, James C. (d 1889 [33])
vaudevillian EA/90*
ROONEY, J. P. (d 1870) comic
singer, dancer EA/71*
ROONEY, Mickey [Joe Yule] (b
1920) American actor SR
ROONEY, Pat, Sr. (1880-1962)
American actor TW/7-14, 19
ROONEY, Mrs. Pat see Bent,
Marion
ROONEY, Mrs. Pat see Nolan,
Pattie
ROONEY, Patrick (1844-92) Irish
actor, dancer CDP
ROONEY, William (b 1945) Ameri-
can actor TW/26
ROOP, Reno Estonian actor TW/
29-30
ROOS, Joanna (b 1901) American
actress BE, WWT/7-9
ROOS, Patricia (b 1945) American
actress TW/29-30
ROOSE, Olwen (b 1900) English ac-
tress WWT/5-9
ROOSE-EVANS, James (b 1927)
English director AAS, WWT/
14-16
ROOSEVELT, Blanche (d 1898)
composer, singer CDP
ROOT, Arabella (fl 1881?) singer,
song composer CDP
ROOT, Mrs. E. B. see Root,
Ivy Ashton
ROOT, George Frederick (1820-95)
American songwriter BE*

ROOT

ROOT, Ivy Ashton [Mrs. E. B.
Root] (b 1872) American dram-
atist WWM
ROOT, John (b 1904) American
scene designer ES, TW/2,
5-8
ROOT, Lynn (b 1905) American
dramatist, actor BE
ROPER, Mrs. (d 1835) actress
HAS
ROPER, Eric (d 1916) revue
comedian EA/17*
ROPER, Samuel Henry (d 1890)
performer? EA/91*
ROPER, Susannah (d 1908 [67])
EA/09*
ROPES, Arthur Reed see Ross,
Adrian
ROPES, Bradford (d 1966 [60])
performer BP/51*
ROQUEMORE, Henry (1890-1943)
actor SR
ROQUEVERT, Noel (d 1973 [81])
performer BP/58*
ROREM, Ned (b 1923) American
composer CB
RORIE, Yvonne (1907-59) Scot-
tish actress WWT/6-11
RORKE, Cecilia (d 1877 [17])
actress EA/78*, WWT/14*
RORKE, John (d 1908) EA/09*
RORKE, John (d 1957 [65]) actor
BE*, WWT/14*
RORKE, Kate [Mrs. Douglas
Cree] (1866-1945) English ac-
tress CDP, COC, DP, EA/
95, GRB/1-4, OC/1-3, WWT/
1-9, WWW/4
RORKE, Margaret Hayden (d
1969 [85]) performer BP/53*
RORKE, Mary [Mrs. Frank St.
Aubyn] (1858-1938) English
actress DP, EA/96, GRB/
1-4, OAA/2, WWT/1-8
ROSA, Mme. de (d 1897) dancer
EA/98*
ROSA, Carl (1843-89) German
conductor, musician CDP,
DNB, ES
ROSA, Mrs. Carl see Rosa,
Parepa
ROSA, H. C. (d 1917) EA/18*
ROSA, Madeline [Mrs. Frank
Travis] (d 1907) ventriloquist
EA/08*
ROSA, Nera (d 1920 [80]) actress
BE*, BP/5*
ROSA, Parepa [née Euphrosyne

Parepa; Mrs. Carl Rosa] (1836-
74) Scottish actress, singer
CDP, DNB, HAS
ROSA, Patti (d 1894) actress, sing-
er CDP
ROSALIND, Myra [Myra MacKenzie
Lloyd] (d 1908 [49]) actress
EA/09*
ROSAR, Annie (d 1963 [75]) per-
former BE*
ROSATI, Carolina (1826-1905)
Italian dancer, mimist ES
ROSAY, Françoise (1891-1974)
French actress BE, BTR/74,
ES, WWT/11-15
ROSCOW, Eleanor [Mrs. George
B. Roscoe] (d 1899) EA/91*
ROSCOW, G. B. (d 1904) agent
EA/05*
ROSCOW, Mrs. George B. see
Roscow, Eleanor
ROSE, Mr. (fl 1612) actor DA
ROSE, Mr. (fl 1839) English actor
HAS
ROSE (d 1893) gymnast EA/94*
ROSE, Miss (fl 1770?) actress
CDP
ROSE, Miss (fl 1854) actress HAS
ROSE, Mlle. [Mrs. E. Harris]
(d 1887 [29]) EA/88*
ROSE, Annie [Mrs. Frederick
Bond] (d 1892 [48]) actress
EA/93*
ROSE, Annie (d 1902 [58]) actress
EA/97*
ROSE, Arthur see Rose, Clarkson
ROSE, Betty Clarke (d 1947) ac-
tress BE*
ROSE, Billy [né William Samuel
Rosenberg] (1899-1966) American
actor, producer BE, CB,
COC, NTH, SR, TW/2-8, 22,
WWA/4, WWT/10-14
ROSE, Mrs. Cecil see Thomas,
Dorothy
ROSE, Clark (1838-87) American
actor? circus performer? circus
proprietor NYM
ROSE, Clarkson (1890-1968) Eng-
lish actor COC, OC/3, WWT/
9-14
ROSE, Clifford (b 1929) English
actor TW/22-23
ROSE, Edward (1849-1904) English
dramatist WWW/1
ROSE, Edward Everett (1862-1939)
Canadian dramatist, director
GRB/3-4, WWA/1, WWM,

WWT/1-7

ROSE, Francis A. (b 1849) American actor, prompter HAS

ROSE, George (b 1920) English actor AAS, BE, TW/22-30, WWT/12-16

ROSE, George see Sketchley, Arthur

ROSE, George Thomas (d 1893) EA/94*

ROSE, Harry (d 1962 [70]) performer BE*, BP/47*

ROSE, Heloise Durant (fl 1890-1921) American dramatist WWA/5

ROSE, Henry (d 1971 [61]) performer BP/55*

ROSE, Jane American actress BE, TW/9, 13, 15, 23-24, 29

ROSE, Rev. John (fl 1788-93) dramatist CP/3

ROSE, Kathleen Mary ["Dolores"] (d 1975 [83]) Ziegfeld girl WWT/16*

ROSE, L. Arthur (1887-1958) Scottish dramatist WWT/10-12

ROSE, Lieut. Manfred (d 1908) manager EA/09*

ROSE, Marie [Marie Leavett] (1856-1919) actress SR

ROSE, Nancie (d 1917) EA/18*

ROSE, Norman (b 1917) American actor TW/9, 23, 25

ROSE, Patrick Latham (d 1896) actress EA/97*

ROSE, Peter librettist CD

ROSE, Philip [né Rosenberg] (b 1921) American producer BE, WWT/15-16

ROSE, Mrs. P. L. see Boone, Lizzie

ROSE, Reginald (b 1920) American dramatist BE

ROSE, Reva (b 1940) American actress TW/23-24

ROSE, Rufus C. (d 1975 [70]) marionettist BP/60*

ROSE, Tom (d 1976 [51]) dramatist BP/60*

ROSEAU, Emé (fl 1870s?) singer CDP

ROSEBERY, Arthur (d 1928) producer, dramatist, manager BE*, WWT/14*

ROSELIE, William (1882-1945) actor SR

ROSELLA, Mlle. (d 1906 [19])

gymnast EA/08*

ROSELLE, Agnes see Knott, Roselle

ROSELLE, Amy [Mrs. Arthur Dacre] (1854-95) English actress CDP, DP, OAA/2

ROSELLE, Emily [Mrs. Gustave Roselle] (d 1882) EA/83*

ROSELLE, Mrs. Gustave see Roselle, Emily

ROSELLE, Julia (fl 1871-78) actress OAA/2

ROSELLE, Percy (b 1856) actor CDP

ROSELLE, W. H. [William Hawkins] (d 1878) actor? EA/80*

ROSELLE, William (d 1945 [67]) American actor BE*, BP/29*

ROSEMONT, Walter (d 1969 [91]) composer/lyricist BP/53*

ROSEN, Abigail (b 1946) Swiss/American actress TW/25

ROSEN, Albert H. (d 1974 [82]) manager BP/59*

ROSEN, Frederick (d 1912 [46]) music-hall agent EA/13*

ROSEN, Irwin (b 1936) American actor TW/26

ROSEN, Jerry M. (d 1972 [60]) agent BP/56*

ROSENBAUM, Edward, Sr. (d 1927 [72]) manager BE*, BP/12*

ROSENBERG, George (d 1969) agent BP/53*

ROSENBERG, Marvin (b 1912) American educator BE

ROSENBERG, Michel (d 1972 [71]) performer BP/57*

ROSENBERG, Philip see Rose, Philip

ROSENBERG, Sarah (d 1964 [90]) actress BE*

ROSENBERG, William Samuel see Rose, Billy

ROSENBLOOM, Maxie (d 1976 [71]) performer BP/60*

ROSENBLUM, M. Edgar (b 1932) American producer, manager BE

ROSENBURGH, Carleton F. (d 1974 [69]) theatre construction BP/59*

ROSENE, Charles F. (b 1844) American actor HAS

ROSENFELD, Jay C. (d 1975 [80]) critic BP/60*

ROSENFELD, Jerome M. producer,

publisher, executive BE

ROSENFELD, John, Jr. (d 1966 [66]) critic BP/51*

ROSENFELD, Juliet see Juliet

ROSENFELD, Sydney (1855-1931) American dramatist GRB/2-4, WWA/1, WWM, WWS, WWT/1-6

ROSENGREN, Frank Duane see Duane, Frank

ROSENHAIN, Jacob (d 1894 [81]) composer, musician EA/95*

ROSENSTOCK, Joseph (b 1895) Polish conductor, composer CB

ROSENSTOCK, Milton (b 1917) American musical director BE

ROSENTHAL, Andrew (b 1917) American dramatist, composer BE

ROSENTHAL, Edmund [Thomas Edmund Metcalf] (d 1902 [77]) singer EA/03*

ROSENTHAL, Harry (d 1953 [60]) Irish composer, musician, actor BE*, BP/37*

ROSENTHAL, Jean (1912-69) American lighting designer BE, TW/25, WWA/5

ROSENTHAL, J. J. (d 1923 [60]) American manager, talent representative BE*, BP/8*

ROSENTHAL, Laurence (b 1926) American composer BE

ROSENTHAL, Moriz (1863-1946) Polish pianist SR

ROSENTHAL, Steven (b 1946) American actor TW/28

ROSETTI, Marie (fl 1872) singer CDP

ROSEWALD, Julie (b 1850) singer CDP

ROSHANARA (d 1926) Indian dancer BE*, BP/11*

ROSICH, Sig. (fl 1825) singer HAS

ROSICH, Signora (fl 1825) singer HAS

ROSIER, Mlle. (fl 1837?) dancer CDP

ROSIER, Fitz William (fl 1881?) musician CDP

ROSIER, Jack (d 1909) actor EA/10*

ROSIERE, J. G. (d 1870) actor WWT/14*

ROSING, Vladimir (1890-1963)

Russian singer, director WWA/4

ROSINI, Victor (d 1910 [56]) variety performer EA/11*

ROSKAM, Cathryn (b 1943) American actress TW/27

ROSMER, Milton (1881/82-1971) English actor, producer, director AAS, WWT/2-14

ROSQUI, Tom (b 1928) American actor BE, TW/22-24, 26-29

ROSS, Adelaide [Mrs. T. W. Ford] (b 1842) English actress GRB/1

ROSS, Adrian [Arthur Reed Ropes] (1859-1933) English dramatist, lyricist, librettist DNB, GRB/1-4, WWT/1-7, WWW/3

ROSS, Alan (b 1920) American actor TW/5-6

ROSS, Anna see Brunton, Mrs. John

ROSS, Ann Boothby American actress TW/27

ROSS, Annie (b 1930) English actress, singer WWT/16

ROSS, Anthony (1906-55) American actor TW/1-12, WWT/11-12

ROSS, Babs (d 1973 [62]) performer BP/58*

ROSS, Bertie (d 1905 [30]) pantomimist EA/06*

ROSS, Bill (b 1915) American stage manager, director BE

ROSS, Charles [Charles Edward Cobb] (b 1880) English actor, singer GRB/1

ROSS, Charles Cowper (b 1929) English actor, director, producing manager WWT/15-16

ROSS, Charles H. [Charles H. Thornton] (b 1882) English actor, pantomimist GRB/1

ROSS, Charles Henry (d 1897) dramatist CDP

ROSS, Charles J. (1859-1918) Canadian actor SR, WWM, WWS

ROSS, Charlie [William George Gant] (d 1893) actor EA/95*

ROSS, Chris (d 1970 [24]) performer BP/54*

ROSS, Corinne Heath Sumner (d 1965 [86]) performer BP/50*

ROSS, Danny (d 1976 [45]) performer BP/60*

ROSS, David (1723/28-90) English actor CDP, DNB, GT, TD/1-2

ROSS, David (1922/24-66) American

director, producer, actor BE,
TW/13-18, 22

ROSS, Mrs. David see Ross,
Frances

ROSS, Dorothy (b 1912) American
press representative BE

ROSS, Elizabeth (b 1926/28)
American actress BE, TW/
2-3, 10

ROSS, Eva Florence (d 1887) actress NYM

ROSS, F. Clure (1874-1942) English actor, stage manager
GRB/1

ROSS, Frances (d 1770?) actress?
CDP

ROSS, Frederick (b 1879) English
actor WWT/1-7

ROSS, Fred Q. (1858-1942) actor
SR

ROSS, George (b 1911) American
producer, dramatist, press
representative BE

ROSS, George A. (d 1916 [42])
EA/17*

ROSS, George I. (b 1907) South
African dramatist AAS, WWT/
14-16

ROSS, Gertrude Mary see Gitana,
Gertie

ROSS, Harriet (fl 1900s) American
actress WWM

ROSS, Henry (b 1913) English actor WWT/10-14

ROSS, Hector (b 1915) English
actor WWT/11

ROSS, Helen (b 1914) American
actress TW/23, 26, 29

ROSS, Herbert [Herbert Tait]
(1865-1934) Indian/English
actor WWT/2-7

ROSS, Herbert (b 1927) American
choreographer, director, dancer
BE, ES

ROSS, Irene English actress
GRB/1-2

ROSS, Isabel (d 1881 [24]) EA/
83*

ROSS, Jack [Jack Snyder] American actor, dancer GRB/1

ROSS, James (d 1873) strolling
player & showman EA/74*

ROSS, Jamie (b 1939) Scottish
actor TW/27-30

ROSS, Jan (b 1948) American
actress TW/28

ROSS, Jerry (1926-56) American
librettist, composer TW/12

ROSS, John E. (d 1859 [54]) English actor HAS

ROSS, John Wilson (d 1887 [69])
dramatist EA/88*

ROSS, Justin (b 1954) American
actor TW/30

ROSS, Kate see Windley, Mrs.
John

ROSS, Katherine (b 1930) American
actress TW/13

ROSS, Larry (d 1973 [65]) performer BP/57*

ROSS, Larry (b 1945) American
actor TW/26-29

ROSS, Lenny (d 1976 [71]) performer BP/60*

ROSS, Mabel Fenton (d 1931 [63])
American actress BE*, BP/15*

ROSS, Marion (d 1966 [68]) performer BP/51*

ROSS, Martin (b 1938) American
actor TW/24-25, 27

ROSS, Minnie (d 1892 [25]) actress? EA/94*

ROSS, Oriel [Muriel Swinstead]
(b 1907) actress WWT/8-13

ROSS, Robert (d 1954 [52]) Canadian actor, director TW/10

ROSS, Robert (d 1974 [65]) performer BP/59*

ROSS, Ronnie (d 1965 [25]) performer BP/50*

ROSS, Rosalind (b 1934) English
actress TW/26

ROSS, Roy Irving (d 1968 [56])
composer/lyricist BP/53*

ROSS, Shirley (d 1975 [62]) performer BP/59*

ROSS, Steven (b 1941) American
actor TW/25

ROSS, Thomas W. (1875/78-1959)
American actor GRB/2-4, TW/
16, WWM, WWS, WWT/1-11

ROSS, T. J. (d 1975 [81]) public
relations BP/59*

ROSS, Weedon (b 1878) English
actor GRB/1

ROSS, W. G. actor CDP

ROSS, Lieut. William (fl 1790)
dramatist CP/3

ROSS, William (d 1963 [38]) performer BE*, BP/47*

ROSS, Mrs. William see Brown,
Mrs. J.

ROSSBOROUGH, H. T. (d 1887)
music-hall proprietor EA/88*

ROSS-CATTANACH, William see
Windsor, Albert C.

ROSS-CLARKE, Betty American
actress WWT/6-7
ROSSE, Frederick (d 1940 [73])
composer BE*, WWT/14*
ROSSE, Mrs. Frederick see
Lichtenstein, Ethel
ROSSE, Herman (d 1965 [78])
designer TW/21
ROSSE, Matthew Russell (d 1910)
manager EA/11*
ROSSE, Russell (d 1910) actor,
producer, manager BE*,
WWT/14*
ROSSEN, Carol American actress
TW/18, 20
ROSSEN, Robert (1908-66) Amer-
ican director, dramatist
WWA/4
ROSSET, Barney (b 1922) Amer-
ican editor BE
ROSSETER, Philip (c. 1575-1623)
English musician, lessee,
composer COC, DA, OC/1-3
ROSSI, Ernesto Fortunato Giovanni
Maria (1827/29-96) Italian actor
CDP, COC, ES, OC/1-3
ROSSI, Gloria (b 1946) American
actress TW/30
ROSSI, Settimio (d 1864) Italian
singer HAS
ROSSI LEMENI, Nicola (b 1920)
Italian singer ES
ROSSILL (fl 1597) actor? DA
ROSSIN, Alfred A. (d 1976 [57])
producer/director/choreographer
BP/60*
ROSSITER, Leonard (b 1926) Eng-
lish actor AAS, TW/20,
WWT/15-16
ROSSLYN, Earl of [James Fran-
cis Harry St. Clair-Erskine]
(1869-1939) English actor
GRB/1-2
ROSSLYN, Lady see Robinson,
Anna
ROSSLYN, Elaine (d 1964) per-
former BE*
ROSSMAN, Edward (d 1876 [36])
musician EA/77*
ROSS-SELWICKE, Ethel (d 1906)
actress, dancer EA/07*,
WWT/14*
ROSTAND, Edmond (1868-1918)
French dramatist COC, GRB/
1-4, MWD, OC/3, SR, WWT/1
ROSTAND, Maurice (d 1968 [76])
performer BP/52*
ROSTEN, Norman (b 1914) Amer-

ican dramatist BE, CB
ROSTOVA, Mira (b 1919) Russian
actress TW/10
ROTCHLEY, Minnie [Sarah Ann
Woollams] (d 1902 [46]) actress
EA/03*
ROTH, Al (d 1972 [68]) musical
director BP/57*
ROTH, Albert A. (d 1969 [71])
performer BP/54*
ROTH, Ann costume designer
WWT/16
ROTH, Carl Heins (d 1972 [62])
producer/director/choreographer
BP/56*
ROTH, Lillian (b 1910) American
actress, singer BE, TW/18,
22, 27, WWT/7-8, 16
ROTH, Wolfgang (b 1910) German
designer TW/3-8
ROTHA, Wanda Austrian actress
WWT/9-16
ROTHAFEL, Samuel Lionel (1881-
1936) American showman DAB,
WWA/H, 4
ROTHE, Anita (d 1944 [77]) Amer-
ican actress BE*, BP/28*,
WWT/14*
ROTHENBERG, David (b 1933)
American press representative
BE
ROTHENSTEIN, Albert Daniel (b
1883) English designer WWT/4
ROTHIER, Leon (1874-1951) French
singer TW/8, WWA/5
ROTHMAN, Benjamin (d 1973 [76])
producer, manager BP/58*,
WWT/16*
ROTHMAN, Lawrence (b 1934)
American manager, producer
BE
ROTHSCHILD, Alfred (d 1972 [83])
editor BP/57*
ROTHWELL, Joan Dorothy see
Benesh, Joan Dorothy
ROTTER, Fritz Austrian dramatist
BE
ROUDENKO, Lobov Russian dancer
TW/2
ROUGH, William (fl 1797) drama-
tist CP/3
ROUGHWOOD, Owen (1876-1947)
English actor GRB/4, WWT/
1-8
ROUKE, Andy (d 1881 [31]) min-
strel EA/83*
ROUND, Henry (d 1905 [66]) com-
poser EA/06*

ROUNDS, David (b 1938) American actor TW/26-30

ROUNSEVILLE, Robert (1914/19-74) American actor, singer BE, TW/9-10, 13-15, 22-29, WWT/12-16

ROURKE, E. (d 1878 [71]) comedian EA/79*

ROURKE, Georgiana (d 1870 [42]) EA/71*

ROUS, Helen [Miss Shaw] (d 1934 [71]) Irish actress GRB/1-4, WWT/1-7

ROUSBEY, Arthur (d 1899) singer EA/00*, WWT/14*

ROUSBEY, Mrs. Arthur see Rousbey, Margaret

ROUSBEY, Margaret [Mrs. Arthur Rousbey] (d 1895 [48]) EA/96*

ROUSBY, Alfred (d 1905 [50]) actor EA/06*

ROUSBY, Alice [Mrs. Walter] (d 1883 [24]) actress EA/84*

ROUSBY, Clara Marion Jessie (1852-79) English actress CDP, DNB, OAA/1-2

ROUSBY, Mrs. Walter see Rousby, Alice

ROUSBY, Wybert (1835-1907) actor, manager DNB, GRB/3, OAA/1-2

ROUSE, Mrs. [Sarah Ann Gale; Mrs. William Charles Gale] (d 1893 [53]) actress EA/94*

ROUSE, Fanny Denham (1837-1912) English actress SR

ROUSE, John (d 1891?) actor, singer CDP

ROUSE, John Frederick Taylor (d 1902) music-hall chairman EA/03*

ROUSE, Thomas (d 1852 [68]) actor EA/72*, WWT/14*

ROUSILLION, W. see Hatt, W.

ROUSSEAU, Gladys (d 1975 [76]) designer BP/59*

ROUSSET SISTERS, The (fl 1851) dancers HAS

ROUSSIN, André (b 1911) French dramatist BE, MWD

ROUTLEDGE, Calvert (1869-1916) English actor, manager GRB/1-3

ROUTLEDGE, Mrs. Calvert see Jocelyn, Mary

ROUTLEDGE, Edmund J. P. (d 1899 [56]) actor EA/00*

ROUTLEDGE, Patricia (b 1929)

English actress AAS, TW/23-24, WWT/14-16

ROUTLEDGE, Mrs. William see Schofield, Laura

ROUVAUN (d 1975 [36]) performer BP/60*

ROUVEROL, Mrs. Aurania (d 1955 [69]) American dramatist BE*, BP/40*

ROVERE, Sig. (d 1865 [60]) singer HAS

ROVIN, Robert H. American actor TW/27

ROWAN, Lansing (1881-1912) actress SR

ROWBOTHAM, Mrs. see Hamilton, Mrs. Robert

ROWBOTHAM, H. H. (d 1837) English actor, manager CDP, HAS

ROWBOTHAM, Mrs. H. H. actress CDP

ROWCROFT, Emma (fl 1860) actress? singer? HAS

ROWDEN, Elizabeth (d 1908) EA/09*

ROWDON, George (d 1917) athlete, trick performer EA/18*

ROWE, Alice E. (d 1916) EA/17*

ROWE, Earl (b 1920) American actor TW/7-8

ROWE, Frances [or Fanny] (b 1913) English actress TW/4-6, WWT/10-14

ROWE, George (fl 1826) American actor HAS

ROWE, George Fawcett (1834-89) American actor, dramatist CDP, COC, HAS, OC/1-3, SR

ROWE, Mrs. George Fawcett see Girard, Kate

ROWE, George T. (d 1880 [81]) American comedian EA/81*

ROWE, Hansford (b 1924) American actor TW/25, 28-29

ROWE, Harry (1726-1800) English puppeteer, commentator, dramatist CDP, CP/3, DNB

ROWE, Harry [James Rowe] (d 1891 [39]) comedian EA/92*

ROWE, James see Rowe, Harry

ROWE, Louisa (b 1805) American actress HAS

ROWE, Mary Alice (1851-87) English actress NYM

ROWE, Nicholas (1674-1718) English dramatist CDP, COC, CP/1-3, DNB, ES, GT, HP,

MH, NTH, OC/1-3, PDT, RE, SR, TD/1-2

ROWE, Sir Reginald (d 1945 [75]) executive BE*, WWT/14*

ROWE, Mr. W. (d 1867) scene artist EA/68*

ROWELLA, William (d 1896) pantomimist EA/97*

ROWLAND (fl 1631) actor DA

ROWLAND, H. W. (d 1937 [70]) producer BE*, WWT/14*

ROWLAND, Mabel (d 1943 [61]) American actress BE*, BP/27*

ROWLAND, Margery (1910-45) English critic WWT/9

ROWLAND, Richard (d 1880 [21]) musician EA/81*

ROWLAND, Samuel (fl 1615) dramatist CP/3

ROWLAND, Toby (b 1916) American producing manager WWT/15-16

ROWLAND, William (d 1905 [62]) EA/06*

ROWLANDS, Cecil see Raleigh, Cecil

ROWLANDS, Elizabeth see Raine, Bessie

ROWLANDS, Gaynor (d 1906) actress, dancer BE*, EA/07*, WWT/14*

ROWLANDS, Gena (b 1936?) American actress BE, CB, TW/12-15

ROWLANDS, Patsy (b 1935) English actress WWT/15-16

ROWLES, Polly (b 1914) American actress BE, TW/7-20, 23, 25-26, 28-29, WWT/14-16

ROWLEY, Cpt. [William Duncan] (d 1910) lion tamer EA/12*

ROWLEY, Alec (1892-1958) English composer WWW/5

ROWLEY, Anne [Mrs. J. W. Rowley] (d 1874 [27]) EA/75*

ROWLEY, Joseph [Sig. Eurardo] (d 1871 [26]) spiral ascensionist EA/72*

ROWLEY, J. W. (d 1925 [78]) actor, singer CDP

ROWLEY, Mrs. J. W. see Rowley, Anne

ROWLEY, Samuel (c. 1575-1624) English actor, dramatist COC, CP/1-3, DA, DNB, FGF, HP, OC/1-3, RE

ROWLEY, Thomas (fl 1602) actor DA

ROWLEY, William (c. 1585-1637/42?) English actor, dramatist COC, CP/1-3, DA, DNB, FGF, HP, MH, NTH, OC/1-3, PDT, RE

ROWNTREE, Mrs. Bert see Rowntree, Edna

ROWNTREE, Edna [Mrs. Bert Rowntree] (d 1916) EA/17*

ROWSELL, Mary Catharine (fl 1884-1911) English dramatist WWW/2

ROWSON, Mr. (fl 1794) actor HAS

ROWSON, Miss (b 1787) English singer HAS

ROWSON, Jane see Crowe, Mrs. William

ROWSON, Susanna H. (1761?/62-1824) English actress, dramatist CDP, DAB, EAP, HAS, HJD, RJ, SR, WWA/H

ROX, John Jefferson (d 1957 [50]) lyricist, composer BE*

ROXBOROUGH, Picton [Picton Gaunt] (1875-1932) English actor GRB/1-4

ROXBURY, Mrs. Harry see Fenton, Kitty

ROXBY, Robert (d 1866 [58]) actor, stage manager EA/72*, WWT/14*

ROXBY, Samuel (d 1863 [58]) actor, manager EA/72*, WWT/14*

ROXBY, Wilfred see Collett, Thomas George

ROXBY, William, Jr. (1814-89) English designer ES

ROY, Agnese (d 1964 [69]) dancer BE*

ROY, Herbert (b 1880) English actor, singer GRB/1

ROY, John (d 1975 [77]) performer BP/60*

ROY, Renee (b 1935) American actress TW/26

ROYAARDS, William (d 1929 [62]) actor, director BE*, WWT/14*

ROYAL, Creed (d 1876 [68]) musician EA/77*

ROYAL, Harry (d 1903) circus performer EA/04*

ROYAL, Harry (d 1904) comedian EA/05*

ROYAL, Ted (b 1904) American composer BE

ROYAL BALLET ES
ROYAL-DAWSON, O. S. (d 1917
[32]) dramatist, manager EA/
18*
ROYALE, Harry M. (d 1963 [88])
performer BE*
"ROYAL PUNCH MAN, The" see
Dean, Thomas
ROYAL SHAKESPEARE CO. pro-
ducing manager WWT/14
ROYCE, Brigham (d 1933 [69])
American actor BE*, BP/17*
ROYCE, Edward (1870-1964) Eng-
lish stage manager, producer
WWT/3-11
ROYCE, Edward William (1841-
1926) English actor, stage
manager OAA/1-2, WWT/2-5
ROYCE, Julian [Julian Gardener]
(1870-1946) English actor
WWT/1-8
ROYCE, Mrs. Julian see Day,
Nora
ROYCE, Virginia (d 1962 [30])
actress BE*
ROYCE, Mrs. W. [née Emily
Watson] (d 1871 [22]) actress
EA/73*
ROYDE, Frank (b 1882) English
actor WWT/6-14
ROYDE-SMITH, Naomi (d 1964
[89]) English dramatist WWT/
8-9
ROYELLE, Charles [E. O.
Bauemann] (d 1894) EA/95*
ROYLE, Edwin Milton (1862-
1942) American actor, drama-
tist CB, GRB/2-4, HJD,
MH, PP/3, WWA/2, WWM,
WWS, WWT/1-9
ROYLE, Frederick Powis (d
1884) EA/85*
ROYLE, Josephine American
actress WWT/7-8
ROYLE, Selena (b 1904) Ameri-
can actress WWT/7-10
ROYLE, Selena Fetter [née
Selena Fetter] (d 1955 [95])
American actress PP/3,
TW/11
ROYS, Lyman P. (b 1815) Amer-
ican actor HAS
ROYSTON, Viscount see Yorke,
Philip
ROYSTON, Laura Eugenie [Mrs.
Frank Jefferson] (d 1884 [27])
EA/85*
ROYSTON, Roy [Roy Crowden]

(1899-1976) English actor WWT/
4-13
ROYSTON, Thomas (d 1889 [19])
actor EA/90*
ROYTON, Helen [Mrs. Walter G.
Douglas] (fl 1900s) Irish ac-
tress, singer WWM
ROYTON, Velma (d 1974 [81]) per-
former BP/59*
ROZAKIS, Gregory (b 1943) Amer-
ican actor TW/22-25, 27
ROZANT, Ina [Theodora Zorn]
American actress, singer
GRB/1-4
ROZE, Eliza Barker (d 1912)
EA/13*
ROZE, Marie (1846/50-1926)
French singer CDP, ES, GRB/1
ROZE, Raymond (1875-1920) Eng-
lish composer, conductor
WWT/3
ROZEWICZ, Tadeusz (b 1921)
Polish dramatist MWD
ROZIER, Mlle. (fl 1830?) dancer
CDP
ROZOV, Victor (b 1913) Russian
dramatist PDT
RUBBER, Violla (b 1910) producer,
personal manager BE
RUBEN, José (1886-1969) Belgian
actor, director, dramatist
TW/25, WWT/4-11
RUBEN, Neal (d 1969 [38]) writer,
producer BP/54*
RUBENS, Alma (1898-1931) Ameri-
can actress BE*
RUBENS, Maurie [or Maury] (d
1948 [55]) American composer
BE*
RUBENS, Paul A. (1875/76-1917)
librettist, composer GRB/1-4,
WWT/1-3, WWW/2
RUBIE, Jennie [Mrs. Tom Fan-
court] (d 1910) comedian EA/11*
RUBIN, Joel E. (b 1928) illuminat-
ing engineer BE
RUBIN, Menachem (d 1962 [67])
Polish actor, director BE*
RUBINI, Adelaide (d 1874 [79])
EA/75*
RUBINI-SCALISI, Mme. (d 1871)
singer CDP
RUBINSTEIN, Harold F. (1891/92-
1975) dramatist WWT/4-10
RUBINSTEIN, Ida (d 1960) dancer,
actress WWT/8-11
RUBINSTEIN, John (b 1946) Amer-
ican actor TW/29-30

RUBINSTEIN, Leon J. (d 1972
[83]) publicist BP/56*
RUBY, Harry (1895-1974) Amer-
ican composer, lyricist BE,
TW/30, WWT/6-11
RUBY, Thelma [née Wigoder]
(b 1925) English actress
WWT/14-16
RUCKER, Sim G. (d 1865) Amer-
ican actor? HAS
RUDD, Henry (d 1872 [50]) con-
ductor EA/73*
RUDD, Paul (b 1940) American
actor TW/25-26, 30
RUDD, Sam (d 1905) comedian
EA/06*
RUDDOCK, John (b 1897) Peru-
vian/English actor WWT/11-16
RUDEL, Julius (b 1921) Austrian
musical director BE, CB
RUDERSDORFF, Hermine (1822-
82) Ukranian singer CDP,
WWA/H
RUDGE, Albert (d 1892 [25])
manager EA/93*
RUDGE, J. F. (d 1873) acting
manager EA/74*
RUDGE, Letty see Lind, Letty
RUDGE, William (d 1893) music-
hall proprietor EA/94*
RUDICH, Nathan M. (d 1975
[56]) executive, publicist
BP/60*
RUDKIN, David (b 1936) English
dramatist CD, CH, MH, RE,
WWT/16
RUDMAN, Michael (b 1939)
American director, stage
manager WWT/16
RUDNER, Reta (b 1953) American
actress TW/30
RUDNEY, Edward (b 1939) Amer-
ican actor TW/23, 25
RUDY, Martin (b 1915) American
actor TW/3, 8, 25
RUFFO, Titta (1877-1953) Italian
singer ES
RUGE, Williams acrobat CDP
RUGG, William Augustus see
Conway, William Augustus
RUGGERI, Ruggero (1871-1953)
Italian actor COC, OC/3
RUGGLE, George (1575-1622)
English dramatist COC, CP/
1-3, FGF, OC/1-3
RUGGLES, Miss (fl 1890?)
dancer CDP
RUGGLES, Aubrey see Reeves,
Arnold
RUGGLES, Carl (d 1971) com-
poser/lyricist BP/56*
RUGGLES, Charles (1892-1970)
American actor BE, ES, TW/
27, WWA/5, WWT/6-11
RUHL, Arthur Brown (d 1935 [58])
American critic BE*, BP/19*,
WWT/14*
RUHLAND, Stanley see Gaige,
Truman
RUICK, Barbara (d 1974 [42]) per-
former BP/58*
RUICK, Melville (b 1898) American
actor TW/5, 8
RUISINGER, Thomas (b 1930)
American actor TW/29
RUIZ, Enrique (d 1975 [67]) per-
former BP/60*
RULE, Charles (b 1928) American
actor TW/24-26
RULE, Janice (b 1931) American
actress BE, TW/11-12, 27,
WWT/16
RULE, John (fl 1766) dramatist
CP/2-3, GT
RUMANN, Sig. (d 1967 [82]) Ger-
man actor TW/23
RUMFORD, Kennerley (b 1871)
English singer GRB/1
RUMFORD, Mrs. Kennerley see
Butt, Clara
RUMLEY, Edward actor HAS
RUMLEY, Jerry (b 1930) American
educator, choreographer, di-
rector BE
RUMMELL, Joseph (d 1880 [62])
professor of music EA/81*
RUMSEY, Charles Ernest (d 1905
[33]) advance agent EA/06*
RUNCIE, Constance Fauntleroy
(1836-1911) American composer
WWA/1
RUNNEL, Albert F. (d 1974 [82])
performer BP/58*
RUNNELS, Bonnie (1857-84) come-
dian, circus performer CDP
RUNNELLS, Burnett American cir-
cus performer SR
RUNYON, Damon (1884-1946)
American dramatist MWD,
NTH, SR, WWA/2
RUPERT, Mike (b 1951) American
actor TW/24
RUPP, Elmer Kohler (b 1871)
American critic WWM
RUSCHENBERGER, Mrs. dramatist
RJ

RUSH, Bert [John A. G. Sims]
(b 1883) English actor, variety
artist GRB/1
RUSH, Cecile (fl 1856-59) actress
HAS
RUSH, Edward F. (b 1864) Aus-
trian manager WWM
RUSHBURY, W. T. (d 1909)
manager EA/10*
RUSHFORTH, Elizabeth [Mrs.
Willie Rushforth] (d 1907) EA/
08*
RUSHFORTH, Mrs. Willie see
Rushforth, Elizabeth
RUSHTON, Lucy [Mary Wilde]
(1844-1909) actress, manager
CDP, COC, HAS
RUSKIN, Leonard (d 1973 [51])
producer TW/30
RUSKIN, Shimen (1907-76) Polish
actor TW/25-26, 28
RUSKIN, Sybil [Miss Raphael]
(1880-1940) English actress
GRB/1-4
RUSS, Giannina (1878-1951) Italian
singer ES
RUSS, Mrs. L. J. see Russ,
Meta Anderson
RUSS, Meta Anderson [Mrs. L.
J. Russ] (d 1905 [28]) EA/06*
RUSS, William R. see Har-
land, Fred
RUSSAK, Gerard (b 1927) Ameri-
can actor TW/23, 25, 30
RUSSEL, Mark (b 1948) American
actor TW/27
RUSSEL, William (1746-94) Scot-
tish dramatist CP/3
"RUSSELL" see Craythorne,
James
RUSSELL, Mr. circus performer?
HAS
RUSSELL, Master (fl 1831) actor
CDP
RUSSELL, Countess (d 1908 [37])
actress GRB/4
RUSSELL, Mrs. [Grace Hamilton]
(d 1883) pantomimist EA/85*
RUSSELL, Miss singer CDP
RUSSELL, Agnes [Mrs. C. W.
Somerset] (d 1947 [73]) actress
BE*, WWT/14*
RUSSELL, Andy (d 1867) Negro
performer EA/68*
RUSSELL, Ann see Bullock,
Mrs. Hildebrand
RUSSELL, Anna [Anna Claudia
Russell-Brown] (b 1911/13)

English performer BE, CB,
COC, OC/3, TW/10
RUSSELL, Annie [Mrs. Oswald
Yorke] (1864-1936) English ac-
tress COC, DAB, GRB/2-4,
OC/1-3, PP/3, WWA/1, WWM,
WWS, WWT/1-8
RUSSELL, Bernard (d 1910 [34])
actor, singer CDP
RUSSELL, Billy (d 1971) performer
BP/56*
RUSSELL, Byron (d 1963 [79])
Irish actor BE*, BP/48*
RUSSELL, Charlotte (d 1901 [64])
singer EA/02*
RUSSELL, David Forbes (d 1969
[77]) performer BP/54*
RUSSELL, Diarmuid (d 1973 [71])
agent BP/58*
RUSSELL, Dorothy (b 1881) Ameri-
can actress WWS
RUSSELL, Edd X. (d 1966 [88])
performer BP/51*
RUSSELL, Edith [Mrs. Irton] (d
1897 [27]) actress, lessee EA/
98*
RUSSELL, Edward Haslingden (d
1906 [46]) EA/07*
RUSSELL, Sir Edward Richard
(1834-1920) English critic
GRB/3-4, WWT/1-3
RUSSELL, Ella [Countess di Rhigini]
American actress CDP, GRB/1
RUSSELL, Ethel English actress
GRB/1
RUSSELL, Evelyn (d 1976 [49]?)
American actress TW/29
RUSSELL, Frank (d 1883) comedian
EA/84*
RUSSELL, Fred [Thomas Frederick
Parnell] (1862-1957) ventriloquist
COC, OC/3
RUSSELL, Fred H. (d 1974 [73])
critic BP/59*
RUSSELL, F. W. see Barry,
H. C.
RUSSELL, Gail (d 1961 [36]) Amer-
ican actress BE*, BP/46*
RUSSELL, George (d 1896 [78])
equestrian EA/97*
RUSSELL, George Henry (fl 1857?)
CDP
RUSSELL, George William see
A. E.
RUSSELL, Harold (fl 1884-1908)
American actor WWS
RUSSELL, Mrs. Harold see
Dwyer, Ada

RUSSELL, Harriet Ellis (d 1912
[66]) actress, proprietor EA/
13*
RUSSELL, Henry (d 1874) musi-
cian EA/75*
RUSSELL, Henry [Henry Falconer]
(d 1887 [49]) actor? EA/88*
RUSSELL, Henry (1812-1899/1900)
American singer, composer
CDP, DNB, HAS
RUSSELL, Henry (d 1900 [87]?)
English actor, composer EA/
02*, HAS
RUSSELL, Henry (fl 1900s) Eng-
lish opera director WWM
RUSSELL, Henry (d 1909) stage
manager EA/10*
RUSSELL, Herbert M. (d 1907)
singer EA/08*
RUSSELL, Howard (1835-1914)
English actor OAA/1-2
RUSSELL, Mrs. Howard (d 1880
[30]) EA/81*
RUSSELL, H. Scott (1868-1949)
English actor, singer WWT/
6-10
RUSSELL, Irene (b 1899/1901)
Tasmanian actress, singer
WWT/6-8
RUSSELL, Iris (b 1922) English
actress WWT/11-16
RUSSELL, J. (fl 1846) actor
HAS
RUSSELL, James (d 1845 [79])
EA/72*
RUSSELL, James (1789-1859)
English actor CDP, OX
RUSSELL, James Howell (d 1909)
scene painter EA/10*
RUSSELL, Jane (b 1921) Amer-
ican actress TW/27-28
RUSSELL, Jay (d 1970 [57])
publicist BP/55*
RUSSELL, J. Fritz Scottish actor
GRB/2
RUSSELL, Jim (b 1927) American
actor TW/13
RUSSELL, John (fl 1617-19)
gatherer DA
RUSSELL, John (d 1925 [69])
comedian BE*, BP/9*
RUSSELL, Mrs. John see
Fanchette, Kate
RUSSELL, Mrs. John see
Huddart, Fanny
RUSSELL, Kathleen actress
GRB/1-2
RUSSELL, Kenna (d 1907) ac-

tress EA/08*
RUSSELL, Lewis (d 1961 [76])
actor BE*
RUSSELL, Lillian [Louise Leonard]
(1861-1922) American actress,
singer CDP, ES, GRB/2-4,
HJD, NTH, OC/1-3, SR, WWA/
1, WWM, WWS, WWT/1-4
RUSSELL, Mabel (d 1908 [36])
actress GRB/4*, WWT/14*
RUSSELL, Mabel (1887-1951) ac-
tress, dancer WWT/2-9
RUSSELL, Maria (d 1905 [77])
EA/06*
RUSSELL, Marian (b 1929) Amer-
ican actress TW/7-8
RUSSELL, Marie (d 1969 [86])
performer BP/53*
RUSSELL, Marie Booth [Mrs. R.
B. Mantell] (d 1911) American
actress GRB/3-4
RUSSELL, Mary (d 1891) EA/93*
RUSSELL, Mary Ann see Far-
ren, Mrs. George Percy
RUSSELL, R. (d 1849) English ac-
tor, manager HAS
RUSSELL, Robert (b 1912) Ameri-
can dramatist BE
RUSSELL, Rosalind (1911/12-76)
American actress AAS, BE,
CB, ES, SR, TW/13, WWT/
13-16
RUSSELL, Samuel Thomas (1769?-
1845) English actor CDP, DNB,
GT, OX, TD/1-2
RUSSELL, Sol Smith (1848-1902)
American actor, manager CDP,
DAB, NTH, OC/1-3, PP/3,
SR, WWA/1
RUSSELL, Thomas (d 1891 [49])
proprietor EA/92*
RUSSELL, Tom H. (d 1892) music-
hall comedian EA/93*
RUSSELL, Violet actress DP
RUSSELL, Walter actor GRB/1
RUSSELL, William (1777-1813)
English composer DNB
RUSSELL, William (1884-1929)
actor, director BE*
RUSSELL, William Clark (d 1911
[67]) writer BE*, WWT/14*
RUSSELL, William H. (d 1871
[49]) stage manager EA/72*
RUSSELL-BROWN, Anna Claudia
see Russell, Anna
RUSSELL-DAVIS, Arthur (d 1917)
EA/18*
RUSSO, Sarett Rude (d 1976 [58])

dramatist BP/60*

RUSSOM, Leon (b 1941) American actor TW/25-28

RUSSON, Joseph (d 1911) minstrel EA/12*

RUST, Alan American actor TW/30

RUST, Gordon A. (1908-77) American executive BE

RUSTON, Ernest (b 1864) English actor GRB/1

RUTH, Jack (b 1921) American actor TW/5, 10

RUTH, Josephine see Taylor, Mrs. J. G.

RUTHERFORD, Mr. (fl 1807) actor HAS

RUTHERFORD, John [Mrs. Evelyn Greenleaf Sutherland] (d 1909) dramatist EA/10*

RUTHERFORD, Dame Margaret (1892-1972) English actress AAS, BE, CB, COC, ES, OC/3, PDT, TW/3, 28, WWA/5, WWT/8-15

RUTHERFORD, Mary (b 1945) Canadian actress WWT/16

RUTHERFORD, Tom (d 1973) actor TW/29

RUTHERSTON, Albert Daniel (1881/83-1953) English designer ES, WWT/5-9

RUTHVEN, Edgar (d 1909 [22]) actor EA/10*

RUTLAND, Ruth [Mrs. W. H. Crosland] (d 1892) actress EA/93*, WWT/14*

RUTLEY, Henry (d 1874 [58]) lessee EA/75*

RUTT, Mrs. Fred see Hayes, Blanche

RUTTER, Grace see Elliston, Grace

RUTTER, Joseph (fl 1635-40) dramatist CP/1-3, FGF

RUTTER, William (fl 1503) actor DA

RUTTLEDGE, Annie (d 1894) EA/95*

RUTTLEDGE, Frances [Mrs. F. Lumsden Hare] English actress GRB/1-3

RUTTY, Herbert Waring see Waring, Herbert

RUYMEN, Ayn (b 1947) American actress TW/27

RUZT-NISSEN, Grethe see Nissen, Greta

RYAN, Mr. (fl 1787) actor HAS

RYAN, Mr. (fl 1850) American actor HAS

RYAN, Belvil (d 1878 [48]) comedian EA/80*

RYAN, Ben (d 1968) performer BP/53*

RYAN, Cecil (b 1886) New Zealand actor, singer WWM

RYAN, Charlene American actress TW/26-29

RYAN, Charles V. (b 1913) American talent representative BE

RYAN, Conny (d 1963 [62]) performer BE*, BP/47*

RYAN, Dennis (d 1786) Irish actor, manager WWA/H

RYAN, Desmond (d 1868 [54]) critic EA/69*

RYAN, Dick (d 1969 [72]) performer BP/54*

RYAN, Edmon (b 1910) American actor TW/7-9, 14-15

RYAN, Grace M. (d 1972 [82]) performer BP/57*

RYAN, Herbert (d 1898 [22]) actor EA/99*

RYAN, Herbert Henry (b 1875) American editor WWM

RYAN, Irene (d 1973 [70]) actress TW/29

RYAN, Jack (d 1850 [53]) prompter, lessee EA/72*

RYAN, James (d 1875 [76]) circus proprietor EA/76*

RYAN, James E. (d 1976 [35]) performer BP/60*

RYAN, John P. (b 1938) American actor TW/26, 28-29

RYAN, Kate (d 1922 [65]) American actress BE*, BP/7*

RYAN, Lacy (1694-1760) English actor, dramatist COC, CP/1-3, DNB, GT, OC/1-3, TD/1-2

RYAN, Madge (b 1919) Australian actress WWT/14-16

RYAN, Mary (1885-1948) American actress SR, TW/5, WWT/4-6

RYAN, Michael (b 1929) American actor TW/19

RYAN, Redmond (d 1855) Irish comedian HAS

RYAN, Richard Nesbitt (d 1865 [46]) actor, manager EA/72*

RYAN, Robert (1909/13-73) American actor AAS, BE, ES, TW/10, 19, 25-27, 30, WWT/14-15

RYAN, Mrs. Robert see Cad-

walader, Jessica
RYAN, Samuel (b 1834) American
actor, stage manager HAS
RYAN, Sheila (d 1975 [54]) per-
former BP/60*
RYAN, Sophie see Eyre, Sophie
RYAN, Sue American actress
TW/1
RYAN, T. E. (d 1920) scene
artist BE*, WWT/14*
RYAN, Thomas (d 1928 [73])
comedian CDP
RYBNER, Martin Cornelius (1853-
1929) Danish composer DAB
RYDE, Will (d 1917) EA/18*
RYDELL, Charles (b 1931) Amer-
ican actor TW/21, 23
RYDER, Alfred [né Alfred Jacob
Corn] (d 1919) American actor,
director BE, TW/3, 7-13,
WWT/15-16
RYDER, Arthur W. (d 1938 [61])
American educator, translator
BE*
RYDER, Emma [Mrs. Edward
Price] (d 1889) actress EA/
90*
RYDER, G. V. M. (fl 1844-61)
American actor HAS
RYDER, Jessie Henry [Mrs. A.
D. McNeill] (d 1904 [70])
lessee EA/05*
RYDER, John (1814-85) English
actor CDP, DNB, OAA/1-2
RYDER, Mrs. John (d 1874)
EA/75*
RYDER, T. (d 1872 [61]) actor
EA/74*
RYDER, Thomas (1735-1790/91)
English actor, dramatist
CDP, CP/3, DNB, GT, TD/
1-2
RYDER, William (d 1871 [24])
musician EA/72*
RYDER, William John (d 1917)
EA/18*
RYDER, Willie (d 1899 [27])
music-hall comedian EA/00*
RYDON, Nita [Mrs. John Vil-
liers] (d 1899) actress EA/
00*
RYE, Mr. (fl 1834) property man
CDP
RYE, Daphne (b 1916) English
producer WWT/11-12
RYER, George (fl 1847-63) Amer-
ican actor, stage manager
CDP, HAS

RYERSON, Florence (b 1892)
American dramatist BE
RYERSON, Margaret see Arling-
ton, Maggie
RYES, Elizabeth (d 1797) dramatist
CP/2-3, GT
RYGA, George (b 1932) Canadian
dramatist CD
RYKEN, Mabel (d 1968 [77]) per-
former BP/53*
RYLAND, Ann (d 1907 [74]) EA/
08*
RYLAND, Cliff (fl 1895?) actor,
singer CDP
RYLAND, Jack (b 1935) American
actor TW/22, 24, 26, 29
RYLANDS, George (b 1902) English
producer, director AAS, COC,
WWT/10-16
RYLESTON, Mrs. Edward A. see
Forde, Emmie
RYLEY, Charles (d 1897) actor,
singer EA/98*
RYLEY, J. H. (d 1922 [81]) actor
BE*, WWT/14*
RYLEY, J. T. (d 1876 [49]) per-
former? EA/77*
RYLEY, Madeleine Lucette (1865-
1934) English actress, drama-
tist, singer GRB/1-4, SR,
WWS, WWT/1-7, WWW/3
RYLEY, Samuel William (1759-
1837) English dramatist CDP,
CP/3
RYMAN, Add (d 1896 [55/59])
American minstrel manager &
performer CDP
RYMER, Thomas (1641-1713) Eng-
lish dramatist CDP, CP/1-3,
GT, HP, NTH
RYNER, Mrs. H. [née Kate
Meadows] (fl 1835) actress HAS
RYSANEK, Leonie (b 1926/28)
Austrian singer CB, ES
RYSKIND, Morrie (b 1895) Ameri-
can librettist, dramatist BE,
CD, MWD, NTH, WWT/8-11
RYVES, Elizabeth see Ryes,
Elizabeth

- S -

S., Mr. see Still, John
S., E. (fl 1607) dramatist CP/1-3
S., J. dramatist CP/1-3, FGF
S., S. (fl 1616) dramatist CP/2-3,
FGF

S. , T. (fl 1671-80) dramatist
CP/3

S. , W. (fl 1619) dramatist FGF

SAAL, Alfred P. (d 1962 [70])
magician BE*

SAARI, Charles (b 1944/47)
American actor BE, TW/14

SAARINEN, Aline B. (d 1972
[58]) critic BP/57*

SABATINI, Rafael (1875-1950)
Italian/English dramatist
NTH, WWT/5-10, WWW/4

SABEL, Josephine (d 1945 [79])
American actress, singer
WWS

SABIN, David (b 1937) American
actor TW/24-26, 29

SABIN, Robert (d 1969 [57])
critic BP/53*

SABINE, Martin (b 1876) English
manager, producer WWT/8-9

SABINSON, Harvey B. (b 1924)
American press representative
BE

SABINSON, Lee (b 1911) American producing manager BE,
TW/2-8, WWT/11-12

SABLON, Jean (b 1909) French
singer, composer BE

SABOL, Dick (b 1937) American
actor TW/22

SABU (d 1963 [39]) Indian actor
BE*

SACCHETTI, Lorenzo (1759-1830)
Italian scene artist ES

SACCOMANI, Signora (fl 1833)
actress HAS

SACCONI, Rosalinda musician
CDP

SACHEVERELL, Mrs. John see
Charke, Mrs. Richard

SACHS, Ann (b 1948) American
actress TW/30

SACHS, Arthur L. (b 1913) American actor TW/3

SACHS, Leonard (b 1909) South
African actor, producer, director WWT/11-16

SACHS, Mary P. K. (d 1973
[91]) dramatist BP/58*

SACK, Nathaniel (d 1966 [84])
actor TW/23

SACK, Penelope American actress TW/4

SACKETT, Millie (b 1842) American actress HAS

SACKLER, Howard (b 1929)
American dramatist, director
CD, MH

SACKS, Joseph Leopold (1881-1952)
Russian/English manager WWT/
4-11

SACKVILLE, Thomas (1536-1608)
English dramatist COC, CP/
1-3, DNB, FGF, HP, MH, OC/
1-3

SACKVILLE, Thomas (d 1628) actor
DA

SADAKICHI, Thomatzu (fl 1867)
acrobat CDP

SADDLER, Donald (b 1920) American choreographer, director,
dancer BE, TW/7, WWT/16

SADLER, Anthony (c. 1610-c. 80)
English dramatist CP/1-3

SADLER, Dudley (b 1918) American
actor TW/1, 3

SADLER, Frank (d 1873) performer
EA/74*

SADLER, Ian (d 1971 [69]) performer BP/56*

SADLER, J. (fl 1640) dramatist
CP/2-3, FGF

SADLER, James (d 1828) aeronaut
CDP

SADLER, Mary Ann [Mrs. Thomas
Sadler] (d 1890 [54]) EA/91*

SADLER, Michael dramatist CD

SADLER, Stella see Mayhew,
Stella

SADLER, Thomas (fl 1766) dramatist CP/3

SADLER, Mrs. Thomas see
Sadler, Mary Ann

SADLER, Thomas H. (d 1893)
American comedian EA/95*

SADOFF, Fred E. (b 1926) American actor, director, producer
BE

SAEMAN, Cecelia see Paez,
Cecelia de

SAENGER, Oscar (b 1868) American
singer, teacher WWM

SAFIER, Gloria (b 1921) American
talent representative BE

SAGAL, Sara Macon (d 1975 [47])
producer/director/choreographer
BP/60*

SAGAN, Leontine (1889/95-1974)
Austrian actress, producer
BTR/74, WWT/8-11

SAGE, Mons. (fl 1859) actor HAS

SAGE, Edward (d 1969 [41]) performer BP/54*

SAGE, John Sylvester (d 1908 [55])
gymnast EA/09*

SAGE, Letitia Anne aeronaut
CDP
SAGER, Max (d 1975 [82]) BP/
60*
SAHARA, Tilly (d 1884) American
singer EA/86*
SAHL, Mort (b 1927) Canadian
comedian CB
SAIDY, Fred (b 1907) American
dramatist, director, lyricist
BE
SAINER, Arthur (b 1924) Ameri-
can dramatist, director, actor
CD
SAINT, Eva Marie (b 1924/29)
American actress BE, ES,
TW/10-15, 29
ST. ALBIN, Mr. (fl 1826?)
dancer CDP
ST. ALBYN, Alfred (d 1871)
singer CDP
ST. ALBYN, E. (d 1872) actor?
EA/73*
ST. ANGE, Josephine (d 1892)
actress, singer CDP, DP
ST. AUBIN, Mrs. (d 1895) EA/
96*
ST. AUBYN, Cpt. (d 1917 [29])
EA/18*
ST. AUBYN, Mrs. Frank see
Rorke, Mary
ST. AUBYN, Harry (d 1906)
EA/07*
ST. AUDRIE, Stella (d 1925
[49]) actress BE*, WWT/14*
ST. CASSE, Clara (b 1841)
singer CDP
ST. CLAIR, Mme. [Mary Mar-
shall] (d 1884 [42]) actress,
manager EA/85*
ST. CLAIR, F. V. (fl 1895?)
singer, composer CDP
ST. CLAIR, Ivy (d 1916) EA/17*
ST. CLAIR, Lydia (d 1970) ac-
tress TW/26
ST. CLAIR, Maurice (d 1970
[67]) performer BP/54*
ST. CLAIR, Norman (d 1910
[44]) actor EA/11*
ST. CLAIR, Robert (d 1967 [57])
dramatist BP/52*
ST. CLAIR, Rosa see Leland,
Rosa
ST. CLAIR, Sallie (1831-67)
English dancer HAS
ST. CLAIR, Stuart (d 1907 [57])
actor EA/08*
ST. CLAIR, Yvonne (d 1971

[57]) performer BP/56*
ST. CLAIR-ERSKINE, James Fran-
cis Harry see Rosslyn, Earl
of
ST. CLARE, Edith (d 1917) pro-
prietor, actress, performer
EA/18*
ST. CYR, Lillian Red Wing (d
1974 [90]) performer BP/58*
ST. CYR, Mimi (fl 1896?) singer
CDP
SAINT-DENIS, Michel (1897-1971)
French actor, dramatist, pro-
ducer AAS, BE, COC, ES,
OC/1-3, PDT, WWA/5, WWT/
8-15
ST. DENIS, Ruth [née Ruth Denis]
(1878-1968) American dancer,
choreographer CB, ES, TW/
25, WWA/5
ST. DENIS, Teddie [June Catherine
Church Denham] (b 1909) Scot-
tish actress, singer WWT/9-10
ST. GEORGE, Julia (d 1903 [79])
actress CDP
ST. GEORGE, Rosie (d 1901) ac-
tress EA/02*
ST. HELIER, Ivy [Ivy Aitchison]
(d 1971) English actress, singer
WWT/3-12
SAINTHILL, Loudon (1919-69) Tas-
manian designer COC, ES,
PDT, WWT/13-14, WWW/6
ST. JOHN, Al (d 1963 [70]) actor
BE*
ST. JOHN, Beatrice (d 1974 [60s])
performer BP/59*
ST. JOHN, Betta (b 1929) American
actress TW/5-8
ST. JOHN, Christopher Marie (d
1960) dramatist GRB/2-4,
WWT/1-12
ST. JOHN, Florence [Florence
Greig] (1854-1912) English ac-
tress, singer CDP, DP, GRB/
1-4, OAA/2, WWT/1
ST. JOHN, George Keller see
Campbell, J. C.
SAINT JOHN, Hon. Henry (fl 1789)
dramatist GT, TD/1-2
ST. JOHN, Herbert [W. H. St.
John Walter] English actor
GRB/1
ST. JOHN, Howard (1905-74)
American actor BE, TW/3,
8-14, 30, WWT/11-15
ST. JOHN, Miss J. [Mrs. J.
Dwight] (d 1897) variety per-

former EA/98*
ST. JOHN, John (d 1793) dramatist CP/3
ST. JOHN, Lily [Lilian Clara Johnson] (b 1895) English actress, singer WWT/4-7
ST. JOHN, Marco (b 1939) American actor TW/21, 23-26, 28
ST. JOHN, Margaret Florence see St. John, Florence
ST. JOHN, Marguerite (d 1940 [79]) English actress BE*, WWT/14*
ST. JOHN, Nelson B. (b c. 1865) manager SR
ST. JOHN, Norah (d 1962 [58]) performer BE*
ST. LEDGER, Annie (d 1891 [43]) EA/92*
ST. LEDGER, Catherine M. [née Williams] (fl 1799-1802) Irish actress CDP, GT, TD/1-2
ST. LEDGER, Harry (d 1906) EA/07*
ST. LEGER, Clara [Mrs. Charles Raynor] (d 1896 [38]) EA/97*
ST. LEON, Arthur M. (1821-70) French dancer, ballet master, musician CDP, ES
ST. LEON, Mr. W. (d 1867) bottle equilibrist, pantomimist EA/68*
ST. LEONARD, Florence (fl 1901-13) Canadian actress WWM
ST. LUKE, Mr. (d 1850) English actor HAS
ST. LUKE, Miss (fl 1837) actress HAS
ST. MARIE, Blanche (fl 1900?) actress, singer CDP
ST. MAUR, John (d 1888 [40]) manager EA/89*
ST. ODY, M. (fl 1853) English dancer HAS
SAINTON, Charlotte Helen (1821-85) singer CDP, DNB
SAINTON-DOLBY, Charlotte Helen see Sainton, Charlotte Helen
ST. PIERRE, Louis (d 1971 [82]) designer BP/56*
SAINT-SAENS, Camille (1836-1921) French composer GRB/1, WWM
SAINTSBURY, H. A. (1869-1939) English actor, dramatist WWT/2-8

ST. SERFE, Sir Thomas (fl 1668) Scottish dramatist CP/1-3, GT
SAINT-SUBBER, Arnold (b 1918) American producer BE, WWT/13-16
ST. VINCENT, Arthur music-hall singer CDP
SAIVI, Sig. (fl 1850) singer HAS
SAKALL, S. Z. (d 1955 [67]) Hungarian actor BE*, BP/39*
SAKAROFF, Clothide (d 1974 [80]) performer BP/58*
SAKER, Mr. actor CDP
SAKER, Ann [Mrs. Horatio Saker] (d 1885 [58]) EA/86*
SAKER, Annie (1882-1932) Scottish actress GRB/1-4, WWT/1-6
SAKER, Master C. R. (fl 1836?) actor CDP
SAKER, Edward (1831-83) English actor, manager CDP, DNB
SAKER, Mrs. Edward [Marie O'Brien] (1847-1912) Irish actress, dramatist, manager CDP, GRB/4, WWT/1
SAKER, Horace (d 1861 [34]) actor BE*, WWT/14*
SAKER, Horatio (d 1902 [54]) actor DNB
SAKER, Mrs. Horatio see Saker, Ann
SAKER, Maria [Mrs. T. G. Mortimer] (d 1902) actress BE*, EA/03*, WWT/14*
SAKER, Marie see Saker, Mrs. Edward
SAKER, Richard Henry (d 1870 [28]) actor, producer BE*, EA/71*, WWT/14*
SAKER, Rose [Mrs. Charles Hay] (d 1923) English actress DP
SAKER, William (d 1849 [59]) actor BE*, WWT/14*
SAKER, Mrs. William (d 1877 [77]) EA/78*
SAKREN, Jared (b 1950) American actor TW/29
SAKS, Gene (b 1921) American actor, director BE, WWT/15-16
SALA, Mme. (d 1860 [67]) singer CDP
SALA, Mrs. George A. (d 1885) EA/87*
SALA, George Augustus (d 1895 [67]) dramatist, journalist, critic BE*, EA/97*, WWT/14*
SALACROU, Armand (b 1899) French dramatist COC, OC/2-3

SALAMAN, Charles Kensington (d 1901 [87]) musician, composer EA/02*

SALAMAN, Malcolm C. (d 1940 [84]) critic BE*, WWT/14*

SALBERG, Derek S. (b 1912/22) English manager, stage manager AAS, WWT/14-16

SALBERG, Leon (d 1937 [62]) producer, manager BE*, WWT/14*

SALBERG, Valérie French actress GRB/2

SALE, Charles (1885-1936) American actor WWA/1, WWT/7-8

SALE, Sara [Mrs. Frank Pacey Buck] (d 1899 [30]) singer EA/00*

SALES, Sammy (d 1967 [61]) performer BP/51*

SALIG, Louis (d 1876 [25]) acting manager EA/77*

SALINGER, Conrad (d 1962 [59]) composer BE*

SALISBURY, Charles (1821-64) American actor HAS

SALISBURY, Leah (d 1975) American literary representative BE

SALKIND, Michel (d 1974 [83]) producer/director/choreographer BP/58*

SALLE, Marie (1707/10-56) French dancer ES, OC/1-2

SALLERT, Ulla Swedish actress TW/21

SALLIS, Peter (b 1921) English actor AAS, TW/22, WWT/13-16

SALMAGGI, Alfredo (d 1975 [89]) producer/director/choreographer BP/60*

SALMI, Albert (b 1928) American actor BE, TW/25

SALMON, Eliza (1787-1849) English singer DNB

SALMON, Scotty (b 1943) American actor TW/24, 28

SALMON, T. H. (d 1867 [54]) band leader EA/68*

SALMOND, Norman (1858-1914) English singer, actor GRB/2-4

SALOMON, Johann Peter (1745-1815) German/English musician CDP, DNB, ES

SALSBURY, Nathan (1846-1902) American actor, manager, showman CDP

SALT, Charles H. (d 1904) acrobat EA/05*

SALT, Jennifer (b 1944) American actress TW/26-27

SALT, Samuel (d 1890) equestrian EA/91*

SALTER, Mr. (fl 1818) actor CDP

SALTER, Henry (d 1892 [51]) variety theatre proprietor EA/93*

SALTER, Mrs. James see Rignold, Lilian

SALTERNE, George dramatist FGF

SALTIKOV-SHCHEDRIN, Mikhail Evgrafovich (1826-89) Russian dramatist OC/3

SALTOUN, Walter (d 1965 [84]) dramatist, manager, critic WWT/14*

SALTZBERG, Geraldine (d 1972 [80]) critic BP/57*

SALVI, Mlle. singer CDP

SALVI, Lorenzo (1810-79) Italian singer CDP, ES

SALVINI, Mme. (d 1868 [37]) Italian actress EA/69*

SALVINI, Alexander (1861-96) Italian actor CDP

SALVINI, Gustavo (d 1930) actor WWT/14*

SALVINI, Tommaso (1829-1916) Italian actor CDP, COC, ES, GRB/1-4, NTH, OC/1-3, SR, WWT/1-3

SALVIO, Robert (b 1942) American actor TW/23-26

SALVIONI, Sig. (fl 1855) singer HAS

SALVIONI, Enrichetta (fl 1833) singer HAS

SALZBERG, Louisa Ann [Miss L. A. Phillips] (b 1812) English actress CDP, HAS

SALZER, Eugene (d 1964 [c. 80]) musical director, conductor BE*

SAM (fl 1590?) actor DA

SAMARY, Jeanne (d 1890 [33]) actress BE*, WWT/14*

SAMARY, Marie (d 1941 [93]) actress WWT/14*

SAMEGO-BRUGNOLI, Amalia (fl early 19th cent) Italian dancer, mimist ES

SAMINSKY, Lazare (1882-1959) Russian composer WWA/3

SAMMARCO, Mario (1868/73/74-
1930) Italian singer ES,
WWA/5, WWM, WWW/3
SAMMIS, George W. (d 1927
[72]) manager BE*, BP/11*
SAMMON, Matilda (d 1898 [34])
wardrobe mistress EA/99*
SAMOILOFF, L. S. (b 1877)
Russian singer, teacher WWM
SAMPLE, Forrest (d 1975 [76])
performer BP/60*
SAMPSON, Selma (d 1965 [53])
performer BP/49*
SAMPSON, William (1590?-1636?)
dramatist CP/1-3, DNB,
FGF
SAMPSON, William (d 1922 [63])
actor BE*, BP/6*
SAMROCK, Victor (b 1907) Amer-
ican manager, producer BE
SAMS, William Raymond (d 1872
[52]) actor? EA/73*
SAMSON, George see Alex-
ander, Sir George
SAMSON, Ivan (1894-1963) Eng-
lish actor WWT/7-13
SAMUEL, Mrs. Emanuel see
Davies, Anna
SAMUEL, Joe (d 1868 [32]) dram-
atic & equestrian agent EA/
69*
SAMUEL, Leopold (d 1975 [92])
composer/lyricist BP/59*
SAMUELL, L. L. (d 1893 [35])
music-hall lessee EA/94*
SAMUELL, W. J. (d 1916) singer
EA/17*
SAMUELLS, Alexander R. mana-
ger CDP
SAMUELS, Maurice Victor (1873-
1945) American dramatist
WWA/2, WWM
SAMUELSON, Julian see Wylie,
Julian
SAMUELSON, Morris Laurence
see Wylie, Lauri
SAMWELL, W. equestrian CDP
SAMWELLS, John (d 1883 [63])
equestrian EA/84*
SAMWELLS, Mrs. John (d 1907
[95]) performer? EA/08*
SAMWELLS, Roland (d 1908 [49])
ringmaster, scene artist
EA/10*
SAMWORTH, Mrs. see Bride,
Elizabeth
SANCHEZ, Jaime (b 1938) Puerto
Rican actor TW/22, 24, 30

SANCHIOLI, Mlle. singer CDP
SAND, Inge (d 1974 [45]) performer
BP/58*
SAND, Paul (b 1935) American ac-
tor TW/20-23, 27, WWT/16
SAND, Tom Hughes (b 1927) West
Indian actor TW/8
SANDE, Walter (d 1971 [63]) per-
former BP/56*
SANDEEN, Darrell (b 1930) Amer-
ican actor TW/17, 25
SANDEMAN, Christopher (1882-
1951) dramatist WWW/5
SANDEMAN, Eleanor Brady (d 1971
[73]) performer BP/55*
SANDER, Ian American actor
TW/28
SANDERS, Albert (b 1943) Ameri-
can actor TW/25, 29-30
SANDERS, Alfred (d 1876) musician
EA/77*
SANDERS, Betty (d 1975 [53]) per-
former BP/60*
SANDERS, Byron (b 1927) Ameri-
can actor TW/12-18, 21
SANDERS, Charlotte (fl 1797)
dramatist CP/3
SANDERS, Dirk actor TW/15-18
SANDERS, Donna American actress
TW/26
SANDERS, Edward S. see Ab-
bott, Edward S.
SANDERS, Felicia (d 1975 [53])
performer BP/59*
SANDERS, George (1906-72) Rus-
sian/English actor CB, ES
SANDERS, Henry Charles (d 1879
[43]) professor of music EA/81*
SANDERS, Honey (b 1928) Ameri-
can actress TW/24, 28
SANDERS, John (d 1865 [66]) actor
EA/72*
SANDERS, Mary (fl 1885-1901)
American actress PP/3
SANDERS, Richard (b 1940) Amer-
ican actor TW/30
SANDERS, Scott (d 1956 [68]) mu-
sic-hall comedian BE*, WWT/
14*
SANDERS, William (fl 1624) actor
DA
SANDERSON, Mr. (fl 1805) actor
HAS
SANDERSON, Mrs. (d 1872) singer
EA/73*
SANDERSON, George (fl 1640) actor
DA
SANDERSON, Gregory (fl c. 1619)

actor DA
SANDERSON, Harry S. actor
 CDP
SANDERSON, James (1769?-1841?)
 musician DNB
SANDERSON, Julia [Mrs. J. T.
 Sloan] (1887-1975) American
 actress, singer BE, GRB/
 3-4, WWM, WWS, WWT/1-8
SANDERSON, Mary see Better-
 ton, Mrs. Thomas
SANDERSON, Sibyl (1865-1903)
 American singer CDP, DAB,
 SR, WWA/1, WWW/1
SANDFORD, Mr. actor, manager
 TD/2
SANDFORD, Mr. (fl 1724) dram-
 atist CP/2-3
SANDFORD, Mr. (fl 1812) Eng-
 lish actor HAS
SANDFORD, Charles J. (d 1917)
 actor EA/18*
SANDFORD, Charles V. (d 1917)
 actor EA/18*
SANDFORD, Charles W. (1796-
 1878) proprietor, lawyer
 CDP
SANDFORD, Mrs. C. W. see
 Holman, Mrs. Joseph George
SANDFORD, E. (b 1825) Ameri-
 can actor HAS
SANDFORD, Edith see Roger-
 son, Mrs. Whit
SANDFORD, Joseph J. (d 1879)
 gymnast EA/80*
SANDFORD, Marjorie (b 1910)
 English actress, singer WWT/
 10-13
SANDFORD, Samuel (fl 1660-99)
 English actor DNB, OC/1-3
SANDILANDS, George Sommerville
 (1889-1961) Scottish dramatist
 WWW/6
SANDILANDS, W. S. (fl 1881?)
 singer CDP
SANDISON, Gordon (1913-58)
 English executive WWT/11-
 12
SANDLE, Floyd (b 1913) Ameri-
 can educator BE
SANDLER, Jacob Koppel (1856-
 1931) Russian/American com-
 poser, conductor DAB
SANDLER, Jesse (d 1975 [57])
 producer/director/choreographer
 BP/59*
SANDOE, Alfred (d 1911 [46])
 actor EA/12*

SANDONI, Signora Pietro Giuseppe
 see Cuzzoni, Francesca
SANDOR, Alfred (b 1918) Hungari-
 an/American actor BE, TW/
 23-25
SANDOW, Eugene (d 1925 [58])
 Prussian athlete GRB/1
SANDROCK, Adele (d 1937 [73])
 German actress CDP
SANDS, Diana (1934-73) American
 actress AAS, BE, ES, TW/19-
 22, 24-25, 28, 30, WWT/15
SANDS, Dick (1840-1900) English
 clog dancer CDP, HAS
SANDS, Dorothy (b 1893/1900)
 American actress, director
 BE, TW/2-3, 9-17, 20, 24-26,
 WWT/13-16
SANDS, Edward (d 1887) American
 actor NYM
SANDS, George E. (d 1887) Amer-
 ican manager EA/88*
SANDS, James (fl 1605-17) actor
 DA
SANDS, Larry (d 1974 [42]) pro-
 ducer/director/choreographer
 BP/59*
SANDS, Leslie (b 1921) English
 actor, dramatist WWT/15-16
SANDS, Richard (1814-61) Ameri-
 can circus performer CDP,
 HAS
SANDS, Thomas (fl 1635) actor
 DA
SANDT, Bernhardt (fl 1600) actor
 DA
SANDY, Little [Alexander Coleman]
 (d 1903 [53]) circus clown EA/
 04*
SANDYS, George (1577-1643) Eng-
 lish dramatist CP/1-3
SANFORD, Jane (b 1943) Ameri-
 can actress TW/26, 30
SANFORD, Jim [Thomas Pynes]
 (d 1891) minstrel EA/93*
SANFORD, John L. (fl 1866)
 comedian HAS
SANFORD, Robert (1904-71) Amer-
 ican talent representative BE
SANFORD, Samuel S. (1821-1905)
 American singer, minstrel, cir-
 cus clown CDP, HAS
SAN FRANCISCO DANCERS' WORK-
 SHOP CD
SAN FRANCISCO MIME TROUPE
 CD
SANG, Leonard B. (b 1904) Amer-
 ican manager BE

SANGALLI, Rita (b 1849) Italian dancer CDP, HAS

SANGER, Alfred (d 1880 [60]) stage manager EA/81*

SANGER, Mrs. Alfred (d 1889 [69]) EA/90*

SANGER, Elizabeth [Mrs. John Sanger] (d 1893 [67]) EA/94*

SANGER, Ellen [Mrs. George Sanger] (d 1899 [67]) EA/00*

SANGER, Eugene (fl 1881) actor CDP

SANGER, Frank W. (d 1904) manager EA/05*, WWT/14*

SANGER, Fred (d 1923 [72]) performer BE*

SANGER, George (1825/26-1911) English circus manager, performer DNB, SR

SANGER, Mrs. George see Sanger, Ellen

SANGER, John (1816-89) English circus proprietor DNB, HP

SANGER, Mrs. John see Sanger, Elizabeth

SANGER, Rachel [Mrs. James Scanlan] (d 1884 [34]) actress, singer CDP

SANGER, Rachel Mary (fl 1851-79) English actress OAA/2

SANGER, William (d 1901 [74]) circus proprietor EA/02*

SANGER, Mrs. William (d 1893) EA/95*

SANGIOVANNI, A. (fl 1852) singer CDP

SANGSTER, Alfred (1880-1972) English actor, dramatist WWT/8-11

SANNA, Johnny (d 1965 [64]) performer BP/50*

SANSBURY, Vernon J. (d 1913) EA/14*

SANSOM, Mrs. Charles (d 1871) singer EA/72*

SANSONE, Charles (d 1968 [63]) composer/lyricist BP/52*

SANTANGELO, Melody (b 1946) American actress TW/28-29

SANTE, Mrs. (d 1912 [86]) EA/13*

SANTE, George Testo (d 1916 [58]) proprietor, circus & music-hall performer, gymnast EA/17*

SANTELL, Marie American actress TW/26-27, 30

SANTINI, Gabriele (b 1886)

Italian conductor ES

SANTLEY, Sir Charles (1834-1922) English singer CDP, DNB, ES, GRB/1-4, WWW/2

SANTLEY, Frederic (1887-1953) American actor, singer TW/9, WWT/7-8

SANTLEY, H. R. (d 1888) advance agent EA/89*

SANTLEY, Joseph (1889-1971) American actor, producer TW/ 28, WWT/3-10

SANTLEY, Kate (d 1923 [86]) American actress, singer, manager CDP, GRB/1-4, OAA/1-2, WWT/1-4

SANTLEY, Mabel (fl 1879) actress CDP

SANTLEY, Marie [Marie Elizabeth Day] (d 1898) actress EA/99*

SANTLEY, William (d 1891 [82]) musician EA/92*

SANTLOW, Hester see Booth, Mrs. Barton, II

SANTLY, Joseph H. (1886-1962) American performer, songwriter BE*, BP/47*

SANTORO, Dean (b 1938) American actor TW/25-27

SANYEAH, Mme. (d 1910 [68]) gymnast CDP

SAPHRINI, Mrs. see Bower, Miss E.

SAPIGNOLI, Francesco (fl 1833) singer HAS

SAPIO, Antonio (d 1868 [64]) professor of music EA/69*

SAPIO, Lewis (1792-1851) English actor CDP, OX

SAPORITI, Mme. see Codesaca, Mme.

"SAPPER" [Lieut.-Col. Cyril McNeile] (d 1937 [48]) dramatist BE*, WWT/14*

SAPPINGTON, Fay (b 1906) American actress TW/8, 22, 24, 28

SAPPINGTON, Margo (b 1947) American actress TW/26-27

SAPPIR, Gerald (b 1939) American actor TW/25

SAQUI, Mme. (d 1866 [80]) rope dancer CDP

SARACCO, Prof. inventor, dancer, teacher CDP

SARAGO, Theo (d 1970 [33]) performer BP/55*

SARANDON, Chris (b 1942) American actor TW/27-29

SARANDON, Susan (b 1946)
American actress TW/28
SARANOFF, Jules (d 1967 [80])
BP/52*
SARCIUT, Mrs. see Victor,
Mary Ann
SARDI, Vincent, Sr. (d 1969
[83]) restauranteur BP/54*
SARDI, Vincent, Jr. (b 1915)
American restauranteur, actor
BE
SARDOU, Victorien (1831-1908)
French dramatist COC, GRB/
1-4, MWD, NTH, OC/1-3
SARG, Tony (1880/82/83-1942)
English marionettist CB,
DAB, SR
SARGANO [John Holloway Bright]
(d 1892) EA/94*
SARGEANTSON, Kate see
Serjeantson, Kate
SARGENT, Mrs. (d 1889) EA/90*
SARGENT, Brent (b 1914) Amer-
ican actor TW/5-7
SARGENT, Epes (1813/14-80)
American dramatist CDP,
DAB, HJD, RJ, SR, WWA/H
SARGENT, Franklin Haven (1856-
1923) American director GRB/
3, WWM
SARGENT, Frederic[k] (b 1879)
English actor GRB/1-2, WWT/
4-8
SARGENT, Herbert C. (b 1873)
English dramatist WWT/6-8
SARGENT, H. J. (1843-96)
actor, manager, magician
CDP
SARGENT, John (fl 1785) drama-
tist CP/3
SARGENT, Sir Malcolm (1895-
1967) English conductor CB
SARGENT, Margherita (d 1964
[81]) actress TW/21
SARGENT, Mary American ac-
tress TW/1
SARGOOD, James J. (b 1875)
English conductor, pianist
GRB/1
SARIDIS, Angelo (b 1932) Greek
actor TW/25
SARINA, Mrs. (d 1883 [21])
EA/84*
SARL, Ernest James [Ernest
Sutton] (d 1887 [33]) actor
EA/88*
SARL, Sydney Claude (d 1916)
EA/17*

SARMENT, Jean (b 1897) French
actor, dramatist MWD
SARNER, Alexander (1892-1948)
English actor WWT/8-10
SARNO, James (d 1972 [62]) pub-
licist BP/57*
SARNOFF, Dorothy (b 1919) Amer-
ican singer, actress BE, TW/
5-13
SARONI [William Frederick Short]
(d 1888 [38]) musical clown
EA/90*
SARONI, Rose [Rose Bell] (d 1881
[29]) EA/82*
SARONY, Leslie (b 1897) English
actor, singer WWT/6-10
SARONY, Oliver (d 1879) propri-
etor, photographer EA/80*
SAROYAN, Lucy American actress
TW/26
SAROYAN, William (b 1908) Amer-
ican dramatist, director AAS,
BE, CB, CD, COC, ES, HJD,
MD, MH, MWD, NTH, OC/1-3,
PDT, RE, WWT/10-16
SARRACINI, Gerald (d 1957 [30])
actor TW/14
SARRATT, Mrs. Jacob Henry see
Dufour, Camilla
SARTLEE Hottentot Venus CDP
SARTORIS, Mrs. E. T. see
Kemble, Adelaide
SARTRE, Jean-Paul Charles Ay-
mard (b 1905) French dramatist
BE, CB, COC, OC/2-3
SARZEDAS, Mr. (fl 1827) actor,
stage manager HAS
SASS, Edward (d 1916 [58]) actor,
manager GRB/1-4, WWT/1-3
SASS, Mrs. Edward see Gwynne,
Emma
SASS, Enid (1889-1959) English
actress WWT/4-8
SATCHELL, Catherine Mary see
Duill, Mrs. John Lewis
SATCHELL, Susanna see Benson,
Mrs. Robert
SATTER, Gustav (b 1832) Austrian
pianist HAS
SATTIN, Lonnie American actor,
singer BE
SATZ, Lillie (d 1974 [78]) per-
former BP/58*
SAUBERE, Mr. (fl 1805) actor
HAS
SAUERS, Patricia (b 1941) Ameri-
can actress TW/23-24
SAUMAREZ, Cissie [Mrs. Arthur

Whitby] English actress, singer GRB/1-3

SAUNDERS, Mrs. (d 1875) singer EA/76*

SAUNDERS, Master (fl 1801?) equestrian CDP

SAUNDERS, Ann see Matthew, Ann

SAUNDERS, C. H. dramatist RJ

SAUNDERS, Charles (fl 1681) dramatist CP/1-3, GT

SAUNDERS, Charles H. (1818-57) American actor HAS

SAUNDERS, Charlotte (d 1899 [73]) English actress OAA/2

SAUNDERS, Clara Verrinder (d 1909 [47]) EA/10*

SAUNDERS, Dan (d 1883) music-hall manager EA/85*

SAUNDERS, Edward (d 1876) comedian EA/77*

SAUNDERS, E. G. (d 1913 [51]) producer BE*, EA/14*, WWT/14*

SAUNDERS, Elizabeth (d 1909 [90]) actress WWT/14*

SAUNDERS, Emily see Don, Lady Emilia Eliza

SAUNDERS, F. J. (d 1917) EA/18*

SAUNDERS, Florence (1890-1926) Chilean/English actress WWT/4-5

SAUNDERS, George (d 1871) comedian EA/72*

SAUNDERS, George Lemon (d 1870 [53]) dramatist EA/71*

SAUNDERS, Mrs. Heath see Hayden, Maud

SAUNDERS, Henry Hooper (d 1905 [49]) circus clown EA/06*

SAUNDERS, Henry Martin (fl 1794) dramatist CP/3

SAUNDERS, James (b 1925) English dramatist AAS, CD, CH, COC, MH, PDT, WWT/14-16

SAUNDERS, Joe see Leybourne, George

SAUNDERS, John (d 1879 [62]) comedian EA/80*

SAUNDERS, John (d 1895 [84]) dramatist BE*, EA/96*, WWT/14*

SAUNDERS, Joseph George (d 1882 [55]) dramatist EA/83*

SAUNDERS, Lanna (b 1941)

American actress TW/28-29

SAUNDERS, Madge (1894-1967) South African actress, singer WWT/4-8

SAUNDERS, Margaret (b 1686) actress DNB

SAUNDERS, Marie [Mrs. Sam Saunders] (d 1894) EA/95*

SAUNDERS, Marilyn (b 1948) American actress TW/26-29

SAUNDERS, Nicholas (b 1914) Russian actor TW/2, 26

SAUNDERS, Peter (b 1911) English producing manager BE, WWT/11-16

SAUNDERS, Sam (d 1893) EA/94*

SAUNDERS, Mrs. Sam (d 1884) EA/85*

SAUNDERS, Mrs. Sam see Saunders, Marie

SAUNDERS, William (fl c. 1517) member of the Chapel Royal DA

SAUNDERSON, Mary see Betterton, Mrs. Thomas

SAURIN, Bernard Joseph (1706-81) French dramatist OC/1-3

SAUSS, Everhart (fl 1592) actor DA

SAUTEREAU, Barry see Kent, Barry

SAVAGE, Miss (fl 1851) actress HAS

SAVAGE, Amelia Jane (d 1887) EA/88*

SAVAGE, Courtenay (1890-1946) American dramatist WWA/2

SAVAGE, David D. (d 1975 [62]) producer/director/choreographer BP/60*

SAVAGE, Mrs. E. G. see Gilbert, Lizzie

SAVAGE, George (b 1904) American educator, dramatist BE

SAVAGE, Henry Wilson (1859/65-1927) American manager DAB, SR, WWA/1, WWM, WWT/2-5

SAVAGE, J. (fl 1707) translator CP/3

SAVAGE, Jerome (fl 1575-79) actor DA

SAVAGE, John (1792-1834) West Indian actor HAS

SAVAGE, John (1828-88) Irish dramatist WWA/H

SAVAGE, Mrs. John [Elizabeth White] actress HAS

SAVAGE, John Dawson (d 1879

[66]) custodian EA/80*
SAVAGE, Rafe DA
SAVAGE, Richard (1697-1743)
English dramatist CP/1-3,
DNB, GT, HP
SAVALAS, Telly (b 1924?) Amer-
ican actor CB
SAVAN, Bruce (b 1927) American
talent representative BE
SAVELLA, Marcia (b 1947) Amer-
ican actress TW/30
SAVEREY, Abraham (fl 1604-06)
actor DA
SAVERY, Marion Castleray (d
1967 [62]) performer BP/52*
SAVIGNY, Mr. (fl 1770) actor
CDP
SAVILE, Geoffrey (d 1969 [87])
performer BP/54*
SAVILE, Mrs. J. H. see
Rhodes, Marie
SAVILL, Arthur (fl 1631) actor
DA
SAVILL, Ethel actress GRB/1
SAVILLE, Alfred (d 1885 [72])
actor EA/86*
SAVILLE, Edmund Faucit (1811-
57) actor CDP
SAVILLE, Mrs. E. Faucit [Miss
Grant] (d 1879) actress, pro-
ducer BE*, EA/80*, WWT/
14*
SAVILLE, Eliza Helena (fl 1870-
79) actress OAA/2
SAVILLE, Helena see Faucit,
Helen
SAVILLE, Henry Faucit (d 1871
[26]) dramatist EA/72*
SAVILLE, J. F. (d 1853 [70])
manager, dramatist EA/72*
SAVILLE, J. Faucit (d 1855
[48]) actor BE*, WWT/14*
SAVILLE, Mrs. J. Faucit (d
1889 [77]) actress, producer,
manager BE*, EA/90*,
WWT/14*
SAVILLE, John (fl 1603) drama-
tist CP/3, FGF
SAVILLE, Kate (d 1922) actress
OAA/2
SAVILLE, May (b 1846) Canadian
actress HAS
SAVILLE, T. G. (d 1934 [31])
actor BE*, WWT/14*
SAVINA, Maria (d 1915 [61])
actress BE*, WWT/14*
SAVINO, Domenico (d 1973 [91])
composer/lyricist BP/58*

SAVINO, Frank (b 1936) American
actor TW/26
SAVO, Jimmy (1895-1960) American
actor TW/2-12, 17, WWT/9-11
SAVOIR, Alfred (d 1934 [51]) dra-
matist WWT/14*
SAVORY, Gerald (b 1909) English
actor, dramatist AAS, MD,
PDT, WWT/9-16
SAVORY, Kenneth see Douglas,
Kenneth
SAVOY, Bert (d 1923 [35]) Ameri-
can comedian BE*, BP/8*
SAVOY, Harry (d 1974 [76]) per-
former BP/59*
SAWFORD, Mr. (b 1818) actor
CDP
SAWFORD, Samuel (d 1891 [81])
EA/92*
SAWIN, George Arthur (b 1842)
American actor, prompter HAS
SAWIN, Mrs. George Arthur [Katie
Gardner] (b 1845) American ac-
tress, dancer HAS
SAWYER, Carl (b 1921) American
producer, manager BE
SAWYER, Charles P. (d 1935 [80])
American critic BE*, BP/19*
SAWYER, Dorie (b 1897) English
actress WWT/6-8
SAWYER, Frank (d 1895 [32]) vari-
ety performer EA/96*
SAWYER, Ivy (b 1896/97) English
actress, singer WWT/4-8
SAWYER, Jeanette (d 1971) publi-
cist BP/56*
SAWYER, Laura (d 1970 [85]) per-
former BP/55*
SAWYER, Lemuel (d 1844) Ameri-
can dramatist EAP, RJ
SAWYER, William (b 1828) English
dramatist EA/68
SAWYER, William Kingston (d
1882 [54]) dramatist EA/83*
SAXE, Serge (d 1967 [67]) com-
poser/lyricist BP/52*
SAXE, Templer [or Templar]
(1866/68-1935) English singer,
actor WWM, WWS
SAXE, Thomas, Jr. (d 1975 [72])
actor? executive? BP/60*
SAXON, Kate (d 1863 [36]) lecturer,
actress CDP, HAS
SAXON, Marie (d 1941 [37]) American actress BE*, BP/26*
SAXON, Thomas A. [Thomas Ell-
more] (fl 1867-69) actor HAS
SAXTON, Luther (b 1916) American

actor TW/1-3

SAYAO, Bidu (b 1906?) Brazilian singer CB

SAYERS, Dorothy L. (1893-1957) English dramatist DNB, ES, HP, MD, MWD, WWA/3, WWT/9-12, WWW/5

SAYERS, Frank (fl 1790) dramatist CP/3

SAYERS, Harry (d 1934 [77]) producer, songwriter BE*

SAYERS, Tom (1826-65) clown, pugilist CDP

SAYLER, Oliver Martin (1887-1958) American critic TW/15, WWA/3, WWT/5-11

SAYLOR, Sid (d 1962 [67]) performer BE*

SAYRE, Jeffrey (d 1974 [73]) performer BP/59*

SAYRE, Theodore Burt (1874-1954) American dramatist GRB/2-4, WWA/3, WWS, WWT/1-7

SBRIGLIA, Giovanni (fl 1859) singer CDP

SCACCIATI, Bianca (1894-1948) Italian singer ES

SCAIFE, Gillian (d 1976) Turkish/English actress WWT/3-11

SCALA, Gia (d 1972 [38]) performer BP/56*

SCALCHI, Sofia (1850-1922) Italian singer CDP, ES

SCALES, Caroline see Miskel, Caroline

SCALES, Prunella [née Illingworth] (b 1932) English actress WWT/15-16

SCALLAN, Miss see Stoneall, Mrs.

SCAMMELL, Terence (b 1937) English actor TW/21, 24

SCANLAN, James (d 1909 [76]) manager, singer EA/10*, WWT/14*

SCANLAN, Mrs. James see Sanger, Rachel

SCANLAN, James C. (d 1897) actor, stage manager EA/98*

SCANLAN, James F. (d 1973 [51]) publicist BP/58*

SCANLAN, John (b 1924) American actor TW/24-25

SCANLAN, William J. (1856-98) American actor, singer, songwriter CDP, SR

SCANLON, William J. see

Scanlan, William J.

SCAPILLON freak CDP

SCARBOROUGH, Earl of (d 1969 [72]) former Lord Chamberlain BP/54*

SCARBOROUGH, George (b 1875) American dramatist WWA/5, WWT/4-11

SCARDINO, Don (b 1949) American actor TW/30

SCARDON, Paul (d 1954 [79]) actor, director BE*

SCARIA, Emil (1838-86) Austrian singer ES

SCARISBRICK, Mrs. [née M. Whitnall] (d 1874 [45]) singer EA/75*

SCARISBRICK, Alice Mary (d 1912) actress EA/13*

SCARISBRICK, C. J. (d 1918) EA/19*

SCARLETT, John (fl 1605) actor DA

SCARLETT, Kathleen (b 1943) American actress TW/24

SCARLETT, Richard (d 1609) actor DA

SCARPINATI, Nicholas (b 1944) American actor TW/30

SCATES, Fred L. (d 1900 [45]) actor EA/01*

SCATES, Joseph (d 1899 [80]) professor of music EA/01*

SCAWEN, John (fl 1773-90) dramatist CP/3, GT, TD/1-2

SCHAAF, Helen (fl 1851) musician? HAS

SCHAAL, Richard American actor TW/23, 27

SCHACHT, Sam (b 1936) American actor TW/25-27, 29-30

SCHACHTER, Leon (d 1974 [74]) performer BP/59*

SCHADER, Freddie (d 1962 [77]) press representative, journalist BE*

SCHADLEUTNER, Sebastian (fl 1623) actor DA

SCHAEFER, George (b 1920) American director, producer BE, CB, WWT/14-16

SCHAEFER, Louis (b 1931) American actor TW/29-30

SCHÄFER, Mrs. Albert see Schäfer, Lily

SCHAFER, John K. (d 1970 [51]) composer/lyricist BP/55*

SCHÄFER, Lily [Mrs. Albert

Schäfer] (d 1903 [22]) EA/04*
SCHAFER, Milton (b 1920) American composer, lyricist BE
SCHAFER, Natalie (b 1912) American actress BE, TW/ 14-19, 24, 30, WWT/10-11
SCHALK, Franz (1863-1931) Austrian conductor ES
SCHALKENBACH, J. B. (d 1910 [85]) inventor of electric orchestra EA/11*
SCHALLERT, William (b 1925) American actor TW/27
SCHALLMAN, Sidney M. (d 1972 [82]) agent BP/57*
SCHARF, Erwin (d 1972 [71]) designer BP/56*
SCHARF, Henry (1822-87) English actor HAS, NYM
SCHARF, Herman (d 1963 [62]) performer BE*
SCHARY, Doré (b 1905) American dramatist, director, producer, actor AAS, BE, CD, MWD, WWT/13-16
SCHATTNER, Meyer (b 1911) American publisher BE
SCHATZ, Johanna (fl 1888) German actress CDP
SCHAUFFLER, Elsie T. (d 1935 [47]) American dramatist BE*, BP/20*, WWT/14*
SCHEAR, Robert (b 1936) American stage manager BE
SCHECHNER, Richard (b 1934) American producer, director, scholar BE, WWT/15-16
SCHECHTMAN, Saul (b 1924) American musical director, composer BE
SCHEERER, Bob (b 1928) American actor TW/5-15
SCHEERER, Maud (d 1961 [80]) American actress TW/13-15, 18
SCHEFF, Fritzi [Baroness Fritz von Bardeleben] (1879/ 80-1954) Austrian actress, singer GRB/2-4, SR, TW/1, 3-10, WWA/3, WWM, WWS, WWT/1-8
SCHEIDEMANTEL, Karl (1859-1923) German singer ES
SCHEIDER, Roy R. (b 1935) American actor TW/22, 25, 27
SCHEINFELD, Lou (d 1974 [72]) lawyer BP/59*

SCHELL, Maximilian (b 1930) Austrian actor BE, CB, TW/26
SCHELLER, Marie (fl 1858-64) German actress HAS
SCHELLOW, Erich (b 1915) German actor WWT/14
SCHENCK, Joseph (1892-1930) American variety performer, actor SR
SCHENCK, Nicholas (d 1969) Russian/American? executive WWA/5
SCHENELING, Gertrude Elizabeth see Mara, Gertrude Elizabeth
SCHENK, Frances Victoria see Day, Frances
SCHENK, Al (d 1966 [61]) performer BP/51*
SCHENKER, Joel (b 1903) American producer BE
SCHEPARD, Eric talent representative BE
SCHERER, Susan (b 1948) American actress TW/30
SCHERTZINGER, Victor (d 1941 [52]) composer, conductor WWT/14*
SCHEUER, Philip (b 1902) American critic, editor BE
SCHEVILL, James (b 1920) American dramatist CD
SCHIAPARELLI, Elsa (d 1973 [83]) designer BP/58*
SCHIESKE, Alfred (d 1970 [61]) performer BP/55*
SCHIFF, David (d 1917) actor, minstrel SR
SCHIFFMAN, Frank (d 1974 [80]) operator BP/58*
SCHILDKRAUT, Joseph (1895/96-1964) Austrian actor AAS, BE, CB, ES, NTH, TW/2-18, 20, WWA/4, WWT/5-13
SCHILDKRAUT, Rudolf (1862-1930) German actor ES, SR, WWT/2
SCHILLER, Friedrich von (1759-1805) German dramatist COC
SCHILLER, Leon (1887-1954) Polish director COC
SCHILLER, Mrs. Max see Guilbert, Yvette
SCHILLING, Berthe-Agnès-Lisette see Bréval, Lucienne
SCHINDLER, Ellen (b 1942) American actress TW/28-29
SCHINDLER, Kurt (1882-1935) German composer, conductor DAB

SCHINHAN, Jan Philip (d 1975
[87]) composer/lyricist BP/
59*
SCHINK, A. (fl 1798) translator
CP/3
SCHINOTTI, Mr. actor HAS
SCHINOTTI, Mrs. (d 1829 [22])
actress HAS
SCHIOTZ, Aksel (1906-75) Danish
singer CB
SCHIPA, Tito (1888-1965) Italian
singer ES, WWA/4
SCHIPPERS, Thomas (1930-77)
American conductor CB, ES
SCHIRMER, Albert (b 1790)
German actor CDP
SCHIRMER, Gus, Jr. (b 1918)
American director, talent
representative BE
SCHISGAL, Murray (b 1926)
American dramatist BE, CB,
CD, CH, ES, MH, MWD,
PDT, WWT/15-16
SCHLAMME, Martha (b 1930?)
Austrian actress, singer CB
SCHLANGER, Ben (1904-71)
American architect, lecturer
BE
SCHLEE, Robert (b 1938) Amer-
ican actor TW/29
SCHLENTER, Dr. Paul (d 1916
[62]) producer, actor, manager
BE*, WWT/14*
SCHLESINGER, Florence Augusta
(d 1906) EA/07*
SCHLESINGER, John (b 1926)
English director CB, WWT/
15-16
SCHLESINGER, Isidore (d 1949
[78]) theatre owner & manager
WWT/14*
SCHLETTER, Annie (d 1944) ac-
tress BE*, WWT/14*
SCHLISSEL, Jack (b 1922) Amer-
ican manager BE
SCHMEISSER, Martin (d 1878
[29]) musician EA/79*
SCHMELING, Walter B. (d 1973
[73]) performer BP/58*
SCHMERTS, Robert W. (d 1975
[77]) composer/lyricist BP/
60*
SCHMIDT, Art (d 1969 [68])
public relations BP/54*
SCHMIDT, Charles A. (b 1923)
American educator BE
SCHMIDT, Douglas W. (b 1942)
American designer WWT/

15-16
SCHMIDT, Harvey (b 1939) Ameri-
can composer BE
SCHMUCK, A. (d 1871) musical
director EA/72*
SCHNABEL, Stephan (b 1912) Ger-
man actor TW/9, 11-15, 22,
25-26, 28-29, WWT/16
SCHNEE, Charles (d 1962 [46])
dramatist BP/47*
SCHNEE, Thelma actress WWT/
10-12
SCHNEEMANN, Carolee kinetic
theatre works CD
SCHNEIDEMAN, Robert Ivan (b
1926) American educator, di-
rector BE
SCHNEIDER, Alan (b 1917) Rus-
sian/American actor AAS, BE,
CB, ES, WWT/14-16
SCHNEIDER, Gunther see Ar-
nold, Edward
SCHNEIDER, Hortense (1833-1920)
French singer ES
SCHNEIDER, Stanley (d 1975 [45])
producer/director/choreographer
BP/59*
SCHNIEBER, Dolph J. (fl 1873?)
composer, actor, singer CDP
SCHNITZER, Robert (b 1906) ad-
ministrator, educator, actor
BE
SCHNITZLER, Arthur (d 1931
[69]) Austrian dramatist BP/
16*, WWT/14*
SCHOEFFEL, John B. (d 1918)
impresario SR
SCHOEN, Judy (b 1941) American
actress TW/25, 29-30
SCHOENFELD, William C. (d 1969
[75]) composer/lyricist BP/53*
SCHOFIELD, Alfred (d 1906 [37])
musician EA/07*
SCHOFIELD, Dick (d 1903 [48])
music-hall performer EA/04*
SCHOFIELD, James A. (d 1903)
contortionist EA/05*
SCHOFIELD, Johnny (d 1921 [65])
actor, minstrel BE*, WWT/
14*
SCHOFIELD, Laura [Mrs. William
Routledge] (d 1894) music-hall
performer EA/95*
SCHOFIELD, Robert W. (d 1970
[69]) manager BP/55*
SCHOFIELD, William (d 1901 [40])
EA/02*
SCHOLES, Charles Henry [Charles

Henry Duval] (d 1883 [52])
lessee EA/84*

SCHOLEY, Anne see Hield,
Anne

SCHOLL, Danny (b 1921) American actor TW/2-3, 6

SCHOMBERG, Ralph (d 1792 [78])
dramatist CP/2-3

SCHOMER, Nahum Meir (1849-
1905) Russian/American dramatist DAB

SCHONBERG, Rosalyn (d 1973
[60]) critic BP/58*

SCHONCEIT, Louis (d 1970 [74])
ticket agent BP/54*

SCHONTHAN, Franz von (d 1913)
German dramatist SR

SCHOOLCRAFT, Alfreda see
Chippendale, Alfreda

SCHOOLCRAFT, Luke (1847-93)
minstrel CDP

SCHOOLER, Lee (d 1975 [52])
publicist BP/60*

SCHOPRGER, James (d 1884
[56]) actor EA/85*

SCHORR, Friedrich (1888-1953)
Hungarian singer CB, ES,
WWW/5

SCHOTT, Angie actress, dramatist CDP

SCHOTT, Helena Cecile see
Ernstone, Helena Cecile

SCHRADER, Frederick Franklin
(1857/59-1943) German/Amer-
ican critic, dramatist WWA/
2, WWM, WWS, WWT/3

SCHRATT, Katharina (d 1940
[84]) Austrian actress CDP,
SR

SCHREINER, Wilfred P. (d 1901
[28]) music-hall agent EA/02*

SCHRIFT, Shirley see Winters,
Shelley

SCHROCK, Robert (b 1945)
American actor TW/27-28

SCHRODER, Friedrich (d 1972
[62]) composer/lyricist BP/
57*

SCHRODER, Friedrich Ludwig
(1744-1816) German actor
OC/1-3

SCHRODER-DEVRIENT, Wil-
helmine (1804-60) German
singer ES

SCHROEDER, Mme. (d 1868
[87]) German actress EA/
69*

SCHROEDER, Michael (b 1943)

Australian actor TW/24

SCHROER, Joseph (b 1943) American actor TW/25

SCHROTT, Eugene (d 1973 [62])
publicist BP/58*

SCHUBERT, Georgina (d 1878)
singer EA/80*

SCHUBERT, Vivian Curtis (d 1967
[75]) performer BP/52*

SCHUDY, Frank (d 1963 [59])
manager BE*

SCHUENZEL, Reinhold (d 1954
[68]) German actor, director
TW/11

SCHULBERG, B. P. (1892-1957)
American producer BE*

SCHULBERG, Budd (b 1914) American dramatist, producer, librettist BE, CD, ES

SCHULMAN, Arnold (b 1925) American dramatist BE

SCHULMAN, Max (d 1964 [65])
performer BP/49*

SCHULT, Minnie (fl 1886?) singer
CDP

SCHULTZ, Cecelia (d 1971 [92])
impresario BP/55*

SCHULTZ, Jack (b 1936) American
actor TW/29-30

SCHULTZ, Michael A. (b 1938)
American director WWT/15-16

SCHULTZ, William H. (b 1889)
American actor EA/90*

SCHULZ, Fritz (d 1972 [76]) German actor BP/57*, WWT/16*

SCHULZE, Herr (d 1876) entertainer EA/77*

SCHUMAN, William Howard (b
1910) American composer, educator BE, ES

SCHUMANN, Elisabeth (1888-1952)
German/American singer ES,
WWW/5

SCHUMANN, Joseph (d 1870) actor? EA/71*

SCHUMANN, Walter (1913-58)
American composer, conductor
BE*

SCHUMANN-HEINK, Ernestine
(1861-1936) Austrian/American
singer DAB, ES, WWA/1,
WWM, WWS

SCHUMANN-HEINK, Henry (b
1886) German actor WWM

SCHUMER, Henry (b 1914) American hauler, producer BE

SCHUMER, Yvette (b 1921) American manager, producer BE

SCHUNZEL, Reinhold (b 1886)
German actor TW/3, 5-6

SCHUSTER, Milton (d 1975 [92])
booking agent BP/60*

SCHUTTE, Ethel see Shutta,
Ethel

SCHUYLER, Philip (b 1921) American actor TW/6

SCHWAB, Laurence (1893-1951)
American dramatist, producing
manager TW/7, WWT/6-11

SCHWANNECKE, Ellen (d 1972)
performer BP/57*

SCHWARTZ, Abe (d 1963 [75])
composer, conductor BE*

SCHWARTZ, Arthur (b 1900/02)
American composer, producer
BE, WWT/7-16

SCHWARTZ, Delmore (1913-66)
American dramatist WWA/4

SCHWARTZ, Evgeny Lvovich
see Shwartz, Evgeny Lvovich

SCHWARTZ, Ida (d 1976 [80s])
performer BP/60*

SCHWARTZ, Jean (1878-1956)
Hungarian/American composer
WWT/6-11

SCHWARTZ, Maurice (1888/89/
90-1960) Russian/American
actor, manager, director, producer COC, CB, ES, NTH,
OC/1-3, TW/16, WWA/4,
WWT/6-12

SCHWARTZ, Oscar see Shaw,
Oscar

SCHWARTZ, Phil (d 1964 [74])
composer/lyricist BP/49*

SCHWARTZ, Ruth (b 1908) American executive, lecturer BE

SCHWARTZ, Stephen L. (b 1948)
American composer WWT/16

SCHWARTZ, Wendie Lee (d 1968
[45]) performer BP/53*

SCHWARZ, Emil (1880-1946)
American impresario ES

SCHWARZKOPF, Elisabeth (b
1915) Polish/English singer
CB, ES

SCHWEID, Mark (d 1969 [78])
actor TW/26

SCHWEIGHOFER, Felix (fl 1900)
German actor CDP

SCHWEYER, Emil (1880-1947)
showman SR

SCHWEZOFF, Igor (b 1904)
Russian dancer, choreographer
ES

SCHYMACHER, Eli (d 1975 [87])

theatrical mover BP/59*

SCIORTINO, Pat (b 1951) American
actor TW/28

SCOBIE, Lizzie [Mrs. J. B. Gor-
don] (d 1912) actress EA/13*

SCOFIELD, Paul (b 1922) English
actor AAS, BE, CB, COC,
ES, OC/2-3, PDT, TW/20,
WWT/11-16

SCOGIN, Robert (b 1937) American
actor TW/26

SCOGNAMIGLIO, Vincent see
Gardenia, Vincent

SCORDLEY, Jack (d 1973 [59])
performer BP/58*

SCOTT, Miss (fl 1829) actress
CDP

SCOTT, Mrs. A. see Ethair,
Emily

SCOTT, A. C. (b 1909) English
educator, writer BE

SCOTT, Agnes Elliot (fl 1900s)
actress WWM, WWS

SCOTT, Allan (b 1909) American
dramatist, producer BE

SCOTT, Arthur (d 1968 [66])
secretary BP/52*

SCOTT, Bonnie (b 1941) American
actress, singer, dancer BE

SCOTT, Bruce (b 1947) American
actor TW/25, 27

SCOTT, Mrs. Clement see
Scott, Isabel

SCOTT, Clement William (1841-
1904) English critic, dramatist
COC, DNB, ES, GRB/1, OC/
1-3, WWW/1

SCOTT, Clifford B. see Bruce,
Clifford

SCOTT, Cyril (1866-1946) Irish
actor GRB/2-4, TW/2, WWM,
WWS, WWT/1-9

SCOTT, Dorothy [Griffiths] (b
1884) English actress GRB/1-2

SCOTT, Ellen Jane [Mrs. William
Scott] (d 1905 [65]) EA/06*

SCOTT, Eric English actor GRB/
1-3

SCOTT, Frances Emily [Mrs.
Walter Egerton] (d 1893) EA/
94*

SCOTT, George (d 1909) English
manager GRB/1-4

SCOTT, George C. (b 1927) American actor AAS, BE, CB, ES,
TW/14-20, 24-25, 29-30, WWT/
14-16

SCOTT, George Henry (d 1910

[29]) EA/11*

SCOTT, Gertrude [Mrs. Norman McKinnell] (d 1951) English actress GRB/3-4, WWT/1-5

SCOTT, Hal (d 1969 [73]) performer BP/54*

SCOTT, Harold (1891-1964) English actor WWT/5-13

SCOTT, Harold (b 1935) American actor BE, TW/24-25, 27

SCOTT, Harry (d 1947 [67]) English actor GRB/1-3

SCOTT, Hazel (b 1920) West Indian singer CB

SCOTT, Helena American actress, singer BE

SCOTT, Henri (1876-1942) American singer WWA/2

SCOTT, Isabel [Mrs. Clement Scott] (d 1890) EA/91*

SCOTT, Ivy (d 1947 [61]) actress TW/1, 3

SCOTT, Mrs. James see Scott, May

SCOTT, James M. (d 1849) actor, manager CDP

SCOTT, Jane (d 1899) EA/00*

SCOTT, Jay Hutchinson (b 1924) English designer ES, WWT/15-16

SCOTT, Jeannie see Ford, Mrs. Martin

SCOTT, Mrs. Joe G. see Morley, Charlotte

SCOTT, John (fl 1503-28) actor DA

SCOTT, John (d 1912 [57]) circus proprietor EA/13*

SCOTT, Mrs. John see Scott, Nellie

SCOTT, John see Pickles, Little

SCOTT, John M. ["Long Tom Coffin"] (d 1849) American actor HAS

SCOTT, John Randolph (1808-56) American actor CDP, HAS, WWA/H

SCOTT, Mrs. John R[andolph] (fl 1851) American actress HAS

SCOTT, Joshua (d 1893 [46]) music-hall proprietor EA/94*

SCOTT, Kay (d 1971 [43]) composer/lyricist BP/55*

SCOTT, Kevin (b 1928) American actor TW/10-13

SCOTT, Lea American actress

TW/28

SCOTT, Leslie (d 1969 [48]) performer BP/54*

SCOTT, Louie [Mrs. Frank S. Strickland] (d 1908 [42]) actress EA/09*

SCOTT, Malcolm (d 1929 [57]) comedian BE*, WWT/14*

SCOTT, Margaret Clement actress GRB/3-4, WWT/1

SCOTT, Margaretta (b 1912) English actress AAS, WWT/7-16

SCOTT, Martha (b 1914) American actress BE, ES, TW/1-8, 10-22, WWT/10-16

SCOTT, May [Mrs. James Scott] (d 1884 [64]) EA/85*

SCOTT, Nan (d 1970 [72]) performer BP/55*

SCOTT, Nellie [Mrs. George Elliott] (d 1890 [33]) music-hall singer EA/91*

SCOTT, Nellie [Mrs. John Scott] (d 1906 [47]) EA/07*

SCOTT, Noel (1889/90-1956) English dramatist WWT/6-12, WWW/5

SCOTT, Norman (1928-68) American singer WWA/5

SCOTT, Peter (b 1932) English actor WWT/11

SCOTT, Pippa (b 1935) American actress BE, TW/13-16

SCOTT, Richard L. (d 1962 [36]) performer BE*

SCOTT, Robert (d 1871 [36]) clown EA/72*

SCOTT, Robert Adrian (d 1972 [61]) producer/director/choreographer BP/57*

SCOTT, Rosemary (b 1914) English actress WWT/9-14

SCOTT, Sam (d 1841 [27]) American diver EA/72*

SCOTT, Seret (b 1949) American actress TW/30

SCOTT, Stephen (b 1928) English actor TW/26, 28

SCOTT, Steve (b 1949) American actor TW/29-30

SCOTT, Thomas (fl 1696-97) dramatist CP/1-3, GT

SCOTT, Thomas (fl 1793) dramatist CP/3

SCOTT, Tom (b 1912) American singer, composer CB

SCOTT, Mrs. W. (d 1907) EA/08*

SCOTT, Walter (fl 1799) Scottish

translator CP/3
SCOTT, Sir Walter (1771-1832)
Scottish dramatist HP, SR
SCOTT, Walter (d 1909 [66])
circus proprietor EA/10*
SCOTT, Mrs. Walter see Morrell, Millie
SCOTT, Walter, Jr. (d 1896
[15]) EA/97*
SCOTT, Cpt. W. E. (d 1893 [25])
EA/94*
SCOTT, Mrs. William see
Scott, Ellen Jane
SCOTT, William Hamilton (d
1886 [36]) musician EA/87*
SCOTT, Winnie (b 1883) English
actress, dancer GRB/1
SCOTT, W. T. (d 1899 [58]) musician EA/00*
SCOTT, Zachary (1914-65) American actor TW/15-16, 22
SCOTT-DALGLEISH, Mrs. D.
see Brooke, Marie
SCOTT-FISHE, Mr. (d 1898) actor, singer EA/99*
SCOTT-GATTY, Sir A. (d 1918
[71]) EA/19*
SCOTT-GATTY, Alexander (1876-
1937) English actor WWM,
WWT/2-8
SCOTTI, Antonio (1866/68-1936)
Italian singer ES, WWA/1
SCOTTI, Joe (d 1972 [57]) performer BP/56*
SCOTT-SIDDONS, Mary Frances
(1844-96) Indian/English actress CDP, HAS, OAA/2
SCOTT-SIDDONS, Sarah (d 1896)
actress OAA/1, SR
SCOTT-SMITH, Peter (b 1932)
English actor TW/6
SCOTT-WARING, Mrs. see
Esten, Harriet Pye
SCOULER, Willie (d 1892 [36])
EA/93*
SCOURBY, Alexander (b 1913)
American actor BE, CB,
TW/23, 28, WWT/15-16
SCOVEL, Chevalier (b 1852)
American singer, actor DP
SCOVILLE, William H. (d 1858)
actor HAS
SCRACE, Miss (fl 1784) actress
CDP
SCRAGGS, William Beckwith (d
1886) music-hall proprietor
EA/87*
SCRASE, Patty Ann see Bates,

Mrs. James
SCRIBE, Eugène (1791-1861) French
dramatist COC, OC/3
SCRIBNER, Samuel A. (d 1941 [82])
American manager BE*, BP/
26*
SCROPPO, Dennis (b 1940) Italian
actor TW/17
SCRYMGEOUR, Lizzie (d 1878)
musician EA/80*
SCUDAMORE, Frank A. (d 1904
[56]) dramatist, actor BE*,
EA/05*, WWT/14*
SCUDAMORE, Margaret (1884-1958)
English actress WWT/5-12
SCUDDER, John proprietor CDP
SCUDERY, Georges de (1601-67)
French dramatist OC/3
SCULLION, James H. J. (d 1920)
treasurer BE*, BP/5*
SCULLY, Barbara singer, actress
TW/1
SCULLY, Frank (d 1964 [72])
columnist BP/49*
SCULLY, Tim (d 1897) music-hall
performer EA/98*
SCULTHORPE, F. (d 1916) musician EA/17*
SCUTT, Charles E. (b 1868) English business manager, actor
GRB/1
SEABERT, Charles F. (c. 1836-87)
actor NYM
SEABROOK, Jeremy (b 1939) English dramatist CD
SEABROOKE, Thomas (fl 1629)
actor DA
SEABROOKE, Thomas Q. [Thomas
Quigley] (1860-1913) American
actor, singer CDP, GRB/2-4,
SR, WWA/1, WWS, WWT/1
SEABROOKE, Mrs. Thomas Q.
see Crox, Elvia
SEABROOKE, Mrs. Thomas Q.
see Lowrie, Jeanette
SEABURY, Ynez (d 1973 [65])
performer BP/57*
SEACOMBE, Dorothy (b 1905) English actress WWT/6-9
SEADER, Richard (b 1923) American manager, musician BE
SEAFORTH, Harriet, Countess of
(d 1779) actress CDP
SEAGLE, Oscar (1877-1945) American singer WWA/2
SEAGRAM, Wilfrid (1884-1938)
English actor WWT/5-8
SEAL, Miss see Bellamy, Mrs.

SEAL, David Abbey (d 1898)
circus jester EA/99*

SEAL, Elizabeth (b 1933) Italian/
English actress, dancer,
singer AAS, BE, WWT/13-16

SEALBY, Mabel (b 1885) English
actress, singer WWT/3-8

SEALBY, Walter (d 1904 [43])
actor, manager EA/05*,
WWT/14*

SEALBY, Mrs. Walter see
Taylor, Agnes

SEALE, Douglas (b 1913) English
director, actor AAS, BE,
WWT/12-16

SEALE, Kenneth (b 1916) English
newspaper executive WWT/16

SEALLY, John (b c. 1747) English dramatist CP/3

SEAMAN, Isaac (d 1923 [88])
critic BE*, WWT/14*

SEAMAN, Julia (1837-1909) actress CDP

SEAMAN, Sir Owen (1861-1936)
critic GRB/2-4, WWT/1-8

SEAMAN, William (d 1883 [74])
actor EA/85*

SEAMAN, Mrs. William (d
1906 [94]) actress EA/07*

SEAMON, Helen (b 1929) American actress TW/6

SEAMORE, T. F. see Sneath,
Thomas F.

SEARELLE, Luscombe (d 1907
[47]) actor, singer, dramatist
GRB/3

SEARLE, Caroline (b 1799) English actress, dancer CDP,
OX

SEARLE, Mrs. C. F. (d 1880)
actress? EA/81*

SEARLE, Cyril (1840-87) English actor CDP, NYM

SEARLE, Mrs. Cyril see Eytinge, Rose

SEARLE, Eliza [Mrs. William
Searle] (d 1886) EA/87*

SEARLE, Kate [Mrs. Harry
Fischer] (d 1892) actress EA/
93*

SEARLE, Louise actress, singer
CDP

SEARLE, Townley [W. F. D.
Townley-Searle] (b 1882)
English actor GRB/1

SEARLE, Walter (d 1885) comedian EA/86*

SEARLE, William (d 1864 [49])

comedian EA/72*, WWT/14*

SEARLE, Willis (b 1857) English
actor EA/97, GRB/1

SEARS, Heather (b 1935) English
actress WWT/15-16

SEARS, Zelda (1873-1935) American actress WWA/1, WWM,
WWT/1-7

SEATON, John (d 1875) master of
ceremonies EA/76*

SEATON, Mrs. R. J. see
Clifford, Marie

SEATON, Scott (d 1968 [97]) performer BP/53*

SEAWELL, Donald R. American
producer, publisher WWT/15-16

SEBASTIAN (b 1837) Italian circus
performer HAS

SEBASTIAN, Dorothy (d 1957 [52])
American actress BE*, BP/41*

SEBASTIAN, Paul (b 1943) American actor TW/27

SEBECK, Henry (fl 1617) actor
DA

SEBRING, Paul E. (d 1974 [84])
performer BP/59*

SECOMBE, Harry (b 1921) Welsh
actor, singer AAS, TW/22,
WWT/14-16

SECOND, Mrs. [née Matron] (fl
1796) singer TD/1-2

SECRETAN, Lance (b 1939) English
actor WWT/12-13

SECUNDA, Sholom (d 1974 [79])
composer BP/59*, WWT/16*

SEDDON, W. Payne English actor,
manager GRB/1-3

SEDGER, Horace (d 1917 [63/64])
lessee EA/18*, WWT/14*

SEDGER, Mrs. Horace see
Harris, Nelly

SEDGWICK, Mr. (d 1803) singer
TD/2

SEDGWICK, Mrs. (d 1868 [79])
EA/69*

SEDGWICK, Amy [Mrs. Charles
Goostry] (1830/35-97) actress
CDP, DNB, OAA/1-2

SEDGWICK, Edie (d 1971 [28])
performer BP/56*

SEDGWICK, Ellen (d 1894) EA/95*

SEDGWICK, Josephine (d 1964 [92])
performer BP/49*

SEDGWICK, Josie (d 1973 [75])
performer BP/57*

SEDGWICK, Ruth (d 1974 [82])
journalist BP/58*

SEDGWICK, Mrs. Sam (d 1877)

EA/78*
SEDLEY, Sir Charles (c. 1639-
1701) English dramatist COC,
CP/1-3, DNB, GT, HP, OC/
1-3
SEDLEY, Henry (fl 1855-61)
American actor HAS
SEDLEY, William Henry see
Sedley-Smith, William Henry
SEDLEY-SMITH, William Henry
(1806-72) English/American
actor CDP, COC, DAB,
HAS, OC/1-3, WWA/H
SEDLEY-SMITH, Mrs. William
Henry [née Riddle] (d 1861)
American actress HAS
SEEBERG, Harry (d 1975 [61])
composer/lyricist BP/60*
SEEBOHM, E. V. (d 1888) dram-
atist BE*, EA/88*, WWT/
14*
SEEBOLD, Mrs. Jack see
Dent, Lizzie
SEED, Phil (d 1971 [70]) per-
former BP/56*
SEEFRIED, Irmgard (b 1919)
Bavarian singer CB, ES
SEEL, Charles [Frederick
Charles Brown] (d 1903) mu-
sic-hall comedian CDP
SEELEN, Arthur (b 1923)
American bookseller, actor
BE
SEELEY, Blossom (d 1974 [82])
singer, vaudevillian TW/30
SEELEY, Frank (d 1913) actor,
singer CDP
SEELEY, James L. (d 1943
[76]) American actor BE*,
BP/27*
SEELIN, Elpha (d 1975 [62])
dramatist BP/60*
SEETZ, George (1888-1944)
American actor, dramatist
SR
SEFF, Manuel (d 1969 [74])
critic BP/54*
SEFF, Richard (b 1927) Amer-
ican talent representative,
actor BE, TW/7
SEFTON, Angela (b 1840) Amer-
ican actress HAS
SEFTON, Annie see Sefton,
Mrs. Joseph
SEFTON, Ernest (d 1954 [71])
actor BE*, WWT/14*
SEFTON, John (1805-68) English
actor, dancer CDP, HAS

SEFTON, Mrs. John [Miss Wells]
(fl 1827-31) English actress
HAS
SEFTON, Joseph (fl 1836) English
actor HAS
SEFTON, Joseph (d 1881) actor,
manager CDP
SEFTON, Mrs. Joseph [Mrs. J.
A. Leonard; Annie Eberle]
(1833-74) American actress
CDP, HAS
SEFTON, Mrs. John [Mrs. Watts]
(1810-95) English actress HAS
SEFTON, L. J. (d 1876 [45])
lessee EA/77*
SEFTON, Marion see Sefton,
Mrs. John
SEFTON, Philip (d 1917 [48]) ac-
tor, singer EA/18*
SEFTON, William (1810/13-39)
English actor HAS, SR
SEFTON, William (d 1866 [25])
scene artist HAS
SEFTON, Mrs. William see
Wallack, Mrs. James William
SEGAL, Alex (1915-77) American
director BE, ES
SEGAL, George (b 1936) American
actor CB
SEGAL, Vivienne (b 1897) Ameri-
can actress, singer BE, TW/
2-9, WWT/4-13
SEGALL, Harry (d 1975 [78])
dramatist BP/60*
SEGER, Lucia Backus (d 1962
[88]) actress BE*
SEGUIN, Ann see Seguin, Mrs.
Arthur Edward Sheldon
SEGUIN, Arthur Edward Sheldon
(1809-52) English singer CDP,
DNB, HAS, SR
SEGUIN, Mrs. Arthur Edward
Sheldon [née Ann Child] (1814-
88) English singer CDP, DNB,
HAS
SEGUIN, Edward (1836-79) Ameri-
can singer CDP, HAS
SEGUIN-WALLACE, Zelda (fl 1876-
83) singer CDP
SEHAIS, Jehan (fl 1598) actor DA
SEIDEL, Tom (b 1917) American
actor TW/1-3
SEIDEN, Stanley (b 1922) American
producer, press representative
BE
SEIDENBERG, Mrs. Edgar see
James, Millie
SEIDL, Anton (1850-98) Hungarian

conductor DAB, ES, WWA/H
SEIDL, Lea [Caroline Mayrseidl]
(b 1902) Austrian actress,
singer WWT/7-11
SEIDMAN, J. S. (b 1901) Ameri-
can investor BE
SEIGER, Marvin L. (b 1924)
American educator, dramatist,
director BE
SEITZ, Dran (b 1928) American
actress, singer, director,
producer BE
SEITZ, Tani (b 1928) American
actress BE, TW/12
SEITZ, Wayne T. (b 1932) Amer-
ican costume designer, execu-
tive BE
SEJOUR, Victor (1817-74) Amer-
ican dramatist DAB
SEKI, Hoshin (b 1941) American
actor TW/27-28
SELBERT, Marianne (b 1946)
American actress TW/25
SELBOURNE, David (b 1937)
English dramatist CD
SELBY, Charles (1802?-63) actor,
dramatist DNB
SELBY, Mrs. Charles see Sel-
by, Clara
SELBY, Clara [Mrs. Charles
Selby] (d 1873 [76]) actress
CDP
SELBY, Henry C. (d 1903 [49])
actor EA/04*
SELBY, Nicholas (b 1925) English
actor AAS, WWT/15-16
SELBY, Percival M. (1886-1955)
English actor, executive
WWT/10-12, WWW/5
SELBY, Tony (b 1938) English
actor WWT/15-16
SELBY, Wilton J. (d 1906) actor
EA/07*
SELDEN, Albert (b 1922) Amer-
ican producer, composer, ly-
ricist BE
SELDEN, Almira (fl 1820?)
dramatist EAP
SELDEN, Samuel (b 1899)
Chinese/American educator,
director, actor BE
SELDES, Gilbert (1893-1970)
American dramatist, critic
BE, NTH
SELDES, Marian (b 1928) Ameri-
can actress BE, TW/7-12,
23-24, 26-27, 30, WWT/14-
16

SELDON, George (d 1894 [28])
actor EA/96*
SELIG, William N. (1864-1948)
American magician, minstrel
TW/5
SELIGER, Mrs. Madison see
Beveridge, Ray
SELIGMAN, Marjorie (1900-74)
American dramatist, bookseller,
editor BE
SELIGMAN, Minnie (1869-1919)
American actress SR
SELIGMANN, Lilias Hazewell Mac-
Lane (d 1964 [71]) dancer BE*
SELIGMANN, Prosper (d 1882 [65])
musician EA/83*
SELKIRK, William (d 1911 [79])
EA/12*
SELL, Janie (b 1941) American
actress, singer TW/26, 29-30,
WWT/16
SELLAR, Robert J. B. (d 1960
[67]) dramatist BE*, WWT/14*
SELLARS, Elizabeth (b 1923) Scot-
tish actress WWT/12-16
SELLERS, Arthur D. (b 1945)
American actor TW/26, 29
SELLERS, Peter (b 1925) English
actor CB
SELLERS, Virginia (d 1973 [51])
performer BP/57*
SELLMAN, Hunton D. (b 1900)
American educator, director
BE
SELLS, Lewis (d 1907 [65]) Amer-
ican manager GRB/3*, WWT/
14*
SELMAN, Linda American actress
TW/26
SELMORE, William see Norton,
William Henry
SELOUS, Angiolo Robson (d 1883
[71]) dramatist EA/84*
SELOUS, H. Courtney (d 1890
[87]) painter EA/91*
SELTEN, Morton [Morton Richard
Stubbs] (1860-1939) actor WWT/
5-8
SELWART, Tonio (b 1896/1906)
German actor BE, TW/3-9,
13-16, WWT/9-15
SELWICKE, Ethel Ross actress
EA/97
SELWOOD, Ethel (d 1916) EA/17*
SELWYN, Archibald (d 1959 [82])
Canadian producing manager
TW/15, WWT/6-11
SELWYN, Edgar (1875-1944) Amer-

ican actor, dramatist CB,
ES, GRB/2-4, SR, WWA/2,
WWM, WWS, WWT/1-9

SELWYN, John H. (1836-73) English actor, manager, scene
artist CDP, HAS

SELWYN, Ruth (d 1954 [49]) producer, actress BE*, BP/39*

SELZNICK, Irene Meyer (b 1910/
11) American producer BE,
TW/5-8

SELZNICK, Myron (d 1944 [45])
American talent representative
BE*

SEMBRICH, Marcella (1858-1935)
Polish singer CDP, DAB,
ES, WWA/1

SEMES, Renee (b 1947) American
actress TW/30

SEMPER, Gottfried (d 1879) architect EA/80*

SEMPLE, Robert (fl 1570-71)
dramatist CP/3

SENDELBECK, Annie see Boudinot, Annie

SENECA, Lucius Annaeus (c. 4
B. C. -65 A. D.) Roman dramatist COC, ES, OC/3, PDT

SENN, Herbert (b 1924) American
designer WWT/16

SENN, Ken (d 1973 [51]) performer BP/58*

SENNETT, Ada see Norris, Ida

SENNETT, Blanche (d 1896)
EA/97*

SENNETT, Charles (d 1905 [73])
actor CDP

SENNETT, Mrs. Charles see
Merton, Annie

SENNETT, Edwin (d 1891 [51])
actor EA/92*

SENNETT, Mack (1880-1960)
Canadian actor TW/17

SENNETT, Thomas (d 1897 [54])
actor EA/98*

SENNETT, Mrs. Thomas [née
Blanche Ford] (d 1875 [32])
actress EA/76*

SENNETT, W. H. (d 1871) comedian, lessee EA/72*

SENNETT, William (d 1875 [76])
actor EA/76*, WWT/14*

SENNETT, Mrs. William (d 1876
[69]) EA/77*

SENSENDERFER, Robert E. P.
(d 1957 [73]) American critic
BE*, BP/41*

SENTER, Annie see Langdon,

Mrs. Henry A. , II

SENZ, Edward (d 1973 [74]) make-
up man BP/58*

SERABIAN, Lorraine (b 1945)
American actress TW/21, 25,
29

SERAFIN, Tullio (b 1878) Italian
conductor ES

SERBAGI, Roger Omar (b 1937)
American actor TW/26, 30

SERGAVA, Katharine (b 1918)
Russian dancer TW/1-4

SERGEANT, Mrs. (fl 1847) actress
HAS

SERGENT, John W. (d 1920) magician BE*, BP/5*

SERGINE, Vera (d 1946 [62])
French actress WWT/3-4

SERGUEEFF, Nicholas Grigorievich
(1876-1951) Russian dancer,
ballet master ES

SERJEANT, Will (d 1912 [60]) music-hall manager EA/13*

SERJEANTSON, Kate (d 1918) actress GRB/3-4, WWT/1-3

SERLE, Thomas James (1798-1889)
English dramatist, actor, acting
manager CDP, EA/69

SERLIN, Edward (d 1968 [56]) publicist BP/52*

SERLIN, Oscar (1901-71) Russian/
American producing manager
BE, CB, TW/2-8, 27, WWA/5,
WWT/10-13

SERLING, Rod (d 1975 [50]) dramatist BP/60*

SERNEAU, Gunther (d 1976 [51])
producer/director/choreographer
BP/60*

SEROFF, Muni (b 1905) Russian
actor TW/23-24, 26

SERON, Orie (b 1945) American
actress? TW/27

SERRANO, Lupe (b 1931) Mexican
dancer ES

SERRANO, Vincent (1870-1935)
American actor WWM, WWT/
4-7

SERRES, Olivia (fl 1805) dramatist
CP/3

SERVAIS, Jean (d 1976 [65]) performer BP/60*

SERVAIS, Joseph (d 1885 [35])
musician EA/86*

SERVANDONY, Jean-Nicholas
(1695-1766) French scene artist
COC

SERVOSS, Mary (d 1968 [80])

American actress BE, TW/
2-7, 25, WWT/7-13

SESSI, Mathilde (fl 1815) singer
CDP

SESSIONS, Almira (d 1974 [85])
actress BP/59*, WWT/16*

SESSIONS, Roger (b 1896) American composer CB, ES, HJD

SESTINI, [Giovana] (fl 1783)
singer CDP, TD/1-2

SETCHELL, Daniel (1831-66)
American actor, manager
CDP, HAS, SR

SETH, Will (d 1964) performer
BE*

SETON, Bruce (d 1969 [60]) performer BP/54*

SETTERBERG, Carl Douglas (d
1973 [54]) performer BP/57*

SETTI, Corrodi (fl 1850) singer
HAS

SETTI, Giulio (1869-1938) Italian
conductor WWA/2

SETTIMIO, Al (b 1945) American
actor TW/24

SETTLE, Elkanah (1648-1724)
English dramatist COC, CP/
1-3, DNB, GT, HP, OC/1-3

SETTLE, Maurice (b 1912) American executive BE

SETTLE, Nellie [Mrs. C. M.
Rodney] (d 1891) actress EA/
92*

SEURAT, Claude A. (b 1798)
freak CDP

SEVAREID, Michael (b 1940)
French actor TW/19, 25

SEVENING, Dora (b 1883) ac-
tress, secretary of Royal
Academy of Dramatic Art
WWT/8-10

SEVENING, Nina English actress
WWT/1-5

SEVERIN-MARS, Mons. (d 1921)
actor WWT/14*

SEVERI, Juan B. (fl 1847)
singer HAS

SEVERN, A. [Herr Hengler] (d
1916 [79]) conjurer EA/17*

SEVERN, Gerry (d 1974) pro-
ducer/director/choreographer
BP/59*

SEVIER, Clara Driscoll (b 1881)
American composer WWM

SEVRA, Robert (b 1945) American actor TW/28

SEWALL, Jonathan Mitchell
(1748-1808) American drama-

tist EAP

SEWARD, Billy (d 1899 [46]) Negro
comedian EA/00*

SEWARD, Emily [Mrs. E. M.
Holland] actress CDP

SEWARD, John (d 1884) EA/85*

SEWELL, Mrs. (fl 1785) actress
HAS

SEWELL, Charles (b 1878) English
actor GRB/1

SEWELL, E. J. (d 1916) EA/18*

SEWELL, Dr. George (d 1726)
dramatist CP/1-3, DNB, GT

SEWELL, Hetty Jane (d 1961)
American dramatist BE*

SEYLER, Athene (b 1889) English
actress AAS, COC, ES, OC/
3, WWT/1-16

SEYMOUR, Mr. (fl 1797-98) actor
HAS

SEYMOUR, Mr. (fl 1803) actor
TD/2

SEYMOUR, Mrs. (fl 1717-23) actress DNB

SEYMOUR, Mrs. (fl 1797-98) actress HAS

SEYMOUR, Mrs. [née Allison] (b
1819) English actress HAS

SEYMOUR, Miss see Reeve,
Mrs. James

SEYMOUR, Alan (b 1927) Australian
dramatist, director CD

SEYMOUR, Anne (b 1909) American
actress BE, TW/14-21

SEYMOUR, Charles Guilfoyle (d
1904) actor EA/05*

SEYMOUR, Clarine (1900-19) actress BE*

SEYMOUR, Cy (d 1973 [70]) performer BP/57*

SEYMOUR, Frank (d 1891) comedian EA/92*

SEYMOUR, Fred (d 1968 [68])
producer/director/choreographer
BP/52*

SEYMOUR, George actor CDP

SEYMOUR, Mrs. Guilfoyle [née
Harriet Hunter] (d 1875 [20])
actress EA/76*

SEYMOUR, Harry (1821-83) actor,
costumier CDP, HAS

SEYMOUR, Harry (d 1877) musician EA/78*

SEYMOUR, Harry (d 1967 [77])
composer/lyricist BP/52*

SEYMOUR, Henry (d 1868) stage
manager EA/69*

SEYMOUR, James [James Cun-

ningham] (1823-64) Irish actor
COC, HAS, OC/1-3

SEYMOUR, James (d 1976 [80])
dramatist BP/60*

SEYMOUR, James (b 1948) American actor TW/30

SEYMOUR, Jane (d 1956 [64])
Canadian actress TW/12

SEYMOUR, John D. (b 1897)
American actor BE, TW/4-
20, 24, 29

SEYMOUR, Katie [Katherine Phoebe
Mary Athol] (d 1903 [33]) actress, dancer EA/04*, WWT/
14*

SEYMOUR, Laura (d 1879 [59])
actress, producer, manager
BE*, EA/80*, WWT/14*

SEYMOUR, Linda (d 1877 [18])
music teacher EA/78*

SEYMOUR, Lynn (b 1939) Canadian dancer ES

SEYMOUR, Madeline (b 1891)
English actress WWT/3-9

SEYMOUR, May Davenport (1883-
1967) American actress, curator BE, TW/24

SEYMOUR, Milly see Fuell,
Emelia

SEYMOUR, Mollie [Mrs. Sim-
mons] (b 1884) English actress,
dancer GRB/1

SEYMOUR, Nelse (1835-75) minstrel CDP

SEYMOUR, Phoebe (d 1912 [75])
EA/13*

SEYMOUR, Robert William (d
1877 [77]) musician EA/78*

SEYMOUR, Thomas Orlando (d
1909) EA/10*

SEYMOUR, Will actor, singer
CDP

SEYMOUR, William Gorman (1855-
1933) American actor, stage
manager, director COC,
DAB, GRB/3-4, OC/1-3, PP/
3, WWA/1, WWM, WWS,
WWT/1-7

SEYMOUR, W. J. see Birchell,
William John

SEYTON, Charles (d 1894) actor
WWT/14*

SEYTON, Clara dramatic reader,
singer CDP

SEYTON, John C. (d 1867 [45])
comedian, manager EA/68*

SHACKELL, Frank (d 1917)
musician EA/18*

SHACKLETON, Robert (d 1956
[42]) American actor TW/7-8

SHADE, Ellen (b 1945) American
actress TW/24

SHADE, Lillian (d 1962 [51]) performer BE*

SHADWELL, Charles (d 1726)
dramatist CP/1-3, DNB, GT

SHADWELL, Thomas (c. 1642-92)
English dramatist CDP, COC,
CP/1-3, DNB, ES, GT, HP,
MH, NTH, OC/1-3, PDT, RE

SHAFER, Robert American actor
TW/1

SHAFF, Monty American producer,
manager BE

SHAFFER, Anthony (b 1926) English dramatist AAS, CB, CD,
COC, WWT/15-16

SHAFFER, Oscar (fl 1876?) singer
CDP

SHAFFER, Peter Levin (b 1926)
English dramatist AAS, BE,
CD, CH, COC, ES, MD, MH,
MWD, PDT, RE, WWT/14-16

SHAHN, Ben (b 1898) American
designer ES

SHAINMARK, Lou (d 1976 [75])
producer/director/choreographer
BP/60*

SHAIRP, Alexander Mordaunt
(1887-1939) English dramatist
MWD, NTH, WWT/6-8

SHAKAR, Martin (b 1940) American
actor TW/23, 25-30

SHAKERLEY, Edward (fl 1620s)
actor DA

SHAKESPEARE, Edmund (d 1607)
actor DA

SHAKESPEARE, Edward (d 1607)
actor DA

SHAKESPEARE, William (1564-1616)
English dramatist, actor CDP,
COC, CP/1-3, DA, DNB, ES,
FGF, HP, MH, NTH, OC/1-3,
PDT, RE, SR

SHAKSHAFTE, William (fl 1581)
actor DA

SHALDERS, Charles William (d
1862 [43]) scene artist, actor
EA/72*, WWT/14*

SHALDERS, William (d 1872 [72])
manager EA/73*

SHALE, T. A. (1867-1953) English
actor WWT/3-9

SHALEK, Bertha (b 1884) American
actress, singer WWS

SHALER, Anna (b 1940) American

actress TW/29
SHANAHAN, Elva (d 1973 [48])
performer BP/58*
SHANAHAN, James A., Sr. (d
1970 [82]) performer BP/55*
SHANBROOKE, John (d 1618)
actor DA
SHANCKE, John see Shank,
John
SHAND, Ernest (fl 1900-04?) ac-
tor, singer CDP
SHAND, John (1901-55) English
critic, journalist WWT/8-10
SHAND, Phyllis (b 1894) English
actress WWT/9-10
SHANDY, Tristram [Michael
Keating] (d 1895) manager
EA/96*
SHANE, Jerry (d 1974 [42]) per-
former BP/58*
SHANE, Peggy (d 1965 [69]) dra-
matist BP/50*
SHANK, John (d 1636) English
actor, dramatist COC, CP/
3, DA, DNB, FGF, NTH,
OC/1-3
SHANK, John, the Younger (fl
1630-42) actor DA
SHANK, Theodore J. (b 1929)
American educator, director
BE
SHANKS, Alec (b 1904) English
director WWT/12-16
SHANNON, Effie [Mrs. Herbert
Kelcey] (1867-1954) American
actress ES, GRB/2-4, PP/3,
SR, TW/2-6, 11, WWA/3,
WWM, WWS, WWT/1-11
SHANNON, Frank (d 1959 [83])
Irish actor WWT/6-10
SHANNON, Harry (d 1964 [74])
performer BP/49*
SHANNON, Mark (b 1948) Amer-
ican actor TW/26
SHANNON, Michael (b 1943)
American actor TW/28-30
SHANNON, Nance (d 1965) per-
former BP/50*
SHANNON, Peggy (1907-41)
American actress CB, WWT/
7-9
SHANNON, Ray (d 1971 [76])
comedian TW/27
SHANNON, Wayne (b 1948) Amer-
ican actor TW/29
SHANNON, William J. (d 1973
[62]) performer BP/57*
SHANNON, Winona (d 1950

[76]) American actress TW/7
SHAPIRO, Herman (b 1898) Amer-
ican stage manager BE
SHAPTER, Mr. (fl 1802) actor
HAS
SHARAFF, Irene (b 1908) Ameri-
can designer BE, ES, TW/2,
4-8, WWT/10-16
SHARKEY, Susan (b 1943) Ameri-
can actress TW/27-29
SHARLAND, Reginald (1886-1944)
English actor, singer WWT/
5-8
SHARMA, Barbara (b 1942) actress
TW/24-25, 27
SHARON, Fran (b 1939) American
actress TW/19
SHARON, Muriel (b 1920) Ameri-
can director, educator, drama-
tist, actress BE
SHARP (d 1894 [72]) music-hall
performer EA/95*
SHARP, Anthony (b 1915) English
actor, director, dramatist
WWT/12-16
SHARP, Arabella (fl 1793) actress
CDP
SHARP, Eileen (b 1900) English
actress, singer WWT/5-8
SHARP, F. B. J. (b 1874) English
actor WWT/4-7
SHARP, Henry (1889-1964) Latvian
actor TW/2, 10
SHARP, Janet Achurch see
Achurch, Janet
SHARP, John W. (d 1856 [38])
singer, musical director CDP
SHARP, Margery (b 1905) drama-
tist WWT/10-14
SHARP, Oliver (d 1969 [38]) pro-
ducer/director/choreographer
BP/54*
SHARP, Richard (fl 1618-29) actor
DA
SHARP, Theodore (d 1882) librarian
EA/83*
SHARP, Mrs. W. [née Bella Men-
age] dancer GT
SHARP, William (b 1924) American
educator, director BE
SHARPE, Mrs. [née Le Sugg] (d
1863) English actress CDP,
HAS
SHARPE, Miss see Kneass,
Mrs.
SHARPE, Miss actress CDP
SHARPE, Albert (b 1885) Irish
actor TW/3-4

SHARPE, A. N. (d 1865 [24])
actor HAS
SHARPE, Belle (d 1913 [40])
EA/14*
SHARPE, Don (d 1975) producer/
director/choreographer BP/
60*
SHARPE, Edith (b 1894) English
actress WWT/7-15
SHARPE, Gyda (d 1973 [65])
performer BP/57*
SHARPE, John (fl 1791) drama-
tist CP/3
SHARPE, John (b 1932) American
actor TW/8, 11-13, 22-24
SHARPE, J. W. (d 1856) comic
singer HAS
SHARPE, L. [Launcelot Sharpe
Abram] (d 1891) musician EA/
92*
SHARPE, Lewis (fl 1640) drama-
tist CP/1-3, FGF, GT
SHARPE, Lizzie see Thompson,
Eliza
SHARPE, Louisa (d 1801) musi-
cian CDP
SHARPE, Richard (c. 1602-32)
English actor COC, OC/1-3
SHARPHAM, Edward (d 1608
[32]?) dramatist CP/1-3,
DNB, FGF, GT
SHARPLES, William (d 1876
[56]) juggler, cannon-ball per-
former EA/78*
SHARPLEY, Sam (1831-75)
American Ethiopian comedian,
minstrel manager CDP, HAS
SHARPMAN, Edward see
Sharpham, Edward
SHATNER, William (b 1931)
Canadian actor BE, TW/12-
20, WWT/16
SHATTERELL, Edward (fl
c. 1640-54) English actor
COC, OC/2-3
SHATTERELL, Robert (d c. 1684)
English actor COC, DA,
OC/2-3
SHATTUCK, Charles F. (d 1905
[69]) minstrel CDP
SHATTUCK, Ethel (d 1963 [73])
performer BE*
SHATTUCK, Robert (b 1940)
American actor TW/24-26
SHATTUCK, Truly [Mrs. Stephen
A. Douglas] (1876-1954)
American actress, singer
GRB/3-4, WWM, WWS,

WWT/1-7
SHAUB, Edna E. (d 1975 [98])
performer BP/60*
SHAVER, Bob (b 1932) American
actor TW/13
SHAVER, C. L. (b 1905) American
educator BE
SHAW, Mr. (fl 1786) musician,
conductor CDP
SHAW, Mr. (b 1794) dwarf CDP
SHAW, Mrs. (fl 1800) actress
HAS
SHAW, Mrs. [née Eliza Marian
Trewar; Mrs. Thomas Sowerby
Hamblin, IV] (fl 1817-39) ac-
tress SR
SHAW, Miss (b 1790) dwarf CDP
SHAW, Miss see Rous, Helen
SHAW, Mrs. Alfred [née Mary
Portans] (1814-76) English singer
CDP, DNB
SHAW, Annie Isabel [Mrs. Tom
Shaw] (d 1900 [23]) EA/01*
SHAW, Anthony (b 1897) actor
WWT/8-13
SHAW, Arthur (d 1946 [65]) Amer-
ican actor TW/2
SHAW, Miss C. (fl 1846) actress
HAS
SHAW, Charles (d 1879 [33]) EA/
80*
SHAW, Charles A. (b 1835) show-
man HAS
SHAW, Charlotte (fl 1842) actress
CDP
SHAW, Claude [David Macgregor
Shaw] (d 1891) business manager
EA/92*
SHAW, David Macgregor see
Shaw, Claude
SHAW, Dennis (d 1970 [50]) per-
former BP/55*
SHAW, Dora (fl 1849-63) American
actress HAS
SHAW, E. J. (fl 1839-51) Irish
actor HAS
SHAW, F. W. (d 1901 [47]) singer
EA/03*
SHAW, George Bernard (1856-1950)
Irish dramatist, critic AAS,
CB, COC, DNB, ES, GRB/1-4,
HP, MD, MH, MWD, NTH,
OC/1-3, PDT, RE, TW/7,
WWA/3, WWM, WWS, WWT/1-
10, WWW/4
SHAW, Mrs. George Bernard [née
Charlotte Frances Payne-Town-
shend] (1857-1943) Irish drama-

SHAW 842

tist BE*, WWT/14*

SHAW, Gerald (b 1950) American
actor TW/30

SHAW, Glen Byam (b 1904) English actor, director AAS,
BE, COC, ES, OC/3, WWT/
7-16

SHAW, G. Tito (b 1943) American actor TW/24

SHAW, Harry E. (d 1903) American minstrel comedian EA/
04*

SHAW, Henry W. see Billings,
"Josh"

SHAW, Irwin (b 1913) American
dramatist, producer AAS,
BE, CB, CD, ES, HJD,
MD, MH, MWD, NTH,
WWT/10-16

SHAW, J. A. (d 1880) actor?
EA/81*

SHAW, Jack (d 1970 [88]) performer BP/54*

SHAW, Joe (d 1898 [29]) actor?
EA/00*

SHAW, John (d 1867 [85]) actor?
EA/68*

SHAW, John (d 1886) proprietor,
manager EA/87*

SHAW, John (d 1890) professor
of music EA/91*

SHAW, Joseph English actor
TW/24

SHAW, Josephine see Hoey,
Mrs. John

SHAW, Lewis (b 1910) English
actor WWT/6-10

SHAW, Mary [Mrs. T. S. Hamblin?] (d 1873 [56]?) actress,
singer CDP, HAS

SHAW, Mary (d 1894) actress,
singer CDP

SHAW, Mary (1854-1929) Amer-
ican actress DAB, ES,
GRB/3-4, PP/3, WWA/1,
WWS, WWT/1-5

SHAW, Montague (d 1968 [85])
performer BP/52*

SHAW, Oscar [Oscar Schwartz]
(1889-1967) American actor,
singer TW/23, WWT/6-9

SHAW, Mrs. Oscar see Givler,
Mary Louise

SHAW, Paula (b 1941) American
actress TW/22-23, 25

SHAW, Ray (b 1926) American
actor TW/11

SHAW, Reta (b 1912) American

actress TW/9-15

SHAW, Robert (fl 1597-1602) actor
DA

SHAW, Robert (d 1908 [55]) actor
EA/09*

SHAW, Robert (b 1927) English
actor, dramatist AAS, BE,
CB, CD, CH, MH, TW/18,
21, 26, 28, 30, WWT/13-16

SHAW, Robert Gould (d 1931 [80])
curator BE*, WWT/14*

SHAW, Rosina see Watkins,
Mrs. Harry

SHAW, Sala (d 1972 [66]) performer
BP/57*

SHAW, Sam (d 1968 [50]) critic
BP/52*

SHAW, Samuel (1635-96) English
dramatist CP/1-3

SHAW, Sebastian (b 1905) English
actor AAS, WWT/7-16

SHAW, Sidney (d 1969 [45]) com-
poser/lyricist BP/54*

SHAW, Sydney (d 1910 [45]) composer, conductor EA/11*

SHAW, Tom (d 1912 [45]) English
agent GRB/1

SHAW, Mrs. Tom see Shaw,
Annie Isabel

SHAW, W. B. (d 1880) musician
EA/81*

SHAWE, Robert (fl 1602) dramatist
CP/3

SHAWHAN, April (b 1940) American actress TW/23-26, 29-30

SHAWLEY, Robert (b 1932) American actor TW/7-9

SHAWN, Dick American actor
TW/24, 27, WWT/16

SHAWN, Michael (b 1944) American
actor TW/25-28

SHAWN, Ted (1891-1972) American
dancer, choreographer CB, ES

SHAWN, Wallace (b 1943) American dramatist, director CD

SHAYNE, Al (d 1969 [82]) performer BP/54*

SHAYNE, Alan (b 1925) American
actor TW/6-16

SHEA, Mrs. [née Blanche Kemble]
(d 1851) actress HAS

SHEA, Jack (d 1970 [70]) performer
BP/55*

SHEA, Joe (d 1970 [72]) publicist
BP/55*

SHEA, Patrick (b 1946) American
actor TW/26-27

SHEA, Thomas E. (d 1940 [79])

American actor, dramatist
BE*, BP/24*, WWT/14*
SHEAHAN, John J. (d 1952
[60]) American actor BP/36*
SHEALDEN (fl 1594) actor DA
SHEAN, Al (1868-1949) German/
American actor DAB, TW/
1, 4, 6, WWT/9-10
SHEARD, Charles Henry (d 1913
[60]) EA/14*
SHEARER, Mrs. (d 1872) propri-
etor EA/73*
SHEARER, Denny (b 1941) Amer-
ican actor TW/25
SHEARER, James (d 1868) pro-
prietor EA/69*
SHEARER, Juanita (b 1919)
American educator, director
BE
SHEARER, Moira (b 1926) Scot-
tish dancer, actress CB,
ES, WWT/11-14
SHEE, Sir Martin Archer (1769-
1850) Irish dramatist DNB
SHEEAN, Vincent (d 1975 [75])
writer BP/59*
SHEEHAN, Bailie (d 1975 [74])
producer/director/choreographer
BP/59*
SHEEHAN, Jack (1890-1952)
American actor TW/8
SHEEHAN, Jack (d 1958 [67])
actor TW/1, 15
SHEEHAN, Jack (d 1973 [53])
performer BP/58*
SHEEHAN, Joseph F. (fl 1892-
1907) American singer WWS
SHEEHAN, Margaret Flavin (d
1969 [88]) Welsh actress
TW/25
SHEEHY, T. J. M. (d 1974
[56]) critic BP/59*
SHEEN, Martin [né Ramon Es-
tevez] (b 1940) American
actor TW/20-24, 26, WWT/
15-16
SHEEN, Pauline (d 1909) variety
performer EA/10*
SHEERING, James (d 1906 [86])
boxkeeper EA/07*
SHEFFIELD, Flora (b 1902)
English actress WWT/6-9
SHEFFIELD, John, Duke of
Buckingham (1649-1720) dram-
atist CP/2-3
SHEFFIELD, Leo (1873-1951)
English actor, singer WWT/
4-11

SHEFFIELD, Nellie (d 1957 [84])
actress BE*, WWT/14*
SHEFFIELD, Reginald (1900/01-
57) English actor WWT/3-9
SHEFFIELD, Thorpe [Robert
Thorpe Wilson] (d 1908 [42])
actor, singer EA/09*
SHEFFIELD, Wilson (d 1903 [38])
actor, singer EA/04*
SHEIL, Richard Lalor (1791-1851)
Irish dramatist CDP, DNB
SHELASKY, George Irving see
Irving, George S.
SHELBY, Daniel manager CDP
SHELBY, Jeanne (d 1964 [71])
performer BP/49*
SHELDON, A. H. (b 1847) Ameri-
can actor HAS
SHELDON, Charles (d 1870 [28])
musician EA/71*
SHELDON, David (b 1931) Ameri-
can producer, director, drama-
tist, actor BE
SHELDON, Edward (d 1878 [58])
bill poster EA/79*
SHELDON, Edward Brewster (1886-
1946) American dramatist CB,
COC, ES, MD, MH, MWD,
NTH, OC/1-3, RE, TW/2,
WWA/2, WWT/1-9
SHELDON, Georg (b 1864) English
actor, musician, stage mana-
ger, producer, dramatist
GRB/2
SHELDON, Herb (d 1964) American
performer BE*
SHELDON, H. Sophus (d 1940
[63]) Danish dramatist WWT/
6-9
SHELDON, Jerome (d 1962 [71])
actor BE*
SHELDON, Jerry (d 1962 [61])
actor BE*
SHELDON, Lechmere (d 1907
[29]) EA/08*
SHELDON, Marie [Mrs. R. B.
Mantell] (d 1939 [83]) Scottish
actress BE*, WWT/14*
SHELDON, Sidney (b 1917) Amer-
ican dramatist, director, pro-
ducer BE
SHELDON, Suzanne [Mrs. Henry
Ainley] (1875-1924) American
actress GRB/1-4, WWS,
WWT/1-4
SHELLE, Lori (b 1955) American
actress TW/25
SHELLEY, Master (fl 1847) actor

HAS

SHELLEY, Carole (b 1939) English actress TW/23-27, WWT/15-16

SHELLEY, Evelyn (d 1918) EA/19*

SHELLEY, Herbert (d 1921 [50]) actor, producer, manager BE*, WWT/14*

SHELLEY, Joshua (b 1920) American producer, director, actor BE, TW/3-4, 6-8, 10-12

SHELLEY, Percy Bysshe (1792-1822) English dramatist CDP, COC, DNB, ES, HP, MH, NTH, OC/1-3, PDT, RE

SHELLY, Norman (b 1921) American actor TW/6, 25-28

SHELTON, Benjamin (d 1885 [73]) EA/86*

SHELTON, Bertie (d 1920) stage manager, actor WWT/14*

SHELTON, George (1852/53-1932) English actor GRB/1-4, WWT/1-6

SHELTON, George (d 1971 [87]) comedian TW/27

SHELTON, Mrs. George (d 1908) GRB/4*

SHELTON, James (d 1975 [62]) performer BP/60*

SHELTON, Kenneth E. (d 1962 [37]) performer BE*

SHELTON, Laura Blanche [Mrs. Tom Diacoff] (d 1917 [40]) EA/18*

SHELTON, Reid (b 1924) American actor TW/23, 25, 28-30

SHELTON, Sloane (b 1934) American actor TW/23-24, 27-28, 30

SHELVING, Paul (1888-1968) English designer ES, WWT/6-11

SHEMELDS, Minnie see Rogers, Mrs. J.

SHENAR, Paul (b 1936) American actor TW/26

SHENBURN, Archibald A. (1905-54) English manager WWT/10

SHENSTON, E. (d 1885 [46]) EA/86*

SHENTON, J. W. (d 1886 [34]) dramatist EA/87*

SHENTON, Thomas Bartlett (d 1887 [74]) actor EA/88*

SHEPARD (fl 1582) doorkeeper DA

SHEPARD, Burt (d 1913 [58]) singer CDP

SHEPARD, Frank (d 1899) American comedian EA/01*

SHEPARD, Grove Burt (d 1913 [58]) EA/14*

SHEPARD, Joan (b 1933) American actress TW/1, 3, 23

SHEPARD, Red American actor TW/27-28

SHEPARD, Sam (b 1943) American dramatist, musician, actor CD, WWT/16

SHEPARD, William J. (d 1965 [74]) performer BP/50*

SHEPEARD, Jean (b 1904) English actress WWT/6-11

SHEPERD, Mr. (fl 1810?) actor CDP

SHEPERD, Mrs. actress CDP

SHEPHARD, Firth (1891-1949) English dramatist, producing manager TW/5, WWT/6-10, WWW/4

SHEPHARD, Rensselaer Albert (1832-54) American actor HAS

SHEPHERD, Mrs. [Mrs. Pope] (d 1862 [65]) actress EA/72*

SHEPHERD, Edward (c. 1670-1747) English architect COC, OC/1-3

SHEPHERD, Elizabeth (b 1936) English actress TW/26-27

SHEPHERD, Henry (fl 1800) dramatist CP/3

SHEPHERD, Jack (b 1940) English actor WWT/15-16

SHEPHERD, Mrs. J. C. see Neverist, Kate

SHEPHERD, Joseph (d 1887 [71]) musician EA/88*

SHEPHERD, Leonard (b 1872) English actor WWS, WWT/4-11

SHEPHERD, R. D. see McLean, R. D.

SHEPHERD, Richard (fl 1757-72) dramatist CP/2-3

SHEPHERD, Richard (d 1886 [76]) actor, manager EA/87*, WWT/14*

SHEPHERD, William Walton (d 1891 [41]) actor EA/92*

SHEPLEY, Ida (d 1975) performer BP/59*

SHEPLEY, Michael (1907-61) English actor WWT/8-13

SHEPLEY, Ruth (1889/92-1951) American actress TW/8, WWT/4-10

SHEPMAN, Louis Evan see Shipman, Louis Evan

SHEPPARD, Miss see Cowell, Mrs.

SHEPPARD, Billy (d 1872) minstrel CDP

SHEPPARD, E. (d 1892) musician EA/93*

SHEPPARD, Edwin James (d 1908 [76]) actor GRB/4*

SHEPPARD, Guy (b 1912) English designer ES

SHEPPARD, Hattie see Hallam, Mrs.

SHEPPARD, S. (fl 1647) dramatist CP/1-3

SHEPPARD, Sarah Amelia [Mrs. W. C. Sheppard] (d 1880) EA/81*

SHEPPARD, Mrs. W. C. see Sheppard, Sarah Amelia

SHEPPARD, William (fl 1602) actor DA

SHERAR, John [Sam Honey] (d 1888) EA/89*

SHERBROOKE, Michael (1874-1957) actor GRB/2-4, WWT/1-8

SHERBURNE, Sir Edward (b 1616) English translator CP/1-3

SHERBURNE, Ernest O. (1878-1952) American critic WWA/3

SHERBURNE, Col. John B. (fl 1844?) dramatist RJ

SHEREK, Henry (1900-67) English manager, producer AAS, BE, WWT/9-14, WWW/6

SHERIDAN, Mr. actor TD/2

SHERIDAN, Miss (fl 1781) dramatist CP/3

SHERIDAN, Amy [Mrs. Preston] (d 1878 [39]) burlesque actress CDP

SHERIDAN, Ann (1915-67) American actress ES

SHERIDAN, Brinsley (d 1890 [55]) comedian, proprietor EA/91*

SHERIDAN, Dinah (b 1920) English actress WWT/16

SHERIDAN, Elizabeth Ann see Linley, Elizabeth Ann

SHERIDAN, Elizabeth Francis [Mrs. Henry Brinsley Sheridan] (d 1893) EA/94*

SHERIDAN, Emily Brinsley English actress EA/97

SHERIDAN, Emma V. (b 1864) American actress PP/3

SHERIDAN, Esther Jane [Mrs. Richard Brinsley Sheridan, II] (1776-1817) CDP

SHERIDAN, Frances [née Chamberlaine] (c. 1724-66) Irish dramatist CDP, CP/1-3, DNB, GT

SHERIDAN, Frank (1869-1943) American actor SR

SHERIDAN, Helen Selina (1807-77) dramatist, songwriter DNB

SHERIDAN, Henry Brinsley (d 1907) actor GRB/2*

SHERIDAN, Mrs. Henry Brinsley see Sheridan, Elizabeth Francis

SHERIDAN, Mrs. J. see Sheridan, Zoe Simeon

SHERIDAN, John (d 1869 [29]) property man EA/70*

SHERIDAN, John (d 1911 [69]) manager EA/12*

SHERIDAN, John Francis (d 1908 [64]) actor, manager CDP, GRB/4

SHERIDAN, J. T. (d 1906 [34]) electrician EA/07*

SHERIDAN, Margaret (1889-1958) Irish singer ES

SHERIDAN, Mark (d 1917) English music-hall performer CDP, COC, OC/1-3

SHERIDAN, Mary [Daphne Graham] (b 1903) English actress WWT/7-10

SHERIDAN, Richard Brinsley (1751-1816) English dramatist, manager CDP, COC, CP/2-3, DNB, ES, GT, HP, MH, NTH, OC/1-3, PDT, RE, SR, TD/1-2

SHERIDAN, Mrs. Richard Brinsley, I see Linley, Elizabeth Ann

SHERIDAN, Mrs. Richard Brinsley, II see Sheridan, Esther Jane

SHERIDAN, Dr. Thomas (c. 1684-1738) Irish translator CP/2-3, DNB

SHERIDAN, Thomas (1719/21-88) Irish manager, dramatist CDP, CP/1-3, DNB, ES, GT, TD/1-2

SHERIDAN, Mrs. Thomas see Sheridan, Frances

SHERIDAN, William Edward (1839/40-87) American actor CDP, COC, HAS, NYM, OC/1-3

SHERIDAN, Mrs. William Edward actress COC

SHERIDAN, Zoe Simeon [Mrs. J. Sheridan] (d 1909 [67]) EA/10*

SHERIFF, Jane see Sherriff, Jane

SHERIN, Edwin (b 1930/32) American actor, director TW/19, WWT/16

SHERINGHAM, George (1885-1937) English designer WWT/6-8

SHERK, Theresa (fl 1868) actress HAS

SHERLOCK, William (fl first half of 17th cent) English actor DA, OC/1-3

SHERMAN, Allan (d 1973 [49]) performer BP/58*

SHERMAN, Allan (d 1973 [76]) composer/lyricist BP/58*

SHERMAN, Frederick (d 1969 [64]) actor TW/25

SHERMAN, Geraldine English actress TW/29

SHERMAN, Henry (fl 1840) American singer HAS

SHERMAN, Hiram (b 1908) American actor BE, TW/3-19, 22, 24, WWT/11-16

SHERMAN, James B. (d 1975 [67]) composer/lyricist BP/60*

SHERMAN, Joe (d 1970 [76]) performer BP/55*

SHERMAN, John K. (1898-1969) American critic BE

SHERMAN, Lowell J. (1885-1934) American actor SR, WWT/4-7

SHERMAN, Margaret American executive BE

SHERMAN, Maud (d 1900) American singer EA/01*

SHERMAN, Noel (d 1972 [41]) composer/lyricist BP/57*

SHERMAN, William (b 1924) American educator, scene designer BE

SHERRATT, Mrs. William (d 1877) EA/78*

SHERRIFF, Jane (fl 1831-39) English singer, actress HAS, SR

SHERRIFF, Robert Cedric (1896-1975) English dramatist AAS, BE, CH, COC, ES, HP, MD, MH, MWD, NTH, OC/2-3,

PDT, WWT/6-15

SHERRIN, Ned (b 1931) English producer, director, dramatist CD, WWT/15-16

SHERRINGTON, Mme. Lemmens (1834-1906) English singer CDP

SHERRINGTON, Louie actress, singer CDP

SHERRY, Miss (d c. 1800?) actress TD/1-2

SHERRY, Katherine (d 1782) actress CDP

SHERWELL, Yvonne (b 1934) American actress TW/26

SHERWIN, Amy (d 1935 [81]) Tasmanian singer WWW/3

SHERWIN, Jeanette (d 1936 [42]) actress WWT/6-7

SHERWIN, Louis (b 1880) German/American critic WWM

SHERWIN, Mrs. Louis F. see Fealy, Maude

SHERWIN, Maude (1903-74) American composer WWT/10-14

SHERWIN, Ralph (1799-1830) English actor BS, CDP, DNB, OX

SHERWOOD, Mrs. (d 1917) proprietor EA/18*

SHERWOOD, Charles E. (b 1825) American actor, circus performer HAS

SHERWOOD, Mrs. Charles E. [Virginia] (1832-88) Irish equestrienne CDP, HAS

SHERWOOD, Garrison P. (1902-63) American actor, historian, journalist WWT/10-13

SHERWOOD, Henry (d 1967 [83]) actor TW/24

SHERWOOD, Henry (b 1931) English presenting manager WWT/15-16

SHERWOOD, James (b 1927) American actor TW/4

SHERWOOD, James Peter (1894-1973) English presenting manager WWT/15

SHERWOOD, Josephine (fl 1906-07) American actress WWS

SHERWOOD, Josephine see Hull, Josephine

SHERWOOD, Lydia (b 1906) English actress WWT/6-13

SHERWOOD, Madeleine [née Thornton] (b 1926) Canadian actress TW/9, 11-12, 21-22, 27-30,

WWT/14-16

SHERWOOD, Robert Emmet (1896-1955) American dramatist AAS, CB, COC, ES, HJD, MD, MH, MWD, NTH, OC/1-3, PDT, RE, TW/12, WWA/3, WWT/6-11, WWW/5

SHERWOOD, Virginia see Sherwood, Mrs. Charles E.

SHERWOOD, Wayne American actor TW/25, 27-28

SHERWOOD, William American actor TW/26

SHESGREEN, James (fl 1890-1913) Canadian press representative WWM

SHEVELOVE, Burt (b 1915) American director, dramatist, librettist BE, CD, WWT/15-16

SHEWELL, Livingston Robert (1833-1904) American actor CDP, HAS

SHEWELL, Mrs. L. R., I [née Henrietta Wilks] (1838-57) American dancer HAS

SHEWELL, Mrs. L. R., II [née Rose Skerrett] (b 1840) American actress HAS

SHIEL, Julia Lalor (d 1902) actress EA/04*

SHIEL, Lalor (b 1869) Canadian actress EA/97

SHIELD, Harry (d 1875 [38]) dramatist EA/76*

SHIELD, William (1748-1829) English composer, musician CDP, DNB, ES, TD/1-2

SHIELDS, Albert Charles (d 1870) advance agent EA/71*

SHIELDS, Arthur (1900-70) Irish actor WWT/9-11

SHIELDS, Ella (d 1952 [73]) American music-hall performer TW/9

SHIELDS, Helen (d 1963) actress BE*, BP/48*

SHIELDS, Robin Neilance (b 1872) Scottish actor GRB/1

SHIELDS, Rose (d 1916) EA/17*

SHIELDS, Sydney (d 1960 [72]) American actress TW/17

SHIELDS, William Joseph see Fitzgerald, Barry

SHIELS, George (1886-1949) Irish dramatist COC, MWD, MH, OC/1-3, RE, WWT/9-10

SHIFFRIN, Helen (d 1975 [55])

performer BP/59*

SHIFRIN, Nisson Abramovich (1892-1959) Russian designer COC

SHILKRET, Jack (d 1964 [67]) American composer, bandleader BE*, BP/49*

SHILLEN, Joseph P. (d 1971 [55]) performer BP/55*

SHILLING, Ivy Australian dancer WWT/4-7

SHILLITO, Charles (fl 1789) dramatist CP/3

SHIMIZU, Dana (b 1958) American actor TW/27

SHIMIZU, Keenan (b 1956) American actor TW/30

SHIMONO, Sab American actor TW/25-27, 30

SHINDELL, Dario (d 1974 [67]) performer BP/59*

SHINE, Bill [né Wilfred William Dennis] (b 1911) English actor WWT/10-16

SHINE, Giles (1860-1912) American actor SR

SHINE, Harry comedian GRB/2

SHINE, J. Myer (d 1971 [78]) theatre owner BP/55*

SHINE, Joe (d 1973 [70]) performer BP/57*

SHINE, John L. (1854-1930) actor CDP, DP, EA/96, GRB/1-4, WWT/1-6

SHINE, Wilfred E. (1864-1939) English actor GRB/1-4, WWT/1-8

SHINE, Wilfred William Dennis see Shine, Bill

SHINE, William H. (d 1909 [40]) EA/10*

SHINER, Ronald (1903-66) English actor AAS, WWT/10-14, WWW/6

SHINGLER, Helen (b 1919) English actress WWT/11-14

SHINTON, John (b 1870) English actor GRB/1

SHIPLEY, Joseph T. (b 1893) American critic NTH, WWT/11-16

SHIPLEY, Mrs. Sam see Worth, Beatrice

SHIPMAN, Ernest (b 1871) Canadian/American manager GRB/3-4, WWT/1-2

SHIPMAN, Louis Evan (1869-1933) American dramatist GRB/2-4, WWA/1, WWM, WWS, WWT/

1-7, WWW/3

SHIPMAN, Samuel (1883-1937)
American dramatist WWA/1,
WWT/4-8

SHIPMAN, Thomas (d c. 1691)
dramatist CP/1-3, GT

SHIPP, Cameron (d 1961 [57])
American writer BE*

SHIPP, Edward (d 1945) circus
manager, performer SR

SHIPP, Julia Lowande (d 1962
[81]) performer BE*

SHIPSTAD, Roy (d 1975 [64])
co-founder of Ice Follies
BP/59*

SHIRA, Jerry (d 1973 [28]) critic
BP/58*

SHIREBURN, Frances see
Cross, Mrs. Richard

SHIRLEY, Mr. (fl 1858) actor
HAS

SHIRLEY, Arthur (1853-1925)
English actor, dramatist
GRB/1-4, WWT/1-5

SHIRLEY, Bill (b 1921) American
actor, singer BE

SHIRLEY, Florence actress TW/1

SHIRLEY, Henry (fl 1638-53)
dramatist CP/1-3, FGF

SHIRLEY, James (1596-1666)
English dramatist CDP, COC,
CP/1-3, DNB, ES, FGF,
GT, HP, MH, NTH, OC/
1-3, PDT, RE

SHIRLEY, James Elliott (d 1892
[61]) EA/93*

SHIRLEY, Madge actress, musician, singer CDP

SHIRLEY, Nellie (b 1882) English actress GRB/1-2

SHIRLEY, Peg American actress
TW/28

SHIRLEY, Thomas P. (d 1962
[62]) actor BE*, BP/46*

SHIRLEY, Walter, Sr. (d 1963
[67]) performer BE*

SHIRLEY, William (fl 1739-80)
dramatist CP/1-3, DNB, GT

SHIRLING, Jack (d 1916) EA/17*

SHIRO, James A. (d 1975) performer BP/60*

SHIRRA, Edmunston (d 1861) actor BE*, WWT/14*

SHIRREFF, Jane [Mrs. Thomas
Walcott] (1811-83) singer CDP

SHIRREFS, Andrew (fl 1790-96)
dramatist CP/3

SHIRVELL, James (1902-62)

English manager WWT/10-14

SHOECRAFT, Ruth see McDevitt,
Ruth

SHOEMAKER, Ann (b 1891) American actress BE, WWT/13-16

SHOLEM ALEICHEM (1859-1916)
Russian dramatist MH, MWD,
RE

SHONE, Minnie Marion [Mrs.
Robert V. Shone] (d 1898 [33])
EA/99*

SHONE, Robert V[ictor] (d 1901
[45]) manager, agent, business
manager EA/02*, WWT/14*

SHONE, Mrs. Robert V[ictor]
see Shone, Minnie Marion

SHONE, W. (fl 1810) editor CP/3

SHOR, Miriam Craig (d 1971
[54]) performer BP/55*

SHORE, Dinah (b 1917) American
singer CB

SHORE, J. G. [James Gregory
McLoughlin] (d 1885 [58]) actor
OAA/1-2

SHORE, Katherine see Cibber,
Mrs. Colley

SHORT, Antrim (d 1972 [72]) performer BP/57*

SHORT, Bobby (b 1924) American
performer CB

SHORT, Ernest (1875-1959) Australian writer WWW/5

SHORT, Frank Lea (d 1949 [75])
American actor, director
BE*, BP/34*

SHORT, Hassard (1877-1956) English producer, director, actor
CB, TW/2-8, 13, WWT/5-12

SHORT, Joe (d 1974 [91]) performer BP/59*

SHORT, Sarah (d 1970 [95]) performer BP/55*

SHORT, Sylvia (b 1927) American
actress, singer BE, TW/11-12

SHORT, William Frederick see
Saroni

SHORT, William Saroni (d 1886)
musical clown EA/87*

SHOSHANO, Rose (d 1968 [73])
performer BP/53*

SHOTTER, Ralph Champion see
Michael, Ralph

SHOTTER, Winifred (b 1904) English actress WWT/6-14

SHOTWELL, Marie (d 1934) American actress WWS

SHOWALTER, Edna Blanche (b
1888) American singer WWM

SHOWALTER, Max [Casey Adams]
(b 1917) American actor TW/
3-5, 22-24, 28

SHOWERISKEY, Ivan slack-rope
dancer HAS

SHRADER, Frederick Franklin
(1859-1943) German/American
dramatist, critic GRB/3-4,
WWT/1-2

SHRAPTER, Thomas (fl 1790)
dramatist CP/3

SHREVE, Tiffany (d 1964 [31])
actress BE*

SHRINER, Herb (1918-70) American humorist, monologist,
musician BE, TW/26

SHRIVAL, Mr. (fl 1843) singer
HAS

SHUARD, Amy (1924-75) English
singer ES

SHUBERT, Jacob J. (1880-1963)
American manager AAS,
COC, ES, NTH, OC/2-3,
SR, TW/2-8, 20, WWA/4,
WWM, WWT/3-13

SHUBERT, John (1908-62) American executive TW/19

SHUBERT, Lee (1875-1953)
American manager AAS,
COC, GRB/2-4, ES, NTH,
OC/2-3, SR, TW/2-8, WWA/
3, WWS, WWT/1-11

SHUBERT, Milton (d 1967 [66])
producer TW/23

SHUBERT, Sam S. (1876-1905)
American manager AAS,
COC, ES, GRB/1, NTH,
OC/2-3

SHUCKBOROUGH, Charles (fl
1740) English? dramatist
CP/2-3

SHUKSHIN, Vasily (d 1974 [75])
producer/director/choreographer
BP/59*

SHULL, Leo (b 1913) American
publisher, producer, journalist
BE, WWT/15-16

SHULL, Richard B. (b 1929)
American actor TW/26

SHULMAN, Max (b 1919) American dramatist BE, CB

SHULMAN, Milton (b 1913) Canadian critic, dramatist AAS,
WWT/14-16

SHULMAN, Thomas (d 1971)
writer? BP/56*

SHUMAN, Roy (d 1973 [48]) actor
TW/30

SHUMER, Harry (d 1965) theatrical
haulier BP/50*

SHUMLIN, Carmen (d 1970) performer BP/55*

SHUMLIN, Herman E. (b 1896/98)
American producing manager
BE, CB, ES, NTH, TW/2-8,
WWT/8-16

SHUNMUGHAM, T. K. (d 1973
[61]) performer BP/57*

SHURR, Lester H. (d 1971) talent
agent BP/55*

SHURR, Louis (d 1967) talent
representative BE, TW/24

SHURTLEFF, Michael American
dramatist, casting director BE

SHUTER, Mr. actor TD/2

SHUTER, Edward (1728-76) English
actor CDP, COC, DNB, ES,
GT, OC/1-2, TD/1-2

SHUTTA, Ethel [née Schutte] (1896-
1976) American actress, singer
TW/20, 27-29, WWT/15

SHUTTLEWORTH, Miss (fl 1805)
actress TD/2

SHWARTZ, Evgenyi Lvovich (1896-
1961) Russian dramatist COC

SHWARTZ, Martin (b 1923) American press representative BE

SHY, Gus (d 1945 [51]) comedian
TW/2

SHYRE, Paul (b 1926/29) American
director, producer, dramatist,
actor BE, TW/13-14, 21, 27,
WWT/15-16

SIAMESE TWINS, The (1810/11-74)
freaks CDP, HAS

SIBBS, John (d 1886) Negro comedian EA/87*

SIBLEY, Antoinette (b 1939) English dancer CB, ES

SIBLEY, Lucy [Mrs. Edgar Smart]
(d 1945) English actress EA/
96, GRB/1

SIBONI, Erik (d 1892 [63]) composer EA/93*

SIBTHORPE, Edward (fl 1608)
share-holder DA

SICARD, Clara (d 1876) reader
EA/77*

SICARI, Joseph R. (b 1939) American actor TW/24-26, 29

SICKELMORE, Richard (fl 1797-
1805) dramatist CP/3

SICKERT, Walter Richard (d 1942
[81]) actor BE*, WWT/14*

SIDAY, Eric (d 1976 [71]) com-
poser/lyricist BP/60*

SIDDLE, S. B. (d 1889) music-
hall proprietor EA/90*

SIDDONS, Harriett see Siddons,
Mrs. Henry

SIDDONS, Harry see Palmer,
Henry

SIDDONS, Henry (1774-1815) English actor, manager, dramatist
CP/3, DNB, ES, GT, TD/1-2

SIDDONS, Mrs. Henry [née Mur-
ray] (c. 1783-1844) actress
CDP, DNB, TD/1-2

SIDDONS, Sarah (1755-1831) Eng-
lish actress CDP, COC,
DNB, ES, GT, HP, NTH,
OC/1-3, OX, PDT, TD/1-2

SIDDONS, William J. (d 1890
[59]) musician EA/91*

SIDELLE, Mr. singer, change
artist CDP

SIDGWICK, Ethel (1877-1970)
English dramatist WWW/6

SIDNEY, Mr. actor CDP

SIDNEY, Miss (d 1833) actress
CDP

SIDNEY, Fred W. (d 1910) English actor, dramatist, stage
manager WWS

SIDNEY, George (1876/78-1945)
American actor ES, SR,
TW/1

SIDNEY, H. C. (d 1890) actor
EA/91*

SIDNEY, Irene (d 1970) performer BP/55*

SIDNEY, Mabel (d 1969 [85])
performer BP/54*

SIDNEY, Minnie [Mrs. Milano]
(d 1873) actress EA/74*

SIDNEY, Sir Philip (1554-86)
English writer DNB, ES,
FGF, NTH

SIDNEY, P. Jay (b 1934) actor
TW/22

SIDNEY, Suzan (b 1946) American actress TW/25, 27

SIDNEY, Sylvia [Sophia Kosow]
(b 1910) American actress
AAS, BE, ES, TW/22-24,
WWT/7-16

SIDNEY, William (d 1895) stage
manager EA/96*

SIDUS, Georgina see Mrs.
Oldmixon

SIEBERT, Charles (b 1938) American actor TW/25, 27-30

SIEBERT, Ronald H. American
actor TW/29-30

SIEDENBERG, Mme. (fl 1852)
singer CDP

SIEGEL, Arthur (b 1923) American
composer, musician, actor BE

SIEGEL, Harvey (b 1945) American
actor TW/28

SIEGEL, Mark (b 1947) American
actor TW/29

SIEGEL, Max (d 1958 [57]) producer BE*, BP/43*

SIEGEL, William (d 1966 [73])
dramatist BP/50*

SIEGLER, Ivy American actress
TW/27

SIEGMEISTER, Elie (b 1909)
American composer, musical
director, educator BE

SIEGRIST AND LEVANION acrobats
CDP

SIENKIEWICZ, Henry (1846-1916)
Polish actor SR

SIEPI, Cesare (b 1922/23) Italian
singer BE, CB, TW/19

SIERRA, Gregorio Martinez (d
1947 [66]) Spanish dramatist
BP/32*, WWT/14*

SIERRA, Margarita (d 1963 [26])
performer BP/48*

SIEVEKING, Margot English actress
WWT/8

SIEVIER, Mary Jane [Mrs. W. R.
Sievier] (d 1868 [22]) EA/69*

SIEVIER, Mrs. W. R. see
Sievier, Mary Jane

SIFACE (1653-97) Italian singer
ES

SIFF, Ira (b 1946) American actor
TW/30

SIFTON, Paul (1898-1972) American dramatist MD, MWD

SIGGINS, Jeff (b 1943) American
actor TW/22-24

SIGNORET, Gabriel (1878-1937)
French actor WWT/4

SIKS, Geraldine B. (b 1912) American educator, director BE

SILBER, Don (b 1936) American
actor TW/23-24, 26

SILBERT, Lisa (d 1965 [85]) performer BP/50*, WWT/14*

SILBON, Cornelius (d 1891) performer? EA/92*

SILBON, Fred [Little Ebor] (d
1876) gymnast EA/77*

SILBON, Minnie [Mrs. Walter Sil-
bon] (d 1905 [34]) EA/06*

SILBON, Walter (d 1903 [37]) acrobat EA/04*

SILBON, Mrs. Walter see
Silbon, Minnie
SILBURNE, Edward (d 1888 [48])
actor EA/89*
SILETTI, Mario (b 1935) Amer-
ican actor TW/27
SILETTI, Mario G. (d 1964 [60])
actor BE*
SILL, William Raymond (1869-
1922) American press repre-
sentative, manager WWM,
WWS
SILLMAN, Leonard (b 1908)
American producer, actor,
director BE, TW/24, 26,
WWT/15-16
SILLS, Beverly (b 1929) Ameri-
can singer CB
SILLS, Gladys Wynne (d 1964
[78]) performer BP/49*
SILLS, Milton (1882-1930) Amer-
ican actor DAB, ES, WWA/1,
WWM
SILLS, Pawnee American actress
TW/25, 30
SILLWARD, Edward (d 1930)
actor BE*, WWT/14*
SILLY, Lea French singer CDP
SILSBEE, Joshua S. (1813/15-53)
American actor CDP, HAS,
SR
SILSBEE, Mrs. Josiah see
Chapman, Mrs. William A.
SILVA, Nina de see De Silva,
Nina
SILVAIN, Mons. (d 1856 [50])
dancer EA/72*
SILVANO, Mme. Alfonso (d 1917)
EA/18*
SILVANO, Jack (d 1917) EA/18*
SIL-VARA, G. (d 1938 [62])
dramatist WWT/14*
SILVER, Mrs. see Kingston,
Gertrude
SILVER, Christine [Mrs. Walter
Maxwell] (1883/84-1960) Eng-
lish actress GRB/4, WWT/
1-12
SILVER, Joe (b 1922) American
actor BE, TW/22-24, 27-28,
30
SILVER, Monty (b 1933) Ameri-
can talent representative BE
SILVER, Ronald (b 1946) Amer-
ican actor TW/30
SILVER, Stuart (b 1947) Ameri-
can actor TW/29
SILVERA, Frank (1914-70)

Jamaican actor, director BE,
TW/27, WWA/5
SILVERBLATT, Howard see Da
Silva, Howard
SILVERMAN, Harriet (d 1975
[100]) columnist WWT/16*
SILVERMAN, Jack (d 1974 [86])
restaurateur BP/59*
SILVERMAN, Sid (1898-1950)
American publisher BE*, BP/
34*
SILVERMAN, Sime (1872-1933)
American editor, publisher
BE*, BP/18*, WWT/14*
SILVERMAN, Syd (b 1932) Ameri-
can newspaper publisher BE
SILVERS, Louis (d 1954 [64])
American composer BE*, BP/
38*
SILVERS, Phil (b 1911/12) Ameri-
can actor BE, CB, ES, TW/
4-5, 8-20, 27-29, WWT/16
SILVERSTONE, Jonas T. (b 1906)
American attorney, producer
BE
SILVESTER (fl 1625) actor DA
SILVESTER, Mr. (fl 1788) drama-
tist CP/3
SILVIA, Leslie (b 1958) American
actress TW/26-27
SILVO, William (d 1880 [17])
gymnast EA/81*
SIM, Alastair (1900-76) Scottish
actor AAS, ES, WWT/9-16
SIM, Henry Edward Clulow (d 1901
[29]) EA/03*
SIM, Millie (b 1895) English ac-
tress WWT/6-9
SIM, Sheila (b 1922) English ac-
tress WWT/11-13
SIM, William (d 1885) musical
director EA/86*
SIMANEK, Otto (d 1967 [66]) per-
former BP/52*
SIMEON, Mrs. J. H. see
Simeon, Mrs. L.
SIMEON, Mrs. L. [Mrs. J. H.
Simeon] (d 1886) EA/87*
SIMEON, Louisa see Chatterley,
Louisa
SIMEONS (fl 1802) dramatist CP/3
SIMIONATO, Giulietta (b 1910/16)
Italian singer CB, ES
SIMKINS, William (d 1870) actor
EA/71*
SIMMONDS, Benjamin (d 1910
[84]) musician EA/11*
SIMMONDS, James (d 1882 [98])

EA/83*
SIMMONDS, John (d 1874 [45])
actor EA/75*
SIMMONDS, J. Rewe (d 1886)
treasurer EA/87*
SIMMONDS, Morris (1836-96)
American agent, manager SR
SIMMONDS, Stanley (b 1907)
American actor TW/24-26
SIMMONS, Mr. (fl c. 1802-04)
actor OX, TD/1-2
SIMMONS, Mrs. see Seymour,
Molly
SIMMONS, Charles (d 1872 [71])
musician, composer EA/73*
SIMMONS, Connie (b 1952)
American actress TW/24-25
SIMMONS, Ernest Romaine (d
1954 [80+]) casting director,
dance director, business
manager, musician BP/38*
SIMMONS, Georgia (b 1884)
American actress TW/23
SIMMONS, James Wright (fl
early 19th cent [68]) Ameri-
can dramatist EAP, RJ
SIMMONS, Joseph (d 1875 [50])
music-hall proprietor EA/
76*
SIMMONS, Keith (b 1955) Amer-
ican actor TW/30
SIMMONS, Lavinia [Miss Lavine]
(d 1872) actress EA/73*
SIMMONS, Lew (1838-1908)
minstrel manager, actor
CDP
SIMMONS, Nat (b 1936) Ameri-
can actor TW/22-24
SIMMONS, Samuel (1777?-1819)
English actor CDP, DNB,
EA/92, GT
SIMMONS, Viola Bowers see
Bowers, Viola
SIMMONS, William Arthur see
Little Simmy
SIMMS, Mrs. C. H. (d 1885)
EA/86*
SIMMS, Don[ald] (b 1934) Amer-
ican actor TW/26, 28
SIMMS, Henrietta (d 1887) ac-
tress WWT/14*
SIMMS, Hilda (b 1920) American
actress BE, CB, TW/1-3,
26, WWT/11-16
SIMMS, John (d 1885) marionette
proprietor EA/86*
SIMMS, Lizzie (d 1886) dancer
EA/87*

SIMMS, Sheryl American actress
TW/30
SIMMS, Willard (fl 1900-06) Amer-
ican actor WWS
SIMMS, William Gilmore (1806-70)
dramatist CDP
SIMON dramatist CP/3, FGF
SIMON, Mme. actress CDP
SIMON, Bernard (1904-77) Ameri-
can press representative BE
SIMON, Charles (d 1910 [60])
dramatist BE*, WWT/14*
SIMON, Harry (d 1976 [87]) in-
surer BP/60*
SIMON, Henrietta (fl 1858) singer
HAS
SIMON, Henry W. (d 1970 [68])
critic BP/55*
SIMON, Herb (b 1946) American
actor TW/27
SIMON, Herb see Braha, Herb
SIMON, Joan Baim (d 1973 [41])
performer BP/58*
SIMON, John (b 1925) Jugoslav/
American BE, WWT/15-16
SIMON, Joseph (1594-1671) English
dramatist OC/3
SIMON, Leila (d 1876) American
reader WWM
SIMON, Louis M. (b 1906) Ameri-
can stage manager, executive
WWT/11-16
SIMON, Michel (d 1975 [80]) actor
BP/59*, WWT/16*
SIMON, Neil (b 1927) American
dramatist AAS, BE, CB, CD,
COC, ES, MH, MWD, WWT/
15-16
SIMON, William J. (d 1971 [80s])
composer/lyricist BP/56*
SIMONE, Mme. [Simone Le Bargy]
(b 1880) French actress GRB/
1-4, WWM, WWT/1-4
SIMONET, Mme. (fl 1781?) dancer
CDP
SIMONET, Miss (fl 1796?) ac-
tress, aeronaut CDP
SIMONIAN, Ronald (b 1948) Amer-
ican actor TW/28
SIMONOV, Konstantin Mikhailovich
(b 1915) Russian dramatist OC/
1-3
SIMONOV, Ruben (d 1968 [69])
performer BP/53*
SIMONS, Beverley (b 1938) Canadian dramatist CD
SIMONS, Eva H. (d 1974 [77])
producer/director/choreographer

BP/59*
SIMONS, Lucy American singer
HAS
SIMONS, Seymour (d 1949 [53])
songwriter TW/5
SIMONSEN, Fanny (d 1896 [61])
Australian singer EA/97*
SIMONSENS, Christie see
Farthing, Maud
SIMONSON, Lee (1888-1967)
American designer, executive
BE, CB, COC, ES, NTH,
OC/1-3, TW/3-8, 23, WWA/
4, WWT/7-14, WWW/6
SIMPLE, Pete (b 1908) circus
clown EA/09*
SIMPSON, Mr. (d 1827) Ameri-
can actor HAS
SIMPSON, Mr. (fl 1796-97)
actor HAS
SIMPSON, Mr. ["Irish Simpson"]
(fl 1797) actor HAS
SIMPSON, Mrs. see Thomas,
Mrs.
SIMPSON, Mrs. (d 1832) actress
HAS
SIMPSON, Mrs. [née Louisa
Dalby] (d 1872 [34]) singer
EA/73*
SIMPSON, Catherine Raynor
[Mrs. Jack Raynor] (d 1912)
EA/13*
SIMPSON, C. H. (1771-1835)
master of ceremonies CDP
SIMPSON, Charles (d 1879 [27])
variety artist EA/80*
SIMPSON, Charles (d 1894 [80])
pantomimist EA/95*
SIMPSON, Mrs. Charles see
Simpson, Emma Ann
SIMPSON, Cheridah (d 1922 [58])
American singer, actress
SR
SIMPSON, Christopher (fl 1610-
12) actor DA
SIMPSON, Clifford (d 1906
[35]) performer? EA/07*
SIMPSON, Cuthbert (fl 1616)
actor DA
SIMPSON, Dennis (b 1950) West
Indian actor TW/29-30
SIMPSON, Mrs. E. [née Jones]
(fl 1809-22) actress HAS
SIMPSON, Edmund Shaw (1784-
1848) American actor, mana-
ger CDP, COC, DAB,
HAS, OC/1-3, SR, WWA/H
SIMPSON, Edward (d 1868) pro-

prietor EA/69*
SIMPSON, Elizabeth see Inch-
bald, Elizabeth
SIMPSON, Emma Ann [Mrs.
Charles Simpson] (d 1881) EA/
82*
SIMPSON, Harold lyricist, librett-
tist WWT/5-11
SIMPSON, Harry (d 1872) actor?
EA/73*
SIMPSON, Ivan (1875-1951) English
actor TW/1-8
SIMPSON, James (d 1877) music-
hall proprietor EA/78*
SIMPSON, John (fl 1616) actor
DA
SIMPSON, John Dempster see
Mite, Mjr.
SIMPSON, John Henry (d 1878
[37]) comedian EA/79*
SIMPSON, John Palgrave (1807-87)
English dramatist CDP, EA/
68, NYM
SIMPSON, Joseph (fl 1785) drama-
tist CP/3
SIMPSON, Joseph (d 1869 [69])
actor? EA/70*
SIMPSON, Mrs. L. [née Woodling]
(d 1873 [26]) EA/74*
SIMPSON, Maria see Liston,
Mrs. W. H.
SIMPSON, Marion (d 1913 [56])
EA/14*
SIMPSON, Mercer Hampson (d
1902 [66]) lessee, manager
EA/03*, WWT/14*
SIMPSON, N[orman] F[rederick]
(b 1919) English dramatist
AAS, BE, CD, CH, COC, ES,
MH, MWD, PDT, WWT/14-16
SIMPSON, Pamela English actress
TW/8
SIMPSON, Peggy (b 1913) English
actress WWT/10-14
SIMPSON, Reginald (d 1964 [68])
performer BP/49*
SIMPSON, Richard (fl 1616) actor
DA
SIMPSON, Robert (fl 1616) actor
DA
SIMPSON, Ronald (1896-1957)
English actor WWT/7-12
SIMPSON, Russell (d 1959 [81])
actor BE*
SIMPSON, Sean (b 1944) American
actor TW/25
SIMPSON, Sloan American actor
TW/13

SIMPSON, Steve (b 1947) American actor TW/29-30

SIMPSON, Thomas Bartlett (d 1872 [66]) proprietor EA/73*

SIMPSON, Timothy Ogilvie (d 1880 [22]) comedian EA/81*

SIMPSON, T. P. (d 1877 [64]) proprietor EA/78*

SIMPSON, Mrs. T. P. (d 1885 [76]) proprietor EA/86*

SIMPSON, T. W. (d 1875) actor EA/76*

SIMPSON, Mrs. William (d 1877 [37]) EA/78*

SIMPSON, William Robert (d 1878 [33]) stage manager EA/79*

SIMS, Mrs. (d 1892) EA/93*

SIMS, Miss (fl 1797) actress TD/1-2

SIMS, Christine (d 1878) dancer EA/79*

SIMS, Mrs. Fred see Taylor, Ada

SIMS, Mrs. George see Clifford, Mrs.

SIMS, George R[obert] (1847-1922) English dramatist CDP, GRB/1-4, WWS, WWT/1-4, WWW/2

SIMS, Mrs. George R[obert] see Sims, Sarah Elizabeth

SIMS, Joan (b 1930) English actress WWT/13-16

SIMS, John A. G. see Rush, Bert

SIMS, Mamie see Williams, Mrs. Alan

SIMS, Marley (b 1948) American actor TW/29-30

SIMS, S. (fl 1797) actress CDP

SIMS, Sarah Elizabeth [Mrs. George R. Sims] (d 1886 [36]) EA/88*

SIMS, Violet (b 1883) English actress GRB/3

SIMS, William (d 1841 [53]) agent EA/72*

SIMS REEVES, Constance Emma (d 1901) EA/02*

SINATRA, Frank (b 1917) American singer CB

SINCKLER, William (fl 1629) musician DA

SINCLAIR, Anna (fl 1846) actress HAS

SINCLAIR, Arthur (1883-1951) Irish actor COC, ES, OC/1-3, TW/8, WWT/2-11

SINCLAIR, Barry (b 1911) English actor, singer WWT/10-16

SINCLAIR, Betty (b 1907) English actress TW/4, 9, 11-14, 22-23, 28

SINCLAIR, Caroline N. [Mrs. Edwin Forrest] (d 1891 [74]) American actress EA/92*

SINCLAIR, Catherine (fl 1837-59) American actress HAS, SR

SINCLAIR, Prof. Charles (d 1890 [63]) ventriloquist EA/91*

SINCLAIR, Mrs. Charles see Sinclair, Eliza

SINCLAIR, Eliza [Mrs. Charles Sinclair] (d 1887 [63]) EA/88*

SINCLAIR, Eric (b 1922) American actor TW/8-17

SINCLAIR, E. V. (d 1887) EA/88*

SINCLAIR, George (b 1858) English agent, composer GRB/1

SINCLAIR, H. (d 1886) actor EA/87*

SINCLAIR, Mrs. Harry [Fanny Vernon] (d 1887 [34]) EA/88*

SINCLAIR, Henry (b 1834) actor OAA/1-2

SINCLAIR, Henry (d 1879 [50]) actor EA/81*, WWT/14*

SINCLAIR, Hugh (1903-62) English actor AAS, TW/19, WWT/7-13

SINCLAIR, Sir John (b 1754) Scottish? dramatist CP/3

SINCLAIR, John (1790/91/93-1857) Scottish singer BS, CDP, DNB, HAS, SR

SINCLAIR, J. P. (d 1871) singer EA/72*

SINCLAIR, Mabel (d 1916 [36]) ventriloquist EA/17*

SINCLAIR, Moray (d 1964 [63]) Canadian actor, press representative BE*

SINCLAIR, Nellie (d 1897) actress EA/98*

SINCLAIR, Polly see Robinson, Mrs.

SINCLAIR, Rebecca [Mrs. Nixon] (d 1875) actress EA/76*

SINCLAIR, Robert B. (1905-70) American director, actor BE, TW/26

SINCLAIR, Tom (b 1941) American actor TW/25, 30

SINCLAIR, Upton (1878-1968) American dramatist CB, HJD

SINCLAIR-HILL, Gerald Arthur Lewin see Hill, Sinclair

SINCLER, John (fl 1590-1604) actor DA

SINDEN, Burt (d 1911) comedian, dancer EA/12*

SINDEN, Donald (b 1923) English actor AAS, WWT/13-16

SINDEN, Topsy (b 1878) actress, singer, dancer GRB/1-4, WWT/1-6

SINGER, Arthur R. (d 1967 [66]) manager BP/52*

SINGER, Campbell (1909-76) English actor, dramatist WWT/14-16

SINGER, Israel J. (1893-1944) dramatist CB

SINGER, John (fl 1598-1602) dramatist, actor CP/3, DA, DNB, FGF

SINGER, Teresina (1850-1928) Moravian singer CDP, ES

SINGERMAN, Bernard (d 1973 [61]) performer BP/58*

SINGHER, Martial (b 1904) French singer CB, ES

SINGLETON, Mr. (fl 1752-53) English actor HAS

SINGLETON, Mr. (fl 1826) actor HAS

SINGLETON, Catherine (d 1969 [65]) performer BP/54*

SINGLETON, Charles W. (d 1880) EA/81*

SINGLETON, Miss E. (fl 1839) actress HAS

SINGLETON, Kate (fl 1864) actress HAS

SINGLETON, Sam (b 1940) American actor TW/26-27

SINGLETON, Rev. Thomas (fl 1656-83) dramatist CP/3

SINNOTT, Catherine (d 1911) EA/12*

SIODMAK, Robert (d 1973 [72]) producer/director/choreographer BP/57*

SIPLE, S. M. (d 1854) actor HAS

SIPPERLEY, Ralph (d 1928 [38]) actor BE*, BP/12*

SIPPLE, John James (d 1905) music-hall comedian EA/06*

SIPPLE, Rosina [Mrs. George Aytoun] (d 1906 [47]) EA/07*

SIRCOM, Arthur R. (b 1899) American director, actor BE, TW/2

SIRE, Henry B. (d 1917) pro-ducer, manager BE*, WWT/14*

SIRKIN, Stephen (d 1974 [30]) dramatist BP/58*

SIROLA, Joseph (b 1929) American actor TW/24

SISSLE, Noble (d 1975 [86]) composer WWT/16*

SITES, G. (fl 1829) American actor HAS

SITGREAVES, Beverley (1867-1943) American actress CB, WWM, WWS, WWT/4-9

SIVADO, Robert (d 1908) music-hall performer EA/09*

SIVRONI, Amy (d 1910 [39]) performer? EA/11*

SIVY, Michael (b 1921) American actor TW/3

SIZEMORE, Asher (d 1975 [69]) performer BP/60*

SIZOVA, Alla (b 1939) Russian dancer ES

SKAIFE, William (d 1892) acting manager, actor EA/93*

SKALA, Lilia Austrian actress TW/7-8, 25, 27, WWT/16

SKEAF, Joseph (d 1884 [46]) professor of music EA/85*

SKEAPING, Mary (fl 1925-59) English dancer ES

SKEFFINGTON, Sir Lumley St. George (1771/78-1850) English dramatist CDP, CP/3, DNB, GT, HP

SKEGGS, Matthew (d 1773) actor CDP

SKEIN, Farmer (b 1877) actor GRB/1

SKELLEY, Henry (d 1904 [49]) property master EA/05*

SKELLEY, Joseph Harold see Skelly, Hal

SKELLY, Hal [Joseph Harold Skelley] (1891-1934) American actor WWT/7

SKELLY, James (d 1969 [33]) performer BP/53*

SKELLY, Madge (b 1904) American actress, producer, director, educator BE

SKELTON, Herbert Sleath see Sleath, Herbert

SKELTON, Mrs. Herbert Sleath see Jeffreys, Ellis

SKELTON, John (c. 1460-1529) English dramatist COC, CP/2-3, DNB, HP, MH, OC/2-3

SKELTON, Red (b 1913) American

comedian CB, ES
SKELTON, Thomas lighting designer, stage manager WWT/16
SKEMP, Arthur Rowland (1882-1918) English dramatist, educator WWW/2
SKERRETT, Emma see Skerrett, Mrs. George
SKERRETT, Fanny (b 1849) American actress HAS
SKERRETT, George (1810-55) English actor CDP, HAS
SKERRETT, Mrs. George [Emma; Mrs. Henry L. Bascomb] (1817-87) Scottish actress CDP, HAS, NYM
SKERRETT, Rose see Shewell, Mrs. L. R., II
SKETCHLEY, Arthur [George Rose] (d 1882 [64]) English dramatist, actor CDP, DNB, EA/68, HAS
SKIBINE, George (b 1920) Russian/American dancer, choreographer ES
SKIKNE, Laurence see Harvey, Laurence
SKILES, Steve (b 1945) American actor TW/24
SKILLAN, George (b 1893) English actor WWT/6-14
SKINNER, Cornelia Otis (b 1901) American actress AAS, BE, CB, COC, ES, HJD, NTH, OC/1-3, TW/1-17, WWT/7-16
SKINNER, Edith Warman (b 1904) Canadian educator, acting coach BE
SKINNER, Edna (b 1922) American actress TW/1
SKINNER, Frank (d 1968 [69]) composer/lyricist BP/53*
SKINNER, George (d 1896) actor EA/97*
SKINNER, Harold Otis (d 1922 [33]) actor BE*, BP/7*
SKINNER, Howard K. (d 1971) American executive WWA/5
SKINNER, Mrs. H. R. see Zimmer, Maggie
SKINNER, Maud Durbin (b 1873) American actress GRB/3-4
SKINNER, Otis (1858-1942) American actor CB, CDP, COC, DAB, ES, GRB/2-4, HJD, NTH, OC/1-3, PP/3, SR,

WWA/1, WWM, WWS, WWT/1-9
SKINNER, Mrs. Otis see Durbin, Maud
SKINNER, Richard (fl 1547-59) actor DA
SKINNER, Richard (1900-71) American producer, manager, actor BE, TW/28
SKINNER, Mrs. Robert see Bristow, Mrs.
SKINNER, Ted (b 1911) American educator BE
SKINNER, W. (d 1906) music-hall stage manager EA/07*
SKIPITARIS, Loukas Greek actor TW/25
SKIPPER, Bill (b 1922) American actor, dancer? TW/2-6, 12
SKIPWORTH, Alison (1863-1952) English actress TW/9, WWS, WWT/8-11
SKIRPAN, Stephen J. (b 1930) American equipment designer, lighting consultant, inventor BE
SKLAR, George (b 1908) American dramatist BE, MH, MWD, NTH
SKLAR, Michael (b 1944) American actor TW/28
SKOURAS, George P. (d 1964 [68]) Greek executive BE*
SKOURATOFF, Vladimir (b 1925) French dancer ES
SKRINE, Mary Nesta see Farrell, M. J.
SKULNIK, Menashe (1894/98-1970) Polish actor BE, TW/11-20, 22-23, 27, WWA/5, WWT/13-14
SLACK, Ben (b 1937) American actor TW/28-29
SLADE, Alfred George (d 1907) circus manager EA/08*
SLADE, John (d 1760) dramatist CP/2-3
SLADE, Julian (b 1930) English composer, dramatist, actor AAS, PDT, WWT/13-16
SLADE, Olga (d 1949) actress BE*, WWT/14*
SLANE, Eva Weith (b 1929) German talent representative BE
SLATE, Henry (b 1915) American actor TW/5-6
SLATE, Syd (d 1976 [68]) performer BP/60*
SLATER, Mr. actor HAS
SLATER, Arthur [Arthur Stewart] actor, variety artist GRB/1

SLATER, C. Dundas (d 1912
[60]) manager WWT/14*
SLATER, Chris (d 1880) music-
hall chairman & manager
EA/81*
SLATER, Daphne (b 1928) English
actress AAS, WWT/11-14
SLATER, Elizabeth [Mrs. Thomas
Slater] (d 1870) EA/71*
SLATER, George M. (d 1949
[79]) actor, producer, mana-
ger BE*, WWT/14*
SLATER, Hartley (d 1964 [63])
performer BE*
SLATER, Mrs. J. H. [Louisa
Pereira] (d 1885 [39]) actress
EA/87*
SLATER, John (d 1886 [43])
stage manager EA/87*
SLATER, John (1916-75) English
actor WWT/12-15
SLATER, Martin (d 1625?) ac-
tor, dramatist CP/3, DA
SLATER, Samuel (fl 1679) dra-
matist CP/3
SLATER, Mrs. Thomas see
Slater, Elizabeth
SLATKIN, Felix (d 1963 [47])
composer, conductor BE*
SLATTERY, Daniel G. (d 1964
[91]) manager BE*
SLATTERY, James (d 1974
[26]) performer BP/58*
SLAUGHTER, Harriet (b 1937)
American actress TW/26-29
SLAUGHTER, Henry (d 1882
[38]) manager EA/83*
SLAUGHTER, Martin see Slater,
Martin
SLAUGHTER, N. Carter (1885-
1956) English actor, manager
WWT/6-11
SLAUGHTER, Ted see Slaughter,
N. Carter
SLAUGHTER, Walter (1860-1908)
English composer, conductor
GRB/1-3
"SLAUGHTER, William" actor
DA
SLAVENSKA, Mia (b 1914/17)
Yugoslav dancer, choreographer
CB, ES
SLAVIN, John C. (d 1940 [71])
American actor BE*, BP/
25*, WWT/14*
SLAVIN, Susan American actress
TW/26
SLEAP, Ellen Caroline [Mme.

Helena; Mrs. William S. Sleap]
(d 1884) EA/85*
SLEAP, Mrs. William S. see
Sleap, Ellen Caroline
SLEATH, Herbert [Herbert Sleath
Skelton] (1870-1921) English
actor, producer GRB/1-4,
WWM, WWS, WWT/1-5
SLEE, John (fl 1537-40) actor DA
SLEEPER, Martha (b 1910/11)
American actress BE, TW/1-3,
WWT/9-11
SLEIGH, J. P. (d 1905 [54]) actor
GRB/1
SLEIGH, Louise Elizabeth [Mrs.
W. H. Sleigh] (d 1869 [24])
EA/70*
SLEIGH, Mrs. W. H. see Sleigh,
Louise Elizabeth
SLEMONS, Frederica (d 1964 [90])
performer BP/49*
SLEZAK, Leo (1873-1946) Austrian
singer ES, TW/3, WWA/2
SLEZAK, Walter (b 1902) Austrian
actor, singer AAS, BE, CB,
ES, TW/15-16, WWT/8-10, 15-
16
SLINGSBY, Mary (d 1694) actress
DNB
SLINGSBY, Simon (fl 1758-85)
English dancer ES
SLITER, Dick (d 1861) jig dancer
HAS
SLOAN, Fern (b 1940) American
actress TW/29
SLOAN, John T. K. (1832-61) Eng-
lish actor, manager HAS
SLOAN, Mrs. John T. K. [née
Ploughman] (fl 1849-68) English
actress HAS
SLOAN, Mrs. J. T. see Sander-
son, Julia
SLOAN, Mimi American actress
TW/24
SLOANE, Alfred Baldwin (1872-
1924) American composer GRB/
3-4, WWA/1, WWM, WWS,
WWT/1-5
SLOANE, Everett (1909-65) Ameri-
can actor CB, TW/22
SLOANE, Olive (1894/96-1963) ac-
tress WWT/5-13
SLOCUM, Edwin N. (1836-95)
minstrel, minstrel manager
CDP
SLOMAN, Charles (1808-70) English
music-hall performer COC,
OC/1-3

SLOMAN, Henry (d 1869 [72])
machinist EA/71*
SLOMAN, Henry (d 1873 [80])
comedian EA/74*, WWT/
14*
SLOMAN, John (d 1873 [79])
English comic singer CDP,
HAS
SLOMAN, Mrs. John [née
Whitaker; Mrs. H. Darton]
(d 1858 [59]) English actress
CDP, HAS, OX
SLONIMSKY, Nicolas (b 1894)
Russian composer, conductor
CB
SLOPER, Edward Hugh Lindsay
(1826-87) composer, musician
CDP
SLOPER, Lindsay see Sloper,
Edward Hugh Lindsay
SLOSSER, Pauline Hall (d 1974
[83]) performer BP/59*
SLOUS, A. R. (d 1883 [71])
dramatist EA/68
SLOWACKI, Juliusz (1809-49)
Polish dramatist COC
SLY, William (d 1608) English
actor DA, ES, GT, NTH,
OC/1-3
SLYE, Thomas actor DA
SMALE, Mrs. T. E. see El-
liott, Charlotte
SMALE, Thomas E. (d 1890)
acting manager, business
manager EA/91*, WWT/14*
SMALE, Mrs. Tom see Elliott,
Charlotte
SMALL, Dick (d 1972 [58]) per-
former BP/56*
SMALL, Jack (d 1962 [52]) Amer-
ican manager BE*, BP/46*
SMALL, Lillian Schary (d 1961
[60]) talent representative
BE*
SMALL, Michael (b 1939) Amer-
ican manager BE
SMALL, Neva (b 1952) American
actress TW/22-28, 30
SMALL, Paul (d 1954 [45]) Amer-
ican talent representative
BE*
SMALL, Seldon (d 1974 [72])
costume supplier BP/58*
SMALL, William (d 1969 [84])
secretary BP/54*
SMALLENS, Alexander (1889-1972)
Russian/American conductor
CB, WWA/5

SMALLEY, Eugene B. (d 1968
[46]) composer/lyricist BP/53*
SMALLEY, John (d 1881 [61])
actor? EA/82*
SMALLS, Ed (d 1974 [92]) showman
BP/59*
SMALLWOOD, Mr. (fl 1786) actor
HAS
SMALLWOOD, Ernest Edward
see Wood, Ernest
SMALLWOOD, William (d 1897)
composer EA/98*
SMART, Christopher (1722-71)
English dramatist CP/2-3,
DNB
SMART, Dick (b 1915) Hawaiian
actor TW/3, 5-6
SMART, Edgar (d 1896 [47]) EA/
97*
SMART, Mrs. Edgar see Sibley,
Lucy
SMART, Sir George Thomas (1776-
1867) English conductor, com-
poser CDP, DNB
SMART, Henry (d 1879 [66]) com-
poser, musician EA/80*
SMART, Henry Edward (d 1894
[50]) EA/95*
SMART, Mary (d 1869) EA/70*
SMEAD, Mr. (fl 1850) actor HAS
SMEATON, Mary (d 1893) EA/94*
SMEDLEY, Arnold (d 1908 [28])
actor EA/09*
SMEDLEY, Constance (1881-1941)
dramatist CB
SMEDLEY, Morgan T. (d 1964
[46]) American actor BE*,
BP/48*
SMEDLEY, William Ellis (d 1916)
actor SR
SMILEY, Brenda (b 1947) Ameri-
can actress TW/24-25
SMILEY, Ralph (b 1916) American
actor TW/2
SMILEY, Red (d 1972 [47]) per-
former BP/56*
SMITH, Mr. actor TD/2
SMITH (fl 1798) dramatist CP/3
SMITH, Dr. dramatist CP/2-3
SMITH, Mrs. [née Parr] (fl 1831)
Welsh dancer HAS
SMITH, Mrs. [née Ellen Mortimer]
(d 1874) actress EA/75*
SMITH, Mrs. see Dixon, Clara
Ann
SMITH, A. B. (d 1896) acting
manager EA/97*
SMITH, Adam (fl 1776) actor,

singer, dramatist CP/3
SMITH, Albert (1816-60) English
dramatist, actor CDP, COC,
DNB, OC/1-3
SMITH, Mrs. Albert see Smith,
Mary Lucy
SMITH, Alexis (b 1921) Canadian
actress TW/27-29, WWT/16
SMITH, Alf E. (d 1917) EA/18*
SMITH, Alfred (d 1870 [19])
acrobat EA/71*
SMITH, A. Montem (d 1891 [73])
singer EA/92*
SMITH, Anthony (fl 1616-28)
actor DA
SMITH, Archie American actor
TW/6-10
SMITH, Art (d 1973 [73]) actor
TW/29
SMITH, Arthur Corbett (d 1945
[65]) dramatist, composer
BE*, WWT/14*
SMITH, Arthur W. W. (1825-61)
English entertainer DNB
SMITH, Sir Aubrey see Smith,
Sir C. Aubrey
SMITH, Barrey American per-
former TW/30
SMITH, Beasley (d 1968 [67])
composer/lyricist BP/52*
SMITH, Betty (1904/06-72) Amer-
ican dramatist, educator BE,
CB, HJD
SMITH, Betty Jane (d 1973 [49])
performer BP/57*
SMITH, Billie see Bard, Wilkie
SMITH, Billy (d 1963 [60]) per-
former BE*
SMITH, Bruce (d 1942 [87])
scene artist BE*, WWT/14*
SMITH, Sir C. Aubrey (1863-
1948) English actor CB,
GRB/1-4, TW/5, WWS, WWT/
1-9
SMITH, C. F. (1813-64) Ameri-
can manager HAS
SMITH, Charles (1786-1856) Eng-
lish dramatist, singer CP/3,
DNB, EAP, RJ
SMITH, Charles F. (d 1894 [43])
secretary of Guildhall School
of Music EA/95*
SMITH, Charles Frederick
[Charles North] (d 1889 [29])
EA/90*
SMITH, Charles T. (1817-69)
English actor, manager HAS
SMITH, Charles W. (d 1971

[74]) performer BP/56*
SMITH, Chris (1879-1949) Ameri-
can composer BE*
SMITH, Christopher John (d 1888
[80]) pantomimist EA/89*
SMITH, C. J. (fl 1851) actor HAS
SMITH, Clara (fl 1803) actress
TD/2
SMITH, Clay (b 1885) American
actor WWT/4-7
SMITH, Constance M. see
Grafton, Cecil
SMITH, Cyril (1892-1963) Scottish
actor WWT/7-13
SMITH, Delos V., Jr. (b 1906)
American actor TW/24, 26
SMITH, Dodie [C. L. Anthony]
(b 1896) English dramatist, ac-
tress, director AAS, BE, CD,
ES, MH, NTH, PDT, WWT/7-
16
SMITH, Doyle R. (b 1924) Ameri-
can producer, director, actor,
educator BE
SMITH, E. dramatist CP/3
SMITH, Eddie (d 1964 [70]) talent
representative BE*
SMITH, Edgar McPhail (1857-1938)
American librettist GRB/3-4,
WWA/1, WWS, WWT/1-8
SMITH, Mrs. Edith see French,
Edie
SMITH, Edmund (1668/72-1710)
dramatist CP/1-3, DNB, GT
SMITH, Edward A. (d 1974 [85])
manager BP/58*
SMITH, Edward Tyrrell (1804-77)
English manager CDP, COC,
OC/1-3
SMITH, Elihu Hubbard (1771-98)
American dramatist CDP,
CP/3, EAP, HJD, RJ
SMITH, Eliza (d 1913 [58]) EA/14*
SMITH, Eliza see Groves, Eliza
SMITH, Elizabeth [Mrs. Sol Smith]
(d 1887 [75]) EA/88*
SMITH, Elizabeth see Arnold,
Mrs. Henry
SMITH, Elmer (d 1963 [71]) per-
former BE*
SMITH, Elsie Linehan (d 1964
[86]) actress BE*
SMITH, Mrs. Ernest J. (d 1975
[77]) dramatist BP/59*
SMITH, Fanny see Higginbottom,
Frances Ann
SMITH, F. H. (d 1869) acting
manager EA/70*

SMITH, Frank L. (d 1953 [67])
American press representa-
tive, manager BE*, BP/37*,
WWT/14*

SMITH, Frank M. (d 1976 [70])
composer/lyricist BP/60*

SMITH, Frederica (d 1910 [28])
EA/11*

SMITH, Frederica C. (d 1911)
lady superintendent of Guildhall School of Music EA/12*

SMITH, Frederick Wilson (d
1944 [64]) actor TW/1

SMITH, F. W. (d 1917) acting
manager EA/18*

SMITH, G. Albert (1898-1959)
American actor TW/2-3, 16

SMITH, Garnett (b 1937) American actor TW/25, 29-30

SMITH, Geddeth (b 1934) American actor TW/23

SMITH, George American actor
HAS

SMITH, George (1777-1836) English actor, singer BS, CDP,
EA/92

SMITH, George (d 1877 [78])
actor? EA/79*

SMITH, George Frederick (fl
1821) American actor HAS

SMITH, George T. (d 1947
[45]) producer, manager BE*,
WWT/14*

SMITH, George Totten (b 1871)
American dramatist WWM

SMITH, George W. (fl 1849)
maître de ballet HAS

SMITH, Gerald (d 1974 [81])
performer BP/59*

SMITH, Gladys Mary see Pickford, Mary

SMITH, Harold Montague see
Montague, Harold

SMITH, Harry Bache (1860-1936)
American librettist, dramatist
DAB, GRB/3-4, NTH, SR,
WWA/1, WWM, WWS, WWT/
1-7

SMITH, Harry James (1880-1918)
American dramatist DAB

SMITH, Harvey (b 1904) American teacher of stage lighting,
theatre consultant BE

SMITH, Helen S. (b 1909) American educator BE

SMITH, Helen Zenna see Price,
Evadne

SMITH, Henry (fl 1699) drama-

tist CP/1-3, GT

SMITH, Mrs. Henry B. see
Bentley, Irene

SMITH, Henry Oscar (d 1882)
EA/83*

SMITH, Henry Richard (b
1861) English manager
GRB/4

SMITH, Howard (1894/95-1968)
American actor, director BE,
TW/1-3, 5-14, 23-24, WWT/
11-14

SMITH, H. Reeves (1862-1938)
English actor EA/95, GRB/3-4,
WWT/1-8

SMITH, Hugh (d 1874) music-hall
lessee EA/75*

SMITH, Jack (1898-1950) American
vaudevillian TW/6

SMITH, James (fl 1796) dramatist
CP/3

SMITH, James (d 1876 [29]) musician EA/77*

SMITH, James Samuel see
Mendel

SMITH, J. C. (d 1888 [80]) American actor HAS

SMITH, J. C. (d 1889 [58]) stage
manager EA/90*

SMITH, Mrs. J. C. see Burchell, Clara

SMITH, Jenny (d 1865) dancer
HAS

SMITH, Jim see Dale, Jim

SMITH, Joe (d 1952) performer
BE*

SMITH, John (fl 1547-80) actor
DA

SMITH, John (fl 1609) actor
DA

SMITH, John (fl 1677) dramatist
CP/1-3

SMITH, John (d 1909) manager
EA/10*

SMITH, John Christopher (1712-95)
musician, composer CDP

SMITH, John N. (fl 1840) dramatist RJ

SMITH, John P. (d 1897 [65])
manager CDP

SMITH, John Washington (1815-77)
American minstrel, minstrel
manager CDP

SMITH, Jonathan S. (fl 1823?)
dramatist EAP

SMITH, Joseph (fl 1834-50) American actor HAS

SMITH, Joseph (d 1871 [42])

acrobat EA/72*
SMITH, Joseph (d 1903 [59])
    music-hall managing director
    EA/04*
SMITH, J. Rawson (1813-64)
    American scene painter HAS
SMITH, J. Sebastian (1869-1948)
    English actor WWT/5-10
SMITH, J. Sidney (d 1865)
    manager HAS
SMITH, J. Stanley (d 1974 [69])
    performer BP/58*
SMITH, Julia actress CDP
SMITH, J. W. (d 1864) Ethiopian
    comedian HAS
SMITH, Kate (fl 1879) singer SR
SMITH, Kate (b 1909) American
    singer, actress CB
SMITH, Kent (b 1907) American
    actor BE, TW/3-13, WWT/
    9-16
SMITH, Lemuel (d 1832) actor
    HAS
SMITH, Len, Jr. (b 1925) Amer-
    ican actor TW/4-6
SMITH, Leonard (fl 1640) actor
    DA
SMITH, Lester (d 1970 [77])
    publicist BP/55*
SMITH, Lewis Worthington (1866-
    1947) American dramatist
    WWA/2
SMITH, Lillian (b 1897) American
    dramatist HJD
SMITH, Mrs. Lillian Boardman
    see Boardman, Lillian
SMITH, Lois (b 1930) American
    actress BE, TW/12-13, 27,
    29-30, WWT/16
SMITH, Loring (b 1895) American
    actor BE, TW/8-15, 20,
    WWT/14-15
SMITH, Maggie (b 1934) English
    actress AAS, CB, COC, ES,
    WWT/13-16
SMITH, Maggie see Power,
    Mrs. Fred
SMITH, Marcus see Smith,
    Mark
SMITH, Margaret Armstrong (d
    1971 [73]) composer/lyricist
    BP/55*
SMITH, Mark (1829-74) American
    actor CDP, COC, DAB, HAS,
    OC/1-3, WWA/H
SMITH, Mark (b 1855) American
    actor PP/3
SMITH, Mark (b 1877) American

comedian WWM
SMITH, Mark, III (d 1944 [57])
    American actor BE*, BP/28*
SMITH, Mary Lucy [Mrs. Albert
    Smith] (d 1870 [39]) EA/71*
SMITH, Mary Sedley [Mrs. Sol
    Smith, Jr.] (d 1917 [87]) ac-
    tress CDP
SMITH, Matthew (fl 1631-38) actor
    DA
SMITH, Matthew (d 1875 [36]) les-
    see EA/76*
SMITH, Maybelle (d 1972 [48])
    performer BP/56*
SMITH, Mrs. M. E. (d 1867 [27])
    EA/68*
SMITH, Mrs. M. E. [Mrs. George
    Smith] (d 1880 [70]) EA/81*
SMITH, Merritt (b 1920) American
    actor TW/23
SMITH, Michael (b 1935) American
    dramatist, director CD
SMITH, Mildred Joanne (b 1923)
    American actress TW/3, 5-6
SMITH, Millicent Granville see
    Granville, Millicent
SMITH, Milton (b 1890) American
    educator, director BE
SMITH, Moses (d 1964 [63]) writer
    BE*
SMITH, Muriel (b 1923) American
    actress, singer BE, TW/1-6,
    12
SMITH, Nicholas (b 1934) English
    actor TW/24
SMITH, Norwood (b 1915) American
    actor, singer BE, TW/27, 30
"SMITH, O." see Smith, Richard
    John
SMITH, Oliver (b 1918) American
    designer, producer BE, CB,
    ES, PDT, TW/2-8, WWT/13-16
SMITH, Oscar (d 1971 [74]) critic
    BP/55*
SMITH, Patricia (b 1930) American
    actress BE, TW/8-9, 14
SMITH, Paul (b 1939) American
    actor TW/15
SMITH, Paul Gerard (1894-1968)
    American librettist, dramatist,
    actor, director WWT/7-9
SMITH, Queenie (b 1898/1902)
    American actress, singer,
    dancer TW/2, 6-8, WWT/6-10
SMITH, Ralph Errolle see
    Errolle, Ralph
SMITH, R. F. (d 1881) actor,
    lessee, manager EA/82*

Sedley-Smith, William Henry
SMITH, Mrs. William Henry
see Sedley-Smith, Mrs.
William Henry
SMITH, William N. (d 1869)
bone soloist HAS
SMITH, Winchell (1871/72-1933)
American actor, dramatist,
manager, director DAB, ES,
GRB/3-4, HJD, MD, MWD,
SR, WWA/1, WWT/1-7
SMITH, Wingate (d 1974 [79])
producer/director/choreographer
BP/59*
SMITH, Winifred (d 1967 [88])
educator BP/52*
SMITH, W. R. dramatist RJ
SMITHERS, Charles (d 1879
[46]) scene artist EA/81*
SMITHERS, Emily (d 1887 [27])
music-hall performer EA/88*
SMITHERS, Florence [Mrs. W.
H. Owen] English actress
GRB/1-3
SMITHERS, William (b 1927)
American actor TW/7-16, 20
SMITHSON, Florence (1884-1936)
English actress, singer GRB/
1-4, WWT/1-8
SMITHSON, Frank (d 1949 [88])
Irish actor, director BE*,
WWT/14*
SMITHSON, Frederick (d 1892
[68]) actor EA/93*
SMITHSON, Georgie (d 1899)
actress EA/00*
SMITHSON, Harriet Constance
(1800-54) English actress
BS, CDP, COC, DNB, EA/
92, OC/1-3, OX
SMITHSON, Laura (1885-1963)
English actress WWT/5-11
SMITHSON, Will (d 1927 [67])
producer, manager BE*,
WWT/14*
SMITH-THOMAS, Eleanor Mary
Tydfil see Fayre, Eleanor
SMOLKO, John (b 1928) Ameri-
can actor TW/14, 22-23
SMOLLETT, Tobias (1720/21-71)
Scottish dramatist CDP,
CP/1-3, DNB, GT, HP,
TD/1-2
SMYCH, J. Anthony (d 1966 [80])
performer BP/50*
SMYGHT, William (fl 1595) actor
DA
SMYTH, Dame Ethel Mary (1858-

1944) English composer DNB,
ES, WWW/4
SMYTH, John (1662-1717) English
dramatist CP/3, DNB, GT
SMYTH, Mrs. W. G. see
Armstrong, Sydney
SMYTHE, George (fl 1796) drama-
tist CP/3
SMYTHE, George see Davies,
George
SMYTHE, James Moore (1702-34)
English dramatist CP/1-3,
DNB
SMYTHE, Paul (d 1961 [79]) di-
rector WWT/14*
SMYTHE, William G. (d 1921 [66])
producer, manager BE*, BP/6*
SMYTH-PIGGOTT, A. (d 1936
[73]) manager WWT/14*
SMYTHSON, George (d 1883 [70])
actor EA/84*
SMYTHSON, Miss Montague [Amelia
Jane James; Mrs. P. R.
James] (d 1891) EA/92*
"SNAPDRAGON, Hector" (fl 1813?)
dramatist EAP
SNAPE, Fred A. (d 1900 [41])
actor EA/01*
SNAPE, Mrs. George (d 1878)
EA/79*
SNAPE, Louis (d 1899) actor
EA/00*
SNAZELLE, Annie T. [Mrs.
George H. Snazelle] (d 1911
[50]) EA/13*
SNAZELLE, George H. (d 1912
[63]) singer, entertainer, actor
EA/13*, WWT/14*
SNAZELLE, Mrs. George H. see
Snazelle, Annie T.
SNAZELLE, Lionel James (d 1907
[33]) EA/08*
SNEATH, Thomas F. [T. F. Sea-
more] (d 1875 [28]) actor EA/
76*
SNELL, David (b 1942) American
actor TW/30
SNELLING, Thomas (fl 1651)
dramatist CP/3
SNOW, Amanda (d 1972 [67]) per-
former BP/56*
SNOW, C[harles] P[ercy] (b 1909)
English dramatist PDT
SNOW, Davis (d 1975 [62]) drama-
tist BP/60*
SNOW, Ellen Rebecca (d 1912)
EA/13*
SNOW, Harry David (b 1928)

American actor TW/15-16, 21

SNOW, Marguerite (d 1958 [69]) actress BE*

SNOW, Norman (b 1950) American actor TW/30

SNOW, Ross (1868-1947) comedian SR

SNOW, Sophia see Baddeley, Sophia

SNOW, Ted (d 1903) minstrel CDP

SNOW, Valaida see Valaida

SNOWDEN, Mrs. (fl 1800) actress HAS

SNOWDON, Launcelot Marshall (d 1902 [44]) lessee EA/03*

SNOWDON, Mary J. see Chippendale, Mary J.

SNOWDON, Walter (d 1912 [50]) music-hall performer EA/13*

SNYDER, Agnes Tilton (d 1974 [90s]) composer/lyricist BP/58*

SNYDER, Arlen Dean (b 1933) American actor TW/25-29

SNYDER, Bert N. (d 1975) performer BP/60*

SNYDER, Denton (b 1915) American educator, director, designer BE

SNYDER, Drew (b 1946) American actor TW/25, 27-30

SNYDER, Gene (d 1953 [45]) American dance director BE*, BP/37*

SNYDER, Glyde (d 1972) performer BP/56*

SNYDER, Harold (d 1974) manager BP/59*

SNYDER, William (b 1929) American dramatist, educator CD

SOANE, George (d 1860 [69]) dramatist BE*, EA/72*, WWT/14*

SOARES, Frank (d 1868) actor? EA/69*

SOBEL, Bernard (1887/90-1964) American dramatist, critic BE, NTH, TW/20, WWA/4, WWT/9-13

SOBOL, Edward (d 1962 [70]) producer BE*

SOBOLEWSKI, J. Friedrich Eduard (1808-72) Prussian conductor, composer DAB

SOBOLOFF, Arnold (b 1930) American actor, singer BE, TW/22-26, 29-30, WWT/16

SOBOTKA, Ruth (d 1967 [42]) designer BP/52*

SODEN, Mrs. John see Forrest, Ella

SODERO, Cesare (1886-1947) Italian conductor, composer CB

SÖDERSTRÖM, Elisabeth (b 1927) Swedish singer ES

SODI, Pietro (c. 1716-c. 75) Italian dancer, choreographer ES

SOFAER, Abraham (b 1896) Burmese/English actor AAS, WWT/7-16

SOHLKE, Gus (1865-1924) producer, director WWT/4

SOKOLOFF, Vladimir (1889-1962) Russian actor TW/4-6, 18

SOKOLOVA, Lydia [Hilda Munnings] (1896-1974) English dancer, actress BTR/74, ES, WWT/9-12

SOKOLOVA, Natasha (b 1917) Brazilian actress, dancer WWT/10-11

SOKOLOW, Anna (b 1912/15) American choreographer BE, CB

SOLANO, Solita (d 1975 [86]) critic BP/60*

SOLAR, Willie (d 1956 [65]) comedian, dancer BE*, WWT/14*

SOLDENE, Emily (1840/44-1912) English actress, singer CDP, COC, GRB/1-4, OC/1-3, WWW/1

SOLEE, Mr. (fl 1797) French manager HAS

SOLEM, Delmar E. (b 1915) American educator BE

SOLEN, Paul (b 1941) American actor TW/29-30

SOLER, Antonio Ruiz see Antonio

SOLIN, Harvey American actor TW/29

SOLOMAN, Mrs. Neil see McEvoy, Nellie

SOLOMON, Charles (d 1890 [71]) composer EA/91*

SOLOMON, Edward (d 1895 [36]) musical director, composer CDP

SOLOMON, Edward (d 1976 [64]) publicist BP/60*

SOLOMON, Max see Rogers, Max

SOLOMON, Neal (d 1917) comedian EA/18*

SOLOMON, Solomon [Cpt. F. Athya] (d 1886 [44]) actor? EA/87*

SOLOMON, Steve (d 1972 [24]) agent BP/56*

SOLOTAIRE, George (d 1965 [62]) ticket broker BP/49*

SOLOV, Zachary (b 1923) American actor TW/5

SOLOVYOV, Vladimir Aleksandrovich (b 1907) Russian dramatist MWD

SOLOWAY, Leonard (b 1928) American manager BE

SOLTERS, Lee (b 1919) American press representative BE

SOLTI, Sir Georg (b 1912) Hungarian conductor CB, ES

SOMACK, Jack (b 1918) American actor TW/23, 25, 27, 30

SOMAN, Claude (1897-1960) English manager WWT/10-12

SOMERBY, Rufus (b 1833) American showman HAS

SOMERFIELD, Fred C. (d 1910 [39]) actor EA/11*

SOMERFIELD, Tom (d 1918 [59]) EA/19*

SOMERS, Brett (b 1927) Canadian actress TW/14

SOMERS, Dalton actor EA/97

SOMERS, Jimsey (b 1937) American actor TW/2

SOMERS, John Isaac (d 1899 [44]) music-hall agency manager EA/00*

SOMERSET, C. W. (1847-1929) actor EA/97, GRB/2-4, WWT/1-5

SOMERSET, Mrs. C. W. see Russell, Agnes

SOMERSET, Mrs. C. W. see Somerset, Fanny

SOMERSET, Fanny [Mrs. C. W. Somerset] (d 1900) EA/01*

SOMERSET, Patrick (b 1897) English actor WWT/4-8

SOMERSETT, George (fl 1600-24) actor DA

SOMERVILE, William (d 1743) English translator CP/2-3

SOMERVILLE, Mr. English singer HAS

SOMERVILLE, Henry (d 1884) reciter EA/85*

SOMERVILLE, Mrs. Henry (d 1867) EA/68*

SOMERVILLE, John Baxter (1907-63) English manager WWT/8-13

SOMERVILLE, Margaret Agnes see Bunn, Margaret Agnes Somerville

SOMERVILLE, Marjorie (d 1916 [19]) EA/18*

SOMERVILLE, Randolph (1891-1958) American director WWA/3

SOMES, Michael (b 1917) English dancer CB, ES, WWT/11-12

SOMLO, Josef (d 1973 [89]) producer/director/choreographer BP/58*

SOMLYO, Roy A. (b 1925) American manager BE

SOMMER, Edith dramatist BE

SOMMER, Henry (fl 1740) dramatist CP/1-3, GT

SOMMER, Josef (b 1934) German actor TW/27-30

SOMMERLAD, A. (d 1909 [46]) conductor EA/10*

SOMMERS, Ben (b 1906) American executive BE

SOMMERS, Harry G. (1870-1953) American dramatist, manager, treasurer SR

SOMNES, George (d 1956 [68]) American director, producer, actor TW/12

SONDERGAARD, Edith Holm see Sondergaard, Gale

SONDERGAARD, Gale [née Edith Holm] (b 1901) American actress BE, TW/23, WWT/15-16

SONDHEIM, Stephen (b 1930) American composer, lyricist AAS, BE, CB, ES, WWT/14-16

SONDHEIMER, Hans (b 1901) German stage manager, lighting director BE

SONNEMANN, Emmy (d 1973 [80]) performer BP/58*

SONNENTHAL, Adolf Ritter von see Von Sonnenthal, Adolf Ritter

SONNEVELD, Wim (d 1974 [56]) performer BP/58*

SONTAG, Carl (d 1900) actor WWT/14*

SONTAG, Henrietta (1805-64) German singer CDP, ES, HAS

SONTAG, Nina (fl 1829?) singer CDP

SOO, Kim Yen (d 1963 [72]) magician BE*

SOPER, Paul (b 1906) American educator BE

SOPHOCLES (c. 497-406 B. C.) Greek dramatist ES

SORAKICHI, Motsada (d 1891 [32]) Japanese wrestler EA/ 92*

SOREL, Cecile (d 1966 [92]) performer BP/51*

SOREL, Felicia (d 1972 [66]) American choreographer, dancer TW/3-4

SOREL, Sonia (b 1921) American actress TW/3, 8

SORELL, Doris (d 1971) dramatist BP/56*

SORIN, Louis (1893-1961) American actor TW/4

SORMA, Agnes [Duchess of Minotta] (1865-1927) German actress ES, GRB/4, OC/1-3, WWT/1-2

SOROKIN, Rachel (d 1969 [84]) performer BP/54*

SORVINO, Paul (b 1939) American actor WWT/16

SOTHEBY, William (fl 1790-1802) dramatist CP/3, GT, TD/2

SOTHERDEN, Betsy see Vernon, Flo

SOTHERN, Ann (b 1909/12) American actress, singer, producer CB, WWT/8-10

SOTHERN, Mrs. E. A. (d 1882) EA/83*

SOTHERN, Edward Askew (1826-81) English actor CDP, COC, DAB, DNB, ES, HAS, HJD, NTH, OAA/1-2, OC/1-3, WWA/H

SOTHERN, Edward Hugh (1859-1933) American actor, dramatist CDP, COC, DAB, ES, GRB/2-4, HJD, NTH, OAA/2, OC/1-3, PP/3, WWA/1, WWM, WWT/1-7, WWW/3

SOTHERN, Mrs. Edward Hugh see Harned, Virginia

SOTHERN, Harry (1883/84-1957) English actor ES, TW/2-3, 13

SOTHERN, Hugh [Roy Sutherland] (d 1947 [65]) actor BE*, WWT/14*

SOTHERN, Janet Evelyn English actress WWM, WWT/1-5

SOTHERN, Jean (d 1964) actress

BE*

SOTHERN, Lytton Edward (1851/56-87) American actor CDP, DNB, NYM

SOTHERN, Sam [George Evelyn Augustus T. Sothern] (1870-1920) English actor ES, GRB/1-4, WWT/1-3

SOTHERNE, David (fl 1538) actor DA

SOTO, Senorita (fl 1852) dancer CDP, HAS

SOTO, Luchy (d 1970 [50]) performer BP/55*

SOUDEIKINE, Serge (d 1946 [60]) Russian designer TW/3

SOULE, Robert (b 1926) American designer BE

SOUPER, G. Kay (d 1947) actor BE*, WWT/14*

SOURAY, Eleanor (1880-1931) English actress GRB/1-3

SOURIS, Andre (d 1970 [70]) composer/lyricist BP/54*

SOUSA, John Philip (1854-1932) American composer, conductor DAB, ES, GRB/1-4, HJD, SR, WWS, WWT/1-6, WWW/3

SOUSSANIN, Nicholas (d 1975 [86]) actor BP/59*, WWT/16*

SOUTAR, Andrew (d 1941 [61]) dramatist BE*, WWT/14*

SOUTAR, J. Farren (1870/74-1962) English actor GRB/1-4, WWT/ 1-9

SOUTAR, Robert (1827-1908) English dramatist, actor, stage manager COC, EA/69, GRB/4, OAA/1-2

SOUTAR, Mrs. Robert see Farren, Ellen

SOUTH, Barbara (d 1975 [45]) producer/director/choreographer BP/60*

SOUTH, Eddie (1904-62) American musician BE*, BP/46*

SOUTH, Richard W. (d 1892 [48]) actor, entertainer EA/93*

SOUTHALL, Carrie see Aldridge, Carrie

SOUTHAMPTON, Henry Wriothesley, Third Earl of (1573-1624) English patron NTH

SOUTHARD, Lucien H. (1827-81) American composer DAB

SOUTHBY, Mr. (fl 1835?) actor CDP

SOUTHERN, Colette (d 1965 [73])

performer BP/50*

SOUTHERN, John (d 1893) manager WWT/5-7

SOUTHERNE, Thomas (1660-1746) Irish dramatist CDP, COC, CP/1-3, DNB, ES, GT, HP, NTH, OC/1-3, PDT

SOUTHEY, Thomas (fl 1547-56) actor DA

SOUTHGATE, Howard S. (d 1971 [76]) performer BP/56*

SOUTHWELL, Henry (d 1841) Irish actor HAS

SOUTHWELL, Maria (fl 1828) Irish actress HAS

SOUTHWORTH, Robert (d 1870 [59]) musician EA/71*

SOUTHWORTH, S. S. dramatist RJ

SOUTHYN, Robert (fl 1550) actor DA

SOUTTEN, Mme. [Millie Barnett] (d 1883 [77]) actress EA/84*

SOUTTEN, Ben professor of dancing GRB/3

SOUTTER, Lillie (fl 1903?) actress, singer CDP

SOUZAY, Gérard (b 1920) French singer CB

SOVEY, Raymond (1895/97-1966) American designer actor BE, ES, TW/2-8, 23, WWT/7-14

SOWARDS, Len (d 1962 [69]) actor BE*

SOWDEN, Margaret see Neilson, Perlita

SOWDON, Thomas (d 1789) Irish actor CDP

SOWELL, Ione M. (d 1975 [62]) performer BP/60*

SOWERBY, Ann (d 1883) EA/84*

SOWERBY, F. (d 1849) English actor HAS

SOWERBY, Katherine Githa English dramatist NTH, WWT/2-7

SOWERBY, Leo (d 1968 [73]) composer/lyricist BP/53*

SOWINSKI, Albert (d 1880 [74]) musician EA/81*

SOYINKA, Wole (b 1934) Nigerian dramatist, director CB, CD, COC, MWD

SOYLES, William (fl 1636) actor DA

SPACHNER, Leon (d 1971 [87]) manager BP/55*

SPAIN, Elsie (d 1970 [91]) ac-

tress WWT/1-5

SPAIN, Katharine Stewart see Stewart, Katharine

SPAISMAN, Zipora (b 1920) Polish actress TW/29-30

SPALDING, Gilbert R. (d 1880 [68]) circus manager & proprietor CDP

SPAMER, Richard (1856-1938) American critic WWA/1

SPANISH DANCERS, Troupe of (fl 1855) HAS

SPAR, Herbert (d 1976 [35]) agent BP/60*

SPARER, Paul actor WWT/16

SPARK, Dr. William (d 1897 [71]) musician EA/98*

SPARKES, Thomas (fl 1622) lessee DA

SPARKS, Mrs. (d 1837 [83]?) actress GT, TD/1-2

SPARKS, Charles actor CDP

SPARKS, Hugh (d 1816 [64]) actor WWT/14*

SPARKS, Isaac (d 1776) Irish actor CDP, TD/1-2

SPARKS, John G. (d 1922 [70]) comedian BE*, BP/6*

SPARKS, Joseph M. (b 1856) American actor WWS

SPARKS, Luke (d 1768 [57]) actor TD/2

SPARKS, Ned (d 1957 [73]) Canadian comedian TW/13

SPARROW, Fanny (d 1903 [76]) EA/04*

SPARROW, Frank (d 1888 [42]) American actor EA/89*

SPARROW, G. (d 1878 [74]) actor EA/79*

SPARROW, Jesse (b 1849) English music-hall singer GRB/1-4

SPARROW, John William (d 1898 [72]) EA/99*

SPATEMAN, Thomas (fl 1742) dramatist CP/2-3

SPAULDING, Georgie Dean [née Georgie Dean] (b 1845) American musician HAS

SPAULDING, George Lawson (1864-1921) American composer WWA/1

SPAULDING, John F. (b 1833) American musician, musical director HAS

SPAULDING, Kim American actor TW/1

SPAULDING, William P. (1836-

87?) American musician HAS,
NYM
SPAULL, Guy (b 1904) American
actor TW/30
SPEACHLEY, John (d 1869) mu-
sician EA/70*
SPEAIGHT, James (d 1874) per-
former CDP
SPEAIGHT, Robert (1904-76)
English actor AAS, ES,
WWT/7-16
SPEAKMAN, James T. (d 1908)
EA/09*
SPEAKMAN, Walter (d 1886 [42])
actor CDP
SPEAKS, Oley (1874-1948) Amer-
ican songwriter TW/5
SPEAR, Felix P. (1836-69)
American actor, property
man HAS
SPEAR, George Gaines (1809-87)
American actor HAS, NYM
SPEAR, Harry (d 1969 [56])
performer BP/53*
SPEARE, Dorothy (d 1951) Amer-
ican dramatist WWA/3
SPEARS, Anna Maria [Mrs.
Tom Spears] (d 1897) EA/98*
SPEARS, Margaret (d 1892 [73])
EA/93*
SPEARS, Sammy (d 1966) per-
former BP/50*
SPEARS, Mrs. Tom see
Spears, Anna Maria
SPECTOR, Edward (d 1974 [73])
American producer BE,
TW/30
SPECTOR, Joel producer BE
SPEECHLEY, Billy (b 1911)
English actor WWT/6-7
SPEED, John (d 1640) English
dramatist CP/2-3, FGF
SPEEDY, George (d 1880)
music-hall proprietor EA/81*
SPEEDY, Henry (d 1883) music-
hall performer? EA/84*
SPEICHER, Ann Drew (d 1974
[83]) performer BP/58*
SPEIGHT, Fred (d 1916) EA/18*
SPEIGHT, Johnny (b 1921/22)
English dramatist CD, MH
SPELMAN, Leon (b 1945) Amer-
ican actor TW/29
"SPELVIN, George" BE, NTH
SPENCE, Beatrice [Mrs. Frank
Cooton] (d 1908 [44]) EA/09*
SPENCE, Edward F. (1860-1932)
English critic GRB/2-4,

WWT/1-6
SPENCE, Harry (d 1898) Negro
comedian EA/99*
SPENCE, Henry (d 1902 [58]) vari-
ety performer EA/03*
SPENCE, James William (d 1873)
music-hall proprietor EA/74*
SPENCE, Margaret (d 1881 [73])
EA/82*
SPENCE, Ralph (d 1949 [59]) di-
rector, producer BE*, WWT/
14*
SPENCE, Tom [Tom Dillon] (d
1884) Negro comedian EA/85*
SPENCER, Mr. (d 1804) actor
TD/2
SPENCER, Mr. (d c. 1836) English
actor HAS
SPENCER, Mrs. (fl 1794) actress
HAS
SPENCER, Bob (b 1938) American
actor TW/27, 29-30
SPENCER, Mrs. Clarence S. see
Ashley, Helen
SPENCER, Colin (b 1933) English
dramatist CD
SPENCER, Edmund (fl 1798) dram-
atist CP/3
SPENCER, Franz (d 1971) drama-
tist BP/56*
SPENCER, Gabriel (d 1598) Eng-
lish actor COC, DA, OC/1-3
SPENCER, George (d 1906) musi-
cian EA/07*
SPENCER, George (d 1907) propri-
etor EA/08*
SPENCER, Mrs. George (d 1876)
actress EA/78*
SPENCER, Mrs. George Preston
[Flora McDonald] (d 1916 [65])
singer EA/17*
SPENCER, Helen (b 1903) English
actress WWT/5-8
SPENCER, Mrs. Herbert H. see
Conway, Helen
SPENCER, Isabella (d 1911) per-
former? EA/12*
SPENCER, Jessica (b 1919) English
actress WWT/10-14
SPENCER, John (fl early 17th
cent) English actor COC, DA,
OC/1-3
SPENCER, Kenneth (d 1964 [51])
American singer BE*, BP/48*
SPENCER, Lillian (fl 1880) actress
CDP
SPENCER, Lou (d 1972 [56]) per-
former BP/57*

SPENCER, Lucy (b 1884) American actress, dramatist WWS
SPENCER, Mabel (fl 1907) American actress WWS
SPENCER, Marian (b 1905) English actress WWT/10-16
SPENCER, Willard (1852-1933) American composer BE*
SPENCER, William (fl 1589) payee DA
SPENCER, William (d 1880 [56]) bill inspector EA/81*
SPENCER, William Robert (fl 1796-1802) dramatist CP/3
SPENCER-BRUNTON, Enid [Mrs. Richard F. L. Lambart] English actress GRB/1-2, 4
SPENDER, Stephen (b 1909) English dramatist CB, ES, HP, MD, MWD, NTH
SPENS, Andrew William (d 1917 [45]) EA/18*
SPENSE (fl 1592?) dramatist FGF
SPERANZA, Adelina (fl 1859) singer HAS
SPESSIVTZENA, Olga (b 1895) Russian dancer ES
SPEWACK, Bella (b 1899) Hungarian/American dramatist, librettist AAS, BE, CD, MD, MH, MWD, NTH, WWT/9-14
SPEWACK, Samuel (1899-1971) Russian/American dramatist AAS, BE, MD, MH, MWD, NTH, WWA/5, WWT/9-14
SPEYSER, Paul J., III (b 1941) American actor TW/24
SPIEGAL, Barbara American actress TW/26
SPIEGEL, Henry (d 1971 [61]) publicity director BP/56*
SPIELBERG, David (b 1940) American actor TW/27-28, 30
SPIER, William H. (d 1973 [66]) producer/director/choreographer BP/57*
SPIERS, Mrs. (d 1893) EA/94*
SPIERS, Harry F. (d 1902 [30]) manager EA/04*
SPIERS, Helen Bateson [Mrs. J. H. Spiers] (d 1878) EA/80*
SPIERS, Mrs. J. H. see Spiers, Helen Bateson
SPIGELGASS, Leonard (b 1908)

American dramatist BE, WWT/15-16
SPIKER, Ray (d 1964 [62]) actor BE*
SPILLANE, Dan (d 1884) musical director EA/85*
SPILLER, Mr. (fl 1811) actor CDP
SPILLER, Mr. (d 1826) English actor HAS
SPILLER, Anne (d 1906 [72]) EA/07*
SPILLER, Emily (d 1941 [81]) actress BE*, WWT/14*
SPILLER, Isaac (d 1905 [77]) EA/06*
SPILLER, James (1692-1727/30) English? actor CDP, DNB
SPILLER, James, Jr. (d 1871) musician EA/72*
SPILSBURY, Percy (d 1895 [25]) actor EA/96*
SPINACUTA, Sig. animal trainer? CDP
SPINELLI, Andree (b 1891) French actress WWT/4
SPINETTI, Victor (b 1933) Welsh actor AAS, TW/21-22, 27, WWT/14-16
SPINK, Beatrice Mary see Bertoldi, Ena
SPIRA, Francoise (d 1965 [30s]) performer BP/49*
SPIRES, James (d 1887) EA/88*
SPITZ, Mrs. Leo (d 1974 [72]) performer BP/58*
SPIVAK, Alice (b 1935) American actress TW/26, 28, 30
SPIVAK, Irene Daye (d 1971 [53]) performer BP/56*
SPIVY (d 1971 [64]) performer BP/55*
SPLANE, Elza K. (d 1968 [63]) performer BP/52*
SPLATT, W. F. (d 1893 [83]) licensee EA/94*
SPOFFORD, Charles M. (b 1902) American executive BE
SPOFFORTH, Reginald (1770-1827) English composer, musician DNB
SPONG, Hilda (1875-1955) Australian actress CDP, GRB/1-4, PP/3, TW/11, WWM, WWS, WWT/1-9
SPONG, W. B. (d 1929 [79]) scene artist BE*, WWT/14*
SPONSELLER, Howard L., Jr. (b

1945) American actor TW/30

SPOONER, Cecil American actress WWT/1-5

SPOONER, Edna May (d 1953 [78]) American actress TW/10, WWT/1-4

SPOONER, Mary G. (d 1940 [87]) manager WWT/14*

SPORLE, Nathan James (d 1853 [42]) composer EA/72*

SPOTTSWOOD, James (1882-1940) American actor CB

SPRACHER, Dwight L. (1903-70) American executive WWA/5

SPRAGG, John C. (d 1886 [56]) musician EA/87*

SPRAGUE, Mrs. see Drummond, Dolores

SPRAGUE, H. N. (1818-58) American actor HAS

SPRAGUE, Mrs. H. N. (b 1833) Irish actress HAS

SPRAKE, Charlotte Amelia [Mrs. Herbert Sprake] (d 1898 [42]) EA/99*

SPRAKE, Frederick (d 1887 [78]) EA/88*

SPRAKE, Herbert (d 1904) music-hall proprietor EA/06*

SPRAKE, Mrs. Herbert see Sprake, Charlotte Amelia

SPRAKE, Herbert Arthur (d 1917) music-hall assistant manager EA/18*

SPRAKE, Thomas (d 1877) musician EA/78*

SPRANGE, Adnam (d 1919) English actor, business manager, stage manager GRB/1

SPRAY, William actor GRB/1-3

SPRIGGE, Elizabeth (1900-74) English translator, director, producer BE

SPRIGGS, Elizabeth (b 1929) actress AAS, WWT/16

SPRIGGS, Mrs. James see Brangin, Rhoda

SPRIGHTLY, William (fl 1780) musician CDP

SPRING, Samuel (d 1839 [62]) box book-keeper EA/72*

SPRINGER, J. H. (fl 1854) actor HAS

SPRINGETT, Freddie (b 1915) English actor WWT/7

SPRINGMEYER, Charles see Durand, Charles

SPROULES, Edwin (d 1873 [42])

actor? EA/74*

SPRUNG, Sandy (b 1937) American actor TW/25, 27

SPRY, Mrs. A. G. see Loftus-Leyton, Rosie

SPRY, Henry (d 1904 [69]) dramatist, manager BE*, EA/05*, WWT/14*

SPRY, Mrs. Henry see Claremont, Lizzie

SPURIN-CALLEIA, Joseph see Calleia, Joseph

SPURLING, John (b 1936) Kenyan/English dramatist CD

SPURR, Mel B. (d 1904) entertainer EA/05*

SPURR, Mrs. Mel B. (d 1910 [59]) EA/11*

SPURWAY, Thomas see Hatton, Walter

SPURWAY, William (d 1890 [79]) EA/91*

SQUIBB, June (b 1935) American actress BE, TW/24

SQUIRE, J. C. (1884-1958) English dramatist, writer MWD

SQUIRE, John (fl 1620) dramatist CP/3, FGF

SQUIRE, Katherine (b 1903) American actress BE, TW/19, 23, 25, WWT/14-16

SQUIRE, Lawrence (fl 1486-93) master of the Chapel Royal DA

SQUIRE, Ronald (1886-1958) English actor AAS, TW/15, WWT/3-12, WWW/5

SQUIRE, Tom (d 1891) actor, singer CDP

SQUIRE, William (b 1920) Welsh actor AAS, BE, WWT/13-16

SQUIRES, Mr. (fl 1827?) actor CDP

SQUIRES, John (d 1889 [49]) musician EA/90*

SRNEC, Jiri (b 1931) Czech actor TW/23

STABILE, Mariano (b 1888) Italian singer ES

STABLES, Harry [John Keogh] (d 1878 [35]) comic singer EA/80*

STACEY, Alexander (d 1897 [63]) proprietor EA/98*

STACEY, R. F. W. (d 1916 [38]) EA/17*

STACEY, Walter [Thomas Wick] (d 1877) comedian, singer EA/78*

STACK, James (d 1973 [65])
performer BP/57*
STACK, William (b 1882) Amer-
ican actor WWT/4-8
STADLEN, Lewis J. (b 1947)
American actor TW/26-27,
29-30, WWT/16
STAFFORD, Alfred (d 1906)
EA/07*
STAFFORD, Altona (d 1965 [78])
actress BP/49*, WWT/14*
STAFFORD, C. (fl 1837) English
actor HAS
STAFFORD, Emily [Mrs. Albert
Bernard] (d 1907 [59]) actress
GRB/3*
STAFFORD, Grey (b 1920) Eng-
lish actor TW/2
STAFFORD, Hanley (d 1968 [69])
performer BP/52*
STAFFORD, John Gascoigne (d
1917 [66]) printer EA/18*
STAFFORD, William (d 1897
[37]) actor CDP
STAFFORD-CLARK, Max (b 1941)
English director WWT/15-16
STAFFORD SMITH, Mary [Mrs.
Charles F. Lloyd] (d 1917
[34]) actress EA/18*
STAGG, Charles (d 1735) Eng-
lish/American actor COC,
OC/1-3, WWA/H
STAGG, Mary (fl early 18th cent)
American actress OC/1-3
STAGNO, Sig. (d 1879) singer
EA/80*
STAHL, Herbert M. (b 1914)
American educator, director
BE
STAHL, Max theatre owner BE
STAHL, Rose (1873-1955) Amer-
ican actress CDP, GRB/3-4,
SR, TW/12, WWM, WWS,
WWT/1-7
STAHL, Stanley theatre owner
BE
STAIGER, Libi (b 1928) Ameri-
can actress, singer BE
STAINES, Thomas (d 1870)
master carpenter EA/71*
STAINFORTH, Frank (d 1899)
dramatist, songwriter EA/01*
STAINSTREET, James (d 1874)
musician EA/75*
STAINTON, Philip (1908-61) Eng-
lish actor WWT/11-13
STAKHOUSE, Roger (fl 1554)
actor DA

STALEY, George actor, singer
CDP
STALEY, James (b 1948) American
actor TW/28-30
STALLING, Carl W. (d 1972 [84])
performer BP/57*
STALLINGS, Laurence (1894-1968)
American dramatist, librettist
BE, HJD, MH, MWD, NTH,
SR, WWT/6-11
STALMAN, Julia [Mrs. Sidney
Lacy] (d 1898) actress EA/99*
STAMFORD, Annie [Mrs. John
Stamford] (d 1878) EA/79*
STAMFORD, Mrs. John see
Stamford, Annie
STAMFORD, John J. (d 1899 [50])
music-hall manager EA/00*
STAMMERS, Blanche see Garner,
Mrs. Arthur
STAMMERS, Frank (d 1921) com-
poser BE*, BP/6*
STAMMERS, Joseph (d 1871) im-
presario EA/72*
STAMPER, Dave (1883-1963) Amer-
ican composer WWT/6-10
STAMPER, F. Pope (1880-1950)
English actor WWT/3-8
STAMPER, Francis (fl 1751) dram-
atist CP/3
STAMP-TAYLOR, Enid (b 1904)
English actress, singer WWT/
6-7
STANDER, Hollice (b 1944) Ameri-
can actress TW/24
STANDER, Lionel (b 1908) Ameri-
can actor, producer BE
STANDIDGE, John (d 1890 [74])
EA/91*
STANDING, Charles Wyndham (b
1880) English actor WWT/4-5
STANDING, Ellen (d 1906 [50])
actress EA/07*, GRB/2*,
WWT/14*
STANDING, Emily (d 1899) actress
BE*, EA/00*, WWT/14*
STANDING, Sir Guy (1873-1937)
English actor GRB/2-4, WWS,
WWT/1-8
STANDING, Mrs. Guy see
Urquhart, Isabelle
STANDING, Herbert [Crellin] (1846-
1923) English actor DP, GRB/
1-4, OAA/2, WWS, WWT/1-4
STANDING, Herbert (d 1955 [71])
English actor TW/12
STANDING, Mrs. Herbert (d 1887)
EA/88*

STANDING, Jack (d 1917) EA/18*

STANDING, John [né Leon] (b 1934) English actor WWT/15-16

STANDING, Michael (b 1939) English actor TW/20

STANDING, Mrs. Percy Cross see Wright, Ellen

STANDISH, Pamela (b 1920) English actress WWT/9-10

STANDISH, Walter (d 1888 [35]) American actor EA/90*

STANDON, Harriet (b 1886) American singer, actress WWM

STANDREN, Charles (d 1891 [40]) musician, musical director EA/92*

STANFIELD, Agnes see Clare, Ada

STANFIELD, Alfred D'Arcy (d 1902 [41]) actor EA/03*

STANFIELD, Clarkson (1793-1867) English scene designer COC, OC/1-3

STANFIELD, James Field (d 1824) Irish dramatist, actor CP/3, DNB

STANFORD, Arthur (b 1878) American actor WWM

STANFORD, Sir Charles Villiers (1852-1924) Irish composer DNB, ES

STANFORD, Henry B. (1872-1921) Egyptian/English actor GRB/1-4, WWM, WWT/1-3

STANFORD, Mrs. H[enry] B. see Burt, Laura

STANFORD, Henry (b 1872) Egyptian/English actor WWS

STANFORD, Jack (d 1968 [67]) performer BP/52*

STANG, Arnold (b 1925) American actor BE, TW/25-26

STANGE, Stanislaus (1861-1917) English actor, dramatist GRB/2-4, SR, WWT/1-3

STANHOPE, Adeline [Mrs. Amory Sullivan] (fl 1872-79) actress OAA/2

STANHOPE, Frederick [Frederick Stanhope Counter] (b 1875) English manager, producer GRB/1

STANHOPE, O. H. Butler (d 1917) EA/18*

STANHOPE, Robert Butler (d 1917) EA/18*

STANILAND, Albert (d 1973 [71]) theatre operator BP/58*

STANISLAUS, Frederick (d 1891 [47]) composer, conductor BE*, EA/92*, WWT/14*

STANISLAVSKY, Konstantin Sergeivich (1863-1938) Russian actor, director, acting teacher COC, NTH

STANLEY, Mr. (fl 1823) actor CDP

STANLEY, Mr. (d 1841) actor HAS

STANLEY, Mrs. [née Wattle; Mrs. Twistleton] (d c. 1808/09) actress CDP, HAS, TD/1-2

STANLEY, Mrs. (d 1834) see Hill, Mrs.

STANLEY, Mrs. (1796?-1861) see Fleming, Miss

STANLEY, Mrs. (fl early 19th cent) actress CDP

STANLEY, Miss (b 1795) actress CDP

STANLEY, Adelaide (b 1906) actress, singer WWT/9-10

STANLEY, Alma (1854-1931) English actress, dancer DP, EA/96, OAA/2, WWT/6

STANLEY, Bessie [Mrs. E. T. Stanley] (d 1880 [39]) EA/82*

STANLEY, Blanche [Mrs. S. Major Jones] English actress GRB/1-2

STANLEY, Charles (b 1851) American actor PP/3

STANLEY, Charles actor, singer CDP

STANLEY, Charlotte Mary actress CDP

STANLEY, Edward (fl 1790) dramatist CP/3

STANLEY, Emma (1823-81) English actress CDP, HAS

STANLEY, Eric (b 1884) English actor WWT/8-9

STANLEY, Mrs. E. T. see Stanley, Bessie

STANLEY, Flora Middleton see Alleyne, Muriel

STANLEY, Florence American actress TW/26-30, WWT/16

STANLEY, Frederic Arthur manager GRB/2-3

STANLEY, F. W. (d 1917) EA/18*

STANLEY, Gase (d 1965 [75]) performer BP/50*

STANLEY, George (b 1786) English

actor BS, CDP

STANLEY, George (d 1820) English actor HAS

STANLEY, George (d 1898 [75]) actor, manager EA/99*

STANLEY, Mrs. George (fl 1806-20) English actress HAS

STANLEY, George B. (d 1850) stage manager HAS

STANLEY, Gladys B. (d 1971) performer BP/56*

STANLEY, Gwladys (d 1974) actress BTR/74

STANLEY, Harry (d 1896) manager EA/97*

STANLEY, Harry (d 1901) actor EA/02*

STANLEY, Helen (1889-1966) American singer WWA/4

STANLEY, Hodson [Charles Henry Hodson] (d 1885 [42]) actor, music-hall singer EA/86*

STANLEY, Hubert Rudolph Gordon (d 1916) EA/17*

STANLEY, Jack (d 1916 [30]) EA/17*

STANLEY, Jean [Joseph Haynes] (d 1904 [52]) music-hall performer EA/05*

STANLEY, Jean see Hosmer, Jean

STANLEY, Jocelyn (d 1883 [32]) singer EA/84*

STANLEY, John (1714-86) English musician DNB

STANLEY, Kim [née Patricia Reid] (b 1921/25) American actress AAS, BE, CB, TW/8-21, WWT/13-16

STANLEY, Laura [Mrs. S. E. Bernard] (d 1893) EA/94*

STANLEY, Lilian M. [Mrs. Charles Vernon] (d 1943 [65]) English actress GRB/1

STANLEY, Marion (fl 1903-07) American actress WWS

STANLEY, Martha (b 1879) American dramatist WWT/6-9

STANLEY, Montague (1809-44) Scottish actor DNB

STANLEY, Nelly [Mrs. Harry Diamond] (d 1902) EA/03*

STANLEY, Pamela (b 1909) English actress WWT/8-11

STANLEY, Pat (b 1931) American actress, dancer, singer BE, TW/15

STANLEY, Phyllis (b 1914) English actress, singer, dancer WWT/9-11

STANLEY, Raymond (d 1973 [54]) performer BP/57*

STANLEY, Rose [Mrs. Fred H. Constable] (d 1899 [38]) EA/00*

STANLEY, Samuel (d 1870 [77]) EA/71*

STANLEY, S. Victor (1892-1939) English actor WWT/7-8

STANLEY, Thomas (d 1678) English dramatist CP/2-3

STANLEY, Walter (fl 1902?) actor, singer CDP

STANLEY, William (fl 1599) dramatist FGF

STANMORE, Frank (1878-1943) English actor GRB/1, 4, WWT/1-4

STANMORE, James (d 1901 [87]) actor EA/02*

STANNARD, Miss see Lewis, Mrs. John

STANNARD, Mrs. Arthur see Winter, John Strange

STANNARD, Heather (b 1928) actress WWT/11-13

STANNARD, Rachel (b 1800) English actress HAS

STANNARD, Sarah (fl 1827) English actress HAS

STANNARD, Will (d 1905 [26]) music-hall performer EA/06*

STANNERS, J. H. (d 1917) actor EA/18*

STANNUS, Edris see De Valois, Ninette

STANSBURY, George (d 1846 [50]) composer EA/72*

STANSBURY, Hope (b 1945) actress TW/23

STANSFIELD, Mrs. (d 1907) EA/08*

STANSFIELD, Agnes see Clare, Ada

STANSFIELD, Grace see Fields, Gracie

STANSFIELD, Mrs. W. (d 1916) EA/17*

STANTLEY, Ralph (d 1964 [67]) actor BE*

STANTLEY, Ralph (d 1972 [58]) actor TW/28

STANTON, Alfred (d 1918) EA/19*

STANTON, Charlotte see Goodall, Charlotte

STANTON, Frank (b 1908) American executive BE

STANTON, Kate (d 1865) jig dancer HAS

STANTON, William (d 1875) actor EA/76*

STANWELL, Mrs. (fl 1804) actress GT

STANWOOD, Moody (fl 1847?) minstrel CDP

STANWYCK, Barbara [Ruby Stevens] (b 1907) American actress, dancer BE, CB, ES, SR, WWT/7-10

STANWYCK, Jay (d 1967 [58]) producer TW/24

STANYON, Brian (b 1941) English actor TW/20

STAPELTON, Ray (d 1974 [52]) performer BP/59*

STAPLES, Arthur Durnford (d 1917) EA/18*

STAPLES, George (d 1898) music-hall stage manager EA/99*

STAPLETON, Jean (b 1923) American actress BE, CB, TW/10-15, 20-21, WWT/16

STAPLETON, Maureen (b 1925) American actress AAS, BE, CB, TW/6-30, WWT/13-16

STAPLETON, Sir Robert see Stapylton, Sir Robert

STAPLETON, Vivian see Blaine, Vivian

STAPLETON, Zoë Margaret see Gail, Zoë

STAPYLTON, Sir Robert (d 1669) dramatist CDP, CP/1-3, DNB, FGF, GT

STARBUCK, James American choreographer, director, actor, dancer BE

STARK, Douglas (b 1916) actor TW/24

STARK, Harold W. (d 1975 [61]) performer BP/60*

STARK, James (d 1875 [57]) actor CDP, HAS

STARK, Mrs. James [Mrs. Kirby] (fl 1850-58) manager, actress HAS

STARK, Joy (b 1952) American actress TW/25

STARK, Molly American actress TW/30

STARK, Ray (b 1915) producer, literary agent BE

STARK, Sally (b 1938) American actress TW/25-27

STARKAND, Martin American actor TW/26

STARKE, Mariana (1762?-1838) dramatist CP/3, DNB, TD/1-2

STARKEY, Walter (b 1921) American actor TW/2-4

STARKIE, Martin (b 1925) English director, dramatist, presenting manager WWT/15-16

STARKWEATHER, A. (fl 1859) actor HAS

STARKWEATHER, David (b 1935) American dramatist, director CD

STARLING, Lynn (1891-1955) American dramatist WWT/6-10

STARMER, Richard (d 1870 [85]) actor EA/71*

STARMER, Mrs. Richard (d 1874 [85]) actress EA/75*

STARR, Bill American actor TW/28-29

STARR, Frances Grant (1886-1973) American actress BE, ES, GRB/3-4, SR, TW/5-19, 30, WWM, WWS, WWT/1-13

STARR, Mrs. Harry see Danbury, Ethel

STARR, Muriel (1888-1950) Canadian actress TW/6, WWT/4-10

STARR, Stanley (fl 1890?) singer, songwriter CDP

STARR, Sylvia (b 1879) American actress WWS

STASHEFF, Edward (b 1909) American educator, writer BE

STATHAM, Jonathan (d 1895 [42]) acting manager EA/96*

STATHER, Frank [H. Stather-Dunn] (b 1869) manager GRB/3

STATHER-DUNN, H. see Stather, Frank

STATTEL, Robert (b 1937) American actor TW/24-26, 29-30

STAUFFER, Ivan Rex (d 1974 [72]) publicist BP/58*

STAUNTON, Alexander (d 1878) Irish comedian, singer, dancer EA/80*

STAUNTON, Alice see Tyrrell, Ruby

STAUNTON, Bernard (d 1888 [34]) EA/89*

STAUNTON, Ella [Elizabeth Ann Nye] (d 1896 [57]) actress EA/98*

STAUNTON, Howard (1810-74)
scholar DNB
STAVIS, Barrie (b 1906) American dramatist BE, CD
STAW, Sala (d 1972 [66]) Polish actress TW/29
STAYLEY, George (1727-79?/ 80) English dramatist, actor CP/2-3, DNB, GT
STAYTON, Frank (1874-1951) English dramatist WWT/2-7
STEAD, James Henry (d 1886) English music-hall performer CDP, COC, OC/1-3
STEAD, James Hurst (d 1886) music-hall singer EA/87*
STEADMAN, Walter (d 1900 [45]) actor EA/01*, WWT/14*
STEAGLES, Mr. (d 1867) actor? EA/68*
STEARNS, Charles (1753-1826) American dramatist EAP
STEARNS, Edith Bond (d 1961 [77]) producer BE*
STEARNS, Kate Palmer (d 1900) EA/01*
STEARNS, Myron Morris (d 1963 [78]) writer, producer BE*
STEARNS, Theodore (1880-1935) American composer WWA/1
STEARNS, William H. (1828-61) American actor HAS
STEBBING, Robert (d 1830) actor CDP
STEBBINS, Rowland [Laurence Rivers] (1882-1948) American producer TW/5
STEBBINS, Walter C. (d 1969 [70]) executive BP/54*
STEBER, Eleanor (b 1916) American singer CB
STECK, Olga (d 1935 [38]) American singer BE*, BP/20*
STEDMAN, Lincoln (d 1948 [41]) actor, producer BE*
STEDMAN, Myrtle (1888-1938) American actress BE*
STEEL, Edward (d 1965 [68]) performer BP/50*
STEEL, John (d 1971 [71]) singer TW/28
STEEL, Susan (1906-59) American actress TW/10, 16
STEEL, Vernon (1882-1955) Chilean actor WWT/2-8
STEEL, Willis (b 1866) American dramatist GRB/3

STEELE, Albert (d 1887) actor, music-hall manager NYM
STEELE, Mrs. Albert Richard see Steele, Ellen
STEELE, Archibald (fl 1789) Scottish? dramatist CP/3
STEELE, Barbara (b 1938) English actress ES
STEELE, Bill American actor TW/25
STEELE, Blanche (d 1944 [80]) actress BE*, WWT/14*
STEELE, David (b 1944) American actor TW/27
STEELE, Dora Gordon singer CDP
STEELE, Ellen [Mrs. Albert Richard Steele] (d 1881) EA/82*
STEELE, Mrs. J. B. see Bowering, Adelaide
STEELE, Lizzie see Palmer, Mrs. David S.
STEELE, Marjorie American actress TW/13-15
STEELE, Michael (b 1921) American actor TW/10-12
STEELE, Sir Richard (1672-1729) English dramatist CDP, COC, CP/1-3, DNB, ES, GT, HP, MH, NTH, OC/1-3, RE, SR, TD/1-2
STEELE, Richard (d 1887 [51]) actor, music-hall singer EA/89*
STEELE, Mrs. R. P. (d 1888) EA/89*
STEELE, Sarah Maria (b 1837) American actress HAS
STEELE, Silas S. (b 1812) American actor, dramatist HAS, RJ
STEELE, Tommy [né Hicks] (b 1936) English actor TW/20, 22, WWT/14-16
STEELE, Vernon (1882-1955) American actor TW/12
STEELE, Vickie (d 1975 [28]) performer BP/60*
STEELE, Wilbur Daniel (1886-1970) American dramatist HJD
STEELL, Willis (1859?-1941) American dramatist CB, WWA/1-2
STEEN, Marguerite (d 1975 [81]) English dramatist, actress CB
STEET, Alban Thomas see Carrick, Tom
STEEVENS, George (1736-1800) English commentator CDP, DNB, GT, HP, TD/1-2

STEFAN, Virginia (d 1964 [38])
actress BE*
STEFFANI, Sig. (fl 1859) singer
CDP
STEFFANONE, Balbina (fl 1850)
singer CDP, HAS
STEGER, Julius (1870-1959) Aus-
trian/American actor, stage
manager WWA/3, WWM,
WWS
STEGGALL, Charles (d 1905 [79])
musician EA/06*
STEGMEYER, William J. (d 1968
[51]) composer/lyricist BP/
53*
STEHLI, Edgar (1884-1973)
French/American actor BE,
TW/6-9, 13-15, 22-23, 30
STEHMAN, Jacques (d 1975 [62])
critic BP/59*
STEIGER, Rod (b 1925) American
actor BE, CB, ES, TW/9
STEIN, Ann R. (d 1970 [72])
lawyer BP/55*
STEIN, Carl (d 1890 [57]) lessee
EA/91*
STEIN, Gertrude (1874-1947)
American dramatist CB,
DAB, ES, HJD, MD, MWD,
PDT, WWW/4
STEIN, Joseph (b 1912) American
dramatist, librettist BE, CD,
WWT/15-16
STEIN, Michael (b 1933) American
actor TW/25-26
STEINBECK, John (1902-68)
American dramatist AAS,
BE, CB, COC, ES, HJD,
MD, MH, MWD, NTH, OC/
1-3, WWT/9-14
STEINBERG, Amy (d 1920 [70])
actress BE*, WWT/14*
STEINBERG, William (b 1899)
German/American conductor
CB
STEINER, George (d 1967 [67])
composer/lyricist BP/52*
STEINER, Ira (b c. 1915) talent
representative BE
STEINER, Max (1888-1971)
Austrian composer WWA/5
STEINFIRST, Donald S. (d 1972
[68]) critic BP/57*
STEININGER, Franz (d 1974
[69]) composer, conductor
BP/60*, WWT/16*
STEINKE, Hans (d 1971 [78])
performer BP/56*

STEINMAN, Harold (d 1975 [70])
producer/director/choreographer
BP/60*
STEINMAN, Morris W. (d 1976
[65]) publicist BP/60*
STEINMETZ, Joseph S. (d 1913)
EA/14*
STELLA, Antonietta (b 1929) Italian
singer CB, ES
STELLA, Nina [Marie Nina de
Harven Duval] (b 1886) New
Zealand actress GRB/1
STELOFF, Frances (b 1887) Amer-
ican bookseller BE
STEMBRIDGE-RAY, Mr. (d 1893)
EA/94*
STENBORG, Helen (b 1925) Ameri-
can actress TW/23, 28-30
STENDER, Doug (b 1942) American
actor TW/29-30
STEPAN, Carl (d 1887) singer
NYM
STEPAN, Celeste (d 1909 [85])
dancer EA/10*
STEPANEK, Karel (b 1899) Czech
actor WWT/10-15
STEPHAN, Mlle. (fl 1839) actress
HAS
STEPHAN, Petit (fl 1843) dancer
CDP
STEPHAN, Celeste (d 1909 [85])
dancer WWT/14*
STEPHEN, John (d 1974 [62]) actor
TW/30
STEPHEN, Stainless (d 1971 [79])
performer BP/55*
STEPHENS (d 1901) dramatist, ac-
tor EA/02*
STEPHENS, Mrs. [née Elizabeth
Taft] (d 1858) English circus
performer, actress HAS
STEPHENS, Miss (b 1794) English
singer, actress BS
STEPHENS, Miss (fl 1798-1801)
actress TD/1-2
STEPHENS, Miss (d 1882) see
Stephens, Catherine
STEPHENS, Alfred (d 1900) musi-
cal director EA/01*
STEPHENS, Alfred George Gower
(d 1933) Australian dramatist
WWW/3
STEPHENS, Ann Sophia (1813-86)
dramatist CDP
STEPHENS, Mrs. B. N. (d 1970
[78]) performer BP/55*
STEPHENS, Catherine, Countess of
Essex (1794-1882) English

singer, actress CDP, DNB
STEPHENS, C. E. (d 1892 [71])
composer EA/93*
STEPHENS, E. B. (d 1884 [31])
manager EA/85*
STEPHENS, Frances (b 1906)
English critic WWT/11-14
STEPHENS, Francis John (d
1917) EA/18*
STEPHENS, Fred W. (fl 1893?)
actor, singer CDP
STEPHENS, Garn American ac-
tress TW/28-30
STEPHENS, George (1800-51)
English dramatist DNB
STEPHENS, Harvey (b 1902)
American actor TW/1, 3,
5-9
STEPHENS, Henry (d 1892 [77])
EA/93*
STEPHENS, Henry Pottinger (d
1903) dramatist BE*, EA/04*,
WWT/14*
STEPHENS, Jane (1813?-96)
actress DNB, OAA/2
STEPHENS, J. Frank (d 1950
[72]) executive TW/6
STEPHENS, John (fl 1613) dram-
atist CP/1-3, FGF
STEPHENS, Kitty see Stephens,
Catherine
STEPHENS, Mrs. Lyne see
Duvernay, Pauline Yolande
Marie Louise
STEPHENS, Olga Worth (d 1964
[75]) performer BP/49*
STEPHENS, Peter (d 1872) circus
proprietor EA/73*
STEPHENS, Richard (1817-69)
English actor HAS
STEPHENS, Robert (b 1931)
English actor, director AAS,
COC, WWT/14-16
STEPHENS, Stephanie (b 1900)
actress WWT/6-8
STEPHENS, Mrs. W. H. (d 1896
[83]) actress BE*, WWT/14*
STEPHENS, William Henry (d
1888) English actor HAS,
OAA/2
STEPHENS, Yorke (1856/60/62-
1937) English actor DP, EA/
97, GRB/1-4, WWT/1-8
STEPHENSON, B. C. (d 1906
[67]) dramatist WWT/14*
STEPHENSON, Charles A. (b
1879) English actor GRB/1
STEPHENSON, Charles Henry

(d 1905 [82]) actor GRB/1
STEPHENSON, Charlotte (d 1905
[54]) EA/06*
STEPHENSON, Frank (d 1890 [31])
actor EA/91*
STEPHENSON, Henry (1874-1956)
English actor TW/12, WWT/
7-11
STEPHENSON, James (1898/1900-
1941) English actor CB, WWA/2
STEPHENSON, Jane (d 1893 [89])
EA/94*
STEPHENSON, John (d 1963 [74])
performer, producer BE*
STEPHENSON, Orlistus Bell (b
1867) American manager
WWA/4
STEPHENSON, Robert (d 1887)
manager EA/88*
STEPHENSON, Robert Robinson
(d 1970 [69]) performer BP/55*
STEPHENSON, William (d 1891
[65]) "spotted man" EA/92*
STEPPAT, Ilse (d 1969 [52]) per-
former BP/54*
STEPT, Sammy (d 1964 [67]) com-
poser/lyricist BP/49*
STERICKER, Hilda (d 1916 [41])
EA/17*
STERLING, Mrs. see Dixon,
Clara Ann
STERLING, Antoinette (1843/50-
1904) American singer CDP,
DNB
STERLING, Edyth (d 1962 [75])
actress BE*
STERLING, Ella [Emma Sophia
Homfray] (d 1898 [38]) actress
EA/99*
STERLING, Ford (c. 1884-1939)
American actor BE*, WWT/14*
STERLING, Frank B. (d 1970
[84]) performer BP/55*
STERLING, James (1701?-63) Irish
dramatist CP/1-3, DNB, GT,
HJD
STERLING, Jan (b 1923) American
actress BE, SR, TW/2-3, 5,
13, 19-20, 26, WWT/16
STERLING, John (d 1916) EA/17*
STERLING, Philip (b 1922) Amer-
ican actor TW/23-24, 28-29
STERLING, Richard (1880-1959)
American actor TW/1, 3, 15,
WWT/6-12
STERLING, Robert (b 1917) Ameri-
can actor BE, TW/7-8
STERLING, Roy (b 1933) American

actor   TW/2

STERN, Ernest (1876-1954)
Rumanian designer   ES, WWT/
10-11

STERN, G[ladys] B[ertha] (b
1890) English dramatist
WWT/7-11

STERN, Harold (d 1972 [65])
lawyer   BP/57*

STERN, Harold S. (d 1976 [53])
critic   BP/60*

STERN, Henry R. (d 1966 [91])
producer/director   BP/50*

STERN, Jean (d 1974 [84]) performer   BP/59*

STERN, Joseph (b 1940) American
actor   TW/28, 30

STERN, Joseph William (1870-
1934) American songwriter
DAB

STERNBERG, Ann (d 1975 [42])
composer/lyricist   BP/60*

STERNDALE-BENNETT, T. C.
(d 1944) composer, performer
BE*, WWT/14*

STERNE, Eleanor (d 1873) singer
EA/74*

STERNE, Morgan (b 1926) American actor   BE, TW/16

STERNE, Richard (b 1942) American actor   TW/24, 30

STERNER, Ernest (d 1891 [21])
actor   EA/92*

STERNFELD, Tommy (d 1974
[65]) producer/director/chore-
ographer   BP/59*

STERNHAGEN, Frances (b 1930/
32) American actress   BE,
TW/15, 20, 22-23, 25, 27-
30, WWT/15-16

STERNHEIM, Carl (1878-1943)
German dramatist   COC,
OC/3

STERNROYD, Vincent (1857-1948)
English actor   WWT/1-10

STETSON, Ada [née Parker] (fl
1847) actress   HAS

STETSON, E. T. (b 1836)
American actor   CDP, HAS

STETSON, John (d 1892 [96])
manager   WWT/14*

STETSON, John (1830/35-95)
American actor, manager,
dramatist?   CDP, SR

STETSON, Mrs. John [née Kate
Stokes] (d 1896) actress,
equestrienne   CDP, SR

STETTHEIMER, Florine (d 1944)

designer   BE*

STETTITH, Olive (d 1937) actress
BE*, WWT/14*

STEVENS, Mr. (fl 1834?) dramatist   RJ

STEVENS, Miss   see   Kemble,
Eugenie

STEVENS, Miss   see   Stavart,
Mrs. H. E.

STEVENS, Alfred Peck   see
Vance, Alfred Glenville

STEVENS, Ashton (1872-1951)
American critic   NTH, TW/8,
WWA/3, WWM, WWT/10-11

STEVENS, Charles (d 1964 [71])
actor   BE*

STEVENS, Charles E. (d 1910)
actor   EA/11*

STEVENS, Clifford (b 1936) American talent representative   BE

STEVENS, Connie (b 1938) American actress   TW/23

STEVENS, Constance Vera   see
Gray, Sally

STEVENS, Craig American actor
BE, TW/20

STEVENS, Edwin (b 1860) American
actor   GRB/3-4, WWM, WWT/
1-6

STEVENS, Emily (1882-1928)
American actress   DAB, WWM,
WWT/4-5

STEVENS, Mrs. Ernest   see
Deering, Rebekah

STEVENS, Ferriss Percival (d
1917 [50]) actor   EA/18*,
WWT/14*

STEVENS, Fran American actress
TW/24-26, 28-30

STEVENS, Frank R. (d 1887) actor
NYM

STEVENS, Frank S. (d 1966 [43])
performer   BP/51*

STEVENS, George   see   Steevens,
George

STEVENS, George (d 1889 [32])
elephant keeper   EA/91*

STEVENS, George (d 1975 [70])
producer/director/choreographer
BP/59*

STEVENS, George Alexander (d
1784 [49]) English actor, dramatist   CDP, CP/1-3, GT, TD/1-2

STEVENS, H. C. G. (1892-1967)
English press representative,
composer   WWT/5-14

STEVENS, Henry Edmund (1814-54)
English actor, stage manager

HAS
STEVENS, Inger (1934-70) Swedish
actress BE, TW/26, WWA/5
STEVENS, Jenny (d 1897) actress
CDP
STEVENS, Jeremy (b 1938)
American actor TW/25
STEVENS, John (fl 1744) drama-
tist CP/1-3
STEVENS, Cpt. John (d 1726)
dramatist CP/1-3, GT
STEVENS, John A. (d 1916 [73])
actor, dramatist, manager
CDP
STEVENS, Jon (b 1946) American
actor TW/26
STEVENS, Julia Warren (d 1903)
actress EA/04*
STEVENS, Katherine (b 1794)
English actress, singer OX
STEVENS, K. T. (b 1919) Amer-
ican actress TW/4, WWT/11
STEVENS, Leith (d 1970 [60])
composer/lyricist BP/55*
STEVENS, Leon B. (b 1926)
American actor TW/23
STEVENS, Leslie (b 1924) Amer-
ican dramatist, director, pro-
ducer BE
STEVENS, Marie (d 1881 [24])
music-hall performer EA/83*
STEVENS, Mark (b 1922) Amer-
ican actor TW/9
STEVENS, Morton L. (d 1959
[69]) actor TW/16
STEVENS, Nan (b 1921) Ameri-
can owner of theatrical secre-
tarial service BE
STEVENS, Onslow [Onslow Ford
Stevenson] (1906-77) American
actor, director BE, TW/4,
WWT/9-14
STEVENS, Pat American actress
TW/27-28
STEVENS, Paul (b 1924) Ameri-
can actor BE, TW/9, 15,
19-20, 22, 24
STEVENS, Risë (b 1913) Ameri-
can singer CB
STEVENS, Robert (d 1963 [83])
actor, director BE*
STEVENS, Robert E. (1838-1918)
American manager, actor SR
STEVENS, Roger (b 1938) Amer-
ican actor TW/10-12
STEVENS, Roger L. (b 1910)
American producer AAS, BE,
CB, WWT/13-16

STEVENS, Ronnie (b 1925) English
actor WWT/15-16
STEVENS, Rose (d 1887) actress
NYM
STEVENS, Rowena (d 1975 [68])
producer/director/choreographer
BP/59*
STEVENS, Ruby see Stanwyck,
Barbara
STEVENS, Sara [Mrs. John C.
Heenan] (d 1904 [70]) American
actress CDP, HAS, PP/3
STEVENS, Sydney (d 1888) EA/89*
STEVENS, Mrs. T. see Alzar,
Mme.
STEVENS, Thomas (fl 1586-87)
actor DA
STEVENS, Thomas Wood (1880-
1942) American producer, coach
SR
STEVENS, Tony (b 1948) American
actor TW/26-28
STEVENS, Ursula (b 1936) German/
American actress TW/15
STEVENS, Victor (d 1925 [72])
actor, dramatist BE*, WWT/
14*
STEVENS, Wallace (1879-1955)
American dramatist HJD
STEVENS, Walter (d 1887 [62])
musician EA/88*
STEVENSON, Mr. (fl 1824-52)
English actor HAS
STEVENSON, Miss (fl 1819?) ac-
tress CDP
STEVENSON, Charles Alexander
(1851-1929) Irish actor CDP,
PP/3, SR
STEVENSON, Douglas (d 1934 [52])
American actor BE*, BP/19*
STEVENSON, Ebenezer (d 1886
[56]) manager EA/87*
STEVENSON, Edward (d 1968 [62])
designer BP/53*
STEVENSON, George Alexander
(d 1869) manager EA/70*
STEVENSON, Hugh (1910-56) Eng-
lish designer ES
STEVENSON, James (d 1894 [27])
variety performer EA/95*
STEVENSON, Mrs. James see
Stevenson, Julia
STEVENSON, Janet MacIntyre Mac-
Kenzie see Norma, Hettie
STEVENSON, John Andrew Irish
composer TD/1-2
STEVENSON, Julia [Mrs. James
Stevenson] (d 1896) EA/97*

STEVENSON, Margot (b 1914/18)
American actress BE, TW/
5-6, 12, 22-23, WWT/9-16
STEVENSON, Onslow Fred see
Stevens, Onslow
STEVENSON, Percy Malcolm
(d 1909 [26]) actor EA/10*
STEVENSON, Robert Louis (1850-
94) Scottish dramatist DNB,
HP
STEVENSON, William (d 1575)
English dramatist COC, MH,
OC/1-3
STEVENSON, W. S. (b 1867)
Scottish actor GRB/1
STEVENSON, Mrs. W. S. see
Robson, Evelyn Stuart
STEWART, Mr. comedian CDP
STEWART, Alfred (b 1843) Eng-
lish actor, singer HAS
STEWART, Anita (d 1961 [65])
American actress BE*
STEWART, Anna Bird American
actress, writer CB
STEWART, Arthur see Slater,
Arthur
STEWART, Athole (1879-1940)
English actor, producer GRB/
1-4, WWT/1-9
STEWART, Caroline (d 1863)
actress HAS
STEWART, Carolyn Hill Ameri-
can actress TW/2
STEWART, Charles (b 1887)
American manager BE
STEWART, Charlotte (d 1855)
actress HAS
STEWART, Clare [Mrs. James
Stewart] (d 1907) EA/08*
STEWART, Danny (d 1962 [55])
actor, musician, composer
BE*
STEWART, David J. (1918-66)
American actor BE, TW/2,
4, 8, 10-15, 18-23
STEWART, David Ogilvie (d 1870
[57]) comedian EA/71*
STEWART, Don (b 1935) Ameri-
can actor TW/20-21
STEWART, Donald Ogden (b
1894) American actor BE,
WWT/7-14
STEWART, Douglas (fl 1852)
actor HAS
STEWART, Douglas (b 1913)
Australian/New Zealand drama-
tist CD
STEWART, Mrs. E. F. [Mrs.

Woodward] (fl 1851) actress
HAS
STEWART, Ellen American pro-
ducer, manager, director CB,
WWT/16
STEWART, Emily (fl 1855?) dancer
CDP
STEWART, Emma (b 1849) English
actress HAS
STEWART, Ernie (d 1974 [61])
composer/lyricist BP/59*
STEWART, Florence Lenora see
Carleton, Billie
STEWART, Fred (1906-70) Ameri-
can actor, director AAS, BE,
TW/4, 9, 11-13, 23-24, 26-27,
WWA/5, WWT/14-15
STEWART, Grant (1866-1929) Eng-
lish actor, dramatist SR, WWS
STEWART, Gwen actress GRB/1
STEWART, Mrs. H. E. [Miss
Stevens] (b 1820) English actress
HAS
STEWART, Henry (b 1842) English
actor HAS
STEWART, Henry E. (d 1917 [22])
EA/18*
STEWART, Hilda (b 1881) Aus-
tralian actress GRB/1-4
STEWART, Humphrey John (1854/
56-1932) English musician, com-
poser DAB, WWM
STEWART, James (fl 1774-79)
dramatist CP/2-3, GT
STEWART, James (d 1881 [61])
music-hall performer? EA/82*
STEWART, James (b 1908/11)
American actor BE, CB, ES,
SR, WWT/9-16
STEWART, Mrs. James see
Stewart, Clare
STEWART, James Lablache see
Granger, Stewart
STEWART, Jean-Pierre (b 1946)
American actor TW/25-26, 30
STEWART, Job (b 1934) South Af-
rican actor TW/23
STEWART, John (d 1957 [58]) di-
rector OC/3
STEWART, John[ny] (b 1934) Amer-
ican actor TW/8-19, 23, 29-30
STEWART, Julia (b 1862) English
actress OAA/2
STEWART, Katharine [Katharine
Stewart Spain] (d 1949 [81])
English actress GRB/1-3,
TW/5
STEWART, Maggie (d 1903) ac-

tress EA/04*

STEWART, Mary (d 1916) actress SR

STEWART, Maud (d 1892 [18]) actress EA/93*

STEWART, Melville (b 1869) English singer, actor WWM

STEWART, Michael (b 1929) American dramatist, librettist BE, CD, ES, WWT/16

STEWART, Nancye (b 1893) English actress WWT/7

STEWART, Nellie [Mrs. George Musgrove] (1860-1931) Australian actress GRB/1-4, WWT/1-6

STEWART, Patrick (b 1940) English actor AAS, TW/27, WWT/15-16

STEWART, Paula (b 1933) American actress, singer BE

STEWART, Ray (b 1932) American actor TW/23-26, 28, 30

STEWART, Richard (d 1902 [75]) actor, manager WWT/14*

STEWART, Rowland (d 1907) manager EA/08*

STEWART, Sophie (b 1908) Scottish actress AAS, WWT/8-16

STEWART, Thomas (fl 1772) dramatist CP/3, GT

STEWART, Thomas (b 1928) American singer CB

STEWART, William G. (1869-1941) American singer, producer, manager CB, WWS

STEWER, Jan [né A. J. Coles] actor, dramatist WWT/8

STEYNE, Adele [Mrs. Charles Steyne] (d 1893) EA/94*

STEYNE, Charles (d 1897 [65]) actor EA/98*

STEYNE, Mrs. Charles see Steyne, Adele

STEYNE, E. T. (d 1912) stage manager, producer, actor EA/13*, WWT/14*

STEYNE, Nelson [Richard Nelson Sutcliffe] (d 1901 [80]) actor EA/03*

STICH RANDALL, Teresa (b 1930) American singer ES

STICKNEY, Mr. (d 1840) American actor HAS

STICKNEY, Mrs. see Buttersby, Mrs.

STICKNEY, Benjamin (d 1860 [40]) equestrian EA/72*

STICKNEY, Dorothy (b 1900/03) American actress BE, CB, TW/2-21, 24, 26, 29-30, WWT/7-16

STICKNEY, Mrs. E. M. [Mrs. Jones] (d 1864 [58]) English actress HAS

STICKNEY, Robert (b 1846) American equestrian CDP, HAS

STICKNEY, Sallie (fl 1861-69) American equestrienne HAS

STICKNEY, Samuel P. (1808-77) equestrian CDP

STIEFEL, Milton (b 1900) American director, producer, actor BE

STIERS, David Ogden (b 1942) American actor TW/30

STIGANT, Arthur (b 1871) English actor GRB/1

STIGELLI, Sig. (fl 1859) singer? HAS

STIGNANI, Ebe (b 1907) Italian singer CB

STILES, Leslie (b 1876) English actor, dramatist, composer, producer WWT/1-8

STILES, Mrs. Leslie (d 1913) EA/14*

STILL, John (d 1607 [63]) English dramatist COC, CP/1-3, FGF, OC/3

STILL, John A. (d 1849) actor? singer? HAS

STILLINGFLEET, Benjamin (1700-71) dramatist CP/2-3, GT

STILLMAN, David B. (d 1963 [57]) attorney BP/47*

STILLMAN, Marsha (d 1962 [23]) actress BE*, BP/47*

STILLSBURY, Agnes (fl 1858) English actress HAS

STILT, Richard (d 1878 [59]) pantomimist EA/79*

STIMSON, Fred J. (d 1884 [27]) actor EA/85*

STINCHCOMBE, William Campbell (d 1886 [48]) costumier EA/88*

STINE, Lawrence (b 1912) American educator BE

STINNETT, Ray J. (d 1974 [92]) theatre owner BP/58*

STINTON, Mrs. (d 1894) EA/95*

STINTON, John Arthur (d 1876 [22]) musician EA/77*

STIRLING, Mr. actor CDP

STIRLING, Earl of see Alexander, William

STIRLING, Mrs. [Fanny Clifton;

Lady Charles Gregory] (1816-95) English actress CDP, OAA/1

STIRLING, Mrs. actress CDP

STIRLING, Alfred (d 1872 [22]) actor EA/73*

STIRLING, Arthur (d 1898 [71]) actor OAA/2

STIRLING, Mrs. Arthur [née Cleveland] (d 1902) actress OAA/2

STIRLING, Charles [Charles Davies] (b 1878) English actor GRB/1

STIRLING, Edward [Edward Lambert] (1809/11-94) English dramatist, actor CDP, EA/68, OC/1-3

STIRLING, Edward see Stirling, W. Edward

STIRLING, Fanny [Mary Anne Kehl] (1813/15-95) English actress CDP, COC, DNB, DP, OAA/1-2, OC/1-3

STIRLING, Fanny (fl 1860-61) actress OAA/2

STIRLING, W. Edward (1891-1948) English actor, manager, dramatist WWT/5-10, WWW/4

STIRLING, William Alexander see Alexander, William

STIRLING, William Fitzgerald (d 1917) EA/18*

STITH, Calvert G. (b 1883) American editor WWM

STITT, Jesse (d 1971 [67]) play sponsor BP/56*

STIX, John (b 1920) American director BE

STIX, Thomas L. (d 1974 [78]) agent BP/59*

STOCK, Charles (d 1891 [68]) steam circus proprietor EA/92*

STOCK, Frederick A. (1872-1942) German conductor WWA/2

STOCK, Jack (d 1954 [60]) actor BE*, WWT/14*

STOCK, Nigel (b 1919) Maltese/English actor AAS, WWT/9-16

STOCK, Thomas dramatist EAP, RJ

STOCKDALE, Ann (b 1943) American actress TW/23

STOCKDALE, Rev. Percival (1736-1811) translator CP/2-3, GT

STOCKEN, Agnes (d 1909) EA/10*

STOCKER, Nannette dwarf CDP

STOCKFIELD, Betty (1905-66) Australian actress WWT/6-13

STOCKHAUSEN, Mons. (d 1868) musician EA/69*

STOCKHAUSEN, Mme. (d 1877) EA/78*

STOCKHOFF, Walter C. (d 1968 [91]) composer/lyricist BP/52*

STOCKING, Robert (b 1941) American actor TW/28

STOCKTON, Fanny (1844-70) American singer CDP, HAS

STOCKTON, Martha Hughes see Brush, Mrs. Clinton E.

STOCKTON, Reginald (d 1898) actor EA/99*

STOCKWELL, Miss see Barrett, Mrs. George Horton

STOCKWELL, Harry American actor TW/1-3

STOCKWELL, Jeremy American actor TW/26, 28

STOCKWELL, L. R. (1851-1912) actor, manager CDP

STOCKWELL, Martha [Mrs. Walter Stockwell] (d 1910) EA/11*

STOCKWELL, Walter (fl 1894?) actor, singer CDP

STOCKWELL, Mrs. Walter see Stockwell, Martha

STOCQUELER, Fanny (b 1847) English actress CDP, HAS

STODARE, Col. (d 1866 [35]) illusionist EA/72*

STODDARD, Mrs. Carlos French see Milliken, Sandol

STODDARD, George (1875-1944) librettist SR

STODDARD, Mrs. George (1832-1911) English actress SR

STODDARD, George D. (b 1897) American educator BE

STODDARD, George William (1826-88) actor CDP

STODDARD, Haila (b 1913/14) American actress, producer, director BE, TW/2-16, WWT/11-16

STODDART, Alexandra (b 1947) American actress TW/28

STODDART, George (fl 1850s) English actor HAS

STODDART, Mrs. George (fl 1850s) English actress HAS

STODDART, J. (fl 1798) translator CP/3

STODDART, James Henry (d
1867 [71]) actor EA/68*
STODDART, James Henry (1827-
1907) English actor CDP,
DAB, HAS, PP/3, SR, WWA/1
STODDART, Mrs. James Henry
[Matilda Phillips] (fl 1856-61)
actress CDP, HAS
STODDART, Marie Scottish ac-
tress GRB/1
STODDART, Mary [Mrs. Richard
D. Stoddart] (d 1892) EA/93*
STODDART, Mrs. Richard D.
see Stoddart, Mary
STOEPEL, Robert [or Richard]
(1821-87) German/American
musician, composer NYM
STOESSEL, Albert Frederic
(1894-1943) American con-
ductor DAB
STOGEL, Syd (d 1974 [60]) pub-
licist BP/58*
STOKEDALE, Edmund (fl 1550)
actor DA
STOKER, Mrs. (d 1885 [84]) ac-
tress EA/86*
STOKER, Bram (1858-1912)
Irish manager, secretary
GRB/1-4, WWW/1
STOKER, Hew Gordon Dacre
(1885-1966) Irish actor WWT/
5-13
STOKER, Willard [né William
Richard] (b 1905) English ac-
tor, producer, director
WWT/11-16
STOKER, William Richard see
Stoker, Willard
STOKES, Ann (d 1894) EA/95*
STOKES, Annie Elizabeth (d
1891 [49]) EA/92*
STOKES, Caroline Ann [Carrie
Romer; Mrs. W. S. Hardy
Stokes] (d 1883) singer? EA/
84*
STOKES, Emma equestrienne
CDP
STOKES, Ernest L. (d 1964
[57]) actor BE*
STOKES, Mrs. Fred see
Ethlo, Maggie
STOKES, Mrs. Henry see
Stokes, Laura Adelaide
STOKES, J. (fl c. 1820) drama-
tist EAP
STOKES, James (d 1833) slack-
rope vaulter HAS
STOKES, John (d 1877) dancer

EA/78*
STOKES, Kate see Stetson, Mrs.
John
STOKES, Laura Adelaide [Mrs.
Henry Stokes] (d 1882) EA/83*
STOKES, Sewell (b 1902) English
dramatist WWT/9-11
STOKES, Thomas (d 1900 [35])
dancer EA/01*
STOKES, Mrs. W. S. Hardy see
Stokes, Caroline Ann
STOLBER, Dean (b 1944) American
actor TW/28
STOLL, Blanche [Mrs. Brukerwich]
(d 1896) EA/97*
STOLL, Harriet [Mrs. Oswald
Stoll] (d 1902 [27]) EA/03*
STOLL, Sir Oswald (1866-1942)
Australian managing director
COC, DNB, GRB/1-4, OC/1-3,
WWT/4-9, WWW/4
STOLL, Mrs. Oswald see Stoll,
Harriet
STOLL, Roderick (d 1890) variety
agent EA/91*
STOLTZ, Rosine (d 1903) singer
EA/04*
STOLZ, Don (b 1919) American
producer, director BE
STOLZ, Robert (1880/86-1975)
Austrian composer, conductor
BE, CB, WWT/10-14
STONE, Alix (b 1918) English de-
signer ES, WWT/15-16
STONE, Amelia (b 1879) American
actress, singer WWS
STONE, Amy actress CDP
STONE, Ann Eliza [née Phillips]
(b 1830) American actress HAS
STONE, Barton (b 1920) American
actor TW/24
STONE, Bentley (b c. 1908) Ameri-
can dancer, choreographer,
costume designer ES
STONE, Carol (b 1915/16) Ameri-
can actress, director BE, TW/
1, 5-19, WWT/10-14
STONE, Charles actor WWT/6-8
STONE, Charles R. [Madelle
Stone] (b 1859) English actor,
producer, stage manager
GRB/1
STONE, Mrs. Charles R. see
Kelsey, Emily
STONE, Christopher Lucius (b
1819) American actor HAS
STONE, Mrs. C[hristopher] L[ucius]
see Drew, Mrs. Frank Melson

STONE, Mrs. C[hristopher]
L[ucius] see Johnston, Mrs.
T. B.

STONE, Dorothy (1905-74) American actress, singer BE,
TW/1-7, WWT/6-11

STONE, Eaton (b 1818) American
equestrian CDP, HAS

STONE, Edward Durell (b 1902)
American architect, educator
BE

STONE, Emma (d 1910) EA/11*

STONE, Ezra (b 1917) American
director, actor, producer,
writer BE

STONE, Florence Oakley [Mrs.
Lewis Stone] (d 1956 [65])
actress BE*, WWT/14*

STONE, Fred Andrew (1873-1959)
American actor GRB/3-4,
SR, TW/1-7, 15, WWA/3,
WWT/1-11

STONE, George (d 1889 [32])
comedian EA/90*, WWT/14*

STONE, George (b 1861) English manager GRB/1

STONE, George E. (d 1967
[64]) performer BP/51*

STONE, Harvey (d 1974 [61])
comedian TW/30

STONE, H. F. (fl 1851) American actor HAS

STONE, Isabel Diaz (d 1924)
singer CDP

STONE, John Augustus (1801-34)
American dramatist, actor
CDP, COC, DAB, EAP, HAS,
HJD, OC/1-3, RJ, WWA/H

STONE, Leonard (b 1923) American actor TW/14-15

STONE, Lewis (1878/79-1953)
American actor TW/10,
WWA/3, WWT/7-10

STONE, Mrs. Lewis see
Stone, Florence Oakley

STONE, Louis H. (d 1972 [76])
producer/director/choreographer
BP/57*

STONE, Mary Anne (d 1883 [58])
EA/84*

STONE, Maxine (d 1964 [54])
performer BP/49*

STONE, Paddy (b 1924/25)
Canadian dancer, choreographer, director AAS, WWT/14-
16

STONE, Paula (b 1916) American
producer, actress BE,

WWT/12-14

STONE, Peter H. (b 1930) American dramatist, librettist BE,
CD, WWT/15-16

STONE, Phil (d 1863 [65]) property
man CDP

STONE, Philip (fl c. 1612-13) lessee DA

STONE, Robinson (b 1919) American actor TW/2, 4

STONE, Sarah see Elliston,
Louise

STONE, Thomas Frederick (d
1895) EA/96*

STONE, William Pidcock (d 1912)
EA/14*

STONEALL, Mrs. [née Scallan]
(fl 1839-49) actress HAS

STONEBURNER, Sam (b 1934)
American actor TW/28

STONEHAM, Adelaide (d 1890
[68]) actress EA/92*

STONEHOUSE, Ruth (1894-1941)
actress BE*

STONER, Mrs. Joe see Stoner,
Marion

STONER, Joseph (d 1889) singer
EA/90*

STONER, Marion [Mrs. Joe Stoner]
(d 1882) EA/84*

STONETTE, Alfred (d 1874 [30])
clown EA/75*

STONETTE, Tom (d 1873) pantomimist EA/74*

STOODLEY, Charles (d 1888)
equestrian EA/89*

STOODLEY, Mrs. G. (d 1878
[37]) EA/79*

STOODLEY, George (d 1903 [69])
circus proprietor EA/04*

STOPPARD, Tom [né Straussler]
(b 1937) Czech/English dramatist, director AAS, CB, CD,
CH, COC, MH, MWD, PDT,
WWT/15-16

STORACE, Anna Selina (1766-
1817) English singer, actress
CDP, DNB, ES, GT, TD/1-2

STORACE, Stephen (1763-96) English musician, proprietor, dramatist, translator CP/2-3,
DNB, ES, TD/1-2

STORCH, Arthur (b 1925) American actor, director TW/10,
12-15, 29, WWT/15-16

STORCH, Larry (b 1923) American
actor BE, TW/12, 14

STORDAHL, Axel (d 1963 [50])

American composer, conductor
BE*

STORER, Mrs. (fl 1760) singer,
actress TD/2

STORER, Miss see Henry,
Mrs. John, I

STORER, Ann see Hogg, Mrs.
John

STORER, Maria (c. 1760-95) actress COC

STOREY, David [Malcolm] (b
1933) English dramatist AAS,
CB, CD, CH, COC, WWT/
15-16

STOREY, Fred (1861-1917) English actor, dancer, scene
painter DP, GRB/1-4, WWT/
1-3

STOREY, F. T. (d 1892) circus
performer? EA/93*

STOREY, John (d 1870 [21])
equestrian EA/71*

STOREY, John (d 1885 [47])
EA/86*

STOREY, Sylvia Lilian (d 1947)
English actress BE*, WWT/
14*

STOREY, Wilson see Bolero

STORM, Howard (b 1939) American actor TW/28

STORM, Lesley (1903-75) Scottish dramatist BE, WWT/
9-15

STORM, Violet (d 1911) performer? EA/12*

STORMONT, Leo (d 1923) actor
BE*, WWT/14*

STORRI, Sadrenne (d 1918 [19])
EA/19*

STORRS, Caryl B. (b 1870)
American editor WWM

STORY, Aubrey (d 1963 [c. 75])
literary representative BE*

STORY, Bob (d 1973 [47]) performer BP/57*

STORY, Mrs. Julian see
Eames, Emma

STORY, Robert (d 1973 [47])
actor TW/29

STORY, Ted (b 1942) American
actor TW/26

STORY, William (d 1870 [86])
actor EA/71*

STORY-GOFTON, Edward English
actor, producer GRB/2-3

STOSSEL, Ludwig (d 1973 [89])
Austrian/American actor
BP/57*, WWT/16*

STOTHART, Herbert P. (d 1949
[64]) American composer WWT/
6-10

STOTT, Judith (b 1929) English actress AAS, WWT/13-15

STOTT, Mike (b 1944) English
dramatist, stage manager CD

STOVALL, Babe (d 1974 [66])
performer BP/59*

STOVALL, Count (b 1946) American
actor TW/30

STOWE, Carl F. (d 1964 [90]) performer BP/49*

STOWELL, Margaret see Rogers,
Maggie

STOYLE, James D. (d 1880 [49])
comedian EA/82*, WWT/14*

STRACCIARI, Riccardo (1875-1955)
Italian singer ES

STRACHAN, Alan (b 1946) Scottish
director WWT/16

STRACHEY, Jack (1894-1972) English composer WWT/11-14

STRADNER, Rose (1913-58) Austrian
actress BE*

STRAHAN, C. G. (fl 1853) actor
HAS

STRAIGHT, Beatrice (b 1918)
American actress, producer
BE, TW/4-15, 24, 29, WWT/
11-16

STRAKER, John Robert (d 1898)
manager EA/99*

STRAKOSCH, Mme. [née Amalia
Patti] (fl 1848) singer HAS

STRAKOSCH, Charles G. (d 1965
[82]) assistant manager, manager
BP/50*

STRAKOSCH, Maurice (1825?-87)
Moravian musician, composer,
manager CDP, ES, HAS, NYM

STRAKOSCH, Max (1835-92) manager CDP

STRANACK, Wallace (d 1950 [78])
actor, business manager BE*,
WWT/14*

STRANGE, Frederick (d 1878 [51])
manager EA/79*

STRANGE, Glenn (d 1973 [74])
performer BP/58*

STRANGE, Michael (1890-1950)
American actress DAB, TW/7,
WWA/3

STRANGE, Robert (d 1975 [61])
actor WWT/7-10

STRASBERG, Lee (b 1901) American director, actor, producer,
coach AAS, BE, CB, COC,

ES, NTH, PDT, WWT/15-16
STRASBERG, Paula (d 1966 [55])
American actress, director,
coach BE, TW/22
STRASBERG, Susan (b 1938)
American actress BE, CB,
ES, TW/12-20
STRASSBERG, Max (d 1968 [55])
performer BP/53*
STRASSBERG, Morris (1897-1974)
actor TW/26, 30
STRASSER, Ilona (d 1976 [55])
performer BP/60*
STRASSER, Robin (b 1945)
American actress TW/23,
29
STRATEN, Mary M. (b 1940)
American actress TW/29
STRATER, Christopher (b 1943)
American actor TW/23
STRATFORD, Dr. (fl 1784) Irish?
dramatist CP/3
STRATFORD, Robert (fl 1631)
actor DA
STRATFORD, William (d 1625)
actor DA
STRATHMORE, Countess of
see Bowes, Mary Eleanor
STRATTON, Charles see
"Thumb, Tom"
STRATTON, Chester (1915-70)
American actor TW/4-8, 27
STRATTON, Eugene (1861-1918)
American variety artist CDP,
COC, GRB/1-4, OC/1-3
STRATTON, John (b 1925) Eng-
lish actor WWT/11-16
STRATTON, John American
actor TW/28
STRATTON, Lottie (d 1907)
EA/08*
STRATTON, Nellie (fl 1900?)
singer CDP
STRATTON, Sam (d 1967 [80])
publicist BP/52*
STRAUS, Oskar (1870-1954)
Austrian composer CB, ES,
TW/10, WWA/3
STRAUS, Sylvie (b 1923) Amer-
ican actress TW/26
STRAUSBAUGH, Warren L. (b
1909) American educator BE
STRAUSBERG, Morris O. (d
1974 [62]) executive BP/58*
STRAUSS, Helen American lit-
erary representative BE
STRAUSS, John (b 1920) Amer-
ican composer, conductor,

musician BE
STRAUSS, Joseph (d 1870 [42])
composer EA/71*, WWT/14*
STRAUSS, Richard (1864-1949)
German composer CB, ES,
WWM
STRAUSS, Robert (1913-75) Amer-
ican actor BE
STRAUSSLER, Tom see Stoppard,
Tom
STRAVINSKY, Igor (1882-1971)
Russian composer, conductor
CB, ES
STRAYCOCK, J. (fl 1804) drama-
tist CP/3
STREAMER, Volney (b 1853) Amer-
ican actor WWM
STREATER, Robert (1624-80) Eng-
lish painter COC, OC/1-3
STREDHELER, Josephine (b 1847)
English dancer HAS
STREET, Ann see Barry, Mrs.
Spranger
STREET, Mrs. Fred see Cousins,
Rosie
STREET, George Slythe (1867-
1936) English examiner of plays
WWT/3-8, WWW/3
STREETER, F. (fl 1778) dramatist
CP/3
STREETER, George Wellington (d
1921) circus proprietor WWA/4
STREIFORD, Hobart A. (d 1974
[63]) performer BP/59*
STREISAND, Barbra (b 1942)
American actress, singer AAS,
BE, CB, ES, TW/18-22, WWT/
14-16
STREIT, Pierre (d 1975 [52]) pro-
ducer/director/choreographer
BP/60*
STRENGTH, William T. (d 1973
[45]) performer BP/58*
STRETCH, John (fl 1635) actor
DA
STRETTON, George (fl 1835) singer
CDP
STRICKLAND, Cowles (d 1971
[68]) director TW/28
STRICKLAND, Enfield (d 1964
[94]) performer BE*, BP/49*
STRICKLAND, Mrs. Frank S.
see Scott, Louie
STRICKLAND, Helen (d 1938 [75])
American actress BE*, BP/22*
STRICKLAND, Robert (d 1845 [47])
actor CDP
STRICKLER, Jerry (b 1939) Amer-

actor BE, TW/19, 22, 24

STRICKLYN, Ray (b 1930)
American actor TW/9-16

STRIDE, James (d 1891 [74])
box office keeper EA/92*

STRIDE, John (b 1936) English
actor TW/18-20, WWT/14-16

STRIDEL, Gene (d 1973 [46])
performer BP/57*

STRIKER, Joseph (d 1974 [74])
actor TW/30

STRIKER, Richard (d 1974 [42])
performer BP/59*

STRIMPEL, Stephen (b 1937)
American actor TW/18-20,
25-26

STRINDBERG, August (1849-
1912) Swedish dramatist
COC, GRB/1-4, OC/3, WWT/1

STRINGER, Emma [Mrs. John
H. Stringer] (d 1877) EA/78*

STRINGER, Mrs. John H. see
Stringer, Emma

STRINGER, John Henry (d 1890
[40]) manager EA/91*

STRINGER, Richard (d 1897
[78]) manager EA/98*

STRINGFIELD, Lamar (1897-
1959) American composer
WWA/3

STRINGHAM, Edwin (d 1974 [83])
composer/lyricist BP/59*

STRINI, Severo (fl 1848) actor?
singer? HAS

STRITCH, Elaine (b 1925/26)
American actress, singer
AAS, BE, TW/4, 11-15,
23-24, 26-28, WWT/14-16

STROBEL, Heinrich (d 1970
[72]) critic BP/55*

STRODE, Warren Chetham (1897-
1974) English dramatist BTR/
74, WWT/10

STRODE, Dr. William (1602-45)
English dramatist CP/1-3,
FGF

STROLLO, Angie (d 1964) costumier BE*

STROMBERG, John (1853-1902)
composer BE*

STRONG, Austin (1881-1952)
American dramatist HJD,
MWD, TW/9, WWA/3, WWM,
WWT/1-11, WWW/5

STRONG, Henry C. (1842-87)
actor NYM

STRONG, Henry K. (fl 1823?)
dramatist EAP, RJ

STRONG, Jay (d 1953 [57]) actor,
director, producer BE*, BP/
38*

STRONG, Michael (b 1918/23)
American actor TW/3, 5-6, 9,
12, 21, 27

STRONG, Rudolph H. (c. 1847-77)
English actor NYM

STROOCK, Bianca (b 1896) American costume designer BE, TW/
3, 6-8

STROOCK, Geraldine (b 1925)
American actress TW/2

STROOCK, James E. (1891-1965)
American executive BE, TW/22

STROUD, Mrs. (d 1872) actress?
EA/73*

STROUD, Clarence G., Sr. (d
1973 [66]) performer BP/58*

STROUD, Gregory (b 1892) English
actor, singer WWT/5-9

STROUD, Henry Charles (d 1888
[61]) singer EA/89*

STROUDE, Mr. (fl 1662-71?)
dramatist CP/2-3

STROUSE, Charles (b 1928) American composer AAS, BE, ES,
WWT/15-16

STROWDEWIKE, Edmund (fl 1559-
68) actor DA

STROZZI, Kay American actress
WWT/7-9

STRUDWICK, Shepperd (b 1907)
American actor BE, TW/3,
9-16, 22-23, 25, 28, 30, WWT/
14-16

STRUGNELL, W. J. (d 1888)
musician EA/89*

STRUTHERS, Robert (b 1837) Scottish actor HAS

STRUTHERS, Sally (b 1948) American actress CB

STRUTT, Joseph (d 1802 [55])
dramatist CP/3

STUART, Mrs. (fl 1800) actress
HAS

STUART, Mrs. [née Vos] (1815-54)
actress HAS

STUART, Mrs. A. B. [Mrs. R.
B. Stuart] (d 1889 [39]) EA/90*

STUART, Aimée (d 1890) Scottish
dramatist WWT/6-14

STUART, Alexander (d 1877) actor
EA/78*

STUART, Alexander (d 1909) stage
manager EA/11*

STUART, Alexander fat boy CDP

STUART, Alicia A. (d 1889 [83])

EA/90*

STUART, Mrs. A. M. see Newham, Rose

STUART, Ann (d 1809) actress CDP

STUART, Barney (d 1913 [41]) EA/14*

STUART, Mrs. C. see Lee, Katie

STUART, C. Douglas (b 1864) English secretary of music-hall artists' railway associa-tion GRB/1-3

STUART, Charles (fl 1777-91) Scottish dramatist CP/3, GT, TD/1-2

STUART, Charles (d 1882) music-hall manager EA/83*

STUART, Charles fat boy CDP

STUART, Colin (b 1825) Cana-dian actor HAS

STUART, Cora (d 1940 [83]) actress BE*, WWT/14*

STUART, Cosmo [Cosmo Stuart Charles Gordon-Lennox] (1869-1921) actor, dramatist COC, DD, GRB/1-4, WWS, WWT/1-3, WWW/1

STUART, Donald (d 1972 [52]) producer BP/56*

STUART, Donald Clive (1881-1943) American dramatist WWA/3

STUART, Dora [Dora Bradford] (d 1887) American actress NYM

STUART, Edward Patrick [James Gray] (b 1867) Scottish dancer GRB/1

STUART, Eliza (d 1877 [74]) actress WWT/14*

STUART, Ella (d 1902) gymnast, trapezist EA/03*

STUART, Frank (d 1917 [54]) EA/18*

STUART, Harry [Harry Stuart Hawkins] (b 1880) English ac-tor GRB/1

STUART, Henri (d 1891 [46]) actor WWT/14*

STUART, Henry Robson see Robson, Stuart

STUART, Ian John (b 1940) Eng-lish actor TW/28

STUART, James (d 1901 [36]) conjuror EA/02*

STUART, Jay American actor TW/30

STUART, Jeanne (b 1908) English actress WWT/7-11

STUART, Joel (b 1938) American actor TW/23

STUART, John (b 1804) actor CDP

STUART, John (b 1898) Scottish actor WWT/8-16

STUART, Laura (b 1938) American actress TW/25-28

STUART, Leslie [T. A. Barrett] (1864/66-1928) English composer GRB/1-4, WWT/1-5

STUART, Louisa (d 1867) actress? equestrienne? EA/68*

STUART, Lynne American actress TW/29

STUART, Madge (b 1897) actress WWT/6-7

STUART, Maggie (d 1897 [23]) ac-tress EA/98*

STUART, Nick (d 1973 [69]) per-former BP/57*

STUART, Otho [Otto Stuart Andreae] (1865-1930) manager, actor GRB/2-4, WWT/1-6

STUART, Philip (1887-1936) Indian/English dramatist WWT/6-8

STUART, Ralph (1860-1910) actor, dramatist SR

STUART, Mrs. R. B. see Stuart, Mrs. A. B.

STUART, Thomas (d 1878 [76]) actor EA/79*, WWT/14*

STUART, William (1821-86) mana-ger, critic CDP

STUBBE, Mr. (fl 1632) dramatist CP/3, FGF

STUBBS, Morton Richard see Selten, Morton

STUBBS, Una actress, dancer WWT/16

STUBBS, William (d 1877) con-ductor EA/78*

STUCKEY, Phyllis actress WWT/4-7

STUCKMANN, Eugene (b 1917) American actor TW/3-4, 10, 26, 28

STUDHOLME, Marie (1875-1930) English actress GRB/1-4, WWT/1-6

STUDLEY, John B. (1831-1910) American actor HAS

STUDLY, John (d 1587) translator CP/1-3

STUDT, John Peter (d 1912) amuse-ment caterer EA/13*

STUDT, Katherine see Broxup,
Katherine
STUDT, Mary Ann (d 1917) EA/
18*
STURANI, Giuseppe (1877-1940)
Italian conductor WWA/1
STURCKEN, Frank W. (b 1929)
American educator BE
STURGES, Charley (fl 1871?)
dancer, singer CDP
STURGES, Preston (1898-1959)
American dramatist ES,
MWD, SR, TW/16, WWA/3,
WWT/7-12
STURGESS, Arthur (d 1931)
librettist, dramatist BE*,
WWT/14*
STURGIS, Julian (1848-1904)
American dramatist, librettist
WWW/1
STURM, Justin (1899-1967) Amer-
ican dramatist, producer
WWA/4
STURMY, John (fl 1722-28) dram-
atist CP/2-3, GT
STUTCHKOFF, Nahum (d 1965
[73]) dramatist BP/50*
STUTFIELD, George (fl 1632-35)
actor DA
STUTHMAN, Fred (b 1919) Amer-
ican actor TW/28-30
STUTZ, Dick (d 1969 [60]) com-
poser/lyricist BP/54*
STYLER, Alan (d 1970 [44])
performer BP/55*
STYLER, Charlotte (d 1971 [75])
performer BP/56*
STYLES, Edwin (1899-1960) Eng-
lish actor WWT/8-12
STYNE, Jule (b 1905) English
composer, producer AAS, BE,
ES, WWT/12-16
STYRES, Earle E. (d 1966 [69])
performer BP/51*
SUBTEL, Walter (d 1918 [37])
EA/19*
SUCHER, Joseph (1844-1908)
conductor CDP
SUCHER, Mrs. Joseph see
Sucher, Rosa
SUCHER, Rosa [Mrs. Joseph
Sucher] (1849-1927) German
singer CDP, ES
SUCKLING, Sir John (1609-42)
English dramatist CP/1-3,
DNB, FGF, HP, OC/3, RE
SUCKLING, John see Wyckham,
John

SUCKLING, Robert see Chetwyn,
Robert
SUDBURY, Thomas (d 1546) actor
DA
SUDERMANN, Hermann (1857-1928)
German dramatist COC, GRB/
1-4, OC/3, WWT/1
SUDLOW, Bessie (d 1928 [78])
singer, actress CDP
SUDLOW, Eliza (d 1906 [87]) EA/
07*
SUDLOW, Joan (d 1970 [78]) per-
former BP/54*
SUES, Leonard (d 1971 [50]) per-
former BP/56*
SUETT, Richard (1755-1805) Eng-
lish actor CDP, COC, DNB,
GT, OC/1-3, OX, TD/1-2
SUGARMAN, Harry (d 1972 [72])
theatre owner BP/56*
SUGDEN, Charles (1850-1921)
English actor DP, GRB/1-4,
OAA/1-2, WWT/1-3, WWW/2
SUGDEN, Mrs. Charles [Helen
Vane] (d 1940 [79]) actress
WWT/2-4
SUGG, Catharine Lee see Hackett,
Mrs. James Henry
SUGG, Lee (d 1831 [85]) ventrilo-
quist EA/72*
SUGRUE, Frank (b 1927) American
producer BE
SULKA, Elaine American actress
TW/30
SULLAVAN, Margaret (1911-60)
American actress CB, COC,
ES, OC/3, TW/5-6, 9-12, 16,
WWA/3, WWT/8-12
SULLIVAN, Mr. see Sylvian,
Mons.
SULLIVAN, Mrs. (d 1882) EA/83*
SULLIVAN, Mrs. Amory see
Stanhope, Adeline
SULLIVAN, Annette Kellerman (d
1975 [87]) performer BP/60*
SULLIVAN, Sir Arthur (1842-1900)
English composer CDP, DNB,
ES, HP, PDT, WWW/1
SULLIVAN, Barry (1821-91) Irish
actor CDP, COC, DNB, HAS,
OAA/1-2, OC/1-3
SULLIVAN, Barry (b 1912) Ameri-
can actor BE
SULLIVAN, Mrs. Barry see
Sullivan, Mary
SULLIVAN, Brian (1919-69) Ameri-
can singer, actor CB, TW/2-3,
6, 26

SULLIVAN, Charles see Gas-
coigne, Charles
SULLIVAN, Mrs. Charles see
D'Alton, Marion
SULLIVAN, Deirdre (b 1925)
American actress TW/24
SULLIVAN, D. J. see Sullivan,
Jeremiah
SULLIVAN, Ed (d 1974 [73])
critic BP/59*
SULLIVAN, Rev. Edward S. (d
1970 [72]) circus priest BP/
54*
SULLIVAN, Elliott (1907-74)
American actor, director,
producer BE, TW/3
SULLIVAN, Francis L. (1903-56)
English actor TW/4, 6, 11-
13, WWA/3, WWT/7-12,
WWW/5
SULLIVAN, Frederic (d 1877
[39]) actor, singer CDP
SULLIVAN, Gael (1904-56) Amer-
ican executive WWA/3
SULLIVAN, George (d 1971) de-
signer BP/55*
SULLIVAN, James see Carney,
Pat
SULLIVAN, James E. (d 1931
[67]) American actor CDP,
GRB/2-4, WWT/1
SULLIVAN, James Francis (b
1880) American actor WWS
SULLIVAN, James W. (d 1974
[65]) designer BP/59*
SULLIVAN, Jeremiah [D. J.
Sullivan] (b 1937) American
actor TW/17-20, 23, 25-28
SULLIVAN, J. F. (d 1866 [25])
balladist HAS
SULLIVAN, Mrs. J. F. see
Clarke, Della
SULLIVAN, Jo American actress,
singer BE, TW/12-16
SULLIVAN, John A. (d 1964
[75+]) ticket broker BE*,
BP/49*
SULLIVAN, John Amory (d 1897)
actor EA/98*
SULLIVAN, John Florence see
Allen, Fred
SULLIVAN, John J. (d 1882)
actor CDP
SULLIVAN, Joseph ["Yankee"
Sullivan] (d 1917 [100]) show-
man, musician, clown, music-
hall proprietor EA/18*
SULLIVAN, Joseph (b 1918)

American actor TW/7, 11, 21-
24, 26-29
SULLIVAN, Kate (d 1912 [56])
burlesque actress EA/13*
SULLIVAN, Liam (b 1923) Ameri-
can actor TW/8-9, 24, 28-29
SULLIVAN, Mary [Mrs. Barry
Sullivan] (d 1908) EA/09*
SULLIVAN, Mella (d 1963 [87])
voice-drama coach BE*
SULLIVAN, Mike (d 1895 [40])
music-hall performer EA/97*
SULLIVAN, Pamela W. (d 1969
[30]) dramatist BP/53*
SULLIVAN, Patrick (b 1848) Eng-
lish actor HAS
SULLIVAN, Richard (d 1877) Irish
comedian EA/78*
SULLIVAN, Rose [Mrs. Arthur
Reece] (d 1895 [32]) Irish singer
EA/97*
SULLIVAN, Thomas Russell (1849-
1916) dramatist BE*
SULLIVAN, Master Tim (d 1904
[13]) actor EA/05*
SULLIVAN, William Francis (fl
1792-97) actor, dramatist TD/2
SULLON, Paul (d 1975 [55]) per-
former BP/60*
SULLY, Daniel [Daniel Sullivan]
(1855-1910) American actor,
dramatist CDP, GRB/3-4,
WWA/1, WWS
SULLY, Frank (d 1975 [67]) actor
BP/60*, WWT/16*
SULLY, Mariette (b 1878) French
actress, singer WWT/1-4
SULLY, Mathew (d 1812) English
actor HAS
SULLY, Robert (b 1918) American
actor TW/2-3
SULLY, Ruby (d 1971 [51]) drama-
tist BP/55*
SULLY, Thomas F. (fl 1870?)
dancer, singer CDP
SULLY, William (d 1969) performer
BP/54*
SULZER, Elmer G. (d 1976 [72])
educator, publicist BP/60*
SUMAC, Yma (b 1927) Peruvian
singer CB, TW/8
SUMMERFIELD, Eleanor (b 1921)
English actress WWT/11-14
SUMMERS, Ann (d 1974 [54]) per-
former BP/58*
SUMMERS, Arthur (d 1969 [59])
agent BP/53*
SUMMERS, Mrs. Charles see

Summers, Emily Jane
SUMMERS, David (b 1952) American actor TW/30
SUMMERS, Dorothy (d 1964 [70]) actress BE*
SUMMERS, Emily Jane [Mrs. Charles Summers] (d 1882) actress EA/84*
SUMMERS, J. W. (d 1893) American comedian EA/94*
SUMMERS, Louisa (d 1879 [42]) burlesque actress EA/80*
SUMMERS, Madlyn Jane American actress, dancer WWS
SUMMERS, Montague (1880-1946/48) English critic, historian COC, OC/1-3, WWT/5-10
SUMMERS, Oliver (d 1878) comedian, buffo singer EA/79*
SUMMERS, Peter (d 1888 [47]) EA/89*
SUMMERS, Styles Joseph (d 1917 [69]) musician EA/18*
SUMMERS, Vikki American actress TW/26
SUMMERS, Walter (d 1905 [38]) dramatist GRB/1
SUMMERSON, James Henry (d 1875 [36]) music-hall performer EA/76*
SUMMERTON, Peter (d 1969 [40]) producer/director/choreographer BP/54*
SUMMERVILLE, Amelia (d 1934 [71]) Irish actress, singer WWA/1, WWM, WWS
SUMMERVILLE, Annie actress CDP
SUMMERVILLE, Hamilton S. [James H. Drew] (d 1888) Negro minstrel EA/89*
SUMMERVILLE, Slim (d 1946 [54]) American actor BE*
SUMNER, Geoffrey (b 1908) English actor WWT/15-16
SUMNER, John (d 1651) actor DA
SUMNER, John (b 1924) English director WWT/16
SUMNER, Mary (1888-1956) English actress WWT/4-7
SUMNER, Reginald (d 1897 [46]) manager EA/98*
SUMNER, Stanley (d 1971 [81]) manager BP/56*
SUNDBERG, Clinton (b 1906) American actor BE, TW/12

SUNDERLAND, Nan (d 1973) actress TW/30
SUNDERLAND, Scott (b 1883) English actor WWT/5-11
SUNDGAARD, Arnold (b 1909) American dramatist BE
SUNDSTEN, Lani (b 1949) American actress TW/30
SUNDSTROM, Florence (b 1918) American actress BE, TW/3
SUNDSTROM, Frank Swedish? actor TW/2
SUNGHAM, Harry ["The Nubian King"] (d 1893) Negro comedian EA/94*
SUNSHINE, Marion (d 1963 [66]) actress, singer TW/19
SURATT, Valeska (fl 1900s) American vaudevillian WWM
SURMAN, Joseph (d 1871 [66]) singer? EA/72*
SUROVY, Nicholas (b 1944) American actor TW/21, 30
SUSANN, Jacqueline (1921-74) American actress CB
SUSINI [Agostino Guillano] (d 1883 [60]) singer HAS
SUSINI, Isabella (d 1862) singer CDP
SUSSKIND, David (b 1920) American producer BE, CB
SUTCLIFFE, Mrs. Alfred (d 1910 [34]) EA/11*
SUTCLIFFE, Richard Nelson see Steyne, Nelson
SUTER, Frederick (d 1896 [21]) actor EA/97*
SUTER, W. E. (d 1882 [70]) dramatist, comedian BE*, EA/83*, WWT/14*
SUTER, William see Suter, W. E.
SUTHERD, Mrs. Arthur (d 1888) singer EA/89*
SUTHERLAND, A. Edward (d 1974 [77]) performer BP/58*
SUTHERLAND, Agnes M. (fl 1857) English singer HAS
SUTHERLAND, Alec (d 1973 [35]) designer BP/57*
SUTHERLAND, Annie [Mrs. Charles Harding] (1867-1942/43) American actress GRB/3-4, WWA/2, WWT/1-9
SUTHERLAND, Birdie (d 1955 [81]) actress BE*, WWT/14*
SUTHERLAND, Efua (b 1924) Ghanaian dramatist CD

SUTHERLAND, Evelyn Greenleaf
(1855-1908) American dramatist
GRB/2-4, WWS

SUTHERLAND, Mrs. Evelyn
Greenleaf see Rutherford,
John

SUTHERLAND, Frank (d 1894
[57]) acting manager EA/95*

SUTHERLAND, Fred [Fred Ander-
son] (d 1889) acrobat EA/90*

SUTHERLAND, Joan (b 1926)
Australian singer CB, ES

SUTHERLAND, Marie [Marie
King] (d 1898) actress EA/
99*

SUTHERLAND, Robert C. (d
1962 [79]) theatre operator
BE*

SUTHERLAND, Roy see Sothern,
Hugh

SUTHERLAND, Victor (1894-1968)
American actor TW/4, 25

SUTHERLAND, Will see Bel-
asco, Will

SUTHERLAND, William A. (d
1969 [52]) performer BP/54*

SUTHERLAND, W. R. (d 1904
[50]) actor EA/97

SUTORIUS, James L. (b 1944)
American actor TW/26, 28-30

SUTRO, Alfred (1863-1933) Eng-
lish dramatist DNB, ES,
GRB/1-4, MH, MWD, WWS,
WWT/1-7, WWW/3

SUTTON, Mrs. (fl 1841-45)
singer HAS

SUTTON, Charles [H. Bunth]
(d 1904) performer? EA/05*

SUTTON, Dolores American actress TW/28

SUTTON, Dudley (b 1933) English
actor TW/22

SUTTON, Emily (fl 1841) singer
CDP

SUTTON, Ernest see Sarl,
Ernest James

SUTTON, Frank (d 1908 [42])
actor EA/09*

SUTTON, Frank (d 1974 [51])
performer BP/59*

SUTTON, Henry (d 1911) managing director EA/12*

SUTTON, Henry (b 1926) American actor TW/30

SUTTON, John P. (d 1887) actor
NYM

SUTTON, Paul (d 1970 [58]) performer BP/54*

SUTTON, Robert (fl 1550) actor
DA

SUTTON, Sam (d 1896 [58]) music-
hall chairman EA/97*

SUTTON, Sambo [James Henry Pat-
terson] (d 1902) Negro comedian
EA/03*

SUTTON, Tom (b 1874) English
conductor, composer, pianist
GRB/1

SUTTON, Will (d 1907) performer?
EA/08*

SUTTON-VANE, Frank (d 1913)
EA/14*

SUTTON-VANE, Vane (1888-1963)
actor, dramatist, stage manager
WWT/4-8

SUZMAN, Janet (b 1939) South African actress AAS, CB, WWT/
15-16

SUZUKI, Pat (b 1930?/34) American
singer CB, TW/14, 16, 30

SVANHOLM, Set (1904-64) Swedish
singer, director CB, WWA/4

SVELTO (d 1895 [13]) musician
EA/96*

SVENDSEN, Olaf (d 1888 [56]) musician EA/89*

SVERDLIN, Lev (d 1969 [57]) performer BP/54*

SVOBODA, Josef (b 1920) Czech
scene designer COC, WWT/16

SWAFFER, Hannen (1879-1962)
English critic, journalist WWT/
5-13, WWW/6

SWAIN, Elizabeth (b 1941) English
actress TW/25, 27, 30

SWAINE, G. B. (fl 1849) actor,
singer CDP

SWALLOW, Fred (d 1900) circus
performer EA/01*

SWALLOW, John (d 1895 [76])
circus performer EA/96*

SWALLOW, J. T. (d 1871) concert
speculator EA/73*

SWALLOW, Margaret (1896-1932)
English actress WWT/6

SWALLOW, William Charles (d
1900 [22]) EA/01*

SWAN, Bradford F. (d 1976 [68])
critic BP/60*

SWAN, Charles (d 1908 [80]) actor
EA/09*

SWAN, John (d 1861) actor WWT/
14*

SWAN, Lew (d 1964 [69]) performer
BE*

SWAN, Mark Elbert (1871-1942)

American dramatist WWT/ 4-9

SWAN, Paul (d 1972 [88]) American dancer, actor WWA/5

SWANBOROUGH, Ada (d 1893 [48]) English actress CDP, OAA/1-2

SWANBOROUGH, Arthur (d 1895 [58]) manager EA/97*, WWT/ 14*

SWANBOROUGH, Mrs. Arthur see Bufton, Eleanor

SWANBOROUGH, Edward (d 1908 [67]) music-hall manager GRB/4*

SWANBOROUGH, Fanny [Fanny Hughes] (d 1888 [45]) actress EA/89*

SWANBOROUGH, Louisa (fl 1856) actress CDP

SWANBOROUGH, Mary Ann (d 1889 [85]) lessee, actress EA/90*, WWT/14*

SWANBOROUGH, William Henry (d 1886 [56/57]) actor, manager EA/88*, WWT/14*

SWANN, Caroline Burke (d 1964 [51]) American producer, director, dramatist, actress BE, TW/21

SWANN, Donald [Ibrahim] (b 1923) English composer, songwriter, entertainer AAS, BE, CB, COC, ES, OC/3, TW/ 23, WWT/13-16

SWANN, Elaine American actress TW/20-21

SWANN, Francis (b 1913) American dramatist, director BE

SWANN, William (d 1872 [15]) gymnast EA/73*

SWANSEN, Larry (b 1930) American actor TW/30

SWANSON, Britt (b 1947) American dancer, actress? TW/ 29-30

SWANSON, Gloria (b 1899) American actress BE, ES, TW/1, 8, 28-29, WWT/16

SWANSON, Larry (b 1930) American actor TW/25-26, 28

SWANSON, Marcella (d 1973 [80s]) performer BP/58*

SWANSTON, Eliard [or Hilliard] (d 1651) English actor COC, DA, OC/1-3

SWANTON, John G. (d 1886 [48]) actor EA/87*

SWANTON, Mary (d 1918 [76]) EA/19*

SWANWICK, Anna (1813-99) English translator DNB

SWARTHOUT, Gladys (1904-69) American singer CB, TW/26, WWA/5

SWARTOUT, Norman Lee (b 1879) American dramatist WWM

SWASH, Bob (b 1929) English producing manager WWT/16

SWAYNE, Eleanor American actress TW/2

SWEARINGEN, John (b 1935) American actor TW/26-27

SWEARS, Herbert (d 1946 [77]) dramatist BE*, WWT/14*

SWEASEY, John Samuel (d 1890) music-hall performer? EA/91*

SWEATMAN, Willis P. (1864-1930) American minstrel, actor, minstrel manager CDP, SR

SWEENEY, Andrew (d 1892) cannon-ball performer EA/93*

SWEENEY, Claire see Degener, Claire S.

SWEENEY, John J. (d 1892 [28]) music-hall performer EA/93*

SWEENY, Joel Walker (1813-60) actor, musician, minstrel manager CDP

SWEENY, J. W. (d 1900) Irish comedian EA/01*

SWEET, Blanche (b 1896) American actress BE, TW/2-3, 6

SWEET, Dolph (b 1920) American actor, director BE, TW/22-26, 28, 30

SWEET, Mrs. H. see Howard, Carrie

SWEET, Sam (d 1948 [27]) actor TW/4

SWEETEN, Robert G. (d 1972 [59]) publicist BP/57*

SWEETLAND, Reynolds (d 1970 [79]) critic BP/54*

SWEETMAN, Robert (d 1892 [57]) actor EA/93*

SWEETMAN, Mrs. Robert (d 1886) actress EA/87*

SWEETMAN, Mrs. Robert see Sweetman, Rose

SWEETMAN, Rose [Mrs. Robert Sweetman] (d 1871) EA/72*

SWEIGARD, Lulu E. (d 1974) dance educator? BP/59*

SWENDALL, Mr. (fl 1790-1803) actor, manager TD/1-2

SWENSON, Alfred G. (1883-1941) actor CB

SWENSON, Inga (b 1932/34) American actress, singer BE, TW/13-17, 20-22, 25, WWT/14-16

SWENSON, Karl actor TW/1

SWENSON, Linda (b 1945) American actress TW/29

SWENSON, Swen (b 1932/34) American actor, singer, dancer BE, TW/16-20, 23, 30, WWT/14-16

SWERLING, Jo (b 1897) Russian/American dramatist BE

SWETE, E. Lyall (1865-1930) English actor, dramatist, producer GRB/1-4, WWT/1-6

SWIFT, Mr. (fl 1806) dramatist CP/3

SWIFT, Mr. (fl 1869) singer EA/70*

SWIFT, Alexandra see Carlisle, Alexandra

SWIFT, Clive (b 1936) English actor WWT/15-16

SWIFT, Eva (d 1901 [24]) EA/02*

SWIFT, Jonathan (1667-1745) Irish author CP/2-3

SWIFT, Joseph (d 1869) singer CDP

SWIFT, Joseph (d 1888 [37]) EA/89*

SWINARSKI, Konrad (d 1975 [46]) Polish director WWT/16*

SWINBOURNE, Mr. (fl 1858-59) English actor HAS

SWINBOURNE, Ann Elizabeth [Mrs. Thomas Swinbourne] (d 1886 [57]) EA/87*

SWINBOURNE, Charlotte Elizabeth see Vandenhoff, Charlotte Elizabeth

SWINBOURNE, Harriett (d 1883 [79]) EA/84*

SWINBOURNE, Thomas (d 1895 [72]) English actor OAA/1-2

SWINBOURNE, Mrs. Thomas see Swinbourne, Ann Elizabeth

SWINBURNE, Algernon Charles (1837-1909) English dramatist DNB, HP, NTH, WWW/1

SWINBURNE, John [J. P. Edwards] (fl 1868) English actor HAS

SWINBURNE, Mercia (b 1900) Australian actress WWT/6-11

SWINBURNE, Nora (b 1902) English actress WWT/5-16

SWINBURNE, Thomas (d 1895 [72]) actor CDP

SWINDEN, Edward (d 1887 [77]) EA/88*

SWINDLEHURST, Lizzie see Lillie, Miss

SWINERD, Esther (d 1899 [67]) EA/00*

SWINERD, Henry (d 1909 [57]) manager EA/11*

SWINERD, Mrs. Henry (d 1906 [51]) EA/07*

SWINEY, J. M. dramatist CP/3

SWINEY, Owen (c. 1675-1754) Irish actor, manager COC, CP/1-3, DNB, GT, OC/1-3, TD/1-2

SWINGLER, Randall (d 1967 [58]) dramatist BP/52*

SWINHOE, Gilbert (fl 1658) English dramatist CP/1-3, FGF

SWINLEY, E. Ion (1891-1937) English actor AAS, WWT/2-8

SWINNERTON, Abel (fl 1628) actor DA

SWINNERTON, Thomas (fl 1603-28) actor DA

SWINNY, Owen Mac (d 1754) manager CDP

SWINSTEAD, Joan (b 1903) English actress WWT/9-13

SWINSTEAD, Muriel see Ross, Oriel

SWINY, Owen Mac see Swiney, Owen

SWIRE, Willard (b 1910) American actor TW/4

SWITZER, Carl (d 1959 [33]) actor BE*

SWOPE, Herbert Bayard, Jr. American director, producer BE

SWOPE, Tracy Brooks (b 1952) American actress TW/25

SWOR, Burt (1873-1947) American minstrel SR

SWOR, John (d 1965 [87]) performer BP/50*

SYDENHAM, Ernest (d 1875 [25]) comic singer EA/76*

SYDENHAM, George English manager, actor GRB/1

SYDNEY, Basil (1894-1968) English actor AAS, BE, TW/24, WWT/4-14

SYDNEY, Harry (d 1870 [45])
singer, composer, songwriter
CDP
SYDNEY, Lewis (d 1941) come-
dian BE*, WWT/14*
SYDNEY, Sir Philip (1554-86)
English dramatist CP/1-3
SYDNEY, Vernon (fl 1874?)
minstrel, singer CDP
SYDOW, Jack (b 1921) American
director, dramatist BE
SYERS, Morris Robert (d 1876
[58]) music-hall proprietor
EA/77*
SYFERWESTE, Richard (fl 1602)
actor DA
SYKES, Mrs. Arthur see
Ganthony, Nellie
SYKES, George Edward see
Murray, J. K.
SYKES, Jerome H. (d 1903
[35]) American singer, come-
dian WWA/1
SYKES, Percival H. T. see
Murray, Percy
SYLOS, Frank Paul (d 1976
[75]) designer BP/60*
SYLVA, Eloi (fl 1885) Russian
singer CDP
SYLVA, Ilena (b 1916) English
actress WWT/10
SYLVA, Marguerite (d 1957 [81])
Belgian singer TW/13,
WWA/3
SYLVA, Vesta (b 1907) English
actress WWT/5-7
SYLVAIN, Mons. (fl 1840)
dancer CDP
SYLVAIN, Eugène (d 1930 [79])
actor WWT/14*
SYLVAIN, Louise (d 1930 [56])
actress BE*, WWT/14*
SYLVAINE, Vernon (1897-1957)
English actor AAS, WWT/
6-12, WWW/5
SYLVESTER, A. B. (d 1878
[37]) Negro comedian EA/79*
SYLVESTER, Bernard see
Petronj, Egidio
SYLVESTER, Bob (d 1975 [68])
columnist WWT/16*
SYLVESTER, Frank see
Franks, Sydney
SYLVESTER, Louisa (b 1851)
American singer, actress
CDP, HAS
SYLVESTER, Robert (d 1975 [68])
critic BP/59*

SYLVESTER, William (b 1922)
American actor TW/12-13,
WWT/11-15
SYLVESTER, William George (d
1916) caterer EA/17*
SYLVESTRE, Cleo English actress
TW/30
SYLVIA, Estrella (d 1895) dancer
EA/96*
SYLVIAN, Mons. [Sullivan] (fl 1833-
40) dancer HAS
SYLVIE (d 1970 [88]) performer
BP/54*
SYMCOCKES (fl 1604-05) actor
DA
SYMINGTON, Donald (b 1925)
American actor TW/10-13, 24,
27-29
SYMMONDS, Rev. Charles (fl 1796)
dramatist CP/3
SYMMONS (fl 1800) dramatist CP/3
SYMNS, Thomas Kelly (d 1873
[52]) comedian, comic singer
EA/74*
SYMONDS, Emily Morse see
Paston, George
SYMONDS, Margaret see Davey,
Nuna
SYMONDS, Robert (b 1926) Ameri-
can actor, director, producer
BE, TW/22-30, WWT/15-16
SYMONS, Arthur William (1865-
1945) Welsh dramatist, critic
DNB
SYMONS, Beatrice [Mrs. David
Symons] (d 1905) EA/06*
SYMONS, Daniel (fl 1865-69) mana-
ger, actor, business manager
HAS
SYMONS, Mrs. David see Sy-
mons, Beatrice
SYMONS, John (fl 1583-99) tumbler
DA
SYMPSON, Tony (b 1906) English
actor WWT/12-16
SYMS, Algernon [Syms-Wilcox]
(d 1915 [71]) English actor
GRB/1-3
SYMS, Mrs. Algernon see Syms,
Rosina
SYMS, Robert John (d 1895) EA/
96*
SYMS, Rosina [Mrs. Algernon
Syms] (d 1901) EA/02*
SYMS, Sylvia English actress ES
SYMS, Sylvia (b 1920) American
actress TW/15, 26
SYMS, Walter (d 1903) EA/04*

SYMS-WILCOX, Algernon see
Syms, Algernon
SYNGE, Mrs. see Granville,
Charlotte
SYNGE, John Millington (1871-
1909) Irish dramatist COC,
DNB, ES, HP, MD, MH,
MWD, NTH, OC/1-3, PDT,
RE, WWW/1
SYPHER, Willie (b 1905) Amer-
ican educator BE
SYRUS, Napoleon [James Syrus
Tully] (d 1891 [63]) comic
singer EA/92*
SYSE, Glenna (b 1927) Canadian
critic BE
SZABO, Sandor (b 1915) Hungarian
actor BE
SZELL, George (1897-1970) Hun-
garian conductor CB

- T -

T., J. (fl 1662) dramatist CP/3
T., R. (fl 1619) actor DA
TAAFF, Joseph Pierce (d 1890
[56]) music-hall performer
EA/91*
TAAFF, Mrs. J. P. (d 1867)
singer? EA/68*
TABACHNIK, Abraham Ber (d
1970 [68]) critic BP/55*
TABBERT, William (1921-74)
American actor, singer BE,
TW/2-17, WWT/11-14
TABELAK, John-Michael libret-
tist CD
TABER, Richard (1891-1957)
American actor TW/3, 5-6,
14
TABER, Robert (1865-1904)
American actor PDT, SR
TABOR, Disiree (d 1957 [57])
actress, singer TW/13
TABOR, Ethel F. (d 1972 [70s])
costumier BP/56*
TABOR, Joan (d 1968 [35]) per-
former BP/53*
TABORI, George (b 1914) Hun-
garian dramatist, director
BE, CD, WWT/15-16
TABORI, Kristoffer (b 1952)
American actor TW/25-26,
30
TABRAR, Joseph (1857-1931)
English composer WWW/3
TABRAR, Tom (d 1904 [50])

music-hall comedian EA/05*
TACAGNI, Benedict (d 1880 [6])
actor EA/81*
TACCHINARDI, Nicola (1772-1859)
singer CDP
TACKABERRY, John (d 1969 [55])
dramatist BP/54*
TACKNEY, Stanley (b 1909) Amer-
ican actor, director, producer
BE
TACKOVA, Jarmilla (d 1971 [59])
performer BP/56*
TADEMA, Sir Laurence Alma see
Alma-Tadema, Sir Laurence
TADLOCK, Renee (b 1949) Ameri-
can actress TW/30
TADOLINI, Eugenia (b 1810) singer
CDP
TAFLER, Sidney (b 1916) English
actor TW/2
TAFT, Elizabeth see Stephens,
Mrs.
TAFT, James Gordon (d 1971 [42])
lawyer BP/56*
TAGG, Alan (b 1928) English de-
signer AAS, ES, WWT/15-16
TAGGART, Hal (d 1971 [79]) per-
former BP/56*
TAGGER, Theodor see Bruckner,
Friedrich
TAGLIAVINI, Ferruccio (b 1913)
Italian singer CB
TAGLIONI, Mons. (d 1868) EA/69*
TAGLIONI, Amalie see Taglioni,
Mme. Paul
TAGLIONI, Filippo (d 1871 [94])
dancer, choreographer WWT/14*
TAGLIONI, Louise dancer CDP
TAGLIONI, Luigia (d 1893 [70])
dancer EA/94*
TAGLIONI, Marie (1804/09-84)
Swedish dancer CDP, DNB, ES
TAGLIONI, Marie P. dancer CDP
TAGLIONI, Paul (1808-84) dancer
CDP, HAS
TAGLIONI, Mme. Paul (d 1881)
dancer CDP, HAS
TAHSE, Martin (b 1930) American
producer BE
TAILLADE, Paul (d 1898 [72]) actor
BE*, WWT/14*
TAILOR, Robert (fl 1597-1601)
actor DA
TAILOR, Robert (fl 1614) dramatist
CP/1-3, DNB, FGF
TAIT, Annie (d 1886) composer
EA/87*
TAIT, Edward J. (c. 1879-1947)

Australian producer SR
TAIT, Sir Frank (d 1965 [81])
Australian manager WWT/14*
TAIT, Herbert see Ross,
Herbert
TAIT, James N. (d 1961 [85])
Australian manager WWT/14*
TAJIRI, Larry S. (b 1914) Amer-
ican editor, critic BE
TAJO, Halo (b 1915) Italian
singer ES
TALBERT, Rose Hershfield (d
1975 [91]) performer BP/59*
TALBOT, Mr. [Mr. Montague]
(fl 1800) actor TD/1-2
TALBOT, Mr. (fl 1820) Irish ac-
tor HAS
TALBOT, Mrs. [Mrs. Charles
Page] (d 1838) Irish actress
HAS
TALBOT, Mrs. see Clifford,
Miss E.
TALBOT, Miss (d 1865 [39]) ac-
tress EA/72*, WWT/14*
TALBOT, Charles (fl 1827?)
dramatist EAP, RJ
TALBOT, Evelyn [Mrs. Arthur
Keand] (d 1910) EA/11*
TALBOT, Hayden (b 1882)
American dramatist WWM
TALBOT, Henry (d 1894 [61])
actor, architect EA/95*
TALBOT, Howard [Howard Mun-
kittrick] (1865-1928) American
composer, conductor GRB/
1-4, WWA/1, WWT/1-5,
WWW/2
TALBOT, Mrs. Howard see
Bellamy, Ada
TALBOT, J. (fl 1686?) trans-
lator CP/2-3
TALBOT, John (d 1831) Irish
manager EA/72*
TALBOT, Lyle (b 1902) American
actor, director BE
TALBOT, Montague (1774-1831)
American/English actor,
manager CDP, DNB
TALBOT, Nita (b 1930) Ameri-
can actress TW/8-13, 25
TALBOT, Rupert (d 1917) singer
EA/18*
TALBOT, Slim (d 1973 [77])
stand-in BP/57*
TALBOT, William C. (d 1866
[27]) manager HAS
TALCOTT, Michael (b 1939)
American actor TW/26

TALENT, Bill (d 1974 [81]) per-
former BP/59*
TALFOURD, Francis (1828-62)
English? dramatist DNB
TALFOURD, Sir Thomas Noon
(1795-1854) English dramatist
CDP, COC, DNB, HP, NTH,
OC/1-3, SR
TALIAFERRO, Edith (1892/93-
1958) American actress ES,
TW/14, WWM, WWT/1-10
TALIAFERRO, Mabel (b 1887)
American actress BE, ES,
TW/1-9, WWM, WWS, WWT/
1-13
TALLCHIEF, Maria (b 1925) Amer-
ican dancer CB, ES, WWT/11-
12
TALLEY, William Edgar (d 1975
[64]) executive BP/60*
TALLIOTT, James (d 1877) ring
master EA/79*
TALLIS, Sir George (1867-1948)
manager WWT/5-9
TALLMAN, Ellen (d 1963 [73])
performer BE*
TALLMER, Jerry (b 1920) Ameri-
can critic, journalist BE
TALLON, Annie [Mrs. William
Tallon] (d 1897) EA/98*
TALLON, William (d 1910 [66])
actor EA/12*
TALLON, Mrs. William see
Tallon, Annie
TALMA, Charlotte (1771-1861)
actress CDP
TALMA, François-Joseph (1763-
1826) French actor CDP, COC,
OC/3, OX
TALMADGE, Constance (d 1973
[73]) actress BP/58*, WWT/16*
TALMADGE, Natalie (d 1969 [70])
performer BP/54*
TALMADGE, Norma (1897-1957)
American actress BE*
TALMAN, William (d 1968 [53])
performer BP/53*
TALMON-GROS, Walter (d 1973
[62]) performer BP/58*
TALOT, Alex (d 1861) actor HAS
TALVA, Galina (1930-68) American
actress TW/7-8, 25
TAMAGNO, Francesco (1850-1905)
Italian singer ES
TAMANTI, Mme. Bastatelli (d
1869 [100]) singer EA/70*
TAMANY, Mary (1856-1918) Amer-
ican comedienne SR

TAMARA [Tamara Drasin] (1907-43) Russian/American actress WWT/9-10

TAMBERLIK, Enrico (1820-89) Italian singer CDP, ES

TAMBURINI, Antonio (1800-76) Italian singer ES

TAMIRIS, Helen (1905-66) American choreographer, dancer BE, ES, TW/2-8, 23, WWA/4, WWT/11-14

TAMIROFF, Akim (1901-72) Russian actor BE, TW/29

TAMKIN, David (d 1975 [68]) composer/lyricist BP/60*

TAMS, Arthur W. (b 1848) American musical director WWM

TANDY, Jessica (b 1909) English/American actress AAS, BE, CB, ES, TW/4, 6-23, 26-27, 29-30, WWT/7-16

TANDY, Valerie (1921-65) English actress, singer WWT/11-12

TANGUAY, Eva (1878-1947) Canadian actress, singer DAB, GRB/3-4, SR, TW/3, WWS, WWT/1-5

TANNEHILL, Frances actress TW/1

TANNEN, Don (d 1974 [60s]) performer BP/58*

TANNEN, Julius (d 1965 [84]) performer BP/49*

TANNER, Miss see Robertson, Mrs. Brougham

TANNER, Annie Louise (d 1921 [65]) singer BE*, BP/5*

TANNER, Beatrice Stella see Campbell, Mrs. Patrick

TANNER, Carolyn (b 1927) American actress TW/4

TANNER, Cora (fl 1880-98) actress CDP, PP/3

TANNER, George (d 1870) pantaloon EA/71*

TANNER, Gordon (b 1918) Canadian actor TW/12

TANNER, James T. (d 1915 [56]) librettist WWT/2

TANNER, Jill (b 1943) English actress TW/29

TANNER, Tony (b 1932) English actor TW/22-23, 26-27, 29

TANNETT, Mrs. A. [Mrs. Charles S. Tanner] (d 1888 [38]) EA/89*

TANNETT, Mrs. B. (d 1882) actress EA/84*

TANNETT, Mrs. Charles S. see Tannett, Mrs. A.

TANNETT, Edward Harley (d 1875 [52]) songwriter EA/76*

TANNYHILL, Francis A. (b c. 1830) American actor HAS

TANNYHILL, Mrs. Francis A. [née Ella Clayton] (fl 1855) American actress HAS

TANSLEY, Derek (b 1917) English actor TW/9

TANSWELL, Bertram (b 1908) English director, actor BE

TAPLEY, Douglas (d 1916 [14]) EA/17*

TAPLEY, Joseph (fl 1885-90) actor DP

TAPLEY, Mrs. Joseph see Varley, Violet

TAPLIN, Mrs. William see Chambers, Harriet

TAPLINGER, Robert (d 1975 [66]) publicist BP/60*

TAPPING, Mrs. A. see Tapping, Lavinia

TAPPING, Alfred (d 1880) actor EA/82*, WWT/14*

TAPPING, Alfred B. (d 1928 [77]) actor, stage manager WWT/3-5

TAPPING, Mrs. Alfred B. [Florence Cowell] (1852-1926) actress EA/95, ES, OC/1-3, WWT/3-5

TAPPING, Lavinia [Mrs. A. Tapping] (d 1873) EA/74*

TARA, Sheila (d 1969 [81]) performer BP/54*

TARAS, John (b 1919) American choreographer, dancer ES

TARASOVA, Alla Konstantinovna (1898-1973) Russian actress WWT/13-14

TARBOCK, John (fl 1610) patentee DA

TARBUCK, Barbara (b 1942) American actress TW/26-27, 30

TARIOL-BAUGE, Anna (b 1872) French actress, singer WWT/1-4

TARJAN, George (d 1973 [63]) performer BP/58*

TARKINGTON, Newton Booth (1869-1946) American dramatist CB, COC, DAB, ES, GRB/3-4, HJD, HP, MH, MWD, NTH, OC/1-3, SR, TW/2, WWA/2, WWM, WWT/1-9, WWW/4

TARKINGTON, William O. (d 1962

[89]) talent representative, manager BE*

TARLETON, Diane American actress TW/29

TARLETON, Richard (1530-88) English clown, dramatist CDP, COC, CP/2-3, DA, DNB, ES, FGF, GT, NTH, OC/1-3

TARLOW, Florence (b 1929) American actress TW/24-29

TARN, Adam (d 1975 [73]) dramatist BP/60*

TARPEY, Tom (b 1943) American actor TW/26-27, 29-30

TARR, Edward Sinclair (b 1842) American actor HAS

TARRANT, George [Paul Pietro] (d 1880) clown EA/81*

TARRANT, L. Newell (b 1911) American director, manager, actor BE

TARRI, Suzette (d 1955 [74]) performer BE*, WWT/14*

TARTEL, Michael (b 1936) American actor TW/26

TASHMAN, Lilyan (1899-1934) American actress WWT/7

TASISTRO, Fitzgerald (fl 1841) actor HAS

TASK, Maggie American actress TW/24, 26, 28

TASKER, William (1740-1800) English dramatist CP/3

TASKER, William see Lee, Edgar

TASSEL, Hazel Mae (d 1973 [80]) performer BP/57*

TATE, Alfred (d 1908) EA/09*

TATE, Dennis (b 1938) American actor TW/24, 26-27, 29

TATE, Harry [Ronald Macdonald Hutchison] (1872-1940) Scottish actor COC, ES, OC/1-3, PDT, WWT/4-9

TATE, James W. (1875-1922) English composer, manager WWT/4

TATE, Margaret see Teyte, Maggie

TATE, Nahum (1652-1715) English dramatist COC, CP/1-3, DNB, GT, HP, NTH, OC/1-3

TATE, Reginald (1896-1955) English actress WWT/7-11

TATE, Mrs. Thomas C. see Busch, Mae

TATE, William Henry Gilbert (d 1900 [50]) agent EA/01*

TATHAM, John (fl 1632-64) dramatist CP/1-3, DNB, FGF

TATIN, Mons. (fl 1822) pantomimist HAS

TATNALL, Mrs. [Mrs. Pemberton] (fl 1822) actress HAS

TATTERDELL, Hugh (fl 1629) actor DA

TAUBE, Evert (d 1976 [85]) composer/lyricist BP/60*

TAUBENHAUS, Eugene see Doyle, Gene

TAUBER, Richard (1890/91/93-1948) Austrian/English actor, singer, composer, conductor ES, TW/4, WWA/2, WWT/7-10

TAUBIN, Amy (b 1939) American actress TW/23-24, 29

TAUBMAN, Howard (b 1907) American critic AAS, BE, WWT/14-15

TAUBMAN, Matthew (fl 1685-89) dramatist CP/3

TAULEE, Gladys (d 1975) performer BP/60*

TAUPIER, Gerald (b 1941) American actor TW/26

TAVARIS, Eric (b 1939) American actor TW/29

TAVARY, Mme. (d 1893 [34]) singer EA/94*

TAVEL, Ronald (b 1941) American dramatist, lyricist, director, actor CD, WWT/15-16

TAVERNER, William (d 1731) dramatist CP/1-3, DNB, GT, TD/1-2

TAWDE, George (b 1883) Scottish actor WWT/4-9

TAWYER, William (d 1625?) actor DA

TAYLEURE, Miss (fl 1842) actress, dancer HAS

TAYLEURE, Clifton W. (1830/31/32-1887/91) American actor, manager CDP, HAS, NTH

TAYLEURE, Harriet [Mrs. Joseph Tayleure] (d 1891 [50]) EA/92*

TAYLEURE, Jane (fl 1834?) actress CDP

TAYLEURE, John (1782-1861) actor CDP

TAYLEURE, Joseph (d 1894) EA/95*

TAYLEURE, Mrs. Joseph see Tayleure, Harriet

TAYLOR dramatist RJ

TAYLOR (fl early 17th cent) actor DA

TAYLOR, Mr. (b 1777) English singer, actor BS, GT

TAYLOR [of Norwich] (fl 1793-1805) dramatist CP/3

TAYLOR, Mr. (fl 1794-1837) actor HAS

TAYLOR, Mrs. [nee Valentine] (fl 1789) actress TD/1-2

TAYLOR, Miss (d 1857) dancer HAS

TAYLOR, Ada (d 1890 [17]) EA/91*

TAYLOR, Ada [Mrs. Fred Sims] (d 1900) actress EA/01*

TAYLOR, Agnes [Mrs. Walter Sealby] (d 1898) actress EA/99*

TAYLOR, Alfred (d 1906 [61]) doorkeeper EA/07*

TAYLOR, Alma (d 1974 [79]) performer BP/58*

TAYLOR, Annie [Mrs. E. C. Corlesse] (d 1896 [48]) actress EA/97*

TAYLOR, Ashworth (d 1917) musical director EA/18*

TAYLOR, Ben (d 1901) music-hall comedian EA/02*

TAYLOR, Bianchi (d 1876) musician EA/77*

TAYLOR, Mrs. Billee see Mayhew, Stella

TAYLOR, Cecil P. (b 1929) Scottish dramatist CD, WWT/15-16

TAYLOR, Charles (1781-1847) English actor CDP, TD/2

TAYLOR, Charles (fl 1865) actor HAS

TAYLOR, Charles (b 1940) American actor TW/10

TAYLOR, Mrs. Charles [nee Herbert] (fl 1804) actress TD/2

TAYLOR, Charles A. (1864-1942) American producer, dramatist CB, DAB

TAYLOR, Charles H. (d 1907 [46]) lyricist, dramatist GRB/3

TAYLOR, Charles Western (fl 1819) English actor HAS

TAYLOR, Christopher (d 1913) EA/14*

TAYLOR, Clarice (b 1927) American actress TW/25-30, WWT/16

TAYLOR, Mrs. C. R. [née Nellie Browne] (d 1864) actress HAS

TAYLOR, C. W. (b 1845) English actor HAS

TAYLOR, David Joseph (d 1917) EA/18*

TAYLOR, Deems (1885-1966) American composer ES, HJD, TW/23, WWA/4, WWT/8-10

TAYLOR, Don (b 1920) American actor TW/11-12

TAYLOR, Don dramatist CD

TAYLOR, Dwight (b 1902) American dramatist BE

TAYLOR, Edward Fenton (b 1817) English actor HAS

TAYLOR, Elizabeth (d 1874) performer? EA/75*

TAYLOR, Elizabeth see Bayzand, Mrs. William

TAYLOR, Emma Elizabeth (1838-63) American actress CDP, HAS

TAYLOR, Enid Stamp (1904-46) English actress, singer WWT/8-9

TAYLOR, Estelle (1899-1958) American actress BE*, BP/42*, WWT/14*

TAYLOR, Ethel S. (d 1975 [80]) dramatist BP/59*

TAYLOR, Florence [Mrs. Herbert Taylor] (d 1911 [34]) EA/12*

TAYLOR, Frederica (fl 1869-76) American/English actress OAA/1-2

TAYLOR, Frederick see Bush, Fred

TAYLOR, Frederick Gray (d 1889 [45]) comic singer EA/90*

TAYLOR, G. Bartholomew (d 1890 [36]) director EA/91*

TAYLOR, Geoffrey (b 1945) American actor TW/27-28

TAYLOR, George (b 1930) English actor TW/29-30

TAYLOR, George Henry (d 1876) musician EA/77*

TAYLOR, Gerhard (b 1827) musician CDP

TAYLOR, Greene (d 1907) actor, singer EA/08*

TAYLOR, Harriet D. [Mrs. Walter Lacy] (1808-74) actress CDP

TAYLOR, Harry (d 1889) comedian, singer CDP

TAYLOR, Harvey (d 1975 [63])
critic BP/59*

TAYLOR, Helen Marie American actress, director, educator
BE

TAYLOR, Sir Henry (1800-86)
dramatist HP

TAYLOR, Mrs. Henry see
Taylor, Margaret

TAYLOR, Henry J. P. (d 1910
[67]) proprietor EA/11*

TAYLOR, Herbert see Rolyat,
Dan

TAYLOR, Mrs. Herbert see
Taylor, Florence

TAYLOR, H. J. (d 1917) manager
EA/18*

TAYLOR, Holland (b 1943) American actress TW/24-26, 29-30

TAYLOR, Howard P. (b 1851)
dramatist SR

TAYLOR, Isaac (d 1880) musician EA/81*

TAYLOR, James (fl 1868) English
comic singer HAS

TAYLOR, James (d 1872 [31])
"second-sighted youth" EA/73*

TAYLOR, James (d 1889) conjuror EA/90*

TAYLOR, James (d 1895) musichall comedian EA/96*

TAYLOR, James Goulde (d 1904
[67]) English actor OAA/2

TAYLOR, James H. (d 1884)
lessee EA/85*

TAYLOR, James H. (1825-97)
American actor CDP, HAS

TAYLOR, Mrs. James V. see
Joyce, Laura

TAYLOR, Jennie see Edgar,
Mrs. Richard

TAYLOR, Mrs. J. G. [née
Josephine Ruth] (d 1877) EA/
78*

TAYLOR, John (fl 1561-57)
choirmaster DA

TAYLOR, John (1580-1654) English dramatist CP/3, FGF,
GT, HP

TAYLOR, John (fl 1594-98) actor
DA

TAYLOR, John (fl 1599?) actor
DA

TAYLOR, John actor TD/2

TAYLOR, John (1757-1832) critic
CDP

TAYLOR, Mrs. John, I see
Duill, Mrs. John Lewis

TAYLOR, John Russell (b 1935)
English critic AAS, WWT/15-16

TAYLOR, Joseph (c. 1585-1652)
English actor COC, DA, DNB,
GT, NTH, OC/1-3

TAYLOR, June (b 1918) American
choreographer BE

TAYLOR, Kate (fl 1852) actress
HAS

TAYLOR, Laurette [Laurette
Cooney] (1884-1946) American
actress AAS, CB, COC, DAB,
ES, NTH, OC/1-3, PDT, TW/
1-3, WWA/2, WWT/3-10

TAYLOR, Louise (d 1965 [57])
performer BP/49*

TAYLOR, Louise (d 1974 [89])
performer BP/58*

TAYLOR, Mabel (d 1970) actress
TW/27

TAYLOR, Madeline (d 1870 [19])
actress EA/71*

TAYLOR, Margaret (fl 1815-19)
actress CDP

TAYLOR, Margaret [Mrs. Henry
Taylor] (d 1901) EA/03*

TAYLOR, Mary [Cecilia] (1825-66)
American actress, singer CDP,
HAS, SR

TAYLOR, Maude (d 1886) actress
EA/87*

TAYLOR, Mitch (b 1936) American
actor TW/25

TAYLOR, Nellie (1894-1932) English actress, singer WWT/4-6

TAYLOR, Noel (b 1917) American
designer BE, WWT/15-16

TAYLOR, Pat (b 1918) English actress, singer WWT/10-11

TAYLOR, Paul (b 1930) American
dancer, choreographer CB, ES

TAYLOR, Raynor (c. 1747-1825)
English musician, composer,
musical director DAB, WWA/H

TAYLOR, Robert (d 1969 [57])
performer BP/54*

TAYLOR, Mrs. Robinson actress,
manager TD/2

TAYLOR, Sam (d 1958 [62]) director BE*

TAYLOR, Samuel (d 1888 [42])
EA/89*

TAYLOR, Samuel (b 1912) American dramatist AAS, BE, CD,
ES, MH, WWT/14-16

TAYLOR, Sylvia (d 1973 [50])
producer/director/choreographer
BP/57*

TAYLOR, Tom (1817-80) English dramatist CDP, COC, DNB, EA/68, HP, MH, NTH, OC/1-3, SR

TAYLOR, Tom (d 1911 [28]) musician EA/12*

TAYLOR, V. (fl 1819?) dramatist EAP

TAYLOR, Valerie (b 1902) English actress AAS, WWT/6-16

TAYLOR, Vaughn (b 1911) American actor TW/11-12

TAYLOR, Walter W. (d 1896) actor EA/97*

TAYLOR, Weston (d 1975 [47]) critic BP/60*

TAYLOR, William (d 1836 [70]) critic BE*, WWT/14*

TAYLOR, William (d 1898) equestrian business manager EA/99*

TAYLOR, William (d 1901 [60]) music-hall proprietor EA/02*

TAYLOR, William G. (d 1859) actor, costumier HAS

TAYLOR, William S. (b 1925) American manager, director BE

TAYLOR-PLATT, E. (d 1946 [75]) business manager WWT/14*

TAZEWELL, Charles (d 1972 [72]) actor TW/29

TCHERNICHEVA, Lubov (b 1890) Russian dancer ES

TEAGARDEN, Jack (d 1964 [58]) American musician BE*, BP/48*

TEAGUE, Anthony (b 1940) American actor TW/28-29

TEAGUE, Brian (d 1970 [33]) performer BP/55*

TEAGUE, Terri (b 1946) American actress TW/25

TEAL, Ben (d 1917 [55]) stage manager, director, producer BE*, WWT/14*

TEAL, Ray (d 1976 [74]) performer BP/60*

TEARLE, Conway (1878-1938) American actor ES, WWT/2-8

TEARLE, Edmund (1856-1913) English actor, producer, manager BE*, EA/14*, WWT/14*

TEARLE, George (d 1896 [73]) EA/98*

TEARLE, Mrs. George Osmond see Tearle, Mary Alice

TEARLE, Sir Godfrey (1884-1953) English actor AAS, COC, DNB, ES, OC/1-3, TW/4-8, 10, WWT/1-11

TEARLE, Malcolm (d 1935 [47]) actor BE*, WWT/14*

TEARLE, Marianne [Marianne Levy; Marianne Conway] (1854-96) English actress CDP, OC/1-3

TEARLE, Mary Alice [Mrs. George Osmond Tearle] (d 1887 [37]) EA/88*

TEARLE, Osmond (1852-1901) English actor CDP, COC, DNB, EA/96, OAA/1-2, OC/1-3

TEARLE, Mrs. Osmond see Conway, Marianne

TEASDALE, Verrée (b 1906) American actress WWT/7-10

TEATRO CAMPESINO, El theatre collective CD

TEBALDI, Renata (b 1922) Italian singer CB, ES

TEBBUTT, Joseph (d 1901 [56]) manager EA/03*

TECOSKY, Morton see Da Costa, Morton

TEDDER, Aynscomb (d 1897 [38]) actor EA/98*

TEDDER, George (d 1896 [77]) singer EA/97*

TEDESCO, Fortunata (fl 1847) singer CDP, HAS

TEED, John (b 1911) English actor WWT/8-10

TEEGE, Joachim (d 1969 [44]) performer BP/54*

TEER, Barbara Ann (b 1937) American actress TW/23

TEESDALE, Henry Robert (b 1841) English actor OAA/1-2

TEICHMANN, Howard (b 1916) American dramatist, educator BE, MH

TEITEL, Carol [née Carolyn Sally Kahn] (b 1929) American actress BE, TW/14-20, 23-24, 26, 30, WWT/15-16

TEIXEIRA DE MATTOS, Alexander Louis (1865-1921) Dutch dramatist, translator WWT/1-3, WWW/2

TELBIN, Rose (d 1849 [22]) English actress CDP, HAS

TELBIN, William (1813-73) English scene painter COC, OC/1-3

TELBIN, William Lewis (1846-1931) English scene painter

COC, OC/1-3
TELESHOVA, Elizabeth (d 1943) actress WWT/14 *
TELFORD, Richard (d 1912) actor EA/13 *
TELFORD, Robert S. (b 1923) American director BE
TELL, Alma (1892-1937) American actress WWT/5-8
TELL, Olive (1894-1951) American actress TW/8, WWT/4-8
TELLEGAN, Lou (1881-1934) Dutch actor? SR
TELLET, Clara Anne (d 1887 [67]) actress CDP
TELLINGS, Mr. (fl 1847) actor HAS
TELVA, Marion (1897-1962) American singer TW/19, WWA/4
TEMPEST, Amy [Mrs. Charles Darrell] (1860-1908) English actress GRB/1
TEMPEST, Florence (b 1873) actress GRB/1-4
TEMPEST, Mabel Emily (d 1899 [23]) actress EA/00 *, WWT/14 *
TEMPEST, Dame Marie Susan [Mrs. C. Cosmo Gordon-Lennox] (1864-1942) English actress AAS, CB, CDP, COC, DNB, DP, ES, GRB/1-4, NTH, OC/1-3, PDT, SR, WWA/2, WWM, WWS, WWT/1-8, WWW/4
TEMPLE, Clarence (d 1911 [42]) actor EA/12 *
TEMPLE, Edward P. (d 1921 [60]) American director BE *, BP/6 *
TEMPLE, Mrs. Edward P. see Temple, Mary
TEMPLE, Mrs. Fred see Graham, Gertrude
TEMPLE, G. (fl 1872) actor CDP
TEMPLE, Helen (b 1894) English actress WWT/4-7
TEMPLE, Henrietta [Mrs. Charles Morton] (d 1890) actress EA/91 *
TEMPLE, Joan (d 1965 [78]) English dramatist, actress WWT/6-13
TEMPLE, Madge (d 1943) actress, singer BE *, WWT/14 *

TEMPLE, Mary [Mrs. Edward P. Temple] (d 1883 [22]) EA/84 *
TEMPLE, Nora see Turner, Florence
TEMPLE, Richard [Richard Cobb] (1847-1912) English actor, singer DP, EA/97, GRB/1-4, OAA/2, WWT/1
TEMPLE, Mrs. Richard see Emmett, Bessie
TEMPLE, Mrs. Richard, Jr. see Greene, Evie
TEMPLE, Rose [Mrs. John Donald] English actress GRB/1-3
TEMPLE, William Clarence (d 1870) comedian EA/71 *
TEMPLEMAN, Samuel (d 1867 [27]) comedian, harlequin EA/68 *
TEMPLETON, Mr. (fl 1831) Scottish singer HAS
TEMPLETON (d 1888) stage manager EA/89 *
TEMPLETON, Alec Andrew (1910-63) Welsh composer, performer, musician BE *, BP/47 *
TEMPLETON, Andrew (d 1896) music-hall comedian EA/97 *
TEMPLETON, C. Mercer (d 1973 [83]) performer BP/57 *
TEMPLETON, Fay [Mrs. William Patterson] (1865-1939) American actress, singer CDP, GRB/2-4, NTH, SR, WWA/1, WWS, WWT/1-9
TEMPLETON, Harry (d 1890 [62]) singer CDP
TEMPLETON, Isabella [Mrs. Robert Templeton] (d 1879) EA/80 *
TEMPLETON, James (fl 1801) dramatist CP/3
TEMPLETON, John (1802-86) Scottish singer CDP, DNB
TEMPLETON, John (d 1907 [69]) American actor, manager CDP, GRB/3
TEMPLETON, Robert (d 1892 [60]) music-hall performer EA/93 *
TEMPLETON, Mrs. Robert see Templeton, Isabella
TEMPLETON, Robert Williamson (d 1883 [82]) proprietor EA/84 *
TEMPLETON, William (d 1868) comedian, pantomimist EA/69 *
TEMPLETON, Willie (d 1886 [43]) circus clown EA/87 *

TEMPLETON, W. P. (b 1913/15) Scottish dramatist BE, WWT/ 11-13

TEN BROECK, May singer, songwriter CDP

TENDUCCI, Giusto Ferdinado (1736?-90) singer, dramatist CDP, CP/3

TENNANT, Mrs. see Millett, Maude

TENNANT, Dorothy (fl 1900s) American actress WWM

TENNANT, Edmund H. (d 1916) EA/17*

TENNANT, Francis (d 1907 [67]) EA/08*

TENNANT, Philip (d 1916) EA/ 17*

TENNENT, Hector Norman (d 1904 [62]) director EA/05*

TENNENT, Henry M. (1879/87-1941) English manager WWT/ 8-9

TENNENT LTD., H. M. producing managers WWT/10-16

TENNEY, Caryl Jeanne American actress TW/24, 28, 30

TENNY, Marion H. (d 1964 [73]) performer, actress BE*

TENNYCK, Egbert Fairchild [Tom E. Egbert] (d 1888 [50]) American actor EA/89*

"TENNYSON" see O'Brien, Edward

TENNYSON, Alfred Lord (1809-92) English dramatist COC, ES, HP, MH, NTH, OC/1-3, PDT, RE

TENNYSON, Ann (d 1887 [68]) EA/88*

TENNYSON, Joe (fl 1903?) singer CDP

TENNYSON, Thomas (d 1887 [80]) EA/88*

TEODOR, Jacob (fl 1627-28) actor DA

TERAN, Fernando Arrabal see Arrabal, Fernando

TER-ARUTUNIAN, Rouben (b 1920) Russian/American designer BE, CB, ES, WWT/ 13-16

TERENCE (c. 190-159 B.C.) Roman dramatist COC

TERES, T. (fl 1769?) translator CP/2-3, GT

TERESIA, Mme. ["The Corsican Fairy"] (b 1743) dwarf CDP

TERHUNE, Albert Payson (b 1872) American dramatist WWM

TERHUNE, Anice (d 1964) American composer WWA/4

TERHUNE, Max (d 1973 [82]) performer BP/58*

TERMINI, Joe (d 1964 [72]) performer BE*

TERNAN, Fanny (b 1837) American actress HAS

TERNAN, Frances Eleanor see Ternan, Mrs. Thomas

TERNAN, Thomas (1804-46) Irish actor HAS

TERNAN, Mrs. Thomas [Frances Eleanor Jarman] (1805-73) English actress CDP, DNB, HAS, OX

TERNINA, Milka (1864-1941) Croatian singer ES

TERRANOVA, Dino (d 1969 [65]) actor TW/25

TERRAUX, L. H. du (d 1878) dramatist WWT/14*

TERRELL, St. John (b 1916) American producer, actor, theatre owner BE, CB

TERRIS, Malcolm (b 1941) English actor TW/25

TERRIS, Norma (b 1904) American actress, singer WWT/7-12

TERRISS, Ellaline [Mrs. Seymour Hicks] (1871-1971) English actress COC, EA/94, ES, GRB/ 1-4, OC/1-3, TW/27, WWT/1-11

TERRISS, Tom [Thomas Herbert F. Lewin] (1874-1964) English actor ES, GRB/4, WWT/1-8

TERRISS, W. (d 1916) EA/17*

TERRISS, William (1847-97) English actor CDP, COC, DNB, DP, OAA/1-2, OC/1-3, WWW/1

TERRISS, Mrs. William see Fellowes, Amy

TERROTT, William Mulready (d 1899 [74]) EA/00*

TERRY, Mrs. (d 1892) EA/93*

TERRY, Alice (b c. 1896) American actress ES

TERRY, Beatrice (b 1890) English actress COC, GRB/2-4, OC/3, WWT/1-11

TERRY, Benjamin (1818-96) English actor COC, ES, OC/1-3

TERRY, Mrs. Benjamin see Terry, Sarah Ballard

TERRY, Charles (1857-1933)

manager COC

TERRY, Daniel (1789-1829) English actor, manager, dramatist BS, CDP, COC, DNB, HAS, OC/1-3, OX

TERRY, Dennis (1895-1932) English actor OC/1-3

TERRY, Mrs. Edward see Terry, Ellen

TERRY, Edward O'Connor (1844-1912) English actor, manager CDP, COC, DP, EA/95, GRB/1-4, OAA/1-2, OC/1-3, SR, WWM, WWS, WWT/1, WWW/1

TERRY, Eliza [Mrs. H. Lewis] (d 1878 [61]) actress BE*, EA/80*, WWT/14*

TERRY, Ellen [Mrs. Edward Terry] (d 1897) EA/98*

TERRY, Dame Ellen Alice (1847-1928) English actress CDP, COC, DNB, DP, ES, GRB/1-4, NTH, OAA/1-2, OC/1-3, PDT, SR, WWA/1, WWM, WWS, WWT/1-5, WWW/2

TERRY, Ethelind (b 1900) American actress, singer WWT/6-10

TERRY, Florence [Mrs. William Morris] (1854-96) English actress CDP, COC, ES, OAA/1-2, OC/1-3

TERRY, Fred (1863-1933) English actor COC, DNB, DP, ES, GRB/1-4, OC/1-3, WWM, WWS, WWT/1-7, WWW/3

TERRY, Mrs. Fred see Neilson, Julia

TERRY, George (1850-1928) manager COC

TERRY, George (b 1938) American actor TW/25

TERRY, Hazel (1918-74) English actress BTR/74, ES, WWT/9-14

TERRY, Herbert E. (b 1875) English actor, manager, dramatist GRB/1-2

TERRY, J. E. Harold (1885-1939) English dramatist WWT/3-8

TERRY, Mrs. John see Lambert, Mabel

TERRY, John S. (b 1870) English actor GRB/1-2

TERRY, Kate [Mrs. Arthur Lewis] (1844-1924) English actress

COC, ES, GRB/1-4, OAA/1-2, OC/1-3, SR, WWS, WWT/1-4

TERRY, Mabel (1872-1957) actress ES

TERRY, Marian (d 1904 [63]) EA/06*

TERRY, Marion (1852/56-1930) English actress CDP, COC, DP, EA/95, ES, GRB/1-4, OAA/1-2, OC/1-3, WWS, WWT/1-6, WWW/3

TERRY, Megan (b 1932) American dramatist, actress, director CD, CH, WWT/16

TERRY, Minnie [Mrs. Edmund Gwenn] (1882-1964) English actress COC, DP, GRB/2-4, OC/3, WWT/1-8

TERRY, Muriel (d 1947 [62]) singer WWT/14*

TERRY, Olive (b 1884) English actress GRB/2-4, WWT/1-5

TERRY, Phyllis (b 1892) English actress OC/1-3

TERRY, Sarah Ballard [Mrs. Benjamin Terry] (1819-92) English actress COC, OC/1-3

TERRY, Teresa (fl 1856) actress HAS

TERRY, Walter (d 1932) editor BE*, WWT/14*

TERRY, Walter (b 1913) critic NTH

TERRY, Mrs. Warwick (d 1913) EA/14*

TERRY, W. Benson (b 1927) American actor TW/25

TERRY, William (b 1914) American actor TW/2-3

TERRY-LEWIS, Mabel [Mrs. R. C. Batley] (1872-1957) English actress COC, GRB/1-4, OC/1-6, WWT/1-11, WWW/5

TERRY-THOMAS (b 1911) English performer ES

TERSHAY, Joe (d 1970) performer BP/55*

TERSI, Maria Theresa Catherine see Bland, Mrs. George

TERSON, Peter [Peter Patterson] (b 1932) English dramatist AAS, CD, CH, COC, PDT, RE, WWT/16

TESTER, Desmond (b 1919) English actor WWT/8-13

TESTO, Charles (d 1872 [54]) equestrian director EA/73*

TETHERINGTON, Mrs. see

Collet, Catherine
TETLEY, Dorothy Argentinian actress WWT/4-8
TETLEY, Glen (b 1926) American dancer, choreographer CB, ES
TETLEY, Walter (d 1975 [60]) performer BP/60*
TETRAZZINI, Louisa [or Luisa] (1871/74-1940) Italian singer CB, ES, SR, WWA/1
TETRAZZINI CAMPANINI, Eva (1862-1938) Italian singer ES
TETU, Princess (d 1971 [79]) circus performer BP/56*
TETZEL, Joan (1921-77) American actress BE, TW/4-8, 10-11, WWT/10-16
TEXAS, Temple (b 1925) American actress TW/3
TEYTE, Maggie [Margaret Tate] (1889-1976) English actress, singer CB, WWT/4-13
THACKER, John see Montrose, Jack
THACKER, Rusty [or Russ] (b 1946) American actor TW/ 24-25, 28-30
THALBERG, Franceska (d 1895 [84]) EA/96*
THALBERG, Sigismund (1812-71) Swiss musician CDP, HAS
THALBERG, T. B. (1864-1947) English actor EA/96, GRB/ 3-4, WWT/1-4
THALIN, Vivien Parker (d 1974 [77]) performer BP/58*
THALL, Al (d 1973 [63]) publicist BP/58*
THANE, Adele (b 1904) American actress, dramatist, director, educator BE
THANE, Elswyth [Elswyth Thane Ricker] dramatist WWT/8-10
THARE, John (fl 1602-03) actor DA
THARP, Twyla (b 1941?) American dancer, choreographer CB
THARPE, Rosetta (d 1973 [57]) performer BP/58*
THATCHER, Billy (d 1964 [43]) performer BP/49*
THATCHER, George (1846/49-1913) American minstrel CDP, SR
THATCHER, Heather English actress, singer WWT/4-14

THATCHER, Torin (b 1905) Indian/ English actor AAS, BE, TW/ 5-8, 14-16, WWT/10-15
THAW, Evelyn Nesbit (1884-1967 [82]) American showgirl TW/ 23, WWA/4
THAW, John (b 1942) English actor WWT/15-16
THAXTER, Phyllis (b 1920) American actress BE, TW/18-19, WWT/14-16
THAXTER, Phyllis Schuyler (d 1966 [74]) performer BP/51*
THAYER, Miss see Walstein, Mrs. Westervelt
THAYER, Agnes (d 1873) actress CDP
THAYER, Ambrose A. (d 1863/64) minstrel CDP, HAS
THAYER, Amidon L. (d 1864 [41]) manager, minstrel CDP, HAS
THAYER, Mrs. Edward [Mrs. Palmer Fisher] (fl 1824) English actress HAS
THAYER, Edward Niles (b 1798) American actor CDP, HAS
THAYER, Tiffany Ellsworth (1902-59) American actor WWA/3
THAYER, William (fl 1594-98) actor DA
THEAKER, John (d 1870 [45]) EA/71*
THEARLE, Nellie [Mrs. Stanley Hope] (d 1910) actress EA/11*
THEATRE GUILD, The TW/2-8
THEATRE INCORPORATED TW/ 2-5
THEATRE WORKSHOP theatre collective CD
THEBOM, Blanche American singer CB
THECLA, Maud [Mrs. Gaston Mayer] American singer GRB/ 1-3
THEILADE, Nini (b 1915) Dutch dancer, choreographer ES, WWT/8-9
THEILMANN, Helen (d 1956 [41]) actress BE*, WWT/14*
THEISE, Mortimer M. (b 1866) American manager WWS
THEISEN, Mme. see Ploux, Edith
THELWALL, John (fl 1794-1802) dramatist CP/3
THENON, George see "Rip"
THEOBALD, John (d 1760) trans-

lator CP/2-3

THEOBALD, Lewis (1688-1744)
English dramatist, editor CP/
1-3, DNB, GT, HP, TD/1-2

THEODORE, Mme. see D'Aub-
erval, Mme. Jean

THEODORE, Mlle. [Mrs. A. B.
Narpier] (fl 1851) dancer HAS

THEOHAROUS, Ted (b 1930)
American actor TW/29

THERESA, Mlle. (b 1837) actress, singer CDP

THESIGER, Ernest (1879-1961)
English actor AAS, ES, TW/
6, 14-15, 17, WWT/4-13,
WWW/6

THIDBLAD, Inga (d 1975 [73])
performer BP/60*

THIEL, Mrs. Leonard see
Welling, Nellie

THIELE, William J. (d 1975
[85]) producer/director/chore-
ographer BP/60*

THILLON, Anna (1812/13/19-
1903) English singer CDP,
HAS, SR

THIMIG, Helene [Mrs. Max Rein-
hardt] (d 1974 [85]) actress
BP/59*, WWT/16*

THIMM, Daisy English actress
WWT/2-5

THIODON, Alfred Aspinall (d
1902 [48]) music-hall manager
EA/03*

THIRER, Irene (d 1964 [59])
critic BP/48*

THIRLWALL, Annie [Mrs. E.
Dussek Corri] (d 1881 [51])
EA/82*

THIRLWALL, John (d 1887 [42])
musician EA/88*

THIRLWALL, John Wade (d 1876
[67]) musician EA/77*

THIRWALL, Connop (1797-1875)
critic, historian, musician
CDP

THOM, Richie (d 1902) music-
hall manager EA/03*

THOMA, Carl (b 1947) American
actor TW/26-28

THOMA, Mike (b 1926) American
director, stage manager, actor
BE

THOMAN, Jacob Wonderly (b 1816)
American actor HAS

THOMAN, Mrs. Jacob Wonderly,
I [Elizabeth Anderson] (b 1818)
American actress HAS

THOMAN, Mrs. Jacob Wonderly,
II [Julia Pelby] (1832-66) American actress HAS

THOMAS, Mrs. [Mrs. Simpson]
(d 1802) actress TD/2

THOMAS, Mrs. [Mrs. Kite] (d
1879 [57]) equestrienne EA/80*

THOMAS, Miss see Jefferson,
Mrs. Joseph

THOMAS, A. E. see Thomas,
Albert E.

THOMAS, Agnes actress WWT/
2-7

THOMAS, A. Goring (d 1892 [40])
composer BE*, EA/93*,
WWT/14*

THOMAS, Mrs. A. K. see
Brophy, Annie

THOMAS, Albert E. (1872-1947)
American dramatist NTH, SR,
TW/4, WWA/2, WWM, WWT/
4-10

THOMAS, Mrs. Alex see
Thomas, Emily

THOMAS, Mrs. Allen see Neilson, Ada

THOMAS, Ambroise (1811-96)
French composer CDP

THOMAS, Ann (b 1920) American
actress TW/2-15, 30

THOMAS, Annie (d 1905) EA/06*

THOMAS, Arthur Goring see
Thomas, A. Goring

THOMAS, Augustus (1857-1934)
American dramatist COC,
DAB, ES, GRB/2-4, HJD, MH,
MWD, NTH, OC/1-3, RE, SR,
WWA/1, WWS, WWT/1-7,
WWW/3

THOMAS, Basil (1912-57) English
dramatist WWT/12

THOMAS, Berte (b 1863) actor
WWT/2-3

THOMAS, Brandon (1856-1914)
English actor, dramatist CDP,
COC, DP, EA/97, ES, GRB/
1-4, MH, MWD, OC/3, PDT,
SR, WWT/1-2, WWW/1

THOMAS, Buddy (d 1967 [55])
producer/director/choreographer
BP/52*

THOMAS, Calvin (d 1964 [79])
American actor TW/1, 11-13,
21

THOMAS, Charles Henry (d 1941
[76]) business manager BE*,
WWT/14*

THOMAS, Christian Friedrich

Theodore (1835-1905) German conductor DAB

THOMAS, Clara Amelia (d 1899) EA/01*

THOMAS, Mrs. Dan see Dare, Dulcie

THOMAS, Danny (b 1914) American actor CB

THOMAS, Dick (d 1910 [37]) quick-change sketch artist EA/11*

THOMAS, Dorothy [Mrs. Cecil Rose] (b 1882) English actress GRB/3-4, WWS, WWT/1-7

THOMAS, Dylan (1914-53) Welsh dramatist DNB, ES, HP, MD, MH, MWD, WWW/5

THOMAS, E. (d 1893) secretary EA/94*

THOMAS, Edna (d 1974 [88]) actress BP/59*, WWT/16*

THOMAS, Mrs. Edward (d 1871) dramatist EA/72*

THOMAS, Elizabeth (fl 1762) dramatist CP/3

THOMAS, Emily [Mrs. Alex Thomas] (d 1886) EA/88*

THOMAS, Emily [Mrs. W. P. Thomas] (d 1893) EA/95*

THOMAS, Evan (b 1891) Canadian actor TW/3, 24-25, WWT/5-14

THOMAS, E. W. (d 1892) musician EA/93*

THOMAS, Frank, Jr. (b 1926) American actor, producer, director, writer BE

THOMAS, Frank M. (b 1890) American actor TW/2-3, 10-13

THOMAS, Fred (d 1909 [75]) actor EA/10*

THOMAS, Freyda-Ann (b 1943) American actress TW/30

THOMAS, Gwyn (b 1913) Welsh dramatist CD, CH, WWT/14-16

THOMAS, Harding (b 1861) Welsh actor, manager GRB/1

THOMAS, Henry (d 1872 [49]) singer EA/73*

THOMAS, Herbert (b 1868) actor WWT/4-6

THOMAS, Hilda (fl 1885?) actress, singer CDP

THOMAS, Jamieson (d 1939 [45]) actor BE*, WWT/14*

THOMAS, Jess (b 1927) American

singer CB

THOMAS, Joel (b 1919) American actor TW/6-9

THOMAS, John (d 1877 [56]) lessee EA/78*

THOMAS, John (d 1913) EA/14*

THOMAS, John Charles (1887/91?-1960) American actor, singer CB, SR, WWA/4

THOMAS, J. R. (b 1830) Welsh singer, composer HAS

THOMAS, J. W. (d 1878) publisher, editor, journalist BE*, EA/79*, WWT/14*

THOMAS, Les (d 1967 [71]) business manager BP/52*

THOMAS, Lewis (d 1896 [70]) singer, critic EA/97*

THOMAS, Lily (d 1916) EA/17*

THOMAS, L. S. dramatist RJ

THOMAS, Marlo (b 1938) American actress TW/30

THOMAS, Minna L. [Mrs. Theodore Thomas] (d 1889 [50]) EA/90*

THOMAS, Olive (1898?-1920) actress BE*, BP/5*

THOMAS, Philip M. (b 1949) American actor TW/28

THOMAS, Phyllis (b 1904) English actress WWT/7-11

THOMAS, Rhys Arthur D. (d 1917) EA/18*

THOMAS, Richard (b 1951) American actor CB, TW/22-24

THOMAS, Ruth (d 1970 [59]) performer BP/54*

THOMAS, Sandra (d 1972) founder of stage mothers' club BP/56*

THOMAS, Stephen (d 1961 [63]) director of drama, British Council BE*, WWT/14*

THOMAS, Theodore (1835-1905) German/American conductor, musician CDP, GRB/1, SR, WWW/1

THOMAS, Mrs. Theodore see Theodore, Minna L.

THOMAS, Tony American actor TW/26-27, 29

THOMAS, Vyvian [Vyvian Laverton] English actor GRB/1

THOMAS, Wally (d 1864 [26]) minstrel HAS

THOMAS, William (d 1870) music-hall proprietor EA/71*

THOMAS, William (d 1872 [74]) musician EA/73*

THOMAS, William [William
Thomas Quarrel] (d 1891)
music-hall manager EA/92*
THOMAS, William, Jr. Ameri-
can actor TW/29-30
THOMAS, William Freeman (d
1898 [54]) EA/99*
THOMAS, W. Moy (d 1910 [81])
critic BE*, WWT/14*
THOMAS, W. P. (d 1882 [47])
Negro comedian EA/83*
THOMAS, Mrs. W. P. see
Thomas, Emily
THOMASHEFSKY, Bessie (d 1962
[88]) actress WWT/14*
THOMASHEFSKY, Boris (d 1939
[71/75]) Russian actor, pro-
ducer, impresario BP/24*,
WWT/14*
THOMASSIN, Jeanne French ac-
tress WWT/1-4
THOME, Francis (d 1909 [59])
composer BE*, WWT/14*
THOMKINS, John (fl 1598) actor
DA
THOMMEN, Edward director,
actor BE
THOMPSON, Mr. (fl c. 1800?)
actor BS
THOMPSON, Mjr. (d 1900) EA/
01*
THOMPSON, A. (fl 1799) dram-
atist CP/3
THOMPSON, Alexander M. (1861-
1948) dramatist WWT/2-10
THOMPSON, Alfred (d 1895)
dramatist, designer BE*,
WWT/14*
THOMPSON, Augusta (d 1877
[36]) actress WWT/14*
THOMPSON, A. W. (b 1878)
Scottish actor, stage manager
GRB/1
THOMPSON, Benjamin (1776?-
1816) translator, dramatist
CDP, CP/3, DNB
THOMPSON, C. dancer CDP
THOMPSON, Charles (d 1869
[86]) actor, dramatist EA/70*
THOMPSON, Charles H. (d
1867 [28]) minstrel EA/68*
THOMPSON, Charles H. (d 1871)
acting manager EA/72*
THOMPSON, Mrs. Charlie see
Thompson, Sarah
THOMPSON, Charlotte (1843-98)
English actress CDP, HAS
THOMPSON, Charlotte American

dramatist WWM
THOMPSON, Clisbia (d 1868 [c.
100]) actress HAS
THOMPSON, Creighton (b 1889)
American actor TW/3
THOMPSON, Denman (1833-1911)
American actor, dramatist
CDP, DAB, GRB/2-3, HJD,
MWD, PP/3, SR, WWA/1,
WWS
THOMPSON, Edward (d 1786) Eng-
lish dramatist CP/2-3, GT,
TD/1-2
THOMPSON, Edward (1817-65)
American actor HAS
THOMPSON, Mrs. Edward (b 1817)
American actress HAS
THOMPSON, Eliza [née Lizzie
Sharpe] (d 1875 [35]) singer
EA/76*
THOMPSON, Emma see Fox,
Emma
THOMPSON, Emma Janet [Mrs.
W. Thompson] (d 1877) EA/78*
THOMPSON, Ephraim (d 1909)
animal trainer EA/10*
THOMPSON, Eric (b 1929) English
actor, director WWT/16
THOMPSON, Evan (b 1931) Ameri-
can actor TW/26-27
THOMPSON, Foster D. (d 1976
[63]) production manager BP/
60*
THOMPSON, Francis Michael see
Melton, J. Rexton
THOMPSON, Frank costume de-
signer WWT/16
THOMPSON, Fred (1884-1949)
English dramatist WWT/3-10,
WWW/4
THOMPSON, Frederick W. (1872-
1919) American manager WWT/
1-3
THOMPSON, George (d 1889 [75])
music-hall singer? EA/90*
THOMPSON, George W. (1838-
1901) American actor, drama-
tist, manager CDP, HAS
THOMPSON, Gerald Marr (1856-
1938) English/Australian critic
GRB/2-4, WWT/1-3, 5-8
THOMPSON, H. (fl 1852) actor
HAS
THOMPSON, Harlan (d 1966 [76])
writer, director TW/23
THOMPSON, Harry (d 1873 [44])
comedian EA/74*
THOMPSON, Henry O'Neil J. (b

1866) Australian press manager
GRB/2-3
THOMPSON, Jack (d 1966 [59])
critic BP/50*
THOMPSON, James E. (d 1900
[34]) actor EA/01*
THOMPSON, Jay (b 1927) Amer-
ican dramatist, composer,
lyricist BE
THOMPSON, Jean M. (b 1867)
American juvenile dramatist
WWA/5
THOMPSON, J. Lee (b 1914)
English dramatist WWT/10-13
THOMPSON, John (c. 1600-34)
English actor COC, DA,
OC/1-3
THOMPSON, Lydia [Mrs. Alex-
ander Henderson] (1836-1908)
English actress CDP, COC,
DNB, DP, GRB/1-4, HAS,
NTH, OAA/1-2, OC/1-3
THOMPSON, Lysander (d 1892)
American actor EA/93*,
WWT/14*
THOMPSON, Lysander Steel
(1817-54) English actor CDP,
HAS
THOMPSON, Marshall (b 1925)
American actor TW/10
THOMPSON, Mary (b 1844)
American actress HAS
THOMPSON, Palmer (d 1969
[51]) producer/director/chore-
ographer BP/54*
THOMPSON, Percy Harry see
Honri, Percy
THOMPSON, Peter American
actor TW/27, 30
THOMPSON, Rebecca (b 1942)
American actress TW/26-27
THOMPSON, Rex (b 1942) Amer-
ican actor TW/10, 18, 27-28
THOMPSON, Richard D. (b 1933)
American lighting consultant
BE
THOMPSON, Ronnie (b 1941)
American actor TW/26
THOMPSON, Sada (b 1929) Amer-
ican actress AAS, BE, CB,
TW/24-29, WWT/15-16
THOMPSON, Sam (d 1965 [48])
performer BP/49*
THOMPSON, Sarah [Mrs. Charlie
Thompson] (d 1890 [35]) EA/
92*
THOMPSON, Tazewell (b 1948)
American actor TW/24

THOMPSON, Thomas J. (d 1881)
actor EA/82*
THOMPSON, Vance (1863-1925)
dramatist WWA/1
THOMPSON, Venie actress CDP
THOMPSON, W. (d 1891 [93])
EA/92*
THOMPSON, Mrs. W. see
Thompson, Emma Janet
THOMPSON, Mrs. Walter see
Carsoni, Marie
THOMPSON, William (fl 1738-51)
dramatist CP/1-3
THOMPSON, William (d 1869)
music-hall chairman EA/70*
THOMPSON, William (d 1881 [32])
musician EA/82*
THOMPSON, William (d 1894)
EA/95*
THOMPSON, William (d 1971 [58])
performer BP/56*
THOMPSON, William A. (fl 1832-
61) American actor HAS
THOMPSON, William C. (d 1868)
actor, manager HAS
THOMPSON, W[illiam] H. (1852-
1923) Scottish/American actor
CDP, GRB/2-4, SR, WWM,
WWT/1-3
THOMPSON, Mrs. W[illiam] H.
see Irving, Isabel
THOMPSON, William Henry see
Merson, Billy
THOMPSON, Woodman (1889-1955)
American designer ES
THOMPSON, W. T. (d 1940) actor
BE*, WWT/14*
THOMS, Virginia American mana-
ger BE
THOMSON, Adam (fl 1738) drama-
tist CP/3
THOMSON, Alexander (fl 1791)
dramatist CP/3
THOMSON, Augusta (d 1877 [36])
actress, singer EA/78*
THOMSON, Barry American actor
TW/2-4
THOMSON, Beatrix (b 1900) Eng-
lish actress WWT/6-13
THOMSON, Brenda (b 1944) Amer-
ican actress TW/28
THOMSON, Mrs. George (d 1870
[70]) actress? EA/71*
THOMSON, James (1700-48) Eng-
lish dramatist CDP, COC,
CP/1-3, GT, HP, OC/1-3,
TD/1-2
THOMSON, Jane Elizabeth see

Vezin, Jane Elizabeth
THOMSON, John (d 1877 [33])
  critic EA/79*
THOMSON, Lesly (d 1902) actor
  EA/03*
THOMSON, Lysander (d 1854
  [37]) comedian EA/72*
THOMSON, R. H. (b 1947) Cana-
  dian actor TW/30
THOMSON, Thomas (fl 1668)
  dramatist CP/1-3
THOMSON, Virgil (b 1896) Amer-
  ican composer, musical di-
  rector BE, CB, ES
THOMSON, Vivien see Merchant,
  Vivien
THOR, Jerome P. (b 1915) Amer-
  ican actor TW/1-3
THOR, Larry (d 1976 [59]) per-
  former BP/60*
THORBORG, Kerstin (1897?/
  1906-1970) Swedish singer
  CB, TW/26, WWA/5
THORBURN, H. M. (1884-1924)
  English business manager
  WWT/4
THORN, Geoffrey see Town-
  ley, Charles
THORNBURY, Cecil H. actor
  EA/97*
THORNDIKE, Arthur Russell
  see Thorndike, Russell
THORNDIKE, Eileen (1891-1953)
  English actress COC, OC/
  1-3, WWT/7-11
THORNDIKE, Frank (d 1917
  [23]) actor EA/18*
THORNDIKE, Louise [Mrs. Dion
  Boucicault, II; Mrs. Fred G.
  Calhoun] actress CDP
THORNDIKE, Russell (1885-
  1972) English actor, drama-
  tist AAS, COC, OC/1-3,
  WWT/4-14
THORNDIKE, Dame Sybil (1882-
  1976) English actress, mana-
  ger AAS, BE, CB, COC,
  ES, NTH, OC/1-3, PDT,
  TW/13-15, WWT/2-16
THORNE, Alice [Mrs. Crayford]
  (d 1896 [40]) actress EA/97*
THORNE, Mrs. Ambrose see
  Kranske, Violet
THORNE, Amelia see Newton,
  Amelia
THORNE, Ann Maria [née Mestay-
  er] (d 1881 [69]) American
  actress CDP, OC/1-3

THORNE, Charles (d 1893 [70])
  actor WWT/14*
THORNE, Charles R. (d 1882)
  American actor EA/83*
THORNE, Charles Robert, Sr.
  (c. 1814-93) American actor,
  manager CDP, DAB, HAS,
  OC/1-3, SR, WWA/H
THORNE, Mrs. Charles Robert,
  Sr. [Maria Ann Mestayer] (d
  1881) American actress, singer
  HAS
THORNE, Charles Robert, Jr.
  (1840-83) American actor CDP,
  COC, DAB, OC/1-3, WWA/H
THORNE, Clara (d 1915 [63]) ac-
  tress BE*, WWT/14*
THORNE, Edwin F. (b 1845)
  American actor HAS
THORNE, Emily (d 1907) actress
  CDP, GRB/3, HAS, OAA/2, SR
THORNE, Eric (d 1922 [60]) actor
  BE*, WWT/14*
THORNE, Frances [Mrs. J.
  Thorne] (d 1874 [42]) EA/75*
THORNE, George (1856-1922)
  English actor DP, GRB/1-4,
  OC/1-3
THORNE, Ivy Ellaline (b 1888)
  English actress GRB/1
THORNE, Mrs. J. see Thorne,
  Frances
THORNE, James (d 1843) English
  actor, singer CDP, HAS
THORNE, James (d 1882 [60])
  pantomimist, scene artist EA/
  83*
THORNE, John N., Jr. (d 1972
  [56]) journalist BP/56*
THORNE, J. W. (d 1860) actor?
  HAS
THORNE, Marguerite (d 1917)
  EA/18*
THORNE, Mary English actress
  GRB/2
THORNE, Maude actress GRB/2
THORNE, May [Mrs. Clifton Ald-
  erson] (d 1898) actress EA/99*
THORNE, Raymond (b 1934) Amer-
  ican actor TW/23, 26, 29
THORNE, Richard (d 1873 [34])
  actor EA/74*, WWT/14*
THORNE, Richard (d 1891 [61])
  musician EA/92*
THORNE, Richard Samuel (d 1875
  [62]) actor, manager WWT/14*
THORNE, Mrs. Richard Samuel
  (d 1896) EA/97*

THORNE, Robert (d 1965 [84])
actor TW/22
THORNE, Sarah (1837-99) Eng-
lish actress, manager COC,
OAA/1-2, OC/1-3
THORNE, Sylvia (d 1922 [55])
singer BE*, BP/6*
THORNE, Thomas (d 1864) actor
HAS
THORNE, Thomas (1841-1918)
English actor CDP, DP,
GRB/1-4, OAA/1-2, OC/1-3,
WWT/1-3
THORNE, Mrs. Thomas see
Newton, Amelia
THORNE, Thomas Wilson (d
1879 [25]) actor OAA/1
THORNE, W. S. (d 1868 [64])
actor? EA/69*
THORNTON, Miss see Martyr,
Margaret
THORNTON, Angela English ac-
tress TW/22-23, 29
THORNTON, Arthur J. (d 1967)
performer BP/51*
THORNTON, Bonnell (c. 1726-
68) English dramatist, trans-
lator CP/2-3, DNB
THORNTON, Bonnie (d 1920
[47]) American comedian BE*,
BP/4*
THORNTON, Charles (d 1881 [60])
music-hall proprietor EA/82*
THORNTON, Charles H. see
Ross, Charles H.
THORNTON, Edna (d 1964) Eng-
lish singer WWW/6
THORNTON, Ellen (d 1900 [83])
actress EA/01*
THORNTON, Emma [Mrs. R.
Thornton] (d 1869 [24]) EA/
70*
THORNTON, Emma (d 1882)
singer EA/83*
THORNTON, Frank (d 1918 [73])
English actor, manager CDP,
SR
THORNTON, Frank [né Ball] (b
1921) English actor WWT/
15-16
THORNTON, George (d 1880)
actor EA/81*
THORNTON, Harry (d 1918)
EA/19*
THORNTON, Henry manager,
actor TD/1-2
THORNTON, James (1861-1938)
English vaudevillian WWM

THORNTON, Kate see Kingsley,
Mrs. A. F.
THORNTON, L. M. (d 1888) EA/
89*
THORNTON, Louis Edmund (d 1908)
EA/09*
THORNTON, Madeleine see Sher-
wood, Madeleine
THORNTON, Margaret see
Martyr, Margaret
THORNTON, Percy (d 1891 [37])
journalist EA/92*
THORNTON, Mrs. R. (d 1893 [49])
EA/94*
THORNTON, Mrs. R. see
Thornton, Emma
THOROGOOD, John [Johnny Johns]
(d 1872 [21]) clown EA/73*
THORP, Mrs. J. see Edgar,
Alice
THORP, Joseph Peter (1873-1962)
English critic WWT/2-8
THORPE, Mrs. Charles H. see
Mountcastle, Fanny
THORPE, Clinton (d 1916) EA/17*
THORPE, George (1891-1961) Eng-
lish actor WWT/10-13
THORPE, Henry (d 1884 [37])
equestrian EA/85*
THORPE, Henry see Alvo, Henry
THORPE, Richard (b 1896) Ameri-
can actor ES
THORPE, Thomas (1570?-1635?)
English publisher DNB
THORPE, Thomas (d 1871) amuse-
ment caterer EA/72*
THORPE-BATES, Peggy (b 1914)
English actress WWT/12-16
THOURLBY, William (b 1924)
American actor TW/10-15
THRASHER, Ethelyn (b 1912)
American producer BE
THRELKELD, Budge (b 1922)
American educator BE
THROCKMORTON, Cleon (1897-
1965) American designer BE,
CB, NTH, TW/22, WWA/4,
WWT/8-10
THROPP, Clara (1875-1960) Amer-
ican actress SR, WWM
THULIN, Ingrid (b 1929) Swedish
actress TW/23
"THUMB, Tom" [Charles Stratton]
(1832/37/38-83) American midget
CDP, HAS, SR, WWA/H
"THUMB, Mrs. Tom" [Lavinia
Warren] (b 1842) HAS
THURBER, James (1894-1961)

American dramatist ES, HJD, MH

THURBURN, Gwynneth (b 1899) Argentinian/English educator WWT/14-16

THURE, Hanson (d 1871) ceiling walker EA/72*

THURLOW, Lady see Bolton, Mary

THURLOW, James Edgar (d 1903 [50]) actor EA/04*

THURMOND, John (fl 1724-49) dancing master, dramatist CP/2-3, GT, TD/1-2

THURMOND, Mrs. John [née Lewis] (fl 1715-37) actress DNB

THURNER, Georges (d 1910 [32]) dramatist BE*, WWT/14*

THURNHILL, Fred Raymond (d 1875 [40]) comic singer EA/76*

THURRELL, Frederick (d 1869) trapezist EA/70*

THURSBY, Emma Cecilia (1845/57-1931) American singer CDP, DAB, WWM

THURSTON, Ernest Temple (1879-1933) Irish dramatist WWT/3-7

THURSTON, Fred (b 1920) American actor TW/23

THURSTON, Harry (d 1955 [81]) English actor BE*, BP/40*, WWT/14*

THURSTON, Howard (1869-1936) American magician DAB, SR, WWA/1

THURSTON, Ted (b 1920) American actor TW/25-26, 28-29

THURTON, John Robert (d 1886 [54]) performer? EA/87*

THURTON, Mrs. Robert see Thurton, Susan

THURTON, Susan [Mrs. Robert Thurton] (d 1880 [57]) EA/81*

THURY, Ilona (d 1953 [77]) Hungarian actress BE*, BP/37*

TIANO, Lou (b 1935) American actor TW/26, 30

TIBBALS, Seymour Selden (1869-1949) American dramatist WWA/3

TIBBETT, Lawrence (1896-1960) American actor, singer CB, ES, TW/17, WWA/4, WWT/7-9

TIBBITTS, Mrs. (d 1888) EA/89*

TIBBITTS, James (d 1890) EA/91*

TIBERINI, Sig. (1807-85) singer CDP, HAS

TICEHURST, James (d 1889) musician EA/90*

TICEHURST, John (d 1871 [76]) musician EA/72*

TICH, Little [Harry Relph] (1868-1928) English variety artist COC, ES, GRB/1-4, OC/1-3, PDT

TICHBOURNE, S. W. L. (d 1879) secretary EA/80*

TICHENOR, Tom (b 1923) American puppeteer, dramatist, actor, director, composer, designer BE

TICKELL, Richard (d 1793) dramatist CP/3, GT, TD/1-2

TICKLE, Frank (1893-1955) English actor WWT/10-11

TICKTON, Dick (d 1907 [58]) topical singer EA/08*

TIDD, John Dunstone (d 1900 [76]) secretary EA/01*

TIDEN, Fritz (d 1931 [54]) actor BE*, BP/16*

TIDMARSH, T. U. (d 1866) circus advertizer HAS

TIDMARSH, Vivian (1896-1941) English dramatist, critic WWT/9

TIDSWELL, [Charlotte?] (d c. 1846) English actress TD/1-2

TIECK, Ludwig (1778-1853) dramatist, director, critic BE*, EA/72*

TIERNEY, Agnes (d 1975 [60s]) performer BP/60*

TIERNEY, Eliza (d 1912 [80]) housekeeper EA/13*

TIERNEY, Harry (1890/94-1965) American composer BE, WWA/4, WWT/5-10

TIERNEY, John T. (1863-1913) American comedian SR

TIERNEY, William A. (d 1974) performer BP/59*

TIETJENS, Paul (d 1943 [66]) American composer, conductor BE*, WWT/14*

TIETJENS, Therese (1831/34-77) Hungarian singer CDP, DNB, ES

TIFFANY, Annie Ward [Mrs. Charles C. Greene] actress CDP

TIFFIN, Pamela (b 1942) American

actress TW/23

TIGAR, Ken (b 1942) American actor TW/29-30

TIGHE, Edward (fl 1786-88) dramatist CP/3

TIGHE, Harry (d 1935 [50]) American actor BE*, BP/19*

TIGHE, James (d 1893 [40]) stage manager EA/94*

TIHMAR, David (1918-71) American actor, dancer, director TW/2, 27

TILBERY, John (fl 1405) member of the Children of the Chapel Royal DA

TILBURY, William Harries (1806-64) actor CDP

TILBURY, Zeffie [Mrs. L. D. Woodthorpe] (1862/63-1950) English actress GRB/2-4, WWT/1-10

TILDEN, Miss (fl 1824-52) actress HAS

TILDEN, Miss see Bernard, Mrs. Charles

TILDEN, Bill (1893-1953) German actor BE*, BP/38*

TILDEN, Milano C. (d 1951 [73]) French performer BE*, BP/36*

TILDSLEY, Peter (d 1962 [64]) performer, manager BE*

TILKIN, John see Caryll, Ivan

TILL, John (d 1910) marionettist EA/11*

TILL, John (d 1963 [77]) American puppeteer BE*

TILLBROOK, Oscar (d 1872) actor EA/73*

TILLER, John (d 1925 [73]) English dancing master, director, designer BE*

TILLEY, John (d 1935 [35]) actor BE*, WWT/14*

TILLEY, Vesta [Mrs. Walter de Frece] (1864-1952) English variety artist CDP, COC, DNB, ES, GRB/1-4, OC/1-3, PDT, TW/9, WWS, WWT/4-11, WWW/5

TILLINGER, John (b 1938) Iranian actor TW/23-27, 29

TILLSTROM, Burr (b 1917) American puppeteer CB

TILNEY, Sir Edmund (d 1610) master of the Revels COC, DNB, OC/3

TILSTON, Jennifer (b 1947) English actress TW/23-24, 26

TILSTON, Kate (b 1851) American dancer HAS

TILTMAN, Nan (d 1912 [38]) EA/13*

TILTON, Edward Lafayette (1824-87) American actor, manager CDP, HAS, NYM

TILTON, James F. (b 1937) American designer WWT/15-16

TILTON, Webb (b 1915) American actor, singer BE

TILZER, Albert von (d 1956 [78]) producer, songwriter WWT/14*

TIMBLIN, Slim (d 1962 [70]) performer BE*

TIMM, Henry Christian (1811-92) German/American musician, conductor, composer CDP, DAB, WWA/H

TIMM, Sarah H. (d 1854) actress CDP

TIMMONS, Mary see Hawthorne, Louise

TINDALL, Loren (d 1973 [52]) performer BP/57*

TINGAY, Mrs. Charles F. see Reynolds, Carrie

TINGAY, Mrs. Charles S. see Gray, Ada

TINNEY, Frank (1878-1940) American actor CB, WWA/1, WWT/4-9

TINNEY, Henry James (d 1896 [50]) conductor, musician EA/98*

TINSLEY, Arthur (d 1894 [29]) comedian EA/95*

TINSLEY, Edith see Robertson, Mrs. Lionel

TINSLEY, Tom (1853-1910) English music-hall manager, comedian GRB/1

TIPPETT, Sir Michael (b 1905) English composer CB, ES

TIPPING, Frank Blamphin (d 1917) musician EA/18*

TIPPIT, Wayne (b 1932) American actor TW/25-26

TISDALE, Benjamin (d 1888 [64]) EA/89*

TISSIER, Jean (d 1973 [77]) performer BP/57*

TISSOT, Alice (d 1971 [81]) French actress BP/55*, WWT/16*

TISSOT, Mme. Jules (d 1898 [38]) EA/99*

TITBITS, Mjr. [William Part-
ridge] (d 1898 [31]) dwarf
comedian EA/99*

TITHERADGE, Dion (1889-1934)
Australian dramatist, actor
WWT/4-7

TITHERADGE, George S[utton]
(1848-1916) English actor
GRB/1-4, OAA/1-2, WWT/
1-3

TITHERADGE, Lily (d 1937) actress BE*, WWT/14*

TITHERADGE, Madge (1887-1961)
Australian actress AAS,
COC, GRB/3-4, TW/18,
WWT/1-11, WWW/6

TITHERINGTON, Ellis (d 1908)
conductor EA/10*

TITHERINGTON, Lilian (d 1894
[23]) EA/95*

TITMAN, Mrs. S. A. (d 1897
[54]) proprietor EA/98*

TITMUSS, Phyllis (1900-46)
English actress, singer WWT/
4-8

TITTELL, Charlotte (d 1941 [60])
actress BE*, WWT/14*

TITTERTON, Frank (1882-1956)
English singer WWW/5

TITTERTON, William Richard
(1876-1963) English critic,
press representative WWT/
5-7

TITUS, Lydia Yeamans (d 1929
[63]) comedian BE*, BP/14*

TITUS, Tracy (c. 1846-87) American ticket-seller, actor?
NYM

TOBANI, Theodore Moses (1855-
1933) German/American composer, musician DAB

TOBIAS, George (d 1970 [72])
composer/lyricist BP/55*

TOBIN, Genevieve (b 1901/02)
American actress WWT/5-11

TOBIN, John (1770-1804) English
dramatist CP/3, DNB, GT

TOBIN, Matthew (b 1933) American actor TW/26-28, 30

TOBIN, Vivian (b 1903/04)
American actress WWT/5-9

TOBYE, Edward (fl 1623) actor
DA

TOCH, Ernst (1887-1964) Aus-
trian/American composer
WWA/4

TOCHE, Raoul (d 1895 [45])
dramatist WWT/14*

TODD, Little acrobat CDP

TODD, Ann (b 1909/10) English actress BE, ES, TW/14-15,
WWT/7-16

TODD, F. C. (d 1877 [32]) secretary EA/78*

TODD, Rev. Henry John (fl 1798)
editor CP/3

TODD, James actor TW/1

TODD, J. Garrett business manager
WWT/4-7

TODD, Michael [né Goldbogen]
(1907/09-58) American producing
manager CB, TW/2-8, 14,
WWA/3, WWT/10-12

TODD, Richard (b 1919) Irish actor, producing manager CB,
ES, WWT/16

TODD, Thelma (1905-35) actress
BE*

TODD-STEWART, James (d 1916)
EA/17*

TODHUNTER, Dr. John (1839-
1916) Irish dramatist WWW/2

TOFT, William (d 1904 [44])
roundabout proprietor EA/05*

TOFTS, Katherine (d 1756 [76])
actress, singer WWT/14*

TOGURI, David Canadian dancer,
director, choreographer WWT/
16

TOKELY, James (d 1819 [29])
actor CDP

TOLAN, Michael American actor
BE, TW/14-15, 22-23, 28

TOLAND, John (b 1926) American
actor TW/23

TOLANO, Raphael (d 1896) Australian lessee EA/97*

TOLER, Sidney (1874-1947) American actor, dramatist SR, TW/
3, WWM, WWT/7-10

TOLHURST, G. W. (d 1877) musician EA/78*

TOLKEIN, Alfred [Boleno Marsh]
(d 1867 [32]) clown EA/68*

TOLL, David (b 1943) American
actor TW/26, 30

TOLLER, Ernst (1893-1939) German dramatist COC, MWD,
NTH, OC/1-3, WWA/4

TOLLER, James (b 1795) giant
CDP

TOLLER, Rosalie (b 1885) actress
WWT/1-5

TOLLET, Elizabeth (1694-1755)
dramatist CP/2-3

TOLLET, George (1725-79) English? critic DNB

TOLLETT, Henrietta Maria see Crisp, Mrs. Samuel

TOLLETT, John [Pat O'Leary] (d 1882) EA/83*

TOLLINGER, Ned (d 1972 [69]) performer BP/56*

TOLSON, Francis (d 1745/46) dramatist CP/1-3, GT

TOLSTOY, Count Leo Nikolaevich (1828-1910) Russian dramatist COC

TOM, Blind (b c. 1848) American musician CDP, HAS

TOMACK, Sid (d 1962) American performer BE*

TOMKINS, Gregory C. (d 1895) lessee EA/96*

TOMKINS, Gregory Styles (d 1893 [63]) journalist EA/94*

TOMKI[N]S, John see Tomkis, Thomas

TOMKINS, Robert (d 1897) proprietor EA/98*

TOMKINSON, Annie (d 1908 [57]) EA/09*

TOMKIS, Thomas (fl 1594-1615?) dramatist CP/2-3, DNB, FGF, HP

TOMLIN, Blanche (b 1889) English actress, singer WWT/4-8

TOMLIN, Felicity see Douglas, Felicity

TOMLINS, Frederick Guest (d 1867 [63]) critic, journalist, dramatist BE*, EA/68*, WWT/14*

TOMLINSON, Mr. (fl 1759-61) actor HAS

TOMLINSON, Miss (fl 1829?) actress CDP

TOMLINSON, David (b 1917) English actor AAS, WWT/12-16

TOMLINSON, John (fl 1792) dramatist CP/3

TOMLINSON, Kellom (fl 1754?) dancing master CDP

TOMPKINS, Eugene (1850-1909) manager, proprietor CDP

TOMPKINS, Toby (b 1942) American performer TW/29

TOMS, Mr. (fl 1796) actor CDP, GT, TD/1-2

TOMS, Carl (b 1927) English designer WWT/15-16

TOMS, Edward (d c. 1779) drama-

tist CP/2-3

TOMSON, Sam (fl early 17th cent) actor DA

TOMSONE, John (fl 1598) actor DA

TONDESILLA, Jesus (d 1973 [80]) Spanish actor WWT/16*

TONE, Franchot (1905/06-68) American actor BE, CB, SR, TW/1-20, 24-25, WWA/5, WWT/7-14

TONER, Tom (b 1928) American actor TW/29

TONGE, H. Asheton (d 1927 [55]) actor BE*, WWT/14*

TONGE, Philip (1892-1959) English actor GRB/3-4, TW/4-16, 15, WWT/1-12

TONKS, John (d 1867 [48]) EA/68*

TONSON, Jacob (d 1736 [80]) publisher BE*, WWT/14*

TONY, Little (d 1918 [43]) EA/19*

TONY, Will (fl late 16th cent) actor DA

TOOHEY, John Latham (1916-75) American press representative BE

TOOHEY, John Peter (d 1947 [66]) American press representative BE*, BP/31*

TOOKER, Guy (d 1975 [83]) performer BP/60*

TOOKER, Joseph Henry (1830-96) manager CDP

TOOKEY, William see Vol Becque, William

TOOLE, Mrs. Alec see Toole, Maggie

TOOLE, Florence Mabel (d 1888 [22]) EA/89*

TOOLE, Frank (d 1889 [70]) EA/90*

TOOLE, Frank Laurence (d 1879 [23]) EA/80*

TOOLE, Harry (d 1892 [23]) EA/93*

TOOLE, J. E. (fl 1872-86) American actor SR

TOOLE, Mrs. John L. see Toole, Susan

TOOLE, John Lawrence (1830-1906) English actor, manager CDP, COC, DNB, DP, ES, GRB/1, OAA/1-2, OC/1-3, WWW/1

TOOLE, Kate (d 1903) music-hall singer EA/04*

TOOLE, Maggie [Mrs. Alec Toole] (d 1917) EA/18*

TOOLE, Susan [Mrs. John L. Toole] (d 1889) EA/90*

TOOLEY, Nicholas [né Wilkinson] (c. 1575-1623) English actor COC, DA, GT, NTH, OC/1-3

TOOMER, Mr. actor HAS

TOONE, Geoffrey (b 1910) Irish actor WWT/10-16

TOOSEY, George Philip (d 1795) dramatist CP/2-3, GT

TOOTLE, Milton (c. 1824-87) manager NYM

TOPA, John A. (b 1909) American actor TW/24

TOPAZ, Murial (b 1932) American dancer, choreographer BE

TOPHAM, Edward (1751-1820) dramatist CDP, CP/3, DNB, GT, TD/1-2

TOPHAM, Frederic (1858-1908) English actor GRB/1-3

TOPHAM, Thomas (1710?-49) strong man CDP, DNB

TOPHOFFS, Mons. (d 1865) ballet master HAS

TOPOL, Chaim (b 1934) Israeli actor COC

TOPPING, Melinda see Jones, Melinda

TORDESILLA, Jesus (d 1973 [80]) performer BP/57*

TORETZKA, Ludmilla (b 1903) Russian actress TW/9

TORMEY, John (b 1937) American actor TW/23-24, 26

TORN, Elmore Rual see Torn, Rip

TORN, Rip [né Elmore Rual Torn] (b 1931) American actor, director BE, TW/20, 23, 25-27, 30, WWT/15-16

TORNATORE, Michael (d 1973 [53]) performer BP/58*

TORR, Clara music-hall singer CDP

TORR, Sam (d 1899 [53]) music-hall singer & manager CDP

TORR, Mrs. Sam (d 1899 [53]) proprietor EA/00*

TORRE, Della (fl 1887?) singer, songwriter CDP

TORREN, Frank (b 1939) American actor TW/26

TORRENCE, David (b 1870) Scottish actor WWT/7-9

TORRENCE, Ernest (1878-1933) Scottish actor, singer WWT/7

TORRENCE, Frederick Ridgely (1874-1950) American dramatist DAB, HJD

TORRENCE, Marietta S. (b 1813) HAS

TORRES, Andy (b 1945) Puerto Rican actor TW/29-30

TORREY, Susan (d 1968 [61]) actress TW/24

TORRIANI, Aimee (d 1963 [73]) performer BP/48*, WWT/14*

TORRIANI, Astava (fl 1874) singer CDP

TORRIANI, Charles (1852-98) musician CDP

TOSCANINI, Arturo (1867-1957) Italian conductor CB, ES, TW/13, WWA/3, WWW/5

TOSEDALL, Roger (fl 1635) actor DA

TOSTI, Sir Paolo (d 1916 [70]) composer EA/18*

TOTHEROH, Dan (1894/95/98-1976) American dramatist HJD, MD, MWD, WWT/9-11

TOTIEN, Henry (d 1878 [63]) actor EA/79*

TOTTEN, Mrs. Henry (d 1889 [73]) EA/90*

TOTTEN, John J. (d 1969 [83]) executive BP/53*

TOTTEN, Joseph Byron (1875-1946) American dramatist, director WWA/2

TOTTEN, Mrs. Joseph Byron see Bingham, Leslie

TOTTERTON CDP

TOTTNELL, Harry (d 1593?) actor DA

TOUBEL, Philippe see Alcidor

TOULIATOS, George (b 1929) American director, manager BE

TOULMOUCHE, Frederic (d 1909 [58]) composer WWT/14*

TOUMANOVA, Tamara [Tamara Khacidovitch] (b 1917) Russian dancer WWT/9-12

TOURBUTTS, Richard (d 1905) conductor EA/06*

TOUREL, Jennie (1910-73) Canadian/French singer CB

TOURNEUR, Cyril (1575-1626) English dramatist COC, CP/1-3, DNB, ES, FGF, HP, MH, NTH, OC/1-3, PDT, RE

TOURNEY, Minna (fl 1854) French singer? musician? HAS

TOURNIAIRE, Benoit (d 1865)
circus performer? CDP, HAS
TOURNIAIRE, Louise (fl 1851)
equestrienne CDP
TOURNOUR, Millie (fl 1868)
aerial bar performer CDP
TOURS, Frank E. (1877-1963)
English musical director,
composer GRB/4, WWT/1-
11, WWW/6
TOUSSAINT, Marie American ac-
tress TW/25-26
TOUSSARD, E. J. (fl 1897?)
music-hall singer CDP
TOUTAIN, Blanche (d 1932)
French actress WWT/2-4
TOVATT, Ellen American ac-
tress TW/29-30
TOVEY, Sir Donald Francis
(1875-1940) English composer
DNB
TOVEY, Henry (d 1885) assistant
stage manager EA/86*
TOVSTONOGOV, Georgyi Alex-
androvich (b 1915) Russian
producer COC
TOWB, Harry (b 1925) Irish actor
TW/23, WWT/15-16
TOWBER, Chaim (d 1972 [70])
dramatist BP/56*
TOWBIN, Beryl (b 1938) Amer-
ican actress TW/24, 26
TOWELL, Miss see Miller,
Mrs. W. Christie
TOWELL, George (d 1894 [21])
musical director, musician
EA/95*
TOWER, Allen (d 1963) American
performer BE*
TOWER, W. C. (fl 1881?) singer,
songwriter CDP
TOWERS, Constance (b 1933)
American actress, singer
TW/22-24, 26-28, WWT/16
TOWERS, Edward (d 1918 [76])
EA/19*
TOWERS, Harry (fl 1897?) singer
CDP
TOWERS, Harry P. (b 1873)
English business manager
WWT/2, 5-7
TOWERS, John (b 1836) English
writer WWM
TOWERS, Johnson (d 1891 [78])
dramatist, manager, actor
BE*, EA/92*, WWT/14*
TOWERS, Susan (b 1948) Ameri-
can actress TW/23

TOWNE, Charles Hanson (1877-
1949) American editor, actor,
writer BE*, BP/33*
TOWNE, Edward Owings (b 1869)
American dramatist WWA/1,
WWM, WWS
TOWNE, John (fl 1583-97) actor
DA
TOWNE, Thomas (d 1612?) actor
DA
TOWNES, Harry (b 1918) American
actor TW/6-9, 25-26
TOWNE'S BOY (fl 1600-01) actor
DA
TOWNLEY, Charles [Geoffrey
Thorn] (d 1905 [62]) pantomime
writer, dramatist BE*, EA/
06*, WWT/14*
TOWNLEY, Rev. James (1714-78)
English dramatist CDP, CP/3
TOWNLEY, James (d 1882 [66])
EA/83*
TOWNLEY, Richard Thomas (d
1889 [31]) EA/90*
TOWNLEY, William (d 1894 [65])
singer EA/95*
TOWNLEY-SEARLE, W. F. D.
see Searle, Townley
TOWNLY, Charles (fl 1760) drama-
tist CP/3
TOWNSEND, Mr. actor, singer
TD/1-2
TOWNSEND, Mrs. (fl 1796) actress
CDP
TOWNSEND, Alice (1860-90) singer
CDP
TOWNSEND, Aurelian (fl 1601-43)
dramatist CP/3, FGF
TOWNSEND, Barbara American
actress TW/23
TOWNSEND, C. (d 1909 [41])
property master EA/10*
TOWNSEND, Daniel E. (b 1823)
American actor HAS
TOWNSEND, Mrs. E. (d 1908)
EA/09*
TOWNSEND, Horace (1859-1922)
English dramatist WWA/1
TOWNSEND, J. E. (d 1899 [44])
actor? EA/00*
TOWNSEND, John (fl 1611-34) ac-
tor DA
TOWNSEND, John Frederick (d
1888) music-hall performer
EA/89*
TOWNSEND, Sarah [Mrs. William
Thompson Townsend] (d 1885)
EA/86*

TOWNSEND, Mrs. Stephen see
Burnett, Frances Hodgson
TOWNSEND, Thompson (d 1870
[64]) dramatist EA/71*,
WWT/14*
TOWNSEND, Mrs. William Thompson see Townsend, Sarah
TOWNWAY, Mrs. George see
Herbert, Annie
TOWSE, John Rankin (1845-1927)
English/American critic COC,
OC/1-3, WWA/1
TOY (fl 1592) actor DA
TOY, Agnes (d 1899) EA/01*
TOY, Beatrice (d 1938 [64]) actress BE*, WWT/14*
TOYE, Geoffrey Edward (b 1889)
conductor WWT/4-9
TOYE, Wendy (b 1917) English
actress, dancer, director
AAS, WWT/8-16
TOYNE, Gabriel (1905-63) English actor, producer WWT/
8-13
TOZER, Annie [Mrs. Henry
Tozer] (d 1899 [47]) EA/01*
TOZER, Sir Henry (d 1918 [67])
EA/19*
TOZER, Mrs. Henry see
Tozer, Annie
TOZER, J. B. (fl 1850s) comedian HAS
TOZERE, Frederic (1901-72)
American actor BE, TW/1-4,
8-9, 16, 26, 29, WWA/5,
WWT/10-15
TOZZI, Giorgio (b 1923) American singer CB
TRACEY, Andrew (b 1936) South
African actor TW/22-23
TRACEY, Herbert (b 1877) English singer GRB/1
TRACEY, Paul (b 1939) South
African actor TW/22-23,
27-28
TRACEY, Sid (d 1970 [70])
performer TW/27
TRACEY, Thomas F. (d 1961
[86]) Irish actor BE*, BP/
46*
TRACT, Jo (b 1939) American
actress TW/21, 25-26
TRACY, Agnes Ethel (fl 1868-75)
actress PP/3
TRACY, Douglas [Jack Graham
Lindsay] (d 1895 [38]) manager
EA/96*
TRACY, Helen (fl 1870-1908)

American actress WWS
TRACY, Hettie [Mrs. Jesse Williams] (d 1907) actress EA/08*
TRACY, John (d 1735) dramatist
CP/1-3
TRACY, John (b 1938) American
actor TW/20
TRACY, Lee (1898-1968) American
actor BE, TW/5-8, 22, 25,
WWA/5, WWT/7-14
TRACY, Lisa (b 1945) American
actress TW/26
TRACY, Spencer (1900-67) American actor BE, CB, ES, SR,
TW/24, WWA/4, WWT/7-11,
WWW/6
TRACY, Virginia (d 1946 [72])
American actress BE*, BP/
30*, WWT/14*
TRACY, William (d 1967 [48]) performer BP/52*
TRADER, Mrs. George Henry see
Augarde, Gertrude
TRAHAN, Al (d 1966 [69]) comedian
TW/23
TRAILL, George (b 1853) Scottish
actor GRB/1
TRAILL, Peter [Guy Mainwaring
Morton] (1896-1968) English
dramatist WWT/6-8
TRAIN, Arthur (1875-1945) American dramatist WWA/2, WWW/4
TRAJETTA, Philip (c. 1776-1854)
Italian/American composer,
manager DAB, WWA/H
TRANSFIELD, Cpt. (d 1887) performer? EA/89*
TRANSFIELD, Mrs. (d 1907 [75])
EA/08*
TRANSFIELD, Bellamina [Mrs. T.
G. Transfield] (d 1899 [39])
EA/00*
TRANSFIELD, Mrs. T. G. see
Transfield, Bellamina
TRANSFIELD, Thomas George (d
1911 [54]) circus proprietor
EA/12*
TRANSFIELD, Tilly (d 1890) EA/
91*
TRANUM, Charles B. (b 1916)
American talent representative
BE
TRAPANI, Lou (b 1947) American
actor TW/28-30
TRAPIDO, Joel (b 1913) American
educator, director BE
TRAPP, Dr. Joseph (1679-1747)
English dramatist CP/1-3, GT

TRASK, Franklin (b 1907) American producer, actor, educator BE

TRASK, Kate Nichols (d 1922) American dramatist WWA/1

TRAUBE, Shepard (b 1907) American manager, producer, director BE, WWT/10-16

TRAUBEL, Helen (1899/1903-1972) American singer, actress CB, ES, TW/12, 29, WWA/5

TRAUTMAN, William E. (d 1973 [75]) critic BP/58*

TRAUX, Sarah [Mrs. C. S. Albert] (b 1877) American actress GRB/3-4, WWT/1

TRAVER, Julia Merrick (fl 1900s) American editor WWM

TRAVER, Lee (d 1975 [70]) performer BP/60*

TRAVER, Sharry (b 1922) American actress TW/4

TRAVERS, Ben (b 1886) English dramatist AAS, BE, CD, CH, COC, MH, PDT, WWT/6-16

TRAVERS, Bill (b 1922) English actor TW/18-20

TRAVERS, Eliza see Brent, Bessie

TRAVERS, Ernest (d 1891) actor EA/92*

TRAVERS, Henry (1874-1965) English actor WWT/7-11

TRAVERS, Linden (b 1913) English actress WWT/10-11

TRAVERS, Nat (fl 1902?) music-hall singer CDP

TRAVERS, Roland (d 1970 [88]) performer BP/54*

TRAVERS, William (d 1880) English actor, dramatist EA/69

TRAVERS, Mrs. W. M. see Walsh, Blanche

TRAVERSE, Madlaine (d 1964 [88]) American actress BE*

TRAVIS, Mrs. Frank see Rosa, Madeline

TRAVIS, Jan R. (d 1975 [23]) performer BP/60*

TRAVIS, Joe (d 1879 [46]) manager EA/80*

TRAVIS, Michael (b 1928) American costume designer BE

TRAVOLTA, John (b 1954) American actor TW/28-30

TRAYLOR, William (b 1930) American actor TW/14-15, 23

TRAYNOR, Edward (d 1886 [31]) actor EA/87*

TRAYNOR, Tom (d 1907) variety comedian EA/08*

TREACHER, Arthur (1894-1975) English actor BE

TREACY, Emerson (d 1967 [66]) performer BP/51*

TREADWAY, Charlotte (d 1963 [68]) actress BE*

TREADWAY, Sophie (1890-1970) American dramatist MD, MH, MWD

TREBELLI, Zelia (1838-92) singer CDP

TREBLE, Sepha (b 1908) English actress, dancer WWT/9-10

TRECHMAN [or Treckman], Emma (b 1909) English actress WWT/9-13

TRECKMAN, Emma see Trechman, Emma

TREE, Miss (fl 1821?) dancer CDP

TREE, Anne (fl 1823) actress CDP

TREE, Ann Maria see Bradshaw, Ann Maria

TREE, David (b 1915) English actor WWT/9-11

TREE, Ellen see Kean, Mrs. Charles

TREE, Sir Herbert Beerbohm (1853-1917) English actor, manager CDP, COC, DNB, DP, ES, GRB/1-4, NTH, OC/1-3, PDT, SR, WWA/1, WWM, WWS, WWT/1-3, WWW/2

TREE, Iris (d 1968) dramatist BP/52*

TREE, Maria see Bradshaw, Ann Maria

TREE, Maud Beerbohm [Maud Holt] (1863-1937) English actress CDP, COC, DP, ES, GRB/1-4, NTH, OC/1-3, WWT/1-8, WWW/3

TREE, Viola (1884-1938) English actress ES, GRB/1-4, NTH, OC/1-3, WWT/1-8

TREES, Amanda American actress TW/25

TREFFZ, Henriette (fl 1850?) singer CDP

TREFOURET, Jeanne Alfredine see Hading, Jane

TREGETOUR, Prof. (d 1899 [32]) juggler, shadowgraphist EA/00*

TREGETOUR, Mrs. C. see

Tregetour, Mary
TREGETOUR, Mary [Mrs. C.
Tregetour] (d 1890 [31]) EA/
91*
TREGRE, George P. (b 1939)
American actor TW/25
TREHERNE, Bernard [Herbert
B. Cooper] (d 1898 [34]) actor
EA/99*
TRELAWNEY, R. S. [Thomas
Reid Strachan Hicks] actor
GRB/1
TREMAINE, Mr. (fl 1759) actor
HAS
TREMAINE, Annie see Amadi,
Mme.
TREMAINE, John (b 1946) Amer-
ican actor TW/30
TREMAYNE, Bella [Mrs. Henry
J. Butler] (d 1900) actress
EA/01*
TREMAYNE, Les (b 1913) Eng-
lish actor TW/7
TREMAYNE, Maude English ac-
tress GRB/1
TRENAMAN, John (b 1932) Aus-
tralian actor TW/25
TRENCH, Herbert (1865-1923)
Irish director, dramatist
DNB, WWT/1-4
TRENCH, Mrs. Ormsby (d 1902)
EA/03*
TRENCHARD, Sarah (1864-87)
actress NYM
TRENHOLME, Helen (1911-62)
Canadian actress WWT/9-11
TRENT, Bruce English actor,
singer WWT/12-16
TRENT, Edie (d 1888) dancer
EA/89*
TRENT, Sheila (d 1954 [46])
actress TW/10
TRENTINI, Emma (d 1959 [74])
Italian actress, singer TW/
15, WWT/4-5
TRESAHAR, John (d 1936 [76])
actor GRB/1-4, WWT/1-5
TRESCOTT, Virginia Drew (d
1911 [41]) American actress
SR
TRESKO, Elsa Austrian actress
TW/30
TRESMAND, Ivy (b 1898) Eng-
lish actress, singer WWT/
4-11
TRESSIDDER (d 1890) stage mana-
ger EA/91*
TRESSIDDER, Mrs. Arthur (d

1889) EA/91*
TRESSIDER, John Arthur (d 1894
[33]) manager EA/95*
TRETYAKOV, Sergei Mikhailovich
(1892-1939) Russian dramatist
COC
TREVANION, Edward (d 1887 [38])
lessee, proprietor EA/88*
TREVANION, Harry (d 1917 [58])
manager, actor EA/18*
TREVELL, William (fl 1608-21)
share-holder DA
TREVELYAN (d 1892 [25]) EA/93*
TREVELYAN, Florence see
Brough, Mrs. Robert
TREVELYAN, Hilda [née Tucker]
(1877/79/80-1959) English ac-
tress COC, DNB, GRB/1-4,
OC/3, WWT/1-11, WWW/5
TREVILLE, Roger (b 1903) French
actor, singer WWT/9
TREVISAN, Vittorio (b 1868) Italian
singer WWA/4
TREVOR, Ann [Annie Trilnick]
(1899-1970) actress WWT/4-9
TREVOR, Austin (b 1897) Irish ac-
tor AAS, WWT/6-15
TREVOR, Claire (b 1909) American
actress ES, WWT/8-11
TREVOR, Enid (d 1965) actress
BP/49*, WWT/14*
TREVOR, Francis (b 1827) English
singer HAS
TREVOR, Leo (d 1927 [62]) drama-
tist GRB/4, WWT/1-5
TREVOR, Norman (1877-1929) In-
dian/English actor WWT/1-6
TREVOR, Spencer (1875-1945)
French/English actor WWT/1-9
TREVOR, Theodore [Herbert Theo-
dore Garland] (d 1909 [56]) EA/
10*
TREVOR, Vaughan (b 1880) English
actor WWM
TREVOR, William [William Trevor
Cox] (b 1928) Irish dramatist
CD
TREVORI, Sig. (d 1916 [89]) per-
former, conjuror, ventriloquist,
musician EA/18*
TREW, Christine Patti [Lady Long-
ford] (fl 1933-40) dramatist,
translator COC
TREWAR, Eliza Marian see
Shaw, Mrs.
TREWIN, John Courtenay (b 1908)
English critic AAS, COC,
PDT, WWT/10-16

TREWREN, Emily M. see
Marmion, Emily M.
TRIANA, Rafael (b 1947) American actor TW/27
TRIBUSH, Nancy (b 1940) American actress TW/26-29
TRIEGLE, Norman (d 1975 [47]) performer BP/59*
TRIEVE, Richard Ernest (d 1916) EA/17*
TRIGG, William (fl first half of 17th cent) actor COC, DA, OC/3
TRIGGER, Ian J. (b 1942) English actor TW/30
TRIGGS, Alfred Standen (d 1910 [62]) EA/11*
TRILLING, Ossia (b 1913) English actor, director, stage manager, critic WWT/13-16
TRILNICK, Annie see Trevor, Ann
TRIMBLE, Byron A. (d 1976 [61]) executive BP/60*
TRIMBLE, Jessie (d 1957 [83]) American dramatist BE*, BP/41*
TRIMBLE, Lawrence (d 1954 [69]) director BE*
TRIMMER, Sarah (1741-1810) English dramatist CDP, CP/3
TRIMMINGHAM, Ernest (d 1942 [63]) actor BE*, WWT/14*
TRINDER, Tommy (b 1909) English comedian WWT/10-16
TRIPLETT, Erna La Quer (d 1964 [66]) equestrian BE*
TRIPP, Emily (d 1893 [70]) EA/95*
TRIPP, Frederick (d 1968 [76]) performer BP/53*
TRIPP, June Howard see June
TRIPP, Susan fat girl CDP
TRIPPAS, Henry (d 1874) music-hall manager EA/75*
TRIPPELLO, Sig. see Goodliffe, John Herbert
TRIQUET, M., Jr. (d 1876) aeronaut EA/77*
TRITSCHLER, Conrad (d 1939 [71]) scene artist WWT/14*
TRITSCHLER, Henry Joseph (d 1917 [19]) EA/18*
TRITTIPO, James (d 1971 [43]) designer TW/28
TRIVIER, Pierre-Olaf see Olaf, Pierre
TRIX, Helen (d 1951 [59]) actress

BE*, WWT/14*
TROCHON, Marie see Aimée, Marie
TROLLOPE, Fred James (d 1910) EA/11*
TRONTO, Rudy (b 1928) American actor TW/21, 27-29
TROOBNICK, Eugene (b 1926) American actor TW/24, 26, 28, WWT/16
TROTERE, H. (d 1912) composer EA/13*
TROTMAN, William C. (b 1930) American administrative director BE
TROTTER, Catharine see Cockburn, Catharine
TROTTER, Thomas actor, manager TD/2
TROUBAT, Francis dramatist RJ
TROUGHTON, Adolphus Charles English dramatist EA/69
TROUNCER, Cecil (1898-1953) English actor COC, OC/3, WWT/9-11, WWW/5
TROUTMAN, Ivy (b 1883) American actress WWM, WWS, WWT/4-11
TROW, William (d 1973 [82]) performer BP/58*
TROWBRIDGE, Mr. (d 1838) manager, actor HAS
TROWBRIDGE, Mrs. see Chapman, Mrs. William A.
TROWBRIDGE, Annie (d 1886 [21]) singer EA/87*
TROWBRIDGE, Hester (d 1890) music-hall performer EA/91*
TROWBRIDGE, Will (d 1911 [74]) music-hall performer EA/13*
TROWER, Carlos (d 1889 [40]) "African Blondin" EA/90*
TROY, Hector (b 1941) American actor TW/25-26
TROY, John J. (d 1975 [56]) performer BP/60*
TROY, Louise American actress, singer BE, WWT/15-16
TROY, Rachel Finney see Denvil, Rachel
TRUAX, Sarah (b 1877) American actress WWM, WWS, WWT/2-6
TRUE, Oswald (d 1899) manager EA/00*
TRUEBA, Don (d 1835) dramatist BE*, WWT/14*
TRUEMAN, Mr. actor TD/1-2
TRUEMAN, Paula (b 1907) Ameri-

can actress BE, TW/1, 8,
12-13, 20, 23-24, 26, WWT/
15-16
TRUESDELL, Frederick (d 1937
[64]) actor BE*, BP/21*
TRUESDELL, Mrs. Frederick
see Hall, Laura Nelson
TRUEX, Ernest (1889/90-1973)
American actor BE, CB,
SR, TW/1-19, 22, 30, WWT/
4-15
TRUEX, Philip (b 1911) American
actor TW/2-5
TRUFFI, Teresa (fl 1848) singer
CDP, HAS
TRUMBO, Dalton dramatist CD
TRUMBO, Nancy (b 1945) Amer-
ican actress TW/29
TRUSSELL, Alvery (fl 1600-01)
actor DA
TRUSSELL, Fred (1858-1923)
English manager, conductor
GRB/1-4
TRZCINSKI, Edmund (b 1921)
American dramatist, director,
actor BE
TSEGAYE GABRE-MEDHIN (b
1936) Ethiopian dramatist,
director CD
TSIANG, H. T. (d 1971 [72])
performer BP/56*
TSOUTSOUVAS, Sam (b 1948)
American actor TW/29-30
TUBBS, Arthur Lewis (1867-
1946) American dramatist
WWA/2, WWM
TUBBS, Mrs. Charles see
Arnold, Mrs. Henry
TUCCI, Maria (b 1941) Italian
actress TW/22-27, WWT/16
TUCHIN, John see Tutchin,
John
TUCK, Mrs. Albert see
Cullen, Rose
TUCKER, Mr. (d 1874) musician
EA/75*
TUCKER, Forrest (b 1919)
American actor, writer BE,
TW/20, 30
TUCKER, Frederick C. (d 1917
[40]) managing director EA/
18*
TUCKER, George Loane (d 1921
[49]) American actor, director
BE*, BP/6*
TUCKER, Hilda see Trevelyan,
Hilda
TUCKER, Ian (b 1946) American

actor TW/30
TUCKER, Johnny (d 1971 [73])
composer/lyricist BP/55*
TUCKER, Richard (1913-75) Ameri-
can singer CB, ES
TUCKER, Sophie [Sophie Abuza]
(1884-1966) American actress,
singer BE, CB, ES, NTH,
TW/2-7, 18-19, 22, WWA/4,
WWT/7-14
TUCKER, William T. (d 1881
[32]) EA/82*
TUCKERMAN, Maury (1905-66)
American director, stage mana-
ger, actor BE
TUCKETT, Harvey (d 1854) English
actor HAS
TUCKETT, Mrs. Harvey (fl 1850s)
English actress, manager HAS
TUCKETT, Margaret see Tuckett,
Mrs. Harvey
TUCKFEILD, Thomas (fl 1624)
actor DA
TUDOR, Alice (d 1876 [29]) eques-
trienne EA/77*
TUDOR, Annie (1855-87) English
actress NYM
TUDOR, Anthony (b 1909) English
dancer, choreographer BE,
CB, ES, WWT/10-12
TUDOR, Carry (d 1879) actress
EA/80*
TUDOR, Rowan (b 1905) American
actor, singer, director BE
TUDOR, Valerie (b 1910) Welsh
actress WWT/9-10
TUERK, John (d 1951 [62]) Ameri-
can producer TW/7
TUESKI, Sophie H. (d 1892 [46])
musician EA/93*
TUFFLEY, Eric see Lewis, Eric
TUFTS, Sonny (d 1970 [59]) per-
former BP/55*
TUKE, Miss see Hallam, Mrs.
Lewis
TUKE, Richard (fl 1672) dramatist
CP/1-3
TUKE, Sir Samuel (d 1674) English
dramatist CDP, CP/1-3, GT,
OC/1-3
TULA, John (d 1906 [58]) gymnast
EA/07*
TULL, Patrick (b 1941) English
actor TW/23
TULLETT, Fred (d 1889) EA/90*
TULLOCK, William (d 1899) EA/
00*
TULLOCK, William, Jr. (d 1886

[23]) musician EA/87*

TULLY, Emily Jane (d 1887 [58]) EA/88*

TULLY, Ethel (d 1968 [70]) performer BP/53*

TULLY, George F. (1876-1930) Irish actor GRB/1, WWT/3-6

TULLY, James H. (d 1868 [53]) musical director EA/69*

TULLY, James Syrus see Syrus, Napoleon

TULLY, May (1884-1924) Canadian actress, dancer SR

TULLY, Richard Walton (1877-1945) American dramatist, producer HJD, WWA/2, WWT/4-9

TUMARIN, Boris [né Tumarinson] (b 1910) Latvian actor, director, teacher BE, TW/24-25, WWT/15-16

TUMARINSON, Boris see Tumarin, Boris

TUNBRIDGE, Joseph A. (1886-1961) English composer, conductor WWT/8-11

TUNE, Tommy (b 1939) American actor TW/29-30

TUNNELL, George N. (d 1975 [62]) performer BP/59*

TUNSTALL, Catherine (1796-1846) actress, singer CDP

TUNSTALL, James (fl 1583-97) actor DA

TUPLIN, Lily [Mrs. T. A. Edge] (d 1898) actress EA/99*

TUPOU, Manu (b 1935/39) Fijian actor TW/26, 28, WWT/16

TUPPER, Martin Farquhar (d 1889 [78]) dramatist EA/90*

TUPPER, Mary (d 1964 [86]) American actress BE*

TURBUTT, Mr. (d 1746) actor CDP

TURGENEV, Ivan Sergeivich (1818-83) Russian dramatist COC, OC/3

TURGEON, Peter (b 1919) American actor, director, writer BE

TURKISH ROPEDANCER CDP

TURLE (d 1882 [80]) musician EA/83*

TURLEIGH, Veronica (1903-71) Irish actress COC, WWT/6-14

TURNBULL, Mr. (fl 1799) actor HAS

TURNBULL, Miss C. (fl 1826) American actress HAS

TURNBULL, Dixon (d 1917) EA/18*

TURNBULL, Jill (b 1963) American actress TW/30

TURNBULL, John (1880-1956) Scottish actor, stage manager WWT/9-11

TURNBULL, John D. (fl 1799?) dramatist EAP, RJ

TURNBULL, Julia (1822?-87) American actress HAS, NYM

TURNBULL, Julia (d 1887 [65]) dancer CDP

TURNBULL, Margaret (d 1942) Scottish dramatist WWA/2

TURNBULL, Stanley (d 1924) English actor WWT/4

TURNER, Aidan (1908/16-68) Indian actor TW/4

TURNER, Alfred (1870-1941) English manager GRB/4, WWT/1-9

TURNER, Annie [Mrs. H. J. Turner] (d 1872) EA/73*

TURNER, Anthony (fl 1st half of 17th cent) English actor COC, DA, OC/1-3

TURNER, Arthur see Rigby, Arthur, Jr.

TURNER, Bob (b 1922) American actor TW/4

TURNER, Bridget English actress WWT/16

TURNER, Carrie (d 1897) actress WWT/14*

TURNER, Charles (d 1894) singer EA/95*

TURNER, Cicely [Mrs. W. H. Leverton] (d 1940) actress BE*, WWT/14*

TURNER, Claramae American actress, singer BE

TURNER, David (b 1927) English dramatist AAS, CD, CH, ES, MH, PDT, WWT/15-16

TURNER, Dorothy (1895-1969) actress WWT/6-9

TURNER, Douglas (b 1930) American actor TW/22-26

TURNER, Drewe (fl 1633) actor DA

TURNER, Eardley (d 1929) actor, journalist BE*, WWT/14*

TURNER, Ella (fl 1866) actress HAS

TURNER, Ellen (d 1872) American

actress HAS

TURNER, Florence [Nora Temple] (d 1917) EA/18*

TURNER, Florence (1887/88-1946) American actress ES, TW/3

TURNER, George (b 1902) English actor BE, TW/13, 22

TURNER, George (d 1968) performer BP/53*

TURNER, G. G. (1844-69) American actor HAS

TURNER, Harold (1909-62) English dancer WWT/9-12

TURNER, Harry (d 1916) music-hall singer CDP

TURNER, Helena [Hélène Crosmond] (d 1888 [35]) singer EA/89*

TURNER, H. J. (d 1891 [85]) actor EA/92*, WWT/14*

TURNER, H. J. (d 1898 [36]) EA/00*

TURNER, Mrs. H. J. see Turner, Annie

TURNER, Jim (b 1947) American actor TW/29

TURNER, John (d 1881) actor EA/82*

TURNER, Mrs. John (d 1881) actress EA/82*

TURNER, John Hastings (1892-1956) English dramatist, producer WWT/4-11, WWW/5

TURNER, Julia (fl 1832) actress HAS

TURNER, J. W. (d 1913 [68]) singer, producer, manager BE*, WWT/14*

TURNER, Kitty see Pryce, Catharine Gompertz

TURNER, Leon (d 1900) musical director EA/01*

TURNER, Maidel (d 1953 [72]) American actress TW/1-6, 9

TURNER, Margaret (fl 1790) translator? CP/3

TURNER, Marion actress GRB/1-2

TURNER, Maurice Clark (1878-1953) American manager WWA/3

TURNER, Michael (b 1921) South African actor WWT/15-16

TURNER, Montague [Raymond Dudley] (d 1917) EA/18*

TURNER, Percy M. (d 1971)

performer BP/55*

TURNER, Richard J. (d 1857) American singer CDP, HAS

TURNER, Robert (d 1970) performer BP/55*

TURNER, Terry (d 1971 [79]) publicist BP/56*

TURNER, W. (d 1872) minstrel EA/73*

TURNER, William see Rigby, Arthur

TURNER, William A. (fl 1810) English actor HAS

TURNER, Mrs. William A. (fl 1810) English actress HAS

TURNER, Willis Lloyd (b 1927) American educator, director BE

TURNER, W. J. (1889-1946) English dramatist MD

TURNEY, Catherine (b 1906) American dramatist BE

TURNEY, John (d 1853) HAS

TURPIN, Mr. actor TD/2

TURPIN, Miss (fl 1837) actress HAS

TURPIN, Ben (1868/69/74-1940) American vaudevillian ES, WWA/4

TURPIN, George (d 1872 [60]) box book-keeper EA/73*

TURPIN, Mrs. George see Turpin, Isabella

TURPIN, Isabella [Mrs. George Turpin] (d 1872 [59]) EA/73*

TURPIN, Maria see Wallack, Mrs. Henry John

TURPIN, S. Hart (d 1899 [62]) scene artist EA/00*

TURQUE, Mimi (b 1939) American actress TW/22-24

TURRELL, Thomas Edward (d 1903) musical director EA/04*

TURTON-BROWNE, Margaret actress GRB/1

TUSHINGHAM, Rita (b 1942) English actress CB, ES, WWT/15-16

TUSON, Isabella [Miss George] (d 1870 [25]) actress EA/71*

TUSSAUD, Mme. (d 1850 [90]) wax-work, exhibitor EA/72*

TUSSAUD, Dorothy Allen (d 1897) EA/98*

TUSSAUD, Francis (d 1873 [73]) waxwork exhibitor? EA/74*

TUSSAUD, Joseph (d 1892 [61]) EA/93*

TUSSER, Thomas (fl c. 1540) actor DA

TUSTIN, John T. (d 1886 [40]) musician EA/87*

TUTCHIN, John (d 1707 [47]) dramatist CP/1-3, GT

TUTE, Agnes Clare [Mrs. James T. Tute] (d 1886 [33]) EA/88*

TUTE, James (d 1870) proprietor EA/71*

TUTE, Mrs. James T. see Tute, Agnes Clare

TUTE, John (d 1885) musician EA/86*

TUTE, Mrs. John see Tute, Mrs. M. M.

TUTE, Mary Elizabeth [Mrs. Sam Tute] (d 1894) EA/95*

TUTE, Mrs. M. M. [Mrs. John Tute] (d 1876 [26]) EA/77*

TUTE, Mrs. Sam see Tute, Mary Elizabeth

TUTHILL, Harry (d 1863) Irish actor HAS

TUTIN, Dorothy (b 1930) English actress AAS, BE, ES, PDT, TW/24, WWT/12-16

TUTON, E. S. (d 1867 [64]) proprietor EA/68*

TUTTLE, Day (b 1902) American director, actor, dramatist, educator BE

TUTTON, Mrs. George S. see Leslie, Grace

TWAIN, Mark (1835-1910) American dramatist ES, NTH

TWAIN, Michael (b 1936) American actor TW/25

TWAIN, Norman (b 1930) American producer, director BE

TWAITS, William (c. 1770-1814) English actor COC, OC/1-3, SR

TWAITS, William (1781-1814) English actor CDP, HAS

TWAITS, Mrs. William [Miss E. A. Westray; Mrs. Villiers] (1787-1813) English actress HAS

TWEDDELL, Frank (1895-1971) Indian actor TW/5, 7, 28

TWEDDELL, Oliver L. (d 1898) scene artist EA/99*

TWEED, Tommy (d 1971 [64]) performer BP/56*

TWEEDALE, Harold (d 1909) manager EA/10*

TWELVETREES, Helen (d 1958 [49]) actress TW/14

TWIBELL, Mrs. (d 1893) EA/94*

TWIBELL, Miss (fl 1842) American actress HAS

TWIBELL, William (d 1890 [56]) EA/91*

TWIGG, Lieut. James (d 1884 [66]) business manager EA/85*

TWINBERROW, William Henry see Wolston, Henry

TWINEM, Leo L. (d 1968 [78]) performer BP/53*

TWISS, Mrs. see Kemble, Frances

TWIST, John (d 1976 [77]) producer/ director/choreographer BP/60*

TWISTLETON, Mrs. (d c. 1808/09) see Stanley, Mrs.

TWOMEY, John (b 1948) American actor TW/28

TWYBELL, Miss see Flynn, Mrs. Thomas

TWYFORD, J. Henry (b 1880) English actor, stage manager GRB/1-2

TWYFORD, Warner (d 1968 [57]) critic BP/52*

TYARS, Frank (1848-1918/19) English actor GRB/3-4, OAA/1-2, WWT/1-3

TYERS, Jonathan (d 1767) proprietor DNB

TYLER, Mr. (d 1851) actress HAS

TYLER, Charles (d 1972 [32]) performer BP/57*

TYLER, Elizabeth Priscilla see Tyler, Mrs. Robert

TYLER, George (d 1878) musician EA/79*

TYLER, George Crouse (1867-1946) American producing manager DAB, GRB/2-4, NTH, TW/2, WWA/2, WWM, WWS, WWT/1-9

TYLER, George H. (d 1884) actor, manager CDP

TYLER, Gladys (d 1972 [79]) performer BP/56*

TYLER, Janet American actress TW/1

TYLER, Joseph (1751-1823) actor HAS

TYLER, Joseph (d 1883) musician EA/84*

TYLER, Joseph (d 1904 [93]) musical director EA/05*

TYLER, Mrs. Joseph (fl 1795-96) English actress HAS

TYLER, Joseph Saunders (b 1811) actor CDP

TYLER, Judy (d 1957 [24]) actress TW/14

TYLER, Leslie (d 1912 [48]) singer EA/13*

TYLER, Marie [Mrs. Leo Dryden] (d 1905 [30]) burlesque actress EA/06*

TYLER, Odette [Mrs. R. D. McLean] (1869-1936) American actress GRB/3-4, SR, WWA/2, WWS, WWT/1-5

TYLER, Parker (d 1974 [70]) critic BP/59*

TYLER, Richard (b 1932) American actor TW/3

TYLER, Mrs. Robert (1816-89) actress CDP, SR

TYLER, Royall (1757-1826) American dramatist CDP, COC, DAB, EAP, ES, HJD, MH, NTH, OC/1-3, RE, RJ, SR, WWA/H

TYLER, Thomas (1826-1902) English scholar DNB

TYLER, Tom (d 1954 [50]) actor BE*

TYLER, T. Texas (d 1972 [55]) composer/lyricist BP/56*

TYLER, William (d 1864 [65]) EA/72*

TYNAN, Brandon (1879-1967) Irish/American actor, dramatist TW/23, WWT/4-10

TYNAN, Kenneth [Peacock] (b 1927) English critic AAS, BE, CB, CH, COC, NTH, PDT, WWT/13-16

TYNDALL, Kate (d 1919) actress BE*, WWT/14*

TYNE, George (b 1917) American actor TW/2, 13-15

TYRA, Dan (b 1936) American actor TW/24-25

TYREE, Bessie (b 1870) American actress WWM

TYREE, Elizabeth (fl 1889-1907) American actress PP/3, WWS

TYRER, Miss (fl 1800-05) singer TD/1-2

TYRER, Sarah see Liston, Mrs. John

TYRREL, Mrs. M. A. (b 1815) English actress HAS

TYRREL, Thomas Moore (fl 1852) English actor HAS

TYRRELL, Brad (b 1943) American actor TW/30

TYRRELL, David (b 1916) American actor TW/3

TYRRELL, Henry (b 1865/66) American dramatist GRB/3, WWM

TYRRELL, Mrs. H. F. see Holt, Issy

TYRRELL, Mrs. Joseph see Tyrrell, Lucy Alice

TYRRELL, Kittie [Mrs. Harry Ewins] (d 1894 [35]) actress EA/96*

TYRRELL, Lucy Alice [Mrs. Joseph Tyrrell] (d 1869) EA/70*

TYRRELL, Rose (d 1934 [75]) dancer BE*, WWT/14*

TYRRELL, Ruby [Alice Staunton] (d 1895) actress EA/96*

TYRRELL, Susan American actress TW/26

TYSALL, Harriett (d 1881 [21]) singer EA/82*

TYSON, Caroline (fl 1854-56) American actress HAS

TYSON, Cicely (b 1939?) American actress CB, TW/24, WWT/16

TYSON, Davey (d 1976 [73]) performer BP/60*

TYSON, Josephine see Kent, Mrs. Fred S.

TYSON, Ruth M. (d 1971 [58]) producer/director/choreographer BP/56*

TYSON, Tara American actress TW/27

TYZACK, Margaret actress WWT/15-16

- U -

UBALDINI, Petruccio (fl 1576) Italian actor DA

UDALL, Charles (d 1884) proprietor EA/85*

UDALL, Nicholas (1505-56) English dramatist COC, CP/2-3, DNB, ES, FGF, HP, MH, NTH, OC/1-3, PDT

UDELL, Peter lyricist CD

UFFNER, Frank manager CDP

UGARTE, Floro M. (d 1975 [91]) composer/lyricist BP/60*

UGGAMS, Eloise (d 1972 [75])
performer BP/57*
UGGAMS, Leslie (b 1943) Amer-
ican singer, actress CB,
TW/23-25
UHDE, Hermann (1914-65) Ger-
man singer WWA/4
UHL, May see Buckley, May
ULANOVA, Galina (b 1910)
Russian dancer CB
ULLENDORF, Jacquie (b 1945)
American actress TW/29
ULLMAN, Bernard manager
CDP
ULLMAN, James Ramsey (d 1971
[63]) dramatist BP/56*
ULLMAN, Robert (b 1928) Amer-
ican press representative BE
ULLMAN, S. George (d 1975
[82]) agent BP/60*
ULMANN, Doris (d 1972 [56])
performer BP/57*
ULMAR, Geraldine (1862-1932)
American actress, singer
CDP, DP, WWT/6
ULMER, Edgar G. (d 1972 [68])
producer/director/choreographer
BP/57*
ULMER, Lizzie May actress CDP
ULMER, Roch (d 1975) producer/
director/choreographer BP/
59*
ULPH, Mrs. Harry see Lauri,
Stella
ULPH, Henry (d 1897 [37]) pro-
prietor EA/98*
ULRIC, Lenore (1892/94-1970)
American actress BE, TW/
3-13, 27, WWT/4-11
ULRICH, Charles (1859?-1941)
dramatist CB
ULRICH, Pauline (b 1835) actress
CDP
ULRICO, Pietro (d 1888 [40])
musician EA/89*
UMANN, Olga (d 1972 [57]) per-
former BP/57*
UMEKO, Miyoshi (b 1929) Japan-
ese actress BE
UNDERELL (fl 1602) actor DA
UNDERHILL, Cave (c. 1634-
c. 1710) English actor CDP,
COC, DNB, OC/1-3
UNDERHILL, Edward (d 1964
[65]) actor BE*
UNDERHILL, John Garrett (1876-
1946) American dramatist,
critic, producer WWA/2

UNDERHILL, Nicholas (fl 1624)
actor DA
UNDERWOOD, Cecil (d 1906) actor
EA/07*
UNDERWOOD, Frank (d 1917)
actor EA/18*
UNDERWOOD, Franklyn (d 1940
[63]) American actor BE*,
BP/25*
UNDERWOOD, Grace see Barry,
Christine
UNDERWOOD, Isabelle (fl 1895-
1907) American actress, singer
WWS
UNDERWOOD, John (c. 1590-1624)
English actor COC, DA, GT,
NTH, OC/1-3
UNDERWOOD, T. (fl 1782) drama-
tist CP/3
UNGER, Gladys B. [Gladys B.
Goodman] (d 1940 [55]) Ameri-
can dramatist GRB/4, WWM,
WWT/1-9, WWW/3
UNGER, Stella (d 1970 [65]) dram-
atist BP/54*
UNRUH, Walther (1898-1973) Ger-
man theatre technician, educator
BE
UNSWORTH, Evelyn [Mrs. J. B.
Ashley] (d 1892 [26]) actress
EA/93*
UNSWORTH, James (1838-75) Eng-
lish minstrel HAS
UNWIN, George actor, manager
GRB/1
UPSHER, Peter (d 1963 [70]) per-
former BE*
UPTON, Frances (d 1975 [71])
performer BP/60*
UPTON, Leonard (b 1901) English
actor WWT/6-9
UPTON, Robert (fl 1750-52) English
actor, manager WWA/H
UPTON, Robert Michael Garbois
(d 1891 [16]) musician, com-
poser EA/92*
URBAN, Joseph (1872-1933) Aus-
trian/American architect, de-
signer COC, DAB, ES, NTH,
OC/1-3
URE, Mary (1933-75) Scottish ac-
tress BE, ES, TW/28, WWT/
12-15
URICH, John (1849-1939) West In-
dian composer WWW/3
URICH, Tom Canadian actor TW/
23, 26-28
URQUHART, Isabelle [Mrs. Guy

Standing] (1865-1907) American
actress CDP, WWS
URQUHART, Mary Sinclair see
Urquhart, Molly
URQUHART, Molly [née Mary
Sinclair Urquhart] (d 1977)
Scottish actress WWT/11-14
URSO, Camilla (1842-1902) musi-
cian CDP
USCO CD
USERA, Ramon (d 1972 [67])
composer/lyricist BP/57*
USHER, Dora (d 1881 [27]) ac-
tress EA/82*
USHER, Graham (d 1975 [36])
performer BP/59*
USHER, Lancelot (d 1916 [44])
EA/17*
USHER, Luke (d 1815) American
actor, manager HAS, WWA/H
USHER, Noble B. (b c. 1770)
actor SR
USHER, Richard (1785-1843)
pantomimist, clown CDP,
DNB
USTINOV, Peter [Alexander] (b
1921) English actor, dramatist,
producer, director AAS, BE,
CB, CD, CH, COC, ES, MD,
MH, MWD, OC/2-3, PDT,
TW/14-19, WWT/10-16
USTINOV, Tamara English ac-
tress TW/30

- V -

VACCARO, Brenda (b 1939) Amer-
ican actress BE, TW/18-20,
22-25, 27, WWT/15-16
VACHE, William A. (d 1849)
American actor HAS
VACHELL, Horace Annesley
(1861-1955) English dramatist
GRB/3, WWT/3-11, WWW/5
VAGUE, Vera (d 1974) actress
BP/59*, WWT/16*
VAHANIAN, Marc (b 1956) Amer-
ican actor TW/26
VAIDIS, Lizzie [Mrs. J. H. Al-
len] (d 1911 [46]) trapezist
EA/12*
VAIL, Mr. American circus
performer HAS
VAIL, Lester (d 1959 [59])
American actor, director
WWT/7-8
VAILE, Amy see Fanchette,

Amy
VAILLAND, Roger (d 1965 [57])
dramatist BP/49*
VAJDA, Ernest (1887-1954) Hun-
garian dramatist TW/10, WWT/
8-11
VAL, Mons. (fl 1796) English actor
HAS
VAL, Mme. (fl 1796) English ac-
tress HAS
VAL, Paul (d 1962 [75]) actor,
producer BE*
VALAIDA [Valaida Snow] American
actress, singer WWT/8-10
VALASCO, David see Belasco,
David
VALDARE, Sunny Jim (d 1962
[88]) American performer BE*
VALDO, Mrs. H. see Chadwick,
Sophia
VALDO, Harry (d 1917) EA/18*
VALDO, Pat (d 1970 [89]) circus
director BP/55*
VALE, Michael (b 1922) American
actor TW/22-26, 28-29
VALE, Samuel (1797-1848) English
actor CDP, OX
VALE, Mrs. W. (d 1882 [42])
EA/83*
VALE, Will (d 1889) music-hall
acting manager EA/90*
VALENCEY, Miss (fl 1812?)
dancer CDP
VALENCY, Maurice (b 1903) Amer-
ican educator, dramatist BE
VALENTI, Michael (d 1943) Amer-
ican actor TW/24-26
VALENTIA, George, Lord Viscount
(b 1769) dramatist CP/3
VALENTINE, Miss (fl 1789) see
Taylor, Mrs.
VALENTINE [Archibald Thomas
Pechey] (b 1876) lyricist, dram-
atist WWT/5-8
"VALENTINE" see D'Iffanger,
Thomas Howard Paul
VALENTINE, Dickie (d 1971 [41])
performer BP/55*
VALENTINE, Gertrude [Mrs.
Lauderdale Maitland] (d 1907
[26]) actress EA/08*
VALENTINE, Grace (1884/91-1964)
American actress TW/3, 5-12,
21, WWT/6-13
VALENTINE, James (b 1933)
American actor TW/18
VALENTINE, James see Balen-
tyne, James

VALENTINE, Paul (d 1924 [85]) dancer, ballet master BE*, WWT/14*

VALENTINE, Paul (b 1919) American actor, dancer, choreographer BE, TW/1-3, 9-12, 14-16

VALENTINE, Sidney [or Sydney] (1865-1919) actor EA/95, GRB/1-4, WWT/1-3

VALENTINE, T. C. (d 1909) actor WWT/14*

VALENTINE, Thomas (d 1878 [87]) composer EA/79*

VALENTINE, Dr. William (d 1865/66) actor CDP, HAS

VALENTINI, Eliza (fl 1856?) CDP

VALENTINO, Rudolph (1895-1926) Italian dancer, actor WWA/1

VALENTINOFF, Val see Valentine, Paul

VALENTY, Lili Polish actress TW/2

VALERIO, Theresa (d 1964 [70+]) performer BE*

VALERO, Fernando (1854/57-1914) Spanish singer ES

VALERIUS, John (fl 1819?) freak CDP

VALINOTE, Merrick D. (d 1976 [78]) conductor BP/60*

VALK, Frederick (d 1956 [55]) German/Czech actor AAS, WWT/10-11

VALLANCE, W. S. (d 1903) teacher of elocution EA/05*

VALLEE, Henrietta see De Bar, Mrs. Benedict

VALLEE, Rudy (d 1901) American actor, singer, musician, composer BE, CB

VALLEE SISTERS, The (fl 1836) American actress HAS

VALLENTINE, Benjamin Bennaton (1843-1926) English/American dramatist DAB, WWA/2

VALLERIA, Alwina Lohmann (b 1848) singer CDP

VALLETTI, Cesare (b 1922) Italian singer ES

VALLI, Valli [Valli Knust] (1882-1927) German actress GRB/4, WWM, WWT/1-5

VALLI, Virginia (d 1968 [70]) performer BP/53*

VALLIERE, Florence actress CDP

VALLIN, Ninon (d 1961 [75]) singer BE*

VALLIQUIETTO, Margaret Rose see Knight, June

VALLO, Domenico (b 1803) musician, writer CDP

VALLON, Michael (b 1897) American actor TW/2

VALOIS, Ninette de see De Valois, Ninette

VALOR, Henrietta American actress TW/29-30

VALPY, Richard (fl 1795-1803) dramatist CP/3

VALROSE, Lizzie singer, actress CDP

VAMP, Hugo see O'Neill, J. R.

VAN, Billy (d 1973 [61]) performer BP/58*

VAN, Billy B. (1870-1950) American actor SR, TW/7, WWA/3, WWT/5-7

VAN, Bobby (b 1930/32) American dancer, singer, actor TW/27-29, WWT/15-16

VAN, Charley (d 1963 [80]) performer BE*

VAN, Gus (1887-1968) American actor TW/3, 24

VAN, Samye (d 1972 [61]) performer BP/57*

VAN, Shirley (b 1927) American actress TW/3

VAN AKEN, Gretchen (b 1940) American actress TW/23, 28-29

VAN ALSTYNE, Egbert Aanson (1882-1951) American songwriter BE*, BP/36*

VAN AMBURGH, Isaac A. (1812-65) American actor CDP, HAS, ES

VAN ARK, Joan (b 1943) American actress TW/27

VAN BEERS, Stanley (1911-61) English actor WWT/12-13

VAN BENSCHOTEN, Stephen (b 1943) American actor TW/28, 30

VAN BEUREN, Mrs. A. H. see Bernard, Dorothy

VAN BEUREN, Archbold (d 1974 [68]) publisher BP/59*

VAN BIENE, Auguste (1850-1913) Dutch actor, composer GRB/1-4, WWM, WWT/1

VANBRUGGEN, Mrs. [Mrs. Mountford] actress GT, TD/2

VANBRUGH, Dame Irene [Mrs. Dion G. Boucicault] (1872-1949) English actress AAS, CDP, COC, DNB, EA/95, ES, GRB/1-4, OC/1-3, TW/6, WWT/1-10, WWW/4

VANBRUGH, Sir John (1664-1726) English dramatist, architect CDP, COC, CP/1-3, DNB, ES, GT, HP, MH, NTH, OC/1-3, PDT, RE, SR, TD/1-2

VANBRUGH, Prudence (b 1902) English actress WWT/5-7

VANBRUGH, Violet [Mrs. Arthur Bourchier] (1867-1942) English actress CB, CDP, COC, DNB, DP, EA/96, ES, GRB/1-4, OC/1-3, SR, WWS, WWT/1-9, WWW/4

VAN BUREN, A. H. (1879-1965) American actor TW/22, WWM

VAN BUREN, Mabel (d 1947 [69]) actress TW/4

VAN BUSKIRK, June [Mrs. Percival J. Mitchell] (b 1880/82) American actress GRB/2-4, WWS, WWT/1-5

VANCE, Alfred Glenville [Alfred Peck Stevens] (d 1888 [49/50]) comic singer EA/90*, WWT/14*

VANCE, Charles [né Goldblatt] (b 1929) Irish actor, director, producing manager WWT/15-16

VANCE, Eunice singer, dancer CDP

VANCE, The Great (1839-88) English music-hall performer COC, OC/1-3

VANCE, Kate [née Warwick] (1840-67) French actress HAS

VANCE, Nina American producer, director BE

VANCE, Thomas (d 1889 [57]) pantomimist, singer EA/90*

VANCE, Vivian (b 1914) American actress TW/4

VAN CLEAVE, Nathan (d 1970 [60]) composer/lyricist BP/55*

VAN CLEVE, Edith (b 1903) American talent representative, actress, director BE

VANDAMM, Florence (d 1966

[83]) English photographer TW/22

VAN DAMM, Vivian (d 1960 [71]) manager BE*, WWT/14*

VANDEGRIFT, B. F. (d 1888) aeronaut EA/89*

VANDENBURGH, Theodore H. [Jack Bunsby] (d 1869 [33]) actor HAS

VANDENHOFF, Charles H. (d 1890) English actor BE*, EA/91*

VANDENHOFF, Charlotte Elizabeth (1818-60) English actress CDP, COC, DNB, ES, HAS, OC/1-3

VANDENHOFF, George (b 1839) English actor HAS

VANDENHOFF, Mrs. George [née Makeath] (1835-85) actress CDP, HAS

VANDENHOFF, George Charles (1813-85) English actor CDP, COC, DAB, ES, OC/1-3, SR, WWA/H

VANDENHOFF, Mrs. H. (d 1870) actress EA/71*

VANDENHOFF, Henry (d 1888) English actor SR

VANDENHOFF, Mrs. Henry (d 1870) actress BE*, WWT/14*

VANDENHOFF, John M. (1790-1861) English actor CDP, COC, DNB, ES, HAS, OC/1-3

VANDENHOFF, Kate (d 1942 [73]) actress BE*, WWT/14*

VANDENHOFF, Mary E. see Vandenhoff, Mrs. George

VANDERBILT, Cornelius, Jr. (d 1974 [76]) journalist BP/59*

VANDERBILT, Gertrude (d 1960 [70]) American actress, singer TW/16

VANDERBILT, Gloria (b 1924) American actress, writer BE, TW/11

VANDERBILT, Jeanne Murray American actress TW/24

VANDERCOOK, John W. (d 1963 [60]) English writer BE*

VANDERFELT, E. H. (d 1900) actor EA/02*, WWT/14*

VANDERGRIFT, Howard Anderson see Kyle, Howard

VANDERMERE, John Byron (d 1786 [43]) actor TD/1-2

VANDERPOOL, Frederick W. (1877/86-1947) American actor, composer, singer SR, WWA/2

VANDERSTOP, Cornelius (fl
1777) dramatist CP/3
VAN der VLIS, Diana (b 1935)
Canadian actress BE, TW/
15, 30
VANDERVORT, Philip (b 1945)
American actor TW/22-23
VAN-DE-VELDE (d 1890 [36])
acrobat, clown EA/91*
VANDEVER, Michael American
actor TW/16
VAN DEVERE, Trish (b 1947)
American actress TW/23
VANDIS, Titos (b 1917) Greek
actor TW/22-24, 26-29
VAN DOREN, Mark (1894-1972)
American dramatist BE
VAN DREELEN, John (b 1922)
Dutch actor TW/7
VAN DRESSER, Marcia (d 1937
[60]) American singer WWA/1
VAN DRUTEN, John (1901-57)
English/American dramatist
AAS, CB, COC, ES, HJD,
MD, MH, MWD, NTH, OC/
1-3, PDT, TW/5-8, 14,
WWA/3, WWT/6-12, WWW/5
VAN DYCK, Ernest (1861-1923)
Belgian singer CDP, ES,
WWA/3
VAN DYKE, Dick (b 1925) Amer-
ican actor, comedian CB, ES
VAN DYKE, Marcia American
actress TW/7-12
VANE, Daphne (d 1966 [49])
dancer TW/23
VANE, Dorothy (d 1947 [76])
actress, singer BE*, WWT/
14*
VANE, Helen see Sugden, Mrs.
Charles
VANE, Richard Scottish actor
GRB/1
VANE, Sutton (1880/85-1963)
English dramatist, actor ES,
MH, MWD, NTH
VANE, W. H. [James Doran]
(d 1891 [33]) banjoist EA/92*
VANE-TEMPEST, Francis Adolphus
(1863-1932) actor GRB/1-4,
WWT/1-5
VAN EYCK, Peter (d 1969 [56])
performer BP/54*
VAN FLEET, Jo (b 1922) Amer-
ican actor AAS, BE, ES,
TW/22, WWT/13-16
VAN GORDON, Cyrena (d 1964
[67]) American singer TW/20,

WWA/4
VAN GRIETHUYSEN, Ted [né
Theodore André] (b 1934) Amer-
ican actor, director, designer
BE, TW/22-23, 25-26, 29,
WWT/15-16
VAN GYSEGHEM, André (b 1906)
English actor, producer, director
WWT/7-16
VAN HAGEN, Peter Albrecht (fl
1774-1800) Dutch composer
WWA/H
VAN HEUSEN, James [né Edward
Chester Babcock] (b 1913) Amer-
ican composer, producer BE,
CB, WWT/15-16
VANHOOK, Mrs. W. F. [née Mary
Ann Lee] (fl 1847) dancer
CDP, ES, HAS
VAN HORN, Rollin (1882-1964)
American costumier, designer,
director BE
VANINI, Francesca see Boschi,
Signora Giuseppe Maria
VANISON, Dolores (b 1942) Ameri-
can actress TW/27-28
VAN ITALLIE, Jean-Claude (b 1936)
Belgian/American dramatist,
director CD, CH, MH, MWD,
WWT/15-16
VAN LEER, Arnold (d 1975 [80])
performer BP/60*
VANLEER, Jay (b 1931) American
actor TW/28-29
VAN LENNEP, William (1906-62)
American curator, scholar BE*
VANLOO, Albert (d 1920) drama-
tist BE*, WWT/14*
VAN MILL, Arnold (b 1921) Dutch
singer ES
VANN, Al (d 1973 [73]) composer/
lyricist BP/58*
VANNE, Marda (d 1970) South Afri-
can actress WWT/6-14
VAN NOORDEN, P. E. (d 1896
[70]) EA/97*
VAN NOORDEN, Walter (d 1916
[50]) managing director EA/17*
VAN NOSTRAND, Morris Abbott (b
1911) American publisher, liter-
ary representative BE
VANNUYS, Ed (b 1930) American
actor TW/25-26, 28, 30
VAN NUYS, Eric (b 1933) American
actor TW/18
VANONI, Marie (fl 1892?) dancer,
singer CDP
VAN ORDEN, Charles (d 1918)

EA/19*
VAN ORE, Harry (b 1944) Ameri-
can actor TW/26
VAN PARYS, Georges (d 1971
[68]) composer/lyricist BP/
55*
VAN PATTEN, Dick (b 1928)
American actor BE, TW/2-4,
25-26, 30, WWT/11-16
VAN PATTEN, Joyce (b 1934)
American actress BE, TW/
2-4, 12-13, 20, WWT/15-16
VAN PEEBLES, Melvin actor,
dramatist, composer, lyri-
cist, director, producer CD,
WWT/16
VAN PELT, Homer (d 1973)
photographer BP/58*
VAN ROOTEN, Luis (1906-73)
Mexican actor BE, TW/30
VAN ROOY, Anton (d 1932 [62])
Dutch singer BE*, BP/17*
VAN ROSEM, Robert E. (b 1904)
Russian/American designer
ES
VAN SABER, Mrs. Lilla Alex-
ander (d 1968 [56]) performer
BP/53*
VAN SCOTT, Glory actress
TW/24-27
VAN SCOYK, Robert (b 1928)
American writer BE
VAN SICKLE, Raymond (d 1964
[79]) American actor, drama-
tist TW/3, 8, 21
VANSITTART, Sir Robert G.
(b 1881) dramatist WWT/
3-4, 9
VAN SLOAN, Edward (d 1964
[82]) American actor BE*
VANSTAVOREN, Jackson P.
(fl 1836) American call boy,
actor? HAS
VANSTAVOREN, Joseph (d 1852)
American call boy, actor
HAS
VAN STUDDIFORD, Grace [Grace
Quive] (1873-1927) American
actress, singer SR, WWT/
1-5
VAN THAL, Dennis (b 1909)
English composer, conductor
WWT/8-10
VAN TULY, Helen (d 1964 [73])
actress, educator BE*
VAN VECHTEN, Carl (1880-
1964) American critic HJD
VAN VOLKENBURG, Ellen

American actress, producer
WWT/7-9
VAN VOOREN, Monique (b 1933)
Belgian actress, singer BE
VAN WILDER, Philip (fl 1550)
musician DA
VAN ZANDT, Mrs. [Jenny Elitz]
(fl 1863-67) singer HAS
VAN ZANDT, Marie (1858/61-
1918/19) American singer ES,
WWA/1
VAN ZANDT, Porter (b 1923)
American stage manager, di-
rector, actor BE
VAN ZILE, Edward S. (b 1863)
American dramatist WWM
VANZINI, Jenny Van Zandt (fl
1864) singer CDP [see also:
Van Zandt, Mrs.]
VARDEN, Dorothy [Mrs. James
Dallas] (d 1913) EA/14*
VARDEN, Evelyn (1893/95-1958)
American actress TW/2-13,
15, WWT/9-12
VARELA, Nina (b 1917) American
actress TW/23
VARENNES, Julie de (fl 1821-23)
dancer CDP
VARESI, Gilda (b 1887) Italian ac-
tress WWT/4-9
VARLEY, Louisa Rose (d 1908
[75]) actress EA/09*
VARLEY, Nelson (d 1883 [39])
actor? singer? EA/85*
VARLEY, Tom F. (d 1895 [49])
actor? EA/96*
VARLEY, Violet [Mrs. Joseph
Tapley] (d 1895) actress EA/96*
VARNA, Elizabeth (d 1895) EA/
96*
VARNAY, Astrid (b 1918) American
singer CB, ES
VARNEL, Marcel [né Marcel Le-
Bozec] (1894-1947) French pro-
ducer, director WWT/10
VARNEY, Louis (d 1908) American
composer ES
VARRATO, Edmond (b 1919) Amer-
ican actor TW/28-29
VARREY, Edwin (d 1907 [80])
American actor BE*, GRB/3*,
WWT/14*
VARVARO, Gloria (d 1976 [61])
performer BP/60*
VASCO [E. A. Bedford] (b 1869)
English vaudevillian WWM
VASNICK, Andrew (b 1926) Ameri-
can actor TW/25-26

VASQUEZ, Manuel (d 1970 [19])
performer BP/54*
VASQUEZ, Myrna (d 1975 [40])
performer BP/59*
VASSAR, Queenie (d 1960 [89])
Scottish actress, singer
TW/17
VASSEUX, Jean-Claude (b 1940)
Venezuelan actor TW/25
VATSKE, Roberta (b 1945) Amer-
ican actress TW/25
VATTELLINA, Sig. (fl 1847)
singer HAS
VATTEMARE, Alexander see
Alexandre
VAUGHAN, Miss see Christian,
Mrs.
VAUGHAN, Ada [Edith Donnahey]
(d 1893) burlesque actress
EA/94*
VAUGHAN, Arthur C. (d 1900
[45]) actor EA/01*
VAUGHAN, Blanche (1859-1919)
American actress SR
VAUGHAN, David (b 1924) Eng-
lish actor TW/14-16, 25-27
VAUGHAN, Gladys American
director BE
VAUGHAN, Gus see Julien,
Paul
VAUGHAN, Henry (d 1779) actor
COC
VAUGHAN, Henry (d 1881 [37])
actor EA/82*
VAUGHAN, Herbert (d 1896
[27]) music-hall performer
EA/97*
VAUGHAN, Hilda Welsh dramatist
WWT/9-13
VAUGHAN, James Jones (d 1871
[59]) comic singer EA/72*
VAUGHAN, Kate [Catherine
Candelon] (c. 1852-1903) Eng-
lish actress CDP, COC,
DNB, DP, OAA/2, OC/1-3
VAUGHAN, Olea Bull (d 1911)
actress SR
VAUGHAN, Sarah (b 1924) Amer-
ican singer CB
VAUGHAN, Stuart (b 1925) Amer-
ican director, actor, drama-
tist AAS, BE, WWT/14-16
VAUGHAN, Susie [Susan Mary
Charlotte Candelin] (1853-
1950) English actress DP,
EA/96, WWT/3-10
VAUGHAN, T. B. (d 1928) pro-
ducer, manager BE*, WWT/
14*

VAUGHAN, Thomas (fl 1772-1820)
dramatist CP/2-3, DNB, GT,
TD/1-2
VAUGHAN, William Russell see
Vaun, Russell
VAUGHAN WILLIAMS, Ralph (1872-
1958) English composer CB,
DNB, ES, WWA/3, WWW/5
VAUGHN, Heidi American actress
TW/24
VAUGHN, Hilda (d 1957 [60])
American actress TW/3-8, 14
VAUGHN, Theresa [Mrs. William
H. Mestayer] (d 1903 [43])
comedienne CDP
VAUGHT, George (d 1975 [46])
producer/director/choreographer
BP/59*
VAUL, Polly [Mrs. F. Fredericks]
(d 1894) actress EA/95*
VAUN, Russell [William Russell
Vaughan] (b 1872) English actor,
dramatist GRB/1-4
VAZ DIAS, Selma (b 1911) Dutch
actress WWT/8-15
VAZQUEZ, Vicente (b 1975 [60])
performer BP/60*
VEAL, George see Collier, Joel
VEBER, Pierre (b 1869) French
dramatist, critic WWT/4
VEDOVELLI, Umberto (b 1972
[60]) conductor BP/57*
VEDRENNE, John E. (1867-1930)
English manager AAS, COC,
ES, GRB/1-4, OC/1-3, WWT/
1-6, WWW/3
VEDRENNE, Mrs. John E. see
Blair, Phyllis
VEGA, Jose (b 1920) American
manager, producer, director
BE
VEGERIUS, Paul (fl 1693) translator
CP/1-3
VEIDT, Conrad (1893-1943) German
actor BE*, WWT/14*
VEIDT, Lily Hungarian talent
representative BE
VEILLER, Anthony (b 1903) Ameri-
can manager ES
VEILLER, Bayard (1869/71-1943)
American dramatist CB, ES,
WWT/4-9
VEJAR, Harry (b 1968 [78]) per-
former BP/52*
VELANCHE, Harry [G. H. Wills]
(d 1916 [38]) animal trainer
EA/17*

VELAZQUEZ, Conchita (d 1974)
  performer BP/58*
VELEX, Lupe [Guadeloupe Velez
  de Villabos] (1909-44) Mexican
  actress, dancer TW/1,
  WWT/9
VELIE, Jay (b 1892) American
  actor TW/7-8, 23-24, 27, 30
VENABLE, Reginald (d 1974
  [48]) performer BP/59*
VENABLES, Ann see Arne,
  Mrs. Michael, III
VENAFRA, M. (fl 1836) actor
  CDP
VENARD, Celeste (d 1909) dancer
  EA/10*
VENDOME, Sidney (d 1907) per-
  former? EA/08*
VENESS, Amy (d 1960 [84]) ac-
  tress BE*, WWT/14*
VENN, Topsy (d 1897) actress
  CDP
VENNARD [or Vennar], Richard
  (fl 1602) dramatist FGF
VENNE, Lottie (1852-1928)
  English actress CDP, COC,
  DP, GRB/1-4, OAA/2, OC/
  1-3, WWT/1-5
VENNING, Kate (d 1917) critic
  EA/18*
VENNING, Una (b 1893) English
  actress WWT/5-14
VENOI, Jeannie [Jeannie Elliott]
  (d 1892) music-hall singer
  EA/93*
VENORA, Lee (b 1932) American
  singer, actress BE, TW/22
VENTANTONIO, John (b 1943)
  American actor TW/26-27
VENTH, Carl (1860-1938) Ger-
  man composer WWA/1
VENTO, Harry (d 1899 [66])
  ventriloquist EA/00*
VENTO, Lillie (d 1918) EA/19*
VENTON, F. W. (d 1918) EA/
  19*
VENTURA, Dick (d 1973 [80s])
  performer BP/58*
VENUA, Frederic Marc Antoine
  (d 1872 [86]) composer EA/
  73*
VENUTA, Benay [née Venuta Rose
  Crooke] (b 1911/12) American
  actress, singer BE, TW/9,
  14-15, 22-23, 29, WWT/15-16
VERA, Mme. (d 1867 [83])
  singer CDP
VERA-ELLEN (b 1926) American

dancer, actress CB
VERBRUGGEN, John (d 1708) actor
  DNB
VERBRUGGEN, Mrs. John see
  Mountfort, Susanna Percival
VERCHININA, Nina dancer WWT/
  9-12
VERDI, Ruby (d 1918) actress
  GRB/1
VERDON, Gwen (b 1925/26) Ameri-
  can actress, singer, dancer
  AAS, BE, CB, TW/9-20, 22-23,
  28, WWT/14-16
VERDY, Violette (b 1933) French
  dancer CB
VERE, Charles (d 1876) actor
  EA/77*
VERE, Edward, Earl of Oxford
  dramatist FGF
VERE, Fred R. [Frederick Vere
  Podmore] (d 1897) actor EA/98*
VEREEN, Ben (b 1946) American
  actor, singer, dancer TW/28-
  30, WWT/16
VERGA, Giovanni (1840-1922) Italian
  dramatist COC
VERGERIUS, Paul (fl 1693) see
  Vegerius, Paul
VERHOEVEN, Paul (d 1975 [74])
  performer BP/59*
VERITY, Agnes actress CDP
VERITY, Sarah (d 1850) American
  actress HAS
VERITY, Mrs. William (d 1890)
  EA/91*
VERLINO, Charles [George
  Brookes] (d 1906 [64]) harlequin
  EA/07*
VERMILYE, Kate Jordan (d 1926)
  Irish dramatist WWA/1
VERMILYEA, Harold (1889-1958)
  American actor TW/2-3, 14,
  WWT/9-11
VERNE, Arthur (d 1912 [48]) come-
  dian EA/13*
VERNE, Fred (d 1902) comedian
  EA/03*
VERNE, Jules (d 1905) French
  writer GRB/1
VERNER, Charles (d 1869 [39])
  actor EA/70*, WWT/14*
VERNER, Charles Erin (fl 1887)
  Irish comedian, singer SR
VERNER, Linda (d 1892) actress?
  singer? EA/93*
VERNER, Thomas (d 1900) actor
  EA/01*
VERNEUIL, Louis (1893-1952)

French dramatist, actor, manager TW/9, WWT/4, 8-11, WWW/5

VERNEY, Guy (d 1970) performer BP/55*

VERNO, Jerry (1895-1975) English actor WWT/7-15

VERNO, Jess (d 1908 [38]) variety performer EA/09*

VERNON, Mr. (d c. 1800?) actor TD/1-2

VERNON, Mr. (fl 1827-49) actor HAS

VERNON, Anne [Mrs. W. H. Vernon] (d 1912 [77]) EA/13*

VERNON, Anne (b 1926) French actress TW/10

VERNON, Charles [George E. J. Williams] (b 1875) English actor GRB/1

VERNON, Mrs. Charles see Stanley, Lilian M.

VERNON, Clari singer, actress CDP

VERNON, Mrs. Darville see Vernon, Louie

VERNON, E. R. (d 1880) actor EA/81*

VERNON, Fanny see Sinclair, Mrs. Harry

VERNON, Flo [Betsy Sotherden] (d 1912 [34]) variety performer EA/13*

VERNON, Frank (1875-1940) Indian/English actor, director, producer WWT/2-9, WWW/3

VERNON, George (fl 1624-29) actor DA

VERNON, George (d 1830 [33]) manager, actor HAS

VERNON, Mrs. George [née Jane Marchant] (1796-1869) English actress CDP, HAS

VERNON, Mrs. George see Fisher, Jane

VERNON, Harriet (d 1923 [71]) actress, singer CDP

VERNON, Harry J. (d 1902) actor EA/03*

VERNON, Harry M. (b 1878) American dramatist WWT/3-9

VERNON, Harvey (b 1927) American actor TW/28

VERNON, Hilary (d 1973 [52]) performer BP/57*

VERNON, Ida (1843-1923) American actress CDP, HAS, WWS

VERNON, Jane Marchant see Vernon, Mrs. George

VERNON, John H. (d 1893) sketch artist EA/94*

VERNON, John William (d 1913 [25]) EA/14*

VERNON, Joseph (1738?-82) English actor, singer CDP, DNB

VERNON, Kate Olga (d 1939 [71]) actress BE*, WWT/14*

VERNON, Louie [Mrs. Darville Vernon] (d 1906) EA/07*

VERNON, Percy see Lyveden, Lord

VERNON, Richard (b 1925) English actor WWT/15-16

VERNON, Virginia [Virginia Fox Brooks] (b 1893) American actress, singer, dramatist WWT/4-9

VERNON, Wally (d 1970 [64]) performer BP/54*

VERNON, Walter (d 1884) comedian EA/85*

VERNON, W. H. (d 1905 [71]) actor EA/07*, WWT/14*

VERNON, Mrs. W. H. see Vernon, Anne

VERRECKE, Mons. (b 1834) Belgian circus performer? HAS

VERREN, Milner (d 1908 [34]) singer EA/09*

VERRETT, Shirley (b 1933?) American singer CB

VERT, Henirato (d 1893) acting manager EA/94*

VERT, N. (d 1905 [62]) impresario EA/06*

VERTES, Marcel (d 1961 [66]) scene designer BP/46*

VERTIPRACH, Vietti (fl 1856) singer HAS

VESEY, Clara dancer CDP

VESEY, Katie (b 1883) English actress, singer, dancer GRB/2

VESSELLA, Oreste (b 1877) Italian composer WWA/5

VESTOFF, Floria (d 1963 [c. 43]) Russian choreographer, dancer BE*

VESTOFF, Valodja (d 1947 [45]) Russian dancer TW/4

VESTOFF, Virginia (b 1940) American actress TW/22-29

VESTRIS, Mme. [Lucia Elizabeth Bartolozzi; Mrs. Charles James Mathews] (1797-1856)

Italian actress, manager BS, CDP, COC, DNB, ES, HAS, OC/1-3, OX, PDT, SR

VESTRIS, Armand (1788-1825) Italian dancer OC/1-2

VESTRIS, Caroline Mary Theresa (b 1802) dancer CDP

VESTRIS, Gaetano Apollino (1729-1808) ballet master CDP

VESTRIS, Marie Jean Augustin (1760-1842) Italian dancer CDP, OC/1-2

VESTVALI, Felicita (1839-80) singer CDP, HAS

VESTVALI, Henry (d 1863) HAS

VEZIN, Arthur (b 1878) English actor WWT/2-8

VEZIN, Hermann (1829-1910) American actor CDP, COC, DAB, DNB, DP, EA/97, ES, GRB/1-4, HAS, OAA/1-2, OC/1-3, WWW/1

VEZIN, Mrs. Hermann see Vezin, Jane Elizabeth

VEZIN, Jane Elizabeth [Mrs. Charles Young; Mrs. Hermann Vezin] (1827-1902) American actress COC, DNB, HAS, OAA/1-2, OC/1-3

VIALETTI, Sig. (d 1870) singer EA/71*

VIAN, Boris (1920-59) French dramatist COC

VIARDOT-GARCIA, Pauline (1821-1910) singer CDP

VIBART, Henry (1863-1939) Scottish actor EA/96, GRB/3-4, SR, WWT/1-9

VICKERS, Henry (d 1871 [64]) comic singer EA/73*

VICKERS, Jon (b 1927?) Canadian singer CB, ES

VICKERS, Martha (d 1971 [46]) performer BP/56*

VICKERS, Mrs. W. G. (d 1880) EA/81*

VICKERY, Mrs. J. G. [née Richardson] (fl 1850-52) actress HAS

VICOTT, Connie (d 1903 [39]) actress EA/04*

VICTOR, Benjamin (d 1778) dramatist, manager CP/1-3, DNB, GT, TD/1-2

VICTOR, Charles (1896-1965) English actor WWT/11-14

VICTOR, C. Leonard (d 1974 [94]) producer/director/chore-

ographer BP/59*

VICTOR, Elizabeth (d 1893) EA/95*

VICTOR, Emma actress EA/96

VICTOR, Eric Swiss actor TW/4-6

VICTOR, Ethel [Mrs. Charles Murray] (d 1902 [45]) serio-comic singer EA/03*

VICTOR, Ethel actress, singer CDP

VICTOR, Frederick [Frederick Clarke] (b 1869) actor GRB/1

VICTOR, Josephine (b 1885) Hungarian/American actress WWS, WWT/5-10

VICTOR, Lionel (d 1940) actor BE*, WWT/14*

VICTOR, Lucia American stage manager, director, dramatist BE

VICTOR, M[ary] A[nn] [Mrs. Sarciut] (d 1907 [67/76]) actress GRB/3

VICTORELLI, John (d 1902) acrobat EA/03*

VICTORELLI, William (d 1897 [52]) acrobat EA/99*

VICTORIA (b 1874) aerial velocipedist CDP

VICTORIA, Vesta (d 1951 [77]) English variety artist CDP, GRB/1-3, WWS

VIDAL, Gore (b 1925) American dramatist AAS, BE, CB, CD, CH, ES, HJD, MD, MH, MWD, PDT, WWT/14-16

VIDAL, Henri (d 1959 [40]) actor WWT/14*

VIDAL, Leonard (d 1906 [45]) acting manager EA/07*

VIE, Florence (d 1939 [63]) actress BE*, WWT/14*

VIEHMAN, Theodore (1889-1970) American director, educator BE

VIEHOEVER, Joseph (d 1973 [47]) producer/director/choreographer BP/58*

VIELLER, Bayard (1869-1943) American dramatist SR

VIENNOISE, The Children (fl 1847) dancers HAS

VIERI, Sig. (fl 1857) musician? HAS

VIETTI, Sig. (fl 1850) singer HAS

VIEUXTEMPS, Mme. (d 1868 [52]) EA/69*

VIEUXTEMPS, Henry (1820-81)

musician HAS

VIEUXTEMPS, Jules Joseph Ernest (d 1896 [64]) musician EA/97*

VIGNA, Arturo (1863-1927) Italian conductor ES

VIGNOLA, Robert G. (d 1953 [71]) Italian actor, director BE*

VIGODA, Abe (b 1921) American actor TW/23, 25-26, 28

VILAR, Jean (1912-71) French actor, manager, director, producer BE, TW/27, WWT/13-14

VILDRAC, Charles Messager (b 1882) French dramatist COC, NTH

VILES, H. A. (d 1894 [78]) EA/95*

VILLA, Alba (d 1976 [55]) performer BP/60*

VILLA, Danny (b 1934) American actor TW/29-30

VILLECHAIZE, Herve (b 1943) French actor TW/27-28

VILLELLA, Edward (b 1936/37) American dancer CB, ES, TW/24

VILLENEUVE, Le Blanc de (fl 1753?) dramatist EAP

VILLETARD, Edmond (d 1890 [78]) dramatist WWT/14*

VILLIERS, Mr. (d 1805) English actor HAS

VILLIERS, Mrs. (1787-1813) see Twaits, Mrs. William

VILLIERS, Edwin (d 1904 [73]) actor, music-hall manager WWT/14*

VILLIERS, Ernest E. (d 1891) business manager EA/92*

VILLIERS, Frederick (d 1885 [59]) actor EA/86*

VILLIERS, George see Buckingham, Duke of

VILLIERS, Mrs. George see Flange, Dora

VILLIERS, Harry (d 1906) music-hall performer EA/07*

VILLIERS, James (d 1863 [76]) actor EA/72*, WWT/14*

VILLIERS, James (b 1933) English actor WWT/15-16

VILLIERS, J. C. (fl 1789) dramatist CP/3

VILLIERS, Mrs. John see Rydon, Nita

VILLIERS, Lizzie [Elizabeth Villiers Bullock] (d 1901 [41]) music-hall dancer EA/02*

VILLIERS, Lyon (fl 1812) actor CDP

VILLIERS, Mavis (d 1976) Australian actress TW/22-23

VILLIERS, R. Edwin (d 1904 [73]) music-hall proprietor EA/05*

VILLION, Lizzie [Mrs. V. Villion] (d 1895) EA/96*

VILLION, Mrs. W. see Villion, Lizzie

VILNER, David (b 1941) American actor TW/24

VINAVER, Steven (d 1968 [31]) producer/director/choreographer BP/53*

VINCENT (fl 1590) musician DA

VINCENT, Mrs. [née Birchill] (d 1802) actress TD/1-2

VINCENT, Miss CDP

VINCENT, Charles (fl 1777) actor CDP

VINCENT, Charles see Viner, Charles Penrucker

VINCENT, Charles T. (1858-1935) English actor, dramatist WWM

VINCENT, Eliza [Mrs. Benjamin Crowther] (1815-56) actress, manager CDP

VINCENT, Ellen Harriet [Mrs. G. A. Vincent] (d 1876 [43]) EA/77*

VINCENT, Mrs. Ernie see Melrose, Doris

VINCENT, E. S. (d 1907 [53]) actor EA/08*, WWT/14*

VINCENT, Mrs. E. S. see Lee, Jenny

VINCENT, Eva (1849-1914) actress SR

VINCENT, Felix A. (1831-1912) English actor CDP, HAS, SR

VINCENT, Fred (d 1904 [54]) manager EA/06*

VINCENT, Mrs. G. A. see Ellen, Harriet

VINCENT, Gene (d 1971 [36]) performer BP/56*

VINCENT, George (d 1876) actor EA/77*

VINCENT, Henry (d 1873 [23]) actor EA/74*

VINCENT, Henry Bethuel (d 1941) American composer WWA/1

VINCENT, H. H. (1848-1913) English actor, stage manager EA/97

VINCENT, Isabella (d 1802 [67])
actress, singer WWT/14*
VINCENT, James (d 1957 [74])
American actor, director
BE*, BP/42*
VINCENT, James R. (d 1850)
actor CDP, HAS
VINCENT, Mrs. J[ames] R.
[née Mary Ann Farley] (1818-
87) English/American actress
CDP, COC, DAB, HAS, NYM,
OC/1-3, WWA/H
VINCENT, Larry (d 1975 [50])
performer BP/59*
VINCENT, Leon John (d 1925
[91]) actor CDP
VINCENT, Madge (b 1884) Eng-
lish actress, singer WWT/
1-6
VINCENT, Mary Ann see Vin-
cent, Mrs. James R.
VINCENT, Naomi (1816-33)
American actress CDP, HAS
VINCENT, Nellie [Mrs. George
Barrett] (d 1886) actress
EA/87*
VINCENT, Romo (b 1909/12)
American actor TW/2, 15
VINCENT, Ruth [Mrs. John
Fraser] (1877-1955) English
actress, singer GRB/1-4,
WWS, WWT/1-8
VINCENT, Thomas (fl c. 1600)
prompter DA
VINCENT, Thomas (fl 1627)
dramatist CP/3, FGF
VINCENT, Virginia (b 1924)
American actress TW/8
VINCENT, Mr. W. (d 1869 [28])
pantomimist EA/70*
VINCENT, Walter (1868-1959)
American actor, producer,
writer TW/15
VINEER, Edmund John (d 1889)
EA/90*
VINER, Charles Penrucker (d
1868 [45]) actor? EA/69*
VINES, Margaret (b 1910) Eng-
lish actress WWT/7-14
VINING, Mr. (d 1881) EA/83*
VINING, Mrs. [née Johannet]
(fl 1820) English actress,
dancer BS, OX
VINING, Mrs. (d 1868) actress?
EA/69*
VINING, Mrs. A. [Rose Bella]
(d 1876) music-hall performer
EA/77*

VINING, Amelia see Wilde,
Amelia
VINING, Arthur (d 1895) music-
hall performer EA/96*
VINING, Charles William (fl 1819)
actor CDP
VINING, Fanny Elizabeth see
Davenport, Fanny Elizabeth
VINING, Frederick (1790-1871)
actor BS, CDP, DNB
VINING, Mrs. Frederick (d 1853
[61]) actress WWT/14*
VINING, George James (1823/24-
75) actor, manager CDP, DNB
VINING, Mrs. Henry (d 1874 [69])
actress EA/76*, WWT/14*
VINING, James (d 1870 [74]) EA/
72*
VINING, James (1795-1870) actor
DNB
VINING, Johannot (fl 1813) actress,
dancer CDP
VINING, Louisa actress CDP
VINING, Matilda Charlotte see
Wood, Mrs. John
VINING, William (d 1861 [78])
actor EA/72*, WWT/14*
VINSON, Helen (b 1907) American
actress WWT/8-10
VINT, Mrs. Leon (d 1917 [40])
EA/18*
VINTNER, Gilbert (d 1969 [60])
composer BP/54*
VINTON, Arthur R. (d 1963)
American actor BE*
VINTON, Stanley (d 1976 [63])
conductor BP/60*
VIOLETTI, Eva Maria CDP
VIOLINSKY [Sol Ginsberg] (1888-
1963) Russian musician, vaude-
villian WWM
VIPOND, Neil (b 1929) Canadian
actor TW/12
VIRNIUS, Johann Friedrich (fl
1615) actor DA
VIRSKY, Pavel (d 1975 [70]) Rus-
sian choreographer BP/60*,
WWT/16*
VIRTO, Albert (d 1890 [29]) EA/
91*
VISCONTI, Luchino (1906-76)
Italian director, designer CB,
ES, PDT
VISHNEVSKAYA, Galina (b 1926)
Russian singer CB
VISSCHER, William Lightfoot (1842-
1924) American actor DAB
VITA, Luis (fl 1847) singer HAS

VITA, Signora Luis (fl 1847) singer HAS

VITA, Michael (b 1941) American actor TW/28

VITALE, Joseph actor TW/1

VITELO see Cryer, Charles Henry

VITU, Auguste (d 1891 [67]) critic EA/92*

VIVIAN, Anthony Crespigny Claud (b 1906) English press representative, producing manager WWT/8-12

VIVIAN, Charles Algernon (b c.1830) English actor SR

VIVIAN, Edward (d 1900) actor EA/01*

VIVIAN, George (d 1970 [85]) performer BP/54*

VIVIAN, Percival (d 1961 [70]) English actor, director BE*

VIVIAN, Robert (d 1944 [85]) English actor BE*, BP/28*, WWT/14*

VIVIAN, Ruth (d 1949 [60]) English actress BE*, BP/34*, TW/6, WWT/14*

VIVIAN, Violet (d 1960 [74]) English actress BE*, BP/45*

VIVIAN-REES, Joan Welsh actress WWT/5-8

VIOLETTI, Eva Maria [Mrs. David Garrick] (1724-1822) dancer COC

VITRAC, Roger (1899-1952) French dramatist COC, OC/3

VIVASH, Henry (d 1879) actor EA/80*

VIVASH, Sarah see Buchanan, Mrs. J.

VIZARD, Harold (b 1871) English actor WWM, WWS

VLADIMIROFF, Pierre (d 1970 [77]) performer BP/55*

VOELLER, Emmeline (fl 1865) actress HAS

VOELLER, Will H. (d 1975 [75]) producer/director/choreographer BP/59*

VOELPEL, Fred designer WWT/16

VOGEL, Eleanore (d 1973 [70]) performer BP/58*

VOGEL, Henry (d 1925 [60]) actor BE*, BP/10*

VOGEL, John W. (1862-1951) American minstrel, manager SR

VOGELING, Mrs. Frederick see Roberts, Florence

VOGHT, Alexander (fl 1854) actor? HAS

VOGL, Heinrich (1845-1900) German singer ES

VOGRICH, Max Wilhelm Karl (1852-1916) composer DAB

VOGT, Gustav (d 1870 [90]) musician EA/71*

VOIGHT, Jon (b 1938) American actor CB, TW/23, WWT/16

VOKES, Fawdon (d 1890) actor CDP, OAA/2

VOKES, F. M. T. (d 1890 [74]) pantomimist, dancer BE*, EA/91*, WWT/14*

VOKES, Frederick Mortimer (1846-88) English actor COC, DNB, OAA/1-2, OC/1-3

VOKES, George (d 1895 [43]) comedian EA/96*

VOKES, George Henry (d 1910 [32]) EA/11*

VOKES, Harry (d 1922 [56]) comedian BE*, BP/6*

VOKES, Jessie [Mrs. Neddy Vokes] (d 1912 [33]) EA/13*

VOKES, Jessie Catherine (1851-84) English actress, dancer CDP, COC, DNB, OAA/1-2, OC/1-3

VOKES, John Russell (d 1924 [52]) Australian vaudevillian BE*, BP/8*

VOKES, May (d 1957 [70+]) comedienne TW/14

VOKES, Neddy see Vokes, Jessie

VOKES, Robert (d 1912 [56]) pantomimist, dancer BE*, EA/13*, WWT/14*

VOKES, Rosina [Mrs. Cecil Clay] (1854-94) actress CDP, COC, DNB, OAA/1-2, OC/1-3

VOKES, Victoria (1853-94) English actress, singer CDP, COC, DNB, OAA/1-2, OC/1-3

VOKES, Walter [né Fawdon] (d 1904) English actor COC, OAA/1, OC/1-3

VOKES, William (d 1894 [83]) circus agent EA/95*

VOLA, Vicki American actress BE

VOL BECQUE, William [William Tookey] (d 1892 [40]) EA/93*

VOLIER, Frank (d 1893) gymnast

EA/94*
VOLKERT, Erie T. (b 1913)
American educator, director
BE
VOLKMAN, Ivan (d 1972) mana-
ger, director BP/57*
VOLKOVA, Vera (d 1975 [71])
ballet teacher BP/59*
VOLLAIRE, Harry (d 1897 [42])
actor EA/98*
VOLLAIRE, John (1820-89)
English actor OAA/2
VOLLAND, Virginia (b 1909)
American costume designer
BE
VOLLMER, Lula (1898-1955)
American dramatist ES, HJD,
MD, MWD, TW/11, WWA/3,
WWT/5-11
VOLMOELLER, Karl (d 1948
[69]) German dramatist BP/
33*, WWT/14*
VOLPE, Frederick (1865-1932)
English actor GRB/1-4,
WWT/1-6
VOLTA, Charlotte E. M. [Mrs.
Edwin Volta] (d 1910 [51])
EA/11*
VOLTA, Mrs. Edwin see
Volta, Charlotte E. M.
VOLTAIRE, Jeanne (d 1970 [70])
performer BP/54*
VOLTAIRE, Nellie (d 1905)
music-hall performer EA/06*
VOLTERRA, Leon (d 1949 [61])
manager, producer WWT/14*
VOLTYNE, Edwin (d 1895) gym-
nast? EA/96*
VON BARDELEBEN, Baroness
Fritz see Scheff, Fritzi
VON BERKEL, Mme. (fl 1856-
57) German singer HAS
VON BERLIN, Ivan Emanuel
Julian see Berlyn, Ivan
VON BONHORST, Julius A. (d
1869) banjo player HAS
VON BUSING, Fritzi (d 1948
[64]) American actress, singer
TW/4
VON DER FINCK, Herman see
Finck, Herman
VONE, William (fl 1807) drama-
tist CP/3
VON ELTZ, Theodore (d 1964
[70]) performer BP/49*
VON FIELITZ, Andrew (b 1860)
German conductor WWA/4
VON FURSTENBERG, Betsy (b

1931/35) German/American ac-
tress BE, TW/7-10, 12-19,
23-24, 27, WWT/15-16
VON HATZFELDT, Olga [Mrs.
Irving Brooks] (b 1884) Ameri-
can actress WWM
VONLEER, Sarah [Mrs. J. M.
Hardie] (d 1916) actress, mana-
ger SR
VON MEYERINCK, Herbert (d 1971
[74]) performer BP/55*
VONNEGUT, Kurt, Jr. (b 1922)
American dramatist CD
VONNEGUT, Walter (d 1940 [56])
American actor, director BE*,
BP/25*
VON NIESSEN-STONE, Matja (b
1870) Russian singer WWM
VON OSTFELDEN, Maria (d 1971
[75]) producer/director/chore-
ographer BP/55*
VON POSSART, Ernst Ritter (1841-
1921) German actor, manager
GRB/4, OC/1-3, WWT/1-2
VON REINHOLD, Calvin (b 1927)
Canadian dancer, choreographer,
singer, actor BE
VON SCHERLER, Sasha (b 1939)
American actress TW/22-24,
26-28, WWT/15-16
VON SONNENTHAL, Adolf Ritter
(1834-1909) German actor,
manager GRB/4
VON STERNBERG, Josef (d 1969
[75]) producer/director/chore-
ographer BP/54*
VON STROHEIM, Erich (1885-1957)
Austrian/American actor WWA/3
VON TILZER, Albert (1878-1956)
American composer, performer
TW/13
VON TILZER, Harry (1873-1946)
American vaudevillian, lyricist
CB, DAB
VON TILZER, Jules (b 1869)
American vaudevillian WWM
VON TWARDOWSKI, Hans Heinrich
(d 1958 [60]) German actor,
director BP/43*
VON UNRUH, Fritz (d 1970 [85])
dramatist BP/55*
VON WITT, Joseph (1843-87)
Bohemian singer NYM
VON ZERNECK, Peter (b 1908)
Hungarian actor TW/1, 3
VOORHEES, Donald (b 1903)
American conductor, musical
director CB

VORSTIUS, Louisa Ann (d 1893 [46]) EA/95*

VOS, Miss (1815-54) see Stuart, Mrs.

VOSBURGH, David (b 1938) American actor TW/25

VOSE, Val [Thomas Davis Eaton] (d 1887) ventriloquist CDP

VOSKOVEC, George (b 1905) Czech actor, producer, director BE, MD, TW/10, 12, 18-27, 30, WWT/14-16

VOSOFF, Hellen Howes (d 1975 [79]) playhouse founder BP/59*

VOSPER, Frank (1899-1937) English actor, dramatist AAS, ES, WWT/6-8

VOSS, Stephanie (b 1936) English actress, singer WWT/13-16

VOTION, Jack (d 1975 [75]) producer/director/choreographer BP/60*

VOTIPKA, Thelma (1898-1972) American singer WWA/5

VOULLAIRE, Andrew Leonard [A. V. Campbell] (d 1870 [80]) actor EA/71*

VOUSDEN, Francis Valentine (d 1905 [43]) musician EA/06*

VOWLES, Mrs. J. (d 1890) EA/91*

VOX, Horace (d 1881 [28]) comedian EA/82*

VOY, Lawrance (d 1868 [42]) Negro comedian EA/69*

VROOM, Lodewick (d 1950 [66]) Canadian producer, press representative BE*, BP/35*

VROOM, Paul (b 1917) American producer, manager BE

VYE, Murvyn (1913-76) American actor TW/1-8, 22-23

VYNER, R. G. (d 1918) EA/19*

VYVYAN, Jennifer (d 1974 [49]) performer BP/58*

- W -

W., J. (fl 1637) dramatist CP/3, FGF

W., J. (fl 1743-50) dramatist CP/3

W., L. (fl 1658) dramatist CP/3, FGF

W., M. (fl 1662) dramatist CP/3, FGF

W., R. (fl c. 1548?) dramatist CP/3

W., R. (fl 1680) dramatist CP/3

W., T. (fl 1662?) dramatist FGF

WACHTEL, Theodor (1823-93) singer CDP

WADBROOK, Mrs. (d 1889) EA/90*

WADDINGTON, Patrick (b 1901/03) English actor, singer BE, WWT/7-16

WADDINGTON, Mrs. W. H. (d 1892 [29]) EA/93*

WADDS, Elijah (d 1875 [68]) box-office keeper EA/77*

WADDY, Mr. (fl 1798-1802) Irish actor GT, TD/1-2

WADE, Mrs. (d 1888) EA/89*

WADE, Allan (1881-1954) English business manager, producer, actor, manager COC, OC/1-3, WWT/5-11

WADE, Cecily (d 1916) actress EA/17*

WADE, Florence (d 1896) actress EA/97*

WADE, Gene (d 1917) comedian EA/18*

WADE, George Edward see Robey, George

WADE, John P. (b 1876) American actor WWM

WADE, Joseph Augustine (1796?-1845) Irish composer, conductor DNB

WADE, Julia see Harwood, Mrs.

WADE, Peter J. (b 1850) Irish actor HAS

WADE, Philip (d 1950 [54]) actor BE*, WWT/14*

WADE, Samuel (d 1878 [67]) musician EA/79*

WADE, Thomas (1805-75) English dramatist DNB

WADE, Tom (d 1908 [47]) music-hall performer EA/09*

WADE, Walter (d 1963 [52]) performer, songwriter BE*

WADE, Warren (d 1973 [76]) actor, director BP/57*, WWT/16*

WADESON, Antony (fl 1601) dramatist CP/3, DNB, FGF

WADKAR, Hansa (d 1971 [47]) performer BP/56*

WADMAN, Miss (fl 1878-90) actress DP, OAA/2

WADMAN, Miss [Mrs. St. Vincent Jervis] (d 1892) singer EA/94*

WADMORE, Mr. (d 1878) singer

EA/79*

WADSWORTH, Handel (d 1964)
English director BE*

WADSWORTH, Henry (d 1974
[72]) actor BP/59*, WWT/
16*

WADSWORTH, Jessie (d 1973
[81]) talent agent BP/57*

WAGENHALS, Lincoln A. (1869-
1931) American producing
manager GRB/2-4, WWT/1-6

WAGER, Lewis (fl 1567) dramatist
CP/1-3, FGF

WAGER, Michael [né Emanuel
Weisgal] (b 1925) American
actor, director BE, TW/7,
23, 25, 27-28, 30, WWT/
15-16

WAGER, W. (fl Elizabethan
period) dramatist CP/2-3

WAGHORN, William (d 1883)
theatrical laceman EA/84*

WAGNER, Arthur (b 1923) American educator BE

WAGNER, Calvin (b 1840) American comedian HAS

WAGNER, Carl (b 1865) German
actor WWT/2

WAGNER, Rev. C. Everett (d
1969 [73]) BP/54*

WAGNER, Charles L. (d 1956
[87]) American producing
manager TW/12, WWA/3,
WWT/6-7

WAGNER, Frank American choreographer, director BE

WAGNER, Harold (b 1885) English actor GRB/1

WAGNER, Jack (d 1965 [68])
performer BP/49*

WAGNER, Johanna (1828-94)
singer CDP

WAGNER, Joseph (d 1974 [74])
composer/lyricist BP/59*

WAGNER, Joseph (b 1913) American educator BE

WAGNER, Leopold (b 1858) English actor, dramatist GRB/1

WAGNER, Nathaniel M. (d 1961
[65]) actor, singer TW/18

WAGNER, Richard Cyril (d
1916 [23]) actor EA/17*

WAGNER, Robin (b 1933) American designer BE, WWT/
15-16

WAGNER, William (d 1964 [79])
actor BE*, WWT/14*

WAHL, Walter Dare (d 1974

[78]) performer BP/59*

WAINRIGHT, Hope (d 1972 [30])
performer BP/56*

WAINWRIGHT, Dr. (fl 1801) dramatist CP/3

WAINWRIGHT, Miss (fl 1767-69)
English actress HAS

WAINWRIGHT, Jane [Mrs. John
Wainwright] (d 1888) EA/89*

WAINWRIGHT, John (d 1911 [69])
actor, producer, manager BE*,
EA/12*, WWT/14*

WAINWRIGHT, Mrs. John see
Wainwright, Jane

WAINWRIGHT, Marie [Mrs. Franklyn Roberts] (1853-1923) American actress CDP, COC, GRB/
2-4, PP/3, SR, WWA/1, WWS,
WWT/1-4

WAITE, Annie (b 1843) American
actress HAS

WAITE, Edward Willoughby (d 1906)
musician EA/07*

WAITE, Harriett [Mrs. Harry
Waite] (d 1886) EA/88*

WAITE, Harry (d 1900 [71]) EA/01*

WAITE, Mrs. Harry see Waite,
Harriett

WAITE, Margaret [Mrs. William
Waite] (d 1880) EA/81*

WAITE, Salome B. (d 1890) EA/91*

WAITE, Mrs. William see
Waite, Margaret

WAKE, Ada Eliza (d 1903) actress
EA/04*

WAKE, Maria [Mrs. Richard Wake]
(d 1911) EA/13*

WAKE, Richard (d 1918) EA/19*

WAKE, Mrs. Richard see Wake,
Maria

WAKEFIELD, Ann (b 1931) English
actress TW/11-12

WAKEFIELD, Douglas (1899-1951)
English actor WWT/7-10

WAKEFIELD, Edward (fl 1597-1602)
actor DA

WAKEFIELD, Gilbert Edward (1892-
1963) English dramatist WWT/
6-13

WAKEFIELD, Henrietta (d 1974
[96]) performer BP/59*

WAKEFIELD, Hugh (1888-1971)
English actor WWT/5-14

WAKEFIELD, J. H. (d 1900) music-
hall comedian, lessee EA/01*

WAKEFIELD, Willa Holt American
entertainer WWM

WAKELIN, Sarah see Baker, Sarah

WAKELING, Mrs. A. C. see
Wakeling, Emma
WAKELING, Emma [Mrs. A.
C. Wakeling] (d 1878) EA/79*
WAKEMAN, Annie (fl 1867) ac-
tress CDP
WAKEMAN, Antoinette von Hoesen
(b 1856) American dramatist
WWA/4
WAKEMAN, Emily [Mrs. Randolph
Hartley] (fl 1900s) American
actress WWM
WAKEMAN, Keith (1866-1933)
American actress EA/96,
WWA/1, WWT/2-5
WAKER, Mr. actor CDP
WAKER, Joseph (fl 1785) drama-
tist CP/3
WAKLEY, Ronald Ford (d 1918
[27]) EA/19*
WALBERG, Betty (b 1921) Amer-
ican composer, dance arranger,
educator, musician BE
WALBOURN, William H. (fl
1821) actor CDP
WALBOURNE, Mr. (fl 1837-40)
English actor HAS
WALBRAN, Kate (d 1916) actress
EA/18*
WALBROOK, Anton [Adolph Anton
Wilhelm Wohlbrück] (1900-66)
Austrian actor WWT/9-14,
WWW/6
WALBROOK, Henry Mackinnon
(1863-1941) Irish dramatist,
critic WWT/1-9, WWW/4
WALBURN, Raymond (1887-1969)
American actor BE, TW/22,
26
WALCOT, Mrs. (fl 1797) actress
TD/1-2
WALCOT, Charles Melton (1816-
68) English/American actor,
dramatist CDP, COC, DAB,
HAS, OC/1-3, SR, WWA/H
WALCOT, Charles Melton [or
Melcot] (1840-1921) American
actor COC, DAB, HAS,
OC/1-3, PP/3, WWS
WALCOT, Isabella [née Nickinson]
(1847-1906) American actress
COC, HAS, OC/1-3, PP/3
WALCOTT, Mrs. see Shirreff,
Miss
WALCOTT, Alexander (1887-
1943) actor SR
WALCOTT, Derek (b 1930) West
Indian dramatist CD

WALCOTT, Mrs. Thomas see
Shirreff, Jane
WALDECK, Elise von (d 1898 [60])
EA/99*
WALDEGRAVE, Cecile (d 1838)
dancer, actress HAS
WALDEGRAVE, Lilias actress
GRB/2-4, WWT/1-6
WALDEGRAVE, Robert [Robert
James Penny Wilson] (d 1894
[37]) EA/95*
WALDEN, Harry (1875-1921) Ger-
man actor BE*, WWT/14*
WALDEN, Robert (b 1944) Ameri-
can actor TW/25
WALDIS, Otto (d 1974 [68]) per-
former BP/58*
WALDMANN, Antoinette (d 1892
[75]) singer EA/93*
WALDO, Fullerton Leonard (b
1877) American dramatist
WWA/5
WALDO, Helen (fl 1900s) American
entertainer WWM
WALDON, Mrs. (d 1886) EA/87*
WALDON, Charles see Escamo
WALDORF, Wilella Louise (1899-
1945) American critic TW/2,
WWA/2
WALDRON, Mr. (fl c. 1839?) actor
CDP
WALDRON, Charles D. (1874-
1946) American actor TW/2,
WWT/7-9
WALDRON, Daniel Gilman (b 1833)
American manager HAS
WALDRON, Fanny see Christian,
Frances Ann
WALDRON, Francis Godolphin
(1744-1818) actor, manager,
dramatist, prompter CDP,
CP/2-3, DNB, GT, TD/1-2
WALDRON, Mrs. Francis G. see
Harlowe, Sarah
WALDRON, Georgia [Mrs. Edward
Emery] (1872-1950) American
actress BE*, WWT/14*
WALDRON, Jack (1893-1969) Amer-
ican actor, comedian BE,
TW/26
WALDRON, James A. (d 1931 [79])
editor BE*, WWT/14*
WALDRON, Isabel see Waldron,
Georgia
WALDRON, May see Robson,
Mrs. Stuart
WALDRON, William R. (d 1910
[88]) manager EA/11*

WALDROP, Gid (b 1919) American educator, conductor, composer BE

WALENN, Cecil see Barth, Cecil

WALENN, Charles R. (d 1948) actor BE*, WWT/14*

WALENN, James Farquharson (d 1884) conductor EA/85*

WALES, Gary American actor TW/25

WALFORD, Ann (b 1928) Indian/English actress WWT/12-14

WALFORD, Marie Henry (d 1906 [21]) EA/07*

WALFORD-HENRY, Marie (d 1912 [23]) EA/13*

WALKEN, Christopher [Ronald Walken] (b 1943) American actor TW/19, 22-30, WWT/16

WALKEN, Ronald see Walken, Christopher

WALKER, Alfred actor, singer CDP

WALKER, Alice Johnstone (b 1871) American dramatist WWA/5

WALKER, Allan (d 1970) performer BP/55*

WALKER, Anna see O'Doherty, Eileen

WALKER, Arlene (d 1973 [54]) actress, casting director TW/29

WALKER, Benjamin (d 1910 [72]) EA/11*

WALKER, Mrs. Benjamin see Walker, Sarah Ann

WALKER, Betty (d 1976 [81]) performer BP/60*

WALKER, Bob (1918-51) American actor BE*

WALKER, Charles (d 1882) scene artist EA/83*

WALKER, Charlotte [Mrs. Eugene Walter] (1878-1958) American actress GRB/3-4, TW/14, WWM, WWS, WWT/1-11

WALKER, Danton (d 1960 [61]) columnist TW/17

WALKER, Diana (b 1942) American actress TW/23-26, 30

WALKER, Don (b 1907) American composer, conductor BE

WALKER, Dorothy Casson see Christie, Dorothy

WALKER, Elizabeth (b 1947) American actress TW/26

WALKER, Eva (d 1889) EA/90*

WALKER, F. S. (d 1917) EA/18*

WALKER, George F. (b 1947) Canadian dramatist CD

WALKER, Hal (d 1972 [76]) producer/director/choreographer BP/57*

WALKER, Harry (d 1896 [65]) actor EA/97*

WALKER, Mrs. Harry see Leechman, Katie

WALKER, Heather Eulalie see Walker, Polly

WALKER, James J. (d 1946) songwriter SR

WALKER, Jeremy see Kemp, Jeremy

WALKER, John (1732-1807) actor CDP

WALKER, John (d 1889 [26]) EA/90*

WALKER, John (d 1890 [61]) musician EA/91*

WALKER, John (d 1910) roundabout proprietor EA/11*

WALKER, John A. (b 1916) American educator BE

WALKER, John Henry (d 1883 [31]) equestrian EA/84*

WALKER, Johnny (1894-1949) actor BE*

WALKER, Joseph A. American dramatist, director CD

WALKER, June (1899/1904-1966) American actress BE, ES, TW/1-8, 10-16, 22, WWT/5-14

WALKER, Kathryn American actress TW/29-30

WALKER, Laura English actress GRB/1

WALKER, Laura (d 1951 [57]) actress, dramatist TW/7

WALKER, Lillian (d 1975 [88]) actress BP/60*, WWT/16*

WALKER, Martin (1901-55) English actor WWT/7-11

WALKER, Maynard Chamberlain (fl 1771) dramatist CP/3

WALKER, Muriel see Ashwynne, Muriel

WALKER, Nancy (b 1921/22) American actress, singer BE, CB, TW/2-6, 15, 17-19, 25, WWT/10-16

WALKER, Norman (1907-63) English singer WWW/6

WALKER, Polly [Heather Eulalie Walker] (b 1908) American

actress, singer WWT/7-9

WALKER, Rhoderick (b 1920)
English actor TW/4

WALKER, Robert Francis (d
1906 [29]) EA/07*

WALKER, Sarah Ann [Mrs.
Benjamin Walker] (d 1873)
EA/74*

WALKER, Sidney see Walker,
William Sidney

WALKER, Stanley (d 1962 [64])
journalist BP/47*

WALKER, Stuart (1880/86/88-
1941) American actor, di-
rector, manager, dramatist
CB, DAB, NTH, WWA/1,
WWT/7-9

WALKER, Syd (1886-1945) English actor WWT/7-9

WALKER, Sydney (b 1921) American actor TW/22-30, WWT/
16

WALKER, T. (fl 1705) dramatist
CP/2-3, GT

WALKER, T-Bone (d 1975 [64])
performer BP/59*

WALKER, Thomas (1693/98-
1744) English actor, dramatist
CDP, CP/1-3, DNB, GT,
TD/1-2

WALKER, Thomas ['Whimsical
Walker''] (d 1934 [84]) clown
BE*, WWT/14*

WALKER, Thomas Henry (d 1901
[41]) musical director EA/02*

WALKER, Wally (d 1975 [74])
performer BP/60*

'WALKER, Whimsical'' see
Walker, Thomas

WALKER, William (d 1726) West
Indian dramatist CP/1-3, GT

WALKER, William Sidney (1795-
1846) Welsh critic DNB

WALKER, Dr. W. Miller (d
1881 [47]) actor EA/82*

WALKER, Zena (b 1934) English
actress TW/24, WWT/15-16

WALKES, W[illiam] R[obert] (d
1913 [59]) dramatist BE*,
EA/14*, WWT/14*

WALKINGTON, John Augustus
(d 1916 [77]) entertainer
EA/18*

WALKLEY, Arthur Bingham
(1855-1926) English critic
COC, DNB, GRB/1-4, OC/
1-3, PDT, WWT/1-5, WWW/2

WALKUP, Fairfax Proudfit (b

1887) American educator, costumier BE

WALL, Mr. (fl 1767) actor HAS

WALL, Prof. (d 1906) EA/07*

WALL, Mrs. (fl 1767) actress
HAS

WALL, Geraldine (d 1970 [57]) actress TW/27

WALL, Mrs. H. see Adams,
Annie

WALL, Harry (b 1838) American
actor CDP, HAS

WALL, Harry (1886-1966) English
dramatist WWT/5-10

WALL, Mrs. Harry [née Louisa
Clarkson] (1846-67) American
actress HAS

WALL, Horace (1837-99) actor,
manager, agent CDP

WALL, Joe (d 1895 [29]) phantoscope proprietor EA/96*

WALL, Max [né Maxwell George
Lorimer] (b 1908) English actor,
dancer WWT/10-16

WALLACE, Agnes (b 1851) English
dancer HAS

WALLACE, Agnes (b 1851) actress
CDP

WALLACE, Alfred E. (d 1866
[33]) comedian EA/72*

WALLACE, Annie Adelaide [Mrs.
Fitzroy Wallace] (d 1881 [45])
EA/83*

WALLACE, Art (b 1935) American
actor TW/23-25, 28-29

WALLACE, Charles (d 1903) Negro
comedian EA/04*

WALLACE, Mrs. Claude see
Belmore, Lily

WALLACE, David (d 1955 [66])
American dramatist BE*,
BP/40*

WALLACE, Mrs. Edgar (d 1933
[36]) producer, manager BE*,
WWT/14*

WALLACE, Edgar Horatio (1875-
1932) English dramatist AAS,
COC, DNB, ES, HP, OC/1-3,
PDT, WWT/6

WALLACE, Lady Eglantine (d 1803)
dramatist DNB, GT

WALLACE, Eustace (d 1916 [40])
EA/17*

WALLACE, Fitzroy (d 1883 [45])
actor, manager EA/84*

WALLACE, Mrs. Fitzroy see
Wallace, Annie Adelaide

WALLACE, Frank (d 1966 [73])

performer BP/51*
WALLACE, George (d 1883 [49])
EA/84*
WALLACE, George (b 1917/24)
American actor, singer BE,
TW/27
WALLACE, George Carlton actor
GRB/1
WALLACE, Harry (d 1920) mana-
ger BP/5*
WALLACE, Hazel Vincent (b
1919) English managing director
WWT/15-16
WALLACE, J. (fl 1835) American
actor HAS
WALLACE, James actor HAS
WALLACE, Lady James [née
Maxwell] (fl 1780s) dramatist
CP/3, TD/1-2
WALLACE, James S. (fl 1833-38?)
dramatist RJ
WALLACE, Jenny (b 1852) English
dancer CDP, HAS
WALLACE, John (fl 1802) drama-
tist CP/3
WALLACE, John J. (1831-92)
American actor HAS
WALLACE, Lee (b 1930) American
actor TW/27, 29-30
WALLACE, Gen. Lew (1827-1905)
American dramatist GRB/1
WALLACE, Lionel [Lionel Saund-
ers] (b 1872) English actor,
agent GRB/1
WALLACE, Louise Chapman (d
1962 [80]) actress BE*
WALLACE, Marcia (b 1942)
American actress TW/26
WALLACE, Marie (b 1939)
American actress TW/22, 29
WALLACE, Mike (b 1918) Amer-
ican actor TW/11
WALLACE, Minnie actress CDP
WALLACE, Mrs. M. M. (d 1889)
EA/90*
WALLACE, Morgan (d 1953 [72])
American actor BE*, BP/38*
WALLACE, Nat (d 1891) come-
dian EA/92*
WALLACE, Nellie (1870/82-
1948) Scottish actress, singer
COC, OC/1-3, PDT, WWT/
5-10
WALLACE, Paul (b 1938) Amer-
ican actor, dancer, singer
BE
WALLACE, Percy (d 1916) EA/
17*

WALLACE, Regina American ac-
tress BE
WALLACE, Rosa (d 1904) EA/05*
WALLACE, Ruby Ann see Dee,
Ruby
WALLACE, Vincent (d 1865 [51])
composer EA/72*
WALLACE, William Henry (d 1893
[28]) EA/94*
WALLACE, William Vincent (1814-
65) Irish composer, musician
CDP, DNB
WALLACE SISTERS, The HAS
WALLACH, Edgar (d 1953 [68])
American manager BE*, BP/
37*
WALLACH, Eli (b 1915) American
actor AAS, BE, CB, ES, TW/
2, 4, 7-22, 24, 28, 30, WWT/
12-16
WALLACH, Ira (b 1913) American
dramatist, lyricist BE
WALLACH, Joseph (d 1974 [62])
stage manager BP/59*
WALLACK, Miss see Jones,
Mrs.
WALLACK, Ann Duff see Wallack,
Mrs. James William
WALLACK, Arthur J. (d 1940
[91]) manager BE*, WWT/14*
WALLACK, Elizabeth [Mrs. Wil-
liam Wallack] (d 1850 [90]) ac-
tress CDP, ES
WALLACK, Fanny [Mrs. Charles
Moorhouse] (d 1856 [34]) actress
CDP, ES
WALLACK, George actor CDP
WALLACK, George Gordon (fl 1858)
actor HAS
WALLACK, Mrs. Henry (d 1845)
English actress HAS
WALLACK, Henry John (1790-1870)
English actor BS, CDP, COC,
DAB, DNB, ES, HAS, HJD,
OC/1-3, WWA/H
WALLACK, Mrs. Henry John [née
Turpin] (d 1860) English actress
CDP, HAS
WALLACK, James H. (d 1908
[64]) actor, manager GRB/4*
WALLACK, Mrs. James W. see
Johnstone, Susan
WALLACK, James William (1791-
1864) English actor, manager
CDP, COC, DAB, DNB, ES,
HAS, OC/1-3, OX, WWA/H
WALLACK, James William (1818-
73) English actor CDP, COC,

DAB, ES, HAS, OC/1-3,
SR, WWA/H

WALLACK, Mrs. James William
[Mrs. William Sefton; née Ann
Waring] (d 1879 [64]) American
actress CDP, HAS

WALLACK, Julia see Harland,
Julia

WALLACK, Lester [John Johnstone Wallack] (1820-88) Eng-
lish/American actor, stage
manager, manager CDP, COC,
DAB, DNB, ES, HAS, NTH,
OC/1-3, SR, WWA/H

WALLACK, Mrs. Lester (d 1909
[84]) actress BE*, WWT/14*

WALLACK, William (d 1805)
actor CDP

WALLACK, Mrs. William see
Wallack, Elizabeth

WALLACK, William H. W. (1760-
1850) actor ES

WALLENDA, Yetta (d 1963 [42])
performer BE*

WALLER, Alma see Waller,
Maggie

WALLER, Arthur (d 1898 [35])
actor EA/99*

WALLER, Mrs. Arthur see
Cawthorn, Lily

WALLER, Carl (d 1900 [28])
pantomimist EA/01*

WALLER, Mrs. Carl see
Waller, Mary

WALLER, Daniel Wilmarth (d
1882 [58]) actor, manager
CDP

WALLER, David (b 1920) English
actor AAS, WWT/15-16

WALLER, D. W. (d 1882 [58])
American actor HAS

WALLER, Mrs. D. W. see
Waller, Emma

WALLER, Edmund (1605-87)
English dramatist CP/1-3,
GT

WALLER, Edmund Lewis (b
1884) English actor GRB/
3-4, WWT/1-8

WALLER, Mrs. Edmund [Lewis]
see Warwick, Ethel

WALLER, Emma (1820-99) American actress CDP, COC,
DAB, HAS, OC/2-3, WWA/H

WALLER, Guy (d 1907 [34]) actor
EA/08*

WALLER, Henry (b 1864) Scottish
composer, conductor WWA/4

WALLER, Jack (1885-1957) English
producing manager, composer,
actor WWT/6-12

WALLER, John (d 1908 [59]) manager EA/09*

WALLER, J. Wallet (d 1951 [69])
director BE*, WWT/14*

WALLER, Lee (d 1974 [59]) pro-
ducer/director/choreographer
BP/59*

WALLER, Lewis (1860-1915)
Spanish/English actor CDP,
COC, DNB, EA/97, ES, GRB/
1-4, OC/1-3, SR, WWA/1,
WWM, WWT/1-3, WWW/1

WALLER, Mrs. Lewis [Florence
West] (1862-1913) actress
EA/97, GRB/1-4, OC/2-3,
WWT/1

WALLER, Maggie [Alma Waller]
(d 1909) EA/10*

WALLER, Mary [née Mary Milford;
Mrs. Carl Waller] (d 1876)
EA/77*

WALLER, Pauline (d 1907) EA/08*

WALLETT, Mrs. (d 1872 [84])
EA/73*

WALLETT, Edgar (d 1906 [23])
EA/07*

WALLETT, John (d 1869 [79])
EA/70*

WALLETT, Russell (d 1912 [44])
comedian EA/13*

WALLETT, William Frederick
(1808-92) English clown CDP,
HAS

WALLFORD, W. C. P. (d 1866)
Yankee comedian HAS

WALLICK, John M. actor, manager
SR

WALLING, Roy (d 1964 [75])
American dramatist, actor BE*

WALLINGTON, James S. (d 1972
[65]) performer BP/57*

WALLIS, Miss see Campbell,
Mrs.

WALLIS, Bella [Mrs. Hugh Moss]
(d 1960) actress BE*, WWT/
14*

WALLIS, Bertram (1874-1952)
English actor, singer GRB/4,
WWT/1-11

WALLIS, Ellen (d 1895) EA/96*

WALLIS, Ellen Lancaster [Mrs.
Walter Reynolds] (1856-1940)
actress CDP, DP, GRB/1-4,
OAA/1-2, WWT/1-8

WALLIS, Fanny see Lowe, Mrs.

William
WALLIS, Fritz (d 1900 [71])
scene artist EA/01*
WALLIS, Mrs. Fritz see
Wallis, Sabina
WALLIS, Dr. George (1740-1802)
English dramatist CP/2-3,
GT
WALLIS, George Ambrose (d 1895)
director EA/97*
WALLIS, Gladys (b c. 1772) ac-
tress SR
WALLIS, Gladys (d 1953 [80])
American actress TW/10
WALLIS, Mrs. H. see Water-
house, Mrs. John
WALLIS, Mrs. Hal see Fazenda,
Louise
WALLIS, Joseph L. (d 1860)
American actor HAS
WALLIS, Sabina [Mrs. Fritz
Wallis] (d 1910 [83]) EA/11*
WALLIS, Samuel H. (d 1890)
EA/91*
WALLIS, Shani (b 1933) English
actress, singer WWT/12-15
WALLIS, Walter (fl 1901?)
actor, singer CDP
WALLIS, William H. (b 1825)
English actor HAS
WALLMAN, Lawrence A. (b
1902) American educator BE
WALLNER, Agnes (1824-1901)
actress CDP
WALLON, T. E. see Dunville,
T. E.
WALLOP, Douglass (b 1920)
American dramatist BE
WALLS, Tom (1883-1949) Eng-
lish actor, manager, producer
AAS, COC, DNB, WWT/3-10
WALLY, Gus (d 1966 [62]) per-
former BP/50*
WALMISLEY, Blanche [Mrs.
Frank Williams] (d 1888)
actress EA/89*
WALPOLE, Mr. actor CDP
WALPOLE, Frances (fl 1616-17)
actor DA
WALPOLE, Horace, Earl of
Orford (c. 1717-97) English
author CDP, CP/2-3, DNB,
GT
WALPOLE, Sir Hugh (1884-1941)
New Zealand dramatist CB,
WWT/8-9
WALSH, Bill (d 1975 [61]) pro-
ducer/director/choreographer

BP/59*
WALSH, Blanche [Mrs. W. M.
Travers] (1873-1915) American
actress DAB, GRB/2-4, PP/3,
SR, WWA/1, WWM, WWS,
WWT/1-3
WALSH, Eliza see Breyer, Mrs.
J. E.
WALSH, Ellen (d 1917) EA/18*
WALSH, Emmet (b 1935) American
actor TW/25, 30
WALSH, Flora see Hoyt, Mrs.
Charles Hale
WALSH, Frederick G. (b 1915)
American educator, dramatist,
director BE
WALSH, Harry (b 1875) Irish actor,
stage manager, singer GRB/1
WALSH, John (d 1736) Irish? editor
ES
WALSH, John (d 1868 [28]) come-
dian, dancer EA/69*
WALSH, Joseph F. (d 1972 [76])
performer BP/56*
WALSH, Kate (d 1903) variety per-
former EA/04*
WALSH, Katherine actress SR
WALSH, Lionel (1876-1916) English
actor WWS
WALSH, Michael (d 1866 [27])
banjoist HAS
WALSH, Michael (d 1917) EA/18*
WALSH, Michael (d 1974 [70])
British stage manager BP/59*
WALSH, Miriam Cooper (d 1976
[84]) performer BP/60*
WALSH, Sam (d 1920 [42]) actor
BE*, WWT/14*
WALSH, Sean J. (b 1938) American
actor TW/25-26
WALSH, Shelford (b 1862) English
producer GRB/1
WALSH, Thomas H. (d 1925 [62])
actor BE*, BP/9*
WALSH, Thomas J. (d 1962 [59])
executive BE*
WALSH, Tom (b 1926) American
actor TW/4, 10
WALSH, Tom Hector see Hector,
"Little"
WALSH, William Thomas (1891-
1949) American dramatist
WWA/2
WALSHAM, Henry (d 1898) singer
EA/99*
WALSHE, William Sesnan (d 1910
[50]) EA/11*
WALSINGER, Bertha singer SR

WALSTEIN, Eliza (d 1833) actress CDP

WALSTEIN, Westervelt (d 1836) American actor HAS

WALSTEIN, Mrs. Westervelt [née Thayer] (d 1856) actress HAS

WALSTON, Ray (b 1917/18/19) American actor, director AAS, BE, TW/8-17, 23, WWT/15-16

WALTER, Mrs. see Bellamy, Mrs.

WALTER, Bruno (1876-1962) German conductor CB, ES, TW/18, WWA/4, WWW/6

WALTER, Charles (d 1883) acting manager, treasurer EA/84*

WALTER, Edwin (d 1953 [82]) American actor TW/10

WALTER, Emilie singer CDP

WALTER, Eugene (1874-1941) American dramatist, actor, manager CB, COC, DAB, ES, HJD, MH, MWD, NTH, OC/1-3, SR, WWA/1, WWM, WWT/1-9

WALTER, Mrs. Eugene see Walker, Charlotte

WALTER, Nancy (b 1939) American dramatist CD

WALTER, Olive (b 1898) English actress, manager WWT/8-13

WALTER, Tracey (b 1950) American actor TW/29

WALTER, W. H. St. John see St. John, Herbert

WALTER, Wilfrid (1882-1958) English actor WWT/5-12

WALTER, Wilmer (1884-1941) actor CB

WALTER-BRIANT, Fredda (b 1912) American wardrobe supervisor BE

WALTER-ELLIS, Desmond (b 1914) English actor WWT/11-16

WALTERS, Mr. (fl 1836) actor HAS

WALTERS, Annie see Jordan, Mrs. George

WALTERS, A. S. (d 1903 [47]) director EA/04*

WALTERS, Bessie see Cooke, Mrs. James

WALTERS, Casey (b 1916) American actor TW/4

WALTERS, Charles American actor, dancer, choreographer ES

WALTERS, Clara (fl 1859) actress HAS

WALTERS, Henry Arnold (d 1872 [13]) gymnast EA/73*

WALTERS, Maud see Walters, Polly

WALTERS, Patricia Wheeler (d 1967) performer BP/52*

WALTERS, Polly [née Maud] (b 1910) American actress, dancer WWT/8-10

WALTERS, Robert see Roberts, George

WALTERS, Thorley (b 1913) English actor TW/4-6, WWT/11-16

WALTERS, Walter H. (b 1917) American educator BE

WALTERS, W. H. (d 1880 [50]) comedian EA/81*

WALTERS, Mrs. W. H. [Ellen Bertram] (d 1867) dancer EA/68*

WALTERS, Wilmarth (fl 1851) American actor HAS

WALTERS-CRAWFORD, William (d 1916) EA/18*

WALTHALL, Henry Brazeal (1878-1936) American actor DAB

WALTHER, Gretchen (b 1938) American actress TW/19

WALTON, Mr. (fl 1827) English actor, stage manager HAS

WALTON, Douglas (d 1961 [51]) Canadian actor BE*

WALTON, Edith (d 1975 [71]) critic BP/59*

WALTON, Elsie [Miss Hemming] (b 1888) English actress GRB/1

WALTON, Eugene A. (d 1967 [76]) theatrical haulier BP/52*

WALTON, Fred (d 1886 [57]) stage manager EA/87*

WALTON, Fred (d 1903 [52]) juggler EA/04*

WALTON, Fred (d 1936 [71]) actor BE*, WWT/14*

WALTON, George (d 1903) comedian EA/04*

WALTON, George Everett (d 1917) EA/18*

WALTON, H. B. [Harry Moffitt] (d 1917) manager EA/18*

WALTON, Henry Everett (d 1917) EA/18*

WALTON, Herbert (d 1954 [74]) actor BE*, WWT/14*

WALTON, J. K. (d 1928 [79])
actor BE*, WWT/14*

WALTON, Mrs. J. K. [Maude
Osmond] (d 1917) EA/18*

WALTON, Mrs. J. K. see
Walton, Sarah Ann

WALTON, John (d 1847) actor,
singer WWT/14*

WALTON, Lottie [Mrs. Robin-
son] (d 1904 [27]) EA/05*

WALTON, Mary (fl 1845) actress
HAS

WALTON, Minnie [Mrs. Frederick
Lyster] (d 1879) actress,
singer CDP

WALTON, Sarah Ann [Mrs. J.
K. Walton] (d 1888 [37])
EA/89*

WALTON, Tony (b 1934) English
designer, producer BE,
WWT/14-16

WALTON, Vera (d 1965 [74])
actress TW/22

WALTON, Mrs. W. see
Craston, Annie

WALTON, Welmouth (fl 1852)
actor HAS

WALTON, William (d 1878 [23])
music-hall performer? EA/
79*

WALTON, William (d 1904 [44])
EA/05*

WALTON, Sir William (b 1902)
English composer ES, HP

WALTON-HEMMING, Mrs. Richard
see Walton-Hemming, Sarah

WALTON-HEMMING, Sarah [Mrs.
Richard Walton-Hemming] (d
1910) EA/11*

WALTZER, Jack (b 1936) American actor TW/29

WALWYN, B. (b 1750) English
dramatist CP/3

WAMBOLD, David (1836-1889)
American minstrel CDP, HAS,
SR

WAMBUS, Francis (fl 1611-24)
actor DA

WANAMAKER, Sam (b 1919)
American actor, director,
producer AAS, BE, PDT,
TW/2-8, WWT/11-16

WANDESFORD, Osborne Sydney
(fl 1730) dramatist CP/2-3,
GT

WANDREY, Donna (b 1947)
American actress TW/26

WANGER, Walter (1894-1968)

American producer ES

WAPUL, George (fl 1576) dramatist
CP/1-3, FGF

WARAM, Percy (d 1961 [80]) English actor TW/1, 3-4, 9, 11-
13, 18, WWT/9-13

WARBOYS, Thomas (fl 1770-77)
actor, dramatist CP/2-3, GT

WARBURTON, A. Hornby (d 1910)
actor? EA/11*

WARBURTON, Charles M. (1887-
1952) English actor WWT/4-7

WARBURTON, Edward A. (b 1867)
Irish actor GRB/1-2

WARD, Mrs. [née Hoare] actress
GT, TD/1-2

WARD, Mrs. (d c. 1770) actress
TD/1-2

WARD, Miss see Guerrabella,
Mme.

WARD, Albert (b 1869) English
actor GRB/1

WARD, Albert (d 1956 [86]) actor
BE*, WWT/14*

WARD, Alfred William (d 1894)
tank performer EA/96*

WARD, Annie (fl 1867) actress
HAS

WARD, Annie [Mrs. James Moor
Ward] (d 1910) EA/11*

WARD, Annie (d 1918 [72]) actress
BE*, WWT/14*

WARD, Anthony (fl 1603) actor
DA

"WARD, Artemus" see Browne,
Charles Farrar

WARD, Arthur Sarsfield see
Rohmer, Sax

WARD, Sir A. W. (d 1924 [86])
historian BE*, WWT/14*

WARD, Bedelia [Mrs. John Ward]
(d 1879) EA/80*

WARD, Betty Australian actress
WWT/4-7

WARD, Charles (b 1761) property
man HAS

WARD, Clara (d 1973 [48]) performer BP/57*

WARD, Dolph (d 1891 [41]) EA/92*

WARD, Dorothy (b 1890) English
actress, singer COC, OC/3,
WWT/3-13

WARD, Douglas Turner (b 1930)
American actor, dramatist,
director, producer CB, CD,
TW/28-30, WWT/15-16

WARD, E. D. (d 1889 [36]) actor
CDP

WARD, Edgar (d 1901) musical
director EA/02*
WARD, Edward ["Ned"] (1667-
1731) English dramatist CP/
1-3, GT
WARD, E. L. (d 1916) EA/17*
WARD, Ethel (d 1955 [75]) actress
BE*, WWT/14*
WARD, Evelyn (d 1895 [32])
EA/96*
WARD, Fanny [or Fannie; Mrs.
Joe Lewis] (1872/75-1952)
American actress COC,
GRB/1-4, OC/3, TW/8,
WWM, WWS, WWT/1-11
WARD, Fleming (d 1962 [75])
actor TW/1, 19
WARD, Dame Geneviève [Countess
de Guerbel] (1838-1922) Amer-
ican actress CDP, COC, DP,
ES, GRB/1-4, OAA/1-2, OC/
1-3, WWA/1, WWM, WWS,
WWT/1-4, WWW/2
WARD, Hap (d 1944 [76]) Amer-
ican performer, producer
BE*, BP/28*
WARD, Henry (fl 1736) actor,
dramatist CP/1-3, GT
WARD, Henry [Arthur W. Dud-
ley] (1868-1913) American
minstrel, manager SR
WARD, Henry Rohadehouse (d
1886) EA/87*
WARD, Hettie (d 1892 [12]) ac-
tress EA/93*
WARD, Hugh J. (1871-1941)
American manager WWT/
3-8
WARD, Mrs. Humphrey (1851-
1920) Tasmanian dramatist
WWW/2
WARD, James M. (d 1892 [41])
actor EA/93*
WARD, Mrs. James Moor see
Ward, Annie
WARD, Jane [Mrs. Tom Ward]
(d 1892 [56]) EA/93*
WARD, Janet American actress
BE, TW/14-17, 22-23, 26-29
WARD, John (d 1893) EA/95*
WARD, Mrs. John see Ward,
Bedelia
WARD, Mrs. John see Ward,
Sarah
WARD, Joseph (1867-1946) actor,
minstrel, vaudevillian SR
WARD, Kate (d 1872) actress
EA/73*

WARD, Lem (1907-42) director
CB
WARD, Lewis J. (d 1903) actor
EA/05*
WARD, Mrs. Lewis J. (d 1893
[30]) EA/94*
WARD, Mackenzie (b 1903) English
actor WWT/8-12
WARD, Mary (d 1966 [78]) Ameri-
can press representative, ac-
tress BE, TW/22
WARD, Ned see Ward, Edward
WARD, Penelope Dudley (b 1914)
English actress TW/3-4, WWT/
9-11
WARD, Polly (b 1909) English ac-
tress WWT/9-11
WARD, Richard (b 1915) American
actor TW/25, 30
WARD, Richard H. (d 1970 [59])
producer/director/choreographer
BP/54*
WARD, Ronald (b 1901) English
actor WWT/8-14
WARD, Samuel actor HAS
WARD, Col. Samuel (d 1879 [70])
EA/80*
WARD, Sarah (d 1771 [39]) actress
WWT/14*
WARD, Sarah [Mrs. John Ward]
(d 1786) actress CDP
WARD, Simon (b 1941) English ac-
tor WWT/15-16
WARD, Solly (1891-1942) actor SR
WARD, Sydney (d 1902) musical
director EA/03*
WARD, Thomas (b 1799) English
actor HAS
WARD, Thomas (1807-73) American
composer, dramatist CDP,
DAB
WARD, Thomas H. (d 1886 [35])
clog dancer EA/87*
WARD, Mrs. Tom see Ward,
Jane
WARD, W. (fl 1785) dramatist
CP/3
WARD, William (d 1972 [62]) per-
former BP/56*
WARD, William H. [Marvin Morton
Mallison] (b 1852) minstrel,
comedian CDP
WARD, William Melmoth (b 1822)
English actor HAS
WARD, Winifred (d 1975 [95])
music-hall performer, male
impersonator BP/60*, WWT/
16*

WARD, W. M. (d 1879) American pantomimist EA/80*

WARDALE, R. (d 1904) lessee
EA/05*

WARDE, Annie [Mrs. John
Warde] (d 1876) EA/77*

WARDE, Anthony (d 1975 [66])
performer BP/59*

WARDE, Eleanor [Mrs. John
Warde] (d 1881 [69]) EA/82*

WARDE, Ernest C. (d 1923
[49]) actor, stage manager
BE*, BP/8*

WARDE, Frederick Barkham
(1851-1935) English actor,
manager CDP, COC, DAB,
GRB/2-4, OC/1-3, PP/3,
SR, WWA/1, WWM, WWS,
WWT/1-7

WARDE, George (d 1917 [80])
actor EA/97

WARDE, Mrs. George [née
Priscilla Lemmon] (d 1877)
actress EA/78*

WARDE, George Faulkner (d
1898 [41]) scene artist EA/99*

WARDE, George Henry [Harry
Lemmon] (d 1888) actor EA/
89*

WARDE, Mrs. G. F. [Tilly
Poole] (d 1884) EA/85*

WARDE, James Prescott (1792-
1840) English actor CDP,
DNB, OX

WARDE, J. G. (d 1887 [85])
EA/88*

WARDE, Mrs. John see Warde,
Annie

WARDE, Mrs. John see Warde,
Eleanor

WARDE, Johnny (d 1892) music-
hall comedian EA/93*

WARDE, Trevor (d 1899 [36])
EA/00*

WARDE, William (fl 1756) dramatist CP/2-3

WARDE, William (d 1859 [48])
comic singer EA/72*

WARDE, Willie (1857-1943) English actor, dancer CDP,
GRB/1-4, WWT/2-8

WARDE, W. Lemmon (b 1870)
English actor GRB/1

WARDELL, Charles see Kelly,
Charles

WARDELL, Charles Clavering
see Kelly, Charles

WARDELL, Chrystabel Elizabeth

[Chrissy Levens] (d 1888 [16])
music-hall performer EA/89*

WARDELL, Mrs. Robert see
Reeve, Emma Louisa

WARDEN, Mrs. (d 1884) EA/85*

WARDEN, Edward Adams (b 1822)
English singer, actor HAS

WARDEN, Edwin Adams (d 1880
[60]) minstrel EA/81*

WARDEN, Fred W. (d 1929 [68])
actor, producer, manager BE*,
WWT/14*

WARDEN, Gertrude [Mrs. Wilton
Jones] (b 1862) English actress
CDP, EA/96, GRB/1-3

WARDEN, Jack (b 1920) American
actor BE, TW/10, 12-15, 25

WARDEN, Jenny [Mrs. J. F.
Warden] (d 1912) EA/13*

WARDEN, J. F. (1836-98) English
actor, managing director OAA/2

WARDEN, Mrs. J. F. [née Jenny
Bellair] (b 1837) English actress
OAA/2

WARDEN, Mrs. J. F. see
Warden, Jenny

WARDEN, Samuel (d 1884 [18])
EA/85*

WARDEN, Sydney (d 1901) actor
EA/02*

WARDEN-REED, Frank [Fritz E.
A. Weiste] (b 1879) English actor GRB/1

WARDHAUGH, Mathew (d 1888
[75]) actor EA/89*

WARDLE, Irving (b 1929) English
critic AAS, WWT/15-16

WARDROPER, Henry (d 1910)
EA/11*

WARDROPER, John [Johnny Lee]
(d 1880) Scottish comedian
EA/81*

WARDWELL, Geoffrey (1900-55)
English actor, director WWT/
10-11

WARDWELL, John American actor
TW/30

WARE, Dr. dramatist RJ

WARE, Albert see Cartini, Albert

WARE, Bill (b 1943) American
actor TW/28

WARE, Charles (fl 1858) actor
HAS

WARE, Courtney (d 1878) manager
EA/79*

WARE, Mrs. Courtney see
Willmore, Lizzie

WARE, George (d 1895 [66])
singer, agent EA/97*

WARE, Harriet (d 1962 [84])
American composer WWA/4

WARE, Helen [Helen Remer]
(1877/79-1939) American actress GRB/3-4, WWA/1,
WWM, WWT/1-8

WARE, Irene [Mrs. J. F. Cli-
burn] (d 1909) EA/10*

WARE, Nettee (d 1913 [29])
EA/14*

WARE, William Hibbert (d 1908
[36]) EA/09*

WAREING, Alfred (1876-1942)
English business manager,
manager, producer, librarian
GRB/3, WWT/2-9

WAREING, Lesley (b 1913) English actress WWT/8-12

WAREING, Robert (d 1888 [39])
proprietor EA/89*

WARFAZ, Georges de (1889?-
1959) Belgian actor BE*

WARFIELD, David (1866-1951)
American actor CDP, COC,
ES, GRB/2-4, HJD, NTH,
OC/1-3, SR, TW/8, WWA/3,
WWM, WWS, WWT/1-11

WARFIELD, Joel (b 1937) American actor TW/19, 25

WARFIELD, Marlene (b 1941)
American actress TW/25-26

WARFIELD, William (b 1920)
American singer, actor BE,
TW/22-23

WARIK, Josef American actor
TW/26-27

WARING, Mrs. (fl 1822-24)
English actress HAS

WARING, Ann see Wallack,
Mrs. James William

WARING, Barbara (b 1912) English actress WWT/10-11

WARING, Bertha [Mrs. John
Wilson Musante] (d 1904)
EA/05*

WARING, Claire (b 1917) American actress TW/25

WARING, Dorothy May Graham
(b 1895) English actress,
singer WWT/3-6

WARING, Herbert [Herbert Waring Rutty] (1857-1932) English
actor EA/95, GRB/1-4,
WWT/1-6, WWW/3

WARING, James (d 1975 [53])
producer/director/choreographer

BP/60*

WARING, Leigh (d 1817) English
actor, stage manager HAS

WARING, Mary (d 1964 [72]) actress BE*

WARING, Noel E. (d 1854) circus
manager HAS

WARING, Richard (b 1912) English
actor BE, TW/3-11, 13-19,
24, WWT/10-16

WARLEY, May English actress
GRB/2-4

WARMINGTON, Stanley J. (1884-
1941) English actor WWT/6-9

WARMINGTON, William (fl 1880)
actor CDP

WARNE, George (d 1868 [71])
musician EA/69*

WARNE, Harry (d 1884) equestrian
clown EA/85*

WARNE, Thomas B. (d 1891 [39])
EA/93*

WARNER, Mrs. see Warner,
Mary Amelia

WARNER, Andrew J. (d 1965 [81])
critic BP/50*

WARNER, Anne [Anne Warner
French] (1869-1913) American
dramatist WWM, WWS

WARNER, Charles (d 1865 [34])
circus showman HAS

WARNER, Charles [Charles Lick-
fold] (1846-1909) English actor
CDP, COC, DNB, DP, GRB/
1-4, OAA/2, OC/1-3

WARNER, David (b 1941) English
actor AAS, WWT/14-16

WARNER, Elizabeth [Mrs. Richard
Warner] (d 1884 [29]) EA/85*

WARNER, Ernest A. (b 1882)
English agent GRB/1

WARNER, Fred (d 1900) EA/01*

WARNER, George Frederick (d
1867 [32]) comic singer EA/68*

WARNER, Grace [Mrs. Franklin
McLeay] (1873-1925) English
actress, manager GRB/1-4,
WWT/1-5

WARNER, Mrs. H. [Emmie d'Este]
(d 1874 [29]) burlesque actress
EA/75*

WARNER, Harry (d 1908) scene
artist EA/09*

WARNER, Henry Byron (1876-1958)
English actor ES, GRB/1-4,
SR, TW/15, WWA/5, WWM,
WWS, WWT/1-11

WARNER, Mrs. H[enry] B[yron]

see Paullin, Louise
WARNER, Hugh L. (d 1894
  [41]) EA/95*
WARNER, Jemmy (fl 1777?) clown
  CDP
WARNER, Jennie (fl 1858) HAS
WARNER, J. L. (d 1871 [26])
  actor EA/72*
WARNER, Kate L. (d 1899 [70])
  EA/00*
WARNER, Marsha (b 1949) Amer-
  ican actress TW/29
WARNER, Mary Amelia [née
  Huddart] (1797/1804-1854)
  Irish actress CDP, DNB,
  HAS, SR
WARNER, Neil (d 1901 [71])
  Australian actor HAS
WARNER, Richard (d 1775) trans-
  lator CP/2-3
WARNER, Mrs. Richard see
  Warner, Elizabeth
WARNER, Rick (b 1943) American
  actor TW/30
WARNER, W. A. (b 1826) Amer-
  ican actor HAS
WARNER, William (d 1608/09)
  dramatist, translator CP/3
WARNICK, Clay (b 1915) Amer-
  ican composer, musical di-
  rector, producer BE
WARNOW, Helen (d 1970 [46])
  performer BP/55*
WARRAL, Mrs. (fl 1777) singer
  CDP
WARRE, Michael (b 1922) English
  actor, designer AAS, TW/
  2-3, WWT/10-16
WARRELL, Master (fl 1793-1812)
  Scottish actor HAS
WARRELL, Mrs. (fl 1790) ac-
  tress TD/1-2
WARRELL, Eliza see Atkins,
  Mrs. William
WARREN, Mr. actor CDP
WARREN, Mrs. (fl 1786?) ac-
  tress CDP
WARREN, Miss see Price,
  Mrs.
WARREN, Albert H. (fl 1876-79)
  actor OAA/1-2
WARREN, Anna see Marble,
  Mrs. Danforth
WARREN, Betty [Babette Hilda
  Hogan] (b 1905) English ac-
  tress, singer WWT/9-14
WARREN, Bob (d 1892) circus
  performer EA/93*

WARREN, Brett (b 1910) American
  director BE
WARREN, C. Denier (1889-1971)
  American actor WWT/4-15
WARREN, Mrs. Charles see
  Fish, Marguerite
WARREN, Mrs. Duane (fl 1866)
  actress HAS
WARREN, Edward Alyn (d 1974
  [54]) manager BP/59*
WARREN, Ella (fl 1850) dancer
  HAS
WARREN, Ernest (d 1887 [45])
  dramatist NYM
WARREN, F. Brooke (d 1950 [83])
  actor BE*, WWT/14*
WARREN, Georgiana [Mrs. Philip
  Warren] (1829-96) actress CDP
WARREN, Harry (b 1893) American
  composer BE, CB
WARREN, Hester see Proctor,
  Mrs. Joseph
WARREN, Mrs. H. L. see
  Frost, Edith
WARREN, Iris (d 1963) speech
  teacher WWT/14*
WARREN, James (d 1876) comedian
  EA/77*
WARREN, Jeff [né Jones] (b 1921)
  American actor, director, singer
  BE, WWT/12-16
WARREN, Jennifer (b 1941) Amer-
  ican actress TW/29
WARREN, Jimmy (d 1972 [50])
  performer BP/57*
WARREN, John Byrne Leicester
  (1835-95) dramatist HP
WARREN, Joseph (b 1916) Ameri-
  can actor TW/22-24, 26, 29
WARREN, J. V. (fl 1848) actor
  HAS
WARREN, Kenneth J. (1929-73)
  Australian actor TW/20,
  WWT/15-16
WARREN, Lavinia see "Thumb,
  Mrs. Tom"
WARREN, Leonard (1911-60)
  American singer CB, ES,
  TW/16, WWA/3
WARREN, Lesley Ann (b 1946)
  American actress TW/20, 22,
  30
WARREN, Mary Ann see Rice,
  Mrs. John B.
WARREN, Mercy Otis (1728-1814)
  American dramatist CP/3,
  DAB, EAP, HJD, NTH, RJ
WARREN, Minnie (fl 1877?) dwarf

CDP

WARREN, Mirian Howell (d 1972 [72]) agent BP/56*

WARREN, Mrs. Philip see Warren, Georgiana

WARREN, Richard Henry (1859-1933) American composer DAB, WWA/1, WWM

WARREN, Robert Penn (b 1905) American dramatist MD, MWD

WARREN, Suzanne Le Mesurier (d 1969 [75]) performer BP/54*

WARREN, T. Gideon (d 1919 [65]) actor, dramatist BE*, WWT/14*

WARREN, Wade (d 1973 [76]) actor, director TW/29

WARREN, W. H. (d 1878 [35]) circus stud groom EA/79*

WARREN, William (1767-1832) English/American actor CDP, COC, DAB, HAS, OC/1-3, SR, WWA/H

WARREN, William (d 1878 [32]) musician EA/79*

WARREN, William (1812-88) American actor CDP, DAB, HAS, OC/1-3, WWA/H

WARREN, Mrs. William see Brunton, Anne

WARREN, William Henry see Atom, Willie

WARRENDER, Harold (1903-53) English actor WWT/7-11

WARRENER, Warren (d 1961 [73]) actor BE*

WARREN-SMITH, Mrs. P. see Loftus, Kitty

WARRICK, Elizabeth (d 1974 [60]) performer BP/59*

WARRICK, Ruth (b 1915) American actress BE, TW/27-30, WWT/16

WARRILOW, John (d 1906 [70]) comedian EA/07*

WARRINER, Annie (d 1900 [44]) EA/01*

WARRINER, Frederic (b 1916) American actor TW/7-8, 11-15, 22-25, 27-28, WWT/14-16

WARRINGTON, Ann [Mary L. Woods] (fl 1895-1909) American actress WWM

WARRINGTON, William (d 1887 [44]) music-hall performer EA/88*

WARRISS, G. A. (d 1893 [52]) journalist EA/94*

WARTENBERG, P. (b 1867) Dutch acrobat GRB/1

WARTENBERG, W. (b 1871) Dutch acrobat GRB/1

WARTON, Elizabeth Hines (d 1971 [76]) performer BP/55*

WARWICK, Ethel [Mrs. Edmund Waller] (1882-1951) English actress GRB/1-4, WWT/1-9

WARWICK, Giulia (d 1904 [47]) singer, actress DP

WARWICK, J. H. (fl 1847-57) English actor HAS

WARWICK, John (d 1972 [67]) performer BP/56*

WARWICK, Kate see Vance, Kate

WARWICK, Robert (d 1964 [85]) actor WWT/14*

WARWICK, Robert [Robert Taylor Bien] (1878-1964) American actor TW/21, WWM, WWT/4-11

WARWICK, Rev. Thomas (fl 1784) dramatist CP/3

WARWICK-MOORE, J. (b 1868) English musical director, composer GRB/1

WASE, Christopher (d c. 1690) translator CP/2-3

WASHBOURNE, Mona (b 1903) English actress AAS, TW/14-15, 27, WWT/13-16

WASHBURN, Bryant (1889-1963) American actor BE*, BP/47*

WASHBURN, Charles (d 1972 [82]) dramatist BP/56*

WASHBURN, Jack (b 1927) American singer, actor BE, TW/19

WASHER, Ben (b 1906) American press representative BE

WASHINGTON, Dinah (d 1963 [39]) performer BP/48*

WASHINGTON, Florence (d 1872) dancer EA/73*

WASHINGTON, Lamont (d 1969 [24]) actor, singer TW/25

WASHINGTON, Vernon (b 1927) American actor TW/24-25

WASSERMAN, Dale (b 1917) American dramatist, librettist BE, CD

WATERFIELD, Charles singer, composer CDP

WATERHOUSE, Mr. singer TD/1-2

WATERHOUSE, Frederick G.
(d 1904) EA/05*

WATERHOUSE, Mrs. John [Mrs.
H. Wallis] (d 1871) actress
EA/72*

WATERHOUSE, Keith (b 1929)
English dramatist CD, CH,
WWT/14-16

WATERLOW, Marjorie (1888-
1921) English actress WWT/
2-3

WATERMAN, Dennis (b 1948)
English actor WWT/15-16

WATERMAN, Ida (d 1941 [89])
actress BE*, WWT/14*

WATERMAN, Willard (b 1914)
American actor TW/23-26,
30

WATEROUS, Allen H. (d 1965
[61]) performer BP/50*

WATEROUS, Herbert L. (1868-
1947) American singer TW/4,
WWM

WATERS, Ethel (1900-77) American actress, singer BE,
CB, COC, OC/3, TW/1,
3-20, WWT/9-16

WATERS, James (d 1923 [68])
critic WWT/1-4, WWW/2

WATERS, James R. (d 1945)
Hungarian/American comedian
CB

WATERS, Jan (b 1937) English
actress, singer WWT/15-16

WATERS, Paulette (b 1947)
American actress TW/22-23

WATERS, T. Hadley (d 1964
[67]) dramatist BP/49*

WATERS, Thomas (fl 1607) actor
DA

WATERSON, J. (d 1893) bandmaster EA/94*

WATERSON, Samuel A. (b 1940)
American actor TW/24-30,
WWT/15-16

WATERSTREET, Edmund (b 1943)
American actor TW/25-26

WATFORD, Gwen (b 1927) English actress WWT/15-16

WATHALL, Alfred G. (d 1938
[58]) English composer BE*,
BP/23*

WATHEN, Mr. (fl c.1792?) actor
CDP, GT, TD/1-2

WATKIN, Alexander see Afrique

WATKIN, Pierre (d 1960) actor
BE*

WATKINS, Catherine (d 1916

[72]) EA/17*

WATKINS, Charles (d 1882) photographer EA/83*

WATKINS, Mrs. Charles A. see
Gray, Ada

WATKINS, Charles W. (d 1892)
EA/93*

WATKINS, Dick (d 1864 [36]) comic
singer, comedian HAS

WATKINS, Elizabeth [Mrs. Pio
Watkins] (d 1894) EA/95*

WATKINS, Harry (1825-94) American actor, manager CDP, HAS

WATKINS, Mrs. Harry [Mrs.
Charles Howard; née Rosina
Shaw] (1829-1904) English ac-
tress CDP, HAS

WATKINS, Helen W. (d 1972 [84])
performer BP/56*

WATKINS, Henry (d 1875 [38])
singer EA/76*

WATKINS, John (d 1905 [68]) EA/
06*

WATKINS, John see Rivalli

WATKINS, Linda (1908/14-76)
American actress TW/2-4,
WWT/7-11

WATKINS, Maurine (d 1968 [68])
dramatist BP/54*

WATKINS, Perry R. (d 1974 [67])
producer/director/choreographer
BP/59*

WATKINS, Mrs. Pio see Watkins,
Elizabeth

WATKINS, Rosina see Watkins,
Mrs. Harry

WATKINS, Thomas (d 1911) EA/12*

WATKINS, William (fl 1802) dramatist CP/3

WATKYN, Arthur (1907-65) Welsh
dramatist WWT/12-14

WATKYN-WYNNE, Nora (d 1908)
EA/09*

WATLING, Dilys [née Rhys-Jones]
(b 1946) English actress WWT/
15-16

WATLING, Jack (b 1923) English
actor WWT/11-16

WATLING, Peter (d 1961 [40])
dramatist WWT/14*

WATSON, Mrs. [Mrs. Dodge] (fl
1835-36) actress HAS

WATSON, Mrs. (d 1871) actress?
EA/72*

WATSON, Mrs. (d 1883) EA/84*

WATSON, Miss actress CDP

WATSON, Miss see Bailey, Mrs.

WATSON, Miss see Brooks, Mrs.

WATSON, Alfred Edward Thomas (1849-1922) critic GRB/2-4

WATSON, Alfred R. (d 1903 [58]) musical director, composer EA/04*

WATSON, Ann [née Wells] (d 1854) actress? HAS

WATSON, Mrs. Barney see Watson, Kate

WATSON, Betty Jane (b 1926/28) American actress, singer BE, TW/5-6, WWT/11

WATSON, Billy (d 1945 [78]) American performer, producer BE*, BP/29*

WATSON, Bobby (d 1965 [77]) performer BP/49*

WATSON, Charles (d 1851) American actor HAS

WATSON, Charlotte see Bailey, Mrs. Thomas

WATSON, David Scott [D. W. Servius] (d 1889 [51]) music-hall performer EA/90*

WATSON, Douglas [or Douglass] (b 1921) American actor AAS, BE, TW/4-21, 23-24, 28-30, WWT/12-16

WATSON, E. Bradlee (d 1961 [82]) American educator, editor BE*

WATSON, Eleanor (fl 1861) singer HAS

WATSON, Elizabeth (d 1931) Scottish actress WWT/5-6

WATSON, Elizabeth see Boman, Mrs. John

WATSON, Ellen Maria see Williams, Nelly

WATSON, Emily see Royce, Mrs. W.

WATSON, Fanny (d 1970 [80]) vaudevillian BP/54*

WATSON, Fanny Mary (d 1874 [92]) manager EA/75*

WATSON, F. Groves (d 1907 [53]) comedian EA/08*

WATSON, F. H. (d 1882 [50]) acting manager EA/83*

WATSON, Florence English actress, singer GRB/1

WATSON, Frederick (d 1874 [21]) pantomimist EA/76*

WATSON, George (fl 1795) dramatist CP/3

WATSON, George (d 1896) registrar & secretary of Royal College of Music EA/97*

WATSON, George M. (d 1971 [51]) publicist BP/55*

WATSON, G. Howard see Manders, Lucy

WATSON, G. L. (d 1872 [46]) music-hall proprietor EA/73*

WATSON, Harry actor CDP

WATSON, Henrietta [Mrs. Walter Thornton Radcliffe] (1873-1964) Scottish actress EA/96, GRB/1-4, WWT/1-12

WATSON, Horace (1867-1934) English manager WWT/4-6

WATSON, Master I. L. Z. juvenile prodigy CDP

WATSON, Ivan Vernon (d 1904 [48]) actor EA/05*

WATSON, Jack Bowles (d 1906 [36]) EA/07*

WATSON, Mrs. J. B. (d 1892) actress EA/93*

WATSON, Dr. J. C. (d 1889) EA/90*

WATSON, John (1520-83) English dramatist CP/2-3, FGF

WATSON, John (d 1867 [63]) stage manager EA/68*

WATSON, John (d 1889 [55]) proprietor EA/90*

WATSON, Mrs. John (fl 1835) actress, singer CDP

WATSON, John Boel (d 1881 [43]) comedian EA/82*

WATSON, John Bowles (d 1804) manager TD/1-2

WATSON, J. R. (d 1887) architect EA/88*

WATSON, Kate [Mrs. Barney Watson] (d 1894 [45]) EA/95*

WATSON, Kitty (d 1967 [80]) performer BP/51*

WATSON, Lee (b 1926) American lighting designer BE

WATSON, Leona (fl 1900s) American actress, singer WWM

WATSON, Lucille (1879-1962) Canadian actress CB, TW/2-11, 19, WWT/7-13

WATSON, Malcolm (1853/57-1929) Scottish critic, dramatist GRB/2-4, WWT/1-5

WATSON, Margaret (d 1940 [65]) actress WWT/4-9

WATSON, Margaret Sarah (d 1913) EA/14*

WATSON, Maria (d 1869 [66]) costumier EA/70*

WATSON, Michael (d 1889) com-

poser EA/90*
WATSON, Minor (1889-1965)
American actor TW/2-4, 22,
WWT/6-11
WATSON, Moray (b 1930) English
actor TW/20
WATSON, Paddy (d 1908 [62])
comedian, circus clown EA/
10*
WATSON, Ralph Haines see
Granville, Fred
WATSON, Rosabel (d 1959 [94])
conductor WWT/14*
WATSON, Rosabel Grace (d 1940
[65]) actress BE*
WATSON, Sammy (b 1854) Irish
animal trainer WWM
WATSON, Solomon Lancelot
Inglis see Lister, Lance
WATSON, Stuart (d 1956 [64])
producer, lessee, manager
BE*, WWT/14*
WATSON, Susan (b 1938) Ameri-
can actress, singer, dancer
BE, TW/21-23, 25-29
WATSON, Thomas (d 1886 [81])
actor? EA/87*
WATSON, Thomas (d 1896 [49])
comedian EA/97*
WATSON, Thomas M. (d 1963
[62]) dramatist, critic BE*
WATSON, Tilly (d 1898) serio-
comic EA/99*
WATSON, Tom (d 1860) English
circus clown HAS
WATSON, Tony (d 1913 [23])
EA/14*
WATSON, Vernon (d 1949 [62])
performer BE*, WWT/14*
WATSON, William (fl c. 1782?)
dramatist CP/3
WATSON, Wylie [John Wylie
Robertson] (1899-1966) Scottish
actor WWT/8-10
WATSON-SCOTT, Mr. (d 1909)
EA/10*
WATT, Billie Lou (b 1924)
American actress TW/2-3, 28
WATT, Hannah (d 1969) performer
BP/54*
WATTERS, George Manker (d
1943 [52]) American dramatist,
producer BE*, WWT/14*
WATTERS, Hal (b 1943) Ameri-
can actor TW/25, 27, 29
WATTERSON, George (1783-1854)
American dramatist EAP
WATTIS, Richard (1912-75) Eng-

lish actor WWT/12-15
WATTLE, Miss see Stanley, Mrs.
WATTS, Mrs. (d 1876 [45]) EA/77*
WATTS, Mrs. see Sefton, Mrs.
John
WATTS, Charles (d 1883) comedian
EA/84*
WATTS, Charles (d 1966) actor
TW/23
WATTS, Dodo (b 1910) English
actress WWT/7-9
WATTS, Elizabeth (d 1967 [79])
actress, singer TW/24
WATTS, Francis Walter [Frank
Clifford] (d 1874) actor EA/75*
WATTS, Henry (d 1881 [70]) music-
hall proprietor EA/82*
WATTS, John see Hanson, John
WATTS, Jonathan (b 1934) American
dancer ES
WATTS, Joseph Albert (d 1881 [29])
musician EA/82*
WATTS, Norman (d 1891) actor
EA/92*
WATTS, Peter (d 1972 [72]) pro-
ducer/director/choreographer
BP/57*
WATTS, Richard, Jr. (b 1898)
American critic AAS, BE,
NTH, OC/1-3, WWT/9-16
WATTS, Stephen (b 1910) Scottish
critic WWT/11-16
WATTS, Weldon (d 1902 [45])
proprietor, director EA/03*
WATTS-PHILLIPS, Mrs. Basil
see Watts, Sophie
WATTS-PHILLIPS, John Edward
(1894-1960) Welsh manager
WWT/9-11
WATTS-PHILLIPS, Sophie [Mrs.
Basil Watts-Phillips] (d 1894)
EA/95*
WAUGH, Amelia (1836-87) Ameri-
can actress NYM
WAUGH, Mrs. De Witt (fl 1843)
actress HAS
WAVER, Robert see Wever,
Robert
WAXMAN, Arthur (b 1921) Ameri-
can manager, producer BE
WAXMAN, Morris D. (d 1931 [55])
actor BE*, WWT/14*
WAY, Mrs. (fl 1843) actress HAS
WAYBURN, Ned (1874-1942) Amer-
ican director, producer WWA/
2, WWT/7-9
WAYER, William (fl 1598-1605)
dramatist CP/1-3

WAYHO, Jack (d 1917) variety performer EA/18*

WAYLETT, Harriet (1798-1851) English actress, singer BS, CDP, DNB, OX

WAYNE, Burt (d 1879) minstrel, songcomposer CDP

WAYNE, David (b 1914) American actor AAS, BE, CB, TW/3-6, 10-24, WWT/11-16

WAYNE, Fredd (b 1923) American actor TW/6-8

WAYNE, Horace Stokes (b 1858) American dramatist WWM

WAYNE, Naunton (1901-70) Welsh actor, entertainer AAS, WWT/9-14, WWW/6

WAYNE, Paula (b 1937) American actress, singer BE

WAYNE, Rollo (1899-1954) American scene designer WWT/7-10

WAYNE, Thomas (d 1971 [31]) performer BP/56*

WAYT, Lizzie (b 1841) American lecturer HAS

WEAD, Frank W. (1894-1947) dramatist SR

WEADOCK, Mrs. Louis see Bergere, Ouida

WEADON, Percy (d 1939 [79]) American producer, press representative BE*, BP/23*

WEALES, Gerald (b 1925) American educator BE

WEAR, Millard (d 1970 [73]) journalist BP/55*

WEATHERBURN, Elizabeth (d 1905 [63]) EA/06*

WEATHERBURN, William (d 1886 [32]) pantomimist EA/87*

WEATHERHEAD, Elizabeth K. (d 1892) EA/93*

WEATHERLEY, Alec (1874-1910) English business manager, stage manager GRB/1-2

WEATHERLY, Alec see Weatherley, Alec

WEATHERS, Roscoe (d 1976 [55]) composer/lyricist BP/60*

WEATHERSBY, Eliza [Mrs. Nat C. Goodwin] (1849-87) English actress CDP, HAS, NYM, SR

WEATHERSBY, Eliza Jane (d 1904 [67]) actress EA/05*

WEATHERSBY, Miss Ernie (d 1884 [22]) actress EA/85*

WEATHERSBY, Frank (b 1870) English agent, manager GRB/1-3

WEATHERSBY, George (d 1911 [81]) actor EA/13*

WEATHERSBY, Helen (d 1943 [80]) actress BE*, WWT/14*

WEATHERSBY, Jennie actress CDP

WEAVER, Affie (1855-1940) actress CB

WEAVER, "Doddles" (b 1914) American actor TW/2-3

WEAVER, Fritz (b 1926) American actor BE, CB, TW/12-22, 25-27, WWT/14-16

WEAVER, Henry A., Sr. (b 1832) English actor PP/3

WEAVER, Henry A., Jr. (b 1858) American actor PP/3

WEAVER, John (1673-1760) English dancing-master, dramatist COC, CP/1-3, DNB, ES, GT, OC/3, TD/1-2

WEAVER, Mrs. John (d 1916) EA/17*

WEAVER, John H. (fl 1833) American actor HAS

WEAVER, John V. A. (1893-1938) American dramatist, critic HJD

WEAVER, Paul Fred see Ford, Paul

WEBB, Mr. (fl 1822) actor CDP

WEBB, Mrs. [née Child] (d 1793) English actress CDP, GT, TD/1-2

WEBB, Mrs. (fl 1808?) actress CDP

WEBB, Mrs. A. (d 1905) EA/06*

WEBB, Ada (b 1845) American actress CDP, HAS

WEBB, Alan (b 1906) English actor, director AAS, BE, TW/4, 8-9, 14, 18, 20, 22-24, WWT/8-16

WEBB, Alfred (d 1899) EA/00*

WEBB, Alfred (d 1901 [48]) comedian EA/02*

WEBB, Alice [Mrs. Will Smith] (d 1904) swimmer EA/05*

WEBB, Alyce Elizabeth (b 1934) American actress TW/26-27, 29-30

WEBB, Arthur Cecil (d 1907) actor EA/08*

WEBB, Charles (d 1851) American actor HAS

WEBB, Charles (d 1889) actor, manager CDP

WEBB, Charles (d 1906) actor, scene artist EA/08*

WEBB, Clifton (1891/93/94-1966) American actor, singer CB, ES, SR, TW/2-6, 23, WWA/4, WWT/7-11

WEBB, Constance (d 1872 [31]) singer EA/72*

WEBB, Edmund (d 1899) journalist EA/00*

WEBB, Elizabeth [Mrs. J. J. Webb] (d 1906) EA/07*

WEBB, Emma (b 1843) American actress CDP, HAS

WEBB, Ernest Henry (d 1868 [16]) EA/69*

WEBB, George John (d 1911 [74]) musician EA/12*

WEBB, Harry [or Henry] (1814-67) actor CDP

WEBB, Harry (d 1903) advance agent EA/04*

WEBB, Henry Berry (d 1867 [52]) comedian EA/68*

WEBB, Jack (d 1954 [65]) manager BE*, WWT/14*

WEBB, James A. (d 1859) actor HAS

WEBB, James Curtois (d 1893) EA/94*

WEBB, James Watson (1802-84) critic CDP

WEBB, Mrs. J. J. see Webb, Elizabeth

WEBB, John (1611-72) English scene painter, scene designer COC, ES, NTH, OC/1-3

WEBB, John (d 1913 [49]) actor EA/14*, WWT/14*

WEBB, Joseph James (d 1917) EA/18*

WEBB, Kenneth Seymour (1885-1966) American dramatist WWA/4

WEBB, Leonard (b 1930) English dramatist, actor CD

WEBB, Lizabeth (b 1926) English actress, singer WWT/11-12

WEBB, Lizzie see Fraser-Brunner, Queenie

WEBB, Mary (fl 1881) actress, singer CDP

WEBB, Nella (d 1954 [78]) American actress, singer TW/11, WWS

WEBB, Ruth (b 1923) American talent representative, singer, actress BE

WEBB, Sidney F. (d 1956 [64]) producer BE*, WWT/14*

WEBB, William (d 1903) scene artist EA/04*

WEBB, Little Willie (d 1878 [6]) actor EA/79*

WEBBE, Samuel (1740-1816) composer CDP

WEBBER, Carrie actress SR

WEBBER, Charles (d 1954 [79]) conductor BE*, WWT/14*

WEBBER, Eliza [Mrs. Arthur Wood] (d 1896) actress EA/97*

WEBBER, John F. (b 1867) American actor WWM

WEBBER, Lisa (c. 1842-87) English actress NYM

WEBBER, M. (d 1893 [57]) manager EA/94*

WEBBER, Mrs. M. A. (d 1893) EA/94*

WEBBER, Robert American actor BE, TW/12-18

WEBB SISTERS, The HAS

WEBER, Carl Maria von (1786-1826) German composer ES

WEBER, Edmund (d 1885) musician, composer EA/86*

WEBER, Edwin J. (d 1968 [75]) composer/lyricist BP/53*

WEBER, Fredricka (b 1940) American actress TW/26-27

WEBER, Henry William (1783-1818) Russian?/English editor DNB

WEBER, Mrs. Joe [Lillian Friedman] (d 1951 [76]) actress BE*, BP/36*

WEBER, Joseph (1867-1942) American actor, manager COC, DAB, ES, GRB/3-4, NTH, OC/3, SR, WWA/2, WWM, WWS, WWT/1-9

WEBER, Karl (b 1916) American actor TW/4-6

WEBER, Leonard S. (d 1973 [45]) producer/director/choreographer BP/58*

WEBER, Liza [Mrs. Robert Britton] (d 1887 [45]) actress CDP

WEBER, L. Lawrence (1872-1940) American producing manager CB, WWT/6-9

WEBER, William (b 1915) American actor TW/2-3

WEBER AND FIELDS COC, OC/3

WEBERN, Anton von (1883-1945) Austrian composer, conductor ES

WEBLEY, John (d 1971 [24])
performer BP/56*
WEBSTER, Mr. actor HAS
WEBSTER, Mr. (d c. 1784)
actor TD/1-2
WEBSTER, Anthony (d c. 1785)
actor CDP
WEBSTER, Mrs. Anthony see
Davies, Elizabeth
WEBSTER, Ben (1864-1947)
English actor COC, DNB,
EA/95, ES, GRB/1-4, OC/
1-3, TW/3, WWT/1-10, WWW/4
WEBSTER, Mrs. Ben see
Whitty, May
WEBSTER, Benjamin Nottingham
(1797-1882) English dramatist,
actor, manager CDP, COC,
DNB, EA/68, OAA/1-2, OC/
1-3
WEBSTER, Byron (b 1933) Eng-
lish actor TW/23, 25, 27
WEBSTER, Clara (1821/23-44)
English dancer CDP, ES
WEBSTER, Florence (d 1893
[28]) EA/94*
WEBSTER, Florence Ann (1860-
99) English actress, dancer
COC, OC/1-3
WEBSTER, Frederick (1802-78)
English stage manager COC,
OC/1-3
WEBSTER, George (fl 1598-
1603) actor DA
WEBSTER, Henry Kitchell (1875-
1932) American dramatist
WWA/1
WEBSTER, Jean [Mrs. Glennford
McKinney] (1876-1916) Amer-
ican dramatist WWA/1
WEBSTER, John (c. 1580-1634)
English dramatist COC, CP/
1-3, DNB, ES, FGF, HP,
MH, NTH, OC/1-3, PDT,
RE
WEBSTER, John (fl 1596) actor
DA
WEBSTER, John (b 1813) actor
CDP
WEBSTER, John actor CDP
WEBSTER, Mrs. John see
McHenry, Nellie
WEBSTER, Lizzie (fl 1878) ac-
tress CDP
WEBSTER, Margaret (1905-72)
American actress, producer,
director AAS, BE, CB, COC,
ES, OC/1-3, SR, TW/2-8,

23, 29, WWA/5, WWT/7-16
WEBSTER, Margaret Davies Eng-
lish actress GRB/1-3
WEBSTER, Marion Litonius (d
1971 [62]) performer BP/56*
WEBSTER, Paul Francis (b 1907)
American lyricist BE
WEBSTER, Thomas (d 1913 [80])
EA/14*
WEBSTER, Mrs. W. H. see
Greville, Mabel
WEBSTER, Wilfred H. Irish actor
GRB/1
WEBSTER-GLEASON, Lucile (1888-
1947) American actress WWT/
6-8
WEBSTER-POWELL, Alma Hall
(b 1874) American singer WWM
WECKER, Gero (d 1974 [51]) pro-
ducer/director/choreographer
BP/59*
WEDDELL (fl 1737-42) dramatist
CP/3
WEDDELL, George Hill (d 1867
[35]) drummer EA/68*
WEDEKIND, Frank (1864-1918)
German dramatist, actor COC,
ES, NTH, OC/3, PDT
WEDGEWORTH, Ann American ac-
tress TW/20-22, 27, 30
WEDWER, William (fl 1627-40)
actor DA
WEED, Leland T. (d 1975 [74])
performer BP/60*
WEEDE, Robert (1903-72) American
actor, singer BE, CB, TW/12-
13, 26, 29
WEEDEN, Evelyn (d 1961 [86])
English actress WWT/2-5
WEEKES, H. (d 1838) comedian
EA/72*, WWT/14*
WEEKES, James Eyre (fl 1743)
dramatist CP/3
WEEKES, Richard (fl 1629-36)
manager, actor DA
WEEKS, Barbara (d 1954 [47])
American actress BE*, BP/39*
WEEKS, Charles [Butler Wentworth]
(fl 1850-59) actor CDP, HAS
WEEKS, Frank (d 1906 [56]) mana-
ger EA/07*
WEEKS, James Ayre (fl 1791)
dramatist CP/3
WEEKS, James Ray (b 1942) Amer-
ican actor TW/29-30
WEEKS, Marion (1887?/1903-68)
American actress TW/4, 24
WEEKS, William J. (d 1972 [71])

composer/lyricist   BP/57*

WEEMS, Nancy (b 1948) American actress   TW/28

WEEMS, Ted (d 1963) conductor BP/47*

WEGENER, Paul (d 1948 [73]) actor   WWT/14*

WEGUELIN, Thomas N. (b 1885) English actor   WWT/2-8

WEHLE, Billy (d 1968 [73]) performer   BP/52*

WEHLEN, Emmy (b 1887) German actress, singer   CDP, WWT/1-5

WEHLI, James M. (fl 1865) pianist   CDP, HAS

WEHLING, Will (d 1975 [47]) producer/director/choreographer BP/59*

WEICHSEL, Elizabeth see Billington, Mrs. James

WEICHSEL, Frederica (d 1786) singer   CDP

WEIDLER, Virginia (b 1927) American actress   TW/2

WEIDMAN, Charles (1901-75) American dancer, choreographer BE, CB, ES

WEIDMAN, Jerome (b 1913) American dramatist, librettist   BE, CD, HJD, WWT/15-16

WEIGEL, Helene (1900-71) Austrian actress   WWT/14

WEIGELT, Lizzie (d 1910)   EA/11*

WEIGHELL, Christopher William (d 1897) music-hall manager EA/98*

WEIGHELL, R. (d 1893) proprietor EA/94*

WEIGHT, Hannah Louisa (d 1908 [56]) actress?   EA/09*

WEIGHT, Michael (1906-73) South African designer   WWT/11-14

WEIGHTMAN, John Albert (d 1884 [23]) acrobat   EA/85*

WEIGHTON, Louis English actor, acting manager   GRB/1

WEIL, Harry (d 1974 [84]) performer   BP/59*

WEIL, Joe (d 1974 [57]) performer   BP/59*

WEIL, Mrs. Leonard (d 1963 [62]) theatre operator, puppet collector   BE*

WEIL, Oscar (b 1840) American composer   WWA/4

WEIL, Robert E. (b 1914) Amer-

ican actor   TW/26-30

WEILER, Berenice (b 1927) American producer, manager, director BE

WEILER, Constance (d 1965 [47]) performer   BP/50*

WEILL, Kurt (1900-50) German composer   CB, DAB, ES, NTH, PDT, TW/6, WWA/3, WWT/9-10

WEIMAN, Ruth [or Rita] (d 1954) American dramatist   WWA/3

WEINBERG, Gus (d 1952 [86]) American actor   GRB/3-4, WWT/1-5

WEINBERG, Myron K. (d 1971 [43]) manager   BP/56*

WEINER, Ann (b 1931) American actor   TW/23, 29

WEINER, Lawrence A. (d 1961 [62]) advertising executive   BE*, BP/46*

WEINER, Robert American producer   BE

WEINGARTEN, Lawrence (d 1975 [77]) producer/director/choreographer   BP/59*

WEININGER, Lloyd (d 1971 [78]) scene designer, teacher   BP/56*

WEINRIB, Leonard (b 1935) American actor   TW/16

WEINSTEIN, Arnold (b 1927) American dramatist, lyricist, director, educator   BE, CD

WEINSTOCK, Herbert (d 1971 [65]) critic   BP/56*

WEINSTOCK, Jack (1909-69) American dramatist   BE, TW/25

WEINTRAUB, Frances (d 1963 [62]) treasurer   BE*

WEINTRAUB, Milton (b 1897) American manager   BE

WEIPPERT, Mr. (fl 1797?) musician?   CDP

WEIPPERT, John Charles (d 1867 [44]) musician   EA/68*

WEIR, Charles (d 1916) actor   EA/17*

WEIR, George R. (d 1909 [56]) actor   BE*, EA/10*, WWT/14*

WEIR, Milton R. (d 1973 [75]) lawyer   BP/58*

WEIR, Walter (d 1876 [54]) scene artist   EA/77*

WEIR, Walter V. (d 1887 [27]) scene artist   EA/88*

WEIRE, Sylvester (d 1970 [60]) performer   BP/55*

WEISBERG, Sylvia (d 1962) actress BE*

WEISER, Grethe (d 1970 [67]) performer BP/55*

WEISFELD, Zelma H. (b 1931) American costume designer, educator BE

WEISGAL, Emanuel see Wager, Michael

WEISMAN, Rita (d 1954 [71]) dramatist TW/11

WEISS, Karl (d 1911) manager WWT/14*

WEISS, Kenneth (b 1947) American actor TW/28

WEISS, Paul (b 1933) American actor TW/2

WEISS, Peter (b 1916) German dramatist CB, COC, MWD, PDT, RE, WWT/14-16

WEISS, Willoughby Hunter (d 1867 [47]) singer EA/68*, WWT/14*

WEISSBERGER, L. Arnold (b 1907) American lawyer BE

WEISSMAN, Dora (d 1974) actress TW/30

WEISSMULLER, Don (b 1923) American actor TW/1, 3

WEISTE, Fritz E. A. see Warden-Reed, Frank

WEISZ, Herbert see Wise, Herbert

WEITZEL, Thomas (d 1975 [50]) producer/director/choreographer BP/60*

WEITZENKORN, Louis (1893-1943) American dramatist BE*, WWT/14*

WELBES, George M. (1934-74) American actor TW/26-29

WELCH, Ben (d 1926) comedian BE*, BP/11*

WELCH, Charles (b 1921) American actor TW/24-25, 27-30

WELCH, Constance American educator BE

WELCH, Deshler (d 1920 [65]) critic BE*, BP/4*

WELCH, Elisabeth (b 1904/08/09) American actress, singer BE, WWT/8-16

WELCH, Harry Foster (d 1973 [74]) performer BP/58*

WELCH, James (1865-1917) English actor GRB/1-4, WWT/1-3, WWW/2

WELCH, Mrs. James see Ford, Audrey

WELCH, James B. (d 1965 [54]) producer/director BP/50*

WELCH, John Bacon (d 1887 [47]) professor of singing EA/88*

WELCH, Lew (d 1952 [67]) actor TW/9

WELCH, Loren (b 1923) American actress TW/4

WELCH, Mary (d 1958 [35]) American actress TW/10-14

WELCH, Robert Gilbert (d 1924 [45]) critic BE*, BP/9*

WELCH, Rufus (1800-65) American circus performer HAS

WELCH, William (1849-87) minstrel CDP, NYM

WELCH, William Addams (d 1976 [61]) dramatist BP/60*

WELCHMAN, Harry (1886-1966) English actor, singer AAS, WWT/2-13

WELD, Arthur Cyril Gordon (1862-1914) American musician, composer, conductor DAB

WELDEN, Ben (b 1901) American actor WWT/7-10

WELDON, Ann (b 1938) American actress TW/26

WELDON, Charles (b 1940) American actor TW/26-29

WELDON, Duncan Clark (b 1941) English producing manager WWT/16

WELDON, Fay dramatist CD

WELDON, John see MacNamara, Brinsley

WELDON, Miss P. see Clifton, Lina

WELFARE STATE theatre collective CD

WELFORD, Dallas (1874-1946) English actor GRB/4, TW/3, WWS, WWT/1-7

WELITSCH, Ljuba (b 1913) Bulgarian singer CB

WELLAND, Colin actor, dramatist CD

WELLBY, William George (d 1879 [34]) musician EA/80*

WELLER, Miss (fl 1778) actress CDP

WELLER, Bernard (1870-1943) English critic GRB/2-4, WWT/1-9, WWW/4

WELLER, Carrie (d 1954 [84]) American actress TW/11

WELLER, Michael (b 1942) American dramatist CD

WELLER, Peter (b 1947) American actor TW/30

WELLER, Sam (d 1907 [47]) stage manager EA/08*

WELLES, Orson (b 1915) American actor, producer, director AAS, BE, CB, COC, ES, NTH, PDT, TW/2-6, WWT/9-15

WELLES, Violet American press representative BE

WELLESLEY, Arthur (d 1906) actor EA/07*

WELLESLEY, Arthur (b 1890) English actor WWT/5-8

WELLESZ, Egon (d 1974 [89]) composer/lyricist BP/59*

WELLING, Nellie [Mrs. Leonard Thiel] (d 1907 [27]) EA/08*

WELLING, Sylvia (b 1901) English actress, singer WWT/10-11

WELLMAN, Emily Ann [Mrs. H. W. Wellman] (d 1946) English actress TW/2, WWM

WELLMAN, Mrs. Francis L. see Juch, Emma

WELLMAN, Mrs. H. W. see Wellman, Emily Ann

WELLMAN, Pearl see Argyle, Pearl

WELLMAN, William A. (d 1975 [79]) producer/director/choreographer BP/60*

WELLS, Mme. (d 1885) singer EA/86*

WELLS, Miss see Sefton, Mrs. John

WELLS, Albert (d 1909) equestrian EA/10*

WELLS, Amelia see Butler, Mrs. Robert

WELLS, Amos (d 1911 [50]) musician EA/12*

WELLS, Ann see Watson, Ann

WELLS, Benjamin (d 1899 [73]) EA/00*

WELLS, Mrs. Benjamin see Wells, Elizabeth

WELLS, Charles B. (d 1924 [73]) actor BE*, BP/9*

WELLS, Miss Clarence (fl 1839) actress HAS

WELLS, Deering (1896-1961) English actor WWT/7-8

WELLS, Doreen (b 1937) English

dancer ES

WELLS, Elizabeth [Mrs. Benjamin Wells] (d 1893 [66]) EA/94*

WELLS, H. (fl 1856) actor HAS

WELLS, Harriet Emma [Mrs. John Wells] (d 1886 [64]) EA/88*

WELLS, Herbert (b 1859) actor SR

WELLS, John (d 1880) equestrian manager EA/81*

WELLS, Mrs. John see Wells, Harriet Emma

WELLS, John Grimaldi (d 1852) circus clown HAS

WELLS, Julia Elizabeth see Andrews, Julie

WELLS, Louisa (b 1927) English actress HAS

WELLS, Malcolm (d 1970 [51]) dramatist BP/55*

WELLS, Marie (d 1949 [55]) actress TW/6

WELLS, Mary [née Davis] (d 1826?) English actress CDP, DNB, GT, TD/1-2

WELLS, Mary (1829-78) English actress CDP, HAS, SR

WELLS, Mary K. American actress TW/24, 26-27

WELLS, Minnie (fl 1872?) "Lion Queen" CDP

WELLS, Roxanna (d 1964 [70]) executive, agent BE*

WELLS, Samuel (d 1864 [38]) comedian HAS

WELLS, Tony (b 1940) American actor TW/29

WELLS, T. W. (d 1902) EA/03*

WELLS, Victor Thaddeus (d 1905 [50]) equestrian EA/06*

WELLS, William (d 1956 [72]) American actor, writer BE*

WELLS, William G. (d 1841) English dancer CDP, HAS

WELLS, Wilmot (fl 1801) manager, actor TD/1-2

WELMHURST, Anne see Howard, Anne

WELSH, Edward see Edwards, Welsh

WELSH, Jane (b 1905) English actress WWT/6-14

WELSH, Thomas (1781-1848) English singer DNB

WELSH, Mrs. Thomas see Wilson, Mary Ann

WELSH, Violet [Mrs. Harold

Clements] (b 1884) English ac-
tress GRB/1
WELSON, Mr. [né Bland] (fl 1802)
English actor HAS
WELSTED, Leonard (d 1747)
dramatist CP/1-3, GT
WELTON, Mrs. James see
Cavanna, Elise
WEMMS, Joe (d 1899) music-hall
comedian EA/00*
WEMYSS, Catherine (b 1821)
actress CDP
WEMYSS, Francis Courtney (1797-
1859) English actor, manager
CDP, COC, DAB, HAS, OC/
1-3, RJ, WWA/H
WEMYSS, Kate see Duffield,
Kate
WEMYSS, Thomas Courtney (b
1831) American actor HAS
WEMYSS, W. C. (b 1841) Amer-
ican actor HAS
WENBURN, Mrs. Harry see
Haynes, Jennie
WEND, John (fl 1627-40) actor
DA
WENDELL, Howard David (d 1975
[67]) performer BP/60*
WENDELL, Jacob (b 1868) actor
SR
WENDLING, Charles (d 1971
[72]) talent agent BP/55*
WENDLING, Pete (d 1974 [85])
performer BP/58*
WENGRAF, John E. (1907-74)
Austrian actor, director TW/
2-3, 5-6, 30
WENHAM, Jane [née Figgins]
English actress WWT/15-16
WENMAN, Henry N. (1875-
1953) English actor WWT/
4-10
WENMAN, Thomas Edmund
[Thomas Edmund Newman]
(1844-92) English actor OAA/2
WENNING, Thomas H. (1903-62)
American critic NTH
WENRICH, Percy (1887-1952)
American composer, per-
former BE*, BP/36*
WENSLEY, Emma (b 1799) ac-
tress CDP
WENSLEY, Frank (d 1889 [22])
singer EA/91*
WENTWIG, Mrs. Benjamin see
Nielsen, Alice
WENTWORTH, Bessie (d 1901
[27]) actress, singer CDP

WENTWORTH, Butler see Weeks,
Charles
WENTWORTH, Clayton (d 1969
[62]) performer BP/54*
WENTWORTH, Fanny (d 1930 [70])
English entertainer CDP, GRB/
1-4
WENTWORTH, Maude (d 1889)
American actress EA/90*
WENTWORTH, Stephen (d 1935)
actor BE*, WWT/14*
WENTZ, John K. (d 1964 [40])
educator, critic BE*
WERBA, Louis F. (d 1942) pro-
ducer, director BE*, WWT/14*
WERDON, George (d 1882 [32])
EA/83*
WERFEL, Franz (1890-1945) Aus-
trian dramatist CB, COC,
MWD, NTH, OC/1-3, WWA/2
WERRENRATH, George (d 1898)
singer EA/99*
WERRENRATH, Reinald (1883-1953)
American singer WWA/3
WERY, Carl (d 1975 [77]) per-
former BP/59*
WESFORD, Susan [79] American
actress BE*
WESKER, Arnold (b 1932) English
dramatist, director AAS, BE,
CB, CD, CH, COC, ES, MD,
MH, MWD, OC/3, PDT, RE,
WWT/13-16
WESNER, Ella actress CDP
WESS, Richard (d 1973 [43]) com-
poser/lyricist BP/57*
WESSEL, Richard (d 1965 [52])
performer BP/49*
WESSELS, Florence (d 1971 [72])
performer BP/56*
WESSON, Gene (d 1975 [54]) per-
former BP/60*
WEST, Mr. (fl 1816) equestrian
manager HAS
WEST, Miss (fl 1848) actress HAS
WEST, Algernon (b 1886) English
actor WWT/7-8
WEST, Arthur (d 1894 [30]?)
singer, song composer CDP
WEST, Bernard [or Bernie] (b 1918)
American actor BE, TW/26
WEST, Billy (d 1975 [82]) performer
BP/60*
WEST, Buster (d 1966 [64]) per-
former BP/50*
WEST, Christopher (1915-67) Eng-
lish director, actor, producer
WWW/6

WEST, Con (b 1891) English
librettist, dramatist WWT/
6-13
WEST, Edna Rhys (d 1963 [76])
American performer BE*,
BP/47*
WEST, Florence see Waller,
Mrs. Lewis
WEST, Florrie (d 1908) burlesque
actress EA/09*
WEST, Gilbert (b 1706) dramatist
CP/2-3
WEST, Henry St. Barbe (1880-
1935) English actor WWT/6-7
WEST, Mrs. H. G. see West,
Sarah
WEST, J. (fl 1809) English? HAS
WEST, Jane (1758-1852) English
dramatist CP/3, DNB
WEST, Jennifer (b 1939) Ameri-
can actress TW/20-21, 23-24
WEST, John (d 1871 [52]) actor?
EA/72*
WEST, Lillie [Amy Leslie] ac-
tress, writer CDP
WEST, Lockwood (b 1905) Eng-
lish actor WWT/14-16
WEST, Mae (b 1892/93) Ameri-
can actress, dramatist BE,
CB, COC, ES, MWD, NTH,
SR, TW/1-13, WWT/6-16
WEST, Rev. Matthew (fl 1769-
1803) dramatist CP/2-3, GT
WEST, Olive [Althea Olive Bow-
man] (b 1871) American ac-
tress WWM
WEST, Paul (1871-1918) Amer-
ican dramatist GRB/3-4,
WWA/1, WWM, WWS
WEST, Paul (d 1965 [75]) per-
former BP/50*
WEST, Richard (d 1726) drama-
tist CP/2-3, DNB
WEST, Sarah [Mrs. William
West] (1790-1876) English ac-
tress BS, CDP, DNB, OX
WEST, Sarah [Mrs. H. G. West]
(d 1886) EA/88*
WEST, Timothy (b 1934) English
actor WWT/15-16
WEST, Mrs. W. (d 1876 [86])
actress EA/78*, WWT/14*
WEST, W. H. C. (d 1876) come-
dian, songwriter EA/77*
WEST, Will (1867-1922) actor
WWT/4
WEST, William (1796-1888) Eng-
lish actor BS, CDP, DNB

WEST, William (d 1890 [77]) EA/
91*
WEST, Mrs. William see West,
Sarah
WEST, William C. (1837-1913)
English minstrel CDP, SR
WEST, William H. (1855-1902)
minstrel, dancer CDP, SR
WEST, William W. (d 1902 [48])
minstrel EA/03*
WESTBOURNE, E. see Layland,
Edward
WESTBROOK, John (b 1922) English
actor AAS, WWT/11-16
WESTCOTT, Emily (d 1903 [59])
EA/04*
WESTCOTT, John Smith (d 1908)
EA/09*
WESTCOTT, Lynda (b 1942) Amer-
ican actress TW/25-26, 28
WESTCOTT, Netta (d 1953 [60])
English actress WWT/10-11
WESTCOTT, Sebastian (fl 1557-82)
Master of the Children of Paul's
DA
WESTE, Humphrey (fl 1594) actor
DA
WESTE, Thomas (fl 1594) actor
DA
WESTERFIELD, James (1916-71)
American actor TW/12, 28
WESTERN, George (d 1969 [74])
performer BP/54*
WESTERN, Helen (1844-68) Amer-
ican actress CDP, COC, HAS,
OC/1-3, SR
WESTERN, Kenneth (d 1963 [62])
performer BE*
WESTERN, Lucille (1843-77) Amer-
ican actress CDP, COC, DAB,
HAS, OC/1-3, SR, WWA/H
WESTERTON, Frank H. (d 1923)
English actor BE*, BP/8*,
WWT/14*
WESTFORD, Owen (d 1908) actor
GRB/4*
WESTFORD, Susanne (1865-1944)
American actress, singer BE*,
BP/28*, WWT/14*
WESTGATE, Rebecca see Cl8ful-
lia, Josephine Fortune
WESTLAND, Henry (1838-1906)
English actor OAA/1-2
WESTLEY, Helen (1875/79-1942)
American actress CB, DAB,
ES, WWT/7-9
WESTLEY, John (d 1948 [70])
actor TW/5

WESTMAN, Lolita Ann (d 1965
[65]) performer BP/50*
WESTMAN, Nydia (1902/07-70)
American actress BE, TW/1,
3-7, 9-10, 13-19, 26, WWT/
7-14
WESTMAN, Theodore (d 1927
[24]) actor BP/12*
WESTMORE, George (d 1973 [55])
makeup man BP/58*
WESTMORE, Walter J. (d 1973
[57]) makeup man BP/58*
WESTMORELAND, Miss M. B.
(fl 1856) actress HAS
WESTON, Mr. (fl 1803-04) actor
TD/2
WESTON, Mrs. [Mrs. Edmund
Falconer] (d 1864) actress
EA/72*
WESTON, Ada [Mrs. Arthur
Weston] (d 1909 [44]) EA/10*
WESTON, Arthur see Boz,
Sig.
WESTON, Mrs. Arthur see
Weston, Ada
WESTON, Charles (d 1870) musi-
cal director EA/71*
WESTON, Charles H. (d 1904)
music-hall performer EA/06*
WESTON, Eddie (b 1925) Ameri-
can actor, dancer, singer BE
WESTON, Edward (d 1874 [54])
music-hall proprietor EA/75*
WESTON, Ellen (b 1939) Ameri-
can actress BE
WESTON, Emmeline Montague
Falconer [Mrs. T. W. Ben-
son] (d 1887) EA/88*
WESTON, Ferdinand Fullerton
(fl 1808) dramatist CP/3
WESTON, Frank (b 1849) actor
CDP
WESTON, George (d 1857) come-
dian HAS
WESTON, George Howarth (d
1901 [58]) EA/02*
WESTON, Graham (b 1944) Eng-
lish actor TW/27
WESTON, Harold [Fred Neatt]
(d 1917 [36]) performer? EA/
18*
WESTON, Jack actor WWT/16
WESTON, James [or Jim] (b
1942) American actor TW/
25, 27-30
WESTON, James Pitney (d 1902)
lessee EA/03*
WESTON, Mrs. James Pitney

see Weston, Marian
WESTON, John (fl 1667) dramatist
CP/1-3
WESTON, Joseph J. (d 1972 [84])
performer BP/56*
WESTON, Julia see Blake, Mrs.
Orlando
WESTON, Mrs. J. W. (fl 1877-
80?) singer CDP
WESTON, Lizzie see Mathews,
Mrs. Charles James
WESTON, Lottie [Mrs. John P.
Cooke] (d 1877 [35]) EA/78*
WESTON, Louise Caroline [née
Laidlaw] (d 1871 [23]) actress
EA/72*
WESTON, Marian [Mrs. James
Pitney Weston] (d 1884) EA/85*
WESTON, Robert P. (1878-1936)
English dramatist, lyricist,
composer WWT/7-8
WESTON, Ruth (1908/11-55) Amer-
ican actress TW/1, 3-6, 12,
WWT/10-11
WESTON, Thomas (1737-76) English
actor CDP, COC, DNB, GT,
OC/1-3, TD/1-2
WESTOVER, Robert (d 1916) actor
BE*
WESTOVER, William H. (d 1905
[58]) musician EA/07*
WESTRAY, Mrs. Anthony (d 1836)
actress COC, OC/3
WESTRAY, Miss E. A. see
Twaits, Mrs. William
WESTRAY, Ellen see Darley,
Mrs.
WESTRAY, Juliana see Wood,
Mrs. William Burke
WESTRUP, Jack A. (d 1975 [70])
critic BP/59*
WESTWOOD, Ellen [Mrs. W. H.
Westwood] (d 1917) EA/18*
WESTWOOD, Mrs. W. H. see
Westwood, Ellen
WESTWOOD, William Henry (d
1918 [67]) EA/19*
WESTZEL, Charles (d 1970 [79])
producer/director/choreographer
BP/55*
WETHERALL, Frances (d 1923)
English actress WWT/4
WETHERBY, Eliza see Weathers-
by, Eliza
WETHERBY, James (fl 1730) dram-
atist CP/1-3
WETHERELL, E. G. (d 1889)
EA/90*

WETHERELL, Joseph (d 1884 [57]) printer EA/85*

WETMORE, Alphonso dramatist EAP, RJ

WETMORE, Joan (b 1911) Australian actress BE, TW/1, 7, 10-11, 22, WWT/10-15

WETTACH, Adrien see Grock

WETTON, Mary see Millar, Mary

WEVER, Robert (fl 1561?) dramatist CP/1-3

WEWITZER, Miss (fl 1772-89) actress CDP, DNB

WEWITZER, Ralph (1748-1825) actor, manager, dramatist CP/3, DNB, GT, TD/1-2

WEXLER, Peter (b 1936) American designer WWT/16

WEXLEY, John (b 1902/07) American dramatist, actor HJD, MD, MWD, NTH, WWT/8-9

WEYAND, Roland (b 1929) American actor TW/14, 23-25

WEYMARK, James (d 1882 [34]) comedian EA/83*

WEYMER, Marguerite-Joséphine see George, Mlle.

WHAITE, Henry (d 1890) marionettist? EA/91*

WHAITE, John (d 1892 [53]) artist EA/93*

WHAITE, Septimus (d 1892 [84]) scene artist EA/93*

WHALE, James (1896-1957) English actor, producer, designer ES, WWT/6-12

WHALE, W. dancer CDP

WHALEN, David Barry (d 1967 [58]) publicist BP/52*

WHALEN, Michael (1899-1974) American actor TW/1

WHALING, Harry (d 1896) comic singer EA/97*

WHALLEY, Caroline see Barclay, Caroline

WHALLEY, J. S. (fl 1799) dramatist TD/1-2

WHALLEY, Norma Australian actress WWT/2-6

WHALLEY, Rev. Thomas Sedgwick (fl 1799) dramatist CP/3

WHALLEY, W. H. (b 1837) Irish actor HAS

WHAMBOULT, Leo (d 1917 [62]) EA/18*

WHAREHAM, William (d 1849) HAS

WHARTON, Anne (d 1685) dramatist CP/2-3

WHARTON, Anthony P. [Alister P. McAllister] (1877-1943) Irish dramatist GRB/3-4, WWT/1-7

WHARTON, Carly [Mrs. John F. Wharton] American producer TW/2

WHARTON, Mrs. Charles (d 1881 [67]) actress EA/82*

WHARTON, John F. (1894-1977) American lawyer BE

WHARTON, Mrs. John F. see Wharton, Carly

WHARTON, Philip, Duke of (1699-1731) dramatist CP/2-3

WHARTON, Thomas Edmond see Edmonds, T. W.

WHATFORD, William Starr (d 1887 [94]) comedian EA/88*

WHATMORE, A. R. (1889-1960) English actor, producer AAS, WWT/7-12

WHATTON, W. (d 1878 [33]) actor EA/79*

WHAUTKINS, Pio (d 1879 [50]) juggler EA/80*

WHEAT, Laurance (b 1876) American actor WWM

WHEATCROFT, Adeline Stanhope (1856-1935) French/English actress GRB/3-4

WHEATCROFT, Nelson (1852-97) English actor SR

WHEATLEIGH, Charles (fl 1848-65) English actor HAS, SR

WHEATLEY, Miss (fl 1796) actress, singer TD/1-2

WHEATLEY, Alan (b 1907) English actor WWT/9-16

WHEATLEY, Emma [Mrs. James Mason] (1822-54) American actress CDP, COC, HAS, OC/1-3

WHEATLEY, Frederick (d 1836) Irish entertainer COC, HAS, OC/1-3

WHEATLEY, Horace English comedian GRB/2

WHEATLEY, Jane (1881-1935) American actress WWT/4-7

WHEATLEY, Mrs. S. (fl 1815) Irish actress HAS

WHEATLEY, Sarah Ross (1790-1872) Irish/American actress COC, HAS, OC/1-3

WHEATLEY, William (1816-76)

American actor, manager CDP, COC, DAB, HAS, OC/1-3, WWA/H

WHEATON, Anna (d 1961 [65]) actress, singer TW/18

WHEATON, Elizabeth (fl 1627) gatherer DA

WHEEL, Patricia (b 1925) American actress TW/6, 8-10, 24, 27-29

WHEELER, Mrs. (d 1893) EA/95*

WHEELER, Miss (b 1781) English actress, singer TD/1-2

WHEELER, Mrs. Andrew C. see Wheeler, Anna

WHEELER, Andrew Carpenter (d 1903 [67]) critic BE*, WWT/14*

WHEELER, Anna [Mrs. Andrew C. Wheeler] (d 1888) EA/89*

WHEELER, Arthur (d 1907) acting manager EA/08*

WHEELER, Benjamin F. (d 1934 [74]) producer, manager BE*, WWT/14*

WHEELER, Benjamin H. (d 1908 [73]) manager EA/09*

WHEELER, Bert (1895-1968) American actor, vaudevillian BE, TW/24

WHEELER, Charles (d 1894) EA/95*

WHEELER, Desmondoe (d 1966 [67]) performer BP/51*

WHEELER, Fanny (fl 1840-49) American actress HAS

WHEELER, H. (d 1895) lessee EA/96*

WHEELER, Hugh (b 1912/16) English/American dramatist BE, CD, WWT/16

WHEELER, Jimmy (d 1973 [63]) performer BP/58*

WHEELER, Lois (b 1920/22) American actress BE, TW/ 1, 3, 9-11, WWT/11-14

WHEELER, Mark (d 1899) living statue EA/00*

WHEELER, Mary Ann (d 1898 [53]) living statue EA/99*

WHEELOCK, Mrs. J. F. [Anna France] (d 1866) actress HAS

WHEELOCK, Joseph (1839-1908) actor CDP, GRB/4

WHEELOCK, Joseph, Jr. (d 1910 [38]) American actor GRB/3-4

WHEELWRIGHT, Rev. C. A. (fl

1810) translator CP/3

WHELAN, Albert (1875-1961) English music-hall performer COC, OC/1-3

WHELAN, Tim (d 1957 [63]) American actor BE*

WHELEN, Frederick (b 1867) English secretary GRB/3-4, WWT/ 1-6

WHERRY, John (d 1876 [34]) singer EA/77*

WHETSTONE, George (1544?-87?) dramatist, actor CP/2-3, DA, FGF, HP

WHIFFIN, Blanche [Mrs. Thomas Whiffin] (1845-1936) English actress CDP, GRB/3-4, PP/3, SR, WWA/4, WWM, WWS, WWT/1-8, WWA/H

WHIFFIN, Thomas (1845-97) English actor SR

WHIFFIN, Mrs. Thomas see Whiffin, Blanche

WHILEY, Manning (b 1915) English actor WWT/10-11

WHINCOP, Thomas (d 1730) dramatist CP/1-3

WHIPPER, Leigh (d 1975 [98]) performer BP/60*

WHIPPLE, Sidney Beaumont (1888-1975) American critic NTH, WWT/9

WHISENANT, Elijah (d 1973 [62]) manager BP/57*

WHISTLER, Rex (1905-44) English designer ES, WWT/9

"WHISTLING COMEDIAN, The" see Mill, Paul

WHISTON, J. W. humorist CDP

WHITAKER, Miss see Sloman, Mrs. John

WHITAKER, Grenna (b 1948) American actress TW/29-30

WHITAKER, Sam (d 1890) actor EA/91*

WHITAKER, Willette [Mrs. F. Wilbur Hill] American musician, singer WWM

WHITAKER, William (fl 1680) dramatist CP/1-3

WHITBECK, Frank L. (d 1963 [81]) press representative BE*

WHITBREAD, Isabel Louisa (d 1916) EA/17*

WHITBREAD, J. W. (d 1916 [68]) dramatist BE*, EA/17*, WWT/ 14*

WHITBREAD, Samuel (1758-1815)

executive CDP

WHITBY, Miss (fl 1856) actress
HAS

WHITBY, Arthur (1869-1922)
English actor GRB/1-4,
WWT/1-4

WHITBY, Mrs. Arthur see
Saumarez, Cissie

WHITBY, Elsie (d 1911) actress
EA/12*

WHITBY, Gwynne (b 1903) English actress WWT/5-16

WHITE, Alfred H. (d 1972 [89])
actor TW/29

WHITE, Archie (1847-1912)
minstrel SR

WHITE, Beatrice [Beatrice Cur-
tis] (d 1963 [62]) performer
BE*

WHITE, Bertie actor GRB/1

WHITE, Bradford (b 1912) American educator, director, designer BE

WHITE, Miss C. (fl 1836-39)
American actress HAS

WHITE, Caroline [Mrs. Harold
White] (d 1893 [58]) EA/95*

WHITE, Charles (1821-91) American comedian, manager,
minstrel CDP, HAS

WHITE, Charles (d 1897) comedian EA/98*

WHITE, Charles (b 1920) American actor TW/25-26, 29

WHITE, Charles A. (d 1892
[62]) American composer,
publisher EA/93*

WHITE, Charles O. (d 1889)
manager EA/90*

WHITE, Christine (b 1926) American actress TW/8

WHITE, Clarence Cameron (1880-
1960) American composer
WWA/4

WHITE, Clement (d 1873) singer
EA/74*

WHITE, Cool (1821-91) actor
CDP, HAS

WHITE, Mrs. Cool [née Eliza
F. Bonnet; Mrs. W. M.
Foster] (d 1887) American
actress HAS, NYM

WHITE, Dana (b 1930) American
actor TW/14

WHITE, Danny (d 1974 [67]) talent
agent BP/59*

WHITE, Donald (b 1925) American
actor TW/2, 5-6

WHITE, Edgar Charles (d 1909)
EA/10*

WHITE, Edward J. (d 1973 [76])
producer/director/choreographer
BP/58*

WHITE, Elizabeth see Hartley,
Elizabeth

WHITE, Elizabeth see Savage,
Mrs. John

WHITE, Ellen F. (d 1900) manager
EA/01*

WHITE, Elmore (d 1964 [75]) performer, songwriter BE*

WHITE, F. B. (1817-68) American
actor HAS

WHITE, Frances (d 1969 [71]) actress, singer, vaudevillian
TW/25

WHITE, Fred (d 1872) harlequin
EA/73*

WHITE, George (d 1876 [38]) actor?
EA/77*

WHITE, George (d 1905 [54])
comedian EA/06*

WHITE, George (1890-1968) Canadian actor, producer, dancer,
dramatist BE, COC, ES, NTH,
PDT, TW/25, WWT/6-11

WHITE, George W. (1816-86) singer, minstrel CDP, HAS

WHITE, Mrs. Harold see White,
Caroline

WHITE, Harry (d 1898) actor EA/
99*

WHITE, Henry (d 1900 [88]) publisher EA/01*

WHITE, J. (d 1871 [72]) comedian
EA/72*

WHITE, James (fl 1759-61) translator CP/2-3

WHITE, Rev. James (d 1862 [77])
dramatist BE*, WWT/14*

WHITE, James (d 1882) EA/83*

WHITE, James (d 1927 [49]) manager WWT/5

WHITE, Mrs. James H. see
Kemble, Myra

WHITE, Jane (b 1922) American
actress BE, TW/2-3, 9-10,
15-18, 20-21, 25, 28, WWT/15-
16

WHITE, Jenny (d 1897) actress
EA/98*

WHITE, Jesse (b 1918/19) American actor, comedian BE, TW/
4-6, 21, 25-26

WHITE, J. Fisher (1865-1945)
English actor GRB/1-4, WWT/

1-9

WHITE, Joan (b 1909) Egyptian/
English actress, producer,
director, teacher BE, TW/
24, WWT/8-16

WHITE, Joan (d 1975 [43]) performer BP/59*

WHITE, John (d 1910 [76]) showman EA/11*

WHITE, John (b 1919) American
dramatist, actor CD

WHITE, John Blake (1781/83-
1859) American dramatist
CDP, DAB, EAP, RJ, SR,
WWA/H

WHITE, John J. (fl 1830) actor
HAS

WHITE, Josh (1908/15-69) American actor TW/6, 26

WHITE, Josias (fl 1628) actor
DA

WHITE, J. W. (d 1898) music-
hall proprietor EA/99*

WHITE, Kitty see Burden,
Kitty

WHITE, Laura [Mrs. Leonard
White] (d 1895 [24]) EA/96*

WHITE, Lee (1886-1927) American actress, singer WWT/4-5

WHITE, Lemuel G. (b 1792)
American actor HAS

WHITE, Leonard (b 1916) English actor TW/8

WHITE, Mrs. Leonard see
White, Laura

WHITE, Mary see Durang,
Mrs. Charles

WHITE, Mary Ann (d 1860) actress HAS

WHITE, Melvin R. (b 1911)
American educator, director
BE

WHITE, Michael Simon (b 1936)
Scottish producing manager
AAS, WWT/15-16

WHITE, Miles (b 1914/17/20)
American costume designer
BE, ES, TW/3-8, WWT/15-16

WHITE, Mrs. M. J. see Hyde,
Marion

WHITE, M. M. dramatist RJ

WHITE, Onna Canadian dancer,
choreographer, director BE,
WWT/15-16

WHITE, Patrick (b 1912) Eng-
lish/Australian dramatist
CD, ES

WHITE, Paul T. (d 1973 [77])

composer/lyricist BP/58*

WHITE, Penny American actress
TW/27

WHITE, Princess (d 1976 [95])
performer BP/60*

WHITE, R. B. (d 1872) musician
EA/73*

WHITE, Rebecca (d 1911) actress?
EA/12*

WHITE, Robert (fl 1617?) dramatist
FGF

WHITE, Robert (b 1926) American
actor TW/5-6

WHITE, Robert, Jr. (d 1881 [30])
EA/82*

WHITE, Ruth (d 1969 [55]) American actress BE, TW/22-26

WHITE, Sammy (1896-1960) American actor TW/3, 16

WHITE, Sidney see Drew, Sidney

WHITE, Tom (d 1900 [42]) music-
hall comedian EA/01*

WHITE, Tommy (b 1943) American
actor TW/13

WHITE, Valerie (1915-75) South
African actress TW/4, WWT/
10-16

WHITE, Watson (b 1888) American
actor TW/3

WHITE, Wilfred Hyde (b 1903) English actor TW/8, 13-14, WWT/
10-13

WHITE, William Charles (fl 1797-
1806) American actor, dramatist
CDP, EAP, HAS, RJ

WHITE, William Henry (d 1911
[57]) treasurer EA/12*

WHITE, Willoughby (d 1917) actor
EA/18*

WHITEBREAD, Mr. (d 1875) EA/
76*

WHITECAR, W. A. actor SR

WHITEHALL, Clarence (1871-
1932) American singer DAB,
WWA/1, WWW/3

WHITEHEAD, Allen (b 1921) American producer BE

WHITEHEAD, Charles (1804-62)
dramatist DNB, HP

WHITEHEAD, Douglass (d 1968
[93]) drama instructor BP/52*

WHITEHEAD, E. A. (b 1933) English dramatist AAS, CD, WWT/
16

WHITEHEAD, James (d 1885) musician EA/86*

WHITEHEAD, John (d 1962 [89])
actor BE*

WHITEHEAD, Paxton English actor
TW/26

WHITEHEAD, Robert (b 1916)
Canadian producer BE, TW/
6-8, WWT/14-16

WHITEHEAD, Robert M. (d 1880
[33]) actor EA/81*

WHITEHEAD, Virginia (d 1965
[84]) executive BP/49*

WHITEHEAD, Virginia Bolen (d
1965 [49]) designer BP/50*

WHITEHEAD, William (1714/15-
85) English dramatist CDP,
CP/1-3, GT, TD/1-2

WHITEHEAD, William (d 1867
[32]) musician EA/68*

WHITEHILL, Jane American actress TW/25, 28

WHITEHOUSE, Mrs. C. (d 1887
[46]) EA/88*

WHITEHOUSE, Esther (d 1946
[51]) actress BE*, WWT/14*

WHITEHOUSE, Florence Brooks
(fl 1894-1904) American dramatist WWA/5

WHITEHOUSE, Freeman H. (d
1865) singer HAS

WHITEHOUSE, William J. (d
1887 [28]) regisseur EA/88*

WHITELAMB, Kelham (fl 1787)
dwarf CDP

WHITELAW, Arthur producer
WWT/16

WHITELAW, Billie English actress AAS, WWT/14-16

WHITELEY, A. (d 1909 [36])
carpenter EA/10*

WHITELEY, James see Whitley,
James Augustus

WHITELEY, John Allen (d 1888
[45]) equestrian EA/89*

WHITELEY, Larry (b 1936)
American actor TW/27

WHITELEY, Leonora C. (d 1969
[93]) performer BP/54*

WHITELOCKE, James actor DA

WHITELY, James see Whitley,
James Augustus

WHITEMAN, George Frederick
Carl see Carroll, Sydney
W.

WHITEMAN, Paul (1890-1967)
American performer BE,
TW/24

WHITESIDE, Ann American actress TW/12, 26-27

WHITESIDE, Walker (1869-1942)
American actor CDP, SR,

WWA/2, WWM, WWT/1-9

WHITFIELD, Mr. (fl 1776) actor
CDP, TD/1-2

WHITFIELD, Howard (b 1914)
American stage manager, director, actor BE

WHITFIELD, James (d 1880) musician EA/81*

WHITFIELD, Joseph (d 1916 [69])
EA/17*

WHITFIELD, Louise (fl 1865) actress HAS

WHITFIELD, Walter W. (d 1966
[78]) performer BP/50*

WHITFORD, Annabelle (d 1961
[83]) actress, singer TW/18

WHITHAM, George (d 1883) circus
performer EA/84*

WHITHORNE, Emerson (b 1884)
American composer HJD

WHITING, Charles (d 1903 [36])
proprietor EA/04*

WHITING, David (1811-81) actor
CDP

WHITING, Edward (fl 1633) actor
DA

WHITING, Frank M. (b 1907)
American educator, director,
designer BE

WHITING, George Elbridge (1842-
1923) American composer DAB,
WWA/1

WHITING, Jack (1901-61) American
actor, singer TW/2-15, 17,
WWT/8-12

WHITING, John (1917-63) English
dramatist, actor AAS, CD,
CH, COC, ES, MD, MH,
MWD, OC/3, PDT, RE, WWT/
13, WWW/6

WHITING, Joseph (fl 1852) American
actor HAS

WHITING, Joseph E. (1842-1910)
American actor CDP, PP/3

WHITING, Richard (fl 1633) actor
DA

WHITING, Richard A. (1891-1938)
American composer BE*

WHITING, Sadie Burt (d 1966)
performer BP/51*

WHITLEY, Bert American actor
TW/3-4

WHITLEY, Clifford (b 1894) English
producing manager WWT/6-10

WHITLEY, James Augustus (c. 1724-
81) Irish manager, dramatist
COC, CP/3, GT, TD/2

WHITLEY, Larry (b 1936) American

actor TW/25

WHITLING, Townsend (1869-1952) English actor WWT/5-11

WHITLOCK, Mr. (d 1812) English actor HAS

WHITLOCK, Billy (d 1951 [76]) composer, performer BE*

WHITLOCK, E. Clyde (d 1970 [84]) critic BP/55*

WHITLOCK, Elizabeth see Kemble, Elizabeth

WHITLOCK, Henry (b 1787) English actor HAS

WHITLOCK, William M. (1813-78) minstrel CDP

WHITMAN, Chance Halliday (d 1974 [39]) performer BP/59*

WHITMAN, Essie (d 1963 [81]) performer BE*

WHITMAN, Estelle (d 1970) performer BP/55*

WHITMAN, Frank (1826-62) English actor? HAS

WHITMAN, John P. (d 1963 [91]) performer BE*

WHITMAN, Robert painter, sculptor CD

WHITMAN, Stuart (b 1929) American actor ES

WHITMAN, William (b 1925) American actor TW/8-12, 15

WHITMEE, Mrs. Alfred see Whitmee, Clara B.

WHITMEE, Clara B. [Mrs. Alfred Whitmee] (d 1912) EA/13*

WHITMORE, Mr. (d 1916) EA/17*

WHITMORE, James (b 1921/22) American actor BE, CB, TW/4-5, 26, 30, WWT/16

WHITNALL, Miss M. see Scarisbrick, Mrs.

WHITNER, Edwin (d 1962 [53]) actor BE*, BP/46*

WHITNEY, Mr. (fl 1839) actor, lecturer HAS

WHITNEY, Art (d 1972 [60]) stage manager, booking agent BP/57*

WHITNEY, Bert C. (1869-1929) American producer, manager SR

WHITNEY, Clark J. (b 1832) American manager SR

WHITNEY, Fred C. (1865-1930) American manager, producer

WWT/1-5

WHITNEY, Iris American actress TW/22

WHITNEY, Myron W. (1835-1910) American singer CDP, DAB, WWA/1

WHITNEY, Peter (d 1972 [55]) performer BP/56*

WHITROW, Benjamin (b 1937) English actor WWT/16

WHITSUN-JONES, Paul (1923-74) Welsh actor BTR/74, TW/14

WHITTAKER, Arthur (d 1914) producer, manager BE*, WWT/14*

WHITTAKER, Francis Warren (1818-87) American circus performer, actor? NYM

WHITTAKER, Herbert (b 1911) Canadian critic WWT/13-16

WHITTAKER, Jack (d 1847) equestrian HAS

WHITTAKER, James (d 1964 [73]) journalist, critic BE*, BP/48*

WHITTAKER, Patrick (d 1826) circus performer HAS

WHITTAKER, William H. B. (1888 [50]) American manager EA/89*

WHITTINGHAM, John (d 1875 [26]) comic singer EA/77*

WHITTLE, Charles R. (d 1947 [73]) English music-hall performer OC/1-3

WHITTLE, James (b 1939) American actor TW/24-25, 29

WHITTLE, Margaret (d 1917 [11]) EA/18*

WHITTLESEY, White (d 1940 [79]) American actor PP/3, WWS

WHITTON, Leon (d 1899 [42]) "Canadian colossus" EA/00*

WHITTON, Peggy (b 1950) American actress TW/29

WHITTY, J. Edward Irish actor, manager, proprietor GRB/1

WHITTY, Dame May [Mrs. Ben Webster] (1865-1948) English actress CB, COC, DP, EA/96, ES, GRB/1-4, OC/1-3, TW/2-4, WWA/2, WWT/1-10, WWW/4

WHITWORTH, Geoffrey (1883-1951) English secretary of the British Drama League COC, DNB, OC/1-3, WWT/7-11

WHOMES, Frederick (d 1878) professor of music EA/79*

WHORF, Richard (1906/07-66) American actor BE, TW/4-13,

23, WWA/4, WWT/9-14
WHYATT, Mrs. George Goddard
  see Willmore, Jenny
WHYLEY, William (d 1893 [53])
  proprietor EA/94*
WHYTAL, Russ (1860-1930)
  American actor, dramatist
  WWT/2-6
WHYTAL, Mrs. Russ [Mary Ade-
  laide] American actress WWT/
  1-7
WHYTE (fl 1779) dramatist CP/3
WHYTE, Bettina F. (d 1974 [87])
  critic BP/59*
WHYTE, Mrs. Carl (d 1907)
  EA/08*
WHYTE, Donn (b 1941) American
  actor TW/26-29
WHYTE, Frederic (d 1941 [74])
  dramatist WWW/4
WHYTE, George (d 1888 [44])
  comedian EA/90*
WHYTE, Harold (d 1919 [73])
  dramatist, actor BE*,
  WWT/14*
WHYTE, Jerome (1908-74) Amer-
  ican stage manager BE
WHYTE, Robert, Jr. (1874-1916)
  English actor GRB/4, WWT/
  1-3
WHYTE, Stirling (d 1911 [72])
  actor EA/12*
WIBURNE, D. (fl 1597?) dram-
  atist FGF
WICK, Thomas see Stacey,
  Walter
WICKER, Ireene (b 1905) Ameri-
  can actress CB
WICKES, Mary (b 1916) American
  actress TW/1-3, 5-8, WWT/
  11
WICKHAM, Florence (fl 1900s)
  American singer WWM
WICKHAM, Glynne (b 1922) South
  African director, scholar BE,
  WWT/15-16
WICKHAM, Tony [Anthony Wick-
  ham-Jones] (1922-48) English
  actor WWT/9-10
WICKHAM-JONES, Anthony see
  Wickham, Tony
WICKMAN, Sally (d 1963 [49])
  American dancer, choreograph-
  er, producer BE*
WICKWIRE, Nancy (1925-74)
  American actress AAS, BE,
  TW/11-21, 24, WWT/14-16
WIDDECOMB, Wallace (b 1878)

English actor TW/2
WIDDECOME, Wallace (d 1969
  [100]) actor TW/26
WIDDELL, Mrs. Tessy see
  Hilton, Tessy
WIDDELL, Joseph (d 1896) actor
  EA/97*
WIDDICOMB, Harry [or Henry]
  (1813-68) actor CDP, DNB
WIDDICOMB, Jarvis (d 1898 [43])
  comedian EA/99*
WIDDICOMBE, John Esdale (d 1854
  [66]) pantomimist, actor BE*,
  WWT/14*
WIDDICOMBE, R. H. (d 1854 [67])
  actor EA/72*, WWT/14*
WIDDICOMBE, Victor (d 1912)
  English actor GRB/3
WIDDOES, Kathleen (b 1939) Amer-
  ican actress BE, TW/14, 22-
  23, 25, 28-30, WWT/15-16
WIDEMAN, Julia see Hache,
  Mlle.
WIDERMAN, Robert see Clary,
  Robert
WIDMARK, Richard (b 1914/15)
  American actor CB, ES, TW/
  1-3
WIDNER, Randell C. (d 1971 [47])
  managing director BP/56*
WIDOM, Leonard (d 1976 [58])
  performer BP/60*
WIEBEN, Michael (b 1944) Ameri-
  can actor TW/28
WIEHE, Charlotte [Mrs. Henry
  Bereny] (b 1875) Danish dancer,
  actress, pantomimist GRB/1-4
WIEHE, Dagmar Indian/English ac-
  tress WWT/1-3
WIELAND, Adelaide see Zaeo
WIELAND, Clara (fl 1900?) ac-
  tress, singer CDP
WIELAND, George (1810-47) actor
  CDP, HAS
WIELAND, H. W. (d 1922 [80])
  pantomimist, dancer BE*,
  WWT/14*
WIELAND, Mrs. H. W. see
  Zaeo
WIELAND, James (d 1890 [43])
  actor, musical artist EA/92*
WIELAND, W. H. (d 1866 [35])
  Negro singer EA/72*
WIELEPP, Kurt O. (d 1962 [80])
  German performer BE*
WIEMAN, Mathias (d 1969 [67])
  performer BP/54*
WIER, Mrs. (b c. 1724) actress

TD/1-2
WIESE, Henry William (1903-74)
American talent representative
BE
WIEST, Stan (b 1943) American
actor TW/27
WIETH, Mogens (1920-62) Danish
actor COC, OC/3
WIETHOFF, Mons. (fl 1848)
dancer HAS
WIGAN, Mrs. Alfred see
Wigan, Leonora
WIGAN, Alfred Sidney (1818-78)
English dramatist, actor
CDP, DNB, EA/68, ES,
OAA/1-2
WIGAN, Horace (1818?-85) actor,
dramatist DNB, OAA/1-2
WIGAN, Leonora [Mrs. Alfred
Wigan] (1805-84) actress, stage
manager CDP, DNB, ES,
OAA/2
WIGGIN, Kate Douglas [Mrs.
George C. Riggs] (1856/59-
1923) American writer HJD,
WWM
WIGGLESWORTH, Hugh (d 1908
[44]) manager EA/09*
WIGGLESWORTH, Mrs. Hugh
see Wigglesworth, Mary G.
WIGGLESWORTH, Mary G. [Mrs.
Hugh Wigglesworth] (d 1895
[28]) EA/96*
WIGHT, Frederick Coit (1859-
1933) American musician,
composer DAB
WIGHTMAN, Mr. actor CDP
WIGHTMAN, T. C. (d 1874)
equestrian EA/75*
WIGHTON, David see Devant,
David
WIGLEY, Alfred (d 1916) stage
manager, actor EA/17*,
WWT/14*
WIGMAN, Mary (1886-1973)
German dancer, choreographer
CB
WIGNELL, J. (d 1774) actor,
dramatist CP/2-3, GT,
TD/1-2
WIGNELL, Thomas (1753-1803)
American actor, manager
CDP, COC, DAB, HAS,
OC/1-3, SR, WWA/H
WIGODER, Thelma see Ruby,
Thelma
WIGPITT, Thomas (fl 1622)
lessee DA

WIKLIN, Stan (b 1938) American
actor TW/30
WILBER, Mabel [Mrs. Madison
Corey] (b 1882) American singer
WWM
WILBRAHAM, Alfred (d 1875 [46])
carpenter EA/76*
WILBRAHAM, Edward [Earl of
Lathom] (1895-1930) English
dramatist WWT/6
WILBRAHAM, Tilly see Bram-
hall, Mrs. Walter
WILBRAHAM, William (fl 1635-40)
actor DA
WILBUR, Mrs. (fl 1861) actress
HAS
WILBUR, Claire American actress
TW/27
WILBUR, Crane (1889-1973) Amer-
ican actor, dramatist, producer
TW/30, WWT/6-10
WILBUR, Richard (b 1921) Ameri-
can critic, translator, teacher
BE, HJD, WWT/15-16
WILCOX, Art (d 1974 [50]) publi-
cist BP/59*
WILCOX, Barbara (b 1906) English
actress WWT/7-10
WILCOX, Collin (b 1935) Amer-
ican actress BE, TW/15-16,
18-19, 21
WILCOX, Frank (d 1974 [66]) actor
TW/30
WILCOX, Ralph (b 1951) American
actor TW/28-30
WILCOX, Richard (d 1889) minstrel
EA/90*
WILCOX, Robert (d 1955 [44])
American actor TW/12
WILCOX, R. Turner (b 1888)
American costumier BE
WILCOXON, Henry (b 1905) West
Indian/English actor TW/4-6,
WWT/8-10
WILD, George (1805-56) actor,
manager CDP
WILD, George (d 1894) EA/95*
WILD, Harold (d 1917) musical
director EA/18*
WILD, James (d 1801 [52]) prompt-
er, dramatist, actor CP/3,
TD/1-2
WILD, James (fl 1804) translator,
dramatist CP/3
WILD, James (d 1867 [57]) eques-
trian clown EA/68*
WILD, John (1843-98) minstrel
CDP

WILD, Louisa (d 1874 [56])
actress EA/75*

WILD, Dr. Robert (fl 1689)
dramatist CP/1-3

WILDBERG, John J. (1902-59)
American producing manager
TW/2, 6-8, WWT/11

WILDE, Al (d 1970 [60]) personal
manager BP/55*

WILDE, Amelia [née Vining] (d
1869) EA/70*

WILDE, Cornel (b 1915/18)
American actor, director,
producer BE, ES

WILDE, Edwin (d 1909) actor
EA/10*

WILDE, George (b 1609) English
dramatist CP/2-3, FGF

WILDE, Hagar (d 1971 [67])
dramatist BE

WILDE, Henry J. (d 1911) English business manager, acting
manager GRB/1

WILDE, Lilla (b 1865) English
actress GRB/1

WILDE, Mary see Rushton,
Lucy

WILDE, Oscar Fingal O'Flahertie
Wills (1854-1900) Irish drama-
tist CDP, COC, DNB, ES,
HP, MD, MH, MWD, NTH,
OC/1-3, PDT, RE, SR

WILDE, Patricia (b 1928) Canadian dancer, choreographer
CB, ES

WILDE, Percival (1887-1953)
American dramatist NTH,
WWA/3

WILDE, W. J. (d 1868 [45])
treasurer EA/69*

WILDER, Alec (b 1907) American
composer BE

WILDER, Clinton (b 1920) American producer, stage manager
BE, WWT/14-16

WILDER, David (b 1936) American actor TW/25, 28-29

WILDER, Gene (b 1934) American actor BE

WILDER, Ian (b 1939) American
actor TW/27

WILDER, James (fl 1750-c. 1810)
actor, dramatist CDP, CP/
1-3, GT, TD/1-2

WILDER, Mrs. Jay L. (d 1975
[82]) promoter BP/60*

WILDER, John C. (1826-69)
American showman HAS

WILDER, Joseph (d 1871) pyrotechnist EA/73*

WILDER, Lilyan American actress
TW/25

WILDER, Marshall Pinckney (1859-
1915) American entertainer
GRB/3-4, SR, WWA/1, WWM

WILDER, Robert (d 1974 [73])
dramatist BP/59*

WILDER, Sophia [Mrs. William
Wilder] (d 1884 [28]) EA/85*

WILDER, Thornton Niven (1897-
1975) American dramatist, actor
AAS, BE, CB, CD, CH, COC,
ES, HJD, MD, MH, MWD,
NTH, OC/1-3, PDT, RE, WWT/
6-15

WILDER, Mrs. William see
Wilder, Sophia

WILDING, Michael (b 1912) English
actor ES, WWT/10-11

WILDISH, Charles Henry (d 1874
[27]) property man EA/75*

WILDMAN, Clara (fl 1875?) singer
CDP

WILDMAN, Edward (d 1886) EA/
87*

WILDMAN, Mrs. F. J. (d 1867
[32]) actress HAS

WILEY, Dora [Mrs. Richard
Golden] (d 1924 [71]) actress,
singer CDP

WILEY, John A. (d 1962 [78])
actor BE*

WILEY, Lee (d 1975 [60]) performer BP/60*

WILEY, Major American actor
TW/23

WILFORD, Miss A. J. (d 1865)
actress HAS

WILFORD, Charles see Dukes,
Charles William

WILFORD, Isabel New Zealand actress WWT/7-8

WILFORD, Mary see Bulkley,
Mrs. George

WILHELM, C. (1858-1925) English
designer, ballet-inventor ES,
WWT/4

WILHELM, Theodore (d 1971 [62])
performer BP/56*

WILHORST, Cora de [née Withers]
American singer HAS

WILKE, C. actor CDP

WILKE, Hubert (d 1940 [85]) German singer, actor BE*, BP/
25*

WILKERSON, Arnold (b 1943)

American actor TW/24-25,
28-30
WILKERSON, Guy (d 1971 [70])
performer BP/56*
WILKERSON, William R. (d 1962
[72]) American publisher BE*
WILKES, Sarah (d 1881) EA/83*
WILKES, Thomas Egerton (d 1854
[42]) dramatist BE*, EA/72*,
WWT/14*
WILKIE, Allan (1878-1970) Eng-
lish actor, manager WWT/7-8
WILKINS, George (fl 1607) drama-
tist CP/1-3, DNB, FGF
WILKINS, John (d 1853 [26])
actor, dramatist BE*, WWT/
14*
WILKINS, Margaret (d 1886 [68])
EA/88*
WILKINS, Marie (d 1883 [70])
English actress CDP, HAS
WILKINS, Mrs. Sidney (d 1878)
American actress EA/79*
WILKINSON, Mr. equestrian
CDP
WILKINSON, Mrs. (fl early 19th
cent) actress CDP
WILKINSON, Mrs. see Allen,
Marie
WILKINSON, Miss see Moun-
tain, Mrs.
WILKINSON, Anna see Carteret,
Anna
WILKINSON, Arthur John (d 1894
[34]) actor EA/95*
WILKINSON, Charles De Witt
Clinton (1830-88) American
actor, stage manager CDP,
HAS
WILKINSON, Christopher (b 1941)
British dramatist, director
CD
WILKINSON, Flossie see Heriot,
Mrs. Wilton
WILKINSON, Harry see O'Con-
nor, John
WILKINSON, Henry Spencer (1853-
1937) English critic GRB/2-
4, WWT/1-3
WILKINSON, James Pimbury (b
1787) English actor BS, CDP,
HAS, OX
WILKINSON, Jan see Holden,
Jan
WILKINSON, J. Benjamin (d 1891
[37]) manager EA/92*
WILKINSON, John Edward (d
1910 [50]) EA/11*

WILKINSON, Kate American ac-
tress TW/26-30
WILKINSON, Leslie (d 1971 [72])
performer BP/56*
WILKINSON, Lillie [Mrs. Charles
De Witt Wilkinson] (d 1920?)
English? actress CDP
WILKINSON, Lillie M. (d 1971
[90]) performer BP/55*
WILKINSON, Marc (b 1929) French
composer, conductor WWT/15-
16
WILKINSON, Marcus (d 1892) music-
hall comedian EA/93*
WILKINSON, Marguerite Ogden
Bigelow (1883-1928) Canadian
dramatist WWA/1
WILKINSON, Nicholas see
Tooley, Nicholas
WILKINSON, Norman (1882-1934)
English artist, designer COC,
DNB, OC/1-3, WWT/4-7
WILKINSON, Richard (fl 1703)
dramatist CP/2-3
WILKINSON, Sarah Scott (d 1894
[55]) EA/95*
WILKINSON, Tate (1739-1803) Eng-
lish actor, manager CDP, COC,
DNB, ES, GT, OC/1-3, TD/1-2
WILKINSON, Tom see O'Connor,
Thomas
WILKINSON, William (fl 1699)
dramatist CP/1
WILKS, Mrs. [née Packard] (fl
1834-57) American dancer, ac-
tress HAS
WILKS, Annie (1840-63) American
actress HAS
WILKS, Benjamin G. S. (fl 1836)
English actor, musician HAS
WILKS, Henrietta see Shewell,
Mrs. L. R., I
WILKS, Robert (1665-1732) English
actor CDP, COC, DNB, ES,
GT, OC/1-3, TD/1-2
WILKS, Thomas Egerton see
Wilkes, Thomas Egerton
WILKS, William (fl 1717-23) actor
DNB
WILL (fl c. 1590) actor DA
WILL (fl 1597) actor DA
WILLA, Suzanne (d 1951 [58]) ac-
tress TW/7
WILLAN, Healey (d 1968 [87])
composer/lyricist BP/52*
WILLAN, Leonard (fl 1651) drama-
tist CP/1-3, FGF
WILLARD, Catherine Livingston

(1895-1954) American actress
TW/1-3, 5-6, 8, 11, WWT/
4-7, 10-12

WILLARD, Edmund (1884-1956)
English actor COC, OC/3,
WWT/5-12

WILLARD, E[dward] S[mith]
(1853-1915) English actor
CDP, COC, DP, EA/95,
GRB/1-4, OC/1-3, SR,
WWA/1, WWM, WWS, WWT/
1-3, WWW/1

WILLARD, Fred American actor
TW/25-26

WILLARD, George Owen (d 1893
[61]) journalist, historian CDP

WILLARD, Harry Francis (d
1970 [74]) performer BP/55*

WILLARD, Helen D. (b 1905)
American curator BE

WILLARD, Henry E. (1802-78)
American? manager CDP

WILLARD, James (b 1871) English actor, manager GRB/
1-3

WILLARD, John (1885-1942) American dramatist WWT/5-9

WILLAT, Irvin V. (d 1976 [84])
producer/director/choreographer
BP/60*

WILLEMETZ, Albert (d 1964
[77]) composer/lyricist BP/
49*

WILLEMS, Miss see Greene,
Mrs.

WILLEMS, Elizabeth see Addison, Mrs. John

WILLENENS, Mme. (d 1871)
EA/72*

WILLERBY, Arthur [Arthur
Gostling Eggington] (d 1911)
actor EA/12*

WILLES, Louise [Mrs. B. Gray
Heald] (d 1889) American actress OAA/1-2

WILLET, Thomas (fl 1778) dramatist CP/2-3

WILLETT, Joseph M. (d 1864)
performer HAS

WILLETT, Mittens (1864-93)
actress CDP

WILLETT, Miss W. [Mrs. H.
Aveling] (d 1893 [29]) American actress EA/94*

WILLEY, Olive (d 1968 [80])
performer BP/52*

WILLEY, Robert (b 1920) American actor TW/3

WILLIAM, David [né Williams] (b
1926) English actor, director
AAS, WWT/14-16

WILLIAM, Earl (b 1924) American
actor TW/6-9

WILLIAM, Robert (d 1931 [34])
American actor BE*

WILLIAM, Warren (1895-1948)
American actor TW/5, WWT/
7-10

WILLIAMES, Mr. [Matthew?] (d
1801) Welsh actor TD/1-2

WILLIAMS, Mr. Welsh actor TD/
1-2

WILLIAMS, Mr. (fl early 19th
cent) actor CDP

WILLIAMS, Mr. (d 1878) musician
EA/79*

WILLIAMS, Mrs. [Fanny Wright]
(d 1883 [43]) singer, dancer,
actress EA/84*

WILLIAMS, Master (fl 1813) singer
CDP

WILLIAMS, Miss see Brougham,
Mrs. John, II

WILLIAMS, Miss see Davis, Mrs.

WILLIAMS, Miss see St. Ledger,
Mrs.

WILLIAMS, A. B. (d 1964 [67])
performer BE*, BP/49*

WILLIAMS, Agnes [Mrs. Alfred
Williams] (d 1894) EA/95*

WILLIAMS, Mrs. Alan [Mamie
Sims] (d 1917) EA/18*

WILLIAMS, Alf (d 1904) ghost
illusion proprietor EA/05*

WILLIAMS, Mrs. Alfred see
Williams, Agnes

WILLIAMS, Ann (b 1935) American
actress BE

WILLIAMS, Anna (d 1783) translator CP/2-3

WILLIAMS, Annabelle Rucker (d
1967 [63]) performer BP/52*

WILLIAMS, Annie (d 1890) singer
EA/91*

WILLIAMS, Arthur (d 1893 [41])
pantomimist EA/94*

WILLIAMS, Arthur (1844-1915)
English actor CDP, DP, GRB/
1-4, WWT/1-3

WILLIAMS, Audrey (d 1975) performer BP/60*

WILLIAMS, Avril see Elgar,
Avril

WILLIAMS, Barbara American actress TW/20, 28

WILLIAMS, Barney (1823-76)

American actor CDP, COC,
DAB, HAS, OC/1-3, SR,
WWA/H

WILLIAMS, Mrs. Barney [née
Maria Pray] (1826-1911)
American dancer, actress
CDP, COC, HAS, PP/3, SR

WILLIAMS, Bernie (d 1971 [60])
publicist BP/56*

WILLIAMS, Bert A. (c. 1876-
1922) West Indian/American
performer CDP, COC, DAB,
ES, SR, WWA/4

WILLIAMS, Betty (d 1967) performer BP/51*

WILLIAMS, Billy (d 1972 [62])
performer BP/57*

WILLIAMS, Billy Dee (b 1937/
38) American actor BE,
TW/17, 24-26, WWT/15-16

WILLIAMS, Bransby (1870-1961)
English actor, mimic COC,
GRB/1-4, OC/1-3, WWT/
4-13

WILLIAMS, Camilla (b c. 1922?)
American singer CB

WILLIAMS, Campbell (b 1906)
English producing manager
WWT/13

WILLIAMS, Celeste (b 1830)
American dancer HAS

WILLIAMS, Charles (d 1877 [33])
comedian EA/78*

WILLIAMS, Charles [Charles
Thomas Howard] (d 1880 [27])
topical singer EA/81*

WILLIAMS, Charles (1815-83)
actor CDP

WILLIAMS, Mrs. Charles see
Moody, Mary

WILLIAMS, Charles B. (1829-
1915) American actor SR

WILLIAMS, Charles Walter
Stansby (1886-1945) English
dramatist HP, MWD

WILLIAMS, Clarence, III (b 1939)
American actor TW/21-24,
WWT/15-16

WILLIAMS, Clark American actor
TW/7

WILLIAMS, Claud (d 1972 [81])
performer BP/57*

WILLIAMS, C. Leonard (b 1943)
American actor TW/24

WILLIAMS, Clifford (b 1926)
Welsh director AAS, ES,
WWT/14-16

WILLIAMS, Clyde American actor

TW/22

WILLIAMS, Mrs. Daniel see
Arthur, Mrs. John, II

WILLIAMS, Daniel James (d 1871
[55]) actor EA/72*

WILLIAMS, David see William,
David

WILLIAMS, Derek (b 1910) English
actor WWT/9-10

WILLIAMS, Dick (d 1962 [46])
journalist, editor BE*

WILLIAMS, Dick (b 1926) American
actor TW/14

WILLIAMS, Dick Anthony (b 1938)
American actor, director, producer TW/25, 28-30, WWT/16

WILLIAMS, Dorian American actor
TW/29

WILLIAMS, Dorothy Trilby (d 1901)
EA/02*

WILLIAMS, Earle (1880-1927)
American actor BE*, BP/11*

WILLIAMS, E. B. [né Adam
Brock] (1824-67) American actor
HAS

WILLIAMS, Edward (d 1908 [64])
musical director EA/09*

WILLIAMS, Edwin (d 1880 [56])
music-hall proprietor EA/81*

WILLIAMS, Egbert Austin (c. 1876-
1922) actor OC/1-3

WILLIAMS, E. Harcourt (1880-
1957) English actor, producer
AAS, COC, GRB/1-4, OC/1-3,
WWT/1-12, WWW/5

WILLIAMS, Miss E. L. (fl 1857)
Welsh singer CDP, HAS

WILLIAMS, Elizabeth (d 1869)
EA/70*

WILLIAMS, Ellwoodson (b 1937)
American actor TW/28-30

WILLIAMS, Emlyn (b 1905) Welsh
actor, dramatist, producer
AAS, BE, CB, CD, CH, COC,
ES, MD, MH, MWD, NTH,
OC/1-3, PDT, SR, TW/8-15,
18-21, 27, WWT/7-16

WILLIAMS, Emma [Mrs. Henry D.
Burton] (d 1890) EA/91*

WILLIAMS, Espy (1852-1908) American dramatist WWA/1

WILLIAMS, Evelyn M. (d 1959
[63]) executive of British Drama
Council BE*, WWT/14*

WILLIAMS, Fanny (d 1909) performer? EA/10*

WILLIAMS, Florence (b 1912) American actress WWT/9-11

WILLIAMS, F. Osborne (d 1890) professor of music EA/91*

WILLIAMS, Frances [Frances Jellineck] (1903-59) American actress, singer TW/15, WWT/9-11

WILLIAMS, Frank see Hepton, William Thomas

WILLIAMS, Mrs. Frank see Walmisley, Blanche

WILLIAMS, Fred (d 1916) music-hall performer, actor EA/17*

WILLIAMS, Mrs. Fred (d 1890) EA/91*

WILLIAMS, Fritz (1865-1930) American actor PP/3, SR, WWT/1-6

WILLIAMS, George (fl 1629-35) actor DA

WILLIAMS, George (d 1890) musician EA/91*

WILLIAMS, George E. J. see Vernon, Charles

WILLIAMS, Guinn (d 1962 [62]) American actor BE*

WILLIAMS, Gus (1847-1915) American actor, singer CDP, SR

WILLIAMS, Gwen (d 1962) performer BE*

WILLIAMS, H. A. (fl 1817) actor HAS

WILLIAMS, Harcourt see Williams, E. Harcourt

WILLIAMS, Harry (fl 1860s) manager, actor SR

WILLIAMS, Harry (d 1886 [53]) actor EA/87*

WILLIAMS, Hattie (1874-1942) American actress, singer GRB/3-4, SR, WWM, WWT/1-5

WILLIAMS, H. B. (fl 1868-69) English clown CDP, HAS

WILLIAMS, Heathcote (b 1941) English dramatist AAS, CD

WILLIAMS, Henry (d 1891) EA/92*

WILLIAMS, Herb (d 1936 [52]) American comedian BE*, BP/21*, WWT/14*

WILLIAMS, Herbert (d 1876) clown EA/77*

WILLIAMS, Herbert see Pete

WILLIAMS, Herschel (b 1909) American dramatist, director BE

WILLIAMS, Hope (b 1901) Amer-

ican actress WWT/7-9

WILLIAMS, Hugh (1904-69) English actor AAS, MH, TW/26, WWT/7-14, WWW/6

WILLIAMS, Ina (d 1962 [65]) Australian performer BE*

WILLIAMS, I. R. (fl early 19th cent) actor CDP

WILLIAMS, Irene (d 1970 [38]) performer BP/55*

WILLIAMS, Jennifer American actress TW/25, 27

WILLIAMS, Mrs. Jesse see Tracy, Hettie

WILLIAMS, Jesse Lynch (1871-1929) American dramatist DAB, ES, GRB/3-4, HJD, MD, MH, MWD, NTH, WWA/1, WWT/5-6

WILLIAMS, Joey (fl 1822) circus performer HAS

WILLIAMS, John (fl 1509-11) member of the Chapel Royal DA

WILLIAMS, John (fl 1723) dramatist CP/2-3

WILLIAMS, John (fl 1784) dramatist CP/3

WILLIAMS, John [Antony Pasquin] (1761/65-1818) English dramatist CDP, CP/3, EAP

WILLIAMS, John (fl 1885?) dancer, singer CDP

WILLIAMS, John (d 1887 [58]) actor EA/88*

WILLIAMS, John (b 1903) English actor AAS, BE, TW/8-13, 18-20, 27, WWT/4-16

WILLIAMS, John D. (1886?-1941) American producing manager CB, WWT/6-7

WILLIAMS, Joseph (fl 1673-1700) actor DNB, GT

WILLIAMS, Joseph (fl 1694) dramatist CP/3

WILLIAMS, Joseph (d 1875 [79]) musician EA/76*

WILLIAMS, Kate (fl 1869?) actress, singer CDP

WILLIAMS, Kathlyn (d 1960 [72]) actress TW/17

WILLIAMS, Kenneth (b 1926) English actor AAS, WWT/13-16

WILLIAMS, Le Roy A. (d 1962 [70]) American performer BE*

WILLIAMS, Lottie [Mrs. George Lashwood] (d 1907) EA/08*

WILLIAMS, Louise (d 1872) actress EA/73*

WILLIAMS, Lucas translator CP/3

WILLIAMS, Mack (d 1965 [58])
performer BP/50*
WILLIAMS, Malcolm (d 1937
[67]) American actor BE*,
BP/21*, WWT/14*
WILLIAMS, Maria Kathleen
see Williams, Mrs. Barney
WILLIAMS, Marie (d 1891) burlesque
actress CDP
WILLIAMS, Marjorie (d 1975
[92]) producer/director/chore-
ographer BP/59*
WILLIAMS, Mattie [Mattie Wood]
(c. 1862-87) actress NYM
WILLIAMS, Michael (b 1935) English
actor TW/20, WWT/15-16
WILLIAMS, Minnie (d 1878) ac-
tress EA/79*
WILLIAMS, Miss M. J. (d 1873
[79]) Welsh singer EA/74*
WILLIAMS, Molly (d 1967) per-
former BP/52*
WILLIAMS, Montague (1835-92)
actor, dramatist CDP
WILLIAMS, Mrs. Montague [née
Louise Keeley] (d 1877 [41])
actress EA/78*
WILLIAMS, Nellie (d 1906 [41])
music-hall comedian EA/07*
WILLIAMS, Nellie see Dauvray,
Helen
WILLIAMS, Nelly [Ellen Maria
Watson] (d 1897) actress EA/98*
WILLIAMS, Noel (b 1919) Irish
actor TW/8
WILLIAMS, Norman (d 1938
[57]) singer WWT/14*
WILLIAMS, Odell (d 1902) Amer-
ican actor EA/03*
WILLIAMS, O. T. (d 1976 [68])
performer BP/60*
WILLIAMS, P. (d 1873) actor,
stage manager EA/74*
WILLIAMS, Paul (d 1973 [34])
performer BP/58*
WILLIAMS, Percy (1857-1923)
American actor, manager SR
WILLIAMS, Peter (b 1915) Amer-
ican actor TW/7
WILLIAMS, Randall (d 1898
[50]) showman EA/99*
WILLIAMS, Rex (b 1914) Ameri-
can actor TW/2, 6
WILLIAMS, Rhys (1897-1969)
Welsh actor, dancer, producer
TW/1-3, 5-6, 25, WWT/10-11
WILLIAMS, Richard see Earle
WILLIAMS, Rico (b 1963) Amer-

ican actor TW/27
WILLIAMS, Rita (d 1971 [51]) per-
former BP/56*
WILLIAMS, Robert (fl 1837) actor?
HAS
WILLIAMS, Robert (d 1901) show-
man EA/02*
WILLIAMS, Robert (d 1931 [34])
American actor BE*, BP/16*,
WWT/14*
WILLIAMS, Robert N. American
educator BE
WILLIAMS, R. S. (d 1880) come-
dian EA/81*
WILLIAMS, Ruth (d 1897 [85]) wax-
work proprietor EA/98*
WILLIAMS, Sailor see Winshurst,
George
WILLIAMS, Sonia (b 1926) English
actress WWT/12-13
WILLIAMS, Stephen (1900-57) Eng-
lish critic WWT/8-12
WILLIAMS, Tennessee [Thomas
Lanier] (b 1914) American dram-
atist, actor AAS, BE, CB,
CD, CH, COC, ES, HJD, HP,
MD, MH, MWD, NTH, OC/1-3,
PDT, RE, TW/28-29, WWT/11-
16
WILLIAMS, Thomas (d 1881 [56])
mechanical exhibition proprietor
EA/82*
WILLIAMS, Thomas H. (d 1888)
American circus performer
EA/89*
WILLIAMS, Thomas J. (1824-74)
English dramatist EA/68
WILLIAMS, Tom (d 1910) stage
manager EA/11*
WILLIAMS, Tony (d 1891) American
actor SR
WILLIAMS, Vanilla (d 1973 [35])
performer BP/58*
WILLIAMS, Walter (d 1882 [68])
actor EA/83*
WILLIAMS, Walter (1887-1940)
English actor, singer WWT/4-9
WILLIAMS, William A. (b 1893)
American actor, singer, director
BE
WILLIAMS, William Carlos (1883-
1963) American dramatist MD,
MWD
WILLIAMS, William Henry (1797-
1846) English actor, magician
CDP, HAS, OX, SR
WILLIAMS, William Henry see
Williams, John

WILLIAMS, William T. (d 1906
[72]) musical director EA/07*
WILLIAMSON, Mr. (fl 1783)
actor, dramatist CP/3, TD/
1-2
WILLIAMSON, Mr. actor CDP
WILLIAMSON, Mr. (fl 1795-97)
English actor HAS
WILLIAMSON, Miss see Bart-
ley, Mrs. George
WILLIAMSON, A. J. (fl 1800?)
dramatist EAP
WILLIAMSON, Audrey (b 1913)
critic AAS
WILLIAMSON, David Irish actor,
prompter TD/2
WILLIAMSON, David (b 1942)
Australian dramatist CD,
WWT/16
WILLIAMSON, Henry William
(d 1899 [60]) dramatist EA/
00*
WILLIAMSON, Hugh Ross (b 1901)
English dramatist BE, WWT/
9-14
WILLIAMSON, James (d 1881 [67])
musician EA/82*
WILLIAMSON, J[ames] C[assius]
(1845-1913) American actor,
manager CDP, GRB/1-4,
HAS, SR, WWT/1-2
WILLIAMSON, Mrs. James Cas-
sius see Williamson, Maggie
WILLIAMSON, J. Brown (d 1802)
actor HAS
WILLIAMSON, Mrs. J. Brown
[née Fontenelle] (d 1799) ac-
tress CDP, HAS, TD/1-2
WILLIAMSON, L. B. (fl 1800?)
dramatist RJ
WILLIAMSON, Maggie [Mrs.
James Cassius Williamson]
(1847-1926) actress CDP
WILLIAMSON, Nicol (b 1937/38)
English actor AAS, CB, PDT,
TW/29-30, WWT/14-16
WILLIAMSON, William Charles
(d 1872 [33]) Negro singer
EA/73*
WILLIARD, Carol (b 1947) Amer-
ican actress TW/29
WILLIG, Steven (d 1975 [30])
producer/director/choreographer
BP/60*
WILLING, Mr. actor CDP
WILLING, Bella [Mrs. J. O'Con-
nor] (d 1894) music-hall per-
former EA/95*

WILLING, James (d 1915 [77])
dramatist BE*, WWT/14*
WILLINGHAM, Calder (b 1922)
American dramatist BE, MD
WILLIS, Prof. (d 1901) comical
conjuror EA/02*
WILLIS, Mrs. see Proctor, Mrs.
Joseph
WILLIS, Constance (d 1940) singer
WWT/14*
WILLIS, Daniel (d 1901) music-hall
comedian EA/02*
WILLIS, Dave (d 1973 [78]) vaude-
villian BP/57*, WWT/16*
WILLIS, H. O. (d 1972) performer
BP/57*
WILLIS, Horton (b 1946) American
actor TW/26
WILLIS, Kirk (d 1966 [60]) director,
actor TW/23
WILLIS, Nathaniel Parker (1806-
67) American dramatist, critic
CDP, DAB, ES, HP, MH, NTH,
OC/3, RJ, SR
WILLIS, Oscar [né McLain] (b
1843) American banjoist, come-
dian HAS
WILLIS, Richard (fl 1628) actor
DA
WILLIS, Sally (b 1948) Welsh ac-
tress TW/29-30
WILLIS, Sam (d 1879 [58]) duologue
artist EA/81*
WILLIS, Susan American actress
TW/24-25
WILLIS, Ted [Baron Willis of
Chislehurst] (b 1914/18) English
dramatist, director CD, COC,
PDT, WWT/14-16
WILLIS-CROFT, Stanley (d 1969)
producer/director/choreographer
BP/53*
WILLISON, James (d 1888) music-
hall singer EA/89*
WILLISON, Walter (b 1947) Ameri-
can actor TW/26-30
WILLMAN, Noel (b 1918) Irish
actor, producer BE, WWT/
11-16
WILLMORE, Ernest (d 1892 [17])
music-hall performer EA/93*
WILLMORE, Jenny [Mrs. George
Goddard Whyatt] (d 1894) English
actress HAS
WILLMORE, Lizzie [Mrs. Courtney
Ware] (d 1877 [29]) actress
EA/78*, WWT/14*
WILLMORE, Lizzie (d 1894) English

actress CDP, HAS
WILLMORE, William (d 1876)
actor EA/77*
WILLMOTT, W. C. (d 1894 [53])
stage manager EA/95*
WILLNER, A. M. (d 1929 [71])
librettist BE*, WWT/14*
WILLOTT, William (d 1870 [53])
lessee EA/71*
WILLOUGHBY, Mr. actor TD/2
WILLOUGHBY, Mrs. Digby (d
1891) actress EA/93*
WILLOUGHBY, Hugh (b 1891)
English designer WWT/4-10
WILLOUGHBY, J. M. (d 1872)
actor? EA/73*
WILLOUGHBY, Kathleen Indian/
English actress GRB/1
WILLS, Betty Chappele (d 1971
[63]) performer BP/56*
WILLS, Beverly (d 1963 [29])
actress BE*, BP/48*
WILLS, Bob (d 1975 [70]) per-
former BP/59*
WILLS, Brember (d 1948 [65])
English actor WWT/4-9
WILLS, Drusilla (1884-1951)
English actress WWT/5-11
WILLS, Rev. Freeman Irish
dramatist GRB/1-3
WILLS, G. H. see Velanche,
Harry
WILLS, Harry (d 1879 [33])
comic singer EA/80*
WILLS, Ivah see Coburn, Ivah
WILLS, James (d 1839) Ameri-
can actor CDP, HAS
WILLS, John S. (1862-1943)
actor, manager SR
WILLS, Lou, Jr. actor TW/2
WILLS, Lou (b 1928) American
actor TW/27
WILLS, Nat M. (1873-1917)
American performer BE*
WILLS, Tommy (d 1962 [59])
performer BE*
WILLS, Walter (d 1967 [86])
performer BP/51*
WILLS, W. G. (1828-91) Irish
dramatist DNB, EA/69
WILLSON, Henry (d 1883)
music-hall proprietor EA/84*
WILLSON, Meredith (b 1902)
American composer, lyricist,
comedian AAS, BE, CB,
CD, NTH
WILLSON, Osmund (b 1896) Eng-
lish actor WWT/6-14

WILLSON, Rini Zarova (d 1966
[54]) Russian/American actress,
singer TW/23
WILLY, J. H. (d 1869) professor
of music EA/70*
WILLYAMS, Walter (fl 1635) actor
DA
WILMER, Douglas (b 1920) English
actor WWT/13-16
WILMER, Lambert A. (1805-63)
American dramatist EAP, RJ
WILMER, Sydney actor, dramatist,
manager SR
WILMER-BROWN, Maisie (d 1973
[80]) performer BP/57*
WILMORE, Ernest see Woollams,
Ernest
WILMOT, Mrs. [Mrs. Marshall]
(fl 1793) English actress HAS
WILMOT, Annie see Hastings,
Annie
WILMOT, Charles (d 1896 [57])
actor, producer, proprietor
BE*, EA/97*, WWT/14*
WILMOT, Fred [James Miller] (d
1917 [50]) performer, managing
director EA/18*
WILMOT, Mrs. George (d 1890)
actress? singer? EA/92*
WILMOT, John, Earl of Rochester
(1648-80) English dramatist
CDP, CP/1-3, GT
WILMOT, John (d 1911) showman
EA/12*
WILMOT, Lottie (d 1903) EA/04*
WILMOT, Maurice (b 1883) English
actor, variety artist GRB/1
WILMOT, Robert (fl 1568-1608)
dramatist CP/1-3, DNB, FGF,
HP
WILMOTT, Charles (d 1955 [95])
songwriter BE*, WWT/14*
WILMOTT, Uriah [J. W. Duriah]
(d 1873 [44]) comic singer
EA/74*
WILSHERE, Austin M. (d 1918)
EA/19*
WILSHIN, Sunday (b 1905) English
actress WWT/6-10
WILSON, Mr. actor GT
WILSON, Mr. (b 1801) Scottish
singer HAS
WILSON, Mrs. [née Adcock] (d
1786) actress DNB
WILSON, Mrs. (fl 1773-91) actress
CDP
WILSON, Mrs. see Davenport,
Ruth

WILSON, Miss (fl 1814) actress
HAS
WILSON, Ada (d 1908) EA/09*
WILSON, Al (d 1964 [76]) per-
former BP/49*
WILSON, Albert C. (d 1974
[98]) performer BP/59*
WILSON, Albert Edward (1885-
1960) English critic, journalist
WWT/5-12
WILSON, Alexander (d 1854)
actor, manager CDP, HAS
WILSON, Mrs. Alexander [née
Brobston] (d 1855) American
actress HAS
WILSON, Rev. Alex M. (d 1895
[51]) professor of music
EA/96*
WILSON, Al H. (b 1868) Ameri-
can singing comedian WWM
WILSON, Ann (fl 1783) dramatist
CP/3
WILSON, Ann (d 1902 [84])
EA/03*
WILSON, A. R. (d 1875) musician
EA/76*
WILSON, Arthur (1595-1652)
English dramatist CP/2-3,
DNB, FGF
WILSON, Beatrice (d 1943 [63])
Indian/English actress, pro-
ducer GRB/1-3, WWT/4-9
WILSON, Billy (d 1887 [29])
Negro comedian EA/88*
WILSON, Carrie (b 1944) Amer-
ican actress TW/26
WILSON, Mrs. C. Baron (d
1846 [49]) dramatist BE*,
WWT/14*
WILSON, Cecil Frank Petch
(b 1909) English critic
WWT/11-13
WILSON, Charles (d 1909 [49])
stage manager, producer,
maître de ballet GRB/2-4
WILSON, Charles Henry (d 1808
[52]) Irish? translator CP/3
WILSON, Charles Hooper see
Milton, Charles
WILSON, Christopher (d 1919
[43]) composer, conductor
BE*, WWT/14*
WILSON, David (d 1917) EA/18*
WILSON, Demond (b 1946) Amer-
ican actor TW/27
WILSON, Diana (1897-1937) Eng-
lish actress WWT/5-8
WILSON, Dooley (b 1895) Amer-

ican actor TW/1
WILSON, Mrs. E. see Wilson,
Mary Elizabeth
WILSON, Earl, Jr. (b 1942) Amer-
ican actor TW/27
WILSON, Edith American actress,
singer WWT/8-9
WILSON, Edmund (1895-1972)
American critic, dramatist BE,
CB, MD, MWD, WWA/5
WILSON, Mrs. Edward (d 1877
[90]) equestrian EA/78*
WILSON, Edwin L. (fl 1900s)
American singer WWM
WILSON, Eleanor American actress
TW/3, 11, 24
WILSON, Elizabeth (b 1925) Amer-
ican actress TW/12-13, 23,
25-30, WWT/16
WILSON, Florence see McKinley,
Mrs. W. J.
WILSON, Frances Annie [Mrs.
Robert Wilson] (d 1885 [45])
EA/86*
WILSON, Francis (1854-1935)
American actor, manager, dram-
atist CDP, COC, DAB, GRB/
2-4, OC/1-3, PP/3, SR, WWA/
1, WWM, WWT/1-7
WILSON, Frank (1890/91-1956)
American actor, dramatist
TW/5-6, 12, WWT/9-11
WILSON, Fred (b 1827) minstrel,
manager CDP
WILSON, Fred C. see Fax, Max
WILSON, Garstin Parker see
Murray, Gaston
WILSON, Gene A. (b 1920) Ameri-
can educator, director BE
WILSON, George (d 1874 [21])
musician, composer EA/75*
WILSON, George (d 1876 [22])
musician EA/77*
WILSON, George W. (1844/49-1930)
American actor, minstrel CDP,
PP/3, SR
WILSON, Germaine (fl 1594) actor
DA
WILSON, G. J. minstrel CDP
WILSON, Grace (b 1903) Scottish
actress WWT/6-8
WILSON, Mrs. Harry (d 1888)
EA/89*
WILSON, Harry Leon (1867-1939)
American dramatist DAB,
HJD, MWD, WWA/1, WWM,
WWT/1-8, WWW/3
WILSON, Harry T. (d 1890) advance

agent EA/91*

WILSON, Harvey L. (d 1972 [72]) performer BP/57*

WILSON, Henry (fl 1624) actor DA

WILSON, Mrs. Henry see Maynard, Lizzie

WILSON, Mrs. H. F. see Wilson, Ruth

WILSON, Hilda (d 1918) EA/19*

WILSON, Jack (b 1876) American comedian WWM

WILSON, Jack (d 1966 [49]) performer BP/51*

WILSON, Jack (d 1970 [76]) performer BP/55*

WILSON, Jane dramatist RJ

WILSON, Jessie (d 1867 [52]) actress EA/68*

WILSON, Joe (d 1875 [33]) writer, singer EA/76*

WILSON, John (1585-1641?) English actor DA, COC, OC/1-3

WILSON, John (1627?-96) Irish? dramatist CP/1-3, DNB, GT, HP

WILSON, John (1800/01-49) Scottish actor, singer CDP, DNB, SR

WILSON, John (d 1885) circus director EA/86*

WILSON, John see Hill, John Henry

WILSON, John C. (1899-1961) American manager, producer, director TW/2-8, 18, WWT/8-13

WILSON, John Crawford (b 1826) Irish dramatist EA/69

WILSON, John Dover (1881-1969) English scholar BE, WWW/6

WILSON, John Henry (d 1913) EA/14*

WILSON, John S. (b 1913) American critic BE

WILSON, Joseph (1858-1940) Irish actor, manager, singer GRB/1-4, WWT/2-6

WILSON, Josephine [Lady Bernard Miles] actress COC

WILSON, Joseph Maria (1872-1933) designer NTH

WILSON, Julia (b 1860) actress, singer CDP

WILSON, Katherine (b 1904) American actress WWT/7-9

WILSON, Lanford (b 1937) American dramatist, director, actor

CD, WWT/15-16

WILSON, Lee (b 1948) American actress TW/27-28

WILSON, Leigh singer CDP

WILSON, Leigh see Cockram, William Edward

WILSON, Lillian Brown (d 1969 [83]) performer BP/54*

WILSON, Lionel (b 1924) American actor TW/1-4, 11-12

WILSON, Lisle (b 1943) American actor TW/24-26

WILSON, Lois (b 1898/1900) American actress BE, TW/2-4, 6-7, 26

WILSON, Lucy (b 1876) actress WWT/3-6

WILSON, Marie (d 1972 [54/56]) actress BP/57*, WWT/16*

WILSON, Mary Anne [Mrs. Thomas Welsh] (1802-67) singer CDP, DNB

WILSON, Mary Elizabeth [Mrs. E. Wilson] (d 1877) EA/78*

WILSON, Mary Louise (b 1936) American actress TW/25-30

WILSON, Matthew (d 1886) actor EA/87*

WILSON, Nellie (fl 1896?) actress, singer CDP

WILSON, "Old" (d 1853 [102]) actor EA/72*

WILSON, Paul (b 1873) English actor, variety artist GRB/1

WILSON, Perry (b 1916) American actress TW/1, 3-4, 10-11, WWT/10-13

WILSON, Ray (d 1963 [56]) director, producer BE*

WILSON, Richard (d 1796/c. 1802) actor, dramatist CDP, CP/3, DNB, TD/2

WILSON, Mrs. Richard (fl 1773-86) actress WWT/14*

WILSON, Robert (d c. 1600) English actor, dramatist COC, CP/1, 3, DA, DNB, FGF, NTH, OC/1-3

WILSON, Robert (1579-1610) dramatist DNB, FGF

WILSON, Mrs. Robert see Wilson, Frances Annie

WILSON, Roberta (d 1972 [68]) performer BP/56*

WILSON, Robert James Penny see Waldegrave, Robert

WILSON, Robert M. [Byrd Hoffman] (b 1944) American dramatist,

director, designer CD
WILSON, Robert Thorpe see
Sheffield, Thorpe
WILSON, Ruth [Mrs. H. F. Wil-
son] (d 1906) EA/07*
WILSON, Samuel T. (d 1971 [71])
critic BP/55*
WILSON, Sandy (b 1924) English
dramatist, composer AAS,
BE, CD, PDT, WWT/12-16
WILSON, Snoo (b 1948) English
dramatist, director, actor
CD, WWT/16
WILSON, T. H. (d 1879) music-
hall manager EA/80*
WILSON, Theodore (b 1943)
American actor TW/25
WILSON, Thomas (d 1882 [49])
musician EA/83*
WILSON, Thomas (d 1887 [73])
EA/88*
WILSON, Tom (d 1887) actor
EA/88*
WILSON, Tom (d 1905) EA/06*
WILSON, Ural (b 1930) American
dancer, singer TW/24
WILSON, Virginia de Luce see
De Luce, Virginia
WILSON, Mr. W. (d 1867) musi-
cal director EA/68*
WILSON, Walter M. (d 1926
[52]) actor, director BE*,
BP/11*
WILSON, Wayne (d 1970 [71])
actor TW/26
WILSON, W. Cronin (d 1934)
actor WWT/4-7
WILSON, William (fl 1617) actor?
DA
WILSON, William (d 1875) musi-
cian EA/77*
WILSON, William (d 1916 [44])
EA/17*
WILSON, William J. (d 1936
[62]) Scottish director WWT/
4-8
WILSON, William John (d 1909
[73]) scene artist EA/10*
WILSON, William Woodrow (d
1972 [60]) performer BP/57*
WILSTACH, Frank Jenners (1865-
1933) American manager
WWA/1
WILSTACH, Paul (1870-1952)
American dramatist, business
manager GRB/3-4, WWT/1-9
WILT, Marie (1833-91) Austrian
singer ES

WILTON (fl 1789) dramatist CP/3
WILTON, Amelia [Mrs. F. Wilton]
(d 1873) stage manager EA/74*
WILTON, Augusta (d 1926) actress
BE*, WWT/14*
WILTON, Clara Goldsby see
Hundon, Mrs. T. J.
WILTON, Edwin (d 1879 [29]) actor?
EA/80*
WILTON, Ellie [Mrs. Thomas C.
Doremus] (d 1902 [50]) actress
CDP
WILTON, Mrs. F. see Wilton,
Amelia
WILTON, Mrs. Frank see Wilton,
Kate
WILTON, Fred (d 1890 [30]) topical
singer EA/92*
WILTON, Fred C. J. (d 1889 [87])
stage manager EA/90*
WILTON, Henry Dolan (d 1871 [28])
agent EA/72*
WILTON, Jenny [Mrs. Louis Bat-
ten] (d 1890) music-hall per-
former EA/91*
WILTON, J. Hall (d 1862 [50])
agent CDP, HAS
WILTON, John (d 1881) music-hall
proprietor EA/82*
WILTON, Kate [Mrs. Frank Wilton]
(d 1888 [27]) EA/89*
WILTON, Marie (fl 1899?) actress,
singer CDP
WILTON, Marie Effie see Ban-
croft, Lady
WILTON, Robb (d 1957 [75]) Eng-
lish music-hall comedian BE*,
WWT/14*
WILTON, Robert Pleydell (d 1873
[75]) actor EA/74*, WWT/14*
WIMAN, Anna Deere (1924-63)
American producer, manager
WWT/13
WIMAN, Dwight Deere (1895-1951)
American producing manager
CB, NTH, TW/3-7, WWT/6-11
WIMPERIS, Arthur (1874/76-1953)
English dramatist, lyricist
WWT/2-11, WWW/5
WINANS, John (1817-59) American
actor CDP, HAS, SR
WINANS, Mrs. John (fl 1843)
actress HAS
WINANS, John, Jr. (d 1861) come-
dian HAS
WINANT, Forrest (1888-1928)
American actor WWM, WWT/
4-5

WINANT, Haim (b 1927) American
actor TW/8-12
WINCELBERG, Shimon (b 1924)
German writer BE
WINCHELL, Mr. (fl 1841) enter-
tainer CDP
WINCHELL, Walter (1897-1972)
American critic, journalist,
vaudevillian CB, NTH, TW/
28, WWT/7-14
WINCHELL, Mrs. Walter [June
Magee] (d 1970 [64]) performer
BP/54*
WINCHESTER, Barbara (d 1968
[70s]) performer BP/52*
WINCHILSEA, Countess of see
Finch, Anne
WINCOTT, Mrs. Charles see
Bridges, Gertrude Agnes
WINDE, Beatrice American ac-
tress TW/28-29
WINDEATT, George (1901-59)
English musical director,
composer WWT/9-10
WINDEL, Lina dancer CDP
WINDER, E. (d 1893 [75]) music-
hall proprietor EA/94*
WINDER, Mrs. Edwin see
Winder, Mrs. E. S. Bovey
WINDER, Mrs. E. S. Bovey
[Mrs. Edwin Winder] (d 1887
[66]) EA/88*
WINDERMERE, Charles [Charles
F. Todd] (1872-1955) English
actor, dramatist, manager
GRB/1-3, WWT/4-8
WINDGASSEN, Wolfgang (d 1974
[60]) performer BP/59*
WINDHAM, Donald (b 1920)
American dramatist BE
WINDLEY, Emily [Mrs. John
Windley] (d 1876 [37]) EA/77*
WINDLEY, John (d 1901 [67])
lessee EA/02*
WINDLEY, Mrs. John [Kate
Ross] (d 1913) EA/14*
WINDLEY, Mrs. John see
Windley, Emily
WINDOM, William (b 1923) Amer-
ican actor BE, TW/3, 10-12
WINDOW, Muriel (d 1965) per-
former BP/50*
WINDSOR, Mrs. see Daniels,
Alicia
WINDSOR, Albert C. [William
Ross-Cattanach] (d 1908 [58])
EA/09*
WINDSOR, Barbara [née Deeks]

(b 1937) English actress WWT/
15-16
WINDSOR, Claire (1898-1972) Amer-
ican actress TW/2
WINDSOR, Flo see Resdan, Rita
WINDSOR, John Peter (d 1976 [60])
composer/lyricist BP/60*
WINDSOR, Lilly (b 1924) American
singer SR
WINDUST, Bretaigne (1906-60)
French director CB, TW/2-4,
16, WWT/11-12
WINDUST, Penelope American ac-
tress TW/24, 28
WINELL, Mr. (fl 1752) English
actor HAS
WINES, Christopher (b 1939) Amer-
ican actor TW/25
WINFREE, Richard (d 1975 [76])
composer/lyricist BP/59*
WING, Dan (d 1969 [46]) performer
BP/54*
WINGARD, Prof. (d 1912) EA/14*
WINGETT, Edwin see Wingett,
Harry
WINGETT, Harry [Edwin Wingett]
(d 1905 [60]) comic singer EA/
06*
WINGFIELD, Conway (d 1948 [81])
actor TW/4
WINGFIELD, Lewis Strange (1842-
91) actor, designer DNB
WINGFIELD, M. (fl 1631) dramatist
CP/3, FGF
WINGHAM, Thomas (d 1893 [47])
composer EA/94*
WINIK, Edna Mae (d 1971) per-
former BP/56*
WINIK, Leslie (d 1975 [72]) pro-
ducer/director/choreographer
BP/59*
WINKELMANN, Hermann (1845-
1912) singer CDP
WINKELMEIER, Herr (d 1887 [20])
Austrian giant CDP
WINKLER, Frank (d 1964 [64])
performer BE*
WINKLER, Henry (b 1945) American
actor CB
WINKWORTH, Mark J. (b 1948)
American actor TW/29-30
WINN, Anona Australian actress,
singer WWT/11-12
WINN, Florence singer CDP
WINN, Godfrey (1906-71) English
actor WWT/6
WINN, H. (d 1880) EA/81*
WINN, Kitty (b 1944) American

actress TW/28-29

WINNEMORE, Tony (fl 1846)
actor HAS

WINNER, Septimus (1827-1902)
American songwriter BE*

WINNETT, Thomas (1851-1912)
American minstrel, agent SR

WINNING, Mrs. Lawrence see
Winning, Marie

WINNING, Marie [Mrs. Lawrence
Winning] (d 1890 [24]) EA/91*

WINNINGER, Charles (1884-
1969) American actor BE,
SR, TW/25, WWT/4-10

WINOGRADSKY, Barnet see
Delfont, Bernard

WINPENNY, Mabel see Audre,
Olga

WINROW, Samuel (d 1969 [89])
performer BP/54*

WINSCOTT, Dudley A. (d 1972
[70]) manager BP/57*

WINSHIP, George (b 1830) American comedian HAS

WINSHIP, Loren (b 1904) American educator, director BE

WINSHURST, George [Sailor
Williams] (d 1873 [48]) nautical
singer & dancer EA/74*

WINSLOW, A. H. (fl 1852) actor
HAS

WINSLOW, Catherine Mary (d
1911) English actress WWA/1

WINSLOW, Herbert Hall (1865-
1930) American actor, dramatist SR, WWM

WINSLOW, Kate Reignolds [Mrs.
Harry Farren] (b 1814) actress WWA/H

WINSTANLEY, Mr. dramatist
RJ

WINSTANLEY, Mrs. (d 1899 [84])
EA/00*

WINSTANLEY, A. N. [Mrs. J.
A. Winstanley] (d 1908 [42])
EA/10*

WINSTANLEY, Eliza (fl 1849)
actress CDP, HAS

WINSTANLEY, Mrs. J. A.
see Winstanley, A. N.

WINSTON, Mr. actor, manager
TD/2

WINSTON, C. Bruce (1879-1946)
English actor, designer WWT/
4-9

WINSTON, Hattie (b 1945) American actress TW/24, 26-30

WINSTON, Helen (d 1972 [40])

performer BP/57*

WINSTON, Helene Canadian actress
TW/26

WINSTON, Jackie (d 1971 [56])
performer BP/56*

WINSTON, James (1773-1843) English actor, manager CDP, GT

WINSTON, Jane (d 1959 [51]) actress BE*

WINSTON, Jeannie (fl 1876) singer
CDP

WINSTONE, Eric (d 1974 [61]) performer BP/58*

WINSTONE, Richard (d 1788) actor
GT, TD/1-2

WINTER, Banks (1857-1936) minstrel, songwriter CDP

WINTER, Mrs. E. C. (fl 1863-69)
actress HAS

WINTER, Edward (b 1937) American
actor TW/22-29

WINTER, Jessie (1885-1971) English
actress WWT/2-9

WINTER, John Strange [Mrs. Arthur
Stannard] (d 1911) writer EA/13*

WINTER, Joseph P. (fl 1865) actor
CDP

WINTER, Keith (b 1906) Welsh
dramatist WWT/8-11

WINTER, Percy (1861-1928) Canadian
actor, stage manager PP/3

WINTER, Richard (fl 1571) actor?
DA

WINTER, Rose Hélène see
Hélène

WINTER, Tom (d 1876) singer
EA/77*

WINTER, Wenonah Gordon (1888-
1940) American actress, singer
GRB/1

WINTER, William (1836-1917)
American critic CDP, COC,
DAB, ES, GRB/2-4, HJD, NTH,
OC/1-3, WWA/1, WWM, WWT/
1-3, WWW/2

WINTER, Winona see Winter,
Wenonah Gordon

WINTER, Mrs. W. J. see Leslie, Elsie

WINTERBOTTOM, W. (d 1889)
bandmaster, composer EA/90*

WINTERFELD, M. see Gilbert,
Jean

WINTERS, Banks (fl 1880s) actor,
singer, songwriter SR

WINTERS, David (b 1939) English
actor TW/18

WINTERS, Lawrence (1915-65)

American actor TW/2-3, 10-
11, 22
WINTERS, Marian (b 1924) Amer-
ican actress, dramatist BE,
TW/8-20, 22, WWT/14-16
WINTERS, Roland (b 1904) Amer-
ican actor BE, TW/18-19,
26, 28
WINTERS, Shelley [née Shirley
Schrift] (b 1922/23) American
actress AAS, BE, CB, ES,
TW/23, 26, WWT/14-16
WINTERSEL, William see
Wintershall, William
WINTERSHALL, William (d 1679)
actor DA, DNB
WINTERSOLE, Bill (b 1931)
American actor TW/30
WINTHROP, Adelaide (d 1923
[32]) actress BE*, BP/8*
WINTHROP, Robert see Flana-
gan, Bud
WINTON, Ethel Alice see
Balfour, Ethel
WINTOUR, Ernest (d 1907) actor
EA/08*
WINWOOD, Estelle (b 1883) Eng-
lish actress AAS, BE, SR,
TW/1-16, 22, WWT/3-15
WIRES, Rodney S. (d 1887) ad-
vance agent NYM
WIRGES, William (d 1971 [77])
composer/lyricist BP/56*
WISDOM, Norman (b 1920) Eng-
lish actor, comedian ES,
WWT/12-16
WISE, Edward J. (b 1876) Eng-
lish composer, agent GRB/1
WISE, Herbert [né Weisz] (b
1924) Austrian director,
actor WWT/15-16
WISE, James Peter (d 1889)
acrobat EA/90*
WISE, Mrs. John [née Pattie
Lincoln] (d 1879 [27]) music-
hall performer EA/80*
WISE, Joseph (fl 1766-79) drama-
tist CP/3, GT
WISE, Patricia Doyle (d 1975
[60]) performer BP/60*
WISE, Thomas A. (1862/65-1928)
English actor DAB, SR,
WWA/1, WWM, WWT/1-5
WISEMAN, Charles (d 1916) EA/
17*
WISEMAN, Emily (fl 1870?) ac-
tress, singer CDP
WISEMAN, Jane (fl 1702) drama-

tist CP/1-3, GT
WISEMAN, Joseph (b 1918) Cana-
dian actor AAS, BE, TW/3-9,
12-13, 21, 25-26, 28-29, WWT/
14-16
WISEMAN, Robert (d 1917) EA/18*
WISHENGRAD, Morton (d 1963 [50])
American dramatist BE*, BP/
47*
WISSLER, Anna (fl 1860) American
actress HAS
WISTER, Owen (b 1860) American
dramatist WWM
WITCHETT, Hawkins see Cowell,
Joseph Leathley
WITCOVER, Walt (b 1924) Ameri-
can director, actor BE
WITHALL, Mrs. C. see Fitzwil-
liam, Kathleen Mary
WITHALL, Charles Edward (d 1886
[65]) lawyer EA/87*
WITHAM, Miss (b 1801) actress
CDP
WITHAM, John (b 1947) American
actor TW/28-29
WITHAM, Marjorie Alexandra see
Aubrey, Madge
WITHEE, Mabel (d 1952 [55])
American singer, actress TW/9
WITHERS, Charles (d 1947 [58])
American vaudevillian TW/4
WITHERS, Googie (b 1917) Indian/
English actress AAS, WWT/
10-16
WITHERS, Grant (d 1959 [55])
American actor BE*
WITHERS, Henry (d 1879 [27])
clown EA/81*
WITHERS, Iva (b 1917) Canadian
actress, singer BE, TW/25-27,
WWT/11-16
WITHERSPOON, Cora (1890-1957)
American actress TW/14, WWT/
8-11
WITHERSPOON, Herbert (1873-1935)
American singer, manager DAB,
WWA/1
WITMARK, Edward (fl 1891) singer
CDP
WITMARK, Frank (fl 1891) singer
CDP
WITMARK, Isidore (1869-1941)
American publisher, composer
DAB
WITMARK, Julius P. (d 1929 [58])
actor, singer CDP
WITMARK, Marcus (d 1910 [76])
publisher EA/11*

WITT, Max Siegfried (1871-1914) German composer WWA/1, WWM

WITT, Peter (b 1911) German talent representative BE

WITTENBERG, Philip (b 1895) American executive, lawyer, writer BE

WITTOP, Freddy [né Fred Wittop Koning] (b 1921) Dutch designer, dancer BE, WWT/ 15-16

WITTSTEIN, Ed (b 1929) American designer BE, WWT/15-16

WIZARD OF THE NORTH see Anderson, John Henry

WIZIARDE, Lou (d 1973 [83]) performer BP/58*

WODEHOUSE, Sir Pelham Granville (1881-1975) English dramatist AAS, BE, CB, ES, HP, MH, NTH, PDT, SR, WWT/4-11

WODERAM, Richard (fl 1586-87) actor? DA

WODHULL, Michael (fl 1782) translator CP/3

WOFFINGTON, Peg [Margaret] (c. 1714-60) English actress CDP, COC, DNB, ES, GT, HP, NTH, OC/1-3, PDT, TD/1-2

WOHLBRUCK, Adolph Anton Wilhelm see Walbrook, Anton

WOHLMUTH, Alois (b 1852) German actress WWT/2

WOIZIKOVSKY, Leon (b 1897) dancer WWT/9-12

WOLCOT, John [Peter Pindar] (fl 1778-82) English? dramatist CP/3

WOLF, Gerd (d 1973 [50]) producer/director/choreographer BP/58*

WOLF, Jack (d 1965 [56]) performer BP/50*

WOLF, Jay (b 1929) American talent representative BE

WOLF, Lawrence (b 1934) American actor TW/28

WOLF, Louis J. (d 1972 [67]) critic BP/57*

WOLF, Rennold (1874-1922) American dramatist, journalist SR, WWA/1, WWM, WWT/3-4

WOLF, Mrs. Rennold see Booth, Hope

WOLF, Thomas E. (d 1864) actor HAS

WOLF, Van (d 1972 [44]) producer/ director/choreographer BP/56*

WOLFE, Mr. (d 1877) Australian actor EA/78*

WOLFE, Clarence (d 1963 [75]) performer BE*

WOLFE, Humbert (1886-1940) Italian dramatist BE*, WWT/14*

WOLFE, Joel (b 1936) American actor TW/26, 28

WOLFE, Karin (b 1944) American actress TW/23, 30

WOLFE, R. Driskill (d 1973 [72]) performer BP/58*

WOLFE, Thomas (1900-38) American dramatist MWD

WOLFENDEN, Joseph (d 1883 [34]) actor EA/84*

WOLFF, Albert (d 1891 [64]) critic EA/93*

WOLFF, Edward (d 1880 [64]) musician EA/81*

WOLFF, Frank (d 1971 [43]) performer BP/56*

WOLFF, Laura Sawyer (d 1970 [85]) performer BP/55*

WOLFF, William (1858-1936) German performer BE*

WOLFINGTON, Iggie (b 1920) American actor BE

WOLFIT, Sir Donald (1902-68) English actor, manager AAS, CB, COC, ES, OC/2-3, PDT, TW/ 3-4, 21, 24, WWA/4, WWT/7-14, WWW/6

WOLFOWSKY, Boris (d 1910) dancer? EA/11*

WOLFSON, Abraham (d 1973 [65]) agent BP/58*

WOLFSON, Billy (d 1973 [75]) performer BP/57*

WOLFSON, Martin (1904-73) American actor BE, TW/4-13, 15, 26, 30

WOLFSON, Victor (b 1910) American dramatist BE

WOLHEIM, Louis Robert (1881-1931) American actor AAS, DAB, OC/1-3, SR

WOLKIND, Phoebe see Ephron, Phoebe

WOLLHEIM, Eric (1879-1948) impresario WWT/7-10

WOLPE, Stefan (d 1972 [69]) composer/lyricist BP/56*

WOLPER, David (1901-64) American producer TW/2

WOLSELEY-COX, Garnet (d 1904

[32]) composer WWT/14*

WOLSK, Eugene V. (b 1928)
American producer WWT/16

WOLSTENHOLME, Frederick
see Newbury, Pollie

WOLSTON, Henry [William Henry
Twinberrow] (b 1877) English
actor WWT/7-8

WOLVERIDGE, Carol (b 1940)
English actress WWT/12-13

WOMACK, George (d 1912 [30])
stage manager EA/13*

WOMACK, Joyce see Ebert,
Joyce

WOMBLE, Andre (b 1940) American actor TW/24-27

WOMBWELL, Miss see Bostock,
Mrs.

WOMBWELL, George (d 1909)
circus showman EA/10*

WOMBWELL, Jeremiah (1780-
1850) menagerie manager CDP

WOMEN'S THEATRE GROUP
theatre collective CD

WONDER, The Little see
Fraser, Kate

WONDER, Tommy American actor
TW/6-9

WONG, Anna May (1908-61) American actress TW/17, WWT/
6-9

WONTNER, Arthur (1875-1960)
English actor AAS, WWT/
1-12, WWW/5

WOOD, Mrs. dramatist EAP, RJ

WOOD, Miss see Meadows,
Connie

WOOD, Alfred (d 1876 [46]) Negro
comedian EA/77*

WOOD, Annie (d 1905 [64]) actress CDP

WOOD, Arthur (1875-1953)
English conductor, composer
WWT/4-11

WOOD, Mrs. Arthur see Webber,
Eliza

WOOD, Arthur Augustus (d 1907
[83]) actor GRB/3

WOOD, Arthur O. (d 1908) EA/
09*

WOOD, Audrey (b 1905) American
literary representative BE

WOOD, Britt (d 1965 [70]) performer BP/49*

WOOD, Charles (d 1902 [68])
manager EA/03*

WOOD, Charles (d 1917) scene
artist EA/18*

WOOD, Charles (b 1932/33) English
dramatist AAS, CD, CH, COC,
PDT, RE, WWT/16

WOOD, Mrs. Charles (b 1840) English actress GRB/1

WOOD, Mrs. Charles see Wood,
Clara

WOOD, Charles Octavius (d 1887
[21]) scene artist EA/88*

WOOD, Clara [Mrs. Charles Wood]
(d 1879) actress EA/80*

WOOD, David (b 1944) English actor, dramatist WWT/15-16

WOOD, David James (d 1889 [31])
musical director EA/90*

WOOD, Edna (b 1918) English actress, singer WWT/10-11

WOOD, Elizabeth (fl 1839) American
actress HAS

WOOD, Elizabeth E. [Mrs. W. H.
Wood] (d 1883 [37]) EA/84*

WOOD, Ernest [Ernest Edward
Smallwood] (d 1897 [37]) actor
EA/99*

WOOD, Eugene R. (1903-71) American actor TW/18-19, 21-23,
25-27

WOOD, Florence [Mrs. Ralph R.
Lumley] English actress GRB/
1-4, WWT/1-9

WOOD, Frank (fl 1866?) dancer,
singer CDP

WOOD, Frank (d 1876) actor EA/
77*

WOOD, Frank Motley (d 1919 [75])
actor BE*, WWT/14*

WOOD, Frank Percy (d 1912) EA/
13*

WOOD, Fred W. (d 1913 [57])
EA/14*

WOOD, G. (fl 1845) Irish comedian
HAS

WOOD, G. (b 1919) American actor
TW/23, 26

WOOD, George (d 1886 [63]) manager CDP

WOOD, George (d 1963 [63]) agent
BP/48*

WOOD, George (d 1970) performer
BP/55*

WOOD, Master H. (fl 1863?) singer
CDP

WOOD, Harry H. (b 1845) English
actor, ballet master HAS

WOOD, Helen (b 1933/35) American
actress TW/8-9, 13

WOOD, Henry minstrel manager
CDP

WOOD, Henry J. (b 1870) English
conductor GRB/1

WOOD, Mrs. Henry J. see
Wood, Olga

WOOD, Herbert (d 1916) advertising manager EA/17*

WOOD, H. J. (d 1910) EA/11*

WOOD, Jane (b 1886) English
actress WWT/6-9

WOOD, J. C. (d 1871 [49]) actor
EA/72*

WOOD, Col. J. H. (d 1900)
manager, proprietor CDP

WOOD, J. H. (d 1906 [64]) music-
hall manager EA/07*

WOOD, J. Hickory (d 1913 [54])
dramatist BE*, EA/14*,
WWT/14*

WOOD, John (d 1863) English
actor CDP, HAS

WOOD, John English actor AAS,
WWT/16

WOOD, Mrs. John [Matilda Char-
lotte Vining] (1831/33/45-1915)
English actress, manager
CDP, COC, DP, GRB/1-4,
HAS, OC/1-3, OAA/2, WWT/
1-2

WOOD, Mrs. John D. (d 1865)
actress HAS

WOOD, John S. (d 1911 [80])
actor EA/12*

WOOD, Joseph (1801-90) English
actor, singer CDP, SR

WOOD, Mrs. Joseph [Mary Ann
Wood; Mary Ann Paton]
(1802-64) Scottish actress,
singer CDP, HAS, SR

WOOD, Juliana see Wood, Mrs.
William Burke

WOOD, Kelly (b 1943) American
actress TW/28, 30

WOOD, Lizzie (fl 1846-65) American dancer HAS

WOOD, Marie see Lloyd, Marie

WOOD, Marjorie (1887-1955)
English actress TW/12

WOOD, Mary see Clarke, Mary

WOOD, Mary Ann see Wood,
Mrs. Joseph

WOOD, Mattie see Williams,
Mattie

WOOD, Metcalfe dramatist, actor
WWT/1-8

WOOD, Rev. Nathaniel (fl 1581?)
dramatist CP/1-2

WOOD, Norma Jean (b 1942)
American actress TW/26

WOOD, N. S. (fl 1876) actor CDP

WOOD, Olga [Mrs. Henry J. Wood]
(d 1909) singer EA/11*

WOOD, Mrs. Paddy see Bennett,
Lily

WOOD, Peggy (b 1892/94) American
actress, singer AAS, BE, CB,
TW/2-16, 20-21, 24, 26-27,
WWT/4-16

WOOD, Peter (b 1927) English director AAS, WWT/13-16

WOOD, Philip (1895-1940) actor,
dramatist CB

WOOD, Ralph dramatist CP/3

WOOD, Richard (fl 1613) actor
DA

WOOD, Roland (d 1966 [70]) actor
TW/23

WOOD, Rosabel (b 1845) American
dancer, actress HAS

WOOD, Rose [Mrs. Lewis Morri-
son] actress CDP

WOOD, Stuart Craig (b 1945) American actor TW/27, 29

WOOD, Thomas (d 1913) EA/14*

WOOD, Tom (d 1898 [27]) comedian
EA/99*

WOOD, Victor (b 1914) actor TW/8

WOOD, W. H. (d 1882) minstrel
EA/83*

WOOD, Mrs. W. H. see Wood,
Elizabeth E.

WOOD, William (fl 1615) actor DA

WOOD, William (d 1855) English
actor CDP, HAS

WOOD, William A. (1833-62) English actor HAS

WOOD, William Burke (1779-1861)
American actor, manager CDP,
COC, DAB, HAS, OC/1-3, SR,
WWA/H

WOOD, Mrs. William Burke [née
Juliana Westray] (d 1836) actress CDP, HAS

WOOD, Zilpha Barnes (b 1871)
American teacher, musician,
conductor WWM

WOODALL, Doris (d 1954 [76])
singer WWT/14*

WOODALL-BIRD, John (d 1917)
actor EA/18*, WWT/14*

WOODBRIDGE, George (1907-73)
English actor WWT/9-13

WOODBRIDGE, James (d 1893 [41])
EA/94*

WOODBRIDGE, Robert (fl 1793)
dramatist CP/3

WOODBURN, James (1888-1948)

Scottish actor WWT/10

WOODBURY, Mr. (fl 1838) actor
HAS

WOODBURY, Clare (d 1949 [69])
American actress TW/5

WOODBURY, Miss J. B. see
Perrin, Mrs.

WOODBURY, Katie L. see
Riley, Mrs. W. H.

WOODBURY, Lael J. (b 1927)
American director, producer,
educator BE

WOODBURY, Miss S. [Mrs. Mc-
Farland] (fl 1853) actress HAS

WOODES, Nathaniel (fl 1581)
dramatist CP/3, FGF

WOODFALL, Miss (fl 1804) actress TD/2

WOODFALL, Henry Sampson
dramatist CP/3

WOODFALL, Mrs. Thomas see
Collins, Clementina

WOODFALL, William (1746-1803)
dramatist, critic CP/3, DNB,
TD/1-2

WOODFORD, Francis D. (d 1892)
scene artist EA/93*

WOODFORD, J. C. (d 1873 [56])
scene artist EA/74*

WOODFORD, Jennie (b 1940)
actress TW/25

WOODFORD, John (d 1878 [51])
musician EA/79*

WOODFORD, Margaretta (d 1913)
EA/14*

WOODFORD, Thomas (fl 1600-
20) lessee DA

WOODGER, Ben (d 1918) EA/19*

WOODGER, Harry (d 1890 [54])
EA/91*

WOODHAM, Mr. (fl 1806-16)
actor HAS

WOODHAM, Mrs. (1743-1803)
singer, actress DNB

WOODHAM, Mrs. Charles Somerset see Daniel, Mrs.
William

WOODHEAD, John (d 1891) EA/
92*

WOODHEAD, Mrs. William (d
1886) EA/87*

WOODHEAD, W. W. (d 1910
[74]) musician EA/11*

WOODHOUSE, J. H. (d 1906)
comedian EA/07*

WOODHOUSE, Vernon (1874-1936)
English dramatist, critic,
journalist WWT/5-8, WWW/3

WOODHULL, Clara (d 1837) actress
SR

WOODHULL, Fred [William Blanch]
(b 1843) English actor HAS

WOODHULL, Jacob (d 1832 [40])
American actor, manager HAS

WOODHULL, John (d 1838) American actor HAS

WOODHULL, Victoria C. actress
CDP

WOODHULL, Zula Maud American
dramatist WWA/5

WOODIN, William Samuel (d 1882
[62]) entertainer CDP

WOODLEY, Jane see Hill, Jenny

WOODLEY, John Wilson see
Pasta, Johnny

WOODLING, Miss see Simpson,
Mrs. L.

WOODMAN, Alex Haines see
Romer, Alec

WOODROFFE, S. H. see Woodroffe-Boyce, S.

WOODROFFE-BOYCE, S. [S. H.
Woodroffe] (b 1877) English actor, singer GRB/1

WOODRUFF, Edna (d 1947 [73])
actress BE*, WWT/14*

WOODRUFFE, Henry Mygatt (1869/
70-1916) American actor GRB/
3-4, PP/3, SR, WWA/1, WWT/
1-3

WOODS, Albert Herman (1870-1951)
American producing manager,
proprietor NTH, SR, TW/7,
WWT/4-11

WOODS, Allie (b 1940) American
actor TW/25-27

WOODS, Annie Louise (d 1917)
EA/18*

WOODS, Aubrey librettist CD

WOODS, Donald Canadian actor
BE, TW/21

WOODS, Col. George H. (fl 1865-
71) manager SR

WOODS, Graham (d 1918 [44])
EA/19*

WOODS, Harry L. (d 1968 [79])
performer BP/53*

WOODS, Harry M. (d 1970 [73])
composer/lyricist BP/54*

WOODS, Henry (d 1889 [29]) comic
singer EA/90*

WOODS, James (d 1947) American
actor TW/26-29

WOODS, J. M. (fl 1884?) singer
CDP

WOODS, John (fl 1604) actor DA

WOODS, Lesley American actress TW/18-19

WOODS, Maria (d 1909) EA/10*

WOODS, Mary L. see Warrington, Ann

WOODS, Richard (b 1930) American actor TW/21-30

WOODS, Robert stage manager BE

WOODS, Rupert (d 1893 [42]) EA/94*

WOODS, William (1760-1802) actor, dramatist CDP, CP/3, TD/2

WOODS, William (d 1909) property master EA/10*

WOODTHORPE, Peter (b 1931) English actor AAS, WWT/14-16

WOODTHROPE, Mrs. L. D. see Tilbury, Zeffie

WOODVILLE, W. F. (d 1875) actor EA/76*

WOODVINE, John (b 1929) English actor AAS, WWT/15-16

WOODWARD, Mrs. (d 1869 [43]) singer EA/70*

WOODWARD, Mrs. see Stewart, Mrs. E. F.

WOODWARD, Charles, Jr. producer WWT/16

WOODWARD, Charles E. (d 1904 [38]) actor EA/05*

WOODWARD, Edward (b 1930) English actor AAS, BE, WWT/14-16

WOODWARD, Mrs. Eugene Lindeman (1859-1947) actress SR

WOODWARD, Grace [Mrs. Warner Hagen] (d 1907) actress EA/08*

WOODWARD, Harry [or Henry] (1714/17-77) English actor, dramatist CDP, COC, CP/2-3, DNB, ES, GT, OC/1-3, TD/1-2

WOODWARD, Horace L. (d 1973 [68]) producer/director/choreographer BP/57*

WOODWARD, Joanne (b 1930/31?) American actress BE, CB, ES

WOODWARD, Mary S. (b 1819) actress HAS

WOODWARD, Milton (d 1964) magician BE*

WOODWARD, Robert (d 1972 [63]) performer BP/56*

WOODWARD, William Jarman (d 1903 [27]) animal trainer EA/04*

WOODWORTH, Samuel (1785-1842) American dramatist COC, DAB, EAP, MH, OC/1-3, RJ, SR

WOOLAND, Norman German/English actor WWT/16

WOOLCOTT, May (fl 1884-88) actress CDP

WOOLDRIDGE, Mrs. (d 1887 [67]) actress EA/88*

WOOLER, John Pratt (d 1868 [44]) dramatist BE*, EA/69*, WWT/14*

WOOLERY, Miss (fl 1784-66) actress TD/1-2

WOOLF, Barney (d 1972 [95]) performer BP/56*

WOOLF, Benjamin Edward (1836-1901) English/American critic, dramatist, musician CDP, DAB

WOOLF, Edgar Allan (1881-1943) American dramatist, actor SR, WWT/4-9

WOOLF, Jack (d 1918) EA/19*

WOOLF, Kitty (d 1944 [73]) actress BE*, WWT/14*

WOOLF, M. actress CDP

WOOLF, Michael Angelo (1837-99) actor CDP

WOOLF, Stanley (d 1959 [59]) producer, performer BE*, BP/43*

WOOLF, Walter (b 1899) American actor, singer WWT/7

WOOLFENDEN, Guy Anthony (b 1937) English musical director, composer WWT/15-16

WOOLFORD, Louise [Mrs. Andrew Ducrow] (d 1901 [86]) rope dancer, equestrienne CDP

WOOLGAR, Elizabeth [Mrs. W. Woolgar] (d 1883) EA/84*

WOOLGAR, Ellen (d 1875 [24]) actress EA/76*

WOOLGAR, Sarah Jane see Mellon, Mrs. Alfred

WOOLGAR, Mrs. W. see Woolgar, Elizabeth

WOOLGAR, William (d 1885 [84]) actor EA/87*

WOOLLAMS, Ernest [Ernest Wilmore] (d 1887 [38]) actor? EA/88*

WOOLLAMS, Sarah Ann see Rotchley, Minnie

WOOLLARD, Robert (d 1971 [83]) performer BP/55*

WOOLLCOTT, Alexander (1887-1943) American critic, actor AAS, CB, COC, DAB, ES, HJD, MWD, NTH, OC/1-3, WWT/5-9, WWW/4

WOOLLEY, Monty (1888-1963) American actor, producer BE, CB, SR, TW/19, WWA/4, WWT/10-11

WOOLLIDGE, Mrs. (d 1863 [63]) actress WWT/14*

WOOLRICH, Cornell (d 1968 [64]) dramatist BP/53*

WOOLRIDGE, Lestocq Boileau see Lestocq, William

WOOLS, Stephen (1729-99) English actor HAS, SR

WOOLSEY, Robert (1889-1938) American actor WWT/7-8

WOOTTWELL, Thomas (fl 1900?) actor, singer, song composer CDP

WORBOYS, William (d 1877 [48]) comedian EA/79*

WORDSWORTH, Richard (b 1915) English actor AAS, WWT/11-16

WORDSWORTH, William (1770-1850) English dramatist HP

WORDSWORTH, William Derrick (b 1912) English press representative WWT/10-13

WORGAN, T. D. (fl 1808) dramatist CP/3

WORK, Henry Clay (1832-84) American songwriter BE*

WORK, William (b 1923) American executive, educator, director BE

WORKMAN, Miss (fl 1828) English actress HAS

WORKMAN, C. Herbert (1873-1923) English actor, singer GRB/4, WWT/1-4

WORKMAN, Gertrude (d 1972 [87]) performer BP/56*

WORKMAN, James (fl 1803) dramatist EAP, RJ

WORKMAN, John William (d 1895) acrobat EA/96*

WORLAND, Jerry (d 1864 [32]) circus performer HAS

WORLEY, Jo Anne (b 1937) American actress, singer BE, TW/22-23

WORLOCK, Frederick G. (1886-1973) English actor BE, TW/8-12, 30, WWT/4-15

WORLOCK, Kitty Ann see Armstrong, Elizabeth

WORLOOU, Lambros see Guetary, Georges

WORLOW, Percy (d 1918) EA/19*

WORM, A. Toxen (d 1922 [55]) Danish producer, press representative BE*, BP/6*, WWT/14*

WORMSER, Andre (d 1926 [75]) composer BE*, WWT/14*

WORONOV, Mary (b 1946) American actress TW/30

WORRALL, Lechmere (b 1874/75) English dramatist WWT/2-11

WORRELL, Irene (b 1849) actress CDP

WORRELL, Jennie (1850-99) actress CDP

WORRELL, Sophia see Knight, Mrs. George S.

WORRELL, Thomas J. (fl 1848) American actor HAS

WORRELL, William (fl 1851) clown HAS

WORRELL SISTERS, The (fl 1848-68) American dancers HAS

WORRENBERGH, Hans (b 1650) Swiss dwarf CDP

WORSDALE, James (d 1767) dramatist, composer, singer CP/1-3, GT

WORSLEY, Bruce (b 1899) English manager WWT/9-14

WORSLEY, T. C. (b 1907) critic AAS

WORSTER, Howett (b 1882) English actor, singer WWT/6-8

WORSWICK, Alfred (d 1917) EA/18*

WORSWICK, James (d 1903) conductor EA/05*

WORSWICK, John (d 1906 [66]) proprietor EA/07*

WORSWICK, Mrs. John (d 1911) EA/12*

WORTH, Beatrice [Mrs. Sam Shipley] (d 1907) variety performer EA/08*

WORTH, Billie (b 1917) American actress BE, TW/8-12

WORTH, Ellis (fl 1615-35) actor DA

WORTH, Irene (b 1916) American actress AAS, BE, CB, ES, TW/21, WWT/11-16

WORTHING, Frank (1866-1910) Scottish actor GRB/2-4

WORTHING, Helen Lee (d 1948
[43]) American actress BE*,
BP/33*
WORTHINGTON, Mrs. actress
TD/2
WORTHINGTON, Thomas (d 1868
[25]) star diver EA/69*
WORTHINGTON, William (d 1966
[69]) performer BP/50*
WORTMAN, Don A. (b 1927)
American talent representative,
actor, director, producer BE
WORTON, Mrs. Erskine [Mrs.
Israel Worton] (d 1886) EA/
87*
WORTON, Mrs. Israel see
Worton, Mrs. Erskine
WOTTON, Sir Henry (1568-1639)
English dramatist CP/2-3,
FGF
WOTY, William (d 1791) drama-
tist CP/3
WOUK, Herman (b 1915) American
dramatist BE, CH, ES, HJD,
MD, MWD
WRANGHAM, Rev. Francis (fl
1792-1801) dramatist CP/3
WRAY, Ada English singer
CDP, HAS
WRAY, Edward A. (d 1866 [27])
comedian HAS
WRAY, Fay (b 1907) Canadian
actress ES
WRAY, George (d 1900 [60]) actor
EA/01*
WRAY, John (1888-1940) American
actor CB, WWT/7-9
WRAY, Louisa Payne (b 1835)
English singer, performer
HAS
WRAY, Maxwell (1898-1972) Eng-
lish producer, actor WWT/
7-15
WRAY, Samuel (d 1886) Negro
comedian EA/87*
WRAY, William A. American
comedian HAS
WREGHITT, George (d 1884 [36])
manager EA/85*
WREN, Alice (d 1880) actress,
singer EA/81*
WREN, Sir Christopher (1631-
1723) English architect, de-
signer NTH, OC/1-3
WREN, Fred R. (1848-1917)
American actor SR
WREN, George (b 1837) English
actor HAS

WREN, Harry (d 1973 [57]) show-
man BP/58*
WREN, Sam (d 1962 [65]) American
actor, director BE*
WRENCH, Benjamin (1778-1843)
English actor BS, CDP, DNB,
OX
WRENCH, James (d 1884) actor
EA/85*
WRIGHT, Mr. (fl 1736) actor CDP
WRIGHT, Mr. (fl 1834-69) Ameri-
can actor HAS
WRIGHT, Mrs. Alex see Wright,
Margaret
WRIGHT, Alexander (d 1878) musi-
cian EA/79*
WRIGHT, Alexander (d 1902 [75])
manager EA/03*
WRIGHT, Alice (d 1892 [59]?)
actress, singer CDP, EA/93*
WRIGHT, Amanda (d 1968 [78])
performer BP/52*
WRIGHT, Belinda (b 1929) English
dancer ES
WRIGHT, Bob (b 1911) American
actor TW/23, 25-28
WRIGHT, Brittain (d 1877 [40])
actor CDP
WRIGHT, Catherine (b 1948) Amer-
ican actress TW/26
WRIGHT, C. B. (d 1892) treasurer
EA/93*
WRIGHT, Charlotte see Blanchard,
Mrs. Thomas
WRIGHT, Cowley (1889-1923) Eng-
lish actor WWT/4
WRIGHT, David (b 1941) English
dramatist, director WWT/15-16
WRIGHT, Edward (1813-59) actor
CDP, DNB
WRIGHT, Mrs. Edward see
Wright, Rose Olivia
WRIGHT, Edwin (d 1916 [60]) EA/
17*
WRIGHT, E. H. (b 1950) American
actor TW/29
WRIGHT, Elizabeth see Arne,
Mrs. Michael, II
WRIGHT, Ellen (fl 1865) actress
HAS
WRIGHT, Ellen [Mrs. Percy Cross
Standing] (d 1904) composer
EA/05*
WRIGHT, Ethel (b 1886) Canadian
actress WWM
WRIGHT, Fanny (d 1954) actress
BE*, WWT/14*
WRIGHT, Fanny see Williams,

Mrs.

WRIGHT, Frances (1795-1852) Scottish/American dramatist EAP, RJ

WRIGHT, Fred, Sr. (1826-1911) English actor, manager GRB/ 1-4

WRIGHT, Mrs. Fred [Sr. ?] (d 1919 [72]) actress BE*, WWT/14*

WRIGHT, Fred, Jr. (1871-1928) English actor EA/97, GRB/ 3-4, WWM, WWT/1-5

WRIGHT, George see Wright-man, George

WRIGHT, George Edward see Bealby, George

WRIGHT, Georgie (d 1937 [79]) English actress BE*, WWT/ 14*

WRIGHT, G. Harry (b 1901) American educator, director BE

WRIGHT, Haidée (1868-1943) English actress GRB/2-4, WWM, WWT/1-9

WRIGHT, Harold Bell (1878-1944) writer SR

WRIGHT, Harry (d 1877) panto-mimist EA/78*

WRIGHT, Hazel (d 1971 [70s]) performer BP/56*

WRIGHT, Henry (fl 1900?) actor, singer CDP

WRIGHT, Henry (d 1905) EA/06*

WRIGHT, Horace (b 1876) English actor, singer WWM

WRIGHT, Hugh E. (1879-1940) French actor, dramatist WWT/4-9

WRIGHT, Huntley (1869-1941/43) English actor CB, GRB/1-4, WWT/1-9, WWW/4

WRIGHT, Jack (d 1917) EA/18*

WRIGHT, Jane (d 1905) EA/07*

WRIGHT, John (fl 1631) actor DA

WRIGHT, John (fl 1674) drama-tist CP/1-3

WRIGHT, John (d 1890) musician EA/91*

WRIGHT, John (d 1900) variety comedian EA/01*

WRIGHT, John B. (b 1814) American call boy, stage manager HAS

WRIGHT, Mrs. John B. (d 1857) American actress? HAS

WRIGHT, John W. (b 1899) American educator, director BE

WRIGHT, Jonas S. (d 1874 [35]) manager EA/75*

WRIGHT, Lawrence (d 1964 [76]) publisher, songwriter BE*

WRIGHT, Mrs. Leonard see Wright, Minnie

WRIGHT, Lloyd, Jr. (d 1964 [65]) lawyer BE*

WRIGHT, Louis B. (b 1899) American educator, library director BE

WRIGHT, Margaret [Mrs. Alex Wright] (d 1899) EA/00*

WRIGHT, Marie (d 1949 [87]) actress BE*, WWT/14*

WRIGHT, Martha (b 1926) American actress, singer BE, CB, TW/ 4-10

WRIGHT, Mary Ann (d 1902 [64]) EA/03*

WRIGHT, Maudie [Mrs. Ernest Mansell] (d 1911 [28]) actress EA/12*

WRIGHT, Minnie [Mrs. Leonard Wright] (d 1906) EA/08*

WRIGHT, Nelly [Mrs. Alfred Baker] (d 1888 [26]) actress EA/89*

WRIGHT, Nicholas (b 1940) South African director WWT/16

WRIGHT, Richard (d 1891) EA/92*

WRIGHT, Richard (1908-60) American dramatist BE*

WRIGHT, Robert (b 1911) American actor, singer BE

WRIGHT, Robert (b 1914) American lyricist, composer BE

WRIGHT, Roger (d 1786) actor TD/1-2

WRIGHT, Rose Olivia [Mrs. Edward Wright] (d 1888 [61]) EA/ 89*

WRIGHT, Teresa (b 1918/19) American actress BE, CB, ES, TW/ 24, 26-27, 29, WWT/15-16

WRIGHT, Mrs. Theodore (d 1922) actress GRB/3-4, WWT/1-4

WRIGHT, Thomas (fl 1693) machinist, dramatist CP/1-3

WRIGHT, Will (d 1962 [68]) American actor BE*, BP/47*

WRIGHT, William Aldis (1831-1914) scholar DNB

WRIGHT, William W. (d 1885 [56]) journalist EA/86*

WRIGHT, Wynn (d 1965 [68]) performer BP/49*

WRIGHTEN, Miss (fl 1848?) actress CDP

WRIGHTEN, James (d 1793) prompter GT, TD/1-2

WRIGHTEN, Mrs. James see Wrighten, Mary Ann

WRIGHTEN, Mary Ann [Mrs. James Wrighten] (d 1796 [40]) actress CDP

WRIGHTMAN, George [né Wright] (d 1866) comedian HAS

WRIGHTON, Norman H. F. (d 1917) actor EA/18*

WRIGHTON, W. T. (d 1880 [83]) composer, musician EA/81*

WRIGHTON, Frank Henry see Wrighton, Norman

WRIGHTON, Norman [Frank Henry Wrighton] (b 1887) English actor GRB/1-2

WRIGHTSON, Earl actor TW/1

WRIGLEY, H. C. (d 1918) EA/19*

WRIXON-BECHER, Lady Eliza see O'Neill, Eliza

WROTHE, Edwin Lee (d 1922 [54]) American comedian BE*, BP/7*

WROUGHTON, Richard (1748-1822) English actor, manager CDP, DNB, GT, TD/1-2

WRUBEL, Allie (d 1973 [68]) composer/lyricist BP/58*

WUELLNER, Ludwig (b 1858) German musician WWM

WULFRIES, Mrs. [née Gunn] (fl 1843) English actress HAS

WUNDERLICH, Fritz (1930-66) German singer WWA/4

WUPPERMANN, Claudia see Morgan, Claudia

WUTKE, Louis M. (d 1974) theatre equipment specialist BP/59*

WYATT, Agnes (d 1932) actress, singer BE*, WWT/14*

WYATT, E. actress, singer CDP

WYATT, Euphemia van Rensselaer (b 1884) American critic BE

WYATT, Frances (d 1897) actress EA/98*

WYATT, Frank, Jr. (1890-1933) producer, manager BE*, WWT/14*

WYATT, Frank Gunning (1852-1926) actor, manager COC, DP, EA/95, GRB/1-4, WWT/1-5

WYATT, George H. (d 1860) actor CDP

WYATT, George W. (d 1860) actor HAS

WYATT, Jane (b 1912) American actress BE, CB, WWT/8-15

WYBERT, Charles (d 1906 [60]) actor EA/07*

WYBROW, Mrs. (fl 1808?-13) actress, dancer CDP

WYBROW, Waller actress, singer CDP

WYCHERLEY, William (1640-1716) English dramatist CDP, COC, CP/1-3, DNB, ES, GT, HP, MH, NTH, OC/1-3, PDT, RE

WYCHERLY, Margaret (1881-1956) English actress GRB/3-4, ES, TW/2-7, 10-12, WWT/1-12

WYCKHAM, John [né Suckling] (b 1926) English lighting designer, theatre consultant WWT/15-16

WYCKOFF, Evelyn (b 1917) American actress, singer TW/1, WWT/10-15

WYCKOFF, Robert Fletcher see Fletcher, Robert

WYES, William (d 1903 [46]) actor BE*, EA/04*, WWT/14*

WYETTE, Charlotte (fl 1858) actress HAS

WYKE, Byam (d 1944 [84]) dramatist BE*, WWT/14*

WYLDE, Dr. Henry (d 1890 [68]) conductor, professor EA/91*

WYLE, Edwin A. (d 1964 [86]) manager, press representative BE*

WYLE, Larry (d 1975 [53]) performer BP/59*

WYLER, Gretchen (b 1932) American dancer, singer, actress BE, TW/11-12

WYLER, Hillary (b 1946) American actress TW/28

WYLER, James (b 1922) American actor TW/8

WYLEY, George (b 1879) English actor GRB/1

WYLIE, Arthur (d 1903) music-hall comedian EA/04*

WYLIE, David B. (d 1868) Scottish singer HAS

WYLIE, James (d 1941 [65]) critic BE*, WWT/14*

WYLIE, Julian [Julian Samuelson] (1878-1934) English producer, manager COC, OC/1-3, WWT/4-7

WYLIE, Lauri [Morris Laurence Samuelson] (b 1880) English dramatist, librettist WWT/6-8

WYLIE, Max (d 1975 [71]) dramatist BP/60*

WYLIE, William (d 1973 [44]) general manager BP/57*

WYLKYNSON, John (fl 1549) DA

WYLLYAMS, Adeline (d 1880 [22]) actress EA/81*

WYMAN, Prof. (d 1904 [40]) illusionist EA/05*

WYMAN, John (fl 1854?) magician CDP

WYMARK, Olwen [Mrs. Patrick Wymark] American dramatist CD

WYMARK, Patrick (1926-70) English actor WWT/14, WWW/6

WYMARK, Mrs. Patrick see Wymark, Olwen

WYMETAL, William (d 1970 [80]) producer/director/choreographer BP/55*

WYMORE, Patricia [or Patrice] (b 1927) American dancer TW/4-8

WYN, Marjery (b 1909) English actress, singer WWT/7-9

WYNDGARDE, Peter French/English actor, director WWT/16

WYNDHAM (d 1911 [34]) wire performer EA/12*

WYNDHAM, Lady see Moore, Mary

WYNDHAM, Arthur (d 1888 [47]) dramatic sketch artist EA/89*

WYNDHAM, Sir Charles (1837-1919) English actor, manager CDP, COC, DNB, DP, EA/97, ES, GRB/1-4, HAS, OAA/1-2, OC/1-3, SR, WWM, WWT/1-3, WWW/2

WYNDHAM, Lady Charles see Moore, Mary

WYNDHAM, Dennis (b 1887) South African actor WWT/4-13

WYNDHAM, Fanny (fl 1838?) actress, singer CDP

WYNDHAM, Fred W. (d 1930 [77]) producer, manager BE*, WWT/14*

WYNDHAM, Gwen actress WWT/6-9

WYNDHAM, Horace (d 1878 [17]) EA/80*

WYNDHAM, Howard (1865-1947) English manager, actor OC/2-3, SR, WWT/8-10

WYNDHAM, Louise Isabella (d 1942) actress BE*, WWT/14*

WYNDHAM, Olive (b 1886) American actress WWM, WWT/2-9

WYNDHAM, R[obert] H[enry] (1814/17-94) Scottish manager, actor COC, DNB

WYNDHAM, Mrs. R[obert] H[enry] (d 1901 [82]) EA/02*

WYNN, Ed (1886-1966) American actor, producer BE, CB, NTH, TW/2-7, 23, WWA/4, WWT/5-11

WYNN, Henry S. (d 1890) proprietor, manager EA/91*

WYNN, Kennan (b 1916) American actor BE

WYNN, Mabel Emily Swinton (d 1916) EA/17*

WYNN, Nan (d 1971 [55]) actress TW/27

WYNN, W. S. (d 1899) manager EA/00*

WYNNE, Mr. (fl 1836) English actor HAS

WYNNE, Augusta see Angelelli, Augusta

WYNNE, Cybel [Mrs. Charles Rock] English actress GRB/1-2

WYNNE, Edith (d 1897 [55]) singer EA/98*

WYNNE, Evelyne [Lotta Brightling] (d 1887) EA/88*

WYNNE, George (d 1846) actor CDP

WYNNE, Jane [Mrs. Johnny Wynne] (d 1892 [38]) EA/93*

WYNNE, Mrs. Johnny see Wynne, Jane

WYNNE, Kate see Matthison, Mrs. H.

WYNNE, Watkin Wyatt see De Glorion, William

WYNNE, Wish (1882-1931) English actress WWT/2-6

WYNTER, Amy [Mrs. George Harker] (d 1906) actress EA/08*

WYNTER, Edyth (d 1910) musician EA/11*

WYNTER, Florrie [Mrs. Charles E. Derwood] (d 1894) EA/95*

WYNTOUR, Bernard (d 1908 [27]) actor EA/09*

WYN WEAVER, A. E. (b 1872)

English actor GRB/1
WYNYARD, Diana [Dorothy Isobel
  Cox] (1906-64) English ac-
  tress AAS, COC, ES, OC/3,
  TW/20, WWT/7-13, WWW/6
WYNYARD, John (b 1915) English
  actor TW/3, WWT/11-16
WYSE, John (b 1904) English ac-
  tor WWT/7-16
WYVLLE, Amber English singer
  GRB/1

- X -

XIFO, Ray (b 1942) American
  actor TW/30

- Y -

YAHNE, Mlle. [Marie Léonie
  Eugénie Jahn] French actress
  GRB/1-4
YAKKO, Sada Japanese actress
  GRB/2-4, WWT/1-4
YAKOBSON, Leonid (d 1975 [71])
  producer/director/choreographer
  BP/60*
YALE, Charles H. (d 1920 [64])
  actor, manager SR
YAMAMOTO, Kajiro (d 1974 [72])
  producer/director/choreographer
  BP/59*
YANKOWITZ, Susan (b 1941)
  American dramatist CD
YANNIS, Michael (b 1922) Greek
  actor WWT/11-12
YAPP, Cecil (b 1879) Canadian/
  American actor WWM, WWT/
  7-8
YARBOROUGH, Bertram (d 1962
  [58]) director BE*, BP/47*
YARDE, Margaret (1878-1944)
  English actress WWT/5-9
YARDE-BULLER, Mrs. John
  see Orme, Denise
YARDLEY, Miss see Kent,
  Mrs. John
YARDLEY, William (d 1900 [51])
  dramatist, critic BE*, EA/
  01*, WWT/14*
YARMOUTH, Earl of [Eric
  Hope] (b 1871) English actor
  GRB/1
YARNELL, Bruce (1935-73)
  American actor, singer TW/
  17-19, 22-23, 26, 30

YARNOLD, Mrs. [née Grove] (fl
  1836) actress HAS
YARNOLD, Anna Maria [Mrs.
  George Yarnold] (d 1895 [80])
  EA/96*
YARNOLD, Edwin (d 1848 [58])
  actor EA/72*, WWT/14*
YARNOLD, Mrs. Edwin [Emma
  Yarnold] (1822-67) CDP
YARNOLD, Emma see Yarnold,
  Mrs. Edwin
YARNOLD, G. (b 1817) actor CDP
YARNOLD, C. B. (d 1891 [41])
  scene artist EA/92*
YARNOLD, George (d 1878 [63])
  comedian EA/80*
YARNOLD, Mrs. George see
  Yarnold, Anna Maria
YARRINGTON, Robert (fl 1601)
  dramatist CP/1-3, DNB, FGF
YARROW, Duncan (b 1884) English
  actor WWT/10
YARROW, Joseph (fl 1742) actor,
  dramatist CP/2-3, GT
YARROW, Susannah see Davies,
  Mrs. Thomas
YARWOOD, George Julian (d 1909)
  musical director EA/10*
YASSIN, Ismail (d 1972 [60])
  Egyptian actor BP/57*, WWT/
  16*
YATES, Anna Maria see Yates,
  Mary Ann
YATES, Benjamin (d 1891 [74])
  English/American actor, dancer,
  manager CDP
YATES, Edmund Hodgson (1831/32-
  94) English dramatist, journalist
  CDP, DNB, EA/68, OC/1-3
YATES, Elizabeth [Mrs. Frederick
  Henry Yates; Elizabeth Brunton]
  (1799-1860) English actress
  CDP, DNB, ES, OX
YATES, Ellen [née Benson] (d 1890
  [26]) EA/91*
YATES, Frederick Henry (1795-
  1842) English actor BS, CDP,
  COC, DNB, ES, OC/1-3, OX
YATES, Mrs. Frederick Henry
  see Yates, Elizabeth
YATES, George [William Cleghorn]
  (d 1907 [81]) actor EA/08*,
  WWT/14*
YATES, Irving (d 1969 [75]) vaude-
  ville booker BP/54*
YATES, John Lowndes (d 1889
  [34]) EA/90*
YATES, Miss M. dancer CDP

YATES, Mark (d 1885) treasurer, acting manager EA/86*

YATES, Mary Ann [née Graham] (1728-87) English actress CDP, COC, DNB, ES, GT, OC/1-3, TD/1-2

YATES, Peter B. (d 1976 [66]) critic BP/60*

YATES, Richard (1706-96) English actor CDP, COC, DNB, ES, GT, OC/1-3, TD/1-2

YATES, Mrs. Richard see Yates, Mary Ann

YATES, Stephen (d 1972 [43]) agent BP/57*

YATES, Theodosia (d 1904 [89]) actress BE*, WWT/14*

YAVORSKA, Lydia (1874-1921) Russian actress WWT/1-3

YAW, Ellen Beach (1869-1947) American singer SR, WWA/2

YAZINSKY, Jean (d 1973 [81]) performer BP/57*

YEAGER, Robert (d 1976 [64]) publicist BP/60*

YEAMAN, George (d 1827) Scottish equestrian? HAS

YEAMANS, Annie (1835-1912) English actress CDP, GRB/3-4, PP/3, SR, WWT/1

YEAMANS, Jennie (1862-1906) Australian actress CDP

YEARSLEY, Anne (d 1806) dramatist CP/3

YEARSLEY, Claude Blakesley (1885-1961) manager, composer WWT/4-5

YEATON, Kelly (b 1911) American educator, director BE

YEATS, Jack B. (1871-1957) Irish dramatist MD, WWW/5

YEATS, Murray F. (d 1975 [65]) performer BP/59*

YEATS, William Butler (1865-1939) Irish dramatist AAS, COC, DNB, ES, GRB/3-4, HP, MD, MH, MWD, NTH, OC/1-3, PDT, RE, WWM, WWT/1-8, WWW/3

YELDING, Harry (d 1918 [50]) EA/19*

YELDING, John (d 1892) EA/93*

YELDING, Mrs. John (d 1903 [80]) circus performer? EA/04*

YELLAND, Estelle D'Arcy [Estelle D'Arcy Bodenham] (d 1871 [27]) actress EA/72*

YELLAND, Willie [George D'Arcy] (d 1886) dramatist EA/87*

YELLEN, Jack (b 1892) Polish lyricist, dramatist BE

YELVINGTON, Ramsey (d 1973 [60]) dramatist BP/58*

YEO (fl 1790) dramatist CP/3

YEOLAND, Edith (d 1901) actress EA/02*

YEOLAND, Ida (d 1901) actress EA/02*

YEOMANS, Thomas (1826-55) American call boy, actor? HAS

YEOMANS, Mrs. Thomas [Miss Marshall; Mrs. Edmonds] HAS

YEZBAK, John J. (d 1965 [53]) dramatist BP/49*

YOELSON, Asa see Jolson, Albert

YOHE, May (1869-1938) American actress, singer EA/94, GRB/1, WWT/2-8

YOHN, Erica American actress TW/25, 27-29

YOKEL, Alexander (1887/89-1947) American producing manager TW/4, WWT/9-10

YONGE, Sir William (fl 1731) dramatist CP/3

YORDAN, Phillip (b c. 1914) American dramatist BE

YORK, Cecil Morton (b 1864) English actor EA/95

YORK, Dick (b 1928) American actor ES

YORK, Elizabeth (d 1909 [90]) EA/10*

YORK, Elizabeth (d 1969 [46]) performer BP/53*

YORK, Michael (b 1942) English actor CB, TW/29

YORK, Richard (b 1930) American producer, actor, dancer, singer BE

YORKE, Alan see Feinstein, Alan

YORKE, Augustus (d 1939 [79]) actor WWT/4-9

YORKE, Augustus see Danemore, A.

YORKE, Dallas (d 1963) performer BE*

YORKE, Harry singer CDP

YORKE, Oswald (1885?-1943) English actor CB, EA/96, GRB/3-4, WWT/1-9

YORKE, Mrs. Oswald see Russell, Annie

YORKE, Philip, Viscount Royston (1784-1808) English translator

CP/3

YORKE, Philip English manager, agent GRB/1-4

YORKE, Tommy (d 1965 [73]) performer BP/49*

YOST, Agnes Scott American actress TW/1

YOST, Herbert A. (d 1945 [65]) American actor TW/2

YOUDAN, Thomas (d 1876 [60]) proprietor EA/77*

YOUENS, Cpt. John Henry (d 1879 [33]) aeronaut EA/80*

YOULL, Jim (d 1962) stage manager BE*

YOUMANS, Vincent (1898-1946) American composer, producer AAS, CB, DAB, ES, PDT, TW/2, WWT/6-9

YOUNG, Mr. (fl 1792-1800) actor, dramatist CP/3

YOUNG, Mr. (fl 1801) dramatist CP/3

YOUNG, Mrs. see Hughes, Mrs.

YOUNG, Miss (fl 1849) actress HAS

YOUNG, A. tight-rope walker CDP

YOUNG, Alfred (d 1883 [54]) manager EA/84*

YOUNG, Alfred W. (d 1876) actor EA/77*

YOUNG, Anne (b 1773/75) English actress CDP, GT, TD/2

YOUNG, Arthur (d 1917) comedian EA/18*

YOUNG, Arthur (1898-1959) English actor WWT/9-11

YOUNG, Aston S. (b 1930) American actor TW/26, 28-29

YOUNG, Benjamin (fl 1838-50) American actor HAS

YOUNG, Bertram Alfred (b 1912) English critic WWW/15-16

YOUNG, Bryan (b 1945) American actor TW/26

YOUNG, Carleton G. (d 1971 [64]) performer BP/56*

YOUNG, Cecilia see Arne, Mrs. Thomas Augustine

YOUNG, Charles (b 1854) minstrel CDP

YOUNG, Charles (d 1874) American actor COC, HAS, OC/1-3

YOUNG, Mrs. Charles [née Foster] (d 1831) actress HAS

YOUNG, Mrs. Charles see Vezin, Jane Elizabeth

YOUNG, Charles Frederick (d 1874) comedian EA/75*

YOUNG, Sir Charles Lawrence (1839-87) dramatist NYM

YOUNG, Charles Mayne (1777-1856) English actor BS, CDP, COC, DNB, ES, GT, OC/1-3, OX

YOUNG, Mrs. Charles Wayne see Grimani, Julia

YOUNG, Charlie Oswald see Oswald, Charlie

YOUNG, Charlotte Elizabeth see Hope, Charlotte

YOUNG, Christopher B. (d 1975 [67]) producer/director/choreographer BP/60*

YOUNG, Clara (1890-1960) American actress ES, TW/17, WWA/4

YOUNG, Daniel (d 1888) EA/89*

YOUNG, David R. (1832-1918) American actor SR

YOUNG, D. B. [D. B. Buchan] Scottish actor, singer GRB/1

YOUNG, Edgar Berryhill (b 1908) American executive BE

YOUNG, Dr. Edward (1681/83-1765) English dramatist CDP, CP/1-3, GT, HP, TD/1-2

YOUNG, Elizabeth see Dorman, Mrs. Ridley

YOUNG, F. (d 1867 [45]) actor? EA/68*

YOUNG, Felix (d 1976 [80]) producer/director/choreographer BP/60*

YOUNG, Florence (d 1920) actress, singer BE*, WWT/14*

YOUNG, Francis Brett (1884-1954) English dramatist WWW/5

YOUNG, Frank (d 1968 [56]) press agent BP/53*

YOUNG, George (d 1896 [30]) actor EA/97*

YOUNG, Mrs. George (d 1917) EA/18*

YOUNG, George Ralph (d 1894 [58]) property man, actor EA/95*

YOUNG, Gig [né Byron Ellsworth Barr] (b 1917) American actor BE, TW/10-15, 17-19, 24, WWT/15-16

YOUNG, Gilbert (d 1874) actor EA/75*

YOUNG, Gladys (d 1975 [70]) performer BP/60*

YOUNG, Harry L. (b 1910) Ameri-

can stage manager, actor,
director BE

YOUNG, Henry (d 1890 [76]) actor
EA/91*

YOUNG, Mrs. H. F. see Henderson, Bessie

YOUNG, Howard Irving (b 1893)
American dramatist WWT/8-11

YOUNG, Howard L. (b 1911)
American producing manager
BE, TW/3-6, WWT/11-12

YOUNG, H. Richard (b 1930)
American actor TW/30

YOUNG, Mrs. H. Wilmot see
Adams, Margie

YOUNG, Isabella Jane (d 1901)
EA/02*

YOUNG, James, Jr. American
actor WWM

YOUNG, James (b 1878) American actor ES

YOUNG, James (d 1974 [51])
performer BP/59*

YOUNG, James L. (d 1975 [58])
performer BP/60*

YOUNG, Janis American actress
TW/24

YOUNG, J. Arthur (d 1943 [63])
American actor BE*, BP/28*

YOUNG, Mrs. J. F. (d 1886)
EA/87*

YOUNG, J. Falconer (d 1887)
actor NYM

YOUNG, Joan (b 1903) English
actress WWT/11-16

YOUNG, Joe (b 1905) American
actor TW/25, 29-30

YOUNG, John (fl 1537-70) actor
DA

YOUNG, John (fl 1626-35) actor
DA

YOUNG, John (d 1909) EA/10*

YOUNG, John Wray (b 1909)
American director, educator
BE

YOUNG, La Monte composer
CD

YOUNG, Louisa see Prior,
Mrs. James J.

YOUNG, Madonna American actress TW/28

YOUNG, Margaret (d 1969 [69])
performer BP/53*

YOUNG, Margaret Mary (b 1911)
American designer, director
BE

YOUNG, Mary Marsden (d 1971
[92]) actress TW/28

YOUNG, Noel American actor
TW/29

YOUNG, Ollie (b 1876) American
vaudevillian WWM

YOUNG, Percival (d 1917) EA/18*

YOUNG, Ralph (b 1923) American
actor TW/15

YOUNG, Richard (d 1846 [55]) actor
CDP

YOUNG, Richard (d 1869 [31])
comic singer EA/70*

YOUNG, Richard W. (d 1887 [65])
actor EA/88*

YOUNG, Rida Johnson (1875-1926)
American dramatist SR, WWA/
1, WWM, WWT/1-5

YOUNG, Robert (b 1907) American
actor CB

YOUNG, Roland (1887-1953) English
actor AAS, ES, TW/10, WWA/
3, WWT/6-11

YOUNG, Ron[ald] (b 1941) American
actor TW/22-24, 28

YOUNG, Sophie (fl 1869-79) actress OAA/2

YOUNG, Stanley (1906-75) American
dramatist, executive BE

YOUNG, Stark (1881-1963) American
dramatist, critic, director
COC, ES, HJD, NTH, OC/1-3,
PDT, WWA/4, WWT/5-13

YOUNG, T. B. (d 1918) EA/19*

YOUNG, Thomas actor TD/2

YOUNG, Victor (1900-56) American
composer, musical director
WWA/3

YOUNG, Victor (d 1968 [79]) com-
poser/lyricist BP/53*

YOUNG, William (1847-1920) American dramatist GRB/3-4,
WWA/1, WWM

YOUNG, Winifred (d 1964 [86])
actor BE*

YOUNGE, A. (b 1806) actor CDP

YOUNGE, Fred (d 1870 [45]) actor,
manager EA/71*, WWT/14*

YOUNGE, Margaret [Mrs. Richard
W. Younge] (d 1883) EA/84*

YOUNGE, Richard (d 1846 [55])
actor EA/72*, WWT/14*

YOUNGE, Mrs. Richard W. see
Younge, Margaret

YOUNGE, R. W. (1822-87) English
actor NYM

YOUNGE, William (d 1897 [39])
actor, author EA/98*

YOUNGER, Elizabeth (1699?-1762)
actress DNB

YOUNGER, Joseph (fl 1774)
   prompter, manager TD/1-2
YOUNGER, Thomas actor CDP
YOUNGSON, Robert (d 1974 [56])
   producer/director/choreographer
   BP/58*
"YOUNG SWEENEY" see Buckley,
   George Swayne
YOUSKEVITCH, Igor (b 1912)
   Russian dancer CB
YOW, Joe (d 1964 [70]) American
   performer BE*
YUILL, Mrs. James, Jr. see
   Plimmer, Annie
YULE, Joe see Rooney, Mickey
YULIN, Harris (b 1937) American
   actor TW/25
YURGEV, Yuri (d 1948 [77]) ac-
   tor WWT/14*
YURIKO (b 1920) American dancer,
   choreographer BE
YURKA, Blanche (1893-1974)
   American actress, director
   AAS, BE, BTR/74, COC,
   TW/3-7, 12-16, 18-20, 23,
   26, WWT/4-15

- Z -

ZABELLE, Flora (d 1968 [88])
   Turkish actress, singer TW/
   25, WWT/1-8
ZACCHINI, Ernest (d 1975 [83])
   performer BP/59*
ZACCHINI, Hugo (d 1975 [77])
   performer BP/60*
ZACCHINI, Ildebrando (d 1948
   [79]) circus performer BP/33*
ZAEO [Adelaide Wieland; Mrs.
   H. W. Wieland] (d 1906 [43])
   gymnast EA/07*
ZAHL, Eda (b 1948) American
   actress TW/28
ZAHL, Ephraim (d 1975 [48])
   agent BP/60*
ZAINNCZEK, Mr. (fl 1853) Polish
   actor HAS
ZAKOWSKI, Rita (d 1974 [43])
   agent BP/58*
ZAKS, Jerry (b 1946) German/
   American actor TW/30
ZALA, Nancy (b 1936) American
   actress TW/29
ZALOOM, Joe (b 1944) American
   actor TW/28
ZALTZBERG, Charlotte Singer (d
   1974 [49]) writer of musicals

CD, TW/30
ZALUD, Sam (d 1963 [77]) designer
   BE*
ZAMBRA [John Buxton] (d 1898)
   acrobat EA/99*
ZAMEZOU, Mons. [Thomas Jame-
   son] (d 1885 [66]) equestrian
   EA/86*
ZAMPI (d 1905 [49]) one-legged
   gymnast EA/06*
ZANFRETTA, Josephine [née Josie
   Dupree] (fl 1863) dancer HAS
ZANFRETTA, Marietta (fl 1858)
   French tight-rope dancer CDP,
   HAS
ZANFRETTA, Rosita (fl 1863)
   tight-rope dancer HAS
ZANFRETTI, Francesca (d 1952
   [90]) dancer BE*, WWT/14*
ZANG, Edward (b 1934) American
   actor TW/24-28, 30
ZANGWILL, Israel (1864-1926)
   English dramatist CDP, COC,
   DNB, ES, GRB/1-4, HP, MWD,
   NTH, OC/1-3, SR, WWM,
   WWT/1-5, WWW/2
ZANTE, Mme. (d 1890) pantomimist,
   dancer EA/91*
ZARATE, Lucia (1864-90) dwarf
   CDP
ZARAZA, Mme. [Mrs. George
   Helton] (d 1898) rifle shot EA/
   99*
ZARIT, Pam (b 1944) American
   actress TW/26-28
ZAVADSKY, Yuri Alexeivich (1894-
   1977) Russian actor, director
   COC
ZAVISTOWSKI, Mons. (fl 1848)
   dancer CDP
ZAVISTOWSKI, Alice (b 1851)
   American dancer HAS
ZAVISTOWSKI, Christine [née
   Ludlam] (fl 1848-69) English
   dancer, actress CDP, HAS
ZAVISTOWSKI, Emeline (b 1850)
   American dancer HAS
ZAVISTOWSKI SISTERS, The (fl
   1850-69) American dancers HAS
ZEANI, Virginia (b 1928) singer
   ES
ZEDORA, Adèle (d 1902 [32]) acro-
   bat EA/03*
ZEFFIRELLI, Franco (b 1923)
   Italian director, scene designer
   BE, CB, COC, ES, OC/3,
   PDT, WWT/14-16
ZEIGER, Mme. see Alboni,

Marietta

ZEIGLER, Clara see Ziegler, Clara

ZEISLER, Peter (b 1923) American managing director BE

ZEITZ, Daisy (d 1974 [67]) performer BP/58*

ZELLER, Mark (b 1932) American actor TW/27, 30

ZEMACH, Nahum L. (1887-1939) Russian producer, director BE*

ZENATELLO, Giovanni (1876-1949) Italian singer ES

ZENIDA, Mme. (d 1891 [28]) lion tamer EA/92*

"ZENO" see Cook, Francis Edward

ZENTO (d 1894 [48]) bicyclist EA/95*

ZERBINI, Mrs. (d 1884) EA/85*

ZERBINI, Carlotta [Mrs. John Harvey] (d 1912 [69]) English actress, singer GRB/1-4

ZERMAN, Mrs. see Marshall, Polly

ZERR, Anna (1822-81) singer CDP

ZERRAHN, Carl (1826-1909) German/American conductor CDP

ZETTERLING, Mai (b 1925) Swedish actress WWT/11-14

ZIBORAN, George (b 1931) American actor TW/11

ZIDES, Max (d 1975 [70]) performer BP/59*

ZIEGFELD, Florenz, Jr. (1867-1932) American manager AAS, COC, DAB, ES, GRB/4, HJD, NTH, OC/1-3, PDT, SR, WWA/1, WWM, WWT/1-6

ZIEGFELD, Mrs. Florenz see Held, Anna

ZIEGLER, Anne [née Irene Frances Eastwood] (b 1910) English actress, singer WWT/10-13

ZIEGLER, Clara (1844-1909) actress, dramatist BE*, WWT/14*

ZIEGLER, Edward (1870-1947) American manager BE*, BP/32*

ZIEGLER, Jules (b 1900) American talent representative, manager BE

ZIEGLER, Larry (d 1974 [27]) assistant stage manager

TW/30

ZIGA, Casey (d 1974 [56]) performer BP/58*

ZILAHY, Lajos (b 1891) Hungarian dramatist MD

ZILLA, Mme. [Eliza Lind] (d 1900 [49]) clairvoyant EA/01*

ZIMBALIST, Al (d 1975 [59]) producer/director/choreographer BP/60*

ZIMBALIST, Efrem, Jr. (b 1913/23?) American actor, producer, composer BE, CB

ZIMBALIST, Sam (d 1958 [54]) producer BE*

ZIMMER, Dolph M. (d 1975 [75]) producer/director/choreographer BP/60*

ZIMMER, Maggie [Mrs. H. R. Skinner] (d 1893) EA/94*

ZIMMERL, Christl (d 1976 [36]) performer BP/60*

ZIMMERMAN, Mlle. [née Anchutz] (fl 1858) actress HAS

ZIMMERMAN, J. Fred (d 1925 [84]) manager BE*, WWT/14*

ZIMMERMAN, J. Fred, Jr. (d 1948 [77]) director, producer BE*, WWT/14*

ZIMMERMANN, Ed (1935-72) American actor TW/22-24, 26-27, 29

ZIMMERMANN, Jacob F. (d 1877) treasurer CDP

ZINDEL, Paul (b 1936) American dramatist CB, CD, MH, WWT/15-16

ZINKEISEN, Doris Clare Scottish designer WWT/7-14

ZIPPRODT, Patricia costume designer WWT/16

ZISKE, Carol Anne (b 1946) American actress TW/28

ZOBOLI, Alessandro (d 1896 [68]) singer EA/97*

ZOE, Marie (1840-86) Cuban dancer, pantomimist CDP, HAS

ZOELLER, Carli (d 1889 [49]) bandmaster EA/90*

ZOELLNER, Peter Lee (d 1971) dramatist BP/56*

ZOFF, Otto (b 1890) Austrian dramatist MD

ZOFFANY, John (1733/35-1810) Bohemian painter COC, OC/1-3

ZOHN, Chester E. (d 1975 [71]) performer BP/59*

ZOLA, Miss (d 1901) gymnast EA/02*

ZOLA, Emile-Edouard-Charles-
Antoine (1840-1902) French
dramatist COC, OC/3
ZONIS, Stuart Michael see
Damon, Stuart
ZORICH, Louis (b 1924) American
actor TW/22-23, 25-26, 28-29
ZORINA, Vera [Brigitta Hartwig]
(b 1917) German/American ac-
tress, dancer AAS, BE, CB,
TW/1-7, WWT/9-16
ZORN, Fritz (b 1871) English
dramatist GRB/2-3
ZORN, Theodora see Rozant,
Ina
ZORRAN (d 1976 [60s]) performer
BP/60*
ZOUCH, R. (fl 1631-38?) drama-
tist FGF
ZOUZE, Emilie see Polaire,
Mlle.
ZOYARA, Ella see Ella Zoyara,
Miss
ZUCCHINI, Giovanni (d 1892)
singer EA/93*
ZUCCO, George (1886-1960) Eng-
lish actor WWT/6-11
ZUCKERBERG, Regina (d 1964
[76]) performer BP/49*

ZUCKMAYER, Carl (1896-1977)
German dramatist COC, NTH,
OC/3, WWT/14-16
ZULIMA, Mme. [Mrs. Navarro]
(d 1903 [52]) circus performer
EA/04*
ZUNSER, Jesse (b 1898) American
critic BE
ZUSSIN, Victoria (b 1927) Amer-
ican actress TW/24
ZWAR, Charles (b 1914) Aus-
tralian composer, lyricist
AAS, WWT/11-16
ZWEIBELSHARF, David see
Dank, David
ZWEIG, Stefan (d 1942 [60])
Austrian dramatist BP/26*,
WWT/14*
ZWERDLING, Allen (b 1922)
American publisher, director
BE
ZWERLING, Darrell American
actor TW/26
ZWICK, Joel (b 1942) American
actor TW/23, 28
ZWISSIG, William (b 1905) Amer-
ican manager, producer BE
ZYLBERCWEIG, Zalmen (d 1972
[77]) historian BP/57*